shakespearean criticism

"Thou art a Monument without a tomb,
And art alive still while thy Book doth
   live
And we have wits to read and praise to
   give."

*Ben Jonson, from the preface
to the First Folio, 1623.*

Mr. WILLIAM SHAKESPEARES

COMEDIES, HISTORIES, & TRAGEDIES.

Published according to the True Originall Copies.

Martin Droeshout sculpsit London.

LONDON
Printed by Isaac Iaggard, and Ed. Blount. 1623.

Frontispiece to the First Folio (1623). By permission of the Folger Shakespeare Library.

ISSN 0883-9123

Volume 2

shakespearean criticism

Excerpts from the Criticism of
William Shakespeare's Plays and Poetry,
from the First Published Appraisals
to Current Evaluations

Laurie Lanzen Harris
Mark W. Scott

Editors

Gale Research Company
Book Tower
Detroit, Michigan 48226

STAFF

Laurie Lanzen Harris, Mark W. Scott, *Editors*

Michael S. Corey, Melissa Reiff Hug, Mark Koch, Michele Roberge-Polizzi,
Sandra L. Williamson, *Assistant Editors*

Phyllis Carmel Mendelson, Anna C. Wallbillich, *Contributing Editors*

Lizbeth A. Purdy, *Production Supervisor*
Denise Michlewicz Broderick, *Production Coordinator*
Eric Berger, *Assistant Production Coordinator*
Robin DuBlanc, Kelly King Howes, *Editorial Assistants*

Victoria B. Cariappa, *Research Coordinator*
Jeannine Schiffman Davidson, *Assistant Research Coordinator*
Vincenza G. DiNoto, Daniel Kurt Gilbert, Maureen Richards, Filomena Sgambati,
Valerie J. Webster, *Research Assistants*

Linda Marcella Pugliese, *Manuscript Coordinator*
Donna Craft, *Assistant Manuscript Coordinator*
Colleen M. Crane, Maureen A. Puhl, Rosetta Irene Simms, *Manuscript Assistants*

Jeanne A. Gough, *Permissions Supervisor*
Janice M. Mach, *Permissions Coordinator*
Susan D. Nobles, *Assistant Permissions Coordinator*
Patricia A. Seefelt, *Assistant Permissions Coordinator, Illustrations*
Margaret A. Chamberlain, Sandra C. Davis, Mary M. Matuz, *Senior Permissions Assistants*
Kathleen J. Grell, Josephine M. Keene, *Permissions Assistants*
H. Diane Cooper, Dorothy J. Fowler, Yolanda Parker,
Mabel C. Schoening, *Permissions Clerks*

Frederick G. Ruffner, *Publisher*
James M. Ethridge, *Executive Vice-President/Editorial*
Dedria Bryfonski, *Editorial Director*
Christine Nasso, *Director, Literature Division*
Laurie Lanzen Harris, *Senior Editor, Literary Criticism Series*

Copyright © 1985 by Gale Research Company

ISBN 0-8103-6126-4
ISSN 0883-9123

Computerized photocomposition by
Typographics, Incorporated
Kansas City, Missouri

Printed in the United States

10 9 8 7 6 5 4 3

Contents

Preface

The works of William Shakespeare have delighted audiences and inspired scholars for nearly four hundred years. Shakespeare's appeal is universal, for in its depth and breadth his work evokes a timeless insight into the human condition.

The vast amount of Shakespearean criticism is a testament to his enduring popularity. Each epoch has contributed to this critical legacy, responding to the comments of their forebears, bringing the moral and intellectual atmosphere of their own era to the works, and suggesting interpretations which continue to inspire critics of today. Thus, to chart the history of criticism on Shakespeare is to note the changing aesthetic philosophies of the past four centuries.

The Scope of the Work

The success of Gale's four existing literary series, *Contemporary Literary Criticism (CLC), Twentieth-Century Literary Criticism (TCLC), Nineteenth-Century Literature Criticism (NCLC),* and *Children's Literature Review (CLR),* suggested an equivalent need among students and teachers of Shakespeare. Moreover, since the criticism of Shakespeare's works spans four centuries and is larger in size and scope than that of any author, a prodigious amount of critical material confronts the student.

Shakespearean Criticism (SC) presents significant passages from published criticism on the works of Shakespeare. Seven volumes of the series will be devoted to aesthetic criticism of the plays. Performance criticism will be treated in separate special volumes. Other special volumes will be devoted to such topics as Shakespeare's poetry, the authorship controversy and the apocrypha, stage history of the plays, and other general subjects, such as Shakespeare's language, religious and philosophical thought, and characterization. The first seven volumes will each contain criticism on four to six plays, with an equal balance of genres and an equal balance of plays based on their critical importance. Thus, Volume 2 contains criticism on one major tragedy *(King Lear)*, one major comedy *(Measure for Measure)*, one minor comedy *(Love's Labour's Lost)*, one history *(Henry VIII)*, and one romance *(Pericles)*.

The length of each entry is intended to represent the play's critical reception in English, including those works which have been translated into English. The editors have tried to identify only the major critics and lines of inquiry for each play. Each entry represents a historical overview of the critical response to the play: early criticism is presented to indicate initial responses and later selections represent significant trends in the history of criticism on the play. We have also attempted to identify and include excerpts from the seminal essays on each play by the most important Shakespearean critics. We have directed our series to students in late high school and early college who are beginning their study of Shakespeare. Thus, ours is not a work for the specialist, but is rather an introduction for the researcher newly acquainted with the works of Shakespeare.

The Organization of the Book

Each entry consists of the following elements: play heading, an introduction, excerpts of criticism (each followed by a bibliographical citation), and an additional bibliography for further reading.

The *introduction* begins with a discussion of the date, text, and sources of the play. This section is followed by a critical history which outlines the major critical trends and identifies the prominent commentators on the play.

Criticism is arranged chronologically within each play entry to provide a perspective on the changes in critical evaluation over the years. For purposes of easier identification, the critic's name and the date of the essay are given at the beginning of each piece. For an anonymous essay later attributed to a critic, the critic's name appears in brackets at the beginning of the excerpt and in the bibliographical citation.

Within the text, all act, scene, and line designations have been changed to conform to *The Riverside Shakespeare,* published by Houghton Mifflin Company, which is a standard text used in many high school and college English classes. Most of the individual essays are prefaced with *explanatory notes* as an additional aid to students using *SC.* The explanatory notes provide several types of useful information, including: the importance of the critics in literary history, the critical schools with which they are identified, if any, and the importance of their comments on Shakespeare and the play discussed. The explanatory notes also identify the main issues in the commentary on each play and include cross references to related criticism in the entry. In addition, the notes provide previous publication information such as original title and date for foreign language publications.

A complete *bibliographical citation* designed to facilitate the location of the original essay or book follows each piece of criticism.

Within each play entry are *illustrations,* such as facsimiles of title pages taken from the Quarto and First Folio editions of the plays as well as pictures drawn from such sources as early editions of the collected works and artist's renderings of some of the famous scenes and characters of Shakespeare's plays. The captions following each illustration indicate act, scene, characters, and the artist and date, if known. The illustrations are arranged chronologically and, as a complement to the criticism, provide a historical perspective on Shakespeare throughout the centuries.

The *additional bibliography* appearing at the end of each play entry suggests further reading on the play. This section includes references to the major discussions of the date, the text, and the sources of each play.

Each volume of *SC* includes a cumulative index to plays that provides the volume number in which the plays appear. *SC* also includes a cumulative index to critics; under each critic's name are listed the plays on which the critic has written and the volume and page where the criticism appears.

An appendix is also included that lists the sources from which the material in the volume is reprinted. It does not, however, list every book or periodical consulted for the volume.

Acknowledgments

No work of this scope can be accomplished without the cooperation of many people. The editors wish to thank the copyright holders of the excerpts included in this volume, the permissions managers of the book and magazine publishing companies for assisting us in securing reprint rights, and the staffs of the Detroit Public Library, the University of Michigan libraries, and the Wayne State University Library for making their resources available to us. We would especially like to thank the staff of the Rare Book Room of the University of Michigan Library for their research assistance and the Folger Shakespeare Library for their help in picture research. We would also like to thank Jeri Yaryan and Anthony J. Bogucki for assistance with copyright research.

Suggestions Are Welcome

The editors welcome the comments and suggestions of readers to expand the coverage and enhance the usefulness of the series.

shakespearean criticism

Henry VIII

DATE: Although several critics have speculated that Shakespeare composed *Henry VIII* as early as 1593 or 1602, most scholars agree that the play was written in late 1612 or early 1613. Stylistic and thematic similarities between *Henry VIII* and Shakespeare's romances suggest the later dates, as do the drama's parallels to controversial issues that were contemporary with the early Stuart era. For example, Henry's role as prosecutor or judge in the four trial scenes reflects the debate over the king's relationship to common law prevalent during the first decades of the seventeenth century, and his divorce from Katharine in the play suggests the divorce proceedings conducted against the Earl of Essex in 1613. In addition to the internal evidence, there exists a letter written by Sir Henry Wotton on July 2, 1613, in which he refers to "a new play called *All Is True*"—a title critics generally accept as the original one Shakespeare applied to *Henry VIII*. Scholars also rely on Wotton's letter to determine the first performance of the play, which is suggested as June 29, 1613, the date the original Globe Theater burned down. Wotton writes that the accident occurred when "certain Cannons" were fired at the appearance of King Henry at Wolsey's masque, a fact which further substantiates the assertion that *All Is True* and *Henry VIII* are the same play, since stage directions in the Folio edition of the play call for the firing of cannons at the beginning of that scene. Finally, most commentators suggest that, although it is not listed among the fourteen plays performed to celebrate the wedding of England's Princess Elizabeth and Germany's Prince Frederick on February 4, 1613, it is likely that *Henry VIII* was composed specifically for this occasion, but was withdrawn after its tone and subject matter were deemed unsuitable for a wedding celebration.

TEXT: No quarto edition of *Henry VIII* exists. It was originally published as the last history play in the First Folio of 1623 as *The Famous History of the Life of King Henry the Eight*. Accumulated evidence indicates that the Folio edition was based on a fair copy—a corrected version of the author's manuscript—rather than a prompt-copy. The text contains act and scene divisions, with complete and intricate stage directions that are often directly quoted from Shakespeare's historical sources. Variations in the speech prefixes assigned to characters in *Henry VIII* can be attributed to the compositors of the Folio, but the discrepancies of characters' names within the text are probably the fault of the original manuscript. These irregularities indicate that the text could not have been taken from a prompt-copy, which would have required definite, distinct speech headings.

Although the text of *Henry VIII* presents few difficulties that can be ascribed to textual corruption, its various verse patterns have prompted an important controversy surrounding the play. In 1850, James Spedding proposed that John Fletcher had collaborated with Shakespeare on *Henry VIII*, thereby accounting for what the critic perceived as two different styles in the drama. He based his theory on an analysis of the play's language and meter, and for the next eighty years scholars generally accepted his hypothesis. However, most recent critics either deny the dissimilarities in style or regard them as intentional on Shakespeare's part, and many attribute the play totally to Shakespeare.

Title page of King Henry VIII taken from the First Folio (1623). By permission of the Folger Shakespeare Library.

SOURCES: Critics agree that Raphael Holinshed's *Chronicles of England, Scotland, and Ireland* (second edition, 1586-87) served as the primary source for the first four acts of *Henry VIII*, while John Foxe's *Acts and Monuments* (1597) supplied Shakespeare with Cranmer's story, which appears in Act V. Several passages in *Henry VIII* closely resemble lines from Edward Hall's *Chronicle of the Union of the Two Noble and Illustre Famelies of Lancastre and Yorke* (1540), and portions of Wolsey's farewell speeches were apparently taken from John Speed's *The History of Great Britain* (1611). Many scenes in the play closely follow their sources; in fact, some are simply the prose passages of Holinshed or Foxe transcribed into verse. Critics have also noted numerous alterations in the chronology of certain historical events. For example, Katharine's death actually occurred in 1536, three years after the birth of Elizabeth, and Cranmer's trial took place after 1540; in *Henry VIII*, Elizabeth is born after Katharine dies, and Cranmer's trial takes place before Elizabeth is christened. Scholars generally attribute this rearrangement of events to dramatic license and consider it of little importance other than providing a sense of temporal continuity to the play's action.

CRITICAL HISTORY: Opinion of the value of *Henry VIII* has ranged from Samuel Pepys's comment that the drama is a simple patchwork of little merit, to Hermann Ulrici's complaint that it offends historic and poetic justice, to the assertion of G. Wilson Knight that it is the ultimate statement unifying Shakespeare's "whole life-work." The fundamental point of contention behind this diversity of interpretation appears to be the question of structural unity. Prior to the twentieth century, most commentators characterized the play as disjointed, a premise that led directly to the authorship controversy and to arguments over its date of composition. Since the 1930s, however, an increasing number of critics have argued that *Henry VIII* is more structurally and thematically cohesive than earlier commentators perceived. To demonstrate this point they have focused on the role of King Henry in the drama, the meaning of the tragedies of Buckingham, Wolsey, and Katharine, and the relation of Cranmer's prophecy to the rest of the play.

The air of controversy that permeates criticism of *Henry VIII* began in the seventeenth century with conflicting assessments of the play's pageantry. Wotton complained that the majesty and splendor in the play are made "very familiar, if not ridiculous," whereas Pepys considered the masques and processions the only parts "good or well done," an opinion echoed by Samuel Johnson in the following century. Critics of both the seventeenth and eighteenth centuries also debated over characterization in *Henry VIII,* as well as Shakespeare's moral purpose. Although most praised Shakespeare for his portraits of Katharine of Aragon and Wolsey, they nevertheless questioned his presentation of these two figures in the same play— since both appear to contend for our sympathy—and, more importantly, the appearance of such characters in a drama that seemed concerned with other matters. Neoclassical critics like Johnson and Charlotte Lennox cited these shortcomings as the reason for the disunity they perceived in *Henry VIII.*

Most eighteenth-century critics devoted their attention to examinations of the characters in *Henry VIII.* Unlike Rowe and Lennox, Edward Capell studied Henry's portrait and declared that it was a "finish'd" representation. By pointing out Anne Boleyn's "addiction to levities," Capell was also the first critic to question the traditional acceptance of that character's innocence. Both Nicholas Amhurst and Elizabeth Griffith focused on Wolsey's role in the play, the former claiming that he represents greed and ambition in human nature, the latter interpreting his tragedy as a depiction of the instability of worldly greatness. Katharine was the only character in *Henry VIII* who elicited universal admiration. Rowe praised her virtue and dignity and wished that she had received a more pleasing fate, while Johnson considered her portrait, along with the pageantry, the only redeeming aspects of the play. Griffith regarded Katharine as the central figure in *Henry VIII,* the one character whose tragedy eclipses even the play's final celebration.

Critics did not examine the stylistic and thematic complexities in *Henry VIII* until the middle of the eighteenth century. Richard Roderick was the first commentator to notice "peculiar" measures in the poetry. He insisted that the instances of extrasyllable line endings in *Henry VIII* are double the number contained in any other Shakespearean play. He also discovered "unusual" pauses and remarked that Shakespeare's dramatic emphasis often clashes with the rhythm of the verse. Roderick's assessment significantly influenced the conclusions of James Spedding, the nineteenth-century critic who firmly established the theory of dual authorship that has influenced *Henry VIII*

criticism to the present day. Roderick himself, however, did not regard the play as the work of any writer other than Shakespeare. That idea was first suggested by Johnson, who maintained that the prologue, epilogue, and other portions of the play show the characteristics of Ben Jonson's work. Over a decade later, Edmond Malone—the first scholar to attempt to establish the original date of *Henry VIII*—concurred with Johnson on the possibility of dual authorship. Malone asserted that the favorable portraits of Henry and Anne and the fact that Elizabeth, rather than James I, is the main subject of Cranmer's prophecy all indicate that the play was composed as a tribute to Queen Elizabeth in 1603. He also suggested that Jonson later added the pageantry and the references to James I in Cranmer's prophecy prior to the first performance of the play in 1613.

Critical discussions of the structural and thematic unity of *Henry VIII* continued in the nineteenth century, with many commentators attempting to ascertain the play's meaning as well as offering numerous theories on its lack of cohesiveness. However, the most influential nineteenth-century discussion of the play is Spedding's "Who Wrote Shakspere's *Henry VIII*?" In this essay—the first disintegrationist reading of *Henry VIII*—Spedding examined the inconsistent verse structure that had been described by Roderick nearly a hundred years earlier. After a close analysis of the play, he concluded that Shakespeare had not written it alone and suggested that John Fletcher had worked alternately upon portions of it. Spedding's study included a chart that illustrated his contention, attributing introductory scenes to Shakespeare and the remainder to Fletcher. Until the middle decades of the twentieth century, Spedding's theory was widely accepted. Algernon Charles Swinburne was the only commentator of the nineteenth century to totally reject Spedding's ideas. An avid reader of Elizabethan and Jacobean literature, Swinburne regarded Spedding's verse-analysis test as misguided and his conclusion unfounded. He considered Fletcher incapable of creating many of the scenes that Spedding attributed to him, and therefore believed that Shakespeare was the sole author of *Henry VIII.*

In their interpretations of the major critical issues surrounding *Henry VIII,* nineteenth-century critics introduced several new topics. August Wilhelm Schlegel initiated the theory that Shakespeare's ten English histories form "an historical heroic poem" that "furnishes examples of the political course of the world, applicable at all times." He perceived *Henry VIII* as the epilogue to this series and saw it as a dramatization of the transition in Europe from feudalism to modern governmental policy. Hermann Ulrici interpreted *Henry VIII* as a comment on the beginning of an absolute monarchy in England and "a new era in history." Ulrici also introduced another important idea to criticism of the play: he was the first critic to examine the disparity between its joyful ending and the suffering experienced by Buckingham, Katharine, and Wolsey. Ulrici asserted that the final scenes of the play, in which Henry wins a new wife and the blessings of a great daughter, violate both poetic justice and the justice of God, and therefore discredit the entire play. G. G. Gervinus put forth a similar interpretation some years later, and it has since become a major topic of contention in twentieth-century criticism of *Henry VIII.*

Characterization, an important subject in the Neoclassical criticism of *Henry VIII,* continued to receive substantial consideration during the nineteenth century. Katharine was the most frequently discussed character, although both Wolsey and King Henry acquired greater interest among commentators on the play. The most important character studies included those by William Hazlitt, Anna Brownell Jameson, H. N. Hudson, Karl Elze, and Denton J. Snider. Hazlitt referred to Katharine as ''the most perfect delineation of matronly dignity'' and commended Shakespeare's unflattering portrait of Henry. Jameson was the first commentator to compare Katharine with Hermione, the heroine of *The Winter's Tale*, a topic that received further consideration in the essays by G. Wilson Knight, R. A. Foakes, and Hugh M. Richmond in the following century. Jameson was also the first critic to emphasize the contrast between Katharine's ''truth as a quality of the soul'' and Anne's ''absolute femalities.'' Hudson further developed this point when he argued that Shakespeare specifically designed Anne as a foil to Katharine, the young, impetuous bride illuminating the rejected Queen's personality through her inability to achieve or understand ''womanly principle and delicacy.'' Elze maintained that the fates of Katharine and Wolsey represent the fall of Catholicism, while the rise of Cranmer and Anne symbolize ''the approaching dawn of Protestantism.'' Snider advanced a similar idea when he suggested that the central concern of *Henry VIII* is the conflict generated by the political and moral impact of the Reformation, represented on the political level by the defeat of Wolsey, and on the moral level by the divorce of Katharine and the coronation of the Protestant queen Anne.

Discussion of the composition date of *Henry VIII*, a topic introduced by Malone in the eighteenth century, continued into the nineteenth and the twentieth centuries. Schlegel supported Malone's theory that Shakespeare first wrote the play in 1603, and that Ben Jonson revised it in 1613. Elze combined the conclusions of Malone and Spedding, claiming that Shakespeare wrote *Henry VIII* in 1603 and that both Fletcher and Jonson revised it ten years later. Taking an opposing view, Ulrici, Charles Knight, Spedding, and Hudson all contended that *Henry VIII* was originally composed in 1613. Ulrici explored the possibility that the play was written as a ''court piece'' for James I and that Shakespeare had planned to add a second part in which the play's conflicts would be resolved. Knight believed that evidence was inadequate to support those hypotheses that attributed an earlier date to the play, and he accepted Wotton's reference to *Henry VIII* as ''a new play'' as meaning just that. Spedding argued that Shakespeare and Fletcher collaborated on *Henry VIII* to celebrate the wedding of Princess Elizabeth in 1613. Hudson concurred with both Knight's and Spedding's findings, pointing to the information presented in Wotton's letter and to other internal matter as evidence for the later composition date.

The focus of *Henry VIII* criticism in the twentieth century shifted from questions of disunity to the recognition and analysis of its structural and thematic integrity. This gradually led critics to dispute the dual authorship theory and to regard Shakespeare as the sole author of *Henry VIII;* it also led to the discovery of internal parallels to contemporary issues that indicate 1613 as the date of composition. Critical debate in recent years has centered on the exact relationship between *Henry VIII* and Shakespeare's earlier plays. A number of critics emphasized the thematic and symbolic links with the romances, while others concentrated on the structural and thematic parallels to the histories; still others have interpreted the play as a synthesis of both the histories and the romances. Scholars have also discussed the play's examination of the nature of truth, the importance of the mythic wheel of fortune motif, the dramatic function of the pageantry and spectacle, the meaning of the play in light of the tragedies of Buckingham, Katharine, and Wolsey, and the work's prophetic ending.

The shift in critical emphasis in the first half of the twentieth century began as a reaction against Spedding and his supporters. Peter Alexander was one of the earliest modern critics to maintain that Spedding's assumptions were either unsubstantiated or contradicted by available evidence. In naming Shakespeare the sole author of *Henry VIII*, Alexander prepared the foundation for much of the twentieth-century criticism of the play. He based his conclusion on the contention that those linguistic characteristics which Spedding ''claimed as peculiar to Fletcher'' are often found in Shakespeare's later works, and that many of Spedding's ''Fletcherian'' oddities can be found even in those parts of the play he assigned to Shakespeare. However, a number of critics continued to question the authorship, and therefore the integrity, of the play. Sir John Squire referred to *Henry VIII* as ''one of the worst-shaped plays that was ever put upon the stage''; for this reason, he regarded Shakespeare's contribution as minimal, though he offered no other suggestions concerning a possible second author. Caroline F. E. Spurgeon explained that the imagery in the play exemplifies Shakespeare's habit of seeing ''emotional or mental situations'' as continually repeated pictures of physical activity, but she attributed only a few of Spedding's ''Fletcherian'' scenes to Shakespeare. Mark Van Doren labelled *Henry VIII* ''an imitation of Shakespeare,'' but he was unable to ascertain whether Shakespeare had imitated himself or had been emulated by another dramatist. Clifford Leech, reflecting a more current attitude, stated that a definite answer to the authorship question is impossible. Robert Ornstein, the only critic in the past two decades who has supported Spedding's argument, was convinced that Fletcher had a ''preeminent'' collaborative role in the play's composition. He considered *Henry VIII* an aimless and dissatisfying work and attributed to Fletcher its lack of motivation and psychological insight, its element of self-abasement, its indefinite structure, and its contrived ending.

G. Wilson Knight's detailed discussion, one of the most important studies of *Henry VIII* in the twentieth century, greatly influenced critics' recognition of the structural and thematic unity in the play. He examined the major topics that had been treated in previous years, such as the authorship controversy, the relationship of *Henry VIII* to Shakespeare's earlier plays, and the meaning of the play itself and put forth his own theory that the drama recapitulates Shakespeare's earlier histories while it is ''modulated and enriched by the wisdom garnered during intermediate works,'' such as *Macbeth, Timon of Athens,* and *Pericles.* Knight based several points of his argument on the findings of Edgar I. Fripp, who was the first critic to note a parallel between the imagery of *Henry VIII* and that of Shakespeare's romances and tragedies. Besides discussing the relation of *Henry VIII* to Shakespeare's other plays, Knight also argued that the ''broken metre'' of the drama, which such critics as Roderick and Spedding had claimed was so unlike Shakespeare, is in reality reflective of the ''deeper, spiritual aristocracy that underlies all Shakespeare's noblest thought.'' He also defined the pageantry in the play as a ''realistic and more directly social'' extension of the natural tempests in the romances and maintained that the themes of reconciliation and self-awareness display Shakespeare's abiding concern for England as a nation. Knight concluded his essay by stating that Shakespeare, in Cranmer's final prophecy, not only defines the ''indwelling spirit of his nation'', but also represents the culminating statement of Shakespeare's ''whole life-work.''

Although many twentieth-century critics employed an eclectic method of analysis to classify the genre and achieve a fuller understanding of *Henry VIII,* they often emphasized single aspects of the play. Utilizing a historical approach, Frank Kermode characterized *Henry VIII* as ''an anthology of falls'' from the grace of God, and as a seventeenth-century descendant of the medieval morality play, *Mirror for Magistrates.* Northrop Frye employed the methods of myth criticism and found that the wheel of fortune motif organizes the drama into an unending series of falls. Lee Bliss and Frank V. Cespedes investigated the mythic wheel of fortune motif in connection with the ambiguity, linguistic complexity, and historic irony inherent in *Henry VIII.* Bliss discovered that Cranmer's vision offers ''a solution to the world's political sickness and corruption and an escape from the endless repetitions of history'' represented in the fates of Buckingham, Katharine, and Wolsey. Cespedes, like Frye, maintained that fortune's wheel continued to turn, and that the ending of the play still proclaims ''the alarming ambiguities of history.'' Paul Bertram and C. B. Purdom interpreted the play as a depiction of the political education of a king and as a study of the value of kingship to English society.

Many twentieth-century critics, including R. A. Foakes, Howard Felperin, and Bernard Harris, regarded the structural, thematic, and linguistic elements that define *Henry VIII* as similar to those in the late romances. Foakes contended that the ''heart of the play'' presents the conflict between ''public interest and private joy and suffering,'' which is illustrated in the juxtaposition of the pageantry and the personal visions. Like the romances, Foakes argued, *Henry VIII* contains the repeated suggestion that self-awareness is gained only through the exercise of patience, and it is toward this realization that the characters evolve. Felperin remarked that the fall-conversion structure of the play is a Christian adaptation of the mythic process of reconciliation developed in the romances. Echoing G. Wilson Knight, Felperin concluded that ''truth'' in *Henry VIII* resides in ''the eternal relevance of the great Christian myth upon which it rests.'' Harris proposed that Cranmer's prophecy patiently rebukes the belief among Shakespeare's contemporaries that England's destined struggle with the Catholic Church would be troublesome and violent. He equated the expansion of peace under Elizabeth with the prophecy of peace that concludes the final reconciliation scene in *Cymbeline.*

A number of recent critics have maintained that *Henry VIII* combines the political conflicts and motives of Shakespeare's earlier histories with the symbolism, self-conscious searching, and masques characteristic of the romances. Frances A. Yates explored the relationship between the presentation of mythical history in *Cymbeline* and the evidence of Tudor imperialism in *Henry VIII.* She concluded that Shakespeare's view of history in *Henry VIII* combines ''the ancient purity of British chivalric tradition'' and the ''purity of royal and Tudor reformation'' within the conciliatory atmosphere of the romances. Tom McBride claimed that the moral disparity in the play, especially surrounding the actions of King Henry, can be resolved if we see the drama as positing ''two ultimately valid moral codes''—one Christian, the other Machiavellian. McBride considered *Henry VIII* primarily a study of Henry's development into a Machiavellian ruler; he thus characterized the play as a ''Machiavellian romance'' in that it achieves romantic ends through the political manipulations of its protagonist. Hugh M. Richmond analyzed the characters of Anne, Katharine, and Elizabeth as illustrations of the feminine approach to life that Shakespeare explored in the romances. In the character of Katharine, as well as in the reign of Queen Elizabeth alluded to in the play, Richmond sees Shakespeare expressing his model for earthly existence—an ideal which stresses the values of

virtue, honesty, compassion, and the acceptance of providential will beyond human understanding. Eckhard Auberlen identified in *Henry VIII* a number of political issues prominent during the Stuart reign. He contended that the play's themes of patience and reconciliation—concepts which, he noted, *Henry VIII* shares with the romances—offer a compromise solution to the political conflicts of the period.

The complex linguistic and thematic design of *Henry VIII,* its stylistic anomalies, and its relation to both the earlier histories and the later romances have inspired disparate interpretations and have made the play one of the most controversial in Shakespeare's canon. Although the focus of recent criticism has shifted from external questions, such as the play's authorship, to an examination of its aesthetic merits, critics generally agree that much remains to be explored in the play. The only accepted certainty is that *Henry VIII* is no longer considered an inferior drama. In fact, many modern scholars maintain that its concluding vision reveals Shakespeare's plan for the future of England and outlines, as G. Wilson Knight stated, ''that greater peace . . . whose cause that nation was, and is, to serve.''

SIR HENRY WOTTON   (letter date 1613)

[*Wotton's reference to ''a new play called* All Is True'' *in his account of the June 29, 1613 Globe Theater fire is often quoted by critics attempting to date the first performance of* Henry VIII. *''All is True'' is considered by most critics to be the original subtitle of* Henry VIII. *In the following excerpt, Wotton complains about the excess of pageantry in the play—an objection that is countered by Samuel Pepys (1664), Samuel Johnson (1765), and many twentieth-century commentators.*]

Now, to let matters of State sleep, I will entertain you at the present with what hath happened this Week at the Banks side. The King's Players had a new Play, called *All is true,* representing some principal pieces of the Reign of *Henry* the *8th,* which was set forth with many extraordinary Circumstances of Pomp and Majesty, even to the matting of the Stage; the Knights of the Order, with their Georges and Garter, the Guards with their embroidered Coats, and the like: sufficient in truth within a while to make Greatness very familiar, if not ridiculous. Now, King *Henry* making a Masque at the Cardinal *Wolsey*'s House, and certain Cannons being shot off at his entry, some of the Paper, or other stuff, wherewith one of them was stopped, did light on the Thatch, where being thought at first but an idle smoak, and their Eyes more attentive to the show, it kindled inwardly, and ran round like a train, consuming within less than an hour the whole House to the very ground.

This was the fatal period of that virtuous Fabrique; wherein yet nothing did perish, but Wood and Straw, and a few forsaken Cloaks; only one Man had his Breeches set on fire, that would perhaps have broyled him, if he had not by the benefit of a provident wit put it out with Bottle-Ale.

> *Sir Henry Wotton, in a letter to Sir Edmund Bacon on July 2, 1613, in* The Shakspere Allusion-Book: A Collection of Allusions to Shakspere from 1591-1700, Vol. I, *edited by John Munro, Books for Libraries Press, 1970; distributed by Arno Press, Inc., p. 239.*

SAMUEL PEPYS   (diary date 1664)

[*A diversified background of travel, intellectual pursuits, and public office gave Pepys both the opportunity and the initiative to act as a close observer of English society in the seventeenth century. His unique* Diary *is an unreserved study of the affairs and customs of his time. His personal revelations create a document of unusual psychological interest and also provide a history of the Restoration theater. The excerpt below comes from his* Diary *in which he states that the pageantry in* Henry VIII *is the only aspect of the play that is "good or well done." This comment contradicts that of Sir Henry Wotton (1613) but is supported by Samuel Johnson (1765).*]

Went to the Duke's house, the first play I have been at these six months, according to my last vowe, and here saw the so much cried-up play of "Henry the Eighth;" which, though I went with resolution to like it, is so simple a thing made up of a great many patches, that, besides the shows and processions in it, there is nothing in the world good or well done.

> *Samuel Pepys, in a diary entry of January 1, 1664, in* The Shakspere Allusion-Book: A Collection of Allusions to Shakspere from 1591 to 1700, *Vol. II, edited by John Munro, revised edition, 1932. Reprint by Books for Libraries Press, 1970; distributed by Arno Press, Inc., p. 91.*

NICHOLAS ROWE   (essay date 1709)

[*Rowe was the editor of the first critical edition of Shakespeare's plays and the author of the first authoritative Shakespeare biography. In his edition of* The Works of William Shakespeare, *Vol. I, published in 1709, Rowe became one of the first critics to regard Shakespeare as an "untutored genius" and to excuse his often-cited violation of the Neoclassical rules for correct drama on grounds that he was unaware of their existence. In the following excerpt, taken from his biographical and critical preface to his edition of Shakespeare, he justifies Shakespeare's rather favorable portrait of Henry VIII as conceived out of respect for Queen Elizabeth, a view also supported by Charlotte Lennox (1754), Edmond Malone (1778), and Karl Elze (1874). Shakespeare's treatment of King Henry is a major topic of contention in* Henry VIII *criticism; he has been variously interpreted as an uncivilized ruler, a divine agent of providence, the historical counterpart to Shakespeare's Prospero, and the definitive expression of Shakespeare's fascination with kingship. For examples of these readings, see the excerpts by William Hazlitt (1817), Denton J. Snider (1890), Frank Kermode (1947), G. Wilson Knight (1947), R. A. Foakes (1957), Paul Bertram (1962), and Howard Felperin (1966).*]

In [Shakespeare's] *Henry VIII* that Prince is drawn with that Greatness of Mind and all those good Qualities which are attributed to him in any Account of his Reign. If his Faults are not shewn in an equal degree, and the Shades in this Picture do not bear a just Proportion to the Lights, it is not that the Artist wanted either Colours or Skill in the Disposition of 'em. But the truth, I believe, is that he forbore doing it out of regard to Queen *Elizabeth,* since it could have been no very great Respect to the Memory of his Mistress to have expos'd some certain Parts of her Father's Life upon the Stage. He has dealt more freely with the Minister of that Great King, and certainly nothing was ever more justly written than the Character of Cardinal *Wolsey.* He has shewn him Tyrannical, Cruel, and Insolent in his Prosperity; and yet, by a wonderful Address, he makes his Fall and Ruin the Subject of general Compassion. The whole Man, with his Vices and Virtues, is finely and exactly described in the second Scene of the fourth Act. The Distresses likewise of Queen *Katharine* in this Play, are very movingly touch'd; and tho' the Art of the Poet has skreen'd

King *Henry* from any gross Imputation of Injustice yet one is inclin'd to wish the Queen had met with a Fortune more worthy of her Birth and Virtue. (pp. 199-200)

> *Nicholas Rowe, in an extract from* Shakespeare, the Critical Heritage: 1693-1733, *Vol. 2, edited by Brian Vickers, Routledge & Kegan Paul, 1974, pp. 190-202.*

[NICHOLAS AMHURST?]   (essay date 1727)

[*The following character sketch of Cardinal Wolsey is taken from an anonymous article in the November 18, 1727 issue of the* Craftsman. *This political journal was established in 1726 by Nicholas Amhurst, who opposed the Whig administration of Prime Minister Sir Robert Walpole. To illustrate his contempt for Walpole and the Whigs, Amhurst filled the* Craftsman *with numerous literary and historical examples of political corruption, particularly from the works of Shakespeare; for this reason, the essay below is generally attributed to him. In it, he declares that Wolsey's role demonstrates that greed and ambition are inherent in human nature, a maxim that exemplifies the Neoclassical penchant for extracting a moral lesson from a work of art.*]

I went the other Night to the Play called *The Life of Henry VIII,* written by *Shakespeare,* designing not only to treat my Eyes with a *Coronation* in Miniature and see away my *three Shillings,* but to improve my Understanding by beholding my Countrymen who have been near two Centuries in Ashes revive again, and act and talk in the same Manner as they then did. Such a Representation as This, given us by so great a Master, throws one's Eye back upon our Ancestors; and while I am present at the Action I cannot help believing my self a real Spectator and Contemporary with our old *Huff-bluff English* Monarch, *Henry VIII,* so much does the useful Delusion of a well-written Play delight and instruct us beyond the cold Narrations of a dry Historian. But the principal Figure, and that which stood fullest out to me, was the great *Minister.* There you see an ambitious, proud, bad Man of Parts, in the Possession of a wise and brave Prince, amassing Wealth, taxing the griev'd Commons, and abusing his Trust and Power to support his Vanity and Luxury. As it is usual with this Sort of *great Men,* all the Errors *He* commits are his *Master's,* and every Thing that may be praise-worthy *his* own. We find a very remarkable Instance of This in the second Scene of this Play. Good Queen *Katharine* intercedes with the King that some *heavy Taxes* might be mitigated, which the People complained were levied upon them by the Order of this *wicked Minister.* . . . The *King,* very justly alarmed and moved with the Recital of these Hardships which his People laboured under, commands the *Cardinal* to write into the several Counties forthwith, and gives his Orders that these *Taxes* should immediately cease, and free Pardon be granted to all who had denied the Payment of them; upon which the *Minister* turns to *Cromwell* and gives his Instructions in these Words:

> —*A Word with you.*
> *Let there be Letters writ to ev'ry Shire,*
> *Of the* King's *Grace and Pardon. The griev'd Commons*
> *Hardly conceive of Me. Let it be noised,*
> *That thro'* OUR INTERCESSION *this Revokement*
> *And Pardon comes.*   [I. ii. 102-07]

There cannot be an Instance of a more shocking Insolence. The *Minister* injures, and the *Minister* forgives. He wrongs the People, and is so gracious as to forgive the People whom he has wrong'd. What a Figure does a great and a brave Prince make under the Wing and Tutelage of such a Servant! A *Min-*

ister like This *is a Spunge* (as the same excellent Author says in *Hamlet*) *who sucks up the King's Countenance, his Rewards, his Authorities.*

Shakespeare has chosen to bring this *Minister* upon the Stage in his full Lustre, when he was in high Favour and just after the *Peace* and *League* concluded with *France.* . . . (pp. 443-44)

Buckingham describes the *Minister* as a partaking of the Natures of a *Fox* and a *Wolf* (equally ravenous and subtle, prone to Mischief and able to perform it) and compares this *Peace* to *a Glass that broke in rinsing;* and then he says

<blockquote>

          This cunning Cardinal
Th' Articles of the Combination *drew*
As himself pleased, and they were ratify'd
As he cry'd, thus let be, to as much End
As give a Crutch to the Dead.   [I. i. 168-72]

</blockquote>

A little after This he says the *Emperor* grew jealous of this new Amity between *France* and us for that

<blockquote>

          From this League
Harms peep'd that menac'd him. He privately
Deals with our Cardinal; *and, as I trow,*
Which I do well, for I am sure the Emperor
Paid ere he promised, whereby his Suit
Was granted ere 'twas ask'd; but when the Way was made
And paved with Gold; the Emperor *thus desired*
That he would alter the King's Course
And break the aforesaid Peace. Let the King know
(As soon he shall by me) that thus the Cardinal
Does buy *and* sell *his Honour as he pleases,*
And for his own Advantage.   [I. i. 182-93]

</blockquote>

At length we behold this *great Administrator* declining. The Favour of the King is gone. . . . (pp. 444-45)

He is found guilty of a *Praemunire,* and all his Goods seized into the King's Hand. And now this Man, who made so very bad a Figure as a *Minister,* makes a very good one as a *Philosopher.* He became his Disgrace very well; and *Shakespeare* has put some Words into his Mouth which all *good Ministers* will read with Pleasure and *bad ones* with Pain. *Wolsey* says to *Cromwell,*

<blockquote>

Mark thou my Fall, and That which ruin'd me.
Cromwell, *I charge thee fling away* Ambition.
By that Sin fell the Angels. How can Man then
(The Image of his Maker) hope to win it?
Love thyself last. *Cherish those Hearts that hate thee.*
Corruption *gains no more than* Honesty.
Still in thy right Hand carry gentle Peace,
To silence envious Tongues. Be just, and fear not.
Let all the Ends thou aim'st at be thy Country's;
Thy God's and Truth's.   [III. ii. 439-48]

</blockquote>

Thus, Sir, I have thrown together some of the Out-lines by which the Character of this ambitious, wealthy, bad *Minister* is described in the very Words of *Shakespeare.* Reflecting People may observe from this Picture how like human Nature is in her Workings at all Times. (pp. 445-46)

[*Nicholas Amhurst?*], in an extract from Shakespeare, the Critical Heritage: 1693-1733, Vol. 2, *edited by Brian Vickers, Routledge & Kegan Paul, 1974, pp. 442-46.*

[CHARLOTTE LENNOX]   (essay date 1754)

[Lennox was an American-born novelist and Shakespearean scholar who compiled a three-volume edition of translated texts of the sources used by Shakespeare in twenty-two of his plays, including some analyses of the ways in which he used these sources. The following excerpt is taken from her study Shakespear Illustrated, *first published in 1754. Lennox devotes the majority of her essay to demonstrating Shakespeare's dependence on Holinshed's* Chronicles, *but she also argues that Shakespeare's combination of both Katharine's and Wolsey's personal tragedies in* Henry VIII *destroys "the Unity of his Fable." Lennox further maintains that Shakespeare purposely left his portrait of King Henry incomplete in order not to offend Queen Elizabeth. This opinion was also voiced by Nicholas Rowe (1709), Edmond Malone (1778), and Karl Elze (1874); however, Edward Capell (1779), as well as most nineteenth-century critics—including August Wilhelm Schlegel (1808), William Hazlitt (1817), Hermann Ulrici (1839), and H. N. Hudson (1872)—regard Shakespeare's treatment of King Henry as realistic.]*

[*King Henry VIII*] might be properly called the Fall of Cardinal *Wolsey,* if the Action had closed with the Marriage of the King to *Anna Bullen.* . . .

[But] the Action could not be considered as one and entire, while Queen *Catharine*'s Sufferings make so large a Part of it, and which, from the Dignity of her Character, and the great and sudden Reverse of her Fortune, cannot, with any Propriety, form only a subordinate Incident in a Play, whose Subject is the Fall of a much less considerable Person than herself. (p. 225)

The Fate of this Queen, or that of Cardinal *Wolsey,* each singly afforded a Subject for Tragedy. *Shakespear,* by blending them in the same Piece, has destroyed the Unity of his Fable, divided our Attention between them; and, by adding many other inconnected Incidents, all foreign to his Design, has given us an irregular historical Drama, instead of a finished Tragedy. (p. 226)

Tho' the Character of King *Henry* is drawn after [the historian *Holinshed*], yet *Shakespear* has placed it in the most advantagious Light, in this Play he represents him as greatly displeased with the Grievances of his Subjects and ordering them to be relieved, tender and obliging to his Queen, grateful to the Cardinal, and in the Case of *Cranmer,* capable of distinguishing and rewarding true Merit. If, in the latter Part of the Play, he endeavours to cast the disagreeable Parts of this Prince's Character as much into Shade as possible, it is not to be wondered at. *Shakespear* wrote in the Reign of Queen *Elizabeth,* a Princess who inherited more of the Ambition of her Father *Henry,* than of the Tenderness and Delicacy of her Mother *Anne Bullen:* And however sensible she might be of the Injuries her Mother endur'd would not have suffered her Father's Character to have been drawn in the worst Colours, either by an Historian or a Poet. *Shakespear* has exerted an equal degree of Complaisance towards Queen *Elizabeth* by the amiable Lights he shews her Mother in, in this Play. . . . (pp. 229-30)

[*Charlotte Lennox*], "The Life and Death of 'King Henry the Eighth'," in her Shakespear Illustrated; or, The Novels and Histories, on Which the Plays of Shakespear Are Founded, *Vol. 3, A. Millar, 1754, pp. 171-230.*

MR. [RICHARD] RODERICK   (essay date 1756?)

[Roderick was the first critic to suggest that two apparently different writing styles are evident in Henry VIII. *The following excerpted essay, believed to have been first published in 1756, is often cited by critics who, like James Spedding (1850) and Karl*

Elze (1874), maintain that the play was a collaboration between Shakespeare and John Fletcher. Roderick, however, did not find another author's hand in Henry VIII. *He concluded that the peculiarities he discovered were deliberate—an idea supported by most twentieth-century scholars—and that any irregularities in the play are due to the alterations of numerous editors.*]

It is very observable, that the measure throughout [*Henry VIII*] has something in it peculiar; which will very soon appear to any one, who reads aloud; though perhaps he will not at first discover wherein it consists. Whether this particularity has been taken notice of by any of the numerous commentators on Shakespear, I know not; though I think it can scarcely escape the notice of any attentive pronouncer. If those, who have published this Author, have taken no notice of it to their readers, the reason may be, that they have chosen to pass-by in silence a matter, which they have not been able to account for. I think, however, 'tis worth a few words.

1. There are in this Play many more verses than in any other, which end with a redundant syllable—such as these:—

Healthful / and e/ver since / a fresh / admi/rer
Of what / I saw / there an / untime/ly a/gue
I was / then pre/sent saw 'em / salute / on horse/back
In their / embrace/ment as / they grew / toge/ther, &c.
[I. i. 3-4, 8-10]

The measure here ends in the syllables—mi—a—horse—ge— and a good reader will by a gentle lowering of the voice, and quickening of the pronunciation, so contract the pairs of syllables—mirer—ague—horseback—gether—as to make them have only the force of one syllable each to a judicious hearer.

This Fact (whatever Shakespear's design was in it), is undoubtedly true; and may be demonstrated to Reason, and proved to Sense; the first by comparing any Number of Lines in this Play, with an equal number in any other Play; by which it will appear, that this Play has very near *two* redundant verses to *one* in any other Play. And, to prove it to Sense: Let any one read aloud an hundred lines in any other Play, and an hundred in This; and, if he perceives not the tone and cadence of his own voice to be involuntarily altered in the latter case from what it was in the former, I would never advise him to give much credit to the information of his ears. (pp. 66-7)

2. Nor is this the only peculiarity of measure in this play. The *Caesurae*, or Pauses of the verse, are full as remarkable. The common Pauses in English verses are upon the 5th or the 6th syllable (the 6th I think most frequently). In this Play a great number of verses have the Pause on the 7th syllable, such as . . . are these:

Which time shall bring to ripeness—she shall be
A pattern to all princes—living with / her.
More covetous of wisdom—and fair vir/tue.
[V. iv. 20, 22, 24]
(p. 67)

3. Lastly, it is very observable in the measure of this Play; that the emphasis, arising from the sense of the verse, very often clashes with the cadence that would naturally result from the metre: *i.e.* syllables that have an emphasis in the sentence upon the account of the *sense* or *meaning* of it, are put in the uneven places of the verse; and are in the scansion made the first syllables of the foot, and consequently short: for the English foot is Iambic.

Take a few instances from the aforesaid speech.

And all that shall succede. Shĕbā was ne/ver.
Than this blĕst sōul shall be: ăll prīncely gra/ces.
Her foes shăke, līke a field of beaten corn.
[V. iv. 23, 25, 31]

What Shakespear intended by all this I fairly own myself ignorant; but that all these peculiarities were done by him advertently, and not by chance, is, I think, as plain to all sense; as that Virgil intended to write Metre, and not Prose, in his Aeneid.

If, then, Shakespear appears to have been careful about measure, what becomes of that heap of emendations founded upon the presumption of his being either unknowing or unsolicitous about it? Alterations of this sort ought surely to be made more sparingly than has been done, and never without great harshness indeed seems to require it, or great improvement in the sentiment is obtained by it. (p. 68)

Mr. [Richard] Roderick, ''Appendix: On the Metre of 'Henry VIII','' in The New Shakspere Society's Transactions, *No. 1, 1874, pp. 66-8.*

ARTHUR MURPHY   (essay date 1757)

[*Like Nicholas Rowe (1709), Murphy regards Shakespeare as a natural genius whose transgressions of the Neoclassical rules for correct drama are compensated for by the beauty of his work. In the following excerpt on* Henry VIII, *first published in the* London Chronicle *on February 17, 1757, he praises Shakespeare for his ability to adapt his source material and create characters both life-like and original.*]

In treating Facts so well ascertained, and Characters in general so well understood, Shakespeare's Invention was fettered [in writing *Harry the Eighth*], and he could not make any considerable Departure from authenticated Tradition. However, he seems upon most Occasions, as has been remarked of a celebrated French Poet, to create the Thoughts of others: Every Thing comes from him with an Air of Originality. When we once forgive him the Violation of all the Rules of the Drama we must allow that he greatly compensates for this want of Regularity by very striking Beauties. The Incidents in *Harry the Eighth* are very interesting. The Death of the Duke of Buckingham, the Divorce of Queen Catharine, the Wedding of Anne Bullen, and the Fall of Woolsey are important Events, which cannot fail to attract our Attention. The Character of the King is set off in such a Glow of Colouring that though the Poet has faithfully taken it from Holinshed it seems a Personage of his own Invention.

The haughty Churchman is likewise admirably drawn. . . . A well imitated sacerdotal Pride appears in every Cast of his Countenance and in his whole Manner; his subtlety, his unfeeling Stiffness, and a certain mean Kind of Craft are preserved amidst all his Grandeur. The Dejection of Spirits which takes Possession of him afterwards has still a Sort of fallen Dignity. . . . (pp. 278-79)

Arthur Murphy, in an extract from Shakespeare, the Critical Heritage: 1753-1765, Vol. 4, *edited by Brian Vickers, Routledge & Kegan Paul, 1976, pp. 278-79.*

SAMUEL JOHNSON (essay date 1765)

[Johnson has long held an important place in the history of Shakespearean criticism. He is considered the foremost representative of moderate English Neoclassicism and is credited by some literary historians with freeing Shakespeare from the strictures of the three unities valued by strict Neoclassicists: that dramas should have a single setting, take place in less than twenty-four hours, and have a causally connected plot. More recent scholars portray him as a critic who was able to synthesize existing critical theory rather than as an innovative theoretician. Johnson was a master of Augustan prose style and a personality who dominated the literary world of his epoch. The following excerpt comes from Johnson's editorial notes to Henry VIII *included in his 1765 edition of Shakespeare's plays. In it he argues that only the pageantry of* Henry VIII *and the tragedy of Katharine contribute to the play's success. His appreciation of the pageantry opposes the view of Sir Henry Wotton (1613), who regarded the pomp as overdone, but supports that of Samuel Pepys (1664). Johnson's claim that Shakespeare's genius goes "in and out" with the character of Katharine was a popular opinion in the eighteenth century, but one which drew considerable attack from William Hazlitt (1817) and later commentators. Also, Johnson's suggestion that Ben Jonson wrote both the prologue and epilogue to* Henry VIII *was among the earliest speculation concerning the authorship of the play. The question of whether Shakespeare was the sole author of* Henry VIII *or whether he collaborated with another dramatist has also been discussed by Edmond Malone (1778), Charles Knight (1843), James Spedding (1850), G. G. Gervinus (1863), Karl Elze (1874), Algernon Charles Swinburne (1880), E. K. Chambers (1908), Peter Alexander (1931), G. Wilson Knight (1947), and Robert Ornstein (1972).]*

> To rank our chosen truth with such a show
> As fool and fight is, besides forfeiting
> Our own brains   [Prologue. 18-20]

This is not the only passage in which Shakespeare has discovered his conviction of the impropriety of battles represented on the stage. He knew that five or six men with swords give a very unsatisfactory idea of an army, and therefore, without much care to excuse his former practice, he allows that a theatrical fight would destroy all "opinion" of "truth," and "leave" him "never an understanding friend." . . . Yet I know not whether the coronation shewn in this play may not be liable to all that can be objected against a battle. (p. 633)

> BUCKINGHAM. A beggar's book
> Out-worths a noble's blood.
>
>   [I. i. 122-23]

That is, the literary qualifications of a bookish beggar are more prized than the high descent of hereditary greatness. This is a contemptuous exclamation very naturally put into the mouth of one of the antient, unlettered, martial nobility. (p. 637)

> BUCKINGHAM. Ye few, that lov'd me,
> And dare to be bold to weep for Buckingham,
> His noble friends and fellows, whom to leave
> Is only bitter to him, only dying,
> Go with me, like good angels, to my end:
> And as the long divorce of steel falls on me,
> Make of your prayers one sweet sacrifice,
> And lift my soul to heav'n.—Lead on, o'God's name.
>
>   [II. i. 71-8]

These lines are remarkably tender and pathetick. (p. 642)

> QUEEN CATHARINE. The more shame for you;
> holy men I thought you,
> Upon my soul, two rev'rend cardinal virtues,
> But cardinal sins, and hollow hearts, I fear you.
>
>   [III. i. 102-04]

If I mistake you, it is by your fault, not mine; for I thought you good. The distress of Catharine might have kept her from the quibble to which she is irresistibly tempted by the word "cardinal." (p. 649)

> [Stage direction] Changes to Kimbolton. Enter
> Catharine Dowager, sick, led between Griffith,
> her gentleman usher, and Patience her woman.
>
>   [IV. ii. 1]

This scene is above any other part of Shakespeare's tragedies, and perhaps above any scene of any other poet, tender and pathetick, without gods, or furies, or poisons, or precipices, without the help of romantick circumstances, without improbable sallies of poetical lamentation, and without any throes of tumultuous misery. (p. 653)

> CRANMER. God shall be truly known, and those about
>   her
> From her shall read the perfect ways of honour,
> And claim by those their greatness, not by blood.
> Nor shall this peace sleep with her; but as when
> The bird of wonder dies, the maiden Phoenix,
> Her ashes new-create another heir,
> As great in admiration as herself;
> So shall she leave her blessedness to one,
> When heav'n shall call her from this cloud of
>   darkness,
> Who from the sacred ashes of her honour
> Shall star-like rise, as great in fame as she was,
> And so stand fix'd. Peace, Plenty, Love, Truth,
>   Terror,
> That were the servants to this chosen infant,
> Shall then be his, and like a vine grown to him;
> Where-ever the bright sun of heav'n shall shine,
> His honour and the greatness of his name
> Shall be, and make new nations. He shall flourish,
> And, like a mountain cedar, reach his branches
> To all the plains about him: childrens' children
> Shall see this, and bless heav'n.
> KING. Thou speakest wonders.
> CRANMER. She shall be, to the happiness of England,
> An aged Princess; many days shall see her,
> And yet no day without a deed to crown it.
> 'Would, I had known no more! but she must die,
> She must, the Saints must have her; yet a Virgin,
> A most unspotted lily she shall pass
> To th' ground, and all the world shall mourn her.
>
>   [V. iv. 36-62]

These lines, to the interruption by the King, seem to have been inserted at some revisal of the play after the accession of King James. If the passage, included in crotchets, be left out, the speech of Cranmer proceeds in a regular tenour of prediction and continuity of sentiments; but by the interposition of the new lines, he first celebrates Elizabeth's successor, and then wishes he did not know that she was to die; first rejoices at the consequence, and then laments the cause. Our authour was at once politick and idle; he resolved to flatter James, but neglected to reduce the whole speech to propriety, or perhaps intended that the lines inserted should be spoken in the action, and omitted in the publication, if any publication ever was in his thoughts. Mr. Theobald has made the same observation.

The play of *Henry the Eighth* is one of those which still keeps possession of the stage, by the splendour of its pageantry. The coronation about forty years ago drew the people together in multitudes for a great part of the winter. Yet pomp is not the only merit of this play. The meek sorrows and virtuous distress of Catherine have furnished some scenes which may be justly numbered among the greatest efforts of tragedy. But the genius of Shakespeare comes in and goes out with Catherine. Every other part may be easily conceived, and easily written.

EPILOGUE.

Though it is very difficult to decide whether short pieces be genuine or spurious, yet I cannot restrain myself from expressing my suspicion that neither the prologue nor epilogue to this play is the work of Shakespeare. . . . It appears to me very likely that they were supplied by the friendship or officiousness of Jonson, whose manner they will be perhaps found exactly to resemble. There is yet another supposition possible: the prologue and epilogue may have been written after Shakespeare's departure from the stage, upon some accidental revisal of the play, and there will then be reason for imagining that the writer, whoever he was, intended no great kindness to him, this play being recommended by a subtle and covert censure of his other works. There is in Shakespeare so much of "fool and fight,"

    the fellow
In a long motley coat, guarded with yellow,
                              [Prologue. 15-16]

appears so often in his drama, that I think it not very likely that he would have animadverted so severely on himself. All this, however, must be received as very dubious, since we know not the exact date of this or the other plays, and cannot tell how our authour might have changed his practice or opinions.

The historical dramas are now concluded, of which the two parts of *Henry the Fourth,* and *Henry the Fifth,* are among the happiest of our authour's compositions; and *King John, Richard the Third,* and *Henry the Eighth,* deservedly stand in the second class. (pp. 656-58)

> *Samuel Johnson, in an extract from "Notes on Shakespeare's Plays: 'Henry VIII',"* in his The Yale Edition of the Works of Samuel Johnson: Johnson on Shakespeare, Vol. VIII, *edited by Arthur Sherbo, Yale University Press, 1968, pp. 633-58.*

MRS. [ELIZABETH] GRIFFITH (essay date 1775)

[*Griffith exemplifies the seventeenth- and eighteenth-century preoccupation with searching through Shakespeare's plays for set speeches and passages that could be read out of dramatic context for their own sake. Griffith, however, avoided the more usual practice of collecting and commenting on poetic "beauties" and concentrated instead on the "moral" presented in the text. In the following excerpt, first published in* The Morality of Shakespeare's Drama Illustrated *in 1775, Griffith comments on the tragedies of Katharine and Wolsey. She argues that the former is meant to arouse our sympathy, whereas the latter is supposed to stir our forgiveness for a repentant sinner.*]

As Cardinal Wolsey stands a distinguished character in history, having raised himself from the meanest origin to the highest pitch of power, consideration, and station, that a subject could well arrive at, by the sole advantages of learning and natural endowments; and whose end was unfortunate, through vanity, insolence, and the unstable favour of princes; there may be an useful lesson deduced from every circumstance of his life, respecting either his rise, grandeur, or decline.

In a dialogue between Buckingham and Norfolk, in this Scene, the former speaking of his vanity and presumption, with that contempt which persons of *noble families and hereditary fortunes* are sometimes too apt to express towards men *whose whole worth is centered in themselves,* the latter engages in his defence, upon a very just and liberal argument.

> *Norfolk.* Yet, surely, Sir,
>   There's in him stuff that puts him to these ends;
>   For not being propt by ancestry, whose grace
>   Chalks successors their way; nor called upon
>   For high feats done to the crown; neither allied
>   To eminent assistants; but spider-like
>   Out of his self-drawing web—This gives us note,
>   The force of his own merit makes his way;
>   A gift that Heaven gives to him, which buys
>   A place next to the king.   [I. i. 57-66]
>   (p. 325)

In the continuation of this dialogue, the impatient spirit of Buckingham is finely contrasted with the calm temper of Norfolk, who illustrates his documents of prudence to him, with equal philosophy and poesy. (p. 326)

The character of Queen Catharine is finely drawn in this Play. A becoming demeanour is preserved throughout every situation and circumstance she is placed in. She discovers that dignity and spirit which become the wife and daughter of a king, shews the duty and obedience which a husband and a sovereign have a right to claim, and speaks, on her own part, with such a noble confidence, as injured innocence may fully warrant. One can never be too much assured, in a just cause, either of their own, or of others; for whoever defends the rights of the oppressed, fights under the banner of Providence. (pp. 331-32)

[Wolsey, in his disgrace,] presents us with a second object of compassion, which though it interests us after a different manner from the former [Catharine], as neither being so innocent, nor suffering so unjustly; yet, shall I hazard the expression? affects us almost as much. We do not, indeed, feel our minds impressed with such a tender sensibility towards the latter, as the first; but, for the honour and dignity of human nature, let me say, that our commiseration, in the second case, arises from principles of a nobler kind; from our forgiveness of the penitent, and our compassion for his misfortunes, softened still more by our sorrow for his guilt: so that, upon the whole, the generosity of our sentiment, in one instance, nearly equals the sympathy of it, in the other.

The true supputation of the precariousness and instability of all worldly happiness and greatness, with the fit temper and resignation to bear their loss, are most pathetically and poetically set forth, in . . . [this] beautiful and affecting scene. (p. 340)

> *Mrs. [Elizabeth] Griffith, "'Henry the Eighth',"* in her The Morality of Shakespeare's Drama Illustrated, *1775. Reprint by Frank Cass & Co. Ltd., 1971, pp. 325-47.*

EDMOND MALONE (essay date 1778)

[*An eighteenth-century Irish literary scholar and editor, Malone was the first critic to establish a chronology of Shakespeare's plays. He was also the first scholar to prepare a critical edition of Shakespeare's Sonnets and the first to write a comprehensive history of the English stage based on extensive research into original sources. As the major Shakespearean editor of the eigh-*

teenth century, Malone collaborated with George Steevens on Steevens's second and third editions of Shakespeare's plays and issued his own edition in 1790. His importance resides not so much in textual emendation as in his unrivaled knowledge of primary sources. The following excerpt is taken from Malone's Attempt to Ascertain the Order in Which the Plays of Shakespeare Were Written, *first published in Steevens's second edition of Shakespeare's plays in 1778. In it he claims that the majority of* Henry VIII *was written in 1602 or 1603, and that only the prologue, epilogue, and the portions of Cranmer's prophecy that deal with America and James I were added later. In a portion of the essay not included here, Malone agrees with Samuel Johnson (1765) in suggesting Ben Jonson as the author who later revised the text. For more commentary on the authorship question in* Henry VIII, *see the excerpts by Charles Knight (1843), James Spedding (1850), G. G. Gervinus (1863), Karl Elze (1874), Algernon Charles Swinburne (1880), E. K. Chambers (1908), Peter Alexander (1931), G. Wilson Knight (1947), and Robert Ornstein (1972).]*

[*King Henry VIII*] was probably written, as Dr. Johnson and Mr. Steevens observe, partly before the death of Queen Elizabeth, which happened on the 24th of March, 1602-3. The elogium on King James, which is blended with the panegyrick on Elizabeth, in the last scene, was evidently a subsequent insertion, after the accession of the Scottish monarch to the

Act III. Scene ii. Norfolk, Suffolk, Surrey, Henry VIII, and Wolsey. Frontispiece to the Rowe edition (1709). By permission of the Folger Shakespeare Library.

throne: for Shakspeare was too well acquainted with courts, to compliment, in the life-time of Queen Elizabeth, her presumptive successor, of whom history informs us she was not a little jealous. That the prediction concerning King James was added after the death of the Queen, is still more clearly evinced, as Dr. Johnson has remarked, by the aukward manner in which it is connected with the foregoing and subsequent lines.

The following lines in that prediction may serve to ascertain the time when the compliment was introduced:

> Wherever the bright sun of heaven shall shine,
> His honour and the greatness of his name
> Shall be, and make new nations.   [V. iv. 50-2]

Though Virginia was discovered in 1584, the first colony sent out went there in 1606. In that year the king granted two letters patent for planting that country, one to the city of London, the other to the cities of Bristol, Exeter, and Plymouth. . . . In 1606 also a scheme was adopted for the plantation of Ulster in Ireland. I suspect, therefore, that the panegyrick on the king was introduced either in that year, or in 1612, when a lottery was granted expressly for the establishment of English Colonies in Virginia.

It may be objected, that if this play was written after the accession of King James, the author could not introduce a panegyrick on him, without making Queen Elizabeth the vehicle of it, she being the object immediately presented to the audience in the last Act of *King Henry VIII.:* and that, therefore, the praises so profusely lavished on her, do *not* prove this play to have been written in her life-time; on the contrary, that the concluding lines of her character seem to imply that she was dead, when it was composed. The objection certainly has weight; but, I apprehend, the following observations afford a sufficient answer to it.

1. It is more likely that Shakspeare should have written a play, the chief subject of which is, the disgrace of Queen Catharine, the aggrandizement of Anne Boleyn, and the birth of her daughter, in the life-time of that daughter, than after her death: at a time when the subject must have been highly pleasing at court, rather than at a period when it must have been less interesting.

Queen Catharine, it is true, is represented as an amiable character, but still she is *eclipsed;* and the greater her merit, the higher was the compliment to the mother of Elizabeth, to whose superior beauty she was obliged to give way.

2. If *King Henry VIII.* had been written in the time of King James I. the author, instead of expatiating so largely in the last scene, in praise of the Queen, which he could not think would be acceptable to her successor, who hated her memory, would probably have made him the principal figure in the prophecy, and thrown her into the back-ground as much as possible.

3. Were James I. Shakspeare's chief object in the original construction of the last Act of this play, he would probably have given a very short character of Elizabeth, and have *dwelt* on that of James, with whose praise he would have *concluded,* in order to make the stronger impression on the audience, instead of returning again to Queen Elizabeth, in a very aukward and abrupt manner, after her character seemed to be quite finished: an aukwardness that can only be accounted for, by supposing the panegyrick on King James an after-production.

4. If the Queen had been dead when our author began to write this play, he would have been acquainted with the particular circumstances attending her death, the situation of the kingdom

at that time, and of foreign states, &c. and as Archbishop Cranmer is supposed to have had the gift of prophecy, Shakspeare, probably, would have made him mention some of those circumstances. Whereas the prediction, as it stands at present, is quite general, and such as might, without any hazard of error, have been pronounced in the life-time of her Majesty; for the principal facts that it foretells, are, that she should die aged, and a virgin. Of the former, supposing this prediction to have been written in 1602, the author was sufficiently secure; for she was then near seventy years old. The latter may perhaps be thought too delicate a subject, to have been mentioned while she was yet living. . . . [But] if Shakspeare knew, as probably most people at that time did, that she became very solicitous about the reputation of virginity, when her title to it was at least equivocal, this would be an additional inducement to him to compliment her on that head.

5. Granting that the *latter part* of the panegyrick on Elizabeth implies that she was dead when it was composed, it would not prove that this play was written in the time of King James; for *these latter lines* in praise of the Queen, as well as the whole of the compliment to the King, might have been added after his accession to the throne, in order to bring the speaker back to the object immediately before him, the infant Elizabeth. . . . I do not, however, see any *necessity* for this supposition; as there is nothing, in my apprehension, contained in *any* of the lines in praise of the Queen, inconsistent with the notion of the *whole* of the panegyrick on her having been composed in her life-time.

In further confirmation of what has been here advanced to show that this play was partly written while Queen Elizabeth was yet alive, it may be observed (to use the words of an anonymous writer), that ''Shakspeare has cast the disagreeable parts of her *father's* character as much into shade as possible; that he has represented him as greatly displeased with the grievances of his subjects, and ordering them to be relieved; tender and obliging [in the early part of the play] to his queen, grateful to the cardinal, and in the case of Cranmer, capable of distinguishing and rewarding true merit'' [see the excerpt above by Charlotte Lennox, 1754].—''He has exerted (adds the same author) an equal degree of complaisance, by the amiable lights in which he has shown the *mother* of Elizabeth. Anne Bullen is represented as affected with the most tender concern for the sufferings of her mistress, queen Catharine; receiving the honour the king confers on her, by making her marchioness of Pembroke, with a graceful humility; and more anxious to conceal her advancement from the queen, lest it should aggravate her sorrows, than solicitous to penetrate into the meaning of so extraordinary a favour, or of indulging herself in the flattering prospect of future royalty.'' (pp. 388-93)

Our author had produced so many plays in the preceding years, that it is not likely that *King Henry VIII.* was written *before* 1603. It might perhaps with equal propriety be ascribed to 1602, and it is not easy to determine in which of those years it was composed; but it is extremely probable that it was written in one of them. (p. 394)

The Globe play-house, we are told by the continuator of Stowe's *Chronicle,* was burnt down, on St. Peter's day, in the year 1613, while the play of *King Henry VIII.* was exhibiting. Sir Henry Wotton . . . says, in one of his letters [see excerpt above, 1613], that this accident happened during the exhibition of a *new* play, called *All is True;* which, however, appears both from Sir Henry's minute description of the piece, and from the account given by Stowe's continuator, to have been our au-

thor's play of *King Henry VIII.* If indeed Sir H. Wotton was accurate in calling it a *new* play, all the foregoing reasoning on this subject would be at once overthrown: and this piece, instead of being ascribed to 1603, should have been placed ten years later. But I strongly suspect that the only novelty attending this play, in the year 1613, was its title, decorations, and perhaps the prologue and epilogue. The Elector Palatine was in London in that year; and it appears from the MS. register of Lord Harrington, treasurer of the chambers to King James I. that many of our author's plays were then exhibited for the entertainment of him and the princess Elizabeth. . . . Princes are fond of opportunities to display their magnificence before strangers of distinction; and James, who on his arrival here must have been dazzled by a splendour foreign to the poverty of his native kingdom, might have been peculiarly ambitious to exhibit before his son-in-law the mimick pomp of an English coronation. *King Henry VIII.* therefore, after having lain by for some years unacted, on account of the costliness of the exhibition, might have been revived in 1613, under the title of *All is True,* with new decorations, and a new prologue and epilogue. . . . [The] prologue has two or three direct references to this title; a circumstance which authorizes us to conclude, almost with certainty, that it was an occasional production, written some years after the composition of the play. *King Henry VIII.* not being then printed, the fallacy of calling it a new play on its revival was not easily detected. (pp. 395-96)

The play, thus revived and new-named, was probably called in the bills of that time, a *new* play; which might have led Sir Henry Wotton to describe it as such. And thus his account may be reconciled with that of the other contemporary writers, as well as with those arguments which have been here urged in support of the early date of *King Henry VIII.* Every thing has been fully stated on each side of the question. The reader must judge. (p. 400)

Edmond Malone, ''Mr. Malone's Life of Shakspeare, Comprehending an Essay on the Chronological Order of His Plays,'' in The Plays and Poems of William Shakspeare, Vol. II *by William Shakespeare, edited by James Boswell, AMS Press, Inc., 1966, pp. 1-528.*

EDWARD CAPELL   (essay date 1779)

[*Capell was the first Shakespearean editor to employ the practice of using good quarto texts as the basis for his edition of the plays, published between 1768 and 1783. In the following excerpt, taken from the first volume of his* Notes and Various Readings to Shakespeare, *published in 1779, he argues that the character of Anne Boleyn is neither naive nor innocent. Although Anna Brownell Jameson (1833) and G. G. Gervinus (1863) also stress this point, most commentators on* Henry VIII *describe Anne as a typically romantic heroine. Like August Wilhelm Schlegel (1808), William Hazlitt (1817), Hermann Ulrici (1839), and H. N. Hudson (1872), Capell considers Shakespeare's portrait of King Henry ''a finish'd one.''*]

[The words of the bawdy toast by Lord Sands in I.iv. 46 ff. of *Henry VIII*] are in character, and so is the health that follows: and in [Lady Anne's] reply to it (however we may condemn it as gross at this time of day) the Poet shews his great insight; for in this addiction to levities lay her character, or that which distinguish'd her, and she bled for them shortly. He gives us only this *trait* of it, his purpose leading him contrary; but 'tis a strong one, and may serve instead of a million. The King's portrait has always been acknowledg'd a finish'd one; and all who rise from the reading of it, rise with a full persuasion that they have seen the identical Henry lay'd on paper. One minute part of it, is a certain coarseness of diction, that has its dignity too; of this the concluding words of this act exhibit a specimen, and there is another before it in his reply to the Chamberlain. (p. 222)

> *Edward Capell, in an extract from* Shakespeare, the Critical Heritage: 1774-1801, Vol. 6, *edited by Brian Vickers, Routledge & Kegan Paul, 1981, pp. 218-71.*

AUGUST WILHELM SCHLEGEL   (lecture date 1808)

[A prominent German Romantic critic, Schlegel holds a key place in the history of Shakespeare's reputation in European criticism. His translations of thirteen of the plays are still considered the best German editions of Shakespeare. Schlegel was also a leading spokesman for the Romantic movement, which permanently overthrew the Neoclassical contention that Shakespeare was a child of nature whose plays lacked artistic form. In the following excerpt, taken from a lecture delivered in 1808, Schlegel compares Henry VIII *and* King John, *calling the latter the prologue and the former the epilogue to Shakespeare's ten-play epic dramatization of English history. The idea that Shakespeare envisioned his ten history plays as one sustained dramatic portrait of English history, with* Henry VIII *serving as the epilogue, has also been suggested by Hermann Ulrici (1839). Schlegel also considers Shakespeare's treatment of King Henry to be more realistic and less idealized than such earlier critics as Nicholas Rowe (1709), Charlotte Lennox (1754), and Edmond Malone (1778) contended. In a footnote to his essay, Schlegel asserts that* Henry VIII *was written during the reign of Queen Elizabeth and that it was revived years later by Ben Jonson, who contributed the prologue and epilogue and inserted material on James I in Cranmer's final speech. For a similar interpretation of the authorship question in* Henry VIII, *see the excerpts by Samuel Johnson (1765) and Edmond Malone (1778). Other critics who have examined the authorship of* Henry VIII *include Charles Knight (1843), James Spedding (1850), G. G. Gervinus (1863), Karl Elze (1874), Algernon Charles Swinburne (1880), E. K. Chambers (1908), Peter Alexander (1931), G. Wilson Knight (1947), and Robert Ornstein (1972).]*

The dramas derived from the English history, ten in number, form one of the most valuable of Shakspeare's works, and partly the fruit of his maturest age. I say advisedly *one* of his works, for the poet evidently intended them to form one great whole. It is, as it were, an historical heroic poem in the dramatic form, of which the separate plays constitute the rhapsodies. The principal features of the events are exhibited with such fidelity; their causes, and even their secret springs, are placed in such a clear light, that we may attain from them a knowledge of history in all its truth, while the living picture makes an impression on the imagination which can never be effaced. But this series of dramas is intended as the vehicle of a much higher and much more general instruction; it furnishes examples of the political course of the world, applicable to all times. This mirror of kings should be the manual of young princes; from it they may learn the intrinsic dignity of their hereditary vocation, but they will also learn from it the difficulties of their situation, the dangers of usurpation, the inevitable fall of tyranny, which buries itself under its attempts to obtain a firmer foundation; lastly, the ruinous consequences of the weaknesses, errors, and crimes of kings, for whole nations, and many subsequent generations. Eight of these plays, from *Richard the Second* to *Richard the Third*, are linked together in an uninterrupted succession, and embrace a most eventful period of

nearly a century of English history. The events portrayed in them not only follow one another, but they are linked together in the closest and most exact connexion; and the cycle of revolts, parties, civil and foreign wars, which began with the deposition of Richard II., first ends with the accession of Henry VII. to the throne. (pp. 419-20)

[Two] historical plays taken from the English history are chronologically separate from this series: King John reigned nearly two centuries before Richard II., and between Richard III. and Henry VIII. comes the long reign of Henry VII., which Shakspeare justly passed over as unsusceptible of dramatic interest. However, these two plays may in some measure be considered as the Prologue and the Epilogue to the other eight. In *King John,* all the political and national motives which play so great a part in the following pieces are already indicated: wars and treaties with France; a usurpation, and the tyrannical actions which it draws after it; the influence of the clergy, the factions of the nobles. *Henry the Eighth* again shows us the transition to another age; the policy of modern Europe, a refined courtlife under a voluptuous monarch, the dangerous situation of favourites, who, after having assisted in effecting the fall of others, are themselves precipitated from power; in a word, despotism under a milder form, but not less unjust and cruel. By the prophecies on the birth of Elizabeth, Shakspeare has in some degree brought his great poem on English history down to his own time, as far at least as such recent events could be yet handled with security. He composed probably the two plays of *King John* and *Henry the Eighth* at a later period, as an addition to the others. (pp. 422-23)

Shakspeare was as profound a historian as a poet; when we compare his *Henry the Eighth* with the preceding pieces, we see distinctly that the English nation during the long, peaceable, and economical reign of Henry VII., whether from the exhaustion which was the fruit of the civil wars, or from more general European influences, had made a sudden transition from the powerful confusion of the middle age, to the regular tameness of modern times. *Henry the Eighth* has, therefore, somewhat of a prosaic appearance; for Shakspeare, artist-like, adapted himself always to the quality of his materials. If others of his works, both in elevation of fancy and in energy of pathos and character, tower far above this, we have here on the other hand occasion to admire his nice powers of discrimination and his perfect knowledge of courts and the world. What tact was requisite to represent before the eyes of the queen subjects of such a delicate nature, and in which she was personally so nearly concerned, without doing violence to the truth!

> [Schlegel adds in a footnote:] It is quite clear that *Henry the Eighth* was written while Elizabeth was still alive. We know that Ben Jonson, in the reign of King James brought the piece again on the stage with additional pomp, and took the liberty of making several changes and additions. Without doubt, the prophecy respecting James the First is due to Ben Jonson: it would only have displeased Elizabeth, and is so ill introduced that we at once recognize in it a foreign interpolation.

He has unmasked the tyrannical king, and to the intelligent observer exhibited him such as he was actually: haughty and obstinate, voluptuous and unfeeling, extravagant in conferring favours, and revengeful under the pretext of justice; and yet the picture is so dexterously handled that a daughter might take it for favourable. The legitimacy of Elizabeth's birth depended on the invalidity of Henry's first marriage, and Shakspeare has placed the proceedings respecting his separation from Catharine of Arragon in a very doubtful light. We see clearly that Henry's scruples of conscience are no other than the beauty of Anne Boleyn. Catharine is, properly speaking, the heroine of the piece; she excites the warmest sympathy by her virtues, her defenceless misery, her mild but firm opposition, and her dignified resignation. After her, the fall of Cardinal Wolsey constitutes the principal part of the business. Henry's whole reign was not adapted for dramatic poetry. It would have merely been a repetition of the same scenes: the repudiation, or the execution of his wives, and the disgrace of his most estimable ministers, which was usually soon followed by death. Of all that distinguished Henry's life Shakspeare has given us sufficient specimens. But as, properly speaking, there is no division in the history where he breaks off, we must excuse him if he gives us a flattering compliment of the great Elizabeth for a fortunate catastrophe. The piece ends with the general joy at the birth of that princess, and with prophecies of the happiness which she was afterwards to enjoy or to diffuse. It was only by such a turn that the hazardous freedom of thought in the rest of the composition could have passed with impunity: Shakspeare was not certainly himself deceived respecting this theatrical delusion. The true conclusion is the death of Catharine, which under a feeling of this kind, he has placed earlier than was comfortable to history. (pp. 439-40)

August Wilhelm Schlegel, "Criticisms on Shakspeare's Historical Dramas," in his A Course of Lectures on Dramatic Art and Literature, *edited by Rev. A.J.W. Morrison, translated by John Black, revised edition, Henry G. Bohn, 1846, pp. 414-45.*

WILLIAM HAZLITT   (essay date 1817)

[*Hazlitt is considered a leading Shakespearean critic of the English Romantic movement. A prolific essayist and critic on a wide range of subjects, Hazlitt remarked in the preface to his* Characters of Shakespear's Plays, *first published in 1817, that he was inspired by the German critic August Wilhelm Schlegel and was determined to supplant what he considered the pernicious influence of Samuel Johnson's Shakespearean criticism. Hazlitt's criticism is typically Romantic in its emphasis on character studies. Unlike his fellow Romantic critic Samuel Taylor Coleridge, Hazlitt was a dramatic critic whose experience of Shakespeare in the theater influenced his interpretations. In his comments on* Henry VIII, *taken from the work mentioned above, Hazlitt calls the portrait of Katharine "the most perfect idealization of matronly dignity, sweetness, and resignation, that can be conceived." Yet, at the same time, he takes direct issue with Samuel Johnson's remark that other than the tragedy of Katharine* Henry VIII *could have been written by anyone (see excerpt above, 1765). Hazlitt regards this interpretation as misguided, pointing to the scenes of Buckingham's execution and Wolsey's fall from grace as other powerful and moving episodes in the play. Also, like Schlegel (1808), Hazlitt considers the vulgarity and arrogance in Shakespeare's portrait of King Henry quite realistic. This view of the king opposes that offered by Nicholas Rowe (1709), Charlotte Lennox (1754), Edmond Malone (1778), and Karl Elze (1874), all of whom see in him an incomplete and idealized characterization.*]

[*Henry VIII.*] contains little action or violence of passion, yet it has considerable interest of a more mild and thoughtful cast, and some of the most striking passages in the author's works. The character of Queen Katherine is the most perfect delineation of matronly dignity, sweetness, and resignation, that can be conceived. Her appeals to the protection of the king, her remonstrances to the cardinals, her conversations with her

women, shew a noble and generous spirit accompanied with the utmost gentleness of nature. What can be more affecting than her answer to Campeius and Wolsey, who come to visit her as pretended friends.

> Nay, forsooth, my friends,
> They that must weigh out my afflictions,
> They that my trust must grow to, live not here;
> They are, as all my comforts are, far hence,
> In mine own country, lords.   [III. i. 87-91]

Dr. Johnson observes of this play, that "the meek sorrows and virtuous distress of Katherine have furnished some scenes, which may be justly numbered among the greatest efforts of tragedy. But the genius of Shakespear comes in and goes out with Katherine. Every other part may be easily conceived and easily written." This is easily said; but with all due deference to so great a reputed authority as that of Johnson, it is not true. For instance, the scene of Buckingham led to execution is one of the most affecting and natural in Shakespear, and one to which there is hardly an approach in any other author. Again, the character of Wolsey, the description of his pride and of his fall, are inimitable, and have, besides their gorgeousness of effect, a pathos, which only the genius of Shakespear could lend to the distresses of a proud, bad man, like Wolsey. There is a sort of child-like simplicity in the very helplessness of his situation, arising from the recollection of his past overbearing ambition. After the cutting sarcasms of his enemies on his disgrace, against which he bears up with a spirit conscious of his own superiority, he breaks out into that fine apostrophe—

> Farewell, a long farewell, to all my greatness!
> This is the state of man; to-day he puts forth
> The tender leaves of hope, to-morrow blossoms,
> And bears his blushing honours thick upon him;
> The third day comes a frost, a killing frost;
> And—when he thinks, good easy man, full surely
> His greatness is a ripening—nips his root,
> And then he falls, as I do.   [III. ii. 351-58]
>   (pp. 146-47)

There is in this passage, as well as in the well-known dialogue with Cromwell which follows, something which stretches beyond commonplace; nor is the account which Griffiths gives of Wolsey's death less Shakespearian; and the candour with which Queen Katherine listens to the praise of "him whom of all men while living she hated most" adds the last graceful finishing to her character. (p. 148)

The character of Henry VIII. is drawn with great truth and spirit. It is like a very disagreeable portrait, sketched by the hand of a master. His gross appearance, his blustering demeanour, his vulgarity, his arrogance, his sensuality, his cruelty, his hypocrisy, his want of common decency and common humanity, are marked in strong lines. His traditional peculiarities of expression complete the reality of the picture. The authoritative expletive, "Ha!" with which he intimates his indignation or surprise, has an effect like the first startling sound that breaks from a thunder-cloud. He is of all the monarchs in our history the most disgusting: for he unites in himself all the vices of barbarism and refinement, without their virtues. . . . It has been said of Shakespear—"No maid could live near such a man." It might with as good reason be said— "No king could live near such a man." His eye would have penetrated through the pomp of circumstance and the veil of opinion. As it is, he has represented such persons to the life— his plays are in this respect the glass of history—he has done them the same justice as if he had been a privy counsellor all his life, and in each successive reign. Kings ought never to be seen upon the stage. In the abstract, they are very disagreeable characters: it is only while living that they are "the best of kings." It is their power, their splendour, it is the apprehension of the personal consequences of their favour or their hatred that dazzles the imagination and suspends the judgment of their favourites or their vassals; but death cancels the bond of allegiance and of interest; and seen *as they were,* their power and their pretensions look monstrous and ridiculous. The charge brought against modern philosophy as inimical to loyalty is unjust, because it might as well be brought against other things. No reader of history can be a lover of kings. We have often wondered that Henry VIII. as he is drawn by Shakespear, and as we have seen him represented in all the bloated deformity of mind and person, is not hooted from the English stage. (pp. 148-49)

William Hazlitt, "Henry VIII", in his Characters of Shakespear's Plays & Lectures on the English Poets, Macmillan and Co. Limited, 1903, pp. 146-49.

MRS. [ANNA BROWNELL] JAMESON (essay date 1833)

[*Jameson was a well-known nineteenth-century essayist. Her essays and criticism span the end of the Romantic age and the beginning of the Victorian era of realism and reflect elements from both periods. She is best remembered for her study* Shakespeare's Heroines, *a work which demonstrates both her interest in history and her sympathetic appreciation of Shakespeare's female characters. In the following excerpt, first published in her* Shakespeare's Heroines *in 1833, Jameson calls Katharine the heroine of* Henry VIII *and, along with Wolsey, its center of interest. She considers the distinct attribute of Katharine's character, as presented by Shakespeare, to be her virtue of truth; not only truth to nature or historic fidelity, but "truth as a quality of the soul." Jameson was the first critic to compare Katharine to Hermione of* The Winter's Tale, *a similarity also noted by G. Wilson Knight (1947), R. A. Foakes (1957), and Hugh M. Richmond (1979).*]

[The] action of the play of "Henry VIII." includes events which occurred from the impeachment of the Duke of Buckingham, in 1521, to the death of Katherine in 1536. In making the death of Katherine precede the birth of Queen Elizabeth, Shakspeare has committed an anachronism not only pardonable, but necessary. We must remember that the construction of the play required a happy termination; and that the birth of Elizabeth, before or after the death of Katherine, involved the question of her legitimacy. By this slight deviation from the real course of events, Shakspeare has not perverted historic facts, but merely sacrificed them to a higher principle; and in doing so has not only preserved dramatic propriety and heightened the poetical interest, but has given a strong proof both of his delicacy and his judgment.

If we also call to mind that in this play Katherine is properly the heroine, and exhibited from first to last as the very "Queen of earthly queens;" that the whole interest is thrown round her and Wolsey—the one the injured rival, the other the enemy of Anna Bullen; and that it was written in the reign and for the court of Elizabeth, we shall yet further appreciate the moral greatness of the poet's mind, which disdained to sacrifice justice and the truth of nature to any time-serving expediency. (pp. 293-94)

Katherine of Arragon may rank as the triumph of Shakspeare's genius and his wisdom. There is nothing in the whole range

of poetical fiction in any respect resembling or approaching her; there is nothing comparable, I suppose, but Katherine's own portrait by Holbein, which, equally true to the life, is yet as far inferior as Katherine's person was inferior to her mind. Not only has Shakspeare given us here a delineation as faithful as it is beautiful, of a peculiar modification of character, but he has bequeathed us a precious moral lesson in this proof that virtue alone (by which I mean here the union of truth or conscience with benevolent affection—the one the highest law, the other the purest impulse of the soul)—that such virtue is a sufficient source of the deepest pathos and power without any mixture of foreign or external ornament: for who but Shakspeare would have brought before us a queen and a heroine of tragedy, stripped her of all pomp of place and circumstance, dispensed with all the usual sources of poetical interest, as youth, beauty, grace, fancy, commanding intellect; and without any appeal to our imagination, without any violation of historical truth, or any sacrifices of the other dramatic personages for the sake of effect, could depend on the moral principle alone to touch the very springs of feeling in our bosoms, and melt and elevate our hearts through the purest and holiest impulses of our nature?

The character, when analysed, is, in the first place, distinguished by *truth.* I do not only mean its truth to nature, or its relative truth arising from its historic fidelity and dramatic consistency, but *truth* as a quality of the soul; this is the basis of the character. . . . With this essential truth are combined many other qualities, natural or acquired, all made out with the same uncompromising breadth of execution and fidelity of pencil, united with the utmost delicacy of feeling. For instance, the apparent contradiction arising from the contrast between Katherine's natural disposition and the situation in which she is placed; her lofty Castilian pride and her extreme simplicity of language and deportment; the inflexible resolution with which she asserts her right, and her soft resignation to unkindness and wrong; her warmth of temper breaking through the meekness of a spirit subdued by a deep sense of religion, and a degree of austerity tinging her real benevolence—all these qualities, opposed yet harmonising, has Shakspeare placed before us in a few admirable scenes.

Katherine is at first introduced as pleading before the king in behalf of the commonalty, who had been driven by the extortions of Wolsey into some illegal excesses. In this scene, which is true to history, we have her upright reasoning mind, her steadiness of purpose, her piety and benevolence, placed in a strong light. The unshrinking dignity with which she opposes without descending to brave the cardinal, the stern rebuke addressed to the Duke of Buckingham's surveyor, are finely characteristic; and by thus exhibiting Katherine as invested with all her conjugal rights and influence and royal state, the subsequent situations are rendered more impressive. She is placed in the first instance on such a height in our esteem and reverence, that in the midst of her abandonment and degradation, and the profound pity she afterwards inspires, the first effect remains unimpaired, and she never falls beneath it. (pp. 294-96)

The annotators on Shakspeare have all observed the close resemblance between this fine passage—

> Sir,
> I am about to weep; but thinking that
> We are a queen (or long have dreamed so), certain
> The daughter of a king—my drops of tears
> I'll turn to sparks of fire—   [II. iv. 69-73]

and the speech of Hermione

> I am not prone to weeping as our sex
> Commonly are, the want of which vain dew
> Perchance shall dry your pities; but I have
> That honourable grief lodged here, which burns
> Worse than tears drown.
>
> [*Winter's Tale*, II. i. 108-12]

But these verbal gentlemen do not seem to have felt that the resemblance is merely on the surface, and that the two passages could not possibly change places without a manifest violation of the truth of character. In Hermione it is pride of sex merely; in Katherine it is pride of place and pride of birth. Hermione, though so superbly majestic, is perfectly independent of her regal state; Katherine, though so meekly pious, will neither forget hers nor allow it to be forgotten by others for a moment. Hermione, when deprived of that "crown and comfort of her life," her husband's love, regards all things else with despair and indifference except her feminine honour; Katherine, divorced and abandoned, still with true Spanish pride stands upon respect, and will not bate one atom of her accustomed state—

> . . . . . . Though unqueen'd, yet like
> A Queen, and daughter to a king, inter me!
>
> [IV. ii. 171-72]
> (pp. 300-01)

On the wonderful beauty of Katherine's closing scene we need not dwell, for that requires no illustration. In transferring the sentiments of her [last letter to Henry VIII] to her lips, Shakspeare has given them added grace and pathos and tenderness without injuring their truth and simplicity; the feelings, and almost the manner of expression, are Katherine's own. The severe justice with which she draws the character of Wolsey is extremely characteristic. The benign candour with which she listens to the praise of him "whom living she most hated" is not less so. How beautiful her religious enthusiasm!—the slumber which visits her pillow as she listens to that sad music she called her knell. Her awakening from the vision of celestial joy to find herself still on earth—

> Spirits of peace! where are ye? are ye all gone,
> And leave me here in wretchedness behind ye?
>
> [IV. ii. 83-4]

how unspeakably beautiful! And to consummate all in one final touch of truth and nature, we see that consciousness of her own worth and integrity which had sustained her through all her trials of heart, and that pride of station for which she had contended through long years—which had become more dear by opposition, and by the perseverance with which she had asserted it—remaining the last strong feeling upon her mind to the very last hour of existence—

> When I am dead, good wench,
> Let me be us'd with honour; strew me over
> With maiden-flowers, that all the world may know
> I was a chaste wife to my grave: embalm me,
> Then lay me forth: although unqueen'd, yet like
> A queen, and daughter to a king, inter me.
> I can no more.   [IV. ii. 167-73]

In the Epilogue to this play, it is recommended—

> To the merciful construction of good women,
> For *such a one* we show'd them: [Epilogue. 10-11]

alluding to the character of Queen Katherine. Shakspeare has, in fact, placed before us a queen and a heroine, who in the first place, and above all, is a *good* woman; and I repeat that in doing so, and in trusting for all his effect to truth and virtue, he has given a sublime proof of his genius and his wisdom—for which, among many other obligations, we women remain his debtors. (pp. 308-09)

> *Mrs. [Anna Brownell] Jameson, "Historical Characters: Katherine of Arragon," in her* Shakspeare's Heroines: Characteristics of Women, Moral, Poetical, & Historical, *second edition, George Newnes, Limited, 1897, pp. 288-309.*

HERMANN ULRICI   (essay date 1839)

[*A German scholar, Ulrici was a professor of philosophy and an author of works on Greek poetry and Shakespeare. The following excerpt is from an English translation of his* Über Shakspeares dramatische Kunst, und sein Verhältnis zu Calderon und Göthe, *first published in 1839. This work exemplifies the "philosophical criticism" developed in Germany during the nineteenth century. The immediate sources for Ulrici's critical approach appear to be August Wilhelm Schlegel's conception of the play as an organic, interconnected whole and Georg Wilhelm Friedrich Hegel's view of drama as an embodiment of the conflict of historical forces and ideas. Unlike his fellow German Shakespearean critic G. G. Gervinus, Ulrici sought to develop a specifically Christian aesthetics, but one which, as he carefully points out in the introduction to the work mentioned above, in no way intrudes on "that unity of idea, which preeminently constitutes a work of art a living creation in the world of beauty." Ulrici considers* Henry VIII *one of Shakespeare's final plays and the epilogue to his series of dramas on the history of the English monarchy—an idea originally suggested by August Wilhelm Schlegel (see excerpt above, 1808). Although such later commentators as Charles Knight (1843), Denton J. Snider (1890), G. Wilson Knight (1947), Paul Bertram (1962), and C. B. Purdom (1963) also regard* Henry VIII *as Shakespeare's final history play, covering the same themes and concerns examined in the earlier plays, other critics—including Edgar I. Fripp (1938), R. A. Foakes (1957), Howard Felperin (1966), and Francis A. Yates (1974)—interpret the play as closer to Shakespeare's late romances, particularly in its examination of personal suffering and human spirituality. This conflict over the exact nature of* Henry VIII *is one of the major issues in both nineteenth- and twentieth-century criticism of the play. Ulrici was also one of the first critics to suggest a symbolic correspondence between the divorce proceedings in* Henry VIII *and the religious reformation initiated during King Henry's reign—a point more fully developed by Denton J. Snider (1890). Ulrici concludes his essay by discussing what he regards as the major flaw in* Henry VIII: *its lack of "moral vitality." For Ulrici, the implication that Henry is blessed with a great ruler in his daughter Elizabeth contradicts poetic justice and, more significantly, refutes the manifest justice of God and history. The idea that the prophetic ending of* Henry VIII *contradicts the dramatic action of the play is also discussed by A. A. Parker (1948) and Robert Ornstein (1972); attempts to reconcile this contradiction can be found in the excerpts by Frank Kermode (1947), Paul Bertram (1962), C. B. Purdom (1963), Tom McBride (1977), and Frank Cespedes (1980).*]

If we . . . turn to the conclusion—the epilogue—of the great dramatic cycle of English histories ["Henry the Eighth"], we find ourselves still within the same historical domain [as "Richard the Third"], but having been carried over an interval of thirty years, we come to a new and altered prospect. The prayer for peace with the seventh Henry, offered up at the end of "Richard the Third" has been heard. His long reign sufficed to heal the deep wounds which the civil wars and the tyranny of Richard had inflicted on his country. Its importance in the general history of the world is derived from this fact, and from its forming for England the passage and introduction of it into the new and essentially altered political relations of Europe, which commenced with the sixteenth century. However, it was ill suited for scenic representation, since by its very character it was deficient in dramatic action. It was only episodically, as it had been done in ''Richard the Third,'' that its spirit and influence could be indicated, and poetical considerations therefore appear fully to justify our poet in choosing the reign of *Henry the Eighth* for the close of his dramatic cycle. It is well suited to form the conclusion of it, because it is at the same time the *commencement* of a new era in history.

The monarchial principle had gradually gained strength during the long troubles of the civil wars, and the peaceful reign of the seventh Henry now appears to be approaching its culmination. The great estates of the kingdom—nobility, clergy, and commons, are now accustomed to obedience; and the arbitrary power of the sovereign is apparently unlimited. The poet has indicated this state of things in several significant scenes (Act V. Sc. 2 and 3, for instance), which simply on this account could ill be spared. The power of the monarch manifests itself outwardly in the splendour and luxury of his court, which the higher nobles are stimulated to emulate; the attempt of the latter to maintain a strong political position, independently of, and in opposition to, the throne, has sunk into a mere competition for the honours of the court, or to rivalry with it in riches and magnificence. This change in the character of the age is ably pointed out in the first introductory scenes. The Church, after obtaining under John the claims which she had so zealously asserted and so vigorously prosecuted, was now reaping the fruits of her unprincipled efforts. Her just influence, which is internal and spiritual, is broken—the power of the crown has outgrown the ecclesiastical. She no longer dares to put forward her former arrogant pretensions; it is only by intrigue, by double dealing, and double speaking, that she can hope to establish them. This truth is most strikingly illustrated by the relation in which Wolsey stands to the King and the State. The middle ages, with their knightly combats, their impetuous deeds, and the strongly marked objective shape which they gave to all classes, are fast sinking in importance. The general life of man has become more inward and more spiritual, while the theological disputations on Henry's divorce seem to intimate the approaching great reformation of religion, which, by gradually dissolving the objective development which the middle ages had given to mind and intellect, was destined to establish more securely the rights of subjectivity. Accordingly, in his representation of the general state of things, in his characterization of the age, and his delineation of its peculiar interests and tendencies, the poet has preserved the truth of history, and has exhibited the same skill here as elsewhere in unveiling its inmost core.

But is this the case with details also? In spite of the long defence of the poet, by F. Horn and others, I feel compelled to answer this question in the *negative*. Henry's character, it is true, is by no means spared: he appears throughout the same capricious, ill-humoured, selfish, and heartless tyrant, the same creature of his passions and favourites, that he really was. That Shakspeare does not *expressly* describe him in this light, but rather allows him to characterize himself by his own acts and deeds, while he purposely and wittingly puts his best traits into the foreground of the picture, is only what we should look for from a national poet who lived in the reign of Henry's daughter—the all-beloved Elizabeth. That, further, he has not painted Anne Boleyn in her true colours, who, after rejecting Henry's addresses, nevertheless lived with him for three years in open adultery, and was pregnant by him as she stood at the altar,

may perhaps be pardoned, since Anne was the mother of Elizabeth, and her true conduct was not generally known, or at least was not so described in the popular histories and chronicles of Shakspeare's day. And further, if the opinions of the eminent theologians consulted by Henry were not so unanimously in his favour as Shakspeare supposes—if Cranmer was not quite the noble and amiable christian character he here appears—these are inaccuracies which may well be left out of consideration. It is not in them that the fault lies of which we complain: they are mere trifles and secondary matters, of which the poet was free to dispose as he might. The objection to which he justly lies open is, that he has not given us the fate and fortunes of Henry and Anne *fully* and *entirely*. By this defect he has rendered the representation *ideally* untrue. Not only does it offend against poetical justice—though that, indeed, is nothing more than the creature of human thought—but he has also unpardonably done indignity to the natural and manifest justice of God, as it is revealed in the history of the world. When we see Henry—that slave of passion, caprice, and pleasure, the puppet of a favourite like the ambitious, intriguing, revengeful Wolsey—condemn to death, without cause or justice, the Duke of Buckingham, (a rash zealot no doubt) and to gratify a sinful lust repudiate his pious, noble, and amiable consort—when we see such a man rewarded with the possession of his beloved, and rendered happy by the birth of his child, the natural sense of right is offended. And as little agreeable to justice does it seem, to behold Anne Boleyn, who, even in the drama itself, appears any thing but free from deep criminality, intruded into the place of the injured Katharine, and apparently the happy, envied mother and wife, and in undisturbed enjoyment of her unrighteous usurpation. Such is *not* the justice of *History*. It is well known, and must have then been known, that Henry died in the prime of life, to speak mildly, in a most disturbed state of mind, and of diseases which were the effects of his mental and bodily excesses; we know it, and it cannot even then have been a secret, that Anne Boleyn, after a short space of happiness, was accused of levity, and put to death in prison, by the command of her own husband.

Such poetical violations of the ideal truth of history, work however their own punishment. The whole drama is poetically untrue and without life—a poetic abortion, since it wants, what alone could give it an intrinsic organization and shape, *moral vitality*. It cannot pretend even to be a perfect whole. At best it is a shewy piece of patchwork, and consequently without true mind—a mere semblance, since it is without any fundamental idea which alone could give it life and organization. Wherever the conclusion stands out in such stiff and irreconcileable opposition to the beginning and middle, as it does in the play of ''Henry the Eighth,'' there it is vain to look for totality, or a pervading idea, since the latter is nothing less than the intrinsic unity of all the parts, and consequently the very essence of the whole. The character of Wolsey, of Katharine, of Henry, and severally of all the other personages of the drama, may, no doubt, be sketched and filled up with wonderful verisimilitude and pathos; but still, this only tends to confirm the opinion we have already advanced, that characterization and well-drawn characters do not alone make a dramatic work. Turn the piece as we may—whether we take the life of Katharine or of Wolsey for the centre of interest—we shall be unable to discover, without forcing and untruth, that which is the first requisition of art, and without which it must forfeit its pretensions to the title of art. (pp. 416-20)

Even against the greatest poet, perhaps of any age, we must maintain the truth, that art cannot *flatter* with impunity—even where, as in the case of Elizabeth, a glorious and successful reign, and general esteem, might urge so fair a plea. I forbear to adduce any more definite reasons for my unfavourable judgment, even because it would hardly grieve me to be shewn to be in error. But until this shall have been done, I shall indulge a belief, that it was Shakspeare's intention to write a *second* and concluding part to "Henry the Eighth," but was prevented by external circumstances from accomplishing his design. On the supposition that such a continuation was contemplated, I should not hesitate to place "Henry the Eighth" by the side of the best works of this great master of the stage. (p. 420)

> Hermann Ulrici, "Criticisms of Shakspeare's Dramas: 'Henry VIII'," in his Shakspeare's Dramatic Art: And His Relation to Calderon and Goethe, *translated by Rev. A.J.W. Morrison, Chapman, Brothers, 1846, pp. 416-22.*

CHARLES KNIGHT   (essay date 1843)

[*Knight, an English author and publisher, dedicated his career to providing education and knowledge to the Victorian working class. In the following excerpt, drawn from his comments on* Henry VIII *in the 1843 edition of* The Library Shakespeare, *Knight identifies the major theme of the play as the process of change— the wheel of Fortune—and the effect of change on the lives of*

Act III. Scene ii. Wolsey, Norfolk, Henry VIII, the Lord Chamberlain, Suffolk, and Surrey. Frontispiece to the Hanmer edition by H. Gravelot (1744). By permission of the Folger Shakespeare Library.

both great and poor. The idea of change, transmutation, or the wheel of Fortune as a structural motif in Henry VIII *is also discussed by Northrop Frye (1965), Lee Bliss (1975), and Frank Cespedes (1980). Following in the tradition of August Wilhelm Schlegel (1808) and Hermann Ulrici (1839), Knight also considers* Henry VIII *the last of Shakespeare's histories—the one in which he examines political corruption and foreshadows the advent of just government under Queen Elizabeth. Lastly, Knight examines the style of* Henry VIII, *concluding that the inclusion in the play of numerous run-on lines is not the result of revisions by another author, but an experiment on Shakespeare's part to approximate the idiomatic speech of his age. In fact, Knight considers the play too unified to be the work of more than one dramatist. For further commentary on the authorship of* Henry VIII, *see the excerpts by Samuel Johnson (1765), Edmond Malone (1778), James Spedding (1850), G. G. Gervinus (1863), Karl Elze (1874), Algernon Charles Swinburne (1880), E. K. Chambers (1908), Peter Alexander (1931), G. Wilson Knight (1947), and Robert Ornstein (1972).*]

> I come no more to make you laugh; things now,
> That bear a weighty and a serious brow,
> Sad, high, and working, full of state and woe,
> Such noble scenes as draw the eye to flow,
> We now present.   [Prologue. 1-5]

This is the commencement of the most remarkable prologue of the few which are attached to Shakspere's plays. It is, to our minds, a perfect exposition of the principle upon which the poet worked in the construction of this drama. . . . He had to offer weighty and serious things, sad and high things, noble scenes that commanded tears; state and woe were to be exhibited together: there was to be pageantry, but it was to be full of pity; and the woe was to be the more intense from its truth. And how did this master of his art profess to be able to produce such deep emotion from the exhibition of scenes that almost came down to his own times; that the fathers and grandfathers of his audience had witnessed in their unpoetical reality; that belonged not to the period when the sword was the sole arbiter of the destinies of princes and favourites, but when men fell by intrigue and not by battle, and even the axe of the capricious despot struck in the name of the law? There was another great poet of this age of high poetry, who had indicated the general theme which Shakspere proposed to illustrate in this drama:

> What man that sees the ever-whirling wheel
>   Of change, the which all mortal things doth sway,
> But that thereby doth find, and plainly feel,
>   How Mutability in them doth play
> The cruel sports to many men's decay?
>   [Edmund Spenser, *The Faerie Queene*]

From the first scene to the last, the dramatic action seems to point to the abiding presence of that power which works

> Her cruel sports to many men's decay.

We see the "ever-whirling wheel," in a succession of contrasts of grandeur and debasement; and even when the action is closed, we are carried forward into the depths of the future, to have the same triumph of "Mutability" suggested to our contemplation. This is the theme which the poet emphatically presents to us under its aspect of sadness. . . . (pp. 257-58)

[With 'Henry VIII.'] Shakspere has closed his great series of 'Chronicle Histories.' This last of them was to be "sad, high, and working." It has laid bare the hollowness of worldly glory; it has shown the heavy "load" of "too much honour." It has given us a picture of the times which succeeded the feudal strifes of the other 'Histories.' Were they better times? To the mind of the poet the age of corruption was as "sad" as the age of force. The one tyrant rides over the obligations of justice, wielding a power more terrible than that of the sword. The poet's consolation is to be found in the prophetic views of the future. The prophecy of Cranmer upon the reigns of Elizabeth and James is the eulogy of just government—partially realized in the age of Shakspere, but not the less a high conception, however beyond the reality, of

What makes a nation happy and keeps it so.

We have a few words to add on the style of this drama. It is remarkable for the elliptical construction of many of the sentences and for an occasional peculiarity in the versification, which is not found in any other of Shakspere's works. The Roman plays, decidedly amongst the latest of his productions, possess a colloquial freedom of versification which in some cases approaches almost to ruggedness. But in the 'Henry VIII.' this freedom is carried much farther. We have repeated instances in which the lines are so constructed that it is impossible to read them with the slightest pause at the end of each line:— the sentence must be run together, so as to produce more the effect of measured prose than of blank-verse. (p. 263)

A theory has been set up that Jonson "tampered" with the versification. We hold this notion to be utterly untenable; for there is no play of Shakspere's which has a more decided character of unity—no one from which any passage could be less easily struck out. We believe that Shakspere worked in this particular upon a principle of art which he had proposed to himself to adhere to wherever the nature of the scene would allow. The elliptical construction, and the licence of versification, brought the dialogue, whenever the speaker was not necessarily rhetorical, closer to the language of common life. Of all his historical plays, the 'Henry VIII.' is the nearest in its story to his own times. It professed to be a "truth." It belongs to his own country. It has no poetical indistinctness about it, either of time or place: all is defined. If the diction and the versification had been more artificial it would have been less a reality. (pp. 263-64)

> *Charles Knight, ''Supplementary Notice: 'King Henry VIII','' in* The Comedies, Histories, Tragedies, and Poems of William Shakspere, Vol. VII *by William Shakespeare, edited by Charles Knight, second edition, 1843. Reprint by AMS Press, 1968, pp. 257-64.*

JAMES SPEDDING (essay date 1850)

[*The following excerpt is taken from Spedding's influential essay on* Henry VIII, *which was originally published in* The Gentleman's Magazine *in 1850. In it, he follows the supposition of Richard Roderick (1756) and maintains that the numerous stylistic inconsistencies and structural deficiencies in* Henry VIII *can be attributed to the fact that two authors worked on the play: Shakespeare and the Jacobean dramatist John Fletcher. Spedding's essay was one of the first demonstrations of ''disintegrationist'' criticism—a method by which textual scholars ''scientifically'' assigned troublesome passages, scenes, or even acts in Shakespeare's work to the efforts of other playwrights—and his arguments were supported by such critics as Samuel Hickson, F. G. Fleay, and F. J. Furnivall (see Additional Bibliography). With the exception of Algernon Charles Swinburne (1880), nineteenth- and early twentieth-century critics were strongly influenced by Spedding's theory. Most commentators during this time merely repeated his findings or simply proposed other dramatists as possible collaborators. However, beginning with the essay by Peter Alexander (1931), an increasing number of critics began to reject Spedding's theory and to consider Shakespeare the sole author*

of Henry VIII, *usually on grounds that the play was more structurally cohesive than had originally been assumed and that the scenes attributed to Fletcher were not unlike Shakespeare. For more commentary on the authorship of* Henry VIII, *see the excerpts by G. G. Gervinus (1863), Karl Elze (1874), E. K. Chambers (1908), G. Wilson Knight (1947), and Robert Ornstein (1972).*]

[Several] of our most considerable critics have incidentally betrayed a consciousness that there is something peculiar either in the execution, or the structure, or the general design of [*Henry VIII.*], which should naturally suggest a doubt [on the authorship of the play]. Dr Johnson observes that the genius of Shakspere comes in and goes out with Katharine, and that the rest of the play might be easily conceived and easily written— a fact, if it be a fact, so remarkable as to call for explanation [see excerpt above, 1765]. Coleridge, in one of his attempts to classify Shakspere's plays (1802), distinguished *Henry VIII.* as *gelegenheitsgedicht* [''poem for an occasion'']; in another (1819) as ''a sort of historical masque or show-play;'' thereby betraying a consciousness that there was something singular and exceptional about it. Ulrici, who has applied himself with a German ingenuity to discover in each of Shakspere's plays a profound moral purpose, is obliged to confess that he can make nothing of *Henry VIII.*, and is driven to suppose that what we have was meant only for a first part, to be followed by a second in which the odds would have been made even [see excerpt above, 1839]. Mr Knight, whose faith is proof against such doubts, does indeed treat *Henry VIII.* as the perfect crown and consummation of the series of historical plays [see excerpt above, 1843], and succeeds in tracing through the first four acts a consistent and sufficient moral; but when he comes to the fifth, which should crown all, he is obliged to put us off with a reference to the historians; admitting that the catastrophe which history had provided as the crowning moral of the whole is not exhibited in the play, ''but who (he asks) can forget it?''—an apology for the gravest of all defects which seems to me quite inadmissible. (pp. 1-2)

The truth is that the interest [in *Henry VIII.*], instead of rising towards the end, falls away utterly, and leaves us in the last act among persons whom we scarcely know, and events for which we do not care. The strongest sympathies which have been awakened in us run opposite to the course of the action. Our sympathy is for the grief and goodness of Queen Katharine, while the course of the action requires us to entertain as a theme of joy and compensatory satisfaction the coronation of Anne Bullen and the birth of her daughter; which are in fact a part of Katharine's injury, and amount to little less than the ultimate triumph of wrong. For throughout the play the king's cause is not only felt by us, but represented to us, as a bad one. We *hear*, indeed, of conscientious scruples as to the legality of his first marriage; but we are not made, nor indeed asked, to believe that they are sincere, or to recognize in his new marriage either the hand of Providence, or the consummation of any worthy object, or the victory of any of those more common frailties of humanity with which we can sympathize. The mere caprice of passion drives the king into the commission of what seems a great iniquity; our compassion for the victim of it is elaborately excited; no attempt is made to awaken any counter-sympathy for *him*: yet his passion has its way, and is crowned with all felicity, present and to come. (pp. 2-3)

This main defect is sufficient of itself to mar the effect of the play as a whole. But there is another, which though less vital is not less unaccountable. The greater part of the fifth act, in which the interest ought to be gathering to a head, is occupied with matters in which we have not been prepared to take any interest by what went before, and on which no interest is reflected by what comes after. The scenes in the gallery and council-chamber, though full of life and vigour, and, in point of execution, not unworthy of Shakspere, are utterly irrelevant to the business of the play; for what have we to do with the quarrel between Gardiner and Cranmer? Nothing in the play is explained by it, nothing depends upon it. It is used only (so far as the argument is concerned) as a preface for introducing Cranmer as godfather to Queen Elizabeth, which might have been done as a matter of course without any preface at all. The scenes themselves are indeed both picturesque and characteristic and historical, and might probably have been introduced with excellent effect into a dramatised life of Henry VIII. But historically they do not belong to the place where they are introduced here, and poetically they have in this place no value, but the reverse.

With the fate of Wolsey, again, in whom our second interest centres, the business of this last act does not connect itself any more than with that of Queen Katharine. The fate of Wolsey would have made a noble subject for a tragedy in itself, and might very well have been combined with the tragedy of Katharine; but, as an introduction to the festive solemnity with which the play concludes, the one seems to me as inappropriate as the other. (pp. 3-4)

I know no other play in Shakspere which is chargeable with a fault like this, none in which the moral sympathy of the spectator is not carried along with the main current of action to the end. In all the historical tragedies a providence may be seen presiding over the development of events, as just and relentless as the fate in a Greek tragedy. Even in *Henry IV.*, where the comic element predominates, we are never allowed to exult in the success of the wrongdoer, or to forget the penalties which are due to guilt. And if it be true that in the romantic comedies our moral sense does sometimes suffer a passing shock, it is never owing to an error in the general design, but always to some incongruous circumstance in the original story which has lain in the way and not been entirely got rid of, and which after all offends us rather as an incident improbable in itself than as one for which our sympathy is unjustly demanded. The singularity of *Henry VIII.* is that, while four-fifths of the play are occupied in matters which are to make us incapable of mirth, . . . the remaining fifth is devoted to joy and triumph, and ends with universal festivity:

—This day let no man think
He has business at his house; for all shall stay:
This little one shall make it holiday.   [V. iv. 74-6]

Of this strange inconsistency, or at least of a certain poorness in the general effect which is amply accounted for by such inconsistency, I had for some time been vaguely conscious; and I had also heard it casually remarked by a man of first-rate judgment on such a point that many passages in *Henry VIII.* were very much in the manner of *Fletcher.* (pp. 5-6)

I determined upon this to read the play through. . . . The result of my examination was a clear conviction that at least two different hands had been employed in the composition of *Henry VIII.*; if not three; and that they had worked, not together, but alternately upon distinct portions of it.

This is a conclusion which cannot of course be established by detached extracts, which in questions of style are doubtful evidence at best. The only satisfactory evidence upon which it can be determined whether a given scene was or was not by

Shakspere, is to be found in the general effect produced on the mind, the ear, and the feelings by a free and broad perusal; and if any of your readers care to follow me in this inquiry, I would ask him to do as I did,—that is, to read the whole play straight through, with an eye open to notice the larger differences of effect, but without staying to examine small points. The effect of my own experiment was as follows:—

The opening of the play,—the conversation between Buckingham, Norfolk, and Abergavenny,—seemed to have the full stamp of Shakspere, in his latest manner: the same close-packed expression; the same life, and reality, and freshness; the same rapid and abrupt turnings of thought, so quick that language can hardly follow fast enough; the same impatient activity of intellect and fancy, which having once disclosed an idea cannot wait to work it orderly out; the same daring confidence in the resources of language, which plunges headlong into a sentence without knowing how it is to come forth; the same careless metre which disdains to produce its harmonious effects by the ordinary devices, yet is evidently subject to a master of harmony; the same entire freedom from book-language and commonplace; all the qualities, in short, which distinguish the magical hand which has never yet been successfully imitated.

In the scene in the council-chamber which follows (Act i. Sc. 2), where the characters of Katharine and Wolsey are brought out, I found the same characteristics equally strong.

But the instant I entered upon the third scene, in which the Lord Chamberlain, Lord Sands, and Lord Lovel converse, I was conscious of a total change. I felt as if I had passed suddenly out of the language of nature into the language of the stage, or of some conventional mode of conversation. The structure of the verse was quite different and full of mannerism. The expression became suddenly diffuse and languid. The wit wanted mirth and character. And all this was equally true of the supper scene which closes the first Act.

The second act brought me back to the tragic vein, but it was not the tragic vein of Shakspere. When I compared the eager, impetuous, and fiery language of Buckingham in the first Act with the languid and measured cadences of his farewell speech, I felt that the difference was too great to be accounted for by the mere change of situation, without supposing also a change of writers. The presence of death produces great changes in men, but no such change as we have here.

When in like manner I compared the Henry and Wolsey of the scene which follows (Act ii. Sc. 2) with the Henry and Wolsey of the council-chamber (Act i. Sc. 2), I perceived a difference scarcely less striking. The dialogue, through the whole scene, sounded still slow and artificial.

The next scene brought another sudden change. And, as in passing from the second to the third scene of the first Act, I had seemed to be passing all at once out of the language of nature into that of convention, so in passing from the second to the third scene of the second Act (in which Anne Bullen appears, I may say for the first time, for in the supper scene she was merely a conventional court lady without any character at all,) I seemed to pass not less suddenly from convention back again into nature. And when I considered that this short and otherwise insignificant passage contains all that we ever see of Anne (for it is necessary to forget her former appearance) and yet how clearly the character comes out, how very a woman she is, and yet how distinguishable from any other individual woman, I had no difficulty in acknowledging that the sketch came from the same hand which drew Perdita.

Next follows the famous trial-scene. And here I could as little doubt that I recognized the same hand to which we owe the trial of Hermione. When I compared the language of Henry and of Wolsey throughout this scene to the end of the Act, with their language in the council-chamber (Act i, Sc. 2), I found that it corresponded in all essential features: when I compared it with their language in the second scene of the second Act, I perceived that it was altogether different. Katharine also, as she appears in this scene, was exactly the same person as she was in the council-chamber; but when I went on the first scene of the third Act, which represents her interview with Wolsey and Campeius, I found her as much changed as Buckingham was after his sentence, though without any alteration of circumstances to account for an alteration of temper. Indeed the whole of this scene seemed to have all the peculiarities of Fletcher, both in conception, language, and versification, without a single feature that reminded me of Shakspere; and, since in both passages the true narrative of Cavendish is followed minutely and carefully, and both are therefore copies from the same original and in the same style of art, it was the more easy to compare them with each other.

In the next scene (Act iii. Sc. 2) I seemed again to get out of Fletcher into Shakspere; though probably not into Shakspere pure; a scene by another hand perhaps which Shakspere had only remodeled, or a scene by Shakspere which another hand had worked upon to make it fit the place. The speeches interchanged between Henry and Wolsey seemed to be entirely Shakspere's; but in the altercation between Wolsey and the lords which follows I could recognize little or nothing of his peculiar manner, while many passages were strongly marked with the favourite Fletcherian cadence; and as for the famous 'Farewell, a long farewell,' &c., though associated by means of Enfield's Speaker with my earliest notions of Shakspere, it appeared (now that my mind was opened to entertain the doubt) to belong entirely and unquestionably to Fletcher.

Of the 4th Act I did not so well know what to think. For the most part it seemed to bear evidence of a more vigorous hand than Fletcher's, with less mannerism, especially in the description of the coronation, and the character of Wolsey; and yet it had not to my mind the freshness and originality of Shakspere. It was pathetic and graceful, but one could see how it was done. Katharine's last speeches, however, smacked strongly again of Fletcher. And altogether it seemed to me that if this Act had occurred in one of the plays written by Beaumont and Fletcher in conjunction it would probably have been thought that both of them had had a hand in it.

The first scene of the 5th Act, and the opening of the second, I should again have confidently ascribed to Shakspere, were it not that the whole passage seemed so strangely out of place. I could only suppose (what may indeed be supposed well enough if my conjecture with regard to the authorship of the several parts be correct), that the task of putting the whole together had been left to an inferior hand; in which case I should consider this to be a genuine piece of Shakspere's work, spoiled by being introduced where it has no business. In the execution of the christening scene, on the other hand (in spite again of the earliest and strongest associations), I could see no evidence of Shakspere's hand at all; while in point of *design* it seemed inconceivable that a judgment like his could have been content with a conclusion so little in harmony with the prevailing spirit and purpose of the piece. (pp. 6-10)

Supposing the inequality of the workmanship in different parts of the play to be admitted, as by most people I think it will,

may not this be sufficiently accounted for by supposing that it was written by Shakspere at different periods? May it not have been an early performance of his own, which in his later life he corrected, and in great part rewrote; as we know he did in some other cases?

I think not; for two reasons. First, because if he had set about the revisal of it on so large a scale in the maturity of his genius, he would have addressed himself to remove its principal defect, which is the incoherence of the general design. Secondly, because the style of those parts which upon this supposition would be referred to the earlier period does not at all resemble Shakspere's style at any stage of its development. (p. 11)

It has been observed, as I said, that lines with a redundant syllable at the end occur in *Henry VIII.* twice as often as in any of Shakspere's other plays. Now, it will be found on examination that this observation does not apply to all parts of the play alike, but only to those which I have noticed as, in their general character, un-Shaksperian. In those parts which have the stamp of Shakspere upon them in other respects, the proportion of lines with the redundant syllable is not greater than in other of his later plays—*Cymbeline,* for instance, and the *Winter's Tale.* In the opening scene of *Cymbeline,* an unimpassioned conversation, chiefly narrative, we find twenty-five such lines in sixty-seven; in the third scene of the third Act, which is in a higher strain of poetry but still calm, we find twenty-three in one hundred and seven; in the fourth scene, which is full of sudden turns of passion, fifty-three in one hundred and eighty-two. Taking one scene with another, therefore, the lines with the redundant syllable are in the proportion of about two to seven. In the *Winter's Tale* we may take the second and third scenes of the third Act as including a sufficient variety of styles; and here we find seventy-one in two hundred and forty-eight; the same proportion as nearly as possible, though the scenes were selected at random. (pp. 13-14)

[In *Henry VIII.*] we have, out of sixteen separate scenes, six in which the redundant syllable occurs (taking one with another), about as often as in *Cymbeline* and the *Winter's Tale;* the proportion being never higher than two in five, which is the same as in the opening scene of *Cymbeline;* never lower than two in seven, which is the same as in the trial scene in the *Winter's Tale;* and the average being about one in three; while in the remaining ten scenes the proportion of such lines is never less than one in two; in the greater number of them scarcely more than two in three. Nor is there anything in the subject or character of the several scenes by which such a difference can be accounted for. The light and loose conversation at the end of the first Act, the plaintive and laboured oration in the second, the querulous and passionate altercation in the third, the pathetic sorrows of Wolsey, the tragic death of Katharine, the high poetic prophecy of Cranmer, are equally distinguished by this peculiarity. A distinction so broad and so uniform, running through so large a portion of the same piece, cannot have been accidental; and the more closely it is examined the more clearly will it appear that the metre in these two sets of scenes is managed upon entirely different principles, and bears evidence of different workmen. To explain all the particular differences would be to analyze the structure first of Shakspere's metre, then of Fletcher's; a dry and tedious task. But the general difference may easily be made evident by placing any undoubted specimen of Shakspere's later workmanship by the side of the one, and of Fletcher's middle workmanship by the side of the other; the identity in both cases will be felt at once. (pp. 14-15)

Assuming then that *Henry VIII*. was written partly by Shak-spere, partly by Fletcher, with the assistance probably of some third hand, it becomes a curious question, upon what plan their joint labours were conducted. It was not unusual in those days, when a play was wanted in a hurry, to set two or three or even four hands at work upon it; and the occasion of the Princes Elizabeth's marriage (February 1612-13) may very likely have suggested the production of a play representing the marriage of Henry VIII. and Anne Bullen. Such an occasion would sufficiently account for the determination to treat the subject not tragically; the necessity for producing it immediately might lead to the employment of several hands; and thence would follow inequality of workmanship and imperfect adaptation of the several parts to each other. But this would not explain the incoherency and inconsistency of the main design. Had Shak-spere been employed to make a design for a play which was to end with the happy marriage of Henry and Anne Bullen, we may be sure that he would not have occupied us through the four first Acts with a tragic and absorbing interest in the decline and death of Queen Katharine, and through half the fifth with a quarrel between Cranmer and Gardiner, in which we have no interest. On the other hand, since it is by Shakspere that all the principal matters and characters are *introduced,* it is not likely that the general design of the piece would be laid out by another. I should rather conjecture that he had conceived the idea of a great historical drama on the subject of Henry VIII. which would have included the divorce of Katharine, the fall of Wolsey, the rise of Cranmer, the coronation of Anne Bullen, and the final separation of the English from the Romish Church, which, being the one great historical event of the reign, would naturally be chosen as the focus of poetic interest; that he had proceeded in the execution of this idea as far perhaps as the third Act, which might have included the establishment of Cranmer in the seat of highest ecclesiastical authority (the council-chamber scene in the fifth being designed as an intro-duction to that); when, finding that his fellows of the Globe were in distress for a new play to honour the marriage of the Lady Elizabeth with, he thought that his half-finished work might help them, and accordingly handed them his manuscript to make what they could of it; that they put it into the hands of Fletcher (already in high repute as a popular and expeditious playwright), who finding the original design not very suitable to the occasion and utterly beyond his capacity, expanded the three acts into five, by interspersing scenes of show and mag-nificence, and passages of description, and long poetical con-versations, in which his strength lay; dropped all allusion to the great ecclesiastical revolution, which he could not manage and for which he had no materials supplied him; converted what should have been the middle into the end; and so turned out a splendid 'historical masque, or shew-play,' which was no doubt very popular then, as it has been ever since.

This is a bold conjecture, but it will account for all the phe-nomena. Read the portions which I have marked as Shakspere's by themselves, and suppose them to belong to the first half of the play, and they will not seem unworthy of him; though the touches of an inferior hand may perhaps be traced here and there, and the original connection is probably lost beyond re-covery in the interpolations. Suppose again the *design* of the play as it stands to have been left to Fletcher, and the want of moral consistency and coherency needs no further explanation. The want of a just moral feeling is Fletcher's characteristic defect, and lies at the bottom of all that is most offensive in him, from his lowest mood to his highest. That it has not in this case betrayed him into such gross inconsistencies and in-delicacies as usual may be explained by the fact that he was

following the Chronicles and had little room for his own in-ventions. (pp. 16-18)

James Spedding, "Appendix: Shakspere's Share in 'Henry VIII','" in The New Shakspere Society's Transactions, *No. 1, 1874, pp. 1-18.*

G. G. GERVINUS   (essay date 1863)

[*One of the most widely read Shakespearean critics of the latter half of the nineteenth century, Gervinus was praised by such eminent contemporaries as Edward Dowden, F. J. Furnivall, and James Russell Lowell; however, he is little known in the English-speaking world today. Like his predecessor Hermann Ulrici, Ger-vinus wrote in the tradition of "philosophical criticism" devel-oped in Germany in the mid-nineteenth century. Under the influ-ence of August Wilhelm Schlegel's literary theory and Georg Wilhelm Friedrich Hegel's philosophy, German critics like Ger-vinus tended to focus their analyses around a search for a literary work's organic unity and ethical import. Gervinus believed that Shakespeare's works contained a rational ethical system inde-pendent of any religion—in contrast to Ulrici, for whom Shake-speare's morality was basically Christian. The excerpt below comes from* Shakespeare Commentaries, *an English translation of the 1863 edition of Gervinus's* Shakespeare. *In his criticism of* Henry VIII, *Gervinus agrees with James Spedding (1850) that the irregularities in the play—its lack of a coherent design, its loosely connected scenes, its languid expression, and its diversity in meter—all suggest dual authorship; also like Spedding, he senses the work of Fletcher in the play. Other critics who consider* Henry VIII *a collaboration between Shakespeare and Fletcher include Karl Elze (1874), E. K. Chambers (1908), and Robert Ornstein (1972). Like many previous commentators, Gervinus has difficulty determining the intent of the play. Although he hypoth-esizes that the central idea may be found in Cranmer's prophetic final speech, he ends by doubting that this is feasible, especially since the meaning of this final speech would discredit the re-mainder of* Henry VIII *as "only the symbolic precursor to the real aim of the piece." For further discussions of the apparent contradiction presented by Cranmer's prophecy in the context of the play, see the excerpts by Hermann Ulrici (1839), A. A. Parker (1948), and Robert Ornstein (1972).*]

A long time ago, [Richard Roderick] . . . hesitated at some peculiarities in the versification of *Henry VIII.* [see excerpt above, 1756], but never since then has the genuineness of the play been doubted, and at the most the prologue and epilogue were all that were denied as the work of the poet's pen. Indeed, the strictly logical design of the four main characters suffered no doubt to arise, as no other poet of the time could have sketched their psychological outline with such sharpness, how-ever much assistance the historical sources . . . , and two pre-vious dramatic works upon Wolsey . . . , might have afforded. (p. 819)

No one [upon examining] . . . the main characters of *Henry VIII*. will mistake the certain hand of our poet. It is otherwise when we approach closer to the development of the action and attentively consider the poetic diction. The impression of the whole becomes then at once strange and unrefreshing; the mere external threads seem to be lacking which ought to link the actions to each other; the interest of the feelings becomes strangely divided, it is continually drawn into new directions, and is nowhere satisfied. At first it clings to Buckingham and his designs against Wolsey; but with the second act he leaves the stage; then Wolsey attracts our attention in an increased degree, and he too disappears in the third act; in the meanwhile our sympathies are more and more strongly drawn to Katharine, who then likewise leaves the stage in the fourth act; and after we have been thus shattered through four acts by circumstances of a purely tragic character, the fifth act closes with a merry festivity, for which we are in nowise prepared, crowning the king's base passion with victory, in which we could take no warm interest. In the course of the play, the marriage of the king and Anne Bullen is only casually linked with the person of the cardinal, who seemed outwardly as if he ought to form the connecting central point of the action, and the enmity between Cranmer and Gardiner is not at all related to this; both circumstances again apparently stand in no relation to each other. The birth and christening of Elizabeth follow at the conclusion as a new by-work, linked to the preceding merely by a natural but not aesthetic sequence, and connected with the character of Cranmer only by the christening spoons which the godfather has to give to the infant. And in this same way, as we stumble at the loose development of the action, we become doubtful also of the poetic diction, as soon as we compare it with any other of Shakespeare's plays. The English critic [James Spedding (see excerpt above, 1850)] perceived only in single scenes . . . that freshness of life and nature, that perfect freedom from all the conventional language of the stage or of books, those concise expressions, that bold and rapid turn of thought, that impatient activity of mind and imagination, which so perceptibly distinguish Shakespeare's language; and even in these scenes we fancy we can feel a certain gloss of varnish, weakening these peculiarities of Shakespeare's diction; in the remaining parts, where whole scenes appear as unnecessary stop-gaps, there often prevails a languid expression of shallow conversation, which seems in scarcely one trait to remind of Shakespeare, though all the more frequently of Beaumont's and Fletcher's style of writing. Fletcher's rhythmic manner is strikingly conspicuous throughout in these very passages of the play; verses with double endings are much more constant in the whole play than in almost any other of Shakespeare's works; in the parts that appear genuine they stand in the proportion of two weak to seven strong endings, but in the less genuine the proportion is of one to two, or two to three; the spondaic double endings, so characteristic of Fletcher's versification, are met with in many passages consecutively. All these peculiarities determined our English critic in the supposition that the play had been consigned by Shakespeare in a mere sketch to Fletcher, whose influence in the completion of the work would at once explain the want of moral and aesthetic consistency and coherence in the drama.

It is striking, and it seems to us of a deciding importance, that this result of philological inquiry fully accords with the result of the utterly opposite aesthetical test of the unity of idea in this historical play. Formerly, indeed, I believed that the key to the play might be found in Cranmer's prophetic speech at the christening of Elizabeth, which in broad touches predicts the blessed fruits of the queen's future government: the establishment of peace, the security of Protestantism, and the consideration of merit before birth and blood; and I have thought that the essential idea of the drama might be referred to the glorification of the house of Tudor by an historical abstraction of the main merit and value of the rule of this house. I was induced to admit that the real action, the victory of Protestantism, which the poet had for this aim placed as the central point of his play of Henry VIII., he could not have ventured to represent on the stage in any deep view or detailed treatment; that this might have compelled him (and this history moreover justified) to make the casual outward causes which have had this great result for England the subject of representation in his drama, which in many passages, it seems unintentionally, hints at the experience that great results often arise from the

smallest and most unexpected causes. But in this attempt to obtain for the play a unity of idea as its foundation, I have not been able to conceal from myself that, even supposing the justice of such an interpretation, the whole play would evaporate into a formal dramatic spiritualising of the subject. The action represented would in this case be only the symbolic precursor to the real aim of the piece, which would not lie in the central point of the play, but in its conclusion, in that prophesying of a period and a condition, lying far behind the present, in which the scene is placed,—in a speech for which, and for the cause of which, few indeed of the facts of the play had prepared in any tangible manner. It seems, therefore, in every way more just simply to confess the lack of dramatic unity and of an ethical focus in the play, and to explain it in the manner of the considerations we have just alleged. (pp. 825-27)

> G. G. Gervinus, "'Henry VIII'," in his Shakespeare Commentaries, *translated by F. E. Bunnètt, revised edition, 1877. Reprint by AMS Press, Inc., 1971, pp. 818-29.*

Rev. H. N. HUDSON (essay date 1872)

[*An American clergyman and literary scholar, Hudson substantially promoted the growth of Shakespeare's popularity in America during the latter half of the nineteenth century, particularly with his* Shakespeare: His Life, Art, and Characters, *a two-volume series originally published in 1872. In the following excerpt, taken from that work, Hudson undertakes an examination of the major characters in* Henry VIII. *Like such earlier commentators as August Wilhelm Schlegel (1808), William Hazlitt (1817), and Hermann Ulrici (1839), Hudson contends that Shakespeare presented an unflattering, and therefore realistic, portrait of King Henry, allowing the character's actions to indicate his numerous faults and thereby establishing his true character through all the seemingly positive rhetoric.*]

[The] interest of [*Henry VIII*] is broken and scattered by incoherences of design and execution. The interest, however, of the several portions is deep and genuine while it lasts; at least, till we come to the fifth Act. We are carried through a series of sudden and most afflicting reverses. One after another, the mighty are broken and the lofty laid low; their prosperity being strained to a high pitch, as if on purpose to deepen their plunge, just when they have reached the summit with their hearts built up and settled to the height of their rising, and when the revolving wheel of time seems fast locked with themselves at the top.

First, we have Buckingham in the full-blown pride of rank and talents. He is wise in counsel, rich in culture and accomplishment, of captivating deportment, learned and eloquent in discourse. A too self-flattering sense of his strength and importance has made him insolent and presumptuous; and his self-control has failed from the very elevation that rendered it most needful to him. . . . Thus he puts forth those leaves of hope which, as they express the worst parts of himself, naturally provoke the worst parts of others, and so invite danger while blinding him to its approach; till at length all things within and around are made ripe for his upsetting and ruin; and, while he is exultingly spreading snares for the Cardinal, he is himself caught and crushed with the strong toils of that master-hand.

Next, we have the patient and saintly Catharine sitting in state with the King, all that she would ask being granted ere she asks it; sharing half his power, and appearing most worthy of it when most free to use it. . . . Yet even now the King is cherishing in secret the passion that has already supplanted her from his heart, and his sinister craft is plotting the means of divorcing her from his side, and at the same time weaving about her such a net of intrigue as may render her very strength and beauty of character powerless in her behalf; so that before she feels the meditated wrong all chance of redress is foreclosed, and she is left with no defence but the sacredness of her sorrows.

Then we have the overgreat Cardinal, who, in his plenitude of inward forces, has cut his way and carried himself upward over whatever offered to stop him. . . . His very power, however, of rising against all opposers serves, apparently, but to aggravate and assure his fall when there is no further height for him to climb; and at last, through his own mere oversight and oblivion, he loses all, from his having no more to gain.

Yet in all these cases, inasmuch as the persons have their strength inherent, and not adventitious, therefore they carry it with them in their reverses; or rather, in seeming to lose it, they augment it. For it is then seen, as it could not be before, that the greatness which was in their circumstances served to obscure that which was in themselves. Buckingham is something more and better than the gifted and accomplished nobleman, when he stands before us unpropped and simply as ''poor Edward Bohun''; his innate nobility being then set free, and his mind falling back upon its naked self for the making good his title to respect. Wolsey, also towers far above the all-performing and all-powerful Cardinal and Chancellor who ''bore his blushing honours thick upon him'' [III. ii. 354], when, stripped of every thing that fortune and favour can give or take away, he bestows his great mind in parting counsel upon Cromwell; when he comes, ''an old man broken with the storms of State,'' to beg ''a little earth for charity''; and when he has really ''felt himself, and found the blessedness of being little'' [IV. ii. 21, 23, 65-6].

Nor is the change in our feelings towards these men, after their fall, merely an effect passing within ourselves: it proceeds in part upon a real disclosure of something in them that was before hidden beneath the superinducings of place and circumstance. Their nobler and better qualities shine out afresh when they are brought low, so that from their fall we learn the true causes of their rising. (pp. 191-94)

The delineation of Catharine differs from the two foregoing, in that she maintains the same simple, austere, and solid sweetness of mind and manners through all the changes of fortune. Yet she, too, rises by her humiliation and is made perfect by suffering, if not in herself, at least to us: for it gives her full sway over those deeper sympathies which are necessary to a just appreciation of the profound and venerable beauty of her character. She is mild, meek, and discreet; and the harmonious blending of these qualities with her high Castilian pride gives her a very peculiar charm. Therewithal she is plain in mind and person; has neither great nor brilliant parts; and of this she is fully aware, for she knows herself thoroughly: but she is nevertheless truly great,—and this is the one truth about her which she does not know,—from the symmetry and composure wherein all the elements of her being stand and move together: so that she presents a remarkable instance of greatness in the whole, with the absence of it in the parts. How clear and exact her judgment and discrimination! yet we scarce know whence it comes, or how. (p. 196)

Her power over our better feelings is in no small degree owing to the impression we take, that she sees through her husband

perfectly, yet never in the least betrays to him, and hardly owns to herself, what mean and hateful qualities she knows or feels to be in him. It is not possible to over-state her simple artlessness of mind; while nevertheless her simplicity is of such a texture as to be an overmatch for all the unscrupulous wiles by which she is beset. Her betrayers, with all their mazy craft, can neither keep from her the secret of their thoughts nor turn her knowledge of it into any blemish of her innocence; nor is she less brave to face their purpose than penetrating to discover it. And when her resolution is fixed, that ''nothing but death shall e'er divorce her dignities'' [III. i. 141-42], it is not, and we feel it is not, that she holds the accidents of her position for one iota more than they are worth; but that these are to her the necessary symbols of her honour as a wife, and the inseparable garments of her delicacy as a woman; and as such they have so grown in with her life, that she cannot survive the parting with them; to say nothing of how they are bound up with her sentiments of duty, of ancestral reverence, and of self-respect. Moreover many hard, hard trials have made her conscious of her sterling virtue: she has borne too much, and borne it too well, to be ignorant of what she is and how much better things she has deserved; she knows, as she alone can know, that patience has had its perfect work with her: and this knowledge of her solid and true worth, so sorely tried, so fully proved, enhances to her sense the insult and wrong that are put upon her, making them eat like rust into her soul. (p. 197)

Catharine in her seclusion, and discrowned of all but her honour and her sorrow, is one of the authors' noblest and sweetest deliverances. She there leads a life of homely simplicity. Always beautiful on the throne, in her humiliation she is more beautiful still. She carries to the place no grudge or resentment or bitterness towards any; nothing but faith, hope, and charity; a touching example of womanly virtue and gentleness; hourly in Heaven for her enemies; her heart garrisoned with ''the peace that passeth all understanding.'' Candid and plain herself, she loves and honours plainness and candour in others; and it seems a positive relief to her to hear the best spoken that can be of the fallen great man who did more than all the rest to work her fall. Her calling the messenger ''a saucy fellow'' [IV. ii. 100], who breaks in so abruptly upon her, discloses just enough of human weakness to make us feel that she is not quite an angel yet; and in her death-scene we have the divinest notes of a ''soul by resignation sanctified.''

The portrait of the King, all the circumstances considered in which it was drawn, is a very remarkable piece of work, being no less true to the original than politic as regards the authors: for the cause which Henry had been made to serve, though against his will, and from the very rampancy of his vices, had rendered it a long and hard process for the nation to see him as he was. The authors keep the worst parts of his character mainly in the background, veiling them withal so adroitly and so transparently as to suggest them to all who are willing to see them: in other words, they do not directly expose or affirm his moral hatefulness, but place it silently in facts, and so make him characterize himself in a way to be felt: nay, they even make the other persons speak good things of him, but at the same time let him refute and reprove their words by his deeds. At all events, the man's hard-hearted and despotic capriciousness is brought to points of easy inference; yet the matter is carried by the authors with such an air of simplicity as if they were hardly aware of it; though, when one of the persons is made to say of Henry, ''His conscience has crept too near another lady'' [II. ii. 17-18], it is manifest that the authors understood his character perfectly. (pp. 199-200)

Act I. Scene iv. Anne Bullen, King Henry VIII, Cardinal Wolsey, and a Page. By F. Pecht. The Department of Rare Books and Special Collections, The University of Michigan Library.

In the whole matter of the divorce, Henry is felt to be acting from motives which he does not avow: already possessed with a criminal passion for which he is lawlessly bent on making a way, he still wants to think he has strong public reasons for the measure, and that religion and conscience are his leading inducements; and he shows much cunning and ability in pressing these considerations into view: but it is plain enough that he rather tries to persuade himself they are true than really believes them to be so; though there is no telling how far, in this effort to hide the real cause from the world, he may strangle the sense of it in his own breast. All this, however, rather heightens the meanness than relieves the wickedness of his course. The power or the poison of self-deceit can indeed work wonders; and in such cases it is often extremely difficult to judge whether a man is wilfully deceiving others or unconsciously deceiving himself: in fact, the two often slide into each other, so as to compound a sort of honest hypocrisy, or a state between belief and not-belief: but Henry wilfully embraces and hugs and holds fast the deceit, and rolls all arguments for it as sweet morsels under his tongue, because it offers a free course for his carnal-mindedness and raging self-will. But the history of his reign after the intellect of Wolsey and the virtue of Catharine were removed is the best commentary on the motives that swayed him at this time; and there I must leave him.

In the brief delineation of Anne Boleyn there is gathered up the essence of a long story. She is regarded much less for what she is in herself than for the gem that is to proceed from her; and her character is a good deal screened by the purpose of her introduction, though not so much but that it peeps significantly through. With little in her of a positive nature one way or the other; with hardly any legitimate object-matter of respect or confidence, she appears notwithstanding a rather amiable person; possessed with a girlish fancy and hankering for the vanities and glitterings of state, but having no sense of its duties and dignities. . . . I can well imagine that, with those of the audience who had any knowledge in English history,—and many of them no doubt had much,—the delineation of Anne, broken off as it is at the height of her fortune, must have sent their thoughts forward to reflect how the self-same levity of character, which lifted her into Catharine's place, soon afterwards drew upon herself a far more sudden and terrible reverse. And indeed some such thing may be needful, to excuse the authors for not carrying out the truth of history from seedtime to harvest, or at least indicating the consummation of that whereof they so faithfully unfold the beginnings.

The moral effect of this play as a whole is very impressive and very just. And the lesson evolved, so far as it admits of general statement, may be said to stand in showing how sorrow makes sacred the wearer, and how, to our human feelings, suffering, if borne with true dignity and strength of soul, covers a multitude of sins; or, to carry out the point with more special reference to Catharine, it consists, as Mrs. Jameson observes, in illustrating how, by the union of perfect truth with entire benevolence of character, a queen, and a heroine of tragedy, though "stripped of all the pomp of place and circumstance," and without any of "the usual sources of poetical interest, as youth, beauty, grace, fancy, commanding intellect, could depend on the moral principle alone to touch the very springs of feeling in our bosoms, and melt and elevate our hearts through the purest and holiest impulses" [see excerpt above, 1833]. (pp. 200-02)

> Rev. H. N. Hudson, "Historical Plays: 'King Henry the Eighth'," in his Shakespeare: His Life, Art, and Characters, Vol. II, revised edition, Ginn & Company, 1872, pp. 170-202.

KARL ELZE (essay date 1874)

[Elze was a nineteenth-century German literary historian who specialized in English literature and philology and was one of the first editors of the German Shakespeare Society's Jahrbuch. In the following excerpt, first published in German in 1874, Elze theorizes that Shakespeare originally wrote Henry VIII in late 1602 or early 1603 to commemorate three important occasions: the seventieth anniversaries of Anne Boleyn's marriage (April, 1603) and coronation (June, 1603), and Queen Elizabeth's seventieth birthday (September, 1603). Elze speculates, however, that the play was not performed at that time—perhaps because Elizabeth died in March of 1603—and was left forgotten until 1613, when it was revised to suit James I. Elze claims that two other writers, Ben Jonson and John Fletcher, added the prologue and epilogue, expanded Katharine's role, and, most importantly, incorporated the laudatory references to James I in Cranmer's final speech. Elze's hypothesis is thus a combination of Edmond Malone's theory that Henry VIII was first written in 1602 or 1603 and James Spedding's argument that two or more authors contributed to the play (see excerpts above, 1778 and 1850). Perhaps the most unusual aspect of Elze's theory is his claim that Shakespeare ceased writing altogether in 1604—a fact which, if true, would make Henry VIII one of his final plays.]

[In] our conviction, 'Henry VIII.,' though written in Elizabeth's lifetime, was not brought upon the stage during that period; had such been the case, perhaps [certain] objectionable points might have been touched up, nay we do not at all feel sure but that some of them were inserted at a later revisal. (p. 164)

Taking everything into consideration, it seems to allow of no doubt that the play, with its apology for Henry, its glorification of Anne Boleyn, and its apotheosis of Elizabeth, was not only written in the reign of Elizabeth, but written expressly for her, to commemorate some festive occasion towards the end of her reign. (pp. 180-81)

Now what was this festive occasion? It seems most natural to think of the day of Elizabeth's birth or baptism, in which case Henry's joy in the birth of the child would have appeared in its fullest light; a joy which in reality did by no means answer the poet's lively description, for the King's ardent desire was to have a son. This deviation from history . . . , is a hint for the right understanding of the play; in fact all the poet's deviations from historical truth point to the same goal. The enthusiastic prophecy with which, like a brilliant piece of firework, Cranmer closes the drama, would on no other day have sounded more splendid, and have transported the audience to greater joy, than on the birthday of the aged Queen, when she herself and her people would look back with a feeling of universal pride and happiness upon her glorious reign, and when all the dangers and inconveniences which had arisen for them

from her father's numerous marriages were happily removed. The play would then have appeared as a last reconciliation of feelings and, as it were, a mellow evening halo of her life. That Cranmer's prophecy is not merely an accidental appendage is clear from the whole structure of the play; it has been interwoven in it from the beginning, and is introduced by previous hints. The Chamberlain, who informs Anne of her promotion in rank, cannot refrain from expressing the presentiment:—

> But from this lady may proceed a gem
> To lighten all this isle,   [II. iii. 78-9]

and the Duke of Suffolk is convinced that she will bring many a blessing to the land 'which shall in it be memorized' [III. ii. 51-2].

And yet we feel convinced that the play was not intended to celebrate the Queen's birthday, but some other festival. For if indeed it had been performed on Elizabeth's last birthday, what would then become of [Henry] Wotton's statement that in 1613 it was a new play? [see excerpt above, 1613]. . . . The eulogy upon James might be a later addition, but what then about the death-scene of Katherine, and the undeniable fact that her character is placed so prominently in the foreground, and delineated so lovingly, that it surpasses the other characters of the play in moral and tragic grandeur, and claims the especial sympathy of the spectator and reader? . . . We here meet with an intrinsic contradiction, an almost inconceivable discord, such as is found in no other of the poet's plays. For we consider it to be impossible that this glorification of Katherine can be blended into an internal unity with that bestowed on Anne Boleyn and her newly born daughter. Shakespeare cannot have aimed at giving a representation of both sides of the picture at one and the same time. Even those critics who recognise Katherine as the inner moral or dramatic centre of the play, must feel as great an objection to this contradiction as we do, for they are after all unable to deny the whitewashing of Anne's character, and the consequent apotheosis of Elizabeth. . . . From whatever point of view we may regard the play, we find in it an evident discord which, in our opinion, can only be explained in one way, and that is the following.

On the 12th of April, 1603, exactly seventy years had elapsed since Anne Boleyn's public nuptials, and this was the day for which the play, written in the winter of 1602-3, was destined. It might indeed have been repeated no less appropriately on Anne's seventieth coronation day (1st of June of the same year), and on Elizabeth's seventieth birthday (7th of September), days which might as well be celebrated by theatrical entertainments as the anniversary of the Queen's accession, in honour of which in 1595 a masque was represented at Essex House. Unfortunately however Elizabeth was no longer alive on these days, but died on the 24th of March. The play had thus lost its object, and was laid aside. Perhaps it was now to be published, so as not to have been written altogether in vain; at least, according to Steevens, in 1604 a play, under the title of 'Henry VIII.,' was entered on the Stationers' Register by the well-known publisher Nathaniel Butter. It is indeed there called an 'Enterlude,' and it may justly be asked whether this designation allows us to think of Shakespeare's play. . . . It is highly probable that this entry refers to Samuel Rowley's 'When You See Me, You Know Me,' which was really published by Butter in the year 1605, and although it bears the name of a Chronicle-history on the title-page, yet much more readily admits of being styled an 'Enterlude' than Shakespeare's work. A second edition of this play appeared in 1613, and thus reminded the company of the Globe Theatre of the Shakespearean drama in their possession, which they now resolved to bring upon the stage. That for this purpose it had to undergo a remodelling is obvious. First of all the prophetic eulogy on Elizabeth had to lose its point by being transferred to James. This was, so to say, the lightning conductor to intercept James' displeasure, which the play would otherwise have incurred, the actors perhaps not excepted. The great majority of English and German critics are now unanimous in considering this second part of the prophecy as an incongruous, awkwardly inserted interpolation, and nothing seems more plausible than that the allusion to the age and death of Elizabeth was likewise inserted at the same time. For how could the poet or adapter have made the transition to James without first causing Elizabeth to die? But the adapter was not content with extending the prophetic eulogy to James, he felt very well that the actual object of the play must be somewhat disguised. This he did by giving greater proportions and a tragic turn to Katherine's character, whereas it no doubt previously stood in perfect accordance with the other characters, as also with the whole tendency of the play. . . . It was only now that Katherine became a martyr. The scene between her and the two Cardinals is so loosely connected with the plot, and can so easily be dispensed with, that it may unhesitatingly be regarded as a subsequent interpolation. The same applies . . . to the death-scene of Katherine, although its substance cannot be cut out from the play as completely as that of the scene just mentioned. For that Katherine's death must have been mentioned in the original form of the play seems unquestionable from what has been said above.

A confirmation of this interpretation, and one which has as yet not been noticed, seems to be discoverable in the epilogue, no matter by whom it may have been composed. Here we read the remarkable lines:—

> I fear
> All the expected good we're like to hear
> For this play at this time, is only in
> The merciful construction of good women;
> For such a one we show'd 'em.   [Epilogue. 7-11]

What is the meaning of 'at this time?' Can it be otherwise interpreted than thus: 'At the representation of this play, written ten years ago, and now remodelled, we hope principally to obtain the approbation of good women, for such a one we have now introduced to them in the person of Katherine;—had the play been represented at the time of its composition, we should have reaped a different praise for it.' That women must sympathise most with the part of Katherine is obvious, and in spite of the advantageous light in which the poet has placed Anne Boleyn, yet the melancholy fate of the former, and the dignity with which she bears it, ensure for her the undisputed preference among women. The prologue admits this with a distinctness which leaves nothing to be desired:—

> Such noble scenes as draw the eye to flow,
> We now present. Those that can pity, here
> May, if they think it well, let fall a tear;
> The subject will deserve it.

Further:—

> Be sad, as we would make ye.

And in conclusion:—

> And, if you can be merry then, I'll say
> A man may weep upon his wedding day.
>   [Prologue. 4-7, 25, 31-2]

This latter expression once more calls to mind the hypothesis that 'Henry VIII.' was composed for the nuptials of the Count Palatine, which for this reason alone ought to have been excluded: could Shakespeare or any one else have wished to draw tears from the eyes of the audience, if the play was intended for the celebration of such a joyful event? The contradiction is evident. At the same time the lines quoted seem to prove that the author of the prologue and the reviser of Katherine's part were one and the same person. (pp. 181-87)

Both the prologue and epilogue, as Dr. Johnson has remarked, are quite in B. Jonson's manner; if they stood in his works nobody would think of ascribing them to Shakespeare; both were certainly added in 1612-13. The death-scene of Katherine, which we have shown must in all likelihood be ascribed to the author of the prologue, would do B. Jonson the highest credit, even if he should have been favoured with oral instructions from the poet respecting it; perhaps it is due to Fletcher, who was better able to enter upon a foreign intention and diction than B. Jonson, so that indeed three hands were at work on the play. At all events the scene is carried out completely in the spirit of Shakespeare.

In conclusion we cannot avoid touching once more on the circumstance that we indeed possess no kind of trustworthy information as to when Shakespeare may have ended his poetical career, but that from several reasons it appears as if in the general opinion much too long a duration were assigned to it. If Shakespeare's regular production ceased as early as 1604 . . . then 'Henry VIII.,' in spite of this alteration of the chronological arrangement, must be reckoned as one of his latest plays, and its loose versification would then in no way cause a difficulty. (pp. 191-92)

Karl Elze, "'King Henry VIII'," in his Essays on Shakespeare, *translated by L. Dora Schmitz, Macmillan and Co., 1874, pp. 151-92.*

ALGERNON CHARLES SWINBURNE   (essay date 1880)

*[Swinburne was an English poet, dramatist, and critic who devoted much of his literary career to the study of Shakespeare and other Elizabethan writers. His three books on Shakespeare—*A Study of Shakespeare *(1880),* Shakespeare *(1909), and* Three Plays of Shakespeare *(1909)—all demonstrate his keen interest in Shakespeare's poetic talents and, especially, his major tragedies. In the following excerpt, taken from the first work mentioned above, Swinburne rejects James Spedding's theory that Shakespeare and John Fletcher collaborated on* Henry VIII *(see excerpt above, 1850). In so doing, Swinburne became one of the only critics in the latter half of the nineteenth century to accept Shakespeare as the sole author of the play; thus, he is the precursor of such twentieth-century commentators as Peter Alexander (1931), Edgar I. Fripp (1938), G. Wilson Knight (1947), and R. A. Foakes (1957). Swinburne maintains that the structure of* Henry VIII *suggests only one author and that the very best of Fletcher's work can never compare to those scenes Spedding attributes to him, particularly the death of Katharine. Most recent twentieth-century scholars accept Swinburne's conclusions on the authorship of* Henry VIII, *but for an opposing view see the excerpts by A. A. Parker (1948) and Robert Ornstein (1972).]*

There can be few serious students of Shakespeare who have not sometimes felt that possibly the hardest problem involved in their study is that which requires for its solution some reasonable and acceptable theory as to the play of *King Henry VIII*. None such has ever yet been offered; and I certainly cannot pretend to supply one. Perhaps however it may be possible to do some service by an attempt to disprove what is untenable, even though it should not be possible to produce in its stead any positive proof of what we may receive as matter of absolute faith.

The veriest tiro in criticism who knows anything of the subject in hand must perceive, what is certainly not beyond a schoolboy's range of vision, that the metre and the language of this play are in great part so like the language and the metre of Fletcher that the first and easiest inference would be to assume the partnership of that poet in the work. In former days it was Jonson whom the critics and commentators of their time saw good to select as the colleague or the editor of Shakespeare; but a later school of criticism has resigned the notion that the fifth act was retouched and adjusted by the author of *Volpone* to the taste of his patron James. The later theory is more plausible than this; the primary objection to it is that it is too facile and superficial. It is waste of time to point out what any intelligent and imaginative child with a tolerable ear for metre who had read a little of the one and the other poet could see for himself—that much of the play is externally as like the usual style of Fletcher as it is unlike the usual style of Shakespeare. The question is whether we can find one scene, one speech, one passage, which in spirit, in scope, in purpose, bears the same or any comparable resemblance to the work of Fletcher. . . . The speech of Buckingham, for example, on his way to execution, is of course at first sight very like the finest speeches of the kind in Fletcher; here is the same smooth and fluent declamation, the same prolonged and persistent melody, which if not monotonous is certainly not various; the same pure, lucid, perspicuous flow of simple rather than strong and elegant rather than exquisite English; and yet, if we set it against the best examples of the kind which may be selected from such tragedies as *Bonduca* or *The False One,* against the rebuke addressed by Caratach to his cousin or by Caesar to the murderers of Pompey—and no finer instances of tragic declamation can be chosen from the work of this great master of rhetorical dignity and pathos—I cannot but think we shall perceive in it a comparative severity and elevation which will be missed when we turn back from it to the text of Fletcher. There is an aptness of phrase, an abstinence from excess, a ''plentiful lack'' of mere flowery and superfluous beauties, which we may rather wish than hope to find in the most famous of Shakespeare's successors. But if not his work, we may be sure it was his model; a model which he often approached, which he often studied, but which he never attained. It is never for absolute truth and fitness of expression, it is always for eloquence and sweetness, for fluency and fancy, that we find the tragic scenes of Fletcher most praiseworthy; and the motive or mainspring of interest is usually anything but natural or simple. Now the motive here is as simple, the emotion as natural as possible; the author is content to dispense with all the violent or far-fetched or fantastic excitement from which Fletcher could hardly ever bring himself completely to abstain. . . . [In] any of the typical tragedies of Fletcher, in *Thierry and Theodoret,* in *Valentinian,* in *The Double Marriage,* the scenes which for power and beauty of style may reasonably be compared with this of the execution of Buckingham will be found more forced in situation, more fanciful in language than this. Many will be found more beautiful, many more exciting; the famous interview of Thierry with the veiled Ordella, and the scene answering to this in the fifth act where Brunhalt is confronted with her dying son, will be at once remembered by all dramatic students; and the parts of Lucina and Juliana may each be described as a continuous arrangement of passionate and pathetic effects. But in which of these parts and in which of these plays shall we find a scene so simple, an effect so modest, a

situation so unforced as here? where may we look for the same temperance of tone, the same control of excitement, the same steadiness of purpose? If indeed Fletcher could have written this scene, or the farewell of Wolsey to his greatness, or his parting scene with Cromwell, he was perhaps not a greater poet, but he certainly was a tragic writer capable of loftier self-control and severer self-command, than he has ever shown himself elsewhere.

And yet, if this were all, we might be content to believe that the dignity of the subject and the high example of his present associate had for once lifted the natural genius of Fletcher above itself. But the fine and subtle criticism of Mr. Spedding [see excerpt above, 1850] has in the main, I think, successfully and clearly indicated the lines of demarcation undeniably discernible in this play between the severer style of certain scenes or speeches and the laxer and more fluid style of others; between the graver, solider, more condensed parts of the apparently composite work, and those which are clearer, thinner, more diffused and diluted in expression. If under the latter head we had to class such passages only as the dying speech of Buckingham and the christening speech of Cranmer, it might after all be almost impossible to resist the internal evidence of Fletcher's handiwork. Certainly we hear the same soft continuous note of easy eloquence, level and limpid as a stream of crystalline transparence, in the plaintive adieu of the condemned statesman and the panegyrical prophecy of the favoured prelate. If this, I say, were all, we might admit that there is nothing— I have already admitted it—in either passage beyond the poetic reach of Fletcher. But on the hypothesis so ably maintained by [Spedding] . . . there hangs no less a consequence than this: that we must assign to the same hand the crowning glory of the whole poem, the death-scene of Katherine. Now if Fletcher could have written that scene—a scene on which the only criticism ever passed, the only commendation ever bestowed, by the verdict of successive centuries, has been that of tears and silence—if Fletcher could have written a scene so far beyond our applause, so far above our acclamation, then the memory of no great poet has ever been so grossly wronged, so shamefully defrauded of its highest claim to honour. But, with all reverence for that memory, I must confess that I cannot bring myself to believe it. Any explanation appears to me more probable than this. . . . Pathos and concentration are surely not among the dominant notes of Fletcher's style or the salient qualities of his intellect. Except perhaps in the beautiful and famous passage where Hengo dies in his uncle's arms, I doubt whether in any of the variously and highly coloured scenes played out upon the wide and shifting stage of his fancy the genius of Fletcher has ever unlocked the source of tears. (pp. 81-8)

[Looking] back upon those passages of the play which first suggest the handiwork of Fletcher, and which certainly do now and then seem almost identical in style with his, I think we shall hardly find the difference between these and other parts of the same play so wide and so distinct as the difference between the undoubted work of Fletcher and the undoubted work of Shakespeare. What that difference is we are fortunately able to determine with exceptional certitude, and with no supplementary help from conjecture of probabilities. In the play which is undoubtedly a joint work of these poets the points of contact and the points of disunion are unmistakable by the youngest eye. In the very last scene of *The Two Noble Kinsmen,* we can tell with absolute certainty what speeches were appended or interpolated by Fletcher; we can pronounce with positive conviction what passages were completed and what parts were left unfinished by Shakespeare. Even on Mr. Spedding's theory it can hardly be possible to do as much for *King Henry VIII*. The lines of demarcation, however visible or plausible, are fainter by far than these. . . . But in *King Henry VIII*. it should be remarked that though we not unfrequently find the same preponderance as in Fletcher's work of verses with a double ending—which in English verse at least are not in themselves feminine, and need not be taken to constitute, as in Fletcher's case they do, a note of comparative effeminacy or relaxation in tragic style—we do not find the perpetual predominance of those triple terminations so peculiarly and notably dear to that poet; so that even by the test of the metremongers who would reduce the whole question at issue to a point which might at once be solved by the simple process of numeration the argument in favour of Fletcher can hardly be proved tenable; for the metre which evidently has one leading quality in common with his is as evidently wanting in another at least as marked and as necessary to establish—if established it can be by any such test taken singly and apart from all other points of evidence—the collaboration of Fletcher with Shakespeare in this instance. And if the proof by mere metrical similitude is thus imperfect, there is here assuredly no other kind of test which may help to fortify the argument by any suggestion of weight even comparable to this. In those passages which would seem most plausibly to indicate the probable partnership of Fletcher, the unity and sustained force of the style keep it generally above the average level of his; there is less admixture or intrusion of lyric or elegiac quality; there is more of temperance and proportion alike in declamation and in debate. And throughout the whole play, and under all the diversity of composite subjects and conflicting interest which disturbs the unity of action, there is a singleness of spirit, a general unity or concord of inner tone, in marked contrast to the utter discord and discrepancy of the several sections of *The Two Noble Kinsmen*. We admit, then, that this play offers us in some not unimportant passages the single instance of a style not elsewhere precisely or altogether traceable in Shakespeare; that no exact parallel to it can be found among his other plays; and that if not the partial work it may certainly be taken as the general model of Fletcher in his tragic poetry. On the other hand, we contend that its exceptional quality might perhaps be explicable as a tentative essay in a new line by one who tried so many styles before settling into his latest; and that, without far stronger, clearer, and completer proof than has yet been or can ever be advanced, the question is not solved but merely evaded by the assumption of a double authorship. (pp. 90-4)

> *Algernon Charles Swinburne, "Second Period: Comic and Historic," in his* A Study of Shakespeare, *R. Worthington, 1880, pp. 66-169.*

FRANCES ANNE KEMBLE   (essay date 1882)

[*The following excerpt is taken from Kemble's* Notes Upon Some of Shakespeare's Plays, *first published in 1882. In it, she undertakes a character study of Katharine and Wolsey, arguing that each of these two figures is dominated by an abundance of pride—the former motivated by "pride of birth," the latter by "pride of power." Kemble's relatively harsh judgment opposes the views of such earlier critics as Samuel Johnson (1765), William Hazlitt (1817), and Anna Brownell Jameson (1833).*]

The Queen [Katherine] and Wolsey in *Henry VIII*. are both types of pride, and yet there is an essential difference in the pride which they each represent. Undoubtedly, the pride of birth and the mere pride of power (whether that power be derived from wealth, intellect, or exaltation of station) are very different things. Katharine represents the pure pride of birth, and Wolsey that of power. Pride of birth, the noblest species of the vice, is not incompatible with considerable personal humility, and the proof that Shakespeare thought so may be found in the Queen's frequently modest and humble mention of herself, her infinite deference to the King, and the repeated reference by the other characters in the play to her meek and quiet spirit. That this pride sometimes consorts with humbleness arises from the fact that it does not rest on any personal, individual quality or achievement, and is therefore less directly egotistical and selfish than the other; and being of a less gross quality is oftener the snare of noble and refined minds, from which, when once possessed by it, it will hardly endure to be eradicated. . . . Of this lofty-seeming sin, this pride of birth, Shakespeare's Queen Katharine is a most perfect type, as well as an instance of the (almost) impossibility of a mind once infected with it ever losing the taint. No change of outward circumstance can affect it, and loss of fortune and decline of station can only tend to increase, in those who have it, their veneration for a species of distinction compatible with the narrowest means and lowliest obscurity. The pride of power, that pride which Wolsey exhibits, is, on the contrary, almost invariably arrogant, and very seldom co-exists with any personal humility; for it springs generally from a consciousness of personal merit, strength, capacity, good fortune or achievement, and thus is necessarily grossly egotistical. (pp. 83-6)

Those who "achieve greatness" do not always . . . encounter with perfect equanimity those who are "born great:" it takes a spirit of rather unusual natural nobility to do so, and the dignity which is not shaken by falling is as nothing to the dignity which is not fluttered by rising. Wolsey, though he had made himself cardinal and hoped to make himself pope, could not unmake himself a butcher's son; and the serene sense of social superiority which men of high and princely birth had over him in this respect galled his consciousness of general power, in which he so greatly excelled them, with a bitter sense of utter impotence in this one particular. To this species of aggressive pride may be attributed the insane arrogance of his "Ego et Rex meus" ["I and my king"]. . . . In the grossminded, low-born "fellow of Ipswich," whose vigorous intellect and powerful will had raised him to strange heights of glory, it was the mere excess and intoxication of the sense of self-made greatness, which had learned to look upon coronets and crowns, and the papal tiara itself, as the instruments or prizes of its daring ambition, to be used or won, but never respected by him with that religious veneration which men of true nobility have felt for them. To him they were merely the noble means of base self-aggrandisement.

On the other hand, though this species of pride is so much grosser and more vulgar and offensive, I believe it will always be found more easily capable of cure and eradication than the other. . . . Thus, Wolsey might have become humble when once hopelessly fallen from his high fortune, because, ruined, he was nothing in the world's account but the butcher's son, all whose personal ability had not sufficed to retain his great position, and might not suffice to regain it. In this predicament the nobler powers of his mind, shifting their point of view so as to take in more than the mere worldly value of his lost prosperity, might present to him a higher and holier standard by which his estimate of the earthly greatness he had forfeited would become more just, and his wisdom and learning and powerful intellectual faculties, chastened in their action by the sweet uses of adversity, might finally produce in him the grace of meekness and humility. . . . Not so Katharine. All the virtue and wisdom she was mistress of could not make her humble, because she was, and remained through ruin and disgrace, even unto "beggarly divorcement" and death, the daughter of the king of Spain, the wife of two kings of England, and felt herself bound, by all the religion and superstition of early training and long habit, to honour her station in herself. So with disgraces *grew* her pride; and with one dying hand stretched out to receive the heavenly crown she was about to put on, with the other she imperiously commanded homage to that earthly one which had been rudely snatched from her brows. Wolsey honoured himself in his station: it was to him the palpable proof of his own great powers of achievement, and when he lost it his confidence in himself must have been shaken to its foundations, and he may almost have fallen into the hopelessness of self-contempt. With what a poisonous bitterness of absolute defeat does he utter the words—

> O Cromwell,
> The king has gone beyond me: all my glories
> In that one woman I have lost for ever.
> [III. ii. 407-09]
> (pp. 87-92)

Frances Anne Kemble, "Notes on 'Henry VIII'," in her Notes upon Some of Shakespeare's Plays, *Richard Bentley & Son, 1882, pp. 81-100.*

DENTON J. SNIDER (essay date 1890)

[*Snider was an American teacher, philosopher, and poet who followed the precepts of the German philosopher Georg Wilhelm Friedrich Hegel and contributed to the dissemination of Hegel's philosophy in America. In the following excerpt, Snider contends that the key to understanding* Henry VIII *resides in the ambiguous presentation of the political reformation in England during Henry's reign. He regards the political and moral conflict of the Reformation as a central concern in the play—represented on the political level by the dominance and defeat of Wolsey, and on the domestic level by the divorce of the Catholic queen Katharine and the coronation of the Protestant queen Anne. For Snider, the major flaw in* Henry VIII *is Shakespeare's failure to reconcile the antagonism between the play's moral and political spheres; in other words, he fails to resolve the sympathy we feel toward the characters of Buckingham, Wolsey, and Katharine with the political exigencies that make the tragedies of these individuals inevitable. For further commentary on the political nature of* Henry VIII, *see the excerpts by Frank Kermode (1947), G. Wilson Knight (1947), R. A. Foakes (1957), Paul Bertram (1962), C. B. Purdom (1963), Tom McBride (1977), and Eckhard Auberlen (1980).*]

Henry the Eighth brings to a close the English Historical Drama, though its connection with that series cannot be termed intimate. The subordination of the turbulent nobility, which created so much trouble in the Wars of the Roses, is manifested in the fate of Buckingham; the crown has attained an unquestioned supremacy. The revival of letters and the importance of culture are often indicated; learning has even come to the point of contesting the palm with rank. But the main point which is sought for by every reader as the very marrow of this period is the great religious revolution—the transition of England from Catholicism to Protestantism. Every other issue of that age sinks into insignificance in comparison; there is no meaning in the reign of Henry the Eighth without the Reformation.

The present drama has, undoubtedly, the change of religion as its fundamental theme, for it could hardly have any other, but the event is portrayed with that dimness and ambiguity so characteristic of almost everything else in the work. The revolution of conscience is made to depend on a guilty passion of the King; the only morally heroic character is immolated to a movement whose essence was, if anything, the revolt of morality against corruption. Indeed, it must be confessed that in this moral and religious revolution, as here portrayed, morality and religion are quite left out. It is the *political* element which is brought into prominence, for the Reformation was also a political revolution.

Here is the key of the play—the standard by which it is to be judged—and every other test is inadequate. The political object of the See of Rome was the subordination of State to Church; all nations of Christendom had ultimately to be subjected to the Pope—not alone in religious, but also often in civil matters. The result was a perpetual strife between Church and State, even in ages of universal Catholic ascendency; which strife finally cumlinated in a separation from the Church on the part of certain nations which were determined to be absolute, even in ecclesiastical matters. This gave rise to the Reformation, whose political principle was subordination of Church to State. To be sure, moral and religious freedom was coupled with political freedom, though the former is, not merely omitted, but repeatedly violated, in the present drama.

The action of *Henry the Eighth,* in general, moves from Catholic England to Protestant England; from Catherine of Aragon to Anne Boleyn as Queen; from Henry the instrument of Wolsey to Henry the uncontrolled arbitrary monarch; from the State ruled by its own King. The revolution is purely political—at least, as here represented—though it is accomplished in the name and by means of the clerical profession. (pp. 489-91)

It will, accordingly, be manifest that there is a culmination in the play which separates it into two movements, notwithstanding its otherwise disjointed character. This culmination is, in a general way, the fall of Wolsey and the marriage of Anne Boleyn; the one movement shows Henry, who is the central figure of the play as the instrument of Wolsey, till his enfranchisement; the second movement shows Henry freely acting in his religious, domestic, and political relations. The two movements may, hence, be named the Wolseiad and Henriad. Also, the threads should be taken as two—the King in his political relations, which manifest a variety of forms, and the King in his domestic relations towards the two Queens. (p. 492)

The first thread of the first movement opens with the conflict between Wolsey and Buckingham; Henry stands in the background—the dupe and the instrument of the Cardinal's ambition. Buckingham is the central figure of a group of high-born relatives and friends; he represents the pride and privileges of the nobility against the new encroachments of "this butcher cur" (Wolsey) and of the men of learning, for now "a beggar's book outworths a noble's blood." Buckingham is himself learned, eloquent, and popular; his birth places him next to Henry in the line of succession to the throne; he is, therefore, a very manifest object of the King's suspicion. (pp. 492-93)

Buckingham proceeds boldly, in spite of the warnings of his friends, and seems on the point of publicly accusing the Cardinal of treason, when suddenly he is arrested himself on the same charge. He sees his fate—"the net has fallen upon me;" he was open and reckless, while Wolsey proceeded with perfect secrecy till he was prepared with proof at every point. It is hard to tell the extent of Buckingham's guilt, in view of his denials; quite as difficult is it to discover the extent of Wolsey's suborning of the witnesses. It is a great blemish in the characterization of these two leading men that the guilt of each is thus left in doubt. (pp. 493-94)

We must next try to find the supreme aim of Wolsey's striving, and therefrom obtain a judgment of the man. His great object in this life is the Papacy. Hither every look bends; every act, however contorted its course, ultimately leads to the Chair of Saint Peter. He says in the hour of humiliation that ambition ruined him; the highest object of ambition in Christendom was the Papal Chair. Thus he would be above all monarchs in name as well as reality—above Henry, who would have to submit to him without disguise. Such, then, was his ambition—the love of supreme arbitrary domination, which the headship of the Church alone could confer.

The acts of Wolsey must always be viewed with this supreme end before the mind of the reader; it is a weakness of the play that Wolsey himself is not made to indicate his object more definitely, for we have to gather it from the mouths of his most vindictive enemies. . . . Wolsey is utterly unscrupulous in his means of attaining his personal end; it is plain that he intends employing bribery at Rome. His immense accumulation of wealth at home is declared to be for the same purpose as his political combinations abroad.

Wolsey is, therefore, the very strongest representative of external domination over the State by the Church. He cares little or nothing for the spiritual purposes of the great religious organization; he wants it for its political supremacy. To be the head of Christendom is his ambition, to which he is just now immolating England. (pp. 494-95)

After Buckingham, Wolsey's next conflict is with Queen Catherine. She has interfered strongly in favor of Buckingham; she has also caused through her influence certain onerous taxes to be repealed, the merit of which repeal Wolsey tries to turn to his own advantage when he cannot obtain the proceeds in money. But the chief ground of his hatred is that she is a Spaniard, and a relation of the Emperor; she thus stands in the way of Wolsey's highest ambition. The Cardinal had already infused into the King's mind certain doubts about the rightfulness of his marriage with Catherine, and the doubts were favored by the unhappy loss of all the male offspring of the royal pair. It is a subtle poison well calculated to work upon a character half hypocritical and half superstitious, like that of Henry. Yet here the drama again leaves us in a haze of uncertainty; the Queen unquestionably looks upon Wolsey as the author of her downfall, though he denies, and seems to disprove her charges from the mouth of the King. Wolsey, therefore, if Catherine's charge be true, must have instigated the Bishop of Bayonne to question the legitimacy of the marriage—so the reader with hesitation inclines to decide, though such an inference lies wholly outside of the play. The object of the Cardinal was to form a matrimonial alliance with France, in order to further his own plan. He uses the King as an instrument, yet Henry must not be permitted to know his own situation, for his arbitrary temper would render him exceedingly intractable. The time has now arrived when Henry's capricious passion and Wolsey's secret purpose will conflict. The King's love for Anne Boleyn suddenly falls athwart the Cardinal's scheme; the latter undertakes furtively to overreach the King; he is found out—then comes his fall. The eyes of the King are opened; henceforth he is resolved to reign untrammeled by any restraint. This makes him an immoral tyrant, but also it makes him the hero of English Protestantism. He is as little governed by ethical ties as by the authority of the Church.

Thus Wolsey with his great hopes is wrecked—wrecked upon a caprice of the King. His end is hostile to England, at least external to England; though its chief minister, he has his eye upon another object than his country. Thus the political relation of Rome to the State has become intolerable; it must be broken. Though we may think little of Henry's motives, the result is in the highest degree commendable, indeed necessary. (pp. 496-97)

So much for the King in his political relations; we may now consider the second thread of his life—his domestic relations—though they cannot be wholly separated from the political thread. (p. 498)

The change of Queens . . . runs parallel to the change of religion—and each Queen may to a certain extent be taken as the symbol of her faith. Anne is represented as an artless maid, full of sympathy with Catherine in her trial; she says that she would not be a queen, reading her destiny in Catherine's:—

> —'Tis better to be lowly born,
> And range with humble livers in content,
> Than to be perk'd up in a glistering grief,
> And wear a golden sorrow.   [II. iii. 19-22]

The unexpected honors of the King overwhelmed her; she does not desert the Queen, yet she cannot resist the King—a simple maid, full of devotion and tenderness, yet without any strength of will or intellect.

Queen Catherine is the most beautiful character—the true heroine of the drama. In her double relation, as queen and as wife, she has been supremely true to both State and Family. She interfered for justice in the case of Buckingham; she came to the aid of the oppressed subjects in their grievances. Her devotion to her husband has been absolute—indeed, too great; she has suppressed all her likes and dislikes in his favor; it has been her great aim in life to dwell in complete unity with him. She combines two traits rarely found conjoined in woman—strength and sweetness; her force of character conflicts not in the least with her amiability. But in her person, though not through her fault, the two relations collide—political necessity demands a new queen for England. This horrible necessity tears asunder the conjugal bond—unqueened is unwifed. Again the Family is sacrificed to the State; domestic life is swept away by a national requirement.

Such is the historical justification of her fate, though there is no justification for the conduct of Wolsey and Henry. The decree of History is that England must change religions in order to attain to her true destiny. . . . Catherine is a Catholic, a Spanish Catholic, and relative of the Emperor, Charles the Fifth, the great supporter of the Papacy; hence her political influence must be eliminated if England is to be free from external domination. But her political influence rests upon her being wife of the monarch—thus the domestic bond is involved. The reader may think that this result does not necessarily follow, but the poetic significance of Catherine is to be a representative of some principle; the divorce from her is the symbol of the divorce from the Church. (pp. 498-500)

The antagonism between the moral and political spheres, which we have noticed everywhere in the Historical Plays, reaches in *Henry the Eighth* its culmination. It divides the work into two unreconciled spiritual tendencies which clash in the soul with an infernal discord. Undoubtedly all dramas have or ought to have some ethical conflict as the basis of the action, but the conflict ought in some way to be harmonized in its own, that is, ethical domain. We may grant in the present case, that the end attained was the true end of History; but the means employed seems quite to balance the grand historical result. In this respect *Henry the Eighth* has in it an ethical scission which corresponds to that felt in *All's Well that Ends Well*. We may be reconciled at last to the outcome, but it is a forced reconciliation. (p. 501)

The second movement shows Henry as absolute master, both in the political and domestic thread. Wolsey, Cardinal Prime Minister, ambitious of the Papacy, has come to an untimely end. The King's predilection now goes out towards Cranmer, a prelate who did not want the Papacy, but quite the opposite, namely, its annihilation. But Wolsey has left behind a faint reflection of himself in Gardiner, Bishop of Winchester, who is seeking to extirpate the "new opinions divers and dangerous," the main supporter of which he sees to be Cranmer. That there may be no doubt about the matter, the home of these new opinions is distinctly indicated to be Upper Germany. So the religious conflict comes out into bold prominence—the two prelates being the two champions of the respective sides.

Cranmer is on the point of being sent to the Tower by the Council at the instigation of his enemy, when King Henry suddenly enters and takes the part of Cranmer. This is the end of the politico-religious struggle—the King sides with the promoter of the new opinions. As before said, it is less a matter of Church than of State; with Henry it is not even a matter of State, but an arbitrary caprice of passion. Still he receives the support of the nation; his successors to this day have upheld the same policy, or had to surrender the crown; the separation from the Papal family was, therefore, a national act. The ground thereof lies patent: England thus attains complete national autonomy—the supreme object of her striving since the beginning of her history; King Henry, therefore, was acting in harmony with the nation, which supported him; this is his historical justification. But as individual, judged by moral tests, he is a wretch, a bigot, yet a hypocrite—his deepest ruling principle being his passion. Defense there is for his deed—none at all for his motives. There ought, doubtless, to be punishment for his moral violation; his career, as shown in this drama, looks too much like a career of successful villainy. If Henry had consciously subordinated moral to political considerations, he might have attained the rank of a Hero, as is the case with a number of Shakespeare's characters. But the mainspring of his actions is capricious passion; the good results are an accident, and in no sense come from his intention.

It is possible to regard Henry as possessed of a subtle political sense, deeper than all his caprices; he may have dimly felt that his individual wish coincided with England's will. At any rate the World-Spirit seemed to take a fantastic delight in clothing

Act I. Scene i. Wolsey and Buckingham. By Solomon Hart. The Department of Rare Books and Special Collections, The University of Michigan Library.

itself in the unrighteous whims of this monarch. His temporary fickleness bore in it a change which has been lasting; his caprice was a strange caper of history itself.

The domestic thread, showing the Queens, remains to be considered. As Anne rises, Catherine descends; the brilliant coronation of the former and the mournful retirement of the latter stand side by side in the drama. Their connection with the general thought of the play is that each Queen is, to a certain extent, the representative of the colliding religions; the change of Queens is a reflection of the change of faiths. (pp. 503-05)

Catherine remains the heroine in defeat, she is successful in her want of success. She combines supreme queenliness with humility; meekness and pride in her do not conflict, but really unite to make one character. She never gives up her right, yet never is uncharitable. Morally she is without a flaw; but politically she is selected as the flawless sacrifice to the new age.

But the counterpart to this tragic side is the coronation of the beautiful Anne Boleyn, amid brilliant ceremonies and the hearty applause of the people. Another festival is held at the christening of the new-born daughter, Elizabeth, terminated by the fervid prophecies of Cranmer. For she will inherit the blessings of the present victory; wisdom, virtue, and peace shall reign in her name. A glance into the future reveals the prospect of untold happiness; still, in the somber background is beheld the domestic tragedy, which deeply tinges the feelings. But political enfranchisement has been reached; no foreign domination of the Church will hereafter fetter the souls of Englishmen; here we arrive at the true reconciling result of this struggle, which reconciliation, however, is not without a twinge. (pp. 506-07)

> *Denton J. Snider, " 'King Henry VIII'," in his* The Shakespearian Drama, a Commentary: The Histories, *Indiana Publishing Company, 1894, pp. 485-508.*

E. K. CHAMBERS   (essay date 1908)

[*Chambers occupies a transitional position in Shakespearean criticism, one which connects the biographical sketches and character analyses of the nineteenth century with the historical, technical, and textual criticism of the twentieth century. While a member of the education department at Oxford University, Chambers earned his reputation as a scholar with his multivolume works,* The Medieval Stage *and* The Elizabethan Stage, *while he also edited* The Red Letter Shakespeare. *Chambers investigated both the purpose and limitations of each dramatic genre as Shakespeare presented it, and speculated on how the dramatist's work was influenced by contemporary historical issues and his own frame of mind. The excerpt below is taken from his introduction to the 1908 Red Letter edition of* Henry VIII. *In it, Chambers contends that, although the existing text of the play indicates two separate writers, it is more likely that the original version of* Henry VIII *was written completely by Shakespeare in the early 1590s, then revised by both Shakespeare and Fletcher in 1613. Chambers tentatively suggests that Shakespeare's original* Henry VIII *was entitled* Buckingham, *a play known to have been written in 1593 by an anonymous dramatist. No other critic accepts this theory, and Chambers himself altered his opinion in his* William Shakespeare: A Study of Facts and Problems *(1930), stating that* Buckingham *"is more likely to be* Richard III *than an early* Henry VIII."]

Modern criticism has long ago made up its mind that *Henry the Eighth,* in the form in which it has come down to us, cannot be classed as a complete and unaided work of Shakespeare. It was the acute analysis of James Spedding, the biographer of Bacon, which first assured the existence of a second hand,

recognized it as the hand of John Fletcher, and after distinguishing on grounds of general aesthetic feeling between the two elements of the play, succeeded in confirming the result by the more mechanical application of the so-called metrical tests. (p. 316)

But the critical difficulties of *Henry the Eighth* begin rather than end with the establishment of Fletcher; since if there is substantial agreement as to this, there is the widest diversity of opinion as to the relations of Shakespeare to the younger dramatist, and as to the conditions under which their work came to be presented in combination. . . . The non-Fletcherian half of the play comprises portions of each Act and touches upon all the various motives, the fall of Buckingham, the rise of Anne Boleyn, the repudiation of Katherine, the disgrace of Wolsey, the intrigue against Cranmer, which succeed each other in the plot. Its scenes are closely dove-tailed into those assigned to Fletcher; and it is difficult to see why, if Shakespeare had started the play independently, he should have selected just those scenes to be written first. You can write a play from beginning to end, or you can write the most significant scenes first and then work round them. But the non-Fletcherian scenes follow neither of these methods, and their distribution seems hardly intelligible except on the hypothesis of collaboration. I do not think that any importance is to be attached to the view that it would be beneath Shakespeare's dignity to collaborate with Fletcher. Those who hold it are imperfectly acquainted with the literary conditions of the sixteenth and seventeenth centuries.

But does the attribution of the non-Fletcherian scenes to Shakespeare carry with it a responsibility for the structure and the meaning of the play? That is a more serious question; for, in spite of its fine rhetorical passages, it would be impossible to maintain that *Henry the Eighth* reaches a high level of excellence. It suffers from the multiplicity of its issues, taken straight over from the chronicle; and in especial from the want of dramatic sense, which spoils the balance of its parts by laying the highest colour upon precisely those elements which should have been kept in the background. The contrast between the overthrow of Wolsey's overweening ambition and the triumphant emergence of Anne Boleyn, bearing with her the destinies of Elizabethan England, was an effective scheme enough. The Buckingham and the Cranmer episodes are perhaps sufficiently subordinated to the two main motives which they respectively support. But there is almost an ethical obtuseness in the stress placed upon the sorrows of the admirable Katherine, and in the failure to observe that dramatic sympathy won for her could only militate against the dramatic sympathy which the whole purpose of the play made it the duty of the writers to win for her more fortunate rival. And thus the interest is over with the death-bed at Kimbolton, and the closing scenes, which should have clinched the dynastic and patriotic theme, inevitably assume the air of an irrelevant and superfluous pageant. This is just the sort of mistake which it was natural for Fletcher to make. Ungifted with the true dramatist's faculty for seeing his design as a whole, he had the instinct for pathos which led him to lavish his poetry upon Katherine's fate without regard to the havoc thereby wrought in the planes of the composition. (pp. 317-20)

It seems implied that Fletcher, whose strong point was not plotting, took the lead in a collaboration with Shakespeare to the extent not only of writing all the most telling scenes, but also of drafting the plot; but, although this is not inconceivable, it is just possible that there may be another alternative. All

Shakespeare's historical plays, apart from *Henry the Eighth*, belong to the earlier periods of his dramatic career. He seemed to have worked out the vein with *Henry the Fifth* in 1599, and one is rather at a loss to imagine why he should have troubled to return to it, fourteen years later. Then again, one is haunted by the feeling that, if Shakespeare had written *Henry the Eighth* at about the time at which he was writing *Henry the Sixth*, its structure would not have been very different from that of the play before us. This does not, of course, extend to the manners of rhythm and phrasing, which, in so far as they are those of Shakespeare, are clearly those of his latest and not of his earliest development. But there is nothing which might not be his early work in the choice of scenes, in the relation to the chronicle, or in that want of the finer spiritual insight in the handling of the emotional issues to which attention has already been drawn. A good deal in the play would become intelligible through the conjecture that it was originally written by Shakespeare during the early 'nineties, as a play on the subject might so naturally have been, to take its place in the series which also contained *Henry the Sixth* and *Richard the Third,* and that it was afterwards rewritten by Shakespeare and Fletcher, upon the old *scenario* but with new dialogue, to meet the demand of 1613. . . . I had arrived at the hypothesis sketched above on *a priori* grounds and without any idea that there was so much as a glimmer of external evidence to support it, when, on turning up *Henslowe's Diary,* I found that there had been a play, which might quite possibly have been just the one I was in search of. This was *Buckingham,* which was played by the Earl of Sussex's men under Henslowe's management on the 30th of December, 1593, and on three other occasions during the following January. There is no evidence that it was then a new play, and it does not appear to have belonged to Henslowe's own stock. It is quite possible that, like *Titus Andronicus,* which was acted by the same company at about the same time, it passed ultimately into the hands of the Chamberlain's men. It might have been Shakespeare's, just as *Richard the Confessor,* which comes next to it in the *Diary,* might have been his *Richard the Third.* I do not assert that it was. Francis Meres does not include a *Henry the Eighth* in his list of Shakespeare's plays in 1598, but that is not quite conclusive, because we are not bound to take the list as exhaustive, especially as regards the earliest journey-work plays, and in fact it does not include *Henry the Sixth.* (pp. 320-22)

> *E. K. Chambers, "'Henry the Eighth'," in his* Shakespeare: A Survey, *Oxford University Press, New York, 1925, pp. 316-24.*

PETER ALEXANDER   (essay date 1931)

[*In a portion of his essay not included here, Alexander presents a detailed examination of the mistakes produced by scholarly conjecture on the history of Shakespeare's life and work. He contends that "historical study has shown that in the history of the text, as in the biography of the poet, the truth is the very opposite of what conjecture has imagined." In the excerpt below, Alexander argues that such editors and scholars as Richard Roderick (1756), James Spedding (1850), and Robert Boyle (see Additional Bibliography) erred significantly in their assessments of* Henry VIII. *Specifically, Alexander questions Spedding's assumption that John Fletcher contributed a large portion of the verse to* Henry VIII, *claiming that the facts demonstrate otherwise. In an argument similar to that of Algernon Charles Swinburne (1880), Alexander states that Spedding's emphasis on the play's double-endings, redundant verse, and run-on lines is not a valid test, especially since many of Shakespeare's plays possess similar elements, including the portions of* Henry VIII *that Sped-*

ding ascribed to Shakespeare. Alexander also maintains that the ideas presented in the play—the self-destructiveness of pride and vanity, the glorification of death, and the inspired prophecy of Elizabeth's reign—are closer in spirit and temperament to Shakespeare than to Fletcher. Alexander was the first twentieth-century critic to assign Henry VIII *solely to Shakespeare's pen; in so doing he prepared the way for such subsequent critics as Edgar I. Fripp (1938), G. Wilson Knight (1947), R. A. Foakes (1957), and other modern scholars who consider the play completely Shakespeare's.*]

[As] a piece of objective criticism designed to make good the presence of other hands in a play assigned to Shakespeare, stands Spedding's essay *On the Several Shares of Shakespeare and Fletcher in the Play of Henry VIII* [see excerpt above, 1850]. As this . . . piece of criticism is still generally considered to provide a safe retreat for the opinion that maintains itself there, it may now be examined in passing to illustrate how facts can be manipulated to accommodate conjecture. (p. 100)

Working on a suggestion made to him by Tennyson that the verse of *Henry VIII* was in places like that of Fletcher, Spedding applied a test borrowed from Hickson, and showed that in some scenes the lines with double endings are considerably in excess of what is found till this time in Shakespeare's verse, and that Fletcher is the only other dramatist that can be shown to have used them so freely. This peculiarity in the verse of *Henry VIII* had already been indicated by Roderick [see excerpt above, 1756]. . . . Roderick, however, exaggerated this peculiarity of *Henry VIII:* there are 1,266 double endings in the 2,666 blank verse lines of *Henry VIII,* while *Coriolanus* has 710; and if *Henry VIII* has 47 per cent. of this type of line there is 35 per cent. in *The Tempest.* Nor is it difficult to find 17 redundant verses in 50 lines in the later plays: the closing scene of *The Winter's Tale* has 21 in the first 50 lines, and there are 17 in the 27 lines of an episode in *The Tempest,* III. iii. 83-109, or 1 in 1·6 lines against the 1 in 1·5 of Cranmer's speech. The mere number of double endings therefore in *Henry VIII* would not entitle Spedding to conclude that Shakespeare's verse could not have developed in this way. But he went on to show that they are arranged within the play so that it may be divided in two on a purely numerical basis: scenes where the proportion of double endings varies from 1 in 2 to 1 in 1·5, and those where it lies between 1 in 2·5 and 1 in 3·5.

Nor is this division an arbitrary one. Spedding also pointed to a difference in the proportion of run-on lines in the two parts, these varying inversely with the double endings. (pp. 103-04)

But these attempts to prove that the kind of verse employed in 'Fletcher's' part is not Shakespeare's break down under two considerations.

An examination of the verse in other plays in the First Folio shows that these characteristics, claimed as *peculiar* to Fletcher, are also found quite frequently in Shakespeare. (p. 106)

But not only are all these features of the verse so confidently pointed to as decisive evidence of Fletcher's style frequently found in Shakespeare, they are also found in those parts of *Henry VIII* assigned to Shakespeare. . . . (p. 107)

Spedding's clear dividing line between the collaborators, so persuasive a feature in his argument, is gone. (p. 108)

Spedding's conjecture that *Henry VIII* was largely by Fletcher involved him in assumptions which he made no attempt to prove, and having committed himself to this view he had to go on to further assumptions that are contradicted by the evidence at our disposal. He imagines another occasion for the play than that, mentioned by Wotton and others, at the Globe, when the house was accidentally set on fire and completely destroyed. . . . This was almost certainly its first performance, for Wotton calls it a 'new' play, and the internal evidence confirms his statement and so does the Prologue. As two years had passed since the last Shakespeare première, and there had been no such interval between his plays for fifteen years and more, it would not be surprising to find that this had been regarded as an important occasion worthy of a special effort by the author as well as the company. The players clearly spared no expense and the play was obviously designed on imposing lines. But Spedding conjectured that it was hastily improvised for the marriage of the Princess Elizabeth, in February 1613, and that Fletcher had to be called in to hasten its completion. There is no record, however, of any such performance among the Lord Treasurer's accounts, which are still preserved.

But Spedding ventured further and was prepared to show how the play would have been written had Shakespeare finished it himself:

> I should conjecture that he had conceived the idea of a great historical drama on the subject of Henry VIII which would have included the divorce of Katherine, the fall of Wolsey, the rise of Cranmer, the coronation of Anne Bullen, and the final separation of the English from the Romish Church, which, being the one great historical event in the reign, would naturally be chosen as the focus of poetic interest.

Shakespeare, however, did not write *King John* round the signing of Magna Carta; and when Spedding shows how the play could have been given a greater unity had Shakespeare carried it through himself, either by his reproving Henry for his unfaithfulness in marriage at the conclusion, as in Nathan's rebuke to David, by the death of his son, or on the other hand by his keeping Katherine in the background, emphasizing the personal attractions of Anne Boleyn, and representing Henry as the champion of the Protestant cause, we can only be glad Shakespeare's idea of poetic interest was so different from Spedding's.

The play has as it stands the compassionate outlook so characteristic of the Fourth Period. It is, as the Prologue suggests, on the familiar theme of the vanity of worldly place and greatness, with Buckingham, Wolsey, and Katherine as strongly contrasted variations. The very pomp and pageantry of the play is justified artistically as a foil to the sombre realities of the situation. On this scene appears as by Providence the child Elizabeth. . . . To a dramatist, on Spedding's lines, who could write, 'God shall be truly known' of the English Reformation, the sympathetic portrait of the Catholic Katherine would be impossible. But they cannot be separated. If Fletcher wrote these lines he also wrote the great scene at Kimbolton that captivated such opposite temperaments as Johnson's and Swinburne's, where Katherine is glorified in death. And in two scenes ascribed to Shakespeare, one of which reminds us directly of Katherine's wrongs, the birth of Elizabeth is clearly anticipated as the wonderful consummation of the whole sorry business. The lines, therefore, on which Spedding's metrical tests divide the play cut right across any division that might be indicated, as he also suggests, by divided minds on the subject-matter. Whether Shakespeare wrote the closing lines or not it is clear from what he did write that he meant to conclude on the note on which the play does in fact end.

And the survey of Elizabeth's times is what might be expected from Shakespeare. In Cranmer's prophecy as in Gaunt's dying thoughts for his country the enthusiasm of the language is in keeping with the speaker's feelings and situation. But there can be no doubt that these speeches are also meant to be taken as essentially truthful, for both Gaunt and Cranmer are represented as men divinely inspired; and that the dramatist's own sympathies were engaged is made certain by this consideration were it not otherwise abundantly clear. But why should Fletcher show such an interest in the age that had just passed away. He was born in 1579 and did not come to manhood till Elizabeth's reign was in its last dark days and all but over. He had not seen with the eyes of maturity any of its memorable events, or shared as a man its anxieties and triumphs. Yet there must have been some strong inward urge to lead the dramatist to recall the triumph of Elizabeth's reign in 1613 with a jealous successor within hearing. . . . [And] though it is difficult to understand why Fletcher should do so, Shakespeare's praise of his own times is more easily understood. (pp. 112-15)

[If] Shakespeare had known some of the asperities of [Queen Elizabeth's] reign as well as enjoyed its blessings, there had been time since it ended for him to see in its place in the history that he had studied so passionately, and, remembering the material at his disposal, so attentively. If this is Shakespeare speaking of that part of the story which he had seen with his own eye and in which he had played his own part, it is easy to understand the inspiration in his words. Every commentator is permitted to remind us that those were indeed the halcyon days, free from the worst of civil distraction past and to come, that brought forth a brood of men and poets whose like has yet to come again. Why then should we not receive as Shakespeare's such a tribute to the time as might be expected from the greatest of them all. . . . The times were worthy of it, and this has all the force of genuine recollection.

The initial guess which started the disintegration of *Henry VIII* can now be seen as a further instance of conjectural history. . . . The similarity between the verse of Fletcher and that of *Henry VIII* in certain externals suggested to Spedding, since it was the received opinion that there were two hands in the play, that Shakespeare's partner was Fletcher. This is a guess, however—for no mathematical or statistical probability attaches to Spedding's argument—that explains one feature of the play but raises many other difficulties. What is required is an explanation that will meet this difficulty and at the same time satisfy the other requirements of the problem. That the ascription of the entire play to Shakespeare solves the difficulties so far considered more satisfactorily than Spedding's suggestion is all that is claimed. It is clear, however, that this is the only solution that the external evidence permits. (pp. 116-17)

Peter Alexander, "Conjectural History or Shakespeare's 'Henry VIII'," in Essays and Studies, Vol. XVI, 1931, pp. 85-120.

SIR JOHN SQUIRE (essay date 1935)

[Squire was a poet and an influential London critic with a reputation for objective analysis. In the following excerpt, he describes Henry VIII *as "one of the worst-shaped plays" ever performed, and for this reason considers it "in the main" not Shakespeare's. Like Robert Ornstein (1972), Squire regards the gravest fault of the play to be its lack of a unifying theme.]*

The three parts of *Henry VI* and *Henry VIII* are patently, to anyone with any sense of character, morality and style, in the main not Shakespeare's. . . . *Henry VIII* . . . is one of the worst-shaped plays that ever was put upon the stage—redeemed by its fine passages and its pageantry. Had every line satisfied the syllable counters (who note Fletcher everywhere) as being Shakespeare's, the construction would still have given us pause. What is the theme? At the beginning we might have thought it the tragedy of Catherine of Aragon, with the figures of Henry and the Cardinal as her opposites, the Cardinal being synchronously ruined by the remorseless King who, in the end, has discarded both, the old wife and the old servant. But no. The Cardinal dies. Catherine dies. Buckingham, quite incidentally, dies—perhaps no play can properly be ranked as an English historical play in which somebody called Buckingham does not get killed. And then the play sails on to Anne Boleyn, a happy marriage, a happy childbirth, Cranmer, cheering crowds, and a characterless Henry desperately whitewashed. Anyone strongly moved by the first part of the play would wish Henry to be punished. Since history does not permit of that, a sensible playwright would obviously have dropped the curtain when the tragedy of Catherine and Wolsey had been worked out. Instead of that the invertebrate thing sprawls on, relying on costumes and physical movement for its hold; without a theme, without a hero, without a designated villain, without an end, happy or unhappy, and leaving us with so dim a picture of Henry VIII that it does not even pretend to displace or supplement the conception we have drawn from other sources. (pp. 64-6)

Sir John Squire, "Plot, Construction, Device," in his Shakespeare As a Dramatist, *Cassell and Company, Ltd., 1935, pp. 59-137.*

CAROLINE F.E. SPURGEON (essay date 1935)

[*Spurgeon's* Shakespeare's Imagery and What It Tells Us *inaugurated the "image-pattern analysis" method of studying Shakespeare's plays, one of the most widely used methods of the mid-twentieth century. In this work, she interpreted the thematic structure of the plays through an examination of patterns in the imagery. Spurgeon also sought to learn about Shakespeare's personality from a study of his images, a course which few of her disciples followed. Since publication of her book, earlier works on image patterns in Shakespeare have been discovered, but none was so important in the history of Shakespearean criticism as Spurgeon's. In the following excerpt, she finds that the "dominating image" in* Henry VIII *is the same as that in* King John: *"the body and bodily action." But in* Henry VIII, *according to Spurgeon, the "continuous picture" is one of "a mere physical body in endlessly varied action," whereas* King John *is concerned with emotional characteristics and personification. Spurgeon states that the imagery of* Henry VIII *exemplifies Shakespeare's habit of seeing "emotional or mental situations" as a continually recurring picture of physical activity.*]

In *Henry VIII*, so far removed in treatment and spirit from *King John*, the dominating image, curiously enough, is again the body and bodily action . . . , but used in an entirely different way and at a different angle from that in the earlier play. The continuous picture or symbol in the poet's mind is not so much a person displaying certain emotions and characteristics, as a mere physical body in endlessly varied action. Thus I find only four 'personifications' in the play, whereas in *King John* I count no less than forty. (pp. 252-53)

There are three aspects of the picture of a body in the mind of the writer of the play: the whole body and its limbs; the various parts, tongue, mouth and so on; and—much the most con-

stant—bodily action of almost every kind: walking, stepping, marching, running and leaping; crawling, hobbling, falling, carrying, climbing and perspiring; swimming, diving, flinging and peeping; crushing, strangling, shaking, trembling, sleeping, stirring, and—especially and repeatedly—the picture of the body or back bent and weighed down under a heavy burden. Except for this last, I see no special symbolic reason for the lavish use of this image, other than the fact that it is a favourite one with Shakespeare, especially the aspect of bodily movement, and we find it in the imagery from various points of view in *King Lear, Hamlet, Coriolanus, King John*, and in a lesser degree, in *Henry V* and *Troilus and Cressida*.

The opening scene—a vivid description of the tourney on the Field of the Cloth of Gold when Henry and Francis met—with its picture of bodily pomp and action, may possibly have started the image in the poet's mind. . . . [The] utter uselessness of the treaty which was the avowed object of the costly Cloth of Gold meeting is brought home by the amazingly vivid picture of a support or means of walking offered to the human body when no longer capable of any movement at all: the articles were ratified, says Buckingham, 'to as much end as give a crutch to the dead'. At the end of the scene the original image returns, and the plot against the king is thought of as a body, so that when the nobles are arrested Buckingham exclaims,

These are the limbs o' the plot: no more, I hope.
[I. i. 220]

We note as we read that many of the most vivid images in the play are those of movements of the body, such as Norfolk's description of Wolsey diving into the king's soul, and there scattering dangers and doubts, Cranmer, crawling into the king's favour and strangling his language in tears, Anne's ejaculation about Katharine's deposition, and her divorce from the majesty and pomp of sovereignty, and Katharine's

sufferance panging
As soul and body's severing. [II. iii. 15-16]

Wolsey thinks constantly in terms of body movement: among his images are those of a soldier marching in step with a 'file', a man scratched and torn by pressing through a thorny wood, or set on by thieves, bound, robbed and unloosed; and in his last great speeches, which, in spite of falling rhythm, I incline to believe are Shakespeare's, he speaks of having *trod* the ways of glory, sees Cromwell *carrying* peace in his right hand, urges him to *fling away* ambition, and pictures himself successively as a rash *swimmer* venturing far beyond his depth with the meretricious aid of a bladder, a man *falling* headlong from a great height like a meteor or like Lucifer, and finally, standing bare and *naked* at the mercy of his enemies.

The image of the back bent under the load recurs five times, and is obviously and suitably symbolic of Wolsey's state, as well as of the heavy taxation. Wolsey complains that the question of the divorce was 'the weight that pulled him down', and after his dismissal, sees himself as a man with an unbearable burden suddenly lifted off him, assuring Cromwell that he thanks the king, who has cured him, 'and from these shoulders' taken 'a load would sink a navy',

a burden
Too heavy for a man that hopes for heaven!
[III. ii. 385]

The idea of a man falling from a great height is constant in the case of both Wolsey and Cranmer; and the remonstrances made with their accusers are in each case exactly alike:

Press not a falling man too far; . . .
                                    [III. ii. 333]

                    'tis a cruelty
To load a falling man.   [V. ii. 111-12]

The queen draws on the same range of bodily similes. She speaks of unmannerly language 'which breaks the sides of loyalty', 'bold mouths' and 'tongues' spitting their duties out, and her description of the great cardinal, with the king's aid going swiftly and easily over the shallow steps until mounted at the top of the staircase of fame, is extraordinarily vivid.

The king also uses it with great force when relating his mental and emotional suffering and the self questioning that followed on hearing the French ambassador demand a 'respite' [an adjournment] in order to determine whether the Princess Mary were legitimate, thus raising the whole question of the divorce.

He draws a picture of the word 'respite' and its effect on him as of a rough and hasty intruder rushing noisily into a quiet and guarded place, shaking and splitting it, forcing a way in so ruthlessly that with him throng in also from outside many other unbidden beings, pressing and pushing, dazed and puzzled with the commotion and the place wherein they find themselves. . . . A little later, as he tells the court how he sought counsel from his prelates, he, like Wolsey, pictures himself as a man almost unbearably burdened, groaning and sweating under his load, when he turns to the bishop with the query,

            my lord of Lincoln; you remember
            How under my oppression I did reek,
            When I first moved you.   [II. iv. 208-10]

When we trace out in detail this series of images, we recognise that it is a good example of Shakespeare's peculiar habit of seeing emotional or mental situations throughout a play in a repeatedly recurring physical picture, in what might more correctly indeed be called a 'moving picture'; because having once, as here, visualised the human body in action, he sees it continuously, like Wolsey's 'strange postures' in every form of physical activity. (pp. 253-57)

> *Caroline F.E. Spurgeon, "Leading Motives in the Histories," in her* Shakespeare's Imagery and What It Tells Us, *Cambridge at the University Press, 1935, pp. 213-58.*

EDGAR I. FRIPP (essay date 1938)

[In the excerpt below, taken from his critical study Shakespeare, Man and Artist, *Fripp opposes most earlier commentators and contends that* Henry VIII *is indeed a unified work, its central idea discernable when one views Cranmer's prophecy on the future reign of Elizabeth "as the providential purpose" of the play. The idea that Cranmer's final speech unifies* Henry VIII *has been disputed by such critics as Hermann Ulrici (1839), G. G. Gervinus (1863), A. A. Parker (1948), and Robert Ornstein (1972), usually on grounds that Shakespeare would never have attempted to justify the tragedies of Buckingham, Wolsey, and Katharine as the inevitable design of providence. Yet, Fripp's interpretation echoes the findings of such later scholars as Frank Kermode (1947), G. Wilson Knight (1947), and Frank V. Cespedes (1980), all of whom see in the ending of* Henry VIII *the explanations of the tragedies of the major characters. Fripp was also one of the first critics to link* Henry VIII *to Shakespeare's romances, a comparison more fully developed by R. A. Foakes (1957), Howard Felperin (1966), and Frances A. Yates (1974).]*

The pageantry [in *Henry VIII*], so far from being superfluous, as some critics would have us believe, a concession to 'popularity', is an essential feature of the drama. Amid scenes of worldly magnificence great personages, severally fit to be the central figure of the story, are presented and cast down—Buckingham, Wolsey, Queen Katharine. They occupy the first four acts, and hold us with moving interest. And we wonder, as these heroic souls depart, what sequel, what 'blessing' from time to time foreshadowed in their calamities—'a blessing to this land which shall in it be memorized' [III. ii. 51-2], 'a gem to lighten all this Isle' [II. iii. 78-9]—can compensate, still more justify, their loss. In the fifth act, however, is the promised and, for Shakespeare in 1612, all-sufficient, providential end. In an atmosphere, still charged with emotion but no longer of lament and retrospect, of bustling energy and homely humour, we witness a great denouement. A little child is brought from her christening in Westminster Abbey, 'richly habited' beneath a canopy, preceded by the Archbishop of Canterbury and followed by her father, the King, in the presence of a surging multitude of citizens. Her name is ELIZABETH. Cranmer, his voice (and the verse richly responding) nearer tears of gladness than mere jubilation, prophesies the glory of her reign—peace, prosperity, the settlement of the Reformation, triumph over Spain, poetry and song, chivalry, colonization, empire. He says:

            This royal in/fant,—Heaven still move abóut / her!
            Though in her crád/le, yet now promises
            Upon this land a thousand, thousand blés/sings,
            Which time shall bring to rípe/ness. She shall be—
            But few now living can behold that góod/ness—
            A pattern to all princes living wíth / her
            And all that shall succeed: Saba was név/er
            More covetous of wisdom and fair vír/tue
            Than this pure soul shall be: all princely grá/ces
            That mould up such a mighty piece as thís / is,
            With all the virtues that attend the good, /
            Shall still be doubled on her.   [V. iv. 17-28]

Was ever a babe so called? 'A Mighty Piece!' And here is a hall-mark Shakespeare term, of endearment and excellence, again and again in his last plays—'this *piece* of your dead queen, a little daughter', for Marina [*Pericles*, III. i. 17]; 'a *piece* of tender air', for Imogen [*Cymbeline*, V. v. 446]; 'a *piece* of beauty rare', 'fresh *piece* of excellent witchcraft', 'the most peerless *piece* of earth that ere the Sun shone bright on', for Perdita [*Winter's Tale*, IV. iv. 32; IV. iv. 422-23; V. i. 94-5]; 'royal *piece*', for Hermione [*Winter's Tale*, V. iii. 38]; and 'a *piece* of virtue', for the mother of Miranda [*The Tempest*, I. ii. 56]. (pp. 770-72)

Henry VIII, as we know him, looking down from Heaven is an anti-climax; but as conceived by the Elizabethan puritan he was the giver of the Bible and the Truth to England, and her deliverer from the Pope and the mass. Shakespeare represents him as not unworthy of his illustrious daughter. He shows us Katharine's love for him [III. i. 180], and his love for Katharine [II. iv. 133-41], whatever his passion for Anne Boleyn and desire for male issue; Buckingham's allegiance—'my vows and prayers yet are the King's' [II. i. 86]; Wolsey's devotion to the last—'I know his noble nature' [III. ii. 419]; and whatever the monarch's failings as a man, his 'sacred person' [II. iv. 41].

The play ends in rejoicing—

            This little one shall make it holiday.
                                            [V. iv. 76]

It could only end so, whatever critics may say of a second hand giving a conclusion other than Shakespeare intended. Politically it is a great finale.

Here is the Poet's tribute—and there is none finer, though some regarded it as belated—to Queen Elizabeth. It would delight the hearts of Raleigh and the old Earl of Nottingham, and thousands who remembered their late Sovereign with adoration, and contrasted her virile and adventurous personality with the mean effeminacy of King James.

But if *Henry VIII* by its 'happy ending' has affinity with the Dramatic Romances—*Pericles, Cymbeline, The Winter's Tale, The Tempest*—it has in it not a little of the great tragedies. It reminds us of *Lear,* and the problem that drama raises, the outstanding problem of Shakespearean tragedy, of personal suffering, and spiritual attainment. Buckingham, Wolsey, and Katharine rise to magnitude in misfortune which is beyond them, and even foreign to them, in worldly greatness, and which we may doubt whether 'children's children' will achieve in the palmy days of Elizabethan 'Peace' and 'Truth'.

Shakespeare had been reading, among other authorities (Holinshed, Hall, Foxe), the *Life of Wolsey,* in manuscript, by Cavendish, one of the few choice classics of Mary's reign, wherein the author sought to replace the 'light tales' and 'innumerable lies' with the 'truth' (whence *All is True* as the second title to *Henry VIII*), and to convey the lesson, as he regarded it, of the Cardinal's fate. . . . (pp. 773-74)

[Cavendish] quotes Psalm xxxix. 7, thus rendered in the Prayer Book: 'Man walketh in a vain shadow and disquieteth himself in vain; *he heapeth up riches, and cannot tell who shall gather them.*'

In Shakespeare's hands King Henry is the god Fortune. He smiles, men rise; he frowns, they fall—Buckingham, Wolsey, Katharine. And echoes of Cavendish's moral may be heard again and again in the play [III. ii. 356-60, 366-67]. But while the biographer can see no 'end in all', Shakespeare both contemplates Elizabeth's reign as the providential purpose and *transforms the sacrificed lives into ends in themselves, noble and worthy of immortality.* The 'meekness, humility and charity' which Cavendish regretted Wolsey had not, the Poet gives him at last in overflowing measure. Such is his treatment also of Buckingham and Katharine. Not only is there national blessing from their sufferings by the Will of God ('the Will of Heaven be done, in this and all things!' [I. i. 209-10], 'Heaven has an end in all' [II. i. 124], 'Heaven is above all yet' [III. i. 100], 'It's Heaven's Will' [III. ii. 128]), but personal faith, strong and convinced through a changed heart, in the life to come. (pp. 774-75)

The portrait of Katharine is beautiful at the beginning and only more beautiful at the close. Not a fault is left in her—save a pardonable touch of the old Spanish pride—

Garlands I am not worthy yet to wear—*I shall, assuredly*.
[IV. ii. 91-2]

We are drawn to Henry for what she says of him:

In death I bless'd him;   [IV. ii. 163]

and to Wolsey by her forgiveness:

So may he rest; his faults lie gently on him!
[IV. ii. 31].
(p. 775)

She is one of Shakespeare's perfect women, and (what artists have so rarely drawn or had the power to draw) the perfect Wife.

Buckingham's development is finely sketched, from a haughty, headstrong, young aristocrat to the model of Christian patience:

he fell to *himself* again, and sweetly
In all the rest showed a most noble patience.
[II. i. 35-6]

Wolsey learns to 'know *himself*'. The picture of his transformation is one of the very greatest of the Poet's achievements.

Nothing can excel the speeches, in soliloquy and in confidence to Cromwell, wherein he lays bare his soul after his fall. It has been the ambition of nearly every great actor to pronounce them. In sensitiveness of feeling, in thought so true and deep, in metrical expression so subtle in its changes, and moving in cadence, they are unsurpassed. . . . (p. 776)

Here, in perfection, is the 'broken metre' we have noted from time to time in the later plays. It occurs in a few lines in *Antony and Cleopatra,* throughout a scene in *Timon of Athens,* in a passage in *Coriolanus,* a passage in *Cymbeline,* and a great speech in *The Winter's Tale.* It occurs also in *The Tempest* in Ferdinand's speech in Act III, Scene i, and the dialogue of Prospero and Miranda in Act I, Scene ii. In *Henry the Eighth* it appears frequently, is so conspicuous, indeed, that it calls for explanation. This may be found in the peculiar sentiment of the drama,

Those that can pity, here
May, if they think it well, let fall a tear;
The subject will deserve it.   [Prologue. 5-7]

For such a theme as fallen greatness and noble grief no metre could be more appropriate. . . . (p. 777)

Shakespeare, moreover, has intensified the effect of this rhythm by the skilful interspersal of lines which contain none of its features and throw them into relief by contrast. There is no penultimate stress, or extra, overhanging syllable, in the direct, challenging declaration,

I have been to you a true and humble wife.
[II. iv. 23]

It has no sob in it or at the end of it; and it is from Holinshed. Of the same character are the lines in Wolsey's soliloquy:

The third day comes a frost, a killing frost . . .
But far beyond my depth: my high blown pride . . .
And when he falls, he falls like Lucifer.   [III. ii. 355,
361, 371]

And if there is a penultimate stress within, a sharp emphasis suitable to the thought, like a knife, concludes the line:

His greatness is a-rípe/ning, *nips his root*.
[III. ii. 357]
(p. 779)

In *The Tempest* Shakespeare observed scrupulously the 'dramatic unities'. The scene shifts but a few yards, and the time of the story is that of the performance at the *Globe*—from a little after two o'clock until shortly before six. Doubtless he had heard of his breaches as a playwright of the laws of Classical Drama. For once he worked within its restrictions, and demonstrated to the critics his capacity to do so as triumphantly as the Ancients. But he had small respect for such rules and limits. Life was too large and incalculable; and having made his obeisance to the idol of classical correctness, he cast it down and trampled it to pieces. In *Henry VIII* he revelled in the freedom of Gothic art, of medieval sculpture and building and painting. While the spirit of history, for once almost contemporary, is preserved, its mere chronology is thrown to the winds, and the events of twenty-four years are gathered up into as many or fewer days. *Men,* not happenings, and what is written on the faces and the hands of them, the marks of the *Soul* or the lack of it, are the Poet's concern. (p. 780)

> Edgar I. Fripp, "1612-13: 'King Henry the Eighth'," in his Shakespeare, Man and Artist, Vol. II, *Oxford University Press, 1938, pp. 770-80.*

MARK VAN DOREN   (essay date 1939)

[*Van Doren was a Pulitzer prize-winning poet, American educator, editor, and novelist. In the introduction to his* Shakespeare, *first published in 1939, he states that he "ignored the biography of Shakespeare, the history and character of his time, the conventions of his theater, the works of his contemporaries" to concentrate on the interest generated by the plays themselves. In the following excerpt, taken from the work mentioned above, Van Doren calls* Henry VIII *an "imitation of Shakespeare"; however, he qualifies this theory by stating that it is impossible to know whether Shakespeare imitated himself or was imitated by another author. Van Doren also maintains that the characters of Buckingham, Wolsey, and Katharine all display a certain "smugness" in their adversity.*]

It has become a tradition to say that only five or six scenes [of "Henry VIII"] are [Shakespeare's], and that Fletcher, or possibly Massinger, is responsible for the remainder; although one extreme theory gives him the entire work, and another takes it all away. The question has interest, not because "Henry VIII" is important in itself but because in any view it is an imitation of Shakespeare; it is at the same time like him and unlike him. And the question will not be answered because in such cases we cannot know whether the poet has imitated himself or been imitated by another.

A certain resemblance to Shakespeare's later plays is all too obvious. Tempests, shores, flowers, music, and peace are incidental themes. Henry knows how to praise Katherine in the idiom of Pericles and Florizel: she is "the queen of earthly queens" [II. iv. 141], and her saint-like meekness is most rare. And reconciliation is rampant—several dramas, rather than one, busily develop it into a kind of orthodoxy.

Just there the resemblance ceases; or overleaps its limits and lands in imitation. For the successive dramas in which Buckingham, Katherine, Wolsey, and Cranmer submit their wills to Henry's are not dramas of reconciliation. The theme has been watered down; resignation is now the word, and its repetition through a series of unmotivated surrenders suggests machinery. Either Shakespeare has lost the impulse which gave his final stories their mellow power, or some other poet has never felt it. Three proud persons break suddenly and bow before a dummy king who represents England, and a fourth who has never been "unsound," Archbishop Cranmer, basks weeping in the sun of his accepted monarch. It is like ninepins going down, nor can we miss a tone of smugness in the proud ones as they pray. This is Buckingham:

> Go with me, like good angels, to my end;
> And, as the long divorce of steel falls on me,
> Make of your prayers one sweet sacrifice,
> And lift my soul to heaven.   [II. i. 75-8]

This is Katherine:

> Remember me
> In all humility unto his Highness.
> Say his long trouble now is passing
> Out of this world; tell him, in death I bless'd him,
> For so I will.   [IV. ii. 160-63]

And this is Wolsey:

> Nay then, farewell!
> I have touch'd the highest point of all my greatness;
> And, from that full meridian of my glory,
> I haste now to my setting. I shall fall
> Like a bright exhalation in the evening,
> And no man see me more. . . .   [III. ii. 222-27]
> (pp. 332-33)

The smugness of their tone goes with a smoothness in their verse such as Shakespeare had long ago outgrown. Not for years had he let his lines roll like this, or ripened his metaphors to rottenness. "Highest point," "meridian," "setting," "bright exhalation in the evening"—there is too much of it by Shakespeare's final standard, and although it is excellent in its way it bears no resemblance to the unique elliptical poetry he had recently been writing. "Swim on bladders," "sea of glory," "high-blown pride," "rude stream"—any competent poet could have developed the image thus, just as any workman of 1612 or 1613 could have worked out the vegetable autobiography of Wolsey in terms of his tender leaves, his blossoms, his blushing honors, his greatness ripening, and his root nipped on the third day by a killing frost [III. ii. 352-58].

The style of any good poet moves from simplicity to congestion, and once this end is reached return is difficult if not impossible. If Shakespeare returned in "Henry VIII" he was performing an extraordinary feat. He had performed many feats in his history, but not this one, of which nevertheless he was perhaps capable. At the same time, however, and in the same play, he imitated—or someone did—his last nervous style. It crops out everywhere, not only in the scenes assigned to him but in some that are assigned to his collaborator.

> The tract of everything
> Would by a good discourser lose some life,
> Which action's self was tongue to.   [I. i. 40-2]

> Of her that loves him with that excellence
> That angels love good men with.   [II. ii. 34-5]

> And which gifts,
> Saving your mincing, the capacity
> Of your soft cheveril conscience would receive,
> If you might please to stretch it.   [II. iii. 30-3]

. . . These are imitations in the sense that their virtue has no bulk, their involutions no excuse. They may or may not have been written by Shakespeare, but it does not matter. They do not save the play for distinction any more than its gorgeous pageants make up for an absence of drama, or than its external compliments to Oxford and Cambridge, Elizabeth and James, have continued after three centuries to be interesting. The two styles in "Henry VIII" are two currents of water, one tepid and the other icy. The difference is to be noted, but it is also to be noted that the water is never wine. (pp. 333-35)

> Mark Van Doren, "'Henry VIII'," in his Shakespeare, *Henry Holt and Company, 1939, pp. 332-36.*

"Fall of Cardinal Wolsey," by Westall. The Department of Rare Books and Special Collections, The University of Michigan Library.

FRANK KERMODE (essay date 1947)

[*In the excerpt below, Kermode considers* Henry VIII *a seventeenth-century descendant of the medieval morality play* Mirror for Magistrates; *thus, he claims that King Henry acts as a flawed agent of divine punishment and mercy whose involvement in the tragedies of Buckingham, Katharine, and Wolsey must not be interpreted too harshly, since his actions ultimately result in "the birth of a great queen and the establishment of the reformed church." In his essay, Kermode attempts to resolve the apparent contradiction between the tragedy of the three falls from power and God's grace and the optimistic ending of the play. This interpretation counters the arguments of Hermann Ulrici (1839), G. G. Gervinus (1863), A. A. Parker (1948), and Robert Ornstein (1972), all of whom declare that the vision of Elizabethan England fails to justify the fates of Buckingham, Katharine, and Wolsey.*]

[*Henry VIII*] is a new kind of play, and very unlike the other histories, but no so unlike that they cannot help us to understand it. Long before drama replaced the morality *rex* with the King of England, but all about him stood the incarnate agents of his and his land's good and evil. The Tudor king was God's deputy, and so, of course, were the kings of the History Plays. But in every case there was something wrong with their title and their rule; they were punished, or their children's children were punished. Henry VIII, on the other hand, had nothing wrong with his title, nor with his rule (if Halle and the absence of

judgment upon him may be believed) and as God's deputy was a minister of grace. It is not he who rises and falls or merely falls for the instruction of the audience; it is the Queen and various great men under his rule. The play is concerned with the old tragic theme of the great man's fall, and the King has a special place in that theme; he is the centre of the drama (and therefore it is pointless to talk of having to get to know new characters at the end of the play) but he is not simply the old *rex* who was the owner of the vices and virtues doing battle about him; he is a representation of an exalted view of kingship fostered by the Tudors out of expedience perhaps, but accepted by James and his subjects as a natural law. If we recall that James himself is often (especially in Court Masques) practically equated with God, and that this is not to be written off as disgusting flattery, we may find it easier to believe that Henry VIII is represented in this play as exercising certain God-like functions.

The Arden editor [Charles Knox Pooler] got nearer than most to seeing what the play was about.

> In comparison with *When you see me you know me* the play may be regarded as history, but it is rather a new "Mirror for Magistrates" in the form of a drama, interspersed or interrupted by pageants. Those that can pity may, if they think

it well, let fall a tear over the successive fates
of Buckingham, of Wolsey, of Katharine; and
for the sightseers there are the processions.

No doubt the processions were conceived to meet a demand
for spectacle, but they also have a simple function in the drama,
which is to illustrate the circumstance from which the great
ones fell. This is self-evident, and needs no labouring; the
detail of the stage-directions indicates further that all is true.
It is in regarding the play as a collection of tragedies that Pooler
came near to the heart of the matter. For this is a collection
of falls (Miss Spurgeon conscientiously notes the iterative imagery of falling) and there are not three falls, but four, Katharine's, Buckingham's, Wolsey's, and Cranmer's.

The tragedy of Katharine is the one which has provoked most
indignant comment in the critics. We are made to sympathise
with her; she clearly doesn't deserve to fall; Henry himself
confesses her virtue—

> That man i' the world who shall report he has
> A better wife, let him in nought be trusted,
> For speaking false in that: thou art, alone
> If thy rare qualities, sweet gentleness,
> Thy meekness saint-like, wife-like government,
> Obeying in commanding, and thy parts
> Sovereign and pious else, could speak thee out,
> The queen of earthly queens. She's noble born,
> And like her true nobility she has
> Carried herself towards me.   [II. iv. 135-44]

It is impossible to deny an element of hypocrisy in the King's
character in this part of the play, or that he was too easily
managed by flatterers. But this ought not to obscure the equal
fact that there was reason in his stated motives for seeking the
annulment, and that one of these, which would weigh powerfully with the Shakespearean audience, was the continued
failure of Katharine to produce an heir. This was the reason,
in so far as reason was needed, for the stage-fall of this virtuous
queen. In fact, the purely historical reason—after all, she did
fall—was enough for the dramatist's purpose.

The *Mirror for Magistrates,* itself the product of a long medieval tradition, had a numerous progeny. The theme continued
popular until well into the Seventeenth Century; and by the
turn of the century . . . it was beginning to show its vitality
and adaptability once more by allowing a discreet sentimentality to creep into it, especially when it was concerned with
the Falls of Women. . . . Women were more likely to be the
passive agents of evil than men, and philosophical considerations of the working of Fate, the natural concomitants of the
De Casibus theme, could in these cases be suspended. (pp.
50-1)

Katharine's fall is surely exactly of this fashionable kind. She
is presented happy and virtuous, confident of the King's attention, free-spoken and above all very much alive. At the
prelates' enquiry she behaves much as Hermione does in *The
Winter's Tale;* she firmly retains the sympathy of the audience
which she won by her just forthrightness in the first Act. But
she falls; there is no malice in the King when he considers it,
and he sends her his good will before she dies. Griffith makes
it clear that she deserves no reproach, and her death is heralded
by a dance of blessed spirits. The whole scene in which the
famous song is sung, and the death-scene itself, are full of
carefully organised appeals to pity; the mood is elegiac; they
are scenes of great beauty, but for all that they remain what
are now known as ''tear-jerkers.'' . . . [And] this fall is the

more pathetic in that it is *true*. Long before the *Mirror* itself
had shown that British history was a rich storehouse of *De
Casibus* exempla; no fiction could match history in this respect,
for history shows what has happened and what therefore can
and will happen again. Virtuous women fall; they are not without sin, and may be, as Katharine was, party to an offence
perhaps incurring God's displeasure; but there is little suggestion in this kind of tragedy that the fall is deserved. Fashion
has, in this corner of the traditional theme, ousted the customary moralising and speculation. Katharine's ultimate beatitude
is not in doubt; but on earth she fell from greatness, though a
queen and a king's daughter, and a heavy spectacle it is.

The fall of Buckingham is a relatively simple affair. The spite
of Wolsey is the cause of it, and the sufferer, though a good
and learned man, is splenetic and undisciplined. The ultimate
pathos of all such falls is heavily underlined in this play. Buckingham makes a noble end, in the tradition of English noblemen. (pp. 51-2)

In some ways the fall of Buckingham is the male equivalent
of Katharine's fall, but it is altogether more conventional,
closely resembles the kind of all experienced in the original
Mirror by Clarence, and lacks the elaborate fashionable circumstances of the Queen's tragedy. The pathos is certainly
there; against the splendour of masquing and procession Buckingham has become plain Bohun; but, of course, we are not
mulcted of so much sympathy for him as for the Queen, and
he falls as great men will as the heterodox wheel turns.

Wolsey certainly does not fall ''like a blessed martyr,'' and
there is no difficulty in accounting for his tragedy in a perfectly
orthodox way. He had been the protagonist of *De Casibus*
tragedy long before this play was written. The prose *Life* of
Cavendish, a gentleman usher in Wolsey's household, deliberately shaped the Cardinal's incredible rise and rapid fall on
the Boccaccian model. Endowed with nothing but brains and
a capacity for learning his master rose on Fortune's wheel, to
the positions of King's chaplain, Archbishop of York, and
Cardinal, to Chancellor of the Exchequer and the most powerful
man in the kingdom, lavishing a great fortune on luxurious
furnishings and entertainments of all kinds; but all this incurred
him the animosity of powerful men, and he was in an instant
swept away. (The play with its device of the inopportune discovery by the King of Wolsey's private accounts is not here
historical, for it borrows the tale from another fall, of a Bishop
of Durham who made this error and was exposed by Wolsey.)
Finally the fallen man dies, broken by sickness. Cavendish,
whose work was still in manuscript in 1613, though the author
of this play must have had access to it, emphasises the odd
fact that Wolsey's body was discovered to be clad in a hair
shirt; and he makes it clear that in his view the Cardinal deserved his fame as well as his fall. In the play there is an
obvious attempt in the speech of the gentle Griffith to do justice
to the extraordinary magnanimity which was an aspect of Wolsey's obsession with power and greatness, but the author's
animus is equally clear: Wolsey is associated with Rome, as
Cranmer is with the Church of England; he calls Anne a spleeny
Lutheran, whereas the well-disposed think of her as a jewel of
worth. . . . [It] is the discovery of his traffic with the Pope
which brings about his fall, and the fall was almost undoubtedly
associated with the fall of the Roman Church in England. But
it is basically as simple as the simplest and most orthodox falls
in the *Mirror,* for Wolsey's acts of conspiracy and treachery
are directly responsible for his tragedy, in that when they were
discovered they provoked the just condemnation of the King,

and also in that they roused the outraged earls who so gleefully accuse him (III. ii.). This, then, is the completely orthodox fall, in accordance with contemporary Christian moral philosophy, and in a sense all the others are variants of it.

The most curious of these is the arrested fall of Cranmer. This seems to me the only possible description of it. Associated with it is the merely adumbrated fall of Gardiner, which is the product of the operation of Mercy in its negative mirror-image, Justice. For Cranmer (whose piety is heavily emphasised in the first three scenes of the last Act) is evidently headed for the same kind of fall as Buckingham's; he displays exemplary resignation even before the event, exhibiting the humility and the traditional noble attitude of a man about to suffer. . . . But the King, observing everything down to the indignities which Cranmer is made to endure, makes an impressive entry and, having by use of the ring-token made it clear to the enemies of the just cleric that he proposes personal intervention, redeems Cranmer from falling and indicates a displeasure with Gardiner and a recognition of his injustice which foreshadow retribution on this arrogant (and Romish) antagonist.

This royal act is an exercise of mercy; and there is a connexion between the part here played by the King and the role of Mercy in the earlier Moralities—that is, those written before the *tragic* theme usurped the form, and in which *homo* in his extremity is preserved from Hell by precisely such an act. It does not seem to me relevant to speak of inconsistency in the character of the King, nor indeed to posit some act of *depersonalisation* as so many modern critics might; for there is nothing out of character in the exercise of divine grace by a Tudor or Stuart sovereign. Here Henry is God's deputy, and it is well known that this office was in Tudor political philosophy a property of all kings by divine law. Cranmer and the Church of England redeemed, it is proper that he should sponsor and prophesy over Elizabeth, the first personally effective Protestant monarch, and the fact that she could not have existed but for the tragedy of a good woman must not be allowed to detract from the pleasure the auditors are expected to feel at the end of the play, which is of course related to the happy dynastic progress of English history since that birth, a progress which might have been very different if Henry had not put away Katharine.

So the Arden editor is not far out when he suggests that this play is an anthology of falls, like the *Mirror*. It is, however, as I see it, necessary to count four of them. The last, Cranmer's, is different from the others. It shows that a man having risen may avoid a fall because Mercy (and perhaps Wisdom as in the Plutarchian theory) intervene. It is not that retribution ceases to function; Cranmer was undeserving the treatment of Wolsey. His fall would have been the kind which yields with any conviction only to the Pyrrhonist reading which was, though extant, heterodox. These four falls, all different, might well be regarded as an attempt to present in the closest possible interrelation as many entertaining variants on the popular theme as the dramatic convention permitted.

Nevertheless, one should beware of regarding the play as episodic. It is called *Henry VIII* and it is about Henry VIII. Notoriously, kings were men as well as divine agents. Here is a king susceptible to flattery, to adulterous passions, choleric and extravagant. His rejection of Katharine is influenced by some of those human flaws; but it is not quite unconnected with a proper kingly concern over the health of the state. The result is the tragedy of a good woman, a type well understood, and for which the dramatist had exemplars. Human justice lacks the certainty of its divine counterpart; so, in spite of a fair trial,

Buckingham, not without sin, falls. The man who caused this tragedy falls as a result of his treachery in the treatment of the affair of the Queen; he knows very well what the moral of his tragedy is, and urges it on Cromwell at some length. ''Fling away ambition,'' he says, already seeing himself as an example or a Mirror. He was never happy until the fall occurred, for God has so disposed it that the evildoer has that in his own breast which destroys his peace. Here punishment is visited on the offender through the King; he is the agent of the divine retribution. As Wolsey falls in sin, Cranmer rises in virtue, and they clearly represent Popery and the English Church as much as they do great men vicious and virtuous. In his turn, Cranmer falls, and we have a pattern whereby to understand the nature of his tragedy; but there is no need for it; Mercy intervenes, and virtue is saved from such a tragedy by the King himself. The guilt or virtue of the King in respect of these happenings should be judged primarily by their fruits. These are the birth of a great queen and the establishment of the reformed church. It is unthinkable that these should be dismissed as the workings of chance; such a position would be both heterodox and treasonable. The play may be regarded as a late morality, showing the state from which great ones may fall; the manner of their falling, be they Good Queen, Ambitious Prelate, Virtuous Prelate, or merely Great Man; and the part played in their falls for good or ill by a King who, though human, is *ex officio* the deputy of God, and the agent of divine punishment and mercy. (pp. 52-4)

Frank Kermode, ''What Is Shakespeare's 'Henry VIII' About?'' in The Durham University Journal, *n.s. Vol. IX, No. 1, December, 1947, pp. 48-54.*

G. WILSON KNIGHT   (essay date 1947)

[*Knight is one of the most influential Shakespearean critics of the twentieth century; he helped shape a new interpretive approach to Shakespeare's work and promoted a greater appreciation of many of the plays. In his studies* The Wheel of Fire *(1930) and* The Shakespearian Tempest *(1932), Knight rejected criticism which emphasizes sources, character analysis, psychology, and ethics and outlined his principles of interpretation which, he claimed, would ''replace that chaos by drawing attention to the true Shakespearian unity.'' Knight argued that this unity lay in Shakespeare's poetic use of images and symbols—particularly in the opposition of ''tempests'' and ''music.'' He also maintained that a play's spatial aspects, or ''atmosphere,'' should be as closely considered as the temporal elements of the plot if one is ''to see the whole play in space as well as time.'' In the following excerpt, Knight attacks the use of verse-analysis tests on* Henry VIII *and rejects any possible contribution to the play by the Jacobean dramatist John Fletcher. Instead, he compares* Henry VIII *to many of Shakespeare's plays, stating that it recapitulates the earlier histories while it is ''modulated and enriched by the wisdom garnered during the intermediate works.'' According to Knight,* Henry VIII *both summarizes and expands ideas present in all of Shakespeare's dramas: Buckingham's and Wolsey's fall from power and grace reflect Shakespeare's concern with authority and betrayal in the tragedies, while Katharine's fall epitomizes his ''feminine sympathies'' apparent in the romances. Knight also argues that* Henry VIII *is more vitally concerned with ritual than its predecessors, and he considers its pageantry a ''realistic and more directly social'' extension of the ''natural phenomena'' in the romances. Knight concludes by stating that Shakespeare, in* Henry VIII, *defines ''the indwelling spirit of his nation'' and outlines ''that greater peace . . . whose cause that nation was, and is, to serve.'' He claims that the play's conclusion reflects Shakespeare's ''whole life-work to this point, with cumulative force and authority.'' Many scholars were significantly influenced by Knight's essay, particularly Hugh M. Richmond (1979), and*

Eckhard Auberlen (1980). However, other critics disputed certain aspects of his study, especially his assessment of the thematic unity of Henry VIII *and his evaluation of the play in light of Shakespeare's earlier histories. For examples of these reactions, see the excerpts by A. A. Parker (1948) and Howard Felperin (1966).]*

The Tempest would scarcely have been quite satisfying as Shakespeare's last play, since despite its many subtle recapitulations, it might yet seem to dissolve the stern political and national interest of earlier works into a haze of esoteric mysticism. One expects, from such a poet, a less visionary and enigmatic conclusion.

Shakespeare seems continually to have been forced backwards as his historical interest developed and plots became exhausted. . . . There is profound examination throughout the Tragedies and Final Plays of such ever-vital and contemporary matters as state-order, warrior honour, kingship and tyranny; many of which are worked . . . into *The Tempest.* Finally the poet, copying his analogue Prospero, returns deliberately to a national and contemporary theme, and writes *Henry VIII.* He may, indeed, have originally purposed such a conclusion, holding it in reserve for his crowning work.

The difficulties would appear great. After *The Tempest,* the poet cannot well be content with anything less comprehensive. The tenour of his recent work precludes, moreover, war, enthusiasm for which was, as it were, scotched by the noble conclusion to *Cymbeline* and the general statement of *The Tempest.* Something at least of a corresponding serenity is demanded. As for the visions and recognitions, the eternal whisperings and thunderings, all such wondrous things as Cerimon, Apollo's oracle, Hermione's resurrection, Jupiter, Prospero's white magic, what comparable themes can be elicited from a realistic and near-distance story? Can a Christian mythology be impregnated with the necessary dramatic force without sacrilege or bathos? Can the more tragic facts of this well-known plot be rendered worthy successors of *Hamlet* and *King Lear?* And what of comedy? Finally, Shakespeare has of late tended more and more to rely on symbol and ritual, ending with *The Tempest,* a play made throughout of such substance. Can this be continued? Are there any possible analogies? (pp. 256-57)

[*Henry VIII*] is as massively conceived and constructed as the peculiarly massive *Richard III,* while showing correspondences in pageant and group-work to the other play's theatric formalism of lamenting women and fatalistic ghosts. Both plays are concerned with the punishment of inordinate ambition. We have something of the royalism of *Richard II* and much, as we shall see, of its sense of fallen greatness followed by religious mysticism. *Richard II* contains one of Shakespeare's two lengthy passages of national praise; *Henry VIII* contains the other. The balance of humour against law, of Falstaff and the Lord Chief Justice, in the two parts of *Henry IV,* finds here not merely expression, but synthesis. *Henry V,* the patriotic play crowning the earlier sequence, is clearly analogous to *Henry VIII,* the patriotic play crowning the second, the prologues of both being couched in a vein of humble reverence for the high themes to follow. . . . The grand actions of both dramas work up to studied eulogies on peace. But our clearest parallel is *King John.* Here, as in *King John,* we have a central figure whose supreme status as king of England is variously related (i) to his own character and (ii) to Papal control (Cardinals being in both plays important). Yet more interesting is the similarity in structure, whereby the tragic endurance of fine people, Constance and Arthur in the one and Buckingham,

Wolsey and Queen Katharine in the other (Katharine confronted by Wolsey and Campeius closely resembling Constance by the side of Pandulph), is firmly juxtaposed to the King's, or England's, advance, with the same seemingly inhuman faculty shown by the poet in so indulging his sympathies without losing the national perspective. The pattern is more symmetrical and purposeful in *Henry VIII,* and here the concluding national prophecy—both end with a prophecy—is more elaborate. *Henry VIII* is thus a recapitulation of earlier Histories, though itself more sober and more substantial, at once modulated and enriched by the wisdom garnered during intermediate works.

In spite of its greatness, *Henry VIII* has, however, for long been suspected as, in part, non-Shakespearian. . . . Individual commentators have made lists of so called 'weak' or 'feminine' endings, calculated percentages and made their private allotments of this or that scene to Fletcher, Massinger, or some author unknown. The process has gone so far that popular editions are found to state, without qualification or reserve, that the play *is* the work of Shakespeare and Fletcher. This is surely inexcusable. (pp. 257-59)

The most authoritative voice so far lifted on behalf of the play's complete authenticity is probably Swinburne's [see excerpt above, 1880]. . . . It is significant that the main defence of the play's authenticity since suspicion was first aroused during the mid-Victorian era should come from a writer who was at once poet, dramatist, and Elizabethan scholar; and that his arguments should be based not on statistics or collections of phrase-resemblances but on the poetic status of the passages concerned. (pp. 263-64)

In reading Beaumont and Fletcher, say *The Maid's Tragedy* or *Philaster,* one is indeed continually aware of some well-worn Shakespearian emotional theme being used, as here (e.g. 'beware of foul ingratitude'), for a temporary purpose, and next curtly dismissed, with scant respect to the depths involved in the Shakespearian statement, to make way for some new attraction. Each piece, out of its context, may often, indeed, seem as good as Shakespeare; but where in Shakespeare a whole play's impact is behind his greater passages, enforcing them far beyond themselves, Beaumont and Fletcher so aim at getting the maximum of poetic thrill out of each incident in turn irrespective of the rest that no reservoir of significance can accumulate and even the finest separate pieces fail of a maximum effect. Power leaks out into the wide areas of second-rate event and sentiment. . . . [Whereas] Fletcher's greatest things come in haphazardly, Shakespeare writes from that higher dimension of artistic control that not only composes a supreme passage but knows precisely how to place it, maintain its dignity and channel its worth.

But the most important argument of all concerns the strangely reiterated use of feminine endings falling on monosyllables and, especially, pronouns. Here the style of *Henry VIII* is, though certainly Fletcherian, not precisely Fletcher's. Consider an example of Fletcher's use:

> I am thine,
> Thine everlastingly, thy love has won me,
> And let it breed no doubt; our new acquaintance
> Compels this, 'tis the gods decree to bless us.
> The times are dangerous to meet; yet fail not,
> By all the love thou bear'st me I conjure thee,
> Without distrust of danger to come to me,
> For I have purpos'd a delivery
> Both of myself and fortune this blest day
> Into thy hands, if thou think'st good.
>
> [*Bonduca,* III. ii.]

In Shakespeare such turns of speech are limited, roughly, to a certain psychic state; in Fletcher they occur normally, at all times. An ear attuned to the Shakespearian use, indeed, finds even this pleading speech from *Bonduca,* where the rhythms accompany a purpose as near as may be to Shakespeare's in *Henry VIII,* peculiarly dry. Normally, they contribute little or nothing; as though Fletcher were not understanding his own rhythms and what they should be doing. Indeed, how do we know that Fletcher is not copying Shakespeare?

Now in *Henry VIII* this particular mannerism is used with strong dramatic point. When a speaker is ambitious and aspiring to play his part in affairs, he speaks normal Shakespearian verse, packed, metaphoric, allusive, complex; when arguing for himself, or herself, against a hostile community, as with Katharine at her trial, the weak-endings occur with run-on and mid-line pause, in what I have called an 'expostulatory' style; which, though not to be limited to expostulation, is probably most potent when used for such a purpose. . . . But *Henry VIII* shows yet a third style: when the speaker's cause is lost and he is severed from all worldly ambition, the run-on ceases, the lines are simple, falling, units with a delicate but reiterated stress on personal pronouns in collaboration with feminine endings. It is, very roughly, the speech of lonely souls, of persons rejected, thrown back on themselves, concentrating on their own, or someone else's, individual selves, what might be called the essential 'I' or 'thou' of human personality. Though a bitter self-concentration may be involved, it is most naturally used for the language of renunciation and acceptance. (pp. 265-68)

[This] is the note to be sounded by Shakespeare in Buckingham's farewell. I point less to numerical facts than a poetical quality. My arguments are not statistical, and must remain subject to many reservations. But clearly there is in such passages a certain detectable rhythm concerned variously with a poetic self-pity or self-accusation; a turning inward from the community to the individual soul, of oneself or another; and this it is which gives us that peculiar music of prepositional and pronominal endings that has caused so much trouble in *Henry VIII.*

This music we scarcely, I think, detect in Fletcher. Even supposing that Shakespeare (long before the composition of *Henry VIII*) had caught the trick from his junior contemporary —or perhaps from Massinger, or some other—we shall observe that he has turned it to a use to them unknown; he has recognized and released the dormant potentiality, the soul-principle, in these little rhythms, and set them softly burning. (p. 269)

The arguments for spuriousness are, indeed, quite untenable; for, though the suspected scenes may contain some minor phrase-reminiscences from Fletcher's work, they offer many reminders, of far greater force and importance, from Shakespeare's. (p. 270)

Moreover, certain recurring thoughts, images, and themes will be found richly sprinkled throughout, whatever the style used, both the Shakespearian and the 'Fletcherian' parts being crammed with similar matter contributing equally to the whole. . . . An understanding of the whole design and the interweaving of its themes and persons, though it cannot prove Shakespeare to have written every word (who can prove that of *Hamlet*?) must quickly remove all cause for suspicion. Contenders for spuriousness themselves fall back regularly on arguments concerned with the play's supposed looseness, pageantry, and lack of concise dramatic statement; while even Swinburne, though sure of the poetry's merit, admitted . . . that the play, as a whole, baffled him. That is no reason why we, to-day, should remain baffled. A complete defence would, however, demand a treatment at least as long as that to be devoted here to a pure interpretation. To that interpretation we shall now advance, with the reminder that, even were *Henry VIII* proved to have been composed by two, three, or any number of separate authors writing independently, the interpretation here offered would remain substantially no less true than if the play were incontrovertibly known to be the child of Shakespeare's undivided and unprompted invention. (pp. 271-72)

We shall now follow three stories: those of Buckingham, Wolsey, and Queen Katharine. (p. 272)

Buckingham is a strong stage personality; he has spoken vigorous and upstanding Shakespearian language, fiery in resentment, innuendo and sarcasm, and ranging wide over affairs of state. . . . The resentments of pride and ambition give place to resignation, humility and a supervening peace, with a religious phrase automatically enthroned. *At this exact moment of conversion the supposedly Fletcherian touch is first heard:* 'fall'n upon me', 'that dye is on me', showing the precise use of rhythm and phrase . . . on which the main argument for spuriousness has been based. This first scene—there is none finer in Shakespeare —arches up swiftly, gathers sweep and fire, towers, and drops (not unlike the whole first movement of *The Winter's Tale*): this movement is to be reiterated and expanded throughout. (p. 273)

Buckingham's farewell is our first long unit in the style of falling rhythms. . . . The opening shows a quiet dignity and Christian charity. He continues in a yet sweeter strain, embracing in brotherhood of nobility those following crowds who have proved faithful, rather as King Henry V in his Crispin speech attributes royal brotherhood to the meanest soldier who sheds blood on the field of battle:

> You few that lov'd me,
> And dare be bold to weep for Buckingham,
> His noble friends and fellows, whom to leave
> Is only bitter to him, only dying,
> Go with me, like good angels, to my end;
> And, as the long divorce of steel falls on me,
> Make of your prayers one sweet sacrifice
> And lift my soul to heaven. Lead on, o' God's name.
>
> [II. i. 71-8]

The lines are spoken from that deeper, spiritual, aristocracy that underlies all Shakespeare's noblest thought. Buckingham shows here a sweetness and serenity distilled from the finest essence of nobility, courtesy, suffering and religious faith, on which the lilting rhythms, as of a boat lifting and falling on a vast sea, sit strangely appropriate. (pp. 274-75)

Buckingham is successor to many past heroes, their aura is on him, in him they are all but lifted to a nobler status; and yet in him they are, for the first time, accused. Timon scorns to forgive; Prospero forgives, coldly, knowing it 'the rarer action' [*The Tempest,* V. i. 27]. But Buckingham, I think, fingers in his convulsive passion a cross worn on his breast; and it is this that accuses not only him, but all his predecessors in passion, Richard II, Hamlet, Troilus, Lear, Othello, Timon, Prospero— of what? Of wounded pride. . . . This is Shakespeare's one explicitly Christian play; but its Christianity is defined not by theological speculation nor any personification of abstract qualities, but rather by the sharp dramatic confronting of the Shakespearian nobility at its best with the yet nobler ideal. Christianity is not treated as an intellectual scheme: it is brought, through drama, to the bar of life. Can the Shakespearian hero live the Christian way, to the end? The presence of Christ Himself is thus realized through His absence.

Here Shakespeare's genius attains a spiritual sensitivity, a fine point of Christian penetration, beyond anything so far attempted. That alone should answer arguments of spuriousness. Is not every phrase infused, saturated, barbed with Shakespearian feeling? Does Buckingham's passionate outburst not lie in direct descent from *The Tempest, Timon of Athens,* and the rest? Does not the whole structure of semi-Christian resignation, desire to conclude a painful ordeal, maddening interruption and consequent reversal of the original acceptance and releasing of a bitterness formerly controlled, exactly recall the deposition scene in *Richard II*? (pp. 277-78)

The fairest comment on Wolsey is the Queen's charge that he takes more thought for his persons 'honour' than his 'high profession spiritual' [II. iv. 114]. He is a skilful and ambitious politician, with a craving for wealth and power; generous on occasion, but over-proud. He is no criminal like Richard III, though the faults developed to prodigious proportions in the hypocrisy and ruthlessness of the tyrant are here more realistically presented, at once more softened and more subtle, rather as the flamboyances of Richard II are given a reserved presentation in Buckingham. As a man Wolsey ranks high; but—and the contrast resembles that already observed in Buckingham—he fails when judged by the standard of his priestly calling. The valuation throughout *Henry VIII* is specifically Christian. (p. 281)

[Wolsey admits] his guilt; that is, his accumulation of wealth to help him to the popedom; and as the full implications of the miscarried letter become clear, his speech glows with a new tragic power, not quite in Buckingham's idiom of falling units, but in a related, pronominal, style relying on vivid imagery of fall:

> Nay then, farewell!
> I have touch'd the highest point in all my greatness;
> And from that full meridian of my glory,
> I haste now to my setting: I shall fall
> Like a bright exhalation in the evening,
> And no man see me more . . . [III. ii. 223-28]

Though pictorial, as Buckingham's tragic style was not, there is a similar lucidity and simplicity, reaching expression in obvious metaphor only and, even more characteristically, simile. The language of conversion, or reorientation, accompanies the moment of disaster; is to be withheld at the lords' re-entry and during the subsequent argument; and is to attain full flower in Wolsey's famous concluding speeches. Commentators, disregarding *the precise reason for the change,* have here actually split the scene, handing the pre-conversion part to Shakespeare and the great tragic set-pieces to Fletcher. (pp. 282-83)

Wolsey's fall is generalized. We watch, as in *Timon of Athens* and *Pericles,* not a particular disaster merely, but a reading of human disaster as such, exactly recalling *Richard II* [III. ii. 160-70]:

> So farewell to the little good you bear me.
> Farewell! a long farewell, to all my greatness!
> This is the state of man: to-day, he puts forth . . .
>   [III. ii. 350-52]

The following lines [III. ii. 354-73] show the limp, pronominal, rhythms: 'and then he falls, as I do', 'and now has left me', 'that must for ever hide me'. These are accompanied by purest

Shakespearian imagery, comparing man's life to the seasonal budding of a tree, its summer blossoming, and final wintry ruin. . . . We watch the act of rejection, of repentance (in the proper sense of turning, of new orientation); the seeing things afresh, as when convalescent or following some 'mystic' experience. Wolsey's conversion is profounder than Buckingham's in proportion as his fault is greater. He has nothing left, no possible worldly pride or hope, nor any excuse for bitterness. He merely observes that dependance on the insecure favour of princes is a state of wretchedness, and compares his fall—he is to do so again—to that of Lucifer.

But he receives the dramatic honour of Cromwell's entry and their deeply moving conversation:

> *Cromwell.*   How does your Grace?
> *Wolsey.*   Why, well;
> Never so truly happy, my good Cromwell.
> I know myself now; and I feel within me
> A peace above all earthly dignities,
> A still and quiet conscience. [III. ii. 376-80]

Wolsey embraces with full understanding that self-knowledge to which past heroes, such as Richard II [at *Richard II,* III. ii. 98, 175; V. v. 49], Macbeth, Lear, Enobarbus, Coriolanus and Leontes were unhappily forced; a deep religious content like that of Richard II or Henry VI. . . . That both he and Buckingham should be conceived as Timon-like figures of bounty shows how closely Shakespeare is reembodying his favourite tragic theme; and that both, so bitterly opposed as they were, should be shown as basically similar alike in their greatness and in their fall, makes a neat comment on all such personal rivalries. (pp. 284-87)

Queen Katharine expands all that was discovered and created in Hermione, while also recalling more distantly such wronged women as Constance in *King John* and the various lamenting women of *Richard III*. Indeed, nearly all the Histories show the suffering of woman under the march of man's political or warlike ambition; and though in the Tragedies what might be called a feminine force does much to challenge and overturn such masculine values (a pattern explicit in *Antony and Cleopatra* and *Coriolanus*), the women, as persons, are, normally, trodden under too. This conflict is epitomized in the trial of Katharine, whose appeal will clearly be overruled and whose enemies have high-sounding defences for their every move, and indeed may well be, to a final judgement, justified, though in terms whose validity no woman can be expected to admit. (pp. 289-90)

Katharine experiences no sudden conversion, since she has throughout shown a fine balance of charity and righteous anger. But a sterner sacrifice is asked of her: she has to conquer even righteous anger, not as an emotional duty, but through clear sight of its limitations. . . . So she learns to transcend her own, personal, cause; and, from a wider view, her casting off, so apparently unjust, is, as the drama unfolds, shown as necessary. Christian charity is thus found to be no more than is dictated by widest reason. So Katharine wins the vision of Paradise, and has the honour of linking *Henry VIII* to the visions and miracles of earlier works. (pp. 293-94)

Queen Katharine is one of Shakespeare's most striking feminine creations. She is not a 'character' study like the Nurse in *Romeo and Juliet,* nor, to take another extreme, a great emotional force as is Constance in *King John;* nor a sublime hypothesis, like Lady Macbeth; nor just a creature of dignity and virtue, and not much else, like Hermione. She has the power of forceful heroines woven with the warm, domestic, virtues of a Desdemona, the integrity of Cordelia, and the spiritual worth of Imogen. Katharine is made of all the better qualities— not just the best moments, as is Imogen—of earlier women. They present aspects of womanhood; she seems, more than anyone but Cleopatra (whose very *tour de force* complexity renders her rather literary in this comparison), a real woman. Her every phrase comes direct from her woman's soul, her typical woman's plight. She is universalized, not by abstraction, but rather by an exact realization of a particular person only lately dead. (p. 296)

There is nothing in Shakespeare more remarkable than these three similar falling movements, of Buckingham, Wolsey, and Queen Katharine. The two first conform to the two main types of Shakespearian tragedy involving (i) betrayal and (ii) the power-quest; while the Queen sums all Shakespeare's feminine sympathies. The Tragedies culminating in *Timon of Athens* and *The Tempest* (for man) and *Antony and Cleopatra* and the remaining Final Plays (for woman) have developed the Shakespearian humanism to its limit, though with no severing of Christian contacts. Here we face the limits of even that, purified, humanism.

These events are, however, countered by others of a different tone, showing variously a gaiety, romantic warmth, and robust humour most strangely juxtaposed to their sweetly-sombre atmosphere. There is, nevertheless, a relation. Here tragedy is characterized by a prevailing softness, at once a charity in the persons themselves and a lack of bitterness in the poet, showing nothing comparable to the ugliness of Leontes, the villainy of Cymbeline's queen, or even Prospero's severity in forgiveness. Now the comedy shows similarly a new kindliness. While avoiding the chief persons, it refuses to degrade anyone: there is no serio-comic satiric creation like Cloten, no reversals of stage dignity like Autolycus', no burlesque as with Stephano and Trinculo. That 'high seriousness' of late in such stern control of both humour and the intimately related matter of sexual approach, is relaxed. It is as though the puritanical severity, gaining so strongly up to *The Tempest*, is given a holiday; as though the return from individualistic, Nietzschean, assertion and adventure to a national and contemporary subject, with a corresponding use of a Christian mythology, were in itself an act of humility dethroning the innate strictness of the individual's power-quest, and not only allowing the poet all his old freedom, but even letting new warmth stream in. (pp. 296-97)

[The humour in *Henry VIII*] is throughout kindly; it is also characterized by sexual freedom; all, from the lords' conversation on the way to Wolsey's feast, through that feast, its merriment and gay talk, the Old Lady and her willingness to 'venture maidenhead' for a crown, to [the] seething crowds at coronation and christening, all cluster round Anne. Herself a bashful, modest, sensitive girl, she is crowned with the gold of boisterous and comely fun, of broad human understanding, of seething fertility and enthusiastic crowds.

We have accordingly a series of warmly conceived humanistic scenes countering our three falling movements. Those were moralistic, on the pattern of medieval stories of the falls of princes; these are eminently Elizabethan. Effects are deliberately got by juxtaposition, as when Buckingham's execution follows Wolsey's feast and the death of Katharine the coronation of Anne. We attend diversely two views of human existence; the tragic and religious as opposed by the warm, sex-impelled, blood; the eternities of death as against the glow and

thrill of incarnate life, of creation. These two themes meet in the person of the King.

King Henry is the one king in Shakespeare in whom you cannot dissociate man from office. In Henry VI, Richard II, Richard III, King John and Prince Hal there are clear divergences; while Henry V shows as king an idealized literary heroism as national hero followed by an equally literary bluffness as a private person; nor do the national heroism and the bluffness quite coalesce. Claudius is a baffling example of resolute kingship backed by crime. In the tragedies temporal kingship pales before the advance of spiritual powers; and we have our impractical governors of philosophic insight. King Cymbeline is scarcely a personal study at all. Now Henry VIII shows something of the rough manliness, the tough royal essence, of Coeur de Lion's son, the Bastard (and Richard III, too, in his oration), together with the official lustre of Richard II; and here the identity is always exact. He has, if not spiritual understanding, yet clear spiritual sympathies. He is all Shakespeare's more practical royalty rolled into one, and is thus kingliness personified. But it is an eminently human kingliness. He is neither faultless, nor austere: his is not quite the kingliness in whose name Henry V rejects Falstaff—he has almost as much of Falstaff in him as of Hal—nor has he the remote austerity of Prospero. He is to be aligned more nearly with our humour than with our religious inwardness. He is, like everyone here, religious, but his personality is not subdued to religion, he takes it, as it were, in his stride. (pp. 306-07)

The King appears as a tower of strength and sanity above intrigue and theological subtlety. He functions in contrast to the religious inwardness of our tragic themes rather as Theseus in *A Midsummer Night's Dream*, himself a thumbnail sketch of the perfect ruler, responsible, kindly, wise and with feet set firmly on earth, contrasts with the fairy imaginings of which he so uncompromisingly [V. i. 2-22] disposes. Henry VIII is, however, a more inclusive and realistic study: he has a genuine religious understanding, but also the instincts of a very ordinary man, his main fault being a fault natural to warm-blooded humanity. He has something in common with Antony. He is, like Antony, a superb animal as well as being, what Antony was not, a wise ruler. He is contrasted with our tragic heroes and heroine rather as Claudius is contrasted with Hamlet; and it is because of the importance of this particular robustness in contrast to a death-shadowed mysticism that one must recognize a certain merit in Claudius that Hamlet never wins. In Henry we have a strength of life, a social sanity and commonsense, set against the profundities of tragedy and overruling the subtleties of religious disquisition. The conception corresponds clearly to the Crown as head of the Church in England: for Christianity, itself a religion pre-eminently of incarnation, cannot allow man's private and personal spiritual adventures, whatever their eternal import, to govern. For that we must have worldly experience, width of sympathy, common sense, and humour. These are the qualities which Shakespeare shows his king as possessing. (pp. 314-15)

In modern phraseology we can say that Shakespeare throughout *Henry VIII* regards his main issues as human rather than ideological. In watching the King, Buckingham, Wolsey, Katharine and Cranmer we are aware of creatures being themselves and acting as they must, however they deceive themselves with arguments and reasons; in those they appear tangled; while the play shows the untangling, which is also the untangling of England from Continental domination. But little of this is said: the emphasis is on men and women, with the King central and the final rise of a Christian purity and simplicity in Cranmer, who thus becomes a voice for the prophecy of Elizabeth's reign. (p. 316)

It is remarkable that a play so un-melodramatic, so un-Aeschylean and un-heroic, should succeed in housing such high themes. *Henry VIII* is peculiarly true to the normality of human business. Things develop, rather as in *Antony and Cleopatra*, smoothly; men rise and fall, and the comic spirit functions; but all is done with charity, and without violence. One recalls Hamlet's definition of art [*Hamlet,* III. ii. 1-17], the 'smoothness' and 'temperance' there counselled here characterizing not only manner but, as far as may be, matter too. The chief persons are themselves shown as moving within the limits imposed by a charity analogous to the balanced serenities of art; as is clear in the careful weighing of Katharine's and Griffeth's judgements on Wolsey from which a final forgiveness matures. The prevailing spirit faces what Berdaev calls the 'thou' of the other, his own peculiar 'I', whereby all ultimate hostility becomes meaningless; a tendency reflected throughout in the 'Fletcherian' speeches with their use of personal pronouns. The chief persons here show regularly a certain graciousness, expressing, as persons, a more than personal repose.

The language of such self-transcending is poetry and its active expression ritual; at the lowest, just 'manners', but elsewhere rising to some communal drama in which the ego is, as it were, willingly and intentionally lifted beyond itself to share in and contribute to some wider life, not necessarily understood. Ritual is an attempt to *live* for a while the higher, more inclusive, life of poetry and drama, and therefore in its essence religious. Now *Henry VIII* is even more intensely concerned with ritual than its predecessors, though, the ritual being modern, one is apt to pass it over as meaningless show, which it certainly is not. On the contrary, the pageantry of *Henry VIII* is an extension of Shakespeare's earlier reliance on thunder and lightning, other natural phenomena, order and disorder symbolisms of various kinds, battle-sounds, ordnance, trumpets, music and visions. Here, however, the effects presented are realistic and more directly social. Shakespearian drama normally avoids emphasis on the raw mass of common people, as a mass, though as individuals he is liable to give them sovereign rights; communal reference is nevertheless throughout implicit in his kings and symbolisms. Here the crowds are themselves important, while both the royalism and the related symbolisms attain new proportions. (pp. 319-20)

Peace dominates our rituals and our thought. We start with the Field of the Cloth of Gold and thenceforward find at least the desire to resolve conflicts by a general recognition of majestic law. Both social warmth and communal unity receive an emphasis directly contrasted with war, as in the interruption of the feast by cannon and the light comment thereon [I. iv. 44-52]; the contrast of Anne's coronation with 'the old time of war' [IV. i. 78]; and the burlesque war-imagery in the crowd speech of the Porter's man [V. iii.]. Peace is itself a recurring concept: in Buckingham's farewell [II. i. 85, 111], in Wolsey's 'Still in thy right hand carry gentle peace' [III. ii. 446], in Katharine's 'Spirits of peace, where are ye?' [IV. ii. 83], in the emblematic 'bird of peace' at the coronation [IV. i. 89]. As the action draws to its conclusion, peace becomes yet more real to us; at the coronation ceremony; in Cranmer, conceived as its personal embodiment; in the King's insistence on a general friendliness in the Council scene; and, finally, in the christening ceremonial and Cranmer's prophecy. (p. 329)

This, our culminating ceremonial, is of all the most richly conceived. Too often commentators have dismissed the greater part of *Henry VIII* as 'pageantry': it is that, but the mistake lies in ranking it among Hamlet's 'inexplicable dumb shows' [*Hamlet,* III. ii. 14] instead of observing the great architecture of sequent pageants and their deeper meanings. Here our whole action is rendered newly purposeful; the balancing of religious spirituality against the calls of temporal duty, suggested throughout and explicit in one of Wolsey's speeches [III. ii. 144-50], reaches a unity in this at once religious and royalistic splendour; while the King's fault itself is found to be justified, as perhaps such a fault can only be justified, in its creative purpose. That purpose is particularly concerned with England, as a nation. . . . All our long plot of intrigue and suffering, of religious resignation and jovial mirth, the fall of Wolsey and advance of Cranmer, Katharine's righteousness and Anne's sweetness, the grand persons and raucous life-teeming crowds, all are subdued, offer homage to, this vision of Elizabethan England. Especially is the eternity of religious insight at last integrated, as earlier it was not, with the other excellence of seething life (hence the broad fertility references in both our main crowd descriptions); not in the King but, through him, in the child. In laying his final prophetic emphasis on a child Shakespeare follows a long tradition, Vergilian and Christian; while the works of Aeschylus and Sophocles show similar completions in national statement. So our ritualistic drama, opening with transcendental description and direct reference to prophetic utterance [I. i. 92], flowers to its conclusion in prophecy. (pp. 330-31)

This, then, is the crowning act for which the Ariel of Shakespeare's art has been steadily, from play to play, disciplined and matured. Therefore the prophecy cannot be confined to the two sovereigns to whom it is directly offered. Shakespeare thinks poet-wise, drama-wise, through persons or, failing that, ritual and symbol, and has little truck with the abstractions normally current as powers of thought; so here he says nothing of England as a 'nation', still less of a national 'destiny', nothing of the 'community'; and yet, in working his story, with all its tragic, historic and theological undertones, all its humanity and humour, and all its ritual and crowds, to the culminating ceremonial from which the prophecy flowers—as prophecy should flower from poetry, the next newness from the old synthesis—so, in making his Cranmer voice for the reigns of two successive sovereigns, he has not only defined the indwelling spirit of his nation, but also outlined that greater peace, those 'olives of endless age', whose cause that nation was, and is, to serve; has thus pushed his art up to a proclamation and a heralding, lifting his whole life-work to this point, with cumulative force and authority.

So the wheel comes full circle: 'and where I did begin, there shall I end'. *Henry VIII* binds and clasps this massive life-work into a single whole expanding the habitual design of Shakespearian tragedy: from normality and order, through violent conflict to a spiritualized music and thence to the concluding ritual. Such is the organic unity of Shakespeare's world. (p. 336)

G. Wilson Knight, " 'Henry VIII' and the Poetry of Conversion," in his The Crown of Life: Essays in Interpretation of Shakespeare's Final Plays, *Oxford University Press, 1947, pp. 256-336.*

A. A. PARKER (essay date 1948)

[*In the following excerpt, Parker takes direct issue with Edgar I. Fripp (1938) and G. Wilson Knight (1947) and maintains that*

Act III. Scene ii. Cardinal Wolsey, Norfolk, Suffolk, Surrey, and the Lord Chamberlain. By Richard Westall (n.d.).

there is no unifying theme in Henry VIII. *Parker asserts that the purpose of the historical theme of the play—the idea that national unity and well-being follow from the strengthening of the Crown—is refuted by the presentation of the play's political theme in terms of "royal despotism." He argues that* Henry VIII *fails as a drama because its political theme "gives no coherence to the action or unity to the tone." Parker also claims that the play's final vision does not compensate for the tragedies of Buckingham, Katharine, and Wolsey. This conclusion is similar to that reached by Hermann Ulrici (1839), G. G. Gervinus (1863), and Robert Ornstein (1972), all of whom stress that the falls of these characters remain unjustified by Cranmer's prophecy.*]

It is difficult to detect any unifying dramatic idea in *Henry VIII*. Despite its many fine scenes it has generally been judged unsatisfactory as a whole—a mere medley of scenes of spectacular pageantry, of scenes depicting the downfall of the mighty, and of scenes of a tragic pathos, held together only by their historical truth, not by the thread of dramatic necessity. When praised, it has usually been not on dramatic grounds but for its national feeling. E. I. Fripp [see excerpt above, 1938] endeavoured to vindicate it on a deeper level as a great play, but his unconvincing argument has now been relegated to the background by Mr. G. Wilson Knight's much fuller interpretation [see excerpt above, 1947]. Whether or not the latter is successful in proving Shakespeare's authorship and in justifying it as his last play, it seems to me that he has not justified it as a play in itself. (p. 328)

[Mr. Knight's] interpretation of the play seems to me to expose its defects. Buckingham, Wolsey and Katharine all attain to charity and resignation when they face their deaths, but they do not fall because they are proud and uncharitable in the first place, but because they work against or stand in the way of the interests of the State, which are identified with the interests of the King. Cranmer rises not because he is humble but because he is the King's friend; his humility is political servility rather than religious meekness. Henry is indeed 'raised above our criticism', but only because he is more a Jacobean than a Tudor monarch: the absolute monarch by divine right, whose power may be threatened by misguided individuals, but the extent of whose power is questioned by nobody, whatever the moral quality of his acts. To connect him with a 'wide trust in creation', and to detect 'kindliness' and 'warmth' in the non-tragic scenes, is surely special pleading in order to raise the play to the level of *The Winter's Tale*. For the tone of these scenes is rather one of a coarse frivolity that is consonant with the servility befitting the subjects of a despot but in no way in harmony with the serious treatment of Katharine's misfortune.

The significance that the play attaches to the historical theme, the significance that should bind the action into a unity, is that it was to England's advantage that its monarch should be a despot. What precisely the advantages are is by no means clear, except that Henry, by exercising his despotic power in a way that is referred to throughout as 'woeful' and 'cruel', becomes the father of Elizabeth. (p. 329)

We are to understand, therefore, that national unity and well-being follow from the strengthening of the Crown. This, the political fruit of the Reformation, follows directly from the divorce and the break with Rome; and the resulting national well-being is described in Cranmer's prophetic apotheosis of Elizabeth as the bestower of 'a thousand thousand blessings' upon England. In her the significance of her father's reign comes to full fruition.

This does indeed point to the historical importance of Henry VIII's reign, but the significance of the play as historical drama is marred by its presentation of its political theme in terms of royal despotism; for this obscures the actual drama of the events, whose religious and political clashes raised for Henry's subjects issues far deeper than those here presented. But the real defect of the play lies in the fact that its political theme—the advantage to the nation of acquiescing in the despotism of its sovereign—gives no coherence to the action and no unity to the tone.

On the plane of dramatic necessity we find that for the King to be strong, and so for England to be blessed, not only must Wolsey fall and Cranmer rise, but Queen Katharine must also fall and Anne Bullen rise. The chief blemish of the play lies, as has long been recognized, in thus setting Katharine's fall on the same level as Wolsey's. She is an innocent victim, and the fullest demand is made upon our sympathy for her. Everything possible is done to enhance her moral stature, to make her, in Henry's own words, 'the queen of earthly queens'. And as if her domination of the play by her moral superiority were not unambiguous enough, the epilogue stresses that the play's presentation of a 'good woman' is its chief merit. Yet we must both feel deeply the injustice done to her and acquiesce happily in it, for while sympathizing with Katharine we must honour her rival and rejoice in her triumph. (p. 330)

In reading the history of England our sympathies can be with the Queen rather than with the King, while we can at the same time be grateful that Elizabeth was given to England; but we are here not reading history. Drama moves on another plane, on which grave moral errors are not justified by accidental, unforeseeable results unless we are made to feel that the destiny holding the erring, suffering human beings in its grip is a powerful force. But in *Henry VIII* 'historical necessity' is only the capricious will of a powerful despot, who steals a kiss from 'a dainty one' and then proceeds to seek his own 'comfort'. (p. 331)

Shakespeare thus failed to transform his historical theme into successful dramatic art. *Henry VIII*, despite its isolated merits, is a failure as a whole. The conception of the theme lacks any deep significance and quite fails to convey the momentous character of the events. The play is marred by ambiguity and an absence of emotional unity, the action moving on two separate planes which pull our interest and our sympathies in opposite directions. The final vision of Elizabethan England fails to resolve this duality and does not give the play significance as historical drama, for, however fine it may be as a poetic statement, it has no inner relation to the dramatic action: it is not a conclusion that inevitably follows from the interpretation and treatment of the theme. (p. 332)

> *A. A. Parker, "Henry VIII in Shakespeare and Calderón: An Appreciation of 'La Cisma de Ingalaterra'," in* The Modern Language Review, *Vol. XLIII, No. 3, July, 1948, pp. 327-52.*

R. A. FOAKES (essay date 1957)

[*As the editor of the New Arden edition of* Henry VIII, *Foakes collated all of the available information on the text, date, sources, and stage history of the play. In a portion of his introduction to this edition not excerpted here, he presents an overview of the authorship question and concludes by agreeing with Algernon Charles Swinburne (1880), Peter Alexander (1931), Edgar I. Fripp (1938), and G. Wilson Knight (1947), all of whom see Shakespeare as the sole author of* Henry VIII. *Foakes bases his argument on more recent information concerning external evidence and the internal evidence of Shakespeare's use of source material, the structure of the imagery, and the "compassionate tone and outlook" the play shares with the romances. In the excerpt below, Foakes identifies the trials of Buckingham, Katharine, Wolsey, and Cranmer as the "keystones" that present the central concern of the play: the conflict between "public interest and private joy and suffering." He demonstrates how the pageantry visually represents the public view of this conflict, while the three tragedies and Katharine's vision symbolize the private view. Foakes also states that the themes of earthly versus heavenly justice and patience in adversity link* Henry VIII *with Shakespeare's romances. For further discussions of the similarities between* Henry VIII *and the romances, see the excerpts by Edgar I. Fripp (1938), G. Wilson Knight (1947), Howard Felperin (1966), and Frances A. Yates (1974). Also, like Paul Bertram (1962) and C. B. Purdom (1963), Foakes suggests that the action of the play traces the development of King Henry from an ineffectual to a self-conscious and successful ruler.*]

In [the] triumphant ending to *Henry VIII* the rise of the "virtuous" Cranmer compensates for the evil of Wolsey, and the glory and promise of a golden future in an age of peace, as represented in the infant princess, compensate for the death of Katherine. The contrasts between scenes of sombreness and scenes of gaiety, the juxtapositions of the rise of Wolsey and Anne against the falls of Buckingham and Katherine, culminate in joy. But the structure of [*Henry VIII*] is more complex than this. Its keystones are the four trials, each of which is presented in an individual way. Buckingham's trial by his peers is reported, but he is allowed his long farewell and his protestations of innocence, so that there remains with the audience the sense of an earthly and fallible justice at work in the fall of this good

man; yet his fall is not tragic, and his guilt under the law of the realm, if exacerbated by Wolsey, is not disproved, rather is it assured in his trial by his peers who sentence him. Katherine is shown defending herself in full trial against her judges, Wolsey and Campeius, and again there is the sense of wrong done against her by Wolsey in fostering the King's impulse and turning the knife in his "wounded conscience"; a sense too, there is, of the force of circumstances operating against a guiltless creature. For the two later trials there is a vital dramatic shift, in that the King intervenes directly, and now right is done; Wolsey is brought low by the King, and the attack of the nobles on Cranmer is foiled by his appearing to reconcile them.

Katherine and Buckingham, the first two, suffer more than they deserve, whereas Wolsey and Cranmer are treated justly. In no case is there any recrimination, or blame attached to Henry; the law operates in its normal course, and against it is always posed the justice of heaven. . . . Where earthly justice fails, all will be made right in heaven; where it does right, as for Wolsey and Cranmer, it corresponds to heavenly justice; and since in the play earthly justice corresponds to heavenly justice only when Henry acts directly, the dramatic effect is to enhance the stature of Henry as God's deputy.

The character of these trials which form the groundwork of the plot is at once public, as they affect the state, and personal, as they affect the protagonists. The conflict they present between the public interest and private joy and suffering is indeed at the heart of the play, and all the contrasts already discussed between neighbouring scenes relate to it. Two other aspects of the structure of *Henry VIII* play a vital part in establishing this general conflict. One is its pageantry, which represents elements of this general conflict visually. So while Buckingham makes his last plea for sympathy, and for our belief in his goodness, which he wins, the "tipstaves before him, the axe with the edge towards him, halberds on each side", stand grimly on stage as a silent but public affirmation of his guilt and sentence. The pageantry of Katherine's trial makes vivid the opposition between the law's requirements and private suffering; indeed, a pageant alone, without words, like the coronation procession of Anne, witnessed by all, may establish the national or public feeling towards an event, and the value of that event, directing the audience's feelings, too. Against this is opposed Katherine's vision, seen only by her, an inward triumph set against an outward triumph. Henry's appearance disguised as a shepherd in the masque of I. iv also represents an escape from the outside world: it is in his private capacity, as a person, that he falls in love with Anne—and this is the only occasion on which he appears informally, on which we see him otherwise than in his official role as King. But usually, as in the description of the Field of the Cloth of Gold in I. i, in the trial scene of Katherine, the coronation scene, and in the final scene with its procession from the christening, the pageantry reflects the public order and view of things.

This is emphasized in the other aspect of the play's structure, the numerous scenes of walking lords or gentlemen, who discuss what has happened or is to happen, and, what is most important, continually direct or counterbalance the audience's reaction. These often unappreciated scenes are amongst the most deft, even brilliant, in the play, full of quick characterization, and conveying information or carrying forward the action with a remarkable economy of means. . . . In addition to such functions, these scenes provide a commentary at several levels upon the main action. At one level are the figures who are involved or who become involved from time to time in that main action, figures like Buckingham and Abergavenny in the opening scene, who characterize Wolsey, describe his influence with the King, and also set the historical background, before going off under an arrest engineered by the Cardinal. (pp. liii-lv)

At a second level the principal characters are sometimes made to comment on one another, as Henry describes the virtues of Katherine, and does something to counteract the united hostility of the lords to Wolsey by his defence of him. . . . In these and other scenes and instances characters involved in the action as intermediaries, or, occasionally, as principals, comment with a variety of bias on the King, Katherine, Anne, Wolsey, Cranmer, and their relationships. This commentary is personal, in the sense that the characters are all courtiers and speaking their own views, and it helps in particular to establish the private characters and actions of the main personages. (pp. lv-lvi)

This careful organization goes to shape a play radically different from Shakespeare's earlier histories in dealing with peace, and in having for its general theme the promise of a golden future, after trials and sufferings terminating in the attainment of self-knowledge, forgiveness, and reconciliation. Except that the nation's interests are kept to the forefront, and that the promise for the future is more than a promise, having already been realized in the reign of Elizabeth long before the play was first produced, all its links in respect of themes are with the other late plays of Shakespeare. . . . But it is worth emphasizing that, by the nature of the story of *Henry VIII,* two aspects are especially prominent. On one, the theme of justice and injustice, as embodied in the series of trials, with their contrast between heavenly and earthly justice, sufficient has been said. The other is the theme of patience in adversity.

Buckingham's initial anger and hotheadedness in rushing to attack Wolsey is, according to Norfolk, a yielding to passion, "let your reason with your choler question . . ." [I. i. 130]; and his character is tempered through his trial and fall, so that when he has to face death he shows "a most noble patience" [II. i. 30]. So it is with Katherine: she will not listen to the arguments at her trial, and sweeps from the court. "They vex me past my patience" [II. iv. 131]; but patience is the lesson she has to learn, and learns so nobly, that she can boast of her "great patience" as exceptional in woman [III. i. 137]. The patience Wolsey had prescribed for her during her trial is soon needed by him, and acquired through his downfall, which teaches him to overcome his pride. . . . For Katherine's last scene, a new character, a notable addition to the sources, is introduced —her woman, Patience. There is a special meaning and poignancy in Katherine's cries, "Patience, be near me still", and "softly, gentle Patience" [IV. ii. 76, 82], as she awaits her death, as though this quality above all is to be desired. Whereas all these characters have to learn to be long-suffering, to acquire the virtue of patience, Cranmer already possesses it, and the quality that goes with it, humility. He is prepared to "attend with patience" while the lords in council make him wait outside the door, and to bear whatever weight they lay upon his patience; and, unlike the other three, he passes successfully through his trial and is vindicated. But all exercise the active virtue displayed by Hermione in *The Winter's Tale,* and so sadly lacking in King Lear—a virtue important for Shakespeare when he wrote his later plays, and perhaps more significant for his audience than for a modern one.

For by the exercise of patience, Wolsey's "fortitude of soul" [III. ii. 388], man was made able to control the tumultous passions which led to sin, and to overcome the vagaries and reverses of an often malicious fortune. . . . The exercise of patience is, in fact, the way to self-knowledge, and it is again very important in *The Tempest,* where Gonzalo alone among the king's attendants displays it: so when Alonso bewails the loss of Ferdinand, Prospero has his retort ready,

> *Alonso.*   Irreparable is the loss, and patience
> Says it is past her cure.
> *Prospero.*   I rather think
> You have not sought her help, of whose soft grace,
> For the like loss I have her sovereign aid
> And rest myself content.
>   [*The Tempest,* V. i. 140-44]

A recognition of the part this idea has in *Henry VIII* affords an important clue to the presentation of Buckingham, Wolsey, and Katherine, and to an understanding of these characters. What has been seen as an inconsistent sentimentalizing of them may also be considered a reflection of that enlarged humanity which gives Shakespeare's later plays their peculiar tone, and which could allow him in a protestant country, and after a great protestant celebration, to show in the fall of Wolsey patience and charity. In doing this he modified the violent hostility of the Tudor historians to Wolsey. In a similar way the death-scene of Katherine is given rich overtones, and the creation of a character Patience is wholly in accord with the atmosphere of the final plays. Through their falls these characters learn to know themselves; their worldly loss is their spiritual gain. (pp. lviii-lx)

The transition from their rashness, or pride in Wolsey's case, their inability to be patient, to their acquisition of "fortitude of soul", is deliberately and strikingly drawn, and is a variation of a theme constantly returning in Shakespeare's later work. The process is something like a conversion, and wins for them the sympathy of the audience—even for Wolsey, whose readiness to forgive and bless helps to bring us into a readiness to forgive him. Sympathy is necessary for the flow of the play, as a prelude to the triumphant ending; for, like *The Tempest,* it is a study in the ways in which men may be saved. Suffering is a mode of learning, and brings its own rewards, teaching virtue; and it is common to all humanity, for fortune or the machinations of evil men may bring it to anyone. But, in *Henry VIII* at any rate, God is above all, the heaven to which Buckingham and Katherine confidently aspire. The general progress is an optimistic one; forgiveness and reconciliation expiate past misdeeds, and the future, in the hands of the young and the good, offers a golden prospect.

If God alone is stable, he has a kind of high-priest on earth, in the person of Henry, in some respects the most difficult character in the play. He is usually played as bluff King Hal, costumed and paunched as grossly as in the late portraits, with a full swagger, and a nervous eagerness to cry "Ha!". The playwright's conception surely embodies more than such a portrait, which enlarges incidentals, like the King's peremptoriness, into his whole character. All that can be said of his physical appearance is that he is lusty and vigorous, and the dramatic impression if anything is of youth. Much more important than his physical characteristics is his growth in spiritual stature during the play. Henry is shown as a strong, regal figure, the embodiment of authority; but initially this authority is subdued under the sway of Wolsey. Henry's progress in the play is to throw off the domination of Wolsey, fulfilling the confidence of the lords in him ("the king will know him [Wolsey] one day" [II. ii. 21]). As long as Wolsey's sway persists, injustice is done, to Buckingham and then to Katherine, for whose downfall the Cardinal is presented as mainly responsible. At the fall of Wolsey, Henry emerges in the full panoply of kingship; from this point all goes well, and Cranmer is saved through his direct intervention in council. When he administers the law himself, justice as of heaven operates, and in his assumption of control Henry may be compared to Prospero, for he seems to stand above fate, and in all accidents of fortune which befall other characters is praised and blessed.

If his treatment of Katherine leaves a feeling of uneasiness in the modern mind, it is largely Henry's character as fixed by history, rather than by the play, to which this is due, as well as to the huge change that has been made in our historical perspective and religious attitude since Shakespeare wrote. . . . Once the power of Rome is quelled in England, the King assumes his rightful dominance, and Cranmer, symbolically kneeling to Henry, demonstrates the true idea of a protestant kingdom. This state of wellbeing is signalized in the appearance of an heir who was to become the great Queen Elizabeth. Now the religious opposition is not felt so strongly, and the promiscuous Henry of the popular conception is so dominant that in the play he may seem cruel and immoral. This is counteracted dramatically by the continual blessings showered on him, by the reflection of national feeling towards him afforded by the gentlemen and lords, by the blessing even of Katherine in distress. Perhaps more importantly it should be borne in mind that Katherine is in distress in her death scene, not in disgrace, and there is no question of a morally false equation between her downfall and Wolsey's. He is abandoned by God, she suffers only the loss of a husband. (pp. lxi-lxii)

[Henry] is shown as human and fallible, not an ideal ruler; and like all the last plays, *Henry VIII* leaves open the possibility of the repetition of a cycle of events such as it presents. Nevertheless, the most significant aspect of Henry's character, and the most neglected in performance, is his growth in stature. It does not come about through an inward change in him; it is an emergence into authority, the recognition and exercise of powers he has already possessed. In this he comes to have something of the nature of Prospero, in that his function is to control, to intervene in events involving others, to act as an agent or an organizer for most of the play, and this aspect of him, as high-priest, beneficent controller, should appear most strongly at the end of the play and after the fall of Wolsey. Like Prospero, he has a kind of vagueness, not a lack of solidity, but a lack of definition, as a representative of benevolent power acting upon others.

In this respect *Henry VIII* moves furthest away from the earlier histories, which display a growth of kingship with the strongest dramatic interest in the central figure, and shows a relationship with the other late plays of Shakespeare. It would be difficult to decide who is the leading character in any of the late plays, which are constructed from the point of view of themes and ideals rather than of an individual. Henry is the central figure as the controlling influence of the play, just as Prospero is of *The Tempest,* but the place of both of them in the action tends to be in the background, pulling the strings; they are central in as much as they are permanent, influencing others, and uniting a complex plot. And in both plays, as in *Cymbeline, The Winter's Tale,* and *Pericles,* the story is one of a satisfaction for old sins, not through tragic waste, or the perpetual suffering of vengeance, but in the joy and love of a new gen-

eration, bringing harmony to the old, and restitution too; the birth of Elizabeth in prophetic splendour corresponds to the weddings that round off these other plays. In all there is an increased use of symbolism, and an abstraction of character from individualization towards an ideal or quality. (p. lxiii)

> *R. A. Foakes, in an introduction to* King Henry VIII *by William Shakespeare, edited by R. A. Foakes, revised edition, 1957. Reprint by Methuen & Co. Ltd., 1968, pp. xv-lxvii.*

PAUL BERTRAM (essay date 1962)

[*In the following excerpt, Bertram echoes a note sounded by Denton J. Snider (1890) and R. A. Foakes (1957) when he describes the action of* Henry VIII *as depicting "the king who reigns becoming the king who rules." Bertram maintains that those critics who have failed to perceive the difference between "the King as defined by the play and the historical Henry VIII" have not distinguished the drama's unifying principle. The apparent inconsistencies and structural deficiencies are solved, he states, if we view* Henry VIII *as an examination of kingship rather than of a specific monarch. Bertram's argument opposes the negative interpretations of Hermann Ulrici (1839), James Spedding (1850), G. G. Gervinus (1863), A. A. Parker (1948), and Robert Ornstein (1972). For a further discussion of the importance of kingship in* Henry VIII, *see the excerpt by C. B. Purdom (1963).*]

Since the action of [*Henry VIII*] deals with the public and private life of the King from the time he is still influenced by Wolsey until the time Elizabeth is born, the ways in which critics have regarded the character of the King have naturally affected their sense of the dramatic action. Not all critics have distinguished, however, between the King as defined by the play and the historical Henry VIII. . . . Critics who were possessed of the truth about the historical King Henry—and there was apparently only one main truth about him to most nineteenth century minds—would naturally want Shakespeare to share in their perception. (pp. 154-55)

[If] the hostile critics had not usually ignored or misrepresented the hero of the play as they reasoned about its structure, they might have been able to construct a more satisfactory unifying principle. For the play itself, more carefully considered, is as political in its concerns as any of Shakespeare's English histories, and the importance of each major character depends (as usual in the histories) on the relation between that character and the King.

The King in Act I is a monarch whose reign is marked both by the opulence of his court and by the dissatisfaction of his subjects. The opening dialogues describe the state visit to France whose hoped for outcome had been enduring peace and a prosperous England. . . . Since Wolsey was responsible for burdening the nobility with the extravagance of the French meeting, he is to blame for many of them having

> so sicken'd their estates that never
> They shall abound as formerly   [I. i. 82-3]

and for others having sold their lands, "broke their backs with laying manors on 'em," and beggared their children.

Wolsey is first portrayed, then, as a solemn lord of misrule, fat on the body politic, an uncomic Falstaff come to power. His taste for opulence is later to be given as much a personal as a political emphasis—as in I, iv, where he plays the generous host and entertainer—but our initial view of him stresses his relation to the land, his bulky interposition between sun and earth or King and subject. The alliance he has arranged with the "heathen" French . . . is a particular sore point with the nobility; the conference in the vale of Andren had been nothing but waste and "vanity," since the French are not going to keep faith; even before the meeting had been concluded, there had been a great storm which those assembled had taken as "a general prophecy":

> this tempest
> Dashing the garment of this peace, aboded
> The sudden breach on't.   [I. i. 92-4]

And much of the following scene develops Wolsey's effect on the social fabric at home, dramatized in the taxation issue. . . . The desperation of the nobility is matched by the suffering of the lesser classes, and the blame is again placed on Wolsey. The conflicts have been clearly embodied for the audience in a series of striking theatrical climaxes: Wolsey's strange procession across the stage . . . , highlighting the clash between Wolsey and Buckingham around which most of the dialogue in the first scene is built; the destruction of Buckingham with his arrest near the end of the scene, confirming the view of the nobles that Wolsey is at the highest point of his power; and the confrontation in the next scene between Wolsey and Katherine—his proud arrogance opposed to her proud righteousness—with the King as yet a mere arbiter, not deeply interested in the taxation issue, not yet deeply involved in his responsibilities. (pp. 156-59)

Our first encounter with the King and our first direct experience of his relation to Wolsey come in the second scene. He makes his appearance "leaning on the Cardinal's shoulder" and thanking him for apprehending Buckingham's treason, but at once Norfolk and Katherine mount their attack on Wolsey's commissions and the King challenges Wolsey to defend himself. . . . It is not so much the King's revocation of Wolsey's tax as it is the curtly instructive tone of his response that suggests his dependence upon the Cardinal has been exaggerated by commentators:

> Things done well
> And with a care exempt themselves from fear;
> Things done without example, in their issue
> Are to be fear'd. Have you a precedent
> Of this commission? I believe, not any. . . .
>   [I. ii. 88-92]

A moment later the King is speaking to Katherine:

> The gentleman is learn'd, and a most rare speaker,
> To nature none more bound . . .
>   This man so complete,
> Who was enroll'd 'mongst wonders (and when we,
> Almost with ravish'd list'ning, could not find
> His hour of speech a minute) he, my lady,
> Hath into monstrous habits put the graces
> That once were his, and is become as black
> As if besmear'd in hell. . . .   [I. ii. 111-12, 118-24]

These lines follow Katherine's "I am sorry that the Duke of Buckingham / Is run in your displeasure" [I. ii. 109-10], and of course they sum up the King's attitudes toward Buckingham. But Katherine's two lines would not blot out most of the action and dialogue which precede them, and the audience, which at this point knows more than the King, would probably note the ironic appropriateness of the speech to the relation between the King and Wolsey. The opening lines of the scene had already made clear that Buckingham's condemnation was a foregone

conclusion, and the whole focus of the scene—even, indeed especially, during the interrogation of Buckingham's Surveyor—is on the King himself. . . . Buckingham is made to appear sufficiently the innocent victim for Wolsey to appear his cruel tormentor, while he is made to appear sufficiently guilty to keep the audience from blaming the King, or even from regarding him simply as Wolsey's dupe. The actual trial of Buckingham is reduced to a mere offstage report by the walking Gentlemen in II,i, and even in his moving speech of farewell Buckingham himself [II. i. 88-94] is made to identify the health of the land with the success of the King. . . . The action of the play shows us a King who reigns becoming a King who rules, and the principal episodes are made to serve this development.

The portraits of Wolsey and Katherine which have so dominated the imagination of most commentators are brought into surprisingly close association throughout the play. Both Katherine and Wolsey are older than the King, and before Act II is concluded the fortunes of each have become associated with the past. Since responsibility for bringing about the divorce is at first attached almost entirely to Wolsey, and since his later opposition to the divorce is one of the principal causes of his downfall, he and Katherine become instruments, so to speak, of each other's destruction. And it is during Katherine's final scene that (by still another of Shakespeare's many drastic and purposeful rearrangements of historical chronology and event) our last view of Wolsey—Griffith's report in IV,ii—associates his death with Katherine's. The Cardinal and Queen whom Henry inherited are undoubtedly larger and more complex figures than their later counterparts Cranmer and Anne; this is due in part to the broadening of the social vision in the later acts—after the conflicts in which Wolsey and Katherine have played leading parts are resolved and both the new Queen and Archbishop are described and seen against the celebrating crowds of the coronation and christening scenes. Acts II and III dramatize the separation from Wolsey and the divorce from Katherine, and they create a new image of the King. (pp. 159-62)

The moral issue of the divorce from Katherine, so rapidly developed in the first three scenes of Act II, remains ambiguous throughout these scenes while the other characters speculate on the King's motives and reasons; it is resolved in an unexpected way during the fourth scene, after Katherine's appearance at the trial in Black-Friars.

The trial is ostensibly the trial of Katherine. Yet the dialogues in the preceding scenes have fully apprised the audience of Katherine's fate (even to the accurate prediction, at [II. ii. 34-6] of her final attitude toward the King), and the outcome of the trial with respect to Katherine is no longer in itself a live dramatic issue. Near the beginning of the trial, moreover, Katherine addresses herself directly to the King rather than to the court ("Sir, I desire you do me right and justice . . ."), and from the outset of the scene it is upon the trial of Henry, not of Katherine, that the attention of the audience is mainly focused. Each time Katherine and Wolsey contradict one another [II. iv. 73 ff.] they raise questions which the audience must look to the King to answer. After Katherine delivers her final challenge to Wolsey and departs, Henry's warm praise of her [II. iv. 131-41] establishes him in the sympathy of the audience. Then follows his great "conscience" speech, the turning point of the action and (incidentally) the longest speech in the play.

Henry begins by clearing Wolsey of any responsibility for the divorce [II. iv. 154-65]. Since the "inducement" of a "scruple" about his marriage with Arthur's widow had been attributed by others to Wolsey in the earlier scenes, this exoneration of Wolsey comes as a dramatic surprise. The consequence of Henry's taking responsibility, ironically, is to reinforce the effect of Katherine's attacks on Wolsey by diminishing his power in our eyes; we are being prepared to see Wolsey's role reduced to that of the mere ineffectual servant he is to play in III,i. And by removing the blame from Wolsey, Henry's introductory lines also reduce us to a state of blank ignorance about the causes of the divorce itself, and therefore (unless we hasten to fetch our explanation from the irrelevant historical sources adduced by Victorian editors) they prepare us to absorb the explanation which Henry himself proceeds to supply. (pp. 163-64)

The substance of the King's defense—the stillbirths or deaths of his sons and the danger to the succession—is new; yet the language of his defense recalls much of the language and action we have been observing in the two preceding acts (language and action not explicitly concerned with the succession): the conflicts of the opening scenes had been portrayed against the external kingdom; the prophetic tempest of the opening scene had been accompanied by images of a "sicken'd" land, its inhabitants tormented or hungry or fearful of "most poor issue." Wolsey—to cite but one contrasting image—had imagined himself as a "new trimm'd . . . vessel" sailing confidently and unharmed through a sea filled with "malicious censurers" who were "rav'nous" in their lust to destroy him [I. ii. 78-81]. Between the Buckingham episode and the trial in Black-Friars, however, the disorders of the state have become the distemper of the King: "the danger which my realms stood in / By this my issue's fail" [II. iv. 198 ff.] has pierced the conscience of the King, the sickness of the land has "press'd" into "the region of my breast." After "hulling" aimlessly in a "wild sea," the King—independent of Wolsey—now attempts to "steer."

Through a remarkable piece of Shakespearean sleight-of-hand, never in the play are we made aware of Henry rejecting Katherine; indeed, he usually speaks as her advocate. By the introduction of the succession issue in particular, the action of the divorce has been made dramatically indistinguishable from the separation from Wolsey and the King's movement toward full control over his own affairs. (p. 165)

The relationship between the King and Wolsey is most richly explored in the scene in which that relationship is finally dissolved. After the not very successful interview with Katherine, Wolsey arrives at court "moody" and "discontented" [III. ii. 75, 91]. His political navigations have begun to "founder" [III. ii. 38-40]. He sounds edgy and erratic long before the King (at line 201) hands him the two papers revealing that his surreptitious accumulation of wealth and his intervention in the divorce case have been discovered. . . . Wolsey's behavior throughout III,ii, is rather like that of a jealous lover, and the dialogues between Wolsey and the King, as the excerpts below may suggest, amount to a rejection scene (that is, in much the way that *Othello* III,iii, parodies a scene of sexual seduction). Wolsey is only half ignorant that the King is reproaching him in these lines:

> My father lov'd you,
> He said he did, and with his deed did crown
> His word upon you. Since I had my office
> I have kept you next my heart . . .
>
>   as my hand has open'd bounty to you,
> My heart dropp'd love, my power rain'd honour, more
> On you than any; so your hand and heart,

> Your brain and every function of your power,
> Should, notwithstanding that your bond of duty,
> As 'twere in love's particular, be more
> To me your friend, than any.   [III. ii. 154-57, 184-90]

Wolsey's flattering replies are similarly impressive in their warmth and weight of feeling:

>   I do profess
> That for your highness' good I ever labour'd
> More than mine own: that am, have, and will be
> (Though all the world should crack their duty to you
> And throw it from their soul, though perils did
> Abound as thick as thought could make 'em, and
> Appear in forms more horrid) yet my duty,
> As doth a rock against the chiding flood,
> Should the approach of this wild river break,
> And stand unshaken yours.   [III. ii. 190-99]

To this, the ordinary courtly lover is but a kitten. When the unappreciative King hands Wolsey the papers, dryly wishes him good appetite, and departs, we hear a different tone of voice, but the imagery is still Petrarchan:

>   What should this mean?
> What sudden anger's this? How have I reap'd it?
> He parted frowning from me, as if ruin
> Leap'd from his eyes. So looks the chafed lion
> Upon the daring huntsman that has gall'd him . . .
>   [III. ii. 203-07]

Then follows the extraordinary succession of further changes in Wolsey: the confusion as he discovers the inventory, the new round of nervous calculations aimed at restoring himself in favor, the shock as he discovers his letter to the Pope, the jealous reproaches as he is forced to surrender the great seal which the King "with his own hand" gave him (ironically reminiscent of Katherine's reproaches at III. i. 98 ff.)—the progression from voice to voice of this writhing, tortured figure, by turns self-righteous, weak, hectic, worldly-wise, fatuously self-deluding, nobly forgiving, coolly sarcastic, and occasionally resigned. His final soliloquy gives us his own late image of himself—not now the "new trimm'd . . . vessel" of Act I, but a lonely figure "swimming" in a "sea of glory" who has gone "far beyond my depth" and whose "high-blown pride" has "at length broke under me" so that he is left to drown in that same "rude stream" of "rav'nous . . . censurers" [III. ii. 359 ff.] he had feared from the beginning might prevent his devoted service to the King. (pp. 166-68)

The King is kept offstage throughout Act IV (a device of Shakespearean construction, used in maybe a dozen plays, enhancing the stature of the protagonist on his return), and when we encounter him again in Act V he is being drawn into the Gardiner-Cranmer dispute. . . . [The King's] active participation in the dispute—first by testing Cranmer, then by good-naturedly reassuring him, finally by intervening against Gardiner—exemplifies the virtuous exercise of royal authority and dramatizes the final commitment of the King. Again, the structure of the play seems a good deal more coherent once it is allowed that *Henry VIII* is somehow mainly about Henry VIII. But of course wise audiences are not very directly interested in anything so abstract as "structure"; they are attracted, if at all, by the experience of the play, and there is much more to attract them in the Gardiner-Cranmer episode than any schematic diagram can show.

Gardiner had made one appearance before Act V. He had been nominated by Wolsey as the King's secretary, and he entered briefly [at II. ii. 116], where, in his aside to Wolsey ("But to be commanded / For ever by your grace, whose hand has rais'd me"), he was established as Wolsey's creature in the minds of the audience. . . . But if he is a miniature Wolsey, he is a peculiarly ineffectual one. Long before Henry enters the council chamber in V,ii, we had been made aware that Gardiner's actions against Cranmer would fail; the dialogues between Henry and Dr. Butts implied as much [V. ii. 19-34], and even before the end of the preceding scene—at about the same time that Anne's child was delivered—Cranmer had been comforted by the King's words and reassured by the gift of his ring [V. i. 150]. (pp. 169-70)

There is, as we have just seen, little suspense over the outcome of the Gardiner-Cranmer episode. And while both of the scenes which embody that episode do offer a fascinating Shakespearean sketch of political maneuverings, the older critics who read these scenes as if they were seriously concerned with ideology (for example, as if they were intended to introduce a "great ecclesiastical revolution" of which Cranmer was spokesman) completely overlooked the tone of the dialogues. . . . The irascible Gardiner combines the wisdom of Polonius with the modesty of Glendower, and the actor who plays this pint-sized Wolsey needs a tongue as thick as the character's wit: "Hear me Sir Thomas . . . Let me tell you . . . Take't of me . . . Yes, yes, Sir Thomas, / There are that dare, and I myself . . ." [V. i. 27 ff.]. The height and weight of this teller-offer can be measured against his crony Lovell, whose will to be agreeable to whomever he's with (audible also in his earlier scenes) is bridled only by his will to be agreeable to the whole crowd at once ("Now sir . . . two / The most remark'd i'th'kingdom . . ." [V. i. 32-3]). Gardiner pushes his village zealotry to its suicidal limit in the next scene, where he continues to speak as diplomatically in public as he had in private ("That's the plain truth; your painted gloss discovers / To men that understand you, words and weakness") and where, his hands already full with Cranmer, he takes on Cromwell too [V. ii. 104-20]. Perhaps his finest moment, however, comes when the King enters the council chamber "frowning," and this self-proclaimed master of blunt open dealing suddenly does his city-mouse act:

> Dread sovereign, how much are we bound to heaven
> In daily thanks, that gave us such a prince,
> Not only good and wise, but most religious:
> One that in all obedience, makes the church
> The chief aim of his honour, and to strengthen
> That holy duty out of dear respect,
> His royal self in judgement comes to hear

Act III. Scene i. Ladies, Queen Katharine, Cardinal Wolsey, and Cardinal Compeins. By Rev. W. Peters (n.d.).

The cause betwixt her and this great offender.

[V. ii. 148-55]

A few moments earlier we had seen the King literally standing above the councilors and observing them critically—playing Prospero—and the councilors themselves, chastened by Cranmer's display of Henry's ring, had just taken a friendlier tack toward "this great offender"; the cantankerous Gardiner is utterly powerless and cuts an almost pitiably comic figure. For in Act V we entered a new dramatic kingdom—the first scene had even begun with a clock striking the hour of one—in which everything is so under control that petty malice and sinister conspiracy, however realistically they are dramatized, have taken on the air of an Illyrian charade.

The entire last act, in the highly original economy of this play, is a celebration of the new order—first in the political comedy at court, then among the festive crowds for whom the christening is a people's holiday which the Porter's Man can compare to "may-day morning," and finally in Cranmer's utopian "oracle of comfort." The palmy but frustrated hopes of the earlier meeting at Andren, suddenly asserted and as quickly withdrawn in the imagery of the opening scene of the play, now emerge transformed and enlarged in the swelling prophecies of "a thousand thousand blessings, / Which time shall bring to ripeness" [V. iv. 19-20]:

In her days every man shall eat in safety
Under his own vine what he plants, and sing
The merry songs of peace to all his neighbours. . . .

      Peace, plenty, love, truth, terror,
That were the servants to this chosen infant,
Shall then be his, and like a vine grow to him . . .

[V. iv. 33-5, 47-9]

The "chosen infant" who will "lighten all this isle" [II.iii. 79], although she is at the center of the ceremony, is merely the occasion—not the cause—of the "Holy-day" toward which the action of the play has been moving, and the particular identities of the three royal figures in Cranmer's lines coalesce in these final images of ritual communion between King and people. "King Henry is the one king in Shakespeare in whom you cannot dissociate man from office" [see excerpt above by G. Wilson Knight, 1947], and the dénouement of *Henry VIII* invests that office with a breadth and fullness of social and human meaning which transcend the private tragedies of Katherine and Wolsey. The unity of the play should manifest itself to the reader who does not allow "the crowd of notable historical personages" who inhabit it to obscure the role of the King in their midst. (pp. 170-73)

Paul Bertram, "Shakespeare: 'Henry VIII', the Conscience of the King," in In Defense of Reading: A Reader's Approach to Literary Criticism, *edited by Reuben A. Brower and Richard Poirier, E. P. Dutton & Co., Inc., 1962, pp. 153-73.*

CLIFFORD LEECH (essay date 1962)

[*In the excerpt below, Leech theorizes that Cranmer's prophecy was most likely considered ironic, rather than prophetic, by the first audiences of* Henry VIII, *especially since many of Shakespeare's contemporaries had lived through the years of Elizabeth's reign and witnessed its triumphs as well as its shortcomings. He also asserts that "an assured answer" to the question of the play's authorship is impossible, a statement that qualifies the theories of Peter Alexander (1931), G. Wilson Knight (1947),*

R. A. Foakes (1957), and most modern scholars, all of whom view the play as completely Shakespeare's.]

[The dominant concern in *Henry VIII*] is the operation of Mutability in high places. In Act I the Duke of Buckingham is condemned to death; in Act II Queen Katharine is brought before the court which is trying the matter of her divorce, the verdict being fully anticipated by the King; in Act III Wolsey, considered luke-warm in his furthering of the divorce-action, and with the extent of his wealth unluckily made known to the King, falls from the royal favour; in Act IV Anne is crowned and Katharine dies; in Act V Cranmer is saved from falling by the personal intervention of the King, and the infant Elizabeth, daughter of Henry and Anne, is baptized, Cranmer prophesying England's greatness in her reign and in her successor James's. It will be observed how the fourth act breaks the simple sequence of falls, and how the reversal in Act V provides another variation. But, in counterpoint to the generally repeated pattern of falling, there is another thought-current in the play, an idea that the course of history is deviously working its way to a point of high achievement outside the play, in the dramatist's own life-time. Buckingham and Katharine were good people destroyed. Wolsey had his better side, but at the end of his life he had to experience the bitterness of disgrace. And others, who do not fall within the play itself, will fall in the interim between Elizabeth's baptism and her accession. Anne will be beheaded, as an alleged adulteress; Cromwell, fully in the King's favour as we see him here, will go to the block; Sir Thomas More, not a character in the play but mentioned as rising when Wolsey fell, will come to Cromwell's end; Cranmer will be burned. If we could take the play at its face-value, and rejoice simply when it bids us rejoice, we should look without serious question on the historical spectacle, counting lost heads as a necessary price for the bright glories of to-day and yesterday.

But the play gives too sharp a picture of human conduct for us to yield unconditionally to the notion of splendour. The coronation-procession of Anne is grandly presented, but as we watch it we hear the shrill and absurd comments of two nameless Gentlemen. It is immediately followed by Katharine's death-scene, and the vision of heavenly spirits that comes into her mind as she sleeps is a companion-picture, and a devastating one, to the glittering pageant in the London streets. Moreover, the plain dignity of Katharine's household suggests that privacy has much to commend it. And the intrigues of man against man that we see throughout the action, though never displayed with strong satire, have a good deal of shabbiness in them. Wolsey wants Buckingham out of the way: the King accepts the evidence of a single witness against the Duke, and assumes the truth of the charge of treason without hearing any defence from Buckingham. This man, on his way to death, speaks at length of his innocence, of his continuing loyalty to the King, of the lesson that his fall may offer to those who now see and hear him. . . . The magnanimity and eloquence almost dampen our ability to consider the nature of the society in which the speaker was condemned; but later we may remember Buckingham's fall as due to something other than cosmic necessity. And Henry, as we have noticed, is eloquent on the subject of his conscience. With characteristic quietness the play lets the mere juxtaposition of scenes provide its own comment. Act II scene ii ends with Henry proclaiming his anguish at having to abandon Katharine. . . . Act II scene iii begins with Anne and an Old Lady discussing the possibility of great place won by marriage. . . . The juxtaposition would be immediate on the seventeenth-century stage, with no change of setting. In the last act we see the enmity among the lords of the Council, and their crestfallen condition when Henry intervenes on Cranmer's side. And at the ceremony of baptism we are told of the throngs of ordinary people who lose their heads and their hearts in pressing to the show: it is a comic but repellent picture of the monarch's subjects that is left with us, and it brings the ceremony into some question. In the play as a whole we see too intimate a picture of human littleness, self-deception, spite, to be able to respond excitedly to Cranmer's prophecy about the coming glories—glories, moreover, which the first spectators had themselves lived through and whose imperfections were not to be wholly banished from their minds.

Indeed only the most naïve of readers can, on consideration, take Cranmer's words at their face-value. . . . The writer and the spectators were living in James's time, and a moment's look about them would have suggested other aspects than those . . . mentioned [in Cranmer's prophecy]. We need not assume that the speech is mere tongue-in-cheek writing. It gives, after all, part of the truth, for the last years of the sixteenth century and the first of the seventeenth were years of achievement and some splendour. The writer makes us for a moment entertain the fancy that the time was curiously free from tarnish. But then we remember what the play has shown us, and the seventeenth-century spectators could look about them at their own world: Cranmer becomes only a man with a dream.

Henry VIII was written well after the period when the history play flourished, and it differs remarkably from Shakespeare's previous contributions to this dramatic kind. It has no political lesson to offer. Good subjects and bad come equally to grief; there is no real threat to the strong Tudor rule. It may appear to exhort us to take a good deal of rough for the sake of an imperfectly realized smooth, but we have seen that the effect is more complicated than that. The writer or writers look dispassionately at the flux of time; they see goodness and shabbiness and self-deceit; they offer us a sense of a recurring pattern which is comic, reveals an occasional touch of human dignity and sorrow, and finds its arbitrary termination in a dream. (pp. 35-9)

> *Clifford Leech, "'Henry VIII'," in his* William Shakespeare, the Chronicles: "Henry VI," "Henry IV," "The Merry Wives of Windsor," "Henry VIII," *Longmans, Green & Co., 1962, pp. 33-9.*

C. B. PURDOM (essay date 1963)

[*In the following excerpt, Purdom regards* Henry VIII *as "Shakespeare's most important political play" in its depiction of the greatness and value of kingship, as well as its vision of the glory of Tudor England. For further commentary on the political nature of* Henry VIII, *see the excerpts by Denton J. Snider (1890), Frank Kermode (1947), G. Wilson Knight (1947), R. A. Foakes (1957), Paul Bertram (1962), Tom McBride (1977), and Eckhard Auberlen (1980).*]

The theme of [*Henry VIII*] is kingship which is the "chosen Truth". Its protagonist is the King, and the action is as seen through Henry's eyes. It is essentially political, the personal issues being only for the tears of the audience, and altogether it is perhaps Shakespeare's most important political play. The greatness of kingship, its value to England, and the greatness of England are what the play is intended to declare. The King's problem is the future of his country, which is settled with the birth of Elizabeth.

There are three great people who fall in the play, the Duke of Buckingham, for treachery against the King; Cardinal Wolsey, for inordinate ambition conflicting with the function of kingship; and Queen Katherine, because she did not produce an heir. They evoke tears; but the fall of none makes the play a tragedy. It is very much the reverse; for Henry gets his heir, and the foundations of the Church of England are laid, so that the play ends in rejoicing.

If it be accepted as Henry's vision, as his account of the affairs it deals with, the play increases in significance. As a mere story it is touching and impressive, but as an interpretation or meditation upon national events it sounds depths not elsewhere reached. This means that the action cannot be carried out by naturalistic playing, but is required to be dream-like, remote, elevated, and serious. The opening sets the high level of the action. The Duke and the Cardinal meet, their enmity is made obvious, and before the scene ends the Duke is arrested. This is as the King sees it. In the second scene he appears with the Cardinal, Nobles, and the Queen. The King's concern for the people appears, though he goes sharply against the Cardinal:

> We must not rend our Subjects from our Lawes,
> And sticke them in our Will.   [I. ii. 93-4]

Throughout, the King is set in a good light. The present-day popular idea of King Henry as a heavy, gross, greedy, rude, licentious man should not be read into it. He was, indeed, the reverse, intelligent, graceful, cultivated, violent, dictatorial, and much concerned about the succession, a man to be admired. The play is misinterpreted unless this is observed and the popular idea ignored. (pp. 185-86)

In this final play the law of drama has a triumphant justification. Full of faults in the eyes of the critics, the play invariably succeeds on the stage, for it has dramatic effectiveness of the highest order. It is, indeed, a splendid play, fulfilling all that the law of drama demands, and a magnificent conclusion to the work of the dramatist. (p. 186)

> *C. B. Purdom, "The Final Period (1608-1613)," in his* What Happens in Shakespeare: A New Interpretation, *John Baker, 1963, pp. 174-86.*

NORTHROP FRYE (essay date 1965)

[*Frye is considered one of the most important critics of the twentieth century and a leader of the anthropological or mythic approach to literature which gained prominence during the 1950s. As outlined in his seminal work,* An Anatomy of Criticism *(1957), Frye views all literature as ultimately derived from certain myths or archetypes present in all cultures, and he therefore sees literary criticism as a type of science in which the literary critic seeks to decode the mythic structure inherent in a work of art. Frye's effort was to produce a method of literary interpretation more universal and exact than that suggested in other critical approaches, such as New Criticism, biographical criticism, and historical criticism, all of which he finds valuable but also extremely limited in application. As a Shakespearean critic, Frye made perhaps his greatest contribution in the area of the comedies and romances, especially with his definition of the three main phases of Shakespearean comic and romantic structure, which he defines as the initial phase of "the anticomic society," "the phase of temporarily lost identity," and the establishment of a "new society" through either marriage or self-knowledge. In the following excerpt from his study* A Natural Perspective, *he explores how the wheel of fortune motif informs the structure of the traditional history play, particularly* Henry VIII. *The wheel of fortune motif and its role in* Henry VIII *is also discussed by Charles Knight (1843), Lee Bliss (1975), and Frank V. Cespedes (1980).*]

The mythical backbone of all literature is the cycle of nature, which rolls from birth to death and back again to rebirth. The first half of this cycle, the movement from birth to death, spring to winter, dawn to dark, is the basis of the great alliance of nature and reason, the sense of nature as a rational order in which all movement is toward the increasingly predictable. Such a conception of nature was of course deeply rooted in the Elizabethan mind: it extends even to the tendency to call anything natural that the writer is accustomed to, as when Sidney expresses horror at the custom of wearing rings in the nose instead of in "the fit and natural places of the ears." In drama, tragedy, the history play (always very close to tragedy) and pure irony (*e.g. Troilus and Cressida*) are centered on this first half. There may be many surprises in the last act of a Shakespearean tragedy, but the pervading feeling is of something inevitable working itself out. The histories deal similarly with a kind of "karma" or continuous force of evil action which produces its own inevitable consequences. . . . The organizing conception of the history play is the wheel of fortune, which, according to Chaucer's monk, started turning with the fall of Lucifer, and is repeated in the fall of every great man, who discovers with Wolsey that

> When he falls, he falls like Lucifer,
> Never to hope again.   [III. ii. 371-72]

The wheel of fortune is a tragic conception: it is never genuinely a comic one, though a history play may achieve a technically comic conclusion by stopping the wheel turning halfway. Thus *Henry V* ends with triumphant conquest and a royal marriage, though, as the epilogue reminds us, King Henry died almost immediately and sixty years of unbroken disaster followed. In *Henry VIII* there are three great falls, those of Buckingham, Wolsey, and Queen Catherine, and three corresponding rises, those of Cromwell, Cranmer, and Anne Boleyn. The play ends with the triumph of the last three, leaving the audience to remember that the wheel went on turning and brought them down too. Being a strong king, Henry VIII turns the wheel himself, and is not turned by it, like Richard II, but history never can end as a comedy does, except for the polite fiction, found in Cranmer's prophecy at the end of the play, that the reigning monarch is a Messianic ruler. (pp. 119-21)

> *Northrop Frye, "The Return from the Sea," in his* A Natural Perspective: The Development of Shakespearean Comedy and Romance, *Columbia University Press, 1965, pp. 118-59.*

HOWARD FELPERIN   (essay date 1966)

[*In the excerpt below, Felperin takes direct issue with G. Wilson Knight (1947) and Paul Bertram (1962) for their attempts to evaluate* Henry VIII *in light of Shakespeare's earlier histories. In Felperin's opinion,* Henry VIII *presents a Christian translation of the myths Shakespeare presented in the romances rather than the moral or political inquiry evident in the earlier histories. For further discussion of the similarities between* Henry VIII *and the romances, see the excerpts by Edgar I. Fripp (1938), R. A. Foakes (1957), and Frances A. Yates (1974).*]

[That] fraction of commentary on [*Henry VIII*] not worried by the academic question of who wrote it is mostly patronizing and wholly disappointing. Both its foes and its few champions present, to my mind at least, not the play as we have it, but some preconception of what the play should be. When G. Wilson Knight calls *Henry VIII* "a recapitulation of earlier Histories, though itself more sober and substantial, at once modulated and enriched by the wisdom garnered during inter-

mediate works" [see excerpt above, 1947], his enthusiasm is refreshing, but he is mistaking peripheral resemblances to the earlier histories for essential ones. The presence in *Henry VIII* of motifs which appeared before—keening women, a *de casibus* pattern, a cardinal, and the like—tells us scarcely more than that Shakespeare is once again using Holinshed. Such resemblances, however, work to obscure the fact that the received materials of history are now being used to an entirely different set of dramatic purposes. Yet in a recent essay, Paul Bertram contends that *Henry VIII*, "more carefully considered, is as political in its concerns as any of Shakespeare's English histories, and the importance of each major character depends (as usual in the histories) on the relation between that character and the King" [see excerpt above, 1962]. Mr. Bertram proceeds to extract the maximum of political concern from the play and to define [the] King's relation to the various characters, but that maximum still leaves the play but a poor thing and its characters (including the King) not very important—so long as one judges them by the touchstone of the earlier histories, as the critics seem determined to do. (pp. 225-26)

The final romances stand nearly a decade apart from the festive comedies, though both share certain pastoral, ritual, and supernatural elements, as well as what may be crudely termed a comedic, or tragicomedic, vision of experience. Yet the eight or nine years of searching moral inquiry and tragic interrogation between *Twelfth Night* and *Pericles* informs the romances with a mature integrity all their own. The forms of the romances may ultimately derive from the festive comedies, but their concerns derive from the tragedies immediately preceding. *Henry VIII* stands chronologically even beyond the romances, yet it is discussed (when it is discussed) in terms defined by the early histories, in fact, as the terminal history which brings Shakespeare's English Chronicle up to date. The form of *Henry VIII* may ultimately derive from the histories, but its concerns (Mr. Bertram to the contrary) derive from the romances immediately preceding. The same years of visionary growth which divide *Twelfth Night* from *Pericles* also divide *Henry V* from *Henry VIII*.

The strategic position of the play in the Shakespearean canon and its curious place in the history of Jacobean drama inform against regarding it as simply another history play and its concerns as mainly political. . . . Previous deviations from the Tudor chroniclers are explicable in terms of the exigencies which arise when chronicle is converted into drama—compression of time-scheme, omission of minor personages—venial lapses of historicity in any case. But *Henry VIII* departs from history, that is, from Holinshed, more radically than any of the earlier dramas—so much so, that the subtitle of the play, "All Is True," makes one wonder whether Shakespeare is not ironically hinting that we revise our conventional notions of historical truth, even of mimetic truth itself. (pp. 226-27)

If the histories depict a political drama being enacted under God's eyes, *Henry VIII* depicts a metaphysical drama being enacted before men's eyes, and in this respect it most resembles the romances. (p. 233)

The providentially governed pattern of worldly fall and Christian conversion projected in *Henry VIII* is virtually an orthodox translation of the heterodox myths of process rendered in the romances. The symbolic pagan deities who direct those romantic actions with dark omnipotence are superseded by the familiar God of Christianity; classical allusion is replaced by Scriptural allusion; Cerimon and Prospero, the Neoplatonic magi, give place to Henry, God's royal deputy; and perhaps most centrally, the leading motif of the tempest yields to that of the fall.

The predominant symbol of Shakespeare's artistic maturity, the tempest, is, in the tragedies, one of universal breakdown, of the divisive forces operating in the soul and society of man. As Shakespeare aspires, in the romances, to see life steadily and whole from the unperturbed vantage of a divine overview, the tempest takes on a double value as destroyer and preserver, becomes an instrument of division and more perfect reunion, punishment and purgation, at once. (p. 243)

In *Henry VIII*, the symbolic motif of the benign tempest, though persisting in an elaborate imagery of sea, storm, and shipwreck, is displaced by another symbolic motif, also a paradox, that of the fortunate fall. Each of the falling characters of Shakespeare's last play leaves his trial, mounts the scafford, or faces ignominy and death with a new access of spiritual strength and self-knowledge. The falls they painfully endure turn out, after all, to be the means of their spiritual redemption and of their reconciliation to the world which persecutes or punishes them. When Wolsey compares himself to Lucifer (III. ii. 371), he momentarily illumines the Christian myth which serves as background to the action of *Henry VIII*: the whole epic movement from paradise lost to paradise regained through the doctrine of the *felix culpa*. Despite the machinations of Lucifer— and of the unregenerate Wolsey—God, in His benevolence toward man, brings forth good out of seeming ill. Just as Buckingham, Katherine, and Wolsey himself come to possess a paradise within them, happier far, so the golden age of Elizabeth prophesied by Cranmer is seen as a paradise regained, not simply from the civil dissension of the previous century, but from the profane and pervasive worldliness of Wolsey's domination; and in a sense totally beyond Shakespeare's conceiving when he wrote the words, England becomes the "other-Eden, demi-paradise" eulogized by old John of Gaunt. By marrying the medieval tragic formula of the fall from high degree with the divine comedy of Christian myth, Shakespeare is able to recast the tragicomedic vision of the romances with impeccable orthodoxy. (p. 244)

If the play started out in Shakespeare's mind . . . as a return from the realm of myth to the realm of fact, it winds up as an escape from the realm of fact into another realm of myth, with a loss of imaginative intensity in the process. The historical myth which Shakespeare endorses in *Henry VIII*, that of a Tudor golden age emerging under the watchful eye of God from a long ordeal of tyranny and dissension, is barely a step removed from mere propaganda, and is of a palpably lower order, for literary purposes, than the mythic raw materials out of which he crafted the romances. The "chosen truth" (Prologue, 18) presented in *Henry VIII* is, historically speaking, more "chosen" than "true." . . . Shakespeare's exclusion of the nastier aspects of Henry's reign, along with his all too orthodox whitewashing of Henry himself, calls into doubt the artistic validity of the historical myth he employs. Prospero's island or the seacoast of Bohemia may be a legitimate setting for a golden age which is itself a metaphor; but the age of *Henry VIII* is too littered with corpses and haunted by ghosts for it to have been anything but brazen. At the end of *The Winter's Tale*, Mamillius and Antigonus remain dead, and Antonio and Sebastian are still unredeemed, still unredeemable, at the end of *The Tempest*. These myths of rebirth confront and accommodate the facts of death, physical and spiritual— such is their ultimate fidelity to the real world. In *Henry VIII*, however, the circle of redemption is simply too all-inclusive to be true. (pp. 245-46)

Whatever claim to truth *Henry VIII* may have resides not in relentless moral and political inquiry or in complexity of portrayal, but in the eternal relevance of the great Christian myth upon which it rests. Shakespeare, at the age of forty-nine— old age for an Elizabethan perhaps—stills his sacred rage for order and, like so many aging English poets after him, embraces traditional answers to questions which he had spent his career formulating on both sides. His celebrated ''negative capability,'' the gift of remaining in mystery, doubt, and uncertainty without irritably reaching after fact and reason, may not have been enough; but the myths—Tudor and Christian— which serve as answers in *Henry VIII* may not have been enough either—not to many generations of audiences, nor, to judge from the gentle but shrunken cadences of his final blank verse, to Shakespeare himself. (p. 246)

> *Howard Felperin, ''Shakespeare's 'Henry VIII':*
> *History As Myth,'' in* Studies in English Literature,
> *1500-1900, Vol. VI, No. 2, Spring, 1966, pp. 225-*
> *46.*

BERNARD HARRIS   (essay date 1966)

[*Harris echoes R. A. Foakes (1957) by evaluating* Cymbeline *and* Henry VIII *as reflections of Shakespeare's personal vision of English history. He also contends that* Henry VIII *is skillfully crafted to display the rise and fall of human ambition, while it presents both the promise of a golden age and a ''patient rebuke'' for the ''violent interpretations'' of England's destined struggle with the Catholic Church. Thus, Harris's essay sheds further light on the influence of the Reformation on the play, an element discussed earlier by Karl Elze (1874), Denton J. Snider (1890), and G. Wilson Knight (1947). Harris concludes that in* Henry VIII, *Shakespeare equates England's territorial expansion with ''the spreading cedar branches'' of* Cymbeline. *For a further discussion of the parallels between* Henry VIII *and* Cymbeline, *see the excerpt by Frances A. Yates (1974).*]

Henry VIII is a play in which Shakespeare shows himself more at ease in the court of King James than we might wish him to have been, whether or not in the company of Fletcher; as the result there is a longstanding critical and scholarly division about authorship, date, tone, intention, and characterization, and rather more solutions than the play offers problems. . . . But if our repeated sight of the play is in the theatre it can be seen more properly to obey its devised laws. And this is not to fall back on the plea that the play makes good theatre—it is very far from being actor-proof—but simply to acknowledge that the play is supremely conscious of its first audience in a way so explicit that a modern audience can still grasp at its proffered guidance. . . . In such a context of self-consciousness the play's 'chosen truth' is something less than Wilson Knight's 'choice and real thing, which to reduce to ''fool and fight'' would be sacrilege' [see excerpt above, 1947]; but it is certainly not cynically less than it simply states. The play is an historical romance, in which 'All is True' in the sense that all has been derived from chronicle record; but it remains a chosen truth that it expects its audience to find humanly sympathetic, dramatically entertaining, and politically instructive. Probably most of our difficulties in reaching a balanced critical view of the play derive from the play's determination to balance the potentially irreconcilable issues then so partisan and perhaps permanent. (pp. 229-30)

The cross-rhythms of pride and submission, rise and fall, are episodically treated obviously enough by matters of pageant marshalling which juxtapose with no less deftly arranged analyses of the interior life. The play scrupulously attempts no less dexterous adjustments of historical biography, atoning for its difficulties over Katharine's treatment by granting her a private vision of final justice, presenting a double case for Wolsey while maintaining its own verdict, and humanizing Henry's more obsessive traits by treating his lust as love and so directly rehabilitating both Anne Boleyn and helping to set aside that distasteful problem of Elizabeth's bastardy. The play in the theatre makes heavy demands upon sentiment, but it does so in a sophisticated manner, for it contrives to mock the common mob ('what a fry of fornication is at door!'), and allows us to be conscious of our separation from those unpleasant youths

> that no audience but the tribulation of Tower-
> hill, or the limbs of Limehouse their dear broth-
> ers, are able to endure.   [V. iii. 60-2]

And at the same time the play extracts the utmost theatrical appeal from its audience's melancholy acquaintance with scaffold-speeches, breaking into elegies which rival the sententious excitations to virtue made popular in the heroic dramas of political ambition. . . . The pathos, misery, and fears of the play are its strongest theatrical effects, and the epilogue expresses a doubt whether we shall take away more from the play than a legend of a good woman; and it is so doubtful of even this that it concludes in a self-dismissive bawdy jest. Yet the play's final prophecy survives not only the final rather gauche presentation of Henry as a doting father, and any special application it might well have had to the marriage of the Princess Elizabeth. And it is certainly a vision powerful enough to warrant Wilson Knight's interpretation of its panegyric qualities as reaching beyond the play's immediate themes to their continuity and persistent appeal in some continuing concept of Britain's destiny.

But in the context of the play as experienced in the theatre it seems arguable that we are conscious of a more explicit Shakespearian concern. For as editors have shown, the terms of the prophecy are scrupulously derived from contemporary handling of scriptural utterance applied to homiletic understanding of the reigns of Elizabeth and James. . . . The propriety of Cranmer's prophecy is not that of something glued together to flatter James, but nor is it necessarily an ecstatic promise of a new golden age. . . . But to a contemporary audience, asked to listen with particular care to a serious and considered account of their past destiny and future security, the prophecy also contains a patient rebuke to those popular and tendentiously violent interpretations of the nature of England's destiny in the continuing struggle with Rome. (pp. 230-32)

But just as Shakespeare was more concerned in poetically reconciling his private phoenix and the imperial and sacred eagle on the cedar of *Cymbeline,* so he persists, in the determined quietism of *Henry VIII,* in equating the expansion of England with the spreading cedar branches, and sees that they might flourish just as generously if they are free from predators. What's past is not forgotten in *Henry VIII,* but it goes on being a prologue of promise to its first or any audience only so long as it chooses to make new truth. (p. 233)

> *Bernard Harris, "'What's Past Is Prologue':*
> *'Cymbeline' and 'Henry VIII','' in* Later Shake-
> speare, *Stratford-Upon-Avon Studies, No. 8, edited*
> *by John Russell Brown and Bernard Harris, Edward*
> *Arnold (Publishers) Ltd., 1966, pp. 203-34.*

ROBERT ORNSTEIN   (essay date 1972)

[*In the following excerpt, Ornstein, like Algernon Charles Swinburne (1880) compares and contrasts the major themes contained*
*in the works of Fletcher and Shakespeare. He challenges Swin-
burne's conclusion and becomes one of the few critics in recent
times to concur with James Spedding (1850) that Fletcher played
a "preeminent" collaborative role in the writing of* Henry VIII.
Ornstein considers Henry VIII *devoid of thematic unity, blaming
its ambiguity of character, its lack of psychological insight, and
its failure to justify the tragedies of Buckingham, Wolsey, and
Katharine all on Fletcher. Other critics who have discussed or
mentioned the disparity between the ending of* Henry VIII *and the
remainder of the play include Hermann Ulrici (1839), G. G.
Gervinus (1863), Sir John Squire (1935), and A. A. Parker (1948).*]

I am convinced that Fletcher collaborated with Shakespeare in *Henry VIII* and that Fletcher's role in the collaboration was by far the preeminent one. (p. 203)

Retired from the stage and willing to collaborate with Fletcher in *The Two Noble Kinsmen* and the lost *Cardenio,* Shakespeare would not have been reluctant to lend his pen and, more important, his great name to one last History Play commissioned by the King's Men. No doubt it was easier for him to adapt to Fletcher's courtly manner than for Fletcher to imitate his way with history, though Fletcher tried in a superficial way to do so and pieced together his conception of *Henry VIII* from Shakespeare's History Plays. He found the inspiration for Cranmer's vision in the prayer by Richmond that concludes *Richard III;* and he makes a show of dealing in *Henry VIII* with the themes of treason, justice, and royal favoritism, that were of paramount importance in the tetralogies. Even with these Shakespearean flourishes, *Henry VIII* is so lacking in essential substance that critics wonder what it is about. A tour de force, it pretends to seriousness only in the way that a trompe l'oeil painting pretends to depth, and its representation of political issues is so vague that it leaves Wolsey's role in English history very much in doubt. We cannot tell whether he was a force for good or evil because the evidence within the play is quite contradictory, and his personality as well as his deeds are ambiguous. In a like way, the nature and political significance of Buckingham's treason remain elusive, and the very question of his guilt is unresolved. One could forgive Fletcher for blurring or evading the political issues of Henry's reign if he greatly realized the historical figures who appear in his scenes. But, except for Katherine (and she only in the early Shakespearean scenes), the characterizations are either shallow or opaque. More often than not, scenes are fashioned as successions of emotional closeups: one watches the menace of a frown, the welling of a tear, the curling of a lip, or the breathing of a passion. The dramatic portraiture is so conventionalized, however, that it is hard to distinguish Buckingham's noble posture of resignation from that which Katherine and Wolsey finally assume. Instead of character in action, Fletcher provides an artfully choreographed ballet of emotional gestures.

The concern with elegantly contrived surfaces in *Henry VIII* is most apparent in the extraordinarily elaborate stage directions and descriptions of courtly spectacle. This lovingly detailed attention to pageantry and ceremony has no parallel in the earlier History Plays or in the late romances. Although banners, fanfares, processions, and rituals of various kinds play an important part in the staging of the History Plays, and though masques and shows have an integral part in the moral and dramatic actions of *The Winter's Tale* and *The Tempest,* only in *Henry VIII* is the glitter of pageantry its own excuse for being. No strain of discord or act of rage is allowed to mar the graceful forms of ritual at Henry's court; no irony shadows the brilliant displays of pomp or interferes with the audience's pleasure in gorgeous costumery and heraldry. Where the ritual moments of the *Henry VI* plays, of *Richard III* and *Richard II*, engage the minds and emotions of the audience, the spectacles of *Henry VIII* merely feast the eye. The emphasis is not, as in the earlier History Plays, on the decorums symbolized by ritual, but on the niceties which only a connoisseur of courtly spectacle would appreciate: who stands next to the King, who by his right side, who by his left; who enters first in a procession, who last; who wears a golden coronal and who plain circlets of gold. Such authenticity of detail is superfluous to the representation of politics and history; it exists to give an audience or a reader the thrill of a vicarious closeness to luxury and power—to bring them within the charmed circle of the Court, which is in *Henry VIII* a very heaven. (pp. 204-05)

Although Shakespeare's view of men was hardly egalitarian, his ideal of nobility was untainted by the courtly snobbery that is a characteristic of *Henry VIII* and of Fletcher's drama. Identifying nobility with courtliness and caste, Fletcher makes refinement appear a cardinal virtue and boorishness a deadly sin. Thus, the treason attributed to Buckingham in *Henry VIII* seems less dreadful than the *arriviste* greed and insolence of Wolsey, a butcher's cur who has risen above his place and betters. Whatever crime the well-bred Buckingham may have committed, he seems a nobler figure than Wolsey because he has a finer spirit, or at least a finer manner. Even those who learn the vanity of great titles in *Henry VIII* never lose their concern with manner and manners. (pp. 206-07)

Where Shakespeare values the nobility of mind that is expressed in steadfast loyalties and courageous acts, Fletcher finds the quintessence of nobility in exquisite gestures of submission. Thus, while the courtiers of *Henry VIII* strike postures of manly defiance now and then, the highest form of nobility in the play is expressed by "feminine" acquiescences. Where Shakespeare and other Jacobean tragedians celebrate a stoic acceptance and readiness to endure, Fletcher, in *Henry VIII* and other plays, is uniquely the laureate of emotional surrender. He alone enshrines his characters' failures of will and makes the instinct to self-abasement in an Aspatia in *The Maid's Tragedy* or a Katherine in *Henry VIII* seem sublime. In those scenes of Acts I and II which can confidently be attributed to Shakespeare, Katherine has the courage of her convictions. Devoted to the principles of justice and concerned with the welfare of her people, she is a noble queen as well as a loyal wife. Like Hermione in *The Winter's Tale*, she knows her royal worth, and outraged, as Hermione is, by her husband's desire to cast her off, she also refuses to admit the legality of her trial. The lyric pathos of the song which opens Act III, however, announces Fletcher's attenuation of Katherine's nobility. Once again she turns on Wolsey as she did at the arraignment, but her indignation burns low and she lacks the will to defend her place and her dignity. Before the scene ends, she turns from Hermione into patient Griseld, from a dramatic personality into a sentimental stereotype of feminine helplessness. (p. 207)

Fletcher, like Shakespeare, must be granted an artistic freedom with history and a right to conceive of Katherine as an Aspatia rather than a Hermione—or perhaps as a Hermione whose resoluteness is sapped by loneliness and misery. But we must object when Fletcher on the one hand exploits the pathos of Katherine's "wrong," and on the other hand obfuscates Henry's role in the divorce. . . . [Fletcher] contrives the scenes of *Henry VIII* so that the audience shares the mistaken impression that Wolsey, not the King, is Katherine's persecutor. As Paul Bertram observes, "Through a remarkable piece of Shake-

spearean sleight-of-hand, never in the play are we made aware of Henry rejecting Katherine; indeed, he usually speaks as her advocate'' [see excerpt above, 1962]. The sleight-of-hand is remarkable; that it is Shakespearean is extremely doubtful because such manipulation of appearances is the very hallmark of Fletcher's dramaturgy.

Because Shakespeare's political and psychological insights were profounder than those of the Chroniclers, he may invite us to look beneath the surface of the Chronicle account, as he does when he depicts the banishing of Suffolk in *Henry VI Part II*. But if he makes this episode more ambiguous than it seems in Hall, he precisely defines the characters of the Nevils, Suffolk's accusers, and he brings into focus the struggle for power that culminated in Suffolk's banishment. In like manner, he makes the character of Bolingbroke far more distinct in *Richard II* than it is in Holinshed, even though he deepens the ambiguity of Bolingbroke's motive for returning from exile. Fletcher, in contrast, again and again makes the historical personalities in *Henry VIII* more opaque and ambiguous than they appear in the Chronicles. Where Shakespeare seeks to fathom the contradictions of a Richard II, Fletcher deliberately creates contradictory impressions of Buckingham, Wolsey, and Henry, because his goal is to intrigue and tantalize his audience, not to explore the mysteries and paradoxes of human personality. (pp. 208-09)

Fletcher makes his portrait of Buckingham a masterpiece of artistic equivocation. On the one hand there seems to be uncontrovertible proof of Buckingham's treason: a Gentleman who was present at the trial reports that there were evidence, proofs, and "confessions of divers witnesses" [II. i. 16-17], which Buckingham could not fling from him. On the other hand the charges seem to be trumped up by Wolsey, and when Buckingham appears on his way to execution he earnestly protests his innocence and devotion to the King. What shall we say of Buckingham: that he is a wronged innocent? a cunning dissimulator? a dreamer who has convinced himself of the fantasy of his innocence? These questions would be germane if the characterization were by Shakespeare, Chapman, Jonson, Webster, or any dramatist concerned with psychological and moral truths. They are irrelevant to Fletcher's portrait of Buckingham, which is all facade—a study in noble anger and saint-like resignation. (p. 210)

The ambiguity of the portrayal of Buckingham teases an audience only for a handful of scenes. The vagueness of the portrayal of the King is more irritating because it spans the entire length of the plot, and it is more disastrous because Henry's role as monarch and judge is the only connecting link between the first scenes and the last, between Buckingham's fate and Cranmer's. The problem is not just that Henry is a contradictory figure, here seemingly earnest, there seemingly hypocritical, but that the contradictions are all that we know of his nature. Apart from them and from some superficial mannerisms of speech, he does not exist as a man, as do the monarchs of the other History Plays. Critics cannot debate, therefore, whether Henry is compassionate or callous, noble or contemptible; they can only debate whether the amorphousness and ambiguity of his characterization are artistically defensible and appropriate. Although some would have us believe that a certain vagueness of characterization enhances Henry's symbolic role as an earthly providence in the play, attempts to treat him as a Prospero of the History Plays fail, because there is no comparable moral ambiguity in Prospero's nature [see excerpt above by R. A. Foakes, 1964]. . . . Even Frank Kermode [see excerpt above, 1947], who would have us look on Henry as an exemplar of the divine, must admit that there is an undeniable element of hypocrisy in the King's character in the first half of the play; among other flaws to be found in this Godlike figure, Kermode lists susceptibility "to flattery, to adulterous passions," choler and extravagance. As we would expect, Holinshed did not dare to suggest that Elizabeth's father was guilty both of hypocrisy and adulterous lust. It is Fletcher who simultaneously elevates and degrades Henry's character by suggesting here that his acts are divinely graced and there that his behavior is contemptible. (pp. 211-12)

When Shakespeare portrays Henry V, who seems both ruthless in ambition and tender in conscience, he illuminates a particular kind of moral sensibility. When Fletcher deliberately blurs the character of Henry . . . , he sacrifices moral insight and psychological verisimilitude to sophisticated wit. Artfully playing with royalist attitudes in *Henry VIII* as in *The Maid's Tragedy*, he makes an object of veneration of a king whose scruples are questionable and whose "conscience" is a source of amusement to his courtiers. Of course, Fletcher is too politic a playwright to sneer at Tudor monarchs. He does not suggest that the jokes about Henry's lust point to the true motive that lies beneath the King's gestures of piety and scruple. On the contrary, he seems to insist, despite the courtiers' innuendoes, that we take Henry's noble protestations at face value, because his mercy and goodness are attested to by those who have the least reason to venerate him: Buckingham, Katherine, and Wolsey. Yawning over his task in *King John*, Shakespeare is quite capable of pushing aside the question of the King's responsibility for Arthur's fate, but he never seeks to amuse his audience as Fletcher does with equivocal characterizations—with heroes like Philaster and Henry VIII who are both ridiculous and sublime.

To enjoy *Henry VIII* as it was meant to be enjoyed, we first must recognize that it is an extended *double-entendre*. The spiritually inclined will find in it an abundance of conventional piety—of spiritual striving and turning away from the tinsel pleasures of the world. The worldly sophisticate will find in it an intense preoccupation with the magnificence of courtly life. While Wolsey's valedictory speeches strike the proper note of resignation and world-weariness, his beatitudes have, on close examination, a curiously worldly taint. (pp. 212-13)

Deliberately ambiguous, *Henry VIII* can seem different things to different viewers. The sober bourgeois no doubt enjoyed the play because he could gawk at the glitter of the Court (knowing that it is slightly tarnished) and savor the pleasure of pitying great noblemen. He could also rejoice in the apparent glorification of his own moral sentiments and shed a tear at the redemption of even the most hardened of sinners. The more sophisticated viewer could admire the authentic representation of courtly elegance and intrigue and relish the witty innuendoes about the royal conscience. To satisfy both sentimentalist and cynic Fletcher willingly sacrifices the integrity of his characters and of his plot. . . . We no sooner enjoy the emotional satisfaction of witnessing Wolsey's exposure and richly deserved downfall than we are allowed the contrary satisfaction of discovering his saintliness. Where the modern sentimentalist invents a trollop with a heart of gold, Fletcher imagines a Machiavel who lived by the Sermon on the Mount. But having seen not one fleeting sign of Wolsey's devotion to Henry, we can scarcely believe his lament:

> Had I but serv'd my God with half the zeal
> I serv'd my king, he would not in mine age
> Have left me naked to mine enemies.
>
>   [III. ii. 455-57]

The new Wolsey is no more convincing as a human being than the old one; once a cliché of malevolent policy, Wolsey becomes next a cliché of Christian piety, and it is precisely because he has no character at all in a Shakespearean sense but merely a set of rhetorical postures that the impression of his character can be so easily altered. (pp. 214-15)

The way that Henry rescues Cranmer from his persecutors leaves no doubt that the unforgivable sin in *Henry VIII* is bad form, not bad theology. Or, perhaps, in *Henry VIII* bad form demands bad theology, because, having failed to create a unified and coherent plot, Fletcher must pretend in the last scene that his play discovers the providential design of English history and thereby justifies the ways of God (and kings) to men. The tragic falls in *Henry VIII,* we are to think, are fortunate not only because they produce remarkable spiritual benefits, but also because they make possible the blessing of future generations. Who can fail to see that partial evil is general good when it is obvious that Henry's just shall provide England's salvation? (p. 218)

The belief that all in history—the suffering, the brutality, and the injustice—is for the best is a sentimentality alien to Shakespeare's temper. He does not attempt to justify the pattern of the past or of the present. He does not try to explain away the pain and the misery of men's lives, nor would he argue the necessity and utility of callousness or cruelty. Aware that men appeal to the heavens to vindicate their acts and desires, he shows us a Margaret who thanks God for Richard's villainies, a York who sees God's will in Richard II's public degradation, and a Prince John who attributes the "victory" at Gaultree Forest to God. He never intimates, however, that the divine plan is furthered by atrocity and deceit, nor does he ask us to believe that God rewards Henry V for his princely virtue by helping him to despoil the world's best garden.

There is good reason to think that Fletcher derived the inspiration for Cranmer's vision from Richmond's prayer, which similarly links the historical past in *Richard III* with the Elizabethan present. Where Richmond prays that a new era of peace and reconciliation will come to a reunited England, Cranmer envisions an England secure, triumphant, and prosperous under Elizabeth and James. . . . Despite its pious rhetoric, Cranmer's speech lacks the moral substance of Richmond's prayer, which somberly recalls the dreadful anarchy of civil war. Its only purpose is to exploit the nostalgic memories of Fletcher's audience so as to provide the sense of an ending and of mighty consonances which the plot of *Henry VIII* fails to provide. Where Richmond's prayer is but one element in the great design of *Richard III*, Cranmer's prophecy is the only thing that saves *Henry VIII* from trailing off into insignificance. Take that single speech out of the text, and the failure of coherence and meaning in Fletcher's plotting is nakedly exposed.

If we assume that Cranmer's vision is Shakespeare's last comment on English history, we may also assume that in 1613 he decided that the millennium had arrived under the wisest fool in Christendom, whose incompetence to deal with political and religious problems was every year becoming more obvious. If we wisely doubt that Shakespeare wrote Cranmer's speech—if we doubt, in fact, that he was capable of its fulsome flattery of James and of its facile optimism—then we can speak with less certainty of his conclusions about England's destiny. Of one thing I am certain: having made the conscience of the king a central moral concern from *Henry VI Part I* to *Henry V*, Shakespeare would not have made it the subject of titillating jests in *Henry VIII*. The similarities in the portraits of Henry

"The Christening of Queen Elizabeth," by Rev. W. Peters (n.d.).

V and Henry VIII, both of whom can be described as royal paragons whose pious motives are sometimes suspect, are only superficial. Critics have not argued vehemently about the characterization of Henry VIII, because he strikes modern readers as a Jacobean waxwork figure, one that no longer seems lifelike but that can possibly be explained by reference to outworn royalist ideas. But critics continue to argue bitterly about the character of Henry V, because he seems all too contemporary and familiar. Those who see through Henry V's easy talk of brotherhood are eager to point out that the mirror of all Christian kings was not his brother's keeper. They are less eager to admit that Harry is our brother, though evidence of our kinship with him is written in the self-righteous political rhetoric and the bloodstained history of our days. (pp. 219-20)

> Robert Ornstein, "'Henry VIII'," in his A Kingdom for a Stage: The Achievement of Shakespeare's History Plays, *Cambridge, Mass.: Harvard University Press, 1972, pp. 203-20.*

FRANCES A. YATES　(essay date 1974)

[*Yates, acknowledging the influence of R. A. Foakes (1957), maintains that both* Cymbeline *and* Henry VIII *are informed by the renewed interest in Queen Elizabeth which occurred under James I—a revival particularly noticeable in the pagentry surrounding the marriage of Princess Elizabeth. She concludes that, by linking*

the mythical history in Cymbeline *to the Tudor imperialism present in* Henry VIII, *Shakespeare offered a model for the monarchy of James I and expressed his hopes for the future of England. Other critics who have discussed* Henry VIII *in relation to Shakespeare's romances include Edgar I. Fripp (1938), Howard Felperin (1966), and Bernard Harris (1966). The following essay was originally delivered as a lecture in January 1974, at University College, London.*]

[R. A. Foakes's] interpretation of *Cymbeline* as a masque-like reflection of the marriage of the Princess Elizabeth with the Elector Palatine, tends to confirm the total authenticity of *Henry VIII*. The treatment of real figures from English history in *Henry VIII* is parallel to the treatment of figures from mythical ancient British history in *Cymbeline*. And both plays reflect some culmination, or hoped-for culmination, of [their] religious and historical themes in the wedding of the Princess Elizabeth. (p. 67)

[In *Henry VIII*,] Shakespeare is remembering and reviving the symbols of the Elizabeth cult, particularly the phoenix. From his paean on the Elizabethan *pax*, Cranmer passes on to prophesy the rebirth of the phoenix, the rebirth of the Elizabeth tradition in her successor.

> Nor shall this peace sleep with her; but, as when
> The bird of wonder dies, the maiden phoenix
> Her ashes new create another heir

As great in admiration as herself,
So shall she leave her blessedness to one . . .
Who from the sacred ashes of her honour
Shall star-like rise. . . .   [V. iv. 39-46]

This phoenix is James, but the allusion includes his children, through the image of the cedar and its branches:

He shall flourish
And like a mountain cedar, reach his branches
To all the plains about him. . . .   [V. iv. 52-4]

This was the image through which James and his children were described at the end of *Cymbeline.* Though the main branch, Prince Henry, was gone when *Henry VIII* was written, the other branch, Princess Elizabeth, had recently been the centre of the brilliant pageantry of her wedding. (p. 74)

[Foakes] has arrived at a similar core of interpretation as was arrived at in my interpretation of *Cymbeline,* in which the imagery of that play is seen as related to the Elizabethan revival, and particularly to the revival of Elizabeth symbols around Princess Elizabeth. Foakes's interpretation of *Henry VIII* and my interpretation of *Cymbeline* would thus seem to match one another. Both plays belong to the Elizabethan revival at the time of Princess Elizabeth's wedding, and both use the imagery of that revival. I suggest that the new interpretation of *Cymbeline* tends to confirm the full Shakespearean authorship of *Henry VIII.* Two plays so close in mood, in historical outlook, and in imagery, are surely likely to be by the same author.

Foakes notes that the image of the cedar spreading its branches had been used of Princess Elizabeth in sermons, prophesying the advent of children born of her. He does not note a significant point about the cedar image, that it connects with *Cymbeline,* and with the presentation in that play of James as the cedar, with his children as branches. In *Cymbeline* the royal cedar had several branches; since then, one has been lopped off in the death of Prince Henry. All hopes for the future now centre on Princess Elizabeth and on her marriage.

The two plays belong to the hour in which King James seemed whole-heartedly on the side of the Union of Protestant Princes, to the head of which he was marrying his daughter. They seize the moment in which James seemed identified with the Elizabethan revival, with which he was not really in sympathy as was soon to appear. At the time of the wedding the future disasters were not foreseen. All seemed joy and hope, and that the people of the younger generation would repair the mistakes of their elders. The linking of *Cymbeline* with *Henry VIII,* which is now possible through new understanding of the reference of *Cymbeline* to contemporary history, may eventually be seen as a new key with which to unlock many Shakespearean problems.

For *Henry VIII* is a Last Play in which the contemporary references of Last Plays are made explicit. In it we have the theme of the long expanse of time, covering generations, and allowing for the arrival of new generations who will heal and resolve the discords of old times. And here the new generations are historical personages. Queen Elizabeth I arrives in it as a child to renew the times after the preceding convulsions. And yet newer generations are coming through Princess Elizabeth's wedding and its promise. The new generations, alluded to in myths and romances in the romantic plays, are given concrete historical expression in the history play.

Above all, the history play makes clear what were the discords and sadnesses of old times with which the new generations

will do away. They are the discords in religion, the 'jars' between Catholics and Protestants which Prince Henry thought that he knew a way of removing, and which the tolerance and kindliness of Shakespeare to both sides in *Henry VIII* seems to indicate. In the play, this new tolerance and kindliness seems connected with new visions, new revelations of the divine, the 'theophanies' which are typical of Last Plays and of which there are several examples in the last history play. (pp. 75-6)

The good dying Catholic [Katherine] sees the heavenly vision. And the good Protestant, Cranmer, is seized with the spirit of prophecy. It would seem that, beyond all earthly jars, Shakespeare envisaged a union of the good.

It is now possible to compare Shakespeare's mode of referring to a contemporary theme in a history play and in a romance play. In *Cymbeline* and *Henry VIII,* Shakespeare is using the two types of history, the mythical, romantic, 'British' type of history, and straight history of real historical monarchs of England. Through the Tudor myth of British descent he can use a mythical British-History character, Cymbeline, and a real Tudor king, Henry VIII, to make his contemporary points about his hopes for the youngest royal generation. The play on real history shares with the romance the atmosphere of the Last Plays, in which new theophanies, new visions of the divine, are experienced in an atmosphere of reconciliation. The theophanies in *Henry VIII* reveal mystical experience in which the religious discords of the past are reconciled. The vision in *Cymbeline,* and its interpretation by the soothsayer, express a mystical view of expanded religious-imperial destiny. The return to mythical Romano-British imperialism in *Cymbeline* matches the return to Tudor Protestant imperialism in *Henry VIII.*

The comparison of the two plays, as now understood, gives an insight into the Elizabeth outlook, which is being deliberately revived. It shows us how Elizabethan Protestantism and its imagery of purity and chastity implying a pure reformed religion, was inextricably blended with the Elizabethan chivalric idea. The purity of Arthur and his knights, or Protestant chivalric ethics, combines with the theological purity of the reformed religion to form the imagery surrounding the Virgin Queen in the Elizabethan age, and which Shakespeare is still using of Princess Elizabeth in the Jacobean age. It is this double historical line of the ancient purity of British chivalric tradition, combined with the theological purity of royal and Tudor reformation, which informs this poetic view of history. The Reformation line informs it politically, and justifies the break with Rome, the British line joins this with chivalric tradition, with knightly purity, and opens the door to mysticism, myth, and magic. (pp. 78-9)

Frances A. Yates, "'Henry VIII'," in her Shakespeare's Last Plays: A New Approach, *Routledge & Kegan Pual, 1975, pp. 63-84.*

LEE BLISS (essay date 1975)

[*In the following discussion of* Henry VIII, *Bliss concentrates on the "essential ambiguity in the play's truths'." She notes that the "truth in any given situation is exceedingly complicated" and argues that the line separating truth from illusion in the play is often blurred by conflicting perspectives and ambiguous motives— the "divorce between word and deed." She also discusses the wheel of fortune motif first suggested by Northrop Frye (1965) and examined later by Frank V. Cespedes (1980). She interprets Cranmer's prophecy as Shakespeare's ideal solution to the "endless repetitions of history" presented throughout the play, spe-*]

cifically in its image of Elizabeth as the answer to the moral chaos or corruption of Henry's reign. This opposes the conclusions of such earlier critics as Hermann Ulrici (1839), G. G. Gervinus (1863), Sir John Squire (1935), A. A. Parker (1948), and Robert Ornstein (1972), all of whom consider the ending of Henry VIII *contrived or structurally disjointed from the remainder of the play.]*

I do not share [the] heroic view of King Henry as either the champion of the Church of England or as a misled youth, akin to Shakespeare's tragic heroes in his "idealistic and overprompt emotional reactions" [see additional bibliography, H. M. Richmond], who finally attains self-knowledge and with it all the virtues of the ideal monarch. Such a simplification of the central figure implies a more uncomplicated unity of action than in fact exists. Those readings which relate the first four acts of *Henry VIII* to the concerns of the history plays do, however, give valuable attention to the political and moral complexities which the play devastatingly explores. . . . (p. 2)

Confusing perspectives on character and action are more pervasive than has been allowed, and the result is an essential ambiguity in the play's "truths." The last act is not devoted to vindicating Henry; and the reconciliations and restoration through suffering are different in kind from those of the late romances, not an "attempt to create a similar total effect within the ordinary terms of causality and succession" [see excerpt above by R. A. Foakes, 1957]. To read the play fairly, it is necessary both to avoid interpreting it backward, from the vantage point of the final romantic prophecy, and to resist the temptation to approach *Henry VIII* as a culmination which *must* draw on and resolve the problems and interests of an entire career. Thus while it would be unwise to isolate *Henry VIII* from the preceding plays, it is well to keep in mind that distinctively Shakespearean predilection for experiment rather than repetition and conspicuous eagerness to bend and transform conventions. . . . [The] shadowy Henry is both the center of court power within the play and the focal point for a dramatic structure distinguished by constant and alarming shifts in its perspective on character and action. With a clear view of the way in which the play builds its disturbing effects, perhaps the final prophecy will seem less a retreat into fantasy (or obsequious flattery) than a significant, dramatically appropriate discontinuity.

Even before the appearance of the king, the first scene sets up a world in which establishing the "truth" in any given situation is exceedingly complicated; prior certainty repeatedly dissolves in the face of later revelations. As the play progresses, its probable subtitle "All is True" and the references to "truth" in the Prologue become increasingly perplexing and ironic. If the facts of history remain constant, those treaties, taxes, deaths and births, rises and falls, become subject to many, even contradictory, interpretaions. Any artistic work of course "interprets" through necessary selectivity and compression, but Shakespeare has dramatized the essential limitations in our knowledge of "truth" or human motivation through a proliferation of explanations within the play itself.

We are introduced to this pattern of contradiction—as well as to a predilection for personally biased reportage of events—through Norfolk's relation to Buckingham of the events of the Field of the Cloth of Gold. Norfolk maintains that he has been "ever since a fresh admirer / Of what I saw there," and goes on to describe this "view of earthly glory" in lavish terms which suggest that even ugliness was temporarily transformed by the magnificence of the occasion [I. i. 3-4, 18-26]. Eighty

lines later, however, we are told that the whole grandiose display was a hollow sham; the gilded pomp and pageantry in which Norfolk expressed his vision of earthly harmony merely draped a temporary political maneuver. In the beginning all had seemed true to Norfolk and, in his report, to us; only in retrospect can we see how false, how truly unstable and "earthly" that appearance was. Events throughout the play modify our reactions to what has already been seen as well as to subsequent incidents. Even in this first scene, we now realize that "admire" did not signify wonder in the sense of approbation, but rather an ironic sense of amazement at the disparity between a dream of transcendent and transforming harmony and the disconcertingly mutable political realities of an impoverished nobility and a broken treaty. Later events also illuminate the ominous suggestion that at Andren "no discerner / Durst wag his tongue in censure" [I. i. 32-33]. . . . As a paradigm for the pattern and concerns of the play, this scene offers not only empty pomp and friendship, but also a characteristic questioning of the truths established by individuals; personal bias in this play generally determines a character's interpretation of events. . . . This whole complex scene of withheld information, shifting perspectives, and uncertain "truths" influences our expectations; caught once in easy acceptance of what we thought was a conventional report speech, we are now less ready to accept either the grand appearance of the moment or any single person's assertion. This attitude is certainly not discouraged by subsequent events.

The truth of Buckingham's guilt or Wolsey's responsibility for his fall is never clear. . . . Buckingham's hearing before his king leaves us no wiser. Katherine impugns the surveyor's testimony, but Henry ignores her comment. Although the king commits Buckingham to trial by his peers, he has already judged Buckingham a traitor and refused him the royal mercy. Buckingham himself is ambiguous on the matter, and our doubts are encouraged rather than resolved. (pp. 2-4)

The confrontation scene leaves us wondering whether the appearance of treason (or innocence) here is as specious as the initial indications of peace; the apparently impartial description of the trial by the walking gentleman in II. i is tantalizingly non-committal. (p. 5)

Their dialogue pointedly fails to resolve the kinds of questions—truth or deception, guilt or innocence—which the play repeatedly raises. As disinterested observers, the gentlemen thus offer a significant response to the pattern of rises and falls, trials and judgments, which demand the court's attention. Absolute guilt and innocence cannot be established in this world, for both earthly glory and earthly justice seem to express no permanent, immutable values; indeed, Shakespeare capitalizes on the inconsistencies of the chronicles and with them enhances his use of multiple sympathetic perspectives. No one is presented as wholly innocent, or without self-interested motives (except perhaps Katherine, and she is guilty of not having borne Elizabeth and hence must fall); and so, despite the fact that the play is studded with trial scenes, establishment of the truth of guilt or innocence is not the play's prime consideration. The trials themselves and the quality of justice they reflect are important, as their number would suggest, but so too are both the continual process of rise and fall they reveal and the opportunity for self-awareness they offer. (pp. 5-6)

Since Henry's motivation in the matter of the divorce is a constant topic within the play, it is worth noting that in compressing historical time Shakespeare has also artfully multiplied our doubts about Henry's religious scruples. Katherine's trial actually occurred four years before Henry's secret marriage to Anne Boleyn. Thus Henry's obvious impatience to be rid of Katherine is given additional significance by the compressed time scheme: Henry has secretly married Anne—apparently just after Katherine's inconclusive trial—while the question of the divorce is still "unhandled" [III. ii. 58]. Moreover, Suffolk's aside here and the Lord Chamberlain's later pun [II. iii. 76-8] suggest at least a possibility that Anne is pregnant even before Katherine's trial. Since this dramatic situation results from conscious changes in historical chronology, its implications can hardly be fortuitous. Henry's impatience, and the disparity between his public speeches and his private actions and asides, render his motivation ambivalent; we feel that justice, though often mentioned, is really peripheral to the matter in hand. (p. 7)

Henry proceeds to cast doubt on his sincerity by insisting that if they but find the marriage lawful he will gladly spend the rest of his life with Katherine. Henry has remained silent during the trial itself; his "Go thy ways Kate" speech of praise occurs only after Katherine has swept indignantly out of the court— that is, when no one remains to contradict him. In view of his relations with Anne and the fact that, barring the judges, everyone seems to see Katherine's dismissal as inevitable (because Henry has hinted that it is his "pleasure"?), Henry's protest rings a bit hollow. Within ten lines, Henry indicates in an aside that his private plans contradict those purveyed for public consumption:

> King.   [Aside]   I may perceive
> These cardinals trifle with me; I abhor
> This dilatory sloth and tricks of Rome.
> My learn'd and well-beloved servant Cranmer,
> Prithee return; with thy approach, I know
> My comfort comes along.—Break up the court;
> I say set on.   [II. iv. 236-42]

Henry is impatient, frustrated by his failure to receive immediately the verdict he obviously plans to obtain by any means. Most critics gloss over this speech because they wish to see Henry as a good man and, at least potentially, a model ruler. They place the blame for the obvious injustice done to Katherine squarely on Wolsey's shoulders and thereby salvage Henry's moral character: the most Henry can be accused of is "honest simplicity" [see excerpt above by G. Wilson Knight, 1947]. Yet Shakespeare has chosen to complicate Henry's position—and any easy political or historical interpretation of the play—with a jarring personal statement which closes an important scene. Moreover, Henry's speech is not a glaring inconsistency, best ignored or noted only as support for the dubious view that *Henry VIII* focuses on the defeat of Catholicism and the rise of Protestantism. Rather, it is consistent not only with what we have seen of Henry's shifting (and shifty) character and with what Katherine soon says to the cardinals, but also with the whole world of conflicting perspectives and ambiguous motives evident from the first scene. (pp. 9-10)

Wolsey's fall from power and the long-sought triumph of the discontented nobility shift our focus but deepen rather than resolve our questions about Henry and his court. . . . Henry himself admits his tarnished moral position when he jocularly taunts Wolsey just before revealing his full anger: he chides Wolsey for being a bad manager of his earthly affairs and adds "sure in that / I deem you an ill husband, and am glad / To have you therein my companion" [III. ii. 141-43]. Wolsey claims that he has endeavored to match his performance to his professions, and the king replies: "'tis a kind of good deed to

say well, / And yet words are no deeds" [III. ii. 153-54]. We may justly wonder at the extent of conscious irony in Henry's righteous maxim, for Henry himself certainly offers occasions to doubt his credibility. Katherine condemned the English court for just such a divorce between word and deed, appearance and intent. (pp. 11-12)

The disturbing characterization of Henry and the political world he dominates may also be contradicted—or resolved—by the paradisal future predicted in the concluding scene. Heavily biblical in language and reference, Cranmer's inspired prophecy applies a visionary description of a golden age to the world of England under Elizabeth and James I. To accept Cranmer's vision of an earthly paradise as Shakespeare's praise of Elizabeth and James is also to accept its implicit progressive view of history, where a benevolent god provides the instrument (Elizabeth) for accomplishing the perfection of human existence. Yet even within the dramatic fiction of the play, the prophecy appears disjunctive rather than as the climactic revelation of a providential pattern in the events we have witnessed. The preceding play seems predicated on the assumption that merely superficial changes thinly mask repetitive life-cycles which are created and perpetuated by what in any Christian scheme would be understood as the nature of fallen man. (p. 16)

Certainly Shakespeare's analysis of the political world's muddled truths, intrigue, and dubiety, and of the human nature which accepts that world, remains too essentially realistic and compelling to be negated by one final version of earthly harmony. When Cranmer foresees that "all the virtues that attend the good, / Shall still be doubled on her [Elizabeth]" [V. iv. 27-8], we cannot but recall the fate of Katherine's goodness; when Cranmer says that "Truth shall nurse her" [V. iv. 28], we cannot forget our experience of a world in which it is almost impossible to determine the "truth" of even simple, purportedly factual, statements. Rather than dismiss the final scene as escapist fantasy, egregious flattery, or a botched attempt to resolve the private and public tensions which generate the play's historical events, I prefer to view the conclusion as another experiment in providing a suggestion of resolution and finality to counterpoint the sense of fruitless repetition. Instead of attempting with Cranmer's visionary resolution to eclipse and supplant the expectations and mood of the preceding play, Shakespeare emphasizes the total dissimilarity between the England we have seen and the "future" England described. Cranmer prophesies a world which pointedly corrects every moral fault which we have seen exemplified in Henry and the court he dominates; our attention is shifted from the contingent, ambiguous world we inhabit to an idealized one in which truth can be known and justice meted out. This conscious shift in planes of perception contributes to a larger resolution, didactic as well as aesthetic.

Shakespeare offers, in the form of an ideal, a solution to the political world's sickness and corruption and an escape from the endless repetitions of history. His paean to Elizabeth and James I cannot be confined to literally "true" predictions of their actual reigns (already belied by the sublunar world of the original audience), or designed merely to feed nostalgic memories of Elizabeth and satisfy the reigning monarch's taste for flattery. Rather, this praise fulfills the didactic function of panegyric in the Renaissance: idealized portraits which heighten the subject's exemplary traits in order to incite emulation. (p. 20)

Firmly rooted in the language of earlier, private, self-discoveries, Cranmer's prophecy offers an aesthetic rather than a logical sense of resolution and finality. By limning in the ideal king (and his realm) a shining example to the man endowed proleptically, it is hoped, with his virtues, it aspires to transform the public world in its image. . . . The "wonders" in *Henry VIII* are limited to a glimpse of what a transformed England, under an inspired monarch, might be. The vision is hortatory and must explode the play's framework to create a world where humanity's endless, profitless cycle of rise and fall can be translated into the more miraculous image of the death and rebirth of "the maiden phoenix." (pp. 22-3)

> *Lee Bliss, "The Wheel of Fortune and the Maiden Phoenix of Shakespeare's 'King Henry the Eighth',"*
> *in ELH, Vol. 42, No. 1, Spring, 1975, pp. 1-25.*

TOM McBRIDE (essay date 1977)

[*McBride contends that the thematic disunity so often perceived by commentators on* Henry VIII *can be explained if we interpret the play as the juxtaposition of two irreconcilable moral systems, one Christian, the other Machiavellian. He states that the action of the play traces the development of King Henry—through such "impolitic" errors as his sentencing of Buckingham and his reliance on Wolsey—into a ruler who adopts Machiavellian ways in order to achieve his goals. Thus McBride calls* Henry VIII *a political intrigue "whose structure is primarily that of a romance," and he characterizes Henry as a combination of romantic hero and Machiavellian prince. McBride's interpretation of Henry as a ruler who becomes more politically shrewd during the course of the drama recalls the earlier comments of R. A. Foakes (1957), Paul Bertram (1962), and C. B. Purdom (1963). In addition, his theory that* Henry VIII *combines both historical and romantic elements is echoed in the excerpts by Edgar I. Fripp (1938), Frank Kermode (1947), G. Wilson Knight (1947), Hugh M. Richmond (1979), and Eckhard Auberlen (1980).*]

To understand Henry and his play fully . . . is to see that there is presented in *Henry VIII* not one but two moral standards. [Such critics as] Spedding, Felperin, and Ornstein are right to challenge those who label the play a Christian history (where God makes all well) and who thus exonerate Henry. *Henry VIII* is not entirely a Christian play, nor is it meant to be. But at the same time Henry's detractors are wrong to judge him by applying in a different way their own, but still essentially Christian, standards. Actually, Henry can neither be excused nor condemned by such a code, for the task he accomplishes is irrelevant to it. Indeed, once we understand that the play posits two ultimately valid moral codes, we can take a critical view that both includes and rectifies those of the past. *Henry VIII* really juxtaposes two moral systems, the Christian and the Machiavellian, and suggests that, while both are moral, they are also irreconcilable.

Those who view *Henry VIII* as a romance have often overlooked its element of political realism. There is indeed a strong romance element in the play, of which more later; but it is combined with a strong dose of what may be properly termed "Machiavellianism," because many of the characters' triumphs and errors in this play closely parallel central doctrines of *The Prince*. (pp. 28-9)

"Machiavellianism" is a valid and serviceable term for describing the harsher political ambience of *Henry VIII*, especially as it applies, in turn, to Buckingham, Wolsey, and Henry.

The fate of Buckingham is that suffered by a demonstrably poor Machiavellian. He ignores Norfolk's warnings about the dangers of opposing Wolsey too publicly. The hot-headed duke is obviously sincere when he says that the Cardinal is a traitor;

but, when one is also impolitic, sincerity is not enough. There is, to be sure, much Christianity in his final speech on earth. He forgives all. But in his closing words he laments that he fell by the perjury of disloyal servants, and he warns his listeners about the perils of foolishly being too "liberal of your loves and counsels" [II. i. 126]. It is a warning also given by Machiavelli in Chapter XXII of *The Prince*.

Nor is the decline of Wolsey himself free of its Machiavellian factor. The Italian advises his prince that it is better to be feared than loved, but he urges him to avoid hatred, in particular the enmity he will arouse if he appropriates his subjects' worldly goods (Ch. XVII). He also warns him not to incur the hatred of the commoners. But Wolsey ignores this advice by imposing a heavy tax on the commoners, with the pretext that money is needed for Henry's wars in France. . . . Henry wisely cancels the tax, but Wolsey's resentful musing, "The grieved commons / Hardly conceive of me" [I. ii. 104-05], indicates that he has not learned his Machiavellian lesson. There is no shrewd analysis in this remark—only bitterness. (pp. 29-30)

[Wolsey's] fall is finally the work of Fortune. But a man hated by the nobles for his arrogance and for his framing of Buckingham—and also despised by the commoners—will not be gently eliminated. Henry's divesting Wolsey of the Great Seal is knowingly to throw him to the wolves. A man more popular with nobles and commoners alike might have been eased out, with care and mercy; but when Henry lets his nobles rob Wolsey of all his possessions, as well as the King's protection, he need have no fear of trouble. Here is a Machiavellian irony: he who would seize a sixth of each commoner's substance has no commoner's support to help him keep his own. Fortune may be the immediate agent of Wolsey's decline, but a more politic man would have kept conditions that cushion the fall.

Henry, above all, is dangerously impolitic. He allows Wolsey to dupe him about Buckingham; and Buckingham's fall, as evidenced by the two gentlemen's conversation, is unpopular with his subjects. Henry's authority is not enhanced by such events. . . . (pp. 30-1)

But eventually, perhaps none too soon, Henry becomes a shrewder man, and he begins to transform Wolsey from a liability into an asset. Machiavelli says that Kings ought to have someone on whom, when necessary, to shift blame (Ch. XIX). Thus the King initially suggests that Wolsey has persuaded him to divorce Katherine. Before the significant audience of Norfolk and Suffolk, who are irritated by rumors to this effect, Henry plays his part:

> O my Wolsey,
> The quiet of my wounded conscience;
> Thou art cure fit for a King.　　　　[II. ii. 73-5]

By now, Henry seems to realize that he is seen as a magistrate who is not the master of his own house; here he pretends to be what before he actually was—masterless. He therefore uses the nobles' bitter suspicions to his own advantage. Like Prince Hal, he picks his moment to emerge from behind the cloud: like Hal, he knows that princes look best redeeming time when men least think they will. So later, after his crafty remark that Wolsey has many enemies, he announces, with surprising and impressive authority, that it is not Wolsey but the good of the realm that brings forth the divorce decree. His timing is perfect. Having been a fox by shifting blame to Wolsey for a politic period, he now plays the lion, who is king and master after all.

On Henry's part, then, there is considerable learning in Machiavellian ways. Even before his ambitious letters backfire, Wolsey loses influence over an increasingly strong ruler. Henry's discharge of his bad servant and his rescue of Good Counsel Cranmer are a measure of his newly gained political wisdom. He travels a far way from the moment he foolishly sent Buckingham to the block.

Yet such political intrigue occurs in a play whose structure is primarily that of a romance. Ronald Berman notes the play's ripe, sunny pageantry and argues that this romance element, which is less apparent when the play is read rather than seen in the theater, dominates it by producing an impression of superhuman harmony [see additional bibliography]. . . . Yet probably Felperin identifies the essential romance structure of the play when he argues that it is informed by a romantic historical myth: England's emergence from leaden tyranny into a golden freedom. It is a myth worthy of the play's powerful pageantry. But more significant still are the additional elements of this romance structure.

Northrop Frye provides an excellent overview of romance structures in general. The romantic hero, he writes, faces an enemy "associated with winter, darkness, sterility"; the hero himself is associated with "spring, dawn, order, fertility, and youth." Often the romance portrays the importance of a king or the laying waste of a land. . . . The romantic hero thus restores fertility to the earth or leads his people out of bondage into a promised land. . . . The romance itself, then, usually includes cyclical imagery, especially solar imagery. . . . (pp. 31-2)

Henry himself is both romantic hero and Machiavellian prince. He casts off the old, sick Katherine and through the youthful Anne brings the fertile joy of the Elizabethan promise. He casts off the Catholic dragon Wolsey, who loved himself and popery more than he loved England; and through the rescue and elevation of Cranmer, Henry brings forth an independent, nationalistic, Protestant England. Cranmer's closing speech, then, in which he blesses Elizabeth and proclaims the future ideal England, is the capstone of this dramatic romance, so often couched in sunny pageantry.

Solar imagery appears throughout. When poor Buckingham says that he is but the "shadow" of his former self, "Whose figure even this instant cloud puts on / By dark'ning my clear sun" [I. i. 225-26], he unknowingly speaks of more than a personal fall; taken in a Machiavellian context, his decline represents a darkening over the English isle. If Henry is so poor a Machiavel, how can he lead England into a brighter day? Wolsey has too easily duped him about the innocent and loyal Buckingham. Hence, when Henry finally rids England of Wolsey himself, when it is the Cardinal's turn to speak of falling from the "full meridian of my glory" and hasting "now to my setting" [III. ii. 224-25], England at last can see her own sun rise in the political cycle. It is the same sun that nurtures the blessed England, "Which time shall bring to ripeness" [V. iv. 20], predicted by Cranmer. And though Henry, as romantic hero, seems for a while to disappear, irrevocably dominated by the Catholic Wolsey, he reappears as Machiavellian master, casting off Wolsey when he opposes Anne, who will give the Protestant Elizabeth. (pp. 33-4)

Still, the paradox of the Machiavellian romance undeniably remains. The usual goals of the romantic hero are not always easy ones, but he achieves them by means that are clearly moral. . . . To achieve romantic ends as a Machiavellian prince,

however, is to use means of suspect morality and to invite debate over an ethical problem of means and ends. Such is the case with Henry. As romantic hero he is duty-bound to slay the dragons that lay waste his land. In a purely romantic sense, his moral obligations are clear. But one of those "dragons" is a woman who, as Henry himself concedes, is

> alone
> (If thy rare qualities, sweet gentleness,
> Thy meekness saintlike, wife-like government
> . . . could speak thee out)
> The queen of earthly queens.
> [II. iv. 137-39, 141-42]

Still, she is barren, having yielded only the future Queen Mary I (in Henry's mind at this point a poor heir on which to depend for Tudor succession) and cannot yield the male heir needed by the realm. She is also Catholic and wishes to appeal to Rome for judgment in her divorce. She thus represents for England a dangerous sterility, and she allies herself with a foreign encroachment upon England's nationhood. She must be cast off; her removal is a necessity. (p. 34)

It is cruel, but it is also needful. For Katherine the divorce is a sickness unto death. But Henry worries about a potential sickness in the body politic: he is concerned with a larger cure. He can achieve it—but only by actions that also make Katherine sick and kill her. It is a moral conundrum.

At play's end the author's hindsight illuminates the nature of this mythic cure; the playwright (individual or collective) knows of England's future greatness under Elizabeth and so makes Cranmer a mighty prophet in predicting the magnificent England to come. But Henry has no such hindsight; working in a more naturalistic world, where prescience is limited, he cannot know that England will need no other heir than Elizabeth (ironically, another woman) to achieve its mythic self-mastery. Using this-worldly Machiavellian methods, then, he will also reject Anne in an attempt to provide the male heir so badly needed, he thinks, in his realm. Ironically, he gains through Anne's fertility alone the mythic remedy; but, little as he can know of the future, he knows at least that such a desirable goal cannot always be achieved by individual Christian virtue. He can hardly be faulted for being unable to know that after eliminating Katherine he could have ended his Machiavellian ways. From as prophetic a viewpoint as he could possibly take, such ways remained necessary. Private morality, then, yields to public; and moral questions are thus thrown into the darkness of an ambivalent mystery. It is such a mystery—and its unraveling—that provides the profound but disturbing unity of this Machiavellian romance. (p. 35)

Tom McBride, "'Henry VIII' As Machiavellian Romance," in Journal of English and Germanic Philology, *Vol. LXXVI, No. 1, January, 1977, pp. 26-39.*

HUGH M. RICHMOND   (essay date 1979)

[Richmond regards Katharine, Anne, and Elizabeth as those characters who "define the values of and unify" Henry VIII *and who demonstrate the drama's distinct correspondence with earlier plays whose "wholly Shakespearean authorship is unquestioned." Richmond suggests that the feminine approach to life as seen in* Henry VIII *is similar to that in the romances. For further comparison of* Henry VIII *and Shakespeare's romances, see the excerpts by Edgar I. Fripp (1938), R. A. Foakes (1957), Howard Felperin (1966), and Frances A. Yates (1974). Richmond also*

maintains that in Katharine and Elizabeth Shakespeare expressed his model for earthly existence, stressing the values of virtue, honesty, compassion, and the acceptance of providential will beyond human understanding.]

Not only does [*Henry VIII*] clarify Shakespeare's ideas in the romances which it follows, it also completes the review of English history which he began with the *Henry VI* plays. Moreover, *Henry VIII* offsets the disconcertingly negative view of women marking that early series in its portraits of Joan of Arc, the Countess of Auvergne, Margaret of Anjou, and Eleanor, Duchess of Gloucester. The last history play is dominated by a moving account of three magnetic queens: Anne, Katherine, and the infant Elizabeth. Together, they form a powerful triad confirming the artistic unity of the work, displaying a distinctly Shakespearean feminism, and providing further critical commentary on the play's consistent authorship—even if its verse does conform to a fashionable theatrical style like Fletcher's. (p. 11)

The first act of *Henry VIII* thus counterpoints the temperaments of men and women: the hectic and sinister egotism of Buckingham, Wolsey, and Henry is measured against the matronly insight of Katherine on the one hand, while it is fostered by the romantic charm of Anne on the other.

Anne's romantic role has been neglected by critics for the most part, but it is no less crucial for being economically expressed. She appears in only three scenes: in the first speaking only two half-lines, and in the third none at all. Yet, in I. iv. she emerges as wryly witty in her jibes at Sandys, appropriately following the mode of the French ladies of *Love's Labour's Lost;* and in the same scene she also appears quite sexually proficient, in accepting the embraces of various male figures, including a bizarrely-costumed masquer reminiscent of the exotic Russians impersonated by Navarre's court. Anne's ostentatious coronation affords her an apotheosis analogous to Cleopatra's various ceremonious tableaux. The testimony by observers of Anne's fascination is as emphatic as that of Enobarbus when telling how Cleopatra sails past the crowds at Cydnus. . . . Yet the procession which occasions such panegyric is preceded by news of Katherine's degradation, and is followed by her apotheosis in a masque which transcends Anne's earthly glories through its sense of a mystical coronation. Each woman's distinction thus unexpectedly rises from the fickleness of Henry, by an irony true to the paradoxical nature of the men's roles in the play. For only through committing evil and responding to its consequences can full awareness of virtue be achieved by figures like Buckingham and Wolsey, who unexpectedly approach Katherine's spirit of humble endurance as their fall is realized and death impends. As a result of male misconduct both sexes in the play learn to accept their limitations in ways epitomized best in the female characters.

Thus, if Anne imperceptibly evaporates from the play after her coronation and before her ruin, the importance of her ambivalent role is not underestimated by the author. The one scene in which she becomes fully characterized (II. iii) is designed to stress how costly the role of romantic heroine must be to those involved. In exchanges reminiscent of the wry relationship between Juliet and her nurse, Anne unhappily recognizes the treachery committed in supplanting her mistress in Henry's affection. . . . The scene concludes ominously with Anne admitting to herself: "It faints me / To think what follows" [II. iii. 103-04], a thought the audience may project beyond the impending marriage. Yet, with a paradox true to the Shakespearean complexity of this play, the Lord Chamberlain who confers her new title also parenthetically forecasts a truer value for Anne:

> I have perused her well.
> Beauty and honor in her are so mingled
> That they have caught the king; and who knows yet
> But from this lady may proceed a gem
> To lighten all this isle.   [II. iii. 75-9]

The role of this "femme fatale" is explored with the author's characteristic objectivity: sentiment's force is recognized, its penalties and viciousness revealed, but its unexpected positive outcome is equally forecast. . . . Indeed, like Milton's Eve, Anne is both a source of disaster and the initiator of a new corrective influence. The moral and psychological sophistication of Anne's role in *Henry VIII* exceeds in subtlety and providential awareness any other study of romantic sexuality in Shakespeare. Even in so doomed a role as Anne's the importance of feminine influence is fully apparent, though this heroine speaks barely fifty lines all together.

The compactness and inconclusiveness of Anne's part is deliberate. Shakespeare intends no other woman's role to overshadow Katherine's, and he refuses to make the romantic impact of Anne's courtship eclipse the richer feminine values of Katherine's career. Woman as generatrix of passion may be the catalyst of new values born out of the ruins of the old, as we see in plays like *Romeo and Juliet, Troilus and Cressida,* and *Antony and Cleopatra,* but these costly and ambiguous advances in awareness cannot compare in status with those achieved by a Hermione or a Katherine. Neither heroine lacks the nerve for her own defense. Hermione defends herself at her trial vigorously and caps her husband's verdict with calm assurance. . . . The historical wife makes an even more sustained and powerful assertion of her fidelity [II. iv. 13-57], echoing closely the terms of an earlier Katherine in her stress on the extreme of wifely devotion at the conclusion of *The Taming of the Shrew.* . . . The parallel is deeply ironic because the earlier Kate's dutifulness can only be savored by a husband as subtle as Petruchio. Neither Leontes nor Henry is moved from his unwise course in the least by such virtues, though Henry admits his wife's claims even as she storms away from her judges. . . . It is a typically bitter stroke of Shakespearean irony that Henry is capable of repudiating such a wife on specious grounds. The implication is clear: if such are womanly virtues, they are no more secure guarantees of a happy outcome than the contrasting wiliness of a Cleopatra. Nor should we be naively petulant enough to think Shakespeare portrays a merely servile victim in his latest Katherine. . . . Since we have already seen her confront the king and the cardinal in securing the repeal of excessive taxation, and in registering flaws in the case against Buckingham, it is stressed that Queen Katherine's personality cannot be minimized as merely passive by modern feminists. If she is humble, it is, like Katharina Minola, from a deliberate choice made from a position of psychological power, not feebleness. . . . (pp. 12-15)

It is a choice against the grain of modern self-assertiveness, but one made by many of Shakespeare's most fascinating figures: Richard II reluctantly deposing himself and elevating Bolingbroke, thus making a virtue of the necessity his own weakness has brought about: Coriolanus reconciled to the compelling claims of a homeland which has illegally expelled him, at the very moment when he can destroy it; Cymbeline wisely but unpredictably surrendering to a Roman empire which he has just defeated in battle. Even more relevant are the feminine precedents: a Cordelia avowing she has "no cause" for com-

"Queen Katharine's Dream," by William Blake (1807-08).

plaint against Lear; or, most paradoxical of all, Desdemona's dying claim that she was responsible for her own death. These highly un-American patterns of behavior are almost beyond modern comprehension, which tends to dismiss them as contemptible equivocations, just as Othello does: "She's like a liar gone to burning hell" [*Othello*, V. ii. 129]. (p. 16)

It is in this spirit of acceptance of a Providence beyond human understanding that Queen Katherine acquiesces in her ruin, having made every fair and practical effort to avert it. And the play is designed to validate this spirit. (p. 17)

Nothing more alien to the American cult of aggression, ambition, and all the attributes of "machismo" can be found, and the superiority of this ethos is validated by Shakespeare's addition to his sources at this point of the mystical vision of Katherine's coronation by angelic spirits.

Perhaps one may wonder if her final spiritual condition is of any broader significance than Katherine's own reconciliation with Providence. The last act of the play is designed to show that the feminine virtues of the dead queen are the wisest model for both sexes. . . . By defending himself even less forcefully than Katherine, Cranmer alone survives the assaults of foes and fortune, and his misadventures are the concluding cycle of the play, resolved in the honor of baptising the newborn Princess Elizabeth.

Between them, Cranmer and Elizabeth end the play as male and female epitomes of the values which Shakespeare sanctions in his final maturity. These values repudiate virile self-confidence like Buckingham's, and undercut both the Machiavellian

but self-defeating guile of Wolsey and its nemesis, the romantic delusions which drive Henry to marry Anne. Yet out of this tangle of male effrontery, greed, and sentimentality, Providence generates many goods: the salvation of Buckingham and of Wolsey from pride and arrogance; the perfection of Katherine's sanctity; and the survival of Cranmer to bless the ultimate outcome of all their sufferings, the birth of Elizabeth. Just as Sabrina, the infant victim of sexual and political disasters precipitated by her father Locrine, proves the truly feminine spirit which resolves the stalemate at the end of Milton's *Comus,* so the infant Elizabeth is born to heal the discords which ironically also permitted her birth and subsequent reign.

The role of Elizabeth is the coda to the tragedy of Katherine, vindicating the latter's acceptance of her fate, somewhat as the abdication of Richard II receives a kind of vindication in the achievements of his successor's son, Henry V. . . . The play seems to fall into place as the conclusion of Shakespeare's survey of English history when it anticipates the literal coronation of a feminine personality (comparable to Katherine's symbolic one) as the best model of earthly rule, an event inaugurating the auspicious reign of Elizabeth, of which Shakespeare himself is the supreme literary representative. . . . The work stresses the exemplary roles of Katherine and Elizabeth for both men and women, subjects and rulers, thereby bringing at least the appearance of history to parallel the imaginary personality of Hermione in *The Winter's Tale.* The female characters not only serve to define the values and unify the play, as a single author would have planned, they show its congruence with those earlier plays whose wholly Shakespearean authorship is unquestioned. (pp. 18-19)

> *Hugh M. Richmond, "The Feminism of Shakespeare's 'Henry VIII'," in Essays in Literature, Vol. 6, No. 1, Spring, 1979, pp. 11-20.*

ECKHARD AUERLEN (essay date 1980)

[*Auerlen develops the hypothesis that the characters in* Henry VIII *symbolize a number of political issues prominent during the early Stuart era. For example, Buckingham represents the aristocracy that was antagonistic to the policies and influence of the coterie that surrounded the king. Also, Shakespeare's presentation of Henry's manner of kingship and struggles with questions of monarchical authority parallel the debate concerning the power of James I. Auerlen also claims that the themes of patience in adversity, forgiveness, and reconciliation in* Henry VIII *offer "a compromise solution to the conflicts of the period." Other critics who have discussed the political nature of* Henry VIII *include G. Wilson Knight (1947), R. A. Foakes (1957), Paul Bertram (1962), C. B. Purdom (1963), Frances A. Yates (1974), Lee Bliss (1975), and Tom McBride (1977).*]

Scholars like Wilson Knight, Foakes, Felperin, and Berman, who helped to vindicate the aesthetic unity of Shakespeare's [*Henry VIII*], did not think of it primarily as a history play, but emphasized its relationship to the Romances by calling it history turned myth. These critics have, however, tended to forget that in *Henry VIII* Shakespeare made use of chronicle material which was part of the collective memories of the nation. The editors of the Shakespeare-Folio of 1623 placed *Henry VIII* among the group of history plays. Henry Wotton, in his well-known letter, thinks of the play as representing the "principal pieces of the Reign of Henry 8" [see excerpt above, 1613]. The events on which Shakespeare focusses—the fall of Wolsey, Elizabeth's birth, the break with Rome, and Cranmer's work in the Reformation of the Church of England—were regarded by his contemporaries as the ushering in of a new era, the beginning of their own. Thus even though Shakespeare abides by the themes of patience in adversity, reconciliation, and compensation for grievous loss explored in the Romances, these acquired a political meaning in the historical world of *Henry VIII*. The play called for a response essentially different from *Pericles* or *The Winter's Tale*. (pp. 321-22)

Shakespeare's *Henry VIII* may to some extent have . . . profited from the nostalgia for the days of Queen Bess at the time of Princess Elizabeth's wedding, but it also touches on several of the most eminent political issues of the early Stuart period: the Court-Country antagonism; the king's relationship to Common Law; the religious problem; the question of succession; and the more general question of the relationship between ruler and people. From Shakespeare's standpoint on these issues in the play, a coherent picture emerges of the form of monarchy he desired in 1613.

The first part of the play is dominated by the antagonism between Wolsey and a composite body of noblemen and commoners which is alienated from the court and whose complaints in many ways resemble those of the Country party emergent in James' reign. Shakespeare's Wolsey embodies a whole range of traditional court criticism. The pompous meeting of Henry VIII and Francis I, at first spoken of with admiration, is criticized shortly afterwards when it is discovered that Wolsey staged it and that he even decided who should take part. Thus the entire display turns out to involve not the glorification of the King, but the self-glorification of an upstart courtier. (p. 331)

Commonplace as the traditional court criticism and the criticism of the historical Wolsey may have been in Elizabethan and Stuart times, it should not be inferred that this took the edge off the political lesson involved. Apart from the question whether or not parallels were then drawn with Robert Carr and other favourites of James, the play makes a plea for a strong monarchy in celebrating Wolsey's fall from power as the real beginning of Henry's rule, the better part of his reign. The didactic purpose, which for [Irving] Ribner is the criterion of the history play, can be easily recognized here [see Additional Bibliography].

While Wolsey epitomizes a whole tradition of court criticism, his opponents resist him on similar grounds as the Country party emergent in Stuart times which was composed of different social classes and was only gradually developing into an organized and coherent opposition. Buckingham, whose characterization is in tune with the popular 'good Duke Humphrey' in *2 Henry VI*, struggles against Wolsey as a representative of the aristocracy which does not live at court and which, cherishing a conservative and isolationist position, contends against all 'foreign' pomp as being un-English. Parallel to Buckingham's resistance, but independent of it, is the protest of the people against Wolsey's exorbitant taxation. By transferring Buckingham's trial (1521) and the Weaver Rebellion (1525) to the same scene and yet keeping them separate—the discussion about social unrest momentarily interrupts the hearing of Buckingham's case (I. ii.)—Shakespeare creates the impression that there is a widespread and spontaneous reaction against Wolsey which is free from the stigma of conspiracy. . . . It is striking that Shakespeare, in contrast to Holinshed and his own earlier unfavourable presentation of the Jack Cade Rebellion, refrains from depicting the weavers as rebels. Their demands are fair; the Queen becomes the advocate of the people; the

King recognizes the rightfulness of the demands and instructs Wolsey:

> Things done without example, in their issue
> Are to be fear'd. Have you a precedent
> Of this commission? I believe, not any.
> We must not rend our subjects from our laws
> And stick them in our will. Sixth part of each?
> A trembling contribution.   [I. ii. 88-95]

The King recommends a cautious procedure according to precedent as required by Common Law. . . . The question of taxation and the manner in which the King dealt with the opposition must have interested a Stuart audience. Shakespeare's political standpoint must be regarded as moderate: the protest against excessive taxation is presented as justified; the discontented people do not, however, obtain their demands by firmness or sheer obstinacy, but the King acts on his own discretion and in complete freedom when he decides the issue. Though the will of heaven is often referred to in the play, there are no speeches in which the King, like James I, stands on his Divine Right.—The view that there is a connection between Shakespeare's novel emphasis on Henry's adherence to the law—so unlike the autocratic bluffness of Rowley's Harry [in *When You See Me You Know Me*]—and the change of the political situation in the Stuart era can be supported by a glance at the changes in the treatment of King John's reign on the stage. The signing of Magna Carta is not mentioned in any of the King John plays by Tudor playwrights, but it is given considerable eminence in Davenport's *King John and Matilda* (1624) where the King's infringement of Magna Carta is used to characterize him as a ruthless ruler.

Henry's voluntary submission to the law is also emphasized by the many trials in the play. . . . Although history records that Henry sent Thomas Cromwell and others to the scaffold without a trial, that is not the Henry of the play. Shakespeare shows a king with much more self-composure than Rowley's. He does indeed often use the angry 'Ha!', but Henry knows how to control his temper with noble restraint. Slapping his subjects or toying with their fears . . . are traits not to be found in Shakespeare's Henry. The impression of arbitrariness is avoided and the King's voluntary submission to the law is emphasized. Buckingham's comment that he felt happier than his father because he had received a fair trial while his father had been put to death by Richard III without a trial, may seem to us bitter and laconic. A Stuart audience is likely to have taken it literally. Since procedures in the pursuit of justice in the Stuart period were not the same as they are today, the audience had to be satisfied with the trial if not with the sentence. (pp. 333-36)

In *Henry VIII* Shakespeare arouses admiration for the spirit of Tudor confessions. The personal sacrifice assures Buckingham the sympathy of the audience, but this sympathy does not lead to a radical criticism of the constitution. Viewed from the perspective of a Stuart audience, all trials in the play function as an affirmation of the rule of law by king and subject alike. Patience is the supreme virtue required in the subject, moderation and justice in the king.

The Queen's trial poses the question of law and justice in a more complex manner than the Buckingham trial. While in Rowley Henry changes wives between the scenes, Shakespeare is aware of and does not shirk the moral issues of the historical material. . . . Shakespeare confronts the audience with three divergent views on the divorce without ever clearly stating which is the right one:

Cham.   It seems the marriage with his brother's wife
        Has crept too near his conscience.
Suf.   [*Aside*]   No, his conscience
        Has crept too near another lady.
Nor.   'Tis so;
        This is the cardinal's doing.   [II. ii. 16-19]

. . . [While] Henry is shown freeing himself of Wolsey's influence, it is never disclosed whether Wolsey at first urged the divorce. The King clears him in his justification speech, but then this can be because the King was not yet aware of being manipulated. Neither is it possible to discern whether the King is mainly motivated by sexual desire or by qualms of conscience. On the one hand, Shakespeare indicates in II. iii. that the wooing is going on during the divorce negotiations, on the other hand, he makes the King's justification speech very convincing: the King fears that it is God's punishment of his marriage to his brother's widow . . . that he lacks a male heir. (pp. 337-38)

It seems that Shakespeare, with shrewd psychological insight, depicts a Henry who is not able to distinguish between sexual desire and qualms of conscience and who, with a naive kind of innocence, complies with the 'force of circumstance'. . . . In taking a lenient view of Anne's and finally also of Henry's behaviour, Shakespeare does not gloss over the moral issue. On the contrary, he shows the full bitterness of Katherine's fate, and the heavenly consolation she receives in the vision of the dancing angels compensates her for the obvious shortcomings of earthly justice.

Although Shakespeare emphasizes the moral ambiguity in the King's and Anne's attitudes and in accordance with the trend of Jacobean drama towards multiple perspectives divides the sympathy equally between Anne, the mother of Queen Elizabeth, and the suffering Katherine, it is also essential to realize that there is a level where the ambiguity ceases. In fact, too much ambiguity has been read into the play. From a Christian outlook, universally accepted at the time, Shakespeare could be fully aware of the failings of the historical origins of the new order which dated from Anne Boleyn's coronation, and yet accept its beneficent outcome because it was effected by divine providence. . . . Though Shakespeare shows the growth of a better political order, he does not—for all the religious overtones in Cranmer's prophecy—believe that the earthly millennium has come. Critics have thought that Henry would have to have been free of human failings if Shakespeare had really wanted to depict an ideal political order, but neither the King's imperfections nor the limitations of earthly justice, against which Henry warns Cranmer before his trial, contradict the view that Shakespeare pleads for a political order which anticipates traits of the later constitutional monarchy. Though Henry is shown freeing the court from the influence of Rome, he is not presented as a Machiavellian manipulator of the law. (pp. 338-39)

The King's genuine love of justice and new commitment to his office are apparent in Cranmer's trial. Before his tête-à-tête with the bishop, Henry sharply rebukes Lovell who was just about to eavesdrop on the gallery. He is thus characterized as a ruler who has learnt to guard his personal decisions against court intrigues and who is now attending to state affairs with greater diligence than when he was a-masquerading at Wolsey's banquet. Henry dislikes the accusations against Cranmer,

nevertheless he permits the trial. His interference before the sentence as a *deus ex machina* after having witnessed the proceedings from "a window above" strikes us today as characteristic of an absolute form of government. . . . Indeed, the King makes use of his prerogative which on the Continent was to become one of the pillars of absolutism. But in 1613 royal prerogative and Common Law stood beside each other as two concurrent forms of justice with no distinct boundaries between them. The clarification of their relationship was to be a major issue of the political struggle in subsequent decades. In the play the two forms of law equally serve the purpose of justice. Where the court fails as in Cranmer's case, the royal prerogative can step in to prevent a repetition of the calamitous outcome of the Buckingham trial.

Concerning the religious question, the play refrains noticeably from broaching dogmatical issues though such matters were not at all thought unfit for the stage, as can be seen from the discussion between Prince Edward and his tutor in Rowley's play. Instead of Rowley's militant Protestantism we have a Gardiner who warns against disintegration into warring sects. Appropriately enough for an audience in 1613, the appeal to unity—a traditional theme of history plays—refers to the political consequences of religious dissensions:

        and what follows then?
    Commotions, uproars, with a general taint
    Of the whole state, as of late days our neighbours,
    The upper Germany, can dearly witness,
    Yet freshly pitted in our memories.   [V. ii. 62-6]

Gardiner's comparison with Germany had lost nothing of its relevance in 1613: Abroad and at home there were similar tensions as in Henry's times, and James was repeatedly urged to support the Protestants in Germany whose position was in danger. Though Gardiner was very unpopular with the Elizabethans and is shown as an intriguer in the play, his warning must have carried conviction. The royal supremacy over the Church is approved of, as the relationship between the King and the humble Cranmer well shows, and an alliance of the altar and the throne is symbolized in Cranmer's position as godfather to Elizabeth. Thus the play makes a plea for a strong monarchy which takes a moderate stand in the religious controversy of the time. (pp. 339-40)

In his picture of an auspicious political order Shakespeare also portrays an ideal relationship between the ruler and the common people. The omission of "a fellow in a long motley coat guarded with yellow" and with it the rejection of [the fool Will Summers] point to a shift in the image of Henry's popularity. . . . Shakespeare, who had . . . continued to use the fool (for highly complex dramatical purposes) in *Twelfth Night* and *King Lear*, deliberately dismisses him from *Henry VIII*. . . . In a hierarchical society the privileged position of the fool, his freedom of speech and his particular closeness to the monarch, kept up the belief that the people still had an immediate and informal access to the king. To a certain extent the Walking Gentlemen take over what were formerly the functions of the fool, when by their admiring or critical comments they provide for a more complex view of the action. But the Walking Gentlemen never cease to be courtiers. Their language and bearing are too sophisticated for an audience in the public theatres to identify with them. While the fool's outspokenness confronted the king with a divergent opinion which often prevailed, these courtiers only gossip among themselves with no open interaction either with the monarch or with the audience. (pp. 341-42)

Act I. Scene i. Cardinal Wolsey in procession to Westminster Hall. By Sir John Gilbert (1856-58).

As in his earlier Histories Shakespeare, in his image of the monarchy, did not wish to dispense with the people's affection for the sovereign, but now there is no mixing with the tapsters of Boar's Head or the common soldiers, and a well-measured distance is kept. (pp. 342-43)

The pomp with which Henry and his court are presented in the play also emphasizes the distance between the king and the people, and it has a function similar to the pomp of the court masques: it is employed to impress the audience with the splendour of the monarchy and to support the idea that the king is able to arbitrate and, from a lofty position, resolve the inner dissensions which were ever increasing during the Stuart period. . . . The appeal to admiration distinguishes the play from the kind of didacticism we find in *Gorboduc* [by Norton and Sackville] or in the allegorical scenes of *Henry VI* and *Richard II*. As in *Henry V*, admiration has an exhortatory function, but the didactic implications are different: in *Henry VIII* admiration increases the willingness to accept the depicted image of the monarchy, and it teaches the subject reverence and affection, and the king dignity. (p. 344)

Henry VIII—not in abstract terms, but in terms of drama and the theatre—offers a compromise solution to the conflicts of the period: on the one hand, it calls for a strong ruler who is independent of favourites and the court coterie, on the other hand, it presents a monarch who voluntarily submits to the rule of law. The royal prerogative functions as an additional safeguard for emergencies. (p. 345)

[In *Henry VIII*, Shakespeare] adapted the Elizabethan history play to the political problems of the Stuart period. Similar to his contemporaries, the legal historians, [he] projected his views about current political issues upon an earlier epoch, the age of Henry VIII. Since that ruler embodied many of the most gen-

erally accepted opinions of the ideal relationship between king and people and since he was also widely admired as the initiator of a new order, he was particularly suited for Shakespeare's attempt at recasting the popular image of the monarchy. Shakespeare found some support for his views in Holinshed, who praised Henry's "majestie tempered with humanitie." But the main reason for his break with the tradition of the folk-hero king, which had stimulated his intense interest in *Henry IV* and *Henry V,* must be looked for in the fact that his ideas of a desirable and feasible form of monarchy had changed during the intervening years. Shakespeare writing *Henry VIII* must certainly not be seen as a bored old man looking for substance in a "depleted larder", but as a dramatist who was able to open the history play to the problems of the Stuart era. (p. 347)

> *Eckhard Auberlen, " 'King Henry VIII'—Shakespeare's Break with the 'Bluff-King-Harry' Tradition," in* Anglia, *Vol. 98, Nos. 3 & 4, 1980, pp. 319-47.*

FRANK V. CESPEDES   (essay date 1980)

[*Cespedes continues the discussion of the wheel of fortune motif in* Henry VIII *previously examined by Charles Knight (1843), Northrop Frye (1965), and Lee Bliss (1975). Cespedes argues that the play deals specifically with a dramatization of the radical uncertainty of both social and political history. For this reason, he calls* Henry VIII *a historical drama that is not concerned with the evolution of an ideal king—as suggested by Frank Kermode (1947), R. A. Foakes (1957), and Paul Bertram (1962),—but with the portrayal of "the fortunate march of English history toward the reign of Queen Elizabeth."*]

In my view *Henry VIII* is indisputably a history play, but not one that presents, or is even primarily concerned with, "the evolution of the ideal ruler'' [see Additional Bibliography, H. M. Richmond]. Like *Paradise Lost,* which contains a tragedy even while the poem as a whole remains a profoundly qualified ''comedy,'' the dramatic structure of *Henry VIII* is designed to force upon its audience an awareness of two things at once: the fortunate march of English history toward the reign of Elizabeth, and the ''sad,'' ''woeful,'' ''pitiful'' story (see the play's Prologue) of individuals during Henry VIII's reign who unwittingly helped to shape, and perished in the unfolding of, this historical process. The tragic conflict, what lifts the play above Fletcherean melodrama, is not offered within the character of Henry, but in the pattern of the play itself, in the conflict between historical ends and means. . . . Historical irony suffuses the entire play and is consistently built into the presentation of events in the final act. . . . Shakespeare achieves this effect by deliberately emphasizing the disparity between the characters' perceptions of their own situations and the audience's knowledge of later events. The fates of Buckingham, Katherine and Wolsey are prominent in the play and the cumulative effect of their fates, cast in the form of tragedies of Fortune, is to present the historical personages as existing in a state of radical uncertainty. This process continues in the fifth act, where Cranmer's prophecy asserts continuity between the events of the play and the present age [V. iv. 39-55]. Cranmer speaks of a time of milk and honey, but historical irony, present even in Cranmer's own subsequent fate, severely qualifies this comforting vision. To paraphrase a distinction currently made popular by Jacques Derrida [in his *Of Grammatology*], the play *describes* what Cranmer cannoy *say:* that historical change takes place both for the better *and* for the worse, at the same time, and this situation annuls eschatology and teleology. Against the optimistic principle of providential history invoked by Cranmer, the play emphasizes the uncertainties of history in order to question the availability of an ''omniscient'' perspective on historical events. (pp. 415-17)

[The] opening scene of *Henry VIII* invokes both the sixteenth-century political tradition surrounding Henry and the predominantly antipathetic tradition surrounding Wolsey, while the play goes on to deny the former and, in its sympathetic portrayal of the fallen Cardinal, to qualify the latter severely. It is in the context of these traditions that the play asks to be viewed, and the drama can in part be seen as a disillusioned revision of both.

The arrest of Buckingham introduces another theme of *Henry VIII.* The reversal in the play's perspective on the Field and the reversal in the language of the opening scene—from Norfolk's hyperbolic praise of Henry and the Field to Buckingham's guttural diatribe against Wolsey—find their dramatic parallel in the fate of Buckingham. . . . One should add that this structure is the dramatic expression of a Wheel of Fortune, and that the pattern extends outside the play itself: it is present in the historical fates of the ostensibly triumphant figures, Cranmer, Cromwell and Anne, whose subsequent histories receive important emphasis throughout the play.

When Henry enters, he does so in state and ''leaning on the Cardinal's shoulder'' [s.d., I. ii. 1]. It should be emphasized, however, that in this scene Henry decides for himself what is to be done. . . . This negates any sense of Henry's ''development'' or ''education'' which culminates in his ''rejection'' of Wolsey. Rather, the scene depicts Henry as already a decisive and consummate politician. But Henry's response to Wolsey does develop the theme of reversals. . . . [At] the height of his political fortunes, Wolsey, like Buckingham but

with less immediately grave consequences, suffers a reversal. Similarly, a contrast is also established between Katherine's favor and influence with Henry at Buckingham's trial and her situation later at the divorce trial; and Wolsey, whom Katherine now boldly criticizes, will be the ostensible judge at that later trial. This series of interlocked parallel movements, in which events have meaning according to an ironic patterning of human affairs, is the major dramatic action of *Henry VIII.* It creates the world of the play, and it is significantly Wolsey who introduces the play's dominant metaphor for this world of fluid and uncertain fortunes:

> We must not stint
> Our necessary actions in the fear
> To cope malicious censurers, which ever
> As rav'nous fishes, do a vessel follow
> That is new trimm'd, but benefit no further
> Than vainly longing.   [I. ii. 76-81]
>   (pp. 421-23)

[At his execution,] Buckingham's speech, delivered ''as the long divorce of steel falls on me'' [II. i. 76], anticipates the responses of Katherine, after her divorce, and of Wolsey after his fall from power. In each case, events divide the person from an accustomed public identity, and the dignity of the individual, or ''noble patience'' in adversity [II. i. 36], is emphasized as more valuable than the specious dignities of ''state.'' Similarly, in drawing a parallel between his fate and that of his father . . . , Buckingham casts his life according to the rhythm of a Wheel of Fortune and also continues the play's major strand of imagery:

> Yet thus far we are one in fortunes; both
> Fell by our servants, by those men we lov'd most.
> . . . for those you make friends
> And give your hearts to, when they once perceive
> The least rub in your fortunes, fall away
> Like water from ye, never found again
> But where they mean to sink ye.   [II. i. 121-31]

Buckingham's personal history comprises the opening, paradigmatic movement of the play, and it establishes the mutability of public glory and the unanticipated speed of events at Henry's court. After Buckingham's departure, Henry's official attitude toward his divorce is stated and undermined. . . . ''Conscience,'' the central element in Henry's defense of his divorce, is . . . introduced in the tainted context of the papal legates, and its moral worth further depreciates in the next scene where the Old Lady reminds Anne of the ''eminence, wealth, sovereignty'' which ''the capacity / Of your soft cheveril conscience would receive, / If you might please to stretch it'' [II. iii. 29-33]. The Old Lady's puns on queen/quean develop the earlier depiction of Anne as the object of Henry's lust, and there are indications that Anne may already be pregnant. (pp. 424-25)

The play is thus structured to increase our sense of the ongoing ''hatch and brood of time'' and also to underline Henry's hypocrisy: Anne meets Henry, receives substantial proof of his favor, and is possibly carrying his child, *before* the presentation of the divorce trial. This design emphasizes the pathos of Katherine's situation and, at the trial, her integrity dominates the scene. . . . Like Buckingham earlier, Katherine distinguishes between herself, ''a most poor woman,'' and her public role as Queen; and it is significant that Katherine upsets judicial decorum only ten lines after the pageant-filled entrance of the court [s.d., II. iv. 1]. . . .

Following Katherine's assertively dignified speeches, the qualities praised by Henry seem true but beside the point, and the stir created by Katherine's departure suggests that Henry's gracious praise is politically motivated. Moreover, his generous posture is compromised by the acknowledgment that he, not Wolsey, initiated the divorce proceedings [II. iv. 156 ff.]. (p. 426)

The trial scene, then, does not indicate Henry's development, but rather fixes his character in an unflattering manner and makes the first reference to Cranmer as, essentially, the King's compliant ecclesiastical substitute. Subsequent events corroborate this perspective on Henry. The scene concerning Wolsey's fall is the play's longest, and is carefully organized to emphasize the grand éclat of Wolsey's departure and his surprising dignity in adversity. (p. 428)

The emphasis is upon the unanticipated in Wolsey's fall, and this is made prominent by the cause of Wolsey's disfavor with Henry that Shakespeare chooses. Henry enters with an "inventory" listing Wolsey's vast and desirable riches, and this inventory was mistakenly sent to Henry by Wolsey himself, who carelessly included it among some "papers of state" [III. ii. 119-28]. . . . Stressing the "negligent" and incidental, "fit for a fool to fall by" [III. ii. 214], it dramatizes the instability of Fortune. . . . [After] Henry exits on a note of self-righteous sarcasm [III. ii. 199-203], the heroism and glamor in this scene are consistently Wolsey's. He withstands the nobles' taunting, and his "farewell" to "that full meridian of my glory" [III. ii. 222-27] is the play's bravura piece. In that speech, Wolsey's metaphor echoes the earlier "farewell" by Wolsey's enemy, Buckingham, and his description of Wolsey as "dark'ning my clear sun" [I. i. 226]. The wheel has come full circle and, in reminding us of this motif, Wolsey's language is part of that pattern which is the play's emblem for the waves of Fortune that surround the ship of state and its precarious members: "I have ventur'd / Like little wanton boys that swim on bladders, / This many summers in a sea of glory, / But far beyond my depth" [III. ii. 358-61]. . . . Similarly, when Cromwell states that Thomas More has become the new Chancellor, Wolsey remarks:

> May he continue
> Long in his highness' favour, and do justice
> For truth's sake, and his conscience; that his bones,
> When he has run his course and sleeps in blessings,
> May have a tomb of orphan's tears wept on him. . . .
>   [III. ii. 395-99]

[The] anachronistic allusions to the fates of More and Cromwell compress history in order to underline the continuing operation of Fortune's wheel and to emphasize Wolsey's rejection of the "vain pomp and glory of this world" [III. ii. 365] immediately before the presentation of the pomp surrounding Anne's coronation. Wolsey's fate, associated with that of a Catholic martyr and a Protestant hero, becomes somewhat universalized as an especially glaring instance of the "tragedy of state."

Henry, on the other hand, appears as the efficient but unheroic arbiter of events, and the coronation of his new queen unfolds against a sober background. Preceded by Wolsey's fall and followed by a scene detailing Katherine's pain, Anne's procession to "a rich chair of state" [IV. i. 67] becomes part of the latest configuration of Fortune's wheel. Moreover the dramatization of Katherine's "vision" [IV. ii. 82 ff.], without precedent in the sources, shows the former queen crowned with an angelic garland, and enforces a comparison with Anne's

coronation and the public pace of history. Shakespeare increases our sympathy for Katherine, and distaste for Henry, immediately before the climactic fifth act. (pp. 429-30)

As Katherine passes "out of this world," the final act opens with reiterated references to "time" and "necessity." . . . Gardiner's bustling entrance signals a return to the temporal arena of history, where Henry plays at a game of chance while his former queen dies and the present queen suffers the pains of childbirth "in great extremity" [V. i. 18-20]. The final act is a fitting conclusion because it militates against a comforting, "providential" resolution, primarily by continuing to draw our attention to events beyond the play's immediate scope. We are not permitted to see things solely in terms of the birth of Elizabeth and, while celebrating Elizabeth, the play continues to proclaim the alarming ambiguities of history. (pp. 431-32)

In presenting Cranmer's retention of Henry's favor, Shakespeare negates suspense about the outcome and emphasizes instead the reversals of Fortune that characterize the lives of men at the center of power. . . . [Henry himself becomes the] focus of an important reversal. When the Old Lady enters, Henry's first words indicate his anxious concern about a male heir: "Is the queen deliver'd? / Say ay, and of a boy" [V. i. 162-63]. After hearing her breathless announcement of a girl, Henry's curt response—"Give her an hundred marks. I'll to the queen"—and the Old Lady's greedy dissatisfaction with her reward [V. i. 171-76] suggest Henry's pique at the news.

Both Elizabeth's birth and the saving of Cranmer—the political and religious watersheds of the play's chosen historical pattern—are thus dramatized as reversals of Fortune, the unforeseen consequences of Henry's sexual and political maneuvering. With Cranmer's appearance before the council, the play continues to dramatize the discrepancy between people's desires to control events and the power of actual circumstances. . . . I suggest that the focus on Cranmer is intended to increase not suspense about the immediate fate of this Protestant hero, but the sense of contingency surrounding this character and the other historical figures in the play.

While expanding Foxe's account, Shakespeare retains the religious coordinates that inform Foxe's influential work. Cranmer's humility establishes the Archbishop as the antitype to Wolsey, the proud churchman and Gardiner's mentor [V. ii. 96-9]. The charges of "heresy" against Cranmer also make explicit the religious edge to the confrontation [V. ii. 50-65, 105-13]. . . . Henry VIII elides the religious struggle invoked by this scene. Henry's repeated reason for intervening on Cranmer's behalf is that the council's behavior lacked "good manners" and "discretion" and, in mistreating a royal favorite, was an insult to the King [V. ii. 25-33, 169-82]. In this context Henry's observation of the action does not create "a partial identification" of God and Henry, but rather emphasizes the distance between the eventual importance of Cranmer's religious beliefs and the King's temporal, courtly and even petty concerns at that historical moment. . . . Cranmer's later prophecy about Elizabeth further underscores Henry's narrow concerns in this scene. Far from being motivated by "conscience" or religion, Henry's actions are consistent with his character throughout the play: "As I have made ye one lords, one remain / So I grow stronger, you more honor gain" [V. ii. 214-15].

Following this closing injunction to Gardiner and Cranmer to "remain" as "one," the Porter's colloquial comparison of the court and a bear-baiting arena [V. iii. 1-2] functions as a commentary on the previous scene. The repeated references to "gallows" and "hanging" [V. iii. 5-16], the fates of Cranmer and Anne who prominently enjoy Henry's favor at this point, further stress the element of ironic counterpoint built into the celebration of Elizabeth's birth and the promise of a golden age. . . . The emphasis upon the crowd's wild energy—and the specific, parodic echo of Henry's words to Cranmer about the christening spoons [cf. V. ii. 200 and V. iii. 38]—makes the scene a contrast and complement to the stately christening ceremony, where Cranmer's prophecy places events in a sweeping historical perspective. . . . Like the crowd gathered earlier for Anne's coronation, this crowd described as present for the play's historical dénouement is both fecund and ominous. The Porter speaks of the crowds as "a fry of fornication" who have come to see "some strange Indian with the great tool come to court" [V. iii. 32-5]. Placed in conjunction with the Porter's oath, "On my Christian conscience" [V. iii. 36], and the earlier mention of Anne as "the Indies" in Henry's arms [IV. i. 45], the crowd embodies the amoral energy that characterizes Henry and the tide of history. Similarly, the Lord Chamberlain describes the crowd as "a trim rabble" from the disreputable "suburbs" and the Porter agrees that "an army cannot rule 'em" [V. iii. 70-7]. Like the "great-bellied women" at Anne's coronation who were "like rams / In the old time of war" [IV. i. 76-9], the crowd is an uncontrollable force capable of creation and destruction, and is thus analogous to the dynamic of Fortune's Wheel, the central motif of the play's historical plot.

Since this imagery resonates throughout the conclusion, it seems fitting that the christening ceremony itself, the converging point of interest in the final scenes, depends upon the symbolism of the baptismal water. In the context of the crowd as a tumultuous "tide" of Fortune and of the play's sustained metaphor of the ship of state, this final transformation in the imagery identifies Elizabeth's birth as both a natural phenomenon arising out of the historical events and a commentary on those events from a special perspective. The play cannot externalize the logic of its conclusion without anachronism and, viewed in this manner, the conclusion is not "arbitrary" or "escapist" but congruent with the play's vision and its pattern of dramatic expectations. Throughout *Henry VIII,* transcendence of any kind has been achieved only by immersion in the realm of nature, with all its limitations: it is only with their "falls" that Buckingham, Katherine and Wolsey achieve their final superiority to the realm of Fortune and to the events at Henry's court. Similarly, the play's concluding dramatic statement is that even its final transcendence, the heroic promise of Elizabeth as voiced in Cranmer's prophecy, is part of the natural world of flux. (pp. 432-36)

> *Frank V. Cespedes, "'We Are One in Fortunes':*
> *The Sense of History in 'Henry VIII',"* in English
> *Literary Renaissance, Vol. 10, No. 3, Autumn, 1980,*
> *pp. 413-38.*

ADDITIONAL BIBLIOGRAPHY

Baillie, William M. "*Henry VIII:* A Jacobean History." *Shakespeare Studies* XII (1979): 247-66.
    Analyzes the parallels between the dramatic structure of events in *Henry VIII* and contemporary issues prevalent during "the months immediately preceding the play's premier." Baillie describes the similarities as evidence of Shakespeare's political

awareness and his "insight into the complexities" of human motivation.

Berman, Ronald. "*King Henry the Eighth:* History and Romance." *English Studies* XLVIII, No. 2 (April 1967): 112-21.
    Concentrates on the importance of the masques and processions in *Henry VIII,* stating that they serve as a metaphor for the entire play and lend coherence to the action.

Berry, Edward I. "*Henry VIII* and the Dynamics of Spectacle." *Shakespeare Studies* XII (1979): 229-46.
    Discusses the combination of dramatic elements that make *Henry VIII* "a history play that redefines truth, a *de casibus* play that moves beyond tragedy, a masque that questions the value of spectacle."

Boyle, Robert. "*Henry VIII:* An Investigation into the Origin and Authorship of the Play." In *The New Shakspere Society's Transactions: 1880-6,* first series, pp. 443-87. London: Trubner & Co., 1886.
    Examines the "metrical development" of *Henry VIII* and concludes that the work is a collaboration between Fletcher and Massinger.

Bradbrook, M. C. "A Craftsman's Theatre: From Mystery to Chronicle." In her *Shakespeare the Craftsman: The Clark Lectures 1968,* pp. 4-26. London: Cambridge University Press, 1969.
    Traces the development of drama and relates how this formed the basis of Shakespeare's history plays. Bradbrook also examines the structural parallels and thematic links between *Henry VIII* and *King John.*

Candido, Joseph. "Katherine of Aragon and Female Greatness: Shakespeare's Debt to Dramatic Tradition." *Iowa State Journal of Research* 54, No. 3 (May 1980): 491-98.
    Considers Shakespeare's portrait of Katharine an adaptation of a popular Renaissance stage tradition that depicted aristocratic women as strong-willed, courageous, and stoic in adversity.

Chambers, E. K. "Plays of the First Folio: *Henry VIII.*" In his *William Shakespeare: A Study of Facts and Problems,* pp. 495-98. London: Oxford at the Clarendon Press, 1930.
    Revises the conclusions stated in Chambers's 1908 introduction to the Red Letter edition of *Henry VIII.* He determines that the play *Buckingham* was an early version of *Richard III* rather than *Henry VIII,* as he had stated in his 1908 introduction. He also determines that Fletcher collaborated with Shakespeare on the latter play in 1613.

Champion, Larry S. "Shakespeare's *Henry VIII:* A Celebration of History." *South Atlantic Bulletin* XLIV, No. 1 (January 1979): 1-18.
    Focuses on the structure of *Henry VIII* as an extension of the dramaturgical techniques developed in Shakespeare's earlier history plays. Champion argues that these methods strengthen the contemporary historical perspective and reveal a change in Shakespeare's focus in which events become more important than individuals.

Craig, Hardin. "The Last Comedy and the Last History Play." In his *An Interpretation of Shakespeare,* pp. 341-72. Columbia, Mo.: Lucas Brothers Publishers, 1948.
    Defines the criteria of a history play and describes *Henry VIII* as a triple tragedy that ends in a transcendant blessing for England. Craig also discusses the dating and authorship of the play, concluding that Shakespeare composed it in 1613.

Doran, Madeleine. Review of *King Henry VIII,* by William Shakespeare. *Journal of English and Germanic Philology* LIX (1960): 287-91.
    Reviews the New Arden edition of *Henry VIII.* Doran disagrees with the editor R. A. Foakes about the unity of design and the authorship of the play; instead, she accepts the collaboration theory presented by James Spedding.

Dowden, Edward. "Introductions to the Plays and Poems: *King Henry VIII.*" In his *Shakspere,* pp. 153-56. London: Macmillan and Co., 1877.

Accepts the theory of dual authorship for *Henry VIII*, but maintains that Shakespeare introduced the characters of Henry, Katharine, and Wolsey, while Fletcher wrote Wolsey's farewell speech and the scene that presents Katharine's vision.

————. "Shakspere's Last Plays." In his *Shakspere: A Study of His Mind and Art,* third edition, pp. 336-82. New York and London: Harper and Brothers Publishers, 1881.
Perceives in *Henry VIII* two themes apparent in Shakespeare's last plays: remoteness from reality and the concept of the noble sufferer who transcends the self and discovers truth.

Ferguson, Charles W. *Naked to Mine Enemies: The Life of Cardinal Wolsey.* Boston: Little, Brown and Co., 1958, 543 p.
Reveals how closely Shakespeare kept to his sources for the character of Wolsey.

Fleay, F. G. "Shakspere." In *The New Shakspere Society's Transactions: 1874,* first series, pp. 1-16. London: Trubner & Co., 1874.
Discusses the results of Fleay's verse-analysis tests on all of Shakespeare's plays and attempts to prove Fletcher's participation in the composition of *Henry VIII.*

Furnivall, F. J. "Another Fresh Confirmation of Mr. Spedding's Division and Date of the Play of *Henry VIII.*" In *The New Shakspere Society's Transactions: 1874,* first series, p. 24. London: Trubner & Co., 1874.
Concurs with James Spedding's analysis of the authorship and dating of *Henry VIII.*

Hickson, Samuel. "Who Wrote Shakspeare's *Henry VIII*?" *Notes and Queries* II, No. 43 (August 24, 1850): 198.
Agrees with James Spedding regarding the authorship controversy, but considers the prologue and epilogue of *Henry VIII* also to be Fletcher's.

Hosley, Richard. *Shakespeare's Holinshed.* New York: G. P. P. Putnam's Sons, 1968, 346 p.
Discusses Shakespeare's deviations from history and chronology in *Henry VIII* and the history plays in general.

Howarth, Herbert. "An Old Man's Methods: *Henry VIII* and the Late Plays." In his *The Tiger's Heart: Eight Essays on Shakespeare,* pp. 143-64. London: Chatto & Windus, 1970.
Conjectures about Shakespeare's motives and frame of mind while writing *Henry VIII.*

Keeton, George W. "Henry VIII and his Council." In his *Shakespeare's Legal and Political Background,* pp. 334-47. London: Sir Isaac Pitman & Sons, 1967.
Outlines contemporary historical sidelights to enhance the interpretation of *Henry VIII* as a discrete depiction of the controversial issues prevalent during "the latter part of Elizabeth's reign and throughout that of her successor."

Law, Robert Adger. "The Double Authorship of *Henry VIII.*" *Studies in Philology* LVI, No. 3 (July 1959): 471-88.
Maintains that Shakespeare and Fletcher collaborated on *Henry VIII.* Law employs verse-analysis tests and discusses image patterns in the play to support his thesis.

Lorkins, Thomas. Letter to Sir Thomas Puckering. In *The Shakspere Allusion-Book: A Collection of Allusions to Shakspere from 1591 to 1700, Vol. I,* edited by John Munro, p. 238. Freeport, N.Y.: Books for Libraries Press, 1970.
States that Richard Burbage's acting company was performing *Henry VIII* when the Globe Theater caught fire. Lorkins's letter, written June 30, 1613, is often used to help date the play.

Masefield, John. "The Plays: *King Henry VIII.*" In his *William Shakespeare,* pp. 235-38. New York: Henry Holt and Co., 1911.
Presents the theory that a Shakespearean scenario on the reign of Henry VIII was revised and enlarged by Fletcher and Massinger, which resulted in the existing *Henry VIII.* Masefield also speculates on the kind of play Shakespeare "would have written by himself."

Matthews, Brander. "The Plays in Collaboration." In his *Shakspere As a Playwright,* pp. 347-66. New York: Charles Scribner's Sons, 1913.
Describes the collaboration between Shakespeare and Fletcher on *Henry VIII* as a genuine, consulting partnership, similar to the efforts of Molière and Corneille.

Mincoff, Marco. "*Henry VIII* and Fletcher." *Shakespeare Quarterly* XII, No. 3 (Summer 1961): 239-60.
Examines parallels between *Two Noble Kinsmen* and *Henry VIII* to give further evidence in support of a Shakespeare-Fletcher collaboration on the latter play.

Nicoll, Allardyce. "The Inner Life." In his *Shakespeare,* pp. 157-77. London: Methuen & Co., 1952.
Contends that Cranmer's prophecy at the end of *Henry VIII* is a fitting conclusion to Shakespeare's career.

Oman, Sir Charles. "The Personality of Henry the Eighth." *The Quarterly Review,* No. 553 (July 1937): 88-104.
Offers a psychological study of *Henry VIII* based on the private correspondence of the historic King Henry. Oman explains that these letters reveal Henry VIII's change from self-confidence to megalomania.

Partridge, A. C. *The Problem of "Henry VIII" Reopened.* London: Bowes & Bowes, 1949, 35 p.
A linguistic study of grammatical idioms in *Henry VIII.* Although Partridge still advances the theory of collaboration, he attributes more of the play to Shakespeare than did James Spedding.

Pater, Walter. "Shakespeare's English Kings." In his *Appreciations: With an Essay on Style,* pp. 192-212. London and New York: Macmillan and Co., 1890.
Views Shakespeare's portrayal of English kings as depicting "the irony of kingship," in which average human beings are thrust into "the vortex of great events." Pater also remarks that the contrast between Wolsey's ascendance and Katharine's unjust fall controls the interest in *Henry VIII.*

Ribner, Irving. "The History Play in Decline." In his *The English History Play in the Age of Shakespeare,* pp. 266-304. London: Methuen & Co., 1965.
Rejects the theory of collaboration suggested by James Spedding on the grounds that the critic's metrical test produced "dubious evidence" and did not definitely establish the fact of coauthorship. Ribner also describes the play as a "patriotic pageant" in which the quality of universal sympathy reduces its force as a historical portrait.

Richmond, H. M. "Shakespeare's *Henry VIII:* Romance Redeemed by History." *Shakespeare Studies* IV (1968): 334-49.
Supports the theories of both G. Wilson Knight and R. A. Foakes on the relation of *Henry VIII* to Shakespeare's romances. Richmond connects *Henry VIII* to Shakespeare's other plays and contends that its central theme depicts the increase of Henry's wisdom through the benefit of experience.

Robertson, J. M. "Shakespeare and Fletcher: *Henry VIII.*" In his *The Genuine in Shakespeare: A Conspectus,* pp. 146-49. London: George Routledge & Sons, 1930.
Regards *Henry VIII* as Shakespeare's revision of a plot originally written by Fletcher.

Saccio, Peter. "Henry VIII: The Supreme Head." In his *Shakespeare's English Kings: History, Chronicle, and Drama,* pp. 209-28. New York: Oxford University Press, 1977.
Outlines the events of Henry VIII's actual reign. Saccio also argues that Shakespeare conceived *Henry VIII* as a dramatic myth about monarchy—a fact demonstrated in Henry's mythic, rather than historic, portrayal.

Schelling, Felix E. "Plays on Henry VIII and Later Historical Dramas." In his *The English Chronicle Play: A Study in the Popular Historical Literature Environing Shakespeare,* pp. 242-75. New York: The Macmillan Co., 1902.

Discusses other plays written about Henry VIII and compares them with Shakespeare's work.

Stoll, Elmer Edgar. "The Ghosts." In his *Shakespeare Studies,* pp. 187-254. New York: The Macmillan Co., 1927.
　　Defines the difference between objective and subjective interpretations of the numerous dreams in Shakespeare's plays. Stoll claims that the purpose of Katharine's vision in *Henry VIII* is negated if it is regarded as merely a product of her imagination.

Tillyard, E.M.W. "Why Did Shakespeare Write *Henry VIII?*" *The Critical Quarterly* 3, No. 1 (Spring 1961): 22-7.
　　Claims that Shakespeare "read and digested Hall's *Chronicle* in his early years" with the intention of including the reign of Henry VIII in his series of history plays. Tillyard states that the play has been undervalued, "but it is vain to pretend that it shows the consistent vitality one would expect from a truly new creation."

Uphaus, Robert W. "History, Romance, and *Henry VIII.*" *Iowa State Journal of Research* 53, No. 3 (February 1979): 177-83.
　　Suggests that, as a history, *Henry VIII* reaffirms the themes of patience, peace, and reconciliation developed in the romances.

Waage, Frederick O., Jr. "*Henry VIII* and the Crisis of the English History Play." *Shakespeare Studies* VIII (1975): 297-309.
　　Stresses the significance of Prince Henry's death in an interpretation of *Henry VIII.*

Waith, Eugene M. "The Pattern of Tragicomedy in Later Plays: *Henry VIII* and the More Historical Tragedies." In his *The Pattern of Tragicomedy in Beaumont and Fletcher,* pp. 117-32. New Haven, Conn.: Yale University Press, 1952.
　　Credits Fletcher and Beaumont as the authors of *Henry VIII* and blames Fletcher's style for the disunity of the play.

Walleser, Joseph G. "Staging a Tertiary." *Franciscan Studies* n.s. 4, No. 1 (March 1944): 63-78.
　　Compares the character of Katharine with the historical figure and concludes that, both in *Henry VIII* and in reality, Katharine's life reflected her Catholic education.

Warner, Beverley E. "*Henry VIII*—The English Reformation." In his *English History in Shakespeare's Plays,* pp. 244-90. New York: Longman's, Green, and Co., 1903.
　　Relates *Henry VIII* to history and discusses its social and political perspectives as reflecting the English Reformation.

Waters, D. Douglas. "Shakespeare and the 'Mistress-Missa' Tradition in *King Henry VIII.*" *Shakespeare Quarterly* XXIV, No. 4 (Autumn 1974): 459-62.
　　Perceives in *Henry VIII* the practice of the Anglican church during Shakespeare's lifetime of referring to the Catholic mass as a symbol of witchcraft and whoredom.

King Lear

DATE: Scholars generally agree that the broadest possible dates for the composition of *King Lear* are the years 1603 to 1606. It is known that on March 16, 1603, Samuel Harsnett's *Declaration of Egregious Popishe Impostures* was entered in the Stationers' Register and that Shakespeare made considerable use of this book in writing his play, particularly in the characterization of Tom O'Bedlam. It is also known that *King Lear* was performed at court on December 26, 1606—a fact noted on the title page to the First Quarto of 1608—and that it was entered in the Stationers' Register on November 26, 1607, where it also states that it "was played before the kings maiestie at Whitehall vppon St Stephens night at Christmas Last." In an attempt to further limit the actual time-frame, many scholars suggest the winter of 1605-06 as the period when Shakespeare composed *King Lear*. Internal evidence for this date includes the reference by Gloucester in Act I, Scene ii to "these late eclipses in the sun and moon," which numerous critics regard as an allusion to the solar and lunar eclipses that occurred in October and September of 1605, respectively. External evidence includes the parallels between Shakespeare's play and *The True Chronicle History of King Leir and his Three Daughters, Gonerill, Ragan, and Cordella*—the historical Leir story—which was reentered in the Stationers' Register on May 8, 1605, and published shortly thereafter. Yet, some scholars, most notably Kenneth Muir, maintain that it is possible that Shakespeare composed *King Lear* during the winter of 1604-05, rather than the following winter. Muir supports this date with both external and internal evidence, arguing, first, that the so-called source play, *The True Chronicle History of King Leir*, was resurrected after a decade in the hands of the stationers for no other reason than to capitalize on the popularity of Shakespeare's play; this being the case, *King Lear* would have been written and performed by May, 1605. Second, Muir points out that *Macbeth* was completed by the summer of 1606, a date agreed upon by most commentators, and that for Shakespeare to have written *King Lear* between 1605 and 1606 we must believe that he could compose two plays of such stature in less than a year—an accomplishment Muir doubts even Shakespeare could have achieved. Last, Muir links *King Lear* in its language and themes with such other plays as *Othello*, *Measure for Measure*, and *Timon of Athens*, rather than with *Macbeth* and *Antony and Cleopatra*, a point which further supports the 1604-05 composition date.

TEXT: The First Quarto (Q1) of *King Lear* appeared in 1608, printed by Nathaniel Butter at "the signe of the Pide Bull," and has since been known as the "Pied Bull" quarto. William Jaggard issued the Second Quarto (Q2) of *King Lear*, essentially a reprint of Q1, in 1619, but he fraudulently dated the edition 1608. Although the "Pied Bull" quarto was apparently an authorized edition, the text is corrupt in numerous places, including omissions and garbled passages. Because of this, scholars disagree whether it should be classified with other of Shakespeare's "bad quartos," since it shows many of the characteristics of this group. Various attempts have been made to explain the corruption. Some scholars, most notably Leo Kirschbaum, have argued that the copy for the text was supplied by a reporter, possibly the bookkeeper of Shakespeare's company, who had access to the promptbook or actors' copy and imperfectly reconstructed what he saw. The famous textual

scholar G. I. Duthie suggested that the text represents a "memorial reconstruction" made by the entire company during a provincial tour, after they inadvertently left the company promptbook and author's manuscript in London. Other commentators have claimed that the text of Q1 represents a stenographic report surreptitiously taken down during a performance of the play, a hypothesis both Duthie and Madeleine Doran regard as unlikely since the systems of shorthand available at that time were too primitive and clumsy to have provided a text similar to that of the quarto of *King Lear*. Alice Walker theorized that the text was derived from a combination of memorial reconstruction and dictation. She claimed that the two boy actors who played Goneril and Regan, and who had access to Shakespeare's "foul papers," or uncorrected manuscript, dictated to a printer's agent the text of the play, supplementing this dictation with their own recollection of the lines.

In addition to the controversy over the nature and authority of the "Pied Bull" quarto, the copy for the text of the Folio edition of 1623 has also provoked a flurry of speculation. The Folio edition contains one hundred lines not found in Q1; Q1, however, contains about three hundred lines not in the Folio. Neither alone constitutes the authoritative text, and nearly all editors rely on a judicious combination of both. Although there is much disagreement, critics generally believe that the reason for the differences between the two texts is that the Folio edition was printed from pages of Q1, and possibly Q2, that had been edited and corrected through reference to the company's promptbook, or some other common source. As can be seen, the effort to establish the authoritative text for *King Lear* represents an ambitious task that continues to the present day.

SOURCES: Geoffrey of Monmouth, in his *Historia Regum Britanniae,* written around 1137, was the first known writer to recount an integrated story of Lear and his daughters, though the figure of Lyr or Ler dates from ancient British mythology. In the sixteenth century the chronicler Raphael Holinshed adopted the story from Geoffrey and inserted it into his *The Chronicles of England, Scotlande and Irelande,* as did Edmund Spenser in *The Faerie Queene* and John Higgins in *A Mirror for Magistrates,* all of which have been suggested as probable sources for *King Lear*. However, the principal direct source for Shakespeare's play appears to be *The True Chronicle History of King Leir,* despite the differences between the two. Whereas Shakespeare's drama ends on a tragic note, the old chronicle presents a happy ending in which Cordella's forces are victorious against the armies of Gonerill and Ragan, and Leir is restored to his throne, where he reigns for a few years and dies peacefully. Lear's madness was also not a part of the chronicle story, nor was the tragic subplot of Gloucester and his sons, a story Shakespeare adapted from Philip Sidney's "The Tale of the Blind King of Paphlagonia" published in his *The Countess of Pembroke's Arcadia.* Two other important sources for *King Lear* were John Florio's translation of Montaigne's *Essays* and Samuel Harsnett's *A Declaration of Egregious Popishe Impostures.* Critics have pointed out that over one hundred words Shakespeare never used before he wrote *King Lear* can be found in Florio's translation, and that Montaigne's most famous essay, the "Apology for Raymond Sebonde," contains references to the major themes presented in Shakespeare's play. Harsnett's *Declaration,* many commentators have acknowledged, provided Shakespeare with the names of the fiends Tom O'Bedlam mentions in Act IV, Scene i, as well as other features of the three storm scenes. Finally, the true contemporary story of Sir Brian Annesley, who was unjustly treated by two of his daughters in a competency trial and defended by a third (remarkably named Cordell), has also been suggested as a possible source.

CRITICAL HISTORY: Undoubtedly the most important issue in *Lear* criticism is the controversy over the exact meaning of Cordelia's and Lear's deaths and their relation to the remainder of the play. Traditionally, one group of critics has argued that the ending demonstrates the pessimistic vision of life inherent in *King Lear*—the idea that only in madness and death can a suffering soul find release from the tragedy of human existence. A second group has regarded the deaths of Lear and Cordelia as evidence of Shakespeare's half-Christian, half-stoic design; they interpret the tragedy as containing an explicit message of hope and faith in Lear's eventual awareness of divine love, embodied in the figure of Cordelia, and, more importantly, as reflecting the will of Providence in all matters of human salvation. Other issues in the history of *Lear* criticism include the controversy over the propriety of the Gloucester subplot, the nature of Lear's insanity—more specifically, the exact point at which it occurs and the reasons for its development—the question of poetic justice in the play, the role of the Fool, and the comic element as a whole in *King Lear.*

Although references to *King Lear* can be found throughout the seventeenth century, the first extended commentary on the play was supplied by the English dramatist Nahum Tate in the preface to his 1681 adaptation. Tate regarded *King Lear* as a "Heap of Jewels, unstrung and unpolisht," and in his alterations of the drama he hoped to correct what he perceived as some major deficiencies on Shakespeare's part. Foremost of these was the play's catastrophic ending, particularly the death of Cordelia, which many readers found unbearable and, more importantly, a gross violation of the laws of poetic justice. Tate completely rewrote the final scenes of the play, eliminating the deaths of the protagonists and replacing them with the victory of Cordelia's armies and the return of the aged king to the throne. He also contrived a love affair between Edgar and Cordelia in order to account for the latter's behavior in the first scene and the former's need for disguise, and concluded the action by reuniting these two lovers in a vow of marriage. Although Tate made other alterations to Shakespeare's play, such as eliminating the Fool and the tragic blinding of Gloucester, his revision of the ending was the most significant. Tate's version of *King Lear* enjoyed immediate popularity and, in fact, dominated the stage in place of Shakespeare's play for nearly 150 years. It was applauded by such prominent eighteenth-century critics as Charles Gildon, Lewis Theobald, and Samuel Johnson. The only critic of any stature to question Tate's alterations was Joseph Addison, and he was quickly silenced by the majority and never returned to the subject. It is important to realize that such learned men as Theobald and Johnson did not actually judge Tate's version of *King Lear* superior to Shakespeare's, but simply found his work more satisfying with respect to the laws of reason and poetic justice. To the Neoclassicists, art must always affirm a just and ordered universe; the deaths of Lear and Cordelia did not conform to this image of Providence, and the play as a whole, therefore, failed to satisfy the highest demands of art.

During the eighteenth century, other issues besides the question of poetic justice began to dominate criticism of *King Lear*. One, the question of the cause and nature of Lear's madness, was initiated by Joseph Warton and continued in the essays by Arthur Murphy, Thomas Fitzpatrick, Samuel Johnson, and William Richardson. Warton claimed that the king's mental breakdown was due to his "loss of royalty," an interpretation countered by Murphy and Johnson, who attributed it to "filial ingratitude," and by Fitzpatrick and Richardson, who combined the opposing readings and attributed it to filial ingratitude engendered by the king's abdication of authority. The controversy over the onset of Lear's insanity, a debate primarily confined to the nineteenth century, was also introduced in the eighteenth century by Charlotte Lennox. In an attack on what she perceived as Shakespeare's misuse of his sources, Lennox characterized Lear as absurd, improbably drawn, and seemingly insane from his first appearance. Her brief comment sparked a series of investigations into Lear's personality, culminating in the detailed psychological studies of the following century by A. Brigham and John Charles Bucknill—both of whom agreed with Lennox and established the king's disorder as evident from the very beginning of the play. Other important essays of the eighteenth century include those by Johnson and Richardson. Besides discussing the issues mentioned above, Johnson addressed the objections frequently suggested by earlier commentators that the elder daughters in Shakespeare's play seem unnecessarily cruel, and that the Gloucester subplot interferes with the unity of the story; the first objection he regarded as unwarranted since the portraits of both Goneril and Regan were true to historical fact; the second he acknowledged but claimed that the disunity afforded by the subplot was greatly compensated for by the variety and moral emphasis it contributes to the play. However, Johnson did agree with earlier critics that the blinding of Gloucester was too horrid for viewing, and for this reason urged that it be kept offstage. Richardson focused on the character of Lear, arguing that Shakespeare's intention in drawing this figure was to demonstrate that "mere sensibility, undirected by reflection, leads men to an extravagant expression both of social and unsocial feelings."

The nineteenth century marked an abrupt turning point in *Lear* criticism. In the first two decades, such critics as August Wilhelm Schlegel, Charles Lamb, Samuel Taylor Coleridge, and William Hazlitt overturned the suppositions of the previous century and established a perspective on the play unheard of before the Romantic movement. Schlegel was the first major commentator to consider Shakespeare's catastrophic ending both proper and effective, stating that "after surviving so many sufferings, Lear can only die." He was also the first to regard the combination of the two plots as essential to the "sublime beauty of the work." Shortly thereafter, Lamb initiated the view—accepted well into the twentieth century—that *King Lear* cannot be successfully acted, for its greatness "is not in corporal dimensions, but in intellectual." For Lamb, staging the play reduces it to a demonstration of "the impotence of rage," whereas reading it as literature discloses the vastness of Lear's mind and the grandeur of his passion. Lamb also severely criticized Tate's happy ending as ridiculous, claiming that for Lear, death is preferable to survival after all he has endured. Coleridge commented on the so-called "love test" of the opening scene, becoming one of the earliest critics to interpret it as "but a trick," though a selfish and foolish one, on the part of the king. Hazlitt called *King Lear* "the best of all Shakespeare's plays" since it was the one work in which he displayed the depths of his imagination. Hazlitt also became one of the first commentators to stress the importance of the Fool in *King Lear*, arguing that the character transports the pathos to its "highest pitch" by constantly demonstrating the foolishness of Lear's conduct.

In the decades that followed, most commentators simply adopted and developed the interpretations of these influential critics. Anna Brownell Jameson, in a character analysis of Cordelia, also derided earlier attempts to revise Shakespeare's play and construct a love affair between Cordelia and Edgar, as well as a happy ending to the tragedy. She regarded such attempts as "absurd" and "discordant" with all previous impressions of the play. The German scholars Hermann Ulrici and G. G. Gervinus contributed further to the nineteenth-century reappraisal of *King Lear*. Ulrici stressed more than anyone before him the sins of both Lear and Gloucester, justifying the extremity of their suffering as the appropriate response of divine will in its attempt to punish such fundamental transgressions in the mortal world. Ulrici was also one of the first critics to discuss the importance of the theme of love in the play; indeed, he called it the "leading principle" and "center of interest" in *King Lear*, as well as that element which shapes the audience's perception of each character. Gervinus compared *King Lear* to the ancient epic myths of the Niebelungen, the Trojan legends, and particularly the story of Iphigenia in its portrayal of a great barbarous age, and he praised the element of savagery in the play as perhaps its greatest source of power. He also was the first critic of his time to regard Cordelia as a "martyr and savior" and to suggest that her death provides the way for Lear's redemption. Although not an avowedly Christian interpretation of the play, Gervinus's essay includes elements of

the Christian approach developed in the twentieth century by R. W. Chambers, Geoffrey L. Bickersteth, L. C. Knights, and others.

The latter half of the nineteenth century is marked by a wide variety of interpretations of *King Lear*. The French novelist and poet Victor Marie Hugo claimed that the appearance of the "double action," or double plot, in many of Shakespeare's plays, such as *The Tempest, Hamlet*, and *King Lear,* was a sign that the dramatist adhered to the spirit of his age, a time when every idea, every gesture was reflected in a parallel symbol or idea. Hugo's essay is significant for its attribution of a historical, rather than an artistic reason for the double plot in *King Lear,* thereby disputing the majority of earlier critics who addressed this issue. In a more traditional approach, H. N. Hudson undertook a comprehensive analysis of the major characters in the play, particularly Lear and the Fool. Like Charlotte Lennox of the previous century, and like A. Brigham and John Charles Bucknill of his own age, Hudson regarded the king as at least partially insane from his first appearance; and, in an assessment similar to Hazlitt's, he called the Fool a "soul of pathos" and the key to the true meaning of *King Lear* in his Christian-like willingness to forget his own misfortunes in order to share the sufferings of those he loves. J. Kirkman became one of the first critics to attempt an imagery-analysis of any Shakespearean drama in his discussion of the numerous references to beasts and animals in *King Lear*. For Kirkman, the animal imagery in the play suggests a definite moral intention on Shakespeare's part, which he identified as the poet's desire to draw a correlation between the baser examples of human nature, namely, Goneril, Regan, and Edmund, and "the lower nature of beasts, birds, and vermin." Algernon Charles Swinburne presented what is now considered one of the seminal essays on *King Lear*, and the first of the so-called pessimistic readings of the play. Swinburne regarded Shakespeare's drama as "elemental and primeval," "oceanic and titanic in conception," and the darkest, most fatalistic of his tragedies. For Swinburne, the keynote of the entire play is reflected in Gloucester's famous "flies to wanton boys" speech—an interpretation which places, if not a nihilistic universe, at least an indifferent one at the heart of Shakespeare's creation. Swinburne's essay firmly established one side of the controversy over the philosophy presented in *King Lear* that continues to dominate criticism to the present day.

Other nineteenth-century critics who are considered significant to the development of *Lear* criticism include Edward Dowden, Denton J. Snider, and George Brandes. Dowden claimed that although *King Lear* never answers the fundamental questions it presents, such as the reason for Lear's and Cordelia's deaths and the exact nature of the gods, the drama still affirms "human virtue, fidelity, and self-sacrificial love" as necessary moral truths. In reaching this conclusion, Dowden established a middle ground between the pessimism of Swinburne and the more optimistic interpretation favored by some twentieth-century critics—a position adopted with varying degrees of qualification by such later commentators as Arthur Sewell, Maynard Mack, Phyllis Rackin, and Bernard McElroy. Whereas Dowden stressed character and morality, Snider approached *King Lear* primarily as a social, symbolic creation. For him, the play presents the world's history divided into two "movements," each reflected in the experiences of the Lear and Gloucester families. According to Snider, the first movement traces the evolution of the "Perverted World" in which evil reigns; the second movement begins in Act IV and traces, within each family, the destruction of the "Perverted World" and the reestablishment of the "Institutional World." Snider's essay focused readers' attentions on the vast social landscape of the play often ignored by critics. Brandes's discussion of *King Lear,* though brief, represents the biographical approach to Shakespeare's plays popular during the latter half of the nineteenth century. He claimed that *Lear* clearly demonstrates the despair apparent in Shakespeare's life at the time of its composition, a period when he felt overwhelmed by the wickedness and agony of the world.

During the first decade of the twentieth century there appeared perhaps the most influential analysis of *King Lear* ever written, that of A. C. Bradley. Like Charles Lamb nearly a century earlier, Bradley considered *King Lear* an inferior work when regarded strictly as drama, claiming that such scenes as the "love test," the blinding of Gloucester, the mock suicide at Dover Cliffs, and even the deaths of Lear and Cordelia all fail to achieve their full import when acted onstage. But if we approach the play as a product of Shakespeare's poetic imagination, Bradley suggested, all of these events succeed and indeed contribute to our immense appreciation of its overall design. Undoubtedly the most important aspect of Bradley's essay, as attested to by numerous twentieth-century critics, is his interpretation of the action of *King Lear* as essentially purgative; in fact, he wanted to retitle the play *The Redemption of King Lear*. For Bradley, Lear dies of joy, believing Cordelia lives. The reality of her death is essentially unimportant; but what is significant, according to Bradley, is what she has come to represent by the play's conclusion: the vision of the indestructible soul. Bradley's interpretation is important for several reasons: first, it clearly established the hypothesis, accepted by many subsequent critics as crucial to Shakespeare's overall design, that Lear dies believing that Cordelia lives; second, it emphasized the fact of suffering as a major theme of the play; and third, its theological implications set the stage for the Christian interpretation of later critics.

Other notable essays of the early twentieth century include those by Leo Nikolayevich Tolstoy, Sigmund Freud, Stopford A. Brooke, Levin L. Schucking, and Harley Granville-Barker. Tolstoy holds the dubious honor of writing what has been called the most negative assessment of *King Lear* in modern letters. Following a scene-by-scene review of the play, he maintained that the tragedy fails to satisfy even "the most elementary demands of art," and he ridiculed Shakespeare for presenting improbably drawn characters in incredible situations. In fact, Tolstoy so despised Shakespeare's play that he called the old chronicle *King Leir* superior in its delineation of motives and its characterization of Lear and Cordelia. Over forty years later, George Orwell disputed this assessment as subjective and injudicious, and he attributed the Russian's dislike of *King Lear* to elements in the play—such as Lear's misguided attempt to renounce the world—that paralleled events in Tolstoy's own life. Applying a psychoanalytic approach to Shakespeare's play, Freud noted the similarity between the casket scene in *The Merchant of Venice* and the trial scene in *Lear*—in particular, comparing the leaden casket and Cordelia with respect to their qualities of silence and simplicity. These qualities, Freud claimed, symbolize death, and he thus interpreted Lear's renunciation of Cordelia as his refusal to make peace with life and accept the necessity of dying. Brooke, like Swinburne, called *King Lear* the darkest play of Shakespeare's canon, and he defined its underlying ideology as reflecting a hopeless, savage world in which there are neither gods nor justice, and human beings function according to the most primitive principles of behavior. Schucking presented one of the more unusual twentieth-century

readings of *King Lear*, opposing the traditional idea that Lear progresses towards a fuller understanding of human existence and, instead, suggesting that the drama actually demonstrates the king's decay, both physically and mentally, as a result of his sudden contact with the cruelty of the world. The noted critic and director Granville-Barker challenged the popular contention, iterated most forcefully by Charles Lamb and A. C. Bradley, that *King Lear* fails as a work for the stage, and in so doing he helped reestablish the play's success in the modern theater.

The 1930s began a period of enormous productivity in *Lear* criticism, the most prolific in the history of the play. G. Wilson Knight contributed significantly to the pessimistic interpretation of *King Lear* with his analysis of the grotesque humor inherent in Lear's experience. For Knight, this humor transforms the play from a typically pathetic tragedy into a terrible vision of a purposeless and cruel universe. The death of Cordelia he called "the most hideous and degrading" joke of destiny, the most horrible of incongruities in which Lear, at the point of regaining his sanity, must witness the destruction of his only source of stability. In the 1960s, Jan Kott undertook a similar interpretation of *King Lear,* calling it a "tragedy of the grotesque" and comparing it to Samuel Beckett's *Endgame* in its portrait of a universe indifferent to the suffering of humankind. The element of folly and the role of the Fool in *King Lear* were examined in an essay by Enid Welsford. Unlike Knight, she saw the Fool, along with such other "fools" as Lear, Cordelia, Kent, and Edgar, as symbols of that attitude towards life which stresses fellow-love and self-sacrifice over worldly wisdom and personal well-being. This is the fundamental truth expressed in *King Lear,* Welsford asserts, despite the fact that both the good and evil characters suffer, since Shakespeare consistently in his dramas championed fellow-love, rather than self-interest, as the most natural of human responses.

During the 1930s and 1940s a wide variety of approaches came to the forefront in *Lear* criticism, including the studies by Caroline F. E. Spurgeon, John Middleton Murry, R. W. Chambers, Theodore Spencer, Edwin Muir, Geoffrey L. Bickersteth, and Oscar James Campbell. Spurgeon, studying the imagery of the play, defined the central image in *King Lear*—from which all others develop—as that of "a human body in anguished movement." Over ten years later, Robert Bechtold Heilman expanded Spurgeon's methodology and published one of the most extensive studies of the imagery in *King Lear*. He divided the play into a series of image patterns, or clusters, which he claimed interact with and inform each other to define the structure of the drama. Heilman concluded that *King Lear* affirms the existence of order and justice in a world apparently given over to chaos, but in order to perceive this underlying reality we must, as Lear eventually learns, abandon the empirical, modern-world view in favor of the "folly" of faith and love embodied in the characters of the Fool, Cordelia, Kent, and Edgar. Murry offered a biographical interpretation of *King Lear,* at first describing it as the work of a man "possessed" by a pessimistic vision of human nature, but, on reconsideration, characterizing it as a play in which Shakespeare strove after "titanic" effects but ultimately failed to achieve an imaginative commitment to his subject because it was beyond his "depth." Chambers, regarded as the first commentator to propose an avowedly Christian interpretation of *King Lear,* disputed the notion that Shakespeare altered his sources and deliberately imposed a pessimistic ending on his play; instead, he maintained that the conclusion does not dramatize the malevolence of the gods, as suggested by Swinburne, but reflects the victory of love and the equity of divine will on earth despite appearances to the contrary. Spencer was among those scholars who adopted a historical approach to *King Lear,* specifically in his interpretation of the play as Shakespeare's "terrible picture" of the chaos that issues from the dissolution of hierarchal order—the correspondences beween the individual, the state, and the universe—so fundamental to Elizabethan thought and life. George R. Kernodle expanded Spencer's discussion, pointing out elements of the medieval play which Shakespeare used to dramatize the violation of the natural order. Edwin Muir suggested another historical interpretation, that Shakespeare dramatized the conflict between medieval communal morality and Renaissance individualism. Bickersteth continued the Christian interpretation suggested by A. C. Bradley and R. W. Chambers, describing the final scenes of the play as Shakespeare's attempt to portray the Christian concept of redemption. Campbell regarded the structure of *King Lear* as based on a combination of the medieval morality play and the precepts of stoic morality—Lear, in this case, representing the stoic image of the "unwise man" and, following his reunion with Cordelia, becoming the Christian soul willing to sacrifice and suffer for the sake of selfless love.

Although the controversy over the exact meaning of *King Lear*—whether it presents a pessimistic or an optimistic vision of human existence—has continued throughout the twentieth century to the present day, a number of critics have sought to synthesize the various approaches and discover a more unified interpretation of the play. This idea, first suggested in the nineteenth century by Edward Dowden, has received its most intense consideration since the 1950s, particularly in the essays by Arthur Sewell, Richard B. Sewall, John Holloway, Maynard Mack, Phyllis Rackin, and Bernard McElroy. Sewell regarded *King Lear* as a play concerned primarily with personal relationships, and he interpreted its fundamental ideology as neither pagan nor Christian, but a world where "characters are imagined not only as members of each other but also as members of a Nature which is active both within themselves and throughout the circumambient universe." Richard B. Sewall maintained that though the play is infused with Renaissance Christian doctrine, the deaths of Lear and Cordelia do not reflect the victory of good or evil, but the movement of the universe to restore order. Employing a mythic, or archetypal, approach to *King Lear,* Holloway compared the drama to the story of Job—a point also made by Sewall and Jan Kott—and he claimed that the action of the play is not resolved in the affirmation of the principle of love, nor of natural order, but lies strictly in the protagonists' "refusal to hide" from the suffering and pain of life, and in the acknowledgment that this suffering is sometimes necessary in order to restore individuals to their rightful relationships. To Mack, Shakespeare's primary concern in *King Lear* was the unpredictable consequences of every human act and thus the ultimate uncertainty of human fate. Most significantly, Mack claimed that the play supports neither the nihilistic nor the transcendent interpretations of Cordelia's death, but depicts the joy and pain that is part of existence—the maxim that "victory and defeat are simultaneous and inseparable." Rackin interpreted Lear's final vision as a creative "delusion," similar to Gloucester's delusion in the scene at Dover Cliffs and Edmund's final act of "goodness." She regarded Lear's delusion as a triumphant "act of faith," unmotivated and unwarranted, and she claimed that in presenting the play's resolution as a deception Shakespeare anticipated his audience's reluctance to accept either the optimistic or the pessimistic ending. Finally, McElroy concluded that both the optimistic

and pessimistic interpretations of *King Lear* fail to explain the exact nature of the play's ending; he suggested that Shakespeare purposely included the potentialities for both readings within the structure of his drama.

Other commentators who offered various explanations for the uncertainty of the play's conclusion, and who emphasized the limitations of either the Christian or nihilistic interpretations of the drama, include D. G. James, Geoffrey Bush, Barbara Everett, and Robert Ornstein. James concluded that "pessimism and optimism have no relevance here," for Shakespeare sought to present Good and Evil as abstractions, and, most importantly, to affirm the human capacity to create values in the face of suffering and despair. Bush claimed that although Shakespeare's play "includes ironies that prevent the certainty of a religious vision," the death of Cordelia still presents the possibility of transcendence, whether real or imagined, as suggested in Lear's final vision. Everett opposed the Christian interpretation of *King Lear* and argued instead that the action depicts, not the redemption of a lost soul through suffering and love, but the life of a great individual who transforms suffering "into something vital and strong." For Everett, the play does not, as in the Christian interpretation, oppose the world and the soul, but shows the relationship between the two. Ornstein generally viewed *King Lear* as more pessimistic than hopeful, but added that the ambiguity of the play's conclusion reflects Shakespeare's desire to present the mystery and unfathomable nature of God's influence on earth, rather than a neat, comprehensible image of providence.

Despite the shift away from an inclusive optimistic or nihilistic interpretation of *King Lear,* many critics of the 1950s and 1960s continued to support certain aspects of these interpretations. This group includes, among others, Irving Ribner, L. C. Knights, J. Stampfer, and Robert H. West. Ribner regarded Lear's suffering as a redemptive process that eventually teaches him to reject worldly possessions and titles and to accept Cordelia's love—a reflection of divine love—as the only eternal value. In a similar vein, Knights argued that the king's redemption does not cease with his hopeless vision of existence, expressed during the height of his insanity in Act IV, Scene vi, but continues in his reunion with Cordelia, a relationship that confirms for the protagonist the presence of love as the ultimate reality. For Knights, those critics who see the play as pessimistic fail to recognize what he calls "the inclusive vision of the whole"—that which makes *King Lear* an affirmation "in spite of everything." On the other hand, Stampfer contended that the play does not end with Lear's spiritual regeneration, but goes on to demonstrate that no matter how much one suffers, how deeply one repents, once "the machinery of destruction has been let loose" nothing can alter its course; in short, for Stampfer, Lear's death underscores the greatest fear of humankind: that we inhabit an "imbecile universe." West maintained that although it is easy to regard *King Lear* as a nihilistic appraisal of such realities as birth, sex, and death, Lear's experience of selfless love, in the figure of Cordelia, permanently changes his earlier conception of these realities, and his devotion to his youngest daughter guarantees that he dies in a universe not grotesque or without purpose, but one filled with potential meaning.

The ethical import of the conclusion of *King Lear* is by no means the only concern in *Lear* criticism during the mid-twentieth century. Other critics emphasized the question of the structure and meaning of the first scene, the role of Shakespeare's imagery in the play, the design and purpose of the poet's language, and the relation of the scene at Dover Cliffs to the rest of the drama. A host of commentators, most notably Harry V. Jaffa, William Frost, and in the 1970s, John Reibetanz, commented on the structure of the opening scene. Jaffa argued that the ''love test'' of Act I, Scene i is much more complex than earlier critics had imagined; in fact, he regarded the love test not as the gratuitous act of a foolish and selfish old man, as suggested by Coleridge and Bradley, but as a highly developed, politically shrewd plan for the continued success of the kingdom. In the central point of his essay, Jaffa concluded that although Cordelia undermines Lear's political plan for the prosperity of the kingdom in her refusal to hypocritically offer the answer he expects to hear, she actually satisfies his unconscious desire to experience her love, unsolicited, and demonstrate his love for her in a manner, and to a degree, which was impossible to expect in his former state of mind. Frost claimed that Shakespeare designed the opening scene of *King Lear* as ceremonial ritual, rather than realistic exposition. Because of this, he suggested that we approach the scene not naturalistically, but as a highly formalized type of art that contributes much to the tone and meaning of the remainder of the play. Similarly, Reibetanz described the opening scene and the entire play as operating on an archetypal rather than a naturalistic level—a fact, according to him, which helps explain the play's mysterious and larger-than-life quality. On other issues, Wolfgang Clemen and Sigurd Burckhardt continued the exploration of the imagery in *King Lear*, the former contending that the play's numerous images help establish the characters and universalize their experiences, while the latter focused on Shakespeare's use of the concept of ''nothing'' in the drama—specifically, as understood by Lear and Gloucester before their redemption—and the ways in which this concept informs the tragedy to come. The design and importance of Shakespeare's language was discussed by Winifred M. T. Nowottny and Richard D. Fly, both of whom regarded *King Lear* as Shakespeare's attempt to explore the capability of language to communicate extreme depths of human feeling, primarily through the figure of the king. Nowottny and Paul A. Jorgensen also analyzed Lear's search for self-knowledge through his need to constantly question his relationship to those around him. And the question of the relation of the scene at Dover Cliffs to the rest of *King Lear* was examined by Alvin B. Kernan and, briefly, by Phyllis Rackin. Kernan considered this scene a kind of morality play in miniature that reflects both the initial falling movement in the action of the play, dramatized as Lear's fall from grace, and the ascending countermovement, depicted in Gloucester's imaginary ''salvation,'' based on the values of human kindness and love. Rackin, in her study of ''delusions'' mentioned above, regarded the scene as an important clue to Shakespeare's intention in *King Lear*, which she interpreted as the exploration of humanity's ability to creatively deceive itself in order to withstand the suffering and terrible possibilties existence offers.

During the last fifteen years, critics have consistently demonstrated the variety, and even contradictory nature, of *Lear* criticism in the twentieth century. Such prominent commentators as Bernard McElroy and René E. Fortin have continued the examination into the reasons for the destruction of Lear and Cordelia, as well as perpetuating the controversy over the viability of either the optimistic or pessimistic interpretations of the play. Ronald F. Miller, like G. Wilson Knight before him, has analyzed the combination of comic and tragic elements in *King Lear*, labelling the drama an anti-comedy or anti-pastoral romance, because of its dependence on numerous techniques from these genres, rather than a traditional Eliza-

bethan tragedy. And Melvin Seiden undertook a further analysis of the Fool in Shakespeare's play, identifying him as that figure who intensifies the destructive and paradoxical nature of existence which undermines the king's sense of order and who embodies the paradoxes ''that emerge out of the thought and behavior of the principle characters'' as these individuals attempt to make sense out of their experiences.

What *King Lear* has come to mean for the twentieth-century reader or spectator can be seen in the modern reevaluation of those issues that dominated previous centuries. Where *King Lear* was once considered unactable and strictly a work of the poetic imagination, it is now regarded as one of Shakespeare's most popular and effective plays in the theater; where it was once regarded as extreme and beyond comprehension, it is now viewed as remarkably relevant; and where it was once criticized or justified for violating the sensibilities of reason, it is now applauded as one man's courageous effort to confront the fundamental questions of human existence. Many present-day scholars consider the most significant shift in *Lear* criticism as the movement away from a strictly Christian or nihilistic interpretation of the play's ideology, and an attempt to define the drama as a reflection of life itself, with all its mystery and uncertainty, and of humanity's capacity for creating enduring values in the face of suffering, even annihilation. Yet, scholars are quick to point out, no one assessment is adequate when dealing with a play of the stature and complexity of *King Lear*. They see the wide disparity and contradictory interpretations as the hallmark of *Lear* criticism, evident from the very beginning. Many agree with the conclusion of Alfred Harbage that *King Lear*, despite centuries of inquiry, remains an elusive work, in his words, ''Shakespeare's divine comedy which we are still striving to learn to read.''

NAHUM TATE   (essay date 1681)

[*An Irish-born playwright of the seventeenth and early eighteenth centuries, Tate specialized in adaptations of the Elizabethan dramatists, particularly Shakespeare, but also John Webster and Ben Jonson. He is best known for his adaptation of Shakespeare's* King Lear, *completed in 1681. For over a century and a half, Tate's version eclipsed Shakespeare's play and dominated the English stage. In the following excerpt, taken from his preface to that work, Tate calls Shakespeare's* King Lear *''a Heap of Jewels, unstrung and unpolisht,'' and he comments on the major alterations he made, such as his omission of the Fool, his decision to keep Lear and Cordelia alive, and his addition of a love affair between Edgar and Cordelia, which ends in their marriage. For Tate, the alterations provided motivation for much of the action and, more importantly, reestablished that ''poetic justice'' which Shakespeare's play subverts—a point supported by such later critics as Charles Gildon (1710), Lewis Theobald (1715), Samuel Johnson (1765), and even in the twentieth century by A. C. Bradley (1904), though with certain reservations. For commentary opposing Tate's revisions, see the excerpts by Joseph Addison (1711), George Colman (1768), August Wilhelm Schlegel (1808), Charles Lamb (1812), Anna Brownell Jameson (1833), Hermann Ulrici (1839), and G. G. Gervinus (1849-50).*]

To My Esteemed Friend Thomas Boteler, Esq;

Sir,

You have a natural Right to this Piece [*King Lear*], since, by your Advice, I attempted the Revival of it with Alterations. Nothing but the Power of your Perswasion, and my Zeal for all the Remains of *Shakespeare,* cou'd have wrought me to so bold an Undertaking. I found that the New-modelling of this Story, wou'd force me sometimes on the difficult Task of making the chiefest Persons speak something like their Character, on Matter whereof I had no Ground in my Author. *Lear's* real, and *Edgar's* pretended Madness have so much of extravagant *Nature* (I know not how else to express it) as cou'd never have started but from our *Shakespeare's* Creating Fancy. The Images and Language are so odd and surprizing, and yet so agreeable and proper, that whilst we grant that none but *Shakespeare* cou'd have form'd such Conceptions, yet we are satisfied that they were the only Things in the World that ought to be said on those Occasions. I found the whole to answer your Account of it, a Heap of Jewels, unstrung and unpolisht; yet so dazling in their Disorder, that I soon perceiv'd I had seiz'd a Treasure. 'Twas my good Fortune to light on one Expedient to rectifie what was wanting in the Regularity and Probability of the Tale, which was to run through the whole A *Love* betwixt *Edgar* and *Cordelia,* that never chang'd word with each other in the Original. This renders *Cordelia's* Indifference and her Father's Passion in the first Scene probable. It likewise gives Countenance to *Edgar's* Disguise, making that a generous Design that was before a poor Shift to save his Life. The Distress of the Story is evidently heightned by it; and it particularly gave Occasion of a New Scene or Two, of more Success (perhaps) than Merit. This Method necessarily threw me on making the Tale conclude in a Success to the innocent distrest Persons: Otherwise I must have incumbred the Stage with dead Bodies, which Conduct makes many Tragedies conclude with unseasonable Jests. Yet was I Rackt with no small Fears for so bold a Change, till I found it well receiv'd by my Audience. . . . (pp. 344-45)

I have one thing more to Apologize for, which is, that I have us'd less Quaintness of Expression even in the newest Parts of this Play. I confess 'twas Design in me, partly to comply with my Author's Style to make the Scenes of a Piece, and partly to give it some Resemblance of the Time and Persons here Represented. This, Sir, I submit wholly to you, who are both a Judge and Master of Style. . . . Many Faults I see in the following Pages, and question not but you will discover more; yet I will presume so far on your Friendship, as to make the Whole a Present to you, and Subscribe my self

Your obliged Friend and humble Servant,

N. Tate.

(p. 345)

Nahum Tate, in an extract from Shakespeare, the Critical Heritage: 1623-1692, Vol. 1, *edited by Brian Vickers, Routledge & Kegan Paul, 1974, pp. 344-45.*

CHARLES GILDON (essay date 1710)

[*Gildon was the first critic to write an extended commentary on Shakespeare's plays. Like many other Neoclassicists, Gildon regarded Shakespeare as an imaginative playwright who nevertheless lacked knowledge of the dramatic "rules" necessary for correct writing. In the following excerpt, first published in his* Remarks on the Plays of Shakespeare *in 1710, Gildon supports Nahum Tate's substantial revisions of Shakespeare's* King Lear *(see excerpt above, 1681), arguing that the deaths of the king and Cordelia obscure the tragic implications and "disgust the Reader and Audience." For other eighteenth-century reactions to Tate's altered version of* King Lear, *see the excerpts by Joseph Addison (1711), Lewis Theobald (1715), Samuel Johnson (1765), and George Colman (1768).*]

The King and *Cordelia* ought by no means to have dy'd, and therefore Mr *Tate* has very justly alter'd that particular, which must disgust the Reader and Audience to have Vertue and Piety meet so unjust a Reward [see excerpt above, 1681]. So that this Plot, tho' of so celebrated a Play, has none of the Ends of Tragedy moving neither Fear nor Pity. We rejoice at the Death of the *Bastard* and the two Sisters, as of Monsters in Nature under whom the very Earth must groan. And we see with horror and Indignation the Death of the King, *Cordelia* and *Kent;* tho' of the Three the King only cou'd move pity if that were not lost in the Indignation and Horror the Death of the other two produces, for he is a truly *Tragic* Character not supremely Virtuous nor Scandalously vicious. He is made of *Choler,* and Obstinacy, Frailties pardonable enough in an Old Man, and yet what drew on him all the Misfortunes of his Life. (p. 406)

Charles Gildon, "Remarks on the Plays of Shakespear," in The Works of Mr. William Shakespear, Vol. 7, *by William Shakespeare, 1710. Reprint by AMS Press, Inc., 1967, pp. 257-444.*

[JOSEPH ADDISON] (essay date 1711)

[*Addison is remembered mainly for his essays published in* The Tatler *and* The Spectator *from 1709 to 1712. Many critics regard these essays as among the finest examples of periodical literature in English. Neoclassical in concept, they were written in an attempt to improve English taste and manners and to educate the unsophisticated middle class in the rules of "correct writing." In his criticism of Shakespeare, Addison considered the dramatist a wild and natural genius; in fact, Addison found him so extraordinary that he was the first critic of the period to argue that Shakespeare's work could not be judged by classical standards. Although Addison often reproved Shakespeare for a tendency toward obscurity and over elaborateness in his poetry, he was never as categorically strict as several of his Neoclassical contemporaries in his criticism of the playwright. In the excerpt below, Addison argues that the aims and merits of tragic literature have nothing to do with the notion of "poetical Justice," and he praises those plays, both by classical authors and contemporary dramatists, that treat individuals "as they are dealt with in the World." In a passing remark, Addison also criticizes Nahum Tate's altered version of* King Lear *as lacking "half its Beauty" (see excerpt above, 1681). For a direct refutation of this assessment, see the excerpt by Samuel Johnson (1765). Addison's essay was originally published in* The Spectator, *April 16, 1711.*]

The *English* Writers of Tragedy are possessed with a Notion, that when they represent a virtuous or innocent Person in Distress, they ought not to leave him till they have delivered him out of his Troubles, or made him triumph over his Enemies. This Errour they have been led into by a ridiculous Doctrine in modern Criticism, that they are obliged to an equal Distribution of Rewards and Punishments, and an impartial Execution of poetical Justice. Who were the first that established this Rule I know not; but I am sure it has no Foundation in Nature, in Reason, or in the Practice of the Ancients. We find that Good and Evil happen alike to all Men on this Side the Grave; and as the principal Design of Tragedy is to raise Commiseration and Terrour in the Minds of the Audience, we shall defeat this great End, if we always make Virtue and Innocence happy and successful. . . . [The] ancient Writers of Tragedy treated Men in their Plays, as they are dealt with in the World, by making Virtue sometimes happy and sometimes miserable, as they found it in the Fable which they made choice of, or as it might affect their Audience in the most agreeable Manner. *Aristotle* considers the Tragedies that were written in either of these Kinds, and observes, That those which ended unhappily, had always pleased the People, and carried away the Prize in the publick Disputes of the Stage from those that ended happily. . . . Accordingly we find, that more of our *English* Tragedies have succeeded, in which the Favourites of the Audience sink under their Calamities, than those in which they recover themselves out of them. The best Plays of this Kind are the *Orphan, Venice preserv'd, Alexander the Great, Theodosius, All for Love, Oedipus, Oroonoko, Othello,* &c. *King Lear* is an admirable Tragedy of the same Kind, as *Shakespear* wrote it; but as it is reformed according to the chymerical Notion of poetical Justice, in my humble Opinion it has lost half its Beauty.

> [*Joseph Addison*], *in an essay in* The Spectator, *No. XL, April 16, 1711.*

[LEWIS THEOBALD]   (essay date 1715)

[*During the first half of the eighteenth century, Theobald was considered one of the greatest and most competent of Shakespearean critics. However, after his death in 1744 his reputation suffered a severe decline, probably due to his misguided attempts to revise many of Shakespeare's plays according to Neoclassical ideas of unity of action and dignity of character. The following excerpt represents the earliest full-length discussion of* King Lear. *In it, Theobald praises Shakespeare for his sense of morality in the play, as well as his faithfulness to the* Chronicles, *his portrait of Lear's descent into madness, and his language and sentiments. Theobald was also one of the earliest commentators to accept the Gloucester subplot as important to Shakespeare's moral purpose—a point later adopted by Samuel Johnson (1765), August Wilhelm Schlegel (1808), Hermann Ulrici (1839), and G. G. Gervinus (1849-50). However, he also criticizes the play for its subversion of poetic justice in the deaths of Lear and Cordelia, saying that "Virtue ought to be rewarded, as well as Vice punish'd; but in their Deaths this Moral is broke through." Thus, he supports Nahum Tate's altered version of* King Lear (*see excerpt above, 1681)—an assessment later disputed by George Colman (1768), August Wilhelm Schlegel (1808), Charles Lamb (1812), Hermann Ulrici (1839), and G. G. Gervinus (1849-50).*]

When I gave you an Abstract of the real History of *King Lear* in my Paper of last *Monday*, I promis'd on this Day to make some Remarks on the Play; to shew how the Poet, by natural Incidents, has heighten'd the Distress of the History; wherein he has kept up to the Tenor of it; and how artfully preserv'd the *Character* and *Manners* of *Lear* throughout his Tragedy.

How far [Shakespeare] has kept up to the Tenor of the History, most properly comes first under Consideration; in which the Poet has been just, to great Exactness. He has copied the *Annals*, in the Partition of his Kingdom, and discarding of *Cordelia*; in his alternate Monthly Residence with his two Eldest Daughters, and their ungrateful Returns of his Kindness; in *Cordelia*'s marrying into *France*, and her prevailing with her Lord for a sufficient Aid to restore her abus'd Father to his Dominions. Her Forces are successful over those of her two unnatural Sisters; but in some Particulars of the *Catastrophe*, the Poet has given himself a Liberty to be Master of the Story: For *Lear* and *Cordelia* are taken Prisoners, and both lying under Sentence of Death, the latter is hang'd in the Prison, and the former breaks his Heart with the Affliction of it.

I come now to speak of those Incidents, which are struck out of the Story, and introduc'd as subservient to the *Tragick* Action: To examine their Force and Propriety, I must first consult the Poet's Aim in the Play. He introduces a fond Father, who, almost worn out with Age and Infirmity, is for transferring his Cares on his Children, who disappoint the Trust of his Love, and possess'd of the Staff in their own Hands, contemn and abuse the Affection which bestow'd it. Hence arise two practical Morals; the first a Caution against Rash and Unwary Bounty; the second against the base Returns and Ingratitude of Children to an Aged Parent. The Error of the first is to be painted in such Colours as are adapted to Compassion; the Baseness of the latter set out in such a Light, as is proper to Detestation. To impart a proper Distress to *Lear*'s Sufferings *Shakespear* has given him two Friends, *Kent*, and *Gloucester;* the one is made a disguis'd Companion of his Afflictions, the other loses his Eyes by the Command of the Savage Sisters, only for interceeding with them for a Father, and acting in his Favour: The good old King is, by the Barbarity of his Daughters, forc'd to relinquish their Roof at Night, and in a Storm. Never was a Description wrought up with a more Masterly Hand, than the Poet has here done on the Inclemency of the Season; nor could Pity be well mov'd from a better Incident, than by introducing a poor injur'd old Monarch, bareheaded in the midst of the Tempest, and tortur'd even to Distraction with his Daughters Ingratitude. How exquisitely fine are his Expostulations with the Heavens, that seem to take part against him with his Children, and how artful, yet natural, are his Sentiments on this Occasion! . . . What admirable Thoughts of Morality and Instruction has he put in *Lear*'s Mouth, on the Growling of the Thunder and Flashes of the Lightning! (pp. 66-70)

Now when the Poet has once work'd up the Minds of his Audience to a full Compassion of the King's Misfortunes, to give a finishing Stroke to that Passion, he makes his Sorrows to have turn'd his Brain: In which Madness, I may venture to say, *Shakespear* has wrought with such Spirit and so true a Knowledge of Nature, that he has never yet nor ever will be equall'd in it by any succceeding Poet: It may be worth observing that there is one peculiar Beauty in this Play, which is, that throughout the whole the same Incidents which force us to pity *Lear*, are Incentives to our Hatred against his Daughters.

The two Episodes of *Edgar* and *Edmund* are little dependant on the Fable, (could we pretend to pin down *Shakespear* to a Regularity of Plot), but that the Latter is made an Instrument of encreasing the Vicious Characters of the Daughters, and the Former is to punish him for the adulterous Passion, as well as his Treachery and Misusage to *Gloucester;* and indeed in the last Instance, the Moral has some Connection to the main Scope of the Play. That the Daughters are propos'd as Examples of Divine Vengeance against unnatural Children, and as Objects of *Odium*, we have the Poet's own Words to demonstrate; for when their dead Bodies are produc'd on the Stage, Albany says,

> This Judgement of the Heav'ns, that makes us tremble,
> Touches us not with Pity.
>
> [V. iii. 232-33]

As to the General Absurdities of *Shakespear* in this and all his other Tragedies, I have nothing to say; they were owing to his Ignorance of *Mechanical* Rules and the Constitution of his Story, so cannot come under the Lash of Criticism; yet if they did, I could without Regret pardon a Number of them, for being so admirably lost in Excellencies. Yet there is one which without the Knowledge of Rules he might have corrected, and that is in the *Catastrophe* of this Piece: *Cordelia* and *Lear* ought to have surviv'd, as Mr. *Tate* has made them in his Alteration of this Tragedy [see excerpt above, 1681]; Virtue ought to be rewarded, as well as Vice punish'd; but in their Deaths this Moral is broke through. . . . (pp. 70-2).

I must conclude with some short Remarks on the third thing propos'd, which is the Artful Preservation of *Lear*'s Character; had *Shakespear* read all that *Aristotle, Horace,* and the Criticks have wrote on this Score, he could not have wrought more happily. He proposes to represent an Old Man, o'er-gone with Infirmities as well as Years; One who was fond of Flattery and being fair spoken, of a hot and impetuous Temper, and impatient of Controul or Contradiction.

His Fondness of Flattery is sufficiently evidenc'd in the parcelling out his Dominions, and immediate discarding of *Cordelia* for not striking in with this Frailty of his; His Impatience of being contradicted appears in his Wrath to *Kent,* who would have disswaded him from so rash an Action. (pp. 72-3)

The same Artful Breaking out of his Temper is evident on *Gonorill*'s first Affront to him in retrenching the Number of his Followers. There is a Grace that cannot be conceiv'd in the sudden Starts of his Passion, on being controul'd; and which best shews it self in forcing Us to admire it. (pp. 73-4)

I cannot sufficiently admire his Struggles with his Testy Humour, his seeming Desire of restraining it, and the Force with which it resists his Endeavours, and flies out into Rage and Imprecations. . . . The Charms of the *Sentiments,* and *Diction,* are too numerous to come under the Observation of a single Paper; and will better be commended, when introduc'd occasionally, and least expected. (p. 74)

> [*Lewis Theobald*], in an essay in The Censor, *No. 10, May 2, 1715, pp. 66-74.*

JOSEPH WARTON   (essay date 1753-54)

[*An eighteenth-century English poet and critic, Warton is best known for his collection of* Odes (1744-46) *and his critical essay on Alexander Pope entitled* Essay on the Writing and Genius of Pope (2 vols., 1756-82). *He was also a close friend of Samuel Johnson and a major contributor to the popular literary journal* The Adventurer. *As a poet and critic, Warton emphasized "imagination" over "didactic sense" or "wit," and he derided the prevailing habit of his age—best exemplified in the work of Pope— of judging literature by external standards of "correctness." As such, Warton is considered one of the forerunners of the Romantic Movement and one of the first critics of the eighteenth century to free Shakespeare from the strictures of Neoclassicism and praise his imagination, his sense of the sublime, and his consistent characterization. In the excerpt below, taken from three different essays published in* The Adventurer *on December 4 and December 15, 1753, and January 5, 1754, Warton undertakes a scene-by-scene analysis of Lear's descent into madness, a subject, he adds, which Shakespeare succeeded at better than any other writer, including the Greek playwright Euripides. Warton's opinion that the force underlying Lear's eventual madness is his "loss of royalty" was to become an important controversy during the eighteenth century. Arthur Murphy (1754) and Thomas Fitzpatrick (1754) directly responded to Warton's statement, arguing, in the former case, that it was "filial ingratitude" which caused Lear's madness, and in the latter, that it was a combination of his loss of royalty as well as filial ingratitude which contributed to his mental decay. For further commentary on the subject, see the excerpts by Samuel Johnson (1765) and William Richardson (1784).*]

I shall confine myself at present to consider singly the judgment and art of [SHAKESPEARE] in describing the origin and progress of the Distraction of LEAR; in which, I think, he has succeeded better than any other writer, even than EURIPIDES himself,

whom LONGINUS so highly commends for his representation of the madness of ORESTES.

It is well contrived that the first affront that is offered LEAR should be a proposal from GONERIL, his eldest daughter, to lessen the number of his knights, which must needs affect and irritate a person so jealous of his rank and the respect due to it. He is at first astonished at the complicated impudence and ingratitude of this design; but quickly kindles into rage, and resolves to depart instantly. . . . This is followed by a severe reflection upon his own folly for resigning his crown, and a solemn invocation to NATURE to heap the most horrible curses on the head of GONERIL, that her own offspring may prove equally cruel and unnatural. . . . (pp. 69-70)

When ALBANY demands the cause of this passion LEAR answers 'I'll tell thee!', but immediately cries out to GONERIL

> —Life and death! I am asham'd,
> That thou hast power to shake my manhood thus.
> —Blasts and fogs upon thee!
> Th'untented woundings of a father's curse,
> Pierce every sense about thee!
>
>   [I. iv. 296-301]

He stops a little and reflects:

>   Ha! is it come to this?
> Let it be so! I have another daughter,
> Who, I am sure, is kind and comfortable.
> When she shall hear this of thee, with her nails
> She'll flea thy wolfish visage—
>
>   [I. iv. 304-08]

He was, however, mistaken; for the first object he encounters in the castle of the Earl of Gloucester (whither he fled to meet his other daughter) was his servant in the stocks, from whence he may easily conjecture what reception he is to meet with:

>   —Death on my state! Wherefore
> Should he sit here?
>
>   [II. iv. 112-13]

He adds immediately afterwards,

>   O me, my heart! my rising heart!—but down.
>
>   [II. iv. 121]

By which single line the inexpressible anguish of his mind, and the dreadful conflict of opposite passions with which it is agitated, are more forcibly expressed than by the long and laboured speech, enumerating the causes of his anguish, that ROWE and other modern tragic writers would certainly have put into his mouth. But NATURE, SOPHOCLES, and SHAKESPEARE represent the feeings of the heart in a different manner; by a broken hint, a short exclamation, a word, or a look. . . . (pp. 70-1)

In the next scene the old king appears in a very distressful situation. He informs REGAN (whom he believes to be still actuated by filial tenderness) of the cruelties he had suffered from her sister GONERIL, in very pathetic terms:

>   Beloved Regan,
> Thy sister's naught.—O Regan! she hath tied
> Sharp-tooth'd unkindness, like a vulture, here,.
> I scarce can speak to thee—thou'lt not believe,
> With how deprav'd a quality,—Oh Regan!
>
>   [II. iv. 133-37]

It is a stroke of wonderful art in the poet to represent him incapable of specifying the particular ill usage he has received and breaking off thus abruptly, as if his voice was choaked by tenderness and resentment. When REGAN counsels him to ask her sister forgiveness he falls on his knees with a very striking kind of irony, and asks her how such supplicating language as this becometh him. . . . (p. 71)

But being again exhorted to sue for reconciliation the advice wounds him to the quick and forces him into execrations against GONERIL which, though they chill the soul with horror, are yet well suited to the impetuosity of his temper. . . . That the hopes he had conceived of tender usage from REGAN should be deceived, heightens his distress to a great degree. Yet it is still aggravated and increased by the sudden appearance of GONERIL, upon the unexpected sight of whom he exclaims:

> Who comes here? O heav'ns!
> If you do love old men, if your sweet sway
> Allow obedience, if yourselves are old,
> Make it your cause; send down and take my part!
>   [II. iv. 189-92]

This address is surely pathetic beyond expression; it is scarce enough to speak of it in the cold terms of criticism. There follows a question to GONERIL that I have never read without tears:

> Ar't not asham'd to look upon this beard?
>   [II. iv. 193]

This scene abounds with many noble turns of passion, or rather, conflicts of very different passions. The inhuman daughters urge him in vain by all the sophistical and unfilial arguments they were mistresses of to diminish the number of his train. He answers them by only four poignant words;

> I gave you all!
>   [II. iv. 250]

When REGAN at last consents to receive him, but without any attendants, for that he might be served by her own domestics, he can no longer contain his disappointment and rage. First he appeals to the heavens, and points out to them a spectacle that is indeed inimitably affecting:

> You see me here, you Gods! a poor old man,
> As full of grief as age, wretched in both.
> If it be you that stir these daughters hearts
> Against their father, fool me not so much
> To bear it tamely!
>   [II. iv. 272-76]

Then suddenly he addresses GONERIL and REGAN in the severest terms and with the bitterest threats:

> No, you unnatural hags!
> I will have such revenges on you both
> That all the world shall—I will do such things—
> What they are yet, I know not—
>   [II. iv. 278-81]

Nothing occurs to his mind severe enough for them to suffer, or him to inflict. His passion rises to a height that deprives him of articulation. He tells them that he will subdue his sorrow, though almost irresistible, and that they shall not triumph over his weakness. . . . (pp. 72-3)

• • • • •

Thunder and a ghost have been frequently introduced into tragedy by barren and mechanical play-wrights, as proper objects to impress terror and astonishment where the distress has not been important enough to render it probable that nature would interpose for the sake of the sufferers, and where these objects themselves have not been supported by suitable sentiments. Thunder has, however, been made use of with great judgment and good effect by SHAKESPEARE to heighten and impress the distresses of LEAR.

The venerable and wretched old king is driven out by both his daughters, without necessaries and without attendants, not only in the night but in the midst of a most dreadful storm and on a bleak and barren heath. On his first appearance in this situation he draws an artful and pathetic comparison betwixt the severity of the tempest and of his daughters:

> Rumble thy belly full! spit, fire! spout, rain!
> Nor rain, wind, thunder, fire, are my daughters.
> I tax not you, you elements, with unkindness;
> I never gave you kingdom, called you children;
> You owe me no subscription. Then let fall
> Your horrible pleasure. Here I stand your slave;
> A poor, infirm, weak, and despis'd old man!
>   [III. ii. 14-20]

The storm continuing with equal violence, he drops for a moment the consideration of his own miseries and takes occasion to moralize on the terrors which such commotions of nature should raise in the breast of secret and unpunished villainy:

> Tremble thou wretch,
> That hast within thee undivulged crimes
> Unwhipt of justice! Hide thee, thou bloody hand. . . .
>   [III. ii. 51-3]

KENT most earnestly entreats him to enter a hovel which he had discovered on the heath; and on pressing him again and again to take shelter there LEAR exclaims

> Wilt break my heart?
>   [III. iv. 4]

Much is contained in these four words; as if he had said, 'the kindness and the gratitude of this servant exceeds that of my own children. Tho' I have given them a kingdom, yet have they basely discarded me, and suffered a head so old and white as mine to be exposed to this terrible tempest, while this fellow pities and would protect me from its rage. I cannot bear this kindness from a perfect stranger; it breaks my heart.' All this seems to be included in that short exclamation, which another writer less acquainted with nature would have displayed at large: such a suppresion of sentiments plainly implied is judicious and affecting. (pp. 73-5)

The mind is never so sensibly disposed to pity the misfortunes of others as when it is itself subdued and softened by calamity. Adversity diffuses a kind of sacred calm over the breast, that is the parent of thoughtfulness and meditation. The following reflections of LEAR in his next speech, when his passion has subsided for a short interval, are equally proper and striking:

> Poor naked wretches, wheresoe'er ye are,
> That bide the pelting of this pityless storm!
> How shall your houseless heads and unfed sides,
> Your loop'd and window'd raggedness, defend you
> From seasons such as these!
>   [III. iv. 28-32]

He concludes with a sentiment finely suited to his condition, and worthy to be written in characters of gold in the closet of every monarch upon earth:

> O! I have ta'en
> Too little care of this. Take physic, pomp!
> Expose thyself to feel what wretches feel;
> That thou may'st shake the superflux to them,
> And shew the Heav'ns more just!
>
> [III. iv. 32-6]

LEAR being at last persuaded to take shelter in the hovel, the poet has artfully contrived to lodge there EDGAR, the discarded son of Gloucester, who counterfeits the character and habit of a mad beggar haunted by an evil demon, and whose supposed sufferings are enumerated with an imitiable wildness of fancy. . . . (p. 76)

Upon perceiving the nakedness and wretchedness of this figure the poor king asks a question that I never could read without strong emotions of pity and admiration:

> What! have his daughters brought him to this pass?
> Couldst thou save nothing? Didst thou give them all?
>
> [III. iv. 63-4]

And when KENT assures him that the beggar hath no daughters, he hastily answers:

> Death, traitor, nothing could have subdued nature
> To such a lowness, but his unkind daughters.
>
> [III. iv. 69-70]
> (pp. 76-7)

SHAKESPEARE has no where exhibited more inimitable strokes of his art than in this uncommon scene; where he has so well conducted even the natural jargon of the beggar and the jestings of the fool, which in other hands must have sunk into burlesque, that they contribute to heighten the pathetic to a very high degree.

The heart of LEAR having been agitated and torn by a conflict of such opposite and tumultuous passions, it is not wonderful that his 'wits should now begin to unsettle.' The first plain indication of the loss of his reason is his calling EDGAR a 'learned Theban', and telling KENT that 'he will keep still with his philosopher' [III. iv. 176]. When he next appears he imagines he is punishing his daughters. The imagery is extremely strong, and chills one with horror to read it.

> To have a thousand with red burning spits
> Come hizzing in upon them!
>
> [III. vi. 15-16]

As the fancies of lunatics have an extraordinary force and liveliness, and render the objects of their frenzy as it were present to their eyes, LEAR actually thinks himself suddenly restored to his kingdom, and seated in judgment to try his daughters for their cruelties. . . . (p. 77)

A circumstance follows that is strangely moving indeed, for he fancies that his favourite domestic creatures that used to fawn upon and caress him, and of which he was eminently fond, have now their tempers changed and join to insult him:

> The little dogs and all,
> Tray, Blanch, and Sweet-heart, see! they bark at me!
>
> [III. vi. 62-3]

He again resumes his imaginary power, and orders them to anatomize REGAN: 'See what breeds about her heart—Is there any cause in nature that makes these hard hearts! You, Sir,' speaking to EDGAR, 'I entertain for one of my HUNDRED' [III. vi. 76-9]; a circumstance most artfully introduced to remind us of the first affront he received, and to fix our thoughts on the causes of his distraction.

General criticism is on all subjects useless and unentertaining; but is more than commonly absurd with respect to SHAKESPEARE, who must be accompanied step by step and scene by scene in his gradual *developments* of characters and passions, and whose finer features must be singly pointed out if we would do compleat justice to his genuine beauties. It would have been easy to have declared, in general terms, 'that the madness of LEAR was very natural and pathetic;' and the reader might then have escaped what he may, perhaps, call a multitude of well known quotations. But then it had been impossible to exhibit a perfect picture of the secret workings and changes of LEAR's mind, which vary in each succeeding passage, and which render an allegation of each particular sentiment absolutely necessary. (p. 78)

• • • • •

Madness being occasioned by a close and continued attention of the mind to a single object, SHAKESPEARE judiciously represents the loss of royalty as the particular idea which has brought on the distraction of LEAR, and which perpetually recurs to his imagination and mixes itself with all his ramblings. Full of this idea, therefore, he breaks out abruptly in the Fourth Act: 'No, they cannot touch me for coining: I am the king himself' [IV. vi. 83-4]. He believes himself to be raising recruits, and censures the inability and unskilfulness of some of his soldiers: 'There's your press money. That fellow handles his bow like a crow keeper: draw me a clothier's yard. Look, look, a mouse! Peace peace; this piece of toasted cheese will do it' [IV. vi. 86-90]. The art of our poet is transcendent in thus making a passage that even borders on burlesque strongly expressive of the madness he is painting. . . . He then recollects the falshood and cruelty of his daughters, and breaks out in some pathetic reflexions on his old age and on the tempest to which he was so lately exposed: 'Ha! Goneril, ha! Regan! They flattered me like a dog, and told me, I had white hairs on my beard, ere the black ones were there. To say ay, and no, to every thing that I said—ay and no too, was no good divinity. When the rain came to wet me once, and the wind to make me chatter; when the thunder would not peace at my bidding; there I found 'em, there I smelt 'em out. Go to, they're not men of their words; they told me I was every thing: 'tis a lie, I am not ague-proof' [IV. vi. 96-105]. The impotence of royalty to exempt its possessor, more than the meanest subject, from suffering natural evils is here finely hinted at. (pp. 78-9)

I shall transiently observe, in conclusion of these remarks, that this drama is chargeable with considerable imperfections. The plot of EDMUND against his brother, which distracts the attention, and destroys the unity of the fable; the cruel and horrid extinction of GLO'STER's eyes, whch ought not to be exhibited on the stage; the utter improbability of GLO'STER's imagining, though blind, that he had leaped down Dover Cliff; and some passages that are too turgid and full of strained metaphors are faults which the warmest admirers of SHAKESPEARE will find it difficult to excuse. I know not, also, whether the cruelty of the daughters is not painted with circumstances too savage and unnatural: for it is not sufficient to say that this monstrous barbarity is founded on historical truth, if we recollect the just observation of BOILEAU,

Le vrai peut quelquefois n'etre pas vraisemblable.
[''Some truths may be too strong to be believed.'']

(p. 83)

Joseph Warton, in extracts from Shakespeare, the
Critical Heritage: 1753-1765, Vol. 4, *edited by Brian
Vickers, Routledge & Kegan Paul, 1976, pp. 68-83.*

ARTHUR MURPHY   (essay date 1754)

[*An eighteenth- and early nineteenth-century English dramatist
and critic, Murphy is best remembered for his animated, two-act
comedies and his often spurious and untrustworthy biographies
of Henry Fielding and David Garrick. He was also the editor,
and oftentimes sole writer, of the* Gray's Inn Journal, *a periodical
devoted mostly to gossip and scandal but which also included
some instances of serious criticism. In the excerpt below, first
published in that magazine on January 12, 1754 under the pseudonym of Charles Ranger, Murphy focuses on Lear's descent into
madness and offers a direct rebuttal to Joseph Warton's statement
that the primary cause of the King's insanity is his loss of royalty
(see excerpt above, 1753-54). Instead, Murphy maintains that it
is strictly filial ingratitude that obsesses Lear. Other critics who
have commented on this topic include Thomas Fitzpatrick (1754),
Samuel Johnson (1765), and William Richardson (1784).*]

In order to criticise a great poet with any degree of perspicuity
it is requisite to consider the nature of his fable and the moral
scope of the work. Order requires that in the next place we
proceed to observe how he lays on his colouring, the disposition
of each person, the expression of the passions, and which is
the capital figure in the piece. *Lear* being examined in this
manner it will appear that the author intended to exhibit in the
most striking colours the horrid crime of filial ingratitude. To
enforce this he represents an old monarch tired with the cares
of state, and willing to distribute his possessions among his
daughters in proportion to their affections towards his person.
Accordingly the two that flatter him obtain all, the third sister
being disinherited for her sincerity. The king is at length driven
by the ingratitude of his two eldest daughters to an extreme of
madness, which produces the finest tragic distress ever seen
on any stage.

This is the ground-work of the play. A different view of it has
been of late displayed by a writer of known ability. He ascribes
the madness of *Lear* to the loss of royalty [see excerpt above
by Joseph Warton, 1753-54]. That this notion is not only fundamentally wrong but also destructive of the fine pathetic that
melts the heart in every scene will, I think, appear from a due
attention to the conduct of the poet throughout the piece. The
behaviour of *Lear*'s children is always uppermost in the thoughts
of the aged monarch. We perceive it working upon his passions,
till at length his mind settles into a fixed attention to that single
object. This, I think, is evident in the progress of the play.

Lear, in his first scene, shews himself susceptible of the most
violent emotions. The poet has drawn him impetuous to a
degree, proud, haughty, revengeful, and tender-hearted. In such
a mind it is not to be wondered that ill-treatment should excite
the most uneasy sensations. (pp. 94-5)

There have been many poets acquainted in general with the
passions of human nature. Accordingly we find them constantly
describing their effects; but *Shakespeare*'s art shows their impulse and their workings without the aid of definition or flowery
description. Besides the general survey of the heart, *Shakespeare* was more intimately versed in the various tempers of
mankind than any poet whatever. We always find him making

the passions of each person in his drama operate according to
his peculiar habit and frame of mind. In the tragedy in question
there are so many strokes of this nature that in my opinion it is
such a masterpiece. In every speech in *Lear*'s mouth there is
such an artful mixture of opposite passions that the heart-strings
of an audience are torn on every side. The frequent transition
and shifting of emotions is natural to every breast: in *Lear* they
are characteristic marks of his temper:

I pr'ythee, daughter, do not make me mad.
I will not trouble thee, my child. Farewel.
We'll meet no more—no more see one another.
But yet thou art my flesh, my blood, my daughter;
Or rather a disease that's in my flesh, &c.
                        But I'll not chide thee;
Let shame come when it will, I do not call it;
I do not bid the thunder-bearer shoot,
Nor tell tales of thee to high judging Jove.

[II. iv. 218-28]

In this speech every master passion in his temper rises in conflict, his pride, his revenge, his quick resentment, and his
tenderness. The following passage has some of the finest turns
in the world:

O let not woman's weapons, water-drops,
Stain my man's cheeks—no, ye unnat'ral hags—
I will have such revenges on ye both—I'll do such things—
What they are I know not—but they shall be
The terrors of the earth.—You think I'll weep—
No—I'll not weep—I have full cause for weeping—
This heart shall break into a thousand flaws—
Or e'er I'll weep—O fool, I shall go mad.

[II. iv. 277-86]

Here the distressed monarch leaves his daughter's roof. The
next time we see him he is on a wild heath in a violent storm.
In this distressful situation all his reflections take a tincture
from the gloomy colour of his mind. We soon see what is the
principal object of his attention.

Thou all-shaking thunder,
Crack nature's mould; all germins spill at once,
That make UNGRATEFUL MAN.

[III. ii. 6-9]

And again:

The tempest in my mind
Doth from my senses take all feeling else
Save what beats there—Filial ingratitude!

[III. iv. 12-14]

His sudden apostrophe to his daughters must draw tears from
every eye:

O Regan! Goneril!
Your old kind father, whose frank heart gave all.

[III. iv. 19-20]

The break has a fine effect.

O! that way madness lies—let me shun that—
No more of that—

[III. iv. 21-2]

As yet the perturbation of his mind does not seem fixed to a
point. He begins to moralize, but still with a view to his own
afflictions. *Edgar* enters disguised like a madman, and this
seems to give the finishing stroke. *Lear*'s first question is,
'have his daughters brought him to this pass? couldst thou save

nothing? didst thou give them all?' [III. iv. 63-4]. Here we have the first touch of fixed madness in the play. Will the resignation of his sceptre or the mere loss of regal power be any longer urged as the cause of *Lear*'s distraction?

Madness opens a new field to the vast imagination of *Shakespeare*. He had before displayed every movement of the heart: the human understanding now becomes his province. In this, we shall find, he acquits himself with the most masterly skill. Mr *Locke* observes, that *madmen do not seem to have lost the faculty of reasoning; but having joined together some ideas very wrongly, they mistake them for truths; and they err as men do that argue right from wrong principles. For by the violence of their imaginations having mistaken their fancies for realities, they make right deductions from them.*

Agreeably to this account *Lear*, upon the appearance of a madman, takes it for granted that it is owing to his daughters illtreatment. When contradicted, he replies, 'Death! traitor! nothing could have subdued nature to such a lowness, but his unkind daughters' [III. iv. 69-71]. He next takes him for a philosopher, and agreeably to that notion enquires 'what is the cause of thunder?' [III. iv. 155].

To a mind exasperated the desire of revenge is natural: accordingly we find him breaking out with the utmost rage.

> To have a thousand with red burning spits
> Come hizzing in upon 'em!
>
> [III. vi. 15-16]

He proceeds to accuse his daughters in a court of justice. 'Arraign her first, 'tis *Goneril*. I here make oath before this honourable assembly, she kicked the poor king her father. Here is another too, whose warpt looks proclaim what store her heart is made of' [III. vi. 46-8, 53-4].—He continues to dwell in imagination upon the crime of ingratitude, which appears so shocking that he exclaims, 'Let them anatomize *Regan;* see what breeds about her heart. Is there any cause in nature for these hard hearts?' [III. vi. 76-8]. This last stroke cannot fail to draw tears from every eye. The reader will please to observe, that all this time there is not a word said of his royalty; on the contrary, he says to *Edgar*, 'You, Sir, I entertain for one of my hundred; only, I do not like the fashion of your garment' [III. vi. 78-80]. (pp. 96-9)

It was *Shakespeare*'s art to reserve [Lear's] being crowned with straw for the last scene of his madness. Here we have a representation of human nature reduced to the lowest ebb. Had he lost his reason on account of his abdicated throne the emotions of pity would not be so intense as they now are, when we see him driven to that extreme by the cruelty of his own children. A monarch voluntarily abdicating and afterwards in a fit of lunacy resuming his crown would, I fear, border upon the ridiculous. Every topic of parental distress being now exhausted and the master-passions of the king appearing in his madness, the poet, like a great master of human nature, shews him gradually coming to himself. We see the ideas dawning slowly on his soul:

> Where have I been?—where am I? fair day-light!
>
> [IV. vii. 51]

In this recollection of his reason he never once mentions the loss of royalty, but again touches upon the cause of his distress in his speech to *Cordelia*.

> I know you do not love me; for your sisters
> Have, as I do remember, done me wrong;
> You have some cause; they have none.
>
> [IV. vii. 72-4]

Upon the whole, before his madness, in it, and after it, *Lear* never loses sight of the ideas which had worn such traces on his brain. He must be unfeeling to the great art of our poet who can look for any other cause of distress in scenes which are drawn so forcibly and strong, and kept up with the most exquisite skill to the very dying words of the unhapy monarch. (pp. 99-100)

Arthur Murphy, in an extract from Shakespeare, the Critical Heritage: 1753-1765, Vol. 4, *edited by Brian Vickers, Routledge & Kegan Paul, 1976, pp. 94-100.*

[THOMAS FITZPATRICK]　　(letter date 1754)

[*The following excerpt is taken from an anonymously written letter to Charles Ranger (Arthur Murphy) first published in the* Gray's-Inn Journal *on January 19, 1754, and later attributed by the biographer and critic Jesse Foot to Thomas Fitzpatrick. In it, Fitzpatrick responds to both Joseph Warton's and Murphy's interpretations of the cause of Lear's insanity (see excerpts above, 1753-54 and 1754), arguing that it is neither the king's loss of royalty nor his daughters' filial ingratitude alone, that drives him insane, but a combination of these forces.*]

To address a letter to you under the character of Mr *Ranger*, I am persuaded, needs little apology; especially when it goes from one who has a real regard to your reputation as an author, and, having often received pleasure from your weekly essays, takes the liberty of throwing out his thoughts on a piece of criticism in which he differs with you in opinion.

Your paper of last *Saturday* contains an examen of *King Lear* [see excerpt above by Arthur Murphy, 1754]. You seem to think that an ingenious critic who in the *Adventurer* has given a discourse upon that beautiful tragedy has intirely mistaken the principal idea in the old king's mind during his state of madness [see excerpt above by Joseph Warton, 1753-54]. After citing *Lear*'s exclamation on the ingratitude of his daughters, you add, 'this might lead any man to the cause of *Lear*'s madness, without thinking of the resignation of his sceptre.' But certainly, whoever considers *Lear*'s character with attention will from the very passage you quote, beside an hundred others, think there is much to be said on the other side of the question.

I have read with pleasure several of the remarks you make on the speeches in *Lear,* which are such as can arise only in the mind of a reader of taste; but I cannot agree that '*he must be unfeeling to the great art of our poet who can look for any other cause of distress*' in the madness of the king than the ingratitude of his daughters.

I know not in what manner you may treat the remarks I am about to make, but I can sincerely assure you they are only intended as hints to yourself on a subject which I think of some consequence to the admirers of *Shakespeare*.

The critic in the *Adventurer* was somewhat wanting in justice to the poet by mentioning the loss of royalty as the sole cause of *Lear*'s madness, without taking notice at the same time of the forcible idea he must have of the ingratitude of his two daughters. I think Mr *Ranger* also wrong in excluding intirely his opinion. What I purpose here is to point out *both the ideas* working strongly in his mind, and what the author intended as conducive to the moral of his play. (pp. 100-01)

Lear's deportment and sentiments in regard to his daughters in the first act, and what *Goneril* says of him to *Regan* mark very plainly his character, which is that of *a haughty, passionate, inconstant, weak old man.* He does not resign his authority to his daughters so much out of love to them as to rid himself of the cares of government. He retains the name of king, with a suitable train of attendants: he still commands with his former impetuosity of temper, and is jealous even of trifles. This the ill-nature of the daughters will not suffer. We soon find them in consultation, in the most undutiful and unbecoming manner, to deprive him of his remaining shew of power: their behaviour and ingratitude soon appear in the most glaring instances and make the old king sorely sensible that he had *given them* ALL.

Nature was *Shakespeare*'s guide. He describes the imagination affected by concurring causes to pave the way for a scene of the highest distress. *Lear,* as a king and father, feels with great sensibility the shock of his daughters' ingratitude and unnatural treatment. He exhibits a moving picture of the feelings of the heart and the various conflicts of passion expressive of his character and circumstances. If the poet had nothing more in view he might have been well content with the masterly picture he has drawn of his distress, grief, and rage in every scene before the loss of his senses; but he has crowned the distress by making him at last fix his imagination on his own rashness and folly in giving away his ALL. He laments his want of power to avenge himself. It is this reflection chiefly that drives him to madness.

The jesting of the fool wholly turns upon his *unkinging himself* and retaining *nothing,* which *Lear* minutely attends to, and says 'a bitter fool!' [I. iv. 136]. After *Goneril*'s proposal to reduce his train, he breaks out, *'woe! that too late repents'* [I. iv. 257]. The ingratitude of his daughters, and his own folly, strike him deeply. (p. 102)

In the next scene, wrapt up in thought, he says,

> TO TAKE 'T AGAIN PERFORCE!—Monster Ingratitude!
>
> [I. v. 39-40]

In this line the two ideas are strongly blended, and the *loss of power* foremost; for surely that was the obvious reason of the insults he had received. If he had still been in possession, they would have continued to sprinkle him with *court holy-water:* the fool whose phrase the last is, says,

> Fathers that wear rags,
> Do make their children blind;
> But fathers that bear bags,
> Shall see their children kind.
>
> [II. iv. 48-51]

I must here take notice of the different colouring used by our poet, and all good writers, in distinguishing the character of men seemingly agitated by the same passions. *Lear*'s idea of his folly, in divesting himself of his authority, is nicely and artfully distinguished by *Shakespeare* from that kind of regret which an imperious man of a different character would feel from the deprivation of power. He is full of the loss of his dignity only as it was the occasion of the ill treatment he met with, not from a thirst of rule. This idea, and that of the ingratitude of his daughters which he feels as the consequence of it, I cannot help thinking, are as closely united in his madness as two twigs twisted together and growing out of the same stem. (pp. 102-03)

I know it may be insisted on by you, and perhaps by many others, that *Lear* makes use of the sentiment of *giving all* only to tax the ingratitude of his daughters in a higher degree; but

it is possible you may be of a contrary opinion, if you can allow that the moral of this play does not expose the ingratitude of children more than the folly of parents. *This same folly of parents* is also touched with great judgment in the underplot of *Glo'ster.* The characters of *Lear*'s two daughters are finely contrasted with those of *Cordelia* and *Edgar;* and the poet's design in marking out so strongly the folly and ill-judged partiality of parents is confirmed by the behaviour of *Edmund.* (pp. 103-04)

[From] all that we hear in common life (for there are many stories) of old weak parents who have acted much in the manner of *Lear,* and to the reproach of human nature have met with ingratitude and disobedience; these, I say, in their feeling-hours of distress are reported to have reproached themselves with their folly in GIVING ALL as well as to have exclaimed against the ingratitude of their children.

There are many characters, I doubt not, now in the world who retain a heap of treasure useless to themselves from their children on no better motives than to ensure their duty and attention; and some who carry the moral of this play to a ridiculous height by denying their children an independence merely on the same parity of reasoning, without considering the difference between the prudence of parents and their folly.

I forbear making any quotations from *Lear*'s speeches in his madness. I think the whole obvious enough, and that our immortal poet, who had a perfect knowledge of the workings of the human mind, has drawn *both the ideas* in *Lear*'s madness agreeable to the representation he has made of him in the first act. (p. 104)

> [*Thomas Fitzpatrick*], *in a letter to Charles Ranger* [*Arthur Murphy*], *on January 19, 1754, in* Shakespeare, the Critical Heritage: 1753-1765, Vol. 4, *edited by Brian Vickers, Routledge & Kegan Paul, 1976, pp. 100-05.*

[CHARLOTTE LENNOX]   (essay date 1754)

> [*Lennox was an American-born novelist and Shakespearean scholar who compiled a three-volume edition of translated texts of the sources used by Shakespeare in twenty-two of his plays, including some analyses of the ways in which he used these sources. In the following excerpt, Lennox criticizes Shakespeare for his excessive alterations to the original Leir history. Most disputed is his portrait of the king, whom Lennox considers improbably drawn, for his behavior is absurd and seemingly insane from his first appearance. This last opinion was to become a major issue in* Lear *criticism throughout the eighteenth and into the nineteenth centuries, and it has been discussed by such critics as Henry Hallam (1837-39), A. Brigham (1844), John Charles Bucknill (1859), H. N. Hudson (1872), and Stopford A. Brooke (1913). Lennox also devotes a considerable portion of her essay to attacking Shakespeare for the addition of the so-called "love test" in the first scene, which she finds improbable and contrived. For further discussion of this scene and its relation to the rest of* King Lear, *see the excerpts by Samuel Taylor Coleridge (1813), Edward Dowden (1881), A. C. Bradley (1904), Levin L. Schucking (1922), Harry V. Jaffa (1957), William Frost (1957-58), and John Reibetanz (1977).*]

This Fable, although drawn from the foregoing History of King *Lear* is so altered by *Shakespear* in several Circumstances, as to render it much more improbable than the Original: There we are sufficiently disgusted with the Folly of a Man, who gives away one Half of his Kingdom to two of his Daughters, because they flatter him with Professions of the most extravagant Love; and deprives his youngest Child of her Portion for no other Crime but confining her Expressions of Tenderness within the Bounds of plain and simple Truth. (p. 286)

But *Shakespear* has carried this Extravagance much farther; he shews us a King resigning his Kingdom, his Crown and Dignity to his two Daughters; reserving nothing to himself, not even a decent Maintenance; but submitting to a mean Dependance on the Bounty of his Children; whom, by promising Rewards proportionable to the Degree of Flattery they lavish on him, he has stimulated to outvie each other in artful Flourishes on their Duty and Affection toward him. (p. 286)

Lear does not run mad till the third Act; yet his Behaviour towards *Cordelia* in [the] first Scene has all the Appearance of a Judgment totally depraved: he asks *Cordelia* what she has to say to draw a Dowry more opulent than her Sisters.

Thus he suggested to her a Motive for exceeding them in Expressions of Love: the noble Disinterestedness of her Answer afforded the strongest Conviction of her Sincerity, and that she possesed the highest Degree of filial Affection for him, who hazarded the Loss of all her Fortune to confine herself to simple Truth in her Professions of it: yet, for this, *Lear* banishes her his Sight, consigns her over to Want, and loads her with the deepest Imprecations. What less than Phrenzy can inspire a Rage so groundless, and a Conduct so absurd! *Lear,* while in his Senses, acts like a mad Man, and from his first Appearance to his last seems to be wholly deprived of his Reason.

In the History *Lear* Disinherits *Cordelia,* but we read of no other kind of Severity exerted towards her. The King of *France,* as well in the History as the Play, charm'd with the Virtue and Beauty of the injured *Cordelia,* marries her without a Portion.

Shakespear does not introduce this Prince till after the absurd Trial *Lear* made of his Daughters' Affection is over. The Lover who is made to Marry the disinherited *Cordelia* on account of her Virtue, is very injudiciously contrived to be Absent when she gave so glorious a Testimony of it, and is touch'd by a cold Justification of her Fame, and that from herself, when he might have been charm'd with a shining Instance of her Greatness of Soul, and inviolable Regard to Truth.

So unartfully has the Poet managed this Incident, that *Cordelia*'s noble Disinterestedness is apparent to all but him who was to be the most influenced by it. In the Eyes of her Lover she is debased, not exalted; reduced to the abject Necessity of defending her own Character, and seeking rather to free herself from the Suspicion of Guilt, than modestly enjoying the conscious Sense of superior Virtue.

Lear's Invective against her to the King of *France* is conceived in the most shocking Terms.

> I would not from your Love make such a stray,
> To Match you where I Hate; therefore beseech you,
> T'avert your Liking a more worthy Way,
> Than on a Wretch, whom Nature is asham'd
> Almost t'acknowledge her's.
>   [I. i. 209-13]

Well might the King of *France* be startled at such Expressions as these from a Parent of his Child; had he been present to have heard the Offence she gave him to occasion them, how must her exalted Merit have been endeared to him by the extream Injustice she suffered; but as it is, a bare Acquittal of any monstrous Crime, is all the Satisfaction she can procure

for herself; and all the Foundation her Lover has for the Eulogium he afterwards makes on her.

> *Cordelia.* I yet beseech your Majesty,
> (If, for I want that glib and oily Art,
> To speak and purpose not; since what I well intend,
> I'll do't before I Speak) that you make known
> It is no vicious Blot, Murther, or Foulness,
> No unchast Action, or dishonour'd Step,
> That hath depriv'd me of your Grace and Favour.
> But ev'n for want of that, for which I'm richer,
> A still soliciting Eye, and such a Tongue,
> That I am glad I've not; though not to have it
> Hath lost me in your Liking.
>   *Lear.*   Better thou
> Hadst not been Born, than not to have pleased me better.
>   [I. i. 223-33]

From this Speech of *Cordelia*'s, and *Lear*'s Answer, *France* collects Matter for extenuating a supposed Error in his Mistress, not for Admiration of her Worth.

> *France.* Is it but this? a Tardiness in Nature,
> Which often leaves the History unspoke,
> That it intends to do.
>   [I. i. 235-37]

Yet a Moment after, without knowing any more of the Matter, he lavishes the warmest Praises on her Virtues, and offers to make her (loaded as she is with her Father's Curses, and deprived of the Dower he expected with her) Queen of *France.* This Conduct would be just and natural, had he been a Witness of her noble Behaviour; but doubtful as it must have appeared to him in such perplexing Circumstances, 'tis extravagant and absurd.

Shakespear has deviated widely from History in the Catastrophe of his Play; the Chronicle tells us that King *Lear,* having been dispossessed by his rebellious Sons-in-Law of that Half of the Kingdom which he had reserved for himself, and forced, by repeated Indignities from his Daughters, to take Refuge in *France,* was received with great Tenderness by *Cordelia,* who prevailed upon her Husband to attempt his Restoration; accordingly an Army of *Frenchmen* pass'd over into *Britain,* by which, the Dukes of *Cornwal* and *Albany* being defeated, King *Lear* was restored to his Crown, died in Peace two Years after, and left his Kingdom to *Cordelia.* In *Shakespear* the Forces of the two wicked Sisters are victorious, *Lear* and the pious *Cordelia* are taken Prisoners, she is hanged in Prison, and the old King dies with Grief. Had *Shakespear* followed the Historian, he would not have violated the Rules of poetical justice; he represents Vice punished, and Virtue rewarded; in the Play one Fate overwhelms alike the Innocent and the Guilty, and the Facts in the History are wholly changed to produce Events, neither probable, necessary, nor just. (pp. 287-91)

[*Charlotte Lennox*], "*Fable of the Tragedy of 'King Lear',*" *in her* Shakespear Illustrated; or, The Novels and Histories, on Which the Plays of Shakespear Are Founded, Vol. 3, *1754. Reprint by AMS Press Inc., 1973, pp. 279-308.*

SAMUEL JOHNSON (essay date 1765)

[Johnson has long held an important place in the history of Shakespearean criticism. He is considered the foremost representative of moderate English Neoclassicism and is credited by some literary historians with freeing Shakespeare from the strictures of

the three unities valued by strict Neoclassicists: that dramas should have a single setting, take place in less than twenty-four hours, and have a causally connected plot. More recent scholars portray him as a critic who was able to synthesize existing critical theory rather than as an innovative theoretician. Johnson was a master of Augustan prose style and a personality who dominated the literary world of his epoch. In the following excerpt, Johnson ambivalently responds to a number of previously criticized aspects of King Lear, *such as Lear's absurd behavior, the cruelty of the daughters, the addition of the Edmund subplot—all of which he justifies on historical or artistic grounds—and the blinding of Gloucester onstage, which he calls an act "too horrid to be endured." He also comments on the death of Cordelia in Shakespeare's play, agreeing with such earlier critics as Nahum Tate (1681), Charles Gildon (1710), and Lewis Theobald (1715) that it violates the "natural ideas of justice." Finally, Johnson mentions the controversy over the exact cause of Lear's madness, concluding that filial ingratitude, not loss of royalty, accounts for the king's mental breakdown. For more on this subject, see the excerpts by Joseph Warton (1753-54), Arthur Murphy (1754), Thomas Fitzpatrick (1754), and William Richardson (1784). Johnson's essay was originally published in his* The Plays of William Shakespeare *in 1765.]*

The tragedy of Lear is deservedly celebrated among the dramas of Shakespeare. There is perhaps no play which keeps the attention so strongly fixed; which so much agitates our passions and interests our curiosity. The artful involutions of distinct interests, the striking opposition of contrary characters, the sudden changes of fortune, and the quick succession of events, fill the mind with a perpetual tumult of indignation, pity, and hope. There is no scene which does not contribute to the aggravation of the distress or conduct of the action, and scarce a line which does not conduce to the progress of the scene. So powerful is the current of the poet's imagination, that the mind, which once ventures within it, is hurried irresistibly along.

On the seeming improbability of Lear's conduct it may be observed, that he is represented according to histories at that time vulgarly received as true. And perhaps if we turn our thoughts upon the barbarity and ignorance of the age to which this story is referred, it will appear not so unlikely as while we estimate Lear's manners by our own. Such preference of one daughter to another, or resignation of dominion on such conditions, would be yet credible, if told of a petty prince of Guinea or Madagascar. Shakespeare, indeed, by the mention of his earls and dukes, has given us the idea of times more civilised, and of life regulated by softer manners; and the truth is, that though he so nicely discriminates, and so minutely describes the characters of men, he commonly neglects and confounds the characters of ages, by mingling customs ancient and modern, English and foreign.

My learned friend Mr. Warton, who has in the *Adventurer* very minutely criticised this play, remarks, that the instances of cruelty are too savage and shocking, and that the intervention of Edmund destroys the simplicity of the story [see excerpt above, 1753-54]. These objections may, I think, be answered, by repeating, that the cruelty of the daughters is an historical fact, to which the poet has added little, having only drawn it into a series by dialogue and action. But I am not able to apologise with equal plausibility for the extrusion of Gloucester's eyes, which seems an act too horrid to be endured in dramatick exhibition, and such as must always compel the mind to relieve its distress by incredulity. Yet let it be remembered that our authour well knew what would please the audience for which he wrote.

The injury done by Edmund to the simplicity of the action is abundantly recompensed by the addition of variety, by the art

with which he is made to co-operate with the chief design, and the opportunity which he gives the poet of combining perfidy with perfidy, and connecting the wicked son with the wicked daughters, to impress this important moral, that villany is never at a stop, that crimes lead to crimes, and at last terminate in ruin.

But though this moral be incidentally enforced, Shakespeare has suffered the virtue of Cordelia to perish in a just cause, contrary to the natural ideas of justice, to the hope of the reader, and, what is yet more strange, to the faith of chronicles. Yet this conduct is justified by the *Spectator* [see excerpt above by Joseph Addison, 1711], who blames Tate for giving Cordelia success and happiness in his alteration, and declares, that, in his opinion, "the tragedy has lost half its beauty." . . . A play in which the wicked prosper, and the virtuous miscarry, may doubtless be good, because it is a just representation of the common events of human life: but since all reasonable beings naturally love justice, I cannot easily be persuaded, that the observation of justice makes a play worse; or, that if other excellencies are equal, the audience will not always rise better pleased from the final triumph of persecuted virtue.

In the present case the publick has decided. Cordelia, from the time of Tate, has always retired with victory and felicity. And, if my sensations could add any thing to the general suffrage, I might relate, that I was many years ago so shocked by Cordelia's death, that I know not whether I ever endured to read again the last scenes of the play till I undertook to revise them as an editor.

There is another controversy among the critics concerning this play. It is disputed whether the predominant image in Lear's distorted mind be the loss of his kingdom or the cruelty of his daughters. Mr. Murphy, a very judicious critick, has evinced by induction of particular passages, that the cruelty of his daughters is the primary source of his distress, and that the loss of royalty affects him only as a secondary and subordinate evil [see excerpt above, 1754]; he observes with great justness, that Lear would move our compassion but little, did we not rather consider the injured father than the degraded king. (pp. 702-05)

Samuel Johnson, "Notes on Shakespeare's Plays: 'King Lear'," in his The Yale Edition of the Works of Samuel Johnson: Johnson on Shakespeare, Vol. VIII, *edited by Arthur Sherbo, Yale University Press, 1968, pp. 659-705.*

GEORGE COLMAN (essay date 1768)

[Colman was an eighteenth-century dramatist and producer who primarily followed Neoclassical standards in his critical and creative writings. However, he accepted Shakespeare's variations of the classical rules as permissible because, like Joseph Addison, he felt that the poet's genius was greater than his lapses; in fact, Colman ranked Shakespeare with Homer in his degree of supremacy over other poets. In the brief excerpt below, he criticizes Nahum Tate's popular adaptation of King Lear *(see excerpt above, 1681), claiming that Tate's addition of the love affair between Edgar and Cordelia is ridiculous and, furthermore, distracts our attention from the distress of Lear and his youngest daughter. Colman concludes that had it not been for its happy ending, Tate's version would have "quitted the stage long ago." For more commentary on Tate's adaptation of* King Lear, *see the excerpts by Charles Gildon (1710), Joseph Addison (1711), Lewis Theobald (1715), Samuel Johnson (1765), Charles Lamb (1812), Hermann Ulrici (1839), and G. G. Gervinus (1849-50). This excerpt is taken from Colman's preface to his* The History of King Lear.*

As It Is Performed at the Theatre Royal in Covent Garden, *published February 20, 1768.*]

[The] very expedient of *a love* betwixt Edgar and Cordelia, on which Tate felicitates himself, seemed to me to be one of the capital objections to his alteration. For even supposing that it rendered Cordelia's indifference to her father more probable (an indifference which Shakespeare has no where implied), it assigns a very poor motive for it; so that what Edgar gains on the side of romantick generosity Cordelia loses on that of real virtue. The distress of the story is so far from being heightened by it that it has diffused a languor and insipidity over all the scenes of the play from which Lear is absent, for which I appeal to the sensations of the numerous audiences with which the play has been honoured. And had the scenes been affectingly written they would at least have divided our feelings, which Shakespeare has attached almost entirely to Lear and Cordelia in their parental and filial capacities; thereby producing passages infinitely more tragick than the embraces of Cordelia and the ragged Edgar, which would have appeared too ridiculous for representation had they not been mixed and incorporated with some of the finest scenes of Shakespeare.

Tate, in whose days *love* was the soul of Tragedy as well as Comedy, was, however, so devoted to intrigue that he has not only given Edmund a passion for Cordelia but has injudiciously amplified on his criminal commerce with Goneril and Regan, which is the most disgusting part of the original. The Rev. Dr. Warton has doubted 'whether the cruelty of the daughters is not painted with circumstances too savage and unnatural,' even by Shakespeare [see excerpt above, 1753]. Still, however, in Shakespeare some motives for their conduct are assigned; but as Tate has conducted that part of the fable they are equally cruel and unnatural, without the poet's assigning any motive at all.

In all these circumstances it is generally agreed that Tate's alteration is for the worse, and his *King Lear* would probably have quitted the stage long ago had not the poet made 'the tale conclude in a success to the innocent distressed persons.' (pp. 294-95)

> George Colman, in an extract from Shakespeare, the
> Critical Heritage: 1765-1774, Vol. 5, *edited by Brian
> Vickers, Routledge & Kegan Paul, 1979, pp. 294-
> 96.*

WILLIAM RICHARDSON (essay date 1784)

[*Richardson was a Scottish author and educator who focused on the psychological and moral aspects of Shakespeare's major characters, drawing from each a philosophical lesson, or what he termed a "ruling principle." For Richardson, such guiding principles served to establish the psychological aspects of Shakespeare's characters—their motives, fears, delusions—and in the process defined the action of each play. In the following excerpt, first published in his* Essays on Shakespeare's Dramatic Characters of Richard III, King Lear, and Timon of Athens *in 1784, Richardson argues that in the figure of King Lear Shakespeare was attempting to demonstrate the moral axiom that "mere sensibility, undirected by reflection, leads men to an extravagant expression both of social and unsocial feelings." Richardson claims that it is only after Lear's madness that he begins to reflect on his previous actions and to censure himself for his mistreatment of Cordelia—an interpretation which established Richardson as one of the first critics to see Lear as a figure who gains self-knowledge through suffering. For further commentary on Lear's gradual self-knowledge, see the excerpts by Winifred M. T. Nowottny (1957) and Paul Jorgensen (1967). Richardson also touches on the con-*

troversy over the exact cause of Lear's madness, apparently adopting the interpretation put forth by Thomas Fitzpatrick (1754)—that both the ingratitude of his daughters and his loss of royalty contribute to his mental breakdown.]

Those who are guided in their conduct by impetuous impulse, arising from sensibility, and undirected by reflection, are liable to extravagant or outrageous excess. Transported by their own emotions, they misapprehend the condition of others: they are prone to exaggeration; and even the good actions they perform, excite amazement rather than approbation. Lear, an utter stranger to adverse fortune, and under the power of excessive affection, conceived his children in every respect deserving. During this ardent and inconsiderate mood, he ascribed to them such corresponding sentiments as justified his extravagant fondness. He saw his children as the gentlest and most affectionate of the human race. What condescension, on his part, could be a suitable reward for their filial piety? He divides his kingdom among them; they will relieve him from the cares of royalty; and to his old age will afford consolation.

But he is not only extravagant in his love; he is no less outrageous in his displeasure. Kent, moved with zeal for his interest, remonstrates, with the freedom of conscious integrity, against his conduct to Cordelia; and Lear, impatient of good counsel, not only rebukes him with unbecoming asperity, but inflicts unmerited punishment. (pp. 60-1)

Cordelia was the favourite daughter of Lear. [Her] sisters had replied to him, with an extravagance suited to the extravagance of his affection. He expected much more from Cordelia. Yet her reply was better suited to the relation that subsisted between them, than to the fondness of his present humour. He is disappointed, pained, and provoked. There is no gentle advocate in his bosom to mitigate the rigours of his displeasure. He follows the blind impulse of his resentment; abuses and abandons Cordelia. (pp. 63-4)

Lear, in the representation of Shakespeare, possessing great sensibility, and full of affection, seeks a kind of enjoyment suited to his temper. Ascribing the same sensibility and affection to his daughters, for they must have it, no doubt, by hereditary right, he forms a pleasing dream of reposing his old age under the wings of their kindly protection. He is disappointed; he feels extreme pain and resentment; but he has no power. Will he then become morose and retired? His habits and temper will not give him leave. Impetuous, and accustomed to authority, consequently of an unyielding nature, he would wreak his wrath, if he were able, in deeds of excessive violence. He would do, he knows not what. He who could pronounce such imprecations against Goneril, as notwithstanding her guilt, appears shocking and horrid, would, in the moment of his resentment, have put her to death. If, without any ground of offence, he could abandon Cordelia, and cast off his favourite child, what would he not have done to the unnatural and pitiless Regan?

[Here] we have a curious spectacle: a man accustomed to bear rule, suffering sore disappointment, and grievous wrongs; high minded, impetuous, susceptible of extreme resentment; and incapable of yielding to morose silence, or malignant retirement. What change can befall his spirit? For his condition is so altered, that his spirit also must suffer change. What! but to have his understanding torn up by the hurricane of passion, to scorn consolation, and lose his reason! Shakespeare could not avoid making Lear distracted. Other poets exhibit madness, because they chuse it, or for the sake of variety, or to deepen the distress: but Shakespeare has exhibited the madness of Lear, as the natural effect of such suffering on such a character. It was an event in the progress of Lear's mind, driven by such feelings, desires, and passions as the poet ascribes to him, as could not be avoided.

It is sometimes observed, that there are three kinds of madness displayed in this performance: that of Lear, that of Edgar, and that of the Fool. The observation is inaccurate. The madness of Edgar is entirely pretended; and that of the Fool has also more affectation than reality. Accordingly, we find Lear for ever dwelling upon one idea, and reconciling every thing to one appearance. The storms and tempests were not his daughters. The gleams of reason that shoot athwart the darkness of his disorder, render the gloom more horrid. Edgar affects to dwell upon one idea; he is haunted by fiends; but he is not uniform. The feeling he discovers, and compassion in spite of his counterfeit, render his speeches very often pathetic. The Fool, who has more honesty than understanding, and more understanding than he pretends, becomes an interesting character, by his attachment to his unfortunate master.

Lear, thus extravagant, inconsistent, inconstant, capricious, variable, irresolute, and impetuously vindictive, is almost an object of disapprobation. But our poet, with his usual skill, blends the disagreeable qualities with such circumstances as correct this effect, and form one delightful assemblage. Lear, in his good intentions, was without deceit; his violence is not the effect of premeditated malignity; his weaknesses are not crimes, but often the effects of misruled affections. This is not all: he is an old man; an old king; an aged father; and the instruments of his suffering are undutiful children. He is justly entitled to our compassion; and the incidents last mentioned, though they imply no merit, they procure some respect. Add to all this, that he becomes more and more interesting towards the close of the drama; not merely because he is more and more unhappy, but because he becomes really more deserving of our esteem. His misfortunes correct his misconduct; they rouse reflection, and lead him to that reformation which we approve. We see the commencement of this reformation, after he has been dismissed by Goneril, and meets with symptoms of disaffection in Regan. He who abandoned Cordelia with impetuous outrage, and banished Kent for offering an apology in her behalf; seeing his servant grossly maltreated, and his own arrival unwelcomed, has already sustained some chastisement: he does not express that ungoverned violence which his preceding conduct might lead us to expect. He restrains his emotion in its first ebullition, and reasons concerning the probable causes of what seemed so inauspicious. (pp. 76-81)

As his misfortunes increase, we find him still more inclined to reflect on his situation. He does not, indeed, express blame of himself; yet he expresses no sentiment whatever of overweaning conceit. He seems rational and modest; and the application to himself is extremely pathetic:

> Close pent up guilts,
> Rive your concealing continents, and ask
> These dreadful summoners grace.—I am a man
> More sinn'd against than sinning.
>
> [III. ii. 57-60]

Soon after, we find him actually pronouncing censure upon himself. Hitherto he had been the mere creature of sensibility; he now begins to reflect; and grieves that he had not done so before. (pp. 81-2)

At last, he is in a state of perfect contrition, and expresses less resentment against Goneril and Regan, than self-condemnation

for his treatment of Cordelia, and a perfect, but not extravagant sense of her affection. (p. 82)

I have thus endeavoured to shew, that mere sensbility, undirected by reflection, leads men to an extravagant expression both of social and unsocial feelings; renders them capriciously inconstant in their affections; variable, and of course irresolute, in their conduct. These things, together with the miseries entailed by such deportment, seem to me well illustrated by Shakespeare, in his Dramatic Character of King Lear. (p. 83)

> *William Richardson, "On the Dramatic Character of King Lear," in his* Essays on Shakespeare's Dramatic Characters of Richard the Third, King Lear, and Timon of Athens, *1784. Reprint by AMS Press, Inc., 1974, pp. 55-83.*

AUGUST WILHELM SCHLEGEL   (lecture date 1808)

[A prominent German Romantic critic, Schlegel holds a key place in the history of Shakespeare's reputation in European criticism. His translations of thirteen of the plays are still considered the best German translations of Shakespeare. Schlegel was also a leading spokesman for the Romantic movement, which permanently overthrew the Neoclassical contention that Shakespeare was a child of nature whose plays lacked artistic form. The following excerpt is taken from a lecture delivered in Vienna in 1808 and is one of the most important nineteenth-century essays on King Lear. *In it, Schlegel rebukes those critics such as Joseph Warton (1753-54) and Charlotte Lennox (1754), who have questioned the propriety of the Gloucester subplot in* King Lear, *claiming that it is artistically proper because it "contributes to the intrigue or denouement"; indeed, he goes so far as to state that it is the combination of the two plots that "constitutes the sublime beauty of the work." Similar assessments of the Gloucester subplot were later advanced by Hermann Ulrici (1839), G. G. Gervinus (1849-50), and Edward Dowden (1881). Schlegel also became one of the earliest critics to consider the catastrophic ending of* King Lear *to be both necessary and dramatically effective, asserting that "after surviving so many sufferings, Lear can only die." The issue of Lear's and Cordelia's deaths, and their meaning in the play, is perhaps the most controversial and problematical aspect in* King Lear *criticism, dividing critics into what has been called the "pessimistic" and "optimistic" camps—or those who see the catastrophic ending as evidence of Shakespeare's evocation of a meaningless universe, and those who see it as his depiction of the redemptive power of love and the guidance of a divine providence. For leading examples of each of these interpretations, see the excerpts by Hermann Ulrici (1839), G. G. Gervinus (1849-50), Algernon Charles Swinburne (1880), A. C. Bradley (1904), E. K. Chambers (1906), Stopford A. Brooke (1913), G. Wilson Knight (1930), R. W. Chambers (1939), Oscar James Campbell (1948), L. C. Knights (1959), J. Stampfer (1960), Jan Kott (1964), and Robert H. West (1968). Also see the essays by John Danby and William R. Elton in the Additional Bibliography.]*

[In] *King Lear* the science of compassion is exhausted. The principal characters here are not those who act, but those who suffer. We have not in this, as in most tragedies, the picture of a calamity in which the sudden blows of fate seem still to honour the head which they strike, and where the loss is always accompanied by some flattering consolation in the memory of the former possession; but a fall from the highest elevation into the deepest abyss of misery, where humanity is stripped of all external and internal advantages, and given up a prey to naked helplessness. The threefold dignity of a king, an old man, and a father, is dishonoured by the cruel ingratitude of his unnatural daughters; the old Lear, who out of a foolish tenderness has given away every thing, is driven out to the world a wandering

Title page of the Second Quarto of King Lear *(1619). By permission of the Folger Shakespeare Library.*

ingenious and pious fraud from the horror and despair of self-murder. But who can possibly enumerate all the different combinations and situations by which our minds are here as it were stormed by the poet? Respecting the structure of the whole I will only make one observation. The story of Lear and his daughters was left by Shakespeare exactly as he found it in a fabulous tradition, with all the features characteristic of the simplicity of old times. But in that tradition there is not the slightest trace of the story of Gloster and his sons which was derived by Shakspeare from another source. The incorporation of the two stories has been censured as destructive of the unity of action. But whatever contributes to the intrigue or the *dénouement* must always possess unity. And with what ingenuity and skill are the two main parts of the composition dovetailed into one another! The pity felt by Gloster for the fate of Lear becomes the means which enables his son Edmund to effect his complete destruction, and affords the outcast Edgar an opportunity of being the saviour of his father. On the other hand, Edmund is active in the cause of Regan and Gonerill; and the criminal passion which they both entertain for him induces them to execute justice on each other and on themselves. The laws of the drama have therefore been sufficiently complied with; but that is the least: it is the very combination which constitutes the sublime beauty of the work. The two cases resemble each other in the main: an infatuated father is blind towards his well-disposed child, and the unnatural children, whom he prefers, requite him by the ruin of all his happiness. But all the circumstances are so different, that these stories, while they each make a correspondent impression on the heart, form a complete contrast for the imagination. Were Lear alone to suffer from his daughters, the impression would be limited to the powerful compassion felt by us for his private misfortune. But two such unheard-of examples taking place at the same time have the appearance of a great commotion in the moral world: the picture becomes gigantic, and fills us with such alarm as we should entertain at the idea that the heavenly bodies might one day fall from their appointed orbits. To save in some degree the honour of human nature, Shakspeare never wishes his spectators to forget that the story takes place in a dreary and barbarous age: he lays particular stress on the circumstance that the Britons of that day were still heathens, although he has not made all the remaining circumstances to coincide learnedly with the time which he has chosen. From this point of view we must judge of many coarsenesses in expression and manners; for instance, the immodest manner in which Gloster acknowledges his bastard, Kent's quarrel with the Steward, and more especially the cruelty personally inflicted on Gloster by the Duke of Cornwall. Even the virtue of the honest Kent bears the stamp of an iron age, in which the good and the bad display the same uncontrollable energy. Great qualities have not been superfluously assigned to the King; the poet could command our sympathy for his situation, without concealing what he had done to bring himself into it. Lear is choleric, overbearing, and almost childish from age, when he drives out his youngest daughter because she will not join in the hypocritical exaggerations of her sisters. But he has a warm and affectionate heart, which is susceptible of the most fervent gratitude; and even rays of a high and kingly disposition burst forth from the eclipse of his understanding. Of Cordelia's heavenly beauty of soul, painted in so few words, I will not venture to speak; she can only be named in the same breath with Antigone. Her death has been thought too cruel; and in England the piece is in acting so far altered that she remains victorious and happy. I must own, I cannot conceive what ideas of art and dramatic connexion those persons have who

beggar; the childish imbecility to which he was fast advancing changes into the wildest insanity, and when he is rescued from the disgraceful destitution to which he was abandoned, it is too late: the kind consolations of filial care and attention and of true friendship are now lost on him; his bodily and mental powers are destroyed beyond all hope of recovery, and all that now remains to him of life is the capability of loving and suffering beyond measure. What a picture we have in the meeting of Lear and Edgar in a tempestuous night and in a wretched hovel! The youthful Edgar has, by the wicked arts of his brother, and through his father's blindness, fallen, as the old Lear, from the rank to which his birth entitled him; and, as the only means of escaping further persecution, is reduced to assume the disguise of a beggar tormented by evil spirits. The King's fool, notwithstanding the voluntary degradation which is implied in his situation, is, after Kent, Lear's most faithful associate, his wisest counsellor. This good-hearted fool clothes reason with the livery of his motley garb; the high-born beggar acts the part of insanity; and both, were they even in reality what they seem, would still be enviable in comparison with the King, who feels that the violence of his grief threatens to overpower his reason. The meeting of Edgar with the blinded Gloster is equally heart-rending; nothing can be more affecting than to see the ejected son become the father's guide, and the good angel, who under the disguise of insanity, saves him by an suppose that we can at pleasure tack a double conclusion to a tragedy; a melancholy one for hard-hearted spectators, and a happy one for souls of a softer mould. After surviving so many sufferings, Lear can only die; and what more truly tragic end for him than to die from grief for the death of Cordelia? and if he is also to be saved and to pass the remainder of his days in happiness, the whole loses its signification. According to Shakspeare's plan the guilty, it is true, are all punished, for wickedness destroys itself; but the virtues that would bring help and succour are everywhere too late, or overmatched by the cunning activity of malice. The persons of this drama have only such a faint belief in Providence as heathens may be supposed to have; and the poet here wishes to show us that this belief requires a wider range than the dark pilgrimage on earth to be established in full extent. (pp. 411-13)

> August Wilhelm Schlegel, "Criticisms on Shakspeare's Tragedies," in his A Course of Lectures on Dramatic Art and Literature, edited by Rev. A.J.W. Morrison, translated by John Black, revised edition, 1846. Reprint by AMS Press, Inc., 1965, pp. 400-13.

CHARLES LAMB   (essay date 1812)

[Lamb is considered one of the leading figures of the Romantic movement and an authority on Elizabethan drama. Although he was, like William Hazlitt, a theater critic, Lamb argued that the stage was an improper medium for Shakespeare's plays, mainly because visual dramatizations marred their artistic and lyrical effects. Like Samuel Taylor Coleridge, Lamb revered Shakespeare as a poet rather than a playwright. Although many scholars consider his views sentimental and subjective and his interpretations of Shakespeare's characters as often extreme, Lamb remains an important contributor to the nineteenth-century's revaluation of Shakespeare's genius. In the following excerpt, taken from his essay originally published in The Reflector in 1812, Lamb argues that King Lear cannot be successfully acted, because staging the play reduces it to a demonstration of "the impotence of rage," whereas reading it as literature discloses the profundity of Lear's mind and the grandeur of his passion. This point was later supported by A. C. Bradley (1904), but has been disputed by the majority of modern critics, most notably Harley Granville-Barker (1927). Along with such other nineteenth-century critics as August Wilhelm Schlegel (1808), Anna Brownell Jameson (1832), Hermann Ulrici (1839), and G. G. Gervinus (1849-50), Lamb also regards Lear's death as unavoidable, indeed, as preferable to his survival. For this reason, he severely chastises Nahum Tate (1681) and other commentators who have created, or wished for, a happy ending to Shakespeare's play.]

[To] see Lear acted,—to see an old man tottering about the stage with a walking-stick, turned out of doors by his daughters in a rainy night, has nothing in it but what is painful and disgusting. We want to take him into shelter and relieve him. That is all the feeling which the acting of Lear ever produced in me. But the Lear of Shakespeare cannot be acted. The contemptible machinery by which they mimic the storm which he goes out in, is not more inadequate to represent the horrors of the real elements, than any actor can be to represent Lear: they might more easily propose to personate the Satan of Milton upon a stage, or one of Michael Angelo's terrible figures. The greatness of Lear is not in corporal dimension, but in intellectual; the explosions of his passion are terrible as a volcano; they are storms turning up and disclosing to the bottom that sea, his mind, with all its vast riches. It is his mind which is laid bare. This case of flesh and blood seems too insignificant to be thought on,—even as he himself neglects it. On the stage

we see nothing but corporal infirmities and weakness, the impotence of rage; while we read it, we see not Lear, but we are Lear: we are in his mind, we are sustained by a grandeur which baffles the malice of daughters and storms. In the aberrations of his reason we discover a mighty irregular power of reasoning, immethodized from the ordinary purposes of life, but exerting its powers, as the wind blows where it listeth, at will upon the corruptions and abuses of mankind. What have looks, or tones, to do with that sublime identification of his age with that of the heavens themselves, when, in his reproaches to them for conniving at the injustice of his children, he reminds them that "they themselves are old"? What gesture shall we appropriate to this? What has the voice or the eye to do with such things? But the play is beyond all art, as the tamperings with it show; it is too hard and stony; it must have love-scenes, and a happy ending [see excerpt above by Nahum Tate, 1681]. It is not enough that Cordelia is a daughter: she must shine as a lover too. Tate has put his hook in the nostrils of this leviathan, for Garrick and his followers, the showmen of the scene, to draw the mighty beast about more easily. A happy ending!—as if the living martyrdom that Lear had gone through, the flaying of his feelings alive, did not make a fair dismissal from the stage of life the only decorous thing for him. If he is to live and be happy after, if he could sustain this world's burden after, why all this pudder and preparation,—why torment us with all this unnecessary sympathy? As if the childish pleasure of getting the gilt robes and sceptre again could tempt him to act over again his misused station!—as if, at his years and with his experience, anything was left but to die! (pp. 182-83)

> Charles Lamb, "On the Tragedies of Shakespeare," in Critical Essays of the Early Nineteenth Century, edited by Raymond Macdonald Alden, Charles Scribner's Sons, 1921, pp. 172-88.

SAMUEL TAYLOR COLERIDGE   (essay date 1813)

[Coleridge's lectures and writings on Shakespeare form a major chapter in the history of English Shakespearean criticism. As the channel for the critical ideas of the German Romantics and as an original interpreter of Shakespeare in the new spirit of Romanticism, Coleridge played a strategic role in overthrowing the last remains of the Neoclassical approach to Shakespeare and in establishing the modern view of Shakespeare as a conscious artist and masterful portrayer of human character. Coleridge's remarks on Shakespeare come down to posterity largely as fragmentary notes, marginalia, and reports by auditors on the lectures, rather than in polished essays. In the excerpt below, taken from the author's notes and signed January 1, 1813, Coleridge established himself as the first critic to consider Lear's "love test" of the opening scene as an act of self-indulgence, or a mere pretense to trick his daughters into professing their love for him in order to justify his preordained division of the kingdom. Thus, Coleridge regards the test as the act of a foolish old man, a point later made by A. C. Bradley (1904), but opposed by such other twentieth-century critics as Harry V. Jaffa (1957), William Frost (1957-58), and John Reibetanz (1977). The remainder of Coleridge's essay deals with a discussion of Edmund's wickedness and Regan and Goneril's cruelty towards their father, both of which he believes Shakespeare portrays convincingly.]

Of all Shakspeare's plays Macbeth is the most rapid, Hamlet the slowest, in movement. Lear combines length with rapidity,—like the hurricane and the whirlpool, absorbing while it advances. It begins as a stormy day in summer, with brightness; but that brightness is lurid, and anticipates the tempest. . . .

Kent. I thought the king had more affected the Duke of Albany than Cornwall.

Glou. It did always seem so to us: but now, in the division of the kingdom, it appears not which of the dukes he values most; for equalities are so weighed that curiosity in neither can make choice of either's moiety.

[I. i. 1-7]

It was [not] without forethought, and it is not without its due significance, that the triple division is stated here as already determined and in all its particulars, previously to the trial of professions, as the relative rewards of which the daughters were to be made to consider their several portions. The strange, yet by no means unnatural, mixture of selfishness, sensibility, and habit of feeling derived from and fostered by the particular rank and usages of the individual; the intense desire to be intensely beloved, selfish, and yet characteristic of the selfishness of a loving and kindly nature—a feeble selfishness, self-supportless and leaning for all pleasure on another's breast; the selfish craving after a sympathy with a prodigal disinterestedness, contradicted by its own ostentation and the mode and nature of its claims; the anxiety, the distrust, the jealousy, which more or less accompany all selfish affections, and are among the surest contradistinctions of mere fondness from love, and which originate Lear's eager wish to enjoy his daughter's violent professions, while the inveterate habits of sovereignty convert the wish into claim and positive right, and the incompliance with it into crime and treason;—these facts, these passions, these moral verities, on which the whole tragedy is founded, are all prepared for, and will to the retrospect be found implied in, these first four or five lines of the play. They let us know that the trial is but a trick; and that the grossness of the old king's rage is in part the natural result of a silly trick suddenly and most unexpectedly baffled and disappointed. . . . [From] Lear, the *persona patiens* of his drama, Shakespeare passes without delay to the second in importance, to the main *agent* and prime mover—introduces Edmund to our acquaintance, and with the same felicity of judgement, in the same easy, natural way, prepares us for his character in the seemingly casual communication of its origin and occasion. From the first drawing up of the curtain he has stood before us in the united strength and beauty of earliest manhood. Our eyes have been questioning him. Gifted thus with high advantages of *person*, and further endowed by nature with a powerful intellect and a strong energetic will, even without any concurrence of circumstances and accident, pride will be the sin that most easily besets him. But he is the known and acknowledged son of the princely Gloster. Edmund, therefore, has both the germ of pride and the conditions best fitted to evolve and ripen it into a predominant feeling. Yet hitherto no reason appears why it should be other than the not unusual pride of person, talent, and birth, a pride auxiliary if not akin to many virtues, and the natural ally of honorable [impulses?]. But alas! in his own presence his own father takes shame to himself for the frank avowal that he is his father—has 'blushed so often to acknowledge him that he is now braz'd to it' [I. i. 10-11]. He hears his mother and the circumstances of his birth spoken of with a most degrading and licentious levity—described as a wanton by her own paramour, and the remembrance of the animal sting, the low criminal gratifications connected with her wantonness and prostituted beauty assigned as the reason why 'the whoreson must be acknowledged' [I. i. 24]. This, and the consciousness of its notoriety—the gnawing conviction that every shew of respect is an effort of courtesy which recalls while it represses a contrary feeling—this is the ever-trickling

flow of wormwood and gall into the wounds of pride, the corrosive virus whch inoculates pride with a venom not its own, with envy, hatred, a lust of that power which in its blaze of radiance would hide the dark spots on his disk. . . . Add to this that with excellent judgement, and provident for the claims of the moral sense, for that which relatively to the drama is called poetic justice; and as the fittest means for reconciling the feelings of the spectators to the horrors of Gloster's after sufferings,—at least, of rendering them somewhat less unendurable (for I will not disguise my conviction that in this one point the tragic has been urged beyond the outermost mark and *ne plus ultra* of the dramatic)—Shakespeare has precluded all excuse and palliation of the guilt incurred by both the parents of the base-born Edmund by Gloster's confession that he was at the time a married man and already blest with a lawful heir of his fortunes. (pp. 49-51)

By the circumstances here enumerated as so many predisposing causes, Edmund's character might well be deem'd already sufficiently explained and prepared for. But in this tragedy the story or fable constrained Shakespeare to introduce wickedness in an outrageous form, in Regan and Goneril. He had read nature too heedfully not to know that courage, intellect, and strength of character were the most impressive forms of power, and that to power in itself, without reference to any moral end, an inevitable admiration and complacency appertains, whether it be displayed in the conquests of a Napoleon or Tamerlane, or in the foam and thunder of a cataract. But in the display of such a character it was of the highest importance to prevent the guilt from passing into utter *monstrosity*—which again depends on the presence or absence of causes and temptations sufficient to *account* for the wickedness, without the necessity of recurring to a thorough fiendishness of nature for its origination. For such are the appointed relations of intellectual power to truth, and of truth to goodness, that it becomes both morally and poetic[ally] unsafe to present what is admirable—what our nature compels us to admire—in the mind, and what is most detestable in the heart, as co-existing in the same individual without any apparent connection, or any modification of the one by the other. That Shakespeare has in one instance, that of Iago, approached to this, and that he has done it successfully, is perhaps the most astonishing proof of his genius, and the opulence of its resources. But in the present tragedy, in which he [was] compelled to present a Goneril and Regan, it was most carefully to be avoided; and, therefore, the one only conceivable addition to the inauspicious influences on the preformation of Edmund's character is given in the information that all the kindly counteractions to the mischievous feelings of shame that might have been derived from co-domestication with Edgar and their common father, had been cut off by an absence from home and a foreign education from boyhood to the present time, and the prospect of its continuance, as if to preclude all risk of his interference with the father's views for the elder and legitimate son. . . . (p. 52)

It is well worthy notice, that *Lear* is the only serious performance of Shakespeare the interest and situations of which are derived from the assumption of a gross improbability; whereas Beaumont and Fletcher's tragedies are, almost all, founded on some out-of-the-way accident or exception to the general experience of mankind. But observe the matchless judgement of Shakespeare! First, improbable as the conduct of Lear is, in the first scene, yet it was an old story, rooted in the popular faith—a thing taken for granted already, and consequently without any of the *effects* of improbability. Secondly, it is merely the canvas to the characters and passions, a mere *occasion*—not (as in Beaumont and Fletcher) perpetually recurring, as the cause and *sine qua non* of the incidents and emotions. Let the first scene of *Lear* have been lost, and let it be only understood that a fond father had been duped by hypocritical professions of love and duty on the part of two daughters to disinherit a third, previously, and deservedly, more dear to him, and all the rest of the tragedy would retain its interest undiminished, and be perfectly intelligible. (p. 53)

Samuel Taylor Coleridge, *"Notes on the Tragedies of Shakespeare: 'Lear',"* in his Shakespearean Criticism, Vol. 1, *edited by Thomas Middleton Raysor, Dutton, 1960, pp. 49-59.*

WILLIAM HAZLITT   (essay date 1817)

[*Hazlitt is considered a leading Shakespearean critic of the English Romantic movement. A prolific essayist and critic on a wide range of subjects, Hazlitt remarked in the preface to his* Characters of Shakespear's Plays, *first published in 1817, that he was inspired by the German critic August Wilhelm Schlegel and was determined to supplant what he considered the pernicious influence of Samuel Johnson's Shakespearean criticism. Hazlitt's approach is typically Romantic in its emphasis on character studies. Unlike his fellow Romantic critic Samuel Taylor Coleridge, Hazlitt was a dramatic critic whose experience of Shakespeare in the theater influenced his interpretations. In the following excerpt, taken from the work mentioned above, Hazlitt calls* King Lear *"the best of all Shakespear's plays" and claims that the first three acts, along with the third act of* Othello, *contain the highest examples in Shakespeare's canon of the force of individual passions. Hazlitt was also one of the earliest critics to devote any serious attention to the Fool, arguing that the character serves to relieve the reader from the "over-strained excitement" of the play and to transport the pathos to its highest pitch by demonstrating the weakness and consequences of the king's conduct. For further discussion of the Fool, see the excerpts by Hermann Ulrici (1839), H. N. Hudson (1872), G. Wilson Knight (1930), Enid Welsford (1935), and Melvin Seiden (1979).*]

We wish that we could pass this play over, and say nothing about it. All that we can say must fall far short of the subject; or even of what we ourselves conceive of it. To attempt to give a description of the play itself or of its effect upon the mind, is mere impertinence: yet we must say something.—It is then the best of all Shakespear's plays, for it is the one in which he was most in earnest. He was here fairly caught in the web of his own imagination. The passion which he has taken as his subject is that which strikes its root deepest into the human heart; of which the bond is the hardest to be unloosed; and the cancelling and tearing to pieces of which gives the greatest revulsion to the frame. This depth of nature, this force of passion, this tug and war of the elements of our being, this firm faith in filial piety, and the giddy anarchy and whirling tumult of the thoughts at finding this prop failing it, the contrast between the fixed, immoveable basis of natural affection, and the rapid, irregular starts of imagination, suddenly wrenched from all its accustomed holds and resting-places in the soul, this is what Shakespear has given, and what nobody else but he could give. So we believe.—The mind of Lear, staggering between the weight of attachment and the hurried movements of passion, is like a tall ship driven about by the winds, buffetted by the furious waves, but that still rides above the storm, having its anchor fixed in the bottom of the sea; or it is like the sharp rock circled by the eddying whirlpool that foams and beats against it, or like the solid promontory pushed from its basis by the force of an earthquake.

The character of Lear itself is very finely conceived for the purpose. It is the only ground on which such a story could be built with the greatest truth and effect. It is his rash haste, his violent impetuosity, his blindness to everything but the dictates of his passions or affections, that produces all his misfortunes, that aggravates his impatience of them, that enforces our pity for him. The part which Cordelia bears in the scene is extremely beautiful: the story is almost told in the first words she utters. We see at once the precipice on which the poor old king stands from his own extravagant and credulous importunity, the indiscreet simplicity of her love (which, to be sure, has a little of her father's obstinacy in it) and the hollowness of her sister's pretensions. Almost the first burst of that noble tide of passion, which runs through the play, is in the remonstrance of Kent to his royal master on the injustice of his sentence against his youngest daughter—"Be Kent unmannerly, when Lear is mad!" [I. i. 145-46]. This manly plainness, which draws down on him the himself displeasure of the unadvised lady, is worthy of the fidelity with which he adheres to his fallen fortunes. The true character of the two eldest daughters, Regan and Gonerill (they are so thoroughly hateful that we do not even like to repeat their names) breaks out in their answer to Cordelia who desires them to treat their father well—"Prescribe not us our duties" [I. i. 276]—their hatred of advice being in proportion to their determination to do wrong, and to their hypocritical pretensions to do right. Their deliberate hypocrisy adds the last finishing to the odiousness of their characters. It is the absence of this detestable quality that is the only relief in the character of Edmund the Bastard, and that at times reconciles us to him. We are not tempted to exaggerate the guilt of his conduct, when he himself gives it up as a bad business, and writes himself down "plain villain." Nothing more can be said about it. His religious honesty in this respect is admirable. One speech of his is worth a million. . . . The whole character, its careless, light-hearted villainy, contrasted with the sullen, rancorous malignity of Regan and Gonerill, its connection with the conduct of the underplot, in which Gloster's persecution of one of his sons and the ingratitude of another, form a counterpart to the mistakes and misfortunes of Lear,—his double amour with the two sisters, and the share which he has in bringing about the fatal catastrophe, are all managed with an uncommon degree of skill and power.

It has been said, and we think justly, that the third act of *Othello* and the three first acts of *Lear,* are Shakespear's great masterpieces in the logic of passion: that they contain the highest examples not only of the force of individual passion, but of its dramatic vicissitudes and striking effects arising from the different circumstances and characters of the persons speaking. We see the ebb and flow of the feeling, its pauses and feverish starts, its impatience of opposition, its accumulating force when it has time to recollect itself, the manner in which it avails itself of every passing word or gesture, its haste to repel insinuation, the alternate contraction and dilatation of the soul, and all "the dazzling fence of controversy" in this mortal combat with poisoned weapons, aimed at the heart, where each wound is fatal. . . . In [*Lear*], that which aggravates the sense of sympathy in the reader, and of uncontroulable anguish in the swoln heart of Lear, is the petrifying indifference, the cold, calculating, obdurate selfishness of his daughters. His keen passions seem whetted on their stony hearts. The contrast would be too painful, the shock too great, but for the intervention of the Fool, whose well-timed levity comes in to break the continuty of feeling when it can no longer be borne, and to bring into play again the fibres of the heart just as they are growing rigid from over-strained excitement. The imagination is glad to take refuge in the half-comic, half-serious comments of the Fool, just as the mind under the extreme anguish of a surgical operation vents itself in sallies of wit. The character was also a grotesque ornament of the barbarous times, in which alone the tragic ground-work of the story could be laid. In another point of view it is indispensable, inasmuch as while it is a diversion to the too great intensity of our disgust, it carries the pathos to the highest pitch of which it is capable, by shewing the pitiable weakness of the old king's conduct and its irretrievable consequences in the most familiar point of view. Lear may well "beat at the gate which let his folly in" [I. iv. 171], after, as the Fool says, "he has made his daughters his mothers" [I. iv. 172-73]. The character is dropped in the third act to make room for the entrance of Edgar as Mad Tom, which well accords with the increasing bustle and wildness of the incidents; and nothing can be more complete than the distinction between Lear's real and Edgar's assumed madness, while the resemblance in the cause of their distresses, from the severing of the nearest ties of natural affection, keeps up a unity of interest. Shakespear's mastery over his subject, if it was not art, was owing to a knowledge of the connecting links of the passions, and their effect upon the mind, still more wonderful than any systematic adherence to rules, and that anticipated and outdid all the efforts of the most refined art, not inspired and rendered instinctive by genius. (pp. 94-8)

> William Hazlitt, "Lear," in his Characters of Shakespear's Plays & Lectures on the English Poets, *The Macmillan Company, 1903, pp. 94-110.*

JOHN KEATS   (poem date 1818)

[*The following sonnet, titled "On Sitting Down to Read* King Lear Once Again," *was written by Keats in January 1818 and enclosed in his letter of January 23, 1818, to his brothers George and Thomas Keats. It is often referred to in later criticism of* King Lear, *especially Keats's description of the play as a "fierce dispute, / Betwixt Hell torment and impassion'd Clay".*]

O golden tongued Romance with serene Lute!
   Fair-plumed Syren! Queen of far-away!
   Leave melodizing on this wintry day,
Shut up thine olden volume and be mute.
Adieu! for once again the fierce dispute,
   Betwixt Hell torment and impassion'd Clay
   Must I burn through; once more assay
The bitter Sweet of this Shakespeareian fruit.
Chief Poet! and ye clouds of Albion,
   Begetters of our deep eternal theme,
When I am through the old oak forest gone
   Let me not wander in a barren dream
But when I am consumed with the Fire
Give me new Phoenix-wings to fly at my desire.

(pp. 88-9)

> John Keats, in a letter to George Keats and Thomas Keats on January 23, 1818, in his The Letters of John Keats, *edited by Maurice Buxton Forman, third edition, Oxford University Press, 1947, pp. 87-90.*

BLACKWOOD'S MAGAZINE   (essay date 1819)

[*The anonymous critic of the following essay, originally published in 1819, presents one of the earliest interpretations of the catastrophic ending of* King Lear *as depicting an optimistic, rather than a pessimistic, vision of human existence. The commentator maintains that the deaths of Lear and Cordelia represent the "full*

consummation of their reunited love." For many later nineteenth- and twentieth-century critics, the final vision of Cordelia's and Lear's deaths demonstrates not the absurdity of human life, but the power of love to overcome even the most extreme pain and suffering and still give meaning to life. For examples of this interpretation, see the excerpts by Hermann Ulrici (1839), Edward Dowden (1881), J. Dover Wilson (1932), Oscar James Campbell (1948), Arthur Sewell (1951), Irving Ribner (1958), L. C. Knights (1959), Robert Ornstein (1960), and Robert H. West (1968).]

[*King Lear* is] a work for the passionate sympathy of all—young, old, rich, and poor, learned, and illiterate, virtuous, and depraved. The majestic form of the kingly-hearted old man—the reverend head of the broken-hearted father—'a head so old and white as this' [III. ii. 24]—the royalty from which he is deposed, but of which he can never be divested—the father's heart which, rejected and trampled on by two children, and trampling on its one most young and duteous child, is, in the utmost degree, a father's still—the two characters, father and king, so high to our imagination and love, blended in the reverend image of Lear—*both* in their destitution, yet *both* in their height of greatness—the spirit blighted, and yet undepressed—the wits gone, and yet the moral wisdom of a good heart left unstained, almost unobscured—the wild raging of the elements, joined with human outrage and violence to persecute the helpless, unresisting, almost unoffending sufferer; and he himself in the midst of all imaginable misery and desolation, descanting upon himself, on the whirlwinds that drive around him—and then turning in tenderness to some of the wild, motley association of sufferers among whom he stands,—all this is not like what has been seen on any stage, perhaps in any reality, but it has made a world to our imagination about one single imaginary individual, such as draws the reverence and sympathy which should seem to belong properly only to living men. It is like the remembrance of some wild, perturbed scene of real life. Everything is perfectly woeful in this world of woe. The very assumed madness of Edgar, which, if the story of Edgar stood alone, would be insufferable, and would utterly degrade him to us, seems, associated as he is with Lear, to come within the consecration of Lear's madness. It agrees with all that is brought together:—the night—the storms—the houselessness—Glo'ster with his eyes put out—the Fool—the semblance of a madman, and Lear in his madness, are all bound together by a strange kind of sympathy, confusion in the elements of nature, of human society, and the human soul. (p. 425)

There is more justness of intellect in Lear's madness than in his right senses, as if the indestructible divinity of the spirit gleamed at times more brightly through the ruins of its earthly tabernacle. The death of Cordelia and the death of Lear leave on our minds, at least, neither pain nor disappointment, like a common play ending ill; but, like all the rest, they show us human life involved in darkness, and conflicting with wild powers let loose to rage in the world, a life whch continually seeks peace, and which can only find its good in peace—tending ever to the depth of peace, but of which the peace is not here. The feeling of the play, to those who rightly consider it, is high and calm, because we are made to know, from and through those very passions which seem there convulsed, and from the very structure of life and happiness that seems there crushed—even in the law of those passions and that life—this eternal Truth, that evil must not be, and that good must be. The only thing intolerable was, that Lear should, by the very truth of his daughter's love, be separated from her love; and his restoration to her love, and therewith to his own perfect mind, consummates all that was essentially to be desired—a consummation after which the rage and horror of mere matter-disturbing death seems vain and idle. In fact, Lear's killing the slave who was hanging Cordelia—bearing her dead in his arms—and his heart bursting over her,—are no more than the full consummation of their reunited love;—and there father and daughter lie in final and imperturbable peace. Cordelia, whom we see at last lying dead before us, and over whom we shed such floods of loving and approving tears, scarcely speaks or acts in the play at all; she appears but at the beginning and the end, is absent from all the impressive and memorable scenes; and to what she does say there is not much effect given, yet, by some divine power of conception in Shakespeare's soul, she always seems to our memory one of the principal characters; and while we read the play she is continually present to our imagination. In her sisters' ingratitude, her filial love is felt; in the hopelessness of the broken-hearted king, we are turned to that perfect hope that is reserved for him in her loving bosom; in the midst of darkness, confusion, and misery, her form, like a hovering angel, is seen casting its radiance on the storm. (pp. 425-26)

> *An extract from* A New Variorum Edition of Shakespeare: King Lear, Vol. 5 *by William Shakespeare, edited by Horace Howard Furness, J. B. Lippincott Company, 1880, pp. 425-26.*

PERCY BYSSHE SHELLEY (essay date 1821)

[*Shelley's so-called "defense of poetry" and his investigation into its relation to the history of civilization was an important contribution to nineteenth-century aesthetics. Influenced by the French philosopher Jean-Jacques Rousseau and the German theoretician and pre-Romanticist Johann Gottfried Herder, Shelley viewed poetry as a medium of continually evolving ideas—in his words, as a "fountain forever overflowing with the waters of wisdom and delight," which when exhausted by one age, "another and yet another succeeds and new relations are ever developed." He argued that poetry was like a mirror to its age, the history of its manners, and thus he labeled all poets "legislators and prophets" who, even unconsciously or when in least prominence, as in the English Restoration, contributed to the spiritual and political evolution of humankind. In the following excerpt, taken from his* A Defence of Poetry, *written in 1821, Shelley considers* King Lear *superior to the ancient tragedies* Oedipus Tyrannus *and* Agamemnon, *primarily because of Shakespeare's subtle combination of tragic and comic elements; in fact, he goes so far as to call* Lear *"the most perfect specimen of the dramatic art existing in the world." For further discussion of the mixture of comedy and tragedy in* King Lear, *see the excerpts by Hermann Ulrici (1839), G. Wilson Knight (1930), Jan Kott (1964), and Ronald F. Miller (1975).*]

The modern practice of blending comedy with tragedy, though liable to great abuse in point of practice, is undoubtedly an extension of the dramatic circle; but the comedy should be as in *King Lear,* universal, ideal, and sublime. It is perhaps the intervention of this principle which determines the balance in favour of *King Lear* against the *Oedipus Tyrannus* or the *Agamemnon,* or, if you will, the trilogies with which they are connected; unless the intense power of the choral poetry, especially that of the latter, should be considered as restoring the equilibrium. *King Lear,* if it can sustain this comparison, may be judged to be the most perfect specimen of the dramatic art existing in the world; in spite of the narrow conditions to which the poet was subjected by the ignorance of the philosophy of the drama which has prevailed in modern Europe. (pp. 39-40)

> *Percy Bysshe Shelley, in his* A Defence of Poetry, *edited by Mrs. Shelley, The Bobbs-Merrill Company, 1904, 90 p.*

MRS. [ANNA BROWNELL] JAMESON (essay date 1833)

[*Born in Ireland, Jameson was a well-known nineteenth-century essayist. Her essays and criticism span the end of the Romantic age and the beginning of Victorian realism, reflecting elements from both periods. She is best remembered for her study* Shakespeare's Heroines *which was originally published in 1833 as* Characteristics of Women: Moral, Poetical, and Historical. *This work demonstrates both her historical interests and her sympathetic appreciation of Shakespeare's female characters. In the following excerpt, from the work mentioned above, Jameson regards Cordelia as the most perfect of Shakespeare's heroines and a major force in* King Lear *far beyond her few scenes onstage. She also derides Nahum Tate (1681) for his attempt to revise Shakespeare's play and construct a love affair between Cordelia and Edgar, a revision she finds "absurd" and "discordant" with all previous impressions of the heroine. For other interpretations of the character of Cordelia, see the excerpts by G. G. Gervinus (1849-50), H. N. Hudson (1872), and R. W. Chambers (1939).*]

There is in the beauty of Cordelia's character an effect too sacred for words, and almost too deep for tears; within her heart is a fathomless well of purest affection, but its waters sleep in silence and obscurity,—never failing in their depth and never overflowing in their fulness. Everything in her seems to lie beyond our view, and affects us in a manner which we feel rather than perceive. The character appears to have no surface, no salient points upon which the fancy can readily seize: there is little external development of intellect, less of passion, and still less of imagination. It is completely made out in the course of a few scenes, and we are surprised to find that in those few scenes there is matter for a life of reflection, and materials enough for twenty heroines. If "Lear" be the grandest of Shakspeare's tragedies, Cordelia in herself, as a human being governed by the purest and holiest impulses and motives, the most refined from all dross of selfishness and passion, approaches near to perfection; and, in her adaptation as a dramatic personage to a determinate plan of action, may be pronounced altogether perfect. The character, to speak of it critically as a poetic conception, is not, however, to be comprehended at once, or easily; and in the same manner Cordelia, as a woman, is one whom we must have loved before we could have known her, and known her long before we could have known her truly. (pp. 200-01)

Amid the awful, the overpowering interest of the story, amid the terrible convulsions of passion and suffering, and pictures of moral and physical wretchedness which harrow up the soul, the tender influence of Cordelia, like that of a celestial visitant, is felt and acknowledged without being quite understood. Like a soft star that shines for a moment from behind a stormy cloud, and the next is swallowed up in tempest and darkness, the impression it leaves is beautiful and deep, but vague. Speak of Cordelia to a critic, or to a general reader, all agree in the beauty of the portrait, for all must feel it; but when we come to details, I have heard more various and opposite opinions relative to her than any other of Shakspeare's characters—a proof of what I have advanced in the first instance, that, from the simplicity with which the character is dramatically treated, and the small space it occupies, few are aware of its internal power or its wonderful depth of purpose.

It appears to me that the whole character rests upon the two sublimest principles of human action—the love of truth and the sense of duty: but these, when they stand alone (as in the "Antigone"), are apt to strike us as severe and cold. Shakspeare has, therefore, wreathed them round with the dearest attributes of our feminine nature, the power of feeling and inspiring affection. The first part of the play shows us how Cordelia is loved, the second part how she can love. (p. 202)

But it will be said that the qualities [she exemplifies]—as sensibility, gentleness, magnanimity, fortitude, generous affection—are qualities which belong, in their perfection, to others of Shakespeare's characters: to Imogen, for instance, who unites them all: and yet Imogen and Cordelia are wholly unlike each other. Even though we should reverse their situations, and give to Imogen the filial devotion of Cordelia, and to Cordelia the conjugal virtues of Imogen, still they would remain perfectly distinct as women. What is it, then, which lends to Cordelia that peculiar and individual truth of character which distinguishes her from every other human being?

It is a natural reserve, a tardiness of disposition, "which often leaves the history unspoke which it intends to do" [I. i. 236-37]; a subdued quietness of deportment and expression, a veiled shyness thrown over all her emotions, her language and her manner, making the outward demonstration invariably fall short of what we know to be the feeling within. Not only is the portrait singularly beautiful and interesting in itself, but the conduct of Cordelia, and the part which she bears in the beginning of the story, is rendered consistent and natural by the wonderful truth and delicacy with which this peculiar disposition is sustained throughout the play. (p. 205)

In the story of King Lear and his three daughters, as it is related in the . . . romance of Perceforest, and in the Chronicle of Geoffrey of Monmouth, the conclusion is fortunate. Cordelia defeats her sisters, and replaces her father on his throne. Spenser, in his version of the story, has followed these authorities. Shakspeare has preferred the catastrophe of the old ballad, founded apparently on some lost tradition. I suppose it is by way of amending his errors, and bringing back this daring innovator to sober history, that it has been thought fit to alter the play of "Lear" for the stage, as they have altered "Romeo and Juliet"; they have converted the seraph-like Cordelia into a puling love heroine, and sent her off victorious at the end of the play—exit with drums and colours flying—to be married to Edgar. Now anything more absurd, more discordant with all our previous impressions, and with the characters as unfolded to us, can hardly be imagined. "I cannot conceive," says Schlegel, "what ideas of art and dramatic connection those persons have who suppose we can at pleasure tack a double conclusion to a tragedy—a melancholy one for hardhearted spectators, and a merry one for those of softer mould" [see excerpt above, 1808]. The fierce manners depicted in this play, the extremes of virtue and vice in the persons, belong to the remote period of the story. There is no attempt at character in the old narratives; Regan and Goneril are monsters of ingratitude, and Cordelia merely distinguished by her filial piety: whereas, in Shakspeare, this filial piety is an affection quite distinct from the qualities which serve to individualise the human being; we have a perception of innate character apart from all accidental circumstance; we see that if Cordelia had never known her father, had never been rejected from his love, had never been a born princess or a crowned queen, she would not have been less Cordelia, less distinctly *herself*—that is, a woman of a steady mind, of calm but deep affections, of inflexible truth, of few words, and of reserved deportment. (pp. 210-11)

[The] character whch at once suggests itself in comparison with Cordelia, as the heroine of filial tenderness and piety, is certainly the Antigone of Sophocles. As poetical conceptions, they rest on the same basis; they are both pure abstractions of truth, piety, and natural affection; and in both love, as a passion, is kept entirely out of sight; for though the womanly character is sustained by making them the objects of devoted attachment, yet to have portrayed them as influenced by passion would have destroyed that unity of purpose and feeling which is one source of power, and, besides, have disturbed that serene purity and grandeur of soul which equally distinguishes both heroines. The spirit, however, in which the two characters is conceived is as different as possible; and we must not fail to remark that Antigone, who plays a principal part in two fine tragedies, and is distinctly and completely made out, is considered as a masterpiece, the very triumph of the ancient classical drama; whereas there are many among Shakspeare's characters which are equal to Cordelia as dramatic conceptions, and superior to her in finishing of outline, as well as in the richness of the poetical colouring. (p. 212)

[In] the "Antigone" there is a great deal of what may be called the effect of situation, as well as a great deal of poetry and character: she says the most beautiful things in the world, performs the most heroic actions, and all her words and actions are so placed before us as to *command* our admiration. According to the classical ideas of virtue and heroism, the character is sublime, and in the delineation there is a severe simplicity mingled with its Grecian grace, a unity, a grandeur, an elegance, which appeal to our taste and our understanding, while they fill and exalt the imagination. But in Cordelia it is not the external colouring or form, it is not what she says or does, but what she is in herself, what she feels, thinks, and suffers, which continually awaken our sympathy and interest. The heroism of Cordelia is more passive and tender—it melts into our heart; and in the veiled loveliness and unostentatious delicacy of her character there is an effect more profound and artless, if it be less striking and less elaborte than in the Grecian heroine. To Antigone we give our admiration, to Cordelia our tears. Antigone stands before us in her austere and statue-like beauty, like one of the marbles of the Parthenon. If Cordelia remind us of anything on earth, it is one of the Madonnas in the old Italian pictures . . . ; and as that heavenly form is connected with our human sympathies only by the expression of maternal tenderness or maternal sorrow, even so Cordelia would be almost too angelic, were she not linked to our earthly feelings, bound to our very hearts, by her filial love, her wrongs, her sufferings, and her tears. (pp. 214-15)

> *Mrs. [Anna Brownell] Jameson, "Cordelia," in her* Shakspeare's Heroines: Characteristics of Women, Moral, Poetical, & Historical, *second edition, 1833. Reprint by George Newnes, Limited, 1897, pp. 200-15.*

HENRY HALLAM   (essay date 1837-39)

> [*In the following brief excerpt, the nineteenth-century English historian Henry Hallam argues that Lear's madness is neither sudden nor evident from the very beginning, but gradual, culminating in "grief and rage" in the scenes on the heath. Hallam's interpretation countered that of Charlotte Lennox (1754), and was later criticized directly by John Charles Bucknill (1859), both of whom maintained that Lear was insane from the very beginning of the play. The excerpt below was originally published in Hallam's* Introduction to the Literature of Europe in the Fifteenth,

Sixteenth, and Seventeenth Centuries, *issued in four volumes between 1837 and 1839.*]

If originality of invention did not so much stamp almost every play of Shakspeare that to name one as the most original seems a disparagement to others, we might say, that this great prerogative of genius was exercised above all in *Lear.* It diverges more from the model of regular tragedy than *Macbeth* or *Othello,* and even more than *Hamlet;* but the fable is better constructed than in the last of these, and it displays full as much of the almost superhuman inspiration of the poet as the other two. Lear himself is, perhaps, the most wonderful of dramatic conceptions; ideal to satisfy the most romantic imagination, yet idealized from the reality of nature. Shakspeare, in preparing us for the most intense sympathy with this old man, first abases him to the ground: it is not Oedipus, against whose respected age the gods themselves have conspired; it is not Orestes, noble-minded and affectionate, whose crime has been virtue: it is a headstrong, feeble, and selfish being, whom, in the first act of the tragedy, nothing seems capable of redeeming in our eyes; nothing but what follows,—intense woe, unnatural wrong. Then comes on that splendid madness, not absurdly sudden, as in some tragedies, but in which the strings that keep his reasoning power together give way one after the other in the frenzy of rage and grief. Then it is that we find, what in life may sometimes be seen, the intellectual energies grow stronger in calamity, and especially under wrong. An awful eloquence belongs to unmerited suffering. Thoughts burst out, more profound than Lear in his prosperous hour could ever have conceived; inconsequent, for such is the condition of madness, but in themselves fragments of coherent truth, the reason of an unreasonable mind. (pp. 296-97)

> Henry Hallam, "*History of Dramatic Literature from 1600 to 1650,*" *in his* Introduction to the Literature of Europe in the 15th, 16th, and 17th Centuries, *Vols. III & IV, 1837-39. Reprint by A. C. Armstrong and Son, 1891, pp. 271-334.**

HERMANN ULRICI   (essay date 1839)

[*A German scholar, Ulrici was a professor of philosophy and the author of works on Greek poetry and Shakespeare. The following excerpt is from an English translation of his* Über Shakspeares dramatische Kunst, und sein Verhältniss zu Calderon und Göthe, *a work first published in 1839. This study exemplifies the "philosophical criticism" developed in Germany during the nineteenth century. The immediate sources for Ulrici's critical approach appear to be August Wilhelm Schlegel's conception of the play as an organic, interconnected whole and Georg Wilhelm Friedrich Hegel's view of drama as an embodiment of the conflict of historical forces and ideas. Unlike his fellow German Shakespearean critic G. G. Gervinus, Ulrici sought to develop a specifically Christian aesthetics, but one which, as he carefully points out in the introduction to the work mentioned above, in no way intrudes on "that unity of idea, which preeminently constitutes a work of art a living creation in the world of beauty." In his commentary on* King Lear, *Ulrici makes a number of significant points: first, and perhaps foremost, he joins the ranks of such other nineteenth-century critics as August Wilhelm Schlegel (1808), Charles Lamb (1812), Anna Brownell Jameson (1833), and G. G. Gervinus (1849-50) in regarding both Lear's and Cordelia's deaths as necessary to the tragic structure of the play; in fact, he argues that the suffering experienced by such characters as Lear, Gloucester, and Cordelia is entirely the result of their own actions—in the case of the first two, caused by their failure to sustain the "natural" family bond, and in Cordelia's case, the effect of her refusal to humor Lear. For Ulrici, the deaths of these otherwise virtuous characters, and the inability of such noble figures*

as Kent, Albany, Edgar, and the Fool to overcome the moral corruption presented in the drama, demonstrate clearly how both the wicked and the good are equally involved in the same ruin, and that only divine will can set aright such fundamental transgressions in the moral world. Second, Ulrici maintains that the leading principle and center of interest in King Lear *is love—specifically, love as "the natural and most intimate bond of the great organism of society, and consequently as the . . . fundamental condition of all intellectual and moral development." For other discussions of the theme of love in the play, see the excerpts by Edward Dowden (1881), J. Dover Wilson (1932), Oscar James Campbell (1948), Arthur Sewell (1951), Irving Ribner (1958), L. C. Knights (1959), Robert Ornstein (1960), and Robert H. West (1968). Lastly, Ulrici regards Shakespeare's combination of comedy and tragedy in* Lear *as a bold and successful experiment, and he considers the Fool far more important to the thought and structure of the play than any previous commentator. The mixture of comedy and tragedy in* King Lear, *as well as the nature of the Fool's role, has also been discussed by William Hazlitt (1817), H. N. Hudson (1872), G. Wilson Knight (1930), Enid Welsford (1935), Jan Kott (1964), Ronald F. Miller (1975), and Melvin Seiden (1979).*]

In "King Lear," *Love* is once more employed by Shakspeare as a leading principle of human conduct; but under a new and wholly distinct manifestation. It is here exhibited in the last of the three principal forms under which it exercises an immediate and direct influence on the destinies of man, and in that particular one in which it reveals itself as the natural and most intimate bond of the great organism of society, and consequently as the principle and fundamental condition of all intellectual and moral development. . . . In "King Lear," *parental affection* and *filial reverence* are contemplated as the focus towards which all the ties of life converge, and the *family*—in its largest and historical import—is the particular grade of life in which the poet has here taken up his position within the domain of poetry. Such is the particular modification of Shakspeare's general tragic view whch constitutes the groundwork of the present drama.

The high mid-day sun has now sunk into the fresh, glowing, but fast fading tints of evening. The old Lear is still vigorous both in mind and body; his old age has not tempered the faults of his nature; his obstinacy, love of power, passion and rashness, are as strong as ever; his heart still retains all its freshness and impetuosity. The rich measure of love which has fallen to the portion of Lear's heart is blindly lavished by him to the last drops upon his children; he resigns to them his all, in the hope of finding in their love and gratitude repose from the storms and fatigues of his long life. But the affection of Lear leads him to forget the king in the parent, and in a father's care to overlook all other duties. Mistaking the outward sign for the deep internal feeling of affection, he has himself in some measure accustomed his children to flattery and hypocrisy. His error is not momentary, but so wilful and deliberate, that the attempt of Kent (of which the artistic necessity is obvious) to bring him to a better judgment, totally fails, in spite of the pertinacity with which it is repeated. Like the love of Romeo, and Othello, that of Lear is far from being pure from gross and earthly alloy; in him, too, it possesses a character of passionateness, as is shewn in his hasty and unjust banishment of Kent and Cordelia. Its first thought is of the external and terrestrial, not the inward and everlasting welfare of his children. As it has not its root in the divine truth, it consequently mistakes its true nature, and, refusing the genuine return of deep and silent gratitude, accepts in the stead a worthless counterfeit. Such a false, and in fact immoral love of the parent, is, by an intrinsic necessity, closely followed by the perfidy, ingratitude, and guilt of the children. While he judges of true affection, which loves and is silent, by mere outward attentions and protestations; while he apportions to what ought and desires to be its own reward, an external recompense; while he tests it by weight and measure; and thus failing to perceive its intrinsic infinity—its proper essence, and adopting a false standard for the rule of his conduct, he snaps asunder the only stable tie of domestic affection. True family love can only exist in the calm, unconscious, disinterested union of hearts in which outward and inward, objective and subjective, are so perfectly blended into one, that no outward sanction, no notions of right and duty, reward or recompense, are ever pressed into consideration. Accordingly, we must look upon Lear himself as the prime cause of the tragic complication, and the guilty author of his own fate, no less than of the crimes and sufferings of his daughters. He falls the victim of the errors and weakness of his own affectionate heart. Thus invariably does the lovely and noble of this earth hasten to perdition whenever unpurified and earthly: it neglects to look back to its divine origin for its true strength and support.

As Shakspeare everywhere exhibits the most wonderful power in completely exhausting the particular subject he has in hand, so, in the present piece, he is not content with simply exhibiting the fundamental idea in the fortunes of the King and his family. He sets it forth under another aspect. In the same way that he contrasted the passionate ardour of Romeo with the equally guilty but prosaic coldness of Paris, and that the ill-conditioned union of Iago and Emilia is placed side by side of the married bliss of Othello—so pure and genuine, and yet so liable to be disturbed—he has associated the story of Lear and his daughters with the similar but divergent story of Gloster and his sons. In order to shew that a moral corruption is never solitary, but is in its seed and principle *universal,* and ultimately resting on the sinfulness of the whole human race, he has taken the noblest families as representatives of the great family of man, and made them the victims of the moral pestilence. While a passionate unreal tenderness avenges itself on Lear, the fate of Gloster is the consequence of unrepented juvenile excess, on which (as shewn in the first scene) the old man still reflects with wanton pleasure. For the stain of his birth the bastard Edmund punishes his father, who is as credulous and superstitious in his old age as he was light-hearted and thoughtless in youth. While in the one case the open folly of the parent is answered by the open and shameless crimes of the children, in the other secret sins are met by hidden and sanctified enormity. In the former case the family tie is broken, together with the false and rickety foundation on which it rested; in the latter it is annihilated by the retributive poison of a single sin, which from the first had eaten away the only stay of domestic happiness—true purity of heart. With imperious caprice Lear demands the outward semblance for the reality, and his punishment consists, accordingly, in his being stripped of all external splendour, opulence, and power, and reduced to that pure needy nakedness in which the true value of things is first discerned. Gloster, on the other hand, errs *unintentionally.* His light, superficial estimate of marriage, and the other relations of life, which leads him superstitiously to look upon the moral liberty of man as dependent upon a physical necessity, and the actions of man on the phenomena of nature, and the latter itself as a ball in the hand of the gods, has completely blinded him, and for this darkness of the moral vision he is visited with blindness of the physical organ; he is deprived of the sight of his eyes because he was without a pure light of the mind. Lear's stronger and bolder spirit makes head against external troubles; he struggles against the fury of the elements as against the wickedness

of man. It is only from within that he can be conquered; in the violent convulsive effort to master the deep emotions of his heart, the bonds of reason snap asunder, and madness spreads its nightly, veiling darkness over him. The weaker character of Gloster, light-minded in youth, and in old age indiscreet and irresolute, as he indulged in excess during prosperity, so, in misfortune, he mistakes the shadow for the substance: not strong enough for resistance, too weak for madness, and without power to endure, in despair he rushes upon self-destruction.

Nothing, as Schlegel has justly observed, could be a greater mistake than to give a happy close to the play, by restoring the old Lear to the throne he had abdicated [see excerpt above, 1808]. In the opinion of mankind generally, no doubt, the sufferings of both these old men far exceed their transgressions. But, in truth, the exact proportion between the inward sin and its *outward* penalty admits not of very nice determination; for in reality no true ratio subsists between them. This is a truth of daily experience and history, and to illustrate it is our poet's purpose in this and others of his tragedies. Moreover, that retribution which brings the sinner to repentance can never be excessive, simply because thereupon it ceases to be punishment.

Lastly, it was necessary to portray Lear and Gloster as infinitely more sinned against than sinning, in order thereby to point out how sins, such as those of which they were the first cause, spring up like weeds, from small beginnings to an unforeseen magnitude, until they cover the whole soil, and absorb its most precious juices. That their baneful influence should have been stronger on the female mind than on that of men—for Edmund, however guilty, has some palliation to plead in the dishonour of his origin—is but founded on the truth of nature. Since the vocation of woman is domestic life, from which both her character and feelings take their tone, whenever this is corrupt and her sole stay undermined, woman necessarily falls lowers than man, who, by his very nature, is thrown more upon himself, and placed on a wider basis of existence. That the same rank soil should also bear a good and wholesome plant is but another proof of the moral liberty of man, which, independent both of space and time, is restricted neither by relations, parentage, nor circumstance. This truth the poet sets before us in the characters of Cordelia and Edgar on the one hand, and on the other in those of Kent, Albany, and the Fool. But even in these examples virtue has lost something of its proper splendour from contact with the general corruption; as finite human creatures they have not the power to stem the torrent. Cordelia must abandon her home and country; it is only in the meanest disguise that Edgar preserves his life; Kent, with all his love of truth, must stoop to dissimulation to satisfy his unshaken attachment and fidelity to the King; and lastly, Albany, at first weak, irresolute, and inactive, must sink into the very depth of misery before he can rouse his moral energy, and the Fool must hide his compassionate heart, and his correct and profound discernment, beneath the tinsel sparkles of wit. They are not called upon to restore the broken order of right and morality; this nothing less than divine justice can accomplish, which punishes vice at one time by its own hand, at another by the instrumentality of the yet unpolluted virtue. In order to shew forth this truth in its full extent, all these characters were necessary for the development of the fundamental idea of the piece. It is only as such instruments that Edgar and Albany assist in restoring moral order, and healing the disorders of the state, while Kent, after long co-operating with them, is withdrawn, weary of life, from this last business. The Fool, too, and Cordelia, as a woman, can have no part properly in such a task; they retire accordingly from the stage of life as soon as they have fulfilled their part, which was to vindicate the father and the friend, and in his person both morality and justice.

The composition or structure of the piece is here again regulated by the several groups into which the dramatic personages spontaneously fall by reason of their respective characters, or of the predominant relations between them. On one side we have Lear with his family, attended by Kent and the Fool; on the other, Gloster with his two sons Edgar and Edmund. This arrangement of nature is, however, quickly disturbed and altered by the characters of the individuals that compose them. Regan, Goneril, and Cornwall, violently detach themselves from Lear and Cordelia, while Edgar is driven away by the enmity of his father and brother. The realm of darkness separates itself from the region of light. The two old men, though henceforward quite powerless and merely passive, continue nevertheless to be the main-springs of the plot, which by their modes of thinking and acting they originally set in motion. Cordelia and her husband, Edgar and Kent, combine for their assistance, while Edmund, Goneril, Regan, and Cornwall, are allied against them, and between both parties stands Albany, at first indecisive, and vacillating like grey between black and white; but at last, startled out of his culpable inaction by the enormity of crime which surrounds him, he becomes the firm and unwavering representative of the objective dignity of justice and rectitude. Out of the reciprocal action and opposition of these groups the evolution of the plot, and the series of its leading incidents, proceed spontaneously and by an intrinsic necessity. After Lear has disinherited Cordelia, and rendered Kent outwardly powerless by his sentence of banishment, and when Gloster has driven his legitimate and noble son from his home, the two weak old men fall helpless victims to the wickedness and insolence of their enemies. Blow by blow their misery is raised to the highest pitch; wherever the family tie—that foundation of all moral feeling—is so entirely subverted as in the present case, the triumph of evil is necessarily rapid and complete. It is only after it has revelled to the full that a turning point and amelioration can be looked for. Cordelia at last arrives with a French force, and Lear finds refuge with her, while Gloster, in the protection and guidance of Edgar, finds at least an outward peace. But in vain does a foreign power seek to quench the internal disorders of a nation, or to restore the dissevered ties of family and society; it is from within the state itself, and under the punishing and retributive hand of God, that order must spring up anew. Accordingly, Cordelia is defeated, and her enterprise fails of success: on the other hand, Cornwall receives his death-blow from the hand of his own attendant, and by his fall the first step towards restoration is made. Brother next falls by the hand of brother, and the one sister poisons the other, and then slays herself—these horrors, such is the suicidal energy of sin, are the inevitable results of the dissolution of all natural and moral ties. But amidst them all, we clearly trace the guiding finger of God; the officious villain of a steward is providentially delivered into the hands of Edgar, and thereby that discovery of treason brought about which induces Albany to take a decided part against his own wife. In all this there reigns an intrinsic necessity.

But the death of Cordelia: is not this sacrifice of an innocent victim, if not wholly without motive, certainly without poetic justification, and therefore devoid of all ideal necessity? By no means. On closer consideration all such doubt vanishes, and what at first sight looks like a blemish, becomes the highest splendour of perfection. Cordelia pays the penalty of the fault she committed, when, instead of affectionately humouring the weakness of her aged father, she met him with unfilial forwardness, and answered his, no doubt, foolish questions with unbecoming harshness and asperity; a father's curse lights upon her head, and its direful consequences cannot afterwards be avoided. The slighter her failing may appear, the deeper is the tragic effect of its heavy penalty. For the true force of the tragic lies exactly in this, that the trivial faults of the good are overwhelmed in the same ruin as the most revolting offences of the bad; with this difference, however, that whereas to the former purification and atonement (and consequently true life also) is conveyed in its annihilation, to the latter temporary destruction and punishment bring likewise eternal death.

Further: the characters of Lear and the Fool merit a more detailed notice. In no other piece has Shakspeare placed the comic in such close and immediate neighbourhood with the tragic as in this, and with no one has the bold attempt been so successful as with Shakspeare. Instead of disturbing for a moment, by this juxtaposition, the tragic effect, he has contrived, with the most wonderful dexterity, to strengthen and exalt it. Not merely does the wisdom of the Fool gain in depth by its contrast with the madness of the King, whose tragic significance is thereby thrown out in a stronger light; not merely is the mirror held up before the thoughts and deeds of all the personages of the drama, and the light of truth condensed by its reflexion, but even all the profound thoughtfulness of view on which the tragic view of the world ultimately rests, lies hidden in the deep meditative humour of the Fool, against which the tragic form of art is, as it were, broken, in order to display more clearly its inmost core. This genuine humour of the Fool plays, as it were, with the tragical; to it pain or pleasure, happiness or misery, are all the same; it makes a sport of the most heart-rending sufferings and misfortunes of earthly existence; even from death and destruction it can derive amusement. By these qualities he is raised high *above* this earthly existence; and he has already attained to that elevation of the human mind *above* all the pursuits or sorrows of this earthly life, which it is the end of this tragic art to set forth, and which is, as it were, personified in him. The humour itself is, in its very essence, the *sublime* of Comic. Although fully conscious of all the grave seriousness and responsibilities of life, in its profoundest depths, he yet pursues, even with this profundity and seriousness, his sportive mockery, and has no misgivings even because he is raised far above this earth and its interests. Some, we know, have expressed surprise that the poet should have ascribed such greatness and amplitude of mind to a man who could degrade himself by accepting the post of a hired merry-maker. But I, for my part, only see in all this, further cause to admire the profound wisdom of the master-artist. For to one who looks upon the whole of life as nothing, his outward position in it must be immaterial. Accordingly, the Fool departs from this life with a witticism in his mouth— ''He'll go to bed at noon'' [III. vi. 85]. But his sublime elevation is not a mere stoical indifference; it is united with the truest love and fidelity, and the most rare sympathy. His heartfelt sorrow for his dear Cordelia and his beloved King has sapped his life. He cares not to live when the King has lost his senses: his occupation is at an end as soon as he can no longer speak the truth to him who was his sun, and can no longer do him any service; for the King, and no one else, can have any need of him. His sun still stands, no doubt, in the heavens; it is not evening, but it is no longer light, and so the mirror, which it is his duty to hold up to it, cannot now reflect any image. Lastly, it must not be overlooked that Shakspeare has skilfully employed the humour of the Fool, as a motive in the tragic evolution of the plot. For it is evident, that the overthrow of the King's senses is, partly at least, occasioned by the crackbrained fancies with which the Fool keeps constantly mocking the folly of the King, although, no doubt, the assumed madness of Edgar powerfully co-operates in bringing it about. Thus, then, in this as in every other detail, Shakspeare combines the profoundest thought with the most artistic skill, in furnishing adequate cause and motive for all that is said or done in his dramas.

This madness of the King cannot be justified on mere psychological grounds; it would be highly censurable, if it had not a *poetic* justification, in the organic structure of the entire work. But little attention has hitherto been paid to this point. As the family tie—the first and absolutely indispensable foundation of all moral and intellectual development has been irremediably broken, and thereby the whole of human existence completely unsettled, being let loose from its primary source and reality in God; this convulsion and the extreme enormity of sin must be exhibited both internally and externally. Its external and objective manifestation is in the disruption of all human relations, and in the fruitless struggle of good against evil; inwardly and subjectively it attains its climax in the disorganization of the King's mind, whose personality formed the subjective centre of the whole piece. Madness is, as it were, the mind's revolt against itself—the loosening of the bonds between its subjectivity and objectivity, so that the two pass into each other, the merely subjective presentation (imagination) passing into objectivity, and the latter being transformed into merely subjective presentations. Every sin consequently must involve the germ of madness, for it is nothing less than the revolt of the mind from itself, and from its truth and objectivity in God. Nevertheless, as long as the sinner is able to maintain his *Ego*—which in imagination he has set up as the master both of himself and the world—in this untruth, so long does the delusion of sin appear outwardly as consistency, understanding, or truth; the madness remains as yet enclosed in the germ, and in its view of the world and of itself the mind still preserves its adherence. When, however, through the might of circumstance, or the weakness of the body, which must supply the mind with food and vigour for its activity, the sinner's mental energy is broken, and he can no longer maintain his *Ego* in this fancied supremacy, while, at the same time, he is unable to cast off the strong fetters of his sin, and to throw himself upon the mercies of God, then does madness burst from the bud, and becomes total both inwardly and outwardly. It appears no longer a revolt from God alone, but from itself and the world. The mind loses at once its organic centre of gravity, and is chaotically dissolved. This is why madness seizes the King, and not Gloster. For Lear, ''in every inch a king'' [IV. vi. 107], had accustomed himself to the thought of, and set his heart on being the unlimited master of the world; although in boundless love he gives his kingdom away, it is still his sovereign pleasure to measure even affection by his own arbitrary will, and he would lord even over it. Even when he has overthrown this visionary empire by his own folly, he must still command; he fights against the very elements, he is determined to be at least the master of his own sufferings and his own destiny. But for this the necessary powers fail him; and consequently the general disorder of all the moral relations of life terminates in madness. It was only by such an affliction that a character like his could be brought to repentance; and by such means alone could the propitiatory element of tragedy be manifested in his case. It was not until his kingly spirit, his haughty virtue, his energy and sovereignty of will, had been utterly overthrown, that he could be brought to the *humility*

which is the parent of true love, and that love in him could be purified.

Lastly, with what consummate skill has Shakspeare contrived in this drama to place the special in the closest communion with the universal, and to blend the private and domestic fortunes of his dramatic personages with a general historical interest! . . . Lear is depicted as the head not only of a family, but also of the state—as the ruler of a great nation. The more seriously, therefore, and the more directly his domestic circumstances influence the destinies of a whole people, the more clearly does the importance of the family bond appear. The tragedy sets before us the public fortunes of a great nation in the first instance, and ultimately the history of the whole world, as affected by the morality or immorality of private life, and it becomes consequently, not merely in its ideal subject-matter, but also by the course taken by the represented fable, a mirror of history in general. At the same time, the poet's reasons for placing this one alone of his five great tragedies upon the soil of heathenism, and for exhibiting it under a heathenish view of things, becomes apparent. Such a wide-spread corruption of morals, making the highest and noblest families its victims, such an unnatural revolt against the first and most stringent laws and requisitions of nature, could never occur, except in a state of human nature still exposed to the old sin in all its power; among Christians it could only be possible as an exception—as an isolated case. (pp. 199-202)

In the present piece the ground idea of the whole is reflected in all the subordinate parts, more clearly than in any other of Shakspeare's dramas: for the tie between parent and child, which in a high historical sense forms here the basis of the tragic sentiment, has for its foundation wedlock, and the religious sanction of the intercourse of the sexes. Accordingly, strong rays of light are thrown off from this central idea upon both these civilizing influences of human life, and on this account the delineation of Goneril's and Regan's feelings for, and behaviour to their wedded lords, and their adulterous fondness for Edmund, as well as the pure and disinterested affection of the French king for Cordelia, and the selfish conduct of Burgundy, were indispensable. But genuine friendship is a part of domestic life—its sheet-anchor and stay. With as much truth, therefore, as artistic skill, has the poet placed the firm and devoted attachment of Kent and the Fool for Lear, in such prominent contrast with Gloster's tardy and hesitating friendship.

In conclusion, I shall briefly call attention to the thoughtful and appropriate correspondence between the general subject of the drama, and its no less touching than sublime conclusion. Gloster has repented and atoned for his faults. After the failure of his cowardly attempt at self-destruction, by which he weakly sought to rid himself of the burthen of life, he submits and suffers in patience; for man must learn to be patient, or, in other words, to conquer himself. His soul is thus emancipated from its suffering body; in the arms, in the embraces of his long lost son, who repays a father's injustice with child-like love and affection, his heart breaks; the tumult of this his last earthly happiness shakes off the earthly dust from his soul, and it mounts pure and clear to heaven. The weary Kent, too, has fallen asleep; with his sterling, earnest, but rugged virtue, he has lived, struggled, and endured enough; his *softened* heart now longs only for the peace of heaven. Edmund, in his last moments, acknowledges his guilt, and seeks to make all the amends within his power. ''Yet Edmund was beloved,'' *loved* in spite of all his selfishness. These words of comfort convulse him to the soul, and throw upon it the semblance at least of divine love, and we may indulge a hope that he closed his eyes with a sigh of penitence. Goneril and Regan—the unnatural daughters, whose crimes have no ignominy of origin to excuse them, whom their own lust and not circumstances plunged headlong into sin, falling by each other's hands, and are hurried into everlasting misery without hope or pity. How sweet and soothing the contrast, in the filial affection, and the lovely and blissful death, of Cordelia! Lear's madness, too, terminates with his mortal sigh for Cordelia's loss. In this moment of anguish all the rich intensity of love, which sat enthroned in the heart of Lear, has found its worthy object. While the faint sparks of life are extinguishing, his love puts off its last earthly weakness, and ascends purified and refined to heaven. The tragic impression loses its crushing and oppressive horror, and is transmuted into the calm consolatory feeling of a gentle death and a blissful peace. (pp. 203-04)

> *Hermann Ulrici, "Criticisms of Shakspeare's Dramas: 'King Lear'," in his* Shakspeare's Dramatic Art: And His Relation to Calderon and Goethe, *translated by Rev. A.J.W. Morrison, Chapman, Brothers, 1846, pp. 191-204.*

A. BRIGHAM (essay date 1844)

[*Like Charlotte Lennox (1754), John Charles Bucknill (1859), and H. N. Hudson (1872), Brigham regards Lear as insane from the very beginning of the play. In support of his thesis, Brigham claims that the ill-treatment of Lear by his two daughters does not cause his madness, but only accelerates its inevitable course. For an opposing view on the development of Lear's madness, see the excerpts by Henry Hallam (1837-39), Stopford A. Brooke (1913), Harry V. Jaffa (1957), William Frost (1957-58), and John Reibetanz (1977). Brigham's essay was originally published in the* American Journal of Insanity *in July, 1844.*]

Lear's is a genuine case of insanity from the beginning to the end; such as we often see in aged persons. On reading it we cannot divest ourselves of the idea that it is a real case of insanity correctly reported. Still, we apprehend, the play, or *case,* is generally misunderstood. The general belief is, that the insanity of Lear originated solely from the ill-treatment of his daughters, while in truth he was insane before that, from the beginning of the play, when he gave his kingdom away, and banished, as it were, Cordelia and Kent, and abused his servants. The ill-usage of his daughters only aggravated the disease, and drove him to raving madness. Had it been otherwise, the case, as one of insanity, would have been inconsistent and very unusual. Shakespeare and Walter Scott prepare those whom they represent as insane, by education and other circumstances, for the disease,—they predispose them to insanity, and thus its outbreak is not unnatural. In the case of Lear the insanity is so evident before he received any abuse from his daughters, that, professionally speaking, a feeling of regret arises that he was not so considered and so treated. He was unquestionably very troublesome, and by his 'new pranks,' as his daughter calls them, and rash and variable conduct, caused his children much trouble, and introduced much discord into their households. In fact, a little feeling of commiseration for his daughters at first arises in our minds from these circumstances, though to be sure they form no excuse for their subsequent bad conduct. Let it be remembered they exhibited no marked disposition to ill-treat or neglect him until after the conduct of himself and his knights had become outrageous. Then they at first reproved him, or rather asked him to change his course in a mild manner. Thus Goneril says to him: 'I

would you would make use of that good wisdom Whereof I know you are fraught; and put away These dispositions which *of late* transform you From what you rightly are' [I. iv. 219-22]; showing that previously he had been different. This, however, caused an unnatural and violent burst of rage, but did not *originate* his insanity, for he had already exhibited symptoms of it, and it would have progressed naturally even if he had not been thus addressed.

Lear is not after this represented as constantly deranged. Like most persons affected by this kind of insanity, he at times converses rationally.

In the storm-scene he becomes violently enraged, exhibiting what may be seen daily in a mad-house, a paroxysm of rage and violence. It is not until he has seen and conversed with Edgar, 'the philosopher and learned Theban' [III. iv. 157], as he calls him, that he becomes a real maniac. After this, aided by a proper course of treatment, he falls asleep, and sleep, as in all similar cases, partially restores him. But the violence of his disease and his sufferings are too great for his feeble system, and he dies, and dies deranged. The whole case is instructive, not as an interesting story merely, but as a faithful history of a case of *senile insanity,* or the insanity of old age. (pp. 412-13)

> *A. Brigham, in an extract from* A New Variorum Edition of Shakespeare: King Lear, *Vol. 5 by William Shakespeare, edited by Horace Howard Furness, J. B. Lippincott Company, 1880, pp. 412-13.*

G. G. GERVINUS (essay date 1849-50)

[*One of the most widely read Shakespearean critics of the latter half of the nineteenth century, the German critic Gervinus was praised by such eminent contemporaries as Edward Dowden, F.J. Furnivall, and James Russell Lowell; however, he is little known in the English-speaking world today. Like his predecessor Hermann Ulrici, Gervinus wrote in the tradition of the "philosophical criticism" developed in Germany in the mid-nineteenth century. Under the influence of August Wilhelm Schlegel's literary theory and Georg Wilhelm Friedrich Hegel's philosophy, German critics like Gervinus tended to focus their analyses around a search for the literary work's organic unity and ethical import. Generally, Gervinus believed that Shakespeare's works contained a rational ethical system independent of any religion—in contrast to Ulrici, for whom Shakespeare's morality was basically Christian. In the following excerpt, first published in his* Shakespeare Commentaries *in 1849-50, Gervinus compares* King Lear *to the ancient epic myths of the Niebelungen, the Trojan War, and Iphigenia in its portrayal of the passing of a great barbarous age. Within this discussion, Gervinus comments on the savagery of the play, on the extreme nature of its tragedy, and on its central or fundamental theme—which he considers not filial ingratitude, but a dramatization of the effects of moral corruption in the social world. Most later nineteenth- and twentieth-century commentators have since accepted this final point, agreeing that filial ingratitude is only Shakespeare's means of depicting a moral dissolution which is really the essence of his play. For more specific social or political analyses of* King Lear, *see the excerpts by Denton J. Snider (1887), John W. Draper (1937), Theodore Spencer (1942), and Edwin Muir (1946). Gervinus also focuses on the controversy over Cordelia's death, arguing that her destruction is necessary to her role in the play as a "martyr" or "savior" whose mortal sacrifice prepares the way for Lear's redemption. This is one of the earliest allusions to Cordelia as a "Christ figure," an interpretation more fully developed in the essays by R. W. Chambers (1939), Geoffrey L. Bickersteth (1946), Oscar James Campbell (1948), Irving Ribner (1958), L. C. Knights (1959), and René E. Fortin (1979).*]

Shakespeare has heightened the horrors of [the tragedy of *King Lear*] merely by enlarging the original plot. To the story of Lear he has added the episode of Gloster . . . ; the ruin of a second family, the snares laid by an unnatural son for a father and brother, a father incensed against a guiltless son; all these are added to the injustice which Lear commits against one of his children, and which he suffers from the others. This episode, connected as it is by similarity of purport, Shakespeare has linked and united with the main action in the most spirited manner, weaving and combining the double action, as it were, into a single one; but he has not done this without greatly heightening its harshness and cruelty. By placing Gloster's bastard son in the service and affection of the terrible sisters, he causes Goneril's attempt on her husband's life and the poisoning of her sister; he causes, moreover, Cordelia's execution and her father's death. These threefold and fourfold family discords rest further on the broader ground of political intrigues. The degenerate daughters strive by secret designs to re-unite the divided kingdom of the old Lear, while, at the same time, it is threatened by France from without; the secret understanding between Cordelia and the English nobility leads to the cruel blinding of Gloster, and in consequence of this to the death of Cornwall. If this play, therefore, from the excess of wild and unnatural deeds, is more bloody than any other of Shakespeare's tragedies, it becomes even more repulsive from the nature and manner, the form and appearance of its horrors. Even Coleridge, the steady upholder of Shakespeare, called the blinding of Gloster, the actual tearing out of his eyes upon the stage, a scene in which the tragic element is carried to the utmost limits, the *ne plus ultra* of dramatic effect [see excerpt above, 1813]. Not only the mode of Cordelia's death, but her death at all, has been considered unnecessarily cruel. (pp. 612-13)

Is it not a decided proof of the barbarism of the age that a piece of this kind should have been written by Shakespeare, and should have found such decided approbation with his contemporaries? And is it not further an evidence that Shakespeare, however highly we may estimate him, did not wholly escape the infection of this time? At any rate, is it not an evidence that he was only too ready to pander to the coarse taste of the period? We believe in none of these three things. That the age of Shakespeare was rich in manifold culture is proved by its vast literature; that this culture was still defaced by many remnants of barbarism is undeniable from the state of manners generally, and from isolated and not insignificant branches of that literature itself. Nevertheless, we should be wrong in calling an age barbarous, in which the individual could attain to such perfection of culture as that which we admire in Shakespeare . . . . But had Shakespeare, when he wrote *King Lear,* fallen for a time at least into the comparative wildness of this vigorous age? Just as little as the man of fine feeling in our own day, who, having given us proofs of the highest tenderness, of the softest humanity, and of the most melting elegiac sentiment, as Shakespeare has done in *Romeo,* in *Hamlet,* and in *Cymbeline*—just as little as this man of fine feeling and delicate organisation in our own day would have done, if he were to undertake, with competent poetic skill, to hold up to the wilder moments of the present their own image reflected in the mirror of the past. When, however, Shakespeare carried the tragic element to its utmost limits in *Lear,* as Coleridge says is the case, did he not, at any rate, do too much homage to the rude taste of the ruder portion of society, inasmuch as he derogated by this somewhat from the dignity of his art? *If* he had in any wise derogated from the dignity of his art, then certainly he would have deserved the reproach by having un-

justly pandered to the rude taste of the masses. But have we not seen Shakespeare even in comedy using the burlesque caricatures of the low popular farces, and ennobling them by the spirited connection into which he brought them with the finer forms of his comedies? And may not our poet just as well have sought for a means of using the horrors of the coarse tragedy in Marlowe's style for a higher moral and artistic aim, making the wildness and atrocity of passion, carried to the utmost bounds, serve as the true aim and object of a work of art? Must not a mind of this magnitude have felt that the strongest poetic genius finds alone the scope necessary for it in the representation of the strongest passions? Must he not have felt that there was good reason why the ancients took their subjects from the old primitive heroic ages, where they could venture to invest the more grandly-formed natures with mightier powers? And is it not an acknowledged fact that Shakespeare attained the highest excellence of his art in the delineation of this unrestrained humanity, in *Macbeth,* in *Hamlet,* and especially in *Lear*? How often has *Lear* been called the grandest and noblest of all his dramas! How was Schlegel amazed at 'the almost superhuman flight of genius' in this work, 'where the mind loses itself just as much in the contemplation of all its heights and depths, as the first impression overpowers the feelings!' [in his *Course of Lectures on Dramatic Art and Literature*]. These and similar confessions of admiration have been made, partly without hesitating at the harsh matter, and partly in spite of it; but it may be a question whether they are not merited also just as much *on account of* the colossal matter which, in horror and savageness of the events themselves, exceeds all natural greatness, and on account of the extraordinary development of the plot. (pp. 613-15)

In *Hamlet* and *Macbeth,* in *Othello* and *Timon,* everything turns on one single principal character. In *Lear* and *Cymbeline,* Shakespeare takes a much wider subject. If in those tragedies one single passion and its development were essentially treated, in *Lear* and *Cymbeline* whole ages and races are, as it were, represented. We are not here confined especially to individual characters; even in *Lear* this is not really the case, and in *Cymbeline* far less so. Twofold or still more manifold actions are united; characters equally important and fascinating move in greater number, in mutual relation; the actual matter gains greatly thereby in richness, extent, and compressed fulness; and we have only separately to select the enterprises of a Kent or an Oswald, to find what a mass of facts in well-connected order lies almost concealed even in the subordinate parts, though at first glance it may be easily overlooked in the abundance of matter. Both these plays, on this account, are richer in events than all others, and approach more nearly to the character of the epic than even the histories did; and they are, therefore, still more opposed to the ancient drama than Shakespeare's other works. This very extension of the events is the cause why these plays are less rich than others in explanatory sentences, why the actions themselves are left to explain the essential point of the whole, and why the accurate consideration of events is as important here as the psychological development of character. (pp. 615-16)

In *Lear* the poet . . . brings actively before us a whole race endowed with that barbaric strength of passion, in which, almost without exception, the resistance of reason and conscience over the emotions of passion is powerless or dead. In *Cymbeline* he has once again represented the same heathenish race, but in a more advanced period; in that play, in perfect contrast to *Lear,* he has portrayed those rare characters in whom the heroic power of self-command and moral energy displays that superior strength necessary to conquer the mighty passions peculiar to such times. It was intentionally, therefore, that he depicted in *Lear* such full bursts of passion. It was not by chance that he placed in this very play the barbarities of the Duke of Cornwall, a second instance of which is not to be found in the other dramas of the poet. The excessive rudeness and vehemence of Kent have not been given indifferently to every coarse fellow of every other age. The filial ingratitude in the hardened hearts of Lear's daughters, the unnatural breach of the most natural family ties, have not been blindly transferred at pleasure to other races. Such depraved natures, without a trace of conscience, have not been given to the greater number of the characters of other plays as they are in this; nay, the most abandoned individuals in his deepest tragedies, Richard and Iago, are not entirely devoid of this sting of conscience.

'Men are as the time is,' says Edmund in our play; 'to be tender-minded does not become a sword' [V. iii. 30-2]. Nor an iron age either, was the poet's opinion, an age in which impulses grow to ungovernable strength, and crime to a gigantic enormity. . . . Special weight is laid upon the fact that it is a heathenish time; nature is the goddess of Lear as well as of Edmund; chance reigns above, power and force below. The best of this race know of no inner strength, of no noble will, of no calmness and self-command, and of no moral principle, whereby the power of the blood can be broken, the impulse of passion controlled, and immoderate desires bridled. All, and especially the best, with fatalistic feeling attribute the acts of men to the influence of nature and the stars; eclipses of the sun and moon bring, according to Gloster's opinion, those frightful scourges of humanity [I. ii. 103ff]; and to the true-hearted Kent the different dispositions of Lear's daughters are a proof that not education, not inherited blood, but the blind stars 'govern the conditions' of men [IV. iii. 32-5]. It is only the very worst of all of them, the free-thinking Edmund, who ridicules this convenient apology for our crimes and passions by imputing them to planetary influence, because he alone is conscious of inward strength of will and mind, although he turns it to profligate uses. If he, as it were on principle, gives the rein to his selfishness, it is, on the contrary, the rule of the race generally to follow vague instincts and the bent of the inclination, and to give free course to the throng of unchained passions, without any scruple of mind or morality. . . . No sting of conscience pricks most of the evil-doers here either before, or during, or after the deed; no agonised reflection upon consequences restrains from crime; here is no Hamlet, no Macbeth, with exciting fancy, with terrifying powers of imagination, with the tender yearnings of an innate moral nature. These daughters of Lear, this Edmund, this Cornwall, this Oswald, frustrated in their designs, meet death without a symptom of remorse. Better natures, such as Lear and Gloster, when their faults bring on them natural punishments, fall from happiness to despair; the one becomes mad, and the other looks upon men as the sport of the gods. . . . All human nature, in such a generation, goes blindly to extremes. Even goodness, where it does appear, fidelity, uprightness, modesty, and self-rule, are all in the extreme. It is a humanity as yet uncultivated, knowing no religious ordinances, no moral laws, no ripeness of experience; a generation near akin to the 'bare, forked animal' of Edgar [III. iv. 107-08], cast rough out of nature's hand. In this state of nature it is relationship that first imposes a law and sets a limit. The tie of blood everywhere first quenches the thirst for ruling and possessing, and destroys the selfishness of the individual. But here self-love rends even these strongest ties of nature. A passionate father, on the point of sacrificing everything for his children, reaps apparent and real ingratitude

from them; he turns his wrath and persecution against dutifulness and truth, and bestows his benefits on flattery and falsehood, in consequence of which he is subjected to the most terrible ill-treatment. A tender father has begotten an adder in adultery, a natural son, who strives to destroy him, and through him his lawfully born brother. Brother against brother, children against parents, and parents against children, husband against wife, are incensed one against the other in the selfish spirit of persecution—a powerful picture of human brutality. The discords in these families form in a manner the central point of this tragedy, so that we are tempted to perceive at the first glance the ruling idea to be the exhibition of filial ingratitude. But the idea of this work is in truth far more comprehensive, and these family discords are rather the body than the soul of the play. But they add to the horror of the matter: similar things, committed by stranger against stranger, would not have had the same fearful weight. These actions, accumulated as they are in the bosom of the closest relationship, represent, says Schlegel, 'a great rebellion in the moral world: the picture becomes gigantic and creates horror, such as would be excited by the idea of the heavenly bodies escaping from their ordained orbits' [see excerpt above, 1808]. (pp. 618-21)

King Lear, in the extremity of age and desolation, looks back upon a time when he was 'every inch a king' [IV. vi. 107], when enemies fled before his sword; and even in his madness the rays of his royal and heroic mind burst forth. In peaceful circumstances he wears a lordly form and a majesty of aspect that well become him; in moments of provocation, 'when he stared, the subject quaked' [IV. vi. 108]. . . . This was his nature; it had become his habit through power and greatness, through the prosperity which had never left him, and had never permitted a thought of misfortune and misery. . . . If we picture such a man still endowed with that strength of passion which makes him not only the child but the very king of that heroic age, we shall require nothing further for the full understanding of his conduct in the opening scene, which has so often been censured. Goethe called this scene absurd; I consider it as true to nature as any other that Shakespeare has written. The inquiry concerning the degree of his daughters' love was found by the poet ready to his hand, and he sacredly retained it according to his custom; he did not find it necessary to give it an air of greater probability . . . ; he left it to the spectator's imaginative power to explain this singular introduction to the division of the inheritance, by referring it to the manners of the time and to the disposition and age of the king. The old king wishes to resign his rank and possessions in favour of his children; in a character such as his this act is one of great renunciation and affectionate trust. For this sacrifice he expected to receive beforehand expressions of gratitude; the selfishness which accompanied his affection produces in him the desire to enjoy the filial protestations of his daughters, while, as Coleridge says, the rooted habit of ruling changes this desire at once into an actual demand. Thereupon, from his favourite child, 'the balm of his age' [I. i. 215], upon whose filial duty he had especially reckoned he receives in the public solemn assembly a cold 'nothing' in answer to his question [I. i. 87ff], and ashamed and undeceived he gives vent to his 'hideous rashness' [I. i. 151]. The whole ungovernable nature of a man who had never learned to master the ebullitions of his passion bursts violently forth. He gives up his kingdom to the two elder sisters, in order . . . with fierce obstinacy to close the way to repentance and retractation; he banishes the remonstrating Kent, his most faithful servant; he casts off his child and loads her with sudden hate in the place of his old love; keen-sighted in his rage, he easily frightens away her wooer, Burgundy, and endeavours to dismiss the unselfish France. . . . It is a 'poor judgment' [I. i. 290-92] with which, according to the declaration of the other daughters, he has cast off the youngest, but this does not make the scene absurd. It is the character of rash passion to cause violent mental shocks without sufficient grounds. The poet knew this well, and he has, therefore, contrasted this rash passion of Lear with the just and well-founded rage of the brave Kent, who, even while his life is in danger, tells the king plainly of his injustice, and casts upon him the heavy reproach—

> Kill thy physician, and the fee bestow
> Upon the foul disease.
>
> [I. i. 163-64]

This disease is now to seize the old hero; the punishment of his last folly follows close upon it, but the long-deferred strokes belong to a long catalogue of faults, which reach their climax in the act of the division of his kingdom. Now that he has renounced his paternal authority, the long submission of his elder daughters to the humours of his old age gives way at once to the abnegation of all filial piety, and their former hypocrisy and falsehood are changed into open ingratitude. (pp. 622-24)

The similar discord in Gloster's family has arisen from points in Gloster's character entirely opposite to those in Lear's. A good, mild, unexcitable man, of easy mind and manners, lax and superstitious, Gloster has created his own trouble, just as Lear has drawn down his misery upon himself. He has a natural son, through whom his breach of the marriage-vow is to be avenged; he has indeed in addition done everything in education and treatment that could provoke the bastard against him. For nine years he kept him away from his house, and he intends to send him away again; he is ashamed of him, and owns this to a stranger with little delicacy in Edmund's presence. The secret machinations of this base-born second son are in the first place directed against the legitimate first-born, Edgar, but they re-act upon the father, who credulously allows himself to become the bastard's tool. In Edmund, Shakespeare has repeated the main features of Richard III. And Iago; he has rather sketched them, we might say, as if he left the character for granted. He has endowed him with outward beauty, which (to use Bacon's words) is that with respect to his wickedness which a pure garment is to ugliness; he invests him with the premeditated wickedness and bitterness of Richard, a bitterness awakened in Richard by disgust at his natural deformity, and in Edmund by annoyance at the defect of his birth and family prejudices. Like Richard, Edmund aspires (and indeed without declaring it) after the prospect which offers itself with regard to the kingdom; he brings ruin on this account first into his own house, and then by his shameless connection with both Lear's daughters into their two families; subsequently, with Goneril's concurrence, upon Lear and Cordelia herself. With this far-stretching ambition, Edmund unites Iago's cold reason and selfish calculation, his realistic free-thinking, his indifference to any means that suit him, his hypocrisy which considers lack of dissimulation as mental weakness, and his perseverance and skill in changing the modes by which he pursues his ends as opportunity serves. . . . Such is the son by whom the old Gloster allows himself to be led to rob the noble Edgar of his inheritance, just as Lear deprives Cordelia of hers, and to pursue his life with cruel obstinacy. For this purpose he confides in Edmund, as Lear does in his elder daughters, and reaps the most shameless treachery for his true adherence to Lear. We cannot justify the putting out of Gloster's eyes *upon the*

stage; although Shakespeare, by the singular circumstance of making a nameless and unknown servant take instant vengeance on the perpetrator of the deed, has given prompt satisfaction to the natural indignation consequent upon such an atrocity. The blinding indeed was Shakespeare's express intention, but this could certainly have been attained as well if the action had been placed behind the scenes. He stumbled, Gloster himself says, when he saw; and Edgar perceives the judgment of Providence in that 'the dark and vicious place where Edmund was begot cost him his eyes' [V. iii. 173-74]. Poor and blind, Gloster now wanders about like Lear; led *by* the child whom he had cast off, as Lear was led *to* his banished one; in like despair, though it takes different ways. Like Lear, he bethinks himself upon poverty for the first time in his own need, and preaches that community of goods which he had never thought of when he possessed them. . . . Like Lear, also, he despairs of the world and records the triumph of the wicked, expressing it in that fearful sentence—

> As flies to wanton boys are we to the gods;
> They kill us for their sport!
>
> [IV. i. 36-7]

Even before his eyes were put out, when oppressed only by his own and Lear's family troubles, Gloster called himself 'almost mad'; subsequently, at the sight of Lear he wishes for himself the same fate, that 'his thoughts might be severed from his griefs' [IV. vi. 282]. But his softer and more elastic nature prevents this; despair drives the less obdurate but equally abandoned one to contemplate suicide, which never entered the thoughts of the revengeful Lear; thus he would scorn the cruelty of fate and escape its arbitrary will. But from this step Edgar restrains him and becomes to him in his despair a spirit-healer and a ministering angel, just as Cordelia is to Lear. (pp. 632-34)

[Cordelia] is one of the tenderest of Shakespeare's creations, hard to be understood, yet simple and clear to those who feel rightly. . . . The dying Lear gives us a perfect and visible picture of her sweet feminine nature in those few words: 'Her voice was ever soft, gentle, and low, an excellent thing in woman!' [V. iii. 273-74]. Richer in love than in tongue, she possessed not the 'glib and oily art to speak and purpose not'; what she 'well intends, she'll do't before she speaks' [I. i. 224-26]. . . . Feminine simplicity and modesty, a want or 'tardiness in nature' [I. i. 235], as her future husband calls it, helps to chain her tongue in the opening scene, and makes her utter the fatal word which decides her fate. The natural shyness of such a being to speak before a great assembly, and the perfect truthfulness of her soul which directs her to retain half her love for her husband, combine to cause this strange reticence; above all she is actuated in her decision by a sickening contempt and scorn of her sisters, which she cannot longer suppress. In the 'milky gentleness' of her disposition there is mingled a drop of gall from her father's obstinacy; by this delicate stroke Shakespeare has linked her to the age and to the family character. . . . In the progress of the story she now proves how fully her intention was to fulfil her bounden duty to that father; she proves also how it belongs to her nature to do what she intends before she speaks. . . . And thus she acts even in a fatal manner by . . . stepping forward for the restoration of her father. Henceforth she has only the one thought of saving him; filial feeling breaks now as strongly forth into action as at first when words were required it had seemed to draw back. Hence it is that she commits a second and still greater imprudence than before, which makes her now a martyr to her filial love as before to her love of truth. In this unsuspicious-ness, in this involuntary obedience to the promptings of sacred feelings, she resembles Desdemona. At that time, in her con-viction of doing right, she had not weighed in what she did too little for her indeed deceived parent; she does not now weigh in what she does too much for him; what, done other-wise, might have led to another end. Ethical justice is in this play especially emphasised strongly by the poet himself. *Where lies the justice of Cordelia's death?* Why is Edgar to have a better fate, when he is just that to his father which Cordelia is to Lear? It is this very difference, however, in the fate of the two which guides us to the meaning of the poet. It is precisely the wise and prudent forethought, evident in all his actions, which places Edgar as a pure contrast to Cordelia. His means stand ever in well-considered relation to his aims; it is not so with Cordelia's. She attacks *England* with a French force in order to restore her *father*. The whole responsibility of this step falls upon her. . . . Cordelia, like Desdemona, falls a sacrifice to her own nature; but the circumstances that accom-pany her death are of a much more reconciling kind. She is conquered in battle, but she has attained the higher conquest, which is all she thought of; she has outwardly restored and inwardly saved her father. . . . When Lear hears of her arrival, deep shame allows him not to see her. The daughter stands beside him as he sleeps, overflowing with filial feelings and with tender words. He awakes, and glad anxiety surprises her; now again she has no words to say. The awakened Lear speaks wanderingly, yet to the purpose; ashamed in the presence of Cordelia, he feels himself as if in the fires of purgatory; when he is again master of his senses he doubts anew; he recognises her, and falls on his knees before her; he is subdued into a tender mood, which in such a nature agreeably surprises us. Is there anything more touching in poetry or more effective on the stage than this recognition? . . . To me it appears that it alone makes ample amends for all the bitter subject of this tragedy; and indeed the whole of the fourth act of *Lear* is without its equal in dramatic poetry. . . . [Lear's] curse had once been, 'So be my grave my peace, as here I give her father's heart from her!' [I. i. 125-26]. It is fulfilled when he restores his heart to her. Over her corpse the recognition of Kent, the death of his daughters, and the recovery of his throne are but as sounds which scarcely reach his ear; no worldly joy can rebuild this 'great decay.' To Kent's contentment, and we must indeed say to our own, he follows his departed child, set free from 'the rack of this rough world' [V. iii. 315]. . . . [Lear] recognised in her the martyr and saviour—the precursor of a better time. This was Shakespeare's meaning in her death; if, indeed, like Desdemona, she falls partly in consequence of her nature, she falls at the same time a sacrifice to the errors of the age and surounding circumstances. . . . As to these angel forms in Shakespeare's plays, to those pure ones who fall guiltless sacrifices to fate, death is but the entrance to their proper home, so to this being death for her father and the sealing of her filial love with her blood is no misfortune. (pp. 637-41)

The tragic end of a whole generation of a bloody race is thus depicted in *King Lear*. . . . The past ages of ancient and me-diaeval nations have produced those great epic myths, the Tro-jan legend and the 'Niebelungen Lied,' which similarly cele-brate the downfall of barbarous races, whose place is occupied by descendants of more advanced civilisation; and from such periods of Tantalus-like horror arise those Iphigenias and Pe-nelopes, who, like Cordelia in our present play, are the pre-cursors of a better generation. With these tragic epics of old can this epic tragedy alone be compared. The drama has not

space sufficient to depict the struggles of whole races and peoples; it is obliged to limit itself to the representation of a similar catastrophe in families. But in this narrower compass the task of the epos has been accomplished. The poet in this work, in this creation of his own, approaches the most com-prehensive works of epic national poetry, the growth, as it were, of centuries; and Aristotle, could he have seen this, would now more than ever have awarded his praise to tragedy: that with smaller means it attained to the great object of the epos. Though Shakespeare at this time might have read the Homeric poems, he had no idea of emulating these magnificent myths in his drama. At the most his great success was the result of a vague desire to strain the theme of his tragedies higher and higher in emulation of these poetic achievements. He imagined just as little that this work would admit of so bold a comparison, as that his *Hamlet* would be a mirror to generations of centuries to come. But if the uncalculating in-stinct of genius in our poet has anywhere or in any wise pro-duced greater things than his conscious and far-seeing under-standing planned, it is here. (pp. 641-42)

      G. G. Gervinus, "'King Lear'," in his Shakespeare Commentaries, *translated by F. E. Bunnètt, revised edition, 1877. Reprint by AMS Press Inc., 1971, pp. 611-43.*

JOHN CHARLES BUCKNILL (essay date 1859)

[*Bucknill was a nineteenth-century English physician who spe-cialized in mental disorders. He wrote several articles dealing with Shakespeare's knowledge of medicine, psychology, and in-sanity and discussed the dramatist's use of this knowledge in his plays. Bucknill's essay on* King Lear *is the most extensive of those studies devoted to a clinical examination of the development of Lear's madness. In the following excerpt, he claims—as did Char-lotte Lennox (1754) and A. Brigham (1844)—that Lear is ob-viously insane from the very beginning of the play. It is only by viewing the king in this light, Bucknill asserts, that the opening scene makes sense. For opposing interpretations of Lear's mad-ness, as well as reassessments of the play's first scene, see the excerpts by Henry Hallam (1837-39), Stopford A. Brooke (1913), Harry V. Jaffa (1957), William Frost (1957-58), and John Rei-betanz (1977).*]

Essayists upon [*King Lear*] have followed each other in giving an account of the development of Lear's character and madness, which we cannot but regard as derogatory to the one, and erroneous in relation to the other. They have described Lear as an old man, who determines upon abdication, and the par-tition of his kingdom, while he is of sane mind, and fully capable of appreciating the nature of the act. Thence it becomes necessary to view the original character of Lear as that of a vain weak old man; thence it becomes necessary to discuss the point when the faculties first give way; thence it becomes necessary to view the first acts of the drama as a gross im-probability. "Lear is the only serious performance of Shake-speare," says Coleridge, "the interest and situations of which are derived from the assumption of a gross improbability" [see excerpt above, 1813]. Such undoubtedly they would be, if they were the acts of a sane mind; but if, on the contrary, it be accepted that the mind of the old king has, from the first, entered upon the actual domain of unsoundness, the gross im-probability at once vanishes, and the whole structure of the drama is seen to be founded, not more upon "an old story rooted in the popular faith," than upon the verisimilitude of nature. The accepted explanation of Lear's mental history, that he is at first a man of sound mind, but of extreme vanity and feeble power of judgment, and that, under the stimulus of subsequent insanity, this weak and shallow mind develops into the fierce Titan of passion, with clear insight into the heart of man, with vast stores of life science, with large grasp of morals and polity, with terrible eloquence making known as with the voice of inspiration the heights and depths of human nature; that all this, under the spur of disease, should be developed from the sterile mind of a weak and vain old man; this, indeed, is a gross improbability, in which we see no clue to explanation. (pp. 128-29)

Hallam expresses unreservedly the opinion that Lear's wondrous intellectual vigour and eloquence are the result of his madness, and that the foundation of his character is that of a mere "headstrong, feeble, and selfish being" [see excerpt above, 1837-39]. (p. 130)

If this great and sound critic had possessed any practical knowledge of mental pathology, he could not have taken this view of the development of the character. Intellectual energy may, indeed, sometimes be seen to grow stronger under the greatest trials of life, but never when the result of these trials is mental disease. So far as eloquence is the result of passion, excitement of passion may stimulate its display; and it is remarkable that so long as Lear retains the least control over his passion, his imagination remains comparatively dull, his eloquence tame. It is only when emotional expression is unbridled, that the majestic flow of burning words finds vent. It is only when all the barriers of conventional restraint are broken down, that the native and naked force of the soul displays itself. The display arises from the absence of restraint, and not from the stimulus of disease. (p. 131)

The willfulness with which critics have refused to see the symptoms of insanity in Lear, until the reasoning power itself has become undeniably alienated, is founded upon that view of mental disease which has, until recently, been entertained even by physicians, and which is still maintained in courts of law, namely, that insanity is an affection of the intellectual, and not of the emotional part of man's nature. . . . It may suffice to state, that with the exception of those cases of insanity which arise from injuries, blood poisons, sympathetic irritations, and other sources of an unquestionably physical nature, the common causes of insanity are such as produce emotional changes, either in the form of violent agitation of the passions, or that of a chronic state of abnormal emotion, which pronounces itself in the habitually exaggerated force of some one passion or desire, whereby the healthy balance of the mind is at length destroyed. From these and other reasons founded upon the symptomatology and treatment of insanity, upon the definite operation of the reasoning faculties, and their obvious inability to become motives for conduct without the intervention of emotional influence, and also from the wide chasm which intervenes, and must intervene, between all the legal and medical definitions of insanity founded upon the intellectual theory and the facts as they are observed in the broad field of nature, the conclusion appears inevitable, that no state of the reasoning faculty can, by itself, be the cause or condition of madness; congenital idiocy and acquired dementia being alone excepted. (pp. 133-34)

How completely is this theory supported by the development of insanity, as it is pourtrayed in Lear! Shakespeare, who painted from vast observation of nature, as he saw it without and felt it within, places this great fact broadly and unmistakably before us. It has, indeed, been long ignored by the exponents of medical and legal science, at the cost of ever futile attempts

to define insanity by its accidents and not by its essence; and, following this guidance, the literary critics of Shakespeare have completely overlooked the early symptoms of Lear's insanity; and, according to the custom of the world, have postponed its recognition until he is running about a frantic, raving, madman.

Lear is king at a time when kings are kings. Upon his will has hung the life and wealth, the being and the having, of all around. Law exists indeed; the reverend man of justice and his yoke-fellow of equity are benched high in the land, but he is the little godhead below.

> Aye, every inch a king.
> When I do stare, see how the subject quakes!
> [IV. vi. 107-08]

Perilous height, too giddy for the poor human brain! Uneasy lies the head which wears a crown! Unsafely thinks the head which wears a crown! (pp. 134-35)

This fact of royalty in Lear; that he has been eighty years and more a prince and king, that he is not only despotic in authority but in disposition, that his will can tolerate no question, no hindrance; this, if not the primary cause of his lunacy, gives colour and form to it. He strives to abdicate, but cannot; even madness cannot dethrone him; authority is stamped legibly on his brow; he is not alone a mad man but a mad king.

Unhappy king, what was thy preparation for thy crown of sorrows, thy sceptre of woe! Unlimited authority; that is, isolation. To have no equals, that is to say, no friends; to be flattered to the face, and told that there were gray hairs in the beard before the black ones were there, plied with lies from early youth, (for this teaches that Lear was a king before he wore a beard), and therefore to be set on a pedestal apart from his kind, even from his own flesh and blood, until all capacity to distinguish truth from falsehood, affection from hypocrisy is lost, this is thy preparation.

Half a century of despotic power, yielded by a mortal of rash and headstrong temper, and with vivid poetic imagination, may well produce habitudes of mind to which any opposition will appear unnatural and monstrous as if the laws of nature were reversed, to which the incredible fact can be accepted only with astonishment and unbounded rage.

But Lear's mind is conditioned by extreme age as well as by despotism; age which too often makes men selfish, unsympathising, and unimpressible. . . . A sad state, one of labour and sorrow, and dangerous to happiness, honour, and sanity. The natural state of old age is, that the judgment matures as the passions cool; but a tendency of equal force is, that the prevailing habitudes of the mind strengthen as years advance; and a man who, in "the best and soundest of his time hath been but rash" [I. i. 295-96], feels himself, and makes those around him feel, "not alone the imperfections of engrafted condition, but therewithal the unruly waywardness that infirm and choleric years bring with them" [I. i. 296-99]; a maxim not less true because it is the heartless observation of a thankless child, and one capable of being extended to almost all the prevailing emotions and tendencies of man. In old age, the greedy man becomes a miser; in old age, the immoral man becomes the shameless reprobate; in old age, the unchecked passions of manhood tend to develop themselves into the exaggerated proportions of insanity. How stern a lesson is the folly, the extravagance, and the vice of old men, that while it is yet time, passion should be brought into subjection, and the proportions and balance of the mind habitually submitted to the ordinances of the moral law! (pp. 136-37)

Coleridge justly observes, that "it was not without forethought, nor is it without its due significance, that the division of Lear's kingdom is, in the first six lines of the play, stated as a thing determined in all its particulars previously to the trial of professions, as the relative rewards of which the daughters were to be made to consider their several portions" [see excerpt above, 1813]. "They let us know that the trial is a silly trick, and that the grossness of the old king's rage is in part the result of a silly trick suddenly and most unexpectedly baffled and disappointed."

That the trial is a mere trick is unquestionable; but is not the significance of this fact greater than Coleridge suspected? Does it not lead us to conclude, that from the first the king's mind is off its balance; that the partition of his kingdom, involving inevitable feuds and wars, is the first act of his developing insanity; and that the manner of its partition, the mock-trial of his daughters' affections, and its tragical denouement, is the second, and but the second act of his madness? The great mind, so vigorous in its mad ravings, with such clear insight into the heart of man that all the petty coverings of pretence are stripped off in its wild eloquence, not only is unable to distinguish between the most forced and fulsome flattery and the genuineness of deep and silent love; it cannot even see the folly of assuming to apportion the three exact and predetermined thirds of the kingdom according to the professions made in answer to the "silly trick;" cannot even see that after giving away two-thirds, the remainder is a fixed quantity, and cannot be more or less according to the warmth of the professions of his youngest and favorite daughter. . . . (pp. 138-39)

With what courtly smoothness of pretence goes on the mocking scene, until Cordelia's real love, and obstinate temper, and disgust at her sister's hypocrisy, and repugnance perhaps at the trick she may see through, interrupt the old king's complacent vanity; and then the astonishment, the retained breath, the short sentences, the silence before the storm! and then the outbreak of unbridled rage, in that terrible curse in which he makes his darling daughter—her whom he loved best, whom he looked to as the nurse of his age—for ever a stranger to his heart! It is madness or it is nothing. Not, indeed, raving, incoherent, formed mania, as it subsequently displays itself; but exaggerated passion, perverted affection, enfeebled judgment, combining to form a state of mental disease—incipient indeed, but still disease—in which man, though he may be paying for past errors, is for the present irresponsible. (p. 139)

[The scene on the heath] is but the climax of the disease, the catastrophy of the mind history. The malady, which has existed from the first, has increased and developed, until it is now completed. And yet writers generally agree with Coleridge in considering that Lear only becomes actually insane at this point, and some indeed have endeavoured to mark the precise expression which indicates the change from sanity to insanity. That which they (under the vulgar error that raving madness, accompanied by delusion, is alone to be considered real insanity) take to be the first signs, I may enquire into as the signs of the first crisis, or complete development of the disease. It is to be remarked that Lear's first speeches in the storm, beginning

> Blow winds and crack your cheeks; rage, blow!
> Rumble thy bellyfull, spit fire, spout rain!
>
> [III. ii. 1, 14]

Act IV. Scene vi. Attendants, Lear, and Edgar. Frontispiece to the Rowe edition (1709). By permission of the Folger Shakespeare Library.

and even his frantic demeanour, as he contends unbonneted with the elements, are the same in character as his language and conduct have been hitherto. There is no difference in quality, although the altered circumstances make the language more inflated, and the conduct more wild. He has, before this time, threatened, cursed, wept, knelt, beaten others, beaten his own head. Under the exciting influence of exposure to a storm so terrible as to awe the bold Kent who never, since he was a man, remembers the like; under this excitement, it is no wonder that the "poor, infirm, weak, and despised old man" [III. ii. 20], should use the extremest emphasis of his eloquence. These speeches, therefore, do not more appear the frantic rant of insanity than much which has preceded them. Still less can I admit, as evidence of delusion, the accusation directed against the elements, that they are "servile ministers" of his "pernicious daughters" [III. ii. 21, 22]. This seems but a trope of high-flown eloquence, consistent with the character and the circumstances. The real critical point where delusion first shews itself I place a little further on, where Lear for the first time sees Edgar, and infers, with the veritable logic of delusion, that a state of misery so extreme must have been the work of his unkind daughters. Before this point, however, is reached, an event occurs very notable, although likely to escape notice, than which there is nothing in this great case from the poet's note book more remarkably illustrating his profound knowledge of mental disease, not only in its symptomatology, but in its causation and development. It is *the addition of a physical cause* to those moral causes which have long been at work.

Lear's inflated speeches, which indicate resistance to the warring elements, are followed by a moment of resignation and of calm, as if he were beaten down by them. He "will be a pattern of all patience" [III. ii. 37]. He thinks of the crimes of other men, in that speech of regal dignity: "Let the great gods find out their enemies now" [III. ii. 49-51]. He is "a man more sinned against than sinning" [III. ii. 59-60]. The energy of rage and of frantic resistance has passed by. Calmer thought succeeds, and then comes this remarkable admission:

> My wits begin to turn,
> Come on, my boy: How do'st my boy? art cold?
> I'm cold myself.—Where is this straw, my fellow?
> The art of our necessities is strange,
> That can make vile things precious. Come, your hovel;
> Poor fool and knave, I've one string in my heart
> That's sorry yet for thee.
>
> [III. ii. 67-73]

The import of this must be weighed with a speech in the last act, when Lear is incoherent and full of delusion, but calmer than at this time, and with the reason and impertinency mixed of complete mania:

> When the rain came to wet me once, and the wind to make me chatter; when the thunder would not peace at my bidding; there I found 'em, there I smelt 'em out. Go to, they are not men o' their words; they told me I was everything: 'tis a lie: I am not ague proof.
>
> [IV. vi. 100-05]

This is thoroughly true to nature. Insanity, arising from mental constitution, and moral causes, often continues in a certain state of imperfect development; . . . a state of exaggerated and perverted emotion, accompanied by violent and irregular conduct, but unconnected with intellectual aberration; until some physical shock is incurred—bodily illness, or accident, or exposure to physical suffering; and then the imperfect type of mental disease is converted into perfect lunacy, characterised by more or less profound affection of the intellect, by delusion or incoherence. This is evidently the case in Lear, and although I have never seen the point referred to by any writer, and have again and again read the play without perceiving it, I cannot doubt from the above quotations, and especially from the second, in which the poor madman's imperfect memory refers to his suffering in the storm, that Shakespeare contemplated this exposure and physical suffering as the cause of the first crisis in the malady. Our wonder at his profound knowledge of mental disease increases, the more carefully we study his works; here and elsewhere he displays with prolific carelessness a knowledge of principles, half of which, if well advertized, would make the reputation of a modern psychologist.

It is remarkable, that in the very scene where Lear's madness is perfected, his first speeches are peculiarly reasoning and consecutive. Shakespeare had studied mental disease too closely, not to have observed the frequent concurrence of reason and unreason; or the facile transition from one state to the other. In Lear, his most perfect and elaborate representation of madness, he never represents the mental power as utterly lost; at no time is the intellectual aberration so complete that the old king is incapable of wise and just remark. (pp. 153-56)

Lear's first speech in this scene, contains a profound psychological truth: Kent urges him to take shelter in a hovel from the tyranny of the night, too rough for nature to endure; Lear objects that the outward storm soothes that which rages within, by diverting his attention from it; which he may well feel to be true, though the exposure and physical suffering are at the very time telling with fearful effect upon his excited, yet jaded condition. . . .

> *Lear.* Thou thinkst't is much, that this contentious storm
> Invades us to the skin: so 'tis to thee;
> But where the greater malady is fix'd,
> The lesser is scarce felt. Thou'dst shun a bear;
> But if thy flight lay toward the roaring sea,
> Thoud'st meet the bear i' the mouth. When the mind's free
> The body's delicate: the tempest in my mind
> Doth from my senses take all feeling else,
> Save what beats there.—Filial ingratitude!
> O, that way madness lies; let me shun that;
> No more of that—
>
> [III. iv. 6-14, 21-2]

This is the last speech of which there have been so many, expressing the consciousness of coming madness, which now yields to the actual presence of intellectual aberration; the excited emotions of unsound mind giving place to the delusions and incoherence of mania. (pp. 157-58)

And now intellectual takes the place of moral disturbance. It is remarkable how comparatively passionless the old king is, after intellectual aberration has displayed itself. It is true, that even in his delusions he never loses the sense and memory of the filial ingratitude which has been the moral excitant of his madness; but henceforth he ceases to call down imprecations upon his daughters; or with confused sense of personal identity, he curses them, as the daughters of Edgar. It is as if in madness he has found a refuge from grief, a refuge which Gloster even envies when he finds his own wretchedness "deprived that benefit to end itself by death" [IV. vi. 61-2]:

> *Gloster.* The king is mad: How stiff is my vile sense,
> That I stand up, and have ingenious feeling
> Of my huge sorrows! Better I were distract:
> So should my thoughts be severed from my griefs;
> And woes, by strong imaginations lose
> The knowledge of themselves.
>
> [IV. vi. 279-84]

To lose the sovereignty of reason is, indeed, to be degraded below humanity:

> A sight most pitiful in the meanest wretch;
> Past speaking of in a king!
>
> [IV. vi. 204-05]

and yet, like the grave itself, it may be a refuge from intense agony. As the hand of mercy has placed a limit even to physical suffering in senseless exhaustion or forgetful delirium, so in madness it has raised a barrier against the continuance of the extreme agony of the soul. Madness may, as in acute melancholia, be the very climax of moral suffering; but in other forms it may be, and often is, the suspension of misery—the refuge of incurable sorrow. This is finely shewn in Lear, who, from the time that his wits, that is, his intellects, unsettle, is not so much the subject as the object of moral pain. His condition is past speaking of, to those who look upon it, but to himself it is one of comparative happiness, like the delirium which shortens the agony of a bed of pain. (pp. 158-59)

John Charles Bucknill, "'King Lear'," in his The Psychology of Shakespeare, *Longman, Brown, Green, Longmans & Roberts, 1859, pp. 127-87.*

[FRIEDRICH] KREYSSIG   (essay date 1862)

[*The comments excerpted below were first published in 1862, in Kreyssig's* Vorlesungen über Shakespeare.]

Goethe has pronounced the first scene [of *King Lear*] absurd. More recent criticism, certainly in view of that judgment harsh, but not without reason, has defended it as unobjectionable, but yet hardly with a convincing, decisive result. It is doubtless only too natural that a hot-blooded gentleman, long accustomed to the exercise of irresponsible power, should reward his children, as well as his servants, not according to their services, but according to their address in flattering his self-love. When did not the flatterer feather his nest more successfully than the faithful, outspoken, independent servant? But in poetry, and especially in the drama, the subject-matter of a scene is not to be separated by the understanding from its form. And the form, in which Lear's arbitrary humour expresses itself in this scene, finds its natural and true significance only in fact as the symbol of a whole series of presumable precedents. Is it not the behaviour of a man already unsettled in his understanding, when a father, in solemn assembly, sets his children a lesson in flattery, and when he formally proposes for the required display of bombast a downright cash premium, so that for the *blasé* vanity of the monarch grown old in the habit of being worshipped, there is no possibility of delusion? And is the scene the first of the part which he plays? It notifies us to expect a reigning king, and the very first words are the words of a man with a crack in his brain. (p. 461)

It was a monstrous illusion which drove [Lear] to that eventful abdication—the idea of the indestructible, all-embracing nature of his personal authority, which he imagines to be wholly independent of what he possesses and can do. He recognizes no other relation to society but claim, right, mercy on his side, prayer, gratitude, devotion from all others. Naturally, the whole airy edifice tumbles into ruins so soon as the open secret becomes clear to him that that mystic regal greatness falls to the ground with the loss of material power, and that the despot's arbitrary humour educates its favourites, even though they be his own children, to be intriguing slaves, when he sets aside their nobler, self-respecting nature as disagreeable opponents, as creatures without court-manners. To the first contradiction which he has met perhaps for many years, Lear opposes a rage, boundless and incapable of all consideration. He raves and foams like some wild torrent around the rock which has rolled down into its waters. . . . Who does not feel the horror of his position? And yet the reckless outburst of his passion certainly qualifies our tribute of sympathy by the violence to which it drives him. We are involuntarily reminded of the old experience that ingratitude rarely wounds the true, that is, the disinterested, benefactor, or that its poison has no effect upon the blessed consciousness of genuine humanity, which has its foundation in a free devotion to moral necessity, and not in the quicksand of selfish interest, driven hither and thither by the waves of passion. Of that devotion there is no trace in the behaviour of the irascible king. Revenge, violence, a taking back what he has given—these are his first thoughts. That by his abdication he has taken a position no longer wholly inde-

pendent, finds no place in his mind. The presentiment of madness comes over him in the fearful collision of the blind, raging thirst for revenge with the laming consciousness of his lack of power. We are almost tempted to excuse the unfilial fye! fye! of the hard-hearted Regan, when the old man, at the bare mention of the strife with Goneril, breaks out into the well-known curse. And it needs the whole, overpowering impression of his weakness and helplessness, it needs the symbolism of the corresponding uproar of the element, to secure the fulness of tragic sympathy for the despairing old man, exposed on the barren heath to the fury of the storm. The fearful magnificence of this celebrated scene requires no word of praise from the commentator, and its terrible truth to nature makes every word expended upon it sound impertinent. His pain at the ingratitude of those whom he has heaped with favour and fortune, all the keener for the humiliating consciousness of his own unquestionable folly, passes into the fatal stability of the fixed idea, by the hot breath of which the springs of his spiritual life are dried up, until the phantom of madness settles weirdly down upon the dry, burnt-out waste. (pp. 461-62)

[*Friedrich*] *Kreyssig, in an extract, translated by Horace Howard Furness, from* A New Variorum Edition of Shakespeare: King Lear, Vol. 5 *by William Shakespeare, edited by Horace Howard Furness, J. B. Lippincott Company, 1880, pp. 461-62.*

VICTOR MARIE HUGO   (essay date 1864)

[*Hugo was the leading poet and novelist of French Romanticism. In his study* William Shakespeare, *first published in 1864, he maintains that Shakespeare is a reincarnation of Aeschylus and regards the poet as a genius who explored the limits of human experience. Hugo was also interested in Shakespeare's use of the supernatural and claimed that the poet "believed profoundly in the mystery of things." In the following excerpt, from the work mentioned above, Hugo finds a historical basis for Shakespeare's use of the double plot in many of his plays, such as* The Tempest, Hamlet, *and* King Lear. *Whereas such earlier critics as Lewis Theobald (1715), Samuel Johnson (1765), August Wilhelm Schlegel (1808), Hermann Ulrici (1839), and G. G. Gervinus (1849-50), all attributed this device, in* Lear *at least, to Shakespeare's desire to "universalize" his themes, Hugo argues that it developed strictly as a result of the poet adhering to the spirit of his age, a time when every idea, every gesture was reflected in a parallel symbol or idea.*]

All Shakespeare's plays, with the exception of *Macbeth* and *Romeo and Juliet*—thirty-four plays of thirty-six—offer to the observer one peculiarity which seems to have escaped, up to this day, the most eminent commentators and critics; one which is unnoticed by the Schlegels, and even by M. Villemain himself, in his remarkable labors, and of which it is impossible not to speak. It is the double action which traverses the drama and reflects it on a small scale. Beside the tempest in the Atlantic is the tempest in the teacup. Thus, Hamlet makes beneath himself a Hamlet; he kills Polonius, father of Laertes—and there stands Laertes over against him exactly as he stands over against Claudius. There are two fathers to avenge. There might be two ghosts. So, in *King Lear,* side by side and simultaneously, Lear, driven to despair by his daughters Goneril and Regan, and consoled by his Cordelia, is repeated in Gloucester, betrayed by his son Edmund and loved by his son Edgar. The idea bifurcated, the idea echoing itself, a lesser drama copying and elbowing the principal drama, the action attended by its moon—a smaller action like it—unity cut in two; surely the fact is a strange one. These double actions have been strongly condemned by the few commentators who have pointed them out. In this condemnation we do not sympathize. Do we then approve and accept as good these double actions? By no means. We recognize them, and that is all. The drama of Shakespeare . . . is peculiar to Shakespeare; it is a drama inherent in this poet; it is his own essence; it is himself. Thence his originalities, which are abolutely personal; thence his idiosyncrasies, which exist without establishing a law.

These double actions are purely Shakespearean. Neither Aeschylus nor Molière would admit them; and we should certainly agree with Aeschylus and Molière.

These double actions are, moreover, the sign of the sixteenth century. Each epoch has its own mysterious stamp. The centuries have a signature which they affix to masterpieces, and which it is necessary to know how to decipher and recognize. The signature of the sixteenth century is not that of the eighteenth. The Renaissance was a subtle time, a time of reflection. The spirit of the sixteenth century was reflected in a mirror. Every idea of the Renaissance has a double compartment. Look at the rood lofts in the churches. The Renaissance, with an exquisite and fantastical art, always makes the Old Testament an adumbration of the New. The double action is there in everything. The symbol explains the personage by repeating his gesture. (pp. 168-70)

Shakespeare, faithful to the spirit of his time, must needs add Laertes avenging his father to Hamlet avenging his father, and cause Hamlet to be pursued by Laertes at the same time that Claudius is pursued by Hamlet; he must needs make the filial piety of Edgar a comment on the filial piety of Cordelia, and bring out in contrast, weighed down by the ingratitude of unnatural children, two wretched fathers, each bereaved of one of the two kinds of light—Lear mad, and Gloucester blind. (p. 170)

> *Victor Marie Hugo, "From 'William Shakespeare',"*
> *translated by Melville B. Anderson, in* Shakespeare
> in Europe, *edited by Oswald LeWinter, The World*
> *Publishing Company, 1963, pp. 163-70.*

REV. H. N. HUDSON   (essay date 1872)

[*Hudson was a nineteenth-century American clergyman and literary scholar whose Harvard edition of Shakespeare's works, published in twenty volumes between 1880 and 1881, contributed substantially to the growth of Shakespeare's popularity in America. Hudson also published two critical works on Shakespeare, one a collection of lectures, the other—and the more successful—a biographical and critical study entitled* Shakespeare: His Life, Art, and Characters (1872). *In the following excerpt, from that work, Hudson undertakes an analysis of the major characters in* King Lear, *primarily Lear, Cordelia, and the Fool. The first of these he considers partially insane from the beginning of the play, a point made earlier by Charlotte Lennox (1754), A. Brigham (1844), and John Charles Bucknill (1859); the second he sees as a sacred exemplar of filial piety and a shaping force in the drama far beyond her hundred or so lines; the last he calls "the soul of pathos" and the secret to the true meaning of* King Lear *in his Christian-like willingness to surrender his own misfortunes in order to share the sufferings of those he loves. For more detailed interpretations of the Fool and his role in the play, see the excerpts by Herman Ulrici (1839), G. Wilson Knight (1930), Enid Welsford (1935), and Melvin Seiden (1979).*]

In speaking of the characters of [*King Lear*] I hardly know where to begin. Much has been written upon them; and the best critics have been so kindled and raised by the theme as

to surpass themselves. The persons are variously divisible into groups, according as we regard their domestic or their moral affinities. I prefer to consider them as grouped upon the latter. And as the main action of the drama is shaped by the energy of evil, I will begin with those in whom that energy prevails.

There is no accounting for the conduct of Goneril and Regan, but by supposing them possessed with a strong original impulse of malignity. The main points of their action were taken from the old story. Character, in the proper sense of the term, they have none in the legend; and the Poet invested them with characters suitable to the part they were believed to have acted.

Whatever of soul these beings possess is all in the head: they have no heart to guide or inspire their understanding, and but enough of understanding to seize occasions and frame excuses for their heartlessness. Without affection, they are also without shame; there being barely so much of human blood in their veins as may suffice for quickening the brain without sending a blush to the cheek. . . . No touch of nature finds a response in their bosoms; no atmosphere of comfort can abide their presence: we feel that they have somewhat within that turns the milk of humanity to venom, which all the wounds they can inflict are but opportunities for casting.

The subordinate plot of the drama serves the purpose of relieving the improbability of their behaviour. Some have indeed censured this plot as an embarrassment to the main one; forgetting, perhaps, that to raise and sustain the feelings at any great height there needs some breadth of basis. A degree of evil which, if seen altogether alone, would strike us as superhuman, makes a very different impression when it has the support of proper sympathies and associations. This effect is in a good measure secured by Edmund's independent concurrence with Goneril and Regan in wickedness. (pp. 355-57)

There is so much sameness of temper and behaviour in these two she-tigers, that we find it somewhat difficult to distinguish them as individuals; their characteristic traits being, as it were, fused and run together in the heat of a common malice. Both are actuated by an extreme ferocity, which however, up to the time of receiving their portions, we must suppose to have been held in check by a most artful and vigilant selfishness. And the malice of Goneril, the eldest, appears still to be under some restraint, from feeling that her husband is not in sympathy with her. For Albany, though rather timid and tardy in showing it, remains true to the old King; his tardiness probably springing, at least in part, from a reluctance to make a square issue with his wife, who, owing to her superiority of rank and position, had somewhat the advantage of him in their marriage. Regan, on the other hand, has in Cornwall a husband whose heart beats in perfect unison with her own against her father; and the confidence of his sympathy appears to discharge her malice entirely from the restraints of caution, and to give it a peculiar quickness and alertness of action. (pp. 357-58)

Of the conduct ascribed to these ladies after the death of Cornwall, what shall I say? It is true, the Poet prepares us somewhat for their final transports of internecine ferocity, by the moralizing he puts into the mouth of Albany:

> That nature which contemns its origin
> Cannot be border'd certain in itself;
>
> [IV. ii. 32-3]

meaning, apparently, that where the demon of filial ingratitude reigns, there the heart is ripening for the most unnatural crimes, and that there is no telling what it will do, or where it will stop. Nevertheless I hardly know how to approve an exhibition of depravity so extreme. The action of Goneril and Regan, taken all together, seems the most improbable thing in the drama. I cannot quite shake off the feeling, that before the heart could become so thoroughly petrified the brain must cease to operate. I find it not easy, indeed, to think of them otherwise than as instruments of the plot; not so much ungrateful persons as personifications of ingratitude. Yet I have to acknowledge that their blood is of much the same colour as ours.

For the union of wit and wickedness, Edmund stands next to Richard and Iago. His strong and nimble intellect, his manifest courage, his energy of character, and his noble person, prepare us on our first acquaintance to expect from him not only great undertakings, but great success in them. But, while his personal advantages naturally generate pride, his disgraces of fortune are such as, from pride, to generate guilt. The circumstances of our first meeting with him, the matter and manner of Gloster's talk about him and to him, go far to explain his conduct; while the subsequent outleakings of his mind in soliloquy let us into his secret springs of action. With a mixture of guilt, shame, and waggery, his father, before his face, and in the presence of one whose respect he craves, makes him and his birth a theme of gross and wanton discourse; at the same time drawing comparisons between him and "another son some year elder than this" [I. i. 19-20], such as could hardly fail at once to wound his pride, to stimulate his ambition, and to awaken his enmity. Thus the kindly influences of human relationship and household ties are turned to their contraries. He feels himself the victim of a disgrace for which he is not to blame; which he cannot hope to outgrow; which no degree of personal worth can efface; and from which he sees no escape but in the pomp and circumstance of worldly power. (pp. 359-60)

With "the plague of custom" and "the curiosity of nations" [I. ii. 3-4] Edmund has no compact: he did not consent to them, and therefore holds himself unbound by them. He came into the world in spite of them; perhaps he owes his gifts to a breach of them: may he not, then, seek to thrive by circumventing them? Since his dimensions are so well compact, his mind so generous, and his shape so true, he prefers Nature as she has made him to Nature as she has placed him; and freely employs the wit she has given, to compass the wealth she has withheld. Thus our free-love philosopher appeals from convention to Nature; and, as usually happens in such cases, takes only so much of Nature as will serve his turn. (p. 361)

Nevertheless there is not in Edmund, as in Iago, any spontaneous or purposeless wickedness. Adventures in crime are not at all his pastime: they are his means, not his end; his instruments, not his element. Nay, he does not so much make war on Duty, as bow and shift her off out of the way, that his wit may have free course. He deceives others indeed without scruple, but then he does not consider them bound to trust him, and tries to avail himself of their credulity or criminality without becoming responsible for it. True, he is a pretty bold experimenter, rather radical in his schemes, but this is because he has nothing to lose if he fails, and much to gain if he succeeds. Nor does he attempt to disguise from himself, or gloss over, or anywise palliate, his designs; but boldly confronts and stares them in the face, as though assured of sufficient external grounds to justify or excuse them. (p. 362)

Edmund is a free-thinker; not in the right philosophical sense of the term, but in the old historic sense; that is, one in whom the intellect owes no allegiance to the conscience. No awe of Duty, no religious fear to do or think wrong, is allowed to repress or abridge his freedom of thought. Thus it is merely the atheism of the heart that makes him so discerning of error in what he does not like; in which case the subtilties of the understanding lead to the rankest unwisdom.

As a portraiture of individual character, Lear himself holds, to my mind, much the same pre-eminence over all others which I accord to the tragedy as a dramatic composition. Less complex and varied than Hamlet, the character is however more remote from the common feelings and experiences of human life. The delineation reminds me, oftener than any other, of what some one has said of Shakespeare,—that if he had been the author of the human heart, it seems hardly possible that he should have better understood what is in it, and how it was made. (pp. 362-63)

The Poet often so orders his delineations as to start and propel the mind backwards over a large tract of memory. . . . Thus even his most ideal characters are invested with a sort of historic verisimilitude: the effects of what they thought and did long before still remain with them; and in their present speech and action is opened to us a long-drawn vista of retrospection. (pp. 363-64)

Lear is among the Poet's finest instances, perhaps his very finest, in this art of historical perspective. The old King speaks out from a large fund of vanishing recollections; and in his present we have the odour and efficacy of a remote and varied past. The play forecasts and prepares, from the outset, that superb intellectual ruin where we have "matter and impertinency mix'd, reason in madness" [V. vi. 174-75]; the earlier transpirations of the character being shaped and ordered with a view to that end. Certain presages and predispositions of insanity are manifest in his behaviour from the first, as the joint result of nature, of custom, and of superannuation. We see in him something of constitutional rashness of temper, which moreover has long been fostered by the indulgences and flatteries incident to his station, and which, through the cripplings of age, is now working loose from the restraints of his manlier judgment. (p. 364)

Lear has a morbid hungering after the outward tokens of affection: he is not content to know that the heart beats for him, but craves to feel and count over its beatings. The passion is indeed a selfish one, but it is the selfishness of a right-generous and loving nature. Such a diseased longing for sympathy is not the growth of an unsympathizing heart. And Lear naturally looks for the strongest professions where he feels the deepest attachment. "I lov'd her most, and thought to set my rest on her kind nursery" [I. i. 123-24],—such is his declared preference of Cordelia. . . . Thwarted of his hope where he has centered it most and held it surest, his weakness naturally flames out in a transport of rage. Still it is not any doubt of Cordelia's love, but a [trick of his dotage] that frets and chafes him. For the device is a *pet* with him. And such a bauble of strategy would have had no place in his thoughts, had he been of a temper to bear the breaking of it. Being thus surprised into a tempest of passion, in the disorder of his mind he at once forgets the thousand little daily acts that have insensibly wrought in him to love Cordelia most, and to expect most love from her. His behaviour towards her, indeed, is like that of a peevish, fretful child who, if prevented from kissing his nurse, falls to striking her.

It is such a poor old piece of tetchy, impotent waywardness, whose forfeiture of respect no art seems capable of retrieving, that the Poet here repeals home to our deepest sympathies, and invests with the sacredest regards of humanity.

Men sometimes take a strange pleasure in acting without or against reason; since this has to their feelings the effect of ascertaining and augmenting their power; as if they could make a right or a truth of their own. It appears to be on some such principle as this that arbitrariness, or a making of the will its own reason, sometimes becomes a passion in men. . . . The very shame, too, of doing wrong, sometimes hurries men into a barring of themselves off from retreat. And so it appears to be with Lear in his treatment of Cordelia. In the first place, he *will* do the thing because he knows it to be wrong; and then the uneasy sense of a wrong done prompts him to bind the act with an oath; that is, because he ought not to have driven the nail, therefore he *clinches* it. This action of mind is indeed abnormal, and belongs to what may be termed the border-land of sanity and madness; nevertheless something very like it is not seldom met with in men who are supposed to be in full possession of their wits.

How deeply the old King, in this spasm of wilfulness, violates the cherished order of his feelings, appears in what follows, but especially in his shrinking soreness of mind as shown when the Fool's grief at the loss of Cordelia is mentioned. The sense of having done her wrong sticks fast in his heart, and will not let him rest. And his remorse on this score renders him the more sensitive to the wrongs that are done him by others. He could better endure the malice of his other daughters, but that it reminds him how deeply he has sinned against her love who has ever approved herself his best. (pp. 367-69)

But the great thing in the delineation of Lear is the effect and progress of his passion in redeveloping his intellect. For the character seems designed in part to illustrate the power of passion to reawaken and raise the faculties from the tomb in which age has quietly inurned them. And so in Lear we have, as it were, a handful of tumult embosomed in a sea, gradually overspreading and pervading and convulsing the entire mass.

In his conscious fulness of paternal love, Lear confides unreservedly in the piety of his children. The possibility of filial desertion seems never to have entered his thoughts; for so absolute is his trust, that he can hardly admit the evidence of sight against his cherished expectations. Bereft, as he thinks, of one, he clings the closer to the rest, assuring himself that they will spare no pains to make up the loss. Cast off and struck on the heart by another, he flies with still greater confidence to the third. Though proofs that she too has fallen off are multiplied upon him, still he cannot give her up, cannot be provoked to curse her; he *will* not own to himself the fact of her revolt.

When, however, the truth is forced home, and he can no longer evade or shuffle off the conviction, the effect is indeed terrible. So long as his heart had something to lay hold of and cling to and rest upon, his mind was the abode of order and peace. But, now that his feelings are rendered objectless, torn from their accustomed holdings, and thrown back upon themselves, there springs up a wild chaos of the brain, a whirling tumult and anarchy of the thoughts, which, till imagination has time to work, chokes down his utterance. Then comes the inward, tugging conflict, deep as life, which gradually works up his imaginative forces, and kindles them to a preternatural resplendence. The crushing of his aged spirit brings to light its hidden depths and buried riches. Thus his terrible energy of thought and speech, as soon as imagination rallies to his aid,

grows naturally from the struggle of his feelings,—a struggle that seems to wrench his whole being into dislocation, convulsing and upturning his soul from the bottom. (pp. 369-70)

In the transition of Lear's mind from its first stillness and repose to its subsequent tempest and storm; in the hurried revulsions and alternations of feeling,—the fast-rooted faith in filial virtue, the keen sensibility to filial ingratitude, the mighty hunger of the heart, thrice repelled, yet ever strengthened by repulse; and in the turning up of sentiments and faculties deeply imbedded beneath the incrustations of time and place;—in all this we have a retrospect of the aged sufferer's whole life; the abridged history of a mind that has passed through many successive stages, each putting off the form, yet retaining and perfecting the grace of the preceding. (p. 370)

In the trial of professions, there appears something of obstinacy and sullenness in Cordelia's answer, as if she would resent the old man's credulity to her sisters' lies by refusing to tell him the truth. But, in the first place, she is considerately careful and tender of him; and it is a part of her religion not to feed his dotage with the intoxications for which he has such a morbid craving. She understands thoroughly both his fretful waywardness and their artful hypocrisy; and when she sees how he drinks in the sweetened poison of their speech, she calmly resolves to hazard the worst, rather than wrong her own truth to cosset his disease. Thus her answer proceeds, in part, from a deliberate purpose of love, not to compete with them in the utterance of pleasing falsehoods.

In the second place, it is against the original grain of her nature to talk much about what she feels, and what she intends. Where her feelings are deepest, there her tongue is stillest. She "cannot heave her heart into her mouth" [I. i. 91-2], for the simple reason that she has so much of it. And there is a virgin delicacy in genuine and deep feeling, that causes it to keep in the background of the life; to be heard rather in its effects than in direct and open declarations. (pp. 374-75)

It is not strange, therefore, that Cordelia should make it her part to "love and be silent" [I. i. 62]. Yet she is in no sort a pulpy structure, or one whom it is prudent to trifle with, where her forces are unrestrained by awe of duty: she has indeed a delectable smack of her father's quality; as appears in that glorious flash of womanhood, when she so promptly switches off her higgling suitor:

> Peace be with Burgundy!
> Since that respects of fortune are his love,
> I shall not be his wife.
>
> [I. i. 247-49]

Mrs. Jameson rightly says of Cordelia that "every thing in her lies beyond our view, and affects us in such a manner that we rather feel than perceive it" [see excerpt above, 1833]. And it is very remarkable that, though but little seen and heard, she is nevertheless a sort of ubiquity in the play. All that she utters is but about a hundred lines; yet I had read the play occasionally for several years before I could fully realize but that she was among the principal speakers; and even to this day I carry to the reading a vague impression that her speech and presence are to fill a large part of the scene.

It is in this remoteness, I take it, this gift of presence without appearance, that the secret of her power mainly consists. Her character has no foreground; nothing outstanding, or that touches us in a definable way: she is all perspective, self-withdrawn; so that she comes to us rather by inspiration than by vision.

Even when she is before us we rather feel than see her; so much more being meant than meets the eye, that we almost lose the sense of what is shown, in the interest of what is suggested. Thus she affects us through finer and deeper susceptibilities than consciousness can grasp; as if she at once both used and developed in us higher organs of communication than the senses; or as if her presence acted in some mysterious way directly on our life, so as to be most operative within us when we are least aware of it. The effect is like that of a voice or a song kindling and swelling the thoughts that prevent our listening to it. (pp. 375-76)

[All of this] shows a peculiar fitness in Cordelia for the part she was designed to act; which was to exemplify the workings of filial piety, as Lear exemplifies those of paternal love. To embody this sentiment, the whole character in all its movements and aspects is made essentially religious. For filial piety is religion acting under the sacredest of human relations. And religion, we know, or ought to know, is a life, and not a language; and life is the simultaneous and concurrent action of *all* the elements of our being. Which is perfectly illustrated in Cordelia; who, be it observed, never thinks of her piety at all, because her piety keeps her thoughts engaged upon her father. And so she reveals her good thoughts by veiling them in good deeds, as the spirit is veiled and revealed in the body; nay, has to be so veiled in order to be revealed; for, if the veil be torn off, the spirit is no longer there, but hides itself at once in immateriality. (pp. 377-78)

There is a strange assemblage of qualities in the Fool, and a strange effect arising from their union and position, which I am not a little at a loss how to describe. It seems hardly possible that Lear's character should be properly developed without him: indeed he serves as a common gauge and exponent of all the characters about him,—the mirror in which their finest and deepest lineaments are reflected. Though a privileged person, with the largest opportunity of seeing and the largest liberty of speaking, he everywhere turns his privileges into charities, making the immunities of the clown subservient to the noblest sympathies of the man. He is therefore by no means a mere harlequinian appendage of the scene, but moves in vital intercourse with the character and passion of the drama. He makes his folly the vehicle of truths which the King will bear in no other shape, while his affectionate tenderness sanctifies all his nonsense. His being heralded by the announcement of his pining away at the banishment of Cordelia sends a consecration before him: that his spirit feeds on her presence hallows every thing about him. Lear manifestly loves him, partly for his own sake, and partly for hers; for we feel a delicate, scarce-discernible play of sympathy between them on Cordelia's account; the more so perhaps, that neither of them makes any explicit allusion to her; their very reserve concerning her indicating that their hearts are too full to speak.

I know not, therefore, how I can better describe the Fool than as the soul of pathos in a sort of comic masquerade; one in whom fun and frolic are sublimed and idealized into tragic beauty; with the garments of mourning showing through and softened by the lawn of playfulness. His "labouring to outjest Lear's heart-struck injuries" [III. i. 16-17] tells us that his wits are set a-dancing by grief; that his jests bubble up from the depths of a heart struggling with pity and sorrow, as foam enwreaths the face of deeply-troubled waters. . . . There is all along a shrinking, velvet-footed delicacy of step in the Fool's antics, as if awed by the holiness of the ground; and he seems bringing diversion to the thoughts, that he may the better steal

a sense of woe into the heart. And I am not clear whether the inspired antics that sparkle from the surface of his mind are in more impressive contrast with the dark tragic scenes into which they are thrown, like rockets into a midnight tempest, or with the undercurrent of deep tragic thoughtfulness out of which they falteringly issue and play.

Our estimate of this drama as a whole depends very much on the view we take of the Fool; that is, on how we interpret his part, or in what sense we understand it. Superficially considered, his presence and action can hardly seem other than a blemish in the work, and a hindrance to its proper interest. Accordingly he has been greatly misunderstood, indeed totally misconstrued by many of the Poet's critics. And it must be confessed that the true meaning of his part is somewhat difficult to seize; in fact, is not to be seized at all, unless one get just the right point of view. He has no sufferings of his own to move us, yet, rightly seen, he does move us, and deeply too. But the process of his interest is very peculiar and recondite. The most noteworthy point in him, and the real key to his character, lies in that while his heart is slowly breaking he never speaks, nor even appears so much as to think of his own suffering. He seems indeed quite unconscious of it. His anguish is purely the anguish of sympathy; a sympathy so deep and intense as to induce absolute forgetfulness of self; all his capacities of feeling being perfectly engrossed with the sufferings of those whom he loves. He withdraws from the scene with the words, "And I'll go to bed at noon" [III. vi. 85]; which means simply that the dear fellow is dying, and this too, purely of others' sorrows, which he feels more keenly than they do themselves. (pp. 380-82)

Need it be said that such ideas of human character could grow only where the light of Christianity shines? The Poet's conceptions of virtue and goodness, as worked out in this drama, are thoroughly of the Christian type,—steeped indeed in the efficacy of the Christian Ideal. The old Roman conception of human goodness, as is well known, placed it in courage, patriotism, honesty, and justice,—very high and noble indeed; whereas the proper constituents of the Christian Ideal are, besides these, and higher than these, mercy, philanthropy, self-sacrifice, forgiveness of injuries, and loving of enemies. It is in this sense that Shakespeare gives us the best expressions of the Christian Ideal that are to be met with in Poetry and Art. (p. 383)

If the best grace and happiness of life consist, as this play makes us feel that they do, in a forgetting of self and a living for others, Kent and Edgar are those of Shakespeare's men whom one should most wish to resemble. Strikingly similar in virtues and situation, these two persons are notwithstanding widely different in character. Brothers in magnanimity and in misfortune; equally invincible in fidelity, the one to his King, the other to his father; both driven to disguise themselves, and in their disguise both serving where they stand condemned;—Kent, too generous to control himself, is always quick, fiery, and impetuous; Edgar, controlling himself even because of his generosity, is always calm, collected, and deliberate. For, if Edgar be the more judicious and prudent, Kent is the more unselfish of the two: the former disguising himself for his own safety, and then turning his disguise into an opportunity of service; the latter disguising himself merely *in order* to serve, and then perilling his life in the same course whereby the other seeks to preserve it. Nor is Edgar so lost to himself and absorbed in others but that he can and does survive them; whereas Kent's life is so bound up with others, that their death plucks him after. (pp. 383-84)

It is rather curious to note how the characteristic traits of these two men are preserved even when they are acting most out of character: so that, to us who are in the secret of their course they are themselves and not themselves at the same time. For example, in Kent's obstreperous railing at the Steward, and his saucy bluntness to Cornwall and Regan, we have a strong relish of the same impulsive and outspoken boldness with which he beards the old King when the latter is storming out his paroxysm against Cordelia, and meets his threats by daring him to the worst: "Do; kill thy physician, and the fee bestow upon the foul disease" [I. i. 163-64]. Of course, in those transports of abusive speech and of reckless retort, he is but affecting the slang-whanger as a part of his disguise: moreover he wants to raise a muss, and embroil Lear with his two daughters, and thereby draw the latter into a speedy disclosure of what he knows to be in their hearts; because his big manly soul is still on fire at the wrong Lear has done to Cordelia, and he would fain hasten that repentance which he knows must sooner or later come: still it is plain enough to us that his tumultuous conduct is but an exaggerated outcome of his native disposition; or, in other words, that he is truly himself all the while, only a good deal more so; a hiding of his character in a sort of overdone caricature. So too the imitative limberness and versatility which carry Edgar smoothly through so many abrupt shiftings of his masquerade are in perfect keeping with the cool considerateness which enables him to hold himself so firmly in hand when he goes to assume the style of a wandering Bedlamite. He acts several widely different parts, but the same conscious self-mastery and the same high-souled rectitude of purpose, which form the backbone of his character, are apparent in them all. (pp. 384-85)

> Rev. H. N. Hudson, "Tragedies: 'King Lear'," in his Shakespeare: His Life, Art, and Characters, Vol. II, revised edition, Ginn & Company, 1872, pp. 349-88.

REV. J. KIRKMAN   (lecture date 1879)

[The essay from which the following excerpt is drawn, originally delivered as a lecture before the New Shakspere Society on January 10, 1879, is often referred to as the earliest discussion of the animal imagery in King Lear. Its author, the Reverend J. Kirkman, contends that the numerous references to animals in the play, second in frequency only to Timon of Athens, were intended by Shakespeare to suggest the correlation between the baser examples of human nature—namely, Regan, Goneril, Osmond, and Edmund—and "the lower nature of beasts, birds, and vermin." Unusual for the nineteenth century, imagery studies became quite popular in the twentieth, and can be seen in the essays by Caroline F.E. Spurgeon (1935), Robert Bechtold Heilman (1948), and Wolfgang Clemen (1951).]

We find . . . in King Lear, an extraordinary frequence in the mention of the lower animals, a constant allusion to animal nature and its destructive or deceitful instincts, and in a vast majority of the instances with one special reference, the reference of comparison with the ways of men, according to resemblance between the two. (p. 386)

There are 64 different names of animals mentioned, "all well defined," as Coleridge says of the stinks of Cologne: for they are, for the most part, mentioned in a morally unsavoury relation. This is by counting each kind of dog, but the word 'dog' only once; and not counting Tray, Blanche, and Sweetheart. These occur in 133 separate mentions, and by 12 different persons, indeed by all the chief persons in the play—

Lear, Edgar, Fool, Edmund, Albany, Cornwall, Kent, Gloucester, Goneril, Regan, Cordelia, Gentleman. Of these 102, or about 78 decimal something per cent are from the mouths of three persons—King, Edgar, and Fool. To this curious fact, strongly in support of the causation I would suggest, I will draw particular attention. There are more birds in other plays . . . : there may be more beasts in other plays: but on the whole there is only one play which can compete with King Lear as to animals. But in no play is there any approach to so many as indicative of the same moral or psychological law as we have here. The only play which approaches to King Lear in this respect is (as I anticipated before I searched, and at once found to be the case) Timon of Athens, the last two Acts. The resemblance may be seen at a glance, and the overruling law perceived to be precisely the same as here. (pp. 386-87)

But we have to do more than count animals: so, even the comparison between two plays may reveal only a casual or superficial fact after all, or not essential in the moral structure of either of them. We have to ask, why is this a fact in King Lear? What beautiful or sad law was it that was like the igneous rock ever beneath us, cropping up through all sedimentary strata here and there, often commanding attention by the height and sharpness of its peaks? Mr. Darwin would answer infallibly without a moment's hesitation, I would venture to predict: "because of the common nature of man and his lower progenitors in the scale of creation." I mean, without any allusion to Shakspere being of "Darwin's views," Darwin would state on biological grounds precisely the same fact in nature as Shakspere has worked out on moral or psychological principles. Even daily conversation or educated speech at every turn betrays it: and in the ordinary degree it is nothing remarkable; unless the reason for it be denied, out of a mistaken notion of man's isolated nobility. In King Lear it seems to underlie all, to overrule all. Its perpetual reappearance, sometimes with singular intensity of point, is one of the most prevalent colours to be observed in any play whatsoever, like jealousy in Winter's Tale, or the charming side of forest life in As You Like It. Indeed, in order of impressiveness, after the primary feature of the baseness of human nature in Goneril, Regan, Oswald, and Edmund, is, next, this paralleled terrible revolting fact of similar villainy, worthlessness, and treachery or cruelty, in the lower nature of beasts, birds, and vermin. Most of the allusions to them point that way. The law of the play's construction makes this inevitable, if the creatures are to be mentioned at all. . . . To fancy that Shakspere might have given us the evil drama of base humanity without bringing in all the other genera of our "earthborn companions and fellow-mortals," would be no more reasonable than to fancy one of Mendelssohn's Lieder of heavenly strivings without certain sequences and harmonies. Animal nature versus human nature may stand to mean, unless I express it infelicitously or uncourteously, the toss-up which is worse in the lovely creations of our sweet Mother Nature herself. . . . This is the simplest account of the melody of King Lear. And it is heard through all the variations of the several scenes, sometimes with terribly shrill clearness. (pp. 389-90)

> Rev. J. Kirkman, "Animal Nature Versus Human Nature in 'King Lear'," in The New Shakspere Society's Transactions, No. 7, 1877-79, pp. 385-401.

ALGERNON CHARLES SWINBURNE   (essay date 1880)

[Swinburne was an English poet, dramatist, and critic who devoted much of his literary career to the study of Shakespeare and other Elizabethan writers. His three books on Shakespeare—A

Study of Shakespeare *(1880)*, Shakespeare *(1909), and* Three Plays of Shakespeare *(1909)—all demonstrate his keen interest in Shakespeare's poetic talents and, especially, his major tragedies. In the following excerpt, taken from the first work mentioned above, Swinburne calls* King Lear *"elemental and primeval," "oceanic and Titanic in conception," and the darkest, most fatalistic of Shakespeare's tragedies. He finds the keynote of the entire drama not in Cordelia's sacrificial love, but in Gloucester's famous "flies to wanton boys" speech. Thus, Swinburne was one of the earliest critics to suggest that* King Lear *dramatizes the meaninglessness of human existence, a point adopted by such later commentators as E. K. Chambers (1906), Stopford A. Brooke (1913), G. Wilson Knight (1930), J. Stampfer (1960), and Jan Kott (1964).]*

Of all Shakespeare's plays, *King Lear* is unquestionably that in which he has come nearest to the height and to the likeness of the one tragic poet on any side greater than himself whom the world in all its ages has ever seen born of time. It is by far the most Aeschylean of his works; the most elemental and primaeval, the most oceanic and Titanic in conception. He deals here with no subtleties as in *Hamlet,* with no conventions as in *Othello:* there is no question of "a divided duty" or a problem half insoluble, a matter of country and connection, of family or of race; we look upward and downward, and in vain, into the deepest things of nature, into the highest things of providence; to the roots of life, and to the stars; from the roots that no God waters to the stars which give no man light; over a world full of death and life without resting-place or guidance.

But in one main point it differs radically from the work and the spirit of Aeschylus. Its fatalism is of a darker and harder nature. To Prometheus the fetters of the lord and enemy of mankind were bitter; upon Orestes the hand of heaven was laid too heavily to bear; yet in the not utterly infinite or everlasting distance we see beyond them the promise of the morning on which mystery and justice shall be made one; when righteousness and omnipotence at last shall kiss each other. But on the horizon of Shakespeare's tragic fatalism we see no such twilight of atonement, such pledge of reconciliation as this. Requital, redemption, amends, equity, explanation, pity and mercy, are words without a meaning here.

> As flies to wanton boys are we to the gods;
> They kill us for their sport.
>
> [IV. i. 36-7]

Here is no need of the Eumenides, children of Night everlasting; for here is very Night herself.

The words just cited are not casual or episodical; they strike the keynote of the whole poem, lay the keystone of the whole arch of thought. There is no contest of conflicting forces, no judgment so much as by casting of lots: far less is there any light of heavenly harmony or of heavenly wisdom, of Apollo or Athene from above. We have heard much and often from theologians of the light of revelation: and some such thing indeed we find in Aeschylus: but the darkness of revelation is here.

For in this the most terrible work of human genius it is with the very springs and sources of nature that her student has set himself to deal. The veil of the temple of our humanity is rent in twain. Nature herself, we might say, is revealed—and revealed as unnatural. In face of such a world as this a man might be forgiven who should pray that chaos might come again. Nowhere else in Shakespeare's work or in the universe of jarring lives are the lines of character and event so broadly drawn or so sharply cut. Only the supreme self-command of

this one poet could so mould and handle such types as to restrain and prevent their passing from the abnormal into the monstrous: yet even as much as this, at least in all cases but one, it surely has accomplished. In Regan alone would it be, I think, impossible to find a touch or trace of anything less vile than it was devilish. Even Goneril has her one splendid hour, her fire-flaught of hellish glory; when she treads under foot the half-hearted goodness, the wordy and windy though sincere abhorrence, which is all that the mild and impotent revolt of Albany can bring to bear against her imperious and dauntless devilhood; when she flaunts before the eyes of her "milk-livered" and "moral fool" the coming banners of France about the "plumed helm" of his slayer.

On the other side, Kent is the exception which answers to Regan on this. Cordelia, the brotherless Antigone of our stage, has one passing touch of intolerance for what her sister was afterwards to brand as indiscretion and dotage in their father, which redeems her from the charge of perfection. Like Imogen, she is not too inhumanly divine for the sense of divine irritation. Godlike though they be, their very godhead is human and feminine; and only therefore credible, and only therefore adorable. Cloten and Regan, Goneril and Iachimo, have power to stir and embitter the sweetness of their blood. But for the contrast and even the contact of antagonists as abominable as these, the gold of their spirit would be too refined, the lily of their holiness too radiant, the violet of their virtue too sweet. As it is, Shakespeare has gone down perforce among the blackest and the basest things of nature to find anything so equally exceptional in evil as properly to counterbalance and make bearable the excellence and extremity of their goodness. No otherwise could either angel have escaped the blame implied in the very attribute and epithet of blameless. But where the possible depth of human hell is so foul and unfathomable as it appears in the spirits which serve as foils to these, we may endure that in them the inner height of heaven should be no less immaculate and immeasurable.

It should be a truism wellnigh as musty as Hamlet's half cited proverb, to enlarge upon the evidence given in *King Lear* of a sympathy with the mass of social misery more wide and deep and direct and bitter and tender than Shakespeare has shown elsewhere. But as even to this day and even in respectable quarters the murmur is not quite duly extinct which would charge on Shakespeare a certain share of divine indifference to suffering, of godlike satisfaction and a less than compassionate content, it is not yet perhaps utterly superfluous to insist on the utter fallacy and falsity of their creed who whether in praise or in blame would rank him to his credit or discredit among such poets as on this side at least may be classed rather with Goethe than with Shelley and with Gautier than with Hugo. A poet of revolution he is not, as none of his country in that generation could have been: but as surely as the author of *Julius Caesar* has approved himself in the best and highest sense of the word at least potentially a republican, so surely has the author of *King Lear* avowed himself in the only good and rational sense of the words a spiritual if not a political democrat and socialist.

It is only, I think, in this most tragic of tragedies that the sovereign lord and incarnate god of pity and terror can be said to have struck with all his strength a chord of which the resonance could excite such angry agony and heartbreak of wrath as that of the brother kings when they smote their staffs against the ground in fierce imperious anguish of agonised and rebellious compassion, at the oracular cry of Calchas for the innocent blood of Iphigenia. (pp. 170-76)

Algernon Charles Swinburne, ''Third Period: Tragic and Romantic,'' in his A Study of Shakespeare, *1880. Reprint by AMS Press Inc., 1965, pp. 170-230.*

EDWARD DOWDEN   (essay date 1881)

[*Dowden was an Irish critic and biographer whose* Shakspere: A Critical Study of His Mind and Art *(rev. ed. 1881) was the leading example of the biographical criticism popular in the English-speaking world near the end of the nineteenth century. Biographical critics sought in the plays and poems a record of Shakespeare's personal development. As that approach gave way in the twentieth century to aesthetic theories with greater emphasis on the constructed, artificial nature of literary works, Dowden and other biographical critics came to be considered limited. In the following excerpt, taken from the work mentioned above, he touches on a number of different points. First, like William Hazlitt (1817), he suggests that* King Lear *depicts Shakespeare's heart, soul, and imagination, and that being so involved with its deeper meanings the poet cared little for verisimilitude—an idea Dowden stresses to counter those critics who disapprove of the first scene for failing to psychologically justify Lear's conduct. Second, Dowden supports the presence of the Gloucester subplot in the drama, calling it the means by which Shakespeare prepares the reader for the grander tragedy of Lear. Third, and perhaps the most important point of his essay, Dowden maintains that although Shakespeare left a number of questions unanswered—such as the reason for Gloucester's restoration to ''calm and light'' while Lear dies in anguish, the reason for Cordelia's goodness in light of her sisters' evil, and the exact nature of the mortal world, whether it is ruled by chance, by divine will, or by the will of humankind—his ultimate statement in* King Lear *is ''clear and emphatic'': only in the presence of human virtue, fidelity, and self-sacrificial love does life have any meaning. The theme of love in* King Lear *and its importance to the play has also been discussed by Hermann Ulrici (1839), R. W. Chambers (1939), Oscar James Campbell (1948), Arthur Sewell (1951), Irving Ribner (1958), L. C. Knights (1959), Robert Ornstein (1960), and Robert H. West (1968).*]

The tragedy of *King Lear* was estimated by Shelley, in his ''Defence of Poetry,'' as an equivalent in modern literature for the trilogy in the literature of Greece with which the *Oedipus Tyrannus,* or that with which the *Agamemnon* stands connected [see excerpt above, 1821]. *King Lear* is, indeed, the greatest single achievement in poetry of the Teutonic, or Northern, genius. By its largeness of conception and the variety of its details, by its revelation of a harmony existing between the forces of nature and the passions of man, by its grotesqueness and its sublimity, it owns kinship with the great cathedrals of Gothic architecture. To conceive, to compass, to comprehend, at once in its stupendous unity and in its almost endless variety, a building like the cathedral of Rheims, or that of Cologne, is a feat which might seem to defy the most athletic imagination. But the impression which Shakspere's tragedy produces, while equally large—almost monstrous—and equally intricate, lacks the material fixity and determinateness of that produced by these great works in stone. Everything in the tragedy is in motion, and the motion is that of a tempest. A grotesque head, which was peering out upon us from a point near at hand, suddenly changes its place and its expression, and now is seen driven or fading away into the distance with lips and eyes that, instead of grotesque, appear sad and pathetic. All that we see around us is tempestuously whirling and heaving, yet we are aware that a law presides over this vicissitude and apparent incoherence. We are confident that there is a logic of the tempest. While each thing appears to be torn from its proper place, and to have lost its natural supports and stays, instincts, passions, reason, all wrenched and contorted, yet each thing in

this seeming chaos takes up its place with infallible assurance and precision.

In *King Lear,* more than in any other of his plays, Shakspere stands in presence of the mysteries of human life. A more impatient intellect would have proposed explanations of these. A less robust spirit would have permitted the dominant tone of the play to become an eager or pathetic wistfulness respecting the significance of these hard riddles in the destiny of man. Shakspere checks such wistful curiosity, though it exists discernibly; he will present life as it is. If life proposes inexplicable riddles, Shakspere's art must propose them also. But, while Shakspere will present life as it is, and suggest no inadequate explanations of its difficult problems, he will gaze at life not only from *within,* but, if possible, also from an extra-mundane, extra-human point of view, and, gazing thence at life, will try to discern what aspect this fleeting and wonderful phenomenon presents to the eyes of gods. Hence a grand irony in the tragedy of *Lear;* hence all in it that is great is also small; all that is tragically sublime is also grotesque. Hence it sees man walking in a vain shadow; groping in the mist; committing extravagant mistakes; wandering from light into darkness; stumbling back again from darkness into light; spending his strength in barren and impotent rages; man in his weakness, his unreason, his affliction, his anguish, his poverty and meanness, his everlasting greatness and majesty. Hence, too, the characters, while they remain individual men and women, are ideal, representative, typical; Goneril and Regan, the destructive force, the ravening egoism in humanity which is at war with all goodness; Kent, a clear, unmingled fidelity; Cordelia, unmingled tenderness and strength, a pure redeeming ardor. As we read the play we are haunted by a presence of something beyond the story of a suffering old man; we become dimly aware that the play has some vast impersonal significance, like the *Prometheus Bound* of Aeschylus, and like Goethe's *Faust.* We seem to gaze upon ''huge, cloudy symbols of some high romance.''

What was irony when human life was viewed from the outside, extra-mundane point of view becomes, when life is viewed from within, Stoicism. For to Stoicism the mere phenomenon of human existence is a vast piece of unreason and grotesqueness, and from this unreason and grotesqueness Stoicism makes its escape by becoming indifferent to the phenomenon, and by devotion to the moral idea, the law of the soul, which is forever one with itself and with the highest reason. The ethics of the play of *King Lear* are Stoical ethics. Shakspere's fidelity to the fact will allow him to deny no pain or calamity that befalls man. ''There was never yet philosopher that could endure the toothache patiently'' [*Much Ado About Nothing,* V. i. 35-6]. He knows that it is impossible to

> Fetter strong madness in a silken thread,
> Charm ache with air, and agony with words.
> [*Much Ado About Nothing,* V. i. 25-6]

He admits the suffering, the weakness, of humanity; but he declares that in the inner law there is a constraining power stronger than a silken thread; in the fidelity of pure hearts, in the rapture of love and sacrifice, there is a charm which is neither air nor words, but, indeed, potent enough to subdue pain and make calamity acceptable. Cordelia, who utters no word in excess of her actual feeling, can declare, as she is led to prison, her calm and decided acceptance of her lot:

> We are not the first
> Who, with best meaning, have incurred the worst;
> For thee, oppressed king, I am cast down;
> Myself could else out-frown false fortune's frown.
> [V. iii. 3-6]

But though ethical principles radiate through the play of *Lear,* its chief function is not, even indirectly, to teach or inculcate moral truth, but rather, by the direct presentation of a vision of human life and of the enveloping forces of nature, to ''free, arouse, dilate.'' (pp. 229-32)

In the play of *King Lear* we come into contact with the imagination, the heart, the soul of Shakspere, at a moment when they attained their most powerful and intense vitality. ''He was here,'' Hazlitt wrote, ''fairly caught in the web of his own imagination'' [see excerpt above, 1817]. And being thus aroused about deeper things, Shakspere did not in this play feel that mere historical verisimiltude was of chief importance. He found the incidents recorded in history and ballad and drama; he accepted them as he found them. . . . [It] would have been easy for him to have referred the conduct of Lear to ingeniously invented motives; he could, if he had chosen, by psychological fence have turned aside the weapons of those assailants who lay to his charge improbability and unnaturalness. But then the key-note of the play would have been struck in another mode. Shakspere did not at all care to justify himself by special pleading and psychological fence. The sculptor of the Laocoon has not engraved below his group the lines of Virgil which describe the progress of the serpent towards his victims; he was interested in the supreme moment of the father's agony, and in the piteous effort and unavailing appeal of the children. Shakspere, in accordance with his dramatic method, drove forward across the intervening accidents towards the passion of Lear in all its stages, his wild revolt against humanity, his conflict with the powers of night and tempest, his restoration through the sacred balm of a daughter's love.

Nevertheless, though its chief purpose be to get the forces of the drama into position before their play upon one another begins, the first scene cannot be incoherent. In the opening sentence Shakspere gives us clearly to understand that the partition of the kingdom between Albany and Cornwall is already accomplished. In the concluding sentences we are reminded of Lear's ''inconstant starts'' [I. i. 300], of ''the unruly waywardness that infirm and choleric years bring with them'' [I. i. 298-99]. It is evidently intended that we should understand the demand made upon his daughters for a profession of their love to have been a sudden freak of self-indulged waywardness, in which there was something of jest, something of unreason, something of the infirmity which requires demonstrations of the heart. Having made the demand, however, it must not be refused. Lear's will must be opposeless. It is the centre and prime force of his little universe. To be thrown out of this passionate wilfulness, to be made a passive thing, to be stripped first of affection, then of power, then of home or shelter, last, of reason itself, and, finally, to learn the preciousness of true love only at the moment when it must be forever renounced— such is the awful and purifying ordeal through which Lear is compelled to pass. (pp. 232-34)

Of the secondary plot of this tragedy—the story of Gloucester and his sons—Schlegel has explained one chief significance: ''Were Lear alone to suffer from his daughters, the impression would be limited to the powerful compassion felt by us for his private misfortune. But two such unheard-of examples taking place at the same time have the appearance of a great commotion in the moral world; the picture becomes gigantic, and fills us with such alarm as we should entertain at the idea that the heavenly bodies might one day fall from their appointed orbits'' [see excerpt above, 1808]. The treachery of Edmund, and the torture to which Gloucester is subjected, are out of the

course of familiar experience; but they are commonplace and prosaic in comparison with the inhumanity of the sisters and the agony of Lear. When we have climbed the steep ascent of Gloucester's mount of passion, we see still above us another *via dolorosa* [''way of sadness''] leading to that

> Wall of eagle-baffling mountain,
> Black, wintry, dead, unmeasured,

to which Lear is chained. Thus the one story of horror serves as a means of approach to the other, and helps us to conceive its magnitude. The two, as Schlegel observes, produce the impression of a great commotion in the moral world. The thunder which breaks over our head does not suddenly cease to resound, but is reduplicated, multiplied, and magnified, and rolls away with long reverberation.

Shakspere also desires to augment the moral mystery, the grand inexplicableness of the play. We can assign causes to explain the evil in Edmund's heart. His birth is shameful, and the brand burns into his heart and brain. He has been thrown abroad in the world, and is constrained by none of the bonds of nature or memory, of habit or association. A hard, sceptical intellect, uninspired and unfed by the instincts of the heart, can easily enough reason away the consciousness of obligations the most sacred. . . . We can, therefore, in some degree account for Edmund's bold egoism and inhumanity. What obligations should a child feel to the man who, for a moment's selfish pleasure, had degraded and stained his entire life? In like manner, Gloucester's sufferings do not appear to us inexplicably mysterious. (pp. 235-37)

But, having gone to the end of our tether, and explained all that is explicable, we are met by enigmas which will not be explained. We were, perhaps, somewhat too ready to

> Take upon us the mystery of things
> As if we were God's spies.
>
> [V. iii. 16-17]

Now we are baffled, and bow the head in silence. Is it, indeed, the stars that govern our condition? Upon what theory shall we account for the sisterhood of a Goneril and a Cordelia? And why is it that Gloucester, whose suffering is the retribution for past misdeeds, should be restored to spiritual calm and light, and should pass away in a rapture of mingled gladness and grief . . . , while Lear, a man more sinned against than sinning, should be robbed of the comfort of Cordelia's love, should be stretched to the last moment upon ''the rack of this tough world'' [V. iii. 315], and should expire in the climax of a paroxysm of unproductive anguish?

Shakspere does not attempt to answer these questions. The impression which the facts themselves produce, their influence to ''free, arouse, dilate,'' seems to Shakspere more precious than any proposed explanation of the facts which cannot be verified. The heart is purified not by dogma, but by pity and terror. But there are other questions which the play suggests. If it be the stars that govern our conditions; if that be, indeed, a possibility which Gloucester, in his first shock and confusion of mind, declares,

> As flies to wanton boys are we to the gods;
> They kill us for their sport;
>
> [IV. i. 36-7]

if, measured by material standards, the innocent and the guilty perish by a like fate—what then? Shall we yield ourselves to the lust for pleasure? shall we organize our lives upon the principles of a studious and pitiless egoism?

To these questions the answer of Shakspere is clear and emphatic. Shall we stand upon Goneril's side or upon that of Cordelia? Shall we join Edgar or join the traitor? Shakspere opposes the presence and the influence of evil not by any transcendental denial of evil, but by the presence of human virtue, fidelity, and self-sacrificial love. In no play is there a clearer, an intenser manifestation of loyal manhood, of strong and tender womanhood. The devotion of Kent to his master is a passionate, unsubduable devotion, which might choose for its watchword the saying of Goethe, ''I love you; what is that to you?'' Edgar's nobility of nature is not disguised by the beggar's rags; he is the skilful resister of evil, the champion of right to the utterance. . . . We feel throughout the play that evil is abnormal; a curse which brings down destruction upon itself; that it is without any long career; that evil-doer is at variance with evil-doer. But good is normal; for it the career is long. . . . (pp. 237-39)

Nevertheless, when everything has been said that can be said to make the world intelligible, when we have striven our utmost to realize all the possible good that exists in the world, a need of fortitude remains.

It is worthy of note that each of the principal personages of the play is brought into presence of those mysterious powers which dominate life and preside over human destiny; and each, according to his character, is made to offer an interpretation of the great riddle. Of these interpretations, none is adequate to account for all the facts. Shakspere (differing in this from the old play) placed the story in heathen times, partly, we may surmise, that he might be able to put the question boldly, ''What are the gods?'' Edmund, as we have seen, discovers no power or authority higher than the will of the individual and a hard trenchant intellect. . . . It is not until he is mortally wounded, with his brother standing over him, that the recognition of a moral law forces itself painfully upon his consciousness, and he makes his bitter confession of faith:

> The wheel is come full circle, I am here.
> [V. iii. 175]

His self-indulgent father is, after the manner of the self-indulgent, prone to superstition; and Gloucester's superstition affords some countenance to Edmund's scepticism. (pp. 239-40)

Edgar, on the contrary, the champion of right, ever active in opposing evil and advancing the good cause, discovers that the gods are upon the side of right, are unceasingly at work in the vindication of truth and the execution of justice. His faith lives through trial and disaster, a flame which will not be quenched. And he buoys up, by virtue of his own energy of soul, the spirit of his father, which, unprepared for calamity, is staggering blindly, stunned from its power to think, and ready to sink into darkness and a welter of chaotic disbelief. . . . [As] Edgar, the justiciary, finds in the gods his fellow-workers in the execution of justice, so Cordelia, in whose heart love is a clear and perpetual illumination, can turn for assistance and co-operancy in her deeds of love to the strong and gentle rulers of the world. . . . (pp. 240-41)

Kent possesses no vision, like that which gladdens Edgar, of a divine providence. His loyalty to right has something in it of a desperate instinct, which persists, in spite of the appearances presented by the world. Shakspere would have us know

that there is not any devotion to truth, to justice, to charity, more intense and real than that of the man who is faithful to them out of the sheer spirit of loyalty, unstimulated and unsupported by any faith which can be called theological. Kent, who has seen the vicissitude of things, knows of no higher power presiding over the events of the world than fortune. Therefore, all the more, Kent clings to the passionate instinct of right-doing, and to the hardy temper, the fortitude which makes evil, when it happens to come, endurable. (pp. 241-42)

Accordingly, there is at once an exquisite tenderness in Kent's nature, and also a certain roughness and hardness, needful to protect, from the shocks of life, the tenderness of one who finds no refuge in communion with the higher powers, or in a creed of religious optimism.

But Lear himself—the central figure of the tragedy—what of him? What of suffering humanity that wanders from the darkness into light, and from the light into the darkness? Lear is grandly passive—played upon by all the manifold sources of nature and of society. And though he is in part delivered from his imperious self-will, and learns, at last, what true love is, and that it exists in the world, Lear passes away from our sight, not in any mood of resignation or faith or illuminated peace, but in a piteous agony of yearning for that love which he had found only to lose forever. Does Shakspere mean to contrast the pleasure in a demonstration of spurious affection in the first scene with the agonized cry for real love in the last scene, and does he wish us to understand that the true gain from the bitter discipline of Lear's old age was precisely this—his acquiring a supreme need of what is best, though a need which finds, as far as we can learn, no satisfaction?

We guess at the spiritual significance of the great tragic facts of the world, but, after our guessing, their mysteriousness remains. (pp. 242-43)

Of the tragedy of *King Lear* a critic wishes to say as little as may be; for, in the case of this play, words are more than ordinarily inadequate to express or describe its true impression. A tempest or a dawn will not be analyzed in words; we must feel the shattering fury of the gale, we must watch the calm light broadening. And the sensation experienced by the reader of *King Lear* resembles that produced by some grand natural phenomenon. The effect cannot be received at second-hand; it cannot be described; it can hardly be suggested. (p. 244)

> *Edward Dowden, '''Othello', 'Macbeth', 'Lear','' in his* Shakspere: A Critical Study of His Mind and Art, *third edition, Harper & Brothers Publishers, 1881, pp. 198-244.*

DENTON J. SNIDER   (essay date 1887)

[Snider was an American teacher, philosopher, and poet who followed closely the precepts of the German philosopher Georg Wilhelm Friedrich Hegel and contributed greatly to the dissemination of his idealistic philosophy in America. In the excerpt below, Snider interprets King Lear *from a social perspective, claiming that it depicts both the corruption and the restoration of the family unit and, on a larger scale, the human world. He then divides the tragedy into two ''movements,'' each containing two different ''threads'' representing the two plots. The first movement traces the ''breaking up of the Institutional World'' and the development of what he calls the ''Perverted World''; the second movement, beginning in the fourth act, traces the destruction of the ''Perverted World'' and the reestablishment of the ''Institutional World.'' Snider was one of the earliest critics to perceive in* King Lear *such a stark, symbolic structure with*

respect to its social themes. For other social or political readings of the play, see the excerpts by John W. Draper (1937), Theodore Spencer (1942), and Edwin Muir (1946).]

The impression left upon the mind by [*King Lear*] is that of terrific grandeur. In it is found, probably, the strongest language ever written or spoken by a human being. Dante has passages of fiery intensity, Aeschylus has strains of wonderful sublimity, but nothing in either of these poets is equal to the awful imprecations of Lear. The grand characteristic of the play is strength—Titanic strength—which can only be adequately compared to the mightiest forces of Nature. There is a world-destroying element in it which oppresses the individual and makes him feel like fleeing from the crash of the Universe. The superhuman power, passion, and expression can only be symbolized by the tempest or volcano; it is, indeed, the modern battle of the Giants and the Gods. Shakespeare, like other poets, seems to have had his Titanic epoch, and his *King Lear* may well be called, in a certain sense, the most colossal specimen of literary Titanism. Not without a touch of the deepest kinship with Nature is the storm introduced—the fierce violence and struggle of the elements.

Yet the tempestuous character of the play is but one phase of it; there is also a mildness, sweetness, gentleness, charity in it, which belongs of necessity to the complete theme. A one-sided treatment is not the highest; if there is a getting into a storm, there is also a getting out of it. From the Fourth Act the passionate upheavals begin to cease, the work of peace and reconciliation starts, there is a gradual calming down of the volcano, the style has a softer touch; though there still be war and discord, we feel in the very language that they are in the process of being overcome. Two styles, we might say, are employed in the drama, with the subtlest adjustment to the subject-matter. This transition in style is doubtless felt by careful readers; but it must be seen to be in perfect harmony with the transition in thought.

It will be noticed that the action of the play lies mainly in the sphere of the Family, and portrays one of its essential relations—that of parents and children. The conflicts arising from this relation involve also brothers and sisters in strife. The domestic side of life is thus torn with fearful struggles, and its quiet affection and repose are turned into a display of malignant hate and passion. Each element is present. There is on the one hand the most heroic fidelity, and on the other the most wanton infidelity. The parents are both faithful and faithless to their relation; so are the children, taken collectively. Such are its contradictory principles, and hence arises the conflict in which the offending individuals perish, since they destroy the very condition of their own existence, namely, the Family. But those who have been true to their domestic relations, and have not otherwise committed wrong, are preserved. It is essentially the story of fidelity and infidelity to the Family.

Still we must note that the action has a tendency to burst the limits of the Family, and to rise into more universal relations. A commonwealth is also involved, Lear is monarch as well as parent, his children, too are rulers; thus the political element is whirled into the domestic cataclysm, and the wrong of the home becomes the wrong of the government. The classes of society are also infected, as we may see in Gloster; indeed, it is not too much to say that this drama presents a condensed picture out of the World's History; the decline and corruption of a State, and its process of freeing itself from that corruption, through war and tragedy, till final restoration. So the family

of Lear, in its domestic limits, is made, by the cunning of the poet, to cast an image of the Universal Family.

The spirit of *King Lear* belongs emphatically to Shakespeare's own time. The play takes its mythical setting from pre-historic Britain, ''before the building of Rome,'' says Holinshed, the chronicler, from whom the poet, in part at least, derived the story. But the drama, as it now stands, reaches to the very heart of the age of the Tudors and Stuarts, and reveals to us the disease of absolute authority, showing how such an authority wrecks society on the one hand, and, on the other, wrecks the monarch who exercises it. In this sense the present drama is historical, and Shakespeare shows himself the poet of the English, and indeed of the whole Anglo-Saxon consciousness, whose history is largely made up of the attempt to put legal limits upon an absolute sovereignty.

There can be no greater mistake than to explain *King Lear* by referring it to a barbarous period. It is Elizabethan, even in its most revolting incident, the putting out of the eyes of Gloster. Its manifold anachronisms we never think of, except by an effort of erudition; then the entire play becomes one monster of anachronism, which swallows all the rest. The poet himself, in a passage suspected by some editors, laughs at his violations of chronology: ''This prophecy Merlin shall make, for I live before his time'' [III. ii. 95]. Still, the setting is mythical and not historical; the poet takes his mythus from a time before history, and pours into it the thoughts and feelings of his own age. (pp. 126-29)

The drama presupposes in [its] two stories, two deeds, done by two men, Gloster and Lear, which deeds by time have solidified into character, and have been built into the temple of life itself; that is, they have hardened into the spirit's boundary within, and have become the world's environment without, for these two human souls. Gloster's act of incontinence, at which he once blushed, though now he is ''brazed to it,'' has entered not only his outward existence, but has wound itself into his very soul and transformed that, during a score of years and more, till it becomes the source of his punishment. Lear's arbitrary conduct, continued long, till it has ossified into character with age, has made for him a world in which he has to live and take the penalty of his action. Thus man's deed is seen to be the architect of the outer edifice of life, as well as the moulder of the inner spirit.

Authority is excellent and may bring forth the highest offspring of human conduct, but it runs always the danger of giving birth to a demon, insolence, which has no charity. Lear, the man of authority, has begotten its two sides in his two sets of children; he has the good child, yet he is father of the demon also, nay, of two demons, who thus show him the parent of more evil than good. Gloster's act, too, has begotten a demon in a son, Edmund, who destroys him, yet inside the family it is good and begets another son, Edgar, who saves him. Such is Shakespeare's dramatic portraiture of the deed; in its image, cast into a brief play, he shows the whole cycle of human action.

Character, then we behold here in its deepest significance, as it stands in relation to the ethical institutions of man. An individual flings his deed into the roaring stream of Time, he is never the same thereafter, that action is transforming him. But we must rise to the supreme standpoint of the poet; he is not simply depicting single characters, he has his last look upon the society, the totality in which the individual moves, which we may call a world, of which the individuals are but the atoms. This world the poet portrays, showing its rise and fall, the corruption and the recovery, a grand revolution in the spirit's solar system, the process of ages compressed into a three hours' spectacle. Yes, we must rise to this point of view in order to see from the altitude where the poet stands, and look with his vision on what he sees.

Accordingly we shall behold the entire drama separating into two parts or movements, the first of which embraces three acts and shows the breaking up of the Institutional World by an inner disease, which has been introduced by Lear and Gloster. The very persons who have violated institutions have obtained control of them and are administering them, in order to banish and destroy those who have shown most truly the institutional spirit. It is the mighty collapse of society, in which the individual and the social order around him fall into complete discord. This is the Perverted World, in which the wrong ones have the right, and the right ones have the wrong. But with the Fourth Act, the return out of disorder begins; the shattered Institutional World purifies itself in the fire of war; the faithful ones assert their right of control, and the faithless ones become faithless to one another, while their power disintegrates of itself. Such is the second Movement showing the restoration, and the whole drama is a grand social cycle, including the essential process of history, giving a picture of a world destroyed and then restored, the tragedy not merely of individuals, but of institutions, yet with the recovery of the latter from their malady.

Such are the two organic movements of the play, which, however, pass into each other by the finest and most intricate net work, showing a double guilt and a double retribution. The First Movement exhibits the complete disintegration of the Family, with the first guilt and the first retribution—the wrong of the parents and its punishment. Lear banishes his daughter; his daughters, in turn, drive him out of doors. Gloster expels from home and disinherits his true and faithful son, in favor of the illegitimate and faithless son, and is then himself falsely accused and betrayed by the latter. Thus the disruption is complete,—the parents expelled, the false triumphant, the faithful in disguise and banishment. Such is the First Movement in its domestic phase—the wrong done by the parents to their children and its punishment. The Second Movement will unfold the second retribution springing from the second guilt—the wrong done by the children to their parents and its punishment. It must be observed, however, that the deeds of the faithless children, which are portrayed in the First Movement of the drama, constitute their guilt. On the one hand, they are the instruments of retribution, but, on the other hand, their conduct is a violation of ethical principle as deep as that of their parents. They are the avengers of guilt, but in this very act become themselves guilty, and receive punishment. The general result, therefore, of the Second Movement will be the completed retribution. Lear and his three guilty daughters—for we have to include Cordelia in this category—as well as Gloster and his guilty son, perish. Such is this terrible tragedy of the Family, with its double sweep of guilt and penalty; but just through this tragedy comes the purification as well as the restoration of the Institutional World.

The Threads of the drama are fundamentally two, which, however, are differently arranged in the separate Movements. For instance, in the First Movement the one Thread is plainly the family of Gloster, the other is the family of Lear. Both rest upon the same ultimate thought; the one can behold its features in the other, as it were, in a mirror; the drama gives a double

reflection of the same content. Both fathers cause a disruption of their families by their uncharitable passion; they drive off the faithful children and cherish the faithless ones; they hand over to the latter their property and power; upon both falls the penalty. There are, however, many differences of character, situation and incident between the two Threads; at the heart there is unity, on the surface there is variety. The one father has only daughters, the other has only sons; each represents thus a side of the Family. Lear is king, Gloster is subject; both taken together show that the conflict is not limited to one rank, but pervades the chief classes of society. Lear is arbitrary, Gloster is superstitious, both are uncharitable. It is a curious fact that the wife of neither appears; long since she dropped out of this world of domestic discord, possibly was its first victim.

In the Second Movement which is the way out of the conflict, there are still two Threads, but they have to be ordered differently. The faithful of both families come together, in their banishment, in order to protect their parents; this is the First Thread, which . . . has two quite distinct strands, that of Edgar and that of Cordelia. The Second Thread of this Second Movement is made up of the faithless of both families, who now coalesce; they triumph in the battle, in the external conflict, but there necessarily arises an internal conflict, a struggle among themselves; for how can the faithless be faithful to one another? The jealousy of the two sisters leads to a conspiracy which ends in their destruction; Edmund, faithless to both, falls at last by the hand of his brother, whom he has so deeply wronged. (pp. 131-36)

[The First Movement] shows the process of society toward wrong, perversion and dissolution, symbolized by the transition into the storm of the Third Act. The social framework is falling to pieces; a disease, which is bringing death, has taken lodgment in the body politic. Now, if we should name the disease, we would call it the want of charity in human character— charity in its universal sense. There is a tendency to selfishness, and therewith to revenge, which, in the ruling class especially, undermines social order; no patience but intense passion, which seethes up in volcanic fury at any restraint or limit; we behold a world in which there is no endurance of others' weaknesses or wrongs, at least on the part of those in authority. (pp. 137-38)

[The] Second Movement, accordingly, proceeds on the line of restoration; it is the attempt to restore the disrupted Family, and the perverted State. Thus the circle of the action is complete; it begins with the wrongs done to the faithful children, and ends by putting into their hands the means of justice, and of social recovery. But the parents cannot be completely restored to a society which is seeking to heal itself of their deeds; they are tragic in a world which they have made tragic.

Between the First and Second Movements the reader will note many differences corresponding to this difference of thought. There is a change in tone, color, style; the volcanic, defiant, wrathful energy of speech becomes calmer, more soothing and compassionate; the First Movement passes into a storm, the Second gradually passes out of it into a clearing-up; Passion and Revenge are turned to Patience and Love; in the one part, limits are placed, in the other, limits are taken away; the one seems to share in the curse, the other in the blessing. All undergoes transformation, from the outer garment of language to the soul within. But the chief of these changes, and the one to which we must reach down as the ground of the others, is that of institutions, which are broken, shattered, perverted in the First Movement, and then in the Second Movement rise toward recovery. The play shows, not some man or some men, but a society, a world going to pieces, then restoring itself by getting rid of its destructive characters. Thus we behold in the total action the process of social regeneration.

The structure of the Second Movement will, of necessity be somewhat different from that of the First Movement. The good people must separate themselves from the bad, and then unite; such is always the process of purification from social disorder. Hence there will be two main Threads still, but differently arranged. In the First Movement these two Threads were the families of Lear and Gloster; but now the faithless members of each family, have coalesced into one party, and the faithful members of each family are brought together into a union of sympathy, if not of action. . . . These two sides are brought into collision; the faithless children are victorious in the external conflict, as they, under the leadership of Albany, are fighting for the State, but the daughters perish in a struggle among themselves, and Edmund falls in single combat with his brother. At the end, all the characters who have introduced disorder and conflict into the institutional world are eliminated, while the positive characters of the drama remain to build up anew the shattered society. (pp. 183-85)

The action has now completed its revolution, and brought back to all the leading characters the consequences of their deeds; the double guilt and the double retribution have been fully portrayed. The treatment of children by parents, and of parents by children, is the theme; both fidelity and infidelity are shown in their extreme manifestation. Two families are taken—that of the monarch and that of the subject; the former develops within itself its own collisions, free from any external restraint, and, hence, exhibits the truest and most complete result; the latter is largely influenced and determined in its course by authority, but an authority which is itself poisoned with domestic conflict. The exhaustiveness of the treatment is worthy of careful study. Regan is faithless to parent; Goneril is faithless to both parent and husband; Cordelia is true to both, yet assails another ethical principle—the State. The two sons and the two sons-in-law exhibit also distinct phases of the domestic tie; they are still further divided, by the fundamental theme of the play, into the faithful and faithless—that is, a son and a son-in-law belong to each side. But it is a curious fact that one very important relation of the Family is wholly omitted—no mother appears anywhere; sonhood, daughterhood, wifehood, fatherhood, are all present, but the tenderest bond of existence—motherhood—is wanting. The poet evidently does not need it, for the action is already sufficiently full and complicated; perhaps, too, the character of the mother may be supposed to reappear in some of her children, as, for example, in Cordelia, who, in spite of certain similarities, is so different from her father. But one cannot help commending the true instinct, or, what is more likely, the sound judgment, which kept such a mild and tender relation out of the cauldron of passion and ingratitude which seethes with such destructive energy in this appalling drama.

But not alone the domestic, but also the social element must be always present to the thought. A history of society in small is shown in the drama; we see how a period gets corrupt and perverted, then how it is purified. A destructive element, a poison is introduced into the body politic, which passes through wrong, convulsion, revolution to restoration. Society is not tragic in Shakespeare, but the individual may be, if he collides with its interest, and persists in his collision. We notice that

three men are left, the truly positive men of the play, Albany, Edgar and Kent, who are to build up anew the shattered social organism. Thus the tragedy leaves us hopeful of a purified society, and reconciled with the supreme ethical order, which, we feel, cannot perish, though it, too, has to pass through its periods of corruption and purification. (pp. 208-09)

> Denton J. Snider, "'King Lear'," in his The Shake-spearian Drama, a Commentary: The Tragedies, Ticknor & Co., 1887, pp. 125-209.

GEORGE BRANDES   (essay date 1895-96)

[*Brandes was a scholar and the most influential literary critic of late nineteenth-century Denmark. His work on Shakespeare was translated and widely read in his day. A writer with a broad knowledge of literature, Brandes placed Shakespeare in a European context, comparing him with other important dramatists. In the following excerpt, first published in his* William Shakespeare *in 1895-96, Brandes suggests a biographical interpretation of* King Lear, *claiming that when he was composing the play, Shakespeare felt personally the wickedness and agony of the world. For Brandes, Shakespeare's "dark mood" accounts for the grotesque and improbable elements in the tragedy. Although biographical interpretations of Shakespeare's work were generally replaced by other forms of criticism in the twentieth century, one commentator, John Middleton Murry (1936), put forth an opinion similar to Brandes's when he claimed that* King Lear *demonstrates a mind obsessed with the idea of humanity's self-destructive nature. Also see the excerpt by Stopford A. Brooke (1913) for further biographical analysis of* King Lear.]

I imagine that Shakespeare must, as a rule, have worked early in the morning. The division of the day at that time would necessitate this. But it can scarcely have been in bright morning hours, scarcely in the daytime, that he conceived *King Lear*. No; it must have been on a night of storm and terror, one of those nights when a man, sitting at his desk at home, thinks of the wretches who are wandering in houseless poverty through the darkness, the blustering wind, and the soaking rain—when the rushing of the storm over the house-tops and its howling in the chimneys sound in his ears like shrieks of agony, the wail of all the misery of earth. (p. 454)

On such a night was *Lear* conceived. Shakespeare, sitting at his writing-table, heard the voices of the King, the Fool, Edgar, and Kent on the heath, interwoven with each other, contrapuntally answering each to each, as in a fugue; and it was for the sake of the general effect, in all its sublimity, that he wrote large portions of the tragedy which, in themselves, cannot have interested him. The whole introduction, for instance, deficient as it is in any reasonable motive for the King's behaviour, he took, with his usual sovereign indifference in unessential matters, from the old play.

With Shakespeare we always find that each work is connected with the preceding one, as ring is linked with ring in a chain. In the story of Gloucester the theme of *Othello* is taken up again and varied. The trusting Gloucester is spiritually poisoned by Edmund, exactly as Othello's mind is poisoned by Iago's lies. Edmund calumniates his brother Edgar, shows forged letters from him, wounds himself in a make-believe defence of his father's life against him—in short, upsets Gloucester's balance just as Iago did Othello's. (pp. 454-55)

Shakespeare moves all this away back into primeval times, into the grey days of heathendom; and he welds the two originally independent stories together with such incomparable artistic dexterity that their interaction serves to bring out more forcibly

Act III. Scene iv. Edgar, Kent, Fool, and Lear. Frontispiece to the Hanmer edition by Francis Hayman (1744). By permission of the Folger Shakespeare Library.

to bend. And the weaker he grows the heavier load is heaped upon him, till at last, overburdened, he sinks. He wanders off, groping his way, with his crushing fate upon his back. Then the light of his mind is extinguished; madness seizes him.

And Shakespeare takes this theme of madness and sets it for three voices—divides it between Edgar, who is mad to serve a purpose, but speaks the language of real insanity; the Fool, who is mad by profession, and masks the soundest practical wisdom under the appearance of insanity; and the King, who is bewildered and infected by Edgar's insane talk—the King, who is mad with misery and suffering.

As already remarked, it is evident from the indifference with which Shakespeare takes up the old material to make a beginning and set the play going, that all he really cared about was the essential pathos of the theme, the deep seriousness of the fundamental emotion. The opening scenes are of course incredible. It is only in fairy-tales that a king divides the provinces of his kingdom among his daughters, on the principle that she gets the largest share who can assure him that she loves him most; and only a childish audience could find it conceivable that old Gloucester should instantly believe the most improbable calumnies against a son whose fine character he knew. Shakespeare's individuality does not make itself felt in such parts as these; but it certainly does in the view of life, its course and character, which bursts upon Lear when he goes mad, and which manifests itself here and there all through the play. And Shakespeare's intellect has now attained such mastery, every passion is rendered with such irresistible power, that the play, in spite of its fantastic, unreal basis, produces an effect of absolute *truth*. (pp. 455-56)

[The] end of all things seems to have come when we see the ruin of the moral world—when he who is noble and trustful like Lear is rewarded with ingratitude and hate; when he who is honest and brave like Kent is punished with dishonour; when he who is merciful like Gloucester, taking the suffering and injured under his roof, has the loss of his eyes for his reward; when he who is noble and faithful like Edgar must wander about in the semblance of a maniac, with a rag round his loins; when, finally, she who is the living emblem of womanly dignity and of filial tenderness towards an old father who has become as it were her child—when she meets her death before his eyes at the hands of assassins! What avails it that the guilty slaughter and poison each other afterwards? None the less is this the titanic tragedy of human life; there rings forth from it a chorus of passionate, jeering, wildly yearning, and desperately wailing voices.

Sitting by his fire at night, Shakespeare heard them in the roar of the storm against the window-pane, in the howling of the wind in the chimneys—heard all these terrible voices contrapuntally inwoven one with another as in a fugue, and heard in them the torture-shriek of suffering humanity. (p. 460)

> *George Brandes, "'King Lear'—The Feeling Underlying It—The Chronicle—Sidney's 'Arcadia' and the Old Play" and "'King Lear'—The Tragedy of a World-Catastrophe," translated by William Archer with Mary Morison, in his* William Shakespeare, *William Heinemann, 1920, pp. 450-53, 454-60.**

the fundamental idea and feeling of the play. He skilfully contrives that Gloucester's compassion for Lear shall provide Edmund with means to bring about his father's utter ruin, and he ingeniously invents the double passion of Regan and Goneril for Edmund, which leads the two sisters to destroy each other. He fills the tame little play of the earlier writer with horrors such as he had not presented since his youthful days in *Titus Andronicus,* not even shrinking from the tearing out of Gloster's eyes on the stage. He means to show pitilessly what life is. (p. 455)

Shakespeare has nowhere else shown evil and good in such immediate opposition—bad and good human beings in such direct conflict with each other; and nowhere else has he so deliberately shunned the customary and conventional issue of the struggle—the triumph of the good. In the catastrophe, blind and callous Fate blots out the good and the bad together.

Everything centres in the protagonist, poor, old, stupid, great Lear, king every inch of him, and every inch human. Lear's is a passionate nature, irritably nervous, all too ready to act on the first impulse. At heart he is so lovable that he arouses the unalterable devotion of the best among those who surround him; and he is so framed to command and so accustomed to rule, that he misses every moment that power which, in an access of caprice, he has renounced. For a brief space at the beginning of the play the old man stands erect; then he begins

A. C. BRADLEY   (essay date 1904)

[*Bradley was a major Shakespearean critic whose work culminated the method of character analysis initiated in the Romantic era. He is best known for his* Shakespearean Tragedy (1904), *a close analysis of* Hamlet, Othello, King Lear, *and* Macbeth. *Bradley concentrated on Shakespeare as a dramatist, particularly on his characters, excluding not only the biographical questions so prominent in the works of his immediate predecessors but also the questions of poetic structure, symbolism, and thematics which became prominent in later criticism. He thus may be seen as a pivotal figure in the transition in Shakespearean studies from the nineteenth to the twentieth century. He has been a major target for critics reacting against Romantic criticism, but he has continued to be widely read to the present day. The following essay on* King Lear, *taken from the work cited above, is considered the most influential analysis of the play ever written. Bradley's interpretation is important for a number of reasons. First, it expands the idea originally suggested by Charles Lamb (1812), and later disputed by Harley Granville-Barker (1927), that* King Lear *is not suited for the stage. In essence, Bradley argues that the play solicits two different points of view: we can regard it strictly as drama, and in this case Bradley considers it inferior to Shakespeare's other major tragedies; or we can approach it as a product of Shakespeare's poetic imagination, and in this respect Bradley regards it as one of the greatest works ever written. A second important aspect of Bradley's essay is that it was one of the first to suggest that Lear dies of joy, not despair, under the delusion that Cordelia lives—a point later disputed by such other critics as Algernon Charles Swinburne (1880), Stopford A. Brooke (1913), G. Wilson Knight (1930), J. Stampfer (1960), and Jan Kott (1964). Third, Bradley's reading of* King Lear *emphasizes the theme of suffering, in both its ennobling and redemptive qualities, as central to the play. This idea forms the principal assumption in the essays of such later commentators as J. Dover Wilson (1932), Oscar James Campbell (1948), D. G. James (1951), Irving Ribner (1958), L. C. Knights (1959), and Robert H. West (1968). Last, Bradley's interpretation clearly suggests that the play is ultimately theological in its implications. Although stopping just short of a Christian metaphysics, Bradley's assessment prepared the way for such Christian interpretations as those by R. W. Chambers (1939), Geoffrey L. Bickersteth (1946), Oscar James Campbell (1948), Irving Ribner (1958), L. C. Knights (1959), Robert H. West (1968), and René E. Fortin (1979).]*

King Lear has again and again been described as Shakespeare's greatest work, the best of his plays, the tragedy in which he exhibits most fully his multitudinous powers; and if we were doomed to lose all his dramas except one, probably the majority of those who know and appreciate him best would pronounce for keeping *King Lear.*

Yet this tragedy is certainly the least popular of the famous four. The 'general reader' reads it less often than the others, and, though he acknowledges its greatness, he will sometimes speak of it with a certain distaste. It is also the least often presented on the stage, and the least successful there. And when we look back on its history we find a curious fact. Some twenty years after the Restoration, Nahum Tate altered *King Lear* for the stage, giving it a happy ending, and putting Edgar in the place of the King of France as Cordelia's lover [see excerpt above, 1681]. From that time Shakespeare's tragedy in its original form was never seen on the stage for a century and a half. . . . In 1823 Kean, 'stimulated by Hazlitt's remonstrances and Charles Lamb's essays,' restored the original tragic ending. At last, in 1838, Macready returned to Shakespeare's text throughout.

What is the meaning of these opposite sets of facts? Are the lovers of Shakespeare wholly in the right; and is the general reader and playgoer, were even Tate and Dr. Johnson, altogether in the wrong? I venture to doubt it. When I read *King Lear* two impressions are left on my mind, which seem to answer roughly to the two sets of facts. *King Lear* seems to me Shakespeare's greatest achievement, but it seems to me *not*

his best play. And I find that I tend to consider it from two rather different points of view. When I regard it strictly as a drama, it appears to me, though in certain parts overwhelming, decidedly inferior as a whole to *Hamlet, Othello* and *Macbeth.* When I am feeling that it is greater than any of these, and the fullest revelation of Shakespeare's power, I find I am not regarding it simply as a drama, but am grouping it in my mind with works like the *Prometheus Vinctus* and the *Divine Comedy,* and even with the greatest symphonies of Beethoven and the statues in the Medici Chapel. (pp. 243-44)

The stage is the test of strictly dramatic quality, and *King Lear* is too huge for the stage. Of course, I am not denying that it is a great stage-play. It has scenes immensely effective in the theatre; three of them—the two between Lear and Goneril and between Lear, Goneril and Regan, and the ineffably beautiful scene in the Fourth Act between Lear and Cordelia—lose in the theatre very little of the spell they have for imagination; and the gradual interweaving of the two plots is almost as masterly as in *Much Ado.* But (not to speak of defects due to mere carelessness) that which makes the *peculiar* greatness of King Lear,—the immense scope of the work; the mass and variety of intense experience which it contains; the interpenetration of sublime imagination, piercing pathos, and humour almost as moving as the pathos; the vastness of the convulsion both of nature and of human passion; the vagueness of the scene where the action takes place, and of the movements of the figures which cross this scene; the strange atmosphere, cold and dark, which strikes on us as we enter this scene, enfolding these figures and magnifying their dim outlines like a winter mist; the half-realised suggestions of vast universal powers working in the world of individual fates and passions,—all this interferes with dramatic clearness even when the play is read, and in the theatre not only refuses to reveal itself fully through the senses but seems to be almost in contradiction with their reports. This is not so with the other great tragedies. No doubt, as Lamb declared, theatrical representation gives only a part of what we imagine when we read them; but there is no *conflict* between the representation and the imagination, because these tragedies are, in essentials, perfectly dramatic. But *King Lear,* as a whole, is imperfectly dramatic, and there is something in its very essence which is at war with the senses, and demands a purely imaginative realisation. It is therefore Shakespeare's greatest work, but it is not what Hazlitt called it, the best of his plays [see excerpt above, 1817]; and its comparative unpopularity is due, not merely to the extreme painfulness of the catastrophe, but in part to its dramatic defects, and in part to a failure in many readers to catch the peculiar effects to which I have referred,—a failure which is natural because the appeal is made not so much to dramatic perception as to a rarer and more strictly poetic kind of imagination. For this reason, too, even the best attempts at exposition of *King Lear* are disappointing; they remind us of attempts to reduce to prose the impalpable spirit of the *Tempest.* (pp. 247-48)

[Let me begin] by referring to two passages which have often been criticised with injustice. The first is that where the blinded Gloster, believing that he is going to leap down Dover cliff, does in fact fall flat on the ground at his feet, and then is persuaded that he *has* leaped down Dover cliff but has been miraculously preserved. Imagine this incident transferred to *Othello,* and you realise how completely the two tragedies differ in dramatic atmosphere. In *Othello* it would be a shocking or a ludicrous dissonance, but it is in harmony with the spirit of *King Lear.* And not only is this so, but, contrary to expectation, it is not, if properly acted, in the least absurd on the stage. The imagination and the feelings have been worked upon with such effect by the description of the cliff, and by the portrayal of the old man's despair and his son's courageous and loving wisdom, that we are unconscious of the grotesqueness of the incident for common sense.

The second passage is more important, for it deals with the origin of the whole conflict. The oft-repeated judgment that the first scene of *King Lear* is absurdly improbable, and that no sane man would think of dividing his kingdom among his daughters in proportion to the strength of their several protestations of love, is much too harsh and is based upon a strange misunderstanding. This scene acts effectively, and to imagination the story is not at all incredible. It is merely strange, like so many of the stories on which our romantic dramas are based. Shakespeare, besides, has done a good deal to soften the improbability of the legend, and he has done much more than the casual reader perceives. The very first words of the drama, as Coleridge pointed out, tell us that the division of the kingdom is already settled in all its details, so that only the public announcement of it remains [see excerpt above, 1813]. Later we find that the lines of division have already been drawn on the map of Britain [I. i. 37ff], and again that Cordelia's share, which is her dowry, is perfectly well known to Burgundy, if not to France [I. i. 197, 242]. That then which is censured as absurd, the dependence of the division on the speeches of the daughters, was in Lear's intention a mere form, devised as a childish scheme to gratify his love of absolute power and his hunger for assurances of devotion. And this scheme is perfectly in character. We may even say that the main cause of its failure was not that Goneril and Regan were exceptionally hypocritical, but that Cordelia was exceptionally sincere and unbending. And it is essential to observe that its failure, and the consequent necessity of publicly reversing his whole well-known intention, is one source of Lear's extreme anger. He loved Cordelia most and knew that she loved him best, and the supreme moment to which she looked forward was that in which she should outdo her sisters in expressions of affection, and should be rewarded by that 'third' of the kingdom which was the most 'opulent.' And then—so it naturally seemed to him—she put him to open shame. (pp. 248-50)

The first scene, therefore, is not absurd, though it must be pronounced dramatically faulty in so far as it discloses the true position of affairs only to an attention more alert than can be expected in a theatrical audience or has been found in many critics of the play.

Let us turn next to two passages of another kind, the two which are mainly responsible for the accusation of excessive painfulness, and so for the distaste of many readers and the long theatrical eclipse of *King Lear*. The first of these is much the less important; it is the scene of the blinding of Gloster. The blinding of Gloster on the stage has been condemned almost universally; and surely with justice, because the mere physical horror of such a spectacle would in the theatre be a sensation so violent as to overpower the purely tragic emotions, and therefore the spectacle would seem revolting or shocking. But it is otherwise in reading. For mere imagination the physical horror, though not lost, is so far deadened that it can do its duty as a stimulus to pity, and to that appalled dismay at the extremity of human cruelty which it is of the essence of the tragedy to excite. Thus the blinding of Gloster belongs rightly to *King Lear* in its proper world of imagination; it is a blot upon *King Lear* as a stage-play.

But what are we to say of the second and far more important passage, the conclusion of the tragedy, the 'unhappy ending,' as it is called, though the word 'unhappy' sounds almost ironical in its weakness? Is this too a blot upon *King Lear* as a stage-play? The question is not so easily answered as might appear. Doubtless we are right when we turn with disgust from Tate's sentimental alterations, from his marriage of Edgar and Cordelia, and from that cheap moral which every one of Shakespeare's tragedies contradicts, 'that Truth and Virtue shall at last succeed.' But are we so sure that we are right when we unreservedly condemn the feeling which prompted these alterations, or at all events the feeling which beyond question comes naturally to many readers of *King Lear* who would like Tate as little as we? What they wish, though they have not always the courage to confess it even to themselves, is that the deaths of Edmund, Goneril, Regan and Gloster should be followed by the escape of Lear and Cordelia from death, and that we should be allowed to imagine the poor old King passing quietly in the home of his beloved child to the end which cannot be far off. Now, I do not dream of saying that we ought to wish this, so long as we regard *King Lear* simply as a work of poetic imagination. But if *King Lear* is to be considered strictly as a drama, or simply as we consider *Othello*, it is not so clear that the wish is unjustified. In fact I will take my courage in both hands and say boldly that I share it, and also that I believe Shakespeare would have ended his play thus had he taken the subject in hand a few years later, in the days of *Cymbeline* and the *Winter's Tale*. If I read *King Lear* simply as a drama, I find that my feelings call for this 'happy ending.' I do not mean the human, the philanthropic, feelings, but the dramatic sense. The former wish Hamlet and Othello to escape their doom; the latter does not; but it does wish Lear and Cordelia to be saved. Surely, it says, the tragic emotions have been sufficiently stirred already. Surely the tragic outcome of Lear's error and his daughters' ingratitude has been made clear enough and moving enough. And, still more surely, such a tragic catastrophe as this should seem *inevitable*. But this catastrophe, unlike those of all the other mature tragedies, does not seem at all inevitable. It is not even satisfactorily motived. In fact it seems expressly designed to fall suddenly like a bolt from a sky cleared by the vanished storm. And although from a wider point of view one may fully recognise the value of this effect, and may even reject with horror the wish for a 'happy ending,' this wider point of view, I must maintain, is not strictly dramatic or tragic.

Of course this is a heresy and all the best authority is against it. But then the best authority, it seems to me, is either influenced unconsciously by disgust at Tate's sentimentalism or unconsciously takes that wider point of view. When Lamb—there is no higher authority—writes, 'A happy ending!—as if the living martyrdom that Lear had gone through, the flaying of his feelings alive, did not make a fair dismissal from the stage of life the only decorous thing for him' [see excerpt above, 1812], I answer, first, that it is precisely this *fair* dismissal which we desire for him instead of renewed anguish; and, secondly, that what we desire for him during the brief remainder of his days is not 'the childish pleasure of getting his gilt robes and sceptre again,' not what Tate gives him, but what Shakespeare himself might have given him—peace and happiness by Cordelia's fireside. (pp. 251-54)

A dramatic mistake in regard to the catastrophe, however, even supposing it to exist, would not seriously affect the whole play. The principal structural weakness of *King Lear* lies elsewhere. It is felt to some extent in the earlier Acts, but still more (as from our study of Shakespeare's technique we have learnt to expect) in the Fourth and the first part of the Fifth. And it arises chiefly from the double action, which is a peculiarity of *King Lear* among the tragedies. By the side of Lear, his daughters, Kent, and the Fool, who are the principal figures in the main plot, stand Gloster and his two sons, the chief persons of the secondary plot. Now by means of this double action Shakespeare secured certain results highly advantageous even from the strictly dramatic point of view, and easy to perceive. But the disadvantages were dramatically greater. The number of essential characters is so large, their actions and movements are so complicated, and events towards the close crowd on one another so thickly, that the reader's attention, rapidly transferred from one centre of interest to another, is overstrained. He becomes, if not intellectually confused, at least emotionally fatigued. The battle, on which everything turns, scarcely affects him. The deaths of Edmund, Goneril, Regan and Gloster seem 'but trifles here'; and anything short of the incomparable pathos of the close would leave him cold. There is something almost ludicrous in the insignificance of this battle, when it is compared with the corresponding battles in *Julius Caesar* and *Macbeth;* and though there may have been further reasons for its insignificance, the main one is simply that there was no room to give it its due effect among such a host of competing interests.

A comparison of the last two Acts of *Othello* with the last two Acts of *King Lear* would show how unfavourable to dramatic clearness is a multiplicity of figures. But that this multiplicity is not in itself a fatal obstacle is evident from the last two Acts of *Hamlet,* and especially from the final scene. This is in all respects one of Shakespeare's triumphs, yet the stage is crowded with characters. Only they are not *leading* characters. The plot is single; Hamlet and the King are the 'mighty opposites'; and Ophelia, the only other person in whom we are obliged to take a vivid interest, has already disappeared. It is therefore natural and right that the deaths of Laertes and the Queen should affect us comparatively little. But in *King Lear,* because the plot is double, we have present in the last scene no less than five persons who are technically of the first importance—Lear, his three daughters and Edmund; not to speak of Kent and Edgar, of whom the latter at any rate is technically quite as important as Laertes. And again, owing to the pressure of persons and events, and owing to the concentration of our anxiety on Lear and Cordelia, the combat of Edgar and Edmund, which occupies so considerable a space, fails to excite a tithe of the interest of the fencing-match in *Hamlet.* The truth is that all through these Acts Shakespeare has too vast a material to use with complete dramatic effectiveness, however essential this very vastness was for effects of another kind. (pp. 254-56)

No one of [these] defects is surprising when considered by itself, but their number is surely significant. Taken in conjunction with other symptoms it means that Shakespeare, set upon the dramatic effect of the great scenes and upon certain effects not wholly dramatic, was exceptionally careless of probability, clearness and consistency in smaller matters, introducing what was convenient or striking for a momentary purpose without troubling himself about anything more than the moment. In presence of these signs it seems doubtful whether his failure to give information about the fate of the Fool was due to anything more than carelessness or an impatient desire to reduce his overloaded material.

Before I turn to the other side of the subject I will refer to one more characteristic of this play which is dramatically disad-vantageous. In Shakespeare's dramas, owing to the absence of scenery from the Elizabethan stage, the question, so vexatious to editors, of the exact locality of a particular scene is usually unimportant and often unaswerable; but, as a rule, we know, broadly speaking, where the persons live and what their journeys are. The text makes this plain, for example, almost throughout *Hamlet, Othello* and *Macbeth;* and the imagination is therefore untroubled. But in *King Lear* the indications are so scanty that the reader's mind is left not seldom both vague and bewildered. Nothing enables us to imagine whereabouts in Britain Lear's palace lies, or where the Duke of Albany lives. In referring to the dividing-lines on the map, Lear tells us of shadowy forests and plenteous rivers, but, unlike Hotspur and his companions, he studiously avoids proper names. The Duke of Cornwall, we presume in the absence of information, is likely to live in Cornwall; but we suddenly find, from the introduction of a place-name which all readers take at first for a surname, that he lives at Gloster [I. v. 1ff]. This seems likely to be also the home of the Earl of Gloster, to whom Cornwall is patron. But no: it is a night's journey from Cornwall's 'house' to Gloster's, and Gloster's is in the middle of an uninhabited heath. Here, for the purpose of the crisis, nearly all the persons assemble, but they do so in a manner which no casual spectator or reader could follow. Afterwards they all drift towards Dover for the purpose of the catastrophe; but again the localities and movements are unusually indefinite. . . . Something of the confusion which bewilders the reader's mind in *King Lear* recurs in *Antony and Cleopatra,* the most faultily constructed of all the tragedies; but there it is due not so much to the absence or vagueness of the indications as to the necessity of taking frequent and fatiguing journeys over thousands of miles. Shakespeare could not help himself in the Roman play: in *King Lear* he did not choose to help himself, perhaps deliberately chose to be vague.

From these defects, or from some of them, follows one result which must be familiar to many readers of *King Lear.* It is far more difficult to retrace in memory the steps of the action in this tragedy than in *Hamlet, Othello,* or *Macbeth.* The outline is of course quite clear; anyone could write an 'argument' of the play. But when an attempt is made to fill in the detail, it issues sooner or later in confusion even with readers whose dramatic memory is unusually strong.

How is it, now, that this defective drama so overpowers us that we are either unconscious of its blemishes or regard them as almost irrelevant? As soon as we turn to this question we recognise, not merely that *King Lear* possesses purely dramatic qualities which far outweigh its defects, but that its greatness consists partly in imaginative effects of a wider kind. And, looking for the sources of these effects, we find among them some of those very things which appeared to us dramatically faulty or injurious. Thus, to take at once two of the simplest examples of this, that very vagueness in the sense of locality which we have just considered, and again that excess in the bulk of the material and the number of figures, events and movements, while they interfere with the clearness of vision, have at the same time a positive value for imagination. They give the feeling of vastness, the feeling not of a scene or particular place, but of a world; or, to speak more accurately, of a particular place which is also a world. This world is dim to us, partly from its immensity, and partly because it is filled with gloom; and in the gloom shapes approach and recede, whose half-seen faces and motions touch us with dread, horror, or the most painful pity,—sympathies and antipathies which we seem to be feeling not only for them but for the whole race.

This world, we are told, is called Britain; but we should no more look for it in an atlas than for the place, called Caucasus, where Prometheus was chained by Strength and Force and comforted by the daughters of Ocean. . . . (pp. 258-61)

Consider next the double action. It has certain strictly dramatic advantages, and may well have had its origin in purely dramatic considerations. To go no further, the secondary plot fills out a story which would by itself have been somewhat thin, and it provides a most effective contrast between its personages and those of the main plot, the tragic strength and stature of the latter being heightened by comparison with the slighter build of the former. But its chief value lies elsewhere, and is not merely dramatic. It lies in the fact—in Shakespeare without a parallel—that the sub-plot simply repeats the theme of the main story. Here, as there, we see an old man 'with a white beard.' He, like Lear, is affectionate, unsuspicious, foolish, and self-willed. He, too, wrongs deeply a child who loves him not less for the wrong. He, too, meets with monstrous ingratitude from the child whom he favours, and is tortured and driven to death. This repetition does not simply double the pain with which the tragedy is witnessed: it startles and terrifies by suggesting that the folly of Lear and the ingratitude of his daughters are no accidents or merely individual aberrations, but that in that dark cold world some fateful malignant influence is abroad, turning the hearts of the fathers against their children and of the children against their fathers, smiting the earth with a curse, so that the brother gives the brother to death and the father the son, blinding the eyes, maddening the brain, freezing the springs of pity, numbing all powers except the nerves of anguish and the dull lust of life.

Hence too, as well as from other sources, comes that feeling which haunts us in *King Lear,* as though we were witnessing something universal,—a conflict not so much of particular persons as of the powers of good and evil in the world. And the treatment of many of the characters confirms this feeling. Considered simply as psychological studies few of them, surely, are of the highest interest. Fine and subtle touches could not be absent from a work of Shakespeare's maturity; but, with the possible exception of Lear himself, no one of the characters strikes us as psychologically a *wonderful* creation, like Hamlet or Iago or even Macbeth; one or two seem even to be somewhat faint and thin. And, what is more significant, it is not quite natural to us to regard them from this point of view at all. Rather we observe a most unusual circumstance. If Lear, Gloster and Albany are set apart, the rest fall into two distinct groups, which are strongly, even violently, contrasted: Cordelia, Kent, Edgar, the Fool on one side, Goneril, Regan, Edmund, Cornwall, Oswald on the other. These characters are in various degrees individualised, most of them completely so; but still in each group there is a quality common to all the members, or one spirit breathing through them all. Here we have unselfish and devoted love, there hard self-seeking. On both sides, further, the common quality takes an extreme form; the love is incapable of being chilled by injury, the selfishness of being softened by pity; and, it may be added, this tendency to extremes is found again in the characters of Lear and Gloster, and is the main source of the accusations of improbability directed against their conduct at certain points. Hence the members of each group tend to appear, at least in part, as varieties of one species; the radical differences of the two species are emphasized in broad hard strokes; and the two are set in conflict, almost as if Shakespeare, like Empedocles, were regarding Love and Hate as the two ultimate forces of the universe.

The presence in *King Lear* of so large a number of characters in whom love or self-seeking is so extreme, has another effect. They do not merely inspire in us emotions of unusual strength, but they also stir the intellect to wonder and speculation. How can there be such men and women? we ask ourselves. How comes it that humanity can take such absolutely opposite forms? And, in particular, to what omission of elements which should be present in human nature, or, if there is no omission, to what distortion of these elements is it due that such beings as some of these come to exist? This is a question which Iago (and perhaps no previous creation of Shakespeare's) forces us to ask, but in *King Lear* it is provoked again and again. And more, it seems to us that the author himself is asking this question. 'Then let them anatomise Regan, see what breeds about her heart. Is there any cause in nature that makes these hard hearts?' [III. vi. 76-8]—the strain of thought which appears here seems to be present in some degree throughout the play. We seem to trace the tendency which, a few years later, produced Ariel and Caliban, the tendency of imagination to analyse and abstract, to decompose human nature into its constituent factors, and then to construct beings in whom one or more of these factors is absent or atrophied or only incipient. This, of course, is a tendency which produces symbols, allegories, personifications of qualities and abstract ideas; and we are accustomed to think it quite foreign to Shakespeare's genius, which was in the highest degree concrete. No doubt in the main we are right here; but it is hazardous to set limits to that genius. The Sonnets, if nothing else, may show us how easy it was to Shakespeare's mind to move in a world of 'Platonic' ideas; and, while it would be going too far to suggest that he was employing conscious symbolism or allegory in *King Lear,* it does appear to disclose a mode of imagination not so very far removed from the mode with which, we must remember, Shakespeare was perfectly familiar in Morality plays and in the *Fairy Queen.* (pp. 262-65)

The influence of all this on imagination as we read *King Lear* is very great; and it combines with other influences to convey to us, not in the form of distinct ideas but in the manner proper to poetry, the wider or universal significance of the spectacle presented to the inward eye. But the effect of theatrical exhibition is precisely the reverse. There the poetic atmosphere is dissipated; the meaning of the very words which create it passes half-realised; in obedience to the tyranny of the eye we conceive the characters as mere particular men and women; and all that mass of vague suggestion, if it enters the mind at all, appears in the shape of an allegory which we immediately reject. A similar conflict between imagination and sense will be found if we consider the dramatic centre of the whole tragedy, the Storm-scenes. The temptation of Othello and the scene of Duncan's murder may lose upon the stage, but they do not lose their essence, and they gain as well as lose. The Storm-scenes in *King Lear* gain nothing and their very essence is destroyed. It is comparatively a small thing that the theatrical storm, not to drown the dialogue, must be silent whenever a human being wishes to speak, and is wretchedly inferior to many a storm we have witnessed. Nor is it simply that, as Lamb observed, the corporal presence of Lear, 'an old man tottering about the stage with a walking-stick' [see excerpt above, 1812], disturbs and depresses that sense of the greatness of his mind which fills the imagination. There is a further reason, which is not expressed, but still emerges, in these words of Lamb's: 'the explosions of his passion are terrible as a volcano: they are storms turning up and disclosing to the bottom that sea, his mind, with all its vast riches.' Yes, 'they are *storms*.' For imagination, that is to say, the explosions of Lear's passion, and the bursts of rain and thunder, are not, what for the senses they must be, two things, but manifestations of one thing. It is the powers of the tormented soul that we hear and see in the 'groans of roaring wind and rain' and the 'sheets of fire' [III. ii. 46, 47]; and they that, at intervals almost more overwhelming, sink back into darkness and silence. . . . [In] the storm we seem to see Nature herself convulsed by the same horrible passions; the 'common mother,'

> Whose womb immeasurable and infinite breast
> Teems and feeds all,
>
> *[Timon of Athens,* IV. iii. 178-79]

turning on her children, to complete the ruin they have wrought upon themselves. Surely something not less, but much more, than these helpless words convey, is what comes to us in these astounding scenes; and if, translated thus into the language of prose, it becomes confused and inconsistent, the reason is simply that it itself is poetry, and such poetry as cannot be transferred to the space behind the foot-lights, but has its being only in imagination. Here then is Shakespeare at his very greatest, but not the mere dramatist Shakespeare.

And now we may say this also of the catastrophe, which we found questionable from the strictly dramatic point of view. Its purpose is not merely dramatic. This sudden blow out of the darkness, which seems so far from inevitable, and which strikes down our reviving hopes for the victims of so much cruelty, seems now only what we might have expected in a world so wild and monstrous. It is as if Shakespeare said to us: 'Did you think weakness and innocence have any chance here? Were you beginning to dream that? I will show you it is not so.'

I come to a last point. As we contemplate this world, the question presses on us, What can be the ultimate power that moves it, that excites this gigantic war and waste, or, perhaps, that suffers them and overrules them? And in *King Lear* this question is not left to *us* to ask, it is raised by the characters themselves. References to religious or irreligious beliefs and feelings are more frequent than is usual in Shakespeare's tragedies, as frequent perhaps as in his final plays. He introduces characteristic differences in the language of the different persons about fortune or the stars or the gods, and shows how the question What rules the world? is forced upon their minds. . . . Almost throughout the latter half of the drama we note in most of the better characters a pre-occupation with the question of the ultimate power, and a passionate need to explain by reference to it what otherwise would drive them to despair. And the influence of this pre-occupation and need joins with other influences in affecting the imagination, and in causing it to receive from *King Lear* an impression which is at least as near of kin to the *Divine Comedy* as to *Othello.*

For Dante that which is recorded in the *Divine Comedy* was the justice and love of God. What did *King Lear* record for Shakespeare? Something, it would seem, very different. This is certainly the most terrible picture that Shakespeare painted of the world. In no other of his tragedies does humanity appear more pitiably infirm or more hopelessly bad. What is Iago's malignity against an envied stranger compared with the cruelty of the son of Gloster and the daughters of Lear? What are the sufferings of a strong man like Othello to those of helpless age? Much too that we have already observed—the repetition of the main theme in that of the under-plot, the comparisons of man with the most wretched and the most horrible of the beasts, the impression of Nature's hostility to him, the irony

of the unexpected catastrophe—these, with much else, seem even to indicate an intention to show things at their worst, and to return the sternest of replies to that question of the ultimate power and those appeals for retribution. . . . Albany and Edgar may moralise on the divine justice as they will, but how, in face of all that we see, shall we believe they speak Shakespeare's mind? Is not his mind rather expressed in the bitter contrast between their faith and the events we witness, or in the scornful rebuke of those who take upon them the mystery of things as if they were God's spies? Is it not Shakespeare's judgment on his kind that we hear in Lear's appeal,

> And thou, all-shaking thunder,
> Smite flat the thick rotundity o' the world!
> Crack nature's moulds, all germens spill at once,
> That make ingrateful man!
>
> [III. ii. 6-9]

and Shakespeare's judgment on the worth of existence that we hear in Lear's agonised cry, 'No, no, no life!' [V. iii. 306]?

Beyond doubt, I think, some such feelings as these possess us, and, if we follow Shakespeare, ought to possess us, from time to time as we read *King Lear.* And some readers will go further and maintain that this is also the ultimate and total impression left by the tragedy. *King Lear* has been held to be profoundly 'pessimistic' in the full meaning of that word,—the record of a time when contempt and loathing for his kind had overmastered the poet's soul, and in despair he pronounced man's life to be simply hateful and hideous. And if we exclude the biographical part of this view, the rest may claim some support even from the greatest of Shakespearean critics since the days of Coleridge, Hazlitt and Lamb. (pp. 269-76)

King Lear is admittedly one of the world's greatest poems, and yet there is surely no other of these poems which produces on the whole this effect, and we regard it as a very serious flaw in any considerable work of art that this should be its ultimate effect. So that Mr. Swinburne's description, if taken as final [see excerpt above, 1880], and any description of *King Lear* as pessimistic in the proper sense of that word, would imply a criticism which is not intended, and which would make it difficult to leave the work in the position almost universally assigned to it.

But in fact these descriptions . . . emphasise only certain aspects of the play and certain elements in the total impression; and in that impression the effect of these aspects, though far from being lost, is modified by that of others. I do not mean that the final effect resembles that of the *Divine Comedy* or the *Oresteia:* how should it, when the first of these can be called by its author a 'Comedy,' and when the second, ending (as doubtless the *Prometheus* trilogy also ended) with a solution, is not in the Shakespearean sense a tragedy at all? Nor do I mean that *King Lear* contains a revelation of righteous omnipotence or heavenly harmony, or even a promise of the reconciliation of mystery and justice. But then . . . neither do Shakespeare's other tragedies contain these things. Any theological interpretation of the world on the author's part is excluded from them, and their effect would be disordered or destroyed equally by the ideas of righteous or of unrighteous omnipotence. Nor, in reading them, do we think of 'justice' or 'equity' in the sense of a strict requital or such an adjustment of merit and prosperity as our moral sense is said to demand; and there never was vainer labour than that of critics who try to make out that the persons in these dramas meet with 'justice' or their 'desserts.' But, on the other hand, man is not represented in these tragedies as the mere plaything of a blind or capricious power, suffering woes which have no relation to his character and actions; nor is the world represented as given over to darkness. And in these respects *King Lear,* though the most terrible of these works, does not differ in essence from the rest. Its keynote is surely to be heard neither in the words wrung from Gloster in his anguish, nor in Edgar's words 'the gods are just.' Its final and total result is one in which pity and terror, carried perhaps to the extreme limits of art, are so blended with a sense of law and beauty that we feel at last, not depression and much less despair, but a consciousness of greatness in pain, and of solemnity in the mystery we cannot fathom. (pp. 277-79)

But there is another aspect of Lear's story, the influence of which modifies, in a way quite different and more peculiar to this tragedy, the impressions called pessimistic and even this impression of law. There is nothing more noble and beautiful in literature than Shakespeare's exposition of the effect of suffering in reviving the greatness and eliciting the sweetness of Lear's nature. . . . The old King who in pleading with his daughters feels so intensely his own humiliation and their horrible ingratitude, and who yet, at fourscore and upward, constrains himself to practise a self-control and patience so many years disused; who out of old affection for his Fool, and in repentance for his injustice to the Fool's beloved mistress, tolerates incessant and cutting reminders of his own folly and wrong; in whom the rage of the storm awakes a power and a poetic grandeur surpassing even that of Othello's anguish; who comes in his affliction to think of others first, and to seek, in tender solicitude for his poor boy, the shelter he scorns for his own bare head; who learns to feel and to pray for the miserable and houseless poor, to discern the falseness of flattery and the brutality of authority, and to pierce below the differences of rank and raiment to the common humanity beneath; whose sight is so purged by scalding tears that it sees at last how power and place and all things in the world are vanity except love; who tastes in his last hours the extremes both of love's rapture and of its agony, but could never, if he lived on or lived again, care a jot for aught beside—there is no figure, surely, in the world of poetry at once so grand, so pathetic, and so beautiful as his. Well, but Lear owes the whole of this to those sufferings which made us doubt whether life were not simply evil, and men like the flies which wanton boys torture for their sport. Should we not be at least as near the truth if we called this poem *The Redemption of King Lear,* and declared that the business of 'the gods' with him was neither to torment him, nor to teach him a 'noble anger,' but to lead him to attain through apparently hopeless failure the very end and aim of life? One can believe that Shakespeare had been tempted at times to feel misanthropy and despair, but it is quite impossible that he can have been mastered by such feelings at the time when he produced this conception. (pp. 284-85)

If to the reader, as to the bystanders, [the final] scene brings one unbroken pain, it is not so with Lear himself. His shattered mind passes from the first transports of hope and despair, as he bends over Cordelia's body and holds the feather to her lips, into an absolute forgetfulness of the cause of these transports. This continues so long as he can converse with Kent; becomes an almost complete vacancy; and is disturbed only to yield, as his eyes suddenly fall again on his child's corpse, to an agony which at once breaks his heart. And, finally, though he is killed by an agony of pain, the agony in which he actually

dies is one not of pain but of ecstasy. Suddenly . . . , he exclaims:

> Do you see this? Look on her, look, her lips,
> Look there, look there!
>
> [V. iii. 311-12]

These are the last words of Lear. He is sure, at last, that she *lives:* and what had he said when he was still in doubt?

> She lives! if it be so,
> It is a chance which does redeem all sorrows
> That ever I have felt!
>
> [V. iii. 266-68]

To us, perhaps, the knowledge that he is deceived may bring a culmination of pain: but, if it brings *only* that, I believe we are false to Shakespeare, and it seems almost beyond question that any actor is false to the text who does not attempt to express, in Lear's last accents and gestures and look, an unbearable *joy.* (p. 291)

A. C. Bradley, ''Lecture VII: 'King Lear''' and ''Lecture VIII: 'King Lear','' in his Shakespearean Tragedy: Lectures on ''Hamlet,'' ''Othello,'' ''King Lear,'' ''Macbeth,'' *second edition, Macmillan and Co., Limited, 1905, pp. 243-79, 280-330.*

E. K. CHAMBERS (essay date 1906)

[*Chambers occupies a transitional position in Shakespearean criticism, one which connects the biographical sketches and character analyses of the nineteenth century with the historical, technical, and textual criticism of the twentieth century. While a member of the education department at Oxford University, Chambers earned his reputation as a scholar with his multivolume works,* The Medieval Stage *(1903) and* The Elizabethan Stage *(1923), while he also edited* The Red Letter Shakespeare. *Chambers both investigated the purpose and limitations of each dramatic genre as Shakespeare presented it and speculated on how the dramatist's work was influenced by contemporary historical issues and his own frame of mind. In the excerpt below, taken from his introduction to* The Red Letter Shakespeare *edition of* King Lear *(1906), Chambers divides Shakespeare's tragedies into two groups: those, such as* Julius Caesar, Hamlet, *and* Antony and Cleopatra, *which he calls psychological tragedies; and those, such as* King Lear *and* Macbeth, *which he calls the ''cosmic kind of tragedy.'' Chambers concludes his essay by claiming that Shakespeare altered the old chronicle* King Leir *from a tragicomedy to a tragedy—by substituting the catastrophic ending for the triumphant one—in order to depict the ''final victory of evil'' in the world. For Chambers, then,* King Lear *presents a pessimistic vision of life, an interpretation that receives further support in the essays by Algernon Charles Swinburne (1880), Stopford A. Brooke (1913), G. Wilson Knight (1930), J. Stampfer (1960), and Jan Kott (1964).*]

Among the tragedies of Shakespeare, *King Lear* stands out as, in the Aristotelian sense of the word, the most tragic. It is the most tremendous in design, brings into play the most elemental forces, makes the most irresistible demand upon those emotions of pity and of awe, the purification of which is the function and deliberate end of tragedy. I say purification, not purgation, since, whatever may be the metaphorical sense which philologists find in [catharsis] as it is used elsewhere than in the treatise *On Poetry,* experience must needs bear it out that the actual effect of tragedy is not to purge away or eliminate pity and awe from the soul of the spectator, and is to purify and ennoble those emotions, by calling them from the personal to the universal and fixing them upon just those elements in the totality of things which, essentially and in themselves, are the most pitiful and the most awful. This ideal of tragedy is realized in *King Lear,* as it has only been realized some dozen times in the history of literature, largely by virtue of the cosmic scope of the play. Like the *Oresteia,* like *Tess of the D'Urbervilles,* it is a philosophical drama…. It is analytic, not constructive; contents itself with an understanding of things, and offers no remedy to make these odds all even. But, for the philosopher, to understand is already to have half the remedy.

King Lear belongs to the later manner of Shakespearean tragedy. All tragedy, of course, depends upon the interplay of two factors; on the one hand human character in its unequal and faulty composition, on the other the environment of conditions within which character moves, and by its reaction upon which it is determined to success or failure. When Shakespeare first began seriously to consider life from a tragic point of view, it was the element of character that claimed his interest and stung his imagination…. In a second group of tragedies, however, Shakespeare's speculation seems to shift from the nature of man to the nature of what is around and above man, and to seek the primary causes of tragic disaster, less in the imperfect mettle of a hero, although that indeed must still contribute, than in external forces which are conceived of, if not as making directly for evil rather than for righteousness, at least as unmoral and blind in their working. Thus in *Macbeth* sin and the retribution of sin are represented as the two closely related parts of a mysterious curse imposed upon the sinner from without, and the symbolism of the witches is used, in characteristic fashion, to indicate its superhuman origin. It is only natural that this change in the dramatist's attitude to tragedy should carry with it an ever-deepening pessimism, for while there is always hope that the frailties of humanity may find amelioration, it would be presumptuous to suppose that the external forces can ever be rendered other than what they are.

Of the second or cosmic kind of tragedy, *King Lear* is perhaps even a more typical example than *Macbeth.* Like the psychological *Hamlet,* it takes its starting-point from the family relations and the human emotions which are built up upon these. Of course it does not disregard psychology, merely because ultimately it is to transcend psychology. Lear himself, in particular, is a most subtle psychological study. He is a man of passionate fibre and unrestrained temper, wholly swayed in his old age by two imperious instincts, that of personal domination and that of natural affection for his daughters. As might be expected, his affection tends to manifest itself, not as self-renunciation, but as one among other forms of domination. His instincts possess him wholly. They warp his judgment of character and drive him to acts of which he has not the imagination to foresee the inevitable results. He abdicates out of an impulse to endear himself to his daughters by a liberal abandonment of everything, and thinks, sincerely enough for the moment, that he will be for ever content to set up his rest in their kind nursery. But it has never entered his head to conceive what abdication really means. His first act after surrendering his kingly prerogative is to exercise that prerogative by ordering Kent into banishment. The same temperament determines his behaviour to Cordelia. Absorbed, as a true egoist, in his own emotions, even when they are most generous, he has no eye for the fine shades of expression and conduct in others, and is thus led into the irony of rejecting the one daughter who would have comprehended and endured. Obviously, with such a father and with pelican children, the attempt to resign power and yet to keep the name and all the additions to a king is doomed to failure. He gives an easy handle to the malevolence of Goneril and of Regan…. Lear, by his own unbalanced act, is helpless.

Goneril and Regan outvie each other in their merciless use of the advantage which his blind impulse has given them. (pp. 240-44)

Outraged affection and outraged self-will find vent in unmeasured denunciations of those who have set the claims of fatherhood at naught. Lear appeals from his daughters to the heavens, to the heavens who surely love old men and must give effect to 'the untented woundings of a father's curse' [I. iv. 300]. He is confident in the justice of his cause. He need hardly formulate his plea, but may leave the stored vengeances of heaven to their inevitable working…. And now comes in the cosmic side of the tragedy; for once more the confident Lear has hopelessly misjudged the position with which he is confronted. The heavens prove as deaf to his call as either Goneril or Regan. They are not on the side of righteousness. The tempest which greets him upon the heath is symbolical; and here, in a scene which surely represents the extremest stretch of Shakespeare's titanic mood, we find him contending with the 'dreadful pudder' of the elements, now calling upon them to—

> Crack nature's moulds, all germens spill at once
> That makes ingrateful man,
>
> [III. ii. 8-9]

and now upbraiding them for joining their high engendered battles with his pernicious daughters against so old and white a head. And in the end it is wind and rain, rather than unkindness, that beat him into submission, and force him to acknowledge what a 'poor, bare, forked animal' is 'unaccommodated man' [III. iv. 106-08]. Then for symbol, once more, of his tragic defeat comes the crash and ruin of his wits, since madness, inadmissible as a motive of tragedy, is here in its right place as an acknowledgment of the culmination and catastrophe of a tragic issue.

It is worth observing with what care Shakespeare has arranged every detail of the play so as to give edge to his indictment of the forces that make sport of man's nothingness. The plot, which deliberately rejects the Christian interpretation of the universe, is set in a pagan environment. The heavens are invoked in a pagan terminology, as Nature, or under the names of the classic deities. Pains are taken, contrary to the usual disregard of anachronisms in the plays, to avoid the introduction of Christian language or Christian sentiments. Again, the story of Lear is not allowed to stand by itself, alone and individual. It is part of the intention that the theme of the play should be of universal significance. And therefore, side by side with the main plot, is set a sub-plot, in which the fortunes of the house of Lear are repeated in the fortunes of the house of Gloucester. The story is less tremendously urged, in order that the main interest of the spectators may not be diverted; but the parallel is complete. (pp. 244-46)

The story of Gloucester is an addition made by Shakespeare to the plot of the old play, known as *The Tragical History of King Leir,* which was doubtless his principal source. Another modification which he introduced is even more significant. The old play was not a tragedy but a tragicomedy. In its conclusion a French invasion confounded the evil-doers, vindicated Providence, reconciled Lear to Cordelia, and restored him triumphantly to his kingdom. But such an ending would not have suited Shakespeare's design, because it would not have borne the burden of the final victory of evil. Therefore he remorselessly altered it. There are forces of good, indeed, in the play— Cordelia and Edgar, the faithful Kent, the generous France, the reluctant Albany; but they are represented as proving in the end quite ineffective agents for the mastering of evil. Emphasis is laid upon this issue by the temporary suggestion shortly after the crisis of a contrary solution. During the Fourth Act things look as if they were tending to a happy close. The fever of Lear's distemper has abated. He is no longer buffeted by the elements, but wanders through the fields, still, no doubt, mad as the vexed sea, but—

> Singing aloud,
> Crowned with rank fumitory and furrow weeds,
> With burdocks, hemlock, nettles, cuckoo-flowers,
> Darnel, and all the idle weeds that grow
> In our sustaining corn.
>
> [IV. iv. 2-6]

There is hope that repose and simples may yet restore him to his senses. Gloucester has fallen in with Edgar and has been saved from destruction on the cliff. Both have made their way to Dover, and at Dover Cordelia, the radiant white soul of the play, awaits them. With her are the armies of France, the righter of wrongs. All seems as if the victims of filial treachery would have their own again, and Goneril, Regan, and Edmund meet with a richly-deserved Nemesis. Only, when it comes to the point, the heavens refuse to have it so. In the last Act, the hopes of tragicomedy are ruthlessly brushed away. High-judging Jove sends down his thunders and lightnings to the end, no less than his rain, upon the just and upon the unjust. There is Nemesis in plenty for the wicked, who are taken in the web of their own devising; but this carries with it no salvation for Lear and for Cordelia. The final reversal of poetic justice is complete. Cordelia and her army are simply defeated. Then, through the ineffectiveness of Albany, Cordelia is murdered, and the tale of Lear's disasters is full.... Here is the tragic awe in abundant measure. And that the tragic pity may not be lacking also, the fate of Cordelia gives the needful touch of pathos in the story of Lear, jsut as the fate of Ophelia gives it in the story of Hamlet. (pp. 246-48)

> *E. K. Chambers, "'King Lear'," in his* Shakespeare: A Survey, *1925. Reprint by Oxford University Press, 1926, pp. 240-48.*

LEO NIKOLAYEVICH TOLSTOY   (essay date 1906)

[*Tolstoy is regarded as one of the greatest novelists in world literature and a master of detail and psychological realism. Following the publication of his famous novels* War and Peace *and* Anna Karenina, *Tolstoy underwent a spiritual upheaval that resulted in his conversion to a radical form of Christianity. The artistic repercussions of this conversion caused him to repudiate nearly all his previous work and to dismiss most of the world's greatest artists, including William Shakespeare and Richard Wagner, as elitist individuals who produced spurious, rather than universal, art. Like George Bernard Shaw, Tolstoy was highly irritated by Shakespeare's reputation, and he wrote several extended attacks against him in an effort to diminish his universal admiration. In his study* What Is Art? *(1898), and even more so in his essay "Shakespeare and the Drama" (1906), he affirmed that even after rereading all of Shakespeare in Russian, English, and German, his response was the same: "repulsion, weariness, and bewilderment." He then undertook to explain the reasons for his negative reaction in a detailed analysis of* King Lear, *where he severely criticizes Shakespeare for his characters' lack of motivation, his lack of realism, and the absence of probability or verisimilitude in his drama. Most reprehensible, for Tolstoy, is Shakespeare's amoralism—a fact the Russian relates to "the irreligious and immoral frame of mind of the upper classes of Shakespeare's time." In the following excerpt, from this essay,*

Tolstoy argues that Shakespeare's King Lear *is so poorly written that, in comparison, the old chronicle* King Leir *stands as a much better play. Over forty years later George Orwell (1947) responded to Tolstoy's charges, claiming that the Russian felt such an aversion to the play because it subconsciously suggested similar failures in Tolstoy's life to achieve peace and happiness.*]

For any man of our time—if he were not under the hypnotic suggestion that [*King Lear*] is the height of perfection—it would be enough to read it to its end (had he sufficient patience for this) to be convinced that far from its being the height of perfection, it is a very bad, carelessly composed production, which, if it could have been of interest to a certain public at a certain time, cannot evoke amongst us anything but aversion and weariness. Every reader of our time who is free from the influence of suggestion will also receive exactly the same impression from all the other extolled dramas of Shakespeare, not to mention the senseless dramatized tales, *Pericles, Twelfth Night, The Tempest, Cymbeline, Troilus and Cressida.*

But such free-minded individuals, not inoculated with Shakespeare worship, are no longer to be found in our Christian society. On every man of our society and time, from the first period of his conscious life, it has been inculcated that Shakespeare is a genius as poet and dramatist, and that all his writings are the height of perfection. Yet however hopeless it may seem, I will endeavor to demonstrate in the selected drama—*King Lear*—all those faults, equally characteristic of all the other tragedies and comedies of Shakespeare, on account of which he is not only no model of dramatic art, but does not satisfy the most elementary demands of art recognized by all.

Dramatic art, according to the laws established by those very critics who extol Shakespeare, demands that the persons represented in the play should be, in consequence of actions proper to their characters, and owing to a natural course of events, placed in positions requiring them to struggle with the surrounding world to which they find themselves in opposition—and in this struggle should display their inherent qualities.

In *King Lear*, the persons represented are indeed placed externally in opposition to the outward world, and they struggle with it. But their strife does not flow from the natural course of events nor from their own characters, but is quite arbitrarily established by the author, and therefore cannot produce in the reader that illusion which represents the essential condition of art.

Lear has no necessity or motive for his abdication, also having lived all his life with his daughters, he has no reason to believe the words of the two elder and not the truthful statement of the youngest; yet upon this is built the whole tragedy of his position.

Similarly unnatural is the subordinate action: the relation of Gloucester to his sons. The positions of Gloucester and Edgar flow from the circumstance that Gloucester, just like Lear, immediately believes the coarsest untruth, and does not even endeavor to inquire of his injured son whether the accusation against him be true, but at once curses and banishes him. The fact that Lear's relations with his daughters are the same as those of Gloucester with his sons makes one feel yet more strongly that in both cases the relations are quite arbitrary and do not flow from the characters nor the natural course of events. Equally unnatural and obviously invented is the fact that, all through the tragedy, Lear does not recognize his old courtier Kent, and therefore the relations between Lear and Kent fail to excite the sympathy of the reader or spectator. In a yet greater degree the same holds true of the position of Edgar, who, unrecognized by anyone, leads his blind father and persuades him that he has leaped off a cliff when in reality Gloucester jumps on level ground.

These positions into which the characters are placed quite arbitrarily are so unnatural that the reader or spectator is unable, not only to sympathize with their sufferings, but even to be interested in what he reads or sees. This in the first place.

Secondly, in this, as in the other dramas of Shakespeare, all the characters live, think, speak, and act quite unconformably with the given time and place. The action of *King Lear* takes place 800 years B.C. and yet the characters are placed in conditions possible only in the Middle Ages: participating in the drama are kings, dukes, armies, and illegitimate children, and gentlemen, courtiers, doctors, farmers, officers, soldiers, and knights with visors, etc. It may be that such anachronisms (with which Shakespeare's dramas abound) did not injure the possibility of illusion in the sixteenth century and the beginning of the seventeenth; but in our time it is no longer possible to follow with interest the development of events which one knows could not take place in the conditions which the author describes in detail. The artificiality of the positions, not flowing from the nature of the characters, and their want of conformity with time and space, is further increased by those coarse embellishments which are continually added by Shakespeare in the places intended to appear particularly touching. The extraordinary storm, during which King Lear roams about the heath, or the grass which for some reason he puts on his head—like Ophelia in *Hamlet*—or Edgar's attire, or the fool's speeches, or the appearance of the helmeted horseman, Edgar—all these effects not only fail to enhance the impression but produce an opposite effect. . . . It often happens that even during these obviously intentional efforts after effect—as for instance the dragging out by the legs of half a dozen corpses with which all Shakespeare's tragedies terminate—instead of feeling fear and pity, one is tempted rather to laugh. (pp. 245-48)

It is generally asserted that in Shakespeare's dramas the characters are especially well expressed, that notwithstanding their vividness, they are many-sided like those of living people; that while exhibiting the characteristics of a given individual they at the same time wear the features of man in general; it is usual to say that the delineation of character in Shakespeare is the height of perfection.

This is asserted with much confidence and repeated by all as indisputable truth; but however much I endeavored to find confirmation of this in Shakespeare's dramas, I always found the opposite. In reading any of Shakespeare's dramas whatever, I was from the very first instantly convinced that he was lacking in the most important, if not the only means of portraying characters: individuality of language, i.e., the style of speech of every person being natural to his character. This is absent from Shakespeare. All his characters speak, not their own, but always one and the same Shakespearean pretentious and unnatural language, in which not only they could not speak, but in which no living man ever has spoken or does speak.

No living man could or can say as Lear says—that he would divorce his wife in the grave should Regan not receive him, or that the heavens would crack with shouting, or that the winds would burst, or that the wind wishes to blow the land into the sea, or that the curled waters wish to flood the shore, as the gentleman describes the storm, or that it is easier to bear one's grief, and the soul leaps over many sufferings when grief finds

fellowship; or that Lear has become childless while I am fatherless, as Edgar says, or use similar unnatural expressions with which the speeches of all the characters in all Shakespeare's dramas overflow. (pp. 248-49)

The perfection with which Shakespeare expresses character is asserted chiefly on the ground of the characters of Lear, Cordelia, Othello, Desdemona, Falstaff, Hamlet. But all these characters, as well as all the others, instead of belonging to Shakespeare are taken by him from dramas, chronicles, and romances anterior to him. All these characters not only are not rendered more powerful by him, but in most cases, they are weakened and spoiled. This is very striking in this drama of *King Lear,* which we are examining, taken by him from the drama *King Leir* by an unknown author. The characters of this drama, that of King Lear, and especially of Cordelia, not only were not created by Shakespeare, but have been strikingly weakened and deprived of expression by him, as compared with their appearance in the older drama.

In the older drama, Leir abdicates because, having become a widower, he thinks only of saving his soul. He asks his daughters as to their love for him—that by means of a certain device he has invented he may retain his favorite daughter on his island. The elder daughters are betrothed, while the youngest does not wish to contract a loveless union with any of the neighboring suitors whom Leir proposes to her, and he is afraid that she may marry some distant potentate.

The device which he has invented, as he informs his courtier Perillus (Shakespeare's Kent), is this: that when Cordelia tells him that she loves him more than anyone or as much as her elder sisters do, he will tell her that she must in proof of her love marry the prince he will indicate on his island. All these motives for Lear's conduct are absent in Shakespeare's play. Then, when according to the old drama, Leir asks his daughters about their love for him, Cordelia does not say, as Shakespeare has it, that she will not give her father all her love, but will love her husband too, should she marry—to say which is quite unnatural—but simply says that she cannot express her love in words and hopes that her actions will prove it. Goneril and Regan remark that Cordelia's answer is not an answer, and that the father cannot meekly accept such indifference, so that what is wanting in Shakespeare—i.e., the explanation of Lear's anger which caused him to disinherit his youngest daughter—exists in the old drama. Leir is annoyed by the failure of his scheme, and the poisonous words of his elder daughters irritate him still more. After the division of the kingdom between the elder daughters there follows in the older drama a scene between Cordelia and [her future husband] the King of Gaul, setting forth, instead of the colorless Cordelia of Shakespeare, a very definite and attractive character of the truthful, tender, and self-sacrificing youngest daughter. . . . Instead of this scene, Lear, according to Shakespeare, proposes to Cordelia's two suitors to take her without dowry, and one cynically refuses, while the other, one does not know why, accepts her. After this, in the old drama, as in Shakespeare's, Leir undergoes the insults of Goneril, into whose house he has removed, but he bears these insults in a very different way from that represented by Shakespeare: he feels that by his conduct toward Cordelia he has deserved this, and humbly submits. As in Shakespeare's drama, so also in the older drama, the courtier—Kent—who had interceded for Cordelia and was therefore banished—comes to Leir and assures him of his love, but under no disguise, simply as a faithful old servant who does not abandon his king in a moment of need. . . . In the older drama there are no tempests nor tearing out of gray hairs, but there is the weakened and humbled old man, Leir, overpowered with grief, and banished by his other daughter also, who even wishes to kill him. Turned out by his elder daughters, Leir, according to the older drama, as a last resource, goes with Perillus to Cordelia. Instead of the unnatural banishment of Lear during the tempest, and his roaming about the heath, Leir, with Perillus, in the older drama, during their journey to France, very naturally reach the last degree of destitution, sell their clothes in order to pay for their crossing over the sea, and, in the attire of fishermen, exhausted by cold and hunger, approach Cordelia's house. Here again, instead of the unnatural combined ravings of the fool, Lear and Edgar, as represented by Shakespeare, there follows in the older drama a natural scene of reunion between the daughter and the father. (pp. 250-53)

However strange this opinion may seem to worshipers of Shakespeare, yet the whole of this old drama is incomparably and in every respect superior to Shakespeare's adaptation. It is so, firstly, because it has not got the utterly superfluous characters of the villain Edmund and the unlifelike Gloucester and Edgar, who only distract one's attention; secondly, because it has not got the completely false "effects" of Lear running about the heath, his conversations with the fool, and all these impossible disguises, failures to recognize, and accumulated deaths; and above all, because in this drama there is the simple natural and deeply touching character of Leir and the yet more touching and clearly defined character of Cordelia, both absent in Shakespeare. Therefore there is in the older drama, instead of Shakespeare's long drawn-out scene of Lear's interview with Cordelia and of Cordelia's unnecessary murder—the exquisite scene of the interview between Leir and Cordelia, unequaled by any in all Shakespeare's dramas.

The old drama also terminates more naturally and more in accordance with the moral demands of the spectator than does Shakespeare's: namely, by the King of the Gauls conquering the husbands of the elder sisters, and by Cordelia, instead of being killed, restoring Leir to his former position. (p. 254)

"Well, but what of the profound utterances and sayings expressed by Shakespeare's characters," Shakespeare's panegyrists will retort. "See Lear's monologue on punishment, Kent's speech about vengeance, or Edgar's about his former life, Gloucester's reflections on the instability of fortune, and in other dramas, the famous monologues of Hamlet, Antony, and others."

Thoughts and sayings may be appreciated, I will answer, in a prose work, in an essay, a collection of aphorisms, but not in an artistic dramatic production, the object of which is to elicit sympathy with what is represented. Therefore the monologues and sayings of Shakespeare, even did they contain very many deep and new thoughts, which is not the case, do not constitute the merits of an artistic poetic production. On the contrary, these speeches, expressed in unnatural conditions, can only spoil artistic works. (p. 261)

[To] say what is superflous is the same as to overthrow a statue composed of separate pieces and thereby scatter them, or to take away the lamp from a magic lantern: the attention of the reader or spectator is distracted, the reader sees the author, the spectator sees the actor, the illusion disappears and to restore it is sometimes impossible—therefore without the feeling of measure, there cannot be an artist, and especially a dramatist.

Shakespeare is devoid of this feeling. His characters continually do and say what is not only unnatural to them, but utterly unnecessary. I do not cite examples of this, because I believe that he who does not himself see this striking deficiency in all Shakespeare's dramas will not be persuaded by any examples and proofs. It is sufficient to read *King Lear* alone, with its insanity, murders, plucking out of eyes, Gloucester's jump, its poisonings, and wranglings—not to mention *Pericles, Cymbeline, The Winter's Tale, The Tempest*—to be convinced of this. Only a man devoid of the sense of measure and of taste could produce such types as Titus Andronicus or Troilus and Cressida, or so mercilessly mutilate the old drama *King Leir.* (p. 262)

Leo Nikolayevich Tolstoy, "Shakespeare and the Drama," translated by V. Tchertkoff and I.F.M., in Shakespeare in Europe, *edited by Oswald LeWinter, The World Publishing Company, 1963, pp. 224-85.*

SIGMUND FREUD (essay date 1913)

[*An Austrian neurologist and the father of psychoanalysis, Freud is considered one of the most influential thinkers of the twentieth century. In the following excerpt, first published in the* Imago *in 1913, he attempts to uncover the meaning underlying the narrative structure of* King Lear. *He opens his commentary by pointing out the similarity in content between the casket scene in* The Merchant of Venice *and the so-called trial scene in* Lear—*in particular, comparing the leaden casket and Cordelia, the least considered but best selections, with respect to their qualities of silence and simplicity. These qualities, Freud claims, symbolize death; interpreted in this light, Lear becomes an aged, dying man whose renunciation of Cordelia signifies his refusal to accept death. In an unusual observation, Freud regards Lear's final entrance—when he comes onstage carrying Cordelia's body—as an emblematic reversal and foreshadowing of his own death. For other psychoanalytic interpretations of* King Lear, *see the essays by F. L. Lucas and Arpad Paunez in the Additional Bibliography.*]

Two scenes from Shakespeare, one from a comedy and the other from a tragedy, have lately given me occasion for setting and solving a little problem.

The former scene is the suitors' choice between the three caskets in *The Merchant of Venice.* The fair and wise Portia, at her father's bidding, is bound to take for her husband only that one among her suitors who chooses the right casket from among the three before him. The three caskets are of gold, silver and lead: the right one is that containing her portrait. Two suitors have already withdrawn, unsuccessful: they have chosen gold and silver. Bassanio, the third, elects for the lead; he thereby wins the bride, whose affection was already his before the trial of fortune. (p. 244)

Shakespeare did not invent this oracle of choosing a casket; he took it from a tale in the *Gesta Romanorum,* in which a girl undertakes the same choice to win the son of the Emperor. Here too the third metal, the lead, is the bringer of fortune. (pp. 244-45)

[In] the tale from the *Gesta Romanorum,* the subject is the choice of a maiden among three suitors; in the scene from *The Merchant of Venice* apparently the subject is the same, but at the same time in this last something in the nature of an inversion of the idea makes its appearacnce: a man chooses between three—caskets. If we had to do with a dream, it would at once occur to us that caskets are also women, symbols of the essential thing in woman, and therefore of a woman herself, like boxes, large or small, baskets, and so on. If we let ourselves assume the same symbolic substitution in the story, then the casket scene in *The Merchant of Venice* really becomes the inversion we suspected. With one wave of the hand, such as usually only happens in fairy-tales, we have stripped the astral garment from our theme; and now we see that the subject is an idea from human life, a man's choice between three women.

This same content, however, is to be found in another scene of Shakespeare's, in one of his most powerfully moving dramas; this time not the choice of a bride, yet linked by many mysterious resemblances to the casket-choice in *The Merchant of Venice*. The old King Lear resolves to divide his kingdom while he yet lives among his three daughters, according to the love they each in turn express for him. The two elder ones, Goneril and Regan, exhaust themselves in asseverations and glorifications of their love for him, the third, Cordelia, refuses to join in these. He should have recognized the unassuming, speechless love of the third and rewarded it, but he misinterprets it, banishes Cordelia, and divides the kingdom between the other two, to his own and the general ruin. Is not this once more a scene of choosing between three women, of whom the youngest is the best, the supreme one?

There immediately occur to us other scenes from myth, folk-tale and literature, with the same situation as their content: the shepherd Paris has to choose between three goddesses, of whom he declares the third to be the fairest. Cinderella is another such youngest, and is preferred by the prince to the two elder sisters; Psyche in the tale of Apuleius is the youngest and fairest of three sisters. . . . Anyone who cared to look more closely into the material could undoubtedly discover other versions of the same idea in which the same essential features had been retained.

Let us content ourselves with Cordelia, Aphrodite, Cinderella and Psyche! The three women, of whom the third surpasses the other two, must surely be regarded as in some way alike if they are represented as sisters. It must not lead us astray if in *Lear* the three are the daughters of him who makes the choice; this means probably nothing more than that Lear has to be represented as an old man. An old man cannot very well choose between three women in any other way: thus they become his daughters.

But who are these three sisters and why must the choice fall on the third? If we could answer this question, we should be in possession of the solution we are seeking. We have once already availed ourselves of an application of psycho-analytic technique, in explaining the three caskets as symbolic of three women. If we have the courage to continue the process, we shall be setting foot on a path which leads us first to something unexpected and incomprehensible, but perhaps by a devious route to a goal.

It may strike us that this surpassing third one has in several instances certain peculiar qualities besides her beauty. They are qualities that seem to be tending towards some kind of unity; we certainly may not expect to find them equally well marked in every example. Cordelia masks her true self, becomes as unassuming as lead, she remains dumb, she 'loves and is silent' [I. i. 62]. Cinderella hides herself, so that she is not to be found. We may perhaps equate concealment and dumbness. . . . But there is an intimation of the same thing to be found, curiously enough, in two other cases. We have decided to compare Cordelia, with her obstinate refusal, to lead. In Bassanio's short speech during the choice of the caskets these are his words of the lead—properly speaking, without any connection:

> Thy paleness moves me more than eloquence
> ('plainness', according to another reading)
> [*The Merchant of Venice*, III. ii. 106]

Thus: Thy plainness moves me more than the blatant nature of the other two. Gold and silver are 'loud'; lead is dumb, in effect like Cordelia, who 'loves and is silent'. (pp. 245-48)

If we decide to regard the peculiarities of our 'third one' as concentrated in the 'dumbness', then psycho-analysis has to say that dumbness is in dreams a familiar representation of death. (p. 248)

Concealment, disappearance from view, too, which the prince in the fairy-tale of Cinderella has to experience three times, is in dreams an unmistakable symbol of death; and no less so is a striking pallor, of which the paleness of the lead in one reading of Shakespeare's text reminds us. (p. 249)

[Numerous] proofs could undoubtedly be gathered from fairy-tales that dumbness is to be understood as representing death. If we follow these indications, then the third one of the sisters between whom the choice lies would be a dead woman. She may, however, be something else, namely, Death itself, the Goddess of Death. By virtue of a displacement that is not infrequent, the qualities that a deity imparts to men are ascribed to the deity himself. Such a displacement will astonish us least of all in relation to the Goddess of Death, since in modern thought and artistic representation, which would thus be anticipated in these stories, death itself is nothing but a dead man.

But if the third of the sisters is the Goddess of Death, we know the sisters. They are the Fates, the Moerae [of Greek mythology], the Parcae or the Norns [of German mythology], the third of whom is called Atropos, the inexorable. (p. 250)

And now it is time to return to the idea contained in the choice between the three sisters, which we are endeavouring to interpret. It is with deep dissatisfaction that we find how unintelligible insertion of the new interpretation makes the situations we are considering and what contradictions of the apparent content then result. The third of the sisters should be the Goddess of Death, nay, Death itself; in the Judgement of Paris she is the Goddess of Love, in the tale of Apuleius one comparable to the goddess for her beauty, in *The Merchant of Venice* the fairest and wisest of women, in *Lear* the one faithful daughter. Can a contradiction be more complete? Yet perhaps close at hand there lies even this, improbable as it is—the acme of contradiction. It is certainly forthcoming if every time in this theme of ours there occurs a free choice between the women, and if the choice is thereupon to fall on death—that which no man chooses, to which by destiny alone man falls a victim.

However, contradictions of a certain kind, replacements by the exact opposite, offer no serious difficulty to analytic interpretation. We shall not this time take our stand on the fact that contraries are constantly represented by one and the same element in the modes of expression used by the unconscious, such as dreams. But we shall remember that there are forces in mental life tending to bring about replacement by the opposite, such as the so-called reaction-formation, and it is just in the discovery of such hidden forces that we look for the reward of our labours. The Moerae were created as a result of a recognition which warns man that he too is a part of nature and therefore subject to the immutable law of death. Against this subjection something in man was bound to struggle, for it is only with extreme unwillingness that he gives up his claim to an exceptional position. We know that man makes use of his imaginative faculty (phantasy) to satisfy those wishes that reality does not satisfy. So his imagination rebelled against the recognition of the truth embodied in the myth of the Moerae, and constructed instead the myth derived from it, in which the

Goddess of Death was replaced by the Goddess of Love and by that which most resembles her in human shape. The third of the sisters is no longer Death, she is the fairest, best, most desirable and the most lovable among women. (pp. 252-53)

The same consideration answers the question how the episode of a choice came into the myth of the three sisters. A wished-for reversal is again found here. Choice stands in the place of necessity, of destiny. Thus man overcomes death, which in thought he has acknowledged. No greater triumph of wish-fulfilment is conceivable. Just where in reality he obeys compulsion, he exercises choice; and that which he chooses is not a thing of horror, but the fairest and most desirable thing in life.

On a closer inspection we observe, to be sure, that the original myth is not so much disguised that traces of it do not show through and betray its presence. The free choice between the three sisters is, properly speaking, no free choice, for it must necessarily fall on the third if every kind of evil is not to come about, as in *Lear*. The fairest and the best, she who has stepped into the place of the Death-goddess, has kept certain characteristics that border on the uncanny, so that from them we might guess at what lay beneath.

So far we have followed out the myth and its transformation, and trust that we have rightly indicated the hidden causes of this transformation. Now we may well be interested in the way in which the poet has made use of the idea. We gain the impression that in his mind a reduction to the original idea of the myth is going on, so that we once more perceive the original meaning containing all the power to move us that had been weakened by the distortion of the myth. It is by means of this undoing of the distortion and partial return to the original that the poet achieves his profound effect upon us.

To avoid misunderstandings, I wish to say that I have no intention of denying that the drama of *King Lear* inculcates the two prudent maxims: that one should not forgo one's possessions and privileges in one's lifetime and that one must guard against accepting flattery as genuine. These and similar warnings do undoubtedly arise from the play; but it seems to me quite impossible to explain the overpowering effect of *Lear* from the impression that such a train of thought would produce, or to assume that the poet's own creative instincts would not carry him further than the impulse to illustrate these maxims. Moreover, even though we are told that the poet's intention was to present the tragedy of ingratitude, the sting of which he probably felt in his own heart, and that the effect of the play depends on the purely formal element, its artistic trappings, it seems to me that this information cannot compete with the comprehension that dawns upon us after our study of the theme of a choice between the three sisters.

Lear is an old man. We said before that this is why the three sisters appear as his daughters. The paternal relationship, out of which so many fruitful dramatic situations might arise, is not turned to further account in the drama. But Lear is not only an old man; he is a dying man. The extraordinary project of dividing the inheritance thus loses its strangeness. The doomed man is nevertheless not willing to renounce the love of women; he insists on hearing how much he is loved. Let us now recall that most moving last scene, one of the culminating points reached in modern tragic drama: 'Enter Lear with Cordelia dead in his arms' [s.d. V. iii.]. Cordelia is Death. Reverse the situation and it becomes intelligible and familiar to us—the Death-goddess bearing away the dead hero from the place of

battle, like the Valkyr in German mythology. Eternal wisdom, in the garb of the primitive myth, bids the old man renounce love, choose death and make friends with the necessity of dying.

The poet brings us very near to the ancient idea by making the man who accomplishes the choice between the three sisters aged and dying. The regressive treatment he has thus undertaken with the myth, which was disguised by the reversal of the wish, allows its original meaning so far to appear that perhaps a superficial allegorical interpretation of the three female figures in the theme becomes possible as well. One might say that the three inevitable relations man has with woman are here represented: that with the mother who bears him, with the companion of his bed and board, and with the destroyer. Or it is the three forms taken on by the figure of the mother as life proceeds: the mother herself, the beloved who is chosen after her pattern, and finally the Mother Earth who receives him again. But it is in vain that the old man yearns after the love of woman as once he had it from his mother; the third of the Fates alone, the silent goddess of Death, will take him into her arms. (pp. 254-56)

> Sigmund Freud, "The Theme of the Three Caskets," translated by C.J.M. Hubback, in his Collected Papers: Papers on Metapsychology, Papers on Applied Psychoanalysis, Vol. 4, *authorized translation under the supervision of Joan Riviere, 1925. Reprint by The Hogarth Press and The Institute of Psycho-analysis, 1956, pp. 244-56.*

STOPFORD A. BROOKE (essay date 1913)

[*In the excerpt below, Brooke regards* King Lear *as the darkest play in Shakespeare's canon, a product of its author's "personal suffering," with its underlying ideology reflecting a hopeless, savage world in which there are no gods and no justice, and human beings function according to the most primitive principles of behavior. This pessimistic view of the play recalls the assessment of Algernon Charles Swinburne (1880) and anticipates the interpretations of such later critics as G. Wilson Knight (1930), J. Stampfer (1960), and Jan Kott (1964). Brooke also takes issue with those critics, such as Charlotte Lennox (1754), A. Brigham (1844), John Charles Bucknill (1856), and H. N. Hudson (1872), who claim that Lear was insane from the very beginning of the play; instead, he attributes Lear's initial behavior to an excess of vanity that will not allow contradiction to his authority.*]

There is no drama in the whole range of modern literature, perhaps of ancient, which can equal *King Lear* in the tragic imagination which has there clothed with chaotic darkness and godless sorrow not only Lear and all the characters that make his mighty pains, but also the whole of humanity, even the gods themselves. The eternal Justice which, we trust, lives beyond and above our sorrow and our crime; which the Greek Drama permits us to feel as holding in its hands a far-off hope— is not to be found in *King Lear*. Its outlook over the world that was, and is, and shall be, is of blackness and darkness for ever. The gods have not only forgotten man; the gods seem dead. The stars alone—the destroying planets who hate the human race—rule the world. And the loveliness of Cordelia's love, and the loyal truth of Kent, and the tenderness of the Fool, and the pity of Lear's madness, while they redeem human nature from the horror of Regan and Edmund, Goneril and Cornwall, only deepen the dreadful aspect of the world, for they suffer for their goodness more than these vulture-men and women for their crimes. The world of *King Lear* is a world from which all the conceptions which create a just God are expunged. In it also Nature herself is as blind, as pain-stricken, as helpless, as left to herself as Lear; and if she is not blind, she is as wicked, as pitiless as Goneril and Regan.

What brought Shakespeare to this dread? How came it to pass that, like Dante, he went down into Hell, and with, it seems, even more personal suffering than Dante? I do not know that we have any right to inquire (though we cannot help it), and certainly it is quite fair that we should not know. (pp. 197-98)

Whatever it was, it took him down, in imagination, not only into the infinite tenderness of Cordelia, but into the primeval brutalities of uncivilised man, into the unrestrained lust, cruelty, and greed of savage humanity; even into their unnatural violation of natural piety. Moreover, during these years he went down into the slums of human nature. And there, in his realism, he found Thersites, and Pandarus, and the vile things he made men in *Measure for Measure*. And these, Thersites and the rest, belonged to a decaying, but a civilised society. The vices in *Troilus and Cressida*, in *Measure for Measure,* and in *Timon of Athens* are the vices of a decadence.

In *King Lear* the social scenery is quite different. The evils are those which characterise the beginnings of a society when men are emerging from savagery and retain much of its brutality. Gloucester's light talk before his bastard son of his lust with his mother is a slight instance of this. The tearing out of Gloucester's eyes by Cornwall and Regan (the woman urging on the hateful deed) is a piece of primeval cruelty. The hanging of Cordelia belongs to a brutal society. So does the lust for Edmund of both the sisters in its bold expression. And the unnatural absence in Goneril and Regan of any shred of filial piety towards their father, combined with cruelty to him, and plotted against him by both from the beginning, is such guilt as could not be openly practised in a society which had been civilised. But here it is open, boasted of, rejoiced in by its doers, claimed to be statesmanlike. This is pure savagery developing itself with frank selfishness in the atmosphere of irresponsible power. We are at the beginning, not at the end of a nation, midst of antique barbarities. Whether Shakespeare deliberately put in this local colour (knowing that his story belonged to early Britain), we cannot tell, but we are certainly placed in the midst of a primeval society, where gigantic figures and gigantic pains pass across the stage, and speak a gigantic language; where all that is said and done arises out of the first unmodified elements of human nature. And this last is as true— on the other side—of Cordelia's love and Kent's loyalty as it is of Regan's hardheartedness and Cornwall's treachery. The good in the play is also of early human nature.

The tragedies of Aeschylus do not place us in quite so savage, so unmoral a world as we are in *King Lear*. Their world is more civilised. The murder of Agamemnon is accounted for. It is by no means unnatural, as the conduct of Goneril and Regan. A Greek audience would not have borne to look on this drama.

It may be said that the central horror which drives the Oedipus of Sophocles into a desolate world is as ghastly as the cruelty which drives Lear into a ruined world, but Oedipus takes with him his daughters' love; and in the end the just gods give him peace. There is no such close to Lear. We are left in darkness that may be felt. Cordelia suffers for her goodness as Goneril and Regan for their guilt.

There is reason for Orestes' slaying of his mother, and a rude Justice demanded her death, yet the sinner against natural piety is driven to madness by the Furies, till, after terrible days, he

is solemnly judged and purified. But no Furies, not even the inward snake of Remorse, pursue the unnatural impiety of Goneril and Regan. They die of their own lust. And no God lives in *King Lear;* no divine Justice interposes to save Cordelia. There are many who think Shakespeare might have saved her. But he was not in the temper to do that justice. As the world is, the best for her, he thought, is that she should leave it. (pp. 198-200)

[Before] the terror and sorrow of [Lear's] tragedy one feels incompetent to speak. The genius who created it soars beyond our ken. When we meet him first, he is that wretched thing— an old man who, because he has, without one check, ruled for many years his kingdom and his household, thinks that his will is absolute wisdom. The serene vanity of this is only equalled by the folly into which his vanity leads him. He is blind to his own folly; blind to the fact that his two daughters hate him; blind when, with the embroidered eloquence of hatred, they tell him that they love him; blind to the character of Cordelia, though she has truly loved him; blind to the worth of Kent; blind to the political results which (even if his daughters loved him) would inevitably follow on the partition of the kingdom; and equally blind to the personal results which were sure to follow on an irresponsible person like himself, with a train of a hundred knights and with a violent temper, wandering about from one petty court to another. Inevitable then would be the irritation, the quarrels, and finally the fury of the situation. There are critics of the medical profession who say that Lear was already mad when he did this; and base their explanation of his character on this supposed fact. But Lear was no more mad now than thousands of persons, perfectly sane in society, are, when, by long dwelling on themselves, they have become compact of vanity. (pp. 205-06)

[Many] unthinking persons have wished for a happy ending to this play. There have been such remakings put upon the stage by audacious persons who did not know themselves or Shakespeare. He was in no mood for this. In the dark unbelief in any just gods which now, as I think, possessed him, he slays the guiltless, after in fierce justice he has slain the guilty. Goneril, Regan, Cornwall, Edmund have died violently. Cordelia and Lear meet as violent a death. Cordelia is hanged, ignobly hanged by one as merciless as Regan. Nor is she alone in her fate. The course of affairs is cruel not only here, but everywhere. So Shakespeare thought in these sunless days. . . . Yet, the indelible sweetness of Shakespeare's nature reasserts itself in the redemption of the soul of Lear. Cordelia has breathed upon him and he has received the Spirit. In the last sane things he says as he is led away to prison, his violence, love of luxury, hatred of the world, are far behind him, gone for ever. Love is best and the simple life. Prison and pain are nothing to love. Even the mystery of the world is solved by it. He is like a happy child. . . . It is his last hour of happiness. When we next see him he comes in, seized again by frenzy, with Cordelia dead in his arms. All the world knows that heart-cracking scene, where in the face of Lear's Titan grief, all the rest speak only broken words. At last his heart breaks asunder. . . . And Kent to Edgar who lifts the King, crying,

> Look up, my Lord,
>
> [V. iii. 313]

says the last word that thousands and thousands of men, in this wild world, have said to such a sorrow—

> Vex not his ghost: O, let him pass! he hates him
> That would upon the rack of this tough world
> Stretch him out longer.
>
> [V. iii. 314-16]
> (pp. 223-24)

Stopford A. Brooke, "'King Lear'," in his Ten More Plays of Shakespeare, Constable and Company Ltd., 1913, pp. 197-224.

LEVIN L. SCHUCKING (essay date 1922)

[*The following excerpt represents one of the most atypical interpretations of* King Lear *in the twentieth century. Whereas nearly all commentators on the play see Lear as progressing towards a fuller understanding of human existence as a result of his suffering, Schucking instead argues that the drama demonstrates the king's decay, both physically and mentally. In the process of this argument, Schucking also derides the attempts of numerous critics—such as Charlotte Lennox (1754), Samuel Taylor Coleridge (1813), and A. C. Bradley (1904)—to explain Lear's behavior in the trial scene. He claims that it is not necessary to justify the king's actions towards Cordelia and Kent and that we should focus instead on whether the character is consistent throughout the play; at every point Schucking believes it is.*]

Though Shakespeare usually to a surprising degree adapts himself to the given action, we yet see in a few instances that he departs from the course prescribed by it. The most remarkable case of this kind is *King Lear*. It is true that here the playwright found a story which was of very doubtful value as a dramatic plot, a king who makes the division of his realm among his children depend on the magniloquence of their protestations of love—the idea strikes one as though it had been invented by the author of *The Playboy of the Western World*, and can, indeed, have arisen only in a nation which is inclined to be intoxicated by fine and well-set phrases. The various versions and arrangements of this theme in existence before Shakespeare's time had not attempted to render the subsequent course of the action psychologically consistent with the initial situation. Everywhere the King is treated cruelly by the daughters he has preferred, until he flees, degraded to the condition of a beggar, to the daughter who had been disowned by him, but who wins back his kingdom for him and puts him on the throne again. The strangeness of the introductory action compelled the dramatist either to provide different motives for the issue of the conflict, or to adjust the subsequent course of the action to the first part of it. The author of the older play of *King Leir*, which was hardly used by Shakespeare, adopted the former alternative, Shakespeare the latter. Many details of this perplexing tangle of vicissitudes may have suited his mood at the time. It was that period of his creative activity when his aim was to represent the overthrow of a great nature brought about by a certain blindness to things which to the common sense of the average mind cannot appear for a moment otherwise than in their true aspect. In this way, for example, his Othello works his own ruin and his infatuated Antony runs his head against the wall.

Not only in the world of the poet's own thoughts do we find figures closely related to King Lear. The suggestions to which this character is due, at least in its most comprehensive outlines, came to him from the works of other poets, a very common occurrence with him, as we know. The old man who goes mad with continual fretting had already fascinated the public in the guise of Kyd's old marshal Hieronimo, and to a lesser degree in that of Titus Andronicus. Furthermore, it is evident that immediately before the creation of Lear the author's mind had had stamped upon it the image of another strong-willed old man who believes himself superior to his whole environment, and then, struck by Fate just where he is most vulnerable, knows no limit to his rage, kicks against the pricks, and is driven into madness by his futile resistance to his destiny. This is the Atheist in Tourneur's drama.

The decisive impression, however, of his figure of Lear Shakespeare had received from the story itself. There the behaviour of the King, especially in the initial action, shows an extraordinary irascibility. On this fundamental trait Shakespeare based the whole character. Only a short, though important, passage is devoted to giving reasons for Lear's behaviour, the device employed being the reflection of his character in the minds of Goneril and Regan. We learn that he was hot-headed, "the best and soundest of his time hath been but rash," that "he hath ever but slenderly known himself" [I. i. 293ff]. . . . Though this review of the situation is given by the two wicked sisters, yet the poet's technique . . . leaves no doubt that it is to be taken as substantially correct. Still, this is not much; we are not given more than a hint, which is not sufficient to explain the much disputed introductory action. (pp. 176-78)

[A. C. Bradley] finds a good reason for Lear's behaviour in the "unfortunate speech" of Cordelia, who, he thinks, is not quite aware that saying less than the truth may also be equivalent to *not* telling it, and who is also partly to blame for the consequences on account of the disappointment and disgrace she has caused her father at the great moment he had so carefully planned [see excerpt above, 1904]. To this view we must object that it misjudges the problem. Nobody will dispute that the thwarting of his most eccentric plan by Cordelia was apt to put her father out of humour, even to anger him, but that it should change his love for his daughter to savage hate would be inconceivable, even if his love for Cordelia had been on a par with that which he felt for his other daughters. The fact that she is his darling, however, shows that he is well aware of her superior worth. How is it possible, then, that this knowledge could be extinguished by a single outburst of ill-humour and be replaced by the most senseless misconception of her character? Bradley replies: The King has a long life of absolute power behind him, in which he has been flattered to an almost incredible extent; as a consequence, an arrogant self-will has been bred in him, the slightest opposition to which makes him fly into a passion. But a domineering spirit and an excessive vanity need not necessarily destroy all power of judgment. For the rest, the dragging in of previous events not mentioned by the poet is always a most questionable undertaking. Besides, all those critics who are so fond of depicting a reign of the King which was filled with flattery seem entirely to forget the fool and the good Kent, no less than the honest Gloster.

The problem cannot be solved in this way. What we have to decide is rather *whether the behaviour of the King toward his daughter can be brought into agreement, not with the laws of reason, but with the rest of his conduct*. The question whether this behaviour itself is reasonable or lunatic, whether the assumption of madness might eventually be detrimental to the tragic effect, etc., may in the meantime be left out of consideration altogether.

Now it is impossible to overlook the fact that Shakespeare has certainly tried very carefully to bring out an agreement between the behaviour of Lear in the introductory scene and the subsequent part of the action. The first indication of this endeavour is found in the conversation of the sisters, who report what we are told again later on, that the abnormal excitement and exaltation is now beginning to be much more noticeable in his behaviour than before. Then in the banishment of the faithful Kent we witness a further instance of this change, which is hardly less remarkable than the preceding incident had been.

In both he is equally immoderate. He is not satisfied with banishing Kent, but must, in addition, threaten him with capital punishment. He does not merely withdraw his favour from Cordelia, but immediately goes so far as to treat her like the scum of the earth; the ''barbarous Scythian'' is as dear to him as she, and he spitefully designates her as ''new adopted to our hate'' [I. i. 203]. This attack is not followed by any return to a saner attitude.

The same traits are manifested by Lear when, after his abdication, he is living on the charity of others. His impatience, lack of self-control, capriciousness, and arrogance remain unchanged. When the fool fails to respond to a sign given by him he reviles the whole world for being asleep. To the remarks made by the faithful fool he repeatedly replies by threatening him with a whip. When Kent, in disguise, applies to him in order to rejoin his service, unknown to him, he uses such language as a policeman might use to a burglar, and then promises magnanimously to take him into his service if, after he has dined, he finds that he still likes him. Such being his treatment of his faithful followers, he naturally behaves with still greater rudeness toward those who provoke him. He strikes Goneril's gentleman-in-waiting . . . and is delighted when Kent trips the fellow up and throws him to the ground. Thereupon, when Goneril dares to remonstrate with him, certainly not out of any feeling of kindness, but at least provisionally observing the forms of outward politeness, he considers himself highly offended in his dignity even by this slight rebuke, and breaks out in a paroxysm of fury that makes him weep with rage and hurl a veritable flood of execrations at his daughter. . . . Then, after Regan has finally disillusioned him, he is seized and shaken in every limb by such a fit of frenzy that even he perceives himself to be struggling with a malady, and makes violent efforts to free himself from the ''hysterica passio.'' . . . The enormous excitement of the ensuing scenes, in which he is degraded to the condition of a beggar, throws his reason completely out of gear.

Every one of these actions shows a remarkable lack of moderation, just as his behaviour to Kent and his undiminished confidence in Regan despite his experiences with Goneril betray, to put it midly, a total lack of judgment, and both of these qualities are in perfect harmony with his conduct in the opening scene. Nevertheless, the poet evidently does not wish him to forfeit thereby the sympathy of the spectator, though it is put to a very severe test. There are several things not only in the mental condition but also in the character of Lear which at first sight repel our modern feeling and which are not quite compatible with the ideal picture, gradually evolved by a long tradition, of the poor, noble, dignified King who is so cruelly treated by his children, We have already drawn attention to the traits which are indicative of a certain brutality, fierceness, arrogance, and capriciousness; to them we must add also a distinctly vindictive spirit which makes him find consolation in the hope that he will one day be able to pay back his daughters in their own coin. . . . [To] be so unspeakably offended by ingratitude is not a sign of a very noble character. Though ingratitude hurts, yet one who does good merely from inward compulsion, to whom the generous deed is an end in itself— and only such a character can we call truly unselfish—will find no venom in his disappointment. None will become incensed and embittered by ingratitude but he who has acted from calculation and has seen his calculation fail. There can be no doubt that Lear is embittered to a high degree. Lastly, we may see an unpleasant trait in the habit which the old King has of

pitying himself. No one speaks so much of his venerable white hairs as he.

All these things might induce us to regard Lear from a point of view different from what the poet intended. For this reason it is important to bear in mind that in the play itself no sympathetic figure reproaches Lear for any of the traits mentioned; they all look at the situation entirely from his standpoint, and this is also what Shakespeare wishes the spectator to do. The predominant impression is to be that of the monstrous irreverence shown to three of the most venerable human qualities here united in one person: fatherhood, old age, and kingship. Stress is laid, above all, on the unspeakable insult offered to the pride of a king who yet retains his dignity in his association with beggars as well as in his madness. This trait has been given an especial prominence. It agrees with the thought we constantly find in Shakespeare, that the true king is best shown by the way in which he preserves his dignity. (pp. 180-84)

Lear thus appears like an old, gnarled, stubborn oak-tree, vigorously resisting the tempest, unyielding, majestic, deep-rooted, upheld only by its own strength, and towering above all its fellows. His weaknesses may almost be said to be the necessary concomitants of his strong qualities. His vindictiveness appears to be a result of his strength, his savage maledictions seem due to his fiery temperament, his behaviour to people of lower rank would not have dishonoured him in that period, when, as is

Act V. Scene iii. Lear and Cordelia. By V. W. Bromley.
The Department of Rare Books and Special Collections, The
University of Michigan Library.

well known, Queen Elizabeth herself boxed her servants' ears with her own hands. . . . King Lear, therefore, is meant to be a sublime and truly noble figure, and the Earl of Gloster has good reasons for designating him in his madness as a "ruin'd piece of nature" [IV. vi. 134]. (p. 184)

It is true that a number of expositors . . . see in Lear's tragedy a great process of purification, by means of which he is freed from the dross of vanity and selfishness and is led out of his blindness to a proper recognition of the true values of life. It is just his sufferings, they think, which draw him closer to us by bringing out his true human nature. By way of proof they adduce the words in which he shows for the fool a sympathy formerly unknown to him, and further the passage in which, being himself exposed to the inclemency of the weather, he for the first time remembers the houseless wretches who have to roam about with no protection. . . . (p. 185)

They also point to the recognition and contempt of empty appearance which are the products of his madness, his magnificent trenchant criticism of authority that lacks true moral sanction: "Thou hast seen a farmer's dog bark at a beggar? And the creature run from the cur? There thou might'st behold the great image of authority: a dog's obeyed in office" [IV. vi. 155-59]. Lastly, his deepened sensibility is mentioned, as revealed by his preferring the company of Cordelia in his prison to all other joys in the world.

But the question is whether it is really consistent with Shakespeare's philosophy to see in this sequence of events an ascent of the character to a higher plane, a process of purification and perfection.

If we take up and examine singly the supposed stages of this upward evolution we cannot unreservedly agree with this conception. Does Shakespeare, for instance, associate compassion for the poor and wretched with a higher moral standpoint? We know that the social sense was very little developed in him. If in this manifestation of pity for the poor naked wretches the emergence of a higher morality was to be shown, we ought really to wonder why it stands quite alone in his works. . . . There is no passage where Shakespeare formulates a demand corresponding to the spirit of Lear's reflection in describing an ideal figure or laying down rules of life (like those given to Laertes by his father). It is quite probable that Lear's words are intended to furnish him with a sympathetic trait—that, as Edgar in the same drama once says of himself. . . , he is "by the art of known and feeling sorrows" "pregnant to good pity" [IV. vi. 222-23]. But we may be quite sure that Shakespeare, for the reasons adduced, would never have taken this matter so seriously as to see in it a purification from adherent dross, whatever his interpreters may do!

That Lear in the further course of his madness comes to reject all that is unnatural and all claims that are morally unjustified, though sanctioned by tradition and authority, cannot be disputed. But it must be noticed that in this he does little more than follow the beaten track of the melancholy type, whose 'humour' especially delights in unmasking all kinds of shams; and the fact of his being greatly attracted by the naked Edgar, the "thing in itself," is a further manifestation of the Melancholy Man's predilection for the Diogenes attitude. Lear shows himself a truer representative of the melancholy type in yet another respect, viz., in his arguing and railing against women. . . . His furious tirade against the unchastity of women—

> Down from the waist they are Centaurs
> Though women all above . . .
>
> [IV. vi. 124-25]

—has really nothing to do with his own affairs.

Undoubtedly Lear's criticism shows profound insight; but this recognition, as it stands here, is but an aspect of a mood and dependent on a state of mental derangement which may under certain circumstances disappear again, as is shown by the example of other melancholy characters. It would have to be confirmed by him in some form or other after his reason had been restored to sanity in order to make us see in it a real revolution of his philosophic outlook and a stage of his development.

This condition seems perhaps to be fulfilled indirectly by his behaviour to Cordelia, whose love he accepts with the unrestrained happiness of one who has got to know the world too well to expect from it anything further. But even his relation to Cordelia, when regarded from this point of view, would appear in a false light. What attracts Lear to Cordelia and makes him regard a life with her in the quiet dungeon as supremely desirable is doubtless the recognition of the true worth of her love, and his deeply pathetic cry when she is dead, "Howl, howl, howl, howl! O! you are men of stones!" [V. iii. 258] shows that by her death the innermost core of his existence has been destroyed. But this change is not to be regarded as a development of his character. That he has completely given up every idea of his kingdom, that he shows no further outburst of vindictiveness or indignation at the insults he has received, is really contrary to his nature and is due to the state of physical decrepitude into which he has fallen after his madness has left him. The thunderstorm has felled the oak. *His predominant feeling is one of weariness.* He is no longer able completely to grasp what is happening. He must make an effort to render the course of events clear to himself. When he recognizes Cordelia, who tenderly and with hot tears in her eyes bends over him, he so misunderstands the situation that he says: "If you have poison for me I will drink it" [IV. viii. 71]. Gradually his mind becomes more lucid again. But when he says of himself, "Pray you now, forget and forgive: I am old and foolish" [IV. vii. 84], this recognition contains a sad truth, especially in view of his former high opinion of himself. Nothing is more touching than the fact that he is no longer the old Lear. (pp. 186-88)

This is not a purified Lear from whose character the flame of unhappiness has burnt away the ignoble dross, but a nature completely transformed, whose extraordinary vital forces are extinguished, or about to be extinguished.

This is the whole course of the drama: the story of a breakdown, of a decay accompanied by the most wonderful and fascinating phenomena comparable to the autumn decline of the year when the dying leaves appear in their most beautiful colours. It is not a development, but a decadence manifesting itself in a variety of forms, among others in that feeling of weakness which creates in the masterful old man, who so far has been centred entirely in himself, a sympathetic interest in the distress of others which he has never known before. Shakespeare's astonishing wisdom and experience of life are shown by the fact that he does not describe the great mental revolutions without reference to the corresponding physical alterations.

It is therefore a complete misunderstanding of the true state of affairs to regard Lear as greater at the close than at the beginning. He has become a different person; he is nearing his end. This is why Shakespeare had no use for the conclusion of the story of Lear as it had been handed down by tradition. . . . For Shakespeare's broken old man this was unthinkable. The conflict between the action and the character would have been too patent, even grotesque. He had therefore to bring Lear's life to an end. This he did, anticipating at the same time the end of Cordelia, but still maintaining a certain connexion with the original source, because from Spenser's *Faerie Queene* we learn that after a long and happy reign, when smitten at last by misfortune, she had hanged herself in prison. By converting her voluntary death into a murder which cost Lear his life he did indeed heap a load of tragedy on the spectator's mind, a thing against which the latter had been rebelling for centuries as against an intolerable excess of horror. On the other hand, however, he secured by this issue, better than by any other, the possibility of working out the process of dissolution in Lear to its last stage. His master-hand even succeeded in building up on this foundation the most tragic effects of the whole play. A soul-stirring anti-climax is produced as his mental fire, which is slowly flickering out and again and again being obscured by the clouds of insanity, is once more fanned into a short, violent flame by the cruelty of the injuries he receives, a flame in which the last sparks of the powerful self-consuming passions flash forth, followed by eternal night. Here the action and the character-drawing are harmoniously blended in one perfect close. (pp. 188-90)

> Levin L. Schucking, "Character and Action," in his Character Problems in Shakespeare's Plays: A Guide to the Better Understanding of the Dramatist, *1922. Reprint by Peter Smith, 1959, pp. 111-202.*

HARLEY GRANVILLE-BARKER   (essay date 1927)

[*Granville-Barker was a noted actor, playwright, director, and critic. His work as a Shakespearean critic is at all times informed by his experience as a director, for he treats Shakespeare's plays not as works of literature better understood divorced from the theater, as did many Romantic critics, but as pieces meant for the stage. As a director, he emphasized simplicity in staging, set design, and costuming. He believed that elaborate scenery obscured the poetry which was of central importance to Shakespeare's plays. Granville-Barker also eschewed the approach of directors who scrupulously reconstructed a production based upon Elizabethan stage techniques; he felt that this, too, detracted from the play's meaning. In the following excerpt, he responds directly to Charles Lamb and A. C. Bradley's contention that* King Lear *fails as a work for the stage because its poetic, imaginative qualities—those attributes that make it great literature—cannot be successfully reenacted in the theater (see excerpts above, 1812 and 1904). Granville-Barker counters Bradley's opinion that too much in* Lear *refuses to reveal itself in a single viewing in the theater, claiming that Bradley errs in assuming that drama "ought in a single performance to make a clear, complete, and final effect on the spectator." Next, he opposes Lamb's condemnation of the three storm scenes as demonstrative of the performance problems presented by the play as a whole. Instead, Granville-Barker maintains that these scenes were highly effective on the Elizabethan stage, and would be just as effective on any stage were poetry and gesture all the director supplied the audience in order to sustain the illusion.*]

Scholars, in the past, have been apt to forbid [*King Lear*] the theatre; it is my business now to justify its place there. Shakespeare meant it to be acted, one might plead. Acted it undoubtedly was in his time, and seemingly with success, for his company took it to play at Whitehall before the King. Does not this settle the question? But no less a voice than Charles Lamb's is heard: Lear is essentially impossible to be represented on the stage. And, something like a century later, Dr. A. C. Bradley, though he qualifies his judgment, concludes

that it is "too huge for the stage." It may be, then, that Shakespeare, "fairly caught in the web of his own imagination" (to quote Hazlitt for a third objector, as he quotes Lamb with approval) [see excerpt above, 1817], broke all bounds, and wrote the play, shall we say, for some perfect theatre laid up for him in heaven. It is not likely, we may admit, that, his mind aflame with the writing of this play or another, he stopped to measure scene after scene to the chances of a perfect performance here on earth. Such consideration makes for competent craftsmanship, no more. The greater a play the less likelihood of its perfect performing; yet, strangely enough, the less need for it. But he certainly meant this play to be acted, as acted it was. . . . (p. 133)

Lamb's denunciation, indeed, was occasioned not by Shakespeare's play at all, but by Tate's perversion of it. And though he may declare that neither will he have Shakespeare's *King Lear* in the theatre, it is from nothing like Shakespeare's theatre that he bans it. Lamb's was the stage of spectacle; I do not know that he ever imagined any other. And if it was not yet the stage of hypnotic visual illusion to which the late nineteenth century accustomed us (also to be remembered when the nineteenth-century scholar is dogmatising), it had parted far enough from the stage upon which the speaker and his spoken word were all but the sole power—an audience, in the true sense, being what they swayed—from the theatre in which a blind man lost little. Visual illusion, and realism so called (though this is but the absorbing of one convention in another) have tended to make the technique of the spoken word, of rhetoric and poetry, absurd; they have shamed it to death. Lamb's theatre had not quite brought Shakespeare to this. Yet rhetoric by his time had mostly become mere rhetoric, and the great passages arbitrary occasion for vocal and emotional display. It was the age of "the beauties of Shakespeare." That, its beauty beside, this dynamic verse and prose held secrets of stagecraft does not seem to have been considered. How indeed, with Shakespeare's stage hardly a memory, should care for its craft survive? As witness of Lamb's theatre's oblivion to it the current treatment of the text is enough; and contemporary criticism of the abuse is less of the damage done to Shakespeare than of the embellishments by which the damage is covered. The playwright was all but forgotten in the dramatic poet. And, despite our recapture of some sense of the seventeenth-century theatre and our restoration of texts, we still are disposed to think we can appreciate the plays, all appreciation of their craftsmanship apart. But Shakespeare built his castles upon a firm, familiar stage, not in the air.

We need not claim for him impeccability as a playwright. His work abounds in improvisations of technique; he is skilful, and never more skilful than when he is in a difficulty, though often enough even then it is the vitality behind the skill which pulls him through. As to rhetoric, he is capable on occasion of the wantonest use of it, and of a little fine sound and fury purely for its own sake. But when he sets himself such a task as *King Lear*, when, his imagination kindling, the full scope of such a theme opens out to him, we may expect him to be at his best—why not?—as craftsman and poet too, and to find him rallying every resource of craftsmanship to his help. For the hugeness of *Lear* these resources may still have been too few, they may have failed him at need. But of this we can be sure; it will be a case of failure, not avoidance, for his admitted task was to make his play stageworthy. In his greatest drama we should at least look for his greatest stagecraft, nor have we a right to pronounce its failure without the fullest understanding, without making the completest test of it. Further, the test must be made in the strict terms of *his* stagecraft; in no other need we expect success.

Bradley's objections to the play's staging are more carefully considered than Lamb's (which were indeed a part of a rather childish outburst against the idolatry of actors and acting in general), and they are pretty comprehensive. He holds that while ''it has scenes immensely effective in the theatre''—and he quotes Lear's scene with Goneril, the later scene with her and with Regan and the reconciliation with Cordelia,—yet that ''the immense scope of the work, the mass and variety of intense experience which it contains . . . the half-realised suggestions of vast universal powers working in the world of individual fates and passions—all this interferes with dramatic clearness even when the play is read, and in the theatre not only refuses to reveal itself fully through the senses but seems to be almost in contradiction with their reports.'' This objection as a whole involves, I fancy, a fallacy about the theatre in general, and the extreme sensibility shown in the last phrase gives us, perhaps, a clue to it. Dr. Bradley seems to assume that every sort of play, when acted, ought in a single performance to make a clear, complete and final effect on the spectator. But this is surely not so. We need no more expect to receive—lapses of performance and attention apart—the full value of a great drama at a first hearing than we expect it of a complex piece of music. And what preliminary study of the music, with its straiter laws and more homogeneous material, will effect, study of drama will not. A play's interpretation is an unrulier business, and we must face it rather as we face life itself. . . . Now, it is the business of the dramatist, doubtless, in turning actuality to art, to clarify all this sort of thing and bring it to terms. But if he aimed only at its clear statement he would produce no illusion of life at all; and this it is his art to do. Comedy does aim at as much clarity as is consistent with character kept in action. Greek tragedy blends thought and emotion very equably; and, with music to help, keeps the power, but keeps the constraint too, of ritual. Does it follow, however, that Shakespeare's method in *King Lear* is not a method like any other, if he sets out—as I suggest he does—to provoke in us, as we listen and look, the very confusion of feeling and chaos of mind which will best bring us into immediate sympathy with the play's happenings, while, every now and then, he lodges thoughts with us (what play is fuller of memorable phrases?) which, with the story told, will remain for a memory when the emotion has subsided? Why should not the ultimate effect of this be coherent and balanced enough? There may well be even more meaning in *King Lear* than will come to us thus; matter we may pick out of the text, speculate and argue over; as, no doubt, much stayed still unexpressed in Shakespeare's own mind when he had done writing. But, again, a work of art must aim first at producing its immediate effect. And this (it is true of great art, if a negligible truth of all other) will be made a little differently upon each of us, and for each of us may differ from time to time. Abundance of power, then, there must be, and a certain waste must be allowed for. *King Lear* does perhaps over-abound in sheer power, and will be apt to excite and confuse our emotions unduly. But the corrective of thought is strongly and currently applied. And I believe we may abandon ourselves to the emotions raised by a performance, confident that the complete and final effect produced on us will be fruitful and equable enough, and that, though we may lose at the time in fullness of understanding, we shall gain in conviction.

The error—as I am bold enough to think it—of Dr. Bradley's contention springs possibly from a too sophisticated approach to the play. I should be surprised to hear that he first made acquaintance with it in the theatre, as Shakespeare would have had him do. Whether or no, he seems to have grown so concerned with its metaphysics that its 'physics' have become repellent to him, and their effect, as he says, contradictory. But this is a paradox, and æsthetically not a very wholesome one. It illustrates the danger that besets all scholastic study of such an abundantly, even crudely, vital art as the art of the theatre must be. There is great delight, there is much profit in such study; but it is, in a sense, a study of causes rather than effects, not a study of the work of art itself. This, when all is said, must still be given its chance. *King Lear* was meant to be acted. Inadequate and misdirected acting of it there may be, by which we must not judge it; and no perfect performance of any play by imperfect human beings can there ever be. Shakespeare may have been wrong to make a play of it. Nor, if he did strain his medium of expression beyond endurance, would he be the first great artist to do so. But he put his purpose to the proof; and so should we—to every proof, before we ignore this for the sake of disparate gains beyond.

Lamb rests his condemnation of the play's acting upon the third act and the scenes in the storm. The passage is always being quoted. ''So to see Lear acted—to see an old man tottering about the stage with a walking-stick, turned out of doors by his daughters on a rainy night—has nothing in it but what is painful and disgusting. . . . But the Lear of Shakespeare cannot be acted. The contemptible machinery by which they mimic the storm which he goes out in, is not more inadequate to represent the horrors of the real elements than any actor can be to represent Lear. . . . The greatness of Lear is not in corporal dimension, but in intellectual. . . . On the stage we see nothing but corporal infirmities and weakness, the impotence of rage; while we read it, we see not Lear but we are Lear. . . .'' [see excerpt above, 1812].

Lamb states the case, let us admit, about as simply and as well as it can be stated, and he fixes upon the supreme moments of dramatic achievement and theatrical difficulty. If we meet the challenge here and make good answer, may not the rest of the play claim a verdict too? Well, Lamb's case, as I suggest, is a bad case because it shows no recognition at all of Elizabethan stagecraft; his case, in fact, is not against Shakespeare the playwright, but against his betrayal. (pp. 134-40)

Now there are plays, and passages of any play, in which convention may seem negligible. One could pick scenes from Shakespeare, from Euripides, from Ibsen that can be made to suit any stage and almost any sort of acting. But when a dramatist has set himself a task to tax all his resources we may look for him to fortify himself within his theatre's strongest convention. So it is, at any rate, with this third act of *King Lear*. The chief strength of Elizabethan stagecraft lay in its comprehensive use of poetry. Plot was carried on, character developed and environment created, by the aid of poetry, emotion was sustained by it and illusion held. And Shakespeare can achieve the multiple task with an abundance of skill, and conceal the achievement in beauty, often (and the better) in an amazing simplicity too. Now no such crisis as this third act presents could be compassed and wrought out in any theatre, surely, without its every technical resource being called in aid. We might look, then, to find this centre of the play a very epitome of Shakespeare's stagecraft—and we do.

What is his exact dramatic need here, and how does he turn to its account this comprehensive use of verse? Be it verse or prose, he has no other resource, we must remember, than the spoken word of the actor, such action as will not mar it, and a negative background to this action. He has no accessories worth mentioning. The shaking of a thunder sheet cannot be said to count for emotional effect. It is little more than symbolic, strikes on the emotions hardly more than do the 'alarums' and 'retreats' which mark the progress of a battle, and less, probably, than the sounding of a trumpet or a 'drum far off.' Music he might command, it is true, but none that could help him to the raising of this storm. Lear, Kent and the rest must *act* the storm then; there is no other way. They must not lose themselves in its description; it will not do for us to be interested in the storm at the expense of our interest in them, the loss there would be more than the gain. For the effect of the storm upon Lear is Shakespeare's true objective. So he has to give it magnitude without detracting for one precious moment during the crisis from Lear's own dramatic supremacy. And he solves his problem by making the actor impersonate Lear and the storm together, by identifying Lear's passion with the storm's. Mere association will not serve; there must be no chance left of a rivalry of interest. For that again might set the sensations of the audience at odds and dissipate the play's power upon them. This puts the thing crudely, and Shakespeare's skill in enriching and masking his main effect with minor ones (lest we grow too conscious of what he is doing and resist him) is amazing. But this is the basis of his stagecraft, to make Lear and the storm as one. And if Lamb saw "an old man tottering about the stage with a walking-stick" he did not see the Lear of Shakespeare's intention.

> Blow winds, and crack your cheeks! rage! blow!
> You cataracts and hurricanoes, spout
> Till you have drench'd our steeples, drown'd the cocks!
> You sulphurous and thought-executing fires,
> Vaunt-couriers to oak-cleaving thunderbolts,
> Singe my white head! And thou, all-shaking thunder,
> Strike flat the thick rotundity o' the world!
> Crack nature's moulds, all germens spill at once,
> That make ingrateful man!
>
> [III. ii. 1-9]

This is the storm itself in its tragic purpose, as Shakespeare's imagination gives it voice. And any actor who should try to speak the lines realistically in the character of a feeble old man would be a fool. There is no realism about it. No real man could or would talk so. But the convention enables Shakespeare to isolate Lear for the time from all pettier circumstance, to symbolise the storm in him, and so to make him the great figure which the greater issues of the play demand. (pp. 140-43)

To heighten even this heroic height by contrast, we have next the shrill, pitiful chatter of the Fool:

> O nuncle, court holy-water in a dry house is
> better than this rain-water out o' door. Good
> nuncle, in, ask thy daughters' blessing; here's
> a night pities neither wise men nor fools.
>
> [III. ii. 10-13]

Then, again, the Promethean Lear:

> Rumble thy bellyfull! Spit, fire! spout, rain!
> Nor rain, wind, thunder, fire, are my daughters:
> I tax not you, you elements, with unkindness;
> I never gave you kingdom, call'd you children,
> You owe me no subscription: then let fall
> You horrible pleasure; here I stand, your slave,
> A poor, infirm, weak, and despis'd old man.
>
> [III. ii. 14-20]

Does it matter that, compassing the grandeur of the defiance, he will not seem of a sudden, as he says it, either poor, infirm, or weak? Not one bit. Shakespeare gains the effect he needs here by the plain meaning of the words and the change in their music, by the quick shift from magniloquence to a line of perfect simplicity. There, by virtue of that effect, stands the man Lear restored to us again, and with interest; pathetic by contrast with these elements, yet still terribly great by his identity with our sense of them. And this is the Lear, great not in corporal but in intellectual dimensions, the Lear of Lamb's demand. (pp. 143-44)

> Harley Granville-Barker, "'King Lear'," in his Prefaces to Shakespeare, first series, *Sidgwick & Jackson, Ltd.*, 1927, pp. 133-231.

G. WILSON KNIGHT   (essay date 1930)

[*Knight, is one of the most influential Shakespearean critics of the twentieth century; he helped shape a new interpretive approach to Shakespeare's work and promoted a greater appreciation of many of the plays. In his studies* The Wheel of Fire *(1930) and* The Shakespearian Tempest *(1932), Knight rejected criticism which emphasizes sources, character analysis, psychology, and ethics and outlined his principles of interpretation which, he claimed, would "replace that chaos by drawing attention to the true Shakespearian unity." Knight argued that this unity lay in Shakespeare's poetic use of images and symbols—particularly in the opposition of "tempests" and "music." He also maintained that a play's spatial aspects, or "atmosphere," should be as closely considered as the temporal elements of the plot if one is "to see the whole play in space as well as time." The following excerpted essay, taken from the first work mentioned above, is considered one of the seminal studies of* King Lear *in the twentieth century. Knight maintains that Shakespeare's play is based squarely "on the incongruous and the fantastic" and depicts a universe in which the actions of humanity are but the comic sport of the gods. Like Jan Kott after him (see excerpt below, 1964), Knight analyzes the grotesque humor that informs the play and transforms it from a typical pathetic tragedy into a vision of the purposelessness and cruelty of the universe. This presence of the absurd and the incongruous he identifies as the central theme of* Lear's *world, one apparent in Lear's descent into madness, in the humor of the fool—whom Knight sees as the comic arbitrator of the play's "unresolved incompatibilities"—and in the Gloucester subplot, particularly the scene at Dover Cliffs. Last, Knight interprets the ignoble death of Cordelia as "the most hideous and degrading" joke of destiny, the most horrible of incongruities in which Lear, at the point of regaining his sanity, must witness the destruction of his only source of stability. For a similar reading of Cordelia's death and its relation to the play, see the excerpts by Algernon Charles Swinburne (1880), Stopford A. Brooke (1913), J. Stampfer (1960), and Jan Kott (1964). It is important to note that a second essay in Knight's* The Wheel of Fire, *entitled "The* Lear *Universe" (see Additional Bibliography), significantly modifies the findings of the essay excerpted below. In that study, Knight maintains that* King Lear *depicts a purgatorial experience of "creative suffering" and that the drama as a whole moves toward that ideal personified in Cordelia—an "awakening into love"—as its ultimate goal.*]

King Lear is great in the abundance and richness of human delineation, in the level focus of creation that builds a massive oneness, in fact, a universe, of single quality from a multiplicity of differentiated units; and in a positive and purposeful working out of a purgatorial philosophy. But it is still greater in the perfect fusion of psychological realism with the daring flights of a fantastic imagination. The heart of a Shakespearian tragedy is centred in the imaginative, in the unknown; and in *King Lear,* where we touch the unknown, we touch the fantastic.

The peculiar dualism at the root of this play which wrenches and splits the mind by a sight of incongruities displays in turn realities absurd, hideous, pitiful. This incongruity is Lear's madness; it is also the demonic laughter that echoes in the *Lear* universe. In pure tragedy the dualism of experience is continually being dissolved in the masterful beauty of passion, merged in the sunset of emotion. But in comedy it is not so softly resolved—incompatibilities stand out till the sudden relief of laughter or its equivalent of humour: therefore incongruity is the especial mark of comedy. Now in *King Lear* there is a dualism continually crying in vain to be resolved either by tragedy or comedy. Thence arises its peculiar tension of pain: and the course of the action often comes as near to the resolution of comedy as to that of tragedy. So I shall notice here the imaginative core of the play, and, excluding much of the logic of the plot from immediate attention, analyse the fantastic comedy of *King Lear*.

From the start, the situation has a comic aspect. It has been observed that Lear has, so to speak, staged an interlude, with himself as chief actor, in which he grasps expressions of love to his heart, and resigns his sceptre to a chorus of acclamations. It is childish, foolish—but very human. So, too, is the result. Sincerity forbids play-acting, and Cordelia cannot subdue her instinct to any judgement advising tact rather than truth. The incident is profoundly comic and profoundly pathetic. It is, indeed, curious that so storm-furious a play as *King Lear* should have so trivial a domestic basis: it is the first of our many incongruities to be noticed. The absurdity of the old King's anger is clearly indicated by Kent:

> Kill thy physician, and the fee bestow
> Upon the foul disease.
>
> [I. i. 163-64]

The result is absurd. Lear's loving daughter Cordelia is struck from his heart's register, and he is shortly, old and grey-haired and a king, cutting a cruelly ridiculous figure before the cold sanity of his unloving elder daughters. Lear is selfish, self-centred. The images he creates of his three daughters' love are quite false, sentimentalized: he understands the nature of none of his children, and demanding an unreal and impossible love from all three, is disillusioned by each in turn. But, though sentimental, this love is not weak. It is powerful and firm-planted in his mind as a mountain rock embedded in earth. The tearing out of it is hideous, cataclysmic. A tremendous soul is, as it were, incongruously geared to a puerile intellect. Lear's senses prove his idealized love-figments false, his intellect snaps, and, as the loosened drive flings limp, the disconnected engine of madness spins free, and the ungeared revolutions of it are terrible, fantastic. This, then, is the basis of the play: greatness linked to puerility. Lear's instincts are themselves grand, heroic—noble even. His judgement is nothing. He understands neither himself nor his daughters. . . . He has fed his heart on sentimental knowledge of his children's love: he finds their love is not sentimental. There is now a gaping dualism in his mind, thus drawn asunder by incongruities, and he endures madness. Thus the theme of the play is bodied continually into a fantastic incongruity, which is implicit in the beginning—in the very act of Lear's renunciation, retaining the 'title and addition' of King, yet giving over a king's authority to his children. As he becomes torturingly aware of the truth, incongruity masters his mind, and fantastic madness ensues. . . . (pp. 160-63)

From the first signs of Goneril's cruelty, the Fool is used as a chorus, pointing us to the absurdity of the situation. He is indeed an admirable chorus, increasing our pain by his emphasis on a humour which yet will not serve to merge the incompatible in a unity of laughter. He is not all wrong when he treats the situation as matter for a joke. Much here that is always regarded as essentially pathetic is not far from comedy. (p. 163)

[The Fool] sees the potentialities of comedy in Lear's behaviour. . . . [The] situation is excruciatingly painful, and its painfulness is exactly of that quality which embarrasses in some forms of comedy. In the theatre, one is terrified lest some one laugh: yet, if Lear could laugh—if the Lears of the world could laugh at themselves—there would be no such tragedy. . . . The situation is summed up by the Fool:

> *Lear.* When were you wont to be so full of
> songs, sirrah?
> *Fool.* I have used it, nuncle, ever since thou
> madest thy daughters thy mother: for when thou
> gavest them the rod, and put'st down thine own
> breeches. . . .
>
> [I. iv. 170-74]

The height of indecency in suggestion, the height of incongruity. Lear is spiritually put to the ludicrous shame endured bodily by Kent in the stocks: and the absurd rant of Kent, and the unreasonable childish temper of Lear, both merit in some measure what they receive. Painful as it may sound, that is, provisionally, a truth we should realize. The Fool realizes it. He is, too, necessary. Here, where the plot turns on the diverging tugs of two assurances in the mind, it is natural that the action be accompanied by some symbol of humour, that mode which is built of unresolved incompatibilities. Lear's torment is a torment of this dualistic kind, since he scarcely believes his senses when his daughters resist him. He repeats the history of Troilus, who cannot understand the faithlessness of Cressid. In *Othello* and *Timon of Athens* the transition is swift from extreme love to revenge or hate. The movement of Lear's mind is less direct: like Troilus, he is suspended between two separate assurances. Therefore Pandarus, in the latter acts of *Troilus and Cressida*, plays a part similar to the Fool in *King Lear*: both attempt to heal the gaping wound of the mind's incongruous knowledge by the unifying, healing release of laughter. They make no attempt to divert, but rather to direct the hero's mind to the present incongruity. The Fool sees, or tries to see, the humorous potentialities in the most heart-wrenching of incidents. . . . [It] is a cruel, ugly sense of humour. It is the sinister humour at the heart of this play: we are continually aware of the humour of cruelty and the cruelty of humour. But the Fool's use of it is not aimless. If Lear could laugh he might yet save his reason. (pp. 164-65)

Just as Lear's mind begins to fail, the Fool finds Edgar disguised as 'poor Tom'. Edgar now succeeds the Fool as the counterpart to the breaking sanity of Lear; and where the humour of the Fool made no contact with Lear's mind, the fantastic appearance and incoherent words of Edgar are immediately assimilated, as glasses correctly focused to the sight of oncoming madness. Edgar turns the balance of Lear's wavering mentality. His fantastic appearance and lunatic irrelevancies, with the storm outside, and the Fool still for occasional chorus, create a scene of wraithlike unreason, a vision of a world gone mad. . . . To Lear [Edgar's] words are easily explained. His daughters 'have brought him to this pass'. He cries:

> *Lear.* Is the fashion that discarded fathers
> Should have thus little mercy on their flesh?

> Judicious punishment! 'twas this flesh begot
> Those pelican daughters.
> *Edgar.* Pillicock sat on Pillicock-hill:
> Halloo, halloo, loo, loo!
> *Fool.* This cold night will turn us all to fools
> and madmen.
>
> [III. iv. 72-9]

What shall we say of this exquisite movement? Is it comedy? Lear's profound unreason is capped by the blatant irrelevance of Edgar's couplet suggested by the word 'pelican'; then the two are swiftly all but unified, for us if not for Lear, in the healing balm of the Fool's conclusion. It is the process of humour, where two incompatibles are resolved in laughter. The Fool does this again. Lear again speaks a profound truth as the wild night and Edgar's fantastic impersonation grip his mind and dethrone his conventional sanity:

> *Lear.* Is man no more than this? Consider him
> well. Thou owest the worm no silk, the beast
> no hide, the sheep no wool, the cat no perfume.
> Ha! Here 's three on 's are sophisticated! Thou
> art the thing itself: unaccommodated man is no
> more but such a poor, bare, forked animal as
> thou art. Off, off, you lendings! come unbutton
> here. (*Tearing off his clothes.*)
> *Fool.* Prithee, nuncle, be contented; 'tis a
> naughty night to swim in.
>
> [III. iv. 102-11]

This is the furthest flight, not of tragedy, but of philosophic comedy. The autocratic and fiery-fierce old king, symbol of dignity, is confronted with the meanest of men: a naked lunatic beggar. In a flash of vision he attempts to become his opposite, to be naked, 'unsophisticated'. And then the opposing forces which struck the lightning-flash of vision tail off, resolved into a perfect unity by the Fool's laughter, reverberating, trickling, potent to heal in sanity the hideous unreason of this tempest-shaken night: ''tis a naughty night to swim in'. Again this is the process of humour: its flash of vision first bridges the positive and negative poles of the mind, unifying them, and then expresses itself in laughter. (pp. 166-67)

The unresolved dualism that tormented Troilus and was given metaphysical expression by him [*Troilus and Cressida*, V. ii. 137-60] is here more perfectly bodied into the poetic symbol of poor Tom: and since Lear cannot hear the resolving laugh of foolery, his mind is focused only to the 'philosopher' mumbling of the foul fiend. Edgar thus serves to lure Lear on: we forget that he is dissimulating. Lear is the centre of our attention, and as the world shakes with tempest and unreason, we endure something of the shaking and the tempest of his mind. The absurd and fantastic reign supreme. . . . Lear's curses were for a short space terrible, majestic, less controlled and purposeful than Timon's but passionate and grand in their tempestuous fury. Now, in madness, he flashes on us the ridiculous basis of his tragedy in words which emphasize the indignity and incongruity of it, and make his madness something nearer the ridiculous than the terrible, something which moves our pity, but does not strike awe:

> Arraign her first; 'tis Goneril. I here take my
> oath before this honourable assembly, she kicked
> the poor king her father.
>
> [III. vi. 46-8]

This stroke of the absurd—so vastly different from the awe we experience in face of Timon's hate—is yet fundamental here.

The core of the play is an absurdity, an indignity, an incongruity. In no tragedy of Shakespeare does incident and dialogue so recklessly and miraculously walk the tight-rope of our pity over the depths of bathos and absurdity.

This particular region of the terrible bordering on the fantastic and absurd is exactly the playground of madness. Thus the setting of Lear's madness includes a sub-plot where these same elements are presented with stark nakedness, and no veiling subtleties. The Gloucester-theme is a certain indication of our vision and helps us to understand, and feel, the enduring agony of Lear. As usual, the first scene of this play strikes the dominant note. Gloucester jests at the bastardy of his son Edmund, remarking that, though he is ashamed to acknowledge him, 'there was good sport at his making' [I. i. 23]. That is, we start with humour in bad taste. The whole tragedy witnesses a sense of humour in 'the gods' which is in similar bad taste. Now all the Lear effects are exaggerated in the Gloucester theme. Edmund's plot is a more Iago-like, devilish, intentional thing than Goneril's and Regan's icy callousness. Edgar's supposed letter is crude and absurd. . . . But then Edmund, wittiest and most attractive of villains, composed it. One can almost picture his grin as he penned those lines, commending them mentally to the limited intellect of his father. Yes—the Gloucester theme has a beginning even more fantastic than that of Lear's tragedy. And not only are the Lear effects here exaggerated in the directions of villainy and humour: they are even more clearly exaggerated in that of horror. The gouging out of Gloucester's eyes is a thing unnecessary, crude, disgusting: it is meant to be. It helps to provide an accompanying exaggeration of one element—that of cruelty—in the horror that makes Lear's madness. And not only horror: there is again something satanically comic bedded deep in it. The sight of physical torment, to the uneducated, brings laughter. Shakespeare's England delighted in watching both physical torment and the comic ravings of actual lunacy. The dance of madmen in Webster's *Duchess of Malfi* is of the same ghoulish humour as Regan's plucking Gloucester by the beard: the groundlings will laugh at both. Moreover, the sacrilege of the human body in torture must be, to a human mind, incongruous, absurd. This hideous mockery is consummated in Regan's final witticism after Gloucester's eyes are out:

> Go, thrust him out at gates, and let him smell
> His way to Dover.
>
> [III. vii. 93-4]

The macabre humoresque of this is nauseating: but it is there, and integral to the play. These ghoulish horrors, so popular in Elizabethan drama, and the very stuff of the *Lear* of Shakespeare's youth, *Titus Andronicus,* find an exquisitely appropriate place in the tragedy of Shakespeare's maturity which takes as its especial province this territory of the grotesque and the fantastic which is Lear's madness. We are clearly pointed to this grim fun, this hideous sense of humour, at the back of tragedy:

> As flies to wanton boys are we to the gods;
> They kill us for their sport.
>
> [IV. i. 36-7]

This illustrates the exact quality I wish to emphasize: the humour a boy—even a kind boy—may see in the wriggles of an impaled insect. So, too, Gloucester is bound, and tortured, physically; and so the mind of Lear is impaled, crucified on the cross-beams of love and disillusion.

There follows the grim pilgrimage of Edgar and Gloucester towards Dover Cliff: an incident typical enough of *King*

Lear. . . . Gloucester has planned a spectacular end for himself. We are given [his] noble descriptive and philosophical speeches to tune our minds to a noble, tragic sacrifice. And what happens? The old man falls from his kneeling posture a few inches, flat, face foremost. Instead of the dizzy circling to crash and spill his life on the rocks below—just this. The grotesque merged into the ridiculous reaches a consummation in this bathos of tragedy: it is the furthest, most exaggerated, reach of the poet's towering fantastically. We have a sublimely daring stroke of technique, unjustifiable, like Edgar's emphasized and vigorous madness throughout, on the plane of plot-logic, and even to a superficial view somewhat out of place imaginatively in so dire and stark a limning of human destiny as is *King Lear*; yet this scene is in reality a consummate stroke of art. The Gloucester-theme throughout reflects and emphasizes and exaggerates all the percurrent qualities of the Lear-theme. Here the incongruous and fantastic element of the Lear-theme is boldly reflected into the tragically-absurd. The stroke is audacious, unashamed, and magical of effect. (pp. 167-71)

The Gloucester-theme has throughout run separate from that of Lear, yet parallel, and continually giving us direct villainy where the other shows cold callousness; horrors of physical torment where the other has a subtle mental torment; culminating in this towering stroke of the grotesque and absurd to balance the fantastic incidents and speeches that immediately follow. At this point we suddenly have our first sight of Lear in the full ecstasy of his later madness. Now, when our imaginations are most powerfully quickened to the grotesque and incongruous, the whole surge of the Gloucester-theme, which has just reached its climax, floods as a tributary the main stream of our sympathy with Lear. Our vision has thus been uniquely focused to understand that vision of the grotesque, the incongruous, the fantastically-horrible, which is the agony of Lear's mind. . . . (p. 172)

But indeed this recurrent stress on the incongruous and the fantastic is not a subsidiary element in *King Lear:* it is the very heart of the play. We watch humanity grotesquely tormented, cruelly and with mockery impaled: nearly all the persons suffer some form of crude indignity in the course of the play. I have noticed the major themes of Lear and Gloucester: there are others. Kent is banished, undergoes the disguise of a servant, is put to shame in the stocks; Cornwall is killed by his own servant resisting the dastardly mutilation of Gloucester; Oswald, the prim courtier, is done to death by Edgar in the role of an illiterate country yokel. . . . Edgar himself endures the utmost degradation of his disguise as 'poor Tom', begrimed and naked, and condemned to speak nothing but idiocy. Edmund alone steers something of an unswerving tragic course, brought to a fitting, deserved, but spectacular end, slain by his wronged brother, nobly repentant at the last. . . . Edmund is given a noble, an essentially tragic, end, and Goneril and Regan, too, meet their ends with something of tragic fineness in pursuit of their evil desires. Regan dies by her sister's poison; Goneril with a knife. They die, at least, in the cause of love—love of Edmund. Compared with these deaths, the end of Cordelia is horrible, cruel, unnecessarily cruel—the final grotesque horror in the play. Her villainous sisters are already dead. Edmund is nearly dead, repentant. It is a matter of seconds—and rescue comes too late. She is hanged by a common soldier. The death which Dostoievsky's Stavrogin singled out as of all the least heroic and picturesque, or rather, shall we say, the most hideous and degrading: this is the fate that grips the white innocence and resplendent love-strength of Cordelia. To be hanged, after the death of her enemies, in the midst of friends.

It is the last hideous joke of destiny: this—and the fact that Lear is still alive, has recovered his sanity for this. The death of Cordelia is the last and most horrible of all the horrible incongruities I have noticed. . . . (pp. 173-74)

The tragedy is most poignant in that it is purposeless, unreasonable. It is the most fearless artistic facing of the ultimate cruelty of things in our literature. That cruelty would be less were there not this element of comedy which I have emphasized, the insistent incongruities, which create and accompany the madness of Lear, which leap to vivid shape in the mockery of Gloucester's suicide, which are intrinsic in the texture of the whole play. Mankind is, as it were, deliberately and comically tormented by 'the gods'. He is not even allowed to die tragically. . . . *King Lear* is supreme in that, in this main theme, it faces the very absence of tragic purpose: wherein it is profoundly different from *Timon of Athens*. Yet, as we close the sheets of this play, there is no horror, nor resentment. The tragic purification of the essentially untragic is yet complete.

Now in this essay it will, perhaps, appear that I have unduly emphasized one single element of the play, magnifying it and leaving the whole distorted. It has been my purpose to emphasize. I have not exaggerated. The pathos has not been minimized: it is redoubled. Nor does the use of the words 'comic' and 'humour' here imply disrespect to the poet's purpose: rather I have used these words, crudely no doubt, to cut out for analysis the very heart of the play—the thing that man dares scarcely face: the demonic grin of the incongruous and absurd in the most pitiful of human struggles with an iron fate. It is this that wrenches, splits, gashes the mind till it utters the whirling vapourings of lunacy. And, though love and music—twin sisters of salvation—temporarily may heal the racked consciousness of Lear, yet, so deeply planted in the facts of our life is this unknowing ridicule of destiny, that the uttermost tragedy of the incongruous ensues, and there is no hope save in the broken heart and limp body of death. This is of all the most agonizing of tragedies to endure: and if we are to feel more than a fraction of this agony, we must have sense of this quality of grimmest humour. We must beware of sentimentalizing the cosmic mockery of the play.

And is there, perhaps, even a deeper, and less heart-searing, significance in its humour? Smiles and tears are indeed most curiously interwoven here. Gloucester was saved from his violent and tragic suicide that he might recover his wronged son's love, and that his heart might

> 'Twixt two extremes of passion, joy and grief,
> Burst smilingly.
>
> [V. iii. 199-200]

Lear dies with the words

> Do you see this? Look on her, look, her lips,
> Look there, look there! . . .
>
> [V. iii. 311-12]

What do we touch in these passages? Sometimes we know that all human pain holds beauty, that no tear falls but it dews some flower we cannot see. Perhaps humour, too, is inwoven in the universal pain, and the enigmatic silence holds not only an unutterable sympathy, but also the ripples of an impossible laughter whose flight is not for the wing of human understanding; and perhaps it is this that casts its darting shadow of the grotesque across the furrowed pages of *King Lear*. (pp. 174-76)

G. Wilson Knight, "'King Lear' and the Comedy of the Grotesque," in his The Wheel of Fire: Interpretations of Shakespearian Tragedy, *Methuen & Co. Ltd., 1949, pp. 160-76.*

J. DOVER WILSON (essay date 1932)

[*Dover Wilson was a highly regarded Shakespearean scholar who was involved in several aspects of Shakespeare studies. As an editor of the* New Cambridge Shakespeare, *he made numerous contributions to twentieth-century textual criticism of Shakespeare, making use of the scientific bibliography developed by W. W. Greg and Charlton Hinman. As a critic, Dover Wilson combines several contemporary approaches and does not fit easily into any one critical "school." He is concerned with character analysis in the tradition of A. C. Bradley; he delves into Elizabethan culture like the historical critics, but without their usual emphasis on hierarchy and the Great Chain of Being; and his interest in visualizing possible dramatic performances of the plays links him with his contemporary, Harley Granville-Barker. In the excerpt below, Dover Wilson characterizes* King Lear *as the work in which Shakespeare best demonstrated his dramatic "balance"—"the tragic balance between truth and beauty, between the inexorable judgment and divine compassion." He claims that the final scene transforms the apparent moral of the drama, couched in Gloucester's pessimistic "flies to wanton boys" speech, for Lear becomes "an eternal and sublime symbol of the majesty of humanity, of the victory of spirit over the worst that fate can do against it." The idea that Cordelia's death redeems the play from its overall pessimistic vision was first suggested by G. G. Gervinus (1849-50) and more fully developed in the essay by A. C. Bradley (1904). It is also evident in the essays by Oscar James Campbell (1948), D. G. James (1951), Irving Ribner (1958), L. C. Knights (1959), and Robert H. West (1968).*]

[Shakespeare always] kept his balance, the tragic balance between truth and beauty, between inexorable judgment and divine compassion. And this balance was at once a supreme spiritual achievement and a triumph of dramatic technique, since it was a development and a consummation of all the accumulated skill and knowledge of the ten previous years. In 1599 he little knew what awaited him; yet when the storm burst he displayed what Bridges has called "masterful administration of the unforeseen". Finally, his victory was a victory for the whole human race. *King Lear* is a piece of exploration, more dearly won and far more significant than that of a Shackleton or an Einstein; for, while they have enlarged the bounds of human knowledge, *Lear* has revealed the human spirit as of greater sublimity than we could otherwise have dreamed.

The tragic balance may, of course, be seen in all the great tragedies, is indeed the clue to their true interpretation. I must, however, be content here to illustrate its relevance by a closer study of the greatest, the play just mentioned. . . . *King Lear* combines the method of *Hamlet* with that of *Othello*; that is to say, it is at once a drama of character and a drama of destiny. Lear is a king "more sinned against than sinning" [III. ii. 60]. Hell, in the person of his two daughters and in the symbol of the storm, seems to rise up in full panoply, first to crush the old man's pride, then to overthrow his intellect, and last of all to break his heart. And yet Lear *has* sinned, so that the play is not a picture only of goodness overwhelmed by evil but also . . . of an irascible old tyrant, spoilt by a long life of uncontrolled and immoderate use of power, rising through the discipline of humiliation and disaster to a height unequalled elsewhere in Shakespeare. Gloucester's cry

> As flies to wanton boys, are we to the gods,
> They kill us for their sport—
>
>   [IV. i. 36-7]

is for many, perhaps for most, the moral of the play, and there is much to support it. Lear invokes the heavens against filial ingratitude, but instead of hearing his appeal for justice they join "with two pernicious daughters" their "high engendered battles" [III. ii. 22-3] of storm and rain, thunder and lightning, to chastise him. At every turn destiny, or God, pursues him as with hatred until, when we hear of Cordelia's army being crushed and herself taken prisoner with her father, we feel, as in the book of Job or in a novel by Thomas Hardy, that we human beings are puppets. . . . (pp. 123-25)

And then the heavens open to discharge their last dreadful bolt, and for some of us at least the mood changes. When Lear enters, in that final and most terrible scene, with Cordelia dead in his arms, we cannot think of him any longer as a fly or a puppet or a chessman. What the meaning of Life may be we know no more than before, but we marvel at the greatness of man and at what man can endure. Lear is like some peak of anguish, an eternal and sublime symbol of the majesty of humanity, of the victory of spirit over the worst that fate can do against it. This last scene reminds us, inevitably, of Calvary. But it is a human Calvary; there is no resurrection to follow, not a hint of a Father in heaven. And yet the universe in which Lear is possible cannot be wholly evil, since he is part of it, and Cordelia is part of it, and the possibility of such souls may even be a clue to its meaning.

And there is something more. The Lear that dies is not a Lear defiant, but a Lear redeemed. His education is complete, his regeneration accomplished. The headstrong, ungovernable, tempestuous old despot, after passing through the purgatory of insanity and the brief heaven of reconciliation with his Cordelia, has become "a very foolish, fond old man" [IV. vii. 59], with no claim except for forgiveness and no desire except for love. This is not the last stage of imbecility and dotage, but recovery. Never is Lear greater, more tremendous, more his real self, than in the final moment, when he confronts "high-judging Jove" not with

> the unconquerable will,
> And study of revenge, immortal hate,
> And courage never to submit or yield,

but with the oblation of a broken heart. And as we turn our eyes from a scene too terrible and pitiable to be endured, is it our weakness or a hint of the Truth that brings back to us words uttered by Lear himself on the way to prison just before:

> Upon such sacrifices, my Cordelia,
> The gods themselves throw incense?
>
>   [V. iii. 20-1]

Men will discuss the meaning of *King Lear* to the end of time, as they will discuss the meaning of the universe, for the two meanings are the same. The one certain message of the play is that nothing is certain. Shakespeare has no solution to offer, but he gives us something far greater. He has fashioned a mirror of art in which, more successfully than any man before or since, he has caught the whole of Life and focused it to one intense and burning point of terror and beauty. And in so doing he found salvation. For, though the ravings of *Timon of Athens* show how near he came to plunging headlong into the abyss, *Macbeth,* which is almost a morality play, and the marvellous *Antony and Cleopatra,* in which love lifts a libertine and a harlot into the sublime atmosphere of Romeo and Juliet, prove that he kept his balance and passed on. (pp. 125-27)

J. Dover Wilson, "The Razor-Edge," in his The Essential Shakespeare: A Biographical Adventure,

Cambridge at the University Press, 1932, pp. 108-27.

CAROLINE F. E. SPURGEON (essay date 1935)

[*Spurgeon's* Shakespeare's Imagery *(1935) inaugurated the "image-pattern analysis" method of studying Shakespeare's plays, one of the most widely used methods of the mid-twentieth century. In this work, she interprets the thematic structure of the plays through an examination of patterns in the imagery. Spurgeon also sought to learn about Shakespeare's personality from a study of his images, a course which few of her disciples followed. Since publication of her book, earlier works on image patterns in Shakespeare have been discovered, but none was so important in the history of Shakespearean criticism as Spurgeon's. In the following excerpt, Spurgeon maintains that the central image in* King Lear, *from which all others develop, is that of "a human body in anguished movement." She also comments, as did the Reverend J. Kirkman (see excerpt above, 1879), on the presence of animal imagery in the play; but whereas Kirkman saw it strictly as an emblem of humanity regressing to bestiality, Spurgeon also regards its presence as augmenting "the sensation of horror and bodily pain." Other critics who have studied the imagery in* King Lear *include Robert Bechtold Heilman (1948) and Wolfgang Clemen (1951).*]

The intensity of feeling and emotion in *King Lear* and the sharpness of its focus are revealed by the fact that in Shakespeare's imagination there runs throughout only one overpowering and dominating continuous image. So compelling is this that even well-marked different and subsidiary images are pressed into its service, and used to augment and emphasise it.

In the play we are conscious all through of the atmosphere of buffeting, strain and strife, and, at moments, of bodily tension to the point of agony. So naturally does this flow from the circumstances of the drama and the mental sufferings of Lear, that we scarcely realise how greatly this sensation in us is increased by the general 'floating' image, kept constantly before us, chiefly by means of the verbs used, but also in metaphor, of a human body in anguished movement, tugged, wrenched, beaten, pierced, stung, scourged, dislocated, flayed, gashed, scalded, tortured and finally broken on the rack.

One can scarcely open a page of the play without being struck by these images and verbs, for every kind of bodily movement, generally involving pain, is used to express mental and abstract, as well as physical facts. (pp. 338-39)

This use of verbs and images of bodily and generally anguished motion is almost continuous, and it is reinforced by similar words used in direct description, as in the treatment of Gloucester; he is *bound* to a chair, *plucked* by the beard, his hairs are *ravished* from his chin, he is *tied to a stake,* like a bear to *stand the course,* and with his eyes blinded and bleeding, he is *thrust out* of the gates to *smell his way* to Dover.

All through the play, the simplest abstract things are described in similar terms. Even in a scene, pleasant in itself, such as the gentleman's ornate but delightful description of Cordelia's reception of his news [IV. iii], this sense of bodily movement and strain is constant. The letters *pierced* her to a demonstration of grief, her passion

> most rebel-like
> Sought to be king o'er her;
>
> [IV. iii. 14-15]

it *moved* her, patience and sorrow *strove,* she *heaved* the name of 'father' *pantingly forth,* as if it *press'd her heart;* she *shook* the tears from her eyes, and away she *started*

> To deal with grief alone.
>
> [IV. iii. 32]

Look at the six lines which follow, in which Kent, having declared that Lear will not *yield* to see his daughter, describes his master's mental and emotional suffering in a series of pictures of physical buffeting, pain and opposition, which, in addition to the two images of brutal dogs and poisonous serpents, have a cumulative and almost overwhelming effect on the mind. . . . (pp. 340-41)

The idea of unnatural horrors, of human beings *preying on themselves* 'like monsters of the deep', or like wolves and tigers tearing one another's flesh, is also constantly before us. (p. 341)

The large number of animal images, and their effect in the play, have often been noticed. . . . I would only point out here that in addition to the feeling they give us that 'humanity' is 'reeling back into the beast', they also, because portrayed chiefly in angry or anguished action, very distinctly augment the sensation of horror and bodily pain. In addition to savage wolves, tigers and other animals, there are *darting* serpents, a *sharp-toothed* vulture and *detested* kite, *stinging* adders and insects, *gnawing* rats, the *baited* bear, as well as *whipped, whining, barking, mad* and *biting* dogs. All this helps to create and increase an unparalleled atmosphere of rapine, cruelty and bodily pain.

To this is added an overtone running through the crisis of the tragedy, the fury of the elements, described, be it remarked, wholly in terms of the human body. They are *wild, fretful, unquiet;* the wind and rain are *to and fro conflicting;* with these, the old king, with his *heart-struck injuries,* is contending, *tearing* his white hair

> Which the *impetuous* blasts, with *eyeless rage,*
> *Catch* in their *fury;*
>
> [III. i. 8-9]

and bidding the winds to blow and *crack their cheeks,* until, at the height of his half-demented passion, he commands the *all-shaking* thunder to 'smite flat the thick rotundity o' the world' [III. ii. 7]. This last amazing image is one of several in Shakespeare, notably in *Antony and Cleopatra,* which evoke the spectacle of devastating bodily action on so stupendous a scale that the emotions which give rise to it are lifted to a similar terrific and vast intensity. So the picture which follows here, of the great gods, through the bursts of thunder and groans of roaring wind and rain, remorselessly seeking and finding out their enemies, while 'close *pent-up* guilts' *rive* their concealing continents, and *cry*

> These dreadful summoners grace,
>
> [III. ii. 59]

seems natural and only in keeping with the feeling aroused in the imagination of a being or a force mighty enough to remould the shape of the globe with one resounding blow.

The sense of bodily torture continues to the end. Gloucester catches the recurrent theme of the tragedy, and crystallises it for ever in the terrible picture of men being torn limb from limb by the gods in sport, to whom they are but as 'flies to wanton boys' [IV. i. 36]. Lear tells Cordelia he is bound

> Upon a wheel of fire, that mine own tears
> Do scald like molten lead;
>
>   [IV. vii. 46-7]

Edgar sees the gods making instruments of torture with which to plague men; and, at the close, when Kent, who loves him, breathes the only valediction possible over his dead master's body, it is still the same metaphor which rises to his lips:

> O, let him pass! he hates him
> That would upon the rack of this tough world
> Stretch him out longer.
>
>   [V. iii. 314-16]
>   (pp. 342-43)

> *Caroline F. E. Spurgeon, "Leading Motives in the Tragedies," in her* Shakespeare's Imagery and What It Tells Us, *Cambridge at the University Press, 1935, pp. 309-56.*

ENID WELSFORD (essay date 1935)

[*The following excerpt is taken from one of the most important discussions of the purpose of the Fool, and to a larger extent the purpose of folly and wisdom, in* King Lear. *Welsford regards the Fool as a direct descendant of the "sage-fool," or that disinterested truth-teller whose primary purpose is to question the audience on the nature of folly. She divides the other characters into fools, who are the good characters capable of "fellow-feeling," and the evil figures, who possess intellect but lack the capacity for love. In the former group Welsford places—besides the Fool—Lear, Kent, Edgar, and Cordelia; to the latter group she relegates Goneril, Regan, and Edmund. Welsford culminates her discussion by maintaining that although Shakespeare appears to suggest a relativist position with respect to these opposing moral principles, especially since both the good and evil characters pay the same price for their actions, either by suffering or by death, in actuality he affirms the philosophy of the fools. Welsford bases this conclusion on Shakespeare's use of the accepted convention of the Fool as "the mouthpiece of real sanity," the spokesman of the truth in the drama—a truth which values disinterested "loving-kindness" over "self-interest" because it is more natural to the human condition. Welsford constructs much of her interpretation on the traditional Christian vision she finds reaffirmed throughout the play, specifically in the idea of the "holy fool" who places fellow-love over self-interest, but she acknowledges that Shakespeare's vision omits the comforting message of the Scriptures. For further analysis of the Fool and his role in* King Lear, *see the excerpts by William Hazlitt (1817), Hermann Ulrici (1839), H. N. Hudson (1872), G. Wilson Knight (1930), and Melvin Seiden (1979).*]

[When] Shakespeare made Lear and his Fool companions in misfortune, he may have broken the canons of classical art, but he certainly was not destroying verisimilitude. On the contrary, if he was catering for the popular taste for clownage, he was doing so by creating a figure who was sufficiently life-like to be tragically convincing. The human truth and pathos of the situation is indeed so appealing that it has sometimes distracted attention from the deeper purpose of the dramatist in this juxtaposition of King and Clown. Lear's Fool is not merely a touching figure who might easily have been drawn from life, he is also the fool of the sottie, and, although evidently half-witted, is endowed with a penetration deeper and more far-reaching than that superficial sharp-wittedness and gift for smart repartee which went to the making of a successful court-jester. He is in fact the sage-fool who sees the truth, and

his role has even more *intellectual* than emotional significance. For *King Lear* is not merely a popular play. If it offends against classical decorum, it is nevertheless true to a definitely intellectual tradition and makes use of the conventions of 'fool-literature' which were . . . clerical rather than popular in origin, and were used as the vehicle for a reasoned criticism of life. The Fool, therefore, as I shall endeavour to prove, is here used both as a commentator whose words furnish important clues to the interpretation of a difficult play; and also as a prominent figure caught up into the drama, whose rôle and nature form a vital part of the central tragic theme.

Lear's Fool, like Touchstone and Feste, is an 'all-licensed' critic who sees and speaks the real truth about the people around him. His business, however, is not to deal out satirical commonplaces, but to emphasize one peculiarly dreadful instance of the reversal of position between the wise man and the fool; indeed he labours this point with a maddening reiteration which is only excusable because his tactless jokes and snatches of song spring so evidently from genuine grief. (pp. 253-54)

When King Lear made his daughters his mothers he committed an act of indubitable folly of which his fool is only too ready to remind him; but the same fool comments on folly of a very different order, when the disguised Kent offers his services to his helpless master:

> FOOL. Sirrah, you were best take my coxcomb.
> KENT. Why, fool?
> FOOL. Why, for taking one's part that's out of favour
>   [I. iv. 97-100]

The same point is made even more forcibly when the Fool finds Kent in the stocks. . . . (p. 254)

In treating the Fool as the disinterested truth-teller, the 'punctum indifferens' of the play, Shakespeare was not making any new departure from his earlier comic method as shown in the handling of Touchstone; and, as a piece of realistic character-drawing, Lear's 'Good boy' with his lovable, sympathetic qualities is only a profounder study of a type already exemplified in the jester of *Twelfth Night*. Nevertheless, Shakespeare's tragic fool differs very profoundly from his comic brethren. In Arden and Illyria it is regarded as a sufficiently good joke that the madman should be the spokesman of sanity, that the ostensible fool should find it so easy to draw out the latent folly of the wise. But Lear's Fool goes further than this. Like others of his profession he is very ready to proffer his coxcomb to his betters, but in doing so he does not merely raise a laugh or score a point, he sets a problem. 'What am I? What is madness?' he seems to ask, 'the world being what it is, do I necessarily insult a man by investing him with motley?'

With this apparently comic question the Fool strikes the keynote of the tragedy of Lear. It is a critical, a crucial question which effects a startling division among the dramatis personae—it being for instance obvious that Goneril, Regan and Edmund are not candidates for the cap and bells. It is also a central question which at once resolves itself into a question about the nature of the universe. For the full understanding of its import it is necessary to leave for awhile our meditation on the meaning of the words of the Fool, and to consider instead their reverberation in the play as a whole: examining firstly the disposition of the characters, and secondly the movement of events.

It is a critical commonplace that in *King Lear* Shakespeare deals with the tragic aspect of human life in its most universal form. The conflict of good with evil, of wisdom with folly, the hopeless cry to the deaf Heavens for justice, are presented with something of the simplicity of a morality play. For just as in that type of drama the central figure was the soul of man competed for by the conflicting forces of good and ill; so in *King Lear* the two heroes are erring men, warm-hearted but self-willed, whose ruin or salvation depends on the issue of a conflict between two sharply opposed groups of people painted far more uncompromisingly in black and white than is customary in Shakespearian tragedy. But if *Lear* has something of the structural simplicity of the morality play it has none of its moral triteness. Where the medieval playwright furnishes answers, Shakespeare provokes questions and reveals ambiguities. Whether he ever suggests a solution is disputable; but there can be little doubt as to the urgency with which he sets the problem of the nature and destiny of goodness.

In *King Lear* all the 'good' characters have one striking quality in common, they have the capacity for 'fellow-feeling' highly developed. . . . Perfect and imperfect alike take it for granted that the capacity for sympathetic love is a very valuable but quite normal attribute of human nature. This attribute makes the good characters peculiarly vulnerable and sometimes almost stupidly helpless. In the first place they instinctively trust their fellows, and this trustfulness does not sharpen their powers of discrimination. The imperfect who crave for affection are particularly liable to make silly mistakes, and their suffering and anger when they think themselves deceived make them still more unable to distinguish friend from foe. The perfectly sympathetic are foolish in a different way. They are blind to their own interests. They save others but themselves they cannot save.

The 'bad' characters are the exact opposite of the good in that they are abnormally devoid of 'fellow-feeling'. They may be hardly more egoistic than some of their opponents, but they differ from them in that they are no more anxious to receive sympathy than they are to give it. They seek only to gratify their physical lust and their will-to-power. . . . For Goneril, Regan and Edmund the world is the world of Hobbes, a world where every man's hand is against every man's, and the only human ties are contracts which reason and self-interest prompt people to make as the only alternative to mutual annihilation, and which no moral scruple need hinder them from breaking when by doing so they defend their own interests. Up to a point the evil are invulnerable. Their activities are never hampered by a distaste for other peoples' sufferings, trustfulness never dims their powers of observation, and above all they never put themselves into anyone else's power by a desire for his affection. (pp. 256-59)

On the whole, and this is true of other plays besides *King Lear*, Shakespeare tends to give more intellectual ability to his sinners than to his saints. Edmund, for instance, is so shrewd and witty that he almost wins our sympathy for his unabashed cruelty. To such an one goodness is simply stupidity. . . . But this is trite; Shakespeare penetrates more profoundly than this into the nature of evil. Sympathy and trustfulness make men easily gullible, and consistently egoistic utilitarians ought to value gulls. But strangely enough they find them most distasteful. 'Well you may fear too far', says Albany, when Goneril suggests that it would be prudent to dismiss her father's train. 'Safer than trust too far' [I. iv. 328], is his wife's characteristic reply. This difference of outlook soon ripens into a real antipathy. . . . (p. 259)

Goneril's attitude reminds us of the wise advice which the Fool ironically offered to Kent. To Goneril it is the only conceivable kind of wisdom, to Albany it is just plain knavery, to the Fool it is either wisdom or folly according to your point of view. For the puzzle about evil is not that men do not live up to their principles; it is that men can reverse values and say: 'Evil, be thou my good', and that by reason alone it is not possible to prove them wrong. The bad characters in *Lear* have no fellow-feeling, and therefore act consistently from motives of self-interest. The analytic intellect cannot prove that 'fellow-feeling' is a possibility, still less that it is a duty. Respectable philosophers have founded their systems (though not their practice) on the notion that altruism can always be resolved into egoism. Are not Edmund and Goneril, then, justified in seeing the world as they do see it and acting in accordance with their insight? What have the good to say on this subject? Well, they have no intellectual arguments to offer, but two intuitions or convictions, on which they are prepared to act even at the cost of their own lives. Firstly, if love is lunacy so much the worse for sanity: the good will merely in their turn reverse values and say, 'Folly, be thou my wisdom'. Secondly, love or 'fellow-feeling' is a normal attribute of humanity, and as such it does not need proof, for it is its absence, not its presence, that requires explanation. 'Let them anatomize Regan, see what breeds about her heart. Is there any cause in nature that makes these hard hearts?' [III. vi. 76-8]. Recurrent throughout the play is the sense that the breaking of human ties, especially ties of close blood or plighted loyalty, is so abnormal and unnatural that it must be a symptom of some dread convulsion in the frame of things that must bring about the end of the world unless some Divine Power intervenes to redress the balance before it is too late. And more than that, it is so fundamentally abnormal and inhuman that the mere contemplation of it upsets the mental balance of a normal man. As Lear looks into Goneril's heart his wits begin to turn. To Edmund, on the other hand, it is the most natural thing in the world that he should pursue his own interests, whatever the expense to other people.

Which of these parties sees the truth, or rather, to speak more accurately, which point of view does Shakespeare mean us to adopt as we experience his tragedy? Or is this an instance of his notorious impartiality? Is he giving us a tragic illustration of moral relativity? Do Goneril and Cordelia separate good from evil, wisdom from folly, with very different results, only because they have different but equally valid frames of reference for their measurements? If we join the good characters in the play in asking Heaven to decide, that would seem to be the inescapable conclusion, for both Cordelia and Goneril die prematurely. And if it is a fact that some of the good survive, whereas the evil are shown to be by their nature mutually destructive; yet we may set against this the fact that the good suffer more than the evil, that love and suffering, in this play, are almost interchangeable terms and the driving force of the action is derived from the power of the evil to inflict mental agony upon the good. This is particularly important, because the physical death of the hero is not really the tragic climax of this play. Lear, after all, is an old man, and the poignant question about him is not: 'Will he survive?' but rather 'What will happen to his mind?' The real horror lies not in the fact that Goneril and Regan can cause the death of their father, but that they can apparently destroy his human integrity. (pp. 260-62)

It has often been pointed out that Lear has a more passive rôle than most of Shakespeare's tragic characters. Nevertheless he is involved in an event, and his relationship with the Fool is no mere static pictorial contrast, but part of the tragic movement of the play; the movement downwards towards that ultimate exposure and defeat when the King is degraded to the status of the meanest of his servants. We watch the royal sufferer being progressively stripped, first of extraordinary worldly power, then of ordinary human dignity, then of the very necessities of life, deprived of which he is more helpless and abject than any animal. But there is a more dreadful consummation than this reduction to physical nakedness. Lear hardly feels the storm because he is struggling to retain his mental integrity, his 'knowledge and reason', which are not only, as he himself calls them, 'marks of sovereignty', but the essential marks of humanity itself:

> O, let me not be mad, not mad, sweet heaven!
> Keep me in temper, I would not be mad! . . .
> O fool, I shall go mad!
>
> [I. v. 46-7, II. iv. 286]

Lear's dread is justified, 'sweet heaven' rejects his prayer, and the central scenes on the heath are peopled by a blind, half-crazy nobleman, guided by a naked beggar supposed to be mad, and by an actually mad King served by a half-witted court-jester—an amazingly daring version of the culminating moment of the sottie: the great reversal when the highest dignitaries appear as fools, and the World or even Holy Church herself is revealed in cap and bells.

Do we then find at the heart of this greatest of tragedies the satire of the sottie transmuted into despair? That depends on what happens when we test the quality of Lear's unreason, and on how we answer the question already suggested by his brother in folly: 'Do I insult a man by investing him with motley?'

From the time when Lear's agony begins and he feels his sanity threatened he becomes gradually aware of the sufferings of other people. . . . And not only are Lear's sympathies aroused, they are broadened. Goneril and Regan break the closest, most fundamental of human ties, they cannot feel even that kind of parental-filial relationship that the animals feel; whereas in his agony, Lear, who had himself been unnatural to Cordelia, suddenly realizes that all men are one in pain. . . . As Lear's brain reels, his agony increases and his sympathies expand. The same thing happens to Gloucester, whose blindness parallels Lear's madness. . . . (pp. 262-63)

In several passages *seeing* and *feeling* are compared and contrasted with one another. It is feeling that gives the true sight. 'I stumbled when I saw' [IV. i. 19]. Again we are confronted with the paradoxical reversal of wisdom and folly. . . . But now that the worst has happened, now that Lear has lost his sanity, he has enlarged his vision. As his wits begin to leave him, he begins to see the truth about himself; when they are wholly gone he begins to have spasmodic flashes of insight in which, during momentary lulls in the storm of vengeful personal resentment, he sees the inner truth about the world. 'Thou wouldst make a good fool' [I. v. 38], said the Fool to his master at the beginning of his misfortunes, and he spoke as a prophet. In his amazing encounter with the *blind* Gloucester, the *mad* Lear has something of the wit, the penetration, the quick repartee of the court-jester. From the realistic point of view it is no doubt a dramatic flaw that Shakespeare does not account more clearly for the fate of the real man in motley; but his disappearance was a poetic necessity, for the King having lost everything, including his wits, has now himself become the Fool. He has touched bottom, he is an outcast from

society, he has no longer any private axe to grind, so he now sees and speaks the truth.

And what is the truth? What does the mad Lear see in his flashes of lucidity? Does he see that Goneril was more sensible than Cordelia? . . . Certainly his vision is a grim one. He sees not one particular event but the whole of human life as a vast sottie. . . . (pp. 263-64)

The statement that Shakespeare tends to give more intellectual ability to the evil than to the good needs modification. In this play, at least, the loving characters when they are perfectly disinterested or when they have lost everything see equally clearly and more profoundly than do the cold-hearted. But the good and evil react very differently to the same facts seen with equal clearness, and it must not be forgotten that the blind Gloucester and mad Lear have come to know that to see truly 'how the world goes' is to 'see it feelingly'. And when the world is seen feelingly, what then? Why then we must be patient. That is all.

'Patience', like 'wisdom', 'folly', 'knavery', 'nature', is one of the key words of this tragedy. As soon as Lear begins to realize the nature of his misfortune, he begins to make pathetic attempts to acquire it, and when his mental overthrow is complete he recommends it as the appropriate response to the misery of life. . . . Patience, here, seems to imply an unflinching, clear-sighted recognition of the fact of pain, and the complete abandonment of any claim to justice or gratitude either from Gods or men; it is the power to choose love when love is synonymous with suffering, and to abide by the choice knowing there will be no Divine Salvation from its consequences.

And here, I think, is the solution of the problem set by the fool; the problem of apparent moral relativity, 'Wisdom and goodness to the vile seem vile, filths savour but themselves' [IV. ii. 38-9], so that Albany and Goneril have not even sufficient common ground to make a real argument possible. Nevertheless, Shakespeare does not allow us to remain neutral spectators of their debate, he insists that although Goneril's case is as complete and consistent as that of Albany it is *not* equally valid, *not* equally true. In the first place Shakespeare's poetry persuades and compels us to accept the values of the friends rather than of the enemies of Lear. Secondly, Shakespeare makes the fullest possible use of the accepted convention that it is the Fool who speaks the truth, which he knows not by ratiocination but by inspired intuition. The mere appearance of the familiar figure in cap and bells would at once indicate to the audience where the 'punctum indifferens', the impartial critic, the mouthpiece of real sanity, was to be found.

Now the Fool sees that when the match between the good and the evil is played by the intellect alone it must end in a stalemate, but when the heart joins in the game then the decision is immediate and final. 'I will tarry, the Fool will stay—And let the wise man fly' [II. iv. 82-3]. That is the unambiguous wisdom of the madman who sees the truth. That is decisive. It is decisive because, so far from being an abnormal freakish judgement, it is the instinctive judgment of normal humanity raised to heroic stature; and therefore no amount of intellectual argument can prevent normal human beings from receiving and accepting it, just as, when all the psychologists and philosophers have said their say, normal human beings continue to receive and accept the external world as given to them through sense perception. (pp. 266-67)

It would seem, then, that there is nothing contemptible in a motley coat. The Fool is justified, but we have not yet a complete answer to his original query: 'What is folly?' Which is the wise man, which is the fool? To be foolish is to mistake the nature of things, or to mistake the proper method of attaining to our desires, or to do both at once. Even Edmund and Edgar, even Goneril and Albany, could agree to that proposition. But have the perfectly disinterested made either of these mistakes and have not the self-interested made them both? The evil desire pleasure and power, and they lose both, for the evil are mutually destructive. The good desire to sympathize and to save, and their desires are partially fulfilled, although as a result they have to die. Nor have the good mistaken the nature or 'mystery of things' which, after all, unlike Edmund, they have never professed either to dismiss or to understand. It is, indeed, as we have seen, the good who are normal. Lear, in his folly, is not reduced, as he fears, to the level of the beasts, but to essential naked humanity, 'unaccommodated man', 'the thing itself'. (pp. 267-68)

That Shakespeare's ethics were the ethics of the New Testament, that in this play his mightiest poetry is dedicated to the reiteration of the wilder paradoxes of the Gospels and of St Paul, that seems to me quite certain. But it is no less certain that the metaphysical comfort of the Scriptures is deliberately omitted, though not therefore necessarily denied. The perfectly disinterested choose loving-kindness because they know it to be intrinsically desirable and worth the cost, not because they hope that the full price will not be exacted. It is Kent's readiness to be unendingly patient which makes him other than a shrewder and more far-calculating Edmund. If the thunder had ceased at Lear's bidding, then Lear would not have become a sage-fool. What the thunder says remains enigmatic, but it is this Divine ambiguity which gives such force to the testimony of the human heart. Had the speech of the gods been clearer, the apparently simple utterances of the Fool would have been less profound. . . . (pp. 268-69)

And so we reach the final reversal of values. 'Ay every inch a king' [IV. vi. 107], says Lear in his madness, and we do not wholly disagree with him. The medieval clergy inaugurated the Saturnalia by parodying the Magnificat: Shakespeare reverses the process. Lear's tragedy is the investing of the King with motley: it is also the crowning and apotheosis of the Fool. (p. 269)

Enid Welsford, "The Court-Fool in Elizabethan Drama," in her The Fool: His Social and Literary History, *1935. Reprint by Farrar & Rinehart Incorporated, 1936, pp. 243-70.*

JOHN MIDDLETON MURRY (essay date 1936)

[A twentieth-century English editor and critic, Murry has been called the most "level-headed" of Shakespeare's major biographical critics. Unlike such other biographical scholars as Frank Harris and Edward Dowden, Murry refused to attribute to Shakespeare a definite personality or creative neurosis which determined all his work, but regarded the poet as a man of powerful insights rather than of character, an individual possessing Keats's negative capability—a man "capable of being in uncertainties, mysteries, doubts, without any irritable reaching after fact and reason." What Murry sees as Shakespeare's greatest gift was his ability to uncover the true spirit of Elizabethan England, to fuse "not merely the poet and dramatist in himself," but to establish "a unique creative relation between himself, his dramatic material, his audience, and his actors." In the following excerpt, Murry presents a biographical interpretation of King Lear *based on both his initial and his retrospective reactions to the play. His "immediate impression" leads him to argue that Shakespeare*

must have been "possessed" with the idea of humanity's self-destructive, negative tendencies during the writing of King Lear. *He claims that this possession interfered with Shakespeare's usual spontaneous imagination and imparted to the play a sense of "hesitation, uncertainty, and a constant interruption of the 'predominant passion'," and for this reason Murry ranks it below the other major tragedies. On reconsideration, however, Murry alters his initial response and states that* Lear *is better understood as a work in which Shakespeare strove to represent obsession, rather than as a play reflecting the dramatist's own struggles. Still, he regards it as a drama of less stature than* Hamlet *or* Macbeth, *because in order to present his material, Shakespeare was forced to take an external approach, to control his material from a safe distance; thus, as Murry states, the "creative was not creating itself," and Shakespeare's imagination was something less than that which produced his other great tragedies, where he was able to identify with his protagonists completely. It is also for this reason, according to Murry, that* King Lear *seems so incoherent, as if Shakespeare was "out of his depth" in writing the play. Nearly twenty years later, Murry was to recant his position, stating that it was "preposterous" to suggest that Shakespeare was out of his depth, "when the evidence stares me in the face that I was out of mine." For a more traditional biographical interpretation of* King Lear, *see the excerpt by George Brandes (1895-96).]*

King Lear is to me always something of a problem, a crux. With the tragedies which preceded it, *Hamlet, Othello, Macbeth,* I feel, rightly or wrongly, that I can penetrate to their imaginative centre; and I feel this with the tragedies which succeeded it, *Coriolanus* and *Antony.* But with *King Lear* it is different. My immediate impression of the play is always to some extent in conflict with my considered retrospection; and this is anomalous in my experience of Shakespeare's greater plays. Something of the same effect is produced upon me by *Troilus and Cressida,* and *Timon of Athens;* but they are not of the same power and magnitude as *King Lear.* If they, too, are finally problematical, I can dismiss them from my consciousness. King Lear is insistent. (p. 337)

I am something of a heretic in regard to *King Lear.* It seems to me definitely inferior to the other three 'great' tragedies of Shakespeare. Not that it is not terribly moving at its climax; nor should I care to deny that its positive theme is more tremendous than that of the others. That positive theme, as I understand it, is no less than the death of the Self and the birth of Divine Love. That comes to pass in Lear, through absolute isolation, through his becoming 'the thing itself', through 'madness'.

But in the handling of the theme, I feel that Shakespeare was, if not perfunctory, uncertain. I could almost believe that Shakespeare was on the verge of madness himself when he wrote *King Lear,* and perhaps—if I attached much importance to these speculations—I should put *King Lear* and *Timon* and *Troilus* together as the evidence of a period of uncontrollable despair, lit by gleams of illumination. I mean a period different, in essential nature, from what is generally called 'the tragic period'. *Hamlet, Othello* and *Macbeth* are tragedies; but they are evidence of entire imaginative mastery in their author. That which is creative is creating itself undisturbed in them. But in *King Lear,* I find disturbance, hesitation, uncertainty, and a constant interruption of the 'predominant passion'. The major and the minor intensities are continually flagging. The imagination of the theme becomes perfunctory or strained, the imagination of the verse spasmodic. There is weariness, and a flagging of the invention.

It is one of the things which has become, by convention, impossible to say; but *King Lear* makes upon me the impression

Act V. Scene iii. The Death of Cordelia; inset, Act III. Scene iv. Lear on the Heath. By Ch. Geofroy. The Department of Rare Books and Special Collections, The University of Michigan Library.

of the work of a Shakespeare who is out of his depth. He does not really know what he wants to say: perhaps he does not know whether he wants to say anything. One is conscious of the strange sexual undercurrent which disturbs the depths of his 'uncontrolled' dramas—a terrible primitive revulsion against sex, or sexuality, which may have been natural to the imaginative man in the days when the ravages of venereal disease were a new thing in Western Europe. And by means of two crucial episodes in *King Lear,* the theme of venery is entwined with the theme of filial ingratitude. In Edmund's relation to Gloucester, the two themes are united; and Edgar insists upon their union.

>   EDG. The gods are just, and of our pleasant vices
>   Make instruments to plague us:
>   The dark and vicious place where thee he got
>   Cost him his eyes. . . .

>   [V. iii. 171-74]

It was not that which cost Lear his reason, or Cordelia her life. But Shakespeare seems to have felt what he puts in the mouth of Albany:

>   It will come:
>   Humanity must perforce prey upon itself

>   Like monsters of the deep.

>   [IV. ii. 48-50]

It is some vast upsurge of the animal, destroying humanity, of which Shakespeare is apprehensive: a non-human welter of bestiality. And the connection of the two themes is made once more apparent in the naked lust of Regan and Goneril for Edmund.

It is tremendous, as it is horrible; and it seems that a man who peered into this pit for long must needs lose his reason. He would be (one conjectures) in a condition when every sight of 'a French crown' or a decayed nose—matters on which, let it be well remembered, Shakespeare had jested again and again—was a glimpse into a sickening abyss, where animal humanity was eating itself away. And this element is so strong, so all-pervasive in *King Lear* that it could credibly be asked whether this was not indeed the really dominant negative theme in Shakespeare's unconsciousness, taking precedence in sensational immediacy over the more conscious negative theme of filial ingratitude.

What is fairly plain to me is that this vision of humanity self-destroyed by its own animality was one that Shakespeare's imagination did not dominate into a drama, as he was wont to do. It may be said that *King Lear* is the drama into which he dominated it. In which case, I reply that there is a difference in kind between *King Lear* and the tragedies with which it is generally ranked, and to which it is forcibly assimilated. That this difference in kind was due to some essential intractability in the material itself, I can readily allow. But to speak of imaginative mastery in *King Lear* in the same sense in which it can be applied to *Hamlet*, or *Othello* or *Macbeth* or *Anthony and Cleopatra,* or even *Coriolanus,* is to me impossible.

Here, I feel, was a vision which Shakespeare did not master; and by that I mean that the Imagination in him did not master it. It may have been a vision which took possession of him, in a sense essentially the same as that in which the Gospel and Christian tradition speak of a man being possessed by the devil. 'An ounce of civet, good apothecary, to sweeten my imagination!' [IV. vi. 130-31] is, to my ear, the voice of the man through whom *King Lear* was uttered. And there is a vital difference between such possession and the spontaneous self-abeyance which is the attitude of Imagination. A man imagines . . . with his whole being. A man possessed, as Shakespeare may have been possessed, during the writing of *King Lear,* by the vision that is continually breaking forth in it, cannot imagine with his whole being. It is his wholeness of being which is incessantly being destroyed.

To use such terms as these, *King Lear* impresses me as a constant struggle of Imagination against Possession—a struggle in which, in the main, the Imagination is defeated. And Possession does not make for poetry. The 'mad' scenes of *King Lear* have been over-estimated in this regard. In texture and expressiveness they are, on the whole, inferior to what Shakespeare had elsewhere achieved. To my sense, the lapse of creative vigour in them is palpable; and I am inclined to suspect that some such impression is the solid basis of the traditional romantic theory that the difficulty which is always found in making the mad scenes convincing on the stage is due to their very magnificence. The conception is too 'titanic', the poetry too 'sublime'.

I do not feel that. On the contrary, I believe that many of the scenes are evidently the work not so much of a tired, as of a divided man—and a man divided in the sense I have tried to indicate: intermittently possessed by a vision that is inimical to the spontaneity of Imagination. Probably this enduring impression of mine could be expressed in terms more congruous with critical tradition by saying that Shakespeare's conception was so tremendous that his art broke under the strain. But, in the first place, that is not how I feel it; and, in the second—even if such a notion were intrinsically credible to me, which it is not—it would make it impossible to explain how *King Lear* came to be followed by *Coriolanus* and *Antony and Cleopatra*. I can conceive, without difficulty, that these plays followed a period of obsession and possession by a vision of life which Shakespeare himself felt and knew could not be final; but I cannot conceive that, if Shakespeare had felt that this vision, while it lasted, was ultimate, the sequel would have been *Coriolanus* and *Antony and Cleopatra*.

The distinction may be hard to establish objectively, but it is very real to me. It is indeed the difference between the tragic and the diseased vision of life; or again, it is the difference between a despair which engulfs the whole man, and a despair which some part of the man refuses to acknowledge. It seems to me that much of *King Lear* derives from an exaggeration, or exploitation of partial despair. It is a kind of enforced utterance, in a period when—from the ideal point of view—silence was more wholesome and more natural.

A poet of genius creates not how he should, but how he can. I am not saying that it would have been better if Shakespeare had not written *King Lear;* and I wish to safeguard myself in advance against a misinterpretation so preposterous. I am merely demurring to the almost inveterate habit of Shakespeare criticism with regard to the play, which is to represent it as the sublime and transcendent culmination of a 'tragic period'. It is not that, to my mind, at all. It does not belong to the same order as *Hamlet, Othello* and *Macbeth*; or as *Coriolanus* and *Antony and Cleopatra*. It is, in that sequence, an anomaly. Compared to them, it is lacking in imaginative control, it is lacking in poetic 'intensity'. It belongs rather to a group of plays—to which *Timon* and *Troilus* belong—which are the work of a man struggling with an obsession. Amongst these plays it is, indubitably, supreme; but it is with them that it belongs.

That is the substance of the immediate impression; it is mixed up with impressions that are not immediate. In attempting to convey the impression, it attempts to account for it. But that is inevitable in criticism. It is the necessary language *of* criticism. Now for the conflicting retrospection.

It may be that Shakespeare wrote *King Lear* much more in the spirit of a 'professional' than I can easily imagine. That he did much careful construction in making the plot is certain. The outline of the story of Gloucester and Edmund comes from the *Arcadia,* and Shakespeare wove it, very cunningly, into the bare 'nursery-tale' of Lear and his daughters: obviously because the 'nursery-tale' had not substance enough to make a drama. Further, both Lear's madness and the completely fatal ending to the play are of Shakespeare's own invention. In the 'nursery-tale', Lear and Cordelia lived happy ever after. There is no doubt that Shakespeare was very much in conscious technical control of the play, at any rate during its first conception.

So much is firm ground. There is nothing perfunctory in his building of the plot: quite the reverse. The question is: May not all that I quarrel with in *King Lear*—perfunctoriness in the poetry, obsession in the psychology—be simply the outcome of Shakespeare's effort to work out his conception? To take the second—the obsession in the psychology, is it not Shake-speare's striving to *represent* obsession which my feeling misrepresents as obsession in Shakespeare himself? Was he not merely trying to answer to himself his own question: What would be the thoughts of a mad king—one 'every inch a king'—driven mad by such means as Lear?

And again, still more to the point, would not such an approach to *King Lear* supply a better explanation of what I find unsatisfying in the immediate impression of the play? Is not *King Lear* pre-eminently an artefact?

If I admit this, of course I must also admit that the plays of which the immediate impression satisfies me may also be artefacts, in the same sense. The difference between them and *King Lear* (assuming that my obstinate difference of impression does correspond to a difference in the object) will be a difference in Shakespeare's power of self-identification with his characters. The nature of the fable in *King Lear* is such that such a difference might be expected. To identify oneself completely with a character in the process of going mad is perhaps inherently impossible. . . . Precisely here, it may be, is set a limit to the self-identifying power of the Imagination. And, if that be so, one's awareness of the artefact must necessarily be more acute than in cases where the passion, however extreme, is one into which the poetic genius can project itself.

Lear's madness is exhibited as a process. He is represented as aware of the menace of impending madness. At Regan's rejection of him . . . , when the savagery of his two daughters is completely revealed to him, he cries: 'O fool, I shall go mad!' [II. iv. 286]. And a little after, on the heath: 'My wits begin to turn' [III. ii. 67]. . . . But, immediately after, when Edgar emerges from the hovel as a Tom o' Bedlam, Lear is mad. Up to that point there has been a definite progress, not merely in suffering, but towards wisdom and charity: there has been extremity of passion, but no hallucination. Lear's thoughts are comprehensible enough. . . . He knows exactly his own condition, and how precarious is his own lucidity. To Kent's appeal to him to enter the hovel, he replies: 'Wilt break my heart?' [III. iv. 4] and does not leave it there. He explains his meaning:

> This tempest will not give me leave to ponder
> On things would hurt me more.
>
> [III. iv. 24-5]

And at the last he comes to his conclusion and his change of heart:

> Poor naked wretches, wheresoe'er you are,
> That bide the pelting of this pitiless storm,
> How shall your houseless heads and unfed sides,
> Your loop'd and window'd raggedness, defend you
> From seasons such as these? O, I have ta'en
> Too little care of this!
>
> [III. iv. 28-33]

It is to the same conclusion, the same change of heart, that Gloucester is driven by his suffering. (pp. 337-46)

By that reduplication, the nature of the spiritual progress is emphasized. It is unmistakable, nor has it been mistaken. From one point of view it might be said that it is now unnecessary to make Lear mad: he has learned his lesson. But that is the point of view of morality and religion, not of art. Shakespeare is concerned with a change beyond this change. Lear's final innocence is not that of a man who has experienced a spiritual revolution through suffering, but that of one who has suffered too much as well. That his final innocence is terrible and wonderful when it comes is beyond dispute. But it is no more than a flash; and there are flashes everywhere in Lear's process: flashes in the period of his total madness.

But Shakespeare's imagination is not wont to be a thing of flashes. There is in general something splendidly sustained about it. And it is irrelevant to say that madness *is* a thing of flashes. For we are concerned not with madness itself, but with the poetic representation of it. That must be steady and sustained, whatever the condition in fact may be. True, I cannot imagine what a poetic representation of madness would be; but I am pretty certain that madness is not poetically represented in Lear in at all the same sense as jealousy is poetically represented in Othello, or hesitation in Hamlet, or guilt in Macbeth.

To put it bluntly, Lear's 'madness'—including in it his desperate sanity as well—is splendidly worked out; but it is worked out. It may, for ought I know, mark the limit of what is possible in this direction. But that would merely show that there is a great difference between the limit of what is possible in a certain direction, and what Shakespeare achieved in certain other directions. I refuse to be overawed by epithets. *King Lear* may be 'sublime' and 'titanic'; and, if those adjectives are used to imply that there is a difference in kind between *King Lear* and the other tragedies, I am willing to submit to them. But the adjective I should choose to convey and define that impression would be less ambiguous; it would suggest that Shakespeare, in being 'titanic', was being unnatural.

To use my own terms, I find *King Lear* lacking in poetic spontaneity. I suspect that this is in the main due to the simple fact that he was attempting the impossible: or rather that he was working against his natural bent, *invita Minerva.* It was not in his natural method to compose a drama as he composed *King Lear.* The creative was not creating itself. He was spurring his imagination, which in consequence was something less than imagination.

But, if this in turn was due to the inherent quality of his theme, which forbade the kind of imaginative identification with his characters which was natural to Shakespeare, I suppose we cannot forbear to speculate upon the reason why he chose the theme. The answer to that question may be quite commonplace: as, for example, that he wanted to do something new. Perhaps the necessity of novelty, of striking out in a new direction, of presenting the public with a new sensation, pressed harder upon Shakespeare than we willingly conceive. Hitherto, his novelties had been of a kind which enabled his imagination to function freely; but *King Lear* obstinately remained in the condition of a *tour de force*. That he took great pains with it in the beginning, the story of its construction is evidence; perhaps he took great pains with it throughout. But great pains is not enough.

That is only to push the question farther back. Why did he choose a novelty of a kind to which his attitude was bound to be external? And here one might conjecture some interruption of his power of instinctive and intuitive proceeding. It may be that there was, after all, some correspondence between the obsession that is given in the immediate impression of *King Lear,* and the condition of mind of Shakespeare himself. I have often felt that *King Lear* is the successful achievement of that towards which *Timon of Athens* is an unsuccessful attempt. It is not part of my argument that *King Lear* is not successful, *in its kind;* it is its kind, which seems to me lacking in the supreme Shakespearian qualities of spontaneity and naturalness. And it may be that we should see in *King Lear* the nearest

that Shakespeare got to a complete expression of the attitude of mind which was less completely expressed in *Timon* and *Troilus;* and that we should regard it, primarily, as a tremendous effort towards control.

In some such conclusion as this, I believe, my conflict of impressions is reconciled. In *King Lear* there is an effort towards control in the elaborate process of construction, and the careful re-duplication of the theme; there is effort towards control in the careful working-out of Lear's progress towards madness. The very externality of Shakespeare's approach, the obstinate sense of *tour de force* which the conduct of the drama and the texture of the language leaves in me, are, on this theory, only additional evidence of some basic incoherence in Shakespeare's own mood and attitude. So we seem to return, almost, to the traditional conception of *King Lear.* But there is a difference. To put it crudely, *King Lear,* on this theory of mine, is to be understood somewhat as Shakespeare's deliberate prophylactic against his own incoherence.

That was not Shakespeare's method. Therefore *King Lear* is obstinately anomalous in the sequence of his tragedies. It is pre-eminently an artefact; and its significance lies in the fact that it is an artefact. If this be so, there is nothing at all surprising in the fact that his next play was *Coriolanus,* which is so conspicuously no resolution at all of the kind of tragic conflict which is traditionally discovered in *King Lear.* To *King Lear,* taken at its conventional face value, as a culmination of the so-called 'tragic period', *Coriolanus* is a highly anomalous successor. But to *King Lear* as artefact and prophylactic, *Coriolanus* is a natural sequence—a magnificent outflow of disinterested imagination, expressed through sustained poetry, of a theme so essentially reposeful (for Shakespeare) that it is generally regarded as dull and uninteresting. That is, of course, nonsense. *Coriolanus* is merely non-melodramatic. As Imagination, dramatic and poetical, it is magnificent. Shakespeare's self-identification with his hero is strangely complete, and completely satisfying. Intrinsically, *Coriolanus* is to me a much finer Shakespearian drama than *King Lear,* and as the prelude to *Antony and Cleopatra* of the highest significance for an understanding of Shakespeare's development. It marks the return from effort to spontaneity, from artefact to creation, from inhumanity to humanity. That is a paradoxical way of regarding the succession of *Coriolanus* to *King Lear.* By the conventional reckoning, *King Lear* is the warm and human, *Coriolanus* the cold and inhuman drama. I think and believe and maintain almost the opposite. (pp. 347-51)

> *John Middleton Murry, "The Paradox of 'King Lear'," in his* Shakespeare, *Jonathan Cape, 1936, pp. 337-51.*

JOHN W. DRAPER   (essay date 1937)

[*An American critic, editor, and poet, Draper is best known for his studies into the background of Shakespeare's plays, particularly with respect to Elizabethan character-types. These include* The Hamlet of Shakespeare's Audience *(1938),* The Humors and Shakespeare's Characters *(1945), and* The "Twelfth Night" of Shakespeare's Audience *(1950). All of these studies stress the influence of contemporary life and thought on Shakespeare's drama and as such attempt to provide new interpretations unavailable to the strictly aesthetic or psychological critic. Draper's efforts reflect the popularity during the mid-twentieth century of historical interpretations of Shakespeare's plays, an approach also apparent in the works of E.E. Stoll and E.M.W. Tillyard. In the excerpt below, Draper argues that the central theme of* King Lear, *that which Shakespeare truly wanted to impress upon his audi-*

ence, is not filial ingratitude or the indifference of the gods, but the danger of renouncing the "divine right of kings" and dividing a kingdom against the will of God. Ultimately, Draper posits a political motive behind Shakespeare's writing of King Lear, *suggesting that it was meant to be both a propaganda piece in support of the union between Scotland and England being debated at that time, and a courtly compliment to James I in the character of Albany. Other critics who have attempted a similar historical interpretation of* King Lear *with regard to contemporary Elizabethan thought and manners include Theodore Spencer (1942), George R. Kernodle (1945), and Edwin Muir (1946).]*

The question of a divided, as opposed to a united, Britain is fundamental in [*King Lear*]. According to Holinshed, and obviously in Shakespeare, Lear is King of all Britain: the play refers to "a British man," the "British powers" as opposed to France, and the quarto of 1608 to the "British party." The dividing of Lear's realm is the first action depicted on the stage, and has every appearance of theatrical significance. . . . The entire plot depends on this division of the kingdom: the quarrels of Goneril and Regan, the disasterous French invasion, the madness and death of Lear, and the distraction of the whole commonwealth that cannot but ensue. Chaos from conflict of authority is the very essence of the play. . . . The situation of Albany toward the end of the play illustrates the *impasse* to which events have come: he is against his wife because of her cruelties to Lear and Gloucester; but he is perforce also against Cordelia because she has brought a foreign army upon British Soil. The skein is so entangled that death is the one way left.

Albany, indeed, has a unique significance in the drama. According to Shakespeare, Lear divided his kingdom into three, and then, after Cordelia's answer, he re-divided her share between the other two, thus leaving two parts in his final division of the realm. Since the island of Great Britain is long and rather narrow north and south, the lines of demarcation must have cut across it east and west, separating it, in the first division, into a southern, a middle, and a northern section. Cordelia's must have been the middle part; for it is later divided between the other two. Thus, in the final division, the two realms of Goneril and of Regan, must roughly have corresponded to England and to Scotland. The titles of the respective husbands bear this out, Cornwall and Albany. Cornwall in ancient times was more extensive than the modern shire; and Lear seems appropriately to have given to this Duke the southern half of his dominions; for Cornwall's capital is the city of Gloucester in the south-central section of the island. Albany then, apparently received the northern half of Britain; and his title at the opening of the play suggests that he was already duke of ancient "Albany," the region north of the Firths of Clyde and Forth, including all the Scottish Highlands. . . . [When] Shakespeare wrote *King Lear*, there was a Duke of Albany, and that Duke was James I. Heraldry in the seventeenth century was much too practical and widely known a subject for Shakespeare's audience—at least the courtly part of it—not to guess at this relationship, just as they must have known that Banquo in *Macbeth* was James's reputed ancestor. Is it this glance at Shakespeare's royal patron that made the playwright change the Albany of Holinshed from a character consistently good and virtuous? Is this why, at the conclusion of the play, the distracted kingdom seems to be happily re-united under his sovereign power? At all events, a drama that contrasted England and Scotland separate and miserable over against a united Britain happy and prosperous, must have had a timely meaning; and a Duke of Albany, who, after many trials, is apparently left at the end, benign and powerful, in sole possession, to "Rule in this realm and the gored state sustain" [V. iii. 321]—

this Duke of Albany was surely not a figure displeasing to the eyes of the contemporary holder of that name and title.

Shakespeare's treatment of his sources suggests that he intended his play to illustrate the evils of disunion. . . . Neither Holinshed, nor *Leir*, nor Shakespeare's other possible sources, the *Mirour for Magistrates* and the *Faerie Queene*, portray the misery of the nobles and the people that result from this division, or the scandalous rivalry of Goneril and Regan for the love of Edmund. Almost all this matter of the last two acts is Shakespeare's own addition; and its plots and counterplots are the dramatic reflection of a realm torn between two equal queens—so equal that Edmund vacillates betweem them. In Holinshed, the two dukes finally seize all of Lear's kingdom by committing the sin of rebellion—the theme that Shakespeare develops in *Macbeth*—but, in *King Lear*, he omits this material as irrelevant to the purpose of the tragedy. The old play, *Leir*, had a happy ending, with Cordelia and the King restored as they are in Holinshed; and many actors and critics have felt that poetic justice required such a conclusion for Shakespeare's drama also; but Shakespeare clearly intended no such thing: does not Lear's division of the kingdom, so contrary to the practice and the political theory of the Renaissance, and so foolish and even wicked in the eyes of James I—does not this division of the kingdom, a grievous sin to the believer in the Divine Right of Kings, provide sufficient cause for the old man's tragic end? May one fly in the face of Providence and refuse the station in life that God has thrust upon one?

The efforts of scholars to discover and to state the theme of Shakespeare's *Lear*, have been somewhat inconclusive and chaotic. Moralists have been especially perturbed; for, as Dr. Johnson remarked, "the wicked prosper and the virtuous miscarry" [see excerpt above, 1765]. But is the theme of the play a matter of mere personal morals? The Elizabethans considered public life, the fall of kings and nations, the proper subject for tragedy; and one should look for a theme that is national rather than domestic. Many critics have taken the pathetic story of Cordelia as overwhelmingly preponderant in the play; but she has a speaking part in only three of the twenty-six scenes, and altogether only a little over a hundred lines. If she is the main figure, and the tragedy be mainly hers, this is crassly stupid dramaturgy. . . . Most nineteenth-century critics seem to consider the tragedy all pathos and no ethos—and so tacitly put it in the class of mere melodrama. Hallam remarked that it "diverges more from the model of regular tragedy than *Macbeth* or *Othello*, and even more than *Hamlet*" [see excerpt above, 1837-39]. Snider takes it as the story of ruptured family relationships, and Gervinus thinks it a picture of filial ingratitude [see excerpts above, 1887 and 1849-50]; but what does the play actually *predicate* about family life or about ingratitude? One does not know *why* or by what degrees Goneril and Regan became ungrateful; and the occasion (if not the cause) of the family disruption was Lear's division of his authority. . . . Professor Bradley is a sort of summary of these nineteenth century critics: he finds "structural weakness" in the play arising apparently from the loose relation of the episodes to the conclusion [see excerpt above, 1904]. . . . Most of these views have been stated only incidentally to other matters; and, up to the present, those who have given the theme of *King Lear* any systematic study end either in doubt or in some conclusion that makes of the tragedy no more than melodrama.

The present writer would see the play as one of a series of studies in statecraft that Shakespeare wrote during the early years of the seventeenth century, studies not conducted entirely in the academic calm of theoretical politics but also to some degree in the arena of actual live issues. Perhaps it was composed as direct propaganda to develop a public sentiment in favor of the Union, perhaps only as a courtly compliment to Shakespeare's patron; but, that it contained such propaganda, that it constituted such a compliment, and that any courtier must have taken it as such, the present writer cannot doubt: the issue was all too timely; Shakespeare changed the events and characters of his sources to emphasize the dangers of disunion; and James I himself had urged, in precept and in practice, that British chronicle history be used for an understanding of the science of government. (pp. 180-85)

> John W. Draper, "The Occasion of 'King Lear'," in Studies in Philology, Vol. XXIV, No. 1, January, 1937, pp. 176-85.

R. W. CHAMBERS   (lecture date 1939)

[*Chambers was a twentieth-century English scholar and critic whose primary emphasis of study was in medieval literature and thought and in the medieval influence on later centuries. In the following excerpt from a lecture originally delivered at the University of Glasgow on November 27, 1939, he presents what many critics consider the most comprehensive refutation of those commentators who attacked Shakespeare for his alteration of the traditional Leir story. Chambers maintains that these critics have misrepresented Shakespeare's sources for* King Lear, *particularly in their assumption that all of the earlier versions of the story end on a happy note, when in fact only the old chronicle play* King Leir *concludes thus. Chambers emphasizes this point in order to disprove the argument that Shakespeare deliberately contrived an unhappy ending to reinforce his pessimistic vision in the play, an interpretation put forth most notably by Algernon Charles Swinburne (1880), E. K. Chambers (1906), Stopford A. Brooke (1913), G. Wilson Knight (1930), J. Stampfer (1960), and Jan Kott (1964). Chambers argues that the ruling principle of the play is not the malevolence of the gods inherent in Gloucester's "flies to wanton boys" speech, as critics have suggested, but that human love and divine justice emerge triumphant, as evidenced in Cordelia's death and Lear's response to it. Chambers's essay was extremely influential as one of the first avowedly Christian interpretations of* King Lear, *an approach further developed in the essays by Geoffrey L. Bickersteth (1946), Oscar James Campbell (1948), Irving Ribner (1958), L.C. Knights (1959), Robert H. West (1968), and René E. Fortin (1979).*]

I am trying to argue to-day that much of our difficulty with *King Lear* comes from our having read about Shakespeare's sources, instead of having read Shakespeare's sources. It is fashionable nowadays to deride the study of Shakespeare's sources, and (since they cannot be altogether ignored) to make that study perfunctory. Critics seem sometimes to resent the fact that Shakespeare *had* sources, and speak as if they needed to 'defend him' from some accusation of want of originality. But to speak thus is absurd. It is to ignore the fact that nearly all the great dramas of the world have been written on themes which were not the free invention of the dramatist, but were given to him by earlier tradition or literature. . . . (p. 10)

The habitual statement about the sources of *King Lear* runs something like this: 'Shakespeare revamped an old play on the subject of *King Lear*.' Some authorities add that Shakespeare, not content with examining merely the old play, examined some other sources as well. But they agree that it was in spite of all his sources that Shakespeare gave an unhappy ending to his play. (p. 11)

Now I submit that the story of Lear and Cordelia had existed in its own right for four centuries and a half before either Shakespeare's *King Lear,* or the old play which he is said to have 'revamped', were thought of. It is dangerous thus to neglect the continuity of literature, and to forget the long series of chronicles and poems which had told Cordelia's story. The story deserves to be read for its own sake, not to be read about as 'one of Shakespeare's sources'. The old play, which is assumed to be Shakespeare's source, will then appear in its true, and small, proportions.

The story of King Lear and Cordelia appears first in that wonderful Twelfth Century in which so many things make their first appearance. The Latin *History of the Kings of Britain* by Geoffrey of Monmouth, composed about the beginning of the troubled reign of King Stephen, rapidly became one of the most popular books of England and of Europe. Geoffrey tells the story of Leir's division of his kingdom among his daughters by a love-test; how Cordeilla refuses to flatter her father and is disinherited; how Aganippus, King of the Franks, marries her without a dowry. The elder daughters, Gornorilla and Regau, and their husbands, treat Leir so ill that he flees across the Channel to Cordeilla, who receives him with great honour. With the help of Aganippus and Cordeilla, Leir invades Britain and wins back his kingdom. So far, Geoffrey's story has affinities with a widespread folk-tale, which ends happily. But Geoffrey's story of Cordeilla does not end happily. In the third year after his restoration Leir dies. Cordeilla's husband, Aganippus, dies likewise, and Cordeilla, left a widow, becomes ruler of Britain. But the children of her wicked sisters rise in rebellion, defeat her armies, and imprison her. Overwhelmed with her sorrows, Cordeilla slays herself, and the kingdom of Britain is left to the descendants of the wicked Regau.

It is, indeed, a depressing story. Cordeilla, who has been the comfort of her parent in his old age, is left without father, husband or child, to perish in despair by her own hand. Life, I admit, sometimes *is* rather like that. It *does* happen that a daughter rejects prospects of worldly happiness in order to comfort her father's old age, and is then left destitute, dependent on the grudging charity of her more selfish and more prosperous kinsfolk. There have been many mute, inglorious Cordeillas.

Such a tale is always sad, sometimes sordid; but seldom, indeed, does it reach the horror of Cordeilla's tragic self-murder. Cordeilla's suicide in prison contradicts painfully the promise to the children who honour their father and their mother, that their days may be long in the land. Therefore it is small wonder that those who retold the story between Geoffrey in the Twelfth Century and Shakespeare in the Seventeenth have in certain cases sought to humanize and soften it. (pp. 11-13)

Most of these versions of the Lear-story follow the tale as Geoffrey of Monmouth told it. None of them takes any such liberty with the original as to depict Cordelia as dying in peace and length of days, surrounded by her children and her children's children. Some of them, however, *do* break off the story when Lear has been restored to his kingdom, and tell us nothing of what happened to Cordelia afterwards, whether good or evil. But only one of these truncated versions is of much use to the student of Shakespeare: that is the old play of *King Leir*. . . . (pp. 13-14)

There were then three ways in which the tale of Cordelia was treated by the scores of chroniclers or poets who told her story during more than four centuries: her death is narrated as suicide, as murder, or is simply ignored. Most accounts, including nearly all the serious ones, tell the story as they have received it from Geoffrey, directly or indirectly. Cordelia's self-murder is a tale too firmly rooted in history and saga to be materially changed. But a few (mostly trivial) versions break off the account with Lear's restoration or his death, and tell us no more about Cordelia. Yet what satisfaction can those who know her story derive from that? Suppose that the story of *The Tempest* had been based upon a history known to all educated and to many uneducated Englishmen: a history which told us that Prospero died three years after being restored to his dukedom, and Ferdinand a year or two later; that Miranda, left a widow, was seized by the children of the wicked Antonio and Sebastian till, worn out by long imprisonment, she slew herself in despair. If we knew *that* to be the full story of Miranda, what satisfaction could we feel in the happy ending of *The Tempest?* What but mockery? . . . The story of Cordelia's self-murder can only be effectually contradicted by giving her some other death. And so we have the version in which Cordelia is murdered by her foes. And this version . . . was often told in English literature of the Fourteenth and Fifteenth Centuries: in Higden [*Mirror for Magistrates*], in the *Bruts,* and in 'Caxton's' Chronicle.

But under the influence of supposed historical truth this gentler ending gave way in Tudor times to the old story of Cordelia's suicide. In this form the story was familiar to Elizabethans from a dozen sources. Above all, Cordelia's self-murder was known to readers of Holinshed's *Chronicles,* of the *Mirror for Magistrates,* and of the *Faerie Queene.* And these books, in the words of that great American critic and scholar, Kittredge, were familiar to every Elizabethan who read anything. It is clear that Shakespeare had read all three, and they have left their mark upon his play. (pp. 17-19)

Shakespeare probably felt it permissible to treat his authorities more freely than he would have done in a more authentic period of history. But, broadly, he follows the practice, usual in his history plays, of preserving the essential facts of his original, but dealing as he chooses with chronology. In Act V of his *King Lear* Shakespeare telescopes, as it were, two battles into one. The battle begins as the battle fought by Cordelia to restore her father to the throne: it ends as the battle in which Cordelia is captured by her foes. By thus combining the two battles, Shakespeare is able to give to Cordelia one who will comfort her distress and mourn her death. Her comforter is the father whom she herself has saved from despair.

Thus Shakespeare's manipulation of the plot humanizes it, by removing the cruel feature which Geoffrey's story shares with the Greek tale of Antigone as Sophocles tells it, in which the faithful girl, after all her pious care for her kinsfolk, is herself left lonely in her own despair. Cordelia is slain. *But not by herself;* there Shakespeare *does* depart from historic fact, as he had received it. For it is extremely unlikely that Shakespeare could have known any of the Fifteenth Century versions in which Cordelia is saved from suicide by being murdered. Nor would many of his audience have known them, except perhaps stray antiquarian students. There was, in Shakespeare's day, no living tradition of Cordelia's death, save by her own hand. She was the most illustrious, most innocent, and most pitiful suicide in British or English story.

I can imagine that some of Shakespeare's audience, as they watched the play drawing to its end, may have asked themselves: How will the poet finish this? Will he break off Cordelia's story in the middle, and refuse to follow her to the end?

Or will be make this brave gentle girl slay herself in despair? (pp. 21-2)

Shakespeare does neither of these unbearable things. For suicide would be unbearable in the case of Shakespeare's Cordelia. (p. 22)

When Cordelia is brought on the stage a prisoner, Shakespeare's audience, as I have said, may have feared that the story would end (as in the versions they knew) by her despair and suicide. Shakespeare makes it clear at once that he is not conceiving the story so. Cordelia turns to Lear:

> For thee, oppressed king, am I cast down;
> Myself could else outfrown false Fortune's frown.
>   [V. iii. 5-6]

This, Professor Raleigh complains, is a rhyming tag, which might have been addressed by a chorus to the audience:

> For the oppressed king is she cast down;
> Herself could else outfrown false Fortune's frown.

To Raleigh it seemed hardly in character that Cordelia, who cannot heave her heart into her mouth even to tell of her love to her father, should tell of her courage to all and sundry in this way. Raleigh felt that Shakespeare is 'making one of his most cherished characters do the menial explanatory work of a chorus.' But (even if this be so) a study of the sources shows us (what Raleigh did not see) that there is a reason for this 'menial, explanatory work'. The Attic dramatists sometimes did the same. They, too, retold stories familiar to their audience in other forms: and they sometimes put words into the mouth of a speaker, expressly to show that the poet's conception is different from that of some predecessor.

Then Shakespeare makes his point still clearer. The dying Edmund confesses that his writ 'is on the life of Lear and on Cordelia'. The Captain, he continues, has commission from Goneril and him

> To hang Cordelia in the prison and
> To lay the blame upon her own despair
> That she fordid herself.
>   [V. iii. 254-56]

But, since Lear is also to be slain, *his* death has also to be accounted for. Logically the words should surely therefore be '*their* own despair, that *they* fordid themselves'. Why only Cordelia's despair? Because Shakespeare's mind is going back to the current story in which (after Lear has died a natural death) a lonely Cordelia slays herself. That, he says, is not true of the Cordelia of my play: it is the kind of libel an Edmund or a Goneril might have invented. So intent is he on contradicting this current story that he allows Lear (for the moment) to slip out of the memory of his audience.

If anyone still doubts that Shakespeare remodels the story to save Cordelia from despair, let him consider this fact. Shakespeare has provided in *King Lear* a sub-plot which simply repeats the theme of the main story. And, as critic after critic has pointed out, this is done that we may feel that we are witnessing something universal—a conflict not so much of particular persons as of the powers of good and evil in the world. Shakespeare, accordingly, looked round for some second story which should support his main theme, and his choice is significant. He chose, from Sidney's *Arcadia,* the story of the Blind Paphlagonian King who was saved from despair by his son. And here again we see the use of reading Shakespeare's sources. We are told by Sir Edmund Chambers that Shakespeare's design was to make his play bear the burden of the final victory of evil [see excerpt above, 1906]. Sir Edmund also tells us that Shakespeare added this sub-plot so that the theme of his play should be of universal significance. Yet the theme of the sub-plot which Shakespeare deliberately chose from the *Arcadia* is the final victory of good.

My argument, then, is that Shakespeare, by taking his usual liberties with time, has remodelled the story of Cordelia: that he makes it end, not in the final victory of evil, as it does in the chronicles, but in the final victory of good: that he saves Cordelia from despair, and gives her to console her, in her captivity, the father whom she has herself consoled.

Such, I admit, is not the view usually held about Shakespeare's treatment of his sources in *King Lear*. The key, I think, will be found in this sub-plot which Shakespeare has added from the *Arcadia*. And that is naturally so, because the sub-plot, we all agree, was added to drive home the meaning of the main plot.

The Blind Paphlagonian King, with his kind and unkind son, is renamed by Shakespeare Gloucester, with his loyal son Edgar and his wicked son Edmund. And it is in the words of Gloucester in his despair that 'many, perhaps most', have found the meaning of the whole of Shakespeare's *King Lear*:

> As flies to wanton boys are we to the gods;
> They kill us for their sport.
>
> [IV. i. 36-7]

Mr. Granville-Barker, to whom we are all of us under such a heavy debt, tells us that it was to the tune of these words that Shakespeare's dramatic mind was working when he wrote *King Lear* [see excerpt above, 1927]. (pp. 23-6)

Now I submit that, in any great drama, however vigorous a sentence may be, we should ask:

Firstly, *Who* speaks it: a wise man or a rash one?

Secondly, *How* does he speak it: in haste, like Hippolytus at first, or deliberately, like Hippolytus later? And

Thirdly, above all, What light does the sequel throw upon it? (p. 27)

Now apply this test to Gloucester's words. What sort of a man is Gloucester? In what circumstances does he speak? Above all, what is the sequel? (p. 28)

The character of Gloucester has been sketched with much skill by Mr. Granville-Barker. He is 'the average sensual man': 'The civilized world is full of Gloucesters': 'An egoist, knowing least of what he should know most, of his own two sons': 'With his pother about "these late eclipses of the sun and moon"', the sort of man who might at any moment be taken in by any sort of tale'. His son Edmund ridicules his superstition. He is a cheap commonplace type, but . . . he is very much alive. It is easy to despise such a man; yet there may be in him possibilities which we did not suspect. But, even so, he is hardly the man from whose mouth we should expect Shakespeare's deepest thoughts on the ways of God to man.

And though Gloucester is foolish, timid, unheroic, unwilling to take sides, nevertheless, when compelled, he defies the tyrants with a resolution which surprises us. Such men often do surprise us. Blinded, he learns that it is his bastard son Edmund, on whom he has relied, who has betrayed him. Then he surprises us still more. He leaps at once to the truth, that the bastard Edmund, who has thus wronged his father, must

have been likewise wronging his brother Edgar, when he accused him to his father.

Yet Gloucester never utters one word of reproach against the 'unkind' son who has betrayed him to blindness, and who would betray him to death. He only blames himself. His whole being goes out in love for his loyal son, for whom he has been pining even whilst seeking to inflict death on him for his supposed attempt at parricide:

> Ah, dear son Edgar,
> The food of thy abused father's wrath!
> Might I but live to see thee in my touch,
> I'ld say I had eyes again.
>
> [IV. i. 21-4]

Edgar, disguised as Poor Tom, is watching Gloucester as he says these words. It is here, just before Edgar links his arm with him to guide his body and his soul, that Gloucester utters those despairing lines about the gods killing us for their sport. Yet the gods *are* giving Gloucester his wish, and, if he can but be saved from despair, he will live to know it. Shakespeare's irony runs deep: too deep, indeed, for some of his critics to perceive.

So much for the circumstances under which Gloucester speaks these words. Let us turn then to the sequel, which is the change that comes over Gloucester through the love which is between him and Edgar. (pp. 29-30)

Gloucester's growth in patience under Edgar's guidance is shown in his prayer, 'You mighty gods' [IV. vi. 34ff]. Edgar tells him that his life is a miracle (as, indeed, the life of every one of us is). Edgar persuades Gloucester that 'the clearest gods' have preserved him: that he must 'bear free and patient thoughts' [IV. vi. 73, 80], till to Gloucester the gods become 'You evergentle gods' [IV. vi. 217]. Then comes the final catastrophe; at the news of Lear's defeat Gloucester would remain on the battlefield to die:

	A man may rot even here.
Edgar.	What, in ill thoughts again? Men must endure
	Their going hence, even as their coming hither;
	Ripeness is all. Come on.
Gloucester.	And that's true too.
	[V. ii. 8-12]

Those are his last words in the play. But we are told what happens when he knows that it has been his son Edgar who

> became his guide
> Led him, begg'd for him, sav'd him from despair.
>
> [V. iii. 191-92]

Gloucester, whom we first met as a commonplace, sensual egoist, dies from a love too great to sustain.

Edgar shows himself becoming gradually 'in this pagan play, a very Christian gentleman'. (The words are those of Mr. Granville-Barker.) And it is Edgar who, by the discovery of the plot against Albany, frustrates the villains. Few characters carry, so obviously as does Edgar, the marks of their author's approval. And Edgar's strength lies in his optimism, and his optimism in the conviction that 'The gods are just' [V. iii. 171]. Edgar never gets cold feet. It is in such men that Shakespeare sees the salvation of the state. And Albany, who begins as a neutral character, comes to share Edgar's belief in the 'justicers above', and to share his task of saving the state. (pp. 31-2)

'The gods are just,' says Edgar. How far can man be a judge of the justice of the gods? On the one hand, we must obviously take our own highest standards of justice as valid, as a sacred revelation. . . . Nevertheless, we must be very careful how we measure the gods by the yardstick of our fallible human justice. Human justice has persistently imprisoned and put to death the noblest men and women, from the Hebrew prophets or Socrates, through the long roll of apostles and martyrs to Joan of Arc or Thomas More or William Tyndall, and so to the tens of thousands who are suffering martyrdom to-day.

Lear, in his madness (or rather his illumination), said of human justice:

> Plate sin with gold,
> And the strong lance of justice hurtless breaks;
> Arm it in rags, a pygmy's straw does pierce it.
>
> [IV. vi. 165-67]

Edgar, a young man, speaks of the justice of the gods: Lear, of fourscore and upward, speaks of the injustice of man. Conscious of his own injustice, Lear comes to think of the sufferings of others, not of his own, and to see that what we call the 'injustice' of the gods is often in fact the injustice of men to each other. (pp. 33-4)

It is a commonplace that in *King Lear* Shakespeare reminds us of Aeschylus. In fact, he reminds us not only of Aeschylus, but also of some of the Old Testament prophets and of the 'Wisdom' books of the Apocrypha. Our modern critics do not remark this Biblical parallel quite so frequently. That is because it is well for the critic to show that he knows his Aeschylus, whilst it is fashionable to pretend that Shakespeare did not know his Bible. Yet, as an intelligent church-going Elizabethan, Shakespeare must have known his Bible better than most of us do to-day.

We are reminded in *King Lear* of Aeschylus, or of the *Apology of Socrates,* or of the Prophets, or the Psalms, or Job, or the 'Wisdom' Books, because of the underlying problem which they all face: How can we reconcile the suffering of man with the justice and mercy of God? (p. 35)

By suffering, wisdom has come to the aged Lear and to Gloucester, to young Edgar too, and to Albany. Kent realizes how suffering opens men's eyes. 'Nothing almost sees miracles but misery' [II. ii. 165-66]. Yet there is a mystery beyond this. The miracle which has been revealed to Kent in his misery is the depth of the love which Cordelia bears to Lear. Why, then, should Cordelia be killed? Why should Socrates be killed? (p. 36)

Socrates, on the day of his death, surprised and shocked his friend Simmias by saying that the right study of philosophy was about nothing but dying and being dead. And surely that is the right study of tragedy. Why then be surprised and shocked at Cordelia's death? It is the nature of tragedy to lead up to the death of hero or heroine. The question is, *how* they die. Shakespeare found in the chronicles a grim story of a noble girl who comforted her father's old age and then, separated from him by death, was left to despair and suicide. Instead of this, he shows us an ancient sage and his great-hearted daughter led to prison together, the father consoling his child by the words which, in one form or another, have consoled all the noble army of martyrs, from the time of Socrates; and which will continue to console them so long as there are martyrs,

which seems likely, by all present indications, to be long enough: The gods are not unmindful; they have received our sacrifice. The gods do indeed give their rewards, but it is 'not as the world giveth'. (pp. 38-9)

Brave men and women may face death without flinching: but to live to see heroic effort tumble to disgraceful ruin whilst foes triumph and deride—is not that the uttermost sacrifice which the gods can demand from proud souls like Lear and his daughter? Yet such sacrifices are demanded; and often. 'We are not the first' [V. iii. 3], says Cordelia. No: nor the last. 'Upon such sacrifices the gods themselves throw incense' [V. iii. 20-1], Lear replies. Cordelia makes no answer: as before, she loves and is silent. (pp. 39-40)

Lear had prayed: 'You heavens, give me that patience, patience I need' [II. iv. 271]. The heavens have indeed given him patience. But his patience is not the mark of an enfeebled mind. Lear's deep words, at the moment of his greatest humiliation, when with Cordelia he is led captive behind Edmund 'in conquest', are no more an expression of weakness than are the words of Kent, at the moment of *his* greatest humiliation, in the stocks: 'Nothing almost sees miracles but misery' [II. ii. 165-66]. Lear is heroic to the end; he will live to avenge his daughter single-handed, as he now lives to console her.

In the old play of *King Leir* the pitiful bourgeois king is shoved back by his benevolent daughter and son-in-law upon a throne which he is ludicrously incapable of occupying. That is what is called 'a happy ending'. Shakespeare's play shows us a mighty old warrior-king suffering intolerable wrong, learning thereby to blame himself because he has allowed others to go hungry and naked, learning to pity the victims of the arrogant 'justice' of the rich . . . : learning to think rather of the sufferings of his poor jester than of his own:

> Poor fool and knave, I have one part in my heart
> That's sorry yet for thee. . . . In, boy; go first.
>
> [III. ii. 72-3]

The old King finds that the love of Cordelia, which he has renounced, has never renounced him.

And such is the power of this love that it matters nothing to Lear, when a sudden change of fortune makes him the prisoner of those who have most wronged him. He is still the old proud warrior-king. He forbids Cordelia to weep in the presence of her foes:

> The goodyears shall devour 'em, flesh and fell,
> Ere they shall make us weep.
>
> [V. iii. 24-5]

But what do the battle and his crown matter? We are moving in the same plane of thought as was that stout soldier Socrates, when he judged the judges who had condemned him, and comforted those who had voted for his acquittal by showing them the meaning of what had happened to him. Lear does not blame the gods because he has again lost his crown, or because the succour which Cordelia has sought to bring to him has brought nothing but disaster on her. He shows her the meaning of what has happened, as Socrates showed his friends that his fate was not the terrible thing they thought—they must grasp this one truth, that the gods are not disregardful:

> Upon such sacrifices, my Cordelia,
> The gods themselves throw incense.
>
> [V. iii. 20-1]

And that . . . is what illustrious critics call 'the final victory of evil', 'a stony black despairing depth of voiceless and inexplicable agony' [see excerpt above by E. K. Chambers, 1906]. (pp. 40-2)

I can imagine a critic replying to all that I have urged: 'Yes, I grant that Shakespeare has saved Cordelia from the horror of despair which the chronicles depicted as her fate: but he has done this only by heaping horror and despair on Lear himself, though the chronicles allowed Lear to die a king, with Cordelia watching over his death-bed, and burying him when dead.'

But Shakespeare gives us as much of this as is consistent with Cordelia being preserved from further danger and distress. It is true that the chronicles represented Lear as restored to his throne and dying 'every inch a king'. Well: Shakespeare also gives us this consolation. That is the explanation of Albany's words, uttered over the dying Lear:

> We will resign,
> During the life of this old Majesty,
> To him our absolute power.
>
> [V. iii. 299-301]

Shakespeare's Lear, then, dies a king. But he could not have continued to live a king. After what he has suffered, and still more after what he has learnt, it would be, as Charles Lamb has said, 'a childish pleasure' to 'get his gilt robes and sceptre again' [see excerpt above, 1812].

Bradley asks that Shakespeare should at least have given Lear 'peace and happiness by Cordelia's fireside' [see excerpt above, 1904]. And it is never safe to differ from Bradley. Nevertheless, I submit that what really matters in the play is neither gilt robes and sceptre, nor yet a peaceful fireside, but the thought that is passing in the soul of Lear under the influence of Cordelia—and likewise in the soul of Gloucester, under the guidance of his pious son. (pp. 42-3)

Lear had challenged the power of Love. He had renounced Cordelia:

> So be my grave my peace, as here I give
> Her father's heart from her. . . .
>   We
> Have no such daughter, nor shall ever see
> That face of hers again.
>
> [I. i. 125-26, 262-64]

In the last scene this is answered by Lear's cry of desolation: 'Thou'lt come no more', followed by the five times repeated 'never' [V. iii. 308-09]. Nothing else could express the length and breadth and depth and height of the victory of Cordelia and of Love. To anyone who doubts this, I would put the question: Would we sacrifice those lines which Lear, dying, utters after he has entered with the dead Cordelia in his arms? Would we barter them for any picture of Lear, peaceful and happy, by Cordelia's fireside? (p. 43)

> *R. W. Chambers, in his* King Lear, *Jackson, Son & Company, 1940, 52 p.*

THEODORE SPENCER (essay date 1942)

[*Spencer, an American literary critic, editor, poet, and educator, is best known for his studies of Elizabethan drama and metaphysical poetry. Concurrently with E.M.W. Tillyard, Spencer elucidated and examined the traditional religious, moral, and social doctrines that he felt informed Elizabethan literature. His most important work,* Shakespeare and the Nature of Man (1942), *explores Shakespeare's dramatic technique and attempts to explain how the playwright resolved the tension between the forces of order and chaos—which Spencer defined as the conflicting attitudes of the Elizabethan world view—in his tragedies. In the following excerpt, taken from the work named above, Spencer regards* King Lear *as Shakespeare's "terrible picture" of the chaos that results from the disruption of the hierarchal order—the correspondences among the individual, the state, and the universe—so fundamental to Elizabethan thought and life. Spencer calls the play itself a "study in relationships," specifically, the relationships of parent and child, state and citizen, and gods and mortals, and he considers among its central themes the inevitability of humanity's descent to "animal" nature once this precarious balance of relationships is upset. Like John W. Draper's study (see excerpt above, 1937), Spencer's is an attempt to determine the influence of contemporary thought on Shakespeare's play. For a similar interpretation of* King Lear, *see the excerpts by George R. Kernodle (1945) and Edwin Muir (1946).*]

Shakespeare uses the three inter-related hierarchies given him by the assumptions of his age to make *King Lear* the largest and the most profound of all his plays. Nowhere else does he so completely fuse the contemporary concepts of the world, the individual and the state into a single unity; correspondences and parallels between them, amalgamations of one concept with another, are everywhere; they embody the vision of life and they form the texture of the style. At the height of his career, with his dramatic craftsmanship developed to a remarkable pitch of virtuosity, daring and assurance, Shakespeare uses the old story of Lear to present his terrible picture of the microcosm and the macrocosm, the picture which shows how, under the good appearance, the evil in man's nature can bring chaos in a kingdom and a soul, and be reflected in the chaos of the external world.

As we think of the technique of this play, and it is with technique that we should begin, two words come at once to mind: re-inforcement and expansion. The sub-plot re-inforces the main plot; it is not, as in all the other plays where a sub-plot occurs, a contrast to it. Both Lear and Gloucester are the victims of filial ingratitude; the blinding of Gloucester is the physical equivalent to the madness of Lear; and both, as a result of their terrible experiences—though in very different degrees—achieve more wisdom at the end than they had at the beginning. The assumed madness of Edgar re-inforces the real madness of Lear, and the character Edgar assumes, that of a man who was once well off in the world, re-inforces, as he stands by Lear on the heath, the situation of the man who was once a king. The bareness of the heath itself . . . re-inforces and reflects what the king discovers there, that "unaccommodated man is no more" than "a bare, forked animal" [III. iv. 106-08]. . . . [Even] more obviously than in *Othello*, the storm in outer nature is meant to be a reflection of the storm in man. The Fool does more than *distract* the king; he calls attention, from another emotional angle, to Lear's situation, and hence emphasizes it. . . . In the same fashion, the mad speeches of Edgar on the heath have again and again a bearing on Lear's situation, and affect us like probings into an open wound.

The main action is also re-inforced in this play by more characters than in any other who act as a chorus. . . . [In] *Lear*, in addition to such minor figures as Curan, two or three Gentlemen and Cornwall's servants, we have Kent, the Fool, Edgar and Albany—all of whom, in various ways, comment on the action and both re-inforce and expand its implications. Even Lear himself in his madness—and at this point Shakespeare uses to the fullest possible extent the resources of the Elizabethan stage convention of presenting mad scenes—even Lear himself acts as a chorus to his own situation, and in the fourth act, his madness giving him an extra personality, he comments with desperate irony on the general evil and injustice which for the moment are more universal than the particular evil and injustice that have driven him insane.

Every cruelty in the action is re-inforced. There is not one evil daughter, there are two; in the scene of the blinding of Gloucester, Regan invariably presses her husband's violence as far as possible by adding to it—it is she, for example, who, immediately after one of Gloucester's eyes is put out, eagerly urges Cornwall to put out the other. . . . And there is the final overwhelming re-inforcement of cruelty in the death of Cordelia; when all the villains are destroyed, and everything seems to be settled, Lear suddenly enters "with Cordelia dead in his arms" [s.d. V. iii.]. (pp. 135-38)

In Lear, says Mr. Wilson Knight, as others have also said, "a tremendous soul is, as it were, incongruously geared to a puerile intellect" [see excerpt above, 1930]. And the greatness of Lear's soul is as clearly indicated by his way of speaking and his use of images, as the smallness of his intellect is shown by his division of the kingdom and his testing of his daughters' love. He naturally and invariably sees himself both in relation to large natural forces and to the gods that control them. (p. 138)

With characteristic violence Lear universalizes his own experience; it is no wonder that other characters in the play think of him in macrocosmic terms. Before he appears on the heath, a Gentleman tells us what to expect, that the king . . .

> Strives in his *little world of man* to out-scorn
> The to-and-fro conflicting wind and rain.
> [III. i. 10-11]

So Gloucester, in the fourth act, as he contemplates the destruction of Lear's sanity, at once associates Lear with the macrocosm:

> O ruin'd piece of nature! This *great world*
> Shall so wear out to naught.
> [IV. vi. 134-35]

At the close of the play, for the third time, Lear is seen as a reflection of the universe. When he enters with Cordelia's body, the sight so affects Kent and Edgar that they think of the Last Judgment; the overwhelming terror and pity of Lear's individual situation makes them imagine the end of the whole world. (pp. 139-40)

The destruction which Lear invokes the elements to accomplish in the macrocosm, "that things might change or cease" [III. i. 7], actually occurs, of course, in the microcosm of Lear himself. Even when he is sane, he is a man quite lacking in wisdom; nothing he does in the first act is good or sensible, and we can easily believe Regan when she says that her father "hath ever but slenderly known himself" [I. i. 293-94]. *Nosce teipsum* was a piece of advice to which King Lear had never paid any attention. The division of the kingdom and the testing of his daughters are only the climax to a life composed of hasty imperious decisions, based on an unthinking acceptance of his own importance and of what was due to him as king and father—a life that has had this acceptance ingrained in it for many years. No wonder that when he gives up the reality of kingly power, he believes that he can still keep the appearance. . . . And no wonder that when the appearance of kingly authority—his retinue of a hundred knights—turns into a rabble of "epicurism and lust" [I. iv. 244], and is taken from him,

or that when the daughters whom he had expected to fulfill the natural law by honoring their father, fail him by turning out to be either, like Cordelia, too honest, or like her sisters, too cruel (Cordelia's appearance of cruelty covering the reality of love, and her sister's appearance of love covering the reality of cruelty)—no wonder that his reason should crack, and the false, insecure order he had lived by, should disrupt into such chaos and madness that the hierarchy of his being should disintegrate, and everything be turned loose.

That is what happens in *King Lear: everything* is turned loose. Lear's own passions, the fury of the elements, the lustful desires of Regan and Goneril, all are horribly released from order. The chaos is more widespread, less local, than in *Hamlet,* for Hamlet himself, in spite of what he may say about the general human situation, is always the prince of Denmark. "This is I; Hamlet the Dane" [V. i. 257-58]. Lear's kingdom, on the other hand, is only irrelevantly Britain; it is any kingdom, or all kingdoms, as Lear, granted his circumstances, is any king, or all kings. And the chaos is more universal than in *Othello,* for *Othello* is a play of intensification, and the turmoil in Othello's mind breaks only an individual world, however splendidly it may be conceived. *King Lear* is orchestrated more broadly, and the instruments for which Shakespeare wrote his score are stretched to the limits of their tonal capacity. Re-inforcement through expansion, expansion through re-inforcement, in the worlds of nature, of the individual and of the state, each inseparably linked to the others so that when one falls, they all fall—such is Shakespeare's technique in *King Lear.* It is a technique that would have been impossible without the picture of man's nature and the conflict it included that was taken for granted in Shakespeare's intellectual and emotional background. Shakespeare's mastery of his craft, at the service of his own deep vision, enabled him to use that picture to create a huge portrayal of devastation that, more excruciatingly than any other, moves us to pity and terror for the protagonists and for ourselves.

King Lear may also be described as a study in relationships. It is concerned with the relations of children to their parents, with the relation of man to the state, and with the relation of the gods to man. Natural law, justice and religion are concepts which permeate the play, the validity of which the action seems to violate. Lear . . . violates natural law—and the law of nations as well—by dividing his kingdom, and his daughters violate natural law by their ingratitude, a vice which, like the bestial jealousy that overcomes Othello, is called "monstrous"—it is outside the order of Nature. (pp. 140-42)

The unnaturalness, the upsetting of order, which is illustrated by the fact that Goneril and Regan, the children, are dominating Lear, the father, is re-inforced by one of the chief themes which run through the apparently irrelevant speeches and songs of the Fool. The fact is another illustration of how one character or *motif* re-inforces the others. For the Fool is continually referring to things that are upside-down or backside-foremost, or out of the natural order, as things are in Lear's erstwhile kingdom. (p. 143)

Goneril and Regan not only violate natural law by their behavior to their father, they also violate their proper functions as human beings by their lust for Edmund, a lust which ends in murder and suicide, and which makes the description of them as animals doubly appropriate. . . . The lust of Regan and Goneril is the clearest indication of their degeneration; here, as in *Hamlet, Troilus* and *Othello,* lust is, to Shakespeare, apparently the chief element in humanity that drags men and women (particularly women) down to the level of animals in the natural hierarchy. Like everything else that is presented in *King Lear* lust is emphasized both by specific action and by universalizing comment; we see Regan and Goneril lusting for Edmund, and the universality of lust in the world is made peculiarly appalling because the eighty-year old Lear himself is the character who generalizes about it. . . . Lust, to Lear, is the evil truth under the false appearance of virtue. . . . And this destructive generalization about the world of the individual, which re-inforces and expands what we have seen exemplified in the lustful behavior of Goneril and Regan, is developed . . . to include the world of the state. There too, the appearance is false, order is broken, and what pretends to be justice is corruption. . . . Lear, whose specifically human property, reason, has been destroyed in a storm of passion and who has unnaturally abandoned his kingly function as the administrator of justice, is the fittingly ironic commentator on a world of government that has also lost all distinction, that has no justice, that cannot authorize any discrimination between good and evil. . . . Lear's mad generalizations are a kind of indirect comment on what has happened in his own kingdom when he selfishly and arrogantly gave up his proper office.

His act has had further ramifications. Almost as soon as he has broken political order by dividing Britain between Cornwall and Albany, we hear from Gloucester that because of disorder in the heavens, there is disorder and disaster in the realm of politics and of nature:

> These late eclipses in the sun and moon portend
> no good to us: though the wisdom of nature
> can reason it thus and thus, yet nature finds
> itself scourged by the sequent effects. Love
> cools, friendship falls off, brothers divide: in
> cities, mutinies; in countries, discord; in pal-
> aces, treason; and the bond cracked between
> son and father.
>
> [I. ii. 103-09]

And this generalization, which, incidentally, might be considered as a particular illustration of what Ulysses, in *Troilus and Cressida,* had said about how disorder can corrupt the world—this generalization is borne out by what we shortly hear of the civil war in the state. . . . Shakespeare has so many other things to show us that he cannot show us these wars in actual operation, but he refers to them three times, and that is enough. The political chaos is as obvious as the chaos in man and in the universe.

Man's relation to the gods, the forces that should order him supernaturally, is as much emphasized as his relation to the state that should order him politically and the self-control by reason that should order his own nature. In fact Shakespeare seems in this play deliberately to use the way a man thinks of the gods as an indication of character. All the characters with whom we are meant to sympathize—Lear, Gloucester, Edgar, Kent and Albany—continually appeal to the gods, and in their different ways think of human affairs as controlled by supernatural power. The bad characters, particularly Edmund (in this respect, as in others, he resembles Richard III and Iago), are incorrigible individualists and egoists. (pp. 143-46)

Yet though the sympathetic figures in the play, unlike Edmund, call frequently upon the gods, and see human affairs in relation to divine control, the gods are highly ambiguous figures, and their rule is not necessarily beneficent. As Dowden says, Shakespeare's *King Lear* differs from the old play which was

its main source, in being deliberately placed in heathen times, "partly, we may surmise, that [Shakespeare] might be able to put the question boldly, 'what are the gods?'" [see excerpt above, 1881] The gods are mentioned many times, in relation to circumstances that are invariably evil; but God, the God that would have meant something to Shakespeare's audience, is mentioned only once, when Lear is delusively looking forward to a blissful life with Cordelia. (pp. 147-48)

What is most characteristic of *King Lear* is, on one occasion, summed up by Albany. The animal imagery, the interweaving of relationships, the rapid shift of thought from man as an individual to man as a prince and from man to the heavens, the re-inforcement of the degeneracy in one hierarchy by the degeneracy in another, the doubt concerning divine control of man's affairs, the monstrous chaos and destruction into which man's unassisted nature will lead him—all these things which form the macrocosm of the play are woven in a typical fashion into the microcosm of a single speech. "What have you done?" Albany asks Goneril,

> Tigers, not daughters, what have you perform'd?
> A father, and a gracious aged man,
> Whose reverence the head-lugg'd bear would lick,
> Most barbarous, most degenerate! have you madded.
> Could my good brother suffer you to do it?
> A man, a prince, by him so benefited!
> If that the heavens do not their visible spirits
> Send quickly down to tame these vile offences,
> It will come,
> Humanity must perforce prey on itself,
> Like monsters of the deep.
>
> [IV ii. 40-50]

As we have seen, Shakespeare uses his consciousness of the difference between appearance and reality in many places and in many connections throughout the play; it is particularly striking in relation to what happens to Lear himself. He begins with all the assurance of long-established authority, his speeches are nearly all imperatives, but one by one his pretensions are stripped away. . . . And on the bare heath life does become as "cheap as beast's." For when he sees the disguised Edgar, as the storm still thunders, Lear finds out what man is really like, and he starts to tear off even the covering of his garments:

> Is man no more than this? Consider him well.
> Thou owest the worm no silk, the beast no hide,
> the sheep no wool, the cat no perfume. Ha!
> here's three on's are sophisticated; thou art the
> thing itself; unaccommodated man is no more
> but such a poor, bare, forked animal as thou
> art. Off, off, you lendings! Come; unbutton
> here.
>
> [III. iv. 102-09]

This stripping off of layers of appearance to arrive at the bare truth is the final and tragic expression of that common Shakespearean theme which derides all affectation. . . , which questions the validity of ceremony. . . , and which tries to describe man as he really is. Lear's description is a terrible one, but even in this play, dark as it is, it is not the whole answer. The movement is not all downward, there is a counter-movement upward. Lear himself is not merely stripped, he is purged, and hence there is a possibility of redemption. The storm makes him think, for the first time in his eighty years, of what happens to "poor naked wretches" in "seasons such as these" [III. iv.

28ff]. . . . And thoughts of this kind make possible his later recovery into love.

But if we are to understand the full dramatic force of the scenes on the heath, we must imagine their effect in the theater. . . . And these particular scenes should be imagined in relation to the opening of the play; the contrast of visual impression, the contrast in *tableau,* must be as concretely perceived by the eye as the contrasts of rhythm and word are heard by the ear. In the opening scene Lear is surrounded by his court: a page holds the gold crown on a velvet cushion, the King of France, the Duke of Burgundy and a crowd of brilliantly dressed courtiers all wait upon his imperious commands. But in the heath scenes his only companions are a fool and a madman. Kent and Gloucester may be looking out for him, but one is in disguise and the other is in disgrace; on the heath it is to the ''bitter Fool'' and the ''loop'd and window'd raggedness' of Edgar that Lear must turn for companionship. . . . We see him reduced to relying on the lowest dregs of human nature, his mind in pieces, trying to get to reality by stripping off his clothes.

Never before or since has there been such dramatic writing as this. In presenting man's nature as below any rational level, Shakespeare's control of poetic and dramatic counterpoint enables him as it were to transcend man's nature. Though Lear, Edgar and the Fool are human beings in whom we can believe, what Shakespeare makes them say is beyond normal human speech, and we are in a world where comedy and tragedy are the same. The real madness of Lear, the assumed madness of Edgar, the half-madness of the Fool all play against one another to make out of chaos an almost incredible harmony. These scenes suggest the technique of music as well as the technique of drama, the use of a dramatic orchestration so broad that it stretches our comprehension as no drama had stretched it before. It would have been impossible to foretell that the tradition of the morality play . . . could ever be used and transcended as Shakespeare transcends it in *King Lear.* (pp. 148-51)

> *Theodore Spencer, '''Othello' and 'King Lear','' in his* Shakespeare and the Nature of Man, *Macmillan Publishing Company, 1942, pp. 122-52.*

GEORGE R. KERNODLE   (essay date 1945)

[*In the excerpt below, Kernodle acknowledges Theodore Spencer and others who analyzed* King Lear *in the light of the Elizabethan concept of the natural order (see excerpt above, 1942). He concurs that the play dramatizes on three planes—the individual, the state, and the universe—the chaos resulting from the violation of that order. Kernodle applies this model to Shakespeare's artistic method in the play, claiming that the dramatic structure of* King Lear *is organized according to principles used in numerous Elizabethan plays. These principles he identifies as the concepts of parallelism and correspondence, both in character and action, derived from medieval drama and based on the Christian doctrine of prefiguration in which figures and events in the Old Testament are paralleled with those in the New Testament. In the nineteenth century, Victor Hugo (1864) applied a similar idea in his attempt to explain Shakespeare's frequent use of double-plots; other commentators who have used historical bases to explain certain aspects of* King Lear *include John W. Draper (1937), Edwin Muir (1946), and Hardin Craig (see Additional Bibliography).*]

In artistic methods, no less than in basic themes, *King Lear* is an epitome of the age. Professor Hardin Craig has shown how the basic themes of *Lear* were the recognized attributes of Natural Law. More recently Professors Spencer and Tillyard have shown how deeply rooted in the thought of the age was the belief, dramatized in *King Lear,* that a breach in the natural bonds of duty, affection, gratitude, and sincerity was of world-shaking importance and would be reflected not only in the domain of man—dethroning his reason and lowering him to the level of beasts—but also in the domain of the state—causing civil war—and in the very stars and elements themselves—causing disorder, eclipses, storms, and tempests. According to the philosophical thought inherited from the Middle Ages, the patterns of order could be traced equally in the human body to the mind, in the state, in the elements of the earth, and in the spheres of the heavens. The microcosm of man was in all details parallel to the macrocosm of the world. If we study the artistic habits inherited from the Middle Ages, we discover that *King Lear,* in its aesthetic organization no less than in its basic thought, has this same dependence on the repetition, in different domains, of a basic pattern.

The medieval basis for this artistic principle of parallelism was the doctrine of prefiguration. Incidents in the Old Testament were paired with corresponding incidents in the life of Christ: the sacrifice of Isaac and the Crucifixion, the story of Jonah and the Resurrection, the tree of Paradise and the Cross. In stained-glass windows, in carved and painted altars, in manuscript illuminations, in the woodcuts of the ''Poor Man's Bible,'' in the *tableaux vivants,* and in the processional pageants, artistic units were organized in pairs or groups by the repetition of a single pattern. (pp. 185-86)

King Lear is built on this same artistic principle of correspondence or parallelism. Each motif is repeated in as many ways as possible. Each character repeats or balances some other character; each event is the prefiguration of some other event; and structural units are balanced against each other. Further, each theme is repeated in the wit and imagery. Just as the main theme of violation of natural law is explored in three domains—the individual character, the social state, and the wider universe of stars and tempests—so the artistic method may be traced in its three domains—the alignment of characters, the structure of scenes, and the verbal imagery.

The parallelisms of character are obvious enough. In almost every point the Gloucester story is parallel to that of Lear. Lear and Gloucester finally appear together in similar plight, and the wicked son and the wicked daughters are involved in a mutual destruction. The contrast between the plain speaking of Cordelia and the flattery of Goneril and Regan is reinforced not only by the plain speaking of the Fool but by the contrast between the honest Kent and the sycophantic Oswald.

In the structure of scenes, likewise, *King Lear* is built on the principle of parallelism. As in many Elizabethan plays, the principle is applied both to the opening scene and to the play as a whole. The symphonic pattern called for an overture of two parallel opening scenes and then two parallel movements, the second movement starting at the fourth act.

The twofold beginning has its origin in medieval drama, doubtless from the custom of presenting the characters to the audience before they were put into action. Especially in the moralities, the separate presentation of the good characters and the bad characters led to closely parallel opening scenes. . . . *King Lear,* likewise, led with two separate sets of characters, presents each in turn before bringing them together. (pp. 186-87)

In *King Lear* the twofold organization . . . [is also] the basic structure of the play. It is marked partly by the key position of Cornwall in the first part and of Albany in the second part. The difference between Cornwall and Albany is indicated in the very first line of the play. After the beginning Albany drops out: it is Cornwall who becomes increasingly dominant. He aligns himself with Oswald, the sycophant, against Kent, the plain-spoken and sincere. He takes charge at the end of Act II and triumphs over Gloucester at the end of Act III. In the second part Albany takes his place, aligns himself against Oswald, and denounces Goneril. While the first part ends with the bloody deed of Cornwall, the second part ends under the leadership of Albany, as man of peace. The Quartos gave Albany the final speech, with its reaffirmation of truth and sincerity: "Speak what we feel, not what we ought to say."

More important in giving a twofold structure to the play than the balance of Cornwall against Albany is the compact and bold outline of Part One. From act I, Scene iii (after the twofold overture), through Act III, the first part forms a single rising action. It in turn is divided into two movements, reaching one climax with the thrusting out of Lear at the end of Act II and another with the thrusting out of Gloucester at the end of Act III. It is a structure of mounting tension, built by alternation of instruments, contrasts, and counter-movement. From the time Goneril sets Oswald, the extreme sycophant, on to oppose Lear, and Lear accepts Kent, the extreme honest man, the fight is on. The tension begun by Oswald and Kent reaches its first peak with Lear denouncing Goneril and departing for Regan. Again the minor instruments take up the theme. Cornwall and Kent confront each other. There is a quiet moment while Kent reads Cordelia's letter and Edgar appears in disguise. Then it is time to bring on the main instruments—Lear facing both Goneril and Regan. The conflict mounts. As he turns from one to the other, they close in on him. With shorter and shorter speeches and the staccato repetition of the word *need,* they drive him to the breaking point. His long impassioned protest at being stripped of all that makes man better than beast is a full musical arrival—a recapitulation of the themes of unnatural daughters and the terrors of the earth. The storm of his anger and madness is taken up by the full orchestra of backstage thunder, wind, and tempest.

The wicked daughters have triumphed over Lear, but Gloucester is still to be dealt with. In the third act the rising scenes of Edmund and Cornwall, leading to the blinding of Gloucester, continue the pattern of the first part and tie together Acts II and III. Act III has an even more interesting structure than the earlier scenes of Part One—a structure built on the contrapuntal balance between the three scenes of Edmund and Cornwall that rise to a terrific climax and the three scenes of Lear in the storm that start at a climax and get progressively quieter. When the first scene of Act III has built the storm to a peak, Lear is brought on, the tempest within equal to that without. The second tempest scene, Scene iv, is a little quieter; the king is more contemplative and is praying rather than defying the elements. . . . The third storm scene, Scene vi, is still more subdued: it is under cover, and the storm is in the distant background. After the trial of the joint stools, the scene is lowered to a whisper, and Lear, exhausted, sleeps.

In contrast to this decrescendo, the alternate scenes—iii, v, and vii—form a bloody and violent crescendo, leading to the blinding of Gloucester, the wounding of Cornwall, and Regan's stabbing of the servant. The first two scenes, rather short, give contrast to the Lear scenes they follow and build up the plot, with Cornwall taking over from Edmund. It is the third, scene vii, coming just after the Lear scenes have subsided, that carries this crescendo to its climax. . . . Gloucester's long speech corresponds to that of Lear at the end of Act II and, like that,

is concerned with the theme of unnatural actions that make "man's life as cheap as beast's" [II. iv. 267]. Now man's life is lower than beast's. Gloucester's eyes are put out, and, like Lear at the end of Act II, he is thrust out of doors.

In the domain of verbal imagery, no less than in the characters and in the structure, Shakespeare reinforces his main themes. . . . Often enough the reflection is not an echo, after the motif, as we would expect, but before the motif—another kind of prefiguration. (pp. 188-89)

King Lear has, of all the plays, the richest direct and indirect reinforcement of themes by verbal imagery. In the lines of Lear it is easy to trace the prefiguration, reinforcement, and echoing of the themes. Lear's recurring fear of madness marks the progressive surges toward madness itself. Especially in the storm and the fourth-act mad scene, he echoes the themes of filial ingratitude, the broken bonds of nature, sincerity and flattery, the contrast between outer appearance and naked reality, and the corruption of human nature, of the social order, and of the elements themselves by unnatural crimes. It has long been recognized how the Fool reinforces the themes not only of madness but also of the foolishness of trust, the unnaturalness of the daughters, and the need of patience. Miss Welsford would go even further and make the Fool the keynote of the whole play—in the traditional medieval ambiguity of the words *fool* and *foolish* [see excerpt above, 1935]. In one sense the good are "foolish" to love, to feel sympathy, to expect gratitude or crave affection. The King is brought to the position of the Fool and learns the patience that is the power to choose love even when love is synonymous with suffering.

Edgar likewise serves for more than a reinforcement of the madness. Both his plight and his words illustrate a condition of man that is lower than beast's. Lear, Gloucester, Cordelia, and Albany compare the sisters to beasts in vivid terms, and Edgar's ravings are full of the wild images of bestiality—fiends, nightmares, whirlpools, cold winds, false and wicked women. . . . His companions are the lowest of animals: frogs, toads, tadpoles, rats, and ditch dogs. The sight of him makes his father "think a man a worm" [IV. i. 33] and inspires Lear's "unaccommodated man is no more but such a poor, bare, forked animal as thou art" [III. iv. 106-08]. Here, too, Edgar reinforces the theme of the stripping off of the layers of appearance to find the naked reality.

In their published plays, the Elizabethans were beginning to use the division into five acts that was called for by the best authorities. But the division was mostly afterthought. It was easy to write "Act IV" where the main break came. In their actual composition, most dramatists used the old native habits built on the principle of parallel reinforcement—reinforcing character by character, opening scene by a second opening scene, first part by second part, and the themes of the main action by the verbal imagery of even the minor characters. In *King Lear* these native principles, deeply based in medieval habits of thinking, are brought to their highest perfection. One of the most profound of all visions of the nature of man and his relation to the universe is bodied forth with consummate artistry. Out of extremely complex material Shakespeare created a unity of theme, structure, and texture that is scarcely approached by even the best symphonies. (pp. 190-91)

George R. Kernodle, "The Symphonic Form of 'King Lear'," in Elizabethan Studies and Other Essays in Honor of George F. Reynolds, *University of Colorado, 1945, pp. 185-91.*

GEOFFREY L. BICKERSTETH (lecture date 1946)

[*In the following excerpt, taken from the annual Shakespeare lecture delivered before the British Academy in London on April 24, 1946, Bickersteth suggests that we interpret* King Lear *according to Philip Sidney's memorable dictum on the transmutation of the natural world, what Sidney calls "brazen," into the "golden" world of the poet's creation. He then discusses the depiction of evil in the play, especially as represented in the death of Cordelia, and recapitulates what numerous critics in the past have voiced: that the deaths of Cordelia and Lear serve neither an artistic nor a moral purpose. However, Bickersteth refutes this centuries-old argument, claiming that, from a moral standpoint,* King Lear *should have ended after the reconciliation scene between Lear and Cordelia; that it does not demonstrates that its purpose is other than moral persuasion. Beyond the point of the reconciliation scene, Bickersteth argues, Shakespeare was attempting a fusion of the Promethean and the Christian myths; but it is the Christian myth that dominates, for it affirms the most important principle of the play, namely, love. For Bickersteth, the symbol of that love is Cordelia: like Christ, her prototype, she is the only one who can redeem "nature from the general curse." Her so-called "resurrection"—that is, A. C. Bradley's idea that Lear dies believing Cordelia lives (see excerpt above, 1904)—causes Lear's heart to break in an ecstasy of joy. Bickersteth's interpretation of the final scene of* King Lear *continues the Christian analysis first implied by Bradley, and later developed by R. W. Chambers (1939), Oscar James Campbell (1948), Irving Ribner (1958), L. C. Knights (1959), Robert H. West (1968), and René E. Fortin (1979).*]

Sir Philip Sidney, in his *Apology for Poetry*, draws a memorable distinction between the two worlds created respectively by Nature and by the poets. 'Her world', he says of Nature, 'is brazen, the poets only deliver a golden.' This famous tribute, itself and in its own sense 'golden', paid to the poet's art by a poet who was also the first great English critic of poetry, affords me a text here. For I propose to consider *King Lear* in the light of it. . . . *King Lear* is by common consent our greatest poet's greatest creation. It follows, therefore, that the world of which Shakespeare delivered himself in this stupendous drama, though admittedly the most painful of all his tragedies, should have a better right to be called, in Sidney's sense, 'golden' than any other we can name, whether among his own works or in the whole galaxy of poems that glorify our literature. Which is only another way of putting what Hazlitt said when he observed of *King Lear* that 'it is the best of Shakespeare's plays', since it is 'the one in which he is most in earnest: he was here fairly caught in the web of his own imagination' [see excerpt above, 1817]. (p. 147)

The dramatic conflict which the play submits for our contemplation is . . . truly universal. It involves the microcosm no less comprehensively than the macrocosm; the two worlds at war with one another, since each is divided against itself. Nature material, human, and divine—each is here revealed to us in all its most significant aspects; Matter, inanimate and animate, vast, primitive, and brutal: Man, a 'natural', like the Fool, or a creature of impulse merely, as Lear is to begin with, old but a child in intellect, or of reason controlling impulse, whether like Edmund to selfish, or like Cordelia, who 'thinks justly', to unselfish ends: and God, variously figured according to the requirements of the action, as Fate, Necessity, or Law of the universe, as the Stars or Fortune, as Deities just or unjust or careless of mankind, or—though on one occasion only—simply as God, the supreme and inscrutable Providence, in connexion with whom we are told that men take upon them the mystery of things, as if they were his spies. (p. 150)

[The] 'mystery of things'—that is, of Nature in this all-inclusive sense, material, human, and divine—is precisely what Shakespeare dares to take upon him in *King Lear*. And of these three the mystery of human nature is, as always for him, central. *Othello* concerns itself predominantly with the mystery of man's emotional, *Hamlet* of his reflective, *Macbeth* of his moral, nature. But *King Lear* confronts us with the mystery of human nature, the wonder of it, simply as such. It would fain see into, and to us reveal, the 'thing itself', when stripped of its 'lendings' and laid bare to the core. 'Does any here *know* me—Who is it that can tell me who "I am"'? [I. iv. 226, 230]. *King Lear* is unique among Shakespearian dramas because it alone makes us one with a world which poses this ultimate question and answers it, not by means of a moral fable invented to be tropologically interpreted (though the play does in fact contain much deliberate symbolism of this kind), but mythically—by means, that is, of a story so composed as to induce in us an amplitude of mind . . . in which there comes to us, if only by flashes, a vision symbolic of human life and destiny, sombre because tragic, but for the same reason not so sombre as to kill hope, and felt immediately and without question to be, in itself, the guarantee of its own truth. The effect of *King Lear,* as thus regarded, can only be known by being actually experienced, and, however explained, has never been denied even by critics, like Charles Lamb and Andrew Bradley [see excerpts above, 1812 and 1904], who were persuaded (though wrongly, according to Granville Barker [see excerpt above, 1927]) that by no mere stage-representation of the play could it ever be more than dimly suggested, if indeed by this means it could be communicated at all.

But at least this may be said without fear of contradiction: the effect once experienced, to inquire into its cause should be of special interest to us at the present time, since the world of *King Lear* happens to resemble so closely the actual world in which we are now alive. (pp. 150-51)

[Our] own recent experience of 'total' warfare, and the hell to which the devildoms of Germany and Japan between them have reduced more than half the civilized world by their monstrous crimes, must surely by now have opened our eyes to the credibility of that vision of life which, however he came by it, inspired Shakespeare to write *King Lear*. The naked Evil, that stalks through it with unashamed effrontery from act to act, we with our own eyes have beheld no less brazenly flaunting itself among ourselves. (pp. 151-52)

It is, of course, true that this 'brazen' world of Shakespeare's imagination also resembles ours, as it must to be credible, in containing besides evil much that is good, even supremely such. For it contains Cordelia, not to mention Kent, Edgar, and the Fool. Indeed, of the *dramatis personae* the righteous and the wicked seem, on balance, to be about equally matched both in number and in their respective degrees of virtue and vice. If, then, we abstract from the play the world it depicts, we might be tempted to account for its 'golden' effect by arguing that the bad in it, by reason of its very hideousness, actually enhances the beauty of the good and—what is still more satisfactory—even brings fresh good into existence, whereas it ends by destroying itself. The argument is familiar; but even those most inclined to employ it in explanation of the aesthetic pleasure we take in Shakespearian tragedy seem dubious of its validity here. Not because this moral is not contained in the play. For it is obvious that Lear's sufferings and therefore, indirectly, the evil that causes them, do in fact reform his character; just as Edmund's defeat—unlike, for example,

Iago's in *Othello*—brings him 'despite of his own nature' to repentance, while of the two principal villains one is murdered by the other, who herself commits suicide. Nor can it be objected that the playwright himself when selecting his theme had no such didactic purpose in view. For Shakespeare, like all tragic poets of his age (or, for that matter, of all previous ages) did not regard his art, except in its purely technical aspect, as an end itself, but as the handmaid of ethics, an illustrative guide to the unphilosophical of the practical difference between living virtuously and otherwise. And precisely because in *King Lear* he is from this point of view 'more in earnest' than in any other of his great tragedies he here perhaps more frequently, and therefore more noticeably, than ever before or afterwards uses his characters both dramatically and (like the chorus in a Greek play) extradramatically to point a moral: whether by what they say as—to take one example out of many—in Edgar's oft-quoted apophthegm:

> The gods are just, and of our pleasant vices
> Make instruments to plague us;
>
> [V. iii. 171-72]

or by what they do, as in Gloucester's mock-suicide, which is as it were an acted 'morality' in miniature, with Edgar for 'angel' or 'prolocutor' (the whole to be regarded rather as interpretative of the plot than as essential to it); or by speech and action simultaneously, as in the highly dramatic utterance of the dying Edmund, when he realizes that Fortune has betrayed him:

> The wheel has come full circle, I am here.
>
> [V. iii. 175]

Granted, then, that for the reason just stated we are justified in attributing to Shakespeare as dramatic artist a consciously didactic purpose; and that there can in fact be found in *King Lear* much to support the theory that he intended it to express his vision of a world whose beauty should depend upon its being made to appear by nature so constituted that its morally evil elements, however real and potent, and the suffering they entail, however intense and prolonged, never fail in the end to be generally beneficial or, as the phrase goes, to work together for good; yet the final issue of the action would seem to have been deliberately so ordered—for the catastrophe was the poet's own invention—as to make it, on this showing, extremely difficult to explain why so *much* evil should have been deemed necessary, when in the play, as we have it, so much less would actually suffice for the complete realization of the aesthetic effect aimed at. The action issues in the death of Cordelia, which is the immediate cause of her father's: but in what respects can either event be shown to serve any good, whether immediate or remote? Cordelia's death—to consider hers first—cannot be necessary to Lear's spiritual reformation (which might have justified it dramatically), since this has been completed before it takes place. So, too, has the overthrow of her enemies, to which, therefore, it contributes nothing. Foully evil itself, and the cause, not of good, but of fresh evil (Lear's death), is it even pathetic? . . . If the moral of the play be indeed that suggested, it has surely been so conclusively pointed, at an earlier moment in the action, as to make the introduction of yet further evil—and *such* evil—quite superfluous and, consequently, a grave artistic error. I refer to the moment when Lear himself makes it plain, at the very nadir of his own and Cordelia's misfortunes, that the evil, which by their military defeat seems to have won its final victory over good, has in fact, so far from destroying the latter, only succeeded in creating the very conditions required for its triumphant survival

in the blissful existence which he imagines himself and his beloved daughter thenceforward enjoying together in prison:

> We two alone will sing like birds i' the cage:
> When thou dost ask me blessing, I'll kneel down,
> And ask of thee forgiveness; so we'll live,
> And pray and sing—
>
> [V. iii. 9-12]

A life of sins forgiven, of reciprocated charity, of clear vision, and of joyous song—what is this but the traditional heaven transferred to earth? The only place for it, be it noted, for which the world of *King Lear* allows room. For, as imagined by Shakespeare, it includes no heaven beyond the grave to 'make good' the injustices and undeserved miseries for which this life has failed to provide any, or any remotely adequate, compensation. However it may be with Hamlet, there are no flights of angels to sing Cordelia to her rest. Once she is dead there remains nothing to relieve the depressing reflection that in her, dying when and how she does, moral rectitude, in the highest manifestation of it which this or any play of Shakespeare affords, meets with final and ignominious defeat.

It may be objected, however, that in thus reacting to her death we merely convict ourselves of having succumbed to the natural temptation to be sentimental about Cordelia and make too much of the function assigned to her in the drama. . . . [But] the importance of the role played by Cordelia in contributing to the effect produced by the play as a whole is not to be measured by the frequency and length of her speeches or by the number of her stage-appearances. To avoid the risk of sentimentalizing her there is surely no need to go the length of reducing her to a mere technical device for getting the action begun and not too gloomily ended. But, apart from Cordelia, and regarded as Lear's tragedy alone, the last act of this play still jars on critics who hold that no poet's world can properly be termed 'golden' unless it be so rounded off as to satisfy at once and in full claim that it shall be not only aesthetically complete, but morally so as well. To fulfil this twofold condition, had not the drama gone far enough, they ask, and would it not therefore, if left to itself, have inevitably ended, at the point near the close of the third act, where, with his wits now wholly gone, but having saved his soul alive, Lear falls asleep—'make no noise, make no noise; draw the curtains: so, so, so' [III. vi. 83-4]? Or, if not drawn there, perhaps better still (since maybe no tragic hero should die insane) immediately after his reconciliation with Cordelia? . . . Surely, if its 'moral' be the one suggested, *King Lear* demands, at one or other of the points just mentioned, the kind of sad but solemn close which, after the hero's last pathetic farewell to his daughter, the poet of Colonus gave to the sequel of his *King Oedipus*. What now remains, or can possibly reconcile us to the sufferings of a man who, when all is said and done, has been far more sinned against than sinning, except to see him fall asleep for ever, thus attaining at long last to peace after storm and, his Purgatory duly endured, to fruition, though but transient, of an Earthly Paradise, since his passage by death to a Heavenly is here out of the question. Had the drama then and thus terminated, there would have been no occasion for Tate to restore to his stage-version of it the happy ending of the original Lear-legend [see excerpt above, 1681]; nor for Johnson to feel that, without transgression of tragic law, such an ending was here not wholly without justification, since even for the most shocking events life does *sometimes* provide compensations and such, moreover, as really do compensate [see excerpt above, 1765]; nor, lastly, for Bradley, who rejected with horror the wish for a

Act III. Scene iv. Gloucester, Fool, Lear, Kent, and Edgar. By B. West (n.d.). The Department of Rare Books and Special Collections, The University of Michigan Library.

happy ending, to hold nevertheless that the final catastrophe, as Shakespeare imagines it, does not seem at all inevitable, and is therefore not strictly either dramatic or necessary, however indispensable it may be—and, as he thought, actually was—to the effect of the play when considered primarily not as a drama but as a poem [see excerpt above, 1904].

The truth is that difficulties of this kind are bound to crop up for critics who insist on treating a work of art as a means to an end, whether moral or otherwise. *King Lear*, like every genuine product of the imagination, is its own end and possesses no meaning other than itself. No 'moral', or 'morals', already belonging to the material out of which it is composed, or read into it by the poet himself, *qua* moralist, with a consciously didactic purpose, can, therefore, as such, though necessarily present *in* the play, be the true determinant of its form. . . . Whatever its defects as a drama the world of *King Lear* has been so created that, as actually experienced, it can justly claim to meet every demand which the mind, when active as a whole, makes upon its object. Whether we choose to call this activity Imagination or Reason or Love, it will be found, under all three modes alike, at once informing and reflected by the world of the play, so that, however ugly, irrational, wicked, and therefore painful this world may seem in itself (and it seems never so much all these at once as in its final dealings with Cordelia and her father), it does, in fact, when

spiritually lived with, compel us to accept without question its beauty, its reasonableness, and its moral worth. (pp. 152-57)

[The] object of Shakespeare's imagination here is a world characterized above all by the fact that it suffers. Its whole being is summed up in that term. Therein lies its 'brazenness' and, as I said earlier, its close resemblance to the world as experienced by countless millions of human beings at the present time. Shakespeare allows no one to exist in this drama except on condition that he suffers. . . . No one acts in it except to react to things done to him or to her, and those things always such as directly or indirectly to cause pain. It is a hideous world, in which Edmund alone seems to enjoy himself (there must, of course, be one such person in the play by way of contrast); and even he suffers in the end. Albany and Edgar, the sole survivors of the tragedy—for one cannot count Kent as such—are among those who have suffered worst. The suffering too, is of every kind, physical, mental, and moral; and all of them, at their acutest, are, as they must be, concentrated in Lear, the protagonist. (pp. 157-58)

But suffering, which in experience, even when deserved, often seems unreasonable because excessive, and when undeserved grossly unjust, in order to be accepted as at once aesthetically and morally 'fair', must, together with the evil that causes it, be intuitively apprehended as integral to the one spiritual system of the universe seen variously figured by the poet's imagination in the scenes and events of this temporal world that in symbol his drama reflects. To consider the world of *King Lear* from this angle of vision is to adopt the view taken by the ancient Greek dramatists of the world as by them imagined. It seems peculiarly appropriate here, since both in style and content *King Lear* more closely resembles an Aeschylean tragedy than any other of Shakespeare's dramas. . . . The artistic necessity of the catastrophe in *King Lear* has, as we have seen, been questioned, on the ground that it does not seem to be the *inevitable* result of preceding events (or actions) in the story as Shakespeare tells it. It seems due, rather, to the intervention of Fortune or chance. . . . But apart from the fact that careful study of the events immediately preceding the catastrophe shows that they do sufficiently account for it, there is no reason to suppose that Cordelia's death (which causes Lear's), even if it *had* seemed accidental, would have troubled a Greek audience. For the Greeks held that Fortune, if not identical with Destiny, subserves it; as the latter in turn subserves Zeus if it be not itself Zeus, or, rather, his mind active under the form of Divine Providence, man's name for that which determines the Law of the universe as he sees it at work in the world ordering inexorably the course of events. The Law, being ultimate, is rational and just—how could it be otherwise?—but it is impersonal and works on the impersonal level. As such, its concern is with humanity, not with individual men, if the latter (as they alone can) happen to break it. Cordelias, therefore, merely because they are innocent, and Lears, merely because they are more sinned against than sinning, since both are human, cannot escape the suffering with which it penalizes mankind in general for any breach of itself. In short, the nature of the Lear-world is the nature of things as Shakespeare's imagination saw it; and Cordelia's death, like her father's, lies in the nature of things, as thus seen. To have spared either of them to live happily ever afterwards would have been to falsify the course of nature quite arbitrarily and on purely sentimental grounds, a weak surrender to the demands of a so-called 'poetic' justice—poetic, that is, in the Coleridgian sense of fanciful, rather than truly imaginative. Humanly speaking, there is no fault in Cordelia. Even if there were, her death, let alone the manner of it, would still be objected to by sentimentalists as a punishment far in excess of that due to her sole discoverable *hamartia,* the supposed *hybris* which, whether consciously to herself or not, prompted her initial reply to her father's question. She is hanged, because that is the doom reserved for her by a relentless Nemesis, which, concerned as it is only with human deeds, not their doers, visits indifferently the sins of the guilty upon the guiltless, though it ensures that the former also shall be condignly punished in the end. Is this unreasonable, unfair? No, because to condemn the law which makes the death of Cordelia inevitable is to condemn the law under which alone she comes into existence and which makes her what she is. For the two laws are the same law. No Edmunds, no Cordelias. Yet if Edmunds exist, Cordelias must perish. That is the tragedy. (pp. 162-63)

[As the tragedy of *King Lear*] deepens, it slowly dawns upon us that all suffering is *in its true nature* at once sacrificial and redemptive. It is sacrificial and such that the gods themselves throw incense upon it, in so far as it comes to be accepted and patiently endured for others' sake and not for the advantage, even though it be the moral advantage, of the sufferer alone. It is redemptive, in that, when thus accepted and endured, it is felt to deliver from the evil that inflicts it, either by converting the evil to good or by depriving it, not indeed of its reality, but of all its effective power. Herein lies the sole beauty of

suffering, the beauty that can alone reconcile us to it, and in revealing which, be it only by flashes, lies the 'golden' effect of this most 'brazenly' painful of all Shakespeare's great tragedies. I say 'by flashes'; but how are these to be explained? Only, I suggest, by supposing that within the practical realities of the world of *King Lear* as the dramatist imagines them, there is set, like a jewel, the image of a deeper dream-world than that to which they belong: deeper because it expresses a profounder intuition than they do of the true meaning of human life and destiny. Within those 'brazen' realities this image is set in such a way that, at certain moments, catching the light of emotion—the emotion that Lear's sufferings excite—it reflects it and illumines or (to retain Sidney's metaphor) gilds them without interfering with their reality as such. Indeed, at these moments, the 'brazen' realities he is imagining are real for the dramatist only because they reveal the real presence of the image called up from the depth by his *alta fantasia* with a power which, we may well believe, comes to a great poet only, as Plato would say . . . , 'by a divine dispensation'.

The image in the presence of which, as it springs spontaneously out of his emotion, the poet sees the familiar Lear-legend enacting itself before his inner eye, and which that legend, as thus dramatized, nowhere directly expresses but by suggestion calls up to mind, is the myth of the sufferer to whose sufferings we become reconciled because his patience of them is such as to convince us *either* that the evil which causes them must inevitably in due time be overcome *or*—what is a greater 'wonder' still—that it has, virtually, already met with defeat. In the former case, set within the story of *King Lear,* we shall recognize the Greek myth of Prometheus (or some variant thereof) and in Lear himself a hero who, like Aeschylus' Titan, is partly responsible for his own sufferings; in the latter we shall recognize, but associate with Cordelia rather than with her father, the Christian myth—for a myth need not always be untrue to history—of the wholly innocent sufferer who saved others while himself apparently, but only apparently, he could not save. By the end of the play, however, the two myths will have merged into one.

Contemplated in the light of the Prometheus-myth, Lear is the symbol of Man sinning through a 'hideous rashness' against the moral order of Nature, which, since he is the chief expression of it, thereby become divided against itself and justly hostile to him. But in the case of both heroes alike, the error was rooted in love, the love of Prometheus for the children of men, of Lear for his own children, but above all, his love for Cordelia, the reality of which Shakespeare never for a moment intends us to doubt and adds, indeed, the last act of the tragedy with the express purpose of emphasizing. Although, therefore, it is true that

> Love is not love
> When it is mingled with regards that stand
> Aloof from the *entire* point
>
> [I. i. 238-40]

as their love was, yet in the case of both alike, as the play proceeds, and they learn by suffering . . . to recognize this truth, their progressive apprehension and acceptance of it cause us . . . to regard them as more sinned against than sinning, so that we find ourselves at last unable to justify their punishment, except on the assumption that it is largely vicarious. As such, it takes on in our eyes, if not consciously in their own, an increasingly redemptive character and gives ground for the hope (obscurely present from the first, and actually realized at last, in the Aeschylean trilogy) that it will eventually—though how we know not—end in the re-atonement of man's nature with the nature of things.

If, on the other hand, in the act of experiencing the world of *King Lear,* there come to us moments, when by means hard to analyse—some fleeting gesture, perhaps, or tone of voice, or turn of phrase—we are suddenly made aware of beng confronted with suffering made *divinely* beautiful, because felt to be in itself a victory over evil, won by a love that sticks to the entire point, 'nor bends with the remover to remove', then we must suppose that Shakespeare (who was in fact a Christian, though he was here imagining a purely pagan world) was unconsciously inspired by a story taken not from Greek, but from Christian mythology, and explain the 'golden' effect of the play by relating it to some such myth as the Harrowing of Hell, which was, of course, familiar enough to the dramatist. Divine love, symbolized by Cordelia, enters a kingdom already divided against itself, which is the Christian definition of hell. (Lear's kingdom had been divided before the play begins.) And though we normally and rightly think of love as a harmonizing power—it is, indeed, ultimately the only one there is—yet Shakespeare here reminds us that, when it descends into hell, it enters there first as a disorganizing force, which must needs make the confusion yet more confounded before it can restore all things to order, as in the end it certainly will. . . . That is, in fact, Cordelia's function in the 'brazen' world of *King Lear.* (Nor was this, I would here note, the first occasion, witness *Richard II,* on which Shakespeare had used symbolism of this kind.) As symbol of love she must be regarded as an alien power in hell, a power which can never be at home there, its very presence boding ruin to such a realm. Nevertheless, it is by her suffering and felon's death for others' sake (she, like her prototype, was hanged) that she not only rescues her *chosen* ones from the dominion of evil, but also 'redeems nature from the *general* curse' [IV. vi. 206], just as, were she to return from hell to the world she has saved, live again and thereby reap in due course the full fruits of her victory, her resurrection—the mere chance of it—would 'redeem all sorrows that ever man has felt' [V. iii. 267-68]. If Bradley be right, it is not the chance, but the certainty that she does indeed so live which causes even Lear's hitherto indomitable heart to break, and the great sufferer dies at last, not of sorrow, but in an ecstasy of joy. (pp. 168-71)

Geoffrey L. Bickersteth, "The Golden World of 'King Lear'," in Proceedings of the British Academy, Vol. XXXII, *1946, pp. 147-71.*

EDWIN MUIR   (lecture date 1946)

[The following excerpt is taken from a lecture Muir originally delivered at the University of Glasgow in 1946. He calls Shakespeare a political writer, not in the sense of his involvement in any type of political organization, but because he was greatly concerned with the quality of human life in society. In this vein, Muir interprets King Lear *as a drama in which Shakespeare depicted the social, political, and moral evolution of his culture—an evolution which brought the decay of medieval communal society and the rise of the Renaissance concept of the individual as preeminent. Muir argues that in* Lear *Shakespeare set these opposing attitudes in conflict: the medieval order represented by Lear, Edgar, Kent, and Cordelia, and the Machiavellian individualism reflected in the characters of Edmund, Goneril, and Regan. Muir's approach is a combination of symbolic analysis and historical interpretation; for examples of more conventional historical methodology, see the excerpts by John W. Draper (1937), Theodore Spencer (1942), and George R. Kernodle (1945).]*

In what I say to-day I do not intend to touch upon the more profound aspects of *King Lear,* though I hope my argument may have some reference to them. I want to speak of the politics of the play, and these naturally must have some relation to Shakespeare's politics. That, of course, is a difficult problem, and a great deal has been written about it by critics ancient and modern, from Coleridge to the late John Palmer and Dr. Tillyard in his last two volumes. I shall not try to summarise the arguments of these writers. But one point is crucial, and has been brought up repeatedly, and I should like to say a few words about it. Briefly, it has been maintained that Shakespeare had no politics. Now this may be true in a sense, if it means that he cannot be put down either as a Conservative, or a Liberal, or a Socialist, or whatever the counterparts of these modern classifications were in his time. I shall not use these terms, or adopt Swinburne's opinion that *King Lear* is the work of Shakespeare the Socialist: Swinburne was speaking rhetorically. But a man may have political sense, and political sense of a high kind, without falling into any of these categories; for his mind, while working politically, may not think in terms of any of them. To say that Shakespeare had no politics—if one takes the statement seriously—can only mean that he had no conception of what is good in society; and to assert that would bring an immediate denial from everybody. It has been said that he was above the conflict; it would be more true to say that he was above the classification. For he had very strongly a conception of what is good in society, just as he had very strongly a sense of what is good in conduct. Professor Caroline Spurgeon demonstrates this in her analysis of the Histories; but it seems to me that the play in which it is most clearly evident is *King Lear.*

To understand the Tragedies and the Histories one has to keep in mind the historical background of Shakespeare's age. I cannot attempt to describe that background, and must indicate it in a sort of historical shorthand by enumerating a few dates. . . . *King Lear* was written round about 1605-6, six or seven years after the birth of Cromwell and forty-three before the execution of Charles I. In the interval between the first and the last of these dates the medieval world with its communal tradition was dying, and the modern individualist world was bringing itself to birth. Shakespeare lived in that violent period of transition. The old world still echoed in his ears; he was aware of the new as we are aware of the future, that is as an inchoate, semi-prophetic dream. Now it seems to me that that dream, those echoes, fill *King Lear* and help to account for the sense of vastness which it gives us, the feeling that it covers a far greater stretch of time than can be explained by the action. The extreme age of the King brings to our minds the image of a civilisation of legendary antiquity; yet that civilization is destroyed by a new generation which belongs to Shakespeare's own time, a perfectly up-to-date gang of Renaissance adventurers. The play contains, therefore, or has taken on, a significance which Shakespeare probably could not have known, and without his being aware, he wrote in it the mythical drama of the transmutation of civilisation. One is reminded of the scene in the second part of Goethe's *Faust* where the temples of the ancient world change and crumble and rise again in the towering Gothic structures of the Middle Ages.

Of the great tragedies *King Lear* is the only one in which two ideas of society are directly confronted, and the old generation and the new are set face to face, each assured of its own right to power. *Macbeth* is a drama of murder and usurpation and remorse; it changes the succession of the crown and brings guilt upon the offender, the guilt showing that the old order is still accepted, and the old laws still valid, since Macbeth feels that he has done wrong both as the killer of a man and the supplanter of a king. But Regan, Goneril and Cornwall never feel that they have done wrong, and this is because they represent a new idea; and new ideas, like everything new, bring with them their own kind of innocence. *Hamlet,* although it deals with a dynastic and therefore a political problem, is essentially a personal drama, perhaps the most personal of them all: there is no relationship in *King Lear* so intensely intimate as that of Hamlet to his mother. Lear's own relation to his daughters is most nearly so; yet Goneril and Regan are curiously equal in his estimation, indeed almost interchangeable; he is willing to accept either if she will only take his part against her sister; and as if his rage had blotted out their very names, he confounds them indistinguishably in his curses upon his daughters. . . . The almost impersonal equivalence of the two women in their father's eyes gives a cast to the play which is not to be found in any of the others, and makes us feel, indeed, that Lear is not contending with ordinary human beings but with mere forces to which any human appeal is vain, since it is not even capable of evoking a response. He, the representative of the old, is confronted with something brand new; he cannot understand it, and it does not even care to understand him.

There is something more, then, than ingratitude in the reaction of Lear's daughters, though the ingratitude, that 'marble-hearted fiend', strikes most deeply into his heart. This something more is their attitude to power, which is grounded on their attitude to life. It is this, more than the ingratitude, that estranges Lear from them. His appeals cannot reach them, but, worse still, his mind cannot understand them, no matter how hard he tries. As this attitude of his daughters violates all his ideas of the nature of things, it seems to him against nature, so that he can only cry out against them as 'unnatural hags'. 'Unnatural' is the nearest he can come to a definition of the unbridgeable distance that divides him from them; his real struggle is to annihilate that distance, but he never succeeds; in his most intimate conflict with them he never comes any closer to them. When Regan shuts him out in the storm her action is symbolical as well as practical. His daughters are inside; he is outside. They are in two different worlds.

The story of *King Lear* tells how an old man parts his kingdom between his daughters when he feels no longer able to rule. . . . His daughters, having got what they want, that is the power, and not caring much for the name or the additions, turn against him. As daughters, their act is one of filial ingratitude; as princesses and vice-regents, it is an act of 'revolt and flying off'. These two aspects of their policy are inseparable; in turning against their father they subvert the kingdom; by the same deed they commit two crimes, one private and one public.

But there is a complication. For Goneril and Regan's idea of rulership is different from their father's, and so, on the anguish caused by their ingratitude, is piled the bewilderment of one who feels he is dealing with creatures whose notions are equally incomprehensible to his heart and his mind. In the later stages of the conflict it is the tortures of his mind that become the most unbearable, since they make the nature of things incomprehensible to him, and confound his ideas in a chaos from which the only escape is madness. (pp. 33-7)

In the new conception of society, that of Goneril and Regan, nature plays an important part; the number of references to nature in the play, almost always as images of cruelty or horror, has often been commented upon. Bradley in his book on Shake-

spearean tragedy tries to make a list of the lower animals which are mentioned in the drama, a list which had afterwards to be completed by Professor Spurgeon [see excerpt above, 1935]. (p. 38)

After looking on this picture of nature, turn to the first speech of Edmund, the mouthpiece of the new generation:

> Thou, Nature, art my goddess; to thy law
> My services are bound. Wherefore should I
> Stand in the plague of custom, and permit
> The curiosity of nations to deprive me,
> For that I am some twelve or fourteen moonshines
> Lag of a brother? Why bastard? wherefore base?
> When my dimensions are as well compact,
> My mind as generous, and my shape as true,
> As honest madman's issue? . . .
>
> [I. ii. 1-9]

Goneril and Regan and Cornwall, though they do not have Edmund's imaginative intellect, worship nature in the same spirit. For it gives them the freedom they hunger for, absolves them from the plague of custom, justifies them when they reflect that their dimensions are well-compact and their shape true, as if that were all that was needed to make human a creature in human shape. They rely confidently on certain simple facts of nature: that they are young and their father old, strong while he is infirm, and that their youth and strength give them a short cut to their desires. They are so close to the state of nature that they hardly need to reflect: what they have the power to do they claim the right to do. Or rather the power and its expression in action are almost simultaneous. (pp. 39-40)

The two daughters ignore all the complexities of what to them is merely a situation, and solve it at once by an abominable truism. They are quite rational, but only on the lowest plane of reason, and they have that contempt for other ways of thinking which comes from a knowledge of their own efficiency. As they are rational, they have a good conscience, even a touch of self-righteousness; they sincerely believe their father is in the wrong and they are in the right, since they conceive they know the world as it is, and act in conformity with it, the source of all effective power. They do not see far, but they see clearly. (pp. 40-1)

The new generation may be regarded then as the embodiment of wickedness, a wickedness of that special kind which I have tried to indicate. But can it also be said that they represent a new conception of society? If we had not lived through the last twenty years, had not seen the rise of Fascism in Italy and Germany and Communism in Russia, and did not know the theory and practice by which they were upheld, we might be disposed to deny this. As it is we cannot. We know, too, that Shakespeare was acquainted with the Renaissance man, and that his plays abound in references to 'policy', which stood in his time for what the Germans dignify by the name of *Realpolitik;* that is, political action which ignores all moral considerations. (p. 42)

To regard things in this way is to see them in a continuous present divested of all associations, denuded of memory and the depth which memory gives to life. Goneril and Regan, even more than Edmund, exist in this shallow present, and it is to them a present in both senses of the word, a gift freely given into their hands to do with what they like. Having no memory, they have no responsibility, and no need, therefore, to treat their father differently from any other troublesome old man.

This may simply be another way of saying that they are evil, for it may be that evil consists in a hiatus in the soul, a craving blank, a lack of one of the essential threads which bind experience into a coherent whole and give it a consistent meaning. The hiatus in Lear's daughters is specifically a hiatus of memory, a breach in continuity; they seem to come from nowhere and to be on the way to nowhere; they have words and acts only to meet the momentary emergency, the momentary appetite; their speech is therefore strikingly deficient in imagery, and consists of a sequence of pitiless truisms. Bradley complains of the characters in the play that, 'Considered simply as psychological studies few of them are of the highest interest' [see excerpt above, 1904]. This is true of Goneril and Regan, for the human qualities of highest interest are left out of them. But that was Shakespeare's intention; he had to interest us in two characters who were both evil and shallow. Their shallowness is ultimately that of the Macchiavellian view of life as it was understood in his age, of 'policy', or *Realpolitik,* whichever we may choose to call it. The sisters are harpies, but as rulers they act in the approved contemporary Macchiavellian convention. If we . . . reflect that Macchiavellianism was a current preoccupation in Shakespeare's time, and consider further that the Renaissance gave to the individual a prominence he had not possessed since classical times, and that personal power, especially in princes, appeared sometimes to be boundless, we need not shrink from regarding Edmund and his confederates as political types. Poets of Shakespeare's time had espoused the liberated hero, the glorious individual, among them Marlowe, and Chapman with his ideal of 'royal man'. But Shakespeare did not: his political sense put him on the opposite side.

To understand his attitude to the new generation we must finally consider his identification of them with nature. Their life in the moment, their decisions based on what the mere moment presents, their permanent want of continuity, their permanent empty newness, are sufficient in themselves to involve them with nature, for nature is always new and has no background; it is society that is old. Their position may be defined by saying that they claim a liberty which is proper to nature but not to society. This is what makes them in a sense unnatural; and this is what makes it impossible for Lear with his traditional beliefs to understand them. (pp. 43-5)

Against this idea of society what had Lear to set? His conception is nowhere clearly formulated, for it is old, and it is to him the accepted conception. But in almost everything he says, whether in anger or kindness, we can feel what it is: he sets against the idea of natural freedom the sacred tradition of human society. (p. 45)

[In] Lear and his friends there exists an order of society so obviously springing from the nature and needs of man that it can also be called natural, though not in Edmund's sense. When it is subverted, the universal frame seems to be wrenched from its place, and the new chaos can be explained only as the result of a portent. (p. 46)

The tradition of society which Lear represents is difficult to reconstruct from anything that is said in the play. Its nature is implied in Lear's appeals to Regan:

> 'Tis not in thee
> To grudge my pleasures, to cut off my train,
> To bandy hasty words, to scant my sizes,
> And, in conclusion, to oppose the bolt
> Against my coming in: thou better know'st
> The offices of nature, bond of childhood,
> Effects of courtesy, dues of gratitude.
>
> [II. iv. 173-79]

It is to such things that Lear appeals when he is trying to find a way to his daughters. He appeals to a sentiment which to him means everything, but which to them means nothing: they do not even understand it. His conception of society can be guessed at again in the words which he says to his Fool out of his own grief:

> Poor fool and knave, I have one part in my heart
> That's sorry yet for thee.
>
> [III. ii. 72-3]

We can guess at it again in these words which made Swinburne write of Shakespeare the Socialist:

> Poor naked wretches, whereso'er you are,
> That bide the pelting of the pitiless storm,
> How shall your houseless heads and unfed sides,
> Your loop'd and window'd raggedness, defend you
> From seasons such as these? O! I have ta'en
> Too little care of this. Take physic, pomp;
> Expose thyself to feel what wretches feel,
> That thou mayst shake the superflux to them,
> And show the heavens more just.
>
> [III. iv. 28-36]

The difference between that and . . .

> Go thrust him out at gates, and let him smell
> His way to Dover,
>
> [III. vii. 93-4]

is the difference between the two worlds described in the play. Lear is an imperfect king; he has taken too little care for his subjects; but he admits the obligation; and the social realities on which he relies, and to which he appeals as if they were self-evident, are purely human, not realistic in the modern sense:

> The offices of nature, bond of childhood,
> Effects of courtesy, dues of gratitude.

If we discern a conception of society behind such fragmentary utterances, and behind Lear himself, it appears to us a society bound together not by force and appetite, but by a sort of piety and human fitness, a natural piety, one would feel inclined to say, if the word were not used in the play as inimical to society.

Lear is very old, almost Saturnian in his legendary age; the kingdom in him exists as a memory and no longer as a fact; the old order lies in ruin, and the new is not an order. The communal tradition, filled with memory, has been smashed by an individualism that exists in its perpetual shallow present. The judgment on the new generation is passed by a member of it who does not belong spiritually to it: Edgar. It is remarkable that in the scenes where Lear, the Fool and Edgar are together, it is Edgar, the only sane man, who conjures up the deepest images of horror. For he is of the new generation, and knows it as Lear cannot. When Lear asks him who he is, he replies by giving a portrait of his brother Edmund. . . . [It] is a picture of an animal with human faculties, made corrupt and legendary by the proudly curled hair. It is a picture, too, of the man of policy in the latest style, who regards the sacred order of society as his prey, and recognises only two realities, interest and force, the gods of the new age. (pp. 47-9)

Edwin Muir, "The Politics of 'King Lear'," in his Essays on Literature and Society, *revised edition, Cambridge, Mass.: Harvard University Press, 1965, pp. 33-49.*

GEORGE ORWELL (essay date 1947)

[*Orwell was an English novelist and essayist who has been consistently praised for his unwavering commitment, both as a man and an artist, to personal freedom and social justice. His unpretentious self-examination and his ability to perceive the social effects of political ideologies inspired Irving Howe to call him "the greatest moral force in English letters during the last several decades." Orwell's prose style, especially that of his essays, has become a model for its precision, clarity, and vividness. Many of his essays, which combine observation and reminiscence with literary and social criticism, are considered modern masterpieces. In the following excerpt, first published in the journal* Polemic *in March, 1947, Orwell responds directly to Leo Tolstoy's famous essay on* King Lear, *in which the Russian severely criticizes the play as inane, improbable, filled with anachronisms, and inferior to the old chronicle play* King Leir *(see excerpt above, 1906). Orwell regards Tolstoy's interpretation of the play as subjective and injudicious and, in fact, as demonstrative of certain unconscious feelings towards* King Lear *related to Tolstoy's failure to achieve happiness at the end of his life. Orwell maintains that it is likely that specific elements in Shakespeare's drama, particularly Lear's act of renunciation, his misguided attempts at achieving peace through a false sense of selflessness, and his ill-treatment by others, reflected incidents in Tolstoy's later life and unconsciously perverted his reading of the play and warped his appreciation.*]

Properly speaking one cannot *answer* Tolstoy's attack [on *King Lear*]. The interesting question is: why did he make it? But it should be noticed in passing that he uses many weak or dishonest arguments. Some of these are worth pointing out, not because they invalidate his main charge but because they are, so to speak, evidence of malice.

To begin with, his examination of *King Lear* is not "impartial", as he twice claims. On the contrary, it is a prolonged exercise in misrepresentation. It is obvious that when you are summarising *King Lear* for the benefit of someone who has not read it, you are not really being impartial if you introduce an important speech (Lear's speech when Cordelia is dead in his arms) in this manner: "Again begin Lear's awful ravings, at which one feels ashamed, as at unsuccessful jokes." And in a long series of instances Tolstoy slightly alters or colours the passages he is criticising, always in such a way as to make the plot appear a little more complicated and improbable, or the language a little more exaggerated. . . . None of these misreadings is very gross in itself, but their cumulative effect is to exaggerate the psychological incoherence of the play. Again, Tolstoy is not able to explain why Shakespeare's plays were still in print, and still on the stage, two hundred years after his death . . . ; and his whole account of Shakespeare's rise to fame is guesswork punctuated by outright mis-statements. And again, various of his accusations contradict one another: for example, Shakespeare is a mere entertainer and "not in earnest", but on the other hand he is constantly putting his own thoughts into the mouths of his characters. On the whole it is difficult to feel that Tolstoy's criticisms are uttered in good faith. In any case it is impossible that he should fully have believed in his main thesis—believed, that is to say, that for a century or more the entire civilised world had been taken in by a huge and palpable lie which he alone was able to see through. Certainly his dislike of Shakespeare is real enough, but the reasons for it may be different, or partly different, from what he avows; and therein lies the interest of his pamphlet.

At this point one is obliged to start guessing. However, there is one possible clue, or at least there is a question which may point the way to a clue. It is: why did Tolstoy, with thirty or more plays to choose from, pick out *King Lear* as his especial target? True, *Lear* is so well known and has been so much praised that it could justly be taken as representative of Shakespeare's best work: still, for the purpose of a hostile analysis Tolstoy would probably choose the play he disliked most. Is it not possible that he bore an especial enmity towards this particular play because he was aware, consciously or unconsciously, of the resemblance between Lear's story and his own? But it is better to approach this clue from the opposite direction—that is, by examining *Lear* itself, and the qualities in it that Tolstoy fails to mention.

One of the first things an English reader would notice in Tolstoy's pamphlet is that it hardly deals with Shakespeare as a poet. Shakespeare is treated as a dramatist, and in so far as his popularity is not spurious, it is held to be due to tricks of stagecraft which give good opportunities to clever actors. Now, so far as the English-speaking countries go, this is not true. . . . Those who care most for Shakespeare value him in the first place for his use of language, the "verbal music" which even Bernard Shaw, another hostile critic, admits to be "irresistible". Tolstoy ignores this, and does not seem to realise that a poem may have a special value for those who speak the language in which it was written. However, even if one puts oneself in Tolstoy's place and tries to think of Shakespeare as a foreign poet it is still clear that there is something that Tolstoy has left out. Poetry, it seems, is *not* solely a matter of sound and association, and valueless outside its own language-group: otherwise, how is it that some poems, including poems written in dead languages, succeed in crossing frontiers? Clearly a lyric like "Tomorrow is Saint Valentine's Day" could not be satisfactorily translated, but in Shakespeare's major work there is something describable as poetry that can be separated from the words. Tolstoy is right in saying that *Lear* is not a very good play, as a play. It is too drawn out and has too many characters and sub-plots. One wicked daughter would have been quite enough, and Edgar is a superfluous character: indeed it would probably be a better play if Gloucester and both his sons were eliminated. Nevertheless, something, a kind of pattern, or perhaps only an atmosphere, survives the complications and the *longueurs*. *Lear* can be imagined as a puppet show, a mime, a ballet, a series of pictures. Part of its poetry, perhaps the most essential part, is inherent in the story and is dependent neither on any particular set of words, nor on flesh-and-blood presentation.

Shut your eyes and think of *King Lear*, if possible without calling to mind any of the dialogue. What do you see? Here at any rate is what I see: a majestic old man in a long black robe, with flowing white hair and beard, a figure out of Blake's drawings (but also, curiously enough, rather like Tolstoy), wandering through a storm and cursing the heavens, in company with a Fool and a lunatic. Presently the scene shifts, and the old man, still cursing, still understanding nothing, is holding a dead girl in his arms while the Fool dangles on a gallows somewhere in the background. This is the bare skeleton of the play, and even here Tolstoy wants to cut out most of what is essential. He objects to the storm, as being unnecessary, to the Fool, who in his eyes is simply a tedious nuisance and an excuse for making bad jokes, and to the death of Cordelia, which, as he sees it, robs the play of its moral. . . . In other words the tragedy ought to have been a comedy, or perhaps a melodrama. It is doubtful whether the sense of tragedy is compatible with belief in God: at any rate, it is not compatible with disbelief in human dignity and with the kind of "moral demand" which feels cheated when virtue fails to triumph. A tragic situation exists precisely when virtue does *not* triumph but when it is still felt that man is nobler than the forces which destroy him. It is perhaps more significant that Tolstoy sees no justification for the presence of the Fool. The Fool is integral to the play. He acts not only as a sort of chorus, making the central situation clearer by commenting on it more intelligently than the other characters, but as a foil to Lear's frenzies. His jokes, riddles and scraps of rhyme, and his endless digs at Lear's high-minded folly, ranging from mere derision to a sort of melancholy poetry . . . , are like a trickle of sanity running through the play, a reminder that somewhere or other, in spite of the injustices, cruelties, intrigues, deceptions and misunderstandings that are being enacted here, life is going on much as usual. In Tolstoy's impatience with the Fool one gets a glimpse of his deeper quarrel with Shakespeare. He objects, with some justification, to the raggedness of Shakespeare's plays, the irrelevancies, the incredible plots, the exaggerated language: but what at bottom he probably most dislikes is a sort of exuberance, a tendency to take—not so much a pleasure, as simply an interest in the actual process of life. It is a mistake to write Tolstoy off as a moralist attacking an artist. He never said that art, as such, is wicked or meaningless, nor did he even say that technical virtuosity is unimportant. But his main aim, in his later years, was to narrow the range of human consciousness. One's interests, one's points of attachment to the physical world and the day-to-day struggle, must be as few and not as many as possible. Literature must consist of parables, stripped of detail and almost independent of language. The parables—this is where Tolstoy differs from the average vulgar puritan—must themselves be works of art, but pleasure and curiosity must be excluded from them. . . . Clearly [Tolstoy] could have no patience with a chaotic, detailed, discursive writer like Shakespeare. His reaction is that of an irritable old man who is being pestered by a noisy child. ''Why do you keep jumping up and down like that? Why can't you sit still like I do?'' In a way the old man is in the right, but the trouble is that the child has a feeling in its limbs which the old man has lost. And if the old man knows of the existence of this feeling, the effect is merely to increase his irritation: he would make children senile, if he could. Tolstoy does not know, perhaps, just *what* he misses in Shakespeare, but he is aware that he misses something, and he is determined that others shall be deprived of it as well. (pp. 290-94)

However, Tolstoy is not simply trying to rob others of a pleasure he does not share. He is doing that, but his quarrel with Shakespeare goes further. It is the quarrel between the religious and the humanist attitudes towards life. Here one comes back to the central theme of *King Lear,* which Tolstoy does not mention, although he sets forth the plot in some detail.

Lear is one of the minority of Shakespeare's plays that are unmistakably *about* something. As Tolstoy justly complains, much rubbish has been written about Shakespeare as a philosopher, as a psychologist, as a ''great moral teacher'', and what not. Shakespeare was not a systematic thinker, his most serious thoughts are uttered irrelevantly or indirectly, and we do not know to what extent he wrote with a ''purpose'' or even how much of the work attributed to him was actually written by him. . . . It is perfectly possible that he looked on at least half of his plays as mere pot-boilers and hardly bothered about purpose or probability so long as he could patch up something, usually from stolen material, which would more or less hang together on the stage. However, that is not the whole story. To begin with, as Tolstoy himself points out, Shakespeare has a habit of thrusting uncalled-for general reflections into the

mouths of his characters. This is a serious fault in a dramatist but it does not fit in with Tolstoy's picture of Shakespeare as a vulgar hack who has no opinions of his own and merely wishes to produce the greatest effect with the least trouble. And more than this, about a dozen of his plays, written for the most part later than 1600, do unquestionably have a meaning and even a moral. They revolve around a central subject which in some cases can be reduced to a single word. For example, *Macbeth* is about ambition, *Othello* is about jealousy, and *Timon of Athens* is about money. The subject of *Lear* is renunciation, and it is only by being wilfully blind that one can fail to understand what Shakespeare is saying.

Lear renounces his throne but expects everyone to continue treating him as a king. He does not see that if he surrenders power, other people will take advantage of his weakness: also that those who flatter him the most grossly, i.e. Regan and Goneril, are exactly the ones who will turn against him. The moment he finds that he can no longer make people obey him as he did before, he falls into a rage which Tolstoy describes as ''strange and unnatural'', but which in fact is perfectly in character. In his madness and despair, he passes through two moods which again are natural enough in his circumstances, though in one of them it is probable that he is being used partly as a mouthpiece for Shakespeare's own opinions. One is the mood of disgust in which Lear repents, as it were, for having been a king, and grasps for the first time the rottenness of formal justice and vulgar morality. The other is a mood of impotent fury in which he wreaks imaginary revenges upon those who have wronged him. . . . Only at the end does he realise, as a sane man, that power, revenge, and victory are not worth while. . . . But by the time he makes this discovery it is too late, for his death and Cordelia's are already decided on. That is the story, and, allowing for some clumsiness in the telling, it is a very good story.

But is it not also curiously similar to the history of Tolstoy himself? There is a general resemblance which one can hardly avoid seeing, because the most impressive event in Tolstoy's life, as in Lear's, was a huge and gratuitous act of renunciation. In his old age he renounced his estate, his title and his copyrights, and made an attempt—a sincere attempt, though it was not successful—to escape from his privileged position and live the life of a peasant. But the deeper resemblance lies in the fact that Tolstoy, like Lear, acted on mistaken motives and failed to get the results he had hoped for. According to Tolstoy, the aim of every human being is happiness, and happiness can only be attained by doing the will of God. But doing the will of God means casting off all earthly pleasures and ambitions, and living only for others. Ultimately, therefore, Tolstoy renounced the world under the expectation that this would make him happier. But if there is one thing certain about his later years, it is that he was *not* happy. On the contrary, he was driven almost to the edge of madness by the behaviour of the people about him, who persecuted him precisely *because* of his renunciation. Like Lear, Tolstoy was not humble and not a good judge of character. He was inclined at moments to revert to the attitudes of an aristocrat, in spite of his peasant's blouse, and he even had two children whom he had believed in and who ultimately turned against him—though, of course, in a less sensational manner than Regan and Goneril. His exaggerated revulsion from sexuality was also distinctly similar to Lear's. . . . And though Tolstoy could not foresee it when he wrote his essay on Shakespeare, even the ending of his life—the sudden unplanned flight across country, accompanied only by a faithful daughter, the death in a cottage in a strange village—seems to have in it a sort of phantom reminiscence of *Lear*.

Of course, one cannot assume that Tolstoy was aware of this resemblance, or would have admitted it if it had been pointed out him. But his attitude towards the play must have been influenced by its theme. Renouncing power, giving away your lands, was a subject on which he had reason to feel deeply. Probably, therefore, he would be more angered and disturbed by the moral that Shakespeare draws than he would be in the case of some other play—*Macbeth,* for example—which did not touch so closely on his own life. But what exactly *is* the moral of *Lear*? Evidently there are two morals, one explicit, the other implied in the story.

Shakespeare starts by assuming that to make yourself powerless is to invite an attack. This does not mean that *everyone* will turn against you (Kent and the Fool stand by Lear from first to last), but in all probability *someone* will. If you throw away your weapons, some less scrupulous person will pick them up. If you turn the other cheek, you will get a harder blow on it than you got on the first one. This does not always happen, but it is to be expected, and you ought not to complain if it does happen. The second blow is, so to speak, part of the act of turning the other cheek. First of all, therefore, there is the vulgar, common-sense moral drawn by the Fool: "Don't relinquish power, don't give away your lands." But there is also another moral. Shakespeare never utters it in so many words, and it does not very much matter whether he was fully aware of it. It is contained in the story, which, after all, he made up, or altered to suit his purposes. It is: "Give away your lands if you want to, but don't expect to gain happiness by doing so. Probably you won't gain happiness. If you live for others, you must live *for others,* and not as a roundabout way of getting an advantage for yourself."

Obviously neither of these conclusions could have been pleasing to Tolstoy. The first of them expresses the ordinary, belly-to-earth selfishness from which he was genuinely trying to escape. The other conflicts with his desire to eat his cake and have it—that is, to destroy his own egoism and by so doing to gain eternal life. Of course, *Lear* is not a sermon in favour of altruism. It merely points out the results of practising self-denial for selfish reasons. Shakespeare had a considerable streak of worldliness in him, and if he had been forced to take sides in his own play, his sympathies would probably have lain with the Fool. But at least he could see the whole issue and treat it at the level of tragedy. Vice is punished, but virtue is not rewarded. The morality of Shakespeare's later tragedies is not religious in the ordinary sense, and certainly is not Christian. Only two of them, *Hamlet* and *Othello,* are supposedly occurring inside the Christian era, and even in those, apart from the antics of the ghost in *Hamlet,* there is no indication of a "next world" where everything is to be put right. All of these tragedies start out with the humanist assumption that life, although full of sorrow, is worth living, and that Man is a noble animal—a belief which Tolstoy in his old age did not share. (pp. 295-98)

If we are to believe what he says in his pamphlet, Tolstoy had never been able to see any merit in Shakespeare, and was always astonished to find that his fellow writers, Turgenev, Fet and others, thought differently. We may be sure that in his unregenerate days Tolstoy's conclusion would have been: "You like Shakespeare—I don't. Let's leave it at that." Later, when his perception that it takes all sorts to make a world had deserted him, he came to think of Shakespeare's writings as something

dangerous to himself. The more pleasure people took in Shakespeare, the less they would listen to Tolstoy. Therefore nobody must be *allowed* to enjoy Shakespeare, just as nobody must be allowed to drink alcohol or smoke tobacco. True, Tolstoy would not prevent them by force. He is not demanding that the police shall impound every copy of Shakespeare's works. But he will do dirt on Shakespeare, if he can. He will try to get inside the mind of every lover of Shakespeare and kill his enjoyment by every trick he can think of, including . . . arguments which are self-contradictory or even doubtfully honest.

But finally the most striking thing is how little difference it all makes. As I said earlier, one cannot *answer* Tolstoy's pamphlet, at least on its main counts. There is no argument by which one can defend a poem. It defends itself by surviving, or it is indefensible. And if this test is valid, I think the verdict in Shakespeare's case must be "not guilty". Like every other writer, Shakespeare will be forgotten sooner or later, but it is unlikely that a heavier indictment will ever be brought against him. Tolstoy was perhaps the most admired literary man of his age, and he was certainly not its least able pamphleteer. He turned all his powers of denunciation against Shakespeare, like all the guns of a battleship roaring simultaneously. And with what result? Forty years later, Shakespeare is still there, completely unaffected, and of the attempt to demolish him nothing remains except the yellowing pages of a pamphlet which hardly anyone has read, and which would be forgotten altogether if Tolstoy had not also been the author of *War and Peace* and *Anna Karenina.* (p. 302)

           George Orwell, "Lear, Tolstoy and the Fool," in his The Collected Essays, Journalism and Letters of George Orwell: In Front of Your Nose, 1945-1950, *Vol. IV, edited by Sonia Orwell and Ian Angus, Harcourt Brace Jovanovich, Inc., 1968, pp. 287-302.**

OSCAR JAMES CAMPBELL   (lecture date 1948)

[*An American scholar and critic, Campbell is best known for his* Comicall Satyre and Shakespeare's "Troilus and Cressida" *(1938), an influential study in which he argues that in* Troilus and Cressida *Shakespeare was imitating a new genre invented by Ben Jonson. In his next book,* Shakespeare's Satire *(1943), Campbell continued his emphasis on the satiric elements in Shakespeare's plays and established himself as an innovative interpreter of Elizabethan drama, particularly his characterization of* Timon of Athens *as a tragic satire, rather than a tragedy. Campbell was also the editor of* The Living Shakespeare, *an edition of twenty-one of Shakespeare's most popular plays, and* The Reader's Encyclopedia of Shakespeare, *an indispensable guide to features of the poet's life and work. In the following excerpt, taken from his Annual Tudor and Steward Club lecture given April 30, 1948, Campbell interprets the structure of* King Lear *as based on a combination of the medieval morality play and the precepts of stoic morality—two religious traditions, one Christian, the other pagan, that informed the work of Elizabethan and Jacobean dramatists. Campbell sees the transformation of Lear from an "unwise man," in stoic terms, in his lack of reason, his desire to unburden himself of the cares of government, and his zealous attachment to worldly possessions and titles, into an "unaccommodated" man willing to sacrifice and even suffer for the sake of selfless love. Thus, Campbell's essay is a mixture of the Christian interpretations of R. W. Chambers (1939) and Geoffrey L. Bickersteth (1946) and the later emphasis on the play's stoic morality by such critics as D. G. James (1951) and John Holloway (1961). Campbell's focus on the importance of love in the play is also apparent in the essays by Hermann Ulrici (1839), Edward*

Dowden (1881), Arthur Sewell (1951), Irving Ribner (1958), L. C. Knights (1959), and Robert Ornstein (1960).]

The *Tragedy of King Lear* moves to its catastrophe on a higher plane than any other of Shakespeare's great tragedies. Most critics of the play have sensed its wider moral range and its greater sublimity. And in their efforts to apprehend what has been called the "metaphysical meaning" of the action and to convey its essence to their readers, they have lavishly expended all the resources of their vocabularies. Yet they have succeeded only in invoking a sense of grandeur both for the unlocalized space which serves as the stage for Lear's woes and for the nature of his conflicts. Their utterances have been oracular rather than precise. . . .

The romantic critics were content to express their wonder at the sense of infinitude which the play inspired. Lamb's verdict that "The Lear of Shakespeare cannot be acted" is familiar to everyone [see excerpt above, 1812]. . . . Schlegel, for his part, finds that the action of the play represents "a great insurrection in the moral world . . . and that the horror it awakens is akin to that which would be felt were the heavenly bodies to rush away from their appointed course" [see excerpt above, 1808]. Gervinus is less cosmic but hardly more precise when he writes "while other tragedies treat of single passions, this tragedy deals with passion in general" [see excerpt above, 1849-50]. (p. 93)

More recent critics have employed their own far-sought terms to express the conviction that Shakespeare designed *King Lear* to be a tragedy of universal significance. But in their attempts to explain the cosmic symbolism of the play most of them are as vague as the romanticists. Many modern commentators are convinced that Shakespeare in this tragedy depicts evil as a monstrous daemonic force. Once caught in its iron grip, so Shakespeare seems to say, man is as pitiful and helpless a creature as is Lear in the grip of the terrible storm on the heath. But if the drama were only an expression of blind and tragic fatalism, it could not produce the sense of sublimity that all thoughtful readers of the play feel. It must possess a more positive moral or religious significance than this.

For *King Lear* is, in my opinion, a sublime morality play, the action of which is set against a back-drop of eternity. Lear's problem and his career resemble those of the central figure in the typical morality play, who is variously called Genus Humanum, Mankind or Everyman. And the action of Shakespeare's play is his greatly modified version of man's endless search for true and everlasting spiritual values, rewarded, in this case, by the final discovery of them just before he must answer Death's awful summons. *The Tragedy of King Lear* differs however from the usual Morality first, in being cast in a much deeper tragic mould and second, in presenting the salvation of Mankind not in orthodox theological terms nor even in strictly Christian terms. For Lear is not so much an erring Christian as a completely unstoical man and he is converted to a state of mind which is a mixture of Stoic insight and Christian humility. Furthermore the methods by which his conversion and redemption are accomplished are similar to those advocated by the great stoic philosophers. (p. 94)

This is not the place to review even the major tenets of later stoicism. It is sufficient to mention one or two of its controlling ideas which will appear in our study of Lear. The Stoics believed

1. That there are only two kinds of men, the completely wise and good and the completely unwise and bad.

2. That no outward calamity is a misfortune, but a divine instrument for the development and training of a man in virtue.

3. That the good man gives Reason his undivided devotion and rejects passion and even emotion as a disease of the intellect.

4. That the good life must be sought in the soul (the God within) where it can be untouched by those vicissitudes of Fortune which are beyond human control.

5. That the good man must therefore (a) resign himself to the will of the Universe, (b) treat his fellow men with forebearance and humility, and (c) willingly accept his Destiny.

These main tenets of stoicism, well known in Elizabethan and Jacobean England, seem to have appealed with peculiar force to some of the dramatists. . . . Shakespeare revealed his interest in the stern moral system as early as 1599, the year in which he wrote *Julius Caesar*. For Brutus' career is a history of the mistakes in which his rigid application of stoical principles involve him. (p. 95)

It is not surprising then that Shakespeare in his version of the Summoning of Everyman should have put a stoical unwise or bad man in the place of the Christian sinner, particularly when we remember that Shakespeare definitely sets his play in pre-Christian times and that stoicism was probably the only pagan philosophy with which he was familiar. In fusing these two alien elements, one a product of mediaeval piety the other a Renaissance recovery of a classical philosophy, Shakespeare was illustrating what some modern critics believe to be the distinguishing feature of baroque art. (p. 96)

When we first see Lear, he is the typical unwise man, for he has disobeyed all the Stoic's rules for right conduct. He values his kingship not for the responsibilities it places upon him but for the possessions and outward shows which attend it. Indeed he has run so directly counter to the injunction to detach himself from the things of this world that he has come to value even love only as it can serve his vanity.

Moreover he is the complete slave of the most violent and uncontrollable of his passions—anger. In his unbridled anger he is as far as may be from the stoic ideal of "Keeping an unruffled temper, an unchanging mien and the same cast of countenance in every condition of life." . . . Reason, being identical with Nature and the will of God, was the one safe guide to every sort of human action, and Lear's conduct during the first two acts of the play insults reason in every respect. In particular all his actions run directly counter to the Stoic's advice to old men. "There is nothing," writes Cicero, "against which old age should be more carefully on guard than surrendering to listlessness and violence." . . . In his very first speech Lear announces his intention of ignoring this article of the stoic faith:

> Know we have divided
> In three our kingdom; and 'tis our fast intent
> To shake all cares and business from our age,
> Conferring them on younger strengths, while we
> Unburden'd, crawl toward death.
>
> [I. i. 37-41]

The division of his territory among his daughters is but an inevitable consequence of his decision to ignore one of the most solemn of stoic injunctions.

Lear's actions in the first scene of the play thus show him to be so completely the slave of his uncontrolled emotions that he can neither follow the guidance of reason nor subordinate his impulses to the demands of moral obligation. His two elder daughters realize that their father's craving for flattery has drowned his reason and so they truckle to his senile vanity. But Cordelia, oblivious of the turbulent state of her father's mind, directs her reply to his buried reason and so unleashes only a torrent of anger. The terrifying burst of wrath erases from his mind every trace of justice, of judgment and of wisdom. He throws to the winds his carefully planned scheme for turning his abdication into a pageant of adulation. Even low cunning must yield to anger. Thus does Lear illustrate the folly and wickedness of a truant from stoicism. (pp. 100-01)

All of the clashes with his unfilial daughters which follow his abdication are further exhibitions of unstoical conduct. His wrath explodes at their every attempt to strip him of the hundred knights who form his body guard. Intemperate insistence on retaining these symbols of luxury and pride is a combination of impulses which the stoics stigmatized as evil. . . . Frustrated in his efforts to retain these things which the Stoics despised, he violently turns from the satisfaction of these condemned appetites and begins his frantic search for the truth that will free him from his slavery to passion. Thereafter he shows his abhorrence of passion by the violence of his anathemas against lust, one of the impulses which most surely degrades man because it most completely submerges reason.

On his pilgrimage he is accompanied by two companions, and commentators, both of whom are creatures of Cynic-Stoic primitivism introduced into Elizabethan literature by way of Roman satire. These two are Kent, the Stoic plain man, and the Fool, or the wise innocent—each a child of Nature. . . . Kent's plain speaking, an expression of his devotion to his Master, ironically has the effect of increasing rather than allaying Lear's passions. The fool's strange mixture of irrelevance and wisdom is similarly ironical. His efforts to outjest his master's woes only increase their poignancy, for he keeps Lear reminded of his folly in surrendering the rule of his kingdom to his wicked daughters. . . . (pp. 102-03)

In a situation turned topsy turvy by unleashed passions, plain speaking in the Cynic-Stoic manner is utterly ineffectual. It only intensifies Lear's mental turmoil. Here, as elsewhere in the play, Shakespeare insists that the stoic way to salvation from turbulent and unworthy emotion is psychologically unsound—that passion cannot be conquered by force of Reason, but only by the substitution for the destructive emotion of a stronger and nobler passion. In other words, erring man can be freed from attachment to the ephemeral treacherous values of this world only by utter devotion to the eternal blessings of the spirit.

When Shakespeare sends Lear accompanied by Kent and the Fool out upon the barren heath to be tormented by the storm blown from Eternity, he enormously extends the canvas of the Morality play. Lear's endurance of such terrible suffering as the storm brings him is an essential part of both the Christian and the stoical scheme for salvation. The stoic believed that adversity purifies, that outward calamity is a divine instrument for teaching the wise man to be indifferent to external conditions, so that he may confine his efforts to exercising the powers of his soul. This is not unlike the Christian doctrine that sinful man is made fit for Heaven by passing through the torments of purgatory. However, even though it be difficult to establish a precise difference between the two forms of salvation, largely because the Roman stoics endowed the severe principles of Stoicism with an emotion akin to religious conviction, still Lear's purgatorial experiences result in a form of salvation

more Christian than Stoical. Earlier in the play Lear had appealed to Nature as his "dear goddess." It is natural then that he should flee to her for comfort when human aid failed him.

The chaotic Nature to which Lear flees is, like him, utterly unlike that predicated by the stoics. Far from being an expression of cosmic harmony established and controlled by reason, it is a revelation of universal discord. That is, the storm on the heath corresponds to the chaos in Lear's nature, in that at this moment both the microcosm and the macrocosm are utterly beyond the control of reason. They have both become expressions of disruptive energy. In no corner of such a chaos of natural forces can the poor old wanderer of the dark find peace, security or moral value. Driven to insane rage by the failure of his quest, Lear enacts a mad version of stoical reformation. If it be true, as the philosophers say, that all external possessions smother the spirit, he will follow their teaching to its bitter end by casting away the last remnants of such superfluities—the clothes that cover his nakedness. By tearing them off perhaps he may be able to discover what place in her realm Nature can offer to pure unaccommodated man. (pp. 103-04)

In the course of this mad experiment, Lear meets Gloucester's good son Edgar who is now disguised as Tom, a bedlam beggar, that is, a poor harmless insane fellow who has been allowed to beg on the roads in order to collect money to pay for his keep in the mad house. Lear asks this grotesque creature, "What is your study." Edgar's answer is, "How to prevent the fiend and kill the vermin" [III. iv. 158-59], a reply which means, as Joseph Wood Krutch once pointed out, how to attain comfort of body and peace of mind. Yet in the situation in which he finds himself, neither he nor Lear can attain either blessing. The rain continues to drench them both and the wind to lash them. "'Tom's acold" and Lear's wits are crazed. Nature proves to be no kind fostering mother to unaccommodated man, but a relentless enemy. Lear's frantic search cannot end on the heath. To the will of the natural universe thus revealed Lear cannot resign himself. These scenes show that the pessimism of seventeenth-century England has superseded traditional stoic pessimism in Shakespeare's conception of the human situation. (p. 105)

Yet the suffering Lear is now enduring begins to show itself as purgatorial. It forces him to realize his own humanity and awakens the philanthropic disposition which was the attitude the stoics cultivated toward their fellow men. Lear expresses his conversion to this ethical position in very famous lines:

> Poor naked wretches, whereso'er you are,
> That bide the pelting of this pitiless storm,
> How shall your houseless heads and unfed sides,
> Your loop'd and window'd raggedness, defend you
> From seasons such as these? O, I have ta'en
> Too little care of this! Take physic, pomp;
> Expose thyself to feel what wretches feel,
> That thou mayst shake the superflux to them
> And show the heavens more just.
>
> [III. iv. 28-36]

A. C. Bradley says that these lines mark the redemption of Lear [see excerpt above, 1904]. But they report only his first hesitant step in that direction, for the old man's moment of humility is fleeting; it has no immediate effect upon his conduct or upon his madness.

The real redemption of Lear comes when he awakens from the delusions of his frenzied mind to discover Cordelia and her unselfish enduring love. The mere sight of her kills "the great rage" in him, the unstoical emotional turmoil from which all his sins and sufferings have sprung. Now he is calmly receptive to the healing power of Christian love. For he has not arrived at utter indifference to external events, at that complete freedom from emotion, the disease of the intellect, which produces true stoic content. On the contrary Lear finds his peace in an active emotion—in all absorbing love. That it is which at last renders him independent of circumstance. Even shut within the narrow walls of a prison, he can now find utter peace and happiness if only Cordelia and her love be with him there. . . . In the first scene of the play he showed himself so exclusively devoted to the external shows of his position that he had come to value even love only in so far as it augmented his earthly glory. But his passage through purgatory has made him realize that beside love all the baser uses of this world seem utterly unprofitable. (pp. 105-07)

If Lear's reunion with Cordelia brings about his salvation, one may well ask why Shakespeare snatches her so suddenly from him? And why does he put Lear to death so soon? The answers to the two questions are closely related. It is not what the earthly creature Cordelia *is,* but what she *represents* that is important for the meaning of the play. It is her spirit not her bodily presence that redeems her father. . . . [She] is hanged, as Christ was crucified, so that mankind might be saved.

For since this is a sublime morality play its action prepares Lear not for a life of stoic tranquility on this earth, but for the heavenly joy of a redeemed soul. The meaning of Cordelia's execution comes to Lear slowly and painfully. At first he is filled with despair at losing her:

> Thou'lt come no more
> Never, never, never, never, never.
>
>   [V. iii. 308-09]

But suddenly he makes the blessed discovery that Cordelia is not dead after all, that the breath of life still trembles on her lips:

> Do you see this? Look on her, look, her lips,
> Look there! look there!
>
>   [V. iii. 311-12]

In the joy of this discovery the old man's heart breaks in a spasm of ecstasy. For only to earthbound intelligence is Lear pathetically deceived in thinking poor Cordelia alive. Those familiar with the pattern of the morality play realize that Lear has discovered in her unselfish God-like love the one companion who is willing to go with him through Death up to the throne of the Everlasting Judge. This knowledge enables Lear to meet Death in a state of rapture. (p. 107)

Even if the basic form of *King Lear* be that of a morality play upon which has been grafted a view of the unwise man of stoic morality, we must not expect to find in the drama either the stiff schematism or the obvious ethical teaching of the naive morality play. The bare outlines of the dramatic type have been overlaid and often obscured by the fullness of the plot and the intricacies of the relationship between the characters. The personifications of the mediaeval play have grown into human beings as complicated and unpredictable as men and women usually are. Finally, the simple stage on which the morality was set suggested a high road between two villages, while Shakespeare's poetic imagination persuades us that the action of *King Lear* takes place on a vast darkling plain, swept by trade-winds from eternity. (pp. 108-09)

It must not be thought strange that in the year 1606 Shakespeare wrote a play which was a grandiose development of a mediaeval model. Jacobean drama is swollen by the resurgence of mediaeval concepts. After the turn of the century attitudes prevalent in the later middle ages took newly intense and newly imposing forms of expression. . . . In this context we can see that Shakespeare's grandiose version of Mankind's pilgrimage marked his participation in a well defined Jacobean movement in tragedy. Most of his fellow dramatists who constructed tragedies through a romantic heightening of mediaeval concepts produced effects of turgidity and morbidity, but Shakespeare, stretching a mediaeval pattern almost to the breaking point, produced a sense of utter sublimity. The superior reach of his imagination and the deeper poignancy of his emotion makes of Lear's agonized journey towards death the most sublime of all Renaissance transformations of simple mediaeval art forms. (p. 109)

> *Oscar James Campbell, "The Salvation of Lear,"*
> *in ELH, Vol. 15, No. 2, June, 1948, pp. 93-109.*

ROBERT BECHTOLD HEILMAN   (essay date 1948)

[*The following excerpt is taken from Heilman's* This Great Stage: Image and Structure in "King Lear," *the first book-length study devoted to an image analysis of Shakespeare's play. Heilman's thesis is that* King Lear *is made up of a series of "image patterns" or clusters which interact with and inform each other and which, together, define the structure of the drama. Each chapter in Heilman's study consists of an in-depth examination of each of these image patterns, including the patterns of sight, clothes, justice, value, nature, and madness, the last of which, Heilman argues, unifies all the others in its concern with the ways in which humanity interprets the world. In the excerpt below, Heilman focuses on the "fool pattern" as a subsidiary cluster of images of the madness pattern, and demonstrates the major paradox Shakespeare developed in* King Lear. *He claims that Shakespeare actually inverts the expectations of the practical world by making the so-called "fools" of the play—Lear, the Fool, Kent, Cordelia, and Edgar, in other words, all of those figures who renounce the world of rational, self-serving thought for the spiritual world of the imagination—the sympathetic, wise characters, while he presents the apparently rational, worldly wise Goneril, Regan, and Edmund as the real "fools" in their lack of humanity, imagination, and right-mindedness. This contradiction of terms has also been discussed by Enid Welsford (1935). In light of this pattern of folly and wisdom, Heilman sees the spiritual salvation of Lear in his descent into madness—a state of experience that frees his imagination from the bonds of reason in order to confront the realities of the world, such as the suffering of humanity, the evil often hidden behind false appearances, and the moral corruption of worldly possessions and pride. Lear's progress, his spiritual rejuvenation, according to Heilman, starts in the first scene with his disruption of the social world and his grand mistake of renouncing his imaginative faculties and attempting to control reality through rational thought; it ends with the unleashing of his imagination in madness and his final union with Cordelia. Heilman's study has been praised as a valuable illustration of the verbal complexity that contributes to the style and effectiveness of* King Lear, *but it has also been criticized, most notably by M. R. Keast (see Additional Bibliography), as misleading and subject to Heilman's own ethical and religious values rather than those in the play.*]

Lear's madness overshadows [*King Lear*]—because it is shocking and terrible, of course, but in a more fundamental manner because it is at the center of the meaning of the play. It is too easy merely to be aware of the pathos of the scenes of madness; and indeed pathos alone, even at such an exalted level, would be incapable of creating the overwhelmingly powerful impression which for centuries has been made by the mad king. Nor could even terrifying madness, and a terrifying storm, of themselves create much of the force of the central scenes of the play. Beneath the superficial aspects of these scenes there must be felt, by even a casual student, a reverberation of underlying meanings which constitute the inner reality of the scenes.

The reader soon becomes aware that the madness functions in more ways than one. In its most palpable aspect it is a psycho-physiological phenomenon, the ultimate collapse of a high-strung but unstable personality brought, by a habitual unrestrained emotional violence, to a pitch of utterly frustrating discords at which it can no longer maintain its identity. But seen from another point of view—which the play presents with equal fullness—madness is an intellectual phenomenon, the expression of a failure of understanding before the extraordinarily complex situation in which the problem of evil is embodied. . . . The madness, however, exists not only at the naturalistic level but also at the moral: here it is a part of the vital middle link in the tragic process—the expiatory phase which in *Lear* is of such bitter intensity as to confound sentimental critics. Finally, the madness is also a symbol, a symbol of a disordered and distraught world where expectancies are defeated and norms contemned; it is and it signifies a ''breach in nature.'' Here it collaborates with the storm: these two phenomena so often thought of as existing primarily in relationship to each other are actually most important in their common function as indices of the spiritual state of the world.

To go still further, we find that the madness is not an isolated fact, any more than are the storm, the nakedness of Edgar, and the blindness of Gloucester. Just as the blindness focuses the sight imagery of the play and the nakedness the clothes imagery, so the madness brings together and is to be read along with the assumed madness of Edgar, the folly and wisdom of the Fool, a great many comments on madness and folly throughout the play, and, finally, the powers of reason of those of whose technical sanity there is no doubt. . . . To the other patterns of meaning [in the play], then, we must add a madness pattern, and we must trace the interrelationships of this pattern and the meaning which they appear to set forth. What we must come to, it is obvious, is some consideration of the kinds of mental balance, the kinds of human wisdom.

The configuration of verbal and dramatic elements of which Lear's madness is the center is of course not a solitary system the meaning of which is to be added to the meanings of the other systems within the play to produce, as a sort of sum, the total meaning of the play. The various systems are constantly interrelated, are often scarcely distinguishable parts of a whole, and should not undergo the separation which is one of the dangers of the present schematized discussion. But since the separation is inevitable here, it may be well to review . . . the mode of interrelationship and interdependence of the constituent thematic elements. With the exception of the sight symbolism the other image and word patterns . . . have, as their general function, the setting forth of the complex universe with which man, as a perceptive and understanding creature, must deal—a universe which includes, in one aspect, humanity, and, in another, the principles, whether natural, moral, or theological, which he invokes in the determination of order; a universe, too, in which, in a variety of phenomenal emergences, the problem of evil is always the ultimate irreconcilable antagonist. The clothes imagery suggests some of the intricacies of the human reality—the disguise and trickery which must be pen-

etrated, the defenses needed for preservation, the nakedness which means not only defenselessness but a kind of loss of the minimal tokens of humanity; so that here we have figured forth, in wonderfully apt concrete form, a paradoxical truth at the center of human conduct, namely, that the necessary protective movement has in it the seeds of, and can with deceptive ease slide over into, the cynical aggrandizement of self. The animal imagery, which is plentiful, is used almost exclusively to emphasize another complication in humanity—its capacity for abjuring its especial characteristics and taking on the rapacity and ruthlessness of the beast; the animality in man receives further expression in the direct and figurative use of sex. The problem of age serves to amplify our picture of a scarcely accountable moral variability in man, in whom this one phase of experience may evoke responses that range from tender compassion to a hard sense of opportunity for profitable manipulation. Such, says the language of the play, are the enigmas of man as a moral agent. On the other hand, viewed with respect to his status in the world, man seems hardly to justify the complacency with which he often regards himself: the animal imagery says repeatedly that his position—the result of his treatment by fellow beings—is like that of animals; and often it seems possible to describe him only in the language of disease, decay, and injury. Does man, then, live in an ordered universe, or is he simply buffeted about in a meaningless chaos? The justice pattern points out not only the miscarriage of principles of justice by deliberation, but the liability to act unjustly even in those who do not intend evil. This is of course not to deny that justice exists or to assert cynically that it is always accidental or too little or too late, but rather to point out that in practice it is far less simple than as an abstract conception. Likewise the value pattern, although incidentally it may assert the preciousness of the compassion and power of seeing which are not the most frequent of human gifts, is largely devoted to showing how ''honest confusion'' may in its effects coincide rather closely with the most clear-minded intention to govern all considerations of value by the possibilities of immediate profit. The distinction of false and true is not easy, and the discovery of an infallible method of making the distinction is still more difficult. If man is unwilling to deal, or incapable of dealing, with experience imaginatively, and substitutes rationalistic procedures where they cannot be successfully used, he will get into trouble: rational man is in the greatest danger of rationalizing essential values out of existence. Finally there is the nature pattern, which includes on one hand the symbolic storm and on the other, direct, literal philosophic inquiries. What appears to be implied by the nature pattern is that trickery, cruelty, injustice, a value system dominated by the spirit of calculation, though real and ever-present to be reckoned with, are to be regarded as disorder, a violation of the nature of things, ab-normal. ''Nature'' still *is*, even though obscure and elusive; it is ever the measure of the world of accident.

What we have here is an immensely inclusive anthropology, an effort unequaled in drama to get at the problem of man from every side and in every aspect, to give it the fullest and most variegated possible expression in differentiable and yet collaborating strands of poetic and dramatic structure; so we have an almost overwhelmingly complex accumulation of phenomena and of the metaphysical problems which they introduce. The play does not attempt, at least in prosaic and logical form, final answers to the problems; it is primarily bent upon evoking a sense of their magnitude and of the well-nigh intolerable burden which they place upon the human mind. But if the play, since it is not didactic, does not announce answers, it at least implies answers; and its method of implication is a very elaborate system of contrasts. The materials of practically all the patterns . . . are presented dualistically; life resolves itself into alternatives. This is not only to say that we always have options, but it is to say that a man in search of understanding finds alternatives as empirical realities. Nearly every pattern has its dichotomy, and the dichotomies tend to coincide and even coalesce into a general definition of reality. There are two natures—Lear's Nature which is order, and Edmund's which is impulse and will. There are the two views of man—that man may be a human being (by conforming with order) or an animal (falling into Edmund's view of nature). Man may view age as the possessor of certain prerogatives (established in Nature) or as mere obsolescence, to be utilized for the profit of the fittest, the up-to-date (the view consistent with Nature as defined by Edmund). There are the two aspects of the problem of justice—the belief in an eternal, unswerving justice (Nature as order), and the fact of actual injustice (inflicted by man as animal). There are the naked and the overdressed—both of whom represent different contradictions of Nature. What we are always kept aware of is the qualitative distinction between the two opposing possibilities: to be on one side of the fence may mean being terribly beset in an actual world, but what happens in the world is never allowed to obscure our sense of intrinsic absolute value. By such means the play moves toward its final statement. Indeed, we are always reminded of the paradoxes of experience: the naked may survive better than the well-protected, those who become beasts of prey may perish before their victims, age may endure and come to a saving understanding, the hidden justice may upset the insuperable temporary power.

Then there is the paradox of man's grasp of the complex world. Again we have the dualism: there are the clearsighted in the world, and those who are blind. But the blind come to sight, and the clear-sighted do not see far enough. The rational may be too rational. But the imaginative may be reduced to complete incompetence in affairs, even to mental incompetence. What is said about them is the burden of the madness pattern.

The clothes, nature, animal, age, and justice patterns present the complex *world that is to be understood;* the sight and madness patterns (of which the values pattern is an auxiliary) are concerned with the *process and method of understanding* and coming to terms with that complex world. What means does man have to cope with its complexity? The shift is from humanity as object to humanity as subject. In the living drama, of course, the two are one, and the present separation is necessarily artificial; but it should serve to show that the objectively single drama is ambivalent, and that the problem of understanding is brilliantly illuminated from two points of view.

The very extensive imagery of sight that permeates the play keeps our attention focused on the quality, and especially the failure, of man's seeing; thus we are aware of Lear's and Gloucester's blindness to important circumstances, symbolized in Gloucester's subsequent real blindness, and of the scornful eyes and tearful eyes, respectively, of Goneril and Cordelia, which represent the kind of seeing, that is, grasp, of experience of which the individual sisters are capable. Since sight is constantly the symbol of insight and comprehension, it may seem that the sight pattern exhausts the possibilities of comment upon man as an observer and student of man and the world and of the evil in man. It is true, indeed, that the sight pattern and the madness pattern often do coincide functionally, and that the kind of sight man has keeps turning our attention toward

the kind of wisdom he has; yet, as a general thing, the sight pattern tends to take man at the level of the *recognition and identification of phenomena,* that of the immediate practical decision. . . . The madness pattern, however, is concerned with the ways in which men *interpret phenomena,* the meanings which they find in experience, the general truths which they consciously formulate or in terms of which they characteristically act, the kind of wisdom, or sophistication, which they achieve. What men see and what men believe, of course, are intimately related; yet it is possible to focus attention on what goes on in the foreground or on what lies behind. The latter is the special area of the madness pattern. Its materials are men's philosophic attitudes to the world of which they are a part, their grasp, more specifically, of the problem of evil. Lear's madness is, in one respect, a result of his inability to bring an obdurate universe under intellectual control: the difficulty is too great, and his mind fails. Gloucester, the typical man of despair, formulates a pessimistic position which makes only suicide meaningful. The implied metaphysics of Lear's elder daughters is, as we shall see, something quite different. Other minds mould the materials of life in still other ways. The play, indeed, puts together an almost schematic pattern of the relationships of minds to experience. In this structure, the madness of Lear is focal; hence the term *madness pattern.*

Of certain fairly obvious structural relationships among Lear's madness, Edgar's assumed madness, and the Fool's ambiguities, much has been said by many commentators. What we may profitably notice here is the patterns of internal structure in the three characters, the varying relationships between the sound and the unsound or quasi-unsound state. Edgar, who gradually becomes a sententious, almost formally philosophical moralist, makes a meaningless hash of his mad speeches (though Shakespeare makes some of Edgar's language support several meaning patterns of the play); his highest integration is at the level of conscious, logical formulations. Lear, who in the normal state is a man of feeling passionately aware of the immediate object but weak on implication and synthesis, shows, amid the irrelevancies of madness, an organizing imagination of considerable power and actually puts together a coherent general view of experience, a symbolic formulation of the problem of evil as set forth in the world of the play; the mental failure caused by the pressure of circumstances is not only a failure but an escape, a means of liberating for full flight an imagination that was hampered before. Edgar's gifts are logical and disappear when he takes to antilogic; Lear's are imaginative and are freed by his departure from the world of normal order and logic. The Fool has the imaginative power which the mad Lear achieves—that is, the ability to read image and symbol, to leap from the concrete manifestation to the meaning, to the values implied; but by definition the Fool is outside the world of normal order and logic, so that his imaginative insight into the meaning of phenomena is always free to find immediate expression. He both forgoes the prerogatives and is free of the responsibilities of the normal everyday world; thus he is known by a term of contempt, lives at the mercy of others, and is hardly taken seriously in the great workaday world of adults; but at the same time no conventions restrain him from putting his grasp of realities into words. In view of the evidence of Lear and the Fool, and of other evidence to be considered later, we might almost treat *King Lear* as a dramatic presentation of the fate of the imaginative grasp of truth in a wholly practical world. Lear's own imagination failed in Act I; the rest of the time his really powerful imagination is contrasted with the rationalistic spirit—for the introduction of which, by his imposition of the love test, he was responsible—of Goneril, Regan, and Edmund. The man of imagination does not have an easy time in the world. But that, as we shall see, is not the only truth that may be told about him—nor the most important truth.

The play says a good deal about fools and folly, nearly all of it useful in determining the attitude of the play to the problem of man's mode of understanding experience. Once again, in fact, we find the characteristic union of the dramatic fact and the verbal pattern: the dramatic fact is the role of the Fool himself, and the verbal pattern is what the Fool and other characters have to say about fools and folly. The different elements work together closely in contributing to the meaning of the play, so that within the madness pattern we have actually a complete Fool pattern. (pp. 173-83)

In the scenes with Lear, the Fool functions in a number of ways. At one level he may be understood as the conscience of Lear, the inner voice—externalized, as Empson says—which will not cease in its condemnation of error. At another level he is a tutor, the intellectual master of the world who lessons Lear in the way of the world. In this role he accents the irony hinted in Kent's earlier phrase, ''when majesty falls to folly'' [I. i. 149]. Lear falls to folly; the fool rises to wisdom. He becomes king in the sense that he sees things in the perspective which ideally should always belong to royalty—a counterpoint which is always emphatically present in the scenes between the two. But there is still something more in the Fool: it is his love for Lear and his devotion to Lear when there was every ''practical'' *reason* for his getting aboard the political band wagon. . . . Here the fool is the man of imagination who by imagination grasps a value that cannot be demonstrated rationally and whose deed is the dramatic opposite of the conduct of the rationalists in the play. His speech is consistently the imaginative speech of poetry: he is always ironic, he depends on symbols (the coxcomb, the crowns of the egg, ''the hedge-sparrow fed the cuckoo so long'' [I. iv. 215]), on riddles and analogies, on similes (''like the breath of an unfee'd lawyer'' [I. iv. 129]), metaphors (''truth's a dog'' [I. iv. 111]), and paradoxes (''thou mad'st thy daughter thy mother'' [I. iv. 171-72]). The Fool's education of Lear is in part a re-education of his imagination, an implied attack upon the calculating rationalism by which Lear had inaugurated all his troubles. Lear's imagination is recovering: he understands the Fool's poetry, he is learning rapidly to grasp the symbolic meaning of action (as he could not at the beginning), and he is moving toward the imaginative syntheses which he will make in his madness. The closer Lear moves to madness, the more he comes to exercise the gifts of the Fool.

The most inclusive paradox, then, is that the despised Fool . . . exposes the folly of the supposedly wise master of men, the King. Now, within the confines of the Fool pattern, we find a great many remarks about folly made by the Fool himself, and we need to examine them briefly to see how they comment upon the concepts of folly held by Kent, Lear, and Lear's daughters. The Fool first offers his coxcomb to Kent for ''taking one's part that's out of favour'' [I. iv. 99-100], and he adds, ''If thou follow him, thou must needs wear my coxcomb'' [I. iv. 103-04]. In this passage he is reasoning exactly as Goneril and Regan might: folly is not looking out for oneself in terms of immediate, material opportunities. Later the Fool returns to this theme—when he and Lear have found Kent in the stocks before Gloucester's castle. . . . At the end of [his lecture to Kent] the Fool becomes explicit: though knavish, it is wise to run away from one's loyalty to a lost cause, and foolish to

adhere to it. But the Fool and Kent, whom we admire, do adhere: and folly thus becomes admirable, and the wisdom of the world itself folly (''the knave turns fool''). The Fool's jingle imperceptibly slides into the complexity of poetry, and it imposes upon us the task of the reader of poetry: the Fool uses *fool* ambiguously, and his communication is complete when we have disentangled and distinguished his two senses.

The Fool is parodying the rationalistic wisdom of Goneril, Regan, and Edmund. Wisdom ultimately lies in loyalties, or in adherence to tradition. At the same time, however, there is an actual world in which one lives, and in it one may conduct oneself in such a way as to be very foolish about one's own interests. The Fool chooses, as his wisdom, the folly of staying with a King who has fallen from power; but he berates the King for the folly of his falling from power. *Folly,* as it is used to describe the King's conduct, implies as its opposite a good sense in the world which nevertheless the Fool himself eschews and which he stigmatizes as knavish folly. Nearly all of his lines on fools and folly, and there are many of them, are a chastisement of Lear for this bad management in the world. (pp. 186-89)

The Fool pattern constantly poses questions: what is folly? who is fooling whom? And precisely as in the areas of meaning developed by the other patterns, Shakespeare presents the relevant material in all its complexities, with all the ironic contradictions that may easily lead us to conclude that he is resting in a detached presentation of the ambiguities of experience. But eventually he resolves—or at least suggests a resolution of—the equivocal. Folly is, as we have seen, the ignoring of worldly interests; but inattention to the world may take quite different forms. The Fool parodies the cynical *un*foolishness of Goneril and Regan; but he also ridicules Lear's folly. In following Lear, he himself is not doing well in the world; but he attacks Lear for foolishly not doing well in the world. But in one lyric he concludes that worldly wisdom, being knavish, is folly. Thus worldliness is folly, and unworldliness is folly.

But we are not caught in an insoluble dilemma. Actually, the words and deeds of the Fool develop further the meaning of the values pattern: the real problem is not at all one of worldly success, which is secondary, but of the values in accordance with which one acts. This is where one is basically wise or foolish. Goneril's and Regan's worldly wisdom is folly because their values are wrong; Lear's failure in the world is also folly, not because it is failure, but because it is the result of wrong values. He has unnecessarily introduced a calculating spirit which incidentally has ruined his worldly position; but what is worse is that he has thus given full scope to the ability of his daughters to profit by acting in terms of this spirit. He has made a qualitatively inferior choice. As we have seen, he failed imaginatively, failed to understand Cordelia in terms of the action symbols of her love—the reason why he had come to love her most; in another sense he failed in his imaginative awareness of loyalties—to both his office and Cordelia—precisely as Kent and the Fool retain their imaginative grip upon their loyalty to the King. They unquestioningly accept it, in the only possible way, as an absolute and undemonstrable value. Lear, in his folly, lost sight of essentials, and thus turned the world upside down. . . . (pp. 189-90)

The Fool is the center of the folly pattern, and what he says takes us close to the heart of the play. But the heart of the play must appear finally in the Lear plot. Now Lear is dealt with both by the folly pattern and by the larger madness pattern of which the treatment of fools and folly is really a subdivision;

and there is some difference between Lear as fool and Lear as madman. His whole career, of course, is of a piece; it is the record of a mistake and the consequences of that mistake, and we need not attempt too-finicky distinctions between what is foolish and what is mad. But it is safe to say that Lear's folly is his mistake, and his madness is the consequence—and at the same time, paradoxically, the rectification—of that mistake. As fool, Lear loses his imaginative grasp of truth, and tries to express truth in the wrong way; he fails to discriminate between the kinds of truth and the ways in which they may be apprehended. The horror of the world that his folly creates, the senselessness and meaninglessness of it, drives him to madness; yet in that very madness there is a powerful lucidity, a tremendous exercizing of the imagination that failed him before. Even before the madness comes on we are made to see it as a potentiality; in fact there is throughout the play a special awareness of mental states—brought about not only by Foolishness and madness as dramatic facts but by the large amount of talk about folly and madmen—which is itself a symbolic way of stressing the problem of understanding which is structurally the center of the play. (pp. 192-93)

I have already noted . . . the various levels of meaning in Lear's madness. In this rich complex of meanings there is still one other possibility: considered as a product, the madness is expression of a certain conflict within Lear. Throughout Acts I and II Lear still tries to act in terms of his original rationalistic disposition of the territory; he still tries to sustain what I have called his heresy of material equivalents. That is, he still believes that the larger share of property which he gave to Goneril and Regan ought to guarantee him his stipulated privileges, and this belief determines all his major actions in Acts I and II. Even after he is out in the storm he cannot wholly get rid of this logic; that actual fact is at variance with logic preys upon his mind. Were he able to renounce his untenable expectations, to recognize that the treatment of him is a logical consequence of his treatment of Cordelia, and to meet this terrible disappointment with resignation, his purgatory would be of a different sort. It is of course not his nature to act in such a way. He still holds, dimly but tenaciously, to his original calculation. Yet at the same time he undergoes a great deal of enlightenment before he goes mad; the Fool, as we have seen, stirs him to a better perception of truth: and two sets of values conflict in him. He is told that he is a fool, yet he still hopes his folly will pay off. He begins to read his daughters in terms of their actions rather than their words, but still hopes for actions that will conform to their original words of assurance. He calls on Nature for punishment of his daughters, but still tries to argue with them. . . . By the end of Act II, as we have seen, his reason-not-the-need speech [II. iv. 264ff] in effect repudiates his philosophy of calculation. His imaginative apprehension of truth is constantly becoming better. In the storm [III. ii. and iv.] he becomes more and more both the philosophic observer and the sympathetic human being; in the farmhouse near Gloucester's castle [III. vi] he conducts the trial which manifests an insight into the world far superior to that which he had at the beginning of the play. His conflict is being resolved in madness: the closer he comes to it, the further he is from his original fallacy: in his madness he exhibits an acute vision; and after his madness he has forgot about Goneril and Regan and thinks only of his relationship with Cordelia and of the truths which they may perceive together. (pp. 195-96)

[The] center of the [madness] pattern is the powerful culmination of Lear's madness in IV. vi, in which Lear appears for the first time since he conducted the imaginary trial in a farmhouse in III. vi. In the interim Gloucester has been tried, blinded, reunited with Edgar, who is still Poor Tom; Albany and Goneril have quarreled; the French forces are ready for battle; Cordelia is searching for Lear near Dover. In IV. vi. we have the climax of the Gloucester plot and the climax of the Lear plot; Gloucester, won from despair by Edgar, reaches his philosophic heights, and Lear comes to his most penetrating vision. Not only are their experiences parallel, but the men are then brought together physically—a dramatic indication of the unifying function of the scene. It is just after Gloucester has promised Edgar to ''bear / Affliction till it do cry out itself'' [IV. vi. 75-6] that Lear enters, crowned with weeds, and, with Gloucester and Edgar as audience, speaks about one hundred lines—his most important in the play.

In these lines there are few irrelevancies; almost every phrase of Lear's relates in some significant fashion to the experiences which he has had. What we become aware of first is the irony of his demonstrating a kind of ''understanding'' of the very world which had been too much for him when he was in possession of his mind; before, he could but exclaim in anguish, now he incisively goes to the heart of the Goneril-Regan world, of all human evil as it is incarnate in them, and even apparent in himself. Outside the limits of everyday rationality he displays immense imaginative resources and finds exact forms for his devastating insight into the moral reality of the world, and, by implication, into himself and the situation of mankind generally. The language of his disillusionment, and of his compassion, makes one of the most powerful scenes in the play. At the most obvious level this is true because his image and symbol are neither conventional nor timid, because they are exactly adapted to the effects, and because the different kinds of image and symbol, instead of being isolated media of expression, collaborate among themselves in the production of those effects. But there is a still greater source of strength in these speeches by Lear, and that is the fact that they are *a nexus of all the main lines of development in the play;* all the patterns of image and symbol are focused here. . . . Almost every line of Lear's, instead of having, by the relations within itself and with the rest of the passage, to create its own poetic momentum, has a very strong initial impulse; this impulse is the prepared meaning and suggestion that can come only from the author's utilization of language patterns already developed and therefore eliciting a special kind of imaginative co-operation from the reader. For Lear expresses himself almost entirely by drawing upon patterns which, at this late time in the play—the next-to-last scene of Act IV—have been well established. Here we find, united in a single impact, the sight, smell, clothes, sex, animal, and justice themes that move throughout the play. And they are organized by means of the madness theme; through them the mad Lear, in what is virtually a soliloquy, gives verbal form to his bitter comprehension of an ugly and deceptive world and of the human capacity for evil that has made it so and to his pity for the sufferers in the world. In his madness there is unity. (pp. 197-99)

Lear's original failure, we have seen, has an intellectual form: he endeavors to introduce quantitative norms where the questions are entirely qualitative. This mistake may be rephrased: Lear himself paves the way for the breakup of the organic order, represented in comparatively unadulterated form by Cordelia and Kent, by making contractual relationships basic. In his *quid-pro-quo* rationalism, however, he fails to provide substitutes for the old sanctions; thus his new system allows infinitely greater scope to latent human evil. Lear thinks badly, unimaginatively. Were he not content to pause at the appearance of things, he would understand that it is impossible to be king-in-name without being king-in-fact (not that this error justifies those who take advantage of the king-in-name-only); he attempts an abstract, theoretic separation characteristic of his early rationalistic temper, and for stability counts upon a contract which cannot be enforced. As he *divests* himself of the symbols of royalty, he forgets that there are no naked kings; he neglects both himself and his society. It is ironic that Lear—and Gloucester too, for that matter—is terribly put upon just at the moment when he feels he is being very clever. Like Faustus, he proposes to beat the game in which the nature of man is his opponent. Thus he evinces his pride. It is not the conscious pride in reason of, say, Oedipus or Faustus; but it is implied by his arbitrary imposition of his scheme of values and relations. He takes on too much. Precisely by being too clever he evades his adult responsibility, which should be intensified in one of position and authority, not to be gulled by every Mr. Plausible bent on profit, and not to give the Mr. Plausibles political power.

But having taken the world apart, Lear very soon has a terrifying vision of what he has done; and he tries, intellectually and morally, to put it together again. He calls upon the certainties of the old organic world (from which Kent and Cordelia derive their impulses), but he has invalidated the old imperatives, and disintegration has gone so far that nothing happens in accordance with his expectations. . . . The old order is gone, and under the shock of its loss, Lear loses the powers of reason which he has not used well.

But Lear's un-reason accommodates a kind of reasoning; we see, in place of his earlier calculative spirit, a restored imagination which, even though at his death he is still battling fundamental enigmas, is capable of effecting austere syntheses out of the materials of the new disorderly world. In place of his old myopia there is a new uncompromisingness of insight. In the experiences before his madness, in the storm scenes during which he goes mad, but most of all in the synthesis scene [IV. vi] . . . , Lear has developed an imaginative awareness of evil which he did not have when he was making the trial of his daughters; he has come to a compassion for humanity—a compassion which, as Cordelia's tears indicate symbolically, is a kind of insight; and, as both his direct statements and his figures show, he has come to some knowledge of himself and his liability to error. He is a very different man from the Lear of Act I; and it is safe to say that if the Lear of Act I had had the kinds of awareness to which he has now come, he would not have acted as he did. At the start, he had no insight into, nor did he question, himself; if he had the power of compassion, he did not show it; and he was so confused that he had no real sense of evil. He was the man of calculation instead of the man of imagination.

But his imagination is restored. If such a process were not going on, the madness scenes would have been merely pathetic or grotesque or sardonic. Yet they are no such thing. Not that the madness is not real; but it is ambivalent, and the meaningfulness is as authentic as the clinical detail. Shakespeare takes pains to point out literally that Lear is as much a man of understanding as he is a raving lunatic, or rather that lunacy of demeanor can co-exist with a most penetrating insight. The key speech is significantly given to Edgar, who, after his pretended madness, has already begun to exhibit the force and clarity of mind which are his to the end of the play. His words are: "O, matter and impertinency mix'd! / Reason in madness!" [IV. vi. 174-75]. *Reason madness:* no single line has a more important bearing on the structure of the whole play.

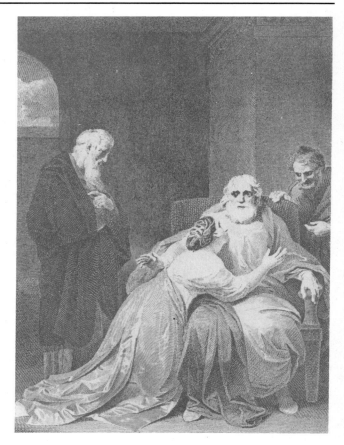

Act IV. Scene vii. Doctor, Cordelia, Lear, and Kent. By Robert Smirke (n.d.).

Shakespeare so qualifies and amplifies *reason in madness* that he avoids having, at one polar extreme, a mere surrealistic laudation of lunacy. Along with Lear's burning knowledge we must take the insight of the Fool and Edgar, which is an essential part of the madness pattern. Madness becomes, then, not merely clinical insanity but the whole realm of what is, from the conventional point of view, mental and worldly incompetence. Shakespeare takes three very "unlikely specimens," as the world might view them—a crazy old man long told that he is in his dotage, a Fool who may be clever but is probably unbalanced and is certainly a no-account, a naïve young man who manages so ill that he can save himself only by becoming an outcast bedlam—and makes them, as far as the reflective and imaginative world is concerned, his three wise men. Lear's interpretative union of symbolic patterns, the Fool's keen perceptions of fact and imaginative inferences from fact, and Edgar's gnomic observations constitute, certainly not a formal philosophic commentary on experience, but a very solid aggregation of wisdom about it. That it should come from the humble, the scorned, and the exiled produces almost a Christian transvaluation of the values of Lear's pagan world. This is Shakespeare's central paradox, by which he unites the other paradoxes into an inclusive paradox: the blind see, the naked survive, and wisdom belongs to the mad. By these paradoxes he presents the dilemma of the World: humanity must live in it, and wishes to do well in it, yet the better man does in it, the more likely he seems to come to ultimate grief. To have little and to be outside the sphere of the great seem the surest way to salvation. (pp. 217-22)

Robert Bechtold Heilman, in his This Great Stage: Image and Structure in ''King Lear,'' Louisiana State University Press, 1948, 339 p.

ARTHUR SEWELL   (essay date 1951)

[Sewell's Character and Society in Shakespeare (1951) is regarded as one of the leading character studies of the twentieth century and an important refutation of the Romantic and neo-Romantic approach to Shakespeare's plays. Sewell focuses on the biographical, the psychological, and the psychoanalytic interpretations of Shakespeare's characters, criticizing all these methods as inappropriate and, at times, misleading, to the extent that each one forces the reader or spectator to attribute certain actions to biographical or psychological motives which are either vague, at best, or not even present in the text. For Sewell, Shakespeare was a moralist, not a psychologist, and his plays demonstrate the manner in which his characters choose to orient themselves to life—whether it be social life, as in the comedies, political life, as in the histories, or metaphysical life, as in the tragedies. In the following excerpt, from the work cited above, Sewell argues that King Lear is primarily a play about personal relationships— the only one in Shakespeare's canon, he asserts, that depicts character as totally determined by its relationship to others. In an interpretation similar to that of Robert Bechtold Heilman (1948), though using different terminology, Sewell claims that the movement of King Lear is from conduct based on self-regarding reason, through social disruption, to conduct based on compassion and love. Ultimately, he regards the play's world and fundamental ideology as neither pagan nor Christian, but a vast arena where "characters are imagined not only as members of each other but also as members of a Nature which is active both within themselves and throughout the circumambient universe." Sewell's essay represents a formidable attempt to transcend the pagan/Christian, pessimistic/optimistic polarity of previous Lear criticism by discovering a methodology that synthesizes, or even goes beyond, that of past critical analyses. This trend in modern and current interpretations of the play can also be seen in the essays by Richard B. Sewall (1959), John Holloway (1961), Maynard Mack (1965), Phyllis Rackin (1970), and Bernard McElroy (1973).]

King Lear is the play in which Shakespeare returns once again to see man as a human soul, not in opposition to society, not rejecting society, but finding in society the sphere of fulfilment. Order is now seen, for the first time, and perhaps imperfectly, 'not merely negative, but creative and liberating'. It is a vision of society very different from that discovered in Othello. In Othello we cannot suppose that society is ever moral or good. Othello and Iago die, but future Othellos will find themselves betrayed in Venice, and future Iagos will still prey upon its profligates. In King Lear the conflict is no longer apprehended as a conflict between the individual and society; the conflict is now within society itself. Disorder in the human soul is both the agent and the product of disorder in society. Social order is the condition, as it is the resultant, of sweet and affirmative being, without which man relapses into a beastly and self-destructive individualism.

The play gives an impression of towns and villages and castles, on which the barren moor and the wild marshland are ever ready to encroach. Outside the walls lies the realm of brutishness, of animals and roots, of standing pools and naked madmen. Certain of the characters become exiles from comfort, from decent living, from politeness. Lear, in the wind and the rain and the thunder, and in the hovel, is such an exile. So is Edgar, in the rags of Tom o'Bedlam. So are the fool and, afterwards, the blind Gloucester. The beastly life is very close, near neighbour to civilized man; and man has not much to do to resume the life of the beast.

He has only to cast off his clothes—for in this symbolism Shakespeare dramatically anticipates Carlyle. Clothes alone divide men from the animals. . . . (pp. 108-09)

The imagery of clothes—and many other things in the play— reinforce the notion that in society 'institutions are necessary'; and character in the play is certainly conceived in terms of social rank and function, as well as in terms of the family. We expect trouble, indeed, when at the beginning of the play we learn that Lear intends to continue rank without function, has subscribed his power, and confined it merely to 'exhibition', and would manage those 'authorities' which he has given away. The bastardy of Edmund ('there was good sport at his making' [I. i. 23] has such results that we see a 'fault', where a woman has 'a son for her cradle ere she [has] a husband for her bed' [I. i. 15-16]. Ironically enough, it is an insistence on the rightness and reasonableness of institutions which gives some point to the sisters' complaint that Lear's hundred retainers are intolerably more than 'nature' needs. There is nothing in the play to cast suspicion upon the rightness of external order—there is much in the play to make us feel that without it we are lost, to affirm that not discipline, but indiscipline destroys. But there is also much to support the view that even discipline will destroy where it is not involved in self-discipline and in love.

King Lear—this is a large claim to make—is the only one of Shakespeare's plays in which personal relationship is treated as an end and not as a means; the only play in which personal relationships seem to determine character rather than to have an effect upon character. It is not merely that, say, in Hamlet the relationships between Hamlet and his mother and Hamlet and Ophelia are subsidiary in the major vision of the play; it is rather that what these characters are, and especially Hamlet, in his personal relationships, is important and enriches the vision, but the relationship in itself plays no necessary part in that vision and is incidental to it. . . . In King Lear, however, all the characters are conceived—and this is central to the vision—in their relationships with other people, in their relationships with each other, and society is a vital complex of such relationships. In King Lear, then, not only is individual character differently conceived, but also living society itself.

The question is one of priority, not psychological but imaginative. In Hamlet (to continue the example) the nature of personal relationship is dependent on the nature of the characters: in King Lear, in a large measure, the nature of the character is revealed in the personal relationship. In Hamlet relationship and character are separable: in King Lear they are wholly bound up with each other. So it is that in King Lear personal relationships are the field of character-fulfilment.

None other of Shakespeare's plays contains such moving and dramatic references to personal loyalty and love. This play opens with the grand and, perhaps, grotesque announcement of the major theme in Lear's demand that his daughters shall declare their love. I do not find this opening difficult to accept; it is a bold enlargement of that morbidity which can poison affection, when affection gives nothing and asks everything. Lear's need to be told is matched by the two elder daughters' readiness in the telling; and it is seen, not wholly but in part, for what it is, in Cordelia's inability to tell. There follow immediately many variations of the theme; for Burgundy personal relationship is a matter of use, whereas to the King of France it is a matter of value. Kent is loyal, Goneril and Regan whisper together because, for a while, their interests are in common. The King of France finds words for the theme, when he says:

> Love is not love
> When it is mingled with regards that stand
> Aloof from the entire point.
>
> [I. i. 238-40]

More subtly and more movingly, Cordelia's conduct quickens and illuminates the vision; for her love, which cannot speak, has some regards—she cannot help it—which stand 'aloof from the *entire* point'. She is to blame, although she can do no other, for keeping herself blameless.

There is no need to rehearse the way in which Shakespeare deepens and develops this vision in the creation of his characters in *King Lear*. One or two of the minor characters catch a vivid if momentary life from it. I think of the servant who bids Cornwall hold his hand. . . . Or of the old man who brings the blinded Gloucester to Edgar. . . . Such a man sweetens and fortifies institutions with loyalty and service. Loyalty is found in Oswald, too—and in Kent. Lear himself—although this is too large a matter to do more than hint at—insists on his hundred followers, but comes to the moment when he bids the fool go first into the hovel; thinks of 'poor naked wretches' [III. iv. 28ff]; will make a little society of affection in prison with Cordelia; thanks a gentleman for undoing his button. And is not something darker suggested, related to this same vision, when the two sisters both desire Edmund? (pp. 110-13)

Personal relationships, however, are conceived in two ways—in loyalty and consideration which are owed according merely to the 'bond', and in that going out of oneself which makes of love and loyalty something more than is demanded by the bond. So, in the first Act, Lear does a terrible thing to Cordelia; he inhibits in her that love which has no need of a bond. So we apprehend that moral behaviours are inseparably bound up with each other, hers with his, for it is Lear who puts Cordelia in the position of relying merely on the bond. In similar fashion, Kent's honesty shows a loyalty something more than his commitment—and this honesty has in it a bluntness something more than the mere requirement of its occasion. There is, indeed, throughout the play a deep sense of the evil that must mix with goodness—and of the 'reason' that may mix with evil; and Shakespeare makes it clear that the admixture of good with evil, of evil with 'reason', is both proof and product of the fact that, morally, we are members of each other. There is, indeed, in *King Lear,* a kind of irony which is not, to any important extent, to be found in any other play: the irony which lies in the contradiction beteen the rightness of what is said and the wrongness of its being said by that particular character, or in that particular situation, or in that particular manner. Lear is old, and his age is full of changes, but his daughters should not say so. There is no reply—no reply but 'Nothing'—to Lear's request that Cordelia should outdo her sisters in protestation of her love; but Cordelia should not make that reply. Kent should warn the king, but loyalty asks for more mannerly phrasing. The vision that is discovered in character in the early part of the play is that vision which sees, in all its complexities, the play in conduct of mere 'reason' and 'rightness', at odds with that other play of something more than 'reason', something more than 'rightness'. So much is this the theme of the first Act that we may risk the judgement that this is what the play is about. Nature, we are to learn, needs more than reason gives.

Except for the King of France, the first Act shows all the other characters—this is the manner in which they were conceived—

determining their conduct and their speech either by self-regarding 'reason' or by a sense of 'rightness' which has in it something of self-regard. At any rate, conduct in them is determined, in one way or another, according merely to the need or the letter, and, because of this, has in it an admixture of evil and necessary imperfection. Whether the regard for self be 'proper' or 'improper', at the beginning of the play the impulse in conduct is almost universally self-regarding, or has in it something self-regarding as a presiding element. Something in self, something inhibitory in the conduct of another combining with something in self, prevents a 'going out' of the self. Even where the spirit is generous, it is forced to seek refuge in 'reason', in the letter, and is thereby frustrated and impoverished. At the end of the play, however, conduct—again in one way or another—becomes something more than 'reason' needs. There is, for example, a kind of generosity, a certain 'going out' of the self, in Goneril, when she says, 'I have been worth the whistle' [IV. ii. 29]. There is, in this, release from the self, and much more than 'reason' needs. So, too, in Edmund's 'Yet Edmund was belov'd' [V. iii. 240]; and it is significant that this is followed immediately by something very much like remorse for others. Edmund—and Goneril, too, for that matter—shows himself for a moment as man enough to be damned. When Lear thinks of the 'poor naked wretches', there is a most subtle play on all these themes—for such compassion in him has been in the past more than reason has seemed to need and is now a 'going out' of himself; and yet in this compassion there is a higher reason, which shows the heavens 'more just'. . . . The movement of the play seems to be from conduct (and character) in which reason is governed by self-regard, to conduct (and character) in which reason is transformed by compassion. In an image, this compassion becomes a healing and medicinal balm. (pp. 113-16)

'Institutions are necessary', but they are administered by men, and, necessary though they are, they are no guarantee against viciousness and evil. Lear, in his madness, has a terrible picture of what may lie beneath the façade of social and political institutions, and for a moment we have a vision of all society itself, in its forms and customs, rotten and hypocritical. It is a picture of society in which institutions are all false-seeming, and justice itself is so perverted that it lends itself as a disguise to those very ills on which it passes judgement. The image of clothes is still used by Shakespeare:

> Through tatter'd clothes small vices do appear;
> Robes and furred gowns hide all.
>
> [IV. vi. 164-65]

Here is society, as Lear in his madness sees it, without grace, without sweetness. The law conceals what it cannot prevent, and, by stealth, luxury goes to it, pell-mell. As we envisage such a society, we have a physical nausea, which makes us wish, like Lear, 'an ounce of civet' to sweeten our imaginations [IV. vi. 130-31]. We have raised the stone and seen the maggots. Shakespeare never gave us a clearer clue—and there is another in that travesty of justice as Lear arraigns the jointstools in the hovel—to the vision of the play from which the characters draw their identities.

But it is not a merely secular society in which these characters are conceived to have their being. Nor, on the other hand, do I think it can be said (even through allegory) to be a society understood in terms of Christian theology. Nevertheless, to put the matter quite simply, we certainly get the impression in the play that the characters are imagined not only as members of each other but also as members of a Nature which is active both within themselves and throughout the circumambient universe. Man is nowhere so certainly exhibited as a member of all organic creation and of the elemental powers. Man's membership of society is more than legal, is more than political, because it is subtended by a wider membership, in which plants and animals, the wind and the thunder, are also included. And is it too extravagant to suggest that this natural universe is, in the earlier part of the play, peopled not only by men but also by beings of a primitive pagan belief—by Hecate, by Apollo, by Jupiter, by 'the gods'; and that the dominion of these beings is, in the action of the play, superseded? Is it, indeed, too extravagant to suggest that in the play we have a veritable change in dispensation? That, at any rate, is the impression given as the imagery changes and one store of images gives way to another. What the final dispensation is, however, it is difficult to determine, for Shakespeare seems not to specify it. The most we can say is that, like the promise of rain in Mr. T. S. Eliot's *The Waste Land,* there are moments and images towards the end of *King Lear* which give promise of grace and benediction. (pp. 117-18)

> Arthur Sewell, ''Tragedy and 'The Kingdom of Ends','' in his *Character and Society in Shakespeare, Oxford at the Clarendon Press, 1951, pp. 91-121.*

WOLFGANG CLEMEN   (essay date 1951)

[*A German Shakespearean scholar, Clemen was among the first critics to consider Shakespeare's imagery an integral part of the development of his dramatic art. J. Dover Wilson described Clemen's method as focusing on ''the form and significance of particular images or groups of images in their context of the passages, speech or play in which they occur.'' This approach is quite different from that of the other leading image-pattern analyst, Caroline F. E. Spurgeon, whose work is more statistical in method and partly biographical in aim. In the excerpt below, taken from his* The Development of Shakespeare's Imagery (1951), *Clemen presents a more general discussion of the important role imagery plays in* King Lear *than do such earlier critics as the Reverand J. Kirkman (1879), Caroline F. E. Spurgeon (1935), and Robert Bechtold Heilman (1948). Clemen argues that imagery contributes more to the meaning of* King Lear *than that in any other Shakespearean play. He bases this conclusion on two points: first, because of the highly psychological nature of the play, particularly with respect to the character of Lear, the numerous images serve as the imaginative perceptions of the characters themselves into their own, as well as the world's, essential nature; second, they also serve to universalize the experience of any one character. Yet, like Heilman, Clemen makes a definite distinction between those imaginative, thoughtful figures whose speech is grounded in the world of imagery—such as Lear, Edgar, Cordelia, and the Fool—and those whose speech reveals a rejection of imaginative perception for a rational, utilitarian outlook on the world, such as Edmund, Goneril, and Regan.*]

An attempt to interpret a Shakespearian play solely on the basis of its imagery—a risky undertaking—would have the greatest chance of success if *King Lear* were the play in question. The imagery here seems to be more fully integrated into the structure of the drama and for that reason to play a more meaningful rôle than in other plays. Not only do the various sequences of imagery offer important clues to what Shakespeare sought to represent in *King Lear,* but the distribution of the images among the characters, their interrelation and their significance for the illumination of certain themes and trends of the action also help us to a better insight into the meaning of the drama. In *King Lear,* action and imagery appear to be particularly closely dependent upon each other and are reciprocally illuminating;

the imagery, in fact, seems to have taken over some functions which so far—in Shakespeare's earlier plays—belonged to other mediums of dramatic expression. In the development of Shakespeare's imagery, *King Lear* therefore represents an important new stage. (p. 133)

At the very first glance we perceive that the form of most of the images and their connection with the context differ from those in the earlier plays. Formerly, the images were used as illustrations, or the metaphorical element was fused with the train of thought as a means of enhancement or elucidation. In *King Lear* we can seldom speak of such an illustrative function. The image is presented as if it existed for its own sake; it serves no other aim but to speak for itself alone. Let us look at Lear's speeches in III. ii. or in IV. vi. from this point of view: he sets image after image as independent, direct visions. The same thing holds true of the fool. Up to now, we have found characters speaking exclusively in imagery only in moments of the greatest excitement. In *King Lear,* however, this is the case throughout many scenes; imagery is for Lear his most characteristic form of utterance.

The reason for this becomes clear if we trace Lear's development during the early scenes. The first shows us Lear still in possession of his power; he is still a member of society. He makes decisions, gives orders and makes plans, addresses the other characters of this scene, his daughters, Kent, France, etc. But the very first scene gives us a hint of how Lear is going to lose contact with this natural relation to his environment. The dialogue which he carries on with his daughters is at bottom no true dialogue, that is, no dialogue based on a mutual will to mutual understanding. Lear determines in advance the answers he will receive; he fails to adapt himself to the person with whom he is speaking. Hence his complete and almost incomprehensible misunderstanding of Cordelia. Lear takes no pains to understand what Cordelia is really trying to say; he does not consider whether her words could not have quite another meaning. He catches up only their superficial form and, because he had expected another answer, different from this, he repels the one person who in reality is nearest and dearest to him. More and more Lear loses contact with the outside world; words become for him less a means of communication with others than a means of expressing what goes on within himself. His utterances, even when addressed to other persons, take on, increasingly, the character of a monologue and become less and less part of the dramatic dialogue, although Lear (which is typical) never speaks an actual monologue himself.

The wealth of images in his speech results from this process and gives it expression; we have seen that in Shakespeare, the monologue is always the form of utterance richest in imagery. Lear gazes within himself; he no longer sees people nor what goes on about him. In madness a man is alone with himself; he speaks more to his own person than to others; where he does not speak to himself, he creates for himself a new and imaginary partner. Lear speaks to people not present, he speaks to the elements, to nature, to the heavens. Men have forsaken him; so he turns to the non-human, superhuman powers. It is one of the functions of the imagery in *King Lear* to awaken these elemental forces and to open to them the way into the play. (pp. 133-35)

If we glance, however, at the other group of characters, Edmund, Goneril, Regan, Cornwall, we note how seldom they employ images, how different their whole language is. In contrast to Lear and his followers, we never find that peculiar form of ''monologic dialogue'' between them. They speak rationally; they address their words to their partner, and converse in a deliberate and conscious manner. They have a goal which they seek to attain and everything they have to say is bent upon this. Their language does not betray to us what is taking place within them—in the form of ''imaginative visions''; it reveals to us solely their aims and attitudes, and how they intend to put these into practice. Thus their language scarcely changes throughout the course of the play, whereas Lear's, Edgar's and Kent's way of speaking is constantly varied. Goneril, Regan and Edmund are the calculating, cool and unimaginative people who are incapable of ''creative'' imagery. They have no relationship to nature, to the elemental powers. Their world is the world of reason; they live and speak within the narrow limits of their plans, within the limits drawn by the plot and the given moment of the action. Lear's language continually points beyond these limits. Thus the distribution of the images among the characters also gives us a hint as to their position within the play.

The middle acts of the tragedy, Acts II.-IV., are the richest in imagery. The outer action is less important here and is relegated to the background. The main emphasis does not fall upon the outer course of events, upon what Regan or Goneril are planning, or what Edmund is about, but rather upon what is passing in Lear himself. The outer drama has become an inner drama. Beneath the surface of the plot lies the deeper level of inner experience which gradually frees itself more and more from the sparse events of the action. The latter becomes a frame and an occasion in order that the former may take on living reality. In truth, Shakespeare has not treated this outer action with the same thoroughness and care as he usually employed in the construction of the plot. . . . But Shakespeare was concerned not with the ''outer'', but with the ''inner'' drama. The important thing is not what Lear does, but what he suffers, feels and envisions with his inner eye. One of the greatest and deepest truths of this play is that we must first go through suffering before we can recognize our real selves and the truth. ''I stumbled when I saw'', Gloucester cries out [IV. i. 19]; he only learned to see when he was blind. Thus Lear, too, sees through the world of appearances not with his physical eyes; it is rather with his inner eye—in madness—that he penetrates to the very bottom of things and recognizes their true nature, whereas he formerly let himself be blinded by their outward appearance. It is obvious that imagery is the only adequate form of expression for such an inner process.

But the term ''inner drama'' is not sufficient to describe accurately the peculiar shifting of emphasis—from the level of human action to another level. Much of what Lear utters in the central scenes points beyond the limits of his personal fate. Indeed, Lear's suffering and experience, although represented to us as an individual case, is meant to signify much more than something merely personal; it is meant to be an archetype of the universal. More than in any other play, the human events in *King Lear* are related to the happenings of the whole world. . . . This inclusive action is made clear to us by means of the imagery. The imagery gives the horizon of the individual occurrence a comprehensive perspective; it transforms human matters into mighty universal events. The elemental forces and the things of nature, as they appear so profusely in the language of Lear and his followers from the second act on, often seem to grow beyond the speakers. They assume, as it were, an individual existence, they become almost independent of the speakers. The imagery becomes the means by which these forces of nature enter into the play and take part therein as

active agents. These sequences of imagery, such as are to be found, for example, in Edgar's long list of animals and plants, are not to be interpreted as the ''expression'' of individual inner experiences, but rather as the appearance of independent forces which belong to the play just as much as to the people. The words ''atmosphere'', ''background'', no longer suffice to designate how nature, landscape and the animal world are evoked by the imagery. This ''atmosphere'' here becomes a world in itself; we almost forget that it is only through the words of certain characters that life is given to this world of nature.

The non-human nature-world enters into the play in the same measure as the human world breaks down and falls to pieces. This occurs when the father is expelled by his daughters, when the son is persecuted by the father and madness dissolves human order; the firm bonds and laws of human society are destroyed; so now non-human powers, heavenly forces, lightning, thunder, rain and wind, animals and plants, enter in rich variety. This interrelationship is to be seen clearly in the structure of the play; the first act contains relatively little nature-imagery; in the second act it begins to grow, and it attains to its height in the third and fourth acts, which show us the forsaken Lear in his madness. (pp. 135-38)

The figure in the play for whom the image is an even more characteristic form of expression than for Lear, is that of the Fool. The Fool never speaks in blank verse, indeed he never comes near the more conventional, measured and dignified manner of speech such as we find, for example, in the first part of the first scene. From the very beginning he has his own peculiar way of expressing himself, a manner which marks him as an outsider. In the speech of the Fool, Shakespeare has given the images wholly new functions. But what is the significance of the image in his case?

We have already stated that in the very first scene Lear loses the capacity for really understanding others in conversation; he cannot carry on a real dialogue. The words of the others no longer reach him or, if they do, in an ill-conveyed meaning. Lear shuts himself off; he becomes isolated in his speech, which from now on, even in the dialogue, bears the stamp of a monologue. The usual manner of speech can therefore no longer move him; such words can neither help nor heal Lear who, in his madness, needs help more and more. The Fool knows this from the very beginning, and he speaks to the King in simile, proverb and image and in rhymed adages and sayings which have the same purpose as his rhymed images. Much of what the Fool says Lear neither hears nor grasps, for much is indeed spoken more to the audience than to the King. But part comes home to him and this he does comprehend. Even if Lear replies to only a few of the Fool's utterances, that is still no proof of what Lear may really have heard and understood. For much of the Fool's talk expects no answer. He inserts his sayings and comparisons between the speeches of the others, and he sings his little songs as an outsider, as it were—in this respect his position is often similar to the chorus of the classical tragedy—and formulates most of what he says not as if it were coined to fit a particular case, or were directed at a particular person. ''He that hath ears to hear let him hear!'' It is the image which makes this unobtrusive parenthetical way of speaking possible. The image clothes the individual and particular case in a more general form; it may take away the sting. Between Lear and the Fool a new form of the dialogue develops which is no longer based upon rational communication, upon the simple play of question and answer, but which is a finer and more subtle interplay of shifting meanings and hints.

The more Lear becomes a victim of self-delusion and madness, the more it becomes the task of the Fool to express in epigrammatic images the unreality of Lear's behaviour, his self-deception and his error. The images of the Fool are the dry and almost trivial language of reality which is continually contrasted with Lear's separation from the outside world. In the great scenes on the heath Lear reaches heights of fantasy and emotion which far transcend human proportions; he becomes a gigantic superhuman figure whose huge dimensions threaten to overstep the limits of what may be represented upon the stage and within the scope of a drama. . . . [But] no matter how tremendously the horizon spread out before us in these scenes may widen, the presentation of the play never loses itself in a sphere of the fantastically unreal. Lear himself . . . returns again and again to intimate, earthly things, he again and again resorts to simplicity and actuality. But it is especially the little sayings and similes of the Fool pertaining to the triviality of every day which counterbalance the gigantic dimensions of Lear's feelings and ideas. The Fool understands how to reduce Lear's behaviour to the simplest, most uncomplicated images of actuality, so that the state of affairs becomes perfectly obvious. (pp. 141-43)

At first glance, the images of the Fool, gathered as they are from the unexciting sphere of everyday common sense and often expressing trivial commonplaces, seem to stand in contrast to the great issues of the Lear drama. Fateful predestinations, even aberrations of such tragic weight and such great pathos—thus we could argue—may not be viewed from a merely utilitarian or common-sense standpoint. But it is precisely these simple, uncomplicated conclusions which form the path by which Lear and we, the audience, are led to a deeper and more moving recognition of the ultimate truth.

The effect of image, rhymed proverb and maxim is different from the effect of the direct admonition. Images as well as proverbs can convey a meaning in a manner more impersonal and universally valid. Images, as they are employed by the Fool, free the action from the narrow restrictions of the moment—they assist in producing a detached attitude of mind. The little songs which the Fool sings, further enhance this quieting effect which liberates us and creates this detachment. . . . The songs of the Fool as well as his images indicate a relaxation and a diminution of the suspense in the structure of the scenes—this being, indeed, to a large degree the function of the Fool. If we recall to mind the early Elizabethan tragedies, the *Spanish Tragedy* or *Titus Andronicus*, we see that such relaxation and counterbalancing are there entirely wanting: everything moves in extremes, every gesture, every word, every action is aimed at achieving the highest possible degree of glaring and bloody effect. In the later Elizabethan drama the Fool with his songs belongs, of course, to the conventions. But nowhere else are he and his forms of utterance employed in so profound a manner, at one and the same time creating detachment and positing beyond the immediate issue, as here in *King Lear*. (pp. 143-44)

Lear's inner development is portrayed in images more than that of any other character in Shakespeare. The great apostrophes to the elemental forces of nature in the scenes on the heath have already revealed a significant change in Lear. The images of the next scenes, in which the King goes mad, are again illuminating for Lear's state of mind. The swiftly passing images, logically unconnected with each other, which we hear Lear utter, correspond to the abnormal mental state of the King; they are the adequate form of perception and expression of a

lunatic. "It is his mind which is laid bare", Charles Lamb said as an interpretation of these strange speeches—especially in the fourth act [see excerpt above, 1812]. Lear's insanity should not be dismissed as simple craziness. It is rather another manner of perception, by means of which, however, Lear now sees and recognizes what formerly remained concealed from him, as long as he was sane. These images are the fragments of his inner visions, which have not yet attained to the form of thoughts; they have not yet been transformed, ordered and connected in logical sequence and in the service of clear statement. Many images in the fourth act become more comprehensible if light is thrown upon them from previous passages. In the great scene on the heath we hear Lear cry out:

> Let the great gods,
> That keep this dreadful pother o'er our heads,
> Find out their enemies now. Tremble, thou wretch,
> That hast within thee undivulged crimes,
> Unwhipp'd of justice: hide thee, thou bloody hand;
> Thou perjured, and thou similar man of virtue
> That art incestuous:
>
> [III. ii. 49-55]

The sins of earth pass before Lear's inner eye as visionary images—the thanklessness of his daughters brings him to the thanklessness and unrighteousness of the whole world. At first judge of his daughters . . . , Lear becomes in the fourth act the judge of all creatures. . . . Lear, having experienced in his personal world the destruction of human right and order, thus gains insight into the common injustice and frailty of all mankind. His fancy now sees examples of this everywhere in the world. . . . Lear has won eyes for reality. His inner eye pierces the outer appearance and penetrates to the true nature of things. (pp. 150-52)

> *Wolfgang Clemen, "'King Lear'," in his* The Development of Shakespeare's Imagery, *second edition, Methuen and Co. Ltd., 1977, pp. 133-53.*

D. G. JAMES (essay date 1951)

[*The following excerpt is taken from James's* The Dream of Learning: An Essay on "The Advancement of Learning," "Hamlet," *and* "King Lear." *James's thesis in this study is that poetry has value as a special mode of comprehension in which reason and imagination are united. James cites Francis Bacon as a representative of those Renaissance thinkers who conceived of poetry as strictly noncognitive and dependent on the laws of "poetic justice" rather than the demands of reality. In juxtaposition, he offers* Hamlet *and* King Lear *as examples of works of art which demonstrate a definite knowledge of the world and refute Bacon's theory. In the excerpt below, James describes Shakespeare's method in* King Lear *as an attempt to represent life "by the creation of extreme simplicities of both good and evil." He discerns within the structure of* King Lear *a continuation of the medieval allegory; in this respect, he justifies Shakespeare's numerous faults in the play—such as those points where plot and characterization conflict with each other—as resulting from his desire to dramatize abstract ideals rather than to present dramatic or psychological consistency. James perceives evil as the dynamic force in the play, that which destroys the virtuous and good, but which destroys itself as well. Out of this process, however, Cordelia and Lear achieve a stoic acceptance of events—"a certain power in human nature to overcome the world and to make the world fade in our imaginations and leave not a rack behind." For James, the fundamental truth* King Lear *reveals to us is the recognition of the capacity of humankind to create enduring values in the face of extreme sorrow and suffering. Other critics who have interpreted* King Lear *as an extension of the medieval morality or allegory include Oscar James Campbell (1948) and Irving Ribner (1958). Also, see the excerpts by Oscar James Campbell (1948) and John Holloway (1961) for further examination of the role of stoic ideology in the play.]*

[Bacon noted in his *The Advancement of Learning* that] 'true history propoundeth the successes and issues of actions not so agreeable to the merits of virtue and vice, therefore poesy feigns them more just in retribution, and more according to revealed providence'; and therefore poetry 'was ever thought to have some participation of divineness, because it doth raise and erect the mind, by submitting the shows of things to the desires of the mind; whereas reason doth buckle and bow the mind unto the nature of things'. These famous words naturally send our minds forward to similar observations of Johnson and to the strictures he passed on Shakespeare in this point of view.

Now in the year in which *The Advancement* was published, *King Lear* was being written; and *King Lear* clearly shows Bacon's statement for untrue. No one will say of *King Lear* that it submits 'the shows of things to the desires of the mind'; this is precisely what it does not do; and if we want a witness we have only to call up Dr. Johnson. But if *King Lear* does not do what a neoclassical theory of poetry requires, what does it do, and what is its justification?

The answer is that it represents a great labour of knowledge: not indeed of understanding but of perception. Bacon requires of us a submissive faith, a strenuous natural philosophy, and a belief that poetry satisfies the desires of the mind to which reality is submitted. Shakespeare has no blind faith; he does not exhibit natural philosophy for important; and he writes poetry which does not satisfy the desires of the mind but offends them instead. We ordinarily believe that in *King Lear* Shakespeare is doing something very important; and this important thing is something for which Bacon makes no allowance in his scheme of knowledge and art. Now what is at stake here is whether or not we allow the imagination as a form of genuine knowledge. I am aware that I am here nearing very large matters which embrace nothing less than the structure of human knowledge. But we cannot, I take it, if we are committed to believing that literature is important, fail to argue that poetry is not chiefly an affair either of the intellect or of the emotions; we must say that it issues from a peculiar labour of knowing; and we must declare that the merits of any literary work belong to it as an act of knowledge. A play such as *King Lear* exhibits human life as it is known by its author; our judgement on it is necessarily a judgement on its veracity, on its rendering of the features of things. It is not a matter of submitting the shows of things to the desires of the mind; it is a matter of seeing things as they really are; and if things are not conveyed as they really are by the poet, the play, whatever else it may be, is a bad play. Now we all believe no doubt that *King Lear* is one of the greatest works of literary art, if not the greatest, ever composed; its creator is with Homer and Dante: a trinity of the greatest writers; and Shakepeare, we say, is the greatest writer our modern civilization has had. Now if we all think so, Shakespeare must, or so it seems to me, show things more as they really are than all other modern writers. Here, we say, life is more fully rendered than in any other modern works; here, we say, the secular imagination of modern Europe has reached the top of its bent. We therefore take *King Lear,* to say the least, seriously, as a contribution to human knowledge; and this in spite of the fact that it is not an expression of faith, nor a work of metaphysic, nor a piece of natural philosophy. Besides, it does not set out to please our desires or seek to submit the shows of things to them; it has nothing to do with what we

happen to want; it is a genuine exploration of experience and the issue of a labour of knowledge. Now Bacon declares that reason, unlike imagination, buckles and bows the mind unto the nature of things; but we declare that Shakespeare's imagination in *King Lear* also buckles and bows the mind unto the nature of things, and that he is certainly not titillating agreeable or other emotions. And if this is so, we need to acknowledge that the imagination is a part of the life of reason, and that it may proceed with all the impersonality, the bleak labour of discovery, which animates the scientist or the philosopher; it has its own rational life; and the only desire which masters it is the desire, shared by saint, philosopher, and scientist, to see things as they really are.

Now because Shakespeare was a poet and not a philosopher, the question is not, What did he believe or declare? but What did he see and show? He was not explicating and theorizing, but merely labouring to see more clearly and to show what he saw. And here, we have to judge Shakespeare's greatest play with its inevitable claim to be a just rendering of mortal life, when life is seen not through the eyes of faith or of the intellect, but merely through the eyes of the most powerful secular imagination the world has yet known. Shakespeare's mind had no prepossessions; his imagination was pure and disinterested; and I do not know therefore that there can be any historical labour more important for us than to try to raise our minds to the height, not of his great argument in *King Lear,* for he had none; but to the height of his bleak and merely exploratory vision. (pp. 77-80)

In *King Lear* . . . Shakespeare's eyes turn to behold more fully what had caused Hamlet's dismay and reluctance, to see more clearly than Hamlet had seen or been able to see; and if this is so, we might expect that now his imagination, keeping its autonomy indeed, should yet seek such compromise with the intelligence as its sovereignty could rightly suffer. Shakespeare has turned from Hamlet's mind to see more clearly, in other plays as well, but for our purposes chiefly in *King Lear,* what it was before which Hamlet had stumbled. The great question of *Hamlet,*

> Whether 'tis nobler in the mind to suffer . . .
> Or to take arms . . .?

[III. i. 56ff]

will also be the great question which gives purpose to the play of *King Lear.* But it will be answered, if at all, not by speculation and thinking precisely on the event, but by a labour of perception. Shakespeare turns, with a question which is not upon his lips but in his eyes; and his eyes, and not his or Hamlet's thought, must be the instruments of discovery. He will not resolve, but behold. But, in what manner is possible to perception which will not suffer itself to be over-intellectualized, he must yet probe and test; he must abstract and classify and separate out; he must simplify in something of the manner of an experimenter; he must deal drastically with his material; he must play boldly, in violence; he must put things to the encounter and commit himself to the extreme; he must not squint at his object, mitigate, and soften down. There is much here that could be said on the infinitely delicate compromises and adjustments to which the imagination and the intelligence may come; and it would of course be absurd to suggest that the one can ever operate without the other, or that they are in their essences set over against each other. I am suggesting only that when Shakespeare has come to the phase in his writing of which I am now speaking, and which is most clearly illustrated in *King Lear,* a new balance of power between them is effected and a subtle reaccommodation; and in this balance and accommodation the intelligence is given more play than formerly. But it is also firmly held and its exercise finely controlled and obscured; it is a free ally, but is also jealously watched. For Shakespeare has a purpose now; he is consciously engaged in a task of imaginative discovery; and the intelligence must yield every possible tittle of support which does not also, in the sum, threaten the imagination's integrity. Like the scientist or the philosopher he has an aim; he also, and pre-eminently, remains an artist; he also becomes, and hereby, a still greater artist. He will push the powers of art to their last encounter; and he will use, in it, a dangerous support. The material, which is the material of life in its extremes, will be intractable enough; he will also risk an uneasy and difficult alliance.

What I mean in speaking in this way will, I trust, become clearer when I say how this readjustment and alliance shows itself in *King Lear*. It shows itself in what I shall call for the present a form of allegory; but in an allegorizing which is cunningly obscured and controlled, so that we hardly know it for what it is. The old Morality is not dead; it survives into Shakespeare's greatest work to become a powerful instrument of discovery. I will not try to estimate its scope and play in Shakespeare's earlier work; but it seems to emerge unmistakably in *All's Well* and then in *Measure for Measure;* and here, in these two plays, we are even uncomfortably aware of it; or perhaps better, we feel it must be there in order to give the plays a coherence which, in a naturalistic point of view, they do not possess. . . . And yet Shakespeare was moving forward; in these two plays he is approaching his greatest period; he has not acquired the new reaccommodation of imagination to intelligence, of creation to purpose, of naturalism to allegory, which he must have if he is to fulfil the highest requirements which can be placed upon the art of literature; but he is experimenting and learning; and soon the solution is reached: we are at the phase where *Othello, King Lear,* and *Macbeth* come quickly. (pp. 82-5)

[Shakespeare] now engaged in what I can only call a poetical experimentation with life by the creation of extreme simplicities of both good and evil. This he has to carry on now, and succeeds in carrying on; but he has to do so in a spirit of temporization with the requirements of representational drama. I am not concerned to argue that something of the tradition of the morality play lived on in Shakespeare alone of the playwrights of the time; I remark only that there came a time in Shakespeare's life when he falls back on it after writing many plays in which he had felt and shown less need of it. I add that he comes to employ it extensively now only under the compulsion of a personal need and as a means of experiment and discovery; and that the tradition of the Morality and of allegory was not so dead as not to be able to give aid to what he now sought to do. Only, it will be active in his writing as a hidden method personal to his needs; it will be subtly renewed, incorporated, and controlled in plays which belong naturally enough to Jacobean England. (pp. 85-6)

In the light of what I have just said and for a conclusion before going on to speak of *King Lear,* I must recoil upon myself and my use of the word 'allegory' in speaking of this phase of Shakespeare's writing. I have tried indeed to soften it down in my employment of it, and to suggest that in these plays it is so obscure or employed with such care as not to interfere with Shakespeare's great gifts in the creation of highly individual character. But the fact is that it is better not to use the word

at all; for so long as we use the word and intend a serious and accurate use of it, we imply a certain dichotomy between intellect and imagination; but that such a dichotomy exists in these plays I have been at some pains to deny. For where there is allegory, there is an explicit conceptual scheme accompanying and explaining what is exhibited in story; and there is certainly no such scheme anywhere explicit here. What we have, or so it seems to me, in these great tragedies, is a state of affairs in which any conceptual schemes, any mere significances, never quite break out from the presented situations; they are strictly implicit; they are held, if only barely, in solution; and they are not precipitated in our apprehension of the plays. That is to say, the state of affairs is strictly one of symbolism, not of allegory; one of 'involvement', not of explication. There is indeed a certain tension between what is imaginative and what is intellectual; but the tension never comes to a break; it never snaps the mind into two and concurrent apprehensions. What is exhibited is charged with meaning; but it does not *carry* it. Now this state of affairs, which is not one of allegory proper, is yet one in which intellectual formulation is nearly breaking out from the imaginative unity of the play; the imagination only just succeeds in keeping its supremacy; the ally pressed into service is all but in revolt, but is always just held; and it is in works like *Othello* and *King Lear* where there is an almost intolerable tension of this kind, and where the artistic consciousness comes near to breaking and to losing its autonomy, that we are aware of the very highest artistic power; it is precisely then that imaginative power needs to be strongest. I only ask therefore that in what follows this may be remembered; we are dealing here with an adjustment so delicate and walk so fine an edge, that words, which are better instruments of analysis than synthesis, are apt to be poor instruments in discussions of this kind. (pp. 87-9)

I have taken it as certain that Shakespeare's imagination in these plays was a secular imagination; and here, in *King Lear,* we see the place where Shakespeare's secular imagination puts itself, without any illusion, under the greatest possible strain. In earlier compositions Shakespeare's secularity had a full and comparatively easy play; but the time came, and was bound to come, when it would be put hardly to the test. It came to work only in great labour and difficulty; it came to be called to great undertakings; and there was bound to be stumbling and vacillation. Suddenly, after *As You Like It* and *Twelfth Night* comes *Hamlet;* and then, after what we now call 'the dark comedies', come the tragedies of which *King Lear* is the chief. After *Hamlet* Shakespeare pushes on, trusting to his imagination as an agency of truth; and he will not at all abate his imagination's secularity. Shakespeare is precisely not a religious dramatist; he is committed to being loyal to his art; he must not make any facile surrender to faith; he will not feign 'the successes and issues of actions more just', as Bacon said, 'in retribution, and more according to revealed providence'; his job is to discover and see and show; and what he discovers and sees he will bring home to us as truth which does not stand upon external testimony but is carried alive into the heart. In *King Lear,* more than anywhere else, his imagination takes the greatest strain: Lear will be locked out in the storm, Gloucester blinded, the Fool forgotten, Cordelia hanged from a beam: poetry will not here come between us and the object. (pp. 89-90)

I have said that at the stage to which Shakespeare has now come in the writing of his tragedies, he will, in varying degrees, in what manner is possible to perception which will not suffer itself to be over-intellectualized, probe and test, abstract and separate out, simplify in something of the manner of an experimenter, deal drastically with his material; and I said that these processes are most clearly shown in *King Lear.* I wish now to illustrate this in some detail, and in that way make clearer what I intended. (p. 99)

Let me give first, before turning to speak of the play as a whole, a simple and obvious illustration of the kind of thing I have in mind, by referring to Shakespeare's way of presenting Cordelia to us. In the first scene Cordelia is led away by the King of France to become his Queen. It will be remembered that Cordelia has rejected Burgundy: 'I shall not be his wife' [I. i. 249]. France then speaks and declares, in a moving speech, that he will have her. Cordelia does not reply. It is Lear who replies: 'Thou hast her, France, let her be thine . . .' [I. i. 262]; and then, with Lear and the others gone, Cordelia and France remain behind with Goneril and Regan. . . . There is nothing here which even begins to correspond with the scene in the old play which shows the wooing of Cordelia by France and her loving acceptance of him. Whatever the role of Cordelia in the play is to be, we are not to see her as a lover and a wife. Then, late in the play, France and Cordelia come with their army; but, as everybody knows, and by what Mr. Granville-Barker called the clumsiest lines in the play [see excerpt above, 1927], France is bundled back again home. But why? Because, again, Cordelia must not come in the role of a wife; her role is other, and wholly other, than this; Shakespeare has intentions which the presence of France would drastically interfere with. . . . [What] is certain is that Cordelia's life as a wife and queen are strangely shut out from the play. It is her relation to her father which is alone relevant; and for this reason and in this measure, Cordelia is drastically simplified and, as we may say, dehumanized.

But I turn now to look at the play as a whole; and I shall speak of the play's beginning, and then of its ending.

The division of the kingdom has frequently been regarded as a serious fault in *King Lear;* we must grant Shakespeare this incredible scene, it is said, in order that he may get started. But in fact this violent and outrageous beginning served Shakespeare's purpose well enough: it cuts away from our imaginations any sense of the preceding life of Lear and his family; it makes the beginning of the play as absolute as may be; and Shakespeare gives us very little which helps to make the scene we see continuous with what had gone before. The play begins with more of the abrupt, unquestioning beginning of a fairy story than of a play which is to satisfy naturalistic requirements: 'Once upon a time there was a very old and foolish King; and he had two wicked daughters who hated him and one good one who loved him. . . .' We do not begin from the normality of any previous family life with its typical graces, suppressions, subtle deceptions, forbearances; the family begins here; here it is what it is; from here it must move; what has been in the past is nothing and nowhere. . . . In this respect there is no play of Shakespeare comparable with *King Lear;* only a little inspection of *Macbeth* and *Othello* shows its difference here from them. It is true that we learn that Lear loved Cordelia most and that Lear had ever but slenderly known himself; but these are little more than pieces of information which, in any case, are barely necessary; nowhere is the past conjured up for us and entertained as something out of which this state of affairs had or could have grown. No doubt Shakespeare was helped by his audience's familiarity with the story. But what is more important is that Shakespeare was content with, he wanted, a highly simplified situation. I have said that he abstracted from

his characters; he was no less content to abstract the present from the past; he simplifies drastically by declining to try to make the opening scene begin even to look like a piece of history.

But then, it is not only this. Shakespeare brought in a subplot, the beginnings of which are even more incredible. No good purpose will be served by my recounting the perplexities and absurdities of the scenes showing Edmund's deception of his father. Here again the past must be carved away; here too, as in the main plot, we must connive at the making of as absolute a beginning as may be; we start with something which is cut clean away from the fine and elaborate tissue of the continuing life of a family. Now these things, the first stages in the two stories of Lear and Gloucester and their children, are no doubt big enough faults in the play. But we must assume that they are faults about which Shakespeare had no illusions; they were necessary for what he wanted to do; if these things were faults, they were yet the conditions of the success of his play. Shakespeare then, by its beginning, lifts the play out of history, out of the context of the past; and this is part and parcel of his intention for his characters. The children of these fathers have not grown out of a preceding human situation; they flare out and occur as the eternal powers which play for place and mastery in the human soul. We have not seen them nor imagined them as members of a family life; they are not and will not be clothed in the normality of the trivial or unultimate things which make up so much of living.

We find a similar state of affairs if we look to the play's ending. The reader will recall that Albany, to whom the succession would normally fall, declines any claim to the throne: it is for Kent and Edgar to rule in the realm, he says. But Kent has a journey to go: his master calls him; and Edgar goes on to speak the last four lines of the play which are as weak as they are obscure. I am aware that it has been held by some editors, who follow the Quarto, that these lines are properly Albany's. I cannot believe this; and assuming that the lines are Edgar's, we can only marvel at so wretched an ending for this greatest of plays. I think we must, on reflection, decide that Shakespeare wishes us to understand that Edgar accepts the throne; but Edgar goes on to speak a line which, if it means anything, means that he prophesies his own early death.

In the face of this ending we must, I think, believe that Shakespeare was embarrassed by the close of his play; and it is clear, or it seems so to me, that he was disinclined, if not averse, to giving us any clear sense of Edgar's assumption and exercise of royal power. That is to say, the ending of the play is not, so far as Shakespeare could with any propriety contrive it, an end which looks on to a succeeding order and condition. Fortinbras succeeds Hamlet, Malcolm Macbeth: sanity and justice are restored. But in *King Lear* we are given little of the feeling of this. The play at its end at most looks dimly ahead beyond itself as, at its beginning, it had not looked back to what had gone before. Shakespeare does not choose to set it in an imagined history; it is more like a fable which is told or an image which occurs and fades. Its final note is anticipated death, and not renewed and continuing life.

Before I go on to look at the content, or some of the content, of the plot, I wish to remark briefly on an aspect of Shakespeare's play which is closely connected with what I have been saying. I mean the unusual vagueness of what I may call the spatial and temporal ordering of the plot of *King Lear.* Bradley has written at some length on this matter [see excerpt above, 1904]; and I shall refer to it only in passing. But it is, unless

I am mistaken, a most significant feature of the play, and of a piece with what I conceive to be its prevailing purpose. We are given, for example, no idea of where, in Britain, Lear, or again Albany and Goneril, live; and it is very hard, if indeed it is possible, to get clear about the movements of characters in the play to the homes of Cornwall and Gloucester; afterwards, we have a vague movement of everybody to Dover; and we have little more. It is the same with time: it is very difficult to arrive at any clearly defined temporal sequence, and hard therefore to believe that we are required to imagine one. None of the great tragedies is comparable to *King Lear* in these respects. . . . This consistent disregard for time and space cannot, I suppose, be an accident; it is one of the ways in which the quality of Shakespeare's imagination in this play is shown; it must be explained in the same way as we explain (if we can) the temporal features of the play's beginning and end; and all must be explained by certain other features of the play of which I shall now go on to speak. (pp. 99-105)

I look now to another striking feature of the plot, which may be illustrated from the stories of Edgar and Kent. Edgar, it will be remembered, declines to disclose himself to his father where the plot provides no obvious reason why he should not do so; and if the plot provides no reason why he should not do so, Edgar's compassionate human nature provides reason enough why he should. On meeting his blinded father, Edgar could well have disclosed himself, would in all nature have disclosed himself, given Gloucester comfort and succour, and saved his life. In Sidney's version there is no hiding of the son's identity; but in *King Lear* the reconciliation of father and son is withheld by what Edgar later acknowledged for a fault in himself; and we hear only from Edgar of how Gloucester died on hearing of the truth and after much terrible and unnecessary suffering. Edmund had deceived Gloucester; why must Edgar now also deceive him? What must now deny to father and son the joy they may have in each other, except for a last, heartbroken, fleeting moment? Why must common human nature be so gratuitously and brutally outraged? For we must reflect that Gloucester, led by Edgar, and above all in the cliff scene, is an even more poignant and inexpressibly pitiable figure than when he staggered blinded from the knives of Cornwall; and this is not required by the plot and is strictly unnecessary: it only heaps misery on both Gloucester and Edgar. The natural flow of Edgar's love and forgiveness is brutally stopped to increase his and his father's suffering. Now if I am right in this, we can only conclude that this situation exhibits an intention essential to Shakespeare's imagination of the play.

Consider again now Kent. Here, if you will, is the common stuff of human nature: a man loyal, generous, rash, loving. But why does not Kent, at the opening of the storm and before Lear's madness sets in, disclose himself to Lear? Again, the plot does not at all forbid it; and again, Kent makes himself known to Lear only at the end when Lear is too far gone in grief and desperation to do more than take the barest note of him. Had Kent acted on what must have been his most natural impulse, he would not indeed have averted the main tragedy; but he could and would have brought comfort and companionship to the lonely and distraught Lear.

Now in the face of what I have said of Edgar and Kent, it is natural to say that we have to consider what, when we set ourselves to apprehend Shakespeare's masterpiece, we are undertaking to do. It is not, as I have said, a question of understanding an argument; it is a question of rising to a difficult perception offered by Shakespeare's most mature tragic art.

Now if we think so, we shall not put down these things I have spoken of as mere faults; and we shall be no more disposed to shrug our shoulders, to leave them for a mystery, to take a note of them and leave a question-mark after them. They were, we must suppose, integral to Shakespeare's intention when he wrote the play; they must become integral to ours when we read it or see it. Shakespeare will not allow us to imagine Cordelia in the human context of wifehood and queenship; he also will not allow the goodness of Edgar and Kent the comfort they may give and receive in the world's conflict. Against the pure wickedness of Cornwall and Edmund the beneficence of Edgar and Kent are not allowed to work with any mitigation; they are held firmly and unnaturally in much helplessness and suffering which are gratuitous and beyond the requirements of the plot. (pp. 106-08)

[If] we turn to the large outline of the plot, we come upon a third illustration, to add to what I have said of Kent and Edgar, and perhaps the most striking of the three, of the kind of improbability which may be seen as a gross fault or may, again, be construed as a sign of Shakespeare's intention in the play. I mean, Edmund's inexplicable delay in telling the others of the instructions he has given to kill Lear and Cordelia. Edmund is now defeated; he has played his adventurer's game and lost. In playing it he has some little sympathy from us; he is not in the same class as Cornwall, Goneril, and Regan; he had some reason, they had not; and when he says 'Yet Edmund was beloved' [V. iii. 240], we warm to him in pity. Now, with the game lost, he acknowledges the justice of his fate; he hears the story of his father's death which, he says, moves him to do good. But he knows that he has given orders to execute his victims instantly; and it is incredible that he has forgotten. Why does Shakespeare suffer him to speak only when he is expressly asked by Albany where Lear and Cordelia are? Shakespeare clearly gives us to understand that Edmund is changed, despite of his own nature; why do not common pity and compunction act in him? We may feel exasperation with Albany and Edgar at delaying at this time in a long colloquy; but we are more mystified by Edmund. Here too, then, a natural and generous impulse, even in Edmund, is forbidden; what good there came to be in him came to nothing in the plot's design. The silences of Edgar and Kent occasioned much and unnecessary suffering; the silence of Edmund is even more inexplicable; but it is also more catastrophic. It brings to nothing what Kent and the others had been indeed suffered to do. (pp. 108-09)

[All] three examples I have given, of Edgar, Kent, and Edmund, show Shakespeare removing virtue away from efficacy and power over the course of events. Lear must go on suffering uncomforted by the knowledge of Kent's presence, and Gloucester by the knowledge of Edgar's; and when Edmund at last repents, he is checked from influencing the course of the plot. On the one side, therefore, is surpassing good, and on the other extreme evil; but the scales are hopelessly weighted on one side; against the wickedness of Cornwall, Goneril, and Regan, what beneficence human nature is shown to possess is not allowed to issue in action; it is kept as far as may be in silence and suffering. Here, it will be seen, the simplification which Shakespeare conducts is not only in the characters themselves; it is, so to speak, in the control of the plot by the characters. The characters of Goneril, Regan, and Cornwall are, indeed, simple. The characters of Edgar, Kent, and Edmund are not; but they are controlled by a plot which holds them, and therefore also Lear and Gloucester and Cordelia, in almost unrelieved suffering, and then brings them to their deaths.

Here, or so it seems to me, is the main abstraction whch Shakespeare seems determined to conduct throughout the play: the forcing apart, I mean, of character from circumstance, of virtue from happiness and then of virtue from life itself. In the world which Shakespeare is now rendering, merit is made as powerless as possible and is then destroyed. 'Therefore', Bacon had said, 'poetry feigns [actions] more just in retribution, and more according to revealed providence'; but, as I have said, this is precisely what Shakespeare was not doing; indeed he set himself at all costs, including the cost of clear faults and absurdities, *not* to do so. The play seems to be designed to exhibit suffering and helpless virtue, whether it be the virtue of a Kent, the uncertain virtue of a Lear, or the transcendent virtue of an Edgar and a Cordelia. None of them may come to any happiness. Gloucester and Lear are given, before they die, and by an irony, only a kind of heartbroken joy. Kent and Edgar indeed survive; only, as I said, Kent speaks of imminent death, Edgar of death not long delayed. For them also, life may not go on.

I wish further to emphasize this primary feature of the play by taking account of events in the story which, as the reader will have noticed, I have hitherto ignored; and I can, I think, illustrate in another and very different way what I have in mind. I am looking principally not to character but to plot; and when we consider the plot as a whole, we can see without any great trouble that it has a major flaw in addition to those I have pointed out. I quote Mr. Granville-Barker who, speaking of the play after the third Act, says: 'The rest of the play must be pitched in a lower key . . . The thing stays by comparison pedestrian. . . . The chief fact to face, then, is that for the rest of the play, the best will be incidental and not germane to the actual story. The producer, therefore, must give his own best attention to Albany, Goneril, and Regan and their close-packed contests, and to the nice means by which Edgar is shaped for a hero . . . If he will take care of this, the marvellous moments will tend to take care of him.' . . . In other words, the soul of the play and the body of the plot have fallen apart; they have indeed to be made to look as if they have not; but they have, all the same; the 'marvellous moments' are 'not germane to the actual story'. To say nothing of the deaths of Goneril and Regan and to speak only of the most vital things in the plot, the combat of Edgar and Edmund, and then the battle, seem somehow to mean nothing to us. The duel is indeed made as stagy as may be; Mr. Granville-Barker spoke (a little uneasily, I suggest) of the 'nice means whereby Edgar is shaped for a hero'; but are they 'nice'? The combat is nearer to being a piece of hollow stage trumpery. Compare it, as Bradley urged us to do, with the duel in *Hamlet*. Everything turns on the battle; but was there ever such a battle so perfunctorily and shoddily treated? Compare it, as again Bradley urged us to do, with the battle in *Macbeth;* it is obvious that, like the duel, it has no life in it. But when Lear, or Lear and Cordelia, are on, the scenes surpass anything even in Shakespeare.

What is the cause of this state of affairs? We may say, no doubt, as Bradley does, that because of the double plot Shakespeare has too much on his hands, and that we are wearied by all that is going on. But this is not, I think, the real reason, or certainly the whole reason; it hardly explains our attitude to the decisive fighting that occurs. I suggest that the reason lies deeper than this: deeper in Shakespeare's imagination and in ours. But it is also simple enough. Edgar has to be made into a fighting man, Cordelia into the leader of an army; and it simply will not do. Shakespeare could not take it; we cannot take it. The Cordelia and the Edgar whom we know are one

thing; the Cordelia and the Edgar who fight battles and engage in combats are another; and they cannot be reconciled. The souls of Cordelia and Edgar are not in the stage figures who in battle and combat thus serve the purposes of a plot which a dramatist has to get on with and bring to a conclusion. In Cordelia and Edgar Shakespeare is contemplating figures of spiritual perfection who cannot move, with any substance of reality, at this level of the plot's working. Who can see Cordelia (or Lear, for that matter, in the state to which he has now come) at the head of an army, whether the army she leads be victorious or defeated? And the whole bent and direction of Edgar's spiritual bearing is away from this kind of thing; make him do this, and whether *he* be victorious or defeated, he is no longer Edgar. (pp. 110-14)

The reader will recall that my argument has been that Shakespeare contrives to allow his virtuous characters as little influence on the course of events as possible; he holds them in a kind of silent and helpless suffering. But now, at the place in the play to which we have now come, Cordelia and Edgar, types of spiritual perfection if ever there were such, are suddenly required to take arms against their troubles. Hitherto they have been figures of patience; they have suffered the slings and arrows of outrageous fortune; Edgar is indeed an Horatio, not spoken of and described merely, but manifested in the detail of life; and Cordelia will be cast down only for Lear's sake: for herself she could outfrown false fortune's frown. But now Cordelia must lead an army against her sisters and Edgar fight his brother; they have now, in all conscience, to take a hand in the plot. But in doing so, they become stage-figures and not what they have been. They become no longer images of suffering; whether they are victorious or defeated is neither here nor there; they no longer ring true. Here again, therefore, as in the illustrations I have given earlier, character and plot are ill-adjusted to each other. Formerly Kent and Edgar were forbidden to do much they might have done for Lear and Gloucester; this is unnatural and inexplicable; and their suffering and the suffering of Lear and Gloucester is thereby increased indefinitely. Now, late in the play, Cordelia and Edgar are required to do things no less unnatural. In either case, plot and character are irreconcilable; in either case, our apprehension of character is offended by the course of the action in which it is set.

I must now ask, Why does this come about? Why is the plot of *Lear* so unsatisfactory in the way I have tried to explain? What explains this severance of character and circumstance? I quote A. C. Bradley: 'When I regard *King Lear* strictly as drama, it appears to me, though in certain parts overwhelming, decidedly inferior as a whole to *Hamlet, Othello,* and *Macbeth*' [see excerpt above, 1904]; and I cannot doubt that Bradley is right. But we must understand the cause of its comparative failure; and its cause lies in just this ill-adjustment of plot to character and character to plot of which I have been speaking. Only, we must assume, I think we can do no other, that Shakespeare knew what he was doing. I part company from A. C. Bradley only when he is content to leave the improbabilities, inconsistencies, and the rest as things due to Shakespeare's carelessness; they must, or so it seems to me, arise from the workings of Shakespeare's imagination here, which for its purposes is willing to manhandle plot and character and wrest them sharply apart. Bradley is willing to believe, in the face of the play's improbabilities and therefore, as he thinks, carelessness of design, that the Fool was forgotten not by Kent and the others, but by Shakespeare. But if I have been at all right in what I have said, the Fool is at the centre of the play's imagination: his virtue is pitiable in its helplessness; he, like others, is an image of helpless and suffering love; he exerts no influence upon the course of events; the course of events passes him by.

For the truth is, or so it seems to me, that in this play Shakespeare is little enough concerned with strict dramatic plot or with character in the ordinary sense. He is, above all, concerned to exhibit certain moral ideas or states, imaginatively apprehended indeed, yet still ideas of evil and of good. His imagination sifts out these essences. To Evil he gives the initiative, the force, the driving power of the plot. Over against it he sets Good; but he forbids it, so far as he may, to interfere with and control the action and consequences of Evil; it is made silent and patient; it is suffering love; it has little influence upon the executive ordering of the world; it merely *is* and suffers; it is not what it does but what it is, as it is shown in a Cordelia and an Edgar, that we contemplate. Evil drives on, dynamic and masterful, but to its own destruction; Good is still, patient, and enduring, but is also destroyed; no limit, not even that of death, is put to what it must endure.

Now that this is so is, I think, shown by the way in which we ordinarily think of the play. It is truer of *King Lear* than of the other tragedies, that we think above all of certain scenes: the plot is comparatively dim to us. We think of Cordelia's silence before Lear; Lear on the heath and in the storm; then, in the last two Acts, what Mr. Granville-Barker calls the 'marvellous moments' which look after themselves; and these, like those earlier, are scenes of pity and suffering. In comparison with these, the course of the plot with its combats and battles engages little enough of our attention. What Shakespeare was concerned above all to contemplate were the figures of suffering; around these figures in their suffering the plot swirls its tragic way. But it is the figures themselves that hold our minds; and where Edgar and Cordelia are suddenly changed into martial shapes and take, or try to take, a strong hand in the direction of affairs, they interest us little; they are no longer at the play's centre. The play then is one which exhibits, above all in Cordelia and Edgar, 'patient merit', to use Hamlet's phrase; and Shakespeare's mind is not dwelling now on the spirit of Hamlet, but of Horatio. . . . 'Bear free and patient thoughts', says Edgar [IV. vi. 80]:

> Men must endure
> Their going hence, even as their coming hither:
> Ripeness is all.
>
>   [V. ii. 9-11]

This is the centre of Shakespeare's perception of life in his greatest play; and it will not do to speak of pessimism and gloom in the face of it; the crass opposites of pessimism and optimism have no relevance here. There could be no question of Cordelia's being brought, with the play, to some happy ending; to give her some thirty years of life in this world would have been as silly as to give us some assurance of temporal immortality for her in another. She, and through her Shakespeare, had come to a sense of life, and therefore of death, in which the soul makes no demand either of life or death. It is here, in all truth, that we may rightly say, The rest is silence. (pp. 114-19)

> *D. G. James, "Poetic Experiment" and "Poetic Discovery," in his* The Dream of Learning: An Essay on "The Advancement of Learning," "Hamlet," *and* "King Lear," *Oxford at the Clarendon Press, 1951, pp. 69-98, 99-126.*

GEOFFREY BUSH   (lecture date 1955)

[*In the following excerpt, taken from a series of lectures originally delivered in Boston in January, 1955, Bush claims that* King Lear *deals primarily with the problem of belief and is presented in terms of such paradoxes as duty in disguise, love in exile, reason in madness, sight in blindness, life in death, and so on. Although paradox is central to Christian belief, Bush argues that in Shakespeare's play "it includes ironies that prevent the certainty of a religious vision, and that suggest a different way of describing what it means to believe." The most troubling of these ironies he sees as Cordelia's death and Lear's reaction to it—his belief that she lives when in fact she's as "dead as earth." For Bush, the final scene dramatizes "the darkest possibility" of the play: that only through deception is "natural misfortune tolerable." Yet, Bush adds, there is comfort at the end of* King Lear *because Shakespeare suggests it is not wrong to believe in what appears to be, whereas at the beginning of the play it was wrong to act on appearances—indeed, the tragedy evolves from Lear's misguided attempt to base his belief on what his daughters seem to be. Bush suggests that this experience foreshadows the vision of Shakespeare's last romances, where rashness of action produces a flight into creative illusion, and where we are "no longer shaken by the difference between what is and what is not." The idea that Cordelia's death presents the possibility of transcendence, whether real or creatively imagined, has also been discussed by Phyllis Rackin (1970) and Bernard McElroy (1973).*]

Shakespeare's exploration of belief in *King Lear* is conducted in terms of paradox: duty in disguise, love in exile, reason in madness, sight in blindness, joy in sorrow, life in death, and heaven in a woman. Paradox is a manner of describing the natural condition that is central to Christian belief; but in *King Lear* it includes ironies that prevent the certainty of a religious vision, and that suggest a different way of describing what it means to believe. Nothing in *King Lear* is what it seems to be. At the division of the kingdom the children are not what they appear; Kent and Edgar assume disguises; and at the end the miracle that saves Gloucester from despair is not a miracle at all, but his child's pretense, an apparent miracle contrived by human affection. Lear dies in happiness, if Bradley is right, thinking that Cordelia lives [see excerpt above, 1904]: his last words are, "Look! her lips!" [V. iii. 311]. But it is not so; he is deceived; Cordelia is dead as earth. The play begins with the deception of the two old men, and at the end they are deceived once more. There is in *King Lear* a bitterly distressing discovery of the incompleteness of natural things in themselves. Something in the anguish of Hamlet's situation drives him to pretending, and the possibility is suggested in *King Lear* that in the face of such natural suffering there is nothing to believe in but pretense and show—a hundred knights or a gorgeous robe or an imagined miracle or a seeming spirit. The darkest possibility of *King Lear* is that only deception makes natural misfortune tolerable, that the unkindness of natural life is endured only through appearances, and that all that human love can offer, to show the heavens more just, is a trick. Yet there is comfort at the end of *King Lear*. What is mysterious about the concluding moments is that our minds are no longer pained by our knowledge that Lear is deceived, that Cordelia is not a spirit, and that there has been no miracle. In the eighteenth century *King Lear* was played with a happy ending. But the ending that we have is somehow beyond unhappiness. There is a necessity to believe, as there is for Hamlet to act; these are engagements to incompleteness for which we can reason not the need. At the beginning it is Lear's tragic mistake to attach his belief to what his daughters seem to be; and the seeming of Edgar, disguised as Poor Tom, is what turns Lear's belief to madness. But at the end it is in some fashion no longer a mistake to believe in what appears to be; Cordelia's seeming is what restores Lear's mind to sanity. It has been said that the tragic protagonist advances through appearances to reality; and this is true of Hamlet's and Lear's discovery of things as they are. But it is true also that at the end of *King Lear* our thoughts come to rest on appearances; it is enough that Cordelia seemed a spirit, and that now she seems to live. We have reached a verge of natural experience at which there are hints of the vision that shapes the last romances: the rashness of action and belief becomes a passage into seeming, and we are no longer shaken by the difference between what is and what is not; time is crossed by the continuance of time. Lear's discovery of the thing itself is supplemented by his discovery of Cordelia; and when he tells her, ''You are a spirit, I know'' [IV. vii. 48], we have reached a moment when what is and what seems come together in a new manner of knowing. (pp. 127-29)

> Geoffrey Bush, ''Tragedy and 'Seeming','' in his Shakespeare and the Natural Condition, *Cambridge, Mass.: Harvard University Press, 1956, pp. 107-35.*

HARRY V. JAFFA (essay date 1957)

[*The following excerpt is drawn from one of the most exhaustive and detailed studies of the first scene of* King Lear *ever published. The central thesis of Jaffa's essay is that the so-called ''love test'' is much more complex than the gratuitous act of a foolish and selfish old man, an interpretation proposed most forcefully by Samuel Taylor Coleridge (1813) and A. C. Bradley (1904). Instead, Jaffa regards it as a carefully developed, politically shrewd plan for the continued success of the kingdom created by a politically wise ruler, Shakespeare's greatest King. Jaffa supports this contention with an extensive elaboration of the motives behind the original love test, claiming that Lear is politically right in dividing the kingdom into three parts, since no single successor to the throne could accomplish the overthrow of the other two rulers; that Lear's plan to marry Cordelia to Burgundy—an intention Jaffa argues is quite obvious from the text—is shrewd in that it would insure a balance of power among the three daughters; and that his willingness to abdicate everything but the crown itself is wise in that it allows Lear to test the results of his plan and to eventually choose his successor. This successor, Jaffa continues, is obviously Cordelia, the person Lear believes is nearest to himself in personality and, therefore, loves him most. Perhaps the most significant aspect of Jaffa's essay, beyond his examination of Lear's political motives, is his assertion that the real reason for the trial scene is not Lear's desire to test Cordelia's love, but to demonstrate the depths of his love for her. For other reactions to the love test in* King Lear, *see the excerpts by Charlotte Lennox (1754), Edward Dowden (1881), Levin L. Schucking (1922), William Frost (1957-58), and John Reibetanz (1977).*]

It is generally agreed that Shakespeare regarded monarchy as the best form of government. It is not generally realized, however, that Lear is the greatest of Shakespeare's kings. For the moment, I submit only this evidence: the supreme object of monarchical policy in the English histories is the unification and pacification of England. Only Henry V even approaches success in this, but in view of his questionable title to the throne, he is compelled to create a dubious national unity by means of an unjust foreign war. Yet the first scene in *King Lear* shows the old monarch at the head of a united Britain (not merely England), and at peace not only with all domestic factions, but with the outside world as well. France and Burgundy, who represent this world, are suitors for the hand of Lear's youngest daughter. Never in the histories does Shakespeare represent his native land at such a peak of prestige and

political excellence: in *King Lear* alone do we find actualized the consummation devoutly wished by all other good Shakespearian kings. . . .

If Lear is, in fact, Shakespeare's greatest king, and if it is true that to perpetuate such a rule is an even greater task than to establish it, then the opening of *King Lear* shows us the old king confronted with the supreme problem of his great career: the problem of providing for the succession to his throne. The action whereby he provides for this succession should, therefore, be his greatest action. Since it would be the greatest action of the greatest king, and since monarchy is the best form of government, such an action would be Shakespeare's presentation of the consummation of the political art, of political virtue, and therewith of political life altogether. But such a presentation could imply even more than this: for if Shakespeare, as a Renaissance classicist, regarded man as a political animal, it is possible that he regarded the fulfillment of man's highest political function as identical with the fulfillment of his highest human function. It is not improbable then that the stage is set, at the opening of *King Lear,* for Shakespeare's presentation of the ultimate in human existence.

The foregoing will, no doubt, strike many as paradoxical. That *King Lear* contains the fullest demonstration of Shakespeare's creative powers, and that these somehow represent the ultimate in man's humanity, is a proposition that would be widely concurred in. Yet I believe that this latter proposition is consistent with, if not identical with, the former ones. For if Shakespeare undertook the fullest revelation of his powers in *King Lear,* then it is entirely probable that the story of the play was selected as the most suitable vehicle for this revelation. In other words, the question as to why we find in *King Lear* the fullest revelation of Shakespeare's genius may be identical with the question, why does Shakespeare reveal himself to us most fully in a play in which his greatest king is confronted with the task of perpetuating the perfect political regime?

Although many critics have opined that *King Lear* is Shakespeare's greatest work, few call it their favorite play, and few fail to remark adversely concerning many of its dramatic properties. . . . According to Coleridge, one can ''Omit the first scene in *Lear,* and everything will remain''; the first scene is a ''nursery tale,'' ''prefixed as the *porch* of the edifice, not laid as its foundation.'' In *King Lear,* says Coleridge, ''the interest and situations . . . are derived from a gross improbability'' [see excerpt above, 1813]. This is but an application of Coleridge's principle that, in a Shakespearian play, the interest does not derive from, indeed is independent of, interest in plot and story. (pp. 405-07)

From the view that the story of *King Lear* is an absurd fairy tale, Coleridge infers that none of the action initiated by Lear in Scene i is to be taken seriously. Yet Coleridge does not fail to observe one fact inconsistent with this general thesis: ''It was not without forethought, and it is not without its due significance, that the triple division is stated here, [I. i. 1-6], as already determined and in all its particulars, previously to the trial of professions, as the relative rewards of which the daughters were to be made to consider their several portions.'' A. C. Bradley, commenting on this observation, says that the love-test is a ''mere form, devised as a childish scheme to gratify his love of absolute power and his hunger for assurances of devotion'' [see excerpt above, 1904]. Yet neither Coleridge nor Bradley has reflected on the possibility that, if the love-test, the trick whereby Lear makes it appear that he is ''dividing his kingdom among his daughters in proportion to the strength of their protestations of love'' is a pretense, then perhaps much more in the scene is also pretense. Coleridge and Bradley rightly assume that to make the division of the kingdom depend upon such protestations could only signify insane vanity and folly, but they also assume that Lear is doing no such thing. Why, then, do they insist that he is vain and foolish nonetheless? May not this pretense be part of a larger system of pretenses? How do we know that this alone is a pretense and nothing else? In truth, we know no such thing. Since Lear in the course of the scene does alter the division of the kingdom to fit the strength of the protestations, one may say that the previously decided division was merely tentative. If we are to maintain the view that the love-test was really intended as a sham, then we must base our view on other and stronger evidence. (p. 407)

But if Lear's sanity, and with it his status as a tragic hero, depends upon the premise that the love-test is a pretense, then the whole meaning of the play, *i.e.,* the meaning of Lear's suffering, depends upon our making this hypothesis intelligible. For we do not know why he must suffer if we do not know why he adopted the pretense which was the efficient cause of that suffering.

The generally accepted explanation is that of Bradley: Lear is a foolish, vain, selfish old man, whose wits are beginning to fail. His failings are extenuated by his ''long life of absolute power, in which he has been flattered to the top of his bent,'' and which ''has produced in him that blindness to human limitations, and the presumptuous self-will, which in Greek tragedy we have so often seen stumbling against the altar of Nemesis.'' Yet this extenuation, besides being contradicted by internal evidence, which I shall present shortly, runs athwart the larger bias of the play. For it is widely admitted that the sufferings of Lear are the most terrible in all Shakespeare and, probably, *a fortiori,* in the whole of the world's literature. But great passion, whether it is that of Lear, of Oedipus, or of Jesus, implies greatness in the soul of the sufferer. A great passion is always, in some sense, compensation for a great error. . . . It seems impossible to suppose that a child, a fool, or a knave would be capable of the passion of a Lear. Is it not, then, as impossible to suppose that the error was childish, foolish, or knavish, which was, in an important way, the cause of such a passion? It is true that the action which precipitated Lear's passion was a sign of the absence of perfect wisdom. But it seems to me that no consistent view of the play as a whole is possible that does not account for Lear's unwisdom in Scene *i* as a defect such as only the very greatest soul could suffer. Bradley's explanation of Lear's failure in Scene *i* is, I think, clearly deficient, in that it is at least compatible with the view that Lear's error was the error of a petty soul.

I have suggested that the stage is set at the beginning of the play for the supreme action of Lear's long and successful reign: the action whereby he provides for its perpetuation. The consciousness of critics has, I believe, been so dominated by Lear's apparent failure in this scene, that they have failed to notice his serious intention. Yet the meaning and extent of Lear's failure can be grasped with precision only in the light of his intentions. We must then try to understand exactly how Lear undertook to solve this paramount political problem. . . . Bradley calls our attention to the fact that catastrophe is the consequence, not of Lear's original plan, but of the alteration of that plan. Bradley assumes, without any attempt at proof, that Lear's original plan was also foolish and rash, although not ''hideously rash.'' In a footnote to the latter phrase, he men-

tions that it is Kent who applies this epithet to the *altered* plan. Yet Bradley does not attempt the possible inference that, if Kent, within the play, was informed concerning the original plan ''in all its particulars'' and had not expressed any objection to it, then perhaps he had approved of it. This, in fact, is a necessary inference, if we are not to suppose that Kent, who does not even express a private doubt to his fellow-councillor Gloucester was, until the penultimate moment of his public service, a time-serving flatterer. But if the original plan had Kent's, and Gloucester's approval, it may not have been foolish at all. It may, indeed, have been a product of sound principles of statecraft.

The proposition that Kent and Gloucester approved of Lear's original plan is a necessary inference for anyone who does not reject the premise that, in general, the relationship of characters in a Shakespearian play is made to appear to flow from their entire lives, and not to start up, *de novo,* with the raising of the curtain. . . . Kent is the King's favorite courtier, as Cordelia is his favorite daughter. Both Kent and Cordelia are, in similar ways, mirrors of the master and father they love. Bradley's statement that Lear has been corrupted by flattery, and has a foolish craving for it, is contradicted by the fact that Lear prefers above all others the two people in the play who are represented as absolutely incapable of flattery or hypocrisy. We can no more suppose that Kent and Cordelia are blunt and plain-spoken to the King for the first time (or that he loved them for anything but their true qualities) than that they have been petty flatterers until the moment the action of the play begins. . . . Moreover, Lear's preference for Cordelia and Kent is consistent with a widely recognized principle of the soul: the principle that self-love is the basis of friendship, and that we prefer as friends those who are most like ourselves. Lear's own nature is not that of a flatterer, and hence, we would expect him to prefer those who were not flatterers. Lear's political success, moreover, would be very difficult to understand, if he did not have about him those who would tell him the truth. (pp. 408-10)

If Kent knew Lear's original plan in all its particulars, he must have approved it, since he is silent concerning any defects it may have possessed, and since we know that he did not hesitate to protest in the most vehement manner when Lear departed from it. If it be objected that Kent may have disapproved the original plan, but acceded to it after he had exhausted his influence in having it rectified, there is this reply: someone as loyal and devoted as Kent would surely have been preoccupied with the danger to his master, if he had anticipated any. Yet, in the moment before the stage fills with the court, we see him and Gloucester turn lightly from state to personal matters, without any sign of apprehension concerning the former. What, then, was the original plan?

The negative view that Bradley and others have taken of the original plan has centered, as has been said, on the love-test. The love-test has already been dismissed as a pretense, as far as the original division of the kingdom is concerned. The real objection has always been to the division of the kingdom itself. It has always been thought that, since the supreme object of monarchical policy in Shakespeare is the unification of England, a British king who deliberately divides a united kingdom is committing the supreme act of monarchical folly. Yet reflection must make us cautious of accepting this view. First of all there looms the paradox of imputing the crime of dividing the kingdom to the one Shakespearian king whose ascendancy appears to have united it, a paradox enforced by Kent's apparent acquiescence. Second is the radical difference between dividing the kingdom into two, as distinct from three. The very number two is, traditionally, the number for strife; as the number three is the number for unity. Without pursuing allegorical possibilities, it is clear that a balance of power can be better preserved where there are three distinct forces, no one of which can overmatch the other two, than where there are only two forces, however evenly matched. The most important reflection, however, concerns whether, in dividing the kingdom, Lear was doing, during his lifetime, what in any event was bound to come to pass after his death. That is, how do we know that the unity achieved by Lear was not itself the result of an equipoise of forces, in unstable equilibrium, rather than a simple unity? In order to understand Lear's policy, one must analyze the problem he faced, the problem of the succession, in terms of the political realities which confronted him. (pp. 410-11)

It is striking that, although Goneril and Regan have been married for some time, they have not yet received dowries. All three daughters must receive their dowries simultaneously. Does this fact not indicate that Lear was thinking in terms of an overall balance of power, each part of which was needed to insure the rest? Had Lear's power been as absolute as it has seemed, why should he have hesitated so long to give the elder daughters their dowries? Lear was certainly using the dowries, and the marriages, as instruments of policy, as was the custom in royal (and not only royal) houses. Burgundy and France have "long" made their amorous sojourn at his court, and presumably it is much longer since Cornwall and Albany first made theirs. Lear has delayed as long as possible making his final disposition, both of the hands and fortunes of his daughters. What then was Lear's matrimonial policy?

First, we must note that Cornwall and Albany represent the geographical extremities of Britain. Cornwall clearly represents the south. Albany, according to Holinshed, originally was the northern part of the island, and included Scotland. . . . Now, anyone who knows only so much of English history as is contained in Shakespeare's histories, knows that English kings found it impossible to exercise control in any region very remote from the center of the royal domains, without the support of the feudal potentates in those regions. The selection of sons-in-law from the remote portions of his kingdom indicates, I believe, that Lear's unification of the kingdom was in part due to his ability to secure the adhesion of the lords of these outlying districts through marriage with the royal house. But the marriage of a daughter involves a dowry: Cornwall and Albany expected more than brides, and the possibility that a descendant might occupy the throne. What could be more natural than that they expected lands that lay in the neighborhood of their ancestral estates?

From this it would seem that Lear's action in dividing the kingdom was not arbitrary or foolish—it was an action predestined by the very means required to bring unity to the kingdom. Lear, it appears, delayed the division as long as possible, but he could not put it off indefinitely, any more than he could put off indefinitely his own demise.

In Lear's speech, announcing to the court the division of the kingdom into three parts, he gives two reasons for his action: first, that he wishes to shake all care and business from his age, conferring them on younger strengths; and second, "that future strife may be prevented now" [I. i. 44-5]. . . . However, if we view these two reasons more superficially, I think it would be correct to say that the second reason is the real

one, and the first primarily an excuse for the latter. For it is difficult to believe that failing strength was a pressing motive for Lear's action: the old man was the most prodigious octogenarian on record, still spending his days hunting, and able, as the last act shows, to kill a man single-handed. The decisive consideration, however, is this: there is no evidence that, in the original plan, Lear intended anything resembling an abdication. On the contrary is the fact that Lear never abandoned the crown. What he divided between his sons-in-law, in the flush of his rage against Cordelia, was a coronet. He himself was to retain, even in the altered plan, "The name, and all th' additions to a king" [I. i. 136]. Yet, as long as Lear retained the name of a king, a name which he in no way shared with a successor, his delegation of authority to his sons-in-law remained fundamentally distinguished from an abdication. . . . To sum up: Lear might have delegated much of his "business" to his sons-in-law in the original plan, but there is no sign of anything resembling an abdication. And as long as he did not abdicate he would, as King, remain the only personage capable of deciding the highest political questions. Since there is no explicit mention, anywhere in the scene, of a successor, the implication is left that Lear would retain the power of naming a successor, and this in turn indicates an intention to retain decisive power. (pp. 411-13)

Concerning the marriage of Cordelia, I think the evidence is overwhelming in favor of the view that she was intended as the bride of Burgundy. First, because Lear offers her to Burgundy, although this is after her disinheritance. Second, because Burgundy has had previous knowledge of Cordelia's dowry. But such knowledge implies at the same time that he has been privy to some, if not all, of Lear's intended scheme. Such a confidential position certainly suggests the status of an intended son-in-law. Now France and Burgundy were traditional enemies. Their presence at Lear's court suggests that Cordelia's dowry would have been an important counter in the balance of power between them. Burgundy is the lesser power, as is shown by Lear's style in addressing him, and by the fact that Lear fears insulting France, but not Burgundy. Now Cordelia's marriage to France would have been a political blunder of the first magnitude, a blunder of which there is no reason to suspect the Lear who drafted the plan approved by Kent and Gloucester. For a French marriage would inevitably have given rise to the French claims to the British throne, such as actually led to the French invasion that occurs in the play. . . . Moreover, such a marriage would have heavily unbalanced the system of powers, as that system is envisaged within the horizon of the play. France, commanding the fairest part of Britain, might easily have overmatched Burgundy, thereafter to hold the remainder of Britain in his power. On the other hand, however, Cordelia's dowry, added to Burgundy, might have aided the balance of power on the continent. And, conversely, Burgundy, added to Cordelia's part of Britain, would have neutralized any combination of the older sisters. (pp. 413-14)

Although the basic problem facing Lear was that of the succession to the throne, there is no direct reference in the text to the subject of a prospective heir. If Cordelia were married to Burgundy, however, it would seem probable that the crown was intended to pass to Cordelia and her descendants. Burgundy would be elevated in the feudal hierarchy by his marriage to a king's daughter, and his ancestral dukedom might become an appendage to the kingdom of Britain, rather than the reverse. Elements in the English tradition would seem to confirm the soundness of this view. The ascent of a foreign duke, William of Normandy, to the throne of England gave English kings claims upon the French throne, but not the reverse. . . . A Burgundian marriage, in short, would have made the succession of Cordelia to the throne a viable political arrangement. Lear's scheme of marrying Cordelia to Burgundy gave good promise of leading to a stable international system, and a peaceful acceptance of Lear's will and testament at home.

It is not clear whether Lear intended to make an announcement concerning the succession at the court we witness in Scene *i*. In our judgment he did not intend to do so. It would have been apparent to everyone, from the preferred treatment of Cordelia, that he intended the crown to pass to her. Yet the precise terms of the inheritance of the crown itself would have left some scope for diplomacy. The absence of evidence on which to decide what these terms might have been suggests that Lear himself was not yet in a position to fix them. The evidence I have cited suggests that Lear, being truly wise in the ways of politics, was not a man to force premature decisions, and that he was in no hurry to give up any more of his authority than necessary. But the announcement of the succession would have involved some further sacrifice of authority. Like any out-going office-holder, Lear's authority would be diminished the moment his successor was known. Those who would be reluctant to oppose the king openly, so long as they had hopes of influencing him in their favour, would lose some of that reluctance the moment they were certain his decision was against them. The succession of Cordelia to the throne had to be accomplished in a succession of steps, each of which required something of a pause, in order to test its firmness. The first step was to be the granting of the dowries, simultaneously with the announcement of the marriage. . . . The realignment of power resulting from the dowries and the marriage would be the essential basis of the future succession. But in a feudal system, in which power depended heavily upon personal loyalties, public pledges would not be a negligible factor in guaranteeing the success of Lear's arrangements. How to secure those pledges was a consideration prior to any plan to announce the succession itself. In our judgment, the love-test was, in one of its meanings, a part of Lear's deliberate system of policy. Its purpose was to supply, at least inferentially, pledges of support for the division of the kingdom which he was in process of announcing. As we shall shortly demonstrate, these pledges were demanded only from Goneril and Regan, not from Cordelia. They were, that is, demanded only from those who might have motives to repudiate his division.

Certainly Lear did not have any practical doubt concerning the nature of his daughters' love for him. He had already arranged things to favor Cordelia as much as possible. Not only was the kingdom divided on the map before the start of the court scene, but Lear gave Goneril, and then Regan, their shares after each had spoken, without hearing the other. Thus Cordelia's "more opulent" third was awaiting her, as the remainder, before she spoke a word. Clearly, Lear's intention was not to weigh the speeches against the shares in any manner or sense. Yet his shrewd knowledge of his elder daughters put them in a position in which it would have been ludicrous for them to repudiate their father's judgment after their fulsome speeches of devotion. (pp. 415-17)

Commentators have long noted the swiftness of the action in Scene *i*, and in the case of the love-test have taken it as additional evidence of Lear's rashness. Yet a sufficient reason for Lear's haste would be his anxiety to have his plan consummated before Goneril and Regan could recover poise enough to object to it. Lear's very haste may be regarded as craftiness.

We know that the professions were not intended to determine the shares, but Goneril and Regan could not know that. As far as Goneril knew, her fortune might depend upon the effect of her speech. Regan may have suspected that this was not the case, but with more than two-thirds of the kingdom remaining, she would take no chance. Cordelia alone of the three, seeing the remainder plainly before her on the map, knew in advance precisely what her share was to be. Cordelia alone therefore knew that her speech was not needed to establish her share. To Cordelia it must have been apparent that the test was a trick devised in her interest, and that Lear, far from demanding that she heave her heart into her mouth, was making his own protestation of love to her. In truth, Lear was not asking Cordelia to flatter him. Lear rightly counted on the hypocrisy of the elder daughters betraying them. But when he turns to Cordelia he seems rather to say, "See how I have turned their greed against them, and reserved the fairest portion for you, whose love I have never doubted."

Our analysis is now exposed to a grave objection. If Lear has, all along, judged correctly the characters of his daughters, as we have maintained, and if the love-test is meant to exploit the hypocrisy of Goneril and Regan in the interest of Cordelia's truth, why does Lear react so violently to that very truth? If his affection for Cordelia is due to the very qualities she here displays in so transcendant a manner, why then does he not place the same interpretation on her behavior that Kent does, and that we do, and tell the court that he sees in her blunt refusal to compete with her sisters the virtue that he all along wished to reward with the greatest share? Would not this have been hailed as a vindication of the old King's judgment, just as Bassanio's choice of the leaden casket vindicated the judgment of Portia's father, in *The Merchant of Venice*? (pp. 417-18)

In brief, it is our thesis that Lear is, on the conscious level, outraged by the injustice of Cordelia's refusal to permit the consummation of his carefully contrived plan. But the violence of his outrage is due to an unconscious sense that that very consummation, which he thinks he desired, would have violated, and forever frustrated, a passion far more profound than the passion for political success. For Lear, in striking at Cordelia, strikes also at his own handiwork. To understand the violence of Lear's eruption, we must understand the unconscious necessity he was under to destroy that political edifice which it had been his life's work to construct.

Starting from Lear's conscious motivation, we can answer the objection we have posed by observing that Lear certainly did not want the love-test to *appear* as a trick. To have done so would have run counter to a host of the political considerations we have advanced. Albany and Cornwall were not to be insulted. Lear wanted the entire scene to be a public "love-feast." In this Lear was acting the role of a hypocrite, we might say, but his hypocrisy was only a concession to his sense of justice. He had devised the best plan for the kingdom, for the common good, and any compromise that he had made with truth was made for the sake of justice. Cordelia's uncompromising, intransigent truthfulness contrasted then with his own willingness to sacrifice for the common good. If we remember the key part that Cordelia was to play in the entire plan, we can begin to understand the sense of outrage, even betrayal, that the old man must have felt.

Although the mere fact of Lear's rage can be accounted for by this surface explanation, its violence, and its tragic consequences, are intelligible only if we relate what occurred on the surface to what occurred beneath it. What occurred beneath the surface may be summarized by saying that, when Cordelia jarred her father by her unexpected response, she not only upset his political plan, but his personal plan, which was to express his love of Cordelia. We must grasp the nature of Lear's need to express this love, if we are to understand the passion loosed when that need was frustrated.

Let us turn again to the love-test, a dramatic device brilliantly adapted to Shakespeare's multiple purpose in Scene *i*. Its function on the level of mere policy has been sketched. Lear asks his daughters to tell him how much they love him. In effect, he commands their love. Yet, in a sense, love cannot be commanded, only professions of love can be. By the love-test Shakespeare establishes one precise limit of Lear's power to command and, thereby, one limit of kingly power and virtue. But Lear asks his daughters to tell him how much they love him that he may proportion his bounty to their merit. He thus proclaims a kingly desire to proceed upon the rules of distributive justice, while also implying that love for himself is a proper test of merit in others. This latter implication is not mere vanity, if Lear is the great ruler we have said he is. For the daughter who loves him most will in all likelihood be the most meritorious, since she will most nearly resemble her father. Yet in proclaiming his desire to make a just distribution, Lear tacitly admits the necessity he is under to know the truth concerning his daughters' love for him. But what the love-test discloses is the impossibility that Lear can ever have such knowledge as long as he remains upon his throne. For if it is true that love cannot be commanded, then he who possesses the power to command professions of love must be at a particular disadvantage in distinguishing genuine from spurious manifestations of love. Because Lear could, as king, command professions of love, it was impossible for him ever to be certain that an expression of love for himself, whether by Cordelia or another, was not in fact a response to his power of command. Lear thought Cordelia loved him most, because he saw in her the reflection of his own kingliness. But if imitation is the sincerest kind of flattery, how could Lear ever distinguish the imitation of flattery from that generated by his virtue in the souls of those who really loved him? Cordelia's defiance in the love-test only brought into the open the king's essential impotence, for it is not impossible to ascribe to Cordelia a very shrewd selfishness in Scene *i*. Consider the consequences of her boldness: she was the intended bride of the "waterish" Burgundy; but, losing her dowry she loses a poor lover and gains a superior one, France. Not only does France exhibit a nobility of character that makes him seem worthy of his bride, but he is a king in his own right and, as we quickly learn, one who has no intention of abandoning his bride's claims. Accordingly, Cordelia's course could be interpreted, not only as a sacrifice of public interest to private happiness, but as a clever scheme to become queen of France and England, thus defeating Lear's just policy, which is national and patriotic. Goneril and Regan were shallow hypocrites, but how could Lear know that Cordelia was not a clever one?

Lear, we have said, implies that love of himself is a test of merit in others. To assume the validity of such a test is, we might say, of the essence of monarchy. Love of justice, in a monarchy, is thought to be identical, in essence, with love of the monarch, because he is thought to incorporate justice. . . . The root of Lear's power is the conviction, in the heart both of king and subjects, that he is justice incarnate. Yet the absoluteness of Lear's power, founded upon this conviction, shuts him off from the very knowledge upon which that justice would

have to be based if it were what it seems to be. For a spontaneous show of love cannot be distinguished from a clever imitation, except by a god who can search men's hearts. Humanly speaking, the power to discern disinterested motives, however limited in the best case, exists in inverse ratio to the power to command. In proclaiming love of himself as the principle of distributive justice Lear in fact proclaimed, as the basis of his justice, a god-like knowledge. Lear, we might say, is compelled by the nature of his situation to pretend to a perfection he does not possess in order to actualize a perfection he does possess.

But what meaning are we to ascribe to the expression "perfection he does possess"? Lear, we have said, is a great ruler. The unity and amity of the kingdom, although seen for the most part retrospectively, and through the attachment to him of all the "good" characters, are witness to this. Yet, granting Lear this superiority, we can still say that Lear never had more than an opinion of his own justice. If we were to assume that such a regime is the best of which human life admits, we would, nonetheless, have to say that the best is, in a decisive sense, an illusion. We would be further driven to conclude that Lear's greatness as a king is an illusion. Lear's supposed knowledge of his daughters' love of him, which was to have been the basis of his greatest and ostensibly most just political action, is of the essence of the illusion.

Now the crux of the situation consists in this: that the illusion which is the basis of Lear's policy, although adequate for all the purposes of political life, becomes intolerable at the decisive moment in the love-test. The old king has need of genuine love. The entire scene, we must remember, is due to his mortality, to the fact that he must provide for a successor. The very insufficiency which necessitates a succession, necessitates love. A god could be loved without loving, but a man cannot. If Lear possessed the perfection which, as king, he pretends to, he would be capable of being loved without loving. But Lear lacks such perfection. His need of love is radical. (pp. 419-22)

We must now analyse the precise impact that Cordelia's refusal had upon her father, and attempt to comprehend the interaction of his conscious and unconscious motivation. At the moment Lear rejects Cordelia, calls her stranger, and dowers her with his curse, she has in fact become a stranger to him. For Lear, in attempting to carry out the well-contrived pretense or deception of the love-test, had not hesitated to compromise with truth, albeit for the sake of justice. Cordelia, in refusing to make any such compromise, showed herself in her intransigence unlike her father. But it is this appearance of unlikeness, rather than the appearance of disobedience, that make a mockery of his plan. For the plan was founded on the assumption of such a likeness. But Lear's assumption that Cordelia loved him, and that she was like him, involved even more than the question of whether he was sound in his intention to make her his successor. For Lear had seen what he thought was the image of his own soul in Cordelia. His passion for Cordelia was his self-love transfigured: in his identification with her he saw his monarchy perpetuated beyond the grave. His faith in the truth of that image caused him to place faith in the bearer of the image. But bewildered by the sudden strangeness of the bearer, Lear could no longer recognize the image, and with this he lost the sheet anchor of what had hitherto been his existence. . . . Lear's alienation from Cordelia involved his alienation from the basis of such self-knowledge as he believed himself to possess. He became alienated not only from her, but from himself, and from the world within which he had seen himself in his own mind's eye. Lear's original, conventional kingliness was intrinsic to the world implied by the image of himself which he saw reflected in Cordelia. The strange image which Cordelia now reflected separated Lear from this world, the world in which he had been king. He could not continue as king, as his original plan required, when he no longer had a basis for faith in that world. Yet some part of the passion of the outburst against Cordelia, like that against his other daughters later in the play, is due to his attachment to that lost world, an attachment not to be overcome lightly or in a moment. For his attachment to justice was at the root of his attachment to that world, and the tragedy of *King Lear* lies in the necessity of Lear to abandon even his attachment to justice, when the claims of love and truth are brought to bear in all their uncompromising imperiousness.

The deeper meaning of the love-test was foreshadowed when we observed that Cordelia, alone of the three sisters, knew in advance of her speech what her share of the kingdom was to be. Cordelia, we said, knew that her father, far from demanding a profession of love from her, was making a profession of love to her. In the test Lear becomes the lover and Cordelia the beloved. But the relation of beloved to lover is that of cause to effect, of superior to inferior. When Lear, responding to Cordelia's "Nothing," tells her that nothing comes of nothing, he expresses the axiom upon which all understanding of causality is founded. He tells her that there is no effect without a cause. He implies that she cannot cause him to be bountiful without obeying him. He does not know, however, that by becoming the lover, the only bounty he has to offer is his love, and that Cordelia, as beloved, can only cause his love by refusing to surrender the sovereignty which he has himself now thrust upon her. For Lear, ironically, is attempting to command Cordelia at precisely the moment, and in the very situation, in which his relation to her has been reversed, and she has become the commanding one. For when Lear turned to Cordelia to bear her profession, she had already ascended a throne. It was not the throne of Britain, but rather the invisible throne prepared by nature for those of surpassing virtue. We have noted above that Lear's choice of Cordelia as his successor was based upon a trans-legal conception of political right, in that he did not proceed upon the legal or conventional rule in accordance with which the eldest, as distinct from the best qualified, inherits. . . . But we now see that Cordelia's precedence over her sisters is also a matter of natural right. But Cordelia's natural right to rule is not an element of political right. It follows not from the wisdom of her father's choice, but from her intransigence in regard to truth. Cordelia's natural right, far from being an element of political right, is destructive of political right. For Lear's policy, which we have shown to be both wise and just, depends upon a small hypocrisy, a relatively slight pretense. Cordelia's nature, refusing to make the concession that policy called for, reveals, at one and the same moment, its transcendant beauty and its superiority to, if not its contempt for justice.

It was Lear's intention that Cordelia become sovereign. That intention is fulfilled within the love-test itself, but in a way that Lear did not anticipate. Nevertheless, we maintain, Cordelia does do what her father wishes her to do, but it is his unconscious wish that she fulfills. It requires the five acts of the tragedy for Lear fully to realize what that true wish was. Strangely enough, Lear, in his outburst against Cordelia, also acts in obedience to her, who is now his sovereign. For in the region beyond that of the political, to which their relationship has now been transferred, the act of obedience, the act of the true subject, is the act of love. To command love in this non-political sense, means to cause loving in the soul of another. Cordelia can be the cause of that love which Lear's great soul needs, only if Lear removes himself from, or removes from himself, every vestige of his monarchy in this world. We may summarize the ironies of Scene *i* by saying that the love-test, which at first glance appears to be a straightforward demand for protestations of love, turns out to be an elaborately contrived deception; but the supreme deception is that of the deceiver himself, who really acts, in the final analysis, albeit unwittingly, for the very purpose for which he says he is acting. Lear, acting to discover the truth about his daughters' love, does what would have been foolish as a political action if it were not a pretense; yet it is not foolish in its deeper, non-pretending meaning, because it is no longer a political action. For Lear's action, but not Lear himself, is thoroughly rational in the rejection of Cordelia. For reason could not have devised a more straightforward way than that actually taken by Lear, to divest himself of all the attributes of worldy monarchy.

We have said that Cordelia's intransigent truthfulness showed her superiority, even to justice. It did indeed show that, on the level of political action, there need be no distinguishable difference between superiority to the claims of justice, and rank injustice. This paradox, far from being merely apparent, is at the core of the tragedy of *King Lear,* and lies in Shakespeare's vision of a universe in which the demands of justice are in an insoluble conflict with the demands of that truth which is, in its turn, the only unconditional motive for justice. The proposition that truth is the motive for justice is symbolized by the fact that Lear's entire policy, his wise and just policy, has as its foundation his conviction in regard to Cordelia. Yet it was impossible for Lear's conviction to be more than a mere opinion within the framework of that policy. Cordelia, responding to Lear's unconscious demand for truth, as distinct from mere opinion, compels him to act in the most unjust manner possible, in order to discover that truth. Thus does the uncompromising quest for truth and love, which can ultimately be understood as different names for the same thing, destroy justice; even as the successful completion of Lear's original plan, while doing justice, that is, serving the common good, would forever have denied him that love and knowledge which alone could link his mighty soul with its source in eternity. (pp. 422-27)

> *Harry V. Jaffa, "The Limits of Politics: An Interpretation of 'King Lear', Act I, Scene 1," in* The American Political Science Review, *Vol. LI, No. 2, June, 1957, pp. 405-27.*

WINIFRED M. T. NOWOTTNY (essay date 1957)

[*Nowottny examines the significance of Lear's questions throughout* King Lear, *from "Which of you shall we say doth love us most?" to "Why should a dog, a horse, a rat have life . . .?" She suggests that all can be placed under one inclusive question: "What is man?" Nowottny argues that in attempting to discover the answer to this question Lear realizes that all a man knows he knows through the flesh; thus the symbol of flesh becomes an ambiguous point of reference for other questions Lear raises during the course of the drama, such as the nature of his own identity, the nature of knowledge, and the nature of the gods. "The whole play is a dramatic answer," Nowottny concludes, which moves towards revelation, not redemption, through suffering. For other comments regarding Lear's achievement of self-knowledge through suffering, see the excerpt by Irving Ribner (1958) and Paul A. Jorgensen (1967).*]

Act V. Scene iii. Edmund, Albany, Edgar, Kent, Goneril, Regan, Cordelia, Lear, and Soldiers. By J. Barry (n.d.).

The greatness of *King Lear* is of a kind that almost disables criticism: in it, Shakespeare has so reconciled opposites as to make it difficult to frame any valid statement about the nature of the play as a whole. The total impression is one of primitive simplicity, of solid rock unfretted by the artist's tool, but whenever, in studying it, the mind is visited by some small insight into its pattern (for of course it is patterned), further reflexion swiftly brings about a rush of critical excitement over the widening significances of what seemed at first a detail of the design, and this not once but many times; life is not long enough fully to explore *King Lear*. These repeated experiences of the play should inure the critic to the idea that whatever element of its design seems at any given moment most fascinating it is none the less merely one element among many, and the critic will do well to think of himself as the groping speleologist who traverses, astonished, one only of the many levels of that rock whose hidden intricacies are no more impressive than its simple mass. . . .

King Lear, as far as his outward fortunes are concerned, is a passive hero, but at the same time he is himself the active cause of what is tragic (as distinct from pathetic) in his experience, and is indeed more truly the maker of his own tragedy, by virtue of the questions he himself raises, than any other Shakespearian tragic hero. The play opens with the *locus classicus* of Lear's questioning: "Which of you shall we say doth love us most?" [I. i. 51]. Goneril's comment that Lear has "put himself from rest" [II. iv. 290] is applicable to this and to almost every subsequent question he asks. It is applicable too, to the essential condition of man, and what in Lear's questioning is wilful is also what (being autonomous) lifts him clear of the particular circumstances of plot and personality and makes him that Everyman that Macbeth with his Witches, Othello with his Iago, even Hamlet with his Ghost, cannot be. In the light of Lear's subsequent questions the first question is seen to be no mere device to get the play started, for his subsequent questions are in a sense as wilful as the first, going beyond the immediate provocation of the moment in which he formulates them. (p. 90)

Before the end of Act II, all the problems that dominate the dialogue of Lear's scenes in Acts III and IV have been posed, and posed by Lear himself: the nature of his own status and identity, the nature of knowing, the nature of need, the nature of the gods; and Lear has also raised, though not as a direct question, the problem of the inherent guilt of the flesh:

> thou art my flesh, my blood, my daughter;
> Or rather a disease that's in my flesh,
> Which I must needs call mine: thou art a boil,
> A plague-sore, an embossed carbuncle,
> In my corrupted blood.
>
> [II. iv. 221-25]

It is the grand achievement of Act III to connect these problems so closely that each increases another's momentum. Lear's own experiences in the storm provide the emotional and logical connexions. The dialogue with the storm is, clearly, a battle with the gods. Pitting himself against the heavens, Lear challenges them to reveal their nature and his own: is he their slave? or is it they who are servile ministers? But this speech, the climax of Lear's resistance to the evil directed against himself by Goneril and Regan, is at the same time but the prelude to deeper issues between the gods and men: are they in their wrath the punishers of covert guilt? and what of the "poor naked wretches" who are involved in "seasons such as these"? Here, though Lear defiantly asserts his own innocence,

> I am a man
> More sinn'd against than sinning—
> [III. ii. 59-60]

this assertion is of short duration, giving place at once to his recognition that he himself has taken too little thought of needy man, and destined to give place again to a deepening of his insight into that "disease that's in my flesh, which I must needs call mine". In this apparently inconclusive struggle with the gods, he does find answers to questions he himself has already raised: that of the nature of man's knowing, and that of his own status. He finds out (as we are told later) that he had been deceived about himself and he finds out also (as we are told immediately) that true knowledge is born of what is felt in the flesh:

> Take physic, pomp;
> Expose thy self to feel what wretches feel.
> [III. iv. 33-4]

From this it is a short step to the notion that the man who must "answer with [his] uncovered body this extremity of the skies" [III. iv. 101-02] is at the heart of truth; Poor Tom because he is most exposed must feel most and so know most, and so he becomes Lear's "philosopher", of whom Lear asks, "What is the cause of thunder?" [III. iv. 155]. Through the impact of the storm Shakespeare has effected one of the most difficult acts of communication necessary to the subsequent development of the play: he has brought home to us Lear's belief that all a man can know is what he knows through the flesh. Further, in Lear's defiance of the storm, his involvement with the problem of guilt has been brought to the fore. By a master-stroke, Shakespeare now establishes an intimate relation between Lear's several preoccupations, by using for them all the one symbol of the flesh: the flesh that suffers, knows, begets, is punished for its guilt. (pp. 91-2)

Henceforward the language takes on the function of binding more closely and exploring more deeply the connexions set up by Lear's experiences in the storm. It is the discovery of the metonymy, "the flesh", wherewith to advert to all the problems vital to the play which gives the language of the latter part of the tragedy its characteristic mark of simplicity charged with power, for within the metonymic structure made possible by the use of this common term, Shakespeare is able to sweep the strings of feeling whilst seeming to make no gesture at all.

The language of the play is further shaped for Shakespeare's purposes by a deliberate exploitation of the ambivalence of this term and of the aptness of the symbol for development through cognate terms such as "heart", "hand", "eyes", "brains", which also, in common usage, have both abstract and concrete significance. Much of the sombre power of the most memorable utterances in the mad scenes is due to the subtle interplay between the flesh as mere flesh and the qualities the flesh embodies, and to the interplay between the different members of that whole complex of ideas of which the flesh has been made the symbol. For instance, Lear's sudden demand,

> Then let them anatomize Regan; see what breeds
> about her heart. Is there any cause in nature
> that makes these hard hearts?
> [III. vi. 76-8]

is macabre, not merely gruesome, because of the interplay between abstract and concrete, coupled with the interplay between the multiple references of the symbol: the flesh itself when dissected will reveal the truth, but an *intellectual* truth ("anatomize" meant not only to dissect but also to give a reasoned analysis or enumeration of qualities); this flesh is also the flesh in which evil things "breed" and the flesh subject to Nature's laws, the flesh in which the physical and spiritual are, according to Lear, so wholly united that the "heart" that breeds wickedness is also the "heart" that can be dissected and its hardness probed to seek the final cause. And the form of this sudden demand is such that we can simultaneously accept it as natural to Lear's way of thinking, and reject it as unnatural to our own. This is but one example of the way in which the language of the mad scenes achieves metaphysical subtlety without breaking the illusion of naturalistic presentation. In the mad scenes Lear again and again has sombre utterances whose power to strike directly at the heart is due to the peculiar dexterity with which they walk the precipice between the figurative and the true. . . . (p. 93)

This technique is, I am convinced, deliberate, and it does much to produce that sense of inexplicable power which we feel in attending a performance of the play. This is of course tricky ground for the critic; Shakespeare here is using means which outstrip our analytical terms. But the belief that the sense of shifting relations between true and false given by these utterances is of definable importance to the total effect of these scenes is strengthened by the evident fact that the mad scene with Gloucester (IV, vi) is a sustained exercise in the deployment of multiple uncertainties, so consistent in this aspect of its technique as to leave no doubt of what is being done. (pp. 93-4)

[In the mad scene with Gloucester] Shakespeare brings to a maximum effect of dissonance all the problems of the play. The problem of suffering is at its rawest in this scene, where mad Lear confronts blinded Gloucester in a visible spectacle of which nothing can be said, save "it is, And my heart breaks at it" [IV. vi. 141-42], a scene in whose fragmented dialogue, which every now and then sharpens to a sliver that stabs the heart and brain, the problems that have brought Lear to this pass are restated in their extremest form. In complete destitution, he claims himself "every inch a king" [IV. vi. 10]; he recalls that Titanic struggle with the gods which taught him he had been flattered like a dog; his sense of the guilt of the flesh takes him down into the pit, and his sense of the guilt of "authority" lifts him to a height of compassion proper only to a suffering god ("None does offend, none, I say, none; I'll able 'em: Take that of me, my friend, who have the power To seal the accuser's lips" [IV. vi. 168-70]). This scene of maximum dissonance leads to that resolution of dissonance which in the reunion with Cordelia brings the play to a penultimate close of pure, still pathos. In that reunion, Lear's passion is over, "the great rage . . . is killed in him" [IV. vii. 77-8], and the plot comes full circle when he is restored to comfort, love and majesty—accepted, humbly, as undeserved gifts, by one claiming no more for himself than

> I am a very foolish fond old man. . . .
> Pray you now, forget and forgive:
> I am old and foolish.
>
>   [IV. vii. 59, 84]

These simple harmonies could not be as effective without the whirling dissonances of the mad scene with Gloucester. The simplicity of Lear's words in this scene could not be so moving were it not instinct with the memory of his long struggle to know the truth. The shifting relations between the false and the true, and between the physical 'real' and the non-physical 'real' now come to rest in such simple physical certainties as "I feel this pin prick" [IV. vii. 55]—certainties the more moving because they are now, to Lear, the only way he knows of settling those searching questions whose racking complexity has been revealed in the course of the play. We have come a long way from "Doth Lear walk thus? talk thus? where are his eyes?" [I. iv. 227] to "I will not swear these are my hands" [IV. vii. 54], from "But goes thy heart with this?" to [I. i. 104] to "Be your tears wet?" [IV. vii. 70]; all the wildness of the long journey is felt, quiescent now, in these questions and the simple physical tests by reference to which Lear finds some sort of answer. Similarly the simplicity of attitude, as in his hesitant, "As I am a man, I think this lady To be my child Cordelia" [IV. vii. 68-9] is powerful because of all Lear has left behind him; he is no longer the wrathful dragon, the outraged king, the impotent revenger, the defiant Titan, the stoic, or the madman, but simply, now, a man. The daring of this is terrible. Shakespeare has made Lear, who has yet to face the worst, exhaust in advance every known tragic attitude (except that of self-destruction, but Gloucester has attempted and rejected that), leaving them all behind him. It is as though Shakespeare sought to write a tragedy which sets itself to present the bitterest experience of all without help of the trappings of tragic style or attitude. It is as man, not as tragic hero, that Lear is to meet the death of Cordelia—as man who has already of his own volition asked all the deepest metaphysical questions about man's condition, suffered all he could suffer because of them, and now, when "nature in [him] stands on the very verge Of her confine" [II. iv. 147-48], confronts the one question he has so far escaped:

> Why should a dog, a horse, a rat, have life,
> And thou no breath at all?
>
>   [V. iii. 307-08]

And here the style, now in "a condition of complete simplicity, costing no less than everything" performs the final miracle of hardening from humble pathos to tragic rock by an intensification of its own simplicity: those same elements of which simple pathos was compounded, are compounded anew. Lear, so recently content to know so little, is now certain of the simplest, sharpest distinction of all: "I know when one is dead, and when one lives" [V. iii. 261]. (pp. 96-7)

The whole play is a dramatic answer to the one question in which all Lear's questions are subsumed: the question, What is Man? Man is that creature whose inherent nature is such as to raise the questions Lear asks; he is at once no more and no less than this, the creature at once vulnerable and tenacious, who must, but can, "answer with [his] uncovered body this extremity of the skies", the "ruined piece of nature" [IV. vi. 134] whose hand, smelling of mortality, is august, the creature whose mere life is so perfectly a value in itself that it redeems

even those sorrows Lear has felt. This conception, explicit at the tragic peaks of the play, tacitly governs its whole structure. The sequence of Lear's deprivations is a sequence of revelations of his tenacity. It is to this end—revelation through suffering (rather than redemption through suffering)—that the whole play moves. (p. 97)

> *Winifred M. T. Nowottny, "Lear's Questions," in Shakespeare Survey: An Annual Survey of Shakespearian Study and Production, Vol. 10, 1957, pp. 90-7.*

WILLIAM FROST (essay date 1957-58)

[*In the following excerpt, Frost maintains that Shakespeare deliberately conceived the opening scene of* King Lear *as ceremonial ritual, rather than realistic exposition. Because of this, he proposes that we interpret the scene as highly formalized art that contributes much to the tone and meaning of the play. For Frost, the scene underscores the mythic quality of the drama and suggests an effect of inevitability in denying the possibility of other developments. It also offers an ironic contrast to the later scenes in the play, specifically, the storm and madness scenes, and thus reflects a progression in the plot from ritualized order to chaos, from highly structured formality to naked humanity. In addition it offers a stark contrast between the royalty and splendor of the opening scene and the humble, self-effacing attitudes of Lear and Cordelia in the final moments of the play. A similar interpretation of the opening scene of* King Lear *can be found in the essay by John Reibetanz (1977).*]

Probably no scene in any of Shakespeare's mature tragedies is more overtly ritualistic in construction and in language than the holding of court that opens *King Lear*; all the force of Dryden's comment on rime in drama—that it will sound as though the speakers in a dialogue had got together and composed it in advance—would seem to apply to this gathering. First Lear speaks, announcing fully and formally what is about to happen; then come the questioning of the daughters in order of age; the breakdown of the four-part liturgy (challenge, response, comment, award) on its third performance; the ceremonial quarrel with Cordelia, followed by formal disinheritance; the ceremonial quarrel with Kent, followed by formal banishment; Kent's elaborate farewells; the public rejection of Cordelia by Burgundy; her ritual wooing by France; and a cluster of antiphonal farewells as the court breaks up. Except for Cordelia's sudden "Nothing"—a violent momentary break in the proceedings—the scene, even at its most passionate moments, is conducted in blank verse of a Byzantine stateliness, if not, indeed, in rime:

> Thy dow'rless daughter, King, thrown to my chance
> Is queen of us, of ours, and our fair France.
> Not all the dukes in wat'rish Burgundy
> Can buy this unpriz'd precious maid of me.
>
>   [I. i. 256-59]

It used to be fashionable to call couplets not unlike those of France—at least when produced a century or so later by Pope or Dryden—frigid and lifeless; and indeed as recently as 1927 Professor Allardyce Nicoll has written that "One could have wished it were possible to prove that these lines were not by Shakespeare or that they were remnants of an earlier *Lear* of his callow youth, but we may accept them I think, as his own, manifesting in their stiffness and mental rigidity the dramatist's recognition of his own failure to make his scene live and his obvious desire to push on to more congenial subject-matter." For Nicoll, as a matter of fact, the whole first scene of

Lear is "a failure" and "easily the most uninteresting long scene of the drama." Here, surely, by contrast to the point of view of some more recent critics, we find modern uneasiness with ritual, and opposition to it, stated in the most uncompromising terms.

What can be said in defense of the scene?

In the first place, if it must be viewed as allegory, then as allegory, at least, it holds together extremely well. Its basic constituents are simply two contests of affection, the first among Goneril, Regan, and Cordelia, the second between France and Burgundy. That the second is a neat and ironic commentary on the first comes out in France's courteous lines to the reluctant Burgundy—

> My Lord of Burgundy,
> What say you to the lady? Love's not love
> When it is mingled with regards that stand
> Aloof from th' entire point. Will you have her?
> She is herself a dowry.
>
> [I. i. 237-41]

The aphorism about the nature of love, though not so intended by France, who was absent from the earlier contest, sums up the moral issue involved in that contest, and prepares for the appropriately religious formality of France's ensuing proposal. . . . (pp. 581-82)

In the second place, the balanced ceremony of the scene accords well with the mythic, the folkloristic nature of the story as it came down from the old chronicles to Shakespeare: the story of an ancient king of Britain who had three daughters, of whom two were evil, and one was good. Such fairy-tale materials, of course, underlie more than one of Shakespeare's plots, and he has various ways of handling them; here, his method is the simplest and boldest possible; all questions of motivation are bypassed at the outset, and we start with the naked myth. For given such a myth, to raise the question of motive would be to undermine dramatic effect in advance. As the earlier play *King Leir* surely demonstrates sufficiently, any conceivable rationalization is bound to be weak and inadequate.

In the third place, the machine-like quality of ritual produces, in the first part of the scene, precisely the effect of nightmarish inevitability most useful, I think, for certain sorts of tragedy. The driver is fully and terrifyingly in control of the car; every piston functions smoothly; and the road ends in a precipice just around the next corner. Any suggestion of deliberation, hesitation, or wavering between alternatives would but confuse and perplex the appalling spectacle.

I have so far mentioned only elements *within* the scene. There is also the question of its relation to the play as a whole, a relation mainly one of several sorts of contrast. In the first place there is the contrast . . . between the rituals and their framework, those brief prose interchanges between Kent and Gloucester before the ceremonies start and between Goneril and Regan after they conclude. The prose dialogues are casual, colloquial, and the reverse of mythic in atmosphere. Because they allude to the motivation of the central figure in the rites, without really attempting to explain it, they give the effect of going backstage and hearing the actors comment on the play. By this means the gap between ritual and more naturalistic drama is bridged, at the same time that ritual itself is thrown into high relief.

Second, there is the contrast between Lear's courtroom and Goneril's household, where we get our second look at the king.

In the household, action and imagery alike are trivial, domestic, and haphazard; again the effect is of going backstage, where fancy dress is partly thrown off, make-up smudged, and wigs awry. This effect is only temporary, however; for tension rises throughout the scene till at its close, in curses and quarrel, Lear is evidently remounting an imaginary throne—how pathetically and ironically imaginary Goneril's reassurances of Albany remind us. The Lear who had disinherited Cordelia and banished Kent retains a power of banishment, but only over himself.

The third contrast is with the storm-and-madness scenes at the center of the play. In these Lear, now unable to distinguish imaginary thrones from real ones, pardons Gloucester for adultery and pronounces a death sentence on Kent for treason:

> KENT [*speaking of Edgar*]—He hath no daughters, sir.
> LEAR—Death, traitor! nothing could have subdu'd nature
> To such a lowness but his unkind daughters.
>
> [III. iv. 69-71]

In these scenes are embodied one enormous parody after another of the ritualistic opening of the play. Of the trial scene in the farmhouse Granville-Barker remarks: "Where Lear, such a short while since, sat in his majesty, there sit the Fool and the outcast, with Kent whom he banished beside them; and he, witless, musters his failing strength to beg justice upon a joint stool. Was better justice done, the picture ironically asks, when he presided in majesty and sanity and power?" . . . The trial scene in the farmhouse, moreover, is followed immediately by a yet more monstrous parody, the justice done on Gloucester by Regan and Cornwall.

Disorder of various sorts is basic to these central scenes. It is no longer as though we had passed backstage to observe the actors in their dressing gowns, but as though the theater itself had suddenly been shaken by an earthquake, and the actors were improvising amid falling masonry. They seem continually to grasp for some shred of ceremony as the boards tremble beneath them and the footlights flicker uncertainly. (pp. 582-84)

The final contrast is between the opening and the conclusion of the play. At this conclusion, both in the reunion with Cordelia and in the final spectacle, ritual has lost all relevance to the King. His "I am a very foolish fond old man, / Fourscore and upward" [IV. vii. 59-60] is like Cleopatra's "No more but e'en a woman, and commanded / By such poor passion as the maid that milks / And does the meanest chares" [*Antony and Cleopatra*, IV. xv. 73-5]; but it is more final than Cleopatra's self-regarding momentary dethronement. We are now in the presence, not of the ceremonies by which human beings encompass their condition, the *rites de passage* of the anthropologists; but of the barest facts of that condition itself. King and daughter, no longer figures in myth or allegory, come before us fragile, irreplaceable, and particular, a pair of jailbirds and losers.

Meanwhile, however, the earthquake is subsiding, and the stage getting swept up so that orderly drama can go forward. Act V is emphatically not without ritual, the chief rite being, of course, the trial by combat which restores Edgar to status and inheritance, eliminates Edmund, and leaves the political field clear for Albany at last. Many commentators have analysed the double plot structure of *King Lear*, mostly in regard to its universalizing effect on the conflict of the generations; another important result of the subplot is that it keeps everybody so busy, especially at the end of the play. Wars have to be fought, traitors unmasked, and a final contest of affection adjudicated between Regan and Goneril, whose love-rivalry for Edmund ironically parallels that of France and Burgundy for Cordelia earlier, just as Edgar's restoration restores some semblance of order to the judicial processes of primitive Britain. So much has been happening, in fact, that Kent creates a sensation by showing up on the stage and asking for his master. "Great thing of us forgot!" cries Albany, stupefied; "Speak Edmund, where's the King? And where's Cordelia?" [V. iii. 237-38].

This moment in the play, which some have criticised as fortuitous, melodramatic, and contrived, needs to be regarded in the light of the ritual which started the whole chain of events in motion. In that opening scene, everything depended on Lear and Cordelia; around the conflict of their wills the fates of nations, literally, revolved. Now, they are of no importance; no role is left to them; what happens to them scarcely matters; it is as though they had been dropped from the play. Contrast the death of Hamlet, in the instant of Claudius's exposure; or the death of Cleopatra, foiling the purposes of Caesar. Left without function in the mechanism of society, Lear will not be, like Hamlet, carried to a stage and exhibited to the tune of a military dead march. He will not be given a few last words, like Othello, about the service he has done the state. Nor can Cordelia be arrayed like Cleopatra in the robes and crown of a princess and made to embrace her death as a bride embraces a bridegroom. . . . [These] two personages have passed beyond ritual altogether at the close. They cannot be expressed or comprehended by any of its forms—this fact is their greatness and their tragedy. (pp. 584-85)

> *William Frost, "Shakespeare's Rituals and the Opening of 'King Lear,'" in* The Hudson Review, *Vol. X, No. 4, Winter, 1957-58, pp. 577-85.*

IRVING RIBNER (essay date 1958)

[*Ribner joins the ranks of such earlier critics as G. G. Gervinus (1849-50), A. C. Bradley (1904), R. W. Chambers (1939), Geoffrey L. Bickersteth (1946), and Oscar James Campbell (1948), all of whom, in different degrees, regard* King Lear *as a dramatic reflection of the redemptive power of love in the world and an affirmation of providential order. Ribner argues that the action of the play deals primarily with the regeneration of Lear through suffering, and to a lesser extent of Gloucester. Like many historical commentators, Ribner claims that Elizabethan audiences would have interpreted Lear's suffering, and the suffering in the play in general, as a direct consequence of his transgression of divine order inherent in his abdication of the throne. Although a political error, the decision has repercussions on the individual as well as the cosmic level. But Lear's suffering serves a redemptive function, teaching him to reject worldly values and to accept Cordelia's love, which Ribner considers a reflection of divine love, as the only eternal principle. The idea that Lear's suffering enriches his self-knowledge and leads him to a final comprehension of Cordelia's divine love has also been suggested by D. G. James (1951), L. C. Knights (1959), and Robert H. West (1968).*]

In *King Lear* Shakespeare's primary emphasis is upon the process of human regeneration. That he chose for the hero of such a play an old man at the very end of physical life was thematically appropriate, for the emphasis is upon a spiritual rebirth for which man never can grow too old. Shakespeare dramatically juxtaposes the physical age of his hero against the new manhood he attains through suffering, and thus he asserts dramatically that Lear's four score years of pride and self-deception were merely the prelude to life, and not life at all.

The savagery of human cruelty and the intensity of human suffering in the play have led some critics to call *King Lear* a secular tragedy in which Shakespeare offers neither insight into the cause of human suffering nor hope for man other than in Stoical submission, divorcing the world of his play from any Christian notion of order or justice. Such a view tends to regard the play's savagery out of its context in the larger intellectual design, to see *King Lear* as a chaotic and disordered mass of impressions, rather than as a neatly unified whole in which every element is designed to support a deliberate intellectual statement. *King Lear*, however, is a highly unified triumph of dramatic construction.

The suffering of Lear and Gloucester must be presented with all of the immediate dramatic intensity of which Shakespeare is capable, for only thus can he emphasize that the process of regeneration is a purgatorial one. And if Shakespeare is to assert the power of man to overcome the evil of the world, the forces of evil must be presented in their most uncompromising terms. I would suggest that in its total effect, *King Lear* is an affirmation of justice in the world, of a harmonious system ruled by a God who in his ultimate purposes is benevolent. (p. 34)

All the elements of *King Lear*—character, action, symbol, and the poetry in which they are embodied—are shaped by the theme of regeneration which dominates the whole. To find a fitting dramatic vehicle for this theme, Shakespeare availed himself of the morality play tradition which was so much a part of his dramatic heritage. The didactic and homiletic tradition of medieval drama, which persisted so strongly in Elizabethan tragedy afforded tools by which Shakespeare might shape a complex of action to reflect the universal role of man on earth in conflict with evil. To make the governing theme of his play even more apparent, Shakespeare employed a new device, the parallel tragedy of Gloucester. The double action, which Bradley called a "structural weakness" [see excerpt above, 1904] offers us another hero who is Lear on a slightly lesser social plane, and his career in paralleling closely that of Lear reinforces the universal validity of the play's central theme.

All of the characters of the play embody symbolic functions. . . . The primary focus of attention is upon Lear, and to a lesser extent upon Gloucester, for together these two aged men represent humanity in the large. All of the other characters serve secondary supporting functions, each symbolic of some force of good or evil acting upon humanity. The theater of the action, moreover, is not the single solitary word of man, but all of its corresponding planes in the great scheme of creation as well: the family, the state and the physical universe itself. This universality of theme is reinforced by the vagueness of the place setting; the audience is observing not only Lear's little kingdom, but the great world at large.

As he faces the purifying storm upon the heath, King Lear . . . speaks of himself as "a man / More sinn'd against than sinning" [III.. ii. 59-60], and a long line of critics have been inclined to take the old man at his word. To do so is to ignore the context in which these lines occur. If *King Lear* is viewed as the story of a foolish old man tortured by those he loves, the play loses its cosmic scope and becomes little more than a pathetic melodrama. In the scheme of regeneration Lear must come to know himself; this he does in the purifying agony of the storm. The first two acts emphasize Lear's lack of self-knowledge, and they exhibit him not as the victim of evil forces, but as the instigator of the evil forces in the play. Our knowledge of the total play sometimes causes us to forget that an audience viewing it for the first time would not at the end of the first two acts regard Lear as a man more sinned against than sinning. . . . Dramatically the speech serves to underscore the self-ignorance of Lear at the beginning of the heath scenes which are to bring him to a contrary self-knowledge through suffering.

Shakespeare reminds us throughout the play that Lear himself has unleashed the forces of evil which cause his suffering, and only when he himself has come to realize this and he no longer sees himself as more sinned against than sinning is his regeneration possible. If evil is symbolized in Goneril and Regan, we must remember that it was Lear himself who brought them into being. . . . To understand the enormity of Lear's sin, which critics like Bradley . . . , Wilson Knight . . . , and others have underestimated, we must recognize the peculiar position of the king in the highly ordered world which Renaissance Christian humanism carried over from the Middle Ages. We must also come to see in its proper perspective the "love contest" which Shakespeare adapted from the old fairy tale play of *Leir*. (pp. 35-6)

To grasp the full significance of Lear's conduct in the opening scene of the play, we must understand the particular use made of such historical legend in Shakespeare's day in order to illustrate large political principles. We must recognize that Lear's division of his kingdom and resignation of his throne would have been regarded by a Jacobean audience with a horror which it is difficult for a modern audience to understand, for these acts constituted a violation of the king's responsibility to God, and they could only result in the chaos on every level of God's creation which is the subject of the play. By his resignation of rule Lear disrupts the harmonious order of nature. It is a denial of God, born out of eighty years of a pride and self-deception which has rendered it impossible for him to distinguish appearance from reality, and which leads him to choose the lesser finite good of power without responsibility, rather than the greater infinite good of God's order which decrees that the king rule for the good of his people until God relieves him of this awful responsibility by death. (pp. 36-7)

Although *King Lear* is more than a history play and the tragedy is more than a political one, the political aspects of Lear's initial act are nevertheless of crucial importance, for they contribute to the cosmic breadth of the whole. The sphere of the state is only one of the levels on which the action of *King Lear* occurs, but in the Elizabethan world view the state was a middle link between the physical universe and individual man, and thus Lear's initial crime may make its reverberations felt both above and below, corrupting the entire scale of God's creation. (p. 37)

Generations of critics have been disturbed by the illogic and inconsistency in the opening scenes of this play, both in the affairs of Lear and of Gloucester. Bradley sought to find a logic in them, but had to admit them dramatically faulty. I would suggest, on the contrary, that they are deliberately illogical, that both Lear's foolish spur-of-the-moment alteration of his careful plans and Gloucester's incredible gulling by Edmund are reflections of the general chaos and irrationality into which society has been plunged by Lear's initial decision to divide his kingdom and abandon his responsibility to God.

Wilson Knight . . . has called Lear, "a tremendous soul . . . incongruously geared to a puerile intellect" [see excerpt above, 1930] and he has pointed to the incongruous and the ludicrous which run through the play. This deliberate illogic is stressed

particularly in the first act, designed to make clear to the audience the magnitude of Lear's initial sin and its effect upon the entire cosmos, perverting both the laws of society and the reason of individual man. It is evident in Lear's delusion, his confusion of appearance with reality, which causes him to accept the flattery of Goneril and Regan and to reject the true love of Cordelia. (p. 38)

The discord unleashed by Lear's wrong moral choice is to be most effectively symbolized in the storm scenes which show the extension of man's corruption to the world of physical nature. It is already evident, however, in the second scene of the play, where we find it breaking out on a lower level of the social scale, in the household of Gloucester. Goneril and Regan, whom so many critics regard as the prime instigators of evil in the play, have not yet begun to act against their father, and Edmund's plan is merely in its incipient stage, but the chaos which is falling upon all nature is already described by Gloucester:

> These late eclipses in the sun and moon portend
> no good to us: though the wisdom of nature
> can reason it thus and thus, yet nature finds
> itself scourged by the sequent effects: love cools,
> friendship falls off, brothers divide: in cities,
> mutinies: in countries, discord; in palaces, trea-
> son; and the bond cracked 'twixt son and father.
> This villain of mine comes under the prediction;
> there's son against father: the king falls from
> bias of nature; there's father against child. We
> have seen the best of our time: machinations,
> hollowness, treachery, and all ruinous disor-
> ders, follow us disquietly to our graves.
>
> [I. ii. 103-14]

It should be noted that the celestial portents by which Shakespeare in his tragedies usually signifies the violation of God's order have already appeared in "these late eclipses of the sun and moon." The "sequent effects" of this corruption in the physical universe extend to all the other levels of creation: in cities, countries, palaces and the individual family, where "brothers divide" and "the bond" is "cracked 'twixt son and father." This is the bond which Cordelia had asserted and Lear had rejected. It is not, however, because of the "late eclipses" as Gloucester supposes, that "the king falls from bias of Nature"; it is Lear's initial falling from this bias which has caused all of the corruptions, both social and natural, which Gloucester enumerates. It is not to be expected that Gloucester at this point should more adequately understand the nature of Lear's sin which so closely parallels his own.

King Lear opens with Lear already fallen, and to account for his wrong moral choice, there is only, as Bradley indicated . . . the suggestion of *hubris*, of long years of absolute rule and subservient flattery during which Lear had forgotten what it means to be a man. In the first two acts Shakespeare shows us the results of the hero's sinful moral choice, and while doing so he develops the parallel career of Gloucester. With the beginning of Act III begins the regeneration of Lear which is not completed until he experiences his beatific vision at the very end, for as Bradley first suggested . . . and as so many others have argued, he dies in a momentary experience of insupportable ecstasy. At the same time, in a lower note, is developed the parallel regeneration of Gloucester, of whose similar death we are told by Edgar.

The structure of *King Lear* is thus designed to place principal dramatic emphasis upon the heath scenes which begin with the opening of Act III. In the third and fourth acts we see the forces of good and evil clearly aligned against one another, for in no other play are the characters divided so unequivocally into good and evil. We have the villainy of Edmund, Cornwall, Oswald, Goneril and Regan to darken our view of humanity, but on the other hand we have the selfless devotion of Cordelia, Edgar, Kent and the Fool to show the potentialities for good still within the human spirit. The evil in the world is mingled dramatically with man's inherent goodness in spite of it. Between the two opposed forces hover Gloucester and Lear, sharing good and evil, and much like the central figures of the old morality plays. Each must make his way from the one side to the other, destroying within himself the force of evil and allowing that of good to emerge triumphant. Gloucester's regeneration will be climaxed by his death in the arms of Edgar, and Lear's by his reunion with Cordelia.

The two sets of characters embody two distinctive philosophies of life. . . . Edgar, who as so many critics have noticed is intensely religious, with Cordelia, Kent and Fool, represents a Christian humanist view of life which sees all of nature as a harmonious order controlled by a benevolent God, and which thus allows for the natural bond of filial affection, of loyalty, duty, and obligation to family and state, of kindness to fellow man. Its greatest good is love, the love of man for man which can unite humanity to an ever-loving God. Opposed to this stands the doctrine of Renaissance skepticism, symbolized primarily in Edmund, with the wicked sisters, Cornwall and Oswald living also by its precepts. Edmund sees nature as a Godless mechanism, governed by impersonal and immutable laws, and unrelated in any way to the mind of man. The universe is without divine guidance. . . . Edmund denies the great system of correspondence between the mind of man and the phenomena of nature, which was so integral a part of the Elizabethan doctrine of order and degree. . . . Human society in Edmund's view is debased, for it consists of villains, fools, knaves, thieves, treachers, drunkards, liars, and adulterers. Only man's body is a part of nature in this view; man's mind is an independent entity by which he can, to some extent, control nature. He may do this by means of "reason," but this is not the "reason" of orthodox Elizabethan doctrine, an attuning of one's will to the will of God. Edmund's "reason" is the ability to manipulate nature and other men for his own advantage. It is utterly selfish in that it recognizes only the dominance of individual will. . . . It is fitting that Edmund should be a bastard, for thus conceived outside of God's harmonious order, with its moral standards, he can set himself outside of this order and deny the benevolent human feelings which are a part of it, proceeding directly from the love of God: loyalty, the bonds of family, and that primogeniture which to Elizabethan and Jacobean Englishmen was the basis of social order.

A principal issue of the play thus becomes the matter of justice, for the side of Edgar invokes what that of Edmund denies, a belief in a benevolent God who visits upon men their desserts. Similarly Edgar and Cordelia stand for the perfection of nature and the magnificence of individual man, while Edmund and his fellows stand for the corruption and ugliness of physical nature and the cheapness of human life. On all of these important issues, the complex double action of the play shows Lear and Gloucester simultaneously rejecting the philosophy of Edmund and learning to embrace that of Edgar. (pp. 39-42)

There is little in the first two acts to win audience sympathy for Lear. His division of his kingdom alone would, as I have indicated, cause a Jacobean audience to view him with horror, for they feared nothing so much as the prospect of a divided England. . . . [When] Lear storms out on the heath at the end of the second act, an audience viewing the play for the first time could not help feeling that however unkind his treatment, it has not been so unkind as what he has meted out to others. If there is anything to keep the audience from total alienation from Lear it is the meanness of Goneril and Regan themselves, which Shakespeare keeps always before us, the pathos of Lear's remorse for his treatment of Cordelia which grows steadily under the cruel, yet loving jibes of the Fool, and the bluff loyalty of the disguised Kent, juxtaposed against the obsequious and effeminate villainy of Oswald. It is also in the very spectacle of an aged man, unaware of his own violations of order which the audience so plainly sees, striving for patience as he holds back his tears. . . . (pp. 42-3)

Under the pressure of his ill-treatment, and unaware of his own responsibility for it, Lear strides out on the heath denying that there is justice in the world, that nature is benevolent, and that there is any difference between man and beast:

> our basest beggars
> Are in the poorest things superfluous:
> Allow not nature more than nature needs,
> Man's life's as cheap as beasts.
>
> [II. iv. 264-67]

Here he suggests in incredulous anger the theme which in his madness is to dominate his thoughts. These are the very convictions of Edmund's philosophy; they are brought out in Lear by his daughters who live by that philosophy, but they are convictions which he must renounce under the opposing influence of Kent, Edgar, the Fool and Cordelia. (p. 43)

And yet, while Lear dwells on the baseness of man and the corruption of nature, at the same time his sufferings cause him to feel a love for his fellow men and a sympathy for humanity which to this time have been alien to his nature. Thus the two motifs run side by side throughout the heath scenes in a kind of grotesque counterpoint. (p. 44)

With the appearance of Edgar as Poor Tom, Lear goes mad. This madness, as Bradley perceived . . . quickens Lear's power of moral perception and reflection and thus contributes to that awareness of himself and his world which, as it grows, is to be the source of his redemption. In this madness the twin motifs of scorn for nature and humanity and an awakening feeling of kinship with humanity at the same time continue to play against one another. Edgar's function as Poor Tom is to serve as a visible symbol of man as Lear in his delusion sees him, reduced to the level of a beast. . . . This is the lowest point of delusion that Lear reaches, as he tries to tear off his clothes and reduce himself to the level of "unaccommodated" man who is no more than naked beast. But even as Lear speaks, Gloucester appears bearing his torch, a light from the world of men who are not beasts, a sign of human kindness and self-sacrifice. The old man who can risk his life to succor his king in the storm is Shakespeare's symbolic reminder that man is more than beast, that he shares, in spite of evil in the world, in the harmony of nature and the love of God which the mad Lear denies.

With such touches of human warmth Shakespeare tempers the savagery of Lear's outbursts, for as his madness progresses he grows wilder and wilder in his indictment of God and man. His madness itself symbolizes a collapse of that reason which differentiates man from beast, but it is also a purgatorial state;

thus we continue to find it in the twin motifs of Lear's rejection of humanity (a collapse of reason) and his recognition of his own fellowship with humanity (the lesson of purgatory). Thus, while the mock trial of Goneril and Regan (III, iv) is a grotesque parody of human justice, it is a posing also of questions which Lear had not before asked, and to which he must learn the answers before the final curtain. (p. 45)

When Lear awakens from his sleep he is, as Bradley . . . and most later commentators have perceived, a regenerated soul. There is a new humility in his speech to Cordelia, and a new awareness of his own nature as a man. . . . The dominant note of [this scene] is recognition of his own ignorance and imperfection. Now he is ready to renounce entirely the power and pomp which he had craved to enjoy without responsibility at the beginning of the play. His only value is the human love which he had before denied, but which he now sees embodied in Cordelia, and for which he will gladly give up the world. . . . Lear has attained an ideal of Christian stoicism through acceptance of human love, which is a reflection of the love of God and of the perfection and harmony of the universe which in his madness he had denied. After such renunciation, which sets its seal upon the after life of heaven, there is no other dramatic possibility than death, and in this instance a reunion in heaven with the Cordelia who has preceded him there. If Lear's final belief, as his heart breaks, that Cordelia lives is contrary to truth, this is of small significance, for Shakespeare's audience could not doubt that she lived, in fact, where her father soon would join her.

That Gloucester has lived a long life of sensual indulgence is obvious from the account of Edmund's origins with which the play opens. We are not to suppose, however, that the fate which overtakes him is mere retribution for lechery, for his sin against the natural order goes deeper than that. Gloucester violates the laws of primogeniture, as surely as Lear violates the duties of kingship. Gloucester's sin is thus also a denial of the law of God and of the harmonious order of the universe on a slightly lower plane than that of Lear; the two sins together work the universal collapse of order with which the play is concerned.

The Gloucester sub-plot represents Shakespeare's unique addition to the ancient Lear story of generically unrelated matter from an alien source, the *Arcadia* of Sir Philip Sidney. It has come to be recognized that the serious political and philosophical implications of Sidney's *Arcadia* were an important shaping force upon the entire play of *King Lear,* that they perhaps first suggested to Shakespeare the means of transforming the simple fairy tale motifs of the old *Leir* play into a sombre tragedy with wide cosmic implications. The dominant theme, not only of the King of Paphlagonia episode which Shakespeare borrowed, but of the entire *Arcadia,* was that of royal responsibility and authority. This concern in Sidney's work coincided perfectly with the vast implications Shakespeare saw in the Lear story and led probably to his fusion of the two stories. (pp. 47-8)

Gloucester must suffer for his violation of order. just as Lear suffers for his, and through suffering he must undergo a similar purgation, learn his own nature as a man, come to a state of Christian stoicism and die finally on a supreme note of joy. This joyful death was part of the Paphlagonian king's story in the *Arcadia,* and it may have suggested to Shakespeare the similar death of Lear. Gloucester's blinding, to which so many critics have objected, is thematically appropriate, for Shakespeare on this lower level wishes to emphasize the physical

aspects of his suffering, just as he had emphasized the mental anguish of Lear. When he had his eyes, Gloucester was mostly blind. With the loss of his eyes he learns for the first time to see the world as it really is, to recognize the perfection of God's total plan. . . . His blinding offers the same pathway to regeneration as Lear's torment on the heath. In typical Shakespearean fashion, however, the brutality of the blinding is tempered by the humanity of the servants' conversation which follows immediately afterwards, and the stabbing of Cornwall seems to represent an intervention of divine justice. In the same manner, while Shakespeare depicts the sins of Gloucester he must also display in him elements of humane feeling so as not utterly to alienate the audience from him, and so as to prepare for his eventual redemption. (p. 49)

As Gloucester wanders blind toward Dover he suffers the same purgation Lear had suffered in his madness, and in the scenes of Gloucester's blindness, we find the same twin motifs which had run through Lear's mad scenes: on the one hand a despair which rejects the order of God, denies justice and sees humanity as utterly debased, and on the other a welling up of love for his fellow men. At the very lowest point of his progression Gloucester speaks words which often have been misinterpreted and quoted out of context:

> As flies to wanton boys, are we to the gods,
> They kill us for their sport.
>
> [IV. i. 38-39]

This does not represent Shakespeare's philosophy or the intellectual statement of the play as even so excellent a critic as Theodore Spencer . . . was led to believe; it represents the very opposite. These lines correspond in the pattern of Gloucester's regeneration to Lear's tearing off his clothes before Poor Tom in the pattern of his. This is the low point from which Gloucester must emerge, just as Lear emerges from his, and Gloucester's recovery is effected by the old man who leads him, and by Edgar, who teaches him the meaning of love and of resignation to divine will. (pp. 49-50)

Gloucester's attempted suicide has been censured by many critics as absurd and impossible, but we must remember that here again Shakespeare is not presenting scientific fact. This episode is a ritual element designed to portray an underlying idea. It is the final step in Gloucester's purgation, for out of his supposed rescue from death, he learns what he must know in order to be redeemed, that "the clearest gods, who make them honours / Of men's impossibilities, have preserved thee" [IV. vi. 73-4]. He acquires a Christian stoicism which recognizes the justice of the divine order and which enables him to bear his lot on earth as every man must. . . . (p. 51)

Edgar sums up an important intellectual statement of the play in his final words to his brother:

> The gods are just, and of our pleasant vices
> Make instruments to plague us:
> The dark and vicious place where thee he got
> Cost him his eyes.
>
> [V. iii. 171-74]

This speech bothered Bradley . . . , who thought it in very poor taste that Edgar should remind his dying brother of his bastardy, and he felt that this would impute to Edgar a coldness and self-righteousness which might alienate an audience from him. Coming from a real, live person, these lines would at once brand the speaker as an insupportable prig. What Bradley did not realize is that Edgar is not a real person, but merely a dramatic tool which Shakespeare uses to perform certain specific functions within his larger design. His speech here is not designed to cast light upon his character, but to assert forcefully at the end of the play the justice and order which Gloucester and Lear had at first denied and then come to accept.

Edgar is adapted to various purposes in various parts of the play. As Poor Tom he serves as a symbol of man reduced to the level of the beast; that he is in disguise symbolically underlines that in reality man is never so. There is no need to search for logical reasons for his assumption of this particular disguise. Shakespeare wishes merely to provide a visual symbol for man as Lear in his delusion conceives him to be. As he leads his blind father, Edgar takes on an entirely different role. Here he becomes a symbol of the very opposite of Poor Tom—of human devotion and love, of those qualities which raise man above the level of the beast and bring him close to God. As such he is able to teach his father the lessons necessary for his redemption.

Finally, in his combat with Edmund, Edgar becomes a symbol of divine justice which will triumph over evil and re-assert the harmony of God's natural order. The blast of his trumpet as he goes into combat is a symbolic echo of the last judgment. . . . That there is little logic in Edgar's behavior from first to last, and that there is but slight psychological consistency in his character are irrelevant considerations in the total design of Shakespeare's play.

Similarly, Cordelia cannot be judged by any standard of psychological verisimilitude. The tendency among critics such as Bradley . . . to censure her for her conduct in the opening scene comes from a failure to perceive that she is not a real person, that her function here is a thematic one, to emphasize the nature of the bond which Lear rejects, and not to humor a foolish father, as a real daughter might have done in such a situation. . . . Throughout the play Cordelia serves as a visible symbol of human love and self-sacrifice, a reflection of the love of God. (pp. 51-2)

We may thus see that in *King Lear* character and action are shaped by a controlling design, which is in itself an intellectual statement. In its totality *King Lear* asserts the perfection of God's harmonious order and the inevitable triumph of justice, with the forces of evil preying upon and destroying themselves. In the process they subvert the good, but ultimately good must be victorious. In such a world man must subject his will to the will of God, patiently enduring whatever may come, with only faith in the perfection of the divine plan to sustain him, for as Edgar instructs his father:

> Men must endure
> Their going hence, even as their coming hither:
> Ripeness is all.
>
> [V. ii. 9-11]

More specifically, in this play, Shakespeare affirms the possibility of human salvation, and he does this by placing in an imaginative setting the regeneration from evil of two aged men. There is a deeper vein of symbol and allegory in *King Lear* than even Bradley . . . hesitatingly perceived, for in the vagueness of the place setting Shakespeare creates the feeling that the stage of *Lear* is the entire world, and in the double action, he reminds us most forcefully that the life journey of Lear may be the life journey of everyman. (pp. 53-4)

> Irving Ribner, "The Gods Are Just: A Reading of 'King Lear'," in The Tulane Drama Review, Vol. 2, No. 3, May, 1958, pp. 34-54.

L. C. KNIGHTS (essay date 1959)

[*A renowned English Shakespearean scholar, Knights followed the precepts of I. A. Richards and F. R. Leavis and sought an underlying pattern in all of Shakespeare's work. His* How Many Children Had Lady Macbeth? *(1933)—a milestone study in the twentieth-century reaction to the Shakespearean criticism of the previous century—criticizes the traditional emphasis on "character" as an approach which inhibits the reader's total response to Shakespeare's plays. In the excerpt below, Knights argues that* King Lear *is an examination and endorsement of traditional Christian values, but one in which all reassurances are overturned and nothing is taken for granted. He begins by analyzing Lear's initial problem as "perverse self-will," an attitude that severely distorts his perception of reality. Deceived by appearances throughout his life, Lear eventually discovers, through his madness, that appetite or lust is universal and that authority is a "sham." However, Knights demonstrates that the king's regeneration, and the play's meaning, do not cease with this pessimistic vision, but continue in the reunion of Lear and Cordelia—a relationship that confirms for the protagonist the presence of love as the ultimate reality. For Knights, those critics who see the play as pessimistic fail to recognize what he calls "the inclusive vision of the whole"— which makes* King Lear *an affirmation "in spite of everything." For further examination of this pessimistic vision in the play, see the excerpts by Algernon Charles Swinburne (1880), E. K. Chambers (1906), Stopford A. Brooke (1913), G. Wilson Knight (1930), J. Stampfer (1960), and Jan Kott (1964). Other critics who have interpreted* King Lear *as a profound endorsement of Christian values include R. W. Chambers (1939), Geoffrey L. Bickersteth (1946), Oscar James Campbell (1948), Irving Ribner (1958), and Robert H. West (1968).*]

If, at the end of *King Lear*, we feel that the King's angry and resounding question, 'Who is it that can tell me who I am?' [I. iv. 230] has indeed been answered, that is because Shakespeare has submitted himself to a process equivalent in the emotional and imaginative sphere to the famous Cartesian intellectual doubt. Some of the most fundamental questions concerning the nature of man are posed in a way that precludes all ready-made answers, that, in fact, so emphasizes the difficulty of the questions as to make any kind of answer seem all but impossible. Only thus could the urgent perplexities of the earlier plays be brought into full consciousness and confronted at the deepest level of significance. For these reasons *King Lear* has the three characteristics of the very greatest works of art: it is timeless and universal; it has a crucial place in its author's inner biography; and it marks a moment of great importance in the changing consciousness of the civilization to which it belongs. (p. 84)

[*Lear*] is a universal allegory (though the word 'allegory' does justice to neither the depth nor the movement within the experience it presents), and its dramatic technique is determined by the need to present certain permanent aspects of the human situation, with a maximum of imaginative realization and a minimum regard for the conventions of naturalism. In the scenes on the heath, for example, we do not merely listen to exchanges between persons whom, in the course of the play, we have got to know; we are caught up in a great and almost impersonal poem in which we hear certain *voices* which echo and counterpoint each other; all that they say is part of the tormented consciousness of Lear; and the consciousness of Lear is part of the consciousness of human kind. There is the same density of effect throughout. One character echoes another: the blinding of Gloucester parallels the cruelty done to Lear; Gloucester loses his eyes, and Lear's mind is darkened; Gloucester learns to 'see better' (as Kent had bidden Lear) in his blindness, and Lear reaches his final insights, the recognition of his supreme need, through madness. But there is not only this mutual re-inforcement *within* the play: there is constantly the felt presence of a range of experience far wider than could be attributed to any of the persons regarded simply as persons. This is achieved partly by the use of simple but effective symbols—the bare heath, the hovel, the nakedness of Poor Tom ('unaccommo-dated man'), the 'cliff' from which Gloucester thinks to cast himself down; partly by the use made of certain organizing ideas such as the Elizabethan conception of a necessary inter-relation between man (the 'little world of man'), the social body, and the cosmos; but above all by the poetry. The poetry of *Lear* is not only vivid, close packed, and wide ranging, involving in the immediate action a world of experience, it has a peculiar resonance that should leave us in no doubt of Shake-speare's intention. (pp. 92-3)

Lear, at the opening of the play, is the embodiment of perverse self-will. Surrounded by obsequious flattery . . . , he knows neither himself nor the nature of things. It is his human self-will that is stressed, and we need not fuss very much about the apparent absurdity of his public test of his daughters' af-fections in the division of the kingdom. It is a dramatically heightened example of something not uncommon—the attempt to manipulate affection which can only be freely given. . . . Now one result of perverse demands is a distorted view of the actual, and one way of discovering that your own lanthorn gives no light is, as Swift put it, by running your head into a post—something that is unquestionably there. Because Lear is perverse he is deceived by appearances; and because he allows himself to be deceived by appearances he sets in motion a sequence of events that finally brings him face to face with an actuality that can be neither denied nor disguised.

The subsequent action of the play is designed not only to force the hidden conflict in Lear into consciousness, and, with the fullest possible knowledge of the relevant facts, to compel a choice, but to force each one of us to confront directly the question put by Lear as Everyman, 'Who is it that can tell me who I am?' One answer to that question is embodied in the group of characters who are most directly opposed to Lear. Edmund, Goneril, and Regan take their stand on the unre-strained self-seeking of natural impulse. The two daughters, by their actions, by what they say, and by the imagery of beasts of prey so consistently associated with them, represent a fe-rocious animality. Their indifference to all claims but those of their own egotism is made explicit by Edmund, who brings into the play conceptions of Nature and human nature, radically opposed to the traditional conceptions, that were beginning to emerge in the consciousness of the age. For Edmund, man is merely a part of the morally indifferent world of nature, and his business is simply to assert himself with all the force and cunning at his command. . . . It is into the world of indifferent natural forces, so glibly invoked by Edmund, that Lear is pre-cipitated by a perversity of self-will that clung to the forms of human affection whilst denying the reality.

We can now see how the play at the personal or psychological level is able to bring to a focus far wider issues. Lear goes mad because he is a mind in conflict; because his conscious view of himself, to which he clings with the whole force of his personality, is irreconcilably opposed to what are in fact his basic attitudes. . . . His talk of love and paternal care, but both his action in casting off Cordelia and—those infallible signs of what a man truly is—his assumptions as they appear in moments of emotional stress, together with his whole tone and manner, reveal a ferocious egotism. . . . Whatever Lear

thinks of himself, one side of his nature is already committed—even before he is thrust into it—to the world that Edmund, Goneril and Regan take for granted, a world where everything that might conceivably be regarded as mere sentimental illusion or the product of wishful thinking is absent, where neither 'humane statute', custom nor religion checks the free play of brute natural force. If Lear is ever, as Kent bids him, to 'see better', this is the world he must see and feel in its full impact.

The storm scenes, and the scenes immediately following, rep-resent a two-fold process of discovery—of the 'nature' without and within. No summary can attempt to do them justice, and perhaps the best way of indicating what goes on in them is to revert to what has been said of Shakespeare's superb and daring technique. The effect is analogous to that of a symphony in which themes are given out, developed, varied and combined. And since one of the characters goes mad, one is an assumed madman, and one is a Fool, there is a freedom without prec-edent in the history of the drama—a freedom only limited by the controlling purpose of the play—to press into service all that is relevant to the full development of the main themes.

The storm itself is vividly presented in all its power to harm; but this is far from being the only way in which the action of Nature is brought home to us. Part of the dramatic function of Edgar is to reinforce the message of the storm. Disguised as one of the lowest creatures to be found in rural England in the sixteenth century (and therefore, for the purpose of the play, becoming one), a wandering madman and beggar . . . , he brings with him continual reminders of rural life at its most exposed and precarious. . . . When Lear with Kent and the Fool surprises him in the hovel, he at once strikes the note of the familiar indifference of Nature—familiar, that is, to those who live close to nature, though not to those who, like Edmund, invoke an abstraction that suits their bent. His talk is of cold and fire, of whirlpool, whirlwind and quagmire, of natural calamity and disease. Nothing he says but has this far-reaching yet precise suggestiveness. (pp. 93-7)

This then is the Nature 'outside'. What of human nature, the nature within? Here too the direct revelation of the action is extended and reinforced—almost overwhelmingly so—by the poetry of allusion. A long catalogue of sins—ranging from the adulteration of beer to usury, slander, perjury and murder—could be collected from the exchanges of Lear, Edgar and the Fool, and as they accumulate they give a sorry enough picture of man in his meanness. But the recurring themes are lust and cruelty. Lust and cruelty are demonstrated in the action of the play; they are harped on in Edgar's 'mad' talk; they are the horrible realities that Lear discovers beneath appearances. (p. 98)

Lear's expression of revulsion and disgust, when, 'a ruin'd piece of nature' [IV. vi. 134], he confronts the blind Gloucester, is, I suppose, one of the profoundest expressions of pes-simism in all literature. If it is not the final word in the play, it is certainly not because Shakespeare has shrunk from any of the issues. Pessimism is sometimes regarded as a tough and realistic attitude. Shakespeare's *total* view of human life in this play has a toughness and actuality that make most pessi-mism look like sentimentality. It is because the play has brought us to this vision of horror—seen without disguise or pallia-tion—that the way is open for the final insights. In the suc-cessive stripping away of the layers of appearance, what re-mains to discover is the most fundamental reality of all. In the play it takes the form of the love and forgiveness of Cordelia. But that love has to be earned in the way in which all things most worth having are earned—by the full admission of a need, the achievement of honesty and humility, the painful shedding of all that is recognized as incompatible with the highest good, by, in short, making oneself able to receive whatever it may be. Now if there is one truth that the play brings home with superb force it is that neither man's reason nor his powers of perception function in isolation from the rest of his personality. . . . *How* Lear feels, in short, is as important as *what* he feels, for the final 'seeing' is inseparable from what he has come to be. For us, as readers or spectators, Lear's vision of life can only be apprehended in close conjunction with the attitudes with which he confronts experience. (pp. 99-100)

In the two great tirades addressed to the blind Gloucester [IV. vi. 107ff. and 150ff.] Lear brings to a head all he has discovered concerning Appetite and Authority. The discovery is that appetite is well nigh universal and that authority is a sham. For the man who knows this, who knows too how little he can dissociate himself from what he denounces, aggression and self-assertion are alike irrelevant: all that is left is a 'patience' hardly distinguishable from despair.

> Thou must be patient; we came crying hither:
> Thou know'st the first time that we smell the air
> We wawl and cry. I will preach to thee: mark . . .
> When we are born, we cry that we are come
> To this great stage of fools.
>
> [IV. vi. 178-83]

There is no immediate way of deciding how we should take these lines. It is important that we should know since it is virtually on this note (after a momentary return to a futile fantasy of revenge) that Lear gives way completely, sleeps, and is carried to Cordelia. The question is whether what we have here is a weary subsidence into the only wisdom that is ultimately possible, or whether, although representing an extreme point of weariness and denial, it masks the possibility of some genuine resilience of the spirit. In order to determine this we must recall the familiar truth that dramatic statements exist in a context, and that their meaning is in relation to— often in tension with—that context. Lear is indeed the central consciousness of the play, but nothing, so far, has put us under any compulsion to accept him as solely qualified as an interpreter of the action. At this point then we must briefly recall the part played by Gloucester, the Fool, Kent, and some others.

Both Gloucester and the Fool powerfully affect our sense of the central experience embodied in Lear, but they belong to two quite different aspects of Shakespeare's wide-embracing dramatic technique. The Gloucester sub-plot is plainly 'a device of intensification' [as stated by J.I.M. Stewart in his *Character and Motive in Shakespeare*], and the progress of Gloucester himself is something like a simplified projection of the Lear experience on to a 'morality' plane: in the bewildering world of the play it helps to give us our bearings. It is commonly recognized that just as Lear finds 'reason in madness' [IV. vi. 175] so Gloucester learns to 'see' in his blindness, and there is no need to rehearse the many parallels of situation, the verbal echoes and cross-references. All that concerns us here can be plainly stated. Gloucester, at the beginning of the play, is sufficiently characterized by his coarse man-of-the-world conversation; he is as blind as Lear to the truth of things, credulous and, one would have said, ineffective. Caught up in the struggle of good and evil his decision to help Lear is deliberate and heroic . . . and his blinding is a kind of martyrdom. It is a martyrdom, however, from which any consolatory vision is completely absent, and his subsequent progress, always so

close to despair, is deliberately deprived of any obvious 'nobility' matching his conduct—as in the grotesque comedy of his attempted suicide. But it is Shakespeare's refusal to romanticize Gloucester that so guarantees the validity of the qualities with which he is endowed. Gloucester learns to suffer, to feel, and in feeling to see; and under Edgar's guidance he comes as near as he may to thoughts that are not only 'patient' but 'free'. . . . The Gloucester who listens to Lear's tirades is someone quite other than his earlier self, someone incredibly— miraculously, the play suggests—better. And the change in him, defined and emphasized by the touching simplicity of the verse he speaks, is something that our imagination completely endorses.

The nature of Gloucester's experience is clearly presented, without ambiguity. The Fool, on the other hand, speaks to (and out of) a quite different order of apprehension: his function is to disturb with glimpses of confounding truths that elude rational formulation. At times he seems like something only partly recognized in the depths of Lear's own personality that will not be kept down . . . , but because he is only licensed, not enfranchised—not, we may say, integrated with the conscious self, which yet has a vein of tenderness towards him— the truth he tells is disguised, paradoxical, sometimes grotesque. . . . Miss Welsford, in the penetrating account she gives of him in her book, *The Fool*, places him firmly in the tradition of 'the sage-fool who sees the truth' [see excerpt above, 1935]. . . . The truths he tells are of various kinds. He can formulate the tenets of worldly wisdom with a clarity that worldly wisdom often prefers to blur. He defines the predatory self-seeking of Goneril and Regan, and has a variety of pithy phrases both for the outward form of Lear's mistaken choice and its hidden causes and results. In relation to these last indeed he shows an uncanny insight, pointing directly to Lear's infantile craving 'to make his daughters his mothers' [I. iv. 173], and hinting at that element of dissociated sexuality that plays into so many human disorders—something that will later rise to the surface of Lear's mind with obsessive force. The world picture he creates is of small creatures in a world too big— and, in its human aspects, too bad—to be anything but bewildering. His sharply realistic, commonplace instances—like Tom's mad talk, though with a different tone—insist on the alien aspect of Nature and on all that detracts from man's sense of his own dignity—corns, chilblains, lice, and the mere pricking of sexual desire. The Fool's meaning, however, lies not merely in what he says but in the way he says it—those riddling snatches which partly reflect the moral confusion of the world, but whose main function is to cast doubt on such certainties as the world (including the audience) thinks it possesses. Not only therefore is he an agent of clarification, prompting Lear towards the recognition of bitter truths: it is he, as Miss Welsford insists, who forces the question, What is wisdom? and what is folly? It is through him, therefore, that we come to see more clearly the sharp distinction between those whose wisdom is purely for themselves and those foolish ones—Kent, Gloucester, Cordelia, and the Fool himself—who recklessly take their stand on loyalties and sympathies that are quite outside the scope of any prudential calculus. Like Gloucester, though in a very different way, the Fool is directed towards an affirmation.

Both the Fool and Gloucester stand in a peculiarly close relation to Lear, but whereas the Fool is inseparable from him, Gloucester also connects with a wider world—a world existing independently of Lear's own consciousness (the alternation of scenes throughout Act III has great dramatic force and significance).

Now that world has so far been dominated by those active promoters of their own fortunes, Goneril, Regan, Edmund and Cornwall, but Shakespeare has also included in it quite other types of representative humanity. Kent, who follows Lear without coming close to him like the Fool or sharing something of the inner nature of his experience like Gloucester, has an especially significant rôle. Even in a play that is far from naturalistic we are bound to reflect that a king who could inspire the dogged devotion of such a man must be remarkable for something else besides perversity: his mere presence helps to check such inclination as we might harbour to regard Lear as foolish and wilful in such wildly improbable ways that we can safely dissociate ourselves. And his headstrong loyalty is a reminder of certain permanent possibilities of human nature. (pp. 106-11)

Even apart from the central movement of Lear's own consciousness, therefore, the development of the play as a whole towards the last great outburst of his pessimism is very far indeed from a simple descent through deepening horrors that would justify an unqualified endorsement of his rejection of the world. There is indeed a full and passionate confrontation of 'the worst', including Edgar's recognition that there is no term that can be set to suffering. . . . But not only does the play compel our recognition of positive values and emerging insights, the same ruthless honesty that has stripped Lear of every rag of illusion is directed also to the brutal 'realism' of his opponents. (p. 111)

When, therefore, Lear 'preaches' to Gloucester on the vanity of human life, there is, as so often in Shakespeare, a clash between the personal or immediate meaning of the words and their full dramatic meaning. . . . [For] Lear, at this point, life is a meaningless comedy of pain. But no more than Macbeth's 'Life is a tale told by an idiot' can this be regarded simply as a summarizing comment emerging from the play as a whole. To be sure the accumulated meaning of the play puts sufficient weight behind the bitterness, but the whole relevant context forbids a simple response. The context of course is not something 'out there' that can be demonstrated in terms of the understanding, it is all that our minds and imaginations, awakened and directed by Shakespeare's art, hold ready to receive and interpret the immediate situation. And what our imaginations now hold is not only a sense of Lear's folly and suffering, of the folly, suffering, cruelty and injustice to be found in the world at large, but a heightened recognition of all that, even in the face of these, the whole personality endorses as clear insight and genuinely human feeling. And behind the widening circle of reference within the play itself there is a context even more extensive. This indeed is slippery ground for interpretation, but it is at least relevant to recall that in other plays of roughly the same period—notably perhaps in *Timon of Athens,* so close to *Lear* in its probing of certain moods of revulsion—Shakespeare was concerned with the way in which the world of the individual is in part created by the nonrational structure of attitudes and feelings that are inseparable from perception. Only an inhibiting fear of life could prevent us from taking the full force of Lear's great indictment: only a refusal to meet honestly—so far as we may—*all* that Shakespeare sets in relation to it could make us blind to the irony—yes, even in this moment of keenest suffering—that plays about it.

What then are the reflections that, with a reversal of the usual effect of dramatic irony, qualify our recognition of all that is valid in Lear's bitterness? Surely they include such thoughts as that the image Lear finds for the world is partly at least a projection of his own folly; that not all the inhabitants of Lear's world are fools in the sense immediately intended here; that folly is a word whose meaning changes according to the standpoint of the speaker, and that in the pain of madness Lear had at least learnt more about human nature than he knew before. With this we bring into focus the three times repeated reference to the birth-cry. Whatever the physiological reasons, the baby's cry at smelling the air (and nothing can deprive that phrase of its disturbing wholesomeness) is commonly taken as a cry of fright and protest. . . . As such it is analogous to the protest, the frightened movement towards headlong regression, of the adult who is called upon to undergo a radical transformation of consciousness. In the subtle and complex interplay of recognitions that surrounds our sympathy with Lear's agony this thought also has its place.

It is through such varied probings, questionings, rejections, recognitions, that a direction is established and a way prepared. Cordelia, though rarely appearing in the play, is very much a positive presence. Her tenderness is rooted in the same strength that enabled her to reject Lear's misconceived demands. Her love is of a kind that, confronted with a real demand, does not bargain or make conditions; it is freely given, and it represents an absolute of human experience that can stand against the full shock of disillusion. When Lear, dressed in 'fresh garments' and to the accompaniment of music (the symbolism is important) is brought into her presence, there follows one of the most tender and moving scenes in the whole of Shakespeare. But it is much more than moving. Since each line engages us to the whole extent of our powers the briefest reminders set vibrating all the chords of the past experience. It is even whilst we respond to the swift sure play of feeling—with a sense as of the actual bodily presence of the protagonists—that we are made to live again the central scenes. . . . [As] recognition dawns in Lear, as consciousness first renews his suffering, then admits it has no terms for a world not known before, we are aware that this still moment is surrounded by nothing less than the whole action of the play; and if questions that have been asked now await their answer, the painful knowledge that has been won will reject anything that swerves a hair's breadth from absolute integrity. (pp. 112-15)

King Lear, however, is more than a purgatorial experience culminating in reconciliation: what it does in fact culminate in we know, and the play's irony, its power to disturb, is sustained. Does this mean, then, that *King Lear* is 'a sublime question, to which no answer is supplied by the play' [as stated by D. G. James in his *The Romantic Comedy*]? I do not think so. What it does mean is that questioning, disturbance, the absence of demonstrable answers, form an essential part of a meaning that lies not in a detachable moral but in the activity and wholeness of the imagination. To the extent therefore that *King Lear* does make a positive affirmation (and I think it does) it is one which takes up into itself the questioning. . . . (pp. 116-17)

In the last act, by the definite withdrawal of Albany from the forces opposed to Lear, the killing of Edmund by Edgar in single combat, and the mutual treachery of Goneril and Regan, the way is apparently cleared for an ending far different from that represented by the stark stage-direction: 'Enter Lear, with Cordelia dead in his arms'. The scene of Lear's final anguish is so painful that criticism hesitates to fumble with it: where no one can remain unaffected the critic's business is to supply something other than his own emotions. What may be said, however, is that there are at least two reasons why no other ending would have been imaginatively right, and for a proper understanding they are of the greatest importance. We do not only look at a masterpiece, we enter into it and live with it. Our suffering, then, and our acceptance of suffering, not simply our sympathy with what we see on the stage, form an intrinsic part of what the play is; for as with Lear and Gloucester our capacity to see is dependent upon our capacity to feel. Now what our seeing has been directed towards is nothing less than *what man is*. The imaginative discovery that is the play's essence has thus involved the sharpest possible juxtaposition of rival conceptions of 'Nature'. In the Edmund-Goneril-Regan group the philosophy of natural impulse and egotism has been revealed as self-consuming, its claim to represent strength as a self-bred delusion. What Lear touches in Cordelia, on the other hand, is, we are made to feel, the reality, and the values revealed so surely there are established in the face of the worst that can be known of man or Nature. To keep nothing in reserve, to slur over no possible cruelty or misfortune, was the only way of ensuring that the positive values discovered and established in the play should keep their triumphant hold on our imagination, should assert that unconditional rightness which, in any full and responsive reading of *King Lear*, we are bound to attribute to them.

Perhaps a final question remains. It has been argued here that at the centre of the action is the complete endorsement of a particular quality of being. We may call it love so long as we remember that it is not simply an emotion, and that, although deeply personal, it has also the impersonality that comes from a self-forgetful concentration—momentary or enduring—upon the true being of 'the other': it is perhaps this kind of impersonality—not a negation of personal consciousness but its heightening and fulfilment—that is most insisted on in Edgar's strange phrase, 'Ripeness is all' [V. ii. 11]. In this sense—so the play reveals—love is that without which life is a meaningless chaos of competing egotism; it is the condition of intellectual clarity, the energizing centre from which personality may grow unhampered by the need for self-assertion or evasive subterfuge; it is the sole ground of a genuinely self-affirming life and energy. But—it may still be asked—how does this apply to Lear when he prattles to Cordelia about gilded butterflies, or when, thinking his dead daughter is alive, his heart breaks at last? For answer, we must consider once more the play's marvellous technique, the particular way in which it enlivens and controls our sympathies and perceptions. King Lear is indeed, for most of the play, 'the centre of consciousness': what he sees we are forced to see. But the question, ultimately, is not what Lear sees but what Shakespeare sees, and what we, as audience, are prompted to see with him. At the end, however poignantly we may feel—Lear's suffering is one of the permanent possibilities, and we know it—we are still concerned with nothing less than the inclusive vision of the whole; and it is that which justifies us in asserting that the mind, the imagination, so revealed is directed towards affirmation *in spite of everything*. Other readings of the play are possible, and have been made. But those who think that it is 'pessimistic', that it is no more than a deeply moving contemplation of man's helplessness, should consider a remarkable and obvious fact: that the tragedies written after *King Lear* everywhere proclaim an intellectual and imaginative energy that, in the firmness of its grasp, the assurance of its sense of life, shows no sign of perplexity, fear, or strain. For what takes place in *King Lear* we can find no other word than renewal. (pp. 117-19)

L. C. Knights, "'King Lear'," in his Some Shakespearean Themes, *1959. Reprint by Stanford University Press, 1960, pp. 84-119.*

RICHARD B. SEWALL   (essay date 1959)

[*Sewall compares* King Lear *to the stories of Job and Oedipus and considers the play a "Christian tragedy," but not in the sense of the term as used by R. W. Chambers (1939), Geoffrey L. Bickersteth (1946), Oscar James Campbell (1948), Irving Ribner (1958), and L. C. Knights (1959). For Sewall, it is Christian only in the sense that it is infused with the characteristic Renaissance Christian atmosphere where the discovery and development of the soul dominated moral thought and literature. In short, the play deals specifically with the "inner workings of human beings under stress" and the recognition through suffering of their own spiritual nature; because of this, he cautions against a "too Christian" reading of elements that are meant to have a more universal significance. The catastrophic ending of* King Lear *Sewall characterizes as the victory of neither good nor evil, but the indifferent movement of the universe to restore balance between these forces, affirming an orderly universe, in accordance with the Elizabethan world view. In this respect, Sewall's essay is similar in approach to those of Arthur Sewell (1951), John Holloway (1961), and Maynard Mack (1965), all of whom have attempted to define* King Lear *in terms other than the traditional pessimistic/optimistic, nihilistic/transcendent dichotomy.*]

Recent scholarship has sufficiently demonstrated the main outlines of the Elizabethan world-view which, inherited from the teachings of the medieval theologians, the tragic dramatists now ventured to put to the full test of action. For all the centrifugal, disruptive forces at work in the Renaissance, what remained deep in the imagination of western man was the sense that, in spite of appearances, there was order in the universe which should find its counterpart (and did, when society was in a healthy state) in the ordered life of man on earth. The terrestrial hierarchy was an emblem of the celestial, with king, priest, father (of the family), and master (of servants) exercising each in his area of influence a divinely sanctioned authority. In man the individual, reason was king and the passions were its subjects. . . . This "great chain of being" was, moreover, a sensitive affair. Disorder in any of the parts might affect the whole; weakness in any link might cause a vital break, even to cutting man off from God and the hope of salvation. (p. 69)

The first actions of [*King Lear*] show hierarchy broken and order imperiled. Lear abdicates, with equivocal provisos, and divides his realm. His youngest and fondest daughter asserts her will against his. In a burst of temper he banishes her and his loyal follower, Kent, who had tried to stay his rashness. His two elder daughters, now emboldened, conspire against him; and in the second scene, as if through spread of contagion, the Earl of Gloucester learns of the supposed treachery of his favorite son, Edgar. Gloucester's despairing soliloquy [I. ii. 112-27] sets the modal background of the play, like the lament of the chorus of Theban citizens in *Oedipus* over their dying city. The series of shocks has given him a glimpse into the depths—a glimpse that throws his world into a new and terrifying perspective. (p. 70)

Although Gloucester is later drawn into the action and transcends himself, his immediate response is to view, like a true pagan or member of the chorus, the present ominous events as signs of a fateful disturbance in the celestial and human orders. All is dark and foreboding: "These late eclipses in the sun and moon portend no good to us. Though the wisdom of nature can reason it thus and thus, yet nature finds itself scourg'd by the sequent effects'' [I. ii. 103-06]. The upshot of such a view, as Edmund promptly points out in sturdy Christian ethical terms, is to lay all our ills to ''the charge of a star'' [I. ii. 128], ''all that we are evil in'' to ''a divine thrusting on'' [I. ii. 125-26]. No tragedy (surely not *Lear*) partakes of such unmixed fatalism. But (on the other hand) the upshot of Edmund's view is, by laying evil to the charge of the sinful will, to turn *Lear* into a morality play. . . . Lear, soon brought to a very Christian sense of guilt by the nagging of the Fool and the twinges of his conscience, finds that the effects of his original hasty action have ramified beyond the question of his guilt, and that he is involved in consequences (the plot of Goneril and Regan against him) which stir in him very different feelings. Had the play been a Christian play, its rationale might have been satisfied with Lear's ''Woe that too late repents'' [I. iv. 257] and with his new and more charitable view of the ''poor naked wretches'' [III. iv. 28] of whom he had taken little care. But the mills of quite unchristian gods seem to be grinding. Lear cannot rest in his own remorse, which at best is never unmixed with hate and hurt feelings. As he feels the pressure from Goneril and Regan ever more insistent, the evil closing in, the question of who is to blame—whether it is the ''most small fault'' of Cordelia or his own ''folly''—ceases to be the issue. Caught up in the action which he had unwittingly precipitated, he refuses to default or compromise (in spite of the pleadings of the Fool) and presses on in heroic pride to justify himself. It is in this mood that he curses Goneril and Regan, vows dreadful vengeance, and plunges into the storm.

Why did Shakespeare choose to dramatize the inferno-purgatory of the subsequent actions? He had a happy ending direct to his hand in the Holinshed account, which tells of the reunion of Lear and Cordelia, the success of their armies, Lear's restoration to the throne, his two-year reign, quiet death, and state burial. Why the painful madness . . .? the blinding of Gloucester? the death of Cordelia? Why did Oedipus dash out his eyes, or why did the people of the late Middle Ages and the Renaissance like to see their Savior suffer and die? Such questions pose basic aesthetic problems, ranging from the mysteries of the creative process and its motivation to problems of the response of audience and spectator, ''catharsis,'' the taste and temper of whole cultures. (pp. 71-3)

The temptation with *King Lear,* as with many tragedies written in the Christian era which inevitably include Christian modes, patterns, and terms, is to give the picture a too-Christian hue: to read the play as reconciling the inferno and purgatory in the perfect goodness of Kent's loyalty, Cordelia's Christlike love, Lear's humility, and (some have even suggested) the reunion of father and daughter after death in a Christian Heaven. But ''Christian tragedy'' is still tragedy. It may turn the Christian conceptions of Hell and Purgatory to metaphoric use as psychological realities; its heroes may ''sin,'' suffer remorse, and (like Lear) know what ''repentance'' is. But whatever redemption the hero wins is not through Divine Grace but, like the Greek hero, through his own unaided efforts. He has no comforter on the dark voyage, no Heavenly City as his destination, where his bundle of sins drops miraculously from his back. What is Christian about Christian tragedy is not eschatological but psychological and ethical. Hamlet's was a soldier's burial, not a saint's or martyr's. When in the final scene of *Lear* the King enters with Cordelia in his arms, Kent, Edgar, and Albany pronounce a choric verdict on the pitiful spectacle:

KENT.   Is this the promis'd end?
EDGAR.   Or image of that horror?
ALBANY.   Fall and cease!
                                              [V. iii. 264-65]

The Christian hope is shattered. The promised Judgment confuses evil and good, and both perish. The original terror looms close, all the more shocking and disillusioning by virtue of the high promises of the Christian revelation. In one sense, this *is* the end. The Chorus, as at the end of Oedipus, have spoken truly. Cordelia is ''as dead as earth'' [V. iii. 262], and the best his friends can wish for Lear is that he be allowed to die:

KENT.   O let him pass! He hates him
That would upon the rack of this tough world
Stretch him out longer.

                                              [V. iii. 314-16]

Loss is as irretrievable and final as that of any pagan tragedy.

So the action concludes. But as Sophocles showed in his presentation of Oedipus, or the Poet of Job of his agonizing hero, there is another action, internal, a ''counter-action,'' which functions vitally in the tragic dialectic and comprises an important part of the meaning. The turn which Christianity gave to tragedy being inward, this counter-action—the inner workings of human beings under stress, the discovery (or rediscovery) of ''soul'' or the lack of it—is more fully developed and given in greater detail in Christian tragedy than any Greek tragedian would have thought justifiable or relevant. The initial action of Scene 1 having been taken, what Lear becomes (rather than what becomes of him), and what each of the other characters becomes or shows himself to be, prove the choric verdict only partly true. The counter-action qualifies the terrible implications of the action and reveals possibilities which make the whole more bearable.

Like Job and Oedipus, Lear shows himself more than sinner, more than sinned against. He does evil, and evil is done to him; but in the course of his ordeal, which in part he brought upon himself, he transcends both these categories. Like the other heroes, he ends victor as well as victim. His victory . . . is pyrrhic and, like everything else about him, ambiguous. His path toward it is tortuous, revealing goods and bads inextricably mixed. It is a pilgrimage (if the term can be dissociated from its Christian promise), and it is presented with characteristic Renaissance-Christian interest in the journey or the process— an interest which foreshadows the harassing ''pilgrimages'' of Dostoevski's heroes and of the protagonists of the modern psychological novel.

Lear's pilgrimage commences true to a pattern now familiar. A man is wounded to the quick—not an ordinary man, but for his age and time ''the first of men.'' His estimate of himself, of his position in the state, in society, in his family, his view of man and the universe, are suddenly called in question. Gloucester's dire thoughts are in part Lear's also, as in Cordelia's action and later in Goneril's and Regan's, he sees his universe tottering. His response is not despair but violence— characteristic, as Goneril and Regan assure each other, of the rashness of old age and of a temperament never stable; but characteristic also, as the developing action of the play shows, of the initial response of the hero. His new and shattering knowledge of the irrational and the demonic forces in himself and in the world around him drives him to the edge of madness. He has moments of fearful nihilism. His curses against his daughters and his railings in the storm recall the dark and destructive mood of Job's opening curse or the frenzy of violence in which Oedipus struck out his eyes. But, like Job and Oedipus, he does not stay long in such a mood, which, even at its worst, is ennobled by his appeal to justice beyond and above the world of man. And in his time of stress new and saving qualities appear—not only his remorse but his increasing efforts toward restraint and patience (hard won from his knowledge of the disastrous effects of his own impatience) and his enlarged sympathies for the humble and the oppressed.

As the Chorus said about Oedipus, Lear is "twice-tormented," in body and mind, and his mental suffering is in itself twofold. As he sees the large consequences of his moment of rashness, he feels guilty and innocent at the same time. He is plunged into the middle of Job's problem: effect is out of all proportion to cause; justice has lost its meaning. "I am more sinned against than sinning" [III. ii. 59-60]. Like Job's, his universe has gone awry, and a recurrent theme of the scenes of his madness, or near-madness, is his longing, like Job's, for instruction. . . . "What is man that thou art mindful of him?" Job had asked, and Lear's questions are of the same kind, the basic and (as here) often explicit question of all tragedy, "Is man no more than this?" [III. iv. 102-03]. "Is there any cause in nature that makes these hard hearts?" [III. v. 77-8]. Finding no answer, he would, in his fantasy, himself bring reason and justice to the world, as in his mad "arraignment" of Goneril and "anatomizing" of Regan. . . . He would himself right the fearful unbalance: "None does offend, none—I say none! I'll able 'em" [IV. vi. 168]. But in another instant this clear insight, even in his madness, into the universal nature of the problem (like the moments, before his mind cracks, of true Christian repentance and enlarged sympathies) reverts to the mad desire for revenge. . . . The cause of justice and suffering humanity is badly mixed with pride and hate—with Job's nihilism and Ahab's vindictiveness. Even the remnants of reason are gone and passion rules. Lear shouting his "Kill, kill, kill . . ." [IV. vi. 187] images the ultimate disaster, when chaos is come again. As with the other heroes, the path is never straight up; the balance is always precarious. Lear is never "born again."

But these are not Lear's final words, nor are they his responsible words. . . . We next see him in the French camp, with Cordelia at his bedside and soft music playing to ease his return to consciousness. The scene of his awakening and reconciliation with Cordelia is as close to redemption as tragedy ever gets. Christian images and spirit pervade it. Lear mistakes his daughter for "a soul in bliss" [IV. vii. 45] and starts to kneel for her benediction as she asks for his. All is repentance, forgiveness, harmony. Here, if ever in tragedy, we are in the presence of the peace that passeth understanding. But it is wrought out of the dialectic of experience and through no conversion or doctrine or miracle—except it be the one miracle that tragedy witnesses, the miracle of the man who can learn by suffering.

But it was fated that Lear learn too late. Fatefully free, Lear was free to choose his own fate. He became by that action freely fated, and fate must run its course. The peace and harmony of the reconciliation were real but momentary. Nothing saves him—not his own hard-won self-knowledge and humility or Cordelia's richer humanity and more expressive love or Gloucester's regeneration or Edgar's bravery or even Edmund's last-minute repentance. The repeated mischances of the last act seem, like Job's misfortunes, systematic. Edmund repented too late. His message revoking Cordelia's execution arrived too late. Lear slew her executioner, but too late to save her life. There is nothing Christian in Lear's response to this awful

Act III. Scene iv. Edgar. Kent, Lear, and Fool. By R. Smirke (n.d.).

fact, and the heaven he invokes as he carries her in is deaf indeed. . . . (pp. 73-7)

Although some have pointed to the redeeming fact that Lear seems to die in an ecstasy of love and hope in his moment of fancy that Cordelia is still alive, the final scene hardly affords such comfort. Nor does the scene say anything about a reunion of father and daughter in a Christian heaven. It says much about loss, decay, suffering, and endurance. "The wonder is," says Kent, "he hath endur'd so long" [V. iii. 317]. . . . It says nothing about salvation, only a wan restoration, after great loss, of a kind of order. The kingdom has, in a sense, been purged—even, indirectly, by Lear, whose defiance of his daughters precipitated the crisis, brought Cordelia back, kept the dialectic of action going and the future still open to possibility. It is not that the "forces for good" triumph over the "forces for evil." Practically speaking, no one triumphs. Lear, Gloucester, and Cordelia die, and they are as dead as Goneril, Regan, and Edmund. Kent sees his own death near. The monstrous and the bestial, the petty and the weak in man have taken a fearful toll, and with these qualities a perverse fate has worked in seeming conspiracy. The play suggests no adequate compensation; there is no discharge in that war, except in death, which, as Edgar pleads for Lear, means only a cessation of pain.

The best that can be said is that human nature, in some of its manifestations, has transcended the destructive element and made notable salvage. Not only Lear, but Cordelia, Gloucester, Edgar, and Albany have grown in knowledge and self-knowledge, have entered a new dimension, achieved a richer humanity. Even the repentant Edmund and the servant who defends Gloucester against his persecutors figure in this repeated pattern. But when Albany says in the concluding moments of the play that "we that are young / Shall never see so much" [V. iii. 326-27], what does he mean? So much evil? So much suffering and endurance? Or so much nobility, self-sacrifice, and love? (The bodies of Lear and Cordelia are there before him as he speaks.) True to the tragic vision, the play answers these questions ambiguously.

But the play embodies tragic truth in another important way. The goods and bads may be shown as inseparable—that is, eternally present in all human actions and in the nature of the universe—but both are real (good as well as evil), and they are distinguishable. Further, though the good cannot be said to triumph, neither can evil. A balance, however precarious, is maintained. If the play denies the comforts of optimism, it does not retreat into cynicism. Its world is hard; evil is an ever-present wolf at the door. But man is free to act and to learn. If Lear never learned what makes these hard hearts, he learned much about the workings of his own heart. He could have found it all in "the old moral catechism," but such is the nature of modern tragic man that he must learn it (like Faustus) in his own way and on his own pulses. He had heard by the hearing of the ear, but at last he saw. What keeps the atmosphere of the play still sweet is just that substance of traditional knowledge, relearned through agonizing experience, an affirmation in the face of the most appalling contradictions. (pp. 77-9)

Richard B. Sewall, "'King Lear'," in his The Vision of Tragedy, Yale University Press, 1959, pp. 68-79.

BARBARA EVERETT (essay date 1960)

[*Everett argues against the strictly Christian or "transcendent" interpretation of* King Lear, *which she traces back to A. C. Bradley (1904) and discerns in later essays by R. W. Chambers (1939) and Oscar James Campbell (1948). She claims that despite the numerous instances and events in the play that can easily be interpreted according to a Christian paradigm, it is more appropriate, as well as more accurate, to view the action as evidence of a great individual who transforms suffering, evil, and chaos "into something vital and strong." Everett further questions those scenes that have been frequently cited as demonstrative of Shakespeare's Christian design—such as the scene at Dover Cliffs, Lear's reconciliation with Cordelia, and the prison scene of the final act—as possibly not religious at all, but as reflective, philosophical points in the action that serve the artistic purpose of resting and preparing the reader's mind for the more tragic scenes. Last, Everett points out that the play does not, as in a Christian interpretation, stress an opposition between the world and the soul, but shows the relationship between the two. Other critics who oppose an exclusively Christian reading of* King Lear *include Arthur Sewell (1951), Richard B. Sewall (1959), and Maynard Mack (1965).*]

It is obviously impossible to decide, simply, whether or not *King Lear* is a "Christian" play. To set it beside a play that uses even so great a degree of Christian context, as *Dr. Faustus*, is to realise what one means by the phrase "a mind naturally Christian"; *King Lear* is not only profoundly concerned with the moral repercussions of desires and actions, nor does it simply present an area of imaginative experience that constantly moves from philosophical into moral and metaphysical spec-

ulation, but it also presents these words, "moral" and "metaphysical", in a peculiarly Christian way. The splendours of pride, passion, aspiration, are constantly mutating, as it were, into the virtues of humility, gentleness, and endurance. Yet, when all this is said, there remains the fact that there are many kinds of art, and many kinds of statement, that a "mind naturally Christian" might make. Montaigne also seems, from his writing, to have loved gentleness and courage; yet it would be difficult to make a case for him as a Christian allegorist. The question is not open to solution either way, nor is it, strictly speaking, the critic's business to answer it. All that might be argued is rather the *kind* of statement which Shakespeare is making in *King Lear;* whether or not it is as doctrinal, and as didactic, as it seems. . . . (p. 332)

Much of the poetry in the play that is quoted as evidence of Lear's apprehension of "Heavenly" things—such as, for instance, the two passages . . . : "We two alone will sing like birds i' th' cage . . ." [V. iii. 9ff] and "Thou art a soul in bliss . . ." [IV vii. 45ff] seems to me to be peculiarly conditioned by the way it is used in the play. These passages are of such great beauty that one realises the degree of imaginative potency that they have. And yet Shakespeare often reserves his most "beautiful" passages, in the tragedies, for a peculiar purpose: to suggest, that is, an imaginative state in ironical opposition to the actual, or to create an atmosphere or a scene that is in some ways irrelevant to the central issues, and heightens them by contrast. . . . In both the *King Lear* passages, imagination is "still, still far wide" [IV. vii. 49]. The beautiful and curiously civilised vision of a purgatorial wheel, or the dream of a shared life in a hermit's cell, are both, with their exquisite rhythm and lucid images, in some way apart from what one thinks of as the "poetic language" of the play, and—to one reader at least—less impressive and moving than this language at its height, as in Lear's and the other characters' speeches in the storm, and Lear's at Cordelia's death. Nor is the poetic vision embodied in such speeches as "We two alone . . ." of such a power as to outweigh, so to speak, the truth of the action in which they occur. The issue at hand is the battle which, being lost, must result eventually in the death of both Lear and Cordelia. In relation to that issue, Lear's speeches have the nature of decorative art, integral perhaps only in the sense that they contribute to the tragedy of a man in love with "our lives' sweetness" in a world that refuses to be sweet. The deliberately child-like tone that enters the second of these speeches especially ("And pray, and sing, and tell old tales, and laugh") certainly can be said to have a divine innocence, but it can also be said to reduce the world of the play to something like a child's playground; to be "God's spies" and to see the flux of human life turn to a game of cards ("wear out packs" may perhaps stand this interpretation) may be a true vision of the "little world of man", but it is very little indeed, compared to the rest of the play.

The scenes which are most full of explicitly "Christian" phrasing, or suggestion, or feeling, are confined, on the whole, to one particular part of the play; that is, to the period between the storm-scenes and the last long scene that contains the meeting of Edgar and Edmund and Lear's entry with Cordelia dead in his arms. It is, perhaps, possible that the mood and tone of these scenes may be caused as much by artistic reasons as by moral design. The storm-scenes form the first climax of the play, to which the whole of the first part proceeds with a speed, violence, and—despite the sense of confusion of time and place—an emotional logic that brings a feeling of complete inevitability: one action of violence generates another with compulsive force. In the storm-scenes Lear is at his most powerful and, despite moral considerations, at his noblest; the image of a man hopelessly confronting a hostile universe and withstanding it only by his inherent powers of rage, endurance, and perpetual questioning, is perhaps the most purely "tragic" in Shakespeare. The last scene of all returns to this mood, and forms a second climax, but the tragic mood is altered by the addition of understanding to Lear's character. The presence of purely tragic pain—the desire to "crack heaven's vault" [V. iii. 260] and deny inevitability by a powerful outcry of feeling—is rarified, as it were, by a more precise knowledge of the source of that pain: the universal issues are intensified and clarified to the form of a single dead body. It is these parts of the play that provide the dominant tragic effect. The quieter scenes on Dover cliff (with the intellectualised memory or echo of violence in Gloster's 'suicide'), the moment of Lear's awakening and first meeting with Cordelia, and the scene in which they are taken away to prison, form a necessary bridge between the more tragic scenes, designed both to rest and to prepare the mind, and to accumulate a sense of the knowledge or understanding necessary to the second climax of the play—that of Lear's death. Hence they will stress not so much what happens, what is seen and felt, but rather what is intellectually understood; and their tone will become necessarily more contemplative and philosophical. (pp. 332-34)

It remains possible that even if one does not lay stress on these particular scenes, and concentrates, rather, on the scenes which show Lear suffering from intense evil, one might make, out of his history, the kind of Christian morality that shows a man "losing the world and gaining his own soul"; and this remains a permanent possibility, in that any picture of good and evil actions must contain suggestions of Christian experience, especially where the good suffer. One can, perhaps, merely remember the strength of Bradley's argument—that in the world of Shakespearian tragedy, one single "nature" generates both good and evil. *King Lear* surely begins, at least, on an assumption that the world of "life" itself—the world, perhaps, of *Twelfth Night* and *Henry IV*—is rich, powerful, beautiful, and important. That the faculties of the mind and body, and the strength and significance of the individual, should be impaired and lost in the course of a play, remains in itself *a* tragedy, if not *the* tragedy. . . . Whatever the structural climax of a Shakespearian tragedy may be, its emotional climax must remain the moment of its hero's death. And the lesser forms of death in a tragedy come with only a slightly smaller impact—loss of profession, loss of love, loss of friends. The worst performance of *King Lear*—and those seen by Lamb were presumably far from good—can at any rate present "an old man tottering about the stage with a walking-stick" [see excerpt above, 1812], and, with this, at least a part of the tragedy. That Lear should be forced, by the evil of two of his daughters, to kneel and plead ironically . . . is terrible, and the moral impact of the moment is great; but that Lear should choose, because of the goodness of his third daughter, to kneel and confess seriously . . . has also something of the terrible in it, and the impact is not, perhaps, what could be called precisely a "moral" one. Shakespearian tragedy often acts, so to speak, under the level of moral responsibility. Lear's "compensation" is said to be that at least he learns from his sufferings: he "loses the world, and gains his soul". But *what* he learns is that he is "not ague-proof", that he is "old and foolish"; and this in itself contains further ranges of common suffering. No moralistic outline that blurs this can be fully satisfying. Such an outline must also, to some degree, blur the character of Lear. A phrase like "he loses the world" suggests a context of

peculiarly Christian experience; that is, it suggests a man . . . who makes a conscious and responsible choice, and is aware of at least some of the unhappiness he is willing to suffer. Lear's character is surely scarcely comparable. His greatness lies not in the choice of "the good", but in the transformation, into something vital and strong, of the suffering that is forced upon him, partly as a result of his own foolishness; and this transformation is a part of that love of the "pride of life" that is involved in his first mistake, and that never leaves him up to his death. (pp. 334-35)

That Lear is represented as a character making perpetual discoveries is certainly true, even if it is hard to accept that the moral weight of these discoveries presents some kind of counterpoint to the sufferings he undergoes; since, if he merely "learns humility", then humility is represented in such a physical way that it contains in itself further active suffering. But perhaps Lear in fact "learns" something rather different from this, or in a rather different way. That society may be corrupt, that justice may become meaningless in the light of this corruption, that both private and public loyalties may be broken and an old order turned into chaos, that humanity is "not ague-proof"—none of these is a particularly new or exciting statement. The interest lies, rather, in the light in which these discoveries show themselves to a certain peculiar character. Lear is divested of that degree of civilised intelligence, subtlety and rationality that Hamlet and Macbeth, and perhaps even Othello, possess: that he shows, often, the consciousness of a child, with immense power and will, is a truism of criticism. The one gift that he possesses is a colossal power of life itself. . . . He is represented as feeling—and not only feeling, but living through, enduring, and becoming consciously and responsibly aware of—actions of profound evil; he feels, with a child's intensity, a range of suffering that a child could never meet. All these forms of evil—the weakness of age, the denial of power, the cruelty of his servants and subjects, social corruption and injustice—present themselves to him as a denial of life, at its profoundest and most simply physical; not, as with the other heroes, as a denial of purity, or of honour, or of imagination, or of the spirit. . . . Lear commands attention continually by the degree to which the simplest discoveries become, through him, a matter of immediate physical experience, felt both intensely and comprehensively.

This faculty to be found in the play, of an imaginative recreation of a physical awareness both intense and wide-ranging, from "I feel this pin prick" [IV. vii. 5], to "this great world shall so wear out to nought"[IV. vi. 134-35], is accompanied by something that is in one sense its diametric opposite, and in one sense an extension of itself: which is an apprehension of nothingness. There is a sense in which this apprehension of absolute cessation of being, appearing whenever the word "nothing" drops into the dialogue, is a worse evil than any of the forms of moral evil that Lear meets. Ironically, the Midas touch of the poet converts even what appals the moral sense into something, if not beautiful, at least intensely interesting, and intensely alive. . . . The only way, perhaps, in which Renaissance art can convey a sense of evil, or death, is by an antithesis of itself. Thus Lear, whose one heroic quality is a habit of totality of experience, demanding absolutes of love, of power and of truth itself . . . is "rewarded" by an apprehension of the one absolute that the tragic world can offer—the absolute of silence and cessation; and even this apprehension is hedged about by a paradoxical and painful vitality: "Why should a dog, a rat, a horse have life And thou no life at all?" [V. iii. 307-08]. The silence of the dead Cordelia is a final summary of the presence of what Donne calls "absence, darkness, death; things which are not," throughout the play, wherever a question is asked and not answered, or a command is not obeyed. That this silence *may* contain, strangely enough, as much potentiality of good as of evil, is suggested by the degree of intense life generated by Cordelia's first "Nothing"; but one thing, at least, it finishes—the idea of the overriding power of heroic and individual experience. The hero is only a hero insofar as he is able to envisage the limits of the heroic world.

It is perhaps in this way that one could make out a case for a "metaphysical" *King Lear;* that it shows a world of extreme power and vitality embracing its antithesis. This sense of startling disparities contained within one imaginative world is much more reminiscent of a mind like Pascal's than of the symbolic clarity of a Morality or the simplicity of a mystery play. Intellectual reflection on the play is more likely to need to quote, as it were, phrase after phrase of Pascal's, than to refine from the play itself a pious summary. . . . [Though] Pascal was a man almost certainly wholly unlike Shakespeare in mind, temperament and way of life, his writing postulates a world in which it is still possible to think both seriously and ironically of "La grandeur de l'homme" ["the grandeur of man"], and to see that the conditions on which such grandeur is based are close to those of tragic experience. One of these conditions is a profound doubt . . . which perpetually accompanies "une idée de la verité" ["an idea of truth"]; the only entire certainty is death. . . . Pascal's image of man—perhaps one learned from Montaigne—is of a creature bewilderingly made "un milieu entre rien et tout" ["a being between nothing and everything"], perpetually conditioned and limited by his senses, and yet able to comprehend "all and nothing".

It is such an image that Lear presents in the closing scene of the play. Whether or not Lear's "Look there" does, as Bradley interprets it [see excerpt above, 1904], suggest a belief that Cordelia is still alive, the last half-dozen lines as a whole condense the poetic experience of the play, whereby the physical and the non-physical are shown in their mysterious relationship.

> Thou'll come no more,
> Never, never, never, never, never!
> Pray you, undo this button. Thank you sir.
> Do you see that? Look on her, look, her lips,
> Look there, look there!
>
> [V. iii. 308-12]

It is natural enough that the central character of a poetic tragedy should finish by directing the attention, as it were, finally to the closed mouth of a dead human being, an image which presents most of what can be said about the physical limitation to an aspiring mind. Each of the great tragedies ends similarly with a momentary directing of the attention to the full effect of the tragic action. . . . That Lear should himself turn chorus . . . is consonant with his rôle throughout the play: his own death is the one thing that cannot be presented through the heroic consciousness.

Perhaps the chief reason, then, why one feels doubt about an extremely allegorical interpretation of the play is not that such an interpretation can be said to be "wrong", but simply that the play succeeds so well in another way. Rather than setting up an absolute dichotomy between "the world" and "the soul", between concretes and abstracts, it shows a continual relation between the two that strengthens and enriches both. . . . It also

fulfils that function by which tragedy makes the unendurable endurable by bringing it within an artistic design, while retaining its essential truth; the forms of suffering in the play are transformed not so much by being seen "*sub specie aeternatis*", but rather by being seen as forms of intense life. If the play exhilarates, it is less because "Cordelia, from the time of Tate, has always retired with victory and felicity", whether temporal or spiritual, than because it exhibits a poetic power in the writing of the play itself, in the consciousness given to its central character, and in the responsive awareness of audience or reader, that can understand and endure imaginatively actions of great suffering, and by understanding can master them. . . . The more terrible the propositions, the greater is the mastery; the greater the degree of the "un-tragic", the "un-sublime", contained—the ugly, the humiliating, the petty, the chaotic, the ridiculous, the mad, the gross, the casual and the carnal—then the greater is the act that can turn these into "the good, the beautiful, and the true", and yet retain the nature of the things themselves. Whether this is, in itself, a highly moral act is a question too difficult to answer; but it is, perhaps, not best answered by turning *King Lear* into a morality play. (pp. 335-39)

Barbara Everett, "The New 'King Lear'," in Critical Quarterly, *Vol. 2, No. 4, Winter, 1960, pp. 325-39.*

J. STAMPFER (essay date 1960)

[Stampfer disputes the interpretation of the ending of King Lear *put forth by A. C. Bradley (1904) and such later critics as R. W. Chambers (1939), Geoffrey L. Bickersteth (1946), Oscar James Campbell (1948), Irving Ribner (1958), L. C. Knights (1959), and Robert H. West (1968), all of whom, in different degrees, regard Lear's death as a moment of "spiritual ecstasy" that transcends the evil in the play and affirms divine justice. Stampfer claims that evidence within the play contradicts this reading on all points. He interprets the play on two levels: the first establishes the necessity of charity or natural law, which he finds reaffirmed in the deaths of those characters who violate the bond between human beings; the second deals with the issue of universal justice, which he maintains is nowhere established in the play. Stampfer supports the latter point by emphasizing that* King Lear *does not end with Lear's spiritual regeneration at the close of what he calls the "middle movement," but demonstrates instead that no matter how much one suffers, how deeply one repents, once the "machinery of destruction has been let loose" nothing can alter its course. In short, for Stampfer, Lear's death underscores the greatest fear of humankind—that we inhabit an "imbecile universe," and it is within the "bounds" of this realization that Stampfer identifies the catharsis of the drama. For a similar interpretation of* King Lear *as a pessimistic tragedy, see the excerpts by Algernon Charles Swinburne (1880), Stopford A. Brooke (1913), G. Wilson Knight (1930), and Jan Kott (1964).]*

The overriding critical problem in *King Lear* is that of its ending. The deaths of Lear and Cordelia confront us like a raw, fresh wound where our every instinct calls for healing and reconciliation. This problem, moreover, is as much one of philosophic order as of dramatic effect. In what sort of universe, we ask ourselves, can wasteful death follow suffering and torture? . . . The problem becomes more overwhelming when we consider that, unlike the problems Shakespeare may have inherited with the plot of *Hamlet,* this tragic ending was imposed by Shakespeare on a story which, in its source, allowed Cordelia's forces to win the war. Moreover, the massive intrusion into *King Lear* of Christian elements of providence, depravity, and spiritual regeneration make it impossible to shunt aside the ending as a coincidence of its pre-Christian setting.

The antiquity of setting may have had the irrelevant effect of releasing certain inhibitions in the playwright's mind; but the playgoers in Shakespeare's audience did not put on pagan minds to see the play. Rather, the constant references to retributive justice, perhaps greater here than in any other of Shakespeare's tragedies, make it an issue in a way that it is not in such 'pagan' plays as *Timon of Athens, Antony and Cleopatra,* and *Coriolanus.* Indeed, part of the poignance of *King Lear* lies in the fact that its issues, and the varieties of evil that it faces, are so central to Christianity, while it is denied any of the mitigation offered by a well-defined heaven and hell, and a formal doctrine of supernatural salvation.

The impression of unreconciled savagery and violence in the ending has been mitigated, in our generation, by a critical reading that would interpret Lear's last emotion as one of joy, even ecstasy, rather than one of unbearable agony. Bradley advances this reading, though hedged with a considerable qualification [see excerpt above, 1904]. . . . Some recent critics have gone much further than Bradley in an attempt to build from Lear's momentary emotion at death a 'chance which doth redeem all sorrows', and make the play's ending a transfigured vision of attained salvation.

Before disputing the weight this penultimate moment in Lear's life can bear in counterbalancing all that precedes it, one must first consider whether the reading itself is defensible; for, in a sense, everything in the play hangs in the balance with Lear's death. If it is one of transfiguring joy, then one might, for all the enormous difficulties involved, affirm that a species of order is re-established. If not, however, then the impression is irresistible that in *King Lear* Shakespeare was confronting chaos itself, unmitigated, brutal, and utterly unresolved. The problems of justice and order, however interpreted, finally rest in the mystery of Lear's last moment, and not in the ambiguity of whether Edgar will or will not take over, by default, the throne of England. Like the news of Edmund's death, the problem of the succession is 'but a trifle' [V. iii. 296] alongside the supreme issue of whether any 'comfort' was applied by Shakespeare to the 'great decay' of Lear, as was evidently applied by him to the deaths of Hamlet and to a lesser extent Othello.

Bradley and those who follow him in this matter rest their case on the observation that Lear died persuaded that Cordelia still lived. He leaves unremarked, however, the fact that this illusion is not a new and sudden turn, but recurs three or four times in the last scene. It is, indeed, the main concern of Lear's first three speeches on re-entering the stage, before he goes temporarily out of his mind:

> She's gone for ever!
> I know when one is dead, and when one lives;
> She's dead as earth. Lend me a looking glass;
> If that her breath will mist or stain the stone,
> Why, then she lives.
>
> [V. iii. 260-64]

The tension here, and it is the underlying tension in Lear until his death, lies between an absolute knowledge that Cordelia is dead, and an absolute inability to accept it. Lear 'knows when one is dead, and when one lives'. His very faculties of reason and knowledge would be in question if he could not distinguish life from death. 'She's gone for ever . . . She's dead as earth', he repeats over and over. If he is to grasp reality in the face of madness, it is the reality of Cordelia's death that he must grasp. But this is the one reality that sears him whenever he

attempts to grasp it, and so he tries, by the test of the looking glass, to prove that she lives, despite his emphatically underlined knowledge to the contrary.

Three brief speeches by Kent, Edgar and Albany intervene between this and Lear's next speech. One would guess that Lear is very active on stage at this point, possibly getting a looking glass, holding it up to Cordelia's lips, registering either momentary hope or immediate despair, then, when this test fails, snatching a feather and trying a second test. He would seem to be oblivious to all reality but Cordelia's body and his attempts to prove that she is alive. His second speech shows what is at stake in the effort:

> This feather stirs; she lives! If it be so,
> It is a chance which does redeem all sorrows
> That ever I have felt.
>
> [V. iii. 266-68]

This effort, too, fails, and Kent's painful attempt, on his knees, to wrest Lear's attention away from Cordelia only makes Lear momentarily turn on his companions with the savage outcry of 'murderers' and 'traitors' before trying again to prove her alive, this time by putting his ear to her lips in the thought that she might be speaking. . . . His outcry, 'Ha!', like his cry 'This feather stirs', registers an illusion that Cordelia has spoken to him. This is a wilder self-deception than the thought that she has breathed, and remains with him beyond the end of the speech. . . . Thus he struggles simultaneously for sanity and for the belief that Cordelia lives. Under the strain of these two irreconcilable psychic needs, his mind simply slips and relaxes into temporary madness. . . . (pp. 1-3)

But agonized sanity breaks through Lear's madness once more, as the words of Kent, Albany and Edgar could not. . . .

> And my poor fool is hang'd! No, no, no life!
> Why should a dog, a horse, a rat, have life,
> And thou no breath at all? Thou'lt come no more,
> Never, never, never, never, never!
>
> [V. iii. 306-09]

The repeated cries of 'Never!' are the steady hammering of truth on a mind unable to endure it. Lear's life-blood rushes to his head. He chokes, and asks someone to undo the button of his collar. . . . Then, against the unendurable pressure of reality, the counterbalancing illusion that Cordelia lives rushes forth once more. Once again, it is at her lips, breathing or speaking, that he seeks life and dies. . . . (p. 3)

Who is to say, given this cycle of despair, insanity, and the illusion of hope, if it really matters at what point of the cycle Lear expires, or even if his last words establish it decisively? On the contrary, on purely aesthetic grounds, we have an indication from another point in Act V that all of Lear's emotions have been gathering to an unendurable head at the moment of death. Gloucester, the counterpart to Lear in the subplot, was, like him, driven out by his false offspring, tormented in the storm, and finally preserved by a faithful, though rejected child. And Gloucester's death, which is described in considerable detail by Edgar, contains just such a welter of conflicting feelings as does Lear's, and might well be the model for understanding Lear's death. . . . Gloucester's heart burst from its inability to contain two conflicting emotions, his psyche torn apart by a thunderclap of simultaneous joy and grief. And such, by aesthetic parallel, we may presume was the death of Lear. . . . But the similarity only serves to accentuate the basic difference between the two deaths. Gloucester died between extremes of joy and grief, at the knowledge that his son was miraculously preserved, Lear between extremes of illusion and truth, ecstasy and the blackest despair, at the knowledge that his daughter was needlessly butchered. Gloucester's heart 'burst smilingly' at his reunion with Edgar; Lear's, we are driven to conclude, burst in the purest agony at his eternal separation from Cordelia.

There is, then, no mitigation in Lear's death, hence no mitigation in the ending of the play. On the contrary, either the play has no aesthetic unity, or everything in it, including Lear's spiritual regeneration, is instrumental to the explosive poignance of Lear's death. Nor can there be any blenching from the implications of Lear's last sane question:

> Why should a dog, a horse, a rat, have life,
> And thou no breath at all? Thou'lt come no more.
> Never, never, never, never, never!
>
> [V. iii. 307-09]

It is only by giving Lear's death a fleeting, ecstatic joy that Bradley can read some sort of reconciliation into the ending, some renewed synthesis of cosmic goodness to follow an antithesis of pure evil. Without it, this is simply, as Lear recognized, a universe where dogs, horses, and rats live, and Cordelias are butchered. There may be mitigations in man himself, but none in the world which surrounds him. Indeed, unless Lear's death is a thoroughly anomalous postscript to his pilgrimage of life, the most organic view of the plot would make almost a test case of Lear, depicting, through his life and death, a universe in which even those who have fully repented, done penance, and risen to the tender regard of sainthood can be hunted down, driven insane, and killed by the most agonizing extremes of passion.

The plot of *King Lear* is generally not read in this fashion. On the contrary, its denouement is generally interpreted as another 'turn of the screw', an added, and unnecessary, twist of horror to round out a play already sated with horrors. If it is defended, it is generally on grounds like those of Lamb, who contended that it was a 'fair dismissal' from life after all Lear had suffered [see excerpt above, 1812], or those of Bradley, that Lear's death is a transfiguration of joy to counterbalance all that has preceded it. Neither reading is satisfactory, Lamb's because it makes the ending, at best, an epilogue rather than denouement to the main body of the action, Bradley's because the textual evidence points to the opposite interpretation of Lear's death. If Lear's spiritual regeneration, however, with the fearful penance he endures, is taken as the play's 'middle', and his death, despite that regeneration, as its denouement, then the catharsis of *King Lear,* Shakespeare's profoundest tragedy, has as yet escaped definition. This catharsis, grounded in the most universal elements of the human condition, can be formulated only when one has drawn together some of the relevant philosophical issues of the play.

Thus, the ending is decisive in resolving the plethora of attitudes presented in the play concerning the relationship between God and man. Set side by side, out of context, and unrelated to the denouement, these attitudes, and their religious frames of reference, can be made to appear an absolute chaos. Certainly almost every possible point of view on the gods and cosmic justice is expressed, from a malevolent, wanton polytheism [IV. i. 36-7] to an astrological determinism [IV. iii. 32-3], from an amoral, personified Nature-goddess [I. ii. 1] to 'high-judging Jove' [II. iv. 228]. But the very multitude, concern, and contradictory character of these references do not cancel each other out, but rather show how precarious is the concept of cosmic justice. Surely if the play's ending is an ending, and cosmic justice has hung in the balance with such matters as Goneril's cruelty [IV. ii. 46-50], and Edmund's death [V. iii. 175], it collapses with Lear's ultimate question: 'Why should a dog, a horse, a rat, have life, / And thou no breath at all?' Despite the pagan setting, the problem of theodicy, the justification of God's way with man, is invoked by so many characters, and with such concern, that it emerges as a key issue in the play. As such, either the denouement vindicates it, or its integrity is universally destroyed. In point of fact, this is implied in the deaths of Lear and Cordelia.

The force of evil, perhaps the most dynamic element in the Christian tragedies, is extended to wide dimensions in *King Lear,* where two distinct modes of evil emerge, evil as animalism, in Goneril and Regan, and evil as doctrinaire atheism, in Edmund. These modes are not to be confused. Goneril, in particular, is, from the point of view of conscience, an animal or beast of prey. She and Regan never discuss doctrine, as does Edmund, or offer motives, as does Iago. Their actions have the immediacy of animals, to whom consideration never interposes between appetite and deed. (pp. 3-5)

Edmund, on the other hand, is a doctrinaire atheist, with regard not only to God, but also to the traditional, organic universe, a heterodoxy equally horrifying to the Elizabethans. This doctrinaire atheism involves an issue as basic in *King Lear* as that of a retributive justice, and that is the bond between man, society and nature. Here, there is no plethora of attitudes, but two positions, essentially, that of Cordelia, and that of Edmund. Cordelia's position is perhaps best expressed by Albany, after he learns of Goneril's treatment of Lear:

> That nature which contemns its origin
> Cannot be bordered certain in itself.
> She that herself will sliver and disbranch
> From her material sap, perforce must wither
> And come to desperate use.
>
> [IV. ii. 32-6]

According to Albany, an invisible bond of sympathy binds human beings like twigs to the branches of a tree. This bond is no vague universal principle, but closely rooted in one's immediate family and society. This is natural law in its most elemental possible sense, not a moral code, but almost a biochemical reaction. Hierarchical propriety is a necessity for life, like sunlight and water, its violation an act of suicide or perversion. . . . This bond, the central concept of the play, is the bond of nature, made up at once of propriety and charity.

In contrast to this concept of Nature is Edmund's soliloquy affirming his doctrinaire atheism [I. ii. 1-15], where natural law is summed up in two phrases, 'the plague of custom', and 'the curiosity of nations'. The bond of human relations, as understood by Cordelia and Albany, is a tissue of extraneous, artificial constraints. Edmund recognizes a hierarchy, but rather than growing out of society, this hierarchy goes wholly against its grain. This is the hierarchy of animal vitality, by which 'the lusty stealth of nature' [I. ii. 11], even in the act of adultery, creates a more worthy issue than the 'dull, stale, tired bed' of marriage [I. ii. 13]. (pp. 5-6)

Strangely enough, however, while the denouement seems to destroy any basis for providential justice, it would seem to vindicate Cordelia with regard to the bond of human nature. Thus, the deaths of Cornwall, Goneril, and Regan are, as Albany prophesied, the swift and monstrous preying of humanity upon itself. Cornwall is killed by his own servant;

Regan is poisoned by her sister; and Goneril finally commits suicide. Even more is Cordelia vindicated in Edmund, who is mortally wounded by his brother, and then goes through a complete, and to this reader, sincere repentance before his death. (p. 6)

But the denouement itself, with the gratuitous, harrowing deaths of Cordelia and Lear, controverts any justice in the universe. Chance kills, in despite of the maidenly stars. It would seem, then, by the denouement, that the universe belongs to Edmund, but mankind belongs to Cordelia. In a palsied cosmos, orphan man must either live by the moral law, which is the bond of love, or swiftly destroy himself. To this paradox, too, Shakespeare offers no mitigation in *King Lear*. The human condition is as inescapable as it is unendurable.

To so paradoxical an ending, what catharsis is possible? This question can be answered only by re-examining the structure of the plot. There can be observed, in *Hamlet,* a radical break from the mode of redemption in such earlier plays as *Romeo and Juliet.* In *Romeo and Juliet,* redemption comes when the tragic hero affirms the traditional frame of values of society, love, an appropriate marriage, peace, and the like, though society has, in practice, ceased to follow them. The result is to enhance the *sancta* of society by the sacrifice of life itself. In *Hamlet,* redemption only comes, finally, when the tragic hero spurns and transcends the *sancta* of society, and appeals to a religious mysticism into which human wisdom can have no entry, and in which, at most, 'the readiness is all'. The final result, however, is none the less the redemption of society and the reconciliation of the tragic hero to it; for Hamlet's last act is to cast a decisive vote for the next king of Denmark. Even *Othello,* domestic tragedy though it is, ends with the reconciliation of the tragic hero and society; and Othello's last act is an affirmation of loyalty to Venice and the execution of judgement upon himself. *King Lear* is Shakespeare's first tragedy in which the tragic hero dies unreconciled and indifferent to society.

The opening movement of *King Lear* is, then, not merely a physical exile from, but an abandonment of the formal *sancta* and institutions of society, which is pictured as even more bankrupt than in *Hamlet.* . . . In this opening movement of abandonment, Lear is stripped of all that majesty and reverence clothing him in the opening scene, of kingdom, family, retainers, shelter, and finally reason and clothing themselves, until he comes, at the nadir of his fortunes, to 'the thing itself . . . a poor bare forked animal' [III. iv. 107-08]. Romeo found his touchstone of truth against the rich texture of the Capulet feast, Lear in an abandoned and naked madman. Romeo and Juliet formed, from the first, an inviolate circle of innocence that was the fulfilment of their previous lives; Lear found no innocence until all his previous life had been stripped away from him.

In contrast to this movement of abandonment, and the basis of the second, counter-movement, stands not, as in *Hamlet,* religious mysticism, but an elemental bond that we can, in this play, indifferently call charity or natural law, one that binds man to man, child to parent, husband to wife, and servant to master almost by a biological impulsion. From first to last, charity is discovered, not as the crown of power and earthly blessing, but in their despite. . . . Indeed, organized society dulls people to an awareness of charity, so that it is only in Lear's abandonment that he becomes bound to all men. . . . (pp. 7-8)

Shakespeare could, of course, have used this more elemental level of charity or natural law as he used the force of love in *Romeo and Juliet,* to redeem and renew society. Had he chosen to do so, it would have become politically effective in Cordelia's invading army, overwhelmed the corrupt elements then in power, and restored the throne to Lear, as is suggested in Shakespeare's conventionally pious source. But society, in Shakespeare, is now no longer capable of self-renewal. And so the counter-movement of the play, the reclothing of Lear, by charity and natural law, with majesty, sanity, family and shelter, after the most terrible of penances, does not close the play. At its close, the completion only of its dramatic 'middle', Lear is utterly purged of soul, while the hierarchy of society is reduced, as at the end of *Hamlet,* to an equation of 'court news' with 'gilded butterflies' [V. ii. 13-14]. At this point, if the universe of the play contained a transcendent providence, it should act as in the closing movement of *Hamlet,* mysteriously to redeem a society unable to redeem itself.

Shakespeare's pessimism, however, has deepened since *Hamlet,* and the deaths to no purpose of Lear and Cordelia controvert any providential redemption in the play's decisive, closing movement, so that another resolution entirely is called for. Narrowing our problem somewhat, the catharsis of any play lies in the relationship of the denouement to the expectations set up in the play's 'middle'. In *King Lear,* this middle movement has to do primarily with Lear's spiritual regeneration after his 'stripping' in the opening movement of the play. These two movements can be subsumed in a single great cycle, from hauteur and spiritual blindness through purgative suffering to humility and spiritual vision, a cycle that reaches its culmination in Lear's address of consolation to Cordelia before they are taken off to prison. . . . The catharsis of *King Lear* would seem to lie, then, in the challenge of Lear's subsequent death to the penance and spiritual transcendence that culminates the play's second movement. (pp. 8-9)

Lear, at the beginning of the play, embodies all that man looks forward to in a world in which, ultimately, nothing is secure. He has vocation, age, wealth, monarchy, family, personal followers and long experience. Like Oedipus and Othello, he would have seemed to have attained, before the play begins, what men strive for with indifferent success all their lives. In this sense, Lear engages our sympathies as an archetype of mankind. And just as Othello discovers areas of experience which he never cultivated and which destroy him, Lear discovers that even in those areas he most cultivated he has nothing. Thus, like Oedipus and more than Othello, Lear activates the latent anxiety at the core of the human conditoin, the fear not only of unexpected catastrophe but that even what seems like success may be a delusion, masking corruption, crime and almost consummated failure.

This opening movement, however, leads not to dissolution, exposure and self-recognition, as in *Oedipus* and *Othello,* but to purgation. And Lear's purgation, by the end of the play's middle movement, like his gifts and his vulnerability at its start, is so complete as to be archetypal. By the time he enters prison, he has paid every price and been stripped of everything a man can lose, even his sanity, in payment for folly and pride. He stands beyond the veil of fire, momentarily serene and alive. As such he activates an even profounder fear than the fear of failure, and that is the fear that whatever penance a man may pay may not be enough once the machinery of destruction has been let loose, because the partner of his covenant may be neither grace nor the balance of law, but malignity, intransigence or chaos.

The final, penultimate tragedy of Lear, then, is not the tragedy of *hubris,* but the tragedy of penance. When Lear, the archetype not of a proud, but of a penitential man, brutally dies, then the uttermost that can happen to man has happened. One can rationalize a passing pedestrian struck down by a random automobile; there is no blenching from this death. Each audience harbours this anxiety in moments of guilt and in acts of penance. And with Lear's death, each audience, by the ritual of the drama, shares and releases the most private and constricting fear to which mankind is subject, the fear that penance is impossible, that the covenant, once broken, can never be re-established, because its partner has no charity, resilience, or harmony—the fear, in other words, that we inhabit an imbecile universe. It is by this vision of reality that Lear lays down his life for his folly. Within its bounds lies the catharsis of Shakespeare's profoundest tragedy. (pp. 9-10)

> *J. Stampfer, "The Catharsis of 'King Lear',"in* Shakespeare Survey: An Annual Survey of Shakespearian Study and Production, *Vol. 13, 1960, pp. 1-10.*

WINIFRED M. T. NOWOTTNY (essay date 1960)

[*In the excerpt below, Nowottny offers an in-depth discussion of Shakespeare's linguistic technique in* King Lear, *claiming that unlike the protagonists of the other great tragedies of Shakespeare's middle period, Lear uses a language that is noticeably sparse in poetic speech and high-style versification. It is closer to that in* Timon of Athens, *she suggests, in its concern with the inadequacy of language to approximate the depths of human feeling. Because of this, Nowottny maintains that Lear's language achieves its effect not through poetic intensification, but through a combination of naturalism and what she terms "contrast of dimension"—a literary technique in which common language is charged with an overabundance of meaning derived from intonation, placement, contrast, and surprise. The idea that* King Lear *deals specifically with the inadequacy of language to communicate human feeling is also discussed by Richard D. Fly (1972).*]

Perhaps one reason why *King Lear* has been mistaken for an unactable play is that it is so nearly an unreadable play: taken passage by passage, it is so flat and grey that the better one knows it the more one feels on reopening its pages that this is almost (as Byron said of *Caractacus*) 'a tragedy complete in all but words'; the style alone might lead one to suppose that what happens in *King Lear* happens in some realm of the imagination beyond ear and eye. This cannot be true, but how is the difficulty of the language to be resolved? The apocalyptic sublime in Lear's defiance of the storm, however much it sticks in the memory, is not the play's climax, nor does this style continue. What of the rest? The 'simplicity' of the closing scenes has been remarked, as has the effective contrast with Lear's former pretensions, but in remarking this we tend to look through the language to what it is 'about', commending it only for transparency and truth to nature, and though we know that such scenes are not to be had by taking a tape-recorder to a deathbed, the terms in which to discuss this style have eluded us. It has been suggested that its art is to be discerned by tracing thematic patterns that give density or bite, but this explanation is vitiated by the fact that other plays by Shakespeare are said to have it too; the case has not been argued that the absence from *Lear* of resplendent imagery, idiosyncrasy of mind expressed in mannered style, indeed of poetry that survives quotation out of context, is deliberately compensated for by an unusually high charge of thematic power. Moreover the suggestion that the play's language draws its power

from a sustained thematic undercurrent conflicts with one's obscure sense that what is really peculiar about the language is the freedom and unexpectedness of its melodic line; Lear himself is unfailingly astonishing, and this property of his words is resistant to explanation in terms of the recurrence of patterns, though, perhaps, in order to maintain this astonishment without having the play fall to bits, Shakespeare might find himself compelled to labour in the vocabulary towards the minimum number and maximum generality of moral and philosophical concepts. For, indeed, the first peculiarity of the style is that its originality is not discernible from its vocabulary, which lays a ground of permanent moral values either instantly identifiable or else so wide as to take their specific colour only from the usage of each speaker; the cultural diversity reflected in the vocabulary of *Hamlet* would be, by the standards of *Lear*, as 'finical' as Oswald seems to Kent; the deeply emotive vocabulary of *Macbeth* or the iridescence of physical and affective experience in *Othello* could have done nothing but obscure, in *Lear*, the terror of a universe whose few simple pillars fall ruining. In this respect *Lear* is at the opposite extreme from that play with which its subject has closest connection, *Timon;* the particularity of detail there, the supple periodicity of syntax sustaining a diction far removed from stereotypes of evaluation, is so much unlike the language of *Lear* that to study the rampant inventiveness of the *Timon* style opens one's eyes wider to the magnitude of the stylistic mystery in *King Lear*. What Timon says of his changed fortunes, Shakespeare might have said of the change that came over his language between the writing of these two plays:

> myself,
> Who had the world as my confectionary,
> The mouths, the tongues, the eyes and hearts of men
> At duty, more than I could frame employment,
> That numberless upon me stuck as leaves
> Do on the oak, have with one winter's brush
> Fell from their boughs and left me open, bare
> For every storm that blows: I, to bear this,
> That never knew but better, is some burden.
> [*Timon of Athens,* IV. iii. 259-67]

What then in the language of *Lear* compensates for its apparent limitations?

First, there is less need for imagery than in other Shakespearian tragedies. Evaluating imagery that projects the conflict or quality of the hero (such as the Pontic sea and the perfect chrysolite images in *Othello,* or the cosmic, heraldic and mythological imagery used for Antony) is unnecessary where the hero is physically the image of his own tragedy. Coleridge observed that Lear has no character and does not need one because old age is itself a character and this peculiarity in the play's subject is repeated at the level of imagery. Lear is visibly old and helpless and later is visibly destitute and mad. The play, to concentrate large issues, need only advert to what the stage has given. . . . The consciousness of this art may be judged by the frequency with which the play resorts to sights recognized as eloquent by the characters who see them, and by Shakespeare's care to point out their significance. There are, however, two very remarkable images of Lear's sufferings: the vulture at the heart and the wheel of fire. Both are aimed at conveying intensity rather than the structure of an experience or the quality of a man; both speak of what cannot be seen, yet is powerfully asserted to be going on here and now in the body: 'she hath tied Sharp-tooth'd unkindness, like a vulture, *here*'; 'Thou art a soul in bliss; but I am bound / Upon a wheel of fire, *that mine own tears / Do scald* like molten lead' [IV. vii. 45-7]. . . . The quality of this writing can best be discussed by way of comparisons. If we put beside it Hamlet's 'I have that within which passeth show', it becomes clear that Lear's language makes the same point whilst avoiding any appearance of concern with the 'show'. If we put beside it Gloucester's 'I am tied to the stake and I must stand the course' [III. vii. 54] it becomes clear that Lear's language is not merely ana-logical; Lear's images of torture are embedded in sentences that bind the suffering body of the speaker to the instrument of his torture and so manage the two terms (what tortures, and what feels) as to achieve maximum impact of the cruelty of the one on the sensitivity of the other. . . . If we put beside these the image used by Kent, 'he hates him much / That would upon the rack of this tough world / Stretch him out longer' [V. iii. 314-16], it is clear that the common idea of the incom-mensurateness of the suffering body to what it has to endure is conveyed not so much by citing the vulture, the wheel or the rack as by making the incommensurateness a reality (rather than an analogical way of speaking). Moreover Kent's image is deployed in a sentence shaped for no other purpose than to support the analogy, whereas Lear's images of wheel and vul-ture seem to erupt from sentences that did not foreknow their ferocity. I labour here under the heavy difficulty of seeking to retrace in language those swift judgements that our common linguistic habits lead us to make without conscious reflection, and I would not attempt so peculiar a task were it not that I think the power of Lear's language is to be located at a level as hard to see, and as inevitably operative, as this. Since it is not to be believed that the play's power operates independently of the art of dramatic language, and since none the less this language is resistant to familiar critical tools, one must examine the possibility that its impact is due not to its displayed de-viations from the language of common life but to its exploi-tation of the common responses we cannot avoid making when confronted by expressively ordered language. One way of breaking through to this level of power in language is to find methods for seeing the apparently simple and inevitable lo-cution as a willed structure of functioning parts. Comparison is one method. Another is substitution for, or disordering of, the parts; when the light of the original language goes out, one knows one has broken the circuit, and where. I am encouraged to believe that so far I am on the right track because comparison has thrown up results that relate themselves to my impression that what is effective in Lear's language is its free line, the apparent absence of contrivance in the sudden blazes that il-luminate the prosy syntax and commonplace vocabulary of Lear's utterances. I am the more encouraged in that these com-parisons, though drawn from the main stratum of the play (the presentation of what it is to suffer), show a difference between the language of Lear and that of other characters treating the same topic. Lear's domination of the play is a linguistic dom-ination; his is the most powerful of the voices that speak out of sufferings. Shakespeare concentrates upon Lear the style that gives a felt experience of the incommensurateness of hu-man nature to what it must endure. (pp. 49-51)

It is of importance in Shakespeare's design that Lear's language though carrying all this power should appear to be uncontrived and matter-of-fact. Gloucester may strain language to express what he conceives . . . or Albany call Goneril fiend, devil and monster, or Lear himself use even more violent language in the cursing episodes, but for Lear's actual prolonged bearing of a suffering to which he is tied, vociferation is useless. A similar contrast obtains between Gloucester's language in the blinding scene and the style in which he speaks in his blind

wanderings; a simplicity is invented for Gloucester which does not trench upon the simple mode of Lear, but is compatible enough with it to make their encounter linguistically possible. The play is deeply concerned with the inadequacy of language to do justice to feeling or to afford any handhold against abysses of iniquity and suffering. . . . *Lear* begins where *Timon* ends, that is with a vision of the futility of language to encompass or direct reality. . . . And fittingly, when Lear enters with the body of Cordelia, his demand for lamentation is not a demand for words—'Howl, howl, howl' [V. iii. 258]. One of the things this play has to say about feeling and suffering is that they are beyond words. This poses the basic problem of the play's dramatic language.

The first steps towards dealing with this problem are taken in the action, characterization and substance of the dialogue rather than in the language itself. The opening scene makes it abun-dantly clear that the deepest feelings do not run out into words. Next, the glib and free-thinking Bastard expresses in soliloquy his rejection of the meanings others attach to words and public forms, and goes on to show how he can manipulate them to betray. In the third scene Goneril is displayed rigging the show-down with Lear; the fourth shows Kent planning to 'defuse' his speech, but reiterates the characterization of him as 'blunt' and 'plain'; we then meet the Fool, giving a pyrotechnic display of the half-riddling form of expression peculiarly his own. Lear is now surrounded by a collection of characters in whom the relation of meaning to verbal expression is in some way de-fective, oblique or trumped-up. The master-stroke of the quar-rel scene with Regan and Goneril is their indifference to all the verbal forms Lear grasps at to fix the chaos of his emotions or to appeal to their supposed better natures. The master-stroke of Lear as outcast was to surround him with characters whose meanings are overlaid by or filtered through some mesh that makes communication indirect—and then to make Lear seek among the utterances of these and among the burning recol-lections of his experiences of the false Regan and Goneril and the misunderstood Cordelia for clues in the effort to understand the nature of things and find a form of response. At the heart of Lear's tragedy there lies the great problem of traditional symbolic forms. These are the only language for love and reverence; they have, however, to be maintained against attack, and the function of authority is to enforce observance of form on those who repudiate it. The play begins by breaking from above and from below the cultural pattern that gives shape to the flux of life. From above, Authority takes the tragic step of asking for a token of love, beyond that reverence for the forms of duty it knows itself able to enforce, whilst at the same time abrogating its power. . . . From below, the Bastard, following in Gloucester's footsteps . . . rejects reverence for forms . . . and acts on his rejection. This double break opens the play's central action: the anatomy of uncontrolled evil and the anat-omy of formless feeling. It is, I believe, from some such point of view that one can best appreciate the linguistic art of the play, and the way in which the minor characters are used to support the language of its hero, who must use language not as the adequate register of his experience, but as evidence that his experience is beyond language's scope.

If the problem is seen in these terms, a technique of *montage* seems the obvious solution. Shakespeare 'mounts' (and of course places) a passage in such a way that its depth of meaningfulness is *inferred* from something not strictly contained within that passage itself. This technique is sustained variously: by con-trasts, by preparatory passages (especially those indicating a turmoil of feeling vaster than any one expression of any one of its forms), and by surprise. Some instances of it have already had their due in criticism, as for instance the way in which Lear's 'I did her wrong' [I. v. 24], striking through the Fool's prattle, indicates feeling running deep under the surface of the dialogue; again, the use of the Fool, harping on the prudent course, to suggest the larger dimensions of Lear's concerns. The technique, however, is continuous throughout. . . . The bluntness of Kent, if it had no other function in the play, would have been worth inventing for the sake of Lear's reactions to it in the scene of the stocks; Kent's reiteration of the brutal truth fights stubbornly with Lear's refusal to admit and face what it must mean, and the tension of the contradictions tells us that Lear's incredulity is a dam over which the chaotic flood of feeling will have to break. . . . It is because so much is at stake that Lear has pitted himself against Kent's bluntness so long, and these exchanges intensify the meaning of the naturalistic speech in which Lear's turmoil of discrete responses breaks out, showing that the attitudes he brings to Regan's behaviour are compounded of the remnants of autocracy . . . , of an appalled sense of what it implies . . . , and a pathetic need for and belief in Regan. . . . Upon the basis of this preparation is mounted the quarrel scene, which is great not by virtue of projecting into heightened language some one strain of emotion, but by bracing through shifts of diction and rhythm the Protean forms Lear's hurt casts up and the tragic failure of all of them to stay fixed or to make any difference to those he tries to reach through them. Is there anywhere in literature a comparable attempt to make us understand from within the one unadmitted compulsion, the need for love, that makes its victim box the compass of attitudes with such rapidity and apparent inconsistency? The language that carries this depends, for effect, on our responding as we do to language heard in ordinary life but—because it is after all the language of art—the cues for response are writ large. And further, we are in advance put upon interpreting it properly by the 'naturalistic' dialogue between Lear and Gloucester that precedes Regan's entry. . . . In these exchanges Lear reacts to and uses language as it is used in common life; his attitudes are expressed not in an overtly heightened theatrical language but through the implications, expressive choices, and significant usages available in the common tongue. But Shakespeare writes into this common speech pointers to what prompts it. For instance, the abrupt shift to a resolutely different attitude is cued by the unfinished state of 'Tell the hot duke that—' and by the explicit 'No, but not yet' [II. iv. 104-05]; the forced nature of this attempted tolerance is brought out by the contrast between its suddenly regular rhythm and syntax, and the exclamatory irregularity of the preceding lines. . . . This style exploits the expressive ranges of common language (cueing it where necessary) and supports the expressiveness by metrical mimesis; it is a style far removed from 'poetic' blank verse that uses the conventional licence of poetry to elaborate a literary equivalent of the state of feeling supposed in the speaker, yet we must admit this style to be, in its own way, far removed from the 'naturalism' that seems merely to transcribe common speech. And though this is by no means the only style used in the play it is one that makes it easy to overlook the art, and to suppose the play to be deficient in heightened language. Upon these exchanges with Kent and Gloucester Shakespeare mounts the great quarrel scene that follows, where Lear's turmoil of conflicting attitudes is conveyed through the obliquities, the expressive choices and nuances and even the extravagances and transparent pretences of language as used by the common man making a scene. But we should not forget how much is done to support this language; especially, that the very shifts of tone illuminate one another

by contrast, and that the whole scene would have been impossible if Lear's hopes of Regan, set off against his despair of Goneril, did not so clearly annotate his ambivalence to both; it was not for nothing that Shakespeare contrived in the plot to get Goneril to Regan's house.

This 'mounting' of great passages on verbal encounters that prepare for them (and even, ultimately, on characterization and plot) is a continuous technique, and to bear it in mind may make some apparent miracles of style less impregnable to commentary. When Lear wakens in the presence of Cordelia and says, 'You do me wrong to take me out of the grave' [IV. viii. 44], though no critical words are needed to draw attention to the astonishing effect of this, it would need a spate of words to trace the cause, but leaving aside considerations of diction, prosody and syllabity, one may observe that what matters very much is that this is precisely the most unexpected thing Lear could have said; it is mounted on the immediate background of Cordelia's prayerful concern and pity, her anxiety for 'restoration' and 'medicine', her sense of the wrong others have done him. This is why Lear astonishes us—but astonishment is as swiftly subsumed into understanding when these words are revealed to be Lear's interpretation of what he sees, an interpretation at once morally true and factually 'still, still, far wide'. 'Thou art a soul in bliss, but I am bound / Upon a wheel of fire, that mine own tears / Do scald' [IV. vii. 45-9]. Indeed, throughout this scene, the language taken line by line or speech by speech resists attempts to trace effect to cause, for each reverberates against the others, whilst at the same time being itself epigrammatic of vast issues in the antecedent action; the language, despite its simplicity of diction, is sculptural and lapidary in effect. Yet this is none the less a linguistic feat: what moves us is written into the language. One cause of our responses I cannot particularize except by some such term as 'contrast in dimension' (as between, for instance, 'wheel of fire' and 'tears'). (pp. 52-6)

A test of the relevance of such suggestions as I have made, is whether they throw light on the langauge which in the last scene conveys that truth to nature all recognize it to have. *'Enter Lear with Cordelia in his armes'*: visual language reaches sublimity here, putting all the play has said into one visible word and bringing the whole plot to its point. Along the receding planes keyed into this tableau we see in an instant of time Lear's sin and its retribution, the wider evil that has struck both, the full fatherhood of Lear bearing his child in his arms whilst at the same time the natural course of life is seen reversed (Lear senile, so lately cared for by Cordelia), the world's destruction of the love and forgiveness that had transcended it— for the reverberation of the reunion is still strong and the language of that scene has opened the way to those suggestions of a saviour's death which now make it inescapable that Cordelia dead in her father's arms and displayed by him to the world, should strike deeply into responses that lie midway between religion and art. 'Howl, howl, howl': there is to be no language for meanings such as these; the point is reiterated in '*Had* I your tongues and eyes, I'd use them so / That heaven's vault should crack' and with the descent to 'She's gone for ever!' [V. iii. 259-60] it is as though Shakespeare announced that the language to come is not heaven-shattering uproar, but the terms of common grief. And perhaps the greatest single reason why such terms become uncommon language is the prosody. Its function is obvious, once one looks; but who does, at such moments? Yet we shall not estimate this language rightly if we ignore it. This almost miraculous prosodic art defeats conjecture as to how far it was consciously contrived or how far it sprang with the certainty of long expertise subserving the fury of creation. . . . Such prosody adds decisively to the expressiveness of the diction; indeed it is as though Shakespeare filled up the blank verse pattern not from what our mere vocabulary offers but from the intonation patterns of expressive English speech. . . . How Shakespeare came to do all this does not matter, but by doing it he wrote the interpretation of the words into the blank verse structure. Lear's 'Never, never, never, never, never!' [V. iii. 309], a recognized stroke of prosodic art, is not isolated; it is the master-stroke of a prosodic brilliance that helps to make the play's language transcend that natural language of human feeling which it so convincingly simulates.

And, as to my final suggestion that a 'contrast of dimension' is a characteristic of the play's tragic vision: surely it hardly needs saying that the heartbreak of the very last scene is in the contrast between infinite concern and the finiteness of its object; put into words, it is all hope and all despair divided by the down of a feather: 'This feather stirs! she lives! if it be so, / It is a chance which does redeem all sorrows / That ever I have felt' [V. iii. 266-68]. (pp. 56-7)

> *Winifred M. T. Nowottny, "Some Aspects of the Style of 'King Lear',"* in Shakespeare Survey: An Annual Survey of Shakespearian Study and Production, *Vol. 13, 1960, pp. 49-57.*

ROBERT ORNSTEIN (essay date 1960)

[*Ornstein is a twentieth-century American critic and scholar and the author of* A Kingdom for the Stage: The Achievement of Shakespeare's History Plays *(1972), which has been called one of the most important contributions to Shakespearean studies in recent years, as well as the most influential study of the history plays since E.M.W. Tillyard's* The Elizabethan World Picture *(1944). The purpose of Ornstein's book was to challenge the popular belief that Shakespeare's histories dramatize not such universal concerns as human nature and the effects of power, but the orthodox view of English history propagated by the Tudor monarchy. Ornstein's efforts to interpret the history plays as drama rather than historical documents contributed to a reappraisal of these works, specifically with regard to their political assumptions, and signified their return to the same standard of evaluation accorded the rest of Shakespeare's canon. In the following excerpt from his* The Moral Vision of Jacobean Tragedy *(1960), Ornstein takes issue with those critics, specifically Robert Bechtold Heilman (1948) and John F. Danby (see Additional Bibliography), who have interpreted* King Lear *as a conflict of such antithetical elements as good versus evil, feudal order versus Machiavellian individualism, and natural versus unnatural. Ornstein believes that such arguments are both overly simple and subtle. More importantly, he argues, none of the so-called good or bad characters in the play can be easily categorized with respect to their attitudes toward the gods. As far as the moral vision of* King Lear, *Ornstein generally views the play as more pessimistic than hopeful; the justice it demonstrates, and the metaphysical order it suggests hold little promise for either the idealist or the self-willed individualist. What it does affirm, according to Ornstein, is the necessity of love and the indestructibility of the human spirit in the face of unimaginable terror. Like René E. Fortin (1979), Ornstein maintains that in* King Lear *Shakespeare refuses to accept simple, comprehensible images of God and the universe, but consistently stresses the mystery of the cosmos and of human existence. For further discussion of the importance of love in the play, see the excerpts by Hermann Ulrici (1839), Edward Dowden (1881), Oscar James Campbell (1948), Arthur Sewell (1951), Irving Ribner (1958), L. C. Knights (1959), and Robert H. West (1968).*]

We do not require an extensive knowledge of Renaissance thought to recognize that *Lear* is deeply concerned with the nature of man and his universe. From a close textual study of the play, conducted with slight reference to Renaissance philosophy, Professor R. B. Heilman reports that its patterns of imagery constitute "a series of implied questions: What is man's nature? What is nature? What in the nature of things may man depend upon? From considerations of what is natural and unnatural it is only a step to the problem of justice, to which the play returns repeatedly . . ." [see excerpt above, 1948]. On the one hand, the ageless contemporaneity of *Lear* rebukes the vanity of those investigators who believe that scholarly research affords a unique revelation of Shakespeare's intention and meaning. On the other hand, the complexity of theme and structure in *Lear* proves the value of historical research as a guide to what is central in Shakespeare's thought and art. At the same time that recent critics [Heilman, John F. Danby, and others] have interpreted *Lear* as an inquiry into the nature of man, they have, to varying degrees, falsified its philosophical and dramatic structure. They read *Lear* as a dramatization of an ideological dichotomy; they classify the characters by their adherence to conflicting philosophies of nature. In one group supposedly are the "idealists," who believe in the classical-Christian concept of natural law: Cordelia, Kent, Edgar, Gloucester, and Lear. Ranged against them are the Machiavellian (or Hobbesian) "realists," who see in nature only amoral physical energy and who view the world as a jungle in which the fittest (i.e., the most ruthless) survive.

While there are undoubted references to the destruction of the feudal ethos in *Lear*, the above interpretation seems at once an oversimplification and oversubtilization of Shakespeare's intention. It construes *Lear* as an analogue of *The Atheist's Tragedy*, more profound in its view of life but puzzling in its dialectic. Despite a crudely literal moral design, Tourneur's play brings its ideological conflict to an unequivocal resolution: D'Amville admits before he dies the error of his philosophy of nature. At the end of *Lear* there is no philosophical conclusion about the nature of the universe on which all agree. Each character interprets the tragic events by the light of his own experience. The dying Edmund admits only that the wheel has come full circle. Goneril and Regan die at each other's throats without philosophical meditation. Edgar and Albany exclaim at the justice of the gods but Lear questions why anything on earth should live when Cordelia must die, and Kent sees that it is the stars that rule men's fates. Surely the deaths of Goneril, Regan, and Edmund do not prove their philosophy invalid when Cordelia, Gloucester, and Lear die with them. In a Morality the conflict between good and evil is implicitly of philosophical importance because it reaffirms the supremacy of God in His universe—a reaffirmation that does not come in the cheerless, dark, and deadly close of *Lear*. Moreover, if Edmund and the evil sisters represent a "modern" order of rationality or individualism, then we must accuse Shakespeare of sentimentally tampering with history in allowing the "wave of the future" to recede before the resurrected traditional idealism of Albany and Edgar.

It is extremely difficult also to think of Goneril and Regan as "rationalists." Cold-bloodedness may be a form of rationality but they are not even cold-blooded. They have the kingdom legitimately in their possession; they own the total reality of power which the Machiavel seeks. But they are not realists enough to tolerate their father's illusions of royalty; they must make him see himself as they see him: aged, weak, defenseless, and dependent on their whim. One imagines that the author of

The Prince would have smiled at the "Machiavellianism" of those who risk secure power to satisfy a purely vicious, irrational impulse. For behind the coldly calculated plan to humiliate Lear lies the feverish desire to subjugate which also expresses itself in almost masculine sexual lusts. To be sure, Goneril and Regan have an air of aggrieved reasonableness but then so do Octavius Caesar, Claudius, and Richard III. (Almost all of Shakespeare's villains are experts at sanctimony.) Their rationalizations are logical, but then all immoralists have a terrifying unspoken logic of their own. They see life more clearly and simply than the rest of humanity. We may, somewhat incorrectly, call Goneril and Regan "Machiavellian" if we remember that Machiavellianism is as old as politics itself and that the *Realpolitik* began with Satan's revolt in heaven. The order whch Goneril and Regan represent began with Cain. If it seems modern it is because ideals of virtue become old-fashioned and disappear while the face of evil is changeless, eternally familiar and "modern."

Edmund, disturbingly enough, is a rationalist. His scheming intellect seems always in control; his reason apparently never gives way to impulse or passion until he is touched by remorse at his death. (pp. 260-62)

Emancipated from the moral superstitions that enslave his naïve brother and father, Edmund finds in libertine naturalism a perfect rationalization for his intended villainy. His first soliloquy immediately defines, by ironic contrast to Lear's invocations of nature, his lawless rebellion against society. . . . (pp. 262-63)

We should not, however, take Edmund's mock-heroic manifesto more seriously than he does. This is no impassioned cry of self-assertion against meaningless convention. His high-spirited wit suggests that he is not so pained by the degradation of his birth as he is contemptuous of the moral code that brands him. He is not so sensitive about his illegitimacy as he is enthusiastic about his plot against Edgar. If Edmund did not have his bastardy, he would no doubt have had to invent it. And his nature philosophy, like his bastardy, seems more a symbol than an explanation of his villainy. Apart from this soliloquy he never mentions his goddess again. Like Richard III, he is a gambler and accepts his defeat as a turn of the wheel, not as proof of intellectual error. (p. 263)

The naturalism to which Edmund makes passing reference is not significant in *Lear*, and the attempt to define Goneril, Regan, and Edmund ideologically merely diverts attention from the true philosophical drama of the play, which is focused in Lear's mind. If we read the play as a conflict between philosophies of nature then Lear becomes a lay figure, a *casus belli* ["cause of conflict"] between warring intellectual factions, or at best a choric voice for Shakespeare's commentary on life. Some critics, I suspect, would like to ignore Lear altogether because they discuss his character with ill-concealed impatience. They acknowledge his greatness of soul and majesty of utterance, the depths and grandeur of his passion. However they find him puerile in intellect, childishly vain and self-deluded, and even criminally stupid. And when they have catalogued all his failings, they still find it impossible to explain his incredible ignorance of the world around him.

Some of the accusations against Lear are unjust. It is customary, for example, to measure his folly against political commonplaces of the Renaissance and to compare his mistake in dividing his kingdom with Gorboduc's. Actually Lear does not commit Gorboduc's unpardonable political sin of destroying the natural succession to the realm. His division of the kingdom among three daughters to "prevent future strife" seems eminently sensible and has disastrous consequences only because two of his daughters are Goneril and Regan. More often than not Lear's assumptions have the weight of theoretical authority behind them. He would no doubt have found good counsel in Erasmus and Elyot, but he needed even more the political realism of Machiavelli.

Part of the misunderstanding of Lear's character stems also from a failure to appreciate the ceremonial quality of the testing scene. Lear walks on stage an absolute monarch whose prerogative is unquestioned and who expects complete obedience. He does not ask his daughters to declare their love; he commands them. When Cordelia refuses to flatter him, he orders her to reconsider. When she refuses again, he banishes her with the outspoken Kent, who dares to intercede, and who would have Lear break a kingly vow. Here is arrogance personified, autocracy, even despotism. Yet Lear does not have the despot's greediness for power or the tyrant's fear of relinquishing authority. We are told directly that the purpose of the testing game is to enable Lear to shrug off peacefully the burden of ruling. He will give up all control of the kingdom, all sway, all instruments of royal authority. He will reserve for himself only the name of king, the respect which it elicits, and a princely retinue of a hundred followers. Before long he learns the fundamental fact of monarchy: that the title of royalty is meaningless without the homage that power demands or that love brings forth unasked.

The opening dialogue between Gloucester and Kent imparts the crucial information that the kingdom has already been equitably divided among Lear's daughters. The testing of their love is purely ritualistic, a last enjoyment of the sway which Lear intends to renounce. It is in fact a tripartite ceremony in which a vain and aging monarch plays the central role. He is, first of all, king, image of authority in the state; he is also father, corresponding ruler in the microcosm of the family; and last but equally important, he is a judge, bearer of the sacred sword of heaven. In all three symbolic roles Lear carries himself with assurance. Is he not the good king, who by dividing power while he lives, will prevent civil war? Is he not the generous father, who, for a small declaration of love (which is in any case his natural due) is prepared to give away a kingdom—to give away "all"? And is he not the perfect judge, who proposes strict, impartial measure for measure: a third of a realm for an appropriate declaration of affection? Of course, the judgment is to be purely symbolic because although Lear knows that Cordelia loves him best, he is quite certain that all his daughters will declare their undying affection—that they are (as they should be) natural children.

In itself Lear's ritual division of the kingdom is no more absurd or potentially tragic than the comparable ritual of marriage. Both ceremonies demand rehearsed answers that are perhaps greatly at variance with the participants' feelings. It would be more honest for those before an altar to state the true nature of their affections, but any declaration other than the customary avowal of eternal devotion would be as shocking as Cordelia's answer is to Lear. It is not Cordelia's "pride" or "tragic reticence" that makes the innocent ritual disastrous in consequence; it is Lear's delight in setting off his daughters against each other and his insulting insinuation that they must buy their inheritance with hyperbole. Even then all might have been well except for the precedent set by Goneril's fulsome flatteries. When Cordelia's turn comes, her plain reply is precisely the answer that Goneril and Lear deserve but it is not the answer which the occasion demands. A less fine nature might have temporized, but Cordelia's revulsion is an almost physical nausea: she cannot heave her heart into her mouth. (pp. 264-66)

[Lear] is a man who very slenderly knows himself and his world in which he has so long and apparently securely lived. He cannot in a crucial instance distinguish between the appearance and the reality of love because his rigid mind cannot adapt to the specific circumstance. He does not know Goneril and Regan, but he knows the natural obligation of love which they owe him; he measures the naturalness of their filial affections by the correspondence of their statements to an ideal which his mind conceives. In a sense Lear is Shakespeare's most paradoxical hero—a man who acts unjustly yet believes implicitly that justice is the rule of the universe, a king and father who acts unnaturally and yet is convinced of the existence of rational, natural order. I do not suggest that Shakespeare uses Lear to present Elizabethan idealism, for Lear's view of nature is narrow, legalistic, egocentric, and supremely naïve; his responses are emotional rather than intellectual. On the other hand, Lear's belief in natural order is, as the play reveals, the deepest certainty of his existence. It is as necessary to him as sanity itself. (pp. 266-67)

Lear, we might say, refuses to accept reality, but this would be too simple an explanation. Before man can accept realities, he must first recognize them; and he has always clung to the belief—written large in the whole of metaphysics—that there is a more stable and enduring reality than the flux of daily experience. His daughters' evil and ingratitude tear at Lear's belief in natural order but do not destroy it. Conceived by reason, that belief can be betrayed only by reason, as it is when Goneril and Regan argue calmly, sensibly, and logically that Lear requires no retinue or outward show of kingly dignity and honor. . . . In a moment of agonized illumination, Lear realizes that Goneril's and Regan's arguments are impeccable. Reason does not require such frivolities as retinue, nor can it measure a king's need for love, loyalty, and devotion. Indeed, when necessity is measured by Goneril's (or Ulysses') reason alone, man's life does become as cheap as beasts'. Reduced by his daughters to emptiness—to the Fool's "O"—Lear rushes out into the storm, maddened with rage and grief.

In one sense Lear's derangement parallels his dethronement of reason in the kingdom, his inversion of justice and family piety. At the same time his growing irrationality also mirrors the destruction of the certainties by which he had lived. After all, the first premise of sanity is that one lives in a somewhat reasonable world. To retain one's sanity one must be able to determine some logical pattern in the disorder of events. One must be able to anticipate with some degree of accuracy the result of actions taken. One must believe, pragmatically at least, in causal relationships. Lear acts "justly" towards his daughters and expects justice in return. He acts "kindly" as king and father and expects kindness in return. Reason and knowledge tell him that he is still king. And when reason and knowledge lie, Lear retreats from an insane world into madness. (p. 268)

In delirium Lear envisions a universe that travesties the orderly, hierarchical cosmos of the Renaissance moral philosophers. But his cynical commentary on hidden guilts and pretended virtue, on the corruption of justice and of family relationships, is double-edged. The bitter pleasure of universalizing his discovery of injustice is chastened by a knowledge of the follies and crimes that were hidden by his own "robes and furr'd

gowns." In madness he can make admissions about himself that were before unthinkable. When he was sane he abused his absolute authority. In madness he claims (as did the Stuarts) a despotic power over all law, civil or moral, only to admit that his omnipotence is counterfeit. (pp. 269-70)

Against the ruins of ancient beliefs, however, stand the unbending loyalties of Kent, Cordelia, and Edgar. Opposed to the staggering disclosure of man's inhumanity is the continuing verbal insistence that evil is a monstrous aberration, an insistence that grows more vehement as evil triumphs. Although we share Albany's horror at Goneril, we are not certain that evil is an aberration or a transient flaw in the design of creation. Who shall we say represents the norm? Cordelia or her sisters? Edgar or Edmund? Albany or Cornwall? the faithful Kent or the equally faithful Oswald? In a Morality, the inevitable triumph of God makes a joke of satanic evil. But instead of the laughter which sounds as angels beat devils off the stage, we hear in *Lear* only the laughter of Edmund, comic interlocutor, as Edgar, Kent, Gloucester, and Lear are forced into hiding. Here is farce of a high order: the politic Edmund and Cornwall exchanging moral platitudes, faithful Kent banished for disloyalty, Cordelia and Edgar slandered and disowned as unnatural children, kindly Gloucester blinded for his "treason"—decency itself made a crime. Yet who dares say in the face of ancient and modern totalitarianisms that such inversion of values is not commonplace in society? In the totalitarian ethic, there is no higher virtue than to inform on one's own father.

The final act of *Lear* brings eventful change, a rift in impenetrable gloom, and a turn of fate that destroys ascendant evil. Still the play does not end, as does *Hamlet*, with a return to normality after a sudden, purgative spasm of violence. The return to normality in *Lear* is a brief delusory interlude between the terror of the storm and the apocalyptic agony of the last scene. For one moment all suffering seems redeemed: Edgar triumphs, the order goes out for the release of Lear and Cordelia, and joyful reunion is at hand. But just when all seems right again with the world, Lear enters with the dead Cordelia in his arms and again all's "cheerless, dark, and deadly" [V. iii. 291]. (pp. 270-71)

That some kind of justice rules the universe of *Lear* is evident, but it is at best a partial justice which metes out exact measure for measure to those who least deserve it: to Goneril, Regan, Cornwall, Edmund, and Oswald. For Cordelia, Edgar, and Kent, the innocents, and for Gloucester and Lear, more sinned against than sinning, there can be no justice. The close of *Lear*, which offended eighteenth-century moral sensibilities, is not made bearable by Albany's belated promise to reward Edgar, or by some impossible hope that the broken Kent will end his years in peace and happiness. For his immeasurable devotion to Lear, Kent seeks only the simplest and humblest satisfaction—to be recognized. This the gods will not allow. As Lear dies we do not regain our confidence in this best of all possible worlds where the torture of the rack produces such remarkable spiritual benefits, nor are we reassured of the existence of universal law. The medieval ideal of nature does not rise phoenix-like out of its ashes any more than it rose again in the scientific world of the seventeenth century. But with loss there is rediscovery; with negation, reaffirmation.

When Lear awakens in Cordelia's presence, he has been cleansed through suffering of vanity and arrogance. Almost literally born again, he is childlike in his weakness and unable to organize his thoughts. Having come to the edge of self-knowledge, he has lost the assurances which formerly made him an imposing ruler. Whereas before he took the measure of all things, now he is unable to predict Cordelia's responses; he is certain only that he is "a very foolish fond old man" [IV. vii. 59]. . . . In the storm Lear had clung to the idea that nature would redeem itself if he were given justice—i.e., if Goneril and Regan were cruelly punished. His unsettled mind was fascinated with legalistic machinery: with courts, arraignments, summoners, and judges. Now he no longer rages against an unjust, "unnatural" world; he no longer hungers for the name and additions to a king. Royal authority, which had seemed a ludicrous pretense in the storm, now appears a childish game of who's in, who's out. Lear needs no other certainty now than Cordelia's love.

Through the vastness of centuries, Lear takes his place beside Job as a man who was confident of the nature of the universe and who knew that measure for measure was the law of God's creation. Like Job he was driven by misery and calamity to question his own beliefs and at last the meaning of life. Like Job he receives no philosophical assurances. The Voice out of the Whirlwind does not explain why the rain falls on the just and the unjust alike. But it restores to Job that sense (close to the heart of all religious belief) of the mystery of suffering, of existence itself. The Voice reminds Job of his insignificance in the cosmic order, of his presumption in defining universal law with his limited comprehension. Lear also gains patience and humility, the stoic resignation that enables man to face the inexplicable with dignity and strength. Even more, he rediscovers the love which redeems all sorrows and without which precise, calculating virtue is brittle and corruptible. Only when he realizes the egocentrism of his ideals and the vanity of his metaphysical formulations, only when he can no longer believe that his petty legalistic conception of justice is the rule of the cosmos, does Lear (and does man) rediscover intuitively and experientially the true nature of his humanity.

Looking backward from *Lear,* we see in the pattern of Jacobean tragedy the turmoil and confusion of Shakespeare's lesser contemporaries, who concern themselves with the broken structure of Renaissance beliefs and who seek new philosophical assurances. Shakespeare alone penetrates beneath the shattered exterior, the outworn cosmology and archaic systems, to bring to light once more the indestructible certainties of the human spirit: its capacity for love, devotion, and joy; its resources of courage and compassion in the face of unimaginable terror. One can of course read *Lear* as a warning against pride, wrath, or relatives. But I suspect that like all great tragedy *Lear* actually celebrates the vulnerability of man, the sublime folly of his "needs" and aspirations, the irrationality of his demands upon the vast inscrutable universe which surrounds him. (pp. 271-73)

Robert Ornstein, "Shakespeare," in his The Moral Vision of Jacobean Tragedy, *The University of Wisconsin Press, 1960, pp. 222-76.**

JOHN HOLLOWAY (essay date 1961)

[*Holloway's* The Story of the Night *includes perhaps the best known and most comprehensive of the mythic or archetypal interpretations of* King Lear. *In the portion excerpted below, he characterizes the play as Shakespeare's dramatization of the Elizabethan belief in the End of the World, the anticipated universal descent into chaos; as evidence, he points to its portrait of human life reduced to bestiality and the breakdown of the structure of both the state and family. Holloway then argues that if* Lear *was a simple tragedy, it would have ended after the third, possibly the fourth act, but that it does not indicate a different desire on*

Shakespeare's part. This intention, Holloway theorizes, was to parallel the Job story, for, like Job, *Lear is made to suffer beyond all notions of orderly justice on his path to self-knowledge. Other critics who have stressed the similarity of* King Lear *to the story of Job include Richard B. Sewall (1959) and Jan Kott (1964). Holloway also claims that the evil in* King Lear *is hardly resolved in the affirmation of the principle of love, as suggested by Hermann Ulrici (1839), Edward Dowden (1881), Oscar James Campbell (1948), Arthur Sewell (1951), Irving Ribner (1958), and L. C. Knights (1959). What affirmation exists in the play, Holloway continues, is that certain "forces of life" guarantee that the natural order will be reestablished and that individuals will return to their proper relationships with each other. Holloway concludes, also, that* King Lear *implicitly presents a pattern of ritual sacrifice—Lear, in this light, representing the scapegoat figure who is isolated, pursued, and eventually destroyed. This idea has also been discussed by Northrop Frye (1967).*]

King Lear, a play set (unlike *Macbeth*) in the legendary prehistory of Britain, depicts a world which is remote and primaeval. This is not to deny that it has life and meaning for all times: its permanent relevance is what follows from having the quality of legend, and the primaeval as subject. Nor is it a merely trite observation about the play. To apprehend this fact is to be led to a decisive truth. The action of *King Lear* comprises an event which today has largely lost its meaning; though one, indeed, which points back to men's original and deepest fears and convictions, and seems to have been part of their consciousness from primitive times.

This by now largely archaic idea is present elsewhere in the tragedies. It is brought before the mind in the guards' words at the death of Antony:

> *Second Guard:*　　　　　　The star is fall'n.
> *First Guard: And time is at his period.*
> 　　　　　　　　[*Antony and Cleopatra,* IV. xiv. 106-07]

It is in Macduff's words at Duncan's murder:

> Shake off this downy sleep, Death's counterfeit,
> And look on death itself. Up, up, and see
> *The great doom's image*! Malcolm! Banquo!
> *As from your graves rise up* and walk like sprites
> To countenance this horror!
> 　　　　　　　　　　[*Macbeth*, II. iii. 76-80]

The point here is that the king's end is like the end of the world: not the Day of Judgement, but the universal cataclysm which was to precede it. Twice, in *Lear,* the idea is mentioned explicitly. Kent, when he sees Lear enter with Cordelia dead in his arms, says:

> Is this the promis'd end?

and Edgar replies:

> Or image of that horror?
> 　　　　　　　　　　　　[V. iii. 264-65]

The mad Lear and the blinded Gloucester meet:

> *Glou:* O, let me kiss that hand!
> *Lear:* Let me wipe it first, it smells of mortality.
> *Glou:* O ruin'd piece of nature! *This great world*
> 　　　*Shall so wear out to nought.*
> 　　　　　　　　　　[IV. vi. 132-35]
> 　　　　　　　　　　(pp. 75-6)

For the Elizabethans, the End of the World was a living conviction and even something of a current fear. We touch here on one of the oldest of traditions: that notion of the world's turning upside down which Archilochus already employs when, having unexpectedly seen a eclipse of the sun, he says that the fish might as well now come and feed on land, or wolves feed in the sea. Repeated incessantly, by Shakespeare's time this was a long-established commonplace. . . . (pp. 76-7)

The reader of Shakespeare has thus to recognize that the 'Elizabethan World Picture' pictured an order quite different from anything which would now come to mind as order. Coherent and providential system as it was, it included within itself a standing potentiality for progressive transformation into chaos. Paradoxically, the more that the world is conceived in religious terms, the easier is it for a potentiality of deflection into chaos to stand as no radical infringement, but a genuine ingredient of order. Further than this, for Shakespeare's time collapse into universal chaos was not merely a permanent possibility in a fallen (though divinely created) Nature: it was a fore-ordained part of created Nature's route to salvation; and to envisage it, to dwell on it, to comprehend what it could be like, was part of what went to make up a comprehension of God's governance of the world.

How *Lear* is in part a rehearsal of this terrible potentiality of Nature becomes plainer, if one bears in mind that what the descent into chaos would be like was delineated by tradition. It already had its familiar contours and features. . . . If we go back, for example, to Mark 13 . . . we see the major concerns of *Lear* emerge one by one: 'There shal nation rise against nation, & kingdome against kingdome: and there shalbe earthquakes . . . the brother shall betray the brother to death, and the father the sonne: and the children shal rise against their fathers and mothers, and shal put them to death.' (pp. 77-8)

Disruption in the kingdom, disruption in the family, linked by tradition, were facets of that universal disruption of Nature, that Descent into Chaos, which for millennia had been a standing dread of mankind and at the same time one of mankind's convictions about providential history in the future.

King Lear is an exploration of this potentiality to quite a different degree from, say, *Macbeth*. The nadir of that play, the point at which Macbeth's own evil nature seems to diffuse evil throughout his whole country, falls short of what happens even at the very start of *Lear*. In *Macbeth* the evil emanates from one man (or one couple) quite alone. In *Lear* it seems, from the first, like an infection spreading everywhere, affecting a general change in human nature, even in all nature. . . . The disease is general; antidotes are helpless or non-existent; the course must be run.

In its details, the play sometimes displays an extraordinary realism. Lear's hesitation before he demands to see the supposedly sick Duke of Cornwall and his inability to believe that his messenger has been set in the stocks, Edgar's impersonation of the peasant, the whole dialogue in Act V scene iii between Albany, Edmund, Goneril and Regan, are all instances of unforgettable rightness and richness in catching the complex and individualized movements of minds vehemently working and intently engaged. Yet for a sense of the play as a whole this has less weight than what is almost its opposite: an action deliberately stylized so that its generic quality and its decisive movement should stand out more than its human detail. This is true, notably, of the division of the kingdom with which the play opens. We must see this as stylized not merely in its quality as it takes place on the stage, but in how it points forward. . . . Its status as decisively misguided or evil is not in doubt; and it is the established sign or first step in a move-

ment which threatens chaos or actually brings it. The direction and nature of what is to happen in *Lear* need not be inferred by the spectator through his detailed response to the behaviour and dialogue of the actors. Richly as it may be confirmed and elaborated in these things, its essence stands starkly before him in the stylization of a known kind of opening event. The intricate complication of the story, the detailed characterization, do nothing to obscure what is clear in the almost folk-tale quality of how the play begins. '*We have seen* the best of our time' [I. ii. 112].

Those words of Gloucester are essentially dynamic words, and this movement and dynamic ought to be seen in an aspect of *King Lear* which has been so much discussed that here it need not be discussed in full: its imagery. That the characters in the play are repeatedly likened to the lower orders of creation, for example, gives no mere general or pervasive tinge to the work, and embodies no merely general idea about humanity at large. It cannot be found in the opening scene. It arrives as the action begins to move, and becomes dominant as the quality of life which it embodies becomes dominant in the play. Just as it is not enough for Professor [Kenneth] Muir to say that the plot of Lear 'expressed the theme of the parent-child relationship'— for it expressed no mere problem or issue, because it depicts a particular movement which begins when that relationship fails in a definite way—so it is not enough for him to refer to 'the prevalence of animal imagery' and to add merely: 'This imagery is partly designed to show man's place in the Chain of Being, and to bring out the subhuman nature of the evil characters, partly to show man's weakness compared with the animals, and partly to compare human life to the life of the jungle' [see Additional Bibliography]. The hedgesparrow that fed the cuckoo, the sea-monster that is less hideous than ingratitude in a child, ingratitude itself sharper than a serpent's tooth, the wolfish visage of Goneril, are not scattered through the play as mere figurative embodiments of those discursive or philosophical interests. They burst upon the audience all together, at the close of Act I. If they throw out some general and discursive suggestion about 'human life', that is far less prominent than how they qualify the phase of the action which comes at that point, crowding the audience's imagination, surrounding the human characters with the subhuman creatures whose appearance they are fast and eagerly assuming. (pp. 79-81)

This descent from humanity, however, is something which cannot be envisaged fully through the idea of the brute and its animal life alone. It is a descent, embodied in the action, enriched by imagery, and confirmed by what is said as comment, far below brutality. Lear does not only 'choose . . . To be a comrade of with the wolf and owl' [II. iv. 208]. He sinks lower still: recreant against Nature and outcast among its creatures:

> This night, wherein the cub-drawn bear would crouch,
> The lion, and the belly-pinched wolf
> Keep their fur dry, unbonneted he runs,
> And *bids what will* take all.
>
> [III. i. 12-15]
> (p. 83)

Regan and Goneril also seem to pass down through, and out of, the whole order of Nature; though they are its monsters not its remnants. The word itself, already recurrent in the present discussion, is explicitly used of each of them . . . ; and Albany, in two of the comments which he makes about his wife, draws attention not only to the kind of movement which the play has displayed so far, but also—and it is an important new point—

to that further movement with which it will close. He asserts that what has happened so far is bringing his society (again the stress is upon the movement, upon its being *brought*) to the condition of the sea, with its universal war, unlimited in savagery, of all against all. . . . Besides this, he indicates what may be expected to ensue:

> That nature which condemns it origin
> Cannot be border'd certain in itself;
> She that herself will sliver and disbranch
> From her material sap, perforce must wither
> And come to deadly use. . . .
>
> [IV. ii. 32-6]
> (p. 84)

Lear's part in this change is a special one. He is not only the 'slave' of the elements; he is also the man to whom Kent said '. . . you have that in your countenance that I would fain call master . . . authority' [I. iv. 27-30]. But his special part is best understood by dwelling upon something which has seldom received much attention: the clear parallel (though it is also a clearly limited one) between the condition of Lear, and that in the Old Testament of Job. (p. 85)

[This parallel] may perhaps best be seen through taking note of something both plain and remarkable about the action of the play: what might be called not its *action,* but its *protraction.* In one sense, *Lear* is a much longer play than it need have been—need have been, that is, to have been less ambitiously tragic. By the middle of Act IV (or even the end of Act III) something of an ordinary tragic action has been completed. Lear has fallen from being the minion of Fortune (when the play opens he is presented as in one sense a king of kings) to being its chief victim. Through the ordeal of this fall, his eyes have been opened. . . . He has learnt, moreover, or re-learnt, the central and traditional lessons that good kings must know:

> Poor naked wretches, wheresoe'er you are,
> That bide the pelting of this pitiless storm,
> How shall your houseless heads and unfed sides,
> Your loop'd and window'd raggedness, defend you
> From seasons such as these? O, I have ta'en
> Too little care of this! Take physic, pomp;
> Expose thyself to feel what wretches feel. . . .
>
> [III. iv. 28-34]
> (pp. 86-7)

[However, the] completeness of this change must not be insisted on beyond a certain point (though that there is something of the same kind in Gloucester's situation seems clear enough). A transition from blindness and injustice, through suffering, to self-knowledge, responsibility and repentance, is not the final import even of this long central section of the play. Nevertheless, it is there plainly enough. The materials exist for a more conventional and less protracted tragedy which could have ended well before the beginning of Act V. If we ask what extends the play further, the Book of Job reveals the answer.

What makes the situation of Job unique may be brought out by starting from the position of Job's comforters: Eliphaz's 'Who ever perished being an innocent? or where were the upright destroyed' . . . , and Bildad's 'if thou be pure and upright, then surely he wil awake up unto thee'. . . . The comforters are orthodox. The men God punishes are sinners. Those who live piously under affliction, he restores; and so far as they are concerned, the sinister implications in Job's case are plain enough. But Job's protracted afflictions are a challenge to this orderly and consoling doctrine. When, despite

his miseries, he 'holdeth fast to his integrity' ('In all this Job sinned not') his miseries are simply re-doubled. This is the extraordinary event, the terrifying paradox indeed, which begins and demands the discussion that occupies the rest of the work. If there is any order of Nature at all, good must now replace evil; instead, evil returns twofold and is prolonged far beyond its proper span.

The action of *Lear* is also prolonged by this same conception. Repeatedly, we are made to think that since Nature is an order (though doubtless a stern one) release from suffering is at hand; but instead, the suffering is renewed. Act IV, the Act in which the play takes on its second and more remarkable lease of life, conspicuously begins with this very turn of thought and situation. Edgar, seeing himself at the very bottom of Fortune's wheel, finds cause for hope (living as he thinks in a world of order) in that fact alone. . . . At this very moment, he encounters his father and sees that he has been blinded; and his response is to recognize the very potentiality of life which was embodied in the story of Job. . . . (pp. 88-9)

The bitter reversal of events comes again and again. It is less than the full truth to say . . . that Lear recovers from his madness during Act IV. The 'great rage' may be killed in him, but among his first words to Cordelia, when he is awakened out of sleep and we hope momentarily for his recovery, are:

> If you have poison for me, I will drink it.
>
> [IV. vii. 71]

Cordelia's army, coming to rescue her father, succeeds only in putting her as well as him into the hands of their worst enemies. Later it seems as if Lear and Cordelia are to find a kind of private happiness in prison together. Yet even as this vision forms in our minds, we recall Edmund's threat, and realize that

> The good years shall devour them, flesh and fell,
> Ere they shall make us weep. . . .
>
> [V. iii. 24-5]

is hopeless fantasy on Lear's part, and only too soon to be proved so. Later still, the threat appears to be removed; for as he is dying Edmund confesses to his plot, and the Captain is sent hurrying to save Cordelia from death. But again, we are worse than e'er we were: the only result, the immediate result, is Lear's entry with Cordelia in his arms.

Perhaps this ironic turn in events, this constant intensifying of disaster at the moment when disaster seems to be over, is represented yet once again in the play: in the very moment of Lear's death. Conceivably, Lear is meant to think for a moment that Cordelia is alive; and dies before he realizes his mistake. Certainly, our hopes for Lear himself are, in a limited sense, raised once more by the words of Albany which immediately precede Lear's last speech. On either or both these counts, it seems as if some kind of remission is at hand; but at this moment Lear suffers the last infliction of all. Nor is it possible to accept, as true in anything but an incomplete and strained sense, R. W. Chambers' opinion that both Lear and Gloucester 'die of joy' [see excerpt above, 1939]. Edgar has already given the audience the exact truth of Gloucester's death:

> But his flaw'd heart—
> Alack, too weak the conflict to support!—
> 'Twixt two extremes of passion, joy and grief,
> Burst smilingly.
>
> [V. iii. 197-200]

The last two words confirm a paradoxical combination of joy and grief, they do not convert it to a state of bliss; and it is a somewhat bold interpretation of the moment of Lear's death, one which without the parallel to Gloucester (and perhaps with it) would be over-bold, to assert that there, joy lies even in equal balance with grief. That Lear's heart breaks is clear from the words of Kent ('Break heart, I prithee break' [V. iii. 313]); and that this is the culmination of an ordeal of torment renewed almost beyond belief, is what we are instructed to see by what this reliable authority says next:

> Vex not his ghost. O, let him pass! He hates him
> That would *upon the rack* of this rough world
> Stretch him out longer.
>
> [V. iii. 314-16]

This in fact is the note sounded throughout the closing scenes. The world can be to mankind, and has been to Lear, a rack: a scene of suffering reiterated past all probability or reason. (pp. 89-90)

At this stage in the discussion, one must try to record the note upon which *King Lear* is resolved. It is not easy to do so, and it is less easy than more than one distinguished critic has allowed. One interpretation, certainly, has attracted many readers. We may frame it, with Professor Chambers, as 'the victory of Cordelia and of Love'; or with Professor Knights, as the 'complete endorsement of love as a quality of being' [see excerpt above, 1959] or with Professor Wilson Knight, as 'the primary persons, good and bad, die into love' [see Additional Bibliography]. It is better to see the play thus, than to regard its close as the embodiment only of cynicism, chaos and despair. But one should remind oneself at this point of what, surely, is familiar knowledge: that love (unless that word is taken, as I fear it is often taken, to mean every good thing) is a value with a great but finite place in human life; and that if it is a full description of the affirmation on which the play closes, that affirmation is a limited one; is indeed, curiously inadequate, curiously out of scale with the range, power and variety of the issues of life on which this incomparable work has touched. Those for whom the word 'love' is a talisman will find this suggestion objectionable. That may be an argument in its favour.

With these considerations in mind, one may incline to see the close of *Lear* in another light. The survivors of Cleopatra, say, and of Brutus and Coriolanus, indeed speak as though these characters enjoyed a kind of victory or triumph even in death. When, at the close of *Lear,* Shakespeare characteristically gives those who survive the protagonist lines which suggest what the audience is to see in his end, it is not to any victory or triumph, through love or anything else, that he makes them direct our attention. He causes them to agree that there has never been such a case of a man stretched out on the rack of the world, and released at last. At the close of *Macbeth* there is much emphasis on a movement of regeneration, a restoration of good at the level of the body politic. Lear ends more sombrely. . . . The last speech of all, that of Edgar, seems peculiarly significant, for all its bald rhyming:

> The weight of this sad time we must obey:
> *Speak what we feel, not what we ought to say,*
> The oldest hath borne most; *we that are young*
> *Shall never see so much nor live so long.*
>
> [V. iii. 324-27]

The ordeal has been unique in its protraction of torment, and the note is surely one of refusal to hide that from oneself,

refusal to allow the terrible potentialities of life which the action has revealed to be concealed once more behind the veil of orthodoxy and the order of Nature. If there is such an order, it is an order which can accommodate seemingly limitless chaos and evil. The play is a confrontation of that, a refusal to avert one's gaze from that. Its affirmation is as exalted, humane and life-affirming as affirmation can be, for it lies in a noble and unflinching steadiness, where flinching seems inevitable, in the insight of its creator.

To turn to a more intimate awareness of the personal bonds on which the play closes is to extend and amplify this, and still to see something other than what deserves the name of 'love' *tout court*. Perhaps there is a clue in the fact that it is Edmund . . . and only Edmund, who speaks of love by itself. We are meant, of course, to see it as embodied always in what Cordelia does; but in her sole reference to this in the later scenes of the play, what she at once goes on to speak of is not her love but, in effect, her duty. . . . Cordelia's first speech of any substance to the re-awakened Lear confirms its relevance for both her and him:

> O look upon me, sir,
> And hold your hands in benediction o'er me.
> No, sir, you must not kneel.
>
> [IV. vii. 568]

What she wants is for him to do what it is a father's duty to do: not what it is *her* duty to do in return. The same kind of thought is prominent in Lear's first speech after capture:

> When thou dost ask me blessing, I'll kneel down,
> And ask of thee forgiveness.
>
> [V. iii. 10-11]

Each of them is to do what (paradoxically, in Lear's case) it is appropriate for them to do: the idea is of service and duteousness, not love in any simple or emotional sense. (pp. 91-3)

[Perhaps] the final import of the reconciliation of Lear to Cordelia, or Gloucester to Edgar, may also be seen as meaning more than the word 'love' can easily mean, at least in our own time; and as being, in the end, one with the whole of what happens at the close of the drama. That the closing phase is one in which the evil in the play proves self-destructive, is well known. Evil has come, it has taken possession of the world of the play, it has brought men below the level of the beasts, it has destroyed itself, and it has passed. Good (I have argued) is far from enjoying a triumphant restoration: we are left with the spectacle of how suffering can renew itself unremittingly until the very moment of death.

If, at the close, some note less despairing than this may be heard, it comes through our apprehending that in an austere and minimal sense, Edmund's words 'the wheel has come full circle' [V. iii. 175] extend, despite everything, beyond himself. Below the spectacle of suffering everywhere in possession, is another, inconspicuous but genuine: that the forces of life have been persistently terrible and cruel, but have also brought men back to do the things that are their part to do. Union with Cordelia barely proves Lear's salvation: his salvation is what Kent says, release from a life of torment. But that union is the thing to which he rightly belongs. He deviated from it, and life itself brought him back. So with Gloucester. To follow the master, to sustain the state, to bless one's child, to succour the aged and one's parents—this idea of being brought back to rectitude is what the play ends with. These are the things which it falls to living men to do; and if the play advances a 'positive', I think it is that when men turn away from how they should live, there are forces in life which constrain them to return. In this play, love is not a 'victory'; it is not that which stands at 'the centre of the action', and without which 'life is meaningless'; it does not rule creation. If anything rules creation, it is (though only, as it were, by a hairsbreadth) simply rule itself. What order restores, is order. Men tangle their lives; life, at a price, is self-untangling at last.

In view of these things, how fantastic it would be to call *King Lear* a play of intrigue! Yet this idea, immediate though its rejection must be, does indeed suggest the many things going on, and being intricately fitted together, which mark the closing scenes of the play. This very fact is what leads back from the attitudes of the play to what is more intimate with its substance, and with the experience which it offers to us in its sequence. The war with France, the intrigue between Edmund and the sisters, the emergence of Albany, Edmund's plot with the captain and his duel with Edgar, densen into a medium of something like quotidian life, through which and beyond which Lear's own situation stands out in isolation. It is the very variety in the strands of life which brings out how, at the end, life as it were stands back from Lear; and affords him a remoteness, a separation from his fellows, in which his ordeal is completed.

This is the culmination, moreover, of how he begins. As in the tragedies which have been discussed already, at the outset the protagonist is at the focal point of all men's regard. But Lear's progressive isolation does not steal upon him, or his audience, unawares. Relinquishing the kingdom, repudiating Cordelia, banishing Kent, cursing Goneril [I. iv. 275-89], departing wrathfully from Regan . . .—all these actions set Lear, of his own free will, apart from his fellows; and are the prelude to how he sets himself apart, first from human contact of any kind whatsoever . . . and then from the whole of Nature. . . . (pp. 94-6)

[The] full currency in Shakespeare's own mind of the image through which we see the king in the later part of the play must be brought to attention and life. Today, the direction 'enter Lear, fantastically dressed with weeds' can easily seem mere fantasy without a background, or have merely some kind of enrichment in generalized associations with fertility and its converse. For Shakespeare, Lear's status in this scene must have been much more exact and significant. The figure . . . is easily recognizable. He is a Jack-a-Green, at once hero and victim of a popular ceremony. For a moment, he is a hunted man literally, as he is in spirit throughout the play. Nor is such a level of interest in any way out of place for Lear. There is much of the quality of folk thinking or acting, of the folk-tale, about his whole career. This shows in the stylized opening scene, in the formality and symmetry of his break with the three sisters, in his mock court in the outhouse and in this Jack-a-Green spectacle, right through to his final entry . . . , in which Lear and Cordelia must appear not as king and princess, but, beyond normal life, as emblems of the extremes of what is possible in life. (pp. 96-7)

Despite the rich detail and realism of this play, the action and the staging are stylized largely throughout. The protagonist (followed, less fully but in some ways more plainly, by Gloucester) pursues a well-marked rôle. He is the man who begins as centre of his whole world, but who is progressively set, both by the other characters and by himself, apart from it and against it. 'Against' means above, in solitary defiance, and below, in an ordeal of protracted suffering which takes on

the quality of a hunt. His response to this may indeed be a growing awareness and comprehension of where he stands; but if this makes the onward movement of the action profounder and more impressive, it in no way retards or re-directs it; and its end is a death which, though realistically the outcome of the human situation of the play, has at the same time the quality of stylized and ritual execution. All is foreseen, nothing can be delayed or hastened or mitigated. We are led, in fact, to envisage a new metaphor for the status of the tragic rôle in these plays; to see running through the work, besides its other interests, its detailed representation of life, its flow of ideas, its sense of good and evil, something which might be called the vertebrate structure of its intrinsic design; the developing line, unabridged, of a human sacrifice. (pp. 97-8)

John Holloway, "'King Lear','' in his The Story of the Night: Studies in Shakespeare's Major Tragedies, *Routledge & Kegan Paul, 1961, pp. 75-98.*

JAN KOTT   (essay date 1964)

[*Kott is a Polish-born critic and professor of English and comparative literature now residing in the United States. In his well-known study* Shakespeare, Our Contemporary, *originally published in Polish as* Szkice o Szekspirze *in 1964, he interprets several of the plays as presenting a tragic vision of history. Kott calls this historical pattern the Grand Mechanism. The following excerpt from that work represents one of the most extreme of the pessimistic or nihilistic readings of* King Lear. *Kott argues that Shakespeare's play is not a tragedy of the traditional type, the "tragedy of the absolute," but a tragedy of the "grotesque." Whereas the former affirms absolute principles and is cathartic, the latter denies the existence of absolutes and offers no hope of consolation. In this light, Kott compares* King Lear *to Samuel Beckett's* Endgame, *for both, he asserts, depict a world devoid of absolutes and hope of redemption, and where all efforts to confront one's existence become absurd. Kott also compares* Lear *to the* Book of Job, *as did Richard B. Sewall (1959) and John Holloway (1961), but he interprets it as a parodical rendering of the parable performed by clowns. Kott's focus on the element of the grotesque in* King Lear *recalls a similar analysis by G. Wilson Knight (1930), and his essay in general, specifically his reading of the play as a pessimistic drama, continues the interpretations of Algernon Charles Swinburne (1880), E. K. Chambers (1906), Stopford A. Brooke (1913), and J. Stampfer (1960).*]

The attitude of modern criticism to *King Lear* is ambiguous and somehow embarrassed. Doubtless *King Lear* is still recognized as a masterpiece, beside which even *Macbeth* and *Hamlet* seem tame and pedestrian. *King Lear* is compared to Bach's *Mass in B Minor*, to Beethoven's *Fifth* and *Ninth* Symphonies, to Wagner's *Parsifal*, Michelangelo's *Last Judgement*, or Dante's *Purgatory* and *Inferno*. But at the same time *King Lear* gives one the impression of a high mountain that everyone admires, yet no one particularly wishes to climb. It is as if the play had lost its power to excite on the stage and in reading; as if it were out of place in our time, or, at any rate, had no place in the modern theatre. (pp. 127-28)

Producers have found it virtually impossible to cope with the plot of *King Lear*. When realistically treated, Lear and Gloucester were too ridiculous to appear tragic heroes. If the exposition was treated as a fairy tale or legend, the cruelty of Shakespeare's world, too, became unreal. Yet the cruelty of *Lear* was to the Elizabethans a contemporary reality, and has remained real since. But it is a philosophical cruelty. Neither the romantic, nor the naturalistic theatre was able to show that sort of cruelty; only the new theatre can. In this new theatre there

Act I. Scene i. France, Cordelia, Burgundy, Lear, Kent, Cornwall, Regan, Goneril, Albany, and Attendants. By Henry Fuseli (n.d.).

are no characters, and the tragic element has been superseded by grotesque. Grotesque is more cruel than tragedy. (p. 130)

Despite appearances to the contrary, this new grotesque has not replaced the old drama and the comedy of manners. It deals with problems, conflicts and themes of tragedy such as: human fate, the meaning of existence, freedom and inevitability, the discrepancy between the absolute and the fragile human order. Grotesque means tragedy re-written in different terms. Maurice Regnault's statement: "the absence of tragedy in a tragic world gives birth to comedy" is only seemingly paradoxical. Grotesque exists in a tragic world. Both the tragic and the grotesque vision of the world are composed as it were of the same elements. In a tragic and grotesque world, situations are imposed, compulsory and inescapable. Freedom of choice and decision are part of this compulsory situation, in which both the tragic hero and the grotesque actor must always lose their struggle against the absolute. The downfall of the tragic hero is a confirmation and recognition of the absolute; whereas the downfall of the grotesque actor means mockery of the absolute and its desecration. The absolute is transformed into a blind mechanism, a kind of automaton. Mockery is directed not only at the tormentor, but also at the victim who believed in the tormentor's justice, raising him to the level of the absolute. The victim has consecrated his tormentor by recognizing himself as victim.

In the final instance tragedy is an appraisal of human fate, a measure of the absolute. The grotesque is a criticism of the absolute in the name of frail human experience. That is why tragedy brings catharsis, while grotesque offers no consolation whatsoever. (pp. 131-32)

In the world of the grotesque, downfall cannot be justified by, or blamed on, the absolute. The absolute is not endowed with any ultimate reasons; it is stronger, and that is all. The absolute is absurd. Maybe that is why the grotesque often makes use of the concept of a mechanism which has been put in motion and cannot be stopped. Various kinds of impersonal and hostile mechanisms have taken the place of God, Nature and History, found in the old tragedy. The notion of absurd mechanism is probably the last metaphysical concept remaining in modern grotesque. But this absurd mechanism is not transcendental any more in relation to man, or at any rate to mankind. It is a trap set by man himself into which he has fallen. (p. 133)

The world of tragedy and the world of grotesque have a similar structure. Grotesque takes over the themes of tragedy and poses the same fundamental questions. Only its answers are different. This dispute about the tragic and grotesque interpretations of human fate reflects the everlasting conflict of two philosophies and two ways of thinking; of two opposing attitudes defined by the Polish philosopher Leszek Kolakowski as the irreconcilable antagonism between the priest and the fool. Between tragedy and grotesque there is the same conflict for or against such notions as eschatology, belief in the absolute, hope for the ultimate solution of the contradiction between the moral order and every-day practice. Tragedy is the theatre of priests, grotesque is the theatre of clowns.

This conflict between two philosophies and two types of theatre becomes particularly acute in times of great upheavals. When established values have been overthrown, and there is no appeal, to God, Nature, or History, from the tortures inflicted by the cruel world, the clown becomes the central figure in the theatre. He accompanies the exiled trio—the king, the nobleman and his son—on their cruel wanderings through the cold endless night which has fallen on the world; through the ''cold night'' which, as in Shakespeare's *King Lear*, ''will turn us all to fools and madmen'' [III. iv. 79].

After his eyes have been gouged out, Gloucester wants to throw himself over the cliffs of Dover into the sea. He is led by his own son, who feigns madness. Both have reached the depths of human suffering. . . . But on the stage there are just two actors, one playing a blind man, the other playing a man who plays a madman. (pp. 141-42)

It is easy to imagine this scene. The text itself provides stage directions. Edgar is supporting Gloucester; he lifts his feet high pretending to walk uphill. Gloucester, too, lifts his feet, as if expecting the ground to rise, but underneath his foot there is only air. This entire scene is written for a very definite type of theatre, namely pantomime.

This pantomime only makes sense if enacted on a flat and level stage.

Edgar feigns madness, but in doing so he must adopt the right gestures. In its theatrical expression this is a scene in which a madman leads a blind man and talks him into believing in a non-existing mountain. In another moment a landscape will be sketched in. Shakespeare often creates a landscape on an empty stage. A few words, and the diffused, soft afternoon light at the Globe changes into night, evening, or morning. But no other Shakespearean landscape is so exact, precise and clear as this one. It is like a Breughel painting thick with people, objects and events. A little human figure hanging halfway down the cliff is gathering samphire. Fishermen walking on the beach are like mice. A ship seems a little boat, a boat is floating like a buoy. (pp. 142-43)

The landscape is now just a score for the pantomime. Gloucester and Edgar have reached the top of the cliff. The landscape is now below them.

> Give me your hand. You are now within a foot
> Of th' extreme verge. For all beneath the moon
> Would I not leap upright.
>
> [IV. vi. 25-7]

In Shakespeare's time the actors probably put their feet forward through a small balustrade above the apron-stage, immediately over the heads of the ''groundlings''. But we are not concerned here with an historical reconstruction of the Elizabethan stage. It is the presence and importance of the mime that is significant. Shakespeare is stubborn. Gloucester has already jumped over the precipice. Both actors are at the foot of a non-existent cliff. The same landscape is now above them. The mime continues.

GLOUCESTER

But have I fall'n, or no?

EDGAR

> From the dread summit of this chalky bourn.
> Look up a-height. The shrill-gorg'd lark so far
> Cannot be seen or heard. Do but look up.
>
> [IV. vi. 56-9]

The mime creates a scenic area: the top and bottom of the cliff, the precipice. Shakespeare makes use of all the means of anti-illusionist theatre in order to create a most realistic and concrete landscape. A landscape which is only a blind man's illusion. There is perspective in it, light, men and things, even sounds. From the height of the cliff the sea cannot be heard, but there is mention of its roar. From the foot of the cliff the lark cannot be heard, but there is mention of its song. In this landscape sounds are present by their very absence: the silence is filled with them, just as the empty stage is filled with the mountain.

The scene of the suicidal leap is also a mime. Gloucester kneels in a last prayer and then, in accordance with tradition of the play's English performances, falls over. He is now at the bottom of the cliff. But there was no height; it was an illusion. Gloucester knelt down on an empty stage, fell over and got up. At this point disillusion follows.

The non-existent cliff is not meant just to deceive the blind man. For a short while we, too, believed in this landscape and in the mime. The meaning of this parable is not easy to define. But one thing is clear: this type of parable is not to be thought of outside the theatre, or rather outside a certain kind of theatre. In narrative prose Edgar could, of course, lead the blind Gloucester to the cliffs of Dover, let him jump down from a stone and make him believe that he was jumping from the top of a cliff. But he might just as well lead him a day's journey away from the castle and make him jump from a stone on any heap of sand. In film and in prose there is only the choice between a real stone lying in the sand and an equally real jump from the top of a chalk cliff into the sea. One cannot transpose Gloucester's suicide attempt to the screen, unless one were to film a stage performance. But in the naturalistic, or even stylized theatre, with the precipice painted or projected onto a screen, Shakespeare's parable would be completely obliterated. (pp. 143-45)

By a few words of dialogue Shakespeare often turned the platform stage, the inner stage, or the gallery into a London street, a forest, a palace, a ship, or a castle battlement. But these were always real places of action. Townspeople gathered outside the Tower, lovers wandered through the forest, Brutus murdered Caesar in the Forum. The white precipice at Dover performs a different function. Gloucester does not jump from the top of the cliff, or from a stone. For once, in *King Lear*, Shakespeare shows the paradox of pure theatre. (p. 146)

Gloucester, falling over on flat, even boards, plays a scene from a great morality play. He is no longer a court dignitary whose eyes have been gouged out because he showed mercy to the banished king. The action is no longer confined to Elizabethan or Celtic England. Gloucester is Everyman, and the stage becomes the medieval *Theatrum Mundi*. A Biblical parable is now enacted; the one about the rich man who became a beggar, and the blind man who recovered his inner sight when he lost his eyes. Everyman begins his wanderings through the world. In medieval mystery plays also the stage was empty, but in the background there were four mansions, four gates representing Earth, Purgatory, Heaven and Hell. In *King Lear* the stage is empty throughout: there is nothing, except the cruel earth, where man goes on his journey from the cradle to the grave. The theme of *King Lear* is an enquiry into the meaning of this journey, into the existence or non-existence of Heaven and Hell.

From the middle of Act II to the end of Act IV, Shakespeare takes up a Biblical theme. But this new *Book of Job* or a new Dantean *Inferno* was written towards the close of the Renaissance. In Shakespeare's play there is neither Christian Heaven, nor the heaven predicted and believed in by humanists. *King Lear* makes a tragic mockery of all eschatologies: of the heaven promised on earth, and the Heaven promised after death; in fact—of both Christian and secular theodicies; of cosmogony and of the rational view of history; of the gods and the good nature, of man made in "image and likeness". In *King Lear* both the medieval and the Renaissance orders of established values disintegrate. All that remains at the end of this gigantic pantomime, is the earth—empty and bleeding. On this earth, through which tempest has passed leaving only stones, the King, the Fool, the Blind Man and the Madman carry on their distracted dialogue.

The blind Gloucester falls over on the empty stage. His suicidal leap is tragic. Gloucester has reached the depths of human misery; so has Edgar, who pretends to be mad Tom in order to save his father. But the pantomime performed by actors on the stage is grotesque, and has something of a circus about it. The blind Gloucester who has climbed a non-existent height and fallen over on flat boards, is a clown. (pp.146-47)

It is not only the suicide mime that is grotesque. The accompanying dialogue is also cruel and mocking. The blind Gloucester kneels and prays:

> O you mighty gods!
> This world I do renounce, and, in your sights
> Shake patiently my great affliction off.
> If I could bear it longer, and not fall
> To quarrel with your great opposeless wills,
> My snuff and loathed part of nature should
> Burn itself out. If Edgar live, O, bless him!
>   [IV. vi. 34-40]

Gloucester's suicide has a meaning only if the gods exist. It is a protest against undeserved suffering and the world's injustice. This protest is made in a definite direction. It refers to eschatology. Even if the gods are cruel, they must take this suicide into consideration. It will count in the final reckoning between gods and man. Its sole value lies in its reference to the absolute.

But if the gods, and their moral order in the world, do not exist, Gloucester's suicide does not solve or alter anything. It is only a somersault on an empty stage. It is deceptive and unsuccessful on the factual, as well as on the metaphysical plane. Not only the pantomime, but the whole situation is then grotesque. From the beginning to the end. It is waiting for a Godot who does not come. (pp. 149-50)

If there are no gods, suicide makes no sense. Death exists in any case. Suicide cannot alter human fate, but only accelerate it. It ceases to be a protest. It is a surrender. It becomes the acceptance of world's greatest cruelty—death. Gloucester has finally realized:

> . . . Henceforth I'll bear
> Affliction till it do cry out itself
> 'Enough, enough,' and die.
>   [IV. vi. 75-7]

And once again, in the last act:

> No further, sir. A man may rot even here.
>   [V. ii. 8]
>   (p. 151)

The theme of *King Lear* is the decay and fall of the world. The play opens like the Histories, with the division of the realm and the king's abdication. It also ends like the Histories, with the proclamation of a new king. Between the prologue and the epilogue there is a civil war. But unlike the Histories and Tragedies, in *King Lear* the world is not healed again. In *King Lear* there is no young and resolute Fortinbras to ascend the throne of Denmark; no cool-headed Octavius to become Augustus Caesar; no noble Malcolm to "give to our tables meat, sleep to our nights" [*Macbeth*, III. vi. 34]. In the epilogues to the Histories and Tragedies the new monarch invites those present to his coronation. In *King Lear* there will be no coronation. There is no one whom Edgar can invite to it. Everybody has died or been murdered. Gloucester was right when he said: "This great world / Shall so wear out to naught" [IV. vi. 134-35]. Those who have survived—Edgar, Albany and Kent—are, as Lear has been, just "ruin'd piece[s] of nature" [IV. vi. 134].

Of the twelve major characters half are just and good, the other half, unjust and bad. It is a division as consistent and abstract as in a morality play. But this is a morality play in which every one will be destroyed: noble characters along with base ones, the persecutors with the persecuted, the torturers with the tortured. Vivisection will go on until the stage is empty. The decay and fall of the world will be shown on two levels, on two different kinds of stage, as it were. One of these may be called Macbeth's stage, the other, Job's stage.

Macbeth's stage is the scene of crime. At the beginning there is a nursery tale of two bad daughters and one good daughter. The good daughter will die hanged in prison. The bad daughters will also die, but not until they have become adulterers, and one of them also a poisoner and murderess of her husband. All bonds, all laws, whether divine, natural or human, are broken. Social order, from the kingdom to the family, will crumble into dust. There are no longer kings and subjects, fathers and children, husbands and wives. There are only huge Renaissance monsters, devouring one another like beasts of prey. Everything has been condensed, drawn in broad outlines, characters are hardly marked. The history of the world can do without psychology and without rhetoric. It is just action. These violent sequences are merely an illustration and an example, and perform the function of a black, realistic counterpart to "Job's stage".

For it is Job's stage that constitutes the main scene. On it the ironic, clownish morality play on human fate will be performed. But before that happens, all the characters must be uprooted from their social positions and pulled down, to final degradation. They must reach rock-bottom. The downfall is not merely a philosophical parable, as Gloucester's leap over the supposed precipice is. The theme of downfall is carried through by Shakespeare stubbornly, consistently and is repeated at least four times. The fall is at the same time physical and spiritual, bodily and social.

At the beginning there was a king with his court and ministers. Later, there are just four beggars wandering about in a wilderness, exposed to raging winds and rain. The fall may be slow, or sudden. Lear has at first a retinue of a hundred men, then fifty, then only one. Kent is banished by one angry gesture of the king. But the process of degradation is always the same. Everything that distinguishes a man—his titles, social position, even name—is lost. Names are not needed any more. Every one is just a shadow of himself; just a man. (pp. 152-54)

A downfall means suffering and torment. It may be a physical or spiritual torment, or both. Lear will lose his wits; Kent will be put in the stocks; Gloucester will have his eyes gouged out and will attempt suicide. For a man to become naked, or rather to become nothing but man, it is not enough to deprive him of his name, social position and character. One must also maim and massacre him both morally and physically. Turn him—like King Lear—into a "ruin'd piece of nature", and only then ask him who he is. For it is the new Renaissance Job who is to judge the events on "Macbeth's stage". (p. 155)

Almost like in Breughel's famous picture, Edgar is leading the blind Gloucester to the precipice at Dover. This is just the theme of *Endgame;* Beckett was the first to see it in *King Lear;* he eliminated all action, everything external, and repeated it in its skeleton form.

Clov cannot sit down, the blind Hamm cannot get up, moves only in his wheel-chair, and passes water only by means of a catheter. Nell and Nagg have "lost their shanks" and are almost breathing their last in dustbins. But Hamm continues to be the master, and his wheel-chair brings to mind a throne. In the London production he was dressed in a faded purple gown and wiped his face with a blood-red handkerchief. He was, like King Lear, a degraded and powerless tyrant, a "ruin'd piece of nature". He was a King Lear in the scene in Act IV, where Lear meets the blind Gloucester and after a great frantic monologue gives the order that one of his shoes be taken off, as it pinches him. It is the same pinching shoe that one of the clowns in *Waiting for Godot* will take off at the beginning of the scene. (p. 157)

The Biblical Job, too, is the ruin of a man. But this ruin constantly talks to God. He curses, imprecates, blasphemes. Ultimately he admits that God is right. He has justified his sufferings and ennobled them. He included them in the metaphysical and absolute order. The *Book of Job* is a theatre of the priests. Whereas in both Shakespearean and Beckettian *Endgames* the *Book of Job* is performed by clowns. But here, too the gods are invoked throughout by all the characters; by Lear, Gloucester, Kent, even Albany. . . .

But the gods do not intervene. They are silent. Gradually the tone becomes more and more ironical. The ruin of a man invoking God is ever more ridiculous. The action becomes more and more cruel, but at the same time assumes a more and more clownish character. . . . (p. 158)

Defeat, suffering, cruelty have a meaning even when gods are cruel. Even then. It is the last theological chance to justify suffering. . . .

From the just God, one can still appeal to the unjust God. Says Gloucester after his eyes have been gouged out:

> As flies to wanton boys are we to th' gods.
> They kill us for their sport.
>
> [IV. i. 36-7]

But as long as gods exist, all can yet be saved. . . . (p. 159)

[But] above "Job's stage", there is in *King Lear* only "Macbeth's stage". On it people murder, butcher and torture one another, commit adultery and fornication, divide kingdoms. From the point of view of a Job who has ceased to talk to God,

they are clowns. Clowns who do not yet know they are clowns. (p. 161)

On "Job's stage" four clowns have performed the old medieval *sotie* about the decay and fall of the world. But in both Shakespearean and Beckettian *Endgames* it is the modern world that fell; the Renaissance world, and ours. Accounts have been settled in a very similar way. (p. 162)

> *Jan Kott, "Tragedies: 'King Lear' or 'Endgame',"*
> *in his* Shakespeare, Our Contemporary, *translated*
> *by Boleslaw Taborsky, 1964. Reprint by W. W. Nor-*
> *ton & Company, 1974, pp. 127-68.*

MAYNARD MACK (essay date 1965)

[*Mack claims that in* King Lear *Shakespeare was most interested in dramatizing the consequences of the human will in action. The extremity of these consequences, he continues, is due to Shakespeare's attempt to demonstrate the power of the unexpected, the imbalance of the effects of one's acts and those acts themselves. In such a world everything is uncertain: one cannot be sure what his or her choices will eventually lead to, as evidenced by the fantastic outcome of both Lear and Gloucester's initial acts. The ultimate uncertainty is humanity's fate, and it is this question that Mack sees as the central concern of* King Lear. *According to Mack, the play depicts Shakespeare's belief that "existence itself is tragic," whether or not it is modified by any act; and it is tragic because existence is inseparable from "relation" or involvement, which in turn guarantees joy as well as pain. This is the knowledge Lear and Gloucester must patiently accept, and thus Mack interprets Cordelia's death as the final necessary experience the king must undergo in order to complete his education. Like such other critics as Arthur Sewell (1951), Richard B. Sewall (1959), John Holloway (1961), Phyllis Rackin (1970), and Bernard McElroy (1973), Mack rejects the traditional interpretations of the final catastrophe of* King Lear *for a middle ground, claiming that the play supports neither the pessimistic nor the Christian, transcendent reading, but simply depicts the joy as well as the suffering necessary to existence—the idea that "victory and defeat are simultaneous and inseparable."*]

As we watch it in the theatre, the action of *King Lear* comes to us first of all as an experience of violence and pain. No other Shakespearean tragedy, not even *Titus*, contains more levels of raw ferocity, physical as well as moral. In the action, the exquisite cruelties of Goneril and Regan to their father are capped by Gloucester's blinding onstage, and this in turn by the wanton indignity of Cordelia's murder. In the language, as Miss Caroline Spurgeon has pointed out [see excerpt above, 1935], allusions to violence multiply and accumulate into a pervasive image as of "a human body in anguished movement—tugged, wrenched, beaten, pierced, stung, scourged, dislocated, flayed, gashed, scalded, tortured, and finally broken on the rack."

Miss Spurgeon's comment tends to formulate the play in terms of passiveness and suffering. But the whole truth is not seen unless it is formulated also in terms of agency and aggression. If the *Lear* world is exceptionally anguished, it is chiefly because it is exceptionally contentious. Tempers in *King Lear* heat so fast that some critics are content to see in it simply a tragedy of wrath. Unquestionably, it does contain a remarkable number of remarkably passionate collisions. Lear facing Cordelia, and Kent facing Lear, in the opening scene; Lear confronting Goneril at her house with his terrifying curse; Kent tangling with Oswald outside Gloucester's castle; Cornwall run through by his own servant . . . ; Edgar and Edmund simulating a scuffle in the first act, and later, in the last act, hurling charge and countercharge in the scene of their duel; the old king himself defying the storm: these are only the more vivid instances of a pattern of pugnacity which pervades this tragedy from beginning to end, shrilling the voices that come to us from the stage and coloring their language even in the tenderest scenes. (pp. 87-8)

It goes without saying that in a world of such contentiousness most of the *dramatis personae* will be outrageously self-assured. The contrast with the situation in *Hamlet,* in this respect, is striking and instructive. There . . . the prevailing mood tends to be interrogative. Doubt is real in *Hamlet,* and omnipresent. Minds, even villainous minds, are inquiet and uncertain. Action does not come readily to anyone except Laertes and Fortinbras, who are themselves easily deflected by the stratagems of the king, and there is accordingly much emphasis on the fragility of the human will. All this is changed in *King Lear.* Its mood, I would suggest (if it may be caught in a single word at all), is imperative. The play asks questions, to be sure, as *Hamlet* does, and far more painful questions because they are so like a child's, so simple and unmediated by the compromises to which much experience usually impels us. . . . (p. 89)

Yet it is not, I think, the play's questions that establish its distinctive coloring onstage. (Some of its questions we shall return to later.) It is rather its commands, its invocations and appeals that have the quality of commands, its flat-footed defiances and refusals: "Come not between the dragon and his wrath" [I. i. 122]. "You nimble lightnings, dart your blinding flames into her scornful eyes!" [II. iv. 165-66]. "Blow, winds, and crack your cheeks! rage! blow!" [III. ii. 1] . . . In the psychological climate that forms round a protagonist like this, there is little room for doubt, as we may see from both Lear's and Goneril's scorn of Albany. No villain's mind is inquiet. Action comes as naturally as breathing and twice as quick. And, what is particularly unlike the situation in the earlier tragedies, the hero's destiny is self-made. Lear does not inherit his predicament like Hamlet; he is not duped by an antagonist like Othello. He walks into disaster head on.

This difference is of the first importance. *King Lear,* to follow R. W. Chambers in applying Keats's memorable phrase, is a vale of soul-making, where to all appearances the will is agonizingly free. As if to force the point on our attention, almost every character in the play, including such humble figures as Cornwall's servant and the old tenant who befriends Gloucester, is impelled soon or late to take some sort of stand—to show, in Oswald's words, "what party I do follow" [IV. v. 40]. One cannot but be struck by how much positioning and repositioning of this kind the play contains. Lear at first takes up his position with Goneril and Regan, France and Kent take theirs with Cordelia, Albany takes his with Goneril, and Gloucester (back at his own house), with Cornwall and Regan. But then all reposition. Kent elects to come back as his master's humblest servant. The Fool elects to stay with the great wheel, even though it runs downhill. Lear elects to become a comrade of the wolf and owl rather than return to his elder daughters. Gloucester likewise has second thoughts and comes to Lear's rescue, gaining his sight though he loses his eyes. Albany, too, has second thoughts, and lives, he says, only to revenge those eyes. (pp. 89-91)

Movements of the will, then, have featured place in *King Lear.* But what is more characteristic of the play than their number is the fact that no one of them is ever exhibited to us in its inward origins or evolution. Instead of scenes recording the genesis or gestation of an action—scenes of introspection or

persuasion or temptation like those which occupy the heart of the drama in *Hamlet, Othello,* and *Macbeth*—*King Lear* offers us the moment at which will converts into its outward expressions of action and consequence; and this fact, I suspect, helps account for the special kind of painfulness that the play always communicates to its audiences. In *King Lear* we are not permitted to experience violence as an externalization of a psychological drama which has priority in both time and significance, and which therefore partly palliates the violence when it comes. This is how we do experience, I think, Hamlet's vindictiveness to his mother, Macbeth's massacres, Othello's murder: the act in the outer world is relieved of at least part of its savagery by our understanding of the inner act behind it. The violences in *King Lear* are thrust upon us quite otherwise—with the shock that comes from evil which has nowhere been inwardly accounted for, and which, from what looks like a studiedly uninward point of view on the playwright's part, must remain uanccountable, to characters and audience alike. . . . (pp. 91-2)

The relatively slight attention given in *King Lear* to the psychological processes that ordinarily precede and determine human action suggests that here we are meant to look for meaning in a different quarter from that in which we find it in the earlier tragedies. In *Hamlet,* Shakespeare had explored action in its aspect of dilemma. Whether or not we accept the traditional notion that Hamlet is a man who cannot make up his mind, his problem is clearly conditioned by the unsatisfactory nature of the alternatives he faces. Any action involves him in a kind of guilt, the more so because he feels an already existing corruption in himself and in his surroundings which contaminates all action at the source. (p. 92)

King Lear, as I see it, confronts the perplexity and mystery of human action at a later point. Choice remains in the forefront of the argument, but its psychic antecedents have been so effectively shrunk down in this primitivized world that action seems to spring directly out of the bedrock of personality. We feel sure no imaginable psychological process could make Kent other than loyal, Goneril other than cruel, Edgar other than "a brother noble." Such characters . . . are qualities as well as persons: their acts have consequences but little history. The meaning of action here, therefore, appears to lie rather in effects than in antecedents, and particularly in its capacity, as with Lear's in the opening scene, to generate energies that will hurl themselves in unforeseen and unforeseeable reverberations of disorder from end to end of the world.

The elements of that opening scene are worth pausing over, because they seem to have been selected to bring before us precisely such an impression of unpredictable effects lying coiled and waiting in an apparently innocuous posture of affairs. The atmosphere of the first episode in the scene, as many a commentator has remarked, is casual, urbane, even relaxed. In the amenities exchanged by Kent and Gloucester, Shakespeare allows no hint to penetrate of Gloucester's later agitation about "these late eclipses," or about the folly of a king's abdicating his responsibilities and dividing up his power. . . . I suspect we are invited to sense, as Lear speaks, that this is a kingdom too deeply swaddled in forms of all kinds—too comfortable and secure in its "robes and furr'd gowns" [IV. vi. 165]; in its rituals of authority and deference . . . ; and in its childish charades, like the one about to be enacted when the daughters speak. Possibly we are invited to sense, too, that this is in some sort an emblematic kingdom—almost a paradigm of hierarchy and rule, as indeed the scene before us seems to be suggesting, with its wide display of ranks in both family and state. Yet perhaps too schematized, too regular—a place where complex realities have been too much reduced to formulas, as they are on a map: as they are on that visible map, for instance, on which Lear three times lays his finger in this scene. . . . Can it be that here, as on that map, is a realm where everything is presumed to have been charted, where all boundaries are believed known, including those of nature and human nature; but where no account has been taken of the heath which lies in all countries and in all men and women just beyond the boundaries they think they know?

However this may be, into this emblematic, almost dreamlike situation erupts the mysterious thrust of psychic energy that we call a choice, an act; and the waiting coil of consequences leaps into threatening life, bringing with it, as every act considered absolutely must, the inscrutable where we had supposed all was clear, the unexpected though we thought we had envisaged all contingencies and could never be surprised. Perhaps it is to help us see this that the consequences in the play are made so spectacular. The first consequence is Lear's totally unlooked-for redistribution of his kingdom into two parts instead of three, and his rejection of Cordelia. The second is his totally unlooked-for banishment of his most trusted friend and counselor. The third is the equally unlooked-for rescue of his now beggared child to be the Queen of France; and what the unlooked-for fourth and fifth will be, we already guess from the agreement between Goneril and Regan, as the scene ends, that something must be done, "and i' th' heat." Thereafter the play seems to illustrate, with an almost diagrammatic relentlessness and thoroughness, the unforeseen potentials that lie waiting to be hatched from a single choice and act: nakedness issues out of opulence, madness out of sanity and reason out of madness, blindness out of seeing and insight out of blindness, salvation out of ruin. The pattern of the unexpected is so completely worked out, in fact, that, as we noticed in the preceding chapter, it appears to embrace even such minor devices of the plot as the fact that Edmund, his fortune made by two letters, is undone by a third.

Meantime, as we look back over the first scene, we may wonder whether the gist of the whole matter has not been placed before us, in the play's own emblematic terms, by Gloucester, Kent, and Edmund in that brief conversation with which the tragedy begins. This conversation touches on two actions, we now observe, each loaded with menacing possibilities, but treated with a casualness at this point that resembles Lear's in opening his trial of love. The first action alluded to is the old king's action in dividing his kingdom, the dire effects of which we are almost instantly to see. The other action is Gloucester's action in begetting a bastard son, and the dire effects of this will also speedily be known. What is particularly striking, however, is that in the latter instance the principal effect is already on the stage before us, though its nature is undisclosed, in the person of the bastard son himself. Edmund, like other "consequences," looks tolerable enough till revealed in full. . . . Like other consequences, too, Edmund looks to be predictable and manageable—in advance. "He hath been out nine years," says Gloucester, who has never had any trouble holding consequences at arm's length before, "and away he shall again" [I. i. 32-3]. Had Shakespeare reflected on the problem consciously—and it would be rash, I think, to be entirely sure he did not—he could hardly have chosen a more vivid way of giving dramatic substance to the unpredictable relationships of act and consequence than by this confrontation of a father with his unknown natural son—or to the idea of consequences come

home to roost, than by this quiet youthful figure, studying "deserving" as he prophetically calls it, while he waits upon his elders.

In *King Lear* then, I believe it is fair to say, the inscrutability of the energies that the human will has power to release is one of Shakespeare's paramount interests. By the inevitable laws of drama, this power receives a degree of emphasis in all his plays, especially the tragedies. The difference in *King Lear* is that it is assigned the whole canvas. The crucial option, which elsewhere comes toward the middle of the plot, is here presented at the very outset. Once taken, everything that happens after is made to seem, in some sense, to have been set in motion by it, not excluding Gloucester's recapitulation of it in the subplot. Significantly, too, the act that creates the crisis, the act on which Shakespeare focuses our dramatic attention, is not (like Lear's abdication) one which could have been expected to germinate into such a harvest of disaster. The old king's longing for public testimony of affection seems in itself a harmless folly: it is not an outrage, not a crime, only a foolish whim. No more could Cordelia's death have been expected to follow from her truthfulnes or Gloucester's salvation to be encompassed by a son whom he disowns and seeks to kill.

All this, one is driven to conclude, is part of Shakespeare's point. In the action he creates for Lear, the act of choice is cut loose not simply from the ties that normally bind it to prior psychic causes, but from the ties that usually limit its workings to commensurate effects. In this respect the bent of the play is mythic: it abandons verisimilitude to find out truth, like the story of Oedipus; or like the *Rime of the Ancient Mariner,* with which, in fact, it has interesting affinities. Both works are intensely emblematic. Both treat of crime and punishment and reconciliation in poetic, not realistic, terms. In both the fall is sudden and unaccountable, the penalty enormous and patently exemplary. . . . When the mariner shots the albatross, the dark forces inside him that prompted his deed project themselves and become the landscape, so to speak, in which he suffers his own nature: it is his own alienation, his own waste land of terror and sterility that he meets. Something similar takes place in Shakespeare's play. Lear, too, as we saw earlier, suffers his own nature, encounters his own heath, his own storm, his own nakedness and defenselessness, and by this experience, like the mariner, is made another man. (pp. 93-8)

The ultimate uncertainty in *King Lear* to which all others point is, as always in tragedy, the question of man's fate. With its strong emphasis on inexorable and unimaginable consequences unwinding to make a web to which every free and willful act contributes another toil, *King Lear* may claim a place near the absolute center, "the true blank" (so Kent might call it), of tragic experience. "The tragedy of Adam," writes Northrop Frye, following Milton in tracing "the archetypal human tragedy" in the narrative of Genesis, "resolves, like all other tragedies, in the manifestation of natural law. He enters a world in which existence is itself tragic, not existence modified by an act, deliberate or unconscious." This is the form of tragedy I think we all sense at the basis of *King Lear,* and the reason why its windows opening on the pilgrimage and *psychomachia* of a king who is also Rex Humanitas are so relevant to its theme. Existence is tragic in *King Lear* because existence is inseparable from relation; we are born from and to it; it envelops us in our loves and lives as parents, children, sisters, brothers, husbands, wives, servants, masters, rulers, subjects—the web is seamless and unending. When we talk of virtue, patience, courage, joy, we talk of what supports it.

When we talk of tyranny, lust, and treason, we talk of what destroys it. There is no human action, Shakespeare shows us, that does not affect it and that it does not affect. Old, we begin our play with the need to impose relation—to divide our kingdom, set our rest on someone's kind nursery, and crawl toward our death. Young, we begin it with the need to respond to relation—to define it, resist it even in order to protect it, honor it, or destroy it. Man's tragic fate, as *King Lear* presents it, comes into being with his entry into relatedness, which is his entry into humanity.

In the play's own terms this fate is perhaps best summarized in the crucial concept of "patience." By the time he meets Gloucester in Dover fields, Lear has begun to learn patience; and patience, as he defines it now, is not at all what he had earlier supposed. He had supposed it was the capacity to bear up under the outrages that occur in a corrupt world to oneself. . . . Now, with his experience of the storm behind him, his mind still burning with the lurid vision of a world where "None does offend, none" [IV. vi. 168], because all are guilty, he sees further. His subject is not personal suffering in what he here says to Gloucester; his subject is the suffering that is rooted in the very fact of being human, and its best symbol is the birth cry of every infant, as if it knew already that to enter humanity is to be born in pain, to suffer pain, and to cause pain. (pp. 110-11)

Lear's words to Gloucester, I take it, describe this ultimate dimension of patience, in which the play invites us to share at its close. It is the patience to accept the condition of being human in a scheme of things where the thunder will not peace at our bidding; where nothing can stay the unfolding consequences of a rash act, including the rash acts of bearing and being born;

> where the worst is not
> So long as we can say 'This is the worst';
> [IV. i. 27-8]

yet where the capacity to grow and ripen—in relation and in love—is in some mysterious way bound up with the capacity to lose, and to suffer, and to endure. . . . (p. 112)

From one half of this tragic knowledge, Lear subsequently wavers—as Gloucester wavers from what Edgar thought he had learned at Dover Cliff. Lear would need no crumbs of comfort after the battle if his sufferings could at last be counted on to bring rewards—if, for example, he could pass his declining years in peace and happiness with Cordelia. He wants to believe that this is possible. He has made the choice that he should have made in the beginning. He has allied himself with those who in the world's sense are fools; and he is prepared to accept the alienation from the world that this requires, as the famous passage at the opening of the last scene shows. In this passage he puts aside Goneril and Regan forever; he does not even want to see them. He accepts eagerly the prison which marks his withdrawal from the world's values, for he has his own new values to sustain. . . . (pp. 112-13)

But to speak so is to speak from a knowledge that no human experience teaches. If it could end like this, if there were guaranteed rewards like this for making our difficult choices, the play would be a melodrama, and our world very different from what it is. So far as human wisdom goes, the choice of relatedness must be recognized as its own reward, leading sometimes to alleviation of suffering, as in the case of Gloucester's joy in Edgar, but equally often to more suffering, as in the case of Lear. For Lear, like many another, has to make

the difficult choice only to lose the fruits of it. Not in his own death . . . but in Cordelia's. Cordelia, our highest choice, is what we always want the gods to guarantee. But to this the gods will not consent. (p. 113)

In his last speech, the full implications of the human condition evidently come home to Lear. He has made his choice, and there will be no reward. Again and again, in his repetitions, he seems to be trying to drive this final tragic fact into his human consciousness, where it never wants to stick:

> No, no, no life!
> Why should a dog, a horse, a rat have life
> And thou no breath at all? Thou'lt come no more,
> Never, never, never, never, never!
> [V. iii. 306-09]

He tries to hold this painful vision unflinchingly before his consciousness, but the strain, considering everything else he has been through, is too great: consciousness itself starts to give way. . . . And with it the vision gives way too: he cannot sustain it; he dies, reviving in his heart the hope that Cordelia lives: "Look on her, look, her lips, Look there, look there!" [V. iii. 311-12].

We are offered two ways of being sentimental about this conclusion, both of which we must make an effort to eschew. One is to follow those who argue that, because these last lines probably mean that Lear dies in the joy of thinking Cordelia lives, some sort of mitigation or transfiguration has been reached which turns defeat into total victory. "Only to earthbound intelligence," says Professor O. J. Campbell, "is Lear pathetically deceived in thinking Cordelia alive. Those familiar with the Morality plays will realize that Lear has found in her unselfish love the one companion who is willing to go with him through Death up to the throne of the Everlasting Judge" [see excerpt above, 1948]. I think most of us will agree that this is too simple. Though there is much of the Morality play in *Lear,* it is not used toward a morality theme, but, as I have tried to suggest in this essay, toward building a deeply metaphysical metaphor, or myth, about the human condition, the state of man, in which the last of many mysteries is the enigmatic system of relatedness in which he is enclosed.

The other sentimentality leads us to indulge the currently fashionable existentialist *nausée* ["nausea"], and to derive from the fact that Lear's joy is mistaken, or, alternatively, from the fact that in the Lear world "even those who have fully repented, done penance, and risen to the tender regard of sainthood can be hunted down, driven insane, and killed by the most agonizing extremes of passion," the conclusion that "we inhabit an imbecile universe" [see excerpt above by J. Stampfer, 1960]. Perhaps we do—but Shakespeare's *King Lear* provides no evidence of it that till now we lacked. . . . Shakespeare can hardly have imagined that in *King Lear*'s last scene he was telling his audiences something they had never known, or was casting his solemn vote on one side or other of the vexing philosophical and theological questions involved in the suffering of the innocent and good. The scene has, besides, his characteristic ambiguity and balance. No world beyond this one in which "all manner of things will be well" is asserted; but neither is it denied: Kent happens to take it for granted and will follow his master beyond that horizon as he has beyond every other: "My master calls me, I must not say no" [V. iii. 323]. Edgar has come to soberer assessments of reality than he was given to making in the forepart of the play, but his instinctive kindness (we may assume) is unabated and has survived all trials. Lear's joy in thinking that his daughter lives (if this is what his words imply) is illusory, but it is one we need not begrudge him on his deathbed, as we do not begrudge it to a dying man in hospital whose family has just been wiped out. Nor need we draw elaborate inferences from its illusoriness about the imbecility of our world; in a similar instance among our acquaintances, we would regard the illusion as a godsend, or even, if we are believers, as God-sent.

In short, to say, with an increasing number of recent critics, that "the remorseless process of *King Lear*" forces us to "face the fact of its ending without any support from systems of moral . . . belief at all" is to indulge the mid-twentieth-century *frisson du néant* ["'sensation of nothingness'"] at its most sentimental. We face the ending of this play, as we face our world, with whatever support we customarily derive from systems of belief or unbelief. If the sound of David crying "Absalom, my son," the image of Mary bending over another broken child, the motionless form of a missionary doctor whose martyrdom is recent, not to mention all that earth has known of disease, famine, earthquake, war, and prison since men first came crying hither—if our moral and religious systems can survive this, and the record suggests that for many good men they do and can, then clearly they will have no trouble in surviving the figure of Lear as he bends in his agony, or in his joy, above Cordelia. Tragedy never tells us what to think; it shows us what we are and may be. And what we are and may be was never, I submit, more memorably fixed upon a stage than in this kneeling old man whose heartbreak is precisely the measure of what, in our world of relatedness, it is possible to lose and possible to win. The victory and the defeat are simultaneous and inseparable.

If there is any "remorseless process" in *King Lear,* it is one that begs us to seek the meaning of our human fate not in what becomes of us, but in what we become. Death, as we saw, is miscellaneous and commonplace; it is life whose quality may be made noble and distinctive. Suffering we all recoil from; but we know it is a greater thing to suffer than to lack the feelings and virtues that make it possible to suffer. Cordelia, we may choose to say, accomplished nothing, yet we know it is better to have been Cordelia than to have been her sisters. When we come crying hither, we bring with us the badge of all our misery; but it is also the badge of the vulnerabilities that give us access to whatever grandeur we achieve. (pp. 114-17)

Maynard Mack, "Action and World," in his King Lear in Our Time, *University of California Press, 1965, pp. 81-117.*

NORTHROP FRYE   (lecture date 1966)

[*Frye has been called one of the most important critics of the twentieth century and a leader of the anthropological or mythic approach to literature which gained prominence during the 1950s. As outlined in his seminal work* An Anatomy of Criticism *(1957), Frye views all literature as ultimately derived from certain myths or archetypes present in the human psyche, and he therefore sees literary criticism as an unusual type of science in which the literary critic seeks only to decode the mythic structure inherent in a work of art. Frye's effort was to produce a method of literary interpretation more universal and exact than that suggested in other critical approaches, such as New Criticism, biographical criticism, historical criticism, and so on—all of which he finds valuable but also extremely limited in application. As a Shakespearean critic, Frye made perhaps his greatest contribution in the area of the comedies and romances, especially with his definition of* the three main phases of Shakespearean comic and romantic structure, which he defines as the initial phase of "the anticomic society," "the phase of temporarily lost identity," and the establishment of a "new society" through either marriage or self-knowledge. In the following excerpt from a lecture delivered in 1966, Frye places* King Lear *in what he terms as Shakespeare's "tragedies of isolation," in which the hero, alienated from society, searches for his lost identity. He sees this as the play's "outer action"; its "inner action" he locates in the Gloucester subplot—what he interprets as a "morally intelligible tragedy" in which retribution is exacted against those who err and order is restored. Frye's comment that* King Lear *ends, with the deaths of Cordelia and Lear, in a "vision of . . . absurd anguish" recalls the so-called pessimistic readings of the play (see the excerpts by Algernon Charles Swinburne, 1880; Stopford A. Brooke, 1913; G. Wilson Knight, 1930; J. Stampfer, 1960; and Jan Kott, 1964). However, for Frye, Lear's experience is not totally pessimistic for it enables us, as in all "authentic tragedy," to recreate that experience. The idea that* King Lear *incorporates the potentiality for an affirmative as well as a negative reaction to life has also been discussed by Maynard Mack (1965), Phyllis Rackin (1970), and Bernard McElroy (1973). Also, for a further examination of the king as a "scapegoat" figure, isolated and pursued, see the excerpt by John Holloway (1961).*]

[Shakespeare's tragic heroes] tend to be attracted to two opposite poles. At one pole is the character who is involved wholly in, and seems to enjoy, the tragic action he brings about, whether he is a tyrant like Richard III or a traitor like Iago and Edmund. He could also be a nemesis-figure, though there is no example in Shakespeare, except for a few moods of Hamlet: a more typical example is Tourneur's Vendice, who surrenders himself to justice as soon as he has established the justice. Such a character is for a time a demonic parody of the successful ruler: Iago, in particular, seems to create the tragedy of Othello with a successful ruler's sense of timing. This type also has about him some feeling of a master of ceremonies or lord of misrule, a perverted artist in crime, a sinister Prospero evoking his own drama, even a kind of macabre clown. The connexion of this last with Richard III is clear enough, and still clearer in Marlowe's Barabas. These "Machiavellian" characters are projections of the author's will to direct the action to a tragic end: they fascinate us and inspire a reluctant admiration, but they are always set over against us.

At the other pole is the character whose isolation from the action has intensified his consciousness. He has withdrawn from the social group and is now seeing it as objective, as facing him with indifference or hostility. But he is seeing it, so to speak, from our own side of the stage, and his thoughts are for the moment ours. Most of the really titanic figures of Shakespearean tragedy are in this position for most of the play, Lear, Othello, Hamlet, and Macbeth included, and it is the presence of this perspective that makes the tragedy authentic. These two poles of dramatic interest are not the moral poles, the simple difference between the right side and the wrong side. The dramatic and the moral placing of characters syncopate against each other, creating a complex pattern of sympathies without confusing us about our ultimate reactions. (pp. 96-7)

At the beginning of *King Lear,* we see the hero preparing to take the fatal step of depriving himself of his own social context. He will exchange the reality for the "name" of king, and instead of being loved by his subjects for his qualities, he will be loved by his daughters for himself alone. All seems to go well until, with Cordelia's "nothing," he finds himself staring into the blankness of an empty world. Those who love Lear love him according to their bond, the tie of loyalty which is their own real life. Who is Lear to be loved apart from that? That is, what is the identity of a king who is no longer a king? Lear starts asking questions about his own identity very early, and he gets a variety of answers. "My lady's father" [I. iv. 79], says Oswald; "Lear's shadow" [I. iv. 231], says the Fool, a much shrewder person than Oswald. The word "shadow" recalls Richard II, seeking his identity in a looking-glass. The substance of Lear and of Richard is royalty and loyalty: their shadows, or spectres as Blake would call them, are the subjective Lear and Richard confronting an objective world which is unreal because they are. They are in the position of the Biblical Preacher who was once king in Jerusalem, and who now knows only that all is "vanity," that is, vapour, mist, shadow. Or, to put the essential paradox more clearly, all things are full of emptiness.

At the beginning of *King Lear* we are introduced to Edmund, making polite murmurs about his duty and services, and immediately after the abdication scene Edmund appears again, saying,

> Thou, Nature, art my goddess: to thy law
> My services are bound.
>
> [I. ii. 1-2]

One of the first points made about Edmund is his contempt for astrology. This contempt has nothing to do with anybody's belief in astrology, but is purely a matter of consistent imagery. The royalty of Lear held his society bound to that greater nature which is symbolized by the stars in their courses, the world of order and reason that is specifically the world of human nature. With the abdication we are now wholly confined to the lower physical nature of the elements, an amoral world where the strong prey on the weak. It is this lower nature, the Dionysian wheel of physical energy and fortune, to which Edmund attaches himself. He is Gloucester's "natural" son, and on that level of nature he will act naturally.

In this situation Lear is joined by the Fool and Kent, Kent being also a fool, as the Fool himself informs him, for we are now in a world where it is folly to be genuinely loyal. The Fool is a "natural" in the sense of representing something still unspoiled and innocent in the middle of a fallen nature. The usual symbol of this natural innocence is the child, the two being associated in the proverb "children and fools tell the truth." Nothing shows the royal nature of Lear more clearly than his tenderness for his "boy"; this tenderness becomes increasingly parental, and the great cry at the end, "And my poor fool is hanged!" [V. iii. 306], represents a blending together in his mind of the two people he loves as a father. Goneril habitually refers to her husband as a fool because he is a "moral fool," full of childish scruples he ought to outgrow. Goneril, of course, does not distinguish the childish from the childlike, and so does not believe that the Fool really is a fool, as she cannot understand innocence. The jokes of the Fool, like those of the clowns in *Hamlet,* consist largely of puns, conundrums, and parodies of syllogisms, and so establish a comic counterpart to the tragic action in which absurdity is made convincing.

The philosopher first isolates himself and then stabilizes himself: he remains a sane, conscious, normal intelligence, and nature therefore appears to him as an order, though a relatively static order or chain of being, not the controlled force that it is to the successful ruler. In the tragic vision whatever isolates the hero pushes him much further than this, into the nausea of Hamlet or the hell-worlds of Othello and Macbeth. Lear is

pushed directly toward the *hysterica passio* ["hysterical passion"] he so dreads, and nature therefore appears to him in the objective form of madness, which is storm and tempest. On the heath, a mad shadow confronts a mad shadow-world, for the storm is described in a way that makes it not simply a storm but chaos come again, the cracking of nature's moulds. The turning point of the scene is Lear's prayer, a prayer which addresses no deity, but the dispossessed of the earth. In this prayer Lear finds his human identity again, though in a very different context from kingship, and immediately after it Poor Tom appears.

No one can study *King Lear* without wondering why Edgar puts on this Poor Tom act for Lear's benefit. He has to go into disguise, of course, but none of Cornwall's spies are likely to be listening, and elsewhere on the heath open conspiracy is discussed under the storm's cover. Just as, in a comic context, Petruchio shows Katherina the reflection of her own shrewishness in himself, so Poor Tom is the providence or guarding spirit that shows Lear the end of his journey to find his own nature. What is the nature of man? There are many answers, but Lear is now in an order of nature so disordered that Edmund is called a "loyal and natural boy" [II. i. 84]. The Fool, who really is a loyal and natural boy, is all that is left of the "desperate train" which Regan pretends to be afraid of. The question then takes the form: what is left of a man when we eliminate his social and civilized context and think of him purely as an object in physical nature? The answer given by satire is the Yahoo, the natural man with his natural vices, of which Gulliver's greater cleanliness and intelligence are merely sophistications. The softer and gentler answer given by comedy is Caliban, nature without nurture, the deformed slave who is loyal to the wrong master and resentful of the right one. The answer given by tragedy is

> Poor Tom, that eats the swimming frog, the
> toad, the tadpole, the wall-newt and the water;
> that in the fury of his heart, when the foul fiend
> rages, eats cow-dung for sallets; swallows the
> old rat and the ditch-dog; drinks the green man-
> tle of the standing pool; who is whipped from
> tithing to tithing, and stock-punished, and im-
> prisoned.
>
> [III. iv. 129-35]

The imagery is deliberately nauseating, and we notice again that nausea is deeply involved in man's contemplation of himself in a physical context. "Is man no more than this?" [III. iv. 102-03] asks Lear wonderingly, but he has had his answer. "Thou art the thing itself" [III. iv. 106], he says, and starts tearing at his clothes to remove what is left of his relation to human society. Poor Tom, a better mirror of identity than Richard had, is trying to stand between Lear in front of him and the abyss of non-being inhabited by the foul fiends behind him, and provide, so to speak, a solid bottom for Lear's fall into nature. If Lear had been granted the few moments of rest he so needed, Edgar's efforts might have preserved his sanity. (pp. 103-07)

The rhetoric of isolation, as we find it particularly in the fourth acts of *King Lear* and *Timon of Athens,* is mainly a bitter denunciation of human hypocrisy, the contrast of reality and appearance. Lear and Timon are in a position to see this hypocrisy because, like the hypocrite, they have separated their real selves from their social relationships. The denunciation has the oracular ring of truth, but of a truth that we cannot do anything about. It is the voice, not of pure detachment, but of a detached consciousness. The feelings are still engaged: Timon is still an outraged idealist and Lear a helpless king. We feel that both Timon and Lear are "unreasonable," that the workings of the sexual instinct in a "simpering dame" hardly call for so much horror, that ingratitude could be shrugged off as well as screamed at. Eliot takes a similar view of the excessive disgust in Hamlet's view of his mother's re-marriage. But in the tragic vision, where one starts with a social order in which reality *is* appearance, the discovery of sin and hypocrisy and corruption cannot be made by the reason, but only by *saeva indignatio* ["fierce wrath"]. (p. 109)

In *King Lear* there is . . . an inner and an outer action. The inner action is a straight tragedy of order, with Gloucester the martyred father, Edmund the rebel-figure, and Edgar the nemesis. Its general context is that of the original sin in which the killing of the father becomes a central symbol of guilt: as Gloucester says in an ironic anticipation of his own betrayal:

> Our flesh, my lord, is grown so vile
> That it doth hate what gets it.
>
> [III. iv. 145-46]

Gloucester's is a morally intelligible tragedy, passing, like the story of Oedipus, through a terrifying blinding and ending, again like Oedipus, in comparative serenity. Gloucester is physically isolated from the action, and, unlike Lear, he tries to make an end of himself physically, by suicide. Edgar appears to him in various disguises, as he does to Lear, and with the same object of guiding him past the abyss of non-being. Everything can be explained in Gloucester's tragedy: he had a moral flaw that made him gullible, and he had a proud mind, shown in his boast about the sexual exploit that produced Edmund. At the moment when Edgar's nemesis is completed, Edgar says:

> The gods are just, and of our pleasant vices
> Make instruments to plague us;
> The dark and vicious place where thee he got
> Cost him his eyes.
>
> [V. iii. 171-74]

For all his courage and devotion Edgar never seems to be able to resist remarks like this, and even as a comment on Gloucester it seems a trifle facile. It is always possible to say that if the hero had acted otherwise (in most cases, more virtuously) the tragedy would not have occurred. The point of saying it about Gloucester is apparently to emphasize the sense of his tragedy as fitting into a moral order.

But the fact that Gloucester's tragedy is morally explicable goes along with the fact that Gloucester is not the main character of the play. If we apply such formulas to Lear they give us very little comfort. What does the good sport at Edmund's making prove when we have Goneril and Regan "got 'tween lawful sheets" [IV. vi. 116]? At the blinding of Gloucester, Cornwall is fatally wounded by a servant. This is again part of the moral sense that Gloucester's tragedy makes, Edgar's axiom "Ripeness is all" [V. ii. 11] being closely related to the view of Job's comforters that a full and completed life is the natural result of virtue. Gloucester appeals for help on this basis, "He that will think to live till he be old" [III. vii. 69] being an ironic anticipation of his later desire to cut his own life short. Another servant remarks of Regan:

> If she live long
> And in the end meet the old course of death,
> Women will all turn monsters.
>
> [III. vii. 100-02]

Well, it is true that Regan is poisoned, but Cordelia is hanged. Regan's death proves nothing, except perhaps the reality of nothingness.

King Lear has been called a purgatorial tragedy, and if that means a structure even remotely like Dante's *Purgatorio*, we should expect to see, as we see in Dante, existence being taken over and shaped by a moral force. Our understanding of the tragedy, then, would have that qualified response in it that is inseparable from a moral or conceptual outlook. It is true that Lear has suffered terribly, but he has thereby gained, etc. Suffering is inevitable in the nature of things, yet, etc. But, of course, Lear is not saying anything like this at the end of the play: what he is saying is that Cordelia is gone, and will never, never come back to him. Perhaps he thinks that she is coming back to life again, and dies of an unbearable joy. But we do not see this: all we see is an old man dying of an unbearable pain. The hideous wrench of agony which the death of Cordelia gives to the play is too much a part of the play even to be explained as inexplicable. And whatever else may be true, the vision of the absurd anguish in which the play ends certainly is true. (pp. 113-15)

If there is anything more than absurdity and anguish in the death of Lear or Othello, it comes, not from anything additional that we can see in or know about the situation, but from what we have participated in with them up to that moment. When Macbeth sees life as a meaningless idiot's tale, we can see that such a vision of absurdity is right for Macbeth at that point, and is therefore true for him. But it is not the whole truth, even for him, because he is capable of articulating it, nor for us, because we have shared with him, however reluctantly, an experience too broad and varied to be identified with its inevitable end, however desired an end. Tragedy finds its ultimate meaning neither in heroic death nor in ironic survival, nor in any doctrine deducible from either, but in its own reenactment as experience. (pp. 117-18)

> Northrop Frye, "Little World of Man: The Tragedy of Isolation," in his Fools of Time: Studies in Shakespearean Tragedy, *University of Toronto Press, 1967, pp. 77-121.*

ALVIN B. KERNAN   (essay date 1966)

[*Kernan argues that the scene at Dover Cliffs, in which Edgar orchestrates Gloucester's attempted suicide, acts as a kind of morality play in miniature and, more importantly, symbolizes that precipitous descent which forms the general movement of the action of* King Lear: *namely, the king's fall from grace into the depths of human misery. However, Kernan perceives a corresponding ascending movement based on the values of human kindness demonstrated in the scenes depicting Gloucester's "salvation" after his imaginative fall, and in Cordelia's reunion with Lear in Act IV, Scene vii. Kernan maintains that these "two interludes—one in the allegorical, the other in the symbolic mode—reconfirm, in surprising and unexpected ways, orthodox, traditional views of the value and meaning of life." Yet, he adds, Shakespeare was obviously not satisfied with these traditional views since he qualifies, if not contradicts them in the final act of the play. For further discussion of the scene at Dover Cliffs and its relation to the rest of* King Lear, *see the excerpt by Phyllis Rackin (1970). Also see the essays by Harry Levin and Bert O. States in the Additional Bibliography.*]

In *King Lear* we seem to be present at the birth of now familiar philosophical and theological concepts, generated under the pressure of suffering and formulated by the characters in a desperate attempt to understand what they have endured. We are, despite intensely formal elements in the play, seldom aware of a poet who has thought his characters' thoughts before them or has forced words and actions on them to illustrate his conceptual scheme. But when Edgar, in IV. vi, places his old blind father on some sort of low step and informs him that he is on the edge of Dover Cliff, allows him to assume a heroic stance and jump off, and then picks him up, after he has tumbled a foot or so, and persuades him that he has miraculously survived, we seem to be back in a morality or miracle play—with grotesque, absurd overtones—in which the poet has used his characters to set up a dramatic demonstration of an abstract idea. But then, this is not quite correct; for it is one of the characters, Edgar, not the poet Shakespeare, who has set up this formal demonstration of the miracle of life. In turn, it is perfectly appropriate and realistic that Edgar should use this dramatic mode, for until his last lines—"speak what we feel, not what we ought to say" [V. iii. 325]—he has a pronounced tendency to the conventional, the formal and the sententious, the formal and theological. Even in his "madness" he explains evil in terms of conventional theories of morality and the devils of folk tale.

The point of Edgar's brief morality play is clear. The last sight that Gloucester *saw* was the diabolic face and the hands of a man reaching to tear out his eyes, and he staggered away from this total denial of humankind, away from the heath and toward the sea, despairing of any value in life. He still believes in the power of the gods, but because of what he has experienced he can no longer believe in their goodness. Suicide seems his only recourse. He engages his son Edgar, still in disguise, to lead him to the cliff at Dover; but Edgar, who despite all he has endured continues to believe in a childlike way, arranges a lesson to persuade his father that life itself, under any conditions, is a miracle to be valued and cherished so long as we still breathe, have heavy substance, speak, and bleed not. Gloucester learns his lesson well—though he forgets it soon afterward when new misfortune comes—and he sums up neatly the moral idea of the scene:

> Henceforth I'll bear
> Affliction till it do cry out itself,
> 'Enough, enough' and die.
>
> [IV. vi. 75-7]

No doubt we should applaud Edgar for teaching and Gloucester for learning such sound doctrine, but *Lear* itself has already shown so many scenes of loss and emptiness and human degradation that by this point it requires more than saying that life is a miracle because the heart still beats to make us believe it. And while Gloucester may be taken in by Edgar's miracle, the grotesque awkwardness on stage of that "miracle" emphasizes the fact that it is only a shabby theatrical device, imposed on a man of less than first-rate intellect to make him go on living some dream of the gods' care for human life which is at odds with what has happened and will happen.

The relevant literary gloss for this scene is the story of the Grand Inquisitor in *The Brothers Karamazov*. There, the Grand Inquisitor berates Christ for leaving the mass of simple mankind, men much like Gloucester, so completely free to choose or not to choose God. The great number of men, says the Grand Inquisitor, cannot bear to be without the miraculous; they "would see a sign," and Christ by his refusal of the Devil's temptations, by his refusal to hurl himself down from the Temple or to come down from the Cross, has denied them the miracles, the mystery, the authority—in short, the proof—that they need in order to endure the hardships of life and

continue to believe in a just and caring God. The church has supplied these solid proofs, requiring of man only the awful freedom that he never wanted anyway. But the Grand Inquisitor, who knows that freedom and certainty are incompatible, regards the miracles his church has engineered as mere tricks designed to ease the minds of the frightened and block the sight of that fearsome emptiness in which true faith must operate.

Edgar, though lacking the Grand Inquisitor's subtle mind, would seem to be supplying his father with the same kind of miracle, at the same expense, and for the same reason. But while Edgar's miracle may be a trick, it is a trick devised to stage and state a truth in such a powerful way that Gloucester can understand that truth *feelingly,* though unable to reason it out for himself. The scene centers around two opposing perspectives, looking down and looking up. By using specific details, Edgar creates both perspectives for his blind father. As the two stand supposedly at the edge of the cliff, the imagination is directed downward and yet farther downward. At first we focus on some birds part way down which "show scarce so gross as beetles" [IV. vi. 14]; then we descend halfway to a man clinging to the cliff, a samphire-gatherer who "seems no bigger than his head" [IV. vi. 16]. Then we plunge to the bottom to look at fishermen who seem no larger than mice, at a ship become as small as her boat, and at last to the idle pebbles of the beach, washed soundlessly and meaninglessly back and forh by the surge of ocean. We have moved by means of details, each of which suggests in several ways the diminution of life, to the point where life vanishes into nothingness and meaninglessness.

This precipitous movement parallels and summarizes the experiences of Lear and Gloucester and Edgar to this point in the play. They have begun on high, certain of their own power and titles, assured of the value of human life, and trusting in the goodness and richness of the world. But as the play proceeds, the world narrows. . . . And as the world constricts, man diminishes in size and importance from King and Father to "the thing itself . . . a poor, bare, forked animal" [III. iv. 106-08].

In the vision from the cliff, Edgar recreates in visual terms the journey that has reduced Gloucester and his fellows from a condition of prosperity and importance, through a series of diminutions, to a condition of animality. In his supposed plunge from the cliff, Gloucester reenacts the downward movement, precipitated by his own act in begetting Edmund out of wedlock, which has brought him from being the great Duke of Gloucester to a blind, ragged beggar seeking his own death.

The leap into the void is a truthful dramatization of what has happened; but what about Gloucester's miraculous survival? It would seem that if Edgar's little morality play is to be accurate, it would have to allow Gloucester to be dashed into nothing—the word that rings through the play as a dreadful threat. But is there not something miraculous in what has happened to Gloucester and Lear? Obviously enough, as one lost his sight he *saw* for the first time, and as the other lost his senses he gained his sanity. But even beyond these ironies, on the heath in the center of the storm, when it looked as if man could be reduced infinitely downward into nothing, man discovered feelingly—not consciously—a basis for his humanity in his concern for other sufferers, both those present and those only imagined: "Poor naked wretches, whereso'er you are" [III. iv. 28]. Man is, they find under pressure, more than a "worm" or a "forked animal." He is a creature capable of pity and therefore cannot be reduced to nothing. The gesture, discovered on the heath, expressing this feeling of shared humanity, "Give me your hand" [III. iv. 41], is picked up and repeated here on the edge of Dover Cliff. Edgar, who has led his blind father by the hand from the heath, repeats the formula of fellowship on the very edge of the void by requesting his father's hand, lest he fall from this fearsome place. In Gloucester's reply, "Let go my hand" [IV. vi. 27], we hear his renunciation of any belief in the possibility of kindness.

But the fall from the cliff ends in miraculous survival and thus dramatizes the truly miraculous salvation found by the wanderers and outcasts on the heath. All their lives *are* miracles in the sense that, just as they thought their humanity was about to disappear into bestiality and nothingness, they discovered their human reality in a way they had never expected. (pp. 60-4)

It has often been noted that Gloucester is a man of the senses, Lear a man of the mind, and that they suffer appropriately by the loss of sight in the first case, the loss of mind in the second. Their regenerative experiences in Act IV follow the same pattern. Since Gloucester is not a thinker, it is necessary that his remarkable survival be translated for him into the solid, sensible terms of miracle. But Lear can experience both his loss and his marvelous recuperation in less miraculous terms. Where Gloucester is "shown" the diminution of life he has endured in terms of a fictional perspective from the cliff, Lear faces unflinchingly what the loss means in more immediate, though less visible, terms. All of society is, he now believes in his madness, corrupt: the great lady is as lustful as the gilded fly, the gods inherit but to a woman's waist, the justice is but a thief dressed in robes of office, the beadle longs for the whore he whips, and the "usurer hangs the cozener" [IV. vi. 163]. (pp. 64-5)

This view of life as bestiality masked by clothes and money, shouted by the old king, presents in social terms the same perspective on life as that which looks downward from the cliff. Again the matter of hands comes up: when Gloucester asks the mad Lear to allow him to kiss his hand, Lear too rejects the saving clasp of fellowship ("Let me wipe it first; it smells of mortality" [IV. vi. 33]) and runs wild in the fields like a hunted animal—his parallel to Gloucester's suicidal leap.

Lear's regeneration, his miracle, also drives home the meaning of his as yet unrecognized salvation on the heath. But where Gloucester's miraculous survival was put to him in the "realistic" terms of the harmless fall from the cliff, Lear's is manifested in the less realistic but more "real" terms of sleep, a change of garments, music, and Cordelia. Each of these speaks to Lear of some healing power in nature which he has already experienced, without knowing, on the heath. Cordelia is the fully realized and humanized form of that ability to care for the suffering of others which all the members of that band of ragged outcasts found in themselves in the storm and, in finding, found the basis of their humanity. When Cordelia bends to kiss Lear and says,

> O my dear father! Restoration hang
> Thy medicine on my lips, and let this kiss
> Repair those violent harms that my two sisters
> Have in thy reverence made,
>
> [IV. vii. 25-8]

the gesture and the sentiments are a pure distillation of all those feelings of compassion which found such rough and abbreviated expression in the night on the heath.

Act IV of *King Lear* is built around these two parallel scenes of regeneration. In both a child arranges for his despairing father to see once again, in terms appropriate to the characters, that man is finally something more than worm or a poor, bare, forked animal and, because he is so, that life is worth living, sanity is bearable. In both cases this new faith is not merely imposed on men too broken and exhausted to resist it but is rather a demonstration, an extension into dramatic form, of a saving reality which Lear and Gloucester have already discovered feelingly at the very point when their humanity seemed to be disintegrating into nothingness.

These two interludes—one in the allegorical, the other in the symbolic mode—reconfirm, in surprising and unexpected ways, orthodox traditional views of the values and meaning of life. But true though they may be, they are not finally in *King Lear* adequate realizations of experience. They sum up life too neatly, round it off too perfectly; and so, in Act V, Shakespeare subjects these visions to the savage test of life as individual man truly experiences it. The right side loses the battle, Gloucester dies, Cordelia dies, and Lear dies. True, the wicked die too, but in the midst of other sorrow their deaths, as Albany says of Edmund's death, seem "but a trifle here" [V. iii. 296]. Generations of readers have testified to their pained doubt as to how to take or sum up this ending. Is it the "promised end" or "image of that horror" [V. iii. 264-65]? It allows some truth still to the "miracles" staged by Edgar and Cordelia— after all, some basis of humanity was discovered, though too late to change events—but it qualifies such optimism severely. In the end the actual experience of life escapes any summation. It can only be presented in a play like *Lear*, not in a morality play like Edgar's. (pp. 65-6)

> *Alvin B. Kernan, "Formalism and Realism in Elizabethan Drama: The Miracles in 'King Lear'," in* Renaissance Drama, *Vol. IX,* edited by S. Schoenbaum, Northwestern University Press, 1966, pp. 59- 66.

SIGURD BURCKHARDT (essay date 1966)

[*In the following excerpt from an essay completed shortly before his death in 1966, Burckhardt recommends a metaphorical rather than a metaphysical reading of* King Lear. *He argues that both Lear's and Gloucester's reactions to the term "nothing," as offered to them by Cordelia and Edmund in the first two scenes of* King Lear, *demonstrate not only their respective attitudes toward reality, but also secure each of their tragic downfalls during the course of the drama. According to Burckhardt, Lear's fault is that he blindly accepts the spoken word as something which carries its own truth. He therefore refuses to consider meanings beyond the words themselves. Lear's response to Cordelia—that "Nothing will come of nothing"—reflects "the very formula of his belief," in Burckhardt's words; a belief that commits him to a mode of action which results in the forsaking of Cordelia, the banishment of Kent, and eventually his confrontation with nature and his descent into madness. The irony of Lear's tragic error, Burckhardt points out, is that he ultimately does realize that "Nothing will come of nothing," that his former conception of supernatural justice, natural law, and right reason—all manifested in the figure of the king—is absurdly false, and that there is nothing between him and chaos except his own belief in justice and truth. When we come to Gloucester, it is the opposite case. According to Burckhardt, he distrusts "mere words" and is constantly "looking beneath" them for the "matter of fact." He trusts only what he sees with his eyes, and, thus, he loses his sight. The irony of Gloucester's tragedy, Burckhardt concludes, is that he is eventually forced to rely totally on the spoken word—an irony underscored especially well in the scene at Dover Cliffs. For further discussion of the language and its function in* King Lear, *see the excerpts by Winifred M.T. Nowottny (1960) and Richard D. Fly (1972).*]

The first two scenes [of *King Lear*] have usually been read as a concentrated exposition of two characters, one rash and despotic, the other weak and gullible, who because of these flaws fall into error. But the scenes are more than that: they are *events*—events which determine the future action. Undoubtedly Lear is rash and Gloster gullible; but since through such different failings they commit exactly the same fault—the banishing of the true and loving child and the preferment of the false one—we are compelled to ask what it is that accounts for the difference in the subsequent fates of the two men—the blindness of one and the madness of the other, for example. If such reasoning sounds forbiddingly rigid in a literary interpretation, I submit that Shakespeare, in this tragedy and in no other, constructed parallel plots of considerable rigor, and that we must assume that he meant something by this structure. He cannot have meant the plots to be merely parallel, one reinforcing the other; for then the subplot would become a mere redundancy, and if ever an action needed no reinforcement of its impact, it is Lear's. There is every reason to think that the apparent similarity of the two plots is like that of controlled experiments, and that the meaning of both lies in the one element which accounts for the difference.

Shakespeare commonly satisfies the positivistic axiom that we can get answers only if we ask the right questions. He certainly does in *Lear*. At the very outset he points up both the sameness and the difference of the two plots by the thematic use of "nothing." This is the word which both Lear and Gloster stumble over; with it, or their response to it, their falls begin. . . . (pp. 237-38)

Had Shakespeare only meant to present us, in the first scene, with a wrathful and imperious old man, he could have found a more plausible way to do so. But what he seized upon in the fairytale motif and makes the substance of his "Let it be granted" is a particular *speech* situation. The king lays down conditions of discourse under which his daughters' words will have an automatic validity; he acts on the premise that what they say will be true by virtue of their saying it. He will not test their professions of love against the matter of fact of their previous behavior, will not treat the words as signs that are true or false to the degree that they correspond to an extraverbal reality. Rather, he treats them as substances, as entities, which carry their own truth within them; they create for him his daughters' loves, as they are to create—a kind of physical precipitate of this verbal creation—their realms. "Which of you shall we say doth love us most?" [I. i. 51] Lear asks and therewith engages to settle this question as though it were a poetry contest. It is false to ascribe to him here a despot's greed for praise or fawning submission; he makes a fearful mistake, but the mistake is the regal one of taking people *at their word* in the most radical and literal sense. He refuses to submit to the demeaning necessity ordinary men are under: the necessity of suspiciously grubbing for facts by which to judge words. Suspicion, the "looking beneath" words for what, as often as not, they hide rather than reveal, would seem to him a diminution of his royal dignity. He *cannot* be lied to by his daughters, because, in transferring his sovereignty to them, he also endows them with its noblest attribute and prerogative; to speak creatively, substantially, with automatic truth.

The error is a noble one, but it compels both Lear and those who wish him well to a disastrous rigor. It is idle to speculate

about Cordelia's pride, her share of responsibility for the consequences of her unbending "plainness." As her asides make clear, she has no choice; the covenant under which she must speak has its own logic. Where there can be no lie, there can be no truth; and since the essential function of speech is to transmit truth, for Cordelia no speech is possible. Her "nothing" is the simple statement of this fact, and her following attempt to return discourse to the sphere where it can be true (or false) is condemned from the start to futility.

For Lear is already committed. . . . [With] his "Nothing will come of nothing" [I. i. 90] he has stated the very formula of his belief. He has no choice either—none, that is, except to give up his conception of himself, his royalty and truth. If words are substantial and creative, then his answer to Cordelia is the only possible one. And by the same token he is compelled to banish Kent. What prompts him is not the vanity of the tyrant who cannot bear criticism, or of the king who cannot bear discourtesy; he does not deign even to notice Kent's desperate ill manners, and he enters into no argument about the substance of Kent's charges. Kent's guilt is that he has sought

> To come betwixt our sentence and our power,
> Which nor our nature nor our place can bear.
> [I. i. 170-71]

Lear here tries to banish the inherent "between-ness" of all discourse; with Kent he means to rid himself of the degrading intrusion of "mere" fact into the gapless identity of "sentence" and "power," of sovereign speech and the power of that speech to create what it states.

Thus the king's wrath and rashness receive the precise definition of a verbal *act*. He has rashly committed himself to a particular conception of himself and his office, his nature and place, has in fact identified the two; and he wrathfully resists all attempts to question this conception as questioning his identity. This he sees in, let us say, *immediacy,* in the possibility of getting at truth directly, without any circuitous "between." . . . [This] "verbal" reading of the first scene makes explicable, not simply Lear's fall (that can be explained in other ways as well), but the specific kind and direction and even depth of his fall. For the remarkable thing about *King Lear* is that in it the tragic error is "made good" as a word is made good: not by contrition and amendment but by an unyielding perseverance in it, a determination to live by it and its bitter consequences until it has yielded its core of truth. (pp. 239-41)

Gloster's analogous stumbling [also] demands attention. Had he responded to Edmund's "Nothing, my lord" as Lear did to Cordelia's—had he taken Edmund at his word—the letter scheme would have come to nothing. But for Gloster speech is the opposite of substantial; he sees in it "mere words," insubstantial signs which, as likely as not, have been made to point in the wrong direction. He is familiar with "the dark and vicious place" [V. iii. 173] of illicit union and has learned the subject's craft of "looking beneath" for the matter of fact. He will not be taken in by words but will trust only to what he can see with his own eyes; there is an ignoble greediness for "the real thing" in his thrice repeated "Let's see" (antiphone to Lear's threefold and royal "Speak!"). And because to him words are merely a medium, he falls victim to a *mediacy* far more abject than Goneril's and Regan's lies; in his eagerness for the matter of fact he gets hold of a forged letter, an indirection squared. . . . Determined as he is to distrust the direct word, he is at the mercy of report, of hearsay, of signs. With this scene, the letter becomes the emblem of the illicit and dangerously mediate—so clearly so that the sight of Lear reading a letter would strike us as somehow incongruous; for a letter is speech reduced to signs, discourse become manifestly indirect. Gloster's belief in signs and portents, ridiculed by Edmund, is further evidence of this affinity; not that it is necessarily wrong, but that it is slavish, implies an abdication of the creative will and a wish to get at the truth by an "outguessing" which Lear would never stoop to.

Gloster, like Lear, will attain his measure of truth—not by abandoning his error, but by being delivered over to it more absolutely than he and we had imagined possible. The problem of immediacy and mediacy, of confrontation and report, of being and meaning, is a true paradox, and the truth of paradoxes does not lie in the golden mean between the extremes; it lies in a man's readiness to penetrate through illusion and despair to his particular extreme and at the pole to find himself.

Shakespeare would be no poet if he gave equal dignity to the two errors; the poet is bound to err on Lear's side: that of thinking speech creatively substantial and truth direct. Every poet, I should guess, is an ironist; knowing, more intimately than the rest of us, the deceptiveness of words, he is condemned to being circuitous, to trying to get the better of his untrustworthy medium by stratagems and indirections. But precisely for this reason the true poet is an ironist *in spite of himself;*

what he longs for is creative immediacy. From Iago to Melville's Confidence Man and Mann's Felix Krull, poets have portrayed themselves as tricksters and sought the release of truth in this self-exposure. But that is the roundabout way, the way of irony.

The difference between Lear and Gloster is to be measured by what one is granted and the other denied: the dignity of direct confrontation. In the end Lear sees Cordelia face to face, and we see both; all Gloster's sufferings never earn him this fulfillment. He can never, literally, *see* Edgar; even in the recognition he is dependent on report, and what is more, this event is withheld from us, buried in Edgar's story. His final release must reach him, and us, mediately.

For this reason it is a mistake to think of Gloster as being, by the loss of his eyes, given "true sight." To be sure, he now becomes aware of things he had been blind to; but we will do well to mind our metaphors in speaking of that awareness. (The trouble with treating *King Lear* under the categories of appearance and reality is not that doing so is false, but that it translates the play's realities too directly into the realm of metaphysics and so loses sight of the metaphorical substance. Both protagonists are deceived by appearance and discover reality; but as their ways of being deceived are not the same, neither are their sufferings and discoveries.) Always a led man, he is now led in the literal sense; always in the dark, he is now

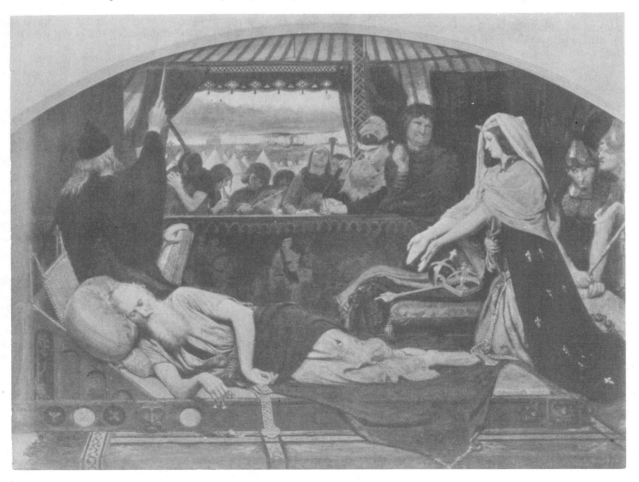

Act IV. Scene vii. Doctor, Lear, Fool, Kent, Cordelia, and Attendants. By Ford Madox Brown (n.d.).

enclosed with darkness and made to *feel* the mediacy of report. He is guided to the truth, not by learning to see with an "inner vision" or "the mind's eye," but by a palpable thickening of the wall between him and reality. . . . There is truth in discovering how densely we are enclosed in darkness; that, fittingly, is Gloster's truth.

Seen this way, his painful progress comes to its proper goal at what he thinks the edge of Dover Cliffs. Here we see him, who had swept aside "nothing" as an insubstantial nothing, totally delivered over to the creative power of the word. Edgar's cliff—a poetic lie creating a purely verbal reality—for Gloster assumes the substantiality of fact, because he no longer has any matter of fact to judge it by. Edgar acts from motives and for ends altogether opposite to Edmund's; but for all that he *does* the same thing: he lies. Though the motives will direct our moral judgment, the fact must determine our interpretation. And the fact is that Gloster is saved from despair and suicide by the very deed that plunged him into them; the difference is that now, he being blind, the lie can be "grosser."

There is another difference: Gloster suffers Edgar's lie, while he invited Edmund's. His assertions of superior insight were as mistaken as his desperate attempt to pit his will against the gods'; *his* truth and wisdom lie in obedience, the virtue of the natural subject. He is compelled by blindness to do what, had he done it when he saw, would have saved him from error: take men at their word. In a sense, therefore, his finding his own truth brings him around to Lear's position; that is the way of paradoxes. But the quality of reaching that point remains radically different; his plus is the product of minuses. There is immediacy in Edgar's summoning up of the cliff; but, as we the spectators know, it is arrived at by squaring mediacy: blindness times lying equals "truth." When the extremes of a paradox meet, a great deal depends on the direction from which the meeting point is approached.

If the metaphor for Gloster's blindness is covering, that for Lear's madness is stripping. Edgar as Tom o' Bedlam is the touchstone. To Gloster his nakedness is an offense. . . . Lear, on the other hand, sees in the naked madman the true pattern of man stripped and essential, and so he eagerly sets about becoming like him. . . . Lear resists the efforts of Kent and Gloster to separate him from this "philosopher" and guide him to the covering of a house; madness and nakedness have come to mean truth to him.

How has he come to this? The Fool's jest tells us:

> This is nothing, Fool.
>
> Then 'tis like the breath of an unfeed lawyer; you gave me nothing for it. Can you make no use of nothing, nuncle?
>
> Why, no, boy; nothing can be made out of nothing.
>
> [I. iv. 128-33]

But the Fool can make use of it:

> Thou wast a pretty fellow when thou hadst no need to care for her frowning; now thou art an O without a figure. I am better than thou art now; I am a Fool, thou art nothing.
>
> [I. iv. 191-94]

Lear discovers that his faith in directness was mistaken because it ultimately did rest on an intervening matter of fact: the sovereign's power to make good his words. The power gone,

so is the immediacy; power was the integer before the zero. The formula "Nothing will come of nothing" is now looked at from the other side. In the first scene it had meant for Lear that the sovereign has, and can endow others with, creative power: Say something, and that something will be. Now the axiom has become the formula of impotence, and so the Fool explicates it. The king, who scorned to construe the meaning of words by indirect evidence, is now under the humiliating necessity of interpreting by signs, by "frowns" and "cold looks," of looking for reasons why his orders are disobeyed and his messengers slighted. In the play's most pitiful scene— the bargaining with Goneril and Regan over the number of retainers—he tries to cling to the illusion, to hold on to the shreds of royalty that will cover the nakedness of the zero he has become; and even as we tremble lest he might fail in this attempt, we tremble lest he might succeed. But he fails, is not left even the shreds. The choice is forced upon him between submitting to the subject's lot, learning the arts of indirection in order to have a roof over his head, and going out to confront reality nakedly, with nothing to interpose between himself and the turmoil of unstructured nature. When he discovers that there *is* a gap between sentence and power, he chooses immediacy, nakedness, the truly royal essence of what his still impure image of himself had been. That is why the "foolish, fond old man" [IV. vii. 59] of the end is more regal than the king was.

It is common to take Lear's compassionate concern for the Fool and his prayer for the "poor, naked wretches" [III. iv. 28] as evidence of his conversion from a blind pride to an understanding of man's common humanity and of the superficiality of rank and power. And so, of course, they are. But they do *not* constitute a turning point in his fall; they only mark a stage. He is now stripped of the title and additions of a king and so learns what it is to be poor and wretched. But he is not naked yet, nor mad. For a moment it seems as though he might find a halt in his prayer, by identifying himself with the common man, finding consolation and support in a kind of Christian pity and humility; but at that moment Edgar's voice first emerges from the hovel and reads the precise and as yet incomplete measure of Lear's descent:

> Fathom and half, fathom and half!
>
> [III. iv. 37]

And Lear's passion for the real and naked immediately instructs him that there are depths yet to be plumbed—those of madness—and a cover yet to be stripped: discourse of reason.

Blindness, since, Homer, Tiresias and Oedipus, has behind it a long tradition as a noble affliction; it is the mark of the seer and poet, of the superior being who has penetrated behind the veils of appearance that enclose ordinary men. Madness is quite another thing. To be sure, the tradition of divine frenzy, of seizure by a higher power, is also an old one; man has long paid the tribute of awe to this kind of madness. But Lear's madness, as Shakespeare portrays it, is of a different sort. It does not issue in dark oracles or hint at mysteries; it is very much of this earth. . . . To convince us that this very ordinary madness is the truly regal affliction was a formidable task— the more so because it is counterposed to what Shakespeare makes us accept, against all tradition, as the servile suffering of blindness. It seems almost perverse for him so to have stacked the cards against himself; my guess is that only the necessity of truth could have brought him to undertake the attempt.

For the truth is that what we call reality comes to us prefabricated, cut to orderly measure and built into orderly structure by language; poets, at least Shakespeare, did not have to wait for [Benjamin Lee] Whorf to discover this truth for them. Discourse of reason, though it may be employed to correct the falsities of this structuring, cannot but remain their victim; every coherent sentence written against the tyranny of words is ultimately a rattling of chains. That is why truth, which cannot reside outside discourse, cannot reside in it either. It is enacted in a confrontation of the real which is either silent and incommunicable or, if it is uttered, madness.

Lear's raving is, as Edgar says, "matter and impertinency mixed, / Reason in madness" [IV. vi. 174-75]. It is natural for the commentator to cling to the reason, to talk about the lines exposing the relativity of justice and the deceptiveness of appearance, and to pass over the "impertinencies." But this is an evasion, not only of the scene's terror but of its truth. Shakespeare makes this point clearly. Directly before the entrance of Cordelia's men, Lear "preaches" to Gloster:

> Thou must be patient; we came crying hither.
> Thou know'st, the first time that we smell the air,
> We wawl and cry. I will preach to thee; mark . . .
> When we are born, we cry that we are come
> To this great stage of fools.—This' a good block.
> It were a delicate stratagem to shoe
> A troop of horse with felt. I'll put't in proof;
> And when I have stol'n upon these son-in-laws,
> Then kill, kill, kill, kill, kill, kill!
>
> [IV. vi. 178-80, 182-87]

The burden of the "preachment" is the same as Edgar's later words about our going hence and coming hither—which means that we should stop quoting them as though they were the distillate of Shakespeare's tragic wisdom. They may be noble to Gloster's ears (and Gloster is most of us most of the time), but Lear knows them for what they are: eloquent commonplaces from the Stoic's repertory. That is why he breaks off in the middle, weary with the formulable precepts of faith or even disillusionment, and turns his mind, or rather perception, back to realities far grimmer, because without any order. Of Gloster's "block," or hat, he sees not the form or social function to which it has been pressed, but the raw material; and this he presses to the purpose of total destruction. (pp. 241-50)

This naked directness and substantiality of perception, this apprehension of the "raw material" which makes all wisdom sound brittle, is one mark of Lear's madness. It applies also to words, which for him assume a phonetic corporeality that strips them of meaning and would, if it were consciously done, be called punning: "Peace, peace; this piece of toasted cheese will do 't" [IV. vi. 89-90]. The same directness leads Lear's mind along the path of free association, in which ideas and images are not functionally ordered in a reasoned chain but assume a body and life of their own. . . . (p. 251)

The second mark, or theme, of his madness is his royalty; it stands at the beginning, middle and end of this scene:

> No, they cannot touch me for coining; I am the
> King himself. . . .
> Aye, every inch a king! . . .
> I will be jovial. Come, come; I am a king,
> My masters, know you that? . . .
>
> [IV. vi. 83-4, 107, 199-200]

Had Lear held on to his discovery of human fellowship, we would have welcomed and pitied him (as we are always ready to do when we see someone brought down to our level); his

tragedy would have been one in the medieval sense: a fall from greatness. We might have been awed, but our awe would have been paid to the eternal powers that make the wheel of fortune turn, not to Lear himself. . . . But Lear is meant, or rather wills, not to o'erskip any sufferance by finding grief-mates; he is the king and has no fellows.

He defines his kingship for us: he cannot be touched for coining. As every coin the king issues is necessarily a true coin, so every word he sovereignly speaks is a true word and every judgment a just judgment. The king can do no wrong—that is what sets him apart from men and forces him, once he understands it, to his fearful directness and confrontation. It is he who justifies:

> None does offend, none, I say, none; I'll able 'em.
>
> [IV. vi. 168]

But who, then, will "able" *him*? Before he saw Edgar, Lear thought he knew. Though powerless, he could call on the "great gods" to send their "dreadful summoners" and bring criminals before the bar of their "higher" justice. At that point he could still speak of himself as more sinned against than sinning, as having a just claim. Then he knew who was guilty and who was not, because then, for a brief moment, he thought he could find refuge in fellowship and the subject's consoling sense of being *under* the law; he could abdicate and become plaintiff before the court of divine law. Now he knows better. First he summons a court of his own, with the Fool and the Madman as justices, to try his daughters. And finally he summons all mankind, judge and felon, beggar and beadle, into the searing light of his discovery that there is nothing and no one to able him, no "natural law" or "right reason" to mediate between him and chaos. He is the *source* of justice and truth and so can receive none.

It is this knowledge that is his madness—not in the sense that he is mad to think so, but rather that no one who penetrates to this point can stay sane. Here words like truth and justice, the comforting constructs under which sane men seek shelter, cease to have meaning. This is the harvest of Lear's proud faith in the substantiality of his words; nothing now *has* come of nothing, the word as entity has created its meaning and drawn the universe into the chaos of universal negation. The "name" has become absolute: Lear, utterly divested of all that gives "meaning" to the name of king, is now king "in name only" and so, paradoxically, king absolute and quintessential. (pp. 251-53)

When Lear awakens from madness and sleep, he no longer is king; all the respectful solicitude of Cordelia and her servants will not persuade him to it. He has earned his release form the frightful office and will not be distracted from the truth he has won—and for which there is no name but Cordelia. His new state is discontinuous with what he was before. . . . (p. 254)

With his fresh garments he has put on a new language—and yet what he speaks is nothing new and dark. It is, rather, wholly private, has the intimate directness of people who believe they stand outside all social orders and need not rely on the mediation of custom and authority to give meaning to what they say. It is as natural as the song of the birds. . . . As natural and as intimate and as remote. Injustice and justice no longer concern him; he does not want to see Goneril and Regan. Cordelia's eight little unstructured words suffice him: "(And so) I am, I am" and "No cause, no cause" [IV. vii. 69, 74]. The first four lifted him from the depth of nothingness, and the last released him from the chain of cause and effect, the iron and ironic consequences of his unchallengeable "Nothing will come of nothing."

It seems as though irony has been vanquished; in the two scenes in which Lear and Cordelia appear before being led to prison, Shakespeare and Lear almost persuade us, against our better judgment, that the plots and armies swirling around them do not matter, that a realm has been won, even if it is only a bird's cage, where the immediate is possible. But it is not only the soldiers and Edmund who warn us that this idyll cannot last; it is something in Cordelia's way of speaking:

> We are not the first
> Who with best meaning have incurred the worst.
> For thee, oppressed king, I am cast down;
> Myself could else outfrown false Fortune's frown.
>
> [V. iii. 3-6]

There is the rhyme, so oddly formal at this point and from this woman; there are the antitheses of reasoned discourse, the coining of epigrammatic wisdom of general currency, the play on words. This might be Edgar speaking to Gloster; it ought not to be Cordelia speaking to the new Lear. If we have understood the play rightly, we will be frightened by these lines more than by Edmund's preceding soliloquy. Lear *is* frightened, as his frantic "No, no, no, no!" [V. iii. 8] shows.

What is he warding off? Ultimately, of course, the loss of his daughter, but more immediately the knowledge that she still belongs to that other realm, still is a queen, cannot extricate herself from the world of war and stratagem. Goneril and Regan are still what she so pointedly calls them: her sisters and Lear's daughters. The almost unspeakable simplicity of directness, purchased by unspeakable suffering, cannot be the last word, or if it is, must literally be the *last* word. For speech remains tied to the social order—and with it truth.

Since almost anything the interpreter can say about the end of *King Lear* is a trivialization, I will risk one that may seem ludicrous: Shakespeare had to write the end because he had to return to living and writing. If the finding of Cordelia had meant the finding, at whatever cost, of a new "style"—the conquest of irony, the beginning of the direct mode—the conclusion could have been triumphant; we might have been dismissed with the lines about the mystery of things. But the end of *Lear* does not yield a new style; it is the absence of all style. Style is the summary term for the way the poet uses "devices"; it is, therefore, the tribute exacted by the "mystery of things." The essence of the experience of direct confrontation—namely its directness—remains uncommunicable; every word violates and distorts it. It is the pain of this insight, I think, which Shakespeare embodies in the play's last scene. (pp. 254-56)

Since I have made so much of immediacy, I may seem to be caught here in a discrepancy. We are made to *see*, with cruel directness, the blinding of Gloster; we are not made to see the killing of Cordelia. But here, too, Shakespeare is rigorously exact. In Gloster's sphere, physical fact is primary; hence the blinding is presented as physical fact, to which the words are a feeble accompaniment. But in Lear's sphere words are primary, so that a physical directness, which with Cordelia's murder would silence all, would be false. *Words* must carry the whole burden, as Lear carries his daughter; to manage things otherwise would have been, for Shakespeare, an evasion of his task and—odd as this may sound—of his pain. Far from sparing himself and us a last, insupportable horror, he makes us bear all of it—in words. For the poet there is, or may be, a release in the abdication from speech; Shakespeare does not

allow himself that release. He must speak, or—if speech refuses its office—"howl."

Lear's "Howl, howl, howl!" [V. iii. 258] as he enters with Cordelia's body should have been enough to keep any English poet from entitling a poem "Howl." To howl is a privilege so bitterly earned that only experiences like Lear's can ever justify it in poetry. There is a quality in the last scene which anywhere else we should have to call indecent—an insensibility to all but that one dead body which, except here, would be subhuman. . . . Lear is not mad, though now we might wish he were. He is totally cut off from everything and everyone, wholly given over to his forlorn hope of a faint breath. It is not even Cordelia as a person that all his senses are fixed on, but only her lips, her breath, her speech. . . . And his final words are the cry of the man who cares for nothing more except the hope that truth has breath and voice and that from it issue visible realities:

> Do you see this? Look on her, look, her lips,
> Look there, look there!
>
> [V. iii. 311-12]

He ends, it might seem, where Gloster, with his "Lets see," began. But he dies believing that he has seen living breath, not letters—words, not signs.

Besides this absorption, all else is what Albany calls Edmund's death: "but a trifle" [V. iii. 296]. We are, all of us, dismissed. At best we are, with Edgar, among those who must "speak what we feel, not what we ought to say" [V. iii. 325]. There can be honesty in speaking what we feel, but what we ought to say is the naked truth, and it cannot be said. Make "nothing" into a substance, and you get Nothing; take it for a mere sign, and you have "nothing." Be king or subject—nothing will be the sum of your earnings. But the uncompromising logic—the logic of life and language, not of syllogisms—with which we work out or more likely let ourselves be led to this sum is, perhaps, something. Since we are dismissed into the stewardship of Edgar, we may be forgiven for covering the shame of silence with saying: "Ripeness is *all*." (pp. 257-59)

> *Sigurd Burckhardt, "'King Lear': The Quality of Nothing," in his* Shakespearean Meanings, *Princeton University Press, 1968, pp. 237-59.*

PAUL A. JORGENSEN   (essay date 1967)

[*Like Winifred M.T. Nowottny (1957), Jorgensen analyzes Lear's habit of posing questions, particularly the meaning of his query: "Who is it can tell me who I am?" Jorgensen claims that the king's questioning precipitates a tortuous self-examination, primarily through the reactions of those around him, that culminates in his final reconciliation with Cordelia. In the chapter excerpted below, Jorgensen traces Lear's gradual understanding of the meaning of Cordelia's love.*]

The opening scene of *King Lear* is one of the most diversely interpreted in all of Shakespeare, even as it is one of the biggest puzzles. Lear's staging of the "love-contest" seems too ridiculous, too transparently wrong, even if Lear were in his dotage. Equally important, it seems inadequaely motivated. Lear gives us only an unsatisfactory explanation for demanding the love protestations:

> Which of you shall we say doth love us most,
> That we our largest bounty may extend
> Where nature doth with merit challenge?
>
> [I. i. 51-3]

Except to a very credulous, simpleminded person, this would seem to be an unreliable way of determining "where nature doth with merit challenge." Another problem presented by the scene is Lear's furious reaction to Cordelia's moderate and honest answer to the question. Probably no other circumstance in the play disturbs him more. (pp. 94-5)

But we may, I think, find some degree of motive in what Lear is doing, a motive that would help to account for the violence of his reaction when "rejected" by Cordelia. . . . Lear is seeking some reassurance of identity. One should note carefully, however, that at this point he is seeking reassurance only; nothing could be further from his mind than the labyrinthine complexity of self-exploration into which so simple a question will lead him.

But it is not, of course, so simple a question as he thinks. Love involves, as the entire first scene makes clear, a great deal more than Lear expected it would. To find out how and why one is loved is to learn some basic, complicated, and sometimes unpleasant truths about oneself. All that Lear has sought is what most old people need: love—the deepest and most certain evidence that they are wanted and needed. No matter how apparently secure a man may be in position, he cannot do without the most basic of emotional needs. (pp. 95-6)

What Lear hears about himself in the first two arias of the love avowal is, in its extravagance, not too much in terms of what he wishes to know. Because he at this point believes, or wants to believe, all these things about himself, he does not question the motives behind the protestations.

Cordelia's unpleasant answer to the question is so monstrously wrong—if we can place ourselves momentarily within Lear's mind—that it can only be cruelty, if not indeed imagined only. He hears his favorite daughter's gentle voice telling him something about himself which could come only from a stranger. Hence she will ever after be "as a stranger to my heart and me" [I. i. 115].

Because of his present hardness of mind, and because Lear cannot see any truth in this view of love, its message is not immediately useful to him, except for its shock value, in reorienting him toward himself. But though he cannot utilize it immediately, it will, like much else in Lear's learning, go underground. What he learns from Cordelia is the nature of his status as a father: that he has begotten, bred, and loved his child; that she will in return obey, love, and honor him; but when she marries, half her love will go to her husband. This, in the *King Lear* world, is merely a logical part, one of the unyielding facts of life. But human relationships in this world *can* go beyond the hard facts; and true love is the most important of the relationships to do so. Both Lear, because of his concept of love, and to a lesser extent Cordelia, because of her tactless manner of expressing only one aspect of it, are at fault in this scene. Lear's error, however, is our concern.

It is, I believe, because the meaning of true love is so crucial to Lear's learning about himself that Shakespeare devoted to it most of the remainder of the scene. We do the opening part an injustice if we do not regard it in the light of what Shakespeare made so deliberately its continuing pattern. Kent, who has always loved Lear "as my father," reinforces the lesson given by Cordelia: that a father, or beloved sovereign, is not privileged to behave unreasonably; more specifically, he must make more modest demands of this kind of world, take a humbler view of himself—a lesson that will prove basic to his final self-image.

In addition to the Cordelia "rejection," the whole episode of France's wooing of Cordelia, which Lear must now witness, could tell the King much about his own actions. After Burgundy balks at accepting a dowerless bride, France defines what true love means:

> Love's not love
> When it is mingled with regards that stands
> Aloof from th' entire point.
>
> [I. i. 238-40]

In accepting Cordelia, France exemplifies a love of what one is rather than what one owns. . . . (pp. 96-7)

This is the meaning of the scene as a whole, if Lear could only see it. Ironically, of course, he cannot. He cannot foresee the prompt applicability to himself of the challenge he throws to Burgundy with his rejected daughter:

> Sir, there she stands:
> If aught within that little-seeming substance,
> Or all of it, with our displeasure piec'd,
> And nothing more, may fitly like your Grace,
> She's there, and she is yours.
>
> [I. i. 197-201]

It will next be Lear himself who, with "that little-seeming substance," will be on the market of appraisal by the world. He will have to learn then, like Everyman, what his essential worth is and who are his abiding friends.

This he will do; it will be part of his education about himself. But he will not quickly change his view about what constitutes love. Even after he has been disabused of his trust in both Goneril and Regan, and is trying to persuade one of them at least to take him with his retinue, he falls back upon his earlier way of calculating love. . . . Even after his long ordeal, when he awakens from his madness to discover Cordelia, Lear cannot believe that she loves him. . . . It is only when he and Cordelia are being led off to prison that he is finally reassured about her love and its independence of worldly circumstances. . . . (pp. 98-9)

For true understanding of love must mean for him a true understanding of himself. As long as his autocratic ego demands protestation of total devotion and as long as he sees love as bound to worldly possessions (as in the distribution of land), he cannot have Cordelia's kind of love and the reliable assurance about his own worth which it can give him. Tragically, of course, human love cannot withstand the exigencies of a ruthless world. And the last scene of the play will implicitly substitute another question for that of the first. It will no longer be, Who loves me most? but rather, Of what final reassurance is even true love? Or, more urgently: What am I if Cordelia is nothing?

In giving up his kingdom, Lear parallels, as we have seen, the plight of Cordelia put dowerless upon the marriage market. What this means for his self-discovery is considerable, for as long as he retains "all the large effects / That troop with majesty" [I. i. 131-32], only his honest counselors will tell him who he is. But it should be noticed that in giving up authority and wealth, he is careful to retain for himself "The name, and all th' addition to a king" [I. i. 136]. Concerning this attribute, he has an anxious need, for it is, as much as "dear father," an important part of his sense of identity. . . . Despite his precautions, Lear will learn that just as he loses one kind of love by giving up authority, so he will forfeit more of his name than he could ever foresee. He will learn that many people indeed do not know him. That is to say, they do not know him as he sees himself. (pp. 99-100)

In [Lear's] new exposure to the world, the first person after Cordelia who does not seem to know him is Kent. By Kent, Lear in his folly is, we recall, addressed bluntly as "old man" [I. i. 146]. The term of address is an accurate augury of the future. Lear is no longer "your majesty." Just how deliberately meaningful Kent's rude term is, we cannot know. But it does seem that the Earl is meant here to be the mouthpiece of the "tough world." A little later in the play, when Kent is disguised as Caius, Lear asks him, "Dost thou know me, fellow?" [I. iv. 26]. Kent replies with another accurate appraisal: Lear has that in his countenance which he would *fain* call master, a possible hint that Lear at present is not the man he once worshiped. But, still, Kent is a symbol of loyalty, of the old recognitions. Kent's answers to what will be Lear's agonized questions are given with love.

Lear's question to the disguised Kent is probably asked with some complacence. He has, except for the distressing Cordelia episode and Kent's earlier candor, had no intimations that he is not everything that he believed himself to be. But by the fourth scene of the play he has begun to perceive "a most faint neglect" [I. iv. 68]. And when he confronts Oswald, already neglectful of him, with a question similar to that he had asked Kent, there may be some uneasiness as well as exasperation in his manner. "Who am I, sir?" he demands [I. iv. 78]. The answer, "My lady's father" [I. iv. 79], gives him his first real view of his new identity. At this stage of disenchantment he meets every new threat to his self-esteem with rage rather than recognition. It will take a series of shocks to make him ask his question of identity with anxious interest. (pp. 101-02)

The most shattering of the new reflections Lear will see of himself is that provided by his two unkind daughters. He "gave [them] all," and to him that is still the definition of what makes for love. He will get from them the most cruelly unflattering of mirrors, much worse than that of Kent . . . because it is given with absolute lovelessness by those from whom he had expected unreserved devotion. (p. 102)

Lear cannot, as we have seen, argue reasonably with his daughters, or with anyone, at this point. Instead, he asks, not without a histrionic manner, "Are you our daughter?" [I. iv. 218]. But the question is more than histrionic; it is, in its most anxious form so far, the question of whether people know who he is. His daughters seem to mean most to him, here and throughout the play. If they do not know him for the "So kind a father" that he is, then he is indeed a stranger to himself.

This is, in fact, the import of his next series of questions about himself, which he seems to address to the world about him rather than merely to Goneril:

> Doth any here know me? This is not Lear.
> Doth Lear walk thus? speak thus? Where are his eyes?
> Either his notion weakens, his discernings
> Are lethargied—Ha! waking? 'Tis not so.
> Who is it that can tell me who I am?
>
> [I. iv. 226-30]

This . . . is one of the real turning points of the play. For the first time Lear is beginning with real anxiety to ask who he is. It is an especially significant inquiry, for he is also beginning to see himself objectively. There is profound psychological insight in Shakespeare's depiction of this perception by having Lear seem to be at a distance from himself. He views his body

and his motions with a mounting panic. Though he is thereby beginning a typically Renaissance study of *nosce teipsum* ["self-knowledge"], the meaning of the episode is timeless. Lear draws away in disbelief from this strange image of himself. This body, which he had always thought himself, cannot really be his. No one recognizes him, and he does not recognize himself.

But of course his daughters, in their coldly limited way, do know him. And they have something to tell him which . . . he will have to incorporate, in part, into his new self-image, once he is capable of doing so. In Goneril's opinion, Lear must

> put away
> These dispositions which of late transport you
> From what you rightly are.
>
> [I. iv. 220-22]

Because her view of people is uniformly biased by selfishness and a cold heart, she does not fully know of Lear "what you rightly are." But she is correctly aware of many of his faults. As he is old, he should be wise. He should keep men about him such "as may besort your age" [I. iv. 251]. But above all, what he must learn from her is something that she cannot consciously teach him: that she is indeed his daughter, and that the way she sees him now does not make her a "degenerate bastard" but one who is flesh of his flesh. This insight, however, comes later in the play. . . . For the present, Lear can only hold desperately to his preferred self-image, cursing Goneril, denying her charges against him, and threatening:

> Thou shalt find
> That I'll resume the shape which thou dost think
> I have cast off for ever.
>
> [I. iv. 308-10]
> (pp. 102-04)

The meeting with that other daughter, however, is even more of a blow to his need for recognition. (p. 104)

Here is his last hope of being known (and loved) as he really is. But once again it is as though "This is not Lear." He hears, instead of the protestations of love he had received from her in their last meeting, cold words to the effect that the fault is perhaps his rather than Goneril's. He should, he is once more told, understand that he is old and unable to judge correctly.

But we should not infer from the daughters' criticisms that they are interested in rehabilitating the old man through his gaining a better self-knowledge. Regan's words are the most significant: "I pray you, father, being weak, seem so" [II. iv. 201]. What the daughters want Lear to become in his senility is a mild, inconspicuous little man, content with a few old retainers. This is the kind of old age they had groomed him for. . . . With a satisfying irony, the daughters prove to be as mistaken about their father as he had been about them. By "slenderly known himself," they have meant partly his failure to behave like a docile old man, attended by a few other docile old men, such as befit his age. Instead, Lear turns out to be an annoyingly assertive senior citizen. Rather than accept the reduced role in life they had planned for him, he resists this diminution, this senility with dynamic wrath. He is no Gloucester being meekly led by the hand through his bad moments. Rather than submit to the humiliating kind of recognition his daughters will give him, he will war against the universe itself. (pp. 105-06)

This is, in fact, what he next tries to do. He confronts the elemental forces of nature in his next assayal of whether anyone knows him. In *As You Like It* Shakespeare had written briefly about the totally impartial kind of tutelage the elements of nature will give a man in self-knowledge, equivalent perhaps to the machine today. . . . Brutal nature will indeed give Lear a feeling sense of what he is; but it will not know him—at least as king and as dear father. . . . Lear later acknowledges that "the thunder would not peace at my bidding" [IV. vi. 102-03], and this is an important lesson learned about what his supposed identity as king means in the storm. But it is not learned without highly dramatic resistance as Lear pleads with the elements to know him. He does not berate their ignorance of him as that of unkind daughters to whom he had given all and who owe him "subscription." Rather:

> Here I stand your slave,
> A poor, infirm, weak, and despis'd old man;
> But yet I call you servile ministers,
> That will with two pernicious daughters join
> Your high-engender'd battles 'gainst a head
> So old and white as this. Oh! Oh! 'tis foul!
>
> [III. ii. 19-24]

What the elements do not know about him is that now he is a pathetic figure of an old man. Kent had also told him that he was an old man, and like the storm he had not told him that he was a pathetic one. The pathos is Lear's new tactic for evading the real truths about himself. To benefit from nature's ignorance of him, he will have to resist self-pity; and in a dramatic struggle he does so—at least sufficiently so that it does not bar more important insights.

By not knowing him in his own self-image, the storm teaches him many things. Most of all . . . it teaches him a Renaissance lesson about himself as unaccommodated man. It makes him question himself in his capacity as king, not only by refusing to heed his commands but also by forcing him to new insights about justice. In Renaissance terms, again, one of the most important things it does for him is to make him aware of sin, a quality in himself never before mentioned:

> Close pent-up guilts,
> Rive your concealing continents, and cry
> These dreadful summoners grace. I am a man
> More sinn'd against than sinning.
>
> [III. ii. 57-60]

The recognition of himself as at least partially a sinner is a remarkable one for a man who has previously admitted only one fault in himself: that he had wronged Cordelia.

There are two later episodes in the play where Lear seems to need further assurance of his identity. Neither is so searching or clear-cut as the preceding ones, but they deserve mention for they suggest how urgent is his need to find from others and from circumstances just who he is.

The first of these episodes is that of Lear in almost complete delirium, when he enters presumably "fantastically dressed with wild flowers." In his madness he is not so anxious about who he is as he was when he felt himself on the brink of madness. Yet the anxiety is there, even beneath some of his seemingly most assured declarations of his identity. With no apparent context, he suddenly announces: "No, they cannot touch me for coining; I am the King himself" [IV. vi. 83-4]. Just what has been going on in his tormented mind, we cannot be sure. But he may well imagine himself in a threatened position, in the midst of an accusing group, perhaps like that in which he officiated in the mad "trial" scene. The accusers

do not know him. He pleads, despite an awareness that he has done wrong, that aspect of his identity which formerly always sustained him: he is a king. Then, in one of his great scenes of merging recognition, he is identified by the blinded Gloucester as the King. Lear's response is a regression to his old imperious manner:

> Ay, every inch a king!
> When I do stare, see how the subject quakes.
>
> [IV. vi. 107-08]

But there is a change from the earlier manner, for he is no longer commanding his familiar subjects. The defendants are monsters of sexual depravity. He is king in an unfamiliar world. Again, in the same scene, when friends enter from Cordelia to relieve him, he imagines himself a prisoner beset without rescue. . . . [Alone] and facing a world that does not know him, he reverts to his one kind of response:

> Come, come; I am a king,
> My masters, know you that?
>
> [IV. vi. 199-200]

It is surely significant that three times in this one scene of greatest madness he should proclaim his identity as king. Perhaps, like Lady Macbeth in her mad scene, he is reliving one of his deepest anxieties. His, of course, is not so much an anxiety of guilt as of who he is, of whether anyone knows him. But beneath an insecurity of identity there is often an anxiety of guilt.

The second episode is that of Lear awakening, after the doctor's ministrations, from his delirium. Here it is natural that he should want to know who he is. It is, in fact, the great recognition scene of the play: the reunion of the shamed, humbled Lear and the solicitous, fully loving Cordelia. . . . When he now sees her, he is once again convinced that he is a captive, and accused, but now in hell past all judgment. He is "bound / Upon a wheel of fire" [IV. vii. 45-6]. Then, with gradual recognition, he becomes aware of himself, but still mainly as an unbelievable stranger. The distancing from himself, noticed when he was losing his wits, is repeated as he returns to sanity. It is as though he is asking himself if he knows this man. . . . But now he does become assured of his condition, though with a tentativeness as he faces the full truth of who he is: one still not in his perfect mind, old, and a *man*. Significantly, he no longer mentions his being king.

Perhaps, though, the principal feature of this recognition scene for him lies not in whether others know him; it is—and this is a sign of great advance—whether he knows others. If he can now see his real friends for what they are, as did Everyman, he will also know himself. Cordelia's "Sir, do you know me?" [IV. vii. 47] is not only one of the most thrilling questions in the play; it is a crucial one in Lear's self-awakening, for . . . its satisfactory answer means that he knows the meaning of true love—a relationship demanding that he can face himself for what he is because he is accepted for what he is. But though others will attempt to reassure him that he is a most royal king, he never, in his own mind, will be able to restore the figure to the "O." (pp. 106-10)

> *Paul A. Jorgensen, in his* Lear's Self-Discovery, *University of California Press, 1967, 154 p.*

ROBERT H. WEST   (essay date 1968)

[*West takes issue with those critics who insist that* King Lear *presents Shakespeare's pessimistic vision of human life. Focusing on the elements of sex and death, specifically Lear's bitter attacks on procreation and the tragic deaths of both him and Cordelia, West admits that it is easy to regard the drama as nihilistic. But he considers this assessment as valid only if one views Lear's mental turmoil as authoritative and the deaths of the protagonists as evidence of a senseless world. Instead, West offers a more positive interpretation, and this he finds in Lear's eventual experience of spiritual love, through the character of Cordelia, and his gradual acceptance of Edgar's doctrine of ''ripeness''—or what West redefines as ''a simple and overmastering certainty of devotion.'' For West, the experience of selfless love permanently changes Lear's conception of sex, and his devotion to Cordelia guarantees that he dies in a universe not grotesque or without purpose, but one filled with potential meaning. In his emphasis on Cordelia's transcendent power in the play, West follows in the tradition of such earlier critics as G. G. Gervinus (1849-50), A. C. Bradley (1904), R. W. Chambers (1939), Geoffrey L. Bickersteth (1946), Oscar James Campbell (1948), Irving Ribner (1958), and L. C. Knights (1959). Also, his final point—that the mystery of life and death that pervades* King Lear *should be seen, not as a lack of moral vision, but as a permanent aspect of human life— can be found in the essays by Robert Ornstein (1960) and René E. Fortin (1979).]*

Most of those who find a cosmic pessimism in *King Lear* think it inescapable there, not only as a feature natural to any tragedy but also as a clear impression and logical inference from the play's particular action and dialogue. Building upon both the discouragement of the afflicted characters and the decisive events of the play, and especially on Cordelia's cruel death and Lear's, they conclude that nothing but sentiment testifies against pessimism. Nature, which the play makes much of, is clearly impersonal, uncaring, nonmoral, these critics say. Of a distinct supernature they find nothing, certainly nothing of outer beneficence. Some of them not only banish Christianity from the play, but also find cosmic pessimism so unrelieved there that *King Lear* does not, in their view, rise to the pitch of tragedy. (p. 149)

Bradley and many others have observed, of course, that the scene of Lear with Cordelia's body has tremendous dignity and even at last tranquility [see excerpt above, 1904]. The quality of the scene is not finally that of unmitigated horror nor yet of outrage at the nature of things nor of a rebellious assertion of man's loneliness and sole worth. It is rather of a poignant awe at the power of Lear's life, seen a near match for the grand finality itself of death. . . . The speeches of the good characters in *King Lear* are certainly full of outrage, sorrow, and despondency, and its events are mostly grievous for the good and the bad alike. But perhaps these things do not add up to an iron mockery of man's state or a defiance of it.

Critics have suggested a long list of themes for *King Lear*: renunciation, the death wish, filial impiety, evil under good appearance, the decay and fall of the world, the meaning of moral chaos. Without trying to name ''the'' theme, I suggest that a subject quite prominent among those that the play touches powerfully is the biological creativeness of nature and its reciprocal destructiveness—generation and death. Of these two death has for obvious reasons received more attention from the pessimistic critics. In the tragedy death seems the inevitable cap and conclusion for inexplicable struggle and undeserved suffering. It is a fitting terminus for nature, that grim totality of things which the characters sense intimately about them and within them and to which some of them ignorantly appeal for a succor that it does not provide. The pessimistic critic takes nature (with emphasis upon death as its characteristic expression) to be about as much suggestion as the play affords of outerness. To both character and critic nature and death in the

world of *King Lear* are vivid but unfathomed. Intimate as the experience of them is, it yet comes upon the characters from without as well as from within. Death is, to use Karl Jasper's term, a ''boundary situation.'' In *King Lear* it is an event in nature on the verge of what may seem beyond empirical nature; it irresistibly suggests the beyond.

Another boundary situation—and on a not wholly different natural boundary—is procreation. The experience of sex, familiar yet extreme, *King Lear* notices as the natural root of death and of its preliminaries that the pessimists find so discouraging: fruitless struggle and inexplicable suffering. The weight and sense of the play's pessimism depend very much on its vision of sex.

Several of Shakespeare's tragedies interest us with virile heroes and alluring heroines. *King Lear*, though, has no female fascinator whose sexiness it dramatically emphasizes, and the protagonist is old. Only in the romance of Cordelia's brief betrothal and later in the repulsive liaisons between Edmund and the evil sisters is the amorous a matter of staged love affairs in *King Lear*. Both main plot and subplot, nevertheless, touch sex as the mating attraction, all the way from Gloucester's elderly bragging in the first scene to Edmund's dying realization that he was beloved and had had of Goneril a slaughterous proof of it. Edgar ties his account of himself as bedlam largely to sexual predation, and the Fool's commentary on Lear's clash with his evil daughters is most wryly knowing on sexual evils. To Edgar copulation is the ''act of darkness'' [III. iv. 87], and to the Fool it is that of the codpiece with which the head must louse. (pp. 150-51)

Yet the sex passages do not mean that the play despairs of sex. They do not express Shakespeare's outrage at the way man reproduces. *King Lear*'s ''fearless artistic facing of the ultimate cruelty of things'' [see excerpt above by G. Wilson Knight, 1930], does not include a moral rejection of sex, much less a merely fastidious one. The play does face, though, such cruel facts of generation as that children may be unkind and that their obligation to be kind has at last an unknown ground, if it has any at all. How does the natural sex act beget, together with children, a moral obligation? Does decency belong to sex naturally, and does the unnatural in sex, perversion of sex, pollute it as source? Does its practice rise sometimes and somehow toward the supernatural, or at least the spiritual?

The major speech on sex is Lear's. To the king, maddened by the offenses of his children against him and his against Cordelia, the act of generation has come to seem an inhuman abyss of the human will. . . . Man begets children by an impulse that Lear now sees as resistless and polluted. That it is natural, too, puts a new face on nature for him. Generation has become to him a most primitive cooperation in which personal knowledge and affection cannot live and out of which they cannot come. We have heard Lear utter a frightful curse on generation in Goneril; finally the conviction of a primordial curse on it in all times and persons ravages his mind. He seems in his madness to imply that sex is an insult to mankind and mercilessly alien—or that a man is a beast. (pp. 152-53)

If Lear's speech can be taken, as Gloucester's on the wanton gods has been, to be a keynote of the play, then clearly *King Lear* is dreadfully pessimistic about sex. If it does indeed say that every man's origin is unredeemed slime, that assertion goes very well with the assertion that his end is the gods' vicious sport. But the fact would seem to be that the play dignifies generation after all, as it does death—dignifies them both largely with the preservation about them of their proper mystery, and with an indication that a sort of miracle may attend them.

To the audience the sex horror of the play comes chiefly by way of the strongly expressed revulsion of the sympathetic characters from a self-evidence foulness. With a kind of shocked Freudian insight the king detects the mating impulse as a brutal power horrifyingly strong just where it is not ordinarily expected. Behind this revulsion in the character we may assume, lies, a kindred one, more sophisticated, in the author. Presumably Shakespeare himself considered the causes of Lear's shock and horror sufficient for their effect in both the king and the audience. Yet they do not move us as they move Lear, any more than the grieved awe we feel at Lear's death is the same as the awed grief that Edgar shows. What is mortal shock to Kent is a tragic pang to the audience. The viewer is detached from the immediate causes of feeling in the characters, and his emotion is refined, furthermore, by the language and spectacle of the play. This well-known benefit from a special purchase on events and from the play's artistry is the audience's share in the sophistication of the author. What for the delirious Lear, then, is a frantic intuition of universal depravity in sex, is for the audience the recognition with pity and terror of a corruption that his world may show—or of Lear's distressed way of seeing whatever it is that his world does show.

The audience's weighing of Lear's distress does not mean that the king's vehemence on sex is unconnected with facts or expresses solely his internal state. However distorted his way of seeing may be, Lear has come through an experience that the dramatic clarity of madness connects directly with sex: the hatefulness of his children belongs to the carnality that made them. (pp. 153-54)

No strict computation of the grounds of Lear's sex raving is either possible or suitable, but plainly it stems in general from his daughters' ill treatment of him, real or fancied. . . . If we are bound by the straight facts of the plot, we can hardly think that Lear spoke from any knowledge of looseness in Goneril's sex life, for he could not have heard of her liaison with Edmund. The audience does know of it, of course, and understands now that the horrid disparity between Goneril's loving profession and her predatory act is matched in her release of a riotous appetite formerly concealed beneath a chaste expression. Perhaps we may suppose that from her uncovered lust for power Lear projects a lust of the flesh as yet undemonstrated to him. Or perhaps Lear's sickness obscured for the moment the sovereign shame that elbowed him about Cordelia and made her seem to him a dame who looked modest yet yearned for fornication. (pp. 154-55)

Whoever the simp'ring dame may be (and of course she need not be anyone we know), the sexual imagery of Lear's long speech recalls powerfully the events and speeches that have gone before it; his sex horror grounds in his sense of tainted generation. Because of unnatural daughters the sex act appears a kind of dreadful seizure. The breeding of man, like that of the wren and the fly, is but a compulsive joining, and the chastest-seeming women are centaurs down from the waist. If these images give justly the nature of propagation, it is no wonder that parent's claim on child and child's on parent do not hold good. Lear's reasoning circles: if—as his experience testifies—these claims do not hold good, then the act of propagation upon which they so mysteriously rest must be as bestial as it seems. The pessimistic suspicion that tears Lear and through him affects the audience is logically naive, but it reflects real

anomalies in sex. It is resistless to the mad king and, in the sight of his suffering, impressive to us.

The audience with its sophistication understands throughout, nevertheless, that children do have a binding obligation to love and to revere their parents, and parents have one to love and to minister to their children. This much the play takes for granted; it is part of the given morality. To plead for Edmund and the evil sisters the vexations and humiliations their fathers troubled them with is to go outside the clear intent of the play. Lear and Gloucester, for their part, are clearly ''wrong'' to reject their good children and then are ''redeemed.'' Edgar and Cordelia are as blameless as dramatic characters can be and still seem human. The play says to the audience with the most moving particularity that the faith of child to father and of father to child does exist and ought to exist. By homely appeal to our human sympathy the play confirms the audience in this fatih and its rightness. The given morality, founded here most elementally, is almost as simple and direct as that morality of condign reward and punishment that Dr. Johnson wished for in *King Lear* [see excerpt above, 1765], and it certainly mitigates the play's pessimism on sex. If some children are kind, then generation cannot be all evil. Cordelia as natural child vindicates nature at least in part and soothes Lear's suspicion about sex. May she soothe ours, too? (pp. 155-56)

Lear is not myopic when he sees the sex act, ''love'' in the natural sense, as a most primitive and abysmal cooperation. Nature compels cooperation as well as predation, and the sex act partakes heedlessly of both. It is, in fact, tainted with the inhuman, with an impersonal force of the vital species, with the bestial. Hence, though among the most basically natural of acts, it may seem unnatural unless a decency of love like that which Cordelia fitly kept for her husband redeems it. In natural love Lear's mad imagination sees most directly humanity's corruptness. As Gloucester suspects that killing is a sport of the gods, so Lear suspects that procreation is a device of the devil. . . . The audience at the same time, however, knows that he has one daughter yet, and it may remember the mystery of a man's natural or unnatural or preternatural growth and cultivation from the slime of his begetting.

The play's given morality has the stamp of naturalness, and in its light Edmund's cynical view of nature seems to be unnatural and to have unnatural consequences. His conviction of man's universal filth repels us, and we see it draw him toward filth. . . . The king's improved understanding of nature, his fresh view of natural faults, gives him in his madness a sense of filth's diffusion through the world. Except for Cordelia as evidence that filth is not universal, Lear's dialectic on nature must have ended much like Edmund's. Does Cordelia, as an exception to natural evil, draw Lear's understanding of nature somehow beyond nature? Lear's understanding rises—as it touches Cordelia, anyway—toward a conscious remission of self-interest, a conscious community with the beloved, that in natural creation only man seems persistently capable of. This feeling concern for another, this surpassing love, is a kind of doubling on nature's tracks, is a transformation of nature's law of self, a departure from the predation so constant in unalloyed nature and a rising superior to it. Through love we can put up with one another's natural faults and filths better than an impartial observer might expect. Is this a kind of supernature, of spirituality, in us and beyond us? Several higher religions have said something of the sort.

Perhaps the question is a loaded one for an inquiry into outerness in *King Lear*. About love in its higher aspects nevertheless—love of God and love of fellows—there does seem something discontinuous with nature, though not oblivious of it, something different in kind from the originating sex act or its biological consequences. With his redemption Lear settles into a transformed faith about love in the universe, so that he and Cordelia may take upon them "the mystery of things" as if they "were God's spies" [V. iii. 16-17]. Here the given morality seems to reach toward a sympathetic outerness. Conversely, Edmund's cynical devotion to filth reaches, like Iago's, toward some negative and hateful outerness. The ruthlessness of the unfilial children in *King Lear* seems, like the love of the filial, to be discontinuous with nature. Their self-seeking breaks with the naturalness of their origin in the sex act (much less with any supernaturalness in it) and is a twisting and perversion of the fruit of loving cohabitation.

But assuredly much of this speculation depends upon interpretation. Whatever benefits of his love for Cordelia Lear may achieve, the play says nothing explicit about his love of God. Cordelia's love may draw Lear to heights, but it would seem to do it by human decency, not by sacramental power. As for the bad children, they may, like Macbeth, feel the contagion of a kingdom of outer evil and may harden their hearts into its inhuman form; but *King Lear* says little directly of outer evil. So far as nonhuman forces are concerned, the play works almost entirely within the concept of nature, with its storm and its calm. Characters call upon "justicers" who are above, but they never get any clearly supernatural response; and, in fact, those who call hardly discriminate justicers, gods, from the stars or great nature. . . . Outerness in *King Lear* remains entirely impersonal, and conceivably the references to it as personal are all ironic.

That Lear achieves a special standing in nature or beyond it, like one of God's spies, the play may seem to contradict, especially by its ending. The serenity of Lear's redemption has not long to last; it is as transient as the honorable retirement he had planned for himself. Obviously Cordelia as object of his love is mortal, and her mortality is quite as prominent dramatically as her love; otherwise her death would not so shatter Lear and us. If some heavenly compensation is operating in the ending of *King Lear,* it is not in a form to blunt the tragic pang. Is it compensation for Lear to prove his love by his mortal anguish? Certainly not a compensation that Lear would have chosen. But then perhaps the true tragic compensation is just in the finality of some such proof, in the good that resistlessly rises out of agony, or at any rate in the clear vision without wavering or indecision with which Shakespeare's protagonists come to their ends. At his end Lear does not need to study his love. For us of the audience the compensation is a sense of something unutterable, not normally manifest. It dignifies the fearful human scene and awes its lesser and surviving participants with a sense of its truth so that they must obey the "weight of this sad time" and "speak what we feel, not what we ought to say" [V. iii. 324-25]. Here—and for others besides Lear and Cordelia—the mystery of things piercingly enters human awareness.

[Jan] Kott's insistence that the wheel of history simply grinds round and round in Shakespeare's plays so that kings rise and fall in bloody and senseless succession leaves us with an outer mystery, true enough; but, as Kott says, this rotation provides no tragic healing. A mystery like a meat grinder is what Kott offers us. Still, outerness as a meat grinder, with men madly pushing one another into the teeth, though a less respectful figure of speech than Gloucester's about the gods killing us

like flies, is no gloomier. Certainly *King Lear* has some passages dark enough to justify pessimism on death. But most of these passages express someone's discouragement with the world, and they are not more authoritative than hopeful ones, like Lear's on the mystery of things.

The mystery of outerness in Shakespeare is like that of the real world in the fact that however secure we may feel in our convictions about it, we must nevertheless acknowledge a vast ultimate inadequacy in whatever dialectic we would use to sustain them. One sign in the play of uncertainty about outerness is the bafflement of some characters. Very clearly Lear and his friends are intellectually unequal to the questions they confront on the natural duties of children and of parents. For Lear piety is at first an unexamined convention: the stars or the gods or nature are our generators, and so duty is natural in the cosmos and on the earth. Lear knows the barbarous unnatural in theory only, without suspecting it in the world around him, much less in his own bosom. (pp. 158-61)

The bafflement of these characters proceeds not only from their intellectual inadequacies but also from real deficiencies in the evidence. The detachment of the audience and their superior knowledge of events gives them here no decisive advantage. We know better than Lear does the evidence from Gloucester's bastard, and we know before Lear that he has "one daughter / Who redeems nature from the general curse / Which twain have brought her to" [IV. vi. 205-07]. But such knowledge just confirms us in the hope of the given morality, not in any sure ground for it. Is this morality given by a greater authority than human yearning? The action does not positively say. After the reunion of Lear and Cordelia we hear no more, it is true, of his disenchantment with generation; we hear rather of his humility before Cordelia and the world and of his bliss in both. But his new mood is only the tenderest assertion of the given morality. It does not, as Dr. Johnson thought it should, ward off death. And it does not answer the question of the unkind child but simply adds the question of the kind one. . . . Lear dies on an ecstatic conviction that Cordelia breathes, but this last delusion does not tell the audience why "a dog, a horse, a rat, have life" [V. iii. 307] and she none. Lear's purified love is no answer, either for him or for us, to the question of how such perversions of nature as unfilial hate and mistreatment can arise from the conditions of nature. In his anguish Lear came again and again to this profound question, and Shakespeare leaves the audience, at least, with it. We cannot find in the nature of Lear's good child an explanation of the nature of his evil ones, and only partial reassurance.

The given morality, then, does not exhaust the sophistication of the author about nature and its boundary experiences of sex and death. The play does not, like a novel of sentiment, come comfortably to rest in the morality. But the painful mystery does not mean that the deaths in the play leave us with a meat grinder outerness any more than the biology of conception leaves us with a slimy one. Whatever the lowliness of human generation, Cordelia and Edgar live as good and noble children, and Lear and Gloucester die as redeemed parents. Whatever death may be, Gloucester finally endured it as he did his coming hither; and Cordelia, too, no doubt died "ripe," though dramatic emphasis is all on her being dead rather than on her dying.

Did Lear die ripe? Or did the pain of his last moments tear ripeness from him and substitute a mockery in a delusion that Cordelia lived? And what, after all, is the meaning of ripeness? A question prefaces Edgar's aphorism: "What, in ill thoughts again?'' [V. ii. 9]. Is this question not notice enough that the ripeness that is all is pious acceptance of life as it comes and the living out of one's time to the end—in submission to Providence, if you like? (pp. 162-64)

The obvious paralleling of Lear's death with Gloucester's suggests Lear's ripeness if, as seems reasonable, we accept Gloucester's. But do we, then, have to think that at the end Lear recognizes his beloved child in another land or at least think that his heart, like Gloucester's "'Twixt two extremes of passion, joy and grief, / Burst smilingly'' [V. iii. 199-200]? To accept Cordelia's survival in another world as part of the play brings all the weight of that heavenly compensation that tragedy cannot exist with. Still we must believe that Lear died in hope when he cried ''Look there! Look on her lips!'' even though our ears yet ring with ''Thou'lt come no more, / Never, never, never, never, never!'' [V. iii. 308-09]. The mighty mystery of ''never'' and the contrary mystery of hope are both in Lear's last words.

But is Lear ripe? . . . If to be ripe is to wrap oneself in a rational hardihood that puts one beyond hurt or at least chokes back outcry, Lear has not attained it. But if it is to die in a simple and overmastering certainty of devotion that redeems one's character, then he has attained it. Such redemption need not mean transformation into an unrecognizable person, but simply that a new and regenerate quality (for Lear perhaps one of love and humility) has assumed control. When Lear brings Cordelia's body in, he is no stranger to us. His old violence and imperiousness are there and also something of a personal prowess that antedates our acquaintance. . . . His courtesy is with him, too, his loyalty to his servants, and his habit of agonized speculation. And does he not have his hardwon humility? . . . We see in him here a shattered epitome of the character we knew, enduring to the end, his purified love for Cordelia now his motive for everything. It dominates Lear, and in its expression as grief alternating with illusory hope it dominates the scene. Does his awful vitality and steadfastness in his knowledge of it suggest the ripeness that is all? I think so. (pp. 164-65)

If Lear achieves and keeps the ripeness that is all, it is a thing for awe, as the survivors find it. It does not seem to encourage them, though, about ''this tough world.'' Shakespeare does not have them translate into outerness whatever glory Lear may have realized by his ripeness, and for us to translate it so is dangerous, though many critics do translate Lear's death back upon outerness as something like objective oppression. If Lear is ripe, his death is, like Cordelia's conception, a pure one. His life before death justifies him in it as Cordelia's life justifies him in fatherhood. We cannot know, of course, as the play stands, why death comes from life any more than we know why evil children grow from good seed; nor can we know, really that death is an evil, however great the shock and grief. The fear of death is, as Socrates says, a ''pretense of wisdom.'' Lear's death is natural, and at the same time, like all death, it is beyond nature. It is a great mystery that we may observe in part with awe and reverence. Love, the play indicates, may be a kind of miracle, so that sex, along with the rest of life and death itself, is transmutable from slime to majesty. We do not find it said that sex is itself naturally majestic or that death is a natural benefit. But the play does say to those who will have it that by the miracle of love, natural sex may be exalted and natural life ripened, so that birth and death alike are confrontable, though mysterious still with the doubt and sorrow that properly go with tragic mystery. (pp. 165-66)

Robert H. West, ''The Christianness of 'Othello' & 'King Lear','' in his Shakespeare & the Outer Mystery, University of Kentucky Press, 1968, pp. 127-66.

PHYLLIS RACKIN   (essay date 1970)

[Rackin focuses on Lear's final vision that Cordelia lives, calling it a ''creative'' delusion similar to Edgar's deception of Gloucester at Dover Cliffs and Edmund's final act of ''goodness'' which runs against his own nature. She considers such a delusion a triumphant lack of faith, unmotivated and unwarranted, and she maintains that Shakespeare, in presenting the play's resolution as he did, anticipated his audience's reluctance to accept either an optimistic or a pessimistic ending. Rackin's essay reflects an apparent trend among many contemporary critics to either synthesize the optimistic and nihilistic interpretations of King Lear or to go beyond this polarity in search of new terms to define the meaning of the play. For examples of this approach, see the excerpts by Arthur Sewell (1951), Richard B. Sewall (1959), John Holloway (1961), Maynard Mack (1965), and Bernard McElroy (1973).]

What Lear sees, or thinks he sees, in the last moment of his life is a question as crucial as it is unlikely to receive a definitive answer. In the absence of a stage direction, Shakespeare's intention remains obscure. Is Cordelia meant to be living or dead? And if dead is she merely dead, or does Lear somehow ''see'' that her soul still lives? (p. 29)

[The] immediate questions raised by the passage—what does Lear see, and how true is his vision—lead, fairly directly, to the much larger questions raised by the play as a whole: ''Is man no more than this?'' [III. iv. 102-03]. ''What is the cause of thunder?'' [III. iv. 155]. ''Is there any cause in nature that make these hard hearts?'' [III. vi. 77-8]. Are we to the gods ''as flies to wanton boys'' [IV. i. 36-7]? Are there just gods above us who speedily punish our crimes? Do the stars really ''govern our conditions'' [IV. iii. 33]? Complex theological questions are constantly being raised in the Lear universe, and by it as well. Before the battle, Edgar tells Gloucester to ''pray that the right may thrive'' [V. ii. 2]. His words ring hollowly in our ears when we learn, almost immediately, that Cordelia's forces have been defeated. After Edmund's confession of the plot to murder Cordelia, Albany says, ''The gods defend her!'' [V. iii. 257]. No sooner has he spoken than Lear enters with Cordelia's corpse in his arms. (pp. 29-30)

Shakespeare seems in King Lear to be confronting every possible thesis about the action and its implications with an antithesis, but never allowing a synthesis to emerge. And, as a matter of fact, the very complexity of the issues raised seems almost to preclude their resolution. The attempt to resolve into unity the extremities of hope and despair, virtue and vice depicted in King Lear must confront an audience that has seen too much by the end of Shakespeare's play to accept either the easy ''poetic'' justice of Tate's ending or the perhaps equally easy pessimism that would deny justice entirely. As a result, any attempt at resolution runs a tremendous danger of looking false. Shakespeare avoids this danger, I think, by presenting his resolutions as false, at least from certain angles of vision. The results look wonderfully true.

Through Edgar, Shakespeare perpetrates delusions—plays practical jokes—on other characters, and these jokes have the effect of resolving the major issues of the play, even though they never fully lose their delusory quality. The first of these delusions, and the most memorable, is the one by which Edgar persuades Gloucester that he has been saved from death by a miracle. Having led the blinded Gloucester to a flat place near Dover, Edgar persuades him that he is at the top of a high cliff. The audience sees that the stage is flat and knows that it represents a flat field. But Edgar persuades his blinded father that it is the high cliff he sought in order to commit suicide. . . . After Gloucester leaps, Edgar, speaking in a changed voice, tells him that he has been miraculously saved from a great fall (''Ten masts at each make not the altitude / Which thou hast perpendicularly fell. / Thy life's a miracle'' [IV. vi. 53-5]) and from an evil spirit who led him to the cliff. . . . What Edgar says, of course, is literally a lie, although symbolically perfectly true. Gloucester has fallen from an enormous height, he has been led by an evil spirit . . . , and he has been saved by a miracle—the miraculous devotion of the son he repudiated. What is more, there is a very important sense in which the gods do here ''make them honours / Of men's impossibilities'' [IV. vi. 73-4], for ''men's impossibilities'' need not mean what superstitious Gloucester probably takes it to mean, ''things impossible to men, done by the gods, who thus acquire honours''. ''Men's impossibilities'' can also mean ''things impossible to men, done by men, with the result that the gods acquire honours''. The second reading is supported by other passages in the play. When Lear says to Cordelia after their capture by the British forces, ''Upon such sacrifices, my Cordelia, / The gods themselves throw incense'' [V. iii. 20-1], he is inverting the customary relationship between gods and men: the men, the worshippers, would ordinarily be expected to throw the incense upon the sacrifice. Similarly, when Lear cries in the tempest,

> Take physic, Pomp;
> Expose thyself to feel what wretches feel,
> That thou mayst shake the superflux to them,
> And show the Heavens more just,
>
> [III. iv. 33-6]

we have a still more explicit case of the same inversion. In each case, the action of a human being has cosmic influence: the status of the gods, and of the heavens, is determined by the actions taken by men on earth.

Edgar's second trick is played on Oswald. (pp. 30-1)

Oswald's fault throughout has been that he is completely the creature of the social and political hierarchy, unaware of any values beyond worldy status or any code beyond manners. Kent tells Oswald early in the play . . . that a tailor made him, and to emphasize the line, Shakespeare has Kent repeat it for Cornwall:

Kent. [to Oswald] You cowardly rascal, nature disclaims in thee: a tailor made thee.
Corn. Thou art a strange fellow; a tailor make a man?
Kent. A tailor, sir: a stone-cutter or a painter could not have made him so ill, though they had been but two years o' th' trade.

[II. ii. 54-60]

This passage takes its meaning from the symbolic association of ''clothes'' in King Lear with the whole structure of values and practices that govern, protect, and disguise men in society. Oswald is so completely and so merely the creature of the social hierarchy that he serves as a perfect revelation of its limitations. Since he is nothing but clothes, he is inhuman—no less so than the unclothed creature that Lear beholds in the storm. If the poor, bare, forked animal needs clothes to distinguish him from the beasts, the thing made by a tailor lacks

even the natural affections that distinguish the beasts from inanimate things. The opportunism that makes Edmund brutal and enables him to betray his own father still lacks, it seems, the sheer deadliness of the pragmatism with which Oswald responds to the sight of the blinded Gloucester:

> A proclaim'd prize! Most happy!
> That eyeless head of thine was first fram'd flesh
> To raise my fortunes. Thou old unhappy traitor,
> Briefly thyself remember: the sword is out
> That must destroy thee.
>
> [IV. vi. 226-30]

Oswald sees a human being as a ''prize'': he is capable of reducing the whole purpose of Gloucester's creation to mechanistic and egotistical terms. Gloucester, to Oswald, is an economic advantage pure and simple.

In view of Oswald's inability to distinguish value from rank, the justice of his death at the hands of a peasant—a person of no rank at all—is very neat. The fact that the peasant is Edgar, dressed in rough clothes and speaking a rustic dialect, complicates the justice and acclimates it to the infinitely complex universe of King Lear, makes it, one would like to say, poetic.

The third of these illusions is, in many ways, the antithesis of the second, and in creating it Edgar assumes a shape exactly the opposite of his previous one. He kills Edmund dressed in all the formal splendor that the hierarchy can afford, and again the manner is perfectly appropriate. For if Oswald is too much the creature of society, Edmund is too much its adversary. Edmund's first major speech, a soliloquy, proclaims his defiance of ''the curiosity of nations'' and ''the plague of custom'' [I. ii. 3-4]. And it is these things that, in the end, cut him down in the person of his despised, legitimate older brother, dressed in armor and fighting in formal knightly combat. Edmund, like Oswald, is finally destroyed by a representative of all the values he has defied and ignored throughout the play; and in both cases the representation is, at least from one point of view, a delusion.

Edmund's final act is an attempt to do ''some good in despite of [his] own nature'' [V. iii. 245]. ''Nature'' here probably has two meanings. First, there is Edmund's own evil disposition, of which he is perfectly aware. . . . Second, there is the ''goddess'' to whom he declares his allegiance in his first major speech, the ''Nature'' who knows no right but the brute strength and ruthless cunning which enable one animal to triumph over another. Edmund's vision of the universe, no less than his disposition, is incapable of explaining a genuinely good act. And yet, Edmund's final statement that he means to do ''some good in despite of [his] own nature'' is not really a refutation of what he has said before, either about his disposition or about the universe; for he does not say that his nature has changed. In fact, his statement that he is acting ''in despite of'' it implies logically that it has not changed. And yet, as is obvious to any audience—and obvious at a level much more immediate than that of discussion—the mere existence of that statement provides the only kind of refutation that really matters on the stage, an existential one. By his attempt to do ''some good'' Edmund cannot help qualifying the picture he has given of his ''own nature'' (in both senses), for that picture completely lacked the means of accounting for such an attempt.

In the case of Lear's final speech, the chief difficulty in interpretation is, I think, that the passage itself seems to support the more optimistic reading, while the play as a whole seems to demand the pessimistic one. The speech begins in despair:

> And my poor fool is hang'd! No, no, no life!
> Why should a dog, a horse, a rat, have life,
> And thou no breath at all? Thou'lt come no more,
> Never, never, never, never, never!
>
> [V. iii. 306-09]

At this point, when despair is total, there is a transition. Lear says, "Pray you, undo this button: thank you, sir" [V. iii. 310]. When he turns his attention back to Cordelia, in the next two lines, he seems to be seeing something new that he had not seen before:

> Do you see this? Look on her, look, her lips,
> Look there, look there!
>
> [V. iii. 311-12]

And yet the first four lines of the speech left nothing new in the way of despair for Lear to perceive. The only new thing he could be seeing, it would seem, is some grounds for hope. It is to her lips that he has looked for hope earlier in the scene, when he called for a looking glass to see if her breath would mist it, when he held a feather up to her lips to see if it would move, and when he imagined she had spoken. All of this tends to suggest that what he now sees on her lips is grounds for hope, whether real or imaginary, but, as the many arguments to the contrary attest, the implication is by no means certain.

What is certain, however, is that the audience has no evidence, other than Lear's word, that Cordelia is anything but dead and that the universe of the play is anything but a meaningless chaos in which a dog, a horse, a rat have life and a Cordelia no breath at all. No evidence, that is, other than Lear's word to the contrary—a word which, as surely as Edmund's final speeches, has the authenticity of an act. Lear has said that if Cordelia lives, "It is a chance which does redeem all sorrows / That ever I have felt" [V. iii. 267-68]. But it is difficult to see how, at this point in the play, mere chance would be adequate to redeem the tremendous weight of sorrows that Lear has felt. The audience has seen too much of the *Lear* universe to regard "a chance" as anything more than a random, and finally meaningless, piece of good luck. There has been far too much evidence that this is a "tough world" for one chance to convince the audience of the existence of an external, benevolent Providence intervening in human events to order human life. Lear, of course, would probably be convinced, for at this point Cordelia is all that matters to him. But Lear matters to the audience, and if Cordelia did live, the contingency of his faith upon a fortuitous occurrence would surely lessen, in their eyes, the triumph of his death. For as it stands, Lear's death is triumphant. It is triumphant because his final assertion of faith, like the delusions Edgar perpetrates and Edmund's final determination to do "some good in despite of mine own nature", is a completely creative act. To use the language of the play, it has no "reason" and no "cause": it is "something" that has come of "nothing". In seeing something on Cordelia's dead lips, Lear triumphs over the destruction that began in the first scene when he failed to see her love because she could not "heave [her] heart into [her] mouth" [I. i. 91-2].

In the *Lear* universe, it is the very absoluteness of the evil that gives force and meaning to the human actions which defy evil. To the extent that Shakespeare provided external grounds for Lear's assertion of faith, Lear's act in making it would be less than fully creative. The greater the evil over which Lear can triumph, the greater, obviously, the meaning of his triumph.

Earlier in the play . . . , a gentleman has told Lear, "Thou has one daughter / Who redeems nature from the general curse / Which twain have brought her to" [IV. vi. 205-07]. If the curse were anything less than general, so much less would be the creative triumph of the good that redeems it. (pp. 31-4)

Phyllis Rackin, "Delusion As Resolution in 'King Lear'," in Shakespeare Quarterly, *Vol. XXI, No. 1, Winter, 1970, pp. 29-34.*

RICHARD D. FLY (essay date 1972)

[In an essay similar to that written by Winifred M.T. Nowottny (1960), Fly regards Shakespeare's central concern in King Lear *as the presentation of moments of extreme suffering and horror that expose the limitations of language. Whereas such earlier critics as A. C. Bradley (1904) considered the breakdown between language and emotion in* King Lear *an indication of Shakespeare's failure to control his material, Fly identified it as crucial to the meaning of the play—an experiment Shakespeare successfully accomplishes by dramtically demonstrating, at numerous points, the conflict between the senses and expression when words are unable to convey the depth of thought and feeling the senses encounter. This breakdown of language Fly regards as only a step, although an important one, in the general movement towards chaos and disintegration that Shakespeare depicts in* King Lear.]

We soon become aware as we watch *King Lear* that we are being swept into a dynamic world that is in an irreversible state of general decomposition, that we are observing the carefully articulated but inexorable disintegration of a complex and manifold universe. Everywhere we look we are confronted with graphic images of a society in the throes of deterioration. In *Troilus and Cressida* Ulysses had spoken eloquently of the irrevocable consequences attending on the neglect of "degree"—"Take but degree away, untune that string, / And hark what discord follows" [I. iii. 109-10]; and now in *King Lear* Shakespeare seems to be tracing dramatically the unavoidable deflection into "chaos" that follows from Lear's initial act of untuning that magical string. . . . The world of *King Lear,* as the Fool never tires of reiterating, is turning topsy-turvy, and the subsequent encroachment of chaos creates in the play an atmosphere of deepening gloom and increasing fragmentation.

The degree to which Shakespeare is able to orchestrate and sustain the motif of the decay and fall of the ordered world testifies to the power behind the conception. For example, the fall can appear sudden and precipitous as in Gloucester's mutilation and symbolic fall from Edgar's Dover Cliff, or it can be more gradual and articulated as in Lear's protracted humiliation. . . . As Lear declines to "an O without a figure" [I. iv. 193] Shakespeare symbolizes his degeneration by means of the analogous action of Goneril's and Regan's gradual reduction of his knights from their initial wholeness of "100" to the diminished numbers of "50," "25," "10," "5," "1," until finally "nothing" remains of his partially symbolic consort. And the reduction of Lear's knightly retinue is only one instance of the general symphonic movement towards the state of "nothing" in the play. The world's disintegration is experienced also in the progression of the action from royal castle to stormy heath to beggarly hovel, in the change in weather from fair to cataclysmic storm, in the dramatically effective change in attire from princely "gorgeousness" to rags and even nakedness, in the rhythmic change of stage movements from ritual and ceremony to the spastic gyrations of devil-ridden madmen, in the auditory change from the solemn pronouncements of royal prerogative to the screams and fragmented utterances of figures of maddened and broken humanity, and in so many other radical reversals which have not gone unnoticed by students of the play. Such alterations of condition from the "best" to the "worst" (and even beyond) may take a variety of shapes, but the process of decomposition remains relatively the same: everything that was thought to distinguish a man from the beasts—his titles, language, "additions" and insignias of rank, social customs, properties, institutions, even names—is cast off or lost.

The symphonic nature of the play's general pattern of disintegration is remarkable, but it should be emphasized that it is Lear who both leads and focuses this progressive change in the human situation. When near the middle of the play Gloucester advises Kent to "take him in thy arms. . . . Take up thy master" [III. vi. 89-92], we may suddenly perceive how the action of the play has taken "Royal Lear" from his initial state of total freedom of motion into a more and more restricted range of movement: from his "castle" to "heath" to "hovel" to "sickbed" to the childlike enclosure of Kent's arms. And as the play continues Lear is seen on his "litter," in a "chair" from which he staggers to kneel at Cordelia's feet, on his way to "prison," and finally, staring with petrifying concentration upon Cordelia's motionless face and struggling against the unspeakable fact of her death. By means of such a brilliant chain of verbal and visual images Shakespeare depicts the gradual removal of space and freedom from his protagonist. . . . By carefully and consistently imaging the shrinkage of Lear's world until he is forced to gaze with heart-stopping horror onto the lips of his dead child, Shakespeare is able to give to Lear's journey the suggestion of something approaching demonic revelation. Lear's quest, that is, tends to lead him into successive encounters with images of his gradual deterioration until this *katagogic* progression is consummated in the vision of his final ruin.

Both the cosmos of *King Lear* and its focal character—both macrocosm and microcosm—participate in the process of general breakdown: "O ruined piece of nature"; Gloucester exclaims when suddenly confronted by the mad old king, "this great world / Shall so wear out to naught" [IV. vi. 134-35]. At the end of the play Lear can be referred to by Albany as "this great decay" [V. iii. 298], and the vision of Lear with his daughter dead in his arms can seem to Kent and Edgar as indicative of the macrocosmic "promised end" or "image of that horror" [V. iii. 264-65].

So pervasive is the sense of universal diminishment in *King Lear,* in fact, that it informs even those few moments of apparent calm and serenity in the play, such as Edgar's beautiful evocation of the view from Dover Cliff. Gloucester, horribly mutilated and in total despair, believes he is positioned on the "extreme verge" of that "cliff, whose high and bending head / Looks fearfully in the confinèd deep" [IV. i. 73-4]. The fearful nature of the imagined situation is deepened by Edgar's exclamation, "How fearful / And dizzy 'tis to cast one's eyes so low!" [IV. vi. 11-12]. Nevertheless, he proceeds calmly and minutely to describe the plunging perspective before them. (pp. 73-6)

Edgar's speech . . . not only participates in the play's general interest in patterns of diminishment but also suggests an important corollary to this motif: the play's deep concern with the exploration of areas of experience seemingly beyond the range of expression or apprehension. The suggestions in Edgar's speech of qualities beyond the capacities of the senses should bring to mind A. C. Bradley's provocative intuition

that "there is something in *King Lear*'s very essence which is at war with the senses," something that "not only refuses to reveal itself fully through the senses but seems to be almost in contradiction with their report" [see excerpt above, 1904]. Somewhat like Edgar peering from Dover Cliff, the play persistently creates diminishing perspectives which allow its characters and its audience to experience areas of "deficient sight" where the brain can turn and one is in danger of toppling down headlong. Bradley implies that the representation of this "essence" is impossible because of the inherent limitations of drama, and that the play is in this regard flawed by the grandeur of its own conception. But I hope to show that this need not be so; for as the lines [mentioned] above partly show, Shakespeare has learned how to use language and the stage so as to produce sudden sharply lit moments of illumination which function dramatically to give body and dimension to the surrounding darkness. Shakespeare can flood our minds with an awareness of this dark and formless essence by gradually bringing us, as in Edgar's speech, to exactly that vanishing point where the senses are forced to capitulate to that essence. (p. 78)

At climactic moments in the play the major characters experience violent juxtapositions of darkness and revelation. The shocking occasion of Gloucester's onstage blinding, for example, is closely followed by his recognition of Edgar's innocence. . . . A quite similar moment occurs at the end of the play when Kent chants "All's cheerless, dark, and deadly" [V. iii. 291] as the ruined figure of the old king stares with life-shattering concentration into the face of his dead daughter and catches glimpses of the truth that "She's dead as earth" [V. iii. 262]. In this manner, the major characters in the play are granted moments of revelation in close conjunction with the gloomy facts of irrevocable error and death. The physical cruelty that darkens the world of *King Lear* . . . is made to symbolize and illuminate the more terrible psychic cruelty which pervades the play. For the primary effect of these flashes of revelation is to give substance and dimension to the darkness out of which they arise; just as the mute tableau of the bodies of Lear and Cordelia at the play's conclusion throws into almost epiphanic clarity the dark nature of their experience. The "essence" of *Lear,* as Bradley says, may be "at war with the senses," but Shakespeare has perfected linguistic and dramatic techniques which permit him to make this warfare a coherent and crucial part of *King Lear*'s peculiar vision.

I am trying to show how the movement of *King Lear* leads by a masterfully orchestrated process of general deterioration to an encounter with a diabolic blackness that appears unfathomable—"a hell-black night" that threatens to engulf the more enlightened forms of humanity. Summing up what he considered to be *King Lear*'s vision, Swinburne said, "We have heard much and often from Theologians of the light of revelation, but the darkness of revelation is here" [see excerpt above, 1880]. Something like "the darkness of revelation," we might recall, occurs at the end of *Troilus* when "the dragon wing of night o'erspreads the earth" [V. viii. 17], plunging that play into apocalyptic darkness. *Timon,* too, concludes on a similarly dark note when Timon, gladly embracing the nothingness of death, exclaims, "Sun, hide thy beams; Timon hath done his reign" [V. i. 223]. The blackness one encounters at the end of these plays gives palpable form and body to the nihilistic vision that informs them. But only in *King Lear*—and this is at once a measure of its formal excellence and a mark of its superiority to *Troilus* and *Timon*—might one properly speak of its "darkness" of vision in terms of "revelation."

These basic aspects of *King Lear*'s vision which I have iso-lated—its focus on a dark reality beyond ordinary represen-tation, and its ability to produce graphic moments of revelation that give shape to that darkness—can be best observed in the linguistic and stylistic qualities of the play. Shakespeare's rep-resentation of human experience in *King Lear* is marked throughout by an intense desire to break through the supposed confines of verbal expression in an effort to confront directly areas of experience that lie beyond words. He seems to be exploiting language primarily to illustrate the final inadequacy of words when confronted by certain kinds of extreme expe-riences. And it was probably this peculiar aspect of the play William Hazlitt was responding to when he expressed his wish "that we could pass this play over, and say nothing about it. All that we can say must fall short of the subject; or even of what we ourselves conceive of it" [see excerpt above, 1817]. Hazlitt's modest demurrer involves more than a sterile and rhetorical use of the age-old "inexpressibility *topos*"; it points, I hope to show, to the heart of Shakespeare's conception of the *Lear* experience.

Throughout the play we are repeatedly compelled to observe language falling "short of the subject" and expression falling mute before the fact of extreme human anguish. Edgar, for instance, coming suddenly upon his blinded father, exclaims, "The worst is not / So long as we can say 'This is the worst'" [IV. i. 27-8]. The emphasis here falls on "say," for Edgar is rather brutally forced to acknowledge what the rest of us are gradually made to perceive, that "the worst" is a condition beyond the capacities of language. When Edgar later observes the "side-piercing sight" of the mad king's grotesque en-counter with his father, he seems to feel himself very close to the speechless condition: "I would not take this from report—it is, / And my heart breaks at it" [IV. iv. 141-42]. The pity and terror contained in the vision he sees can only be suggested indirectly and negatively by the neutral pointer, "it." But even this most slight concession to language is apparently an un-acceptable compromise to the full reality of suffering. For when the king reappears at the end of the play with the strangled Cordelia in his arms, Lear underscores the only legitimate use of language in a universe that can destroy so cruelly and mean-inglessly:

> Howl, howl, howl! O, you are men of stones.
> Had I your tongues and eyes, I'ld use them so
> That heaven's vault should crack.
>
> [V. iii. 258-60]

Shakespeare is repeatedly forcing the dramatic action to these exquisitely anguished moments of experience: moments which he then presents as validly transcending the scope of verbal representation—perhaps a kind of demonic sublime. And it is at these peak moments that we encounter most vividly the revelatory quality of the vision. As the boundaries of language collapse the audience and participants are suddenly given the visual objective equivalent—"the thing itself"—of our emo-tional state. Like Lear confronting the unspeakable fact of his daughter's death, language at these extreme moments can only point beyond itself and expire in silence. . . . (pp. 79-82)

By synchronizing language and stage action in this manner Shakespeare is able to pass beyond the usual confines of his art into areas of experience so intense as to be expressible only by mute suggestion. Perhaps only in *Troilus* and *Timon* does one encounter a similarly emphatic concern with propelling the dramatic action into states of being inaccessible to language. (p. 82)

King Lear differs from these two plays in that Shakespeare seems to have a firmer grasp of the serious problems involved in dramatizing the inadequacy of language. The play is deeply infused from the very outset with the conviction that language cannot do justice to strong feeling or, as Winifred Nowottny aptly puts its, "to afford any handhold against abysses of in-iquity and suffering" [see excerpt above, 1960]. Thus, the full force of the anarchic vision is concentrated and released at exactly those moments when language collapses under the pres-sure of an inexpressible reality—as, for example, Lear col-lapses verbally under the weight of Cordelia's senseless mur-der. . . . As in Lear's cases, and in Edgar's case above, the characters in *King Lear,* when suddenly face to face with ex-treme horror, are forced to fall back upon the barest bones of language, causing these humble and colorless words to be sud-denly charged with miraculously expressive power. . . . [A] powerful example can be found in Lear's sudden mind-crushing encounter with Poor Tom: "Didst thou give all to thy daugh-ters?" he says, "And art thou come to this?" [III. iv. 49-50]. Lear's simple stark question, as he sees the demon-haunted beggar and plunges immediately into madness, reminds one, in its quiet but powerful sublimity, that *King Lear* is exploring moments of experience so terrifying that their exact size is without discernible boundaries. The truly astonishing force of the word "this" in its terminal location at the end of the sentence, as Norman Maclean has demonstrated [see Addi-tional Bibliography], jolts us into a recognition that certain areas of experience have a legitimately unmentionable dimen-sion—spots of experience which, at least in the instantaneous flash of shocked recognition, "cannot be fully faced or exactly spoken of by those who must endure them." That terminal word *this* calls attention to the capitulation of language in the face of this horror and simultaneously directs attention to the visible "image" of this inexpressible horror, "the thing it-self," Poor Tom, the shameful *ne plus ultra* ["furthest possible point"] of human degradation. . . . Such moments, I believe, are graphic occasions of Swinburne's "darkness of revelation" when language falls silent before "the image of that horror" which *King Lear* repeatedly confronts. (pp. 82-4)

> *Richard D. Fly, "Revelations of Darkness: The Lan-guage of Silence in 'King Lear'," in* Bucknell Re-view, *Vol. XX, No. 3, Winter, 1972, pp. 73-92.*

BERNARD McELROY (essay date 1973)

[*McElroy undertakes an in-depth examination of the qualifying elements he claims make up the "Lear-world," which he describes as follows: it is "basic," characterized by an "often ferocious primal energy," tends towards "violently opposed extremes," depicts "shifting identities," and is "complementary." Like such earlier critics as Arthur Sewell (1951), Richard B. Sewall (1959), Maynard Mack (1965), and Phyllis Rackin (1970), McElroy be-lieves that both the so-called optimistic and pessimistic interpre-tations of* King Lear *fail to explain the exact nature of the play's ending. Instead, he suggests that Shakespeare purposely included the potentialities for both readings. For McElroy, this is what contributes more than anything else to the sense of* Lear's *com-plementariness.*]

More than any other of the mature tragedies, *King Lear* has conveyed the unmistakable impression of creating the unique universe in which it takes place. Critics as far removed from each other in time, technique, and point of view as A. C. Bradley, G. Wilson Knight, and Maynard Mack have all ana-lyzed the universe of *Lear* [see excerpts above, 1904, 1930, and 1965], and terms such as "*Lear*-world" or its equivalents

Act I. Scene i. Gloucester, Albany, Goneril, Cornwall, Lear, Burgundy, Cordelia, and France. By Ford Madox Brown (n.d.)

occur again and again in the work of dozens of commentators. Perhaps the reason for the ubiquitous feeling that the world of *King Lear* is self-created and self-defining is that life in that world is so far removed from literal experience not only of Shakespeare's England but also of any historical period which he might have thought he was recreating. In *Hamlet* and *Othello,* the dramatist relied heavily upon the conventions and trappings of life in Renaissance Europe, but, in *King Lear,* he seemed expressly to avoid transposing the old legend into contemporary times, in contrast to the author of the probable source play, *The True Chronicle History of King Leir.* Nor do I think he was attempting to recreate the atmosphere and life style of an ancient civilization, as he so manifestly was in the Roman plays. Rather, it seems to me, the setting of the *Lear*-world is an amalgam in which borrowings from several different eras and civilizations are fused for particular dramatic purposes, the two most important epochs being the Middle Ages and Shakespeare's own time. *King Lear* is, among many other things, a paradigm of the waning medieval hierarchy confronting the onset of pragmatic materialism. (p. 146)

In no play since *Richard II* did Shakespeare so conspicuously incorporate the forms, conventions, and ideas of medieval times. The most obvious examples are the pomp and pageantry of the distinctly feudal court in the first scene and the trial by combat in the last, both of which have close parallels in *Richard II.*

Far more significant, however, is the inclusion of so many medieval attitudes and ideas, beginning with the idea of kingship itself. When he first appears, Lear is an openly absolute monarch of the kind England had not seen in centuries (if, in fact, it had ever seen one). . . . Lear's word, like Richard's, is absolute law, no matter how rash or foolish that word may be. To disobey, or even to disagree, is tantamount to treason and risks the gravest consequences. Hence there is no middle ground between acquiescence and usurpation, a fact as instrumental to Lear's tragedy as to Richard's.

Moreover, the court which Lear convenes is unmistakably medieval and feudal. References to feudal bonds and the dues of hospitality abound throughout the play, and the concepts of familial, political, and social order reverenced by Lear, Cordelia, Gloucester, Edgar, Kent, and Albany are all firmly rooted in the world-picture of medieval times. In style and manner, too, the court of Lear has none of the elegance and polish which characterize a Renaissance court such as Claudius'. Kent is hardly depicted as having mastered the intricacies of Castiglione, and the principal nobles are warriors rather than courtiers. Moreover, the world outside Lear's court has a distinctly medieval cast, lacking the urban society and middle classes so prominent a part of subsequent civilizations. There are no capitals, no universities, no strolling players, no wealthy centers of commerce in *Lear* as there are in *Hamlet* and *Othello.* . . .

We are told that there is a town of Dover, but we never see it; action which is not set in a castle is set in wild, rustic fields, isolated heaths, in hovels, or in the tents of military camps.

Though Shakespeare drew heavily upon the Middle Ages for the setting of *King Lear,* he did not, as in *Richard II,* attempt to give a literal depiction of feudalism in action. Rather, starting from a medieval base, he made certain crucial additions and subtractions. The most significant of the subtractions is, of course, the deletion of the Christian orthodoxy from which the medieval hierarchy had drawn both its rationale and its viability. Instead, the *Lear*-world posits a dubious set of pagan gods drawn anachronistically from Greek and Roman mythology, and an anonymous though energetic principle of Nature. By removing the theological underpinnings of the family and the state, Shakespeare opens for exploration the possibility that such institutions rest not upon immutable order and objective truth, but upon purely human assumptions which sway not as they have power but as they are suffered.

If the removal of the theological basis of hierarchy is Shakespeare's principal subtraction from the basically medieval setting of *Lear,* his most significant addition is the inclusion of an approach to life more characteristic of Renaissance political philosophy than of the court of Edward the Confessor. This view, much in the air in Shakespeare's day, is preached by Edmund and practiced by him, Goneril, Regan, Cornwall, and Oswald. The conflict between good and evil characters is in large measure a conflict between medieval idealism and Renaissance pragmatism. The good characters are deeply concerned about the way things should be, while the wicked ones keep an unblinking eye upon the way things are. Moreover, most members of the good faction, especially Lear, begin with an assumption that there is no discrepancy between the way things should be and the way things are, while the wicked ones, especially Edmund, are acutely aware of the discrepancy and alert to turn it to their advantage.

An understanding of the setting of *King Lear* as an amalgam of medieval and Renaissance cultures and world-views points the way to the definition of those qualities of the *Lear*-world which . . . loom most important. I would summarize them as follows:

> The *Lear*-world is very basic.
> It is charged at every level with an often ferocious primal energy.
> It tends always toward violently opposed extremes.
> It is a world of constantly shifting identities.
> The *Lear*-world is complementary.

"Basic" is perhaps a peculiar word to apply to the world of a play, but I can think of no other which better describes the way that all things in this tragedy, including the dramaturgy itself, have been stripped down, literally, to the essentials. The conflicts and issues are of the most basic kind, centering on the two most fundamental units of society, the family and the state. Moreover, the conflicts which break out within these two basic units are not merely disruptive but tend to annihilate the institutions themselves. The sources of conflict are essential to the human condition and transcend particular details of time, place, or systems of social organization: age versus youth, individualism versus communality, order versus anarchy, moral significance versus emptiness and absurdity, supernaturalism versus empiricism, wealth versus poverty, justice versus injustice, endurance versus despair or rebellion, reverence for tradition versus scorn for convention—the list could be con-

siderably lengthened. Everything is reduced to the lowest denominator for presentation with the utmost clarity and power. From the first scene onward, the action strives relentlessly to peel away layer upon layer of all that is incidental or merely assumed, and to arrive at the bedrock of absolute reality—the true identity of man, the real nature of society, the cause of evil, the value of existing at all. Nothing, absolutely nothing, is given or assumed in the *Lear*-world. Any course of action is judged not upon the correctness of its principles, but upon the consequences it produces. Each belief, system, and individual identity must stand the proof of action, and if it cannot stand that test, not even its right to exist is granted.

The basicness of the *Lear*-world is everywhere evident in the dramaturgy. If the action of *Hamlet* may properly be called elliptical, *King Lear* is unstintingly linear, proceeding without digression or abatement from its startlingly abrupt beginning to its apocalyptic end. Time and space are drastically compressed so that incidents which would require many months seem to take place in a matter of days or even of hours. As if driven by storms and demons, the action plunges headlong to its conclusion. So economical is the dramaturgy of *Lear* that many of its most memorable points are made not through spoken words but through a series of intense visual images. The action is ingeniously wrought to produce situations which I think may be properly called visual metaphors, situations which assume emblematic meaning and communicate directly through the eye, largely bypassing language. For example, there is the mock trial in which a madman, a naked beggar, and a fool sit in judgment on a joint stool, or the image of the madman leading the blind man. Tom O'Bedlam himself becomes such a visual metaphor in Lear's eyes, and in ours, when the King asks us to consider him well. The image of a mad king outlandishly decked and crowned with wild flowers, presiding over a wholly imaginary kingdom is another such metaphor which conveys at least as much meaning visually as by what is spoken. And in the final scene, the stage-direction, "Enter Lear, with Cordelia in his arms," says all that can be said, leaving as the only possible elaboration Lear's inarticulate "Howl, howl, howl!" [V. iii. 258].

In the *Lear*-world, nothing is done either in leisure or in moderation. Violent energy charges the action, the characterization, and the imagery, and is apparent at all levels—in human affairs, in the natural elements, and in the heavens as variously envisioned by Lear, Edmund, and Gloucester. More often than not, the enormous energy of the *Lear*-world is expended in disruption and upheaval. Of course, the most obvious manifestation of violent, primal energies is the storm which rages throughout six of the central scenes; no ordinary tempest this, it seems almost to possess the apocalyptic qualities Lear demands of it. Something of the same energy seems to charge every one of the major characters, conferring upon them extraordinary strength either to inflict or to endure. . . . Even suffering, that most characteristic activity of the *Lear*-world, is imbued with the energy of the *Lear*-world. Gloucester's despair is extraordinarily vigorous; rather than quietly stab or hang himself, he will walk to Dover, climb a hill, address the gods, and hurl himself from a cliff. (pp. 147-52)

The metaphysical universe of *King Lear* is also imbued with the primal force we find in the natural elements and in the characters. In marked contrast to *Othello* and *Macbeth*, there is no clearly defined metaphysical system presumed in the world of *King Lear;* rather, each of the major characters attempts to project upon a neutral and inscrutable universe a particular concept of the forces which presumably govern it. Each defines the universe differently, but they all impute to it the energy and force so characteristic of the play. The King's gods, like the rhetoric of his invocations, have a distinctly Old Testament character, despite the surface trapping of classical paganism. . . . The gods that Gloucester ultimately comes to believe in torture and kill men for their savage sport. The goddess Nature, to whom Edmund's services are bound, is cast in his own energetic image:

> Who, in the lusty stealth of nature, take
> More composition and fierce quality
> Than doth, within a dull, stale, tirèd, bed,
> Go to th' creating a whole tribe of fops
> Got 'tween asleep and wake?
>
> [I. ii. 11-15]

As far as he is concerned, it is the very energy of nature that renders him superior to his conventional, legitimate brother. The values of Christianity—charity, forgiveness, compassion—we identify with Cordelia, but in her they are raised to the status of heroic virtue, the stuff that martyrs are made of. And, of course, towering over all this turbulent and energetic world is the titanic energy of Lear himself—Lear, with his implacable "constant will," vehemently insisting that things be as he demands or cease to be at all; Lear, flying into apocalyptic rages, thundering at the elements, in madness marshalling imaginary forces and furiously indicting his imaginary subjects, and finally, at the threshold of death, killing the rugged soldier Edmund has bribed to hang Cordelia and bearing her body from the prison.

Because the issues of the *Lear*-world are the most basic in human experience, and because the exploration of these issues is animated by surging, primal energy, all elements in the world of the play seem to be pushed almost from the outset to violently conflicting extremes. The middle-ground, which forms so much of life in even turbulent or disruptive times, is eliminated entirely, and life seems to be lived at one or another of its outermost limits. For instance, one main line of development is the conflict between youth and age, and the *Lear*-world seems to be populated largely by people who are either very old or fairly young. (pp. 152-53)

So intent was Shakespeare upon emblemizing the conflict between youth and age by pushing both to extremes and eliminating the middle that he presented us with a rather peculiar family. Lear is over eighty, yet he has only three daughters, the youngest of whom is not yet married and the eldest of whom has not yet borne children. That is, we may assume the dramatist intended them to be played as ranging in age from the late teens to perhaps the middle twenties. While such a situation is not impossible, it is most certainly not usual, especially in royal families. This is not in the least to worry the question of how many wives had King Lear, a question the play does not encourage or permit us to ask. The point is that Shakespeare has set young daughters against a father easily old enough to be their great-grandfather in order to sharpen the basic conflict by pushing it to its extremes. (p. 154)

The same emphasis upon extremes characterizes the social situation of the *Lear*-world. The two boundaries of the social scale are the absolute top and the absolute bottom, royalty and penury, the king and the naked beggar. Toward one or another of these extremes every one of the major characters is inexorably drawn. Goneril, Regan, Edmund, Cornwall, and initially perhaps Albany are locked in a life and death struggle for possession of no less than all. Conversely, when Lear, Cordelia, Gloucester, Kent, and Edgar fall upon ill fortune, they are all reduced, in one way or another to

> the basest and most poorest shape
> That ever penury, in contempt of man,
> Brought near to beast.
>
> [II. iii. 7-9]

Vulnerable, despised, humiliated, and homeless, they all at one time or another possess "nothing," that word that echoes so sepulchrally throughout the world of the play. The epitome of these extremes is Lear himself, who goes with dizzying speed from the pomp and power of the first scene to the desolation of the heath, where he attempts to rip off his "lendings" and become the thing itself, thus traversing the whole social spectrum of the *Lear*-world.

As with the conflict between youth and age, the middle ground of the social spectrum, which might lend some balance and normalcy to the *Lear*-world, has been almost entirely omitted. The nobles are shut up in their castles and the beggars are shut out on the heath. The minor characters, who in the histories and comedies, and in such tragedies as *Hamlet,* lend balance and proportion to the play-world, are kept nameless and faceless in *King Lear*—a gentleman, an officer, servants to Cornwall, an old man, a doctor, a herald. Their appearances are brief and their roles are transparently functional; they are not individuated by the quirks their counterparts so frequently display in the rest of the canon. They are given no opportunity to distract our attention from the conflict between the two significant extremes, king and beggar.

As I suggested at the beginning of this [discussion], the two concepts of social and political organization depicted in *King Lear* are also extreme examples of the political outlooks which coexisted in an uneasy and doomed compromise in Shakespeare's England. In the early scenes of the play, the older hierarchical system is pushed to its extreme and falters. Age and position are given absolute sway, and act with incredible folly. Conversely, in the later scenes, the new order of individualism and ruthless opportunism is also pushed to its extreme, and it, too, falters. Neither the old nor the new can stand the proof of action: when their principles are followed with single-minded determination to their logical conclusions, both finally destroy themselves.

The emotions and attitudes which the various characters register also shun moderation to epitomize extremes. Thus we have the bestial cruelty of Cornwall against the angelic kindness of Cordelia, the apocalyptic rage of Lear against the superhuman patience of Edgar. Kent's loyalty is completely without reservation while Edmund's opportunism is utterly without scruple. Gloucester's despair is abysmal and unmitigated, yet hope is indomitable and unquenchable in the *Lear*-world even at its worst. Joy, what there is of it in this play, is ecstatic, almost celestial, while the sorrow which inevitably displaces it is such as flesh and blood should not be called upon to bear. Frequently the two are placed in stark contrast within a single scene or even within a single speech, as in Lear's comparison of Cordelia to a soul in bliss while he is bound upon a wheel of fire, or in the description of Gloucester's death, or in Lear's final agony where illusory joy is juxtaposed against the all too factual sorrow.

Many critics . . . have pointed out the importance of relatedness in the play; but, as Mack has observed, the problem of identity precedes the problem of relatedness. The basic question is not "how is this related to that," but rather, "exactly what is it that is related to what?" What is a king? What is a father? What is "natural"? Who is a madman? Who is blind? Who is a fool? Is identity fixed and immutable or is it arbitrary and fragile, built from the curiosity of nations and plague of custom and resting upon a foundation of nothing? What is man himself? These questions underlie the rapid, frequent shifts of identity and the search for the bedrock of identity which form such an important part of the action.

Edmund's identity, for instance, is self-defined and self-imposed, and depends upon his ability to manipulate external circumstances to his advantage. He means to become a self-made man in the most literal sense of the term. Man, in his view, starts out with what nature has given him, and what he makes of it is entirely in his own hands. Edmund considers himself distinctly superior raw material, but the identity which the curiosity of nations and the plague of custom have assigned him is wholly unsatisfactory. He makes a steady climb up the social scale of the *Lear*-world, and throughout his changes in fortune, his sense of his own identity never falters as long as his theory of self-definition works out well. (pp. 155-58)

Edgar's career is the opposite of his brother's. He plummets from the rather comfortable position of heir to an earldom to that of a hunted criminal, and rises again agonizingly back to the earldom and perhaps to the throne itself. Superimposed upon this quick fall and slow rise in fortunes is a startling progression of disguises and incognito appearances. . . . As Edgar, son of Gloucester, he is important to the play, but rather uninteresting in himself. His disguises, however, are extraordinary both in conception and execution, and the first identity he assumes, the bare, forked animal, unaccommodated man, becomes a central image of the play. After his meeting with his blind father, his personae progress through peasant, soldier, knight incognito, and perhaps to king. The rapid fall and slow rise of his fortunes suggest that the *Lear*-world, having been dismantled from the top down, must be reassembled slowly and painfully from the bottom up. Moreover, the progression of assumed identities portrays the narrow distance between nobleman and beggar, accommodated man and the forked animal, and provides the context for the most sweeping question of identity which the play poses: "Is man no more than this?" [III. iv. 102-03]. When Lear asks us to consider him well, what we see is not a disguised noble whom the King mistakenly thinks a real Bedlam beggar; we see what Lear sees, man stripped of all his sophistications.

For Gloucester, the problem of identity is twofold, discovering his own identity and correctly identifying the world around him. When we first see Gloucester, he fairly exudes self-satisfaction, making jokes about his earlier exploits and congratulating himself on his own magnanimity. After the agony of his ordeal, however, he redefines the man he was as "the superfluous and lust-dieted man . . . that will not see / Because he does not feel" [IV. i. 67-9]. . . . The problem of correctly identifying external reality is brilliantly dramatized by the conjunction of Gloucester's blindness and Edgar's disguise. Throughout his search for the correct identity of things, Gloucester takes the man who guides him for a naked beggar, one whose speech is suddenly improved, a grotesque fiend, a poor man made tame by fortune's blows, and a trusty peasant, before correctly perceiving him as the man whom he had wanted to encounter more than anyone in the world. So, too, in the great meeting between Lear and Gloucester, blindness, madness, and the inversion of values are all focused upon the

problem of perceiving the true identity of those in the *Lear*-world, of seeing how the world goes and being able to distinguish which is the justice and which the thief.

The problem of identity receives its fullest treatment in the main plot, centering on the figure of Lear. "He hath ever but slenderly known himself" [I. i. 293-94], we are told of him early in the action. Yet, when he first appears, Lear is absolutely certain about who he is: he is *The King*. That the king may be a thing of nothing would never occur to him, and, when it proves to be the case, his identity, which he has defined largely in terms of his place in a supposedly immutable hierarchy, begins rapidly to disintegrate. . . . The Fool has a good deal to say on the subject of Lear's identity, and saying it is one of the principal functions of this fascinating character. Lear has made his daughters his mothers, the Fool informs him in an image both comic and cruel; he has exchanged his position as parent for that of a child awaiting chastisement. The King is by turns a bitter fool, Lear's shadow, a shealed peascod, and, finally, nothing. The destruction of Lear's subjective world, so overwhelmingly complete, begins with the destruction of his identity.

The final quality of the *Lear*-world which I propose to consider here is its complementarity, the way in which Gloucester's "And that's true too" [V. ii. 11], sounds a note which reverberates throughout the length and breadth of the drama. There is no more striking evidence of the complementarity of *King Lear* than the remarkable division of the criticism into two mutually exclusive factions. Of course, all the plays of Shakespeare engender varying interpretations, and there seem to be as many readings of *Hamlet* as there are critics who have commented upon it. But only in the case of *Lear* is criticism so sharply divided between an interpretation which sees it as the most glorious and transcendent dream of human redemption ever conceived, and one that sees it as the most unstintingly pessimistic indictment of the absurd human condition ever written. . . . It seems to me that the only plausible reason for this phenomenon is that *King Lear* embodies two views of life's potentials, and that these views or attitudes are diametrically opposed in such a way that each must logically exclude the other. Yet, there they exist together, side by side, in perfect artistic unity and harmony in the play. The dreadful way things have of working out in the *Lear*-world never allows us to dismiss the possibility that the world as seen by Edmund and Cornwall, by Gloucester in despair and by Lear in madness is, in fact, the *Lear*-world as it really is. Yet, at the same time that this abominable vision is being forced upon us most relentlessly, we are also kept aware of the instrinsic values represented by Cordelia, Edgar, Kent, and by Lear after the reconciliation.

If in one sense *King Lear* is the confrontation between order and chaos, between age and youth, between the waning Middle Ages and ascendant modernism, in a much more fundamental sense it is the confrontation between ethics and experience. Ethics and experience are the two principal poles of the *Lear* dialectic, and that dialectic is complementary in that both elements have inexorable demands to make and there is no resolution or meeting ground between them. As the play clearly demonstrates, there must be ethics if life is to continue, let alone be endurable. But the play no less clearly demonstrates that at every turn experience is an overmatch for ethical values. Though Edgar does kill Edmund and the wicked characters do prey upon themselves like monsters of the deep, yet a dog, a horse, a rat *has* life and Cordelia no breath at all. The *Lear* dialectic forces us at once to assent to both the necessity and intrinsic worth of ethical values, but at the same time to contemplate the utter inability of such values to cope with experience. Thus it seems to me that ''optimism'' and ''pessimism'' as terms to describe the vision behind *Lear* are wholly beside the point. Neither one is capable of including the whole picture. (pp. 158-62)

A comparatively minor incident demonstrates, perhaps even better than Gloucester's ''And that's true too,'' the complementary mode of vision which underlies the tragedy. I refer to the scene in which a messenger reports to Albany the death of Cornwall:

> MESSENGER: O, my good lord, the Duke of Cornwall's
>   dead,
>   Slain by his servant, going to put out
>   The other eye of Gloucester.
> ALBANY: Gloucester's eyes?
> MESSENGER: A servant that he bred, thrilled with
>   remorse,
>   Opposed against the act, bending his sword
>   To his great master; who, thereat enraged,
>   Flew on him, and amongst them felled him dead;
>   But not without that harmful stroke which since
>   Hath plucked him after.
> ALBANY: This shows you are above,
>   You justicers, that these our nether crimes
>   So speedily can venge. But, O poor Gloucester,
>   Lost he his other eye?
> MESSENGER: Both, both, my lord.
>
>   [IV. ii. 70-81]

There is justice in Cornwall's death, though it is achieved not by the supernatural forces envisioned by Albany, but by the common humanity of the servant, thrilled with remorse and opposed against the deed, an opposition which we have no alternative but to admire and share. Yet Gloucester lost both eyes. The promptings of outraged humanity and the ineffectuality of those promptings in experience are the poles of the *Lear* dialectic. From the tension between them arise other complementary oppositions, all centered upon the principal problem of the *Lear*-world, how is existence to be endured. (p. 163)

> *Bernard McElroy, "'King Lear': The Tempest in the Mind," in his* Shakespeare's Mature Tragedies, *Princeton University Press, 1973, pp. 145-205.*

RONALD F. MILLER (essay date 1975)

[*Miller claims that even though numerous critics have commented on the combination of comedy and tragedy in* King Lear, *most notably Percy Bysshe Shelley (1821), Hermann Ulrici (1839), G. Wilson Knight (1930), and Jan Kott (1964), no one has considered the play strictly as a comedy, or rather, as an anticomedy or antipastoral romance which utilizes traditional elements from the comic mode but which subverts the conventional comic ending and offers instead "pain and destruction." Miller supports this hypothesis, and he does so by focusing primarily on the play's numerous improbabilities, the lack of inevitability in its conclusion, and those elements natural to the comic form incorporated in the play, such as its fairytale beginning, the double plot, the use of the Fool, the lack of substantial motivation for the characters, the parody of the Green World, and the "gratuitous" death of Cordelia.*]

King Lear, I would argue, is from a *formal* standpoint a comedy, deriving much of its incomparable power from a radical tension between the emotional texture of the events and the generic form into which the events have been cast. The fairytale beginning, the double plot, the humor of the Fool, the lack of proper motivation, the parody of the Green World, the gratuitous death of Cordelia—anomalies noted by countless critics—are all not simply comic elements embedded in a tragic structure; they are outward signs of Shakespeare's overall strategy of using the comic form to delineate a terrible vision, not the traditional comic image of life triumphant over folly and chance, but quite the opposite. Certainly in this age of Wittgenstein and after it should be superfluous to take too much time conceding that other critics concerned with tragic visions or tragic myths or tragic points of view can quite properly label the play a tragedy. The common reader calls *King Lear* a tragedy, and revisionism can be justified, if at all, only because the relationship between *King Lear* and comedy is far less convoluted than has been suggested by critics interesting themselves primarily with theme. . . .

Incidental comic motifs and devices can of course crop up anywhere in a work to alter the texture or swell a scene or modify the movement of events; in this they differ little from any other set of arrows in a writer's quiver. But overall generic identity must perforce be established rather quickly, for readers and spectators must from the first know, explicitly or intuitively, the requisite mode for receiving and ordering the data. Those paradigms which have so much concerned generic critics since Aristotle are best treated as ex post facto abstractions, consequences of more fundamental clusters of attitudes which enable us to accept certain conventionalities or to assume the necessary moral or intellectual stances toward words and events. (p. 3)

If then we look at the first act of *King Lear,* pretending for a moment to be unaware of the catastrophe to come, matters take on an interesting coloration. The fairy-tale setting, the abrupt and virtually unmotivated actions will be seen as more than noteworthy anomalies or stumbling blocks for the ingenious critic to explain away. These are comic signals generating comic expectations which are after a fashion satisfied. Anyone familiar with romantic comedy should feel right at home. Two rash old men, according to the fairy-tale manner, reject their good children in favor of their bad. One, a choleric humor figure of sorts, first mistakes noble reticence for lack of affection and flattery for love and almost immediately begins to reap the consequences of his rashness while in the company of a wise fool who uses his folly like a stalking horse to take his master to task again and again for imprudence. Meanwhile, back in the other plot the second old man, more senile than conventionally humorous, is incited to folly by a witty Vice figure who persists in preaching the catechism of amorality whenever everyone else is off the stage. The story line involving the choleric old man begins the awaited complications when one of the hypocritical elder daughters (as could have been predicted by anyone familiar with comedy) refuses to back up her flatteries with deeds, and the act ends in the conventional comic disorder with the evil elder daughter prissily complaining about riot in her house and the old man exploding once more with a malediction which parallels exactly the exaggerated curse he had earlier laid upon his reticent but loving younger child.

Obviously, this is hardly an adequate representation of the first act of *King Lear;* all too well it resembles Tolstoy's famous retellings to demonstrate the general absurdity of Shakespear-ean drama [see excerpt above, 1906]. But I am hard-pressed to say exactly at what point the representation falsifies. The mood is wrong, certainly; yet how much do we view the actions in the first act in the shadow of the horror we know is coming? All the conventional signals—the humor figure, the double plot, the rhetoric out of proportion to stimulus, the precipitate beginning—invite other expectations. Perhaps there is in Gon-eril's responses a steely tone hinting of deeper matters, but how much do these intimations weigh when balanced against the broader comic gestures? In fact, the extraordinary power of the first act seems precisely attributable to this disjunction between the insistent comic surface and the sinister hints of what will come. . . . (pp. 4-5)

Nothing could be easier than to imagine a conventional comedy built upon the first act of *King Lear*. Molière could hardly have failed with such material. We would expect the complications to continue and the two plots to begin to interact more strongly. Society and good sense would soon initiate a countermove-ment, and, after several surprises and quick reversals, Cordelia and Edgar would be restored and, at the end, married. Goneril and Regan would get their comeuppance, and Edmund, if not actually converted, might well wander off like Jaques in witty chagrin. We might expect a strategy of disguise on the part of counterattacking good sense, and much of the wisdom to be articulated in the humor of the Fool. Since this is Shakespeare, the conversion of the *senex iratus* figures might well occur amid some kind of pastoral landscape.

Except for the marriage, which Nahum Tate willingly supplied, each of these expectations is met, though in ways that bring little enough delight to anyone. We could well be observing the photographic negative of a pastoral comedy; the shapes are there, but black and white have eerily been transposed. This is more than to say, after Maynard Mack, that the pastoral romance is a "defining source" behind *King Lear* [see excerpt above, 1965]. The play *is* a pastoral romance—or better yet, we might say with Mack that it is "the greatest anti-pastoral ever penned." So long as we acknowledge that an inversion of a comic pattern is structurally quite another thing than trag-edy.

If we look back to the beginning to seek for tragic signals instead, we will find little more than an ominous and ultimately ambiguous tone. Experience with other plays conventionally termed tragic would lead us to expect a fairly extensive ex-position making probable (in the Aristotelian sense) the choices and actions moving toward the tragic end. In *Julius Caesar* the idealism and the personal attachments of Brutus are ex-plored at considerable length, so we may appreciate in full his decision to participate in the events at the Capitol. In *Hamlet*, we are shown the young Prince despondent and withdrawn before we see the Ghost give him his difficult charge to action. The first act of *Macbeth*, for all its precipitate speed, concerns itself mostly with revealing the individual and corporate natures of the Thane of Glamis and his wife. *Othello*, perhaps the tragedy with the cleanest, what might be called the most So-phoclean line of action in the last three acts, spends the first two in tangential matters, shoring up the probability of an action which (as numerous critics attest) teeters on the edge of im-plausibility anyway.

Though the list might be extended almost indefinitely and to other tragic poets, the principle involved seems relatively plain: in order to produce that peculiar blend of dread and sympathy characteristic of tragedy, there must be a well-developed sit-

uation out of which the events proceed, to all appearances inexorably. . . . In many ways, indeed, the actual tragic de-velopment is no more than a corollary to the exposition; even the much-debated tragic mistake of traditional analysis (*ha-martia*: "missing the mark") cannot be the final cause of the fall, though it may well be the immediate and efficient cause of the disaster which comes down upon the hero's head. The egregious and singular mistake—if the play is cooperative enough to supply one—will of necessity be that very event which the exposition was first of all intended to make probable. We accept the mistake as significant because we have been shown that the mistake is precisely the sort of error the protagonist *would* make. To step out into the street and be run over by a truck is perhaps always a considerable mistake, but not a tragic one unless an exposition has prepared us to accept the truck or the driver as integral to the situation confronting the protagonist, and to see the circumstances leading to his stepping out as arising from his distinctive personal nature. (pp. 5-7)

Yet if we turn to *King Lear* for such causal preparations, we find instead—nothing. Neither the old King's outburst against Cordelia nor his choice to stage a public love-test are made probable. They are perhaps, as some apologists have argued, at least conceivable; but Shakespeare makes no attempt to have them seem likely, much less inevitable. It might be objected that so obvious a piece of folk-lore demands no probabilities. Perhaps it doesn't—unless you wish to build a tragic plot out of it, and Shakespeare was never in other cases shy about changing a story to suit his intents. Consider the way he altered the setting for Cinthio's tale of Othello, making a strange match psychologically understandable. Furthermore, it is easy to imagine what would be required to conform the Lear story to the tragic pattern. Lear's willfulness would first be illustrated in another, suitably minor context. His affection for Cordelia would be shown to be intense, though rendered unstable by his inability to separate his roles of king and father. Goneril and Regan would be revealed as smoothly hypocritical and Cordelia as tender but abrupt, her father's daughter. Lear could then be seen rather childishly planning a public ceremony to add pomp to his private designs. Who can doubt that at this late stage in his career, Shakespeare could had he wished have realized these antecedents in scenes full of action and interest? The fatal mistake would then take on a proper inevitability, and critics would have little temptation to extrapolate back from the events to imagined situations, in order in turn to make probable the events themselves.

The deed itself, pure and simple, is the donnee of *King Lear*. To find analogous beginnings we must turn to Shakespeare's comedies. Surprisingly enough, these works begin almost uni-formly with an unprepared-for piece of violence or folly. We ask in vain why Egeus would willingly condemn his daughter to death for the sake of Demetrius, or why Oliver is moved to try to burn Orlando in his lodging, or why a set of healthy young men, less violently though no less rashly, would swear to forsake the world for the cold rigors of the academy. Even when an explanation is given, as in the case of the laws of the Ephesians against the Syracusans in *The Comedy of Errors,* the emphasis falls not on the logic of the situation but on its enormity. . . . Since improbabilities are part and parcel of the conventional comic expectations, few would complain: we all know the focus will fall not upon the inexplicable action but upon the comic potential to be discovered in the upcoming complications. Any unwillingness to grant the generic con-ventions will immediately result in the asking of unanswerable questions. Surely the unfatherly harshness of Egeus, no less than that of Lear, could be psychoanalyzed as a proper tragic flaw, and a flaw none too different from some conventionally attributed to the latter.

And even were we to ignore the problems of motivation in the generative event, there is still difficulty in fitting the King into the pattern of the tragic hero. After the first act and his willful deed, as A. C. Bradley has noted, he is a man more acted upon than acting. He seems more like someone who foolishly leans against a prop and brings his house crashing down around his head than a hero whose character is the agency leading him inexorably to his fall. As a matter of fact, only his decision to place himself in Regan's care—which eventuates in his being turned out onto the heath—of *all* his subsequent decisions has any effect on the action whatsoever. Neither his much-commented-upon recognition of common humanity out in the storm nor the awakening of his humility and love before Cordelia has any issue in action; for all we can tell Lear would have wandered off to Dover and Cordelia would have perished had these transcendent moments never occurred. The marked contrast between Lear and the other putatively tragic figures of Shakespeare, Romeo to Brutus to Coriolanus and everyone in between, should be obvious. What other tragic figure dies from a chance occurrence, unprepared for by the march of previous events? Although Romeo's and Juliet's deaths seem in some ways comparable, they at least kill themselves in direct response to an impulsive passion which has motivated the previous action, and Juliet does have complicity in the scheme that didn't quite work out. And yet the arbitrariness of the undelivered message in the earlier play has often been censured as a flaw, whereas the far more capricious twist that brings death to the King seems to be accepted by critics (albeit often uncomfortably) as somehow the crowning touch to the overall design. (pp. 7-9)

The traditional comic myth portrays life triumphant; spring overcomes winter, the threat to society and good sense is frustrated, chaos and complication miraculously result in those good turns which the audience has willed all along. As Susanne Langer observes, tragedy is the image of Fate whereas comedy is the image of Fortune. The various comic conventions . . . have survived primarily because they promote this sense of beneficent fortune. But when these conventions appear accompanied by pain and destruction, a terrible suggestion is made that life may well not triumph after all, that fortune may well be inimical to our hopes and our feelings. The essentially societal perspective of comedy, usually so affirmative in its implications, has a potential for generalizing this dark vision in a way that the more individualized perspective of tragedy cannot match.

This is shown best by the way the actions of *King Lear* proceed. As was discussed earlier, tragic action is a convergent process; even seemingly chance events take on an aura of inevitability when immersed in the concatenated movement toward the *telos* of the fated end. After the initial impulse in comic plots, however, the complications diverge; they expand rather arbitrarily until some event, almost always signalling the frustration of the original anti-comic threat, brings the expansion to a halt. Though the conventionally fortunate end to the complications is doubtlessly anticipated by every spectator, there is little sense of any ineluctable necessity at work making us view the action as a kind of glacial slide toward the anticipated marriage and reconciliation. I would go so far as to speculate that in comedy the closing on the awaited tonic chord is felt to be so much the more gratifying if it comes by way of an unexpected mod-

ulation. This intimate relation between the comic and the contingent could hardly be better indicated than by the arbitrary strokes ending comedies as diverse as *Tartuffe, The Winter's Tale,* and *Pygmalion.* The latter is particularly instructive, since the finale surprises us by overturning even the comic convention of marriage between principals. I doubt if any tragic plot could survive so willful a resolution. We apparently delight in being "had" by the comic poet, perhaps because the unexpected and the improbable, working always in the long run for the good, are recurrent emblems of the benevolence of the comic world. Traditionally, the comic poet, unaided and unfettered by the probabilities of tragedy, has demonstrated his skill through the ingenuity he displays in uncovering fantastic possibilities inherent in the compounding events.

An unbiased examination of the last four acts of *King Lear* will reveal the action is, like that of the romantic comedies, a fabric of chance events, wandering encounters, unmotivated acts, concealed identities, surprise endings, and gestures leading nowhere. . . . In his remarks in the first lecture on *Lear,* Bradley spends about four or five pages worrying over the inconsistencies, improbabilities, and non sequiturs in the action [see excerpt above, 1904]. Though the totally unexpected last scene seems to present the most puzzling "dramatic flaw" of them all, he finds the play rife with comparable unmotivated events. Why shouldn't Edgar and Kent have revealed themselves earlier, he wonders. Why does everyone happen to descend upon Gloucester's castle the night of the storm? Why does the converted Edmund delay in reversing his orders? And so on. No doubt Shakespeare was never fastidious about plot logic, but this seems to exceed mere carelessness. Bradley could only conclude "that in *King Lear* Shakespeare was less concerned than usual with dramatic fitness." No doubt most of the events Bradley complained of *could* have occurred; Bradley, child of Aristotle, wanted to know why they *should* occur, and that question *King Lear* will never answer.

But on one level the problem is even more radical than Bradley suggests. His complaints deal with unaswerable questions about central moments of the play, not with mere loose ends like the puzzle of Lady Macbeth's children or of Cassio's wife but with events crucial to the sequence of actions. The indispensable gathering at Gloucester's castle, for instance, seems the merest chance. Cornwall and Regan just happen to be passing through on the way home . . . ; Kent and Oswald have been dispatched to intercept them at the castle (for no apparent reason, since Goneril and Lear hotly follow after); and Edgar happens to be playing madman in the vicinity so he can chance upon Lear and, later, upon his father. It might have been otherwise; it was not, and Gloucester is blinded and Lear locked out to go mad. We might as soon ask of *A Midsummer Night's Dream* why the fairies, the mechanicals, and the lovers all troop to the same precincts of the forest near Athens. No doubt both that comedy and *King Lear* progress by a logic of their own, but the logic is thematic and affective, not causal; and therein lies all the difference.

Thus when *King Lear* progresses from improbability to chance meeting to unlikely event, we are observing a comic action stumble its way to catastrophe. Two old men leap to rash conclusions and set off, after the comic pattern, a widening circle of repercussions. . . . Shakespeare's usual comic devices—the journey into nature, the repudiation of the court, the fool, the rash decision, the disguisings, the chance encounters, the children good and bad, and the rest—all reveal a frightening potential. The pastoral landscape becomes the dark night on the heath, rustic simplicity becomes nakedness and squalor, the jokes of the fool become searing insights, and the evil children turn out to be not the petty, malicious step-daughters of *Cinderella* nor such easily thwarted siblings as Oliver or Don John, but Goneril and Regan, who shut their father out to die in the storm, and Edmund, who for advancement gives his father over to torture before ordering his death. Yet apparently no *necessity* obtains for any of this; chance would have it so, and such is the dark underside of comedy. Nahum Tate could affix his happy ending to *King Lear* because there is no structural reason why a romantic ''anticomedy'' could not be converted into a romantic comedy through the choice of other possibilities latent in the situation.

This systematic subversion of generic expectations helps create the peculiar atmosphere of *King Lear*. We are not spectators to the tragic agony of individuation; we watch instead a whole society and perhaps a whole world brought to ruin. The comic norm bears tidings of good cheer, promising that life and society and justice will prevail. *King Lear* whispers that they may not. Those comic motifs so often remarked by critics serve ironically to underscore the great gulf fixed between our fragile humanity and the cruel working of the way things are. Nor is this to embrace a nihilistic reading of the play. The *Lear* universe contains Cordelia as well as Goneril and Regan and sacrifice as well as selfishness. The old King does grow in understanding. Only fashionable posturing would declare these great goods meaningless. But the anticomic world of Lear is utterly devoid of tendermindedness: if the triumphs of the spirit are to be celebrated, they must be celebrated without any illusions about the flesh.

Consider for example the much-commented-upon enlightenment of Lear himself. A process of recognition leading to the purgation of folly has been a comic motif at least since Aristophanes. This recognition, as Northrop Frye has argued, often involves a renewed sense of identity. So it is in *Lear*. In the first act the King inquires, ''Who is it that can tell me who I am?'' [I. iv. 230]. After a journey through a hard pastoral landscape, after disguisings and confusions and symbolic rejections of the Court he has learned enough to say, ''I am a very foolish fond old man, / Fourscore and upward, not an hour more or less; / And, to deal plainly, / I fear I am not in my perfect mind'' [IV. vii. 59-62]. Though the significance and profundity of this transformation could hardly be overstated, on a *formal* level this reflects a run-of-the-mill comic motif, the renunciation of the error producing the original comic blockage. The cruel natural landscape out on the heath proves to be as instructive and corrective in its way as the benign pastoral landscape at the center of Shakespeare's romantic comedies.

Both our hopes and our generic expectations point toward a setting of all things right to chime with this newfound wisdom. In comedy such is the convention; the outer world smiles once self-knowledge prevails. That possibility is dangled before us in Lear's wonderful speech in the last act, ''Come, let's away to prison; / We two alone will sing like birds i' th' cage'' [V. iii. 8ff]—an austere vision perhaps, but nonetheless a perfect image of the earthly good remaining when the superficialities and illusions which blinded Lear at the beginning have been stripped away. A violation of the most fundamental of generic expectations makes the death of Cordelia so agonizing: the old man has seen, confessed, and humbled himself; what was lost by folly has been found; and then chance, unmotivated and arbitrary chance, snatches that away too. A typical comic twist,

more like the close of *Tartuffe* than of *Othello*, robs us of our last-ditch tenderminded hope that somehow the world will finally grant the spirit a physical boon. The world of event in *King Lear* is (in recent parlance) a ''bottom line'' vision of the world in which we live. Like Ivan Karamazov's vision of the suffering of children, the spectacle of Lear with Cordelia in his arms defines a point beyond which must begin our affirmations. All affirmations before this point depend upon the chance benevolence of fortune. Appalled by his vision of what the world of event can be—and therefore what in essence it is—Ivan feels compelled to give his ticket back; the history of the criticism of Shakespeare's play indicates that *King Lear* is far more suggestive and ambivalent than that. (pp. 13-17)

> *Ronald F. Miller, '''King Lear' and the Comic Form,''*
> in *Genre, Vol. 8, No. 1, March, 1975, pp. 1-25.*

JOHN REIBETANZ (essay date 1977)

> [*Reibetanz agrees with A. C. Bradley (1904) that the opening scene of* King Lear *is vastly different from those moments of exposition in Shakespeare's other tragedies, and that it psychologically prepares us for the remainder of the play, with all its mystery and surprise; but he disagrees with Bradley that the scene is faulty because of its ''gross improbability.'' Instead, Reibetanz argues that the first scene operates on an archetypal rather than a naturalistic level, just as the rest of the play does. Because of this, it contributes to the titanic quality of the characters, prepares us for the method of Shakespeare's dramatic presentation, which Reibetanz labels ''explosive'' rather than ''cumulative,'' and intensifies the play's emotive power by keeping us off-balance from the very start. For other commentaries on the first scene of* King Lear, *see the excerpts by Charlotte Lennox (1754), Samuel Taylor Coleridge (1813), Edward Dowden (1881), Levin L. Schucking (1922), Harry V. Jaffa (1957), and William Frost (1957-58).*]

The opening scenes of *King Lear* have fascinated and disturbed generations of critics—Johnson, Coleridge, and Bradley being only the most eminent of many [see excerpts above, 1765, 1813, and 1904]. If one compares their comments on these scenes, one notices a remarkable similarity in their reactions, despite the great differences of approach: words like 'strange,' 'absurd,' 'improbable,' and 'obscure' form the common vocabulary of a shared response. They also share the opinion that, for good or ill, the scenes are highly uncharacteristic of Shakespearean tragedy. An interpretation of *King Lear* must come to terms with these impressions, if only because they articulate the feelings of unease that the play's opening can still evoke.

What are we to make of an opening scene that, after a quick exchange between three apparently level-headed courtiers, thrusts us into a grotesque world of love-tests and wicked sisters? The courtiers' chatty prose accentuates the formality of the ceremonial setting and patterned dialogue that follow: after fanfare and procession, Lear questions and rewards each daughter in turn, proceeding from eldest to youngest. Yet the love-test itself, biased by the promise of reward, and the inexplicable extremes of conduct to which it gives rise, border on the absurd. This blend of ritualism and unreason is less characteristic of Shakespeare than of the brothers Grimm. We may search in vain for similar incidents in *Hamlet* or *Macbeth*, for instance, which confine the grotesque to the supernatural, and which set their main characters on a far more comprehensible course of action. The subplot of *King Lear* gets off to an equally curious start in scene ii, presenting without apology one of the most tenuous intrigues in Shakespearean tragedy: 'and pat he comes'

[I. ii. 134], notes Edmund, calling our attention to the situation's implausibility.

These radical departures from the norm of Shakespearean tragedy were called 'defects' by Bradley, who found them representative of greater lapses, flaws in the play's overall design. . . . Bradley was right in finding the initial effects typical of *King Lear*. The opening scenes form an appropriate gateway to a whole structure of equally bizarre and incongruous incidents, just as remote from the world of common sense. But Bradley was perhaps too quick to censure the structure for violating the canons of that commonsense world. For *King Lear* sets up its own realities and exhibits its own logic.

Undeniably, each of the major tragedies takes us into a distinct world that encourages and satisfies its own different expectations. Each offers its own world where language and action depart from the language and action of the real world primarily by displaying an internal coherence; the outlines of the play-world are familiar enough (except where they make clear departures into the supernatural) to identify with readily, but we are conscious of a shaped unity that creates a more singular atmosphere in each play. But the *Lear* world makes further demands on its audience. Like many of his contemporaries, Shakespeare here creates a play-world where events seem to unfold and characters to present themselves at a much greater remove from real life. (pp. 11-12)

When John Day placed his characters on a well-guarded island at the start of *The Isle of Gulls* (1606), he was being literal about what other Jacobean playwrights were undertaking figuratively: the creation of a special, isolated world that would elicit extreme and entertaining reactions from their protagonists. The dramatist sets up a play-world where settings, time sequences, and behavioural patterns exhibit notable departures from the logic of the real world. Such departures, consistent and mutually supporting, give the writer greater opportunity for the intense, exclusive development of situation and theme than a more naturalistic framework would allow. (p. 12)

The world of *King Lear* is similarly integral and exclusive, and similarly extreme. Bradley perceived the unity of the *Lear* world when he made this sensitive appraisal of Gloucester's attempted suicide at Dover:

> Imagine this incident transferred to *Othello*. . . . In *Othello* it would be a shocking or a ludicrous dissonance, but it is in harmony with the spirit of *King Lear*. And not only is this so, but, contrary to expectation, it is not, if properly acted, in the least absurd on the stage. The imagination and the feelings have been worked upon with such effect . . . that we are unconscious of the grotesqueness of the incident for common sense [see excerpt above, 1904]. . . .

We have intuitively accepted the peculiar logic of the *Lear* world, and recognize the incident as belonging to it. The same might be said of the love-test in the first scene, or of many of the 'defects' that Bradley cited. We feel that they all grow in the same garden, and we usually tend to accept them because we have entered into it. We would not accept other kinds of action, though, because the world of this play is also an exclusive one. In Act IV of Nahum Tate's version, for instance, an officer enters and tells Regan that the peasants have been outraged by Gloucester's blinding and are staging a rebellion; and in the second scene of Act III, Edmund has informed us

that the people are crying out against the unjust rule of Regan and Goneril. These incidents do not ring true to Shakespeare's play. There, the thoughts and activities of the common people never enter the picture, even peripherally. Power plays and outrages occur within a select circle, and their effects are confined to it. A more national scope would, paradoxically, render the action of *King Lear* less cataclysmic, for Shakespeare's characters share their primitive world only with the elements, like the pagan gods they invoke so frequently. (pp. 13-14)

An exploratory survey of the *Lear* world discloses, first of all, that it is almost placeless. One reason Edgar's description of the Dover cliffs . . . is so powerful is that the cliffs loom up out of nowhere. The other places—where Lear holds court, where Gloucester and Cornwall live, and the routes taken by those innumerable messengers—are as vague as the ubiquitous 'plaine' of *The Faerie Queene*. With the suggestive amplitude of allegory, *King Lear* moves us from Court to Heath. We find no memorable details that particularize either place, nothing comparable to the craggy seascape around Elsinore or the nests in Macbeth's walls. . . . The locale shifts, but remains undelineated until all the characters begin to come together at Dover. There is a complete absence of the kind of seemingly irrelevant specifics that provide reassurance.

This impression is fostered right from the opening scene. No editor dares give a more specific scene direction than 'King Lear's Palace,' and even the map Lear uses is apparently unlocalized, being without specific geographical references. . . . The various nebulous locations reinforce our sense of the self-contained yet all-encompassing nature of the *Lear* world. One thinks of Sir Thomas Browne's favourite image of the circle whose centre was everywhere and circumference nowhere.

Within this vague arena a series of suitably improbable incidents occurs: the love-test and its outcome, the tenuous intrigue by which Edmund hoodwinks his father and brother, the famous suicide attempt, the donning and the puzzling retention of real disguises (as opposed to the antic disposition that Hamlet puts on) for the only time in Shakespearean tragedy, and a plethora of less fabulous but similar actions. Critics have probed each of them in detail, but it is enough for our purposes to note how well the incidents complement each other. All of them break upon us in a rather inchoate manner; their unfolding is as nebulous as the localities that contain them; and progression from one incident to the next is often marked by the kind of sequential discontinuity that characterizes our dreams rather than our waking moments. People and things keep taking us by surprise. One feels that there could be no better introduction to this world than the first scene of *King Lear*.

As in the first scene, too, the incidents and characters in the rest of the play present a somewhat impenetrable surface to us. We sense an absence of intimate conversations and situations. Rarely alone on stage, the characters make only oversized gestures, because they are constantly thrust into situations that demand such gestures. The *Lear* world unfolds at such a breakneck speed that there is no time for more familiar views. This perspective stands in contrast to that of *Hamlet,* or even to that of the intensely concentrated *Othello,* both of which proceed at a leisurely enough pace to show us what their characters are like in moments of relaxation. There are no such moments in *King Lear*. We never see the intimacies between Edmund and his two queens, or between *any* of the characters. We never see them off guard. After Edmund's proclamation of villainy the long, ruminative soliloquy disappears, and Lear and his daughters share no soliloquies at all with us. Johnson marvelled at the play's 'quick succession of events' that 'fill the mind with a perpetual tumult' [see excerpt above, 1765]. Shakespeare sets the pace in Act I, and from then on the tempo precludes polite conversation.

Not that these characters would exchange any, even if they had the time. There are more instances of unexpected or indifferent acts of physical violence in *King Lear* than in any other Shakespearean tragedy. Kent beats and trips Oswald, Lear strikes his own head, Edmund stabs himself, Kent beats Oswald again, Regan plucks Gloucester's beard, Cornwall gouges out his eyes, the First Servant stabs Cornwall and is stabbed by Regan, Oswald attacks Edgar and is bludgeoned by him, a Gentleman runs in carrying the bloody knife with which Goneril has stabbed herself, Lear kills the man who hanged Cordelia. Brutality seems to be the common mode of discourse in *King Lear*. These 'most savage and unnatural' acts are the shock waves of a world hurtling out of control. We can never hope that a character's assertion of himself (as in *Hamlet*) or a change of heart (as in *Othello*) will right the situation. Actions and characters in the *Lear* world define themselves at irreversible extremes. When they are good, they are very good, and when they are bad they are unspeakable. (pp. 14-16)

Bradley feels that no stage can hold *King Lear*, that its titanic world is irreconcilable with the demands of theatrical production. The actors will presumably be unable to convey the play's extreme 'poetic atmosphere' to us because we know that they are only 'mere particular men and women.' What the real eye sees must negate the vision of the inward eye. This view shows that Bradley shares the late nineteenth-century conception of the stage as a faithful reproduction of physical reality. Bradley's stage is that of Shaw, with its real rugs, furniture, drapes, and 'particular men and women,' beheld through the wide proscenium window. His Ibsen is the author of *A Doll's House*, rather than of *Peer Gynt*. . . . He tends to separate the world of the imagination from that of the stage.

Today we are in a better position to reconcile the two. In the seventy years since Bradley wrote, we have been conditioned by exposure to such creations as Noh drama, bare open stages, surrealism, and the theatre of the absurd, to be more aware of the dramatic experience as one *projected from* the stage rather than taking place on it. We can therefore appreciate the extremities and improbabilities of *King Lear* without feeling that they disqualify it as a stage play, or that its imaginative effects suffer during performance. Perhaps these changes in expectation help to account for the unprecedented theatrical popularity of *King Lear* in our time. (pp. 16-17)

But in the main the relationship between life and the world of *King Lear* is not so antithetical as the above discussion might suggest. While it is true that the *Lear* world is a self-sustained construct, isolated from many real-world standards of logic and plausibility, it is a critical commonplace that the play is nevertheless charged with profound meaning for that world. Its indirections find directions out. Unburdened of the need to deal with the accidentals of everyday existence, *King Lear* can present essentials with undiminished intensity. (pp. 17-18)

A spectator coming to *King Lear* for the first time, after having seen the other great tragedies, would have good reason to expect its first scene to be expository. He would expect the exposition to unfold subtly and indirectly, in the midst of a gripping theatrical opening, but with perfect clarity. It would present immediately the predominant 'atmosphere' of the play,

reveal in some detail the events leading up to the present situation, and feed our anticipations of the central protagonist through an initial acquaintance with lesser figures. Not until this spadework was complete would the central character make a decisive act. Every other major Shakespearean tragedy meets these conditions, although each play naturally stresses some more than others. (p. 18)

No such exposition awaits the spectator of *King Lear*. The 'choric' scene between Kent, Gloucester, and Edmund, far from preparing us, actually leaves us off guard for both the ritualism and the vehemence of what follows. The main characters act decisively at once, with no clear presentation of background or outline of their motives. Anyone interested in such information must struggle, sometimes in vain, to piece out sequences of causality. Exposition in *King Lear* is an *ex post facto* manoeuvre—and not one the play gives us time to make. Shakespeare does not prepare us for Lear's odd behaviour, or for Cordelia's. It was this aspect of the opening scene that A. C. Bradley found most disturbing. . . . He even postulated that the scene might have suffered from hasty revision: perhaps the present text was merely a careless abridgment of the original version, pared down because Shakespeare found it too bulky for performance. Perhaps so, but not very likely, Bradley admitted.

In fact, the first scene's *lacunae* seem quite deliberate. Shakespeare has thoroughly removed the carefully placed hints about motivation that abound in his primary source, *The History of King Leir*. There, several reasons are given for Leir's strange conduct: he is sad and distraught because his wife has just died, and he wants to resign the throne to live in devout contemplation; he is ignorant of the affairs and characters of his daughters. . . . None of these intimations appears in Shakespeare's version. Obviously, he is not trying to make the same impression that the anonymous *Leir* playwright made, or that Nahum Tate was to make by embroidering the opening scenes with similar motives. Shakespeare simply presents us with the situation, and makes no attempt to acquaint us with its probable causes. (p. 19)

If we assume that there is more method than madness in what Shakespeare is doing here, our investigation becomes a matter of trying to establish the nature of that method, and what he might have hoped to accomplish by using it. Coleridge has provided us with an important hint, in his discussion of the opening scene: 'It is well worthy notice, that *Lear* is the only serious performance of Shakespeare the interest and situations of which are derived from the assumption of a gross improbability; whereas Beaumont and Fletcher's tragedies are, almost all, founded on some out-of-the-way accident or exception to the general experience of mankind' [see excerpt above, 1813]. Associating the opening of *King Lear* with the plays of Beaumont and Fletcher furnishes an illuminating perspective from which to view the scene. For the art of Beaumont and Fletcher is consistently one that sacrifices clarity and plausibility of motive and situation, in order to generate more compelling dramatic moments. This emphasis, like the first scene of *King Lear*, is highly theatrical: it concerns itself more with the immediate forcefulness of the dramatic situation than with tying the causal details of the situation into a realistic pattern. (p. 20)

The 'assumption of a gross improbability' in *King Lear* is, in fact, characteristic of much Jacobean drama, and not just of the plays of Beaumont and Fletcher. Several other playwrights are also much less concerned with establishing a plausible

foundation for each situation than with letting each generate
an entertaining dramatic exhibition. The opening of Day's *The
Isle of Gulls* (1606) illustrates this concern. Duke Basilius takes
his family to an island and issues a general challenge: whoever
outwits him and succeeds in wooing his daughters may have
them in marriage. Day then puts a succession of protagonists
into this contrived situation, which provokes entertaining reactions from them. The situation is, of course, reminiscent of
Shakespeare's own *Love's Labour's Lost*, a play written under
the influence of a man whose art anticipated many features of
early Jacobean drama, John Lyly. (p. 21)

A more exclusively situational interest governs the openings
of Chapman's *Bussy D'Ambois* (1604) and *The Widow's Tears*
(1605), or Field's *Amends for Ladies* (1611), plays written
both before and after *King Lear*. Here, the logic behind the
situation is never at issue, and to ask for more detailed motivation is to miss the point. The same interest characterizes the
deliberately implausible openings of Marston's *Antonio's Revenge* (1600) and *The Malcontent* (1603), and of Jonson's
Cynthia's Revels (1601). It must be emphasized that by no
means all the drama of these playwrights shares this characteristic; in fact, the openings of most of the plays they wrote
before 1605 (the date of *King Lear*) manifest a concern for
plausibility and/or clear exposition. But since the 'gross improbability' becomes increasingly typical of their drama, and
since they seem to point the way to the improbabilities of
Beaumont and Fletcher, I feel justified in associating the emphasis with these writers. Their works provide a wealth of
antecedents and analogues to the opening of *King Lear*.

Shakespeare's dramaturgy in the first scene of *King Lear* seems
to be in keeping with such practice, rather than with the openings of *Hamlet*, *Othello*, and most other earlier plays. . . .
Typical of much Jacobean drama but not of more naturalistic
works, *Lear*'s opening satisfies the question 'How?' while ignoring the 'Why?' When Bradley faults the scene because it
does not clearly establish 'the true position of affairs,' he displays the literary preconceptions of his age. He wants basic
motivations and relationships to be apprehensible right from
the start, as in a nineteenth-century novel. But *King Lear* does
not unfold as a novel transcribed for the stage, and its first
scene does not exhibit the narrative coherence that Bradley
seeks. Tate, not Shakespeare, endows the opening with such
unity and plausibility; and it is perhaps no coincidence that
the rise of Tate's version paralleled the rise of the novel and the
decline of playwriting. Tate's play answered different expectations. But the affinities of Shakespeare's *King Lear* are more
with the world of Chapman, Jonson, and Beaumont and Fletcher.
(pp. 21-2)

Many of the characters of this play, and Lear especially, are
conceived on a titanic scale. Their struggles have repercussions
that are cosmic rather than naturalistic, and that 'Strike flat the
thick rotundity o' th' world!' [III. ii. 7]. . . . For Shakespeare
to place these characters' actions in the framework of normal
human motivation at the outset would be to diminish their
stature irreparably; it would show them too much like us 'particular men and women,' reacting to identifiable stresses rather
than reverberating with archetypal meaning.

Given the quality of these characters, another advantage arises
form the first scene's bold physiognomy: it prepares us for the
play's distinctive method of character presentation. *King Lear*
involves us only in those moments when the essential nature
of a character manifests itself in action designed to typify it.
Instead of planning the dramatic action so that it gradually (and

sometimes indirectly) lets us build composite portraits of the
characters, as we see them reflecting, planning, and acting,
Shakespeare arranges each scene to represent the essence of
those involved in it. The process is explosive rather than cumulative, shocking us into a series of full, intense recognitions.
Finally, the impossibility of complacent, leisurely reactions to
King Lear itself suggests a third advantage of the opening
scene, an emotive one. By thrusting us into an indecipherable
but compelling situation, Shakespeare knocks us off balance.
We are unsure of our position. We cannot respond to the scene
with confidence in our knowledge of its *données*, yet it involves
us immediately and forcefully. And Shakespeare never lets us
regain our composure. *King Lear* keeps springing surprises on
us. The enigmatic opening scene is an introduction to, and an
epitome of, the play's power over us. (p. 22)

> *John Reibetanz, "Gateway to the 'Lear' World," in*
> *his* The "Lear" *World: A Study of* "King Lear" *in*
> *Its Dramatic Context, University of Toronto Press,*
> *1977, pp. 11-32.*

MELVIN SEIDEN (essay date 1979)

[*Seiden, in an assessment differing from that of Enid Welsford
(1935), claims that the Fool in* King Lear *is a figure who is both
more and less than a man—an individual who is "man-like, boy-
like, sage-like, and idiot-like," but can be called neither a man,
a boy, a sage, nor an idiot. In Aristotle's definition of character,
according to Seiden, the Fool is both "pure" character, to the
extent that he lacks all accidents of birth, family, and education,
and "characterless," in the sense that he lacks the "impure*

Fool. By Frank Gillett (n.d.).

accretions of individual and social experience" that contribute to moral purpose—what Aristotle regards as the essence of character. Seiden goes on to describe the Fool's main function as intensifying the destructive and paradoxical nature of existence which undermines the king's sense of order and embodying the paradoxes "that emerge out of the thought and behavior of the principle characters" as these individuals attempt to make sense of their experiences. For further analysis of the Fool and his function in King Lear, *see the excerpts by William Hazlitt (1817), Hermann Ulrici (1839), H. N. Hudson (1872), and G. Wilson Knight (1930).]*

Hamlet is the notorious instance of the failure of the Rosencrantzes and Guildensterns of criticism to "pluck out the heart of [his] mystery"[*Hamlet*, III. ii. 365-66]; but the case of the Fool in *Lear* is not much more encouraging to the aspirations of criticism. We can if we wish speak of the Fool as experiencing grief, dismay, fear, and the like; yet these "emotions" are not quite intelligible; they cannot be understood as the specific responses of an individuated person to a particular situation. Of course the Fool has a "personality"; yet he is not—or cannot be perceived as being—a person. He expresses but does not genuinely experience feeling. He is engaged in the action; yet he is not changed by his engagement in ways that can be understood by any psychology or logic of human behavior. (p. 197)

Lear's past life, though hardly mentioned, can be inferred, at least in broad outline, from the "data" given in the play. The King has been somewhere and been something; he is now journeying elsewhere and will become something different from what he has been; he has a past, a personal history. For him, as for all of us, time makes itself felt in the interplay of *was, is, and will-be*.

With the Fool one has the sense of his being out of time, without a past, miraculously free of the weight of experience. Like a god the Fool has come full blown into the world; he is fated never to have been or to become anything or anyone other than what he eternally is. The Fool incarnates the stasis of Being impervious to the flux of Becoming. (pp. 197-98)

The Fool, let us say, is a supernatural figure in something like the sense in which, for want of a better word, we use this term to describe Ariel or Caliban in *The Tempest*. The Fool is man-like, boy-like, sage-like, and idiot-like; but he is not unequivocally a man, a boy, a sage, an idiot; and no one can fail to perceive this troublesome and disorienting fact about him.

Uncorrupted and incorruptible, the Fool, insofar as he is a person at all, is both less and more than human. Shall we say that the Fool is permanently arrested in a childhood the blessedness of which can be assessed by comparing it with the terrible second childhood of the King's retrograde old age? It seems equally plausible to imagine the Fool as one who, if ever he did live in human time, may once have been a mere man; if so, perhaps he followed the path of his affliction to a "promis'd end" of release from human suffering more healing than anything Lear will ever experience this side of death. Insofar as the Fool is more than a man he is a being for whom there are no precise names, unless these be the only approximate terms, "teacher," "saint," "sage," or "priest." Insofar as he is less than a man he is, literally, what Lear in self-pity calls himself: "the natural fool of fortune" [IV. vi. 191]. (p. 198)

The Fool's "nature" is essentially one of contradiction and paradox. But what do we mean when we speak of the Fool's "nature"? It seems inappropriate to speak of the Fool as having that Bradleyan substratum of "character" which in men like

Hamlet, Othello, and Macbeth gives coherence to their deeds and permits us to impute significance to their "behavior." In Aristotle, "character" seems to allude to a single, intelligible principle "which reveals the moral purpose of the agents, i.e. the sort of thing they seek or avoid, where that is not obvious." What is "not obvious," i.e., problematic, in human personality emerges out of behavior. Thus as Aristotle defines it, "character" is conceived of as a conceptual means of arresting the experiential flux of behavior into a fixed, unchanging idea: the Platonic reduction of the multifariousness of a life being lived to an idea that converts contradiction and chaos into coherence and form.

It seems correct, therefore, to describe the ontological status of the Fool as one of pure character—all the accidents of birth, family, education, and social, economic, and political relationship having been expunged from "the record," if ever such human data can have existed. In another sense, however, the Fool is precisely characterless. If we conceive of Aristotle's "moral purpose" as a kind of common denominator for the sum of all the epiphenomena of behavior, how can there be this pure essence without the impure accretions of individual and social experience? The fundamental difference between the Fool of *King Lear* and Shakespeare's other clowns—the Fool's *soi disant* ["self-styled"] cousins—rests in just this point: a Feste, a Touchstone or a Launcelot Gobbo carries with him the individuating signature of a personal history; each of them thus possesses, however minimally, a character in the same sense in which we use the term in speaking of the character of Macbeth or of Desdemona or of Angelo; the Fool, from one angle of vision, does not. He cannot be imagined to have had a past; no one could possibly be tempted to make Maurice Morgann's error (in speaking of Falstaff) of inventing for the Fool a plausible youth. Perhaps the simplest way of making this point is to say that the Fool, whatever else he is, is not merely a man. . . . Such a being may possess the irreducible essence of character and yet, like the air when it is unmoved and unmoving—or like Ariel, whom the Fool resembles in some crucial respects—the Fool resists our efforts to endow him with a personality that is comprehensible in ordinary human terms. (pp. 198-200)

The Fool's is a saturnalian power. But unlike his archetypal ancestors, the Fool is not licensed to enact his fantasies (which are ours) of unbridled freedom in the shocking or shameful deed; the Fool *does* nothing exceptional, unless it be the negative deed of not abandoning his suffering master. He shares in the impotence of the true king. His license is truly poetic license: the freedom to say what, prudentially, he ought not but must say; the enfranchisement of the uncensored tongue to speak uncensorable thoughts.

In the Fool outrageous action is translated or sublimated into outrageous and subversive speech which, of course, is another kind of action. The Fool speaks the obscenities he cannot enact, never has, and never will perform. He voices as it were the principle of obscenity, the summing up of all those obscenities which lie threateningly beneath the surface of the decencies, pieties, and traditional observances the function of which is to insure the health of individual psyches and of social institutions.

The Fool voices his obscenities with all the ritualistic impersonality of the priest intoning his pieties. But we cannot say how or what the Fool feels about the sexual images which he projects on to the screen of the King's imagination. . . . It is as if the Fool were will-less, projecting verbal pictures not of his own making. The Fool is only the medium through which these images are expressed. Personally (if it is possible to speak of the Fool as a person), he neither enjoys nor is disgusted by these images; he does not judge them; he does not take a moral position in respect to, let us say, the work of the organ housed in the codpiece. Yet neither is the Fool the objective reporter; he is not saying, as Edmund the natural scientist might say: Men and women "make love" just as and for the same reasons that animals couple. After all, that's what they—we—are: animals. (pp. 200-01)

As Act I draws to a close, Lear cries, "O, let me not be mad, not mad, sweet heaven!" [I. v. 46]. The Fool is not as guiltless as he may seem. By forcing the King to look down into the abyss of his own folly, the Fool has contributed to the harm done by the evil daughters and to the King's raging quarrel with himself. "Keep me in temper; I would not be mad!" [I. v. 47] Lear begs. This remorseless, pitiless Fool—perhaps because wise-folly transcends remorse or pity—replies lewdly: "She that's a maid now, and laughs at my departure, / Shall not be a maid long, unless things be cut shorter" [I. v. 51-3]. What is this? The allopathic remedy of medicinal laughter? Can anyone suppose, however, that the Fool's phallic wit does induce laughter or even a smile in Lear? Or, if Lear does succumb to a wry, pained, involuntary smile, can we suppose such smiling to have a purgative effect? Everything that will happen subsequently in the brief, aborted relationship between Lear and the Fool strongly suggests that if the Fool's function is to provide curative laughter, he fails. By undercutting the foundations of Lear's faith and certitudes, the Fool's jests, quibbles, riddles, equivocations and obscenities only intensify the destructive power of the "nothing"'s which prey on the King.

What does this bawdy couplet tell us about the Fool? If the Fool were not a court Fool, we might take it to imply the braggadocio of arrogant virility . . . : beware of the threat lodged between *my* legs. Could anyone ever find this meaning in these lines? The true Saturnalian god-figure is a deflowerer of maidens, a potential rapist, a demon of superhuman sexual energy, pure, untrammeled libido. Our poor Fool is none of these things. He is no Edmund. This Fool who might be breaking his jests on the heads of harem women, this emasculated Fool knows or can imagine with a vividness more painful than the knowledge born of experience how it feels if *your* "things be cut shorter" [I. v. 52].

In one sense nothing could be less appropriate than to address the comedy of castration to an old, beaten, and impotent man. In another sense Lear is a castrated king, indeed, a self-castrated king. And yet kingship is not equivalent to manhood, to manliness, nor to that condition of humanness which cuts across gender. The Fool's sexual jokes, with the genital allusions, serve primarily to remind Lear, who does not always notice the point, and to show us who cannot fail to see the connection, that copulation, birth, and death are the essential, the brute facts of human existence.

The content of these sexual probings is Saturnalian; the message is tragic. The jokes are, as we say, "dirty"; the speaker is of a purity which transcends the human condition. The jokes, as jokes, are perhaps funny; their effect, as moral pointers, is intensely painful.

In an ideal production of the play, Edmund, almost beyond the point of anatomical credibility, will strut the stage with codpiece bulging. The Fool's wrinkled, parti-colored leotard will be as flat at the fork as that of any little girl who is taking her first ballet lesson . . . the visual juxtaposition will enforce the paradox of the bawdy Fool who speaks with the ignorance of one who will never know but must imagine the mysteries of human sexuality.

The Fool embodies irreconcilable contradictions, the central one being the supra-logical phenomenon wherein the Fool is both fool and wise man; he is also rational and irrational, young and old, principled and unscrupulous, bawdy and chaste, friend and foe to his master, the King, and an object of ridicule and of pathos. Were the Fool intelligibly human, we would infer from this lack of integration of personality that he is deranged. In fact, however, we take this psychic state (which is indeed analogous to madness) to be transcendent sanity. . . . Thus it is that when Lear falls into raving and irrationality we attribute to him a Fool-like sanity and wisdom. Just as the Fool teaches Lear so he instructs us in the slippery dialectics of paradoxical truth; it is because of what and who the Fool is that we are able to recognize what Lear has become when, for example, the King babbles his confused but enlightening words about justice, hypocrisy, and reproduction in IV. vi. Even though the Fool has left the play in III. vi. and is never to return again, it is the Fool-principle, we might say, working in and through Lear at this later point in the great "adultery" speech.

Let us then postulate an hypothesis about the Fool: the Fool incarnates in his equivocal person those ambiguities, contradictions, and dilemmas that inhere in the *ideas* expressed by Lear and others about what is natural, unnatural, and supernatural; the paradoxes that inhere in the person of the Fool reflect, symbolize, or objectify (as in Eliot's "objective correlative") the paradoxes that emerge out of the thought and behavior of the principal characters, as these men and women struggle to get what they want out of life and to make sense of what they do and of what is done to them. Insofar as the play raises complex questions about reality, it is no exaggeration to say that the Fool embodies everything that is problematical in the play. (pp. 201-04)

Melvin Seiden, "The Fool and Edmund: Kin and Kind," in Studies in English Literature, 1500-1900, *Vol. XIX, No. 2, Spring, 1979, pp. 197-214.*

RENÉ E. FORTIN   (essay date 1979)

[*In the following excerpt, Fortin compares the contradictory interpretations of the ending of* King Lear *and claims that the so-called pessimistic reading of the play is prone to the same shortcomings as the redemptive reading, since both tend to focus on certain scenes, characters, and themes at the expense of other portions of the drama. Yet, Fortin adds that the current attacks on the Christian interpretation of* Lear *are misleading in that the critics who make these accusations fail to possess a proper understanding of the Christian religion. He explains that specific Christian concepts—most importantly the belief in the mystery of God's ways, but also the ideas of the holy fool and suffering as a redemptive measure—are clearly present in the play and support a Christian reading. Fortin's final thesis, similar to that of Robert Ornstein (1960), is that* King Lear *represents Shakespeare's attempt to "demythologize Christianity, to reassert the hiddenness of God against the presumptuous pieties and shallow rationalism of the Edgars and Albanys of the world."*]

Attempts to redeem *King Lear* by appealing to intimations of Christian transcendence in the play have been summarily, if not vehemently, dismissed by secular critics. Christian critics, we are told by W. R. Elton and others [see Additional Bibliography], are simply wrong because they do not attend to the "facts" of the play; seeking to escape the dire significances of the tragic vision, they are in effect guilty of wishful thinking, of imposing their own a priori assumptions upon the play. (p. 113)

Recently, however, René Wellek has posed an intriguing question: whether it is possible to conclude that there is indeed a single correct interpretation of the tragedies. Wellek's question is worthy of further consideration, for perhaps the root of the controversy between secular critics and "Christian" critics is the fact that our criticism lacks a solid hermeneutical base. It is quite evident that the typical interpretation of *King Lear* (and of the other tragedies as well) is offered as the "right" interpretation, setting forth the meaning of the tragedy all would derive if they would only see the plays aright. But perhaps we are now ready to awaken from our dogmatic slumber and reexamine the implicitly Lockean assumptions which have governed our critical practice. For time after time in the past several decades we have been cautioned that perception and cognition are highly complex activities and that the perceiving eye and mind are actively engaged in constituting or shaping the truth they are naively supposed merely to register. The conceptual model of a purely objective critical encounter, such as that called for by Morris Weitz (a model which would have the critic as spectator attempting to "see the object exactly as it is"), seems highly questionable at this time. It is now almost de rigueur in critical essays to offer ritual obeisance to E. H. Gombrich and his demonstration that our vision is largely a matter of projection, of seeing only what we are prepared to see. Specifically in literature the now familiar paradigm of the "included spectator" indicates an awakening to the creative participation of the viewer of a play, while Norman Rabkin's view of the complementarity of Shakespearean meanings has made remarkable inroads; Shakespearean structure, Rabkin tells us, sets up "the opposed elements as equally valid, equally desirable, and equally destructive, so that the choice the play forces the reader to make becomes almost impossible." (pp. 113-14)

I do not propose . . . that secular readings of *King Lear* are wrong; indeed they are often quite persuasive and should be heeded. I wish rather to suggest that to consider the secular reading as exclusively valid is as much an act of dogmatic assertion as is the comforting vision offered by the Christian interpreters, since the assertion in either case is based upon a selection of evidence as well as a selective interpretation of that evidence. (pp. 114-15)

The final scene of *King Lear* provides the best opportunity to pursue these questions, for in the death of Cordelia lies the most formidable challenge to any affirmative, religious view of the tragic experience. The Christian critic's attempt to wrest comfort from the dire outcome of the play is decisively repudiated by the secular critic because the events of the play—its "facts"—supposedly contradict the central tenets of Christianity. But what specifically are these tenets? If we examine closely the secular arguments, we find (1) that nothing short of poetic justice would validate a religious argument; (2) that a truly Christian play would have to dramatize the miraculous intervention of the gods or otherwise catch them red-handed as they intrude into the affairs of men; and (3) that the universe in which the tragic ordeal takes place would have to be transparently meaningful. Nicholas Brooke, for example, states: "I have never been clear what constitutes a 'Christian play.' I should have supposed that label would involve some effort to

justify God's ways to men, to make the mysterious less inscrutable." . . . He later adds, "Poetical justice has been dealt out to Oswald, but embarrassingly, the gods didn't do it themselves," just as it is Edgar—and not God—who provides the "miracle" that saves Gloucester. . . . [Marvin] Rosenberg joins this chorus with his utter certitude about the vacancy of Lear's final vision: "On this ultimate stage of fools, no one—except possibly Lear dying in illusion—is so foolish as to see any evidence of divinity at work. . . . Death everywhere, of the good as well as the 'bad'" [see Additional Bibliography] . . . . (pp. 115-16)

Such responses cannot be peremptorily dismissed even by the Christian interpreter, for the question of poetic justice and of the benign concern of the gods for man is at the very heart of the play. From the outset of *King Lear* the characters express faith in the concern and loving-kindness of the gods: the gods, Lear feels, will at once take his part against his daughters; Cornwall's servants pray that the blinding of Gloucester be speedily avenged; Albany sees the killing of Cornwall as evidence that the "justicers" are above; and Edgar constantly assures his father that the gods are sensitive to human anguish. . . . (p. 116)

What we notice, however, is a far less hospitable universe. As many commentators have pointed out, a conspicuous feature of the structure of *King Lear* is its irony, the rhythm of expectation and frustration to which the characters are subjected. It has been too infrequently noted, however, that the viewer is himself victimized by the same ironies. Our familiarity with the play—we all know how it ends—has largely blunted these ironies for us; like trained hounds we have been over the course before and are not likely to be led astray by false scents, as Lear, Albany, and Edgar are. But the "naive spectator," the first-time viewer of the play, who lacks our synchronic, spatial sense of the play's form, would hardly be so fortunate—especially if he is familiar with the earlier *Leir*. The naive spectator, rather, is constantly being assured that all will be well; he is comforted by the discreet loyalty of Kent, by the early and persistent rumors of civil wars that will bring down the house divided of Goneril and Regan, by the tender care of Edgar (as Poor Tom) for his father, and especially by the perpetual promise of the return of Cordelia. . . . It is as if the play is taking great pains to buffer the viewer from anguish, assuring him that the darkness is only temporary.

The peculiar cruelty of *King Lear,* of course, is that this promise is violated, most glaringly in the manner in which Cordelia—"Great thing of us forgot" [V. iii. 237]—dies. Though we do see some measure of what could be taken for "rough justice" in the deaths of Cornwall, Oswald, Edmund, Goneril, and Regan, there is in the death of Cordelia no poetic justice, no "dark and vicious place" [V. iii. 173] to account for her murder, no discernible incense thrown upon her sacrifice. The viewer is tempted, after this unconscionable mischief of the wanton gods, to accept as his the "cheerless, dark and deadly" world described by Kent [V. iii. 291].

But does the play insist that we do so? Do the "facts" of the play, particularly its excruciating final scene, make *King Lear* absolutely incompatible with a Christian worldview? Any critic intending to offer an unequivocal reading of its ending should recall that he is witnessing a play that has throughout insisted upon the problematics of seeing and that this theme dominates the final lines of Lear:

> Do you see this? Look on her. Look, her lips,
> Look there, look there.
>
> [V. iii. 311-12]
> (pp. 116-17)

Lear's final statement presents to the viewers the ultimate challenge to vision: everything depends upon what is actually seen—or not seen—in these final moments. But here is perhaps the most devastating irony of the play: we do not and cannot see what Lear sees. What we see is merely Lear seeing. Philip Hobsbaum is at least partially right in arguing that "we cannot, to put it crudely, know whether or not Lear dies smiling. At the end of the play we are in exactly the same position as the spectators on stage. . . . Most of the critics who have dealt with the play seem to me wrong in opting for one or the other of these possibilities [hope and despair]: the values are more complex than that."

Hobsbaum's comment is particularly useful when we consider the scene in the light of Bertrand Evans' concept of discrepant awarenesses, for the concept may be especially relevant, though in a different way than most would imagine. For where comedy typically offers to the viewer a cognitive perspective superior to that of the central figure (*we* know, for example, that Cesario is really Viola), it is possible that in *King Lear* it is the central figure who has the privileged vision, with the viewer able to see only from afar. Such a conclusion would be supported by the logic of the play, which postulates suffering as a precondition to accurate vision. . . . (p. 117)

Lear, because he has suffered, may indeed see more than the survivors (Edgar, Kent, and Albany), who seem to see nothing more than "general woe" [V. iii. 320], and more than the spectators, whose suffering is at best vicarious. . . . [We] must be careful about arrogating to ourselves a clarity of vision superior to that of Lear, for what he sees, or cannot see, must remain for us only a matter of inference.

In order to be convincing, a Christian reading of *King Lear* must bravely push on beyond the "redemption" scenes of Act IV and take in fully the devastatingly ironic death of Cordelia. It is true, as secular critics have argued, that the death of Cordelia suggests the failure of the gods to provide the "chance which does redeem all sorrows" [V. iii. 267], the saving miracle that would attest to their beneficence. Their failure to do so is particularly agonizing because it has occurred in a universe that seemed to support a faith in poetic justice but which instead decisively reasserts its opaqueness; we are left blindly staring at that which passeth all understanding.

But for the Christian critic the opaqueness of the *Lear* world is no insurmountable obstacle, for the very structural ironies which purportedly impeach the Christian worldview provide, when seen from a different perspective, a strong support for a Christian reading. To begin with, if the absence of visible supernatural intervention is to be the cudgel to beat down Christian interpretations—or Christian interpreters—one had better take a second look at the traditional beliefs of Christianity, for it is not at all presumed in the mainstream of Christian orthodoxy that God will intervene on call for his faithful; nowhere is a God of sweetness and light promised to man on this earth. (p. 118)

The ordeal of Lear and the death of Cordelia are, to be sure, hard to cope with, but they do not contradict the image of God held in either Catholic or Protestant Christianity. In fact, an ear attuned to scripture would discern in Lear's ordeal resonances of the Book of Revelation:

> I knowe thy workes, that thou art nether colde
> nor hote;

I wolde thou werest colde or hote. Therefore, because thou art lukewarm, and nether colde nor hote, it will come to passe, that I shall spewe thee out of my mouth.

For thou saist I am riche and increased with goods, and have neede of nothing, and knowest not how thou art wretched and miserable, and poore, and blinde, and naked. . . .

I think it is evident that the verses point to central themes of the play and suggest much about its imagery. The lesson that Lear learns in his suffering is that he has been morally callous; it is a lesson that he learns by becoming himself poor, naked, and—symbolically through his madness—blind. The suffering of Lear, seen against this background is at once punitive and propaedeutic, a necessary condition to his redemption. . . . (p. 119)

There still, of course, remains the death of Cordelia. It is true, as many critics have averred, that Christian interpretations generally ignore the final excruciating scene of the play. . . . It is, however, equally true that secular interpreters tend to view the death of Cordelia as an isolated episode, apart from the rich context that the previous four acts of the play have provided.

Because this context has been effectively explored elsewhere, I shall limit myself to brief remarks about how it may support a Christian reading. First, what is especially remarkable about the final scene is its recapitulatory nature, its gathering up of themes which developed earlier in the play. It should be noted, for example, that the Lear whom we view in the final scene has come full circle, being in much the same position as he was in Act I: calling upon his one true daughter to utter the words needed to sustain value in his life and once again receiving an answer the silence which is the alpha and omega of the play. . . .

But Cordelia's failure to speak now may be no more a denial of value than was her earlier silence, particularly when one construes that silence in the light of other themes and images. Above all, Lear's lament over the dead Cordelia, "And my poor fool is hanged" [V. iii. 306], recalls the motif of folly which has been so prominent earlier in the play. We have seen folly constantly associated with virtue: in the Fool's poignant commitment to Lear despite his own worldly wisdom which counsels a different course; in the supererogatory loyalty of Kent, who serves Lear despite his unjust banishment; and particularly in the superfluity of Cordelia's loving forgiveness. Virtue, for all its foolishness, yet survives in an otherwise bleak world. The Christian reader will have little difficulty seeing in such instances of unlikely goodness reminiscences of the Pauline theme of Christian folly. . . . (p. 120)

[A] prominent feature of *King Lear* is that virtue, in a world overwhelmed by evil, chooses to or is compelled to conceal its presence, to operate covertly. The list of "unpublished virtues" in the play is impressive; it includes Kent and Edgar, who fulfill their obligations in disguise; Gloucester, who summons up unexpected moral strength to assist his king and to bear his own ordeal patiently; the servants of Cornwall, who unexpectedly lash out at the cruelty of their master; and finally, Cordelia, who can publish her love for her father neither at the beginning nor at the end of the play.

But does the list of unpublished virtues end there? No one, I think, will deny that the question Lear addresses to the dead

Cordelia, "Why should a dog, a horse, a rat, have life, / And thou no breath at all?" [V. iii. 307-08], is really addressed to the gods who would allow such an abomination. The Christian interpreter, recognizing that Lear has been throughout his ordeal surrounded by goodness which he has had difficulty perceiving, may have warrant enough to see the dead Cordelia as but a further instance of a pattern which points beyond to the gods, the ultimate unpublished virtues of the world. The apparent absence of redeeming goodness has thus far proven to be no guarantee that it does not exist.

And thus a play which begins with a king announcing "darker purposes" which lead to the temporary loss of a daughter ends with a Higher Power (or powers) announcing infinitely darker purposes and apparently bringing the same victim to distress. The Christian viewer will accept the harsh fact that the world offers no cheap consolations but need not necessarily infer that God has forsaken that world.

Rather, the Christian reader who is responsive to the Biblical echoes of the play may view the play as an attempt to demythologize Christianity, to reassert the hiddenness of God against the presumptuous pieties and shallow rationalism of the Edgars and Albanys of the world. In the death of Cordelia the viewers are once more confronted with the Judaeo-Christian God who, from the Book of Job on, has chosen to remain hidden and refuses to render account of His "darker purposes" to man. . . . The God who emerges in the final events of the play is not the majuscule God as prime mover and creator of all, nor God as supreme justicer, nor even the God of translucent love to whom Cordelia seems to point. He is rather an unaccommodated and unaccommodating God who refuses masks of any kind, who denies us either the explanations we seek or the miracles which would make such explanations unnecessary. He is the miniscule God of Pauline theology who denies both signs and wisdom. . . . (pp. 121-22)

For the Christian interpreter the death of Cordelia need not, cannot be explained away; as "stumbling block" it supports rather than contradicts Revelation, the true Biblical God, even and perhaps especially that of the New Testament, being a God of faith seen but through a glass darkly, whose promises are beheld from afar. The ending of King Lear, in short, presents a demythologized Christianity that offers mystery rather than justice and that is founded upon hope rather than fulfillment. . . .

Such a Christian reading, again, is not intended as the authoritative reading of King Lear; it is offered, rather, in an attempt to show that a Christian response to the play may be in conformity with both the "facts" of the play and with the doctrines of Christianity. Such a response, however, does not invalidate the secular reading, since even the most adamantly Christian of interpreters must feel the force of Edgar's admonition to "speak what we feel, not what we ought to say" [V. iii. 325]. What King Lear strongly suggests is that the lion of tragedy need not be devoured by the lamb of theology. . . . (p. 122)

To assert that King Lear admits both secular and religious interpretations is not, however, to argue for critical relativism, to consider the play as a tabula rasa awaiting any critical impression whatever. . . . It is evident that the play, despite its apparent multivalence, creates its unique frame of discourse, channeling inquiry into specific areas of speculation and compelling attention to clearly-defined overwhelming questions. . . . [It] dramatizes man's quest for justice; the folly,

callousness, and brutality of which humanity is capable; the apparent injustice which man may suffer. It also dramatizes the unlikely perdurance of virtue under the most trying conditions, as well as the moral awakening of several under the pressure of adversity. Calculations about what all of this adds up to may differ, and differ markedly, but it is most probably true that any interpretation of the play which denies that these are central concerns is simply wrong.

The open form of tragedy, its respect for the limits of human experience, allows readers to draw different conclusions: enough is given to allow interpreters to "see feelingly," to infer an interpretation based upon their own personal experience of the play; but enough is withheld to compel respect for the tragic mystery, to remind us that our conclusions are, after all, nothing but inference. If we learn anything from King Lear, it is that we all must see in our way, that a personal response is mandated by the tragic structure, but that our own vision is necessarily limited. Perhaps this humbling truth, hermeneutical as well as theological in its implications, is the play's most valuable revelation. (p. 123)

> René E. Fortin, "Hermeneutical Circularity and Christian Interpretations of 'King Lear'," in Shakespeare Studies: An Annual Gathering of Research, Criticism, and Reviews, Vol. XII, 1979, pp. 113-25.

ADDITIONAL BIBLIOGRAPHY

Barnet, Sylvan. "Some Limitations of a Christian Approach to Shakespeare." ELH No. 2 (June 1955): 81-92.
> An examination of the Christian approach to Shakespeare's tragedies. Barnet isolates and discusses a number of problems apparent in Christian interpretations of Shakespeare's tragedies as a whole. He cites as the most obvious discrepancy the fact that Christian eschatology is essentially optimistic—portraying life as a preparation for death and an eternity of bliss—whereas Shakespeare's tragedies suggest nothing so redeeming or transcendent.

Battenhouse, Roy W. "Moral Experience and Its Typology in King Lear." In his Shakespearean Tragedy: Its Art and Christian Premises, pp. 269-302. Bloomington and London: Indiana University Press, 1969.
> Identifies certain elements in King Lear, such as character, motif, conflict, and theme, in an effort to establish their basis in Christian liturgy. Battenhouse states that the purpose of his study is to justify a Christian reading of the play.

Blok, Alexander. "Shakespeare's King Lear." In Shakespeare in the Soviet Union: A Collection of Articles, edited by Roman Samarin and Alexander Nikolyukin and translated by Avril Pyman, pp. 17-24. Moscow: Progress Publishers, 1966.
> Lecture delivered before the actors of the Bolshoi Drama Theatre on July 31, 1920, instructing them on how to interpret the action of King Lear. Blok argues that any group wanting to be honest to Shakespeare's intentions should present King Lear in all its "cruelty" and "bitterness."

Boas, Frederick S. "The Climax of Tragedy." In his Shakspere and His Predecessors, pp. 409-53. New York: Charles Scribner's Sons, 1896.
> General discussion of King Lear, focusing on Shakespeare's mixture of "titanic vastness and passion with orderly elaboration of detail." Boas also contributes to the controversy over the play's exact meaning, asserting that it is neither overly pessimistic nor optimistic, but a drama in which Shakespeare "boldly recognizes that . . . virtue is not always triumphant nor vice cast down."

Bonheim, Helmut, ed. The "King Lear" Perplex. San Francisco: Wadsworth Publishing Co., 1960, 195 p.

Collection of over seventy essays on *King Lear* written between 1687 and 1960 and including such important critics as Samuel Johnson, William Hazlitt, Samuel Taylor Coleridge, Algernon Charles Swinburne, A. C. Bradley, and Harley Granville-Barker.

Bowers, Fredson. "The Structure of *King Lear*." *Shakespeare Quarterly* 31 (1980): pp. 7-20.
Argues that *King Lear* follows the structural pattern of classical Greek tragedy as demonstrated in such plays as *Oedipus* and the *Oresteia*, rather than the traditional Renaissance five-act tragedy. Bowers claims that such a hypothesis helps to explain the difference between *King Lear* and Shakespeare's other tragedies and answers the questions concerning the exact location of the play's climax and dénouement.

Brooke, C.F. Tucker. "*King Lear* on the Stage." *The Sewanee Review* XXI, No. 1 (January 1913): 88-98.
Claims that *King Lear* fails on the modern stage, not because of its poetic grandeur, but because it deals with a theme of "less than tragic proportions," namely, filial ingratitude.

Burke, Kenneth. "*King Lear*: Its Form and Psychosis." *Shenandoah* XXI, No. 1 (Autumn 1969): 3-18.
Suggests that readers take a very generalized view of *King Lear* in order to discover its underlying "psychosis"—that element or pattern in the play that contributes to its mass appeal. At one point, Burke identifies this pattern as Lear's act of abdication, or "retirement" from the cares of life; however, he further defines the pattern as "the paradox of substance"—a concept in which individual identity exists only in relation to the phenomena, situations, relationships, and social customs that form its foundation.

Calarco, N. Joseph. "The Tragic Universe of *King Lear*." In his *Tragic Being: Apollo and Dionysus in Western Drama*, pp. 81-120. Minneapolis: The University of Minnesota Press, 1968.
Attempts to define *King Lear*'s relation to medieval drama and thought and determine if it is a Christian play in the context of theological doctrine popular during the Middle Ages. Although Calarco bases much of his discussion on the paradigms of the "Apollonian" and "Dionysian" concepts of Greek culture, he transforms these ideas into Christian terminology in his examination of *King Lear*, focusing on the presence of "chaos" or "nothingness" and "order" or "grace" in the play. After concluding that the distinguishing trait of medieval drama, and Christian thought in general, is a paradoxical acceptance of the history of events—the linear movement of time—in conjunction with an ahistorical perspective, or a transcendence of temporality in the symbol of Christ, Calarco claims that Shakespeare's *King Lear* manifests the same paradoxical vision in the death of Cordelia. On one level, Cordelia's death is but an example of the absurdity of human existence; yet, on a higher level, possibly Lear's perspective at the close of the play, it demonstrates the transcendence of time, suffering, and chaos if we accept the illusion that Cordelia lives.

Campbell, Lily B. "*King Lear*: A Tragedy of Wrath in Old Age." In her *Shakespeare's Tragic Heroes: Slaves of Passion*, pp. 175-207. New York: Barnes & Noble, 1970.
Examines the Renaissance view towards anger—its causes, its effect on certain personalities, and its different modes or degrees of expression—then interprets *King Lear* in light of these commonly held opinions, specifically, how the play reflects the Renaissance conception of anger.

Caneiro de Mendonça, Barbara Heliodora. "The Influence of *Gorboduc* on *King Lear*." *Shakespeare Survey* 13 (1966): 41-8.
Argues that the English tragedy *Gorboduc*, written by Thomas Norton and Thomas Sackville, greatly influenced Shakespeare's writing of *King Lear*. Caneiro claims that Shakespeare must have used *Gorboduc* as a model for incorporating the elements of suffering, evil, and disorder in *King Lear*, since nowhere in the traditional sources for Shakespeare's play are these elements so prominent.

Cavell, Stanley. "The Avoidance of Love: A Reading of *King Lear*." In his *Must We Mean What We Say? A Book of Essays*, pp. 267-353. Cambridge: Cambridge University Press, 1976.
Close reading of the variously interpreted scenes in *King Lear*, including the meeting of Gloucester and Lear in IV. vi., the opening scene of the "love test," and the final scene of Cordelia's and Lear's deaths. Cavell suggests the possible motivation for much of Lear's actions in these and other scenes could be an "avoidance of love"—his inability to accept the selfless love of another individual because he cannot repay that love in kind.

Chambers, E. K. "Plays of the First Folio: *King Lear*." In his *William Shakespeare: A Study of Facts and Problems*, Vol. I, pp. 463-70. London: Oxford at the Clarendon Press, 1930.
Commentary on the *King Lear* Quartos and the dating of the play. Chambers concludes that *King Lear* was written in 1605 and, perhaps because of censorship, was not performed until 1606.

Charlton, H. B. "*King Lear*." In his *Shakespearian Tragedy*, pp. 189-229. Cambridge: Cambridge University Press, 1948.
General discussion of *King Lear*. Charlton reviews the different versions of the Leir story and discusses their influence on Shakespeare's *King Lear*. He also examines the characters' relations to the universe of the play, specifically their concepts of the gods.

Colie, Rosalie L., and Flahiff, F. T., eds. *Some Facets of "King Lear": Essays in Prismatic Criticism*. Toronto: University of Toronto Press, 1974, 237 p.
Collection of twelve essays on *King Lear* written by various critics and covering a wide range of topics, including language, structure, textual analysis, and dramatic technique.

Craig, Hardin. "The Ethics of *King Lear*." *Philological Quarterly* IV, No. 2 (April 1925): 97-109.
Claims that the social and religious ethics Shakespeare presents in *King Lear*, such as the acknowledgment of God, the natural love of children and parents, and a comprehensible truth in the natural order, were all widely accepted integral parts of the Elizabethan outlook on life. Craig traces these ethical concepts back to the early Greeks, through the works of Thomas Aquinas, and into Renaissance philosophy and common thought.

———. "The Great Trio: *King Lear*." In his *An Interpretation of Shakespeare*, pp. 206-19. New York: The Citadel Press, 1948.
Interprets *King Lear* as Shakespeare's dramatization of the chaos that ensues in the moral world when the divine sanction of kingship has been violated.

Cunnington, R. H. "The Revision of '*King Lear*'." *Modern Language Review* V (1910): 445-52.
Argues against the majority opinion in modern *King Lear* criticism that the deletions, additions, and revisions apparent in the Folio edition of 1623 were not the work of Shakespeare.

Danby, John F. *Shakespeare's Doctrine of Nature: A Study of "King Lear*." London: Faber and Faber, 1949, 234 p.
Analyzes *King Lear* according to the Elizabethan concepts of nature developed in the play. Danby traces the different attitudes towards nature personified in each of the major characters. Cordelia, for example, he sees as embodying Thomas Hooker's concept of nature as a benign pattern which sustains the universe and represents the ideal toward which humanity strives. On the other hand, Edmund espouses the view of nature as amoral, autonomous, and unrelated to divine plans and to human values. Danby considers Lear the symbol of Everyman, caught between these two visions of the universe, and arriving through pain and suffering at a new perception in the image of Cordelia. For Danby, the result of Lear's experience brings the reader or spectator to the edge of "religious insight," and for this reason he interprets *King Lear* as "our profoundest expression of an essentially Christian comment on man's world and his society."

Danson, Lawrence, ed. *On "King Lear*." Princeton, N.J.: Princeton University Press, 1981, 185 p.
Collection of eight lectures originally delivered at Princeton University in 1978 and 1979 by such prominent critics as Alvin B.

Kernan, Michael Goldman, Theodore Weiss, and Lawrence Danson.

Doran, Madeleine. "Elements in the Composition of *King Lear*." *Studies in Philology* 30, No. 1 (January 1933): 34-58.
  Attempts to reconstruct Shakespeare's composition of *King Lear* by focusing on the textual irregularities in the First Quarto and analyzing them as segments in which Shakespeare revised the original Leir story and developed his own themes.

Draper, John W. "The Old Age of King Lear." *The Journal of English and German Philology* XXXIX, No. 4 (October 1940): 527-40.
  Discusses characteristics apparent in Lear's old age and their relation to Elizabethan theories of the stages of human life.

Duthie, G. I. *Elizabethan Shorthand and the First Quarto of "King Lear."* Oxford: Basil Blackwell, 1949, 82 p.
  Disputes the hypothesis that the copy for the First Quarto of *King Lear* was supplied by a stenographic transcript of a playhouse performance. Duthie maintains that none of the systems of shorthand available at the time *King Lear* was written was capable of reproducing a text as full as the *Lear* Quarto, an argument that has since been generally accepted by textual scholars.

————. Introduction to *King Lear*, by William Shakespeare, edited by G. I. Duthie and John Dover Wilson, pp. ix-lv. Cambridge: Cambridge University Press, 1960.
  Comprehensive discussion of *King Lear*. Duthie answers questions relating to text, date, and source, then focuses on the roles of such characters as Lear, Cordelia, Kent, and the Fool in the action of the play.

Egan, Robert. "Nature's Above Art: *King Lear*." In his *Drama within Drama: Shakespeare's Sense of His Art in "King Lear," "The Winter's Tale," and "The Tempest,"* pp. 16-55. New York: Columbia University Press, 1975.
  Maintains that the ambiguity apparent in *King Lear* between order and chaos, affirmation and absurdity, transcendence and nihilism, is a deliberate element in the play. For Egan, Shakespeare's artistic purpose "is reflected within the play itself through attempts by its characters to deal with, influence, or alter the circumstances of their world directly through exercises of dramatic art."

Elliott, G. R. "The Initial Contrast in *Lear*." *The Journal of English and German Philology* LVIII, No. 1 (January 1959): 251-63.
  Attempts to define the exact nature of the first scene of *King Lear*. Elliott asserts that at the beginning of the play Lear is hardly the senile and foolish ruler that Samuel Taylor Coleridge and A. C. Bradley suggest (see excerpts above, 1813 and 1904); instead, he sees the king as a wise and successful leader whose plan to divide the kingdom and maintain his country's peace and prosperity is a shrewd political undertaking which eventually fails only because of Cordelia's breach of pride.

Ellis, John. "The Gulling of Gloucester: Credibility in the Subplot of *King Lear*." *Studies in English Literature: 1500-1900* 12, No. 2 (Spring 1972): 275-89.
  In-depth analysis of the Gloucester subplot. Ellis argues against those critics who have criticized Edmund's gulling of Gloucester and Edgar as improbable and dramatically unconvincing, suggesting instead that the duping of both of these characters is prepared for in the first scene.

Elton, William R. *"King Lear" and the Gods*. San Marino, Calif.: The Huntington Library, 1966, 369 p.
  Examines *King Lear* in relation to its Renaissance religious background, claiming that the play is structurally and thematically based on a combination of four attitudes towards Providence typically ascribed by the Renaissance public to heathen societies. Elton finds that these attitudes are best delineated in Philip Sidney's *Arcadia*, where they are referred to as those of the *prisca theologia*, or virtuous heathen; the atheistic; the superstitious; and "the shiftingly indeterminate reaction to an inhospitable cosmos." The goal of Elton's investigation is to test the validity of the Christian optimistic interpretation of *King Lear*, which he finds invalid for two reasons: first, no evidence exists to show that Lear arrives at "salvation"; and second, there is nothing in the play to support the idea of a benevolent, just, or special Providence.

Empson, William. "Fool in Lear." In his *The Structure of Complex Words*, pp. 125-57. London: Chatto & Windus, 1979.
  In-depth, scene by scene examination of the concept of folly in *King Lear*. Empson interprets the action of the play and concludes that Lear makes "a fool of himself on the most cosmic and appalling scale possible," for he reveals not only his own folly, but the folly of nature and the gods.

Evans, Bertrand. "Practice as Diversion: *King Lear*." In his *Shakespeare's Tragic Practice*, pp. 147-80. Oxford: Clarendon Press, 1979.
  Discusses the structure of *King Lear* in relation to Shakespeare's other major tragedies. Evans claims that whereas in such plays as *Hamlet* and *Othello* the "discrepant awarenesses" of the protagonists dominate the action, in *King Lear* this dramatic technique plays a far less important role, since the major discrepant awareness—Lear's misperception of Goneril and Regan's hypocrisy and Cordelia's love—is essentially resolved by the second act. Shakespeare was therefore, according to Evans, forced to develop other minor, less intrinsic practices of deception—situated mainly in the Gloucester subplot—in order to maintain interest in the development of his story and to keep the purgation of Lear from becoming too oppressive on the audience.

Freedman, Sanford. "Character in a Coherent Fiction: On Putting *King Lear* Back Together Again." *Philosophy and Literature* 7, No. 2 (Fall 1983): 196-212.
  Surveys *King Lear* criticism from the eighteenth, nineteenth, and twentieth centuries, focusing on the emphasis each century placed on either the internal forces within the text, such as character, structure, or language, or on the external concepts to which the text refers. Freedman's major emphasis is on how the eighteenth and nineteenth century's legacy of "inside/outside" debate affects twentieth-century critical opinion, and how "twentieth-century controversy polarizes 'insides' and 'outsides' without acknowledging the implications of doing so."

Furness, Horace Howard, ed. *A New Variorum Edition of Shakespeare: "King Lear."* Philadelphia: J. B. Lippincott Co., 1880, 503 p.
  Contains useful excerpts on *King Lear* by such prominent critics as August Wilhelm Schlegel, Samuel Johnson, Samuel Taylor Coleridge, and G. G. Gervinus, as well as an in-depth discussion by Furness on the text of *King Lear* and Shakespeare's sources.

Gardner, Helen. *"King Lear."* London: The Athlone Press, 1968, 28 p.
  General discussion of *King Lear* which was originally delivered as a lecture before the University of London on March 2, 1966. Gardner touches on a number of points in her study, such as *King Lear*'s difference from Shakespeare's other tragedies, its use of comic elements, the dialectical relationship of its characters, and the ambiguity of its ending. Gardner concludes that the play espouses no single metaphysical attitude towards life, but simply presents the mystery of existence in both its horror and its profundity.

Goldberg, S. L. *An Essay on "King Lear."* Cambridge: Cambridge University Press, 1974, 192 p.
  In-depth, detailed study of *King Lear* which attempts to reconstruct the logic inherent in the play and which questions the generally accepted findings of A. C. Bradley in an effort to redefine the dramatic action. Goldberg argues that in the post-Bradleyan age of criticism of *King Lear* too many critics have forsaken Bradley's "linear" approach for an analysis of the "spatial" or "organic" kinds of structure in the play. In his own study, Goldberg returns to the methods of Bradley—focusing on the "temporal" rather than the "spatial" structure of *King Lear*—in order to challenge "two basic assumptions" of Bradley's reading: one, "that the drama moves in time only in order to represent the spiritual history of Lear"; and two, that if we are supposed to identify with the hero, so we must "identify the end of his spiritual history as the meaning of the drama."

Greg, W. W. "Time, Place, and Politics in 'King Lear'." *Modern Language Review* XXXV, No. 4 (October 1940): 431-46.
Detailed examination of the setting and progression of events in *King Lear,* as well as a discussion of the politics inherent in France's invasion of England.

Griffith, [Elizabeth]. "*Lear.*" In her *The Morality of Shakespeare's Drama Illustrated,* pp. 350-75. 1775. Reprint. London: Frank Cass & Co., 1971.
Detailed reconstruction of *King Lear* focusing on Shakespeare's moral precepts.

Harbage, Alfred. "Justice in Tragic Fable." In his *As They Liked It: An Essay on Shakespeare and Morality,* pp. 142-52. New York: The Macmillan Co., 1947.
Maintains that *King Lear, Romeo and Juliet, Othello, Hamlet,* and other of Shakespeare's tragedies do not violate poetic justice in their presentation of the success of evil in the world, as many critics have concluded. Harbage suggests instead that these works demonstrate, not a separation of God and humanity, but the worldly effects of human wickedness, cruelty, and sin. By rendering such powerful examples of human cruelty, Harbage continues, Shakespeare does not violate our sense of justice, but shows us situations, painful as they are, true to the nature of the human world.

Harris, Duncan S. "The End of *Lear* and a Shape for Shakespearean Tragedy." *Shakespeare Studies* IX (1976): 253-68.
Considers the four types of resolution present at the conclusion of *King Lear:* the resolution of justice, conveyed in the deaths of the evil characters; the unjust and tragic resolution apparent in the deaths of Gloucester, Lear, and Cordelia; "the return to perilous balance in which the tragedy began"; and that resolution in which the audience and survivors share—what Harris calls "the catharsis of clarity." Harris's hypothesis is that all of these resolutions contribute to a Christian reading of the play; or, in other words, that *King Lear* presents a vision of a Christian cosmos, and not chaos, at the conclusion of its action.

Honigmann, E.A.J. "Lear's Mind." In his *Shakespeare, Seven Tragedies: The Dramatist's Manipulation of Response,* pp. 101-25. London: The Macmillan Press, 1976.
An examination of Lear's mind and the manner in which his perception, as well as the way in which the reader views him at any one moment, shapes the meaning of the play.

Kahn, Sholom J. "'Enter Lear Mad'." *Shakespeare Quarterly* 8, No. 3 (Summer 1957): 311-29.
Primarily a textual study, but with the intention of determining the exact point Lear becomes mad. Kahn compares both the 1608 Quarto and the Folio texts of *King Lear,* the speeches by Lear in Acts II, III, and IV, and the investigations of earlier textual critics, to posit the theory that Lear is not completely insane until his meeting with Gloucester in Act IV, Scene vi.

Keast, W. R. "The 'New Criticism' and *King Lear.*" In *Critics and Criticism: Ancient and Modern,* edited by R. S. Crane, pp. 108-37. Chicago: The University of Chicago Press, 1952.
A refutation of Robert B. Heilman's image-pattern analysis of *King Lear* (see excerpt above, 1948). Keast contends that Heilman frequently in his study sacrifices the obvious or practical for the obtuse or symbolic, and he finds particularly misleading Heilman's interpretation of the text of *King Lear*—its imagery or "image patterns"—according to his own external definitions of tragedy.

Kirschbaum, Leo. "The True Text of *King Lear.*" *Shakespeare Association Bulletin* XVI, No. 3 (July 1941): 140-53.
Argues that the Folio of 1623, and not the so-called "Pied Bull" Quarto of 1608, is the authoritative text of *King Lear.* Kirschbaum bases his conclusion on available evidence, which he says demonstrates that the Quarto is a memorial corruption and that the Folio edition is a corrected copy of the Quarto based on a transcript used by Shakespeare's company.

———. "Banquo and Edgar: Character or Function?" *Essays in Criticism* VII, No. 1 (January 1957): 1-21.
Compares Banquo and Edgar as poetic functionaries in their respective plays, rather than as cohesive psychological portraits. Kirschbaum maintains that the only way we can conceive of a character such as Edgar, who changes throughout *King Lear* from a seemingly simple-minded brother, into a madman, a peasant, and finally the figure of retribution in the play, is to view him not as a psychologically unique individual, but as a poetic "function" in Shakespeare's play—a dramatic device used to facilitate other incidents and to expound certain themes.

———. "Albany." *Shakespeare Survey* 13 (1966): 20-9.
Focuses strictly on the character of Albany to demonstrate Shakespeare's method of using evil or catastrophic events as a device for spiritually and physically elevating certain heretofore "weak" characters.

Knight, Charles. "*King Lear.*" In his *Studies of Shakspere,* pp. 337-52. London: George Routledge and Sons, 1868.
Traces the textual history of *King Lear* and reviews some of Shakespeare's possible sources for the drama. Knight also compares Nahum Tate's seventeenth-century version of *King Lear* and Shakespeare's own adaptation.

Knight, G. Wilson. "The *Lear* Universe." In his *The Wheel of Fire: Essays in Interpretation of Shakespeare's Sombre Tragedies,* pp. 194-226. London: Oxford University Press, 1930.
Interprets *King Lear* as depicting a purgatorial experience of "creative suffering." Knight sees Edmund, Lear, and Cordelia as corresponding to three periods in the development of the human being: the primitive, the civilized, and the idealistic. For Knight, Shakespeare's drama moves toward that ideal personified in Cordelia—an "awakening into love"—as its ultimate goal. He therefore sees the suffering experienced by Lear as "creative" to the extent that it prepares him for a new awareness and transforms his being into a higher level of existence.

Knights, L. C. "*King Lear* as Metaphor." In his *Further Explorations,* pp. 169-85. Stanford, Calif.: Stanford University Press, 1965.
An analysis of the method of Shakespeare's art, specifically as developed in *King Lear.* Knights attributes the problems that "naturalist-inclined" readers have accepting the progression of events in a play like *King Lear* to their wish for verisimilitude rather than poetic representation. Shakespeare, Knights continues, conceived his works metaphorically, not naturalistically: he constructed his plays out of "key-words" which act as symbols, but which also reverberate with meanings both with reference to the surrounding text and with regard to the reader's impressions.

Kreider. P. V. "Gloucester's Eyes." *Shakespeare Association Bulletin* VIII, Nos. 3 and 4 (July-October 1933): 121-32.
Focuses on the imagery of sight and blindness as a continuous and unifying pattern in *King Lear.*

Lawlor, John. "The Truth of Imagination and the Idea of Justice." In his *The Tragic Sense in Shakespeare,* pp. 147-83. London: Chatto & Windus, 1966.
Speculative discussion of the concept of "justice" in *King Lear.* Lawlor's main contention is that *King Lear* demonstrates the indifferent reality of justice beyond the scope of human desires. Unlike "poetic justice," which is controlled by the individual artist and which answers to his or her needs, the justice of the real world satisfies its own ends and refuses the demands or sacrifices of humankind. Applied to *King Lear,* Lawlor argues, this concept of justice explains the necessity for Lear's and Cordelia's deaths, despite their sacrifices and repentance, since their acts, once committed, require that this ultimate justice set all things aright.

Leider, Emily W. "Plainness of Style in *King Lear.*" *Shakespeare Quarterly* 21, No. 1 (Winter 1970): 45-53.
Asserts that the language and style of *King Lear* evolve during the course of the play from elaboration, ornamentation, and affectation, to simplicity, sparseness, and sincerity.

Levin, Harry. "The Heights and the Depths: A Scene from 'King Lear'." In *More Talking of Shakespeare*, edited by John Garrett, pp. 87-103. London: Longmans, Green and Co., 1959.
> Interpretive reading of *King Lear* in which the critic reconstructs the heights and depths apparent in the structure of the play by focusing on the scene at Dover Cliffs.

Lucas, F. L. "Lear, Othello, Macbeth." In his *Literature and Psychology*, pp. 62-78. London: Cassell & Co., 1951.
> A psychoanalytic interpretation of *King Lear*. Lucas characterizes the play as a "tragedy of jealousy" between parents and children, between siblings, and, "above all, of a father's morbid possessiveness towards a favourite daughter."

Maclean, Norman. "Episode, Scene, Speech, and Word: The Madness of Lear." In *Critics and Criticism: Ancient and Modern*, edited by R. S. Crane, pp. 595-615. Chicago: The University of Chicago Press, 1952.
> Focuses on that portion of *King Lear* from Act III, Scene i, to Act IV, Scene vi, as a single dramatic unit in which Shakespeare reveals the onset of Lear's madness, while at the same time preparing the reader or spectator for the king's complete reversal in moral outlook: from his "Reason not the need" speech at the end of Act II to his cynical vision of human life in Act IV, Scene vi.

Markels, Julian. "Shakespeare's Confluence of Tragedy and Comedy: *Twelfth Night* and *King Lear*." In *Shakespeare 400: Essays by American Scholars on the Anniversary of the Poet's Birth*, edited by James G. McManaway, pp. 75-88. New York: Holt, Rinehart and Winston, 1964.
> Argues that *King Lear* and *Twelfth Night* draw upon a common body of intellectual and thematic material, out of which Shakespeare's mind achieves "the forms and effects appropriate to comedy and tragedy."

Masefield, John. "The Plays: *King Lear*." In his *William Shakespeare*, pp. 186-95. New York: Henry Holt and Co., 1911.
> General discussion of the themes, symbolism, characterization, and other elements presented in *King Lear*.

Mason, H. A. "*King Lear*." In his *Shakespeare's Tragedies of Love: An Examination of the Possibility of Common Readings of "Romeo and Juliet," "Othello," "King Lear," and "Anthony and Cleopatra*," pp. 165-226. London: Chatto & Windus, 1970.
> Attempts a total reevaluation of *King Lear* in an effort to discover the "central stream" that flows throughout the play and to determine what it is in the drama that appeals to such a wide spectrum of readers and spectators.

Matthews, Brander. "'King Lear'." In his *Shakspere as a Playwright*, pp. 276-93. New York: Charles Scribner's Sons, 1923.
> Regards *King Lear* as a play ill-suited for the modern stage and admits that its true force can only be appreciated when approached as literature rather than drama.

Maxwell, J. C. "The Technique of Invocation in 'King Lear'." *Modern Language Review* XLV, No. 2 (April 1950): 142-47.
> Examines the manner in which Shakespeare mixes the pagan and the Christian world views in *King Lear*.

McNeir, Waldo F. "The Role of Edmund in *King Lear*." *Studies in English Literature: 1500-1900* 8, No. 2 (Spring 1968): 187-216.
> Focuses on Edmund's role in *King Lear* "in an effort to understand his actions in the final scene in terms of Elizabethan doctrine on the subject of repentance."

Moulton, Richard G. "How Climax Meets Climax in the Centre of 'Lear': A Study in More Complex Passion and Movement." In his *Shakespeare as a Dramatic Artist: A Popular Illustration of the Principles of Scientific Criticism*, rev. ed., pp. 202-24. London: Oxford at the Clarendon Press, 1888.
> An analysis of the plot structure of *King Lear*. Moulton argues that the primary action of the drama—the tragedy of Lear—consists of three subordinate tragedies, all springing from Lear's initial impetuousness: the death of Lear, the deaths of Cordelia and Kent, and the deaths of Regan and Goneril. Similarly, the play's subplot—the tragedy of Gloucester—consists of three subordinate falls: the tribulations of Edgar, the blinding of Gloucester, and the death of Edmund.

Muir, Kenneth. "Madness in *King Lear*." *Shakespeare Survey* 13 (1966): 30-40.
> An examination of Shakespeare's use of madness, in general, and, in particular, Lear's descent into insanity. Muir reconstructs Lear's drift into and out of insanity and praises Shakespeare's insight into the human psyche in order to draw such a convincing spectacle.

——. Introduction to *King Lear*, by Willliam Shakespeare, edited by Kenneth Muir, pp. xiii-lviii. The Arden Edition of the Works of William Shakespeare, edited by Harold F. Brooks and Harold Jenkins. London: Methuen & Co., 1972.
> Supplies information on the date and text of *King Lear*, as well as Shakespeare's possible sources, and traces the major trends in *Lear* criticism. Muir also discusses important themes and motives, plot, characterization, style, and other elements of the play.

Myrick, Kenneth. "Christian Pessimism in *King Lear*." In *Shakespeare, 1564-1964: A Collection of Modern Essays by Various Hands*, edited by Edward A. Bloom, pp. 56-70. Providence, R.I.: Brown University Press, 1964.
> Outlines the doctrine of Christian pessimism popular during the English Renaissance and illustrates its presence as a significant element in *King Lear*.

Nevo, Ruth. "*King Lear*." In her *Tragic Form in Shakespeare*, pp. 258-305. Princeton, N.J.: Princeton University Press, 1972.
> Detailed study of the themes, motives, characterization, and philosophy presented in *King Lear* as they are developed in each act, and, in some instances, in each subsequent scene. Nevo's purpose is to demonstrate that both the optimistic and pessimistic readings of *King Lear* err in their failure to analyze the events properly. Nevo maintains that the death of Cordelia is dramatically necessary because it forms the basis of Shakespeare's purpose, namely, to demonstrate the inadequacy of love to redeem, no matter how pure or powerful that love is. Nevo defines this as "the burden of the play," and for this reason she describes *King Lear* as a "titanic agon rather than a purgatorial progress."

Nosworthy, J. M. "*King Lear*—The Moral Aspect." *English Studies* 21 (1939): 260-68.
> A somewhat detailed, character by character analysis of the moral breakdown Shakespeare dramatizes in *King Lear*. This moral breakdown of the *Lear* universe Nosworthy considers the primary concern of Shakespeare's play.

Oates, Joyce Carol. "'Is This the Promised End?': The Tragedy of *King Lear*." *Journal of Aesthetics and Art Criticism* 33, No. 1 (Fall 1974): 19-32.
> Perceives in the play a conflict between the visionary, or the transcendent, hope offered by Cordelia, and the tragic, or the world caught in historical time. Oates regards Cordelia as an emblem of both "fallen Nature," with all its ramifications of freedom and creativity, and, ironically, of the spiritual bridge through whom the fatal division of the Lear universe could be overcome. However, Oates concludes that Cordelia's death defeats any idea of salvation inherent in the work.

Paunez, Arpad. "Psychopathology of Shakespeare's 'King Lear'." *The American Imago* 9, No. 1 (April 1952): 57-77.
> Further develops the psychoanalytic approach to *King Lear* first suggested by Sigmund Freud (see excerpt above, 1913). Paunez argues that the tragic events which befall Lear are partly the result of his "erotic" love for his daughters, especially Cordelia.

Peck, Russell A. "Edgar's Pilgrimage: High Comedy in *King Lear*." *Studies in English Literature: 1500-1900* 7 (1967): 219-37.
> Detailed discussion of Edgar's development during the course of *King Lear*. Peck considers Edgar rather than Gloucester the major figure of the subplot, and even regards him as the most important character in the play after Lear.

Perkinson, Richard H. "Shakespeare's Revision of the Lear Story and the Structure of *King Lear.*" *Philological Quarterly* XXII, No. 3 (July 1943): 315-29.

A comprehensive refutation of those critics who see in *King Lear,* particularly the first act, a falling off or decay in Shakespeare's talents. Perkinson argues that *King Lear* follows a well-conceived and deliberate plan based on Shakespeare's desire to write a tragedy rather than another chronicle play. Perkinson further maintains that it was Shakespeare's "tragic concept" that caused him to condense the so-called "love test," as well as Lear's changing attitude towards Cordelia, and redirect the effect of Goneril's and Regan's ingratitude—which in the chronicles causes Lear to flee to Cordelia in France—in order to contribute to the tragic dimensions of his hero.

Reid, Stephen. "In Defense of Goneril and Regan." *The American Imago* 27, No. 3 (Fall 1970): 226-44.

Claims that the traditional interpretation of Goneril's and Regan's characters as they are presented in the first act—that both are all too willing and capable of testing their new authority against their father—is erroneous to the extent that it fails to take into account the daughters' development with regard to their "authority." Reid suggests instead that both are extremely insecure as to how far they can manipulate their father, and it is only through the ordeals of Act II—the reducing of Lear's train and the stocking of Kent—that they secure their relations with each other and sense the limitless possibilities of their power.

Rinehart, Keith. "The Moral Background of *King Lear.*" *The University of Kansas City Review* XX, No. 4 (Summer 1954): 223-28.

An examination of the stoic moral background dramatized in *King Lear.* Rinehart considers Cordelia the closest individual to the stoic ideal: reasonable, honest, forebearing, and subservient to the laws of nature. Other characters, such as Lear, Gloucester, Edgar, and Kent, he sees as located on a scale between Cordelia and her evil sisters, Goneril and Regan, both of whom represent the antithesis of the stoic ideal in their abundance of passion and their thirst for self-gratification.

Rosenberg, Marvin. *The Masks of "King Lear."* Berkeley, Los Angeles, and London: University of California Press, 1972, 431 p.

Attempts to juxtapose the major interpretations of *King Lear* presented by literary critics with the theatrical conceptions of the play depicted in past performances by both actors and producers. Rosenberg states that the "history of the play in theatre and criticism was pieced from hundreds of books, essays, periodical reports, memoirs, and acting versions consulted, as well as from my notes on performances and rehearsals attended and actors interviewed."

Siegel, Paul N. "*King Lear.*" In his *Shakespearean Tragedy and the Elizabethan Compromise,* pp. 161-88. New York: New York University Press, 1957.

A close reading of specific characters and events in *King Lear.* Siegel discusses Shakespeare's use of evil in the play and its eventual self-destructive nature, then parallels the trials of suffering and redemption experienced by Lear and Gloucester.

Sisson, C. J. "The Quandary: 'King Lear'." In his *Shakespeare's Tragic Justice,* pp. 74-98. London: Methuen & Co., 1963.

Discusses the role of human and divine justice in *King Lear.* Sisson specifically focuses on the process by which Lear comes to realize that justice and power, on the mortal plane, are hopeless, and that even the justice of the gods is nonexistent. However, out of this despair, Sisson argues, Lear discovers the Christian concept of charity, or divine love, which in itself negates the issue of justice in the play.

Skulsky, Harold. "*King Lear* and the Meaning of Chaos." *Shakespeare Quarterly* 17, No. 1 (Winter 1966): 3-17.

Argues that *King Lear* is Shakespeare's reply to Ulysses's vision of a chaotic universe presented in *Troilus and Cressida.* Skulsky refers to *King Lear* as "the poetic laboratory" in which Shakespeare tested the most basic values of human existence in a world devoid of justice, divinity, dignity, and love.

Snyder, Susan. "Between the Divine and the Absurd: *King Lear.*" In her *The Comic Matrix of Shakespeare's Tragedies: "Romeo and Juliet," "Hamlet," "Othello," and "King Lear,"* pp. 137-79. Princeton, N.J.: Princeton University Press, 1979.

Examines the manner in which Shakespeare relates the grotesque, chaotic comedy of the Fool, Edgar, and Lear—the last during his temporary insanity—with the overall comic pattern of his play. Snyder also addresses the question why such an overall comic scheme—one which traces its protagonist's experience from selfish king, through abasement and suffering, to redemption—should produce in the spectator or reader such a tragic emotional effect.

Soellner, Rolf. "*King Lear:* Valuing the Self" and "*King Lear:* Stripping the Self." In his *Shakespeare's Patterns of Self-Knowledge,* pp. 281-304, pp. 305-26. Columbus: Ohio State University Press, 1972.

Deals, in one chapter on *King Lear,* with the concept of *nosce teipsum,* or "self-knowledge," and its presence in the play. Soellner discusses the numerous paradoxes Shakespeare presents as elements of self-knowledge, all of which are based on the thoughts and writings of Elizabethan England. These include the ideas of creation from nothing, redemption in suffering, wisdom in folly, insight in blindness, and strength in weakness. In the second chapter, Soellner examines Lear's questions on the meaning of existence by comparing them to a systematic consideration of the human condition expanded in Sir James Perrott's *The First Part of the Consideration of the Human Condition* (1600).

Spencer, Benjamin T. "*King Lear:* A Prophetic Tragedy." *College English* 5, No. 5 (February 1944): 302-08.

Maintains that in *King Lear* Shakespeare dramatized the tragedy of Renaissance man as he knew him—naive, complacent, and crudely civilized—and, in Lear and Gloucester, foreshadowed the humanistic philosophy of the twentieth century.

States, Bert O. "Standing on the Extreme Verge in *King Lear* and Other High Places." *Georgia Review* 36, No. 2 (Summer 1982): 417-25.

Examines the manner in which Edgar's speech in the scene at Dover Cliffs, specifically, his visual description to the blind Gloucester of the precipice below, achieves its powerful effect.

Stewart, J.I.M. "The Blinding of Gloster." *The Review of English Studies* XXI, No. 84 (October 1945): 264-70.

Focuses on the issue of Gloucester's blinding and its place on the modern stage. Like most twentieth-century critics, Stewart argues for the inclusion of the blinding scene in any stage production, basing his assessment on two points: first, it was necessary for Shakespeare to show the spectacle on stage, since no amount of narration could produce the horror he sought; second, the scene serves as a vivid actualization of what the play's imagery suggests on an imaginative level.

Tamblyn, William Ferguson. "Tragedy in *King Lear.*" *The Sewanee Review* XXX, No. 1 (January 1922): 63-77.

General discussion of the structure of Shakespeare's tragedies. Tamblyn maintains that although many critics argue that Shakespeare's tragedies are primarily based on character, they are in reality based more on fate. He devotes the remainder of his essay to substantiate this point, using examples from all the major tragedies, including *King Lear.*

Traversi, D. A. "'King Lear': I, II, and III." *Scrutiny* XIX, Nos. 1, 2, and 3 (October 1952; Winter 1952-53; Spring 1953): 43-64, 126-42, 206-30.

In-depth, three-part study of the characters, themes, and structure of *King Lear.* Traversi primarily focuses on each of the characters' interpretations of the concept of nature and then demonstrates how these attitudes, with the exception of the attitudes of Cordelia, Kent, and the Fool, represent distortions of the natural order in their dependence on passion, rather than reason, as the human faculty which shapes actions and determines values. Traversi reconstructs and analyzes each scene, paying particular attention to the conflict raging in Lear's mind—his growing awareness of the faults and misperceptions of his past actions—and the dramatic/

symbolic rift in the physical, moral, and political world that corresponds to and transforms Lear's own crisis of identity.

Van Doren, Mark. "*King Lear*." In his *Shakespeare*, pp. 238-51.
New York: Henry Holt and Co., 1939.
    An imaginative interpretation of *King Lear* in which the critic
    calls the play "lyrical instead of logical, musical instead of moral."

Vickers, Brian. "Tragic Prose: Clowns, Villains, Madmen." In his
The Artistry of Shakespeare's Prose, pp. 331-404. London: Methuen
& Co., 1968.
    Discusses the syntax, as well as the prose and verse styles, Shake-
    speare employs in *King Lear*. Vickers attempts to gain an un-
    derstanding of the play by focusing on Shakespeare's shifts from
    prose to verse, and verse to prose, and on the language used by
    each of the major characters.

Walker, Alice. *Textual Problems of the First Folio: "Richard III,"
"King Lear," "Troilus and Cressida," "2 Henry IV," "Hamlet,"
"Othello."* Cambridge: Cambridge University Press, 1953, 170 p.
    Presents a new theory concerning the origins of the 1608 Quarto
    of *King Lear*. Walker suggests that the text represents a transcript
    of Shakespeare's "foul papers," supplemented with the recollec-
    tions of certain actors. The Folio text of 1623, Walker continues,
    was printed from a copy of the 1608 Quarto which had been
    collated with the acting company's prompt-book. Walker's con-
    clusion is that the Quarto needs to be given much greater authority
    than modern editors have been willing to grant it.

Walton, J. K. "Lear's Last Speech." *Shakespeare Survey* 13 (1966):
11-19.
    Detailed reconstruction of Lear's education in self-knowledge,
    which is at first inflicted on him, but which, after his encounter
    with Poor Tom, he later seeks on his own. Walton argues that
    the theme of self-knowledge must be accepted as essential if we
    hope to understand Lear's final speech. Disputing A. C. Bradley
    (see excerpt above, 1904), he claims that no evidence exists to
    suggest that Lear dies in a moment of ecstasy; instead, Walton
    maintains that Lear's death is a result of both his despair and the
    depth of his newly acquired consciousness at the end of the play.

Watkins, W.B.C. "The Two Techniques in *King Lear*." *The Review
of English Studies* XVIII, No. 69 (January 1942): 1-26.
    Maintains that in *King Lear* Shakespeare consciously attempted
    to fuse two different narrative techniques, psychological realism
    and symbolic stylization, in order to present his grand theme on
    both an individual and universal level. Although for Watkins
    Shakespeare's attempt causes a certain degree of confusion, such
    as some critics interpreting the Fool "psychologically" rather than
    "poetically," as Watkins argues he was meant to be, he still
    claims that the experiment works, primarily because Shakespeare
    manages to retain a complexity in presentation equal to the com-
    plexity of his theme.

Weitz, Morris. "The Coinage of Man: 'King Lear' and Camus's 'L'É-
tranger'." *Modern Language Review* 66 (1971): 31-9.
    Compares *King Lear* and Albert Camus's *L'Étranger* and claims
    that whereas Camus eventually asserts a nihilistic vision of the
    universe, Shakespeare posits a world without metaphysical com-
    fort, yet one which contains the force of human values.

West, Robert H. "Sex and Pessimism in *King Lear*." *Shakespeare
Quarterly* 11, No. 1 (Winter 1960): 55-60.
    A discussion of sex and pessimism in *King Lear*. West argues
    that the pessimistic vision with which Lear contemplates sexual
    procreation is tempered by the audience's knowledge of his frail
    mental state and, further, by the "given morality" in the play
    that stresses the devotion of children to their parents. Still, West
    counters, the play does not support this morality with an obvious
    cosmology or eschatology, but suggests, by the absence of such
    an overriding metaphysical system, that Shakespeare understood
    the "mystery of the world" and the need for basic human values.

Whitaker, Virgil K. "The Rack of This Tough World: *Hamlet* and
King Lear." In his *The Mirror Up to Nature: The Technique of Shake-
speare's Tragedies*, pp. 183-240. San Marino, Calif.: The Huntington
Library, 1965.
    Compares *Hamlet* and *King Lear* as two plays that deal specifically
    with the Christian concepts of patience and redemption.

White, Richard Grant. "*King Lear*." In his *Studies in Shakespeare*,
pp. 183-232. Boston and New York: Houghton, Mifflin and Co., 1896.
    Study of the major characters in *King Lear*. White takes a some-
    what negative view of Lear and Cordelia, blaming both exclu-
    sively for the suffering they experience.

Williams, George W. "The Poetry of the Storm in *King Lear*." *Shakespeare Quarterly* 2 (1951): 57-71.
    In-depth examination of Act III, Scene ii, in *King Lear*. Williams
    maintains that this scene is probably the most important of the
    play, especially for its fusion of the universal and the particular,
    the macrocosm and the microcosm, corresponding to the tempest
    on the heath and the chaos in Lear's mind.

Williams, Philip. "Two Problems in the Folio Text of *King Lear*."
Shakespeare Quarterly 4, No. 4 (October 1953): 451-60.
    Takes issue with two important assumptions accepted by those
    textual scholars who believe the 1608 Quarto of *King Lear* to be
    a "bad" quarto and who regard the Folio edition of 1623—which
    they claim is based on a corrected copy of the First Quarto—as
    the primary authoritative text. First, Williams considers erroneous
    the assumption that only one compositor typeset the Folio edition
    of *King Lear;* second, he finds no evidence that the Folio text
    was set directly from a corrected copy of the 1608 Quarto.

Love's Labour's Lost

DATE: Scholars have variously maintained that Shakespeare composed *Love's Labour's Lost* as early as 1588 and as late as 1596. The title page of the 1598 quarto edition—the earliest extant copy of *Love's Labour's Lost*—states that it was "presented before her Highnes this last Christmas" and that it was "Newly corrected and augmented by W. Shakespere." Although this evidence has helped critics determine a rather precise performance date for *Love's Labour's Lost* of 1597-98, the question of when Shakespeare originally composed the play remains unanswered. Early critical tradition placed *Love's Labour's Lost* among Shakespeare's first dramatic efforts, a position upheld by some recent critics who, examining the structure, language, and style of the play, maintain that it was originally written in 1588. Other scholars proposed that certain topical references in the play—such as allusions to the French civil war (1588-92), to Sir Walter Raleigh's "School of Night," and to the Gabriel Harvey-Thomas Nashe controversy—can be used to date the drama. Raleigh's "School of Night," alluded to by Shakespeare in IV. iii. 251, consisted of a group of scientists and poets organized around 1590 to study astronomy and speculate on the nature of human existence and Christian thought; the Harvey-Nashe controversy—a scurrilous debate between two rival dramatists—lasted from 1592 to 1599 and, according to many critics, served as the model for the disputes between Armado and Moth in Shakespeare's play. Aside from the question of the validity of such historical allusions in *Love's Labour's Lost,* the resultant dates of composition supported by these indentifications range anywhere from 1588 to 1596. In an effort to narrow this time span, most scholars speculate that *Love's Labour's Lost* was written sometime between 1593 and 1595; in support of their conclusion they cite the play's stylistic affinities with other Shakespearean works known to have been composed during this so-called "lyrical period," such as the Sonnets and *Romeo and Juliet.*

TEXT: As mentioned above, the earliest extant copy of *Love's Labour's Lost* appeared in the quarto of 1598 and stated on the title page that it was "Newly corrected and augmented By W. Shakespere." This quarto edition, also referred to as Q, is considered by most textual scholars to be the basis for the later Folio edition of the play and, hence, the only authoritative text. There are, however, numerous variants between the Q and Folio editions of *Love's Labour's Lost,* causing some critics to question whether the former served as the sole source of the latter's composition. Arthur Quiller-Couch and John Dover Wilson explained these variants by proposing that the copy of Q used in the composition of the Folio edition had also served as a company prompt-book and contained changes not made or authorized by Shakespeare. Other critics, most notably H. C. Hart, declared that the texts for both Q and the Folio editions were based on two separate prompt-books presumably based on Shakespeare's manuscript. Still other scholars attributed these variants to editorial alterations on the part of the Folio compositor, or even to changes supplied by the Folio editors, John Heminges and Henry Condell. The text of Q also presents its share of problems, most notably the presence of essentially duplicated lines and speeches and a number of inconsistent or confused speech-headings. Dover Wilson attributed these anomalies to the fact that Shakespeare himself revised the manuscript of *Love's Labour's Lost* years after its original compo-

Title page of Love's Labour's Lost taken from the First Folio (1623). By permission of the Folger

sition, perhaps carelessly, and that the compositor of Q inadvertently included material meant to be deleted or simply misinterpreted some of Shakespeare's revisions. Other critics who support this theory include Henry David Gray, T. W. Baldwin, and Alfred Harbage, the last of whom claimed that the original *Love's Labour's Lost* ended not with the King of France's death but with a settlement of the Princess's territorial claims and marriage, and that the earlier version may have been the play *Love's Labour's Won* which Francis Meres attributed to Shakespeare in 1598. Other scholars have attempted to explain the inconsistencies in Q by suggesting that a "bad quarto," now lost, was used as the sole source of its composition. Although this theory has received considerable attention, most critics consider Q's peculiarities and corruptions too numerous to attribute them to a "bad quarto," claiming that they are more than likely the work of an apprentice compositor.

SOURCES: *Love's Labour's Lost* and *A Midsummer Night's Dream* share the distinction of being the only two Shakespearean plays for which there is no evident source. While it is generally conceded that the dramatic structure of *Love's Labour's Lost* is reminiscent of the works of the Elizabethan playwright John Lyly, and that the low-comedy characters, such as Holofernes, Armado, and Costard, derive ultimately from the Italian *commedia dell'arte*, most critics agree that the original source for the play is now lost. However, some scholars question the existence of such a source and the extent of Shakespeare's indebtedness to it. The suggestion that *Love's Labour's Lost* contains references to French and Russian political events has led several critics to propose a number of historical accounts as possible sources for the drama. The most prominent of these is Pierre de la Primaudaye's *Academie Française* (1577), which describes the self-imposed seclusion of four young scholars. Historical records also indicate that, like his counterpart in Shakespeare's play, Henri of Navarre received visits from a princess of France and, later, from the Queen of France during which a dowry, including the region of Aquitaine, was discussed. The fact that Biron, Longueville, and Duc de Mayenne (Shakespeare's "Dumain") were actual Navarrese nobles has also fueled speculation that Shakespeare based *Love's Labour's Lost* on historical incidents. The Masque of the Muscovites may have been suggested to Shakespeare by similar entertainment held during the Christmas Revels of 1594-95 at Gray's Inn, or, it is sometimes suggested, by a politically embarrassing reception of a Russian ambassador at Elizabeth's court in 1582. The notion that *Love's Labour's Lost* is laced with topical satire also offers some possible background for the characterizations in the play, although most critics agree that such characters as Holofernes, Armado, and Moth owe more to Shakespeare's imagination than to the suggestions of any contemporary figure.

CRITICAL HISTORY: Critics have called *Love's Labour's Lost* Shakespeare's worst play, suffering from weak and haphazard characterization and a feeble plot. Indeed, the play's strengths have rarely been found in its dramatic form. But there is no other Shakespeare play so laced with wit and wordplay, so concerned with the use and misuse of language, a point noted by numerous commentators. Consequently, it is in the language that most critics have discovered the vitality of *Love's Labour's Lost*.

Eighteenth-century critics of *Love's Labour's Lost* seemed primarily occupied with establishing the authorship of the play. Perhaps to check a widely held opinion of their day, Charles Gildon, Samuel Johnson, and Edward Capell all thought it necessary to offer evidence that Shakespeare did indeed write the drama. Gildon claimed that it was Shakespeare's worst play and, therefore, had to be among his earliest works. Francis Gentlemen also commented that *Love's Labour's Lost* was Shakespeare's weakest drama. Johnson, who had called Shakespeare's love of punning his "fatal Cleopatra," considered certain passages in *Love's Labour's Lost*—Shakespeare's most pun-laden play—"mean, childish, and vulgar." Yet, not all of the critical reception of the play in the eighteenth century was so harsh. Gildon was also willing to praise some of the characterization and the more adept dramatic scenes. Lewis Theobald, although critical of much of *Love's Labour's Lost,* was pleased by Shakespeare's rare adherence to the classical rules of drama demonstrated in the work. Johnson noted the "many sparks of genius" scattered throughout the play and, despite its shortcomings, regarded it as the most Shakespearean of the dramatist's entire canon. Capell observed the "ease and sprightliness of the dialogue" and the "truly comick characters" in it, and was the first critic to comment on the similarity between Berowne and Rosaline and their "counter-parts" in *Much Ado About Nothing,* Benedick and Beatrice. The classification of *Love's Labour's Lost* as a topical satire was also

initiated in the eighteenth century when William Warburton identified Holofernes as a parody of John Florio, an Elizabethan scholar who translated into English the works of Montaigne and numerous Italian authors.

With the start of the nineteenth century and the influence of Romanticism, critics began to examine the language and characterization in the play, and were altogether more laudatory than previous commentators. William Hazlitt, although critical of the play as a whole, concluded nonetheless that the personae are indispensable and that "Biron is too accomplished a character to be lost to the world." Coleridge commended the play's "wonderful activity of thought" and Shakespeare's imitation of the linguistic exaggerations of Elizabethan English. This more positive view of *Love's Labour's Lost*'s vivacious display of language was also presented a few years earlier by August Wilhelm Schlegel, who said that the wit and wordplay "resemble a blaze of fireworks." Schlegel's comments anticipated the focus on language which was to become so dominant in subsequent criticism of the play.

Later nineteenth-century critics sought for the moral import of *Love's Labour's Lost* and found it in Shakespeare's satiric presentation of the male characters' affectations and delusions. Whether the men were immoral or merely misdirected, these critics viewed their behavior as essentially unworthy of winning the fruits of "love's labour"—a position supported by the majority of more recent critics. G. G. Gervinus observed that *Love's Labour's Lost* was Shakespeare's first play to have "a single moral aim" and said that the drama does not end with a comic resolution because Shakespeare's ethical system could not reward the men's vanity, ostentation, and thirst for fame. Hermann Ulrici, argued that *Love's Labour's Lost* contrasts the active reality of life with contemplative hermetic study, and he maintained that the play finally asserts that the "highest splendor and pleasures of life, wit and talents, without the earnestness and profundity which a thoughtful mind lends to them, are a mere false tinsel, while learning and science, abstracted from, and undirected to the realities of life, are equally worthless." Ulrici cited the songs of spring and winter which close the play as an example of the play's espousal of the synthesis of these opposing elements. The opposition of the real and the abstract that Ulrici noted was to become an important interpretive approach in the twentieth century and is especially relevant in the essays by Bobbyann Roesen, Ralph Berry, and William C. Carroll. Ulrici was also the first critic to discuss the songs and to point out their integral relation to the play. Another dialectical reading of *Love's Labour's Lost* was offered near the end of the nineteenth century by Denton J. Snider, who argued that the play moves toward a resolution in which the family and society, as the goals of life, triumph over monasticism and learning. Charles Knight called *Love's Labour's Lost* "the Comedy of Affectation," and said that it presents "almost every variety" of this behavior that is "founded upon a misdirection of intellectual activity." Edward Dowden, examining the "serious intention" of the play, claimed that it is a "protest against youthful schemes of shaping life according to notions rather than according to reality, a protest against idealizing away the facts of life."

Not all nineteenth-century critics dwelled upon the moral seriousness of *Love's Labour's Lost.* Walter Pater, in an important essay on the play, wrote, "It is this foppery of delicate language, this fashionable plaything of his time, with which Shakespeare is occupied in 'Love's Labour's Lost'." He noted that this exaggerated type of language also had "its really delightful side,'' and that Shakespeare did not roundly condemn affected speech or prose, but merely subjected it to laughter and, at most, "a delicate raillery." Pater also suggested that Berowne is Shakespeare's self-portrait, a point argued in the twentieth century by John Palmer and Thomas Marc Parrott. Perhaps the greatest significance of Pater's essay is that the majority of recent critics support his assertion that the problem of language is at the heart of Shakespeare's concerns in *Love's Labour's Lost.*

Twentieth-century commentators on *Love's Labour's Lost* introduced sharply contrasting estimations of the play's dramatic qualities. H. B. Charlton complained that the drama is "deficient in plot and in characterization" and concluded that it is really more like a "modern revue, or a musical comedy without music, than a play." S. C. Sen Gupta similarly argued that the play is a "fantasy" and that it suffers from weak and uneven character development. The noted director and critic Harley Granville-Barker, however, regarded *Love's Labour's Lost* as an effective piece when produced, and he found in it much to be admired, particularly the depth of such characters as Costard and Nathaniel, which he called "outcroppings of pure dramatic gold." Granville-Barker's assessment of the play's dramatic power is indicative of the twentieth century's more positive reception of the play. In a similar vein, J. Dover Wilson later argued that *Love's Labour's Lost* is a much better play in performance than in study.

The past one hundred years has been filled with numerous theories on the satire in *Love's Labour's Lost.* S. L. Lee proposed that *Love's Labour's Lost* contains allusions to certain political actions of Henri of Navarre and a visit by a Russian ambassador to the court of Queen Elizabeth. Around the beginning of the twentieth century, Arthur Acheson claimed that Holofernes was a parody of George Chapman, and, more recently, Walter Oakeshott supplied considerable evidence identifying Armado as Walter Raleigh. The 1930s saw the publication of two of the most notable examinations of the topical satire in *Love's Labour's Lost:* Muriel C. Bradbrook's *The School of Night: A Study in the Literary Relationships of Sir Walter Raleigh* and Frances A. Yates's *A Study of "Love's Labour's Lost."* Bradbrook developed the hypothesis that "the school of night" mentioned in *Love's Labour's Lost* at Act IV, Scene iii is a reference to a group of Elizabethan astronomers known as the "School of Atheisme." This group was headed by Walter Raleigh and may have included such other notables as George Chapman and Christopher Marlowe. Bradbrook saw in *Love's Labour's Lost* a parody or satire of the group's academic pretensions, particularly in the figure of Armado, whom she identified with Raleigh. Yates discussed the play's supposed references to John Florio, Gabriel Harvey, Thomas Nashe, Chapman, and other contemporaries of Shakespeare.

One of the most important twentieth-century interpretations of *Love's Labour's Lost* is Bobbyann Roesen's discussion of the opposition of reality and illusion in the play. Roesen argued that from the moment the princess and her ladies enter the court of Navarre the play begins to trace the destruction of illusion and artificiality and the triumph of reality. According to Roesen, the male characters, deluded in their unreal pastoral world, must accept the reality of the outside world if there is to be a comic resolution to the play. Roesen stressed the importance of Marcade's appearance in the final act and the reality of death he represents. A similar view of the significance of death and the movement from illusion to reality in the play was argued

by Philip Parsons; in addition, Ralph Berry traced this progression by exploring the characters' use of language. A number of other critics, most notably Terence Hawkes, Malcolm Evans, and Louis Adrian Montrose, have argued that the illusion and artificial isolation of the male characters prevents their consummation with the natural social reality represented by the women in the play. William C. Carroll, however, has countered that Shakespeare was not upholding the real and natural over illusion and artifice, but was seeking a dialectical balance of their opposition—an interpretation recalling the comments of Hermann Ulrici.

In the late 1950s, C. L. Barber, employing an anthropological approach, detected a different kind of movement in the action of *Love's Labour's Lost.* Barber claimed that Shakespeare's comedies present a "release" from an implied position of restraint and move toward a clarification of humanity's relation to nature and a reestablishment of social or communal life. The release in these comedies, said Barber, is achieved through elements of festivity which parallel actual Elizabethan holiday celebrations. The release in *Love's Labour's Lost* takes the form of wooing games and word games, according to Barber, and he regarded the play as "all too obviously designed to provide a resistance which can be triumphantly swept away by festivity." Barber's essay on *Love's Labour's Lost* is one of the most important considerations of the play in the twentieth century, and his method of interpreting Shakespeare's comedies has had a great influence on the later direction of Shakespearean criticism.

In the last twenty years, critical commentary on *Love's Labour's Lost* has been noticeably influenced by structuralist methodology, a discipline somewhat similar to the anthropological criticism of Barber in that it seeks to discover the underlying structures which determine all works of literature, but different in its emphasis on linguistics rather than archetypal patterns. Such tacitly structuralist precepts as the priority of speech over the written word were discussed by both Terence Hawkes and Malcolm Evans in their analyses of the play. Hawkes and Evans argued that the male characters' hermetic study of books and their use of "speeches penned" to court the female characters removed them from the reality of the organic oral community and, consequently, destined their efforts to failure. There was also much commentary on the denial of the social reality of language in the essays by James L. Calderwood and Louis Adrian Montrose, as well as those by Hawkes and Evans. Montrose claimed that the Navarrese nobles isolate themselves from the real world by denying the reciprocity necessary to the social bond formed by language, sexuality, and art; Calderwood charged them with first overvaluing and then undervaluing the "linguistic currency" of society. Calderwood argued that the male characters must do what Shakespeare himself does: "Instead of removing words from public circulation the dramatic poet allows them truly to become a medium of exchange, circulating freely within the community of the theatre, and indeed by virtue of this circulation *creating* a community of what were merely so many random individuals before the play began." Other considerations of the problem of language in *Love's Labour's Lost* were presented by Gladys Doidge Willcock and William Matthews, who stated that the play is concerned with the state of the English language and that Shakespeare was commenting on the various changes and fashions which were affecting both the written and spoken word of his day. Also noting this phenomenon, Ralph Berry claimed that "words compose the central symbol in *Love's Labour's Lost.*"

Linguistic analyses of *Love's Labour's Lost* have flourished in the last twenty years, and nearly all recent commentary makes some mention of the play's concerns with language. But this aspect of the play also attracted the attention of earlier critics like Schlegel, Coleridge, and Pater; hence, considerations of the wordplay or the parody of affected speech mannerisms have been a traditional aspect of the critical history. Also, the view that *Love's Labour's Lost* presents a conflict between reality and illusion, cited frequently in recent criticism, was pointed out over a century ago by Hermann Ulrici. Critics adopting anthropological or linguistic approaches to the play seem to offer a synthesis of these two approaches and have suggested that Shakespeare was not only occupied with questions of language and reality, but with the necessary link between them. Whatever Shakespeare's concerns may have been in writing *Love's Labour's Lost*, most critics would seem to concur with Bradbrook's comment that "Nowhere else does Shakespeare display so consistent a linguistic interest as here."

R. T. [ROBERT TOFTE]   (poem date 1598)

[*A contemporary of Shakespeare, Tofte was a sonneteer and a translator of French and Italian verse. The following excerpt, taken from his* Alba, or the Monthes Minde of a Melancholy Lover *(1598), represents one of the earliest extant references to* Love's Labour's Lost. *In it, the narrator laments that the grief displayed by the actors in the play is "fained" and "not from the heart," whereas the sorrow he feels is real.*]

Loves Labour Lost, I once did see a Play
Y-cleped so, so called to my paine.
Which I to heare to my small Joy did stay,
Giving attendance on my froward Dame:
    My misgiving minde presaging me to ill,
    Yet was I drawne to see it 'gainst by will. . . .
Each Actor palid in cunning wise his part,
But chiefly Those entrapt in Cupid's snare;
Yet All was fained, 'twas not from the hart,
They seemde to grieve, but yet they felt no care;
    'Twas I that Griefe (indeed) did beare in brest,
    The others did but make a show in Jest.

                                                    (p. 50)

> *R. T. [Robert Tofte], in an extract from* The Shak-spere Allusion-Book: A Collection of Allusions to Shakspere from 1591 to 1700, Vol. I, *edited by John Munro, revised edition, 1932. Reprint by Books for Libraries Press, 1970; distributed by Arno Press, Inc., p. 50.*

WALTER COPE   (letter date 1604)

[*Cope, in a letter to a member of Queen Anne's court, refers to his attempt to secure a play for a performance before the queen, and he mentions the suggestion of "burbage," i.e., Richard Burbage of Shakespeare's company, that* Love's Labour's Lost *would "please her exceedingly."*]

I have sent and bene all thys morning huntyng for players Juglers & Such kinde of Creatures, but fynde them harde to finde, wherfore Leavinge notes for them to seeke me, burbage ys come & Sayes ther ys no new playe that the quene hath not seene, but they have Revyved an olde one, Cawled *Loves Labore lost*, which for wytt & mirthe he sayes will please her

exceedingly. And Thys ys apointed to be played to Morowe night at my Lord of Sowthamptons, unles yow send awrytt to Remove the Corpus Cum Causa to your howse in strande. (p. 139)

> *Walter Cope, in a letter to Lorde Vycount Cranborne in 1604, in* The Shakspere Allusion-Book: A Collection of Allusions to Shakspere from 1591 to 1700, Vol. I, *edited by John Munro, revised edition, 1932. Reprint by Books for Libraries Press, 1970; distributed by Arno Press, Inc., p. 139.*

CHARLES GILDON   (essay date 1710)

[*Gildon was the first critic to write an extended commentary on Shakespeare's plays. Like many other Neoclassicists, Gildon regarded Shakespeare as an imaginative playwright who nevertheless lacked knowledge of the dramatic "rules" necessary for correct writing. In the following excerpt, taken from his "Remarks on the Plays of Shakespeare", Gildon counters a popular notion that Shakespeare did not write* Love's Labour's Lost *and asserts that, although it is Shakespeare's worst play, there are aspects that convince us that it is nevertheless his work, a position reiterated by Samuel Johnson (1765) and Edward Capell (1768).*]

Tho' I can't well see why the Author gave this Play this Name, yet since it has past thus long I shall say no more to it, but this, that since it is one of the worst of *Shakespear's* Play's, nay I think I may say the very worst, I cannot but think that it is his first, notwithstanding those Arguments, or that Opinion, that has been brought to the contrary. (p. 308)

[We] ought to look into *Shakespear*'s most imperfect Plays for his first. And this of *Loves Labour's Lost* being perhaps the most defective, I can see no Reason why we shou'd not conclude, that it is one of his first. For neither the Manners, Sentiments, Diction, Versification, *etc.* (except in some few places) discover the *Genius* that shines in his other plays.

But tho' this Play be so bad yet there is here and there a Stroak, that persuades us, that *Shakespear* wrote it. The Proclamations, that Women shou'd lose their Tongues if they approach'd within a Mile of the Court, is a pleasant Penalty. There are but few Words spoken by *Jaquenetta* in the later End of the first Act, and yet the very Soul of a pert Country Lass is perfectly express'd. The several Characters of the King's Companions in the Retreat, is very pretty, and the Remarks of the Princess very just and fine. . . . *Longaviles* good Epigram furnishes a Proof, that these publish'd in this Volume are Genuine . . . [IV. iii. 58-71]. (pp. 310-11)

The Discovery of the Kings, *Longaviles*, and *Dumain*'s Love is very prettily manag'd, and that of *Biron* by *Costards* mistake, is a well contriv'd Incident. The whole indeed is a tolerable Proof how much in vain we resolve against Nature, nor is *Biron's Casuistry* amiss when he strives to salve their common Breach of Oath. (p. 312)

> *Charles Gildon, "Remarks on the Plays of Shakespear," in* The Works of Mr. William Shakespear, *Vol. 7 by William Shakespear, 1710. Reprint by AMS Press, Inc., 1967, pp. 257-444.*

LEWIS THEOBALD   (essay date 1733)

[*During the first half of the eighteenth century, Theobald was considered one of the greatest and most competent of Shakespearean critics. However, after his death in 1744 his reputation suffered a severe decline, probably due to his misguided attempts to revise many of Shakespeare's plays according to Neoclassical ideas of unity of action and dignity of character. The following comments were first published in Theobald's* The Works of William Shakespeare *in 1733 and are typical of the rigorous application of Aristotelean rules to Shakespeare's plays that was popular during the eighteenth century.*]

Besides the exact Regularity to the Rules of Art which [Shakespeare] has happen'd to preserve in some few of his Pieces [*Love's Labour's Lost*] is Demonstration, I think, that tho' he has more frequently transgress'd the *Unity* of *Time* by cramming Years into the Compass of a Play, yet he knew the Absurdity of so doing, and was not unacquainted with the Rule to the contrary. . . . (p. 498)

> *Lewis Theobald, in an extract from* Shakespeare, the Critical Heritage: 1693-1733, Vol. 2, *edited by Brian Vickers, Routledge & Kegan Paul, 1974, p. 498.*

WILLIAM WARBURTON   (essay date 1747)

[*Warburton, a controversial eighteenth-century English theologian and literary scholar, edited the works of Alexander Pope and Shakespeare. His edition of Shakespeare, based primarily on the work of Lewis Theobald, contained many unsubstantiated and questionable emendations. Because of this, subsequent scholars severely criticized and generally rejected his work. However, Warburton did contribute a few significant textual emendations which are accepted by scholars today. Warburton was also the first critic to suggest that Shakespeare modeled the characters in* Love's Labour's Lost *on contemporary figures, an approach to the play which has since generated speculation on who, if anyone, Shakespeare meant to satirize. Such explications of the play are developed in the excerpt by Muriel C. Bradbrook (1936) and in the Additional Bibliography by such critics as Arthur Acheson, Ray B. Browne, Oscar J. Campbell, Eva Turner Clark, Richard David, Austin K. Gray, S. L. Lee, Walter Oakeshott, Arthur Quiller-Couch and John Dover Wilson, Hugh M. Richmond, W. Schrickx, and Frances A. Yates. Arguments against the validity of such an approach can be found in the essays by J. O. Halliwell-Phillipps (1879), Thomas Marc Parrott (1949), and S. C. Sen Gupta (1950). Warburton's essay was first published in 1747 in his edition of* The Works of William Shakespear.]

There is very little personal reflexion in *Shakespear*. Either the virtue of those times, or the candour of our author, has so effected, that his satire is, for the most part, general, and as himself says,

> . . . his taxing like a wild goose flies,
> Unclaim'd of any man. . . .
> [*As You Like It*, II. vii. 86-7]

The place before us [*Love's Labour's Lost*] seems to be an exception. For by *Holofernes* is designed a particular character, a pedant and schoolmaster of our author's time, one *John Florio*, a teacher of the *Italian* tongue in *London*, who has given us a small dictionary of that language under the title of *A World of words*. . . . (p. 13)

> *William Warburton, in an extract from* A Study of "Love's Labour's Lost" *by Frances A. Yates, Cambridge at the University Press, 1936, p. 13.*

SAMUEL JOHNSON   (essay date 1765)

[*Johnson has long held an important place in the history of Shakespearean criticism. He is considered the foremost representative of moderate English Neoclassicism and is credited by some literary historians with freeing Shakespeare from the strictures of*

the three unities valued by strict Neoclassicists: that dramas should have a single setting, take place in less than twenty-four hours, and have a causally connected plot. More recent scholars portray him as a critic who was able to synthesize existing critical theory rather than as an innovative theoretician. Johnson was a master of Augustan prose style and a personality who dominated the literary world of his epoch. In the following excerpt, taken from his 1765 edition of The Plays of William Shakespeare, *Johnson remarks that the topical satire in* Love's Labour's Lost *inhibits the comprehension and pleasure of the drama for later audiences. Johnson also finds fault with many of the passages in the play, but sees in others the evident genius of Shakespeare, and thus concurs with Charles Gildon (1710) and Edward Capell (1768) on the question of the play's authorship.*]

I am not of the learned [William Warburton's] opinion, that the satire of Shakespeare is so seldom personal [see excerpt above, 1747]. It is of the nature of personal invectives to be soon unintelligible; and the authour that gratifies private malice, . . . destroys the future efficacy of his own writings, and sacrifices the esteem of succeeding times to the laughter of a day. It is no wonder, therefore, that the sarcasms which, perhaps, in the author's time "set the *playhouse* in a roar," are now lost among general reflections. Yet whether the character of Holofernes was pointed at any particular man, I am, notwithstanding the plausibility of Dr. Warburton's conjecture, inclined to doubt. Every man adheres as long as he can to his own preconceptions. Before I read [Warburton's] note I considered the character of Holofernes as borrowed from the Rhombus of Sir Philip Sidney, who, in a kind of pastoral entertainment, [*The Lady of May*,] exhibited to Queen Elizabeth, has introduced a schoolmaster so called, speaking "a leash of languages at once," and puzzling himself and his auditors with a jargon like that of Holofernes in the present play. (pp. 274-75)

In [*Love's Labour's Lost*], which all the editors have concurred to censure, and some have rejected as unworthy of our poet, it must be confessed that there are many passages mean, childish, and vulgar; and some which ought not to have been exhibited, as we are told they were, to a maiden queen. But there are scattered, through the whole, many sparks of genius; nor is there any play that has more evident marks of the hand of Shakespeare. (p. 287)

> *Samuel Johnson, "Notes on Shakespeare's Plays: 'Love's Labour's Lost'," in his* The Yale Edition of the Works of Samuel Johnson: Johnson on Shakespeare, Vol. VII, *edited by Arthur Sherbo, Yale University Press, 1968, pp. 266-87.*

EDWARD CAPELL   (essay date 1768)

[*As an editor of Shakespeare's plays, Capell broke with traditional textual scholarship by proposing that the earliest texts of the plays should be used as the basis for authoritative editions of Shakespeare, a view supported by modern textual critics. The following excerpt is from the introduction to Capell's edition of* Mr. William Shakespeare: His Comedies, Histories, and Tragedies *(1768). Like Charles Gildon (1710) and Samuel Johnson (1765), Capell maintains that* Love's Labour's Lost *is solely the work of Shakespeare; in support of this conclusion, he points to the "sprightliness of the dialogue," the "quick turns of wit," and "the humour it abounds in" as all evidence of Shakespeare's hand.*]

[If SHAKESPEARE] is not visible in *Love's Labour's lost* we know not in which of his comedies he can be said to be so. The ease and sprightliness of dialogue in very many parts of it; it's quick turns of wit, and the humour it abounds in, and (chiefly) in those truly comick characters the pendant and his companion, the page, the constable, *Costard,* and *Armado,* seem more than sufficient to prove SHAKESPEARE the Author of it. And for the blemishes of this play, we must seek their true cause in it's antiquity, which we may venture to carry higher than 1598, the date of it's first impression. Rime, when this play appear'd, was thought a beauty of the drama, and heard with singular pleasure by an audience who but a few years before had been accustom'd to all rime; and the measure we call dogrel, and are so much offended with, had no such effect upon the ears of that time. But whether blemishes or no, or however this matter be which we have brought to exculpate him, neither of these articles can with any face of justice be alledg'd against *Love's Labour's lost,* seeing they are both to be met with in several other plays, the genuineness of which has not been question'd by any one. And one thing more shall be observ'd in the behalf of this play, that the Author himself was so little displeas'd at least with some parts of it that he has brought them a second time upon the stage. For who may not perceive that his famous *Benedick* and *Beatrice* [in *Much Ado About Nothing*] are but little more than the counter-parts of *Biron* and *Rosaline?* All which circumstances consider'd, and that especially of the Writer's childhood (as it may be term'd) when this comedy was produc'd, we may confidently pronounce it his true off-spring and replace it amongst it's brethern. (pp. 317-18)

> Edward Capell, in an extract from Shakespeare, the Critical Heritage: 1765-1774, Vol. 5, *edited by Brian Vickers, Routledge & Kegan Paul, 1979, pp. 303-27.*

FRANCIS GENTLEMAN (essay date 1774)

[*Gentleman, an Irish actor and playwright, contributed the introduction to John Bell's 1774 Edition of Shakespeare's Plays. In the following excerpt from that work, Gentleman, like Charles Gildon (1710), regards* Love's Labour's Lost *as Shakespeare's worst play, attacking its characterization and language and claiming that its sentiments appear "labored" rather than spontaneous.*]

Shakespeare never sported more with his desultory muse than in tacking together the scenes of [*Love's Labour's Lost*]; he certainly wrote more to please himself than to divert or inform his readers and auditors. The characters are by no means masterly, the language is cramp; the scenes possess a wearisome sameness, and the sentiments, except a few, appear at this day much laboured, though we believe they flowed spontaneously from our Author's creative imagination. It must certainly be accounted one of *Shakespeare's* weakest compositions, and does no great credit to his muse. (p. 106)

> Francis Gentleman, in an extract from Shakespeare, the Critical Heritage: 1774-1801, Vol. 6, *edited by Brian Vickers, Routledge & Kegan Paul, 1981, p. 106.*

AUGUST WILHELM SCHLEGEL (lecture date 1808)

[*A prominent German Romantic critic, Schlegel holds a key place in the history of Shakespeare's reputation in European criticism. His translations of thirteen of the plays are still considered the best German editions of Shakespeare. Schlegel was also a leading spokesman for the Romantic movement, which permanently overthrew the Neoclassical contention that Shakespeare was a child of nature whose plays lacked artistic form. In the excerpt below,*

drawn from a lecture given in 1808, Schlegel points out the vivacious display of language in Love's Labour's Lost, *declaring that the wit and wordplay "resemble a blaze of fireworks." This consideration and praise of the play's language anticipates the comments of Walter Pater (1885) and many twentieth-century critics.*]

Love's Labour's Lost is . . . numbered among the pieces of [Shakespeare's] youth. It is a humorsome display of frolic; a whole cornucopia of the most vivacious jokes is emptied into it. Youth is certainly perceivable in the lavish superfluity of labour in the execution: the unbroken succession of plays on words, and sallies of every description, hardly leave the spectator time to breathe; the sparkles of wit fly about in such profusion, that they resemble a blaze of fireworks; while the dialogue, for the most part, is in the same hurried style in which the passing masks at a carnival attempt to banter each other. The young king of Navarre, with three of his courtiers, has made a vow to pass three years in rigid retirement, and devote them to the study of wisdom; for that purpose he has banished all female society from his court, and imposed a penalty on the intercourse with women. But scarcely has he, in a pompous harangue, worthy of the most heroic achievements, announced this determination, when the daughter of the king of France appears at his court, in the name of her old and bed-ridden father, to demand the restitution of a province which he held in pledge. Compelled to give her audience, he falls immediately in love with her. Matters fare no better with his companions, who on their parts renew an old acquaintance with the princess's attendants. Each, in heart, is already false to his vow, without knowing that the wish is shared by his associates; they overhear one another, as they in turn confide their sorrows in a love-ditty to the solitary forest: every one jeers and confounds the one who follows him. Biron, who from the beginning was the most satirical among them, at last steps forth, and rallies the king and the two others, till the discovery of a love-letter forces him also to hang down his head. He extricates himself and his companions from their dilemma by ridiculing the folly of the broken vow, and, after a noble eulogy on women, invites them to swear new allegiance to the colours of love. This scene is inimitable, and the crowning beauty of the whole. The manner in which they afterwards prosecute their love-suits in masks and disguise, and in which they are tricked and laughed at by the ladies, who are also masked and disguised, is, perhaps, spun out too long. It may be thought, too, that the poet, when he suddenly announces the death of the king of France, and makes the princess postpone her answer to the young prince's serious advances till the expiration of the period of her mourning, and impose, besides, a heavy penance on him for his levity, drops the proper comic tone. But the tone of raillery, which prevails throughout the piece, made it hardly possible to bring about a more satisfactory conclusion: after such extravagance, the characters could not return to sobriety, except under the presence of some foreign influence. The grotesque figure of Don Armado, a pompous fantastic Spaniard, a couple of pedants, and a clown, who between whiles contribute to the entertainment, are the creation of a whimsical imagination, and well adapted as foils for the wit of so vivacious a society. (pp. 383-84)

> August Wilhelm Schlegel, "Criticisms on Shakspeare's Comedies," *in his* A Course of Lectures on Dramatic Art and Literature, *edited by Rev. A.J.W. Morrison, translated by John Black, revised edition, 1846. Reprint by AMS Press, Inc., 1965, pp. 379-99.*

SAMUEL TAYLOR COLERIDGE (essay date 1808-18)

[*Coleridge's lectures and writings on Shakespeare form a major chapter in the history of English Shakespearean criticism. As the channel for the critical ideas of the German Romantics and as an original interpreter of Shakespeare in the new spirit of Romanticism, Coleridge played a strategic role in overthowing the last remains of the Neoclassical approach to Shakespeare and in establishing the modern view of the dramatist as a conscious artist and masterful portrayer of human character. Coleridge's remarks on Shakespeare come down to posterity largely as fragmentary notes, marginalia, and reports by auditors on the lectures, rather than in polished essays. In the following excerpt, first published in 1836 but taken from notes and marginalia written between 1808 and 1818, Coleridge maintains that* Love's Labour's Lost *is a "juvenile drama" but nonetheless contains many of Shakespeare's characteristic features. He also states that the affected language of the pedants in the play is meant to satirize the exaggerated style of speech used by the Elizabethan courtiers and other nobles, an issue similarly considered by George Brandes (1895-96).*]

According to internal evidence [*Love's Labour's Lost* is] the earliest of Shakespeare's dramas, probably prior to the *Venus and Adonis,* and sketched out before he left Stratford. [The] characters [are] either impersonated out of his own multiformity, by imaginative self-position, or of such as a country town and a school-boy's observation might supply—the curate, schoolmaster, the Armado (which even in my time was not extinct in the cheaper inns of North Wales). [Note] the satire too on follies of *words.* Add too that the characters of Biron and Rosaline are evidently the pre-existent state of his Beatrice and Benedict. Add too the number of the rhymes, and the sweetness as well as smoothness of the metre, and the number of acute and fancifully illustrated aphorisms. Just as it ought to be. True genius begins by generalizing and condensing; it ends in realizing and expanding. It first collects the seeds.

Yet if this juvenile drama had been the only one extant of our Shakespeare, and we possessed the tradition only of his riper works, or [accounts] from writers who had not even mentioned the *Love's Labor's Lost,* how many of Shakespeare's characteristic features might we not discover, tho' as in a portrait taken of him in his boyhood. (p. 83)

I can never sufficiently admire the wonderful activity of thought throughout the whole of the first scene of the play, rendered natural, as it is, by the choice of the characters, and the whimsical determination on which the drama is founded. A whimsical determination certainly;—yet not altogether so very improbable to those who are conversant in the history of the middle ages, with their Courts of Love, and all that lighter drapery of chivalry, which engaged even mighty kings with a sort of serio-comic interest, and may well be supposed to have occupied more completely the smaller princes, at a time when the noble's or prince's court contained the only theatre of the domain or principality. This sort of story, too, was admirably suited to Shakespeare's times, when the English court was still the foster-mother of the state and the muses; and when, in consequence, the courtiers, and men of rank and fashion, affected a display of wit, point, and sententious observation, that would be deemed intolerable at present,—but in which a hundred years of controversy, involving every great political, and every dear domestic, interest, had trained all but the lowest classes to participate. Add to this the very style of the sermons of the time, and the eagerness of the Protestants to distinguish themselves by long and frequent preaching, and it will be found that, from the reign of Henry VIII. to the abdication of James

II. no country ever received such a national education as England.

Hence the comic matter chosen in the first instance is a ridiculous imitation or apery of this constant striving after logical precision, and subtle opposition of thoughts, together with a making the most of every conception or image, by expressing it under the least expected property belonging to it, and this, again, rendered specially absurd by being applied to the most current subjects and occurrences. The phrases and modes of combination in argument were caught by the most ignorant from the custom of the age, and their ridiculous misapplication of them is most amusingly exhibited in Costard; whilst examples suited only to be gravest propositions and impersonations, or apostrophes to abstract thoughts impersonated, which are in fact the natural language only of the most vehement agitations of the mind, are adopted by the coxcombry of Armado as mere artifices of ornament.

The same kind of intellectual action is exhibited in a more serious and elevated strain in many other parts of this play. Biron's speech at the end of the fourth act is an excellent specimen of it. It is logic clothed in rhetoric;—but observe how Shakespeare, in his two-fold being of poet and philosopher, avails himself of it to convey profound truths in the most lively images,—the whole remaining faithful to the character supposed to utter the lines, and the expressions themselves constituting a further development of that character. . . . [It] is quite a study;—sometimes you see this youthful god of poetry connecting disparate thoughts purely by means of resemblances in the words expressing them,—a thing in character in lighter comedy, especially of that kind in which Shakspeare delights, namely, the purposed display of wit, though sometimes, too, disfiguring his graver scenes;—but more often you may see him doubling the natural connection or order of logical consequences in the thoughts by the introduction of an artificial and sought for resemblance in the words, as for instance, in the third line of the play,—

> And then grace us in the disgrace of death;—
>
> [I. i. 3]

this being a figure often having its force and propriety, as justified by the law of passion, which, inducing in the mind an unusual activity, seeks for means to waste its superfluity,—when in the highest degree—in lyric repetitions and sublime tautology. . . . and, in lower degrees, in making the words themselves the subjects and materials of that surplus action, and for the same cause that agitates our limbs, and forces our very gestures into a tempest in states of high excitement.

The mere style of narration in *Love's Labour's Lost,* like that of Aegeon in the first scene of the *Comedy of Errors,* and of the Captain in the second scene of *Macbeth,* seems imitated with its defects and its beauties from Sir Philip Sidney; whose *Arcadia,* though not then published, was already well known in manuscript copies, and could hardly have escaped the notice and admiration of Shakespeare as the friend and client of the Earl of Southampton. The chief defect consists in the parentheses and parenthetic thoughts and descriptions, suited neither to the passion of the speaker, nor the purpose of the person to whom the information is to be given, but manifestly betraying the author himself,—not by way of continuous undersong, but—palpably, and so as to show themselves addressed to the general reader. However, it is not unimportant to notice how strong a presumption the diction and allusions of this play afford, that, though Shakespeare's acquirements in the dead

languages might not be such as we suppose in a learned education, his habits had, nevertheless, been scholastic, and those
of a student. For a young author's first work almost always
bespeaks his recent pursuits, and his first observations of life
are either drawn from the immediate employments of his youth,
and from the characters and images most deeply impressed on
his mind in the situations in which those employments had
placed him;—or else they are fixed on such objects and occurrences in the world, as are easily connected with, and seem
to bear upon, his studies and the hitherto exclusive subjects of
his meditation. (pp. 84-7)

> Samuel Taylor Coleridge, "Notes on the Comedies
> of Shakespeare: 'Love's Labor's Lost'," in his
> Shakespearean Criticism, Vol. 1, edited by Thomas
> Middleton Raysor, second edition, Dutton, 1960, pp.
> 83-9.

WILLIAM HAZLITT   (essay date 1817)

[Hazlitt is considered a leading Shakespearean critic of the English Romantic movement. A prolific essayist and critic on a wide
range of subjects, Hazlitt remarked in the preface to his Characters
of Shakespear's Plays, first published in 1817, that he was inspired
by the German critic August Wilhelm Schlegel and was determined
to supplant what he considered the pernicious influence of Samuel
Johnson's Shakespearean criticism. Hazlitt's criticism is typically
Romantic in its emphasis on character studies. Unlike his fellow
Romantic Samuel Taylor Coleridge, Hazlitt was a dramatic critic
whose experience of Shakespeare in the theater influenced his
interpretations. In the following excerpt, taken from the work
mentioned above, Hazlitt states that Love's Labour's Lost is the
most dispensable of Shakespeare's comedies, primarily because
in attempting to imitate "the fair, the witty, and the learned" of
his time, rather than create from his own imagination, Shakespeare misused his talents. Yet, Hazlitt finds much to commend
in the play, particularly the characters of Armado, Holofernes,
and Berowne, and the scene in which the hidden amorous intentions of the male characters are successively revealed to the reader
or audience.]

If we were to part with any of the author's comedies, it should
be this. Yet we should be loth to part with Don Adriano de
Armado, that mighty potentate of nonsense, or his page, that
handful of wit; with Nathaniel the curate, or Holofernes the
school-master, and their dispute after dinner on "the golden
cadences of poesy" [IV. ii. 122]; with Costard the clown, or
Dull the constable. Biron is too accomplished a character to
be lost to the world, and yet he could not appear without his
fellow courtiers and the king: and if we were to leave out the
ladies the gentlemen would have no mistresses. So that we
believe we may let the whole play stand as it is, and we shall
hardly venture to "set a mark of reprobation on it." Still we
have some objections to the style, which we think savours
more of the pedantic spirit of Shakespear's time than of his
own genius. . . . It transports us quite as much to the manners
of the court, and the quirks of the courts of law, as to the
scenes of nature or the fairy-land of his own imagination.
Shakespear has set himself to imitate the tone of polite conversation then prevailing among the fair, the witty, and the
learned, and he has imitated it but too faithfully. It is as if the
hand of Titian had been employed to give grace to the curls
of a full-bottomed periwig, or Raphael had attempted to give
expression to the tapestry figures in the House of Lords. Shakespear has put an excellent description of this fashionable jargon
into the mouth of the critical Holofernes "as too picked, too
spruce, too affected, too odd, as it were, too peregrinate, as I
may call it" [V. i. 12-14]; and nothing can be more marked

than the difference when he breaks loose from the trammels
he had imposed on himself, "as light as bird from brake,"
and speaks in his own person. (pp. 180-81)

The character of Biron drawn by Rosaline and that which Biron
gives of Boyet are equally happy. The observations on the use
and abuse of study, and on the power of beauty to quicken the
understanding as well as the senses, are excellent. The scene
which has the greatest dramatic effect is that in which Biron,
the king, Longaville, and Dumain, successively detect each
other and are detected in their breach of their vow and in their
profession of attachment to their several mistresses, in which
they suppose themselves to be overheard by no one. The reconciliation between these lovers and their sweethearts is also
very good, and the penance which Rosaline imposes on Biron,
before he can expect to gain her consent to marrry him, full
of propriety and beauty. (p. 182)

> William Hazlitt, "'Love's Labour Lost'," in his
> Characters of Shakespear's Plays & Lectures on the
> English Poets, Macmillan and Co. Limited, 1903,
> pp. 180-83.

HERMANN ULRICI   (essay date 1839)

[A German scholar, Ulrici was a professor of philosophy and the
author of works on Greek poetry and Shakespeare. The following
excerpt is from an English translation of his Über Shakespeares
dramatische Kunst, und sein Verhältniss zu Calderon und Göthe,
a work first published in 1839. This study exemplifies the "philosophical criticism" developed in Germany during the nineteenth
century. The immediate sources for Ulrici's critical approach
appear to be August Wilhelm Schlegel's conception of the play
as an organic, interconnected whole and Georg Wilhelm Friedrich
Hegel's view of drama as an embodiment of the conflict of historical forces and ideas. Unlike his fellow German Shakespearean
critic G. G. Gervinus, Ulrici sought to develop a specifically
Christian aesthetics, but one which, as he carefully points out in
the introduction to the work mentioned above, in no way intrudes
on "that unity of idea, which preeminently constitutes a work of
art a living creation in the world of beauty." Ulrici's comments
on Love's Labour's Lost reflect a Hegelian influence; he sees the
play as dramatizing the conflict between the "reality of life" and
the "recluse study of science," an opposition which must be
reconciled. For Ulrici, the songs of spring and winter illustrate
the synthesis of two contrarieties that cannot be made "independent of each other, but by their constant interaction and mutual
influence produce life and fertility." The songs of Love's Labour's
Lost are discussed in a similar manner by William C. Carroll
(1976), and in a more general way by Richmond Noble (1923),
Bertrand H. Bronson (1948), Louis Adrian Montrose (1977), and
Catherine McLay (see Additional Bibliography). Also, the opposition Ulrici perceives in the play between reality and the "science which abstracts itself from reality" receives further consideration by such modern critics as Bobbyann Roesen (1953),
E. M. W. Tillyard (1962), Ronald Berman (1964), Ralph Berry
(1969), James L. Calderwood (1971), Terence Hawkes (1973),
William C. Carroll (1976), and Louis Adrian Montrose (1977).]

The leading idea of ["Love's Labour's Lost"] is, in short, the
significant contrast of the fresh, youthful, and ever-blooming
reality of life, and a dry, lifeless, and recluse study of science.
Either member of the contrariety, nakedly opposed to the other,
and placed in hostile opposition to, and wholly uninfluenced
by it, becomes untrue, preposterous, and absurd. The science
which abstracts itself from reality and retires in lonely contemplation, must either quickly entomb itself in the barren sands
of a tasteless and pedantic erudition, or else, overcome by the
gay seductions of life, give itself up to excessive pleasure and

learned trifling, and earn for itself the merited reproach of affectation or pretension. One of these results is embodied in the Curate, Sir Nathaniel, and the Village Schoolmaster, Holofernes—those truthful representatives of the retailers of learned trifles—and in the pompous and bombastic Spanish Knight, Don Adriano de Armado—the Quixote of a high-sounding phraseology. The other is indicated by the King and his companions. From the pursuit of wisdom, which they blindly hope to gain by abstract study, they soon fall into veriest silliness and fooleries of love-making; in spite of their oaths and fraternity, nature and truth quickly make themselves felt, and gain an easy victory. But this victory over false wisdom is fundamentally nothing more than the defeat of folly by folly. For, on the other hand, nature and reality, taken by themselves, are but fugitive and illusory images when apart from the solidity of the cognizant mind; separated from this, the merry sport of love and life is checked and damped; talents, shrewdness, and acquirements, become a mere vain and superficial wit, and love itself, when unassociated with the solidity, earnestness, and moderation, which occasional solitude and contemplative reflection alone can bestow upon the mind, sinks into a tawdry show of tinsel and spangle. And to such meditation the Prince and his courtiers are for a while consigned by the objects of their adoration. We have here the triumph of the fine and correct judgment of a noble woman, which is as complete as that of her social wit and clever management. The speech of the Princess, in which she condemns the Prince to twelve months of seclusion and self-denial, and the words of Rosaline, which indignantly expose the thorough worthlessness of wit and talents when exclusively directed to festive and social amusement, convey, as it were, the moral of the fable. The end of the comedy returns, so to speak, into its beginning: the dialectic of irony has palsied both members of the truth when presented to it in their untenable and one-sided exclusiveness. The highest splendour and pleasures of life, wit and talents, without the earnestness and profundity which a thoughtful mind lends to them, are a mere false tinsel, while learning and science, abstracted from, and undirected to the realities of life, are equally worthless and unsubstantial. The same truth is conveyed by the closing contrast between Spring and Winter; separate from each other they either lose themselves in self-destroying and pernicious excess, or in the cold and stiffness of death; in reality, however, they are not in truth, and cannot be made, thus independent of each other, but by their constant interaction and mutual influence produce life and fertility.

Thus considered the present comedy likewise acquires a profound poetical significance. We have no longer to look about for the meaning of those ridiculous characters, Sir Nathaniel, Holofernes, Armado, and Dull, and of the apparently superfluous and impertinent scenes in which they are introduced. And we also see grounds for the partiality with which Shakespeare evidently regarded this piece, and which led him to submit it to several revisions and corrections. It was a merry parody on the tasteless imitation of [John] Lilly by a pedantic literary clique of his contemporaries, who were doing all in their power to corrupt their native tongue by coquetting with alliteration and antithesis, by introducing orthographical improvements and the most fanciful etymologies, and by an affectation of learning and the constant use of Latin phrases and forms. In scarcely another piece is so great an influence allowed to wit and humour, and to harmless satire and intrigue. In a certain sense the whole is nothing but a lively game at ball with joke and banter, a sparkling of antithesis and pun—a perpetual rivalry of wit between the lists of sense and reason. By this means the contrast between the latter, which otherwise

were too grave and too important for comedy, is resolved into a sportful and amusing antithesis. Over the whole, poetry rises on the light undulations of that dialectic irony which is the soul of the comic view of things; without, however, forgetting the seriousness, which is also an element of it. ''Love's Labour's Lost'' is, however, open no doubt to the objection that it lightly and wickedly trifles with broken oaths. But if we consider that they do not seem to have been meant very seriously—and were really little more than a knightly parole of honour—and that, on the other hand, the violation is made to incur a grave penalty, the charge of irreverence seems to be in fact groundless. By its very nature, comedy must adhere strictly to the ordinary realities of life and the usual estimate of things, and this, we all know, sets but little store by such knightly pledges. Moreover, the drama itself, like all other of Shakespeare's compositions, if we overlook a few low jests and equivoques, is full of the most chaste and reverent meaning. (pp. 281-83)

Hermann Ulrici, ''Criticisms of Shakspeare's Drama: 'Love's Labour's Lost'—'Two Gentlemen of Verona'—'All's Well that Ends Well','' in his Shakspeare's Dramatic Art: And His Relation to Calderon and Goethe, translated by Rev. A. J. W. Morrison, Chapman, Brothers, 1846, pp. 280-88.

CHARLES KNIGHT   (essay date 1849)

[*Knight, an English author and publisher, dedicated his career to providing education and knowledge to the Victorian middle class. Elements of Knight's populist beliefs are suggested in the following excerpt taken from his 1849* Studies of Shakspere, *a collection of the critical notes that accompanied his earlier editions of Shakespeare's plays. Knight calls* Love's Labour's Lost *''the Comedy of Affectations'' and concludes that the play marks the ''triumph of simplicity over false refinement,'' demonstrated specifically in the song of ''the owl and the cuckoo.''*]

Charles Lamb was wont to call 'Love's Labour's Lost' the Comedy of Leisure. It is certain that, in the commonwealth of King Ferdinand of Navarre, we have—

> All men idle, all;
> And women too.
> [*The Tempest*, II. i. 155-56]

The courtiers, in their pursuit of ''that angel knowledge,'' waste their time in subtle contentions how that angel is to be won;—the ladies from France spread their pavilions in the sunny park, and there keep up their round of jokes with their ''wit's peddler,'' Boyet, ''the nice;''—Armado listens to his page while he warbles 'Concolinel;'—Jaquenetta, though she is ''allowed for the day,'' seems to have no dairy to look after;—Costard acts as if he were neither ploughman nor swineherd, and born for no other work than to laugh for ever at Moth, and, in the excess of his love for that ''pathetical nit,'' to exclaim, ''An I had but one penny in the world, thou shouldst have it to buy gingerbread'' [V. i. 71-2];—the schoolmaster appears to be without scholars, the curate without a cure, the constable without watch and ward. There is, indeed, one parenthesis of real business connected with the progress of the action—the difference between France and Navarre, in the matter of Aquitain. But the settlement of this business is deferred till ''to-morrow''—the ''packet of specialties'' is not come [II. i. 163]; and whether Aquitain goes back to France, or the hundred thousand crowns return to Navarre, we never learn. This matter, then, being postponed till a more fitting season, the whole set abandon themselves to what Dr. Johnson calls ''strenuous idleness.'' The King and his courtiers forswear their studies, and every man becomes a lover and a sonneteer; the refined traveller of Spain resigns himself to his passion for the dairy-maid; the schoolmaster and the curate talk learnedly after dinner; and, at last, the King, the nobles, the priest, the pedant, the braggart, the page, and the clown join in one dance of mummery, in which they all laugh, and are laughed at. But still all this idleness is too energetic to warrant us in calling this the Comedy of Leisure. Let us try again. Is it not the Comedy of Affectations? (pp. 124-25)

[In] 'Love's Labour's Lost' Shakspere presents us almost every variety of affectation that is founded upon a misdirection of intellectual activity. We have here many of the forms in which cleverness is exhibited as opposed to wisdom, and false refinement as opposed to simplicity. The affected characters, even the most fantastical, are not fools; but, at the same time, the natural characters, who, in this play, are chiefly the women, have their intellectual foibles. All the modes of affectation are developed in one continued stream of fun and drollery;—every one is laughing at the folly of the other, and the laugh grows louder and louder as the more natural characters, one by one, trip up the heels of the more affected. The most affected at last join in the laugh with the most natural; and the whole comes down to "plain kersey yea and nay,"—from the syntax of Holofernes, and the "fire-new words" of Armado, to "greasy Joan" and "roasted crabs." (p. 125)

[In the final scene the] affectations are blown into thin air. The King and his courtiers have to turn from speculation to action—from fruitless vows to deeds of charity and piety. Armado is about to apply to what is useful: "I have vowed to Jaquenetta to hold the plough for her sweet love three years" [V. ii. 883-84]. The voices of the pedants are heard no more in scraps of Latin. They are no longer "singled from the barbarous" [V. i. 81-2]. But, on the contrary, "the dialogue that the two learned men have compiled, in praise of the owl and the cuckoo" [V. ii. 885-87], is full of the most familiar images, expressed in the most homely language. Shakspere, unquestionably, to our minds, brought in this most characteristic song—(a song that he might have written and sung in the chimney-corner of his father's own kitchen, long before he dreamt of having a play acted before Queen Elizabeth)—to mark, by an emphatic close, the triumph of simplicity over false refinement. (p. 129)

Charles Knight, "'Love's Labour's Lost'," in his Studies of Shakspere, 1849. Reprint by George Routledge and Sons, 1868, pp. 120-29.

G. G. GERVINUS (essay date 1849-50)

[One of the most widely read Shakespearean critics of the latter half of the nineteenth century, the German critic Gervinus was praised by such eminent authors of his day as Edward Dowden, F. J. Furnivall, and James Russell Lowell; however, he is little known in the English-speaking world today. Like his predecessor Hermann Ulrici, Gervinus wrote in the tradition of the "philosophical criticism" developed in Germany in the mid-nineteenth century. Under the influence of August Wilhelm Schlegel's literary theory and Georg Wilhelm Friedrich Hegel's dialectical philosophy, German critics like Gervinus tended to focus their analyses around a search for the literary work's organic unity and ethical import. Gervinus believed that Shakespeare's works contained a rational ethical system independent of any religion—in contrast to Ulrici, for whom Shakespeare's morality was basically Christian. In the following commentary, first published in his Shakespeare (1849-50), Gervinus states that Love's Labour's Lost is the first of Shakespeare's plays to have a "single moral aim in

view." He locates this moral concern in Shakespeare's presentation of the members of King Henry's court and in the failure of their suit for the love of the ladies. According to Gervinus, Love's Labour's Lost ends on a sombre note and, therefore, thwarts the "custom of comedy"; yet, in Gervinus's understanding the play's conclusion is inevitable, since vanity and misdirected intelligence could never be rewarded in a Shakespearean "moral" world. For a similar reaction to the conclusion of Love's Labour's Lost, see the excerpt by August Wilhelm Schlegel (1808).]

The peculiarities of Shakespeare's youthful pieces are perhaps most accumulated in [Love's Labour's Lost]. The reiterated mention of mythological and historical personages; the air of learning, the Italian and Latin expressions, which here, it must be admitted, serve a comic end; the older England versification, the numerous doggrel verses, and the rhymes more frequent than anywhere else and extending over almost the half of the play; all this places this work among the earlier efforts of the poet. . . . The tone of the Italian school prevails more than in any other play. The redundancy of wit is only to be compared with the similar redundancy of conceit in Shakespeare's narrative poems, and with the Italian style in general, which he at first adopted.

This over-abundance of droll and laughter-loving personages, of wits and caricatures, gives the idea of an excessively jocular play; nevertheless everyone, on reading the comedy, feels a certain want of ease, and, on account of this very excess, cannot enjoy the comic effect. In structure and management of subject it is indisputably one of the weakest of the poet's pieces; nevertheless we divine a deeper meaning in it, not readily to be perceived, and which it is difficult to explain. . . . The whole turns upon a clever interchange of wit and asceticism, jest and earnest; the shallow characters are forms of mind, rather proceeding from the cultivation of the head than the will; throughout there are affected jests, high-sounding and often empty words, but no action; nevertheless we feel that this deficiency is no unintentional error, but that there is an object in view. There is a motley mixture of fantastic and strange characters, which for the most part betray no healthy groundwork of nature; and yet the poet himself is so sensible of this, that we might trust him to have had his reason for placing them together—a reason worth our while to seek. And indeed we find, on closer inspection, that this piece has a more profound character, in which Shakespeare's capable mind already unfolds its power. We recognise this as the first of his plays in which, as in all his subsequent works, he has had one single moral aim in view—an aim that here lies even far less concealed than in others of his work. (pp. 164-65)

In the burlesque parts of Love's Labour's Lost we meet with two favourite characters or caricatures of the Italian comedy; the Pedant, that is the schoolmaster and grammarian, and the military Braggart, the Thraso of the Latin, the 'Captain Spavento' of the Italian stage. These stereotyped characters are depicted by Shakespeare with such life, that it has been supposed, and it has been endeavoured to be proved, that the poet portrayed in them persons living at the time [see the excerpt above by William Warburton, 1747]. . . . The characteristics of both are exaggerated, as they could only be in the rudest popular comedy. Armado, the military braggart in the state of peace, as Parolles [in All's Well That Ends Well] is in war, appears in the ridiculous exaggeration and affectation of a child of hot Spanish imagination, assuming a contempt towards everything common; boastful but poor, a coiner of words but most ignorant, solemnly grave and laughably awkward, a hector and a coward, of gait majestical and of the lowest propensities. The schoolmaster Holofernes appears among the many enamoured characters of the comedy as a dry inanimate pedant, an imaginary word-sifter, a poor poet of the school of the Carmelite Mantuan, fantastically vain of his empty knowledge. Both caricatures become still more distorted when they are seen by the light of the contrast which the poet has placed beside them: to the stiff, weak, melancholy Armado is opposed the little Moth, who, light as his name, is all jest and playfulness, versatility and cunning; the pedant Holofernes is placed in opposition to Costard the child of nature, whose common sense ridicules the scholar who lives 'on the alms-basket of words' [V. i. 38]. The two characters, we see, are caricatures, taken from simple nature, exhibited in their effort to attract attention, in their ostentation, vanity, and empty thirst for fame, based upon an appearance of knowledge and a show of valour.

But these two originals, and their gross desire for glory, have been associated by Shakespeare with a society of finer mould, suffering from the same infirmity, only that, from their mind and culture, the poison lies deeper concealed. The court of Navarre had for three years devoted itself to study and retirement; the young king, seized with an ascetic turn, in the spirit of the courts of love and the vow-loving chivalry of those regions, desires that his young courtiers should join him in changing the court and its revels into an academy of contemplation, in mortifying their passions and worldly desires, and

A

PLEASANT

Conceited Comedie

CALLED,

Loues labors loft.

As it vvas prefented before her Highnes
this laft Chriftmas.

Newly corrected and augmented
By W. Shakefpere.

Imprinted at London by *W.W.*
for *Cutbert Burby.*
1598.

Title page of the Quarto of Love's Labour's Lost *(1598).
By permission of the Folger Shakespeare Library.*

in renouncing for the time all intercourse with women. He is in the same danger of erring from a vain desire for glory; he wishes to make Navarre a wonder of the world. (pp. 165-66)

The king has chosen Armado to amuse them by his minstrelsy during their hermit-life; and similar to the contempt with which the king regards his boasting vein is the scorn with which Biron views the learned and ascetic vanity of the king; but he has himself fallen into a still lighter vanity, for which he incurs Rosaline's censure. Endowed with a keen eye and an acute mind, gifted with captivating and touching eloquence, he has habituated himself to see every object in a ridiculous light, and to consider nothing sacred. The ardent black-eyed Rosaline, who is in no wise insensible to such mental gifts, but holds her part victorious in the war of words, considers him at first within the limits of becoming wit; she would not otherwise have loved him. But at last she agrees with the verdict of the world, which condemns him as a man replete with wounding and unsparing satire. And she sees the origin of this evil habit entirely in the vanity which delights in 'that loose grace which shallow laughing hearers give to fools' [V. ii. 859-60]. She looks upon him as abandoned to the same empty desire for unsubstantial applause, as he does upon those who are placed at his side. (p. 167)

[Shakespeare] has given the catastrophe, which concludes the merry comedy, a striking turn, in order to make [his intentions] most glaringly apparent. The nobles order a play to be represented before the ladies by their musicians and attendants, and by this means they revenge themselves on the director Holofernes for their own spoilt masquerade, by spoiling his pageant also, which was one of those simple popular plays such as Shakespeare ridicules in the *Midsummer-Night's Dream*, but which he ridicules in a kindly spirit, honouring the good will—one of those innocent sports which best please because 'they least know how' [V. ii. 516]. In the midst of extravagant jest and folly, however, a discord rings through the piece: the king of France is dead, and sorrow and parting interrupt the mirth. The embarrassed king attempts an unintelligible wooing, the embarrassed Biron endeavours to explain it, and becomes confused and perplexed himself; but the princess banishes the perjured guilt-burdened king for a year to a hermitage, if he wishes to have his request granted; Rosaline sends the mocker Biron to a hospital, where for a twelvemonth he is to jest with the sick, and if possible to be cured of his fault. Love's Labour is lost; 'Jack hath not Jill' [V. ii. 875], contrary to the custom of comedy; it is a comedy that ends in tears. Certainly this conclusion is in opposition to all aesthetic antecedence, but the catastrophe is genuinely Shakespearian; for moral rectitude was ever the poet's aim rather than a strict adherence to the rules of art. (pp. 169-70)

G. G. Gervinus, "Second Period of Shakespeare's Dramatic Poetry: 'Love's Labour's Lost' and 'All's Well that Ends Well'," in his Shakespeare Commentaries, *translated by F. E. Bunnètt, revised edition, 1877. Reprint by AMS Press, Inc., 1971, pp. 164-86.*

ÉMILE MONTÉGUT   (essay date 1867)

[*Montégut was a nineteenth-century French critic and the translator of such eminent English and American authors as Ralph Waldo Emerson, Thomas Macauley, and Shakespeare. As a critic, he is noted for his keen judgment, his practical approach to art, and his intellectual flexibility in all matters of literary discourse. In the following excerpt, taken from his* Oeuvres Complètes de

Shakespeare *(1867), Montégut praises the elements of French style in the dialogue of* Love's Labour's Lost.]

It is something extraordinary to observe Shakespeare's fidelity to the most minute details of historic truth and of local colour. Just as all the details of *Romeo and Juliet,* of *The Merchant of Venice,* of *Othello* are Italian, so all the details of *Love's Labour's Lost* are French. The conversations of the lords and the ladies are thoroughly French; vivacious, sprightly, witty; an unbroken game of battle-dore and shuttle-cock, a skirmish of *bons mots* ["'witticism'"], a mimic war of repartees. Even their bad taste is French, and their language, filed and refined to the utmost, possesses that pungency of elaborate wit which has never been displeasing to the French, especially in the upper classes. The style of their sentiments is equally French; under a disguise of gaiety they conceal the seriousness of their affections; under a veil of scoffing, the sincerity of their passion, and they acknowledge that they are in love only when they talk to themselves or believe that they are alone. In them is reflected, in the most delicate way in the world, that thoroughly French vice, the fear of ridicule, the poltroonery which makes us put a damper on our emotions, and makes us affix a tinkling bell on all our most serious passions in order to put our enemy, that is, the being whom we love, on a false scent, and to hinder him from having that hold on us which would assure him of our love. (p. 374)

> *Émile Montégut, in an extract, translated by Horace Howard Furness, in* A New Variorum Edition of Shakespeare: "Loves Labour's Lost," *Vol. XIV, edited by Horace Howard Furness, J. B. Lippincott Company, 1904, p. 374.*

J. O. HALLIWELL-PHILLIPPS (essay date 1879)

[*A nineteenth-century English bibliophile and scholar, Halliwell-Phillipps originally concentrated on textual criticism in his study of Shakespeare's works. However, later in his career he shifted his interest from textual and critical problems to those of historical import. In so doing, he became the first scholar to make extensive use of town records from Stratford in the study of Shakespeare's life. In his comments on* Love's Labour's Lost, *Halliwell-Phillipps maintains that Shakespeare was not satirizing John Florio in the character of Holofernes but that, because of their common patron, Lord Southampton, Shakespeare and Florio were more likely friends than enemies. According to Halliwell-Phillipps, Shakespeare was not ridiculing any specific person, but was merely satirizing the typical pedant of his day in his depiction of Holofernes. By arguing that the parody in* Love's Labour's Lost *is general and not personal, Halliwell-Phillipps concurs with such critics as Thomas Marc Parrott (1949) and S. C. Sen Gupta (1950), but is in disagreement with a larger critical tradition that includes William Warburton (1747), Muriel C. Bradbrook (1936), and, of special note in the Additional Bibliography, Arthur Acheson, Richard David, Walter Oakeshott, and Arthur Quiller-Couch and John Dover Wilson.*]

In the character of Holofernes, the poet no doubt intended a general satire upon the pedant of his day, a personage elsewhere delineated, in a similar style, by Sir Philip Sydney in the *Lady of the May,* where Rombus the school-master is another individual of the same type. The idea, however, has been entertained, by several eminent critics, that Shakespeare shadowed a real character under the name of Holofernes, and that the personage so satirized was John Florio, an Italian teacher in London contemporary with the great dramatist. The grounds for the formation of such an opinion are singularly inadequate to authorize the dogmatic manner in which it is promulgated

by Warburton [see excerpt above, 1747] and supported by [Richard] Farmer. Florio, it is assumed without the slightest evidence, had affronted Shakespeare by observing that "the plaies that they plaie in England are neither right comedies, nor right tragedies; but representations of histories without any decorum." It is scarcely necessary to say that this remark may be general in its application, without any peculiar reference to Shakespeare, who was not the only writer of historical plays; but even were it admitted that Florio's words were directed against his productions, there is nothing so individually applicable in the character of Holofernes to lead necessarily to the conclusion that it was delineated in the spirit of retaliation. Florio and Shakespeare, moreover, both acknowledged the same patron in Lord Southampton, and they were more probably friends than enemies. There could not have existed any idea of rivalry between two authors whose pursuits were so dissimilar, and Shakespeare would hardly have endangered his position with Lord Southampton by holding up a favorite to ridicule, Florio, in 1598, thus speaking of that nobleman,—"in whose paie and patronage I have lived some yeeres; to whom I owe and vowe the yeeres I have to live." This was in his *Worlde of Wordes,* 1598, in the introduction to which he is supposed to allude to Shakespeare, but without the slightest probability, for the passage in which the presumed allusion occurs is in the midst of a long tirade against a person whose initials are H. S., and other circumstances are mentioned that do not well apply to the great dramatist. Richard Mulcaster, a schoolmaster and scholar of some eminence, also contemporary with Shakespeare, has likewise been conjectured, with as little likelihood, to have been the original prototype of the character of Holofernes. [Edmond] Malone is much more likely to be correct when he gives it as his opinion that "the character was formed out of two pedants in Rabelais: Master Tubal Holophernes, and Master Janotus de Bragmardo. (pp. 12-14)

> *J. O. Halliwell-Phillipps, "'Love's Labour's Lost',"* in his Memoranda on 'Love's Labour's Lost', 'King John', 'Othello', and on 'Romeo and Juliet', *James Evan Adlard, 1879, pp. 5-19.*

ALGERNON CHARLES SWINBURNE (essay date 1880)

[*Swinburne was an English poet, dramatist, and critic who devoted much of his literary career to the study of Shakespeare and other Elizabethan writers. His three books on Shakespeare—*A Study of Shakespeare *(1880),* Shakespeare *(1909), and* Three Plays of Shakespeare *(1909)—all demonstrate his keen interest in Shakespeare's poetic talents and, especially, his major tragedies. In the following excerpt on* Love's Labour's Lost, *Swinburne extols Berowne's speech on love and remarks on the Marlovian flavor of the blank verse. He also praises Shakespeare for being among the first writers to utilize a "higher key" in the mode of poetic or romantic comedy, and he further regards this experiment as preparing the way for the language employed in such later plays as* As You Like It *and* The Tempest.]

[The] real crown and flower of *Love's Labour's Lost,* is the praise or apology of love spoken by Biron in blank verse. This is worthy of Marlowe for dignity and sweetness, but has also the grace of a light and radiant fancy enamoured of itself, begotten between thought and mirth, a child-god with grave lips and laughing eyes, whose inspiration is nothing akin to Marlowe's. In this as in the overture of the play and in its closing scene, but especially in the noble passage which winds up for a year the courtship of Biron and Rosaline, the spirit which informs the speech of the poet is finer of touch and deeper of tone than in the sweetest of the serious interludes of the *Comedy of Errors*. The play is in the main a yet lighter thing, and more wayward and capricious in build, more formless and fantastic in plot, more incomposite altogether than that first heir of Shakespeare's comic invention, which on its own ground is perfect in its consistency, blameless in composition and coherence; while in *Love's Labour's Lost* the fancy for the most part runs wild as the wind, and the structure of the story is as that of a house of clouds which the wind builds and unbuilds at pleasure. Here we find a very riot of rhymes, wild and wanton in their half-grown grace as a troop of "young satyrs, tender-hoofed and ruddy-horned"; during certain scenes we seem almost to stand again by the cradle of new-born comedy, and hear the first lisping and laughing accents run over from her baby lips in bubbling rhyme; but when the note changes we recognise the speech of gods. For the first time in our literature the higher key of poetic or romantic comedy is finely touched to a fine issue. The divine instrument fashioned by Marlowe for tragic purposes alone has found at once its new sweet use in the hands of Shakespeare. The way is prepared for *As You Like It* and the *Tempest;* the language is discovered which will befit the lips of Rosalind and Miranda. (pp. 46-8)

> *Algernon Charles Swinburne, "First Period: Lyric and Fantastic," in his* A Study of Shakespeare, *R. Worthington, 1880, pp. 1-65.*

EDWARD DOWDEN   (essay date 1881)

[*Dowden was an Irish critic and biographer whose* Shakspere: A Critical Study of His Mind and Art *(rev. ed. 1881) was the leading example of the biographical criticism popular in the English-speaking world near the end of the nineteenth century. Biographical critics sought in the plays and poems a record of Shakespeare's personal development. As that approach gave way in the twentieth century to aesthetic theories with greater emphasis on the constructed, artificial nature of literary works, Dowden and other biographical critics came to be considered limited. In his discussion of* Love's Labour's Lost, *Dowden argues that the play is both "a protest against idealizing away the facts of life" and a subtle reminder that practicality, without the capacity for ideas, is also a limiting, reductive philosophy. His comments recall the notion of dialectic irony in the play first noted by Hermann Ulrici (1839), but in giving priority to "the realities of human nature" he anticipates those twentieth-century critics, like Bobbyann Roesen (1953) and Ralph Berry (1969), who perceive a movement in* Love's Labour's Lost *from idealism to reality.*]

Love's Labor's Lost, if we do not assign that place to *The Two Gentlemen of Verona,* is the first independent, wholly original work of Shakspere. Mr. Charles Knight named it "The Comedy of Affectations" [see excerpt above, 1849], and that title aptly interprets one intention of the play. It is a satirical extravaganza embodying Shakspere's criticism upon contemporary fashions and foibles in speech, in manners, and in literature. This probably, more than any other of the plays of Shakspere, suffers through lapse of time. Fantastical speech, pedantic learning, extravagant love-hyperbole, frigid fervors in poetry—against each of these, with the brightness and vivacity of youth, confident in the success of its cause, Shakspere directs the light artillery of his wit. Being young and clever, he is absolutely devoid of respect for nonsense, whether it be dainty, affected nonsense, or grave, unconscious nonsense.

But, over and above this, there is a serious intention in the play. It is a protest against youthful schemes of shaping life according to notions rather than according to reality, a protest against idealizing away the facts of life. The play is chiefly interesting as containing Shakspere's confession of faith with

respect to the true principles of self-culture. The King of Navarre and his young lords had resolved, for a definite period of time, to circumscribe their beings and their lives with a little code of rules. They had designed to enclose a little favored park in which ideas should rule to the exclusion of the blind and rude forces of nature. They were pleased to rearrange human character and human life, so that it might accord with their idealistic scheme of self-development. The court was to be a little Academe; no woman was to be looked at for the space of three years; food and sleep were to be placed under precise regulation. And the result is—what? That human nature refuses to be dealt with in this fashion of arbitrary selection and rejection. The youthful idealists had supposed that they would form a little group of select and refined ascetics of knowledge and culture; it was quickly proved that they were men. The play is Shakspere's declaration in favor of the fact as it is. Here, he says, we are with such and such appetites and passions. Let us, in any scheme of self-development, get *that* fact acknowledged at all events; otherwise we shall quickly enough betray ourselves as arrant fools, fit to be flouted by women, and needing to learn from them a portion of their directness, practicality, and good-sense.

And yet the Princess and Rosaline and Maria have not the entire advantage on their side. It is well to be practical; but to be practical, and also to have a capacity for ideas, is better. Berowne, the exponent of Shakspere's own thought, who entered into the youthful, idealistic project of his friends, with a satisfactory assurance that the time would come when the entire dream-structure would tumble ridiculously about the ears of them all—Berowne is yet a larger nature than the Princess or Rosaline. *His* good-sense is the good-sense of a thinker and of a man of action. When he is most flouted and bemocked, we yet acknowledge him victorious and the master; and Rosaline will confess the fact by-and-by.

In the midst of merriment and nonsense comes a sudden and grievous incursion of fact full of pain. The father of the Princess is dead. All the world is not mirth—"this side is Hiems, Winter; this Ver, the Spring" [V. ii. 891]. The lovers must part—"Jack hath not his Jill" [V. ii. 875]; and to engrave the lesson deeply, which each heart needs, the King and two of his companions are dismissed for a twelvemonth to learn the difference between reality and unreality; while Berowne, who has known the mirth of the world, must also make acquaintance with its sorrow, must visit the speechless sick and try to win "the pained impotent to smile" [V. ii. 854].

Let us get hold of the realities of human nature and human life, Shakspere would say, and let us found upon these realities, and not upon the mist or the air, our schemes of individual and social advancement. Not that Shakspere is hostile to culture; but he knows that a perfect education must include the culture, through actual experience, of the senses and of the affections. (pp. 55-7)

> *Edward Dowden, "The Growth of Shakspere's Mind and Art," in his* Shakspere: A Critical Study of His Mind and Art, *third edition, Harper & Brothers Publishers, 1881, pp. 37-83.*

WALTER PATER   (essay date 1885)

[*An English critic and essayist, Pater is one of the most famous proponents of aestheticism in English literature. Distinguished as the first major writer in England to formulate an explicitly aesthetic philosophy of life, he advocated the "love of art for art's sake'' as life's greatest offering—a belief which can be discerned in the essays collected in his* Studies in the History of the Renaissance *(1873) and* Appreciations *(1889). Pater is also recognized as a master prose stylist and a leading exemplar of impressionist criticism. In his commentary on* Love's Labour's Lost, *which first appeared in* Macmillan's Magazine *in 1885, Pater describes the play as ''an ancient tapestry''—a work unified not through plot or characterization, but through "a series of pictoral groups, in which the same figures reappear, in different combinations, but on the same background." Pater argues that Shakespeare's playfulness with words in* Love's Labour's Lost—*his parody of ''euphuism''—is not trivial but shows a genuine concern with language. Although August Wilhelm Schlegel (1808) had earlier noted the play of words in* Love's Labour's Lost, *Pater's suggestion that Shakespeare is occupied with language in itself anticipates several important twentieth-century interpretations of the play by such critics as Gladys Doidge Willcock (1934), William Matthews (1964), Ralph Berry (1969), James L. Calderwood (1971), Terence Hawkes (1973), and Malcolm Evans (1975). Pater also states that Berowne is a ''reflex of Shakespeare himself''—an observation made earlier by Edward Dowden (1881) and later by John Palmer (1946) and Thomas Marc Parrott (1949).]*

'Love's Labour's Lost' is one of the earliest of Shakspere's dramas, and has many of the peculiarities of his poems, which are also the work of his earlier life. The opening speech of the King on the immortality of fame—on the triumph of fame over death—and the nobler parts of Biron, have something of the monumental style of Shakspere's Sonnets, and are not without their conceits of thought and expression. This connection of the play with his poems is further enforced by the insertion in it of three sonnets and a faultless song; which, in accordance with Shakspere's practice in other plays, are inwoven into the action of the piece and, like the golden ornaments of a fair woman, give it a peculiar air of distinction. There is merriment in it also, with choice illustrations of both wit and humour; a laughter often exquisite, ringing, if faintly, yet as genuine laughter still, though sometimes sinking into mere burlesque, which has not lasted quite so well. And Shakspere brings a serious effect out of the trifling of his characters. A dainty love-making is interchanged with the more cumbrous play; below the many artifices of Biron's amorous speeches we may trace sometimes the ''unutterable longing;'' and the lines in which Katherine describes the blighting through love of her younger sister are one of the most touching things in older literature. . . .

The merely dramatic interest of the piece is slight enough— only just sufficient, indeed, to be the vehicle of its wit and poetry. The scene—a park of the King of Navarre—is unaltered throughout; and the unity of the play is not so much the unity of a drama as that of a series of pictorial groups, in which the same figures reappear, in different combinations, but on the same background. It is as if Shakspere had intended to bind together, by some inventive conceit, the devices of an ancient tapestry, and give voices to its figures. On one side, a fair palace; on the other, the tents of the Princess of France, who has come on an embassy from her father to the King of Navarre; in the midst, a wide space of smooth grass. . . . The same personages are combined over and over again into a series of gallant scenes—the Princess, the three masked ladies, the quaint, pedantic King—one of those amiable kings men have never loved enough, whose serious occupation with the things of the mind seems, by contrast with the more usual forms of kingship, like frivolity or play. Some of the figures are grotesque merely, and, all the male ones at least, a little fantastic. (p. 89)

Play is often that about which people are most serious; and the humorist may observe how, under all love of playthings, there

is almost always hidden an appreciation of something really engaging and delightful. This is true always of the toys of children; it is often true of the playthings of grown-up people, their vanities, their fopperies even—the cynic would add their pursuit of fame and their lighter loves. Certainly, this is true without exception of the playthings of a past age, which to those who succeed it are always full of pensive interest—old manners, old dresses, old houses. For what is called fashion in these matters occupies, in each age, much of the care of many of the most discerning people, furnishing them with a kind of mirror of their real inward refinements, and their capacity for selection. Such modes or fashions are, at their best, an example of the artistic predominance of form over matter; of the manner of the doing of it over the thing done; and have a beauty of their own. It is so with that old euphuism of the Elizabethan age—that pride of dainty language and curious expression, which it is very easy to ridicule, which often made itself ridiculous, but which had below it a real sense of fitness and nicety; and which, as we see in this very play, and still more clearly in the Sonnets, had some fascination for the young Shakspere himself. It is this foppery of delicate language, this fashionable plaything of his time, with which Shakspere is occupied in 'Love's Labours Lost.' He shows us the manner in all its stages; passing from the grotesque and vulgar pedantry of Holofernes, through the extravagant but polished caricature of Armado, to become the peculiar characteristic of a real though still quaint poetry in Biron himself—still chargeable, even at his best, with just a little affectation. As Shakspere laughs broadly at it in Holofernes or Armado, he is the analyst of its curious charm in Biron; and this analysis involves a delicate raillery by Shakspere himself at his own chosen manner.

This ''foppery'' of Shakspere's day had, then, its really delightful side, a quality in no sense ''affected,'' by which it satisfies a real instinct in our minds—the fancy so many of us have for an exquisite and curious skill in the use of words. Biron is the perfect flower of this manner—

> A man of fire new words, fashion's own knight
>
> [I. i. 178]

—as he describes Armado in terms which are really applicable to himself. In him this manner blends with a true gallantry of nature, and an affectionate complaisance and grace. He has at times some of its extravagance or caricature also, but the shades of expression by which he passes from this to the ''golden cadence'' of Shakspere's own chosen verse, are so fine, that it is sometimes difficult to trace them. (pp. 90-1)

As happens with every true dramatist, Shakspere is for the most part hidden behind the persons of his creation. Yet there are certain of his characters in which we feel that there is something of self-portraiture. And it is not so much in his grander, more subtle and ingenious creations that we feel this— in Hamlet and King Lear—as in those slighter and more spontaneously developed figures, who, while far from playing principal parts, are yet distinguished by a certain peculiar happiness and delicate ease in the drawing of them—figures which possess, above all, that winning attractiveness which there is no man but would willingly exercise, and which resemble those works of art which, though not meant to be very great or imposing, are yet, wrought of the choicest material. Mercutio, in 'Romeo and Juliet,' belongs to this group of Shakspere's characters—versatile, mercurial people, such as make good actors, and in whom the

> Nimble spirits of the arteries,
>
>   [IV. iii. 302]

the finer but still merely animal elements of great wit, predominate. A careful delineation of little, characteristic traits seems to mark them out as the characters of his predilection; and it is hard not to identify him with these more than with others. Biron, in 'Love's Labours Lost,' is perhaps the most striking member of this group. In this character, which is never quite in touch with, never quite on a perfect level of understanding with the other persons of the play, we see, perhaps, a reflex of Shakspere himself, when he has just become able to stand aside from and estimate the first period of his poetry. (p. 91)

> *Walter Pater, "On 'Love's Labour's Lost',"* in Macmillan's Magazine, *Vol. LIII, December, 1885, pp. 89-91.*

THOMAS R. PRICE (essay date 1890)

[*Price, an American scholar, prepared an edition of* Othello *(1890) and produced a study called* Shakespeare's Verse Construction *(1889). The following essay on* Love's Labour's Lost *is notable for its emphasis on character analysis, an approach typical of Shakespearean criticism throughout the nineteenth century. In the excerpt below, Price describes the characterization of* Love's Labour's Lost *as "a marvel of delicate art," particularly Shakespeare's insightful portraits of Berowne and Rosaline; the former Price calls the "prince among Shakespeare's group of gentlemen," the latter an example of the dramatist's love for "glorious woman." Price also identifies the "higher purpose" of the play as Shakespeare's attempt to show how the influence of "fashionable life" may help create "healthy and robust natures" such as Berowne and Rosaline represent.*]

[In] Shakespeare's crown of great poems, even when compared with the *Othello,* or with the *Tempest, Love's Labour's Lost* has a charm of its own, a lustre that is not dimmed by others. We love it because it speaks to us so clearly of the most brilliant and most lovable young man that the world ever saw. It shows how Shakespeare felt and thought in his youth, what his own eyes saw in the world, what his observations so far had perceived in men and women; it shows us the kind of verses that he loved—"those golden cadences of poetry" that he caught from others before he had had time to forge his own. It shows us the kind of wit he admired, the form of character that he took delight in, before the pressure of the world had made him grave and thoughtful. If *Love's Labour's Lost* be fantastical, it is joyous and cheery. If its views of life be shallow, they are true and bright. If its characters be unreal, they are delightfully varied and delightfully amusing, and above all the play of youthful poesy there looms the greatness of the poet. The genius that sketched for us the pranks of Moth and the absurdities of Armado had already power to show us in Rosaline and in Biron the depths of tenderness and of wisdom that lie hidden in the noblest men and women. (pp. 67-8)

As interpreter of nature, Shakespeare has not in this play attained the full measure of his artistic growth. Yet his youth had been passed amid country scenes, in close communion with nature, and his observation of nature had been keen, his enjoyment of nature intense. All the play rolls before us in the open air. There is sunshine and bright weather all through it; great trees standing in clumps, gay tents and pavilions shining through the forest vistas of the royal parks. The princess goes forth to hunt the deer in the wild woods; Biron and his fellow-lovers seek the depth of the forest to recite their love-sick

verses. The clowns, when they come forth to show their simple pageant, seem to come out of the bushes, and to play upon the grass. In all this Shakespeare has put the joyousness of lovely natural scenes as fit setting for the joyous activity of human life. The genial manhood of Biron, the graceful womanhood of Rosaline, show brighter in the park of Navarre than if we saw them in palace halls or city streets. (p. 68)

In his presentation of human life there are the same two powers of mind at work as in his presentation of nature; there is the same keenness of observation in seeing what is before him, there is the same art of the imagination in combining what he sees into groups and in interpreting what he does not see by what he sees. Moth and Armado, for example, may each have been the result of mere observation of real persons. The impish smartness of the small boy, the brag and affectation of the low-bred adventurer, are things that even now one can see in the real world. But to combine Moth and Armado into one group, to play them off upon each other, to tell how Moth acts upon Armado, and Armado upon Moth,—this could not be done by observation, however keen. This was the work that only the imagination could achieve. To do this as Shakespeare does it, even in the simplest combination of his simplest play, is a sign, on a small scale, of that imaginative power which makes the poet's work the greatest of intellectual achievements.

Each play of Shakespeare is, above all things else, a vision of some isolated phase of human life; there is a group of characters brought before us, each distinct in itself, and all combining by laws of delicate grouping, to make out an action that involves the development and the destiny of each. The genius of the poet is displayed in every detail; the vision of life that he brings before us is in part, as we have seen, the fruit of poetic observation, in part the fruit of poetic imagination. The facts observed, gathered in from his knowledge of the world, are set forth into novel groups by his imaginative power, and fitted into a marvelous complexity of action by the process of his invention.

In *Love's Labour's Lost* the ardent genius of the young poet is already at its creative work. In spite of his youth he has already great treasures of experience and observation to expend upon his characters. As we embark upon the rippling current of his verses, they bear us on into a world not less novel than it is beautiful. The characters all slip one by one into their places. They touch, they meet, they combine. Swept on by the poet's imagination, we see the characters live before us, we hear them talk. We watch as if all were real the weaving of the many lines of separate action, crossing and re-crossing like the silken threads of woven tapestry, into the lines and colors of the pre-ordained design.

In *Love's Labour's Lost* the characters are in number nineteen. Five of them are women and fourteen are men. Even in their number we can see the amplitude of Shakespeare's imagination—the fearless audacity of his method. He bursts into the world with the full fervor of the innovating romantic impulse on him. He leaps forth from the narrow confines of the classical art. The harmony that his spirit craves is not the narrow and intense harmony of the old world drama, brought forth from the collision of two or three types of humanity. It is the rich and varied harmony that comes from the complex grouping of a large number of sharply discriminated men and women. (pp. 74-5)

Among all the nineteen characters of the *Love's Labour's Lost,* there is not one that is not in its way a marvel of delicate art;

and our delight in Shakespeare's workmanship becomes the intenser for looking sharply into all the mysteries of his character-creation. Costard is, for example, the type of the good-natured, vulgar, sagacious, brave-hearted English bumpkin. Boyet is the type of the selfish, worldly-wise old courtier. The king and the princess, although less strongly marked than the others, are both in conception and in detail nobly portrayed. Don Armado, as a deep study of the reflex action between obliquity of mind and obliquity of character, is at once the most elaborate and the most odious of the lower characters. Passing by them all, we come to the glory of this drama, to the crown and love knot of Shakespeare's youthful poetry, the interwoven characters of Biron and Rosaline.

The full picture of Biron is precious to us as giving the youthful Shakespeare's conception of the gentleman,—a conception not to be eclipsed, perhaps not to be even equaled, by any of his later renderings. To paint him from all sides, in all his attributes, was the chief aim of the poet; and thus the character dominates all, and takes by far the largest space in the canvas. The king, in spite of his rank, speaks only 260 verses; Rosaline herself only 160; but Biron speaks over 600, and fills about one-fourth of the play by his noble presence. In dealing with him, there is no disdain in the poet's mind for even the lighter sides of what in worldly conventionality makes the gentleman. Biron is, indeed, on first acquaintance only the genial, somewhat caustic and satirical, man of the world, the merry, madcap lord,—''not a word with him but a jest'' [II. i. 216]. He is master of all social accomplishments, witty, graceful, easy, unsurpassed in small talk. He shows us right soon how well he knows the way to defend himself against rudeness, how to punish insolence, and put down familiarity and presumption. He has even the faults of the man of fashion; his wit is a little too prone to wound; his calm self-assertion has a touch of dangerous arrogance. But under this external polish of courtier and man of fashion lie the noblest virtues of character and the highest qualities of mind. Alone among the grandees, for example, he has the kindly grace of charity and tenderness toward inferiors. Thus he appreciates and humors the homely merits of the clownish Costard: and he pleads with the king to give gracious audience to the villagers that wish to show him their rural pageant. Akin to this, the virtue rarest among polished and hardened men of the world, is his belief in womanhood, his passionate devotion of himself, mind and heart and soul, to the woman that he loved. Biron is prince among Shakespeare's group of gentlemen; first, because he knows so well whom to love; secondly, because he knows so well how to love. Had he lacked sense, he might have chosen unworthily; had he lacked character, he might have loved feebly or treacherously. Because this man combined the gift of intellect with the gift of true and deep emotion, he stands unsurpassed in the world of the poet's vision, a type of the gentleman. (pp. 86-7)

[In] all this glowing picture of the man there shines above all the radiance of his intellectual qualities. Whenever he speaks he utters himself with the grace, the directness and the simplicity that mark the best style of all the great ages. . . . But, although he had lived among scholars, and drunk deep of the learning of his times, he kept himself as free from the pedantic jargon of Holofernes as from the fashionable jargon of Armado. And along with this true literary taste, and this inborn nobleness of speech, he has, what is akin to it, a marvelous knowledge of the world of men and women, of society in general, and even of his friends and of himself. Thus he moves through the scenes of the play, understanding all, sympathizing with all, and controlling all. Even of those that he best likes he sees the

faults; he understands the weakness of the king, for example, but he loves him for his goodness, and he is faithful to him and gentle with him. When others are deceived, he is clear-sighted. He understands, under the affectations of Armado, the baseness, the lustfulness, the cowardice of the wretched man. He sees, under the ponderous erudition of Holofernes the feebleness of his intellect, and knows him to be a fool. He understands the weak points of his own nature, and struggles keenly and subtly against the mastery of love until he finds that his passion is no whim of fancy, but real and profound emotion. Above all, he understands, under the gay and lively manner of Rosaline, the depth and goodness of the woman's nature. And thus, as the play wears on, the gay young gentleman of the first scene grows before our eyes into intellectual greatness. He rejects all plans for the distorting and mutilation of human life. He ''sees life clearly, and he sees it whole.'' He sees what are its realities, its duties, and its meaning. He sees what are its pleasures and its consolations,—the new birth of the soul in a deep and unselfish love. Thus Biron rises to a conception of human life great enough and perfect enough to be safely taken as Shakespeare's own. The play has its highest significance in the fact that the action and the mind and the qualities of Biron are the revelation to us of the young Shakespeare's idea of manhood. (pp. 88-9)

As compared with the full length description of Biron, the sketch of Rosaline is slight and rapid. Yet each line tells, and many details are supplied that give to Rosaline's picture almost the fidelity of a portrait from life. Even her appearance is described with a detail that Shakespeare does not often afford. All through his treatment of Rosaline there is the caressing touch of love in the poet's mind for the glorious woman, who, in Boyet's old-fashioned phrase, was ''a continent of beauty'' [IV. i. 109]. Her very name, linking her with the poet's best-loved flower, sets the verse into lover-like vibration of tones.

> She is a gentle lady;
> When tongues speak sweetly, then they name her name,
> And Rosaline they call her.
>
> [III. i. 165-67]
> (p. 89)

[Throughout] the play the character of Rosaline, side by side with the character of Biron, expands and rises. At first all that shines in her is her sprightly wit, her ease and dignity and conversational grace. She was very beautiful and very brilliant, fond of teasing her friends, fond of giving cheek and rebuff to impatience and presumption and vanity. But even in her gayest mood she was nice in her jesting, and even in her jesting there was knowledge of the world, discretion and modesty. . . . In her manner of speech she partook, more than Biron, of the fashion of her times. It is perhaps in the nature of women, where other things are equal, to absorb more deeply than men the influence of convention and the taint of fashion. Thus the language shows distinct traces of the antithesis and word-play that Shakespeare turns to scorn in the jargon of Armado. But her wit rose often into genial humor, and she had an epigrammatic power and a skill of innuendo that are peculiar to herself. When, however, her heart was touched, her language sprang upward into beauty and eloquence. Her description of Biron in the second act is a masterpiece of that penetration and refinement which are the intellectual woman's surpassing gifts of expression; and her parting words to Biron are poetry as grand as Biron's own description of the power of love.

As the lower purpose of the play was to show how far honesty and good taste are superior to affectation and bad taste, so its higher purpose was to show how the fashionable life and the gay world may develop healthy and robust natures into the highest forms of human character. Thus the play culminates in the development of Rosaline's character into fitness for Biron's manhood, and in the development of Biron's character into fitness for Rosaline's tender and trustful love. (p. 91)

         Thomas R. Price, "'Love's Labour's Lost'," in Shakespeariana, *Vol. VII, No. 2, April, 1890, pp. 67-91.*

DENTON J. SNIDER   (essay date 1890?)

[Snider was an American teacher, philosopher, and poet who followed closely the precepts of the German philosopher Georg Wilhelm Friedrich Hegel and contributed greatly to the dissemination of his philosophy of absolute idealism in America. Hegel's influence on Snider can be detected in his essay on Love's Labour's Lost, *particularly in the critic's emphasis on the notions of Family and Love and in his dialectical interpretation of the play. Snider identifies a movement in the action of* Love's Labour's Lost *which consists of a "collision of love" with the attempt to live a strictly ascetic existence. This movement is composed of three different conflicts: ethical love (Family) versus study, sensual love versus monasticism, and pedantic learning versus its subsequent renunciation. Snider concludes that the play is a reaction against pastoral seclusion, study, and monasticism, and he maintains that higher social values, such as Family and Love, ultimately triumph.]*

[In *Love's Labour's Lost*] there is shown a re-action against . . . ideal life when it takes an ascetic form for the purpose of mere study. The re-action is given in three leading phases: first, ethical Love, which leads to the Family, assails such a life, overcomes it, and inflicts upon its adherents a penalty; secondly, sensual Love, as the strong protest of Nature, violates the ascetic ordinance from the start; thirdly, Learning, which is the object of the life above mentioned, is shown in its one-sidedness and folly when it is an end unto itself; it simply makes pedantic fools, and thus dissolves in its own absurdity. Biron, who, to a certain extent, is the bearer of the protest against this ascetic world, asks the keen question: What is the end of study? This question is essentially that of the play, which also gives an answer.

Disease of Learning is shown in manifold forms by the various characters, who become comic, self-annulling in the very folly of their pursuit of wisdom. As Biron says:—

> So study evermore is overshot,
> While it doth study to have what it would,
> It doth forget to do the thing it should.
> [I. i. 142-44]

There is Don Armado, who is "a refined traveler of Spain," in whom learning has produced only bombast, who "hath a mint of phrases in his brain" [I. i. 163, 165]. Costard, the ignorant boor, has caught the affectation and uses words and logical forms which he does not understand. Then there is a special class of pedants drawn in broad caricature. The lovers, too, the more elevated characters, are strongly tainted with the prevailing epidemic; they indulge in affected speech, alliteration, conceits, sonnets in which the language of love wears the heaviest bonds. Yet they are men of study, and are eager

in the pursuit of knowledge. The words of the Princess apply to them all:—

> None are so surely caught, when they are catched,
> As wit turned fool; folly in wisdom hatched,
> Hath wisdom's warrant and the help of school,
> And wit's own grace to grace a learned fool.
> [V. ii. 69-72]

Even in this speech we see affectation falling into affectation in censuring itself; the devil is still the devil in reproving sin.

Now this was the condition of the Poet when he wrote the play. He was still under the domination of conceit and affected antithesis, coupled with a certain degree of pedantry, though he was laughing at these follies. If he were outside of them and wholly beyond them, they would be indifferent to him. This gives the flavor of the play with its fantastic humor; the author is still in it, but rises above it with a laugh, which, nevertheless, involves him in his own ridicule. He is aware of this condition. Biron declares penitently:—

> These summer flies
> Have blown me full of maggot ostentation. . . .
> Henceforth my wooing mind shall be expressed
> In russet yeas and honest kersey noes:—
> [V. ii. 408-09, 412-13]

but at once he cannot help violating his good resolution by using an affected word, whereat he confesses:

> Yet I have a trick
> Of the old rage; bear with me, I am sick,
> I'll leave it by degrees.
> [V. ii. 416-18]

This whole play, one thinks, is the process of the Poet in freeing himself from the "rage," which is his own, and that of his time. Like these students he is votary of love rather than of learning; so he will remain during life; he is not going to be a scholar, but a poet. He has here settled his own relation to erudition—a matter which has troubled so many critics. Latin, French, History, Mythology, and other disciplines are touched upon in this drama; but especially we see how profoundly he has studied his own language and his own poetic art on their technical side. Listen to the school master criticising speech and verse; it is doubtless an echo from the Poet's own talk and study, though it be comic and exaggerated. In later works he will not often have much to say about his art—never so much as in this play.

In fact, the relation of the Poet to *Love's Labour's Lost* is very significant. It shows that he had wrought in many departments of learning, even in anatomy, that he is a man of study, yet has seen its vanity when pushed beyond its end. The play is clearly his declaration of war against mere erudition, though he is still involved in its meshes, he is liberating himself, but is not yet wholly free. The struggle has still a strong interest for him, because he is not yet fully master of himself in this direction; he revels with delight in pedantry while ridiculing it; we see the young Shakespeare with vivid reminiscences of his school days—beyond them, yet in them still. He undoubtedly was asking that question of Biron—What is the end of Learning? Those who are fond of dwelling upon Shakespeare's illiteracy, and of drawing conclusions from it, would do well to ponder this play, which shows both learning and its comedy. (pp. 297-300)

Twelfth Night is probably the most perfect comedy written by Shakespeare—viewed from the stand-point of organization—while just the contrary must be asserted of *Love's Labour's Lost*. There is no scaffolding here which adequately supports the entire work; there is no intrigue which gives a backbone to the whole action and makes it a complete unity. It lies before us, to a certain extent, divided into pieces which are not fully articulated. It is like the less perfect animals which may be separated into parts and each part will still remain an animal. It has disguises and concealments, but none which run through and hold together the entire plot. A story it has, undoubtedly, but a story to which precisely the same objections apply. Those of the Poet's readers who find as much delight in the structure of his dramas as in their other great qualities must now expect some disappointment.

So much may be said about its organization, which pertains to the proper employment of dramatic instrumentalities. Still, there is a central thought which controls the work, though often in a very remote and capricious manner. Other merits, too, of a high order must be acknowledged. Characters are drawn with definiteness, though frequently with some extravagance—in fact, the play is thoroughly a comedy of character, and is defective in the element of situation; hence its frame-work is so inadequate. Its coloring is that of unbounded, uncontrollable caprice, which scouts all propriety—even artistic propriety; it bubbles over with puns, conceits, whimsicalities, of every description and under all circumstances; it is a wilderness of jokes and humors. The reader is not expected to be able to keep his face straight for any length of time, and, if the scene momentarily wears a sober look, it is felt to be preparatory to an effervescence. The youthful author shows here his most wanton mood; it is as if he were trying to leap out of his skin from pure mirthfulness. Still, it is worth our trouble to see how far the thought shines through this somewhat tangled mass of dramatic luxuriance, even though we sometimes have to force what is dim into a little stronger light than either the strict language or the immediate connection of the passage may warrant.

It is manifest that the drama mainly springs from a collision of love. But the form of this collision is novel; a new obstacle is introduced—study undertakes to suppress, and, hence, conflicts with, love. The latter is supposed to be an ancient enemy of learning; it distracts the attention, stirs up the passions, muddles the brain. Thus the two hostile powers grapple; the course of the play will show that love is not only triumphant against the pursuit of erudition and philosophy, but also punishes its contemners by a torture peculiar to itself, namely, loss of immediate fruition. Such is unquestionably the leading thread of the drama, supported by the group of elevated characters. But another element must not be omitted; the reverse side of mere erudition is shown when it is not tempered by love, or some other corrective—it makes men comic; they become learned fools. So, from this point of view, study may be said to be triumphant in its one-sided pursuit—triumphant in producing pedants. Hence the complete statement of the work must exhibit the conflict of these two principles, each of which is victorious, though in different groups of characters.

The play will be most easily grasped by dividing it into three movements. The first represents the conflict—love is in a struggle with study, and is not only victorious in this one case, but also in other relations which are introduced. The second is the mutual revelation of the secret passion; its triumph is acknowledged, and even defended; the oath of asceticism is openly

violated, and the violation is supported by all. Here, in particular, the comic effect of the purely studious life is brought in; it results in pedantic folly. The third movement has, in general, the nature of retribution; the higher group are teased, tricked, and cajoled by the ladies—are beaten at their own game of intellectual dexterity, are deferred in their hopes for a year, with some additional penalties. The lower group have their erudition reduced to a comic nullity in the ridiculous farce of the Nine Worthies.

The play opens with the fundamental point—the King has resolved to devote himself for three years to study and contemplation, and for that purpose has drawn up some rigid rules which are to govern him and his associates. . . . . Besides other less important regulations whose object is to enforce abstinence, the main one can be at once given—the complete renunciation of the society of women. Here is the pivot upon which the whole action turns. The ethical basis, too, should not be forgotten—man, in the execution of his plans, abjures the Family; the latter, however, as an institution, must prove itself the more powerful through its emotion, namely, love. Thus the play moves from love violated by study to love triumphant over a one-sided life of erudition. (pp. 301-05)

Thus the conflict opens. Ascetic life undertakes to suppress all desire and passion, and, to make it effective, the supreme ruler of the State enforces it by penalties for violation. But what is this violation which the Poet at once thrusts before our eyes? The scene cannot be told in its details to the reader; suffice it to say that already one of the rigid injunctions has been set flagrantly at naught within the very limits of the "little Academe," and the guilty couple, Costard and Jaquenetta, are brought into the presence of the King. Here we behold the revolt of nature, in its rudest form, against the ascetic ordinance; passion, on its purely animal side, is introduced in all its nakedness, to show one of the Titanic forces with which the realm of discipline has to contend. Love without its ethical elements, as mere natural impulse, has thus assailed this student-world at its very origin. (pp. 306-07)

[Costard and Don Armado] represent, in general, the triumph of love in its sensual phase. Costard is an ignorant boor, while Don Armado is a cultivated fantastic; though so different in other respects, both agree in their fundamental relation to the play—they represent passion in its natural impulse, without its ethical basis. . . . [In the group of elevated characters] love is shown in its higher and purer manifestation—its end is the Family, but its conflict with the cloistered life of learning is brought out in the plainest and most decisive manner.

The Princess of France, with her three attendant ladies, has arrived, and is waiting to be received. They have heard of the vow which the King and his three lords have taken; it were a great pity if such an untoward occurrence would prevent the two triple sets from pairing off. But we are here astonished to learn that each of the three ladies has met her man before, and knows his character. The truth is, therefore, that they are all in love, and the present visit really is a courting expedition; the women are going to storm the castle of learning, and bring its inmates under the yoke of marriage. (pp. 309-10)

The result of their meeting it is not difficult to foretell; love has asserted its power in the breasts of all the students. Biron, in his soliloquy, gives expression to what the others feel; against his will, against his knowledge, he has been conquered and confesses his humiliation. He contemns the act; he berates himself and berates women—it cannot be helped, yield he must. . . . It will thus be seen that love has entered the student-world and destroyed it; the individual purpose is gone, being banished by an intruder. Still, each person is seeking to preserve an outward semblance of fidelity to his oath, and to keep his internal condition from the knowledge of the rest of his associates. Thus ends what was stated to be the first movement—Navarre, which represents the realm of learning and austerity, is in conflict with various phases of love; the latter has already secured its first triumph in the emotional nature of each individual.

We can now pass to the second movement, in which new elements are introduced. The low group is here subordinate in importance, though not entirely dropped; but its peculiar function of representing sensual love quite disappears. . . . [Shakespeare now] proceeds to introduce a new group of comic characters, and with them a new principle. It is pedantry, with its two representatives—Holofernes, and Sir Nathaniel, the curate; to them is added the constable, Dull, who, though ignorant, is also pedantic, as is seen mainly in his use of words. Here learning is exhibited in one of its phases—it has made a monstrous puff-ball out of mediocrity. Such is the possible outcome of a life devoted to mere erudition—of a life which cuts out and throws away the essence of human existence, namely institutions. Learning is only a means; if it be made the absolute end, it produces a Holofernes—that is, it renders man comic. For his object is absurd and nugatory; yet, at the same time, he is supposed to be the most intelligent of human kind, being so highly educated. The relation of this group to the drama must, therefore, be comprehended; the result of the King's cloistered study is here seen—Navarre would become, not an Academe, but the Pedant's Paradise. (pp. 311-12)

In general . . . , the first comic group represented love in its one-sidedness, namely, sensual passion; the second comic group represents erudition in its one-sidedness, namely, pompous pedantry; both taken together show the comic extremes of love on the one hand, and study on the other. The implication seems to be that a judicious admixture of the two is the golden mean.

The elevated group of characters may next be considered. The King and his young lords have been already captivated, though each tried to keep his condition concealed from the others. Now the truth is to be revealed to all, and the new situation to be accepted. Biron is wandering alone in the forest; he is in a deadly struggle with his emotion; he cannot free himself from its power. He hides himself when he sees the King coming; the latter, too, is groaning from Cupid's "bird-bolt under the left pap" [IV. iii. 23-4], and gives vent to his feelings in a sonnet to his mistress. In like manner the King secretes himself when he sees Longaville passing that way, who also confesses to the trees his griefs, and reads his poetical effusion. The latter, too, hides himself when, last of all, Dumaine appears, who does just like the rest, for he also must have a lyrical expression of his passion. At this point each comes out of his hiding-place in order; the revelation has to be made; all are equally guilty of the trespass; all are in love, and are trying to conceal it from one another. Biron—who, on account of being the first one in the forest, thought to escape detection—is also discovered; the fragment of a torn letter tells the whole story.

What now about the oaths? The violation has taken place; is there any defense? Biron—who, it will be recollected, protested against the vow at the beginning—at once undertakes to vindicate their conduct. His lengthy speech contains the best statement in the play concerning its own purport. He declares that,

when they swore "to fast, to study, and to see no woman," they committed "flat treason 'gainst the state of youth" [IV. iii. 288-89]; it was a violation of the right of love. The true objects of study, the real writings over which young men should pore, are those masterpieces of Nature—woman's eyes. . . . The transition is here stated clearly enough—Navarre has turned into a love-land; the Academe has changed to some female eye, into which each one of them is diligently looking. Thus the student-world dissolves apace, and its lofty ambition melts to a cloud. Such is the result on the one side—if study be asserted against love, the latter will be triumphant.

But there is something more in Biron's speech which ought to be considered—"this universal plodding prisons up the nimble spirits" [IV. iii. 301-02]—men become "barren practicers" of learning [IV. iii. 322], who find no reward of their heavy toil; in other words, the product of mere study is the dry pedant—a Holofernes. Thus the second movement gives a double aspect of the two colliding principles of the drama—study triumphs, terminating in pedantry; love triumphs, terminating in the dissolution of the ascetic realm.

The third movement now begins. It brings to a true conclusion what has gone before, and also has a distinct tinge of its own. The notion of retribution gives it the peculiar element which marks it as a separate part. Both the previous comic groups unite, though Holofernes, with his erudition, is the leading character. He suggests the representation of the Nine Worthies of antiquity for the entertainment of the King and Princess; learning proposes to exhibit the heroic personages whose fame is a part of the world's history. . . . The result may be confidently predicted—it is the narrow, ridiculous conception of the pedagogue which is seen in the execution of the plan; the mighty individualities of old are burlesqued—are turned into comic figures of the lowest order. Such are the fruits of mere erudition in its chosen field; it cannot comprehend itself, nor impart to others what is great and true in the Past; it feeds on husks and leaves the kernel untouched. But the retributive element must not be forgotten—subjected to the criticism of his audience, his work perishes; the representation is torn to tatters by the sneers and sarcasms of the spectators. Such is the fate of this product of learning; it is destroyed by the people to whom it is addressed, and who carry into realization what logically lies in such an attempt. Thus mere erudition has received its penalty.

Of the elevated group the men were last seen in the act of mutually acknowledging their passion, and of defending the violation of their oath. The right of love was asserted to be higher than fidelity to a vow. But the greater half of their labor remains to be done; they have not yet won their ladies—off they start to the trial. . . . [The] result is plain—the book-men, with all their learning and wisdom, are made to suffer a defeat, in their own special province, at the hands of the ladies, who worry them with the sharpest sayings, and exhibit the greater intellectual keenness. But the object of wooing is marriage—to which the men are ready to advance at once, making, in the meantime, loud protestations of their love. But they cannot be believed, for they have just broken an oath; the ladies argue that they will be quite as ready to disregard a second vow. Thus the logic of their action is brought home to them; before credence can be given them, they must show by a year's penance the sincerity of their professions, as well as a change of life. Then a marital pledge will be possible. Thus Love's Labor is both lost and won—there is the punishment for the violation by deferring the union; but ultimately this ascetic world is to

Act V. Scene ii. The Masque of the Muscovites. Frontispiece to the Rowe edition (1709). By permission of the Folger Shakespeare Library.

pass into the Family as the higher sphere, in which the true solution of the collision must be found. Both threads of the last movement, however, will be seen to possess a retributive element—pedantic erudition beholds its own achievements reduced to nothing, and the violated oath demands a year's chastisement. (pp. 313-18)

Learning, in the furtherance of its own end, calls for the abnegation of the Family; but the latter, through its all-powerful emotion—love—rises up and puts down its enemy. Institutions are the higher principle; neither culture nor religion must place a bar to their entrance, for they are really the essence of both. It is a theme upon which the Poet has often touched, and in which he shows his fealty to the thought of the modern world. Nor will the attentive reader fail to supply the historical illustration. Monasticism was long supposed to be the chief handmaid of learning; an ascetic life was thought to be the main condition of the pursuit of science. But human progress has solved the conflict—has reconciled a career devoted to study with the Family; the Academe is not found in the secluded cloister, but can exist in the domestic institution. Nor has the drama failed to show the one-sided results of the two conflicting principles: Love, without the Family, is sensuality; and study, without some corrective—that it is the Family which is this

corrective is rather implied than declared—degenerates into fantastic mummery. (pp. 318-19)

> *Denton J. Snider, "'Love's Labor's Lost'," in his* The Shakespearian Drama, a Commentary: The Comedies, *Sigma Publishing Co., 1890? pp. 297-319.*

GEORGE BRANDES   (essay date 1895-96)

[*Brandes was a scholar and the most influential literary critic of late nineteenth-century Denmark. His work* William Shakespeare, *originally published in 1895-96, was translated and widely read in his day. A writer with a broad knowledge of literature, Brandes placed Shakespeare in a European context, comparing him with other important dramatists. In this excerpt, Brandes calls* Love's Labour's Lost *"a play of two motives"—one of love, the other of language. Like Walter Pater (1885), Brandes notes the playfulness of language in the drama, describing the dialogue as "a tournament of words." And like Samuel Taylor Coleridge (1808-18), Brandes attributes the bombastic language, pedantry, and "over-luxuriant and far-fetched method of expression" to the fashion of Shakespeare's age, and he discusses this affected style of speech, known as Euphuism, as a Continental movement. He concludes that Shakespeare, while satirizing specific forms of Euphuism, is unable to rise above it himself and, hence, the parody is as tedious as the object of derision. For further discussion of the play of language in* Love's Labour's Lost, *see the excerpts by William Matthews (1964), Ralph Berry (1969), James L. Calderwood (1971), Terence Hawkes (1973), and Malcolm Evans (1975).*]

[*Love's Labour's Lost*] is a play of two motives. The first, of course, is love—what else should be the theme of a youthful poet's first comedy?—but love without a trace of passion, almost without deep personal feeling, a love which is half make-believe, tricked out in word-plays. For the second theme of the comedy is language itself, poetic expression for its own sake—a subject round which all the meditations of the young poet must necessarily have centred, as, in the midst of a crossfire of new impressions, he set about the formation of a vocabulary and a style.

The moment the reader opens this first play of Shakespeare's, he cannot fail to observe that in several of his characters the poet is ridiculing absurdities and artificialities in the manner of speech of the day, and, moreover, that his personages, as a whole, display a certain half-sportive luxuriance in their rhetoric as well as in their wit and banter. They seem to be speaking, not in order to inform, persuade, or convince, but simply to relieve the pressure of their imagination, to play with words, to worry at them, split them up and recombine them, arrange them in alliterative sequences, or group them in almost identical antithetic clauses; at the same time making sport no less fantastical with the ideas the words represent, and illustrating them by new and far-fetched comparisons; until the dialogue appears not so much a part of the action or an introduction to it, as a tournament of words, clashing and swaying to and fro, while the rhythmic music of the verse and prose in turns expresses exhilaration, tenderness, affectation, the joy of life, gaiety or scorn. Although there is a certain superficiality about it all, we can recognise in it that exuberance of all the vital spirits which characterises the Renaissance. To the appeal—

> White-handed mistress, one sweet word with thee,

comes the answer—

> Honey, and milk, and sugar: there are three.
>
> [V. ii. 230-31]

And well may Boyet say . . . :—

> The tongues of mocking wenches are as keen
> As is the razor's edge invisible,
> Cutting a smaller hair than may be seen;
> Above the sense of sense, so sensible
> Seemeth their conference; their conceits have wings
> Fleeter than arrows, bullets, wind, thought, swifter
> things.

[V. ii. 256-61]

Boyet's words, however, refer merely to the youthful gaiety and quickness of wit which may be found in all periods. We have here something more than that: the diction of the leading characters, and the various extravagances of expression cultivated by the subordinate personages, bring us face to face with a linguistic phenomenon which can be understood only in the light of history.

The word Euphuism is employed as a common designation for these eccentricities of style—a word which owes its origin to John Lyly's romance, *Euphues, the Anatomy of Wit*, published in 1578. Lyly was also the author of nine plays, all written before 1589, and there is no doubt that he exercised a very important influence upon Shakespeare's dramatic style.

But it is a very narrow view of the matter which finds in him the sole originator of the wave of mannerism which swept over the English poetry of the Renaissance.

The movement was general throughout Europe. It took its rise in the new-born enthusiasm for the antique literatures, in comparison with whose dignity of utterance the vernacular seemed low and vulgar. In order to approximate to the Latin models, men devised an exaggerated and dilated phraseology, heavy with images, and even sought to attain amplitude of style by placing side by side the vernacular word and the more exquisite foreign expression for the same object. (pp. 39-40)

Strictly speaking, it is not against Euphuism itself that Shakespeare's youthful satire is directed in *Love's Labour's Lost*. It is certain collateral forms of artificiality in style and utterance that are aimed at. In the first place, bombast, represented by the ridiculous Spaniard, Armado (the suggestion of the Invincible Armada in the name cannot be unintentional); in the next place, pedantry, embodied in the schoolmaster Holofernes, for whom tradition states that [John] Florio, the teacher of languages and translator of Montaigne, served as a model—a supposition, however, which seems scarcely probable when we remember Florio's close connection with Shakespeare's patron, Southampton. Further, we find throughout the play the over-luxuriant and far-fetched method of expression, universally characteristic of the age, which Shakespeare himself had as yet by no means succeeded in shaking off. Only towards the close does he rise above it and satirise it. (p. 44)

But what avails the justice of a parody if, in spite of the art and care lavished upon it, it remains as tedious as the mannerism it ridicules! And this is unfortunately the case in the present instance. Shakespeare had not yet attained the maturity and detachment of mind which could enable him to rise high above the follies he attacks, and to sweep them aside with full authority. He buries himself in them, circumstantially demonstrates their absurdities, and is still too inexperienced to realise how he thereby inflicts upon the spectator and the reader the full burden of their tediousness. (p. 45)

> *George Brandes, "Shakespeare's Conception of the Relation of the Sexes," translated by William Archer,*

in his William Shakespeare, *revised edition, William Heinemann, 1920, pp. 34-46.*

E. K. CHAMBERS   (essay date 1905)

[*Chambers occupies a transitional position in Shakespearean criticism, one which connects the biographical sketches and character analyses of the nineteenth century with the historical, technical, and textual criticism of the twentieth century. While a member of the education department at Oxford University, Chambers earned his reputation as a scholar with his multivolume works,* The Medieval Stage *and* The Elizabethan Stage, *while he also edited* The Red Letter Shakespeare. *Chambers both investigated the purpose and limitations of each dramatic genre as Shakespeare presented it and speculated on how the dramatist's work was influenced by contemporary historical issues and his own frame of mind. In the following excerpt, which first appeared in an introduction to* Love's Labour's Lost *in* The Red Letter Shakespeare *(1905), Chambers discusses the restrictions placed on comedy by the passage of time and says that much of the play is not humorous because of the topical nature of the satire, a point also made by Samuel Johnson (1765) and Harley Granville-Barker (1927), though the latter critic finds other dramatic strengths in the play.*]

Little in Shakespeare is more tedious than certain parts of *Love's Labour's Lost*. Among the verbal antics of 'the pedant, the braggart, the hedge-priest, the fool and the boy,' which form the background of the play, if you occasionally stumble upon a recognizable jest, you more often wander, a disconcerted alien, through impenetrable memorials of vanished humour. Even in the lighthearted scenes in which the skirmishing girls of France uphold the battle of sex against their flouted Navarrese lovers, although the spirit of mirth is undeniably there, the actual savour of mirth has not seldom, for a modern reader, evaporated from the dialogue. One is sometimes tempted to hold that a difference in the sense of humour is the last barrier between age and age, which even the most highly-trained historic consciousness never quite succeeds in overleaping. But the judgment will bear a yet further refinement. Humour has its roots after all in elements of the strange composition of man which are constant enough; his vanity, his mutability, his serious preoccupation with trifles, from shells and feathers to laces and scarves, his ineradicable tendency to pass himself off on himself and on others as that which he is not. These things remain, and, age by age, the remorseless comic spirit makes its game of them. But, by their very nature, their manifestations, or at least their urban manifestations, with which comedy has most to do, are transitory. Follies of speech, follies of dress, fantasies of youth, fantasies of lovers in love with love; they come and go, lighter than a puff-ball, and as they pass into oblivion, the wit and irony of the pursuing humourist pass too. 'A jest's prosperity lies in the ear of him that hears it' [V. ii. 861-62]. You must laboriously exhume, with the aid of the scholiast, what split the sides of Aristophanes and his audiences; and even the London of Elizabeth, or, for the matter of that, the London of Victoria, was alive to absurdities which, for the twentieth century, belong to the region of archaeology. (pp. 58-9)

> *E. K. Chambers, "'Love's Labour's Lost'," in his* Shakespeare: A Survey, *1925. Reprint by Oxford University Press, New York, 1926, pp. 58-67.*

RICHMOND NOBLE   (essay date 1923)

[*In his discussion of* Love's Labour's Lost, *Noble examines the anticlimatic nature of the songs of "the owl and the cuckoo" and* concludes that they were inserted in the play to clear the stage and allow one final opportunity to ridicule the pedants. For a contrary view of the songs' function in the play, see the excerpts by Bertrand H. Bronson (1948), William C. Carroll (1976), Louis Adrian Montrose (1977), and, in the Additional Bibliography, Catherine McLay.]

The two songs [in Love's Labour's Lost] help to clear the stage, and as Epilogues they are used delightfully to sustain, even in the end, the laughing character of the comedy. Evidently the play, in its original form, had ended with Berowne's 'That's too long for a play' [V. ii. 878]. Not only was such an ending too abrupt and ineffective for clearing the stage, but also something had to be done to restore the spirit of comedy, banished by the news of the death of the Princess's father. Accordingly Armado enters with a belated request to hear 'the dialogue that the two learned men have compiled in praise of the owl and the cuckoo' [V. ii. 886-87]. The world 'dialogue' has given rise to misconception on the part of some; its employment here was intentional and significant. The annoucement of the songs as a dialogue or debate between two birds was a sample of pedantry in itself, for it was meant to exhibit Armado's and Holofernes' scholarly knowledge of mediaeval minstrelsy wherein such academic exercises were of frequent occurrence. (p. 34)

The songs relate to three characters—Armado with his 'mint of phrases' [I. i. 165] who presents the songs; Holofernes the Pedant with his Latin and Latinized words, and Sir Nathaniel the Curate, their two authors. Armado announces the songs in Latin as well as in English. . . . The spectators are thus prepared for a learned and tedious argument according to academic precedent.

Instead there follows the inimitable Cuckoo Song, wherein everything is bright and gay, all except married men, whom the Cuckoo's call makes fearful of their freehold. The comic intent, in keeping with the play, is manifest. All the learned men's idealism of the meadow flowers, the shepherds' piping on oaten straws and the merry larks waking the ploughmen is dissipated by the fear of the woeful tragedy with which, as the cuckoo's habits remind them, married men are threatened in the Spring, when inclinations are supposed to be amorous and lovers heedless. The song feigns seriousness in its conceits just like any of the pretty verse of the time, and naturally something like 'Cuckoo, the Sweet Spring' might be expected to follow. Instead there is a fall from the sublime to the ridiculous, a transition from serious conceit to the ludicrous and comic.

> The cuckoo then on every tree,
> Mocks married men; for thus sings he,
> [V. ii. 898-99]

Then there is a long drawn out 'Cuckoo', as is indicated by the full stop, followed by a couple of sly echoing calls—'Cuckoo, Cuckoo'—whereat the singer shivers in pretended fear and shakes his head at the impropriety of such a call being sounded in the presence of married men. A joke of such a kind was dear to Elizabethan hearts and Shakespeare was never tired of resorting to the theme. Here appreciation was enhanced by absurdity.

When the learned men came to compile The Owl Song, obviously the same joke could not carry. In the first stanza romance is contrasted with reality, the picturesque with the disagreeable and, in the second, comic objects are cunningly interspersed among ordinary objects of natural history. Thus in the first, on the one hand we have the icicles hanging by

the wall, and on the other the frozen milk, the nipped blood and the muddy roads, and, in the second, we have the coughing drowning the parson's saw—the use of the word 'saw' is good in itself—and the red and raw condition of Marian's nose. But the most disagreeable of all the sensations to be experienced in Winter is that afforded by the sight and smell of the sluttish Joan keeling the pot, for she makes uncomfortable the farm kitchen, the only refuge from the inclemency of the season. The unmusical laughing hoot of the owl acts as a diversion where all else is depressing. Pastoral romance gives way to pastoral realism. It is difficult for the inhabitants of nineteenth- and twentieth-century England to realize the sixteenth-century rural conditions which Shakespeare was here describing.

The debate between the two birds has not been very decisive—the cuckoo threatens to disturb the peace and the owl depresses the spirits—the burlesque is suitably slight, it is not exhaustive. Spring may induce the amorous, but the greasy Joan of the Winter most assuredly disperses any such thoughts. Both are Elizabethan comic songs, without any serious intention whatever. That the affected learning of the lean and cadaverous-looking Holofernes could evolve nothing more serious enriches the comedy, and there can be no doubt that, when the songs are well and significantly rendered, the fooling is admirable. (pp. 34-6)

> Richmond Noble, ''Separate Plays: 'Love's Labour's Lost','' in his Shakespeare's Use of Song, Oxford at the Clarendon Press, 1923, pp. 32-8.

HARLEY GRANVILLE-BARKER   (essay date 1927)

[Granville-Barker was a noted actor, playwright, director, and critic. His work as a Shakespearean critic is at all times informed by his experience as a director, for he treats Shakespeare's plays not as works of literature better understood divorced from the theater, as did many Romantic critics, but as pieces meant for the stage. As a director, he emphasized simplicity in staging, set design, and costuming. He believed that elaborate scenery obscured the poetry which was of central importance to Shakespeare's plays. Granville-Barker also eschewed the approach of directors who scrupulously reconstructed a production based upon Elizabethan stage techniques, for he felt that this, too, detracted from the play's meaning. In his discussion of Love's Labour's Lost, Granville-Barker notes the problems created by the play's topical satire, an idea discussed earlier by E. K. Chambers (1907). But despite these difficulties, he maintains that the play "abounds in beauties of fancy and phrase, as beautiful today as ever," and that Shakespeare's dramatic genius is evident in his "projection of character in action." Specifically, Granville-Barker points to the development of such characters as Costard and Nathaniel—whom he calls "outcroppings of pure dramatic gold"—as evidence of Shakespeare's effective artistry in the play. Granville-Barker's affirmation of the commendable dramatic qualities in Love's Labour's Lost marks something of a new direction in the reception of the play. John Dover Wilson (1962) modifies but generally concurs with this view of the play's dramatic strengths, while H. B. Charlton (1937) and S. C. Sen Gupta (1950) have argued that the play suffers from weak plot and characterization.]

Here is a fashionable play; now, by three hundred years, out of fashion. Nor did it ever, one supposes, make a very wide appeal. It abounds in jokes for the elect. Were you not numbered among them you laughed, for safety, in the likeliest places. A year or two later the elect themselves might be hard put to it to remember what the joke was.

Were this all one could say of Love's Labour's Lost, the question of its staging to-day—with which we are first and last concerned—would be quickly answered, and Lose no Labour here be the soundest advice. For spontaneous enjoyment is the life of the theatre. (p. 2)

It is true that with no play three hundred years old can we press our 'spontaneous' too hard. For the full appreciation of anything in Shakespeare some knowledge is asked of its why and wherefore. Hamlet and Falstaff [in *1* and *2 Henry IV*] however, Rosalind [in *As You Like It*] and Imogen [in *Cymbeline*], are compact of qualities which fashion cannot change; the barriers of dramatic convention, strange habit, tricks of speech are of small enough account with them. But what is back of these word-gymnastics of Rosaline and Berowne, Holofernes' jargon, Armado's antics? The play is a satire, a comedy of affectations. The gymnastics, the jargon and the antics are the fun. But a play hardly lives by such brilliancies alone. While the humour of them is fresh and holds our attention, actors may lend it a semblance of life; for there they are, alive in their kind! No play, certainly, can count on survival if it strikes no deeper root nor bears more perennial flowers. If its topical brilliance were all, Shakespeare's name tagged to this one would keep it a place on the scholar's dissecting table, in the theatre *Love's Labour's Lost* would be dead, past all question. But there is life in it. The satire beside, Shakespeare the poet had his fling. It abounds in beauties of fancy and phrase, as beautiful to-day as ever. And we find in it Shakespeare the dramatist learning his art. To students the most interesting thing about the play is the evidence of this; of the trial and error, his discovery of fruitful soil and fruitless. The producer, pledged to present an audience with a complete something, cannot, of course, be content with promise and experiment. Measuring this early Shakespeare by the later, we may as well own there is not much more. But the root of the matter is already in him; he is the dramatist born, and all, or nearly all, is at least instinct with dramatic life. It is oftenest his calculations and his cleverness that betray him.

For satire and no more is too apt to prove dramatically fruitless. A play's values are human values, and a playwright's first task is to give his creatures being. Imaginative love for them may help him to; even hate may; but a mocking detachment cannot. If he is to shoot at their follies he must yet build up the target first; and if it is not a convincing one there will be little credit in the shooting. He cannot, of course, in a play, take direct aim himself, unless he use the method of the Moralities or its like. There is the less direct method of twisting a set of familiar heroic figures awry. Shakespeare made this experiment, not too successfully, in *Troilus and Cressida*. But his obvious plan will be to turn one or more of his creatures satirists themselves, and under their cover plant his own shafts. Even so, he must give the victims their chance, or the play will be lopsided and come tumbling down.

The Shakespeare that sets out to write *Love's Labour's Lost* is a very clever young man, a wit, a sonneteer. He is 'in the movement.' He flatters his admirers by excelling in the things they admire; he will flatter his rivals hardly less by this attention he means to pay them. But your clever young man is usually more than a little impressed by the things he mocks at; he mocks at them in self-defence, it may be, lest they impress him too much. Mockery is apt, indeed, to capitulate to the thing mocked, to be absorbed by it. And these academic follies of Navarre, the fantastic folly of Armado, the pedantic folly of schoolmaster and parson—sometimes the satire is so fine that the folly seems the clever young man's own. Yet this weakness of the would-be satirist is the budding dramatist's

strength. Shakespeare cannot resist his creatures; he never quite learned to. He cannot make mere targets of them. He cannot resist his own genius, poetic or dramatic; all through the play we find the leaven of it working.

He has not written ten lines before the poet in him breaks bounds. Is this the voice of that frigid wiseacre Navarre; does this suggest the 'little academe'?

> Therefore, brave conquerors—for so you are,
> That war against your own affections
> And the huge army of the world's desires.
>
> [I. i. 8-10]

But the clever young man recollects himself; and here, soon enough, is the sort of thing he has set out to write.

King.	How well he's read, to reason against reading!
Dumain.	Proceeded well, to stop all good proceeding!
Longaville.	He weeds the corn, and still lets grow the weeding.
Berowne.	The spring is near, when green geese are a-breeding.
Dumain.	How follows that?
Berowne.	Fit in his place and time.
Dumain.	In reason nothing.
Berowne.	Something then in rhyme.
	[I. i. 94-9]

Pretty tricksy stuff! Well enough done to show that he quite enjoyed doing it, but the sort of thing that almost anyone could learn to do. No signpost on the road to *Hamlet,* certainly.

But mark the dramatist in his provision at the outset of the conflict and balance that every play needs, in the setting of Berowne against his companions, one man's common-sense against the crowding affectations (a sporting conflict), an ounce of reality for counterweight to a ton of shams (an instructive balance). (pp. 2-5)

In this earliest essay, then, we may divine the dramatist to be; and we find dramatist putting wit and poet to the proof. Shakespeare will have set out to do his best by his creatures one and all; but while Berowne grows under his hand into a figure, finally, of some dramatic stature, while the Princess, simple, straightforward, shrewd, is made flesh and blood, in the speaking of seven lines, Navarre, though a natural focus of attention and discussing himself unsparingly, remains a bundle of phrases, and Dumain and Longaville have about the substance of echoes. Of the humbler folk; Costard for three-quarters of the play is the stage Fool, but suddenly, when he comes to the acting of his Worthy, we have:

Costard.	I Pompey am, Pompey surnam'd the big—
Dumain.	The great.
Costard.	It is great, sir; Pompey surnam'd the great; That oft in field, with targe and shield, did make my foe to sweat; And travelling along this coast, I here am come by chance, And lay my arms before the legs of this sweet lass of France. If your ladyship would say "Thanks, Pompey," I had done.
Princess.	Great thanks, great Pompey.
Costard.	'Tis not so much worth; but I hope I was perfect: I made a little fault in ''great.''
	[V. ii. 550-59]

And these two last lines have, mysteriously and unexpectedly, given us the man beneath the jester. Then, with another thirty words or so, Costard (and Costard's creator) settles Sir Nathaniel the Curate, till now little but a figure of fun, snugly in our affections.

> There, an't shall please you; a foolish mild
> man; an honest man, look you, and soon dashed!
> He is a marvellous good neighbour, in sooth;
> and a very good bowler: but, for Alisander,
> alas, you see how 'tis;—a little o'erparted.
> [V. ii. 580-84]

And settles himself there the more snugly in the doing it! Throughout the play, but especially towards the end, we find such outcroppings of pure dramatic gold.

Drama, as Shakespeare will come to write it, is, first and last, the projection of character in action; and devices for doing this, simple and complex, must make up three-quarters of its artistry. We can watch his early discovery that dialogue is waste matter unless it works to this end; that wit, epigram, sentiment are like paper and sticks in a fireplace, the flaring and crackling counting for nothing if the fire itself won't light, if these creatures in whose mouths the wit is sounded won't 'come alive.' To the last he kept his youthful delight in a pun; and he would write an occasional passage of word-music with a minimum of meaning to it (but of maximum emotional value, it will be found, to the character that has to speak it). His development of verse to dramatic use is a study in itself. He never ceased to develop it, but for a while the dramatist had a hard time with the lyric poet. The early plays abound, besides, in elaborate embroidery of language done for its own sake. This was a fashionable literary exercise and Shakespeare was an adept at it. To many young poets of the time their language was a new-found wonder; its very handling gave them pleasure. The amazing things it could be made to do! He had to discover that they were not much to his purpose; but it is not easy to stop doing what you do so well. (pp. 7-9)

> Harley Granville-Barker, "'Love's Labour's Lost',"
> in his Prefaces to Shakespeare, first series, Sidgwick
> & Jackson, Ltd., 1927, pp. 1-50.

GLADYS DOIDGE WILLCOCK (essay date 1934)

[In her monograph Shakespeare As Critic of Language, excerpted below, Willcock examines the playwright's concern with language in several of his plays. In her discussion of Love's Labour's Lost, she argues that language in the Elizabethan era was in a crucial stage of development, and that the play, reflecting this change, is "packed with linguistic comment and allusion," and that Shakespeare was acting as a kind of philologist in writing it. Samuel Taylor Coleridge (1808-18) and George Brandes (1895-96) also examined the language style of Elizabethan England, but Willcock's focus on the linguistic concerns in Love's Labour's Lost anticipates an important trend in later criticism of the play, as seen in the essays by William Matthews (1964), Ralph Berry (1969), James L. Calderwood (1971), Terence Hawkes (1973), and Malcolm Evans (1975).]

In the Armada period and during a few subsequent years [in England] language was advancing irresistibly along all fronts. It may be asked, What has Shakespeare to do with most of it except, of course, to use it? The answer is to be found in Love's Labour's Lost. (p. 8)

The dominant theme of this play, as distinct from artificial and symmetrical plot, is the overwhelming event of the English language and all that had been happening to it in the last twenty years or so. In this play the great game of language is played with unfailing verve from the first Act to the last, but the fertile use of language by no means exhausts Shakespeare's interest in it. The play is packed with linguistic comment and allusion.

The main plot of King, Princess, Lords and Ladies is worked out in terms of the courtly wit inherited from Lyly and his school. Into a great deal of it we can only enter as detectives. There can be no doubt that the spirit of the play is sympathetic to that sort of courtly leadership which we can imagine Southampton to have exercised. Shakespeare looked to the best elements in the contemporary noblesse to make a bulwark against divorce from nature and the world, against utilitarian limitation and pedantic interference. The bias against bookishness and University Wit is so marked that it cannot be accidental:

> Small have continual plodders ever won,
> Save base authority from others' books,
> [I. i. 86-7]

The school of this wit, this language, is the world and experience, especially the experience of love—the sonneteer's experience. . . . There was, however, a great deal of froth beaten up on top of all that was virile and liberal. With this Shakespeare enjoys himself by the help of Armado. Armado is, of course, a stage type of Thrasonical pedigree. To be affected was his character. He is 'Fashion's own knight' [I. i. 178]. The critical point to note about Armado is that the mention of fashion flashes the message language to the Elizabethan mind. We make no such automatic connection. Moreover, active cerebration lies behind all Armado's extravagances. His conversation is devoid of clichés and padding and therefore offers the most remarkable contrast to Pistol's. As soon as this refined traveller of Spain is described as 'a man in all the world's new fashion planted' the audience knows that he will have 'a mint of phrases in his brain' [I. i. 164-65]. He is 'a man of compliments'—that is, the 'mere' courtier of no particular age and country—but as an Elizabethan he is also a 'child of fancy' [I. i, 168, 170]. The king keeps him by him in order to enjoy his flow of 'highborn words' [I. i. 172]. Armado, though shirtless, succeeds in maintaining his position as a man of fashion by virtue of his command of language. There was nothing more fashionable than language and fantasy. Boyet I suspect of representing an older type of courtier, for, though he plays with aplomb the same games as the others and picks up wit as a pigeon picks up peas, he inspires no linguistic comment.

Inset in this exposition of the courtly in language are a remarkably well-informed commentary on pedantic influences and a slighter, but adequate, illustration of the clownish corruption of words.

Holofernes is again a stage type of largely foreign antecedents. The pedant was, and is, a recognised butt. But here, as in the case of Armado, the conventional outline is filled in with a wealth of information and observation which must be studied in detail to be appreciated. Practically every remark of Holofernes is a pointer to something going on in the world of language, to the sort of fact with which the linguistic historian fills his book. (pp. 8-11)

The much-disputed inkhorn ["pedantic"] terms were excellent comic grist for Shakespeare's mill. In this play, with suitable discrimination, he divides the responsibility for them between Courtier and Pedant. The attempt to stop all foreign recruitment of the language had by this time broken down. Shakespeare himself has no objection to neologism and was a most prolific coiner of words. In Holofernes' and Armado's polysyllabic extravagances he pillories the brands of affectation and types of pompous perversity which, as a poet and a man of humour, he thought the language could very well do without. (p. 12)

Holofernes and Nathaniel together illustrate a very marked contemporary vice in vocabulary—the synonym habit. This will naturally be rife in an age of translation and rhetorical study. It was fostered by the practice of collecting synonyms in order, theoretically, that the translator or orator might weigh, discriminate, and select the one which gave him his right shade of meaning. Human nature being what it is, he generally found it easier to put them all in to make sure. This habit pervades our translated literature from the Alfredian Bede onwards. It is also a homilist's trick, a lecturer's trick. The man who is making his points orally hopes that if one word is missed the next will go in. The error came, as did so many Elizabethan excesses, from failure to distinguish, from carrying over what has a place in the schoolmaster's method and the rhetorician's oratory into other spheres. Holofernes naturally illustrates the schoolmaster's responsibility:

> ripe as a pomewater, who now hangeth like a
> jewel in the ear of *caelo,* the sky, the welkin,
> the heaven; and anon falleth like a crab on the
> face of *terra,* the soil, the land, the earth.
>
> [IV. ii. 4-7]

But even now the wealth of linguistic commentary offered by Holofernes is not exhausted. The schoolmaster naturally stands for the threat of Latin influence and formalist interference. This was a real menace of which the most striking effects were not to become visible until the next century. Holofernes speaks a precise and pompous English interlarded with Latin words. He possesses the grammatical mind, quick to 'smell' false Latin, that cannot leave a small slip by others uncorrected. Since it was a schoolmaster's business to know and speak good Latin, there is nothing more in this than a harmless professional foible, but men of this stamp tend to have interfering minds. They confuse grammar and nature; they will carry the rules of the schoolroom into life. Owing to the Renascence prestige of classical learning, men in general were in those days less on their guard against this habit than we are. It was allowed to exert potent influences on the language; some of its by-products were destined to have far-reaching effects on the spoken as well as the written language. In one brief paragraph Shakespeare takes Holofernes over the greater part of this ground. It is the paragraph in which Holofernes condemns the rackers of orthography who say *det* when they should say *d e b t.* (pp. 14-15)

The courtly and the pedantic are rounded off by the clownish or simple. Dull, Costard, and Jaquenetta are foils to both Armado and Holofernes. Costard excellently illustrates the almost purely verbal nature of the early fooling. It is a mistake to try to unify the mental processes of a Costard into a consistent character. Such clowns are walking word-games. They are alternately stupid and clever. They must have a pointer's nose for a pun and they must display an astonishing ingenuity in tripping up the words and meanings of others. In their presence "men must speak by the card or equivocation will undo them" [*Hamlet,* V. i. 137-38], yet they can generally be floored by an inkhorn term. It is not in this play but in *Twelfth Night* that Shakespeare goes out of his way to comment on this order of wit. In Act III, Sc. i. Feste gives Viola a little lecture on fooling. He has a perfectly clear notion of the taste of the age in language and wit. Every sentence was a challenge to the new analytical power:

> To see this age! A sentence is but a cheveril
> glove to a good wit: how quickly the wrong
> side may be turned outward!
>
> [III. i. 11-13] . . .

Feste defines the Fool as a corrupter of words and after some neat demonstration goes out, while Viola remains behind on purpose to make this comment:

> This fellow's wise enough to play the fool,
> And to do that well craves a kind of wit:
> He must observe their mood on whom he jests,
> The quality of persons, and the time,
> And, like the haggard, check at every feather
> That comes before his eye. This is a practice
> As full of labour as a wise man's art.
>
> [III. i. 60-6] . . .

Shakespeare's plays up to about 1600 are unified by this sense of language as well as by delight in its exploitation. Certain characters seem to exist in order to express the balance between the critical and creative faculties—they are the characters whom everyone feels in some way to be especially Shakespeare's own: Berowne, Mercutio, Falstaff, Prince Hal, Hotspur, Hamlet. They discourse upon the features and tendencies of language, they listen to it as experts, they chase it like sportsmen. To Berowne we owe this succinct summary of the whole phase of Elizabethan poetic speech, which reached its climax about 1593:

> Taffeta phrases, silken terms precise,
> Three-pil'd hyperboles, spruce affectation,
> Figures pedantical.   [V. ii. 406-08]
>   (pp. 17-18)

Gladys Doidge Willcock, in her Shakespeare As Critic of Language, *Oxford University Press, 1934, 30 p.*

CAROLINE F. E. SPURGEON   (essay date 1935)

[*Spurgeon's* Shakespeare's Imagery *(1935) inaugurated the "image-pattern analysis" method of studying Shakespeare's plays, one of the most widely used methods of the mid-twentieth century. In this work, she interprets the thematic structure of the plays through an examination of patterns in the imagery. Spurgeon also sought to learn about Shakespeare's personality from a study of his images, a course which few of her disciples followed. Since publication of her book, earlier works on image patterns in Shakespeare have been discovered, but none was so important in the history of Shakespearean criticism as Spurgeon's. In the excerpt below, Spurgeon examines the images of war in* Love's Labour's Lost *and concludes that even "in Shakespeare's earliest play" there is a "subtle but decisive" use of imagery.*]

[In] *Love's Labour's Lost,* apart from the nature and animal images, the dominating series [of symbolic images], as is easily seen, is that of war and weapons, emphasising the chief interest and entertainment of the play, the 'civil war of wits' [II. i. 226], the whole being, in Armado's words, little more than 'a quick venue of wit—snip, snap, quick and home!' [V. I. 58-9] The main underlying theme of the confounding and dispelling of the fog of false idealism by the light of the experience of real life, is presented through a series of brilliant encounters, when even the laughter 'stabs', the tongue is keen as 'the razor's edge invisible' [V. ii. 257], and lets missiles fly to right and left—conceits having wings

> Fleeter than arrows, bullets, wind, thought, swifter
>   things,   [V. ii. 261]

and words being pictured throughout as rapier-like thrusts, arrows, bullets fired from a cannon or as combatants tilting with their spears at a tournament. Longaville's wit is described as a sharp-edged sword handled by too blunt a will, Moth carries Armado's message as a bullet from the gun, Boyet and Biron tilt straight and merrily at each other, Boyet's eye wounding like a leaden sword' [V. ii. 481], while the jesting Biron, at the end, in despairing capitulation, stands in front of Rosaline and cries,

> lady, dart thy skill at me;. . .
> Thrust thy sharp wit quite through my ignorance;
> Cut me to pieces with thy keen conceit.
>   [V. ii. 396-99]

In addition to this general 'civil war', we witness three other kinds of combat, that of the little group of scholars in their 'Academe', who, as the king rather prematurely assures them in the opening lines, are 'brave conquerors', warring against their own affections 'and the huge army of the world's desires' [I. i. 8, 10]; the war of the men upon the women in the cause of love, headed by the king when he cries,

> Saint Cupid, then! and, soldiers to the field!

and Biron who adds,

> Advance your standards, and upon them, lords;
> Pell-mell, down with them! but be first advised,
> In conflict that you get the sun of them;
>   [IV. iii. 363-66]

the defence made by the women with their wits, incited by Boyet:

> Arm, wenches, arm! encounters mounted are
> Against your peace: Love doth approach disguised,
> Armed in arguments; you'll be surprised:
> Muster your wits; stand in your own defence;
>   [V. ii. 82-5]

and their final victory with the enforcement of strict terms of probation on their prisoners.

It is all, of course, very obvious running symbolism, but it is interesting to find, in Shakespeare's earliest play, even in this simple form, the tendency which in the great tragedies becomes so marked a feature, and plays in them a definite part—subtle but decisive—in expressing the poet's own conception of his theme, as well as in raising and sustaining the emotions of his audience. (pp. 271-73)

> *Caroline F. E. Spurgeon, "Leading Motives in the Comedies," in her* Shakespeare's Imagery and What It Tells Us, *1935. Reprint by Cambridge at the University Press, 1958, pp. 259-90.*

M[URIEL] C. BRADBROOK   (essay date 1936)

[*Bradbrook is an English scholar specializing in the development of Elizabethan drama and poetry. In her Shakespearean criticism, she combines both biographical and historical research, paying particular attention to the stage conventions popular during the playwright's lifetime. Her* Shakespeare and Elizabethan Poetry *(1951) is a comprehensive work which relates Shakespeare's po-*

etry to that of George Chapman, Christopher Marlowe, Edmund Spenser, and Philip Sidney and describes the evolution of Shakespeare's verse. In an earlier work, The School of Night: A Study in the Literary Relationships of Sir Walter Ralegh *(1936), Bradbrook examines elements of topical satire in* Love's Labour's Lost. *In the excerpt below, taken from that work, she expands upon the notion suggested by Arthur Acheson (see Additional Bibliography) that Shakespeare's mention of "the school of night" at IV. iii. 251 refers to Raleigh's circle of astronomers and poets by contending that Armado is meant to be a parody of Raleigh. Bradbrook's book and Frances A. Yates's* A Study of "Love's Labour's Lost" *(see Additional Bibliography) are considered the two most detailed treatments of the play as a contemporary satire. Since William Warburton's assertion in 1747 that Shakespeare modeled Holofernes after John Florio (see excerpt above), many such studies have been made, and this effort to identify historical figures in* Love's Labour's Lost *constitutes a substantial portion of the criticism on the play. For examples of this approach, see the essays in the Additional Bibliography by Ray B. Browne, Oscar J. Campbell, Eva Turner Clark, Richard David, Austin K. Gray, S. L. Lee, Walter Oakeshott, Arthur Quiller-Couch and John Dover Wilson, Hugh M. Richmond, and W. Schrickx. While most critics have accepted the idea of topical references in the play, this interpretation has met with skepticism from such critics as J. O. Halliwell-Phillips (1879), Thomas Marc Parrott (1949), and S. C. Sen Gupta (1950).*]

Love's Labour's Lost was among other things Shakespeare's account of the School of Night. That is not all that goes to it, even in the way of topical allusion, as Miss Yates' study has shown: and the topical allusion furnishes only a side-line in the play. It may be questioned if anything comes out of Shakespeare's mind recognizably akin to what it was on going in: but assuming that it did, *Love's Labour's Lost* may be partly accounted for as follows.

Ralegh, having been banished from Court, betook himself to study, and even protested that a hermit's life was the life he had always wanted. From any other courtier this would have been a clear case of sour grapes: it probably was from him. Moreover, having been banished for a love affair, he allowed Chapman to write against the pleasure of love-making with great vehemence; and all his following made a parade of study, particularly of astronomy and philosophy.

The situation tempted mockery. Shakespeare drew a very realistic picture of the Court: its games, its sets of wits, its love-tokens and masquing and sonnets and riddles, its submerged money matters and jealous competitions coming to the surface now and then and giving a jar to the gaiety. Being Shakespeare, he also added a closing scene which covers the courtly games and the courtly mode with two narrow words "hic jacet".

Shakespeare was not making a jibe but a joke: he did not aim the whole play at the school, but brought in some hits and hints by the way. The personal caricature was used for the low comedy: Ferdinand and his lords, however like their creeds to Ralegh's, represent the opposite party, from the moment the princess arrives. But there is a tall and fantastic traveller, a knight, who spends his time writing poetry and penning long letters to his sovereign telling of imaginary plots, who rewrites old ballads, who addresses his servant with a West Country "Chirrah" and who writes love-letters in Ercles' vein.

Armado fits Ralegh perfectly. The fact that he is a Spaniard is such an insult to one of the sea-dogs that it also serves as positive evidence. The king gives his character at length: he is a literary man, an orator and a writer:

> A man in *all the world's new fashions planted*
> That hath a mint of phrases in his brain.
> One whom the music of his own vain tongue
> Doth ravish like enchanting harmony. . . .
> How you delight, my lords, I know not, I,
> But I protest *I love to hear him lie.*
>
> [I. i. 164-75]

The dandy and planter of Virginia, spinner of travellers' tales, appears at once in "fashion's own knight". Armado's literary interests distinguish him from the simple braggart-like Bobadil: but they are not detachable from that "humour", for his plausible tongue and complimentary flourishes are the weapons of his pride. He is "the magnificent Armado", upon whose shoulder the king leans, dallying with his mustachio; but to pluck his plumes he is compared to "the fantastical Monarcho", a crazy Italian megalomaniac who haunted the Court in the eighties, and of whom the poet Churchyard wrote an account.

In his letter to the king, Armado announces himself, "besieged with sable-coloured melancholy" [I. i. 231-32]. Soon he appears, still melancholy. We learn that he is in his "old time", a "tough senior" (Ralegh was forty-one, about fifteen years older than Essex. His melancholy was more than a fashion: but he may have helped to set a fashion for it. At all events, Essex' party would treat it as affectation.) The knight is "in love", and with a base wench: as a soldier he resents his captivity, but as a man he submits and desires the comfort of precedents, Hercules and Samson. Armado's military pretensions are very much stressed here, and in all the other scenes; there was nothing of which Essex was so jealous, and later he attempted to hang Ralegh for stealing a successful advance on him during the Islands Voyage.

It is also made plain that Armado is uncomfortably short of money. Costard only gets a three-farthing tip and the knight goes "woolward for penance". Throughout 1592-3 Ralegh was protesting with vigour (and justice) that the queen had taken all the profits of the *Madre de Dios* for herself and her favourites: he had barely recovered his outlay. He wrote desperate letters to her and to Burghley on this subject.

Armado decides to have *King Cophetua and the Beggar-Maid* refashioned for his turn. . . . The next time he appears he is still as melancholy as ever: and his page sings an Irish song. It is in this scene also that he and Moth recite the mysterious rhyme

> The Fox, the Ape and the Humble Bee
> Were still at odds, being but three. . . .
> Until the Goose came out of door
> Staying the odds by adding four.
>
> [III. i. 89-92]

All three animals give aspects of Ralegh: the Fox his Machiavellianism, the Ape court flattery, the Humble Bee court amours. Riddles of three persons in one are common enough. *At odds* is a codpiece joke: *goose* was slang for prostitute. . . . The riddle is thus an indecent statement of the intrigue between Ralegh and Mistress Throckmorton, which stopped all three of his activities. (pp. 153-56)

In the show [of the Nine Worthies] Armado takes the part of Hector of Troy, so that he wears very imposing armour when Costard rushes in with the news that Jaquenetta is "two months upon her way", popularly supposed to be the same predicament

(though there is no evidence for it) which landed Ralegh in the Tower. But Armado discreetly arranges matters so that he does not have to fight. Finally he chooses to retire from court to the country with his wench and hold the plough for her love three years. Ralegh held it for five. (p. 157)

Ralegh's marraige [to Elizabeth Throckmorton] must have seemed to Essex as providential as Berowne's collapse to his wit-riddled companion. For only in 1590, Essex had married [Francis] Walsingham's daughter Frances, widow of Philip Sidney. This was so much more heinous than his habit of getting the maids of honour with child that he concealed it as long as he could: and Elizabeth, when it finally came out, banished him the Court for a time. Lady Sidney, she considered, had been his social inferior: Essex had polluted his blood. The countess lived "very retired in her mother's house", and was never readmitted to Court. How Ralegh's wit was barbed on this occasion may easily be conjectured.

Consequently when Ralegh was discovered in an even more invidious situation, Essex would have the last laugh. This is one more reason for identifying Ferdinand and his companions with Essex, and keeping Ralegh's part to Armado: and it underlines the very positive tone of triumph and achievement that accompanies the breaking of the vow. (p. 159)

Miss Yates has worked out many references in the farcical subplot of the play, some to people unconnected with the School of Night, such as John Florio, tutor to the Earl of Southampton, and as she believes, the subject of caricature in Holofernes. . . .

But the play is on the whole more concerned with theories of living than with personalities: the satire is not sustained and consistent. The convenient masks of the *Commedia dell' Arte*, Braggart, Pedant and Zany, gave a stiff framework into which many different hits could be worked without interference with each other. Shakespeare's real interest was in the general theme of active *versus* contemplative living. That he managed to deal with it without much theorizing is a proof of how thoroughly his methods embodied his convictions. (p. 161)

All the dozens of references to logic and mathematics and astronomy and pedantic Latinisms are not so many separate and spiteful little darts: they function apart from that purpose. Shakespeare, having decided what he was going to make fun of, could go ahead without having to think all the time of that: on the contrary, he wrote a play close-packed enough to be watered down into two or three, and found his "facetious grace in writing" had not needed calculation. Half the pleasure of discovering the allusions lies in finding how perfectly they are digested, and with what ease Shakespeare contrived to do half-a-dozen things at once. The references are just obvious enough to be recognizable where we have the clues, or to produce a slight consciousness of secondary intentions where we have not. But compared with, say, [Ben Jonson's] *The Poetaster*, how masterly it includes both the wood and the trees! (pp. 167-68)

> M[uriel] C. Bradbrook, "Shakespeare, the School, and Nashe," in her The School of Night: A Study in the Literary Relationships of Sir Walter Ralegh, Cambridge at the University Press, 1936, pp. 151-78.

H. B. CHARLTON (essay date 1937)

[*An English scholar, Charlton is best known for his* Shakespearian Tragedy *and* Shakespearian Comedy—*two important studies in*

*Act V. Scene ii. Princess, Boyet, and Ladies. Frontispiece
to the Hanmer edition by Francis Hayman (1744). By permission of the Folger Shakespeare Library.*

*which he argues that the proponents of New Criticism, particu-
larly T. S. Eliot and I. A. Richards, were reducing Shakespeare's
drama to its poetic elements and in the process losing sight of his
characters. In his introduction to* Shakespearian Tragedy, *Charlton described himself as a "devout" follower of A. C. Bradley,
and like his mentor he adopted a psychological, character-oriented approach to Shakespeare's work. This concern with characters and characterization can be seen in his discussion of* Love's
Labour's Lost, *first published in the* Bulletin of the John Rylands
Library *in 1937. Charlton complains that* Love's Labour's Lost
*is "deficient in plot and characterization" and that "the worst
consequences of the poverty of the story appear in the persons
who perform it"—a view in sharp opposition to the comments of
Harley Granville-Barker (1927) and, to a lesser extent, John
Dover Wilson (1962), but in agreement with S. C. Sen Gupta
(1950). More like a "modern revue" than drama, Charlton concludes,* Love's Labour's Lost *offers no "profound apprehension
of life."*]

Love's Labour's Lost is more like a modern revue, or a musical
comedy without music, than a play. It is deficient in plot and
in characterisation. There is little story in it. Its situations do
not present successive incidents in an ordered plot. Holofernes
and Nathaniel could drop out, and yet leave intact the story of
the aristocratic lovers. So, too, Armado, although he is allowed
to purchase a specious entry at the price of his moral character:
his liaison with Jaquenetta brings him into the plot. Even Costard could disappear, for his employment as a bungling postman

is a convenient rather than a necessary way of exposing Biron's
misdemeanours; equally easily, a supernumerary with a staff
could replace Constable Dull. There remains as essential persons for the conduct of the story only the king and his associates
and the princess and her ladies. Four men take an oath to
segregate themselves from the society of woman for a term of
years: circumstance at once compels them to a formal interview
with four women: they break their oath. That is the whole
story. (p. 270)

But the worst consequences of the poverty of the story appear
in the persons who perform it. The four courtiers could not
but resemble each other in a wooden conformity; for they have
all to do the same sort of thing, and have all to be guilty of
an act of almost incredible stupidity. To have attempted human
differentiations would have been to explore a world of the spirit
where deep-rooted passions, conflicting instincts, and complex
promptings mould distinctive personalities: and thereby to have
made the oath-taking humanly impossible. Hence the courtiers
in the play lack personality, and are equally without typical
character of the human sort. They have manners, and beyond
that, nothing but wit. So, when an older Shakespeare, revising
the play of his youth, came again to its end, he despatched his
Biron to a suffering world that thereby he might attain a tincture
of humanity. Whilst, in the earlier version, the King is relegated
for a twelvemonth to a hermitage, and Biron to a hospital
merely as a penance, the later sentence converts the penance
to an act of social service, from day to day visiting the speechless sick, conversing with groaning wretches for the specific
object of forcing the pained impotent to smile. Only so may
wit acquire sympathy and count itself human.

To the eye, at all events, the ladies of *Love's Labour's Lost*
are a little more individualised than are the men; for, being
ladies, the colour of the hair and the texture of the skin are
indispensable items in the inventory. A whitely wanton with
a velvet skin will not be confused with another of a dark
complexion, nor with one so auburn-haired that she stands apart
like the red dominical letter on a calendar. Yet under the skin,
these ladies are as empty and as uniform as are their wooers.
So when Katharine says that she had a sister who died of love,
she is accused by all the commentators of speaking out of her
part, for no one in this play was ever related so closely as that
to the world of real grief. Biron and Rosaline are frequently
said to have something of essential individuality. But in effect,
it is only that more of them is seen than of their associates.
Biron has indeed more wit and perspicuity than have his fellows. But it is a possession which is dramatically more of an
encumbrance than an asset. To save his reputation for wit, he
is allowed to expound the absurdity of the oath before it is
sworn; thus his subscription to it is doubly fantastic; it is entirely without reasonable motive. Moreover, his scoffs at love
and his rhapsodies on its virtues are apparently at haphazard,
and he passes from the one condition to the other without a
trace of conflict in his nature. Rosaline, dramatically, is in
equal plight. To justify her supremacy in wit, she has no time
to be anything but witty. There is apparently neither sentiment
nor passion in her nature, and without these she will scarcely
be taken as a human creature. Like the rest of the courtiers,
she is a figure sporting in a world of fantasy where words are
meat and drink, and where wit alone is law and conscience.
(pp. 271-73)

Nathaniel is a masterpiece in miniature. Every line expresses
both his native quality and his professional habit. He improves
every occasion by a thanksgiving in which the voice of the

curate appropriately phrases his pennyworth of gratitude for a full stomach and a void mind. He has the art of accepting benefits of patronage from his superiors in status or in learning in such a way that the patron is gratified and the recipient suffers no loss of prestige. He snaps up a fine phrase for next week's sermon. The man, and his calling, and his place both in his congregation and amongst his associates, are all revealed in his praise for Holofernes' ''reasons at dinner''. He is grateful to Holofernes for the dinner; he is impressed by the school-master's superior intellect, and he pays his tribute in terms which have just enough of admiring deference to please Hol-ofernes, but not so much as to deprive them of authoritative impressiveness to the vulgar, and which yet have nothing at all in them more substantial than platitudinous common-place.

But the most considerable character of them all is Costard, the unlettered, small-knowing, blundering hind. By sheer lack of every rational gift, he is immune from diseases which are epidemic in the play. Wit and words are not for him, unless, like spades and poles, they make for his immediate and material welfare. If ''remuneration'' is three farthings, it is well to have it, and its worth is just elevenpence farthing less than that of ''guerdon.'' The wit which knocks a rival down is a ponderable possession equivalent at least to a pennyworth of gingerbread, but for the rest, it may be cast to the almsbasket. Horse-sense and mother-wit are sufficient for Costard. His horse-sense smells out his advantage, and his mother-wit secures it. When he fasts it is on a full stomach. No occasion overcomes his imperturb-ability. His stupidity is proof against all shocks. Neither king nor courtier daunts him, and airily misunderstanding, he dis-misses himself with credit from the court. More consummate is his complacent patronage of Nathaniel when the curate fails in the show of the Worthies:

> a conqueror, and afeard to speak! run away for
> shame, Alisaunder. There, an't shall please you;
> a foolish mild man; an honest man, look you,
> and soon dashed. He is a marvellous good
> neighbour, faith, and a very good bowler: but,
> for Alisaunder,—alas, you see how 'tis,—a lit-
> tle o'erparted.
>
> 　　　　　　　　　　　　　　　　　　　[V. ii. 579-84]

This is not mere brag, for Costard justifies his superiority by proving the best Worthy of them all. He will decline to be pushed aside when the intellectual substance of the play is being sought.

No profound apprehension of life will be expected from *Love's Labour's Lost*. That a flagrantly absurd vow will be broken is a proposition too self-evident to call for substantiation. Its reason is as patent as is Moth's deduction that when a man grows melancholy it is a sign that he will look sad. The story of the making and the breaking of the vow needs but to be shown to the eye. For anything deeper than mere observation of the surface of life, there is neither room nor need. The imagination is not called upon to reveal powers working in the deeps, silently controlling the currents on the face of the waters. Moreover, the surface here displayed is that of so remote a backwater that to reveal in it the operation of the great ocean-tides of life would be well-nigh impossible. Of apprehension of life in the dramatic way, therefore, there can be very little; but of opinion prompted by the dramatists' observation of living men there may be much. The course of an action which shows that foolish men are guilty of folly, that the best way to the back-gate is not over the house-top, that we cannot cross the

cause why we were born, will hardly excite its author's passions to flashes of inspired insight. (pp. 274-76)

> *H. B. Charlton, ''The Consummation,'' in his* Shake-spearian Comedy, *Methuen & Co. Ltd., 1938, pp. 266-98.*

JOHN PALMER　(essay date 1946)

[*In his* Comic Characters of Shakespeare *(1946), Palmer, an Eng-lish novelist and drama critic, begins his discussion of* Love's Labour's Lost *by contrasting the play with Molière's* Les Pré-cieuses Ridicules. *Palmer says that while Molière uses his satire derisively in an effort to correct the ''absurdities'' of his society, Shakespeare is less serious and more sympathetic towards the subjects of his ridicule. Shakespeare is especially sympathetic toward Berowne, whom Palmer, like Walter Pater (1885) and Thomas Marc Parrott (1949), sees as an embodiment of the play-wright himself. Palmer concludes that though satire in Shake-speare's time often proved to be politically dangerous,* Love's Labour's Lost *was inoffensive because it was meant to be a hu-morous self-parody rather than a vindictive social commentary. In defining* Love's Labour's Lost *as a parody rather than a satire Palmer sought to refute those critics—specifically Samuel Johnson (1765), whom he mentions by name in his essay, but also such earlier commentators as Hermann Ulrici (1839), Charles Knight (1849), Edward Dowden (1881), and Muriel C. Bradbrook (1936)— all of whom have interpreted the play as contemptuous satire directed at certain individuals or attitudes of Elizabethan life.*]

The greatest comic dramatist since Aristophanes—assuming that Shakespeare is ineligible to compete—sprang into fame with a genial satire upon the metaphysical exquisites of the blue *salon* of the Marquise de Rambouillet. Molière, when he came to Paris in 1658, impudently challenged the established arbiters of literary taste with a comedy as devastating in its effect upon the fashionable wits and poets of the day as the little child's remark upon the Emperor's new clothes in An-dersen's fairy tale. *Les Précieuses Ridicules,* by a young dra-matist who had recently arrived from the provinces, destroyed in a gale of laughter a literary and social sect which no one until that moment had ventured to find ridiculous.

By a happy coincidence Shakespeare, at an almost identical point in his career, came upon the London stage with a 'Pleasant Conceited Comedy Called Love's Labour's Lost', in which the exquisites of his own time and country were brought to book. It is instructive to compare the spirit in which these two men of genius approached a very similar enterprise. Their subject was the same; they had a like intention, which was to be amusing at the expense of the verbal and sentimental affec-tations of the period; their audience in both cases was a select company of persons passionately addicted to the follies at which they were invited to laugh. These follies, moreover, had a superficial resemblance.

Here, then, is a unique opportunity of observing two great comedians at work upon the same theme, writing under much the same conditions, basing their comic appeal on the same conflict of broad humanity with social artifice, of common sense with intellectual extravagance, of truth to nature with the distortions of fancy. Everything seems to be prompting them to the same conclusions and consequences. The result is, never-theless, a contrast at all points between the two achievements and a revelation of essential qualities that divide their authors in everything but their firm grasp of the abiding realities of the human spirit.

The first point of contrast lies in the fact that Molière, in mocking the exquisites of the blue *salon,* was deriding a coterie whose standards of taste and whose approach to literature and life were quite definitely alien and pernicious. . . . In writing his first pugnacious comedy he deliberately challenged and destroyed something for which he felt an actively wholesome contempt. These exquisites were not only corrupters of taste and manners; they were veritable misleaders of youth, setting up false standards of sentiment and behaviour in whose presence common sense and good feeling were almost ashamed to show their honest faces. Molière, moved to a genuine derision, was determined to put out of court and countenance absurdities which were naturally antipathetic to his genius.

Very different was the mood and purpose of Shakespeare in his 'pleasant conceited comedy'. Admittedly he set out to make fun of the sophisticated and metaphysical wits of London. But he was ridiculing absurdities which, on occasion, he was quite happy to share with his contemporaries and he amused his audience with a display of virtuosity in an art of which he was himself a notable practitioner. There is nothing destructive or contemptuous in his handling of these pedantical lords and subtle ladies. Their sentimental encounters, in which phrases and fancies run extravagantly wild for our pleasure, are mocked with an indulgence that implies affection rather than reprobation. Who, after all, was Shakespeare to castigate man or woman for exuberance in 'conceit', extravagance in the manipulation of words, profligacy in the pursuit of a fair image, prodigality in the expense of imagination? How could Shake-, speare, who was one day to present on his stage Benedick and Beatrice [in *Much Ado About Nothing*], allow himself to suggest that Berowne and Rosaline were too silly for words? Admittedly he invites us to laugh at their antics. Berowne is often exquisitely ludicrous. But all this is chaff rather than satire, provoking us to laugh companionably at a fool with whom his author is ready to change shoes at any moment. (pp. 1-3)

[In] this pleasant conceited comedy, simple nature and good sense prevail over subtle sentiment and false conceit. All follies are redeemed and none is left in the stocks. In the conduct of plot and character the author keeps his wonted mean between sympathy and satire. It is yet more significant that in the Euphuistic embroideries of his theme Shakespeare shows the same tendency to identify himself with the object of his derision. He means to mock these fine gentlemen for their preciosity, but, when he comes to write their verses, we are often in doubt whether to admire their skill or smile at their perversity. We begin to laugh and are caught by a melody. We come to scoff and remain to pray that the music may continue. Berowne, of whom it is said that every word is a jest and every jest but a word, suddenly slips a line into his sonnet:

Those thoughts to me were oaks, to thee like osiers bowed;
　　　　　　　　　　　　　　　　　　　　　　[IV. ii. 108]

and we feel that Shakespeare, lost in the object of his mirth, has given him something for which no poet need crave indulgence. The King's sonnet [IV. iii. 25-40], precious enough in all conscience, admirably sustains the conceit on which it is founded and, though we may be jolted into mockery as we ride along, it lands us at last in a crystal coach upon the broad highway of the muses. . . . If this be parody it is such that only a poet, indulgently smiling at a brother's extravagance, could write. It is written in sport, but might have fallen from the sheaf inscribed to Mr. W. H. Shakespeare is smiling at his own excess, standing aside as it were, from the solemn achievement of his younger muse, presenting it for our merriment.

The pure comedian, flouting absurdity, would have written for his poetasters effusions that were wholly ridiculous. . . . There is no fellow-feeling in Molière for Mascarille or in Congreve for Mr. Brisk, as they spout and posture to their coteries of half-wits. The mood, intention and result are entirely different. Shakespeare can laugh at his Euphuists and love them, too.

Nor does Shakespeare's sympathy so generously extended to the finer wits of his comedy stop short at grosser manifestations of the literary fashion at which he aims. His wits 'have been at a great feast of languages and stolen the scraps' and upon such as 'have lived long on the alms-basket of words' [V. i. 36-9] he can be downright satirical:

This fellow pecks up wit, as pigeons pease,
And utters it again when God doth please. . . .
　　　　　　　　　　　　　　　　　　　　　　[IV. ii. 315-16]

But how he delights in Holofernes, the schoolmaster, speaking by the book; Sir Nathaniel, the priest, adoring a text; Don Armado, the fantastical knight, composing a letter; Costard, the clown, who must needs be in the fashion, too! What zest he imparts to the display of their talents! They have all drunk of the cup of Dionysus, and Shakespeare, sharing their intoxication, comprehends their contempt for any dullard to whom the Pierian spring supplies no headier draught than plain mineral water:

Sir, he hath never fed of the dainties that are bred in a book.
He hath not eat paper, as it were; he hath not drunk ink:
His intellect is not replenished, he is only an animal, only sensible in the duller parts:
　　　　　　　　　　　　　　　　　　　　　　[IV. ii. 24-7]

Holofernes blesses God for his gift and Shakespeare enjoys it with him even as he parodies its exercise:

This is a gift that I have, simple, simple; a foolish extravagant spirit, full of forms, figures, shapes, objects, ideas, apprehensions, motions, revolutions. These are begot in the ventricle of memory, nourished in the womb of pia mater, and delivered upon the mellowing of occasion. . . . But the gift is good in those in whom it is acute, and I am thankful for it.
　　　　　　　　　　　　　　　　　　　　　　[IV. ii. 65-72]

These fantastical fellows have their own standard of excellence and Shakespeare enjoys their company. (pp. 15-18)

Molière, satirising a literary fashion in his *Les Précieuses Ridicules,* presented a group of exquisites which were not only true to the period but true of all the exquisites who ever lived. His characters were from life and there was not a phrase or gesture in his comedy which could not be matched from the conversation and behaviour of his originals. So long as complicated fashion is liable to corrupt natural simplicity his play will remain amusing and intelligible. He successfully avoided, in fact, the faults which he was denouncing, refraining from a preciosity which might have tempted him to multiply his local and personal allusions and would in time have rendered much of his comedy incomprehensible to posterity. Shakespeare's 'Love's Labour's Lost', though in essentials it is broader in humanity than Molière's play, has, on the contrary, become in places difficult and here and there forever meaningless even to the scholar. The reason, again, is to be sought in the fact that Shakespeare, less intent than Molière on the 'correction of social absurdity', is absorbed into the game from which Molière held aloof in a more critical frame of mind. Molière looked on at the follies which he denounced. Shakespeare romps whole-heartedly with his fools. His play is more in the nature of a family diversion in which intimate private jests are exchanged for the fun of the thing. To many of these witticisms we have lost the clue. They remain embedded in his play, to use the vivid metaphor of Dr. Dover Wilson, as 'persistent flies in its amber'. . . . Dr. Johnson, discussing these blemishes, charged the author with sacrificing permanent interest to personal satire [see excerpt above, 1765]. Shakespeare, he argues, in presenting Holofernes, was so bent on ridiculing the local schoolmaster that his portrait has little value for those who are unacquainted with the original. . . . Very trenchant and very true; but wholly irrelevant. There is no private malice in the presentation of Holofernes or Moth or Armado. There is not even a sustained criticism of their extravagance. If Shakespeare in this comedy sacrificed the esteem of succeeding time to the laughter of a day, it was not owing to any malice, private or general, but to a warm interest in his characters, and boundless pleasure in their oddities of mind.

It is possible by study and the exercise of imagination to recover something of that laughter of a day which for the casual reader is irretrievably lost. But we are seeking here confirmation that in the topicalities of the play as in its general design Shakespeare, so far from gratifying any private malice, was presenting a picture of contemporary manners to an audience which was more than ready to take everything in good part—that he was offering it, in fact, not a personal invective but, in the words of the title-page, a pleasant conceited comedy. Whether, in point of fact—as seems not at all unlikely—we may identify Holofernes with John Florio, Moth with Thomas Nashe, the little Academe of the King of Navarre with the group of Copernicans and black magicians whose poet was George Chapman, there can be no doubt whatever that 'Love's Labour's Lost', as played before the Queen in 1597, was a topical piece packed with open and covert allusions to a piece of social history in which many members of the distinguished audience had, in fact, themselves participated. His theme, moreover, was not only topical but dangerous. Shakespeare in the comic vein contrived in 'Love's Labour's Lost' to do precisely what he did more seriously, and just as successfully, in 'Richard II' and 'King John', namely to write a play bristling with perilous implications and to escape either censure or calumny because he wrote it with an entire absence of prejudice, putting a natural emphasis upon its broadly human as opposed to its narrowly social, political or sectarian aspects, exhibiting a tolerance that embraced every man in his humour, passions, affections, foibles and infirmities. It was an almost unique achievement. His contemporaries seldom meddled with subjects of public or social interest without paying the penalty. Jonson, Nashe, Kyd, Chapman—all experienced the untender mercies of Star Chamber. To write a topical play under Elizabeth or James was to ask for trouble and in most cases to get it promptly and in full measure. But Shakespeare was never molested. He wandered freely in a world in which neither the Queen who was quite prepared to hang a man for witnessing a play with treason in it, nor the King who put Jonson in prison for a play which made fun of the Scots, ever challenged his conduct or authority.

To those who are unfamiliar with the social background to 'Love's Labour's Lost' it must seem impossible that it should

contain anything perilous to life or liberty. The play is, nevertheless, charged with brimstone:

> Black is the badge of hell,
> The hue of dungeons and the School of Night.
> [IV. iii. 250-51]

The King of Navarre is here treading on dangerous ground and Berowne with his enigmatic praise of black ladies and commendation of ebony as a wood divine is inviting disaster. In the spring of 1593 the Queen's Privy Council were taking a sinister interest in a small society which counted among its initiates Chapman, Kyd and Marlowe, among the dramatists, and no less a person than Sir Walter Raleigh among the nobility. These men studied the stars; they were proficient in the art of numbers and were even suspected of raising the devil. A warrant was issued for Marlowe's arrest, but he was killed in a brawl before he could be brought to trial. Kyd was put to the torture. Raleigh, already in disgrace, was later examined by a special commission appointed to investigate his 'heresies'. Into the thick of all this comes Shakespeare, smiling, with a pleasant conceited comedy in his hand; and the comedy is presented to the Queen at Christmas. In it he presents a little academe of seclusive gentlemen who also study the stars and swear to sleep for only three hours in twenty-four. The play abounds in cryptic allusions to numbers and chapmen's tongues. Berowne sings the praises of sable beauty. But Shakespeare seems not to be in the least aware of his peril. He makes fun of these fantastical gentlemen, but it is all done in pure kindness of heart. His references to certain poets, head-over-heels implicated in some very dangerous proceedings, are not in the least censorious. He seems to be neither of one side nor the other. He promises a satire on the wicked and a castigation of fools; but the wicked prove on acquaintance to be excellent company and the fools are merely diverting. Was there ever a more striking example of charity in genius covering a multitude of sins any one of which was a hanging matter in the eyes of authority?

And so we revert to Berowne himself, who of all the characters in this strangely enchanting medley of wit and poetry most fully expresses its mood and purpose. For Shakespeare in Berowne is smiling not merely at follies with which after the fashion of his comic genius he puts himself for the time being in imaginative sympathy, but at folly to which he was himself as a poet peculiarly liable in his own person. (pp. 21-5)

[Walter Pater] sees in Berowne 'a reflex of Shakespeare himself, when he has just become able to stand aside from and estimate the first period of his poetry' [see excerpt above, 1885]. He is fascinated by that 'foppery' of language which 'satisfies a real instinct in our minds—the fancy so many of us have for an exquisite and curious skill in the use of words'. This, however, is but one aspect of the matter. Berowne is the first of Shakespeare's characters in which the essential quality of his comic genius becomes apparent. He is the first fine product of that imaginative process whereby Shakespeare identifies himself with the object of his mirth, thus combining in a single gesture of the spirit, detachment with sympathy, serene judgment with congenial understanding, the objectivity of a creating mind with an entire subjection of the imagination to the thing created. (p. 25)

John Palmer, "Berowne," in his Comic Characters of Shakespeare, *Macmillan and Co., Limited, 1946, pp. 1-27.*

BERTRAND H. BRONSON   (essay date 1948)

[*Bronson refutes Richmond Noble's interpretation of the two songs that conclude* Love's Labour's Lost *(see excerpt above, 1923).*

*Whereas Noble regards both songs as Shakespeare's ironic rid-
icule of "pretty pastorals and sententious verses," Bronson characterizes them as symmetrically balanced in their contrasting
messages, the first in which spring sings the fear of cuckoldry,
the second in which winter "intensifies one's sense of well-being."
Noble's reading of the songs, according to Bronson, ignores this
sense of balance and paradox which he believes crystalizes the
"bitter-sweet" dénouement of the play. For further commentary
on the songs and their importance in the play, see the excerpts
by Hermann Ulrici (1839), William C. Carroll (1976), and Louis
Adrian Montrose (1977).]*

No songs have been better loved or more admired than the two
which constitute the anti-masque at the end of *Love's Labour's
Lost*:—"When daisies pied" and "When icicles hang." John
Masefield has called them "the loveliest thing ever said about
England," and a small anthology in their praise could easily
be compiled. Yet has any commentator ever called due attention to one of their most remarkable features, or offered to
account for it? I refer to the fact that in the first song . . . the
burden (in all senses) of the song falls upon a consideration
which elsewhere in Shakespeare, as in life, makes toward tragedy. . . . A sour note, undeniably, even though an allowed
Elizabethan jest. Whilst again, in the other song, the poet has
marshaled reminders of the genuine physical discomforts of
winter, adding one to another, to culminate in the hooting of
the "staring" owl, which every generation has concurred in
regarding as unmusical, depressing, even dismal and ill-
omened. And this, for the nonce, he perversely calls "a merry
note."

Let me hasten to acknowledge that the songs in their entirety
convey no despondent impression. Rather, they leave us with
a sense of two contrasting kinds of intense pleasure: the out-
of-door enjoyment of delicious springtide, and the compan-
ionable, snug enjoyment of winter fireside, the satisfying sense
that all things disagreeable are shut out. It is just this paradox
that calls for comment. (pp. 35-6)

Granted that everything flowers to beauty for Shakespeare, is
there no special reason for his introducing not merely an obvious contrast that sets song against song, but also, and more
subtly poised, this further conflict of elements within each
separate song? Reduced to logical propositions, the first song
says, in part, "The sum of vernal delights but serves to remind
husbands of their fears of infidelity in their wives'" and the
second, "The sum of winter's annoyances but intensifies one's
sense of well-being (given fire and a pot)." Not to elaborate,
it is, then, the age-old lesson of the imperfect and paradoxical
condition of human felicity that is resident in this antiphony.
And, surely, the meaning of so equivocal a comedy, with such
a name, with such a denouement, bitter-sweet, could not have
been more exquisitely distilled and quintessentialized. (p. 36)

Mr. Noble sees both songs as 'merciless ridicule' of "pretty
pastorals and sententious verses" [see excerpt above, 1923].
He indicates some clowning on the part of the singer of the
first song. After the "sly, echoing . . . 'Cuckoo, Cuckoo'—
the singer shivers in pretended fear and shakes his head at the
impropriety of such a call." And the second song he interprets
as satire in which "pastoral romance gives way to pastoral
realism." Not only does he regard the owl's hoot as "merry"
only in an ironic sense—"a diversion where all else is depressing"; but proceeds, "the most disagreeable of all the
sensations to be experienced in Winter is that afforded by the
sight and smell of the sluttish Joan keeling the pot." Although
I ought perhaps to find my account with Mr. Noble, who of
all the commentators that I have seen is the only one to discover

any unpleasantness in the intention, yet I can hardly believe
that the poet's humanity was so nice as to consider greasy Joan
a repellent figure, while she busied herself over the fire, with
the kettles steaming and the roasted "crabs" hissing in the
bowl. Rather, as I take it, the aim is to suggest hearty enjoyment, not irony nor burlesque. Moreover, if "merry" be taken
ironically, we spoil the pretty opposition between the boding
bird of spring and the comfortable bird of winter, which itself
makes a delightful surprise and reversal of the traditional "debate" of the birds that Armado has led us to anticipate. Surely,
part of the fun lies in this unexpected flouting of convention;
and if the reversal is not completed, the point is lost. Again,
if "merry" be not honest, the structural parallel and contrast
with the spring song are both obliterated, and our pleasure in
the artistry and logical neatness of the antithesis is correspondingly impaired. (p. 37)

*Bertrand H. Bronson, "Daisies Pied and Icicles,"
in* Modern Language Notes, *Vol. LXIII, No. 1, January, 1948, pp. 35-8.*

THOMAS MARC PARROTT (essay date 1949)

[*Parrott, an American scholar, wrote several critical studies on
Shakespeare and Elizabethan drama and edited a collection of
Shakespeare's plays and sonnets. In the excerpt below, from his*
Shakespearean Comedy (1949), *Parrott argues against the theory
that* Love's Labour's Lost *is actually a veiled attack on Sir Walter
Raleigh and the so-called "School of Night"—an interpretation
put forth most thoroughly by Muriel C. Bradbrook (1936), Arthur
Acheson, and Frances A. Yates (see Additional Bibliography)—
stating that the satire in the play is deeper and more universal
than personal invective. Like Charles Knight (1849), Parrott regards affectation and pedantry as the primary targets of the play's
satire. Also, in a modified version of Walter Pater's and John
Palmer's assessments of the character of Berowne (see excerpts
above, 1885 and 1946), Parrott argues that this figure was not
meant to be a portrait of the youthful Shakespeare himself, but,
instead, is a projection of the ideal personality Shakespeare wished
he could be.*]

Love's Labour's Lost is the first opening of the satiric vein
which flows with greater force than has been generally recognized through more than one of Shakespeare's plays. Many
of the contemporary allusions, such as that to the dancing horse
and to the Harvey-Nashe controversy, require annotation today.
These we may pass by. It is another matter, however, with the
personal satire passing into caricature which has been suspected
in this play. Holofernes has been identified with the Italian
scholar, Florio; Moth is supposed to stand for Nashe, because
among other reasons, his name spelled backward, *Htom*, resembles Shakespeare's spelling of Nashe's Christian name,
Thom; a reflection of the great philosopher, Giordano Bruno,
has been found in the first lord because the old spelling of his
name, Berowne, rhymes in the play with 'moon.' Here, indeed,
be proofs of Shakespeare's ingenuity of malice.

Several recent editors and critics have conceived the whole
play as a thinly veiled attack upon the group of scholars and
studious gentlemen that gathered about Sir Walter Raleigh,
upon which group they have hung the label of 'The School of
Night' [see excerpt above by M. C. Bradbook, 1936]. It is,
however, unfortunate that this label is taken from a line in the
play [IV. iii. 251] where the important word, *school*, has long
been suspected as a misprint and has been emended in all
possible ways: *Scowl, stole, scroll*, et cetera. There is no reason
to believe that Raleigh's coterie was ever known to his contemporaries as 'the school of night.' The charge most fre-

quently brought against them was that of atheism, and to atheism there is not the most remote allusion in the play. As a matter of fact, there is not the slightest possible resemblance between the mathematicians, geographers, and misogynists of Raleigh's group and the 'well-accomplished,' merry, and amorous King of Navarre and his lords.

What Shakespeare aimed at in *Love's Labour's Lost* was something deeper and more permanent than a contemporary 'school of night'; it was the whole body of pedantry, affectation, and formal control of life, which flew in the face of nature. This tendency was, perhaps, especially dangerous in Shakespeare's day when enthusiasm for the newly discovered classics was degenerating into blind pedantry and the new delight in the exploitation of language was blossoming into fantastic affectation. Yet it is not unknown in our time, when academic formalism insists upon a doctor's degree as a *sine qua non* for a post in a college faculty. In our day, too, the passion for novelty of expression is, no doubt, one of the reasons why modern poets indulge in a preciosity of speech unintelligible to the common reader.

Shakespeare's sound sense revolted against this tendency away from nature, and *Love's Labour's Lost* is in essence a laughing philippic against both pedantry and affectation. It is a merry, but none the less vigorous, plea for simplicity and natural behavior. The unnatural vow of the King and his lords to follow learning at the expense of youth, pleasure, and beauty is broken by the natural passion of love. The pedantic Masque of the Worthies is driven from the stage by a quick fire of quips, puns, and broad jests such as rose naturally to the lips of laughter-loving Elizabethans. The pompous Spaniard falls a victim to the charms of a country wench and is 'infamonized among potentates' [V. ii. 679] by a country clown. Berowne himself, too, sensible to yield wholly to fashionable affectation, too courtly to escape them altogether, is beaten from his point device wooing, 'taffeta phrases, silken terms precise,' to 'russet yeas and honest kersey noes' [V. ii. 404, 413]. Everywhere simplicity and common sense triumph over pedantry and affectation; 'Young blood doth not obey an old decree' [IV. iii. 213]. Nature conquers art, and the play closes fitly with a nature lyric rising from the heart of the young poet lately come from rustic Stratford. Amid the follies and fancies and witty affectations of the town, Shakespeare has not forgotten the Warwickshire meadows with 'daisies pied and violets blue' [V. ii. 894], or the homely sights and sounds about the cottages 'when icicles hang by the wall' [V. ii. 912]. This is the conclusion of the whole matter, and 'the words of Mercury are harsh after the songs of Apollo' [V. ii. 931]. (pp. 120-22)

There is . . . a special reason for the attraction *Love's Labour's Lost* exerts upon all lovers of Shakespeare. It is that here, for the first time, he seems to draw aside the veil that conceals his inmost self and to present, as he was later to do in the *Sonnets, Hamlet*, and *The Tempest*, something that might be likened to a painter's self-portrait. There is, of course, a difference. The painter studies his face in a mirror and consciously reproduces on canvas the lineaments that he sees there. Shakespeare was not trying to draw a portrait of himself in the costume of Berowne. On the contrary this character seems to express what Shakespeare wished to be. When in moments of depression he wrote of himself as

> Wishing me like to one more rich in hope,
> Featur'd like him, like him with friends possess'd,
> Desiring this man's art, and that man's scope,
>
> [*Sonnet* 29]

he must have longed to exchange places with one of the hopeful, well-bred, and witty favorites of the Court, an Oxford or a Southampton. . . . [A] man's aspiration often reveals a true portrait of his inner self. And that is the special characteristic of *Love's Labour's Lost;* it reveals, as no other early play does, the promise and to some extent the personality of William Shakespeare. (pp. 124-25)

> *Thomas Marc Parrott, ''Apprentice Work,'' in his* Shakespearean Comedy, *Oxford University Press, 1949, pp. 100-33.*

S. C. SEN GUPTA   (essay date 1950)

[*Sen Gupta, an important Indian Shakespeare scholar, has written several books of criticism on Shakespeare's plays. In his discussion of* Love's Labour's Lost, *taken from his* Shakespearian Comedy *(1950), he calls the play a ''fantasy'' because of its loosely constructed plot. He also argues that, with the exception of Berowne and possibly Boyet,* Love's Labour's Lost *suffers from weak and uneven character development—a conclusion also reached by H. B. Charlton (1937), but opposed by Harley Granville-Barker (1927). Sen Gupta also counters such critics as Muriel C. Bradbrook (1936) and Frances A. Yates (Additional Bibliography) and states that there is little evidence to support the School-of-Night theory.*]

It may be argued that *Love's Labour's Lost* is a fantasy, and, therefore, it is more loosely constructed than an ordinary drama. But a drama must have a well-organized form, which means that even in a dramatic fantasia there must be a plot, however slight it may be, in which there is an evolution from the beginning to the middle and from the middle to the end; and this evolution must serve the dramatic purpose of revealing character. (p. 84)

Critics have for a long time read topical allusions into this play. . . . The editors of the New Cambridge Shakespeare suggest that the play is a topical satire on the School of Atheism of which Ralegh was the chief patron and Marlowe, Chapman and Harriot were members [see essay by Arthur Quiller-Couch and John Dover Wilson in the Additional Bibliography]. This suggestion has been worked out in detail by Miss Frances Yates in *A Study of 'Love's Labour's Lost'* and by Miss M. C. Bradbrook in *The School of Night* [see Additional Bibliography and excerpt above, 1936]. These writers speak of the existence of a School of Atheism, whose doctrines, esoteric and heretical, aroused public scandal and which Shakespeare, who belonged to the rival group of Essex and Southampton, nicknamed The School of Night. (p. 85)

It is idle at this distance of time to speculate what exactly were the circumstances that led Shakespeare to write *Love's Labour's Lost*. A poet is in many ways an extraordinary person, but he is none the less a human being. He cannot create his works out of sheer vacuum. His experiences and observations determine the scope of his art and supply him with hints and materials which enable him to build up plot and portray character. It may be allowed that the School of Atheism, if such a school actually existed, supplied him with some suggestions, but the more important question is whether these suggestions were casual or vital, how far the significance of the comedy, as we have it, depends on the eccentricities Shakespeare may have observed in Ralegh and his associates. And to this question the answer must be that the suggestions were casual and the dependence, if any, is very slight. (pp. 85-6)

[The proponents of the School-of-Night theory] rely chiefly on the King's reply to Berowne in Act IV, Sc. iii, which they, adopting the Folio and the Quarto versions, read as follows:—

> O paradox! Black is the badge of hell,
> The hue of dungeons and the School of Night.
>   [IV. iii. 250-51]

If Shakespeare really wanted to satirize Ralegh and Harriot's School of Atheism, why should he deliver his main onslaught through a casual and not very pointed outburst which has nothing to do with the main plot of the play? He surely knew how to emphasize his satire and make it unmistakable. It may be argued that the allusion, so dim and distant to us, would not have been lost on the Elizabethan audience who were well acquainted with the School. But this does not explain why Shakespeare, if his intention were satirical, should introduce the nickname so casually and in such a light-hearted debate on the value of dark hair and sallow complexion. The Academy of Navarre was a stoical school, and so, for all we know, might have been Ralegh's School of Atheism, but there is not a scrap of evidence to show that the lords and their followers were atheistical. There are a few references to astronomy and to the mathematical incompetence of Holofernes, Costard and Don Armado, but are these enough to connect the Academy with a School which was supposed primarily to be concerned with sceptical metaphysics and esoteric profundities and of which no member except Harriott was an astronomer?

The dramatis personae of this play may be divided into two groups, the lords and the ladies forming one group and the eccentrics, Holofernes, Don Armado, Moth and Costard, the other. Though the lords take an absurd vow, they have been portrayed in the broad humane manner characteristic of Shakespeare who may have found hints for these characters in real life but worked on them in his own way, so that it would be idle to read caricatures of particular individuals into them. In Don Armado and Holofernes we find an isolation and over-emphasis of some particular trait or eccentricity which is so contrary to real life as to make it highly probable that the characters are fictitious. Such an intensive selection of detail points rather to caricature of a type than to caricature of an individual. In fact, Armado and Holofernes are portrayed exactly after those 'humorous' types so prevalant in Elizabethan comedy, and it is less likely that Shakespeare was tilting at an individual than that he was falling in with a literary trend of the times. (pp. 87-8)

Shakespeare is here dealing in the manner of cinquecento comedy with types rather than with individuals. Indeed, in the old texts, Armado and Holofernes are described as the Braggart and the Pedant, which show that they were intended to represent types well known in contemporary drama. The most significant thing in Shakespeare's handling of these stock characters is that he tries, however ineffectively, to endow them with some glimmering of individuality. The most unimportant, from this point of view, is Dull, who does little beyond misapplying and twisting words. This trick persists in the foolish characters of Shakespeare's later comedies but is irradiated by many original traits which give them vitality. Much the same thing can be said of Sir Nathaniel who utters nothing but ineptitudes and does nothing but thank his host for a sumptuous dinner. Moth is talkative and restless and never misses an opportunity of riddling his chief with shafts of ridicule. But he seems to have been designed primarily as an appendage to Don Armado and has no independent existence of his own. It is not in this way that a character becomes living. . . . The other three—Costard,

Holofernes and Don Armado—have been portrayed in greater detail and point to the way in which Shakespeare's genius will begin to move when it has got into its stride. These men were originally intended to represent particular idiosyncrasies, but they exhibit such a variety of traits that very soon we lose sight of generalities in the portraiture of individuals. Costard, for example, appears at first sight to be a fool who does not know the meaning of words and who carries love-letters whose import he does not grasp. But how is it that he delivers Armado's letter to the Princess and Berowne's first to Jaquenetta and then to the King and the lords? Is it, one wonders, pure stupidity or is there a little impishness mixed with his tomfoolery? . . . Indeed, it seems that Shakespeare wants to portray him as a clownish fool but with more than an ordinary fool's share of homely wisdom, but he has failed to make a proper amalgam of stupidity and sense and has been content to stitch together two disparate personalities. (pp. 89-90)

There has been endless discussion about what particular linguistic eccentricity Don Armado represents, whether it is Lyly's euphuism or the affectations of the ladies in Elizabeth's court or highflown Spanish diction or Italian sonneteering. The most important thing from the dramatic point of view is that Don Armado cannot be identified with any particular eccentricity, linguistic or other. For he is more than a mere personification of any one vice or idiosyncrasy; he is a person who has many oddities but knows also how to behave as a sane, normal, honourable gentleman, as we conclude from his conduct in the last scene of the play. . . . The weakness of *Love's Labour's Lost* is that Shakespeare is not yet able to weld all these multifarious traits into one unified whole. It is easy to catalogue all the characteristics of Don Armado, but we do not know the core of personality from which they spring and draw their warmth and vitality.

The protagonists of the play—the lords and the ladies—are not eccentrics, but they, too, meet, make love and then part in exceptional circumstances. The lords, although sane and normal men, take an absurd vow, and Shakespeare shows how they are brought back to the normal ways of life by the promptings of their hearts. The meeting of the lords and the ladies is due to a contingency which the rash votaries did not foresee, but the ridiculous manner in which they readily fall in love is a kind of nemesis for the foolish vows they took in the beginning of the drama. The principal defect of this play is that Shakespeare cannot limn his characters properly. With one remarkable exception, Shakespeare cannot even distinguish between one lord and another, or, for the matter of that, between one lady and another. All the distinction he draws between characters of the same group is external and not fundamental. (pp. 92-3)

The one exception . . . is Berowne in whom we have an example of Shakespeare's art on its way to full bloom. Berowne has a rich and varied individuality. If he is not as prominent as the greater creations of Shakespearian comedy, that is merely because there is no plot through which he can reveal himself; no wonder, therefore, that his most characteristic expression is through lyrical outbursts rather than through dramatic utterance or action. He looks at life from a broad humane point of view and knows that any attempt at the repression of the fundamental instinct of life is not only futile but, if it were practicable, also suicidal. Even on the eve of taking the vow, he inveighs against it:—

> O! these are barren tasks, too hard to keep,
> Not to see ladies, study, fast, not sleep. . . .
>   [I. i. 47-8]

He is a believer in love rather than in asceticism, but as his philosophy of life is broad and humane he does not make a fetish of love. He is well aware of its limitations and pitfalls. Even in the midst of his raptures he is conscious of the fatuity which is at the basis of a lover's ecstasies. Although he glorifies what he considers the most deep-seated and most unescapable of all impulses and lauds his own lady-love to the skies, his self-defence is curiously interpolated with a good deal of self-chastisement. . . . It is this richness of perception and this critical aloofness in the midst of rapturous exaltation which distinguish Berowne from the ordinary lover. His character points to what is best in Shakespearian comedy in which we get a completer picture of the labyrinthine complexity of human life than anywhere else. Shakespeare reveals depths behind superficies, reconciles contradictions and shows that human life is a medley of interpenetrating elements which seem to be incompatible but are held together by the magic of personality. Shakespeare's love for a complex harmony is indeed so strong that there is a gradual development of Berowne's personality through all the stages of this drama in which the plot is too thin and slight to allow of sufficient scope for characterization. Even when the play comes to an end, we feel that Berowne must continue to grow. He must not remain a superficial mocker; his laughter must be rooted in humanity. He must learn 'to enforce the pained impotent to smile' [V. ii. 854], and then only will he be a husband worthy of Rosaline.

Another remarkable creation is Boyet who has not received from critics the attention he deserves. The part he plays in the drama is negligibly small, but he represents what may be regarded as the comedian's point of view. He understands the King sooner than the King understands himself, and at the conclusion of the first interview between the King and the Princess, thus warns the latter:—

> If my observation—which very seldom lies,—
> By the heart's still rhetoric disclosed with eyes,
> Deceive me not now, Navarre is infected. . . .
>
> [II. i. 228-30]

He gives the most adequate description of Don Armado, and when he meets Moth he does the clever page out of his part. He helps the ladies to befool the lords in their amorous expedition, easily turning the sport against them. His forecasts never prove false, his reading of a situation is always correct because, though he has his part to play within the comedy, he is really outside it. He looks at the incidents in a spirit of detachment and thus helps us to find the comic significance of all that happens around him. (pp. 93-7)

> *S. C. Sen Gupta, "Early Comedies," in his* Shake-
> spearian Comedy, *Oxford University Press, 1950,*
> *pp. 82-128.*

M[URIEL] C. BRADBROOK (essay date 1951)

[*In her discussion of* Love's Labour's Lost, *taken from her* Shakespeare and Elizabethan Poetry *(1951), Bradbrook emphasizes the
language and verbal wit in the play, which she believes compensates for the lack of action. She also notes the paradox of Shakespeare's attack on affected and artificial language because his
play remains "the most artificial of all [his] comedies." A similar
point has also been made by George Brandes (1895-96), Harley
Granville-Barker (1927), and John Palmer (1946).*]

The elegance and wit of Shakespeare's courtly comedy is nowhere so polished as in *Love's Labour's Lost*. Although the
relation of this play with *As You Like It* would seem sufficiently

obvious, the earlier drama has not enjoyed the same popularity until quite recently, when Granville Barker's study [see excerpt above, 1927] and a number of stage performances have shown how much life remains in the most fantastic scenes. (p. 212)

The play is as near as Shakespeare ever came to writing satire; and yet there is more than a spice of panegyric behind the ridicule of fine manners. After seeing such a comedy, no one would be ashamed to continue in the use of taffeta phrases, silken terms precise, although they might be a little moderated. The sport is intended for the ears of friends, and like the banter of the 'mocking wenches' it is even a subtle way of establishing good relations. For *Love's Labour's Lost* implies a clever au-dience. It is a bout of verbal fencing, carried out before experts.

The action is slighter than even the slightest of musical com-edies. Gone are the elaborate disguises and mistaking of earlier courtly dramatists like Lyly and Peele. Two masques, a number of songs and a quantity of sonnets fill out the spaces between the wit-combats, the clowning and the passionate soliloquies of Berowne. If some of the actors were indeed young noblemen or gentlemen, the atmosphere of charade would be strong, and the double use of masquers for 'plays within the play' would heighten the sense of a mirror-image, the reflection of the spectators in the glass of comedy.

The lack of action is compensated for by elaborate and intricate style. Many speeches are in the nature of a verbal *tour de force*: quibbling and innuendo flourish. Nowhere else does Shake-speare display so consistent a linguistic interest as here. The varieties of speech set off each other, and are more sharply differentiated than elsewhere: style is a garment indeed, and each character dresses in his own fashion. The play, like Ly-ly's, largely depends on the control of rhythm, the contrasts in vocabulary, and the use of 'figures': it is an artificial consort of voices. (pp. 212-13)

The characters are defined by their individual accent and idiom: Jacquenetta's set of catchphrases . . . are inherited from Lyly's country wenches, and Moth is descended from his pert pages; the tone and imagery of their speech constitutes the characters. The contrast of different characters in terms of their different idiom, played off or chiming in together, constitutes the 'form' of the comedy. In tragedy a recurrent image binds the play together and is the embodiment of the moral, the 'objective correlative' to use Mr. Eliot's perhaps too famous phrase; in comedy the consort of voices is, in itself, the definition of those characters, and the sum of these definitions makes up the play. (pp. 214-15)

Love's Labour's Lost is a play about courtship which turns out to be a play about love, and an attack on fine speech which is consistently full of fine speeches. Even the attack on learning becomes rather paradoxical when the unusually full use of the *trivium* is considered. It is the most artificial of all Shake-speare's comedies and comes nearer than any other to con-taining a manifesto against artifice. The acting is exceptionally formal, with no less than four pairs of lovers—the usual al-lowance was two—and the symmetry of the discovery scene is heightened in the grouping of the dances and shows that fill up the fifth act. Masque and antimasque—the Russians and the Nine Worthies—underline the artifice and give a dramatic perspective to the last scene with its rapid alternations of farce, gravity, lyric pleading and for conclusion the simple, traditional song, old and plain; a medieval debate between Winter and Spring, the Owl and the Cuckoo, which dissolves all the fore-going wit into the simplest country humour, such as even Antony Dull could appreciate. Spring in the meadows and Christmas in the hall are in such a different world from anything else in the play that they carry the listener forward to the more complex world and the richer harmonies of *As You Like It*.

Love's Labour's Lost is unsurpassed for sheer virtuosity of language; language which is always designed for the stage, for finely-turned dramatic speaking. Changing of pace, 'interchangeable variety' of couplet, stanza, blank verse, and prose, the consort of voices is conducted with a masterful ease amounting almost to showmanship. The manage in which an expert horseman displayed his skill, in fencing matches or in hazards of Real Tennis might to its contemporaries best reflect its intricacies. Yet it is completely different from the genuine court poetry of the time by reason of that extra-heightening, that element of make-up which the stage requires. Shakespeare in this play, at least, never wanted Arte. He improved Nature just enough to flatter her. (pp. 217-18)

> M[uriel] C. Bradbrook, ''Comical—Fantastic: 'Love's Labour's Lost', 'As You Like It', 'Twelfth Night','' in her Shakespeare and Elizabethan Poetry: A Study of His Earlier Work in Relation to the Poetry of the Time, *Chatto and Windus, 1951, pp. 212-33.*

BOBBYANN ROESEN (essay date 1953)

[*In her influential essay on* Love's Labour's Lost, *Roesen examines the dichotomy between the illusory, artificial setting of Navarre's Academe and the real, outside world of the Princess, concluding that the play presents a movement from illusion to reality. According to Roesen, the failure of such ''plays within the play'' as the Masque of the Muscovites and the Masque of the Nine Worthies, which she says are themselves illusory and artificial, illustrates this gradual dominance of the real on a dramatic level—a development she also sees in the humiliation of Armado, the most artificial of the play's characters, in the second of the staged masques. Roesen also states that the imposition of reality in Navarre's park comes from the outside world and is felt most strongly when ''Death itself actually enters the park, for the first time, in the person of Marcade''—an interpretation suggested earlier by August Wilhelm Schlegel (1808) and discussed more fully by Philip Parsons (1963). It is the reality of Death, Roesen concludes, that these men must accept if they are to win the fruits of love's labour. Although the conflict between illusion and reality in the play was noted as early as the nineteenth century by Hermann Ulrici (1839), Roesen's development of this idea established an important interpretive trend in later criticism and is evident in the essays by E.M.W. Tillyard (1962), Ronald Berman (1964), Ralph Berry (1969), James L. Calderwood (1971), Terence Hawkes (1973), and Louis Adrian Montrose (1977). The argument that the play champions the real over the artificial has been challenged by William C. Carroll (1976).*]

Walter Pater found *Love's Labour's Lost* particularly charming in its changing ''series of pictorial groups, in which the same figures reappear, in different combinations but on the same background,'' a composition, for him, like that of some ancient tapestry, studied, and not a little fantastic [see excerpt above, 1885]. The grouping of the characters into scenes would appear, however, to have been dictated by a purpose far more serious than the mere creation of such patterns; it is one of the ways in which Shakespeare maintains the balance of the play world between the artificial and the real, and indicates the final outcome of the comedy.

There are, of course, huge differences in the reality of the people who walk and speak together within the limits of the royal park. From the artificial and virtually indistinguishable

Act V. Scene ii. King, Princess, Lords, and Ladies. By G. F. Sargent. The Department of Rare Books and Special Collections, The University of Michigan Library.

figures of Dumain and Longaville, never really more than fashionable voices, the scale of reality rises gradually towards Berowne, in whom the marriage of a certain remote and fantastic quality with the delightful realism which first recognized the flaws in the Academe reflects the comedy as a whole, and reaches its apogee in the utter substantiality and prosaic charm of Constable Dull, who could never in any sense be accused of retreating into unreality, or affecting an elegant pose. Again and again, characters from different levels along this scale are grouped into scenes in a manner that helps to maintain the delicate balance of the play world; thus, in the first scene, with the incredible idea of the Academe and the sophisticated dialogue of Berowne and Longaville, Costard and the bewildered Dull are employed in much the same way that the mocking voice of the cuckoo is in the glowing spring landscape of the closing song, to keep the play in touch with a more familiar and real world, as well as to indicate the ultimate victory of reality over artifice and illusion.

As the first act ends, this theme is repeated again, and the inevitability of future events made even more clear with the abandonment of the edicts of the Academe by the very individual who was responsible for the deliverance of Costard into the righteous hands of Dull, the intense and serious Armado. The grave figure of the Spanish traveller is one of the most interesting and in a sense enigmatic to appear in *Love's Labour's Lost,* and his sudden love for Jaquenetta certainly the strangest of the five romances which develop within the park. Like Berowne, Armado is a very real person who is playing a part, but in his case it is far more difficult to separate the actor from the man underneath, and the pose itself is more complex than the fashionable role of Berowne. Even in his soliloquies, Armado seems to be acting to some invisible audience, and it is only in one moment at the end of the play that we are granted a glimpse of the man without the mask.

Romantic and proud, intensely imaginative, he has retreated into illusion much further than has Berowne, creating a world of his own within the world of the park, a world peopled with the heroes of the past, Samson and Hercules, Hector and the knights of Spain. Somehow, it is among these long-dead heroes that Armado really exists, rather than among the people of the play itself, and his bizarre language, so strange and artificial when placed beside the homely speech of Costard, was created for that remote, imaginative environment and possesses there a peculiar beauty and aptness of its own. . . . The illusion in which the real character of Armado lives has its own beauty and charm, but as the play progresses it becomes evident that this illusion is not strong enough to withstand the pressure of reality and must in the end be destroyed.

With the coming into the King's park of the Princess of France and her companions a new stage in the development of *Love's Labour's Lost* has been reached, and a theme we have not heard before begins slowly to rise in the musical structure of the play. Before the arrival of the ladies, it has been made clear that the Academe must fail, and it is no surprise when in the opening scene of the second act we find each of the four friends stealing back alone after the initial meeting to learn the name of his love from the obliging Boyet. As life itself breaks swiftly through the artificial scholarship of the court, the vitality of the play rises to an amazing height; the Academe is kept constantly before us, the reasons for its failure elaborated and made more plain, but at the same time, while the world of the royal park becomes more and more delightful, while masque and pageantry, sensuous beauty and laughter flower within the walls, it becomes slowly obvious that more than the Academe will be destroyed by the entrance of the ladies. Not only its scholarship, but the entire world of the play, the balance of artifice and reality of which it was formed, must also be demolished by forces from without the walls.

The Princess and her little retinue represent the first penetration of the park by the normal world beyond, a world composed of different and colder elements than the fairy-tale environment within. Through them, in some sense, the voice of Reality speaks, and although they seem to fit perfectly into the landscape of the park, indulge in highly formal, elaborate skirmishes of wit with each other and with the men, they are somehow detached from this world of illusion and artificiality in a way that none of its original inhabitants are. The contrived and fashionable poses which they adopt are in a sense less serious, more playful than those of the other characters, and they are conscious all the time, as even Berowne is not, that these attitudes are merely poses, and that Reality is something quite different. With them into the park they bring past time and a disturbing reminder of the world outside, and from them come the first objective criticisms which pass beyond the scheme of the Academe to attack the men who have formed it. Maria, remembering Longaville as she saw him once before in Normandy, criticizes in her first speech the unreality with which

the four friends have surrounded themselves, and points out for the first time in the play the danger of attitudes which develop without regard for the feelings of others, of wit that exercises itself thoughtlessly upon all.

In the wit of the ladies themselves, it is a certain edge of reality, an uncompromising logic, which cuts through the pleasant webs of artifice, the courtly jests and elaborations in the humor of the men, and emerges victorious with an unfailing regularity. Unlike the women, the King and his companions play, not with facts themselves, but with words, with nice phrases and antithetical statements, and when their embroidered language itself has been attacked, their courteous offers disdained as mere euphemisms, they can only retire discomfited. Even Berowne is utterly defeated when he approaches Rosaline with his graceful conceits.

> Ber. Lady, I will commend you to mine own heart.
> Ros. Pray you, do my commendations;
>   I would be glad to see it.
> Ber. I would you heard it groan.
> Ros. Is the fool sick?
> Ber. Sick at the heart.
> Ros. Alack, let it blood.
> Ber. Would that do it good?
> Ros. My physic says ''ay.''
>
> [II. i. 180-88]

Witty as Berowne, as agile of mind, Rosaline attacks his conventional protestations with a wit based on realism, a ridicule springing from a consciousness of the absurdity of artifice. That Berowne could be expressing a real passion in these artificial terms never enters her mind; he is merely mocking her, and she defends herself in the most effective way she can.

Berowne is, however, like the King, Dumain, and Longaville, suddenly and genuinely in love. The Academe has been thoroughly demolished and now, in the fourth act, Shakespeare introduces, in the characters of Holofernes and Nathaniel, reminders of what such a scheme might have led to, examples of the sterility of learning that is unrelated to life. (pp. 414-16)

Unlike Dull, the schoolmaster and the curate are in some sense mere types, elements of a satire, but Shakespeare is after all not writing a treatise, and even though their absurdity is emphasized, the two have a certain charm of their own, and their interminable quibblings a faint and grotesque beauty. On a lower, less refined level, they reflect the love of words themselves that is visible throughout the play, reveling, not like Armado in the romance and wonder of the past, but in Latin verbs and bits of forgotten erudition, spare and abstract. As Moth says, ''They have been at a great feast of languages and stol'n the scraps'' [V. i. 36-7], and in their conversation the wisdom of ages past appears in a strangely mutilated form, the life drained from it, curiously haphazard and remote.

When in the third scene of Act Four, Berowne appears alone on the stage, we move from the two pedants to a higher level of reality, but one in which artifice is still present. Berowne's love for Rosaline is becoming increasingly intense, and although he seems at first only to be adopting another pose, that of melancholy lover, he is slowly becoming, as the play progresses, a more convincing and attractive figure, and his love more real.

> By heaven, I do love; and it hath taught me to
> rhyme and to be melancholy; and here is part

of my rhyme, and here my melancholy. Well,
she hath one of my sonnets already; the clown
bore it, the fool sent it, and the lady hath it;
sweet clown, sweeter fool, sweetest lady.

[IV. iii. 12-17]

Often, beneath ornament and convention the Elizabethans disguised genuine emotion. (p. 417)

The episode which follows Berowne's introductory soliloquy is, of course, one of the finest in the entire play. It is the first of three scenes in *Love's Labour's Lost* which possess the quality of a play within the play, formal in construction, somehow contrived, always beautifully handled. Here, above the whole scene, Berowne acts as spectator and as Chorus, establishing the play atmosphere in his various asides, crying out upon the entrance of Longaville, "Why, he comes in like a perjure, wearing papers" [IV. iii. 46], or in a more general affirmation,

"All hid, all hid"—an old infant play,
Like a demigod here sit I in the sky,
And wretched fools' secrets heedfully o'er-eye.

[IV. iii. 76-8]

Throughout *Love's Labour's Lost,* the play is a symbol of illusion, of unreality, as it is in *A Midsummer Night's Dream,* and here it is employed to render the artificiality, the convenient but obvious device of having each of the four lovers appear alone upon the stage, read aloud the poem addressed to his lady, and step aside for the advance of the next one, not only acceptable, but completely delightful. In this play environment, a level of unreality beyond that of the comedy as a whole, the multiple discoveries are perfectly convincing, and the songs and sonnets read by the lovers the charming testimonies of a passion that is not to be questioned.

Through the comments of the spectator, Berowne, the scene is still, however, kept in touch with reality. From his wonderful, rocketing line upon the entrance of the King, "Shot, by heaven!" [IV. iii. 22] to the moment when he steps from his concealment in all the splendor of outraged virtue, Berowne's role is again analogous to that of the cuckoo in the closing song . . . , maintaining the balance of the play. When he actually appears among his shamefaced friends to chide them for this "scene of fool'ry," the play within the play ends, as the spectator becomes actor, and we return, with his beautifully sanctimonious sermon, to the more usual level of reality.

The sheer delight of the scene rises now towards its peak as, only a few lines after the close of the play scene, another and even more effective climax is built up. Costard appears with Berowne's own sonnet written to Rosaline, and suddenly the play rises into magnificence. "Guilty, my lord, guilty. I confess, I confess" [IV. iii. 201]. Berowne has become more real and brilliant than ever before, and at the same time, his speech attains a power and a radiance new in the comedy, an utterance still fastidious, still choice, but less self-conscious, as he sums up for Navarre, Dumain, and Longaville all that Shakespeare has been saying long before, in the Costard scene, in the fall from grace of Don Armado.

Sweet lords, sweet lovers, O let us embrace!
As true we are as flesh and blood can be.
The sea will ebb and flow, heaven show his face;
Young blood doth not obey an old decree.
We cannot cross the cause why we were born,
Therefore of all hands must be we forsworn.

[IV. iii. 210-15]

Following these lines, there is a deliberate slackening of intensity, and the scene descends for a moment into a completely artificial duel of wits among the King, Berowne, and Longaville, on a somewhat hackneyed conceit. Berowne's toying with the various meanings of dark and light is as artificial and contrived as anything we have heard from him earlier in the play, but from these lines the scene suddenly rises to its final climax in that speech justifying the breaking of the vows, which is without doubt the most beautiful in the entire play. "Have at you then, affection's men-at-arms" [IV. iii. 286]. Finally and completely, the Academe has crumbled, and it is Berowne, as is perfectly proper, who sums up all that the play has been saying up to this point in his exquisite peroration upon earthly love. (pp. 417-18)

The Academe defeated by life itself on all levels of the park, one might expect that *Love's Labour's Lost* would move now, as *Much Ado About Nothing* does in its final act, into an untroubled close, a romantic ending like that of the Beatrice-Benedick plot. As we have in some sense been told by the title, and by the comments of the ladies, such an ending is, in this case, impossible. From the Academe theme the play turns now to the destruction of the half-real world within the royal park, a destruction which, in the actual moment in which it is accomplished, is unexpected and shocking, and yet has been prepared for and justified by previous events within the comedy. As we enter the Fifth Act, shadows begin to fall across the play world. Life within the park, its brilliance and laughter, mounts higher and higher, yet it is the winter stanzas of the closing song that this act suggests, and a new darkness, a strange intensity forces the harmony of the play into unforeseen resolutions. Vanished now are the untroubled meadows of spring, and the landscape acquires a realism that is somehow a little harsh. (p. 419)

With Act Five, the thought of Death enters the park. The play opened, of course, under the shadow of death, the great motivation of the Academe, but after that opening speech of Navarre's, it vanished altogether, never appearing again even in the imagery of the play until the entrance of the ladies. Significantly, it is they, the intruders from the outside world of reality, who first, in Act Three, bring death into the park itself. In this act, the Princess kills a deer, but in the lines in which the hunt is spoken of, those of Holofernes and the Princess herself, the animal's death is carefully robbed of any disturbing reality. (pp. 419-20)

Not until Act Five does the death image become real and disturbing, and even here, until the final entrance of Marcade, it is allowed to appear only in the imagery, or else in the recollection by some character of a time and a place beyond the scope of the play itself, the country of France where Katherine's sister died of her melancholy and longing, or that forgotten antiquity in which the bones of Hector were laid to rest. Appearing thus softened, kept in the background of the comedy, it is nevertheless a curiously troubling image, and as it rises slowly through the fabric of the play, the key of the entire final movement is altered. . . .

It is the tremendous reality of death which will destroy the illusory world of Navarre as thoroughly as the gentler forces of life destroyed the Academe and the artificial scheme it represented, earlier in the play. At the very beginning of the Fifth Act, it is made apparent why this must happen, why it is completely necessary for the world of the comedy, despite its beauty and grace, to be demolished. The Princess and her gentlewomen have been discussing the favors and the promises showered upon them by the King and his courtiers, laughing and mocking one another gently. Suddenly, the atmosphere of the entire scene is altered with a single, curious comment, a kind of overheard aside, made by Katherine, upon the real nature of Love. Rosaline turns to her, and as she remembers past time and a tragedy for which the god of Love was responsible then, the scene suddenly becomes filled with the presence of death.

> Ros.   You'll ne'er be friends with him: 'a kill'd your
>   sister.
> Kath.   He made her melancholy, sad, and heavy;
>   And so she died. Had she been light, like you,
>   Of such a merry, nimble, stirring spirit,
>   She might have been a grandam ere she died.
>   And so may you; for a light heart lives long.
>   [V. ii. 13-18]
>   (p. 420)

[The masque of the Muscovites] scene is, of course, the second of the plays within the play, less delightful than the one before it, but immensely significant, the part of audience and commentator played in this instance by Boyet. As usual, the men are completely defeated by the ladies, the delicate fabric of their wit and artifice destroyed by the realistic humour of their opponents. . . .

Even when the exposure is complete and the men have asked pardon from their loves, the women think only that they have defeated a mocking jest directed against them, not that they have prevented their lovers from expressing a genuine passion. For the first time, Berowne reaches utter simplicity and humbleness in his love; his declaration to Rosaline at the end of the masque scene is touching and deeply sincere, but for her, this passion is still unbelievable, a momentary affectation, and she continues to mock her lover and the sentiments he expresses. (p. 421)

The masque has failed, and Berowne's more direct attempt to announce to the ladies the purpose behind the performance and detect in them an answering passion has been turned away by the unbelieving Princess. At this point, Costard enters to announce that Holofernes and Nathaniel, Moth and Armado are at hand to present the pageant of the Nine Worthies, and the third and last of the plays within the play begins. As we enter this play scene, the vitality and force of the comedy reaches its apogee, but in its laughter there rings now a discordant note that we have not heard before. The actors themselves are, after all, no less sincere than Bottom and his troupe in *A Midsummer Night's Dream,* and they are a great deal more sensitive and easy to hurt. They are real people whose intentions are of the very best, their loyalty to their King unquestioned, and although their performance is unintentionally humorous, one would expect the audience to behave with something of the sympathy and forbearance exhibited by Duke Theseus and the Athenians. . . .

The players have only the Princess to appeal to in the storm of hilarity which assails them, and it is only she, realistic as she is, who understands that a play is an illusion, that it is to be taken as such and respected in some sense for itself, regardless of its quality. Like Theseus in *A Midsummer Night's Dream,* she realizes somehow that "the best in this kind are but shadows; and the worst are no worse, if imagination amend them" [*A Midsummer Night's Dream,* V. i. 211-12], and when she addresses the players she is wise and sensitive enough to do so not by their own names, which she has read on the playbill, but by the names of those whom they portray, thus helping them to sustain that illusion which is the very heart of a play.

In contrast to that of the Princess, the behaviour of the men is incredibly unattractive, particularly that of Berowne. It is difficult to believe that this is the same man who spoke so eloquently a short time ago about the soft and sensible feelings of love, and promised Rosaline to mend his ways. Costard manages to finish his part before the deluge, and Nathaniel, although unkindly treated, is not personally humiliated. Only with the appearance of Holofernes as Judas Maccabaeus and Armado as Hector is the full force of the ridicule released, and it is precisely with these two characters that the infliction of abuse must be most painful. Costard, after all, is a mere fool; he takes part in the baiting of the others with no compunction at all, and Nathaniel throughout the comedy has been little more than a foil for Holofernes, but the village pedagogue is a more sensitive soul, and not at all unsympathetic.

Holofernes has his own reality, his own sense of the apt and the beautiful which, though perverse, is meaningful enough for him, and it is exceedingly painful to see him stand here on the smooth grass of the lawn, his whole subjective world under merciless attack, a storm of personal epithets exploding about him. (p. 422)

Of all the players, Armado is the one for whom we have perhaps the most sympathy. He is a member of the court itself, has had some reason to pride himself upon the King's favor, and has been good enough to arrange the pageant in the first place. The people represented in it are those who inhabit that strange world of his fancy, and one knows that his anguish is not alone for his personal humiliation, but for that of the long-dead hero he portrays, when he cries, "The sweet war-man is dead and rotten; sweet chucks, beat not the bones of the buried; when he breathed, he was a man" [V. ii. 670-72]. A little grotesque, as Armado's sentences always are, the line is nevertheless infinitely moving in its summoning up of great spaces of time, its ironic relation to the idea of immortality through fame expressed in the opening speech of the comedy. Not since the reference to Katherine's sister have we had such a powerful and disturbing image of death brought before us, death real and inescapable although still related to a world and a time beyond the play itself.

In the remaining moments of the play scene, the hilarity rises to its climax, a climax becoming increasingly harsh. During the altercation between Costard and Armado which results from Berowne's ingenious but unattractive trick, images of death begin to hammer through the fabric of the play. The painfulness of the realism grows as Armado, poor, but immensely proud, is finally shamed and humbled before all the other characters. For the first time in the play, the mask falls from Armado's face, and the man beneath it is revealed, his romanticism, his touching personal pride, the agony for him of the confession that in his poverty he wears no shirt beneath his doublet. Still acting, he tries feebly to pass off this lack as some mysterious and romantic penance, but the other characters know the truth; Armado knows they do, and the knowledge is intensely humiliating. The illusion of the role he has played throughout *Love's Labour's Lost* is destroyed for others as well as for himself, and he stands miserably among the jeers of Dumain and Boyet while complete reality breaks over him, and the little personal world which he has built up around himself so carefully shatters at his feet.

The other people in the play are so concerned with Armado's predicament that no one notices that someone, in a sense Something has joined them. His entrance unremarked by any of the other characters, materializing silently from those shadows which now lie deep along the landscape of the royal park, the Messenger has entered the play world.

> *Mar.*   I am sorry, madam, for the news I bring
>   Is heavy in my tongue. The King your
>   father—
> *Prin.*   Dead, for my life!
> *Mar.*   Even so; my tale is told.
>   [V. ii. 18-20]

There is perhaps nothing like this moment in the whole range of Elizabethan drama. In the space of four lines the entire world of the play, its delicate balance of reality and illusion, all the hilarity and overwhelming life of its last scene has been swept away and destroyed, as Death itself actually enters the park, for the first time, in the person of Marcade. (pp. 423-24)

As vows had begun the play, so vows end it. The King is assigned as his symbol of reality a "forlorn and naked hermitage" [V. ii. 795] without the walls of the royal park, in the real world itself, in which he must try for a twelvemonth if this love conceived in the sunlit landscape of Navarre can persist in the colder light of actuality. (p. 424)

Berowne is condemned to haunt the hospitals and plague-houses of the world outside the park, to exercise his wit upon the "speechless sick," and try the power of his past role, the old artificiality that had no concern for the feelings of others, that humiliated Armado in the play scene, the careless mocks of the old world, upon the reality of the ailing and the dying. "A jest's prosperity lies in the ear / Of him that hears it, never in the tongue / Of him that makes it" [V. ii. 861-63]. It was this reality of actual living that Berowne was unconscious of when he led the unthinking merriment of the play scene just past. Yet, at the end of the year, love's labors will be won for Berowne, and he will receive Rosaline's love, not in the half real world of the park, but in the actuality outside its walls. Thus the play which began with a paradox, that of the Academe, closes with one as well. Only through the acceptance of the reality of Death are life and love in their fullest sense made possible for the people of the play.

The world of the play past has now become vague and unreal, and it is not distressing that Berowne, in a little speech that is really a kind of epilogue, should refer to all the action before the entrance of Marcade, the people who took part in that action and the kingdom they inhabited and in a sense created, as having been only the elements of a play. It is a play outside which the characters now stand, bewildered, a little lost in the sudden glare of actuality, looking back upon that world of mingled artifice and reality a trifle wistfully before they separate in the vaster realm beyond the royal park. Through *Love's Labour's Lost*, the play has been a symbol of illusion, of delightful unreality, the masque of the Muscovites, or the pageant of the Nine Worthies, and now it becomes apparent that there was a further level of illusion above that of the plays within the play. The world of that illusion has enchanted us; it has been possessed of a haunting beauty, the clear loveliness of those landscapes in the closing song, but Shakespeare insists that it cannot take the place of reality itself, and should not be made to. Always, beyond the charming, frost-etched countryside of the pastoral winter, like the background of some Flemish Book of Hours, lies the reality of the greasy kitchen-maid and

her pot, a reality which must sooner or later break through and destroy the charm of the artificial and the illusory. (p. 425)

> Bobbyann Roesen, "'Love's Labour's Lost'," in *Shakespeare Quarterly*, Vol. IV, No. 4, October, 1953, pp. 411-26.

C. L. BARBER   (essay date 1959)

[*An American scholar, Barber is one of the most important contemporary critics of Shakespearean comedy. In his influential study,* Shakespeare's Festive Comedy (1959), *Barber examines the parallels between Elizabethan holiday celebrations and Shakespeare's comedies. In both festival customs and comic plays Barber identifies a saturnalian pattern which, as he explains in his introduction, involves "a basic movement which can be summarized in the formula, through release to clarification." Barber defines release as a revelry, a mirthful liberation, "an accession of wanton vitality" over the restraint imposed by everyday life; the clarification that follows he characterizes as a "heightened awareness of the relation between man and 'nature',," which in comedy becomes a humor that "puts holiday in perspective with life as a whole." Barber's approach is termed "anthropological" because his methodology involves the search for primordial ritual and ceremony in all works of art. This is also indicative of a growing critical trend in the 1960s, as demonstrated in the works by such critics as Francis Fergusson and Northrop Frye. In his discussion of* Love's Labour's Lost, *Barber says that the play "is all too obviously designed to provide a resistance which can be swept away by festivity." Games—wooing games and word games— provide the festive release in this play, he claims, and they show the effervescence of folly in the presence of restraint. That the play does not conclude with marriages Barber finds appropriate and attributes to the failure of the male characters to recognize that "love is not wooing games or talk." The final songs, he concludes, return the festivity to the simplicity of daily life and, in essence, take the place of the traditional wedding ritual in returning the characters to a sense of community and nature.*]

The story in *Love's Labour's Lost* is all too obviously designed to provide a resistance which can be triumphantly swept away by festivity. The vow to study and to see no woman is no sooner made than it is mocked. The French Princess is coming; the courteous king acknowledges that "She must lie here of mere necessity" [I. i. 148]. . . . We know how the conflict will come out before it starts. But story interest is not the point: Shakespeare is presenting a series of wooing games, not a story. Fours and eights are treated as in ballet, the action consisting not so much in what individuals do as in what the group does, its patterned movement. Everything is done in turn: the lords are described in turn before they come on; each comes back in turn to ask a lady's name; each pair in turn exchanges banter. The dancing continues this sort of action; the four lords and four ladies make up what amounts to a set in English country dancing. We think of dancing in sets as necessarily boisterous; but Elizabethan dancing could express all sorts of moods, as one can realize from such a dance as Hunsdon House, at once spirited and stately. The evolutions in *Love's Labour's Lost* express the Elizabethan feeling for the harmony of a group acting in ceremonious consort, a sense of decorum expressed in areas as diverse as official pageantry, madrigal and motet singing, or cosmological speculation about the order of the universe. (pp. 88-9)

A crucial scene, Act IV, Scene iii, dramatizes the folly of release taking over from the folly of resistance. Each lord enters in turn, reads the sonnet love has forced him to compose, and then hides to overhear and mock the next corner. As the last one comes in, Berowne describes their antics as a game of hide and seek:

> All hid, all hid—an old infant play.
> Like a demigod here sit I in the sky
> And wretched fools' secrets heedfully o'er-eye.
> More sacks to the mill. O heavens, I have my wish!
> Dumain transform'd! Four woodcocks in a dish!
>
> [IV. iii. 76-80]

Having wound them into their hiding places one-by-one, Shakespeare unwinds them one-by-one as each in turn rebukes the others. . . . The technique of discovery in this fine scene recalls the *sotties* presented by the French fool societies on their holidays, where the outer garments of various types of dignified pretension were plucked off to reveal parti-colored cloaks and long-eared caps beneath. The similarity need not be from literary influence but from a common genesis in games and dances and in the conception that natural impulse, reigning on festive occasions, brings out folly. Berowne summarizes it all with "O, what a scene of fool'ry I have seen!" [IV. iii. 161]. (pp. 89-90)

The final joke is that in the end "Love" does not arrive, despite the lords' preparations for a triumphal welcome. That the play should end without the usual marriages is exactly right, in view of what it is that is released by its festivities. Of course what the lords give way to is, in a general sense, the impulse to love; but the particular form that it takes for them is a particular sort of folly—what one could call the folly of amorous masquerade, whether in clothes, gestures, or words. It is the folly of acting love and talking love, without being in love. For the festivity releases, not the delights of love, but the delights of expression which the prospect of love engenders—though those involved are not clear about the distinction until it is forced on them; the clarification achieved by release is this recognition that love is not wooing games or love talk. And yet these sports are not written off or ruled out; on the contrary the play offers their delights for our enjoyment, while humorously putting them in their place. (p. 93)

If all we got were sports that fail to come off, the play would indeed be nothing but labor lost. What saves it from anticlimax is that the most important games in which the elation of the moment finds expression are games with words, and the wordplay does for the most part work, conveying an experience of festive liberty. It is all conducted with zest and with constant exclamations about how well the game with words is going. Wordplay is compared to all sorts of other sports, tilting, dueling—or tennis: "Well bandied both! a set of wit well played" [V. ii. 29]. (p. 95)

The aristocratic pastimes with language are set against the fantastic elaborations of the braggart and the schoolmaster, Armado puffing up versions of Euphuistic tautology and periphrasis, Holofernes complacently showing off his inkhorn terms, rhetorical and grammatical terminology, even declensions and alternate spellings. To play up to these fantasts, there are Moth, a quick wit, and Costard, a slow but strong one. And there is Sir Nathaniel, the gull curate, who eagerly writes down in his table-book the schoolmaster's redundancies. Dull and Jaquenetta, by usually keeping silent, prove the rule of Babel. But even Dull has a riddle in his head which he tries out on the schoolmaster. The commoners normally speak prose, the lords and ladies verse; most of the prose is as artificial in its way as the rhymed, end-stopped verses. The effect is that each social level and type is making sport with words in an appropriate

way, just as the lords' infatuation with the ladies is paralleled by Costard's and then Armado's attentions to Jaquenetta. "Away," says the schoolmaster, as he invites the curate to dinner, "the gentles are at their game, and we will to our recreation" [IV. ii. 165-66]. And when they come from dinner, still babbling, Moth observes aside to Costard that "They have been at a great feast of languages and stol'n the scraps" [V. i. 36-7].

This comedy is often described as a satire on various kinds of overelaborate language. It is certainly true that the exhibition of different sorts of far-fetched verbal play becomes almost an end in itself. Armado is introduced as a buffoon of new fashions and "fire-new words." He and the schoolmaster do make ridiculous two main Elizabethan vices of style. But each carries his vein so fantastically far that it commands a kind of gasping admiration—instead of being shown up, they turn the tables and show off, converting affectation and pedantry into ingenious games. "Be it as the style shall give us cause to climb in the merriness," says Berowne in anticipation of Armado's letter [I. i. 199-200]. For a modern reader, the game with high or learned words is sometimes tedious, because we have not ourselves tried the verbal exercises on which the gymnastic exhibition is based. Even the princess and her ladies in waiting, when they talk in terms of copy-book letters, seem just freshly out of school:

> *Rosaline.* O, he hath drawn my picture in his letter! . . .
> *Princess.* Beauteous as ink—a good conclusion.
> *Katherine.* Fair as a text B in a copy-book.
> *Rosaline.* Ware pencils, ho! Let me not die your debtor,
> My red dominical, my golden letter.
>
> [V. ii. 38-44]

This kind of thing does weigh down parts of the play; it is dated by catering to a contemporary rage, a failure rare in Shakespeare's works, and one that suggests that he was writing for a special audience.

But the more one reads the play, the more one is caught up by the extraordinary excitement it expresses about what language can do—the excitement of the historical moment when English, in the hands of its greatest master, suddenly could do anything. Zest in the power of words comes out particularly clearly in the clown's part, as the chief motifs so often do in Shakespeare. As Armado gives Costard a letter to carry to Jaquenetta, he gives him a small tip with big words: "There is remuneration; for the best ward of mine honor is rewarding my dependents" [III. i. 131-33]. When he has gone out, Costard opens his palm:

> Now I will look to his remuneration. Remuneration—O, that's the Latin word for three farthings. Three farthings—remuneration. 'What's the price of this inkle?' 'One penny.' 'No, I'll give you a remuneration!' Why, it carries it! Remuneration. Why, it is a fairer name than French crown. I will never buy and sell out of this word.
>
> [III. i. 136-42]

O brave new world, that has *remuneration* in it! . . . By getting so literal a valuation of the words, Costard both imitates and burlesques the way his superiors value language. (pp. 95-8)

In a world of words, the wine is wit. Festivity in social life always enjoys, without effort, something physical from the world outside that is favorable to life, whether it be food and drink, or the warmth of the fields when they breathe sweet. Exhilaration comes when the world proves ready and willing, reaching out a hand, passing a brimming bowl; festivity signals the realization that we *belong* in the universe. Now in wit, it is language that gives us this something for nothing; unsuspected relations between words prove to be ready to hand to make a meaning that serves us. All of the comedies of Shakespeare, of course, depend on wit to convey the exhilaration of festivity. But *Love's Labour's Lost,* where the word *wit* is used more often than in any of the other plays, is particularly dependent on wit and particularly conscious in the way it uses and talks about it. So it will be useful to consider general functions of wit as they appear in this comedy.

When Moth speaks of 'a great feast of languages,'' Costard continues the figure with ''I marvel thy master hath not eaten thee for a word; for thou art not so long by the head as honorificabilitudinitatibus; thou art easier swallowed than a flapdragon'' [V. i. 39-42].

This is excellent fooling, and sense, too. For the people in *Love's Labour's Lost* get a lift out of fire-new words equivalent to what a tavern-mate would get from swallowing a ''flapdragon''—a raisin floating in flaming brandy. Eating words is apt because the *physical* attributes of words are used by wit: a witticism capitalizes on ''external associations,'' that is to say, it develops a meaning by connecting words through relations or likenesses not noted or used in the situation until found. The ''physical,'' for our purpose here, is whatever had not been noticed, had not been given meaning, until wit caught hold of it and made it signify. The exploitation of physical features of language is most obvious where the wit is forced, where what is found does not really do very well after all. Little or nothing is really found when Jaquenetta mispronounces Parson as ''Person,'' and Holofernes tries to make an innuendo by wrenching: ''Master Person, quasi pers-one. And if one should be pierc'd, which is the one?'' [IV. ii. 83-4]. By contrast, consider Berowne's zooming finale in the speech justifying oath breaking, where successive lines seem to explode meaning already present in what went just before:

> Let us once lose our oaths to find ourselves,
> Or else we lose ourselves to keep our oaths.
> [IV. iii. 358-59]

To appropriate physical relations of sound and position in language, so that it seems that language makes your meaning for you, as indeed it partly does, gives an extraordinary exhilaration, far more intense than one would expect—until one considers how much of what we are is what we can find words for. When wit flows happily, it is as though the resistance of the objective world had suddenly given way. One keeps taking words from ''outside,'' from the world of other systems or orders, and making them one's own, making them serve one's meaning as they form in one's mouth.

In repartee, each keeps jumping the other's words to take them away and make them his own, finding a meaning in them which was not intended. So elusive yet crucial is this subject that it will be worth while to quote a passage of wit where much that is involved in repartee is almost laboriously exhibited. As constantly happens in this play, the nature of wit is talked about in the process of being witty, here by hunting and sexual metaphors:

> *Boyet.* My lady goes to kill horns; but if thou marry,
> Hang me by the neck if horns that year miscarry.
> Finely put on!
> *Rosaline.* Well then, I am the shooter.
> *Boyet.*   And who is your deer?
> *Rosaline.* If we choose by the horns, yourself. Come not near.
> Finely put on indeed!
> *Maria.* You still wrangle with her, Boyet, and she
>   strikes at the brow.
> *Boyet.* But she herself is hit lower. Have I hit her
>   now?
> *Rosaline.* Shall I come upon thee with an old saying,
> that was a man when King Pippen of France was a little
> boy, as touching the hit it?
> *Boyet.* So I may answer thee with one as old, that
> was a woman when Queen Guinover of Britain was a
> little wench, as touching the hit it.
> *Rosaline.*   'Thou canst not hit it, hit it, hit it,
>   Thou canst not hit it, my good man.'
> *Boyet.*   'An I cannot, cannot, cannot,
>   An I cannot, another can.'
> *Costard.*   By my troth, most pleasant. How both did
>   fit it.
> [IV. i. 111-29]

To reapply or develop a given metaphor has the same effect as to reapply or develop the pattern of sound in a given set of words. Costard's comment describes the give and take of the repartee by the sexual metaphor—which the party go on to develop far more explicitly than even our freest manners would allow. The point they make is that to use one another's words in banter is like making love; each makes meaning out of what the other provides physically. They notice in *medias res* that there is the same sort of sequence of taking advantage and acquiescing: the process of taking liberties with each other's words goes with a kind of verbal hiding and showing. (pp. 99-101)

But though one cannot blink the fact that the wit is often a will-o'-the-wisp, the play *uses* its witty extravagance, moves through it to clarification about what one sort of wit is and where it fits in human experience. There are a number of descriptions of the process of being witty which locate such release as an event in the whole sensibility. These usually go with talk about brightening eyes: typically in this play a lover's eyes catch fire just before he bursts into words. There is a remarkable description of the King's first response to the Princess which defines precisely a gathering up of the faculties for perception and expression:

> *Boyet.* If my observation (which very seldom lies),
> By the heart's still rhetoric, disclosed with eyes,
> Deceive me not now, Navarre is infected.
> *Princess.* With what?
> *Boyet.* With that which we lovers entitle 'affected.'
> [II. i. 228-33]

Notice that Boyet does not answer simply ''with love.'' Shakespeare is out to define a more limited thing, a galvanizing of sensibility which may or may not be love; and so Boyet goes round about to set up a special term, ''affected.'' He goes on to describe his observation of ''the heart's still rhetoric'':

> Why, all his behaviours did make their retire
> To the court of his eye, peeping through desire. . . .
> His tongue, all impatient to speak and not see,
> Did stumble with haste in his eyesight to be;

All senses to that sense did make their repair,
To feel only looking on fairest of fair.
Methought all his senses were lock'd in his eye,
As jewels in crystal for some prince to buy,
Who, tend'ring their own worth from where they were
    glass'd,
Did point you to buy them along as you pass'd.
                                        [II. i. 234-45]

This is extremely elaborate; but the dislocation of the language, for example in "to feel only looking" . . . , catches a special movement of feeling important for the whole play, a movement of awareness into the senses and toward expression. (pp. 103-04)

The lords' quality of youthful elation and absorption in their own responses is what lays them open to being fooled as they are by the ladies when they try to set about revelry whole-heartedly. The game they are playing, without quite knowing it, tries to make love happen by expressing it, to blow up a sort of forced-draft passion by capering volubility and wit. . . . The Princess and her ladies are not in any case the sort of nice wenches to be betrayed. The ladies believe, indeed, rather too little than too much. "They do it but in mocking merriment," says the Princess. "And mock for mock is only my intent" [V. ii. 139-40]. . . . The lords' trusting in speeches penn'd, with three-piled hyperboles, has been part and parcel of trusting in the masquerade way of making love, coming in a vizard, in a three-piled Russian habit. And these pastimes are not being dismissed for good, but put in their place: they are festive follies, relished as they show the power of life, but mocked as they run out ahead of the real, the everyday situation. The point, dramatically, is that the lords had hoped that festivity would "carry it," as Costard hoped Armado's fancy word "remuneration" would carry it. (pp. 107-08)

Shakespeare can do without marriages at the end [of Love's Labour's Lost], and still end affirmatively, because he is dramatizing an occasion in a community, not just private lives. News of the French King's death breaks off the wooing game. In deferring the question of marriage, the princess says frankly but graciously that what has passed has been only "courtship, pleasant jest, and courtesy . . . bombast . . . and lining to the time . . . a merriment" [V. ii. 780-84]. . . . The ladies' bizarre commands, by insisting that the men confront other types of experience, invite them to try separating their affections from the occasion to see whether or not their feelings are more than courtly sports. In the elation of the festive moment, the game of witty wooing seemed to be love: now comes clarification.

To draw the line between a pastime and a play is another way of marking limits. Berowne's final ironic joke shows how conscious Shakespeare was that he had made a play out of social pastimes, and one which differed from regular drama.

        Our wooing doth not end like an old play:
        Jack hath not Jill. These ladies' courtesy
        Might well have made our sport a comedy.
                                        [V. ii. 874-76]

Sport would have become drama if something had happened. Berowne almost says what Will Fool said of Nashe's pageant [Summer's Last Will and Testament]: "'tis not a play neither, but a show." Love's Labour's Lost is not a show, because the sports in it are used, dramatically, by people in a kind of history; it is comedy, precisely because Berowne can stand outside the sport and ruefully lament that it is only sport. (pp. 111-13)

The pageant and songs of summer and winter are the finale Shakespeare used instead of a wedding dance or masque; and they are exactly right, not an afterthought but a last, and full, expression of the controlling feeling for community and season. The songs evoke pleasures of the most traditional sort, at the opposite pole from facile improvisations. Nobody improvised the outgoing to the fields in spring or the coming together around the fire in winter. After fabulous volubility, we are looking and listening only; after conceits and polysyllables, we are told a series of simple facts in simple words. . . . (p. 113)

The magic of "When daisies pied and violets blue" and of "When icicles hang by the wall" [V. ii. 894, 912] is partly that they seem to be merely lists, and each thing seems to be dwelt on simply for itself; and yet each song says, in a marvelously economical way, where people are in the cycle of the year, the people of farm, manor or village who live entirely in the turning seasons. . . . Of course these songs are not simply of the world they describe, not folk songs; they are art songs, consciously pastoral, sophisticated enjoyment of simplicity. Their elegance and humor convey pleasure in life's being reduced to so few elements and yet being so delightful. Each centers on vitality, and moves from nature to man. The spring song goes from lady smocks to the maidens' summer smocks, both showing white against the green of the season, from turtle cocks who "tread" to implications about people. The old joke about the cuckoo is made so delightful because its meaning as a "word," as a call to the woods, is assumed completely as a matter of course. In the winter song, the center of vitality is the fire. . . . The fire is enjoyed "nightly," after the day's encounter with the cold. Gathered together "When roasted crabs hiss in the bowl," it is merry to hear the owl outside in the cold—his "Tu-whit, tu-who" [V. ii. 925, 927] come to mean this moment. Even the kitchen wench, greasy Joan, keeling the pot to keep it from boiling over, is one of us, a figure of affection. The songs evoke the daily enjoyments and the daily community out of which special festive occasions were shaped up. And so they provide for the conclusion of the comedy what marriage usually provides: an expression of the going-on power of life. (pp. 117-18)

> C. L. Barber, "The Folly of Wit and Masquerade in
> 'Love's Labour's Lost'," in his Shakespeare's Fes-
> tive Comedy: A Study of Dramatic Form and Its
> Relation to Social Custom, Princeton University Press,
> 1959, pp. 87-118.

BERTRAND EVANS   (essay date 1960)

[In two studies of Shakespearean drama, Shakespeare's Comedies (1960) and Shakespeare's Tragic Practice (1979), Evans examines what he calls Shakespeare's use of "discrepant awarenesses." He claims that Shakespeare's dramatic technique makes extensive use of "gaps" between the different levels of awareness the characters and audience possess concerning the circumstances of the plot. In the following excerpt on Love's Labour's Lost, he notes that these "gaps" of perception are not so frequent here as in Shakespeare's other comedies; but Evans argues that the two scenes in which they are exploited—IV. iii. and V. ii.—represent the most important in the play.]

[In Love's Labour's Lost] Shakespeare tried exploitation of the comic potentialities in language and eccentric humanity. No later comedy relies so much on language as a source of laughter, or exhibits such a collection of human oddities as Armado, Sir Nathaniel, Holofernes, Dull, Costard, Jaquenetta, and Moth. Nor, for that matter, does a later play exhibit so many courtly wits: the King with his lords and the Princess with her ladies make eight, and Boyet, as sharp as any, nine. To the potentialities of language, wit, and eccentric character, add those of satiric allusion to contemporary affairs, and the main resources of fun in *Love's Labour's Lost* are accounted for. In the range of its comic devices, the play differs most from its predecessors.

Since these sources are the primary subjects of experiment, this comedy inevitably relies less for effect on exploitation of discrepant awareness. Such exploitation, in fact, is confined to two of the nine scenes, and—excepting some persons who are afflicted with some form of congenital unawareness—only four of the seventeen named characters ever occupy levels below ours. In terms of such statistics, no comedy, but only *Henry VI*, shows a lower proportion. But of greater import is the fact that the two scenes which *do* exploit discrepant awarenesses are the climactic portions of the play, are the most satisfying dramatically and comically, and, if one excepts the songs of Summer and Winter, are the most memorable artistic moments of *Love's Labour's Lost*.

The first of these scenes is particularly prophetic of Shakespeare's way in its elaboration of a stair-step structure of awarenesses, the first version of which was erected in *The Two Gentlemen of Verona* (III. i) when Thurio, the Duke, and Proteus stood on ascending levels—with ours above all. In the present scene, it is Biron who occupies the level next below ours. Entering 'with a paper in his hand' [IV. iii. s.d.], he tells us that he has broken his oath to the King by falling in love. The King enters 'with a paper', and Biron withdraws. The King reads a sonnet—and we, with Biron, perceive that he, too, has fallen. Next Longaville enters and reads a sonnet while we, Biron, and the King look on. Finally Dumain approaches and reads the lyric 'On a day—alack the day!— / Love, whose month is ever May' [IV. iii. 99-100], and we, with Biron, the King, and Longaville, perceive that he, too, is fallen and foresworn. The King and his three gentlemen make four steps of a stair, Dumain at the bottom, overpeering none, and Biron at the top, crowing above all:

> 'All hid, all hid;' an old infant play.
> Like a demigod here sit I in the sky,
> And wretched fools' secrets heedfully o'er-eye.
>   [IV. iii. 76-8]

Never one to abandon an exploitable situation while possibilities of its exploitation remain, Shakespeare next unbuilds the stair, step by step. First Longaville comes out of hiding to shame Dumain:

> You may look pale, but I should blush, I know,
> To be o'erheard and taken napping so.
>   [IV. iii. 127-28]

After him, in order, come the others. Throughout the process of unbuilding, the boldest effects are the flashes of irony which illuminate the gap between the speaker's ignorance and our knowledge. . . . The flashes grow ever more spectacular as each man descends; the flashiest of all comes last. (pp. 19-21)

The perfection of the jest, of course, is that we overpeer the topmost overpeerer. The scene uses five levels of awareness, from Dumain's upward to ours. The preparation of our advantage was begun in III. i, when Biron ordered Costard to deliver 'This seal'd-up counsel' into the white hands of Rosaline; but, indeed, preparation had begun even earlier, for Costard had previously been ordered to deliver Armado's letter

to Jaquenetta. When the Clown, mistaking, brings this letter to the Princess, it becomes apparent that Biron's sonnet must go wrong, too. In IV. ii it reaches Sir Nathaniel, who reads it aloud for Jaquenetta, and thereafter Holofernes orders wench and clown to 'deliver this paper into the royal hand of the King; it may concern much' [IV. ii. 141-42]. Characteristically, Shakespeare has placed this final instruction immediately before Biron's entrance at the start of the stair-stepped scene, so that it is impossible for us to forget, all the while the stairs are building up and then down again, that Jaquenetta and Costard, sonnet in hand, are running through the park seeking the King. But merely to assure our remembrance of so crucial a point was not enough for Shakespeare. To make assurance doubly sure that we will not forget and thus lose the advantage which is indispensable to the full force of the scene, he gives our awareness repeated sharp prods by means of Biron's repetition of the relevant facts—as far as he knows them—at the opening of the scene: 'Well, she hath one o'my sonnets already; the clown bore it, the fool sent it, and the lady hath it: sweet clown, sweeter fool, sweetest lady!' [IV. iii. 14-17]. Thereafter, each crowing word of Biron's on his lofty perch reminds us also of our advantage and exploits the space between his vantage-point and ours: 'Like a demigod here sit I in the sky, / And wretched fools' secrets heedfully o'er-eye.'

Though obviously contrived, Lyly-mannered in balance and movement, this scene is of enormous significance, for here Shakespeare worked out in detail a structure for the exploitation of discrepancies in awareness: with greater complexity but no essential changes, this structure was to become a central fixture in the comedies.

Similarly artificial in its balance and movement and also featuring a complex pattern of awarenesses is v. ii, the second climactic point of the play. Two episodes compose the heart of this scene, the first running through 100 lines . . . from the entrance of the King's party 'like Muscovites or Russians' to their departure; the second extending through 115 lines . . . from the second meeting of the ladies and their wooers up to the moment of Biron's perception that the gentlemen have twice been the ladies' dupes. The grace and charm of this portion of the scene are remarkable; the wit of the lines and the balanced precision of the physical action make it a treat for eye and ear. But it would hardly excel similar arrangements by Lyly if its effectiveness depended wholly on these qualities. What makes it superior is that more is going on than merely that which directly strikes the eye and the ear. 'There's no such sport', says the Princess to her ladies just before the entrance of the masqueraders, 'as sport by sport o'erthrown' [V. ii. 151]. As in the earlier stair-stepped scene, it is not the decorative effects but the maintenance of exploitable gaps between the awarenesses of the participants and between the participants' awarenesses and ours that makes the scene dramatic.

Here, as usually in the comedies, it is the ladies who hold the advantage; the gentlemen, supposing themselves overpeerers, are from the outset overpeered. Boyet betrays his own sex, revealing to the ladies that the King's men will come

> Like Muscovites or Russians, as I guess;
> Their purpose is to parle, to court, and dance.
> And every one his love-feat will advance
> Unto his several mistress, which they'll know
> By favours several which they did bestow.
>   [V. ii. 121-25]

Forewarned, the ladies exchange favours; says the Princess, justifying the counter-practice and characterizing the spirit in which it is undertaken:

> The effect of my intent is to cross theirs.
> They do it but in mocking merriment,
> And mock for mock is only my intent.
>
> [V. ii. 138-40]

When the gentlemen enter, then, they are twice deceived, being unaware that they are known and their purpose marked and unaware of the identities of their respective mistresses. Each courts the wrong lady and is, as Biron puts it, 'all dry-beaten with pure scoff!' [V. ii. 263]. 'The tongues of mocking wenches are as keen', observes Boyet, 'As is the razor's edge invisible' [V. ii. 256-57]. The retreat ending the first movement is like a rout. Still, the unwitting gentlemen suppose that, though dry-beaten as Russians, they have passed unrecognized; but Boyet, again traitor, tells the ladies that the King's party will return 'In their own shapes' [V. ii. 288], and Rosaline—who might be arguing for Shakespeare's own dramatic method—at once insists that no such fine advantage should be surrendered until its potentialities have been exhausted:

> Let's mock them still, as well known as disguis'd.
> Let us complain to them what fools were here,
> Disguis'd like Muscovites, in shapeless gear.
>
> [V. ii. 301-03]

Re-entering, the gentlemen are still doubly ignorant, being unaware that they were known before and that each had courted and been mocked by the wrong mistress; absurdly clinging to their illusion, they are again dry-beaten one by one—for example, Biron:

> *Ros.* We four indeed confronted were with four
> In Russian habit; here they stay'd an hour,
> And talk'd apace; and in that hour, my lord,
> They did not bless us with one happy word.
> I dare not call them fools; but this I think,
> When they are thirsty, fools would fain have drink.
> *Bir.* This jest is dry to me.
>
> [V. ii. 367-73]

Not until each gentleman's condition has been exploited does the dramatist begin to close the gap that has made all the fun. First the gentlemen learn that their masquerade had fooled no one. Next their ignorance that they had unbosomed themselves 'To loves mistook' is dispelled, but less abruptly, for the ladies want to relish their advantage to the last moment. The denouement, here as usually in the comedies, amounts to a closing of gaps, an equalizing of awarenesses:

> *Bir.* I see the trick on't; here was a consent,
> Knowing aforehand of our merriment,
> To dash it like a christmas comedy.
>
> [V. ii. 460-62]
> (pp. 21-4)

> *Bertrand Evans, "Here Sit I in the Sky: First Explorations," in his* Shakespeare's Comedies, *Oxford at the Clarendon Press, Oxford, 1960, pp. 1-32.*

E.M.W. TILLYARD (essay date 1962)

[*Tillyard is best known for his influential* Shakespeare's History Plays *(1944), considered a leading example of the historical approach to Shakespeare's work that was popular during the twentieth century. In addition to his historical studies, Tillyard also*

Act I. Scene ii. Armado and Jaquenetta. By J. Holmes. The Department of Rare Books and Special Collections, The University of Michigan Library.

published Shakespeare's Last Plays *(1938),* Shakespeare's Problem Plays *(1949), and* Shakespeare's Early Comedies, *a book he was working on at the time of his death in 1962, but which was not published until 1965. In the following excerpt, taken from his study of the comedies, Tillyard breaks with the traditional reading of* Love's Labour's Lost *that states that the love and marriages sought after by the male characters will be achieved when they complete their year of penance; instead, he claims that "the spirit of the play" is riddled with too many uncertainties and irregularities to support such a traditional comic resolution, and that the immature, fickle, and thoughtless nature of the men, combined with the awkward position of the women, runs counter to any assumption of marriage. The idea that the Navarrese nobles, particularly Berowne, will be reunited with the women, and that the fruits of "love's labour" will eventually be won, has been suggested most strongly by Bobbyann Roesen (1953), Arthur Quiller-Couch, and John Vyvyan (see Additional Bibliography).*]

Love's Labour's Lost is neither a farce, nor a picaresque play, nor, in spite of the strangeness of the park of Navarre, a fairy play. It belongs . . . to the central area of social comedy. Four young men, refusing to see things as they are, attempt a feat which common sense could have told them was impossible. That impossibility becomes quickly apparent, but even then they persist in their childish vision of reality. But society, in the form of four clear-sighted women, and the unexpected irruption of the reality of death give them a series of lessons and put them on the way to seeing things as they are. Matching the four young men in their distorted vision of reality are two older men [Armado and Holofernes] and a hanger-on of one of them [Nathaniel]. One of these distorts reality by clothing his spiritual nakedness in fantasies, and they both violate reality by enlarging the distance of words from the things they represent. They are fully grown and set in their habits and, unlike the young men, who are still malleable, they will continue to be comparatively harmless misfits in the society to which they belong; or, to put their case more accurately in terms of the play, they will remain for ever islanded in the park of Navarre which is made to stand so exquisitely for a state of affairs at odds with what prevails beyond its bounds. Whatever becomes of the four young men, they have, by the end of the play, quitted the old enclosure. In contrast, Armado and Holofernes will inhabit it for ever.

How does Shakespeare fabricate the delicate unreality of the park? Is it through making fantastic things happen there? Or is it through using strange words to denote its attributes, for instance, the afternoon there being the posterior of the day? Or are the items of its furniture studiedly unexpected and incongruous? . . . Whatever the means, Shakespeare makes his park into a kind of Cloudcuckooland and by siting his comic action there creates a most unusual kind of comedy. In normal comedy the folk who trangress the social norm are set within it; in *Love's Labour's Lost* the social norm is a visitor breaking through the barriers by which Cloudcuckooland is enclosed. This reversal of the usual procedure renders the play unique; and the only fit response is one of simple admiration for a stroke of genius. (pp. 173-75)

The arrival of Marcade with the news of the French king's death is both a supreme dramatic stroke and has unexpected results. As a dramatic stroke it clearly twins the sudden appearance of the Abbess at the height of the farcical action in the *Comedy of Errors;* and in both plays the appearance of the tall figure in black among the motley of the other persons must as sheer spectacle have been thrilling. But the Abbess introduces no new element, she merely clears up an action whose end was not in doubt. Marcade causes a double reversal and enlightenment. The play had opened with the King of Navarre toying with the idea of cheating death through achieving fame:

> Let fame, that all hunt after in their lives,
> Live regist'red upon our brazen tombs,
> And then grace us in the disgrace of death;
>
> [I. i. 1-3]

The reference to death was quite hollow, for real death was the last thing that Navarre had in his mind; and in the body of the play he and his fellows live in the moment, as regardless of the future as any young men have ever been. The irruption of real and present death into their mood of greatest frivolity shakes them to their depths; they will not be the same men after it. But the process does not end here. It is because they are truly shaken that they can make the women see, as they had not done before, that for all their frivolous behaviour their professed love was not altogether affected; it had some core of truth. And so for the chief characters the world begins to assume a touch of its true colours, and the women are able to dictate the terms under which they will accept their lovers in the setting of true social life.

The contention . . . that Shakespeare left the issue of his action in doubt goes so much against normal opinion that I ought to add something concerning it. The nearest approach to scepticism I have encountered is from Quiller-Couch in his introduction to the *New Cambridge Shakespeare* edition: 'Love's labour has been lost for a while, since mourning in this world often interrupts it, perhaps for its good; but it shall be redeemed anon, we hope' [see Additional Bibliography]. Such a hope

may be legitimate but only if it is balanced by the opposing doubt whether the young men have been shaken and matured enough by the intrusion of death on their world of fantasy to enable them to go through with their penances: is there anything in their past behaviour to justify Quiller-Couch's tentative optimism? Other critics have no qualms about the happy ending. Miss Roesen writes of the young man who has been given the harshest penance and who thus is the least likely to make good:

> At the end of the year, love's labors will be won for Berowne, and he will receive Rosaline's love, not in the half real world of the park, but in the actuality outside its walls [see excerpt above, 1953]. . . .

I yet persist in asking: does the play really make it plain that the young men will seize the possibility referred to? Again, John Vyvyan is quite assured of a happy ending:

> Love's labour is lost in this play because it is a labour of affectation not sincerity. But it will be won—so we are promised at the end—by service and sacrifice [see Additional Bibliography].

I fail to see any sign of such a promise in Shakespeare's text: all we know is that it *could* be won.

But I go further than saying that such certainties are not borne out by the text; I would say that they violate the play's whole complexion. The main substance of the play is of uncertainties and irregularities. The principal men are in the muddy state of adolescence; the principal women, placed in a queer position anyhow, in a kind of campers' or caravan existence, and puzzled by the antics of the men, assume the poses that seem to befit their position and which are not the natural ones of their own choosing. Most of the other characters are freaks, uncertain either of themselves or of the larger world without. It is true that into this world breaks the sobering fact of death but it does not work its complete sobering effect while the play's true action lasts, for the two principal penances imposed are macabre and in their ways as remote from the larger world as have been the actions of those who have to undergo them. They are also perfectly fitted to expiate those actions. In fact they look back into the body of the play more than they look forward to the new life which may or may not emerge. It is perfectly apt that Navarre, promoter of the bogus academy, should have to endure the hardships he had planned in theory. But the setting of those hardships, the 'forlorn and naked hermitage, / Remote from all the pleasures of the world' [V. ii. 795-96], where its occupant will be subject to 'frost and fasts, hard lodging and thin weeds' [V. ii. 801], is strangely grim and remote from the clear light of the common Elizabethan day. As for Berowne,

> You shall this twelvemonth term from day to day
> Visit the speechless sick, and still converse
> With groaning wretches; and your task shall be,
> With all the fierce endeavour of your wit,
> To enforce the pained impotent to smile.
>
> [V. ii. 850-54]

It is an apt penance, for, as Rosaline goes on to explain, the success of Berowne's notorious sallies of satire depended on the applause of fools easily provoked to laughter. Let him now try his luck with another kind of audience. But it is a grotesque and macabre penance, remote from the norm of ordinary life; and Berowne protests against it in horror:

> To move wild laughter in the throat of death?
> It cannot be; it is impossible,
> Mirth cannot move a soul in agony.
>
> [V. ii. 855-57]

And of course it points backward: in its substance to his wild laughter when the actors are being baited and Armado and Costard hooted on to their duel, and in its grotesqueness to the other, if different, grotesquenesses of the past action of the play. To demand clarity just here, to impose on this lovely medley of uncertainties the cut-and-driedness of a happy ending is to offend against the whole spirit of the play; whereas to leave the issue in doubt makes us continue to dwell on all the things that have charmed us before.

Of course full reality does break in; but not through the action of the play. It is the songs of the cuckoo and the owl, about spring and winter, that tell of real life, of a life accepted and enjoyed in spite of its knowledge of death and of the dying in their hospitals, and which release a surprise on us as thrilling as when Mercade interrupted the wild hubbub in the park of Navarre. Miss Roesen would have it that the songs are not contrasted with the substance of the play but echo different parts of it. Thus the embroidery-like picture of the enamelling of flowers echoes the artificial picture of the park of Navarre. But the flowers enumerated—daisies, violets, cuckoo-flowers, and buttercups—are none of them exotic; and I cannot see that in enumerating them Shakespeare meant to evoke anything more remote than an English spring when the weather is fine. It may be legitimate to picture a tapestry background to the Cloudcuckooland that is the park of Navarre, but it certainly did not breed ordinary daisies and buttercups, any more than it was concerned with housekeeping or eating. . . . Nor is the deer that the princess shot a real beast, though it has its function in provoking fantastic thoughts, snobbery, and bad puns from the actors. But the larks and the turtles of the spring song are real birds, while greasy Joan keeling her pot in winter is an emblem of real housekeeping. (pp. 175-80)

What are we to make of the few words of prose that follow the songs? In the traditional texts they run as follows:

> *Arm.* The words of Mercury are harsh after the songs of
> Apollo.
> You thay way: we this way. . . .
>
> [V. ii. 930-31]

[We] are given an exquisitely appropriate ending. The last six words proclaim division; suggest uncertainty. They take us back to the play itself and, a miracle of economy, hint that we must leave things hanging. (p. 181)

> E.M.W. Tillyard, "'Love's Labour's Lost'," in his
> Shakespeare's Early Comedies, *Chatto and Windus,*
> *1965, pp. 137-81.*

JOHN DOVER WILSON   (essay date 1962)

[*Dover Wilson is a highly regarded Shakespearean scholar who was involved in several aspects of Shakespeare studies. As an editor of the* New Cambridge Shakespeare, *he made numerous contributions to twentieth-century textual criticism of the plays, making use of the scientific bibliography developed by W. W. Greg and Charlton Hinman. As a critic, Dover Wilson combined several contemporary approaches and does not fit easily into any one critical "school." He is concerned with character analysis in the tradition of A. C. Bradley; he delves into Elizabethan culture like the historical critics, but without their usual emphasis on hierarchy and the Great Chain of Being; and his interest in visualizing possible dramatic performances of the plays links him with his contemporary, Harley Granville-Barker. This last characteristic can be seen in his comments on* Love's Labour's Lost, *taken from his* Shakespeare's Happy Comedies *(1962). Here, Dover Wilson states that his low estimation of* Love's Labour's*]*

Lost changed when he viewed the play in performance. His observations are presented from "the point of view of a spectator," and he finds the play full of vivacity, dance, rhythm, and pattern— quite a different play than he had perceived through reading. He is in general agreement with Harley Granville-Barker (1927) concerning the play's dramatic qualities, but opposed to H. B. Charlton (1937) on the question of characterization, which Dover Wilson believes does not have to be as complex in a play like Love's Labour's Lost *as in other kinds of drama, such as tragedy or history.*]

The first thing one notices about [*Love's Labour's Lost*] in the theatre is its extraordinary vivacity; it was evidently written in the highest possible spirits, by a dramatist who was thoroughly enjoying himself, and knew how to make his audience enjoy themselves thoroughly also. If the actors catch this spirit of merriment and alertness, as they can hardly help doing, the spectators will be carried right off their feet from the outset; so much so that the sixteenth-century allusions will seem little more than pebbles in the eddying, yet never-ceasing ripples of their laughter. The critics insist that none of the characters are quite human—we shall see presently what is to be said about that—but at least they are one and all exceedingly bright and agile. Even 'most Dull, honest Dull' [V. i. 155], the constable, catches the infection, feels that itching of the toes which all the rest display, so that his last words are

> I'll make one in a dance, or so; or I'll play
> On the tabor to the worthies, and let them dance the
> hay.
>
> [V. i. 153-54]

The spirit of the whole is far more like that of a Mozart opera— quite an interesting comparison might be made with *Còsi fan Tutti*—than anything we are accustomed to in modern drama.

But quotation will give a better idea of the pace of the play than mere description.

'Master', exclaims the page Moth, who dances about the portentous but magnificent Armado like a glistening speck of dust in sunlight, 'will you win your love with a French brawl?'

> ARM. How meanest thou? brawling in French?
> MOTH. No, my complete master—but to jig off
> a tune at the tongue's end, canary to it with
> your feet, humour it with turning up your eye-
> lids, sigh a note and sing a note, sometime
> through the throat as if you swallowed love with
> singing love, sometime through the nose as if
> you snuffed up love by smelling love, with your
> hat penthouse-like o'er the shop of your eyes,
> with your arms crossed on your thin-belly doub-
> let like a rabbit on a spit, or your hands in your
> pocket like a man after the old painting—and
> keep not too long in one tune, but a snip and
> away!
>
> [III. i. 8-22]

Prose—but what rhythm! The speaker's body and feet are constantly on the move; he dances the brawl. 'Snip and away' might be the play's sub-title. Its structure may be mechanical, its plot feeble, its 'apprehension of life' shallow [see excerpt above by H. B. Charlton, 1937]—as the critics allege—but it *goes*, goes with a swing and an impetus which, when seen on the stage, are irresistible. For sheer gaiety none of Shakespeare's other comedies can beat it, not even the golden *As You Like It* or that buck-basket stuffed full of fantastics, *The Merry Wives of Windsor*. (pp. 65-6)

There is of course a great deal of rhyme in *Love's Labour's Lost*—so much so that many have thought it must be Shakespeare's earliest play, on the theory that the passage from rhyme to blank verse is one of the indications of his development in dramatic power. But the rhyme here, as in Dryden and Pope, is part of the wit; it adds just that touch of artificiality required for a pattern-play; it points the jest and gives the grace of an echo to the happy repartee. Without rhyme *Love's Labour's Lost* would lose much of its life and colour. But rhyme is not the only form of verse. When something serious shows through the glitter of the surface, blank verse is used. Thus Berowne, who laughingly defends his black mistress in rhyme, turns to blank verse in his great speech of recantation, while it is noticeable that little but blank verse is spoken after the entry of the messenger of death in V, ii. An analysis of the whole play according to its use of rhyme, blank verse and prose would be instructive. Glance a moment, for instance, at the opening scene. It begins solemnly; the King announcing the oath and the three courtiers giving their respective assents to it. Lines I-48 therefore are in blank verse. Yet the whole thing is artificial, and, as we are intended to feel, a little comic: therefore the blank verse is end-stopped and the speeches terminate in couplets. Then, when Berowne makes his protestation, and the tone becomes lively, even flippant, the blank verse is dropped and the banter of the men, together with Berowne's mock rhetoric, is conveyed in couplets, quatrains and sonnets: a rhyme-pattern that forms a delightful accompaniment to the dialogue, something like the patter of feet on the floor in a Polish mazurka. And even when Costard and Dull enter at l. 181 and prose begins, the patterning is not at an end, for Shakespeare writes his prose as well as his verse in patterned form in this play.

The structure of *Love's Labour's Lost* is of course a pattern also. The two parts are almost exactly equal in length, Berowne's recantation occurring about half-way through. But perhaps the most remarkable instance of parallelism in the two parts is in regard to the oaths. The oaths of the students at the beginning are offset by the oaths of the lovers at the end—with a significant difference, however. The students swear to follow the pagan stoical life for the sake of fame; the lovers are compelled to take *religious* vows as a penance for perjury and as a means of regeneration. And this system of repetition and echo is not confined to the main plot but is carried out in detail of all sorts throughout the play. For example in I, i, Costard's confession concerning Jaquenetta is followed by Armado's letter—both, though in different fashion, going over the same points. Or again, Armado's soliloquy in I, ii is matched by Berowne's in III, i; both have the same theme (contemptuous confession of Cupid's power) and both end with a promise of poetry. Or yet again, we have Armado's letter to Jaquenetta (franked by remuneration) contrasted with Berowne's letter to Rosaline (franked by a guerdon). Or lastly, take once more the famous recantation scene. Each of the four men in turn comes on to the stage, makes his confession of love and perjury, reads aloud his poem and hides himself as his successor appears. And when all have revealed their secrets in the view of their fellows, one by one they step forth again to denounce the perjurer who has last spoken, until at length Berowne the first comer and original spy springs down from his tree to denounce the lot, only to be himself unmasked by the entry of Costard and Jaquenetta with his incriminating letter to Rosaline. The scene winds itself up and unwinds itself again for all the world as if four boys were dancing and reversing about a maypole.

It would be idle to multiply examples, some of them of the subtlest character, so subtle that like the lesser variations upon a theme in music they are felt rather than perceived; suffice it to say that repetition with variations is one of the mainsprings of the play's structure.

But there is another, for there are two elements in every pattern, balance and contrast as well as repetition and variation. These are secured in *Love's Labour's Lost* chiefly by the grouping of characters, and by the shifting colour effects produced by the regrouping.

The play, we are told, is 'deficient in characterization' [Charlton]. But 'characterization' is not one of the purposes of the play. Occasionally the persons fall into character, but as they do they tend to fall out of the pattern.

The minor characters are intended as types—the traditional types of the *commedia dell' arte*—not as rounded human characters at all, and Berowne tells us as much when he sums them up as the pedant, the braggart, the hedge-priest, the fool and the boy. Charlton indeed declared Costard to be 'the most considerable character' in the play and quotes as evidence Costard's oft-quoted words about Sir Nathaniel Alisander as the latter departs discomforted [V. ii. 580-84]. . . . On the other hand, Granville-Barker, who had to think about stage-production and casting, comes to a very different conclusion, that Costard is (as Berowne calls him) 'the fool', i.e. the official jester at the court of Navarre [see excerpt above, 1927]. And had it not been for the Alisander passage there would have been no doubt about it—the mask slips and accidentally reveals a face. For a moment Costard has stepped out of the stage design and become a man, as a Shakespearian Fool is in other plays.

As to the eight principals—the two groups of student lovers and mocking wenches, who 'resemble each other in a wooden conformity', who 'have all to do the same sort of thing' [Charlton]; they constitute of course the most striking feature of the design and they do so the more effectively in that they provide the main element in the colour scheme.

The Elizabethan actors, saved all the cost of scenery and lighting which swells the bill of modern production, are known to have spent lavishly upon dress; and *Love's Labour's Lost*, which contains a sixteenth-century King and three attendant nobles, all in choice costume of similar though not identical cut and design; a French Princess with her three ladies also brilliantly tricked out in dresses of a quasi-uniform style (for when they mask they must look alike); the foppish old courtier Boyet; and 'fashion's own knight', Don Adriano de Armado, with the page Moth at his heels, must have presented a perfect riot of colour and magnificence, to which the pedant and the curate, the patched fool, the frieze cloth constable and the ragged dairymaid acted as foils.

And the scenes are so arranged that the colour-scheme is constantly changing: the King and his lords are outblazoned by Armado and Moth, who after being contrasted with the simplicity of Dull, Costard and Jaquenetta, are in their turn followed by the dapper Boyet and his bevy of dainty ladies. Next, the two main groups are brought together for the splendour of Navarre to confront the grace of France, and this first meeting is followed, of course, by many others. The encounters of the two groups are like dramatic minuets. In the Muscovite scene, indeed, we get what is obviously intended to represent, in a kind of comic ballet, opposing armies with heralds passing to and fro; the men masked and disguised as Russians, on one side of the stage, and the women, likewise masked and disguised by the interchange of 'fairings', on the other. First Moth advances as 'herald' for the men and after a vain attempt to deliver his 'ambassage' retires in confusion. Then Boyet advances to the men and demands their intentions. This business is particularly effective on the stage, because though the two parties are only a few yards apart, the nimble Boyet runs backwards and forwards between them like a busy herald receiving and delivering messages; until at length the ladies line up, dress themselves by the right, make one pace forwards and speak to the enemy face to face.

So the kaleidoscope goes on, until suddenly, with the effect of a smashing hammer-stroke, there appears a figure clothed in black from head to foot. Death enters and the brilliant 'scene begins to cloud' [V. ii. 721].

The extraordinary impression left upon the audience by the entrance of the black-clad messenger upon the court revels was the greatest lesson I took away with me from the [1936 Tyrone] Guthrie production. It made me see two things—(a) that however gay, however riotous a Shakespearian comedy may be, tragedy is always there, *felt*, if not seen; (b) that for all its surface lightness and frivolity, the play had behind it a serious mind at work, with a purpose.

In conclusion then consider this purpose for a moment. First there is the terrible portrait of a renaissance schoolmaster, self-complacent, self-seeking, irascible, pretentious, intolerant of what he calls 'barbarism', and yet himself knowing nothing but the pitiful rudiments, the husks of learning, which he spends his life thrusting down the throats of his unfortunate pupils. Holofernes moves upon Shakespeare's stage as the eternal type of pedant, the 'living-dead man' [in *The Comedy of Errors*, V. i. 242] who will always be with us, because so long as there is a human race to be educated there will always be many to mistake the letter for the spirit.

It is a pity that *Love's Labour's Lost* is in parts so obscure, so topical. Else it might be commended without hesitation to the attention of all teachers, professors, and educationalists to be read once a year—on Ash Wednesday, shall we say?—for their souls' good. For we have here, not only in the figure of Holofernes, but in the play as a whole, Shakespeare's great onslaught upon the Dark Tower, the fortress of the enemies of life and grace and gaiety. . . . the name of which is Pedantry. Against it he hoists the banner of Love. . . . Love for Shakespeare, in short, is a symbol of that passionate apprehension of Life, which sets all five senses afire and is the great gift of the poet and the artist to his fellows. (pp. 69-74)

John Dover Wilson, '' 'Love's Labour's Lost': The Story of a Conversion,'' in his Shakespeare's Happy Comedies, *Northwestern University Press, 1962, pp. 55-75.*

PHILIP PARSONS (essay date 1963)

[*Parsons discusses Shakespeare's use of the device of masking in* Romeo and Juliet *and* Love's Labour's Lost, *stressing its qualities of self-realization and its connection with death. Like Bobbyann Roesen (1953), he maintains that the approaching sense of darkness and images of death in the play generate a deeper self-awareness in the characters and an overall "movement toward reality." Parsons also argues that light imagery in* Love's Labour's Lost *is not necessarily associated with love; in fact, he suggests that the light of Navarre is false, blinding the men from a proper understanding of love and their own identities, and that only in the approaching darkness, both physical and spiritual, do they come to appreciate true love.*]

Man's profound self-identification with the face he wears is reflected in a dozen different cultures, both ancient and modern, where the dead are given masks to help them make their return to earth at the appropriate time. By the same token, to assume a new face is to assume a new personality—the mask imposes its role upon the wearer. But what happens to the wearer of a blank mask? Symbolically, it throws open the whole question of identity. The old self is blotted out and the way left clear for a new to manifest. The blank mask imposes the most challenging role of all, signalling a death and an enigmatic rebirth. Something of this feeling appears in Shakespeare's handling of the black masquing visor in two early plays, probably written within a year of each other, *Love's Labour's Lost* and *Romeo and Juliet*. At their very different levels, each play shows the mysterious unfolding of personal destiny, a creative development from which emerges a deeper and more vital self-awareness. And at the beginning of that jounrey stands the mask. (p. 121)

In *Love's Labour's Lost* the themes of love, death and self-realization run through a full circle in the course of a summer's day. The play begins and ends with a vow of mortification in order to find wisdom, but while the first is taken in the bliss of ignorance, the second springs from sadness and understanding. Youth, summer, light and gaiety surround the vow at the opening of the play, with the King of Navarre looking forward lightheartedly to that Fame which shall

> Live register'd upon our brazen tombs,
> And then grace us in the disgrace of death.
>
> [I. i. 2-3]

The light conceit conveys the care-free mood, when death is very far away and quite unreal. The King and his lords have taken a three-year vow to 'war upon' their 'own affections', forswearing women, eating little and sleeping less, 'living in philosophy': and the grand purpose of all their study is, rather vaguely, 'that to know which else we should not know' [I. i. 56]. But when the Princess of France arrives with her ladies, the young men discover that wisdom is taught not by books but by life itself. They have vowed to ignore their own true nature.

> Let us once lose our oaths to find ourselves,
> Or else we lose ourselves to keep our oaths.
>
> [IV. iii. 358-59]

Their decision to break the vow, marked by Berowne's great panegyric on love, is the serious centre in a comedy of self-realization. And from this moment the dark images begin to gather. (p. 122)

The black mask belongs with the imagery of darkness and cloud which is associated with the themes of death and self-realization. Having decided to 'find themselves', the lords' first thought is to court the ladies in a masque. 'Blackamoors with music' go before them as they advance through the park, masked and disguised as men from the wintery north, come to be thawed by beauty. The ladies, forewarned and suspecting mockery, have put on black visors to receive their Muscovite guests and of course the whole plan miscarries. The lords court the wrong ladies unknowingly, and unknowingly the ladies reject sincere advances.

That masquing has to be seen. The predominant tone will be one of witty contrariety and each figure will be a little unfamiliar and strange. Things are not what they seem, the summer scene is flecked with black. 'Vouchsafe to show the sunshine of your face', asks Berowne, 'that we, like savages, may worship it' [V. ii. 201-02]. 'My face is but a moon', he is told, 'and clouded too' [V. ii. 203]. Even the King's request for the 'bright moon' and 'these stars to shine, (Those clouds removed)' [V. ii. 205-06] is to no avail. Not only do the ladies deny the masquers the traditional courteous welcome. When the lords ask to 'tread a measure with you on the grass' [V. ii. 185]—the essence of every masque—they wittily decline, and the omission of this exercise of love and joy points up the frustrated wooing. By all the rules, the scene ought to be the perfect conventional setting for love. But despite the summer's day, youth, and masquing in the park, it all comes to nothing. The truth of each lover is hidden from his lady, the identity of each lady is hidden from the men, and the real demands of love have yet to appear. The slightly sinister black visor fitly dominates a scene where the reality is disguised by appearance.

So much for the place of the mask in the imagery pattern of *Love's Labour's Lost*. It brings a feeling of the unknown, and its association with winter imagery and darkness connects it with death. But it is also connected with self-realization, a fact which is underlined not only by the imagery but also by the striking position of the masquing theme in the play. When the lords decide to find themselves, they believe the search is already at an end. They need only break their vows, court the ladies and marry them. They are mistaken, yet their decision does lead to self-realization, through a series of quite unforseen events. Those events are causally unrelated—the king's death and the ladies' misunderstanding are matters of chance—but all are touched with the same darkness. And the first sign of this intangible movement towards reality comes with the masquing.

The confrontation of light-hearted youth with death and the need for deeper self-awareness also mark the second masque, or rather pageant, in which the amiable eccentrics present the Nine Worthies for the ladies' delectation. The lords, brilliant, unperceptive and a little cruel in their youthful confidence, revenge their failed masque by making this old-fashioned entertainment a butt for their modish wit. The show comes at the end of the long afternoon, and this sadly burlesque offering for a young princess catches somehow a momentary gleam of the late golden light. It falls kindly on Pompey, 'traveling along this coast' to make his devoir and lay his 'arms before the legs of this sweet lass of France' [V. ii. 555]. It touches with pathos this Alexander, who begins 'When in the world I liv'd. . .' [V. ii. 562]. As the odd, shambling figures relate their legends, they serve only to remind us how long ago, and in how remote a world, they lived.

This sense of things vanished and forgotten is sharpened by the wit of the court into something harsher, a sense of mortality. The liveliness of the lords turns again and again to death. They will have Judas Maccabeus to be Judas Iscariot, a kissing traitor who hanged himself; and the face lent him by Holofernes is a death's face in a ring, the face of an old Roman coin, scarce seen. Their laughter puts him to flight in the dusk, with the boy Moth crying after him 'A light for monsieur Judas, it grows dark, he may stumble' [V. ii. 630]. The echo is a little macabre. The jest will turn back on the lords in a few moments when news arrives from France. Don Armado's gentle rebuke in defence of Hector comes through the shadows with a piercing sadness:

> The sweet war-man is dead and rotten,
> Sweet chucks, beat not the bones of the buried.
>   [V. ii. 660-61]

The Nine Worthies are presented, of course, as a companion piece to the masque made by the lords. But although one entertainment is graceful and the other ludicrous, this difference is less striking than their similarity. Both are laughed at, both are failures, and, as we have seen, the darkness imagery runs through both. Berowne's dismissal of the pageant—'Worthies away, the scene begins to cloud' [V. ii. 721]—recalls faintly the fair moon clouded in the masque. If the Muscovites brought a hint of the coming winter, the Nine Worthies give it weight. The surprising thing is that Don Armado should be allowed to utter words of this peculiar resonance, that the comic characters should carry so grave a meaning. The bones of the buried Hector have the impact of a *memento mori* ["reminder of death"], and in them the serious undertones of the pageant break through the burlesque. Behind the fantastic costumes the dead have come to speak to the young, and as their mouthpiece Don Armado finds a touching, utterly unexepected dignity. Both here and in the Muscovite costumes that expressed more truth than the wearers knew, there is something of the feeling for disguise as a form of possession by unknown powers—a feeling which the Elizabethans never quite lost.

Love's Labour's Lost may be left with a brief reference to Shakespeare's curious hint that light is not necessarily associated with love. The first half of the play is full of light and gaiety but that light is gradually streaked with shadow as the young men come closer to a sober realization of love. Yet the ladies, for all their darkness, seem to move in a peculiar light of their own. Berowne swears that Rosaline is 'born to make black fair' [IV. iii. 257]. His argument, as the King observes, seems a paradox, and Dumaine adds mockingly 'Dark needs no candles now, for dark is light' [IV. iii. 265]. When it is remembered that all the ladies have in fact come out of dying France, a suggestion arises that love is somehow inherent in death, that the true light burns invisibly within darkness. Sunlit Navarre must then appear a land of wanton desire, not love, a place to be rejected, not transformed. There the cuckoo sings on every tree, unpleasing to a married ear; but in true-loving France, Marion's red and raw nose is not unattractive by twilight. In Navarre, the eye is dazzled by a false light which blinds it to the true—or as Berowne remarks in another context, 'Light seeking light, doth light of light beguile' [I. i. 77]. This hint of a dual concept of light is so slight as to have little bearing on the interpretation of the play, but it is interesting as a premonition of the imagery pattern in *Romeo and Juliet*, where . . . love is entirely a thing of the night, a secret rite which, as Juliet says, lovers perform by the light of their own beauties. And in both plays the black masquing visor is one of love's dark images, an element in the creative pattern of self-discovery. (pp. 122-24)

> *Philip Parsons, "Shakespeare and the Mask," in* Shakespeare Survey: An Annual Survey of Shakespearian Study and Production, *Vol. 16, 1963, pp. 121-312.*

WILLIAM MATTHEWS (essay date 1964)

[*Matthews contends that in* Love's Labour's Lost *Shakespeare is concerned with the state of the English language, a suggestion made earlier by Walter Pater (1885) and Gladys Doidge Willcock (1934). In his discussion of the play's linguistic structure, Matthews divides the speech mannerisms of the characters into three distinct social groups, noting the puns and pronunciation of each, and considers the resultant problems of the Elizabethans' pedantic fascination with the written word. For other treatments of language in* Love's Labour's Lost, *see the excerpts by Ralph Berry*

(1969), James L. Calderwood (1971), Terence Hawkes (1973), and Malcolm Evans (1975).]

All Shakespeare's plays exhibit his resource in language, his delight in exploiting its resources, and his preoccupation with its strengths and weaknesses; but it is in *Love's Labour's Lost* that his linguisticism is perhaps most apparent. Not even *Hamlet*, in which 'word' is a dominant theme, is so charged with sensitivity to the processes and uses of language or so rich in linguistic criticism. It might not be excessive indeed to regard *Love's Labour's Lost* as being by emphasis a comedy on the English *état de langue* ["state of language"].

Stylistically, its characters are disposed into three social groups: a large group consisting of the courtiers and their feminine opposites, the academic trio of Armado, Nathaniel, and Holofernes, and the yokel trio of Costard, Dull, and Jaquenetta— Moth, the remaining character, is linguistically an intermediary but closest to the courtiers. Allowing for the peculiarities of poetical theatre and of employing a recent terminology, one may label the three styles U, Would-be-U, and Non-U—although they are not so distinct as that classification might suggest.

What unites the first two groups and also affects the third is an attitude towards language that may fairly be called Elizabethan. In Shakespeare's day, people who wrote books and pamphlets, and even who wrote only letters, were seemingly entranced by language: they approached it with the same speculative and playful eye that an actor turns upon his robes and paint. Some quiet, sober writers there were, of course; men who preferred to work within the limited ranges of well-established usage, but they were few in comparison with the writers who aimed at more striking styles, styles which achieved their effects by drawing upon the more recondite lexicon and semantics of the language, by patterning and playing with its phonology, by assembling its syntactic elements into uncustomary structures, by joining to their jointure of English the riches of alien tongues. From our distance, we may perhaps doubt that so formidable an exuberance was altogether typical of everyday or Everyman's usage: the devices are apt to be too *recherché* ["researched"], smell too much of the book and the lamp, to be normal linguistic practice, especially the practice of speech. Nevertheless, it is the habit of much of the written English of the time, and the playwrights and others who make use of dialogue are too consistent in their linguistic plenitude to warrant a sceptic in questioning that Elizabethans, even speaking ones, were considerably more absorbed by the game of words than were their simpler forebears or their more controlled successors.

Many factors contributed to this lnguistic obsession: schoolmasters, rhetoricians, schoolbooks, dictionaries, travel, translation, the doctrine of limitation, printing, the pulpit, the theatre itself—to mention only some. But the basic drive was an idea that began in the late Middle Ages and continued well into the seventeenth century, not only in England but on the continent too—the idea that the vernaculars whch had taken over the vast literary service that had once been performed by clerical Latin were inadequate to their task and needed to be augmented in all their phases, the rhetorical and semantic as well as the lexicographical and syntactic. . . . One may learn much about an age from the behaviour of its heroes, and in Shakespeare's day the glass of fashion and the mould (or ape) of form was by definition a man of golden and painted words, one adept in playing pleasingly on all the strings and stops of the language.

The most obvious aspect of this plethoric style in *Love's Labour's Lost* is the lexicographical abundance that characterizes both U and Would-be-U speakers. All of them are verbal cornucopias, and sometimes they speak like Florio's dictionary, in which the words are defined by as many synonyms as the lexicographer can muster. . . . The differentiation between U and Would-be-U lis largely in example, degree, and mood. If to the King it was Armado who was the man of linguistic fashion, one whom 'the music of his own vain tongue, Doth ravish like enchanting harmony' [I. i. 166-67], to Biron, the ape of this particular linguistic fashion was 'honey-tongu'd Boyet' [V. ii. 334], the courtier de luxe. All the speakers in fact employ words that must have seemed strange to a large part of a Globe audience—that the *O.E.D.* [Oxford English Dictionary] may now record earlier appearance is of little significance, for the Elizabethan neologist had no such dictionary in which to check the activities of his rivals and Shakespeare's audiences had only their awareness of context to lead them the right way. All of the speakers, too, are inclined to be bookish in their speech—'fair as a text B in a copy book' [V. ii. 42]. But the U-speakers are less obvious, less extreme in neologism than the Would-be's, and more playful and easy in their practice. Holofernes, Nathaniel, and Armado have eaten paper; Armado is 'a man of fire-new words, fashion's own knight' [I. i. 178], Holofernes and Nathaniel are linguistically Artsmen. The courtiers exploit the language at all social levels, the courtliness of their speech is mixed with words and especially meanings that are even more familiar to the proletarians of the play. The Would-be's on the other hand, are dominated by a desire to be 'singuled from the barbarous' [V. i. 81-2], to differentiate themselves linguistically from the non-U's wth whom they are most closely associated in society. In so doing they ape the courtly fashion, but solemnly, excessively, absurdly, and inadequately. For although they flaunt their neologisms and grossly marry Latin with English, they lack the awareness of vulgar usage which links the courtiers to the non-U's; they are more aware of a 'most singular and choice epithet' [V. i. 15] than of the vulgar (and usually unseemly) connotations of words that they themselves use, everyday words like *limb, joint, brawl,* or *cull'd,* and even learned words of their own importing, *posterior,* for instance.

Plays, like sermons and orations, live on the boundary of writing and speech, and it is therefore to be expected that a playwright will exploit the phonology of the language more than, say, a novelist—his equipment, moreover, includes the actor's voice and gesture. So it is that *Love's Labour's Lost* exploits features of the English tongue that would be hard for a writer whose works were meant for silent readers. Pronunciation in its various social styles is every playwright's concern, and in *Love's Labour's Lost,* although there is no attempt at a complete directive, there are hints to the actor in all three classes— hints of the kind that appear in the songs written for the Cockney comedians of the later English music-halls. These spelling hints point to an easy, colloquial style of pronunciation among the courtiers—'Whoe'er 'a was, 'a show'd a mounting mind' [IV. i. 4], says the Princess. Whether they also employed the tone and timbre that is now the most distinctive feature of U-speech—it is obvious even when the words and syntax cannot be distinguished—is something that can only be guessed at, though it is my own guess that part of the 'accent' in which the courtiers instructed Moth when they sent him with their verses was the accent which in the linguist's more exact term is timbre. The yokels are presented as dialect-speakers: towards the end of the play Costard is given words and pronunciations that form directives to the actor to play him as a Northerner.

No such hints are given for Dull: topographical logic might suggest that he too should be played with a Northern pronunciation, but topographical logic was scarcely compelling in Shakespeare's theatre. The pedants may be held to be typified in Holofernes. Unlike the courtiers and yokels, he abhorred many a pronunciation that had been on every Englishman's tongue for generations (*det, dout, cauf, hauf, nebour* are his particular examples), preferring, and doubtless using, pronunciations promulgated by etymological pedants. *Natural: artificial* is the opposition in this area, with the U's and the non-U's joined in opposition to the Would-be's. (pp. 1-6)

The other phonological game that *Love's Labour's Lost* shares with Elizabethan literature in general is the pun, the device of playing upon the homophones and near-homophones of the language. If for Shakespeare (which means Shakespeare's characters too) the pun was a Cleopatra, the reason should be apparent from his dealings with the larger aspects of the language. Abundance of pronunciation doublets within good speech and the variations provided by the speech of different social levels and dialects afforded an infinite variety for both playwright and actor. It is a game that is best played orally, and the virtuoso player is the man who can best exploit the near-homonym or the most variants. In *Love's Labour's Lost*, the courtiers pun upon homonyms provided not only by good usage, *äy* and *eye* for example, but also upon equations that, according to the pronunciation manuals and the practice of Mistress Quickly [in *Henry IV, Henry V, The Merry Wives of Windsor*], were used only by the vulgar—*shooter* and *suitor, qualm* and *calm* are cases in point. The same comic end, they also exploit current variants in stress and juncture. Thus, the Princess achieves a witty commentary on the King's greeting simply by shifting the stress of one word—'You shall be welcome madam' . . . 'I will be welcome then' [II. i. 95-6]—and Dumain plays greasily upon the semantic significance of two different stresses in *Judas*. Costard, as his confusing way with *plantain* shows, shares something of the courtiers' pleasure in phonological gamesmanship, but Holofernes is not only slow in grasping the phonological ploys of others, he is also laboriously exegetical in using them himself:

> Master Person, quasi per-son. And if one should
> be pierc'd, which is the one?
>
> [IV. ii. 82-3]

In semantics, the most striking feature of the play is the fascination of almost all the characters in face of the extremes of meaning that a word may carry. The pedants are prone to express this fascination in synonymical lists. The courtiers are more subtle and varied. Everyday Englsh usage provided them with a great many words that, in Doll Tearsheat's phrase, were excellent good words before they became ill-sorted [in *2 Henry IV*, II. iv. 150]—*yard, horn, prick,* and their like—and these are principal pieces in the courtiers' armoury of wit. But in their gay verbal battles they are busy to add to the common stock. The semantic principles of extension and association are their method, and by its means they contrive *double-entendres* for the most innocent of words—*in, out, mark, howl,* to list only a few. Costard, no fool though a clown, can admire this gay facility in perverting linguistic process:

> O' my troth, most sweet jests! most incony vulgar wit!
> When it comes so smoothly off, so obscenely, as it
>   were, so fit!
>
> [IV. i. 142-43]

but, as the colloquy between Holofernes, Nathaniel and Dull on *pricket* and *haud credo* shows, similar wit in the pedants

and yokels is apt to be accidental rather than deliberate, the playwright's rather than their own. (pp. 6-7)

Most of this essay has dealt with the U's and Would-be's. The Non-U's are not without linguistic interest, however. At bottom they are countrymen, speakers of dialect, users of plain, traditional English. But they are not immune from linguistic fashion either. Jacquenetta is the character of least words, and it may not be insignificant that she is also the woman of speediest action; she is two months gone when the court-ladies have a year and more to go. Dull, whose taciturnity in the midst of general loquacity reminds one of Silence in the company of Shallow and Falstaff [in *2 Henry IV*], is in a way an ironical yardstick. Yokel though he is, 'a twice-sod simplicity, *bis coctus*' [IV. ii. 22], under the pressure of the law and the Artsmen he is nevertheless prone to be seduced from his usual plain speech into learned malapropisms whose wit is none of his own intending (the learned *allusion,* for example, which on his simple tongue is transformed into *collusion* and *pollusion*). Costard, who is a half-way figure, a clown in two senses, is occasionally unconsciously witty in Dull's way though the ground of his speech is sound enough. But he has much of the court manner, too; he is adroit and persistent in puns, he can deliberately tangle a word with a bogus etymology, and in semantic juggling with several balls he is almost as skilful as Biron:

> In manner and form following, sir; all those
> three: I was seen with her in the manor-house,
> sitting with her upon the form, and taken following her into the park; which, put together,
> is in manner and form following. Now, sir, for
> the manner—it is the manner of a man to speak
> to a woman. For the form—in some form.
>
> [I. i. 205-11]

Pondering on the language of the rustics, a solemn critic might even come to think that one of Shakespeare's intentions in *Love's Labour's Lost* was to show how city fashion can linguistically corrupt country simplicity and directness.

Embodied and on stage, *Love's Labour's Lost* can seem a thing of elegant pattern and dancing grace; a ballet of fireflies, as it were. On the page, its tensions are more strained: a delicate reader may think he is attending a Mad Linguists' Party, a brilliant and amusing affair, but strangely narcissistic. Entrancing as the play may be to anyone who is himself touched with its trouble, the compulsiveness of the play's logosophy may still strike him as somewhat neurotic. To others, such an impression may seem anachronistic and certainly over-solemn. But that it is not altogether *malapropos* and even that linguistic disease may be an intended motif of the play, may be supported by some Elizabethan opinions on Elizabethan linguistic fashions, and by Shakespeare's own words.

Punctuating Elizabethan demands for augmenting the language, varying the eulogies on its ever-growing copiousness, is a mutter of protest that grows louder as the Elizabethan Age passes into the Jacobean. The essence of the protest is that contemporary fascination with the language and its processes is a disease, a moral and intellectual disease; that what is an instrument has been made an end in itself. As early as 1570, for instance, Thomas Browne complained of his contemporaries' preference for 'painted word and smooth Rhetoricke' over 'matter good and precious'; some years later, Sir William Cornwallis speaks of their 'disease of words'; Bacon is vehement in asserting that the 'first distemper of learning' begins 'when men study words and not matter' and the title of one of Montaigne's most potent essays is, 'Of the Vanitie of Words'. Shakespeare, throughout his poems and plays, bombards his audience with comments to the like effect, so abundant that they must represent his own opinion as well as that of his puppets. (pp. 8-10)

Love's Labour's Lost is a comedy on books and behaviour, words and matter, and its resolution may be a proposal for therapy. The King is sent into silence for a year; Biron is commanded to speak with the speechless and to apply his witty loquacity to a charitable end. Plain speech becomes the battle-cry. 'Honest plain words best pierce the ear of grief' [V. ii. 753], says Biron. 'Now to plain-dealing, lay these glozes by' [IV. iii. 367], says Longaville. Dull triumphs over Holofernes. And Biron's resolution seeks a cure for linguistic disease in a plain and country-style of speaking:

> O, never will I trust to speeches penn'd
>   Nor to the motion of a school-boy's tongue,
> Nor never come in vizard to my friend,
>   Nor woo in rhyme, like a blind harper's song. . . .
> Henceforth my wooing mind shall be express'd
>   In russet yeas, and honest kersey noes.
>
> [V. ii. 402-13]
> (pp. 10-11)

William Matthews, "Language in 'Love's Labour's Lost'," in Essays and Studies, *n.s. Vol. 17, 1964, pp. 1-11.*

RONALD BERMAN   (essay date 1964)

[*Berman discusses the priority of the physical, sensual "human animal" over the Academe's Platonic ideals in* Love's Labour's Lost *and cites Armado's relations with Jacquenetta as an illustration of this triumph of the body over the mind. The notion that* Love's Labour's Lost *celebrates the victory of the physical or natural over the intellectual or artificial can also be found in the essays by Bobbyann Roesen (1953) and Ralph Berry (1969).*]

[It] is not so much the idea of an academy of imbecile pedants which is ridiculed in *Love's Labour's Lost* as that of the "Platonic" academy. Lyly could have furnished Shakespeare with all the courtiers and pedants he required—he could not have furnished the physical, sensual energy which permeates the play. The world of ideas to be celebrated by the king of Navarre and his companions is unreal in the specific sense that it denies the operation of the blood. The fools in this play—and the women—are otherwise notable. In a milieu of the most incredible etherealization of ideas they assert the power of the senses. When Sir Nathaniel scornfully disposes of Dull he speaks, after the fashion of many Shakespearean characters, better than he knows:

> Sir, he hath never fed of the dainties that are
> bred in a book; he hath not eat paper, as it
> were; he hath not drunk ink: his intellect is not
> replenished; he is only an animal, only sensible
> in the duller parts.
>
> [IV. ii. 23-7]

It is precisely the human animal who is the unseen hero of the play.

The play is conceived in terms of antitheses, all of which bear out to some degree the opposition of "honour" and "affections" stated in the opening speech. Some of these are men against women, mind against body, inhibition against appetite, pedantry against folly. Costard, who is of some importance,

enters a scene in which life has been described as a "fast"; its purpose as the "war against your own affections"; its ethic the mortification of the "world's delights" [I. i. 9, 24, 29]. He enters, in short, a world in which the aristocratic pieties have a recognizably Platonic, not to say Puritan, tinge. He breaks the laws of this suddenly transformed milieu as much by being what he is as by doing what he does. It is not enough that he is caught *in flagrante* ["in the act"] by Armado; he has a ready apology lifted from St. Paul. "Such," he says, "is the simplicity of man to hearken after the flesh" [I. i. 217]. It is an important statement for the play as a whole and for the idea of the comic itself. Costard proves to be a witty and even dangerous reasoner in a world that idealizes a rarefied form of intellect. He has, for example, shown his pragmatic solution for problems like that of Don Armado, who also is in love with Jacquenetta. It is a solution that will not bear much description—but it evidently works. At least Armado has seen its results in the northeast corner of Navarre's garden. (pp. 2-3)

Costard's part of the underplot seems to have a fairly clear application to the situation of the principals. He, Jacquenetta, and Armado form a triangle of male, female, and obtrusive ideal. It is of some interest that Jacquenetta proves eventually to be pregnant by the pedant. This points with some frankness to the larger resolution in the court of Navarre. Woman, it is there discovered, is Nature's answer (or perhaps rebuttal) to ideas. The play ends with the celebration not of seclusion but marriage, not of abstinence but fertility. Renaissance high seriousness could never again be the same. (p. 3)

Ronald Berman, "Shakespearean Comedy and the Uses of Reason," in South Atlantic Quarterly, *Vol. LXIII, No. 1, Winter, 1964, pp. 1-9.*

RALPH BERRY   (essay date 1969)

[*In an interpretation similar to that of Bobbyann Roesen (1953) and Philip Parsons (1963), Berry maintains that the action of* Love's Labour's Lost *progresses from the fantasy world of the king's Academe to the establishment of an inevitable reality, symbolized in the final act by the entry of Mercade. But Berry states that this movement takes place at the level of words, that the men's illusion consists in their misvalue and misuse of words, and that reality will only be reestablished when words reassert "their status as symbols of reality." Like William Matthews (1964), Berry categorizes the characters by their use of language: whereas the courtiers use words only as jests and the pedants use them as self-contained entities, perverting their sense of reality, the Princess's group and the clowns use them as "symbols for things," and thus are linked with the real world. The entrance of Marcade, Berry concludes, not only introduces the world of reality outside the illusory setting of Navarre, but enforces plain and simple language. This concern with language in* Love's Labour's Lost *can also be found in the essays by Gladys Doidge Willcock (1934), James L. Calderwood (1971), Terence Hawkes (1973), Malcolm Evans (1975), and Louis Adrian Montrose (1977); for an argument against Berry's assertion that the play validates words as symbols of reality, see the excerpt by William C. Carroll (1976).*]

Love's Labour's Lost is probably better appreciated today than at any time since its earliest performances. . . . [Critics] have slackened their efforts to expound the play as a sophisticated in-joke, a spoof on Lyly and on the School of Night. No doubt it is all that, but the concentration on the topical interest of *Love's Labour's Lost* tended to obscure its permanent value. The play retains its elusiveness, but is today generally regarded as a delicate and controlled movement towards an acceptance

Act V. Scene ii. Show of the Nine Worthies. The Department of Rare Books and Special Collections, The University of Michigan Library.

of reality. 'Reality' is a term that (however unsatisfactory philosophically) critics agree upon as a convenient designation for the target of the play's probing. The word is not susceptible to exact definition, but it designates all those phenomena of life that are symbolized by the entry of Mercade. That entry is the key fact of the play: it is hardly possible to sustain the argument that it is 'sudden, unprovided for, external to the inner necessity of the plot, and for that reason aesthetically unsatisfactory, though theatrically effective' [see Peter G. Phialas in the Additional Bibliography]. For the play has opened with an assault upon Time/Death [I. i. 1-14], as it closes with the acknowledgement of Time's victory. The death-message is organically present in Scene i, as certain cells die shortly after the body's birth. And the final Act makes sense only as a reversal of the first Act: the themes of light-darkness, folly-wisdom, fantasy-reality are initiated and resolved in the exposition and conclusion. . . . Words compose the central symbol of *Love's Labour's Lost;* it is towards this symbol that the characters are oriented; it is through it that they define themselves. . . . I see the personae in *Love's Labour's Lost* as falling into four main groups, characterized by different attitudes towards words; and the interaction of these groups sets up an intellectual drama that underlies the emotional and personal conflicts.

Navarre, Berowne, Dumain, and Longaville are equivocators. They are concerned with two sorts of words; words as jests, words as oaths. But they do not distinguish absolutely between the two categories; it is a very great error, for an oath cannot exist in the context of a jest, nor a jest in an oath. Essentially, they undermine words, for they see words as projections of their personal whims. The occasion that serves to expose their abuse of words is a fantastic 'study'-project manifestly opposed to 'common sense' [I. i. 57]—a term with a meaning very similar to ours. It is a denial of reality shared by all four. We need not pursue minor distinctions down to the Dumain-Longaville level (though this is possible), but the King and Berowne offer different aspects of the matter.

Navarre has the imperial tendency to want words to match his wishes. Words are his servants. There is a slight, but unmistakable, touch of oafishness about him; a favourite word of his is 'chat'; thus, to Rosaline:

> If you deny to dance, let's hold more chat . . .
>
> [V. ii. 228]

and, more plainly:

> Are we not all in love? . . .
> Then leave this chat; and, good Berowne, now prove
> Our loving lawful, and our faith not torn.
>
> [IV. iii. 278-81]

It is the eternal voice of the superior officer, dismissing with a disdainful monosyllable some business that he does not comprehend, and leaving it to a clever second-in-command to arrange. 'Chat' is the utterance of a man who does not understand words, and does not respect them. Navarre is responsible for the play's most embarrassing moment, when—following the news of the death—he tries, with unbelievable lack of sensibility, to keep the old game going: 'The extreme parts of time extremely forms', and so on through a threadbare string of conceits [V. ii. 740]. It asks for, and gets, the ultimate blank wall of language: 'I understand you not' [V. ii. 752]. His penance will instruct him that words—as oaths—have a meaning and status that lie outside his authority.

Berowne is, however, the focus of the word-attitudes current in his group. He is not deceived by words: he has an ironic appreciation of all modes of language, and can switch easily from plain to tuppence-coloured. He is vitiated by a fundamental lack of faith in words as counters; the jest devalues all currency. When we first encounter him he is trying to back out of an oath, his agreement to study for three years on the King's terms, which seems likely to prove uncomfortable: 'By yea and nay, sir, then I swore in jest' [I. i. 54]. Already he erodes the status of words as oaths. But he is distinguished from the first scene onwards by a highly equivocal attitude to words. 'Necessity will make us all forsworn', he warns prophetically [I. i. 149]: an attitude which the course of the play refutes. The trouble with Berowne is very clearly stated in the exchange between Margaret and Boyet:

> *Margaret:* Not a word with him but a jest.
> *Boyet:*   And every jest but a word.
>
> [II. i. 216]

Boyet's comment is a covert reproach, and a most important one. For Berowne's attack upon the integrity of words leads him to a dilemma, which he himself sees clearly:

> Let us once lose our oaths to find ourselves,
> Or else we lose ourselves to keep our oaths.
>
> [IV. iii. 358-59]

So the reality-principle asserts itself, forcing Berowne to re-examine the bases of his course of conduct. But even though Berowne talks sense, in his praise of love [IV. iii. 286-362], his ready volte-face betrays the true weakness; he accords too little fixed value to words. He has betrayed an oath, and the frivolity of that original oath is itself the fault. . . . We can pass over the oft-quoted rejection of 'Taffeta phrases' in favour of 'russet yeas and honest kersey notes' [V. ii. 406-13]: it is a jesting confession, an adroit attempt to wriggle out of an insupportable situation and, in context, cannot be taken at its face-value. The end, for Berowne, comes when he has to swear *in earnest* to jest—a nice reversal of the opening scene, and a fitting punishment for his besetting vice.

In sum, the King and Berowne typify in their different ways two modes of abusing words. The King wants words to mean what he wants them to mean; Berowne has the opposite tendency, the star debater's readiness to deploy words in any cause, for or against. Wilfulness in one case, frivolity in the other, is the fault. Their common penance is to learn the meaning of oaths, hence of words in general, and to see re-asserted their status as symbols of reality.

The Princess and her court have, for all their gaiety, the utmost respect for words as symbols of reality. 'Through them, in some sense, the voice of Reality speaks', as Miss Roesen remarks [see excerpt above, 1953]. The values of the court are concentrated in its mistress, and we can readily arrive at them by examining the Princess's words. She announces them with her opening lines:

> Good Lord Boyet, my beauty, though but mean,
> Needs not the painted flourish of your praise:
> Beauty is bought by judgment of the eye,
> Not utter'd by base sale of chapmen's tongues.
>
> [II. i. 13-16]

The Princess, gracious and shrewd, stands for sound values arrived at by the senses; and she is utterly opposed to meaningless words. . . . She is beyond question the internal arbiter of the values of *Love's Labour's Lost*.

The Princess is seen at her most commanding in the final Act. Her attitude to words is expressed decisively in her comment on the badinage of Katherine and Rosaline:

> Well bandied both; a set of wit well play'd.
>
> [V. ii. 29]

The metaphor is central, and exact. The Princess and her retinue see words as *games*. This is not at all the same thing as jests. They may indeed make jests, but they never devalue words. The 'game' metaphor implies rules, scrupulously observed by all participants in the contest. The women in *Love's Labour's Lost* use words, but are never used by them.

When, therefore, the women come into contact, and therefore conflict, with the men, they are only superficially sharing the same idiom. In reality, two different modes of language are in collision. The feminine objective is to unmask the *meaning* of the words, that is, to relate words to the motives and purposes of the originators. The poems they regard as 'a huge translation of hypocrisy' [V. ii. 51]. As for the Russian masquerade, the Princess counters this with an unmasking device:

> The effect of my intent is to cross theirs:
> They do it but in mockery merriment;
> And mock for mock is only my intent.
>
> [V. ii. 138-40]

The women will play according to their own rules and on ground of their own choosing:

> *Rosaline:* If they do speak our language, 'tis our will
> That some plain man recount their purposes . . .
>
> [V. ii. 176-77]

And, in the interrogation that follows, the conceit ('. . . we have measur'd many miles / To tread a measure with her on this grass' [V. ii. 184-85]) yields to the ruthless application of the reality-principle. This passage—conceit exposed by reality—figures the whole play.

The Princess's court—and one can legitimately include the epicene Boyet in the group—upholds the value of truth, or reality. The women reason like philosophers. They use words to establish the meaning of words, and hence to relate words to the intentions of the men. This not only accords with their sexual function—the word-game is more serious for women—it expresses an intellectual role, women as realists, that we can see elsewhere in Shakespeare. . . . At all events, they play the word-game with an essentially serious skill that deservedly puts the men to shame.

The Clowns, Costard and Dull (with whom one can associate Moth) are the lower-class equivalent of the women. They, too, are realists of the first order. Within the limits of their education and intelligence, they are not to be deceived. The prime assumption of Costard and Dull is that words symbolize things. (This, be it noted, is a more rudimentary phase of the inquiry initiated by the women, into words as symbols of motives.) Costard, the 'rational hind', is certainly a reality-man. Note his reply to the charge brought against him by Armado: 'Sir, I confess the wench' [I. i. 283]. The words of Armado are not for him, and his own words express a *fact*. Costard, like Moth (and Feste) knows that money is a form of reality. His brief cadenza on 'remuneration' [III. i. 135-42] shows that he is not deceived; words have to symbolize things, and he is aware of their relationship. He is quite clear that one remuneration equals three farthings, and one guerdon equals a shilling [III. i. 170-73], and he has a sardonic awareness—confirmed by Berowne—that a remuneration, in spite of its opulent aura, buys only three-farthings worth of silk [III. i. 139-40]. To Costard, fittingly, are given the words that shortly precede the entry of Mercade: 'she's quick; the child brags in her belly already: 'tis yours' [V. iii. 676-77]. The language, staccato and decisive, prefigures the reality that is shortly to blow the pageant away.

Dull shares Costard's position on words. He is in accord with the view that words must symbolize things. For him, a pricket is a pricket, and not a *haud credo* [IV. ii. 12-21]. The triangular discourse with Holofernes and Sir Nathaniel reveals Dull at his best, stubbornly holding his own; he is like a bridge player, refusing to be psyched out of his hand. . . . It is worth noting that for all the word-play the three are actually discussing a *fact,* i.e. what sort of deer the Princess shot—buck or pricket. These three are by no means such fools as they look, and emerge well from a comparison with their (male) social superiors.

The Clowns, then, form a natural alliance with the ladies. They are intellectual, if not social, complements. . . . In the great work of determining the status of words, the Clowns undertake the primary task: that of establishing the relationship between words and things. Without it no progress at all is possible. And we can, I think, comprehend the importance Shakespeare assigns to the Clowns' role by noting the parallelism he supplies between the Princess and Dull. Both of them use words honestly, and both are ready to admit when words have failed to communicate:

> *Dull:*   Nor understand none neither, sir.
>   [V. i. 151]

> *Princess:* I understand you not.   [V. ii. 752]

Armado, Holofernes, and Nathaniel complete the spectrum of attitudes. They are concerned with words as things in themselves, rather than as symbols for other realities. Such an attitude can be dangerous, if indulged too far; and for Armado it is part of his incessant role-playing. His role as prototype of the dandy requires him to flourish words like ruffles. Since words are the mode, he uses them modishly. . . . It is impossible to determine whether his impulse to Jacquenetta is a genuine yielding to reality, or a decision to incorporate her into his role-playing. He, too, goes the way of Navarre and company: 'I shall be forsworn, which is a great argument of falsehood, if I love' [I. ii. 169-70]—and therefore constitutes a variant of their error. But while the others, at the end, see their roles shattered by reality, Aramdo contrives to incorporate reality into his role. The three-year penance at the plough, clearly, suits him psychologically very well. He is a disturbing testimony to the importance of words as adjuncts to one man's reality. (pp. 69-74)

Predictably, [Holofernes] does not care for Armado, one of his own tribe . . . , and provides an epitome for the two of them (plus the attendant Sir Nathaniel): 'He too is picked, too spruce, too affected, too odd, as it were, too peregrinate, as I may call it' [V. i. 12-14]. This is a great joy for all of us. But Holofernes is not a fool. He is addicted to verbal arabesques, but this is harmless enough. They do not interfere with his sense of reality—he functions perfectly well in the limited society which is his normal milieu. He is, in his scene with Dull and Sir Nathaniel, discussing a fact—one of specialist interest only, to be sure, but a fact nonetheless. And he does not come to grief at the end. His merciless ragging by Berowne and company expresses them, but leaves him, though 'out of countenance', with his essential dignity unshaken. He has a superb final line, in equal command of English and the situation:

> This is not generous, not gentle, not humble.
>   [V. ii. 628]

He has to retire, but the inner man is undefeated. Holofernes' love of words for their own sake is a faculty that Shakespeare—as well he might—treats gently enough here.

Through this grouping of the personae in *Love's Labour's Lost* we can study the intellectual centre of the play: words. *Love's Labour's Lost* is a sustained inquiry into the nature and status of words; and the characters in it embody, define, and implicitly criticize certain concepts of words. Shifting patterns of speakers endlessly debate the propositions, establishing or seeing refuted their word-concepts. The main concepts are these: first, words as jests. Ultimately, this can be a way of rejecting reality—an attempted statement that it is not so. So, though words can be used gaily, they must themselves be treated seriously. The play presents right and wrong models. Those who wish to jest must, like the Princess, use words as in games—that is, adhering strictly to the rules of usage. One must never jest by oath-breaking. An oath is sacred, for it is a wholly laudable attempt to invest words with meaning by submitting policies and actions to the agreed mediation of words. Navarre and his courtiers, then, see their confusion between 'oaths' and 'jests' refuted

by events—and by the ladies. Words as symbols for things is a concept stoutly upheld by the Clowns-realists, who emerge unscathed from the play; their mission is humble, but absolutely necessary. And finally, words as things in themselves is a concept delicately criticized in Armado; they become a part of his role, to the extent that they exclude an awareness of reality. But the concept is allowed to pass with Holofernes, who—whatever his other faults—has his passion for words under control. The pressures of reality test, but do not refute, Holofernes.

And reality is the test to which all the personae must submit. It is there, throughout the play, waiting for them; it begins to throb like a pulse in the last scene, well before Mercade enters. (pp. 75-6)

He, Mercade-Mercury, is the messenger of the gods, bringing the tidings of mortality. His words dissolve the world of illusion, and announce the presence of a reality that must be mediated by words. Armado is the first to see it, and his language is itself a rite of confession: 'For mine own part, I breathe free breath. I have seen the day of wrong through the little hole of discretion, and I will right myself like a soldier' [V. ii. 722-26]. Then the King is rebuked into using 'honest plain words'; and Berowne, the core of the King's party, has to endure the play's central penance. *Words* are the means whereby Berowne is to pass his purgatory, his initiation into the world of reality. His penance sets jokes to work; it restores the meaning of oaths, hence of words, and reasserts their status as symbols of reality. That is the main point established by the close of *Love's Labour's Lost*. And the final songs, perhaps, take up the hint dropped by Armado in Act III:

> it is an epilogue or discourse to make plain
> Some obscure precedence that hath tofore been sain.
>   [III. i. 81-2]

The burden of that epilogue is plain enough. Summer and Winter are both aspects of reality; but Winter is second, and final. The season of death ends the play, as the news of death had stilled the Worthies. It is the final message from the forces that govern the pageant. 'The words of Mercury are harsh after the songs of Apollo' [V. ii. 930-31]. (p. 76)

> *Ralph Berry, "The Words of Mercury," in* Shakespeare Survey: An Annual Survey of Shakespearian Study and Production, *Vol. 22, 1969, pp. 69-76.*

THOMAS M. GREENE   (essay date 1971)

[*Greene argues that* Love's Labour's Lost *is a play about civility and grace in society. He notes that the king and his men are lacking in the social graces and have little sense of civility, as illustrated by their adolescent efforts at courtship, while the women react appropriately to their hosts. Consequently, contends Greene, the women win the "civil war of wits," and the men eventually come to a fuller social awareness through their humiliation. Greene also examines the way in which Shakespeare employs the word "grace" to convey different shades of meaning: grace of entertainment, of love, of wit, and of civility.* Love's Labour's Lost, *he concludes, is about the pursuit of these several kinds of grace.*]

The qualities of *Love's Labour's Lost* determine its limitations. The arabesques of wit, the elaborations of courtly artifice, the coolness of tone—these sources of its charm contribute to that brittleness and thinness and faded superficiality for which some critics of several generations have reproached it. For its admirers, a heavy stress upon these limitations is likely to appear irrelevant. But even admirers must acknowledge that, placed against its author's work, *Love's Labour's Lost* is distinguished by a certain slenderness of feeling, a delicate insubstantiality. It is most certainly not a trivial play, but its subtlety remains a little disembodied.

One source of that impression may be the play's lack, unique in Shakespeare, of any firm social underpinning. Not only is there missing any incarnation of responsible authority, any strong and wise center of political power, but there is equally missing any representative of a stable and dependable citizenry. There is nobody here who, however quirky or foolish or pro-vincial, can be counted on, when he is multiplied enough times, to keep society functioning. Or if there is such a figure in the person of Constable Dull, we are struck with how very marginal a role his creator has permitted him. The patently comic fig-ures—Armado, Holofernes, Costard, Nathaniel, Moth—are all too thin or specialized or socially peripheral to suggest any sort of living society. They may be contrasted with the mechanicals of *A Midsummer Night's Dream,* who, for all their splendid ineptness, do persuade us that a kind of Athenian proletariat exists. The earlier play may owe its peculiar airiness in part to a lack of that social solidity.

Yet despite its lack of a ballasted society, the play is really about ''society'', in a slightly different sense of the word. Its true subject is caught in an offhand remark by one of its funny men: ''Society (saith the text) is the happiness of life'' [IV. ii. 161-62]. The play does not challenge Nathaniel's text, how-ever insubstantial its dramatic sociology. It is much concerned with society, and the happiness of life in society. If it does not present a living society in action, it presents and comments on configurations of conduct which sustain living societies in and out of plays. It is concerned with *styles,* modes of language and gesture and action which befit, in varying degrees, the intercourse of civilized people. And being a comedy, it is concerned with the failures of inadequate styles, since this is the perennial source of elegant comedy from Homer to Proust. Only at the end, and much more surprisingly, does it turn out to reflect the failure of all style.

To distinguish most sensibly the play's hierarchy of moral styles, one may adopt the vantage point of the Princess of France and her three attendant ladies. These four women, being women, cannot provide a strong political center but they do constitute a certain spirited and witty center of social judgment. In their vivacious and spontaneous taste, limited in range and depth but not in accuracy, each is a poised, a Meredithian arbitress of style. This power of discrimination is established by the first speech each lady makes on stage. In the cases of the three attendants, the speech consists in a sketch of the gentleman who is to become the given lady's suitor, and each speech, in its alert and finely qualified appreciation, does credit to the speaker as well as to its subject. . . . As regards the Princess, it is her modesty, her impervious disregard of flattery, the sense of proportion regulating her pride of birth, which betoken most frequently her moral poise. The Princess' first speech opens with a mild rebuke of the spongy Lord Boyet for his gratuitous compliments. . . . She refuses coolly to be hood-winked by the flattery her station conventionally attracts, with an acuteness which sets off the foolish egotism of the King. His first speech, the opening speech of the play, is full of tiresome talk of fame and honor, posturing predictions of im-mortality and glory. The Princess' view of ''glory'' is plain enough after her quick disposal of Boyet, as it is in a later scene when she laughingly dismisses with a tip an unwitting blunder by the forester. Indeed she follows that incident with

reflections which are painfully apposite to the King's foolish enterprise, even if they are ostensibly and deprecatingly di-rected at herself:

> And, out of question, so it is sometimes:
> Glory grows guilty of detested crimes
> When, for fame's sake, for praise, an outward part
> We bend to that the working of the heart.
>
> [IV. i. 30-3]

This last phrase about bending to externals the working of the heart touches very nearly the heart of the play. For *Love's Labour's Lost* explores the relation of feeling and forms, feel-ing and language, feeling and the funny distortions of feeling which our social experience beguiles us to fashion. The four gentlemen, quite clearly, begin by denying the workings of their hearts and libidos for the outward part of fame, just as Armado squirms from his distressing passion for a girl who is outwardly—i.e. socially, his inferior. The distinctions of the ladies is that their feelings and their style, their outward parts, are attuned; they know what they feel and they are in control of its expression. Although they are as quick to admire as the four gentlemen, they are slower to think they are falling in love. They are also, to their credit, far clearer about the phys-iological dimension of their interest. The freedom of their by-play about sex may have lost with time some of its comic sprightliness, but next to the dogged Petrarchan vaporizings of their suitors that freedom still emerges as the more refreshing and healthier mode of speech. The four ladies are, in the best sense, self-possessed, although the play does not try to pretend that the *scope* of their feelings or their experience is any wider than most girls'. An older person with no wider a scope would risk the hollowness of the ambiguous, slightly sterile Boyet. The ladies are so engaging because their spirited and untested freshness is tempered by instinctive good sense.

The roles of the gentlemen—Navarre and his three courtiers—are slightly more complicated. For they must justify to some degree the interest the ladies conceive in them. Longaville may not be quite the ''man of sovereign parts'' [II. i. 44] Maria says he is, but he must remain within hailing distance of that distinguished man she thought she saw and liked. We must always be able to assume that the gentlemen are salvageable as social animals and potential husbands, and need only the kind of education provided by laughter and the penances to which, at the close, they are assigned. But granting them a basic attractiveness, we have to confess that they resemble a little—in their deplorable affectations, their wayward rhetoric, their callow blindness to themselves—the caricatured figures of the sub-plot. There is a difference of degree, not of kind, between the doggerel of, say, Holofernes [IV. ii. 55-61] and the mediocrity of Dumain's verses:

> A huge translation of hypocrisy,
> Vilely compil'd, profound simplicity.
>
> [V. ii. 51-2]

Like Holofernes, Armado, and Nathaniel, the gentlemen ''have been at a great feast of languages and stolen the scraps'' [V. i. 36-7]; all steal indifferently from a common alms-basket of words. They are failures as poseurs because their poses are never original, and as Holofernes himself is able to recognize, ''imitari is nothing'' [IV. ii. 125-26]. The successive defeats of the gentlemen in their sets of wits with the ladies betray an ineptitude of social intelligence and style.

Shakespeare will tolerate cheerfully enough the fashionable inanities of sentimental rhetoric, but he sees the risk of mistaking rhetoric for real sentiment. It is the risk which anguished [Luigi] Pirandello, but it works in this more comical world to expose the gentlemen to their mistresses' ridicule. For the ladies, who are not all wise, know enough to distinguish language in touch with feeling from the language which does duty for feeling, or, more accurately, which papers over adolescent confusions of feeling. The ladies' rhetoric, cooler, more bracing, more alert than the lords', enlivened by the freedom of its casual license, finds a natural recreation in a kind of amiable flyting, a "civil war of wits" [II. i. 226]. The ladies vanquish their suitors unfailingly in this civil badinage because they are, so to speak, in practice. The suitors are not, having attempted to exclude from their still and contemplative academy what they call "the world's debate". Or rather, they have allowed the debate to impinge only at second hand, as a recreative fancy and linguistic toy. (pp. 315-18)

The war of wits is "civil" [II. i. 222] in more meanings than one, since the term *civility* gathers up all of the play's central values. The term as Elizabethans used it embraced all those configurations of political and social and moral conduct which can render society the happiness of life. The gentlemen, in their cocksure unworldliness, have only bungling conceptions of civility, and for all their fumbling efforts toward urbanity, their parochial manners unflaggingly show through. The ideal is defined partly by its breaches: the ascetic breach represented by the academy's austere statutes; or the inhuman breach of the decree which should deprive an interloping woman of her tongue: "A dangerous law against gentility!" [I. i. 128]; or the inhospitable breach which denies the Princess welcome to the court of Navarre; or the rhetorical breaches of the gentlemen's poetastical love complaints; or the fantastical breach of the Muscovite embassy:

> Their shallow shows and prologue vilely penn'd,
> And their rough carriage so ridiculous . . .
>
> [V. ii. 305-06]

or the final blunder which asks the bereaved Princess to listen still to her lover's suit. This variety of gaffes is filled out by the cruder affectations of the minor comic characters. Virtually all the men in the play violate, each in his peculiar way, the values of "civility", which meant at once civilization, social polish, government, courtesy, decorum, manners, and simple human kindness. (p. 318)

The relationship of Berowne to the ideals of civility is rather more complex than his fellows', since he understands so much more than they without ever saving himself from their muddles. He has traits in common with Shaw's John Tanner: both are brilliant, ineffectual talkers who never quite learn how useless are even their best lines. Berowne for all his brilliance is easily put in his place by the securer wit of Rosaline. But despite his frustrations he remains the most original, interesting, and complicated character in the play. He is insincere from the outset; he knows of course that he will sign the articles of the academic oath, even as he calls attention to himself by pretending to refuse. He plays with life, and his life is a play within the play. It is the last word he speaks, in the famous regretful line that gives us—had we been so obtuse as to miss it—the key to his character:

> That's too long for a play.
>
> [V. ii. 878]

Ironist, sophist, scoffer, he has one small, delusory faith: he believes in language, and it fails him. He is almost saved by his capacity to laugh at himself, but not quite; his worst muddle

is his last, when he tries to chasten his rhetoric before the fact of death, and cannot shake his inveterate cleverness. . . . (pp. 319-20)

Berowne's teasing dilettantism is not up to death—nor (more surprisingly?) is it up to sex. His sexuality, like his fellow suitors', is visual, not to say voyeuristic. Their obsession with the eye transcends the Petrarchan cliché; it betokens their callow and adolescent virginity. (p. 320)

The comedy of the gentlemen's sentimental inadequacies is reflected obliquely in the comedy of their inferiors. This reflection receives dramatic expression in Costard's mistaken interchange of Berowne's poem with Armado's letter. The confusion suggests a common element which we recognize as the vice of affectation, a vice which is only a few degrees more marked in the style of Armado and spills over into humor. One might almost say that we are invited to share Costard's error. But from another perspective the gentlemen as gallants emerge from the contrast with even less credit than the ostensible clowns. Costard at least represents the closest thing to good sense in the flights of folly of the opening scene; through his malapropising nonsense a few primitive truths are sounded which shatter all the foregoing silliness about asceticism. . . . Armado of course is more closely parallel to the gentlemen because, unlike Costard, he fancies himself to be in love. Armado is the most suggestive of the comic figures and one of the richest of any in Shakespeare's early comedies, although his potentialities are not consistently developed. There is a resonance to his humor which is lacking, say, in the humor of his fellow pomposity, Holofernes. This is because Shakespeare invests Armado's grandiloquence with a touch of melancholy. We are allowed to catch a bat's squeak of pathos behind the tawny splendor, and a lonely desire for Jaquenetta behind the clumsy condescension to her. The pathos is really affecting when he must decline Costard's challenge and confess his shirtlessness, infamonized among potentates. Nothing so touching overshadows the presentation of the gentlemen. Armado's courtship is more desperate, more clouded, and more believable.

A conventional reading of the play places the main turning point at the end of the fourth act, with the four-fold exposure of the quondam academics and their abjuration of study in the name of Saint Cupid. But to read in this way is to be taken in by the gentlemen's own self-delusions. For their apparent conversion is at bottom a pseudo-conversion, the exchange of one pretentious fiction for another, and we are meant to view ironically their naive release of enthusiasm, as we view Caliban's "Freedom, high-day!" [*The Tempest*, II. ii. 186]. The Muscovite embassy represents the culmination of the gentlemen's clumsy posing, their inept sophistication, and their empty formalism. Never yet in the play have manner and mien been quite so far from feeling, and we learn merely that courtship as performance can be just as silly as the performance of monastic seclusion. The real turning point begins with Berowne's second abjuration and its potentially deeper renunciation of rhetorical affectation. . . . Indeed the remaining action of this rich last scene—almost a one-act play in itself—can be regarded as a progressive and painful exorcism of the gentlemen's pretenses and pretensions. . . . That step leads to the further humbling discovery of the exchanged favors and mistaken identities, and that in turn to the puzzling but clearly important episode of the Worthies' pageant.

The intrusion of this interlude, so cruelly and even pathetically routed at the climax of the action, has troubled more than one reader, and indeed it is not easily justified by our common standards of daily morality. Yet I think that Shakespeare has given us a key to its interpretation, a key which no critic to my knowledge has noticed. The essential point is the reluctance of the gentlemen to watch the pageant, chastened as they already are at this point by their sense of their own absurdity. Yet in fact they do watch. . . . The clumsy pageant will imitate uncomfortably the fumbling Muscovite masquing. The analogy is painfully close, as both the King and Berowne are alert enough to perceive. The Princess' wise insistence on the performance—"That sport best pleases that doth least know how" [V. ii. 516]—creates a small moral dilemma for the lords which they come to resolve by mocking their own unwitting mockers. They recognize, not without a certain rueful courage, that the pageant represents a quintessential parody of their own offenses against propriety; so they choose to follow Boyet in turning upon that parody as though to exorcise their own folly. . . . Unforgivable in itself, the routing of the pageant is dramatically right as ritual action, as a symbolic rejection of a mask beginning to be outworn. Indeed only the savage shame one feels toward an unworthy part of one's self could motivate the gentlemen's quite uncharacteristic cruelty. (pp. 320-23)

The final and most telling chastisement appears with the entrance of Marcade, who brings the fact of death. Even a few minutes earlier, this fact would have shattered the play; now it can be borne. Heretofore death has been itself rhetorical, as in the very first lines:

> Let fame, that all hunt after in their lives,
> Live regist'red upon our brazen tombs
> And then grace us, in the disgrace of death. . . .
>
> [I. i. 1-3]

Then an abstract unreality, death now is a particular event. No one of the characters has the emotional depth fully to command a rhetoric commensurate with the event, but in the speeches following Marcade's entry three degrees of rhetorical inadequacy can be distinguished. The Princess falls short only in the reserve with which she receives her bereavement, a reserve which betrays no feeling and risks the appearance of coldness. Otherwise she is sensible, brief, even, briskly courteous, alert to the relative inconsequence of all the badinage that has preceded. In contrast the poverty of the King's rhetoric is painfully manifest:

> The extreme parts of time extremely forms
> All causes to the purpose of his speed. . . .
>
> [V. ii. 740-41]

a rhetorical failure because it cannot conceal the underlying poverty of sympathy or even of decent respect. . . . Berowne's essay at a valediction . . . opens with a gesture toward the proper simplicity but winds up with an equally inappropriate contortion. Berowne at least recognizes the rhetorical problem; the lesson of *his* failure seems to be that habits of feeling and language are not quickly overcome. (p. 324)

In the light of the lords' inadequacies before the fact of death, the penances set them by the ladies constitute a kind of final prodding toward maturation. Berowne's will test the relevance of his dilettantish jesting to human suffering and thereby purge perhaps the frivolity of his ironies. In these closing moments of the last scene, one has the impression of the comedy turning back upon itself, withdrawing from those modes of speech and laughter which have in fact constituted its distinctiveness. . . . The judgment on Berowne comes to seem like a judgment on the slenderness of a certain moral style that has been outgrown.

There could be no greater mistake than to conclude from this judgment that Shakespeare disliked rhetorics and forms, patterns of words and of experience. He was not, needless to say, in favor of the crude expression of raw passion. He knew that society, the happiness of life, depends on configurations and rituals. He represented the Muscovite masquing to be silly not because it was artificial but because, in his sense of the word, it was not artificial enough; it was "shallow" and "rough" and "vilely penned". This being so, one may ask whether Shakespeare did not provide within the play an instance of authentic artifice, and the answer is that he did provide it, in the form of the two concluding songs. If we regard the presentation of these songs literally, as a part of the pageant they are designed to conclude, then their artistic finish is out of place. But if we regard them as rhetorical touchstones by which to estimate the foregoing funny abuses of language, they form an ideal ending. In their careful balance, elaborate refrain, and lyric poise, the songs are artificial in the good old sense, but in their freshness and freedom from stale tradition, they blithely escape the stilted modern sense. (pp. 324-25)

Society may be, ideally, the happiness of life, but the end of the play has not placed us in it. Perhaps Nathaniel's text is fallacious. But by one very faint, almost surreptitious means, Shakespeare seems to me to remind us repeatedly of the possible felicity into which society can flower. This means is the unusual frequence and special prominence accorded the word "grace"—the word, we remember, with which the opening sentence plays [I. i. 3]. As the play continues, the many extensions and intricate variations of "grace" in all its meanings are explored with deliberate subtlety. In no other play by Shakespeare is the address, "Your Grace", to a sovereign so alive with suggestiveness. The Princess is represented explicitly and emphatically endowed with "grace", from the first mention of her:

> For well you know here comes in embassy
> The French king's daughter with yourself to speak,
> A maid of grace and complete majesty. . . .
>
> [I. i. 134-36]

The Princess' grace has something to do presumably with the comely carriage of her physical bearing, but also with a certain courtesy and sweetness of manner which transcend the body. As the multiple meanings of the word quietly exfoliated, educated Elizabethan playgoers may have remembered the quality of *grazia* in [Baldassare] Castiglione's *Cortegiano*, that indefinable air whch represents the courtier's supreme distinction, and which is repeatedly and emphatically opposed to affectation. Such an echo could only heighten the ironies of the honorific "Your Grace" addressed to the King, and indeed on one occasion his fitness for it is indirectly questioned:

> Good heart, what grace hast thou thus to reprove
> These worms for loving, that art most in love?
>
> [IV. iii. 151-52]

The word in these contexts signifies a virtue a person can possess, but other contexts remind us that it is something that can be given to another. It is what lovers want, as Longaville's poem shows:

> Thy grace being gain'd cures all disgrace in me. . . .
>
> [IV. iii. 65]

Grace is what a wit desires from his audience, perhaps meretriciously:

> For he hath wit to make an ill shape good,
> And shape to win grace though he had no wit . . .
>
> [II. i. 59-60]

Act IV. Scene i. Forester, Princess, Ladies and Lords. By William Hamilton (n.d.).

but it is also the very ability to amuse:

> He is wit's pedlar, and retails his wares
> At wakes and wassails, meetings, markets, fairs;
> And we that sell by gross, the Lord doth know,
> Have not the grace to grace it with such show.
>
> [V. ii. 317-20]

These last passages suggest the paradoxical openness of this ability to perversion or manipulation, and other usages imply the same double-edged danger:

> Folly, in wisdom hatch'd,
> Hath wisdom's warrant, and the help of school,
> And wit's own grace to grace a learned fool.
>
> [V. ii. 70-3]

But all these failures, real or potential, of the virtue never quite suppress the hope which the word embodies: the hope for felicitous human conversation. And although the hope is firmly rooted in the affairs of this world, at least one usage holds the word open briefly to its theological sense:

> For every man with his affects is born,
> Not by might mast'red, but by special grace.
>
> [I. i. 151-52]

That is Berowne on the resilience of human passion, to be echoed later by his flip cynicism: "God give him grace to groan!" [IV. iii. 19-20]. . . . (pp. 326-28)

The grace of entertainment, the grace of love, the grace of wit, the grace of civility—*Love's Labour's Lost* is about the pursuit of all these fragile goals. Its opening adumbrates the need of some ulterior, metaphysical principle to "grace us in the disgrace of death", though the principle of fame proposed there is quickly forgotten. The reader may ask what means the play holds out to us to confront that disgrace, since in fact we are forced at the end to consider it, and the disgrace also of "the speechless sick" and "the painted impotent". Perhaps the upshot is a wry surrender and such a devaluation of grace as [Helge] teaches us to find in the irreverent play of *The Comedy of Errors* on the word's Elizabethan homonym:

> Marry, sir, she's the kitchen-wench, and all grease.
>
> [III. ii. 95-6]

But *Love's Labour's Lost* is not, in the analysis, devaluative, and in a sense its object is to live with the best sort of grace—with enlightened intercourse between the sexes, with gaiety and true wit, with poise, taste, decorum, and charity. The ending does not discredit this object, even if it acknowledges the helplessness of wit before suffering, and even if it extends the realm of grace to unexpected social strata. For the play does not leave us with the Princess; it leaves us with a pun on greasy Joan who keels the pot. (p. 328)

Thomas M. Greene, "'Love's Labour's Lost': The Grace of Society," in Shakespeare Quarterly, *Vol. XXII, No. 4, Autumn, 1971, pp. 315-28.*

JAMES L. CALDERWOOD   (essay date 1971)

[*Calderwood has examined what he calls Shakespeare's "meta-drama" in two studies,* Shakespearean Metadrama *(1971) and* Metadrama in Shakespeare's Henriad *(1979). In the introduction to his earlier book, Calderwood declares that "Shakespeare's plays are not only about . . . various moral, social, political, and other thematic issues," but also about dramatic art itself—"its materials, its media of language and theater, its generic forms and conventions, its relationship to truth and the social order." In his discussion of* Love's Labour's Lost, *Calderwood examines the association of word-play and sexual intercourse in the dialogue, a relation noted earlier by C. L. Barber (1959). Such verbal intercourse, says Calderwood, is potentially procreative and vital, but in the hands of Navarre's men it becomes promiscuous, private, and divorced from social reality. Calderwood cites the men's creation of a verbally oriented monastic society as evidence of this "impulse to take language for one's own." With the breaking of their oaths and the abandonment of the Academe, he continues, the men vacillate from one linguistic extreme to the other—from believing that their words can constitute reality to believing that their words reflect nothing real at all. The women, however, believe in a "valid and reliable" medium of exchange, and this, says Calderwood, is what the men must learn. He observes that they are possessed with a lyric tendency corrected only by the women's satire, which directs language back to a public social body and out of the private, monastic world. Calderwood introduces his notion of metadrama in his conclusion by stating that the play offers an ideal combination of lyric and satire, which both uses and shares language, creating a proper medium of social exchange among a community of individuals. Calderwood's emphasis on the value and exchange of "linguistic currency" and language as the bond of society is echoed in the essays by Terence Hawkes (1973), Malcolm Evans (1975), Louis Adrian Montrose (1977), and, to a lesser degree, in the essays by Gladys Doidge Willcock (1934), William Matthews (1964), and Ralph Berry (1969).*]

Giving a rich and patterned opacity to the clear window of language is one thing Shakespeare is doing in *Love's Labour's Lost.* It is not the only thing he does, and the ending of the play modifies his doing of it very radically, but the doing deserves attention. In perhaps no other play does language so nearly become an autonomous symbolic system whose value lies less in its relevance to reality than in its intrinsic fascination. The referential role of words as pointers to ideas or things is consistently subordinated to their relational role as pointers to other words. (p. 56)

The aesthetic pleasure generated by all this linguistic fooling is "mirth," which in one of the play's dominant metaphors is begotten by the creative intercourse of language with wit. "My father's wit and my mother's tongue, assist me!" [I. ii. 96]—Moth's epic invocation as he girds himself to deliver a definition in song establishes the gender of wit and language, whose issue is wholly verbal. Or to pursue this metaphor a bit, the creative act engaged in by wit and language may take the form of repartee in which the mutual thrust, parry, and riposte of words are associated with hunting, dancing, combat, and most of all the sexual act. . . . (p. 57)

The intercourse between wit and words to which all [the scholars'] energies are devoted is ambiguous in value and effect. On the one hand it is procreative and vital, generating through mirth and amusement a community of feeling that goes at least partway toward binding society together. But on the other hand it is as barren as Dull's intellect because what could be a genuine union of words and thoughts, language and reality, has in their practice degenerated to mere verbal promiscuity, to a splendid but ephemeral dalliance between wit and words.

Such a relationship is fitting enough in a world of holiday and festive release. But in the world of everyday toward which the drama moves, license whether verbal or sexual must give way to the governing forms of social order, promiscuity to marriage. The final attitude which the play takes toward this dalliance of wit and language is suggested in its own punning title, for when words do duty for realities love's labor is truly without issue and in the metadramatics of the play literary form miscarries. But that is to get ahead of the story.

So one of the things this play does is to give words the function not so much of expressing the truth of things or thoughts but of eliciting—through puns, metaphors, rhyme, alliteration, coinage, through all the devices that suggest the substantiality of language—verbal relations that are in themselves aesthetically pleasing. But if Shakespeare runs with the hares of playful speech, he hunts with the hounds of satiric sense as well. In fact most critics have found it easy to regard the hares as existing only to be coursed by the hounds. If so, Shakespeare lines up with the verbal skeptics as a kind of "exteriorized" Berowne feeding the wormwood of burlesque to the linguistic ills of his time—gongorism, preciosity, pedantry, inkhornism, and plain ignorance. As satirist of verbal affectation and related abuses he would presumably aim to purify language, to transform the whore back into a virgin. Thus aggrandizing words as substantive entities and satirizing verbal affectation appear as twin aspects of the same desire, which is to convert the public and corrupt medium into his private and pure property, giving to transient breath a solidity in which he can carve his own enduring shapes.

The impulse to take language for one's own is most obviously figured in the opening scene of the play. To achieve eternal fame in the mouths of men the scholars create a private society by verbal fiat. They bind themselves to one another by giving their words or oaths to each other, they bind themselves to the words of the statutes that define their obligations, and they bind themselves to the study of words. As a result the court "shall be a little Academe, / Still and contemplative in living art" [I. i. 13-14]—a transfixed (still) rather than enduring (still) social unit the central feature of which is its prohibition of women. Since this academe is verbally created its integrity is primarily verbal and must be verbally guaranteed. Therefore "no woman shall come within a mile of [the] court . . . On pain of losing her tongue" [I. i. 119-24], and in the only other item revealed to us from the statutes "If any man be seen to talk with a woman within the term of three years, he shall endure such public shame as the rest of the court can possibly devise" [I. i. 129-32]. Figured in the oaths and statutes the interdependence of language and the social order is complete; neither can exist apart from the other. Even to say that the breakdown of language precipitates the breakdown of the social order is to imply a division between the two that is simply not there. When the scholars one by one break their words, that does not *cause* their private masculine community to disintegrate; it *is* that disintegration.

The major reason for the collapse of the academic society is that the language that created it in the first place was disjoined from the truth of human nature, which is defined in the phrase of that minor lexicographer and master lover Costard—"such is the simplicity of man to hearken after the flesh" [I. i. 217-18]. In the verbal world of academe the word has been set against the word—"will" as moral resolve against "will" as passion and the affections. The brave conquerors who "war against [their] own affections / And the huge army of the world's desires'' place passion under the lock and key of verbal oaths, subjecting will to will [I. i. 8-10]. The function of both Berowne and Costard in the opening scene is to point the fact that language so divorced from realities of human nature can achieve little more than merely verbal triumphs, let alone foster an enduring social order. (pp. 59-61)

Costard even more bluntly reveals the disjunction between language and truth. No sooner have the "deep oaths" been sworn than he "is taken with a wench" in the park and brought to justice. Forecasting the scholars' later devices, he first tries to evade the facts by quibbling with the language of the statutes:

> KING. It was proclaimed a year's imprisonment to be
>   taken with a wench.
> COSTARD. I was taken with none, sir. I was taken with a
>   damsel.
> KING. Well, it was proclaimed damsel.
> COSTARD. This was no damsel neither, sir. She was a
>   virgin.
> KING. It is so varied too, for it was proclaimed virgin.
> COSTARD. If it were, I deny her virginity. I was taken
>   with a maid.
> KING. This maid will not serve your turn, sir.
> COSTARD. This maid will serve my turn, sir.
>
> [I. i. 288-99]

In the last line Costard abandons his attempt to evade the language of the statutes, which he has found is in its own way perfect, an absolutely closed system without verbal loopholes. But his last line underscores the fact that however perfect the system may be on its own grounds it is not grounded in reality; the word "maid" will not serve his turn by giving him a quibbling out, but the maid herself will "serve" him in the overworked sexual sense of the term. Thus when sentenced to a week on "bran and water" Costard can say to Berowne "I suffer for the truth, sir; for true it is I was taken with Jaquenetta, and Jaquenetta is a true girl" [I. i. 311-12]. In being taken with a true girl Costard has revealed himself a true man hearkening as true men do after the flesh. But separating these masculine and feminine truths and preventing their incorporation into the social order is a repressive language in the service of a repressive justice, or rather a language and a justice that are mutually defining, a sterile tautology from which there is no escape and into which reality cannot penetrate. So Costard suffers not only "for the truth," as he claims, but because the truth of human nature goes unreflected in the received language of Navarre.

At his humble level Costard acts as a weathervane pointing the way the dramatic winds blow. In demonstrating that language can neither substitute for nor suppress reality, that the victory of "will" over "will" is spuriously verbal, he exposes more than he himself understands. Not, however, more than the French ladies understand. (pp. 62-3)

The point here is not merely to reaffirm Shakespeare's much-noted verbal skepticism in Love's Labour's Lost. The skepticism is of course there, and the scholars are allowed to feed so fully of the dainties that are bred in a book and to inhale so deeply of fine phrases that they threaten to suffocate on syllables. But Shakespeare's treatment of the scholars suggests not a repudiation of the power of language but an acute awareness of its limits and of the comic consequences of exceeding them. The play has yet to establish a final attitude toward the use and abuse of speech.

Structurally the play divides into three phases—the formation of academe, the abandonment of academe, and a final peripeteia marked by the entrance of Mercade. The dominant theme of the first phase is the aggrandizement of words by the scholars, which makes its way against the abrasive sub-theme of Berowne's dubiety. This phase ends when the scholars' oaths and hence their closed society both collapse under the pressures of human nature. (p. 64)

During the second phase of the play the scholars switch from aggrandizing words to debasing them. Berowne having gone along with them in their ingenuous confidence in verbal power, they now go along with him in his comically cynical view of language:

> KING. Then leave this chat and, good Berowne, now
>   prove
> Our loving lawful and our faith not torn.
> DUMAINE. Ay, marry there—some flattery for this
>   evil.
> LONGAVILLE. O some authority how to proceed—
>   Some tricks, some quillets how to cheat the devil.
> DUMAINE. Some salve for perjury.
>
> [IV. iii. 280-85]

To find flattery for this evil Berowne is most apt, and in his famous exonerating speech he turns the word against the word with such sophistical eloquence that perjury is transformed into charity [IV. iii. 285-362]. . . . Berowne's entire speech, too long to quote, sums up the attitudes expressed a bit earlier by all the scholars in their poem-letters to the ladies. He pits language and vows against reality and nature and concludes with Longaville that "Vows are but breath, and breath a vapour is" [IV. iii. 66].

Thus the scholars drift from one linguistic extreme to the other. Having discovered that language cannot create *ex nihilo* an enduring social order or legislate reality out of existence, they now assume that words are quite without substance—mere breath. Like Costard they have been taken with a wench, language, and like his at first their defense is based on proving language a whore instead of acknowledging themselves lechers. What they had set up with all due formality as a marriage, they now prefer to annul and redefine as a dalliance, demoting language from wife to mistress since in one of the play's recurrent puns words are "light"—not only in the sense of their being brilliantly insubstantial but in the sense of their being loose or promiscuous.

Such a view leads of course to verbal chaos. If words are merely appearances devoid of any intrinsic truth or power then one may do with them as he will. Oaths can be made and broken on the dictate of whimsy ("O who can give an oath?" Berowne cries—[IV. iii. 246]); facts are at the mercy of phrases; and meanings may be created, modified, or dismissed at will. In the dramatic worlds of chronicle and tragedy such a collapse of language generates or at least attends social and political collapse. In the comic world of Love's Labour's Lost, however, a built-in corrective in the form of the French ladies prevents the corruption of language from seriously impairing the social order. For despite their own very considerable talent for fooling in words the ladies have a greater respect for language than the scholars. . . . [When] the King prepares to break his oath by inviting the ladies to enter the court, the Princess replies

> This field shall hold me, and so hold your vow.
> Nor God nor I delights in perjured men.
> KING. Rebuke me not for that which you provoke.

The virtue of your eye must break my oath.
PRINCESS. You nickname virtue—"vice" you should
    have spoke,
For virtue's office never breaks men's troth.
    Now by my maiden honour, yet as pure
As the unsullied lily, I protest,
    A world of torments though I should endure,
I would not yield to be your house's guest;
    So much I hate a breaking cause to be
Of heavenly oaths vowed with integrity.

[V. ii. 345-56]

The Princess's speech here calls attention to the dissolution of language that is corollary to the lords' assumption that words are mere breath. It also, in her insistence on fidelity to oaths, not only associates linguistic integrity with moral integrity but even suggests through references to God and heavenly oaths that language, like the moral order, has a transcendent dimension of meaning to which men must remain faithful. Most important though, her speech constitutes the redemption of the word by the word. Sworn on her "maiden honour" the Princess's vow not to enter the court intercepts the King's intention to break his own vow and thereby preserves his word. . . . [The] King's promiscuous intentions toward his own vow are countered by the Princess's vow and transformed into a genuine marriage between word and meaning. In a play as absorbed in language as this one it is fitting that redemption should take the form not of mercy or love, as it normally does in Shakespearean comedy, but of words themselves.

However, the redemption of language and of the scholars is far from complete. The fact that the King's word is kept true through outside assistance, the Princess's vow shoring up his original vow, reminds us that language is a public medium in which everyone has a stake. Surely the social order needs a true language no less than a true currency. In the marketplace of love—where seller, buyer, and money take the form of lover, beloved, and language—a valid linguistic currency must effectively unite what is meant with what is understood: love must be truly felt, truly expressed, and truly received. This paradigm for the dialogue of love is disregarded in *Love's Labour's Lost,* and love's labor is lost because the scholar-lovers cannot find the verbal *style* in which love can be genuinely expressed and hence genuinely received.

The style the scholar-lovers do adopt during the second phase of the play is that inflationary species of linguistic currency that was flooding the poetic market in the 1590s—the Petrarchan. . . . Exuberantly afflicted with love, holding their own emotional pulses, and calling out their rising temperatures with gleeful woe, the scholars have all become lyric poets singing the praises of their malady less for the benefit of the ladies than for their own wonder and delight. Compared to the pulsing reality of their overheated blood, words have no apparent worth and hence can be lavished in sonnets, declarations of love, flattery, and similar forms of conspicuous improvidence. From the kind of verbal hoarding represented by their Academe project, the scholars have passed to the wildest profligacy.

To the ladies, who advocate a stable currency backed by solid gold reserves, the scholar-lovers look suspiciously prodigal and their verbal coin counterfeit. . . . These new oaths ask to be compared to those in the opening act, for each marks a different form of linguistic abuse. The earlier oaths sought to bring about verbal purity in isolation from the larger social context. The later oaths are the product of a machine-tooled courtly style that parades words too easily and indiscriminately, setting the mask of "goddess of beauty" on dark-skinned Rosalines and blue-eyed Katherines alike. The contrast between the two kinds of oath, one in the service of verbal purity, the other in the service of verbal laxity, is paralleled at the sexual level in that the scholars pass from the self-centered celibacy of Academe to an equally self-centered "love" that bestows itself too readily and freely in all directions. (pp. 64-70)

This underlying stress on language as a social instrument enabling, if the right words were found, subjective experiences like love to be shared by lover and beloved helps explain Rosaline's punishment of Berowne at the end of the play. . . . For his infidelity to language Berowne must learn linguistic decorum, which decrees that words be framed not to his fancy as images of self-love but in accord with the feelings of his audience and the nature of the social, or in this case medical, situation. From his attempt to generate a communion of feeling between self and auditor under these trying circumstances will emerge his awareness of the nature and limits of language. Thus whereas he earlier said that he and the other scholars must lose their words to find themselves, he must now find the truth of words in order to find both himself and Rosaline. For not only do they, like the whole of the human community, have a share in language but through language of the right kind they may come to share one another. (p. 71)

The impulse to construct a self-enclosed verbal context indifferent to outside realities and concerned less to communicate meanings than to exploit them autistically, let me call, with some apologies, lyric. And remembering that at this time, around 1593-94, Shakespeare was also at work on the sonnets, we may see considerable evidence of a lyric impulse operating within and even against the dramatic framework of the play. For the evolution of action and plot is reduced to a series of verbal events: vows made and broken, games of wit and wordplay, penned speeches, songs, epistolary sonnets, and even "sentences" pronounced on the scholars by the ladies. Like Don Armado (and in part by creating him) Shakespeare "draweth out the thread of his verbosity finer than the staple of his argument" [V. i. 16-17]. Thus the play seems almost an experiment in seeing how well language spun into intricate, ornate, but static patterns can substitute for the kinetic thrust of action in drama.

The other major impulse in the play is the satiric: Shakespeare's burlesque of verbal affectation in general and of current linguistic and literary fashions in particular. Lyric seeks to appropriate words from the public structure of language and turn them into mirrors of the self. Its radical emphasis is on the isolated speaker whose words are not directed to an audience and hence are not so much heard as, in Mill's famous phrase, overheard. The episode in Act 4 in which each of the scholars reads his love poem aloud while Berowne sits listening like a demigod in the sky is a perfect illustration of this aspect of lyric. Satire on the other hand turns language back on society, presumably in the interests of sanative castigation. Its radical emphasis therefore is less on the speaker than on the audience under attack. In *Love's Labour's Lost* two kinds of satire are distinguishable: that of the French ladies, which operates on the scholars with the aim of purging them of faults; and that of the scholars and especially Berowne, which, perhaps most obviously in their comments on the unworthiness of the Nine Worthies, functions destructively as a form of self-aggrandizing mockery, punitive rather than purgative.

Perhaps now I can work toward the metadramatic implications of all this. In the scholars we see a lyric appropriation of words, a desire to create through word power a world insulated against such outside realities as women and such inner realities as passion—"the huge army of the world's desires" and "your own affections" [I. i. 9-10]. Against this bubble of lyric seclusion is set the abrasive of the French ladies, the outer world of fact and substance which expresses itself in ridicule, demonstrating through "pure scoff" the futility of words divorced from the public body of language and used only as the kept mistress of private feeling. From this conflict emerges a view of language as a medium of social exchange in the most generous sense, a medium that is true to itself when it enables men and women to share the inner experience of love, thus becoming the verbal sacrament that confirms "the marriage of true minds" [Sonnet 116]. As the characters move toward a recognition of language not as an instrument of either private expression or public attack but as an agency of social communion, so the generic movement of the play itself proceeds through lyric and satire toward the comic vision that reconciles both. The comic form leads to the acceptance of the isolated individual (associated here with lyric) into a society purged of harshness and discord (or the satiric), a social integration for which the conventional symbol is the wedding. (pp. 71-4)

Speculating about Shakespeare's stake in this is of course risky, but perhaps it is not too much to suggest that through his imaginative involvement in this play he has worked out some metaphoric formulations of the poet's responsibilities to his medium and his art. The poet must come to realize that he cannot transform language by force to serve his pleasure. He cannot try like the scholars to seize the Word and inflate it into a self-contained world in the image of his own desires since that is to appropriate the Word to himself, and it does not belong to him. Seeking to virginize language for himself is as futile in the long run as the scholars' attempt to ensconce themselves in celibacy. If language is to serve the poet, he must serve her as well; and that means recognizing not only her generosity to him but also her independence from him. It means recognizing that language is like Nature in that she

> never lends
> The smallest scruple of her excellence
> But like a thrifty goddess she determines
> Herself the glory of a creditor,
> Both thanks and use.
>   [Measure for Measure, I. i. 36-40]

The trouble with lyric celibacy is that it fails to acknowledge that it is taking words on loan and must return "both thanks and use" (that is, interest). The way the poet can return thanks and use to language and enrich her for her enrichment of him is by helping her fulfill her role as the bringer of social communion. In the best sense of liberality he must give in return. The scholars, however, pass from the non-giving of celibacy to the pseudo-giving (license in the guise of liberality) of a "love" that is made to look like promiscuity when they make their vows to the wrong ladies. Two extremes of sexual conduct correspond to two extremes of linguistic usage, and underlying both is an essential selfishness. Sexually both celibacy and promiscuity deny nature her due ("use"), which is children: if man owes God a death as Hal tells the sweating Falstaff at Shrewsbury [in I Henry IV], he owes Nature a child as the first seventeen of Shakespeare's sonnets repeatedly insist. And linguistically both verbal purity that aggrandizes words, as in Academe, and verbal prodigality that degrades them, as in the wooing sequences, deny language her due, which is, Shakespeare seems to feel in this play, the genuine marriage of word and meaning in drama.

For in drama the poet, far from using language selfishly, gives his words to actors who in turn give them to an audience. Instead of removing words from public circulation the dramatic poet allows them truly to become a medium of social exchange, ciruclating freely within the community of the theater, and indeed by virtue of this circulation creating a community of what were merely so many random individuals before the play began. (pp. 74-6)

Purely verbal self-containment cannot cordon art off from reality. It is not enough to carve isolated shapes in words—to solidify as Shakespeare has a line or couplet, a sequence of repartee, even a scene. The "songs of Apollo" are vulnerable to the harsh "words of Mercury" [V. ii. 930-31] precisely because they are individually isolated units. If the "endeavour of this present breath" is to make its author one of the "heirs of all eternity" [I. i. 5, 7] words themselves must be more than breath of the kind that can be blown away by messengers of mortality. The material solidity of words can be stressed by sheer linguistic play, but the result is not an enduring solidity. Linguistic play must graduate into dramatic play, and that involves the collusion of art and nature, language and action. Only when anchored within a context of action, deriving from it and contributing to it, are words finally safe from cormorant devouring Time. Love's Labour's Lost embodies Shakespeare's discovery that drama is the literary form of true liberality and that drama achieves fulfillment when verbal celibacy and verbal prodigality give way to a genuine marriage of words to action.

With this marriage of words and actions within the play an ideal "marriage of true minds"—the minds of poet, actors, and audience—is consummated in the Theatre itself. But it is especially in dramatic comedy where everyone is bound together in the festivity of the ending that the perfect imaginative and social union occurs. To achieve that union in Love's Labour's Lost would take, as Berowne says, "too long for a play" [V. ii. 878]; and Shakespeare realizes full well that "a great feast of languages" [V. i. 37] will not serve as a substitute. But through the raising and purging of linguistic delight, he has perhaps come to realize how language in the service of the comic vision can create an image of social communion shared not only by the characters within but by the audience without as well. That achievement is not to be found here, but like the marriages it stands in the offing. It wants perhaps less than "a twelvemonth and a day" [V. ii. 827] before A Midsummer Night's Dream capitalizes on the rich gains of Love's Labour's Lost to usher in the great train of Shakespearean comedy. (pp. 80-1)

> James L. Calderwood, "'Love's Labour's Lost': A Dalliance with Language," in his Shakespearean Metadrama: The Argument of the Play in "Titus Andronicus," "Love's Labour's Lost," "Romeo and Juliet," "A Midsummer Night's Dream," and "Richard II," University of Minnesota Press, 1971, pp. 52-84.

TERENCE HAWKES (essay date 1973)

[Hawkes notes in Love's Labour's Lost a conflict between "the resonant world of speech" and the "silent world of writing" and argues that the men's social and sexual failures are the result of their rejection of the reality of the oral community. Armado and Holofernes in their scripted and mechanical efforts at courtship he regards as two extreme examples of sterile "bookmen;" while Berowne, in his rejection of "speeches penned," opens the way for "the organic reality" of the oral community and, hence, a *comic resolution. Hawkes is one of the only critics to interpret the actions of Berowne in such a favorable light. He concludes that the written play and the performed play may also be viewed in this opposition. This concern with the social reality of language in* Love's Labour's Lost *is also apparent in the comments of James L. Calderwood (1971), Louis Adrian Montrose (1977), and Malcolm Evans (1975), the last of whom focuses on the dichotomy of writing and speech in the drama. For more general considerations of the play's linguistic concerns, see the excerpts by Gladys Doidge Willcock (1934), William Matthews (1964), and Ralph Berry (1969).]*

In the *Phaedrus,* Plato presents a famous argument against writing. Re-telling the myth of its invention, he recounts the words of the Egyptian King to Theuth, who has invented letters:

> If men learn this, it will implant forgetfulness in their souls: they will cease to exercise memory because they rely on that which is written, calling things to remembrance no longer from within themselves, but by means of external marks. What you have discovered is a recipe not for memory, but for reminder. And it is no true wisdom that you offer your disciples but only its semblance; for by telling them of many things without teaching them, you will make them seem to know much, while for the most part they know nothing; and as men filled, not with wisdom but with the conceit of wisdom, they will be a burden to their fellows.

In essence, that seems to be a reasonable account of what happens in *Love's Labour's Lost,* for in this [play] . . . the resonant world of speech is comically opposed to the silent world of writing. At its simplest, the action concerns a group of men who opt out of active oral society in pursuit of immortality, and in the name of what turns out to be the 'conceit of wisdom'. It tells the story of their realization that true wisdom, true 'civilization', true immortality, resides only within the oral community and its social and sexual processes which they have rejected. As 'bookmen' [II. i. 227] (as the play calls them) the members of Navarre's 'silent court' realize they have betrayed their true nature of 'talking animals'.

On another closely related level, the play also concerns itself with the relationship between the faculty of reason and that of language (the Greek word *logos* is the same for both faculties). A narrow concept of logical, or 'dialectical' reason manifested in the form of the sterile 'reduced' language of books, is set against its oral, rhetorical opposite symbolized by the music of rhyme: that 'fertile' language in which love manifests itself in the play, and which lies beyond the grasp of the reason, appearing in consequence 'mad' or 'foolish' to it. In short, the opposition of the world of speech to the world of books overtly proposed in the play finds itself covertly reinforced by a more contemporary tension between the rival claims of rhetoric and dialectic, itself a version of the immemorial linguistic opposition of rhyme to reason. (pp. 53-5)

Armado's 'high-born' and 'fire-new' words [I. i. 172, 178] parody those of his betters, and constitute the essence of a language which is obviously 'literary' in its origin and function, and comically divorced from the real world of oral interchange. We encounter it first in its most characteristic form, as language written down, in a letter:

> The time when? About the sixth hour; when beasts most graze, birds best peck, and men sit down to that nourishment which is called sup-

per: so much for the time when. Now for the ground which? which, I mean, I walked upon: it is ycleped thy park. Then for the place where? . . .

[I. i. 235-40]

The reduction of the dimensions of nature itself to the level of a horn-book of dialectical 'method' is comic because so much of nature's reality eludes the linguistic structures. . . . Armado's language is a language of the book. As such, it is unable to cope with ordinary life, even on the level of the necessary social and sexual relationship between men and women on which society depends. Holofernes's designation of the 'wench' Jaquenetta as 'a soul feminine' [IV. ii. 81] indicates the same disabling characteristic.

In essence, then, Aramdo embodies a language appallingly, and so comically, 'methodized'. If to speak is to be human, he hardly achieves that status. He does not speak, so much as utter writing. . . . He does not laugh, but announces 'the heaving of my lungs provokes me to ridiculous smiling' [III. i. 77]. And he is ponderously unable to deal with the wit of low-life characters such as Moth. . . . Appropriately, the 'external marks' of the written word engage a good deal of his interest, and 'letters' constitute in great measure his way of communicating, and so his way of life. He writes, characteristically, of his love to Jaquenetta;

> The magnanimous and most illustrate king Cophetua set eye upon the pernicious and indubitate beggar Zenelophon, and he it was that might rightly say, *veni, vidi, vici;* which to annothanize in the vulgar (O base and obscure vulgar!) *videlicet,* he came, saw, and overcame: he came, one; saw, two; overcame, three. Who came? the king: why did he come? to see. . . .

[IV. i. 64-72]

Such 'language' copes with reality by painting it over, in a 'cosmetic' process which requires ordinary experience to fit preconceived 'logical' structures. By means of such a process, the complexities of love can be dialectically 'reduced' to primary colours, and can seem 'most immaculate white and red' [I. ii. 90]. Moth's jocular piercing of this painted linguistic veil notably takes the form as he puts it of setting a 'dangerous rhyme' against this 'reason of white and red' [I. ii. 107-08]. Language used to 'paint over' reality, to reduce its complexities to a sinister simplicity, becomes a major and a tragic theme in Shakespeare's later plays. . . . Here, it is sufficient to remark the process in its light-hearted aspect, as the comic means by which Armado tries rationally to cope with normal but apparently 'irrational' human emotions. His response to the inward animal disturbances of love is hilariously that of the 'book-man'. . . . (pp. 56-8)

Holofernes's contribution to the debate about orthography consists, predictably, of the assertion that the rules of writing ought to dominate and determine speech. (p. 59)

Predictably, Holofernes's critical response to Berowne's beautiful poem to Rosaline is wholly stilted, restricted to observations concerning the breaking of the 'rules':

> You find not the apostrophus, and so miss the accent: let me supervise the canzonet . . .

[IV. ii. 119-20]

As he begins to 'overglance the superscript' [IV. ii. 131] the inability of such literary standards to comprehend genuine emotion, genuinely expressed, is once more reinforced. In fact the play leaves us in no doubt that Armado and Holofernes are buffoons because they are 'lettered', as Armado puts it [V. i. 45] beyond reasonable bounds. They are 'bookmen', not human beings. . . . (p. 60)

Berowne's rejection of 'speeches penned', the 'taffeta phrases, silken terms precise' of 'orthography', and his resolve to embrace their oral apposite, 'russet yeas and honest kersey noes' [V. ii. 406, 413], constitutes an important statement of the play's main theme. Access to reality, he discovers, lies not in books, but in involvement with other people: not in the domain of the eye, reading and writing, but in that of the voice and the ear, talking and listening. (p. 61)

The fundamental irony the play explores is that those who confine themselves to books, and to book-language, end up by being paradoxically and wittily 'caught out' by ordinary human language in its widest sense. In this way, as Berowne predicts from the first,

> . . . study evermore is overshot:
> While it doth study to have what it would,
> It doth forget to do the thing it should;
> [I. i. 142-44]
> (p. 62)

Indeed, much of the comedy derives from the fact that [man's emotions] turn out to constitute an overriding and compelling 'language' of their own which is fundamentally human, though shared with the non-rational animals. The *leitmotif* of hunting scenes in the play carries this message forcefully: we are all animals in part, and should 'listen' to that part of our language. Thus the King's park, the setting of the play, becomes a microcosm filled with beasts and humans, all of whom 'hunt' each other. And of course the rhetoric of the hunting scenes manifests an appropriate sexuality. . . . [Its] profusion of sexual puns on 'hit', 'horns', 'prick' and 'rub' between the Princess, the ladies, Boyet and the rest, constitutes a more genuine language of love (and a highly rhetorical one) than the sterile 'logical' absurdities of Armado's 'methodical' letter, quoted above, which precedes it. Here, as elsewhere in Shakespeare, fruitful linguistic intercourse prefigures and mirrors its sexual analogue.

It also leads, inevitably and naturally, to the comic 'reversal' at the play's core, in which women first usurp, and then metaphorically *become* the books which the 'book-men' admire. In the event, the *real* 'book-mates' turn out to be women. They constitute the only legitimate repositories of knowledge, the only generative source of valid learning, the only fertile stimulus of rhetoric. (pp. 62-3)

Access to reality lies not through study, but through life itself, through language. Berowne's sonnet to Rosaline has this as its theme:

> Study his bias leaves and makes his book thine eyes,
> Where all those pleasures live that art would
>   comprehend.
> If knowledge be the mark, to know thee shall suffice;
> Well learned is that tongue that well can thee commend;
> [IV. ii. 109-12]
> (p. 64)

His long speech in Act IV contains the central thesis of the play; women are in essence the proper object of man's study, for

> They are the ground, the books, the academes,
> From whence doth spring the true Promethean fire.
> [IV. iii. 299-300]

Man, the argument seems to run, is naturally a social being, one that characteristically thrives in and adapts to a changing environment. He should not attempt to impose an unchanging, rationally conceived 'shape' on the world around him, for this violates his and the world's essential condition. The use of language which 'paints over' reality in false colours has been diagnosed as one of the major means by which the 'academe' and the court in this play have attempted to impose a narrowly prescriptive 'rational' scheme of things on the vagaries of nature and human nature; the imposition of reason without rhyme, of dialectic without rhetoric. Berowne's rejection of that involves his acceptance, and embracing, of the nature of the world as it is, for that is to accept and embrace his own nature. Fundamentally, this means embracing other people not books;

> For where is any author in the world
> Teaches such beauty as a woman's eye?
> [IV. iii. 308-09]

Knowledge, this seems to say, lies in life itself, in our interaction with others in the community, that talking-listening involvement which, the play has already made clear, precedes and prefigures its necessary sexual counterpart. Like love, knowledge is no abstract entity that books can 'contain', or reading give access to. In Berowne's words

> Learning is but an adjunct to ourself,
> And where we are our learning likewise is.
> [IV. iii. 310-12]

Our way of life, that is to say, constitutes our knowledge. And in an oral society, as way of life and language are intimately related, so the language embodies, and indeed *is* knowledge for the community. Knowledge thus resides in communal life. There is no other source. (pp. 64-5)

Ultimately, as Northrop Frye says, the play's central theme is one of fruitful reconciliation, the result of Shakespeare's 'impersonal concentration on the laws of comic form' [see Additional Bibliography]. Life itself triumphs over human aridity, as love triumphs over letters. And at the very end of the play the two 'opposites' of nature itself, Spring and Winter, are finally seen to 'complete' each other, as part of the same total process. The songs sung in their name draw, linguistically, on the essence of ordinary experience. They manifest the texture of ordinary life, of icicles, frozen milk, coughing, cooking, birth and marriage; and they advocate acceptance of this life, of things as they are. (p. 67)

[On] the level of the human world of social organization, the ultimate realization borne in upon Navarre and his 'bookmates' is that speech reflects, indeed guarantees the organic reality of the whole community and its way of life; that consideration of 'each thing that in season grows' [I. i. 107] makes of the language of the 'unlettered' a necessary ingredient without which the writing of the 'learned' remains unredeemably sterile; that rhetoric is not alien to dialectic but adds to it its own kind of 'rhyme' as an essential social complement of learning's 'reason'. (pp. 67-8)

Act IV, Scene ii. Holofernes, Nathaniel, Dull, Jacquentta, and Costard. By Francis Wheatly (n.d.).

In his role as messenger of the Gods, Mercury (or Hermes) was also firmly associated with writing, often as its inventor, a connection he shared with his Egyptian and Scandinavian counterparts. As the various avatars of Mercury merge into a single figure in the Renaissance, this association becomes more and more firmly esablished, so that, for example, Nashe's *Summer's Last Will and Testament* (1592-3), in the process of a satirical account of the history of writing, can tell how Hermes/Mercury

> Weary with graving, in blind characters,
> And figures of familiar beasts and plants
> Invented letters to write lies withal. . . .

Apollo, of course, symbolized no less a number of disparate ideas during the same period, but in respect of the contrast with Mercury here postulated will obviously primarily be connected with language in its oral form, and its tonal aspects; a relationship appropriate to his role as god of music and harmony. Robert Stephanus's *Thesaurus Linguae Latinae* (1573) assigns to Apollo the specific role, amongst others, of protector of the vocal chords. In short, both Mercury and Apollo could be said to have a good deal to do with 'what precedes'.

The line 'The words of Mercury are harsh after the songs of Apollo' [V. ii. 930-31] perhaps constitutes not so much a comment on the *subject* of *Love's Labour's Lost*, in which Mercury as Mercade the messenger brings his harsh words into the Apollonian atmosphere of the play, as a comment on the *form* of this play, and on the nature of the drama which it

embodies. The 'words of Mercury' are surely *Love's Labour's Lost* seen in written form; in its printed Quarto version. It is itself part of the world of books which the play has urged us to reject. The 'songs of Apollo' are those oral words heard in the actual performance of the play, of which the book is a 'harsh' shadow. The book cannot 'contain' the play, as Dover Wilson discovered for himself when he was 'converted' by Tyrone Guthrie's production in 1936 [see excerpt above, 1962], and the words are printed in a larger type, separate from the words of the play for this reason. They constitute a comment on the *book* the reader of *Love's Labour's Lost* holds in his hand. Momentarily he is like the ''boookmen' of the play, engrossed in a 'reduced' world of writing, not in the 'real' world of oral interchange, of which the play in performance is a compelling version. The play's epigraph, which these words are, is perhaps intended to jolt him out of that state; to force him to raise his eyes from the 'speeches penned' and to encounter the world with voice and ear, to add the reconciling vocal, auditory dimension of rhyme to the silent world of reason, to temper dialectic with rhetoric in the oral spirit intended by Berowne. The words thus use the functions of Mercury to achieve the purpose of Apollo, uniting these opposites in characteristically Shakespearean fashion. (pp. 69-71)

> Terence Hawkes, ''*Love's Labour's Lost*': Rhyme against Reason,'' in his Shakespeare's Talking Animals: Language and Drama in Society, *Edward Arnold, 1973, pp. 53-72.*

ALEXANDER LEGGATT   (essay date 1974)

[*Leggatt identifies the problem of society's reliance on convention as a major concern in* Love's Labour's Lost. *He suggests that the courtiers' methods of courtship are either used self-consciously in a manipulative manner or are turned to nonsense—or ''dislocated,'' in his term—by a speech which fails to communicate its intended meaning. Consequently, Leggatt continues, the convention of language is questioned throughout the play. He concludes that the viability of the play itself as a dramatic medium is challenged and that, while showing the limits of expression and presenting an image of insecurity, primarily through the imagery of the final songs,* Love's Labour's Lost *also extends the rules of comedy by suggesting ''pleasurable'' possibilities. For a similar consideration of the play's language and the function of the songs, see the commentary by J. Dennis Huston (1981).*]

With its dance movements, its wit combats and its symmetrical teams of wooers, *Love's Labour's Lost* may claim to be Shakespeare's most formal play. The awareness of convention that characterized *The Taming of the Shrew* is here extended in a variety of ways. In that play, we saw the main action, initially at least, as a show put on for a drunken tinker. But that was a play put on by professional actors; *Love's Labour's Lost* is full of enthusiastic amateurs. The performing instinct affects the characters' normal behaviour: not only do they recite poems, adopt disguises and stage shows, but even in what purports to be normal conversation the style may be suddenly heightened and patterned, turned from casual talk into a self-conscious dance of language. When Navarre and his bookmen first meet the Princess and her ladies, they inquire their names of Boyet, one after another, in a passage of jingling rhymes and puns which begins calmly enough but rapidly accelerates, with shorter lines and faster repartee [II. i. 194-213]. The same stylized, lilting, punning dialogue characterizes the encounter between the masked ladies and the men disguised as Russians [V. ii. 195-265]. The two parties seem incapable of approaching each other informally; some convention of behaviour appears to dictate that relations between the sexes should be conducted in a stylized way. But this manner is not confined to the big ensemble scenes of courtship: over and over, individual characters will, at a moment's notice, stage their own little performances, set off by rhyme, and often by a special metre—as when Boyet describes the effect of love on the King, and makes quite a substantial set piece of it [II. i. 234-48]. This capacity is not confined to the courtiers: the comic routines of the clowns, such as the play on the idea of 'l'envoy' [III. i. 71-115], may be coarser in texture, but they are equally stylized. Costard joins with the ladies and Boyet in their bawdy playing with hunting terms, and for the moment they all share the same style [IV. i. 108-39]. The wit game, like village cricket, is a great social leveller. (pp. 63-4)

The characters' sporadic awareness that they are putting on performances recalls the special awareness of Petruchio, Katherina and the Lord in *The Taming of the Shrew*. The characters are not simply creatures of convention: they are also *aware* of conventions, and manipulate them, using them to describe or evoke special states of mind. Again, as in *The Taming of the Shrew*, the special state most frequently evoked is that of the game-player, *homo ludens*. But while the other play suggested a rough outdoor fun, the interest here—even when the same sports are referred to—is more in elegance and precision. . . . Just as, in the bawdy set piece in which Boyet, Costard and the ladies play with hunting, archery and bowling, sex becomes a matter of arrows hitting targets [IV. ii. 108-39], so throughout the wit exchanges the primary value is not feeling but accuracy. However coarse or brutal the joking may be (and the characters are at no pains to spare each other's feelings) what matters is that the shaft should hit its mark. Even the pedants are not as cloistered as we might think, but show some sporting instincts. . . . The play evokes a world of social pastime and recreation, in which courtship and even learning are woven into the figures of a dance; and the play's fascination with the actions of groups, rather than those of individuals, reflects this interest in recreation: the individual surrenders some of his individuality, to become part of a team, a figure in a larger pattern.

In *The Taming of the Shrew* dependence on convention was simply accepted, and the play conveyed a feeling of pleasure and satisfaction in seeing how well the conventions worked, how much could be achieved in human terms by sport and playacting. But in *Love's Labour's Lost* there is a new spirit of edgy suspicion. The Lord and Petruchio were firmly in control, using conventions to manipulate the minds of Sly and Katherina, who responded with increasing eagerness. But here the characters are more sharply in competition with each other: the difference is between teaching someone to use a weapon and seeing if you yourself can use the weapon better. The result is that the conventions which appeared so powerful are now being explored for weaknesses. The show put on for Sly took over the stage and became the play's main reality; the shows put on for the Princess and her ladies are torn to pieces. The men come masked and disguised, only to find that the ladies too are masked and (having changed identities) even more deeply disguised, determined to beat them at their own game. The characters' awareness of convention, which led simply to pleasure in the other play, now produces a more complex and sceptical response.

In discussing earlier plays, I have suggested some of the comic devices by which Shakespeare can dislocate an experience and show its limits; here these devices are skilfully and elaborately deployed in order to dislocate the various conventions on which the characters depend. The most frequently used device is that of addressing a speech to an unsympathetic or uncomprehending audience, as in *The Comedy of Errors*; though in *Love's Labour's Lost* the listener's lack of sympathy usually results not from misunderstanding but from a deliberate refusal to cooperate. Moth meets the problem in its most basic form: 'They do not mark me, and that brings me out' [V. ii. 173]. Attempts at wooing are constantly bedevilled in this way: love letters are read by the wrong people, who comment disapprovingly on the style: protestations of love are either misdirected (as in the Masque of Russians), or rebuffed, or both. The ladies' characteristic tactic is to take the conventional utterances of love at their face value, thereby reducing them to nonsense:

BEROWNE: White-handed mistress, one sweet word with thee.
PRINCESS: Honey, and milk, and sugar; there is three.
[V. ii. 231-32]

You can reduce any convention to nonsense by taking it too literally. . . . (pp. 65-7)

Berowne, as a one-man audience for his fellows' confessions of love, also has a dislocating effect. They are mostly aware of their own private feelings, which seem very important and serious to them. But, from his special vantage point—'Like a demigod here sit I in the sky' [IV. iii. 87] (and whatever that means in stage terms, there is no doubt what it means in psychological ones)—he sees them as we do, losing their individuality, and their seriousness, to a pattern of comic repetition that reduces the importance of individual feeling. . . . (pp. 67-8)

What is high talk to the speakers is, to the listeners, just so much noise. For the most part, this device of playing the speaker off against his listener is used for its obvious comic value; but, as in *The Comedy of Errors*, our failure to reach each other's minds is not always funny. In the last scene the King speaks, as before, in the language of love, but it is embarrassingly out of place, and the Princess replies 'I understand you not; my griefs are double' [V. ii. 752]. To the grief of her father's death is added the pain of watching her suitor behave so tactlessly in a serious situation. Once again the conventional utterance of love is dislocated; but here it is seen, not as laughable, but as painfully inappropriate.

Broken or interrupted ceremonies are another device by which conventions are challenged: one thinks of the ceremony of oath-taking, which Berowne disrupts, and the masque in which the ladies refuse to dance (were this to happen in a real masque, the result would likely be an international scandal). The show of the Nine Worthies is destroyed at the most basic level, as the audience simply refuses to accept the convention of theatrical illusion:

COSTARD: *I Pompey am—*
BEROWNE: You lie, you are not he.
[V. ii. 547]

The players are forced out of their disguises, with particularly humiliating results for Armado's portrayal of Hector. . . . The result is to emphasize how fragile their impersonations are, how far they are from being the great figures of legend they are pretending to be.

Contrasts of style also have their function in this process: we see this in the difference between the formality of the lords and the sharp responses of the ladies; and between Armado's elaborate meditations on love when he is alone, and the blunt utterance he slips into when faced with Jaquenetta, whose mind is incapable of grasping words of more than one syllable. . . . One of the most elaborate and telling effects, however, is in the opening scene. The oath-taking ceremony, and Berowne's rebellion, are written in a more or less uniform style: smooth, formal, self-consciously clever. Berowne is, for all his objections, one of them, and it is no surprise when he finally subscribes. The real challenge to the credibility of the King's legislation comes with the entrance of Dull and Costard, and the reading of Armado's letter. We hear a different range of voices now: Dull's comic, futile self-importance; Costard's cheeky earthiness, which includes a few parodies of the high style . . . ; and, best of all, Armado's delicate hovering several miles above reality. . . . (pp. 69-70)

So radically does the play question conventions that even words themselves, the most basic of conventions, come under suspicion. Language is based on a tacit agreement that certain combinations of sound carry certain meanings. But in the very first encounter of the King and the Princess, his apparently innocuous speech of greeting is seized upon, and his use of words mercilessly dissected:

> KING: Fair Princess, welcome to the court of Navarre.
> PRINCESS: 'Fair' I give you back again; and 'welcome' I have not yet. The roof of this court is too high to be yours, and welcome to the wide fields too base to be mine.
>
> [II. i. 90-4]

Costard, like Dogberry after him [in *Much Ado About Nothing*], uses words with a fine unconcern for their agreed meanings: 'and therefore welcome the sour cup of prosperity! Affliction may one day smile again; and till then, sit thee down, sorrow' [I. i. 313-15]. In another play, this might be an incidental comic effect; but here, a sense that language is unreliable is basic to the play's vision. The mistaking of words is still a comic effect, but it is far from incidental.

The play, in short, shows conventions—even words themselves—as comically vulnerable. And here is where the lovers' problem lies. . . . [Love] depends for its fulfilment on expression, but the means of expression available to it are largely conventional and therefore open to mockery. Standard metaphors are used to decribe love and courtship—metaphors drawn from war [from hunting and from law]. . . . These are all commonplaces of Elizabethan love poetry; and they all have the effect of reducing love to generalizations—conflict, desire, bargaining. They compare love to something which is not love, and they find the common ground in some general experience. The bawdry in the references to war and hunting also reduces love to its physical expression, seen as a subject of mechanical jokes. Moth, in prescribing to Armado the correct behaviour for a lover, recites a series of formulae [III. i. 11-25]. Berowne is aware of how painfully unoriginal love has made him, and expresses this in a cliché rhyme: 'Well, I will love, write, sigh, pray, sue, and groan; / Some men must love my lady, and some Joan' [III. i. 204-05]. The trouble with these conventional expressions of love is that they offer no guarantee that the feelings the lover expresses are his own. The love poems the men produce could be written by anybody, for anybody. The Princess, I think, makes this point when she has her ladies exchange favours, tricking the men into courting the wrong women:

> The effect of my intent is to cross theirs.
> They do it but in mockery merriment,
> And mock for mock is only my intent.
>
> [V. ii. 138-40]

If courtship is simply a game or dance, it does not matter who your partner is, so long as the forms are observed. And indeed one feels that in this scene the speakers could be interchanged in a variety of ways, and it would make no difference: the lines they speak, like the masks they wear, could belong to anyone. (pp. 71-3)

The play itself, in which so many conventions are tested and broken, is one more convention. Our awareness of this is conveyed by a variety of extra-dramatic references. Berowne . . . steps partly outside the dramatic illusion by his awareness that he and his fellows are speaking in rhyme, and his readiness to poke fun at this particular convention:

> KING: How well he's read, to reason against reading!
> DUMAIN: Proceeded well, to stop all good proceeding!
> LONGAVILLE: He weeds the corn, and still lets grow the weeding.
> BEROWNE: The spring is near, when green geese are a-breeding.
> DUMAIN: How follows that?
> BEROWNE: Fit in his place and time.
> DUMAIN: In reason nothing.
> BEROWNE: Something then in rhyme.
>
> [I. i. 94-9]

In IV. iii, eavesdropping on the others, he has some of the function of a 'presenter': 'Now, in thy likeness, one more fool appear!' [IV. iii. 44]. Then, in the final scene:

> BEROWNE: Our wooing doth not end like an old play: Jack hath not Jill. These ladies' courtesy Might well have made our sport a comedy.
> KING: Come, sir, it wants a twelvemonth and a day, And then 'twill end.
> BEROWNE: That's too long for a play.
>
> [V. ii. 874-78]

We are made aware of the limits of the theatrical convention, as of the others, by seeing its fragility in a larger context. Like the show of the Nine Worthies, it rests on a basis of illusion that is perilous and easily broken; and, in the end, it can no more embody the 'world-without-end bargain' of love in a two-hours comedy than Alexander the Great can be embodied in the village curate.

What it *can* show, however, is the problem of expressing love, and it does this with liveliness and grace, and with the joking acceptance of a hopeless dilemma that is shown most clearly in the figure of Berowne. For all its scepticism it is not an austere or bitter play, for it sees the attractions of everything it attacks. The love poems, at their best, have genuine charm; the Masque of Russians can be staged—and there is no reason why not—as a lively and colourful show. There is pleasure to be had even from inadequate conventions; there is fun to be had from demolishing them; and there is pleasure of a deeper kind in pressing beyond them to more satisfying conventions. The solemn anxiety expressed in some individual passages is only part of the play's ultimate effect. The final songs of Spring and Winter lie closer to its heart: they could be called a celebration of mutability. The cuckoo's 'word of fear' sounding through the spring meadows and the 'merry note' of the owl in the cold of winter suggest a comment on the men's final vows: the pleasures of spring, the season of courtship, are fragile; the testing and patience of winter may bring joy. Other comedies may end with an image of security, but this play by its constant questioning of convention—up to and including the convention that at the end of a comedy Jack shall have Jill—has denied itself that. Instead, through the songs, it presents the instability of life as a general experience (everyone can talk about the weather) and a familiar one, all the more familiar for being so precisely described. Just as, in writing conventionalized love poetry, the private feelings of the lover are turned into something public and familiar and cease to be his own, so in the songs the characters' experience of the insecurity of life is embodied in images which seem far away from that experience—images which are, in a sense, public property; and in that way some of the personal pain of the last scene is dissipated. But if this creates a distance between the characters and the audience, by moving us away from them as individuals, it also creates a link. Seen directly, the problems of Berowne, Rosaline and the others were theirs, not ours; but the images of spring and winter provide a meeting point for the characters and the audience, a shared experience of the mutability of life. We should not forget, too, that these vivid and delightful songs were written by the two pedants (now 'the two learned men'—[V. ii. 86]), whose literary efforts have earned so much ridicule throughout the play. It is not so much that they are talented enough to write the songs (which one can hardly believe); rather, Shakespeare is kind enough to say they did, even at some cost to the consistency of the characterizations. This is typical of Shakespeare's generosity to characters who, like himself, labour in the mysteries of art and language: the problems they face are formidable; the chances for folly and misdirected zeal are legion; but in the last analysis, none of them, even the lowest, is to be despised. But the play's ultimate effect is to provide an image of insecurity, and the songs, by conveying a delight in the changes and surprises of life (how many writers would describe an owl as merry?) help to ensure that the image is a pleasurable one, that the play can break the rules of comedy only to extend them. (pp. 86-8)

> *Alexander Leggatt, "'Love's Labour's Lost,'" in his* Shakespeare's Comedy of Love, *Methuen & Co. Ltd., 1974, pp. 63-88.*

MALCOLM EVANS   (essay date 1975)

[*Evans argues that the final statement of* Love's Labour's Lost— *"the words of Mercury are harsh after the songs of Apollo"— refers to a conflict at work throughout the play which he identifies as the opposition of writing and speech. Evans says that the men's hermetic Academe represents the spirit of Mercury, the patron of learning and the inventor of letters. Because writing lacks the social presence that oral communication promotes, continues Evans, the men's binding of personal intercourse to the written word undermines their attempts at courtship. The women, he says, recognize the importance of "the converse of breath" and, hence, represent the Apollonian medium of living speech. It is this exchange of verbal communication, Evans concludes, which must triumph if there is to be a comic resolution to the play. The opposition of writing and speech in* Love's Labour's Lost *is also discussed in a similar fashion by Terence Hawkes (1973), and the emphasis placed on the organic verbal community is also*

found in the essays by James L. Calderwood (1971) and Louis Adrian Montrose (1977).]

By the end of the first scene of *Love's Labour's Lost,* the conflict between the demands of Mercury and Apollo has been firmly established, and the hold of books and reason on the minds of the four young men is no longer unchallenged. But the arrival at Navarre of the Princess and her ladies does *not* herald the immediate and expected unconditional return to love and society—the normality of romantic comedy. Mercury dies hard in the world of the play. Even when the scholars have relinquished their books and their cerebration for the delights of courtly dalliance, Mercury's influence persists, and the conflicting sets of values which are juxtaposed in the opening scene remain throughout the play, as two continually expanding clusters of ideas which finally crystallize in its closing utterance under the symbols "Mercury" and Apollo." The focal point of both clusters is language, and the play's central duality— that of speech and the written word—two intrinsically different and mutually exclusive forms of language—embraces all of its lesser dramatic conflicts. Just as speech pertains to the sphere of "unlettered" barbarism—"rhyme," nature, and sexuality— so the written word is, in the terms of the play, the characteristic medium of reason—book-learning, the quest for fame, and the desire for immortality. Mercury . . . was the inventor of letters; it is therefore fitting that Apollo, no less, is portrayed in the Renaissance dictionaries as patron of speech and the protector of the *chorda vocalis,* the anatomical equivalent of his lyre.

Speech, the medium of the play, is language in its primal and natural form. As sound is essentially transient, so speech, unlike its visual analogue, writing, is necessarily "fit in . . . time and place" [I. i. 98]. Throughout the play speech appears as one of man's natural activities, of a piece with breathing and breeding, living and dying. When the Princess calls speech "the converse of breath" [V. ii. 735], her words recall those spoken earlier by the King, who refers to "this present breath" of life, which is soon to expire in the 'disgrace of death' [I. i. 3-5]. This "breath," as Shakespeare and his audience would know from *Genesis,* was not only the sign of life, but also the means by which God first bestowed life on man having created him in His image. The "breath" of speech is the "breath" of life, and of humanity; it is, like death and sexuality, an archetypal corollary of human existence.

When the courtiers, at the beginning of the play, attempt to escape the fact of mortality, they are compelled to outlaw, at one blow, both speech and women:

> Item: if any man be seen to talk with a woman
> within the term of three years, he shall endure
> . . . public shame.
>
> [I. i. 129-31]

The penalty for breaking their edict is, in a most literal sense, linguistic:

> Item: that no woman shall come within a mile
> of my court . . . on pain of losing her tongue.
>
> [I. i. 119-24]

Their repudiation of speech is an integral element of the withdrawal from "converse" and society, while their espousal of the written word presupposes silence and solitude.

Even when the King and his associates return to society and the joys of courtship, writing remains with them. Although the *tongue*—by which "the air (is) beaten and framed with articulate sound," as La Primaudaye wrote in his *French Academie,* a probable source for *Love's Labor's Lost*—is, in the play, "conceit's expositor" [II. i. 72], the outward manifestation of thought, they show scant respect for the business of speaking and listening. Words spoken are, for them, by no means a commitment, for, as Longaville says, "Vows are but breath, and breath a vapour is" [IV. iii. 66]. But speech, which is, by its transience, grounded in the immediate situation, does demand a certain *decorum* and a degree of commitment to the interlocutor, and the young men's contempt for the decorum of speech is symptomatic of a deeper disrespect for relationship and personality. Their professed love for the ladies is, in essence, *im*personal. Berowne, a pattern for his fellows, veers between the extremes of exaggerated spiritual love for an idealized Rosaline, and an obsessive distaste for the mortal woman who can threaten him with "horns." At one moment, woman has replaced books as the means of beguiling the senses and ecstatically blurring the distinction between mortal, vulnerable self and external nature, while at the next she is the "pitch that defiles" [IV. iii. 3]. But both the idealized *donna sapienza* ["knowledgeable woman"] and the "animal" Rosaline are abstractions, bearing little relation to the "personality" of Rosaline as it is realized in verbal interaction. "Love," as far as the courtiers are concerned, is not, however, an affair of personalities. It is, rather, yet another means of avoiding those facts of mortal existence which are implicit in the very fabric and decorum of speech. The young men use "love" as a catalyst in evoking within them a sense of immortal omnipotence, or, alternatively, as a way of renouncing the responsibilities of selfhood by projecting that fantasy of omnipotence into the loved one.

It is fitting that Berowne and his fellows conduct their wooing through the medium of the written word. Writing, as Socrates had declared, is language in an inherently impersonal form. The truth of his dictum that writing 'does not know how to address the right people and not address the wrong'' [Plato, *Phaedrus*] is demonstrated in dramatic terms when letters written by Berowne and Armado are delivered, by Costard, each to the wrong lady. But even when letters reach the "right people," they are not adequate substitute for speech, as the ladies show in greeting their lovers' sonnets with ridicule. The only message transmitted by writing—which does not embrace the realities of time, place, and personality—is writing itself:

Ros.	. . . he hath drawn my picture in his letter.
Prin.	Anything like?
Ros.	Much in letters, nothing in the praise.
Prin.	Beauteous as ink; a good conclusion.
Kath.	Fair as a text B in a copy-book.

[V. ii. 38-42]

The mockery is warranted. To profess personal sentiment through a medium by nature impersonal is foolish:

Prin.	We are wise fools to mock our lovers so.
Ros.	They are worse fools to purchase mocking so.

[V. ii. 58-9]

When not wooing directly in writing, the courtiers use what is described as "penn'd speech" [V. ii. 147]. Their penned speeches are words uttered not spontaneously, in a spirit of reciprocation, but with a predefined suasive purpose. Shakespeare uses the image of the actor to suggest that the words spoken are not an uttering of the inner self, but a detached "part" which is memorized and remains, like writing, oblivious of the person addressed [V. ii. 150]. Their written speeches serve a dual purpose of warding off the commitments of speech

and enchanting the ladies into a state of acquiescence. Any response to these set-pieces serves only to disrupt their flow, as Moth illustrates in his role as Prologue to the masque of the Muscovites. Although transmogrified into what is, in effect, a piece of writing—his words and even the para-language of gesture and intonation are set in a rigid order which eliminates the variables of oral communication—Moth fails when confronted with a concrete situation and a reacting audience. Caught between the Prologue and the natural reflexes of a speaking, listening, social being, Moth is "put out"[V. ii. 165], and achieves little success in either part.

Throughout this scene, the young men's penned speeches are, like their vizards, a means of tricking and of concealing themselves from their mistresses. They also follow the letters in being unable to address the appropriate person; each courtier in turn, in a stylized piece of verbal choreography, presents his favor and declares devotion to the wrong lady. Through language and disguise they avoid those commitments which bear a reminder of mortality.

The whole concept of "penn'd speech" is taken to the extreme of literal absurdity in the language of the pedant, Holofernes, who believes that words should be spoken as they are written. He reviles Armado and such "rackers of orthography" [V. i. 19] who do not pronounce words as they are spelled. But Armado himself offers a grotesque echo of the courtly "penn'd speech." His letters and speeches are highly formal structures which follow the rhetorical prescriptions concerning *copia* and place argument, becoming that "sweet smoke of rhetoric" [III. i. 63] which, in its confusion and affected circumlocution, is an effective block in the path of communication.

The fusion of writing and rhetoric in the concept of "penn'd speech" reaffirms the bearing of Mercury, even after the collapse of the academy, on the language of the courtiers and pedants. Mercury, inventor of writing, was also regarded as the patron and arch-exponent of rhetoric, a role closely allied to that of protecting swift-talking merchants and their wares (*merces*), and by logical extension liars and confidence-tricksters. In one of a number of rhetorical attacks on rhetoric, Berowne recognizes the connection between penn'd speech and sale:

> Fie, painted rhetoric! O! she needs it not:
> To things of sale a seller's praise belongs.
> She passes praise. . . .

[IV. iii. 235-37]

The language of the seller, its aim being not to elicit personal response but to enchant the buyer into easy acquiescence, uses the concept of objective value to reduce the irreducible person . . . to its quantifiable and superficial attributes, that false appearance symbolized in the play's cosmetic imagery. The Princess' negative response to the "paint" of rhetoric is an indication of her self-knowledge, just as Berowne's ready resort to rhetorical "penn'd speech," which manipulates reality into comforting verbal patterns, is an index of his self-conscious desire to protect a vulnerable self from the alien and nonmanipulable realities of death, sex, and other people.

In *Love's Labor's Lost,* the words of Mercury, both written words in books and rhetorical penned speech, entail a psychic withdrawal from the realities which are figured in the very substance and decorum of speech. The words of Mercury are a disruptive force in the comic world of the play, dividing society into literate and illiterate, the seller and his unsuspecting prey. The comic ideal of society can only be established with the triumph of the Apollonian medium, speech, and the reformation of the old society according to the innate pattern of "the converse of breath," which presupposes a recognition of time, place, and occasion, and of the personality of the interlocutor. Throughout the play, the ladies of France support this decorum. Their "jesting"—a conventional exercise in speaking, listening, and responding, comparable in form to a tennis match . . .—provides a radical contrast to that of Berowne, whose wit, rather than embracing or recognizing its object, excludes and devalues it, all in the cause of a shallow and flattering popularity with the courtly coterie. He has, says Rosaline:

> . . . a gibing spirit,
> Whose influence is begot of that loose grace
> Which shallow laughing hearers give to fools.
> [V. ii. 858-60]

The penances imposed by the ladies on the young men at the end of the play amount to an initiation into their Apollonian world—into everything implied, in the terms of the play, by *speech*. Their first lesson is that speech, unlike writing, is a matter of *reciprocation*:

> A jest's prosperity lies in the ear
> Of him that hears it, never in the tongue
> Of him that makes it.
> [V. ii. 861-63]

In order to prove this on his pulses, Berowne must undertake a salutary exercise in observing the decorum of speech:

> You shall this twelve month term from day to day
> Visit the speechless sick, and still converse
> With groaning wretches. . . .
> [V. ii. 850-52]

His task will be to "enforce the pained and impotent to smile" [V. ii. 854].

Berowne, like Navarre, is to be divested of his protective cloak of rhetoric, and compelled to face nature—its "frosts" and "hard lodging" through "thin weeds" [V. ii. 801]. Only after a year of penitence, having completely abjured the boyish pursuits of book-learning and affecting verbal pyrotechnics, may the four young men become husbands, thus assuming a full adult role in society. To this end, Katharine wishes Dumaine "a beard" before all else [V. ii. 824]. But the first prerequisite of marriage is self-knowledge, and at the end of the play we see the King, Berowne, Dumaine, and Longaville again on the threshold of a venture into learning. This time, however, they will not learn from books, but from speaking and listening. Self-knowledge can be achieved only in society, in "the converse of breath," which exposes the self to relationship and to the actualities of material existence. Resounding behind the penances, which bridge the transition from the solitary sphere of Mercury to the social world of Apollo, is Apollo's Delphic invocation, *Nosce teipsum* ["Know thyself"]. (pp. 119-23)

With *Love's Labor's Lost*, Shakespeare defined his commitment to the oral/aural art of drama, not on paper, but in the theater, which itself embodied the alternative to writing. In the terms of the play, drama, although utilizing in its process the written word and "speeches penned," pertains nevertheless to the sphere of Apollo, by employing these devices to stage a paradigm of the give-and-take of speaking and listening. When Rosaline, at the end of the play, informs Berowne of where a "jest's prosperity" lies, her words are no less applicable to Shakespeare's own medium where, for the obvious artistic and economic reasons, the jest lies or dies in the ear of the audience. But responsibility for the success of drama does not rest wholly with the actors; while the written word's one-way flow of shallow "wisdom" beguiles the acquiescent reader, the contract which links poet, actors, and audience in the theater is reciprocal in nature, demanding a positive act from each sector, particularly from the audience who, to make drama possible, must respect its conventions, listen, and respond. (p. 124)

For Shakespeare, the immortality of the written word was illusory, the social role of the poet being to give his words to the actors who, in turn, would present them to the audience, thus giving them free circulation within the theater and, by extension, the community. Thus, implicit in the art of the dramatic poet is the assumption that living language is an organic force more powerful than the thinking of the individual man. In this sense, the English language is the hero of *Love's Labor's Lost*, a play first performed at a time when the language was an issue of national importance, serving to bind together a community composed of individuals who, like Armado at the end of the pageant, "breathe free *breath*" [V. ii. 722], having achieved discretion and self-knowledge through the heuristic value of human communication and contact with those natural realities which are figured in speech. (p. 125)

Malcolm Evans, "Mercury Versus Apollo: A Reading of 'Love's Labor's Lost'," in Shakespeare Quarterly, *Vol. XXVI, No. 2, Spring, 1975, pp. 113-27.*

WILLIAM C. CARROLL (essay date 1976)

[*In his study* The Great Feast of Language in "Love's Labour's Lost," *Carroll challenges what he views as a general critical tendency to read* Love's Labour's Lost *as depicting the triumph of the real or natural over the illusory or artificial—an interpretation developed most thoroughly by Bobbyann Roesen (1953). Carroll's argument, reminiscent of Hermann Ulrici's (see excerpt above, 1839), is that though Shakespeare was concerned with the opposition of art and nature in* Love's Labour's Lost *he did not finally favor one over the other but was presenting "a balance or dialectic," and in so doing showed their essential interrelatedness. The mediator of art and nature, contends Carroll, is "decorum," and it is this principle that allows a reconciliation to create a "living art." Like Ulrici, Carroll cites the play's final songs as an illustration of this synthesis of contrarieties. For other considerations of the final songs, see the excerpts by Richmond Noble (1923), Bertrand H. Bronson (1948), Louis Adrian Montrose (1977), and Catherine McLay (see Additional Bibliography). The excerpt below begins with an argument against Ralph Berry's interpretation of* Love's Labour's Lost *(see excerpt above, 1969), which Carroll identifies as typical of the critical trend to view the play as presenting a victory of reality, or what he terms Baconian materialism, over art and imagination.*]

Beneath the games of wit and the parodies of style [in *Love's Labour's Lost*] lie conflicting fundamental assumptions about language and what should be done with it. To say, as Ralph Berry does [see excerpt above, 1969], that the play finally asserts the validity of the concept of words as "symbols of reality," or "symbols for things," or as "counters," is to oversimplify. Berry does allow, in Holofernes alone (who, he says, "has his passion for words under control"), that the idea of "words as things in themselves" is allowed by the play to stand. . . . This is backwards: the play stands on the idea. The test of language for Berry, nevertheless, is still its relation to "reality" or "things," and if there is no clearly perceived relationship, then it is condemned, supposedly by the play as a whole, as frivolous, escapist, self-deceiving.

This is essentially a Baconian position, and though there is a grain of truth in it, it rests on a questionable distinction between matter and words, *res* and *verba*. It makes style into mere ornament—the very vice it attacks. The *locus classicus* ["classic passage"] of this concept is Bacon's statement of the first distemper of learning: "when men study words and not matter . . . Pygmalion's frenzy is a good emblem or portraiture of this vanity: for words are but the images of matter; and except they have life of reason and invention, to fall in love with them is all one as to fall in love with a picture." . . . The trouble is, people *do* fall in love with pictures, they do fall in love with language; it is just as unreasonable, and just as much fun, as falling in love with people. Pygmalion's frenzy is an occupational hazard with poets. We can imagine Bacon's reaction to a performance of *Love's Labour's Lost,* full of sound and fury and not signifying enough. A suspicion lingers that Bacon was thinking of this very play when he observed that "the conditions of life of *Pedantes* [Holofernes?] have been scorned upon theatres." . . . (pp. 61-2)

It is tempting to conclude, as we now generally share Bacon's materialism, that at the end of *Love's Labour's Lost* Shakespeare, with Berowne, forswears "taffeta phrases" and "silken terms." That this is simply not so is evident in the continuing use of such phrases in the rest of the play—indeed, in the rest of his plays. And we should recall the impressive range of possible attitudes toward language, no one of which is wholly sufficient in itself. The ideal Bacon aims toward is a perspicuous, presumably transparent language, one with no ambiguities. . . . [In] a wholly referential language—one that approaches the status of symbolic logic—there is no room for ambiguity, for the play of imagination, for the liberty of language. This is a possibility barely conceived of in *Love's Labour's Lost,* much less affirmed.

At the other end of the continuum, there is Costard tossing his "remuneration" in the air, very nearly a total identification between name and thing, in the impressive sound of the word; the two seem inherently connected, in an Adamic sense. The punsters and malaprops treat words as autonomous entities, rhyming and twisting them, jostling them next to one another, taking them apart and reassembling them in intricate patterns. The most important result is the "dislocation" [Sigurd] Burckhardt mentions, the creation of that nagging and fruitful ambiguity so necessary to the poet. Words are slippery things, as Bacon well knew: "Yet even definitions cannot cure this evil in dealing with natural and material things; since the definitions themselves consist of words, and those words beget others." . . . Or as Feste ironically complains, "words are grown so false I am loath to prove reason with them" [*Twelfth Night,* III. i. 24-5]. A vicious circle in which scientists squirm and poets thrive; the mystery of words, the uncanny energy which seems to issue from within them, which causes one word to "beget" another, always in transformation, never remaining still, never fixed—if the play asserts anything, it is just this power.

The energy of language in *Love's Labour's Lost* reminds us that poetry is almost always language used for its own sake as well as language used referentially; not an absolute polarity, but a kind of double exposure. The antinomies . . . of play and judgment, of solipsism and society, of words as things and words as signs . . . constitute a dialectic, a "dialogue," in the play's own terms. The play is a "great feast of languages" [V. ii. 37] in the sense that it gives us everything at once—appetizers and dessert, the "scraps" and the main dish. What

the men come to learn, in their little "academe," is not simply that words must be used as symbols of things, since words are always more than that, nor simply that speech is better than writing, but that there is a time and a place in which different attitudes are required or sanctioned. What the men and the audience "learn," therefore, is the principle of decorum, the way to use words in a variety of situations, in whatever "manner" and "form" the imagination decrees. (pp. 62-4)

The structural movement of *Love's Labour's Lost* takes an expansive form. The play seems to proceed from the inner ring of concentric circles to the outer, from the less to the more inclusive, from "artifice" and "illusion" to "reality." The play begins in Navarre's mind, as he details in his opening speech a plan for defeating time with a "little academe." The constricted world of the academe is forcibly widened, however, by the arrival of the women, and the setting moves to the park, away from the court itself. The introduction of the various low comic characters contributes to a continuing expansion as the play progresses, and more and more reminders of time and death impinge on the secluded park. The Princess' embassy implies another world beyond the court, another dimension where wars are fought, debts must be settled, old men sicken and die. With the entrance of Marcade in the final scene, announcing the death of the Princess' father, death itself enters the play. Whatever remained of the plan for the ascetic academe has long since vanished. The various levels of awareness and self-knowledge so schematically outlined in the sonnet-reading scene are found mirrored in the larger structure of the entire play. We move from the innermost ring, in the opening speech, to something like the outermost with Marcade's entrance and the imposition of the year-long penances.

Recent critics of *Love's Labour's Lost* are virtually unanimous in their appraisals of the meaning and implications of this outward movement. It represents, in its broadest terms, what is usually called the victory of "reality" over "illusion," of "nature" over "art." This verdict is all the easier to reach because of the extraordinary complexity of the play's language; it is simpler to call it "affected" or "artificial" than to understand what it achieves. As Ralph Berry sums it up, the movement of the lay is "towards an acceptance of reality." . . . He concludes that this "movement towards reality" should be seen as "a set of reversals, refutations of the untenable positions taken up in Act I—just as, perhaps, the logic of the final Winter-song refutes Summer." . . . I hope to show that such interpretations severely oversimplify the play's complex balance of opposites.

If there is agreement on the general movement of the play, not everyone is agreed on its precise turning-point. For one thing, the theme of death runs throughout the play, from the opening words of Navarre to Armado's lament for the dead Hector. But death is finally embodied in Marcade, another verbal allusion made flesh. The build-up is gradual, from witty references to plague "tokens" or a "death's-face in a ring" [V. ii. 612] to the movement in the fifth act stage-time from early afternoon to the gathering darkness of twilight, in which Holofernes-Judas stumbles. Most readers of the play, however, see Marcade's entrance, quite properly, as the chilling and dramatic high-point in the play. It never fails to shock in performance.

But the brilliance of Marcade's *coup de théâtre* may blind us to the fact that his entrance is not yet the end of the play, that there are some 200 lines left, and that the play actually ends, not with a chilling note of death or with a harsh penance but with a much more complex tone, in a highly artificial debate or "dialogue." Schematic structures of all sorts are continually being dissolved and re-created during the play—outer circles suddenly become inner, exclusive points of view are shattered into multiplicity. I suggest that a similar enlargement of meaning occurs at the end of *Love's Labour's Lost*, after Marcade's entrance, and that recent criticism of the play has largely failed to take this expansion into account.

The use of multiple rings of perception is a basic principle of construction in the play. It structures the whole and . . . is the governing form of individual scenes. We think of the rings as extending past the audience to the dramatist, occupying the outermost circle, who is the "demi-god," the *primum mobile* ["first mover"] which turns the universe of the play, with the elements near the center (Dull, Costard) slower and heavier than those near the edges (Moth, the ladies). Shakespeare's method everywhere is to set opposites in conflict, worlds in collision, to bring contrary viewpoints into contention with one another. . . . It is an insistence on giving us the many rather than the one, on showing us multiple-colored refractions of Nature rather than a single narrowly focused image. He shifts, to continue the optical metaphor, from telescopic to microscopic views, from a wide scan to a contracted highlight, and then back again. (pp. 167-70)

The final "dialogue" or debate between Hiems and Ver serves as a suggestive emblem of the basic structural principle of *Love's Labour's Lost*. Two opposite powers of myth literally appear on stage to contend in mock-struggle, each making claims for itself which exclude the other. It is a rudimentary form of the dramatic impulse. This "dialogue" is conducted throughout the play on a number of levels. *Love's Labour's Lost* is a debate on the nature of poetry and the imagination in the sense that two or more conflicting attitudes and examples are again and again placed in opposition so that contrary claims can be more starkly revealed and evaluated. . . . I believe that the debate about the use of imagination and language is the chief one in the play, though there are to be sure many more debates conducted at the same time. A list of all the contending dualisms in the play would be long; the following are those most frequently heard:

Spring	vs.	Winter
Learning	vs.	Experience
Rhetoric	vs.	Simplicity
Affectation	vs.	Self-Knowledge
Wearing a Mask	vs.	Revealing Oneself
Playing a Role	vs.	Being Oneself
Style	vs.	Matter
Words	vs.	Things
Form	vs.	Content
Mind	vs.	Body
Paradox	vs.	Common Sense

(pp. 170-71)

If recent criticism of Shakespeare's comedies has taught us anything, surely it is that these plays are more complex than we at first suspect, that Shakespeare's structures and his ideas are occasionally simple but never simple-minded. All the more surprising, then, to find almost unanimous agreement among recent readers of *Love's Labour's Lost* that the play clearly affirms the "victory" of the right side of this list over the left, of russet and honest kersey over taffeta and silk, of Winter-Reality over Spring-Illusion, of, most generally, Nature over Art. At its worst, this traditional reading of the play finds Shakespeare in Berowne, renouncing gimmickry and artificiality once and for all. Some readers continue, moreover, to

say that Shakespeare "prefers" or sides with Winter's song over Spring's on the grounds that it is more realistic. Yet a reading of the tradition of the debate form does not support such conclusions, apart from the evidence of the play itself. (pp. 171-72)

Winter's song comes after Spring's in *Love's Labour's Lost*, but there is no evidence in the text that one song is superior to the other. . . . But Catherine McLay, among others, has recently argued to the contrary, in part by appealing to the play's structure: "Like the Song, the play too moves from spring to winter, from art to nature, from illusion to reality. And the movement in the Song from the folly of the cuckoo to the wisdom of the owl has its counterpart in the handling of the several strands of the play's action, of its plots and subplots" [see Additional Bibliography]. This does justice neither to the play nor to the songs, both of which are far more complex than McLay allows. . . . [No] such either-or decision is made in *Love's Labour's Lost*. It is the interplay between the dualistic forces which is of interest; the stress in the play is now to one side, now to another, but one side never achieves complete dominance over the other—the entrance of Marcade comes close to such a victory, only to fall short.

A similar case may be made for the other dualisms listed above. To stress only the right side of the list—matter, things, experience—is naive, not to say materialistic. It is a curious ontology (and meteorology) which allows "reality" and "nature" to be identified exclusively with Winter. To emphasize only the left side of the list, however—learning, style, words—is equally perverse. Shakespeare advocated neither of these sides alone, though it is not difficult to find theoretical proponents in the Renaissance of one side or the other, from [George] Chapman, say, to Montaigne. But in *Love's Labour's Lost*, easy dualisms are suspect; they are flourished and emphasized, only to be rigorously examined. Differences between the opposites always turn out to be less than we thought. . . . Nowhere is the interrelatedness of apparent opposites more evident than in the most important and inclusive opposition of the play, Art versus Nature. (pp. 173-74)

Most of us are instinctively on the side of Nature rather than of Art. There have never been many anti-primitivists around, and today they are an endangered species. In an argument, or in theory, we tend to side with Perdita rather than Polixenes [*The Winter's Tale*, IV. iv. 79-103]. So too in the Renaissance. But the very perception of a division, or the possibility of one, between Art and Nature, places us in the camp of "Art." Self-consciousness and sophistication are not attributes of even the noblest savage; malaprops cannot consciously make a good pun. . . . We prefer Nature to Art, but to say so is in effect to admit that we exist more in Art than in Nature. In *Love's Labour's Lost*, Shakespeare insists on this paradox. The opposition of Art and Nature, as well as the other contraries associated with them, is formed only to be dissolved. The metaphors of clothes and painting are a case in point. A literal reading of these analogies, a reading which takes the analogy in place of the idea it amplifies, creates a form-content opposition, an absolute distinction between style and subject. But it is the kind of reading that only a Holofernes makes.

We learn from the play's dialectic that all dualisms are suspect, that there is not an opposition but a continuum between the terms, that the relation between Art and Nature is necessarily not static but dynamic. We think of Blake: "Without Contraries is No Progression." The difference is that, unlike Blake, Shakespeare follows a constant impulse toward reconciliation.

The noblemen in *Love's Labour's Lost,* and the audience, come to learn what a "living art" really is. They learn that to deny either of the two terms in the concept is to falsify and destroy both. The noblemen, at the beginning, have denied what is "living"; the critics, with few exceptions, have concluded that the play denies the "art." The women and the songs embody and exemplify both.

The concept which mediates between Art and Nature is decorum. It has been broadly used to refer to living in general, to some natural rhythm, and to a specific poetic requirement. Approaching the play from the standpoint of its views on society, one reader sums up: "Virtually all the men in the play violate, each in his peculiar way, the values of 'civility', which meant at once civilization, social polish, government, courtesy, decorum, manners, and simple human kindness. . . . The play lays particular stress on the virtue of decorum, which becomes here a sense of the conduct appropriate to a given situation" [see the excerpt above by Thomas M. Greene, 1971]. Decorum means all this and even more. Specifically, the play forwards the debate about poetry by affirming a principle of poetic decorum. This can be narrowly construed as simply the process of matching social level with stylistic level, and the play has great fun with this. It can also include the broader suitability of poetic subject for a particular audience (Berowne's penance) or, reversed, the suitability of a poetic subject for a particular artist (the low characters present an imitation of the Nine Worthies). But in *Love's Labour's Lost* Shakespeare goes beyond these somewhat limited senses of decorum to probe the nature of a more mysterious, more significant kind of poetic decorum. This exceptional quality of imaginative propriety is finally elusive and indefinable; it is only suggested by example, and by analogy with other kinds of decorum. (pp. 199-201)

At the end of the play, the verbal debate ceases and the actual principle of decorum, of "imaginative"—not literal—decorum, is exemplified. The women represent the "living art" brought about through decorum in its social and intellectual, as well as verbal, form; the final songs represent "living art" as it applies to poetry in particular. That "grace" which the men so glibly refer to again and again lives only in the art of the women and the songs. (p. 202)

The last songs, the most perfect "marriage" of opposites in the play, take us a final step away from the harsh "reality" of Marcade and the penances toward a realm where dualisms vanish and death is transformed by art. This realm is the ideal form, a true golden world, of which the ascetic academy was only a grotesque parody. It is a place where Art, if only for a moment, on a stage with "living" actors, merges with Nature—where the oxymoronic "living art" finds its incarnation. (p. 204)

The final songs contain everything in the play. Though they are presented almost as an afterthought, *Love's Labour's Lost* is incomplete, and unimaginable, without them. They receive almost unanimous praise, even (or especially) from critics who dislike the rest of the play. The songs represent a magic moment in *Love's Labour's Lost,* a moment which seems of a different quality and order from what has come before it. (p. 206)

The songs are not simple or "natural," in the usual sense, but are perhaps the most carefully crafted things in the entire play. They represent not the rejection of Art for Nature, but the rejection of bad art for good art, for sophisticated stylistic devices are used with assurance in the songs: rhyming, inverted word order, frequent alliteration, punning ("To-it" and "to-

Princess of France. By J. J. Jenkins (n.d.).

wit"), low to middle diction, and an insistent if uncomplicated syntax ("when" = "then," with a free use of "and" connectors that carry us along effortlessly). The meter is a carefully regulated ground-tone of iambic tetrameter, and the planned irregularities—the spondee of "mocks married men" and the anapestic surprise of "When icicles hang by the wall" [V. ii. 908, 912]—are strikingly effective. Holofernes would be astonished.

The point . . . is that, to say anything, we have to use a common body of rhetorical constructs and devices, although some schemes, such as periphrasis, are suspect from the start. *Love's Labour's Lost* in effect has debated the use of such devices, and if the parody and exaggeration in the play show us how not to use them, the last songs show what can be done with them. The rhetorical devices are essentially the same in both cases; what makes the difference is the imagination employing them.

That the songs seem a moment out of or beyond the play constitutes their triumph. They *are* still in the play, in the realm of the imagination, without seeming to be. The play proper, we think, ended some moments ago and this is simply being tacked on. But it isn't. Where the three earlier theatrical sections were self-consciously emphasized, the songs are introduced on a more casual note. It is crucial that they follow immediately upon Berowne's comment, "That's too long for a play [V. ii. 879]," for as the play begins to turn back to artifice, away from the harshness of Marcade's outer world, the songs are offered as the perfect fusion of Art and Nature, inner and outer. And, as Shakespeare announces that his materials are too long for the traditional dramatic model, he concludes his play with one of the most traditional of all dramatic models, the medieval *conflictus*. (pp. 206-07)

It seems fair to say that the songs as a single entity represent the reconciliation of all the opposites in *Love's Labour's Lost*: the perfect marriage of Art and Nature, the play's central example of the transforming power of the imagination. (p. 208)

> *William C. Carroll, in his* The Great Feast of Language in "Love's Labour's Lost," *Princeton University Press, 1976, 279 p.*

LOUIS ADRIAN MONTROSE   (essay date 1977)

[*In his study of* Love's Labour's Lost, *Montrose argues that language, sexuality, and art form the social bond in the play, but that the male characters try to deny the human interaction necessary to these social elements by insulating themselves from the "actual world." Their "second world," which Montrose suggests is an effort to recreate the Garden of Eden, is lost when the women bring to it the harsher realities of an alien, fallen world. Unlike most critics, Montrose does not regard the Princess as an agent of comic resolution, but as the representative of a severe and serious political society. It is Armado, in his dialogue of the owl and the cuckoo, who comes closest to providing a happy ending to the play, for, according to Montrose, it is the final songs that bring together, in a bond of reciprocity, the men, the women, and the theater audience. These songs are also discussed by Richmond Noble (1923), Bertrand H. Bronson (1948), William C. Carroll (1976), and, in the Additional Bibliography, Catherine McLay. The concern with language as a social bond in* Love's Labour's Lost *is also examined in the essays by James L. Calderwood (1971), Terence Hawkes (1973), and Malcolm Evans (1975).*]

The King's quest of heroic wisdom conflates desires for eternal grace and perpetual fame; Berowne's quest of heroic love conflates desires for sexual union and self-display. Both study and courtship are, in practise, means for the avoidance rather than the achievement of their objects. The King's translation of heroic action into reclusive study and Berowne's realization of romantic love as courtly play are obfuscations of the engagement and commitment that each quest necessitates. Navarre's description of Armado extends to himself and his courtiers: each is "One who the music of his own vain tongue / Doth ravish like enchanting harmony" [I. i. 166-67]. They are the captives of their own eloquence.

The King's image of pleasure is built on a metaphor of sexuality turned in upon itself. Shakespeare assimilates and expresses in his drama a value that his society shared with all traditional societies, that the sexual and linguistic are, ideally, homologous dimensions of a basic social bond. (p. 49)

Navarre and Berowne and their cronies use the self-referentiality of language to insulate themselves in a verbal "second world" against whatever is objectionable in the "actual" world from which the ladies come. The ladies' speech is primarily recreative in function when they are among themselves; their goal is "a set of wit well played" [V. ii. 29]. But in her first confrontation with the King, the Princess insists on the bindingly denotative and referential function of language: "We arrest your word" [II. i. 159]. Language is motivated, it is the cardinal form of symbolic action; to avoid the reality that words have consequences is either foolish or dangerous. (p. 57)

The Princess has a potential energy which contrasts very effectively with the kinetic energy of the males. Within the context of the play's fictive world, the lords and their low-plot counterparts conflate the imaginative with the actual, their own "great feast of languages" [V. i. 37] with "the world's debate" [I. i. 173]. The ladies maintain an air of detachment which keeps the imaginative and the actual firmly apart. In doing so, they perform a purgative function in the humorous world of Navarre, but they are far from embodying the spirit of romantic comedy. Theirs is not a simple, witty detachment but a sophisticated irony. They may rate the play's action "At courtship, pleasant jest, and courtesy, / As bombast and as lining to the time" [V. ii. 780-81], while taking advantage of their courtiers' absorbtion in it in order to impose the priorities of the world of work upon the world of play. The Princess and her entourage have received uncritical enthusiasm from nearly all who have written on the play. There has been a consistent tendency to endow the Princess with a normative function in the world of the play or to associate her with some ideal which is presumed to be Shakespeare's. The roles which the Princess does enact in the play are both more complex and more ambivalent than the play's critics usually perceive; their bedazzlement is shared by the courtiers of Navarre.

The character who does perhaps come closest to the central experience of Shakespearean comedy is Rosalind in *As You Like It*. . . . As both Rosalind and Ganymede, she combines and resolves within herself the conflicting attitudes of romance and satire which the other characters project. The conclusion which she engineers in the world of Arden includes the wedding masque and four marriages denied in *Love's Labour's Lost*.

The Princess' very detachment makes such a feminine role impossible in *Love's Labour's Lost*. The Princess and her girls of France bring the concerns of the outside world with them when they invade the enclosure of Navarre. Contemplation and celibacy, the promulgated principles of the academe, are really evasions of social and sexual responsibility disguised as forms of transcendence. The women's participation in the artificial environment of play contaminates it with all that the actual world represents. Thus, while the women may be said to introduce the values of healthy sexuality, common sense, and scorn of pretension into the stilted life of the academe, they also bring the harsher realities of social and political existence. Although the ladies engage in excesses of wit and obscene banter (the Princess herself being carefully excluded from the latter), they remain visitors in the humorous kingdom of Navarre, from a world in which play coexists with power. The Princess comes as "The daughter of the King of France / On serious business craving quick dispatch" [II. i. 30-1], as a political and economic agent, not as an ambassador of love. In the pseudo-erotic action which the arrival of the ladies precipitates, they play at the courtly diversions with the requisite social grace while never losing sight of the object of their mission.

The murky negotiations of the first scene of Act Two would have engaged the active interest of many in an Elizabethan audience, those who were attuned to affairs of war, finance, and diplomacy, and to the intricacies of continental politics which could exert a profound influence on the welfare of England. This would be especially true in the case of a play whose setting and whose chief characters' names recalled the recent, turbulent French religious-political wars. Given such a context of interests at the play's outset, any contemporary audience would undoubtedly have been much more struck than we are that such significant issues seem to evaporate as the play unfolds. The explanation is surely not that Shakespeare's interest wandered but that he was contriving to point up the wavering interest of some of his characters. After Marcade has brought the news that she is now herself a queen, the Princess makes a curious remark in taking her leave of the King: "Excuse me so, coming too short of thanks / For my great suit so easily obtain'd" [V. ii. 738-39]. We are suddenly reminded of the political-economic purpose of her embassy. This has been elaborated with diplomatic formality at their first meeting [II. i.], and casually alluded to by the Princess in the peculiarly predatory context of the hunt:

> Well, lords, to-day we shall have our dispatch;
> On Saturday we will return to France.
> Then, forester, my friend, where is the bush
> That we must stand and play the murtherer in?
>
> [IV. i. 5-8]

The world of "serious business" intrudes allusively into the world of "game" and "recreation" [IV. ii. 166-67] around the beginning, middle, and end of the play. The Princess' parting words to the King suggest that, though he has been diverted, she has been very much aware of her mission all the time.

Boyet had frankly recommended the strategy of the Machiavellian fox in his first assessment of Navarre: "I'll give you Aquitaine and all that is his, / And you give him for my sake but one loving kiss" [II. i. 248-49]. After reading the claims of the King of France, Navarre confesses:

> Dear Princess, were not his requests so far
> From reason's yielding, your fair self should make
> A yielding 'gainst some reason in my breast,
> And go well satisfied to France again.
>
> [II. i. 149-52]

The Princess is the practitioner of a charming power politics. Not only does she fully possess the social and personal grace which represented the quintessence of nobility to [Baldassare] Castiglione [in *The Book of the Courtier*]; she also possesses a personal strength and flexibility, enabling her to control or influence the course of events, akin to the *virtù* which represented to Machiavelli the essential quality of the effective prince. The Princess masters her affects with both "Might" and "special grace." She possesses the courtly grace that the King attempts, with such ineptitude, to affect, and the political *virtù* that he shrinks from exercising.

The darker side of the Princess' strength of character is part of a subliminal counter-theme to the gay romp that makes the play of *Love's Labour's Lost* so immediately appealing. The strategies of language and the dislocations of social bonding engendered by abuses of speech which Shakespeare anatomizes through comedy in *Love's Labour's Lost*, he explores in the harsher light of history in *The Tragedy of King Richard the Second*. Richard's solipsistic lyricism, his self-staging, and the energy with which he verbally embraces each new role thrust upon him, are all characteristics which connect him to Navarre and Berowne. The agreeable faces which face so many follies in Navarre's curious-knotted garden are out-faced in a sexual combat of wits that generates laughter, not pathos. The opposition of lords and ladies in *Love's Labour's Lost* exemplifies a contrast of two linguistic modes, in which the former falls before the superior efficiency of the latter in dealing with the political strategies lurking behind social rituals. Though no comic Bolingbroke, the Princess certainly shares in the ambiguous nature, the characteristic manipulativeness and detachment, of such a Shakespearean political hero as Prince Hal

[in *Henry IV*]. A sojourner among habitués in the anti-temporal play-world of Navarre, the Princess awhile upholds the unyoked humor of their idleness, until sport becomes tedious and the imperatives of the world of time, work, and death must no longer be put aside. Upon inheriting her father's authority, the Princess banishes the King of Navarre to a penitential hermitage; she holds out to him the promise of advancement in her favor if he reforms himself. Shakespeare brings comedy into history in *Henry IV* by a rich and strange transformation of the Renaissance comic structure, shaped by ethical and political themes, of which *Love's Labour's Lost* is a particularly brilliant example. The world of history, conflict, obligation, anxiety, and suffering that the characters' play-world is designed to evade is precisely the context in which Shakespeare's play becomes meaningful for his audience, who are themselves Time's subjects. (pp. 85-90)

If the play can be said to make any doctrinal point, it does so by exposing the discrepancy between the intent of theology and the uses to which the characters put its vocabulary. Berowne's playful blasphemies culminate in a final argument for absolution:

> Our love being yours, the error that love makes
> Is likewise yours. We to ourselves prove false,
> By being once false forever to be true
> To those that make us both—fair ladies, you;
> And even that falsehood, in itself a sin,
> Thus purifies itself and turns to grace.
>
> [V. ii. 771-76]

The Princess resists deification; she insists on the lords' free will, and thus on the culpability of their wanton fancies. Berowne and his fellows thirst for a courtly parody of grace; the Princess and her ladies confront them with a secular and metaphorical use of "sin," "guilt," and "reformation." Attempts to reduce the play to an allegory of theological doctrine are far wide of the mark. The language and doctrines of religion provide a context—a largely ironic context—for the thematic content of the fiction.

Soon after the King concludes his opening speech on the pursuit of grace and eternity, he receives a letter from Armado which he reads aloud [I. i. 231 ff.]. Behind its delightfully preposterous rhetoric is a strangely haunting echo of the third chapter of *Genesis*. 'About the sixt hour," Armado went walking in the King's "park," and witnessed "that obscene and most prepost'rous event": the transgression of the King's "proclaimed edict" by Costard ("that low-spirited swain") and Jaquenetta ("a child of our grandmother Eve") within Navarre's "curious-knotted garden." The King attempts to reestablish a prelapsarian Garden of Eden but the Fall is reenacted almost as soon as the word is promulgated. There is much ado about apples (costard, pomewater, and crab) in the garden of Navarre.

In the Garden of Eden, as described by Milton, there are

> Flow'rs worthy of Paradise which not nice Art
> In Beds and curious Knots, but Nature boon
> Pour'd forth profuse on Hill and Dale and Plain.
>
> [*Paradise Lost* IV. 241-43]

Human art is anomalous in a world of as yet unfallen Nature. In *Love's Labour's Lost*, nature appears in a cultural form (park, garden, field) which seeks to exclude the world of brazen actualities in which fallen man finds himself. Navarre's is a hothouse variety of "green world," with something of the pejorative connotation of "artifice" (Milton's "nice art") about it. The image of Navarre's "curious-knotted garden" [I. i. 246] suggests the labyrinthine self-deceptions of the misguided wits that effloresce within its confines. Here art is an escape from the realities of a state of fallen nature rather than an instrument by which to morally transform them. The alienated world of nature must force its way inside the park in its radical aspects, as sexuality and, more effectively, death. (pp. 132-34)

The spell of the playworld's magic circle is weakened from within before it succumbs to the pressures of an inexorable outer reality. It is threatened from the play's beginning, and is only maintained by an anxious and at times frantic group effort. The play's texture is filled with ominous prolepses and disturbing images, knit together by an undercurrent of lust and obscenity and the symbolism of the hunt. Berowne and his comrades playfully draw their imagery of love and courtship from disease. . . . The obsessive series of these images hints continually at the world of pain and death from which the courtiers try to insulate themselves in living art. (p. 154)

The form of *Love's Labour's Lost* is very much a mutation of the archetypal Shakespearean comic structure: "Our wooing doth not end like an old play: / Jack hath not Gill" [V. ii. 874-75]. The harsh law contrary to the comic spirit—the fact of mortality and the world of pain, struggle, and responsibility which it implies—is enforced at the end of this play, rather than at the beginning. The players have been avoiding the burden of imaginatively coming to terms with the facts of fallen nature, so as to accommodate the fear and anxiety which they arouse. (p. 156)

The tone of the scene between Marcade's entry and the final songs poses a problem of interpretation. The ladies are forcing the lords into a temporal, fallen world of experience which, in the penances of the King and Berowne, is dramatically presented through the tradition of medieval romance. The disdainful lady imposes harsh, long, nigh impossible tasks on the lover who, by undertaking them, aims to perfect his self and prove worthy of the lady. The indeterminacy of the ending, the plot's open form, injects considerable ambiguity into the significance of the action. From one perspective, a new sense of relation is established between the ladies and their courtiers and the action of a romantic comedy has been initiated; from another perspective, the ladies exit the playworld as easily as they had entered it, having fulfilled their function as the collective agency of both a comic nemesis and a diplomatic coup. The follies of the men have been exposed, the illusion broken, the possibilities of self-discovery presented. In either case, the final outcome lies beyond the scope of "our sport," the dramatic fiction of *Love's Labour's Lost*. By explicitly pointing out that "our wooing doth not end like an old play," Shakespeare is conspicuously implying that this is a new kind of play which insists that the audience take seriously the theatre's claim to hold the mirror up to the world's stage upon which the audience are the actors. Shakespeare makes a comedy by refusing to make his characters' sport a comedy. By dooming their "old infant play" from the beginning, he creates an exhilarating and penetrating examination of the modes of playing.

The conclusion of Shakespearean romantic comedy points toward an accommodation of its first and second worlds—the "actual" world of the fiction, in which the characters find themselves, and the imaginative playworld they create within it. The latter is not totally repudiated; we are made to feel that its vision is in some way brought over into the fiction's "ac-

tual" world and will be made to imaginatively inform it beyond the characters' final *exeunt*. The last scene of *Love's Labour's Lost*, however, tends to force these two worlds violently apart, to irrevocably disjoin them. (pp. 158-60)

When Berowne and the King conclude their discussion of the play's dramatic kind, they have closed the borders of the world of *Love's Labour's Lost* and severed its contract with the audience:

> *Ber.* Our wooing doth not end like an old play:
> Jack hath not Gill. These ladies' courtesy
> Might well have made our sport a comedy.
> *King.* Come, sir, it wants a twelvemonth an' a day,
> And then 'twill end.
> *Ber.* That's too long for a play.
> [V. ii. 874-78]

The world of Navarre is now recognized as a playground bounded by a world outside; the larger context of actuality within the fiction is itself implicitly associated with the world of the theatre audience. When Armado re-enters, the Princess asks, "Was not that Hector?" [V. ii. 880]. The characters-as-actors are being separated from their roles in the games which have constituted an elaborate play-within-the-play; all the masquers must resume their true shapes now that the revels are ended. The play seems about to dissolve in unresolved antithesis and dissonance when Armado reconstitutes the fiction, "at the latest minute of the hour" [V. ii. 787], in order to perfect it for the audience, if not for the characters. Armado is the only humorous character for whom the play's catastrophe has been clearly understood as a recognition scene: "For mine own part, I breathe free breath. I have seen the day of wrong through the little hole of discretion, and I will right myself like a soldier" [V. ii. 722-25]. Now he reenters, having "vow'd to Jaquenetta to hold the plow for her sweet love three year" [V. ii. 883-84], the term originally projected for the now defunct academe. This new Adam will labor in the earth, while Jaquenetta ("a child of our grandmother Eve") will labor in childbirth. Armado's shift from martial to pastoral (or, more precisely, georgic) images ushers in the songs which so simply, concisely, and profoundly express the ground of heroic action in the experience and integration of life's most basic contradictions. By presenting the lyric dialogue which "should have followed in the end of our show" [V. ii. 887-88], Armado becomes, in a rudimentary way, the architect of the happy ending typical of Shakespearean romantic comedy but absent from the dramatic fiction of *Love's Labour's Lost*.

For a brief moment, the lords and ladies are again an audience; now they listen and watch together in silent attention. The relation of the theatre audience to the formalized art of the songs is not mediated by the fictive audience on the stage. The theatre audience is led into the dramatic fiction and beyond it, toward the vision of the lyrics. The awareness of the various characters and the members of the theatre audience have been levelled by the entry of the messenger of death; the knowledge of death as an ultimate separator is the bond which brings characters and audience together. Now, game becomes ritual in this moment of song.

The ambiguity of reference characteristic of the play's language is present in the final words which dissolve the playworld— "You that way; we this way" [V. ii. 931]. The director's options in interpretation will create different final effects: Armado may clear the stage by separating the players into two groups on the basis of class distinctions, which gives the effect of distinguishing the unlikely couple for whom love's labors have been won from the four aristocratic pairs who are about to part; he may clear the stage by separating the players into the original groups of Navarrese residents and French visitors, emphasizing the tonality of separation and loss; or he can break through the illusionary actuality of the fictional world to speak directly to the audience an epilogue on behalf of all the players. Though the audience who have been entertained in the play-world of Navarre are now bid to return to their own worlds, it is to be expected that they carry something of its vision home with them. (pp. 169-72)

Art, language, and sexuality are, in *Love's Labour's Lost*, largely devoid of the complex social context and web of kinship so pervasive in the other comedies and the romances. Both kinship and socio-political relations are alluded to only in the most oblique, negative, and fragmentary way. The characters practice a promiscuous abuse of the analogy of creation and procreation, which the playwright uses to negatively reassert the analogy's validity. *Love's Labour's Lost* is an implicit critique of the self-persuading rhetoric and asocial lyricism of which it is largely composed—and, at some level, a critique of the centripetal impulse in Shakespeare's own art. The failure of form at the play's conclusion is genuinely poetic justice; it is the play's own nemesis. *Love's Labour's Lost* demonstrates its own rhetorical logic, which is to deny a conclusion based on the logic of its characters. Rituals of verbal, sexual, and social bonding are denied: the lords deny their own oaths, the ladies deny the lords their favors, the playwright denies the audience the expected conclusion.

That which is "too long for a play" to perfect must be worked out among the members of the audience; the songs are their guide. It is appropriate, and even necessary, that the final festivity be a specifically aesthetic and objectified one. It is not the expression of the characters' own realization but a gift to them—and to the audience—from the playwright. (p. 175)

> *Louis Adrian Montrose, in his* "Curious-Knotted Garden": The Form, Themes, and Contexts of Shakespeare's 'Love's Labour's Lost'," *Institut für Englische Sprache und Literatur, 1977, 222 p.*

A. P. RIEMER   (essay date 1980)

[*Riemer, arguing against the "received opinion" of* Love's Labour's Lost, *contends that the play has no overriding moral or ethical meaning and that to "impose such a scheme on it is to pervert or to overlook several by no means negligible aspects of its structure." Like Walter Pater (1885), Riemer suggests that the language of* Love's Labour's Lost *exists more for its own elaboration than as the vehicle of a coherent moral statement, and he argues that the play itself is "a compendium of poetic, rhetorical and theatrical devices which furnishes its own fascination." He concludes by calling it "a pleasant conceited jest."*]

Love's Labour's Lost is more complex and more ambiguous than received opinion is willing to grant. The relationship between its various facets and the question whether these contribute toward a coherent set of meanings (in the post-romantic sense) are the major problems facing any interpretation or explication of this crucially important comedy.

Certainly the play expresses very fully the allure of this world which, in most modern accounts, it appears to castigate so sternly. Theoretically, the King's opening speech may be taken as a collection of shop-soiled clichés which were as outmoded in the 1590s as they were to become later. But its vitality,

exuberance and rhythmic drive demand recognition. It is possible, of course, that Shakespeare experienced the same difficulties Molière encountered when he found himself incapable of writing a bad sonnet for his poetaster to recite in *Le Misanthrope*. Also, the charm of the King of Navarre's green retreat could be taken to represent an attempt by Shakespeare to establish the strength and force of these aspirations, even though they come, ultimately, to be revealed as foolish or even, perhaps, as immoral. He could be thought to have refused, in other words, to score easy points: the play's effect may be thought to depend on the vitality with which unfortunate practices are depicted, so that their condemnation at the end is not facile but fully justified. These are, however, rationalizations; literature, especially drama, rarely operates in this manner without including specific signs of such ambitions. The opening speech of *Love's Labour's Lost* is an instance of poetic display which neglects to concern itself exclusively or even primarily with demonstrating the nature of its inherent values. . . . In part, of course, this introduction serves to depict the character of the King and the nature of his court—pompous, learned, articulate. The shortcomings of this view of life (with which modern criticism is preoccupied almost to the exclusion of all else) are thereby registered.

But the speech has other important effects and functions. In a way, we are not listening here to the King of Navarre, for, within the structure of the play, his character is merely beginning to exist for us. We attend, indeed, to an actor, and (more importantly, perhaps) to Shakespeare himself fashioning this impressive display of rhetorical skill and traditional imagery. And, because we are attending to a skilled poet, the performance cannot but be enthralling. The poetic display is, moreover, notable for its restraint: this is not merely the young writer of genius showing off his ability, the effect is transcended by the artistry which makes the rhetorical elaboration (as in the play on 'grace' and 'disgrace') merge into the poetic and emblematic commonplaces—'brazen tombs', 'devouring Time', 'scythe's keen edge'. The rhythms of these lines and congruence between the verse structure and the grammar of this complex sentence reveal a shaping and organizing literary intelligence that makes the linguistic members of the passage serve the needs of the passage itself. Moreover, the tactful introduction of the epithet 'cormorant' prevents these commonplaces from becoming too commonplace.

The King's speech is a skilled display by Shakespeare the craftsman; we are in the presence of a sportive performance which is not entirely germane to the suggestions involved in the play, though it is by no means wholly irrelevant to them. The allure of this speech is considerable, and it must remain a memorable and attractive experience for the spectators, no matter what shortcomings are revealed in those that maintain such sentiments. The sportiveness creates its own values of exhilaration and even, perhaps, of joy; these lines are exciting because of their poise; an audience cannot but become involved with the world they depict. A most subtle and complex relationship is established, as in so many other instances, between the audience's enjoyment of the theatrical representation and the moral or ethical judgements it might wish to make. In the earlier scenes of the play, at least, this enjoyment of the poet's skilled performance seems to predominate. The King and his nobles dwell in a linguistic universe which is grandiloquent and polished. Nowhere else, perhaps, in Shakespeare's earlier drama do we find the blandishments of sonorous and elegant speech so beautifully illustrated. . . . A major part of Shakespeare's intention in the early episodes of the play seems, therefore, to have been devoted to the creation of this richness of language that is its own justification.

The elaborately ornamented world of *Love's Labour's Lost* is often regarded as a term within the play's dialectic of ideas. The language created for the King and his nobles is considered to reveal their attitude towards life and to give it substance. This mode of language is thought to enter into a generally dynamic relationship with other attitudes and with other linguistic worlds in the play. By this process, the various worlds are taken to be contrasted, judged, adjudicated and weighed. The purpose of art, according to such views it must be stressed once more, is fundamentally moral; literature is a species of *regulum vitae* ["regular life"]. It is, nevertheless, questionable how far *Love's Labour's Lost* engages with such issues. Naturally, a comparison of its four orders of existence is not entirely avoided. The king and his nobles, the wordy representatives of 'learning', are contrasted against the insistence of the Princess and her ladies on plain-speaking honesty. Standing against these worlds (and against the other types of 'learning' represented by the fantastical Spaniard and the schoolmaster) we find the vernacular village-society of Dull, Costard and Jaquenetta, with Sir Nathaniel as a member of this world who has bettered himself through his association with Holofernes. But the play may not be reduced to a diagrammatic or even to a consistent demonstration of the nature of the world depicted in it. The contrasts do not contribute towards coherent moral or ethical statements, despite certain loud protestations by critics to the contrary. To impose such a scheme on it is to pervert or to overlook several by no means negligible aspects of its structure.

One example is striking. At the end of IV. i., we are given an exchange between Rosaline and Boyet (with some assistance from Margaret) consisting of a series of *risqué* puns in the manner much liked apparently, by sixteenth-century audiences. Some sensibilities find it offensive that the representatives of sincerity should engage in this sort of mild obscenity; comfort may, however, be drawn from the observation that the Princess leaves the stage just before the commencement of this passage. More problematical is the function of this passage within the design of the play. A charactertistic critical response is to ignore it, to regard it, that is, as a piece of stage-business, quite out of harmony with the significance of these characters, intended to indulge the tastes of the audience or the whims of the actors. Refuge may also be taken in the convenient supposition that this part of the play is a theatrical addition by a hand other than Shakespeare's. But these are strategies to avoid the essential issue: this episode is an integral part of the play, and it must therefore have an effect on the total impression the play makes.

It cannot be said (as it may be in the case of the disquisition on child-actors in *Hamlet*) that the passage is so out-of-key with the rest of the play that it may be safely overlooked. The protracted puns on 'hitting' resemble a number of similar passages in the play. Moth and Armado have several contests of this sort (principally at the beginning of III. i.), Holofernes's fantasia on prickets and sorels in IV. ii. and his burlesque scholastic dispute with Sir Nathaniel in V. i. belong to this category of incidents; they occupy a considerable portion of this relatively brief play. While it is possible to see in these cases instances of a critique of the various abuses of language committed by the pedants, euphuists and courtly wits of the late sixteenth century, these passages are, nevertheless, intrinsically the same in effect as the punning exchange between

Rosaline and Boyet: fantastical, elaborate flights of verbal ingenuity in which the 'significances' of literary criticism play a relatively minor part.

These aspects of *Love's Labour's Lost* point towards the possibility that the play consists of a string of bravura set-pieces loosely strung together on a slender narrative frame—a view implicitly held by those that would dismiss it as an immature extravaganza of little artistic merit. But, as a performance of dazzling skill, the changes rung by Shakespeare on the dramatic and poetic modes of the late sixteenth century in *Love's Labour's Lost* are without peer. The play is a compendium of poetic, rhetorical and theatrical devices which furnishes its own fascination; but it incorporates, as well, a rich though evanescent combination of feelings. The play constantly borders on parody, to the extent of its seeming to parody itself; yet this parody involves emotional overtones of surprising complexity. (pp. 18-22)

Love's Labour's Lost, then, is a pleasant, conceited jest. It finds much of its value in its exuberance, variety, display of virtuoso skill, and in its ability to evoke contradictory feelings about the strange, dream-like world of the King's park, flourishing in a perpetual spring yet harbouring the serpent of death. The play is simultaneously flippant, trivial and serious, but its seriousness is not that of the pulpit or of the soap-box; it is, rather, the seriousness to be encountered when an artist arranges his perfectly fashioned pieces into a pleasing shape. The ability of the artist, or of the work of art, to remain unimpressed by artistic achievement, while in no way denying its importance or excellence, is a measure of this curious comic effect. No other play of Shakespeare's demonstrates so clearly or so simply the fundamental qualities of his art of comedy; and, indeed, for all its marvellous freshness, Shakespeare's command of his artistic resources was not mature enough fully to sustain this most difficult of tasks undertaken in *Love's Labour's Lost*. (pp. 22-3)

> A. P. Riemer, "Expounding Bottom's Dream," in his Antic Fables: Patterns of Evasion in Shakespeare's Comedies, *St. Martin's Press, 1980, pp. 1-26.*

J. DENNIS HUSTON (essay date 1981)

[*In the introduction to his* Shakespeare's Comedies of Play, *Huston maintains that "playfulness" is the "defining quality of Shakespeare's early comedies" and refers to Jean Piaget's theory which cites play as the medium between the self and reality. In* Love's Labour's Lost, *argues Huston, Shakespeare is concerned with the play of language and "the uses to which man puts it as he constructs schemes and pageants to suit reality to his desires." He states that the men of Navarre's court, being isolated from the real world, have withdrawn too much into the self and, consequently, substitute language for the reality of experience. Huston contrasts* Love's Labour's Lost *with* The Comedy of Errors, *pointing out that, unlike the latter play,* Love's Labour's Lost *does not have a plot based on a coherent pattern of experience. Instead, Huston continues, it presents a series of interrupted "beginnings," or widening responses on the part of the male characters to changing events, which ultimately move the play toward a more inclusive presentation of life. Huston also interprets the final songs as Shakespeare's demonstration of the unpredictability of events in the world, as well as the medium by which both the characters and the audience experience the realities of life. Yet, for Huston,* Love's Labour's Lost *does not end on a discouraging note, but celebrates "man's unending capacity to build new beginnings upon the broken remains of old ones." Alexander Leggatt (1974)*

Almost nothing about *The Comedy of Errors* prepares us for
what we initially find in *Love's Labour's Lost*. From a play
built almost entirely of plot and modelled on Plautine patterns
of comedy, we move now to one built almost exclusively of
language and modelled on the courtly dramas of John Lyly,
as if Shakespeare were consciously experimenting with a different form of stage comedy—which is almost certainly what
he is doing. In *The Comedy of Errors* Shakespeare exuberantly
celebrates his powers as a maker of dramatic plots; here he
celebrates his powers as a maker of dramatic language. So if
in the first of these comedies the characters often seem like
puppets, guided through carefully choreographed movements
by the hand of the playwright, in the second, the characters
appear at times almost like ventriloquist dummies, deriving
their life not so much from what they do as from what they
say as they speak, in various voices and accents, the words of
their master. In place of the puppets' persistent movement,
they offer constant talk; in place of action, declamation. But
The Comedy of Errors is not the only Shakespearean play
whose structure is at odds with that of *Love's Labour's Lost*.
Almost all of the comedies differ from it in at least one significant way. For when we think of comic action in Shakespearean drama, we think of near tragedy and of violence often
just barely averted. . . . No such violence, though, appears in
Love's Labour's Lost, because the world of this play is carefully
insulated against pain. In it there are no tyrannical parents to
run from, no violence provoked by misunderstanding or malignant wrongdoing, no apparent madness or witchcraft affecting human behavior and threatening the very order of things.
Instead characters engage in the ordinary, everyday activities
of courtly life: they talk, they play games, they receive visitors,
they hunt, they fall in love, they write letters and love poems,
they put on a masque, and they watch a play. No Shakespearean
comedy is so obviously free of violence and potential tragedy
as *Love's Labour's Lost*. It is true that hints of such complications occasionally appear in the play: the King of Navarre
proclaims a law which would treat men who keep company
with women almost as harshly as the laws of Ephesus treat
Syracusians; the pageant of the Worthies is disrupted by potential violence; and Mercade brings sudden, shocking news
of death. But these possible complications are not darkly developed: the king begins to make exceptions to his law almost
as soon as it is proclaimed; the violence at the pageant is all
verbal; and Mercade's message comes suddenly, unexpectedly,
from the world outside Navarre and, as we shall see, almost
from outside the play. Navarre itself remains basically insulated
from the violence, madness, and potential tragedy of other
Shakespearean comedies. (pp. 35-6)

Not even the Forest of Arden [in *As You Like It*], which is the
closest equivalent to Navarre in Shakespearean comedy, is as
sheltered as this world. For Arden has the melancholy Jaques
to remind the Duke of his role as usurper; and immediately
outside of Arden villains, planning to kill their brothers, prepare to disrupt its pastoral serenity. No one, however, is melancholy for long in Navarre, and the world outside is so easily
forgotten that Mercade's entrance and message of death come
as one of the most shocking surprises in Shakespearean drama.

So insulated, in fact, is the world of this play that we feel the
presence of the playwright as conspicuously here as in *The
Comedy of Errors,* though this effect is achieved in a very
different way. Here Shakespeare does not proclaim his un-

bounded delight in his medium by obviously manipulating his
characters and outrageously overgoing the limits of a credible
plot line. Instead he calls attention to his play-making powers,
as a dramatist celebrating the possibilities the theater offers his
creative energies, by presenting a dramatized image of that
sheltered world. Within the world of the theater, temporarily
set off in time and place from the press of reality outside it,
Shakespeare presents his audience with a dramatic world sheltered from the 'reality' of work, responsibility, sorrow, and
death. As a playwright, working within the insulated world of
the theater, his own action thus serves in some ways as the
subject of his play—in which surrogate playwright figures,
living within the sheltered world of Navarre, self-consciously
construct their own staged productions principally by manipulating language in order to shape reality to their desires. (pp.
36-7)

All the commonwealth of Navarre, as it appears in this play,
is an enclosed and cultivated park, playground for the idle king
and his attendant lords, who find there deer to hunt, swains to
laugh at, and ladies to love. Unlike the inhabitants of Ephesus
[in *The Comedy of Errors*], no one in Navarre, during the
course of the play, ever works. Holofernes may have pupils,
but we never see them; Jaquenetta, turned over to the custody
of Constable Dull and ordered to become a dairymaid, very
quickly puts away dairying and the constable for dalliance and
Costard; and Nathaniel may get his living as a curate, but we
never see him administering to the needs of his parish. Everyone in Navarre is on holiday, busily engaged in the manifold
forms of play, from love-making to fool-baiting, offered within
the round of the king's verdant park, and Shakespeare's
wooden O.

Here even the business of ruling a kingdom can be playfully
pushed aside. The king begins by announcing that for the next
three years he will pursue the life contemplative—as if a king
were really free to abandon the worldly concerns of his kingdom. Then when the unavoidable duties of rule do interrupt
Navarre's plans for a perfect academe, he gives the problems
only the most casual attention, consigning Costard the law-
breaker to the keeping of Armado and throwing away Aquitaine
for half of what it is worth as surety. And this latter action,
arising out of the only real business of kingship demanding
Navarre's attention in the play, is of so little concern to him,
and everyone else, that we hear about it only as an afterthought
in the fifth act, when the Princess, called suddenly away by
her father's death, summarily thanks Navarre 'For my great
suit so easily obtain'd' [V. ii. 739].

Problems of abiding concern in Ephesus, where people struggle
with the tyrannous inflexibility of their own constructed systems of time, money, and law, have little place in the holiday
world of Navarre. There time repeatedly shifts its shape to suit
the dictates of human desire: a lifetime in pursuit of fame may
be as short as 'this present breath' [I. i. 5], three years' study
as brief as 'an hour' [I. ii. 37], or the latest minute of an hour
time enough for a king to consider making 'a world-without-
end bargain' in [V. ii. 789]. (pp. 37-8)

Then, too, the world of *Love's Labour's Lost* is almost as free
of concern about money and law as it is about time. The king
has only the most casual interest in the two hundred thousand
crowns he thinks he is owed by France. And the young lords,
in bestowing rich gifts upon their loves, appear so prodigal
that the ladies take this attention as merely 'courtship, pleasant
jest and courtesy, / As bombast and as lining to the time' [V.
ii. 780-81]. For the common people of Navarre money is, of

Act IV. Scene iii. Longaville, Berowne, Dumaine, and King.
By Thomas Stothard (n.d.).

course, of more immediate interest than it is to the lords, but even for these people money is as much a subject for verbal as for material exchange. The poverty of his master regularly provides Moth with opportunities for mockery, and one of Costard's best comic speeches in the play explores the way in which language plays tricks with the intractable substantiality of money.

About the problem of law—man's laws, which are almost always in comedy arbitrary and something to be circumvented, usually at the end of the play by the action of the comedy as a whole—people in Navarre have no problem. There law is only a very temporary sort of inconvenience. We no sooner hear of the king's edict than we see its unworkability. Business of state brings the Princess of France to Navarre, and in negotiating with her about Aquitaine the king will of necessity have to disobey his own decree. 'Necessity,' Berowne reminds them, 'will make us all forsworn / Three thousand times within this three years' space' [I. i. 149-50], and he signs his name to the schedule of oaths while simultaneously talking of the excuses he will find for breaking faith. Then, as if to emphasize the validity of Berowne's perception, Costard is brought in as an offender against the edict. His defense of the naturalness of his crime—'Such is the simplicity of man to hearken after the flesh' [I. i. 217-18]—is merely a more direct assertion of Berowne's earlier claim to 'like of each thing that in season grows' [I. i. 107]: in this world man cannot successfully leg-

islate against the naturalness of sexual desire, nor does he really want to. Not even the king can take his own law seriously, for although his proclamation has promised a year's imprisonment to any man taken with a wench, he sentences Costard only to a week's fasting on bran and water in the custody of Armado. It is little wonder then that in less than a day Armado suspends even this sentence, for if the king cannot bring himself to enforce the rigor of his laws, we can hardly expect his agent to take their enforcement seriously. (pp. 39-40)

The restraints imposed by law, time, and money, then, little affect life in Navarre's kingdom of play. And such problems as they do produce belong properly to others, from a world outside Navarre, where a king may fall into debt fighting wars, bind over part of his kingdom in surety for money borrowed, and then die before he has heard of its successful reacquisition. In the insulated world of Navarre, death—and the ultimate disorder it imposes on all human action—threatens man only from a very great distance, both physically and emotionally: it happens to someone who never appears in the play and who inhabits another realm, outside Navarre. So it can be known only by report.

To the young men of Navarre death is little more than a word, and they (unlike the ladies of France who come from the world outside the king's sheltered park) are at first no more emotionally affected by Mercade's message than they have earlier been by the king's talk of 'brazen tombs,' 'the disgrace of death,' and 'cormorant devouring Time' [I. i. 2-4]. If the ladies would let them, they would continue their courtship uninterrupted, using this news of death as an excuse to move on to the next stage of wooing—betrothal—and so bring their play to a tidy conclusion. Near the end of Love's Labour's Lost the young men would repeat a pattern of behavior they have demonstrated before: they would confront a disruption and potential end to their play by talking it away, by linguistically manipulating it in such a way as to modify the description of their behavior, so that they can continue doing as they please. This is what they have done when they have earlier forsworn their vows of study in order to swear love to ladies who are 'the books, the arts, the academes, / That show, contain and nourish all the world . . .' [IV. iii. 349-50]. And this is what the king tries to do again when he would facilely put away the Princess' sorrow, and the inconvenient interruption it poses to their game of love-making, by turning an aphorism to his advantage:

> . . . since love's argument was first on foot,
> Let not the cloud of sorrow justle it
> From what it purposed; since, to wail friends lost
> Is not by much so wholesome-profitable
> As to rejoice at friends but newly found.
> [V. ii. 747-51]

Such behavior from the king emphasizes again how insulated the inhabitants of Navarre are from sorrow and pain. They cannot really understand the Princess's sorrow because it comes to them indirectly: not in the unmediated action of experience—they have not, like Egeon [in The Comedy of Errors], left the comfort of home to encounter a turbulent sea of sorrow, loss of loved ones, and imminent death—but in the mediating form of language—in their books they have encountered cliches about 'cormorant devouring Time,' and now Mercade softens his message of death as best he can. In the sheltered world of Navarre language often substitutes for the action of experience, perhaps because it substitutes for dramatic action as well. For no Shakespearean play is built so obviously out of words as Love's Labour's Lost. (pp. 40-2)

[Rarely] in a drama does a playwright make the skeletal framework of his art as obvious as Shakespeare does in *Love's Labour's Lost,* where he regularly draws his audience's attention to interrupted plays and pageants. A list of notable examples includes, besides Navarre's disrupted pageant of the first scene: the negotiations over Aquitaine, which are put off until the arrival of the packet of acquittances from France; the lovers' severally assumed stances of shock at their fellows for betraying their academy to love, which are each cut short by evidence of wrong-doing on the part of the accuser; the embassage of Moth and masque of the Muscovites, both disrupted by the mockery of the ladies; and the pageant of the Worthies, interrupted first by the rude remarks of the nobles, then by Costard's challenge to Armado, and finally by the arrival of Mercade. By presenting so many examples of failed drama, of 'form confounded' [V. ii. 519] in this play, Shakespeare is bringing art into more immediate contact with life, dramatizing in the insulated world of Navarre as he creates it the challenge of that other insulated world of the theater as he confronts, and also creates, it. In making a play that repeatedly depicts the attempts of others to make *their* plays, Shakespeare here dramatizes again a theme which he has explored in a somewhat different way in *The Comedy of Errors*—that of the discontinuity of human experience. (p. 48)

In *The Comedy of Errors* he was concerned primarily with the act of interpreting experience, of discovering a coherent pattern in the threateningly discontinuous events of everyday life. And behind the apparent disorder of things in Ephesus there appears at last a discernible order, coherent and miraculous, revealing itself to the characters and delivering them from the bondage of their own mistakings. The pattern may have been long hidden and elusive, discernible in part only by chance, but in Shakespeare's Ephesus there *is* a pattern of coherence—with a beginning, a middle, and an end—to be discovered. In Navarre there is no such pattern. In place of the carefully structured plot which orders the world of *The Comedy of Errors,* Shakespeare has provided a series of apparently haphazard meetings between lords and ladies, lords and commoners, and ladies and commoners. These meetings are not, in fact, altogether unmotivated (the characters do have things to say to one another) or unpatterned (the scenes focus alternately on the nobility and the common people), but they give no clear impression of a single controlled and developing action, building to a conclusion in time. Instead they suggest episodic events, often interrupted and only loosely related. If Shakespeare in *The Comedy of Errors* is giving dramatic emphasis to the difficulty of interpreting experience that *seems* discontinuous, here he is showing how man faces the difficulty of encountering experiences which *are* discontinuous, either psychologically or actually. In Navarre life does not ultimately reveal itself as a coherent pattern, with a beginning, a middle, and an end; rather, it appears as a series of interrupted actions out of which other actions must then be begun: characters constantly meeting with disruptions constantly attempt to overcome them with new beginnings. (pp. 49-50)

[Although] Mercade's entrance brings an end to the commoners' play and, in a sense, interrupts Shakespeare's, it does not finally end *Love's Labour's Lost.* In this drama of grand beginnings that are repeatedly disrupted by unlooked-for endings Shakespeare follows the examples of his characters and builds a new beginning on the ruins of the old one. He concludes his play by turning his characters, as well as his audience, out into a world wider than the insulated confines of the theater. For when the ladies of France impose trials upon their lovers to test the validity of sworn vows, their intent is not only to separate their lovers from the company of former playmates; it is also to force the young men out of the king's sheltered park, where these lords have been free to play at being 'boy eternal' (*The Winter's Tale,* [I. ii. 65]), and into a world of time, where the possibility of their growth is tied also to the inevitability of decay and death. . . . (pp. 53-4)

Shakespeare ends *Love's Labour's Lost* with a beginning for a number of reasons. First, the young men of Navarre, though at the end of a play, are also at the beginning of a new experience, which promises to take them outside the narrow confines of the king's park and their own self-absorption. Second, the ending, by so closely recalling the beginning of the play, emphasizes the dubiousness of the men's new vows. The lords may think their constancy in trial is certain, but they may prove as faithless in love as in study. The ending of the lovers' story is thus shadowed in the unpredictabilities of life not only by being projected forward beyond the bounds of the play but also, paradoxically, by being directed backwards towards its beginning. Third, and most important, Shakespeare is here working with an effect that is a dominating concern of his comedies: he is breaking down the conventional barriers between his play and actuality, between actors and audience, between drama and life. Drama, after all, *is* life for a man who makes his living in the theater, writing and acting in plays and keeping company with other players and playwrights. And life often takes on the qualities of drama, since we all at times see ourselves as characters engaged in an action of some coherence, with a beginning, a middle, and an end. In the process other characters, coming and going around us, make their entrances and exits in our play.

However this may be, the conclusion of *Love's Labour's Lost* offers its characters, and its audience, the promise of all comic endings; that is, a dramatic celebration of man's *un*ending capacity to build new beginnings upon the broken remains of old ones. The world of Navarre may be one in which man's hopes—his great schemes and his little plans alike—come to nothing, but it is not a world in which anyone is easily discouraged or ultimately defeated. Mercade's message, after all, comes from a realm *outside* Navarre, and his appearance, though dark, is fleeting, only briefly suggesting the more imposing shadows which will later darken the worlds of the mature comedies and eventually take full-bodied form in *Hamlet,*—another drama of academic study disrupted, of pageants interrupted, and of great beginnings crossed by unexpected endings. In that play, though, the messenger bringing the news of a father's death comes literally from another world and appears at the beginning of the play. And the shadow he casts is not fleeting but permanent, blackening the clothes and countenance and thoughts of the hero, and taking him at last to the earthy stage of man's inescapable end, where he can feel the worthless dust of all human endeavor slip through his fingers. Such a vision, however, is a long way from the world of *Love's Labour's Lost,* where Mercade enters and leaves almost in a moment and where human failure produces at worst silence and embarrassment—Nathaniel withdrawing from the pageant—and at best either a virtuoso verbal performance—Browne justifying the abandonment of the academy—or a chance to begin again—the king swearing new vows of constancy that make the ending of the play also a beginning. In such a world even the best of beginnings may be threatened by disruption; no spring is without the cuckoo's song and the threat it poses to human relationships. And even the worst of endings may provide opportunities for new beginnings; winter, the season of death, sickness, and cold without, is also the season of communal cooperation, merriment, and warmth within. (pp. 56-7)

J. Dennis Huston, "'Form Confounded' and the Play of 'Love's Labour's Lost'," in his Shakespeare's Comedies of Play, *Columbia University Press, 1981, pp. 35-57.*

ADDITIONAL BIBLIOGRAPHY

Acheson, Arthur. "The School of Night" and "Chapman as Original of Holofernes." In his *Shakespeare and the Rival Poet*, pp. 76-99, 100-15. London: John Lane, The Bodley Head, 1903.
Compares antithetical elements in George Chapman's poem "Shadow of the Night" with lines from *Love's Labour's Lost* and argues that Holofernes is a caricature of Chapman.

Agnew, Gates K. "Berowne and the Progress of *Love's Labour's Lost*." *Shakespeare Studies* IV (1968): 40-72.
Examines the dramatic structure of *Love's Labour's Lost* and Berowne's ambivalent status as a protagonist.

Anderson, J. J. "The Morality of 'Love's Labour's Lost'." *Shakespeare Survey* 24 (1971): 55-62.
Argues that Navarre's men fail to win the love of the women because they show themselves to be morally unworthy of it.

Baldwin, T. W. "*Love's Labour's Lost*" and "Stages of Structure in *Love's Labour's Lost*." In his *Shakespeare's Five-Act Structure*, pp. 579-625, pp. 626-64. Urbana: The University of Illinois Press, 1947.
Discusses the date, sources, and the possible dramatic influences on *Love's Labour's Lost*. Baldwin concludes that the play was modeled on John Lyly's *Endimion* and *Gallathea*, and that it was originally composed in 1588-89.

Berry, Jackson G. "Poem or Speech?: The Sonnet as Dialogue in *Love's Labour's Lost* and *Romeo and Juliet*." *Papers on Language and Literature* 19, No. 1 (Winter 1983): 13-36.
Examines the use of the sonnet as "a natural part of the dialogue" and argues that the sonnet speeches in *Love's Labour's Lost* demonstrate an "unusual but fruitful conjunction of a complex poetic experience with a dramatic one."

Bonazza, Blaze Odell. "*Love's Labour's Lost*." In his *Shakespeare's Early Comedies: A Structural Analysis*, pp. 44-75. The Hague: Mouton & Co., 1966.
Argues that *Love's Labour's Lost* "suffers from a number of structural deficiencies" as a result of its thin plot and its lack of dramatic conflict.

Browne, Ray B. "The Satiric Use of 'Popular' Music in *Love's Labour's Lost*." *Southern Folklore Quarterly* XXIII, No. 3 (September 1959): 137-49.
States that Shakespeare's references to "popular" songs are meant to satirically recall the quarrel between Gabriel Harvey and Thomas Nashe, who themselves referred to contemporary ballads in their polemics.

Bullough, Geoffrey, ed. "*Love's Labour's Lost*." In his *Narrative and Dramatic Sources of Shakespeare, Vol. I*, pp. 425-43. London: Routledge and Kegan Paul, 1966.
Contains reprints of several historical accounts which suggest that contemporary affairs in France and Russia may have served as a source for *Love's Labour's Lost*. Bullough admits that the "source-hunter has little to offer."

Campbell, Oscar J. "*Love's Labour's Lost* Re-studied." In *Studies in Shakespeare, Milton and Donne*, edited by Eugene S. McCartney, pp. 3-45. University of Michigan Publications, 1925. Reprint. New York: Phaeton Press, 1970.
Identifies Armado, Holofernes, and the other low characters in *Love's Labour's Lost* as traditional comic types from the Italian *commedia dell' arte*. Campbell also summarizes several theories on the topical references in the play.

Charlton, H. B. "The Date of 'Love's Labour's Lost'." *Modern Language Review* XIII, No. 3 (July 1918): 257-66.
Uses the references to the French civil wars to argue that 1592 is the earliest possible date for *Love's Labour's Lost*.

Clark, Eva Turner. *The Satirical Comedy "Love's Labour's Lost."* New York: William Farquhar Payson, 1933, 188 p.
Defines *Love's Labour's Lost* as a topical satire and maintains that Jacquenetta represents Mary Queen of Scots and Armado parodies Don John of Austria. Clark's premise is that Shakespeare was a pseudonym used by the Earl of Oxford and that *Love's Labour's Lost* was written by him in 1578 when William Shakespeare, "the Stratford actor . . . was only fourteen years old."

Curtis, Harry, Jr. "Four Woodcocks in a Dish: Shakespeare's Humanization of the Comic Perspective in *Love's Labour's Lost*." *Southern Humanities Review* 13, No. 2 (Spring 1979): 115-24.
Compares *Love's Labour's Lost* to *The Two Gentlemen of Verona* and concludes that the former, by denying the conventional comic ending, is the first of Shakespeare's comedies to offer a vision of the paradoxical complexity of life.

David, Richard. Introduction to *Love's Labour's Lost*, by William Shakespeare, edited by Richard David, pp. xiii-lii. The Arden Edition of the Works of William Shakespeare, edited by Una Ellis-Fermor. London: Methuen & Co., 1951.
Contains valuable information on date, text, and source, as well as a comprehensive discussion of the topical satire in *Love's Labour's Lost*.

Draper, John W. "Tempo in *Love's Labour's Lost*." *English Studies* 29, Nos. 1-6 (1948): 129-37.
Analyzes the tempo of speeches in *Love's Labour's Lost* and concludes that, unlike the speech rhythms in his later plays, this early comedy demonstrates that Shakespeare had not yet mastered a consistent and dramatically effective use of tempo.

Edwards, Philip. "*Love's Labour's Lost*." In his *Shakespeare and the Confines of Art*, pp. 33-48. London: Methuen & Co., 1968.
Emphasizes the force of sexual desire in the conflict between reality and illusion in *Love's Labour's Lost*.

Ellis, Herbert A. *Shakespeare's Lusty Punning in "Love's Labour's Lost."* The Hague: Mouton & Co., 1973, 239 p.
Presents an exhaustive study of semantic and homophonic puns in *Love's Labour's Lost*, most of which have sexual implications according to the author. Ellis states that the fullest comprehension of these puns and also of Shakespeare's work is achieved through an oral-aural study of the plays. He also concludes that Shakespeare's bawdy intent in his punning is much more prevalent than is generally acknowledged and that the humor of *Love's Labour's Lost* was probably intended for a more popular audience than most critics have supposed.

Erickson, Peter B. "The Failure of Relationship Between Men and Women in *Love's Labour's Lost*." *Women's Studies* 9, No. 1 (1981): 65-81.
Argues that the bonding of male characters in *Love's Labour's Lost* promotes a view of women as dangerous outsiders; consequently, the women become inaccessible, domineering, and punitive. Finally, concludes Erickson, neither homosexual nor heterosexual bonds are affirmed in *Love's Labour's Lost* and the play ends in "an uneasy stasis."

Frye, Northrop. *A Natural Perspective: The Development of Shakespearean Comedy and Romance*. New York: Columbia University Press, 1965, 159 p.
Mentions *Love's Labour's Lost* in various passages throughout and uses it specifically as an example of an anti-comic society that is overcome by the erotic pleasure principle.

Godshalk, William Leigh. "Pattern in Love." *Renaissance Papers 1968* (1969): 41-8.

Examines the image of an ordered symmetrical pattern in *Love's Labour's Lost,* and also notes an underlying sense of dissonance and decay in the drama.

Goldstein, Neal L. "*Love's Labour's Lost* and the Renaissance Vision of Love." *Shakespeare Quarterly* XXV, No. 3 (Summer 1974): 335-50.

Discusses the satire in *Love's Labour's Lost* of the Petrarchan and Neoplatonic tradition as well as the schism between sensual and spiritual concerns in the play.

Gray, Austin K. "The Secret of *Love's Labour's Lost*." *PMLA* 39, No. 1 (1924): 581-611.

Presents a hypothesis regarding the topical allusions in *Love's Labour's Lost*. Gray combines historical evidence with conjecture to produce a narrative account of the political circumstances surrounding the play as "it was peformed for the first time in the park of Titchfield House on the afternoon of September 2nd, 1591."

Gray, Henry David. *The Original Version of "Love's Labour's Lost": With a Conjecture as to "Love's Labour's Won."* Palo Alto, Calif.: Stanford University Press, 1918, 55 p.

Offers a reconstruction of the original *Love's Labour's Lost* and concludes that Holofernes and Nathaniel, as well as other elements of the play, were first introduced in Shakespeare's revision of the drama in 1597.

Griffith, Mrs. [Elizabeth]. "*Love's Labour's Lost*." In her *The Morality of Shakespeare's Drama Illustrated,* pp. 93-101, 1775. Reprint. London: Frank Cass & Co., 1971.

Comments on various passages in the play with a special emphasis on the morals presented.

Hamilton, A. C. "The Early Comedies: *Love's Labour's Lost*." In his *The Early Shakespeare,* pp. 128-42. San Marino, Calif.: The Huntington Library, 1967.

Emphasizes the verbal spectacle in *Love's Labour's Lost* and states that the play relies upon its "melody of words."

Harbage, Alfred. "*Love's Labour's Lost* and the Early Shakespeare." *Philological Quarterly* XLI, No. 1 (January 1962): 18-36.

Dates the play in the late 1580s and places it among Shakespeare's earliest work.

Hasler, Jörg. "Enumeration in *Love's Labour's Lost*." *English Studies* 4, Nos. 1-6 (1969): 176-85.

Discusses the balance and symmetry formed by the enumerative speeches in *Love's Labour's Lost*.

Hassel, R. Chris, Jr. "Love Versus Charity in *Love's Labour's Lost*." *Shakespeare Studies* X (1977): 17-41.

Examines the doctrine of charity in the context of its opposition in Protestant and Catholic theologies and discusses Shakespeare's treatment of this doctrine in *Love's Labour's Lost*.

Heninger, S. K., Jr. "The Pattern of *Love's Labour's Lost*." *Shakespeare Studies* VII (1974): 25-53.

Discovers patterns of contrast and continuity in the formal structure of the play.

Hoy, Cyrus. "*Love's Labour's Lost* and the Nature of Comedy." *Shakespeare Quarterly* XIII, No. 1 (Winter 1962): 31-40.

Uses *Love's Labour's Lost* to develop the more general argument that the basic pattern of all Shakespearean comedy "consists in a movement from the artificial to the natural, always with the objective of finding oneself."

Hunter, G. K. "Poem and Context in *Love's Labour's Lost*." In *Shakespeare's Styles: Essays in Honour of Kenneth Muir,* edited by Philip Edwards, Inga-Stina Ewbank, and G. K. Hunter, pp. 25-38. Cambridge: Cambridge University Press, 1980.

Compares and contrasts the effect of identical sonnets in *Love's Labour's Lost* and in *The Passionate Pilgrim,* an Elizabethan anthology of poems, and concludes that the poems in the play do not "lose their potential as mere poems," despite their satirical context.

Kerrigan, John. "*Love's Labour's Lost* and the Circling Seasons." *Essays in Criticism* XXVIII, No. 4 (October 1978): 269-87.

Notes the cyclical pattern and balance of the seasons in *Love's Labour's Lost*.

Knight, G. Wilson. "The Romantic Comedies." In his *The Shakespearian Tempest,* pp. 75-95. London: Oxford University Press, 1932.

Examines Shakespeare's use of imagery and notes that *Love's Labour's Lost,* which is full of gaiety but ends sadly, is a reversal of Shakespeare's later romances which have "tempests first, then the happy conclusion."

Lee, S. L. "A New Study of 'Love's Labour's Lost'." *The Gentleman's Magazine* CCXLVII, No. 1798 (October 1880): 447-58.

Introduces several important notions concerning the topical satire in *Love's Labour's Lost,* including explanations of the Masque of the Muscovites and the members of Navarre's court.

McClumpha, C. F. "Parallels Between Shakespeare's *Sonnets* and *Love's Labour's Lost*." *Modern Language Notes* XV, No. 6 (June 1900): 168-74.

Compares the Sonnets with passages from *Love's Labour's Lost* and concludes that both were written at approximately the same time.

McLay, Catherine M. "The Dialogues of Spring and Winter: A Key to the Unity of *Love's Labour's Lost*." *Shakespeare Quarterly* XVIII, No. 2 (Spring 1967): 119-27.

Contrasts the elements of artificiality in the spring song with the "pure realism" of the winter song, arguing that the imagery of these final songs, like the whole of *Love's Labour's Lost,* "moves from spring to winter, from art to nature, from illusion to reality."

Montrose, Louis A. "'Sport by sport o'erthrown': *Love's Labour's Lost* and the Politics of Play." *Texas Studies in Literature and Language* XVIII, No. 4 (Winter 1977): 528-52.

Discusses the importance of shame and grace in the courtly politics of *Love's Labour's Lost*.

Nelson, Timothy G.A. "The Meaning of *Love's Labour's Lost*." *Southern Review* (Adelaide, Australia) IV, No. 3 (1971): 179-91.

States that Berowne's speech renouncing monastic vows in favor of romantic love is full of irony and sophistry, and thus shows him inconstant and unworthy of that love.

Nosworthy, J. M. "The Importance of Being Marcade." *Shakespeare Survey* 32 (1979): 105-14.

Identifies Marcade as the god Mercury and discusses his role in the play as both "messenger and psychopomp."

Oakeshott, Walter. "Raleigh and 'Love's Labour's Lost'." In his *The Queen and the Poet,* pp. 100-27. London: Faber and Faber, 1960.

Supports the argument that Armado is a caricature of Walter Raleigh by citing internal and external evidence.

Quiller-Couch, Arthur, and Wilson, John Dover, eds. Introduction to *Love's Labour's Lost,* by William Shakespeare, pp. vii-xxxix. Cambridge: Cambridge at the University Press, 1923.

Contributes more hypotheses for the topical references in *Love's Labour's Lost* and concludes that the play "was written in 1593 for a private performance in the house of some grandee who had opposed Raleigh and Raleigh's 'men'—possibly the Earl of Southampton's."

Phialas, Peter G. "*Love's Labour's Lost*." In his *Shakespeare's Romantic Comedies,* pp. 65-101. Chapel Hill: The University of North Carolina Press, 1966.

Includes information on text, source, date, and historical background in an overview of the play.

Richmond, Hugh M. "Shakespeare's Navarre." *Huntington Library Quarterly* XLII (Summer 1979): 193-216.

Relates French historical events involving Henri of Navarre and Catherine de' Medici to the action of *Love's Labour's Lost*.

Schrickx, W. *Shakespeare's Early Contemporaries: The Background of the Harvey-Nashe Polemic and "Love's Labour's Lost."* 1956. Reprint. New York: AMS Press, 1972, 291 p.

Devotes a chapter to *Love's Labour's Lost* as part of a study of polemical tracts written by Elizabethan literary figures. Schrickx concludes that the play is "Shakespeare's deliberate and eminently successful attempt to rival the contemporary output in linguistic ingenuity."

Stevenson, David Lloyd. "Shakespeare's Comedies of Courtship: Shakespeare's First Love-Game Comedy, *Love's Labour's Lost*." In his *The Love-Game Comedy*, pp. 190-98. New York: Columbia University Press, 1946.

Examines John Lyly's influence on the courtship comedy in *Love's Labour's Lost*.

Talbert, Ernest William. "*Love's Labour's Lost* and *A Midsummer Night's Dream*." In his *Elizabethan Drama and Shakespeare's Early Plays*, pp. 235-61. Chapel Hill: The University of North Carolina Press, 1963.

Considers the "comic spirit" of *Love's Labour's Lost* to be embodied in the character of Berowne and in the dramatist's presentation of wit, which "mocks itself and yet in no way invalidates its true virtuosity."

Taylor, Rupert. *The Date of "Love's Labour's Lost."* 1932. Reprint. New York: AMS Press, 1966, 134 p.

Cites such topical allusions in *Love's Labour's Lost* as the Harvey-Nashe controversy and the political relations between England and France to argue that 1596 is the earliest possible date of composition of the play.

Thompson, Karl F. "Shakespeare's Romantic Comedies." *PMLA* 67, No. 7 (December 1952): 1079-93.

Examines the influence of the conventions of courtly love on *Love's Labour's Lost*.

Vickers, Brian. "From Clown to Character." In his *The Artistry of Shakespeare's Prose*, pp. 52-88. London: Methuen & Co., 1968.

Notes the strength of the prose spoken by certain characters in *Love's Labour's Lost* and determines that the play "is Shakespeare's first virtuoso piece in prose," but that it "ultimately disappoints."

Vyvyan, John. "*Love's Labour's Lost*." In his *Shakespeare and the Rose of Love*, pp. 23-67. London: Chatto & Windus, 1960.

Claims that "love's labour" is lost in the play because the men are insincere and lack self-knowledge. Vyvyan also discusses the possible influence of Chaucer's *The Romance of the Rose* and Dante's *Vita Nuova* on *Love's Labour's Lost*.

Westlund, Joseph. "Fancy and Achievement in *Love's Labour's Lost*." *Shakespeare Quarterly* XVIII, No. 1 (Winter 1967): 37-46.

Illustrates the conflict between the illusory world of fancy and the real world of achievement in *Love's Labour's Lost*, highlighting the importance of heroism in the play.

Wilders, John. "The Unresolved Conflicts of *Love's Labour's Lost*." *Essays in Criticism* XXVIII, No. 1 (January 1977): 20-33.

Maintains that *Love's Labour's Lost* is full of irreconcilable opposites and that instead of moving toward reconciliation, as comedy should, it moves toward greater division.

Yates, Frances A. *A Study of "Love's Labour's Lost."* Cambridge: Cambridge at the University Press, 1936, 224 p.

Details fully the historical background of the satire in *Love's Labour's Lost*, offering chapters on the relevance of John Florio, John Eliot, Gabriel Harvey and Thomas Nashe, George Chapman, Giodorno Bruno, and others to Shakespeare's play. Yates's study is generally considered to be one of the most developed and persuasive arguments for reading *Love's Labour's Lost* as a topical satire.

Measure For Measure

DATE: The first recorded performance of *Measure for Measure* appears in an entry of the Revels Accounts, which lists the presentation of a play entitled "Mesur for Mesur" by "Shaxberd" at Whitehall on St. Stephen's Night, December 26, 1604. This play was performed before King James I and his court by "his Maiesties players," the troupe with which Shakespeare was associated from early 1603 until the time of his retirement. However, internal evidence suggests that *Measure for Measure* was originally composed and performed during the summer of 1604. Often cited in support of this date is Lucio's allusion to a peace conference in Act I, Scene ii, accepted by many scholars as a reference to James I's negotiations to end the war between Spain and England's ally, the Netherlands. These deliberations occurred between May 20 and August 19, 1604, at which time a peace treaty was ratified. The reactions in the play of Lucio and his companions to the possibility of peace and an end to the war indicate to most scholars that the treaty had not yet been finalized. Further support for the earlier performance date, critics contend, can be found in the numerous parallels between the Duke and James I during the early years of his reign. Specifically, commentators consider the Duke's speech at I. i. 67-72 and Angelo's soliloquy at II. iv. 20-30 a reflection of the opinion shared by James's public that the king disliked the unrestrained adoration of the people. Certain scholars suggest that this impression of James began after an actual incident during the first royal procession through the streets of London on March 15, 1604. The incident, in which the king and queen were mobbed by a noisy crowd at the Royal Exchange, was reported in *The Times Triumphant* in language similar to that adopted by Shakespeare in the passages noted above. Taking account of this evidence, most critics place the composition of *Measure for Measure* between May and August 1604 and its first performance sometime during the summer months of that year.

TEXT: Since no quarto editions of *Measure for Measure* exist, the only authoritative text is that published in the First Folio of 1623. Most recent critics accept it as a transcription of Shakespeare's "foul papers," that is, an uncorrected manuscript written in the author's own hand. This theory is based on the presence in the text of anomalies often found in uncorrected manuscripts, such as bare stage directions, omitted and transposed words, and mislineations. Other apparent errors, such as redundant or unnecessary characters within the play and stylistic inconsistencies, have led a number of scholars to conclude that *Measure for Measure* went through several major revisions. John Dover Wilson maintained that an unknown playwright altered Shakespeare's original play for the 1604 court performance and that this abridged version was expanded for public viewing in 1606, again by an unknown playwright. Dover Wilson's theory received support from numerous critics when it first appeared, but more recent scholars tend to regard the textual flaws and examples of corruption—evidence that a dramatist other than Shakespeare altered the play—as less pervasive than previously believed. With very few exceptions, Shakespeare's sole authorship of *Measure for Measure* has been accepted throughout the play's critical history.

SOURCES: Two works have long been considered the primary sources of *Measure for Measure*: a novella in the collection of

Title page of Measure for Measure taken from the First Folio (1623). By permission of the Folger

tales entitled *Hecatommithi* (1565) by Giovanni Battista Giraldi (called Cinthio) and George Whetstone's two-part play, *The Right Excellent and Famous Historye of Promos and Cassandra* (1578), which was based on Cinthio's novella. However, Louis Albrecht, Frederick E. Budd, Robert H. Ball, and others identified a number of significant parallels between *Measure for Measure* and *Epitia* (1583), a drama adapted by Cinthio from his novella. These discoveries have led to the generally accepted theory that Shakespeare based the main aspects of his plot on Cinthio's two works and used the structure of Whetstone's drama to organize the action, characterization, and theme in *Measure for Measure*. According to this hypothesis, Shakespeare found the material for the Duke's magnanimous nature, his deputation of Angelo, Isabella's intellectual character and her refusal to accept Angelo's proposition, and the Duke's attraction to Isabella all in the *Hecatommithi*. In the *Epitia*, he found the conflict between justice and mercy and expanded it into a central theme in *Measure for Measure*; Shakespeare also based the character of Mariana on a secondary heroine Cinthio introduced in his *Epitia*. Finally, Shakespeare incorporated into *Measure for Measure* certain alterations of Cinthio's *Hecatommithi* which Whetstone utilized in *Promos and Cassandra*, such as the inclusion of a comic subplot and a change in Claudio's offense from forcible seduction to a consummated love relationship. Shakespeare also introduced two vital alterations to Cinthio's novella in his presentation of Isabella as a novice and in his emphasis on the importance of the Duke. Throughout the history of *Measure for Measure* criticism, commentators have focused on these modifications in an attempt to discover their function and purpose in Shakespeare's overall design.

CRITICAL HISTORY: Measure for Measure has fascinated and perplexed audiences and critics alike for centuries. Robert M. Smith wrote in 1950: "If there is any play, outside of *Hamlet,* that bristles with more problems than *Measure for Measure,* it is not known to Shakespearean criticism." Interpretations range from Samuel Taylor Coleridge's claim that it is "the most painful" Shakespearean play to F. R. Leavis's assertion that it is one of Shakespeare's greatest achievements; indeed, scholars have disagreed on virtually every aspect of *Measure for Measure,* including its central themes, artistic unity and style, genre, and characterization.

Critics of the eighteenth century were primarily concerned with three aspects of *Measure for Measure:* its intended morality, its characterization, and its relation to Shakespeare's sources, especially Whetstone's *Promos and Cassandra.* Charles Gildon considered the play a "just Satire" against social reformers who want to perfect the human species, thus tacitly indicting Angelo for his strict reliance on the law as a means of reforming mankind. He also praised Shakespeare for adhering to the Neoclassical unities of action and setting. Lewis Theobald, Charlotte Lennox, and Arthur Murphy all discussed the issue of Shakespeare's use of his source material, the first commending the dramatist's alterations of Cinthio's novella and Whetstone's *Promos and Cassandra,* the other two criticizing Shakespeare for failing to "mend the moral" of Cinthio's novella and, in Murphy's words, overcharging the play with "supernumerary Incidents" that contribute little to the main plot. In addition, Lennox maintained that *Measure for Measure* lacks a just distribution of rewards and punishments, an issue that was to dominate critical inquiry throughout the eighteenth and nineteenth centuries, and which also forms the basis of later commentators' assessment of the play as a study of mercy and forgiveness, rather than of justice and legal equity. Shortly after Theobald published his commentary on *Measure for Measure,* an anonymous critic in the *Gentleman's Magazine* noted "the exercise of compassion towards offenders" based on an acknowledgment of human sin and weakness, an idea that was taken up again in the beginning of the nineteenth century.

Samuel Johnson generally agreed with Lennox that Angelo's crimes deserve punishment of some sort, thereby opposing Shakespeare's concept of justice in the play. In addition, he questioned the propriety of Isabella's harsh renunciation of her brother and argued that the heroine acts out of vanity rather than selfless virtue in pardoning Angelo. This second point raised questions about Isabella's character and motives, the most important of which shed new light on Shakespeare's moral design in *Measure for Measure*; for, as such twentieth-century critics as Robert Ornstein and Hal Gelb noted, if Isabella does not act out of sincere forgiveness, then the Duke's scheming is all for naught and the play is left unresolved. On other matters, Johnson faulted Shakespeare for inattention to detail and severely criticized the Duke's speech on death in Act III, Scene i, interpreting it as a direct refutation of Christian doctrine. William Kenrick and John, Lord Chedworth took up Johnson's comments, the former attacking Johnson for what

he called "hypercriticism," and the latter agreeing with him only in the opinion that Isabella acts out of personal vanity rather than true mercy in pardoning Angelo.

Towards the end of the eighteenth century, George Steevens returned to a discussion of Shakespeare's sources, calling Whetstone's *Promos and Cassandra* "an almost complete embryo of *Measure for Measure*" and praising Shakespeare for the skill in which he used his source material. Alexander Gerard focused on Claudio's speech on the uncertainties of death, stating that this passage demonstrates, in its combination of "Christian manners" and "pagan notions," that Shakespeare did not always unite necessary judgment with his "fertile imagination." And at the close of the century, George Chalmers put forth one of the first topical interpretations of *Measure for Measure,* identifying the Duke as Shakespeare's portrait of King James I. Specifically, Chalmers examined the Duke's speech at I. i. 67-72 to argue that the dramatist was not attempting an apology for James's supposedly ungracious demeanor, but merely supplying some character traits to make his portrait convincing.

The coming of the nineteenth century saw a shift in emphasis in the critical reaction to *Measure for Measure.* Commentators seemed less concerned with the play's moral and the propriety of the characters' behavior, and more interested in the drama's central themes and the psychological foundation of the major characters. August Wilhelm Schlegel reiterated the idea proposed by the anonymous critic of the *Gentleman's Magazine* that *Measure for Measure* depicts "the triumph of mercy over strict justice," establishing the theme on which most later critics were to base their analyses—especially those twentieth-century scholars, such as G. Wilson Knight, Roy W. Battenhouse, Nevill Coghill, and Tom McBride, who viewed the play as essentially an allegory of Christian doctrine. Ulrici and Gervinus extended Schlegel's interpretation; the former defined Shakespeare's intent in *Measure for Measure* as the dramatization of the Christian concept of mercy, the idea that all of humanity exists in sin and that only through the grace of God can we hope to achieve a truly virtuous and moral life. Ulrici concluded by calling *Measure for Measure* "a perfect comedy" in the Duke's defeat of Angelo's earthly justice and in his championing of the Christian concept of mercy and forgiveness. Gervinus focused more on the play's principal characters than did either Schlegel or Ulrici, but reached a similar conclusion. He described both the Duke and Angelo as two types of ineffective rulers—the Duke because he is lax and sympathetic, Angelo because he is overly zealous in his implementation of the law. Isabella he characterized as the perfect mixture of these attributes, and for this reason he called her the effective mean between the Duke and Angelo. As did Schlegel and Ulrici, Gervinus perceived Shakespeare's controlling idea in *Measure for Measure* as the need for a corrective rather than a punitive form of justice—a system that permits mercy to rule and allows for the opportunity of moral reformation. Unlike many of the eighteenth-century commentators, Gervinus found this type of justice manifested in Isabella's act of selfless mercy in pardoning Angelo.

Other critics of the early nineteenth century continued the debate over issues first discussed by Lennox and Johnson. William Hazlitt contended that despite the evidence of genius and wisdom in *Measure for Measure,* "our sympathies are repulsed and defeated in all directions." He found nothing redeeming in any of the principal characters, with the exception of Claudio. Angelo he described as a hypocrite throughout, an assessment also reached by A. S. Pushkin, Ulrici, Charles Knight, and Walter Bagehot. Hazlitt also questioned the propriety of Isabella's "rigid chastity" at "another's expense," and he regarded the Duke as more of a manipulator than a conscientious ruler. Samuel Taylor Coleridge called *Measure for Measure* "the only painful" play in Shakespeare's canon. To him, Angelo's pardon "merely baffles the strong indignant claim of justice" and is likewise "degrading to the character of woman." On the character of Isabella, Anna Brownell Jameson followed Schlegel in praising her saintly grace, moral grandeur, self-denying generosity, and compassion. Whereas such earlier critics as Johnson and Hazlitt questioned the severity of Isabella's "moral chastity," Jameson found her behavior appropriate and commendable.

Towards the middle of the nineteenth century, Charles Knight offered one of the first interpretations of *Measure for Measure* as a work concerned primarily with political themes. For Knight, Shakespeare was attempting to demonstrate the dangers inherent in a weak government and a society overrun by a "corrupt state of manners," reflected foremost in the characters of Angelo, the Duke, Lucio, and Pompey. Despite Shakespeare's "lessons of tolerance" in the play's final scene, Knight concluded that *Measure for Measure* leaves an unsatisfactory impression, due to the Duke's intervention and the pardoning of all involved. This sense of uneasiness over the play's conclusion was also voiced by H. N. Hudson, who argued that the ending is disappointing mainly because Shakespeare never united his concepts of justice and mercy to form the harmony his resolution demands. In fact, Hudson maintained that a number of incidents in the play, such as the humiliations of Mariana and the ludicrous treatment of Lucio, suggest that Shakespeare was in reality mocking justice rather than honoring mercy. Both Knight's and Hudson's reactions to the conclusion of *Measure for Measure* foreshadowed later critics' concerns over the artistic integrity of Shakespeare's resolution—a controversy that has attracted such twentieth-century commentators as L. C. Knights, F. R. Leavis, Derek A. Traversi, Robert Ornstein, Hal Gelb, R. A. Foakes, and Tom McBride.

Hudson's study of *Measure for Measure* is also significant because it offers one of the first biographical interpretations of *Measure for Measure*. Hudson argued that Shakespeare wrote the play during a turbulent period of his life, a time when he became "fascinated by the appalling mystery of evil that haunts our fallen nature"; to this he attributes the apparent bitterness and cynicism in the drama. Later nineteenth-century critics, such as Edward Dowden, George Brandes, and Frederick S. Boas, also formulated a biographical explanation for the dark quality of the play. Dowden maintained that it reflects the dramatist's farewell to the mirth of his earlier comedies and his acceptance of a dark and tragic vision reflected in his own personal life. Brandes interpreted the play as Shakespeare's bitter attack on the "pharisaic aspect" and "simulated virtue" of Elizabethan Puritanism, specifically in response to the Puritan censorship of his art. As with numerous earlier critics, Brandes contended that *Measure for Measure* should end with the punishment of Angelo and the satisfaction of justice; that it does not, he asserted, is because Shakespeare realized that it "would have been unwise, and perhaps even dangerous, to carry to extremities this question of the punishment of moral hypocrisy." Thus, Brandes maintained that the conclusion of *Measure for Measure* serves two purposes: it establishes the comic resolution of the play while providing Shakespeare with a means of protecting himself and averting the antagonistic design of his entire work. Boas was the first critic to use the

term "problem-plays" to describe *Measure for Measure, All's Well That Ends Well, Troilus and Cressida*, and *Hamlet*—works all characterized by their divergence from Shakespeare's earlier romantic style. This change, Boas suggested, might be attributable to disturbing events in the dramatist's life, such as the execution of the Earl of Essex and the imprisonment of Shakespeare's friend and patron, Lord Southampton, who were both allegedly involved in the plot to overthrow Queen Elizabeth in 1601. Although later critics generally dispute Boas's findings, he is still recognized as the first person to establish a separate category for these plays and to relate them to Shakespeare's development as an artist.

The late nineteenth century saw the publication of two important and influential essays by Walter Pater and Denton J. Snider. Pater explored the relationship between Claudio and Isabella and what he called the "ethical interest" of *Measure for Measure*. Pater identified this as the "intricacy and subtlety of the moral world itself" and the realization of the difficulty of rightful judgment, or "judgment that shall not be unjust." He concluded that the uncertainties and ambiguities of the play develop in the reader or spectator the conception of a finer type of justice, one based on "a finer knowledge through love." The uncertainty of Shakespeare's world and the contradictory manner in which he presents his themes of justice and mercy, law and personal freedom, has received considerable attention in the twentieth century. Many critics, like Pater, have accepted and resolved the ambiguity or contradictions in *Measure for Measure* as fundamental to the logic behind Shakespeare's examination of human justice, whereas others question their necessity and regard them as a clear indication of Shakespeare's inability to resolve the issues raised in the play. Snider's essay includes a detailed interpretation of the action of *Measure for Measure*. Snider divided the play into three movements: the first he argued depicts the spiritual breech in the world of Vienna between the religious and the secular; the second illustrates the attempt to mediate the conflict in the secular world between "extreme law" and "extreme license"; the third depicts the Duke's return to power and the resolution of the preceding conflicts. Within these movements, according to Snider, Shakespeare demonstrates the ineffectiveness of both socially detached religion and absolute law in achieving social and spiritual order—a goal which can only be realized through the application of what Snider termed "true justice," or the combination of mercy and abstract justice that seeks to restore rather than remove the individual from society. Although more systematic than previous studies, Snider's essay follows the tradition established by Schlegel and Gervinus in its appraisal of Shakespeare's ideal combination of justice and mercy dramatized in the play's final scene.

Twentieth-century criticism of *Measure for Measure* is marked primarily by commentators' attempts to justify the inconsistencies in Shakespeare's plot and characterization as well as to analyze the ambiguities inherent in his theme. In an essay reminiscent of that by George Brandes, Mary Suddard interpreted the play as a study of Renaissance Puritanism. Suddard perceived the Puritanical outlook embodied in the characters of Angelo and Isabella, both of whom evidence its qualities of fortitude, loftiness, and resistance, but who also demonstrate, in starkly different ways, the inadequacies of the Puritan code when forced to confront the realities of life. Other twentieth-century critics who focused on contemporary events or issues depicted in *Measure for Measure* include Una Ellis-Fermor and Elizabeth Marie Pope. Ellis-Fermor described the play as a projection of "the lowest depths of Jacobean negation''—a reflection of the belief among Shakespeare's contemporaries that good and evil are inexorably mixed and that chaos and destruction are inherent in every civilization. Pope maintained that Shakespeare was concerned with dramatizing the issue of the divine right of kings and exposing the problematic nature of the Christian concept of justice and mercy combined. She thus explained the Duke's actions in the final scene as Shakespeare's attempt to clarify and resolve the "discrepancy between the concepts of religious mercy and secular justice" prevalent during the Elizabethan and Jacobean eras.

Other important essays of the twentieth century include those by Sir Arthur Quiller-Couch, G. Wilson Knight, Hoxie N. Fairchild, William Witherle Lawrence, H. B. Charlton, and R. W. Chambers. Quiller-Couch maintained that the unsatisfying impression *Measure for Measure* leaves is a result of Shakespeare's inconsistent characterization, particularly his portrait of Isabella. In a comment similar to that of Lennox, Johnson, and Hazlitt, Quiller-Couch declared that she does not gain our sympathy and admiration, and he asserted that her chastity exists only in the strictest sense of the word. As with many critics, Quiller-Couch found it difficult to reconcile Isabella's actions—especially her treatment of Claudio and Mariana—with Shakespeare's final portrait of the heroine as a chaste and virtuous woman. It was in an effort to resolve such discrepancies that Knight put forth his allegorical reading of *Measure for Measure*, one of the most important contributions to twentieth-century commentary on the play. Knight contended that it is possible to account for the "stiffness" and "arbitrariness" of the drama only by viewing it as an allegory structured on certain Christian concepts, particularly the doctrines of tolerance, mercy, and forgiveness stressed in the Gospels and especially in the parables of Jesus. As such, Knight identified the characters according to their allegorical relation to each other: Isabella he described not as Shakespeare's ideal image of truth and chastity, but as an individual deceived by her quest for virtue and purity; he characterized Angelo as neither a hypocrite nor a villain, but as another figure misguided by his own virtuous and noble image of himself; and the Duke Knight regarded as the central charcter of the play, the vessel of Jesus' teachings in the Gospels and, according to Shakespeare's design, a divinity figure who combines "perfected ethical philosophy" with "supreme authority." Knight's study is significant for a number of reasons; most important, it was the first to provide an allegorical interpretation of Shakespeare's design in *Measure for Measure*, and it was among the earliest to view both Angelo and Isabella as generally well-meaning though flawed personalities. Knight's influence can be seen most directly in the essays by Roy W. Battenhouse, Nevill Coghill, A. D. Nuttall, and Tom McBride, all of whom regarded *Measure for Measure* as an allegory of one or more Christian concepts—typically, an allegory of the Atonement, as in the analyses of Battenhouse, Nuttall, and McBride, but also an allegory of human testing similar to the Book of Job, as demonstrated in the study by Coghill.

Shortly after Knight published his analysis of *Measure for Measure*, Hoxie N. Fairchild and William Witherle Lawrence contributed further commentary to the on-going debate over the play's structure and characterization. Fairchild determined that Shakespeare created two different characters in the figure of Angelo: the first—whom the critic considered the more interesting and complex—based on Whetstone's *Promos* and meant to reflect the struggles of a "respectable man tempted by respectability"; the second—whom Fairchild perceived as dominant from the entrance of Mariana to the end of the play—

based on the traditional hypocrite, villain, or "smooth rascal." According to Fairchild, this second Angelo is never expected or prepared for, and for this reason he remains unconvincing and disconnected from the plot. Although Fairchild was concerned with Shakespeare's representation of the deputy in *Measure for Measure*, his remarks suggested a fault in the play's dramatic structure more problematical than the question of one character's psychological consistency. This dilemma was later addressed by E.M.W. Tillyard and J. W. Lever, both of whom determined that the entire structure of *Measure for Measure*—its tone, language, and characterization—is decidedly different in the first half of the drama than in the second. They described the first half as poetic, spontaneous, and complex and the second as abstract, prosaic, and highly conventional, attributing this dramatic breakdown to the Duke's increased involvement and his manipulation of events following the appearance of Mariana. In a related matter, Lawrence justified the inconsistencies of plot and characterization in *Measure for Measure* as an inevitable result of Shakespeare's tendency to combine traditional elements of Elizabethan drama with his own natural genius for characterization and psychological insight. In this way, Lawrence explained the fantastic quality of the Duke and the scene of the bed-trick as popular elements which Shakespeare simply borrowed for the sake of dramatic convenience. In reaction to the interpretation of *Measure for Measure* as a "dark" or cynical play, both H. B. Charlton and R. W. Chambers contended that nowhere does the drama support the assumption that Shakespeare's mood was despondent at the time of its composition. Instead, each critic focused on the character of Isabella and on the play's final pronouncement of mercy over strict justice to assert a more optimistic reading; for Charlton, *Measure for Measure* reflects Shakespeare's desire to discover the basis of human goodness, whereas Chambers regarded the play as ultimately a dramatization of Christian principles.

A number of seminal studies of *Measure for Measure* were published during the 1940s and 1950s. Foremost among these are the essays by L. C. Knights, F. R. Leavis, Derek A. Traversi, E. C. Pettet, Clifford Leech, William Empson, and Robert Ornstein. Also significant are the analyses of Muriel C. Bradbrook, Oscar James Campbell, and Murray Krieger. Bradbrook compared *Measure for Measure* to the late medieval morality plays, particularly with regard to Shakespeare's presentation of his central conflict, which she maintained follows the pattern of the debate in the moralities. In this manner, she characterized Angelo as the archetype of Law and Authority, Isabella as Truth and Mercy, and the Duke as both Humility and Heavenly Justice. The central conflict of *Measure for Measure* thus becomes, according to Bradbrook, the struggle between Mercy and Law or Human Justice, a confrontation which the Duke controls and, in the final scene, resolves in his role as the arbitrator of Heavenly Justice. Bradbrook also examined the different types of marriage contracts depicted in *Measure for Measure*, an area more fully explored by Ernest Schanzer in the 1960s. The three essays by Knights, Leavis, and Traversi brought to light one of the central issues of *Measure for Measure* criticism in the twentieth century, namely, the question of whether Shakespeare resolved the ambiguity inherent in his presentation of justice and mercy, law and personal freedom. Knights focused on the figure of Claudio, specifically his speech in Act I, Scene ii, to argue that the play depicts a genuine ambiguity in that character's response to his predicament, since he condemns his act and recognizes the need for lawful restraint while simultaneously acknowledging the demands of human passion; in addition, Claudio questions the role of the state to punish such transgressions. For Knights, this contradiction reflects the larger paradox of Shakespeare's theme: that human law and justice must be both abstract and personal—the first in order to maintain social harmony, the second in order that compassion or mercy may temper retribution. Knights concluded that in *Measure for Measure* Shakespeare failed to resolve this contradiction, or, at least, did not subject it to the same "process of clarification" with which he treated such later works as *King Lear* and *Antony and Cleopatra*. In response to this assessment, Leavis maintained that Knights's difficulty with Claudio's reaction is unwarranted since it is very probable, indeed preferable, that the character should experience both guilt and indignation—the first as a response to his society's moral code, the second as a necessary reaction to the severity of his sentence. On the broader level of thematics, Leavis asserted that we need not agree with Knights's conclusion that Shakespeare confuses his audience by conveying, in a play specifically about Christian mercy and forgiveness, that law, order, and abstract justice are necessary for society's well-being. Although Knights regarded this as a contradiction of critical importance, Leavis concluded that it is another example of Shakespeare's unique ability to dramatize "complexity of attitude" apart from "contradiction, conflict and uncertainty." In another reaction to this controversy, Traversi argued that Shakespeare suggested rather than developed the resolution to the conflict between law and personal freedom presented in *Measure for Measure*. He identified this underlying supposition as the concept of death introduced by the Duke in his speech to Claudio in Act III, Scene i. According to Traversi, "the universal relevance of death" significantly redefines the question of liberty and moral law in the play and provides the characters—those, that is, who have accepted "the implications of death"—with a freely acknowledged reason for choosing restraint and social responsibility over the demands of human passion. However, Traversi noted, the Duke is the only character to experience this truth; by the end of the drama, he concluded, Shakespeare seemed willing to abandon this concept for a more conventional resolution.

A second important issue in twentieth-century commentary on *Measure for Measure* is the debate over the play's genre. Critics as early as Frederick S. Boas have attempted to determine the exact form of the play, usually designating it along with *All's Well That Ends Well*, *Troilus and Cressida*, and sometimes *Hamlet* as a "problem play." Oscar James Campbell was the first critic since Charles Gildon to describe *Measure for Measure* as a satire, or more specifically a satiric comedy written in the manner of Ben Jonson and John Marston. Campbell maintained that the characterization, structure, and plot of the drama all tend towards the satiric mode. He further contended that the difficulty of reading the play as primarily a satiric comedy occurs because Shakespeare expanded Isabella's role beyond her satiric function and transformed the play's denouement into the more conventional ending characteristic of romantic comedy. In a similar assessment, Murray Krieger attributed the confusion apparent in *Measure for Measure* not to a contradiction of moral thematics, but to Shakespeare's attempt to combine two different types of comedic form: the satiric form of Jonson and Marston with the romantic form of Thomas Greene. Other commentators also contributed to this topic. Elmer Edgar Stoll focused on the ironic elements in *Measure for Measure*, which he suggested Shakespeare incorporated to lessen the tragic effects of his story and to heighten the comic. E. C. Pettet argued that the "unresolved conflict" apparent in each of Shakespeare's problem plays is the result of the dramatist's attempt to accomodate his changing vision

of life and art—a vision that was made manifest in the major tragedies—to the romantic form of his early comedies. Pettet described Angelo as the most obvious example of this dichotomy between form and vision, claiming—as did Fairchild, Tillyard, and Lever—that the character gradually looses his complex or dramatic dimension in order to satisfy "the necessities of a romantic story." Hal Gelb regarded *Measure for Measure* as essentially comic, its structure and vision presented by Shakespeare to establish expectations of a comic resolution; but within this structure Gelb perceived tragic possibilities of evil, suffering, and despair, which he contended never assert themselves over the comic vision but which nonetheless hinder our appreciation of Shakespeare's resolution.

Critics like Clifford Leech, William Empson, and Robert Ornstein took a more atypical approach to *Measure for Measure*. Leech, focusing on the numerous contradictions apparent in Shakespeare's play, called for an eclectic interpretation that combines a variety of methodologies, including the historical, the allegorical or Christian, and the generic. As such, he criticized Pope, Lawrence, Knight, Battenhouse, and Campbell for limiting their perceptions to one set of ideas apparent in the play, while ignoring the complex interconnection of various meanings. Empson examined Shakespeare's use of the word "sense" in *Measure for Measure*, stating that upon Lucio's first ambiguous use of the term in Act I, Scene iv it comes to possess various meanings within the context of each character's speech—including "sensuality," "sensibility," and "sensibleness"—all of which reflect on the broader themes of the play. Ornstein asserted that it is the critics "who ponder the moral dilemmas" in *Measure for Measure*, not the characters themselves, whom he regarded as typically "insignificant" and unheroic individuals dealing with questions of law, judgment, and social behavior in self-centered, pedestrian ways. Importantly, he maintained that none of the characters, except for Claudio, ever approaches self-knowledge and human compassion. Ornstein concluded that the reason why critics find *Measure for Measure* unsatisfactory is because it "disappoints our longing for a more perfect justice than the world affords," and because, on the artistic level, it fails to resolve the questions it raises, such as the conflict between "the high ethic of the Gospel and the necessity of punitive law." Ornstein's final assessment echoes a dissatisfaction with the play's resolution voiced by many other critics. Earlier, Knights and Traversi faulted Shakespeare for failing to resolve the contradiction between abstract justice and Christian mercy or between law and personal freedom; later, such critics as Gelb, R. A. Foakes, and Tom McBride all voiced a similar disappointment. Gelb, as with Ornstein, contended that none of the characters undergoes a personal transformation, and he concluded that although the Duke's final act assures that the play's comic vision remains intact, we end by sensing that this vision "does not fit the world on which it has been imposed." Foakes determined that *Measure*'s resolution remains confusing or uncomfortable primarily because Shakespeare never reconciles the "neatness" of the conclusion with "what remains unexplained and unresolved below the surface." McBride concluded, in an allegorical interpretation of *Measure for Measure* reminiscent of that by Knight, that the Duke as a Christ-figure only technically satisfies the conflicting demands of justice and mercy, whereas spiritually he fails to redeem the souls of Isabella, Angelo, and Claudio.

In the past twenty-five years, critics have continued the controversy over the structure and theme of *Measure for Measure*. Like Knights, Leavis, and Traversi, many have attempted to determine whether Shakespeare resolved the contradictions his play presents, while others have examined the formal elements the dramatist chose to employ. In addition, a host of commentators have discussed the symbolic function of the characters and the significance of the marriages that conclude the play. Terence Eagleton maintained that Shakespeare, through the figure of the Duke, called for a more "personally authentic" system of law, based on the "reciprocity of relationships in society" and united with the qualities of love and knowledge, which are emphasized in the play by the act of marriage and the concept of multiple or changeable identities. Thus, Eagleton viewed the resolution of marriage which concludes the drama as not simply a stock element of romantic comedy, but, more importantly, as emblematic of Shakespeare's prescription for the shortcomings of human justice. Foakes argued that *Measure for Measure* depicts the limitations of both personal license and extreme discipline—what he termed as the absolute quest for either life or death—since each response in the extreme is incomplete. Instead, he concluded that what Shakespeare sought to express is the need for "balance and harmony" symbolized by the act of marriage. James Black focused on Mariana's willingness to substitute herself for Isabella in the bed-trick scene as the most important event in *Measure for Measure*. He regarded her decision as an act of charity which immediately reverses the play's regressive movement—symbolized by Isabella's spiritual isolation and Angelo's withdrawal into the security of the law—and prepares for the "unmasking" of the other characters in the final act. Black also regarded the marriages as a gesture which both "qualifies the 'too much liberty'" of the low characters and ensures that none of the participants will retreat from the world of human experience into a self-enclosed confinement. Lawrence W. Hyman perceived an ethical or philosophical pattern in *Measure for Measure* that resolves the contradictions in the characters' actions and unites the discrepancies between the two parts of the play noted by such earlier critics as Tillyard, Pettet, Lever, and Gelb. This pattern, Hyman noted, is based on the idea that virtue and chastity negate the possibility of life, while life itself is of value only when sin and shame are accepted as necessary. Ultimately, Hyman considered Angelo's pardon not as the victory of love or mercy over strict justice, but as the result of Mariana's and Isabella's acceptance of sin and corruption as part of life. In fact, Hyman maintained that all of the marriages that conclude *Measure for Measure* reflect a realignment of the characters towards the acceptance of life rather than death, and with it the recognition of the realities of sin and human lust. David Sundelson pointed out numerous passages in *Measure for Measure* that demonstrate both Angelo's and the Duke's insecurity over their own power and sexuality, which further exhibit their desire to limit women within a safe, nonthreatening role. Sundelson suggested that the marriages which conclude the play express not the hoped-for ideal relationship of man and woman, but the masculine need to suppress woman's threatening potential within a socially defined and restrictive role.

Twentieth-century commentary has demonstrated critics' growing interest in determining the structural and thematic integrity of *Measure for Measure*. Whereas scholars of previous centuries contented themselves with issues of morality, propriety, and psychological consistency, and because of this were often frustrated by the text, modern analysts have generally abandoned these questions in search of more complex and meaningful assessments. What has emerged is a variety of interpretations and the sense, noted by Clifford Leech and others, that the play defies any single approach. The debate over the drama's generic classification, the critical struggle over the contradiction or ambiguity in Shakespeare's theme of justice tempered by mercy, the contention over the exact role of Christian doctrine in the play, and the success of Shakespeare's resolution all continue to dominate current evaluations of *Measure for Measure*. If Shakespeare's work ultimately disappoints the reader or spectator, as numerous critics allege it does, it still expresses the uncertainty of humanity's moral nature— what H. B. Charlton described as the "effective goodness of all the characters involved in the story." Even Robert Ornstein, who maintained that the play fails to resolve its most fundamental conflict, perceived in *Measure for Measure* "an exalted ethic" which salvages Shakespeare's moral design. For many critics, it is this aspect which makes *Measure for Measure* one of the most dynamic and provocative plays in Shakespeare's canon.

CHARLES GILDON   (essay date 1710)

[*Gildon was the first critic to write an extended commentary on Shakespeare's plays. Like many other Neoclassicists, Gildon regarded Shakespeare as an imaginative playwright who nevertheless lacked knowledge of the dramatic "rules" necessary for correct writing. However, in the excerpt below, Gildon notes that Shakespeare followed the "unities of action and place" in* Measure for Measure. *He also finds a moral in the play that presents a "just satire" against the pretensions of social reformers. For other Neoclassical discussions of the play's morality, see the excerpts from* The Gentleman's Magazine *(1748) and Charlotte Lennox (1753).*]

There are some little under Characters in [*Measure for Measure*], which are produced naturally enough by the Severity of the new Law, as that of the Bawd and the Pimp; as well as of *Lucio,* which Character is admirably mantain'd, as *Shakespear* does every where his Comic Characters, whatever he does his *Tragic.*

The Unities of Action and Place are pretty well observed in this Play, especially as they are in the Modern Acceptation. The Design of the Play carries an excellent Moral, and a just Satire against our present Reformers; who wou'd alter their Course of Nature and bring us to a Perfection, Mankind never knew since the World was half Peopled. (pp. 292-93)

Allowing for some *Peccadillos* the last Act is wonderful, and moving to such a Degree, that he must have very little Sense of Things, and Nature, who finds himself Calm in the reading it.

The Main Story or Fable of the Play is truly *Tragical* for it is Adapted to move Terror, and Compassion, and the Action is one. Its having a Fortunate *Catastrophe,* is nothing to the purpose for that is in many of the Greek Tragedies; tho' *Aristotle* indeed makes the Unfortunate Ending the most beautiful and perfect. (p. 293)

> *Charles Gildon, "Remarks on the Plays of Shakespeare," in* The Works of Mr. William Shakespear, *Vol. 7 by William Shakespeare, 1710. Reprint by AMS Press, Inc., 1967, pp. 257-444.*

LEWIS THEOBALD   (essay date 1733)

[*Theobald, a dramatist and classical scholar, was also one of the most important editors of Shakespeare's plays in the first half of the eighteenth century. Although his reputation as a Shakespearean editor declined after his death and opinion of the value of his work remains divided today, he nonetheless contributed significant emendations which have been adopted by modern editors. However, his adaptations of Shakespeare's plays, revised to adhere to Neoclassical dramatic rules, have been less well received. In his editorial comments on* Measure for Measure, *Theobald praises Shakespeare's use of his sources as well as his creation of the character of Mariana. For further remarks concerning Shakespeare's handling of his sources, see the excerpts by Charlotte Lennox (1753), George Steevens (1773), Hoxie N. Fairchild (1931), and William Witherle Lawrence (1931).*]

> *Prov.* Pardon me, noble lord.
> I thought, it was a fault, but knew it not;
> Yet did repent me, after more advice:
> For testimony whereof, one in th' prison,
> That should by private Order else have dy'd,
> I have reserv'd alive.
> *Duke.* What's he?
> *Prov.* His name is *Barnardine.*
> *Duke.* I would, thou hadst done so by *Claudio:*
> Go, fetch him hither; let me look upon him.
> [V. i. 462-69]
> (p. 396)

The introducing *Barnardine* here, is, seemingly a matter of no Consequence; as he is no Person concern'd in the Action of the Play, nor directly aiding to the *Dénoüement,* as the *French* call it, of the Plot: but, to our Poet's Praise, let me observe, that it is not done without double Art; it gives a Handle for the Discovery of *Claudio* being alive, and so heightens the Surprize; and, at the same time, by the Pardon of *Barnardine,* gives a fine Opportunity of making the *Duke's* Character more amiable, both for Mercy, and Virtue. (pp. 396-97)

I cannot help taking notice, with how much judgment *Shakespeare* has given Turns to this Story, from what he found it in *Cinthio Giraldi's* Novel. In the first place, the Brother, whom our Poet calls *Claudio,* is there actually executed: And the ungrateful *Governor* sends his Head in a Bravado, to the Sister; after he had debauch'd her, on Promise of Marriage. A Circumstance of too much Horror, and Villany, for the Stage. And in the next place, this Sister afterwards is, to solder up her Disgrace, marry'd to the Governor, and begs his Life of the Emperor, tho' he had so unjustly been the Death of her Brother. Both which Absurdities our Poet has avoided by the Episode of *Mariana,* a Creature purely of his own Invention. The *Duke's* remaining *incognito* at home, to supervise the Conduct of his *Deputy,* is also entirely our Author's Fiction.—This Story was attempted for the Scene by one *George Whetstone* (before our Author was fourteen Years old,) in Two *Comical Discourses* (as they are call'd) containing, the right, excellent and famous History of *Promos* and *Cassandra:* and printed in the old Black Letter, in 1578. . . . I could prove to Demonstration, that *Shakespeare* had perus'd these Pieces; but whoever has seen, and knows what execrable mean Stuff they are; I am sure, will acquit him from all Suspicion of Plagiarism. (pp. 398-99)

> *Lewis Theobald, in notes to "Measure for Measure," in* The Works of Shakespeare, Vol. I *by William Shakespeare, edited by Lewis Theobald, 1733. Reprint by AMS Press, 1968, pp. 309-99.*

THE GENTLEMAN'S MAGAZINE   (essay date 1748)

[*The following excerpt comes from "Remarks on* The Tragedy of the Orphan," *an article that appeared in the November and December, 1748 issues of* The Gentleman's Magazine. *The anonymous critic regards Shakespeare as unequalled in the presentation of "moral precepts" and contends that* Measure for Measure *is a "powerful" example of this ability. Further, the critic identifies* Measure's *moral and discusses its negative representation in Angelo. For additional Neoclassical discussion of Shakespeare's handling of the moral of* Measure for Measure, *see the excerpts by Charles Gildon (1710) and Charlotte Lennox (1753).*]

That a tendency to promote the cause of Virtue is essential to Epic and Dramatic poetry will hardly be contested; and accordingly we find the great poets not content with barely holding up *the mirror to Nature,* and exercising the virtuous affections of mankind (which yet, it must be confess'd, are valuable ends of these species of writing) but that they have constantly endeavoured to inculcate some *prudential maxim,* or *moral precept.* In this particular, our admirable *Shakespeare* seems to stand without an equal; in him we find the most instructive lessons inforced with all the art imaginable, and that not by a tedious and intricate deduction of consequences but barely by the necessary result of a well-wrought Fable. . . . *Measure for Measure* contains an argument for the exercise of compassion towards offenders, the most powerful that can be thought of, *The frailty of human nature:* and this argument is exemplified in the character of the merciless *Angelo* in such a manner that we are at once convinced of its force, and excited to a just abhorrence of that cruelly inflexible disposition in magistrates, which is often mistaken for justice. . . . (pp. 328-29)

> *N.S., in an extract from "Remarks on the Tragedy of the 'Orphan'," in* Shakespeare, the Critical Heritage: 1733-1752, Vol. 3, *edited by Brian Vickers, Routledge & Kegan Paul, 1975, pp. 328-33.**

[CHARLOTTE LENNOX]   (essay date 1753)

[*Lennox was an American-born novelist and Shakespearean scholar who compiled a three-volume edition of translated texts of the sources used by Shakespeare in twenty-two of his plays, including some analyses of the ways in which he used these sources. In the excerpt below, she presents a paradigmatic Neoclassical attack against Shakespeare's handling of his sources for* Measure for Measure. *According to Lennox, Shakespeare's alterations weaken the story and fail to "mend the moral" of Cinthio's original tale; she claims that Shakespeare displays "vice not only pardoned, but left in tranquility." She argues that Shakespeare's invented incidents are unnecessary and improbable, and that the comic parts—which contain "none of the requisites of comedy"—are episodes unrelated to the main story. To further illustrate her hypothesis, Lennox condemns Shakespeare's characterization in the play: she states that the Duke is absurd and that Shakespeare's depiction of Angelo is inconsistent. To Lennox, Angelo is a villain rather than a "sanctified hypocrite." She accepts Isabella as an improvement on Cinthio's Epitia, but describes her as a "mere vixen in her virtue," a character who displays "the manners of an affected prude." Lennox concludes that the play's title is misleading, because* Measure for Measure *is "absolutely defective in a due distribution of rewards and punishments." For additional commentary on Shakespeare's handling of his sources, see the excerpts by Lewis Theobald (1733), George Steevens (1773), Hoxie N. Fairchild (1931), and William Witherle Lawrence (1931).*]

There are a greater Diversity of Characters, and more Intrigues in the Fable of [*Measure for Measure*], than the Novel of *Cinthio;* yet I think, whereever *Shakespear* has invented, he is greatly below the Novelist; since the Incidents he has added, are neither necessary nor probable.

The Story of *Juriste* and *Epitia,* of itself, afforded a very affecting Fable for a Play; it is only faulty in the Catastrophe. The Reader, who cannot but be extremely enraged at the Deceit and Cruelty of *Juriste,* and very desirous of his meeting with a Punishment due to his Crime, is greatly disappointed, to find him in the End, not only pardoned, but made happy in the Possession of the beautiful *Epitia.*

Shakespear, though he has altered and added a good deal, yet has not mended the Moral; for he also shews Vice not only pardoned, but left in Tranquility. (pp. 24-5)

Since the Fable in *Cinthio* is so much better contrived than that of *Measure for Measure,* on which it is founded, the Poet sure cannot be defended, for having altered it so much for the worse; and it would be but a poor Excuse, for his want of Judgment, to say, that had he followed the Novelist closer, his Play would have been a Tragedy, and to make a Comedy, he was under a Necessity of winding up the Catastrophe as he has done.

The comic Part of *Measure for Measure* is all Episode, and has no Dependance on the principal Subject, which even as *Shakespear* has managed it, has none of the Requisites of Comedy, great and flagrant Crimes, such as those of *Angelo,* in *Measure for Measure,* are properly the Subject of Tragedy, the Design of which is to shew the fatal Consequences of those Crimes, and the Punishment that never fails to attend them. The light Follies of a *Lucio,* may be exposed, ridiculed and corrected in Comedy.

That *Shakespear* made a wrong Choice of his Subject, since he was resolved to torture it into a Comedy, appears by the low Contrivance, absurd Intrigue, and improbable Incidents, he was obliged to introduce, in order to bring about three or four Weddings, instead of one good Beheading, which was the Consequence naturally expected. (pp. 27-8)

[Why] does not the Poet acquaint us with this extraordinary Accident [the Duke's knowledge of the Story of Mariana], which happens so conveniently for his Purpose? If he is accountable to our Eyes for what he makes us see, is he not also accountable to our Judgment for what he would have us believe? But, in short, without all this Jumble of Inconsistencies, the Comedy would have been a downright Tragedy; for *Claudio*'s Head must have been cut off, if *Isabella* had not consented to redeem him; and the Duke would have wanted a Wife, if such a convenient Person as *Mariana* had not been introduced to supply her Place, and save her Honour.

As the Character of the Duke is absurd and ridiculous, that of *Angelo* is inconsistent to the last Degree; his Baseness to *Mariana,* his wicked Attempts on the Chastity of *Isabella,* his villainous Breach of Promise, and Cruelty to *Claudio,* prove him to be a very bad Man, long practised in Wickedness; yet when he finds himself struck with the Beauty of *Isabella,* he starts at the Temptation; reasons on his Frailty; asks Assistance from Heaven to overcome it; resolves against it, and seems carried away by the Violence of his Passion, to commit what his better Judgment abhors.

Are these the Manners of a sanctified Hypocrite, such as *Angelo* is represented to be? Are they not rather those of a good Man, overcome by a powerful Temptation? That *Angelo* was not a good Man, appears by his base Treatment of *Mariana;* for certainly nothing can be viler than to break his Contract with

a Woman of Merit, because she had accidentally become poor; and, to excuse his own Conduct, load the unfortunate Innocent with base Aspersions, and add Infamy to her other Miseries: Yet this is the Man, who, when attacked by a Temptation, kneels, prays, expostulates with himself, and, while he scarce yields in Thought to do wrong, his Mind feels all the Remorse which attends actual Guilt.

It must be confessed indeed, that *Angelo* is a very extraordinary Hypocrite, and thinks in a Manner quite contrary from all others of his Order; for they, as it is natural, are more concerned for the Consequences of their Crimes, than the Crimes themselves, whereas he is only troubled about the Crime, and wholly regardless of the Consequences.

The Character of *Isabella* in the Play seems to be an Improvement upon that of *Epitia* in the Novel; for *Isabella* absolutely refuses, and persists in her Refusal, to give up her Honour to save her Brother's Life; whereas *Epitia,* overcome by her own Tenderness of Nature, and the affecting Prayers of the unhappy Youth, yields to what her Soul abhors, to redeem him from a shameful Death. It is certain however, that *Isabella* is a mere Vixen in her Virtue; how she rates her wretched Brother, who gently urges her to save him!

> *Isabella.* Oh, you Beast!
> Oh faithless Coward! Oh dishonest Wretch!
> Wilt thou be made a Man out of my Vice?
> Is't not a Kind of Incest, to take Life
> From thine own Sister's Shame? . . .
> Thy Sin's not accidental, but a Trade;
> Mercy to thee wou'd prove itself a Bawd:
> 'Tis best that thou dy'st quickly.
>   [III. i. 135-39, 148-50]

Is this the Language of a modest tender Maid; one who had devoted herself to a religious Life, and was remarkable for an exalted Understanding, and unaffected Piety in the earliest Bloom of Life?

From her Character, her Profession, and Degree of Relation to the unhappy Youth, one might have expected mild Expostulations, wise Reasonings, and gentle Rebukes. . . . [But] that Torrent of abusive Language, those coarse and unwomanly Reflexions on the Virtue of her Mother, her exulting Cruelty to the dying Youth, are the Manners of an affected Prude, outragious in her seeming Virtue; not of a pious, innocent and tender Maid.

I cannot see the Use of all that juggling and Ambiguity at the winding up of the Catastrophe; *Isabella* comes and demands Justice of the Duke for the Wrongs she had received from his Deputy, declaring she had sacrificed her Innocence to save her Brother's Life, whom *Angelo* had, notwithstanding his Promise to the contrary, caused to be executed.

Upon the Duke's telling her, that he believed her Accusation to be false, she goes away in Discontent, without saying a Word more: Is this natural? Is it probable, that *Isabella* would thus publicly bring a false Imputation on her Honour, and, though innocent and unstained, suffer the World to believe her violated?—She knows not that the honest Friar who advised her to this extraordinary Action, is the Duke to whom she is speaking; she knows not how the Matter will be cleared up.

She who rather chose to let her Brother die by the Hands of an Executioner, than sacrifice her Virtue to save his Life, takes undeserved Shame to herself in public, without procuring the Revenge she seeks after.

Mariana's evasive Deposition; Friar *Peter*'s enigmatical Accusation of *Isabella;* the Duke's winding Behaviour; what does it all serve for? but to perplex and embroil plain Facts, and make up a Riddle without a Solution. (pp. 30-5)

The Play sets out with the Moral in the Title, *Measure for Measure;* but how is this made out? the Duke speaking of *Angelo* to *Isabella,* says, . . .

> An *Angelo* for *Claudio;* Death for Death.
> Haste still pays Haste, and Leisure answers Leisure;
> Like doth quit Like, and *Measure* still for *Measure.*
>
> [V. i. 409-11]

Thus it should have been, according to the Duke's own Judgment to have made it *Measure for Measure;* but when *Angelo* was pardoned, and restored to Favour, how then was it *Measure for Measure?*

The Case is not altered, because *Claudio* was not put to death, and *Isabella* not violated; it was not through *Angelo*'s Repentance, that both these Things did not happen; a Woman he was engaged to, supplied the Place of *Isabella,* and the Head of another Man, was presented to him instead of *Claudio*'s. *Angelo* therefore was intentionally guilty of perverting Justice, debauching a Virgin, and breaking his Promise, in putting her Brother to death, whose Life she had bought by that Sacrifice. *Isabella* when pleading for him, says,

> My Brother had but Justice,
> In that he did the Thing for which he dy'd;
> For *Angelo,* his Act did not o'ertake his bad Intent,
> And must be buried but as an Intent,
> That perish'd by the Way; Thoughts are no Subjects:
> Intents, but meerly Thoughts.
>
> [V. i. 448-54]

This, is strange Reasoning of *Isabella;* her Brother deserved Death, she says, because *he did the Thing for which he died;* he intended to do it, and his doing it was the Consequence of his Intention.

Angelo likewise intended to debauch her, and murder her Brother, and he did both in Imagination; that it was only Imagination, was not his Fault, for so he would have had it, and so he thought it was. It is the Intention which constitutes Guilt, and *Angelo* was guilty in Intention, and for what he knew, in fact, therefore, as far as lay in his Power, he was as guilty as *Claudio.*

This Play therefore being absolutely defective in a due Distribution of Rewards and Punishments; *Measure for Measure* ought not to be the Title, since Justice is not the Virtue it inculcates. . . . (pp. 35-7)

[*Charlotte Lennox*] *"Observations on the Use Shakespear Has Made of the Foregoing Novel in His Comedy Called 'Measure for Measure',"* in her Shakespear Illustrated; or, The Novels and Histories, on Which the Plays of Shakespear Are Founded, Vol. I, *1753. Reprint by AMS Press Inc., 1973, pp. 21-37.*

[ARTHUR MURPHY]　(essay date 1757)

[*Like many of his contemporaries, Murphy regarded Shakespeare as a natural genius whose transgressions of the Neoclassical rules for correct drama are compensated for by the beauty of his work. In the excerpt below, which first appeared in a review of* Measure for Measure *in the March 1, 1757 issue of the* London Chronicle,

Murphy commends the "fine Variety of Passions" displayed in Isabella, and he considers the Duke's role both "important and interesting." For opposing interpretations of these characters, see the excerpts by Charlotte Lennox (1753), William Hazlitt (1817), and Arthur Quiller-Couch (1922).]

In the Conduct of the Fable [in *Measure for Measure*] the Poet has made some Mistake, and he has unnecessarily overcharged it with supernumerary Incidents which do not much conduce to the main Business, and he has crouded it with episodical Characters. . . . In Isabella's Character there is a fine Variety of Passions, and a beautiful Struggle between her Virtue and her tender Sentiments for her Brother. The Duke is likewise a very important and interesting Character; and, notwithstanding some farcical Scenes, the Business of the Piece irresistably commands Attention. (p. 284)

[*Arthur Murphy*], *in an extract from a review of "Measure for Measure," in* Shakespeare, the Critical Heritage: 1753-1765, Vol. 4, *edited by Brian Vickers, Routledge & Kegan Paul, 1976, pp. 284-85.*

SAMUEL JOHNSON　(essay date 1765)

[*Johnson has long held an important place in the history of Shakespearean criticism. He is considered the foremost representative of moderate English Neoclassicism and is credited by some literary historians with freeing Shakespeare from the strictures of the three unities valued by strict Neoclassicists: that dramas should have a single setting, take place in less than twenty-four hours, and have a causally connected plot. More recent scholars portray him as a critic who was able to synthesize existing critical theory rather than as an innovative theoretician. Johnson was a master of Augustan prose style and a personality who dominated the literary world of his epoch. The following excerpt is taken from his editorial notes on* Measure for Measure, *originally published in the 1765 edition of his* The Plays of William Shakespeare. *The "Doctor Warburton" to whom Johnson refers is William Warburton, an eighteenth-century Shakespearean editor whose textual emendations and explanations often received adverse criticism from contemporary scholars. Johnson is the first critic to discuss the import of the Duke's "death is only sleep" speech in III.i. 17ff., claiming that this philosophy "in the Friar is impious, in the reasoner is foolish, and in the poet trite and vulgar." With typical Neoclassical attention to form and character, Johnson also comments on Lucio's dialogues with the Duke and specific aspects of the denouement. He argues that Lucio's use of the word "coward" to describe the Duke in V.i. 335 is an example of Shakespeare's inattention to detail. And he contends that Angelo's crimes deserve punishment—an idea that is emphatically reiterated by Samuel Taylor Coleridge (1818)—while Isabella's intercession for the deputy is motivated by her own vanity. Johnson's remarks are specifically debated by William Kenrick (1765) and John, Lord Chedworth (1805). In his conclusion, Johnson states that although the comic parts of* Measure for Measure *are "natural and pleasing," the serious scenes are more labored than elegant, and the plot is more intricate than artful. For additional commentary on Shakespeare's design in* Measure for Measure, *see the excerpts by William Hazlitt (1817), Oscar James Campbell (1943), E.M.W. Tillyard (1949), Murray Krieger (1951), and Nevill Coghill (1955).*]

There is perhaps not one of Shakespeare's plays more darkened than this by the peculiarities of its authour, and the unskilfulness of its editors, by distortions of phrase, or negligence of transcription. . . . (p. 176)

> DUKE. Reason thus with life;
> If I do lose thee, I do lose a thing,
> That none but fools would keep. . . .
>
> [II. i. 6-8]

The meaning seems plainly this, that "none but fools would *wish* to keep life"; or, "none but fools would keep" it, if choice were allowed. A sense, which, whether true or not, is certainly innocent. . . . (pp. 191-92)

> DUKE: Thy best of rest is sleep,
> And that thou oft provok'st; yet grosly fear'st
> Thy death, which is no more. . . .
>   [II. i. 17-19]

Here Dr. Warburton might have found a sentiment worthy of his animadversion. I cannot without indignation find Shakespeare saying, that "death is only sleep," lengthening out his exhortation by a sentence which in the Friar is impious, in the reasoner is foolish, and in the poet trite and vulgar. . . . (pp. 192-93)

> CLAUDIO. If it were damnable, he being so wise,
> Why would he for the momentary trick
> Be perdurably fin'd?
>   [III. i. 112-14]

Shakespeare shows his knowledge of human nature in the conduct of Claudio. When Isabella first tells him of Angelo's proposal he answers with honest indignation, agreeably to his settled principles, "thou shalt not do't." But the love of life being permitted to operate, soon furnishes him with sophistical arguments, he believes it cannot be very dangerous to the soul, since Angelo, who is so wise, will venture it. (p. 196)

> ISABELLA. Is't not a kind of incest, to take life
> From thine own sister's shame?
>   [III. i. 138-39]

In Isabella's declamation there is something harsh, and something forced and far-fetched. But her indignation cannot be thought violent when we consider her not only as a virgin but as a nun. (p. 197)

> CLOWN.   and are now in for the Lord's sake. . . .
>   [IV. iii. 19]

I rather think this expression intended to ridicule the puritans, whose turbulence and indecency often brought them to prison, and who considered themselves as suffering for religion.

It is not unlikely that men imprisoned for other crimes, might represent themselves to casual enquirers, as suffering for puritanism, and that this might be the common cant of the prisons. In Donne's time every prisoner was brought to jail by suretiship. (p. 205)

> LUCIO.   and was the duke a flesh-monger, a fool,
> and a coward, as you then reported him to be?
>   [V. i. 333-35]

So again afterwards,

> You, Sirrah, that know me for a fool, a *coward*,
> One of all luxury—
>   [V. i. 500-01]

But Lucio had not, in the former conversation, mentioned "cowardice" among the faults of the Duke.—Such failures of memory are incident to writers more diligent than this poet. (p. 212)

The Duke has justly observed that Isabel is "importuned against all sense" [V. i. 433] to solicit for Angelo, yet here "against all sense" she solicits for him. Her argument is extraordinary.

> A due sincerity govern'd his deeds,
> 'Till he did look on me; since it is so,
> Let him not die.
>   [V. i. 446-48]

That Angelo had committed all the crimes charged against him, as far as he could commit them, is evident. The only "intent" which "his act did not overtake" [V. i. 451], was the defilement of Isabel. Of this Angelo was only intentionally guilty.

Angelo's crimes were such, as must sufficiently justify punishment, whether its end be to secure the innocent from wrong, or to deter guilt by example; and I believe every reader feels some indignation when he finds him spared. From what extenuation of his crime can Isabel, who yet supposes her brother dead, form any plea in his favour. "Since he was good 'till he looked on me, let him not die" [V. i. 445-48]. I am afraid our varlet poet intended to inculcate, that women think ill of nothing that raises the credit of their beauty, and are ready, however virtuous, to pardon any act which they think incited by their own charms. (p. 213)

> DUKE. By this, lord Angelo perceives he's safe
>   [V. i. 494]

It is somewhat strange, that Isabel is not made to express either gratitude, wonder or joy at the sight of her brother. . . .

> DUKE. And yet here's one in place I cannot pardon.
>   [V. i. 499]

After the pardon of two murderers Lucio might be treated by the good Duke with less harshness; but perhaps the poet intended to show, what is too often seen "that men easily forgive wrongs which are not committed against themselves." (p. 214)

Of this play the light or comick part is very natural and pleasing, but the grave scenes, if a few passages be excepted, have more labour than elegance. The plot is rather intricate than artful. The time of the action is indefinite; some time, we know not how much, must have elapsed between the recess of the Duke and the imprisonment of Claudio; for he must have learned the story of Mariana in his disguise, or he delegated his power to a man already known to be corrupted. The unities of action and place are sufficiently preserved. (p. 216)

> *Samuel Johnson, "Notes on Shakespeare's Plays: 'Measure for Measure'," in his* The Yale Edition of the Works of Samuel Johnson: Johnson on Shakespeare, Vol. VII, *edited by Arthur Sherbo, Yale University Press, 1968, pp. 174-216.*

WILLIAM KENRICK   (essay date 1765)

[An English journalist, translator, essayist, and playwright, Kenrick was notorious for his abusive and acrimonious attacks on Samuel Johnson, Oliver Goldsmith, David Garrick, and others. After the publication of his A Review of Doctor Johnson's New Edition of Shakespeare: In which the Ignorance, or Inattention, of that Editor Is Exposed, and the Poet Defended from the Persecution of his Commentators *in 1765, Kenrick lost his position as a contributor to the* Monthly Review. *He later wrote articles for the* Gentleman's Journal *and in 1775 established his own periodical,* London Review of English and Foreign Literature. *In the excerpt below, which is taken from his review of Johnson, Kenrick quarrels with Johnson's interpretation of certain passages in* Measure for Measure *(see excerpt above, 1765). Kenrick*

argues that the Duke's philosophy of death, rather than contra-
dicting the doctrine of the soul's immortality, as suggested by
Johnson, is merely concerned with the separation of body and
soul. Johnson claims that Lucio's use of the word "coward" in
connection with the Duke is an example of Shakespeare's inat-
tention to detail; Kenrick views this overemphasis on what he
considers marginal issues as "hypercriticism." Finally, Kenrick
interprets Isabella's intercession for Angelo as an example of
"Christian charity" and an attempt to do "poetical justice" on
behalf of the "injured Mariana," rather than "a covert satire
on the fair sex." Additional commentary on Johnson's interpre-
tation of Measure for Measure *can be found in the excerpt by*
John, Lord Chedworth (1805).]

> DUKE.—Reason thus with life;
> If I do lose thee, I do lose a thing
> That none but fools would keep.
>
> [III. i. 6-8]

Dr. Warburton, in order I presume to lay hold of an occasion
for altering the text, excepts against this passage as being a
direct persuasive to *suicide*. The absurdity, however, of supposing that the speaker intended it as such is obvious, since
he is endeavouring to instil into a condemned prisoner a resignation to his sentence. Dr. Johnson observes that the meaning
seems plainly this, that 'none but fools would wish to keep
life; or, none but fools would keep it, if choice were allowed'
[see excerpt above, 1765]. A sense which, whether true or not,
he remarks, is certainly innocent. But though our editor is
graciously leased to exculpate Shakespeare in this particular,
it appears to be only that he may fall upon him with the greater
violence in a page or two after; where Dr. Warburton vouch-
safes to pay the poet a compliment. . . .

> Thy best of rest is sleep,
> And that thou oft provok'st; yet grosly fear'st
> Thy death, which is no more.
>
> [III. i. 17-19]

[Kenrick quotes Dr. Johnson's comment on this passage: 'I
cannot, without indignation, find Shakespeare saying, that *death
is only sleep* . . . ']—Nor can I, Dr. Johnson, without equal
indignation find you misrepresenting Shakespeare, and thence
taking occasion to condemn him for what he is not culpable;
lengthening out your censure with imputations that, being false
in themselves, appear as invidious in the *man* as they are
contemptible in the *critic*. Would not one imagine, from the
warmth with which Dr. Johnson speaks of this passage, that
it militates against the doctrine of the immortality of the soul,
insinuating that in death we close our eyes and sleep for ever?
Nothing, however, can be more foreign from the plain intent
of the speaker and the obvious meaning of the passage. The
duke, in the assumed character of a friar, is endeavouring to
persuade Claudio to acquiesce in the sentence of death passed
on him, and to prepare himself for launching into eternity. . . .
Thou oft provokest sleep, says he, yet absurdly fear to die;
which, with regard to the painful and perplexing vigil of life,
is only to go to sleep. For that he only speaks of the mere
sense of death, the parting of the soul from the body, and that
Claudio understood him so, is very evident by the reply which
the latter makes to his harangue; notwithstanding the very last
words of it seem to be full as exceptionable as those objected
to.

> DUKE.   . . . in this life
> Lie hid a thousand deaths; yet death we fear,
> That makes these odds all even.
>   CLAU. I humbly thank you.
> To sue to live, I find, I seek to die;
> And, seeking death, find *life*: let it come on.
>
> [III. i. 39-43]

If any thing further be necessary to corroborate what is here
advanced we might instance the duke's exhorting him, in scene
III. of the same act, *to go to his knees* and prepare for death.
It is highly inconsistent to think such a piece of advice should
come from one who conceived death to be a perpetual sleep.
Prayers must seem as superfluous to him as the advice must
appear impertinent to the prisoner. But that Claudio had the
strongest notions of a future state after death is not to be doubted
since, speaking of the sin of debauching his sister, and Angelo's
design to commit it, he says

> If it were damnable, he being so wise,
> Why would he for the *momentary* trick
> Be *perdurably* fin'd?
>
> [III. i. 112-14]

Again, when his fears recurring, he tells his sister that 'Death
is a fearful thing' [III. i. 115], it is plain he doth not confine
the meaning of the word, as the Duke did, to the mere act or
circumstance of dying. For when she retorts upon him, 'And
shamed life a hateful,' he goes on, 'Ay, but to die, and go we
know not where' [III. i. 116-17]. As if he had said, I do not
mean the mere pain of dying; it is what is to come after death
that I fear, when we are to

> go we know not where;
> To lie in cold obstruction, and to rot;
> This sensible warm motion to become
> A kneeded clod; and the delighted spirit
> To bathe in fiery floods, or to reside
> In thrilling regions of thick-ribbed ice:
> To be imprison'd in the viewless winds,
> And blown with restless violence round about
> The pendant world; or to be worse than worst
> Of those, that lawless and incertain thoughts
> Imagine howling; 'tis too horrible!
>
> [III. i. 117-27]

Can we think that Shakespeare could so far forget himself as
to be here so very explicit regarding the notion of a future
state, if but two or three pages before he had been inculcating
a contrary doctrine!—What then must we think of his commentator, who affects to be moved with indignation and in
effect presumes to charge him on this account with vulgarity,
folly and impiety! (pp. 202-04)

> Lucio. Do you so, Sir? and was the duke a
> flesh-monger, a fool, and a coward, as you then
> reported him to be?
>
> [V. i. 333-35]

Dr. Johnson, who seems constantly on the watch to catch
Shakespeare tripping, observes here that 'Lucio had not, in the
former conservation, mentioned *cowardice* among the faults
of the duke.' But, says he, very graciously, 'such failures of
memory are incident to writers more diligent than this poet.'—
On this occasion I cannot help remarking that it is somewhat
singular to find our editor so extremely remiss and negligent
in illustrating the beauties of Shakespeare, and so very diligent
in discovering his faults. This carping critic is in this particular,
however, egregiously mistaken; there being no grounds for
charging the poet in this place with want of attention to his
plot. It is true that Lucio does not expresly call the duke a
coward, in that part of their conversation which passed on the
stage, in [III. ii]. Our editor might have observed, however,
that he hath a farther conversation with him in [IV. iii.] where
he begins again to talk of the *old fantastical duke of dark
corners*; and when the duke wants to shake him off by bidding

him farewel and telling him his *company is fairer than honest,* Lucio will not be thus got rid of, but follows him, saying, *By my troth, I'll go with thee to the lane's end. If bawdy talk offend you, we'll have very little of it. Nay, friar, I am a kind of bur, I shall stick* [IV. iii. 177-79]. Is it not very natural to suppose that Lucio might afterwards call the duke a *coward,* considering the many opprobrious names he had already given him? and is the poet to be censured because he hath made the Duke charge Lucio with a single word of detraction which was not actually spoken before the audience? If this be not hyper-criticism, I know not what is. But, to make the matter worse on the part of our unfortunate editor, the Duke doth not charge Lucio with calling him a coward at the time when he runs on enumerating his other vices. For this was in the open street, through which the officers passed in carrying the bawds to prison: but the time is particularly specified when he called him *coward,* which was when the duke met him in the prison and, as I above remarked, could not get rid of him. This is plain from the context.

> LUCIO. Come hither, goodman bald-pate; do you know me?
> DUKE. I remember you, Sir, by the sound of your voice: I met you at the prison in the absence of the duke.
> LUCIO. Oh, did you so? and do you remember what you said of the duke?
> DUKE. Most notedly, Sir.
> LUCIO. Do you so, Sir? and was the duke a fleshmonger, a fool, a coward, as you then reported him to be?
> DUKE. You must, Sir, change persons with me, ere you make that my report: *you* spoke so of him, and much *more,* much worse.
>
> [V. i. 326-38]

Surely Dr. Johnson must have *invidiously sought* occasion to depreciate the merit of Shakespeare, or he could never had laid hold of so groundless a pretext to cavil either at his inattention or want of memory. . . .

> ISAB A due sincerity govern'd his deeds
> Till he did look on me; since it is so,
> Let him not die.
>
> [V. i. 446-48]
> (pp. 206-08)

To expose the several fallacies suggested [by Dr. Johnson throughout his note on this passage], I shall observe first that it was very natural for Mariana to solicit Isabel's intercession for her husband, the man she so much loved. I cannot think also that it is in any respect out of character for Isabel, after repeated solicitations, to be moved to oblige Mariana, who had already obliged her, so far at least as to prevent the apparent necessity of prostituting herself to Angelo: especially if we reflect on the tranquil state of mind she seems to be in with regard to her brother, in whose supposed death she appears to have acquiesced, either from principles of religion or philosophy. For when the Duke, in the foregoing page, speaking of her brother, says

> Peace be with him!
> That life is better life, past fearing death,
> Than that which lives to fear: make it your comfort.
> So, happy is your brother.
>
> [V. i. 396-99]

Isabel answers 'I do, my lord' [V. i. 399]. From a principle of philosophy she must be very conscious that the death of Angelo could not bring her brother to life again; and if to this reflection we suppose her religion might add the suggestion of Christian charity and forgiveness, I do not see any impropriety in Isabel's soliciting Angelo's pardon.

As to the argument she makes use of, and which Dr. Johnson thinks so very extraordinary, it is to be observed that she does not make use of it as a positive plea, but introduces it with 'I partly think/A due sincerity', &c. Again, Dr. Johnson says, 'the only *intent* which *his act did not overtake* was the defilement of Isabel.' Surely Dr. Johnson forgets the intended execution of Claudio! There is no doubt that Angelo's guilty intentions fully deserved punishment; but as the principal of them failed of being carried into execution I do not see why the reader should feel so much indignation at his being pardoned, especially as he must perceive the propriety of doing poetical justice to the injured Mariana; which would not be the case if her new-made husband were to be immediately punished with the severity due to his wicked designs.

As to the sinister meaning he imputes to the poet of intending a covert satire on the fair sex, I think enough is already said to exculpate him; I wish, therefore, Dr. Johnson were equally excusable for giving Shakespeare the appellation of *varlet* poet. Our editor can hardly intend here to confine that term to its simple and ancient meaning: for where is the jest of propriety of calling Shakespeare a yeoman or servant, agreeably to the old meaning of the word *varlet*; which like *fur* in Latin, it is allowed, originally conveyed no base or opprobrious idea?—And yet, if Dr. Johnson did not use the word in this limited and antiquated sense, what can he mean by calling Shakespeare a mean, sorry, or rascally poet? For this is the modern sense of the word; and in this sense the word *varletry* is inserted in a certain folio dictionary, on the authority of Shakespeare himself.—Perhaps, indeed, Dr. Johnson only meant here to express himself in a strain of wit and pleasantry. If so, let him beware how he attempts to be witty again: for surely never was such an aukward attempt made before! It is not in his nature. (pp. 208-09)

> *William Kenrick, in an extract from "A Review of Dr. Johnson's New Edition of Shakespeare," in* Shakespeare, the Critical Heritage: 1765-1774, Vol. 5, *edited by Brian Vickers, Routledge & Kegan Paul, 1979, pp. 200-11.**

GEORGE STEEVENS   (essay date 1773)

[*Steevens was an English scholar who collaborated with Samuel Johnson on a ten-volume edition of Shakespeare's works in 1773. The subsequent revision of this collection, along with Steevens's own edition of 1793, formed the textual basis for the first two Variorum editions of Shakespeare's plays. The following excerpt first appeared in the collaborative 1773 edition. Steevens praises Shakespeare's handling of his sources for* Measure for Measure, *which he identifies as Whetstone's* Promos and Cassandra, *characterizing the earlier work as "an almost complete embryo" of Shakespeare's play, but one in which "it is nearly impossible to detect" the features Shakespeare was to develop. For further discussion of Shakespeare's treatment of his sources, see the excerpts by Lewis Theobald (1733), Charlotte Lennox (1753), Hoxie N. Fairchild (1931), and William Witherle Lawrence (1931).*]

Shakespeare took the fable of this play from the *Promos and Cassandra* of George Whetstone, published in 1598. . . .

A hint, like a seed, is more or less prolific according to the qualities of the soil on which it is thrown. This story, which in the hands of Whetstone produced little more than barren insipidity, under the culture of Shakespeare became fertile of entertainment. The curious reader will find that the old play of *Promos and Cassandra* exhibits an almost complete embryo of *Measure for Measure;* yet the hints on which it is formed are so slight that it is nearly as impossible to detect them, as it is to point out in the acorn the future ramifications of the oak. (p. 521)

> *George Steevens, in an extract from a head-note to "Measure for Measure," in* Shakespeare, the Critical Heritage: 1765-1774, *Vol. 5, edited by Brian Vickers, Routledge & Kegan Paul, 1979, pp. 510-51.*

ALEXANDER GERARD   (essay date 1774)

[*Gerard was a Scottish philosopher and theologian who defined the process of literary creation as an association of ideas. In the following excerpt from his* An Essay on Genius (1774), *he faults Shakespeare's blending of Christian and pagan attitudes about death in* Measure for Measure *for lacking "propriety."*]

A fertile imagination is apt to overload a work with a superfluity of ideas: an accurate judgment rejects all that are unnecessary. Shakespeare was not always able to keep the richness of his fancy from displaying itself in cases where judgment would have directed him to control it. That very exuberance of imagination which commands our admiration is sometimes indulged so far as necessarily to incur our censure. We need not be at a loss for an example. (pp. 113-14)

Sometimes . . . it happens that tho' each of the ideas is subservient to the end in view, yet they are so incongruous that they cannot be all adopted with propriety. Shakespeare describes the terrors of death by a variety of very striking and poetical images:

> [Ay, but to die, and go we know not where;
> To lie in cold obstruction, and to rot;
> This sensible warm motion to become
> A kneaded clod; and the delighted spirit
> To bathe in fiery floods, or to reside
> In thrilling region of thick-ribbed ice;
> To be imprison'd in the viewless winds
> And blown with restless violence round about
> The pendant world; or to be worse than worst
> Of those that lawless and incertain thought
> Imagine howling—'tis too horrible!
> The weariest and most loathed worldly life
> That age, ache, [penury], and imprisonment
> Can lay on nature is a paradise
> To what we fear of death.]
>
> [III. i. 117-31]

All the ideas here introduced are conducive to the poet's design, and might have been suggested by the correctest fancy. It is only judgment that can disapprove the uniting of them in the same description, as being heterogeneous, derived partly from Christian manners, and partly from pagan notions. (p. 114)

> *Alexander Gerard, in an extract from "An Essay on Genius," in* Shakespeare, the Critical Heritage: 1774-1801, *Vol. 6, edited by Brian Vickers, Routledge & Kegan Paul, 1981, pp. 113-14.*

EDWARD CAPELL   (essay date 1780)

[*Capell was the first Shakespearean editor to practice the idea of using good quarto texts as the basis for his editions of the plays, published between 1768 and 1783. The following comments on* Measure for Measure *are taken from the second volume of his* Notes and Various Readings to Shakespeare (1780). *In an approach that reflects the Neoclassical preoccupation with language and style, Capell argues that Shakespeare's rhymed speeches should be viewed as one of "the time's vices." He admits, however, that the Duke's lines at the end of III.ii. do not produce an "ill effect."*]

> He who the sword of heaven will bear
> Should be as holy as severe. . . .
>
> [III. ii. 261-62]

Speeches, and parts of speeches, in rime, (some in measures properly lyrical, like the sententious one here) are found in all parts of Shakespeare; and should be look'd upon as the time's vices, sacrifices of judgment to profit, but not always unwilling ones; for such speeches are not of ill effect in all places, of which the present is instance. But his lovers have cause to wish, notwithstanding, that he had less consider'd his audiences and comply'd less with their taste; for it happens but too often that constraints of rime or of measure operate badly on his expression, causing breaches of grammar, strange and scarce allowable ellipsis's, and usage of terms improper. . . . The concluding lines of this speech owe their darkness to purpose. They are riddles, but not of any great difficulty; nor altogether so free of it that the following short comment should be look'd upon as an affront:—so the feigning Angelo shall, by means of me a feign'd friar, be punish'd with false Isabel for his false attempt on her, and made perform his old contract with Mariana. (pp. 234-35)

> *Edward Capell, in an extract from "Notes and Various Readings to Shakespeare," in* Shakespeare, the Critical Heritage: 1774-1801, *Vol. 6, edited by Brian Vickers, Routledge & Kegan Paul, 1981, pp. 234-35.*

GEORGE CHALMERS   (essay date 1799)

[*A Scottish antiquarian, lawyer, and essayist, Chalmers practiced law in the colonial courts of Maryland from 1763 to 1775. At the outbreak of the American Revolution he returned to England, where he published numerous biographical, historical, and political tracts and essays. One of many scholars duped by the Shakespeare forgeries of William Henry Ireland, Chalmers published two works in defense of his position:* An Apology for the Believers in the Shakspeare-Papers (1797) *and* A Supplemental Apology for the Believers in the Shakspeare-Papers (1799). *Although these works are mainly an attack against Edmond Malone's scholarship concerning the Ireland forgeries, the historical facts upon which Chalmers based his arguments were an important contribution to Shakespearean studies. In the excerpt below, taken from his* A Supplemental Apology, *Chalmers is the first of many scholars to claim that the character of the Duke in* Measure for Measure *is a "very accurate" portrait of James I.*]

The commentators seem not to have remarked, that the character of *the Duke* [in *Measure for Measure*], is a very accurate delineation of that of King James, which Shakspeare appears to have caught, with great felicity, and to have sketched, with much truth. (p. 404)

Several of those characteristics are alluded to throughout *Measure for Measure:*

> ——— I love the people,
> But, do not like to stage me to their eyes:
> Though it do well, I do not relish well
> Their loud applause, and aves vehement:
> Nor, do I think the man of safe discretion,
> That does affect it.   [I. i. 67-72]

This is said, by the commentators, to be intended as a *courtly apology,* for the *stately* and *ungracious* demeanor of King James, on his entry into England. No: The fault of this prince was *too much familiarity,* and not stateliness; he was good natured, and not ungracious; he did not like to *stage* himself to the people's eyes; because, he delighted in retirement, in the company of a few, in study, and in writing. . . . On the contrary, Shakspeare did not intend to make any apology, but merely to give *traits of character,* which the commentators did not comprehend. (pp. 408-09)

> *George Chalmers, "'Measure for Measure', 1604,"*
> *in his* A Supplemental Apology for the Believers in
> the Shakspere-Papers, *1799. Reprint by Frank Cass
> & Co. Ltd., 1971, pp. 402-13.*

JOHN, LORD CHEDWORTH (essay date 1805)

[*In the following extract from his comments on* Measure for Measure, *Chedworth concentrates on elements of the play discussed by both Samuel Johnson (1765) and William Kenrick (1765). He recognizes a similarity between the Duke's death philosophy and Hamlet's view of death as a sleep that ends heartache. Like Kenrick—but without his vitriolic approach—Chedworth disagrees with Johnson about Lucio's use of the word "coward" in connection with the Duke. And finally, he supports Johnson's interpretation of Isabella's intercession for Angelo, describing her motive as "female vanity." For other negative reactions to the character of Isabella, see the excerpts by Charlotte Lennox (1753), William Hazlitt (1817), and Arthur Quiller-Couch (1922).*]

> *Sleep thou provok'st; yet grossly fear'st*
> *Thy death, which is no more.*
>   [III. i. 17-19]

Dr. Johnson's indignation is unjustly excited here . . . : the poet's meaning was no other than that obvious and innocent one . . . occurring in the meditation of Hamlet:

> ——————— To die! to sleep:
> No more; and, by a sleep, to say, we end
> The heart-ach. . . .
>   [*Hamlet,* III. i. 59-61]
>   (p. 95)

> ——————— And a coward.
>   [V. i. 334]

[Dr. Johnson remarks that] Lucio had not, in the former conversation, mentioned coward. I believe it is not necessary, either to the consistency of the character or the humour of the scene, that Lucio should here repeat, with fidelity, the exact terms of the abuse which his invention had produced before; and his mentioning coward now is enough for the Duke to lay hold of it afterwards.

> ——————— Till he did look on me.
>   [V. i. 447]

I believe there are very few who, in contemplating the scene before us, will not agree in the justness of Dr. Johnson's com-

ment upon it: it is true that Isabella is not prompt to comply with the request of Mariana, but when she yields at length female vanity is very conspicuously a motive with her. (p. 104)

> *John, Lord Chedworth, in an extract from his manu-
> script in* Remarks, Critical, Conjectural, and Ex-
> planatory, upon the Plays of Shakspeare, *Vol. I by
> E. H. Seymour, edited by Isaac Reed, Lackington,
> Allen & Co., Longman, Hurst, Rees, and Orme, F.
> and C. Rivington & Others, 1805, pp. 81-105.*

AUGUST WILHELM SCHLEGEL (lecture date 1808)

[*A prominent German Romantic critic, Schlegel holds a key place in the history of Shakespeare's reputation in European criticism. His translations of thirteen of the plays are still considered the best German editions of Shakespeare. Schlegel was also a leading spokesman for the Romantic movement, which permanently overthrew the Neoclassical contention that Shakespeare was a child of nature whose plays lacked artistic form. The excerpt below was originally part of a lecture delivered by Schlegel in 1808 and subsequently published in his* Über dramatische Kunst und Literatur *(1811). Schlegel concentrates on the characters of Isabella and the Duke, describing the former as "the most beautiful embellishment" of* Measure for Measure *and the latter as "an earthly providence" who averts every evil. He finds, however, that the Duke's vanity and capriciousness prove Lucio's slanderous accusations to be ironically true. Schlegel interprets the import of the play as "the triumph of mercy over strict justice," because no one is shown as guiltless enough to act as a judge. For further commentary on Shakespeare's handling of the theme of justice and mercy, see the excerpts by G. G. Gervinus (1849-50), Walter Pater (1874), Denton J. Snider (1890), and Muriel C. Bradbrook (1941).*]

All's Well that Ends Well, Much Ado about Nothing, Measure for Measure, and *The Merchant of Venice,* bear, in so far, a resemblance to each other, that, along with the main plot, which turns on important relations decisive of nothing less than the happiness or misery of life, and therefore is calculated to make a powerful impression on the moral feeling, the poet, with the skill of a practised artist, has contrived to combine a number of cheerful accompaniments. Not, however, that the poet seems loth to allow full scope to the serious impressions: he merely adds a due counterpoise to them in the entertainment which he supplies for the imagination and the understanding. He has furnished the story with all the separate features which are necessary to give to it the appearance of a real, though extraordinary, event. But he never falls into the lachrymose tone of the sentimental drama, nor into the bitterness of those dramas which have a moral direction, and which are really nothing but moral invectives dramatized. Compassion, anxiety, and dissatisfaction become too oppressive when they are too long dwelt on, and when the whole of a work is given up to them exclusively. Shakspeare always finds means to transport us from the confinement of social institutions or pretensions, where men do but shut out the light and air from each other, into the open space, even before we ourselves are conscious of our want. (p. 384)

In *Measure for Measure* Shakspeare was compelled, by the nature of the subject, to make his poetry more familiar with criminal justice than is usual with him. All kinds of proceedings connected with the subject, all sorts of active or passive persons, pass in review before us: the hypocritical Lord Deputy, the compassionate Provost, and the hard-hearted Hangman; a young man of quality who is to suffer for the seduction of his mistress before marriage, loose wretches brought in by the police, nay, even a hardened criminal, whom even the preparations for his execution cannot awaken out of his callousness. But yet, notwithstanding this agitating truthfulness, how tender and mild is the pervading tone of the picture! The piece takes improperly its name from punishment; the true significance of the whole is the triumph of mercy over strict justice; no man being himself so free from errors as to be entitled to deal it out to his equals. The most beautiful embellishment of the composition is the character of Isabella, who, on the point of taking the veil, is yet prevailed upon by sisterly affection to tread again the perplexing ways of the world, while, amid the general corruption, the heavenly purity of her mind is not even stained with one unholy thought: in the humble robes of the novice she is a very angel of light. . . . [In] masterly scenes, Shakspeare has sounded the depths of the human heart. The interest here reposes altogether on the represented action; curiosity contributes nothing to our delight, for the Duke, in the disguise of a Monk, is always present to watch over his dangerous representative, and to avert every evil which could possibly be apprehended; we look to him with confidence for a happy result. The Duke acts the part of the Monk naturally, even to deception; he unites in his person the wisdom of the priest and the prince. Only in his wisdom he is too fond of round-about ways; his vanity is flattered with acting invisibly like an earthly providence; he takes more pleasure in overhearing his subjects than governing them in the customary way of princes. As he ultimately extends a free pardon to all the guilty, we do not see how his original purpose, in committing the execution of the laws to other hands, of restoring their strictness, has in any wise been accomplished. The poet might have had this irony in view, that of the numberless slanders of the Duke, told him by the petulant Lucio, in ignorance of the person whom he is addressing, that at least which regarded his singularities and whims was not wholly without foundation. It is deserving of remark, that Shakspeare, amidst the rancour of religious parties, takes a delight in painting the condition of a monk, and always represents his influence as beneficial. We find in him none of the black and knavish monks, which an enthusiasm for Protestantism, rather than poetical inspiration, has suggested to some of our modern poets. Shakspeare merely gives his monks an inclination to busy themselves in the affairs of others, after renouncing the world for themselves; with respect, however, to pious frauds, he does not represent them as very conscientious. Such are the parts acted by the monk in *Romeo and Juliet,* and another in *Much Ado about Nothing,* and even by the Duke, whom, contrary to the well-known proverb, the cowl seems really to make a monk. (pp. 387-88)

> August Wilhelm Schlegel, "Criticisms on Shakespeare's Comedies," in his A Course of Lectures on Dramatic Art and Literature, *edited by Rev. A.J.W. Morrison, translated by John Black, revised edition, 1846. Reprint by AMS Press, Inc., 1965, pp. 379-99.*

WILLIAM HAZLITT (essay date 1817)

[*Hazlitt is considered a leading Shakespearean critic of the English Romantic movement. A prolific essayist and critic on a wide range of subjects, he remarked in the preface to his* Characters of Shakespear's Plays, *first published in 1817, that he was inspired by the German critic August Wilhelm Schlegel and was determined to supplant what he considered the pernicious influence of Samuel Johnson's Shakespearean criticism. Hazlitt's criticism is typically Romantic in its emphasis on character studies. Unlike his fellow*

Romantic critic Samuel Taylor Coleridge, Hazlitt was a dramatic critic whose experience of Shakespeare in the theater influenced his interpretations. In the excerpt below, taken from his Characters of Shakespear's Plays, *he maintains that despite the genius and wisdom evident in* Measure for Measure, *"our sympathies are repulsed and defeated in all directions." To Hazlitt, Angelo displays a "greater passion for hypocrisy than for his mistress," Isabella's "rigid chastity" diminishes our sympathy for her, the Duke is more concerned with his schemes than his duty, and only Claudio demonstrates natural emotion. For other discussions of the perplexing nature of the main characters, see the excerpts by Charlotte Lennox (1753), Samuel Taylor Coleridge (1818), Arthur Quiller-Couch (1922), and L. C. Knights (1942). Hazlitt also explores the quality of Shakespeare's morality, calling Shakespeare at once the weakest and greatest of moralists, the former because he wrote out of sympathy for his characters and failed to establish the antipathies of human nature, the latter because he "shewed the greatest knowledge of humanity with the greatest fellow-feeling for it." He implies that Shakespeare's depiction of the minor characters in* Measure for Measure *reveals this talent.*]

[*Measure for Measure* is] a play as full of genius as it is of wisdom. Yet there is an original sin in the nature of the subject, which prevents us from taking a cordial interest in it. "The height of moral argument" which the author has maintained in the intervals of passion or blended with the more powerful impulses of nature, is hardly surpassed in any of his plays. But there is in general a want of passion; the affections are at a stand; our sympathies are repulsed and defeated in all directions. The only passion which influences the story is that of Angelo; and yet he seems to have a much greater passion for hypocrisy than for his mistress. Neither are we greatly enamoured of Isabella's rigid chastity, though she could not act otherwise than she did. We do not feel the same confidence in the virtue that is "sublimely good" at another's expense, as if it had been put to some less disinterested trial. As to the Duke, who makes a very imposing and mysterious stage-character, he is more absorbed in his own plots and gravity than anxious for the welfare of the state; more tenacious of his own character than attentive to the feelings and apprehensions of others. Claudio is the only person who feels naturally; and yet he is placed in circumstances of distress which almost preclude the wish for his deliverance. Mariana is also in love with Angelo, whom we hate. In this respect, there may be said to be a general system of cross-purposes between the feelings of the different characters and the sympathy of the reader or the audience. This principle of repugnance seems to have reached its height in the character of Master Barnardine, who not only sets at defiance the opinions of others, but has even thrown off all self-regard,—"one that apprehends death no more dreadfully but as a drunken sleep; careless, reckless, and fearless of what's past, present, and to come" [IV. ii. 142-44]. He is a fine antithesis to the morality and the hypocrisy of the other characters of the play. Barnardine is Caliban transported from Prospero's wizard island to the forests of Bohemia or the prisons of Vienna. He is the creature of bad habits as Caliban is of gross instincts. He has however a strong notion of the natural fitness of things, according to his own sensations—"He has been drinking hard all night, and he will not be hanged that day" [IV. ii. 44-5]—and Shakespear has let him off at last. We do not understand why the philosophical German critic, Schlegel, should be so severe on those pleasant persons, Lucio, Pompey, and Master Froth, as to call them "wretches" [see excerpt above, 1808]. They appear all mighty comfortable in their occupations, and determined to pursue them, "as the flesh and fortune should serve" [II. i. 253-54]. A very good exposure of the want of self-knowledge and contempt for others, which is so common in the world, is put into the mouth of Abhorson, the jailor, when the Provost proposes to associate Pompey with him in his office—"A bawd, sir? Fie upon him, he will discredit our mystery" [IV. ii. 28-9]. And the same answer will serve in nine instances out of ten to the same kind of remark, "Go to, sir, you weigh equally; a feather will turn the scale" [IV. ii. 30-1]. Shakespear was in one sense the least moral of all writers; for morality (commonly so called) is made up of antipathies; and his talent consisted in sympathy with human nature, in all its shapes, degrees, depressions, and elevations. The object of the pedantic moralist is to find out the bad in every thing: his was to shew that "there is some soul of goodness in things evil." Even Master Barnardine is not left to the mercy of what others think of him; but when he comes in, speaks for himself, and pleads his own cause, as well as if counsel had been assigned him. In one sense, Shakespear was no moralist at all: in another, he was the greatest of all moralists. He was a moralist in the same sense in which nature is one. He taught what he had learnt from her. He shewed the greatest knowledge of humanity with the greatest fellow-feeling for it. (pp. 195-97)

> William Hazlitt, "'Measure for Measure'," in his Characters of Shakespear's Plays & Lectures on the English Poets, *Macmillan and Co. Limited, 1903, pp. 195-99.*

S[AMUEL] T[AYLOR] COLERIDGE (lecture date 1818)

[*Coleridge's lectures and writings on Shakespeare form a major chapter in the history of English Shakespearean criticism. As the channel for the critical ideas of the German Romantics and as an original interpreter of Shakespeare in the new spirit of Romanticism, Coleridge played a strategic role in overthrowing the last remains of the Neoclassical approach to Shakespeare and in establishing the modern view of him as a conscious artist and masterful portrayer of human character. Coleridge's remarks on Shakespeare come down to posterity largely as fragmentary notes, marginalia, and reports by auditors on the lectures, rather than in polished essays. His comments on* Measure for Measure, *excerpted below, were originally part of a lecture delivered in 1818 and incorporated in the second volume of his posthumous* Literary Remains *(1837). Coleridge considers* Measure for Measure *"the most painful" Shakespearean play, one in which both the comic and serious parts are detestable. He also states, in more emphatic terms than those of either Charlotte Lennox (1753) or Samuel Johnson (1765), that Angelo's pardon "baffles the strong indignant claim of justice" and degrades "the character of woman."*]

[*Measure for Measure*], which is Shakespeare's throughout, is to me the most painful—say rather, the only painful—part of his genuine works. The comic and tragic parts equally border on the [detestable],—the one being disgusting, the other horrible; and the pardon and marriage of Angelo not merely baffles the strong indignant claim of justice—(for cruelty, with lust and damnable baseness, cannot be forgiven, because we cannot conceive them as being morally repented of); but it is likewise degrading to the character of woman. (p. 115)

> S[amuel] T[aylor] Coleridge, "'Measure for Measure'," in Shakespeare, Ben Jonson, Beaumont and Fletcher: Notes and Lectures, *revised edition, Edward Howell, 1881, pp. 115-16.*

MRS. [ANNA BROWNELL] JAMESON (essay date 1833)

[*Jameson was a well-known nineteenth-century essayist. Her essays and criticism span the end of the Romantic age and the beginning of Victorian realism, reflecting elements from both periods. She is best remembered for her study* Shakspeare's Heroines, *which was originally published in 1833 as* Characteristics of Women: Moral, Poetical, and Historical. *This work demonstrates both her historical interests and her sympathetic appreciation of Shakespeare's female characters. In the excerpt below, Jameson concentrates on the character of Isabella, comparing her "moral grandeur" and "saintly grace" to the wisdom, graciousness, and virtue of Portia, the heroine in* The Merchant of Venice. *Jameson's interpretation typifies the encomiums of many nineteenth-century critics who, unlike Neoclassical commentators, idolized rather than chastized Isabella. To Jameson, Isabella is the only character in* Measure for Measure *that is consistent and the only one that engages our sympathy. She concludes that Isabella's new life as Duchess of Vienna is both deserved and natural. Other favorable interpretations of Isabella can be found in the essays by August Wilhelm Schlegel (1808), Charles Knight (1842), G. G. Gervinus (1849-50), and Frederick S. Boas (1896).*]

The character of Isabella, considered as a poetical delineation, is less mixed than that of Portia [in "The Merchant of Venice"]; and the dissimilarity between the two appears, at first view, so complete, that we can scarce believe that the same elements enter into the composition of each. Yet so it is: they are portrayed as equally wise, gracious, virtuous, fair and young; we perceive in both the same exalted principle and firmness of character, the same depth of reflection and persuasive eloquence, the same self-denying generosity and capability of strong affections. . . . (p. 59)

Isabella is distinguished from Portia, and strongly individualised by a certain moral grandeur, a saintly grace, something of vestal dignity and purity, which render her less attractive and more imposing; she is "severe in youthful beauty," and inspires a reverence which would have placed her beyond the daring of one unholy wish or thought, except in such a man as Angelo—

> O cunning enemy! that to catch a saint
> With saints doth bait thy hook.
>
> [II. ii. 179-80]

This impression of her character is conveyed from the very first, when Lucio, the libertine jester, whose coarse, audacious with checks at every feather, thus expresses his respect for her—

> I would not—though 'tis my familiar sin
> With maids to seem the lapwing, and to jest,
> Tongue far from heart—play with all virgins so.
> I hold you as a thing enskyed and sainted,
> By your renouncement, an immortal spirit,
> And to be talked with in sincerity,
> As with a saint.
>
> [I. iv. 31-7]

A strong distinction between Isabella and Portia is produced by the circumstances in which they are respectively placed. Portia is a high-born heiress, "lord of a fair mansion, master of her servants, queen o'er herself" [*Merchant of Venice*, III. ii. 167-69]; easy and decided, as one born to command, and used to it. Isabella has also the innate dignity which renders her "queen o'er herself," but she has lived far from the world and its pomps and pleasures; she is one of a consecrated sisterhood—a novice of St. Clare; the power to command obedience and to confer happiness are to her unknown. Portia is a splendid creature, radiant with confidence, hope, and joy. She is like the orange-tree, hung at once with golden fruit and luxuriant flowers, which has expanded into bloom and fragrance beneath favouring skies, and has been nursed into beauty by the sunshine and the dews of heaven. Isabella is like a stately and graceful cedar, towering on some Alpine cliff, unbowed and unscathed amid the storm. She gives us the impression of one who has passed under the ennobling discipline of suffering and self-denial: a melancholy charm tempers the natural vigour of her mind: her spirit seems to stand upon an eminence, and look down upon the world as if already enskyed and sainted; and yet, when brought in contact with that world which she inwardly despises, she shrinks back with all the timidity natural to her cloistral education.

This union of natural grace and grandeur with the habits and sentiments of a recluse—of austerity of life with gentleness of manner—of inflexible moral principle with humility and even bashfulness of deportment, is delineated with the most beautiful and wonderful consistency. Thus, when her brother sends to her to entreat her mediation, her first feeling is fear, and a distrust in her own powers—

> Alas! what poor ability's in me
> To do him good?
> *Lucio.* Essay the power you have.
> *Isabella.* My power, alas! I doubt.
>
> [I. iv. 75-7]

In the first scene with Angelo she seems divided between her love for her brother and her sense of his fault; between her self-respect and her maidenly bashfulness. She begins with a kind of hesitation, "at war 'twixt will and will not" [II. ii. 33]: and when Angelo quotes the law, and insists on the justice of his sentence and the responsibility of his station, her native sense of moral rectitude and severe principles takes the lead, and she shrinks back—

> O just but severe law!
> I *had* a brother then—Heaven keep your honour!
>
> [II. ii. 41-2]

Excited and encouraged by Lucio, and supported by her own natural spirit, she returns to the charge—she gains energy and self-possession as she proceeds, grows more earnest and passionate from the difficulty she encounters, and displays that eloquence and power of reasoning for which we had been already prepared by Claudio's first allusion to her—

> In her youth
> There is a prone and speechless dialect,
> Such as moves men; besides, she has prosperous art,
> When she will play with reason and discourse,
> and well she can persuade.
>
> [I. ii. 182-86]

It is a curious coincidence that Isabella, exhorting Angelo to mercy, avails herself of precisely the same arguments and insists on the self-same topics which Portia addresses to Shylock in her celebrated speech; but how beautifully and how truly is the distinction marked! how like, and yet how unlike! Portia's eulogy on mercy is a piece of heavenly rhetoric; it falls on the ear with a solemn, measured harmony; it is the voice of a descended angel addressing an inferior nature: if not premeditated, it is at least part of a preconcerted scheme; while Isabella's pleadings are poured from the abundance of her heart in broken sentences, and with the artless vehemence of one who feels that life and death hang upon her appeal. (pp. 59-62)

In all that Portia says we confess the power of a rich poetical imagination, blended with a quick practical spirit of observation, familiar with the surfaces of things; while there is a

profound yet simple morality, a depth of religious feeling, a touch of melancholy, in Isabella's sentiments, and something earnest and authoritative in the manner and expression, as though they had grown up in her mind from long and deep meditation in the silence and solitude of her convent cell. . . . (pp. 62-3)

Isabella's conscientiousness is overcome by the only sentiment which ought to temper justice into mercy, the power of affection and sympathy.

Isabella's confession of the general frailty of her sex has a peculiar softness, beauty, and propriety. She admits the imputation with all the sympathy of woman for woman; yet with all the dignity of one who felt her own superiority to the weakness she acknowledges—

> *Angelo.* Nay, women are frail too.
> *Isabella.* Ay, as the glasses where they view themselves;
> Which are as easy broke as they make forms.
> Women! help heaven! men their creation mar
> In profiting by them. Nay, call us ten times frail;
> For we are soft as our complexions are,
> And credulous to false prints.
>
> [II. iv. 124-30]

Nor should we fail to remark the deeper interest which is thrown round Isabella by one part of her character, which is betrayed rather than exhibited in the progress of the action; and for which we are not at first prepared, though it is so perfectly natural. It is the strong undercurrent of passion and enthusiasm flowing beneath this calm and saintly self-possession, it is the capacity for high feeling and generous and strong indignation veiled beneath the sweet austere composure of the religious recluse, which, by the very force of contrast, powerfully impress the imagination. As we see in real life that where, from some external or habitual cause, a strong control is exercised over naturally quick feelings and an impetuous temper, they display themselves with a proportionate vehemence when that restraint is removed; so the very violence with which her passion bursts forth, when opposed or under the influence of strong excitement is admirably characteristic. (pp. 65-6)

She places at first a strong and high-souled confidence in her brother's fortitude and magnanimity, judging him by her own lofty spirit—

> I'll to my brother;
> Though he hath fallen by prompture of the blood,
> Yet hath he in him such a mind of honour,
> That had he twenty hearts to tender down
> On twenty bloody blocks, he'd yield them up,
> Before his sister should her body stoop
> To such abhorr'd pollution.
>
> [II. iv. 177-83]

But when her trust in his honour is deceived by his momentary weakness, her scorn has a bitterness and her indignation a force of expression almost fearful; and both are carried to an extreme, which is perfectly in character—

> O faithless coward! O dishonest wretch!
> Wilt thou be made a man out of my vice!
> Is't not a kind of incest to take life
> From thine own sister's shame? What should I think?
> Heaven shield my mother play'd my father fair!
> For such a warped slip of wilderness
> Ne'er issued from his blood. Take my defiance:
> Die! perish! Might but my bending down

Reprieve thee from thy fate, it should proceed.
I'll pray a thousand prayers for thy death,
No word to save thee.

[III. i. 136-46]
(pp. 66-7)

Of all the characters, Isabella alone has our sympathy. But though she triumphs in the conclusion, her triumph is not produced in a pleasing manner. There are too many disguises and tricks, too many "by-paths and indirect crooked ways" [2 *Henry IV*, IV. v. 184], to conduct us to the natural and foreseen catastrophe, which the Duke's presence throughout renders inevitable. This Duke seems to have a predilection for bringing about justice by a most unjustifiable succession of falsehoods and counterplots. He really deserves Lucio's satirical designation, who somewhere styles him "The Fantastical Duke of Dark Corners" [IV. iii. 157]. But Isabella is ever consistent in her pure and upright simplicity, and in the midst of this simulation, expresses a characteristic disapprobation of the part she is made to play—

To speak so indirectly I am loth:
I would say the truth?

[IV. vi. 1-2]

She yields to the supposed Friar with a kind of forced docility, because her situation as a religious novice, and his station, habit, and authority, as her spiritual director, demand this sacrifice. In the end we are made to feel that her transition from the convent to the throne has but placed this noble creature in her natural sphere; for though Isabella, as Duchess of Vienna, could not more command our highest reverence than Isabel the novice of Saint Clare, yet a wider range of usefulness and benevolence, of trial and action, was better suited to the large capacity, the ardent affections, the energentic intellect and firm principle of such a woman as Isabella, than the walls of a cloister. (pp. 68-9)

Such women as Desdemona and Ophelia would have passed their lives in the seclusion of a nunnery without wishing, like Isabella, for stricter bonds, or planning, like St. Theresa, the reformation of their order, simply because any restraint would have been efficient, as far as *they* were concerned. Isabella, "dedicate to nothing temporal" [II. ii. 154-55], might have found resignation through self-government, or have become a religious enthusiast; while "place and greatness" [IV. i. 59] would have appeared to her strong and upright mind only a more extended field of action, a trust and a trial. The mere trappings of power and state, the gemmed coronal, the ermined robe, she would have regarded as the outward emblems of her earthly profession: and would have worn them with as much simplicity as her novice's hood and scapular: still, under whatever guise she might tread this thorny world, the same "angel of light" [see excerpt above by August Wilhelm Schlegel, 1808]. (p. 70)

Mrs. [Anna Brownell] Jameson, "Isabella," in her
Shakespeare's Heroines: Characteristics of Women,
Moral, Poetical, & Historical, second edition, 1833.
Reprint by George Newnes, Limited, 1897, pp. 59-
70.

A. S. PUSHKIN (essay date 1836)

[*Pushkin is considered the greatest poet and dramatist of nineteenth-century Russia. Shakespeare was a dominant influence on his work; he wrote several adaptations of the plays and used Shakespeare's work as the source for a number of his poems and* dramas. *Acknowledging his indebtedness to Shakespeare, he wrote of his drama* Boris Gudonov: *"Not disturbed by any other influence, I imitated Shakespeare in his broad and free depiction of characters, in the simple and careless combination of plots." The following excerpt was first written in 1836 and published in the Russian journal* Sovremenik *in 1837. Pushkin's comments about the complexity and depth with which Shakespeare depicts Angelo's hypocrisy indicates the Romantic celebration of Shakespeare's genius for characterization. For additional discussion of the nature of Angelo's hypocrisy, see the excerpts by William Hazlitt (1817), G. G. Gervinus (1849-50), H. N. Hudson (1872), and G. Wilson Knight (1930).*]

The characters portrayed by Shakspere are not, like Molière's, types of this particular passion or that particular vice, but are living beings filled with many passions, many vices; the circumstances unfold before the spectator their variety and their complex aspects. . . . In Molière the hypocrite trails after the wife of his benefactor—the hypocrite; asks for a glass of water—from the hypocrite. In Shakspere the hypocrite pronounces a court verdict with conceited austerity, but with equity; he justifies his heartlessness with the thoughtful considerations of a statesman; he courts innocence with captivating sophistry and not with ludicrous concoctions of devotion and gallantry. *Angelo* is a hypocrite because his known actions contradict his secret passions! And what depth in this character! (p. 120)

A. S. Pushkin, "Notes on Shylock, Angelo and Falstaff," translated by Albert Siegel, in The Shakespeare Association Bulletin, Vol. XVI, No. 1, January, 1941, pp. 120-21.

HERMANN ULRICI (essay date 1839)

[*A German scholar, Ulrici was a professor of philosophy and the author of works on Greek poetry and Shakespeare. The following excerpt is from an English translation of his* Über Shakespeares dramatische Kunst, und sein Verhältniss zu Calderon und Göthe, *a work first published in 1839. This study exemplifies the "philosophical criticism" developed in Germany during the nineteenth century. The immediate sources for Ulrici's critical approach appear to be August Wilhelm Schlegel's conception of the play as an organic, interconnected whole and Georg Wilhelm Friedrich Hegel's view of drama as an embodiment of the conflict of historical forces and ideas. Unlike his fellow German Shakespearean critic G. G. Gervinus, Ulrici sought to develop a specifically Christian aesthetics, but one which, as he carefully points out in the introduction to the work mentioned above, in no way intrudes on "that unity of idea, which preeminently constitutes a work of art a living creation in the world of beauty." Ulrici is the first critic to state that* Measure *dramatizes a specifically Christian concept, asserting that the main theme of the play rests on the Christian truth that everyone is a sinner in need of mercy. To him, the play's characterization, plot, and circumstances are unified by this fundamental idea. Ulrici concludes that the play's title is an ironic reference to the Mosaic "eye for an eye" code of justice, since it actually expresses a message of Christian forgiveness. Other critics who focus on the Christian aspects of* Measure for Measure *include G. Wilson Knight (1930), R. W. Chambers (1937), Roy W. Battenhouse (1946), and Nevill Coghill (1955).*]

["Measure for Measure,"] in external form, in tone, and colouring, widely differing from the "Merchant of Venice," is nevertheless related to it by its ideal subject-matter. The basis on which its story is constructed is closely allied, and at the same time essentially divergent. (p. 309)

Human virtue and morality, in so far as they pretend to be something in and by themselves, and claim to be self-sufficient, is the mark against which Comedy directs its mockery, and which the dialectic of irony, or rather their own immanent dialectic, soon resolves into absolute nothingness. Virtue and morality are, no doubt (who will pretend to deny it?) the principle and the end of human existence. But they are so merely through and in *God*. Mere *human* virtue, which pretends to a strength of *its own,* and, as if it had with free creative energy made itself, arrogates a self-sufficiency, is but a mere factitious virtue, a nothing, like the glittering soap-bubble which bursts with the first breath of air; nay, it is infinitely lower than nothing, since it is the vilest of sins, and the seed and germ of all wickedness. The whole piece, accordingly, rests on the prime Christian truth—we are all sinners, children of wrath, and in need of mercy; in other words, life is here contemplated in its gravest and profoundest principle of virtue and morality. But even this foundation is found to be frail, hollow, and worm-eaten, when employed exclusively in its earthly and human nature to prop up and support the human and the earthly.

It is not man's moral energy, but the *divine grace,* which is the stay of human life, because it is only in and through the latter, that human virtue becomes practicable, and that it is truly and properly virtue;—a truth similar to that which the "Merchant of Venice" illustrated in the case of law. If it be true that it is only by God's grace, and upon penitent acknowledgment of his own frailty and sinfulness, that man receives the faculty of virtue and perfection, then most assuredly is he bound to shew mercy and not justice; and, for punishment, pardon upon his repentant and sorrowing fellows. . . . (pp. 310-11)

[The] poem itself furnishes such abundant explanations of its deep and pregnant meaning, it would be worse than folly to presume to add one word on the subject. All that remains for me to do is, to point out the manner the fundamental idea is again reflected in the several parts—the characters, the situations, and the circumstances, attracting them all to its magnetic centre, and there arranging them into one organic body. . . . Aescalus stands by the side of Angelo like the mild, peaceful, and aged sage, by impetuous and energetic manhood: his long years have taught and purified him, and he no longer mistakes proud pretension for virtue, nor rigour for justice. His part is indispensable as an organic counterpoise to Angelo; and partly as a mean between him and the Duke. For the Duke and Isabella stand far higher than he does; they have the grace of God with them, while he possesses nothing more than human experience and compassion. With equal wisdom, Claudio and Juliet appear only in the background; they are the well-executed pictures of human weakness which sins from too great liberty, and being brought by constraint and suffering to repentance, on its penitent return is received and forgiven. They stand in contrast to the Pharisaic virtue of Angelo, and are, as it were, the opposite pole of the piece. In Lucio, lastly, and Froth, Pompey the Clown, Barnardine, and Mistress Overdone, we have various shades of human folly, vice, and iniquity. Lucio, without being absolutely depraved or intentionally bad, as we see from his ready co-operation with Claudio and Isabella, becomes, through want of consideration, both vicious and dissolute. Young Master Froth is simply froth; without solidity enough for deep crime, and far too light for virtue. Mistress Overdone loves sin from long habit, and because she gains a livelihood by it. The murderer Barnardine is the type of man's rude sensual nature, which becomes inhuman because civilization has not extended to it the training hand of education;—we see in his crime the sinfulness of the individual, which has its root and nurture within itself, but is at the same time fed and fostered by the universal sinfulness of the human race. Lastly, Pompey is the assistant of vice from mere stupidity; he knows not, nor indeed troubles himself to think what it is he is doing, and his untaught ignorance looks upon life itself as a drinking-room, in which a man may be merry if he will, but not without money: his faults are not so much faults of inclination and commission, as they are the fruit of a criminal want of a right knowledge and of a perverted judgment; he has a conviction that no man is or can be without faults and weaknesses, and so he allows himself to go his own way without thought or care; his crime is his very folly, and therefore it is of the most venial kind. Although he sustains the part of the Clown of the piece, the preceding remarks must have prepared us to find that it is not pre-eminently his vocation to invest in his own individuality the fundamental idea with concrete vitality, or to exhibit it in a parodical form. Ordinary folly is too light to balance the whole weight of the grave view of life, which is here opened before us; and a more reflective and tragic fool, like the friend of "Lear," would be out of place in comedy. Accordingly, Shakespeare has made use of the fool, as one among many other subordinate characters, to throw light upon the leading idea; he has no more weight and importance than any of the other figures with whom we have classed him. But if we ask what common purpose is this—for what end is this register of crime and criminals brought before us—the answer is at hand: as we must gain a real insight into the essence of human virtue and morality, it is to this end necessary to look into the whole depths of man's viciousness and immorality; that is the purpose of the poem. All these sinful creatures, with their various offences, were furthermore requisite to shew how far more deserving of mercy and forgiveness all other evil-doers are, than the harsh, arrogantly virtuous, and hypocritical Angelo. . . . [These figures] were therefore necessary in order that the profound depth of the represented idea might be totally exhausted. For the comic view of things—and comedy, which is its dramatico-poetic form—work only by contrast. It is not true human virtue and morality that it directly exhibits, but rather false virtue, sin, and moral perversity. And even because the latter is broken in pieces before the might of virtue, or else proves its own destruction, truth and justice are by the contrast brought to view, not merely before the mental eye of the spectator, but bodily in the drama itself. And it is simply on this account, and not because of the occasional comic scenes and laughable characters, that "Measure for Measure" merits its title of comedy: it is, in truth, a perfect comedy in Shakespeare's noble style.

I cannot, therefore, understand on what principle this piece has been censured as *gloomy*. This blame could only have proceeded from a mind which had never felt the inexpressible pleasure of melancholy. As to its fundamental idea, that is the most cheerful that could be. An inexhaustible stream of joy wells forth from the thought that, although mere human virtue is absolutely good for nothing, we have only need to confess our weakness to find in the divine grace not only true virtue, but strength likewise, for exercising it. No doubt the way in which *life* leads us to this wisdom, is not always the merriest. But neither art, nor comedy itself, have mere laughter for their end. Indeed, to laugh aright we must even be deeply serious, and the laugh which has not a depth of gravity beneath it, is childish, silly, and most strange to art. This truth must have been felt by all who have understood and found merriment in the comedies of Shakspeare.

A few words, in conclusion, on the title of the piece. It is not intended, as might perhaps be supposed, to convey the meaning that like ought to be repaid with like, according to the old law of *talio*—a limb for a limb, and life for life. Such is its purport in an ironical sense alone. Its true sense is that of the beautiful petition in the prayer which Our Lord has taught us:—"Forgive us our trespasses as we forgive them that trespass against us." None of us, in short, ought mentally even to judge another: for not one of us is without sin, and we are all liable to the very fault which we condemn. As, therefore, each looks for mercy from God, he ought in like manner to shew mercy—to give what he asks, and with the same measure that he wishes it to be meted unto himself, he ought to mete unto others. And in this sense is like to be given for like, and Measure for Measure. (pp. 312-15)

> *Hermann Ulrici, "'Merchant of Venice'—'Measure for Measure'—'Cymbeline'," in his* Shakspeare's Dramatic Art: And His Relation to Calderon and Goethe, *translated by Rev. A.J.W. Morrison, Chapman, Brothers, 1846, pp. 300-22.*

CHARLES KNIGHT (essay date 1842)

[*Knight, an English author and publisher, dedicated his career to providing education and knowledge to the Victorian middle class. The following excerpt is taken from the 1842 edition of his* The Comedies, Histories, Tragedies, and Poems of William Shakspere. *Knight notes that* Measure for Measure *contains scenes and passages not only of great beauty but also of "grossness." Knight maintains that the unpleasant material in* Measure *contributes to Shakespeare's political theme, which he identifies as the disruptive nature of a "weak government" and a corrupt society—a theme established in the play through the contrast of setting and different characters. For further commentary on* Measure for Measure *as a political treatise, see the excerpt by A. D. Nuttall (1968).*]

"Look, the unfolding star calls up the shepherd" [IV. ii. 203]. In the midst of the most business-like and familiar directions occur these eight words of the highest poetry. By a touch almost magical Shakspere takes us in an instant out of that dark prison, where we have been surrounded with crime and suffering, to make us see the morning star bright over the hills, and hear the tinkle of the sheep-bell in the folds, and picture the shepherd bidding the flock go forth to pasture, before the sun has lighted up the dewy lawns. In the same way, throughout this very extraordinary drama, in which the whole world is represented as one great prison-house, full of passion, and ignorance, and sorrow, we have glimpses every now and then of something beyond, where there shall be no alternations of mildness and severity, but a condition of equal justice, serene as the valley under "the unfolding star," and about to rejoice in the day-spring. (p. 476)

> Heaven doth with us as we with torches do;
> Not light them for themselves: for if our virtues
> Did not go forth of us, 't were all alike
> As if we had them not. Spirits are not finely touch'd
> But to fine issues.
>
> [I. i. 32-6]

> Reason thus with life:
> If I do lose thee, I do lose a thing
> That none but fools would keep: a breath thou art,
> (Servile to all the skiey influences,)
> That dost this habitation, where thou keep'st,
> Hourly afflict.
>
> [III. i. 6-11]

> Merciful heaven!
> Thou rather, with thy sharp and sulphurous bolt,
> Splitt'st the unwedgeable and gnarled oak,
> Than the soft myrtle: But man, proud man!
> Dress'd in a little brief authority;
> Most ignorant of what he's most assur'd,
> His glassy essence,—like an angry ape,
> Plays such fantastic tricks before high heaven,
> As make the angels weep.
>
> [II. ii. 114-22]

> The sense of death is most in apprehension;
> And the poor beetle, that we tread upon,
> In corporal sufferance finds a pang as great
> As when a giant dies.
>
> [III. i. 77-80]

We select these, contrary to our usual practice of not separating the parts from the whole, for the purpose of pointing out that there is something deeper in them than the power of expressing a moral observation strikingly and poetically. They are imbued with the writer's philosophy. They form a part of the system upon which the play is written. But, opposed to passages like these, there are many single sentences scattered through this drama which, so far from dwelling on with pleasure, we hurry past—which we like not to look upon again—which *appear* to be mere grossnesses. They are, nevertheless, an integral portion of the drama—they, also, form part of the system upon which the play is written. What is true of single passages is true of single scenes. Those between Isabella and Angelo, and Isabella and Claudio, are unsurpassed in the Shaksperean drama, for force, and beauty, and the delicate management of a difficult subject. But there are other scenes which appear simply revolting, such as those in which the Clown is conspicuous; and even Barnardine, one of the most extraordinary of Shakspere's creations, will produce little beyond disgust in the casual reader. But these have, nevertheless, not crept into this drama by accident—certainly not from the desire "to make the unskilful laugh." Perhaps the effect of their introduction, coupled with the general subject of the dramatic action, is to render the entire comedy not pleasurable. Coleridge says, "This play, which is Shakspeare's throughout, is to me the most painful—say, rather, the only painful—part of his genuine works" [see excerpt above, 1818]. This is a strong opinion; and, upon the whole, a just one. (pp. 477-78)

The leading idea . . . of the character of Isabella, is that of one who abides the direst temptation which can be presented to a youthful, innocent, unsuspecting, and affectionate woman—the temptation of saving the life of one most dear, by submitting to a shame which the sophistry of self-love might represent as scarcely criminal. It is manifest that all other writers who have treated the subject have conceived that the temptation could not be resisted. Shakspere alone has confidence enough in female virtue to make Isabella never for a moment even doubt of her proper course. But he has based this virtue, most unquestionably, upon the very highest principle upon which any virtue can be built. (p. 482)

As a ruler of men the Duke is weak, and he knows his own weakness:—

> *Fri.*   It rested in your grace
> To unloose this tied-up justice when you pleas'd:
> And it in you more dreadful would have seem'd
> Than in lord Angelo.
> *Duke.*   I do fear, too dreadful:

Sith 't was my fault to give the people scope,
'T would be my tyranny to strike and gall them
For what I bid them do.

[I. iii. 31-7]

And yet he does really strike and gall them through another;
but he saves himself the labour and the slander.

And here, then, as it appears to us, we have a key to the
purpose of the poet in the introduction of what constitutes the
most unpleasant portion of this play,—the exhibition of a very
gross general profligacy. There is an atmosphere of impurity
hanging like a dense fog over the city of the poet. The philosophical ruler, the saintly votaress, and the sanctimonious
deputy, appear to belong to another region to that in which
they move. The grossness is not merely described or inferred;—
but we see those who minister to the corruptions, and we are
brought in contact with the corrupted. This, possibly, was not
necessary for the higher dramatic effects of the comedy; but
it was necessary for those lessons of political philosophy which
we think Shakspere here meant to inculcate, and which he
appears to us on many occasions to have kept in view in his
later plays. Mr. [Henry] Hallam has most truly said of 'Measure
for Measure' that "the depths and intricacies of being, which
he (Shakspere) has searched and sounded with intense reflection, perplex and harass him" [see Additional Bibliography].
In this play he manifests, as we apprehend, his philosophical
view of a corrupt state of manners fostered by weak government: but the subject is scarcely dramatic, and it struggles with
his own proper powers. Here we have an exhibition of crimes
of passion, and crimes of ignorance. There stands the Duke,
the representative of a benevolent and tolerant executive power
which does not meddle with the people,—which subjects them
to no harsh restrictions,—which surrounds them with no biting
penalties; but which utterly fails in carrying out the essential
principle of government when it disregards prevention, and
sees no middle course between neglect and punishment. A new
system is to be substituted; the *laissez faire* is to be succeeded
by the "axe upon the block, very ready" [IV. iii. 37-8]; and
then come all the commonplaces by which a reign of terror is
to be defended:—

We must not make a scarecrow of the law,
Setting it up to fear the birds of prey,
And let it keep one shape, till custom make it
Their perch, and not their terror.

[II. i. 1-4]

The law hath not been dead, though it hath slept:
Those many had not dar'd to do that evil,
If the first that did the edict infringe
Had answer'd for his deed; now, 't is awake.

[II. ii. 90-3]

The philosophical poet sweeps these saws away with an indignation which is the more emphatic as coming from the
mouth of the only truly moral character of the whole drama:—

Could great men thunder
As Jove himself does, Jove would ne'er be quiet,
For every pelting, petty officer
Would use his heaven for thunder: nothing but thunder.

[II. ii. 110-14]

But he does more—he exhibits to us the every-day working of
the hot fit succeeding the cold of legislative and executive
power. It works always with injustice. The Duke of the comedy
is behind the scenes, and sees how it works. The weak governor

resumes his authority, and with it he must resume his principles, and he therefore pardons all. The mouth-repenting deputy,
and the callous ruffian, they each escape. We forget; he does
not pardon *all;* the prating coxcomb, who has spoken slander
of his own person, is alone punished. Was this accident in the
poet? Great crimes may be looked over by weak governments,
but the pettiest libeller of power is inevitably punished. The
catastrophe of this comedy necessarily leaves upon the mind
an unsatisfactory impression. Had Angelo been adequately
punished it would have been more unsatisfactory. When the
Duke took the management of the affair into his own hands,
and averted the consequences of Angelo's evil intentions by a
series of deceptions, he threw away the power of punishing
those evil intentions. We agree with Coleridge that the pardon
and marriage of Angelo "baffle the strong indignant claims of
justice" [see excerpt above, 1818]; but we cannot see how it
could be otherwise. The poet, as it appears to us, exhibits to
the end the inadequacy of human laws to enforce public morals
upon a system of punishment. But he has not forgotten to
exhibit to us incidentally the most beautiful lessons of tolerance; not using 'Measure for Measure' in the sense of the *jus
talionis,* but in a higher spirit—that spirit which moves Isabella
to supplicate for mercy towards him who had most wronged
her:—

Most bounteous sir,
Look, if it please you, on this man condemn'd,
As if my brother liv'd: I partly think,
A due sincerity govern'd his deeds,
Till he did look on me; since it is so,
Let him not die.

[V. i. 443-48]
(pp. 483-85)

*Charles Knight, "Supplementary Notice: 'Measure
for Measure'," in* The Comedies, Histories, Tragedies, and Poems of William Shakspere, Vol. III *by
William Shakespeare, edited by Charles Knight, second edition 1842. Reprint by AMS Press, 1968, pp.
476-85.*

G. G. GERVINUS   (essay date 1849-50)

*[One of the most widely read Shakespearean critics of the latter
half of the nineteenth century, the German critic Gervinus was
praised by such eminent contemporaries as Edward Dowden, F.
J. Furnivall, and James Russell Lowell; however, he is little
known in the English-speaking world today. Like his predecessor
Hermann Ulrici, Gervinus wrote in the tradition of the "philosophical criticism" developed in Germany in the mid-nineteenth
century. Under the influence of August Wilhelm Schlegel's literary
theory and Georg Wilhelm Friedrich Hegel's philosophy, German
critics like Gervinus tended to focus their analyses around a search
for the literary work's organic unity and ethical import. Gervinus
believed that Shakespeare's works contained a rational ethical
system independent of any religion—in contrast to Ulrici, for
whom Shakespeare's morality was basically Christian. The excerpt below is taken from the English translation of Gervinus's*
Shakespeare *(1849-50). He contends that Measure for Measure
evidences Shakespeare's concept of moderation, both in "the
exercise of justice"—punishment with measure—and in the application of the Golden Rule in all human relationships. Gervinus
describes the Duke as a "superior scene-shifter" who acts as an
earthly Providence and plays the dramatic part of the classical
Greek chorus. He details Angelo's decline into sin and attempts
to explain why his repentance is believable and his redemption
just. Gervinus also finds that Isabella is the play's only representative of "a complete human nature," serving as a more effective example of leaderhip than the Duke or Angelo in her*

balance of honor and compassion, authority and mercy; Isabella represents what Gervinus describes as the mean between the extremes offered by the Duke and Angelo. For additional commentary on the nature of justice and mercy in Measure for Measure, *see the excerpts by August Wilhelm Schlegel (1808), Walter Pater (1874), Denton J. Snider (1890), and Muriel C. Bradbrook (1941).]*

In spite of [Shakespeare's improvements upon Cinthio's novel and Whetstone's play], most readers at the present day feel that all that is offensive in the tenor of [*Measure for Measure*] is not yet wholly removed. We are not inclined to pardon the poet for having brought upon the stage the cruel subjects of the Italian novelists both here, in *All's Well that Ends Well,* and in *Cymbeline,* and for having required us to look with the more sensitive eye on the representation of that which in narration falls less forcibly on the blunter ear. . . . [The objections of earlier critics] would be indisputable were we convinced, from the course of action and the nature of the actors, that a sincere repentance on the part of Angelo was inconceivable, and were we to admit that 'severe, indignant justice' [see excerpt above by Samuel Taylor Coleridge, 1818] is the only true justice—a justice in this instance well employed. To form a correct judgment on these passions it is necessary that we should as usual go back to the motives of action, and discover their psychological connection.

A novel taken from Shakespeare's play, furnished with all his characteristic touches and with his representation of circumstances, and placed by the side of the original source or by the side of Whetstone's play, would evidence, in the simplest and most striking manner, the wonderful difference from others which renders our poet so unique and distinct. What a richness of reflection do we meet with in Shakespeare when we search into the elements of the facts before us! What a depth in the characters, compelling attention from us even before we see them entangled in such painful intricacies! What a boldness in bringing the very noblest characters into these same odious intricacies, just as if he aimed at multiplying the difficulties and contradictions of the plot! And, moreover, what a careful construction of circumstances, so that from the outset our apprehension is calmed as to the gloomy incidents, and we are allowed to anticipate an end not altogether disastrous!

In the first place, in how masterly a manner is the ground prepared on which the poet has placed the scene of these habits, characters, and incidents! The scene is laid in Vienna. Moral corruption here 'boils and bubbles till it o'erruns' [V. i. 318-19]; society is destroyed by it, and all decorum is lost. . . . Debauchery has become a common custom. Every mind seems occupied with transactions and matters of this kind. The man who, like Angelo, has never exposed himself to evil report, is not regarded as sound and perfect; the Duke, who has never had intercourse with women, escapes not the poisonous tongue of Lucio, the light-minded calumniator; and even in the cloister, where the Duke hides himself, Friar Thomas believes at first that an affair of gallantry drives him to that place of secrecy. Existing restraints are cast down; unbridled liberty plucks justice by the nose; law, like an unused rod to the child, is rather mocked at than feared. (pp. 486-87)

The reigning duke, who had thus allowed this law to slumber, had done so from kindness of heart and innate mildness. . . . His whole nature is that of a man of moderation, gentleness, and calmness, his whole endeavour that of a circumspect philosopher. He loves his people, but he does not relish their loud applause and thronging, nor does he think the man of safe discretion that affects it. He has a leaning to solitude, and plays

Act II. Scene ii. Angelo, Isabella, and guards. Frontispiece to the Rowe edition (1709). By permission of the Folger Shakespeare Library.

the part of a friar perhaps even better than that of a statesman; his earnest endeavour was always to know himself, but it also seemed a kind of necessity with him to know men and to test the instruments of his rule. This circumspect wisdom, never seeing things imperfectly or from one point of view, shows itself also in his conduct respecting the morality or immorality of the people of Vienna, which by degrees had attained to such a height that the prince could no longer remain inactive. (pp. 487-88)

[Angelo] presents the strange phenomenon of an isolated stoic in the midst of a Sybarite city; we see him with a serious suitable bearing, with sober countenance and well-considered words, as if he would frighten away all kind of levity. . . . That this virtue and sobriety in such extreme youth is constrained and exaggerated is evidenced by the anxious care with which Angelo lays greater stress upon outward appearance than upon inward reality. He is continually upon his guard against envy, he has the most nervous ambition never for a moment to lose his irreproachable reputation. This ambition, this pride in his virtue, he hardly even ventures to confess to himself in his soliloquies. This ambition is closely connected with his aspiring endeavour after outward rank and dignity. (pp. 488-89)

These unnaturally strained endeavours are observed by the psychological Duke in the useful, promising young man thus richly endowed by nature. He appears to distrust his political as well as his moral ambition, and he welcomes the opportunity of at once testing both. . . . The manner in which we see the circumspect man watching every incident, and, as it were, playing the part of Providence, has the effect of rendering us prepared and calm as the events unfold before us; all that is painful and severe in them thus becomes much mitigated; in the play itself we perceive the superior scene-shifter and observer, before whom the action seems to pass like a drama within a drama; in this way we are unconcerned for the evil issue of the evil actions. (pp. 489-90)

Now begins the official career of the eager young statesman. He 'picks out' from the dust the Draco-like statutes; the law is no longer to remain a derided scarecrow: unexceptional mercy is no longer to prevail, but unexceptional justice. . . . With the pulling down of [the] abodes of crime, crime is in no wise extirpated, it only changes its place. Habitual sinners do not allow themselves to be frightened by admonition and threatening. Besides, the instruments of justice err: the stout Elbow, of the race of the Dogberrys, apprehends a poor knave who, according to the intimations of the Clown, is indeed not capable of sinning, while in Elbow's own house matters are worse, and his own wife is notoriously more guilty than the imprisoned Froth. This then, according to Shakespeare's method, is the burlesque parody of Angelo's administration of justice, who is at last more open to sin than any of his delinquents. For those who pass unpunished in this system are just the most obdurate and the most crafty, whom the law ought to have touched first of all. A Lucio, the infamous slanderer and liar, whose familiar sin it is 'with maids to seem the lapwing and to jest' [II. iv. 32], who coldly brings his accomplice into misfortune as his sacrifice, but hesitates not to free himself with false oaths, this incorrigible man is just out of reach of the law, he mocks at its severity, and passes unpunished, while a lesser offence is to bring his friend Claudio to the block. (pp. 490-91)

[Claudio] erred because, with a lively and sanguine nature, very different to Angelo's, he surrenders himself to every momentary impression. The poet shows us the excitable and easily influenced nature of the man very distinctly in the scene in which he is at first filled with the Duke's representations of the evils of life and the consolations of death, but immediately afterwards he is overwhelmed by his own ideas of the horrors of death, compared to which even the weariest life seems to him a Paradise. We perceive the same nature subsequently, when, in the first feeling of honour, he utterly rejects the price at which Isabella is to purchase his life, and immediately afterwards, when he pictures to himself the terror of death, he would gladly see her pay the price. (p. 492)

[Isabella] possesses, like the Duke, in well-balanced proportion, that two-sided nature, the capacity to enjoy the world according to circumstances or to dispense with it. . . . Strong as she is, she does not hesitate to take upon herself and her whole sex the show of weakness, a great contrast in this to Angelo, who falls with a show of strength and moral austerity. When her virtue is put to the test she exhibits herself in truth as the hero she had formerly supposed Angelo to be; and, sympathisingly as she had before felt for Claudio, as soon as he wishes to purchase his life with her shame, regardless of her twice-repeated reminder of their honourable deceased father, she indignantly rejects him, for she now regards his sin

not as 'accidental, but a trade' [III. i. 148]. However much this severity and heroism may seem in its asceticism and sobriety similar to Angelo's pride of virtue and show of honour, yet even in this she is the opposite to Angelo, being so far from all false pretensions that, upon the friar-duke's remonstrance that 'virtue is bold and goodness never fearful' [III. i. 208], she hesitates not to take upon herself the appearance of crime for the sake of a truly virtuous object, and agrees to his adventurous plan, which by a pious fraud is to procure safety to her brother, and to restore her faithless lover to the rejected Mariana. Sympathy with her brother does not lead her to disregard the sin, but only the appearance of sin; feeling and womanliness are developed in the very action which seems to demand a masculine renunciation of womanly delicacy. A similar instance is again subsequently to be remarked in her when she is petitioned by Mariana to implore for the life of Angelo, whom she still regards as the murderer of her brother. It may seem to require the strength of masculine asceticism, when she even now calms herself upon her brother's death that he 'had but justice' [V. i. 448]; but it certainly demanded the utmost womanly gentleness and pity, and the absence of every feeling of spite and revenge, when, in the same breath, she petitions for Angelo's life. The whole character of this woman is pervaded by a mixture of commiseration and strength of character, of personal purity and forbearance for the weakness of others, of tenderness and firmness, of womanly timidity, and even mistrust of self and resolute decision of action, of modesty and ability, of humility and the exhibition of mental and moral power. She stands in the midst of the universal depravity, elevated in stainless purity of soul far above all the basenesses of crime, a being whose thoughts were already wafted above the earth, and whose feelings were free from the emotions of all common passion.

However much such a being, from the almost supernatural greatness of her virtue, may forfeit our sympathy, yet, if we are to give a slight symbolic interpretation to poetry, it was in excellent accordance with the poet's plan to present just such an angel as the tempter of Angelo's virtue. (pp. 493-94)

She touches him . . . on the side of his pride of virtue, and at the same time of that hypocrisy and pretence of sanctity which lay deep in the secrets of his bosom; what wonder, then, that all the hitherto quiet feelings of his soul burst forth at last in the expression of deep astonishment: 'She speaks, and 'tis such sense, that my sense breeds with it' [II. ii. 142-43]. He receives in an understanding and ready spirit the pregnant riddles which she utters, since every word is drawn from the innermost system of his own principles, his thoughts, and his whole nature. (p. 497)

He confesses . . . , when we are alone with him, that he is on the way leading to temptation, 'where prayers cross' [II. ii. 159] his wishes. We find him thus again subsequently, when his own prayers and thoughts are at variance; heaven has his empty words, his imagination anchors on Isabella. Suddenly the suppressed feeling revenges itself on the unnatural restraint, and all that has made the man hitherto ambitious and proud fails him, his studies are grown 'feared and tedious' [II. iv. 9] to him, and his virtuous gravity he could change for 'an idle plume' [II. iv. 11]. He who was never in the least exposed to the temptation of light women's art or nature, *he* yields to the dangerous temptation of modesty; the cunning enemy catches the saint with a saint, and goads him on to sin 'in loving virtue' [II. ii. 182]. Isabella herself, after she had surveyed the whole course of Angelo's error and had suffered from it, bears witness to him that she must believe a due sincerity governed his deeds till he met with her. . . . But why is not his first thought of an honourable and lawful love? Why do his thoughts tarry at once upon the picture he so condemns, while he asks himself:—

> Having waste ground enough,
> Shall we desire to raze the sanctuary,
> And pitch our evils there?
>
> [II. ii. 169-71]

If he regards her, as was possible from his knowledge of her, as an already dedicated nun, his designs were all the more criminal. But even without this, his connection with Mariana must have been in his constant remembrance, and he had to fear her protest against every marriage; he avoids the public announcement of this secret history, and loses himself more and more in the intoxication of his passion, which seduces him to take such an advantage of his power and opportunity as allowed him to maintain the appearance of blamelessness, except in the eyes of one whose estimation ought indeed to have out-balanced that of all the rest of the world. His earlier heartless behaviour towards Mariana is thus the source of a second greater outrage; the nature at work in the one influences this new connection also. . . . The vein of tyranny, which had slumbered in this man of cold conventionality, awakes as soon as he is excited and has once cast the mask aside; he torments her now even with the threat of aggravating her brother's death. When he now believes himself to have reached his aim, and has committed the one misdeed, he is drawn still further along the downhill path of crime; and more and more apparent becomes the deep shadow cast by the light of this richly-gifted man, and the evil disposition hitherto concealed within his soul. (pp. 497-99)

As soon as Angelo has reached this extreme, repentance seizes him; he perceives with fear into what evil the loss of virtue is resistlessly carrying him; he stands crippled and incapable for everything; the summons of the Duke, who announces his return and invites public information of all injustice, strikes his heart with anguish. How gladly would he believe that the Duke is mad! What frightful torture must oppress him when he hears the modest Isabella in the open street denouncing fearful accusation of such nameless baseness, and this in the man whose virtue had hitherto appeared unequalled! How must pain and despair seize him when he hears the voice of the rejected Mariana, and sees her veil drop! How disgraced at last he stands before all the world, he who till now has been regarded as a saint! How confounded must he depart, constrained to consummate the formality of marriage with Mariana, after the consummation of which his possessions are to fall to the forsaken one, and his execution is to take the place of Claudio's. A load of dishonour and disgrace is now cast upon him, to whom honour and dignity, or at any rate the mantle and show of dignity and honour, had been beyond everything; and this veiling mantle is now so violently withdrawn that the very body and substance of his honour is also lacerated. How deeply degraded he who hitherto had stood highest in opinion now stands in the estimation of the good, of the Duke and of Escalus! We may thus readily believe him when he says to the latter that 'sorrow sticks so deep in his penitent heart, that he craves death more willingly than mercy' [V. i. 474-76]. For must not death to a criminal of this character have been a greater benefit than a life of shame? His life is, however, to be spared, and he is to be raised from his fall. The poet, in this character, has designed a new variation of his favourite theme of *show*. The task in Angelo is a worthy

sequel for the actor who represented the gross hypocrisy arising from the systematic selfishness of a villain like Richard, and the regardless contempt of all show, based as in Prince Henry on the absence of all selfishness. . . . The task demands that the actor should not allow the mental endowments and the germ of good in this character utterly to be lost sight of in the midst of his fall; that he should let the original nobility of this nature appear through all its immoderate errors, and thus leave open the sure prospect of a radical reformation and repentance. Or could it be true, as Coleridge was of opinion [see excerpt above, 1818], that sincere repentance on the part of Angelo was impossible? Certainly, after this deed, there was no more *show* for this man. The eyes of the tester would no more leave him; he would deceive no one again. He has henceforth only the prospect of becoming a great criminal or of raising himself to lasting virtue and honour. Isabella—she who has most to complain against him—petitions for him, and seems to trust in the germ of good within him. Mariana—she who takes the greatest interest in him—will keep him with all his faults, and she pleads in his behalf that 'men are moulded out of faults, and become much more the better for being a little bad' [V. i. 439-41]. (pp. 499-501)

But the severe indignant justice which Coleridge desired was not executed upon Angelo. Not though he had so solemnly challenged the whole rigour of the law against himself and had uttered his own sentence! Not though he had even deserved a severer doom than Claudio, against whom he had committed a judicial murder when his own greater crime was to go unpunished! . . . Even the Duke's own feeling and sentence seemed unrelentingly to condemn him. If he once pronounced himself a tyrant for suddenly punishing that which he had before overlooked, how must he have regarded Angelo, who punished with death a crime less severe than that which he had himself committed? And, moreover, this severe condemnation had solemnly fallen from the lips of the Duke:—

> And Angelo for Claudio, death for death:
> Haste still pays haste, and leisure answers leisure,
> Like doth greet like, and Measure still for Measure.
>
> [V. i. 409-11]

This equal retribution has ever been the poetical expression of a 'severe and indignant justice,' and its sentence seemed here to be inexorably pronounced. Yet, apart from poetry, Angelo's doom would not be in law altogether in conformity with justice. Angelo's double crime—the disgrace of Isabella and the death of Claudio—had indeed not been carried out. The severest law could have pronounced upon Angelo only the highest chastisement for attempt. Moreover, the Duke is not in earnest as to his sentence of retaliation; it is only one of those exciting tests which he has delighted in inflicting upon Claudio and Isabella and now upon Angelo. . . . And how could the Duke execute the sentence of death on Angelo, when he had himself expressly led him upon this ground of temptation and trial by reviving severe discipline, and by confiding to him so high and slippery a position? . . . And how could *he* execute this severe act of punishment; he who shuddered to consign to death the gipsy Barnardine—a brute, a Caliban, a heavy stubborn malefactor? *he*, in whose heart, not 'severe indignant justice,' but mercy and mildness lay? *he* who demanded of the prince who bears the sword of heaven that he should pay to others neither more nor less than he could justify after weighing his own offences and respecting human weaknesses?

And this indeed is not only the spirit of the Duke, but that of our whole play, in which the Duke is, as it were, the chorus:—

namely, that true justice is not jealous justice, but *that* circumspect equity alone, which suffers neither mercy nor the severe letter of the law to rule without exception, which awards punishment not *measure for measure,* but *with* measure. Neither the lax mildness which the Duke had allowed to prevail and which he himself condemns, nor the over-severe curb which Angelo applied, is to be esteemed as the right procedure; the sluggishness which gives license to sin, and the system of intimidation which destroys the sinner with the sin, meet with the same condemnation. This play, in its strikingly practical character, has become like a defence of the corrective system, the only system of punishment which a poet's moral intuition could pronounce to be suitable to the world. The Duke loves to employ intimidation in suspense, threats, and torments of imagination, but in actual cases of penalty he permits mercy to rule when possible, thus giving opportunity for moral reformation. (pp. 501-03)

But whilst our play in the first place recommends moderation in the exercise of justice, it occupies at the same time a far more general ground, and extends this doctrine to all human relations, exhibiting, as it were, the kernel of that opinion so often expressed by Shakespeare, of a wise medium in all things. It calls us universally from all extremes, even from that of the good, because in every extreme there lies an overstraining, which avenges itself by a contrary reaction. . . . The single character of Angelo, with the unnaturally overstrained exaggeration of his nature, counterbalances a series of contrasts; his severity counterbalances the mildness of the Duke, his sobriety the levity of Claudio, his heartlessness the tender weakness of his faithful Mariana, and his anxious adherence to the appearance of good Lucio's indifference to the basest reputation. Between these extremes stands Isabella alone, a type of a *complete* human nature, rendering it plain that all extreme is but imperfect and fragmentary; that moderation is not weakness and indolence; that far rather it forms in man the true moral centre of gravity, which holds him secure from all waverings and errors, and qualifies him for the highest power which can be required of man. (pp. 503-04)

> G. G. Gervinus, "'Measure for Measure'," in his Shakespeare Commentaries, *translated by F. E. Bunnètt, revised edition, 1877. Reprint by AMS Press, Inc., 1971, pp. 485-504.*

WALTER BAGEHOT (essay date 1853)

[*Bagehot was an English economist, historian, journalist, literary critic, and political philosopher whose analysis of Shakespeare's psychological temperament widely influenced the biographical critics of the nineteenth century. The following excerpt is taken from his study* Shakespeare, the Man, *which was originally published as "Shakspere as Revealed in his Writings" in the August, 1853 issue of* Prospective Review. *He describes Angelo as the dramatic embodiment of Shakespeare's "malevolent pleasure" and a "natural hypocrite," a man whose passionate instincts have been so long submerged that he impresses himself with his own rectitude. The nature of Angelo's hypocrisy is also assessed in the essays by G. G. Gervinus (1849-50), H. N. Hudson (1872), and G. Wilson Knight (1930).*]

[The] malevolence of Shakespeare is to be found in the play of *Measure for Measure.* We agree with Hazlitt, that this play seems to be written, perhaps more than any other, *con amore* ["with love"], and with a relish; and this seems to be the reason why, notwithstanding the unpleasant nature of its plot, and the absence of any very attractive character, it is yet one of the plays which take hold on the mind most easily and most powerfully. Now the entire character of Angelo, which is the expressive feature of the piece, is nothing but a successful embodiment of the pleasure, the malevolent pleasure, which a warm-blooded and expansive man takes in watching the rare, the dangerous and inanimate excesses of the constrained and cold-blooded. One seems to see Shakespeare, with his bright eyes and his large lips and buoyant face, watching with a pleasant excitement the excesses of his thin-lipped and calculating creation, as though they were the excesses of a real person. It is the complete picture of a natural hypocrite, who does not consciously disguise strong impulses, but whose very passions seem of their own accord to have disguised themselves and retreated into the recesses of the character, yet only to recur even more dangerously when their proper period is expired, when the will is cheated into security by their absence, and the world (and, it may be, the "judicious person" himself) is impressed with a sure reliance in his chilling and remarkable rectitude. (pp. 37-8)

> Walter Bagehot, in his Shakespeare, the Man: An Essay, The University Society, *1901, 48 p.*

REV. H. N. HUDSON (essay date 1872)

[*Hudson was a nineteenth-century American clergyman and literary scholar whose Harvard edition of Shakespeare's works, published in twenty volumes between 1880 and 1881, contributed substantially to the growth of Shakespeare's popularity in America. Hudson also published two critical works on Shakespeare, one a collection of lectures, the other—and the more successful—a critical biography entitled* Shakespeare, His Life, Art, and Characters *(1872). In the excerpt below, Hudson attempts to explicate the ethical issues raised in* Measure for Measure *by focusing on the characters. He maintains that Angelo is initially a self-deceiver who fails to accept his own frailties, then, after his confrontation with Isabella and his lustful desires, he consciously falsifies his actions and becomes a hypocrite. He claims that the emphasis on Isabella's chastity heightens both the parallels and the contrasts between her and Angelo; Hudson also considers Isabella the best of "Shakespeare's matchless cabinet of female excellence." He interprets the Duke's motives as pure, but states that his actions reveal that he is too fond of intrigue, and is more a philosopher than a ruler. Hudson concludes that justice and mercy are never in harmony in* Measure for Measure, *a statement that contradicts the interpretations of G. G. Gervinus (1849-50), Walter Pater (1874), and Denton J. Snider (1890).*]

Measure for Measure, in its vein of thought and complexion of character, is the deepest of Shakespeare's comedies,—deeper even than some of his tragedies. The foundation principles of ethics are here explored far as the plummet of thought can sound; the subtleties and intricacies of the human heart are searched with an insight which the sharpest and most inquisitive criticism may strive in vain to follow. The mind almost loses itself in attempting to trace out through their course the various and complicated lines of reflection here suggested. (p. 398)

The strongly-marked peculiarities of the piece in language, cast of thought, and moral temper, have invested it with great psychological interest, and bred a strange desire among critics to connect it in some way with the author's mental history,— with some supposed crisis in his feelings and experience. (p. 399)

[Surely] in the life of so earnest and thoughtful a man as Shakespeare, there might well be, nay, there must have been, times when, without any special woundings or bruisings of fortune, his mind got fascinated by the appalling mystery of evil that haunts our fallen nature.

That such darker hours, however occasioned, were more frequent at one period of the Poet's life than at others, is indeed probable. And it was equally natural that their coming should sometimes engage him in heart-tugging and brain-sweating efforts to scrutinize the inscrutable workings of human guilt, and thus stamp itself strongly upon the offspring of his mind. Thus, without any other than the ordinary progress of thoughtful spirits, we should naturally have a middle period, when the early enthusiasm of hope had passed away, and before the deeper, calmer, but not less cheerful tranquility of resignation had set in. For so it is apt to be in this life of ours: the angry barkings of fortune, or what seem such, have their turn with us; "the fretful fever and the stir unprofitable" work our souls full of discord and perturbation; but after a while these things pass away, and are followed by a more placid and genial time; the experienced insufficiency of man for himself having charmed our wrestlings of thought into repose, and our spirits having undergone the chastening and subduing power of life's sterner discipline.

In some such passage, then, I should rather presume the unique conception of *Measure for Measure* to have been formed in the Poet's mind. I say unique, because this is his only instance of comedy where the wit seems to foam and sparkle up from a fountain of bitterness; where even the humour is made pungent with sarcasm; and where the poetry is marked with tragic austerity. In none of his plays does he discover less of leaning upon pre-existing models, or a more manly negligence, perhaps sometimes carried to excess, of those lighter graces of manner which none but the greatest minds may safely despise. His genius is here out in all its colossal individuality, and he seems to have meant it should be so; as if he felt quite sure of having now reached his mastership; so that henceforth, instead of leaning on those who had gone before, he was to be himself a leaning-place for those who should follow.

Accordingly the play abounds in fearless grapplings and strugglings of mind with matters too hard to consist with much facility and gracefulness of tongue. The thought is strong, and in its strength careless of appearances, and seems rather wishing than fearing to have its roughnesses seen: the style is rugged, irregular, abrupt, sometimes running into an almost forbidding sternness, but everywhere throbbing with life: often a whole page of meaning is condensed and rammed into a clause or an image, so that the force thereof beats and reverberates through the entire scene: with little of elaborate grace or finish, we have bold, deep strokes, where the want of finer softenings and shadings is more than made up by increased energy and expressiveness; the words going right to the spot, and leaving none of their work undone. (pp. 406-07)

Whether from the nature of the subject, or the mode of treating it, or both, *Measure for Measure* is generally regarded as one of the least attractive, though most instructive, of Shakespeare's plays. Coleridge, in those fragments of his critical lectures which now form our best text-book of English criticism, says, "This play, which is Shakespeare's throughout, is to me the most painful—rather say the only painful—part of his genuine works" [see excerpt above, 1818]. From this language, sustained as it is by other high authorities, I probably should not dissent; but when, in his *Table Talk*, he says that "Isabella herself contrives to be unamiable, and Claudio is detestable," I can by no means go along with him. . . . [Though] I do indeed feel that Claudio were rather to be pitied than blamed, whatever course he had taken in so terrible an alternative, yet the conduct of his sister strikes me as every way

creditable to her. Her reproaches were indeed too harsh, if they sprang from want of love; but such is evidently not the case. The truth is, she is in a very hard struggle between affection and principle: she needs, and she hopes, to have the strain upon her womanly fortitude lightened by the manly fortitude of her brother; and her harshness of reproof discovers the natural workings of a tender and deep affection, in an agony of disappointment at being urged, by one for whom she would die, to an act which she shrinks from with noble horror, and justly considers worse than death. So that we here have the keen anguish of conflicting feelings venting itself in a severity which, though unmerited, serves to disclose the more impressively her nobleness of character. (pp. 408-09)

[Henry Hallam], referring to the part of Mariana as indispensable to "a satisfactory termination" of the story, objects, that "it is never explained how the Duke had become acquainted with this secret, and, being acquainted with it, how he had preserved his esteem and confidence in Angelo" [see Additional Bibliography]. But, surely, we are given to understand at the outset that the Duke has not preserved the esteem and confidence in question. In his first scene with Friar Thomas, among his reasons for the action he has on foot, he makes special mention of this one:

> Lord Angelo is precise;
> *Stands at a guard with envy;* scarce confesses
> That his blood flows, or that his appetite
> Is more to bread than stone: *hence shall we see by,*
> *If power change purpose, what our SEEMERS be.*
> [I. iii. 50-4]

Which clearly infers that his main purpose in assuming the disguise of a monk is to unmask the deputy, and demonstrate to others what has long been known to himself. And he throws out other hints of a belief or suspicion that Angelo is angling for emolument or popularity, and baiting his hook with great apparent strictness and sanctity of life; thus putting on sheep's clothing, in order to play the wolf with more safety and success. As to the secret concerning Mariana, it seems enough that the Duke knows it, that the knowledge justifies his distrust, and that when the time comes he uses it for a good purpose; the earlier part of the play thus preparing quietly for what is to follow, and the later explaining what went before. In truth, the Duke is better able to understand the deputy's character than to persuade others of it: this is one of his motives for the stratagem. And a man of his wisdom, even if he have no available facts in the case, might well suspect an austerity so theatrical as Angelo's to be rather an art than a virtue: he could not well be ignorant that, when men are so forward to air their graces and *make* their light shine, they can hardly be aiming at any glory but their own. (pp. 409-10)

Angelo is at first not so properly a hypocrite as a self-deceiver. For it is very considerable that he wishes to be, and sincerely thinks he is, what he affects and appears to be; as is plain from his consternation at the wickedness which opportunity awakens into conscious action within him. . . . Even so Angelo for self-ends imitates sanctity, and then gets taken in by his own imitation. This "mystery of iniquity" locks him from all true knowledge of himself. He must be worse before he will be better. The refined hypocrisies which so elude his eye, and thus nurse his self-righteous pride, must put on a grosser form, till he cannot choose but see himself as he is. The secret devil within must blaze out in a shape too palpable to be ignored. And so, as often happens where the subtleties of self-deceit are thus cherished, he at length proceeds a downright conscious hypocrite, this too of the deepest dye.

Angelo's original fault lay in forgetting or ignoring his own frailty. As a natural consequence, his "darling sin is pride that apes humility." And his conceit of virtue,—"my gravity, wherein (let no man hear me) I take pride" [II. iv. 9-10],— while it keeps him from certain vices, is itself a far greater vice than any it keeps him from; insomuch that his interviews with Isabella may almost be said to *elevate* him into lust. They at least bring him to a just vision of his inward self. The serpent charms of self-deceit which he has so hugged are now broken. . . . So indeed it must be where men turn their virtues into food of spiritual pride; which is the hardest of all sores to be cured, "inasmuch as that which rooteth out other vices causeth this." And perhaps the array of low and loathsome vices, which the Poet has clustered about Angelo in the persons of Lucio, Pompey, and Mrs. Overdone, was necessary, to make us feel how unspeakably worse than any or all of these is Angelo's pride of virtue. (pp. 412-13)

The placing of Isabella, "a thing ensky'd and sainted" [I. iv. 34], and who truly *is* all that Angelo seems, side by side with such a breathing, shining mass of pitch, is one of those dramatic audacities wherein none perhaps but a Shakespeare could safely indulge. Of her character the most prolific hint that is given is what she says to the disguised Duke, when he is urging her to fasten her ear on his advisings touching the part of Mariana: "I have spirit to do any thing that appears not foul in the truth of my spirit" [III. i. 205-07]. That is, she cares not what face her action may wear to the world, nor how much reproach it may bring on her from others, if it will only leave her the society, which she has never parted from, of a clean breast and a pure conscience. (pp. 413-14)

With great strength of intellect and depth of feeling she unites an equal power of imagination, the whole being pervaded, quickened, and guided by a still, intense religious enthusiasm. And because her virtue is securely rooted and grounded in religion, therefore she never thinks of it as her own, but only as a gift from the Being whom she adores, and who is her only hope for the keeping of what she has. Which suggests the fundamental point of contrast between her and Angelo, whose virtue, if such it may be called, is nothing, nay, worse than nothing, because it is a virtue of his own making, is without any inspiration from the one Source of all true good, and so has no basis but pride, which is itself a bubble. Accordingly her character appears to me among the finest, in some respects the very finest, in Shakespeare's matchless cabinet of female excellence. (p. 414)

It is not to be denied, indeed, that Isabella's chastity is rather too demonstrative and self-pronounced; but this is because of the unblushing and emphatic licentiousness of her social environment. Goodness cannot remain undemonstrative amidst such a rank demonstrativeness of its opposite: the necessity it is under of fighting against so much and such aggressive evil forces it into stress, and so into taking a full measure of itself. Isabella, accordingly, is deeply conscious and mindful of her virtue, which somewhat mars the beauty of it, I admit; but in the circumstances it could not be otherwise: with such a strong stew of corruption boiling and bubbling all about her, it was not possible that purity in her case should retain that bland, unconscious repose which is indeed its greatest charm. From the prevailing rampancy of vice, a certain air of oversternness and rigidity has wrought itself into her character, displacing somewhat of its proper sweetness and amiability: but, in the right view of things, this loss is well made up in that she is the more an object of reverence; albeit I have to confess that she would touch me rather more potently, if she had a little more of loveliness and a little less of awfulness. (p. 416)

The Duke has been rather hardly dealt with by critics. Shakespeare—than whom it would not be easy to find a better judge of what belongs to wisdom and goodness—seems to have meant him for a wise and a good man: yet he represents him as having rather more skill and pleasure in strategical arts and roundabout ways than is altogether in keeping with such a character. Some of his alleged reasons for the action he goes about reflect no honour on him; but it is observable that the sequel does not approve them to have been his real ones: his conduct, as the action proceeds, infers better motives than his speech offered at the beginning; which naturally suggests that there may have been more of purpose than of truth in his speaking. His first dialogue with Angelo is, no doubt, partly ironical. A liberal, thoughtful, and merciful prince, but with more of whim and caprice than exactly suits the dignity of his place, humanity speaks richly from his lips; yet in his actions the philosopher and the divine are better shown than the statesman and ruler. Therewithal he seems to take a very questionable delight in moving about as an unseen providence, by secret counsels leading the wicked designs of others to safe and just results. It is indeed true, as Heraud observes regarding him, that so "Divine Providence, while it deputes its authority to the office-bearers of the world, is still present both with them and it, and ever ready to punish the evil-doer": still I doubt of its being just the thing for the world's office-bearers to undertake the functions of Providence in that particular. Probably the Duke should not be charged with a fanaticism of intrigue; but he comes something nearer to it than befits a mind of the first order. Schlegel thinks "he has more pleasure in overhearing his subjects than in governing them in the usual way of princes"; and sets him down as an exception to the proverb, "A cowl does not make a monk" [see excerpt above, 1808]: and perhaps his princely virtues are somewhat obscured by the disguise which so completely transforms him into a monk. Whether he acts upon the wicked principle with which that fraternity is so often reproached, or not, it is pretty certain that some of his means can be justified by nothing but the end. But perhaps, in the vast complexity of human motives and affairs, a due exercise of fairness and candour will find cause enough for ascribing to him the merit of honestly pursuing the good and true according to the best lights he has. (pp. 416-18)

As to the Duke's pardoning of Angelo, though Justice seems to cry out against the act, yet in the premises it were still more unjust in him to do otherwise; the deception he has practised on Angelo in substituting Mariana having plainly bound him to the course he finally takes in that matter. For the same power whereby he works through this deception might easily have prevented Angelo's crime; and to punish the offence after thus withholding the means of prevention were clearly wrong: not to mention how his proceedings here involve an innocent person; so that he ought to spare Angelo for her sake, if not for his own. Coleridge indeed strongly reprehends this act, on the ground that "cruelty, with lust and damnable baseness, cannot be forgiven, because we cannot conceive them as being morally repented of." But it seems to me hardly prudent or becoming thus to set bounds to the grace of repentance, or to say what amount of sin must necessrily render a man incapable of being reformed. All which may in some measure explain the Duke's severity to the smaller crime of Lucio, after his clemency to the greater one of Angelo. (p. 418)

Lucio is one of those mixed characters, such as are often generated amidst the refinements and pollutions of urban society, in whom low and disgusting vices, and a frivolity still more offensive, are blended with engaging manners and some manly sentiments. Thus he appears a gentleman and a blackguard by turns; and, which is more, he does really unite something of these seemingly-incompatible qualities. With a true eye and a just respect for virtue in others, yet, so far as we can see, he cares not a jot to have it in himself. And while his wanton, waggish levity seems too much for any generous sentiment to consist with, still he shows a strong and steady friendship for Claudio, and a heart-felt reverence for Isabella; as if on purpose to teach us that "the web of our life is of a mingled yarn, good and ill together" [*All's Well That Ends Well*, IV. iii. 70-1]. And perhaps the seeming "snow-broth blood" of Angelo puts him upon affecting a more frisky circulation than he really has. For an overacted austerity is not the right way to win others out of a too rollicking levity. (p. 419)

[If the comic] scenes please, it is not so much from any fund of mirthful exhilaration, or any genial gushings of wit and humour, as for the remorseless, unsparing freedom, not unmingled with touches of scorn, with which the deformities of mankind are anatomized. The contrast between the right-hearted, well-meaning Claudio, a generous spirit walled in with overmuch infirmity, and Barnardine, a frightful petrification of humanity, "careless, reckless and fearless of what is past, present, or to come" [IV. ii. 143-44], is in the Poet's boldest manner.

Nevertheless the general current of things is far from musical, and the issues greatly disappointing. The drowsy Justice which we expect and wish to see awakened, and set in living harmony with Mercy, apparently relapses at last into a deeper sleep than ever. Our loyalty to Womanhood is not a little wounded by the humiliations to which poor Mariana stoops, at the ghostly counsels of her spiritual guide, that she may twine her life with that of the execrable hypocrite who has wronged her sex so deeply. That, amid the general impunity, the mere telling of some ridiculous lies to the disguised Duke about himself, should draw down a disproportionate severity upon Lucio, the lively, unprincipled, fantastic jester and wag, who might well be let pass as a privileged character, makes the whole look more as if done in mockery of justice than in honour of mercy. Except, indeed, the noble unfolding of Isabella, scarce any thing turns out to our wish; nor are we much pleased at seeing her diverted from the quiet tasks and holy contemplations where her heart is so much at home; although, as Gervinus observes, "she has that two-sided nature, the capacity to enjoy the world, according to circumstances, or to dispense with it" [see excerpt above, 1849-50].

The title of this play is apt to give a wrong impression of its scope and purpose. *Measure for Measure* is itself equivocal; but the subject-matter here fixes it to be taken in the sense, not of the old Jewish proverb, "An eye for an eye, and a tooth for a tooth," but of the divine precept, "Whatsoever ye would that men should do to you, do ye even so to them." Thus the title falls in with one of Portia's appeals to Shylock, "We do pray for mercy, and that same prayer doth teach us all to render the deeds of mercy" [*Merchant of Venice*, IV. i. 200-02]. The moral centre of the play properly stands in avoidance of extremes,—

the golden means and quiet flow
Of truths that soften hatred, temper strife.

(pp. 419-20)

Rev. H. N. Hudson, " 'Measure for Measure'," in his Shakespeare: His Life, Art, and Characters, *Vol. I, revised edition, Ginn & Company, 1872, pp. 398-420.*

WALTER PATER (essay date 1874)

[*A nineteenth-century essayist, novelist, and fictional portrait writer, Pater is one of the most famous proponents of aestheticism in English literature. Distinguished as the first major English writer to formulate an explicitly aesthetic philosophy of life, he advocated the "love of art for art's sake" as life's greatest offering. He is also recognized as a master prose stylist and a leading exemplar of impressionist criticism, a method in which he expresses what he sees and feels in the presence of a work of art. His essay on* Measure for Measure, *excerpted below, was originally published in an October, 1874 issue of* Fortnightly Review. *Pater begins his assessment of the play by discussing the way in which Shakespeare's idea of justice is revealed in the relationship between Isabella and Claudio. He finds that the play's action develops in the reader or spectator the ideal of "poetical justice," a concept based on a combination of acknowledged law and a "sympathy" or "love" towards individual human nature. He also contends that the ethical interest of* Measure *is primarily the remnant of a medieval morality drama, which forms an integral part of the play's action and characterization. Pater concludes by calling the play "the epitome of Shakespeare's moral judgment." For other interpretations of Shakespeare's ethical intent in* Measure for Measure, *see the excerpts by August Wilhelm Schlegel (1808), G. G. Gervinus (1849-50), H. N. Hudson (1872), Denton J. Snider (1890), and Walter Raleigh (1907).*]

[The] main interest in *Measure for Measure* is not, as in *Promos and Cassandra*, in the relation of Isabella and Angelo, but rather in the relation of Claudio and Isabella.

Greek tragedy in some of its noblest products has taken for its theme the love of a sister, a sentiment unimpassioned indeed, purifying by the very spectacle of its passionlessness, but capable of a fierce and almost animal strength if informed for a moment by pity and regret. At first Isabella comes upon the scene as a tranquillising influence in it. But Shakespeare, in the development of the action, brings quite different and unexpected qualities out of her. It is his characteristic poetry to expose this cold, chastened personality, respected even by the worldly Lucio as "something ensky'd and sainted, and almost an immortal spirit" [I. iv. 34-5], to two sharp, shameful trials, and wring out of her a fiery, revealing eloquence. Thrown into the terrible dilemma of the piece, called upon to sacrifice that cloistral whiteness to sisterly affection, become in a moment the ground of strong, contending passions, she develops a new character and shows herself suddenly of kindred with those strangely conceived women, like [John] Webster's Vittoria, who unite to a seductive sweetness something of a dangerous and tigerlike changefulness of feeling. The swift, vindictive anger leaps, like a white flame, into this white spirit, and, stripped in a moment of all convention, she stands before us clear, detached, columnar, among the tender frailties of the piece. . . . The play, though still not without traces of nobler handiwork, sinks down, as we know, at last into almost homely comedy, and it might be supposed that just here the grander manner deserted it. But the skill with which Isabella plays upon Claudio's well-recognised sense of honour, and endeavours by means of that to insure him beforehand from the acceptance of life on baser terms, indicates no coming laxity of hand just in this place. It was rather that there rose in Shakespeare's conception, as there may for the reader, as there certainly would in any good acting of the part, something of that terror, the seeking for which is one of the notes of romanticism in Shakespeare and his circle. The stream of ardent natural affection, poured as sudden hatred upon the youth condemned to die, adds an additional note of expression to the horror of the prison where so much of the scene takes place. It is not here only that Shakespeare has conceived of such extreme anger and pity as putting a sort of genius into simple women, so that their ''lips drop eloquence,'' and their intuitions interpret that which is often too hard or fine for manlier reason; and it is Isabella with her grand imaginative diction, and that poetry laid upon the ''prone and speechless dialect'' [I. ii. 183] there is in mere youth itself, who gives utterance to the equity, the finer judgments of the piece on men and things. (pp. 183-86)

The many veins of thought which render the poetry of this play so weighty and impressive unite in the image of Claudio, a flowerlike young man, whom, prompted by a few hints from Shakespeare, the imagination easily clothes with all the bravery of youth, as he crosses the stage before us on his way to death, coming so hastily to the end of his pilgrimage. Set in the horrible blackness of the prison, with its various forms of unsightly death, this flower seems the braver. Fallen by ''prompture of the blood'' [II. iv. 178], the victim of a suddenly revived law against the common fault of youth like his, he finds his life forfeited as if by the chance of a lottery. With that instinctive clinging to life, which breaks through the subtlest casuistries of monk or sage apologising for an early death, he welcomes for a moment the chance of life through his sister's shame, though he revolts hardly less from the notion of perpetual imprisonment so repulsive to the buoyant energy of youth. Familiarised, by the words alike of friends and the indifferent, to the thought of death, he becomes gentle and subdued indeed, yet more perhaps through pride than real resignation, and would go down to darkness at last hard and unblinded. Called upon suddenly to encounter his fate, looking with keen and resolute profile straight before him, he gives utterance to some of the central truths of human feeling, the sincere, concentrated expression of the recoiling flesh. Thoughts as profound and poetical as Hamlet's arise in him; and but for the accidental arrest of sentence he would descend into the dust, a mere gilded, idle flower of youth indeed, but with what are perhaps the most eloquent of all Shakespeare's words upon his lips.

As Shakespeare in *Measure for Measure* has refashioned, after a nobler pattern, materials already at hand, so that the relics of other men's poetry are incorporated into his perfect work, so traces of the old ''morality,'' that early form of dramatic composition which had for its function the inculcating of some moral theme, survive in it also, and give it a peculiar ethical interest. This ethical interest, though it can escape no attentive reader, yet, in accordance with that artistic law which demands the predominance of form everywhere over the mere matter or subject handled, is not to be wholly separated from the special circumstances, necessities, embarrassments, of these particular dramatic persons. The old ''moralities'' exemplified most often some rough-and-ready lesson. Here the very intricacy and subtlety of the moral world itself, the difficulty of seizing the true relations of so complex a material, the difficulty of just the judgment, of judgment that shall not be unjust, are the lessons conveyed. Even in Whetstone's old story this peculiar vein of moralising comes to the surface: even there, we notice the tendency to dwell on mixed motives, the contending issues of action, the presence of virtues and vices alike in unexpected places, on ''the hard choice of two evils'' on the ''imprison-

ing'' of men's ''real intents.'' *Measure for Measure* is full of expressions drawn from a profound experience of these casuistries, and that ethical interest becomes predominant in it: it is no longer *Promos and Cassandra;* but *Measure for Measure,* its new name expressly suggesting the subject of *poetical justice.* The action of the play, like the action of life itself for the keener observer, develops in us the conception of this poetical justice, and the yearning to realise it, the true justice of which Angelo knows nothing, because it lies for the most part beyond the limits of any acknowledged law. The idea of justice involves the idea of rights. But at bottom rights are equivalent to that which really is, to facts; and the recognition of his rights therefore, the justice he requires of our hands, or our thoughts, is the recognition of that which the person, in his inmost nature, really is; and as sympathy alone can discover that which really is in matters of feeling and thought, true justice is in its essence a finer knowledge through love. . . . It is for this finer justice, a justice based on a more delicate appreciation of the true conditions of men and things, a true respect of persons in our estimate of actions, that the people in *Measure for Measure* cry out as they pass before us; and as the poetry of this play is full of the peculiarities of Shakespeare's poetry, so in its ethics it is an epitome of Shakespeare's moral judgments. (pp. 187-90)

> *Walter Pater, '' 'Measure for Measure','' in his* Appreciations: With an Essay on Style, *Macmillan and Co., 1890, pp. 176-91.*

EDWARD DOWDEN   (essay date 1881)

[*Dowden was an Irish critic and biographer whose* Shakspere: A Critical Study of His Mind and Art *(1881, rev. ed.) was the leading example of the biographical criticism popular in the English-speaking world near the end of the nineteenth century. Biographical critics sought in the plays and poems a record of Shakespeare's personal development. As that approach gave way in the twentieth century to aesthetic theories with greater emphasis on the constructed, artificial nature of literary works, Dowden and other biographical critics fell out of favor and their analyses came to be regarded as limited and often misleading. In the following excerpt, Dowden states that the gravity of* Measure for Measure *indicates Shakespeare's ''farewell to mirth.'' The focus of his essay is Isabella's nature, and he charts her development. Other critics who see Isabella experiencing a process of development include Walter Pater (1874), Denton J. Snider (1890), G. Wilson Knight (1930), Roy W. Battenhouse (1946), Nevill Coghill (1955), and Lawrence W. Hyman (1975).*]

Of the group of comedies which belong to [the middle period of Shakspere's career], the two latest in date are probably *Measure for Measure* and *All's Well that Ends Well.* When the former of these plays was written, Shakspere was evidently bidding farewell to mirth. Its significance is grave and earnest; the humorous scenes would be altogether repulsive were it not that they are needed to present, without disguise or extenuation, the world of moral license and corruption out of and above which rise the virginal strength and severity and beauty of Isabella. At the entrance to the dark and dangerous tragic world into which Shakspere was now about to pass stand the figures of Isabella and of Helena—one the embodiment of conscience, the other the embodiment of will. Isabella is the only one of Shakspere's women whose heart and eyes are fixed upon an impersonal ideal, to whom something abstract is more, in the ardor and energy of her youth, than any human personality. . . . Isabella's saintliness is not of the passive, timorous, or merely meditative kind. It is an active pursuit of holiness through exercise and discipline. She knows nothing of a Manichæan hatred of the body; the life runs strongly and gladly in her veins; simply her soul is set upon things belonging to the soul, and uses the body for its own purposes. And that the life of the soul may be invigorated, she would bring every unruly thought into captivity, "having in a readiness to revenge all disobedience." (pp. 72-3)

[The] severity of Isabella proceeds from no real turning away, on her part, from the joys and hopes of womanhood; her brother, her schoolfellow Julia, the memory of her father, are precious to her. Her severity is only a portion of the vital energy of her heart. Living actively, she must live purely; and to her the cloister is looked upon as the place where her energy can spend itself in stern efforts towards ideal objects. Bodily suffering is bodily suffering to Isabella, whose "cheek-roses" proclaim her physical health and vigor; but bodily suffering is swallowed up in the joy of quickened spiritual existence:

> Were I under the terms of death,
> The impression of keen whips I'd wear as rubies,
> And strip myself to death, as to a bed
> That longing have been sick for ere I'd yield
> My body up to shame.

> [II. iv. 100-04]

And as she had strength to accept pain and death for herself rather than dishonor, so she can resolutely accept pain and death for those who are dearest to her. (p. 73)

Putting aside from her the dress of religion, and the strict conventual rule, she accepts her place as Duchess of Vienna. In this there is no dropping-away, through love of pleasure or through supineness, from her ideal; it is entirely meet and right. She has learned that in the world may be found a discipline more strict, more awful, than the discipline of the convent; she has learned that the world has need of her. Her life is still a consecrated life; the vital energy of her heart can exert and augment itself through glad and faithful wifehood, and through noble station, more fully than in seclusion. To preside over this polluted and feculent Vienna is the office and charge of Isabella, "a thing ensky'd and sainted" [I. iv. 34]. (p. 74)

> Edward Dowden, "The Growth of Shakspere's Mind and Art," in his Shakspere: A Critical Study of His Mind and Art, third edition, Harper & Brothers Publishers, 1881, pp. 37-83.

DENTON J. SNIDER   (essay date 1890?)

[*Snider was an American scholar, philosopher, and poet who followed closely the precepts of the German philosopher Georg Wilhelm Friedrich Hegel and contributed greatly to the dissemination of his dialectical philosophy in America. Snider's critical writings include studies on Homer, Dante, and Goethe, as well as Shakespeare. Like Hermann Ulrici and G. G. Gervinus, Snider sought for the dramatic unity and ethical import of Shakespeare's plays, but he presented a more rigorous Hegelian interpretation than those two German philosophical critics. In the introduction to his three-volume work,* The Shakespearian Drama: A Commentary, *Snider states that Shakespeare's plays present various ethical principles which come into "Dramatic Collision," but are ultimately resolved and brought into harmony. He claims that these elements can be traced in the plays' various "Dramatic Threads" of action and thought, which together form a "Dramatic Movement," and that the analysis of these "structural elements of the drama" reveal the organic unity of Shakespearean drama. Snider observes two basic movements in the tragedies—guilt and retribution—and three in the comedies—separation, mediation,*

and return. In the following in-depth analysis of the action of Measure for Measure, *Snider divides the play into three movements: the first he maintains depicts the spiritual breech in the world of Vienna between the religious—represented by Isabella and the Duke—and the secular—personified in the figure of Angelo and the characters of the lower class; the second illustrates the attempt to mediate the conflict in the secular world between "extreme law" and "extreme license"; the third movement depicts the Duke's return to power and the resolution of the preceding conflicts. Within each of these movements, according to Snider, Shakespeare demonstrates the ineffectiveness of both socially detached religion and absolute law in achieving social and spiritual order—a goal he asserts can only be realized through the application of "true justice," or the combination of mercy and abstract justice which seeks to restore rather than remove the "individual from society" (and what Snider calls the "Institution of the Family"). Although more systematic than previous studies, Snider's essay follows in the tradition established by August Wilhelm Schlegel (1808) and G. G. Gervinus (1849-50) in its appraisal of Shakespeare's ideal image of justice and mercy dramatized in* Measure*'s final scene.*]

We may consider *Measure for Measure* as the Poet's grand study in which he gets rid of his overwhelming tragic thought of life. Hitherto, in the great tragedies, he has seen mainly the stern retribution of the ethical order; now he sees the inadequacy of that view, as never before. He turns to mercy, but that he had done in previous works, notably in *Merchant of Venice*, where there is also mediation. At present, however, he moves a step further, and shows the inadequacy of mere mercy by itself, divorced from justice. The two must be united, are united in *Measure for Measure*, after a separation in which the insufficiency of both is manifested; in their union lies the salvation of man and of society. The old world of mere justice—the Roman one, say—will not do, it becomes injustice, cruelty; the new world of mere mercy—it may be the monastic or religious one—will not do, it becomes mere sentiment. Only that mercy which follows after the discipline of justice and results from the same, is true mercy; that which relieves man from the return of his deed, is really merciless. The name of the play seems to signify justice, and to connect its thought with that of tragedy rather than with that of mediation. Still, the measure of penalty is meted out to the measure of guilt, and then beneath all and after all is the measure of mercy with which the drama ends. The effect of justice is not to destroy the guilty man and thus make him tragic, but to destroy his guilt and thus save him.

The play, however, is not an abstract treatise on the virtues, but concrete as history itself. In fact, it introduces the historical phases which embody these two principles of mercy and justice—namely, Church and State. The contrast is between the secular and religious spheres; religion furnishes in the present instance the ideal realm of mediation in the cloister. . . . The cloister is just the ideal world placed amid civil institutions, and embodied in a special organization, with the design of reconciling the collisions of the real world, or, at least, of furnishing a place of flight when the conflict is too strong for the individual. . . . This play has its roots in the great transition out of medieval monasticism into modern institutionalism—a transition which belonged to the Poet's own age, and of which he is here the dramatic architect. (pp. 429-31)

Measure for Measure . . . belongs to the class of mediated dramas. The collision has a tragic depth and earnestness; the fundamental tone of the whole work is serious, and even dark, notwithstanding the comic nature of certain portions. The conflict, however, is reconciled and the persons are saved from a tragic fate by the intervention of the World of Mercy. This form of mediation is the main thing to be noticed, and constitutes the distinguishing characteristic of the play. . . . [It] is religion, as an organized system, which is brought in with its principles, and which seeks to determine the affairs and harmonize the conflicts of Family and State. (p. 434)

In the first movement the first thread has its central figure in the person of the Duke. Mercy is his predominating trait, but mercy in its one-sided manifestation. Through the pardon of offenses and their tacit permission he has suffered the law to become of no validity, and, indeed, to fall into utter contempt. The result is universal crime and disregard of all authority. He is aware of the evils, but cannot bring himself to execute those enactments which he has permitted to be violated. (p. 436)

He recognizes his mistake to be excessive leniency; to restore respect for law, and to secure society, there is need of a sharp, decisive remedy. He, therefore, selects as his substitute a man of quite the opposite character, a man who will enforce the law rigidly to the letter. Angelo is taken, whose temperament is cold and inflexible, and whose knowledge of the statutes is most ample. But his chief characteristic is the strictest adherence to formal justice. He is, therefore, the person best fitted by nature to enforce the old enactments which have fallen into desuetude, and, in general, to restore the reign of law which seems to have taken its departure from society. (pp. 436-37)

It would seem, however, that the Duke, notwithstanding his laudation of Angelo, his still a lingering suspicion of his deputy's weakness, or at least believes that mercy cannot be entirely banished from the administration of the law. . . . [He] must remain in the country to watch an experiment whose success he does not regard as absolutely certain, if he be true to his sense of duty and his benevolent character. He cannot deliver his people over entirely to formal justice, if he have any faith at all in his own principle of mercy. His stay is, therefore, necessitated by the situation.

The Duke has also thrown up another bulwark against the extreme tendencies of Angelo's disposition. Escalus has been appointed to the second position in the State, with large authority, and he possesses also great influence on account of his character and his age. In this man the element of mercy again becomes the predominant trait. . . . The Duke, to a certain extent, reappears in him—not as supreme now, but as subordinate; for it is the principle of both of them which has broken down the administration of the State, and, hence, must not again be made paramount. Such seems to be the reason of this double authority, and such the true relation between Angelo and Escalus. Mercy and justice thus form the contrast of their characters, and are supposed to be united in the execution of the law.

But whither will the Duke go when he quits the State, with its laws and institutions? He can only follow the bent of his nature and enter the pure realm of mercy, if there be such in existence. He will find it in the organization of the Christian Church. When, therefore, he abandons secular life, he can betake himself only to a religious life. Accordingly, he enters a monastery—assumes the habit of a holy friar, whose life is devoted to works of benevolence and mercy. . . . He is not of the world, but descends into it as a power from without—as a messenger from Heaven—in order to reconcile its difficulties and to banish its doubts. Religion means mediation, and the priest must mediate, not only between God and man, but also between man

and man. Therefore the Duke, as friar, henceforth becomes the chief mediator of the play.

But we must not fail to notice the other determinations which flow from his situation. He will have to be in disguise, for he remains in his own city; in his ordinary garb he could not help being generally known to the citizens. He is thus compelled to act a species of falsehood from the start. Moreover, his influence is external—comes from a sphere beyond—for he no longer possesses any authority to realize his views and intentions. He is, hence, forced to resort to trickery and deception in order to accomplish his ends. Thus a taint is thrown upon his character and calling which no plea of good results can wholly remove. But his shrewd devices totally fail of their purpose. The lesson seems to be that this separation of the secular and religious worlds has a tendency to pervert both from their true nature, for both thus become immoral, though in different manners; they must be united and reconciled in the institutions of man. (pp. 437-40)

The Duke alone cannot completely represent the dissatisfaction with the present condition of society; he must have his counterpart in the other sex, whose principle is chastity, and whose institution is the Family. Isabella is the embodiment of this element of female virtue; but we observe that she, too, is about to abandon the world for a religious life. . . . Religion is the ideal realm to which she flees in order to avoid the conflicts of life, and to preserve intact her deepest conviction. (p. 441)

To express this thought abstractly, chastity sees itself assailed and disregarded in the world; it can find a solution of the difficulty only by an entire annihilation of the sexual relation—that is, mankind will be pure when it is destroyed. Chastity, therefore, betakes itself to a realm of its own, and leaves behind merely incontinence, which is also destructive of man. Both sides are thus negative, inadequate. (p. 442)

Let us now sum up our results, and mark the necessary transition to the next movement. There has taken place a spiritual breach, which produces two worlds—the religious and secular. The religious world has two principles—mercy and chastity—which principles have been taken away from the secular world. In the latter, therefore, remain abstract justice on the one hand—for mercy has departed, and the illicit sexual relation on the other hand—for chastity has fled from society to the cloister. Such is the logical result of the flight of the Duke and Isabella to their monastic life. In the secular world, therefore, two principles are now found which can produce only the most bitter conflict—formal law undertakes to root out licentiousness.

The second movement unfolds fully the conflict in the secular world between extreme law and extreme license; but chiefly, it shows the attempt to mediate this conflict through the monastic phase of religious life. . . . In accord with the theme, we notice three groups which give the threads of the action: that of religion, that of law, and that of license.

The first thread comprises the religious element—the Duke and Isabella mainly, who seek to be the mediators of the conflicts which are about to arise. They are the heaven overarching this earth; but the heaven is very high and distant, and the earth is very earthy. Isabella, we are told, is "a thing enskied and sainted, by your renouncement an immortal spirit" [I. iv. 34-5]—which is, perhaps, the trouble with her; she must come down from her pure celestial perch, and impart some of her virtue to the world which needs it sorely. Then she will be not merely chaste, but also good. The Duke, too, has entered the celestial realm, from which he seeks to play the part of Providence; he has to descend from his upper ethereal region, and mingle among men in order to save them, and, we may add, in order to save himself. Thus the man and the woman, the two celestial characters, have the same discipline; they find that their very virtue may become narrow, cramping, indeed self-destructive, and must be transcended. (pp. 442-44)

The second thread is made up of the instruments of justice, from the deputy down to the pettiest officer. The characters in this class are contrasted on the principles of mercy and justice. The difference between Angelo and Escalus in this respect was before noted. In the humane Provost of the prison, mercy becomes again the predominant trait, while in the brutal executioner, Abhorson, justice shows its most revolting feature. The constable, Elbow, in a low sphere, is a stickler for legality, like Angelo in a high sphere; both, too, are guilty of a violation of the law which they execute. . . .

One of the primal institutions of man is the Family, whose true existence depends, not only upon the mutual fidelity of husband and wife, but also upon the chastity of man and woman. Hence legislation has always sought to erect barriers against the passions of the human race, in order to protect this institution. But in spite of every effort the evil has not been extirpated, and in all civilized societies there is a despised and outlawed class which has been called the negative Family. (p. 445)

The law against incontinence was the one that was first taken by Angelo, and of whose enforcement there was, of course, the greatest need. An old enactment which had long lain dormant, and which prescribed death as the punishment for the offense, is suddenly raked from its obscurity and executed with rigor. Here was formal justice, undoubtedly. Angelo was technically correct—the law had never been repealed—yet his conduct under the circumstances was palpably unjust. But the character of the deputy is to adhere simply to this formal side, to the neglect of all others.

The third thread is now to be unfolded. The whole world of incontinence, in all its phases, must come up for portraiture, since it is the object against which the law directs its shaft. Angelo proposes to sweep it out of existence; hence it must appear, in order to be swept out of existence. Such is the reason for the introduction of this element; to be exhaustive, the theme had to be treated. (p. 446)

The incontinent world, which the critic has also to consider, is divided into two very distinct groups of people, between whom the Poet makes the greatest difference—quite the difference between guilt and innocence. Yet both are liable to the law, and must suffer punishment. The first group is composed of the most degraded members of the negative Family above mentioned—those who have lost both chastity and fidelity to the individual, these two virtues being an object of purchase and sale. Here we remark that loathsome sore of modern society, popularly known as "social evil." As before stated, it assails the existence of the Family, since the latter depends upon the absolute and unreserved devotion of one man and one woman to each other. "Social evil," therefore, destroys the primitive natural basis of the Family. (p. 447)

It is the second group, however, of this incontinent world which gives rise to the leading incidents of the play. Its persons differ from the persons of the first group in the fact that both parties—men and women—have fidelity, but have lost chastity—that is, they are true to one another, though they have violated the

commandment. It is the class which is often said to love "not wisely, but too well." Such are Claudio and Juliet. It will be noticed that these possess the essential basis of the Family, namely, fidelity to the individual; but their fault, equally with the former case, comes under a violation of law which inflicts the penalty of death upon the man. Claudio is willing to have the marriage rite performed; his intention is to be true to his betrothed; but nothing can help him against the stern deputy. Such is the conflict; Claudio is, in spirit, the husband of Juliet, but has failed to comply with the form, which, however, he is ready to do at once. (p. 449)

In order to rescue him from death, the mediations of the poem are introduced. Claudio's sister, Isabella , . . . is hastily called upon to intercede with the deputy for the life of her brother. She at once strikes the heart of the subject; she pleads the cause of mercy against the rigor of the law; she alludes to the redemption of all mankind through the Savior against the strict demands of justice. . . . In the second interview the deputy says that he will save the life of her brother on condition that she yield up her honor to him, to which proposition she gives an indignant refusal.

Let us consider, for a moment, the logical bearing of these two scenes. Virgin innocence comes to plead for incontinence. Isabella feels the conflict within herself in making such a plea, but, on the other hand, the life of a brother is at stake. She tries to soften the offense in every way—she who has placed chastity the highest in her vow. This is what seduces the deputy, with all his severity of character. Virtue pleading for its own overthrow can alone touch his rigor. Accordingly, he replies in substance, with logical precision: If incontinence be so trivial an offense, yield to me. Thus Angelo falls—becomes the violator of his own deepest principle, namely, legality. The man who adheres to form alone must always exhibit the same weakness. . . . Just the opposite is the case with Isabella. Though inconsistent in her request, she spurns his proposal; for her, chastity is the highest principle. Isabella, therefore, can no longer plead for her brother on such grounds, and Angelo can no longer assert his own innocence. Angelo has lost his integrity, but Isabella has not obtained her request; Claudio's safety must be brought about by some new means.

But another conflict and more anguish await Isabella. She goes to her brother and tells him of her rejection of the base proposition of the deputy, expecting his admiration and approval. Great is her disappointment. But how could she expect that her brother, who cared so little for chastity, would be willing to sacrifice his life for her purity? He asks her to submit, but she, true to her principle, again indignantly refuses, and breaks out into a curse upon her incontinent brother. Thus Isabella passes triumphantly through her double ordeal against deputy and brother.

This plan has now failed to save Claudio; another mediator must be brought to his rescue. This is the Duke, disguised as a friar. He designs to overreach Angelo in his lustful proposal. A young lady once betrothed to, but now abandoned by, the deputy is substituted for Isabella. This is an important turning-point of the drama, and it must be carefully noted. The disguised Duke, in order to save Claudio from death, brings about the very same offense for which Claudio was condemned. It is the demand of mercy to rescue the unfortunate man, for law has inflicted an unjust punishment—has become wrong. To get rid of the injustice of law, the offense is repeated; law thus condemns—indeed, logically destroys—itself, since it forces the very crime which it seeks to punish, in order to thwart its own injustice. Also, the highest officer of the law is made guilty of the same crime which he unrelentingly punishes. Thus the inherent contradiction of the law is shown in the plainest manner. (pp. 449-52)

But even by this last scheme Claudio is not rescued; Angelo violates the agreement to release him. It is perfectly natural that the deputy should act thus. His promise has violated his own deepest principle—why should he now be restrained merely by his promise? In fact, it is just the strength of that principle of abstract justice within him which drives him to disregard his word and to give orders for Claudio's death. The deputy, however, in his own person has broken loose from his principle; now his fall is accomplished in act. He can hardly be called a villain, though he is narrow, bigoted, and even cruel. His conduct springs directly from his conviction, which is adherence to the form rather than regard for the spirit of justice. He loves the law more than the essential object of the law; hence he falls into contradiction just at this point; he becomes a libertine in punishing libertinism. . . . His abandonment of his betrothed was from a formal ground—she did not live up to her contract in furnishing dower. Finally, he exhibits the same trait in the last words which he utters in the play, when he says, in substance: "Execute me according to law." He thus shows what is his ultimate principle, as well his own readiness to have it applied to himself.

The result of the disruption between the secular and religious worlds is now manifest—the one has become criminal, the other helpless. Justice has turned out utterly contradictory of itself, and mercy has sought in vain to mediate the wrong. . . . The purposes and principles of all are shattered and broken, and death is still hanging over Claudio. It is clear that external meditation cannot clear him, nor, indeed, can it save society. There remains one alternative—the return of the Duke to power, to the secular world.

This is the theme of the third movement, which is now to be considered. We shall, therefore, behold the restoration of mercy to the State, which cannot dispense with it. The abstract form of justice grinds the world to death. That form, however, is necessary to society; the purpose here is not to underrate it; only, it is not absolute—it has limits. The question always is to ascertain these limits. Also, mercy without justice is equally impotent—means social disorder and violence. The play starts from an anarchy produced by undue leniency. The Duke must come back from his religious life; the result is true justice, of which mercy is a constituent.

The Duke is now to judge the world before him in accordance with his two principles. The first class of offenders are left in prison to atone for their guilt; the Duke does not discharge them, for they are truly amenable to justice. Their punishment was mild in the first place, compared to the penalties of the law. The gentle Provost and the good Escalus receive his approbation for the happy blending of mercy and justice in their actions. Barnardine, the prisoner from youth and the victim of the forms of law, is brought in and pardoned. This character does not fit well into any particular thread of the play; still, he is a striking illustration of its general theme. Each person gets his dues, yet none perish—not even Angelo, who repents of his deed, and must be forgiven; he has, too, a wife, whose claim cannot be forgotten. The Duke has learned to be just as well as merciful.

Four pairs are brought up before us, representing various phases of marriage. Lowest of all is the union of Lucio, who is com-

pelled to wed one of his kind as a punishment. Men and women are in this case both unchaste and faithless, yet the child born to them necessitates the Family. The second pair is Claudio and Juliet, who love and are willing to comply with the inherent result of their conduct; they have been faithful to one another, but unchaste. The third pair, Angelo and Mariana, represent the same phase in general; the woman here has at least love and fidelity. In all these cases the Duke makes marriage the solution of the difficulty, instead of destroying the offender. The object of the law could have been only the security of the Family; yet that object would certainly not be obtained by killing the husband. Thus the Duke by his decision reaches the great purpose of the law, and at the same time shows mercy in its true sense and limitation. But the fourth pair, the Duke and Isabella, have the indispensable condition of the true union, for they alone possess chastity before marriage. This element has been dwelt upon by the Poet, in other dramas, with great force and beauty. Isabella intended to take the vow of perpetual chastity; that is the best reason why she should enter the Family. It is Mistress Overdone and her class who ought to take such a vow. The Duke has also entered monastic life, but his virtue cannot be spared from a society in which there is none to throw away. He and Isabella are thus modeled after a similar pattern, and go through with quite the same experience. Both of them, independently of each other, fled from the prevailing corruption; they sought to annihilate the sexual relation entirely, since it is productive of so much evil. But they discover their own chastity and fidelity, which form the true ethical basis of marriage; thus they belong together, and are united at the end of the play. Conventual life is inadequate, and passes away; the disruption between the secular and religious worlds is healed; their reconciliation and union are found in the institutions of man, in which religion becomes the most potent principle, but loses its forms, its organization, and even its name. (pp. 452-57)

> *Denton J. Snider, " 'Measure for Measure'," in his* The Shakespearian Drama, a Commentary: The Comedies, *1890? Reprint by Indiana Publishing Co., 1894, pp. 428-58.*

GEORGE BRANDES   (essay date 1895-96)

[*Brandes was a scholar and the most influential literary critic of late nineteenth-century Denmark whose work on Shakespeare, originally published in 1895-96, was translated and widely read in his day. A writer with a broad knowledge of literature, Brandes placed Shakespeare in a European context, comparing him with other important dramatists. He interprets* Measure for Measure *as Shakespeare's attack against the "moral hypocrisy" of the Puritans, but notes how Shakespeare's comic handling of Angelo's hypocrisy deflates both the potentially fierce treatment of the theme and the play's pessimism. For further commentary on* Measure for Measure *as an examination of Puritanism, see the excerpt by Mary Suddard, S.J. (1912).*]

[*All's Well that Ends Well* contained] some incidental mockery of the increasing Puritanism of the time, with its accompaniment of self-righteousness, moral intolerance, and unctuous hypocrisy. The bent of thought which gave birth to these sallies reappears still more clearly in the choice of the theme treated in *Measure for Measure*. . . .

What attracted Shakespeare to this unpleasant subject was clearly his indignation at the growing Pharisaism in matters of sexual morality which was one outcome of the steady growth of Puritanism among the middle classes. It was a consequence of his position as an actor and theatrical manager that he saw only the ugliest side of Puritanism—the one it turned towards him. (p. 401)

He came into contact with Puritanism only in its narrow and fanatical hatred of his art, and in its severely intolerant condemnation and punishment of moral, and especially of sexual, frailties. All he saw was its Pharisaic aspect, and its often enough only simulated virtue.

It was his indignation at this hypocritical virtue that led him to write *Measure for Measure*. He treated the subject as he did, because the interests of the theatre demanded that the woof of comedy should be interwoven with the severe and sombre warp of tragedy. But what a comedy! Dark, tragic, heavy as the poet's mood—a tragi-comedy, in which the unusually broad and realistic comic scenes, with their pictures of the dregs of society, cannot relieve the painfulness of the theme, or disguise the positively criminal nature of the action. One feels throughout, even in the comic episodes, that Shakespeare's burning wrath at the moral hypocrisy of self-righteousness underlies the whole structure like a volcano, which every moment shoots up its flames through the superficial form of comedy and the interludes of obligatory merriment.

And yet it is not really against hypocrisy that his attack is aimed. At this stage of his development he is far too great a psychologist to depict a ready-made, finished hypocrite. No, he shows us how weak even the strictest Pharisee will prove, if only he happens to come across the temptation which really tempts him; and how such a man's desire, if it meets with opposition, reveals in him quite another being—a villain, a brute beast—who allows himself actions worse a hundredfold than those which, in the calm superiority of a spotless conscience, he has hitherto punished in others with the utmost severity.

It is not a type of Shakespeare's opponents that he here unmasks and brands—it is a man in many ways above the average type, as he saw it. The chief character in *Measure for Measure* is the judge of public morality, the hard and stern *Censor morum*, who in his moral fanaticism believes that he can root out vice by persecuting its tools, and imagines that he can purify and reform society by punishing every transgression, however natural and comparatively harmless, as a capital crime. The play shows us how this man, as soon as a purely sensual passion takes possession of him, does not hesitate to commit, under the mask of piety, a crime against real morality so revolting and so monstrous that no expression of loathing and contempt would be too severe for it, and scarcely any punishment too rigorous.

From its nature such a drama ought to end by appeasing in some satisfactory manner the craving for justice awakened in the spectator. But comedy was what Shakespeare's company wanted; and besides, it would have been unwise, and perhaps even dangerous, to carry to extremities this question of the punishment of moral hypocrisy. So the knot in the play was summarily loosed, without any great expenditure of pathos, by the provident care and timely intervention of a wise and invisibly omnipresent prince, an occidental Haroun-al-Raschid. Fastidious in his choice of means this prince was not. With an ingenuity which is profoundly unsatisfactory to any one of the least delicacy of feeling, he substitutes a lovable girl, whom the iniquitous judge had at one time promised to marry, for the beautiful young woman who is the object of his bestial desire. (pp. 402-03)

Shakespeare has imagined one of the men who were the bitterest enemies of his art and his calling invested with absolute power, and using it to proceed against immorality with cruel rigour. The first step is his attack on common prostitution, which he persuades himself he can exterminate. This vain imagination is repeatedly ridiculed. . . .

But besides taking strict proceedings against actual debauchery, Angelo revives an old law which has long been in disuse—according to the Duke for fourteen, according to Claudio for nineteen years—making death the punishment of all sexual commerce without marriage; and by this law young Claudio is condemned to death for his relation to Juliet. (p. 404)

In this very unequally elaborated play, it is evident that Shakespeare cared only for the main point—the blow he was striking at hypocrisy. And it is probable that he here ventured as far as he by any means dared. It is a giant stride from the stingless satire on Puritanism in the character of Malvolio to this representation of a Puritan like Angelo. Probably for this very reason, Shakespeare has tried in every way to shield himself. The subject is treated entirely as a comedy. There is a threat of executing first Claudio, then the humorous scoundrel Barnardine, whose head is to be delivered instead of Claudio's; Barnardine is actually brought on the scene directly before execution, and the spectators sit in suspense; but all ends well at last, and the head of a man already dead is sent to Angelo. A noble maiden is threatened with dishonour; but another woman, Mariana, who was worthy of a better fate, keeps tryst with Angelo in her stead, and this danger is over. Finally, threats of retribution close round Angelo, the villain, himself; but after all he escapes unpunished, being merely obliged to marry the amiable girl whom he had at an earlier period deserted. In this way the play's terrible impeachment of hypocrisy is most carefully glozed over, and along with it the pessimism which animates the whole.

For it is remarkable how deeply pessimistic is the spirit of this play. When the Duke is exhorting Claudio . . . not to fear his inevitable fate, he goes farther in his depreciation of human life than Hamlet himself when his mood is blackest:

> Reason thus with life:—
> If I do lose thee, I do lose a thing
> That none but fools would keep; a breath thou art,
> Servile to all the skyey influences,
> That do this habitation, where thou keep'st,
> Hourly afflict. Merely, thou art death's fool;
> For him thou labour'st by thy flight to shun,
> And yet runn'st toward him still.
>
> [III. i. 6-13]
> (pp. 407-08)

It is clear that in this play the poet was earnestly bent on proving his own standpoint to be the moral one. In hardly any other play do we find such persistent emphasis laid, with small regard for consistency of character, upon the general moral. (p. 408)

[The] moral pointer comes into play wherever there is an opportunity of showing how apt princes and rulers are to be misjudged, and how recklessly they are disparaged and slandered.

Thus the Duke says towards the close of Act iii.:—

> 'No might nor greatness in mortality
> Can censure scape: black-wounding calumny
> The whitest virtue strikes. What king so strong
> Can tie the gall up in the slanderous tongue?
>
> [III. ii. 185-88]

And later [IV. i.] again:—

'O place and greatness! millions of false eyes
Are stuck upon thee. Volumes of report
Run with these false and most contrarious quests
Upon thy doings.

[IV. i. 59-62]

It is quite remarkable how this dwelling on baseless criticism by subjects is accompanied by a constant tendency to invoke the protection of the sovereign, or, in other words, of James I., who had just ascended the throne, and who, with his long-accumulated bitterness against Scottish Presbyterianism, was already showing himself hostile to English Puritanism. Hence the politic insistence, at the close, upon a point quite irrelevant to the matter of the play: all other sins being declared pardonable, save only slander or criticism of the sovereign. Lucio alone, who, to the great entertainment of the spectators, has told lies about the Duke, and, though only in jest, has spoken ill of him, is to be mercilessly punished. To the last moment it seems as if he were to be first whipped, then hanged. And even after this sentence is commuted in order that the tone of comedy may be preserved, and he is commanded instead to marry a prostitute, it is expressly insisted that whipping and hanging ought by rights to have been his punishment. ''Slandering a prince deserves it'' [V. i. 524], says the Duke, at the beginning of the final speech. (p. 409)

> George Brandes, '' 'Measure for Measure'—Angelo
> and Tartuffe,'' translated by William Archer with
> Mary Morrison, in his William Shakespeare, 1898.
> Reprint by William Heinemann, 1917, pp. 401-09.

FREDERICK S. BOAS (essay date 1896)

[Boas was a nineteenth- and early twentieth-century scholar specializing in Elizabethan and Tudor drama. In his Shakespearean criticism, he focuses on both the biographical elements and the historical influence apparent in Shakespeare's works. For this reason, many scholars today regard him as occupying a transitional position in the history of Shakespearean criticism between the biographical methods of Edward Dowden and Frank Harris and the historical approach of E. E. Stoll, Hardin Craig, and E.M.W. Tillyard. Boas is the first critic to categorize Measure for Measure, All's Well That Ends Well, Troilus and Cressida, and Hamlet as Shakespeare's ''problem plays.'' To Boas, these plays are characterized by corrupt, ''highly artificial societies'' and depict ''intricate cases of conscience'' by which ''we are excited, fascinated, perplexed, for the issues raised preclude a satisfactory outcome.'' Further discussion of Measure for Measure as a problem play can be found in the essays by William Witherle Lawrence (1931), H. B. Charlton (1937), E. C. Pettet (1949), E.M.W. Tillyard (1949), Ernest Schanzer (1963), and Hal Gelb (1971). Also, Boas, like G. G. Gervinus (1849-50), Walter Pater (1874), and Denton J. Snider (1890), concludes that the spirit of Measure for Measure negates the meaning of its title, revealing instead that justice must be applied with equity, and that it must seek to reform and not only to punish if it is to achieve its desired end.]

The opening of the seventeenth century coincides almost exactly with a sharp turning-point in Shakspere's dramatic career. On one side of the year 1601 lie comedies of matchless charm and radiance, and histories which are half comedies. On the other appear plays, in which historical matter is given a tragic setting, or in which comedy for the most part takes the grim form of dramatic satire. The change has been compared to the passage from a sunny charming landscape to a wild mountain-district whose highest peaks are shrouded in thick mist. The

causes of this startling alteration in the poet's mood are . . . in great measure obscure. . . . [One] cause that has been suggested for the dramatist's change from gaiety to gloom, is the failure of the conspiracy of Essex, followed by the execution of the Earl and the imprisonment of Shakspere's friend Southampton. . . . It can scarcely be a mere coincidence that Julius Caesar immediately follows the Earl's tragic end, and it is remarkable that most of the plays which with more or less warrant may be assigned to the last three years of Elizabeth's reign, contain painful studies of the weakness, levity, and unbridled passion of young men. This is especially the case with All's Well that Ends Well, Measure for Measure, Troilus and Cressida, and Hamlet. The last-named play is, of course, distinguished from the others by its tragic ending, but it is akin to them in its general temper and atmosphere. All these dramas introduce us into highly artificial societies, whose civilization is ripe unto rottenness. Amidst such media abnormal conditions of brain and of emotion are generated, and intricate cases of conscience demand a solution by unprecedented methods. Thus throughout these plays we move along dim untrodden paths, and at the close our feeling is neither of simple joy nor pain; we are excited, fascinated, perplexed, for the issues raised preclude a completely satisfactory outcome, even when, as in All's Well and Measure for Measure, the complications are outwardly adjusted in the fifth act. In Troilus and Cressida and Hamlet no such partial settlement of difficulties takes place, and we are left to interpret their enigmas as best we may. Dramas so singular in theme and temper cannot be strictly called comedies or tragedies. We may therefore borrow a convenient phrase from the theatre of to-day and class them together as Shakspere's problem-plays. (pp. 344-45)

[Measure for Measure is linked with Hamlet] by its deeply reflective tone, its brooding sense of the pollution spread by lust in the single soul and in society at large, and the shivering recoil of the man of phantasies from the mystery of the unknown hereafter. Claudio's gloomy meditations on death sound like an echo from the soliloquies of the Danish Prince. It is this wealth of philosophic thought, this concern with the deepest issues of life here and beyond the grave, that give the play a massive weight which the original framework of plot might well have seemed too slight to bear. (pp. 357-58)

In Measure for Measure, though undeniably strong meat is served up, the most repulsive details have all their place in the general scheme, which is indisputably noble, while numberless lustrous shafts of poetry and thought pierce the sombre atmosphere in which the action moves. . . .

[Vienna] is, as here portrayed, a city of dreadful night, wherein

Corruption boils and bubbles
Till it o'errun the stew.

[V. i. 318-19]

Lust holds its shameless saturnalia in the open, and society is perishing of inward corruption. Beneath the mild sway of a shy, meditative ruler, animal instincts have broken loose in uncurbed riot. (p. 359)

Up to [the point in III. i, when Isabella and Claudio meet in the prison, and] which forms the exact centre of the play, all has been wrought in Shakspere's mightiest manner, but henceforward, through the remainder of Act iii and Act iv, the workmanship flags. The scenes are written chiefly in prose of a comparatively tame character, and the rapidity with which they succeed one another is confusing. But the action advances in a number of material points. Isabella proves that her outburst of defiance to Claudio does not spring from callousness to his sufferings, for she lends herself to the Duke's strategem whereby her seeming assent to Angelo's overtures is to save her brother and secure the happiness of the forsaken Mariana. The glimpse of the lonely woman at the moated grange gives the outline which the Lincolnshire poet of our own day was to fill in with sombre detail from the landscape of the fens. A pleasanter glimpse is that of Angelo's brick-walled garden, abutting on a vineyard with a planched gate. But the scene lies for the most part in the prison and its precincts, where the disguised Duke adds hourly to his experiences of criminal life, and gathers fresh evidence of the results of his deputy's administration. Once having entered upon the downward path, Angelo finds himself driven ever lower and lower. (p. 367)

The threads thus somewhat loosely scattered are gathered into a knot in the fifth act. This act in its structure closely resembles the final scene of *All's Well that Ends Well*. The ruler again sits in judgement, and there are the same charges, arrests, and threats of death, the same deliberate mystification before guilt is brought home to the evil-doer. But the *dénouement* is more impressive in the present play, which rises once again to something of its earlier power. . . . The shrine of outward respectability at which [Angelo] had worshipped so zealously is shivered, and in the agony of his humiliation he may well crave to be buried among its ruins. Coleridge deplores that he is not taken at his word, that he is not sacrificed to 'the strong indignant claim of justice' [see excerpt above, 1818]. But Angelo's character is not conceived of as irredeemably vile. It was the previous austerity of his life, and the overstrained self-confidence which this begot, that left him prone to the overwhelming temptation that burst upon him from the most unforeseen quarter. Isabella herself admits that 'a due sincerity governed his deeds' [V. i. 446] till he looked upon her, and though she believes that Claudio has died by his command, instead of clamouring for vengeance she petitions Angelo's pardon on the ground that he has sinned but in intent. Mariana, with whom he has been constrained to fulfil his marriage-contract, sues for his life on the plea that 'best men are moulded out of faults' [V. i. 439]. The Duke for a time poses as inflexible:

> An Angelo for Claudio, death for death!
> Haste still pays haste, and leisure answers leisure,
> Like doth quit like, and Measure still for Measure.
>
> [V. i. 409-11]

But the spirit of the play is in reality the negation of the maxim which serves as its title. Even while the Duke thus pronounces judgement he knows that Claudio is alive, and that the capital sentence on Angelo is merely a feint. The deputy is saved by the humane interpretation of the law against which he had battled so tenaciously. In the years passed since *The Merchant of Venice* was written Shakspere had reached a loftier conception of justice. The earlier play had furnished an ideal illustration of 'measure for measure.' Shylock took his stand upon the letter of the law, and by the letter he was overthrown. But here the fanatical worship of the letter is shown to conflict with the genuine principle of equity, and we realize that codes and charters may become a curse instead of a blessing to society, unless they are applied in a remedial and not a nakedly retributive spirit. That such will henceforth be the case in Vienna is guaranteed by Isabella's elevation to a share in the ducal seat. She does not return to the nunnery, yet in her cloistral whiteness of soul she bears abroad the stamp and seal of her noviciate. Her leavening presence at the core of the state

promises a speedier regeneration of the devotees of *Venus genetrix* in her impure form than the most Draconian enactments. In her we salute what Angelo had so miserably failed to become, a 'saviour of society,' and if the light that streams from her countenance is at first dazzling in its pure severity, it turns if we gaze but long enough into a soft, benignant glow. (pp. 367-69)

> Frederick S. Boas, "The Problem-Plays," in his Shakspere and His Predecessors, *Charles Scribner's Sons, 1896, pp. 344-408.*

WALTER RALEIGH (essay date 1907)

[*Raleigh maintains that* Measure for Measure, *more than any other Shakespearean play, "comes nearest to the direct treatment of a moral problem." He states that by presenting every side of the issues involved, Shakespeare allows none of his characters to express his viewpoint; even Isabella is touched by irony. For additional commentary on the moral issues raised in the play, see the excerpts by G. G. Gervinus (1849-50), H. N. Hudson (1872), and Walter Pater (1874).*]

Of all Shakespeare's plays, [*Measure for Measure*] comes nearest to the direct treatment of a moral problem. What did he think of it all? He condemns no one, high or low. The meaning of the play is missed by those who forget that Claudio is not wicked, merely human, and fails only from sudden terror of the dark. Angelo himself is considerately and mildly treated; his hypocrisy is self-deception, not cold and calculated wickedness. Like many another man, he has a lofty, fanciful idea of himself, and his public acts belong to this imaginary person. At a crisis, the real man surprises the play-actor, and pushes him aside. Angelo had underestimated the possibilities of temptation:

> O cunning enemy, that to catch a saint
> With saints dost bait thy hook!
>
> [II. ii. 179-80]

After the fashion of King Claudius in *Hamlet,* but with more sincerity, he tries to pray. It is useless; his old ideals for himself are a good thing grown tedious. . . . When the wickedness of Angelo is unveiled, Isabella is willing to make allowances for him:

> I partly think
> A due sincerity governed his deeds,
> Till he did look on me.
>
> [V. i. 445-47]

But he is dismayed when he thinks of his fall, and asks for no allowance:

> So deep sticks it in my penitent heart,
> That I crave death more willingly than mercy;
> 'Tis my deserving, and I do entreat it.
>
> [V. i. 475-77]

Shakespeare, it is true, does not follow the novel by marrying him to Isabella, but he invents Mariana for him, and points him to happiness.

Is the meaning of the play centred in the part of Isabella? She is severe, and beautiful, and white with an absolute whiteness. Yet it seems that even she is touched now and again by Shakespeare's irony. She stands apart, and loses sympathy as an angel might lose it, by seeming to have too little stake in humanity:

> Then Isabel live chaste, and brother die;
> More than our brother is our chastity.
>
> [II. ii. 184-85]

Perhaps it is the rhyming tag that gives to this a certain explicit and repulsive calmness: at the end of his scenes Shakespeare often makes his most cherished characters do the menial explanatory work of a chorus. When we first make acquaintance with her, Isabella is on the eve of entering a cloister; we overhear her talking to one of the sisters, and expressing a wish that a more strict restraint were imposed upon the order. She is an ascetic by nature, and some of the Duke's remarks on the vanity of self-regarding virtue, though they are addressed to Angelo, seem to glance delicately at her. Shakespeare has left us in no doubt concerning his own views on asceticism; his poems and plays are full of eloquent passages directed against self-culture and the celibate ideal. . . . No man can know himself save as he is known to others. Honour is kept bright by perseverance in action: love is the price of love. It is not by accident that Shakespeare calls Isabella back from the threshold of the nunnery, and after passing her through the furnace of trial, marries her to the Duke. She too, like Angelo, is redeemed for worldly uses; and the seething city of Vienna had some at least of Shakespeare's sympathy as against both the true saint and the false.

In this play there is thus no single character through whose eyes we can see the questions at issue as Shakespeare saw them. His own thought is interwoven in every part of it; his care is to maintain the balance, and to show us every side. He stands between the gallants of the playhouse and the puritans of the city; speaking of charity and mercy to these; to those asserting the reality of virtue in the direst straits, when charity and mercy seem to be in league against it. Even virtue, answering to a sudden challenge, alarmed, and glowing with indignation, though it is a beautiful thing, is not the exponent of his ultimate judgment. His attitude is critical and ironical, expressed in reminders, and questions, and comparisons. When we seem to be committed to one party, he calls us back to a feeling of kinship with the other. . . . Measure for measure: the main theme of the play is echoed and re-echoed from speaker to speaker, and exhibited in many lights. "Plainly conceive, I love you," says Angelo; and quick as lightning comes Isabella's retort:

> My brother did love Juliet; and you tell me
> That he shall die for't.
>
> [II. iv. 142-43]

The law is strict; but the offence that it condemns is knit up with humanity, so that in choosing a single victim the law seems unjust and tyrannical. Authority and degree, place and form, the very framework of human society, are subjected to the same irony:

> Respect to your great place; and let the devil
> Be sometime honour'd for his burning throne. . . .
>
> [V. i. 292-93]

Many men make acquaintance with Christian morality as a branch of codified law, and dutifully adopt it as a guide to action, without the conviction and insight that are the fruit of experience. A few, like Shakespeare, discover it for themselves, as it was first discovered, by an anguish of thought and

sympathy; so that their words are a revelation, and the gospel is born anew. (pp. 169-73)

> *Walter Raleigh, "Story and Character," in his* Shakespeare, *Macmillan and Co., Limited, 1907, pp. 128-208.*

S. J. MARY SUDDARD (essay date 1912)

[*Suddard describes* Measure for Measure *as Shakespeare's exploration of the effect of Puritanism on Renaissance England. To her, the uncompromising ascetic attitudes of Angelo and Isabella reveal their inability to cope with the problems of real life. Suddard states that through a process of growth and development Isabella transcends and condemns her Puritanical feelings. Other critics who regard* Measure for Measure *as Shakespeare's commentary on Renaissance Puritanism include George Brandes (1895-96) and H. B. Charlton (1937).*]

Measure for Measure might indeed be looked upon as a precursor of those bold and often hazardous prophecies with which our modern socialistic literature is overrun. The poet had here undertaken to deliver a message from "the prophetic soul of the wide world dreaming on things to come" [*Sonnet* 107]. . . . The play may be safely accepted as a forecast of the effects of Puritan rule on England.

What gives it its abiding value is its extremely solid basis. . . . Shakespeare exposes with unsparing severity the corruption of Renaissance life among the frivolous middle classes; he admits, in fact insists upon, the necessity of a reform; he already foresees from what quarter it will come; now the question arises: How far is Puritanism fitted to play the part it seems to be on the point of assuming? how far would it be expedient to entrust it with supreme power? He now examines the validity of its titles to authority. In order to remain just, he takes it on its own ground. Puritanism is studied as much in its effects on its own disciples as on outsiders. Shakespeare, with his usual impartiality, continually changes the touch-stone applied. To get an all-round view of the question, he adopts now the standpoint of the initiated, now that of the unbeliever. He investigates now its effect on the individual, now its effect on society. The different methods employed in this psycho-sociological study all, however, as usual in Shakespeare, lead to the same result.

Puritanism is treated by Shakespeare essentially as a moral discipline, divested of all religious peculiarities. None of its distinctive doctrines, opinions, or dialect, varying from sect to sect, from generation to generation, are insisted upon in *Measure for Measure*. . . . [All] its principles, from an ethical point of view, may be summed up in one,—the establishment and maintenance, at any price and under any circumstances, of hard and fast lines of distinction between good and evil, virtue and vice, the saint and the sinner. In this inflexibility, now rising into heroic constancy, now hardening into rigidity, lies its saving strength as well as its fatal weakness. On the one hand it prevents all compromise with sin, on the other it denies all possibility of redemption. The effects of this training on the individual, as displayed in the two main types of mind to which it can appeal, are exemplified on the one hand in Isabella, on the other in Angelo.

Isabella represents Puritanism under its most favourable aspect. . . . All woman's yearning devotion and self-sacrifice, absorbed by passion in Italian Juliet, are absorbed by principle in Isabella. Her intellect delights in vanquishing the difficulties of Puritanic (in the play symbolised as conventual) discipline,

her heart delights in offering itself up, unrewarded and unre-
pulsed, to an unattainable ideal. . . . Isabella, the young disciple of a young religion, exults in multiplying the restrictions
of Puritanic rule. Her very first words strike the key-note of
her character, so intense in its moderation, so passionate in its
self-control:

ISABELLA.	And have you nuns no farther privileges?
NUN.	Are not these large enough?
ISABELLA.	Yes, truly; I speak not as desiring more,
	But rather wishing a more strict restraint
	Upon this sisterhood, the votaries of St Clare.
	[I. iv. 1-5]

A generation of such women would soon ensure the triumph
of Puritanism in England. The chief object of the new discipline
was to establish law, and the very mainspring of Isabella's
nature is obedience to law, whatever suffering such obedience
may imply: "I had rather my brother die by the *law* than that
my son should be *unlawfully* born" [III. i. 189-91].

This obedience to the external law is only the outward sign of
obedience to the moral law within. No considerations of human
affection can weigh against principle. Rather than violate the
virginal ideal of purity imposed by principle, Isabel will stifle
the voice of feeling, sacrifice her brother without a tear: "More
than our brother is our chastity"; indeed, at the very thought,
inspired principle puts into her mouth the language of the Christian virgins fifteen hundred years before. To repel the attacks
of the tempter her voice thrills with the ecstasy of martyrdom:

> Were I under the terms of death
> The impression of keen whips I'd wear as rubies,
> And strip myself to death as to a bed
> That longing have been sick for, ere I'd yield
> My body up to shame.
>
> [II. iv. 100-04]

Contrast this unflinching adherence to principle with the yielding of Isabella's prototype, Cassandra, in the original play,
you will have caught the difference in spirit between the Renaissance ideal of mercy to the individual and the Puritanic
ideal of obedience to the law. Isabella, for the first time perhaps
in English literature, displays the wonderful power of Puritanism in conquering nature, that strength which has become the
backbone of the Englishwoman's character, that implicit obedience to the laws of truth and chastity which silences alike
the casuistry of conscience and the promptings of passion. . . .
(pp. 138-42)

And yet has Isabella so completely broken with the tradition
of the Renaissance? In truth, this strength of principle had
always lain dormant in the Englishwoman's nature. The frankness and fidelity of Chaucer's Dorigen needed little transformation to develop into the Shakespearian heroine, and Shakespeare's women are all Puritans at heart. The latent tendencies
of all are simply brought to consciousness in Isabella. She is
first cousin, if not sister, to Imogen and Desdemona.

As the highest type of Renaissance woman shares Isabella's
austerity of principle, so Isabella shares the other's impulsive-
ness of emotion. As live water may be seen dashing and dancing
along under thin ice, so feeling in Isabella seems always on
the point of bursting through the set coldness of Puritanic or
conventual reserve. Puritanic principles merely fit over the
more delicate impulses of her own nature to shield their purity
from harm. Puritanism for her meant no more than a moral
discipline; it served simply to protect the feeling it could not

repress. When the time comes the husk slips off like the sheath
off a catkin, leaving a silken tenderness beneath, soon to blossom out in fragrant, tremulous beauty.

Had Isabella always remained a voluntary prisoner in her convent, wrapt in silent meditation, only peeping out at the world
through a grating,—in other words, could she have held fast
to her Puritanic principles without bringing them to the test of
fact,—the slumbering warmth of her nature could only have
been divined from an occasional flash; it would never have
burnt through to a steady glow and shone out in its own eventual
radiance. But Isabella is brought into contact with real life,
and with life in the form her training teaches her to most abhor.
She is forced to plead for sin, to become the apologist of human
frailty and human passion. The first moral crisis of her life
reveals to her the inadequacy of her principles to cope with
problems whose magnitude she had never before realised. Her
icicles of logic, which seemed before so fair and firm, thaw,
dwindle, melt away at the first warm breath of feeling. Or, to
be more just, the logic of the intellect is transcended by the
logic of emotion. In Isabella, as in most women, the logic of
the intellect moves in extremely narrow grooves. It had sufficed
to regulate her own personal judgment, opinions and conduct.
But a finer intuition tells her it will no longer apply to the case
she has undertaken to defend. This new need calls forth the
supple logic of emotion, reaching the right solutions by the
wrong means, ignoring all the process of formal reasoning, yet
instinctively working itself out to a result no formal reasoning
could have given. The struggle between the two and her fruitless efforts to reconcile them are what confer its half-pathetic,
half-humorous interest on her first interview with Angelo. . . .
(pp. 142-43)

This contention of principle and feeling, at which she herself
seems frightened and abashed, is leading her into a higher
sphere. In Shakespeare's women feeling always carries principle along with it, not denying its validity, but extending its
application. Struggle as she will, "a something wild within
her breast, A greater than all knowledge" beats her down: not
love, but charity, the divine Amor. It takes her back to the
gracious mercy, the infinite forgiveness of the Redeemer:

> Why, all the souls that were were forfeit once,
> And he who best the 'vantage might have took
> Found out the remedy. . . .
>
> [II. ii. 73-5]
> (pp. 144-45)

But what has become of her Puritanism? In her highest, most
heroic burst, her early training has been not only transcended,
but unconsciously condemned. Contact with real life has thrown
her back on Christianity; before the sorrow and suffering of
humanity, Puritanic morality she had thought so lofty now
seems narrow; its solutions she had thought so just seem almost
flippant. Through Isabella the Renaissance pays Puritanism a
magnanimous tribute, and takes at the same time a worthy and
magnificent revenge.

Shakespeare is, however, very far from wishing to prove the
inability of Puritanism to retain a firm hold on its disciples.
Over against the complex character of Isabella he sets the more
elementary nature of Angelo. On him Puritanism has set its
distinctive and ineffaceable seal. We have said that Isabella
used the austerity of Puritanism as a moral discipline for her
own passionate nature; Angelo turns this purely personal and
spiritual discipline into a mechanical drill, to be applied to all
minds alike. Puritanic principle, as before said, serves rather

as a shell to protect her tenderest feelings from injury; Angelo, carrying his narrow logic to its extreme consequences, tries to assimilate the creature to the shell, to fossilize the living heart within. Puritanism appealed to Isabella through its superhuman difficulty of application; it appeals to Angelo, on the contrary, through its extreme simplicity. What acts as a restraint on a passionate heart serves as a support to a cold intellect. Live entirely by the brain, suppress feeling, and Puritanic morality becomes the easiest of all to follow. The only penalty Angelo will have to pay for his complete surrender to Puritanic rule is loss of power, under any circumstances whatsoever, to shake off the habits of mind he has acquired.

The difference in the effect of such a discipline on the superior and on the average mind can only be brought out by contact with reality. Angelo, like Isabella, brings his Puritanism to the test of fact and, to the credit of the strength if not the liberality of his training, preserves its logical integrity much longer. The paradox of the situation requires one Puritan to convert the other. Isabella, forced by her instinct to desert her own tenets, beckons to Angelo to follow her up to the summit she has reached. In their first interview the faith of both is shaken. But the result of the crisis is widely different in the complex and the elementary nature. Feeling is in both cases brought into play, but feeling of a radically different character. Departure from Puritanic morality in Isabella meant return to Christian grace, in Angelo it means return to Nature in its lowest form. As in intellect he has never advanced beyond the logic of the understanding, so in emotion he has never advanced beyond animal desire.

The worst feature of Puritanism now makes its appearance. In its anxiety to keep virtue from being sullied by the least contact with vice, it denies all possibility of the two being combined in one,—consequently all possibility of redemption. A false step, once taken, can never be retrieved. . . . The knowledge of this essential rule drives Angelo to despair. After the minute and morbid self-analysis Puritanism, to its own great danger, encouraged, Angelo comes to the conclusion he is but as carrion corrupting in the sun. His conduct has always been governed by abstract principle. No sense of human tenderness can restrain him from taking human life. No artistic awe and respect of beauty can prevent him from desecrating Isabella, for the brutality of his proposal is of a piece with the Vandalism which was later to disgrace for ever Puritanic rule. No feeling for "the pity of it" [*Othello*, IV. i. 195], so strong even in uncivilised Othello, can hold him back from shattering the virginal ideal of purity enshrined in Isabella's soul. That is, no consideration but law can keep him from committing the foulest crimes, and Angelo's inner law, once broken, as it admits of no forgiveness and requires no repentance, practically gives the offender scope for all his desires of lust, murder or revenge. . . . Over and above all, may be added the passive hypocrisy of keeping up appearances. Shakespeare takes pains to show that hypocrisy is not the fundamental vice of Puritanism . . . , but he foresees that, on account of its intangible, indefinable character, it offers Puritanic severity the only means of compounding with human weakness. To such a compromise has the severe and upright judge been brought, not from the sin of following Nature, but from the iniquity of the training which, by cutting off all hope of pardon, has urged him on from crime to crime. (pp. 145-48)

In Isabella and Angelo Shakespeare not only embodies the two main types of Puritan, but sets forth all the advantages and defects of Puritanic training. He does full justice to its abstract

loftiness of principle, to its power of resistance, its strength in warding off evil, its straightforward language, its uncompromising divisions between right and wrong, its freedom from all the sophistries of a more indulgent morality. But his praise is emphatically confined to Puritanism in the abstract. Notice that the common test which neither Isabella nor Angelo can resist is coming into contact with real life. Puritanism has done its part as a training and may still last as an ideal; for practical purposes it must give place to a larger and more liberal morality, on pain of falling below itself. Its worthiest disciples will surpass it, its lower ones disgrace it. Different as its result may seem on Angelo and Isabella, the two studies point to the same conclusion: Puritanism, in its present state, unmodified, is unfit to come into contact with society. (p. 149)

How can the general scheme of *Measure for Measure* be interpreted save as an onslaught on Puritanism, if not as an individual yet as a social force? And does not the dénouement mean the downfall of Puritanic rule, the humbling of Puritanic pride, the restoration of the Renaissance? Angelo's delinquencies are all exposed, his decisions all reversed, he himself dismissed with the mercy which he would not show. Like Shylock he is taught "to know the difference of their spirits" [*Merchant of Venice*, IV. i. 368]; Puritanic, like Judaic morality, with which it shows many points of contact, is absorbed and taken up into Christianity. The Duke, enlightened by his experience, after carrying Puritan logic to its barbarous conclusion, declares the futility in life and before reason of "Measure still for Measure."

But in the course of fifty years a change was to take place. The spirit of the nation was to change. Puritanism was to settle down into English character, chiefly, as Shakespeare seems to have foreseen, through the agency of women. What had been the exception was to become the rule. When the Puritans actually came into power the body of the people went with them. Puritanic rule was no longer imposed as a penance, but exacted as a right. Those fifty years' transition between the death of Elizabeth and the founding of the Commonwealth wrought a change Shakespeare could not have foreseen. Reality would have given his play just the opposite dénouement.

Measure for Measure therefore may stand as the supreme study of Puritanism in its essence, detached from all external accidents; to this psychological study it owes its lasting value; it presents the further interest of a record of the reception Puritanism met with from the Renaissance; it must not be accepted on trust as a prophecy of fact. (pp. 151-52)

S. J. Mary Suddard, " 'Measure for Measure' As a Clue to Shakespeare's Attitude towards Puritanism," in her Keats, Shelley, and Shakespeare: Studies & Essays in English Literature, *Cambridge at the University Press, 1912, pp. 136-52.*

[ARTHUR QUILLER-COUCH] (essay date 1922)

[Quiller-Couch was editor with J. Dover Wilson of the New Cambridge edition of Shakespeare's works. In his study Shakespeare's Workmanship *(1918), and in his Cambridge lectures on Shakespeare, Quiller-Couch based his interpretations on the assumption that Shakespeare was mainly a craftsman attempting, with the tools and materials at hand, to solve particular problems central to his plays. He argues that the main problem in interpreting* Measure for Measure *is Shakespeare's treatment of Isabella: there is "something rancid" in her chastity that makes her inconsistent and disappointing. His reaction to the Duke is similar, and he calls the character capricious. Thus, Quiller-Couch bases his*

assessment of the play's major weakness on Shakespeare's in-consistent characterization. He concludes, however, that Measure for Measure *remains a work of genius despite its faults, stating that it "arrests—it impresses while it puzzles—every reader." For similar reactions to Isabella, see the excerpts by Charlotte Lennox (1753), William Hazlitt (1817), and H. B. Charlton (1937).]*

We submit that in *Measure for Measure,* as we have it, [Shake-speare's idea of poetical justice] is not thoroughly clear, has not been thoroughly realised. We take as our test Isabella; the 'heroine' and mainspring of the whole action. Isabella, more than any other character in the play, should carry our sympathy with her, or, at the least, our understanding. But does she? On the contrary the critics can make nothing of her or—which is worse—they make two opposite women of her, and praise or blame her accordingly. (pp. xxvii-xxviii)

We do not set ourselves up for umpires in this dispute. Our point is that the dispute itself—the mere fact that intelligent readers can hold such opposite views of a character which, on the face of it, should be simplicity itself—is proof that the play misses clearness in portraying its most important character.

And our own sense of the play has to admit the perplexity of Isabella. It has annoyed us so that at one time we were almost driven to examine her and Angelo as two pendent portraits or studies in the ugliness of Puritan hypocrisy. We grant, how-ever, that she is honestly conceived as a heroine; and further, if the reader will, that hers (as opposed to Cassandra's in the original) was the righteous choice. Still, it has to be admitted that she is something rancid in her chastity; and, on top of this, not by any means such a saint as she looks. To put it nakedly, she is all for saving her own soul, and she saves it by turning, of a sudden, into a bare procuress. . . . To Isabella the sup-posed Friar (the disguised Duke) would be a holy man: and we are all acquainted with the sort of woman who will commit herself to any deed without question, if it be suggested by a priest. It remains a fact that on the supposed Friar's suggestion, and with no qualm of conscience, but with careful contrivance, Isabella substitutes Mariana for herself in Angelo's bed. Her panegyrists may excuse it: they cannot overlook it: and to us, in our day, it looks as if this virgin 'enskied and sainted' had saved herself by a trick which denudes her own chastity of all but chastity's conventional (or conventual) religious trappings; that she is chaste, even fiercely chaste, for herself, without quite knowing what chastity means. (pp. xxix-xxx)

We put aside the question whether she was a better or a worse woman in refusing to sacrifice her chastity to save a very dear brother's life. . . . We do not condemn it: yet we have no doubt that it lay within Shakespeare's power, at its best, to create an Isabella who should make the refusal and yet keep our sympathy along with our admiration. In the play, as we have it, he has not done this; and the trouble, to our thinking, lies *in his failure to make Isabella a consistent character.* (pp. xxx-xxxi)

She will plead Claudio's lapse as a venial sin: at the first suggestion of her own sinning it is 'O, you beast!'—but by-and-by, to escape this, she is mating a pair without wedlock; while at the end we are left to suppose that for herself mating is mainly a question of marriage-lines; and that, for a Duke, she will throw her novitiate head-dress over the mill. She can be eloquent! She will plead to Angelo for clemency, for mercy, in words that melt the heart: yet when it comes to her own turn to pity and forgive, she casts her own brother from her remorselessly, and never speaks to him again—no, not when he is returned to her from the tomb. Her gift of taciturnity

would seem to be no less wayward, spasmodic, unaccountable, than her gift of golden speech. (pp. xxxi-xxxii)

In effect, Isabella disappoints. The stage has been carefully set for her. Brothel and prison contribute their darkness, all Vienna is taxed of its vice, to throw into higher relief this white ap-parition from the cloister shining in purity, corsletted in virtue. Yet in effect she disappoints: for in effect she writes no lesson on the dark walls, as they teach none to her soul. The true human interest slides away from her contention with Angelo to her contention with her wretched brother; and when that is over (and we have felt that, though her conduct may be ex-emplary, her behaviour has been too hard), she does little benefit to anybody. . . . But for our true release from the stews of Vienna and their foetid atmosphere we turn not to Isabella. We turn rather to Mariana's moated garden beyond the walls, . . . a garden upon the dusk of which Isabella glides with something more sinuous than the innocence of a dove. Mariana has little to say: but Mariana feels as Isabella does not; and with her we have at least the craving to be free of that Viennese world in which Isabella, with her Friar-Duke, is too fatally at home, and destined to be at home for all her vows. . . . Is it extravagant to suppose that Shakespeare invented this remote and exquisite scene, with its sob of the lute, on realising that Isabella had failed, and was henceforth issueless, to deliver the spirit of his dream?

The Duke comports himself no less capriciously. He begins well, and in his exhortation to Claudio upon death he speaks most nobly. But he tails off into a stage-puppet and ends a wearisome man, talking rubbish. From the first no one quite knows why he has chosen to absent himself ostentatiously from Vienna and to come back pretending to be somebody else. His game puzzles Lucio only less completely than it puzzles us. The one thing certain about him, apart from the occasional nobility of his diction, is that, as guardian of the state and its laws, he shirks his proper responsibility and steals back *in-cognito* to play busy-body and spy on his deputy. (pp. xxxiii-xxxiv)

Yet we could forgive, while regretting, that his issues, and Isabella's, fail in fineness and end in staginess, if they were but pursued consistently with character. But they are not. They are pursued capriciously: and this, we suspect—albeit he did not go on to lay his instinct in account with reason—lurks beneath Hazlitt's complaint that 'there may be said to be a general system of cross-purposes between the feelings of the different characters and the sympathy of the reader or the au-dience' [see excerpt above, 1817]. (pp. xxxiv-xxxv)

Measure for Measure is a great play—in parts, and in despite that its parts do not fit. It arrests—it impresses while it puz-zles—every reader. It does not, in our experience, gain new votes when transferred from the library to the stage—as *The Taming of the Shrew,* for example (a vastly less serious play), undoubtedly does. But no play of Shakespeare's carries a stron-ger conviction that, although the goods may be 'mixed,' we are trafficking with genius. (p. xli)

[Arthur Quiller-Couch], *in an introduction to* Mea-sure for Measure *by William Shakespeare, Cam-bridge at the University Press, 1922, pp. vii-xliii.*

G. WILSON KNIGHT   (essay date 1930)

[Knight is one of the most influential Shakespearean critics of the twentieth century; he helped shape a new interpretive approach

to Shakespeare's work and promoted a greater appreciation of many of the plays. In his studies The Wheel of Fire *(1930) and* The Shakespearian Tempest *(1932), Knight rejected criticism which emphasizes sources, character analysis, psychology, and ethics and outlined his principles of interpretation which, he claimed, would "replace that chaos by drawing attention to the true Shakespearian unity." Knight argued that this unity lay in Shakespeare's poetic use of images and symbols—particularly in the opposition of "tempests" and "music." He also maintained that a play's spatial aspects, or "atmosphere," should be as closely considered as the temporal elements of the plot if one is "to see the whole play in space as well as time." Knight contends that* Measure for Measure *explicates "the moral nature of man in relation to the crudity of man's justice, especially in the matter of sexual vice." For Knight, the play is an allegory that, to be understood, must be read in light of the Gospels and the parables of Jesus. He asserts that the Duke, like Jesus, is the "prophet of a new order of ethics," presenting a message of mercy and tolerance that reiterates the moral imperative contained in the Gospels. Knight is also the first critic to elevate the Duke to a prominent and admirable role in* Measure. *His portrait of Isabella continues the negative assessments of that character presented by Charlotte Lennox (1753), Samuel Johnson (1765), William Hazlitt (1817), Arthur Quiller-Couch (1922), and H. B. Charlton (1937), but goes further in its examination of the relationship of sanctity to chastity—a quality which Knight states takes precedence over Isabella's willingness to love. Knight's interpretation of* Measure for Measure *as a Christian allegory initiated a trend in twentieth-century criticism that is reflected in the essays by R. W. Chambers (1937), F. R. Leavis (1942), Roy W. Battenhouse (1946), Nevill Coghill (1955), and Tom McBride (1974).]*

In *Measure for Measure* we have a careful dramatic pattern, a studied explication of a central theme: the moral nature of man in relation to the crudity of man's justice, especially in the matter of sexual vice. There is, too, a clear relation existing between the play and the Gospels, for the play's theme is this:

> Judge not, that ye be not judged.
> For with what judgement ye judge, ye shall be
> judged: and with what measure ye mete, it shall
> be measured to you again.
>
> > (Matthew vii. 1)
> > (p. 73)

Measure for Measure is a carefully constructed work. Not until we view it as a deliberate artistic pattern of certain pivot ideas determining the play's action throughout shall we understand its peculiar nature. . . . We must be careful not to let our human interest in any one person distort our single vision of the whole pattern. The play tends towards allegory or symbolism. The poet elects to risk a certain stiffness, or arbitrariness, in the directing of his plot rather than fail to express dramatically, with variety and precision, the full content of his basic thought. Any stiffness in the matter of human probability is, however, more than balanced by its extreme fecundity and compacted significance of dramatic symbolism. The persons of the play tend to illustrate certain human qualities chosen with careful reference to the main theme. Thus Isabella stands for sainted purity, Angelo for Pharisaical righteousness, the Duke for a psychologically sound and enlightened ethic. Lucio represents indecent wit, Pompey and Mistress Overdone professional immorality. Barnardine is hardheaded, criminal, insensitiveness. Each person illumines some facet of the central theme: man's moral nature. The play's attention is confined chiefly to sexual ethics: which in isolation is naturally the most pregnant of analysis and the most universal of all themes. . . . The atmosphere, purpose, and meaning of the play are throughout ethical. The Duke, lord of this play in the exact sense that

Prospero is lord of *The Tempest,* is the prophet of an enlightened ethic. He controls the action from start to finish, he allots, as it were, praise and blame, he is lit at moments with divine suggestion comparable with his almost divine power of foreknowledge, and control, and wisdom. There is an enigmatic, other-worldly, mystery suffusing his figure and the meaning of his acts: their result, however, in each case justifies their initiation—wherein we see the allegorical nature of the play, since the plot is so arranged that each person receives his desserts in the light of the Duke's—which is really the Gospel—ethic. (pp. 73-4)

The atmosphere of Christianity pervading the play merges into the purely ethical suggestion implicit in the inter-criticism of all the persons. Though the Christian ethic be the central theme, there is a wider setting of varied ethical thought, voiced by each person in turn, high or low. The Duke, Angelo, and Isabella are clearly obsessed with such ideas and criticize freely in their different fashions. So also Elbow and the officers bring in Froth and Pompey, accusing them. Abhorson is severely critical of Pompey:

> A bawd? Fie upon him! He will discredit our mystery.
> > [IV. ii. 29]

Lucio traduces the Duke's character, Mistress Overdone informs against Lucio. Barnardine is universally despised. All, that is, react to each other in an essentially ethical mode: which mode is the peculiar and particular vision of this play. (p. 76)

[The Duke's] government has been inefficient, not through an inherent weakness or laxity in him, but rather because meditation and self-analysis, together with profound study of human nature, have shown him that all passions and sins of other men have reflected images in his own soul. He is no weakling: he has been 'a scholar, a statesman, and a soldier' [III. ii. 146]. But to such a philosopher government and justice may begin to appear a mockery, and become abhorrent. His judicial method has been original: all criminals were either executed promptly or else freely released [IV. ii. 132-34]. Nowhere is the peculiar modernity of the Duke in point of advanced psychology more vividly apparent. It seems, too, if we are to judge by his treatment of Barnardine [IV. iii. 67-9], that he could not tolerate an execution without the criminal's own approval! . . . The Duke's sense of human responsibility is delightful throughout: he is like a kindly father, and all the rest are his children. Thus he now performs the experiment of handing the reins of government to a man of ascetic purity, who has an hitherto invulnerable faith in the rightness and justice of his own ideals—a man of spotless reputation and self-conscious integrity, who will have no fears as to the 'justice' of enforcing precise obedience. The scheme is a plot, or trap: a scientific experiment to see if extreme ascetic righteousness can stand the test of power. (pp. 78-9)

As the play progresses and his plot on Angelo works he assumes an ever-increasing mysterious dignity, his original purpose seems to become more and more profound in human insight, the action marches with measured pace to its appointed and logical end. We have ceased altogether to think of the Duke as merely a studious and unpractical governor, incapable of office. Rather he holds, within the dramatic universe, the dignity and power of a Prospero, to whom he is strangely similar. With both, their plot and plan is the plot and plan of the play: they make and forge the play, and thus are automatically to be equated in a unique sense with the poet himself—since both are symbols of the poet's controlling, purposeful, combined, movement of the chessmen of the drama. Like Prospero, the Duke tends to assume proportions evidently divine. . . . In the rhymed octosyllabic couplets of the Duke's soliloquy in III. ii. there is a distinct note of supernatural authority, forecasting the rhymed mystic utterances of divine beings in The Final Plays. . . .

> He who the sword of heaven will bear
> Should be as holy as severe;
> Pattern in himself to know
> Grace to stand and virtue go;
> More nor less to other paying
> Than by self-offences weighing.
> Shame to him whose cruel striking
> Kills for faults of his own liking!
> Twice treble shame on Angelo,
> To weed my vice and let his grow!
> O what may man within him hide,
> Though angel on the outward side!
> How many likeness made in crimes,
> Making practice on the times,
> To draw with idle spiders' strings
> Most ponderous and substantial things!
> Craft against vice I must apply:
> With Angelo to-night shall lie
> His old betrothed but despised;
> So disguise shall, by the disguised,
> Pay with falsehood false exacting,
> And perform an old contracting.
>
> [III. ii. 261-82]

This fine soliloquy gives us the Duke's philosophy: the philosophy that prompted his original plan. And it is important to notice the mystical, prophetic tone of the speech.

The Duke, like Jesus, is the prophet of a new order of ethics. This aspect of the Duke as teacher and prophet is also illustrated by his cryptic utterance to Escalus just before this soliloquy:

> *Escalus.* What news abroad i' the world?
> *Duke.* None, but that there is so great a fever on goodness, that the dissolution of it must cure it: novelty is only in request; and it is as dangerous to be aged in any kind of course, as it is virtuous to be constant in any undertaking. There is scarce truth enough alive to make societies secure; but security enough to make fellowships accurst: much upon this riddle runs the wisdom of the world. This news is old enough, yet it is every day's news.
>
> [III. ii. 221-30]

This speech holds the poetry of ethics. Its content, too, is very close to the Gospel teaching: the insistence on the blindness of the world, its habitual disregard of the truth exposed by prophet and teacher:

> And this is the condemnation, that light is come into the world, and men loved darkness rather than light, because their deeds were evil.
>
> (John iii. 19)

The same almost divine suggestion rings in many of the Duke's measured prose utterances. There are his supremely beautiful words to Escalus [IV. ii. 203-06]:

> Look, the unfolding star calls up the shepherd. Put not yourself into amazement how these things should be: all difficulties are but easy when they are known.

The first lovely sentence—a unique beauty of Shakespearian prose, in a style peculiar to this play—derives part of its appeal from New Testament associations; and the second sentence holds the mystic assurance of Matthew, x. 26:

> . . . for there is nothing covered, that shall not be revealed; and hid, that shall not be known.
>
> (pp. 79-81)

The Duke's ethical attitude is exactly correspondent with Jesus': the play must be read in the light of the Gospel teaching, if its full significance is to be apparent. So he, like Jesus, moves among men suffering grief at their sins and deriving joy from an unexpected flower of simple goodness in the deserts of impurity and hardness. . . . Now, in that he represents a perfected ethical philosophy joined to supreme authority, the Duke is, within the dramatic universe, automatically comparable with Divinity; or we may suggest that he progresses by successive modes, from worldly power through the prophecy and moralizing of the middle scenes, to the supreme judgement at the end, where he exactly reflects the universal judgement as suggested by many Gospel passages. There is the same apparent injustice, the same tolerance and mercy. The Duke is, in fact, a symbol of the same kind as the Father in the Parable of the Prodigal Son (Luke xv) or the Lord in that of the Unmerciful Servant (Matthew xviii). The simplest way to focus correctly the quality and unity of *Measure for Measure* is to read it on the analogy of Jesus' parables.

Though his ethical philosophy is so closely related to the Gospel teaching, yet the Duke's thoughts on death are devoid of any explicit belief in immortality. He addresses Claudio, who is to die, and his words at first appear vague, agnostic: but a deeper acquaintance renders their profundity and truth. Claudio fears death. The Duke comforts him by concentrating not on death, but on life. In a series of pregnant sentences he asserts the negative nature of any single life-joy. . . . Life is therefore a sequence of unrealities, strung together in a time-succession. Everything it can give is in turn killed. Regarded thus, it is unreal, a delusion, a living death. The thought is profound. True, the Duke has concentrated especially on the temporal aspect of life's appearances, regarding only the shell of life and neglecting the inner vital principle of joy and hope; he has left deeper things untouched. He neglects love and all immediate transcendent intuitions. But since it is only this temporal aspect of decayed appearances which death is known to end, since it is only the closing of this very time-succession which Claudio fears, it is enough to prove this succession valueless. Claudio is thus comforted. The death of such a life is indeed not death, but rather itself a kind of life:

> I humbly thank you.
> To sue to live, I find I seek to die;
> And seeking death, find life: let it come on.
>
> [III. i. 41-3]

Now he 'will encounter darkness as a bride', like Antony [III. i. 83]. The Duke's death-philosophy is thus the philosophy of the great tragedies to follow—of *Timon*, of *Antony and Cleopatra*. So, too, his ethic is the ethic of *King Lear*. In this problem play we find the profound thought of the supreme tragedies already emergent and given careful and exact form: the Duke in this respect being analogous to Agamemnon in *Troilus and Cressida*. Both his ethical and his death thinking are profoundly modern. But Claudio soon reverts to the crude time-thinking (and fine poetry) of his famous death-speech, in which he regards the afterlife in terms of orthodox eschatology, thinking of it as a temporal process, like Hamlet:

> Ay, but to die, and go we know not where . . .
>
> [III. i. 117]

In the Shakespearian mode of progressive thought it is essential first to feel death's reality strongly as the ender of what we call 'life': only then do we begin to feel the tremendous pressure of an immortality not known in terms of time. We then begin to attach a different meaning to the words 'life' and 'death'. The thought of this scene thus wavers between the old and the new death-philosophies.

The Duke's plot pivots on the testing of Angelo. Angelo is a man of spotless reputation, generally respected. . . . Angelo, hearing the Duke's praise, and his proposed trust, modestly declines, as though he recognizes that his virtue is too purely idealistic for the rough practice of state affairs:

> Now, good my lord,
> Let there be some more test made of my metal,
> Before so noble and so great a figure
> Be stamp'd upon it.
>
> [I. i. 47-50]

Angelo is not a conscious hypocrite: rather a man whose chief faults are self-deception and pride in his own righteousness— an unused and delicate instrument quite useless under the test of active trial. This he half-recognizes, and would first refuse the proffered honour. The Duke insists: Angelo's fall is thus entirely the Duke's responsibility. So this man of ascetic life is forced into authority. . . . Angelo, indeed, does not know himself: no one receives so great a shock as he himself when temptation overthrows his virtue. He is no hypocrite. He cannot, however, be acquitted of Pharisaical pride: his reputation means much to him, he 'stands at a guard with envy' [I. iii. 51]. He 'takes pride' in his 'gravity' [II. iv. 10]. Now, when he is first faced with the problem of Claudio's guilt of adultery—and commanded, we must presume, by the Duke's sealed orders to execute stern punishment wholesale, for this is the Duke's ostensible purpose—Angelo pursues his course without any sense of wrongdoing. . . . He feels no personal responsibility, since he is certain that he does right. We believe him when he tells Isabella:

> It is the law, not I, condemn your brother:
> Were he my kinsman, brother, or my son,
> It should be thus with him.
>
> [II. ii. 80-2]

To execute justice, he says, is kindness, not cruelty, in the long run.

Angelo's arguments are rationally conclusive. A thing irrational breaks them, however: his passion for Isabella. Her purity, her idealism, her sanctity enslave him. . . . Good and evil change places in his mind, since this passion is immediately recognized as good, yet, by everyone of his stock judgements, condemned as evil. The devil becomes a 'good angel'. And this wholesale reversion leaves Angelo in sorry plight now: he has no moral values left. Since sex has been synonymous with foulness in his mind, this new love, reft from the start of moral sanction in a man who 'scarce confesses that his blood flows', becomes swiftly a devouring and curbless lust:

> I have begun,
> And now I give my sensual race the rein. . . .
>
> [II. iv. 159-60]

In proportion as his moral reason formerly denied his instincts, so now his instincts assert themselves in utter callousness of his moral reason. He swiftly becomes an utter scoundrel. He threatens to have Claudio tortured. Next, thinking to have had his way with Isabella, he is so conscience-stricken and tortured by fear that he madly resolves not to keep faith with her: he orders Claudio's instant execution. For, in proportion as he is nauseated at his own crimes, he is terror-struck at exposure. He is mad with fear: his story exactly pursues the Macbeth rhythm. . . . This is the reward of self-deception, of pharisaical pride, of an idealism not harmonized with instinct—of trying, to use the Duke's pregnant phrase:

> To draw with idle spiders' strings
> Most ponderous and substantial things.
>
> [III. ii. 275-76]

Angelo has not been overcome with evil. He has been ensnared by good, by his own love of sanctity, exquisitely symbolized in his love of Isabella: the hook is baited with a saint, and the saint is caught. The cause of his fall is this and this only. The coin of his moral purity, which flashed so brilliantly, when tested does not ring true. Angelo is the symbol of a false intellectualized ethic divorced from the deeper springs of human instinct.

The varied close-inwoven themes of *Measure for Measure* are finally knit in the exquisite final act. To that point the action— reflected image always of the Ducal plot—marches

> By cold gradation and well-balanced form.
>
> [IV. iii. 100]

The last act of judgement is heralded by trumpet calls:

> Twice have the trumpets sounded;
> The generous and gravest citizens
> Have hent the gates, and very near upon
> The duke is entering.
>
> [IV. vi. 12-15]

So all are, as it were, summoned to the final judgement. Now Angelo, Isabella, Lucio—all are understood most clearly in the light of this scene. The last act is the key to the play's meaning, and all difficulties are here resolved. I will observe the judgement measured to each, noting retrospectively the especial significance in the play of Lucio and Isabella.

Lucio is a typical loose-minded, vulgar wit. He is the product of a society that has gone too far in condemnation of human sexual desires. He keeps up a running comment on sexual matters. His very existence is a comdemnation of the society which makes him a possibility. Not that there is anything of premeditated villainy in him: he is merely superficial, enjoying the unnatural ban on sex which civilization imposes, because that very ban adds point and spice to sexual gratification. He is, however, sincerely concerned about Claudio, and urges Isabella to plead for him. He can be serious—for a while. He can speak sound sense, too, in the full flow of his vulgar wit:

> Yes, in good sooth, the vice is of a great kindred;
> it is well allied: but it is impossible to extirp it
> quite, friar, till eating and drinking be put
> down. . . .
>
> [III. ii. 101-03]

This goes to the root of our problem here. Pompey has voiced the same thought [II. i. 233-56]. This is, indeed, what the Duke has known too well: what Angelo and Isabella do not know. Thus Pompey and Lucio here at least tell downright facts—Angelo and Isabella pursue impossible and valueless ideals. Only the Duke holds the balance exact throughout. Lucio's running wit, however, pays no consistent regard to truth. To him the Duke's leniency was a sign of hidden immorality. . . . He traduces the Duke's character wholesale. He does not pause to consider the truth of his words. Again, there is no intent of harm—merely a careless, shallow, truthless wit-philosophy which enjoys its own sex-chatter. The type is common. Lucio is refined and vulgar, and the more vulgar because of his refinement. Whereas Pompey, because of his natural coarseness, is less vulgar. Lucio can only exist in a society of smug propriety and self-deception: for his mind's life is entirely parasitical on those insincerities. His false—because fantastic and shallow—pursuit of sex, is the result of a false, fantastic, denial of sex in his world. Like so much in *Measure for Measure* he is eminently modern. Now Lucio is the one person the Duke finds it all but impossible to forgive.

> I find an apt remission in myself;
> And yet here's one in place I cannot pardon.
>
> [V. i. 498-99]

All the rest have been serious in their faults. Lucio's condemnation is his triviality, his insincerity, his profligate idleness, his thoughtless detraction of others' characters. . . . Lucio's treatment at the close is eminently, and fittingly, undignified. He is threatened thus: first he is to marry the mother of his child, about whose wrong he formerly boasted; then to be whipped and hanged. Lucio deserves some credit, however: he preserves his nature and answers with his characteristic wit. He cannot be serious. The Duke, his sense of humour touched, retracts the sentence:

> *Duke.* Upon mine honour, thou shalt marry her.
> Thy slanders I forgive; and therewithal
> Remit thy other forfeits. Take him to prison;
> And see our pleasure herein executed.
> *Lucio.* Marrying a punk, my lord, is pressing to death,
> whipping, and hanging.
> *Duke.* Slandering a prince deserves it.
>
> [V. i. 518-24]

Idleness, triviality, thoughtlessness receive the Duke's strongest condemnation. The thought is this:

> But I say unto you, That every idle word that
> men shall speak, they shall give account thereof
> in the day of judgement.
>
> (Matthew xii. 36)

Exactly what happens to Lucio. His wit is often illuminating, often amusing, sometimes rather disgusting. He is never wicked, is sometimes almost lovable—but he is terribly dangerous.

Isabella is the opposite extreme. She is more saintly than Angelo. And her saintliness goes deeper, is more potent than his. . . . Even Lucio respects her. She calls forth something deeper than his usual wit:

> I would not—though 'tis my familiar sin
> With maids to seem the lapwing and to jest,
> Tongue far from heart—play with all virgins so:
> I hold you as a thing ensky'd and sainted,
> By your renouncement an immortal spirit,
> And to be talk'd with in sincerity,
> As with a saint.
>
> [I. iv. 31-7]

Which contains a fine and exact statement of his shallow behaviour, his habitual wit for wit's sake. Lucio is throughout a loyal friend to Claudio: truer to his cause, in fact, than Isabella. A pointed contrast. He urges her to help. She shows a distressing lack of warmth. It is Lucio that talks of 'your poor brother' [I. iv. 71]. She is cold.

> *Lucio.* Assay the power you have.
> *Isabella.* My power? Alas, I doubt—
> *Lucio.* Our doubts are traitors
> And make us lose the good we oft might win,
> By fearing to attempt.
>
> [I. iv. 76-9]

Isabella's self-centred saintliness is thrown here into strong contrast with Lucio's manly anxiety for his friend. . . . Isabella lacks human feeling. She starts her suit to Angelo poorly enough—she is luke-warm.

> There is a vice that most I do abhor,
> And most desire should meet the blow of justice;
> For which I would not plead but that I must;
> For which I must not plead, but that I am
> At war 'twixt will and will not.
>
> [II. ii. 29-33]

Lucio has to urge her on continually. We begin to feel that Isabella has no real affection for Claudio; has stifled all human love in the pursuit of sanctity. When Angelo at last proposes his dishonourable condition she quickly comes to her decision:

> Then, Isabel, live chaste and, brother, die.
> More than our brother is our chastity.
>
> [II. iv. 184-85]

When Shakespeare chooses to load his dice like this—which is seldom indeed—he does it mercilessly. The Shakespearian satire here strikes once, and deep: there is no need to point it further. But now we know our Isabel. We are not surprised that she behaves to Claudio, who hints for her sacrifice, like a fiend:

> Take my defiance!
> Die, perish! Might but my bending down
> Reprieve thee from thy fate, it should proceed:
> I'll pray a thousand prayers for thy death,
> No word to save thee.
>
> [III. i. 142-46]

Is her fall any less than Angelo's? Deeper, I think. With whom is Isabel angry? Not only with her brother. She has feared this choice—terribly: 'O, I do fear thee, Claudio', she said [III. i. 73]. Ever since Angelo's suggestion she has been afraid. Now Claudio has forced the responsibility of choice on her. She cannot sacrifice herself. Her sex inhibitions have been horribly shown her as they are, naked. She has been stung—lanced on a sore spot of her soul. She knows now that it is not all saintliness, she sees her own soul and sees it as something small, frightened, despicable, too frail to dream of such a sacrifice. Though she does not admit it, she is infuriated, not with Claudio, but herself. 'Saints' should not speak like this. Again, the comment of this play is terribly illuminating. It is significant that she readily involves Mariana in illicit love: it is always her own, and only her own, chastity that assumes, in her heart, universal importance.

Isabella, however, was no hypocrite, any more than Angelo. She is a spirit of purity, grace, maiden charm: but all these virtues the action of the play turns remorselessly against her-

Act V. Scene i. Guards, Mariana, Isabella, Escalus, Angelo, Lucio, and the Duke. Frontispiece to the Hanmer edition by F. Hayman (1744). By permission of the Folger Shakespeare Library.

self. In a way, it is not her fault. Chastity is hardly a sin—but neither, as the play emphasizes, is it the whole of virtue. And she, like the rest, has to find a new wisdom. Mariana in the last act prays for Angelo's life. Confronted by that warm, potent, forgiving, human love, Isabella herself suddenly shows a softening, a sweet humanity. Asked to intercede, she does so—she, who was at the start slow to intercede for a brother's life, now implores the Duke to save Angelo, her wronger:

> I partly think
> A due sincerity govern'd his deeds,
> Till he did look on me.

[V. i. 445-47]

There is a suggestion that Angelo's strong passion has itself moved her, thawing her ice-cold pride. This is the moment of her trial: the Duke is watching her keenly, to see if she has learnt her lesson—nor does he give her any help, but deliberately puts obstacles in her way. But she stands the test: she bows to a love greater than her own saintliness. Isabella, like Angelo, has progressed far during the play's action: from sanctity to humanity.

Angelo, at the beginning of this final scene, remains firm in denial of the accusations levelled against him. Not till the Duke's disguise as a Friar is made known and he understands that deception is no longer possible, does he show outward

repentance. . . . To Angelo, exposure seems to come as a relief: the horror of self-deception is at an end. For the first time in his life he is both quite honest with himself and with the world. So he takes Mariana as his wife. This is just: he threw her over because he thought she was not good enough for him,

> Partly for that her promised proportions
> Came short of composition, but in chief
> For that her reputation was disvalued
> In levity.

[V. i. 219-22]

He aimed too high when he cast his eyes on the sainted Isabel: now, knowing himself, he will find his true level in the love of Mariana. He has become human. The union is symbolical. Just as his supposed love-contact with Isabel was a delusion, when Mariana, his true mate, was taking her place, so Angelo throughout has deluded himself. Now his acceptance of Mariana symbolizes his new self-knowledge. So, too, Lucio is to find his proper level in marrying Mistress Kate Keepdown, of whose child he is the father. Horrified as he is at the thought, he has to meet the responsibilities of his profligate behaviour. The punishment of both is this only: to know, and to be themselves. This is both their punishment and at the same time their highest reward for their sufferings: self-knowledge being the supreme, perhaps the only, good. We remember the parable of the Pharisee and the Publican (Luke xviii).

So the Duke draws his plan to its appointed end. All, including Barnardine, are forgiven, and left, in the usual sense, unpunished. This is inevitable. The Duke's original leniency has been shown by his successful plot to have been right, not wrong. Though he sees 'corruption boil and bubble' [V. i. 318] in Vienna, he has found, too, that man's sainted virtue is a delusion: 'judge not that ye be not judged.' He has seen an Angelo to fall from grace at the first breath of power's temptation, he has seen Isabella's purity scarring, defacing her humanity. He has found more gentleness in 'the steeled gaoler' [IV. ii. 87] than in either of these. He has found more natural honesty in Pompey the bawd than Angelo the ascetic; more humanity in the charity of Mistress Overdone than in Isabella condemning her brother to death with venomed words in order to preserve her own chastity. Mistress Overdone has looked after Lucio's illegitimate child:

> . . . Mistress Kate Keepdown was with child
> by him in the Duke's time; he promised her
> marriage; his child is a year and a quarter old,
> come Philip and Jacob: I have kept it my-
> self . . .

[III. ii. 199-202]

Human virtue does not flower only in high places: nor is it the monopoly of the pure in body. In reading *Measure for Measure* one feels that Pompey with his rough humour and honest professional indecency is the only one of the major persons, save the Duke, who can be called 'pure in heart'. Therefore, knowing all this, the Duke knows his tolerance to be now a moral imperative: he sees too far into the nature of man to pronounce judgement according to the appearances of human behaviour. But we are not told what will become of Vienna. There is, however, a hint, for the Duke is to marry Isabel, and this marriage, like the others, may be understood symbolically. It is to be the marriage of understanding with purity; of tolerance with moral fervour. The Duke, who alone has no delusions as to the virtues of man, who is incapable of executing justice on vice since he finds forgiveness implicit in his wide and sympathetic understanding—he alone wins the 'enskied and sainted' Isabel—more, we are not told. And we may expect her in future to learn from him wisdom, human tenderness, and love:

> What's mine is yours and what is yours is mine.
>
> [V. i. 537]

[If] we still find this universal forgiveness strange—and many have done so—we might observe Mariana, who loves Angelo with a warm and realistically human love. She sees no fault in him, or none of any consequence:

> O my dear lord,
> I crave no other nor no better man.
>
> [V. i. 425-26]

She knows that

> best men are moulded out of faults,
> And, for the most, become much more the better
> For being a little bad.
>
> [V. i. 439-41]

The incident is profoundly true. Love asks no questions, sees no evil, transfiguring the just and unjust alike. This is one of the surest and finest ethical touches in this masterpiece of ethical drama. Its moral of love is, too, the ultimate splendour of Jesus' teaching.

Measure for Measure is indeed based firmly on that teaching. The lesson of the play is that of Matthew v. 20:

> For I say unto you, That except your righteousness shall exceed the righteousness of the scribes and Pharisees, ye shall in no case enter into the Kingdom of heaven.

The play must be read, not as a picture of normal human affairs, but as a parable, like the parables of Jesus. The plot is, in fact, an inversion of one of those parables—that of The Unmerciful Servant (Matthew xviii); and the universal and level forgiveness at the end, where all alike meet pardon, is one with the forgiveness of the Parable of the Two Debtors (Luke vii). Much has been said about the difficulties of *Measure for Measure*. But, in truth, no play of Shakespeare shows more thoughtful care, more deliberate purpose, more consummate skill in structural technique, and, finally, more penetrating ethical and psychological insight. None shows a more exquisitely inwoven pattern. And, if ever the thought at first sight seems strange, or the action unreasonable, it will be ever found to reflect the sublime strangeness and unreason of Jesus' teaching. (pp. 82-96)

> G. Wilson Knight, " 'Measure for Measure' and the Gospels," in his The Wheel of Fire: Interpretations of Shakespearian Tragedy, *Methuen & Co. Ltd.*, 1949, pp. 73-96.

HOXIE N. FAIRCHILD   (essay date 1931)

[*Fairchild argues that Angelo's character is inconsistent, changing from "a harsh precisian" in the first two acts of* Measure for Measure *to a "smooth rascal" in the last three acts. Fairchild contends that this inconsistency is the result of Shakespeare's additions to the character as he is depicted in Whetstone's* Promos and Cassandra, *changes which, in effect, created two Angelos. The first one, according to Fairchild, is an interesting character based on Whetstone's* Promos, *while the second one is a typical Elizabethan villain—what Fairchild describes as the "result of*

the introduction of the Mariana plot." Additional interpretations of Angelo's role appear in the essays by G. G. Gervinus (1849-50), H. B. Charlton (1937), W.M.T. Dodds (1946), Arthur Sewell (1951), Robert Ornstein (1957), and A. D. Nuttall (1968).]

In Elizabethan drama, the baseness of smooth rascals is often concealed from their victims in the play, at least up to the turning-point of the action; but it is very rarely concealed from the audience for any length of time. Until almost the end of II, ii [in *Measure for Measure*], there is no clear indication that Angelo is anything but a harsh precisian without a stain upon his puritanical conscience. In the light of subsequent developments, certain lines in I and in II, i, might be interpreted as hints of Angelo's villainy. These hints, however, are so obscure and dubious that no spectator would be likely to suspect Angelo. His virtue is so extreme that it will probably crack, but it does not at first appear to be the veneer of a hypocrite.

Furthermore, the baseness of smooth rascals is *never* concealed in soliloquies. Elizabethan soliloquies invariably represent the real thoughts of the character. They are not used to mislead the audience or to indicate self-deception on the part of the speaker. When Isabella, in II, ii, leaves Angelo after pleading with him for her brother's life, his inmost thoughts are disclosed in the words:

> What's this, what's this? Is this her fault or mine?
> The tempter or the tempted, who sins most?
> Not she, nor doth she tempt; but it is I,
> That, lying by the violet in the sun,
> Do as the carrion does, not as the flower—
> Corrupt with virtuous season. . . .
> O cunning enemy, that, to catch a saint,
> With saints dost bait thy hook! Most dangerous
> Is that temptation that doth goad us on
> To sin in loving virtue. Never could the strumpet,
> With all her double vigour, art, and nature,
> Once stir my temper; but this virtuous maid
> Subdues me quite. Ever till now,
> When men were fond, I smil'd and wonder'd how.
>
> [II. ii. 162-86]

This is not the soliloquy of a smooth rascal. Scene iv of the same act begins with another self-revelation:

> When I would pray and think, I think and pray
> To several subjects. Heaven hath my empty words,
> Whilst my invention, hearing not my tongue,
> Anchors on Isabel; Heaven in my mouth,
> As if I did but only chew his name,
> And in my heart the strong and swelling evil
> Of my conception. The state whereon I studied
> Is, like a good thing, being often read,
> Grown sear'd and tedious; yea, my gravity,
> Wherein—let no man hear me—I take pride,
> Could I with boot change for an idle plume,
> Which the air beats for vain. O place, O form,
> How often dost thou with thy case, thy habit,
> Wrench awe from fools, and tie the wiser souls
> To thy false seeming! Blood, thou art blood.
> Let's write 'good angel' on the devil's horn,
> 'Tis not the devil's crest.
>
> [I. iv. 1-17]

That he takes pride in his gravity is a thought that he would not wish to be overheard. If this mild secret is to be guarded with particular care, his conscience must be reasonably clear of graver sins.

In the subsequent interview with Isabella, Angelo begins to play the villain, yet there is no suggestion that his wickedness is anything but the sudden collapse of a saint who has been tempted by saintliness. In the first scene of Act III, however, we get a totally different conception of Angelo's character. The Duke says of Mariana:

> . . . [Angelo] Left her in her tears, and dried
> not one of them with his comfort; swallowed
> his vows whole, pretending in her discoveries
> of dishonour; in few, bestow'd her on her own
> lamentation, which she yet wears for his sake;
> and he, a marble to her tears, is wash'd with
> them, but relents not.
>
> [III. i. 225-30]

Angelo, then, has condemned Claudio for behaving chivalrously though rashly in a situation in which Angelo himself had previously behaved like a mercenary cad. The man who jilted Mariana is simply not the same person as he whose thoughts are revealed in the soliloquies.

There are two Angelos. The Angelo of Acts I and II is a cold, harsh, severe, pure prig, "whose blood is very snow-broth" [I. iv. 57-8]. By an interesting psychological development, his unnatural restraint breaks down before the purity of Isabella. Impelled by a hitherto unexperienced lust, he drives his evil bargain with her. The Angelo of Acts III-V is Professor Lawrence's smooth rascal [see excerpt below, 1931]. He has not only broken his trothplight to Mariana, but has foully slandered her. Plainly, he has been a hypocrite from the beginning. Not content with seeking to dishonour Isabella, he breaks his promise to her by ordering Claudio's execution. His final repentance is a theatric convention that cannot figure in an interpretation of the character.

This fundamental inconsistency can hardly be denied, and it is important enough to demand some explanation. The first Angelo, as we shall call him, is one of Shakespeare's most mature and interesting character-studies. Where does he come from, and why does he give place to the much more conventional second Angelo? (pp. 53-5)

The first Angelo of *Measure for Measure*, very different from Promos as he is, is probably derived from that figure. Whetstone's respectable man tempted by respectability, though vaguely outlined, had interesting possibilities which Shakespeare determined to develop.

But the development of those possibilities conflicted with certain changes of plotting which Shakespeare felt to be needful. In Whetstone's play, Cassandra gives in to Promos only after he has promised to spare her brother and has signed an agreement to marry her. He enjoys Cassandra, but keeps neither of his promises. Near the end of the play, the prototype of Shakespeare's Duke forces Promos to marry Cassandra, and then condemns him to death. But marrying Promos transforms Cassandra into a doting wife who loudly laments that her "sweet husband" is to die. Her pleas, added to the fact that her brother Andrugio proves not to have been executed after all, cause the Duke to be merciful. Shakespeare was generally willing to adopt the plots of his sources without sweeping changes, but this was a little too much. Isabella must preserve her chastity, and she must not marry Angelo. Hence Shakespeare, as the reader will remember, introduced Mariana and adapted from *All's Well* the traditional "bed-trick" whereby Isabella remains virtuous and Mariana consummates her trothplight with Angelo. But with the introduction of this device, our second Angelo, the smooth rascal created by the exigencies of the new plot, necessarily appears.

Shakespeare was too fond of the first Angelo to banish him from the play in the interests of consistency. He was not the man to throw away two of the best acts he ever wrote. He accepted his predicament philosophically, and hurried on to the sure-fire tricks of the last act. Perhaps, however, he recognized almost from the first that the sincere precisian must give place to the base hypocrite, and made some rather half-hearted attempts to prepare the audience for the coming change. Thus I, iii, ends with the Duke's words to Friar Thomas,

> . . . . . hence shall we see,
> If power change purpose, what our seemers be.
>
> [I. iii. 53-4]

The word "seemers" hints suspicion, but the Duke apparently fears that power may pervert Angelo's purpose, not that his purpose is essentially bad.

Two passages in Act II might be taken as pointing forward to the disclosure of Angelo's treatment of Mariana. Referring to Claudio's case, Escalus urges Angelo to consider

> Whether you had not sometime in your life
> Err'd in this point which now you censure him.
>
> [II. i. 14-15]

Later Isabella strikes the same note in bidding Angelo

> . . . . . Go to your bosom;
> Knock there, and ask your heart what it doth know
> That's like my brother's fault.
>
> [II. ii. 136-38]
> (pp. 56-7)

Though these passages assume significance when we look back upon them, they do not, as the play develops before our eyes, adequately prepare us for a deliberately villainous Angelo. All the emphatic clues point in the other direction. If Elizabethan villains do not tell the audience that they are villains, other characters provide that information in unmistakable terms.

On the other hand, the only trace of the first Angelo in the latter part of the play appears in Isabella's not very confident words in Act V:

> . . . . I partly think
> A due sincerity govern'd his deeds
> Till he did look on me.
>
> [V. i. 445-47]

This is doubtless a relic of Cassandra's plea on behalf of Promos. (p. 58)

Whether or not Shakespeare revised *Measure for Measure*, my main contention stands. We cannot say that Angelo is a good man who succumbs to temptation, nor can we say that he is a hypocritical villain. There are two Angelos. The first is a characteristically Shakespearian development of Whetstone's Promos. The second is merely the result of the introduction of the Mariana plot. (p. 59)

Hoxie N. Fairchild, "The Two Angelo's," in The Shakespeare Association Bulletin, *Vol. VI, No. 2, April, 1931, pp. 53-9.*

WILLIAM WITHERLE LAWRENCE (essay date 1931)

[Lawrence was an American scholar and author of Shakespeare's Problem Comedies *(1931). In that work he initiated a trend in modern criticism by evaluating Shakespeare's "problem plays" through an explication of his indebtedness to Elizabethan dramatic conventions and social concepts, an approach employed by critics of the historical school. In his analysis of* Measure for Measure, *Lawrence argues that the contradictions and improbabilities identified by earlier commentators result from Shakespeare's unsuccessful blending of artificial plot devices with the realism of the play's basic story and his talent for natural characterization. Lawrence contends, however, that much of the critical confusion surrounding* Measure for Measure *can be resolved if the play is examined in light of Elizabethan customs, and he faults earlier critics—especially Samuel Taylor Coleridge (1818)—for lacking the insight to do so. Lawrence notes, for example, that a contemporary audience would have accepted the so-called bed-trick, because in the eyes of the Elizabethan church, Angelo's betrothal to Mariana was binding. This interpretation counters the charge of immorality presented by William Hazlitt (1817) and Arthur Quiller-Couch (1922). Lawrence also discusses the Duke's artificial nature, stating that he seems to be a puppet in comparison to the "low" characters, who are real enough to make an audience forget the play's improbabilities. For other interpretations that assess* Measure for Measure *in light of contemporary stage devices and social customs, see the excerpts by R. W. Chambers (1937), Muriel C. Bradbrook (1941), Oscar James Campbell (1943), Murray Krieger (1951), Nevill Coghill (1955), and Ernest Schanzer (1963).]*

What Shakespeare failed to do in *All's Well* he achieved in *Measure for Measure,* a play surcharged with emotion, and suffused with sympathy for the frailties of mankind. Here his imagination was kindled by his theme, and flashed forth in white flame, in a brilliance all the greater because of the deep shadows of the background. (p. 78)

This heightened sympathy and realism are undoubtedly due, in part, to the nature of the theme which Shakespeare was recasting. It is commonly said that this theme is of the same sort as that in *All's Well,* but the truth is that it is very different, both in nature and origin. *All's Well* is a composite of archaic and illogical folk-tale situations. The basic theme of *Measure for Measure,* on the other hand, may apparently be ultimately traced to an episode in real life. In any case, such a situation might actually have arisen at any time, and probably has arisen more than once. It is not only poignantly real, but intensely dramatic. It presents one of those dreadful alternatives between conflicting demands of honor and affection which have in them the very essence of tragic drama. (p. 79)

In [*Measure for Measure*] this realistic basic action is combined with plot-material taken from traditional story, and exhibiting the archaisms and improbabilities characteristic of such narrative. The introduction of these artificial elements was chiefly due to Shakespeare, not to his sources. This point seems generally to have been overlooked. The extraordinary thing is that while the main situation apparently stirred Shakespeare very deeply, and while he gave to it a power such as no other writer had attained, he made it in some respects more conventional, less like real life. The result has been confusion among the commentators. They have been puzzled by the contradictions arising from the fusion of realism and artificiality, and they have failed to understand the significance of the changes made by Shakespeare. (pp. 79-80)

The central figure of [*Measure for Measure*], the pivot about which all else turns, is, as in *All's Well,* the heroine. And here,

as in that play, there is the widest diversity of opinion as to the heroine's true character. (p. 81)

Shakespeare radically modified the plot [of Whetstone's *Promos and Cassandra*] in making the heroine refuse to surrender her honor at the price of her brother's life, on the ground that her personal purity is of greater importance. . . . Indeed, the firm insistence of Isabella upon chastity reminds one of the mediaeval heroines of Virtue Stories, who subdue all other considerations to the one perfect quality which they keep ever before them. (p. 93)

Nothing in the play has aroused sharper dissent than the device by which the honor of Isabella is safeguarded, and nothing has been more completely misunderstood. The Duke has been blamed for suggesting it, Isabella for consenting to it, and Mariana for carrying it out. (p. 94)

But Mariana and her adviser are in no wise culpable, nor is Isabella herself. The point of importance to keep in mind is the relation between Angelo and Mariana. The fact that they had earlier been affianced is of the utmost significance in drawing conclusions as to the morality of the story. . . . This simple and obvious point in the Mariana story has been strangely overlooked by those who have censured harshly the gentle lady of the moated grange. (p. 95)

An understanding of the binding force of the Elizabethan betrothal is important. Spousals, or betrothals, and the final celebration of marriage were separate and distinct ceremonies; the latter following after an interval of not less than three weeks. "Private spousals could be accomplished by any of the lovers' formulas of today for becoming engaged, and in public spousals there was also a certain amount of latitude allowed. In the most orthodox form of the latter, a priest was present, and a regular ceremony consisting of vows similar to those of a present-day wedding was gone through with." [C. L. Powell, *English Dramatic Relations, 1487-1653*] Such a union was recognized by both ecclesiastical and state authorities as valid, the law declared the offspring of a troth-plight legitimate, and the church imposed penalties for violation of the contract. (p. 97)

In the light of these considerations, Hazlitt's remark about the virtue that is "sublimely good at another's expense" [see excerpt above, 1817], and Quiller-Couch's assertions that Isabella is "a bare procuress," and that she "is mating a pair without wedlock" [see excerpt above, 1922], collapse like pricked bubbles. We have seen how insistent Shakespeare is upon the purity of Isabella, how he altered the plot, making her refuse to sacrifice her honor even for her brother's life, and how she desires the strictest restraint in the sisterhood which she is about to enter. The moral justification of the Mariana ruse would be shown, if by nothing else, by the instant readiness with which she accepts the plan and puts it into execution. (p. 98)

We may dismiss immediately, in view of what has just been said in regard to betrothals, any doubts which we may cherish as to the morality of the episode. Whether it be a sacrifice of dignity on the part of a woman to entrap her lover, as Helena entrapped her husband, is another matter. . . . Shakespeare was utilizing, as he so often did, a bit of archaic plotting which is hard to reconcile with the naturalness of his characters. His heroines seem so real that we find it hard to accept them in artificial situations. But such situations had been deemed suitable for heroines in the earlier traditions from which Shakespeare was drawing, they were current in the story-telling of his own day, and he therefore accepted them for his own dramatic purposes. How far he was disturbed by them we cannot tell; but it would seem, from the frequency with which he employed them, that he felt far less their lack of reality than we do, even when they seem to involve psychological contradictions. If they were not felt as disturbingly artificial by the people of his own day, they are less likely to have worried Shakespeare. (p. 99)

The great prominence of the Duke is . . . one of Shakespeare's most important additions to the plot. The sources give the ruler of the state a part only at the end of the story; Shakespeare makes him active throughout the play. Whatever shortcomings may be charged to the Duke are, then, due to Shakespeare alone. (p. 102)

In the dramas written before *Measure for Measure,* two agencies stand out prominently as representatives of right and justice in straightening out complications of plot: the State and the Church. The former is represented by the person in supreme lay authority. . . . The latter is represented by priest or friar. . . . The law and authority in these pieces is romantic law and authority; it cannot be judged by strict legal or ecclesiastical standards. The quibbles which are the undoing of Shylock are as much a part of poular story as the sleeping potion which sends Juliet to the tomb. Shakespeare used dukes and friars when the peculiar powers and opportunities afforded by their station would help his narrative. He did not bother himself about the strict legality or rationality of their actions. What they suggest or decide has in his plays the binding force of constituted and final authority, and was so understood by his audiences.

The Duke in *Measure for Measure* combines the functions both of State and Church in his person. As Duke, he is supreme ruler of Vienna, who returns at the end to straighten out the tangles of the action, and dispense justice to all. In his disguise as Frair, he represents the wisdom and adroitness of the Church, in directing courses of action and advising stratagems so that good may come out of evil. But the plots which he sets in motion and the justice which he dispenses are the stuff of story; they cannot be judged as if they were historical occurrences. And the Duke's character cannot be estimated on a rationalistic basis. (pp. 103-04)

The essentially artificial character of the Duke may . . . be well illustrated by comparing him with the "comic relief." . . . Here we have striking studies of the riff-raff of the Southwark bank, the unsavory yet amusing types of the Elizabethan brothels. They are unhampered in the play by incidents or characterization drawn from conventional story; they show us, in naked realism, the unlovely side of London life, etched deep with the penetrating acid of keen observation. But in spite of all their vices, they are likable as well as human. (pp. 108-09)

Beside men and women like these, full of vigorous life, the Duke, with his shifts and tricks, which strain plausibility to the breaking-point, seems a puppet, manufactured to meet the exigencies of dramatic construction. He is more important but quite as artificial as Oliver or the Usurping Duke in *As You Like It,* who are wicked as long as Shakespeare needs them so, and are then, with a grotesque lack of probability, converted, because it helps the plot to have them virtuous at the end. We cannot analyze such characters psychologically. The Duke of Vienna, on account of his great prominence in the play, has just enough plausibility of characterization to make an audience accept him; he has none to spare. Perhaps we may sum the whole matter up by saying that Shakespeare drew the Duke as he did because he needed him, and that he drew the

main protagonists and the low-comedy people as he did because they interested him. Pompey and Mistress Overdone and the rest, in particular, serve an important purpose, in their very detachment from the artificial details of plot; they serve to make us forget the improbabilities which Shakespeare imported into the play, improbabilities which revolve about the Duke and his schemings; and they throw over the whole an illusion of vivid and unforgettable reality.

I imagine that some readers will take issue with me for regarding the Duke as an essentially artificial figure, elaborated to meet the requirements of plot, and as a study in character, of minor importance in himself, or for the play. Critics have frequently regarded him as the mainspring of the action, and his peculiar disposition as having profoundly influenced the development of the plot. This I believe to be quite the reverse of the truth. (pp. 109-10)

We have no right to object to the remodelling of a play, no matter how this has taken place, if it results in a logical and consistent whole. But in *Measure for Measure* no such result has been attained. The art of the expert craftsman has only partially concealed the stages by which his structure has been erected. The picture of the Duke at the very beginning, his retirement, and the appointment of a deputy, are natural and plausible, but what follows is story-book business—Haroun al Raschid disguised, Substituted Bride, Severed Head, and the various mechanical tricks and turnings of a complicated *dénouement.* As soon as the Duke gets into action, the artificiality of his figure is evident. Moreover, his very activity ill accords with his retiring disposition, his desire to lay aside power, and delegate it to another. More than any fictitious character in Shakespeare except Iago, the Duke is the directing force in the intrigues of the plot. Yet, says Lucio, "a shy fellow was the Duke" [III. ii. 130-31], and recent criticism has taught us that such comments from minor characters report truth. In a word, then, Shakespeare has not succeeded in making the Duke both serviceable to the purposes of drama, and psychologically consistent. Not only in origin, but in the effect which he produces upon the spectators, he is entirely different from Angelo and Isabella and Claudio. Their experiences are transcripts of actual human life, and usually in accord with their characters. They are real people. The Duke's part in the plot, excepting for his abdication, is little in accord with his disposition as sketched in the beginning, and little in accord with probability. He is essentially a puppet, cleverly painted and adroitly manipulated, but revealing, in the thinness of his coloring and in the artificiality of his movements, the wood and pasteboard of his composition. (pp. 111-12)

Analysis of the character of Angelo, and of the reasons why he does not get his just punishment, will form an admirable introduction to a discussion of how far the ends of justice are in general served by the decisions of the Duke, once more enthroned in power at the end of the play.

Let us begin at the beginning. Did Shakespeare mean Angelo to be regarded as a good, though narrow, man, suddenly gone wrong through an overmastering sexual temptation? . . . Or was Angelo a villain from the start, who deceived the Duke as to his real character? I do not imagine that there is any way of settling this point. It is even possible that Shakespeare had not made up his mind about the virtue of Angelo, any more than Thackeray had—in a different sense—about the virtue of Becky Sharpe. But it seems more likely that Angelo is to be regarded as having been a smooth rascal, who had been successful in concealing his baseness. His cruel and unjust treatment of Mariana, which has sent that unhappy lady to languish in her moated grange, his readiness not only to put Isabella in her dreadful predicament in order to satisfy his lust, but also to break faith with her and to kill her brother, do not point to native virtue. True, the Duke puts confidence in him, raising him to power above the older and more temperate Escalus, but even if this be regarded as a trial of his character . . . it proves little. Some of the most conscienceless of Shakespeare's characters, Edmund, Goneril, Regan, Iago, seem so effectively to have concealed their wickedness that the virtuous people whom they destroy have no suspicion of their real baseness. True, Mariana pleads for Angelo's life, and even Isabella, greatly as she has suffered, joins in urging that he be spared. But the complete repentance and forgiveness of the villain is a common dramatic convention, which Shakespeare found in Whetstone in this particular instance, and used frequently in other plays. A further piece of evidence seems to point to Angelo's native baseness; his flat refusal to temper justice with mercy, and spare Claudio, long before the dishonorable proposal is made to Isabella. (Act II, Scene ii.) One is reminded of Shylock and the trial scene by Angelo's stand, in this first interview with Isabella, upon the strict letter of the law, and the deaf ear which he turns to her eloquent appeal for mercy for her brother. Rigorous enforcement of the law is indeed no crime, but an audience would hardly see virtue in a man who insisted on sending a youth to death for a venial offence, in the face of moving appeals for mercy uttered by a beautiful heroine.

There can be no doubt, however, that as soon as Angelo has resolved to use his power to satisfy his passion, and at the same time to compass the death of Claudio, he must be regarded as a "strong and fast'ned villain" [*King Lear*, II. i. 77]. (pp. 112-14)

Angelo has made full confession, and asked for death. It turns out, however, that Claudio has not been put to death, after all, and that Angelo has not succeeded in his plot against the honor of Isabella. Both of the women whom Angelo has wronged now plead for his life. What is the Duke to do? What does the strong, indignant claim of justice require?

The whole point of the closing scene is that justice should be tempered with mercy. The mercy which Angelo had refused to Isabella is extended by the Duke in far greater measure, and under far stronger provocation. There is no stickling upon the letter of the law. Claudio is forgiven his venial offence. Even the wretched Barnardine, "unfit to live or die" [IV. iii. 64], is pardoned.

> But, for those earthly faults, I quit them all;
> And pray thee take this *mercy* to provide
> For better times to come.
>
> [V. i. 483-85]

And Angelo is pardoned too. No doubt Shakespeare was influenced by the ending of Whetstone's play, in which Promos is not only forgiven, but restored to his governorship, and he took advantage of the conventional solution of the plot to lift the whole into a higher moral conception of justice than "an eye for an eye and a tooth for a tooth." The ending of the play, then, really contradicts the title. Our modern feeling may be that Angelo gets off altogether too lightly, but the pardon of the repentant villain and his union to a heroine was a commonplace in Elizabethan drama, and would certainly have been readily accepted by a contemporary audience. . . . The claims of strict justice are secondary to those of stage entertainment. *Measure for Measure* is not a tract on equity, any more than

it is on government; it is not an expression of Shakespeare's convictions in regard to the administration of law, but a story of human passion, sin and forgiveness.

In judging this situation, we are likely to be led astray by failing to realize the difference between conceptions of justice in mediaeval and modern times. The mediaeval attitude still persisted in the days of Elizabeth, especially in the minds of the common folk, and in literature reflecting their views. The modern idea of a progressive amelioration of the social body by far-sighted legislation, and its application to particular cases, was anticipated by the best minds of the Renaissance, but had by no means gained acceptance in the days when Shakespeare wrote. . . . Altruistic and advanced social philosophy like that of Coleridge, then, is no touchstone for judging an Elizabethan play. (pp. 116-17)

The transition from the heights of tragic experience to the cheerfulness of a happy ending is too abrupt for the taste of modern critics, who like a play to be psychologically consistent. Shakespeare, however, did not shrink from violating such consistency, and executing a deliberate *volte-face* at the end. This is bitter medicine for those who claim that Shakespeare's works will appear as perfect and well-rounded wholes, if we only have the wit to look at them in the right way. We may as well admit that Shakespeare's art oscillates between extreme psychological subtlety, and an equally extreme disregard of psychological truth, in the acceptance of stock narrative conventions. To attempt to explain away the Shakespearean happy ending seems to me a hopeless task. . . .

Coleridge's objection that Angelo's marriage is "degrading to the character of woman" [see excerpt above, 1818] is that of a nineteenth century philosopher, strong in moral judgments, and weak in knowledge of Elizabethan narrative and social conventions. The same miraculous processes which lead to the forgiveness of erring male characters, and their conversion to the paths of rectitude, also automatically make them perfect husbands. The audience in the Globe Theatre, we may be sure, did not worry their heads over the illogicalities of the situation. (p. 118)

The true interpretation of the whole play, indeed, depends upon constant realization that while it seems real through the brilliancy and veracity of the portraiture of most of its characters, and through the intensely human struggle of the basic plot, it nevertheless exhibits improbabilities and archaisms which must be judged in the light of early traditions and social usages. (p. 121)

William Witherle Lawrence, "'Measure for Measure'," in his Shakespeare's Problem Comedies, *1931. Reprint by Frederick Ungar Publishing Co., 1960, pp. 78-121.*

CAROLINE F.E. SPURGEON (essay date 1935)

[*Spurgeon's* Shakespeare's Imagery and What It Tells Us *inaugurated the "image-pattern analysis" method of studying Shakespeare's plays, one of the most widely used methods of the mid-twentieth century. In this work, she interprets the thematic structure of the plays through an examination of patterns in the imagery. Spurgeon also sought to learn about Shakespeare's personality from a study of his images, a course which few of her disciples followed. Since publication of her book, earlier works on image patterns in Shakespeare have been discovered, but none was so important in the history of Shakespearean criticism as Spurgeon's. She states that the imagery in* Measure *reflects both a serious intention and a "strange brilliance," an idealistic vision of life and a cynical bitterness exemplified in pictures that are grim, grotesque, or shocking. She also hints at a biographical cause for this juxtaposition of "thoughtful poetry and strange brilliance." For additional commentary on the imagery in Measure for Measure, see the excerpts by G. Wilson Knight (1930) and Roy W. Battenhouse (1946).]*

Measure for Measure in several respects stands alone among Shakespeare's plays. There are two points which strike one at once on examining its images. The first is that we find among them, chiefly in the speech of the duke, some of the most beautiful, as well as the most thoughtful similes in the whole of Shakespeare, such as the two in his exhortation to Angelo at the beginning, his descriptions of life, his comparison of the rich man to the heavily laden ass unloaded by death, as well as many of the most brilliant and unusual of Shakespeare's pictures and personifications:

> back-wounding calumny
> The whitest virtue strikes.
>
> [III. ii. 186-87]

> It was the swift celerity of his death,
> Which I did think with slower foot came on,
> That brain'd my purpose.
>
> [V. i. 394-96]
> (pp. 287-88)

The second remarkable point is that out of the hundred and thirty-six images in the play, I feel I can classify eighteen only as 'poetical', because by far the largest group (twenty-seven in number) seem to fall under another category which I can only call vivid, quaint, or grotesque. It is this which is the most noticeable feature about the quality of the images as a whole. Often these latter ones are poetical as well, from sheer force and brilliance, as in Isabella's outburst against man, and her description of his 'glassy essence, like an angry ape', playing

> such fantastic tricks before high heaven
> As make the angels weep;
>
> [II. ii. 120-22]

but what strikes one first is the unusual pictures they conjure up, and their touch of grimness, grotesqueness, or a vividness so piercing as to give one a shock almost as if from lightning.

Many of these are personifications, semi-comic, and very arresting, such as 'liberty plucks justice by the nose' [I. iii. 29], 'bidding the law make court'sy to their will' [II. iv. 175], 'make him bite the law by the nose' [III. i. 108]. Others are marked by what is, even for Shakespeare, an unusually vivid use of concrete verbs and adjectives applied to abstractions:

> Hooking both right and wrong to the appetite,
> To follow as it draws;
>
> [II. iv. 176-77]

> Lent him our terror, dress'd him with our love;
>
> [I. i. 19]
> a purpose
> More grave and wrinkled than the aims and ends
> Of burning youth.
>
> [I. iii. 4-6]

Some are little pictures with a slightly comic touch, such as

> The baby beats the nurse, and quite athwart
> Goes all decorum;
>
> [I. iii. 30-1]

the forfeits in the barber's shop, death's fool, the scarecrow, and the fathers with the birch rods, and there is one which, though frankly grotesque, is still amazingly vivid—Lucio's summary of Claudio's unfortunate position, 'thy head stands so tickle on thy shoulders, that a milkmaid, if she be in love, may sigh it off' [I. ii. 172-74].

Shakespeare seems to be torn in this play, as nowhere else, save in *Troilus and Cressida,* and, to some extent, in *Hamlet,* between deeply stirred idealistic thought and reflection, and a tendency to cynical bitterness and grim realism which delights in a certain violence and even distortion of speech and figure, and sometimes of incident. Just as a man with gnawing toothache takes pleasure in biting on the tooth, and thereby increasing the pain, so one feels in these plays that Shakespeare, whose deepest and purest feelings have somehow been sorely hurt, takes pleasure in hurting them still more by exposing all the horrible, revolting, perplexing and grotesque aspects of human nature.

Whatever experience it was that so deeply stirred him about this time (1602-4?), it led him to ponder much on a certain range of thoughts—the amazing contradictions in man, the strange and often horrible transmutations of physical matter, the meaning and nature of death, and what possibly may constitute the chief value in life; while, going along with these grave reflections, there is ample evidence of a shocked, disillusioned and suffering spirit, taking refuge in mocks and jeers and bitterness.

So these two qualities, for which the images as a whole in *Measure for Measure* are remarkable, thoughtful poetry and strange brilliance, with a touch of the bizarre, are curiously expressive of the peculiar character and mental atmosphere of the play, and help towards the impression left on us of majesty and squalor, of thoughtful gravity and jeering cynicism, of the strange contradictions in life and still stranger contradictions in human nature, with its unexpected flaws and weaknesses and strengths and heroisms. This character, in spite of the intolerable nature of the plot, goes far, so it seems to me, to make it, of all the plays, the one which bears in it most clearly and unmistakably the impress of Shakespeare's mind and outlook. (pp. 288-90)

Caroline F.E. Spurgeon, "Leading Motives in the Comedies," in her Shakespeare's Imagery and What It Tells Us, *1935. Reprint by Cambridge at the University Press, 1971, pp. 259-90.*

UNA ELLIS-FERMOR   (essay date 1936)

[An Irish scholar, critic, and editor, Ellis-Fermor devoted a considerable portion of her literary and academic career to the study of Shakespearean and Jacobean drama, although she also contributed studies on the Irish dramatic movement and on modern drama. She served on the advisory board of Shakespeare Survey *and from 1946 to 1958 was the General Editor of* The New Arden Shakespeare. *At the time of her death, Ellis-Fermor left unfinished her only full-length study of Shakespeare, portions of which were later published by Kenneth Muir in his* Shakespeare the Dramatist and Other Essays *(1961). In her* The Jacobean Drama *(1936), excerpted below, Ellis-Fermor presents her interpretation of the scope and purpose of Shakespeare's works as a whole. She perceives in the plays of Shakespeare's Jacobean era a social and political hierarchy informed by the Jacobean preoccupation with evil and death. To her,* Measure for Measure *represents the lowest point of Jacobean cynicism and negation: the denial of mankind's nobility and the laws made to guide society. She contends that Angelo is not the stage Machiavellian described by earlier critics,*

but rather a decent citizen who has warped his own nature and who symbolizes the ''soul of evil in things good.'' She further states that the impression of an ''ineradicably corrupted'' world order is sealed by the ambivalence and cynicism of Isabella's character.]

[When], by the study of all the plays which bear in any way upon political or social thought, we realize the significance of Shakespeare's repeated pictures of leaders, rulers and their relations with the ruled, we are ready to understand the nature of that social and political hierarchy in whose constitution he so firmly (but not as a result of abstract deduction) believed:

> The Heavens themselves, the Planets, and this Center,
> Observe degree, priority, and place,
> Insisture, course, proportion, season, forme,
> Office, and custome, in all line of Order:
> . . . How could Communities,
> Degrees in Schooles and Brother-hoods in Cities,
> Peacefull Commerce from dividable shores,
> The primogeniture, and due of Byrth,
> Prerogative of Age, Crownes, Scepters, Lawrels,
> (But by Degree) stand in Authentique place?
> Take but Degree away, un-tune that string,
> And, hearke, what Discord followes.
>   [*Troilus and Cressida*, I. iii. 85-8, 103-10]

We understand, moreover, out of many conclusions implicit in these studies why he so often emphasizes certain axioms of state, the almost mystic virtue of an unflawed, hereditary title, the sanctity of law, the difference between the private and the public virtues which allows Henry to reject Falstaff, which would have made of Hamlet an extremely poor ruler and makes of Claudius, the murderer and usurper, an efficient and, on the whole, a beneficent one. (pp. 257-58)

But even this phase of his work, reflecting as it does the double process of penetration and synthesis, is but preliminary to the great Shakespearian resolution of the deeper-lying Jacobean problems of man's nature and his relation to that circumambient reality that shapes his ends.

Because such resolution can only be complete when it has included all things in its experience, and belief in world order only impregnable when all evil has been gathered into its embrace, Shakespeare is supreme (like Sophocles, choosing and transmuting the theme of *Oedipus*) because into him there pours, as perhaps into no other single dramatist, the full flood of the early Jacobean dread of death and horror of life. The significant period opens with *Hamlet, Troilus and Cressida* and *All's Well*, reaches a pausing place in *Measure for Measure* and then leads on to *Macbeth, Lear* and *Timon*. Never was the characteristic doubt of that age more searching, more nearly comprehensive of everything within its reach than in the first of these sequences that leads down to *Measure for Measure;* never did the sense of chaos, of disjunction and flying apart of the very bonds of earth, of mutiny in the spheres themselves, find so nearly apocalyptic expression as in the sequence in which *Macbeth* and *Lear* lead up to *Timon*. . . . For, with Shakespeare, the continual extension of scope and deepening of penetration, joined to an ever-growing tendency to unification, leads, when this incipient universe of half-co-ordinated worlds suffers disruption, to doubt and destruction on a colossal scale, beyond the spiritual anarchy of his contemporaries. The elements then desecrated or destroyed are those most precious and the laws impugned those that reach out beyond the universe of common experience till Mutability lays hands upon the stars themselves. The all-comprehending doubt, the dead disgust of *Measure for*

Measure sounds a lower note than does the burning satanism of [Cyril Tourneur's] *The Revenger's Tragedy*. It is the laws that integrate civilization itself, no less than those that wall in the human mind, that break apart in *Lear* and *Timon*. In these plays 'Natures germens tumble all together, Even till destruction sicken' [*Macbeth,* IV, i. 59-60], and this is possible to perhaps no other English dramatist, because, it would seem, there was no other with the power (the growth of a long habit of simultaneous synthesis and penetration) to lay hold on laws so fundamental. (pp. 258-59)

In *Measure for Measure* the lowest depths of Jacobean negation are touched. Cynicism has taken on a kind of diabolic vigilance; with the exception of the kindly, timid Provost, there is no character who is not suspect, and those whose claims to goodness or decency seem most vigorous are precisely those in whom meanness, self-regard and hypocrisy root deepest. The theme of the main plot is Isabella's triumphant preservation of physical chastity against Angelo's cunning and at the risk of Claudio's life; that of the underplot, the shifts of a company of brothel-keepers to maintain their trade. Before the end of the play we prefer the company of the second group to that of the first. Vile, dull and lacking even in the redeeming virtue of humour, they are at least plain in their intents and practices.

Claudio, selfish and self-indulgent, is another Bertram [from *All's Well*], with something in him, too, of that other Claudio of *Much Ado,* but fortune does not conspire to save him from the consequences of his deeds. To Isabella he is a craven weakling, but Shakespeare, to whom man is now no more than 'an angry Ape', one who

> Plaies such phantastique tricks before high heaven
> As makes the Angels weepe,
>   [II. ii. 120-22]

sees to it that, in his most contemptible abasement, he speaks the language of generic humanity, so that, in his words on death, all men may hear the echo of their own terrors, see him no other than the mirror of their own nothing. In Angelo the elements are more thoroughly mixed and the picture drawn with cynicism, not pity. The man who traps Isabella with a perfidy at which even the intellect staggers, who admits, between his administration of the law and his own observances, a breach so wide that its impudence leaves the beholder breathless, who, finally, refuses the reward for which he has exacted in advance a nefarious payment, this man is no stage Machiavellian, but only an upright, decent citizen who has forced upon his nature a standard beyond its capacity and warped it with the strain. Here is the soul of evil in things good, thus does 'corruption boil and bubble' [V. i. 318], spreading and searching till it tinges the innermost sanctuary of the mind:

> When I would pray, and think, I thinke and pray
> To severall subjects: heaven hath my empty words;
> Whilst my Invention, hearing not my Tongue,
> Anchors on *Isabell*: heaven in my mouth
> As if I did but onely chew his name;
> And in my heart the strong and swelling evill
> Of my conception.
>   [II. iv. 1-7]

This is indeed the very type of that division of mind that beset the Jacobeans; the inseparable mingling of evil with good here is such as Middleton later did indeed perceive, though with him it is mainly a record of scientific observation, while with Shakespeare at the stage of *Measure for Measure* it constitutes the denial, not only of the nobility of man, but of the very laws which pretend to guide him. What seals our impression of a world-order ineradicably corrupted and given over to evil is the character of Isabella, where the same method is followed as in that of Angelo, but with a mingling of the elements so much deeper as to call in question the sanctity of religion, sex, marriage and even 'the holiness of the heart's affections'. Isabella, the novice already entered upon the religious life, pleads, despite her own severe chastity, for the life that Claudio's incontinence has forfeited. When nothing will move Angelo else, she applies the ultimate test of earthly judgement:

> Why, all the soules that were, were forfeit once,
> And he that might the vantage best have tooke,
> Found out the remedie: how would you be,
> If he, which is the top of Judgment, should
> But judge you, as you are?
>
> [II. ii. 73-7]

With the words hardly cold on her lips she meets Angelo again and hears his nefarious offer to release Claudio only if she will commit with him the very deed for which Claudio is condemned. For a moment she feels only normal horror at this duplicity. Then the obsession of 'abhorred pollution' takes hold of her, the virtue of her chastity fills her universe. Hard as an icicle she visits Claudio in prison and lays before him the terms and her decision. She does right to 'fear' him, for primitive humanity is at all times stronger in him than in her. But because of her very inhumanity she can watch unmoved while he faces the awful realization of immediate death, her pitilessness only growing with his pleading. Weak as he is, his self-indulgence cannot stand comparison with hers, with the pitiless, unimaginative, self-absorbed virtue which sustains her.

> Die, perish: Might but my bending doune
> Repreeve thee from thy fate, it should proceede.
> Ile pray a thousand prayers for thy death,
> No word to save thee.
>
> [III. i. 143-46]

This is another divided mind, but more deeply so than Angelo's because unaware of its own division. We know from this moment that a nunnery contains no cure for Isabella's malady and we have a shrewd suspicion that she will not end there. But we are not quite done with her, nor with Shakespeare's final comment. In the next scene or two she agrees contentedly to Mariana taking her place with Angelo, arranges the deception, gets the keys of admission from him, breaks the plan to Mariana and gives her a few last words of business-like admonishment. Finally, when the Duke proposes to make her his Duchess, she gives silent consent, all thought of the religious life abandoned without comment and all backward reflections, apparently, full of self-content.

Before the comprehensiveness of this exposure, the imagination staggers, all the cynicism in individual speeches is as nothing beside the cynicism implicit in this orientation of the material; it is a world in whose fetid air no wholesome thing can grow. It is, in Shakespeare's thought, the very nadir of disgust and cynicism, a world where 'nothing is but what is not', where such order as there is is evil, where all passion and all enterprise is only 'the expense of spirit in a waste of shame' [Sonnet 129].

It is indeed the lowest point. From it we move up into the world of tragedy again, to the great plays that have for their common theme the disintegration of all order, even of a world order that is evil. Poetry returns to these plays, if for no other reason because Shakespeare's fundamental belief in ultimate

co-ordination and in an ordered universe, is marshalling its forces against the uttermost of denial and loathing, against final immersion in the rising tide of Jacobean negation. (pp. 260-63)

> Una Ellis-Fermor, "The Shakespearian Transmutation," in her The Jacobean Drama: An Interpretation, revised edition, Methuen & Co. Ltd., 1953, pp. 247-71.*

H. B. CHARLTON (essay date 1937)

[An English scholar, Charlton is best known for his Shakespearian Tragedy (1948) and Shakespearian Comedy (1938)—two important studies in which he argues that the proponents of New Criticism, particularly T. S. Eliot and I. A. Richards, were reducing Shakespeare's drama to its poetic elements and in the process losing sight of the importance of his characters. In his introduction to Shakespearian Tragedy, Charlton described himself as a "devout" follower of A. C. Bradley, and like his mentor he adopted a psychological, character-oriented approach to Shakespeare's work. In the following excerpt, originally published as "Shakespeare's 'Dark Comedies'" in the Bulletin of the John Rylands Library in 1937, Charlton refutes the biographical critics who assume that Shakespeare wrote his "dark comedies" during a cynical period of his life. Charlton argues instead that these plays reveal Shakespeare seeking the noble and joyful aspects of life. He also conjectures that the "dark comedies" were written prior to, rather than after, Shakespeare's "bright comedies": Twelfth Night, Much Ado about Nothing, and As You Like It. Charlton views Angelo as the villain of Measure for Measure, but one who has been "overtaken" by villainy. He contends that Angelo's major crime is callousness towards human life, and he perceives that Shakespeare created Mariana to heighten Angelo's perfidy. He interprets Angelo's exposure and repentance as the reaffirmation of Shakespeare's belief in the goodness of human nature. To Charlton, Isabella is a dramatic failure because, as Angelo's foil and the apparently positive example of goodness in human nature, she is unconvincing. He states that her virtue is self-righteous, "a formal code of verbal assumption" rather than "an intense spiritual dedication." For examples of the biographical and cynical assessments of Measure which Charlton attacks, see the excerpts by H. N. Hudson (1872), Edward Dowden (1881), George Brandes (1895-96), Caroline F.E. Spurgeon (1935) and Una Ellis-Fermor (1936). Also, for further discussion of the drama as a problem play, see the excerpts by Frederick S. Boas (1896), William Witherle Lawrence (1931), E. C. Pettet (1949), E.M.W. Tillyard (1949), and Ernest Schanzer (1963).]

The epithet "dark" has been almost universally accepted as a right description of [Measure for Measure, All's Well that Ends Well, and Troilus and Cressida]. That epithet is generally taken to mean, not only that in these plays the seamier, indeed the nastiest, side of life obtrudes more persistently than elsewhere in Shakespeare, but that their underlying mood is one of bitter cynicism. (p. 210)

In fact, the spiritual and intellectual temper which is the motive of these plays is in no wise a contempt for life and for its potential worthiness, but on the contrary, an intense impulse to discover the true sources of nobility in man and of joy in life, an intuition so ardent that it frustrates its own artistic fecundity and calls in, as a substitute, the dramaturgical exploration of conscious enquiry and deliberate experiment. These plays are not at all a bridge linking a serene comic mood with the awe-inspiring vision of tragedy. They are the road by which Shakespeare climbed from the misleading comedy of Falstaff to the richer and more satisfying comic air of Twelfth Night, As You Like It, and Much Ado. In brief, I take these three dark comedies to be misleadingly named; I take them to be predecessors and not successors of the three comedies in which Shakespeare's comic triumph is most manifest.

The situation is not, as it might seem, merely a matter of actual chronology. For one thing, Croce has taught us to beware of confusion between the sequences of biographical occurrences, and the ideal chronology of the artist's growth. Moreover, it appears to be generally agreed that no specific date can be allotted to the three dark comedies, since of all of them it is claimed that there is evidence of very considerable revision stretching over a fairly considerable measure of time. But even if it were merely a matter of historical chronology, there is in fact no more solid evidence for placing the dark comedies in the order commonly assigned to them than in that which I suggest. If we knew exactly when Shakespeare first took up and then finished this or that play, all attempts to explain the plays in relation to Shakespeare's artistic development would have to take account of such evidence as primary. But the dating of the dark comedies is, within limits as serviceable to my arguments as to any other, largely a matter of conjecture. Moreover, the trend of that conjecture has been mainly determined by the view that these plays are the expression of a mood of cynical despair. (pp. 211-12)

Measure for Measure may be an eye for an eye, a tooth for a tooth, an Angelo for a Claudio. But look at the plot and its outcome. There is an almost intolerable insistence on meting out reward to the virtuous and punishment to the guilty. And even the punishment is determined in the spirit that it is as much a judge's duty to qualify as to enforce the laws. One remembers Isabella's impassioned plea that neither heaven nor man can grieve at mercy:

> No ceremony that to great ones 'longs,
> Not the king's crown, nor the deputed sword,
> The marshal's truncheon, nor the judge's robe,
> Become them with one half so good a grace
> As mercy does.
>
> [II. ii. 59-63]

This sentiment of mortality and mercy humanises, even sentimentalises, the formal organisation of society. Its rulers are enjoined to remember that whilst it is excellent to have a giant's strength, it is tyrannous to use it like a giant. It is no indifferent pessimist, no bitter cynic, who recalls how man, proud man, drest in a little brief authority, is liable to wrench awe from fools and tie the wiser souls to his false seeming. For these are observations implying that grace is grace despite of all controversy; and that of all graces, the exercise of a beneficent mercy is most gracious. It is a sense of the potential richness of humanity rather than despondency at its neglect of those possibilities. So, too, with life itself. The agonised dread of Claudio as he contemplates death . . . in itself springs from a sense of the immeasurable possibilities of worth in life, though it be in life the mere living. (pp. 213-14)

The whole episode [with Barnardine] is a manifest revelation of Shakespeare's sense of human life; his first scruples only to destroy what manifestly deserves destruction, and then his sudden discovery that the apparently worthless human being still has his humanity with which to excite sympathy in a fellow-mortal. ''Mortality and mercy'' are here palpably the author's sentiments: and they are a complete negation of a mood which could in any sense be called cynical. (pp. 216-17)

Measure for Measure exhibits the conditions under which an ideal is effective in attaining the good it proposes to itself. But in the course of its achievement, the ideal itself is in danger of failing when it lacks the tolerance of sympathy with human beings as such and the good-will to enhance their welfare. *Measure for Measure* is dramatically more successful in exposing the limitations of the ideal of the Puritan than in establishing the effectiveness of the ideal of formal purity: Angelo's fall is a clearer instance of the beneficence of mere human nature than is Isabella's nominal success. But between them, they suggest imaginative conjecture concerning the capacity of simple human kindness as an instrument for multiplying the happiness of humanity. (p. 248)

[In] *Measure for Measure,* the situation is that in this world of ours—

> there is so great a fever on goodness, that the
> dissolution of it must cure it: novelty is only
> in request; and it is as dangerous to be aged in
> any kind of course, as it is virtuous to be con-
> stant in any undertaking. There is scarce truth
> enough alive to make societies secure; but se-
> curity enough to make fellowships accursed.
>
> [III. ii. 222-28]

Hence the riddle which confronts the wisdom of the world. What is goodness? How can real goodness be distinguished from seeming goodness? A well-disposed contemplative man such as the Duke needs confirmation of his trust that things are not as bad as they appear. He devises circumstances with the declared object of discovering what our seemers really are. He rigs the plot; it is a leaven'd and a prepared choice. Explicitly, it is a trial of Angelo's virtue, a deliberate test of his metal. But when this is woven into the dilemmas which constitute a dramatic story, it becomes an experiment in measuring the effective goodness of all the characters involved in the course of the story. The incidents run on and each in succession is the outcome of energies contributed by the will or the judgment of the various people involved in it. In so far as this outcome is palpably for good or for evil, to what energies, and to energies exerted on what sorts of impulse, is it to be set down? The issue of the action is artistically the visible or dramatic answer. And every episode which is part of the plot of *Measure for Measure* appears to be even more plainly than in most of Shakespeare's plays an experimental demonstration of the results proceeding from the operation of given forces. The play is literally an assay of virtue, to practise the author's and the audience's judgment in the matter of the disposition of natures, of the effective worth, that is, of its chosen types of human beings. Each person in the play is seen in the light of his contribution to the sum-total of human welfare: and though many of the people involved add but little, they are nevertheless accessories in a comprehensive judgment which, of course, bases itself primarily on the attainments in this particular of such major characters in the story as Angelo, Isabella, and the Duke.

Angelo plays the villain's part. But he is not primarily shaped for evil-doing. He does not seek villainy; it overtakes and conquers him. He has earned amongst those who know him a high repute for a specific kind of virtue. The Duke chooses him as deputy: he never hints even a suspicion that Angelo has not in fact the sort of virtue which is attributed to him; what the Duke is uncertain of is how far a virtue of that kind is a real virtue. One must remember this, because the issue is later confused by Shakespeare's divergence from the original story. The invention of Mariana . . . involves a retrospective blackening of Angelo's character. His perfidy to Mariana is necessary to the new plot, and is therefore brought in as an episode remembered by the Duke. But it had no place in the Duke's mind when he nominated Angelo for Deputy, nor would it have had any existence in fact if the new form of the denouement had not required it.

Angelo is a man who has governed his life on a rigorous system. He is a man of stricture and firm abstinence. He has not disciplined his human nature to confidence in its active exercise; he has rigidly suppressed it. So completely has he secured control of his instincts, impulses, and emotions, that without boasting he confidently asserts

> What I will not, that I cannot do.
>
> [II. ii. 52]

He has so far conquered impulses of the blood that he seems to have attained passionlessness. (pp. 248-50)

For most of the situations of life, Angelo's is a kind of virtue which seems to serve. But it is fundamentally insecure: blood may at any time assert itself, and the more violently because it has been so rigorously restrained. The way of Angelo's fall, however, almost seems a conspiracy of nature against his calculated probity. He does not lightly step into temptation. Isabella's pleading has a kind of malicious suggestiveness. When she comes to beg her brother's life, Angelo is eager to dismiss her as soon as he can—''Pray you, be gone'' [II. ii. 67]. Her plea that Angelo should knock at his own bosom and ask his heart whether it knows anything in himself like the natural guiltiness of her brother is a telling blow: it recalls to Angelo the temptations of the blood which he has so far overcome. But it recalls them in circumstances which make him fear his mastery. . . . On her departure, Angelo realises how frail are the foundations of his virtue. His monologue is at least an honest diagnosis of his case. He has succumbed: ''This virtuous maid subdues me quite'' [II. ii. 184-85]. . . . Once the system on which he has built up his life has collapsed, there is no limit to the evil of which he is capable. His worst crime is his intent to sacrifice Claudio after the price of his safety has been paid. And that is his worst crime because it displays an absolute callousness towards a human life. It is a clue to his undoing. His virtue has been built on purely formal or intellectual motives of probity: it has discounted all sentiments of human kindness. It has been a virtue in and for itself, the attempt to set up a state of individual well-being, regardless of obligations towards the well-being of others. It has been erected on a denial of the human nature which is the bond of humanity. It has reduced blood to snow-broth.

Yet even Angelo, sunk in sin, comes to truer notions of life. His penitence is absolute, and the sense of his own unfitness to go on living is a mark of his redemption.

> Then, good prince,
> No longer session hold upon my shame,
> But let my trial be mine own confession;
> Immediate sentence then and sequent death
> Is all the grace I beg.
>
> [V. i. 370-74]
> (pp. 251-52)

The action of the play has put him on trial. It has found in him a false virtue, a virtue erected on a nicely-calculated scheme of rigid principles. It has also found the source of his weakness, a disregard of, even a contempt for, the sub-conscious and non-rational impulses which for good and evil are amongst the most potent forces in man's heritage. But a dramatist who finds an attempt at calculated virtue frustrated through the starving of mere human instinct, is surely not a dramatist writing under a sense of life's futility. Like Falstaff, Angelo has a narrow and formal scheme of values, the value to oneself here and now. His pragmatical realism is even more obviously delusive than is Falstaff's: for Falstaff at least had veins through which the blood ran hot. The exposure of Angelo is a stage in the reintegration of belief in the essential goodness of human nature.

The more positive exposition of its goodness in the person of Isabella is dramatically far less satisfying. The action of the play requires her as an active contributor to the happy ending. Her character and her acts are meant to be visibly convincing forces in the overthrow of evil and the triumph of good. . . . Somehow or another, the audience is unpersuaded. Her goodness is, so to speak, traditional. She is to be vowed to chastity: she is to dedicate her life to a mode of living which in the experience of mankind has been the manifestation of a high degree of spiritual well-being. If, in a sense, it is a notion of formal goodness, a fugitive and cloistered virtue, it has nevertheless a wider and a larger sanction than the selfish and individual notion of goodness which is Angelo's puritanism, because it has the approbation of many centuries of human experience. Yet somehow, as if its implicit denial of natural law confused Shakespeare's apprehension of its living reality, the dramatist's embodiment of it does not come to convincing life. Isabella in act does not dramatically compel the results which theoretically her character is cast by the story to achieve. Too frequently she makes the ideal for which she lives seem more like a formal code of verbal presumption than an intense spiritual dedication. When she hears of Claudio's crime, her first recommendation is of no higher order than any other suggestion for making an honest woman of the victim: ''O, let him marry her'' [I. iv. 49]—and all apparently will be well. Moreover, she utters not a single word of doubt when the substitution trick is suggested. . . . An air of self-righteousness attaches itself to her; she professes herself, when she is not called upon to make it, to be capable of extreme sacrifice:

> O, were it but my life,
> I'd throw it down for your deliverance
> As frankly as a pin.
>
> [III. i. 103-05]
> (pp. 252-54)

Somehow she makes herself unattractive: ''I have no superfluous leisure'' [III. i. 157]: that is the sort of self-possessed hussy she sometimes seems. Her own affairs and her own sense of their righteousness are of paramount importance. Her belief begins to look like a narrow formal dogmatism, and her turning on her desperate brother appears as a mere cheap triumph in verbal theatricality. The violence of her denunciation of his cowardice utters itself in language more like that of cruel badinage than of shocked virginal purity—

> O you beast!
> O faithless coward! O dishonest wretch!
> Wilt thou be made a man out of my vice?
> Is't not a kind of incest, to take life
> From thine own sister's shame?
>
> [III. i. 135-39]

Nor is there a spark of humanity in the pose of utter contempt she assumes when she declares herself unwilling to do the slightest thing to save her brother:

> Take my defiance!
> Die, perish! Might but my bending down

Reprieve thee from thy fate, it should proceed:
I'll pray a thousand prayers for thy death,
No word to save thee.

[III. i. 142-46]

But this only means that dramatically she is a failure. Shakespeare has conceived of a sort of goodness efficient to overcome such evil as there is in the play. Nominally, Isabella's virtue does so triumph. But it is a forced triumph: one, that is, which as it proceeds through the story, carries no conviction of its necessity to the minds of the audience. Still, even if Shakespeare's imagination has failed to apprehend a traditional form of goodness as a power demonstrably and compellingly making for a better world, the fact that he chose a story in which goodness is cast for that rôle, is surely no pessimist's view of life. Even the failure is reassuring—for what obstructs his imaginative grasp of Isabella is her lack of the simpler and commoner traits of mere humanity. In a way, her goodness has this in common with Angelo's: it is a condition of the individual soul within the narrow sphere of its own identity. But even in this play, there are other characters who are becoming aware of the imperfection of this limited kind of personal goodness. The Duke has been generally censured. He seems to run away from unpleasant duties: and perhaps he is unfitted for the kind of government which a hard-hearted Henry IV can bring off so well. His humaneness is in fact a hindrance to his practical efficiency. But his instincts are benevolent. . . . His code of goodness is a larger one than any which has hitherto ruled in Shakespeare's comedy. Falstaff's virtue was his aptitude for securing his own welfare. But the Duke's standard is not self, it is service:

> Thyself and thy belongings
> Are not thine own so proper as to waste
> Thyself upon thy virtues, they on thee.
> . . . Spirits are not finely touch'd
> But to fine issues, nor Nature never lends
> The smallest scruple of her excellence
> But, like a thrifty goddess, she determines
> Herself the glory of a creditor,
> Both thanks and use.

[I. i. 29-40]

This is a point of view which not only hopes for a larger nobility in life, but seeks to promote it. (pp. 254-56)

Is it not . . . palpably an error to take *Measure for Measure* as a cynic's play? . . . The mere bulk of evil which is spread across the scene of *Measure for Measure* is in itself no indication of the mood of the author. The greater the evil, the greater the author's faith in the goodness which can overcome it. And the evil in the play is nominally vanquished by the forces of virtue which the Duke and Isabella bring against it. That their conquest is more nominal than real simply means that Shakespeare's dramatic art has not welded his matter into an imaginative organism. But the intention seems patent. There is virtue in man to make life well worth the living. (pp. 257-58)

> H. B. Charlton, "The Dark Comedies," in his *Shakespearian Comedy*, *Methuen & Co. Ltd.*, 1938, pp. 208-65.

R. W. CHAMBERS (lecture date 1937)

[*Chambers was an English scholar and educator who concentrated primarily on medieval literature. His essay on* Measure for *Measure, excerpted below, was originally part of a British Academy Shakespeare Lecture delivered in 1937 and later included in his* Man's Unconquerable Mind *(1939). Expanding upon the historical approach of William Witherle Lawrence (1931), Chambers offers a corrective to those critics who fail to judge the play in light of such Elizabethan theatrical conventions as betrothals, betrayed brides, and disguised monarchs—all of which appear in* Measure for Measure. *He also discusses Shakespeare's alteration of Whetstone's* Promos and Cassandra, *claiming that Shakespeare tempered the barbaric scenes of the earlier work and modified the "crudity" of Cassandra's transformation from vengeful to prayerful penitent. Most importantly, Chambers maintains that we must accept Isabella's nobility to fully understand the play, for in her character he finds the proof against the cynical readings of previous critics. He states that Shakespeare identified himself closely with Isabella, particularly in her speech on the forgiving nature of mercy. Like H. B. Charlton (1937), Chambers also claims that there is no proof that Shakespeare suffered a personal crisis at the time of* Measure's *composition which colored his conception of mankind—an idea put forth by such nineteenth-century critics as H. N. Hudson (1872), Edward Dowden (1881), and George Brandes (1895-96)—and he further agrees with Charlton that the play in no way reflects Shakespeare's cynical vision of life. Instead, Chambers interprets* Measure for Measure *as a play of forgiveness, a dramatization of the Christian principles presented in the Sermon on the Mount. He thus joins G. Wilson Knight (1930) in continuing the tradition of evaluating the play in light of its Christian elements. Other critics who interpret* Measure for Measure *as a play concerned primarily with Christian themes include F. R. Leavis (1942), Roy W. Battenhouse (1946), Nevill Coghill (1955), and Tom McBride (1974). For further discussion of Shakespeare's reliance on contemporary stage conventions in* Measure, *see the excerpts by Muriel C. Bradbrook (1941), Oscar J. Campbell (1943), Elmer Edgar Stoll (1943), Murray Krieger (1951), Nevill Coghill (1955), and Ernest Schanzer (1963).*]

Shakespeare, for all the 'self-laceration', 'disgust', and 'general morbidity' which is supposed to have obsessed him and his Jacobean contemporaries, removes from [Whetstone's *Promos and Cassandra*] the really morbid scene of the heroine kissing the severed head of her supposed brother. Then, he divides the sorrows of the heroine between two characters, Isabel and Mariana. And the object of this duplication is, that, whatever their spiritual anguish, neither of them shall be placed in the 'really intolerable situation' of poor Cassandra. Mariana has been contracted to Angelo formally by oath. It is vital to remember that, according to Elizabethan ideas, Angelo and Mariana are therefore man and wife. But Angelo has deserted Mariana. Now I grant that, according to our modern ideas, it is undignified for the deserted Mariana still to desire union with the husband who has scorned her. *We* may resent the elegiac and spaniel-like fidelity of Mariana of the Moated Grange. *But is that the sixteenth-century attitude?* The tale of the deserted bride seeking her husband in disguise is old, approved, beloved. It is a mere anachronism to assume that Shakespeare, a practical dramatist, told this tale with some deep cynical and self-lacerating intention unintelligible to his audience, but now at last revealed to modern criticism. Shakespeare made Mariana gentle and dignified. She, in all shadow and silence, visits her husband in place of Isabel, to save Claudio's life. (pp. 2-3)

In the sixteenth century the story was a commonplace of romance, and Shakespeare used it in order to make more gentle one of the quite horrible situations of the pre-Shakespearian drama. There was a time when Shakespeare had not shrunk from staging the grossest horrors. It is to avoid them, that he now brings in the substitution which offends 'the modern conscience'. . . .

A second fault of the old play is the crudity of the change from Cassandra's thirst for vengeance to her prayer for forgiveness. Shakespeare had permitted himself similar crudities in the past. Now he sets to work to make the plot consistent: he does this by making it turn, from first to last, on the problem of punishment and forgiveness. It is Shakespeare's addition to the story that the Duke is distressed by this problem. Fearing lest his rule has been too lax, he deputes his office to Angelo, whilst remaining, disguised as a friar, to 'visit both prince and people' [I. iii. 45]. And here many critics, among them . . . Sir Arthur Quiller-Couch, object. It is not seemly for a Duke to 'shirk his proper responsibility, and steal back incognito to play busybody and spy on his deputy' [see excerpt above, 1922]. (p. 4)

Why do critics today bring against *Measure for Measure* this kind of objection, which they would be ashamed to bring against Shakespeare's earlier comedies, or later romances?

Disguise and impersonation and misunderstanding are the very life of romantic comedy. The disguised monarch, who can learn the private affairs of his humblest subject, becomes a sort of earthly Providence, combining omniscience and omnipotence. That story has always had its appeal. 'Thus hath the wise magistrate done in all ages' [Ben Jonson, *Bartholomew Fair*]; although obviously to introduce into our daily life this ancient habit of the benevolent monarch would be to incur deserved satire. There is no doubt how Shakespeare meant us to regard the Duke. 'One that, above all other strifes, contended especially to know himself: a gentleman of all temperance' [III. ii. 232-33], says Escalus. Isabel, in her moment of dire distress, remembers him as 'the good Duke'. Angelo, in his moment of deepest humiliation, addresses him with profound reverence and awe. Lucio (like our moderns) regards the Duke cynically; but he ends by admitting that he deserves a whipping for so doing.

The deputy, Angelo, is not so called for nothing. He *is* 'angel on the outward side' [III. ii. 272]—as ascetic saint in the judgement of his fellow citizens, and despite the meanness of his spirit, nay, because of it, a saint in his own esteem. His soliloquies prove this, and Isabel at the end gives him some credit for sincerity. (p. 5)

Critics speak as if Shakespeare had imagined Claudio a self-indulgent boy, a 'poor weak soul' [see E. K. Chambers in the Additional Bibliography]. Yet it is only Angelo's retrospective revival which makes Claudio's offence capital. 'He hath but as offended in a dream' [II. ii. 4], says the kindly Provost. He 'was worth five thousand of you all' [I. ii. 61], says Mistress Overdone to Lucio and his friends. Claudio is first introduced, bearing himself with great dignity and right feeling, under his sudden arrest. He sends his friend Lucio to his sister in her cloister, to beg her to intercede for him, because, he says,

> in her youth
> There is a prone and speechless dialect,
> Such as move men; beside, she hath prosperous art
> When she will play with reason and discourse,
> And well she can persuade.
>
> [I. ii. 182-86]

Such descriptions of characters before they appear—perhaps before Shakespeare had written a word for them to speak— have surely a great weight. They show how Shakespeare wished the audience to see them. Isabel's characteristic when she does appear is exactly this mixture of winning silence with persuasive speech. (p. 6)

Isabel begins her pleading slowly and with characteristic silences: then she grows eloquent, and to Angelo's stern refusal she at last replies:

> I would to Heaven I had your potency,
> And you were Isabel! Should it then be thus?
> No; I would tell what 'twere to be a judge.
> And what a prisoner.
>
> [II. ii. 67-70]

Isabel has no notion as yet of the depth of sin which may have to be pardoned in Angelo. But there is 'irony' behind these two speeches, and we can forecast that in the end the places will be reversed: the fate of the convicted Angelo depending upon Isabel.

> [Chambers adds in a footnote:] The phrase 'dramatic irony' may be misunderstood. Shakespeare, like Sophocles, puts into the mouths of his characters words which they speak in all sincerity, but which, as the play proceeds, will be found to have a deeper meaning than the speaker knew. Dramatic irony does *not* mean that, at every turn, we are justified in suspecting that Shakespeare may have meant the reverse of what he makes his characters say. When he does that ('honest Iago') he leaves us in no doubt.
>
> (p. 7)

[Isabella's] marvellous and impassioned pleadings, unsurpassed anywhere in Shakespeare, are based on her Christian faith, and upon the Sermon on the Mount: all men are pardoned sinners, and *must* forgive:

> Why, all the souls that were, were forfeit once;
> And he that might the vantage best have took
> Found out the remedy.
>
> [II. ii. 73-5]

'Judge not, that ye be not judged. For, with what measure ye mete, it shall be measured to you again.' *Measure for Measure.* But how is the Sermon on the Mount to be reconciled with the practical necessities of government? That is the problem which puzzles people—and particularly perhaps young people—so much today. In the Tudor Age men met it by exalting Government. The King is 'the image of God's majesty': to him, and to his Government, the divine office of rule and punishment is committed. The private man must submit and forgive. Accordingly, Angelo appeals to his 'function': and there is real force in his answers to Isabel—remembering, as we always must, that, for the purposes of the play, Claudio is supposed guilty of a capital offence.

Never does Shakespeare seem more passionately to identify himself with any of his characters than he does with Isabel, as she pleads for mercy against strict justice:

>   O, it is excellent
> To have a giant's strength; but it is tyrannous
> To use it like a giant. . . .
>   man, proud man,
> Drest in a little brief authority . . .
> Plays such fantastic tricks before high heaven
> As make the angels weep . . .
>
> [II. ii. 107-09, 117-22]

Angelo does not fall without a sincere struggle. But more than one of Isabel's pleadings find a mark which she never meant:

> Go to your bosom;
> Knock there, and ask your heart what it doth know
> That's like my brother's fault . . .
> Hark how I'll bribe you . . .

[II. ii. 136-38, 145]

Angelo has thought himself superior to human weakness, because he is free from the vulgar vices of a Lucio. And the 'beauty of mind' of a distressed, noble woman throws him off his balance. If we fail to see the nobility of Isabel, we cannot see the story as we should. . . . Angelo tempts Isabel in a second dialogue, as wonderful as the first. In her innocence Isabel is slow to see Angelo's drift, and it is only her confession of her own frailty that gives him a chance of making himself clear. 'Nay,' Isabel says,

> call us ten times frail;
> For we are soft as our complexions are,
> And credulous to false prints.

[II. iv. 128-30]

If Shakespeare is depicting in Isabel the self-righteous prude which some critics would make of her, he goes strangely to work.

But when she perceives Angelo's drift, Isabel decides without hesitation. Now whatever we think of that instant decision, it is certainly not un-Christian. Christianity could never have lived through its first three hundred years of persecution, if its ranks had not been stiffened by men and women who never hesitated in the choice between righteousness and the ties to their kinsfolk. We may call this fanaticism: but it was well understood in Shakespeare's day. Foxe's *Martyrs* was read by all; old people could still remember seeing the Smithfield fires; year after year saw the martyrdoms of Catholic men (and sometimes of Catholic women like the Ven. Margaret Clitherow). It was a stern age—an age such as the founder of Christianity had foreseen when he uttered his stern warnings. 'He that loveth father or mother more than me . . .' 'If any man come to me, and hate not his father, and mother, and brethren and sisters, he cannot be my disciple.' (pp. 7-9)

[Isabel] goes to her brother, not because she hesitates, but that he may share with her the burden of her irrevocable decision. Claudio's first reply is, 'O heavens! it cannot be'; 'Thou shalt not do't' [III. i. 98, 102]. But the very bravest of men have quailed, within the four walls of a prison cell, waiting for the axe next day. I am amazed at the way critics condemn Claudio, when he breaks down, and utters his second thoughts, 'Sweet sister, let me live' [III. i. 132]. Isabel overwhelms him in the furious speech which we all know. And I am even more amazed at the dislike which the critics feel for the tortured Isabel. But when they assure us that their feeling towards both his creatures was shared by the gentle Shakespeare, I am then most amazed of all. (p. 10)

Shakespeare has made Isabel say to Claudio

> O, were it but my life,
> I'ld throw it down for your deliverance
> As frankly as a pin.

[III. i. 103-05]

It is standing the play on its head, to say that Shakespeare wrote those words in irony and cynicism. How did he convey that to his audience? If such assumptions are allowed, we can prove anything we like, 'eight years together, dinners and suppers and sleeping-hours excepted'.

Isabel then, as Shakespeare sees her and asks us to see her, would frankly, joyously, give her life to save Claudio: and, let there be no mistake about it, 'greater love hath no man than this'. And now Claudio is asking for what she cannot give, and she bursts out in agony. Have the critics never seen a human soul or a human body in the extremity of torment? Physical torture Isabel thinks she could have stood without flinching. She has said so to Angelo:

> The impression of keen whips I'ld wear as rubies,
> And strip myself to death, as to a bed
> That longing have been sick for, ere I'ld yield
> My body up to shame.

[II. iv. 101-04]

To suppose that Shakespeare gave these burning words to Isabel so that we should perceive her to be selfish and cold, is to suppose that he did not know his job. The honour of her family and her religion are more to her than mere life, her own or Claudio's. (pp. 11-12)

Shakespeare imagined Claudio as a good lad, but not, like his sister, devout; he doesn't keep devout company, exactly. Isabel 'well can persuade'. She is one of a few women in Shakespeare who can persuade. . . . The other great persuaders are: Isabel, Beatrice, and Lady Macbeth. And they all use the same arguments—the arguments which, I expect, the first Cave-woman, when in dire straits, used to her Cave-man: You are a coward; You have no love or respect for me; I have no longer any love for you.

Isabel is the most vehement of the three. Sisterly technique has its own rules; there is a peculiar freedom about the talk of those who have known each other from babyhood. And Isabel can use arguments outside the range of Beatrice or Lady Macbeth. Don't forget that Escalus, when he first pleaded for Claudio, remembered his 'most noble father' [II. i. 7]. Isabel had exclaimed, when she first found Claudio firm,

> there my father's grave
> Did utter forth a voice.

[III. i. 85-6]

And now she cries,

> Heaven shield my mother play'd my father fair.

[III. i. 140]

Isabel appeals to the passion which, in an Elizabethan gentleman, may be presumed to be stronger than the fear of death—pride in his gentle birth and in the courage which should mark it. Don't people see that there are things about which we cannot argue calmly? The fierceness of Isabel's words is the measure of the agony of her soul. . . . And it is our fault if we don't see that Isabel is suffering martyrdom none the less because her torment is mental, not physical.

One of the most significant of Shakespeare's alterations of his original is to make the heroine a 'votarist of St. Clare' [I. iv. 5]. At the root of the movement of St. Francis and St. Clare was the intense remembrance of the sufferings of Christ, in atonement for the sins of the whole world—the 'remedy' of which Isabel in vain reminds Angelo. Isabel, as a novice, is testing herself to see whether she is called to that utter renunciation which is the life of the 'poor Clare'. Whether she remains in the Convent or no, one who is contemplating such a life can no more be expected to sell herself into mortal sin, than a good soldier can be expected to sell a stronghold entrusted to him. (pp. 12-14)

Critics ask, as does Sir Edmund Chambers, whether Isabel too 'has not had her ordeal, and in her turn failed', whether she was 'wholly justified in the eyes of her creator'. They are entitled to ask the question. But they ought to wait for the answer. The Duke enters, takes Claudio aside, and tells him there is no hope for him. And we find that Claudio, who before Isabel's outburst had been gripped by the mortal fear of death, is now again master of his soul:

> Let me ask my sister pardon. I am so out of
> love with life, that I will sue to be rid of it.
>
> [III. i. 171-72]

'Hold you there', says the Duke. Claudio does. Later, we see him quiet and self-possessed when the Provost shows him his death-warrant. To the Provost he is 'the most gentle Claudio' [IV. ii. 72]: and to Shakespeare, the word 'gentle' is a word of very high praise, not consistent with any want of spirit. . . . Claudio, 'most gentle' in his cell, has passed his ordeal well, showing quiet courage equally removed from the hilarity of a Posthumus [*Cymbeline*] and the insensibility of a Barnardine.

Mrs. Lennox says that Isabel ought to have taught Claudio what is due to her honour and his own [see excerpt above, 1753]. She has.

Now, if Isabel's speech had been intended to depict a 'cold' and 'remorseless' woman, 'all for saving her own soul', acting cruelly to her brother in the 'fiery ordeal' which (we are told) 'his frail soul proves ill-fitted to endure', why does Shakespeare show Claudio, far from resenting his sister's reproaches, only wishing to ask her pardon, and henceforth courageous and resolute? Why, above all, does Shakespeare make the Duke, when he overhears Isabel's whole speech, comment on the beauty of her goodness? This is intelligible only if Shakespeare means Isabel's speech as an agonized outcry, working on her brother as no calm reasoning could have done. If Shakespeare's critics think they could have written the scene better, they are welcome to try; but it does not follow that Shakespeare was a disillusioned cynic because he did not write Isabel's speech as Charlotte Lennox would have done. (pp. 16-17)

If Shakespeare's Jacobean audiences were as perverse as his modern critics, I can well understand how 'gloom and dejection' may have driven the poor man 'to the verge of madness', as critics assert that it did. That Shakespeare imagined Isabel as business-like, should be clear to any one who studies with care her words in the earlier scenes. She is a sensible Elizabethan girl, with no nonsense about her, and she knows that it is no sin to bring husband and wife together. (p. 17)

Again, if Shakespeare meant us to regard Isabel cynically, why did he picture her not only as touching by her goodness both Angelo and the Duke, though to different issues, but even as aweing the frivolous Lucio into sobriety and sympathy? To Lucio she is 'a thing ensky'd and sainted' [I. iv. 34]. . . . Sir Arthur [Quiller-Couch] disqualifies Lucio's evidence because Lucio is a sensualist, and sensualists, he says, habitually divide women into angels and those who are 'their animal prey' [see excerpt above, 1922]. Even if that be true, could Shakespeare seriously expect his audience to grasp such a subtlety? Critics see Isabel 'hard as an icicle'. If Shakespeare meant that, why did he make Lucio see her differently: 'O pretty Isabella, I am pale at mine heart to see thine eyes so red' [IV. iii. 151]. Even a sensualist can tell when people's eyes are red.

Angelo's own words make it clear that it is his conviction of the innocence and goodness of Isabel which overthrows him.

As for Claudio—the critics may despise him, but Angelo knows better. He knows that Claudio is a plucky lad who, 'receiving a dishonour'd life with ransom of such shame' [IV. iv. 31-2], might take his revenge in time to come. So he commands Claudio's execution. The Duke, of course, prevents it, and continues to weave his toils round Angelo, till the moment when he will fall on him, and grind him to powder.

And, immediately, Angelo's remorse begins. He realizes what he really is: 'This deed unshapes me quite' [IV. iv. 19]. Yet his state is more gracious now, when he believes himself to be a perjured adulterer, than it was a few days before, when he believed himself to be a saint. (pp. 17-18)

A cold-hearted, self-righteous prig is brought to a sense of what he is, in the sight of his Master. A few hours before, Angelo had turned a deaf ear to the plea 'Why, all the souls that were, were forfeit once' [II. ii. 73]. But now he can conceive no depth of guilt so deep as his own. 'Guiltier than my guiltiness' [V. i. 367]. It is like the repentance of Enobarbus, 'I am alone the villain of the earth' [*Antony and Cleopatra*, IV. vi. 29], or of Posthumus,

> it is I
> That all the abhorred things o' the earth amend
> By being worse than they.
>
> [*Cymbeline*, V. v. 215-17]

For Angelo, as for Enobarbus and for Posthumus, nothing remains save a passionate prayer to be put out of his misery:

> Then, good prince,
> No longer session hold upon my shame,
> But let my trial be mine own confession:
> Immediate sentence then, and sequent death,
> Is all the grace I beg.
>
> [V. i. 370-74]

Surely it is concerning repentance like this that it is written, 'There is joy in the presence of the angels of God'. (p. 19)

Angelo, publicly shamed, longing for death, faces an Isabel who can bring herself to say, after an agony of silent struggle, 'let him not die' [V. i. 448]. It was not in a spirit of 'weariness, cynicism, and disgust' that the Master Craftsman made the whirligig of time bring in revenges like these.

Isabel's sufferings are over. The muffled Claudio is brought in. Sister meets brother with that 'prone and speechless dialect' [I. ii. 183] which moves, or should move, men.

Sir Edmund Chambers asks, Why does the Duke conceal from Isabel in her grief the knowledge that her brother yet lives? Sir Walter Raleigh asked the same question thirty years ago. His answer was that the reason is dramatic; the crisis must be kept for the end. And, as a piece of stage-craft, the ending justifies itself; it is magnificent. But Sir Edmund Chambers is surely right when he says that a play dealing seriously with the problems of life must be taken seriously; the Duke, he thinks, symbolizes the workings of Providence. Is not such treatment of Providence, then, he asks, ironical?

The Duke certainly reminds us of the ways of Providence. And we feel so in the great final scene, where Mariana is imploring the silent Isabel to intercede for Angelo. Why, then, does the

Duke gather up all his authority, as former Friar and present Monarch, and crash it, with a lie, in the path Isabel must tread?

> Should she kneel down in mercy of this fact,
> Her brother's ghost his paved bed would break,
> And take her hence in horror.
>
>   [V. i. 434-36]

Yet all this time the Duke is keeping her brother in reserve, to produce him when Isabel shall have fulfilled her destiny, by making intercession for the man she most hates.

I can only reply that life undoubtedly *is* sometimes like that. There are some souls (Isabel is one) for whom it is decreed that no trial, however agonizing, no pain, however atrocious, is to be spared them. Nevertheless, it is also true that there is no trial so agonizing, no pain so atrocious, but that some souls can rise above it, as Isabel does when, despite the Duke's stern warning, she kneels at his feet to intercede for Angelo. (pp. 22-3)

We must be prepared to accept the postulates of Shakespeare's plays, as we do, for example, of Sophocles' *Oedipus Tyrannus*. And, generally, we are so prepared: we accept the caskets and the pound of flesh, King Lear's love-test and Prospero's art. It is a postulate of our story that Claudio has committed a capital offence. Angelo has not committed a crime in letting the law take its course upon Claudio; he has not committed a crime in his union with Mariana, to whom he has been publicly betrothed; those are assumptions on which the play is based. Angelo would be despicable if he put forward any such plea for himself, and he does not. But the fact remains that Angelo's sin has been, not in act, but in thought, and human law cannot take cognizance of thought: 'thoughts are no subjects' [V. i. 453]. Besides, Isabel is conscious that, however innocently, she herself has been the cause of Angelo's fall:

> I partly think
> A due sincerity govern'd his deeds,
> Till he did look on me; since it is so,
> Let him not die.
>
>   [V. i. 445-48]

And Angelo is penitent. There can be no doubt what the words of the Sermon on the Mount demand: 'Judge not, and ye shall not be judged.' That had been Isabel's plea for Claudio. It is a test of her sincerity, if she can put forward a plea for mercy for her dearest foe, as well as for him whom she dearly loves. (p. 24)

Now, when we mark how evil, and its forgiveness, is depicted in *Measure for Measure* in 1604, can we agree that Shakespeare's philosophy about 1604 was 'obviously not a Christian philosophy'? On the contrary, it seems to me more definitely Christian than that of *The Tempest*, though I don't deny that the philosophy of the Romances can also be called Christian. I would not deny that, on the whole, Shakespeare's last plays *are* 'happy dreams', 'symbols of an optimistic faith in the beneficent dispositions of an ordering Providence' [as stated by E. K. Chambers in the *Encyclopedia Britannica*, 1911]. But I see no ground to believe that there is any 'complete breach' between the mood of 1604 and that of 1611, or that we must assume a 'conversion', caused by 'a serious illness which may have been a nervous breakdown, and on the other hand may have been merely the plague' [as E. K. Chambers claims in his *William Shakespeare*, 1930]. (pp. 27-8)

No woman in Shakespeare is more individual than Isabel: silent yet eloquent, sternly righteous yet capable of infinite forgive-ness, a very saint and a very vixen. But, first and last, she 'stands for' mercy. The Duke is shown to us as a governor perplexed about justice, puzzled in his search for righteousness, seeking above all things to know himself. Is it altogether fanciful to remember once again that *Measure for Measure* was acted before the court at Christmas, 1604: that when Isabel at the beginning urges her plea for mercy (which she also makes good at the end) it is on the ground that

> He that might the vantage best have took
> Found out the remedy.
>
>   [II. ii. 74-5]

The day before *Measure for Measure* was acted, the finding out of that remedy was being commemorated. All sober criticism must remember the part which the accepted theology played in the thought of Shakespeare's day; that the Feast of the Nativity was—is—the union of Divine Mercy and of Divine Righteousness, and was—is—celebrated in the Christmas psalm:

> Mercy and truth are met together: righteousness
> and peace have kissed each other.

Shakespeare's audience expected a marriage at the end: and, though it may be an accident, the marriage of Isabel and the Duke makes a good ending to a Christmas play. (pp. 30-1)

> *R. W. Chambers, "'Measure for Measure'," in* Shakespeare Criticism: 1935-60, *edited by Anne Ridler, Oxford University Press, London, 1963, pp. 1-31.*

MARK VAN DOREN (essay date 1939)

[*Van Doren was an American educator, editor, novelist, and Pulitzer prize-winning poet. In the introduction to his* Shakespeare *(1939), he states that he "ignored the biography of Shakespeare, the history and character of his time, the conventions of his theater, the works of his contemporaries" to concentrate on the interest of the plays and their relevance to the modern reader or spectator. In the excerpt below, Van Doren argues that* Measure for Measure *is an unsatisfactory comedy because Shakespeare was too absorbed with the play's atmosphere of evil and corruption to pay attention to the characters. In an interpretation similar to that of William Witherle Lawrence (1931), he considers the Duke to be both an exploited stage device and a manipulative "dummy." He describes Isabella's character as Shakespeare's "most ponderous" and, therefore, "most negligible" feminine role. Other interpretations of* Measure for Measure *as an unsuccessful comedy appear in the essays by E. C. Pettet (1949) and Murray Krieger (1951).*]

If "Measure for Measure" is . . . unsatisfactory in some way that is difficult to define, the reason can hardly be a lack of serious attention on Shakespeare's part. He has given it thought and care, and he has written for it some of his gravest, most complex, and most effective poetry. The reason is rather that it goes against his grain to make comedy out of such matter; or perhaps that his absorption in the evil background of the tale is of such a sort as to leave his mind unfree either to judge it with detachment or to concentrate with his usual success upon the figures in the foreground, the persons of the play. (p. 217)

Shakespeare, altering his source, disguises [the Duke] as a friar so that he may stand by and watch the tangle of events. His commentary will maintain the sinister tone the poet desires:

> There is so great a fever on goodness, that the
> dissolution of it must cure it. Novelty is only

in request; and it is as dangerous to be aged in
any kind of course, as it is virtuous to be constant in any undertaking. There is scarce truth
enough alive to make societies secure; but security enough to make fellowships accurst. Much
upon this riddle runs the wisdom of the world.

[III. ii. 222-29]

And of course his presence at every crisis is our sign that all
will end well. . . . The Duke does to be sure intervene, and
no one dies. But he is torturously slow about it. His hands are
sluggish in the manipulation of the dummies whose predicament he has wantonly created. Our wonderment will cease
only when we realize that he is a tall dark dummy too; that it
is the atmosphere of Vienna, not the hypothetical perils of
Claudio and Isabella, which interests Shakespeare. It is the
somber spectacle of "a thirsty evil,"

Like rats that ravin down their proper bane,

[I. i. 129]

rather than the motives of the Duke as spectator, or the psychology of any spectator, out of which he has made the poetry
of "Measure for Measure."

That poetry is missing from the significant orations which here
and there are asked to do the work of thought and action.
Angelo's soliloquy when he finds his famous virtue yielding
ground to lust for Isabella is too conscious of itself as document
and case-history to be convincing as revelation.

What's this, what's this? Is this her fault or mine?
The temper or the tempted, who sins most?
Ha!
Not she, nor doth she tempt; but it is I
That, lying by the violet in the sun,
Do as the carrion does, not as the flower,
Corrupt with virtuous season. Can it be
That modesty may more betray our sense
Than woman's lightness? Having waste ground enough,
Shall we desire to raze the sanctuary
And pitch our evils there? O, fie, fie, fie!
What dost thou, or what are thou, Angelo?

[II. ii. 162-72]

These are the morals of melodrama, and we know them by the
questions and exclamations everywhere, the rhetorical mold
that forms on Angelo as he talks. (pp. 218-19)

The trouble with Isabella is partly of course the trouble with
all women in story who have to debate whether they will "give
themselves" for a consideration. The situation in itself makes
virtue theoretical—and makes their own goodness problematical, a thing to be discussed, a commodity to be weighed and
measured. The paradox of goodness is that when it is most
real it weighs the least, and thinks least of itself. Isabella, for
all she is "enskied and sainted" [I. iv. 34], and the words are
Lucio's, is the most ponderous of Shakespeare's good women
and therefore the most negligible. We do not see her in her
goodness; we only hear her talking like a termagant against
those who doubt it. This is because Shakespeare is not primarily
in love with it in his capacity as poet, any more than he is in
love with the subject of Mariana's sorrows. (p. 221)

The atmosphere of Vienna is the thing. It curls like acrid smoke
through all the crannies of the plot, and in more secret ways

than we know presents itself to our senses. The odor of it is
in the Duke's words,

And quite athwart
Goes all decorum.

[I. iii. 30-1]

It is strong in Angelo's words sometimes:

Blood, thou art blood.
Let's write good angel on the devil's horn;
'T is not the devil's crest.

[II. iv. 15-17]

And it hangs like a bitter scent above the humor of the play,
which is as rank and real as anything in Shakespeare. "Measure
for Measure" has for its clown a pimp, a parcel-bawd, whose
twirling tongue is practiced in the art of delaying justice. . . .
But there is a clown beyond Pompey, for there is the cynic
fop Lucio, who does not guess the trouble he is making for
himself when he abuses the Duke as one who would "eat
mutton on Fridays" and "mouth with a beggar though she
smelt brown bread and garlic" [III. ii. 181-84]. . . . The exposure of Lucio is finally more interesting than that of Angelo,
for of the two men Lucio has the greater dramatic integrity and
is the better acclimated to the play. And the Duke's harshness
to him, sentencing him to be whipped and hanged, or at any
rate to marry a punk he has got with child, has no parallel in
Hal's settlement with Falstaff for slander, Henry V's paying
off of Michael Williams, or even Bertram's dismissal of Parolles from his service [*All's Well That Ends Well*]. It is harshness unrelieved, as befits the quality of the evil in which "Measure for Measure" has chosen to steep itself.

Above all there is the prison where Abhorson the executioner
instructs Pompey in the new "mystery" of hanging, and where
one Ragozine, a most notorious pirate, dies of a cruel fever in
time to supply his head in place of Claudio's; and where Barnardine is too drunk to be present at his own execution:

Abhorson. Sirrah, bring Barnardine hither.
Pompey. Master Barnardine! You must rise
and be hang'd, Master Barnardine!
Abhorson. What, ho, Barnardine!
Barnardine. (*Within.*) A pox o' your throats!
Who makes that noise there? What are you?
Pompey. Your friends, sir; the hangman. You
must be so good, sir, to rise and be put to death.
Barnardine. (*Within.*) Away, you rogue,
away! I am sleepy.
Abhorson. Tell him he must awake, and that
quickly too.
Pompey. Pray, Master Barnardine, awake till
you are executed, and sleep afterwards.
Abhorson. Go in to him, and fetch him out.
Pompey. He is coming, sir, he is coming. I
hear his straw rustle.

[IV. iii. 20-36]

The rustling of that straw will be louder in our memory of
"Measure for Measure" than Claudio's outcry in the face of
death, or Angelo's perverse mutterings, or Isabella's pante-
gyrics to her chastity. It is the permanent symbol for a city,
itself all earth and rotting straw, with which Shakespeare at
the moment can do no more than he had been able to do with
the diseased bones of Pandarus's Troy [*Troilus and Cressida*].
All he can do is stir it until its stench fills every street and
creeps even into the black holes of prisons. In a tragedy he

might have done more, for tragedy is a cleansing stroke, like lightning. Perhaps in this year he was not up to tragedy, however soon he was to write ''Othello.'' But comedy has its lightnings too, and none of them strikes Vienna. The bank of dark cloud above her forehead is never burned away. (pp. 221-24)

> Mark Van Doren, '' 'Measure for Measure','' in his Shakespeare, *Henry Holt and Company, 1939, pp. 217-24.*

M[URIEL] C. BRADBROOK (essay date 1941)

[*Bradbrook is an English scholar specializing in the development of Elizabethan drama and poetry. In her Shakespearean criticism, she combines both biographical and historical research, paying particular attention to the stage conventions popular during Shakespeare's lifetime. Her* Shakespeare and Elizabethan Poetry *(1951) is a comprehensive work which relates Shakespeare's poetry to that of George Chapman, Christopher Marlowe, Edmund Spenser, and Philip Sidney and describes the evolution of Shakespeare's verse. In the excerpt below, Bradbrook explores the resemblance between Shakespeare's ''analytic technique'' in* Measure for Measure *and the allegorical debates of the late medieval morality plays. To her,* Measure for Measure *is based on the conflict between justice and mercy presented as a debate that examines the ethical problems of conduct rather than belief. In this light, she describes Angelo as the archetype of Law and Authority, Isabella as Truth and Mercy, and the Duke as both Humility and Heavenly Justice. Bradbrook thus regards the central conflict of the play as the struggle between Mercy and Law or human Justice—a conflict which the Duke eventually resolves through educating the characters, especially Angelo, and his imposition of Heavenly Justice, which seeks to reform the soul rather than to punish the offender. Bradbrook also discusses the importance of Law in* Measure, *specifically civil law as depicted in the contracts of marriage entered into by the characters, and she stresses the legal sanctity of these social contracts in Elizabethan society. For additional commentary on Elizabethan betrothal and marriage customs in the play, see the excerpts by William Witherle Lawrence (1931), R. W. Chambers (1937), and Ernest Schanzer (1963). Bradbrook concludes that the marriage of Isabella and the Duke unites truth and justice, but in terms of the impersonal morality of a social obligation rather than the doctrinal Christian approach of the morality plays. Other interpretations of justice and mercy in* Measure for Measure *appear in the essays by August Wilhelm Schlegel (1808), G. G. Gervinus (1849-50), Walter Pater (1874), and Denton J. Snider (1890).*]

[*Measure for Measure*] is more theoretical than most of Shakespeare's writings, less easy, without his accustomed refusal to theorise or analyse. It differs from *Troilus and Cressida*, the problems of which are epistemological, and the method therefore impersonal but elaborate. In *Measure for Measure* the problems are ethical, and concern conduct rather than belief: the style is barer, sharper, and harder, the language simpler and plainer, and the characters allegorical rather than symbolical. The method, however, is akin to that of *Troilus and Cressida* in being largely based upon the debate: not the massed public debate, but the naked antagonism of conflict, as between Isabel and Angelo, Claudio and Isabel, and Claudio and the Duke.

In this play Shakespeare adopts a technique as analytic as that of Donne to something resembling the late medieval Morality. It might be named The Contention between Justice and Mercy, or False Authority unmasked by Truth and Humility; Angelo stands for Authority and for Law, usurping the place of the

Duke, who is not only the representative of Heavenly Justice but of Humility, whilst Isabel represents both Truth and Mercy.

The first necessity is to grasp the importance of the Duke. Historically he belongs to a familiar dramatic type; that of the omnipotent disguised character who directs the intrigue, often hearing strange things of himself by the way—the type of Malevole, Vindice, the husband in *Eastward Ho!* and the father in *Englishmen for My Money,* a type to which the early Hamlet perhaps also belonged. Wilson Knight sees in him a Christlike figure come from a far country to save Vienna [see excerpt above, 1930]: all powerful, all merciful, and perhaps in his marriage to Isabel only ratifying her position as the Bride of the Church. It is certain that the Duke is more than the average disguised puppet master of which Brainworm is the best known example: he is at least the representative of Heavenly Justice. (pp. 385-86)

As the Duke represents unerring Justice, and in his readiness to live as a poor Friar, helping his meanest and most criminal subjects, represents also Humility as it resides in true authority; so Isabel stands for unerring Truth, and Truth is always merciful.

> How would you be,
> If he which is the top of Judgement should
> But judge you, as you are?
>
> [II. ii. 75-7]

she asks Angelo. The marriage of Truth and Justice resolves the frenzy of lies, prevarications, truths and half-truths which in the last scene records the hollowness of all external judgment, even as in *The Faerie Queene,* the marriage of Truth and Holiness, in the persons of Una and the Red Cross Knight, defeats the calumnious and evil forces represented by Duessa and Archimago.

Angelo stands for the letter of the Law, for a false Authority: he also stands for Seeming or False Semblant. At the very moment he is about to tempt Isabel he says:

> I (now the voyce of the recorded Law)
> Pronounce a sentence on your Brothers life.
>
> [II. iv. 61-2]

But Authority is arbitrary (why pick out Claudio?), it apes a state unfit for humanity, encourages hidden vice in its own representative by endowing him with arbitrary power, and strives to overthrow truth and justice.

Claudio and Juliet stand for human nature, original sin; Mariana for *eros* (as distinct from *agape*); Barnardine is contrasted with Claudio to show how much below panic-struck egoism is mere brute insensibility. Juliet, whom Claudio 'wrong'd', is penitent from the first and therefore absolved by the Duke; nor apparently does she ever stand in peril of her life, and she is not given a judgment in the final scene as all the others are. In the last scene measure for measure is meted out to all; not, perhaps, their measure according to earthly law—for Barnardine is pardoned—but the measure best devised to save their souls. The main purpose of the scene is to bring Angelo to repentance, and to achieve it against so strong a character terrific pressure has to be brought to bear. The Duke, who is as ruthlessly efficient in his means as he is benevolent in his ends, proceeds to apply the third degree with the skill of a Grand Inquisitor: and to this end he is ready to inflict any temporary suffering on Mariana and Isabel. . . . The technique is only an advance upon the enacted lie of Mariana's visit, and that the Duke has justified beforehand: 'Craft against vice I must applie' [III. ii.

277]. He is naturally a merciful character; in theory he can condemn Barnardine, but when he actually sees the murderer, 'A creature unpre-par'd, vnmeet for death', he realizes 'To transport him in the minde he is, Were damnable' [IV. iii. 67-9]. It is not Shakespeare's relenting before the miracle of his own creation, as the critics have sometimes stated, which reprieves Barnardine—in this play Shakespeare is hardly in a relenting mood—but the Duke's instinctive revolt from applying the penalties of the law without regard to their consequences. He gives Barnardine to Friar Peter to receive religious instruction, for he anticipates the maxim of Kant, and considers every human being as an end and never as a means, whether a means to the demonstration of the law or to other ends.

The debate between Justice and Mercy, which is the main theme of the play—see especially II. ii. and V. i.—is conducted mainly between Isabel and Angelo, for of the Duke it might be said as it was of archetype and ectype in *The Faerie Queene:*

He merciful is, but Mercy's self is she (cf. *F.Q.* II. ix. 43).

This debate can also be seen as a debate between Law and Religion, of which Angelo and Isabel are by profession the representatives. The Duke as secular head of the state is bound to punish not only offences but the offenders: yet Christianity, which he also professes, bids condemnation of the sin, not the sinner. . . . The two sides of his dilemma are stated by Isabel and Angelo:

> I haue a brother is condemn'd to die,
> I doe beseech you let it be his fault,
> And not my brother. . . .
> Condemne the fault, and not the actor of it,
> Why, euery fault's condemnd ere it be done:
> Mine were the verie Cipher of a Function.
>
> [II. ii. 34-9]

On the other hand, Angelo's 'devilish mercy' is, as the Duke sees, the very converse of true forgiveness:

> When Vice makes Mercie; Mercie's so extended,
> That for the faults loue, is th' offender friended.
>
> [IV. ii. 112-13]

Yet Isabel pardons Angelo when he is forfeit to the law, and asks the Duke to pardon him also. The Duke deliberately reminds her of the *lex talionis,* as well as appealing to all her feelings of rage and resentment: 'He dies for *Claudio's* death' [V. i. 443]. Yet although Isabel's first and natural impulse on hearing of her brother's execution had been 'Oh, I wil to him, and plucke out his eies!' she kneels 'in mercy of this fact', and perhaps it is this, rather than any of the Duke's ingenious tortures, which finally breaks the spirit of Angelo, though—an exquisite touch—only to the applying of his own legal standard to himself. . . . The retributive aspect of criminal law seems always to have distressed Shakespeare. The cry of the tragedies is 'None does offend, I say: none' [*King Lear,* IV. vi. 168], and in the final plays the penalties of the law are waived for the most flagrant evil-doers—Iachimo [*Cymbeline*], Alonzo, Sebastian [*The Tempest*]. The problem that a law to be just in general, must always be only an approximation to justice in particular cases, is stressed both by Claudio who suffers under it and the Duke who administers it.

> On whom it will, it will,
> On whom it will not (soe) yet still tis iust.
>
> [I. ii. 122-23]

> Lawes, for all faults,
> But faults so countenanc'd, that the strong Statutes
> Stand like the forfeites in a Barbers shop,
> As much in mocke, as marke.
>
> [V. i. 319-22]

Yet here as in other plays Law in the sense of civil law is a constant subject of praise. Ulysses' speech in defence of order and degree (*Troilus and Cressida* I. iii.) is the most comprehensive eulogy, with its assimilation of human institutions, contracts and laws to the universal order of times and seasons. In *Henry IV, Part II,* the Lord Chief Justice stands as the embodiment of everything that's excellent, and clearly represents civil law. (pp. 386-89)

In *Measure for Measure* civil law enters the story chiefly through the marriage contracts. Juliet and Mariana are both contracted: Claudio says,

> Vpon a true contract
> I got possession of *Iulietas* bed,
> You know the Lady, she is fast my wife,
> Saue that we doe the denunciation lacke
> Of outward Order.
>
> [I. ii. 145-49]

which was deferred for financial reasons. It is not clear whether this was a marriage 'per verba de praesenti', as was the Duchess of Malfi's; if so, the child would be legitimate, as the union was customary, and neither party could have married elsewhere according to the English law and habit. Nevertheless the marriage was not regular, and in [George] Chapman's continuation of *Hero and Leander* it may be seen what immense stress was laid on the public nature of the marriage contract, both in the vision of the goddess Ceremony, who descends to rebuke Hero, and in the Tale of Teras, which is a glorification of the social aspect of marriage.

Mariana was publicly affianced 'as strongly as words could make up vows' [V. i. 227-28], and the marriage settlements had been actually drawn up. Angelo is therefore her 'combynate husband', and the Duke envisages that the result of their union may be a child whose existence will 'compell him to her recompense' [III. i. 252]. The fact that the contract had been public and approved by the lady's friends would weigh very strongly with the Elizabethans, for to steal a marriage was almost a misdemeanour, as the case of the Duchess of Malfi demonstrated.

Isabella is the Bride of the Church, and to the horror of proposed violation Angelo adds a direct crime against religion. As a novice she is as it were betrothed, and apparently on the eve of her 'approbation'. If she were a novice she would be subject to the authority of the Mother, would wear the novice's dress, and obey the Rule, which was that of the Poor Clares, an order of great poverty, seclusion, and austerity. . . . Isabel's vows should have been taken between her first and second interview with Angelo; in the second, she is introduced as 'One *Isabell,* a Sister' [II. iv. 18]. and the friar addresses her as 'sister' [III. i. 252], a term he would not use to a novice; but if in the interval she had been given the first veil—it is scarcely likely that she was at a more advanced stage—she would hardly accuse herself publicly of incontinence, considering the disgrace to her order. It seems more reasonable that she should defer her vows, and that in the last scene she should appear in secular clothes, perhaps in mourning for Claudio. The Duke also appears again in secular habit, and changes of clothes had a strong effect upon the Elizabethan stage. An Isabel in a secular habit could be arrested with more propriety than an Isabel in a veil; and the final tableau also would look less unnatural.

Some indication of the Elizabethan view of marriage as a public contract rather than a private relationship may be gained, as has been said, from Chapman; though English youth was more free than that of most countries, the rule was still that marriage should be determined by social equality, family duty, and public advantage rather than by personal inclination. Juliet and Mariana are parallel in misfortune: in the view of the friar Juliet is more guilty than Claudio, but in the view of Isabel the sin is Claudio's:

> Women? Helpe heauen: men their creation marre
> In profiting by them: Nay, call us ten times fraile,
> For we are soft, as our complexions are,
> And credulous to false prints.

> [II. iv. 127-30]

It is the old story, 'Men have marble, women waxen minds', and their fatal vulnerability lies in their sympathetic natures: they lack judgment and intellectual detachment. Hence even the Duke adjures Claudio to marry her he has 'wrong'd', and he insists on a full marriage ceremony for Mariana to 'safeguard' her 'honor' against 'Imputation' [V. i. 419-20]. Even Lucio, though forgiven for his other forfeits, is obliged to make an honest woman of Mistress Kate Keepdown. The four marriages represent, in descending order of dignity, variations upon this basic social contract. In *The Merchant of Venice,* a forerunner of this play in so many ways, the marriage contract is symbolized in the story of the rings, and contrasted with Shylock's purely legal bond. Marriage is the highest form of contract, in that it contains subtler possibilities for good, for evil, for variety than other types of contract: it not only imposes a legal obligation, but contains a promise of personal and general prosperity of the highest kind.

The basis of Justice and of Law is the establishment of truth. Perfect truth resides only in God: the devil is the father of lies, and in the current morality representations of him, his power of disguise, particularly of disguising himself as a virtue, was his subtlest weapon for the destruction of man. Hence the question of Truth apparent and real, of Falsehood conscious and unconscious is crucial to the plot. . . . In *Measure for Measure,* the issue is prominent, but it is not a subject for debate or doubt. The main contrast between seeming and reality lies of course in 'the prenzie Angelo', 'the well-seeming Angelo', 'this outward-sainted deputy'. The Duke's first speech is an ironic comment on this:

> There is a kinde of Character in thy life
> That to th' obsseruer, doth thy history
> Fully vnfold.

> [I. i. 27-9]

But it is made plain in the next scene but one that the Duke is by no means reading Angelo's life in the accepted version.

The 'seeming' of the deputy is echoed so often and so bitterly that to dwell on it would be tedious. Angelo has in him something of the dissembling power of Claudius King of Denmark, and also of his gnawing conscience; he is 'At warre, twixt will and will not' [II. ii. 33]. Isabel, who, like Hamlet, 'knows not "seems"' but is forced to learn it, maintains the truth although Angelo's false outweighs her true: 'Truth is truth To th' end of reckning' [V. i. 45-6]. She is traduced as sorely as the Duke had been traduced by Lucio: yet she remains steadfast, more

steadfast than the Duke would have been, for to him, as to Prospero, life itself is a dream and all its events but 'seeming'.

> Thou hast nor youth, nor age
> But as it were an after-dinners sleepe
> Dreaming on both.

> [III. i. 32-4]

Yet the Duke is capable of turning every occasion to his own purpose, as in his ironic speech to Angelo on his return, which is designed to give a smart lash to the conscience of the deputy, and to express his own scepticism on 'the vanity of wretched fooles'.

> Giue me your hand,
> And let the Subiect see, to make them know
> That outward curtesies would faine proclaime
> Fauours that keepe within.

> [V. i. 13-16]
> (pp. 390-93)

Angelo himself upheld the doctrine of seeming. He admits to Escalus that a jury may contain worse criminals than the prisoner it condemns, yet the known crime must be punished.

> What knowes the Lawes
> That theeues do passe on theeues?

> [II. i. 22-3]

But, he continues,

> When I, that censure him, do so offend,
> Let mine owne Iudgement patterne out my death.

> [II. i. 29-30]

In this alone Angelo is not a seemer; he has the consistency to sentence himself.

> Immediate sentence then, and sequent death,
> Is all the grace I beg.

> [V. i. 373-74]

In his fate, the Elizabethans would recognize the best and indeed the only true justice, that which is invoked by the title: Heaven's justice or Providence. They believed that justice could be left to the magistrate because if he were unable or unwilling to execute it, Heaven would deal justice to the evil-doer. Whoever else forgot his contract God would not, and 'Vengeance is mine, I will repay, saith the Lord'.

The Duke, in his own way, is as great a seemer as Angelo. In his role as a poor Friar he is continually placed in ironic situations, his real and his seeming character being perpetually brought into conflict by unconscious words of Isabella, Escalus, the Provost and Lucio. . . . Some of the situations the Duke enjoys and more he turns to good account, but on one occasion he is rudely disillusioned. He had at least believed that the people loved him, and had retired only to preserve his reputation with them; yet he learns with cruel elaboration from Lucio how little a public man can claim immunity from slander. He is almost driven, in forgetfulness of his habit and his office alike, to challenge Lucio:

> *Duke.* . . . I am bound to call vppon you, and
> I pray you your name?
> *Lucio.* Sir my name is *Lucio,* wel known to the
> Duke.

> [III. ii. 157-59]

In the last scene he suffers defamation from the same quarter in his person as a friar, when Lucio coolly puts into his own mouth all the slanders which he had been obliged to listen to. The Duke is wounded in his one vulnerable point, the dignity of his office, and it requires a second thought before he can pardon Lucio.

The difference between the Duke's seeming and that of Angelo is of course that the Duke's is purely an external change. In one sense he is a benevolent Haroun-al-Raschid; but his purposes are better than mere curiosity, and he is not defaming the cloak of religion.

> Come hither *Isabell*.
> Your *Frier* is now your Prince: As I was then,
> Aduertysing, and holy to your businesse,
> (Not changing heart with habit) I am still,
> Atturnied at your seruice.
>
> [V. i. 381-85]

He who was greatest has been as a servant amongst them.

In the actions of Angelo, Isabel, and the Duke, the question of Truth and Seeming is stated, and they have thus a double burden of symbolism to carry. Nevertheless, the allegorical nature of *Measure for Measure* does not preclude a human interest in the characters. Though based perhaps on the Moralities, it is not a Morality. Angelo has always been recognized as a superb character study; Isabel and the Duke, though less impressive, are subtly presented. She is possibly the most intelligent of all Shakespeare's women; even poor Claudio recognizes her power in 'reason and discourse' [I. ii. 185]; yet she is young, and pitifully inexperienced. (pp. 393-95)

The Duke himself is a type of character whom Shakespeare did not often depict. His relations with his people are comparable with those of Henry V with Bates and Williams—Williams in particular is left rather in the position of Lucio; and, like Henry V, he can be extremely peremptory, is a born administrator, and enjoys probing and investigating into the lives of the common people—he would have appreciated Prince Hal's conversation with the drawer. On the other hand he more resembles Prospero in that all his actions are controlled by one purpose, in that complete self-confidence justifies his seeming cruelties (compare Prospero to Ferdinand), and in his almost unerring moral insight —being only twice deceived or surprised by other people's reactions. He resembles Prospero also in the absolute power which he maintains over the lives of the rest of the characters, except indeed the minor comic characters. These, the human sediment of Vienna, are not capable of being systematized: they exist independently of the moral framework and help further to give the play its naturalism and solidity. The difference between Pompey and Barnardine is the difference between a character and a portent—between the Artful Dodger and Bill Sikes. (pp. 396-97)

Measure for Measure remains a problem play, not because it is shallower, more unfinished or more incoherent than Shakespeare's other plays, but because it is stiffened by its doctrinaire and impersonal consideration of ethical values. The dryness, the pain behind the play, seem to depict a world in which external personal relationships are so hopelessly false and unreliable that it is necessary to cut below them to the moral substratum. To look for happiness is childish: what should be looked for is the good, proper, socially fitting relation; the basis is impersonal morality. (p. 398)

> *M[uriel] C. Bradbrook, "Authority, Truth, and Justice in 'Measure for Measure'," in* The Review of English Studies, *Vol. XVII, No. 68, October, 1941, pp. 385-99.*

L. C. KNIGHTS   (essay date 1942)

[*A renowned English Shakespearean scholar, Knights followed the precepts of I. A. Richards and F. R. Leavis and sought for an underlying pattern in all of Shakespeare's work. His* How Many Children Had Lady Macbeth? *(1933)—a milestone study in the twentieth-century reaction to the Shakespearean criticism of the previous century—criticizes the traditional emphasis on character as an approach which inhibits the reader's total response to Shakespeare's plays. The next two excerpts by Knights and Leavis were published in the same issue of* Scrutiny *and present diametrically opposed interpretations of* Measure for Measure. *In the first essay, Knights argues that the absence of simple answers to "questions of personal conduct" in* Measure for Measure *has led to the conflicting opinions about the main characters. He notes that Shakespeare's examination of "the sexual instinct" is the basis of the action, while the numerous characters represent varying positions regarding the relation of suppression and license. Knights contends that the multiple points of view in the play, especially those of Isabella, the Duke, and Claudio—whom he calls the "central figure of the plot"—confuse us, primarily because these characters are often ambiguous and fail to clearly present their perspectives on law and justice central to the action. He also remarks that the last two acts display signs of "haste," which further contributes to the confusion. Knights concludes that* Measure for Measure *contains "genuine ambiguity," because Shakespeare's "process of clarification"—the recognition and successful dramatization of "conflicting 'truths'"—is not complete. For additional commentary on the ambiguity and Shakespeare's "process of clarification" in* Measure for Measure, *see the excerpts by Walter Raleigh (1907), Una Ellis-Fermor (1936), Derek A. Traversi (1942), and J. W. Lever (1965).*]

It is probably true to say that *Measure for Measure* is that play of Shakespeare's which has caused most readers the greatest sense of strain and mental discomfort. . . . The most obvious reason for this discomfort is to be found in the conflicting attitudes towards the main characters that seem to be forced upon us, and it is easy to list questions of personal conduct for which it is impossible to find a simple answer. (What, to take one example, are we to think of Isabella? Is she the embodiment of a chaste serenity, or is she, like Angelo, an illustration of the frosty lack of sympathy of a self-regarding puritanism?) Hazlitt's explanation of the painful impression created by the play, that 'our sympathies are repulsed and defeated in all directions' [see excerpt above, 1817], is, however, only part of the truth. It is not merely that the play is a comedy, so that the 'general system of cross-purposes between the feelings of the different characters and the sympathy of the reader' can be in part attributed to the needs of the plot—complication, suspense and a conventionally happy ending; the strain and conflict goes much deeper than that, being in fact embedded in the themes of which the characters are made the mouthpiece.

Like many other Elizabethan plays, *Measure for Measure* has an obvious relation to the old Moralities. It is too lively and dramatic—too Elizabethan—to be considered merely as a homiletic debate, but it turns, in its own way, on certain moral problems, the nature of which is indicated by the recurrent use of the words 'scope,' 'liberty' and 'restraint.' What, Shakespeare seems to ask, is the relation between natural impulse and individual liberty on the one hand, and self-restraint and public law on the other?

The mainspring of the action is of course the sexual instinct: Claudio is condemned 'for getting Madam Julietta with child' [I. ii. 72-3], Angelo discovers the force of suppressed impulse, and most of the lesser characters seem to have no other occupation and few other topics of conversation but sex. Angelo on the one hand and Mrs. Overdone and her clients on the other represent the extremes of suppression and licence, and towards them Shakespeare's attitude is clear. The figure of Angelo, although a sketch rather than a developed character study, is the admitted success of the play. In few but firm lines we are made aware that his boasted self-control is not only a matter of conscious will ('What I will not, that I cannot do' [II. ii. 52]), but of a will taut and strained. (pp. 222-23)

Neither Angelo nor the traffickers in sex are the source of the sense of uneasiness that we are trying to track down. It is Claudio—who is scarcely a 'character' at all, and who stands between the two extremes—who seems to spring from feelings at war with themselves, and it is in considering the nature of his offence that one feels most perplexity. Soon after his first appearance, led by a gaoler, he is accosted by Lucio:

Lucio: Why how now, Claudio! Whence comes this
             restraint?
Claudio: From too much liberty, my Lucio, liberty:
             As surfeit is the father of much fast,
             So every scope by the immoderate use
             Turns to restraint. Our natures do pursue,
             Like rats that ravin down their proper bane,
             A thirsty evil, and when we drink we die.
Lucio: If I could speak so wisely under an arrest, I
             would send for certain of my creditors. And yet,
             to say the truth, I had as lief have the foppery
             of freedom as the mortality of imprisonment.
             What's thy offence, Claudio?
Claudio: What but to speak of would offend again.
Lucio: What, is it murder?
Claudio: No.
Lucio: Lechery?
Claudio: Call it so.

                                                    [I. ii. 124-40]

That Shakespeare was aware of an element of sententiousness in Claudio's words is shown by Lucio's brisk rejoinders. The emphasis has, too, an obvious dramatic function, for by suggesting that the offence was indeed grave it makes the penalty seem less fantastic; and in the theatre that is probably all one notices in the swift transition to more explicit exposition. But on coming back to the lines with fuller knowledge of what is involved it is impossible to avoid the impression of something odd and inappropriate. Apart from the fact that Claudio was 'contracted' to Juliet, he does not seem to have 'surfeited,' and he was certainly not a libertine: his 'entertainment' with Juliet was, we learn, 'most mutual'—they were in love with each other—a fact that is emphasized again later [II. iii. 24-8], when the Duke makes it a matter of special reproach to Juliet: 'Then was your sin of heavier kind than his.' And consider the simile by which Claudio is made to express feelings prompted, presumably, by his relations with the woman who—except for 'the denunciation . . . of outward order'—is 'fast my wife' [I. ii. 147-49]:—

          Our natures do pursue,
     Like rats that ravin down their proper bane,
     A thirsty evil, and when we drink we die.
                                                    [I. ii. 128-30]

The illustrative comparison has, we notice, three stages: (i) rats 'ravin down' poison, (ii) which makes them thirsty, (iii) so they drink and—the poison taking effect—die. But the human parallel has, it seems, only two stages: prompted by desire, men quench their 'thirsty evil' in the sexual act and—by the

terms of the new proclamation—pay the penalty of death. The act of ravening down the bane or poison is thus left on our hands, and the only way we can dispose of it is by assuing that 'our natures' have no need to 'pursue' their 'thirsty evils' for it is implanted in them by the mere fact of being human. This of course is pedantry and—you may say—irrelevant pedantry, for Shakespeare's similes do not usually demand a detailed, point by point, examination, and the confusion between desire (thirst) and that from which desire springs does not lessen the general effect. The fact remains, however, that there is some slight dislocation or confusion of feeling, comparable, it seems to me, to the wider confusion of Sonnet 129. 'An expense of spirit in a waste of shame.' . . . And even if you accept the simile as completely satisfactory, nothing can prevent 'our natures' from receiving some share of the animus conveyed by 'ravin,' a word in any case more appropriate to lust than to love, and so used by Shakespeare in *Cymbeline:*

          The cloyed will—
     That satiate yet unsatisfied desire, that tub
     Both fill'd and running—ravening first the lamb,
     Longs after for the garbage.
                                              [*Cymbeline,* I. vii. 47-50]

The sentiments expressed here concerning what, compared with Angelo's abstinence and Lucio's sexuality, looks like a natural relationship, are not the only ones voiced in the course of the play. Shakespeare in fact dramatizes various attitudes, and one would say that our estimate of their relative validity depended on our sense of the character embodying them were it not that some of the characters are themselves either ambiguous or without much dramatic substance. Angelo's unqualified contempt for Juliet—

          See you the fornicatress be remov'd:
          Let her have needful, but not lavish, means
                                                    [II. ii. 23-5]

—is sufficiently 'placed,' as are Pompey's remarks about 'the merriest usury' [III. ii. 6]; and Lucio, embodying a vulgar flippancy that blurs all distinctions, is obviously not disinterested when, pleading for 'a little more lenity to lechery' [III. ii. 97], he complains of Angelo, 'What a ruthless thing is this in him, for the rebellion of a codpiece to take away the life of a man!' [III. ii. 114-15]. But we can feel no such certainty about the Duke or Isabella, who are sure enough of themselves: each of them is disposed to severity towards 'the sin' [II. ii. 29-36; III. i. 148] of Claudio and Juliet, and the Duke seems to regard it as an instance of the 'corruption' that boils and bubbles in the state: 'It is too general vice, and severity must cure it' [III. ii. 103]. To Escalus who, so far as he is anything, is simply a wise counsellor, the 'fault' [II. i. 40] is venial; and the humane Provost describes Claudio as,

                    a young man
          More fit to do another such offence,
          Than die for this.
                                                    [II. iii. 13-15]
                                                    (pp. 225-27)

The play of course is only 'about' Claudio to the extent that he is the central figure of the plot; he is not consistently *created*, and he only lives in the intensity of his plea for life. But I think it is the slight uncertainty of attitude in Shakespeare's handling of him that explains some part, at least, of the play's disturbing effect. Shakespeare, we know, had a deep sense of the human worth of tradition and traditional morality, but his plays do not rely on any accepted scheme of values. Their

Act II. Scene i. Froth, Pompey, Escalus, Angelo, and El-
bow. By Riley (1791). From the Art Collection of the Folger
Shakespeare Library.

morality (if we call it that) springs from the unshrinking exploration of—the phrase is [John] Marston's—'what men were,
and are,' and the standard is, as we say loosely, nature itself.
In the period immediately preceding the greatest plays—the
period of *Measure for Measure, Troilus and Cressida, Hamlet*
and perhaps some of the *Sonnets*—analysis is not completely
pure, and an emotional bias seems to blur some of the natural,
positive values which in *Macbeth* or *Lear* are as vividly realized
as the vision of evil.

The theme of liberty and restraint has, in *Measure for Measure,*
another and more public aspect. The first full line of the play
is, 'Of government the properties to unfold,' and the working
out of the new severity of the law against licence leads to an
examination of more general questions—the relations of law
and 'justice,' of individual freedom and social control, of governors and governed. Here again one finds not only divided
sympathies but the pressure of feelings that fail to reach explicit
recognition, as in the Duke's lines about the folly of keeping
laws on the statute book but not enforcing them:

> We have strict statutes and most biting laws,
> The needful bits and curbs to headstrong weeds,
> Which for this fourteen years we have let slip;
> Even like an o'er grown lion in a cave,
> That goes not out to prey. Now, as fond fathers,

Having bound up the threat'ning twigs of birch,
Only to stick it in their children's sight
For terror not to use, in time the rod
Becomes more mock'd than fear'd; so our decrees,
Dead to infliction, to themselves are dead,
And liberty plucks justice by the nose;
The baby beats the nurse, and quite athwart
Goes all decorum.

[I. iii. 19-31]

What one first notices here is the crisp and lively description
of the disorder resulting from official negligence; but behind
this there are more complex feelings. If the offenders are 'weeds,'
they are also full of natural energy, like the horse that needs
the curb; whilst the concluding lines suggest mischief or childish tantrums rather than deliberate wickedness. And if the unen-
forced law is ludicrous—'a scarecrow,' as Angelo says [II. i.
1]—the law and the lawmakers are not exactly amiable. If the
Duke's metaphors are given due weight ('biting,' 'prey,' 'rod,'
etc.) one begins to sympathize with Lucio's feelings about 'the
hideous law' [I. iv. 63], especially when, a few lines later, the
Duke is explicit that to enforce the laws is, now, 'to strike and
gall' the people. It is, however, a postulate of the play that
laws are necessary; and although Shakespeare's deep—and
characteristically Elizabethan—sense of social *order* is not expressed here with the same force as it is elsewhere, it is not,
I feel, simply Angelo who thinks of the law as 'all-building.'
It is when this epithet is restored to its context that the underlying dilemma of the play becomes apparent: the full phrase
is,

> the manacles
> Of the all-building law.

[II. iv. 93-4]

Once more, Shakespeare presents various possible attitudes and
points of view. The perplexity of the ordinary man confronted
with the application of the laws to a particular fellow human
is expressed by Escalus when, towards the end of Act II, scene
i, he reverts to Angelo's explicit instruction that Claudio shall
'be executed by nine to-morrow morning': . . .

Justice: Lord Angelo is severe.
Escalus: It is but needful:
Mercy is not itself, that oft looks so;
Pardon is still the nurse of second woe.
But yet, poor Claudio! There is no remedy.

[II. i. 282-85]

Whilst laws are necessary, they must be enforced; yet one's
readiness to accept the logic of this is qualified by various
considerations already, in the same scene, brought to our attention. Elbow, chosen constable by his neighbours for seven
years and a half, is not simply a stock figure of fun: those who
are concerned for the validity of the law can hardly ignore the
fact that its instruments may be as foolish as he. . . . 'Robes
and furr'd gowns hide all,' as the mad king says in *Lear* [IV.
vi. 165]. More important still, those who make or administer
the laws may be as corrupt, at least in thought, as those they
sentence. . . . Angelo, self-righteous and unsubtle, claims that
the law is impersonal: equating law with justice, he complacently overlooks the fact that justice has a moral basis, and
that morality is concerned with men's thoughts and desires,
not merely with their acts. . . . Given Angelo's premise, that
law *is* justice, his further contention, that any deviation from
strict law involves injustice to 'those . . . which a dismiss'd
offence would after gall' [II. ii. 101-02], is unassailable. Is-

abella, when her plea for mercy fails, takes the only course open to her and attacks the human motive that sets the logical machine in motion,

> Hooking both right and wrong to the appetite,
> To follow as it draws.
>
> [II. iv. 176-77]

Claudio has already made some bitter comments on 'the demigod Authority' [I. ii. 120], and Isabella, in words that remind us once more of *Lear*, now forces the personal, as opposed to the purely formal, issue:

> So you must be the first that gives this sentence,
> And he, that suffers . . .
> Could great men thunder
> As Jove himself does, Jove would ne'er be quiet,
> For every pelting, petty officer
> Would use his heaven for thunder; nothing but thunder!
>
> [II. ii. 106-14]

That, really, is as far as we get. That Angelo has to reverse his former opinion and to tell himself,

> Thieves for their robbery have authority
> When judges steal themselves,
>
> [II. i. 22-3]

is not a full answer to the questions we have been forced to ask; and it is significant that the last two acts, showing obvious signs of haste, are little more than a drawing out and resolution of the plot. Angelo's temptation and fall finely enforces the need for self-knowledge and sympathy which seems to be the central 'moral' of the play, and which certainly has a very direct bearing on the problems of law and statecraft involved in any attempt to produce order in an imperfect society. But the problems remain. Important in any age, they had a particular urgency at a time when established social forms were being undermined by new forces, and Shakespeare—who in several plays had already pondered 'the providence that's in a watchful state' [*Troilus and Cressida*, III. iii. 196]—was to return to them again with a developed insight that makes most political thought look oddly unsubstantial. The development was, of course, to be in the direction indicated by *Measure for Measure*—the continued reduction of abstract 'questions' to terms of particular human motives and particular human consequences, and the more and more explicit recognition of complexities and contradictions that appear as soon as one leaves the realm of the formal and the abstract. But in this play the paradox of human law—related on one side to justice and on the other to expediency—is felt as confusion rather than as a sharply focussed dilemma. (pp. 228-33)

The play itself—and this is a sign of its limitations—tends to force discussion in the direction of argument; but I certainly do not wish to imply that its admitted unsatisfactoriness is due to Shakespeare's failure to provide neat answers for Social Problems. Even when, later, he probes far more deeply the preoccupations that have been touched on here, he offers no solutions. *Lear, Coriolanus, Antony and Cleopatra,*—each is a great work of clarification, in which there is the fullest recognition of conflicting 'truths'; in these plays, therefore, there is that element of paradox which seems inseparable from any work of supreme honesty. In *Measure for Measure* the process of clarification is incomplete, and one finds not paradox but genuine ambiguity. (p. 233)

> L. C. Knights, "The Ambiguity of 'Measure for Measure'," in Scrutiny, Vol. X, No. 3, January, 1942, pp. 222-33.

F. R. LEAVIS   (essay date 1942)

[*In the following excerpt, Leavis challenges L. C. Knights's interpretation of* Measure for Measure *(see excerpt above, 1942); both essays appeared in the same issue of* Scrutiny, *a literary review founded and edited by Leavis. To Leavis, Shakespeare's ability to display "complexity distinguished from contradiction, conflict, and uncertainty" is the greatest accomplishment of* Measure for Measure. *Contradicting Knights, Leavis finds no ambiguity in the play and he states that its Christian values are firmly defined and established in the "consummately right" denouement. Other commentators who praise Shakespeare's design in* Measure for Measure *include G. G. Gervinus (1849-50), Denton J. Snider (1890), G. Wilson Knight (1930), Roy W. Battenhouse (1946), Bertrand Evans (1960), and James Black (1973).*]

Re-reading, both of the above and of *Measure for Measure*, has only heightened my first surprise that such an argument about what seems to me one of the very greatest of the plays, and most consummate and convincing of Shakespeare's achievements, should have come from the author of *How Many Childen Had Lady Macbeth?* For I cannot see that the 'discomfort' [Knights] sets out to explain is other in kind than that which, in the bad prepotent tradition, has placed *Measure for Measure* both among the 'unpleasant' ('cynical') plays and among the unconscionable compromises of the artist with the botcher, the tragic poet with the slick provider of bespoke comedy. In fact, Knights explicitly appeals to the 'admitted unsatisfactoriness' of *Measure for Measure*. The 'admitted unsatisfactoriness,' I find myself with some embarrassment driven to point out . . . , has to be explained in terms of that incapacity for dealing with poetic drama, that innocence about the nature of convention and the conventional possibilities of Shakespearean dramatic method and form, which we associate classically with the name of Bradley. (p. 234)

Knights judges [Claudio] to be 'not consistently *created*': it is plain that the main critical intention would be rendered by shifting the italics to 'consistently'—he is not 'created' (*i.e.,* 'scarcely a "character"') and, what's more significant, not consistent. This inconsistency, this 'uncertainty of handling,' we are invited to find localized in the half-dozen lines of Claudio's first address to Lucio—here Knights makes his most serious offer at grounding his argument in the text:

> From too much liberty, my Lucio, liberty:
> As surfeit is the father of much fast,
> So every scope by the immoderate use
> Turns to restraint. Our natures do pursue,
> Like rats that ravin down their proper bane,
> A thirsty evil, and when we drink we die.
>
> [I. ii. 125-30]

What problem is presented by these lines? The only problem I can see is why anyone should make heavy weather of them. Knights finds it disconcerting that Claudio should express vehement self-condemnation and self-disgust. But Claudio has committed a serious offence, not only in the eyes of the law, but in his own eyes. No doubt he doesn't feel that the offence deserves death; nor does anyone in the play, except Angelo (it is characteristic of Isabella that she should be not quite certain about it). On the other hand, is it difficult to grant his acquiescence in the moral conventions that barring Lucio and the professionals, everyone about him accepts? A Claudio who took an advanced twentieth-century line in these matters might have made a more interesting 'character'; but such an emancipated Claudio was no part of Shakespeare's conception of his theme. Nor, I think Knights will grant, are there any grounds for supposing that Shakespeare himself tended to feel that the prescription of pre-marital chastity might well be dispensed with.

No perplexity, then, should be caused by Claudio's taking conventional morality seriously; that he should do so is not in any way at odds with his being in love, or with the mutuality of the offence. And that he should be bitterly self-reproachful and self-condemnatory, and impute a heavier guilt to himself than anyone else (except Isabella and Angelo) imputes to him, is surely natural; he is not a libertine, true (though a pal of Lucio's); but, as he now sees the case, he has recklessly courted temptation, has succumbed to the uncontrollable appetite so engendered, and as a result brought death upon himself, and upon Juliet disgrace and misery. Every element of the figurative comparison will be found to be accounted for here, I think, and I can't see anything 'odd' or 'inappropriate' about the bitterness and disgust.

Further, Knights's own point should be done justice to: 'The emphasis has, too, an obvious dramatic function, for, by suggesting that the offence was indeed grave, it makes the penalty seem less fantastic; and in the theatre that is probably all one notices in the swift transition to more explicit exposition.' The complementary point I want to make is that nowhere else in the play is there anything to support Knights's diagnostic commentary. The 'uncertainty of attitude' in Shakespeare's handling of Claudio, an uncertainty manifested in a 'dislocation or confusion of feeling,' depends on those six lines for its demonstration: it can't be plausibly illustrated from any other producible passage of the text. (pp. 235-37)

Actually, no play in the whole canon is remoter from 'morbid pessimism' than *Measure for Measure,* or less properly to be associated in mood with *Hamlet* or *Troilus and Cressida.* For the attitude towards death (and life, of course) that the Friar recommends is rejected not merely by Claudio, but by its total context in the play, the varied positive aspects of which it brings out—its significance being that it does so. In particular this significance appears when we consider the speech in relation to the assortment of attitudes towards death that the play dramatizes. Barnardine is an unambiguous figure. Claudio shrinks from death because, once he sees a chance of escape, life, in spite of all the Friar may have said, asserts itself, with all the force of healthy natural impulse, as undeniably real and poignantly desirable; and also because of eschatological terrors, the significance of which is positive, since they are correlatives of established positive attitudes (the suggestion of Dante has often been noted). Isabella can exhibit a contempt of death because of the exaltation of her faith. Angelo begs for death when he stands condemned, not merely in the eyes of others, but in his own eyes, by the criteria upon which his self-approval has been based; when, it may fairly be said, his image of himself shattered, he has already lost his life.

The death-penalty of the Romantic comedy convention that Shakespeare starts from he puts to profoundly serious use. It is a necessary instrument in the experimental demonstration upon Angelo:

> hence shall we see,
> If power change purpose, what our seemers be.
>
> [I. iii. 53-4]

The demonstration is of human nature, for Angelo is

> man, proud man,
> Drest in a little brief authority,

> Most ignorant of what he's most assured.
> His glassy essence . . .
>
> [II. ii. 117-19]
> (p. 239)

The generalized form in which the result of the experiment may be stated is, 'Judge not, that ye be not judged'—how close in this play Shakespeare is to the New Testament Wilson Knight (whose essay in *The Wheel of Fire* gives the only adequate account of *Measure for Measure* I know) and R. W. Chambers (see *Man's Unconquerable Mind*) have recognized [see excerpts above, 1930 and 1937]. But there is no need for us to create a perplexity for ourselves out of the further recognition that, even in the play of which this is the moral, Shakespeare conveys his belief that law, order, and formal justice are necessary. To talk in this connexion of the 'underlying dilemma' of the play is to suggest (in keeping with the general purpose of Knights's paper) that Shakespeare shows himself the victim of unresolved contradictions, of mental conflict or of uncertainty. But, surely, to believe that some organs and procedures of social discipline are essential to the maintenance of society needn't be incompatible with recognizing profound and salutary wisdom in 'Judge not, that ye be not judged,' or with believing that it is our duty to keep ourselves alive to the human and personal actualities that underlie the 'impersonality' of justice. Complexity of attitude isn't necessarily conflict or contradiction; and, it may be added (perhaps the reminder will be found not unpardonable), some degree of complexity of attitude is involved in all social living. It is Shakespeare's great triumph in *Measure for Measure* to have achieved so inclusive and delicate a complexity and to have shown us complexity distinguished from contradiction, conflict and uncertainty with so sure and subtle a touch. The quality of the whole, in fact, answers to the promise of the poetic texture, to which Knights, in his preoccupation with a false trail, seems to me to have done so little justice.

To believe in the need for law and order is not to approve of any and every law; and about Shakespeare's attitude to the particular law in question there can be no doubt. We accept the law as a necessary datum, but that is not to say that we are required to accept it in any abeyance of our critical faculties. On the contrary it is an obvious challenge to judgment, and its necessity is a matter of the total challenge it subserves to our deepest sense of responsibility and our most comprehensive and delicate powers of discrimination. We have come now, of course, to the treatment of sex in *Measure for Measure,* and I find myself obliged to insist once more that complexity of attitude needn't be ambiguity, or subtlety uncertainty.

The attitude towards Claudio we have dealt with. Isabella presents a subtler case, but not, I think, one that ought to leave us in any doubt. 'What,' asks Knights, 'are we to thnk of Isabella? Is she the embodiment of a chaste serenity, or is she, like Angelo, an illustration of the frosty lack of sympathy of a self-regarding puritanism?' But why assume that it must be 'either or'—that she has to be merely the one or else merely the other? It is true that, as Knights remarks, *Measure for Measure* bears a relation to the Morality; but the Shakespearean use of convention permits far subtler attitudes and valuations than the Morality does. On the one hand, Isabella is clearly not a simple occasion for our feelings of critical superiority. The respect paid her on her entry by the lewd and irreverent Lucio is significant, and she convincingly establishes a presence qualified to command such respect. Her showing in the consummate interviews with Angelo must command a measure of sympathy in us. (pp. 240-41)

To begin with, we note that the momentary state of grace to which her influence lifts Lucio itself issues in what amounts to a criticism—a limiting and placing criticism:

> *Lucio:* I hold you as a thing ensky'd and sainted:
> By your renouncement an immortal spirit,
> And to be talked with in sincerity,
> As with a saint.
> *Isab..* You do blaspheme the good in mocking me.
> *Lucio:* Do not believe it. Fewness and truth, 'tis thus:
> Your brother and his lover have embrac'd:
> As those that feed grow full, as blossoming time
> That from the seedness the bare fallow brings
> To teeming foison, even so her plenteous womb
> Expresseth his full tilth and husbandry.
>
>   [I. iv. 34-44]

This is implicit criticism in the sense that the attitude it conveys, while endorsed dramatically by the exalted seriousness that is a tribute to Isabella, and poetically by the unmistakable power of the expression (it comes, we feel, from the centre), is something to which she, with her armoured virtue, can't attain. We note further that this advantage over her that Lucio has (for we feel it to be that, little as he has our sympathy in general) comes out again in its being he who has to incite Isabella to warmth and persistence in her intercession for Claudio. The effect of this is confirmed when, without demanding that Isabella should have yielded to Angelo's condition, we register her soliloquizing exit at the end of Act II Scene iv, it is not credibly an accidental touch:

> Then, Isabel, live chaste, and, brother, die:
> More than our brother is our chastity.
>
>   [II. iv. 183-84]

The cumulative effect is such that it would need a stronger argument than R. W. Chambers's to convince us that there oughn't to be an element of the critical in the way we take Isabella's parting discharge upon Claudio. . . . It is all in keeping that she should betray, in the exalted assertion of her chastity, a kind of sensuality of martyrdom:

> were I under the terms of death,
> The impression of keen whips I'd wear as rubies,
> And strip myself to death, as to a bed
> That longing have been sick for, ere I'd yield
> My body up to shame.
>
>   [II. iv. 100-104]

Finally, it is surely significant that the play should end upon a hint that she is to marry the Duke—a hint that, implying a high valuation along with a criticism, aptly clinches the general presentment of her.

But at this point I come sharply up against the casual and confident assumption that we must all agree in a judgment I find staggering: 'it is significant that the last two acts, showing obvious signs of haste, are little more than a drawing out and resolution of the plot.' The force of this judgement, as the last sentence of Knights's first paragraph confirms, is that the 'drawing out and resolution of the plot,' being mere arbitrary theatre-craft done from the outside, in order to fit the disconcerting development of the poet's essential interests with a comedy ending that couldn't have been elicited out of their inner logic, are not, for interpretive criticism, significant at all. My own view is clean contrary: it is that the resolution of the plot of *Measure for Measure* is a consummately right and satisfying fulfilment of the essential design; marvellously adroit,

with an adroitness that expresses, and derives from the poet's sure human insight and his fineness of ethical and poetic sensibility.

But what one makes of the ending of the play depends on what one makes of the Duke; and I am embarrassed about proceeding, since the Duke has been very adequately dealt with by Wilson Knight, whose essay Knights refers to. The Duke, it is important to note, was invented by Shakespeare; in *Promos and Cassandra,* Shakespeare's source, there is no equivalent. He, his delegation of authority and his disguise (themselves familiar romantic conventions) are the means by which Shakespeare transforms a romantic comedy into a completely and profoundly serious 'criticism of life.' The more-than-Prospero of the play, it is the Duke who initiates and controls the experimental demonstration—the controlled experiment—that forms the action. (pp. 241-44)

Subtly and flexibly as he functions, the nature of the convention is, I can't help feeling, always sufficiently plain for the purposes of the moment. If he were felt as a mere character, an actor among the others, there would be some point in the kind of criticism that has been brought against him (not explicitly, I hasten to add, by Knights—though, in consistency, he seems to me committed to it). How uncondonably cruel, for example, to keep Isabella on the rack with the lie about her brother's death!

I am bound to say that the right way of taking this, and everything else that has pained and perplexed the specialists, seems to me to impose itself easily and naturally. The feeling about the Duke expressed later by Angelo—

> O my dread lord!
> I should be guiltier than my guiltiness,
> To think I can be undiscernible,
> When I perceive your grace, like power divine
> Hath look'd upon my passes,
>
>   [V. i. 366-70]

the sense of him as a kind of Providence directing the action from above, has been strongly established. The nature of the action as a controlled experiment with the Duke in charge of the controls, has asserted itself sufficiently. We know where we have to focus our critical attention and our moral sensibility: not, that is, upon the Duke, but upon the representatives of human nature that provide the subjects of the demonstration. This, we know, is to be carried to the promised upshot—.

> hence shall we see,
> If power change purpose, what our seemers be,
>
>   [I. iii. 53-4]

which will be, not only the exposure of Angelo, but his exposure in circumstances that develop and unfold publicly the maximum significance.

The reliance on our responding appropriately is the more patently justified and the less questionable (I confess, it seems to me irresistible) in that we can see the promise being so consummately kept. The 'resolution of the plot,' ballet-like in its patterned formality and masterly in stage-craft, sets out with lucid pregnancy the full significance of the demonstration: 'man, proud man,' is stripped publicly of all protective ignorance of 'his glassy essence' [II. ii. 117, 120]; the ironies of 'measure for measure' are clinched; in a supreme test upon Isabella, 'Judge not, that ye be not judged' gets an ironical enforcement; and the relative values are conclusively established—the various attitudes settle into their final placing with regard to one another and to the positives that have been concretely defined. (pp. 244-45)

F. R. Leavis, "The Greatness of 'Measure for Measure'," in Scrutiny, Vol. X, No. 3, January, 1942, pp. 234-47.

DEREK A. TRAVERSI (essay date 1942)

[*Originally planned as a lecture and written before the appearance of the essays by L. C. Knights and F. R. Leavis (see excerpts above, 1942), Traversi's commentary on* Measure for Measure *addresses the same issues. In the excerpt below, he examines Claudio's speech in I. ii. 125-30, citing it as an example of the play's moral seriousness. Traversi emphasizes the importance of death in* Measure, *specifically as that "point of focus" that determines the characters' "moral maturity" in their response to death, and that also serves as the "common destiny" of human beings, hinted at by the Duke, that justifies moral law as an external restraint while simultaneously preserving liberty and personal experience as the foundation on which that law succeeds. He argues that Shakespeare "was elaborating a state of experience" in* Measure for Measure, *offering no real solutions to the problems raised in the play. To Traversi, the play's theme—"the inextricable interdependence of good and evil within human experience as centred in the act of passion"—demonstrates Shakespeare's attempt to understand mankind's contradictory impulses in the quest for moral maturity. Additional discussion of this theme can be found in the essays by Una Ellis-Fermor (1936) and J. W. Lever (1965).*]

Sooner or later, at least in a civilized society, the poet is faced with the problem of putting his experiences together, of moulding them into some intelligible organic structure; and this work of evaluation and selection calls for standards and so, in the broadest sense, for a morality. It is only by recognising the presence of this need in Shakespeare that we can grasp the peculiar spirit of *Measure for Measure*.

That spirit is essentially, uncompromisingly moral. The need for constant standards and for their enforcement by the civil power is everywhere stated and underlined. It is to strengthen it that the Duke, at the beginning of the play, calls upon Angelo; and even Claudio, who is most directly interested in the loosening of bonds that condemn him to immediate death, agrees that the sentence passed upon him is just. When Lucio asks him why he has been arrested, his reply is quite unequivocal. His plight, he says, proceeds—

> From too much liberty, my Lucio, liberty;
> As surfeit is the father of much fast,
> So every scope by the immoderate use
> Turns to restraint. Our natures do pursue,
> Like rats that ravin down their proper bane,
> A thirsty evil; and when we drink we die.
>
> [I. ii. 125-30]

Claudio's speech, however, does more than confirm the necessary ruthlessness of the law. Its verbal qualities point, in the expression, to the motive that compelled the assertion of that ruthlessness. The linguistic power of *Measure for Measure*, far from expanding easily into lyricism or rhetoric, is subordinated to a supple bareness and concentrated most often upon an intense underlining of the value of single words. This does not mean that the effect is necessarily simple. No word in Claudio's speech is logically superfluous, but more than one is, in its context, surprising. The verb 'ravin', for instance, suggests bestial, immoderate feeding, and therefore 'appetite', but the next line proceeds, through a 'thirsty evil', to transfer

the metaphor to drinking; the shift of the image, and the sharp focussing of impressions by which it is accompanied, are characteristic of Shakespeare's mature art. The effect is to transfer attention almost imperceptibly from the idea of Claudio's first condemnation to another which, without directly presuming to question the first, yet profoundly modifies it. The repellent impression of animal appetite summoned up by 'ravin' and maintained by the reference, at once contemptuous and loathing, to 'rats' is unobtrusively transformed into an evocation of natural thirst; the evil remains and is uncondoned, but its relation to the normal human situation has gone through a decisive change. The whole passage is designed to stress the deep-seated contradiction involved in the very nature of passion. (p. 40-1)

The presentation of Vienna in *Measure for Measure* is purposely, inevitably grim; so much so that the 'comic' scenes representing the street life of the city have often been criticised as pedestrian and even degrading performances. Judgments of this kind ignore the moral balance which the play is so concerned to hold. The key to a proper understanding of these passages lies in their unquestionable moral seriousness. A society in the advanced stages of moral dissolution is necessarily ugly. The physical beastliness upon which Shakespeare so insistently dwells is a direct and natural consequence of spiritual decay. Its cause is the gradual corrosion, within Viennese society, of all moral values. Once these values have been undermined the dissolution—the 'ravening' process of self-destruction—follows logically enough from the truths already announced by Claudio; the 'bane', once swallowed, leads inevitably to death. The necessary consequences of allowing complete 'liberty' to the satisfaction of bodily 'appetite' is the spread of disease, physical as well as moral, from the individual to the mass of society. The presentation of such a process is naturally anything but comic. The jesting conversation of the courtiers and men of the world in this play turns insistently, even monotonously, upon the threat of sexual disease; but beneath the levity which springs from long familiarity there appears a deeper note of fear. The courtiers of Vienna are aware of the frightening moral emptiness which their maladies imply. . . . Beneath this hollowness, which is more than physical, lies that fear of death which is in *Measure for Measure* the beginning of wisdom.

Here too, however, dissolution and death are only one side of the picture. The 'bane' that has poisoned Viennese society is still, to return once more to that key phrase of Claudio's, 'proper' to it. It is still a consequence, however tainted by human perversity, of natural human failings. This is a fact with which the law itself must eventually come to terms. When Angelo, in his determination to remove the causes of social disintegration, proceeds to enforce the statutes by pulling down the familiar houses of resort and punishing those who trafficked in them, he challenges instincts which lie at the very root of man's normal nature. The real problem is once more that of liberty. To enforce the law without convincing the guilty that they should freely accept it, that their mode of life involves a tragic neglect of spiritual possibilities which can only lead to ruin, is ultimately to deny all moral responsibility; and this is precisely what Angelo seems forced to do. In the examination of Pompey by Escalus, Shakespeare sets before us in concrete form some of the intricacies which human nature imposes upon the necessary administration of justice. Pompey, challenged by his judge, makes no attempt to deny his trade. He simply denies the utility of trying to suppress it. . . . To re-establish the law in Vienna is, as Shakespeare has shown us in the most concrete form, vitally necessary. Failure to deal with the disease of which Pompey is a symptom involves the consequences so vividly presented in Lucio and his associates; it involves the collapse of society under the double burden of physical disease and moral dissolution. Yet—and here once more is the fundamental question raised by *Measure for Measure*—upon what human instinct, if Pompey is right, can the law be based? To what reality in man can it finally appeal in the effort to make itself, not merely feared without understanding, but accepted with free respect? For Pompey, and for the great unconscious mass of humanity, the law is no more than a matter of verbal caprice. . . . There are men like Angelo—so it appears to him—who, having themselves no experience of carnal desire, are obstinate in repressing the desires of others; but their obstinacy, failing to appeal to more natural instincts, is bound eventually to founder in the face of permanent realities: 'Does our lordship mean to geld and splay all the youth of the city?' [II. i. 230-31]. The question remains unanswered for the simple reason that no character in *Measure for Measure*—except possibly the Duke when, at the end of the play, he has the whole of its moral experience behind him—. . . could conceivably answer it. The others, and more especially Angelo, have no respect for the liberty which all genuine morality presupposes; while the Duke himself only comes gradually to realize the difficulties to which the concession of liberty can give rise. These difficulties bring him face to face with the question of moral sanctions. The force of Pompey's argument depends in the last analysis upon the definition of love as a transitory physical appetite. If it is no more, if there is no superior scale of moral values upon which the restraining law may depend, its application becomes an impossible and baseless imposition which man's more permanent instincts will eventually overthrow. That is one side of the question. The other insists, with equal force, that the law must be imposed in defence of the very structure of society; and this, as events show, is difficult too. To find for the law a necessary sanction in experience without depriving it of the firmness and impartiality upon which its maintenance depends is the task which ultimately faces the Duke in *Measure for Measure*. (pp. 42-4)

The attempt to enforce the law by delegating authority to Angelo fails. It fails because Pompey's estimate of the Deputy's character, springing as it does from the depth of his instinctive normality, is fundamentally just. Angelo's peculiar failure lies ultimately in a lack of self-knowledge. He believes that he has, by the force of his own virtue, dominated passion, where he has in reality simply passed it by. The underlying weakness of his character is brought out, step by step, in his treatment of Claudio. . . . If the moral law is to be enforced at all it must be assumed that man has the power, by the free exercise of firm self-control, to check his own disorderly impulses. This is true, but it is not all the truth. The distinction made by Angelo needs to be drawn, but it must be made with a full grasp of the human issues involved. That Angelo has no such grasp is persistently suggested, not only by Pompey, but by all those around him. . . . Self-deception is only the first stage in Angelo's progress. The ignorance upon which his virtue is so precariously based can turn, with catastrophic suddenness, into the complications of vice. . . . Reason that is not fully harmonized with a rich and free emotional life may easily become an imposition concealing every kind of dangerous thwarted instinct. . . . The forces of passion, denied all natural expression by a man who has never felt their true force, can easily take control of the unprepared will. Angelo's self-control is of the kind which can turn, almost without warning, into a

desire for domination which aims directly and in complete ruthlessness at the goal appointed by his lower instincts.

This is precisely what happens when he meets Isabella. When he finally becomes aware of his feelings towards her he expresses them in terms that are pregnant with sexuality and self-will:

> I have begun;
> And now I give my sensual race the rein;
> Fit thy consent to my sharp appetite;
> Lay by all nicety and prolixious blushes,
> That banish what they sue for; redeem thy brother
> By yielding up thy body to my will.
>
> [II. iv. 159-64]

The most remarkable thing about this speech of Angelo's is the completeness with which it accepts the impulse to evil. . . . The sense of evil expresses itself in Angelo . . . through a conscious and determined orientation of the will in which the whole personality is involved not less fully than it had been in Claudio's passion. It is just this recognition of the personal that gives the play its eminently moral character. For it is not sufficient to say that Angelo is weak-willed or that his normal self-control has been undermined by irrational forces. It is rather that the passion to which he has, in his self-ignorance, denied all natural expression has now taken complete control of his will, which reveals itself as forcibly in the direction of carnal desire as it had previously been affirmed in moral rigour and 'firm abstinence'. (pp. 44-7)

Isabella's virtue, though standing at the other extreme from that of Angelo's, is related to it by a common foundation in inexperience. When the play opens she is about to take her vows of profession as a nun. The fact is in itself significant. Virtue in *Measure for Measure* is habitually on its guard, habitually defending itself by withdrawal against the temptations that so insistently beset it. Isabella's opening dialogue with the nun who accompanies her stresses the note of retreat and mortification. Considering the rules to which she is shortly to submit herself she desires an even stricter seclusion from the world. . . . To grasp the spirit in which this retirement is conceived, we must see it in relation to the necessity for enforcing the law at any cost. Virtue and chastity need to be restored in a world where every natural instinct threatens to violate them; and just as the lawgiver must defend them by imposing 'the needful bits and curbs to headstrong weeds' [I. iii. 20], so must the individual preserve it in himself even at the cost of renouncing a society which seems to incline almost universally to corruption. Isabella, by entering the convent, is simply carrying to its logical extreme the fulfilment of a moral duty.

More restraint, however, is not enough. Isabella's acceptance of this duty, necessary as it is, may spring from a false simplicity no less fatal than Angelo's self-ignorance. Her own virtue is to be severely tested in the light of wider obligations. Before she has taken her vows, human claims of a kind which no seclusion can solve call her away from the cloister. Lucio brings the news that her brother, at the point of death, places his last hope in her intervention. The terms in which this hope is expressed by Claudio himself are an indication of the difficulties, so far unsuspected by Isabella, which beset virtue in this play:

> bid her assay him:
> I have great hope in that; for in her youth
> There is a prone and speechless dialect
> Such as move men; besides, she hath prosperous art.

When she will play with reason and discourse,
And well she can persuade.

[I. ii. 181-86]

The qualities upon which Claudio relies are not, typically enough, those of simple virtue. The gift of persuasion which is so strong in Isabella has little to do with the vocation that has brought her to the cloister. It is simply an unalienable and, as the event will show, a highly dangerous part of her womanhood. Already, in spite of the unquestioned honesty of her intentions, the gift has become a little tarnished in Claudio's description. Isabella can 'play with reason' and mould the wills of men most subtly—even if quite innocently, in complete unconsciousness of artifice—to her purpose. Most significantly of all, her main power lies in the 'prone and speechless' attractions—there is even a faint suggestion of invitation and artful passivity in the adjectives—of her youthful person. It is not, of course, that she is dishonest or that she sets out to appeal deliberately to Angelo's baser instincts. It is simply that she is a woman and that therefore her power over men is one which is bound, whatever her intentions, to become a temptation. . . . If her virtue does not fully satisfy, that is through no clearly defined moral deficiency (though many critics have tried to find one), but simply because the state of simple virtue does not exist in *Measure for Measure*. Chastity there is surrounded by reservations not of its own making, flaws related to the flesh and inherent in the human situation. If Isabella has any fault, it is that she is unaware of these flaws and reservations. Her retirement is too simple, her virtue too little rooted in experience to correspond to the spirit in which Shakespeare conceived this play. In the very confidence with which she accepts her mission—

Commend me to my brother: soon at night
I'll send him certain word of my success

[I. iv. 88-9]

there is a touch of the wilfulness, itself based on inexperience, that proves fatal to Angelo. It is certain that the path to Claudio's salvation will be longer and harder than she yet realizes.

The two scenes which portray the encounter between Angelo and Isabella owe much of their effect to the fact that each is peculiarly fitted to bring out the weakness of the other. The first is devoted substantially to the downfall of Angelo. His fall is as sudden as might be expected in one whose self-knowledge has always been so limited. . . . His utterances, at first short and ambiguous and later, after the departure of Isabella, full and passionate, become charged with the imagery of desire:

she speaks, and 'tis
Such sense, that my sense breeds with it.

The tempter or the tempted, who sins most?
Not she, nor does she tempt, but it is I
That, lying by the violet in the sun,
Do as the carrion does, not as the flower,
Corrupt with virtuous season. Can it be
That modesty may more betray our sense
Than woman's lightness? Having waste ground enough,
Shall we desire to raze the sanctuary,
And pitch our evils there.

[II. ii. 141-42, 163-71]

The peculiar verbal texture of these speeches is already familiar in work of this period. The play, in the first tentative aside, on the double meaning of sense'—'sense' as 'meaning' or

'understanding' and 'sense' as 'sensuality'—conveys perfectly the half-conscious process by which Angelo's self-control has been undermined. . . . His will, clarifying itself in the very process of expression, reveals itself as a destructive instinct perversely incited by the mere presence of virtue to the satisfaction of its corrupt desires. The 'carrion' element of passion, always present beneath his modesty, is breaking out in a form even more dangerous than the evils he had so confidently undertaken to destroy.

The connection between Angelo's 'foulness' and its opposite in Isabella is the key to all that follows. Having abandoned himself irrevocably to his instincts he proceeds at their next meeting to work upon her with consummate dialectic skill. Desire, far from undermining his intelligence, sharpens it, gives it fresh power to penetrate and destroy. He proves step by step from her own words that her pleading is not really consistent with her principles; and in so doing he shows how untested are the foundations upon which these principles rest. . . . The argument, perverse as it is, brings out complexities which Isabella is remarkably unfitted to recognize. She originally brought forward the admission of man's natural weakness as a reason for relaxing the rigour of the law; Angelo, not less logically, though moved by the selfishness of his own desire, bases upon the very same recognition his demand that she should surrender herself to his will.

What are we to conclude from all this? Not certainly that Angelo is right and Isabella wrong. Isabella's main point—the essential distinction between 'ignominy in ransom' and the graciousness of 'free pardon'—stands, and Angelo's lust is clearly the enemy of virtue. Yet we do wrong, beyond this, to falsify Shakespeare's conception by looking for 'solutions' to clear-cut moral problems. The dilemma set before Isabella is one which the play is not concerned to solve. Shakespeare merely gives us two opposed attachments, both right and both involved in contradiction by an evil quite beyond her control. But, granted that the dilemma is beyond any perfect solution, Isabella shows no understanding of the natural root of Claudio's sin. It is hard not to feel in her virtue at least a touch of wilful egoism.

More than our brother is our chastity,

[II. iv. 185]

she says, and the words already anticipate, by the clarity with which they divide the morally indivisible, the revulsion with which she later turns on her brother when he weakens in his resolve to accept untimely death:

Heaven shield my mother play'd my father fair,
For such a warped slip of wilderness
Ne'er issued from his blood. Take my defiance;
Die, perish! might but my bending down
Reprieve thee from thy fate, it should proceed;
I'll pray a thousand prayers for thy death,
No word to save thee.

[III. i. 140-46]

It is not the sentiment that surprises, but the emphasis of its expression. That Isabella should, in such a case, refuse indignantly is natural: that she should turn upon her brother, accuse him of cowardice and even—at the moment of condemning him to death—cast upon him the shadow of bastardy is less so. It is certainly not in harmony with that spirit of deeper understanding towards which Shakespeare is groping all through this play. The ideas of virtue and vice did not present themselves to the author of *Measure for Measure* as clear-cut and opposed issues. They were rather things that tended, however distinct they might appear in *a priori* definition, to merge into one another in the difficult business of living. The egoism which prompted Angelo to will the evil conceived in his 'appetite' is not totally absent from Isabella's defence of her chastity. 'Virtue', as each of them conceives it, is still a partial and abstract thing, still an imposition of the reason planted a little aridly upon a whole world of sentiments and reactions which remain outside it and take refuge in the humanity, corrupt and hollow though it be, of Pompey and Lucio. Both sets of characters, the good not less than the evil, are still partial, still lacking in the self-knowledge which true moral maturity requires. Both are themselves in need of judgment and both, before they can be adequately judged, must be considered in the light of an expereince more mature and impartial than their own.

That experience is provided by the Duke. The figure of the Duke, as Shakespeare conceives him, hesitates between two aspects. He is both inside the action as an indispensable instrument of the plot, and outside it, judging with compassionate detachment of the events to which his own abdication has given rise. The two functions are not always perfectly distinct. As a character within the action his self-confessed weakness, born though it is of a tolerance and understanding which events prove to have been very necessary, has contributed to the intolerable conditions of Viennese social life. As a detached 'symbol' of truth in judgment, whose entry into the remotest corners of the action is covered by his function as 'friar' and confessor, his understanding is absolute, perfect. (pp. 47-52)

In emphasizing this superior detachment we must not think of the Duke's function in terms of providing solutions, more or less clearly defined, to difficult problems. 'Solutions' of this kind are no part of the writer's function. Shakespeare was elaborating a state of experience, not answering an abstract question; and this state was essentially a strife, a disharmony still far from poetic resolution. 'Solutions' in Shakespeare are not intellectual statements; they are only apprehensible in a gradual harmonizing of imagery to which the functions of plot and character become increasingly knitted. The contradictory elements of experience are resolved, if at all, in the process of living them out. The harmony towards which they move is not imposed in abstraction, but slowly and patiently attained through a steady incorporation of the most diverse elements. In *Measure for Measure,* at any rate it is still early to speak of this kind of resolution. The Duke, and therefore Shakespeare with him, is primarily occupied in *understanding,* in trying to bear in mind all the different and contradictory elements which a premature moral solution—such as that ruthlessly and yet, as it seems, necessarily proposed by Angelo—must fatally offend. The Duke, as Escalus remarks, is one that has 'above all other *strifes, contended* especially to know himself' [III. ii. 232-33]. This description is significant. Both Angelo and Isabella had failed in self-knowledge, in awareness of the complex knot of good and evil which centres on human passion. A law-giver must be aware of this complexity, must seek to harmonize the natural sources of experience with the moral 'law'. In *Measure for Measure,* however, this knowledge is still a strife rather than a harmony; the goodness of human inclination, which must be recognized to attain moral maturity, contains also a seed of evil which the moral law must uproot. The Duke's own self-knowledge, however, still hangs in the balance. It is still a 'strife', a 'contention', a matter of working out obscure and even contradictory impulses that refuse, so far, to submit to a common unity. (p. 53)

The Duke's distinctive contribution to *Measure for Measure* really begins when, having assumed the Friar's role, he comes to confess Claudio (III. i.). He introduces, in his great opening speech, a new element, a fresh fact in relation to which the problems raised by the desires of the flesh need to be reconsidered. This fact is the universal relevance of death. . . . Shakespeare makes the Duke assert, before the sentence which hangs over Claudio, the futility of *all* desire. . . . [He] argues to Claudio that the very acceptance of death will free the soul from the burden of its desires. . . . In a world dominated by mutability and fluctuation man is no more than an inconsistent bundle of ephemeral impulses, and the only thing about him which is constant is his destiny of death. . . . He proposes to Claudio a clear-cut moral choice, based upon a reasoned weighing of the possibilities of life and demanding a conscious acceptance of tragic values. . . . Character, on the stage as in life, requires a point of focus round which the various impulses may cohere; and in the figures of Angelo, Isabella, and Claudio that point is provided by the reaction of the mature moral being to the fact of death. Death is the common destiny of man and simply to rebel against it is the act of a child; but to consider in the light of it the passions and appetites which have brought Claudio—and Vienna—to such tragic consequences is the beginning of wisdom.

The beginning, but not the end. Men do well to accept the idea of death as an element inextricably interwoven, through the action of time, with every moment of our living experience. Without that acceptance there is no true maturity; but without a corresponding sense of life there is no vitality at all. The reaction against death, like that against the law, affects *Measure for Measure* at every level in society. The problem of Pompey, as it faces Angelo and Escalus, is balanced for the Duke by that of Barnardine. Like Pompey, like so many other characters in the background of this play, Barnardine has no conception of the moral law. He has, in other words, no understanding of the implications of death upon which the necessity of that law so urgently depends. . . . The Duke whose own sense of the moral law is so closely bound up with his awareness of mortality, cannot consent to his execution in such a state. . . . [The] sense of moral issues implicit in our acts and prolonging themselves inexorably to eternity is throughout distinctive of the Duke's outlook. The acceptance of the moral law, itself based on the recognition of inevitable dissolution, leads to a deeper, profounder respect for human life. This does not, of course, invalidate the law itself, or even diminish the need for its constant enforcement; but it does underline the almost infinite patience and understanding which that enforcement involves. (pp. 54-5)

The reservations represented by Barnardine are taken up on a higher level—as they were with Pompey in the matter of judgment—by Claudio and Isabella. As the dialogue between these two proceeds after the Duke's departure, the emphasis is slowly but decisively shifted from death to its opposite—that is, to Claudio's keen desire for life. . . . The emphasis is no longer where the Duke had left it, upon the peace of death, but rather upon the pain involved in the passage to extinction. The body reacts wth vivid sensual immediacy against the consolation offered to it. The reaction, proceeding as it does from the nervous sensibility, is completely spontaneous; and gradually it communicates itself to Claudio. At first he is resolved to die that his sister's honour may be saved; but the resolution that expresses itself in the phrase—'I will encounter darkness as a bride' [III. i. 83], is really a rhetorical effort to force himself to accept a fate which he still regards as inevitable. It does not live long. As Claudio slowly comes to realize that he *might* live, his resolution palpably wavers. . . .

> Sure, it is no sin;
> Or of the deadly seven it is the least.
>
> [III. i. 109-10]

The phrase already amounts to a plea to Isabella to change her mind. To meet death boldly when no hope of life remains is a thing that a man owes to his self-respect, but to choose it when it might be avoided, even shamefully, is far harder. It calls for a degree of detachment and determination which few young men can claim to possess. Claudio tries to show that he has acquired them, but fails.

In the remark I have just quoted, if anywhere, lies the moral issue beneath the whole incident. The conception of *Measure for Measure* rests upon a balance between two aspects of human passion: the natural and proper instinct upon which it rests, and the dissolution and disease to which its unchecked indulgence leads. Shakespeare's phrase holds the balance perfectly. Let us make no mistake about it. The idea that it would be 'no sin' for Isabella to lie with Angelo is no part of Shakespeare's conception. It *is* a sin, and a *deadly* one, barely redeemable. Claudio himself has committed this same 'deadly sin'—and the phrase has behind it the force of a Christian tradition to which Shakespeare in this play firmly adheres—but he has also committed the most natural, the most spontaneous of the seven. Isabella, when she turns on him in her anger, forgets this. It is not her decision which is wrong, but her expression of it which is—from the Duke's level of compassionate understanding—inadequate; and Claudio's profoundly human observation compels us to recognize it. Having made it he falters and then visibly breaks down. . . . The emphasis in Claudio's tremendous outburst of horror is all upon the sensitive apprehension of life, upon the immediate opposition between the 'sensible warm motion' of the living body and the 'cold', rotted 'obstruction' which reduces it to 'a kneaded clod'; even the life of the 'delighted spirit' in the cosmic obscurity of the afterlife is sensually conceived [III. i. 118-20]. The impending presence of death has brought out in Claudio a fear whose very weakness is natural, human: a fear which Isabella's virtue has not allowed for, but which the Duke in his compassion will understand and accept.

It is from this point, indeed, that his activities of reconciliation really begin to take shape. His 'symbolic' function henceforward overshadows his internal position in the action. Having overheard the dialogue of Isabella and Claudio he realizes the wickedness of Angelo and begins at once to take steps to ward off its practical consequences. These steps are plunged for a time, corresponding roughly to the duration of the fourth Act, in an obscurity during which the issues are delicately balanced, poised between life and death. The Duke's behaviour, often at this stage as tortuous and enigmatic as the realities with which he is contending, does a good deal to justify Lucio's description of him as 'the old fantastical duke of dark corners' [IV. iii. 157]. But this obscurity in the Duke is only a reflection of the situation, moral and spiritual, with which he is struggling. . . . The issue, in short, still hangs in the balance, and evil instead of good may easily come from it. The intricate mechanism of the plot at this point, which is often brought forward as evidence of Shakespeare's lack of interest in his theme, may be more significant than it looks. The Duke, for all his detachment, is not fully in charge of events. He is learning, like the others, from experience, and only differs from them in the wider range of his compassion. The control

of evil is *not* in his hands; its machinations often find him unprepared, leave him groping hastily in the darkness for an improvised remedy. That is why the unfolding of the play, directed towards a clarification which has no place in the outlook of the characters themselves, cannot completely satisfy. The external and the inner situation, the visible action and the spiritual impulse, simply do not correspond. . . . In the confusion which life offers to the seeker after moral clarity the opportunity to do good offers itself in a strangely haphazard way; and the Duke, with no more than an unusually awakened moral sense to see him through the surrounding darkness, grasps it and turns it to his own ends. In so doing, however, he increases the area of his understanding and shows his humanity.

Measure for Measure, then, offers no real 'solution' to the problems it raises. The problems, indeed, still interested Shakespeare more closely than the possible 'solutions'. The ambiguities so essential to the play were to be worked out, with far greater resources and in another style, later. Here the resolution is no more than hinted at. The clearing-up in the last scene is little more than a piece of able manipulation. The full body of experience never really informs it, as it had informed the episodes of anguish and division, to give it a corresponding life. But suggestions of greater clarity can be found. They express themselves, in that very Fourth Act which seems so given over to tortuous obscurities, in a rising series of dawn-images, which become more powerful as the Duke begins to feel his mastery of the situation. It culminates in his great prose speech to the Provost:

> Look, the unfolding star calls up the shepherd.
> Put not yourself into amazement how these things
> should be: *all difficulties are but easy when
> they are known* . . . Yet you are amazed; but
> this shall absolutely resolve you. Come away;
> it is almost clear dawn.
>
> [IV. ii. 203-10]

But the 'symbolism', if such we may call it, remains elementary. All the forces of life and fertility suggested in Lucio's great speech on Claudio's love are not yet behind it to give it life and adequate content. This strengthening has yet to grow out of the whole body of the tragedies. The theme of *Measure for Measure* is still the inextricable interdependence of good and evil within human experience as centred in the act of passion. The mature tragedies which follow are to separate the elements within this complexity; this separation will result in a more adequate projection of the individual experience into a more plastic and sensitive dramatic form. (pp. 55-8)

> D[erek] A. Traversi, in a review of "Measure for Measure," in Scrutiny, Vol. XI, No. 1, Summer, 1942, pp. 40-58.

OSCAR JAMES CAMPBELL (essay date 1943)

[*An American Shakespearean scholar, critic, and professor, Campbell was the editor of* The Living Shakespeare *and a co-editor of* The Reader's Encyclopedia of Shakespeare. *In his* Shakespeare's Satire *(1943), from which the following excerpt is taken, Campbell discusses the influence of contemporary satiric conventions upon Shakespeare's achievement in the satiric mode. He interprets* Measure for Measure *as Shakespeare's second attempt at comical satire, describing it as a play created for popular audiences, whereas he characterizes* Troilus and Cressida *as Shakespeare's first satire which was written for educated audiences. Campbell examines the forbears of Shakespeare's satiric characters, finding a parallel between the Duke and characters from John Marston's* The Malcontent *and* The Fawn —*two plays that contain disguised dukes who act as satiric commentators. To Campbell, the Duke is neither a spectator nor a deus ex machina; rather, he acts as the author's agent to unmask Angelo and Lucio. Campbell argues that the Duke is an intriguer who often acts like an "over-clever stage manager," an aspect of* Measure for Measure *that he perceives as a flaw. He contends that Isabella is not a puppet, but adds that Shakespeare's handling of her character obscures the satiric structure. For further discussion of the comic conventions upon which* Measure for Measure *is based, see the excerpts by Murray Krieger (1951) and Nevill Coghill (1955).]*

The following paragraphs offer a different explanation of the aesthetic confusion caused by [*Measure for Measure*], an explanation which does not attribute mythical woes to the author or find in him resented inner or outer compulsions to fashion a comedy out of unsuitable material. It is simply that *Measure for Measure* is Shakespeare's second attempt to adapt to his genius some of the conventions of comical satire.

According to this view Angelo was first designed as clearly as Malvolio or Troilus to serve as an object of ridicule. The Duke was as certainly a satiric and moral commentator as were similar figures in earlier dramas of Jonson or Marston. Isabella's first duty, then, was to serve as the main agent in the exposure and derision of Angelo. The Viennese background of corruption and moral filth is as harmonious with the sin of the principal culprit as was the disorganization of the Greek and Trojan hosts with the passion which destroyed Troilus and Cressida.

This satiric structure is now obscure because Isabella completely outgrew the role in which she was first cast. A modern audience is properly much more concerned for her fate than for her success in laying bare the hypocrisy of Angelo. Consequently the play does not end as a satire should. Angelo is exposed but not ejected from the play with a final burst of derision. Instead he is shown as purged of his sin, repentant, and ready to make atonement for it. This fact enables Shakespeare to put into Isabella's mouth a final plea for mercy for which she has stood during the entire drama. Once the Duke has granted this prayer, Shakespeare has lost his chance for an effective denouement. So he falls back upon the conventional ending of romantic comedy, a marriage for both the deserving and undeserving. This offers no proper resolution of the emotions aroused by the characters and is a perfunctory and aesthetically unsatisfactory close to the complicated action. For Angelo deserves not a wife, but scornful ridicule. The nature of Isabella and of her problems on the other hand have carried us to the deepest springs of human conduct. They have all along trembled on the verge of tragedy. Her promised marriage to the Duke provides a completely unsatisfactory conclusion to such a dramatic career.

Let us examine then the fundamental satiric structure and temper of the drama. As in *Troilus and Cressida* the social world in which the characters live is in a state of chaos and for the same reason: 'The specialty of rule hath been neglected' [*Troilus and Cressida*, I. iii. 78]. The Duke, as he himself confesses, has disregarded his plain duties as magistrate. . . . (pp. 124-25)

The serious-minded are sore perplexed, but the careless and thoughtless are cynical and irresponsible in the face of the vice and license which flourish around them. Shakespeare, following the earlier satiric dramatists, obeyed a sound aesthetic instinct in setting the characters whose vices he satirizes in a morally chaotic milieu.

The Duke, fearing to be thought tyrannical if he should now begin to correct his people, has chosen Angelo to be his deputy. He disguises himself as a friar in order to observe Angelo's actions. Indeed he intends to conduct a kind of experiment on the fellow in the hope of discovering if his cloistered virtue and untried purity will remain unchanged under the stress of real temptation. The Duke's subsequent actions, however, show that his real dramatic purpose is not to probe Angelo's nature but to expose the man's unconscious hypocrisy and to hold it up for derision.

John Marston had made conventional the casting of a deposed and disguised Duke in the role of satiric commentator. Malevole, who plays this part in *The Malcontent* (1600), is Altofronto, the deposed Duke of Genoa. In *The Fawn* (1602) the ironic commentator is Hercules, the disguised Duke of Ferrara, who has followed his son abroad to watch the young man's wooing of the Princess Dulcimel and to manipulate events as he chooses. The first commentator which Marston introduced into one of his plays was Feliche. He appears in *Antonio and Mellida* (1599), not, to be sure, as a disguised duke, but as no less of a hanger-on at the court. He, like Altofronto, seems to hold a roving commission to ferret out the evils of life there. Now the Duke in *Measure for Measure* bears a close relationship to these figures of Marston. He is also a commentator, one who utters the condemnations of his author as clearly as do Marston's characters. He too, like Hercules in *The Fawn*, manipulates events in such a way as to drive the derided figures into exaggerated displays of their follies.

The Duke, playing the part of a friar, appropriately couches his denunciations of vice in the solemn and elevated language of a churchman. He lashes the bawd Pompey in a tone of suitable indignation:

> Fie, sirrah! a bawd, a wicked bawd!
> The evil that thou causest to be done,
> That is thy means to live. Do thou but think
> What 'tis to cram a maw or clothe a back
> From such a filthy vice. Say to thyself
> 'From their abominable and beastly touches
> I drink, I eat, array myself, and live.'
> Canst thou believe thy living is a life
> So stinkingly depending?
>
> [III. ii. 19-28]

His comments on the rancid condition of his city maintain the critical and sinister tone that Shakespeare desires his play to possess. It is the proper atmosphere for a satiric drama.

> There is so great a fever on goodness, that the
> dissolution of it must cure it. Novelty is only
> in request; and it is as dangerous to be aged in
> any kind of course, as it is virtuous to be constant in any undertaking. There is scarce truth
> enough alive to make societies secure; but security enough to make fellowships accurst. Much
> upon this riddle runs the wisdom of the world.
>
> [III. ii. 222-29]

At the end of the play, just as he is about to remove his disguise, the Duke returns to this general condemnation of the social corruption in Vienna:

> . . . My business in this state
> Made me a looker-on here in Vienna,
> Where I have seen corruption boil and bubble
> Till it o'errun the stew; laws for all faults,

But faults so countenanc'd that the strong statutes
Stand like the forfeits in a barber's shop,
As much in mock as mark.

[V. i. 316-22]

This is sound comment, grave and reverent.

To keep laughter awake, even though it be the sneering sort proper to satire, Shakespeare associates with the Duke a rogue named Lucio, a representative of the second or buffoonish commentator who had become conventional in satiric plays. Lucio is a gay and ribald cynic like Carlo Buffone and all his successors. (pp. 126-29)

Lucio is a much more credible human being than any of Ben Jonson's buffoonish commentators, and much more credible than Thersites [in *Troilus and Cressida*], whose censure is frank calumny. Though a gentleman, Lucio has contact with the bawdy underworld, which frequently erupts into the main action. Sexual promiscuity to Lucio is a joke, and a merry one. This attitude lends to all his comments a careless and cynical tone appropriate to a buffoonish satirist.

In creating this figure Shakespeare seems again to be indebted to John Marston. In his play *What You Will* (1601) Marston presented as an ideal satiric commentator a character called Quadratus [Four Square], a keen-minded debauchee, a gay ribald fellow of whom Pietro Aretino was the prototype and patron. Marston believed that the satiric attitude of his Quadratus was a happy union of the traditionally severe spirit of correction with the traditional gaiety of comedy. Lucio in these respects clearly resembles Quadratus, but he has a more secure place in the plot than Marston's commentator. His appetite for cleverly expressed detraction leads him to slander the Duke to his disguised face and to keep it up with perverse insistence. (pp. 129-30)

The Duke leads Lucio on, to the amusement of the audience, wth the clear purpose of exposing him. When Lucio plucks off the Friar's hood and discovers the Duke, the impudent buffoon also accomplishes his own exposure. He then tries to sneak unobtrusively away, but is arrested and held before the Duke for sentence. Although threatening Lucio with whipping and hanging after he has married the punk whom he has got with child, the Duke relents and remits all the 'forfeits' except his marriage with the courtesan. This deflation of the careless cynic and liar is in exactly the right key. An audience which has been entertained by this genial rascal throughout the play would have been outraged to see him severely punished. But it would accept the libertine's forced marriage to the harlot as an excellent joke. Moreover the sentence arouses in nice proportions the laughter of both comedy and satire.

The satiric treatment of Angelo is conducted in a much more serious mood. The portrait of him which the Duke draws in the very first scene of the play lacks firm outline. Though he knows the fellow's obvious characteristics, he seems perplexed by them and brings them to the bar of general ethical principles for judgment:

Angelo,
There is a kind of character in thy life
That to th' observer doth thy history
Fully unfold. Thyself and thy belongings
Are not thine own so proper as to waste
Thyself upon thy virtues, they on thee.
Heaven doth with us as we with torches do,
Not light them for themselves; for if our virtues

Did not go forth of us, 'twere all alike
As if we had them not. Spirits are not finely touch'd
But to fine issues; nor Nature never lends
The smallest scruple of her excellence
But, like a thrifty goddess, she determines
Herself the glory of a creditor,
Both thanks and use.

[I. i. 26-40]

Later, in a dialogue with the Friar, he clears up some of the obscurity in his portrait:

Lord Angelo is precise
Stands at guard with envy, scarce confesses
That his blood flows, or that his appetite
Is more to bread than stone.

[I. iii. 50-3]

Angelo, he says, follows strictly the dictates of conventional morality. He is an ethical formalist and proud of his way of controlling sexual impulse by ignoring its existence. However, it is Lucio who in his extravagant way makes Angelo's constricted nature clear to the audience. He calls him:

. . . A man whose blood
Is very snow-broth; one who never feels
The wanton stings and motions of the sense
But doth rebate and blunt his natural edge
With profits of the mind, study and fast.

[I. iv. 57-61]

By the time Lucio has made this speech, we understand Angelo so well that we detect the irony in the description and are prepared for the ribald characterization which has already been quoted. The semi-tragic action of the play is devised, then, not so much to test Angelo's undisciplined virtue as to expose the folly of his confident self-righteousness.

Measure for Measure thus begins as a satiric play should. The character who is to be exposed and shamed appears at once. Almost immediately the two contrasted commentators familiar to comical satire reveal their identities. If Shakespeare had adopted the most approved mechanism of the new dramatic type, he would have made the Duke knowingly tempt Angelo by sending Isabella to him. But by the year 1604 he had freed himself from the extreme formalism of the conventional structure of such plays. Besides, Isabella is too noble a character to serve as anyone's puppet. (pp. 131-32)

The subtle plan of tempting the austere Angelo, not through the calculated wiles of an experienced wanton like Cressida but through the cold beauty of an all but dedicated woman, is Shakespeare's own. Angelo, through his utter failure to understand the power of Claudio's temptation, has shown that he is ignorant of one whole range of human experience. For this reason he has developed no defenses against the allurements of Isabella. When he first feels himself aroused, his self-righteous astonishment awakens in us just the sort of scornful amusement that the satirist tries to evoke. He is amazed that he, a kind of saint, should be like other men! (p. 132)

Mark Van Doren voices the opinion of many critics when he says that the Duke is 'tortuously slow' in making everything turn out right. He feels that the Duke's 'hands are sluggish in the manipulation of the dummies whose predicament he has wantonly created' [see excerpt above, 1939]. But if the main purpose of the action is, like that of all satiric plays, to expose and humiliate the foolish and evil characters, the Duke's manipulation of events is not wanton. He is neither a spectator nor a *deus ex machina*. He is rather acting as the author's agent in displaying and unmasking Lucio and Angelo. He thus performs the duties of an intriguer in such plays as this. He sets the traps for the fools and knaves.

It is true that the Duke seems to be sometimes omnipotent and sometimes merely an over-clever stage-manager. At least he seems to delight in tying tangled knots for the mere sake of the strong theatrical effects he can produce while untying them. This is an undoubted flaw in the structure of the play. But the Duke's complicated plotting has the supreme merit of laying bare the ugly scars in Angelo's nature. (pp. 133-34)

Angelo's remorse, particularly over his execution of Claudio, is so deep that he continues to crave 'death more willingly than mercy' [V. i. 476]. And he persists in this feeling until the Duke unmuffles the supposedly dead Claudio. This is the last trick in his program of mystification and correction. Only then does Angelo wish to live, only then does he show that he has been thoroughly purged of his sin. The Duke, too, is satisfied that his craftiness has produced the results he sought. 'Well, Angelo,' he remarks, 'your evil quits you well. Look that you love your wife, her worth worth yours' [V. i. 496-97]. Thus is Angelo cleansed from his evil impulses and pronounced fit to play his part in the triplicate mating at the close of the comedy.

Except for its ending, the plot, as thus far described, is exactly like that of the typical satiric drama. But Shakespeare's development of the character of Isabella and the theatrical skill with which he has written the scenes in which she appears obscure the basic satiric anatomy of the work. This fact has led many commentators to mistake her position in the action. Structurally she is the author's device for bringing Angelo's unsound nature to the judgment seat. In this sense alone is she 'the main-spring of the whole action' [see excerpt above by Arthur Quiller-Couch, 1922]. Poetically she does become the heroine of the play, because her impassioned pleas for mercy are the vehicle for the principal ideal values expressed in the drama. In almost all her appearances in the first three acts, she transcends her appointed service to the plot. This independence has led many critics to charge Shakespeare with failure to make Isabella a consistent character. Like many of Shakespeare's figures she comes to life in the course of the play and escapes from the narrow limits assigned her as a creature of the plot. Her liberation is responsible for much of the perplexity which afflicts most persons who pronounce judgment on *Measure for Measure*.

Shakespeare makes us realize very early in the play that the essence of Isabella's nature is her innate austere purity. Unless all her actions were dominated by this instinct for chastity, the irony of her becoming to Angelo an irresistible temptation to lust would be lost. Though Lucio's tribute to her:

> I hold you as a thing enskied and sainted,
>
> [I. iv. 34]

may be, as Quiller-Couch suggests merely 'the sentimental homage which vice pays to virtue' [see excerpt above, 1922], the buffoon voices the opinion which Shakespeare wished his audience to form at once. Her speeches in the interviews with Angelo and Claudio, all of them subtly and skilfully composed for the stage, possess an elevation and a moral intensity which cynical moderns often mistake for harsh declamation. Most literary critics of our age are contemptuous of any author who places his women on pedestals of any sort. They hold austere

sexual restraint in particular disfavor, putting it down at once as springing from emotional starvation or pathological frigidity.

It must be admitted that Shakespeare has placed Isabella in a dilemma which is excessively cruel. This is a relic of archaic plotting. Medieval story was prone to subject its heroines, in particular, to extravagant trials of virtue. What could be more extreme than the choice which the novice of the sisterhood of St. Clare is forced to make? She must decide whether she will be the innocent cause of her brother's death, or consent to the sacrifice of her virtue and so lose her soul. The choice for the sainted Isabella is inevitable:

> Better it were a brother died at once
> Than that a sister, by redeeming him
> Should die forever.
>
> [II. iv. 106-08]

As her dilemma is extreme, so is the language immoderate with which she rejects the temptation to sell her soul at the dictates of human affection:

> Then Isabel, live chaste; and, brother, die!
> More than our brother is our chastity.
>
> [II. iv. 184-85]

The abuse which she rains upon Claudio for asking her to yield to Angelo also seems to us unjustified. The difficulty, however, is not that her chastity is rancid [see Quiller-Couch], but that she meets the test to her virtue with too adamantine a hardness for our taste. (pp. 134-37)

After the end of the third act, Isabella is almost wholly occupied with fulfilling the dramatic purpose for which she was created. She serves as the Duke's pawn in the elaborate plot which he devises to expose Angelo. She obediently makes an assignation with Angelo and just as obediently induces Mariana, his troth-plight wife, secretly to take her place in the darkness. In arranging this substitution she is no wanton procuress, but a friend helping the rejected Mariana to consummate a union which the authorities of both Church and State in Shakespeare's day recognized as legally valid. It is true that Mariana's willingness thus to trap her fiancé into marriage may now be considered . . . a complete sacrifice of her dignity as a woman. But the Elizabethans did not so regard it. They would have seen in what W. W. Lawrence calls the 'bed-trick' [see excerpt above, 1931] an act of poetic justice for the hypocritical way in which Angelo had abandoned Mariana, and they would have applauded the deception.

Isabella's execution of this part of the Duke's plot does not seem so inconsistent with her saintly nature as her willingness to announce before an assemblage of almost all the *dramatis personae* that she has yielded to Angelo. Here, as often in the last two acts, the character of Isabella, as Shakespeare has built it up in the earlier big scenes, seems to go to pieces. In other words she reassumes the role for which she was created, faithfully discharging her dramatic duty to shame Angelo and force him to repent. She forswears her eloquent expositions of Christian doctrine to become the principal element in the craft which the Duke announces he 'must apply against' [III. ii. 277] Angelo's wickedness.

We can perhaps best understand *Measure for Measure* if we regard it as a form of comical satire designed for a popular audience, as *Troilus and Cressida* was the version of the type suited to the taste of an intelligent audience of barristers. (pp. 138-39)

[The] dramas are in some ways as unlike as the different spectators for which they were written. The complicated structure of *Troilus and Cressida* and the many long passages devoted to the elaboration of ethical and social theory were too heavy for a popular audience. Consequently Shakespeare made the plot which exposes Angelo simple in structure and contrived the philosophical speeches of the Duke and Isabella in such a way that they too advance the plot. Moreover, an ending like that of *Troilus and Cressida* would have confused a popular Elizabethan audience, as it has confused almost every modern reader, just because it is so resolutely consistent with the temper of satire.

Shakespeare took no such chance of perplexing his spectators with the denouement of *Measure for Measure*. Instead of ending it on a note of savage scorn, he gave the drama a conventional close, one that forces satire to effect a self-effacing compromise with comedy. It ends with the inevitable three marriages. None of these is a logical consummation of any part of the story, nor does any one of them give off the slightest aroma of romance. The marriages merely announce to the audience in familiar terms that the play is finished. This pseudo-romantic denouement ought not to divert intelligent spectators from their interest in the exposure and humiliation of Lucio and Angelo. An attentive audience should continue to recognize the correction of the knave and the scamp as the central theme of the drama.

The occasional expansion of Isabella's role forms a more serious barrier to a complete understanding of Shakespeare's purpose in composing *Measure for Measure*. During the first three acts she threatens to make her dilemma the dramatic center of the play. However, the author does not permit her to succeed. The manipulations of the Duke relieve her of the obligation to decide whether to be the innocent cause of her brother's death or to sacrifice her maiden honor. Either of these courses of action would have carried her down the road to a tragic ending. But Shakespeare allows the Duke to save her virtue and at the very end of the play to offer himself to her as a husband. The dramatist, therefore, takes ample precaution against our elevating Isabella into the role of a heroine. He undoubtedly thought that he had given her dramatic career an ending perfunctory enough to keep our interest in her secondary to our concern for Angelo. However as in the case of Cressida, he did not foresee the hypnotic effect that a beautiful woman, whatever her position in the plot, will inevitably make upon sentimental masculine critics. When the woman is also noble and fallen into undeserved distress, she possesses unlimited power to steal the interest from other characters more important for the structure of the work of art. (pp. 139-41)

The diminution of [Isabella's] importance need not diminish our delight in her eloquent ethical tirades, or our admiration for the technical skill with which Shakespeare has made these speeches contribute to the mounting suspense of her great scenes with Angelo and Claudio. This fairer conception of her part in the play does, however, deprive her of the role of heroine, and proves that in *Measure for Measure* there is neither heroine nor hero.

For Angelo cannot fill the hero's place left vacant by Isabella. Her retirement restores him, to be sure, to the central place in the drama, but it is a bad eminence, on which a rain of ridicule falls without intermission. His predicament there should enable us to see that *Measure for Measure* is a comedy which is more than half satiric. We can now recognize it to be Shakespeare's second original development of the distinctive features of the

new type of satiric play which Ben Jonson had invented in *Every Man in His Humour*. (p. 141)

Oscar James Campbell, "'Measure for Measure'," in his Shakespeare's Satire, *1943. Reprint by Archon Books, 1963, pp. 121-41.*

ELMER EDGAR STOLL   (essay date 1943)

[*Stoll was one of the earliest critics to attack the method of character analysis that had dominated nineteenth-century Shakespearean criticism. He maintained that Shakespeare was primarily a man of the professional theater and that his works had to be interpreted in the light of Elizabethan stage conventions and understood for their theatrical effects, rather than their psychological insight. Stoll has in turn been criticized for seeing only one dimension of Shakespeare's art. In the excerpt below, which was written in 1943, Stoll—like William Witherle Lawrence (1931) and R. W. Chambers (1937)—uses a historical approach in his study of* Measure for Measure, *examining the way in which Shakespeare incorporates ironic characters and situations in order to lessen the play's tragic effects and heighten the comic. The comic style of* Measure for Measure *is also investigated by Oscar James Campbell (1943), Murray Krieger (1951), Nevill Coghill (1955), and R. A. Foakes (1971). Stoll also challenges the conclusions of such critics as G. G. Gervinus (1849-50), Denton J. Snider (1890), G. Wilson Knight (1930), L. C. Knights (1942), F. R. Leavis (1942), and Derek A. Traversi (1942), all of whom stress the moral seriousness of* Measure for Measure. *Stoll asserts instead that Shakespeare raised no questions or problems concerning ethical conduct, and that "as usual" there is no moral or thesis apparent in the play.*]

The denouement [of *Measure for Measure*], however unsatisfactory as a social document, is quite in harmony with the rest of the play. The forgiveness of Angelo is, apart from the requirements of a comedy, owing to his penitence, which appears in his repeated outcry for death as his punishment [V. i. 371-74, 474-77]. This, though it does not make reparation to the psychology, does so to the emotional impression; and all the more because it is in keeping with what he had said to Escalus, the other Deputy, at the outset:

> When I that censure him do so offend,
> Let mine own judgment pattern out my death,
> And nothing come in partial.
>
> [II. i. 29-31]

He has at least the virtues of consistency and courage. And the pleading of Mariana, who, like a woman, declares,

> I crave no other, nor no better man,
>
> [V. i. 426]

and that of Isabella, who (though a nun, perilously like a woman too) confesses,

> I partly think
> A due sincerity governed his deeds,
> Till he did look on me,—
>
> [V. i. 445-47]

both of these make the pardon, though not more plausible, more acceptable, if still, for us, not by any means enough so. Nevertheless, according to the Duke's formal and perfunctory principles, not as in life but as in the play it is about the only thing he can well do. . . . In general Shakespeare's notions of justice are like ours, as well as those of his age; but like those of other dramatists in his own day and earlier, not strictly so in comedy, especially, as Mr. Lawrence . . . notices, at the denouement [see excerpt above, 1931]. There the leading likable characters, at least, though faulty, are, by marriage, "dismissed to happiness." Ordinarily in Shakespearean and other Elizabethan comedy there is no such villain; and ordinarily such as there are do not appear in the denouement to trouble it, having fled like Don John in *Much Ado,* or dropped out, after getting their deserts, like Shylock; but Angelo, like Bertram, and like Iachimo in *Cymbeline,* is in the denouement as an essential figure. To justice, moreover, acknowledgments have been made; and it is only after much pleading by those who have suffered injustice, and after the appearance of Claudio, supposed to have been executed, that the sentence of death is recalled. (pp. 251-53)

Of the Duke's psychology, Mr. Lawrence rightly thinks, little or nothing can be made: neither a coward nor a shirk, as others have thought, he serves to produce complications and resolve them. He is a stage figure, mainly. In a real sovereign much of his maneuvering and deceiving, even though good in the long run may come of it, would be indefensible. But it is chiefly owing to him, unreasonable and unplausible, sensational and stagy as he is, that the play is both interesting and exciting and yet, as we shall see, not too much so for comedy. Since we are in the secret of his disguise, and quite aware that he knows all that is going on, we are, when we need to be, reassured. Mr. Lawrence calls him a puppet; and so he is, as the dramatist manipulates him; but he is also, as Mr. Murry says, "a power" [see Additional Bibliography]. The situation has been so prepared for that when he, as the Friar, known, even in that character, by those on the stage to know so much, is stripped of his disguise, he in the very act of appearing accuses Angelo of all his secret iniquity. . . . (pp. 253-54)

[Mariana] serves to relieve Isabella of the opprobrium of falling a prey to Angelo's lascivious treachery; but why is Isabella thereupon made a nun? Both changes [from Whetstone] are, like the disguising of the Duke, meant, though in different ways, to produce in the action a greater effect of compactness and also of comic irony—external irony (that is), not, to be sure, any at the heart of the play or in the background, not the "Romantic" sort, of pessimism or disillusion. The play must be kept a comedy. By the deception practiced upon him, Angelo, who, betrothed like Claudio, had cravenly and brutally deserted Mariana because of her losing the dowry, is now put in exactly the same position (though in a far lower moral level) as the condemned Claudio. . . . And by his disguise the Duke is continually hearing, and comfortably or uncomfortably participating in, discussion favorable or unfavorable of himself; which also (and decidedly) lowers or counteracts the tragic tone.

As a nun, Isabella makes, in a sense, a more exciting (though in another sense a less dramatic) situation of both the proposal and also her refusal, before Angelo and then Claudio in prison; and, besides, she thus gives a more urgent occasion for Mariana's being sought as a substitute. But she thus also furnishes a contrast . . .—one grimly comic, and often somewhat ironical too. A nun receiving such a proposal, or having it urged upon her, a saint unlawfully desired by a saint—"O cunning enemy!" cries Angelo after her first appeal, meaning, of course, the Devil,

> that, to catch a saint,
> With saints dost bait thy hook!
>
> [II. ii. 179-80]

And the preceding portion of the scene is given the same ironical turn through such remarks as these of Isabella's, which touch him up a bit though without her knowledge:

> If he had been as you and you as he,
> You would have slipt like him.
>
> [II. ii. 64-5]

> but man, proud man,
> Dress'd in a little brief authority,
> Most ignorant of what he's most assur'd,
> His glassy essence, like an angry ape,
> Plays such fantastic tricks before high heaven
> As make the angels weep.
>
> [II. ii. 117-22]

> Go to your bosom;
> Knock there, and ask your heart what it doth know
> That's like my brother's fault.
>
> [II. ii. 136-37]

Even with her words, she herself, unaware, now does the knocking. (pp. 254-55)

The comic quality of the . . . scene, with Isabella, is heightened by the presence of Lucio (incongruous companion and adjutant!) and his humorous remarks. Certainly, high-pitched though it is, it is kept nevertheless from being tragic. The next, between the holy Sister and the saintly judge alone, takes on a comic cast, again, through his hypocrisy and his crafty coming out into the open. And the greater—the famous—scene, between the nun and Claudio, is kept from being too tragic for comedy in somewhat the same way as the first between her and Angelo,—through Claudio's making such an appeal to her, the nun, and through our knowledge that the Duke is overhearing it.

In herself, moreover, she is well constituted to serve for the comic contrast—is made not too much of a nun. She is not squeamish, finicky, or sanctimonious; and while she does not participate in the gross talk about her, she does not take much notice of it, either. She serves for a contrast without herself being compromised, and also without jarring upon us. She does no lamenting or grieving over sexual or other sinfulness in Vienna—that in the play is a matter left to the Duke and the Deputies: otherwise, she would not serve for the comic effect and would clash with the humorous scenes noticed by Raleigh, "in which most of the corruption comes to light." If the contrast between the dazzling purity of Isabella and the impurity roundabout her were not a little broken or blurred, the play would approach the aborted tragedy that many of the critics have taken it to be. As she is—not too good for this world—on hearing of the plight Juliet is in because of Claudio, all she says is "O, let him marry her" [I. iv. 49]; and she goes through the necessary arrangements with Angelo for the rendezvous according to the Duke's directions, with (as she reports the matter, but well that it is only reported) no apparent shrinking. Most remarkable of all, at the city gates it is she herself, the nun, that brings the charge of his ravishing and murdering—the effect, because of our inside knowledge, is not tragic!—and with clamorous clearness. Sturdy, downright, and direct, "heroic and noble," she is not, however,—for that again would interfere with the comedy—delicate, pathetic, or tender. She loves her brother but—"There spake my brother" [III. i. 85],—

heroically. When before those words, on her arrival in the prison, he asks what comfort, this is the way she produces it:

> Why,
> As all comforts are; most good, most good indeed.
> Lord Angelo, having affairs to heaven,
> Intends you for his swift ambassador,
> Where you shall be an everlasting leiger;
> Therefore your best appointment make with speed,
> To-morrow you set on.
>
> [III. i. 54-60]

Bitterness outstrips tenderness; and as Claudio inquires, "Is there no remedy?" she replies, facing the facts,

> None but such remedy as, to save a head,
> To cleave a heart in twain.
>
> [III. i. 61-2]

So, when towards the close of the scene he pleads for life at her expense, she calls him a "beast," tells him "'tis best thou diest quickly" [III. i. 150]; and when she hears Angelo has been his death, is not plunged in despair, but is for "direct action," as she might call it:

> O, I will to him and pluck out his eyes!
>
> [IV. iii. 119]

Her own, as Lucio notices a moment later, are "red"; but we are not permitted to take that much more to heart than he does. And it is with such vehemence that later she clamors for justice at the gates. (pp. 256-58)

A vociferous, ironical nun! She is almost a Major Barbara.

The irony, as I have said, is external. It resides mostly in the situation of Angelo, though heightened by his relations to Isabella and Mariana, and in the parallel and contrast with Claudio; but also in the whole death-dealing venture of reform, which is preposterous, and, of course, in the deception and misunderstanding occasioned by the Duke's disguise. And this irony, the comic contrast of the votarist of Saint Clare, at the center of the sexual discussion and action, and the humorousness of the low-life scenes (Pompey, Froth, Lucio, and the constables) in which nature and rude sense assert themselves—all these effects or qualities are in keeping with one another. (p. 258)

As for the irony in the reform, the Duke, or rather Angelo, has, of course, in the character of a Draco, gone prodigiously far. The vice, says Lucio (and the humorous spirit of the play bears him out)—"it is impossible to extirp it quite till eating and drinking be put down" [III. ii. 102-03]—; even the Provost says "all sects, all ages smack of it, and he to die for't" [II. ii. 5]. Isabella herself, who abhors it, but says so little about it, asks Angelo,

> Who is it that hath died for this offence?
> There's many have committed it;
>
> [II. ii. 88-9]

while the Deputy, said by Elbow the constable not to abide a whoremaster, his blood, according to Lucio, being very snow-broth, turns out the greatest offender. Claudio, on the other hand, picked out to suffer death for it, is the most venial one, having been betrothed like Angelo—"upon a true contract . . . she is fast my wife" [I. ii. 145-47]—and both he and Julietta avow their love. Everybody but Angelo, either good or bad (though to keep the tragicomic tone not much is said about it), esteems them and sympathizes with them; and the reformation

has been a fiasco. But as usual in Shakespeare, there is, at the end, no moral, and, throughout, nothing approaching a thesis; for the Duke and the Sister, marrying, seem, quite properly, though absentmindedly, to have abandoned, he the business of reform and she the ascetic ideal. (pp. 258-59)

No question is raised, no "casuistry" is engaged in, no "dilemma," whether intolerable or tolerable, is put. At three points, to be sure, there might have been—the proposal by the judge, the substitution of Mariana, and the forgiveness of the judge at the end; but as we have seen, the last is promptly disposed of according to the expectations of comedy, and the other two as promptly, without hesitation or discussion, according to those of the conventional morality, whether of that day or this. (p. 259)

With [Shakespeare] and other Elizabethans the decisive difference between comedy and tragedy lies in the conclusion: though in comedy it is an unhappy and inharmonious effect if before that the tragic element gets the upper hand or rises anywhere to the heights. So the deeper and more poignant feelings of Isabella, Claudio, and Juliet are left in the background. And the tragicomedy now before us differs from such as *Much Ado* and *The Merchant of Venice,* besides [*Alls Well that Ends Well*], only in that the ambiguous tone or tenor is more continuous. The cloud of suspense concerning Claudio and the Deputy, though now and then thinning, does not quite clear up till the very end. The comic contrast in the role of Isabella is fairly constant, and the Duke is ever at hand, either by our confidence in him to diminish our anxiety or else by his intriguing and deceiving to heighten it. He not only withholds from Isabella the truth concerning her brother's fate to the end but two or three times deliberately falsifies it. . . . The Duke plays his part of Friar for all it is worth; acting as if Claudio's life really depended, and very insecurely, upon the will of Angelo, reconciling him to death in prison, and, after the judicial countermand that turns out a treacherous and bloody command, as if this had been carried out. Even with the Provost he has arranged only for a delay, which keeps the audience uncertain and alert. (p. 260)

As we have noticed in the Isabella scenes the tragic effect is somewhat counteracted by Lucio's running comments and her own saintly garb and condition, or by this together with her free-and-easy speech. In several other scenes Lucio has slandered the Duke (when disguised) to his face, as a whoremaster. And in the long exciting scene of the denouement these comic or ironic elements appear together again and also separately, Lucio now slandering the Friar to the Duke as his slanderer, thus doubling his own guilt. Then, the Duke having left the stage and (as the Friar) re-entered, Lucio eagerly recognizes him—"Here comes the rascal I spoke of . . . This is the rascal" [V. i. 283, 304]—thereupon accuses him again, and, amid insults, helps pull off his hood. Yet even this his self-exposure is not ironical enough—he, too, in conformity with the rules of comedy, and also with the Duke's notions of justice, already sufficiently manifested, must now marry, but a whore.

That, likewise, is pretty strong for our regenerate taste, but not too much so for the Elizabethan; it is comic not merely because of the poetic justice upon the obscene and slanderous Lucio, but also because of the prevailing tone of the denouement, which is comic, certainly, though not entirely so. The Duke knowing all, and all going, as we know, by his arrangement, we are free to be amused by the mystifications and ironical surprises,—not only at Lucio caught in his own trap, and at Angelo in his, but also (if robust enough) at the nun so loudly insisting on the loss of her virtue with no one to believe her, and at the humorous Duke meanwhile indignantly siding with Angelo, calling her, because of the imposture, "this wretched woman" [V. i. 132], and Mariana, "pernicious woman, compact with her that's gone" [V. i. 241-42]. By the various means of comic deception—prevarication, impersonation, and disguise—the Duke, Isabella, Mariana, and Friar Peter play upon the others, to bring Lucio, but above all Angelo, to the point of a bigger and bigger ironical repercussion; and the Duke also plays even upon his partners, though this is to happier effect. It is certainly a better, because a two-sided, role, that Isabella takes up as she accuses Angelo, under the misconception that he has been the death of her brother, and more in consonance with her conduct before this and with the tragicomic tenor of the whole drama. There is a bitterness or indignation in her deception; and even because of that her forgiveness, still in ignorance but in acknowledgement of his penitence, takes on nobler proportions. The cruelty to Lucio, moreover, is no stumbling-block to the audience, just as it would not be to an audience of males and congenial females today. (pp. 262-63)

[Here], as generally in Shakespeare's plays, there is not a spirit of poetry, such as there is in Racine and Sophocles, pervading and informing the whole. Of all Shakespeare's plays, *Othello*, perhaps, comes nearest to that. There is, however, as we have seen above, what is more important for a stage play, a predominant dramatic tone. The ambiguous tragicomic tone prevails; and the audience knows what to expect, how to respond. The Elizabethan, that is to say; an audience simply and frankly receptive, not concerned, as part of a present-day audience is, with implications or motives, with anything such as we can call psychology. "Alive, interesting, exciting"—poetical too—no more than that did the audience ask. And even at the greatest periods of drama no more than that, I think—though often, as here, they got considerably more—did they ever ask. (p. 268)

> *Elmer Edgar Stoll, "'All's Well' and 'Measure for Measure'," in his* From Shakespeare to Joyce: Authors and Critics; Literature and Life, *Doubleday, Doran and Company, Inc., 1944, pp. 235-68.*

W.M.T. DODDS (essay date 1946)

[*Dodds focuses on the character of Angelo, a figure, she contends, on whom Shakespeare "lavished" as much attention as he did on those of Macbeth and Othello. She claims that the form of* Measure for Measure *clearly establishes Angelo's tragic dimensions, but because Shakespeare emphasized the intellectual rather than the emotional aspects of a "soul's tragedy," Angelo's tragic suffering and awareness are suggested rather than fully realized. Dodds insists that if his plight is not regarded as the "crucifixion of a soul," the play becomes "untuned" and the thematic conflict between justice and mercy is weakened. She supports her thesis by explicating the nature of Angelo's speech, concentrating especially on his two soliloquies. For other interpretations of Angelo's role, see the excerpts by G. G. Gervinus (1849-50), Hoxie N. Fairchild (1931), H. B. Charlton (1937), Arthur Sewell (1951), Robert Ornstein (1957), and A. D. Nuttall (1968).*]

The soul's tragedy in Angelo has been much neglected; Angelo is not commonly included in the gallery of great Shakespearean portraits. It seems that in literature as in life it is impossible fully to recover a reputation once lost. . . . The recoilings of nineteenth-century criticism have left their mark and accordingly in the twentieth century Angelo is suspect still. . . . If he is seen either as dissembler or as prig, he cannot at the same time be seen as a man whose soul is large and fine enough to experience tragic intensity of suffering. It is the purpose of this study to aver that Angelo's spirit is indeed, as the Duke remarks, 'finely touched', and to attend, in a detailed analysis, to the care and passion which Shakespeare lavished on this character—a care and passion not less than that given to a Macbeth or an Othello, but different in its manifestations.

More is at stake than merely the interpretation of one character. Angelo's part in the dramatic economy of *Measure for Measure* is an important one: he typifies strict justice. The contention between Angelo and Isabel is, as well as the personal issue, the greater issue of Justice and Mercy; it is therefore of crucial importance that the justice should be as genuine as the mercy. It is of course also part of the argument of the play that the ministers of justice in this mortal life are fallible, but this does not (as Angelo explains to Escalus) reflect upon the quality of abstract Justice itself, and Shakespeare has taken great care to show Angelo as a man whose ideals of abstract Justice are clear, and to be revered, whatever his own practice as a 'justicer' may be. To dismiss these ideals as narrow, priggish, pharisaical, is to destroy the dramatic antithesis upon which the argument turns. It is therefore vital to the understanding of the play as a whole to put from oneself all hostility to the idea of Justice as typified by Angelo before his fall. It is a Christian commonplace to think of justice giving place to mercy, but it is unchristian to decry justice itself.

And indeed there is, at the root of erroneous interpretations of Shakespeare's conception of Angelo, a neglect of Christian thinking on the matter of sin. Christian experience has been that goodness carries no exemption, in this life, from the fury of the Tempter; no man is guaranteed against a sudden fall from grace. It is this truth which is neglected when we argue that Angelo tempting Isabel is Angelo revealing his true nature and that, therefore, the golden opinions he had won from the Duke were always unmerited. The case for branding Angelo dissembler rests on the supposition that nothing but a long course of covert sinning could have fitted him to make his bed in hell with such rapidity. Against that supposition stands the evidence of the play itself and in particular the evidence of the very scene in which Angelo tempts Isabel with the offer of her brother's life in return for the enjoyment of her person. (pp. 246-47)

Angelo reasons with Isabel's conscience, and it is a fair inference that his estimate of her nature is based on his knowledge of his own: he reasons with her because he cannot imagine that she will be brought to commit any action which her conscience does not first approve, any more than he would himself were it not that passion is now 'dispossessing all [his] other parts of necessary fitness' [II. iv. 22-3]. If it be argued that this proceeds, not from the habits of a lifetime of deliberation on right conduct, but from a crafty assessment of his adversary's strength, one passage refutes the allegation. Angelo begins to argue that sins committed under compulsion have no gravamen:

> Our compelled sins
> Stand more for number than accompt
>
> [II. iv. 57-8]

but immediately takes back the words, saying,

> Nay, I'll not warrant that; for I can speak
> Against the thing I say.
>
> [II. iv. 59-60]

Here, plainly, we have a man who cannot, even to compass his own ends, even while knowing himself to be on the way to mortal sin, bring himself to employ an argument which he himself knows to be false. For 'hypocrisy' and 'narrowness' of this calibre all scholars may well pray.

The truth is, of course, that Angelo is exactly as the Duke describes him: a man whose whole way of life bears on it the mark that enables an observer of men to reconstruct the secret history of self-discipline that has gone to its making. . . . To aver that the Duke too was deceived by 'seeming, seeming', and speaks with no authority, is to ignore the care that Shakespeare took in giving the Duke the vocabulary and style of a thinker and also Shakespeare's care in adding weight to the choice of Angelo for the supreme position, by making the Duke first commend and commission Escalus and then top commendation by preferring Angelo to the higher office. It is, also, to ignore Shakespeare's revelation of Angelo in his style of utterance.

There are two striking characteristics of Angelo's speech: one is the absence of that welling imagery associated, in Shakespeare's practice, with the presence of strong passions; the other is the frequency and nicety of the ethical distinctions Angelo makes.

Angelo thinks with concepts, not with impassioned images. The rare images he does use are deliberate illustrations of his thought and these are elaborated without change of metaphor, as in the lines

> We must not make a scarecrow of the law,
> Setting it up to fear the birds of prey,
> And let it keep one shape, till custom make it
> Their perch and not their terror.
>
> [II. i. 1-4]

This intellectual deployment of analogy, radically different from the maelstrom of imagery characteristic of a Macbeth, is no accident, for when Angelo is in the grip of his passion for Isabel the character of his speech changes, and the images which are no more than exempla give place to images jetted out by the spring of emotions within. . . . Evidently, Shakespeare has taken care to give Angelo the imagery of a man in whom passion is not yet awake. (pp. 247-48)

The two things, the character of the imagery and the nicety of distinction, are unmistakeable in the argument with Escalus about the sentence on Claudio. Escalus has urged mercy on the grounds that Claudio succumbed to a universal temptation and that Angelo must have felt in himself the stirrings of the same vice. Angelo replies, with strict logic:

> 'Tis one thing to be tempted, Escalus,
> Another thing to fall,
>
> [II. i. 17-18]

and then demolishes the case that Escalus has put. Granted, the jury may contain some few who are guiltier than the prisoner they condemn, but the consideration is irrelevant, for two reasons: first, justice is concerned only with known facts ('what's open made to justice, that justice seizes' [II. i. 21-2]), secondly, justice is an impersonal autonomy which takes no cognizance of the human instruments who are its executors ('what know the laws that thieves do pass on thieves?' [II. i. 22-3]). . . . And it is typical of Angelo's mental habits that having stated a formed decision, he immediately sees it in terms of its issue in action: 'Sir, he must die' [II. i. 31]. This is the mark of effective thinking: the intention of achieving decision and

promptly converting decision into fact. It is so in his treatment of Isabel. He attempts to persuade; it fails; he therefore proceeds to a plain statement of the alternatives, and demands decision of her as he is accustomed to demand it of himself: 'Answer me tomorrow' [II. iv. 167]. Disciplined and effective thought is not usually the concomitant of slavery to the lusts of the body. (p. 249)

Angelo's consuetude with decisive thinking on ethical matters is nowhere so well revealed as in his reflections on himself when he realizes that he desires Isabel. The sequence of thought reveals the nature of the man, and is in itself so carefully thought out and vividly imagined, that one cannot in face of it deny that Shakespeare valued his creation here.

His very first concern is to apportion moral responsibility:

> What's this? What's this? Is this her fault, or mine?
>
> [II. ii. 163]

He settles his own problem as decisively as he settles the problems of others:

> Not she, nor doth she tempt, but it is I.
>
> [II. ii. 164]

His next question is typical of the reflective moralist: it is an attempt to formulate new experience and to consider how far the personal discovery indicates a general truth:

> Can it be
> That modesty may more betray our sense
> Than woman's lightness?
>
> [II. ii. 167-69]

and immediately after, to pronounce on the moral implications of the experience to place it accurately in the moral scale:

> Having waste ground enough
> Shall we desire to raze the sanctuary
> And pitch our evils there? O fy, fy, fy!
>
> [II. ii. 169-71]

Next—perhaps the greatest revelation of all—comes his immediate impulse to re-value his whole being in the light of new knowledge, re-estimating the old by the light of the new:

> What dost thou, or what art thou, Angelo?
>
> [II. ii. 172]

Here is revealed—and Shakespeare cannot have done this with his eyes shut—Angelo's ability to state a problem correctly with rapid logic and moral simplicity: he is saying, in effect, 'One of two conclusions may be drawn: either I am what I have always thought, in which case the problem is, How can I do this thing? or I am one to whom such a thing *is* natural, in which case the problem is, What evil nature is mine?' The pressure of an intellectual and spiritual agony forces that dilemma into the simple frame, 'What dost thou, or what art thou, Angelo?' This is followed by as full a piece of self-knowledge as any Shakespearean hero ever showed:

> Dost thou desire her foully for those things
> That make her good?
>
> [II. ii. 173-74]

The exhaustion that follows this simultaneous suffering and self-scrutiny reveals itself in the next words, which are a helpless longing to be rid of the whole problem:

> O let her brother live!
> Thieves for their robbery have authority,
> When judges steal themselves.
>
> [II. ii. 174-76]

It is one of the great touches of this play that Shakespeare makes Angelo so desperate in his longing to escape the temptation of Isabel's presence, that he is willing to abandon the position for which he contended in the argument with Escalus; faced with the alternative of betraying his conception of justice or enduring again the compelling presence of Isabel, he weakens so far as to use almost the very instance that he had before dismissed as irrelevant. It is not sufficiently recognized that to Angelo the betrayal of his trust as a servant of justice was as grave a matter as unchastity was to Isabel, and the weakening on this point is evidence of the irresistible force of the temptation that Isabel put in his path. . . . And Angelo's next words show how swiftly the temptation had prevailed, for they reveal that he had (immediately after the thought of avoiding her) felt in prospect that the pang of *not* seeing her again:

> What! do I love her,
> That I desire to hear her speak again,
> And feast upon her eyes?
>
> [II. ii. 176-78]

There is more in this than the mere lust of the body, and in one sense Angelo, in his bid for Isabel, is an object of pity as well as horror. What he feels for her is love—a love begun by the recognition of a complementary mind ('she speaks, and 'tis such sense, that my sense breeds with it' [II. ii. 141-42]), confirmed by the sympathy of one disciplined and virtuous nature for another, and mounting to the inexplicable catalysis of love where the body too is desired, both for itself and as a means to participation in the soul. Isabel's soul is by the nature of her vocation beyond his reach—at least, her soul in the fair state which attracted his, for bodily possession must inevitably have been accompanied by the defacing of the essence that first drew him and so would have been, at best, the expense of spirit in a waste of shame. Something of this tragic impasse is in the concluding passage of this soliloquy:

> O cunning enemy, that to catch a saint
> With saints doth bait thy hook! Most dangerous
> Is that temptation, that doth goad us on
> To sin in living virtue.
>
> [II. ii. 179-82]

That this *is* the concluding passage is surely remarkable: that only now, after the sequence of reflection, Angelo finds a place to remark the severity of his fate. He does not remark it; there is not the outcry that a tragedy would have found scope for. The situation of Angelo is, as it were, a diagram of a tragedy; all the lines of the structure are clearly drawn, but because this is a comedy, the mass and weight are not insisted on; they can, nevertheless, be experienced by imaginative reconstruction.

Shakespeare has here performed an extraordinary artistic feat. He has assured us by external witness (the Duke) that Angelo has spent years in the pursuit of self-knowledge and self-discipline; he has substantiated this by giving Angelo a style of speech that reflects such mental habits; he has in this soliloquy shown 'the thing itself': the very process of self-awareness in the moment of becoming conscious; he has placed a man of this kind in a situation that overthrows him and in which he knows himself overthrown. Yet all this is managed within the frame of comedy, because it is indicated only and is not given full tragic dimensions; the emphasis is on the intellectual diagram, not on the emotional impact.

In Angelo's next soliloquy, Shakespeare combines restraint with lucidity in such a way that the personal agony is held in solution without being precipitated, yet the nature of the precipitation can be known, if one cares to enter into an imaginative experiencing of Angelo's description of his state. It is, when thought upon, the state of a man in hell. Nor Brutus nor Macbeth ever endured such spiritual agony before the commission of a crime. In this soliloquy the extreme of anguish is reached, for in it the will to God and the will to evil do not so much struggle, as co-exist in mutual loathing, while Angelo experiences the external antipathy of these adversaries. . . . Angelo has failed in every stage: he cannot exert his will to the point of recollection, his words are empty, his imagination fails to hold God before his eyes and 'anchors on Isabel', and in his affections there is, not God, but the 'strong and swelling evil' [II. iv. 4, 6] of his conception. In despair of meditation he has turned to study; this too has failed. Mere self-respect, the last strong-point, has dispersed, and his attitude to himself, now, is as chaotic as his attitude to good and eivl. The old things seem false, disparate, and vacuous, the new consciousness of 'blood' (the passions he had dismissed as negligible) is foreign and incorrigibly strong. The last two lines of the speech:

> Let's write good angel on the devil's horn,
> 'Tis not the devil's crest
>
> [II. iv. 16-17]

sum up what he has learned from his reflections on his life and this sudden new light on it: he had writ himself good angel, only to find that the devil within remained, and proved the superscription wrong.

The realization in dramatic terms of a crucial state of mind and soul, which follows this, is one of the finest things in Shakespeare. Angelo's will is temporarily paralysed: it cannot direct him to either of the opposed alternatives, since both are desired at once. And the confusion of his faculties is the more severe since both are also hated at once. (pp. 249-52)

The scene which follows is one difficult to understand if the nature and the predicament of Angelo have not been properly grasped. This scene shows Angelo's will moving, in action, to one of its two poles; this it must show, for it is only in the passion of the spirit that irreconcileables can co-exist. . . . It is when Isabel flatly refuses him and denounces the yielding of the body as 'shame', that he as decisively commits himself to the other extreme. The balance is now struck, and Angelo who so far has hardly known whether he argues with Isabel, or with himself, or whether he is in fact feeling his way to the beginning of the seduction in the only way he knows, now enters the struggle with Isabel and puts into it all the pent-up strength of will that recently in the struggle with himself could find no direction for its power. The veerings from pole to pole now cease, and the whole momentum of a powerful nature, of a will accustomed to browbeat the opposition of the subordinate faculties, of a temper inflexible in decision and rapid in action, flares up to the fuel of this occasion and consumes Isabel. There is the exultation of release as well as the savagery of a desire which is the obverse of love, in Angelo's words:

> I have begun;
> And now I give my sensual race the rein:
> Fit thy consent to my sharp appetite;
> Lay by all nicety and prolixious blushes,
> That banish what they sue for; redeem thy brother
> By yielding up thy body to my will,
> Or else he must not only die the death
> But thy unkindness shall his death draw out
> To lingering sufferance: answer me tomorrow.
>
> [II. iv. 159-67]

Angelo's passion of cruelty is as extreme as the suffering that gave it birth, and it is in his enormities that we see fully what had been the pitch of his agony before; just as in Isabel's rounding on Claudio we see reflected the precedent anguish of her alternatives. This cruelty is further exacerbated by the hell of lusting after the body where primarily the soul is loved. (pp. 252-53)

The subsequent deepening of his villainy, the rapid blunting of a soul once its first fine edge is lost, has its parallel in Macbeth, and no more casts doubt on the validity of Angelo's first estate than does Macbeth's blood-boltered villainy make his earlier scruples incredible. (p. 254)

And this Angelo of Shakespeare's, this crucifixion of a soul, has had few watchers. A fellow of his name, but not of his note, has too long sneaked in his place. In consequence, the harmony of the play has been untuned, the great antithesis of justice and mercy reduced to a shadow of itself, and the complexity of Angelo's character and experience passed over.

It may be that Angelo's breaking-off of the nuptials with Mariana is the mote that has loomed large to the critical eye. But Angelo is not plot-proof; the connection with Mariana is essential to the untying of the dramatic knot; Angelo is not the first of Shakespeare's characters to bestride the narrow world of tidy dénouements like a Colossus, and Shakespeare may have thought, if he gave it a thought at all, that there is no real matter for surprise in the fact that a man whose blood was very snowbroth should have broken off the negotiations for a marriage of convenience which had ceased to offer the conveniences for whose sake it was first contemplated. The delineation of Angelo's character in the scenes that come before we have learned anything of the Mariana business is so passionately done, so consistent in every detail, so speaking a likeness of scrupulous integrity, that it is Mariana who must square with this, not this with Mariana.

It is possible to regard Measure for Measure as an experiment by Shakespeare: an attempt to handle, in a comedy, a character comparable to the characters of the tragedies. It is even possible that the hesitations in the critical attitude to Angelo are in some measure due to the failure to see this—a failure born of the practice of looking for tragic intensity only in those characters who are by their whole nature tragically incompatible with their circumstances. Angelo, like any ordinary character in a comedy, is made to see himself in a new light by the impact of an external accident—in his case, the accident of meeting Isabel. But, unlike the ordinary characters of comedy, he bears the marks of having been imagined intensely in all his complexity and capacity for suffering, just as Shakespeare's tragic characters are imagined, though his suffering is not fully bodied forth. It may be this departure from practice that has crippled the criticism of Measure for Measure. (pp. 254-55)

W.M.T. Dodds, "The Character of Angelo in 'Measure for Measure'," in The Modern Language Review, *Vol. XLI, No. 3, July, 1946, pp. 246-55.*

ROY W. BATTENHOUSE   (essay date 1946)

[*Battenhouse is well known for his studies of religion and literature and for his theory that Shakespeare's works embody a specifically Christian world view. In the excerpt below, Battenhouse examines the language, characterization, structure, and plot of* Measure for Measure *to support his thesis that the play is an "Atonement drama," offering an analogy of the reconciliation between God and man through Christ's sacrifice. He emphasizes* parallels between Measure for Measure *and medieval Atonement stories, especially the portrait of a benevolent sovereign who disguises himself in order to reform his disordered society. Battenhouse also maintains that the imagery in* Measure for Measure *further defines its indebtedness to Atonement drama, specifically in Shakespeare's use of such Christian concepts as the deception of the devil "and elements of" divine romance. For other interpretations of* Measure for Measure *as a form of Christian allegory, see the excerpts by Hermann Ulrici (1839), G. Wilson Knight (1930), R. W. Chambers (1937), F. R. Leavis (1942), Nevill Coghill (1955), and Tom McBride (1974).*]

The present essay is written in the belief that our latter-day critics have approximated a proper focus on *Measure for Measure,* without as yet achieving it precisely or employing it adequately. What Chambers [and] Wilson Knight . . . are assuming is that the drama is thoroughly and properly ethical, if only we will accept Christian ethics [see excerpts above, 1937 and 1930]. If such a solution is argued, it would seem to me right to urge at the same time its corollary: that the drama is esthetically acceptable and sound, if we will but measure it by a Christian esthetics. Our critical problem, then, becomes one of discriminating the patterns by which Christian ethics and Christian art declare themselves; and then testing the relevance of such patterns to the actual texture of Shakespeare's drama. Is there manifest in the poetry, we will ask, any of the imagery, symbol, and myth traditional in Christian story? If so, an attempt to explore these aspects may open up the deeper meaning of the play. (p. 1031)

Now the one pattern which most finally sets the norm for Christian ethics and Christian art is the story of the Atonement. It is told in Scripture and retold in the liturgies of the Church and the commentaries of her theologians. What is this Atonement story? (p. 1032)

Briefly this: a sovereign disguises himself in order to visit his people and reform them. Though he is the Lord of men, he condescends to become their brother. Acting incognito he sows within their history the processes whereby they may be reconciled to him in a just and happy kingdom. By temporarily taking the form of a servant, he is able to mingle intimately in his people's affairs, discover their hearts, prevent and remove sins, intrude wise and far-reaching counsels, and direct all things toward a great Last Judgment when he shall appear with power to establish peace. As setting for this stratagem, Christian story emphasizes certain preconditions: the fact of disorder in the world, resulting from an abuse by men of their free-will; the attitude of the ruler, who desires not punishment but a non-tyrannical restoration of order; and the benevolent readiness of the prince to undertake a remedy for evil when he can no longer overlook it. Starting from these premises, the plot is then unwound with deliberate care, until of a sudden its design is discovered to be, miraculously, accomplished. Along the way many subsidiary themes make the story both fascinating and wondrously complex. We see nobility undergoing shame and royalty going "hooded"; grace working side by side with law; the wisdom of serpents joined to the harmlessness of doves; the power of petition operating within the realm of providence, the virtue of intercession even within the scheme of predestination. (pp. 1032-33)

Bearing in mind the chief features of the Atonement drama, let us note now the points of superficial resemblance to the action of Shakespeare's play. The opening situation in both stories is that of a people in need of reform. In Shakespeare's Vienna "Liberty plucks justice by the nose" [I. iii. 29], decorum goes "quite athwart." The Duke, seeing this, wishes to curb license while preserving liberty. His strategy is twofold: he stirs up the arm of the Law by deputizing Angelo, a zealous legalist; and then concurrently "His Grace" undertakes in disguise to prevent the Law from collecting the penalty he has just newly permitted it to claim. From here on the plot is a contest between Law and Grace, both of course having their authority from the "Lord" of the city. Law serves a providential function, though Grace is ultimately the victor. The disguise chosen by His Grace is that of friar, "spiritual brother" to man. Attired thus, the Duke visits the spirits in prison (cf. *I. Pet.* iii. 19); brings comfort to the captive Claudio, victim of the "just" law; shrives the penitent Juliet; watches over the temptation and "fall" of Angelo; approves the saintly Isabella in her victory over temptation, and encourages her with a plot for outwitting the fallen "angel"; at the same time aids the needy Mariana (a sort of importunate "widow"); strengthens these disciples of his by his reasoning and authority, and finally commits them to Friar Peter (note the name!) until his coming again. Then, when he comes in judgment, all things undergo apocalypse (cf. *I Cor.* iv. 5). Isabella initiates the miraculous denouement by announcing she has news both "strange" and "true." . . . Presently, and suddenly, the seeming righteous are convicted of sin, and the seeming sinners are vindicated. Angelo perceives that to his "dread lord" nothing is indiscernible; that His Grace "like power divine" has looked upon Angelo's trespasses. And for Isabella, on the other hand, there are the words of welcome: "Come hither, Isabel. Your friar is now your prince" [V. i. 381-82]. (Cf. *Mt.* xxv. 34. "Come, ye blessed of my Father, inherit the kingdom prepared for you . . .")

From this point on, the Judgment is enriched by still other themes, traditionally Christian if not specifically Biblical. The manner in which Justice and Mercy seem to contend in the Duke's court as they work their way to a final reconciliation reminds us of the debate among the four daughters of God—Mercy, Truth, Justice, and Peace—which in medieval drama brought the morality of play to its happy conclusion. Medieval teaching regarding the invocation and intercession of saints has its reflection here too; for the saintly Isabella responds to Mariana's plea that she intercede for Angelo, and we who watch the action realize that indeed Isabella is bound by charity to do just this, since Mariana has earlier given her an example by interceding her own body to save Isabella's brother, Claudio. (pp. 1033-35)

Further thinking along the lines of Atonement doctrine is unavoidable, it seems to me, when we call to mind some of the most celebrated passages of the play. None is better known, perhaps, than the lines of Angelo's lament:

Alack, when once our grace we have forgot,
Nothing goes right; we would, and we would not.

[IV. iv. 33-4]

Or again, there is the famous speech . . . in which Isabella is pleading before the judge for her brother's life:

Why, all the souls that were, were forfeit once;
And he that might the vantage best have took
Found out the remedy.

[II. ii. 73-5]

Both these passages carry the ring of profound truth and of Christian apocalypse. . . . "We would, and we would not" calls to mind St. Paul's discussion, in the seventh chapter of *Romans,* of the two wills which contended in him before the advent of, and in the absense of, Grace. The allusion points a

finger at Angelo's lack of Grace as the fundamental cause of his frustration, and at the same time it lets us know that his present agony is but the old story of the Pharisee Saul—a man self-divided by a law within his members at war with the law of the spirit. Isabella's speech, likewise, revolves about the cardinal facts of sin and grace—this time illuminated by the memory of the Atonement. "And he . . . found out the remedy" is a clear allusion to the work of redemption wrought by Christ—God's remedy at a time when all souls were forfeit under the Law. Angelo takes pride in being a "just" judge: and here Isabella is reminding him that the most just of all judges, God Himself, *sought out a means for circumventing his own just* claim upon man. God could not rest content to see man get his just deserts, but provided a way for man to escape from prison!

But Isabella is addressing an "angel" who has forgot that his proper rôle is to aid as well as watch over men: this Angelo neither searches for nor desires a means to release Claudio. It remains for the Duke to do that. He does it by contriving the plot of Mariana's voluntary yet sinless humiliation of herself. When the arranging of this stratagem is finally complete in Act IV. sc. i., the Duke rounds off his counsels with some Scripture-like imagery:

Come, let us go;
Our corn's to reap, for yet our tithe's to sow.

[IV. i. 74-5]

Mariana's laying down of her body is as the sowing of a tithe. It makes for an atonement in several senses: it fulfils the "promise of satisfaction" (the phrase is Shakespeare's at the end of Act III. sc. i.) exacted by the Adversary; it accomplishes her own physical at-one-ment with her estranged husband; and it makes possible the eventual reconciliation between the Prince and his (spiritually) estranged people. Yet the "suffering" of Mariana does not automatically free "fallen" Claudio; it merely establishes a claim for his "redemption"—which the Adversary defies by perfidiously breaking contract (once again!). It is then time for the Duke to return in judgment. But first, his coming is foretold: the Provost is assured by certain secret writings that the Lord of the city will return "within these two days" [IV. ii. 198] (Cf. the Scriptures quoted by Christ to his disciples to assure them of His return "on the third day," i.e., two days after the Crucifixion). (pp. 1036-38)

I have called attention to the finer points of the situation (not over-refining them, I trust) because it is exactly at this moment that the Duke's words rise to an arresting beauty which has made them quoted, by both Knight and Traversi [see excerpt above, 1942], as one of the most haunting passages in the entire play:

Look, th'unfolding star calls up the shepherd.
Put not yourself into amazement how these things
should be; all difficulties are but easy when
they are known . . . Come away; it is almost
clear dawn.

[IV. ii. 203-10]

Not only the imagery of the star and the shepherd but the very syntax of the language is Biblical, and its ring is apocalyptic. . . . [It] seems to me that the "unfolding star" of the Duke's vision is more symbolic than literal (as is his announcement of daybreak), and that it makes best sense when we recall that Christian revelation "unfolds," ushering in "the Day of the Lord." In other words, the star—and the shepherd too—have in the Shakespearean context supernatural overtones. The Duke is exercising a pastoral rôle over his subjects and, even in doing so, interprets his course as that of a shepherd-of-the-sheep summoned now to the fulfilment of his work by the unfolding of the star of predestined plan.

As reinforcement for this interpretation, it should be recalled that the shepherd analogy—whether in St. Luke's parable or in later commentary—is one of the most venerable for describing the work of the Atonement. (pp. 1038-40)

Shepherding, however, is not the only metaphor in terms of which the drama of the Atonement can find expression. The art of fishing furnishes analogy even more fascinating. Christ's promise "Follow me and I will make you fishers of men" had profound implications. Indeed, the imagery of fishing, above all other, appealed to the imagination of disciples in the early centuries, and its homely concepts were readily adopted for communicating the mysteries of the Faith. (pp. 1040-41)

In *Measure for Measure* the imagery of fishing obtrudes in Isabella's soliloquy at the end of Act II:

> O perilous mouths,
> . . . Bidding the law make court'sy to their will;
> Hooking both right and wrong to the appetite,
> To follow as it draws!
>
> [II. iv. 172-77]

She is implying here that the hungry Angelo is like a fish, moved only by appetite, and compelling the law (like a fishline) to condescend to his will. Even more arresting is the use of the fishing metaphor in an earlier speech by Angelo:

> O cunning enemy, that, to catch a saint,
> With saints dost bait thy hook!
>
> [II. ii. 179-80]

Angelo sees himself lured like a fish to the hook. Isabella's beauty is the bait; if he seizes it he will be caught in an act of sin; he will no longer be a "saint." Obscurely he sees that there is, behind Isabella, some "cunning enemy" (Satan, so he thinks; but actually, as we shall see, it is an arrangement of his "lord," the Duke) contriving this temptation of his virtue. The situation is rich in dramatic irony. Angelo's analysis, apparently, is no accidental touch of Shakespearean fancy; rather, the imagery illuminates the whole plot of the play and points the alert reader who wants commentary to a long line of Christian writers on the Atonement. . . .

The particular form of the doctrine of Atonement which Angelo's words point at is commonly known as the "deception of the devil" theory. (p. 1041)

Angelo, when he has succumbed to temptation and fallen, is a devilish angel, a creature who when he hungers hastens to devour—a sort of leviathan. He takes the saintly Isabella as his bait: her humanity luring him, her open confession of infirmity exciting him, while her godly virtue makes her doubly attractive. But his cunning stratagems are perforated by the acute moral sense of Isabella and the sharp counsels of the Duke. Providentially, a line is being spun for his catching: it is the Isabella-Mariana line, arranged marvellously by the Duke. To the corded, seemingly twisted, righteousness of Isabella, the Duke joins the sharp, seemingly "crooked," love of Mariana; then when Angelo strikes he is "hooked" in a double sense, cheated of that which he has desired but caught by that which he has swallowed. The Duke also has put a ring in Leviathan's nose in the sense that he has forged a ring of

heavenly protection which prevents Angelo's cunning from prevailing anywhere, even against Claudio. (pp. 1042-43)

The parleys between Isabella and Angelo present us still another sort of imagery well known to students of the Christian doctrine of the Atonement. It is the concept of "ransom." The first suggestion of it is made, ironically, by the saintly Isabella, who proposes the notion of an "illegal" bargain with her ambiguous, "Hark, how I'll *bribe* you." "How! bribe me!" exclaims Angelo, feeling for the first time a stab of personal interest in the affair. "Ay," responds Isabella, "with such gifts that heaven shall share with you . . . Not with fond shekels . . . but with true prayers" [II. ii. 145-51]. Angelo, however, sees here a gambit other than Isabella intends, and he warms to the play. He replies, at their next meeting, with a challenge to Isabella to "redeem" her brother. And Isabella answers, with fine Christian discrimination, that

> Ignomy in ransom, and free pardon
> Are of two houses: lawful mercy
> Is nothing kin to foul redemption.
>
> [II. iv. 111-13]

Only a devil's logic would confound Christian charity with mortal sin. Isabella must therefore reject the particular means of redemption proffered by the fallen-angel. Still, she would like to rescue her brother; and when by the Duke's counsel she finds how she can do so without endangering her soul, she adjusts herself to Angelo's proposition and the bargain is agreed to. Then Angelo, having (so he is sure) received his goods, refuses to pay and taunts Isabella to prosecute him for violation of contract. In this extremity she does not, thanks to the presence of the Duke, lose faith; inspired by his advice she resolves that if she cannot restore her brother she will at least restore justice. "Justice, justice, justice, justice!" [V. i. 25] she cries, like the importunate widow of the Biblical parable. The returned Duke pretends to brush her off, referring her case to his deputy. Her reply is significant: "You bid me seek redemption of the devil: Hear me yourself" [V. i. 29-30]. For awhile the "royal Duke" does not seem to hear. In the end, however, her insistent petitioning is but the price she has had to pay for a double answer: both justice and her brother are restored. (pp. 1043-44)

Angelo's rôle in the drama is, morally, that of rival prince to the true sovereign, Vincentio. Claudio, by an act of his own free will, is discovered to have fallen within this adversary's power. Unless someone intercedes for Claudio he is lost; but, providentially, he has a holy sister who volunteers for the mission of rescue. She visits the ruling prince, and so stirs him by her beauty (a supremely bewitching beauty because it has in it something of the divine) that he proposes—unfairly—the price of her (spiritual) "death" in exchange for the brother's release. . . . The holy Isabella, like Christ in the wilderness, at once discerns that a laying down of her life in obedience to the will of this Devil is not the allowable answer to the problem posed by the fact of human sin:

> Better it were a brother died at once,
> Than that a sister, by redeemng him,
> Should die for ever.
>
> [II. iv. 106-08]

She emerges unharmed thus from the Temptation. But that is only half the victory: her brother is still in bonds. At this point the teaching of one whom she recognizes as her spiritual Father, one who assures her that in following his teaching she will please her absent lord—for not until the climax of revelation does she discover that *he is the lord—,* shows her how to go beyond the rules of Old Testament law. In the spirit of faith, she consents to play a part in a sort of Passion-play (in an ambiguous sense, being analogous on the one hand to Christ's Passion, on the other to human passion) which culminates in the overcoming and binding of the adversary, and the freeing of sinful man (represented in Claudio), whom the adversary, by a kind of justice, was holding in prison. She saves her honor; and she saves her brother too. She withstands temptation because she obeys the *precepts* binding on a votarist of the Order of St. Clare; more than that, she frees a sinner, because she follows the *counsels* of one who wears the garb of St. Francis. Seeking first the Kingdom of Heaven, she has all things else, even a palace in Vienna (if she will have it), added unto her—but not without agony and action.

It is worth noting that Vincentio, who works as a sort of secret, omniscient, and omnipresent Providence, contrives in his stratagem to make it both beneficial and just. He tricks the adversary for a good purpose and in a fair contest. . . . The Duke aims to see to it that Angelo shall get measure of punishment for measure of fraud, and that Mariana shall get the withheld measure of satisfaction owed her by former contract. (pp. 1046-47)

But some of us with modern tastes are likely to ask, Is deception ever ethical? Shakespeare's Duke very plainly believes it sometimes is. "Virtue is bold," he says, "and goodness never fearful" [III. i. 208]. Or again: "The doubleness of the benefit defends the deceit from reproof" [III. i. 257-58]. His trick is a "remedy" which presents itself "to the love I have in doing good." (p. 1047)

The Christian ethics which we here observe is not a moralistic, or a rationalistic, ethics. Rather, all action is made properly flexible within the framework of the total goal, which is God's victory and man's salvation. The single, fundamental consideration is that of the Atonement. We may recall St. Paul's famous statement that Christians are men who approve themselves ministers of God in a paradoxical fashion: "by honor and dishonor, by evil report and good report; as *deceivers* yet *true.*" A true judgment as to the morality or immorality of any action depends on our asking the leading question, "Why did Christ come down from heaven?" . . . In other words, all Christian action properly takes its "measure" from the story of the Atonement. . . . (p. 1048)

It should by now be evident how relevant this conceptual framework is to the design of *Measure for Measure.* Shakespeare's Vincentio, whose name means Victor, is presented dramatically in the double rôle of Duke and Friar. When his little world, Vienna, needs reform he introduces two lines of action. He gives a commission to the wielders of law, and then he himself descends to undertake the direction of the forces of mercy. Soon it becomes evident that what St. Paul teaches is true: that the way of legal righteousness which the law recommends can never lead to salvation. Rather, the law increases sin—both in Angelo who finds by it his opportunity, and in Claudio who is driven by it into a second sin, the desiring of his own sister's dishonor. But the Duke directs a stratagem by which both Angelo and Claudio are redeemed from the curse of the law. Though the law makes forfeit first the head of Claudio, then the head of Angelo, the good Duke sees to it that the axe never falls. Instead, the "angel" learns that he is but a man, and the "lame man" learns to walk—"Grace to stand, and virtue [to] go" [III. ii. 264]. Reform is achieved,

without almighty *fiat,* and the prince is hailed both as victor and benefactor.

But, finally, Atonement is one thing more: a divine romance. This is the most circumambient metaphor, the most inclusive symbol; for the whole action of atonement is a work of love. Christian thought insists that the Shepherd-Fisherman-Prince is primarily a King of Love, who puts himself in the rôle of humble wooer of the human heart, prospective Bridegroom of his 'elect.' In this rôle he looks forward to a "marriage" (the symbol is used in *Mt.* xxii. 2); but first he must win his beloved by courting and serving her. He must persuade her first to listen, then to obey, then to suffer for him: for she does not see in him the predestined husbander of her resources until shown it by proofs of love. Hence he must fight for her against those who would shame her, safeguard her honor, forward her wishes—and thus attach her to himself. But note: he has the task of making the bride worthy of him at the same time that he wins her; he must bring out the best in her through the very action by which he masters her. His must be a strategic love capable both of taming and of perfecting the bride. (pp. 1049-50)

It is this aspect of the Atonement drama that offers, I think, our best guide for understanding the course and the context of the Duke's relations with Isabella. Her character does indeed develop in the play—not quite, as Wilson Knight has said, "from sanctity to humanity," but rather, from innocence to maturity, from the narrow sanctity and cold humanity of a novice-sister under "law" to the large sanctity and warm humanity of a "sister" to Mariana under "His Grace." Like the Jewish Church which the Messiah came to "free," Isabella requires an enlargement from her moral isolationism into a moral cosmopolitanism.

And how is this accomplished? By a loving stranger's putting in the right word at the right time—or, as the Bible expresses it supernaturally, by a visitation of The Word "in the fulness of time." In the very middle of Shakespeare's play . . . we find Isabella exhibiting a legalistic righteousness in a fashion which would have pained St. Clare:

> Die, perish! might but my bending down
> Reprieve thee from thy fate, it should proceed:
> I'll pray a thousand prayers for thy death,—
> No *word* to save thee.
>
> [III. i. 13-46]

Five lines later we see the Friar-Duke interposing his first speech to her:

> Vouchsafe a *word,* young sister, but one *word.*
>
> [III. i. 151]

To which she replies submissively, "What is *your will?*" She is now about to be tempted into an act of grace—as the Biblical Eve, conversely, was tempted into an act of sin.

The virgin Isabella is at first very cool to her suitor's approach ("I have no superfluous leisure; my stay must be stolen . . ." [III. i. 157-58]); but the stranger's seeming to take her side as against Claudio is indirectly flattering, and his fund of gossip regarding Angelo arouses her interest. He begins then with courtly compliment, couching it in the Euphuistic style of balanced moralizing and entreaty:

> The hand that made you fair hath made you
> good: the goodness that is cheap in beauty makes
> beauty brief in goodness; but grace, being the

Act II. Scene iv. Angelo and Isabella. By R. Smirke (1797). From the Art Collection of the Folger Shakespeare Library.

soul of your complexion, shall keep the body
of it ever fair.

> [III. i. 180-84]

The teasing quality of these lines is that their meaning moves at two levels—the natural and the supernatural—like parable. The supernatural meaning, at the moment no doubt quite unappreciated by Isabella, is that the Creator intends her to be "fair" (i.e. just—and magnanimous) to Claudio as well as "good" (i.e., virtuous—and charitable); that a light measure of the one excellence means a short measure of the other; but that "grace," animating both, will preserve a balanced and immortal beauty.

But note that at the "natural" level the wooing constantly suggests the conventions of chivalric romance. The lover presently has a "remedy" for his lady's distress: a scheme whereby she may "do . . . a benefit" without staining her honor. "I have spirit to do" it, she says; "show me how" [III. i. 205-06, 238]. Then he outlines a plan of "deceit" involving a secret appointment—to which she replies in lover-like fashion, "The image of it gives me content already" [III. i. 200-59]. The element of surface parallel here to the love-compacts of adulterous chivalry serves but to give dramatic heightening to the interplay of false and true, seems and is, which makes up the mystifying texture of the play.

But the remedy proposed by the suitor seems to fail, and Isabella's distress is increased: the reward for which she had hoped is treacherously denied her. Now the Duke deftly fans

her sense of injury in order to increase her desire for satisfaction. (If he takes advantage of her ignorance it's because "all's fair in love.") He plans for her certain "heavenly comforts" which can be made known to her only when she has learned patience; and she can accomplish patience only if she hungers and thirsts for satisfaction—and paces her wisdom in "that good path that I would wish it go" [IV. iii. 133]. What went before was harmless play; what is called for now is humiliating passion. Isabella, prepared by the extremity of her desire, and trusting her suitor, fits herself to the more difficult rôle. She pleads shamelessly and ardently—and is denied, only to be suddenly rewarded! At the moment when she attains her heart's desire she realizes how much she has "employ'd and pain'd" [V. i. 386] her unknown Master, and she then begs and receives his pardon. This is the beginning of her larger awakening. Mariana now asks her to pardon Angelo, and she does so; for she has been made pliable to this most difficult of all love's rôles by discovering her own indebtedness to the mercy of the Duke and of Mariana. Experience has taught her "how to love." At last she is a mature woman fit to be joined to the King of love, whose forethought was meanwhile assembled a considerable wedding party from among the needs of Vienna. Accordingly, he proposes to her in words whose timeworn sound has a timeless meaning:

> Give me your hand, and say you will be mine
> He [the resurrected Claudio] is my brother too . . .
>
> > [V. i. 492-93]

A moment later, as the curtain falls, comes another of love's old refrains:

> if you'll a willing ear incline
> What's mine is yours, and what is yours is mine.
> So, bring us to our place . . .
>
> > [V. i. 536-38]

Here the bracketing phrases of lines 1 and 3, it is interesting to discover, copy verbally from Psalm 45, verses 10 and 15, so that the wondrously "natural" second line is delicately enveloped in its proper atmosphere of a supernatural context. It is the way all true romance, all good comedy, should end. And could there be any more final at-one-ment? (pp. 1051-53)

In Shakespeare's play, so it seems to me, justice, charity, and wisdom are all present, centered in the Duke and richly exhibited in the plotted peace and merciful comedy which he effects. The happy ending is one which may be not inaptly described by borrowing words from Isaiah and St. Luke: there is release for the captive Claudio, a recovering of sight for the blind Angelo, a setting at liberty the bruised Mariana, and a proclaiming of the acceptable year of the lord Vincentio. The mysterious "star" mentioned in the play has called up a "shepherd" who has brought all his sheep safely home; and at the same time the great leviathan has been caught. Vincentio has shown himself the "conqueror" of rebellious wills not by the power of the sword or the whip of the magistrate, but by *hook* and by *crook*! (p. 1055)

Roy W. Battenhouse, "'Measure for Measure' and Christian Doctrine of the Atonement," in PMLA, 61, Vol. LXI, No. 4, December, 1946, pp. 1029-59.

ELIZABETH MARIE POPE　(essay date 1949)

[*Pope examines Renaissance writings on the duties and responsibilities of a ruler to ascertain the era's attitudes toward justice and mercy; she then relates her findings to* Measure for Measure *and its characters. According to the "divine right of kings" theory, sovereigns were considered God's human substitutes, di-*

vinely appointed to rule as He would. Their primary duty was the administration of justice, but they were also expected to cultivate the "virtues" and know themselves. Pope claims that the Duke's character and actions are based on these concepts. She concludes from her exploration of contemporary opinions about justice and mercy that, in Measure for Measure, *Shakespeare attempted to strengthen, clarify, and resolve the conflicting attitudes concerning the relationship between the two concepts. For additional commentary on this theme and the Duke's role in* Measure for Measure, *see the excerpts by G. G. Gervinus (1849-50), Denton J. Snider (1890), G. Wilson Knight (1930), and Roy W. Battenhouse (1946).*]

Sermons and treatises defining the status, privileges, and responsibilities of the Christian governor are plentiful enough during the sixteenth century. . . . [But in 1603 and 1604, an] outburst of concern with the theory of government seems to have been inspired primarily by the accession of James. A certain amount of such preaching and writing would probably have occurred in the arrival of any new monarch, but in this particular case, it must have been greatly stimulated by the fact that the new monarch was himself an authority on the subject, whose work was being eagerly discussed by the public and whose favour the court clergy and *literati* were naturally anxious to gain. . . .

Now *Measure for Measure* is very largely concerned with the "Prince's duty", particularly in regard to the administration of justice. At no time, perhaps, could Shakespeare have presented such a subject without reckoning to some extent on what his audience would be predisposed to think of his characters and their behaviour. But if he *did* write the play about 1603-4, he had unusually good reason to believe the subject would be popular and to consider it in terms of the contemporary doctrine of rule—even if we do not assume that he, like so many others, was seriously concerned over the problems of Christian and godly government and deliberately trying to catch the eye of the King. . . . (p. 70)

According to Renaissance theory, the authority of all civil rulers is derived from God. Hence, they may be called 'gods', as they are in Psalm lxxxii, 6, because they act as God's substitutes, "Ruling, Judging, and Punishing in God's stead, and so deserving God's name here on earth", as Bilson put it in the sermon he preached at King James's coronation. "The Prince", says Henry Smith in his *Magistrates Scripture* . . . , "is like a great Image of God, the Magistrates are like little Images of God", though he is careful to point out that they are not indeed divine: the name is given them only to remind them that they are appointed by the Lord "to rule as he would rule, judge as he would judge, correct as he would correct, reward as he would reward". This doctrine may very well explain why the Duke moves through so much of the action of *Measure for Measure* like an embodied Providence; why his character has such curiously allegorical overtones, yet never quite slips over the edge into actual allegory; and finally, why Roy Battenhouse's theory that Shakespeare subconsciously thought of him as the Incarnate Lord is at once so convincing and so unsatisfactory [see excerpt above, 1946]. Any Renaissance audience would have taken it for granted that the Duke did indeed "stand for" God, but only as any good ruler "stood for" Him; and if he behaved "like power divine" [V. i. 369], it was because that was the way a good ruler was expected to conduct himself.

Furthermore, since the ruler's authority was considered an extension of the same kind of power God delegates to parents, teachers, ministers, masters, shepherds, and husbands, all these

terms were frequently used to describe him, especially 'father' and 'shepherd'. So when the Duke compares himself to a fond father who has not disciplined his children for so long that they have run wild [I. iii. 23-8], the image probably meant rather more to a Renaissance audience than it would mean to a modern one. When later, after his discussion with the Provost, he rises at dawn to go about his work with the remark: "Look, th'unfolding star calls up the shepherd" [IV. ii. 203], one wonders if he may not be thinking of himself and his office. God was, moreover, supposed to endow rulers with what was called "sufficiency of spirit" to carry out their duties, though He might withdraw this gift if they disobeyed Him, as He withdrew it from Saul. (pp. 70-1)

In their capacity as God's substitutes, rulers have four privileges. The first is sanctity of person, especially in the case of an anointed prince. No man may raise his hand against him, or even disparage him in speech or thought. . . . [This belief] must have made Lucio's malicious gossip about the Duke appear a much more serious offence than it seems to a modern audience. Secondly, the ruler has sovereignty of power: all men must obey him without question, except when his commands directly contradict God's ordinances. Even then, disobedience must be entirely passive, and any retaliation from the authorities endured with patience—although Roman Catholics held that open rebellion was sometimes permissible when the ruler was a heretic. As the authorities in *Measure for Measure* are not heretics, this particular question does not arise: there is no doubt that the characters are legally bound to reverence and obey them. But this raised a problem which required—and received—very delicate handling. Since to yield to Angelo would mean breaking a law of God, Isabella is fully entitled to resist him; but the measures taken to circumvent him are by no means passive and might even have been considered to savour dangerously of conspiracy against a lawful magistrate if Shakespeare did not slip neatly away from the whole difficulty by making the chief conspirator the highest officer of the State himself. (p. 71)

The third privilege of rules is the right to enforce the law. In civil matters, the avenging of evil, which God has strictly forbidden to private individuals, is the office and duty of the ruler and his subordinates. . . . The further question of the ruler's title to authority in ecclesiastical as well as civil matters . . . is not brought up in *Measure for Measure.*

Finally, the ruler has the privilege of using extraordinary means. As Gentillet points out, this certainly does not imply that he is entitled to deceive, betray, and commit perjury in the manner recommended by Machiavelli, but only, in the words of William Willymat, that

> Kings, Princes, and governors do use oftentimes to use diverse causes to disguise their purposes with pretences and colours of other matters, so that the end of their drifts and secret purposes are not right seen into nor understood at the first, this to be lawful the word of God doth not deny. . . .

Hence, the Duke in *Measure for Measure* is quite justified in using disguise, applying "craft against vice" [III. ii. 277], and secretly watching Angelo much as King James advises his son in the *Basilicon Doron* to watch his own subordinates: "Delight to haunt your Session, and spy carefully their proceedings . . . to take a sharp account of every man in his office''. . . . There would have been no need to apologize for these practices to a Renaissance audience. . . . (p. 72)

But in the eyes of the Renaissance, the Christian prince had not only authority and privileges, but a clearly defined and inescapable set of duties to perform as well. The first is to remember that he is not really God, but man ''dressed in a little brief authority'' [II. ii. 118], as Isabella reminds Angelo— mere man, whom his God will in the end call strictly to account, although his subjects may not. He cannot make a single decision at which the Lord is not invisibly present and which He does not weigh and record, as He is said to do in Psalm lxxxii. . . . It is to this text (with all its associations) that Angelo is almost certainly referring when he cries at his exposure:

> I perceive your grace, like pow'r divine,
> Hath look'd upon my passes.
>
> [V. i. 369-70]

As ever in his great Taskmaster's eye, therefore, the ruler must labour to be what God would have him. To begin with, he must be sincerely religious—or, as the Duke puts it in his soliloquy at the end of Act III,

> He who the sword of heaven will bear
> Should be as holy as severe.
>
> [III. ii. 261-62]

Furthermore, he must know and be able to govern himself . . . [—a principle we find] in *Measure for Measure,* where it is most clearly stated when the Duke declares in his soliloquy that the ruler must be a man

> More nor less to others paying
> Than by self-offences weighing.
> Shame to him whose cruel striking
> Kills for faults of his own liking!
>
> [III. ii. 265-68]

He should also cultivate all the virtues to the best of his ability. . . . Therefore, when Escalus describes the Duke as ''one that above all other strifes, contended especially to know himself'', and ''a gentleman of all temperance'' [III. ii. 232-33, 237], what may seem rather faint praise to a modern reader would have been regarded as a very high tribute indeed during the Renaissance. (pp. 72-3)

But the highest and most important of the ruler's specific duties is to see well to the administration of justice. Here more than anywhere else he and his deputies must act consciously as the substitutes of God. . . . ''They should think'', [writes] Henry Smith, in his *Magistrates Scripture,* ''how Christ would judge, before they judge, because God's Law is appointed for their Law''. . . . They must not, of course, play favourites, put off decisions, allow their passions to carry them away, accept bribes, give in to fear, be ignorant, listen to slander, or refuse to hear the complaints of the oppressed. But above all, both the chief and the inferior magistrates must cherish the innocent and punish the wicked with all due severity. Bad judges, according to Wiliam Perkins' *Treatise on Christian Equity and Moderation,* are of two kinds: the first are

> such men, as by a certain foolish kind of pity
> are so carried away, that would have nothing
> but *mercy, mercy,* and would . . . have the
> extremity of the law executed on no man. . . .

The second kind are

such men as have nothing in their mouths, but the *law,* the *law:* and *Justice, Justice:* in the meantime forgetting that Justice always shakes hands with her sister mercy, and that all laws allow a mitigation. . . .

Mercy and justice, he goes on to say,

> are the two pillars, that uphold the throne of
> the Prince: as you cannot hold mercy, where
> justice is banished, so cannot you keep Justice
> where mercy is exiled: and as mercy without
> Justice, is foolish pity, so Justice, without mercy,
> is cruelty. . . . (p. 74)

Allusions to the measure-for-measure passage [from *Luke* VI. 36-42] occasionally crop up in the studies of rule, just as references to the doctrine of rule keep recurring in discussions of the measure-for-measure passage. . . . Evidently the passage was one which writers often recalled when working on the doctrine of rule, and frequently brought to the attention of their readers. But Shakespeare would have had special reason to take note of it. The heroine of his play is a private individual wrestling with the very issues raised by the passage: judgment, tolerance, mercy, retaliation in kind, and Christian forgiveness. His hero and his villain are primarily concerned with the same issues as they appear on a different level—to the holder of public office. His villain has, in addition, just those deficiencies of character which form the clearest and most commonly observed link between the doctrine of rule and the commentaries on the passage. And so, centred as *Measure for Measure* is on the very points at which the two are either parallel or interlocked, it is hardly surprising to find that Shakespeare was apparently influenced to some extent by both.

His treatment of the initial situation seems to have been based in part on the crude but picturesque contrast which the Renaissance theorists so often drew between the two types of bad magistrate. The Duke, at the beginning of the play, would be recognized at once as the type who has failed because he was too merciful to enforce the laws properly. . . . The Duke is essentially a wise and noble man who has erred from an excess of good will; he has put an end to his foolishness before the action proper begins, and so can step gracefully into the role of hero and good ruler; but Shakespeare does not disguise the fact that he has been wrong: he himself frankly describes his laxity as a 'vice' [III. ii. 270], and as such any Renaissance audience would certainly consider it.

Angelo, on the other hand, is a perfect case-study in the opposite weakness. Whatever he afterwards becomes, he is not from the first the ordinary venal judge, who is ignorant or cowardly, refuses to hear complaints (for he listens to Isabella), or takes bribes (for his indignation when she unfortunately uses the word sounds quite real). . . . But he is the epitome of all the men who ''have nothing in their mouths but the *law,* the *law:* and *Justice, Justice,* in the meantime forgetting that Justice always shakes hands with her sister mercy''. This harshness Shakespeare traces to the personal flaw described in the measure-for-measure passage: the bitter and uncharitable narrowness in judging others that springs from a refusal to recognize or deal with one's own faults. Unlike the Duke, Angelo has not contended especially to know himself; he has no real conception of the potentialities of his own character. As a result, he thinks so well of himself that he neither has any defence against sudden overwhelming temptation nor possesses the humility and comprehension necessary to deal properly with Claudio.

His treatment of Claudio is from the first inexcusable, even by the strict standards of the Renaissance. For clemency in this particular case would certainly have had ''a good foundation upon reason and equity'' [Perkins]: Claudio and Juliet are betrothed; they fully intend to marry; they are penitent; and the law was drowsy and neglected when they broke it. Furthermore, Claudio comes of a good family; and his fault is, after all, a very natural one. Shakespeare wisely leaves these last points to be made by Escalus and the Provost, both kind, sensible men who represent the normal point of view and whose support of Claudio is therefore significant. But Isabella cannot treat the offence lightly without weakening both the dignity of her calling and the force of her horror at Angelo's proposal. So in the first scene where she implores him for her brother's life, she bases her plea chiefly on modulations and variations of the two great Christian arguments . . . encountered in discussions of the measure-for-measure passage, interwoven with appropriate material from the doctrine of rule. The first is most clearly stated when, after pointing out that clemency is considered a virtue in the ruler, she begs him to remember that we must be merciful, as the Father was also merciful in redeeming us [II. ii. 73-9]. . . . And then, afer reminding him that a ruler is only a man dressed in a little brief authority, she urges him to think of his own faults before he condemns Claudio's [II. ii. 136-41]. . . . But it should be noted that she does not threaten him with retaliation in kind for his cruelty. Indeed, in her eagerness to show him that it *is* cruelty and to convince him that he ought to do as he would be done by, she argues rather that she in his place would not be so severe [II. ii. 66-9]. . . . (pp. 75-7)

Her problem is not, however, to be quite such a simple one. . . . If she is truly so merciful, [Angelo] implies, she should be willing to rescue Claudio even at the expense of breaking what the Renaissance regarded as a most sacred law of God, and one doubly binding upon her because she is not only a virgin but a novice: if she refuses,

> Were you not then as cruel as the sentence
> That you have slandered so?
>
> [II. iv. 109-10]

The modern reader may find it difficult not to echo this question, particularly when Claudio himself breaks down and adds the weight of his own desperate pleading to Angelo's arguments. Why, afer all her talk of charity and forbearance, should Isabella not only decline to save her brother's life by an act of generosity, but condemn him so unsparingly for begging her to do so? When, however, we remember the limitations which Renaissance doctrine set on both charity and forbearance, we have no right to assume that Shakespeare is deliberately and cynically implying that his heroine is, in her own way, as narrow and cold as his villain. He seems rather to be trying to emphasize and illustrate the familiar tenet that neither charity nor forbearance must be carried to the point of permitting or condoning outrage. Like the Duke on the public level, Isabella is not entitled to let Angelo and Claudio use her mercy as their bawd; and, as the commentators on the measure-for-measure passage had made clear, her ''duty is not to wink at them, but to take notice of them, and to show open dislike of them'' [Perkins]. (pp. 77-8)

The conspiracy which follows also has its place in that pattern. It takes the form of a deliberate infliction upon Angelo of like

for like, as the Duke is at pains to inform the audience in his soliloquy:

> So disguise shall, by th' disguised
> Pay with falsehood false exacting
>
> [III. ii. 280-81]

—offence punishing offence just as it is said to do in the measure-for-measure passage and the commentaries upon it. It should be noted, however, that the responsibility for devising and managing the whole plot rests on the shoulders of the Duke, who has a ruler's right to see to retaliation in kind and a ruler's privilege of using extraordinary means to ensure the success of a worthy cause. . . . Unlike the Duke, [Isabella] acts from no special desire to pay Angelo back in his own coin; it is only afterwards, when she hears the news of Claudio's death by his treachery, that she breaks down and very understandably cries for personal and immediate revenge: ''Oh, I will to him and pluck out his eyes!'' [IV. iii. 119]. The calmer Duke then very properly persuades her that she ought instead to turn her cause over to the civil authorities:

> And you shall have your bosom on this wretch,
> Grace of the Duke, revenges to your heart,
> And general honour.
>
> [IV. iii. 134-36]

The audience at the first performance of the play probably took this promise at its face-value, as a prediction that Angelo was to suffer full legal punishment for his offences in the trial to come. Nor would they have disapproved. . . . Although he has not actually succeeded in doing the worst he intended to do, there is still a heavy count against him: attempted seduction, abuse of his authority, deception of his prince, and treachery of the meanest kind; while if he *had* done what he himself and every character on the stage except the Duke believes that he has, there was nothing to be said against the Duke's sentence . . . :

> We do condemn thee to the very block
> Where Claudio stooped to death, and with like haste.
>
> [V. i. 414-15]

The audience, knowing what they knew, probably did not expect that the execution would really take place; but they can hardly have been prepared for what actually follows. (pp. 78-9)

The cruelty of [Mariana's appeal to Isabella] is obvious; and the natural, the instinctive, and (we must remember) the allowed reply to it is implicit in the shocked exclamation of the Duke:

> Against all sense you do importune her.
> Should she kneel down, in mercy of this fact,
> Her brother's ghost his paved bed would break,
> And take her hence in horror.
>
> [V. i. 433-36]

Then Mariana cries out to Isabella again—and she kneels, not in silence, which is all Mariana dares to ask for, but generously to make the best case she can for Angelo. Her act is not natural; it is not (as the Duke has carefully pointed out) even reasonable: it is sheer, reckless forgiveness of the kind Christ advocates in the Sermon on the Mount—the great pronouncement which in Luke immediately precedes and forms part of the measure-for-measure passage. And like Christ, Shakespeare contrasts this sort of forgiveness with another. Mariana is certainly more praiseworthy than the 'sinners' described by the Lord, for Angelo has treated her very badly; but her mercy to him resembles theirs in that it springs primarily from preference and affection: she loves her lover (to quote the common sixteenth-century translation of Luke vi. 32) and she hopes for something again— the renewal of his devotion and a happy marriage with him. Hence, however gracious and commendable her conduct may be, it differs markedly from that of Isabella, who has nothing to sustain her but the conviction that she *must* be merciful and the memory of what she had promised Angelo on the strength of it. And then, almost before the audience at the first performance had time to catch its breath, the Duke, having summoned Claudio and revealed the truth, proceeds not only to pardon him, but to let off Angelo, Lucio, and Barnardine as well, with penalties entirely disproportionate to what their conduct deserved by ordinary Renaissance standards. (p. 79)

[When] we recall the special difficulties and defects of Renaissance doctrine, it seems at least possible that the conclusion of *Measure for Measure* may rather represent a deliberate effort—perhaps a little clumsy, certainly romantic—to "do something" about that disturbing discrepancy between the concepts of religious mercy and secular justice which we find in the commentaries on the measure-for-measure passage and again in the studies of rule. Like the theorists, Shakespeare was apparently prepared to concede that the private Christian should not (in the name of mercy) weakly condone every form of injustice and oppression, and may, if necessary, invoke secular authority to defend what he knows to be right. But it is not enough merely to wash his hands of personal revenge, and— let the secular authority do the dirty work for him. Nor should the secular authority himself forget that "judging as Christ would judge" means something more than weighing each case according to common sense and ordinary good will. He need not make a scarecrow of the law: he must be vigilant to suppress or prevent disorder and evil; and he should see to it that the innocent are properly protected—that Isabella's name is cleared by her traducer; that Barnardine is committed to the friar instead of being turned loose on society; that Claudio makes amends to Juliet, Angelo to Mariana, Lucio to the girl he has wronged. He may even, to a certain extent, use retaliation in kind, or the threat of retaliation in kind, to bring malefactors to their senses: it is no accident that Angelo is paid with falsehood false exacting, or finds himself sentenced to the very block where Claudio stooped to death, and with like haste. But his primary duty is, like God, to show mercy whenever he possibly can, even when the fault is disgusting and the criminal despicable: to remember that Lucio's slanders hurt chiefly the Duke's own personal feelings; that Barnardine is a mere animal,

> A creature unprepared, unmeet for death;
> And to transport him in the mind he is
> Were damnable;
>
> [IV. iii. 67-9]

that Angelo has been blasted and shamed out of his appalling complacency, and may, as Mariana pleads: "become much more the better / For being a little bad" [V. i. 440-41]. It is the difference between the "Like doth quit like" [V. i. 411] with which the Duke begins his sentence on his deputy and the "Well, Angelo, your evil quits you well" [V. i. 496], with which he concludes it.

In all this, Shakespeare is not so much rejecting the ordinary Christian doctrine of the Renaissance as clarifying it, strengthening it, and holding it true to its own deepest implications. (pp. 79-80)

> *Elizabeth Marie Pope, "The Renaissance Background of 'Measure for Measure'," in* Shakespeare

Survey: An Annual Survey of Shakespearian Study and Production, *Vol. 2, 1949, pp. 66-82.*

E. C. PETTET   (essay date 1949)

[*Pettet contends that the cynicism, frustration, and "unresolved conflict" in the artistry of the problem plays reveal the uncertainty with which Shakespeare attempted to revise the romantic vision of his early comedies. He interprets* Measure, *as well as the other problem plays, as transitional works in Shakespeare's development—dramas which include intimations of the darker vision in his later tragedies, framed in the structure of the early comedies, thus accounting for their ambivalent qualities. As an example, Pettet notes that Angelo is initially complex, realistic, and convincing, but is later distorted to meet the exigencies of a romantic plot. According to Pettet, romance was traditionally "framed for lyricism" and concerned with the exalting quality of love; he concludes that, because romantic conventions cannot adequately present serious philosophical concepts,* Measure for Measure *and the other "dark" comedies—*All's Well That Ends Well *and* Troilus and Cressida—*fail as works of art. Other interpretations of* Measure for Measure *as a problem play appear in the essays by Frederick S. Boas (1896), William Witherle Lawrence (1931), H. B. Charlton (1937), E.M.W. Tillyard (1949), Ernest Schanzer (1963), and Hal Gelb (1971).*]

The mood of disgust and disillusionment in *Measure for Measure* . . . has an obvious reference to romantic love. In this play Shakespeare passes beyond scepticism to a cynical and complete disregard of the values and attitudes that had been cherished by romance. Nowhere in the oppressive sultry atmosphere of *Measure for Measure* is there a breath of those delicate zephyrs of love that fan through the earlier comedies. . . . The background, always obtrusive, is a grey, fly-blown one of wenching, 'French crowns', and brothels.

However, this sour spirit of disillusionment and cynicism is only one of the salient features of the 'dark' comedies. Another, no less striking, is the sense of strain, frustration, unresolved conflict in their artistry. We feel that, for once in his life, Shakespeare was uncertain of his medium, that he was struggling, not always with success, to refashion it so that it might correspond with radical changes in his vision.

This cleavage between Shakespeare's mind and art, which is a flaw running through [*Measure for Measure, Troilus and Cressida,* and *All's Well That Ends Well*], stands out conspicuously in *Measure for Measure,* a work which, while it could only have been written by a great poet, certainly falls short of great poetry and great drama. There is, for instance, something peculiarly unsatisfying in the play's treatment of evil. At times Angelo's unbridled lust is impressive and convincing, a disruptive, elemental force that threatens to destroy Angelo himself and spread misery and suffering around him. . . . Yet this passion, at once animal and sophisticated, that might have been one of the lawless, egotistical impulses that devastate the world of the tragedies, is trimmed and adulterated to the needs of an artificial, romantic plot—to the safe, all-knowing supervision of the disguised Duke . . . ; to the fantastic deception by which Mariana substitutes herself for Isabella; and to the conventional happy ending where Angelo is forgiven and tamely paired off with the woman he has so shamefully treated. We feel, and with something of a sense of having been cheated, that what has happened is after all just a game and not to be taken too seriously. . . . (pp. 156-58)

But why, it may be objected, does the wickedness in such romantic plays as *The Two Gentlemen of Verona* and *Much*

Ado About Nothing not affect us in the same way? Why are we never tempted for a single moment to take these plays seriously? Why do we swallow their wildly romantic stories and conventional endings without the slightest sense of a cheat?

The answer to such questions lies in the difference between the characters of Proteus and Don John on the one hand and Angelo on the other. Don John and Proteus are simply puppets, and the evil in each of them has no significance except as a motive in the plot. But Angelo—at least in the first part of *Measure for Measure*—is a convincing character in whom Shakespeare has represented a subtle, complicated working of lust; and Angelo is quickened into life precisely because Shakespeare was vitally interested in that form of wickedness. But barely has life been breathed into Angelo when he has to be distorted to the necessities of a romantic story. In Proteus and Don John there is no such sense of distortion or arrested life, since they are kept throughout in strict subordination to the needs of an incredible story.

Nor, so long as Shakespeare clung to the romantic type of plot, could this frustration that we discern in the treatment of Angelo be easily avoided, for, to be significant in art, evil and the suffering and misery it produces must be terrifyingly near to the stuff of real life. Even when, as in the Shakespearean tragedies, evil is largely transformed into poetic symbolism it must remain rooted in human nature and move in a credible world that is parallel, for all its simplification and heightened intensity, with the real world. The world created by romance, on the other hand, was a realm of unashamed, and often child-like, make-believe. Never had it accommodated more than one important human emotion, and even that had been manipulated to a highly artificial and idealised form.

Moreover this preoccupation with the problem of evil that we glimpse in the figure of Angelo is only one symptom of Shakespeare's changing outlook, which by the turn of the century was becoming more reflective, philosophic and visionary. Time and again in *Measure for Measure* (as in *All's Well* and *Troilus and Cressida*) we come across passages that reveal new impulses of interest and awareness striving for poetic expression. Lines like the following, for instance, might easily have come from one of the great tragedies:

> Merciful heaven,
> Thou rather with thy sharp and sulphurous bolt
> Splitt'st the unwedgeable and gnarled oak
> Than the soft myrtle; but man, proud man,
> Drest in a little brief authority,
> Most ignorant of what he's most assured,
> His glassy essence, like an angry ape,
> Plays such fantastic tricks before high heaven
> As make the angels weep.
>
> [II. ii. 114-22]
> (pp. 158-59)

Such passages are the 'splendid poetry' that every critic wishes to salvage from these dark, enigmatic and rarely acted comedies. Torn from their context they are indeed magnificently impressive. But if we listen to them in the run of the play in which they occur they produce a slight discord. When Macbeth breaks out into 'She should have died hereafter' [*Macbeth*, V. v. 17] or Cleopatra into 'Give me my robe, put on my crown' [*Anthony and Cleopatra*, V. ii. 280], we are under the spell of perfect art: the effect of the words is direct, complete, spontaneous because the words are the essence of the speaker and the speaker a convincing symbol of human experience and

human nature. But when Isabella utters such a speech as the one quoted above we are teased by an irrepressible scepticism that not all Shakespeare's spell can charm away. Could such a shallow, cold-blooded creature as Isabella, aware only of an abstract and formal virtue, ever conceivably utter lines like those, so warm, pitiful and extensive in vision? Could the Duke whom we observe in the rest of the play have uttered such a speech as 'Be absolute for death' [III. i. 5], or was Shakespeare, for the moment, merely using him as a mask? (pp. 159-60)

So long as Shakespeare's mind and sensibility were predominantly lyrical, aerated with wit and a sense of humour, romance was a happy medium in which to work. By its long tradition romance was framed for lyricism, especially of love, while it lent itself admirably, through dramatic adaptation, to wit and comedy of a certain kind. But for the sensibility, thought, and vision that were soon to be expressed in the great tragedies romance was, in its general run, an inadequate and unsuitable mode. In spite of this, whether through conservatism, force of habit, the pressure of keeping his company constantly supplied with plays, or a combination of all these forces, Shakespeare attempted for a time to work inside the old romantic type of story, even when his dynamic poetic impulses were radically changing. Here is a discrepancy that offers us an invaluable clue to the elucidation of one of the mysteries of these three comedies—their failure as works of art. (p. 160)

> E. C. Pettet, "The 'Dark' Comedies," in his Shakespeare and the Romance Tradition, *Staples Press, 1949, pp. 136-60.*

E.M.W. TILLYARD (essay date 1949)

[*Tillyard, whose* Shakespeare's History Plays *(1944) is considered a leading example of historical criticism, studies another group of dramas in his* Shakespeare's Problem Plays *(1949). He argues that in* All's Well That Ends Well, Measure for Measure, Hamlet, *and* Troilus and Cressida *Shakespeare combined "a strong awareness of evil" with his interest in "religious dogma" and abstract speculation about human nature. However, Tillyard states that these interests are not fully absorbed into the design of the four plays, because Shakespeare's religious speculations and explorations of the human mind are presented for their own sake rather than as part of a "great overriding theme." He also asserts that the problem plays exhibit a sense of real life without supplying the "sharp clarity of intention" expected in great art, and that they were developed simply to identify and define the questions they raise without offering any specific solutions. In his commentary on* Measure for Measure, *Tillyard claims that no single critical approach provides an inclusive interpretation of the play; he especially challenges R. W. Chambers (1937) for his positive assessment of Isabella and the denouement, as well as the allegorical analyses of the characters and dramatic action (see excerpts above by G. Wilson Knight and Roy W. Battenhouse, 1930 and 1946). Tillyard contends that the problem in* Measure for Measure *is one of stylistic inconsistency, which he identifies as a contradictory change in tone from the realism in the first half of the play to the folklore and allegory of the second half. Basing his conclusion on William Witherle Lawrence's source study (see excerpt above, 1931), Tillyard conjectures that Shakespeare recognized the dramatic possibilities in Whetstone's play, but his alterations—specifically his decision to save Isabella's chastity by having her refuse Angelo—created a stylistic transformation from the poetic to the prosaic that resulted in "an artistic breach of internal harmony." Additional discussion of* Measure for Measure *as a problem play can be found in the essays by Frederick S. Boas (1896), H. B. Charlton (1937), E. C. Pettet (1949), Ernest Schanzer (1963), and Hal Gelb (1971).*]

Troilus and Cressida, All's Well That Ends Well, and *Measure for Measure* have been called "dark comedies" and "problem comedies," while the first has been called a "satirical comedy." Though not fond of any of these names, I recognize that the plays make a group and that a common name is needed. As a choice of evils "problem comedies" gives least offence. But, finding, however reluctantly, that *Hamlet* goes with these plays (or at any rate with *Troilus and Cressida*) more aptly than with the three undoubted tragedies usually grouped with it, I cannot use "problem comedies" for all four plays; and "problem plays" is the only available term.

It is anything but a satisfactory term, and I wish I knew a better. All I can do now is to warn the reader that I use it vaguely and equivocally; as a matter of convenience. . . . To achieve the necessary elasticity and inclusiveness, consider the connotations of the parallel term "problem child."

There are at least two kinds of problem child: first the genuinely abnormal child, whom no efforts will ever bring back to normality; and second the child who is interesting and complex rather than abnormal, apt indeed to be a problem for parents and teachers but destined to fulfilment in the larger scope of adult life. Now *All's Well* and *Measure for Measure* are like the first problem child: there is something radically schizophrenic about them. *Hamlet* and *Troilus and Cressida* are like the second problem child, full of interest and complexity but divided within themselves only in the eyes of those who have misjudged them. To put the difference in another way, *Hamlet* and *Troilus and Cressida* are problem plays because they deal with and display interesting problems; *All's Well* and *Measure for Measure* because they *are* problems. (pp. 3-4)

Many readers have found in the Problem Plays a spirit of gloom, disillusion, and morbidity that exceeds dramatic propriety and demands some extrinsic explanation in Shakespeare's private life at the time. Others on the contrary think that such readers have unconsciously begun from Shakespeare's supposed biography and have insisted on reading that biography into this group of plays. . . . I take it with those who think such personal explanations superfluous, or at least too uncertain to be worth anything. (pp. 4-5)

However, though it may be vain to conjecture from external evidence how Shakespeare's emotions were behaving at this period, we can infer from the plays themselves that he was especially interested in certain matters. Some of these occur in all plays, some in at least three; and, when pointed out, they will serve to make a genuine group of the four plays which so far I have separated into two pairs.

First, Shakespeare is concerned throughout with either religious dogma or abstract speculation or both. It may be retorted that so he was also when he wrote his later tragedies. Yet there is a difference, in that dogma and speculation are less completely absorbed into the general substance of the Problem Plays; they are felt rather more for their own and rather less for the drama's sake, as if, in this form at least, they were new and urgent in Shakespeare's mind, demanding at this point statement and articulation rather than solution and absoprtion into other material. (pp. 5-6)

Thoughtfulness about man's estate and about religious dogma must be serious to be worth anything, but it need not be pessimistic. And the mood of these plays is serious but not black. . . . [The plays] are powerfully united by a serious tone amounting at times to sombreness; they show a strong awareness of evil, without being predominantly pessimistic. (p. 7)

Now in the Problem Plays Shakespeare was interested in observing and recording the details of human nature for its own sake in a way not found elsewhere. It is as if at that time he was freshly struck by the fascination of the human spectacle as a spectacle and was more content than at other times merely to record his observation without subordinating it to a great overriding theme. . . . Hamlet, Troilus, Bertram, and Angelo are all of them characters embodying their author's powerful interest and pleasure in the varieties and the possibilities of the human mind.

It is these two interests—in speculative thought and in the working of the human mind—pursued largely for their own sake that partly characterize the Problem Plays. And from them spring characteristic virtues and defects. They create a peculiar sense of real life but they prevent the sharp clarity of intention we are apt to demand of very great art. (p. 8)

Much has been added in recent years to our knowledge of Shakespeare's thought, of his imagery, and of his contemporary setting; and it should all be to the good. The danger is that it should blind us to the poetic logic of the actual text. For instance, in learning that a certain type of image occurs frequently in a play we may easily forget that frequency, a mere numerical thing, may mean little compared with poetic emphasis: that a certain type of image occurring once but in a poetically emphatic place may have more weight than another type that occurs ten times in less emphatic places. . . .

Some of the criticism of the Problem Plays seems to me to incur the above danger by abstracting the thought too crudely from its dramatic context. It may not be for me to criticize, since I have probably done the same in writing of Shakespeare's History Plays. But for my present treatment I have tried to follow the poetic and not the mere abstracted significances and to allow the poetic or dramatic effect to dictate the relative emphasis. (p. 13)

Measure for Measure has been singularly apt to provoke its critics to excess; and in the most different manners. Earlier critics vented their excesses on two of the main characters, Isabella and the Duke. Later critics have, in reaction to the earlier, gone to two different extremes. Some, in righteous and justified defence of the play's heroine, have refused to see any fault in the play at all; others, rightly recognizing a strong religious tone, have sought to give the whole play an allegorical and religious explanation. This is not to say that the above critics have not written well of the play. Many of them have; but nearly all have yoked their truths to strong and palpable errors. (p. 124)

I begin with an earlier type of criticism. To an age whose typical mistake in criticism was to judge the persons of Elizabethan plays by the standards of actual life it is very natural that the Duke should be offensive. He is an eavesdropper; he chose as his deputy a man whom he knew to have behaved shabbily to his betrothed lady; and he displayed the utmost cruelty in concealing from Isabella for longer than was strictly necessary the news that her brother still lived. Certainly, as a real person, he is a most unsympathetic character; and though we may feel wiser than the Victorians and find no difficulty in the Duke as an allegorical figure or as a convenient stage machine, we can understand Victorian resentment. With Isabella the case is different. Here is a character who, in those parts of the play where she really counts, will stand up to the test of the most rigid realism; and yet how they hated her!— this hard, smug, self-righteous virgin, preferring her own precious chastity to the actual life of a far more sympathetic person, her brother, and then, having got the utmost kick out of her militant virginity, having it both ways by consenting to marry the Duke at the end of the play. (pp. 124-25).

Why was it that many readers mistook [Isabella's nature and motives]? Partly, I think, because of an unfortunate habit of treating Shakespeare's heroines as a repertory of ideal brides, quite detached, poor things, from their native dramatic settings. . . . Now Isabella comes off very ill on such a criterion. The husbands of such female saints or martyrs as were married have, as far as I know, never been the object of much envy; the role of martyr-consort is a hard one. And such would have been that of Isabella's husband. And so the day-dreaming bride-pickers very naturally found her distasteful and turned and rent her. And yet, in defending her, we must not forget that in the play Isabella marries and in so doing makes herself the more open to irrelevant comparisons. Her enemies have at least that excuse for their attacks; and her friends, like R. W. Chambers [see excerpt above, 1937], however well justified in defending her behaviour towards her brother, have erred in justifying the sum total of her conduct.

This brings me to the other type of error, which is roughly that of seeing nothing wrong with the play. There are several ways of establishing it. One (and I here think mainly of R. W. Chambers) is to begin by making hay of the mythical sorrows of Shakespeare and of the mythical hypocrisy of Isabella and to go on to prove that the high ethical standards set in the first half are maintained and carried through in the second. And the proof can be fascinating. Nothing could be more ingenious and plausible than Chambers's notion of Shakespeare's keeping Isabella ignorant of her brother's survival and filled with justified fury at Angelo's having done him to death, in order that her powers of forgiveness might be tested to the uttermost when she brings herself to join Mariana in pleading for Angelo's life. And how much more creditable to Shakespeare and pleasanter to most of us, to whom his credit is very dear, if he did in fact keep Isabella in the dark for so high and moral a motive and not merely to pander to that appetite for ingenious plot-complications and improbable and strained moments of suspense which was one of the regrettable qualities of an Elizabethan audience. Nothing, too, could help to colour the last part of the play more happily than a truly heartfelt and impressive repentance on the part of Angelo. And, relying on the undoubted truth that Angelo does profess himself very repentant, Chambers does duly find Angelo's repentance very impressive.

The other way to find the play faultless is to cut out all the Bradleian character-stuff from the start and to go straight to ideas or allegory or symbols. There is much thought and much orthodox piety in *Measure for Measure,* and during the time when Shakespeare was writing the Problem Plays he had the Morality form rather prominently in his mind. That in some sort the relation of justice and mercy is treated, that Angelo may stand at one time for the letter of the law or for the old law before Christian liberty and at another for a Morality figure of False seeming, that the Duke contains hints of Heavenly Grace and that he embodies a higher justice than mere legality, that Isabella is Mercy as well as Chastity—all these matters may very likely be concluded from the text and they may help us to understand the play. But they are conclusions which are ineffective in just the same way in which Chambers's theories on Isabella's ignorance and Angelo's repentance are ineffective: they have little to do with the total play, however justi-

fiable they may appear by these and those words or passages in abstraction.

Now the doctrinal or allegorical significance of *Measure for Measure* culminates in the last long scene. And this scene does not really succeed either seen or read. Its main effect is that of labour. Shakespeare took trouble; he complicated enormously; he brought a vast amount of dramatic matter together. . . . In the strain the supposed subtle reason for Isabella's ignorance of Claudio's survival goes unnoticed, while Angelo's repentance is a perfunctory affair amidst all the other crowded doings. Similarly, after reading the play through, how little aware we are of any sustained allegorical motive. Even if the Duke stands for Providence, he does not begin to interpose till after the first and incomparably the better half of the play. (pp. 126-29)

The simple and ineluctable fact is that the tone in the first half of the play is frankly, acutely human and quite hostile to the tone of allegory or symbol. And, however much the tone changes in the second half, nothing in the world can make an allegorical interpretation poetically valid throughout.

Recent critics, in their anxiety to correct old errors, have in fact gone too far in the other direction and ignored one of the prime facts from which those old errors had their origin: namely that the play is not of a piece but changes its nature half-way through. It was partly through their correct perception of something being wrong that some earlier critics felt justified in making the Isabella of the first half of the play the scapegoat of the play's imperfections. (pp. 129-30)

Briefly, the inconsistency is the most serious and complete possible, being one of literary style. Up to III. 1. 151, when the Duke enters to interrupt the passionate conversation between Claudio and Isabella on the conflicting claims of his life and her chastity, the play is predominantly poetical, the poetry being, it is true, set off by passages of animated prose. And the poetry is of that kind of which Shakespeare is the great master, the kind that seems extremely close to the business of living, to the problem of how to function as a human being. One character after another is pictured in a difficult, a critical, position, and yet one which all of us can imagine ourselves to share; and the poetry answers magnificently to this penetrating sense of human intimacy. Up to the above point the Duke, far from being guide and controller, has been a mere conventional piece of dramatic convenience for creating the setting for the human conflicts. Beyond that he is just an onlooker. And, as pointed out above, any symbolic potentialities the characters may possess are obscured by the tumult of passions their minds present to us. From the Duke's entry at III. 1. 151 to the end of the play there is little poetry of any kind and scarcely any of the kind just described. . . . Where in the first half the most intense writing was poetical, in the second half it is comic or at least prosaic. While the elaborate last scene . . . is, for all its poetical pretensions, either a dramatic failure or at best a Pyrrhic victory, it is the comedy of Lucio and the Duke, of Pompey learning the mystery of the executioner from Abhorson, of Barnardine (for Shakespeare somehow contrives to keep his gruesomeness this side the comic), that makes the second half of the play possible to present on the stage with any success at all. And the vehicle of this comedy is prose, which, excellent though it is, cannot be held consistent with the high poetry of the first half. Another evident sign of tension relaxed in the second half of the play is the increased use of rhyme. . . .

[There] are many short passages, like this soliloquy of the Duke after hearing Lucio's scandalous remarks on his character . . . :

> No might nor greatness in mortality
> Can censure 'scape; back-wounding calumny
> The whitest virtue strikes. What king so strong
> Can tie the gall up in the sland'rous tongue?
>
> [III. ii. 185-88]

or the couplet containing the title of the play:

> Haste still pays haste, and leisure answers leisure;
> Like doth quit like, and measure still for measure.
>
> [V. i. 410-11]

Here an antique quaintness excuses the lack of poetic intensity. Most characterstic of this quality in the last half of the play are the Duke's octosyllabic couplets at the end of III. 2:

> He who the sword of heaven wll bear
> Should be as holy as severe:
> Pattern in himself to know,
> Grace to stand, and virtue go;
> More nor less to others paying
> Than by self-offences weighing—
>
> [III. ii. 261-66]

and the rest. Far from being spurious, the Duke's couplets in their antique stiffness and formality agree with the whole trend of the play's second half in relaxing the poetical tension and preparing for a more abstract form of drama.

A similar inconsistency extends to some of the characters. From being a minor character in the first half, with no influence on the way human motives are presented, the Duke becomes the dominant character in the second half and the one through whose mind human motives are judged. (pp. 130-32)

Nowhere does the change in the Duke's position show so strikingly as in Isabella. There is no more independent character in Shakespeare than the Isabella of the first half of the play: and independent in two senses. The essence of her disposition is decision and the acute sense of her own independent and inviolate personality. . . . At the beginning of the third act, when she has learnt Angelo's full villainy, her nature is working at the very height of its accustomed freedom. She enters almost choked with bitter fury at Angelo, in the mood for martyrdom and feeling that Claudio's mere life is a trifle before the mighty issues of right and wrong. Her scorn of Claudio's weakness is dramatically definitive and perfect. To his pathetic pleas, "Sweet sister, let me live" [III. i. 132] . . . , comes, as it must, her own, spontaneous retort from the depth of her being,

> O you beast,
> O faithless coward, O dishonest wretch!
> Wilt thou be made a man out of my vice?
> Is't not a kind of incest to take life
> From thine own sister's shame? What should I think?
> Heaven shield my mother play'd my father fair,
> For such a warped slip of wilderness
> Ne'er issued from his blood. Take my defiance.
> Die, perish! Might but my bending down
> Reprieve thee from thy fate, it should proceed.
> I'll pray a thousand prayers for thy death,
> No word to save thee.
>
> [III. i. 135-46]

That is the true Isabella, and whether or not we like that kind of woman is beside the point. But immediately after her speech, at line 152, the Duke takes charge and she proceeds to exchange her native ferocity for the hushed and submissive tones of a well-trained confidential secretary. To the Duke's inquiry of how she will content Angelo and save her brother she replies in coolly rhetorical prose:

> I am now going to resolve him: I had rather
> my brother die by the law than my son should
> be unlawfully born. But, O, how much is the
> good duke deceived in Angelo! If ever he return
> and I can speak to him, I will open my lips in
> vain or discover his government.
>
> [III. i. 189-94]

But such coolness is warm compared with her tame acquiescence in the Duke's plan for her to pretend to yield to Angelo and then to substitute Mariana:

> The image of it gives me content already, and
> I trust it will grow to a most prosperous perfection.
>
> [III. i. 259-60]

To argue, as has been argued, that the plan, by Elizabethan standards, was very honourable and sensible and that of course Isabella would have accepted it gladly is to substitute the criterion of ordinary practical common sense for that of the drama. . . . [Isabella] has been bereft of significant action . . . , and she has turned into a mere tool of the Duke. In the last scene she does indeed bear some part in the action; but her freedom of utterance is so hampered by misunderstanding and mystification that she never speaks with her full voice: she is not, dramatically, the same Isabella. That the Duke is in his way impressive, that he creates a certain moral atmosphere, serious and yet tolerant, in the second half of the play need not be denied; yet that atmosphere can ill bear comparison with that of the early part of the play. To this fact Lucio is the chief witness. He is now the livest figure and the one who does most to keep the play from quite falling apart, and he almost eludes the Duke's control. He is as it were a minor Saturnian deity who has somehow survived into the iron age of Jupiter; and a constant reminder that the Saturnian age was the better of the two.

The fact of the play's inconsistency, then, seems to me undoubted: the reason for it must be conjectural, yet conjectural within not excessive bounds of probability. I believe it may be found through considering Shakespeare's originals. (pp. 133-36)

There is a lot about justice in [Whetstone's] play including disquisitions on the true meaning of what Shakespeare called measure for measure. But there is more about the wickedness of bribery in the government and the need for the magistrate to be a pattern of virtue. It is in the narrative that the theme of what true justice is predominates. That Shakespeare was drawn to that theme, and possibly in the first stages of roughing out his plot, may be conjectured.

But there were things in Whetstone's play that kindled his imagination more warmly than the theory of justice, whether derived from narrative or drama. . . . However feeble the [best scene in *Promos and Cassandra*], it does present to the reader or the recaster certain simple and basic human passions and conflicts: Promos's dilemma betwen justice and lust; Andrugio's instinct to save his life at almost any cost; Cassandra's dilemma between the desires to save her brother's life and to save her honour. The human interest and the dramatic possibilities of these passions and conflicts kindled Shakespeare's imagination and he proceeded in the first half of *Measure for Measure* to give his version of them.

But in so doing he altered Whetstone in one very important matter: he made his heroine resist the appeal of her brother to save his life. In accordance with this change he turns his heroine into a much more decided and uncompromising person. In Whetstone the chief dramatic interest is the heroine's divided mind, her struggle with herself: Shakespeare's heroine has a whole mind and has no struggle with herself; all her struggles are outside, with her brother and her would-be seducer. It looks as if Shakespeare had been carried away by his conception of Isabella without realizing the dramatic difficulties it involved. Whetstone's Cassandra, however inferior in execution to Shakespeare's Isabella, was through her very weakness a more flexible dramatic character. . . . Shakespeare by altering the plot and by recreating his heroine, however superb the immediate result, could only ruin the play as a whole. Not having been violated, Isabella has no call to meditate suicide. Not having become Angelo's wife, she has no reason to recommend him to mercy as well as to justice. Her one possible line of action was to appeal outright to the Duke; and that would be to sabotage most of the substance of the last half of the play. With significant action denied to Isabella, Shakespeare must have seen that to carry the play through in the spirit in which he began it was impossible; and after III. 1. 151 he threw in his hand.

Whether in the second half Shakespeare reverted to an original plan from which he had played truant, or whether he began to improvise when he found himself stuck, we shall never know. But conjecture may be easier when we recognize the large differences in the material from which he derived the two portions of his play. That we can do so is largely due to W. W. Lawrence. Lawrence distinguishes two kinds of material in *Measure for Measure* [see excerpt above, 1931]. The central episode of a sister having to decide whether to save her brother's life at the expense of her honour may go back to an historical incident and anyhow is related to real life and not to folk-lore. Similarly the setting in the low life of a city not found in Whetstone, is realistic and not traditional or magical. But Shakespeare grafted onto the realistic material of Whetstone two themes that belong to the world of the fairy tale: first, the disguised king mingling with and observing his own people and second, the secret substitution of the real bride in the husband's bed. At first sight the case seems to be very much that of *All's Well*. There we have a highly realistic setting and array of characters, to which are attached the folk themes of the person who by healing a king obtains a boon, of the setting of certain seemingly impossible tasks, and of the substitute bride. But actually the cases are very different and suggest that the plays were differently put together. In *All's Well* realism and folk-lore are blended from beginning to end; in *Measure for Measure* realism admits no folk-lore for half of the play, while all the folk-lore occurs in the second half. The same is true of allegory. The notions of Helena standing in some way for an emissary of heaven and of Bertram as a Morality figure drawn on one side by his mother and bride to good and on the other by Parolles to evil, faint in themselves, are yet spread throughout the play. Corresponding notions of the Duke as Heavenly Justice, or Isabella as Mercy, and so forth, though in themselves more evident and stronger than their parallels in *All's Well*, are quite absent from the first part of the play and appear quite suddenly in the second. It looks therefore as if *All's Well*, however deficient in execution, was conceived and executed consistently and with no change of

mind, but as if the two types of material from which *Measure for Measure* was drawn betoken two different types of execution, and an abrupt change from one to the other. Exactly what happened in Shakespeare's mind we shall never know. He may or may not have meant initially to write a play on the great themes of justice, mercy, and forgiveness. If he did, he seems to have changed his mind and sought above all to give his own version of the human potentialities of Whetstone's theme. Self-defeated half-way, through the turn he gave that theme, he may have reverted to his original, more abstract intentions, to help him out. More likely, to my thinking, he sought help from the methods and the incidents of the play, written shortly before and still in temper akin to his present self, *All's Well That Ends Well*.

It is, incidentally, because the folk material is so differently spaced and blended in the two plays that the theme of the substitute bride is quite seemly in *All's Well* and is somehow rather shocking in *Measure for Measure*. In *All's Well* we have been habituated to the improbable, the conventional, and the antique: in *Measure for Measure* the change to these from the more lifelike human passions is too violent; and it is here a case not of a modern prudery unaware of Elizbethan preconceptions but of an artistic breach of internal harmony. (pp. 137-41)

E.M.W. Tillyard, "Introduction" and "'Measure for Measure'," in his Shakespeare's Problem Plays, *University of Toronto Press, 1949, pp. 3-13, 124-45.*

CLIFFORD LEECH (essay date 1950)

[*In the excerpt below, Leech discusses the limitations of various critical approaches and states that no single method can resolve the contradictions and discrepancies in meaning that exist in all of Shakespeare's plays. He argues that the historical analysis of Elizabeth Marie Pope (1949), with its focus on the strictures of Christian doctrine and Elizabethan political theory, does not explain why we are repelled by the actions of the characters in* Measure for Measure. *Leech claims that the Christian coloring of the play is "intermittent" rather than pervasive, and that interpreting the Duke's role as that of Divine Providence or a deus ex machina neglects the perplexing nature of his character. Leech also contends that* Measure for Measure *is not a dramatic satire, because the play does not contain a simple thesis; rather, the juxtaposition of secondary and primary meanings argues for a more complex interpretation. In discussing these different readings of the play, Leech thus qualifies the analyses of such critics as G. Wilson Knight (1930), William Witherle Lawrence (1931), Oscar James Campbell (1943), and Roy W. Battenhouse (1946).*]

The realization that the greatness of [Shakespeare] lies, partly at least, in the scope of his mind has led in recent years to a close study of the ideas communicated through the plays. We now tend to see the histories as dramatic essays on a political theme, the final romances as embodiments of religious truth. Even the tragedies are dredged for underlying 'meanings'. But in one characteristic these searchers for theses do not differ from the stage-conditions men of a generation ago. They, too, emphasize the Elizabethanism of Shakespeare, and relate the significance of his plays to the general current of Elizabethan thought on political and religious themes. . . . If we accept these interpretations unreservedly, we may see Shakespeare as the superb expositor of his age's thought, but perhaps we shall be giving both to the Shakespeare plays and to the Elizabethan age a consistency of texture that they can hardly claim. Historically it was a time of important social transition, and the birth-pangs of the new order often induced doubt of old premise and new practice: the Homilies are of necessity orthodox, but we would do violence to *Tamburlaine* to interpret it exclusively in their light; Chapman's tragedies and Jonson's comedies are the products of independent minds, ever ready to scrutinize an accepted code; in *Troilus and Cressida* the traditional values of Hector and Ulysses are seen as unavailing in a world given over to disorder. If, then, we are to think of Shakespeaare as the dramatic champion of the Tudor supremacy and the Anglican Church, we must recognize that this makes him, not the complete Elizabethan, but the sturdy partisan.

Yet it would appear particularly strange for Shakespeare's plays to be the embodiments of theses. In all matters of detail we find contradictions between one part of a play and another: the time-schemes are hardly ever consistently worked out; the manner of the dialogue may be rhetorical, intimate, sententious, euphuistic, compact, staccato, orotund, facetious, according to the particular demands of the individual scene; the statement of one passage may be at odds with others in the play, as with the differing accounts of Ophelia's death, the riddle of Macbeth's children, and Prospero's claim that he has raised men from the dead on his enchanted isle. Of course we can argue that contradictory time-schemes will fuse in the theatre, that the style in the best plays brings diversity into unity, and that incidental contradictions of statement will go unnoticed by an audience under a poet's spell. It remains significant that there are these discrepancies, for they may lead us to expect to find contradictory 'meanings' juxtaposed in the plays, to see the ending of *Macbeth* as simultaneously the destruction of a brave spirit and the reassertion of a political and moral order. (pp. 66-7)

In Miss Pope's account of *Measure for Measure* [see excerpt above, 1949] we have, I think, a corresponding simplification. Her relation of certain utterances in the play to Elizabethan statements of Christian doctrine does indubitably throw light on those utterances, and on the strands in the play's thought and feeling that they represent. But the total impression she leaves with us hardly coheres with the effect produced by the play in the theatre or when read as a whole. We are disturbed by it, not because its Christian doctrine is strict and uncompromising—as we may be disturbed by François Mauriac or Graham Greene—but because the very spokesmen for orthodoxy in the play repel us by their actions and the manner of their speech: they are not too hard for us, but rather too shifty, too complacent, too ignorant of their own selves, and for these failings they are nowhere explicitly reproved. That there is a Christian colouring in the play Miss Pope has securely demonstrated, particularly in the prayer of Isabella for Angelo's life and in the ultimate transcendence of justice by mercy. But this Christian colouring is, I hope to show, not more than intermittent in the play: it wells up, as it were, from Shakespeare's unconscious inheritance, and it does not determine the play's characteristic effect.

We should note first of all that *Measure for Measure* is not free from those incidental contradictions of statement that are to be found in almost all of Shakespeare's plays. Dover Wilson has observed gross inconsistency in the time-references and has drawn attention to the way in which Mistress Overdone in I, ii first tells Lucio and the others of Claudio's imprisonment and immediately afterwards, in her talk with Pompey, displays ignorance of it. A much more serious puzzle is provided by the Duke's statements about Angelo in different parts of the play. In I, i the Duke is presumably serious in his profession

of trust in Angelo. If he were not, the appointment of Angelo would be inexcusable. Moreover, he professes that Angelo's high character is fully manifest:

> There is a kind of character in thy life,
> That to th' observer doth thy history
> Fully unfold;
>
> [I. i. 27-9]

and he adds that such merit should not go unused. Yet, in his conversation with Friar Thomas, the Duke is by no means so sure: part of his object in deserting his post and turning spy is to find out whether Angelo is all that he appears. . . . We will not stay to consider whether, in view of these suspicions, the appointment of Angelo should have been made. In III, i, however, the Duke professes himself amazed at Angelo's fall from grace:

> but that frailty hath examples for his falling,
> I should wonder at Angelo;
>
> [III. i. 186-87]

and then, some forty lines later, tells Isabella of Angelo's former relations with Mariana. We should in particular note the Duke's assertion that Angelo, wishing to escape from his dowerless bride, pretended "in her discoveries of dishonour" [III. i. 227]. . . . Yet the Duke knew all this long before, we must assume. Not only, therefore, does Angelo's appointment reflect on the Duke, but we must find Shakespeare curiously engaged in deceiving his spectators: we have been led to believe that Angelo was honest in his puritanism, was convinced of his own strength against temptation, was horrified when Isabella was used to bait vice's hook. It is difficult to see how even a revision-theory could explain these inconsistencies. Rather it seems likely that, as so often, it was the immediate situation that primarily engaged Shakespeare's attention.

If that is the case, however, should we expect to find consistency of thought and feeling through the play? Are we to try to reconcile the deeply Christian cry of Isabella:

> Why, all the souls that were were forfeit once;
> And He that might the vantage best have took,
> Found out the remedy;
>
> [II. ii. 73-5]

with the Duke's speech on death in III, i? In this connexion we should remember that, though Miss Pope will not accept Roy Battenhouse's view of the Duke as representing "the Incarnate Lord" [see excerpt above, 1946], she does see him as the good ruler, doing God's work and moving through the play as "an embodied Providence." Yet, despite his Friar's gown, the Duke offers no hint of Christian consolation: Claudio must welcome death because there is no real joy to be found in life: he denies even personality itself:

> Thou art not thyself;
> For thou exist'st on many a thousand grains
> That issue out of dust. . . .
>
> [III. i. 19-21]

And there could hardly be a more dreadful or more sober denunciation of human lovelessness than we are offered here:

> Friend hast thou none;
> For thine own bowels, which do call thee sire,
> The mere effusion of thy proper loins,
> Do curse the gout, serpigo, and the rheum,
> For ending thee no sooner.
>
> [III. i. 28-32]

We can, of course, see the dramatic reason for this speech. It provides the thesis to which Claudio's shrinking from death is the antithesis. But it cleaves too near the bone to be regarded as a mere dramatic convenience. We have to recognize that the ideas in the speech reverberated in Shakespeare's own mind, that they could co-exist with echoes of redemption and of a human as well as divine forgiveness.

The Duke, ultimately the dispenser of pardon, has something of Prospero's magisterial place and nature, is indeed at certain moments a morality-figure, a god out of the playwright's pigeonhole. G. Wilson Knight assures us that "Like Prospero, the Duke tends to assume proportions evidently divine" [see excerpt above, 1930], while W. W. Lawrence argues that the Duke is but "a stage Duke", a mere instrument in the play's economy [see excerpt above, 1931]. Both these judgements, however, overlook the strong antipathy which the Duke has aroused in many readers during the past hundred years. (pp. 67-9)

Raleigh pointed out how the Duke plays at cat-and-mouse with Angelo in the last act, and indeed his supreme indifference to human feeling is as persistent a note as any in the play. In II, iii he catechizes Juliet, and in bidding her farewell casually breaks the news of Claudio's imminent execution:

> Your partner, as I hear, must die to-morrow,
> And I am going with instruction to him.
> Grace go with you! *Benedicte!*
>
> [II. iii. 37-9]

We should note perhaps that as yet there is no hint that the Duke will interfere with the sentence: he has no criticism of Angelo's severity to make here, and in IV, ii he insists that the sentence would be unjust only if Angelo fell short of the standards he is imposing on others. If, however, we are to assume that the Duke undergoes a 'conversion' which brings him to the exercise of mercy, we should be given some clear token of this in the play: as things stand, it appears as if the Duke pardons because he has not the strength to be severe and because he enjoys the contriving of a last-minute rescue. He is indeed like Prospero in this, who pretends sorrow for Alonso's loss of his son, and then extracts a stage-manager's thrill from the sudden discovery that Ferdinand is safe. When Lucio refers to "the old fantastical duke of dark corners" [IV. iii. 156-57], he gives us a phrase that our memories will not let go: it comes, too, most appropriately in IV, iii, just after the Duke has told us that he will proceed against Angelo "By cold gradation and well-balanc'd form" [IV. ii. 100] and has informed Isabella that Claudio is dead. Of course, he gives us a reason for this behaviour: Isabella shall have "heavenly comforts of despair, When it is least expected" [IV. iii. 110-11], but this implies an odd principle of conduct, which we should challenge even in "an embodied Providence". Indeed, it appears that there is nothing the Duke can do directly. After he has spied on the interview between Isabella and her brother in III, i, he tells Claudio that Angelo has merely been testing Isabella's virtue: one can see no reason for this beyond the Duke's love of misleading his subjects. Having, moreover, hit upon the Mariana-plan, he still urges Claudio to expect immediate death. We should note, too, that he claims to know Angelo's mind by virtue of being Angelo's confessor. One does not have to be deeply religious to be affronted by this piece of impertinence, but later we find that the Duke takes a special delight in the confessor's power which his disguise gives him: in Angelo's case he doubtless lied, but in IV, ii he is prepared to shrive Barnardine immediately before execution

and in the last speech in the play he recommends Mariana to Angelo as one who has confessed to him. We have reason to believe that the home of Shakespeare's childhood was one in which the old religion was adhered to: be that as it may, however, it is difficult to believe that he could look with favour on a man who deceived a condemned criminal with a pretence of priestly power and who tricked Mariana into giving him her confidence. (pp. 69-70)

It may be argued that we are taking the last act too seriously, that here, as Raleigh put it, we have "mere plot, devised as a retreat, to save the name of Comedy". Indeed, there is evidence that Shakespeare's mind was not working at full pressure in this part of the play: Isabella tells Mariana in IV, vi that the Friar may "speak against me on the adverse side" [IV. vi. 6]: this he does not do and we may assume that when writing IV, vi Shakespeare had not fully worked out the conduct of the final scene. Nevertheless, the stage-managing Duke of V, i is of a piece with the man we have seen eavesdropping and contriving throughout the play. But now he forsakes his 'dark corners', focuses the light on himself as Richard did at Coventry, gives pardon to all, even to Escalus for being shocked at the Friar's seeming impudence, and promises himself an added delight in further discourse of his adventures.

We should not forget in this last scene that the Duke is still outraged by the manner of Viennese life. Speaking as the Friar, he puts forward the same view as at the beginning of the play:

> My business in this state
> Made me a looker-on here in Vienna,
> Where I have seen corruption boil and bubble
> Till it o'er-run the stew: laws for all faults,
> But faults so countenanc'd, that the strong statutes
> Stand like the forfeits in a barber's shop,
> As much in mock as mark.
>
> [V. i. 316-22]

Apart from his desire to spy on Angelo, his whole object in abandoning his ducal function was that the law should be exercised with greater rigour; yet at the end all are forgiven—except Lucio, whose punishment is grotesque rather than stern—and it would seem inequitable to discriminate between Barnardine and Mistress Overdone. But perhaps at the end, like the Duke himself, we forget Vienna and the governmental function: it may be that a *coup de théâtre* should not supply a legal precedent.

There is, moreover, something odd in the relations between the Duke and Lucio. Miss Pope, in exalting the Duke's ultimate dispensation of mercy, says that Lucio has to make amends "to the girl he has wronged". This is a sententious way of putting it, for Shakespeare seems to take it much less seriously: in III, ii Mistress Overdone gives us the lady's name, and 'wronging' seems too romantic a term for Lucio's association with her. Our reaction to the Duke's punishment of the one man he could not forgive is compounded of amusement at Lucio's discomfiture and astonishment at the intensity of the Duke's spite. When Lucio protests against the sentence, the Duke's reply is "Slandering a prince deserves it" [V. i. 524]: this is a different matter from righting a wrong done to Mistress Kate Keepdown. . . . Critics, searching for ethical formulations, are apt to forget that in the theatre the low life of Vienna and Lucio's persevering wit can arouse our sympathetic laughter. And because we have earlier tended to side with Lucio against the Duke, we are amused when the Duke is petulant at Lucio's interruptions in the final scene. As for the judgement, we may remind ourselves as we hear it that, about this time, Shakespeare wrote in *Lear* of a judge and a condemned thief who might exchange places.

But much in this play seems to provide a comment on the administration of justice. The law's instruments include Abhorson, Elbow and, as a recruit from the stews, Pompey: their combined efforts take something away from the law's majesty. During Shakespeare's middle years he made much use of trial-scenes and other ceremonial unravellings. There is the Venetian court in *The Merchant of Venice*, the dismissal of Falstaff by the newly crowned Prince in *2 Henry IV*, the King's putting of things to rights in *All's Well*, and the Duke's similar exercise of his function in this play. In each instance the sentence given can be justified; some clemency is allowed to mitigate the letter of the law; the way is cleared for the return of common conditions. And yet in every case our feeling is hardly of complete satisfaction. Shylock, Falstaff, Lucio arouse some resentment on their behalf, and we have little pleasure in the assertion of the law. It is frequently argued that we are too sensitive in our attitude to these victims of justice, and Miss Pope suggests that Shakespeare's first audience would have been at least as well contented if Angelo, Lucio and Barnardine had been, like Shylock, punished severely. But perhaps the attitude of the audience is not so necessary to an understanding of Shakespeare's purpose as his own attitude must be, and it is in *Measure for Measure* that we are given one of the clearest statements of his wide-reaching sympathy: Isabella herself reminds us that

> the poor beetle, that we tread upon,
> In corporal sufferance finds a pang as great
> As when a giant dies. . . .
>
> [III. i. 78-80]

It would be dangerous to base a judgement of Shakespeare's purpose on the assumption that his feelings were less fine than ours.

No more than the other plays incorporating 'trial-scenes' is *Measure for Measure* to be interpreted as a dramatic satire. It is indeed the overt purpose of the play to demonstrate, as Miss Pope has suggested, a governor's duty to practise mercy, to requite evil with forgiveness or with the gentler forms of punishment. Even the Duke's cat-and-mouse tricks with Claudio and Angelo may be justified as the mitigated punishment for their wrongdoing. Miss Pope has judiciously drawn attention to the Duke's soliloquy at the end of Act III, where in gnomic octosyllabics he speaks with chorus-like authority: here, indeed, the morality-element in the play is uppermost, and Wilson Knight has noted the resemblance of these lines to the theophanic utterances of the last plays. But, as so often with Shakespeare, the play's 'meaning' is not to be stated in the terms of a simple thesis: there are secondary as well as primary meanings to be taken into account, and the secondary meanings may largely determine the play's impact. We can see *2 Henry IV* as a play with a morality-outline, with the Prince tempted by disorder and finally won over to the side of Royalty. At the same time, that play seems a dramatic essay on the theme of mutability, with sick fancies, the body's diseases, senile memories, and lamentations for a lost youth constituting its lines of structure. And we can see it, too, as part of the great historical design, of the chain of actions that led from Gloucester's murder to Bosworth Field. There is a satiric element as well, which appears uppermost when Prince John teaches us not to trust the word of a noble, and which is perhaps latent in Falstaff's rejection-scene.

It is this complexity of meaning that makes it possible for us to see and read these plays so often, that enables the theatrical producer to aim at a new 'interpretation'. We are tempted always to extract a meaning, and the undertaking may be profitable if it leads us to inquire into the bases of Elizabethan thought and does not limit our perception to those things in the play that are easy to fit in place. In *Measure for Measure* in particular we should be careful of imposing a pattern on Shakespeare's thought, for the silence of Isabella in the last hundred lines suggests either a corrupt text or a strange heedlessness of the author. But we should always be ready for the by-paths which Shakespeare's thoughts and feelings may take at any moment of a play. If we would penetrate into his state of mind during the composition of *Measure for Measure*, we should not, I think, overlook the name he gave to Claudio's young mistress and the light thrown on Isabella's childhood when she cries that she would rather think her mother a strumpet than her father Claudio's begetter. Shakespeare cannot have forgotten an earlier Juliet when he used her name again, and the words of Isabella illuminate her cult of chastity. In our search for the play's 'meaning', we should not neglect these hints of a suppressed but deep sympathy with Juliet and of an almost clinically analytic approach to Isabella. In *Measure for Measure* we have a morality-framework, much incidental satire, a deep probing into the springs of action, a passionate sympathy with the unfortunate and the hard-pressed. Only if we concentrate our attention on one of these aspects will the play leave us content. (pp. 70-3)

> *Clifford Leech, "The 'Meaning' of 'Measure for Measure',"* in Shakespeare Survey: An Annual Survey of Shakespearian Study and Production, *Vol. 3, 1950, pp. 66-73.*

MURRAY KRIEGER (essay date 1951)

> [*Krieger identifies and contrasts two comedic traditions prevalent during Shakespeare's era, and he discusses their influence on* Measure for Measure. *In addition to Jonsonian satire—the dramatic form analyzed and applied by Oscar James Campbell (1943) in his study of* Measure for Measure—*Krieger finds similarities between Shakespeare's play and the pastoral-romantic comedies of Robert Greene. To Krieger, the technical problems created by this combination are the source of the ambiguity and the critical confusion surrounding* Measure for Measure. *He concludes that Shakespeare obscured the play's meaning by mingling these antithetic comedic styles. For further interpretations of the ambiguities present in the play, see the excerpts by Arthur Quiller-Couch (1922), L. C. Knights (1942), and Clifford Leech (1950).*]

Commentators on Shakespeare's *Measure for Measure*, in addressing themselves to a variety of problems, have arrived at equally varied conclusions about the quality of the play. Behind all of these comments, however, whether favorable or unfavorable, lies one common assumption: that the play, on the surface at least, is not entirely satisfactory and therefore requires a somewhat exceptional elucidation. (p. 775)

Those who condemn the play often wish to spare Shakespeare while they attack his work, striving particularly to ensure that Shakespeare receive full credit for the passages of poetic brilliance. Thus they claim that the play breaks into two historically separate parts at the point where the Mariana plot is introduced, and that Shakespeare, in a hasty revision of his own work or, preferably, of that of an inferior dramatist, had to allow the weaknesses to remain. (pp. 775-76)

Even the more favorably disposed commentators seem to be somewhat uncomfortable when confronted by the difficulties in the play. They all feel the need to explain away the two incongruous elements which somehow have made their home in a single work by our master playwright, whether these elements be seen as textual inconsistencies, as the conflict between moral meaning and dramatic effect, or as the clash between realistic satire and romantic melodrama. That they should so often reduce the central and crucial moral perplexities to such quibbles as, for example, those about the contemporary importance of betrothals, further indicates their uneasiness before the obvious aspects of the action. It is possible, however, that these studies have not fully utilized all that can be recovered about Shakespeare's dramatic intention, and that a further consideration of the play in relation to the kinds of comedy current around 1604 will clarify some of the problems which have provoked such diverse solutions. I propose, therefore, first to examine this context of Elizabethan comedy and then to see with what relevance it may be brought to bear upon the ambiguities of *Measure for Measure*. (pp. 776-77)

In moving from Elizabethan dramatic theory to dramatic practice, we find, first, that the plays of the neo-classicists, of course, were dedicated to the classic ideal. The form of comedy which they established is [one] of the various traditions I want to examine here. It is comedy completely controlled by the desire to hold folly up to ridicule. Thus it leads quite naturally to the comedy of "humours" in which every character is sharply defined and clearly "typed" so that the satiric implications of his folly are evident. The tradition seems to begin with [George] Chapman's *An Humourous Day's Mirth* or *Comedy of Humours* (1597) or at least with [Ben] Jonson's *Every Man in his Humour* (1598). In the Chapman play, Lemot is a mischief-maker who manipulates all the characters in order to exhibit their folly. His principal aim, however, seems to be the joy he gets out of making trouble. In Jonson the formula is similar, if greatly refined. Even more accentuated here is the foolishness of those who are to be gulled, and the desire to expose this foolishness becomes more completely the motivation of those who do the gulling. When we move to [John] Marston's *Antonio and Mellida* (1599), *The Malcontent* (1604), and *Parasitaster* or *The Fawn* (1606), we find, in addition to these other ingredients, that here, even more than in Jonson, there is emphasized the element of moral corruption of which the gulls are examples and against which the intriguer rails. . . . These plays follow a similar pattern: we have the introduction of the gull or gulls along with the intriguer who may also be the moral commentator; the main action involves the successful perpetration of the intriguer's plot to frustrate and expose the gull, ending in his cure or his being hooted off the stage. Character is stressed rather than plot, and the audience is forced to assume an objective attitude which frees it from any emotional involvement and allows it a detached aloofness from the fools they see displaying themselves. (pp. 778-79)

[But] the bulk of Elizabethan dramatists did not intend to pursue this kind of comedy. Since, unlike the classicists, they did not formulate a fully developed dramatic theory to which we may look for their comedies to conform, we must try to find plays with enough common elements to allow us to piece together this non-classical tradition, which, we may assume, also had a certain focus and certain limitations. Perhaps the basis of this tradition is to be found in the pastoral dramas of the last two decades of the sixteenth century. . . . [The broad characteristics of the pastoral play are:] the idyllic, simple life of the country (often opposed to urban corruption), the sophisticated

manners of the court which intrude upon it, and the magic of mythology which manipulates the action. While few dramas closely adhere to this pattern in its entirety, the general conception of drama embodied in the pastoral does help to fashion many plays toward the end of the century.

In this connection it is especially significant to study the work of Greene, because he seems to have transformed certain basic pastoral attributes to formulate a kind of romantic comedy which in many respects resembles Shakespeare's. . . . In *Friar Bacon and Friar Bungay* (about 1590) and *James IV* (about 1591), Greene has modified the pastoral elements he employs. Magic, although it is not mythologically derived, is used in both plays, functioning as a major structural device in *Friar Bacon and Friar Bungay* and as a background to the action in *James IV;* in both plays rural virtues are extolled and courtly vice condemned, and disguised nobles add the courtly touch to the country scenes. These plays also incorporate several incidental features generally common to the pastorals. Like the pastorals, they are primarily concerned with the telling of a romantic and fanciful story. It is significant in this connection that both plays are called "histories" (that is, stories) and that only *James IV* is even secondarily called a comedy. Because of this exclusive interest in the story for its own sake, consistency of character is not taken very seriously, so that we never see the process by which a character changes his mind but rather are forced to accept such vacillation on the spot so long as it moves the plot interestingly along toward the desired ending. Since we are to become emotionally involved in the action, we are hardly to regard the characters objectively or ironically. Rather our attitude is to be one of sympathy toward them: we take seriously what they take seriously. Thus, concerned about the fortunes of the characters and heedless of their psychological consistency, we can accept improbabilities in keeping with our hope for all to turn out well. (pp. 779-80)

It should be clear that the two lines of Elizabethan comedy we have traced are completely opposed to each other. In addition to their different attitudes toward such superficial structural principles as the three unities, there are two antithetical concepts of drama involved here. In one there is the primacy of character-consistency, in the other the primacy of fanciful plot. In one, no perilous element is allowed to obfuscate the purely comic effect; in the other even the most tragic possibilities may enter along the way, provided that all ends well. One demands from its audience an attitude of detachment, of disdainful superiority; the other demands so sympathetic a concern for the fortunes of its characters that the audience will tolerate anything so long as the obstacles to a happy ending are cleared away. (p. 781)

It seems likely that the two conflicting varieties of Elizabethan comedy, that of Jonson and that of Greene, are combined in *Measure for Measure,* and that their incompatibility has caused the critical confusion which still exists about the play. Recognizing this duality, we also . . . would see the play as having two incongruous elements, but these would not be so easily separated at any one point in the action as [commentators] would have us believe. Rather Shakespeare seems to be doing two things at once throughout this work. Campbell, in his *Shakespeare's Satire,* has carefully examined the play in terms of the elements in it of the comedy of ridicule [see excerpt above, 1943]. He concludes, however, that the play fails because Isabella, who structurally is the Duke's device to gull Angelo, outgrows her function and, in outgrowing it, threatens to become the heroine of a serious play. It should be added to this analysis, I believe, that Isabella's development is not so much an accident or loss of control during playwriting as it is a manifestation of a clearly defined variety of romantic comedy which had its hold on Shakespeare and which he could not or would not shake off even as he was introducing the currently popular Jonsonian characteristics. As a result, he tried to graft the latter elements on to the fundamentally different tradition of comedy to which he formerly was devoted, but failed to blend the two. Perhaps the two concepts, being too opposed, inevitably involved too many incongruities to allow an organic union or, for that matter, to allow anything more than an un-integrated superimposition of one on the other. Be that as it may, it is important, in returning to Isabella, that we see how she is shaped by both traditions. In addition to and simultaneously with the conventional satiric function attributed to her by Campbell, Isabella, as the supremely virtuous woman whose purity is threatened by a vicious ruler, is called upon to function as an equally conventional counterpart of Greene's heroines. (pp. 781-82)

In light of Campbell's presentation and in view of the fact that there are no pastoral elements as such in the play, one may say that *Measure for Measure* is farther from Greene and closer to Jonson than are Shakespeare's earlier and more obviously romantic comedies. Nevertheless it is also evident that his earlier romantic characteristics are there constantly to battle the classical ones for supremacy. For example, the puritanical Angelo, Campbell states, is the Jonsonian gull, and the entire play is so constructed as to expose his hidden vices. On the face of it, this would indeed seem to differentiate him from Shylock [*The Merchant of Venice*] or Don John [*Much Ado about Nothing*], who are the purely romantic villains. But it must be noted on the other side that his vices take on a far more serious aspect than Jonson would permit, and that in this respect he shows a close resemblance to the Scotch king in *James IV*, as well as to Shylock and Don John. Consequently, at the same time as he is the gull, he is the conventional villain of romantic comedy whose defeat is necessary. And his final repentance has a similar duality about it. On the one hand there is evidence that he is purged of his vice in Jonsonian fashion; on the other hand he appears to undergo the unforeseen and unjustifiable change-of-heart that is characteristic of a comedy by Greene or an earlier one by Shakespeare.

If we add to this analysis of Angelo's role the ambiguous function of Isabella as romantic heroine and as tool for the Duke's plot—a point which has already been touched upon—the contradictory character of the play becomes clear. Seen in this light, the play reveals how complete a struggle it is between the two opposed patterns of comedy. The one has Angelo as the main character and gull, with Isabella as the means of gulling him (and would not Jonson rather use a courtesan, the classic functional type?). The other is a story of romantic adventure presenting Isabella as the pure heroine and Angelo as the lustful villain who repents after he is overcome. And, as we have seen, our emotional response can hardly cope with such divergent demands. By studying the play in terms of the framework suggested here, we can also account for the many critical objections to Isabella's moral consistency. True to her romantic counterparts, she must withstand Angelo's advances at all costs and rebuke Claudio for pleading that she yield herself in order to save him. But as the instrument of Jonsonian intrigue, she must turn around and engineer the Mariana "bed trick." Thus the inconsistency of the play, as well as the difficulty of critics with it, does not, as it is commonly claimed, spring from a confusion of moral principles so much as it

springs from a confusion of two technical patterns, each of which makes different moral demands. At their source, then, the problems are revealed as formal rather than thematic.

The Duke and Lucio seem to have more consistently Jonsonian functions than the others. From the outset the Duke has determined to test Angelo. And once Angelo has committed himself, the Duke directs all his efforts toward exposing him. Here, perhaps, is the clearest answer to those who become annoyed as the Duke persists in his intrigues and delays despite the fact that he can act at any time. Yet we need not explain his waywardness in terms of the prerogatives allowed the ruler in Elizabethan political tradition. The explanation would seem to lie solely in the realm of dramatic convention. For it is the essence of the comedy of ridicule to push the gull, by means of intrigue, as far as possible until his self-exposure is most painful. It should be noted that the Duke's continuous and assuring presence, demanded by his function as intriguer, does prevent the romantic element from involving too dangerous a situation; we see here how a Jonsonian device helps maintain the play as comedy.

The Duke also has some qualities which remind us of Malevole, hero of Marston's *The Malcontent*. For example, even while testing Angelo, his prize gull, he continually prods the other characters as well. But Isabella stands firmly merciful, Claudio is taught the proper attitude toward death, and only Lucio remains also to be gulled. In addition, the Duke, again like Malevole, moralizes from time to time about the vicious atmosphere which envelops the action. (This background of moral corruption would fit into both traditions of comedy: it is the courtly depravity about which Bohan laments in *James IV* and which is contrasted to rural virtue in all the pastorals, and it is the ugliness, personified by the gulls, about which the satiric commentator complains in the comedy of ridicule.) It would seem, from the similarities between the Duke and Malevole, that certain consistent developments and alterations of the formula for realistic comedy were taking place and that less restricted horizons for political and moral dramatic satire were being revealed. . . . In any case, Shakespeare's mingling of the satirical elements with those descended from pastoralism seems to have obscured any possible single intention in his play. (pp. 782-84)

When viewed in the context of contemporary dramatic genres, *Measure for Measure* is seen to be an unsatisfactory product of conflicting fashions in dramatic construction. It is thus possible to establish more clearly the author's artistic intention and to estimate more accurately the relevance of the problems which critics have raised. There may be much to be said about the meaning of the play, if we choose to consider it a moral-political tract. But its unified significance as drama must elude us as, indeed, it may have eluded even Shakespeare. (p. 784)

Murray Krieger, " 'Measure for Measure' and Elizabethan Comedy," in PMLA, *66, Vol. LXVI, No. 5, September, 1951, pp. 775-84.*

ARTHUR SEWELL (essay date 1951)

[*Sewell's* Character and Society in Shakespeare *(1951) is regarded as one of the leading character studies of the twentieth century and an important refutation of the Romantic and neo-Romantic approach to Shakespeare's plays. Specifically, Sewell focuses on the biographical, the psychological, and the psychoanalytic interpretations of Shakespeare's characters, criticizing all these methods as inappropriate and, at times, misleading, because each one forces us to attribute certain actions to biographical or psychological motives which are either vague or the extrapolation of the critic. For Sewell, Shakespeare was a moralist, not a psychologist, and his plays demonstrate the manner in which his characters choose to orient themselves to life—whether it be social life, as in the comedies, political life, as in the histories, or metaphysical life, as in the tragedies. Sewell begins his essay on* Measure for Measure *with a discussion of characters from* The Winter's Tale *and* The Tempest; *he notes that Leontes, Alonzo, and Sebastian experience an "inner transformation," a change in attitude that forms a believable part of each play's comprehensive vision and corresponds to the reader or spectator's "social judgment." In* Measure, *however, Sewell maintains that Angelo's sudden transformation from self-control to an obsessive fascination with possessing Isabella is unacceptable, because there is no "inner motivation" that causes his change in attitude. Sewell asserts that Angelo's character proved to be "intractable" to Shakespeare's design and is an example of the uncertainty of his vision in* Measure for Measure. *For additional discussion of Angelo's function in the play, see the excerpts by G. G. Gervinus (1849-50), Hoxie N. Fairchild (1931), H. B. Charlton (1937), W.M.T. Dodds (1946), Robert Ornstein (1957), and A. D. Nuttall (1968).]*

There is a general agreement that in Shakespeare's tragedies we witness a process of 'chemical change' in the hero's spirit, brought about by a situation which makes demands upon him which he cannot fulfil and by a moral failure which has its issue at last in a reorganization of his whole being. Character-change and character-development, at any rate, are fundamental elements in Shakespeare's great tragic dramas. He was not only concerned with what happens to a man; he was also concerned with what happens within a man. (p. 64)

[It also] seems to me useful to consider the nature of 'change' in certain other characters created in another mode.

In *The Winter's Tale* and *The Tempest* the characters of Leontes, Alonzo, and Sebastian undergo what certainly appears to be character-development, going hand in hand with repentance and reconciliation at the end of the play. Leontes, having learned the truth, repents immediately, but has to wait sixteen years for reconciliation. Alonzo and Sebastian are taught a brief but bitter lesson by Prospero. We would say, in everyday language, that they become changed men, and it is part of the optimism of tragi-comic effect that we should suppose the change to be lasting. The motivation of the change, and the evidence for its probable permanence, do not seem to be wholly adequate and are, at least, mainly mechanical. How mechanical it is we may illustrate perhaps from the extreme case of Iachimo [*Cymbeline*]. The inner transformation (if we suppose there to be one) is only conveniently brought about: in Leontes by the words of the oracle declaring Hermione to be chaste, and in Alonzo and Sebastian by the discomforts and distresses which Prospero imposes upon them. Attitude before and attitude after are really opaque to each other, although they are credibly represented as belonging to the one character. Personality is not reorganized but metamorphosed. (pp. 64-5)

Why, then, are we convinced by the change—or, at least, why do we accept it?

For two reasons, I think. In the first place, these characters change in a manner directly and unambiguously derived from the comprehensive (and ultimately optimistic) vision of the play. In the play's magnetic field, as it were, we do not doubt that all the characters will be drawn towards the pole. Just as character itself may be directly determined by the moral vision of the play, so also in the same way what happens to character and within character may be so determined and made credible.

Secondly, the change in character is one which we approve and which agrees with the social judgement. It is a return to what is more desirable by way of nature; for in the Romances evil in man is an accident and not the original condition of his being. Repentance and forgiveness, after all, conserve order and harmony in society. Such changes need no deeper motivation than the persuasion of external events. If a man is punished, we grant that he will do better in future. If a man is undeceived, we grant that he will not persist in folly. It is the assumption of comedy that men and women are capable of being educated, and in comedy the Law (as it were) is often a schoolmaster to bring men to their senses. At least, as with Lucio in *Measure for Measure*, they can be restrained. We do not, then, in characters such as these discover any real change. We discover rather a change of attitude, the result not of any inner motivation but of the teaching of external events. (pp. 65-6)

[Angelo in *Measure for Measure*] undergoes changes, and changes of a very dramatic kind; and he has always been something of a puzzle to the critics. It is possible that the groundlings saw Angelo as a mere hypocrite, who sent them back to their viciousness with the comfortable feeling that the seeming best of men have the itch as much as they. But it is quite clear that Shakespeare intended something more serious than that. It is also possible to see in Angelo the study of a man whose appetites have been too tightly reined, and who is overwhelmed by a 'fetichistic' lust for a girl who comes in the robes of the nunnery to plead for her brother's life. (p. 67)

We learn enough about Angelo, even though he is not the central character, to know that he is involved in the most awful moral crisis of the play; a moral crisis in which might well have been represented the universal crisis of man, in which there might have been a particular exposure of man's fall from grace. Indeed, the main responsibility for representing this case of man is laid on Angelo; but Angelo cannot properly represent it, just because he is not the central character of the play.

Nor is it at all the concern of *Measure for Measure* to make such a study of 'awful consciousness'. The world of the play is not really the world of human souls. It is true that in the last act there is some play with the notions of penitence and forgiveness; the Law is threatened and then remitted. But the play is called *Measure for Measure*, and the deeper seriousness of penitence and forgiveness are uneasily accommodated in the treatment of such a theme. The final concern of the play is not with redemption or with grace but with the Law, and when the Law seems at the end of the play to be abrogated it is surely an error to suppose that its place has been taken by a covenant of grace. For the Law, in fact, is not abrogated. The marriages imposed—Angelo's as much as Lucio's—are salutary, not blessed. This so-called forgiveness, this remission of the Law, is in some ways more terrible than the rigour of the law suspended; for it implies that lust may, after all, be bridled as well by marriage as by death. Angelo's marriage is not very different from Lucio's; it is not, surely, the marriage of a man who has undergone a 'saving experience'. It is a marriage which will conserve (and perhaps continuate) the society to which both Angelo and Lucio belong.

No world of evil makes a bid in *Measure for Measure* for the soul of a man, for such a world always both is and is not the creation of man. The lust that overwhelms Angelo seems to spring, psychologically, from within, but in a truer sense it overwhelms him from without. It does not come to him as a revelation of himself, as Macbeth's ambitious purpose both surprises and convicts him and makes him tremble as at a revelation of himself. There is always a separateness between Angelo and his lust; and the lust is simple and opaque, except after psychological analysis, to the earlier nature of the man. Angelo's lust has no more poetry in it than rape in a court of law; and had he indeed belonged to the world of human souls the lust would have been pitifully, terribly, in the poetry. And so in Angelo, changed and remorseful, what was this lust, never having been other than separate from him, can only be destroyed. In a human soul all may be transformed, but nothing destroyed.

Nevertheless, the implied agony and the moral seriousness of Angelo's case are such that they cannot be sustained unless he is seen—unless in Shakespeare's vision he has been apprehended—as a human soul. For we refuse to accept him either as a study in morbid psychology or as a canting hypocrite. We must conclude, then, that in Angelo Shakespeare has introduced a situation, a case, and a character, intractable to the working out of the comprehensive vision of the play. And this is as much as to say that the vision itself is uncertain, for vision seeks to discover itself in character.

In Angelo, vision does not so discover itself, and it is instructive to note in what manner and measure it fails. The imagery in which Angelo expresses himself scarcely ever reveals the darker recesses of his being; nothing rises from the centre. The promptings of his lust express themselves in external figures, in the very language of the Law, and the appetite has no status or activity in the world of the spirit. Once recognized, it turns outward to explain itself, using language which takes its substance and its currency from secular society.

> O heavens!
> Why does my blood thus muster to my heart,
> Making both it unable for itself,
> And dispossessing all my other parts
> Of necessary fitness?
>
> [II. iv. 19-23]

Then, immediately, Angelo turns to a mere simile, a memory from social experience, elaborating but not enriching, not generating the emotion:

> So play the foolish throngs with one that swounds;
> Come all to help him, and so stop the air
> At which he would revive.
>
> [II. iv. 24-6]

This is not the appetite speaking, but the man about the appetite. So, later, lust takes its language from the Law, and loses thereby its nature, since it takes this language and leaves it untransformed. It speaks of 'accusation', 'calumnies', 'seeing', 'banishment', and 'lingering sufferance'. Even after the satisfaction, Angelo does not see the evil he has done except in these terms of Law and reputation—and some doubts about his own safety:

> This deed unshapes me quite, makes me unpregnant
> And dull to all proceedings. A deflower'd maid,
> And by an eminent body that enforc'd
> The Law against it! But that her tender shame
> Will not proclaim against her maiden loss,
> How might she tongue me! Yet reason dares her no;
> For my authority bears so credent bulk,
> That no particular scandal once can touch;
> But it confounds the breather.
>
> [IV. iv. 20-8]

There is no penitence here; there is no exhaustion of lustful appetite; the lawyer is talking about the lecher. It is not for nothing that at the end of the last Act the Duke says, when Claudio is known to be still alive:

> By this, Lord Angelo perceives he's safe:
> Methinks I see a quickening in his eye.
>
> [V. i. 494-95]

The Duke speaks here of a man not redeemed but reprieved. But there is something in Angelo's case, and in the treatment of that case, which would make us wish him both redeemed and reprieved. (pp. 69-72)

Arthur Sewell, "Change in the Tragic Character," in his Character and Society in Shakespeare, *Oxford at the Clarendon Press, 1951, pp. 64-90.*

WILLIAM EMPSON (essay date 1951)

[*An English poet, critic, and scholar, Empson is considered one of the most influential theorists of modern criticism. In his two important studies,* Seven Types of Ambiguity *(1930) and* The Structure of Complex Words *(1951), Empson adapted the ideas of I. A. Richards, the English critic and forerunner of New Criticism, and argued that the value of poetic discourse resides not in any ultimate critical evaluation, but in the correspondences and contradictions of the creative structure itself. In short, Empson has been more interested in the manner in which poetic elements work together in a literary piece than in assessing the final value of a creative work as a whole. As a Shakespearean critic, Empson has focused mainly on the emotive and connotative aspects of Shakespeare's language, as well as on the ambiguity of his verse. Although many critics have attacked his methods and questioned the practicality of his theories, Empson contributed significantly to the development of New Criticism in the twentieth century. In the excerpt below, Empson concentrates on an explication of the word "sense" in* Measure for Measure. *He finds that as the play progresses, the term takes on different meanings within the context of each character's speech, and can be construed to mean "sensuality," "sensibility," and "sensibleness." He also argues that Shakespeare's use of the word reflects "an examination of sanity itself," especially in Angelo's soliloquies and in Isabella's reaction to Angelo's threat to her chastity. Additional commentary on the ambiguity of* Measure for Measure *appears in the essays by L. C. Knights (1942), Derek A. Traversi (1942), and J. W. Lever (1965).*]

There are only about ten uses of the word ["sense" in *Measure for Measure*], but I think almost all of them carry forward a puzzle which is essential to its thought. It is not denied that the word then covered (1) "sensuality" and (2) "sensibility", and I maintain that it also covered (3) "sensibleness", though in a less direct way, through the ideas of "a truth-giving feeling" and "a reasonable meaning". Clearly the equations between these three could carry very relevant ironies, though the effect is not so much a covert assertion as something best translated into questions. Are Puritans hard? . . . Are they liable to have crazy outbreaks? . . . Is mere justice enough? . . . To be sure, these questions look very unlike the flat false identity of one idea with another, but I think the state of the word then made them easier to impose. It seems to have been neither analysed nor taken as simple; it points directly into the situation where it is used, implying a background of ideas which can be applied to the situation, but somehow as if the word itself did not name them; it is a shorthand term, rather than a solid word in which two of the meanings can be equated. And yet, as the play works itself out, there is a sort of examination of the word as a whole, of all that it covers in the cases where it can be used rightly; or rather an examination of sanity itself, which is seen crumbling and dissolving in the soliloquies of Angelo. (p. 270)

The first use of the word in the play is by the gay Lucio, when he goes to Isabella at her nunnery to tell her about the pregnancy and ask her to beg for her brother's life. . . . He wants to respect her highmindedness, but he has to treat the scandal as trivial to induce her to help, so he falls into a verbose style which the bitter woman thinks is mocking her virtue.

> A man whose blood
> Is very snow-broth: one who never feels
> The wanton stings and motions of the sense;
> But doth rebate, and blunt his natural edge
> With profits of the mind; Study, and fast . . .
>   . . . hath pick'd out an act,
> Under whose heavy sense your brother's life
> Falls into forfeit: he arrests him on it. . . .
>   [I. iv. 57-66]

He clearly feels, though he cannot say outright, that Angelo's habits have cost him his "common sense". However we must guard against taking this as part of his intended meaning for *sense;* the meaning "sensuality" is very unequivocal. Indeed one might say that this clear-cut use of the word is put first in the play to thrust the meaning "sensuality" on our attention and make us treat it as the dominant one. Yet the word acts as a sort of euphemism, and this suggestion is supported by the jauntiness of Lucio's whole tone. The form implies that sensuality is only one of the normal functions of the senses, and the rest of the speech implies that to neglect them is to become *blunted, heavy* (cruel) and so forth. Lucio does not want to annoy Isabella by saying this plainly, even by the relative plainness of a covert assertion; but it can hang about in his mind, and there is evidence that it does so when *sense* crops up again as the "meaning" or "intention" of the heavy Act. (pp. 273-74)

The next use is an aside of Angelo when first fascinated by Isabella (he will bargain to give her her brother's life in exchange for her body).

> She speaks and 'tis
> Such sense, that my Sense breeds with it. Fare you
> well. . . .
>   [II. ii. 141-42]

Angelo's first use of the word is "wise or reasonable meaning", and then the meaning "sensuality", which Lucio has made dominant for this stage of the play, pokes itself forward and is gratified by the second use of the word as a pun. Even in the second use I am not sure that "sensuality" can be called the chief meaning of the word; the suggestion of *breeds* is rather that both the "meanings in his mind" and his "sense-data" have sensuality growing inside them—added to them, so to speak, as an Implication. (p. 274)

In real life it seems rather unlikely that this pun would occur to Angelo. It occurred to Shakespeare, and was wanted; to Lucio it could occur spontaneously, with a cheerful feeling that sensuality goes with sensibleness; but to Angelo the combination of meanings in the word can only appear as a hideous accident. The only touching side of Angelo is that he is genuinely astonished by his desires. (It is taken for granted that he could not make love to her in the ordinary way, though there is nothing to prevent him.) Yet the real irony, apart from the verbal accident, is that her coldness, even her rationality,

is what has excited him; the two things are patently connected as in the word, though not in his system of ideas. (pp. 274-75)

In the next use, after the interview is over, Angelo is not thinking of the word as a pun, and indeed the possible connections have become so elaborate that the meanings are hard to tie down.

> What's this? What's this? is this her fault or mine?
> The Tempter or the Tempted, who sins most?
> Not she: nor doth she tempt: but it is I
> That, lying by the violet in the Sun,
> Do as the Carrion does, not as the flower,
> Corrupt with virtuous season. Can it be,
> That Modesty may more betray our sense
> Than woman's lightness? . . .
>   [II. ii. 162-69]

The Arden edition's note says, very properly, that *sense* here means "sensuality, desire"; that of course is the most prominent idea in Angelo's mind. But the recent punning may easily be recalled, and the immediately preceding metaphor is not obvious. . . . I am begging a question when I translate one of the meanings as "sensuality", because that tends to imply that the sexual desire in question is of an evil kind, whereas *sense* in itself does not have to add this Emotion. In the play it seems to be added insistently, not only by Angelo but by the presence of Isabella at the first use of the word; but perhaps Angelo is trying to exorcise this Emotion by the picture of the violet. There is a parallel confusion to that of *sense*, I think, in *season;* indeed part of the strength of a ready-made puzzle like that of *sense* is that it can impose itself as pattern on neighbouring words. The Arden note gives "benign influence of summer" for *virtuous season*—the warmth rots the carrion but makes the flower sweet. This idea is certainly present and gives a tidy metaphor. But it would make Isabella the sun, whereas she is clearly the modest violet, which he is lying by. If the sun is the natural strength which causes sexual desire, that itself can be good, the metaphor will imply. But if the violet is giving the *season*, the idea seems to be the smell of it, like "*seasoning*" in food, pepper for instance. Unlike the public and clear sunlight, this brings in ideas of privacy and of exciting the senses. He is no longer sure what the natural process can be, to which he contrasts himself, and has gone far towards accepting the confusion of meanings as a single and "profound" one. . . . (pp. 275-76)

The next use of the word is in his second interview with Isabella.

> ANG.:   Nay, but hear me,
> Your sense pursues not mine; either you are ignorant,
> Or seem so craftly; and that's not good.
>   [II. iv. 73-5]

The pathetic or disgusting assumption of superior morality, in this rebuke to her for not understanding the bargain, finds an echo in the stock pun. . . . In "your sense pursues not mine" the immediate context very definitely imposes "interpretation" ("the sense you put on my words") as the chief meaning, indeed to suppose it means "sensuality" is a satire on Angelo; but by this time it is so strong a dominant meaning that it arises easily.

Act III. Scene i. Claudio and Isabella. By Henry Fuseli (1803). From the Art Collection of the Folger Shakespeare Library.

There is a long pause before the next use of the word; Angelo has now settled down into crime, and can combine the meanings harmoniously enough in a way of his own.

> He should have lived
> Save that his riotous youth with dangerous sense
> Might in the times to come have ta'en revenge
> By so receiving a dishonour'd life
> With ransome of such shame.
>
> [IV. iv. 28-32]

It is still with superior morality that he looks back on the most repulsive of his supposed actions. . . . The *danger* of keeping the bargain and letting Claudio live would be that he would feel too deeply about it; *sense* covers "sensibility" here. But the reason why he is sure to have a keen sense of honour is that he is *riotous,* he is "sensual", for that either shows that you have strong feelings or develops them. In either case Angelo despises him for it; he is himself one of the cold people. The idea "meaning, purpose" is still possible in the word, but it is unimportant beside this startling irony.

There is no need to make these interpretations rigid, especially in so fluid a word. The simple view of the uses by Angelo is that he always means "sensuality" when in soliloquy and always pretends to mean something else when talking to other people. But this corresponds to the view of him as a hypocrite and villain all through; if you take the character as capable of struggle and development you need to suppose that his language carries the marks of it. . . . I think "sensuality" is the idea that comes first in his mind, and acts as chief meaning of the word; if you had to choose only one meaning, what the logic of the passage requires is "sensibility", but it is regarded as a consequence. This is the order of the terms in the equation; the idea is "sensuality entails sensibility". He seems indeed to have moved the idea "sensuality" from being an intrusive dominant to being what he considers the head meaning of the word. He has no more to say with it, and does not use it again; the main force of its irony now turns against Isabella, and "sensuality", till now so prominent, becomes only a solemn paradox making a darkness in the background.

> DUKE: Away with her; poor soul
> She speaks this in th'infirmity of sense.
>
> [V. i. 46-7]
> (pp. 276-77)

The use is simple enough, but the Duke is teasing Angelo, and a double meaning would be in order. . . . I think it is possible that the voice of Shakespeare behind him is preparing an irony of another kind. The Duke is still toying with the word a few lines later:

> By mine honesty,
> If she be mad, as I believe no other,
> Her madness hath the oddest frame of sense,
> Such a dependency of thing on thing,
> As ere I heard in madness.
>
> [V. i. 59-63]

If [Isabella] has reason it is of a queer kind, not common sense but the obscure wisdom that Shakespeare expected in clowns and the half-mad. It is true that she would put an odd construction on *sense* (give it an odd *frame*); she is too otherworldly to use it in the common way. There is no pressure behind the passage, but I think it adds to the cumulative effect. Then Mariana has a use, important because free from irony; and her rhetoric (it is like that of Troilus) gives the word a fine chance to spread the peacock tail of its meanings. . . .

> Noble Prince,
> As there comes light from heaven, and words from breath,
> As there is sense in truth, and truth in virtue,
> I am affianced this man's wife, as strongly
> As words could make up vows: And my good Lord,
> But Tuesday night last gone, in's garden house,
> He knew me as a wife.
>
> [V. i. 224-30]

There is meaning in a true statement; there is purpose in making one; it is wise to tell the truth frankly. But the series goes from *sense* to *virtue,* and this tends to call out another part of the word's range. The kind of truth that is in virtue seems rather to be constancy or correspondence to natural law. Desire or passion, sensuality or sensibility, may make her constant; and she can decently assert them both in public; to be constant is to have the common sense of our normal feelings. The meanings are not merely compatible but undivided here; this is what the whole word is meant to do.

The next and final use raises a question about what Shakespeare himself thought of the play. . . .

MARI.:   Sweet Isabell, take my part:
             Lend me your knees, and all my life to come,
             I'll lend you all my life to do you service.
DUKE: Against all sense you do importune her:
             Should she kneel down, in mercy of this fact,
             Her Brother's ghost, his paved bed would break,
             And take her hence in horror.
                                    [V. i. 430-36]

In the Duke's earlier plotting with Isabella, the chief impulse
he appeals to in her is the desire to be revenged on Angelo,
not to save her brother; indeed in her first revulsion when he
begs for his life she says "'tis best that thou diest quickly"
[III. i. 150]. . . . But Isabella does not apply it to Angelo. We
are given a further test of the quality of her feeling, in the
appeal of Mariana for his life. She does react with the mercy
enjoined by her religion, and this is certainly meant to be to
her credit, but she attains this height by an impulse of personal
vanity so repulsive as to surprise even Dr. Johnson [see excerpt
above, 1765].

             I partly think,
             A due sincerity govern'd his deeds
             Till he did look on me.
                                    [V. i. 445-47]

She knows the history of Mariana, who is appealing for Angelo's life beside her; in fact the Duke has told her that when
Mariana lost most of her marriage portion Angelo "swallowed
his vows whole, pretending in her discoveries of dishonour"
[III. i. 226-27]. Afterwards, when Isabella's brother is presented to her still alive, she does not speak to him at all; no
doubt the plot gave no room for a long speech, but the Bard
is not as tongue-tied as all that if he can think of anything for
a character to say. The apologists have objected that flippant
modern critics merely do not understand the old reverence for
virginity if they dwell on such points. But it is impossible to
suppose all these details are accidental; they are not even clumsy;
they are pointed. It seems to me the only working theory to
suppose that Shakespeare could not quite stomach the old reverence either.

And on this view the final use of *sense* can carry a good deal
of meaning, though if you suppose the Duke meant all of it
he is not likely to have married her afterwards. "Against all
reason"—"all normal decent feeling"—"all depth or delicacy
of feeling"; whatever kind of *sense* is meant here, she lacks
it. For a moment, in the elaborate and teasing balance of the
play, Shakespeare turns even against mercy, or at least against
the abstract rule of mercy from which she acts. She is too
otherworldly to feel the thing like a sane person; she is not
sensual enough, the word might argue, to have tolerable human
feelings.

This is certainly not what the Duke thinks; here as always,
however savagely he tests her, he finds her ideally right. If he
means any irony in the word, apart from the general triumph
in knowing better than his audience which he is enjoying in
all these uses of *sense*, it is that she is altogether above "sense",
above the whole view of life which even a good use of the
suggestions of the word would imply. Miss M. C. Bradbrook,
in an essay on the play [see excerpt above, 1941], has maintained that the Duke did not expect Isabel to forgive Angelo,
but accepts her superior wisdom when "her justice recognises
the one grain of good in him". I am not sure how much a
verbal analysis can prove, and I would think this view wrong
without one, but surely those who support it must find it less

plausible when they notice that this use of the word is the last
of a series of uses by the Duke in this scene, and that the
previous ones (whatever else they mean) have both carried
secret boasts of superior knowledge. It does not seem to me
that there was any subtle unconsciousness about the matter; I
think Shakespeare felt he was "polishing off" the series of
puns on *sense* by this very dramatic final use of it. But if he
meant to kick away his key word at the end, it seems to me,
he could not manage to do it. This is not to say that he took
the same cheery view of the affair as Lucio; the play repeatedly
tells us that Lucio took venereal disease for granted, and I think
this practical argument gave the basic emotional drive in favour
of purity. Claudio ends the old story with a brave and generous
action, giving himself up in the expectation of death to save
the life of Angelo, now married to his sister; Shakespeare would
not allow him so much dignity, and altered the plot. This seems
good evidence that he found the behaviour of Claudio disgusting. But he could not convince himself, it seems to me,
even that the Duke was agreeable, let alone that Isabella was.
The pomposity of the man he probably found natural, but the
touchiness, the confidence in error, the self-indulgence of his
incessant lying, must I think always have been absurd. (pp.
277-80)

What makes the Duke ridiculous on the stage is the fuss he
makes about the backbiting of Lucio, that is, precisely what
makes Mr. Knight think him so high and pure [see excerpt
above, 1930]. The Duke of course is in disguise when Lucio
tells him these things, and he answers by boasting about himself, in a phrase which seems an obvious dramatic irony, "let
him but be testimonied in his own bringing forth, and he shall
appear to the envious a scholar, a statesman and a soldier"
[III. ii. 144-46]. He anxiously questions Escalus in the hope
of hearing something better, and continues to drag the subject
up when we are thinking about the plot. The soliloquy "Oh
place and greatness" [IV. i. 59-64], while Isabella is trying
to induce Mariana to play her part, is so much out of key that
at first we think he is talking about Angelo. In the final scene,
the mutual petty accusations of Lucio and the Duke, working
up to "yet here's one in place I cannot pardon" [V. i. 499],
are good farce and nothing else. No doubt there was a casualness and good-humour about the Elizabethan stage, so that
the great man could be laughed at for a bit and resume greatness
when required; but this is only to say that there was room for
Shakespeare to put in mixed feelings of his own.

But it is true, I think, that there is an agreeable side of the
Duke; it becomes dramatically prominent on the occasions when
he is proved absurdly wrong. He is certain (IV. iii) that Angelo
will be sending a pardon for Claudio to the prison (thinking
he has enjoyed Isabella); and he keeps boasting to the provost
of his superior knowledge. When the letter is opened it orders
an earlier execution under cover of night. The Duke immediately starts plotting again, apparently unperturbed, but the
fact that he could not imagine the depth of evil that he is playing
with does, I think, operate on us as somehow to his credit.
From then on his tricks seem less offensive; the claim to divine
foreknowledge has been broken. Also by this time it has become clear that nothing less than the fantastic behaviour of the
Duke could have kept the play from being a tragedy. The whole
force of the case against Angelo is that, in the ordinary way,
he would have been completely safe; he is a symbol of justice
itself, as Escalus points out (III. ii, end); he can only be imagined as vulnerable if he is handled by very strange means. In
the same way the Duke's final test of Isabella, that she must
forgive Angelo still beliving he killed her brother treacherously,

is a result of his general expectation of mercy; the fact that she agrees to it for bad reasons is not one that he is likely to realise. One might even find it pathetic that the intended nun should say "I partly think A due sincerity governed his deeds Till he did look on me". Her new sensual vanity seems meant to imply a partial awakening of her senses after the battering she has gone through; and her decision to marry the Duke is perhaps not so grossly out of character as critics have supposed. (pp. 282-83)

William Empson, *"Sense in 'Measure for Measure',"* in his The Structure of Complex Words, *1951. Reprint by Rowman and Littlefield, 1979, pp. 270-88.*

HAROLD S. WILSON   (essay date 1953)

[*Wilson compares* Measure for Measure *with* The Tempest, *presenting a number of structural similarities in an attempt to prove that Shakespeare's technique in* Measure for Measure *is both "logical and consistent."*]

If we compare the dramatic methods of *Measure for Measure* and *The Tempest* with reference to the directing roles that their two dukes play—Vincentio of Vienna and Prospero of Milan and the Magic Island—we may observe a notable difference in their procedures. Both of them seem to supervise and control the action of their respective plays. But whereas Prospero takes us immediately into his confidence and explains his purpose as he goes along, Duke Vincentio never explicitly states his purpose in *Measure for Measure* and we are left to deduce it from the course and outcome of the action. The result has been that Prospero's aims and methods have puzzled no one; but the reticence of Duke Vincentio has given rise to widespread complaint, if not misunderstanding as well, and *Measure for Measure* accordingly has often been thought to present a "problem" by reason of its doubtful morality, its discordant techniques, or both. The purpose of this paper is to argue that the technique of *Measure for Measure* is logical and consistent, and to support this opinion by comparing *Measure for Measure* with *The Tempest.* The two plays have much in common, and the one may be used to shed light upon the other. (p. 375)

[The pattern in *Measure for Measure*] is revealed cumulatively and held in some suspense until the very end, when everything falls into place as an effect of the culminating action; hence there can be no real explanatory comment from the Duke by way of preparation—according to the way the play is designed—and no one else is in a position to supply it. The Duke's purpose must remain something of an enigma till his final action of forgiveness makes it as explicit as it can be made. . . . [If the Duke had explained his motives at the beginning of the play,] the whole ensuing action would have been prejudged. Our sense of conflict would have been lessened. The Duke, to be sure, does not really control anyone's actions; on the contrary, he constantly prepared choices for others; but our reliance upon his revealed purposes would lessen the suspense and there would be virtually no surprise in the outcome. Thus all the author's skill goes to maintaining the suspense of the action through the Duke's reticence and the implied ambiguity of his motives and conduct, through the very ambiguity of the play's title, and the significance of the action is revealed through the recurrence of a single theme which builds a symbolic design. The method of *Measure for Measure* might thus be called "symbolic action"; that is, the theme of the play emerges out of the pattern of the action, as a conception and effect embodied

in the action without the help of any anticipatory hint or clue. (p. 379)

The Duke has prompted the action from the beginning, and none of the other characters has realized the full scope and significance of his operations. He has deceived them all for their own good, this "duke of dark corners" [IV. iv. 157], and, in the end, as Wilson Knight has suggested, the Duke seems almost like the author himself telling us a story, speaking for the puppets and pulling the strings before our eyes, to show us how the mercy of the Sermon on the Mount transcends the limitations of human justice and fills human life with the radiance of love. And yet, while the action is going forward, Angelo and Isabel and Claudio, Lucio and Pompey and Barnardine and the rest, all seem real enough; and everyone, under the Duke's direction, makes some kind of choice, even Barnardine, who chooses not to be bothered. The play is not a parable or an allegory, unless we regard it in only one aspect, its symbolic aspect; it is an action, a drama of men and women lusting and hating, loving and suffering, as well. But it has great dramatic suspense and a most happy ending, and the Duke's conduct, until the end, seems very mysterious and arbitrary; and all this makes the play seem something like a fairy tale too. It is this mingling of effects of successful realism with the more obvious artifice of the Duke's role that apparently sits so ill with some critics; though the same mingling of "art" and "artifice"—to use Professor Stoll's distinction [see excerpt above, 1943]—is to be found in *The Tempest.* (pp. 380-81)

When we reflect upon it, we cannot help noticing how close the parallel is [between *The Tempest* and] *Measure for Measure.* In each play, the action is set going and guided throughout by its duke; yet neither Duke Vincentio nor Prospero controls anyone else's choice; rather, they prepare the conditions in which others choose while taking precautions that no one shall give effect to a choice injurious to others. As Vincentio guides Claudio and Angelo to choose penitence and Isabel to prefer mercy to revenge or justice, so Prospero guides Alonso to choose penitence, Ferdinand to choose the love of Miranda, while he himself forgoes revenge or even justice in favor of mercy; and even Caliban shows signs of amendment at the end. As Barnardine and Lucio in *Measure for Measure* are given the chance to repent, though they remain unmoved, so with Antonio and Sebastian; but though all four are pardoned, they are also curbed of their evil propensities.

The parallelism is not precise—nor should we expect it to be; Shakespeare does not repeat himself—but it is fundamental, arising as it does out of the identical ruling conception of the two plays: the virtue of forgiveness and the tempering of justice with mercy; and the parallel may be carried further. In the two dukes, there is the suggestion of an earlier unworldliness and a consequent failure to anticipate evil or cope with it—Prospero in failing to anticipate his brother's plot against him, Vincentio in failing to curb the evil conditions of Vienna. When each duke begins to act effectively, his conduct seems to invoke a certain supernatural aid and sanction. Duke Vincentio's arrangements are compared with the operation of Divine Grace [*Measure for Measure,* V. i. 369], while Prospero's "white-magic" is explained as divinely sanctioned: Ariel and his fellows are "ministers of fate" [*The Tempest,* III. iii. 60ff], and their powers cannot be used to serve an evil purpose. . . . Thus each duke is seen as the human agent who gives effect to the moral order of things as divinely authorized. And appropriately, after the wrongs have been righted and the reconciliations effected, Duke Vincentio lays aside his friar's robe and returns to his appointed role as ruler of Vienna; Prospero breaks his staff, drowns his book, and resumes his natural function as Duke of Milan. Prospero's method throughout *The Tempest* has been to deceive men for their own good; so with Duke Vincentio; and *The Tempest* shows us the same design of "measure for measure": the suffering visited upon Prospero is in turn meted to his enemies; but the grace that preserved Prospero also preserves them.

When each duke puts off his disguise and stands revealed in his true temporal status, the Duke of Vienna and the Duke of Milan, each is seen as a *temporal* authority, the good governor who knows how to mingle mercy with justice. Mr. Wilson Knight has associated *Measure for Measure* with the text: "Judge not, that ye be not judged," and has further written: "The central idea of *Measure for Measure* is this: 'And forgive us our debts as we forgive our debtors.' Thus 'justice' is a mockery: man, himself a sinner, cannot presume to judge. That is the lesson driven home in *Measure for Measure*" [see excerpt above, 1930]. But this way of putting it overlooks an important point. Duke Vincentio and Duke Prospero are both temporal rulers; that is, to a sixteenth-century way of thought, they are divinely constituted authorities whose duty it is to rule and judge other men, according to the precept and example of Scripture, with justice and mercy. This is precisely the problem with which *Measure for Measure* deals, how to do this; and it is likewise the difficulty that confronts Prospero. Each of them solves the problem, though by different means. Duke Vincentio relies upon a conveniently impenetrable disguise and a certain ubiquitousness that makes it possible for him to influence people's purposes strongly for good; and Prospero has his magic; but each of them stands revealed at the end in his proper role as an earthly ruler who judges his subjects with authority. Each is a type and model of the Christian governor. (pp. 382-83)

These affiliations between the two plays can hardly be inadvertent on Shakespeare's part. *Measure for Measure* is an important "source" for *The Tempest*. The later play is a reworking of the theme of the former, employing a different dramatic method and calculated for a different dramatic effect. *Measure for Measure* is all action; *The Tempest* is largely spectacle invested with some of the finest poetry Shakespeare ever wrote. The significance of the one emerges from the pattern of the action, without commentary; of the other, from a succession of magic spells accompanied by the magician's interpretive comment. The method of *The Tempest* is less dramatic, less deeply moving, perhaps; it is pictorially static, "spatial," as Mr. Wilson Knight calls it; and this effect is in remarkable contrast with the temporal, dynamic movement of *Measure for Measure*. But the method of *The Tempest* affords very much greater scope for the decorating of the theme, with the panoply of the court masque, its gorgeous properties of costume and music and setting, graceful dances and tableaux, and the richer texture of poetic image and symbol. None of these compete with the action of the developing thought of *The Tempest*, made crystal clear in Prospero's explanations. In *Measure for Measure*, the method is indirect and more economical of decoration; and by the same token it is the more deeply stirring; the action contains the thought, the symbolic effect, which is achieved wholly by implication. (pp. 383-84)

> Harold S. Wilson, "Action and Symbol in 'Measure for Measure' and 'The Tempest'," in Shakespeare Quarterly, Vol. IV, No. 4, October, 1953, pp. 375-84.

NEVILL COGHILL   (essay date 1955)

[*In the following excerpt, Coghill initially defines the two conflicting comic traditions popular during Shakespeare's lifetime. The first he identifies as the medieval comic convention exemplified in the works of Dante, Chaucer, and John Lydgate and founded on a pattern similar to that in the Book of Job; its primary characteristics—God's testing of human faith and the strengthening of virtue through suffering and trial—reflect its Christian origins. The second he identifies as the Latin comic convention exemplified in the works of Philip Sydney and Ben Jonson and based on the ridicule of human folly or sin. Coghill claims that all of Shakespeare's comedies, including* Measure for Measure, *are founded on the medieval comic tradition. He calls* Measure for Measure *a study of human testing, like Chaucer's "Clerk's Tale," and he disputes Clifford Leech's assessment that the structure of the play is not necessarily allegorical (see excerpt above, 1950), claiming that the characters of the Duke and Isabella attest to its religious meaning. Within this allegorical framework, Coghill describes the Duke as the primum mobile, or "prime mover" of the action, and Isabella, Angelo, and Claudio as the primary figures the Duke "tests." Importantly, Coghill is one of the only critics to assign Lucio a relatively significant role in the play, describing him as something of a Satan figure, specifically since he stands out as the Duke's adversary and the instrument by which Isabella and Angelo "are led into temptation." For further discussion of* Measure for Measure's *indebtedness to contemporary comic traditions, especially the satiric convention employed by Jonson, see the excerpts by Oscar James Campbell (1943) and Murray Krieger (1951).*]

Long before there was any inkling that Shakespeare had ever written a 'dark' comedy, *Measure for Measure* had been judged morally shocking, a play horrible in its tragedy, disgusting in its comedy and scandalous in its conclusion. . . .

Since the discovery of a working Shakespeare chronology this view has strengthened, for the play falls squarely in the 'Tragic Period' thereby revealed; it lies deep in what Dowden called 'The Depths'. The turbid sexual anguish, the manifold treacheries, the squalor and injustice of the play found in this fact their explanation.

Then came a tendency to account for Shakespeare's seven-year contemplation of Evil in terms of some disaster in his private life, some huge personal despair, of which the plays (it was thought) might be in some sense a record; and, after that, it seemed that the despairs of our own age chimed in so readily with those attributed to him that it was almost as if a full understanding of these plays was a privilege reserved for the sorrowful century in which we live. (p. 14)

The argument from chronology, however, can lead by a series of doubtful premises and false syllogisms into many dangerous superstitions; such as that Shakespeare's tragic vision, being concerned with self-torture and waste, is a vision of disillusion and despair; that Art is Self-expression and that therefore a man capable of such a vision must himself be in a condition of disillusion and despair; that such a man will eschew comedy altogether unless he can find in it a further means to vent his edifying blasphemy at the Abyss and die, or a chance to extend Timon's welcome to his theatre-patrons:

> Uncover, dogs, and lap.
> [*Timon of Athens*, III. vi. 85]

But if a 'dark' interpretation of *Measure for Measure* is a lawless conjecture, what is the alternative? May we trust the Christian context to which it has been so movingly referred by other critics—Wilson Knight, the late R. W. Chambers, Roy

Battenhouse and Miss Pope? [See excerpts above, 1930, 1937, 1946, and 1949.] Clifford Leech thinks not . . . :

> This Christian colouring is . . . not more than intermittent in the play: it wells up, as it were, from Shakespeare's unconscious inheritance, and it does not determine the play's characteristic effect [see excerpt above, 1950].
>
> (p. 16)

But if these claims are true, the Christian colouring of the play can hardly be "no more than intermittent"; on the contrary it must certainly "determine the play's most characteristic effect"; it must even be pervasive, for to be pervasive is the nature of the theme in any great work of art. Leech wisely bids us beware of "imposing a pattern on Shakespeare's thought"; and so we must. But what if the pattern is really there? May we not recognize it? He also seems to commend in the play "a complexity of meaning . . . that enables the theatrical producer to aim at a new 'interpretation'". But, as it seems to me, what is here involved is not complexity but contradiction. We have two sharply-defined and widely-held views diametrically opposed to each other; at least one of them must be wrong, and by 'wrong' I mean 'hostile or contrary to Shakespeare's understanding of it'—an understanding which it is often the excellent foppery of producers to ignore, or to dismiss as unascertainable.

The evidences advanced, and for which considerable objectivity can be claimed, are pointers towards an understanding of the play which is at least likely to have been his, and it is my hope that by bringing the test of comic form to bear upon it, that likelihood will seem a certainty. (pp. 16-17)

[There] existed in the sixteenth century two opposed conventions as to the nature of comedy; the first, then losing ground among the critics, was the medieval. . . . This is comedy as Dante, Chaucer and Lydgate knew and understood it. *The Divine Comedy* was its greatest exemplar, and it is to Dante also that we owe a very full exposition of its nature, in his famous letter to Can Grande.

Such a comedy, then, has this known, certain and necessary shape, that it starts in trouble and ends in joy, and this is the convention manifestly followed by Shakespeare in almost every instance. . . . (p. 17)

The other and opposed convention, though in fact of equal antiquity with the medieval form (for both . . . go back to the Latin grammarians of the fourth century) first came to the fore at the Renaissance and may be defined in the words of Sir Philip Sidney [in "An Apologie for Poetrie"].

> Comedy is an imitation of the common errors of our life, which he representeth in the most ridiculous and scornefull sort that may be; so that it is impossible that any beholder can be content to be such a one.

This was the tradition of comedy embraced by Ben Jonson.

To return, however, to Dante. He explains that his work (the *Paradiso*) is a comedy and is to be interpreted allegorically, according to the usual medieval fourfold scheme; and he gives us an example of how to do this: *(a)* The Children of Israel (he reminds us) went from servitude in Egypt to the milk and honey of the Promised Land; their story is therefore a comedy as defined. *(b)* So we, in our redemption made through Christ, passed from the bondage of ignorance to the light of the Gospel.

(c) So the soul, in its exchange of the state of sin for a state of grace, is also to be understood in the image of the Exodus. *(d)* So the righteous pass at death from this body of corruption into eternal glory. Comic form was, in other words, a picture of ultimate reality, as Dante knew it. Comic form was cosmic form. Its heart was love.

Shakespeare's comedies also begin with trouble, end in joy and are centred in love, albeit human love. The joyful *solemnitas* of marriage is an image of happiness that ends his comedies almost as invariably as death ends a tragedy. Unless *Measure for Measure* be an exception in his use of this image, there are no exceptions. Wherever else it comes in his comedy, it betokens joy.

To draw argument from allegory, we must follow, as Dante did, the narrative movement. It is here that we will find the pattern, if there is a pattern, that we are not to impose. (pp. 17-18)

Measure for Measure is in an older and better tradition than any mere morality play; it is, as Wilson Knight has pointed out, in the tradition of the parables of Christ, that is, something fully human, like the narrative of the Prodigal Son . . . , which has moral overtones easily perceived . . . and pictures a typical human situation in which we find the likeness of our own personal situations. . . . In short it shows a human world in an eternal situation, not a series of abstractions in a contrived predicament, like a Morality Play or like the comedies of Ben Jonson.

In our own literature Chaucer showed the way to this kind of allegory; he too excelled in the gift of creating character and could intermix allegory with comedy upon occasion; the *locus classicus* is the Clerk's Tale of Patient Griselda, one of the most tenderly and barbarously human in all Chaucer, yet with overtones on every plane. . . . (p. 18)

Now this is like, and it is not like, *Measure for Measure*. It is like it in that both are stories of human testing, trial·or assay, seen in relation to both God and man. It is unlike in that the reason given by Chaucer for God's testing us is that we must exercise our virtues as an athlete exercises his muscles, not to know if they are there, but to keep them fit. In *Measure for Measure* the reason is the one given in the Sermon on the Mount:

> Let your light so shine before men that they may see your good works and glorify your Father which is in heaven.

Or, to use the Duke's words:

> Heaven doth with us as we with torches do,
> Not light them for themselves; for if our virtues
> Did not go forth of us, 'twere all alike
> As if we had them not.
>
> [I. i. 32-5]

Now these words govern the entire action of the play, which pictures the world as a place where all are continually liable to tests, and some to tests increasingly severe, that they may show their virtues. Isabella and Angelo are tested to the core.

Of course the Duke knows, before the play begins, that there is some reason to suspect Angelo's integrity; indeed he gives him the strongest possible hint that he knows of his not wholly creditable past when he tells him that one who has observed his history could unfold his character. The hint wears a polite veil of ambiguity, but it is a warning to him none the less:

> There is a kind of character in thy life,
> That to the observer doth thy history
> Fully unfold.
>
> [I. i. 27-9]

Angelo's mettle is to be tested. Of course he falls at the first fence, though I believe the point has not been noted. He falls at the test of his faithfulness in elementary matters of justice, when he is to adjudicate in the case of Mr. Froth and Pompey Bum; instead of doing his duty he exhibits the insolence of office, refuses the tedium of sifting evidence and departs with a pun and a flick of cruelty, leaving the patient Escalus to do his work for him:

> This will last out a night in Russia,
> When nights are longest there: I'll take my leave,
> And leave you to the hearing of the cause;
> Hoping you'll find good cause to whip them all.
>
> [II. i. 134-37]

Then comes the greater testing when he is confronted by the pleading beauty of Isabella, and the anguish of his spirit expresses itself in two soliloquies of a quality not inferior to those of Hamlet. From then on he continues to fail and fall under successive test, more and more hideously up to the instant of discovery.

It was the action of the devious Lucio in persuading Isabella to intercede for her brother with Angelo that had brought him to this pass; it also brought Isabella to the test of her chastity. The fact that she resisted in that brought her to the further test of her courage: she had to tell her condemned brother that he must die. She could easily have lied to him, need never have told him of the one condition upon which life had been promised to him. But she preferred to tell the truth. In these two tests she is seen to triumph. . . . She has still, as Chambers has so well noted, to be searched for charity of heart. When the time comes, she is found to have that also; perhaps she learnt it during the play.

Isabella is in turn a means of testing Claudio. Does he value her soul above his own life? At first he does, nobly responding

> Thou shant not do't.
>
> [III. i. 102]

He had been prepared for this test by the Friar Duke, who had sought to give him what he needed most—the cardinal virtue of fortitude—but he could not hold on to it. Down he went at the third step, like St. Peter when he left the boat and tried to walk on the waters. He does not drown, for the Duke steps in to save him with a white lie, so offensive even to those not deeply religious:

> Son, I have overheard what hath past between
> you and your sister. Angelo had never the pur-
> pose to corrupt her; only he hath made an assay
> of her virtue. . . . I am confessor to Angelo,
> and I know this to be true; therefore prepare
> yourself to death.
>
> [III. i. 160-67]

The Duke has been criticized by some for preaching a stoical rather than a Christian sermon; yet John Donne was a Christian preacher, and one has only to finger through his sermons to find passages of no less stoical admonition on the contempt of life. . . . The white lie remains an offence to critics, but apparently without evil effect in the play. Indeed it sets the stricken Claudio upon his feet again, for he replies to it:

> Let me ask my sister pardon. I am so out of
> love with life, that I will sue to be rid of it.
>
> [III. i. 171-72]

He is safely back in the boat.

(pp. 19-20)

[Juliet is also put to test, and she] responds with what by Christian standards, or by whatever standards may be invoked, is the answer of a soul in a state of grace:

> I do repent me, as it is an evil,
> And take the shame with joy.
>
> [II. iii. 35-6]
>
> (p. 20)

To return to the narrative design; we have seen who the tested are. Who is the tester? In all cases, sometimes directly and sometimes at one or two removes, it is the Duke. He is the *primum mobile* ["prime mover"] of the play.

What else do we know of him? We know that he had long since ordained laws the breach of which he has never himself punished, because his personal intervention would seem 'too dreadful' [I. iii. 34]; he has withdrawn himself into invisibility from the world of which he is the Lord, but remains as it were omnipresent and omniscient, in the guise of a priest, seeking to draw good out of evil; he reappears "like power divine" [V. i. 369] in righteousness, majesty and judgement in the last scene. It is not very difficult to see what is here suggested on the anagogical plane, without taking away a particle of the Duke's humanity on the literal plane. One has to think both thoughts at once, to be 'multi-conscious' as S. L. Bethell has so well explained. (p. 21)

It is of course intellectually possible to twist the story of the Incarnation so as to make it seem as if God the Father and God the Holy Ghost had conspired to slay God the Son. That is what Langland calls "drivelling on the dais" and "gnawing God with the gorge". In like manner we are drivelling on the dais if we accent what is irrelevant or distort what is apparent in the behaviour of the Duke—if we complain that he pretends to be what he is not, that he lies to Claudio, that he pimps for Mariana, and so on. What is important to notice in the 'bed-trick' (as it has been called) is not what happens to Mariana, but what happens to Angelo. The bed-trick puts him in exactly the same position (with regard to the law which he is charged to administer) as Claudio, whom he had condemned, is in. Both have lain with their contracted wives before marriage; both are equally guilty. That is the whole point, and to glance wryly at the morality of substituting Mariana for Isabella is to refuse proper attention to what Shakespeare is trying to do with the story he found. It is to underline what is accidental and irrelevant instead of what is pertinent and essential, the very core of the situation, long since announced with unconscious but self-condemning irony by Angelo himself:

> When I, that censure him, do so offend,
> Let mine own judgement pattern out my death,
> And nothing come in partial. Sir, he must die.
>
> [II. i. 29-31]

Handy-dandy, which is the justice, which is the thief? With the marvellous adroitness noted by F. R. Leavis [see excerpt above, 1942] of the last Act, the irony is brought home, full circle, in the denouement:

'An Angelo for Claudio, death for death!'
Haste still pays haste, and leisure answers leisure;
Like doth quit like, and MEASURE still for MEASURE . . .
We do condemn thee to the very block
Where Claudio stoop'd to death, and with like haste.

[V. i. 409-15]

Would it be sensible at such a moment to remark that the Duke is lying again, since, as well he knows, Claudio is alive and just about to be pardoned? It would not. More sensible would be to note that Angelo, like Claudio, is repentant, and, like him, is forgiven. That is the only block on which they have to stoop. The parallel between them is maintained to the end. . . . Marriage seems at least to be the Duke's idea of a right solution for problems of incontinence. Lucio, no less guilty in this kind, as Mistress Overdone tells us,

Mistress Kate Keep-Down was with child by him in the Duke's time, he promised her marriage . . .

[III. ii. 199-201]

is obliged to keep his promise.

The mention of Lucio at last raises the question where he is to be fitted into the grand allegorical design. Before this can be answered there are some strange things to be noted about him that, I think, have not received proper attention. (pp. 21-2)

He is, as I have said, the instrument by which Isabella is led into temptation, in a scene which shows him gallant and agreeable; he treats her brother's sin as a thing for which, in his opinion, Claudio should be rewarded rather than punished, and when he is rebuked by Isabella for this levity, he tells her that he holds her "as a thing ensky'd and sainted" [I. iv. 34], which, from the general tone of his conversation, seems hardly probable. It is rather a piece of alluring humbug, for, as he says himself, it is his familiar sin to play the lapwing with maids; and here he is at his lapwing tricks. The next time we see him he has brought her to Angelo and is warming her to her work with him, with worldly-wise asides.

Thereafter his function in the play is virtually confined to being rude to the Duke; if anyone in the audience has felt an impulse to "drivel on the dais", for instance by criticizing the Duke for duplicity, the crudity of Lucio's slanders ought to throw him back onto the Duke's side of the fence. Amusing as he is, Lucio is a foul-mouthed liar, and that fact should restore us to our senses; but it may not succeed with everybody. Some of the mud will cling perhaps. "I am a kind of burr; I shall stick" [IV. iii. 179], as he says himself. Whether or not this be so, his function is that of comic adversary to the Duke.

All this is fairly straightforward, but now there must be mentioned a point in the presentation of Lucio that is both startling and difficult to argue, more especially as the authenticity of his character has been impugned by Dover Wilson, who thinks him largely the product of a revising botcher, and is especially suspicious of the passages of prose dialogue in which he occurs [see Additional Bibliography]. It may therefore be that Lucio's part in the allegorical design has been obscured; nevertheless I hope to recover it. I would first draw attention to the fact that both in the verse and in the prose he speaks, Lucio gives us reason to think that he knows all the time who the Friar-Duke is. (pp. 22-3)

The duke is very strangely gone from hence;
Bore many gentlemen, myself being one,
In hand and hope of action: but we do learn

By those that know the very nerves of state,
His givings-out were of an infinite distance
From his true-meant design.

[I. iv. 50-5]
(p. 23)

It was a mad fantastical trick of him to steal from the state, and usurp the beggary he was never born to.

[III. ii. 92-4]

The beggary he was never born to. How did Lucio know the Duke had become a mendicant? No one else thought so. The only answer we have is his own, that he knew what he knew; and that is a line that can hardly be said without searching innuendo:

Come, sir, I know what I know.

[III. ii. 152]

If Lucio did not know, but was pretending to, it was an amazing guess, just as it was a rare coincidence that he should broach such a subject to the Duke himself, and to him only. Is it a wholly satisfactory explanation to say the coincidence is no more than a stage-situation contrived to raise a laugh? It seems to carry a hint beyond that.

Let me gather together these observations about Lucio. He is never tempted himself: he is the instrument by which Isabella and Angelo are led into temptation: he is the Duke's adversary and mocker: it is hinted that he has recognized the Duke in the Friar, and he is not afraid of him. It seems almost too obvious what part Lucio plays in the parable of the play. Like the Duke, he suggests an anagogical plane of meaning, on which he stands for what Hardy would have called the Spirit Ironic or the Spirit Sinister; or Satan, as he is called in that other play of testing, *The Book of Job*. He is very far, of course, from Milton's Satan. . . . Lucio is not of his calibre, not even of that of Lucifer, though the name is suggestive; he is hardly more than a minor fiend, like that fiend in *The Friar's Tale,* who claims to be sometimes an instrument of God. . . . (p. 24)

This suggestion, grounded in the text such as we have it, completes the shadowy shape of the human world as a testing-ground, and of an even shadowier world above it which together make the meaning of the play. The allegorical should neither supplant nor overbear the literal, human meaning; it should on the contrary enrich it by such touches in production as will make audiences imaginatively conscious of an extra depth. They need not be able clearly to define it, but it should remain an overtone which hearing they may hear and not understand. There is no need to be heavy-handed in the matter.

What then happens at the end, when Lucio unmasks the Duke? If Lucio knew all along who the 'Friar' was, how can that be reconciled with his tearing off his cowl? Job's Satan and Chaucer's fiend, being comedy characters as well as Immortals, should be able to pass the situation off; and so can Lucio. He makes a joke of it. After calling him a "bald-pated, lying rascal" [V. i. 352] and bidding him show his "sheep-biting face" [V. i. 354] he reveals his Duke to the assembly. There is a general movement of stupefaction. For an instant Lucio strikes the pose of a conjuror who has produced a white rabbit out of a black hat, and then he slinks tiptoe away, leaving stage-centre to more important characters, with a line that carries a grimace and raises a laugh:

This may prove worse than hanging.

[V. i. 360]

And indeed Shakespeare concludes the play in a comic and a forgiving mood; Lucio must of course be kept down, but only by Kate Keep-Down. What matters more is that we are in a swift mood of general amnesty and the uniting of lovers; and the Duke will govern them and lift them up for ever. (pp. 24-5)

It seems worth adding, for the sake of objectivity, that in *Promus and Cassandra* there is no character that corresponds to Mariana, no character that corresponds to Lucio, and no character that corresponds to the Friar-Duke; for the King of Hungary who comes so tardily in towards the end of Whetstone's double-decker ten-act play is a mere *Deus ex machina*. The omnipresent Friar-Duke is Shakespeare's invention; so are Lucio, Mariana and Barnardine. There is no scene in the source corresponding to that which shows the penitence of Juliet, and, most significant of all, Shakespeare has turned Cassandra, who is described merely as "a very vertuous and bewtiful Gentlewoman", into Isabella, about to enter the cloister and become a votarist of St. Clare, and the bride of Christ.

Can changes such as these 'well up from the unconscious'? Do they not necessarily indicate some meditated purpose? I have attempted to present a coherent meaning that accounts for them and for other changes in the play; of course there may be some other and better explanation; but it cannot be objected that I have imposed an unwarrantably religious pattern upon it, for it is Isabella and the Friar-Duke who import religion into the play, not I.

I would, however, rather refer the matter once more to that deceptively simple medieval formula for comedy. It will then at once become apparent why a religious basis for the design of this particular play is inevitable; the reason is that the subject-matter is sin.

Exordium triste laeto fine commutans. That is the difference between the *exordium triste* in *Measure for Measure* and in those other, earlier comedies; in them the causes of sadness that haunt their beginnings are separations, misunderstandings, crossings in love, exiles, shipwrecks, paternal wrath, mistaken identity, false report, fickleness, shrewishness and other light afflictions; such things are easily supplied with happy endings, they belong to the "golden World". But can there be happiness for a world bursting with sin and misery? Must Evil always end in Tragedy?

It may call for a mind at the top of its energies and a man in good heart to hold up a mirror to nature so that it reflects what is truly dark and diseased, yet still can show how it may turn to health and joy. To do so was possible to Shakespeare in the midst of his so-called 'Tragic Period', and that it is possible has always been the mainstay of Christian imagination; we live in a fallen world and yet have hope of salvation. It is the comedy of Adam.

If a 'dark' comedy is one in which pessimism or cynicism is uppermost, it has yet to be shown that there is any such thing in Shakespeare. *Measure for Measure* is as easily embraced by the medieval definition of comedy as any other that he wrote, for that definition includes sin as a root-cause of sorrow, as it is also a cause of all Christian joy. (pp. 25-6)

> Nevill Coghill, "Comic Form in 'Measure for Measure'," in *Shakespeare Survey: An Annual Survey of Shakespearian Study and Production, Vol. 8, 1955,* pp. 14-27.

ROBERT ORNSTEIN (essay date 1957)

[*Ornstein is a twentieth-century American critic and scholar and the author of* A Kingdom for the Stage: The Achievement of Shakespeare's History Plays *(1972), which has been called one of the most important contributions to Shakespearean studies in recent years, as well as the most influential study of the history plays since E.M.W. Tillyard's* The Elizabethan World Picture *(1944). Ornstein's purpose was to challenge the popular belief that Shakespeare's histories do not dramatize such universal concerns as human nature and the effects of power, but rather the orthodox view of English history as championed by the Tudor monarchy. Ornstein's attempt to interpret the history plays as drama rather than historical documents contributed to a reappraisal of these works, specifically with regard to their political assumptions, and signified a return to the same standard of evaluation accorded to the comedies and tragedies. In the following excerpt, Ornstein argues that it is the critics rather than the characters of* Measure for Measure *who struggle with questions of morality. To him, Angelo, Isabella, and the Duke are insignificant and unheroic; their soliloquies reveal neither "depth of conviction" nor perplexity, nor do they gain self-knowledge. Ornstein contends that the root of the dissatisfaction with* Measure for Measure *stems from the conflicts and questions Shakespeare leaves unresolved, such as the conflict between "Divine Commandment and human frailty, between the high ethic of the Gospel and the necessity of punitive law." Yet, he maintains that the echoes of Divine Judgment are not meant to mock humanity's attempts at justice and mercy; rather, they suggest "an exalted ethic" which the individual may barely comprehend, but which, on occasion, "illumines his life with a touch of grace beyond the reach of human arts." For additional discussion of the ambiguity in* Measure for Measure, *see the excerpts by L. C. Knights (1942), Derek A. Traversi (1942), and J. W. Lever (1965).*]

So much attention has been paid to the artifices and artificialities of Shakespeare's *Measure for Measure* that it is perhaps time to rediscover the play's essential human truths. Although the fable seems, at first glance, an unreconstructed bit of novella chicanery, it is set in a realistic civic world called "Vienna." . . . Tragedy threatens insignificant lives and sacred honors but is averted by the politic stratagems and unheroic compromises that sustain communal life.

One can find almost anything in this Vienna except greatness, for it is a comic world of little men dwarfed by the minor catastrophes their frailties create. It is the *critics* who ponder the moral dilemmas in Shakespeare's *Measure for Measure*. The characters in the play do not wrestle with problems of moral choice because they do not recognize them. Assured of certain certainties, they hurry down unfamiliar pathways, pausing but a moment at each blind turning. Unaccustomed to examining their own actions, they do not reveal, in soliloquy, unexpected depths of conviction or perplexity. The Duke offers only one formal, semi-choric comment on the responsibilities of office. Isabella pauses to and from her visit with Claudio, but simply to confirm her instinctive, inevitable decision. Angelo three times approaches the edge of self-knowledge only to retreat, first into incredulous dismay, next into despairing but facile cynicism, and last into craven fear.

Because they place themselves at the center of their moral universes (as ruler, virgin, and judge), they never gain that complete awareness of self which redeems the coarser-grained Claudio. Indeed, like most respectable people they are better at deceiving themselves than at deceiving others. (p. 15)

Shakespeare's *Measure for Measure* . . . does not cast off all human lendings to lay bare the soul of depravity or saintliness. Rather it sheds new light on human lendings—on the forms, observances, and values which normalize civic relationships. It dramatizes the ''social mode'' of morality, the counterfeited expression of divine law and judgment, mercy, and love in ordinary life. Its thematic image is, in fact, the counterfeit coin, the debased marker of worldly value which passes undetected until weighed against an uncorrupted standard of worth. Counterfeitings and substitutions are the center of the action as well as the meaning of the play. (pp. 15-16)

Behind the sleights and evasions which surround the administration of Viennese justice, however, rises the ''uncorrupted standard'' of the Morality, evoked in language, metaphor, and dramatic debate, reminding the audience (if not the players) of the angelic compassion and disinterestedness that is scarcely found in human pleadings. In Vienna, Justice is first represented by a ruler who admittedly did not punish offenders, and next by his substitute, a heartless legalist whose passions betray him into worse crimes than those he ruthlessly condemns. Mercy (Isabella) is cold in her plea. She is too willing to accept the harsh sentences of the law and must be prompted by the evil-tongued, evil-minded Lucio. Actually, she is a daughter of Mercy only by an accident of blood. Her motive is not a selfless redeeming love of humanity but the selfish love of sister for brother. Committed to a religious ideal of chastity, she has no pity for Claudio's frailty. She cannot (as Mercy should) forgive him his sin, but she would not have him suffer for it. (p. 16)

She is as strict a moralist as the ''prenzie Deputy'' and as disdainful of other people's weaknesses. Accepting the black and white universe of the medieval sermonist, she seems to recognize only two moral categories: the virtuous and the vicious—those eternally damned for even a single trespass. Thus she does not plead the obvious extenuating circumstances of her brother's crime—his youthfulness, his true affection, and his intention to marry—for these are irrelevant considerations opposed to the irreparable breach of ''all-building law'' [II. iv. 94]. But equating Angelo's role with that of a divine Justice, she eloquently pleads that he perform the God-like office of mercy.

Isabella's pleas fall on deaf ears, not because Angelo is cruel, but because he is a realistic administrator who distinguishes between the divine and human offices which she confuses. He never claims to have judged Claudio with divine omniscience. . . . Angelo, however, has the perfect answer for those who doubt one man's ability to judge another:

'Tis one thing to be tempted, Escalus,
Another thing to fall. I not deny,
The jury, passing on the prisoner's life,
May in the sworn twelve have a thief or two
Guiltier than him they try. What's open made to justice,
That justice seizes. What know the laws
That thieves do pass on thieves? 'Tis very pregnant,
The jewel that we find, we stoop and take't,
Because we see it, but what we do not see
We tread upon, and never think of it.

[II. i. 17-26]

That is to say, in an imperfect world perfection is an absurd criterion of justice. Although Divine Law and the nature of God are inseparable because one springs from and exemplifies the other, civil law is distinct from, and superior to (by its ideality) the nature of any one man. Thus while it would be tyrannical for God to punish man for a vice which He shared, a human judge can rightly punish those weaknesses of the flesh which no man wholly escapes. And though it would be unjust

for God, who sees all, to punish one sinner while a thousand escape, it is not unjust for a human judge, who cannot see all, to punish only those criminals who are caught. (pp. 16-17)

Moral law sets the standard of behavior, civil law maintains the standard; the former condemns, the latter punishes. ''Judge not that ye be not judged'' may be the highest ideal of individual relationships, but as a legal principle it can only subvert society.

Now we can hardly assume that the heartless Angelo speaks for Shakespeare; yet he does speak a kind of partial truth which the Morality framework clarifies rather than contradicts. The Divine Arraignment of the Morality is supremely detached from the mundane problems of earthly society. It is concerned only with the uniquely precious and individual soul. Judgment in Vienna, however, can never escape utilitarian ends. The law's purpose (as Angelo, Lucio, and the Duke remark) is to restrain man's incipient wickedness, to ''fear the birds of prey'' [II. i. 2] and prevent ''future evils [II. ii. 95]. Utility is, in fact, the chief justification of punitive law, without which it would simply presume the judgment which should be only God's. And even with this justification, punitive law remains one of civilization's ugliest necessities, incapable by nature of rising above a *lex taliones* [''law of retaliation'']. (pp. 17-18)

Angelo sees clearly the social function of law but he cannot see beyond it. He worships legality in the name of justice because he has, after all, the viewpoint of a bureaucrat who is supposed to enforce statutes, not interpret them. A consummate prig, he congratulates himself on impersonal administration of justice because he does not realize that only in the divinely perfect Arraignment of the Morality are Legality and Justice one. Like Isabella he sees good and evil as categorical antitheses, but his moral universe does not extend beyond the city limits of Vienna in which mercy cannot be freely given.

Far more humane in his view of crime and punishment is the Duke, who understands the ideal as well as the utility of civil law. He is a kindly ruler, concerned with his people's happiness. He is intelligent and shrewdly knowledgeable about human nature. . . .

[He] is too compassionate to impose directly the severity which must on occasion accompany any form of government. In Vienna, however, the occasion for severity has arisen. The bawds and brothels are prospering, and more innocent indulgences go unreproved. (p. 18)

To the audience it seems as tyrannical to commission severity as to employ it, and cowardly to ''leave town'' allowing a Deputy to absorb public resentment. As the play proceeds, however, we suspect that the Duke appoints Angelo, not to escape unpopularity, but because he knows himself to be incapable of harshness. Though accepting the necessity of punitive law, he prefers, as he demonstrates, to rehabilitate rather than to sentence. And having no illusions about his Deputy, he remains in Vienna in disguise while the reform proceeds.

Critics who fail to see the Duke's personal motive for deputizing Angelo speak cheerfully of him as a ''scientist'' whose laboratory is the world, who empirically tests Angelo's integrity by placing him in high office. But surely no intelligent ruler tests his subordinates by giving them power of life and death when he knows beforehand their lack of simple humanity. Nor does a man as moral as the Duke experiment with human beings simply to discover what they will do. To achieve certain limited moral ends he takes certain calculated risks; he is in some respect weak but never irresponsible. . . . [Vincentio recoils] from Angelo's idea that justice is served when a lecher hangs a lecher. Reversing Isabella's demand, he would have Angelo judge *himself* as he judges others—a patent impossibility. Thus a higher justice than Vienna's demands that Claudio be set free.

To obtain this higher justice, the Duke must circumvent the forms of civil law. He must apply "craft against vice" and "pay with falsehood false exacting" [III. ii. 277, 281]. Lest Mariana shrink from her ignoble role in the deception of Angelo, Vincentio assures her

> . . . fear you not at all.
> He is your husband on a precontract.
> To bring you thus together, 'tis no sin,
> Sith that the justice of your title to him
> Doth flourish the deceit.
>
> [IV. i. 70-4]

These are strange words for one seeking to transcend legal forms. Even worse, they disturbingly echo Claudio's extenuation that his "true contract" lacked but the "formality of outward order" [I. ii. 145, 149]. What kind of morality is it that condemns a sinning lover yet countenances a politic trick compounded of lechery, deceit, and bribery? Actually, the Duke realizes the hollowness of his "comfortable words." Though he tells Mariana "'tis no sin," he later admits that Claudio's pardon is to be

> purchased by such sin
> For which the pardoner himself is in.
>
> [IV. ii. 108-09]

Once again the Duke's clever plan goes awry. Afraid to let Claudio live, Angelo reneges on the illicit bargain, leaving Vincentio no other choice than to halt the execution and render open justice by "returning" to Vienna. Even now, though, he hopes to raise the fallen Angelo. Keeping secret the fact that Claudio lives, he pits Isabella against his Deputy in an open scene of judgment. Again transcending the forms of civil law, he allows Angelo to hear his own case—to wrap himself in the public shame and ignominy that brings sudden, complete repentance.

When the Duke sheds his friar's costume, *Measure for Measure* closes with a second debate of Mercy and Justice, a second moral masque on the exalted theme of sin and redemption. This time Justice (the Duke) is incorruptible and Mercy (Isabella) truly speaks with disinterested tongue—indeed, against all promptings of hatred and revenge. And still the Duke's masque remains an elaborately contrived sham, a woefully imperfect substitute for a Divine Judgment. (pp. 18-20)

Vincentio's indictment is so stern, so just, so pregnant with moral outrage, and so precisely legal that many readers are confounded by the leniency of Angelo's sentence. They fail to see that Vincentio never intended to punish his Deputy—indeed, that his impressive bill of particulars, like his masque of judgment, is merely counterfeit. . . . [The] Duke could not justly punish Angelo *for the crimes listed* without also punishing Marianna for fornication, Isabella for breach of promise, and himself for false accusation. Moreover, the Duke, by his own high moral principles, cannot judge Angelo more severely than he judged himself—an organizer of a sordid, deceitful attempt to purchase the life of a justly sentenced criminal. As a matter of fact, the Duke omits from his indictment the one grave offense which Angelo did commit and for which he could be legally punished: namely, the criminal abuse of high office.

But then the power which corrupted Angelo was thrust upon him, against his will and entreaties, by Vincentio. To force a man to perform a duty for which he is not adequately prepared and then condemn him for his failures would smack too much of tyranny.

The Duke's pose of Justice, then, is a majestic bit of play-acting dedicated to several utilitarian ends. Angelo is shocked into complete, open repentance. Isabella, though her grace is not freely given, triumphs over vindictiveness. Her victory, however, is one of mind rather than heart. She speaks not of divine forgiveness but of the doubtful legality of the Duke's case:

> Let him not die. My brother had but justice,
> In that he did the thing for which he died.
> For Angelo,
> His act did not o'ertake his bad intent,
> And must be buried but as an intent
> That perished by the way. Thoughts are no subjects,
> Intents but merely thoughts.
>
> [V. i. 448-54]

Here is a clarity of legal perception which the precise Angelo might well admire. (Indeed, is not his failure to make these points himself proof of his regeneration?) Isabella's education in the world is nearly complete. Whereas before she confused them, now she nicely distinguishes between the high idealism of the Christian ethic and the practical realism of civil codes. Through her eyes we see that the ending of *Measure for Measure* is not patched together artistically or morally. The Duke does not improbably and arbitrarily reverse a tragic sequence of events. On the contrary, through his early intervention he diverted a potential tragedy towards a comic resolution by thwarting Angelo's criminal intentions and rehabilitating his moral character. Thus for once the claims of mercy and justice accord in a final scene of repentance, reconciliation, and promised joy.

This does not mean that the many readers who find the ending of *Measure for Measure* unsatisfactory are insensitive or mistaken. The ending of the play is unsatisfactory in that it disappoints our longing for a more perfect justice than the world affords—because it avoids the very moral problems which lend reality and meaning to a contrived novella fable. The conflict between Divine Commandment and human frailty, between the high ethic of the Gospel and the necessity of punitive law, is brushed aside, not resolved. To the final scene Angelo's legalistic conception of justice remains valid in the eyes of his fellow citizens and even triumphs in Isabella's "mercy." Civil law, however imperfectly it counterfeits Divine Judgment, must still pass current in the title, sublunary world of Vienna. (pp. 20-1)

One finishes *Measure for Measure* with mixed feelings of amusement, pity, sympathy, and scorn. . . . Yet when all has been said and done on stage, decency and common sense have triumphed over a fanatic attempt to stamp the insignia of an "ideal" morality on intractable human materials. With a little suffering has come a little more wisdom and understanding of man's precarious and tragicomic situation. We need not assume, therefore, that the echoes of parables and Moralities mock man's fumbling attempts at justice or mercy. Instead they whisper of an exalted ethic which man scarcely comprehends but which, on occasion (as even Angelo can testify), illumines his life with a touch of grace beyond the reach of human arts. (p. 22)

Robert Ornstein, ''The Human Comedy: 'Measure for Measure','' in The University of Kansas City Review, *Vol. XXIV, No. 1, October, 1957, pp. 15-22.*

BERTRAND EVANS   (essay date 1960)

[*In two studies of Shakespearean drama*, Shakespeare's Comedies *(1960) and* Shakespeare's Tragic Practice *(1979), Evans examines what he calls Shakespeare's use of ''discrepant awarenesses.'' He claims that Shakespeare's dramatic technique makes extensive use of ''gaps'' between the different levels of awareness the characters and audience possess concerning the circumstances of the plot. In his essay on* Measure for Measure, *Evans concentrates on the omniscient vantage point of the Duke, which we share until the denouement, where he is presented as the only one who understands all the aspects of the plot and controls the action of the play. Additional commentary on the Duke's omniscient and manipulative role can be found in the essays by August Wilhelm Schlegel (1808), Denton J. Snider (1890), G. Wilson Knight (1930), William Witherle Lawrence (1931), and Roy W. Battenhouse (1946).*]

Central, in point of time, among the worlds of *All's Well that Ends Well, Troilus and Cressida, Hamlet, Othello, King Lear,* and *Macbeth,* the world of *Measure for Measure* would inevitably appear as wicked, dark, and dangerous as the unhealthiest of these but that our view of it is profoundly affected by our certainty that all is well and will end well. (p. 186)

Only *The Comedy of Errors,* which has nothing to offer besides, relies more exclusively than *Measure for Measure* on discrepancies in awareness for both action and effect. We hold advantage over all named persons except the Duke and his accomplice friars during thirteen of seventeen scenes—that is, from I. iii to the end except for IV. v, when only the Duke and Friar Peter are present. Throughout this period the gap between our awareness and the participants', like the several secondary differences in the awarenesses of participants, is not only wide but defined with unfailing clarity. Once established our main advantage remains fixed until the abrupt, spectacular denouement. In all, the management of the awareness represents a reversal of the methods of *All's Well* and *Troilus and Cressida* and an emphatic reassertion of the way of *Twelfth Night* and its predecessors. Here no ambiguity is allowed to exist in our understanding of the relation of our vision to that of a participant; we have no moments of uncertainty about where we stand or where participants stand. Here it is unnecessary to review and reinterpret earlier action in the light of later action and belated information, as is repeatedly necessary in *All's Well.* Before a scene begins we are provided with the light by which it is to be seen in a true perspective.

The main cleavage of awareness comes with a single stroke in I. iii, when the Duke tells us that he will stay in Vienna. It is therefore only in the first two scenes that our vision, like the participants', is imperfect. We are deceived by the Duke's remarks in deputizing Angelo:

> Hold therefore, Angelo:
> In our remove be thou at full ourself.
> Mortality and mercy in Vienna
> Live in thy tongue and heart.
>
> [I. i. 42-5]

Though he never actually states that he intends to leave Vienna, the Duke speaks of 'our absence', 'our remove', 'Our haste from hence', and promises to communicate by letters 'How it goes with us, and do look to know / What doth befall you

here' [I. i. 18, 43, 53, 57-8]. From such remarks we must assume, with Angelo and Escalus, that he intends to travel at some distance from Vienna and to depend upon these two for information. We remain under this misapprehension throughout the second scene, along with Lucio, Pompey, Mrs. Overdone, and Claudio—the first representatives of the general world of Vienna whom we meet after Vincentio's supposed departure. We learn from them that the new deputy is tyrannizing the city, and the specific case of Claudio is so presented as to appear as desperate to us as to them. . . . (pp. 186-87)

It is just after we have been shown the peril of the city in general and Claudio in particular that Shakespeare floods our awareness with reassurance; says the mighty Duke:

> . . . to behold his sway,
> I will, as 'twere a brother of your order,
> Visit both prince and people; therefore, I prithee,
> Supply me with the habit and instruct me
> How I may formally in person bear me
> Like a true friar.
>
> [I. iii. 43-8]

This disclosure gives us a new perspective in which the situation appears suddenly and drastically changed. It establishes a climate for comedy by assuring us that a supreme power of good yet watches over this world; that evil has a line drawn around it and will be contained; that though villainy may threaten, it can do no permanent harm. Omniscience and omnipotence are on the side of good: Vincentio, unseen and unknown, will see all and know all. Ill can no more befall good people in the benignly guarded, wicked world of Vienna than in the brutal world of *The Tempest,* snug in the palm of Prospero. These are the indispensable facts that we are not to forget for an instant during the subsequent action, for their light profoundly alters the appearance of every scene. It is noteworthy that in *The Comedy of Errors,* during the entire middle action that is the lightest, most farcical in the comedies, we are asked to remember the tragic plight of Aegeon; and that in *Measure for Measure,* during the whole course of the dark and dangerous action that takes place in one of Shakespeare's worst worlds, we are required to remember that a godlike power has everything in control. Lightness is darkened, and darkness lightened: not only in climactic scenes, but often during whole actions, Shakespeare so manages the awarenesses as to make simple, single responses impossible, and to demand complex, conflicting ones. (pp. 188-89)

The chasm opened between Vienna's awareness and ours by the Duke's announcement of his masquerade is the principal dramatic fact during all subsequent action. It conditions our view of every scene after I. iii. Structurally, because of an unusually strict concentration upon one centre, *Measure for Measure* is most unlike its immediate non-tragic predecessor, *Troilus and Cressida,* in which, lacking a centre, parts have no proper orbits, but meet 'in mere oppugnancy' [*Troilus and Cressida,* I. iii. 111]. Here concentration of our awareness upon the secret shared with Vincentio controls and shapes the play's representation of the world, even as the Duke's centrality controls the world represented in the play. (p. 190)

Besides reassuring us, despite participants' fears, the early scenes serve to impress two ideas upon our consciousness: first, that Angelo's condemnation of Claudio is truly an abuse of authority which a just power would not tolerate; second, that his tyranny cannot be checked unless by the action of a just and superior power. In I. i the Duke himself has advised us of Escalus's wisdom and righteousness; when, therefore, we hear Escalus plead for Claudio, and plead in vain, the two ideas are impressed simultaneously. (p. 191)

Together, the three scenes ending in the rebellion of Angelo's flesh overwhelm our minds with a sense that justice with mercy can triumph in Vienna only if a force greater than Angelo's exists, knows all that we know, and is disposed to intervene. So far we have been advised only that the Duke has not left Vienna; he has not learned of the situation that is shaping. Now, in II. iv—with some evidence of haste in the order of events—Shakespeare brings him in to learn all that we know. Moreover, by having him learn of Claudio's affair from Juliet, the dramatist assures us that the Duke's sympathies are engaged; it is noteworthy, however, that he does not have Vincentio expressly commit himself to Claudio's cause. The Duke makes no such declaration as Oberon's: 'Ere he do leave this grove, / Thou shalt fly him and he shall seek thy love' [*A Midsummer Night's Dream*, II. ii. 245-46]. It is left to be assumed that, being benevolent, Vincentio sides with us and Claudio once he perceives what preceding scenes have made evident to us. Perhaps a declaration such as Oberon's would be both superfluous and demeaning in a force which Shakespeare begins early to elevate to the godlike. So Vincentio, first hearing of Claudio's plight from the Provost, gets the details from Juliet, and is satisfied that her repentance is not 'hollowly put on' [II. iii. 23]. . . . This is a crucial interview: if there is a precise point at which the Duke commits himself to the cause, it is here, when he finds Juliet's penitence honest, and, being so, to merit forgiveness. This is also the first of the great moments in the play during which the predominant effect is exhilaration in the knowledge that a supreme power of good exists and is ready.

At the end of II. iii, then, we know that Vincentio is aware of Claudio's plight, and sympathetic. In the next scene our knowledge briefly outstrips his when we see Angelo yield to the devil in his flesh and confront Isabella with the choice of her chastity or her brother's life. Since we have been advised a moment earlier of what Angelo intends, we hold advantage over Isabella through about a hundred lines of the interview. (pp. 192-93)

At the opening of Act III, with a double practice—eavesdropping and disguise—the Duke again catches up with us, never to fall behind again. His argument urging Claudio to be 'absolute for death' [III. i. 5], with which this scene begins, even though it lacked a context, must stand with the greatest passages in Shakespeare; its innate force, however, is enormously enhanced by the special frame of our awareness. Vincentio clearly does not intend to let Claudio die. Though he does not yet know of Angelo's improper proposal to Isabella, his interview with the penitent Juliet showed him the right and the wrong of the case. Hence the speech urging Claudio to be absolute for death is a simultaneous double practice: neither the speaker nor the argument is truly what it seems. Simply as the speech of a humble friar, the argument has power to persuade Claudio—at least for the present; but our knowledge that the speaker who argues so brilliantly for death has both authority and intent to save the life of the person addressed works a sea-change on the whole utterance. The effect of this combination of message, speaker, and situation is not exactly paralleled elsewhere in Shakespeare; the nearest analogy is the combination in *The Tempest*, when Prospero feigns to condemn the sudden love of Ferdinand and Miranda while he is inwardly overjoyed: 'At the first sight / They have chang'd eyes' [*The Tempest*, I. ii. 441-42].

The anguished scene between brother and sister which follows this introduction is similarly elevated and transformed by our advantage. For the participants it is a time of conflicting emotions, all painful. Claudio, honourable but passionately human, is appalled by thought of death and the grave:

> Ay, but to die, and go we know not where;
> To lie in cold obstruction and to rot;
> This sensible warm motion to become
> A kneaded clod, and the delighted spirit
> To bathe in fiery floods, or to reside
> In thrilling region of thick-ribbed ice;
> To be imprison'd in the viewless winds,
> And blown with restless violence round about
> The pendent world; or to be—worse than worst—
> Of those that lawless and incertain thought
> Imagine howling,—'tis too horrible!
>
> [III. i. 117-27]

All too human, he remains absolute for death only so long as he can conceive it in terms of life: 'If I must die, / I will encounter darkness as a bride, / And hug it in mine arms' [III. i. 82-4]. But his martyr's resolution is overwhelmed by that same flow of warm blood that had first swept him under Angelo's edict. In striking contrast to Claudio's human warmth is his sister's inhuman coldness. Still 'enskied and sainted' [I. iv. 34], confessing to no stirring of blood within, but even yet as frozen in nature as when she spoke her first lines in our hearing, at the entrance of the nunnery—'I speak not as desiring more, / But rather wishing a more strict restraint / Upon the sisterhood, the votaries of Saint Clare' [I. iv. 3-5]—Isabella meets her brother's plea for life with a denial that is shocking in its ferocity:

> O you beast!
> O faithless coward! O dishonest wretch!
> Wilt thou be made a man out of my vice?
> Is't not a kind of incest, to take life
> From thine own sister's shame? What should I think?
> Heaven shield my mother play'd my father fair!
> For such a warped slip of wilderness
> Ne'er issued from his blood. Take my defiance!
> Die, perish! Might but my bending down
> Reprieve thee from thy fate, it should proceed.
> I'll pray a thousand prayers for thy death,
> No word to save thee.
>
> [III. i. 135-46]

This is perhaps the warmest feeling she has ever experienced—but it expresses itself in a shriek of fury.

Like Angelo's, Isabella's veins are filled with snow-broth at first. Angelo's ice gives way in the heat of lust, Isabella's in the heat of anger. The cases run parallel, and perhaps there is no real choice between them. In each an excess of virtue amounting to a form of inhumanity yields to its opposite excess, which is a vice of humanity. Wicked as are lust and rage, they do evince a human potentiality more promising than the 'saintliness' which formerly denied this pair's affinity with humankind. The involuntary surrender of this 'saintliness' to a frailty of humanity is thus, in a sense, a step forward for both Angelo and Isabella.

Yet the precipitation of each from one excess to another evinces also a terrible need for correction—and it is a fact not to be forgotten during subsequent action *that the Duke has seen and heard exactly what we have seen and heard of Isabella's interview with her brother: 'Bring me to hear them speak, where*

I may be conceal'd' [III. i. 52-3], he told the Provost. If the hundred lines of dialogue between brother and sister were presented in another circumstance—the Duke not overhearing, or we ignorant that he overhears—the effect of the scene would be quite different. We would then stand on the participants' level, subject to the emotions that tear them. Our knowledge that the Duke, like power divine, hears both the account of Angelo's moral fall and the furious shriek of Isabella's outraged inhumanity enables us to watch the scene objectively, free of the participants' frenzy. The problem of the scene is intellectual rather than emotional, and the Duke's reassuring presence enables us to view it so. With the Duke hovering at its edge, the scene is a dark and bitter parallel of that in *A Midsummer-Night's Dream* when Oberon overhears the lovers' quarrel and enlists himself in their cause. But though dark and bitter, with the participants more agonized, the scene of Claudio and Isabella should cause us no more genuine anxiety than that of Demetrius and Helena. In each case an 'outside force' equal to the occasion hears all.

During the interview Claudio and Isabella are ignorant both that they are overheard and that the eavesdropper is the one force stronger than Angelo. A fold of their ignorance is stripped off when the Duke interrupts their talk: 'Son,' he says, 'I have overheard that hath pass'd between you and your sister' [III. i. 160-61]. That a mere friar has overheard the report of Angelo's fall and witnessed his own confession of human frailty and his sister's exhibition of inhumanity, however, signifies little to Claudio. The greater secret, which would signify much, the Duke withholds, even at the expense of a series of plain lies:

> Angelo had never the purpose to corrupt your sister; only he hath made an assay of her virtue to practise his judgment with the disposition of natures. She, having the truth of honour in her, hath made him that gracious denial which he is most glad to receive. I am confessor to Angelo, and I know this to be true; therefore prepare yourself to death.
>
> [III. i. 161-67]

The seven lines contain three falsehoods apparent to us: Angelo did indeed mean to corrupt Isabella; the Duke is not Angelo's confessor; and, finally, now aware of all the facts, he cannot truly intend to let Claudio die. These lies appear notably ungodlike, and here the Duke's conduct first raises a question: recognizing the perfidiousness and danger of his deputy, why does he keep up his masquerade, when the removal of his friar's hood would set matters right—or at least as right as before he gave power to Angelo? Continuation of the masquerade is essential, obviously, to the maintenance of the gap between the participants' awareness and ours—and Shakespeare's addiction to the use of an exploitable discrepancy makes him willing, sometimes, to strain probability in order to preserve the discrepancy. (pp. 195-97)

But there are further reasons for him to continue. He had set out to be a looker-on in Vienna, visiting 'both prince and people' [I. iii. 45]. In his perspective the specific case of Claudio and Isabella is part of a whole; to abandon the practice so as to rescue the first persons he finds in trouble under Angelo would be to forfeit the larger purpose. His test of Angelo, announced to Friar Thomas at the outset, designed to discover 'what our seemers be' [I. iii. 54] under the temptation of absolute power, is not yet complete; he must give the deputy rein awhile to find the limit of his propensity.

Finally, the Duke must be considered to have taken a close interest in Isabella as a result of observing her in the interview with Claudio. From what proceeds, to the very end, it is evident that he sees her to be in as great need of rescue as, in another sense, Claudio is. (p. 198)

A benevolent power, becoming ever more godlike, the Duke is concerned for Isabella and Angelo as for the rest of Vienna. Were he to give up the masquerade, neither would be saved. Isabella would withdraw to the nunnery, where an enduring rage at Angelo and Claudio would remain her only human indulgence. As for Angelo, arrested in his course, his blood would again congeal. The Duke's task is grander than merely the saving of Claudio's life: it is the salvation of Angelo and Isabella, and that, in these cases, amounts to the humanization of two 'saints'.

To carry out the purpose he must continue the masquerade. His use of the abandoned Mariana would be an absurdly inefficient method which would hardly occur to him if his purpose were only to free Claudio. The direct way to accomplish that end would be to take off his hood and speak to the Provost. *But Mariana provides a way for the salvation of everyone in need of salvation.* Much is in the Duke's mind when he tells Isabella of Mariana's plight. From his suggestion that she will at least be able to do 'uprighteously' what she is asked to do, he advances gingerly in the education of Isabella's humanity, first seeking to move compassion for Mariana's wretched condition:

> Left her in tears, and dried not one of them with his comfort; swallowed his vows whole, pretending in her discoveries of dishonour; in few, bestow'd her on her own lamentation, which she yet wears for his sake; and he, a marble to her tears, is washed with them, but relents not.
>
> [III. i. 225-30]

His words are heavily laden with the pity of it—and Isabella is sufficiently touched to remark that 'this poor maid' would be better off dead [III. i. 231-32]. On this evidence of promise in his pupil, the Duke entails the practice by which multiple ends can be accomplished: '. . . your brother saved, your honour untainted, the poor Mariana advantaged, and the corrupt deputy scaled' [III. i. 253-55]. These are the only appropriate ends of which he can speak to Isabella. On the deep-lying benefits he intends for her and Angelo he is silent. (p. 200)

Dependent upon discrepancies in awareness for its very existence, the denouement of *Measure for Measure*, in both its workmanship and its effects achieved by workmanship, has few peers and no superiors in Shakespearian comedy. Neither so fantastically complex as that of *Cymbeline* nor so grandly spectacular as that of *The Tempest*, it exceeds both in its clarity and sharpness of detail, in its structure and movement, and in its concentration of power. (pp. 207-08)

Four levels make up its structure of awareness. At the bottom are Escalus, Lucio, and all the officers and citizens gathered at the city gate to greet the Duke. These are the yet-unknowing world, alike ignorant of truth and abused by false report. The one fact known to them is that Claudio was arrested and condemned under Angelo's strict application of the law. . . .

The next level above the unknowing world's is Angelo's alone. His only advantage over Vienna is the knowledge of his improper proposal to Isabella, which proved that blood, and not the snowbroth imagined by Vienna, flows in his veins. He is quite in error in his opinion of the sequel to that proposal, believing that Isabella visited him secretly and that Claudio is now dead. (p. 208)

On the level just above Angelo's stand Isabella and, less significantly, Mariana. Isabella shares with us, the Duke, and Angelo himself an awareness of the seemer's other side. Further, with the 'friar' and Mariana, having perpetrated a midnight fraud on Angelo, she holds advantage over him in knowing the truth of that crucial incident. On the other hand, she remains ignorant of Claudio's survival and, of course, with all Vienna, of the 'friar's identity.

On the highest level, from which every aspect of the situation is open to his vision, ready to proceed with Angelo 'By cold gradation and well-balanc'd form' [IV. iii. 100], stands the Duke. Friar Peter shares all his secrets, and the Provost some of them. . . . (p. 209)

It is one of the shrewdest dramatic strokes in this play, of which the workmanship is everywhere characterized by great shrewdness, that a sense of mystery and suspense is preserved amid absolute assurance that all is and must end well. Our recognition that the Duke's mind grasps the totality of action and holds purposes beyond our certain knowledge heightens his stature during this climactic period, when full effect requires that he loom 'like power divine' [V. i. 369]. Realization that he intends to proceed 'By cold gradation and well-balanc'd form' [IV. iii. 100], joined with uncertainty of precise means and ends, binds us to watch the proceedings with an attentive eye.

Unlike Helena of All's Well, the Duke is himself on hand to direct the movements of his intricate plot—indeed, he is on hand in a triple role, as proprietor of two distinct practices and as himself. As the 'friar' he continues the masquerade begun in Act I. As the Duke who feigns to have returned from some remote country he wears a mask of ignorance. Both roles are essential in the final test of the question, whether truths can be exposed, wrongs redressed, and all set right in Vienna without the intervention of an 'outside' force. Hitherto the Duke has refused to reveal his true identity in spite of all; but once, in order to have the Provost spare Claudio's life, he had to compromise the test by displaying the Duke's hand and seal. Now, as the final action proceeds, he continues his effort to right wrong without having to call upon the supreme power which exists, in effect, apart from both 'friar' and 'newly returned' Duke. As 'friar' he is omniscient, but not omnipotent. As 'newly returned' Duke he is omnipotent, but not omniscient: indeed, his is the same ignorance as all Vienna's. Omniscience and omnipotence are combined only in the Duke in the true identity that we alone perceive, apart from either masquerader. (p. 210)

[From the first phase of the final text] and on until the moment that the friar's hood is snatched from the Duke's head, the most spectacular products of exploitation of the multiple discrepancies in awareness are bursts of irony which flare up in a succession that provides virtually steady illumination. The complex situation has been so devised that the Duke cannot address Angelo, Isabella, or Lucio without striking a shower of sparks. . . . (p. 211)

The flashes [of irony] that accompany the Duke's remarks to Angelo and Isabella, however, are only incidental to the demonstration of the main point—that if the Duke did not already know the truth it would go unregarded. It would not go unheard, but it would be rejected, even as it seems rejected now by the consciously ironical remarks of the Duke, which Angelo and Isabella take as unconsciously ironical. Repeatedly, with rising passion that suggests growth of her human capabilities, Isabella pleads for redress:

> He would not, but by gift of my chaste body
> To his concupiscible intemperate lust,
> Release my brother; and, after much debatement,
> My sisterly remorse confutes mine honour,
> And I did yield to him; but the next morn betimes,
> His purpose surfeiting, he sends a warrant
> For my poor brother's head.
>
> [V. 1. 97-103]
> (p. 212)

For Isabella the dismal affair seems to have ended in that utter defeat which Angelo foretold. But Shakespeare has equipped us with an advantage which enables us to watch objectively: even when the Duke, in his role of ignorant omnipotence, orders Isabella carried off we know that all is well. Such is the use of awareness; even this darkest moment of the play is bathed in comforting assurance that makes the effects of comedy possible.

The second phase of the final test is represented by Mariana's efforts to win the 'newly returned' Duke's belief. Her failure is as conclusive as was Isabella's, and it comes more abruptly, even though she tells perfect truth whereas Isabella mixed truth with practice:

> . . . this is the body
> That took away the match from Isabel,
> And did supply thee at thy garden-house
> In her imagin'd person.
>
> [V. i. 210-13]

Her truth is startling news, of course, to Angelo; but, though he unquestionably believes it, he gives no sign: 'This is a strange abuse' [V. i. 205]. And then, ignorant—pitifully so, in our perspective—that he is lying in the very face of heaven, he goes on boldly:

> I do perceive
> These poor informal women are no more
> But instruments of some more mightier member
> That sets them on. Let me have way, my lord,
> To find this practice out.
>
> [V. i. 235-39]

'And punish them unto your height of pleasure' [V. i. 240], the 'newly returned' Duke answers, putting the case of the women into Angelo's hands—even as he might have done if he were truly as unknowing as the deputy supposes.

In the last phase of the test the 'friar' replaces Isabella and Mariana in striving to win justice without aid from outside. Now masked as impotent omniscience rather than ignorant omnipotence, making a determined final effort, the Duke touches the highest point in his career as masquerader and perpetrator of multiple practices. His first plea hurled back at him, the 'friar' laments for the helpless victims of Angelo's tyranny:

> O, poor souls,
> Come you to seek the lamb here of the fox?
> Good night to your redress! Is the Duke gone?
> Then is your cause gone too.
>
> [V. i. 297-300]

Angelo, of course, could not be expected to heed the appeal of the 'friar' and his fellow petitioners, but Escalus might yet be induced to heed it; hence Shakespeare puts everything on the exchanges between 'friar' and Escalus rather than on 'friar' and Angelo. Moreover, the prior characterization of Escalus gives great significance to his conduct in these last crucial moments. Escalus is the wisest mere mortal in Vienna, and is completely dedicated to the idea of justice. If, therefore, the truths told by Isabella, Mariana, and the 'friar' have failed to reach him, then the final proof is conclusive: *truth and justice cannot prevail in this world without help from without.* Guilt-ridden, Angelo would of course deny the appeal; Escalus, however, has no purpose except to find the truth—and he is one who could find it if it were discoverable by mere mortal wisdom. But like Isabella in her 'Unhappy Claudio! Wretched Isabel!' [IV. iii. 121] lamentation, and like Angelo in his soliloquy—'A deflow'red maid!' [IV. iv. 21]—that just precedes the final act, he is quite mistaken about the situation in which and of which he speaks, and his verdict is therefore appalling:

> Take him hence; to the rack with him! We'll touse you
> Joint by joint, but we will know his purpose.
>
> [V. i. 311-12]

In the frightfully worsened world of *Measure for Measure,* neither awareness without power nor power without awareness is enough to save truth: both 'friar' and 'newly returned' Duke fail. The wisest man of law shouts down the very principle of justice that is dearest to him—and by the blind excess of Escalus's zeal to punish, Shakespeare drives home the ugly fact:

> Away with him to prison! Where is the Provost?
> Away with him to prison! Lay bolts enough
> upon him! Let him speak no more. Away with
> those giglots too, and with the other confederate
> companion!
>
> [V. i. 345-48]

Such would be the fate of truth in a world lacking the control of an external, benevolent, omnipotent, and omniscient force. It is noteworthy that the 'friar' does not end the masquerade voluntarily, but might have allowed himself to be taken to prison, there to continue his efforts to have truth prevail. It is Lucio who, by tearing off the 'friar's' hood, ends the Duke's masquerade. (pp. 213-15)

The main discrepancy in awarenesses which has provided the exploitable condition for almost five acts is thus closed with sensational abruptness. Lucio, suddenly lifted to our vantage-point, tries to sneak away. The wise and just Escalus, who in ignorance has just been shouting loudly in the cause of injustice, is stunned, and the Duke speaks a consoling word. But the coming-to-awareness of these persons is relatively unimportant; in this climactic instant the main attention is on the one to whom the sudden revelation means most. Says Angelo:

> O my dread lord,
> I should be guiltier than my guiltiness,
> To think I can be undiscernible,
> When I perceive your Grace, like power divine,
> Hath look'd upon my passes.
>
> [V. i. 366-70]

Angelo's conversion is effected by shock; his lesson is finished, and the Duke has really nothing more to do with this pupil. But he has not yet finished with Isabella. (p. 215)

She has come a good way from [the 'enskied and sainted' thing who wished the nunnery's rules more rigorous]—or, more precisely, *she has been led by the 'friar'.* But her humane education is not complete—nor will the Duke let it stop short of

completion. Hence he reasserts his lie about Claudio's death, and then proceeds, with the same 'cold gradation and well-balanc'd form' with which he had proceeded with Angelo, to give his pupil a final lesson—and a test. Newly married, Angelo and Mariana return to the scene, and the Duke sentences Angelo to death, making plain—and speaking pointedly to Isabella in doing so—that no malpractice of the deputy *except his execution of Claudio* is responsible for the penalty. . . . Knowing that Claudio lives, the Duke cannot really intend to take Angelo's life for Claudio's. His condemnation of Angelo is, therefore, a practice. But on whom and to what end? It is not on Angelo, already a changed man, ready to accept death, clearly in need of no further lessons. Nor, obviously, is it a practice on Mariana, who has never needed a lesson in humanity. It is a practice on Isabella, the shrewdest and most drastic devised by Vincentio in the entire action. When, speaking directly to her, he says that Angelo must die for Claudio's death, Isabella stands silent. Mariana pleads movingly for her husband's life. The Duke's answer is a harsh 'no'. Isabella stands silent. Again Mariana pleads and again the Duke's reply is cold as stone: 'Never crave him; we are definitive' [V. i. 427]. Isabella stands silent. Once more Mariana pleads, and this time drops on her knees before the Duke. Vincentio could hardly maintain his practice of seeming to intend the death of Angelo merely to prolong the sport of it—or to make Mariana 'heavenly comforts of despair' [IV. iii. 110] a little later; but again his reply is startling in its harshness: 'You do but lose your labour. / Away with him to death!' [V. i. 428-29]. Isabella stands silent. Then Mariana—who might almost perceive the purpose of the Duke's practice, and as if induced to act by his prompting—turns to beg Isabella's help:

> Sweet Isabel, take my part!
> Lend me your knees, and all my life to come
> I'll lend you all my life to do you service.
>
> [V. i. 431-32]

Isabel stands silent. Says the Duke, pointedly,

> Against all sense you do importune her.
> Should she kneel down in mercy of this fact,
> Her brother's ghost his paved bed would break,
> And take her hence in horror.
>
> [V. i. 433-36]

'Should she kneel down in mercy of this fact': it is the prompting of a hesitant pupil. And yet Isabel stands silent. Mariana again picks up her plea—this time rather a plea for Isabella's salvation than for Angelo's:

> Sweet Isabel, do yet but kneel by me.
> Hold up your hands, say nothing; I'll speak all. . . .
> O Isabel, will you not lend a knee?
>
> [V. i. 437-38, 442]

Though with Mariana's help he has led Isabella to the critical point, the Duke does not ease his demand at the last instant: 'He dies for Claudio's death' [V. i. 443]. The proof must be conclusive: if Isabella asks mercy for Angelo, she must do so even with the realization at the forefront of her consciousness that Angelo killed her brother; nothing less will serve. And it is with the words 'Claudio's death' in her ears that, at long last, she goes to her knees:

> Most bounteous sir,
> Look, if it please you, on this man condemn'd
> As if my brother liv'd.
>
> [V. i. 443-45]

It has taken much time, shrewd deception, and sharp nudging at the last moment, but the proof is won on the Duke's uncompromising terms. Working in mysterious ways, he has transformed an erstwhile 'saint' into a creature of human sympathies and forced her to demonstrate them against odds. She who had once shrieked refusal—'Might but my bending down' [III. i. 143]—to save her brother's life has at last humbly knelt to beg mercy for one who, she believes, has done her terrible wrong. Once she has been brought to her knees, no reason remains for the Duke to keep the secret of Claudio's survival—nor does he keep it. (pp. 217-18)

During the remaining eighty lines after her plea for Angelo's life Isabella is notably silent. Even when her brother is unmuffled and the Duke claims her as his bride she says nothing. One of two 'saints' humanized in the course of the action, she is presumably speechless at the sensation of blood flowing in her veins. (pp. 218-19)

> Bertrand Evans, "Like Power Divine: 'Measure for Measure'," in his Shakespeare's Comedies, Oxford at the Clarendon Press, Oxford, 1960, pp. 186-219.

ERNEST SCHANZER (essay date 1963)

[*In the introduction to his* The Problem Plays of Shakespeare *(1963), Schanzer rejects the accepted definitions of the term "problem play." He especially disputes the explanations presented by Frederick S. Boas (1896), William Witherle Lawrence (1931), and E.M.W. Tillyard (1949), arguing that the problems contained in* All's Well That Ends Well, Measure for Measure, Troilus and Cressida, *and* Hamlet *are of too diverse an assortment to be classified in the same category. Schanzer offers a more specific definition of a "problem play" that, to him, describes only* Measure for Measure, Julius Caesar, *and* Antony and Cleopatra: *a play that presents a central ethical problem "in such a manner that we are unsure of our moral bearings." His commentary on* Measure for Measure *includes a detailed study of its five main characters; the following excerpt focuses primarily on Claudio and Angelo. Schanzer, adopting a historical approach, explicates Elizabethan attitudes and customs in an attempt to resolve the perplexities in the play. He contends that Shakespeare exploited contradictions in the Church's position on marriage rites to account for Claudio's ambivalent feelings and to expose Angelo's narrow vision, as well as to heighten the parallels between Angelo and Claudio. Schanzer argues that it is only by recognizing the historical significance of the betrothal contracts in the play, between Claudio and Juliet and Angelo and Mariana, that we can understand Shakespeare's purpose. Elizabethan betrothal customs are also discussed by William Witherle Lawrence (1931), R. W. Chambers (1937), and Muriel C. Bradbrook (1941).*]

There have [been critics], notably, in the last century, such unlikely yoke-fellows as Gervinus in Germany and Walter Pater in England [see excerpts above, 1849-50 and 1874], who have seen [*Measure for Measure*] neither as expressive of cynicism and disgust nor as filled with the spirit of the Gospels, and yet believe it to be no 'meaningless' entertainment but a serious and coherent exploration of certain moral issues. It is in support of this view that the following pages are written. (p. 73)

In *Measure for Measure* Shakespeare has created a greater number of complex characters which are apt to perplex the modern reader than perhaps in any other of his plays. And an understanding of Elizabethan tenets and feelings on certain matters seems particularly necessary in order to dispel or diminish some of these perplexities.

Claudio is not the least puzzling [character]. In a valuable essay on the play, published in 1942, L. C. Knights, discussing the presentation of Claudio, expressed his belief that 'it is the slight uncertainty of attitude in Shakespeare's handling of him that explains some part, at least, of the play's disturbing effect' [see excerpt above]. . . . Apparently alone among commentators, he pointed to 'something odd and inappropriate' in Claudio's attitude towards the offence for which he has been sentenced to death. . . . What are we to make of this young man, who feels deeply sinful because he has cohabited with his wife, and at the same time sees himself as the only nominally guilty victim of a tyrannical ruler? Most commentators escape from the perplexity by ignoring Claudio's remarks about his marriage-contract. But once they are considered, how are we to account for the sense of guilt and shame, felt not only by Claudio but also by Juliet, who is made to declare of her transgression, 'I do repent me as it is an evil, / And take the shame with joy' [II. iii. 35-6]? And, above all, if Claudio and Juliet are man and wife, what legal right has Angelo to arrest them and to sentence Claudio to death for fornication?

An answer to all these questions is, I believe, to be found in the complex and inherently contradictory nature of the contemporary laws and edicts relating to marriage, which had remained basically unchanged since the twelfth century. The contradictions sprang from two opposed and irreconcilable objectives on the part of the Church. On the one hand it wished to make the contraction of a legal marriage as easy as possible in order to encourage people to live in a state of matrimony rather than 'in sin'. It therefore decreed that any *de praesenti* contract (i.e. one in which a man and a woman declared that henceforth they were husband and and wife) constituted a legal marriage. Such a contract did not need the presence of a priest, nor, indeed, of any third person to witness it, nor any deposition in writing. All that was required was the mutual consent of both parties. . . . But to counteract the obvious evils to which such laws were bound to give rise, the Church also insisted that, though valid and binding, such secret marriages were sinful and forbidden, and that, if they took place, the offenders were to be punished and forced to solemnize their marriage *in facie ecclesiae* ["in the presence of the church"]. (pp. 73-6)

If the Church denounced the contraction of clandestine marriages *per verba de praesenti*, it inveighed even more vehemently against their consummation before they had been publicly solemnized, an act which it regarded as fornication and a deadly sin. (p. 76)

We see, then, that Claudio and Juliet are guilty in the eyes of the Church of two transgressions: of having contracted a secret marriage and of having consummated it. Being technically guilty of fornication, Claudio is therefore punishable under the law which Angelo has revived. . . . Angelo's condemnation of Claudio was—and no doubt was intended by Shakespeare to appear—absolutely tyrannical. But it was also unquestionably legal. Claudio knows this only too well, and never suggests that he could save himself by appealing to the legal circumstances of his case. It is by relying on Isabel's power to move the tyrannical ruler to mercy that he hopes to save his life.

We can now understand why it should be possible for Claudio to feel guilt and shame for having cohabited with his own wife, and at the same time to see himself as a judicial victim, condemned to die merely 'for a name' [I. ii. 171]. Claudio is depicted as highly impressionable, easily swayed, and, like his counterpart in Whetstone's play, markedly religious. . . . When he . . . finds himself condemned to death for fornication, and the instrument of Juliet's disgrace, it is not surprising that, in spite of his indignation at Angelo's legal tyranny, he should see himself as the Church saw him, a sinner who must suffer for his transgressions.

It seems to me, then, that the contradictions in Claudio's attitude towards the action for which he has been sentenced are not, as Professor Knights suggested, the result of 'feelings at war with themselves' in the poet, but rather spring from Shakespeare's exploitation, for his own purposes, of the contradictions inherent in the Church's edicts relating to the marriage-contract. What were these purposes? In order to show up in its blackest colours Angelo's legalism, his adherence to the letter rather than the spirit of the law, which is one of the main concerns of the play, Shakespeare needed a case in which the death-penalty could be lawfully imposed for an offence which would not lose for its perpetrator the sympathies of the audience, and one in which a proper regard for its circumstances should have earned him the judge's pardon. . . . The fact that [Shakespeare] should also have chosen to embody in Claudio something of the conflicting emotions which the Church's pronouncements must have aroused in many couples who had consummated an unsolemnized *de praesenti* contract, must, I think, be accounted for on dramatic grounds: apart from making him a more interesting and, to many, a more sympathetic character, it makes him a more perfect foil to Angelo. The self-incriminations of the comparatively innocent and lovable Claudio form a telling contrast to the self-righteousness of the guilty and repellent Angelo. (pp. 77-9)

Next a word about Lucio. He too has been much disliked by commentators. One of them, Dover Wilson, would indeed hand over most of his lines to an unknown reviser [see Additional Bibliography]. . . . To me Lucio seems Shakespeare's throughout, and one of his most masterly and vivid creations. . . . It is strange that critics who profess to delight in Falstaff should sternly refuse to be amused by Lucio. He has not only a touch of Falstaff about him (compare, for instance, the excellent scene in which he slanders the Duke to his face [III. ii.] with the very similar scene in which Falstaff slanders the Prince [*I Henry IV*, II. iv.]), but also of Hal. His frivolities do not claim his entire being: they are partly a cloak for a nobler self which comes out in his conversations with Isabel, above all in his 'by my troth, Isabel, I lov'd thy brother' [IV. iii. 156]. He is a rather complex and, in some ways, contradictory character (which does not make him the less Shakespearian). Towards Claudio he shows himself to be a true and loyal friend, while towards Mrs. Overdone and Pompey he proves callous and perfidious, having them arrested, it would seem, in order to get out of the way these two incriminating witnesses to his own transgressions.

There are two opposite attitudes towards sexual relations expressed through much of the play. There is the view of them as something natural, creative, and desirable. Of this view the chief spokesman is Lucio. And there is the view of them as something which leads to excess and thus to destruction. Of this the chief spokesman is Claudio, who sees this excess in the sexual appetite and the consequent self-destruction as something inherent in human nature:

> Our natures do pursue,
> Like rats that ravin down their proper bane,
> A thirsty evil; and when we drink we die. . . .
>
> [I. ii. 128-30]

The opposite attitude is most fully expressed in the great lines spoken by Lucio to Isabel:

> Your brother and his lover have embrac'd.
> As those that feed grow full, as blossoming time
> That from the seedness the bare fallow brings
> To teeming foison, even so her plenteous womb
> Expresseth his full tilth and husbandry.
>
> [I. iv. 40-4]

The speech is a close counterpart, almost a reply, to Claudio's description of the same event. Again the simile of feeding is used, but here it is shown to lead not to death but to life, not to self-destruction but to self-fulfilment. (pp. 81-3)

Lucio even more than Claudio serves as a foil to Angelo. In a play which relies for many of its effects on contrast of characters the two seem particularly marked out as opposites.

> This outward-sainted deputy,
> Whose settled visage and deliberate word
> Nips youth i' th' head, and follies doth enew
> As falcon doth the fowl,

as Isabel describes him [III. i. 88-91]; who takes pride in his gravity and 'stands at a guard with envy' (i.e. is careful to give no occasion to traducers); who 'scarce confesses / That his blood flows; or that his appetite / Is more to bread than stone', as the Duke puts it [I. iii. 51-3], is the exact opposite of the lapwing and jester, the reckless scandalmonger, the debauchee, and the loving friend. (His opposite, that is, in character. As a ruler and judge Angelo's opposite . . . is the Duke.) (pp. 83-4)

What made Shakespeare devise [the] 'bed-trick', as it is commonly referred to? . . . I do not believe that, had it suited his dramatic conception, Shakespeare would have hesitated to let Isabel follow Cassandra's course. But . . . his desire to make us question Isabel's choice and to turn *Measure for Measure* into a problem play, demanded that she should persist in her refusal, and therefore a substitute had to be found if Angelo was fully to act out his villainy and yet a happy ending was to be contrived. And by means of the 'bed-trick' Shakespeare was able at the same time to avoid the one element which is most repugnant in what critics condescendingly like to call "the barbarous old story' (though I find nothing barbarous in either Cinthio's or Whetstone's treatment of it): the heroine's forced marriage to the villain she hates. . . . (p. 109)

One of the purposes of the 'bed-trick' seems explicable by a point of law which commentators have overlooked. Where, as we have seen, Claudio and Juliet were made husband and wife by a *de praesenti* contract, the marriage-contract between Angelo and Mariana seems to have been a case of sworn spousals *per verba de futuro* (in which the couple promise under oath to become husband and wife at a future date). Now any *de futuro* contract was turned into matrimony and became as indissoluble as a *de praesenti* contract as soon as cohabitation between the betrothed couple took place. This point of law seems to be basic to the Duke's substitution-plot, and appears to be alluded to when he declares, 'If the encounter acknowledge itself hereafter, it may compel him to her recompense' [III. i. 251-52]. And its recognition may make the expedient more acceptable to those who have been distressed by it and by Isabel's immediate consent to it. (pp. 109-10)

Isabel appears to be ignorant throughout of her brother's marriage-contract. Lucio fails to mention it in his report of Claudio's arrest, while the words he uses, 'He hath got his friend with child', 'Your brother and his lover have embraced' [I. iv. 29, 40], would, on the contrary, suggest that there was no matrimonial bond between them. But why did Shakespeare choose to keep Isabel ignorant of the marriage-contract? Because had she known of it her entire plea before Angelo would have had to be different, an appeal to equity rather than to mercy. And it would have much lessened her inner conflict, 'At war 'twixt will and will not' [II. ii. 33]. For not even the 'enskied and sainted' [I. iv. 34] Isabel could have called the consummation of a *de praesenti* contract 'a vice that most I do abhor' [II. ii. 29] and have thought of it as justly deserving the death-penalty. It is apparently the situation of the saintly novice exculpating the seeming libertine which above all kindles Angelo's lust and gives him his opening in the seduction-scene. And all this Shakespeare would have had to forgo, had he made Isabel aware of the circumstances of Claudio's transgression.

To Isabel, therefore, her brother's 'vice' and Mariana's nocturnal encounter with Angelo, with its multiple benefits ('by this', the Duke tells her, 'is your brother saved, your honour untainted, the poor Mariana advantaged, and the corrupt deputy scaled' [III. i. 253-55]) would not have seemed by any means identical, or indeed to have much in common. And the fact that the scheme is put forward by the Friar-Duke as spokesman of the Church would have helped to counteract any possible scruples raised in her mind by the Church's commands in this matter.

And yet there remains a basic contradiction: not between Isabel's attitude to her brother's 'vice' and to the 'bed-trick', but rather between her ready acceptance of the scheme and her equally ready refusal to fulfil herself Angelo's demand. For Mariana is as much guilty of the deadly sin of fornication by her action as Isabel would have been. And the same legalistic view of Divine Justice which made Isabel assume that she would be eternally damned for it ought to have made her postulate the same about Mariana. It is difficult to see how Shakespeare could have avoided this inconsistency once he had decided on the 'bed trick', for which Isabel's consent is needed. Shakespeare at this point required an Isabel with a liberal view of morality; elsewhere one with a narrowly legalistic view.

I do not believe that this inconsistency can be explained by postulating a change of outlook in Isabel. . . . To me Isabel, like the other main *dramatis personae*, with the important exception of Angelo, seems essentially a static character. She possesses that remarkable integrity in the literal sense which would make any great change in her come as a surprise. (pp. 110-12)

Ernest Schanzer, "'Measure for Measure'," in his The Problem Plays of Shakespeare: A Study of "Julius Caesar," "Measure for Measure," "Antony and Cleopatra," Routledge & Kegan Paul, 1963, pp. 71-131.

J. W. LEVER (essay date 1965)

[*Like such earlier critics as S. J. Mary Suddard (1912), G. Wilson Knight (1930), William Witherle Lawrence (1931), R. W. Chambers (1937), Muriel C. Bradbrook (1941), Roy W. Battenhouse (1946), and Nevill Coghill (1955), Lever acknowledges that Measure for Measure "abounds in instances of morality and interlude devices"; but unlike these commentators, Lever contends that these conventional elements supply little meaning to Shakespeare's play, that wherever they are present the dramatist constructs a "deliberate imbalance" in their analogical relationships*

in order to direct attention away from ideas and onto the characters. It is only in this way, Lever continues, that Shakespeare is able to "convey an impression of complete and real human beings." However, Lever perceives a breakdown in this dramatic presentation of character in the second half of Measure; *in an assessment similar to that of E.M.W. Tillyard (1949), he claims that the major characters—Angelo, Isabella, and Claudio—lose their independence, and with it their dramatic interest, in the second half of the play, a circumstance he attributes to the Duke's increased involvement in and manipulation of events. According to Lever, the dynamic characters of the first two acts become, under the Duke's guidance, "animated puppets," whose moral education "seems to proceed through conditioned reflexes rather than through genuine self-discovery." Of the play's language, he states that what was dramatic and spontaneous in the first half becomes, in the second, "sententious" and "uninspired" prose. As a "self-sufficient entity," Lever thus interprets* Measure for Measure *as a "flawed masterpiece"; but as representative of a phase in Shakespeare's artistic development, he regards it as significant in establishing the themes and concerns Shakespeare was to present more successfully in his later tragedies. This final point has also been voiced by Derek A. Traversi (1942) and E. C. Pettet (1949).*]

Measure for Measure is intensely concerned with the nature of authority, the workings of the psyche, and the predicament of man faced with the universal facts of procreation and death: but it is in the nature of Shakespearean drama that all such issues are taken up into the greater mystery of the actual individual. The art is 'incarnational', to borrow Graham Hough's useful term [in his *A Preface to "The Faerie Queene"*]; and the play's true greatness is felt wherever its concepts are, in Hough's phrase, 'completely absorbed in character and action and completely expressed by them'. Isabella is too complex a personality to be thought of as the static embodiment of Holiness or Chastity. At the beginning she aspired to the life of the cloister, but in the end she finds her vocation in marriage to the Duke: the rationale of either way of life turns upon its relationship to the inner laws of her being. Angelo's precisianism is sincere at the outset; under stress he proves to be a 'seemer'; ultimately he repents and is forgiven. Clearly he is much more than a personification of Zeal or Hypocrisy, Puritanism or False Authority, though at times evincing all these traits. Even Pompey, 'a poor fellow that would live' [II. i. 223], is no mere generic bawd but a vividly conceived individual; he is made to change his trade, but he remains Pompey still. As with some Elizabethan mansion built from the stones of a ruined abbey, *Measure for Measure* abounds in instances of morality and interlude devices made to serve new ends. Trials, 'contentions', and statements of 'doctrine' are frequent; yet on each occasion a deliberate imbalance of presentation directs the attention to the characters rather than to the ideas as such. From the dramatic viewpoint, the significance of Pompey's trial is not the exposure of bawdry but the comic ebullience of the private individual undaunted by institutions. Isabel's first interview with Angelo is, in conceptual terms, a 'contention' between Mercy and Justice; its dramatic effect, however, is to strain to breaking-point the tensions in Angelo's psyche. Similarly at their second encounter Angelo's arguments for Charity, unanswered but juxtaposed to Isabella's insistence on Chastity, prepare the way for Isabella's own breakdown. The Duke's perverse homily in contempt of life, matched by Claudio's equally perverse plea for survival at all costs, do not illustrate the respective attitudes of Holy Church and Everyman, but by their very distortions, by the lurid lights and elongated shadows they cast, provide a universal vista to Claudio's tragic impasse. The last act is entirely taken up with a protracted judicial inquiry; but since the true facts are already known, dramatic interest centres not in the substance of the pleas but in what they reveal of the characters who advance them. (pp. xcii-xciii)

[The] attitudes of the three major characters, Angelo, Isabel, and Claudio, are integral to their personalities. The result is to convey an impression of complete and real human beings whose truth, imaginatively conceived, transcends their time and setting. Angelo's taut will-power, belief in his own principles, capacity for anguished soul-searching, and final readiness to face the consequences of his deeds, are qualities one associates with the Puritan cast of mind; likewise his ignorance at the crucial point of 'the dark and hitherto unsuspected forces of his own nature' [W. H. Durham, in his essay ''What Art Thou, Angelo?'']. But they are qualities of the whole man, the individual, and not just the type, who might have identified himself with other doctrines at other times. Isabella's strongly-sexed ardour and impetuosity, combined with her intellectual craving for absolutes, might in one age have led her to a martyrdom like Antigone's, in another to the frustrated life of a Dorothea Brooke: in the world of Shakespeare's play, marriage to the Duke is her true destiny. Claudio, easily affectionate, easily guilt-stricken, dependent on others for his ethical standards, is the average man of his time, and all times; the test-case, then as now, of systems and creeds. Through these characters and their interactions the drama reveals itself as essentially a quest for self-knowledge on the part of individuals who are, in Ulrici's words, 'sinners, children of wrath, and in need of mercy' [see excerpt above, 1839]. Like Lear, all three have ever but slenderly known themselves. In the course of the play their self-ignorance is fully manifested, and they are subjected to a process of moral re-education which would seem to be, in the last analysis, the true purpose of the Duke's experiment.

Yet it is just in this process that the basic defects of the play appear. As the experimenter with human lives, the Duke belongs to quite another level of dramatic presentation than that on which the other characters act and suffer. The representative of true secular and spiritual authority, he typifies the most widely approved models of the age. Political theory, literary tradition, and the precepts of the ruling monarch cast him for the part of an earthly providence who is, if not divinely omniscient, at least sagacious beyond the limits of the subjects he rules. In consequence he stands secure against vicissitude to a degree not known by actual rulers. No threats of war, revolt, or intrigue disturb him or cloud his vision. The result is a sacrifice of full humanity. Some individual traits are allowed him; he is modest, retiring, and scholarly, capable of a certain wry humour, and even given to occasional petulance. But he undergoes no inner development of character and achieves no added self-knowledge. His encounter with Barnardine suggests that even a model ruler may be fallible, but it is too brief to transform his personality; nor do we learn anything of the Duke's inner response to this experience. The offer of marriage to Isabella implies a farewell to hopes of 'the life removed' [I. iii. 8] and an assurance that active virtue is required of rulers as well as subjects; it is, however, a formal decision rather than a change of heart. . . . [The] Duke of Vienna never stoops to inquire into himself. Since, moreover, he must preside over all characters and actions in the latter half of the play, the other main figures lose much of their independent volition. Not only do they tend to behave like animated puppets in furtherance of the Duke's designs; often their moral education, too, seems to proceed through conditioned reflexes rather than through genuine self-discovery. Isabella's consent to the substitution

device is too easily granted; so is Mariana's co-operation. In the last act Isabella's public humiliation is, no doubt, a necessary psychological purge, but her response to this is not very different in tone from the simulated rhetoric in which, under the Duke's coaching, she had previously denounced Angelo. Only in the dénouement, when Angelo repents his sins and Isabel, in defiance of the Duke's warning, pleads for his pardon, do these characters regain some spontaneity. But not for long: the Duke's final verdict is received with silent and general acquiescence. Angelo, about to be pardoned, reveals 'a quickening in his eye' [V. i. 495], and as much may perhaps be allowed to Claudio. But not even the impetuous Isabella, told by the Duke to 'give me your hand and say you will be mine' [V. i. 492], offers any verbal reply. (pp. xciv-xcv)

Lucio's part is extremely heterogeneous. Elements of the slanderous courtier of romance, and the typical Jacobean gallant and 'fantastic', go to his making. He is jester, butt, and intermediary, a cold-blooded lecher, and a kindly, sympathetic friend to both Isabella and Claudio. The exceptional prominence of his role as well as his composite character are best explained by his special dramatic function. In the first two acts he is the indispensable go-between, passing from Claudio to Isabella, from Overdone to the nun Francisca; drawing Isabella from her cloister, leading her to the presence of Angelo, and ensuring that she persists in her suit. In reality it is Lucio, not Escalus or Angelo, who serves here as the Duke's true deputy. Thereafter, his function becomes subsidiary to the Duke's. He supplies his ruler with a comic foil, and his slanders provide emotional relief from the over-exemplary virtues of the supposed Friar. . . . Increasingly he comes to typify the 'slanderous tongues' which perturbed both the Duke of Vienna and King James. In the end he seems to be cast as the solitary scapegoat of the comedy, though at the last minute he too is ignominiously reprieved.

These anomalies and distortions are best understood as results of the special difficulties latent in the Duke's role. In earlier versions of the story the ruler had served as a *deus ex machina*, who appeared at the end and pronounced judgment; here he was conceived as a secular providence immanent in the world of the play. But this great expansion of the part brought with it a new problem. To have made the Duke an active figure in the first half, when the tragic knot was in the course of being tied, would have dissipated his aura of mystery and reduced the suspense by a too overt assurance that all was well. Shakespeare's solution, suggested perhaps by the split ducal personality of [John] Marston's Malcontent, was to project not only an *alter ego* to his own Duke, in the character of the supposed Friar, but also a scoffing polarity, Lucio, who carried out the practical tasks of a dramatic providence in the first two acts and later served to cushion both Duke and 'Friar' against the restiveness of audiences exposed to a prolonged object-lesson in 'the disposition of natures' [III. i. 163-64]. It is likely enough that through Lucio's prattle the exigencies of entertainment were met and interest in the Duke's part sustained. In terms of 'theatre' the exemplary ruler survived; with the support of a lord of misrule.

Yet to understand motives is not wholly to forgive effects. In *Measure for Measure* the tragicomic solution was brought about through the direct, explicit, and continuous intervention of 'the demi-god authority' [I. ii. 120]. The vast speculative themes were knit together, the complex characters guided towards the middle path of virtue, through the transcendent wisdom of a Jacobean paragon. But the price to be paid was a substitution of precept and example for inner development and spontaneity. The dramatic poetry of the first half of the play, with its free-ranging, esemplastic imagery and flexible speech-rhythms, gave way to sententious prose, stiff gnomic couplets, and a blank verse which, though generally dignified, was basically uninspired. The Duke's Apollonian intellect resolved all conflicts in society and stilled all tumults in the soul; but in the process the autonomy of the individual was lost, and with it his innate right to choose as between evil and good. At the same time the Duke himself, a prisoner of his own exemplary image, failed as an authentic human being and remained a stage device, midway between personality and type.

If, as some critics think, each literary work is to be judged as a self-sufficient entity, *Measure for Measure* might fairly be described as a 'flawed masterpiece'. But if we choose to see this play as one phase in an organic creative process, it will have for us a more positive meaning. The enigma of authority vested in flesh and blood, which Shakespeare failed to resolve in the character of his Duke, was not solely a problem of technique, but a challenge to his artist's integrity. It presented itself with mounting urgency in the plays written at the turn of the century, in *Julius Caesar, Hamlet,* and *Troilus and Cressida.* Ultimately the challenge sprang from the central Renaissance paradox of man, 'noble in reason', 'infinite in faculties', yet the 'quintessence of dust'. Tragicomedy on a realistic plane, which turned on the deeds of a wise earthly providence immune to the weakness of common men, seemed theoretically to provide an answer. In practice it supplied only an evasion. Shakespeare's later tragedies, in contrast, looked the issues full in the face. They required that rulers, like other men, should 'in the destructive element immerse'. The king must be a beggar that he might become truly royal: a beggar in fact, not a mendicant friar by way of disguise. He must forfeit his sanity, not merely put an antic disposition on. Only when all outward trappings of authority had vanished could the truth in man be separated from the falsehood, and his reality from his seeming. Tragedy taught the hard lesson that self-knowledge came, not from reason and moderation, but from madness and excess; that evil, though in the end it destroyed itself, was not overcome by good; and that the magnanimous monarch ruled only in a country of the imagination. If *Measure for Measure,* for all its probing of the issues, brought no genuine transcendence, it prepared the way for *King Lear* and *Antony and Cleopatra.* Only after the tragic exploration had been completed did Shakespeare return to the affirmations of tragi-comedy, in the sublimated simplicities of pastoral romance, where time and the cycle of generations restored natural good. (pp. xcvi-xcviii)

> *J. W. Lever, in an introduction to* Measure for Measure *by William Shakespeare, edited by J. W. Lever, revised edition, 1965. Reprint by Vintage Books, 1967, pp. xi-xcviii.*

TERENCE EAGLETON (essay date 1967)

[*In his* Shakespeare and Society *(1967), Eagleton focuses on the relationships and responsibilities of the individual and society in eight of Shakespeare's plays. In the following excerpt, he contends that* Measure for Measure *deals with the conflict between social order and individual freedom and between law and passion, and he further maintains that the inherent design of the play stresses the idea that law must be "personally authentic, so that spontaneous action may also be responsible action." Eagleton reconstructs the development of this concept by focusing primarily on Shakespeare's logic in the play and on those characters—Angelo,*

Claudio, and Lucio—who falsely view the law as either a "reciprocity of condemnation" or judgment, as Angelo does, or as simply an external restraint on individual freedom, as Lucio and Claudio do. Eagleton claims that Shakespeare, through the manipulations of the Duke, calls for a more personal and humane system of law, one which is based on the "reciprocity of relationships in society" and is united with the ideas of love and knowledge, symbolized in the play by the act of marriage and the concept of changing identities. According to Eagleton, Angelo's process is destructive because, as the image of authority in the play, he lacks the knowledge and love of others, and therefore the self-knowledge and self-love necessary to make law a part of his experience, the possibility of which would demonstrate that judgment of others is impossible "in the continuous reciprocity of human society," since such an act amounts to judgment of oneself. Ultimately, Eagleton concludes, Measure for Measure *champions the need for mutual forgiveness based on the actual sharing of another's life through love and knowledge, and the existence of law not as an external restraint, but as an authentic part of one's experience. Other interpretations of the marriages that conclude* Measure for Measure *appear in the essays by Denton J. Snider (1890), R. A. Foakes (1971), and Lawrence W. Hyman (1975).*]

Measure for Measure is about the opposition between law and passion, but nothing in the play can really be understood unless the full significance of 'law' is grasped. Law can be seen as an essential restraint on individual action, and thus as a negative force: it is seen like this frequently in the play, both by those who dispense justice and by those who are its victims. But law has a positive aspect as well, one which makes criticism of those who break the law deeper and more subtle. (p. 66)

The contract by which Claudio gained possession of Julietta's bed may have been true, but it was a private one, made between themselves and without the sanction of society. . . . Their act stands exposed to the judgement of society, and Claudio is condemned by law. But Claudio's way of viewing his own offence is inadequate: he submits to the law's censure but fails to see the real point of the law, its function in verifying private experience, giving social confirmation or censure to individual action. . . . As the play demonstrates, 'the denunciation of outward order' [I. ii. 148-49] is not a marginal element in human action, as Claudio sees it, an additional seal to an already firm contract; until individual action is ratified by society, the private contract does not properly exist. . . . Marriage is a public commitment, a way of relating personal behaviour to a whole society; its physical results are part of that society, children. Claudio and Julietta have ignored this, treating sexuality as a private affair, and their own act has turned against them in Julietta's evident pregnancy. Claudio is condemned not merely for lechery, but for breaking social order by concealing personal action from society's evaluation, trying to live a private reality beyond the law and thus beyond others. Sexual activity, which is at once intimately personal and directly social, is an ideal image of this theme. (pp. 66-7)

Personal identity, personal action, live only in that formal network of communications which is society. This is the meaning of the Duke's remark to Angelo at the beginning of the play:

> . . . Thyself and thy belongings
> Are not thine own so proper as to waste
> Thyself upon thy virtues, they on thee.
> Heaven doth with us as we with torches do,
> Not light them for themselves; for if our virtues
> Did not go forth of us, 'twere all alike
> As if we had them not . . .   [I. i. 29-35]

A man who conceals his qualities wastes himself, in a self-consuming process; the alternatives are self-hoarding or self-spending, free self-giving in action. A man is given natural qualities which he must use and communicate in action, otherwise they hardly exist: he can only know himself in this process of communication. Men are stewards for Nature, responsible to her for their action: Nature hates waste, and demands back from men in precise measure the gifts she lends him:

> Spirits are not finely touch'd
> But to fine issues; nor Nature never lends
> The smallest scruple of her excellence
> But, like a thrifty goddess, she determines
> Herself the glory of a creditor,
> Both thanks and use.   [I. i. 35-40]

There is a poetic tension in this between precision and freedom, scruples and excellence: men must expend freely the qualities Nature gives them, but this bounteousness must take place within the context of a precise weighing, a balancing of credit and debit. Free self-giving must co-exist with a kind of responsibility, to Nature or heaven or society: it is this responsibility which Claudio and Julietta ignore.

The Duke's resignation of government to Angelo and Escalus at the beginning of the play is also done in terms of a fullness of self-expression within a specific responsibility. . . . Angelo is praised as a genuine man, one whose public actions and private self are in complete continuity. He is then given his commission by the Duke:

> In our remove be thou at full ourself;
> Mortality and mercy in Vienna
> Live in thy tongue and heart. . . .
>   [I. i. 43-5]

Angelo, then, is being asked to make personally his the pattern of behaviour which the Duke epitomises, so that his personal action, his real self, will exist only in these terms. And what the Duke epitomises is law, the pattern of social responsibility. The law is to be Angelo's authentic life, so that it will be natural and spontaneous for him to think and act within its terms: he will be a living fusion of social responsibility and authentic, spontaneous self-expression. In him they will be the same life: to be less than good will be to be less than himself.

This is not, of course, how Claudio or Lucio see the law. For Claudio, the law is an external, repressive force, designed to interfere with personal self-fulfilment in the interests of society: it is a regrettable necessity. Lucio doesn't even recognise the necessity: for him, law is merely external, a ludicrous piece of official mechanism which has no relation to the realities of life, the living experience of wit or sex or compassion. As a result, Lucio's view of life is completely private: he lives in the margin of society, contemptuous of the public world, outside the network of roles and relationships. . . . To deny law is to deny society, to reject public experience; but it is only within the controlling network of law and society that individual experience can have meaning. Law is the articulation of the relations between things: particularly of the relations between private and public experience, personal behaviour and society, self and others. Without law, personal experience can only remain fragmentary, socially irresponsible.

Law is a positive force, then, because ideally it is not just part of a society, but actually *constitutes* society: it is a body of communications between men which makes their personal experience present to each other for verification, and thus brings them into relationship with each other; being a member of a society is defined by keeping its laws. In this way, law is very similar to language, and the play brings out, implicitly, the connection. Both law and language are communications which bring men into relationship and community by externalising their private experience, making it open to public judgement and response. This is why there is so great an emphasis, throughout the play, on the fact of speech. Lucio's lack of respect for law is closely tied to his lack of respect for language: both law and language make a man social, relate him dynamically to a society. . . . Lucio is flighty in speech, and his language defines and expresses his whole, opportunist character, his tactical approach to life. His lack of respect for language is a lack of respect for the public world: his public presence, in his speech, is at odds with his real intentions, he is an inauthentic man. (pp. 68-74)

If words are used existentially, differently in different contexts, then no fixed and constant meaning is possible, and no consistent value or communication: inconstancy strikes at the root of society. When Isabella is arguing for Claudio's life, she argues on this kind of shifting, relative basis, in the face of Angelo's inhuman constancy: she uses a situation-ethics, an individualist kind of value, as Troilus did:

> We cannot weigh our brother with ourself.
> Great men may jest with saints: 'tis wit in them;
> But in the less foul profanation.
>   [II. ii. 126-28]

Isabella's rejection of the possibility of weighing and comparing two people, like Cressida's, is a contracting-out of the whole process of public evaluation and the rational establishment of value, an obstinate stand on individuality, uniqueness. But then this becomes the basis of a total relativism: if things lack the intrinsic values which make comparison possible, they become wholly dependant, for meaning and value, on their contexts. . . . A word's meaning depends on who speaks it: there can be no constancy, the constancy which comes from comparing and relating different experiences. Isabella's final attack is precisely in Troilus's terms: she says she will bribe Angelo,

> Not with fond sicles of the tested gold,
> Or stones, whose rate are either rich or poor
> As fancy values them; but with true prayers . . .
>   [II. ii. 149-51]

The echo of Troilus's 'What's aught but as 'tis valued?' is significant: a sense of value as lying primarily in the human response is part of that whole relativism which destroys the continuity of formulated law and language. Angelo's attitude to Isabella's pleading is quite firm: he cannot make an individual exception, because this demolishes the whole meaning of law. Law cannot operate as a kind of situation-ethics, relative to individual and context, any more than language can be altered to suit the whims of individual men. (pp. 74-5)

The idea of proportion, of fitting the word to the action and the action to the word, is a central one in the play, as the title makes clear. The whole man, the man of integrity, will be one whose public presence, in language and action, will be a real, authentic expression of himself, without jar or dislocation; this is the meaning of spontaneity, the ability of a man to give himself fluently to the world, without tension or falsification. But action must be socially responsible as well as spontaneous: wholeness is to be authentically lawful, spontaneously responsible, as Angelo is meant to be. The idea of a proportion between the inward and the public self, experience and action, is close, also, to the idea of proportion between crime and punishment: a man must 'answer' for his deed, otherwise the whole balance of society is upset. Gratuitous, individual forgiveness upsets the balance: there must be weighing and reckoning, measure for measure. Angelo is 'precise', and the word occurs several times in the play: he believes that there must be proportion, not only between what a man is and what he does, but between what he does and society's response to this.

Angelo, to begin with, is totally authentic: there is no dislocation at all between himself and his actions, between what he is and what he does. He represents the living fusion of responsibility and authenticity which we described earlier: he lives personally in terms of the law, of socially responsible behaviour. But total integrity of this kind can be destructive and inhuman, based on a rejection of human experience. . . . Angelo is incapable of acting inauthentically, of acting contrary to his nature: his integrity is total, in that it makes it impossible for him to falsify himself. But in the context of a society which works by human compromise and half-measure, Angelo's authenticity shows up as frightening and destructive. The tension is the tension of *Troilus* and *Hamlet*: to live in society, a man must be prepared to modify his integrity. Isabella's arguments against Angelo . . . are ineffective precisely because they are appeals for him to dislocate his private and public selves, to repress his real instincts in the interests of humanity. She appeals to the concrete, existential circumstances of human life:

> If he had been as you, and you as he,
> You would have slipp'd like him. . . .
>
> [II. ii. 64-5]

But the existential position, as always, involves a complete relativism, a lack of constancy: if all men's virtues are simply contingent on time and place, then all evaluation and all consistent identity seem to be cancelled. Angelo sees that society has to work on the basis of consistent, intrinsic values and identities; if men are simply to be valued according to their circumstances, they are fluid, interchangeable. . . . Angelo sees that this shifting of identities is part of the whole relativism which Isabella's position implies, and which he is concerned to reject; he admits that all men are capable of guilt, including himself, but does not see why this should be made the basis of a disowning of judgement, as long as he himself is ready to undergo the punishments he metes out. His chief wish is to avoid individual particularities of judgement: law must be common and therefore constant, 'and nothing come in partial' [II. i. 31].

For wholeness, a man's public and private selves must be in continuity. But *Measure for Measure* also shows that the way a man sees himself and the way he sees others must be adjusted. This is the Gospel resolution of the problem of the self and others: a man must behave towards others as he would have them behave towards himself, as he would behave towards himself: he must be as close to others as he is to himself. In this way others cease to be tools or objects and become subjects, sharing the same life. The extent to which a man shares in the lives of others is reflected in the extent to which he judges them: he must judge others as he would wish himself to be judged. In this way, the reciprocity of condemnation on which Angelo takes his stand can be replaced by the reciprocity of forgiveness. (pp. 77-80)

Angelo wants himself to be judged in exactly the same measure to which he gives out judgement, and the process is continuous

and enclosed: the man who passes judgement on another is laying down the pattern by which another will pass judgement on him, and that other will himself be judged; in the very moment of condemning another one is condemning oneself. . . . Angelo, in trying to erect an absolute by asking for his own act of judgement to be taken as final precisely because he is open to the same kind of judgement himself, is exposing the very flaw of the argument. The circularity that he offers as a virtue, the reciprocity, is in fact the very thing wrong with the system: it cancels all absolutes, any hope of a constant criterion. . . . If all men share in a community of guilt, simultaneously condemning and being condemned in a circular process, there is no reason why this should not be the ground for a community of forgiveness: all men may forgive each other precisely because all men are guilty. The only act of judgement can then be from someone outside the closed system, not himself open to judgement: for the Christian this is Christ, in *Measure for Measure* it is the Duke.

The reciprocity of relationships in society, the continual intermeshing of men and actions, is a major theme in the play, and two chief ideas are used to mirror this: the idea of marriage, and the idea of changing identities. The Duke's words to Escalus about Angelo in his first speech of the play introduce and emphasise the theme of identity:

> What figure of us think you he will bear?
>
> [I. i. 16]

Angelo is not to be an agent of the Duke, a tool to be manipulated, as men in *Hamlet* are manipulated; he is to be both free and responsible, himself yet related: fully autonomous, but answerable to the Duke for his actions. The relationship he stands in to the Duke is in fact very close to the way the Christian conceives of man's relationship to God: man is both himself and God's, fully free yet fully responsible. This is the fusion we have seen already in the way the Duke resigns power to Escalus and Angelo: they are to be him, and he is to be in them, yet he is separate from them, outside the system of which they are part. The relationship of the Duke to Angelo is thus an ideal model of all relationship: Angelo does not resign his selfhood to the Duke, he remains a source, a subject, but his real self now functions in terms of the Duke, to whom he is responsible. (pp. 80-2)

Reciprocity of characters is imagined throughout in the plot, which makes use constantly of substitution, mistake, disguise, paradox. Substitution is not merely metaphorical but deeply physical, a substitution of heads or bodies: again the central image for this is marriage, where the couple are two in one flesh:

> PROVOST . . . Can you cut off a man's head?
> POMPEY   If a man be a bachelor, sir, I
> can; but if he be a married man, he's his wife's
> head, and I can never cut off a woman's
> head. . . .
>
> [IV. ii. 1-5]

In *Measure for Measure,* the union of two in the flesh is a dominant theme: Julietta and Claudio, Angelo and Mariana, Lucio and his bawd, are physically linked in this way, but so too, metaphorically, are Angelo and the Duke, Julietta and Isabella (as children), and the Duke and the Friar. The union of the Duke and the Friar, of a man with himself, reflects the desired union, the relationship which defeats exploitation. . . . Physical kinship is seen, even by those in authority, as the most powerful prohibition of judgement and condemnation. . . . It is impossible to condemn someone who is one flesh with oneself because this is to condemn oneself: full judgement involves making a man an object, placing oneself over against him as a weighing subject, and this cannot be done when two people are 'in' each other, as Escalus says the Duke is 'in' him [V. i. 295]. A man cannot fully objectify one who is one flesh with him any more than he can objectify himself. To be in one flesh with another is to act towards them as one would act towards oneself: there is thus no need for cerebral effort to act well in this condition, action is spontaneously responsible.

The substitution of Mariana for Isabella images this interchangeability of bodies, and the image is forced home with a peculiar insistence on the significance of *knowledge* of another. The Duke is a man who has 'ever striven to know himself' [III. ii. 232-33], and knowledge of self, for him, involves knowledge of others: a man comes to know himself as he learns to know others. This is the process which Angelo must pass through, coming to self-knowledge through close dealing with others: it is in communication, relationship, that a man finds himself. Angelo begins in ignorance of himself and others, and the fact is brought out specifically in his ignorance of Mariana:

> I have known my husband; yet my husband
> Knows not that ever he knew me.
>
>   [V. i. 186-87]

Angelo's ignorance of Mariana implies ignorance of himself: as he does not know she is his wife he does not know he is her husband. . . . Knowledge must be reciprocal, mutually established, and the deepest image of this is carnal knowledge. Angelo is one flesh with Mariana without knowing it, and this ignorance reflects his general lack of knowledge of men, the ignorance which made him condemn Claudio. To judge others harshly is to show a lack of self-knowledge, because all judgement, in the continuous reciprocity of human society, is judgement of oneself. (pp. 83-6)

It is in loving knowledge of each other that forgiveness can be established, and the fullest image of forgiveness is therefore marriage, the fullest mutual loving knowledge. To slander and falsify another in speech, as Lucio does, is to show a lack of either love or knowledge or both, as the Duke's rebuke to Lucio indicates:

> LUCIO   Sir, I know him, and I love him.
> DUKE   Love talks with better knowledge,
> and knowledge with dearer love.
>
>   [III. ii. 149-51]

Love and knowledge are not distinct, contradictory: they grow in proportion to each other. It is this truth which brings us back to the fusion of freedom and exactness, fullness of self-expression and responsibility, which we saw in the Duke's consigning of power to Angelo. *Troilus and Cressida* ends on a note of incompatibility between wisdom and loving, free, spontaneous action and reflective responsibility. It is these poles which *Measure for Measure* can unify, by taking the ideas of love and forgiveness as central. For in both love and forgiveness there is a shifting of the centre of the self which makes responsiveness and responsibility to another natural and spontaneous: one identifies with the other, and knowledge of and care for the other is then as authentically personal as self-knowledge, self-caring. But the fact that identity is not cancelled in love, but shifted, means that this freedom and fullness operates within a specific context of identity and relationship,

as Angelo's freedom operates within the defining limits of the Duke's personality.

To love is therefore to act within a particular pattern which is public, epitomised in the public fact of marriage. Love and law must be fused: in a good society it is law which is the living, articulated definition of the limits of wisdom, and to step outside these limits is for men to be less than themselves, less than authentic. This is so, clearly, only if the law is truly humane, not external to human experience but responsive to it: love and knowledge are unified when men are authentically lawful, when the law is in their hearts and tongues, and good action therefore spontaneous. In this condition, the law will both create and define the limits of human authenticity and grow from this authenticity: men must not merely authenticate external restraints—an action which can make tyranny easy—but by drawing the law into their personal experience must make it humane, in a reciprocal movement. Responsibility can then become real freedom, creative bondage: the Duke, when going to minister to the Provost's prisoners, says he goes 'bound by his charity' [II. iii. 3], and it is this fusion of defined limits and free self-giving that the play is exploring. (pp. 87-8)

Measure for Measure is about the need to make law personally authentic, so that spontaneous action may also be responsible action. But although much of the play is about the difficulty of making this fusion, it also becomes clear that there is a deep sense in which law and experience are already intimately bound up in a single process before the struggle for synthesis begins. This sense is expressed in the recurrence of processes in which good and evil evolve each other, of paradoxes and entanglements of the two. (p. 95)

Part of the significance of this process seems to lie in the influence of Paul's epistles on the play. Paul sees the law, not only as a restraint on goodness, but as an actual cause of sin: no man will be justified in God's sight by works of the law, since through the law comes knowledge of sin: where there is no law, there can be no transgression. So law is at once a symbol of good and a creator of evil: the fact that it exists means that it can, and will, be broken. This is at the root of Angelo's condition: it is the very purity of Isabella which causes his lust. Good and evil are intertwined, interfeeding, as the law creates the very passions it exists to curb; in this sense

Act V. Scene i. Friar Peter, Isabella, Angelo, the Duke, and Escalus. By H. Howard (n.d.). From the Art Collection of the Folger Shakespeare Library.

there is already a deep relation between law and passion in the actual texture of human life. (pp. 96-7)

Terence Eagleton, "'Measure for Measure'," in his Shakespeare and Society: Critical Studies in Shakespearean Drama, <i>Chatto & Windus, 1967, pp. 66-97.</i>

A. D. NUTTALL (essay date 1968)

[Although Nuttall argues that allegorical interpretations of Measure for Measure *miss the play's political connotations, he examines Roy W. Battenhouse's Atonement theory (see excerpt above, 1946) as a point of departure in his discussion of the play's meaning. Nuttall claims that* Measure for Measure *is a political play that raises questions regarding the ethics of government and judgment, and he defines and explores the Machiavellian nature of the Duke and Angelo. He calls Angelo a "white Machiavellian" because he takes a pragmatic view of government and is willing to have "the ends justify the means"; he calls the Duke a political Machiavel, because he chooses to delegate the unfavorable task of restoring order to Vienna. On the level of metaphysics, which is where he perceives the Atonement pattern recognized by Battenhouse, Nuttall calls Angelo both a Christ-figure—in his role as the Duke's substitute and in his willingness to commit sin by enforcing the law over the Christian doctrine of forgiveness—and a "Devil-figure" or scapegoat. On this level Nuttall calls the Duke a metaphysical Machiavel—or God, the Father—because he protects his soul from sin by substituting Angelo for himself as the figure of Atonement. The pardoning of Angelo by the Duke Nuttall describes as the most Machiavellian of acts because it prevents his death and perpetuates his anguish. For additional commentary on the allegorical nature of the play, see the excerpts by G. Wilson Knight (1930), R. W. Chambers (1937), Roy W. Battenhouse (1946), and Tom McBride (1974).]*

[The Grand Inconsistency of *Measure for Measure* is] the inconsistency between the ethic of government and the ethic of refraining from judgement. But having named this conflict I propose to postpone its discussion. It may profitably be left to germinate for a while in the reader's consciousness.

I [suggest that there is] a discrepancy between the "technical" smartness of this play and its ideological discordancy. The application of this distinction to, say, the character of Angelo is straightforward. Its effect is greatly to weaken the force of the plain man's argument against him . . . : "Angelo is the technical villain; therefore it makes good sense to hold that he is contemptible." Isabel is the technical heroine, but she is not permitted to survive unmarked. Perhaps a correlative dispensation is extended to Angelo. (pp. 234-35)

Angelo is, in the inherited story of the play, a deputy, the Duke's Vicar. But Shakespeare has extended this notion to color the very essence of Angelo. He is in himself a sort of surrogate human being. The Duke, gazing at Angelo on his first appearance, observes that the virtue of so excellent a man requires and merits public exercise. The sentiment is ordinary enough. But also present in the speech is the merest hint of a much more radical—indeed, a philosophical—idea, namely that virtue is essentially a matter of behaviour, that the man whose virtue is invisible cannot meaningfully be said to be virtuous at all. . . :

Thyself and thy belongings
Are not thine own so proper as to waste
Thyself upon thy virtues, they on thee.

Heaven doth with us as we with torches do,
Not light them for themselves; for if our virtues
Did not go forth of us, 'twere all alike
As if we had them not. . . .

[I. i. 29-35]

Through all the proliferating substitutions of the play, Angelo remains (so to speak) the supreme vicar. Yet he has his own kind of solidity (and it is a moral kind). Professor Coghill makes much of his refusal personally to sift the evidence in the case of Froth and Bum [see excerpt above, 1955]—

This will last out a night in Russia
When nights are longest there. I'll take my leave,
And leave you to the hearing of the cause;
Hoping you'll find good cause to whip them all.

[II. i. 134-37]

It is, however, doubtful whether there is anything discreditable in the delegation of this tedious business to Escalus. Physical chastisement has acquired in modern times an added character of traumatic outrage and thus Angelo's parting words may shock a present-day audience where they would earn a sympathetic laugh in a Jacobean theatre. Nevertheless, the line retains a distinctly unpleasant force, which is principally located in the word "hoping." A certain relish of anticipation is implied. Perhaps we might say that this is the first faint sign in Angelo of the lust which will destroy him. But the real tenor of the speech is missed if we stop here. There is a further phrase in the line which, coming from the lips of Angelo, has the power to check and channel the suggestion of "hoping": I mean the phrase "good cause." At the very moment when Angelo's blood quickens, his grip tightens on the law. Although the tension of this speech is so gently hinted and so soon over, it is really present and foreshadows the later development of Angelo. Our dominant impression is still that of a hollow man, a sort of lay-figure. But as the play progresses we see that there persists in Angelo, even through the usurpation of his own soul by lust fully revealed and irresistible, a kind of integrity.

Which is more than can be said for the Duke. The Duke is a ruler who has let things slide. In order to restore good order in Vienna he appoints a substitute who will bear on his shoulders all the odium of renewed severity. This is the Grand Substitution of the play at the purely political level.

For this play is profoundly political. Roy Battenhouse described it (but without any consciousness of paradox) as "a Mirror for Magistrates founded on Christian love" [see excerpt above, 1946]. We can now look a little more closely at the conflict I have already alluded to—the conflict between the ethic of government and the ethic of refraining from judgement. (pp. 235-37)

[What] of the Prince, who, in his own person, is the State? Presumably he should not indulge a promiscuous clemency. Of course the Prince who condemns does so not in his own name but as the minister and vicar of God. This in a way reproduces the dual morality of those Scriptural passages which lie behind the title "Measure for Measure." For example, in the verses from *Matthew*, vii we are told to refrain from judgement, not because judgement must be transcended by love, but "that ye be not judged." In *Mark*, iv the over-riding context of divine retribution is even clearer. So the Prince *qua* man has no duty save to love and forgive his fellow creatures, but as God's substitute he must hunt out and punish the malefactor.

If we press hard on the argument, the ruler might appear to be metaphysically in a cleft stick. As the bloodless instrument of God's will he must perform actions which in a human creature count as sins; his office is eschatologically a millstone round his neck, for the obligation it confers is an obligation to sin.

There is, of course, a short way to resolve this difficulty. The only disquieting thing about it is that if we adopt it we come near to absolving Angelo of guilt in his treatment of Claudio. . . . Thus God, not the Prince, bears the responsibility for official executions. Now Angelo certainly condemns Claudio in the Duke's name. So whose is the responsibility now? It may be replied that this is sheer sophistry since the Duke never authorised Angelo to do *that*. But is it? The Duke was fully aware of Angelo's character. Hence, indeed, his appointment as substitute. The Duke wants Angelo for the job just because he will condemn people like Claudio. And to condemn the Claudios of Vienna is not just politically imprudent; it is too dirty a job for the Duke's squeamish conscience. (pp. 237-38)

There are two arguments here: the first is straight Machiavelli: delegate unpopular actions. (p. 238)

Of course, to show that a character is Machiavellian is not *ipso facto* to prove him a villain. The idea that a ruler should delegate odious offices is Aristotelian and was referred to with approval by Erasmus before it was adopted by Machiavelli. Mario Praz has shown how Machiavellian principles were implicitly approved by Thomas More, Montaigne and Spenser. Mary Lascelles notes that the ideal governor in Elyot's *The Image of Governaunce* (1541) is allowed to use subterfuge to ensure a just outcome. There is a whole essay to be written round what might be called the "White Machiavel" in Shakespeare. Such an essay might begin from Sonnet 94 ("They that have power to hurt") and end in a discussion of the supreme White Machiavel, Prince Hal. . . . Plainly, any writer with as strong an interest as Shakespeare's in government could not long escape seeing the bitter duties of a prince whose care for his people was more than sentimental. But have we a White Machiavel in *Measure for Measure*? I think perhaps we have, but the Duke is not he.

The good Machiavellian ruler, if we allow him to be saveable at all, is saved by his resolute dedication to a good end. No such powerful direction is discernible in the tergiversations of the Duke. Certainly, he preserves the luxury of a technically uncorrupted conscience; certainly he ensures that the laws are reinforced, even if he proceeds by his orgy of clemency at the close to undo all the good achieved. Note that we can approve his behaviour at the end of the play only at the cost of condemning his behaviour at its outset. . . . At whichever end of the ethical spectrum you begin, you will never make a satisfactory hero of the Duke. I suspect that the essential frivolity of his nature really shows itself in the speech with which he ends I. iii—

> Lord Angelo is precise;
> Stands at a guard with Envy; scarce confesses
> That his blood flows; or that his appetite
> Is more to bread than stone. Hence shall we see
> If power change purpose, what our seemers be.
> 　　　　　　　　　　　　　　　　[I. iii. 50-4]

Is it too curious to detect in this speech a certain relish of anticipation? Is there not a slight shifting of ground from the opening scene in which the Duke professes his trust in, and grave respect for, the ascetic probity of Angelo? Is there not

the merest shadow of a Lucio-like sneer at the chastity of Angelo? . . . As Clifford Leech has observed [see excerpt above, 1950], the Duke cannot *both* be testing a suspected nature and tightening up the administration of Vienna by the most reliable means to hand. But perhaps this is too dubious an instance to hang an entire interpretation on. A surer index is the Duke's unblushing readiness to hear confessions (and talk about them afterwards). The priestly disguise holds no embarrassment for him: "I have confess'd her, and I know her virtue" [V. i. 527]. The Duke in *Measure for Measure* is, at the political level, at best an off-white Machiavel, incongruously elevated to the position of Presiding Genius. At the metaphysical level he is, perhaps, mere Machiavel.

The bare mention of Machiavelli, however, raises the ethical question of ends and means. Ought we to perform an action in itself wicked in order that a greater good may come of it? . . . [We find] in *Measure for Measure* two fundamental ethical views, tender and tough, of which the first must be subdivided into two further sections. Let us label them *Ia, Ib* and *II.*

Ia may be expressed as follows: No man who is not himself perfect has the right to judge a fellow creature. Man can only forgive and exercise charity. . . . Persons who hold to this opinion tend in practice to believe that the end cannot justify the means. The connection between these two notions is not immediately obvious. My own guess is that both stem from a powerful awareness of the supernatural authority of God and a correspondingly low estimate of man. To such a mind ethics tends to consist of a series of God-given imperatives. These imperatives cannot be appraised or placed in order of value by merely human intelligence. . . . View *Ia* almost certainly lies behind the repulsion Escalus feels at Angelo's account of the law as a scarecrow, which if left unchanged will become the object of contempt [II. i. 1f]. Note that if we side with Escalus here we place ourselves in opposition to the Duke whose loving state-craft is very fairly represented by Angelo's words. But we are growing accustomed to these uncomfortable choices. Such then is ethic *Ia*; the high Christian variant of the tender view.

Ib is on the contrary, low and non-Christian, though still, of course, tender. It goes something like this: anybody without a bit of generous vice in him isn't properly human. The sexual appetite is in itself good; it is of the heart, and heart is more than head. This has a very twentieth-century flavour but is certainly present in *Measure for Measure* —most obviously in the "low" dialogue of the play. . . . (pp. 239-41)

Ethic *II*, the tough-minded one, has much less power (it will be noticed at once) to give us warm feelings. To begin with, it is white Machiavellianism. Ends (in this fallen world) justify means; to resist this is to lapse into sentimentalism; *of course* none of us is perfect but *of course* we must judge; the man who is willing to abolish the police force in order to luxuriate in a private orgy of conscience is less merciful than the magistrate who administers the law in the interests of the community. This ethic is impersonalist, pragmatic and anti-sentimental. Above all it is the ethic of Angelo. (p. 241)

Now concerning these rival ethics I should like to put what might well be thought an indecorous question. Which of them, *as argument*, cuts deepest? . . . In order to obtain a fair hearing for Angelo I must ask the reader to consider the moral questions before him not as if they were in a romance (where we should all applaud indiscriminate clemency without a moment's compunction) but as if they were a part of real life. *Measure for*

Measure deserves no less. Now, do we really think that because none of us is perfect so no one should judge—that is, in hard terms, there should be no law-courts, no penal system, no juries, no police? Certainly judges are imperfect, but equally certainly it is a job that someone has to do. Men of tender conscience may preserve their charity intact, but only so long as others are willing to tarnish theirs a little.

Angelo grants at once that those who judge are not themselves free from sin. This may mean that they lack, at the metaphysical level, a "right" to judge, but it certainly does not mean that they cannot, at the practical level, do it:

> I not deny
> The Jury passing on the prisoner's life
> May in the sworn twelve have a thief, or two,
> Guiltier than him they try. . . .
>
> [II. i. 18-21]

The naked intelligence of this transfixes the naive casuistry of the Duke's evasion of guilt at I. iii. 36-40. (p. 242)

Where, then, does this leave us? The judgement of the law must be imposed (all agree to that, except perhaps Lucio and his associates). To the question: Who shall impose the law since none of us is perfect? Angelo and the Duke return different answers. Angelo's answer is that men must sink their individuality in the law; that men must judge according to the law, and, when they err, submit to the same law; if it seems grotesque that a man should sit in judgement on other men, one should remember that the judge also is subject to the same rules. The Duke's answer is: Get someone else to do it.

This brings us back to the Duke's speech of explanation at I. iii. 34f. I said that there were two arguments in this speech, the first being the Machiavellian thesis that unpopular actions should be delegated, according to the example of Cesare Borgia. The second argument I have yet to discuss. At first sight it looks more respectable.

> Sith 'twas my fault to give the people scope.
> 'Twould be my tyranny to strike and gall them
> For what I bid them do.
>
> [I. iii. 35-7]

That is to say, it is not only imprudent for me to enforce the law personally, it would also be immoral; I should be a tyrant in so switching from indulgence to rigour. That this argument is slightly more poisonous than the other appears on a very little reflection. For the Duke *is* switching from indulgence to rigour. Such a process is hard on the more sentimental sort of conscience, and the Duke is struggling to keep his untroubled by wrapping it in a tissue of evasions. Angelo would say at once that if rigour is really what is required then no tyranny but rather benevolence is involved in its exercise (as he argues to Isabel at II. ii. 101-105 that there is a more genuine mercy in the enforcement of the law than in its neglect). But the Duke's intelligence, unlike Angelo's, is cunning rather than comprehensive. Morals to him are not contextual. Every action is intrinsically good or bad. To release a prisoner is to be charitable. Actually to prosecute a prisoner is uncharitable. Such an atomistic view of morals rapidly breeds what might be called meta-ethical situations. Thus, it is uncharitable suddenly to change course and enforce the law (that is basic ethics) but somehow it seems as if that is what *ought* to be done (meta-ethics!). The contextual view of an Angelo, whereby ends justify means, instantly resolves this dilemma, of course. But which view does *God* incline to, the atomistic or the contextual?

The thunderingly simple commands in the Gospels, urged with such power by Isabel, suggest that God is more than half an atomist, and, by implication, that the eschatological structure of the universe will reflect an atomistic ethic. In plain terms they suggest that a man who does not perform charitable actions (like releasing criminals)—for whatever reason—is a sinner, and may go to Hell.

It is, of course, a primitive ethic, but it is deeply embedded in the ritual comedy-story of the play. To perceive its presence is to learn that the Duke is not merely a political Machiavel; he is also (so to speak) a metaphysical one. The device which saves his reputation also preserves his soul. Certain kinds of practical virtue (being technical sins) are beneath the saintly charity of the Duke, so someone else must be found as a surrogate. This situation is exactly paralleled by Isabel's adoption of Mariana as her substitute.

The idea of substitution is paramount. One might map it with reference to two poles, Machiavelli in the south and Christ in the north. For, as Roy Battenhouse saw, the Grand Deception of the Atonement moves beneath the surface of the drama just as certainly as does the bloody subterfuge of Cesare Borgia. It is explicitly conveyed in some of the most moving words of the play:

> Why, all the souls that were, were forfeit once,
> And he that might the vantage best have took
> Found out the remedy.
>
> [II. ii. 73-5]

If we contemplate the structure of the Atonement for a while, we may be willing to draw the last, and most terrifying, lesson from this play. Mankind lay groaning under a burden of sin, of which the wages are death. The Son of God took these sins away from us, bore them on his own shoulders, and by his death on the Cross, discharged our debt. Thus Christ, by taking our sins, was the supreme substitute.

Battenhouse, with some difficulty, sought to identify the God of the Atonement with the Duke. This can be done as long as we restrict our attention to God the Father—as long, that is, as we ignore the cardinal fact of substitution, which above all else connects *Measure for Measure* with the Atonement. Suppose we ask, who, in this play, most obviously corresponds to the figure of Christ? It is not surprising that this question has been avoided. The answer is both unthinkable and only too plain. (pp. 244-45)

One element in the traditional doctrine which is obstinately unclear is the phrase "took upon his shoulders our sins." How could this be, since Christ was without sin? Of course one can deal with the phrase by saying that it simply means that Christ took upon his shoulders the *consequences* of our sins. But as soon as one substitutes this account one gets the feeling that something has been lost—that the central mystery of Christ's incarnation has been removed. If God really became man, if the crucifixion really involved the voluntary self-humiliation of God, then—we feel—"took upon his shoulders our sins" must bear a slightly stronger sense. But then we are confronted once more by the first difficulty. The good Christian cannot say that Christ *became a sinner* just like the rest of us. It is too much to require of God that he should deny his nature.

Yet that is what is required of Angelo. In the atonement of *Measure for Measure* the implications of vicarious guilt are followed out to the very end. Angelo takes on his shoulders the necessary sins of human judgement. But in the morality of this comedy there is no such area of uncertainty as we found in the Christian doctrine of the Atonement. Angelo, unlike Christ, really sins. His hands do not remain clean.

Under the pressure of Shakespeare's genius the figure of the atoning sufferer begins to take on the lineaments of his anthropological ancestor, the scapegoat. Thus, while I must plead guilty to introducing the *bête noire* of present day criticism, the Christ-figure, yet Angelo is certainly a Christ-figure with a difference. For he is also a Devil-figure. We are now in a position to account for the strange resonance of Isabel's cry in the last scene—"You bid me seek redemption of the devil" [V. i. 29]. Angelo is at once a Redeemer and the polluted. Earlier in this essay I was forced to acknowledge (for what it was worth) that Angelo at the close of the play is forgiven by the Duke. At the civil level this must be seen as a mitigation of the Duke's Machiavellianism. But the Duke is also, as we have seen, a metaphysical Machiavel. And I am not sure that, at this level, his forgiveness of Angelo is not his finest stratagem. It had always been a necessary consequence of Angelo's view of law that that administrator should desire for himself, if found guilty, the same punishment he would impose on others:

> When I that censure him do so offend,
> Let mine own judgement pattern out my death,
> And nothing come in partial.
>
> [II. i. 29-31]

Angelo (how different, here, from Hazlitt's arch-hypocrite! [see excerpt above, 1817]) is absolutely consistent on this point when the crisis comes:

> No longer session hold upon my shame
> But set my trial be mine own confession.
> Immediate sentence, then, and sequent death
> Is all the grace I beg. . . .
>
> [V. i. 371-74]

Angelo is pleading for justice. The ending of *Measure for Measure* is really not very like the ending of *The Winter's Tale* or *Cymbeline*. For Angelo the Duke's indulgent benevolence does not confer felicity; rather, it perpetuates his anguish. . . . The play leaves him in a state of torture, mitigated only by the fact that Claudio is not, after all, dead. . . . He longs to discharge his debt, to rest his burden. The Duke makes sure that he carries it to the end. (pp. 246-47)

At the beginning of this essay I expressed dissatisfaction with those critics who make *Measure for Measure* sound like a naive morality play. I now find myself concerned lest, in my reaction, I have fallen into the far grosser error of making it sound like something by Bernard Shaw. Curiously, the charge of making it sound like Graham Greene frightens me far less. The ingenious structure of Machiavellian redemption, of substitution and atonement which I discern in this play is only an element in a larger whole. There is an exploratory reverence, a diffidence before the indefinitely recessive humanity of the persons of the play, which excludes all Shavian facility. Yet if the play has a fault it is perhaps a Shavian one. The vertiginous paradoxes with which the dramatist assaults his audience are achieved at some cost to reality. For example, we are led to suppose that the duties of government place man in a simple dilemma; either he must punish all, or he must forgive all. Some glimmerings of a third, less dramatic course appear in the person of Escalus but that is all. A great part of the tension of the play consists in the clash of theoretic absolutes.

Yet no play of Shakespeare is so moving in its assertion of concrete fact. The imminent death of Claudio and his fear entirely transcend the theoretic extravagance of Isabel. I am aware that in saying this I may offend some historical critics who will tell me that to the Jacobean mind death was unreal compared with becoming a nun. I can only ask such readers to listen to the verse. The poetry given to Isabel works as hard for Claudio as it does for her:

> The sense of death is most in apprehension;
> And the poor beetle that we tread upon
> In corporal sufferance finds a pang as great
> As when a giant dies.
>
> [III. i. 77-80]

Let the historicist have his say: "Taken in their context, the lines clearly mean that even a giant feels at death no more pain than a beetle does." Of course. But is it pure accident that the common reader has always taken it to mean just the opposite? (p. 248)

> *A. D. Nuttall, "'Measure for Measure': Quid Pro Quo?" in* Shakespeare Studies: An Annual Gathering of Research, Criticism, and Reviews, Vol. IV, *1968, pp. 231-51.*

HAL GELB (essay date 1971)

[*Gelb examines Shakespeare's use of comic devices in* Measure for Measure *and claims that the play's comic vision—which is supplied by the "low" characters in the sub-plot—is almost undermined by the terror and darkness of the main plot. He states that these shifting angles of vision make us uneasy and raise unanswered questions. Like numerous earlier commentators, Gelb criticizes the Duke's manipulations, and the despair and suffering experienced by the characters as a result of them, as hardly worthy of the achieved ends, because no character truly undergoes a change in outlook and the Duke himself never understands the people he controls. The play's resolution, although it satisfies the comic vision, "does not fit the world on which it has been imposed." For additional commentary on the comedic form in* Measure for Measure, *see Oscar James Campbell (1943), Murray Krieger (1951), Nevill Coghill (1955), and R. A. Foakes (1971).*]

[*Measure for Measure*] capitalizes, for its own purposes, on the expectations raised by certain comic devices and motifs found in others of Shakespeare's comedies: the quitting of a particular society, disguise, an eiron figure, low comic scenes, the enforcement of arbitrary laws, a barrier to the union of young lovers and finally a wedding that fulfills the expectations raised. In *Measure for Measure*, certain of these devices and motifs are used to create expectations that will be fulfilled within the course of the play, and others that will be thwarted; some control our attitude toward the tragic possibilities which are introduced into the play.

Like *A Midsummer Night's Dream* and *As You Like It, Measure for Measure* begins with a departure from one society and removal to another. In *Measure for Measure*, however, this abandonment—as we discover after two scenes—is merely a ruse. In fact, there is never a suggestion that there is some other society, pastoral or otherwise, to flee to. Instead, the Duke returns to his own vice-ridden Vienna, a society full of the appearance of virtue, where those responsible for the care of the law are at least as immoral as the lawbreakers. There, he plays a game which eventually exposes *some* of the appearances.

His returning to view his own society places a frame about that society, allows an audience to view it from a distance, intellectually and critically. Comic distancing is a matter of dramatic irony; the audience feels it knows more than the characters, and what the audience knows makes it feel safe. The Duke in his disguise as Friar knows more than the other characters, indeed seems to be an eiron—or plays at being an eiron—and that role makes us feel safe in his hands. (pp. 25-6)

Similarly, the comic characters control in part the audience's reaction, keep the audience from becoming unduly concerned by the threat of pain. Lucio's remarks during Isabella's first interview with Angelo call the critical faculties into play and distance us from whatever pain she may be feeling; his intrusions in the final act, notably at [V. i. 179-80], break the tension and seriousness of that scene.

At the same time, in their rough foolery and play of wit, the low comic characters attack the arbitrary laws which unnaturally restrain the sexual urge: they undermine Claudio's arrest, the plucking down of the whorehouses, and Angelo's, Isabella's, and the Duke's denial of sexuality; indirectly they support the union of the young lovers which, as in Shakespeare's romantic comedies, has been blocked, thereby creating the expectation that the barrier will be removed, and that in the end the lovers will be joined. (p. 26)

While he is establishing comic possibilities, Shakespeare is also unleashing possibilities that may become tragic. So intense is the evil of Angelo's lust and treachery; so impossible is Isabella's dilemma; so dark is her telling Claudio he will have to die, his at first accepting it, and then pleading with her against his death; so great is the suffering to which the Duke subjects Isabella; and so great is our empathy in these scenes, that the protection provided by the comic frame falls away for their duration. Unleashed suffering and evil, rupturing all boundaries of comedy.

But the comic vision will probably restrain them after all.

Yet if the expectation of a comic resolution is so strong that it seems to restrain the tragic, shifting angles of vision make us less certain of that restraint, more uneasy. The shifting angles of vision cause us to lose our moral bearings. We more or less know which actions are right and which are wrong, but it is nearly impossible for us to assess the morality of any of the complex characters. . . .

Their actions are extremely difficult to assess because we have merely the action and its consequences; the intent is either missing entirely or is made ambiguous. For example, why does Isabella consent to the bed-trick? Never explained. Why does Mariana love Angelo? Never really explained. Why does Angelo decide to proceed with Claudio's execution? Never explained. Or for that matter, why does Hamlet hesitate to kill Claudius, and why does Lear decide to divide his kingdom? Possible reasons may be hinted at, but they are never established. The words that create our knowledge of the inner being are missing; we have only actions. (p. 27)

In other words, Shakespeare's omission of motivation not merely confuses our moral vision but also allows many different playgoers to identify with characters with whom they could not identify if the characters' motivations were more specifically defined.

Finally, lack of motivation leads us to a sense of the opaqueness of the characters. With the possible exception of Angelo, we

don't really know the characters at the end. In a play which constantly forces its audience to make moral judgments, this is extremely important, for one is forced to realize he is judging people, as in life, without knowing them. (pp. 27-8)

The use of shifting perspectives and dead-end expectations contributes to the questioning of the appearance of virtue and of the entire system of law and values. Angelo seems good, has the outward appearance of an angel. . . . Isabella and the Duke similarly appear virtuous, and some of that illusion is never wholly dispelled. In fact "those whose claims to goodness or decency seem most vigorous are precisely those in whom meanness, self-regard and hypocrisy root deepest" [see excerpt above by Una Ellis-Fermor, 1936]. Those characters, the comic characters, who make no claim to goodness and decency, live outside the law; Shakespeare uses them to collapse the appearance of a system of moral order. Words in their mouths are shown to signify appearances, and in collapsing the meaning of words Shakespeare equates the self-righteous moral world with the brothel crew outside the law, a law established by that self-righteous moral world. (pp. 28-9)

Finally, the Duke's own actions make us question his morality. Unless the end will justify his means, how can we accept the suffering he causes Isabella? Unlike Rosalind [in *As You Like It*] or Portia [in *The Merchant of Venice*], who likewise maintain their disguises when they are no longer necessary, the Duke hurts people and treats them as if they were inhuman cogs to be manipulated. He even considers executing the marvelous Barnardine merely to provide himself with a head for his plot. Nevertheless, though the Duke's scheme makes us uneasy, the momentum of our expectation that he is good and will make things work out makes us go along with the scheme, even wink at the suffering involved. Shakespeare further prepares us to overlook the consequences of the Duke's plotting by having him act in ways that win audience sympathy. . . .

But whether the ending is a truly appropriate comic ending hinges not so much on the Duke's morality as on his vision, though his morality is a reflection of that vision. One must ask whether the Duke, manipulating the action, is an eiron, and if so, how good an eiron is he? (p. 29)

We have only to watch the contrast between the passionate, fearful Claudio and the calm and balance of the Duke's *consolatio* to understand that the Duke lacks knowledge of suffering and of the fear of death. We have only to remember that he is taken by surprise when Angelo orders the Provost to proceed with Claudio's execution to realize that he had not taken Angelo's measure as well as he thought, that the depth of evil in the world eluded him, and that his first plan as eiron-plot manipulator just didn't work out. Perhaps the problem is that he is not dealing with folly, but with evil.

The real test of his ability as eiron-plot manipulator comes in the quadruple wedding, the comic resolution he has contrived for the play. And it is in the wedding scene that we may best judge whether the expectations, first created, then confused and qualified, are ever fulfilled.

In terms of comic expectation, the marriage of Claudio and Juliet is the only satisfying one. Claudio and Juliet are the young lovers we have wanted to see together since the beginning. Now that the barrier preventing their union has been removed, we are glad to see them joined.

In contrast, the marriage of the Duke and Isabella fulfills no expectations, for no expectations had been raised. Even though we feel Isabella must be wedded to the world, the first suggestion of a marriage to the Duke is in the last fifty lines of the play. . . . Had Shakespeare wanted to suggest the fitness of this union . . . all he needed to do was give the Duke a line or two to make us aware he was contemplating such a marriage. As it stands, there is no overwhelming sense of dramatic necessity.

It has been argued that the Duke's cruelty, putting Isabella through the flames to wring from her wisdom and mercy, is justified in this final scene. But no speech of another character, no, not Isabella herself in soliloquy, tells us that she has changed. In fact, her earlier pleas for Claudio are based more on arguments for mercy than is her prayer for mercy for Angelo. Her first argument alone in the latter plea offers Angelo's intent as an extenuating circumstance. Her last two reasons argue for Angelo's life on purely legalistic grounds: Claudio had done the thing for which he died, and Angelo did not accomplish the rape. But by a Shakespearian sleight of hand, we are led to believe that she is arguing for mercy.

The Duke, legislating a wedding between Mariana and Angelo, ignores the problem of how such a marriage may be both punishment for Angelo and reward for Mariana. . . . Knowing Angelo does not want to marry Mariana, remembering his recent anger with her, and knowing Angelo's character, we feel that the Duke has created a marriage for Mariana in which hell is the other person. In effect, the Duke has observed the letter of the law—a marriage contract has been drawn up and now must be executed—and once again shows himself blind to the human situation.

Again, it seems doubtful whether the Duke's elaborate scheming has wrought a change in a character; doubtful that the end was worth the suffering. For one thing, it could be argued that Angelo was no self-deceiver to begin with. When Vicentio offered him the regency, he rejected the role the Duke was making him play:

> Let there be some more test made of my metal,
> Before so noble and so great a figure
> Be stamp'd upon it.
>
> [I. i. 48-50]

For another thing, it is doubtful that Angelo changes in the play. In terms of the Duke's own definition of a true repentance—

> Showing we should not spare heaven as we love it,
> But as we stand in fear,—
>
> [II. iii. 33-4]

—Angelo's repentance is insincere, for he fears his "dread" lord's omniscience [V. i. 366-70]. Certainly, Angelo has not learned to be merciful: he now calls for the same death punishment that earlier in the play he saw as just should he transgress his own law [II. i. 27-31; V. i. 373-74, 476-77]. (pp. 30-2)

There is another technical reason for feeling that the marriage of Mariana and Angelo is inappropriate. The Mariana plot and the bed-trick—which Shakespeare adapted, not from his source, but from his own *All's Well That Ends Well*—are not well integrated into the plot. Mariana is not mentioned until III. i and does not come onstage until Act IV. In using her and the bed-trick, whose very elaborateness and lack of spontaneity make it stick out, the Duke chooses a device for resolution that may resolve the action but does not arise from the action it resolves. Had Shakespeare, who had already satisfactorily resolved a few plays in his time, wanted to integrate the Mariana plot with the earlier action, I think he might have managed to introduce her a little earlier. But he did not, and hence the marriage seems legislated and unnatural.

The marriage of Lucio and Kate Keepdown is less of a problem. Though it bothers us that the Duke is punishing Lucio largely for personal reasons, there is something enjoyable about this wedding. It is a joke on Lucio, who has previously controlled all the scenes in which he appeared, a disquieting of him; and because he is a comic character, we do not worry about any suffering in this marriage. At the same time, the charges against Lucio remind us, as the play ends, that the Duke, by a neat trick of prestidigitation, by making us look elsewhere, by judging everyone else, has not himself been judged for the faults Lucio found in him. (pp. 32-3)

The play as I see it then deals with characters who are consumed with self, who have insulated themselves from the world, who are blind and cannot see in themselves the faults they see in others. Oedipus too was a ruler who "above all strifes contended to know himself" [III. ii. 232-33]. As Hazlitt said, the Duke "is more absorbed in his own plots and gravity than anxious for the welfare of the state; more tenacious of his own character than attentive to the feelings and apprehensions of others" [see excerpt above, 1817]. The Duke, by ever studying himself, is not, however, the only one to exclude himself from touch with his society. Angelo's virtue until now has been untried; Isabella was about to escape to a nunnery; Mariana lives in a moated grange; Bernardine is happy in sleep and his womb-cell. . . . The Duke, however, for a time makes the characters touch life, and though he does not have the ability or the vision to touch life himself, we can admire his attempt. (p. 33)

Measure for Measure is a play in which comic elements and a comic structure are used to create expectations usually associated with a comic vision. Throughout the play, however, they are interspersed with tragic possibilities, and both possibilities are viewed through shifting perspectives, so that they confuse the audience's moral vision and finally leave the audience with a vision similar to the protagonist's, the would-be eiron, Duke Vincentio. Like him, they feel that everything has been resolved for the best in a comic resolution, but unlike him they are made to feel that the comic vision does not fit the world on which it has been imposed and that their comic expectations have been fulfilled in form rather than in substance. Hence, Shakespeare has used a primarily comic structure to create a form that is neither comedy nor tragedy, and which questions the comic vision itself. And through this form, an audience is made to feel purely neither the joy of comedy nor the cathartic fear and pity of tragedy, but some inseparable blending of the two. (p. 34)

> Hal Gelb, "*Duke Vincentio and the Illusion of Comedy; or, All's Not Well That Ends Well*," in Shakespeare Quarterly, *Vol. XXII, No. 1, Winter, 1971, pp. 25-34.*

R. A. FOAKES (essay date 1971)

[*Foakes concentrates on the "tonality" of Shakespeare's plays, a term he defines in the introduction to his* Shakespeare, the Dark Comedies to the Last Plays: From Satire to Celebration *(1971) as the "pattern of expectations established by the sum of relations existing between the parts of the action at any given point.'' In the excerpt below, he maintains that the tonality of* Measure for Measure *is provided by the repeated ironic contrasts between the freedom, vitality, and licence of the secondary characters and the extreme discipline and restraint of Angelo and Isabella. He finds that as the play progresses, it displays the limitations of ''being absolute'' for either life or death, revealing that Claudio, Pompey, and Lucio are as flawed as Angelo and Isabella in their exaggerated and unhealthy behavior. Instead,* Measure *demonstrates, through the figure of the Duke, the need for a ''full acceptance of the natural inclinations and responsibilities of a human being,'' symbolized by the institution of marriage. Foakes concludes, as have such earlier critics as E.M.W. Tillyard (1949), Robert Ornstein (1957), J. W. Lever (1965), and Hal Gelb (1971), though for varying reasons, that Shakespeare's resolution remains uncomfortable and confusing because he never resolves the ''neatness'' of the conclusion and ''what remains unexplained and unresolved below the surface.''*]

In *Measure for Measure* . . . a striking feature of the play almost from the beginning is the powerful presence of a clown, Pompey, and a corrupting lover of words, like Parolles [in *All's Well That Ends Well*], in the figure of Lucio. They enter in the second scene, where Mistress Overdone is introduced also; their liveliness, good humour, and freedom are important in establishing the tonality of the play. . . . [What] is primary in the presentation of these characters is not their nature as sinners, or their licentiousness, but simply their vitality, their zest for life. The action of the first part of the play, as it involves Angelo, Claudio and Isabella, develops in relation to Pompey's exuberant existence and defiance of repression, and against a world of bawdy talk and of bawdy houses where there is no lack of clients.

Measured against this, the actions of Angelo and Isabella appear harsh, extreme, even absurd. Claudio, contracted to Juliet, is sentenced to death for lack only of what he calls 'the denunciation . . . of outward order' [I. ii. 148-49]; they are married, in other words, according to English common law, though the religious ceremony and public announcement are lacking. For Claudio to be sentenced to prison on this account, while bawds walk free, is outrageous; for him to be sentenced to death is nothing short of monstrous. As Claudio is marched off unwillingly to prison, so his sister Isabella is seen complaining that the rules of the votarists of St Clare are not strict enough; chastity, poverty, obedience, silence and virtual imprisonment are something less than she desires, 'wishing a more strict restraint Upon the sisterhood' [I. iv. 4-5]. The juxtaposition of, on the one hand, freedom, common vitality, licence and lechery, against, on the other hand, Angelo's urge to impose extreme penalties, and Isabella's drive to inflict on herself the maximum discipline and restraint, provide the tonality of the play.

These ironic contrasts are developed further in Act II, which opens with the long scene of the trial of Pompey. It seems that when Claudio was arrested, he did not try to defend himself, but admitted the offence, to the extent of having had too much liberty in getting Juliet with child; at any rate we do not see him tried, but he enters already sentenced, and on his way to prison. In II. i, however, Angelo and Escalus sit in full state as judges to determine the case of those two 'notorious benefactors', Pompey the bawd and Froth a foolish gentleman. . . . It appears that Pompey has provided Froth with a mistress in Elbow's wife, who has been pretty free in her favours anyway; as Pompey says, 'There was nothing done to her once' [II. i. 141]. If they have offended, then, in making a whore of Elbow's wife, Pompey and Froth have committed a much worse

crime than Claudio and Juliet; but the whole thing is a tangle, and is presented so comically that even Escalus as judge can only join in the fun . . . ;

Escalus Truly, officer, because he hath some offences in him which thou wouldst discover if thou couldst, let him continue in the courses till thou know'st what they are.

[II. i. 185-88]

This comic perspective on the demands of the flesh is followed at once by the meeting of Isabella, come to plead for Claudio's life, and Angelo. As in the scene in *All's Well* in which Helena cures the King, Shakespeare changes the key, so to speak, endowing the earnestness of Angelo and Isabella with a religious colouring. . . . As their interchanges develop through the second act, Angelo sees himself becoming a devil, and the overtones of his name seem to allude to the fall of Lucifer. Locally this is powerful, and Angelo's self-amazement and temporary disgust at the discovery of his lust are strongly realized. The whole sequence, however, is tempered by what has gone before. If Pompey's licence in sexual matters needs to be restrained, at least his instinct as 'a poor fellow that would live' [II. i. 223] seems healthier than Angelo's and Isabella's shrinking from the demands of the flesh. Angelo indeed, tormented by Isabella's beauty, comes in these scenes to admit that his blood, far from being 'snow-broth' as Lucio had said, is as hot as other men's; 'Blood, thou art blood' [II. iv. 15], he cries in pained acknowledgment of what in the arrogance of conscious virtue he had denied. So Isabella's chastity is rather a repudiation of the flesh than an acceptance of Christ.

It is striking that in her first interview with Angelo, Lucio stands looking over her shoulder, a kind of Mephistopheles, egging her on not from any interest in virtue, or in the rescue of Claudio, but simply in the enjoyment of the game of winning Angelo over, through the exercise of rhetoric and the warmth of her personality. He is a strange companion for the 'saintly' Isabella. It is true that the scenes in which Angelo confronts Isabella with his demand that she sleep with him to save her brother, and the scene in which Claudio begs Isabella to save his life at the cost of her virginity, are written with a poetic intensity, and here the inflexibilities of character come into serious collision with the inflexibilities of the law. Nevertheless, it is important to distinguish between the way the characters see themselves, and the pattern of expectations set up from the start of the action, with its promise of a comic resolution. Angelo's inflexible addiction to the letter of the law in the case of Claudio is followed by his equally outrageous demand that Isabella commit with him the very offence for which he has sentenced Claudio to death. Isabella's absolute valuation of her chastity above life . . . is followed by her terrible and total rejection of Claudio when he begs her to save him. . . . Angelo and Isabella are off balance, lacking a sense of proportion, or a sense of humour, as is brought out by the contrast between them and Pompey and Mistress Overdone.

Their inflexible stances are further set off against the bearing of the Duke, who has already appeared in his disguise as a Friar in I. iii, where he indicates some suspicion of Angelo. He returns in II. ii to advise Juliet, and again in III. i, to see Claudio and deliver his famous exhortation to him to be 'absolute for death'. . . .

Thou hast nor youth nor age,
But as it were an after-dinner's sleep,
Dreaming on both; for all thy blessed youth
Becomes as aged, and doth beg the alms

Of palsied eld: and when thou art old and rich,
Thou hast neither heat, affection, limb, nor beauty
To make thy riches pleasant. What's yet in this
That bears the name of life?

[III. i. 32-9]

The Duke's rhetoric is splendid, and the speech justly celebrated, for it strikes plangently a chord to which all human
beings respond, and which echoes Christian homilies on the
vanity of this world, and on the art of dying well. (pp. 17-22)

[Yet, if] life corresponds to the Duke's description of it here,
there would be little point in Angelo and Isabella taking their
peremptory and rigid attitudes; Angelo's lust to possess Isabella, and her concern for chastity, have become more important to them than life or death. These drives in them, together with Angelo's anxiety to preserve his 'unsoil'd name',
are what make their lives important to them, and yet paradoxically make them careless of life in others. The attitudes they
take would result in the death of Claudio, and both are destructive of life. Claudio's initial acceptance of the Duke's
counsel, 'To sue to live, I find I seek to die' [III. i. 42] is a
contradiction of that natural urge that brought him and Juliet
together to create new life. . . . His repudiation of this acceptance of death, and cry to Isabella to save him, are not in this
context the appeals of a coward, but cries from the heart of
one who loves life, whose life is love, a love that contrasts in
its warmth with the chill austerity of Angelo and the frigid
chastity of Isabella. Shakespeare, however, does not let him
get away with it and command our sympathy thus easily. Claudio does not mention Juliet in his pleading with Isabella, but
thinks only of himself; what's more, his appeal to her, 'Ay,
but to die, and go we know not where . . .' [III. i. 117], springs
not from a love of life, but from a horror of death and dread
of what comes after. To be absolute for life in this way is as
perverse as to be absolute for death in the Duke's way.

The inadequacies of the Duke's homily, and of Claudio's plea
for his life, help to maintain an uneasy balance of sympathies
in the scene, and Isabella's final shrill denunciation of Claudio
seems almost warranted. For a moment it appears that no solution is possible, and the harsh polarities established in the
action and in the speeches in this scene reflect in their bleakest
extremity the oppositions which form the basis of the dramatic
shaping of the play. In fact, the return of the Duke in disguise
to watch over Angelo's rule in Vienna is itself sufficient indication that all will be set to rights in the end; and at the very
point when a resolution of conflict seems impossible, the Duke
appears again, immediately after Claudio's interview with Isabella, dropping into prose and effecting another change of
key to restore something of an earlier tone and mood. He
produces the solution in Mariana of the moated grange, married
to Angelo as truly as Juliet is married to Claudio, by civil
contract, and a happy outcome is assured. This confirms the
drift of the action from the opening scenes, which is on the
side of life, not death. The development of the conflicts between Angelo and Isabella, and between Isabella and Claudio,
to the crisis of III. i shows horrifyingly the limitations of being
absolute for death in the way Isabella and Angelo are, and
displays also the inadequacies of being absolute for life in the
way Claudio and, by implication, Pompey and his fellows are.
So now we see Pompey and Mistress Overdone conveyed to
prison as bawd and prostitute, and the prison, emblem of the
law's restraint upon the lusts of men, remains the centre of the
play's action almost until the final unravelling in Act V. The
prison is curiously also a centre of life. Pompey exchanges the

role of cheerful bawd for that of equally cheerful hangman.
Lucio appears there, refusing to bail Pompey, and slandering
the disguised Duke; he too, it seems, may be condemned for
lechery, and has, like Angelo and Claudio, promised marriage:
'Mistress Kate Keep-down was with child by him in the Duke's
time, he promised her marriage' [III. ii. 199-201]. It seems
that on all sides the demands of the flesh, or the natural drive
of life, asserts itself. . . . Even the Duke carries some smack
of mere humanity in his long interchange with Lucio; it is not
that he is, as Lucio says, a lecher who would 'mouth with a
beggar, though she smelt brown bread and garlic' [III. ii. 183-
84], but that he is a man of flesh, subject to common lusts and
desires. . . . The Duke deceives and lies, deceives Claudio
and Escalus by concealing his plot from them, usurping a
beggary he was never born to, as Lucio says, and the tricks
that go with it. The dialogue puts him and Lucio on an equal
footing for a time, as Lucio nudges him, and takes him by the
elbow in confidential gossip. This is why Act III has to end
with the Duke's choric speech in rhymed couplets:

He who the sword of Heaven will bear
Should be as holy as severe. . . .

[III. ii. 261-62]

This is designed to restore his authority as ruler and justice,
and comes as a reminder of the undisguised Duke in the middle
of his performance in another role, that of intriguing Friar.
(pp. 22-5)

The last act unravels all with its series of confrontations and
revelations, enabling the play's title to exert a quibbling meaning in several ways; the obvious significance, of punishment
to fit the crime, relates to Angelo chiefly, though, more lib-
erally interpreted, it fits the case of Lucio at the end; the phrase
also suggests plot countering plot, as the Duke's measures work
against those of Angelo; and also dance or movement for movement, implying a balance in plot and rhythm, a balance worked
out in the comic resolution of pardon and marriage. Of that
world of bawdy vitality so prominent in the earlier part of the
play, only two representatives, Lucio and Barnardine, are seen
in the last act, and the latter has no speaking part. . . . Lucio's
lechery is as harmful and unbalanced as the prim rigour of
Angelo and Isabella, and the balance and harmony symbolized
by marriage terminate the action for him as for Angelo and
Isabella—and for all three marriage may have the nature of a
recovery of health, a punishment, and an expiation, or a full
acceptance of the natural inclinations and responsibilities of a
human being. The play leaves us to determine in just what
'measure' any of these applies. (p. 27)

Like All's Well, Measure for Measure is in the end an uncomfortable play because in spite of the marriages that round it
off, it forces on us a sense of the gap between belief and act,
between what people would be and what they are, or between
justice and charity. So, for instance, there is no way of accounting judicially or ethically for the stubborn Barnardine; it
is not clear whether the marriage of Angelo to Mariana is more
a reward or a punishment to both of them; the Duke's impending marriage to Isabella goes unexplained; and all through
virtue gains no notable victories in opposition to licentiousness,
but rather loses out in its strictness, while licentiousness carries
in it a love of life that wins sympathy and seems generous by
contrast. If 'liberty plucks justice by the nose' [I. iii. 29] this
tends to prove beneficial in curbing the harshness of the law,
and shows how there can indeed be 'a charity in sin' [II. iv.
63], as Angelo and Isabella agree there may, but without seeing
the implications of what they are saying. The last act is neat

in its contrivance of measure for measure, but the dramatic effect of the play stems from the gap between that neatness and what remains unexplained and unresolved below the surface. Some see mere confusion in this, and not an effect sought by Shakespeare; and some regard the play as limited in its achievement because 'the "incarnation" of ideas, principles, beliefs is not at all points consistent and complete' [see excerpt above by J. W. Lever, 1965]. A study of the dramatic shaping of the play suggests rather that such a reading is made too plausible by some aspects of what is not basically a drama attempting such consistency. In other words, the weakness of *Measure for Measure* lies not in its failure to maintain the 'incarnation' of beliefs found in Act II and the beginning of Act III, but rather in the overweighting of these scenes. The strong religious feeling here seems to invite too close an involvement with some characters in an action which is generally more concerned with a critical placing of them. The change of key in Act III seems too marked and too abrupt, the revelation of Mariana too easy a way out, and the Duke has too much responsibility as a character here in holding the action together. If Shakespeare had given a serious weight to the action in wholly secular terms, he might have been able to control the play's balance more easily. (pp. 30-1)

> R. A. Foakes, "Shakespeare and Satirical Comedy," in his Shakespeare, the Dark Comedies to the Last Plays: From Satire to Celebration, The University Press of Virginia, 1971, pp. 7-62.*

JAMES BLACK (essay date 1973)

[*Black attempts to justify Shakespeare's use of the bed-trick convention and to prove that* Measure for Measure *"turns upon the positive virtue" of Mariana's action through an exploration of the characters' moral experiences. He examines the atmosphere of confinement and retreat, such as Isabella's spiritual isolation and Angelo's seclusion within the safety of the law, stating that the play is about "human beings who in an uncertain world are shut up against themselves and from one another." He claims that the play accentuates the inadequacy of "splendid talk" and stresses the need for physical action. Thus, Mariana performs the "first act of whole-hearted substitution," which dispels the darkness and turns the play toward "light and freedom." Black concludes that all of the characters, through Mariana's example, find release and fulfillment in substituting themselves for another, thereby achieving "self-abnegation and forgiveness." For additional discussion of the importance of "substitution" in* Measure, *see the excerpts by Terence Eagleton (1967) and A. D. Nuttall (1968). Also, for further interpretations of the theme of forgiveness in* Measure for Measure, *see the excerpts by August Wilhelm Schlegel (1808), G. G. Gervinus (1849-50), Walter Pater (1874), G. Wilson Knight (1930), Roy W. Battenhouse (1946), and Nevill Coghill (1955).*]

The 'bed-trick' in *Measure for Measure* has always caused embarrassment of one sort or another. 'This thing of darkness' [*The Tempest*, V. i. 275] must be acknowledged, but no critic has managed to assimilate the device fully into his view of the play or quite been able to come to terms with what has seemed to be an 'incompatibility of the intrigues of comedy with the tone of what has gone before' [see Philip Edwards in the Additional Bibliography]. (p. 119)

My own approach to *Measure for Measure* is going to be from the point of view that Shakespeare did not simply forget to justify his use of the bed-trick device, nor did he adopt in this play a policy of 'never apologise, never explain'. I believe that he intended the play as it stands (textual corruptions aside) to

convey the sense that Mariana in sleeping with Angelo has done something right, and that the play turns upon the positive virtue of her action.

Measure for Measure is set largely in a series of places of confinement or retreat. Claudio is under the strict restraint of prison, as are Barnardine and, to a lesser extent, Pompey. Julietta also is in prison and the late stages of pregnancy, and much of the action takes place in the gaol. . . . Escalus and Angelo try Pompey, and Isabella and Angelo face one another, in antechambers to this prison. There also is the St Clare nunnery, on whose threshold we first encounter Isabella. The ethos of this place is conveyed only through the quoting of a single rule, but it is a curious either-or prescription whose terms compel notice:

> When you have vow'd, you must not speak with men
> But in the presence of the prioress;
> Then, if you speak, you must not show your face;
> Or if you show your face, you must not speak.
>
> [I. iv. 10-13]

Though Isabella never completes this vow there is no doubt that she has prescribed for herself an ideal kind of nunnery whose rules transcend in strictness those of the actual sisterhood. These rules she wishes for herself, and it appears she would extend them to others as well:

> I speak not as desiring more [privileges],
> But rather wishing a more strict restraint
> Upon the sisters stood, the votarists of St. Clare.
>
> [I. iv. 3-5]

Isabella is not alone in wishing to impose her self-restraints upon others. Angelo would do this as well through his application of the law, of which he is not just a representative but the actual embodiment, for 'Mortality and mercy in Vienna Live in [his] tongue, and heart' [I. i. 44-5]. . . . Angelo has adopted gravity as his role, and over the years has carefully built a *persona*, persuading the world—and himself—of 'a kind of character in [his] life' [I. i. 27]. His reading of the law has been and is closely tied up with his creation of this character, as is suggested in his reference to 'the state whereon I studied' [II. iv. 7]. The setting through which he moves—we may as well call it the courtroom—is dominated by this *persona*, for, as the play never lets us forget, the law exists as it is applied and as it begins to be applied to Vienna it takes on the peculiar stamp of Angelo's repressive character. Thus his courtroom and his very presence stand, like the nunnery of Isabella's ideal, for 'a more strict restraint' [I. iv. 4]. (pp. 120-21)

Clearly, in his use of the law he does not *want* room for manoeuvre. The inflexible statute, the irreversible sequence of procedure ('He's sentenc'd, 'tis too late' [II. ii. 55]), the judge's anonymity (Escalus never addresses him by name while discussing this case, and Isabella calls him Angelo for the first time only when his carnal intentions are clear to her [II. iv. 151])—all of these conventions shield him from the necessity of taking decisions on individual circumstances. In sum, he is as circumscribed and secure in the law as Isabella in her ideal nunnery. And we scarcely need Angelo's admission that he takes pride in his gravity to make us see that these two people, each bounded in his or her chosen nutshell, count themselves kings of infinite space.

But there is no suppressing what is for them the bad dream of sexuality. It breaks through just where Angelo has every expectation of security: a courtroom, a legal debate, the appellant a religious novice. All that passes between them is words, which Angelo always has been able to use to bind with or hide in. While words hold to the meanings their users intend, so long as Angelo can positively label and anathematise 'these filthy vices' [II. iv. 42] in others, and so long as 'be tempted' keeps its proper distance from 'to fall', his legalistic enclosure is secure. Very early in the play, however, it is shown that words are very shaky foundations upon which to build a system of absolute law. The trial of Pompey in II, i degenerates into farce because of the way language lends itself to misuse. The continual malapropisms of Elbow, the prosecuting officer, undermine the dignity of these proceedings from the beginning; and no sooner have the judges Escalus and Angelo attuned their ears to his 'misplacings' than Pompey offers his side of the case in a run of bawdy equivocations, giving hilariously suggestive connotations to the most innocent-seeming words. (pp. 121-22)

The scene suggests that it is impossible to apply—or to take refuge in—the letter of the law when letters themselves will not yield to organisation or discipline.

In this trial of Pompey the tone also is set for the scene which follows, where in an antechamber to the courtroom Angelo hears Isabella appeal on Claudio's behalf and where despite the terrible gravity of the occasion words soon again begin to veer into equivocation and suggestiveness. Isabella 'speaks, and 'tis such sense That [Angelo's] sense breeds with it' [II. ii. 141-42]. He has just come from a courtroom where *double-entendre* reigned, and now, approached by a beautiful girl whose intellect itself stimulates him, and who directs his attention to his own human frailty—

> Go to your bosom,
> Knock there, and ask your heart what it doth know
> That's like my brother's fault—
>
> [II. ii. 136-38]

he finds his legal world of words unbalanced and betraying, his security threatened. Misconstruction follows misconstruction in a run of the kind in which one verbal slip is compounded by another as the speaker continues unaware or even as he tries to correct the impression. . . . (pp. 122-23)

Words are associated with the law and with rank: condemnation and reprieve live in Angelo's tongue, and Isabella says 'That in the captain's but a choleric word / Which in the soldier is flat blasphemy' [II. ii. 130-31]. The play began with the Duke's test to see 'if power change purpose, what our seemers be' [I. iii. 54], and now as Angelo goes further into temptation both power *and* words change purpose. In this moral whirligig, which exemplifies Lear's 'change places, and, handy-dandy, which is the justice, which is the thief?' [*King Lear*, IV. vi. 153-54], Angelo changes from judge to ravisher, Pompey from bawd to hangman—'a feather will turn the scale', says the Provost [IV. ii. 30-1]. Angelo may well ask, 'The tempter, or the tempted, who sins most?' [II. ii. 163], and Abhorson expatiate upon how 'every true man's apparel fits your thief' [IV. ii. 43-7]. (p. 123)

It is little wonder that in a world of such shifting possibilities the prison has no lack of inmates, or that Isabella and Angelo should seek refuge in the nunnery and the self-constructed enclosure of reputation and legal absoluteness. Despite these precautions, however, Isabella finds herself eventually in the confine of a terrible dilemma which delimits movement as effectively as any actual chain. When she and Claudio come together for the first time, in III, i, they are like the claustro-

phobe of Angelo's fancy [II. iv. 19-26], struggling in ever-growing panic against the press of dreadful alternatives.

The philosophy which will free all from their confinements is never far to seek in the play. It is stated at the outset:

> If our virtues
> Did not go forth of us, 'twere all alike
> As if we had them not. Spirits are not finely touch'd
> But to fine issues.
>
> [I. i. 33-6]

There is repeated insistence that not only must the professor of virtue 'issue' their talents, but also they must stand-in for others and do so in such a way as wholly to be the person substituted for. 'In our remove, be thou at full ourself', says the Duke [I. i. 43] when commissioning Angelo to 'supply [his] absence' [I. i. 18]. . . . The meaning is not restricted to that of office-bearing: Angelo soon is invited by Escalus to put himself in Claudio's shoes and to ask himself whether, if he had been given the opportunity, he 'had not sometime in [his] life / Erred in this point. . .' [II. i. 8-16]. . . . [By] graded steps, as it were, the dialogue comes to the great of all examples of substitution for others:

> Why, all the souls that were, were forfeit once,
> And He that might the vantage best have took
> Found out the remedy . . .
>
> [II. ii. 73-5]

It is all splendid talk of the necessity of loving and feeling for one's neighbour as oneself. But fired as it may be by desperation and danger, it is still—it seems we may say *only*—talk. . . . As they do in the Gospels, words must find enactment, else

> Heaven in my mouth,
> As if I only did but chew his name.
>
> [II. iv. 4-5]

As Angelo has put the letter of the old law into effect, so Mariana sets the letter of forgiveness and love in act. This she does through the bed-trick. In its simplest terms this is a liberating action for her: it initiates her release from the moated grange, where for five years she has hidden herself away. . . . In sleeping with Angelo she acts as a substitute, literally giving her body in place of someone else's. She is more than a convenient body, however, for in Angelo's apprehension she *is* Isabella. Hers is the first act of wholehearted substitution: although Angelo was enjoined to be 'at full' the Duke he has not exercised power as the Duke would do, nor can Isabella substitute for her brother in the manner which Angelo has proposed. Putting herself so fully in another's place, Mariana makes good the moral dicta that till now have been not much more than splendid pronouncements, and makes of the bed-trick—to quote Isabella talking theory—'no sin at all, but charity' [II. iv. 66].

If Shakespeare needed the bed-trick to resolve his plot, he has made a virtue of necessity. We also should note that this action of Mariana's takes place in the most confined of settings. . . . This setting—the bed within the garden-house [V. i. 212] within the walled and locked garden within the gated and locked vineyard—would seem to pattern out the labyrinth of dilemma into which Isabella, Claudio and Angelo have wound. It answers also, keys and all, to the confines and wards of Claudio's prison; while the very arrangements for Angelo's deception—the 'repair in the dark' [IV. i. 42] which will have 'all shadow and silence in it' [III. i. 247]—also suggest restrictions which go beyond even the nunnery's. . . . It is as if Mariana, encountering darkness like a bride, has reached into all those confines where the others are enthralled: from this bedroom of darkness and silence events turn back toward light and freedom. The 'repair' in the dark is a remedy as well as an assignation. (pp. 123-25)

The public setting of the final scene is heavily stressed [IV. iii. 95-6; IV. iv. 5-6, 10; IV. v. 9; IV. vi. 13-15]. From the pent-up atmosphere of court, prison, and grange the action is removed to the open and public space by the city gates, where under the Duke's stage-management [cf. IV. vi. 1-8] each character in turn is made to play out actions of self-enfranchisement. Mariana is first: after Isabella has, on the Duke's prior instructions, accused Angelo and then been 'arrested' for slander, Mariana enters heavily veiled. The Duke's command both echoes and overrides the nunnery's rule:

First, let her show her face, and after, speak.

[V. i. 168]

Mariana fulfils this command both literally and symbolically, showing her face and declaring herself in public for the first time in five years. The Duke also 'shows his face' when, after leaving and returning in his Friar's habit, he is unhooded by Lucio. These two dramatic enactments of 'coming out' lead of course to the unmasking of Angelo.

But an even more dramatic issuing-forth has yet to be undertaken by Isabella. Still with every reason to hate Angelo, believing her brother to be dead, and with Angelo's own ordainment of his penalty and the Duke's legalistic explication of the case fresh in her ears—'An Angelo for Claudio; death for death' [V. i. 409]—Isabella is begged by Mariana to take Angelo's part. The play suddenly compresses into two brief speeches the opposites that have warred throughout:

Mariana.   Sweet Isabel, take my part;
        Lend me your knees, and all my life to come
        I'll lend you all my life to do you service.
Duke.
        Against all sense you do importune her.
        Should she kneel down in mercy of this fact,
        Her brother's ghost his paved bed would break,
        And take her hence in horror.

[V. i. 430-36]

The Duke invokes the 'sense' of the law, the 'fact' of an unjustly dead brother and natural as well as legal revenge, family honour (which counted much with Isabella before, [II. iv. 179 and III. i. 71]), and even the superstition of a certain kind of morbid religiosity. Mariana appeals as Isabella formerly pleaded with Angelo, in the terms of redemptive substitution and self-sacrifice: 'take my part' and 'all my life to come I'll lend you all my life' [V. i. 430-32]—offering her own life in place of what Isabella may in justice demand, Angelo's death. Mariana, 'craving no other nor no better man' [V. i. 426] than Angelo and offering herself thus, is spiritually at one with Juliet, who earlier in prison answered the Duke's question so affirmatively: 'Love you the man that wrong'd you? Yes, as I love the woman that wrong'd him' [II. iii. 24-5]. It is now Isabella's turn to join their company; and she who talked so much about mercy is again being asked to *do* something, indeed something physical. For the whole scope of Mariana's plea should be noticed: she asks only a silent gesture:

Sweet Isabel, do yet but kneel by me;
Hold up your hands, say nothing; I'll speak all.

[V. i. 437-38]

This to Isabella, whom we remember to have been not only morally but also physically unyielding. . . . Therefore it is an act of self-conquest (and a great stage gesture) when Isabella falls on her knees.

She does more than kneel, however. Mariana asked only for a silent appeal—'Say nothing; I'll speak all'—but Isabella goes the second mile to speak on Angelo's behalf:

Look, if it please you, on this man condemn'd
As if my brother lived.

[V. i. 444-45]

The legalism of her plea for Angelo has been strongly denounced. . . . But such a response overlooks at least three factors. First, so far as Isabella knows she is addressing in the Duke a judge who up to now has invoked the strict letter of the law, and so she must plead the letter if Angelo is to have any chance. Second, it is in itself a striking reversal that the letter is being cited, not to kill as in Claudio's situation, but to save. And third, it ought to be recognized that the real force of this plea lies not so much in its terms as in the fact that Isabella is interceding for Angelo at all. The stubborn Barnardine is rightly admired for his determined refusal to cooperate with his executioners: he is 'absolute for life'. But the formerly stubborn Isabella has now surpassed Barnardine in that she is absolute for someone else's life, and that life her enemy's. Perhaps Barnardine and Isabella together illustrate the Duke's distinction between a grace that 'stands' and a virtue that 'goes' [III. ii. 264]; this is the distinction between the 'old' and 'new' Isabella as well.

So Isabella's own enfranchisement from the exactness of 'measure still for measure' [V. i. 416] is being enacted when she pleads for Angelo. The reciprocal virtue of her action is expressed in Romeo and Juliet's joyful realisation that in loving Juliet, his 'enemy': 'My intercession likewise steads my foe' [*Romeo and Juliet,* II. iii. 54]. Kneeling in public with Mariana, Isabella has 'shown her face', and she has spoken as well. . . . She sees the narrowness and irreversible nature of justice. Having formerly cried out for 'Justice! Justice! Justice!' [V. i. 25], she now can say 'My brother had but justice' [V. i. 448]. The 'but' contains a whole statute of limitations.

Just as Isabella shows her face so too has Angelo's been shown, and what he knows about himself painfully revealed to the world. No-one who feels that Angelo is treated too leniently has fully taken into account the city-gate setting and the public humiliation there endured (to Shakespeare's contemporaries it was a recognised factor in punishment). The exposure of so essentially withdrawn a man and the breaking through of his *persona* is in itself a punishment which if it does not exactly fit the crime certainly fits the offender. To Angelo execution would be preferable, entailing as it does the concealment of prison and the oblivion of death: it is the public session he wants curtailed:

No longer session hold upon my shame.
But let my trial be mine own confession.
Immediate sentence, then, and sequent death
Is all the grace I beg.

[V. i. 371-74]

The soul-searching Angelo underwent before sinning, his remorse and fear when his villainy has, as he thinks, succeeded [IV. iv. 19-34], and the penitence he expresses when caught [V. i. 474-77]—all these cannot be left out of the reckoning; and as his public humiliation is prolonged the audience may sum up, with the Duke, 'Your evil quits you well' [V. i. 496]. (pp. 125-27)

But although the Duke 'like power divine, Hath looked upon [Angelo's] passes' [V. i. 369-70], it does not follow that he should be seen as God. It is not so much divine power as resourcefulness and good luck which enable him to counter Angelo's attempted double-cross [IV. ii. 115f.]. In becoming the Friar he undergoes, like others, his own process of self-removal: though he does this voluntarily, some sort of drastic action obviously has been dictated by Vienna's condition. The Duke has been a secretive man—'I love the people', he says, 'But do not like to stage me to their eyes' [I. i. 67-8]—and only Escalus seems to know him well. Retiredness encourages rumour, and even Friar Thomas seems to think that this ruler's disguise may have a nefarious motive [I. iii. 1-6]. It is therefore salutary that the Duke-Friar must perforce listen to Lucio's slanders, as well as see his prison. At the play's end he indicates that he is not God (or even a Friar) by making himself one partner in the marriage-pairings which have the earthy membership of Lucio and his paramour. The emphasis, in this final scene, upon action and gesture makes it fairly clear that although Isabella is silent after the Duke's proposal she may not necessarily be equivocal in accepting. 'Give me your hand and say you will be mine' is followed directly and conclusively by 'He [Claudio] is my brother too' [V. i. 492-93], a firm indication that the Duke has received the sign he asked for. In the marriage-pairings he is associated with men and women: wedlock qualifies the 'too much liberty' which formerly turned to restraint [I. ii. 125-28], and is the best assurance that none of them will any longer 'forswear the full stream of the world and . . . live in a nook, merely monastic' [As You Like It, III. ii. 419-21]. (pp. 127-28)

Measure for Measure, as I see it, is about human beings who in an uncertain world are shut up against themselves and from one another. They find release and fulfilment in 'going forth' through self-abnegation and forgiveness. The play illustrates that a fugitive and cloistered virtue is of equal uselessness with a buried talent, and that noble ideals are supposed to be put into action. In making Mariana's trick an important part of the ethical fabric of *Measure for Measure* Shakespeare has wedded a traditional comic device to a serious moral intention. They are not at all strange bedfellows. (p. 128)

> *James Black, "The Unfolding of 'Measure for Measure'," in* Shakespeare Survey: An Annual Survey of Shakespearian Study and Production, *Vol. 26, 1973, pp. 119-28.*

TOM McBRIDE (essay date 1974)

[*In an interpretation similar to that of G. Wilson Knight (1930), R. W. Chambers (1937), Roy W. Battenhouse (1946), and A. D. Nuttall (1968), McBride contends that* Measure for Measure *is a secular reenactment of the medieval allegory "Parliament of Heaven," a drama that "explained to medieval and Renaissance man the ineffable reality of Christian salvation." He compares the characters in Shakespeare's play to their counterparts in the allegory; however, he concludes that whereas Christ in the medieval story both technically and spiritually saves humankind, the Duke, who performs a similar function in* Measure for Measure, *technically satisfies the demands of justice and mercy, but spiritually fails to redeem the souls of Isabella, Angelo and Claudio. For this reason, McBride refers to him as a "God that fails." Other critics who regard the Duke as a dramatic failure include Charles Knight (1842), William Witherle Lawrence (1931), Clif-*

ford Leech (1950), Robert Ornstein (1957), J. W. Lever (1965), and Hal Gelb (1971).]

Two scholars have commented extensively on the allegory of which *Measure for Measure* is a secular re-enactment. Hope Traver and Samuel Chew provided overwhelming evidence of the popularity, both literary and visual, of the "Parliament of Heaven," an allegorical drama that explained to medieval and Renaissance man the ineffable reality of Christian salvation. In its simplest form this allegory depicts the fallen Adam and Eve before God's throne, where the Four Daughters of God—Justice, Truth, Mercy, and Peace—debate in a law-court trial the punishment to befall the original sinners. Justice and Truth argue that Adam and Eve knew God's command but broke it; for their disobedience they therefore must die. But Mercy and Peace counter that God should view this disobedience in the context of extenuating circumstances: Adam and Eve had no evil intent, and they were no match for the brilliant tempter Satan. Therefore, they must be spared. God then reconciles this dilemma between justice and mercy by sending His Son, who, clothed in man's flesh, satisfies Justice by taking man's punishment for him; but since man himself is spared, Christ also satisfies Mercy. Thus are reconciled the conflicting claims of allegorized virtues, and thus did man better understand the meaning of Christian salvation as a deliverance from the dilemmas of a fallen world.

This allegory provides the foundation on which Shakespeare constructed *Measure for Measure*. From its beginning to the middle of Act III (about the first half of the play), a complex dilemma develops between the demands of justice and mercy. In the second half of the play, a providence-like figure, the Duke, intervenes to resolve the dilemma. Since he saves Isabella's chastity and yet spares both Claudio and Angelo, his external resolution seems successful; but since the "Parliament of Heaven" ideal demands not only external rescue but also internal reform, his resolution is really a failure. The "Parliament of Heaven" thus becomes an ironic commentary on the fallen Parliament of Earth. This most basic structure, the analogue to an allegory well-known in Shakespeare's time and before, is a simple one. The details, flesh hung on the bare skeleton, are more complicated.

But for Lord Angelo, it seems, nothing is complicated. He sees little conflict between justice and mercy. Much like Justice in the allegory, he feels it enough to insist that disobedience be punished. (pp. 265-66)

But his view of strict justice is an inadequate one, for there is evidence everywhere of a larger context that he fails to see. Lucio and the two gentlemen are full of bawdy talk and unrepent sexual license; but only Claudio is to be judged by Angelo's hard new justice. And Claudio's disobedient adultery involves no Mistress Overdone but rather a lady who is

> fast my wife
> Save that we do the denunciation lack
> Of outward order.
>
> [I. iv. 147-49]

So the justice Claudio deserves for his disobedience conflicts with the mercy he deserves because of his circumstances. Escalus, who cannot make Angelo recognize this conflict, sees an even larger unresolved dilemma. On the one hand, Vienna needs severity to curb Viennese license. On the other, it should acknowledge the peculiar context of Claudio's situation. (pp. 266-67)

But Angelo has already revealed why he will grant no mercy to poor Claudio: unlike the judged, the judge has felt no sexual temptation. . . . Mercy requires empathy; Angelo has none. But he is ironically tempted by an equally chaste Isabella, about to take vows that forbid her to "speak with men / But in the presence of the prioress" [I. iv. 10-11]. Indeed, Isabella agrees with Angelo's dictum that adulterers should receive severe justice:

> There is a vice that most I do abhor,
> And most desire should meet the blow of justice.
> [II. ii. 29-30]

Were it not for a peculiar context—that the offender happens to be her own brother—Isabella would be supporting Angelo's justice; she would not be pleading with him for mercy. Hers too, then, is the temperament of justice. And though Angelo's ultimatum would seem to place her in a brutal dilemma, her immediate decision, that chastity comes before brother, is for justice. There, with justice and severity, her ultimate loyalties reside. (p. 267)

Claudio's entire situation is a quandry. So far he is the Adam in this "Parliament." But his situation might have been an instructive one for Angelo and Isabella, who badly need lessons in mercy. Isabella might have learned that the ethical contest between chastity and brother is at least a hard one to decide. And Angelo might have learned, especially since he has been tempted, how powerful are the forces that array against many of his brothers' chastity. But neither learns anything. Both cling to the cruel justice consistent with their similar temperaments. (pp. 267-68)

The situation corresponds to the first part of the "Parliament of Heaven" allegory, for here, as in the allegory, there is a seemingly unresolvable conflict between the claims of justice and mercy. Justice demands that Angelo limit Viennese license, even by the harsh punishment of death; mercy demands that he take into account the extenuating circumstances of Claudio's license. Justice demands that the postulant Isabella support efforts to limit sexual excesses; mercy demands that she do all she can, perhaps even surrender her own chastity, to save her brother's life. The play, at about its mid-point, shifts, as does the allegory, into its last half, when an external agent intervenes to reconcile the dilemma between justice and mercy. In the allegory the agent is Christ; in the play it is the Duke.

In the allegory Mercy concedes that Adam and Eve are "technically" guilty of disobedience, but she insists that one must see the spirit, as well as the letter, of their disobedience. Christ's subsequent intervention, then, must satisfy not only the technical, literal side of the dilemma—saving their lives by substituting His own body—but also its spiritual side. . . . In intervening, the Duke should want to help Angelo become a man who practices self-control not in the letter of stern duty but in the spirit of happy inclination. The same goes for Isabella.

It is according to the standards of this ideal that the Duke's intervention should be judged. On the technical side, he intervenes with success, for he substitutes Ragozine for Claudio and Mariana for Isabella, and saves both brother and chastity. But on the spiritual side, since Mercy demands more than the simple preservation of the body, the issue involves souls and becomes more subtle. Here the Duke's intervention is suspect. In viewing the two couples, Claudio and Juliet, Angelo and Mariana, he looks but with "technical" eyes, quite opposite the true insight of mercy. Since Angelo and Mariana are "tech-

nically" betrothed, it seems, the Duke happily tricks Angelo into fornication with her. Were he to view the situation with more spiritual eyes, he would be less quick to blame Claudio for "technical" adultery with a woman he loves, while tricking Angelo into fornication with a woman he dislikes. . . . [The] obvious gap between the spirit and the letter of the law, as the Duke applies it to Claudio and Angelo, seems quite wrong for a Viennese government in need of distinctions between the law's letter and its spirit. Hence, if the final destination is to be a reconciliation between letter and spirit, justice and mercy, the Duke's early direction is not a promising one.

And there is another way in which he provides unethical leadership. Sexual license is not his city's only, or even its worst, problem; Vienna also lacks those bonds of trust that hold citizens together. . . . With Lucio typifying its malaise, the last thing Vienna needs is more deception, especially from its ruler. His "bed-trick" intervention not only strikes the wrong balance between the letter and spirit of the law; it is also in itself dishonest—hardly the way to restore trust in the realm.

Unaware of these failures, however, the Duke enthusiastically proceeds to arbitrate justice for Angelo. Having played the Christ of this earthly "parliament," he now plays its God. His role combines Christ the intervener with God the Judge. In prideful posture, he will be both Father and Son. A narcissistic God, he continues to be fascinated by the aesthetics of his interventionist drama. Just as in the Abraham-Isaac story (an Old Testament variation of the "Parliament of Heaven"), where the angelic intervener does not save Isaac until the last possible second, the Duke will not tell Isabella of Claudio's safety until later, so as

> To make her heavenly comforts of despair
> When it is least expected.
> [IV. iii. 110-11]

As he knowingly bumbles on earth, the Duke finds much pleasure in his "heavenly" role.

But soon he begins to play his other role—the judging God. Here he no longer plays the disguised priest-intervener but returns as the Duke. He has a costume for both parts. In terms of the "Parliament of Heaven," one costume is for Father, the other, for Son. As the Duke plays God, then, so does Isabella play Lady Justice. She approaches him to demand Angelo's punishment. . . . (pp. 268-70)

At this point there is no Lady Mercy to argue that the court should view the extenuating circumstances of Angelo's deed. If there were, she might note that Angelo has at least blamed no one for his crimes but himself, or that he would naturally be attracted to a woman of similar temperament. But Isabella takes no account of these circumstances. She is not Lady Mercy but, understandably enough, Lady Justice.

Still, however, she does not see justice forthcoming. . . . But just at the moment of her despair, the Duke unmasks, revealing himself as agent on behalf of Isabella and as righteous judge of Angelo and Lucio. Lady Justice is satisfied. But like Adam and Eve, Angelo and Lucio stand in judgment; at hand is the climax of their earthly "parliament."

The Duke first begins to deal with Angelo. But before he can pronounce condemnation on his deputy, Angelo condemns himself. His righteous temperament does not mercifully deal with his very self. Ironically, his refusal to make excuses is already an extenuating circumstance arguing for mercy; but Angelo views himself in the fixed light of justice. . . . The

Duke agrees. Taking the phrase "measure for measure" out of its New Testament context of forgiveness, he plans for Angelo the "just" penalty of Old Testament law. (pp. 270-71)

But at last Angelo hears, on his behalf, a voice of mercy. It is Mariana, who yet loves him, and who also appeals to Isabella to join her plea:

> They say best men are molded out of faults,
> And, for the most, become much more the better
> For being a little bad; so may my husband.
> O Isabel, will you not lend a knee?
>
> [V. i. 439-42]

She views Angelo with a wider vision than that of narrow justice. And since he does take sole responsibility for his son, she is probably right that he can become a better man for his experience—if he is allowed to live and learn.

Mariana's plea obviously reminds Isabella of the desperate time when she too pleaded mercy for a loved one, for now she leaves justice and comes to mercy. In the "Parliament of Heaven" one of Mercy's main characteristics is her ability to make distinctions. Traver tells us, for instance, of a late fifteenth-century mystery play by Greban, *Mystere de la Passion*, in which "Misericorde" argues that man's punishment should not be equal to Satan's since Satan sinned out of pride, while man only sinned out of ignorance. . . . As a new Lady Mercy for Angelo, Isabella makes her own distinction. Her brother, she argues, died rightly because he was an actual adulterer; Angelo should be spared because he only intended to be one.

Logically, she misses the point. Logically, her argument remains on the side of justice: it makes Angelo, who only intended to do evil, technically innocent, but Claudio, who intended no evil, technically guilty. Besides, it is for ordering Claudio to his death that Angelo is really to be punished. Still, questionable as the letter of Isabella's logic may be, its spirit is not: she has performed her first genuine act of mercy. The Duke, with romantic longings for her, does not deny her request. In characteristically surprising drama he sends for Claudio, unmasks him, and pardons Angelo, instructing him to make Mariana a good husband. But for this grant of mercy the credit goes solely to Isabella. As for the Duke, he seems to act out of romance, not mercy. Technically, he has bestowed mercy upon Angelo; spiritually, Isabella has done it.

And when the Duke begins to deal with the slandering and salacious Lucio, no merciful voice ever appears to dissuade his harsh judgment. This self-dramatizing governor, whose love of popularity has contributed, by his own admission, to the excessive "scope" [I. iii. 35] and hedonism of his realm, cannot bring himself to forgive anyone who has slandered him. He has forgiven Angelo's intended murder (a worse crime than Lucio's), and his own misgovernance has helped make the atmosphere in which the Lucios thrive; but these facts do not impress him. In the end he spares Lucio from death only because the offender pleads that cuckoldry is worse than death. So the Duke has him cuckolded. Perhaps because he has offended his duke's intemperate desire for popularity, the vice that first led to Vienna's decadence, there is little mercy for Lucio.

In neither his arbitration of justice and mercy for Angelo nor Lucio, then, has the Duke shown good judgment. Technically, his intervention succeeds in that it saves Claudio's life and Isabella's chastity; but spiritually he does not concern himself

with the souls of Angelo, Isabella, or Lucio. Such redemption as Angelo finds is due in part to Isabella, and such redemption as she finds is due in part to Mariana. The Duke plays no spiritual part in the redemption of either. Lucio, representative of licentious and hypocritical Vienna, gets no opportunity for redemption; and Vienna itself gets no new leadership. In the "Parliament of Vienna," as he gives out "measure for measure," the Duke plays a God that fails. (pp. 271-72)

On the basis of this analysis . . . one cannot logically reach E. K. Chambers' conclusion that in the play "the searchlight of irony is thrown" on those who pridefully assume providential powers. In *Measure for Measure* the Duke blunders badly; but his creator—the playwright—understood exactly his own task, and performed it well. (p. 273)

> *Tom McBride, " 'Measure for Measure' and the Unreconciled Virtues," in* Comparative Drama, *Vol. 8, No. 3, Fall, 1974, pp. 264-74.*

LAWRENCE W. HYMAN (essay date 1975)

[*Hyman identifies an ethical or philosophical pattern in* Measure for Measure *that explains the contradictory actions of the characters and unifies the discrepancies between the first and second parts of the play, a discontinuity noted by such earlier critics as E. C. Pettet (1949), E.M.W. Tillyard (1949), J. W. Lever (1965), and Hal Gelb (1971). He argues that Shakespeare composed a drama in which the concepts of virtue and chastity—symbolized by the characters of Angelo and Isabella—negate the possibility of life, while life itself is of value only when sin and shame are accepted as necessary parts of existence, an idea he finds convincingly displayed in the attitudes and conversations of the secondary characters. For this reason, he regards Angelo's stay of execution not as the victory of love or mercy over strict justice, an interpretation that has dominated both nineteenth- and twentieth-century evaluations of the play, but as the result of Mariana's and Isabella's acceptance of sin and corruption as inseparable from life. In fact, Hyman maintains that all of the marriages that conclude* Measure *reflect an alignment of the characters, managed by the Duke, towards the acceptance of life rather than death, and with it the acknowledgement of realities of sin and human lust. For a similar assessment of the characters in the play and the polarities of life and death they represent, see the excerpt by R. A. Foakes (1971). Also, for further discussion of the final marriages and their relevance to the play's meaning, see the excerpts by Muriel C. Bradbrook (1941), Terence Eagleton (1967), R. A. Foakes (1971), and James Black (1973).*]

The contradictory actions of the characters [in *Measure for Measure*] can be understood . . . if we depart from psychological realism and look for a philosophical or a thematic development, an ethical equation that is not allegorical (in the sense of being imposed on the action) but that arises out of the distinctive actions of this particular play. By tracing out such a pattern, I hope to show a hitherto undiscerned unity in this powerful and disturbing play.

From the premarital relationship between Claudio and Juliet that opens the play to the four marriages at the end, we see sexuality as the source of life, whereas its absence, chastity, leads to death. Neither the sexuality nor the life to which it leads is necessarily good or desirable, and hardly ever do we see sexuality or its results as anything but sinful and shameful. But sexuality is the only force for life. Virtue, on the other hand, arising from chastity and being enforced by Justice, may often seem heroic and desirable; but it always results in death. Of course the death that is a consequence of the desire for Virtue is not necessarily an evil to be shunned, any more than the life that arises from lust and sin is necessarily desirable. *Measure for Measure* is not a didactic play; it does not have a humanistic, Lawrentian, "life affirming" ethic any more than it has a Christian ethic. It is a sardonic comedy that derives its distinctive tone and mood from its ability to defeat whatever sympathies or ethical values we may bring to it. Not only does the play forge a link between sexuality and shame, and between virtue and death, but the action and the language often compound the paradox by playing with the Elizabethan ambiguity of the word *die,* to bring together at one level of our mind what it separates at a more conscious level—sexuality and death. It is only by "dying" in the sexual sense that life can come about.

From the beginning we see that the wages of sin is life, not eternal life, of course, or even a virtuous life, but the natural life of ordinary sinful man. The shameful and immoral act of Claudio and Juliet brings about life, literally, in Juliet's womb, whereas the claims of virtue and justice, as exemplified in Angelo's decree, would result in death for Claudio. Such a statement does not indicate that any reader should approve of Angelo's decree. The response of the common reader is right: we must be shocked at Angelo's perversion of justice, and our shock deepens as the play develops. For Shakespeare makes us see that Claudio's death is not the result of a monstrous action, of a judge who has gone berserk, but the logical outcome of his strict adherence to virtue and justice. To see Claudio's fate as a result of Angelo's wickedness is to see only the melodrama. But *Measure for Measure* is obviously more. It is, to use Stevenson's phrase, an "intellectual comedy" in which our deepest feelings are disturbed and, in a serious sense, played with. . . . (pp. 4-5)

For it is not only Angelo but Virtue itself that is presented to us as frightening, as well as something that is necessary if society is to move beyond the level of Lucio and Pompey. No reader can deny that Angelo is cruel and almost unnatural. But we are not allowed to forget that he is also *virtuous* in at least one sense of that word. The Duke himself says so in his confidential remarks to Friar Thomas:

> Lord Angelo is precise;
> Stands at a guard with Envy; scarce confesses
> That his blood flows; or that his appetite
> Is more to bread than stone. Hence shall we see
> If power change purpose, what our seemers be.
>   [I. iii. 50-4]
>   (p. 5)

What is frightening about Angelo is not his failure but his success in living up to a "Christ-like" behavior. For to be "Christ-like" in the context of *Measure for Measure* is to be inhuman, not in the theological sense of transcending the flesh, but in the ordinary sense of being inhumane. Both senses of the word are always present, and we are and should be disturbed by the play's insistent reminder that to be like Christ allows Angelo to embrace death rather than life.

The corollary is just as disturbing: to embrace life is to accept sin and shame. We may be as sympathetic to Claudio and Juliet as we are horrified by Angelo. But Claudio's passion for Juliet is presented as Lust, and Shakespeare insists upon this lust and shame. . . . [We] are allowed to recognize that Claudio and Juliet are in love; but we are not allowed to forget that their relationship is very much like that between Lucio and his prostitutes. . . . Claudio accepts the word "Lechery" [I. ii. 138] in referring to his relationship, and the whole atmosphere con-

spires to force us to recognize the common factor in all sexuality. That is why our sympathy for Claudio is expressed most clearly by Lucio, whose chief characteristic is his inability or his unwillingness to discriminate between one form of sexuality and another. To Lucio all sexuality is lechery; and it is significant that he is the first one who asks that Claudio be allowed to live. For as the play goes on we see that the death of Claudio can be prevented only by some form of sinful sexuality. (pp. 6-7)

[In *Measure for Measure*] human procreation is never divorced from the religious, moral, and legal restraints and attitudes that are usually associated with sexuality. Lucio, it is true, compares Juliet's "plenteous womb" to the coming of spring [I. iv. 41ff.], but in everyone else's eyes her pregnancy is sinful. The Duke (in the guise of a friar) deems her to be as guilty as Claudio; and Juliet accepts his reference to the embryo in her womb as a "sin" [II. iii. 19]. He is emphatic in stating that her sin in the creation of this child was of a "heavier kind" [II. iii. 28] than Claudio's.

Of course, Juliet also sees her "sin" as a "joy," and this feeling on her part is significant in moving the play toward a more complex attitude toward the sinful behavior of both her and her lover. In answer to the Duke's question as to whether she repents, her reply is, "I do repent me as it is an evil. / And take the shame with joy" [II. iii. 35-6]. But there is never any doubt that the "joy" comes out of the "evil" and "shame." (p. 7)

As a corollary to this equation of life and shame, the death that we are constantly trying to fend off, from the first scene to the end of the play, is seen as the inevitable consequence of a strict adherence to virtue and justice. There is no difficulty in seeing Isabella as an embodiment of virtue, but is Angelo an embodiment of justice rather than of perverted justice? I believe that he is, and that he does honestly attempt to remove the worst effects of immorality from Vienna. Whatever layers of irony may be present in the Duke's opening speeches, there is no doubt that corruption in Vienna is real enough, and that whatever else he may have in mind the Duke wants to put an end to a state of affairs where "Liberty plucks Justice by the nose, / The baby beats the nurse" [I. iii. 29-30]. There is no real question as to the virtuous intentions of both Isabella and Angelo. What is at issue is whether the virtues of these two people, the novice nun and the reformer, are compatible with the nature—the "blood" and "appetites"—of ordinary human beings. (p. 8)

Angelo's desire for justice, as the second act opens, means death for Claudio, as he makes clear to Escalus. But this death has wider implications, as we see when we go on to the rather wild scene in which Angelo and Escalus try to interrogate Pompey. The first effect of this change from Claudio's plight to Pompey's is to allow us to sympathize, if not with Angelo, at least with the Virtue that he represents. . . . Even Escalus, who earlier in the scene had pleaded for mercy in Claudio's case, has no doubt that prostitution is an evil that the law should not and "will not allow" [II. i. 228].

But Escalus still does not want to admit that the abolition of the worst corruptions of lust must lead to death. He tries to convince Pompey that just to be aware of the shame and the legal consequences of prostitution should be enough to stop it. But Pompey is not convinced. Just as Angelo had made Escalus (and the audience) uncomfortable by his insistence that if justice is really to prevail we must be prepared to act harshly, so

Pompey confronts Escalus (and us) with the fact that if we want life to go on we must accept the immorality and shame of sexuality. (pp. 8-9)

Escalus does not want to accept this unpleasant reciprocity between life and sin, any more than we do. But Pompey insists that you must have lechery if you are going to have life, that is, if you are not "to geld and splay all the youth" [II. i. 230-31]. . . . Whenever we deal with sexual incontinence (and it is this kind of sexuality that dominates *Measure for Measure*), we are confronted with the same dilemma: to allow it to go unchecked breeds corruption and shame; to control it results in death. This death can be joked at by Pompey, and is quite serious with respect to Claudio. But the same equation holds, as we see in the confrontation between Angelo and Isabella.

Most readers have acknowledged that Isabella's chastity, despite her sincere desire to use it to save her brother, leads to his death, even according to her own logic:

> There is a vice that most I do abhor,
> And most desire should meet the blow of justice:
> For which I would not plead, but that I must:
> For which I must not plead, but that I am
> At war 'twixt will and will not.
>
> [II. ii. 29-33]

To "abhor" the "vice" leads to a desire to punish, and this desire, as Isabella realizes in her next speech, leads her to ask that the "fault" be condemned, but "not my brother" [II. ii. 36]. Angelo quickly points out the obvious weakness in this kind of reasoning, and Isabella is reduced to a vain hope that Angelo will show the same compassion for Claudio that she has. It is clear that in so far as the plea for mercy comes from the virtuous maid, Claudio is doomed. (pp. 9-10)

[What] is significant about her speeches in terms of the action of this play is that (as so often in Shakespeare) the arguments have absolutely no effect. For one thing, Angelo's replies are also quite logical and have a force of their own: "I show [pity] most of all when I show justice; / For then I pity those I do not know" [II. ii. 101-02]. But what is most important in negating the power of Isabella's plea for mercy is her unconscious arousal of Angelo's sexuality:

> Go to your bosom,
> Knock there, and ask your heart what it doth know
> That's like my brother's fault. If it confess
> A natural guiltiness, such as is his,
> Let it not sound a thought upon your tongue
> Against my brother's life.
>
> [II. ii. 136-41]

Of course Angelo finds in his bosom much more than Isabella had intended. But the lustful desire is, ironically, what Isabella wanted Angelo to become aware of. Wretched, cowardly, and cruel as this desire may be, whatever the "expense of spirit" that Angelo's lust may incur, it is only this feeling that holds out the possibility of life for Claudio. And, conversely, it is Isabella's virtue, her fierce (but surely understandable) desire to maintain her chastity, that spells out her brother's death. (pp. 10-11)

Conversely, the more sinful Angelo becomes in allowing full rein to his "sharp appetite" the greater is the possibility of life, not only for the doomed Claudio but for Angelo himself. His long-dormant sexuality, although it does not make him a better man, does allow him to come alive emotionally and intellectually, as well as physically. As we learn from his

soliloquies (at the end of II. ii and the beginning of II. iv), Angelo looks more deeply into his life and, consequently, comes to a greater awareness of the hollowness of his previous existence. (p. 11)

Of course there is something inhumane in Isabella's choice, and most modern critics no longer defend her resolve to "live chaste" and have her "brother die" as a sentiment that Shakespeare's audience would have accepted. What has not yet been seen is that Isabella's action in preferring her chastity to her brother's life (as well as her own) is the culmination of all the previous actions, and that when she asks Claudio, "Wilt thou be made a man out of my vice?" [III. i. 137], she is striking the dominant note in the theme of *Measure for Measure*. For the play tells us, in a dozen different ways, that the answer is: "Yes, life not only can but *must* come out of vice, shame, and dishonor." . . . It is not, therefore, a matter of seeing Isabella as a villain but of recognizing that a strict adherence to virtue and chastity—whatever form it takes in Angelo or in Escalus or in Isabella—leads to death. (p. 12)

At this point the Duke comes out of one of his "dark corners" and moves the entire play in another direction, toward life rather than death. . . . [He] tells Claudio that Angelo "had never the purpose to corrupt" his sister, that Isabella had made him a "gracious denial which he is most glad to receive," and that Claudio must prepare himself for a certain death [III. i. 160ff.]. All three statements are completely false, and critics have had a difficult task in discovering just why the Duke feels he must lie so brazenly to a man who has suffered enough and whom he is determined to save. (pp. 12-13)

[The] Duke's false statements to Claudio, far from restoring the traditional virtues, provide one more example of how these virtues would still lead to certain death for the victim. It is only in the *absence* of honor, as we see in the Duke's speech to Isabella (which immediately follows his speech to Claudio), that we see a possibility for life. For the Duke now is truthful about Angelo's proposal and asks Isabella to pretend acceptance so that Mariana can be substituted as Angelo's bedmate. (p. 13)

[Isabella's] answer to the Duke's request, however, an answer that involves deceit as well as lust, leads to life. There is some resistance, as we would expect, before Isabella can make this change. When she first hears about the previous relationship between Angelo and Mariana, one that involved perfidy and slander on Angelo's part and shame for Mariana, Isabella responds as she has always done. She would destroy evil even at the cost of life. "What a merit were it in death to take this poor maid from the world! What corruption in this life, that it will let this man live!" [III. i. 231-33]. But the Duke obviously prefers life, with all of its corruption, to death, no matter how honorable. He proceeds to employ the "violent and unruly" passions of Mariana, the lust of Angelo, and the deceit of Isabella, in an effort to save Claudio's life. And he persuades Isabella to follow him.

Seen in this way, the substitution of Mariana for Isabella is . . . the climax of a series of actions that remind us with increasing force that life in this play not only can but must come out of vice and shame. In such a perspective, the comic scenes are also developments, in another key, of the main theme, and not signs that Shakespeare is no longer interested in the ethical dilemmas of the first half of the play. (p. 14)

We expect, of course, that Angelo will free Claudio. As the Duke predicted, "When vice makes mercy, mercy's so extended / That for the fault's love is th'offender friended'' [IV. ii. 112-13]. Angelo, however, *does not love* the fault, as we learn later on: ''This deed unshapes me quite'' [IV. iv. 20]. As might be expected, Angelo felt no real satisfaction after the deed was over. His lust is ''perjured, murderous, bloody, full of blame'' *after* the action as well as before. But, paradoxically enough, it is precisely this *revulsion* from the sinfulness of his lust that makes him ''murderous'':

> This deed unshapes me quite; makes me unpregnant
> And dull to all proceedings. A deflower'd maid;
> And by an eminent body, that enforc'd
> The law against it! But that her tender shame
> Will not proclaim against her maiden loss,
> How might she tongue me! . . .
>   He should have liv'd;
> Save that his riotous youth, with dangerous sense,
> Might in the times to come have ta'en revenge
> By so receiving a dishonour'd life
> With ransom of such shame. Would yet he had lived.
>   [IV. iv. 20-32]

To read these lines carefully is to see that the immediate result of Angelo's lust was to let Claudio live. What reversed this impulse was Angelo's sense of the ''shame'' and the loss of honor that, he imagined, would cause Claudio to seek his death. Thus it is still the demands of honor and the revulsion from shame that move Angelo's mind toward death. Only the acceptance of his own lust and the acceptance of shame on Isabella's and Claudio's part could result in life for Claudio. But Angelo cannot imagine life on such terms. That is why we hear the order for Claudio's death, rather than a reprieve. (p. 15)

Of course we know all along that Claudio is alive and that the Duke knows the truth about Angelo. Our knowledge enables us to maintain enough distance not to be overwhelmed, as Isabella is, by the complete absence of justice or mercy. At the same time, however, we should recognize that in the real world there may not be a *deus ex machina* and that real dukes and judges may very well be taken in by the appearance of virtue in an Angelo and be blind to the truth. Thus, Shakespeare allows us to enjoy our superiority to Isabella because of our greater knowledge, while at the same time we share her intellectual development to the extent that we also see the terrible results of ''Justice! Justice! Justice!'' [V. i. 25]

But Isabella's painful lesson is not over. She is betrayed not only by the Duke but also by Mariana, who testifies that it was she, not Isabella, who lay with Angelo:

> She that accuses him of fornication
> In self-same manner doth accuse my husband,
> And charges him, my lord, with such a time
> When I'll depose I had him in mine arms
> With all th'effect of love.
>   [V. i. 195-99]

There is obviously a literal truth in what Mariana says; but it is surely not a virutous or honorable act to use a literal truth to make a liar out of Isabella—her accomplice in the most important action of her life—in order to protect a man whom Mariana herself, a few lines later, describes as ''thou cruel Angelo'' [V. i. 207]. How can we possibly be sympathetic to Mariana at this point? Only, I maintain, if we see her as the exemplification of our paradoxical equation: Mariana, more obviously than any other character in the play, is not concerned with justice or virtue, only with life. And she is willing to

accept life even at the price of Angelo's lust and her own shame.

Angelo, of course, exemplifies the opposite principle, even at the end. . . . [He] confesses everything. But unlike Mariana, and in conformity with her previous actions, he wants virtue and justice more than life:

>   Then, good prince,
> No longer session hold upon my shame,
> But let my trial be mine own confession.
> Immediate sentence, then, and sequent death
> Is all the grace I beg.
>   [V. i. 370-74]
>   (pp. 17-18)

It should be observed, in answer to those critics who stress mercy or true justice as the concluding note, that it is not a perverted justice that calls for ''An Angelo for Claudio; death for death'' [V. i. 409], but ''The very mercy of the law'' [V. i. 407]. And what prevents the execution of Angelo is not mercy so much as an acceptance of shame and corruption. Or, to put it another way, the mercy arises not from any concept of ''Law,'' divine or human, New or Old, but from a willingness to accept sin as a necessary part of life. Appropriately, it is Mariana who again exemplifies this principle. Replying to the Duke's offer ''To buy [her] a better husband,'' she renounces any desire for virtue or honor: ''O my dear lord, / I crave no other, nor no better man'' [V. i. 425-26]. It is precisely this craving to be ''better'' than our nature allows us, and to make others ''better'' in the same way, that has led to death throughout the play. Like Claudio before him, Angelo is to be made a man out of a woman's shame. The literal, biological sense is, of course, present, and it reinforces the inevitability of the equation. (p. 18)

It is only Angelo who upholds honor. Almost afraid to look Escalus in the eye, Angelo in his final words represents, as always, the principles of virtue and justice:

> I am sorry that such sorrow I procure,
> And so deep sticks it in my penitent heart
> That I crave death more willingly than mercy:
> 'Tis my deserving, and I do entreat it.
>   [V. i. 474-77]

This is the last attempt of the ''penitent heart'' to bring about mercy and justice. For Isabella, who had been Angelo's ally in virtue, has deserted him, or rather his cause, and has joined Mariana in pleading for his life [V. i. 443ff.].

Her reasons are indeed shallow and have not endeared her to many readers from Samuel Johnson to Quiller-Couch [see excerpts above, 1765 and 1922]. . . . But if we see Isabella not as an angel of mercy but as one who takes off her wings to live in the sinful world of natural men and women—as Mariana has done—we will not be troubled by her legalistic reasoning. Saving Angelo's life may be indicative of mercy, and mercy may be truly ''angelic.'' But obviously the mercy that saves Angelo comes not from heaven but from earth, from Mariana's natural desire for a man, even if he is a scoundrel. . . . What Isabella brings about by her plea is not justice or even mercy (in the noble sense) but simply life with all of its corruptions.

Nor do the marriages which close the play bring about the triumph of mercy, love, or any noble or virtuous principle. . . . There is undoubtedly a sharp difference between Claudio's feeling for Juliet and Lucio's feeling for the prostitute, as there is also, presumably, between the Duke's feeling toward Isabella and Angelo's toward Mariana. Yet it is not the differences but the similarities that are significant. These four marriages are announced in one breath, as it were, because marriage is the great symbol, at least in this play, of the acceptance of human lust. Whatever the feelings, all "marriages," whether legally consummated or not, bring about life. (pp. 19-20)

The tracing of such a thematic pattern enables us to see the second half of the play as integrally related to the first. . . . [The] concluding acts of *Measure for Measure* move away from the death that would have resulted from the virtue of Angelo and Isabella to the life that results from the acceptance of sin. Everyone lives in the second half of the play. Not only is the possibility of life literal, as it is for Claudio and Barnardine, but there is a resurgence of life in a wider sense for Mariana, Angelo, and Isabella. (p. 20)

> Lawrence W. Hyman, "The Unity of 'Measure for Measure'," in Modern Language Quarterly, Vol. 36, No. 1, March, 1975, pp. 3-20.

DAVID SUNDELSON   (essay date 1981)

[*Sundelson argues that* Measure for Measure *integrates "anxieties about political and sexual power" in a manner that reveals the precariousness of male identity. To him, the play presents a vision of misogyny, which is exemplified in the attitudes of the Duke and Angelo, both of whom are insecure about the destructive power of women. Sundelson also suggests that the marriages that conclude the play express not the desired love between man and woman, but the masculine need to suppress woman's threatening potential within a socially defined and restrictive role. For further discussion of the importance of the theme of marriage in* Measure, *see the excerpts by Muriel C. Bradbrook (1941), Terence Eagleton (1967), R. A Foakes (1971), James Black (1973), and Lawrence W. Hyman (1975).*]

When Hamlet welcomes the Players to Elsinore, he pays special attenton to one of them. "What, my young lady and mistress! by'r lady, your ladyship is nearer to heaven than when I saw you last by the altitude of a chopine. Pray God your voice, like a piece of uncurrent gold, be not cracked within the ring" [*Hamlet*, II. ii. 424-28]. Although the repetition of "lady" and the bawdy puns ("cracked," "ring") may betray a certain uneasiness about what is female, Hamlet can joke comfortably enough about a farewell to it, about a boy actor who will soon be unable to play a woman's role. For Shakespeare, the movement from androgyny to a clearer, more certain masculinity is evidently not disturbing.

What can be very disturbing indeed is the idea of reversing this movement. The idea haunts *Measure for Measure;* at its heart are grave fears about the precariousness of male identity and, linked to them, fears of the destructive power of women. Together, these fears explain much of what seems most puzzling about the play. Take for example its central problem: the behavior of Duke Vincentio. To mention only two of the questions it raises, why does he entrust Angelo with power, and why does he allow Isabella to believe that her brother is dead? I want to show that the answers to these questions are related. *Measure for Measure* fuses anxieties about political and sexual power, and I believe that the Duke's actions, which have struck readers as mysteriously benign or haphazard or even perverse, belong instead to the coherent defensive strategy of a shrewd prince and an insecure man. (p. 83)

The executioner Abhorson is a convenient emblem of the play's preoccupations. With his highly suggestive name ("abhor,"

"whore," "whoreson") and his pride of office, his ax and his assistant the bawd, he reflects a network of fantasies about power, sex, degradation and punishment. Only the Deputy learns all the connections in the network, learns how easily the throneroom can become the bedroom or the block. But even Escalus, kindly and disinterested as he is, finds that power brings out an impulse in him that smacks of Angelo's ugly proposition: "Pray you, my lord, give me leave to question; you shall see how I'll handle her . . . I will go darkly to work" [V. i. 270-78]. Judicial office is dangerous to hold; as if to avoid being compromised by working darkly, Elbow's neighbors pay him to serve their terms as constable.

Instead of buying a surrogate as they do, the Duke appoints one.

> I have on Angelo impos'd the office:
> Who may in th' ambush of my name strike home,
> And yet my nature never in the fight
> To do in slander.
>
>   [I. iii. 40-3]

"Ambush," "strike," and "fight" make government aggressive and violent. "To do in slander" is unclear (the text may be corrupt), but the phrase adds an erotic dimension to the power the Duke is unwilling to wield. If the fear of sadistic impulses, of the temptation to let the body politic "straight feel the spur" [I. ii. 162] is one reason for his abdication, he also dreads humiliation, the moment when "the rod / Becomes more mock'd than fear'd" [I. iii. 26-7] and "Liberty plucks Justice by the nose" [I. iii. 29]. He seems to equate rule and exhibition—"to stick it in their children's sight / For terror" [I. iii. 25-6]—and ranges nervously from one vulnerable appendage to another. To save his nose from plucking, he confers on Angelo "all the organs / Of our own power" [I. i. 20-1] in the hope that his double, "one that can my part in him advertise" [I. i. 41], will perform the exhibition for him, and with more vigor than he himself is willing to risk. . . . (pp. 84-5)

"Part" suggests both a role and an organ, but Angelo finds that to advertise his parts is to jeopardize them. While he gives every sign of being the aggressor with Isabella, her very approach makes his heart "unable" [II. iv. 21] and, even worse, "dispossesses" all his "other parts / Of necessary fitness" [II. iv. 22-3]. "I would to heaven I had your potency, / And you were Isabel" [II. ii. 67-8], the lady exclaims in their first interview, and a similar notion of exchange or androgyny surfaces in Pompey's answer when the Provost asks if he can cut off a man's head: "if he be a married man, he's his wife's head; and I can never cut off a woman's head" [IV. ii. 3-5]. With a joke, Pompey can pluck the flower, safety, from the nettle, danger, but in Angelo's second meeting with Isabella, uncertain sexual identity becomes more and more unsettling.

We see the uncertainty in the deputy's description of his desire as "the strong and swelling evil / Of my conception" [II. iv. 5-6]; the metaphor seems male and female at once. Similarly, a wish for passivity lies beneath his assault. "Teach her the way" [II. iv. 19] he says when Isabella returns, as if he wanted to be seduced, and complains openly: "your sense pursues not mine" [II. iv. 74]. If at first Isabella has "too tame a tongue" [II. ii. 46] to affect him, she soon grows more assertive, and her increasingly penetrating rhetoric corresponds to Angelo's growing doubt. (p. 85)

These warnings of female potency make Angelo's violence seem like a defense, as if he resorted to rape so as not to confront his own weakness.

YOV·MVST·RISE · &
BE·HANGED ACT·IV SCENE·III

*Act IV. Scene iii. Pompey, the Clown. By Byam Shaw (1901).
From the Art Collection of the Folger Shakespeare Library.*

Angelo	Be that you are,
	That is, a woman; if you be more, you're none.
	If you be one—as you are well express'd
	By all external warrants—show it now,
	By putting on the destin'd livery.
Isabella	I have no tongue but one: gentle my lord,
	Let me entreat you speak the former language.
Angelo	Plainly conceive, I love you.

[II. iv. 134-41]

Love has nothing to do with the case, of course, the nightmare intensity of this dialogue comes from its barely suppressed anxieties. "If you be one," Angelo says, and the doubt persists; he fears that Isabella may really be a man. She tries to convince him that she hides nothing beneath the "external warrants" of her gender—"I have no tongue but one"—but the reassurance is not enough, and "gentle my lord" is hardly tactful at such a moment. She must wear the "livery" that announces submission and, more important, "plainly conceive": only by bearing a child can she dissolve Angelo's fear that their encounter has made him a woman.

In the light of Angelo's ordeal, the rules of Isabella's convent seem designed to protect men more than women. . . . Men must not confront the double danger of a pretty face and a confident tongue, and the play as a whole reinforces these rules by keeping a tight rein on female energy and initiative. No Portia or Rosalind wears male clothing. Isabella is quite dependent on the Duke and needs Lucio's urgent coaching—"You are too cold" [II. ii. 56]—in her interview with Angelo. Juliet and Mariana are conspicuously submissive. . . . As needy or compliant as they are, however, the women still threaten. "O, I will to him and pluck out his eyes" [IV. iii. 119], Isabella cries when she learns of Angelo's perfidy. Describing Mariana, the Duke begins with pity and ends with something close to fear: "His unjust unkindness, that in all reason should have quenched her love, hath, like an impediment in the current, made it more violent and unruly" [III. i. 240-43]. Mistress Overdone—"Overdone by the last" [II. i. 202] of her husbands, according to Pompey—has in fact survived all nine of them. "Women?—Help, heaven!" [II. iv. 127] Isabella exclaims; like Pompey's joke, her remark leaves the weaker sex's identity in doubt and gives an ironic turn to her wish that "a more strict restraint / Upon the sisters stood, the votarists of Saint Clare" [I. iv. 4-5].

This nervousness helps to explain the play's considerable misogyny. Its expressions range greatly in intensity and self-consciousness; they include Lucio's casual reference to Mistress Kate Keepdown, who has borne him a child, as "the rotten medlar" [IV. iii. 174] and Elbow's malapropism: "My wife, sir, whom I detest before heaven" [II. i. 69]. Less humorous is Angelo's metaphor when he predicts what will happen to Isabella if she tries to accuse him: "you shall stifle in your own report, / And smell of calumny" [II. iv. 158-59]. Angelo must bear the pain of recognizing that his own sexuality is inseparable from his wish to annihilate women, although self-awareness at least gives him a certain moral stature: "Shall we desire to raze the sanctuary / And pitch our evils there? O fie, fie, fie!" [II. ii. 170-71].

Far more painful to Isabella than his attempted extortion ironically—and it is perhaps the central irony in the play, the one that makes us most uneasy—is her protracted torment at the hands of the Duke, who never for an instant admits that he has anything at heart but her good. . . . "Look," the Duke tells the Provost, "th' unfolding star calls up the shepherd" [IV. ii. 203]. He invites us to regard him as that kindly guardian, guided by a star, but his rationale for lying to Isabella suggests that the lamb this shepherd tends best is himself. . . . Isabella has wished for her brother's death—"Take my defiance, / Die, perish!" [III. i. 142-43]—and the lie punishes her for that wish, in fairy tale fashion, by pretending to grant it. The lie also feeds the rage which can make Isabella so threatening, directs it once again at Angelo, and enables the Duke to dispel it and belittle its power: "This nor hurts him, nor profits you a jot. / Forbear it therefore; give your cause to heaven" [IV. iii. 123-24]. What happens is not unlike an exorcism: a woman's hidden and unpredictable menace is exposed and then tamed by the controlling wisdom of her husband to be.

The Duke proposes to Isabella only after explosions at the Deputy and Claudio have exhausted her rage, and he makes sure that Angelo will marry Mariana, whose love is so violent and unruly. With a deputy to act out the play's most dangerous fantasies, both aggressive and passive, the Duke is free to define his own identity in safer terms. Concealing the truth about Claudio will let the Duke restore him to his sister as if resurrecting him from the dead. . . . The synthetic miracle will earn Isabella's perpetual gratitude, but this strategy, surely, is at the heart of our disappointment in their union. It establishes control where we hope for playfulness and freedom, fixes permanently what ought to be flexible, and defines a hierarchy—patron and debtor—which precludes any marriage of true minds. It makes us feel, in short, that Isabella leaves one sort of convent only to enter another.

The Duke's method with his other subjects is much the same; the purity of his own motives is his constant theme, even with Barnardine, Pompey, and Abhorson for an audience. . . . He wants obedience without recourse to the spur, and the note of piety hallows what would otherwise be only a prince's bidding. In addition, this "most bounteous sir" [V. i. 443], as Isabella learns to call him, finds a novel strategy: he rules by forgiving. As the play ends he pardons not only the obvious offenders Angelo, Claudio, Lucio, and Barnardine, but the Provost, Escalus, and Isabella as well. It is startling to hear Isabella, after all her needless suffering, ask forgiveness for having "employ'd and pain'd / Your unknown sovereignty" [V. i. 386-87], but such is the power of his spell.

Measure for Measure leaves us nevertheless with mutually exclusive resolutions: a Duke both retiring and worldly, who sounds like an altruist but serves only himself. "Your friar is now your prince" [V. i. 382], he tells Isabella, but the transformation is incomplete; he clings to both roles at once, as his language sways doubtfully between courtliness and piety.

> As I was then,
> Advertising and holy to your business,
> Not changing heart with habit, I am still
> Attorney'd at your service.
>
> [V. i. 382-85]

The Duke's weakness at least makes him a reassuring husband for Isabella—no threats of rape are likely from a man who "can do you little harm" [III. ii. 166], even if he is the "more mightier member" [V. i. 237] Angelo perceives behind Mariana's accusation. But what are we to think of a bridegroom who referred earlier to "the dribbling dart of love" [I. iii. 2] and whose most passionate words, even now, are "Dear Isabel, / I have a motion much imports your good" [V. i. 534-35]? Such excessively modest overtures are hardly the occasion for comic rejoicing. Indeed, if Isabella's plea for the deputy's life balances her wish for Claudio's death, the anxieties about women are too strong to be completely resolved. Angelo has tried once to define a woman in a limited, reassuring way—"if you be more, you're none"—and the attempt continues in the Duke's catechism of Mariana.

Duke	What, are you married?
Mariana	No, my lord.
Duke	Are you a maid?
Mariana	No, my lord,
Duke	A widow, then?
Mariana	Neither, my lord.
Duke	Why, you are nothing then; neither maid, widow, nor wife!

> [V. i. 171-78]

Once again, we see the play's fearfulness about women and its willingness to obliterate their mystery ("You are nothing") rather than embrace it, features which anticipate the explosion of violence against them in subsequent Jacobean drama. (pp. 85-90)

David Sundelson,, "Misogyny and Rule in 'Measure for Measure'," in Women's Studies, *Vol. 9, No. 1, 1981, pp. 83-91.*

ADDITIONAL BIBLIOGRAPHY

Altieri, Joanne. "Style and Social Disorder in *Measure for Measure*." *Shakespeare Quarterly* 25, No. 1 (Winter 1974): 6-16.
    Studies Shakespeare's development of contrasting dramatic and linguistic patterns to ascertain the relationship between *Measure for Measure* and the earlier comedies. Altieri notes that the "discontinuous speech styles," which reflect the fragmented society in *Measure for Measure*, situate the play at the midpoint between the "social order" of the early comedies and the "metaphysical harmony" of the romances.

Bache, William B. *"Measure for Measure" As Dialectical Art*. Lafayette, Ind.: Purdue University Studies, 1969, 66 p.
    Considers *Measure for Measure* a dialectical argument in which Shakespeare demonstrates the proper relationship between the individual and society. Bache examines the play as a learning experience through which all of the characters discover the meaning of human existence, their obligations to themselves, and their duty to society.

Bald, R. C. Introduction to *Measure for Measure* by William Shakespeare. In *William Shakespeare: The Complete Works*, edited by Alfred Harbage, pp. 400-02. Baltimore: Penguin Books, 1969.
    Introduction that outlines the date, text, and sources of *Measure for Measure*. Bald concludes that Shakespeare recognizes human frailty in the play without despairing of mankind.

Ball, Robert Hamilton. 'Cinthio's *Epitia* and *Measure for Measure*." In *Elizabethan Studies and Other Essays in Honor of George F. Reynolds*, pp. 132-46. Boulder: University of Colorado Studies, Series B: *Studies in the Humanities* 2, No. 4, 1945.
    Discusses significant parallels between *Measure for Measure* and *Epitia*, a drama adapted by Cinthio from his *Hecatommithi*.

Barton, Anne. Introduction to *Measure for Measure* by William Shakespeare. In *The Riverside Shakespeare*, edited by G. Blakemore Evans, pp. 545-49. Boston: Houghton Mifflin Co., 1974.
    Introduction containing an overview of the date, text, and sources of *Measure for Measure*. Barton contends that the forced happy ending and the confusion of values in the play reveal Shakespeare's disenchantment with the comic form.

Bennett, Josephine Waters. *"Measure for Measure" As Royal Entertainment*. New York: Columbia University Press, 1966, 208 p.
    Stresses the importance of the date of the first recorded performance—December 26, 1604—for an understanding of *Measure for Measure*. Bennett interprets the play's Christian aspects in light of the spirit of Christmas.

Berman, Ronald. "Shakespeare and the Law." *Shakespeare Quarterly* 18, No. 2 (Spring 1967): 141-50.
    Compares the themes of forgiveness, mercy, and self-awareness in *Measure for Measure* with Pauline doctrine.

Berry, Ralph. "Language and Structure in *Measure for Measure*." *University of Toronto Quarterly* XLVI, No. 2 (Winter 1976-77): 147-61.
    Examines the imagery and setting of *Measure for Measure* and maintains that the conflict between freedom and restraint is expressed in terms of repressed sexuality. Berry argues that the final scene is "a public exorcisement by the Duke of impulses in himself."

Bowden, William R. "The Bed-Trick, 1603-1642: Its Mechanics, Ethics, and Effects." *Shakespeare Studies* V (1969): 112-23.
    Investigates the use and import of the "bed-trick" as a conventional plot device employed by Renaissance dramatists.

Brown, John Russell. "Love's Ordeal and the Judgements of *All's Well that Ends Well, Measure for Measure*, and *Troilus and Cressida*." In his *Shakespeare and His Comedies*, pp. 183-200. London: Methuen & Co., 1964.
    Regards the problem comedies as "imperfect responses" to the "ideals of love" established in the early comedies. Brown states that they focus instead on the "follies and ignorance"—the in-

compatibility—of lovers, revealing characters who are "dwarfed by the possibility of perfection."

Bryant, J. A., Jr. *"Measure for Measure."* In his *Hippolyta's View: Some Christian Aspects of Shakespeare's Plays,* pp. 86-108. Lexington: University of Kentucky Press, 1961.

> Analyzes the interrelationships of the characters and assesses *Measure for Measure* as a Christian allegory that concludes with "Duke Vincentio's transformation of sinful Vienna."

Budd, Frederick E. "Material for a Study of the Sources of Shakespeare's *Measure for Measure.*" *Revue de Litterature Comparée* XI, No. 4 (October-December 1931): 711-36.

> Documents known sixteenth-century crimes similar to Angelo's and lists dramatic and nondramatic accounts of such offenses. Budd emphasizes the relevance of Cinthio's *Epitia* in addition to his *Hecatommithi* and Whetstone's *Promos and Cassandra* as the sources of *Measure for Measure.*

Chambers, E. K. *"Measure for Measure."* In his *Shakespeare: A Survey,* pp. 208-17. New York: Oxford University Press, 1926.

> Discusses Shakespeare's apparent cynicism while writing the problem comedies. Chambers argues that *Measure for Measure* contains "the form of comedy," but strains the limits of humor with its "remorseless analysis" of human nature.

Champion, Larry S. "The Problem Comedies." In his *The Evolution of Shakespeare's Comedy: A Study in Dramatic Perspective,* pp. 96-153. Cambridge: Harvard University Press, 1970.

> Views the problem comedies as carefully constructed experiments in which Shakespeare attempted to control his expanding concept of character and human emotion. Champion describes *All's Well* and *Measure for Measure* as intermediate steps in "Shakespeare's comic evolution"; he considers the two plays to be structural failures that contain a "blurring of the comic perspective."

Cisson, C. J. "The Mythical Sorrows of Shakespeare." In *Proceedings of the British Academy,* pp. 45-70. London: Oxford University Press, 1934.

> Refutes the biographical criticism concerning Shakespeare's cynical frame of mind while writing *Measure for Measure.* Cisson asserts that Isabella is "one of Shakespeare's greatest creations," representing an ideal that Shakespeare "reveres with all his heart."

Craig, David. "Love and Society: *Measure for Measure* and Our Own Time." In *Shakespeare in a Changing World,* edited by Arnold Kettle, pp. 195-216. New York: International Publishers, 1964.

> Compares Shakespeare's psychological approach to the social problems presented in *Measure for Measure* with D. H. Lawrence's treatment of similar topics.

Craig, Hardin. *"Measure for Measure."* In his *An Interpretation of Shakespeare,* pp. 228-35. New York: The Citadel Press, 1948.

> Appraises *Measure for Measure* as one of Shakespeare's worst plays.

Doran, Madeleine. "The Fable: Complication and Unraveling." In her *Endeavors of Art: A Study of Form in Elizabethan Drama,* pp. 295-340. Madison: The University of Wisconsin Press, 1954.

> Traces the development of the debate form in dramatic dialogues from the Middle Ages to the Renaissance. Doran notes that despite "Shakespeare's habit of seeing both sides of a question," he is "never ambiguous in the fundamental bases of ethical judgment."

Drake, Nathan. "Observations on *Measure for Measure.*" In his *Shakespeare and His Times,* pp. 556-58. 1838. Reprint. New York: Burt Franklin, 1969.

> Eulogizes Isabella as "a being of a higher order" sent to minister to a corrupt world. Drake's work was originally published in 1817.

Draper, John W. "Political Themes in Shakespeare's Later Plays." *Journal of English and Germanic Philology* XXXV, No. 1 (January 1936): 61-93.

> Outlines the Renaissance concepts of government and the Divine Right of Kings. Draper comments that *Measure for Measure* displays the need for the legitimate ruler's constant presence as the

head of state and depicts the potential harm that results from the absence of "God's Anointed."

———. "Patterns of Tempo in *Measure for Measure.*" *Philological Papers of the West Virginia University Bulletin* IX, No. 6 (June 1953): 11-19.

> Ascertains a correlation between the characters and the "tempo-pattern" of their responses to events in *Measure for Measure.*

Dryden, John. An extract from his *A Defense of the Epilogue, or, an Essay on the Dramatique Poetry of the Last Age* (1672). In *Shakespeare, the Critical Heritage, Vol. 1: 1623-1692,* edited by Brian Vickers, pp. 143-52. London: Routledge & Kegan Paul, 1974.

> Claims that the drama and poetry of the Restoration is superior to that of the Jacobean era. In passing, Dryden condemns *Measure for Measure* as an example of poor writing.

Edwards, Philip. "The Problem Plays (ii)." In his *Shakespeare and the Confines of Art,* pp. 109-20. London: Methuen & Co., 1968.

> Considers *Measure for Measure* a dramatic failure because it is "not strong enough to bear the weight of the human problems pressed on to it, nor the weight of their religious solution."

Fisch, Harold. "Shakespeare and the Puritan Dynamic." *Shakespeare Survey* 27 (1974): 81-92.

> Explores Shakespeare's treatment of Angelo, Shylock, and Malvolio as "studies in the use or abuse of power." To Fisch, the characterization of Angelo depicts the Puritan abuse of power.

Fripp, Edgar I. *"Measure for Measure."* In his *Shakespeare: Man and Artist, Vol. II,* pp. 612-18. London: Oxford University Press, 1938.

> Recounts the influence of contemporary customs and events on the setting of *Measure for Measure* and briefly relates Montaigne's religious philosophy to Shakespeare's handling of his theme.

Frye, Northrop. "Mouldy Tales." In his *A Natural Perspective,* pp. 1-33. New York: Columbia University Press, 1965.

> Argues that *Measure for Measure* is not an attempt at realism, but is rather a "disturbing fantasy" and that the characters must be interpreted in this context. Frye observes that the Duke's experiment possesses an unrealistic quality because it revolves around Angelo's claim to untested virtue.

Gentleman, Francis. An extract from *Bell's Edition of Shakespeare's Plays* (1774). In *Shakespeare, the Critical Heritage, Vol. 6: 1774-1801,* edited by Brian Vickers, pp. 89-112. London: Routledge & Kegan Paul, 1981.

> Condemns the versification in the Duke's soliloquy that ends Act III.

Gless, Darryl J. *"Measure for Measure,"* the Law, and the Convent. Princeton: Princeton University Press, 1979, 282 p.

> Examines contemporary political and religious documents as a guide for understanding *Measure for Measure.* Gless states that the nature of the play is religious, but Shakespeare "appears consistently to have selected and dramatized doctrines that are especially flexible and tolerant of adjustment to particular circumstances."

Goddard, Harold C. *"Measure for Measure."* In his *The Meaning of Shakespeare,* pp. 436-54. Chicago: Univeristy of Chicago Press, 1951.

> Contends that *Measure for Measure* demonstrates the effect of power on those who govern.

Godshalk, W. L. *"Measure for Measure:* Freedom and Restraint." *Shakespeare Studies* VI (1970): 137-50.

> Emphasizes that the conflict between freedom and restraint in *Measure for Measure* is resolved when the major characters learn to balance these opposing forces within themselves and realize "their place in the human community." Godshalk concludes that the marriages in the denouement are a precarious, temporary solution that will require further adjustments by each character to maintain internal balance.

Greco, Anne. "A Due Sincerity." *Shakespeare Studies* VI (1970): 151-74.

Analyzes Isabella and contends that Shakespeare presents her as an "extraordinary woman" whose chosen vocation and intellectual abilities do not parallel conventional seventeenth-century female behavior. Greco maintains that Shakespeare carefully prepares an audience for the change in Isabella's attitude that allows her to gain self-knowledge and "a better understanding" of God and mankind.

Griffith, Elizabeth. *"Measure for Measure."* In her *The Morality of Shakespeare's Drama Illustrated,* pp. 38-48. 1775. Reprint. London: Frank Cass & Co., 1971.
> Finds no moral in *Measure for Measure.*

Grillparzer, Franz. *"Measure for Measure* (1849)." In *Shakespeare in Europe,* edited by Oswald LeWinter, pp. 137-39. Cleveland: Meridian Books, 1963.
> Claims that *Measure for Measure* is a mediocre work despite its excellent characterization because it is dramatically unconvincing as a "scene from life."

Hallam, Henry. "History of Dramatic Literature from 1600 to 1650: *Measure for Measure.*" In his *Introduction to the Literature of Europe in the 15th, 16th, and 17th Centuries, Vol. III,* pp. 83-4. 1837-39. Reprint. New York: Frederick Ungar, 1970.
> Indicates that Shakespeare's "contemplative philosophy" in *Measure for Measure* is difficult to understand due to the play's complex, obscure language.

Hamilton, Donna B. "The Duke in *Measure for Measure:* 'I Find an Apt Remission in Myself'." *Shakespeare Studies* VI (1970): 175-82.
> Postulates that the Duke is subjected to a learning process through which he discovers the meaning of true mercy, an ideal that is as antithetical to his original soft-heartedness as it is to Angelo's concept of strict justice.

Hawkes, Terence. "The Problem Plays." In his *Shakespeare and the Reason: A Study of the Tragedies and the Problem Plays,* pp. 72-99. London: Routledge & Kegan Paul, 1964.
> Stresses the difference between the rational valuations of human justice and the intuitive, emotional quality of divine mercy in *Measure for Measure,* noting that the play demonstrates the conflict between these concepts and emphasizes the world's need for mercy.

Holland, Norman N. *"Measure for Measure:* The Duke and the Prince." *Comparative Literature* XI, No. 1 (Winter 1959): 16-20.
> Contends that the Duke's actions resemble those of Cesare Borgia in an "Anti-Machiavel" tract written in 1602.

Howarth, Herbert. "Puzzle of Flattery." In his *The Tiger's Heart: Eight Essays on Shakespeare,* pp. 120-42. London: Chatto & Windus, 1970.
> Conjectures that Shakespeare wrote *Measure for Measure* to flatter the recently-crowned James I, incorporating many of the king's ideas about government into the play.

Hunter, Robert Grams. *"Measure for Measure."* In his *Shakespeare and the Comedy of Forgiveness,* pp. 204-26. New York: Columbia University Press, 1965.
> Links *Measure for Measure* and *All's Well That Ends Well* with Shakespeare's romances, stating that all six plays promote charity based on self-knowledge and the recognition of mankind's inherent evil nature.

Jaffa, Henry. "Chastity As a Political Principle: An Interpretation of Shakespeare's *Measure for Measure.*" In *Shakespeare As Political Thinker,* edited by John Alvis and Thomas G. West, pp. 181-213. Durham, N.C.: Carolina Academic Press, 1981.
> Examines chastity as a political ideal, maintaining that it represents the integrity of the family. Jaffa asserts that this ideal provides the method for the Duke's goal of social reform in *Measure for Measure.*

Kirsch, Arthur C. "The Integrity of *Measure for Measure.*" *Shakespeare Survey* 28 (1975): 89-105.

Interprets *Measure for Measure* as a work that demonstrates the relationship between human and divine truths through the process of Christian experience.

Kirschbaum, Leo. "The Two Angelos." In his *Character and Characterization in Shakespeare,* pp. 119-26. Detroit: Wayne State University Press, 1962.
> Declares that Angelo changes from a noble, tragic figure to an "avaricious and small-minded creature" during the course of the action in *Measure for Measure.* Kirschbaum concludes that this alteration changes the nature of the play from "great drama" to theatrical convention and artificiality.

Kott, Jan. "Head for Maidenhead, Maidenhead for Head: The Structure of Exchange in *Measure for Measure.*" *Theatre Quarterly* VIII, No. 31 (Autumn 1978): 18-24.
> Explores the interrelationship between *Measure for Measure* and Whetstone's *Promos and Cassandra.*

Lascelles, Mary. *Shakespeare's "Measure for Measure."* 1953. Reprint. New York: AMS Press, 1970. 172 p.
> Studies the plot of *Measure for Measure,* meticulously comparing Shakespeare's design with that of his sources and speculating about their structural and thematic impact on Shakespeare. Lascelles interprets the play as a fairy tale or "moral apologue" in which the Duke symbolizes the Renaissance concept of a good ruler. She concludes that Shakespeare's "unconfined thought transcends the bounds" of his story, leaving many unanswered questions.

Levin, Richard A. "Duke Vincentio and Angelo: Would 'A Feather Turn the Scale'?" *Studies in English Literature, 1500-1900* 22, No. 2 (Spring 1982): 257-70.
> Illustrates how the Duke processes as many faults as Angelo.

Makaryk, Irene Rima. "The Problem Plays: *Measure for Measure.*" In her *Comic Justice in Shakespeare's Comedies, Vol. 2,* pp. 244-77. Salzburg Studies in English Literature: Jacobean Drama Studies, edited by James Hogg, vol. 91. Salzburg, Austria: Institut fur Anglistik und Amerikanistik, Universität Salzburg, 1980.
> Reiterates the interpretations of those critics who view *Measure for Measure* as a play concerned with justice that goes beyond retribution and is based on the Golden Rule. To Makaryk, the experiences of the Duke, Isabella, and Angelo demonstrate this concept as well as the relationship between judgment and self-awareness; all three characters initially deny human nature, love, and passion, but undergo a learning process through which they recognize their own faults and the purpose of mercy and forgiveness. Makaryk also notes that the play is a tragicomedy in which the concept of moderation—"a balanced relationship between crime and punishment and between inward and public self"—is explicated by the juxtaposition of "virtuous characters" whose actions are morally questionable and "unvirtuous" characters who display elements of goodness.

Malone, Edmond. "An Attempt to Ascertain the Order in which the Plays of Shakespeare Were Written: *Measure for Measure,* 1603." In *The Plays and Poems of William Shakespeare, Vol. II,* edited by Edmond Malone and James Boswell, pp. 383-87. 1821. Reprint. New York: AMS Press, 1966.
> Investigates external evidence and topical allusions within *Measure for Measure* and concludes that the play was written late in 1603. Malone's essay was originally published in 1778.

Masefield, John. "The Plays: *Measure for Measure.*" In his *William Shakespeare,* pp. 174-80. New York: Henry Holt & Co., 1911.
> Compares Angelo's concept of chastity to Isabella's, characterizing both types as obsessions "that exalt a part of life above life itself."

Matthews, Brander. "The Comedy-Dramas." In his *Shakespeare As a Playwright,* pp. 219-36. New York: Charles Scribner's Sons, 1913.
> Describes the characters in *Measure for Measure* as "wooden" and claims that the play's appeal is due wholly to Isabella, who is not equal to the burden.

Maxwell, J. C. "The Middle Plays." In *The Age of Shakespeare: Vol. II of the Pelican Guide to English Literature,* edited by Boris Ford, pp. 201-27. Baltimore: Penguin Books, 1955.

Suggests that *Measure for Measure* is a parable that blends the clarity of realism with the complexity of symbolism in a Christian interpretation of life. Maxwell states that the marriage between the Duke and Isabella is "a Holy union between Justice and Mercy."

Miles, Rosalind. *The Problem of "Measure for Measure": A Historical Investigation.* New York: Barnes & Noble, 1976, 349 p.

Interprets *Measure for Measure* as "a play of emotional collapses, of the unpredictability of human nature under stress, and of the disintegration of the carefully-erected self-image."

Millet, Stanton. "The Structure of *Measure for Measure.*" *Boston University Studies in English* II, No. 4 (Winter 1956-57): 207-17.

Contends that *Measure for Measure* examines the function of government by contrasting the false concepts of law and justice held by Angelo, Isabella, and Claudio with the Duke's true principles of justice.

Mincoff, Marco. "*Measure for Measure:* A Question of Approach." *Shakespeare Studies* II (1966): 141-52.

Regards *Measure for Measure* as a "gallery of portraits"—an intricate system of character interactions designed to make an audience feel the characters' emotions—rather than a philosophical discussion of ideas.

Moulton, Richard G. "Moral Problems Dramatised." In his *The Moral System of Shakespeare: A Popular Illustration of Fiction As the Experimental Side of Philosophy,* pp. 14-57. New York: Macmillan, 1903.

Identifies a dual antithesis underlying the plot of *Measure for Measure*: the relationship between purity and passion and the dichotomy between inner and outer life. Moulton argues that the Duke's "scientific experiment" reconciles these diverse elements and solves the moral problems raised.

Murry, John Middleton. "The Problem Comedies." In his *Shakespeare,* pp. 295-310. London: Jonathan Cape, 1936.

Disputes William Witherle Lawrence's theory that Angelo is "a villain by nature" and that the Duke is a stage puppet (see excerpt above, 1931).

Nagarajan, S. Introduction to *Measure for Measure* by William Shakespeare. In *The Complete Signet Classic Shakespeare,* edited by Sylvan Barnett, pp. 1137-42. New York: Harcourt, Brace, Jovanovich, 1964.

Presents brief plot summaries of Shakespeare's sources for *Measure for Measure* and outlines the major points of critical controversy surrounding the play.

Owen, Lucy. "Mode and Character in *Measure for Measure.*" *Shakespeare Quarterly* 25, No. 1 (Winter 1974): 17-32.

Studies the dramatization of the characters' moral experiences and concludes that repentance and forgiveness "are part of the process of coming to terms with oneself."

Paris, Bernard J. "The Inner Conflicts of *Measure for Measure:* A Psychological Approach." *Centennial Review* 25, No. 3 (Summer 1981): 266-76.

Argues that the Duke's internal conflicts, and those of "the implied author," create a thematic confusion in *Measure for Measure* in which justice and mercy are not reconciled.

Parker, M.D.H. "The First Testing—Corruption and Salvation." In his *The Slave of Life: A Study of Shakespeare and the Idea of Justice,* pp. 76-124. London: Chatto & Windus, 1955.

Observes that "the metaphysical and allegorical meaning alternates with the ethical and personal" in *Measure for Measure.* To Parker, the play concentrates on human conduct and describes "the relation of this world to the other" as one of coherence rather than analogy.

Parrott, Thomas Marc. "*Measure for Measure.*" In his *Shakespearean Comedy,* pp. 355-65. New York: Oxford University Press, 1949.

States that the realistic background and Shakespeare's tragicomic technique clash with the essentially tragic theme in *Measure for Measure,* producing a lack of inner harmony.

Price, Jonathan R. "*Measure for Measure* and the Critics: Towards a New Approach." *Shakespeare Quarterly* 20, No. 2 (Spring 1969): 179-204.

Highlights the major trends and individual interpretations in *Measure for Measure* criticism and stresses the need for an investigative approach that combines and improves upon the methods used thus far.

Riefer, Marcia. " 'Instruments of Some More Mightier Member': The Constriction of Female Power in *Measure for Measure.*" *Shakespeare Quarterly* 35, No. 2 (Summer 1984): 157-69.

Claims that *Measure for Measure,* more than any other Shakespearean play, "exposes the dehumanizing effect on women" of living in a patriarchal society where men "re-create womanhood according to their fantasies."

Rosenberg, Marvin. "Shakespeare's Fantastic Trick: *Measure for Measure.*" *The Sewannee Review* LXXX, No. 1 (Winter 1972): 51-72.

Concentrates on the relationship between Isabella and the Duke, examining their "layers of seeming" and their unmasking.

Rosenheim, Judith. "The Stoic Meaning of the Friar in *Measure for Measure.*" *Shakespeare Studies* XV (1982): 171-215.

Ascertains that the Duke initially possesses a "Stoic rather than Christian ethic" and argues that the action of *Measure for Measure* condemns that philosophy, forcing the Duke to accept a Christian ideology.

Rossiter, A. P. "The Problem Plays" and "*Measure for Measure.*" In *Angel with Horns and Other Shakespeare Lectures,* edited by Graham Storey, pp. 108-28, 152-70. New York: Theatre Arts Books, 1961.

Defines the problem plays as tragicomedies. Rossiter also notes that the ambiguities in *Measure for Measure* cannot be resolved because their double meanings are part of the play's structure. He maintains that the Christian ethic intended for the play is never fully realized because the quality of the writing "goes thin" and lacks "inner conviction."

Sachs, Hanns. "The Measure in *Measure for Measure.*" In *The Creative Unconscious: Studies in the Psychoanalysis of Art,* edited by A. A. Roback, pp. 63-99. Cambridge, Mass.: Sci-Art Publishers, 1951.

Describes Angelo as "an obsessional neurotic" whose ultimate feelings of guilt, humiliation, and shame are a worse punishment than death. Sachs concludes that the moral of *Measure for Measure* demonstrates that everyone is a sinner, because mental acts are as permanent as reality; they can be suppressed, but not destroyed.

Schanzer, Ernest. "The Marriage Contracts in *Measure for Measure.*" *Shakespeare Survey* 13 (1960): 81-9.

Documents several types of Elizabethan marriage contracts to clarify the difference between Claudio's union with Juliet and Angelo's bond with Mariana. Schanzer incorporated this essay with other remarks on *Measure for Measure* in his *The Problem Plays of Shakespeare* (see excerpt above, 1963).

Sen Gupta, S. C. "Dark Comedies." In his *Shakespearian Comedy,* pp. 174-200. Calcutta: Oxford University Press, 1950.

Regards "the acceptance of life with all its dirt and immorality" as the main theme of *Measure for Measure.*

Shaw, Bernard. "Preface." In his *Plays: Pleasant and Unpleasant, Vol. I,* pp. v-xxvii. New York: Brentano's, 1906.

Conjectures that the unpopularity of the problem comedies during the nineteenth century was caused by the absence of elaborated prompt copies—descriptive stage directions and character sketches—that would have better conveyed Shakespeare's actual meaning. Shaw argues that without this "process of elaboration," interpreting Shakespeare's essentially "nineteenth-century" approach to character and society is hampered by seventeenth-century concepts and theatrical conventions.

Siegel, Paul N. "*Measure for Measure*: The Significance of the Title." *Shakespeare Quarterly* 4, No. 3 (July 1953): 317-20.

Claims that "measure for measure" is distributed according to the justice of comedy: punishment is administered, but with mercy.

Smith, Robert M. "Interpretations of *Measure for Measure*." *Shakespeare Quarterly* 1, No. 4 (October 1950): 208-18.

Surveys twentieth-century criticism of *Measure for Measure*, concentrating on character interpretations.

Soellner, Rolf. "*Measure for Measure*: Looking into Oneself." In his *Shakespeare's Patterns of Self-Knowledge*, pp. 215-36. Columbus: Ohio State University Press, 1972.

Analyzes the manner in which Angelo, Isabella, and the Duke gain self-knowledge.

Stauffer, Donald A. "The Unweeded Garden." In his *Shakespeare's World of Images: The Development of His Moral Ideas*, pp. 110-62. New York: W. W. Norton & Co., 1949.

Indicates that the Duke is an embodiment of divinity who provides the necessary learning experience for the moral development of both Angelo and Isabella. To Stauffer, *Measure for Measure* is a morality play that demonstrates the Aristotelian concept of moderation.

Stevenson, David L. "Design and Structure in *Measure for Measure*: A New Appraisal." *ELH* 23, No. 4 (December 1956): 256-78.

Maintains that *Measure for Measure* is an intellectual comedy that resembles Jonsonian satire in its concentration on irony and paradox. Stevenson comments that the play tests its auditors' ability to respond to the dramatic design as well as the "demonstration of the enormous range of human response" as the characters are "caught between justice and mercy."

Swinburne, Algernon Charles. "Third Period: Tragic and Romantic." In his *A Study of Shakespeare*, pp. 170-223. 1879. Reprint. London: William Heinemann, 1920.

Argues that *Measure for Measure* fails because Angelo is unpunished and that the addition of the Mariana plot is an "evasion of a natural and proper end."

Sypher, Wylie. "Shakespeare As Casuist: *Measure for Measure*." *The Sewannee Review* LVIII, No. 2 (April-June 1950): 262-80.

Examines *Measure for Measure* as an experiment in casuistry in which the opposing concepts of mercy and justice appear illusory, and the result of the experiment is inconclusive.

Toole, William B. "*Measure for Measure*." In his *Shakespeare's Problem Plays*, pp. 159-97. The Hague: Mouton & Co., 1966.

Asserts that the Christian elements are an insistent, functional part of *Measure for Measure*. Toole describes the play's morality structure as "the medieval comic pattern in dramatic form."

Watson, Curtis Brown. "Shakespeare and the Renaissance Concept of Honor." In his *Shakespeare and the Renaissance Concept of Honor*, pp. 206-26. Princeton: Princeton University Press, 1960.

Argues that Shakespeare's characters must be judged on two levels: the Renaissance ideals of moral philosophy and Shakespeare's own "naturalistic attitude." Watson interprets Claudio primarily by employing Shakespeare's own approach.

Weisser, David K. "The Ironic Hierarchy in *Measure for Measure*." *Texas Studies in Literature and Language* XIX, No. 3 (Fall 1977): 323-47.

Determines that Lucio, Angelo, Isabella, and the Duke "compose an ascending moral hierarchy" in which each character "is defined by his success or failure in combining detached ironic tolerance with active moral judgment."

West, E. J. "Dramatist at the Crossroads: A Suggestion Concerning *Measure for Measure*." *Shakespeare Association Bulletin* XXII, No. 3 (July 1947): 136-41.

Remarks that although Shakespeare records the manners and problems of his age in *Measure for Measure*, "it is a play of shreds and patches" because Shakespeare did not combine this record with a psychological character analysis.

Williamson, Marilyn L. "Oedipal Fantasies in *Measure for Measure*." *Michigan Academician* IX, No. 2 (Fall 1976): 73-84.

Presents a psychoanalytical interpretation of the main characters in *Measure for Measure*, concentrating on the relationship between the "father-figure" (the Duke) and his "children" (the citizens of Vienna). Williamson notes that Shakespeare clearly differentiates between intentions and actions in the play, demonstrating that only actions can be judged.

Wilson, John Dover. "The Copy for *Measure for Measure*, 1623." In *The Works of Shakespeare: "Measure for Measure,"* edited by Arthur Quiller-Couch and John Dover Wilson, pp. 97-113. London: Cambridge at the University Press, 1922.

Examines internal evidence and the history of the text, theorizing that *Measure for Measure* was revised in 1604 and 1606 by unknown playwrights.

DATE: External evidence suggests a date for *Pericles*'s composition and first performance between 1606-08. The play was entered in the Stationers' Register by Edward Blount on May 20, 1608, apparently to discourage unauthorized publication. Subsequently, however, in 1609 a quarto text was published, which most scholars consider an unauthorized version because of its corruptions. It was reported that the Venetian ambassador to England, Zorzi Giustinian, attended a performance of *Pericles* sometime during his tour between January 5, 1606, and November 23, 1608.

TEXT: *Pericles* was not included in the First Folio edition of Shakespeare's works (1623). The only authoritative text is the quarto version of 1609, believed by modern scholars to have been printed in more than one print shop by three separate compositors, and to have been based on a faulty copy of the author's manuscript. The play was subsequently included in the Third Folio of 1664 as "Written by W. Shakespeare, and published in his lifetime." Given the anomalous publishing history and the marked stylistic differences within the play, many scholars have concluded that Shakespeare was not the sole author of *Pericles*. The usual practice has been to assign Acts I and II to some other playwright—most commonly George Wilkins, though William Rowley, Thomas Heywood, and John Day have also been considered—and to credit Shakespeare with Acts III, IV, and V.

SOURCES: The story of Pericles is derived from the legend of Apollonius of Tyre. The legend has its roots in Greek and Roman antiquity and is found in numerous Romance and Slavic manuscripts. Elizabethans were introduced to the Apollonius legend through John Gower's treatment of it in his *Confessio Amantis* (1385-93). Lawrence Twine published a prose rendering of the tale in 1576, *The Patterne of Paynfull Adventures*, which, it is often suggested, was accessible to Shakespeare. In 1608, the minor playwright George Wilkins produced another prose version, entitled *The Painfull Adventures of Pericles, Prince of Tyre, the True History of the Play of Pericles, as it was lately presented by the worthy and ancient poet, John Gower.* The fact that Wilkins's novel follows the first quarto text closely, often transcribing the play verbatim, and the curious titular mention of Gower's presentation of the tale (the play employs Gower as a chorus, introducing scenes and filling in plot details) has inspired debate concerning Wilkins's share in and responsibility for the play as it has survived. Without a specific date of composition, there is little evidence and great speculation as to whether the Wilkins novel was a source for Shakespeare, or conversely, whether Wilkins borrowed from Shakespeare and Twine. Kenneth Muir has further proposed the existence of a lost source, an Ur-*Pericles,* that was used by both Wilkins and Shakespeare.

CRITICAL HISTORY: The history of *Pericles* criticism is marked by the controversy over the play's authorship: some commentators stoutly refuse to accept the work as part of Shakespeare's canon, primarily because of its inferior quality, while others defend the play as indicative of Shakespeare's genius in its unity, complexity, and evocative vision.

Although *Pericles* was evidently popular with Shakespeare's audiences, its early reception was mixed. The play was praised

by playwrights Samuel Sheppard and George Lillo, yet Shakespeare's contemporary Ben Jonson denigrated it in the phrase, "a mouldy tale like *Pericles*," and, in the next generation, Owen Feltham referred to the play as containing the epitome of an ill-constructed plot. John Dryden, in a poem in which he pardoned the initial works of all dramatists, no matter how weak, cited *Pericles* among this category.

Writing in the eighteenth century, the editor George Steevens doubted that "even the irregular and lawless Shakespeare" could have composed the disjointed *Pericles*. Edmond Malone agreed with Steevens's estimate of *Pericles*'s relative formlessness, but he took exception to Steevens's view that the play was not solely by Shakespeare. Although Malone later acceded to Steevens's position, the debate between these two was only the first in a long series of discussions on the authorship of *Pericles* that has dominated later criticism of the play. Such questions as whether Shakespeare revised an earlier *Pericles,* written by himself or by another dramatist, most likely George Wilkins, or that he simply penned a three-act play which some other playwright extended into five acts, have occupied scholars since Steevens first introduced the issue.

In the nineteenth century, Samuel Taylor Coleridge argued that Shakespeare revised an already existing play, making changes sparingly at first, but then more substantial as he became fascinated by the subject. Coleridge confidently asserted that "the last two acts are almost altogether by him." Nikolas Delius concurred with Coleridge, stipulating that George Wilkins was the author of the play Shakespeare revised. F. G. Fleay countered with the hypothesis that Shakespeare had originally created the Marina episodes, with the exception of the Gower choruses and the brothel scenes, to which Wilkins and William Rowley attached the remaining portions. Many Victorian critics contended that Shakespeare could not have written the indecorous brothel scenes, but others, like George Brandes, Walter Raleigh, and K. Deighton, pointed out the parallels between these scenes and similar ones in *Measure for Measure,* concluding that they were distinctly Shakespearean. The authorship controversy continued into the twentieth century with H. Dugdale Sykes's analysis of Wilkins's hand in the play and Henry David Gray's assertion that Thomas Heywood—not Wilkins—wrote the earlier version of *Pericles.* More recently, F. D. Hoeniger added another twist in the authorship conundrum by arguing that it was John Day's play that Shakespeare revised. Thus, the question of authorship posed two centuries ago remains unresolved.

Not all nineteenth-century criticism neglected consideration of *Pericles*'s dramatic qualities in order to engage in the debate over authorship. G. G. Gervinus claimed that although the play was definitely revised by Shakespeare it nonetheless lacks a "unity of idea." By contrast, Gervinus's fellow German Shakespearean, Hermann Ulrici, regarded the play as wholly Shakespeare's and, on the question of structure, maintained that it is "intrinsically held together by the thread of a single idea"—the triumph of love. A similar aesthetic evaluation of *Pericles* was given by William Watkiss Lloyd, who found "much to admire in the skill with which the play . . . is constructed and put together." The play's most prominent and enthusiastic champion in the nineteenth century however, was Algernon Charles Swinburne. In praise of those portions of the play he favored, Swinburne spoke of "unsurpassable pathos and sublimity," and he characterized the storm scene in Act III, Scene i as the greatest "ever raised in poetry." Edward Dowden, while admitting the play's weak dramatic structure, categorized *Pericles,* along with *Cymbeline, The Winter's Tale,* and *The Tempest,* as a "Romance" play, noting the themes of reunion, reconciliation, and atonement which these four plays have in common. Later, George Brandes, who shared Swinburne's enthusiasm for the storm description, also commented on the similarity between *Pericles* and Shakespeare's other romances and observed that the "germs of all his latest works lie in this unjustly neglected and despised play"—a view still held by many critics today and developed in the commentaries by E.M.W. Tillyard, Clifford Leech, W. B. Thorpe, and Alan Velie.

Brandes began the investigation into the biographical nature of *Pericles,* suggesting that the play represents Shakespeare's emergence from an artistic period of gloom. This suggestion was further developed at the turn of the century in the criticism of E. K. Chambers and Frank Harris, both of whom argued that Shakespeare had experienced some "conversion" as he passed from the despairing themes of the tragedies to the more hopeful visions of the romances. Harris even speculated that Shakespeare's conversion was initiated by a reunion with his daughter, Judith, in 1608. Despite the conjectural essence of such biographical criticism, the notion that Shakespeare's ro-

mances contain a brighter vision of the world—and that this vision is first seen in *Pericles*—became important to twentieth-century appreciation of the play.

G. Wilson Knight was also instrumental in bringing about a new appreciation of *Pericles.* Disregarding the questions of authorship and biography, Knight analyzed the play as a symbolic drama embodying a mystical, post-tragic vision. Knight claimed that, with the exception of *The Tempest* and the second half of *Antony and Cleopatra,* "the latter half of *Pericles* has no equivalent in transcendental apprehension in all of Shakespeare." D. G. James made a similar case for the play's depth of vision by analyzing Shakespeare's use of symbolism and contending that the drama is unified by the myth of resurrection, as well as that of lost and recovered royalty.

Several critics identified patience as another unifying theme in *Pericles.* John F. Danby claimed that patience in adversity is the dominating motif in the play, while J.M.S. Tompkins stated that Pericles is the most patient of all of Shakespeare's heroes, noting that Shakespeare's sources did not contain a quietly suffering protagonist. F. D. Hoeniger contrasted the tolerant behavior of Pericles with the wild ragings of Lear. Conversely, Ernest Schanzer contended that Pericles is not an exemplary embodiment of patience and that it is accident—not divine Providence—that directs his tribulations. The question of whether Pericles's misfortunes are caused by divine retribution or mere accident has also been considered by William Watkiss Lloyd, G. Wilson Knight, and F. D. Hoeniger.

Other twentieth-century critics have discovered elements of the medieval miracle play in *Pericles.* Donald Stauffer called it a "miracle play based upon a Renaissance romance," while Howard Felperin, noting Shakespeare's use of allegory in the drama, maintained that it resembles a miracle play in offering "a timeless parable for our spiritual enlightenment." Richard Wincor discerned another historical dramatic form in *Pericles,* namely the festival play. Wincor compared Shakespeare's romances to these ritual dramas which celebrate the cycle of the seasons, pointing out the motifs of rebirth, fertility, and barren incest in *Pericles.* C. L. Barber also considered the problem of Antiochus's incestuous relationship with his daughter, stating that Shakespeare's romances are concerned with "freeing family ties from the threat of sexual degradation" and showing how the threat of incest is overcome in *Pericles.* Phyllis Gorfain's structuralist analysis similarly traced the incest motif, laying heavy emphasis on the importance of kinship in the riddles posed by Antiochus's daughter, Thaisa, and Marina. Lastly, Northrop Frye illustrated the archetypal form of the Pericles tale by showing its parallels with a variety of other works of literature, such as T. S. Eliot's *The Waste Land.*

Although some twentieth-century critics have continued to view *Pericles* as a dramatic failure, a number of other commentators, with their various analyses of the play's mythic form, have achieved a new understanding of the work. It is perhaps through these interpretations of *Pericles* as a universal tale that modern readers can most appreciate the qualities of the play which made it so popular in Shakespeare's age.

BEN JONSON (essay date 1629)

[*Shakespeare's contemporary and fellow playwright, Jonson was the first writer to comment on Shakespeare's work, often respond-*

ing directly to the dramatist on certain scenes and plays. He is best known among Shakespearean critics for his famous dedicatory verses to the First Folio and for his scattered remarks and allusions elsewhere. The following uncomplimentary allusion to Pericles *occurs in a context of bitter and scornful rejection of the theatrical audience of his day, occasioned, according to Jonson scholars, by the failure of his play* The New Inn *in 1629. The verses suggest that* Pericles *was still a popular play some twenty years after its probable first performance. The phrase "the shrieve's crust" refers to jail bread. Jonson's labeling of* Pericles *as a "mouldy tale" caught the eye and ears of numerous critics in subsequent centuries, and the phrase is a commonly cited one in later* Pericles *criticism.*]

> Come leave the loathèd stage,
>   And the more loathsome age,
> Where pride and impudence in faction knit,
>   Usurp the chair of wit:
> Indicting and arraigning every day,
>   Something they call a play. . . .
>
> Say that thou pour'st them wheat,
>   And they would acorns eat:
> 'Twere simple fury, still thyself to waste
>   On such as have no taste:
> To offer them a surfeit of pure bread,
>   Whose appetites are dead:
> No, give them grains their fill,
>   Husks, draff to drink, and swill:
> If they love lees, and leave the lusty wine,
> Envy them not, their palate's with the swine.
>
> No doubt a mouldy tale,
>   Like *Pericles*, and stale
> As the shrieve's crust, and nasty as his fish,
>   Scraps out of every dish,
> Thrown forth and raked into the common tub,
>   May keep up the play club.
>   (pp. 282-83)

Ben Jonson, "Ode to Himself," in his Ben Jonson: The Complete Poems, *edited by George Parfitt, Penguin Education, 1975, pp. 282-84.*

OWEN FELTHAM   (essay date 1630?)

[*In the following excerpt, written around 1630, Feltham refers to* Pericles *as a play evoking as much displeasure as Ben Jonson's* The New Inn. Jug, Pierce, Peck *and* Fly *are characters from Jonson's play.*]

> Jug, Pierce, Peck, Fly, and all
>   Your Jests so nominal,
> Are things so far beneath an able Brain,
>   As they do throw a stain
> Through all th' unlikely plot, and do displease
>   As deep as *Pericles*,
>   Where yet there is not laid
>   Before a Chamber-maid
> Discourse so weigh'd, as might have serv'd of old
> For Schools, when they of Love & Valour told.

Owen Feltham, in an extract from The Shakspere Allusion-Book: A Collection of Allusions to Shakspere from 1591 to 1700, Vol. I, *edited by John Munro, revised edition, Oxford University Press, London, 1932, p. 346.*

SAMUEL SHEPPARD   (essay date 1646)

[*In an excerpt from his* The Times Displayed in Six Sestyads *(1646), Sheppard, an English playwright, compares Shakespeare to such Greek dramatists as Sophocles and Aristophanes and cites* Pericles *as evidence of his power of "Fancy."*]

> With Sophocles we may
> Compare great Shakespeare: Aristophanes
> Never like him his Fancy could display,
> Witness the *Prince of Tyre*, his *Pericles*.

Samuel Sheppard, in an extract from The Library of Literary Criticism of English and American Authors: 680-1638, Vol. I, *edited by Charles Wells Moulton, Peter Smith, 1959, p. 531.*

JOHN TATHAM   (essay date 1652)

[*The following reference to* Pericles, *written by Tatham in 1652, reflects the tendency of many seventeenth-century critics to group Shakespeare in the same class of dramatists as Ben Jonson, Francis Beaumont, and John Fletcher. Tatham alludes to* Pericles *as Shakespeare's weakest play—the ship in which he "Founder'd."*]

> There is a Faction (Friend) in Town, that cries,
> Down with the *Dagon-Poet, Johnson* dies.
> His Works were too elaborate, not fit
> To come within the Verge, or face of *Wit*.
> Beaumont and *Fletcher* (they say) perhaps, might
> Passe (well) for currant Coin, in a dark night:
> But *Shakespeare* the *Plebean* Driller, was
> Founder'd in 's *Pericles*, and must not pass.
> And so, at all men flie, that have but been
> Thought worthy of Applause; therefore, their spleen
> Ingratefull *Negro-kinde*, dart you your Rage
> Against the Beams that warm'd you, and the Stage!

John Tatham, in an extract from The Shakspere Allusion-Book: A Collection of Allusions to Shakspere from 1591 to 1700, Vol. II, *edited by John Munro, revised edition, Oxford University Press, London, 1932, p. 23.*

JOHN DRYDEN   (essay date 1684)

[*Dryden, the leading poet and playwright of Restoration England, helped form the Neoclassical view of Shakespeare as an irregular genius whose native talent overcame his ignorance of the classical "rules" of drama. The following verses are written in the tone of sly malice cultivated by Dryden in the epilogues and prologues of his plays and reveal the assumption that* Pericles *was the earliest, rather than among the latest, of Shakespeare's dramatic works. The poem is a rewritten version of Dryden's prologue to Charles D'Avenant's* Circe, A Tragedy *(1677), which made no mention of* Pericles. *The version below was first published in the 1684* Miscellany Poems *by Dryden and others.*]

> Were you but half so Wise as y'are Severe,
> Our youthful Poet shou'd not need to fear:
> To his green Years your Censures you would suit,
> Not blast the Blossom, but expect the Fruit.
> The Sex that best does pleasure understand,
> Will always chuse to err on t'other hand.
> They check not him that's awkard in delight,
> But Clap the young Rogues Cheek, and set him right.
> Thus heart'nd well and flesh'd upon his prey,
> The Youth may prove a Man another day.
> Your *Ben* and *Fletcher* in their first young flight
> Did no *Volpone*, no *Arbaces* write.

But hopp'd about, and short excursions made
From Bough to Bough, as if they were afraid,
And each were guilty of some *slighted Maid*.
Shakespear's own Muse her *Pericles* first bore,
The Prince of *Tyre* was elder than the *Moore:*
'Tis miracle to see a first good Play,
All Hawthorns do not bloom on *Christmas-day*.
A slender Poet must have time to grow,
And spread and burnish as his Brothers do.
Who still looks lean, sure with some Pox is curst,
But no Man can be *Falstaff* fat at first.
Then damn not, but indulge his stew'd essays,
Encourage him, and bloat him up with praise,
That he may get more bulk before he dyes;
He's not yet fed enough for Sacrifice.
Perhaps if now your Grace you will not grudge,
He may grow up to Write, and you to Judge.

> John Dryden, "Prologue to 'Circe'," in his The
> Poems and Fables of John Dryden, *edited by James
> Kingsley, Oxford University Press, London, 1970,
> p. 160.*

GERARD LANGBAINE   (essay date 1691)

[*Langbaine, an English biographer and critic, comments here on
the popularity of* Pericles *in Shakespeare's time and suggests a
source for the play.*]

[*Pericles Prince of Tyre*] was published in the Author's Life-
time, under the title of The Much Admired Play of *Pericles;*
by which you may guess the value the Audience and Spectators
of that Age had for it. I know not whence our Author fetch'd
his Story, not meeting in History with any such Prince of Tyre;
nor remembering any of that Name, except the Famous Athenian, whose Life is celebrated by Plutarch.

> Gerard Langbaine, in an essay in his An Account
> of the English Dramatick Poets; or, Some Obser-
> vations and Remarks on the Lives and Writings of
> All Those That Have Publish'd Either Comedies,
> Tragedies, Tragi-Comedies, Pastoral, Masques, In-
> terludes, Farces, or Operas in the English Tongue,
> 1691. Reprint by Garland Publishing, Inc., 1973,
> p. 33.

GEORGE LILLO   (essay date 1738)

[*The following excerpt is from the prologue to Lillo's play* Marina,
an adaptation of Shakespeare's Pericles *published in 1738. Lillo
says that* Pericles *is not solely Shakespeare's work but is "mix'd
with baser metal"—a position upheld by the bulk of critical commentary on the play's authorship.*]

We dare not charge the whole unequal play
Of *Pericles* on him; yet let us say,
As gold tho' mix'd with baser metal shines,
So do his bright inimitable lines
Throughout those rude wild scenes distinguish'd stand
And shew he touch'd them with no sparing hand.

> George Lillo, in an extract from The Library of Lit-
> erary Criticism of English and American Authors:
> 668-1638, Vol. I, *edited by Charles Wells Moulton,
> Peter Smith, 1959, p. 531.*

RICHARD FARMER   (essay date 1767)

[*In Farmer's* An Essay on the Learning of Shakespeare *(1767),
from which the following excerpt is taken, he argued that Shakespeare's knowledge of classical literature came through English
translations. Thus, in the case of* Pericles, *Farmer concludes that
Shakespeare based his story on "Apollonius of Tyre" by the
English poet John Gower.*]

Mr. *Langbaine* [see excerpt above, 1691] could not conceive
whence the Story of Pericles could be taken, . . . yet his legend
may be found at large in old *Gower*, under the name of *Ap-
polynus*.

Pericles is one of the Plays omitted in the later Editions, as
well as the early Folios, and not improperly; tho' it was published many years before the death of *Shakespeare*, with his
name in the Title-page. *Aulus Gellius* informs us that some
Plays are ascribed absolutely to *Plautus* which he only retouched and *polished;* and this is undoubtedly the case with
our Author likewise. The revival of this performance, which
Ben Johnson calls *stale* and *mouldy* [see excerpt above, 1629]
was probably his earliest attempt in the Drama. (p. 462)

> Richard Farmer, in his An Essay on the Learning of
> Shakespeare, *1767. Reprint by T. and H. Rodd, 1821,
> 114 p.*

EDMOND MALONE   (essay date 1780)

[*An eighteenth-century Irish literary scholar and editor, Malone
was the first critic to establish a chronology of Shakespeare's
plays. He was also the first scholar to prepare a critical edition
of Shakespeare's Sonnets and the first to write a comprehensive
history of the English stage based on extensive research into
original sources. As the major Shakespearean editor of the eighteenth century, Malone collaborated with George Steevens on
Steevens's second and third editions of Shakespeare's plays and
issued his own edition in 1790. The collaboration with Steevens
in 1780 resulted in a disagreement between the two editors over
the authorship of* Pericles. *Malone initially maintained that Shakespeare was the play's sole author, Steevens that Shakespeare had
revised the work of an unknown playwright. Ten years later (see
excerpt below, 1790), Malone acquiesced to Steevens's position.
The initial 1780 debate, which can be followed in the two excerpts
immediately below, took the form of two "dissertations," one by
Malone, the other by Steevens, published with an introduction by
Malone explaining that the two pieces were written more or less
simultaneously, each editor keeping the other informed of his
progress "till one of us should acquiesce in the opinion of his
opponent, or each remain confirmed in his own." Malone added,
"The reader is therefore requested to bear in mind, that if the
last series of arguments be considered as an answer to the first,
the first was equally written in reply to the last. . . ."*]

Mr. Steevens's intimate acquaintance with the writings of
Shakspeare renders him so well qualified to decide upon this
question, that it is not without some distrust of my own judgment that I express my dissent from his decision; but as all the
positions that he has endeavoured to establish in his ingeious
disquisition on the merits and authenticity of *Pericles* do not
appear to me to have equal weight, I shall shortly state the
reasons why I cannot subscribe to his opinion with regard to
this long-contested piece.

The imperfect imitation of the language and numbers of Gower,
which is found in the choruses of this play, is not in my
apprehension a proof that they were not written by Shakspeare.
To summon a person from the grave, and to introduce him by
way of Chorus to the drama, appears to have been no uncom-

mon practice with our author's contemporaries. Marlowe, before the time of Shakspeare, had in this way introduced Machiavel in his *Jew of Malta;* and his countryman Guicciardine is brought upon the stage in an ancient tragedy called *The Devil's Charter.* In the same manner Rainulph, the monk of Chester, appears in *The Mayor of Quinborough,* written by Thomas Middleton. Yet it never has been objected to the authors of the two former pieces, as a breach of decorum, that the Italians whom they have brought into the scene do not speak the language of their own country; or to the writer of the latter, that the monk whom he has introduced does not use the English dialect of the age in which he lived.—But it may be said, ''nothing of this kind is attempted by these poets; the author of Pericles, on the other hand, has endeavoured to copy the versification of Gower, and has failed in the attempt: had this piece been the composition of Shakspeare, he would have succeeded.''

I shall very readily acknowledge, that Shakspeare, if he had thought fit, could have exhibited a tolerably accurate imitation of the language of Gower; for there can be little doubt, that what has been effected by much inferior writers, he with no great difficulty could have accomplished. But that, because these choruses do not exhibit such an imitation, they were therefore not his performance, does not appear to me a necessary conclusion; for he might not think such an imitation proper for a popular audience. Gower, like the persons above mentioned, would probably have been suffered to speak the same language as the other characters in this piece, had he not written a poem containing the very story on which the play is formed. . . . Hence, Shakspeare seems to have thought it proper (not, to copy his versification, for that does not appear to have been at all in his thoughts, but) to throw a certain air of antiquity over the monologues which he has attributed to the venerable bard. Had he imitated the diction of the *Confessio Amantis* with accuracy, he well knew that it would have been as unintelligible to the greater part of his audience as the Italian of Guicciardine or the Latin of Rainulph; for, I suppose, there can be no doubt, that the language of Gower (which is almost as far removed from that of Hooker and Fairfax, as it is from the prose of Addison or the poetry of Pope,) was understood by none but scholars, even in the time of Queen Elizabeth. Having determined to introduce the contemporary of Chaucer in the scene, it was not his business to exhibit so perfect an imitation of his diction as perhaps with assiduity and study he might have accomplished, but such an antiquated style as might be understood by the people before whom his play was to be represented.

As the language of these choruses is, in my opinion, insufficient to prove that they were not the production of Shakspeare, so also is the inequality of metre which may be observed in different parts of them; for the same inequality is found in the lyrical parts of *Macbeth* and *A Midsummer-Night's Dream.* It may likewise be remarked, that as in *Pericles,* so in many of our author's *early* performances, *alternate rhymes* frequently occur; a practice which I have not observed in any other dramatick performances of that age, intended for publick representation.

Before I quit the subject of the choruses introduced in this piece, let me add, that, like many other parts of this play, they contain some marked expressions, certain *ardentia verba,* that are also found in the undisputed works of our great poet; which any one who will take the trouble to compare them with the choruses in *King Henry V.* and *The Winter's Tale,* will readily

perceive. If, in order to account for the similitude, it shall be said, that though Shakspeare did not compose these declamations of Gower, he might have *retouched* them, as that is a point which never can be ascertained, so no answer can be given to it.

That the play of *Pericles* was originally written by another poet, and afterwards improved by Shakspeare, I do not see sufficient reason to believe. It may be true, that all which the improver of a dramatick piece originally ill-constructed can do, is, to polish the language, and to add a few splendid passages; but that this play was the work of another, which Shakspeare from his friendship for the author revised and corrected, is the very point in question, and therefore cannot be adduced as a medium to prove that point. It appears to me equally improbable that Pericles was formed on an unsuccessful drama of a preceding period; and that all the weaker scenes are taken from thence. We know indeed that it was a frequent practice of our author to avail himself of the labours of others, and to construct a new drama upon an old foundation; but the pieces that he has thus imitated are yet extant. We have an original *Taming of a Shrew,* a *King John,* a *Promos and Cassandra,* a *King Leir,* &c. but where is this old play of *Pericles?* or how comes it to pass that no memorial of such a drama remains? Even if it could be proved that such a piece once existed, it would not warrant us in supposing that the less vigorous parts of the performance in question were taken from thence; for though Shakspeare borrowed the fables of the ancient dramas just now enumerated, he does not appear to have transcribed a single scene from any one of them. (pp. 244-47)

The conduct of *Pericles* and *The Winter's Tale,* which have several events common to both, gives additional weight to the supposition that the two pieces proceeded from the same hand. In the latter our author has thrown the discovery of Perdita into narration, as if through consciousness of having already exhausted, in the business of Marina, all that could render such an incident affecting on the stage. Leontes too says but little to Hermione, when he finds her; their mutual situations having been likewise anticipated by the Prince of Tyre and Thaisa, who had before amply expressed the transports natural to unexpected meeting after long and painful separation.

All the objections which are founded on the want of *liaison* between the different parts of this piece, on the numerous characters introduced in it, not sufficiently connected with each other, on the various and distant countries in which the scene is laid,—may, I think, be answered, by saying that the author pursued the story exactly as he found it either in the *Confessio Amantis* or some prose translation of the *Gesta Romanorum;* a practice which Shakspeare is known to have followed in many plays, and to which most of the faults that have been urged against his dramas may be imputed.—If while we travel in *Antony and Cleopatra* from one country to another with no less rapidity than in the present piece, the objects presented to us are more beautiful, and the prospect more diversified, let it be remembered, at the same time, that between the composition of these plays there was probably an interval of at least fifteen years. . . . (pp. 248-49)

If this play had come down to us in the state in which the poet left it, its numerous ellipses might fairly be urged to invalidate Shakspeare's claim to the whole or to any part of it. But the argument that is founded in these irregularities of the style loses much of its weight, when it is considered, that the earliest printed copy appears in so imperfect a form, that there is scarcely a single page of it undisfigured by the grossest corruptions. As many words have been inserted, inconsistent not only with the author's meaning, but with any meaning whatsoever, as many verses appear to have been transposed, and some passages are appropriated to characters to whom manifestly they do not belong, so there is great reason to believe that many words and even lines were omitted at the press; and it is highly probable that the printer is answerable for more of these ellipses than the poet. The same observation may be extended to the metre, which might have been originally sufficiently smooth and harmonious, though now, notwithstanding the editor's best care, it is feared it will be found in many places rugged and defective.

On the appearance of Shakspeare's name in the title page of the original edition of *Pericles*, it is acknowledged no great stress can be laid; for by the knavery of printers or booksellers it has been likewise affixed to two pieces, of which it may be doubted whether a single line was written by our author. However, though the name of Shakspeare may not alone authenticate this play, it is not in the scale of evidence entirely insignificant; nor is it a fair conclusion, that, because we are not to confide in the title-pages of two dramas which are proved by the whole colour of the style and many other considerations not to have been the composition of Shakspeare, we are therefore to give no credit to the title of a piece, which we are led by very strong internal proof, and by many corroborating circumstances, to attribute to him. Though the title-pages of *The London Prodigal* and *Sir John Oldcastle* should clearly appear to be forgeries, those of *Henry VI.* and *Othello* will still remain unimpeached. (pp. 249-50)

Why this drama was omitted in the first edition of Shakspeare's works, it is impossible now to ascertain. But if we shall allow the omission to be a decisive proof that it was not the composition of our author, we must likewise exclude *Troilus and Cressida* from the list of his performances: for it is certain, this was likewise omitted by the editors of the first folio, nor did they see their error till the whole work and even the table of contents was printed; as appears from its not being paged, or enumerated in that table with his other plays. I do not, however, suppose that the editors, Heminge and Condell, did not know who was the writer of *Troilus and Cressida*, but that the piece, though printed some years before, for a time escaped their memory. The same may be said of *Pericles*. Why this also was not recovered, as well as the other, we can now only conjecture. (p. 250)

After all, perhaps, the internal evidence which this drama itself affords of the hand of Shakspeare is of more weight than any other argument that can be adduced. If we are to form our judgment by those unerring criterions which have been established by the learned author of *The Discourse on Poetical Imitation*, the question will be quickly decided; for who can point out two writers, that without any communication or knowledge of each other ever produced so many passages, coinciding both in sentiment and expression, as are found in this piece and the undisputed plays of Shakspeare? Should it be said, that he did not scruple to borrow both fables and sentiments from other writers, and that therefore this circumstance will not prove this tragedy to be his, it may be answered, that had *Pericles* been an anonymous production, this coincidence might not perhaps ascertain Shakspeare's title to the play; and he might with sufficient probability be supposed to have only borrowed from *another;* but when, in addition to all the circumstances already stated, we recollect the constant tradition that has accompanied this piece, and that it was printed with

his name, in his life-time, as acted at his own theatre, the parallel passages which are so abundantly scattered throughout every part of *Pericles* and his undisputed performances, afford no slight proof, that in the several instances enumerated in the course of the preceding observations, he borrowed, as was his frequent practice, from *himself;* and that this contested play was his own composition.

The testimony of Dryden [see excerpt above, 1684] to this point does not appear to me so inconsiderable as it has been represented. If he had only meant to say, that *Pericles* was produced before *Othello*, the second line of the couplet . . . would have sufficiently expressed his meaning; nor, in order to convey this idea, was it necessary to call the former the *first* dramatick performance of Shakspeare; a particular which he lived near enough the time to have learned from stage-tradition. . . . [Whether], when Dryden entitled *Pericles* our author's first composition, he meant to be understood literally or not, let it be remembered, that he calls it *his Pericles;* that he speaks of it as the legitimate, not the spurious or adopted, offspring of our poet's muse; as the sole, not the partial property of Shakspeare.

I am yet, therefore, unconvinced, that this drama was not written by our author. The wildness and irregularity of the fable, the artless conduct of the piece, and the inequalities of the poetry, may, I think, be all accounted for, by supposing it either his first, or one of his earliest essays in dramatick composition. (pp. 251-52)

Edmond Malone, in an essay in The Plays and Poems of William Shakspeare, Vol. I *by William Shakspeare, edited by James Boswell, F. C. and J. Rivington, 1821, pp. 245-52.*

GEORGE STEEVENS (essay date 1780)

[*Steevens, a Shakespearean scholar and editor, collaborated with Samuel Johnson on a ten-volume edition of Shakespeare's works in 1773. The subsequent revision of this collection, along with Steevens's own edition of 1793, formed the textual basis for the first two Variorum editions of Shakespeare's plays. In the following excerpt, Steevens presents his case for the dual authorship of* Pericles *and challenges Edmond Malone's assertion that Shakespeare was the sole author of the play (see excerpt above, 1780). Steevens's conclusion that* Pericles *was probably composed by some other writer and "improved" by Shakespeare, especially in the last act, remains the prevailing critical opinion of the play's authorship.*]

That this tragedy has some merit, it were vain to deny; but that it is the entire composition of Shakspeare, is more than can be hastily granted. I shall not venture . . . to determine that the hand of our great poet is *only* visible in the last Act, for I think it appears in several passages dispersed over each of these divisions. I find it difficult, however, to persuade myself that he was the original fabricator of the plot, or the author of every dialogue, chorus, &c. and this opinion is founded on a concurrence of circumstances which I shall attempt to enumerate, that the reader may have the benefit of all the lights I am able to throw on so obscure a subject.

Be it first observed, that most of the choruses in *Pericles* are written in a measure which Shakspeare has not employed on the same occasion, either in *The Winter's Tale, Romeo and Juliet,* or *King Henry the Fifth.* If it be urged, that throughout these recitations Gower was his model, I can safely affirm that their language, and sometimes their versification, by no means

resembles that of Chaucer's contemporary. One of these monologues is composed in haxameters, and another in alternate
rhymes; neither of which are ever found in his printed works,
or those which yet remain in manuscript; nor does he, like the
author of Pericles, introduce four and five-feet metre in the
same series of lines. If Shakspeare therefore be allowed to have
copied not only the general outline, but even the peculiarities
of nature with ease and accuracy, we may surely suppose that,
at the expence of some unprofitable labour he would not have
failed so egregiously in his imitation of antiquated style or
numbers.—That he could assume with nicety the terms of affectation and pedantry, he has shown in the characters of Osrick
[*Hamlet*] and Armado, Holofernes and Nathaniel [*Love's Labour's Lost*]. That he could successfully counterfeit provincial
dialects, we may learn from Edgar and Sir Hugh Evans; and
that he was no stranger to the peculiarities of foreign pronunciation, is likewise evident from several scenes of English
tinctured with French, in *The Merry Wives of Windsor,* and
King Henry the Fifth.

But it is here urged by Mr. Malone [see excerpt above, 1780],
that an exact imitation of Gower would have proved unintelligible to any audience during the reign of Elizabeth. If it were
(which I am slow to admit) our author's judgment would scarce
have permitted him to choose an agent so inadequate to the
purpose of an interpreter; one whose years and phraseology
must be set at variance before he could be understood, one
who was to assume the form, office, and habit of an ancient,
and was yet to speak the language of a modern. (pp. 224-25)

If the inequalities of measure which I have pointed out, be also
visible in the lyrick parts of *Macbeth,* &c. I must observe that
throughout these plays our author has not professed to imitate
the style or manner of any acknowledged character or age; and
therefore was tied down to the observation of no particular
rules. Most of the irregular lines, however, in *A Midsummer-
Night's Dream,* &c. I suspect of having been prolonged by
casual monosyllables, which stole into them through the inattention of the copyist, or the impertinence of the speaker.—
If indeed the choruses in *Pericles* contain many such marked
expressions as are discoverable in Shakspeare's other dramas,
I must confess that they have hitherto escaped my notice; unless
they may be said to occur in particulars which of necessity
must be common to all soliloquies of a similar kind. Such
interlocutions cannot fail occasionally to contain the same modes
of address, and the same persuasive arguments to solicit indulgence and secure applause. As for the *ardentia verba*
[''burning words''] celebrated by Mr. Malone, (to borrow Milton's phrase,) in my apprehension they *burn* but *cold and frore.*

To these observations I may add, that though Shakspeare seems
to have been well versed in the writings of Chaucer, his plays
contain no marks of his acquaintance with the works of Gower,
from whose fund of stories not one of his plots is adopted. . . .
I ought not to quit the subject of these choruses without remarking that Gower interposes no less than six times in the
course of our play, exclusive of his introduction and peroration.
Indeed he enters as often as any chasm in the story requires
to be supplied. I do not recollect the same practice in other
tragedies, to which the chorus usually serves as a prologue,
and then appears only between the Acts. Shakspeare's legitimate pieces, in which these mediators are found, might still
be represented without their aid; but the omission of Gower in
Pericles would render it so perfectly confused, that the audience
might justly exclaim with Othello:—''Chaos is come again''
[III. iii. 92].

*Act III. Scene ii. Thaisa, Cerimon, and Gentlemen. From
the Rowe edition (1709). By permission of the Folger Shakespeare Library.*

Very little that can tend with certainty to establish or oppose
our author's exclusive right in this dramatick performance, is
to be collected from the dumb shows; for he has no such in
his other plays, as will serve to direct our judgment. These in
Pericles are not introduced (in compliance with two ancient
customs) at stated periods, or for the sake of adventitious splendor. They do not appear before every Act, like those in Ferrex
and Porrex; they are not, like those in Jocasta, merely ostentatious. Such deviations from common practice incline me to
believe that originally there were no mute exhibitions at all
throughout the piece; but that when Shakspeare undertook to
reform it, finding some parts peculiarly long and uninteresting,
he now and then struck out the dialogue, and only left the
action in its room: advising the author to add a few lines to
his choruses, as auxiliaries on the occasion. Those whose fate
it is to be engaged in the repairs of an old mansion-house, must
submit to many aukward expedients, which they would have
escaped in a fabrick constructed on their own plan: or it might
be observed, that though Shakspeare has expressed his contempt of such dumb shows as were *inexplicable,* there is no
reason to believe he would have pointed the same ridicule at
others which were more easily understood. I do not readily
perceive that the aid of a dumb show is much more reprehensible than that of a chorus. . . . (pp. 225-27)

Next it may be remarked, that the valuable parts of *Pericles* are more distinguished by their poetical turn, than by variety of character, or command over the passions. Partial graces are indeed almost the only improvements that the mender of a play already written can easily introduce; for an error in the first concoction can be redeemed by no future process of chemistry. A few flowery lines may here and there be strewn on the surface of a dramatick piece; but these have little power to impregnate its general mass. Character, on the contrary, must be designated at the author's outset, and proceed with gradual congeniality through the whole. In genuine Shakspeare, it insinuates itself every where. . . . (p. 227)

But the drama before us contains no discrimination of manners (except in the comick dialogues,) very few traces of original thought, and is evidently destitute of that intelligence and useful knowledge that pervade even the meanest of Shakspeare's undisputed performances. To speak more plainly, it is neither enriched by the gems that sparkle through the rubbish of *Love's Labour's Lost,* nor the good sense which so often fertilizes the barren fable of *The Two Gentlemen of Verona.*—*Pericles,* in short, is little more than a string of adventures so numerous, so inartificially crowded together, and so far removed from probability, that, in my private judgment, I must acquit even the irregular and lawless Shakspeare of having constructed the fabrick of the drama, though he has certainly bestowed some decoration on its parts. Yet even this decoration, like embroidery on a blanket, only serves by contrast to expose the meanness of the original materials. That the plays of Shakspeare have their inequalities likewise, is sufficiently understood; but they are still the inequalities of Shakspeare. He may occasionally be absurd, but is seldom foolish; he may be censured, but can rarely be despised.

I do not recollect a single plot of Shakspeare's formation (or even adoption from preceding plays or novels) in which the majority of the characters are not so well connected, and so necessary in respect of each other, that they proceed in combination to the end of the story; unless that story (as in the cases of Antigonus [*The Winter's Tale*] and Mercutio [*Romeo and Juliet*]) requires the interposition of death. In *Pericles* this continuity is wanting. . . . And even with the aid of Gower the scenes are rather loosely tacked together, than closely interwoven. We see no more of Antiochus after his first appearance. His anonymous daughter utters but one unintelligible couplet, and then vanishes. Simonides likewise is lost as soon as the marriage of Thaisa is over; and the punishment of Cleon and his wife, which poetick justice demanded, makes no part of the action, but is related in a kind of epilogue by Gower. This is at least a practice which in no instance has received the sanction of Shakspeare. From such deficiency of mutual interest, and *liaison* among the personages of the drama, I am further strengthened in my belief that our great poet had no share in constructing it. Dr. Johnson long ago observed that his real power is not seen in the splendor of particular passages, but in the progress of his fable, and the tenour of his dialogue: and when it becomes necessary for me to quote a decision founded on comprehensive views, I can appeal to none in which I should more implicitly confide.—Gower relates the story of *Pericles* in a manner not quite so desultory. . . . Mr. Malone indeed observes that our author has pursued the legend exactly as he found it in [Gower's] *Confessio Amantis,* or elsewhere. I can only add, that this is by no means his practice in any other dramas, except such as are merely historical, or founded on facts from which he could not venture to deviate, because they were universally believed. Shakspeare has deserted his

originals in *As You Like It, Hamlet, King Lear,* &c. The curious reader may easily convince himself of the truth of these assertions.

That Shakspeare has repeated in his later plays any material circumstances which he had adopted in his more early ones, I am by no means ready to allow. Some smaller coincidences with himself may perhaps be discovered. Though it be not usual for one architect to build two fabricks exactly alike, he may yet be found to have distributed many ornaments in common over both, and to have fitted up more than one apartment with the same cornice and mouldings. If *Pericles* should be supposed to bear any general and striking resemblance to *The Winter's Tale,* let me enquire in what part of the former we are to search for the slightest traces of Leontes' jealousy (the hinge on which the fable turns) the noble fortitude of Hermione, the gallantry of Florizel, the spirit of Paulina, or the humour of Autolycus? Two stories cannot be said to have much correspondence when the chief features that distinguish the one, are entirely wanting in the other.

Mr. Malone is likewise willing to suppose that Shakspeare contracted his dialogue in the last Act of The Winter's Tale, because he had before exhausted himself on the same subject in Pericles. But it is easy to justify this distinction in our poet's conduct, on other principles. Neither the king or queen of Tyre feels the smallest degree of self-reproach. They meet with repeated expressions of rapture, for they were parted only by unprovoked misfortune. They speak without reserve, because there is nothing in their story which the one or the other can wish to be suppressed.—Leontes, on the contrary, seems content to welcome his return of happiness without expiating on the means by which he had formerly lost it; nor does Hermione recapitulate her sufferings, through fear to revive the memory of particulars which might be construed into a reflection on her husband's jealousy. The discovery of Marina would likewise admit of clamorous transport, for similar reasons; but whatever could be said on the restoration of Perdita to her mother, would only tend to prolong the remorse of her father. (pp. 227-31)

Mr. Malone is likewise solicitous to prove, from the wildness and irregularity of the fable, &c. that this was either our author's first, or one of his earliest dramas. It might have been so; and yet I am sorry to observe that the same qualities predominate in his more mature performances; but there these defects are instrumental in producing beauties. If we travel in *Antony and Cleopatra* from Alexandria to Rome—to Messina—into Syria—to Athens—to Actium, we are still relieved in the course of our peregrinations by variety of objects, and importance of events. But are we rewarded in the same manner for our journeys from Antioch to Tyre, from Tyre to Pentapolis, from Pentapolis to Tharsus, from Tharsus to Tyre, from Tyre to Mitylene, and from Mitylene to Ephesus?—In one light, indeed, I am ready to allow *Pericles* was our poet's first attempt. Before he was satisfied with his own strength, and trusted himself to the publick, he might have tried his hand with a partner, and entered the theatre in disguise. Before he ventured to face an audience on the stage, it was natural that he should peep at them through the curtain.

What Mr. Malone has called the *inequalities of the poetry,* I should rather term the *patchwork of the style,* in which the general flow of Shakspeare is not often visible. An unwearied blaze of words, like that which burns throughout [Racine's] *Phaedra and Hippolitus,* and [Voltaire's] *Mariamne,* is never attempted by our author; for such uniformity could be maintained but by keeping nature at a distance. Inequality and wildness, therefore, cannot be received as criterions by which we are to distinguish the early pieces of Shakspeare from those which were written at a later period.

But one peculiarity relative to the complete genuineness of this play, has hitherto been disregarded, though in my opinion it is absolutely decisive. I shall not hesitate to affirm, that through different parts of *Pericles,* there are more frequent and more aukward ellipses than occur in all the other dramas attributed to the same author; and that these figures of speech appear only in such worthless portions of the dialogue as cannot with justice be imputed to him. Were the play the work of any single hand, or had it been corrupted only by a printer, it is natural to suppose that this clipped jargon would have been scattered over it with equality. Had it been the composition of our great poet, he would be found to have availed himself of the same licence in his other tragedies; nor perhaps, would an individual writer have called the same characters and places alternately Perìcles and Perícles, Thaïsa and Thaïsa, Pentapŏlis and Pentapōlis. Shakspeare never varies the quantity of his proper names in the compass of one play. In *Cymbeline* we always meet with Posthūmus, not Posthŭmus, Arvirāgus, and not Arvirăgus.

It may appear singular that I have hitherto laid no stress on such parallels between the acknowledged plays of Shakspeare and *Pericles,* as are produced in the course of our preceding illustrations. But perhaps any argument that could be derived from so few of these, ought not to be decisive; for the same reasoning might tend to prove that every little piece of coincidence of thought and expression, is in reality one of the petty larcenies of literature; and thus we might in the end impeach the original merit of those whom we ought not to suspect of having need to borrow from their predecessors. . . . I therefore attempt no deduction from premises occasionally fallacious, nor pretend to discover in the piece before us the draughts of scenes which were afterwards more happily wrought, or the slender and crude principles of ideas which on other occasions were dilated into consequence, or polished into lustre. . . . I admit without reserve that Shakspeare,

> —whose hopeful colours
> Advance a *half-fac'd sun striving to shine.*
> [2 *Henry VI,* IV. i. 97-8]

is visible in many scenes throughout the play. But it follows not from thence that he is answerable for its worst part, though the best it contains may be, not dishonourably, imputed to him. Both weeds and flowers appear in the same parterre, yet we do not infer from their being together, that they were planted by the same hand. (pp. 231-37)

To conclude, the play of *Pericles* was in all probability the composition of some friend whose interest the ''gentle Shakspeare'' was industrious to promote. He therefore improved his dialogue in many places; and knowing by experience that the strength of a dramatic piece should be augmented towards its catastrophe, was most liberal in his aid of the last act. (p. 242)

Before I close this enquiry, which has swelled into an unexpected bulk, let me ask, whose opinion confers most honour on Shakspeare, my opponent's or mine? Mr. Malone is desirous that his favourite poet should be regarded as the sole author of a drama which, collectively taken, is unworthy of him. I only wish the reader to adopt a more moderate creed, that the

purpurei panni are Shakspeare's, and the rest the productions of some inglorious and forgotten play-wright. (p. 244)

On the whole, were the intrinsick merits of *Pericles* yet less than they are, it would be entitled to respect among the curious in dramatick literature. As the engravings of Mark Antonio are valuable not only on account of their beauty, but because they are supposed to have been executed under the eye of Raffaelle, so *Pericles* will continue to owe some part of its reputation to the touches it is said to have received from the hand of Shakspeare.

To the popularity of the *Prince of Tyre* . . . we may impute the unprecedented corruptions in its text. What was acted frequently, must have been frequently transcribed for the use of prompters and players; and through the medium of such faithless copies it should seem that most of our early theatrical pieces were transmitted to the publick. There are certainly more gross mistakes in this than in any other tragedy attributed to Shakspeare. Indeed so much of it, as hitherto printed, was absolutely unintelligible, that the reader had no power to judge of the rank it ought to hold among our ancient dramatick performances. (pp. 244-45)

> *George Steevens, in an essay in* The Plays and Poems of William Shakspeare, Vol. I *by William Shakspeare, edited by James Boswell, F. C. and J. Rivington, 1821, pp. 224-45.*

EDMOND MALONE   (essay date 1790)

[*Ten years after his debate with George Steevens on the authorship of* Pericles *(see excerpts above, 1780), Malone conceded to his opponent's argument on the question and enunciated what remains the majority opinion of twentieth century scholars on Shakespeare's part in writing the play. The following remarks first appeared as an end-note to the text of* Pericles *in Malone's 1790 edition of the plays.*]

To a former edition of this play were subjoined two Dissertations; one written by Mr. Steevens, the other by me. In the letter I urged such arguments as then appeared to me to have weight, to prove that it was the entire work of Shakspeare, and one of his earliest compositions. Mr. Steevens on the other hand maintained, that it was originally the production of some elder playwright, and afterwards improved by our poet, whose hand was acknowledged to be visible in many scenes throughout the play. On a review of the various arguments which each of us produced in favour of his own hypothesis, I am now convinced that the theory of Mr. Steevens was right, and have no difficulty in acknowledging my own to be erroneous.

[In all questions of authorship,] internal evidence is the best that can be produced, and to every person intimately acquainted with our poet's writings, must in the present case be decisive. The congenial sentiments, the numerous expressions bearing a striking similitude to passages in his undisputed plays, some of the incidents, the situation of many of the persons, and in various places the colour of the style, all these combine to set the seal of Shakspeare on the play before us, and furnish us with internal and irresistible proofs, that a considerable portion of this piece, as it now appears, was written by him. The greater part of the three last Acts may, I think, on this ground be safely ascribed to him; and his hand may be traced occasionally in the other two divisions.

To alter, new-model, and improve the unsuccessful dramas of preceding writers, was, I believe, much more common in the time of Shakspeare than is generally supposed. This piece having been thus new-modelled by our poet, and enriched with many happy strokes from his pen, is unquestionably entitled to that place among his works which it has now obtained. (pp. 221-22)

Edmond Malone, in a note on "Pericles," in The Plays and Poems of William Shakspeare, *Vol. XXI by William Shakspeare, edited by James Boswell, F. C. and J. Rivington, 1821, pp. 220-22.*

SAMUEL TAYLOR COLERIDGE [as reported by H. C. Robinson] (essay date 1810)

[*Coleridge's lectures and writings on Shakespeare form a major chapter in the history of English Shakespearean criticism. As the channel for the critical ideas of the German Romantics and as an original interpreter of Shakespeare in the new spirit of Romanticism, Coleridge played a strategic role in overthrowing the last remains of the Neoclassical approach to Shakespeare and in establishing the modern view of the dramatist as a conscious artist and masterful portrayer of human character. Coleridge's remarks on Shakespeare come down to posterity largely as fragmentary notes, marginalia, and reports by auditors on the lectures, rather than in polished essays. The following excerpt is from the memoranda of H. C. Robinson. Robinson was a friend and admirer of Coleridge, and his Diary, begun in 1811, is a source of valuable comment on Coleridge's lectures on Shakespeare. Coleridge's assertion that Shakespeare merely reworked the first three acts of* Pericles, *but wrote the last two acts himself, is in general agreement with modern opinion of the play's composition.*]

[Coleridge] dined with us. . . . His remarks on Shakespeare were singularly ingenious. S., he said, delighted in portraying characters in which the intellectual powers were found in a preëminent degree, while the moral faculties were wanting, at the same time that he taught the superiority of moral greatness. . . . He considered *Pericles* as illustrating the way in which S. handled a piece he had to refit for representation. At first he proceeded with indifference, now and then only troubling himself to put in a thought or an image, but as he advanced he interested himself in his employment, and the last two acts are almost altogether by him. (p. 209)

Samuel Taylor Coleridge [as reported by H. C. Robinson], in a detached memoranda of December 23, 1810, in his Shakespearean Criticism, *Vol. II, edited by Thomas Middleton Raysor, Constable & Co. Ltd., 1930, pp. 208-30.*

WILLIAM HAZLITT (essay date 1817)

[*Hazlitt is considered a leading Shakespearean critic of the English Romantic movement. A prolific essayist and critic on a wide range of subjects, Hazlitt remarked in the preface to his* Characters of Shakespear's Plays, *first published in 1817, that he was inspired by the German critic August Wilhelm Schlegel and was determined to supplant what he considered the pernicious influence of Samuel Johnson's Shakespearean criticism. Hazlitt's approach is typically Romantic in its emphasis on character studies. Unlike his fellow Romantic critic Samuel Taylor Coleridge, Hazlitt was a dramatic critic whose experience of Shakespeare in the theater influenced his interpretations. In the excerpt below, Hazlitt states that the "movement of thoughts and passions" in* Pericles *is Shakespearean, but the "grammatical construction" is not.*]

The circumstance which inclines us to reject the external evidence in favour of [*Titus Andronicus*] being Shakespear's is, that the grammatical construction is constantly false and mixed up with vulgar abbreviations, a fault that never occurs in any of his genuine plays. A similar defect, and the halting measure of the verse are the chief objections to *Pericles of Tyre,* if we except the far-fetched and complicated absurdity of the story. The movement of the thoughts and passions has something in it not unlike Shakespear, and several of the descriptions are either the original hints of passages which Shakespear has ingrafted on his other plays, or are imitations of them by some contemporary poet. The most memorable idea in it is Marina's speech, where she compares the world to "a lasting storm, hurrying her from her friends" [IV. i. 19-20]. (p. 211)

William Hazlitt, "Doubtful Plays of Shakespear," in his Characters of Shakespear's Plays & Lectures on the English Poets, *Macmillan and Co. Limited, 1903, pp. 204-11.*

HERMANN ULRICI (essay date 1839)

[*A German scholar, Ulrici was a professor of philosophy and the author of works on Greek poetry and Shakespeare. The following excerpt is from an English translation of his* Über Shakespeares dramatische Kunst, und sein Verhältniss zu Calderon und Göthe, *a work first published in 1839. This study exemplifies the "philosophical criticism" developed in Germany during the nineteenth century. The immediate sources for Ulrici's critical approach appear to be August Wilhelm Schlegel's conception of the play as an organic, interconnected whole and Georg Wilhelm Friedrich Hegel's view of drama as an embodiment of the conflict of historical forces and ideas. Unlike his fellow German Shakespearean critic G. G. Gervinus, Ulrici sought to develop a specifically Christian aesthetics, but one which, as he carefully points out in the introduction to the work mentioned above, in no way intrudes on "that unity of idea, which preeminently constitutes a work of art a living creation in the world of beauty." In the following analysis of* Pericles, *Ulrici argues against George Steevens's case for a dual authorship of the play (see excerpt above, 1780), and concludes that "this play can have come from no other hand than Shakespeare's." Like John Dryden (1684), Richard Farmer (1767), and Edmond Malone (1780), Ulrici claims that, in addition to being Shakespeare's own composition,* Pericles *was also one of his first dramatic works. He notes that all of the principal parts of the play are "held together by the thread of a single idea" which reflects a view of "pure and genuine love" as life's supreme good.*]

Shakspeare's authorship of this lovely drama [*Pericles*] is now admitted by most English critics. Even Malone was originally of this opinion [see excerpt above, 1780], and ably enough refuted Steevens, who held it to be an older drama which Shakspeare had merely retouched. . . . Subsequently, however, he changed his views, and concurred with Steevens [see excerpt above, 1790]. But this is only a further proof how ill qualified Malone was, by reason perhaps of the very extent of his learning, to judge of genuine poetry. For, in fact, Steevens's reasons . . . are those of a mere philologist, and even as such not tenable. Thus, in the first place, he objects that the chorus (prologue) in "Pericles" is cast quite differently from that in the "Winter's Tale," "Romeo and Juliet," and "Henry the Fifth." But this only proves that it was composed at a different and earlier date. Again, dumb-shows are employed in "Pericles," but this is not the case with any other unquestionable piece of Shakspeare. . . . The remark is quite correct: but again it is only a proof that the piece was written at a time when dumb-show was still in vogue, and that Shakspeare, with his usual fine tact and artistic judgment, felt that if pantomime was to continue available for dramatic purposes, it must cease to be a mere spectacle, and must somehow or other be interwoven with the development of the action. Further, Steevens argues that the asserted resemblance between the ''Pericles'' and the ''Winter's Tale'' is not decisive, and that no safe conclusion can be drawn from parallel passages, between it and other genuine pieces, since it would be quite as easy to find as many between Shakspeare and other poets—Fletcher, for instance, in the ''Two Noble Kinsmen.'' The diction too, he asserts, varies greatly from that of his other productions—ellipses, for instance, are frequent in ''Pericles.'' The observation is true again, but at the same time it is only another proof that ''Pericles'' is much older than the ''Winter's Tale,'' and that the juvenile productions of Shakspeare, like that of most other writers, are not faultless. The last objection is, that the author has here followed his authority (the old poet Gower in his ''Prince Apolyn'') much more closely than Shakspeare usually does; as, for instance, in ''As You Like It,'' ''Hamlet,'' ''Lear,'' &c. This is also correct, though only in part, and even if wholly true it would not decide the point at issue, since in other pieces, as the ''Romeo and Juliet,'' ''Othello,'' ''Macbeth,'' &c. he has adhered quite as closely to his originals.

Only two, therefore, of all Steevens' reasons remain worth considering. The first is drawn from the fact that the ''Pericles'' was not admitted into the first folio by [John] Heminge and [Henry] Condell. But in answer to this, Malone and [Nathan] Drake . . . rightly object that Heminge and Condell also forgot the ''Troilus and Cressida,'' and only remembered this unquestionably genuine piece after the whole work, including the table of contents, had been printed—an oversight which even the second edition blindly repeated. It follows therefore—a remark which we here make once for all—that the absence of a piece from the first folio edition is no proof of its spuriousness; not however conversely, for the English critics maintain that the adoption of a piece, even by Heminge and Condell, by itself is no warranty of its genuineness. (pp. 428-29)

The last argument of Steevens applies to the composition and characterization. The best parts of ''Pericles,'' he observes, are more remarkable for their poetical tone than for the variety of the characters, or for the forcible delineation of passion. It contains, he says, nothing like true portraiture of manners, and few original thoughts, and the fable is at best but a complication of many highly improbable and ill-connected adventures; the scenes do not run naturally into each other, and are tacked but loosely together: after the first appearance, for instance, of ''Antiochus,'' we see nothing more of him, and his unnamed daughter in like manner disappears; Simonides is lost immediately after the marriage of Thaisa, and the punishment of Cleon and his wife is but slightly noticed. Even the old Gower is less desultory in his story of Prince Apolyn, which even as related by him could have had little attractions for a dramatist at all acquainted with the rules of his art. Shakspeare, therefore, Steevens concludes, can have had no hand in the composition of this piece. In this deduction again the premises are perfectly true. In fact, this play does fall apart into a number of detached scenes, which have only an external connexion with each other; it is without any such living and organic fundamental idea as, pervading all the parts, can alone adjust and combine them into a whole. Human life is not contemplated in its inmost centre, which determines the whole circle of surrounding circumstances, but outwardly rather, and in its periphery;—the poetry seems to proceed in a circular line, and touches nothing but what is directly in its way, and several figures are thus extrinsically included in the action, which again drops them as it proceeds: in fine, the composition is not in Shakspeare's manner in the highest sense of the term. So, too, the characters

are depicted in their outward more than in their inward features; *i.e.* they are illustrated by the circumstances and incidents of their lives, by their outward deeds and sufferings, rather than portrayed in the dispositions and feelings of their minds: they do not stand out roundly from the canvas, but like the figures in old paintings are flat and superficial. With all these defects the diction is perfectly correspondent: although a genuine air of poesy breathes in every line it yet wants true Shakspearean depth of thought, his vigorous delineation of passion, and his intense and lofty utterance of feeling. Steevens is, in fact, fully justified when he asserts, that in every respect—choice of subject, characterization, and composition—the work betrays a writer as yet imperfectly acquainted with the rules of his art. And yet his conclusion is, to speak mildly, most precipitate. In short, this play can have come from no other hand than Shakspeare's; but in truth the youthful Shakspeare's, and must have been, if not the very first, among the earliest of his essays. . . . The composition, although externally (formally) it is perfectly epical, is nevertheless intrinsically held together by the thread of a single idea. All the principal parts of the piece, either immediately or mediately (by contrast), reflect the same view of life, as spent in the search after and the acquisition, and in the loss again and recovery, of its fancied supreme good—pure and genuine love. Such a view is no doubt defective, as being in itself more epical than dramatic. Accordingly, the action, instead of being condensed, hangs loosely together, and proceeds flatly and diffusely. Lastly, the diction, although occasionally heavy, and without the vigour and terseness of Shakspeare's later works, possesses nevertheless so much grace, life, and ease, so much of harmony and rhythm, so many pregnant and lovely images, and contains so many golden grains of profound thought, that even in this respect [Robert] Greene is far from coming up to the lofty poetical genius, whose presence the reader is sensible of throughout the ''Pericles.'' But the comic scenes especially—those, for instance, with the fishermen—are . . . perfectly in Shakspeare's style. . . . (pp. 430-32)

''Pericles,'' which is composed in Greene's style, suffers . . . from a preponderance of the *epic* element. It was necessary, in fact, that even a genius like Shakspeare should at first be one-sided and partial in his labours, and pass successively through each of the two tendencies, whose organic fusion first constitutes the drama in its highest signification, in order that he might at last penetrate the true secret of dramatic excellence. (p. 432)

> Hermann Ulrici, ''Of Certain Pieces and Plays Ascribed to Shakspeare,'' in his Shakspeare's Dramatic Art: And His Relation to Calderon and Goethe, *translated by Rev. A.J.W. Morrison, Chapman, Brothers, 1846, pp. 422-63.*

GULIAN C. VERPLANCK (essay date 1847)

[*Verplanck was a nineteenth-century American lawyer, journalist, politician, scholar, and editor, and one of the earliest American Shakespearean scholars. His major contribution to American letters was a three-volume biographical edition of Shakespeare's plays in 1847. In his comments on* Pericles, *Verplanck, in agreement with George Steevens (1780), says that Shakespeare improved but did not originally compose the play.*]

Pericles having, from its first appearance, by means of its story, its dumb-show, and by its comparative merit relatively to its rivals for popular favour, succeeded and kept possession of the stage, the author would not feel himself called upon to rewrite a play which answered its main end, and the subject of which presented no peculiar attractions to him, while the re-examination of his own boyish, half-formed thoughts would naturally expand and elevate them into nobler forms, and re-clothe them in that glowing language he had since created for himself. . . . Nevertheless, the other solution of the difficulty . . . may still be the true one: that the original *Pericles* was by some inferior hand, perhaps by a personal friend of Shakespeare's, and that he, without remodelling the plot, undertook to correct and improve it, beginning with slight additions, and his mind, warming as it proceeded, breaking out towards the close of the drama with its accustomed vigour and abundance. (p. 8)

> *Gulian C. Verplanck, in introductory remarks in* Shakespeare's Plays, with His Life: Tragedies, Vol. III *by William Shakespeare, edited by Gulian C. Verplanck, Harper & Brothers, Publishers, 1847, pp. 5-9.*

G. G. GERVINUS (essay date 1849-50)

[*One of the most widely read Shakespearean critics of the latter half of the nineteenth century, the German critic Gervinus was praised by such eminent contemporaries as Edward Dowden, F. J. Furnivall, and James Russell Lowell; however, he is little known in the English-speaking world today. Like his predecessor Hermann Ulrici, Gervinus wrote in the tradition of the "philosophical criticism" developed in Germany in the mid-nineteenth century. Under the influence of August Wilhelm Schlegel's literary theory and Georg Wilhelm Friedrich Hegel's philosophy, German critics like Gervinus tended to focus their analyses around a search for the literary work's organic unity and ethical import. Gervinus believed that Shakespeare's works contained a rational ethical system independent of any religion—in contrast to Ulrici, for whom Shakespeare's morality was basically Christian. In his commentary on* Pericles, *first published in his* Shakespeare *(1849-50), Gervinus, unlike Ulrici (1839), does not find a "unity of idea" in the play. He suggests that Shakespeare reworked the play to develop the character of the "romantic sufferer," Pericles, "only to prepare a difficult theme" for actor Richard Burbage. Gervinus also claims that* Pericles *was Shakespeare's response to a demand for more popular plays and that its inferior quality is attributable to Shakespeare's efforts to "do homage to the multitude."*]

The relation of Shakespeare to his contemporaries is illustrated by the fact that his early plays were only elaborations of older existing dramas, some of which we possess for comparison; the elaborator, however, soon raised himself above his prototypes, and after a few years towered like a giant over them. *Pericles* and *Titus*—the one from internal evidence, the other from a transmitted record—are amongst these plays by another hand which were only elaborated by Shakespeare. (p. 101)

If it be asked, how it were possible that Shakespeare with [his fine] nature could ever have chosen such a play [as *Titus Andronicus*] even for the sake alone of appropriating it to his stage, we must not forget that the young poet must always in his taste do homage to the multitude, and that in the beginning of his career he would be stimulated by speculation upon their applause, rather than by the commands and laws of an art ideal. This must explain likewise the choice of *Pericles,* even though it were proved that Shakespeare did not undertake the elaboration of this play until a riper period. How readily the great genius delights for a time in trifling with the puny subject of which he sees the public susceptible! . . . Such pieces as *Titus* and *Pericles* lay within the horizon of common hearers; we know from express testimony that *Pericles* by good fortune

obtained great applause—upon the titles of different editions it is called a 'much admired play'; in prologues of other dramas it is spoken of as a fortunate piece; the prologue of *Pericles* itself says that this song 'had been sung at festivals,' and that 'lords and ladies in their lives have read it for restoratives.' This popularity proceeded from the subject, which was originally taken from a Greek romance of the fifth or sixth century. . . . The fondness for the subject of Pericles was thus transferred from the epic form to the dramatic, however rudely it was here treated. The art of transforming a narrative into a lively dramatic action—that art in which Shakespeare was from an early period entirely a master—is in *Pericles* quite in its infancy. The epos is only partly transposed into scenes; what could not be represented, as the prologue itself says, was made 'plain with speech' or pantomimic action; the prologues are very significantly placed in the lips of the old narrator Gower; he introduces the piece, as it were, and carries it on with narrative when the scene ceases; like a balladsinger with his puppets, he explains the mute scene in iambics of four feet and in the antique language of the old sources, which sounded in Shakespeare's time just as the droll verses of Hans Sachs do to us. Good-humouredly the prologue himself smiles at the quickly changing scene, in which the spectator rapidly passes over the life of the hero from his youth to extreme age. . . . There is here no unity of action, but only unity of person; there is here no inner necessity for the occurrences, but an outer force; a blind chance shapes the adventures of the hero. Nor does a unity of idea, such as Shakespeare ever took as the soul of his pieces, unite the parts of the play; at the most a moral tendency connects the beginning and the end of it. At the close of the piece itself the dramatic poet places in the lips of Gower, in whose narrative he had already met with this same moral, a demonstration of the glaring moral contrast between the daughter of Antiochus, who in the midst of prosperity, without temptation and allurement, lived in 'monstrous lust,' and the daughter of Pericles, who 'assailed with fortune fierce and keen,' amid the snares of power and seduction, preserves her virtue and makes saints out of sinners. As in *Titus Andronicus,* the idea of representing the passion of revenge, in its pure and impure motives and forms, is adhered to in its repeated gratification, so here the contrast of chastity and unchastity is the moral lesson, which, after the manner of the Moralities, glances forth plainly and glaringly at the beginning and end of the piece; far from that artistic refinement with which Shakespeare usually conceals his moral lessons under the veil of actions. Yet, however forcibly in *Pericles* the moral is brought forward, the middle scenes of the play have no connection with this idea, unless it be by explaining how the heroine of the second part of the play was born, or by conducting the hero from his youth through a series of poor and barren scenes to his old age. All English critics are agreed in refusing Shakespeare the outline of this fantastic, rude, and badly versified play. We know that there was an older drama of the same name; to this, then, Shakespeare added a few passages, which can be more justly termed 'master-touches' than those which he may have placed to *Titus*.

Whoever reads *Pericles* with attention readily finds that all these scenes in which there is any naturalness in the matter, or in which great passions are developed—especially the scenes in which Pericles and Marina act—stand forth with striking power from the poorness of the whole. Shakespeare's hand is here unmistakable. . . . The profound character of the speeches, the metaphors, the significant brevity and natural dignity, all the peculiar characteristics of Shakespeare's diction, are here exhibited. Yet these more perfect and richer scenes are only

Frontispiece to the Verplanck edition (1847). By permission of the Folger Shakespeare Library.

sketches; the delineation even of the two principal characters is also a sketch; but they are masterly sketches, standing in a strange contrast of delicacy with the broad details of the barberous characters in *Titus*. It is an unusual part which Marina has to play in the house of crime. The poet found these scenes in the old narrations; it was for him to verify them in the character. As this Marina appears before us, arming envy with her charms and gifts and disarming persecution . . . as we see her throughout, she is indeed a nature which appears capable of remaining unsullied amid the impurest, and, as her persecutor says, of making 'a puritan of the devil' [IV. vi. 9]. This character is sufficiently apparent; that of Pericles lies deeper. . . . This romantic sufferer exhibits far rather features of character entirely opposed to chivalrous feeling. His depth of soul and intellect and a touch of melancholy produce in him that painful sensitiveness, which indeed, as long as he is unsuspicious, leaves him indifferent to danger; but after he has once perceived the evil of men, renders him more faint-hearted than bold, and more agitated and uneasy than enterprising. The motives which induce him to venture the dangerous wooing of Antiochus' daughter have not been previously depicted by the poet, but are subsequently intimated. . . . And he, whose imagination, after fear has been once excited in him, is filled with ideas of a thousand dangers, whose mind is seized with the darkest melancholy, appears also in these touches to be a nature of

such prominent mental qualities that, trusting rather to these than to chance, he ventured to undertake to guess the dangerous riddle of the daughter of Antiochus. . . . The tender nature of his character, which makes him anxious in moments of quiet action, renders him excited in misfortune, and robs him of the power of resistance in suffering. The same violent emotion, the same sinking into melancholy, the same change of his innermost feelings, which he remarks in himself in the first act, after his adventure in Antiochia, we see again rising in him after the supposed death of his wife and child; as at that time he again casts himself upon the wide world and yields to immoderate grief, forgetful of men and of his duties, until the unknown daughter restores him to himself, and he at the same time recovers wife and child. The ecstatic transition from sorrow to joy is here intimated in the same masterly manner as the sudden decline from hope and happiness to melancholy and mourning was before depicted. As we said above, this is only sketched in outline; but there is a large scope left to a great actor to shape this outline into a complete form by the finishing touches of his representation. We therefore before suggested that Shakespeare may have chosen this play, in all other parts highly insignificant and trifling, only to prepare a difficult theme for his friend Burbage, who acted this character. (pp. 106-11)

> *G. G. Gervinus, ''Shakespeare's First Dramatic Attempts: 'Titus Andronicus' and 'Pericles','' in his* Shakespeare Commentaries, *translated by F. E. Bunnètt, revised edition, 1877. Reprint by AMS Press Inc., 1971, pp. 101-48.*

WILLIAM WATKISS LLOYD (essay date 1858)

[*In the excerpt below, Lloyd, a Shakespearean scholar, says that all of Pericles's troubles spring from his suit of Antiochus's daughter, an assertion similarly put forth by G. Wilson Knight (1947)— who defined the act as Pericles's ''consequent fall'' from ''adolescent fantasy''—but countered by F. D. Hoeniger (1963) and Ernest Schanzer (1965). Lloyd also notes the stylistic similarities between* Pericles *and* The Winter's Tale, *a point often discussed by later critics.*]

Of Shakespeare's skill in the creation of individual character I think we may agree that [*Pericles*] contains no indications whatever, nothing therefore of his best excellence; but in this respect is not much inferior to the *Comedy of Errors,* and it is perhaps not more destitute than that play of the effusions of his vein of impassioned and fanciful poesy. Still the play has characteristics which have led critics, without exception, to recognize the hand of Shakespeare. . . . Speaking from impression, I am disposed to think that Shakespeare remodelled a play of another writer from beginning to end, and that the discrepancies we observe are due to his sometimes contenting himself with lopping and abridging, sometimes taking the trouble to alter and insert words and lines, and sometimes recasting speeches, and perhaps scenes entirely. We do not meet in the play with the doggerel verses that are so frequent in his known earlier plays, and what rhymed couplets occur are scarcely introduced with the judgment and system that are observable where he is even most lavish of them, but they seem rather interspersed and scattered like vestiges of an earlier half and only half obliterated creation. Again, the play is quite free of his youthful tendency to redundance, and various and manifold as are its materials and incidents, its characters and combinations, its scenes and speeches have, to my mind, little of the goutiness, so to speak, and unwieldiness that are so contrasted with the correctness and sweep of outline, the cleanness of limb and mastery of the articulations that were realized by his pencil in his finished works. The style of the play is indeed remarkable for elliptical expressions that may in some instance have been the necessities of another writer in his metrical difficulties. . . . Looking, therefore, at those parts of the play where the hand of Shakespeare declares itself most markedly, I find that of all other of his plays *The Winter's Tale* is called most forcibly to my mind, by the combined effect of style, metrical tendencies and principle of versification, and the current of association generally. . . .

The scenes of coarser comedy among the fishermen and panders are, perhaps, so far beyond the capabilities of any other dramatist of the day, both in what they set forth and what they abstain from, as any other portion of the drama. After these I would indicate as another unapproachable characteristic, the steady flow and unfaltering progress by which Shakespeare could conduct a scene unflagging from its commencement to its end, with none of those flaws of unrhythmical hastiness and tardiness that mar so much of the otherwise fine music of the secondary Elizabethan dramatists. And more I think of this harmonizing power is observable in the general distribution of the subject matter of the play at large than has hitherto been supposed.

A play which has such various and frequently shifting scenes as *Pericles* must always be read to a certain degree of disadvantage beyond the fortune of others of less diversified stage accident. These changes furnish a source of fatigue and refreshment to the spectator, which an experienced dramatist knows how to manage and control. . . . Taking however, as well as one may, the point of view of the parterre, I confess I find much to admire in the skill with which the play of *Pericles* is constructed and put together. Whether we take the outline of the story in the form of argument, or read it in the verses that furnished it to the playwriter, we may be honestly struck with the ingenuity that could group, divide and connect it for dramatic purposes, with the requisite clearness and facility that are successfully attained. The story rambles dispersedly in various countries and by sea and by land, and the incidents are of every degree of importance and insignificance; but the stages of the story as enacted are cleverly made to correspond with the relief of the divisions of the acts. Old Glover interposes in each case, like the guard and sign and bound of the compartment, and his narrative both bridges intervals and renders them defined, while the dumb show that he interprets is an intermediate term of the narrated and the enacted. . . .

[Not] alone our desires, but somewhat also of our experience, is gratified when justice that is poetic, but not therefore utterly unreal, is fulfilled in the fate of Pericles. His original difficulties spring from his suit to the daughter of Antiochus, a suit unblessed by any better passion, than deceptive beauty stimulates, and the politic desire to furnish his realm with an heir. His error, for by the standard of Shakespeare's moral feeling so it must stand, is recognized soon, but not so as to evade all its consequences; hence his exile and wanderings and vicissitudes; prudence and noble sensibility, and patience when fortune admits no better, help and preserve him, and weariness and melancholy are aroused at last to renewed enjoyment of affection and prosperity.

> *William Watkiss Lloyd, "Critical Essay on 'Pericles, Prince of Tyre'," in his* Essays on the Life and Plays of Shakespeare, *C. Whittingham, 1858.*

F. G. FLEAY   (lecture date 1874)

[*Fleay was an English clergyman, scholar, and critic who, as a member of the New Shakspere Society, joined F. J. Furnivall as a pioneer in the area of standardized verse analysis tests, a method in which critics "scientifically" investigated the metrical variations in Shakespeare's verse. Fleay constructed a statistical table that evaluated each of Shakespeare's plays with a numerical breakdown of blank verse, prose, rhyme, short and long lines, and redundant syllables. The results of his tests indicated that a number of passages that had been accepted as Shakespeare's were the work of another author. Fleay and Furnivall laid the foundation for succeeding disintegration theorists. Despite its initial appeal, most twentieth-century scholars have come to reject Fleay's verse analysis method and the conclusions both Fleay and Furnivall drew from their experiments. In his analysis of* Pericles, *first delivered as a lecture before the New Shakspere Society in 1874, Fleay argues that Shakespeare could not have written either the Gower chorus or the brothel scenes and further asserts that "Shakespeare certainly never had any management or arrangement of the play." Fleay continues that the objectionable brothel scenes and other non-Shakespearean parts of the play were probably added to Shakespeare's original Marina story by George Wilkins and William Rowley. For further commentary on the possible coauthors of* Pericles, *see the excerpts by George Steevens (1780), H. Dugdale Sykes (1919), Henry David Gray (1925), and F. D. Hoeniger (1960).*]

With regard to the authorship of [*Pericles*], we may, I think, take it at once for granted, that the first two Acts are not by Shakespeare. It has been so long admitted by all critics of note that this is the case, that it cannot be worth while to go over the evidence again in detail. In order, however, to extinguish any lingering doubt, I give the metrical evidence; which will, at the same time, show how much more easily and certainly this result would have been arrived at had this method of investigation been earlier adopted. The play consists of verse scenes, prose scenes, and the Gower chorus. Considering at present only the first of these three parts, we shall find so marked a difference between the first two, and last three, Acts, as to render it astonishing that they could ever have been supposed to be the work of one author. . . .

[The] difference of the numbers of rhymes, the proportion being 14 in the one part to 1 in the other, is such as the most careless critic ought to have long since noticed. With regard to this main question, then, there can be no doubt: the three last Acts alone can be Shakespeare's; the other part is by some one of a very different school. But we have minor questions of some interest to settle. The first of these is, Who wrote the scenes in the brothel? . . . I say decidedly, not Shakespeare; for these reasons: These scenes are totally unlike Shakespeare's feeling on such matters. He would not have indulged in the morbid anatomy of such loathsome characters; he would have covered the ulcerous sores with a film of humour, if it were a necessary part of his moral surgery to treat them at all—and, above all, he would not have married Marina to a man whose acquaintance she had first made in a public brothel, to which *his* motives of resort were not recommendatory, however involuntary *her* sojourn there may have been. A still stronger argument is the omission of any allusion in the afterscenes to these three. (pp. 209-10)

But if these scenes are not Shakespeare's (and repeated examination only strengthens my conviction that they are not), the clumsy Gower chorus is not his either. And this brings us to the only hypothesis that explains all the difficulties of this play. The usual hypothesis has been that Shakespeare finished a play begun by some one else: that is, that he deliberately chose a story of incest, which, having no tragic horror in it, would have been rejected by [John] Ford or [Philip] Massinger; and grafted on to this a filthy story, which, being void of humour, would even have been rejected by [John] Fletcher. This arises from the fallacy which I noted in a previous paper, caused by the inveterate habit of beginning criticism from the first pages of a book, instead of from the easiest and most central standpoint. The theory which I propose as certain, is this:—Shakespeare wrote the story of Marina, in the last three acts, minus the prose scenes and the Gower. This gives a perfect artistic and organic whole; and, in my opinion, ought to be printed as such in every edition of Shakespeare: the whole play, as it stands, might be printed in collections for the curious, and there only. But this story was not enough for filling the necessary five acts from which Shakespeare never deviated; he therefore left it unfinished: and tried the arrangement of much of the later part in the end of *Winter's Tale,* which should be carefully compared with this play. The unfinished play was put into the hands of another of the ''poets'' attached to the same theatre, and the greater part of the present play was the result; this poet having used the whole story as given in Gower and elsewhere.

It is somewhat confirmatory of this theory that the play was not admitted into the first Folio; nor published before 1623, except in Quarto, first by [Henry] Gosson, then by [Thomas] Pavier, whose dealings in *scarcely anything but* surreptitious editions are so conspicuous. It is difficult to understand how such poetry as is contained in the Shakespeare part of this play could have been neglected, had there not been some reason for the editors of the Folio to leave it out of their edition; either some tradition of Shakespeare's disgust at the way in which his work had been completed, or some strong feeling that its publication in their authorized edition would be no credit to its author. One thing is certain, that it was absolutely neglected by Shakespeare himself: no pity of his, however carelessly printed, has its text in so wretched a condition; nor has the way in which modern editors have arranged its verse—which is for the most part printed as prose in the old editions—been much more creditable to them than the disarrangement of it was to the older editors. (pp. 210-11)

[Nikolaus Delius] says that ''the original Composer of this Drama, later on withdrew in favour of his co-worker Shakespeare—so to say, allowing himself to be eclipsed.'' Imagine Shakespeare in his best period allowing this stuff to stand in a play over which he had the full control! It is impossible. Shakespeare certainly never had any management or arrangement of the play: he only contributed the Marina story, which I have tried to separate and restore to him. Read that by itself: then turn to any of the other portions, and see how you like the flavour! (p. 214)

Surely, we may conclude that there were three authors. But who were they?

The original manager and supervisor of the whole work was, as Delius says, George Wilkins: he made the play as far as he *wrote* it from Twine's novel: he calls it ''a poore infant of my braine;'' he plumes himself on this arrangement of the Gower choruses as his own invention. In this, Delius is undoubtedly right. . . .

The second author was, I think, unquestionably W. Rowley. I have not just now access to complete plays of this author in verse, but comparison of the prose with that of *A Match at Midnight,* and of the verse with that of the plays he wrote in

conjunction with Fletcher and Massinger, assures me absolutely of the truth of this conjecture. (p. 215)

Since writing the above, I find that, just about the time that *Pericles* was written, George Wilkins was joined with John Day and W. Rowley in writing *''The Travels of the Three English brothers, Sir Thomas, Sir Anthony, and Sir Robert Shirley, an Historical Play, printed in Quarto, 1607.''* This makes assurance doubly sure, that Rowley and Wilkins were also joint-writers in the *Pericles.* Moreover, the impudent use of Shakespeare's name in 1653 on the title-page of *The Birth of Merlin,* in conjunction with Rowley's, indicates a tradition that Shakespeare and Rowley had worked on the same piece or pieces at some period. (p. 216)

The fact is, that Wilkins in his novel and in his play (*Miseries of Inforced Marriage*) has many blank-verse lines in the midst of his prose, and not lines only, but passages. (p. 218)

These passages occur in *all* parts of the story, and quotations can be multiplied of them: but these already given would be too numerous, were it not that I wished to show that they not only occur in the parts of the novel corresponding to the Wilkins, Rowley, and Shakespeare parts of the play indiscriminately, but also in passages of pure narrative, as well as in the speeches of the characters. In fact they are inseparable from Wilkins's style. . . . (pp. 219-20)

F. G. Fleay, '''Pericles','' in his Shakespeare Manual, *Macmillan and Co., 1876, pp. 209-23.*

EDWARD DOWDEN   (essay date 1877)

[*Dowden was an Irish critic and biographer whose* Shakspere: A Critical Study of His Mind and Art *(rev. ed., 1881) was the leading example of the biographical criticism popular in the English-speaking world near the end of the nineteenth century. Biographical critics sought in the plays and poems a record of Shakespeare's personal development. As that approach gave way in the twentieth century to aesthetic theories with greater emphasis on the constructed, artificial nature of literary works, Dowden and other biographical critics came to be considered limited. In the following excerpt, Dowden proposes four distinct periods for classifying Shakespeare's plays. The four plays of the final period—* Pericles, Cymbeline, The Winter's Tale, *and* The Tempest—*Dowden identifies as ''Romances'' and cites* Pericles *as the first of these. Dowden's observations are important not only because of his popularization of the term ''Romances,'' but because he also examines the similarities of these final plays, stating, in an unexcerpted passage of this essay, that they are ''all concerned with the knitting together of human bonds, the reunion of parted kindred, the forgiveness of enemies, the atonement for wrong—not by death but by repentance—the reconciliation of husband with wife, of child with father, of friend with friend.'' In noting the essential similarities between* Pericles *and the other romances, Dowden anticipates George Brandes (1895-96) and most later commentators on these plays.*]

Pericles is the first of the group of plays which I have named Romances. Shakspere's portion of the play has something of the slightness of a preliminary sketch. The first two acts are evidently by another writer than Shakspere, and probably the scenes in Act IV. (Sc. ii., v., and vi.), so revolting to our moral feeling, are also to be assigned away from him. What remains (Acts III., IV., V., omitting the scenes just mentioned), is the pure and charming romance of Marina the sea-born child of Pericles, her loss, and the recovery of both child and mother by the afflicted Prince. (p. 144)

The drama as a whole is singularly undramatic. It entirely lacks unity of action, and the prominent figures of the opening scenes quickly drop out of the play. A main part of the story is briefly told in rhymed verse by the presenter, Gower, or is set forth in dumb show. But Shakspere's portion is one and indivisible. It opens on shipboard with a tempest, and in Shakspere's later play of storm and wreck he has not attempted to rival the earlier treatment of the subject. . . . To this rage of storm succeeds the hush of Cerimon's studious chamber, in which the wife of Pericles, tossed ashore by the waves, wakens wonderingly from her trance to the sound of melancholy music. Cerimon, who is master of the secrets of nature, who is liberal in his "learned charity,' who held it ever

> Virtue and cunning were endowments greater
> Than nobleness and riches,   [III. ii. 27-8]

is like a first study for Prospero [*The Tempest*]. In the fifth act Marina, so named from her birth at sea, has grown to the age of fourteen years, and is, as it were, a sister of Miranda [*The Tempest*] and Perdita [*The Winter's Tale*] (note in each case the significant name). She, like Perdita, is a child lost by her parents, and, like Perdita, we see her flower-like with her flowers—only these flowers of Marina are not for a merry-making, but a grave. The melancholy of Pericles is a clear-obscure of sadness, not a gloom of cloudy remorse like that of Leontes [*The Winter's Tale*]. His meeting with his lost Marina is like an anticipation of the scene in which Cymbeline recovers his sons and daughter; but the scene in *Pericles* is filled with a rarer, keener passion of joy. And again, the marvellous meeting between Leontes and Hermione is anticipated by the union of Pericles and his Thaisa. Thus *Pericles* containing the motives of much that was worked out more fully in later dramas, may be said to bear to the Romances somewhat of the same relation which *The Two Gentlemen of Verona* bears to the comedies of love which succeeded it in Shakspere's second dramatic period. (pp. 145-46)

> *Edward Dowden, "Introductions to the Plays and Poems: 'Pericles'," in his* Shakspere, *Macmillan and Co., 1877, pp. 144-46.*

ALGERNON CHARLES SWINBURNE (essay date 1880)

[*Swinburne was an English poet, dramatist, and critic who devoted much of his literary career to the study of Shakespeare and other Elizabethan writers. His three books on Shakespeare—A Study of Shakespeare (1880), Shakespeare (1909), and Three Plays of Shakespeare (1909)—all demonstrate his keen interest in Shakespeare's poetic talents and, especially, his major tragedies. In the excerpt below, Swinburne ridicules those critics, like F. G. Fleay (1874), who have censored the brothel scenes in their consideration of* Pericles. *Noting the play's "purple" passages, Swinburne maintains that Shakespeare wrote the last three acts, including the brothel scenes, and that even the first two acts show "evident and positive traces of a passing touch from the hasty hand of Shakspere."*]

It is of course inexplicable, but it is equally of course undeniable, that the mention of Shakespeare's *Pericles* would seem immediately and invariably to recall to a virtuous critical public of nice and nasty mind the prose portions of the fourth act, the whole of the prose portions of the fourth act, and nothing but the prose portions of the fourth act. To readers and writers of books who readily admit their ineligibility as members of a Society for the Suppression of Shakespeare or Rabelais, of Homer or the Bible, it will seem that the third and fifth acts of this ill-fated and ill-famed play, and with them the poetical parts of the fourth act, are composed of metal incomparably more attractive.

But the virtuous critic, after the alleged nature of the vulturine kind, would appear to have eyes and ears and nose for nothing else. It is true that somewhat more of humour, touched once and again with subtler hints of deeper truth, is woven into the too realistic weft of these too lifelike scenes than into any of the corresponding parts in *Measure for Measure* or in *Troilus and Cressida;* true also that in the hands of imitators, in hands so much weaker than Shakespeare's as were [Thomas] Heywood's or [Robert] Davenport's (who transplanted this unlovely episode from *Pericles* into a play of his own), these very scenes or such as they reappear unredeemed by any such relief in all the rank and rampant ugliness of their raw repulsive realism; . . . but after all it remains equally true that to senses less susceptible of attraction by carrion than belong to the vultures of critical and professional virtue they must always remain as they have always been, something very considerably more than unattractive. I at least for one must confess myself insufficiently virtuous to have ever at any time for any moment felt toward them the very slightest touch of any feeling more attractive than repulsion. And herewith I hasten to wash my hands of the only unattractive matter in the only three of Shakespeare's plays which offer any such matter to the perceptions of any healthy-minded and reasonable human creature.

But what now shall I say that may not be too pitifully unworthy of the glories and the beauties, the unsurpassable pathos and sublimity inwoven with the imperial texture of this very play? the blood-red Tyrian purple of tragic maternal jealousy which might seem to array it in a worthy attire of its Tyrian name; the flower-soft loveliness of maiden lamentation over the flower-strewn seaside grave of Marina's old sea-tossed nurse, where I am unvirtuous enough (as virtue goes among moralists) to feel more at home and better at ease than in the atmosphere of her later lodging in Mitylene? What, above all, shall be said of that storm above all storms ever raised in poetry, which ushered into a world of such wonders and strange chances the daughter of the wave-worn and world-wandering prince of Tyre? Nothing but this perhaps, that it stands—or rather let me say that it blows and sounds and shines and rings and thunders and lightens as far ahead of all others as the burlesque sea-storm of Rabelais beyond all possible storms of comedy. . . . None other most assuredly than [Shakespeare] alone could have mingled with the material passion of the elements such human passion of pathos as thrills in such tenderly sublime undertone of an agony so nobly subdued through the lament of Pericles over Thaisa. As in his opening speech of this scene we heard all the clangour and resonance of warring wind and sea, so now we hear a sound of sacred and spiritual music as solemn as the central monochord of the inner main itself.

That the three last acts of *Pericles*, with the possible if not over probable exception of the so-called Chorus, are wholly the work of Shakespeare in the ripest fullness of his latter genius, is a position which needs exactly as much proof as does his single-handed authorship of *Hamlet, Lear, Macbeth,* and *Othello*. In the fifth act is a remarkable instance of a thing remarkably rare with him; the recast or repetition in an improved and reinvigorated form of a beautiful image or passage occurring in a previous play. The now only too famous metaphor of "patience on a monument smiling at grief"—too famous we might call it for its own fame—is transfigured as from human beauty to divine, in its transformation to the comparison of Marina's look with that of "Patience gazing on kings' graves, and smiling Extremity out of act'' [V. i. 138-39]. (pp. 206-10)

In the two first acts of *Pericles* there are faint and rare but evident and positive traces of a passing touch from the hasty hand of Shakespeare. . . . It has been said that those most unmistakable verses on "the blind mole" [I. i. 91 ff.] are not such as any man could insert into another man's work, or slip in between the lines of an inferior poet: and that they occur naturally enough in a speech of no particular excellence. I take leave decisively to question the former assertion, and flatly to contradict the latter. The pathetic and magnificent lines in dispute do not occur naturally enough, or at all naturally, among the very poor, flat, creeping verses between which they have been thrust with such over free-handed recklessness. No purple patch was ever more pitifully out of place. There is indeed no second example of such wanton and wayward liberality; but the generally lean and barren style of these opening acts does not crawl throughout on exactly the same low level. (pp. 211-12)

> *Algernon Charles Swinburne, "Third Period: Tragic and Romantic," in his* A Study of Shakespeare, *1880. Reprint by William Heinemann, 1920, pp. 170-230.*

GEORGE BRANDES (essay date 1895-96)

[*Brandes was a scholar and the most influential literary critic of late nineteenth-century Denmark. His work on Shakespeare was translated and widely read in his day. A writer with a broad knowledge of literature, Brandes placed Shakespeare in a European context, comparing him with other important dramatists. In his* William Shakespeare: A Critical Study (1895-96), *Brandes, like Algernon Charles Swinburne (1880), argues that Shakespeare wrote the last three acts of* Pericles, *including the brothel scenes, and portions of the first two acts. The rejection of Shakespeare's hand in these brothel scenes by critics like F. G. Fleay (1874), Brandes claims, is a "pandering to the narrow-mindedness of the clergyman," and he supports his contention by noting the parallels between these scenes and similar ones in* Measure for Measure, *an observation also made by K. Deighton (1907) and Walter Raleigh (1907). Brandes also challenges Fleay's contention that* Pericles *is a Shakespearean play reworked by another dramatist, maintaining instead that it is actually another dramatist's play reworked by Shakespeare at a time when he was emerging from a period of melancholy and pessimism—a suggestion later developed by E. K. Chambers (1908) and Frank Harris (1911). Brandes calls the character of Pericles a "romantic Ulysses" and discusses the affinities between the play and Shakespeare's other romances, stating that the "germs of all his latest works lie in this unjustly neglected and despised play."*]

[To] ascribe to Rowley the two prose scenes in *Pericles* which take place in the brothel is made more on moral than aesthetic grounds, and can have very little weight. My own opinion is that they were entirely written by Shakespeare. They are plainly presupposed in certain passages which are unmistakably Shakespearian; they accord with that general view of life from which he is but now beginning to escape, and they markedly recall the corresponding scenes in *Measure for Measure*. . . . (p. 282)

[That Shakespeare] should have made the first sketch of the play, as Fleay so warmly maintains [see excerpt above, 1874], seems very improbable upon a careful study of the plot. To write such a beginning to an already finished end would have been an almost impossible task for Wilkins and his collaborator, involving a terribly active vigilance; for the setting of the Shakespearian scenes, Gower's prologues, interludes, and epilogues, &c., is a frame of their own making. Everything

favours the theory that it was Shakespeare who undertook to shape a half- or wholly-finished piece of patchwork.

He hardly touched the first two acts, but they contain some traces of his pen—the delicacy with which the incest of the Princess is treated, for example, and Thaisa's timid, almost mute, though suddenly-aroused love for him who at first glance seems to her the chief of men. The scene between the three fishermen, with which the second act opens, owns some turns which speak of Shakespeare, especially where a fisherman says that the avaricious rich are the whales "o' the land, who never leave gaping till they've swallowed the whole parish, church, steeple, bells, and all," and another replies, "But, master, if I had been the sexton, I would have been that day in the belfry."

> *Second Fisherman.* Why, man?
> *Third Fisherman.* Because he should have swallowed me too: and when I had been in his belly, I would have kept such a jangling of the bells, that he should never have left till he cast bells, steeple, church, and parish up again.
>
> [II. i. 33-43]

It is not impossible, however, that these gleams of Shakespearian wit are mere imitations of his manner. (pp. 283-84)

An awkwardly introduced pantomime interrupts the prologue [to the third act], which is tediously renewed; then suddenly, like a voice from another world, a rich, full tone breaks in upon the feeble drivel, and we hear Shakespeare's own voice in unmistakable and royal power:

> Thou God of this great vast, rebuke these surges,
> Which wash both heaven and hell; and thou, that hast
> Upon the winds command, bind them in brass,
> Having called them from the deep! Oh, still
> Thy deafening, dreadful thunders; gently quench
> Thy nimble, sulphurous flashes!—Oh, how, Lychorida,
> How does my queen?—Thou stormest venomously:
> Wilt thou spit all thyself? The seaman's whistle
> Is as a whisper in the ears of death,
> Unheard. . . .   [III. i. 1-10]
>   (p. 284)

There is so mighty a breath of storm and raging seas, such rolling of thunder and flashing of lightning in these scenes, that nothing in English poetry, not excepting Shakespeare's *Tempest* itself, nor Byron's and Shelley's descriptions of Nature, can surpass it. The storm blows and howls, hisses and screams, till the sound of the boatswain's whistle is lost in the raging of the elements. (p. 285)

The effect is tremendously heightened by the struggles of human passion amidst the fury of the elements. The tender and strong grief expressed in Pericles' subdued lament for Thaisa is not drowned by the storm; it sounds a clear, spiritual note of contrast with the raging of the sea. (pp. 285-86)

It is not until the birth of Marina in the third act that Shakespeare really takes the play in hand. Why? Because it is only now that it begins to have any interest for him. It is the development of this character, this tender image of youthful charm and noble purity, which attracts him to the task.

How Shakespearian is the scene in which Marina is found strewing flowers on the grave of her dead nurse just before Dionyza sends her away to be murdered; it foreshadows two scenes in plays which are shortly to follow—the two brothers laying flowers on the supposed corpse of Fidelio in *Cymbeline*, and Perdita, disguised as a shepherdess, distributing all kinds of blossoms to the two strangers and her guests in *The Winter's Tale.* (p. 286)

The words are simple, and not especially remarkable in themselves, but they are of the greatest importance as symptoms. They are the first mild tones escaping from an instrument which has long yielded only harsh and jarring sounds. There is nothing like them in the dramas of Shakespeare's despairing mood.

When, weary and sad, he consented to re-write parts of this *Pericles,* it was that he might embody the feeling by which he is now possessed. Pericles is a romantic Ulysses, a far-travelled, sorely tired, much-enduring man, who has, little by little, lost all that was dear to him. When first we meet him, he is threatened with death because he has correctly solved a horrible riddle of life. How symbolic this! and he is thus made cautious and introspective, restless and depressed. There is a touch of melancholy about him from the first, accompanied by an indifference to danger; later, when his distrust of men has been aroused, this characteristic despondency becomes intensified, and gives an appearance of depth of thought and feeling. His sensitive nature, brave enough in the midst of storm and shipwreck, sinks deeper and deeper into a depression which becomes almost melancholia. Feeling solitary and forsaken, he allows no one to approach him, pays no heed when he is spoken to, but sits, silent and stern, brooding over his griefs. . . . Then Marina comes into his life. When she is first brought on board, she tries to attract his attention by her sweet, modest play and song; then she speaks to him, but is rebuffed, even angrily repulsed, until the gentle narrative of the circumstances of her birth and the misfortunes which have pursued her arrests the king's attention. The restoration of his daughter produces a sudden change from anguished melancholy to subdued happiness.

So, as a poet, had Shakespeare of late withdrawn from the world, and in just such a manner he looked upon men and their sympathy until the appearance of Marina and her sisters in his poetry. (pp. 287-88)

As Shakespeare, with the greater susceptibility of genius, was more keenly alive to the joyousness of youth, so more intensely than others he felt the quiet, half-sad pleasures of convalescence.

Wishing to accentuate the sublime innocence of Marina's nature, he submits it to the grimmest test, and gives it the blackest foil one could well imagine. The gently nurtured girl is sold by pirates to a brothel, and the delineation of the inmates of the house, and Marina's bearing towards them and their customers, occupies the greater part of the fourth act.

As we have already said, we can see no reason why Fleay should reject these scenes as non-Shakespearian. When this critic (whose reputation has suffered by his arbitrariness and inconsistency) does not venture to ascribe them to Wilkins, and yet will not admit them to be Shakespeare's, he is in reality pandering to the narrow-mindedness of the clergyman, who insists that any art which is to be recognised shall only be allowed to overstep the bounds of propriety in a humorously jocose manner. These scenes, so bluntly true to nature in the vile picture they set before us, are limned in just that Caravaggio colouring which distinguished Shakespeare's work during the period which is now about to close. Marina's utterances, the best he has put into her mouth, are animated by a sublimity which recalls Jesus' answers to his persecutors. Finally, the whole *personnel* is exactly that of *Measure for Measure,* whose

genuineness no one has ever disputed. There is also an occasional resemblance of situation. Isabella, in her robes of spotless purity, offers precisely the same contrast to the world of pimps and panders who riot through the play that Marina does here to the woman of the brothel and her servants. (pp. 289-90)

At a somewhat earlier period such a subject would have assumed, in England, the form of a *Morality,* an allegorical religious play, in which the steadfastness of the virtuous woman would have triumphed over *Vice.* At a somewhat later period, in France, it would have been a Christian drama, in which heathen wickedness and incredulity were put to confusion by the youthful believer. Shakespeare carries it back to the days of Diana; his virtue are alike heathen, owning no connection with church or creed. (p. 292)

The calm dignity of Marina's innocence has none of that taint of the confessional which was plainly obnoxious to Shakespeare, and which neither the mediaeval plays before him, nor Corneille and Calderon after, could escape. . . . Shakespeare's Marina, the tenderly and carefully outlined sketch of the type which is presently to wholly possess his imagination, is purely human in her innate nobility of nature.

It is deeply interesting to trace in this sombre yet fantastically romantic play of *Pericles* the germs of all his succeeding works.

Marina and her mother, long lost and late recovered by a sorrowing king, are the preliminary studies for Perdita and Hermione in *A Winter's Tale.* Perdita, as her name tells us, is lost and is living, ignorant of her parentage, in a strange country. Marina's flower-strewing suggests Perdita's distribution of blossoms, accompanied by words which reveal a profound understanding of flower-nature, and Hermione is recovered by Leontes as is Thaisa by Pericles.

The wicked stepmother in *Cymbeline* corresponds to the wicked foster-mother in *Pericles.* She hates Imogen as Dionyza hates Marina. Pisanio is supposed to have murdered her as Leonine is believed to have slain Marina, and Cymbeline recovers both sons and daughter as Pericles his wife and child.

The tendency to substitute some easy process of explanation, such as melodramatic music or supernatural revelation, in the place of severe dramatic technique, which appears at this time, betrays a certain weariness of the demands of the art. Diana appears to the slumbering Pericles as Jupiter does to Posthumus in *Cymbeline.*

But it is for *The Tempest* that *Pericles* more especially prepares us. The attitude of the melancholy prince towards his daughter seems to foreshadow that of the noble Prospero towards his child Miranda. Prospero is also living in exile from his home. But it is Cerimon who approaches more nearly in character to Prospero. (pp. 293-94)

The position in which Thaisa and Pericles stand in the second act towards the angry father, who has in reality no serious objection to their union, closely resembles that of Ferdinand and Miranda before the feigned wrath of Prospero. Most notable of all is the preliminary sketch we find in *Pericles* of the tempest which ushers in the play of that name. Over and above the resemblance between the storm scenes, we have Marina's description of the hurricane during which she was born . . . and Ariel's description of the shipwreck. . . . (pp. 294-95)

[The] germs of all his latest works lie in this unjustly neglected and despised play, which has suffered under a double disadvantage: it is not entirely Shakespeare's work, and in such portions of it as are his own there exist, in the dark shadow cast by her hideous surroundings about Marina, traces of that gloomy mood from which he was but just emerging. But for all that, whether we look upon it as a contribution to Shakespeare's biography or as a poem, this beautiful and remarkable fragment, *Pericles*, is a work of the greatest interest. (p. 295)

George Brandes, "'Pericles': Collaboration with Wilkins and Rowley—Shakespeare and Corneille," in his William Shakespeare: A Critical Study, Vol. II, *translated by Diana White with Mary Morison, Wm. Heinemann, 1898, pp. 275-95.*

SIDNEY LEE   (essay date 1905)

[*Lee, a Renaissance and Shakespearean scholar, wrote an important biography of Shakespeare,* Life of Shakespeare *(1898), as well as several other books on Shakespeare and his milieu. In the excerpt below, he discusses the dramatic weaknesses of* Pericles.]

The play of *Pericles, Prince of Tyre* dramatizes a tale of great antiquity and world-wide popularity. . . . The vein is frankly pagan. (p. 7)

The play, whatever literary merit attaches to a small portion of it, proves, as a whole, that the old story of Apollonius' travels is ill adapted to drama. The action is far too multifarious to present a homogenous effect. The scene rambles confusedly by sea from Antioch to Tyre, Tarsus, Mytilene, Ephesus, and Pentapolis. The events cover too long a period of time to render them probable or indeed intelligible in representation. At least nine months separate the last scene of Act iii, where his first child is born; a year elapses between scenes 2 and 3 of the latter Act, and as many as fourteen years pass between its close, where the child figures as an infant of one year, and the opening of Act iv, where she is a full-grown woman. The choruses, which are themselves interrupted by dumb-shows, supply essential links in the narrative. They "stand i' the gaps to teach the stages of the story" [IV. iv. 8-9]. The whole construction gives the impression of clumsy incoherence. (pp. 10-11)

Sidney Lee, in an introduction to Shakespeare's "Pericles": Being a Reproduction in Facsimile of the First Edition 1609 *by William Shakespeare, Oxford at the Clarendon Press, 1905, pp. 7-48.*

K. DEIGHTON   (essay date 1907)

[*Like George Brandes (1895-96) and Walter Raleigh (1907), Deighton discusses the parallels between the disputed brothel episodes in* Pericles *and similar scenes in* Measure for Measure *and concludes that Shakespeare wrote all of the scenes in which Marina appears.*]

I go much farther than [Frederick S.] Boas [see Additional Bibliography], and believe that throughout the three [brothel scenes] Shakespeare's presence is distinctly visible in characteristic expressions and turns of thought. These, indeed, are to my mind so striking and abound so largely that while space does not admit of my instancing them, I am astonished at their being supposed to come from any mint but one. What, however, impresses me even more forcibly is a consideration of structure. . . . Pericles is shown us as cheerfully giving his daughter in marriage to a man of notoriously evil life. To Shakespeare such a *dénouement* was impossible. While there-

fore he was bound to the brothel episode, he has, I maintain, taken upon himself to give us his own reading of Lysimachus's character. It has been pointed out that in their general scope these scenes have much in common with certain others in *Measure for Measure*. This likeness may, I think, be extended to a particular fact. The Duke there uses his disguise, assumed for a special purpose, as a means of informing himself upon the manner of life of his subjects, who owing to the laxity of his rule had fallen into dissolute ways. Similarly, it seems to me, Shakespeare may have conceived Lysimachus as wishing to probe the plague-sores of the city of which he was governor. . . . [Whatever] the object that led Lysimachus to visit the brothel, his conduct there is quite in keeping with motives other than those by which he is actuated in the prose narratives of the story. With the Bawd and Pander he naturally assumes the *rôle* of an ordinary trafficker in the wares they had to utter and talks to them in their own language. Towards Marina his attitude is wholly different. While making trial of her virtue, he gives vent to none of the threats, displays none of the coarseness and violence, which Wilkins plentifully imputes to him. (pp. xx-xxii)

Of course it is not necessary to my view that Shakespeare should have written the whole of these scenes. Indeed, if he had originally taken the plot into his hands, I can imagine that he would have omitted certain details, would have brought the

Act II. Scene i. By Byam Shaw (1902). From the Art Collection of the Folger Shakespeare Library.

different parts into more complete harmony, and left us in no doubt as to points that have given rise to debate. While, therefore, as regards the dialogue I hold that wherever Marina is on the stage, Shakespeare is present too, and that throughout the rest his contributions are manifold, my main contention is that not without set purpose did he pourtray Lysimachus as we have him in the sixth scene, nor without a motive sufficiently obvious. (pp. xxiii-xxiv)

[Shakespeare's] work *concludes* the play. Now, while he would not have considered these three Acts sufficient in themselves for an acting drama, it is almost equally beyond belief that he should have begun in the middle, or that, having so far worked out the details of the plot as to put its climax into final shape, he should have left himself the task of adapting the earlier portions to the incidents that follow. To a piece of work so preposterous, in the strict sense of the word, so useless for theatrical purposes, so unsuitable for publication, the history of literature affords, I think, no parallel. Had the fragment been one commencing the story, we could account for its being laid aside for various reasons: a reversal of the process is to my mind inconceivable. Nor can I admit that the Marina portion "gives a perfect artistic and organic whole," especially when stripped of the Gower parts, which Fleay repudiates as non-Shakespearean [see excerpt above, 1874]; for some introduction of the characters and some outline of previous events would be necessary to the understanding of the story.

If, then, we may take it for granted that Shakespeare wrote the greater part of the last three Acts; that he could not have left behind him a headless torso; that metrical tests, coupled with considerations of style, prove almost the whole of the first two Acts to be by some other author; and that in the brothel scenes there are abundant manifestations of Shakespeare's hand: there seems to me no option left but to believe that he furbished up a play already in the possession of the Globe Theatre—a play which as it stood did not in the opinion of the company promise to be a success. That he did at times revise the work of other dramatists is admitted; and, since he would regard such revision as little else than a matter of business, we need feel no surprise at his handling a theme that would have been repugnant to his own free choice. (pp. xxiv-xxv)

> *K. Deighton, in an introduction to* The Works of Shakespeare: Pericles, *Vol. 28 by William Shakespeare, edited by K. Deighton, Methuen & Co. Ltd., 1907, pp. vii-xxix.*

WALTER RALEIGH   (essay date 1907)

[*Raleigh, like George Brandes (1895-96) and K. Deighton (1907), notes the affinities between the brothel scenes in* Pericles *and* Measure for Measure, *concluding that Shakespeare was familiar with "the darker side of the life of the town."*]

Measure for Measure, and the Fourth Act of *Pericles* (which no pen but his could have written), prove Shakespeare's acquaintance with the darker side of the life of the town, as it might be seen in Pickt-hatch or the Bankside. He does not fear to expose the purest of his heroines to the breath of this infection; their virtue is not ignorance; "'tis in grain: 'twill endure wind and weather'' [*Twelfth Night,* I. v. 237-38]. In nothing is he more himself than in the little care that he takes to provide shelter for the most delicate characters of English fiction. They owe their education to the larger world, not to the drawing-room. . . . Shakespeare's heroines are open-eyed;

therein resembling himself, who turned away from nothing that bears the human image. (p. 53)

> *Walter Raleigh, "Stratford and London," in his* Shakespeare, *1907. Reprint by The Macmillan Company, 1909, pp. 29-62.*

E. K. CHAMBERS   (essay date 1908)

[*Chambers occupies a transitional position in Shakespearean criticism, one which connects the biographical sketches and character analyses of the nineteenth century with the historical, technical, and textual criticism of the twentieth century. While a member of the education department at Oxford University, Chambers earned his reputation as a scholar for his multivolume works,* The Medieval Stage *and* The Elizabethan Stage, *and he also edited* The Red Letter Shakespeare. *Chambers both investigated the purpose and limitations of each dramatic genre as Shakespeare presented it and speculated on how the dramatist's work was influenced by contemporary historical issues and his own frame of mind. In the excerpt below, from his edition of* Pericles *in* The Red Letter Shakespeare *(1908), Chambers argues that Shakespeare's world view underwent a "conversion" between the composition of* Timon of Athens *and* Pericles *and that the latter play "is like the first fresh outlook of a sick man." A similar biographical explanation of the more optimistic feeling in* Pericles *was first suggested by George Brandes (1895-96) and later developed by Frank Harris (1911).*]

It is true that *Pericles* is cast in a very different vein from that of *Timon;* but it is a characteristic of the group of romances to which it belongs, not to ignore the black possibilities of human nature, but rather to acknowledge these, and to transcend them in the strength of a boundless and confident optimism. . . . On the other hand, I find it difficult to trace in the first two Acts any touch whatever of Shakespeare, beyond the single simile which he must have inserted with a vagrant pen in the first scene of all—

The blind mole casts
Copped hills towards heaven, to tell the earth is thronged
By man's oppression; and the poor worm doth die for it.
[I. i. 100-02]

But even when Shakespeare's share in the play has been satisfactorily marked off, the literary problems which it suggests are far from done with. . . . The tone and temper of Shakespeare's contribution, no less than its rhythmical qualities, are too obviously those of his latest and not those of his earliest work. You cannot dissociate the storm of *Pericles* from the storm of *The Tempest,* or Cerimon from Prospero, or the double recovery of Marina and Thaisa from the double recovery of Perdita and Hermione. . . . It would be tempting to take *Pericles* as an early work of Shakespeare, partly rewritten by him in 1608. . . . But this again is an hypothesis which will not for a moment bear comparison with the facts. The rhythm of the first two Acts, with their frequent double endings and curiously interspersed rhymes, is no more like Shakespeare's early rhythm than it is like his rhythm in 1608. It is not like anything which he ever wrote at any time in his life. It is a little more difficult to say to what undistinguished writer it should be credited. . . . I see no reason to differ from the common conclusion that on the whole the probabilities are in favour of the authorship of George Wilkins, who is known to have been employed upon other work for the King's men about the date of *Pericles,* and who published a prose story with the title of *The Painful Adventures of Pericles, Prince of Tyre* in 1608. This is admittedly based upon the play, and in many places adopts its very phrasing. . . . There is not much dramatic work by Wilkins upon which to base a comparison, but such as there is does not discredit the hypothesis that the first two Acts of *Pericles* may be his. (pp. 278-81)

Clearly, we are upon a ground where, at the best, nothing but a more or less plausible conjecture is attainable. But I do not think that it is possible to advance even upon the lines of conjecture, without taking into account, in addition to the presence of two hands in *Pericles* itself, two other considerations. One is the unfinished state of its immediate predecessor, *Timon of Athens;* the other is the complete contradiction which these two fragments present to each other, when considered in the light of the spiritual tempers which they reveal and the judgments of life which they convey. *Timon of Athens* is the last word in that pessimistic analysis of man and man's place in eternity which is the underlying motive of all the long range of Shakespearean tragedies. . . . Compared to *Timon of Athens,* the Shakespearean part of *Pericles,* with its touches of exquisite poetry, and its happy dreams of purity that triumphs over sin and of wrongs that all come to be righted in the process of time, is like the first fresh outlook of a sick man, as the besetting fancies drop away from him, upon the green fields of his convalescence. Within the bounds of permissible conjecture, I find it hard not to believe that the metaphor comes very near to being a statement of literal fact. The change from the Shakespeare of the last tragedies to the Shakespeare of the romances is so fundamental and above all so sudden, as to need some exceptional and drastic explanation. It is not a mere transition, such as took place when Shakespeare gradually laid aside the unreflecting optimism of his high-hearted comedies and entered upon the tragic view of things. It is rather a conversion, a complete reversal of standards and values, which at once betrays itself through the whole man, in his sense of rhythm no less than in his spiritual outlook. Something happened when he laid aside *Timon of Athens,* some crisis of overwrought brain and nerve; and when he recovered, lying there, let us hope, in the great chamber of New Place in Stratford, it was no longer the Shakespeare of *Timon* who regarded a new-washed world. And when he came back to work, he took up the silly piece which George Wilkins had been allowed to begin for the King's men in his absence, and put in the latter end of it the beautiful idyll which centres round the figure of the good physician Cerimon. . . . (pp. 283-84)

> E. K. Chambers, "'Pericles',," in his *Shakespeare: A Survey, Sidgwick & Jackson, Ltd., 1925, pp. 277-85.*

FRANK HARRIS (essay date 1911)

[*An Irish-born American journalist and biographer, Harris attempted to find a pattern in Shakespeare's work that would shed light on the nature of his life. His approach is considered rather flamboyant and unreliable, and his theories have been either ignored or ridiculed by most Shakespearean scholars. The conjectural nature of his criticism is clearly illustrated in his comments on* Pericles. *Harris further extends suggestions by George Brandes (1895-96) and E. K. Chambers (1908) that* Pericles *indicates a conversion or new world view in Shakespeare and argues that a visit to his daughter in Stratford initiated this change. Thus, claims Harris, Shakespeare's subsequent plays feature maiden-heroines and reunited families, and, in this light,* "Pericles is an incarnation of Shakespeare himself."]

[In] *Pericles, The Winter's Tale* and *The Tempest* we have a totally new figure that of a young innocent girl. As we have seen Shakespeare showed his grief for the death of his mother and the death of his son very plainly; we are now to learn what a profound impression his young daughter Judith made on him.

In that fatal year, 1608, Shakespeare's mother died. He was probably called back to Stratford by the news of his mother's illness, and there he came to know his daughter Judith intimately. . . . From this time on she lives for us in his art. To find her portrait in Marina of *Pericles,* in Perdita of *The Winter's Tale,* and in Miranda of *The Tempest* will surprise some readers, but the evidence is really quite sufficient. It should strike everyone that all these plays are warmed, so to speak, with the joy of reunited kinsfolk. All these maiden-heroines, too, have abstract names and are all manifestly portraits of the same girl, who was lost to her father (Perdita) and is now admired by him (Miranda). She is dutiful and sweet tempered, but above all modest in mind and body. . . . [All] Shakespeare's pictures of girls before his breakdown were tainted with coarseness which often reached the impossible of uncharacteristic lewdness; but Miranda, Perdita, and Marina proclaim themselves virtuous at all costs. Instead of Juliet's and Portia's astounding freedom of speech we have now a careful avoidance by his maidens of suggestive allusions.

The change is abrupt and marked, and in itself extraordinary. I can only explain it by the supposition that it was his daughter who brought Shakespeare to better knowledge. (pp. 228-30)

I find the master on almost every page in *Pericles.* The character of Pericles is manifestly Shakespeare's work from beginning to end: he is, indeed, an incarnation of Shakespeare himself, and his words are curiously characteristic and beautiful. Take almost his first speech in the first scene of the first act, when the daughter of Antiochus enters:

> See where she comes *apparell'd like the spring,*
> *Graces her subjects, and her thoughts the king*
> *Of every virtue gives renown to men!*
>
> Her face the book of praises, where is read,
> Nothing but curious pleasures as from thence,
> Sorrow were ever raz'd, and testy wrath
> Could never be her mild companion. . . .
>
> [I. i. 12-18]

Where else but in Shakespeare could one find anything like the magnificent lines I have put in italics? Swinburne's idea of a "lean and barren style" [see excerpt above, 1880] is amusing. I wonder how many finer lines there are in all the treasury of English verse than this:

> See where she comes apparell'd like the spring

The very soul of Shakespeare is in the divine phrase; and what an optimist he was even to the end; he will always have it that it is "virtue gives renown to men," whereas surely it is the extraordinary, the abnormal whether for good or evil; the "sport," in fact. Nero will probably be remembered for his crimes as long as Marcus Aurelius for virtue. (pp. 231-32)

Once we accept the fact that Pericles is an incarnation of Shakespeare himself and that the play is his, two points must interest us. First of all, *Pericles* was one of Shakespeare's most popular plays; it was therefore condemned by the envious Jonson as "a mouldy tale" [see excerpt above, 1629]. Its popularity was chiefly due to the scenes in the brothel. Did Shakespeare deliberately invent these scenes to win the applause of the many. I believe he did just as he beat the patriotic drum in *Henry V.,* long after he had ceased to feel very patriotic. Secondly, what most surprised Shakespeare in his daughter Judith-Marina was her modesty. Her innate purity, indeed, astonished him to such a degree, impressed him so sincerely, that he shows it to us by placing her in a brothel and depicting her as immediately converting all comers and even the lewd servant to belief in her angelic innocence. And she carries it all through with a high hand. In spite of his disillusions and despairings, Shakespeare still idealizes life to an extraordinary extent. (pp. 236-37)

> *Frank Harris, ''Shakespeare's Daughter As Marina, Perdita, Miranda,'' in his* The Women of Shakespeare, *Methuen & Co. Ltd., 1911, pp. 227-53.*

H. DUGDALE SYKES   (essay date 1918)

[*In the following excerpt, Sykes challenges F. G. Fleay's argument that* Pericles *was originally composed by Shakespeare and altered by George Wilkins and William Rowley (see excerpt above, 1874), proposing instead that the play was first written by Wilkins and later revised by Shakespeare. The position that* Pericles *is Shakespeare's revision of Wilkins's play remains popular among critics, but Henry David Gray (1925) and F. D. Hoeniger (1960) have both argued that other Elizabethan dramatists wrote the original* Pericles.]

Though there are still critics who, like Professor [George] Saintsbury [see Additional Bibliography], are disposed to regard any attempt to allocate parts of *Pericles, Prince of Tyre,* to a dramatist other than Shakespeare as a ''hazardous piece of hariolation,'' the view that George Wilkins, the author of *The Miseries of Enforced Marriage,* was associated with him as part-author of the play is one that has gradually gained ground. If it cannot be said to have won general acceptance, it has at least secured a substantial following of competent Shakespearean scholars.

The evidence in support of this view has never yet been presented in anything like a complete form. Even if that already adduced by [Nikolas] Delius and [Robert] Boyle [see Additional Bibliography] had been collated—as it might have been thirty-five years ago—it would have been seen that the presence of Wilkins' hand in *Pericles* was not a matter open to question. The precise *extent* of his share in its composition is another matter, and one that necessarily presents a problem difficult to solve. Nevertheless, . . . it is possible without resort to anything in the nature of ''hariolation'' to allocate certain parts of *Pericles* to Wilkins. It is possible, for instance, to demonstrate his authorship of the whole of the first two Acts (including the Gower choruses) to the satisfaction of any person not obstinately determined to shut his eyes and ears to the evidence. To this task I shall first devote myself. But I hope to do more than this, and to show conclusively that Wilkins was also concerned in the later part of the play. The conclusion at which I have arrived, as the result of a prolonged study of its text, is that it was originally planned and written by Wilkins throughout, that as it now stands the first two acts are his unaided work, and that the rest of the play, though freely revised by Shakespeare, nevertheless contains a substantial substratum of Wilkins material. . . . If Shakespeare's concern in the play is as small as I believe it to have been, it was not without good reason that [John] Heminge and [Henry] Condell omitted it from the folio edition of his works. (pp. 143-44)

Wilkins' avowed authorship of *The Painful Adventures of Pericles* makes the relation between that prose narrative and the play of *Pericles* a matter of prime importance in the enquiry

before us. . . . The point now to be considered—obviously one of great importance in its bearing upon the authorship of the play—is as to how far the language of the novel coincides with that of the play.

On this subject there is a direct conflict of testimony between [J. Payne] Collier [see Additional Bibliography] and Fleay [see excerpt above, 1874]. Collier says that the novel ''very much adopts the language of the play.'' This statement Fleay, for some inexplicable reason, has thought fit to deny. Collier has doubtless many crimes to answer for in the way of falsification of evidence and misrepresentation of fact, but this is not one of them. Not only does the novel of Pericles ''very much adopt the language of the play,'' but it contains a number of passages (some of them of a considerable length) almost word for word as they appear in the play. (pp. 146-47)

[The] ellipsis of the relative, the excessive use of antithesis, repetition of words within the line, and repetition of rimes,—which are the distinguishing characteristics of Wilkins' dramatic work, are to be noted throughout the first two acts of *Pericles,* including the choruses. When, added to this, we find that in *The Painful Adventure of Pericles* Wilkins gives us a fuller treatment in prose of the same version (or perversion) of the story of Apollonius of Tyre as that given in the drama, it will at least be admitted that the grounds for presuming his authorship of these two acts are very strong. But there is much stronger evidence yet to come. It remains to be shown that, apart from the ellipses, antitheses, and repetitions already noted, these acts are from beginning to end full of Wilkins' metaphors, allusions and tricks of style, and that there is scarcely a single distinctive feature of the text of this portion of the play that cannot be paralleled in Wilkins' work elsewhere. (pp. 158-59)

The Gower parts of acts I and II, as well as that of act III, differ from those of acts IV and V in that they are written in lines of four measures as against five measures in the later acts. Their language is so crabbed and elliptical, and the lines themselves are so destitute of poetic merit, that it is surprising that anyone could believe them to be Shakespeare's. . . . If, at least, the qualities common to these choruses and any authentic Shakespearean verse are held to justify a presumption of Shakespeare's authorship, it seems to me that there is no contemporary poet or poetaster whose claims are not entitled to consideration. But as an actual fact there is no reason to suppose that anyone has ever written verses like them. Their author has made an attempt to reproduce the language of a bygone age with a dismal lack of success—for anything less in the style of Gower than the affected, unnatural diction of the *Pericles* choruses it would be difficult to imagine—and this attempt bears the impress of Wilkins' hand as plainly as everything else that he wrote. (pp. 159-60)

The author of these two acts was some person who was well acquainted with Sidney's *Arcadia.* Three passages derived from that romance have been noted by Steevens. (p. 174)

It will be admitted that the borrowing of another man's figures of speech in this way is unlike Shakespeare; at any rate there is not a single play in the folio that contains verbal echoes of Sidney's romance. Is there any reason to identify Wilkins with this person who introduces scraps of the *Arcadia* into his text? There is: for he does the same thing in his novel. (pp. 174-75)

Here is the crowning proof of Wilkins' authorship of the first two acts of the play. They were written by a man who has all his tricks of style and grammar, who uses his favourite metaphors and allusions and who, finally, borrows, as he does, from the *Arcadia*. I shall assume that no further evidence is needed. That Wilkins wrote every word of this part of the play, as I firmly believe, is of necessity not capable of demonstration, but for my part nowhere in these acts do I find a single line or image bearing the Shakespearean stamp, nor anything beyond the power of Wilkins to execute. . . .

Having established the point that the author of the "true history of the play of Pericles" was the author of a large portion of the text of the play itself, I will now give the reasons for my belief that the novel was not—as is commonly supposed—based upon the play, but that, on the contrary, the play is a dramatization of the novel. (p. 176)

It is commonly assumed that the novel cannot have been written until after the play because of the words that appear on the title page of the novel: "*The Painfull Adventures of Pericles, Prince of Tyre*. Being the true History of the play of Pericles, as it was lately presented by the worthy and ancient Poet, John Gower."

Let it first be noted that both this title "The Painfull Adventures of Pericles" and the running title "A patterne of the painefulle Adventures of Pericles Prince of Tyre" are taken from that of Twine's earlier work "The Patterne of Painefulle Adventures," thus at once giving us notice that Wilkins was directly acquainted with Twine's book, and that his knowledge of the story of Apollonius was not derived merely from the play. Now what does Wilkins mean when he describes his novel as being "the true history of the play of *Pericles*?" The words "*true history*" are surely somewhat curious. Whatever else they may mean, they do not mean that the novel accurately reproduces the story of the play, nor that it presents merely a fuller treatment of the incidents set forth in the play. On the contrary, the story given in the novel differs in many important respects from that found in the play, especially towards the close. Obvious as it may seem at first sight that in his title-page he avows his indebtedness to the play, I feel confident that Wilkins never intended anything of the kind. If he had meant to imply that his novel contained an account of the story of Pericles as told in the play, surely he would have called it simply "the history of the play of Pericles." He does not so describe it because it is *not* the history of the play of *Pericles,* i.e. it is the true and original version of the story of Pericles used in the play. It is not, I think, putting a strained construction upon the title to take it in this sense, indeed if it is construed otherwise the word "true" is worse than meaningless, it is grossly misleading. . . . Wilkins' only references to the play are on the title-page and in the "argument" prefixed to his "history." No doubt in offering his original prose version to the public he desired to profit by the popularity of the play, and it would be then that he would add the references to the stage version that have been construed as an admission that he had based his narrative upon it.

Let us look at the allusions to *Gower* in the novel and see how they fit in with the hypothesis that the references to the play were added afterwards to help the sale of the novel. Gower, as we know, is the "presenter" of the play, appearing before every act and at other points during its progress to tell us of incidents in the story of Pericles that it is essential for us to know in order that we may comprehend what is presented on the stage. . . . At any rate, whether his introduction is due to Shakespeare's skill or to Wilkins' lack of it, in the play as it stands, Gower is the *deus ex machina;* his presence is indispensable. But there is obviously no need for him at all in the novel, and only if it describes the story as given in the play shall we expect to find Gower figuring as a character in the novel. And what part does Gower in fact play in the novel? Wilkins makes a great parade of his *name*, it is true. It appears on the title-page, together with a picture of the poet, and again in the concluding lines of the prefatory "argument." . . . After this advertisement of his name, and the prominence given to it in the list of characters, is it not somewhat surprising to find that nowhere in the text of "this historie" is Gower's name once mentioned? Observe that I say in the *text*, for there is indeed one more reference to him. It is in the first words of the title to the first chapter. Almost all Wilkins' chapter headings are copied from those in Twine's novel, and here he has altered the heading of Twine's first chapter by inserting the words "Wherein *Gower* describes" before Twine's "How Antiochus committed incest with his owne daughter and beheaded such as sued to her for marriage if they could not resolve his questions." But for this addition to the title we could have no idea that it was Gower who was describing these things, or any of the ensuing adventures of Pericles. He does not even appear at the end of the narrative to give us his blessing or bid us farewell. The prefatory announcement to the contrary notwithstanding, Gower is in no sense the "presenter" of the prose story, nor is his name as a fact "mentioned in the history."

The next point is one that has been much discussed and its significance as bearing upon Wilkins' claim to a share in the play—to my mind, unconvincingly—contested. It is that Wilkins, in the dedication of his novel, speaks of it as "a poor infant of his brain." . . . (pp. 177-80)

What else can Wilkins mean when he terms this story an "infant of his brain" and himself its "father" but that he was responsible for its *conception*? . . .

In what sense can it be said to be his "infant," if the story was lifted bodily from the play? If all Wilkins did was to cast it into narrative form, contributing only a few embellishments, then nothing but the clothing of the infant was his, and not all of that. That he should claim the parentage of a story that had formed the plot of a contemporary play, *and was based upon that play,* is all but incredible. The story is "a poor infant of his brain" and it comes "naked" to its patron, with no clothing but its father's love,—in the condition, that is, in which it was born. If my theory is the right one, this infant had already appeared in public, but then it was not naked, it wore dramatic clothing, part of which had been supplied by Shakespeare. (p. 181)

As I read the evidence, the 'true history' of the play is this:

1. It was planned and drafted by Wilkins throughout.

2. Wilkins founded it upon a prose romance he had himself composed, but which he did not publish until after the play was performed—*The Painful Adventures of Pericles Prince of Tyre*.

3. He hit upon the device of the Gower choruses as a means of escaping the difficulties, which he had not sufficient skill to overcome, of representing the whole story in regular dramatic form.

4. The play as printed in the quarto represents Wilkins' draft as revised by Shakespeare. All the Gower choruses and Acts I and II are Wilkins' unaided work, the remainder of the three later acts having been altered and improved by Shakespeare.

Whether my theory is accepted in its entirety or not, I hope I have at least removed any possible doubt of the accuracy of the view that Wilkins was substantially the author of *Pericles*, and that Shakespeare's part in it did not extend beyond a hasty and incomplete revision of the later acts of the play. (pp. 202-03)

> H. Dugdale Sykes, "Wilkins and Shakespeare's 'Pericles, Prince of Tyre'," in his Sidelights on Shakespeare, The Shakespeare Head Press, 1919, pp. 143-203.

HENRY DAVID GRAY (essay date 1925)

[*In the excerpt below, Gray continues the debate on the authorship of* Pericles, *arguing that it was Thomas Heywood, not George Wilkins, who wrote the non-Shakespearean parts of the play. For further commentary on the authorship of* Pericles, *see the excerpts by George Steevens (1780), F. G. Fleay (1874), H. Dugdale Sykes (1919), and F. D. Hoeniger (1960).*]

The best proof, to me, that Wilkins did not write the first two acts of *Pericles* is the proof that Heywood did. I wish to examine his claim to the first two acts as they stand; to the choruses and brothel scenes; and to the substratum of the scenes which Shakespeare revised, which I shall call for convenience the Shakespearean scenes. If I succeed in establishing this claim, I feel that I shall be adding as much to Shakespeare's credit by subtraction as to Heywood's by addition. (pp. 508-09)

Pericles, Prince of Tyre, belongs in the group of romantic adventure dramas of which *Fortune by Land and Sea* and *The Fair Maid of the West* are examples. These follow somewhat the chronicle-play method in which each episode is given for its own sake. Such a method is essential if the dramatist follows his source closely and his source is a narrative of incidents. . . . The most obvious similarity of *Pericles* to many of the plays of Heywood is in the particular use it makes of the chorus and dumb show. "Old Gower" presents *Pericles* in just the way that "Old Homer" presents the first three [plays of Heywood's pentalogy] the *Ages*. There is a special problem in connection with the choruses, as some of them are in a different meter, and have been claimed for the reviser. But those which admittedly go with the original drama are sufficient to show the structural similarity, with which I am now concerned.

In addition to the dumb shows, there are several bits of pageantry which are in accordance with Heywood's practice. . . . It has often been observed that Heywood was fond of storms; and banquets are served in so many of his dramas that the absence of one forms rather an [exception]. My point is merely that *Pericles* is fairly typical of Heywood in that it is a loosely connected series of episodes, that it keeps close to its source, that it supplies the incidents not otherwise given by choruses which introduce dumb shows midway, and that it attempts to supply a dramatic lack by a liberal use of the spectacular. (pp. 509-10)

The illustrations from *Pericles* which I have thus far used have been drawn from Acts I and II. In these acts we see a brave and generous hero driven from his country by misfortune and through no fault of his own (*Fair Maid of the West, Fortune by Land and Sea*). We find him as an unknown knight overcoming all the others in battle (*Four Prentices of London*). We find him, thus unknown, chatting in friendly fashion with honest and hard working commoners (*Edward IV*). We have in Helicanus the perfectly submissive and loyal henchman (*Royal King and Loyal Subject*); in Thaisa a lady who tells her love without being asked and, in despite of her father's apparent (but not real) opposition, engineers her marriage (*Fair Maid of the Exchange*). These are characters and situations with which Heywood loves to deal. (p. 512)

The particular characteristic of the brothel scenes which has made it difficult or impossible for some of us to regard them as Shakespeare's is that they dwell upon a harrowing situation for its own sake, that they pile up filthy details in order to squeeze out of the situation all the sensational appeal that there is in it. That this is particularly the way of Heywood becomes increasingly apparent on a more careful analysis of his plays. Heywood is equally fond of portraying wantonness luxuriating in indulgence, and of showing innocence and virtue triumphant over tyranny and temptation. He is also capable of representing a good woman as yielding with scarcely a struggle and repenting most pathetically. This situation comes first to mind because of its employment in *A Woman Killed with Kindness, The English Traveller*, and *Edward IV*. We recall, also, that he employs wantonness for humorous effects. But the *Pericles* method is entirely in accordance with his genius. (pp. 514-15)

Now the brothel scenes in *Pericles* are derived not from Gower, the primary source, but from Twine; for it is only there that Marina (I use the *Pericles* name to avoid confusion) meets in a brothel the man whom she is destined to marry. In Twine's narrative Marina has a genuinely pathetic and moving appeal, and the response of Lysimachus is much more credible and effective. Here for once the story is finer than the drama. It is not the way of Shakespeare to sink below the level of his source; nor would it be, so far as I am aware, like any other Elizabethan dramatist than Heywood to sacrifice a really pathetic scene for a set speech and an incredible response to the power of eloquence. . . . (pp. 515-16)

If it is like Heywood [to] dwell upon these scenes for their sensational value, to play up the dramatic contrast of innocence in the grip of tyranny and vice, and to rescue Marina by a speech to Boult which is a mixture of the didactic and disgusting . . . it is also like him to alter his manner in the latter part of the play. (p. 516)

There are smaller similarities between the dramatic action and characterization of *Pericles* and Heywood's recognized dramas, such as the "aside" information that a character "must dissemble," or the frequent inquiring of the country parentage, and birth of a character, but these may be safely neglected. I mention them only as among the things one notices in *Pericles* when he has Heywood in mind; it is the frequency with which similar expedients are used that deepens one's conviction as he reads. (pp. 516-17)

One who investigates a problem of this sort usually comes upon some matters that make against his thesis. I have never tried to hold back such considerations, nor will I now. It is strange that a man who placed so high a value upon learning should give the name of Pericles to Apollonius; Heywood's sense of fitness would be shocked, it seems, by all the connotations which such a name would carry with it. Pericles himself is named in *The Man-Hater* . . . as shielding Anaxagoras from the vengeance of Jupiter; the author who could make such a reference would not be likely to choose so inappropriate a name for the hero of a medieval romance. Or was Heywood thinking of Sidney's Pyrocles, associated in the *Arcadia* with Musidorus?

I offer this as an argument on the other side; but weighing it fairly against the evidence for Heywood, I cannot find that it is by any means sufficient to reverse my judgment. I know of no other objection. As Professor [Joseph Quincy] Adams has said, we know so little of Heywood's early activities that there can be no serious objection to attributing to him a play which by internal evidence seems to be his. How the King's men came into possession of the play cannot be told, but that they did so is not without precedent. (pp. 527-28)

Is it not possible, therefore, that Jonson was thinking of "Heywood's *Pericles*" in his contemptuous reference to the play [see excerpt above, 1629],—as little concerned with Shakespeare's revision of it as were the Folio editors? . . . None of Jonson's references to the man he loved and honored "this side idolatry as much as any" has the tang of the *Pericles* slur. It is difficult to believe that between the high tribute in the Folio and the critical admiration in *Timber,* Jonson should have made so vicious a gibe at the dead Shakespeare. It seems . . . that he must have thought of *Pericles* as the distinctive work of an imitative but successful living playwright. The somewhat fatuous, eminently successful, and blandly pilfering Heywood was apparently a leading member of the "Play-club" at the time when *The New Inn* scored its failure; in 1633 he had had "either an entire hand or at least a main finger" in 220 plays. If he did as much work in *Pericles* as seems like him, neither Jonson nor the Folio editors can be held to account for ignoring Shakespeare's connection with this drama. (pp. 528-29)

> *Henry David Gray, "Heywood's 'Pericles,' Revised by Shakespeare," in* PMLA 40, Vol. XL, No. 3, September, 1925, pp. 507-29.

G. WILSON KNIGHT (essay date 1929)

[*Knight is one of the most influential Shakespearean critics of the twentieth century; he helped shape a new interpretive approach to Shakespeare's work and promoted a greater appreciation of many of the plays. In his studies* The Wheel of Fire *(1930) and* The Shakespearian Tempest *(1932), Knight rejected criticism which emphasizes sources, character analysis, psychology, and ethics and outlined his principles of interpretation which, he claimed, would "replace that chaos by drawing attention to the true Shakespearian unity." Knight argued that this unity lay in Shakespeare's poetic use of images and symbols—particularly in the opposition of "tempests" and "music." He also maintained that a play's spatial aspects, or "atmosphere," should be as closely considered as the temporal elements of the plot if one is "to see the whole play in space as well as time." In the following excerpt from his study* Myth and Miracle *(1929), which was later republished as a chapter in his* The Crown of Life *(1947), Knight discusses the significance of these images of tempest and music. In* Pericles, *says Knight, "the author is moved by vision, not fancy," and he adds that, with the exception of* The Tempest *and parts of* Antony and Cleopatra, *"the latter half of* Pericles *has no equivalent in transcendental apprehension in all Shakespeare." Knight notes many similarities of theme and image between* Pericles *and the other romances, and his overall positive assessment is indicative of the growing appreciation of the play in the twentieth century. For additional commentary by Knight on* Pericles, *see the excerpt below (1947).*]

In this essay I shall consider the Final Plays, whose significance has not yet been recognized, as the culmination of a series which starts about the middle of Shakespeare's writing career and exposes to a careful analysis a remarkable coherence and significance; and, by throwing them into direct relation with their predecessors, show that those improbabilities of plot texture and curiosities of the supernatural descending on the purely human interest—as in *Pericles* and *Cymbeline*—are not the freaks of a wearied imagination, as has been usually supposed; nor the work of that convenient 'incompetent coadjutor' who is too often at hand when necessary to solve the difficulties of Shakespeare interpretation; but rather the inevitable development of the questioning, the pain, the profundity and grandeur of the plays they succeed. (p. 9)

The stories of *Pericles* and *The Winter's Tale* are remarkably alike. In both the hero loses his wife and daughter just after the birth of his child; in both the idea of a child's helplessness is synchronized with a sea-storm of the usual Shakespearian kind; in both the wife and child are miraculously restored after a long passage of time; and the revival of Thaisa, and the restoration of Marina and Hermione are accompanied by music. These plays are throughout impregnated by an atmosphere of mysticism. The theology is pseudo-Hellenistic. The Delphic oracle and a prophetic dream occur in *The Winter's Tale;* Hermione is restored to Leontes in a 'chapel' to the sound of music, Thaisa to Pericles in the temple of Diana, with the full circumstance of religious ceremonial. The goddess Diana appears to Pericles. A reader sensitive to poetic atmosphere must necessarily feel the awakening light of some religious or metaphysical truth symbolized in the plot and attendant machinery of these two plays.

Cerimon, who raises Thaisa from the dead, is a recluse and visionary. . . . The body of Thaisa, supposed dead, is cast ashore by the tempest in a coffin. Cerimon, by his magic, and with the aid of fire and music, revives her. . . . This incident, with the exquisite conception of the character of Cerimon, and the reviving of Thaisa, is one of the pinnacles of Shakespeare's art: this scene and those of the restoration to Pericles of his long-lost daughter and consort which follow, are alone sufficient to establish my thesis that the author is moved by vision, not fancy; is creating not merely entertainment, but myth in the Platonic sense. . . . The blindness of past Shakespearian criticism is at no point more completely in evidence than in the comments on this play. To the discerning mind it will be evident that we are here confronted with the furthest reach of Shakespeare's poetic and visionary power: if we except *The Tempest,* the latter half of *Pericles* has no equivalent in transcendental apprehension in all Shakespeare but the latter half of *Antony and Cleopatra* which on the plane of myth and symbolism it may be considered to interpret.

Almost of an equal beauty is the restoration of Thaisa in the Temple of Diana. . . .

> *Pericles.*   Immortal Dian!
> *Thaisa.*   Now I know you better.
> When we with tears parted Pentapolis,
> The king, my father, gave you such a ring.
>   *(Shows a ring)*
> *Pericles.* This, this: no more, you gods! your present kindness
> Makes my past miseries sport. . . .
>   [V. iii. 37-41]

That last thought of Pericles is to be echoed again, with clear religious and universal significance, in the Vision of Jupiter in *Cymbeline.* Now if, as is probable, the greater part of *Pericles* is the work of Shakespeare grafted on to an earlier play of different authorship, of which signs are apparent in some of the early scenes, it is not surprising that, after his composition of these supreme latter acts, he found another plot of the same kind for his next play; nor is it surprising that that next play,

The Winter's Tale, though more perfect as a whole, lacks something of the paradisal radiance of *Pericles.* The great artist does not well to repeat himself: in *Pericles,* as the writer handles an old theme, some mystic apprehension of a life that conquers death has sprung to vivid form, as it were, spontaneously: a shaft of light penetrating into the very heart of death. . . . It will be sufficient here to point the recurrence of the themes of birth, restoration, tempest, and music, and to speak shortly of their significance in both plays. (pp. 14-17)

In Shakespeare the failing of love's faith is essentially a metaphysical difficulty, and one with the difficulty of loss in death: conversely, 'perfect love casteth out fear'. The infidelity-theme of *The Winter's Tale* is thus not essentially different from the loss of Thaisa at sea. In both we see the tempests of temporal conditions seemingly at war with the otherness of a purely spiritual experience.

In both these plays we have the theme of a child bereft of its mother and threatened by storm and thunder. The emphasis on tempests is insistent, and the suggestion is clearly that of the pitifulness and helplessness of humanity born into a world of tragic conflict. That the tempest is percurrent in Shakespeare as a symbol of tragedy need not be demonstrated here at length. Its symbolic significance is patent from the earliest to the latest of the plays—in metaphor, in simile, in long or short description, in stage directions. The individual soul is the 'bark' putting out to sea in a 'tempest': the image occurs again and again. . . . The theme of helpless childhood synchronized with storm in *Pericles* and *The Winter's Tale* . . . is significant, just as the tempests in *Julius Caesar, Macbeth* and *Lear* are significant: poetic symbols of the storm and stress of human life, the turbulence of temporal events reflecting and causing tempestuous passion in the heart of man. Lastly, in these two plays we have the music which accompanies resurrection and reunion. This music may seem to perform a dual function: first, to suggest, as a symbol of pure aesthetic delight, the mystic nature of the act being performed; second, to anaesthetize the critical faculty, as does the overture in a theatre, and prepare the mind for some extraordinary event. But these are in reality twin aspects of the same function: for music, like erotic sight, raises the consciousness until it is in time with a reality beyond the reach of wisdom. . . . Music in Shakespeare is ever the solace and companion of love, and love in Shakespeare the language of mysticism. For this reason the mystic happenings in these plays are accompanied by the theme of music. (pp. 17-19)

[In the] plots of *Pericles* and *The Winter's Tale,* . . . these miraculous and joyful conquests of life's tragedy are the expression, through the medium of drama, of a state of mind or soul in the writer directly in knowledge—or supposed knowledge—of a mystic and transcendent fact as to the true nature and purpose of the sufferings of humanity. My primary intention here is not to insist on the truth of the immortality shadowed forth in these plays; but simply to indicate that they are of this mystic kind, so that we may allot them their proper place in our assessment of Shakespeare's achievement. . . . Now the supreme value to man is always love. What more perfect form, then, could such a myth take than that of the restoration to Pericles of his Thaisa and Marina, so long and so mistakenly supposed lost? It is, indeed, noticeable that these plays do not aim at revealing a temporal survival of death: rather at the thought that death is a delusion. What was thought dead is in reality alive. In them we watch the fine flowers of a mystic state of soul bodied into the forms of drama. The

parables of Jesus, which, through the medium of narrative, leave with the reader what is pre-eminently a sense of quality rather than a memory of events, are of the same kind. *Pericles* and *The Winter's Tale* show us the quality of immortality in terms of victorious love welling up in the beautiful plot of loss and reunion. . . . (p. 22)

> G. Wilson Knight, ''Myth and Miracle,'' in his The Crown of Life: Essays in Interpretation of Shakespeare's Final Plays, *Methuen & Co. Ltd., 1948, pp. 9-31.*

CAROLINE F.E. SPURGEON   (essay date 1935)

[*Spurgeon's* Shakespeare's Imagery *(1935) inaugurated the ''image-pattern analysis'' method of studying Shakespeare's plays, one of the most widely used methods of the mid-twentieth century. In this work, she interprets the thematic structure of the plays through an examination of patterns in the imagery. Spurgeon also sought to learn about Shakespeare's personality from a study of his images, a course which few of her disciples followed. Since publication of her book, earlier works on image patterns in Shakespeare have been discovered, but none was so important in the history of Shakespearean criticism as Spurgeon's. Her view that*

Act IV. Scene i. Leonine, Marina, and Pirates (1796). From the Art Collection of the Folger Shakespeare Library.

Pericles *lacks the kind of "running motive" she discerns in the other plays is challenged by James Wood (1970).*]

Pericles alone of the romances has no sign of any running 'motive' or continuity of picture or thought in the imagery, a fact sufficient in itself to throw grave doubts on its authorship.

The proportion and subjects of the images in *Pericles* are, however, quite in keeping with Shakespeare's other plays: though as a whole they seem rather thin, and there is a very small proportion (eleven of the hundred and nine) of poetical images. A certain selection, though they fall under Shakespeare's usual headings, are flat, general, uninteresting and un-Shakespearian (e.g. the diamonds round a crown, spring and summer, the unplucked flower, 'groves, being topp'd', storm, snowball, 'pretty wrens', 'angel-eagle'). On the other hand, we find quite a fair number of images which are markedly 'Shakespearian' in quality. (p. 291)

> Caroline F.E. Spurgeon, *"Leading Motives in the Romances,"* in her Shakespeare's Imagery and What It Tells Us, *1935. Reprint by Cambridge at the University Press, 1971, pp. 291-308.*

D. G. JAMES (essay date 1937)

[*James argues that because myth can express supernatural meaning, Shakespeare's romances contain a mythology that gives the plays "a degree of explicit significance . . . not present in the comedies or the tragedies." The essential myth in these plays, James says, is that of lost and recovered royalty. He states that "it is in* Pericles *that we have the most perfect presentation" of this pattern, which creates a unity of symbol and meaning not found in the later romances. James also comments on the myth of resurrection in* Pericles. *He notes that throughout the romances there is an alternation "between a sense of Shakespeare's high metaphysical symbolism and a sense of the silly."*]

Our chief concern is with what is beyond the tragedies, that is to say, with what happened after the failure of Shakespeare's imagination to 'idealize and unify' the world of human experience as he faced it in the tragedies. For Shakespeare's 'tragic period' ended as Shakespeare became, like Wordsworth's soldier, one

> Remembering the importance of his theme
> But feeling it no longer.

He had failed to solve the 'problem' which he 'presented' in his tragedies, to apprehend unity and harmony informing human affairs; he had seen the necessarily tragic character of human life. In that apprehension lay, for Shakespeare, as for Keats and Wordsworth, peace of mind. And it was this peace of mind which gave us the last plays. But these last are not among the greatest of Shakespeare's plays, for the simple reason that they are not plays; they are no longer, that is to say, of the order of imagination which is 'human and dramatic'—they are of the order of imagination which is 'enthusiastic and meditative.' In them he is no longer interested in humanity—his interest is elsewhere. It is a platitude of criticism that the later plays are the writings of a man careless of what he is doing; poetry is no longer a passion or a necessity to him, and he finally gives it up and goes home. (p. 207)

Shakespeare, having failed to see human life as a neat, orderly, and satisfying unity, had resort to myth for the conveyance of his new imaginative apprehension of life. But his mythology was not Christian; as long as he wrote poetry he tried to maintain its independence of traditional forms. Yet he must quickly have come to see the impossibility of what he was trying to do. Several times he tried to recast the essential symbols which are present in all the later plays. But however highly we may praise the plays, they exert, as attempted mythologies, little of the sheer compulsion exerted by the comedies and tragedies as conveying Shakespeare's former sense of life. No doubt Shakespeare's instinct in endeavouring to avoid a frankly mythical form which would use the language of religion was a sound one; he wanted a poetry which would, as far as possible, show forth his final attitude to life and death, without surrendering to traditional religious language. But the result is necessarily unsatisfactory. The plays are comparatively formless (with the exception of *The Tempest,* in which he made his last supreme effort), and thereby show a failure of expressiveness. The symbols are there; but they rarely liberate compulsive significances. We hover between apprehension of momentous significances, of a luxurious imagination, and of absurdities. And if we need a sign that Shakespeare was aware of this failure of expressiveness, we need only observe the ways in which he repeatedly used a single theme for his purpose—a curious lack of versatility for the man who wrote the comedies and tragedies with all their great variety of plot. Labouring, with the true instinct of the great artist, to avoid direct expression of belief, he failed nevertheless to create a mythology of adequate expressiveness. The making of a mythology is too great a work for one mind, though that mind be Shakespeare's. Moreover a mythology implies an accompanying belief; and Shakespeare sought to keep his symbols pure, uncontaminated by assertion. (pp. 210-11)

Yet the last plays are a renewal; a new light had somehow been borrowed, a light difficult of conveyance, but which Shakespeare nevertheless struggled to shed. But the light was not merely the destroyer of tragic darkness; it was not the light which the comedies shed. And its difference demanded a new kind of artistic creation, unique in drama, so unique that it can hardly be called drama. For it is not concerned with expression of imagination of the human situation. And its uniqueness may be said to consist in this, that for the first time in his poetic life, Shakespeare seems to be concerned to *say* something with a degree of explicitness greater than ever before. For if we are right in believing that in the later plays there is an essential mythology; and if a mythology be a mode of saying something which evades lucid and intelligible expression in the prose of statement; then we may believe that in the last plays is a degree of explicit significance and meaning which is not present in the comedies or the tragedies. . . . But in the last plays we feel Shakespeare is no longer primarily concerned to show forth a human situation, from which we can, if we will, extract a meaning; we feel rather that while what is set forth is done in a way to capture our imagination, the plots yet contain a direct significance which is intended to be released in the course of imaginative effort. For myth is essentially the point at which dream and exposition, imagination and conviction, meet; the two aspects are essential to its existence. And if therefore there is myth in these plays we cannot fail to be sensitive to them both. The purpose of myth is the showing forth of that which cannot be set out by the representation of a merely human situation; its function is the conveyance, to whatever degree possible, of the divine as well as the human. Yet it is the case that to try to extract its significances, and to convey them in the prose of statement, is at once a desecration of the work of art, and, in any case, an impossibility; for the justification of the work of art is that it is only thus that an adequate conveyance of the writer's mind can be made. (pp. 212-13)

The essential myth which runs throughout the last plays, *Pericles, Cymbeline, The Winter's Tale,* and *The Tempest,* is the finding of what is lost. Pericles loses and finds Marina; Cymbeline loses and finds his sons; Leontes loses and finds Perdita; Alonso loses and finds Ferdinand. This myth, however, is complicated in certain ways. There is throughout the plays another myth, which is run into the first, namely, the bringing to life of what is dead. Thaisa is literally raised from the dead; Imogen revives from what is taken for death, and Posthumous too had been thought to be dead; Hermione comes to life, and Ferdinand had been thought dead by Alonso. So closely run together are the two myths that it is difficult, if at all possible, to pick them apart. Thus Pericles finds Marina after thinking she had died; the sons of Cymbeline were thought to have been dead; Perdita was thought to be dead, as was Ferdinand. These two myths, essentially one in idea, are again fused with a third, namely, that of the recovery of a lost royalty. Pericles is compelled to relinquish his throne, but later returns; the sons of Cymbeline live as wild huntsmen, but finally are restored to royal estate; Posthumous too in a measure fits in here, for he was of noble descent, at one time favourite of the court, is banished, and returns to Imogen; Perdita lives as a shepherdess; Prospero and Miranda are outcasts from a kingdom but are finally restored. This again, it will be seen, runs into the former mythical elements and becomes an integral part of it. Again, there is a fourth element, namely, that of the seeking of what is lost by a royal personage; if what is lost be royal, a royal person seeks it out, or is at least instrumental in its recovery. Thus, in *Pericles,* Pericles is brought back through the agency of Helicanus who has refused the princedom of Tyre in the absence of Pericles; Marina is restored to Pericles largely through the help of Lysimachus, the governor of Mytilene; Posthumous is sought by Imogen, and it is she who falls in with Belarius and the sons of Cymbeline; Perdita is sought out by Florizel and Miranda wooed by Ferdinand. Between these pairs are ties of strongest attachment, even when, as in the case of Imogen and her brothers, they are ignorant of each other's identity; and Lysimachus finally marries Marina, Florizel Perdita, and Ferdinand Miranda.

The mythical situation is however not yet fully described. There is constant repetition of situations in which a lost person is placed in a position of peculiar helplessness. Marina is born at sea and, her mother dead, is parted from her father; the sons of Cymbeline are stolen as small children, and no mention is made throughout the play of their mother; Posthumous' name is significant; Perdita is carried away and exposed, and her mother is powerless in prison; Miranda, motherless, is also exposed to the greatest danger. Such is their condition as little children; and on growing up further grave dangers await them. . . . Yet from these dangers they are rescued. Moreover about them all is an essential royalty of character; indeed the praises of them, sung by other characters, seem to throw about them something of divinity.

Finally, we must observe that in these plays all the disturbing events recorded are, by the hatred, suspicion, jealousy which give rise to them, a striking contrast to an original condition of peace, harmony, love and friendship, which is suddenly disrupted. *Pericles* indeed begins with Antiochus; but immediately and in contrast appears the friendship of Pericles for Cleon and Dionyza and theirs for Pericles. But this strong and confident friendship is suddenly broken in upon by Dionyza's hatred of Marina. . . . The stories of the plays issue from a state of peace and love into which, after suffering and disloyalty, they again pass. (pp. 214-16)

Now it is to be observed that it is in *Pericles* that we have the most perfect representation of the myth of lost and recovered royalty; in none of the three later plays is it set out with the same simplicity and single-mindedness. This simplicity is achieved by the careful avoidance of a love story. Lysimachus does not become Marina's lover until after she is known for what she is. Indeed Lysimachus, if we look at him through the eyes of Florizel and Ferdinand, has a chilliness and conscious sense of royalty which is distasteful. . . . Lysimachus does not gain our admiration, as do the later heroes. And he does not do so because Shakespeare is strenuously keeping the issue of the play to Marina's restoration to royal status. For in the other plays the love interest is contradictory to the myth of royalty. . . . In other words, the introduction of the love stories acts against the significance which Shakespeare is attaching to his symbol of which Imogen, Florizel, and Ferdinand, so far from suffering a loss of royalty, would gladly yield it up. To this extent is the efficacy of the myth weakened; in *Pericles* alone did Shakespeare maintain the myth of royalty uncontaminated. And in the succeeding plays he had to run together his myth of royalty, of its loss and recovery, with another element, namely, that of willingness to abandon royalty in the presence of eclipsing beauty. This gives to them a lack of the simple significance which we derive from *Pericles.* (pp. 219-20)

Throughout these plays the heroes and heroines, whether or not they have suffered loss of royalty, take on 'a more than mortal seeming'. If in the tragedies the leading characters be kings, princes, leaders of state who show in the course of the play a certain and frail mortality, in these last plays the heroes and heroines are princes and princesses who, whether or not they bear the robes of royalty, are royal; who in poverty and suffering take on a divine bearing, and, so far from suffering death and disaster, are given at the close the full attributes of royalty. But in the reading of them it is the perfect beauty of these men and women in contrast to all others, not their mere royalty in contrast to the humble condition of all others, which occupies the eye of imagination. The external royalty is seen as an inadequate symbol to a superlative spiritual beauty. (p. 222)

In *Pericles* the symbol and significance are one; we are aware of the high destiny of the soul in and through the symbol of royalty. But in the later plays symbol and significance have fallen apart; the symbol is manifestly inadequate. (p. 223)

Thus whereas in *Pericles* the world which does not give recognition to Marina's royalty is a storm, or a bondage, to her; in *The Tempest* bondage is enough if it be bondage with Miranda. And it is to be noted that this double significance does not merely mark a difference in the usage of the symbol in *Pericles* on the one hand, and in the last three plays on the other. It is present in the last three plays themselves. For Shakespeare took over from *Pericles* the myth of royalty; it remains in all three essential to the plot of each. (pp. 223-24)

We may pass at this point to the theme of finding that which is lost. The circumstances in which the characters in each of the four plays are lost differ in each case. . . . It is, it need hardly be said, dangerous to seek a precise symbolism in all that is to be found in these plays. Yet here again, where a situation is repeated, in essence, four times, it is difficult to avoid the conclusion that in it is a clue to an important element in what Shakespeare was, in his last work, labouring to convey. We may believe therefore that in this part of his mythology, he is seeking to body forth his sense of the loss by man, through his own evil, of his most treasured possession, 'the jewel of his soul'. It is impossible to avoid the parallel with the constant use of the theme in the Gospels, the theme of the finding of that which is lost.

But let us in the first place concentrate on the loss. The loss is due to man's evil, which in each case is a sudden, inexplicable evil arising out of a former state of happiness, love, and loyalty. (pp. 227-28)

It is from outbursts of sheer evil, on the part of characters who in their former nature were otherwise, Dionyza and Cleon, Cymbeline, Leontes, Antonio, that the loss occurs. (p. 228)

In each case what is lost through the agency of this evil is a person of the greatest beauty and incomparable worth. And that person is in each case restored; and with that restoration comes the recovery, to those who have lost them, of their true nature. Pericles has no active evil to be purged from his nature; but he is brought out of desolation, and also sees the characters of Cleon and Dionyza in their true light. . . . Clearly, the most satisfactory interpretation we can place upon this striking repetition, in four plays, of a single theme, is Shakespeare's imagination of human life as a descent into a necessary tragedy and evil which is seen as a sudden irruption into what is originally perfect, and as a sudden loss of innocence; and as the recovery of a lost perfection, the achievement of a condition which is not merely an innocence but which, in its achievement, is an 'affliction' having

> a taste as sweet
> As any cordial comfort.
> [*The Winter's Tale*, V. iii. 76-7]
> (p. 229)

Such restoration, occasioning so 'notable a passion of wonder', does not however occur by accident. It is, in each case, however indirectly, brought about either by a royal personage or by a child of royal personage—a child who has not been lost. In all the plays royalty seeks out royalty, or, if it does not seek it out, recognizes it for what it is. It is the offices of Lysimachus, a royal person, which restore Marina to Pericles; and though Lysimachus does not love Marina at first sight, he recognizes her all-excelling worth. (p. 230)

Finally, we must notice the constant repetition of situations in which the dead return to life. (p. 231)

In *Pericles* [Shakespeare] literally resurrects Thaisa; but he resurrects her into the incredible stupidity of not attempting to find Pericles. Had she sought and found Pericles his plot would have been ruined, for she would have also sought Marina who would then never have been lost. Having been saved from tempest and transfigured by death, she at once becomes a more than usually silly mortal and is stored away in a temple. . . . Such situations, which he was under necessity to create, cut across the expression of his momentous purpose in these plays. And if we ask why he was under such necessity, the answer is because, although concerned primarily to convey his sense of the more than human, he struggled, as hard as he could, to do so without resorting, as Wordsworth and Keats in differing degrees did, to a mythology which frankly involves religious belief and language. He was right in refusing to do so. Yet by not doing so, he set himself the impossible task of conveying a sense of what lies beyond humanity through the use of human symbols. . . . So long as he was using men and women characters his purpose in seeking to convey imagination of something more than mortal was necessarily obscured. We alternate throughout the plays between a sense of Shakespeare's high metaphysical symbolism and a sense of the silly. His purpose

and his art were in conflict, and there was no resolution of it. For if his purpose was to command our imagination with a sense of 'worlds unrealized', he had also to write a story about men and women who, to serve his purpose, must at once be symbolic of 'worlds unrealized' and behave with an almost more than mortal silliness. Refusing to use, for by far the greater part, a frankly religious imagery and language, he has to use his symbol of resurrection in a trivial way, so that though we feel his purpose, his means of expressing it are inadequate, and pathetically so. When we read the story of the resurrection of Thaisa we feel the greatness of Shakespeare's significance and so far it becomes adequately symbolic. But when we view the incident from the point of view of Thaisa's later behaviour it is a piece of tawdry magic. And when, in the later plays, Shakespeare refused to repeat so frank a piece of symbolism, he has to resort to a form of it in which characters are 'resurrected' from what was only thought to be death. But this enfeebles the symbolism; and it is still more enfeebled if, as sometimes happens, the assumption that they are dead is made on little or no grounds, or when their 'death' has a complete artistic irrelevance. (pp. 233-34)

> *D. G. James, "The Failure of the Ballad-Makers,"*
> *in his* Scepticism and Poetry: An Essay on the Poetic
> Imagination, *George Allen & Unwin Ltd, 1937, pp.*
> *205-41.**

E.M.W. TILLYARD   (essay date 1938)

[*Tillyard is perhaps best known for his* Shakespeare's History Plays *(1944), one of the most influential twentieth-century works in Shakespearean scholarship. But he also produced studies on Shakespeare's comedies, problem plays, and romances. In the following excerpt, from his* Shakespeare's Last Plays *(1938), Tillyard claims that* Pericles *is not a fully formed romance and, in addition, that one can conclude nothing more than the fact that* "Shakespeare at the time of Pericles was being impelled along some *new way of expression."*]

[It] may be asked why I am not considering [*Pericles*] along with the other three romances. Although it is likely that the last three acts are mainly Shakespeare, there is no proof that he handled them seriously enough to justify our basing any elaborate theorising upon them. The scene of Marina's birth . . . does indeed touch the height of Shakespearean art, while the recognition of Pericles and Marina is very fine. The brothel scenes, though probably by Shakespeare, are not ultimately effective. The brothel is superbly described, but, seeing it primarily through Shakespeare's own sympathetic eyes, we can find little use for Marina in that setting. When Marina preaches at Boult and he replies:

> What would you have me do? go to the wars,
> would you? where a man may serve seven years
> for the loss of a leg and have not money enough
> in the end to buy him a wooden one,
> [IV. vi. 170-73]

it is Boult rather than Marina who catches our sympathy. We cannot indeed be at ease simultaneously with Marina and the other inmates of the brothel; and end by thinking her a prude, however strongly our reason insists that she would in point of fact and in all decency have been horrified at her plight and have behaved precisely as she is made to behave. If the brothel scenes are ineffective, except in isolation, the end, with the vision of Diana and the recognition of Thaisa in Ephesus, is scanty and ridiculous. Some of the play's versification, however, is important for our present purposes. In general, it quite lacks the fullness and complexity that mark most of the verse of the three last plays. On the other hand, there is heard now and then, and perhaps for the first time in Shakespeare, that simple yet strained, remote and magical note that sounds from time to time in the last plays and helps to give them their unique character. . . . The last of these lines from Pericles's farewell speech to Thaisa will serve to illustrate its early appearance in Shakespeare:

> A terrible childbed hast thou had, my dear;
> No light, no fire: the unfriendly elements
> Forgot thee utterly; nor have I time
> To give thee hallow'd to thy grave, but straight
> Must cast thee, scarcely coffin'd, in the ooze,
> Where, for a monument upon thy bones
> And aye-remaining lamps, the belching whale
> And humming water must o'erwhelm thy corpse,
> Lying with simple shells.
>
> [III. i. 56-64]

Still, it is wrong to extract from this novelty of music any more complex fact than that Shakespeare at the time of *Pericles* was being impelled along *some* new way of expression. The other features of the play are too haphazard and ill-organised to give any sure information whither that way was tending. . . . That Shakespeare handled the Pericles story may have been the merest accident. He may have approached it with the vaguest notion of what he might make of it. Nor is there the least reason to be sure that an incident occurring in *Pericles* bears the same significance as it does when repeated in a later play. . . . As a seminal play, rich in undeveloped possibilities, we may heed it, but not as something embodying any fully formed experience in Shakespeare's mind. (pp. 22-5)

> *E.M.W. Tillyard, "The Tragic Pattern," in his* Shakespeare's Last Plays, *Chatto and Windus, 1938, pp. 16-58.*

HARDIN CRAIG   (essay date 1942)

[*Craig's* The Enchanted Glass *(1936), which describes the intellectual background of the Elizabethan age, was an important contribution to the historical school of criticism, whose exponents attempted to analyze Shakespeare's works in the context of their age and audience. Craig also edited two editions of Shakespeare's works and wrote a second volume of criticism,* An Interpretation of Shakespeare *(1948). In the excerpt below, Craig notes the affinity between the character of Pericles and Prospero of* The Tempest, *and comments, "If Shakespeare wrote* Pericles, *he did, relatively speaking, a bad job."*]

Pericles seems to belong to the same impulse and has the same kind of interest which gave us the great romances of Shakespeare's latest period. You are asked to accept the milieu of the Greek novel with its sailors, shipwrecks, pirates, abandoned infants, separated families, shepherds, tyrants, and thieves of mercy, and yet over the whole there rests the peace and serenity of old romance. *Pericles,* like the other late plays, defies metrical standards, disregards probabilities and considerations of time and place, delights in the sensational, and displays the obscure compact style of Shakespeare's latest period. It has, moreover, passages of such poetic power that it is difficult to attribute them to anybody but Shakespeare. But the greatest argument of all to indicate that Shakespeare had experience with the plot of *Pericles* is the figure of Pericles himself. Pericles is almost patently an earlier sketch of Prospero. He

is, like Prospero, a wise, competent, superior man who dominates and unifies the drama, and with his gentle, forbearing, clear-surfaced melancholy sets its tone. Back of him lies the great figure of Apollonius of Tyre, a great figure in the minds of many ages, whom Shakespeare or another has renamed after the greatest Athenian of the greatest age of Athens.

If Shakespeare wrote *Pericles,* he did, relatively speaking, a bad job. I believe that he did write the play, not exactly in its extant form, and that he had difficulties with the new milieu. It is probable that his genius mastered the new material and atmosphere, that the experience helped to give a new form and temper to his latest plays, and that it enabled him with a more certain hand to create Prospero. (pp. 237-38)

> *Hardin Craig, "Shakespeare's Development As a Dramatist in the Light of His Experience," in* Studies in Philology, *Vol. XXXIX, No. 2, April, 1942, pp. 226-38.*

THEODORE SPENCER   (essay date 1942)

[*Spencer, an American poet, educator, literary critic, and editor, is best known for his studies of Elizabethan drama and metaphysical poetry. Concurrently with E.M.W. Tillyard, Spencer elucidated and examined the traditional religious, moral, and social doctrines that he felt informed Elizabethan literature. His most important work,* Shakespeare and the Nature of Man *(1942), explores Shakespeare's dramatic technique and attempts to explain how the playwright resolved the tension between the forces of order and chaos—which Spencer defined as the conflicting attitudes of the Elizabethan world view—in his tragedies. In his comments on* Pericles, *Spencer states that the setting of the play is "the tragic world turned inside out," in which "the reality is invariably good."*]

The world of *Pericles,* like the world of all the later plays, is the tragic world turned inside out. (p. 186)

At the tragic height of *King Lear,* when the mad king meets the blind Gloucester, Edgar comments:

> I would not take this from report; it is,
> And my heart breaks at it.
>
> [IV. vi. 141-42]

But in the final plays, that which *is,* the reality, does not break hearts; on the contrary, it is a cause for thanksgiving. . . . Rebirth through spring, through woman, acceptance of things as they are, but with a glory round them—that is what we find in all the plays from *Pericles* on. In the tragedies the appearance may be good, but the reality—the lust of Gertrude [*Hamlet*], the faithlessness of Cressida, the hypocrisy of Regan and Goneril [*King Lear*], the crown of Scotland, and, to Timon, all mankind—is evil. In the last plays the appearance may be evil, but the reality is invariably good. Marina and Thaisa are alive, not dead, Imogen is faithful [*Cymbeline*], Hermione and Perdita are restored to Leontes [*The Winter's Tale*], and Miranda's view of man is the opposite of Timon's:

> How beauteous mankind is! O brave new world
> That has such people in 't!
>
> [*The Tempest,* V. i. 183-84]
> (pp. 186-87)

Shakespeare's later vision of man and his place in the scheme of things, the vision that grows out of an inner turmoil, is different from the first unthinking acceptance of youth. Rebirth is another thing than birth, since the memory of evil is behind it. In Shakespeare's last plays the memory and the possibility of evil are reflected in the belief of Posthumus, in *Cymbeline*, that Imogen has betrayed him, in Leontes' fury of jealousy at the beginning of *The Winter's Tale,* in the storm and shipwreck of *The Tempest.* And because the possibility of evil is still in the background, the theme of rebirth is often expressed in a tone of incredulous wonder, as if it could hardly be believed. (p. 187)

Theodore Spencer, ''Shakespeare's Last Plays,'' in his Shakespeare and the Nature of Man, *The Macmillan Company, 1942, pp. 177-202.*

G. WILSON KNIGHT   (essay date 1947)

[*In the following commentary on* Pericles, *Knight continues his consideration of the opposing images of tempest and music in the play first noted in his earlier essay (see excerpt above, 1928). Again stressing the visionary nature of the play, Knight says that Shakespeare has gone* ''beyond psychological lessons and social comment'' *in* Pericles *and concludes that it represents* ''Shakespeare's total poetry on the brink of self-knowledge.'' *Knight also asserts that the play as a whole* ''is unquestionably dominated by a single mind''—Shakespeare's.]

The problems raised by *Pericles* are unique. In no other Shakespearian play do we find so stark a contrast of (i) scenes of supreme power and beauty with (ii) scenes which no one can accept as Shakespeare's without disquietude. Two more facts must be faced: the first, that the play seems to have been extremely popular; the second, that it alone of the accepted canon was omitted from the First Folio.

The most questionable scenes, which occur early, are strange both in matter and in manner. The first, showing Pericles' suit for the hand of Antiochus' daughter and his reading of the riddle, is peculiar enough; what dramatic interest is raised sags soon after and it is hard to follow his later fears and successive flights with the requisite interest. The verse, too, is troublesome. The thought is clear and pointed, but the language seems weak; at the best, it lacks colloquial grip and condensed power and at the worst sounds like apprentice work; there are few striking metaphors, and rhyme bulks large. . . . Often one suspects the text which may be faulty. And yet, as against these suspicions, we are forced to recognize that everything is organic in story-value; more, that each scene, indeed the early scenes as a single unit, are imaginatively coherent, and the peculiar manner, on the whole, sustained. Moreover, little occurs that is indisputably unauthentic, and the thoughts at least, and even the action, recall other Shakespearian plays. Occasionally we meet lines that sound like late writing of the normal kind. Later, we have long sequences of apparently mature Shakespeare between work of the doubtful sort. . . . Finally, after a number of re-readings one begins to suspect some especial purpose in the passages of stilted verse, lending themselves, as they do, to semi-didactic comment and generalized statement. The style is often gnomic.

It is often supposed that Shakespeare was re-writing someone else's play. This is possible, though it may be wiser to suppose an earlier text of his own. Anyway, the allotment of unauthentic, early Shakespearian and late-Shakespearian passages, if such allotment is attempted, must be left to the reader's private judgement, since no certainty is possible. (pp. 32-3)

There is meaning in Shakespeare's art; but that is not to say that Shakespeare has a meaning in his head and proceeds to express it in his art. His art is more than expression; it is creation, born from a fusion of his own thoughts, dreams and

intuitions with a chosen narrative, the choice of which exists in the order of action, not in the order of thinking. The poet responds, perhaps without knowing why, to a certain tale; and the precise reason for his decision to follow up response with action must be as elusive and unanalysable, to himself and to others, as life itself. (p. 34)

So we have Shakespeare, a working dramatist, with a firm sense of new plays to be written, but no clear knowledge of their nature. The problem has been created by his own past work and to that he probably looked for guidance; to the comedies, the histories, the tragedies; plays Roman and Greek, Nordic and Italian. But the inner or suffusing moods of *Twelfth Night,* of *Henry V,* of *King Lear,* are alike alien to his present, more religious, temper. He may well have looked to the moralities for a precedent. (pp. 35-6)

His choice was, very clearly, in direct line with the central poetic impulse that had carried him so far. In poetry of metaphor and simile, description, atmospheric suggestion, symbol and plot, his imaginative emphasis has, from *The Comedy of Errors* onwards, concentrated primarily on tempests and especially sea-tempests, with fortunate or, more often, ill-starred ship-voyages: in the plots of the comedies, as running imagery throughout the histories, in the grander symbolism of the tragedies . . . the emphasis persists. In choosing the story of *Pericles* Shakespeare is therefore basing his new structure on his own most instinctive symbol. To put it shortly: being at a loss, he chooses a story that gives full rein to his poetic passion for voyages, tempests and wrecks. With these he is thoroughly at home. More, the problem posed by his own poetry is solved by giving that poetry its head. He aims to compose a morality play around his own poetic symbolism as dogma. For the rest, we may expect him to rely here, and in succeeding plays, on his own past accomplishments in comedy, history and tragedy, redistributing and re-knitting their elements into yet more complex designs. (p. 36)

For poetry is now expected to make, rather than to bind and harmonize, his story. The quality which formerly interpenetrated the story now *is* the story. Now the new tale supplies exactly the required looseness, being merely a succession of happenings linked by sea-journeys. We have poetry, as it were, writing itself and are to see what new thing unfolds. The resulting work will be nearer faëry-lore then realistic drama, though, in so far as it becomes interpenetrated with meaning, it will resemble parable; for parable is, precisely, a stringing out into narrative sequence of some single quality not readily definable; here, the essential magic of Shakespeare's world. We are not surprised to find the meaning grow in depth and stature as the narrative progresses. (p. 37)

[The opening scene] is clearly important. Though the verse may at moments recall Shakespeare's early manner, the philosophical impact lies clearly in advance of it. Moreover, the rhymed or otherwise stilted sequences suit the intention of the miniature 'morality'. The meaning is generalized: the King is less man than ogre, the lady less a lady than a ravishing *thing*: she is not even given a name, and her entry to music is correspondingly formal. The whole scene is a moral on the dangers attending visual lust, and recalls the moral undertones of the casket-scene in *The Merchant of Venice.* . . . In both plays failure to read the riddles concerned is to be punished, the penalty in *Pericles* being death. The scene is impregnated with a grimness of intention surpassing anything in the earlier play, the antimony of good and evil transcended in *Antony and Cleopatra* being now again powerfully distinct: the unity has fallen apart, as is, in the new style of myth-making, necessary, since that fine immediacy and coalescence is to be henceforth strung out again into narrative sequence. (pp. 39-40)

The opening of Act II brings us closer than ever before to the Shakespearian tempest: we have, as it were, a close-up of this persistent terror that has for so long burdened the poet's imagination. Pericles enters 'wet' and speaks in the usual tradition. . . . The accent is clearly Shakespearian, though even here the virile tempest-verse tails off into rhyme. Notice that the elements are directly humanized as divine powers. We are made to feel that the hero has endured a series of trials and buffetings; in him mortality is getting a rough passage. The implications are again general. The speech says crisply in Shakespearian terms, 'Tragedy': that is its function. (p. 43)

[The] most insistent impressionistic recurrence in *Pericles*, except for the sea-voyages, concerns the balancing of true and false values. We started with Pericles' infatuation for a deceptive beauty compared to the golden apples of the Hesperides . . . and turning out to be, like Morocco's choice, a 'glorious casket stor'd with ill' [I. i. 77]. . . . We moved next to the paradox of Tarsus once so wealthy with people overdressed and bejewelled and their food arranged more to please the eye [than the taste], . . . but now brought low by savage hunger; brought, that is, to realize its ultimate dependence; brought up against basic fact; such fact as is the natural air breathed by the admirable fishermen of Pentapolis.

Always in Shakespeare riches (gold, jewels, rich clothes, etc.) have two possible meanings: they may be shown as in themselves deceptive or they may, by metaphor, be used to reflect an essential good. So the rusty armour that had so often defended Pericles' father is compared to a 'jewel' . . . and princes are like 'jewels' which need keeping bright to deserve respect. . . . The comparison of a loved person to a rich stone is, of course, among the most frequent of Shakespeare's habitual correspondences. . . . (pp. 48-9)

Music is regularly in Shakespeare the antagonist to tempests; and Simonides' peaceful court thinks automatically in artistic terms. Indeed, there are in *Pericles* many noticeable artistic emphases, some of a new sort to be observed later; and all blend with the moralistic tone of thought, the ceremonious directions, and even the stilted, and often questionable, formality of the verse. Art, as such, seems to be getting a more self-conscious attention than is usual; which is scarcely surprising in a play where the myth-making fantasy seems, as in the recurring voyages, to be functioning with a new freedom. (p. 51)

Pericles' story has clearly been forming itself into a significant design. His first adventure was one of semi-adolescent fantasy bringing him up sharply against disillusion and a realization of evil; he next won merit by charitable deeds; was again rebuffed by fortune, only to find himself on the shores of a hospitable community rich in social wisdom and artistic feeling; and so to a love affair characterized not by daring and aspiration (as was the other) but by a profound humility and crowned with unexpected success. We are watching something like a parable of human fortune, with strong moral import at every turn. (p. 52)

We move to Ephesus, where we meet Cerimon, a descendant of Friar Laurence in *Romeo and Juliet,* deeply versed in the understanding of mineral and vegetable properties, and indeed at home with the inmost 'disturbances that nature works and of her cures' [III. ii. 37-8]. . . . He is a magician, of 'secret art' . . . , like Prospero in *The Tempest*. He is, too, noble, a man of Timon-like lustre, renowned for his generosity, who has, like Timon, 'poured forth' his charity, till 'hundreds' are indebted to his skill, personal labours, and 'purse'. . . . The contrast already suggested between the substantial and the ephemeral, the real and the deceptive, is here more sharply defined and given a personal centre. Cerimon is an almost superhuman figure living out a truth expressed throughout the New Testament, as in the parable of the rich man summoned by death, and such phrases as 'the body is more than clothes', 'consider the lilies of the field'. (pp. 54-5)

The poetic excitement is breathlessly intense: we are watching the key-incident that unlocks the whole range of Shakespeare's later work. His imagery, his poetry, dictates the action. From his earliest plays he has been deeply engaged with sea-tempests and death; with true and false appearance; with riches, real and unreal, in relation to love; and with wealth strewn on the sea's floor (as in Clarence's dream [*Richard III,* I. iv. 9-33]), the treasures it has gorged; and more than once with a jewel thrown into the sea, as a symbol of love, for ever lost; and, continually, with music as an almost mystical accompaniment of love, reunion, and joy. All are together here, as the supreme jewel, Thaisa, is given back. . . .

We have moved very far beyond gnomic rhymes and moral precepts; beyond psychological lessons and social comment; have advanced beyond ethic altogether to a dramatic disclosure metaphysical rather than moral, indeed visionary rather than metaphysical, as we watch life blossom and glow from the very jaws of death, warmed into renewed existence by Cerimon's fire and music. This is the new thing that has come, spontaneously, from Shakespeare's novel attempt in free narrative; something quite unlike any previous incident; which yet could not, perhaps, have been born before *Antony and Cleopatra;* but which, once touched, insists on re-expression till the end. (p. 57)

[Marina's] survival is, of course, given a perfectly water-tight realism. On the plane of logical statement nothing unique has occurred, but such logic has at best a secondary importance in drama. It is what we momentarily live, not what we remember, that counts. Here the experience dramatized is one of a gradual unfurling; an awakening to discovery of life where death seemed certain. The plot has been manipulated specifically to generate this peculiar experience, which next quite bursts its boundaries, and, expanding beyond, automatically clothes itself in semi-transcendental phraseology. The story is, anyway, a fiction; its threaded events, even less than in most stories, count for little; all depends on what the poet makes of them. The most realistic tension in the whole play comes at these moments of amazing tragic reversal, at the restoration of Thaisa by Cerimon and the amazing impact of Marina's survival. In both we attend the unveiling of death from off the features of life: this it is which generates the unique excitement. The discovery is elaborately delayed, expanded, played upon, allowed to grow more and more certain till no doubt remains. . . . (p. 66)

'The gods', 'great miracle', 'power', a 'god': the impressions are piled on. We are directed to feel that a dead person 'relives', and though Cerimon promises, as does Paulina in *The Winter's Tale,* an explanation, we do not hear it, in either play. We are left with a sense of wonder. (p. 69)

One should not, however, regard *Pericles* as a completely new departure. We rather feel as present fact those miracles already hinted by Kent's 'nothing almost sees miracles but misery' and by Lear's dying 'Look there! look there!'. . . . The dim shadowings of *King Lear* are turned to the light. The new play follows naturally on Timon's 'nothing brings me all things.' . . . Nor is the use of a happy ending to a serious purpose wholly new: the earlier comedies, more serious works than is usually supposed, dramatized stories of error dispelled, mistaken identity set right, reunion after separation, generally in direct relation to tempests, as in *The Comedy of Errors* and *Twelfth Night*. . . . The structural elements in *Pericles* are not all new; but the treatment gives them fresh, and explicitly transcendental, meaning. Instead of a happy-ending romance, or ritual, in the tradition of Lyly, with whatever validity such fictions may be considered to hold—and it is probable that they hold more than we normally suppose—we are here confronted by some extra dimension of validity. The depth and realism of tragedy are present within the structure of romance. The two extremes, happy and sad, of Shakespearian art coalesce to house a new, and seemingly impossible, truth; as though the experiences behind or within the composition of *King Lear* and *Timon of Athens* were found not necessarily antithetical to the happy ending but rather reached therein their perfect fulfilment. Hence the sense of breath-taking surprise, of wonder and reverence, in the reunions, and the cogent presentation of the miracle-worker, Cerimon.

Pericles might be called a Shakespearian morality play. The epilogue asserts as much, though it does no justice to the more important scenes, which so tower above the rest and which it would be a great error to relate too sharply to any known type of drama. These, whatever we think of them, are spontaneous, new creations. And yet, in spite of their superiority, they cannot be isolated: *Pericles* is too thoroughly organic a play for that, with all its running coherences of idea, image, and event. (pp. 69-71)

Pericles is the result of no sudden vision: it is Shakespeare's total poetry on the brink of self-knowledge.

It is accordingly not strange that art, as such, should be given greater emphasis than hitherto; in stage-direction, ceremonious procession (as of the tourneying knights) and ritual-setting; in dumb-show; in monumental inscriptions, and metaphors; in musical accomplishment (Pericles' and Marina's); in Marina's dancing and decorative needlework. The arts least emphasized in Shakespeare, the static arts of design, assume a new prominence, giving us the exquisite descriptions of Marina in monumental terms. Shakespeare's drama is aspiring towards the eternal harmony and the eternal pattern.

The new excellences are bought at a cost. Pericles himself is a passive figure, quite unlike Shakespeare's usual dynamic protagonists. He himself does nothing crucial; his fall is purely an awareness of evil, like Hamlet's, his good acts are perfunctorily set down, his repentance in sack-cloth and unshaven hair a repentance for no guilt of his own but rather for the fact of mortality in a harsh universe. He is here for things to happen to and forges little or nothing for himself; his most original actions are a series of escapes or departures; he is too humble to press his suit for Thaisa. He is, indeed, less a realized person than man, almost 'every man', in the morality sense, as the epilogue suggests. We can, however, improve on the epilogue by seeing the whole as a panorama of life from adolescent fantasy and a consequent fall, through good works to a sensible and fruitful marriage, and thence into tragedy, with a re-emergence beyond mortal appearances into some higher recognition and rehabilitation. The medium is myth or parable, supposedly, of course, realistic: we must not expect death to be totally

negated; Thaisa's father dies . . . ; Cerimon cannot restore everyone. . . . But, as in parable always, it is the central person, or persons, that count; and here the deaths of Thaisa and Marina are shown, in the fiction, as false, though with an intensity surpassing fiction. (pp. 73-4)

The obvious conclusion is that some much earlier play, either of Shakespearian or other authorship, shows through, mainly in the first half, but that it has been so modified by incorporation that we need not, from an interpretative view, be seriously disquieted. *Pericles* was published under Shakespeare's name during his life. The high standard of authenticity demanded by the Folio editors is witnessed alike by their own preface and the massive and detailed coherence of the material they published: such things do not happen by chance. But neither can the internal coherence of *Pericles*, far more precise than that of many a more famous Shakespearian work, be dismissed. Nothing is here forgotten: Antiochus' wickedness, Pericles' relief of the famine, the crime of Dionyza and Cleon, all are exactly remembered long after their purpose in the narrative sequence has been fulfilled; from first to last the Gower speeches have the whole action in mind; the various imagistic corre-

Act IV. Scene i. Marina. By T. Stothard (1804). From the Art Collection of the Folger Shakespeare Library.

spondences, cutting across divergences of style, knit the narrative into a unity. Every line, good or bad, serves a purpose: there are probably less extravagant irrelevancies than, say, in *Hamlet* or *King Lear*. . . . The play appears to be carefully and critically composed. . . . Whatever we think of certain parts, the whole, as we have it, is unquestionably dominated by a single mind; that mind is very clearly Shakespeare's; and Shakespeare's, too, in process of an advance unique in literature. (p. 75)

> *G. Wilson Knight, "The Writing of 'Pericles'," in his* The Crown of Life: Essays in Interpretation of Shakespeare's Final Plays, *1947. Reprint by Methuen & Co. Ltd., 1948, pp. 32-75.*

KENNETH MUIR   (essay date 1949)

[*In addition to his editions of* Richard II, King Lear, *and* Macbeth, *Muir also published numerous volumes of Shakespearean criticism and served as the editor of* Shakespeare Survey. *In the following excerpt, Muir makes a case for an "Ur-*Pericles*," a now-lost play which, he argues, both Shakespeare and George Wilkins used as a source for their adaptations of the Pericles story.*]

The resemblances between *The Painfull Aduentures of Pericles*—Wilkins' novel—and [Shakespeare's *Pericles*] are so many that we must assume either that one was based on the other, or that there was a common original, apart from Twine's novel. . . . [I believe that] Wilkins based his novel on a play. If that play was the Shakespearean *Pericles*, it in turn must have been based on an Ur-*Pericles*, or on Twine and Gower. If, on the other hand, Wilkins based his novel on an Ur-*Pericles*, *Pericles* itself may be based on Wilkins' novel, on the Ur-*Pericles*, or on both.

If Wilkins based his novel on the Shakespearean *Pericles*, we must conclude that those passages in the novel which are neither in Twine's novel nor in *Pericles* were *either* (a) omitted by accident from the printed text of the play and preserved by Wilkins—in which case we might suppose that he had access to the playhouse copy, or else that he relied on a shorthand transcript taken down in the theatre; *or* (b) the invention of Wilkins. Now (b) is unlikely, because many passages peculiar to Wilkins seem to be based on blank verse. (pp. 68-9)

The brothel scene in the play is obviously much curtailed, and in the novel there are a number of eloquent speeches, not far removed from blank verse. . . . (p. 69)

There are several reasons for believing that these speeches were originally in verse. In the first place, there are a number of lines which can be extracted from the prose without alteration, and the whole scene could be converted into verse with extraordinarily little change. (p. 70)

The second reason for believing that these speeches were originally in verse is the fact that in the following passage Lysimachus drops suddenly from indirect into direct speech, because Wilkins carelessly neglected to alter his pronouns:

> or his displeasure punish at his owne pleasure,
> which displeasure of *mine, thy beauty shall not
> priuiledge thee from, nor my affection, which
> hath drawen me vnto this place abate, if thou
> with further lingering withstand me.*

Thirdly, there are two passages which contain repetitions of a word, for no apparent reason except to complete the line:

> which too too many feele such houses are. . . .
> let me euen now, now in this minute die. . . .

It will surely be agreed that the Wilkins speeches *must* have been written originally as verse, and there is therefore no reason to think that they were written for the novel. This . . . disproves Sykes' theory that Wilkins based his play on his own novel [see excerpt above, 1874]. If therefore the novel was based on the Shakespearean *Pericles* we are driven back on the alternative explanation—that such speeches were omitted accidentally from an admittedly corrupt quarto and preserved somehow or other by Wilkins.

To judge the possibility of this explanation it will be necessary to [compare] the passages in the brothel scenes which appear both in the novel and in *Pericles*. . . . (p. 71)

As the dialogue of the play is jerky, a mingling of prose and verse with many short and irregular lines, it reads as though it had been condensed. On the other hand, the dialogue in the novel runs smoothly and naturally, although none of the lines of verse fossils correspond to lines of verse in the play. If Wilkins in his verse fossils were merely reproducing lines which had been accidentally omitted by the quarto, it is curious that the reporter was so much less accurate in reproducing a popular brothel scene than he was in reproducing the scene of the reunion of Pericles and Marina. Since some of the verse in the brothel scene is respectable, but nowhere corresponds to the fossil verse in the novel, we must surely assume that the novel was not derived from the Shakespearean *Pericles*, but from its source, which we have called the Ur-*Pericles*. This, I believe, is the only theory that fits the facts.

It is a theory which is supported by a consideration of some differences between the novel and *Pericles*. In the brothel scene in the novel, Lysimachus assumes that Marina's pleading is a trick to squeeze more money out of him. . . . In the play, however, as soon as Marina appeals to Lysimachus he desists from his wooing. It would seem that the novel preserves a more primitive form of the story than the play. If Wilkins were following the Shakespearean *Pericles*, he would have been singularly foolish if he had made Lysimachus thus threaten Marina, especially as there is no trace of the threat in the still more primitive Twine. On the other hand it would have been natural for Shakespeare, working on the Ur-*Pericles*, to tone down the brutality, so as to make Lysimachus a less intolerable husband for the pure Marina. . . . By thus whitewashing Lysimachus' character, Shakespeare leaves us confused about his motives for visiting the brothel at all. Is the Governor a playwright in search of local colour? Or are we meant to assume that like the Duke in *Measure for Measure* or the hero of [Thomas] Middleton's *Phoenix*, he is investigating the underworld of the city? He is not, like them, effectively disguised. Perhaps Shakespeare merely introduced this disclaimer to make Lysimachus into a presentable bridegroom; and members of the audience who thought that the bawdy Lysimachus of the earlier part of the scene was incompatible with the virtuous character of the conclusion could assume that in the later speeches he was lying out of a sense of shame.

In the following scene, where Marina is reunited to her father, there is another example of the difference of tone between Wilkins and the author of *Pericles*. Pericles in the novel strikes

Marina on the face and she swoons. In the play he pushes his daughter back, the incident being twice referred to—

> I sed my Lord, if you did know my parentage,
> you would not do me violence.   [V. i. 99-100]

> Didst thou not say when I did push thee backe,
> which was, when I perceiu'd thee . . .
>   [V. i. 126-27]

In Twine's novel Apollonius kicks Tharsia on the face. Wilkins, and doubtless the Ur-*Pericles*, are midway between the crudity of Twine and the comparative refinement of Shakespeare. We are forced to conclude once more that Wilkins based his novel not on *Pericles*, but on the Ur-*Pericles*.

The numerous verbal parallels between *Pericles* and the novel can mostly be explained on the assumption that Shakespeare himself retained parts of the Ur-*Pericles*, virtually unchanged, in his play. A few passages in the play, for example, corrupt in the quarto, can be emended by reference to the novel. We may assume that Wilkins derived all these readings from the Ur-*Pericles;* and we may likewise assume that passages in Acts III-V of *Pericles* . . . were retained by Shakespeare from the source play. (pp. 72-4)

[The] evidence that Shakespeare had anything to do with the opening acts of the play is inconclusive. My opinion, for what it is worth, is that he made a number of cuts and added the lines about the mole. (p. 80)

Shakespeare's play was based on the Ur-*Pericles;* but he doubtless knew Gower, and had possibly read Twine. There seems to have been some confusion of thought on this subject: critics who believe that Shakespeare's play was based on Wilkins' novel have continued to assume that Shakespeare also used Twine. If the novel were based on Shakespeare's play, then, of course, the latter might have borrowed incidents from Twine's novel. But once we assume that the play is based on Wilkins' novel, then we should conclude that the Twine influence is only indirect; and once we postulate the existence of an Ur-*Pericles*, Twine can be ignored. There are, I believe, no verbal parallels between *Pericles* and Twine's novel; and even if there were any, they might be *via* the Ur-*Pericles*. There is only one scene which appears to be slightly closer to Twine's version than to that of Wilkins: in the play and in Twine's novel, Thaliard is relieved that, owing to the disappearance of Pericles, he does not have to murder him. Wilkins presumably deviated from the Ur-*Pericles* here. Even the Gower influence, for which some critics have argued, may have come *via* the Ur-*Pericles*.

Finally, it may be pointed out that there are a number of passages and phrases in Wilkins' novel, which are not to be found in *Pericles* itself, but which seem in varying degrees to have a Shakespearean flavour. . . . Presumably Wilkins was echoing [passages] . . . from *Othello*, and Shakespeare in turn echoed Wilkins. (p. 81)

I have endeavoured to show the relationship of Wilkins' novel to Twine's, and to prove that it was based on an earlier play, which also served as the source of Shakespeare's *Pericles*, and I have suggested tentatively that the novel has a few interpolations from Shakespeare's play and that the quarto of the latter may have been slightly influenced by the novel. I have accepted Sykes' theory of the authorship of the Ur-*Pericles* [see excerpt above, 1918], though I believe it was written before, and not after, the novel. Elsewhere I have given reasons for believing that the quarto of *Pericles* obscures at least one theme of Shake-

speare's play; but it is clear that he left the first two acts more or less as they stood in the Ur-*Pericles*. Wilkins was not a good dramatist, but he provided Shakespeare with the gangway to his last period. For that he has earned a vicarious immortality. (pp. 82-3)

Kenneth Muir, "The Problem of 'Pericles'," in English Studies, *Vol. XXX, No. 3, June, 1949, pp. 65-83.*

DONALD A. STAUFFER   (essay date 1949)

[*In the following excerpt, Stauffer maintains that* Pericles *is "a miracle play based upon a Renaissance romance" and that it "expresses in visions the archetypal patterns of the human soul, its loneliness and fear and courage and hope for continuing life." For additional commentary on* Pericles *as a miracle play, see the excerpt by Howard Felperin (1967).*]

Pericles is an old story. In Latin and perhaps in Greek, it whiled away the time of readers in the late Roman Empire, and sprang to life again in late Anglo-Saxon, and again in many medieval versions in many countries, and again in Renaissance England. The adventures of Pericles, or of Apollonius King of Tyre (for the name does not matter in the Greek romances or in their descendants), are as complicated, interminable, and about as convincing as those in a modern soap-opera. Whoever writes it, he may once again, "by relating tales of others' griefs, See if 'twill teach us to forget our own" [I. iv. 2-3].

Shakespeare tells it as if it were an old story, watched over by the quaint guardian spirit of the medieval poet John Gower. The glow of his poetry, in the two or three scenes where the play catches fire, contrasts with the flat compressed narrative of most of the play almost as deliberately, it might be argued, as Hamlet's Hecuba soliloquy is set against the stilted rhetoric of the players at Elsinore.

The story, for Shakespeare, is "this great miracle" [V. iii. 58]. (pp. 266-67)

Proud enemies are burned in their palace, or a fire from heaven shrivels their bodies even to loathing. As for the good characters, everyone will turn out to be royal or wedded to nobility. Though Pericles himself cannot but think it the rarest dream that ever mocked sad fools, his lost daughter, his lost wife, are restored to him.

But the real miracles in this fairy-story are miracles of the spirit. They are presented as sudden illuminations; psychological realism, the slow preparation for an inevitable action, are sacrificed—almost purposefully, in order to make the magical changes more purely magical. Shakespeare no longer appears primarily interested in showing the subtle gradations by which a mind takes on new direction and decision. In *Pericles* there are none of those masterful persuasion scenes, no more dialogues of the mind with itself as it reaches toward a painful choice. The reversals in situation come like bolts of lightning. Men are struck without reference to their own wills; their faults and virtues do not lie in themselves, except for a predisposition to evil or good; free will in the piece exists beyond men, in the stars. In thunder and sudden vision, a mysterious moral order actualizes what has been hidden in man's mind; even as Pericles speculates helplessly on what might happen "Were my fortunes equal to my desires" [II. i. 111-12], the sea casts up his deliverance. (pp. 267-68)

Over the rippling surfaces of the plot the dramatist glances as swiftly as a water-spider. The story is merely a plane on which he may set up focal points of rest, not to develop believable characters, but to return to central ideas—of integrity, man's helplessness, immutable order, obedience, patience, prayer, healing, and new life—and to the images which support these recurring and interrelated ideas: the sea and the sun, music and the gods. Or, to say the same thing in another mode, here is another book of the *Faerie Queen,* dramatized, in which the hero is a further aspect of Arthur or Magnificence, his wife the True Florimel, Antiochus a Busirane and his daughter an Acrasia, and Marina—how Spenserian even in name!—playing the rôle of a young Britomart or Belphoebe in the brothel scenes. (pp. 269-70)

Pericles, then, is neither a comedy nor a tragedy nor a realistic drama nor a problem play nor a morality play. It is a miracle play based upon a Renaissance romance. It is a piece of music. And it sets sharply and unwaveringly the mode for Shakespeare's final moral thought. The device upon the hero's shield is "A withered branch that's only green at top" [II. ii. 43]. . . . Many of Shakespeare's own earlier preoccupations still cling like dead leaves—the love-lust contrast, the fatal likeness between hypocrisy and truth, the old sense of sin and tragedy.

But at the top the branch is green. The gods are powerful (though they choose at times to operate through human agents), and they will rescue those of upright mind. (p. 270)

Before the omnipotent gods show their compassion, they test Pericles with trials equal to Job's or Griselda's. "Lady Fortune" orders or disorders the day. Life is envisioned as a sea, fickle, treacherous, always changing, and more tempestuous and ever-present than in that other sea-play *The Tempest.* Man is no more than a sailor "With whom each minute threatens life or death" [I. iii. 24]. The raging battery and huge billows and masked calm of the ocean furnish the images of existence. Sea-tossed Pericles rides out three tempests. Clasped to the mast, he "endures a sea that almost burst the deck," while "from the ladder tackle washes off A canvas climber" [IV. i. 55-61]. In such mastering storms "The seaman's whistle Is as a whisper in the ears of death, Unheard." Oceanic terrors are realized with such prolonged intensity that we may feel with the shuddering fishermen, "Master, I marvel how the fishes live in the sea" [II. i. 25-6]. (p. 272)

Who through his own power can quiet the storm? The bases for building a new life are the recognition of human sin—"the earth is throng'd By man's oppression, and the poor worm doth die for 't" [I. i. 101-02]—the recognition of such sin in one's own nature (since experience teaches "My frail mortality to know itself" [I. i. 42]), and finally the taking on of an absolute humility. Worldly greatness, however exalted, is "no guard To bar heaven's shaft" [II. iv. 14-15], and the villains themselves know that "The gods are quick of ear" [IV. i. 69]. Naked and alone, "having all lost," the lowest and most dejected thing of fortune must constantly acknowledge and submit to the justice of all-powerful gods. The readiness is all.

Having abandoned his wilful pride but not his integrity, man may become, like Helicanus and Cerimon, an instrument "through whom the gods have shown their power" [V. iii. 60]. He may become their voice, their mirror, and their consciousness. This is no play of agonized questionings, of rational debates, and of independent decisions; it is a succession of prayers, from Pericles' second speech in the play . . . to his last: "Heavens make a star of him!" Three of the best scenes

(II, i; III, i; V, iii) open with prayers, and it is the hero who offers them. (p. 273)

The moral outlines of this piece of music are clear: desperate trials borne unflinchingly; the acknowledgment of sin; humility and patience never abandoned; willing obedience to an irresistible order; self-forgetfulness, as man realizes himself to be an instrument played upon by unseen virtues; trustful prayers to gods believed to be just; hope and integrity freely rewarded by unlooked-for compassion and joy.

Such a pattern of themes fails to describe the moral effect of the play adequately, for it is at once too neat and not vivid enough. On one side, all of the elements described are present in full measure . . . , but an inescapable causal sequence and relationship is never distinctly set. Shakespeare realizes, or has here learned to imagine, the sudden descent of unexpected joy; and the play reaches its height of passion in the two scenes of restoration to lost happiness, or more accurately, of discovery of a happiness previously unsuspected. Yet these scenes are revelations, or smiling hypotheses—not the culmination of an ordered analysis and understanding. With the same materials, Shakespeare reaches clearer conclusions—perhaps through the mere reworking of his own thoughts—in the plays yet to be considered. *Pericles* falls short in comparison, because even in this world of miracle, where spiritual mysteries are touched upon by the subtlest of minds, the inevitability of moral cause and effect may be more sharply set forth.

On the other side, the threads of the thought as traced so far are lusterless in comparison with the play itself, which is a tapestry glinting and glowing with colors and shot through with gold. *Pericles* is not an abstract preachment, but an embodied intuition. Part of its moral thought results from its incarnation or visualization of intangible values in human subjects and in the symbols of nature—so that joy is felt, not discussed, and the experience of happiness after grief is set above any arguing about it. (pp. 274-75)

Surely this is a fabric that expresses in visions the archetypal patterns of the human soul, its loneliness and fear and courage and hope for continuing life. It is a romance none of whose parts is so poor but is a race of heaven. And it is a dream from thick slumber. Here, more richly realized than in Spenser's House of Holiness, though their presences are iridescent and they act through human agents, are Faith, Hope, and Charity. "More is won," we learn in a strange tongue, "through sweetness than through force." Nature's lesson of fear and joy is presented through Neptune and Diana. Man's dearest, save in his own mind, is subject to loss; and he must learn to guard his rarest treasure in a world that whirs him from his friends:

> The rough seas, that spare not any man,
> Took it in rage—though, calm'd, have given 't again. . . .
> [II. i. 131-32]

In hac spe vivo ["In this hope I live"] reads the motto on the shield of the hero [II. ii. 44]. The branch may wither, yet it remains green at top. (p. 278)

> Donald A. Stauffer, "A World of Images," in his Shakespeare's World of Images: The Development of His Moral Ideas, *W. W. Norton & Company, Inc., 1949, pp. 266-323.*

RICHARD WINCOR (essay date 1950)

[*Wincor compares Shakespeare's romances to the festival plays of ancient societies that celebrated fecundity, marriage, and the cycle of the seasons. He notes the significant relation of the punishment of Antiochus's ''barren marriage'' and Thaisa's rebirth in* Pericles *to these older festival dramas. Wincor's analogy of Shakespeare's romances to festival plays is suggestive of later anthropological criticism of Shakespeare, especially that of C. L. Barber (1969).*]

I am going to suggest that Shakespeare's last plays may be best understood by comparing them with the old festival plays that celebrate the return of spring after a barren winter. There is little question of direct influence. Truths about life are often lost and rediscovered; even the original symbols for their expression suggest themselves once again. And so it seems entirely natural that they should be the essence both of Shakespeare's sunset masterpieces and the old ceremonies from which drama was born. It was for the more sophisticated art to relate them to all of human experience. Shakespeare had learned that there was more than tragedy in this world. The theme of festivals for over two thousand years took on a sudden poignance. (p. 219)

A festival play may be any dramatic celebration, but the term is here applied to drama growing out of seasonal rites and worship. (p. 220)

The crux or central theme in these plays is strangely the same. Yet there is something far more remarkable behind it. A regular structure of supposed deaths and wonderful rebirths is strikingly familiar. Naturally enough! This is the exact pattern of the old festival Mock Death and Cure.

At first, any such idea may be hard to accept. Yet more details only justify its acceptance. Begin with *Pericles,* of which Shakespeare certainly wrote the greater part. . . .

Marina is first to undergo the Cure. In a sense her release from the brothel where pirates placed her is regenerating, but only to those already contaminated by it; she is untouched. Her real rebirth occurs when Pericles finds her alive to ''the music of the spheres.'' . . . Thaisa's ''Cure'' is less moving but even more a thing done in festival terms. Pericles finds her as a High Priestess in the Temple of Diana, and upon recognizing him she swoons. Then, for the miracle of their finding each other alive, she speaks those great words toward which the entire play has been moving. Thaisa says,

> Did you not name a tempest,
> A birth, and death? . . .   [V. iii. 33-4]

The Cure has been effected, and the story has a happy ending. (p. 224)

Fecundity and symbolic marriage are also part of the festival vision. Of course the idea of fertility is implicit in everything considered so far; but Shakespeare gives it ever plainer expression until with *The Tempest* it seems almost an obsession. *Pericles* begins with an interesting example of Nature veneration. Antiochus lives incestuously with his daughter, a deed so unnatural that both are later blasted by avenging gods. That is a bad and barren marriage. So is the relationship in the brothel which Marina escapes; and as Lysimachus leads her to real marriage, Nature is redeemed again. Interesting, too, is the institution from which reborn Thaisa is removed by her husband. It is the temple of Diana, goddess of chastity. From High Priestess to Bride once more;—so it goes with Thaisa, as with Diana herself in the dim past, when she wedded the Priest-King at Nemi! Austerity gives way before fecundity. (p. 229)

Why do Shakespeare's festival plays take the form of improbable romance? Why this world in which the Russian emperor, Apollo's oracle, and Julio Romano are contemporaneous; this fairyland where tempests upset every plan, where lost brothers and sisters find the same cave, where lovers, family, and friends are reconciled after a generation? In short, why was it the romance that Shakespeare borrowed for his own ends? Perhaps because it was fashionable. Perhaps also, because the unconscious implications of festival drama made the romance his best way of saying what he had to say.

After all, an entire cycle had to be shown. If life is like a dream, details of what happens in it lose their importance. Reconciliation alone is worth while, and a hope of immortality at the other end of this great metamorphosis. What matter, then, if improbabilities and anachronisms exist? Pericles can be wrecked a thousand times if it leads to a happy ending. . . . No longer the individual but the entire picture of the seasons, embracing cities, kingdoms, flowers and men and women as well, is the subject. Shakespeare's protagonist is Supernature. The people in his last plays are sometimes wonderful because he is a great artist who enlarges everything and who always maintains a human balance; but their basic function remains that of characters in a fairy tale. They exist so that all may come out right at the end. This is not always as clear as with Imogen [*Cymbeline*], whose wicked stepmother, poisoned apple, and re-awakening make her like Snow-White. Yet their role in the mightiest fairy tale of all is played upon a stage whose confines are the Dream, the Hope of Immortality, and Reconciliation. (pp. 232-33)

> *Richard Wincor, ''Shakespeare's Festival Plays,'' in* Shakespeare Quarterly, *Vol. 1, No. 4, October 1950, pp. 219-40.*

CLIFFORD LEECH   (essay date 1950)

[*In his comments on* Pericles, *Leech, an Elizabethan drama scholar, discusses the parallels between the play and Shakespeare's later romances. Leech concludes that although Shakespeare initially undertook only a revision of another dramatist's play by the same title, he found the form ''much to his purpose and decided to continue in the same path.''*]

[Marks] of casualness in Shakespeare's last group of plays there undoubtedly are, and they are most evident in the earliest of the group, *Pericles.* As it stands this is a botched affair, and not even Mr. Wilson Knight can claim to find Shakespeare's hand in the whole of it [see excerpt above, 1947]. The commentators are generally agreed that Shakespeare took over another's work and that his hand becomes clearly discernible from the third act. Moreover, Shakespeare's use or preservation of the Gower chorus passages seems, partly at least, to stem from a disinclination to make the story tell itself, though partly too Shakespeare may have desired the effect of greater distance between spectators and actors that the intervention of a narrator effects. In any event, Thaisa's withdrawal to the temple of Diana seems over-hasty: even in the ill-defined days of the play's action, communication between Tyre and Ephesus cannot have been altogether unknown. Perhaps after [*Timon of Athens*] Shakespeare was undecided how to proceed: in that play he had shown signs of weariness and of a general contempt for the nature of mankind. If he could have been left to himself, a longer interval might have come before he resumed his pen. But he was his company's most successful dramatist, he was a sharer in their gains, and doubtless it was difficult for him to resist the clamour for more theatre-stuff. A dramatic romance, by Wilkins or another, lay at hand, at least partially written but woefully unready for playing. The solution of his and the company's problem could be found in setting to work to manipulate another man's material. Had not [Robert] Greene long ago accused him of filching? It was a habit that might be conveniently resumed. Nevertheless, his writing in the completed *Pericles* was sufficiently extensive to make the presence of his hand beyond question and to constitute the play a minor landmark in his development. In it we have clear anticipations of what he was to write later and we have too an extension of certain characteristics that had first become noticeable in *Timon*.

We get, for example, a black-and-white method of characterisation. On the one side, Pericles, Marina, Thaisa, Cerimon; on the other, Antiochus and his daughter, Dionyza, and the keepers of the brothel in Mitylene. The good are incorruptible, so that Pericles can quickly throw off his love for the daughter of Antiochus as soon as he guesses at her sin, and Marina comes no nearer harm than Milton's Lady in *Comus*. And the characters of the bad are not explored but merely exposed: Boult the pandar is not humanised like his cousin Pompey in *Measure for Measure*, he is simply not of Pericles' kin, the dark strain in the world which sets off the light. It is true that Boult is finally won over to Marina's plan for her livelihood and agrees to spare her from the fellowship of the brothel, but that appears only for the convenience of the plot: after he has dropped his demands on her, his character is dropped by the dramatist: it has served its turn, to be Marina's foil, and Shakespeare has no further use for or interest in it. We may come to understand the nature of the last plays if we direct our attention closely to the treatment in them of those who have sinned: sometimes, like Leontes [*The Winter's Tale*] and the enemies of Prospero [*The Tempest*] they are forgiven, but first they are most rigorously tormented; more often, they get no forgiveness but a sharp condemnation. The clearest example in *Pericles* is provided by the presentation of Cleon, the governor of Tarsus, whose wife Dionyza plotted the death of Marina through jealousy: Cleon was ignorant of the plot, and is horrified when the news of Marina's murder is given him: his fault is that he does not denounce his wife and acquiesces in the deception of Pericles. This might be thought an almost pardonable fault, but it is worth while our noticing the references to him in the last act of the play: . . . in scene iii Pericles accuses him of seeking to murder Marina, and in Gower's concluding chorus he is 'wicked Cleon' and we are told that the people rose against him and burned "him and his" in his palace. The reader may conjecture that here we have careless workmanship, a forgetfulness on Shakespeare's part of Cleon's comparative guiltlessness. But this is surely improbable, and indeed the variety of the abusive epithets that are attached to Cleon's name in the last act even suggests a special animus against the character. It is because Cleon has condoned his wife's fault, has not applied the salutary discipline of a Prospero, that he comes under rebuke. (pp. 127-29)

In matters of detail, *Pericles* anticipates the later romances very noticeably. . . . Simonides abuses Pericles as Prospero abuses Ferdinand, each with the same intent, to ensure the wedding of his daughter; Thaisa, moreover, is as forward in admitting her love as Miranda [*The Tempest*] was to be, and Simonides pretends anger with his daughter as Prospero with his. . . . Lychorida rebukes Pericles on shipboard with "Patience, good sir; do not assist the storm", sending our minds forward to the Boatswain's "You do assist the storm" in the opening scene of *The Tempest*. The presentation of Cerimon's

character . . . is a kind of preliminary sketch for Prospero's: both have studied the secrets of nature through their books and learned to do strange things. One might list such resemblances at length, linking the appearance of Diana here with the descent of Jupiter in *Cymbeline*, the frequent references to the passing of time in Gower's speeches with the very appearance of Time as chorus before Act IV of *The Winter's Tale*, the reviving of the apparently drowned Thaisa with the animating of Hermione's statue [*The Winter's Tale*], the omnipresence of the sea in this play with the island setting of *The Tempest*. What should emerge from such a list is the realisation that Shakespeare, stumbling upon this form of play in the rehandling of another man's work, found it much to his purpose and decided to continue in the same path.

Yet doubtless he would not have continued if *Pericles* had not proved popular. . . . [There is] testimony not merely that the fame of *Pericles* had lasted for a few years but that it could be rather condescendingly alluded to, as Ben Jonson might refer to *The Spanish Tragedy* or *Titus Andronicus*. That should not surprise us, for by 1613 Beaumont and Fletcher's tragicomedies had established themselves on the stage, and in technical competency *Pericles* would look strange beside them. It is for us important, seeming to advance Shakespeare on the road from *Timon* to *The Tempest*, but for its contemporaries it might be simply one of his less impressive displays, carelessly put together and a little childish in its flights of fancy. Nevertheless, it pleased. (pp. 130-32)

> *Clifford Leech, "'Timon' and After," in his* Shakespeare's Tragedies: And Other Studies in Seventeenth-Century Drama, *Chatto and Windus, 1950, 113-36.*

J.M.S. TOMPKINS　(essay date 1952)

[*Tompkins, like John F. Danby (1952) and F. D. Hoeniger (1963), argues that patience is an important theme in* Pericles *and states that the protagonist of this play represents Shakespeare's most patient hero. Tompkins also notes that though Shakespeare may have chosen the Pericles tale for the purpose of developing the theme of patience, the character of Pericles in Shakespeare's sources was not so acquiescent. Ernest Schanzer (1965) argues against the interpretation of Pericles as the epitome of patience.*]

Of all Shakespeare's heroes Pericles is the most patient man—one would have said the only patient man but for Brutus [*Julius Caesar*], and Brutus's cheerless patience is part of his Stoic philosophy and is worn and frayed before he finds his rest at Philippi. All the other heroes are dominated, as Elizabethan tragic heroes are bound to be, by impulse, passion, resentment, leading to physical and spiritual violence. They have moods of weary suffering, but this is not patience but numbness and melancholy. They recognize their deprivation. They cry out for patience, like Lear—'You heavens, give me that patience, patience I need!' [*King Lear*, II. iv. 271]—and recognize it enviously in others, like Hamlet; their present state is contrasted with a former time when they exercised patience, as in *Othello*; but for them, in their self-destructive anguish, the heavenly virtue which Othello, with his young wife's face before him, sees as a 'young and rose-lipp'd cherubim' has 'turned [its] complexion' and looks 'grim as hell' [*Othello*, IV. ii. 62-4]. Only Timon and Cleopatra, who dwell in extremities, never salute patience with bruised lips; to her it is 'sottish'; and Coriolanus, least analytic of them all, seems never to perceive that he is impatient. It is, nevertheless, by one of Shakespeare's ironies, Coriolanus who describes that aspect of patience which is presented in the Romances. As he goes into banishment, he turns to console his mother by quoting her own words, reminding her that she has been used to tell him that

> fortune's blows
> When most struck home, being gentle wounded craves
> A noble cunning   [*Coriolanus*, IV. i. 7-9]

To be gentle wounded means, I think, to preserve the temper and training of the spirit under heavy calamity. The word 'wounded' dissociates the conception from the theoretical 'invulnerability' of Senecal man, in which Shakespeare did not believe; not is he thinking of mere submission, still less of a politic and wary self-control. What he means cannot enter the mind of Coriolanus, who throws the phrase with others into the gulf of his mother's grief and then forgets it; but it is beautifully exemplified in Pericles.

In the first two acts his figure is merely outlined, but the poses are in harmony with what is to come. He masters himself to accept quietly the undeserved rebuke of Helicanus and the necessity of exile, and endures a ruinous shipwreck with constancy and cheerfulness. The third act is another matter; here a crushing blow falls in the death of Thaisa in childbed, in the tumult of a storm at sea, and Shakespeare enters into the depth of his subject. What he shows us is not the Stoic discipline under grief; he had dramatized that in Brutus, and then, perhaps, finding his first version morally showy, rewritten the scene. Pericles is no Stoic; there is no theoretical stiffening in his attitude, nor does he take Fortune's buffets and rewards with equal thanks, or call contempt of pain his own. He is wounded to the quick, yet 'gentle'. The scene, enacted, as it were, in the hollow of a great wave of Fate, is instinct with tenderness. There is no human clamour to match the sea's outrage. Lychorida tells him of his loss in the last words of a sentence that begins by offering to him his only consolation, the child of his dead queen; and, after a stunned exclamation and one agonized question of the gods, he obeys her injunction to be manly and take comfort for the child's sake, holding and blessing it in the name of the gods who have robbed him of its mother. Immediately the sailors come, blunt with their necessity and their embarrassment, to insist on clearing the ship of the dead. He remonstrates once—'That's your superstition!' [III. i. 50]—and then yields to their conviction, issuing quiet orders, accepting thankfully the 'caulked and bitumed' chest they offer for a coffin, and still addressing them singly as 'good mariner', 'gentle mariner'. We overhear his intimate address to his wife:

> A terrible child-bed hast thou had, my dear;
> No light, no fire . . .   [III. i. 56-7]

and then he controls himself to say the 'priestly farewell' which we do not hear. And even before he commits her to the 'humming water', he has turned to consider Marina's welfare.

In this picture of what it is to be 'gentle wounded' Shakespeare has done his best with Pericles. It is not an effect that bears much repetition or enlargement. At Tarsus he shows the same sober manhood, and replies to Dionyza's lamentations with an expression of that primitive and universal piety which results from man's sense of his subordination in a world of mysterious forces, and for which the name of philosophy is too pretentious:

> We cannot but obey
> The powers above us. Could I rage and roar
> As doth the sea she lies in, yet the end
> Must be as 'tis   [III. iii. 9-12]

Then, after a touch of sad kindness to Lychorida, he makes for Tyre. (pp. 317-18)

It should be observed that there was little of this Pericles in the versions of the story most accessible to Shakespeare. The Apollonius of Lawrence Twyne's *Patterne of painefull Adventures* . . . is a vehement person. At his wife's death 'like a madman distracted he tore his clothes and rent his hair', and when he learns of the loss of his daughter he falls into an 'outrageous affection'. The push that the barely conscious Pericles gives to Marina is derived from a far more violent demonstration, for Apollonius 'stroke the maiden on the face with his foote, so that she fell to the ground, and the blood gushed plentifully out at her cheekes'. If we turn to Gower's *Confessio Amantis,* as Shakespeare seems to have done, we find less violence but little patience. Appolinus swoons and defies fortune when his wife dies, and at his daughter's tomb 'He curseth and saith all the worst Unto fortune'. There is one suggestive touch of temperance, which Shakespeare did not miss though Twyne did. When the sailors approach the grieving king with their demand, he replies: 'It is al reson that ye preie.' He shares their belief. To Shakespeare's Pericles it is not reason but superstition, and his courtesy is the greater. Gower, however, is not concerned with patience, but with honest, well-placed love, which he is contrasting with the incest of Antiochus and his daughter. There is therefore more coherence and proportion in his story than in Twyne's and it moves logically to its moral, which is that, while the incestuous are foredoomed, there is some hope for the honest lover. . . . To Twyne the attraction of the story lay in the exemplary instability of fortune. It offered him a 'delectable varietie' of strange accidents, and he finishes up with a hearty distribution of punishments and rewards, including, somewhat oddly, the knighting of the pirates who kidnapped the princess. His *Patterne of painefull Adventures* does not presume a pattern endurance, but to Shakespeare it may well have suggested one, and he allowed his imagination to fill the empty niche within the exuberant framework with figures of ideal purity. (pp. 320-21)

> *J.M.S. Tompkins, ''Why Pericles?'' in* The Review of English Studies *n.s., Vol. III, No. 12, October, 1952, pp. 315-24.*

JOHN F. DANBY   (essay date 1952)

[*In the following excerpt, Danby discusses Pericles's misfortunes and his reaction to them, concluding that patience in adversity is the play's dominating motif—a view also held by J.M.S. Tompkins (1952) and F. D. Hoeniger (1963), but challenged by Ernest Schanzer (1965).*]

Pericles is a study of the prince in misfortune. The first two acts show a good man embroiled, swept from security by the tempest of another's wickedness. The misfortunes are external, the loss is the loss of a throne. The second part begins with the more inward loss of a wife, a loss however which brings the gain of a daughter, for Fortune always has a 'doutous or double visage'. Shakespeare is supported by what he has himself learnt about the inner structure of this world as well as guided by what he knows of it from others who have also explored it.

Act III begins with the tempest and ends with Pericles making provision for his daughter, the 'fresh-new seafarer', and bidding 'a priestly farewell' to his wife. Scene i is a lyrical Shakespearian handling of the matter of Patience. In his opening speech Pericles addresses the 'god of this great vast'—a deity higher than Fortune. In the first shock of his grief at hearing of Thaisa's death he is in danger of being overthrown. 'Patience, good sir,' the nurse calls to him, 'do not assist the storm,'—

> Be manly and take comfort.   [III. i. 22]

The force of Lychorida's last words is apt to be lost on a post-renaissance audience. 'Manly' implies the summoning-up of the full fortitude manhood implies, but also assumes in this context the creaturely dependence of that manhood: virtue cannot be self-sufficient however far it exerts itself, and even though it is asserted to the full. Pericles calls out against the gods, but it is a human bewilderment rather than a passionate revolt. Again Lychorida cries, 'Patience, good sir.' Pericles recovers himself and turns to the child. The overflow of compassion is a good augury. Only those can take comfort who can give comfort, and there is immense tenderness in Pericles' words. By the time he is finished he has found a new balance. His reply to the sailor indicates the firm hold he now has on his re-established manliness:

> FIRST SAILOR.   What courage, sir? God save you!
> PER.   Courage enough. I do not fear the flaw:
>   It hath done to me the worst.
>   [III. i. 38-40]

When the sailors tell him his wife must be cast overboard he submits to the necessity. In the great speech . . . [at III. i. 56-69] he fully realizes death's final 'apathie'—away from the storm, on the sea's floor, 'lying with simple shells': an apathy which is the opposite of patience as death is the opposite of life. He bids Thaisa 'a priestly farewell'.

The difference between the first and the second parts of *Pericles* can now be more clearly seen. Instead of reporting moral precepts Shakespeare is presenting moral occasions. The audience

Act V. Scene i. Lady, Marina, and Pericles. By W. Hilton (n.d.). From the Art Collection of the Folger Shakespeare Library.

not only has a map to the territory it can also see the movements of the protagonist across the countryside. In taking over or resuming the play Shakespeare judged rightly that what it needed was a 'voice'—the impression of a living personality, and that personality a centre of sensitive moral consciousness. The unit of communication now is the whole scene. Inside that scene we can see the complete turn or rotation of a person responding to a completely given moral occasion. Lyrically evocative as the scene is, the lyrical imagery would not be sufficient, however, without the clearly mapped territory behind it—which Shakespeare shared both with his audience and his collaborator. 'Belching whale' and 'humming water' [III. i. 62-3], overpoweringly suggestive as they are, are not as illuminatingly definitive as the interchange between the sailor and the bereaved husband. 'Imagery' is a deceptive word to use in connection with occasions such as this. Imagery includes more than metaphor, more even than is usually included in the phrase 'verbal texture'. Shakespeare's main controlling image is the image of a man in certain circumstances speaking from the midst of his situation to another man (Shakespeare, again, gives the Sailor a 'voice'). The flow of meaning that then takes place only has significance within the moral situation that has been presented. The emotive aura of the separable 'images' (what Aristotle called 'diction') is large and maybe vague. The total moral reference of the scene, however, is specific and precise. And the references in this case fall within the field covered by 'patience in adversity'.

The two explaining systems which have been applied recently to the interpretation of the Last Plays miss, I think, the essentially Elizabethan—and for that matter the more deeply human—inwardness of the romance scheme. The first of these has been based on [James George Frazer's] the *Golden Bough* and the fertility cycle and rebirth. The second has been similarly based on the Christian conception of regeneration and resurrection. Neither, I think, is as satisfactory as the contemporary and conventional scheme which Shakespeare used. Anthropology does not take us far enough. By its insidious precipitations it tends to silt over the clear and sharp contours of the renaissance moral world. The second explaining system errs in the opposite direction. It carries us too far and too fast. It particularizes in a field of meaning beyond Shakespeare's intention—though Shakespeare, I have no doubt, would know St. Paul and the burial service, and accepted the New Testament. To theologize the last plays, however, is to distort them. Though patience as Shakespeare conceives it implies St. Paul and the New Testament, patience as Shakespeare realizes it in the Last Plays is a familiar and well-walked parish in a wider diocese. Nor is the parish presided over by the Fisher King, and in it St. Paul is taken for granted but not allegorized in every Whitsun pastoral. And this brings us to a further distortion which over-anxiety about the greatness of Shakespeare's final plays is sometimes responsible for—a distortion of their tone. Shakespeare's last plays are not conceived at the same level of seriousness as Dante's *Paradiso*. They have an *ironia* of their own. Shakespeare during the last period is comparatively relaxed. He makes a toy of thought. Drawing on the full richness of his inner life, sporadically, as they do, executed with the unanxious brilliance of the maestro who has never lost his flair for improvisation, as they are, the final plays are for all that adjusted to the level of entertainment, controlled by an intention 'which was to please'.

The 'resurrection' scene in *Pericles,* for example, follows immediately on the storm and Thaisa's committal to the sea. The casket in which Thaisa has been placed is washed ashore near the house of Cerimon. Cerimon, as the Epilogue says, is a 'reverend' example of 'learned charity': as Mr. Wilson Knight has pointed out, Shakespeare's first sketch for Prospero [see excerpt above, 1947]. Cerimon prefers the power which wisdom gives to that which the mere governor can exercise:

> I held it ever,
> Virtue and cunning were endowments greater
> Than nobleness and riches: careless heirs
> May the two latter darken and expend;
> But immortality attends the former,
> Making a man a god. 'Tis known I ever
> Have studied physic.   [III. ii. 26-32]

With a kind of endearing *pietas* Shakespeare builds up his scene along lines slightly old-fashioned. We are shown Cerimon first in actual fact helping 'some Persons who have been shipwrecked'. We then see him being greeted by two gentlemen who announce his character:

> Your honour hath through Ephesus pour'd forth
> Your charity, and hundreds call themselves
> Your creatures, who by you have been restor'd.
>   [III. ii. 43-5]

Finally Thaisa's coffin is brought in and opened, and the moment of her resuscitation occurs. Again the lyrical note is struck. The verse quickens and pants with wonder:

> Gentlemen,
> This queen will live: nature awakes; a warmth
> Breathes out of her . . . see how she 'gins to blow
> Into life's flower again. . . .
> THAISA.   O dear Diana!
> Where am I? Where's my lord? What world is this?
>   [III. ii. 92-5, 104-05]

When thinking of symbolism we must remember that one of the most important things an apple can mean is simply itself. Thaisa's re-awakening feels to her like a rebirth—and also like a loss. To the spectators it is wonder enough, the more so that Thaisa is a miracle of beauty. But the moment attains its highest significance, I think, when it is brought into relation with Pericles' great speech before the committal, and into the general romance frame of 'doutous fortune' and the Providence that smiles while it seems to frown. We do not need to make it more important than that—nor less. And indeed, while there is a restoration of the seeming dead to breathing warmth, it is still a world of trial and of separation to which Thaisa is brought back. Cut off from Pericles, she must retire to Diana's temple and endure her exile in patience. (pp. 95-9)

In *Pericles* it is patience in adversity which is the dominating *motif*, and in Act V patience returns to hold the stage.

The supposed death of his daughter is the second blow Pericles has sustained. It almost exhausts his reserves of 'manliness' but not quite:

> He bears
> A tempest, which his mortal vessel tears,
> And yet he rides it out.   [IV. iv. 29-31]
>   (pp. 101-02)

There can be little doubt that in *Pericles* Shakespeare is responding richly—and with almost lyrical excitement—to the inward theme of the Romance. It is the inwardness that is important: the externals alone would never explain either

Shakespeare's excitement or the individuality of his accent even when he is handling material that might otherwise be dismissed as merely conventional or 'in the sources'. The tempests of the last plays are Sidneian tempests, too, but that makes them no less Shakespearean.

In *Pericles* Shakespeare has crossed the threshold of the final period. *Pericles* (the last three acts) is the swiftest and most lyrically conceived handling of the romance matter. For one thing, it concentrates on a single aspect only, a single turn of the wheel in the life of a prince who loses wife and daughter and finds them again. The plays that follow *Pericles* are more complex than this, draw on more of the matter, have more than one centre of focus. (p. 103)

> *John F. Danby, "Sidney and the Late-Shakespearian Romance," in his* Poets on Fortune's Hill: Studies in Sidney, Shakespeare, Beaumont & Fletcher, *Faber and Faber, 1952, pp. 74-107.**

BERTRAND EVANS (essay date 1955)

[*Evans's major contribution to Shakespearean scholarship, first outlined in his* Shakespeare's Comedies *(1960), is his examination of Shakespeare's dramatic use of discrepant awareness—a technique which creates different levels of perception among the play's characters. Evans's concern with* Pericles, *however, is with the Gower chorus, which he contends is "uniquely personal" and, hence, does not work in the manner of a traditional chorus, which is generally more objective and abstract. He proposes that this unusual chorus is attributable to Shakespeare's use of a lost poem as a source for the play.*]

Perhaps among Shakespeare's plays none is a better choice than *Pericles* to set aside. Clearly, it is not much of a play; probably no manner of criticism, so it be honest, can make this play look good. In isolated passages the poetry is striking, and in isolated scenes the action is compelling. But as a whole thing it is the most unsatisfactory of Shakespeare's works.

Whatever the point of departure, the ultimate question of *Hamlet* criticism is singular: Why does Hamlet delay? So with *Pericles,* in such attention as it has had or is likely to have, the mystery is singular also: Why is it such a bad play? It is no simple question, answerable by the easier observations— that its characters are bloodless, its actions strung out, event after event, endlessly, as in a narrative which knew no destination when it began. These are facts, of course; but as answers they do not come near the real intent of the question, which is none other than why Shakespeare, in 1607, wrote such a bad play. For him, in or about that year, the feat would have seemed impossible. (p. 35)

When one raises in his mind the image of the total work of *Pericles,* and ponders this image, he becomes aware that of its several unique features as a play of Shakespeare's the most extraordinary is the Chorus. It is not, certainly, the mere presence of the Chorus that is unique. . . . In *Pericles* the moral Gower enters eight times as Chorus, and, all told, speaks 306 lines. The use of the Chorus in this play, then, is more extensive by nearly 100 lines than in any other.

But not only is the Chorus in *Pericles* more extensive; it is also uniquely personal. The Chorus in *Romeo and Juliet* is a nameless, bodiless spokesman; so is that in *Henry V.* In *2 Henry IV* and *The Winter's Tale* the Choruses are personified abstractions, respectively Rumour and Time. In *Pericles,* in possibly significant contrast, the Chorus is a real person, the poet Gower. It is true, of course, that Gower told the story of

Apollonius of Tyre in his *Confessio Amantis* and that this, along with Twine's *Patterne of Painefull Adventures,* was Shakespeare's source. But Arthur Brooke told the tale of *Romeus and Juliet,* to which Shakespeare was not less indebted for his first important tragedy than to the *Apollonius* for his first romance; yet the Chorus of *Romeo and Juliet* is not Brooke, but an impersonal voice. So also the history plays owe most to Holinshed; but when the dramatist requires a Chorus in two of these plays, that Chorus is not Holinshed. (pp. 36-7)

So the Chorus in *Pericles* is both uniquely extensive and uniquely personal. It is also unique in its relation to the play. Elsewhere Shakespeare's Choruses serve a special, limited, and rather obvious purpose; typically they express the dramatist's awareness of some problem which he may have felt himself unable to solve by wholly dramatic means. (p. 37)

[In such instances], the Chorus performs a special task which, fairly obviously, needs to be done. In each, the Chorus is an impersonal extradramatic voice, a supernumerary which accomplishes its special supernumerary function and then steps aside. In contrast, the Chorus in *Pericles*—except on one occasion—performs no special task of obvious character, and yet it is by far the most conspicuous Chorus in Shakespeare, appearing eight times, speaking long each time, and representing the person of a particular man. Such, then, is the paradox of this Chorus: that though the need it serves is less readily apparent than is the need in certain other plays, nevertheless both itself and the role it takes are not, as in these plays, supernumerary and secondary, but principal and primary. (pp. 38-9)

[Often] shifts of time, shifts of place, and masses of incident might, any of them, have been cause to introduce an inconspicuous Chorus. However, the Chorus in *Pericles* is not inconspicuous, but highly conspicuous. And, what is more, though he speaks some three hundred and six lines, Gower does not seem to be concerned with the very matters that could have provided plausible reasons for one or two unobtrusive appearances. So the paradox remains: Gower is the most conspicuous Chorus in Shakespeare, yet he scarcely performs even the more obvious tasks of the usual Chorus. (p. 40)

In the presence of universal belief that some form of retelling intervened between Twine and Shakespeare, and in the absence of proof that the form was dramatic, it is possible to hypothesize the existence of a narrative poem on the subject. If there was such a poem, it is of course lost. But perhaps it is not so completely lost as is the hypothetical drama.

Of the eight passages spoken by Gower as Chorus in *Pericles,* the first four, totaling 194 lines, appear to be substantial remnants of a narrative poem that was once possibly a complete work which stood independent of any drama. The final four of the Gower passages, totaling 112 lines, appear . . . to be increasingly appropriate recastings of longer narrative portions for incorporation into the play. . . . The remaining three passages of the last group appear to be sharply condensed summaries, or précis, clearly devised to be incorporated into the play.

On the evidence of the surviving remnants, it is possible to make a partial description of the lost poem. It was a poem in octosyllabic couplets, in certain lines imitative of the language of Gower, but in far the greater number of lines as modern as the language of 1600. It was a poem approximately one-third to one-half the length of Gower's *Apollonius of Tyre,* if pro-

portions suggested by the surviving, nonsummarized parts of it are representative. (pp. 53-4)

[Some] special effort has been made to fit the first four Chorus passages within the frame of the play. But the very effort reveals itself, and the result is that these parts do not seem to belong inside a play so much as the scenes of the play seem to belong in the spaces left by omission of parts of the poem. Thus the greater frame seems to be not dramatic, but narrative. When the dramatist, at the close of the first narrative bit, adds the pentameter lines,

> What now ensues, to the judgement of your eye
> I give, my cause who best can justify,
>
> [I. Cho. 41-2]

not only is the tacked-on appearance conspicuous, but also the effect is to place what follows (the dramatized episode of Pericles and the riddle) in the subordinate position. This effect gives clearer significance to the title-page advertisement of George Wilkins' novel: "The Painfull Adventures of Pericles Prince of Tyre. Being the true History of the Play of Pericles, *as it was lately presented by* the worthy and ancient Poet Iohn Gower." (Italics mine.) For the play of *Pericles* is indeed "presented" by Gower—even to the extent that it seems to be Gower's play, or, rather, Gower's poem, within which certain episodes are dramatized. These dramatized parts of the story Gower "presents," somewhat as, in our time, a speaker may set illustrative slides into a machine and project them onto a screen.

The result of this relationship between Chorus passages and dramatized episodes is that, in the first three acts of *Pericles,* the poem dominates and the play is subordinate. And in their subordinate role, the dramatized episodes look precisely like what they are. The characters lack blood and the incidents lack reality. Both are quite unlike the full-bodied persons and events with which Shakespeare—or any other notable dramatist of the mature age—packs the stage when these persons and incidents are to carry the main burden of a tale. Having been conceived as subordinate, while the principal role was allotted to sections of an original poetic narrative, the scenes of the first three acts of *Pericles* might be said to play their own role well: they are appropriately bodiless and bloodless.

The change of conception may be marked at the opening of the second scene of the fourth act. Up to this point, the poem of *Pericles* has enclosed and dominated the play of *Pericles.* Gower's long speech in pentameter at the opening of Act IV, scene iv, represents the last struggle for supremacy between poem and play in the final perspective of the total work. The latter, very plainly, wins, for after this point Shakespeare—and there can be no serious doubt in the last two acts that it was he—summarily whips the Chorus into submission and transforms an "illustrated poem" into a play with brief extradramatic links. Thus, rather abruptly, after Gower's last long speech in tetrameter at the opening of Act IV, the poem of *Pericles* ends and the play begins. (pp. 54-6)

Bertrand Evans, "The Poem of 'Pericles'," in The Image of the Work: Essays in Criticism, *Bertrand Evans, Josephine Miles, William R. Steinhoff, eds., University of California Press, 1955, pp. 35-58.*

F. D. HOENIGER (essay date 1960)

[*In the following excerpt, Hoeniger proposes to "keep the fire burning" in the debate over the authorship of* Pericles *by offering evidence that John Day may have written the non-Shakespearean parts of the play. Arguments for a second playwright have also been developed by George Steevens (1780), F. G. Fleay (1874) and H. Dugdale Sykes (1918), who all saw George Wilkins's hand in the drama, and by Henry David Gray (1925), who claimed it was coauthored by Thomas Heywood.]*

[Most] readers of *Pericles* are agreed that the play's literary and dramatic quality is highly uneven. Much of the first two acts is written in doggerel, sometimes flat sometimes twisted, for which no superior dramatist, let alone Shakespeare, can be held responsible. On the other hand, some passages, especially in the last three acts, bear the mark of Shakespeare's consummate verse-artistry and abound in echoes to Shakespeare's last romances, *The Winter's Tale* and *The Tempest*. It is no wonder than, that from early days doubt was cast on the play's authorship. (p. 27)

[The controversy still] stands, unresolved. It is still very hot, and I propose to keep the fire burning by introducing yet another collaborator, one nobody seems ever to have thought of before in connection with *Pericles.*

That such a proposition, if it at all merits attention, will keep the issue hot can hardly be doubted, for while it may echo much of the learned debate of the last hundred years on *Pericles,* it goes counter to the general trend in present-day Shakespearian criticism in at least two ways. For it will be argued, first of all, that at least one of the plays now regularly included among his works is of mixed authorship. And what is even more heretic, if not foolhardy, the evidence for the claim of my new collaborator, John Day (known best for his *Parliament of Bees*), will take mainly the form of textual parallels. (pp. 27-8)

The majority of Day's plays have perished. Many were probably never printed. The extant canon of Day's works consists of *The Blind Beggar* (with Chettle), *The Ile of Gulls, The Travels* (with Wilkins and W. Rowley), *Law-Tricks, Humour out of Breath,The Parliament of Bees,* and a single piece of prose, *Peregrinatio Scholastica.* A close reading of these works revealed to me a strikingly large number of textual parallels to *Pericles.* Further encouraged by the fact that no fewer than four of Day's surviving plays were first printed in 1606-8, that is the three years preceding the publication of the first quarto of *Pericles,* I made a detailed list of all parallels, whether they in themselves seemed significant or not; everything, that is to say, from proverbial phrasing to striking correspondences of several successive lines or clusters of images. The resulting catalogue showed for most scenes of *Pericles* only one or two, and usually insignificant, parallels, but for two scenes, namely II.i and II.iii, a much larger number of parallels, including some remarkable ones.

One of these parallels was pointed out long ago by Bullen and is well-known. It involves the liveliest episode of the first two acts, the dialogue of the fishermen in II.i. The fishermen are overheard by the shipwrecked Pericles whom the stormy waves have tossed ashore near Pentapolis. . . . Bullen discovered that some of the fishermen's very phrases also occur in two scenes of *Law-Tricks.* . . . These remarkable parallels called for some explanation, and considering the *Law-Tricks* was first printed in 1608, the same year in which *Pericles* was entered in the Stationers' Register, Bullen decided that "Day must either have seen the MS of *Pericles,* or must have carried away the words in his memory from the playhouse". (pp. 31-2)

I believe that [such parallels] are remarkable, and that together with Bullen's, they make highly probable some close connec-

tion between the works of Day and the first scene of Act II of *Pericles*—a connection which indeed suggests identical authorship. (pp. 33-4)

As has already been stated, no external evidence can be found which might give direct support for such a conclusion. Yet what we do know about Day's career and about the general character of his work does not go contrary to it in any way. The dates of Day's works fit well, for four of his six extant plays were first printed between 1606 and 1608. Day seems to have been writing mainly for the Children of the Revels, who performed at Blackfriars, and for the Children of Paul's during the first years of King James's reign. Neither company survived beyond 1608, when the Blackfriar's Theatre passed into the possession of Shakespeare's company. We do not know what happened to Day then, for his name is not linked to a single play between 1608 and 1623. (pp. 35-6)

As for the character of his plays, it would be absurd to suggest any close kinship between them and *Pericles.* Some of them remind one rather of Shakespeare's early comedies, whose language is often imitated in them, or of Lyly or Dekker. They owe much to the themes and style of Elizabethan prose romance. . . .

Structurally, the most striking resemblance to *Pericles* is afforded by *Travels* (1607). Like *Pericles* this play sets forth a sprawling action of epic dimension, which the playwrights managed to hold together only by the device of a chorus who acts as prologue and epilogue, and who several times supplies narrative links between scenes, somewhat like the chorus of *Dr. Faustus.* At some points, the resemblance between the Chorus of *Travels* and Gower in *Pericles* is indeed a close one. Yet . . . other factors discourage one from making very much of this similarity. For the present purpose, it will suffice for us to know that Day had a share in a play which employs a device similar to that of Gower in *Pericles.* (p. 36)

These considerations of some of the larger structural features of Day's plays, though in themselves not contributing much direct evidence pointing to a link between Day and *Pericles,* have yet revealed sufficient points of contact for one to feel encouraged to give some weight to the evidence of textual parallels. For the kind of claim made here, no strong support from a comparison of form and structure was to be expected anyhow. If Day did contribute to the planning of the action of *Pericles,* he has not left his personal mark clearly. But he has left his mark, as I have tried to show, in the style of two scenes, II.i and II.iii. In these scenes, echoes to Day are varied and many. And their quantity as well as their multifariousness supports the general, if older, theory that *Pericles* is of composite authorship. For however much Elizabethan reporters of surreptitiously printed plays were prone to fall on their tenacious memories of the works of other playwrights, it is inconceivable that a reporter of *Pericles* should have echoed the work of Day in so many different ways, and so much more in two scenes than in other parts of the play. To say this does not, of course, rule out the likelihood that the quarto text as a whole, including the Day part, is a report. But if Day did write II.i and II.iii, it seems probable that there are other scenes in *Pericles,* particularly in the first two acts, that are not by Shakespeare. But who wrote them is not as yet known. (p. 37)

F. D. Hoeniger, "How Significant Are Textual Parallels? A New Author for 'Pericles'?" in Shakespeare Quarterly, *Vol. XI, No. 1, Winter, 1960, pp. 27-38.*

F. D. HOENIGER (essay date 1963)

[*Unlike William Watkiss Lloyd (1858), Hoeniger claims that Pericles is essentially a guiltless victim of fate, saying, "To seek for a moral cause of Pericles' troubles is to assume the role of Job's comforters," a position similar to that of Ernest Schanzer (1965). In noting the theme of patience as a central concern in* Pericles, *Hoeniger is in agreement with such critics as J.M.S. Tompkins (1952) and John F. Danby (1952).*]

While the leading characters of Shakespeare's comedies and tragedies are drawn as preponderantly active figures, as men and women who make decisions or show fateful indecision, thus contributing to a chain of events which eventually leads to their happiness or ruin, in *Pericles* the events usually happen to the protagonists. One can infer from Pericles' talents and activities that he is a man of unusual gifts, a skilful soldier as well as a great musician, a man of great authority among his subjects, and of generous dealing. But he is revealed mainly as the plaything of Fortune and the gods. He does not create his fortune in any important sense: he endures Fortune's blows and accepts her gifts. Such a manner of characterization is only partly explained by his indirect presentation through Gower. It is inherent in the nature of the play's action, and thus indicative of the view of life which informs it.

Besides being presented mainly passively, Pericles is drawn as an impeccably good man, a man without defect, which constitutes another essential difference from the characterization of Shakespeare's tragic heroes, and foreshadows the idealized figures of Imogen [*Cymbeline*] and Hermione [*The Winter's Tale*]. Pericles cannot be said in any sense to deserve misfortune or suffering, let alone the immensity of loss that lies in store for him. He is drawn without moral weakness—at any rate up to Act IV—and without even any ambivalent passion; that is partly why he does not strike us as especially interesting. Nor is his daughter Marina in any sense responsible for her misfortunes, though her eloquent chastity safeguards her from worse. Both Pericles and Marina undergo intense suffering, though both are wholly good.

My reason for emphasizing this point is that some contemporary scholars have been unwilling to face its implications, but instead have tried, in one way or another, to discover a trace of guilt in Pericles, Thaisa, or Marina. These critics see Pericles following the course of guilt, chastisement, atonement, and restoration, like Leontes in *The Winter's Tale*. G. Wilson Knight, for instance, in an otherwise illuminating essay on *Pericles* [see excerpt above, 1947], argues that Pericles is somehow infected by the evil of Antiochus' daughter whom he tried to woo, and therefore has to undergo purification through suffering. But when was a character ever conceived as worthy of the gods' chastisement whose only wrong had been to discover another's evil and who recoiled from it at once? Pericles is truly a man 'on whom perfections wait' [I. i. 79]. Kenneth Muir's imaginative suggestion that in the original uncorrupted text it was clearly indicated that Thaisa upon suddenly marrying Pericles broke a vow to Diana is equally misleading [see Additional Bibliography]. That Pericles and his family should be chastised by the gods on account of some broken vow or because they have come into contact with evil men—such an interpretation is irreconcilable with any known form of the story and, it seems to me, with the whole spirit of the play. Pericles suffers as a good man and for reasons beyond human comprehension. He is more like Job or like Tobit in the Apocrypha than like Leontes. As Gower puts it simply, Pericles' sufferings serve to show how 'those in troubles reign, Losing

a mite, a mountain gain' [II. Cho. 7-8]. To seek for a moral cause of Pericles' troubles is to assume the rôle of Job's comforters.

When we first encounter Pericles, he is a young prince of already exceptional insight. He solves Antiochus' riddle, which had baffled a hundred suitors, and conveys his solution to Antiochus diplomatically so as to gain time to flee from his murderous wrath. By the end of the play, he has undergone all the practical education a philosopher-king might desire. That aspect of Pericles' career, however, receives only secondary emphasis. It is indicated rather than impressed upon the spectator's mind. What matters is the pattern of sudden changes in Pericles' fortune, his severe losses, the sufferings which ensue, and his restoration to joy. (pp. lxxx-lxxxii)

As is to be expected, the blows Pericles undergoes increase in severity and in their crushing effect upon his happiness. In his first shipwreck he loses his companions and most of his goods, and is reduced to nakedness, begging for help among fishermen. But his armour is soon cast up again by the sea, though heavily rusted, and before long he has not merely achieved victory at the tournament organized by the local king but also gained the affection of his daughter. Pericles' response to the first storm is utterly unlike Lear's. Lear challenges the storm heroically. First he actually encourages it:

> Blow, winds, and crack your cheeks! rage! blow! . . .
> Strike flat the thick rotundity o' th' world.
> Crack Nature's moulds . . .
>
> [*King Lear*, III. ii. 1, 7-8]

Then, after his dramatic exclamation of his own helplessness in the face of the elements—'Here I stand your slave. A poor, infirm, weak, and despis'd old man' [*King Lear*, III. ii. 19-20]—he proceeds to denounce them for collaborating with the forces of ingratitude. . . . (p. lxxxii)

This, by contrast, is how Pericles addresses the gods of thunder:

> Yet cease your ire, you angry stars of heaven!
> Wind, rain, and thunder, remember, earthly man
> Is but a substance that must yield to you;
> And I, as fits my nature, do obey you.
>
> [II. i. 1-4]
> (pp. lxxxii-lxxxiii)

When Lychorida informs him that the queen has died, she implores him: 'Patience, good sir; do not assist the storm' [III. i. 19]. And after his brief outburst,

> O you gods!
> Why do you make us love your goodly gifts,
> And snatch them straight away? We here below
> Recall not what we give, and therein may
> Use honour with you,   [III. i. 22-6]

she again urges him, this time successfully: 'Patience, good sir, Even for this charge' [III. i. 26-7]. Awareness of new responsibilities towards his daughter quickly calms any rebellious mood to which his mind might have been prone. He even yields without long debate to the sailors' request that his queen be at once buried at sea. But his wholehearted submission to inevitable fate finds its clearest expression in the following scene at Tharsus, where, upon recalling the death of Thaisa, he says to Cleon and Dionyza:

> We cannot but obey
> The powers above us. Could I rage and roar
> As doth the sea she lies in, yet the end
> Must be as 'tis.   [III. iii. 9-12]

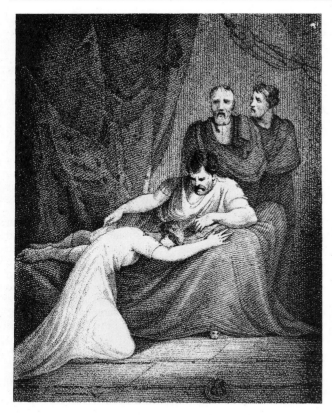

Act V. Scene i. Marina, Pericles, Helicanus and Lysima-chus. By Porter (1800). From the Art Collection of the Folger Shakespeare Library.

His words of stoic resignation recall Edgar's in *King Lear*:

> Men must endure
> Their going hence, even as their coming hither:
> Ripeness is all.   [*King Lear*, V. ii. 9-11]

So far Pericles has borne his misfortunes steadfastly. Yet one more tragedy is to overtake him, for on returning to Tharsus he is led by the tomb erected in her memory to believe that his daughter Marina is dead. Now his patience has reached an end, at least for a while. The occasion is presented in dumb-show only, but the stage-direction clearly conveys the violence of Pericles' grief: '. . . whereat Pericles makes lamentation, puts on sackcloth, and in a mighty passion departs' [IV. iv. 22]. After this event he no longer washes his face, and, as we learn at the beginning of the fifth act, he refuses food. He withdraws from human society altogether, not speaking a word to anyone. (pp. lxxxiii-lxxxiv)

But Marina, aided by the grace of Diana, the play's presiding goddess, becomes the main instrument in the freeing of Peri-cles, her father, from his condition of inward darkness after extreme tribulation. She enables him to see beyond tragedy. The extent of her sufferings bears comparison with his, and her expression, like 'Patience . . . smiling Extremity out of act' [V. i. 138-39], is the living image of her powers of calm endurance, and more, of her capacity to transcend tragic ex-perience. But as his daughter, Marina is part of Pericles' own personality, a symbol of the fruition of his marriage with Thaisa. She clearly represents—though this is probably only part of her function in the play—that hope man can find in the younger

generation, more especially in his children, of renewal, which reconciles him to life even after he has undergone severe dis-illusionment. Some creative power at work in this world can take him beyond tragedy to reaffirmation and joy. But the tragic experience brings with it humility, sympathy, and wisdom, all of which qualities are in the course of the play stressed in both Pericles and Marina. As to Marina, let Pericles' own words speak:

> Falseness cannot come from thee, for thou look'st
> Modest as Justice, and thou seem'st a palace
> For the crown'd Truth to dwell in.   [V. i. 120-22]

To give an expression of this creative, renewing principle closely related to ordinary human experience is the function of the double plot in *Pericles*. (pp. lxxxv-lxxxvi)

> *F. D. Hoeniger, in an introduction to* Pericles *by William Shakespeare, edited by F. D. Hoeniger, re-vised edition, Methuen, 1963, pp. xiii-xci.*

ERNEST SCHANZER   (essay date 1965)

[*In the following excerpt, first published in 1965, Schanzer chal-lenges the critical perception of Pericles as the quintessential embodiment of patience in adversity—a view held by J.M.S. Tompkins (1952), John F. Danby (1952), and F. D. Hoeniger (1963). Schanzer also contends, with Hoeniger, that Pericles's loss and eventual recovery of his family is caused by accident and not by divine Providence, as has been suggested by William Wat-kiss Lloyd (1858).*]

A number of critics in recent years have claimed that Pericles, as Shakespeare depicts him, is an embodiment of patience in adversity, a kind of male Griselda-figure, and that the play presents an *exemplum* of this virtue of patience that leads to restoration and happiness. Now it is true that, compared to his prototypes in the sources, Pericles behaves under the earlier blows of fortune with much moderation and restraint. For in-stance, in his reception of the news of his wife's death, where in Gower and Twine he indulges in the most frantic display of grief, in Shakespeare's scene he expresses it much less ve-hemently. Yet nothing suggests to me here that he is meant to be seen as an embodiment of patience in adversity. The nurse, Lychorida, repeatedly calls upon him to be patient: "Patience, good sir; do not assist the storm" [III. i. 19] (assist, that is, by his loud cries of grief); "Patience, good sir, / Even for this charge" [III. i. 26-7]. . . . It would be odd to be preaching patience to a figure embodying that virtue. (p. 1411)

I find even more misleading the common assertion that Shake-speare presents the main events of the play, both the misfor-tunes and the reunions, as the work of divine Providence. The whole pattern of Pericles' painful adventures, as these critics see it, is a pattern imposed by the gods. But the notion of a divine Providence that persecutes wholly virtuous characters so cruelly and for so long is repugnant, and so several of these critics are driven to discover some offense in the protagonists for which they are punished. Such an attempt to find a pattern of sin, punishment, expiation, and restoration in the play seems to me to violate and distort its whole spirit. It is to assimilate *Pericles* to *The Winter's Tale* and *The Tempest,* where sin and expiation do play an important part. In *Pericles,* as in the miracle plays, we are confronted with the *undeserved* sufferings of the wholly innocent and entirely virtuous—of Pericles, Thaisa, and Marina. And both their misfortunes and their restorations are shown to be mainly due to accident, to chance. The goddess who presides over the play is not Diana but Fortuna. It is by accident that the waves throw up the coffin containing Thaisa at Ephesus near the house of Cerimon, just the person who possesses the rare medical knowledge and skill needed to restore her to life. It is accident that brings Pericles' ship Mytilene and Marina on board this ship, thus enabling father and daughter to be reunited. To see in all this the hand of Providence is indeed to take away from our sense of wonder. Only once in the play is there any clear evidence of supernatural intervention: [when] the goddess Diana appears to Pericles in a vision. Without this vision the final reunion of Thaisa with her husband and daughter would have been difficult to bring about. In both Shakespeare's sources this vision is found, though only in Shakespeare is it the goddess Diana that appears to Pericles. . . . But I can find no suggestion in the play that Diana had any other part in its events. (p. 1412)

> Ernest Schanzer, in his introduction to "Pericles, Prince of Tyre," in The Complete Signet Classic Shakespeare, Sylvan Barnet, General Editor, Harcourt, 1972, pp. 1407-16.

NORTHROP FRYE (essay date 1965)

[Frye is considered one of the most important critics of the twentieth century and a leader of the anthropological or mythic approach to literature which gained prominence during the 1950s. As outlined in his seminal work, An Anatomy of Criticism (1957), Frye views all literature as ultimately derived from certain myths or archetypes present in the human psyche, and he therefore sees literary criticism as an unusual type of science in which the literary critic seeks only to decode the mythic structure inherent in a work of art. Frye's effort was to produce a method of literary interpretation more universal and exact than that suggested in other critical approaches, such as New Criticism, biographical criticism, or historical criticism—all of which he finds valuable, but also limited in application. As a Shakespearean critic, Frye has devoted himself primarily to the comedies and romances, especially with his definition of the three main phases of Shakespearean comic and romantic structure: the initial phase of "the anticomic society," "the phase of temporarily lost identity," and the establishment of a "new society" through either marriage or self-knowledge. The following excerpt is from Frye's essay entitled "Mouldy Tales," an allusion to Ben Jonson's comment on Pericles (see excerpt above, 1629), from his A Natural Perspective: The Development of Shakespearean Comedy and Romance (1965). Frye illustrates the archetypal nature of Pericles by comparing it to a wide range of literary works, including T. S. Eliot's The Waste Land. The story of Pericles, says Frye, "evokes the primitive responses from us that are evoked by popular literature." Other critics who have focused on the archetypal structure of Pericles include Richard Wincor (1950) and C. L. Barber (1969).]

Pericles is a most radical experiment in processional narrative: the action is deliberately linear, proceeding from place to place and from episode to episode. In the background is the Gower story, with its constant "and then" beat, a story we drop into from time to time when a part of it is dramatically manifested. (pp. 27-8)

At the same time the way in which the action of Pericles is presented makes it one of the world's first operas. Apart altogether from the development of the masque, we sometimes forget how operatic the Elizabethan popular theater was, with its sennets and tuckets and flourishes, its "mood music" of viols and hautboys, its interspersed songs. We are reminded of this when we study the texts of a dramatist who was interested in the musical backgrounds of his plays and gave full directions for them. . . . In Pericles Gower provides a narrative continuity, like recitativo, while the main action dram-

atizes the central episodes. In the imagery, music is practically the hero of the play: it is to the action of Pericles what Prospero's magic is to the action of The Tempest.

And just as the structure of Pericles anticipates opera, with its narrative recitativo and its dramatized arias, so it also anticipates the kind of modern poem where, as in Eliot's The Waste Land, the narrative connective tissue is cut out and only the essential scenes are presented. Eliot's debt to Pericles is partly recorded in his Marina, and some of Eliot's readers have felt that the ideal dramatic form he speaks of so often is better represented by The Waste Land, which is close to Pericles not only in its fragmentation but in its symbolism of Phoenician sailors, sterile fornication, and deliberate archaizing, than it is by his more conservative stage plays. (pp. 28-9)

Finally, we notice that the dumb show, along with such visual clichés as the procession of knights with their emblems and mottoes, occupies a prominent place in Pericles, and helps to make it a spectacular as well as an operatic play. . . . The late romances, Pericles in particular, are plays in which a union of the three major arts, melos, lexis, and opsis, to use the Aristotelian terms, give us a drama beyond drama, a kind of ultimate confrontation of a human community with an artistic realization of itself. We remain in a center of action where, as in the commedia dell' arte, the spirit of which is so close to Shakespearean comedy, everything that goes on seems spontaneously improvised, precisely because its general convention is prescribed in advance. (pp. 29-30)

[There] is a great symmetry of design in Pericles and a skillful orchestration of thematic images. One aspect of Gower's role is like that of the manager at the beginning of [Kalidasa's] Sakuntala or [Goethe's] Faust: he reminds us that this is a play, and the effect of the reminder is to shatter the framework of the play and lead us inside it. But the contrast with the prologues in Jonson's plays strikes us at once. In Jonson the prologue, whether monologue or dialogue, is designed to awaken our critical faculties. Gower is an aged figure recalled from the dead, like Samuel by the Witch of Endor; he stands for the authority of literary tradition; he is himself dependent on still older sources, and he is there to put us in as uncritical a frame of mind as possible. The play opens with Pericles attempting to win the daughter of Antiochus, who lives in incest with her father and is consequently his wife as well. It closes with Pericles reunited to his own proper wife and daughter. These two contrasting episodes frame the whole play, and most of the intervening action is contained in two other repetitions of the same theme, which also contrast with each other. (pp. 31-2)

The setting of the play is not only dramatically but psychologically primitive. Antiochus' daughter is surrounded with imagery of forbidden fruit, Hesperidean gardens, and serpents. Pericles' ordeal is the ancient riddle game, which seems to combine the primitive features of the two main stories of the Oedipus legend. If Pericles fails to solve the riddle, he must die; if he succeeds in solving it, he must die. The logic is that of the Arabian Nights. But where so uncritical a participation is demanded from us, the action cannot be lifelike: it can only be archetypal. It evokes the primitive responses from us that are evoked by popular literature: it has a hero's hairbreadth escapes, a heroine's deliverance from death and dishonor, a miraculous curing of someone apparently dead; it appeals to the horror of incest and the tearful joy of reunions. The dramatic construct, for all its symmetry, has been reduced to great simplicity and directness in order to put the strongest possible emphasis on the immediate dramatic experience itself. (pp. 32-3)

Northrop Frye, "Mouldy Tales," in his A Natural Perspective: The Development of Shakespearean Comedy and Romance, *Columbia University Press, 1965, pp. 1-33.*

HOWARD FELPERIN (essay date 1967)

[*Felperin discusses Shakespeare's supposed spiritual "conversion"—noted by George Brandes (1895-96), E. K. Chambers (1908), and Frank Harris (1911)—and its effect on his dramatic style and purpose. According to Felperin, Shakespeare's technique becomes allegorical in* Pericles, *and he maintains that the play offers "a timeless parable for our spiritual enlightenment—like the miracle play." Donald Stauffer (1949) also noted elements of the miracle play in* Pericles.]

The hypothesis that Shakespeare experienced some sort of religious conversion, intuition, vision, or inspiration about 1607-1608, which remained with him until the close of his career, is, of course, merely a critical convenience. It is useful only in so far as it illuminates the marked change of style and change of dramatic purpose in the last plays . . . and it is valid only in so far as it derives from the plays themselves. The change of style which *Pericles* announces seems all the more radical if we remember that it almost certainly follows *Coriolanus.* From the most naturalistically earth-bound of the Tragedies, we move to the stagy fairy-tale of the first of the last plays. A lucid, chaste, Virgilian rhetoric gives place first to a gnomic, archaic, brittle verse and then, by the end of *Pericles,* to Shakespeare's final, magical speech-music; tight dramatic structure to slack, episodic, narrative structure; psychologically complex personalities to simple character-types; and so on. Rather than be baffled or exasperated we must assume that Shakespeare, at this point in his career, knew what he was doing: that the marked change in style is accounted for by a change in dramatic purpose, and the change in purpose, by a change in his poetic vision of life.

When Ancient Gower walked onto the stage as Chorus, a Jacobean audience would have been immediately aware of the archaism of the device. The convention of the poet as Chorus had been all but brushed aside by the momentum of increasing naturalism, and plays at this point in the development of the drama often began in mid-dialogue. . . . (pp. 364-65)

Obviously Shakespeare would not deliberately cultivate an archaic medievalism at this stage in his work without very sophisticated ulterior motives. . . . The imitation of Gower's jingly rhymes, archaic diction, and simpleminded didacticism is itself skilful, and who but Shakespeare could have introduced so unobtrusively, yet purposefully, the main themes of the play, "man's infirmities", resurrection, and restoration, within the first eight lines? The humorous Latin tag, the contrast between "these latter times" and a "song that old was sung", a contrast embodied in the resurrected Gower himself, serve to surround the tale with an air of vague antiquity. . . . In short, Shakespeare is telling us that the story we are about to witness will be a timeless parable for our spiritual enlightenment—like the miracle play—and that to learn from it we must unlearn our sophisticated notions of dramatic storytelling. Aware of the difficulties that this request involves, he makes Gower humorously self-conscious in his demand. Like the long-suspected chorus of Time in *The Winter's Tale,* Gower's speeches are not intended as great poetry—why do we insist that Shakespeare always sound like Shakespeare?—but as dramatically appropriate poetry calculated to persuade us to accept certain impossibilities, to establish on the spur of the moment a convention crucial for our understanding of what is to follow. In the case of Gower, the convention was partly established in the mind of the audience already, trained as it was on an earlier drama. (pp. 365-66)

The technique is to be allegory. Pericles in his first scene is derived from Everyman through *Juventus* of the neo-moralities. Unlike his Christian predecessors, however, he is not culpable but eminently virtuous; yet we shall see that his play also is to be concerned with redemption. (p. 367)

Cataracts of ink have been spilled in the effort to find in Pericles' experience up to [the end of the second act] at least one specific sin which will explain his self-imposed penance. Needless to say, there is none, and that is the very point. Thaisa's death is not simply the death of a wife but the final overpowering evidence of worldly mutability and loss. Like Mankind in *The Castle of Perseverance,* Pericles and Thaisa withdrew from the pain and flux of the Earthly City into a decidedly medieval asceticism. The theme will be climactically realized—and modified—in the terrible penitential figure of Pericles in the last act.

Act IV belongs to Marina, the first of Shakespeare's idealized portraits of young womanhood in the last plays. . . . The underlying myth employed by Shakespeare is that of a figure of innocence transported to a realm of darkness, where she eventually becomes its ruler. The moral allegory is mythologically sustained. . . . Exemplary virtue, though it may strike us as prudish, could not have struck Shakespeare's audience that way. Marina culminates a long tradition of incorruptibly virtuous heroines. . . . (pp. 369-70)

In *Pericles* the eschatological metaphors become reality. The world becomes, ultimately, the place of love's fulfillment rather than defeat, and with an intensity so perfect it becomes salvation, the state which is the goal and justification for all previous states. Cordelia is a figure of grace who redeems the cursed and brutal Nature of the play, but the redemption she offers the ruined Lear is fugitive, lifting him out of purgatory but into no abiding heaven within the play. The salvation that Marina and Thaisa bring to Pericles is absolute and enduring, a beatific love-vision realized on earth, while the gods, previously indifferent, hostile, or non-existent in Shakespeare, become benevolent, working inevitably to bring that final fulfillment about. And as we should expect, allusion to an afterlife disappears. There is no suggestion of Christian eschatology in the last plays—how could there be when salvation becomes an earthly destiny?—while the Christian values of faith, patience, charity, chastity, take on a new teleological significance in Shakespeare's mind. (pp. 372-73)

Despite the considerable theatrical success of *Pericles* in its first days, Shakespeare deviated from the allegorical method in his subsequent efforts and reverted at least part-way back to naturalism. The process of selective simplification which represented life as a tempest, a birth, and a death and human beings as passive emblems in an eternal metaphysical drama may have struck him as inadequate to the increasing complexity of his vision. We value the later plays more highly, I suspect, partly because of their reversion to a causal, consequential, and recognizable world, to a more naturalistic mode—the dramatic style and substance in which *we* have been schooled—and also, perhaps, because they are simply better plays. Yet

Shakespeare's audience did not, alive as it still was to the proposition that the phenomenal world is but the shadow of a magnitude and to the dramatic technique which that proposition implies. (p. 374)

Howard Felperin, ''Shakespeare's Miracle Play,'' in Shakespeare Quarterly, Vol. XVIII, No. 4, Autumn, 1967, pp. 363-74.

C. L. BARBER (essay date 1969)

[*An American scholar, Barber is one of the most important and influential contemporary critics of Shakespearean comedy. In his study* Shakespeare's Festive Comedy *(1959), Barber examines the parallels between Elizabethan holiday celebrations and Shakespeare's comedies. In both festival customs and comic plays Barber identifies a saturnalian pattern which, as he explains in the introduction, involves* ''a basic movement which can be summarized in the formula, through release to clarification.'' *Barber defines release as a revelry, a mirthful liberation,* ''an accession of wanton vitality'' *over the restraint imposed by everyday life; the clarification that follows he characterizes as a* ''heightened awareness of the relation between man and 'nature','' *which in comedy becomes* ''a humor that puts holiday in perspective with life as a whole.'' *In his consideration of the romances, however, Barber observes not simply a release but a transformation of love, and concludes* ''that where regular comedy deals with freeing sexuality from the ties of the family, these late romances deal with freeing family ties from the threat of sexual degradation.'' *Barber thus notes how this threat, specifically the fear of incest, is overcome in* Pericles, *contrasting it with the nature of sexuality as presented in* King Lear. *Phyllis Gorfain (1976) also discusses the incest motif in* Pericles. *For further comparison of* Pericles *with ancient festival customs, see the excerpt by Richard Wincor (1950).*]

In the comedies of [Shakespeare's] youth, the perverse and repressive are laughed out of court while release leads to the embrace of passion, sanctioned by clarification as to its place as part of the natural cycle. In the romances, however, fulfilment for the principal figure requires a transformation of love, not simply liberation of it. One can put this in summary by saying that where regular comedy deals with freeing sexuality from the ties of family, these late romances deal with freeing family ties from the threat of sexual degradation. . . .

I picked out the strange line which I have quoted in my title, 'Thou that beget'st him that did thee beget' [V. i. 195], because, addressed by Pericles to his daughter, it summarizes both the effect of the beloved figures on the protagonists, in bringing them back to life, and the thing that is most emphasized in the feminine figures—their power to create and cherish life, their potential or achieved maternity. The line also recalls, in one direction, the unholy incest of Antiochus which devastated Pericles when he first sought a wife, an incest where both the riddle and Pericles' response stress that the daughter took the place of wife and mother: 'with foul incest to abuse your soul; / Where now you're both a father and a son' [I. i. 126-27]. In the other direction, the line points forward to the mother and wife who is found through Marina when the ecstasy of recognizing her leads Pericles to hear the music of the spheres and fall into a trance-like sleep. Pericles at the beginning of recognition literally sees the mother in the daughter. . . . (p. 61)

It was probably not more than two years before *Pericles* that Shakespeare had written about a tragic king who, in his Fool's words, 'madest thy daughters thy mother'. Here there is no queen, and the tragedy begins with Lear asking for everything from his daughters in return for giving himself away. Regan and Goneril, who we discover have inwardly rejected his de-

mand for tenderness and become cruel and avidly sensual, pretend to give him what he wants—in terms that are almost incestuous. . . . Lear's reunion with Cordelia, for me the most moving scene in all Shakespeare, anticipates, often point by point, the reunion of Pericles and Marina. But even as the tragedy realizes the full value of the love of parent and child, it follows out remorselessly the destructive logic of Lear's possessiveness. . . . The old king has learned to ask forgiveness, learned he is not everything—and ceased to care for that. But he still wants his daughter 'to love [her] father all'. He leads her off with him to death, telling her as he does so that upon such sacrifices as hers 'the gods themselves throw incense' [V. iii. 21].

In *Pericles* the motive which leads to tragedy in *King Lear* finds resolution. Why is not the romance merely a superbly realized wish-fulfilment? Of course the given facts are simply different: Pericles is in middle age: there is a wife; the moment of *her* loss is central. And where Lear is a superb impatient egotist, Pericles is a figure of patience who lives chiefly through his awareness of others. On deeper levels, the final happy ending is earned by moving through a sequence of attitudes which have a spiritual and psychological logic and make the seemingly random adventures a visionary exploration. Components of the motive in Lear are objectified, distanced and so brought under control, with a generalized experience of suffering and misfortune which reflects the psychic cost of the process. Thus at the outset the potentiality of overt incest is recognized and felt as a destructive horror. Later, when Marina is coming to maturity, the possibility of a mother's destructive jealousy of a daughter—another tendency running counter to the final atonement—is enacted in Dionyza's attempt to murder Marina.

The total concentration of Lear on his daughters creates the tragic split between brutal sexual greed in Regan and Goneril and sacrificial tenderness in Cordelia. It fits with Lear's horror of female sexuality. . . . In *Pericles,* the strange, comical scenes in the brothel bring the daughter into relation to brutal sexual desire so as literally to disassociate her from it. Boult and the Bawd and even Lysimachus assault her with brutal imagery and intention, only to be rebuked. (pp. 62-3)

In *Pericles,* the acceptance of the daughter's independent feminity is achieved not by dramatizing her own self-realization as a woman, as is done with Perdita in *The Winter's Tale,* but by seeing her as a new embodiment of the generative powers of her mother. It is the renewed relation with these powers which brings Pericles out of his death-like trance. That the whole scene is elevated to a visionary level at its close fits with the fact that it is the recovery of relation to this power in life which is crucial. In the opening scene, Pericles in describing the perversion of the daughter of Antiochus, described the power of woman to relate man to the ultimate forces of the universe. . . . The recognition of Marina leads to mysterious music which does indeed mediate between human and divine. . . . [Pericles] sleeps—and sees the vision of Diana, goddess of chastity and childbirth, who directs him to her temple at Ephesus. The final scene of recognition with Thaisa is anticlimactic not only because it is foreknown, but also because the symbolic action of recovering the relationship has already been completed. (p. 64)

C. L. Barber, '''Thou that Beget'st Him that Did Thee Beget': Transformation in 'Pericles' and 'The Winter's Tale','' in Shakespeare Survey: An Annual Survey of Shakespearian Study and Production, *Vol. 22, 1969, pp. 59-67.*

JAMES O. WOOD (essay date 1969)

[The following essay is largely a response to Caroline F. E. Spurgeon's claim that Pericles *lacks a consistent image pattern (see excerpt above, 1935). Wood contends that images of vegetation are a unifying element throughout the play.]*

The running metaphor in Shakespeare's five early histories is that of the growing vegetation of garden, orchard, and woodland. This was fully illustrated by Caroline Spurgeon. The same is discernible in simple and apparently more primitive guise in *Pericles.* This was not pointed out by Professor Spurgeon, who thought that

> *Pericles* alone of the romances has no sign of any running "motive" or continuity of picture or thought in the imagery, a fact sufficient in itself to throw grave doubts on its authorship [see excerpt above, 1935].

The metaphor of growing vegetation is recurrent in the first two, the "non-Shakespearean," acts of the play and also, but with a significant difference, in the last three acts, in which Shakespeare's hand is occasionally unmistakable. Since its prevalence is not explained by reference to sources of the play, it must be due to an imaginative penchant of the author or authors. A detailed examination of its occurrences seems necessary. We are concerned for the moment with the "non-Shakespearean" portion.

A conspicuous example occurs in the second scene of the play. Pericles, Prince of Tyre, has returned home from Antioch, where he has detected King Antiochus' incestuous relationship with his daughter. Fearful that the king will inevitably overrun Tyre to silence him, he has withdrawn into a grieving seclusion, forsaking his royal responsibilities. He describes himself as one

> Who once no more but as the tops of trees,
> Which fence the rootes they grow by and defend them. . . .
>   [I. ii. 30-1]

The image of man-as-tree is frequent in the Bible and is a great commonplace; yet an instance fully compatible with this one has not been found in Elizabethan drama outside Shakespeare, though it has been sought for in an effort to identify the first portion of *Pericles.* (p. 240)

After Pericles employs the image, in the same scene his good counsellor Helicanus adapts it to the subject's point of view, kneeling before the angry prince:

> How dares the plants looke vp to heauen
> From whence they haue their nourishment?
>   [I. ii. 55-6]

The image seems to continue. In the next lines Helicanus invites the prince to smite him with an axe. The recently introduced word *propagate,* . . . ("an issue I might propogate"), had its origin in plant husbandry. . . . A little farther on, when Pericles says that "feare so grew in me" [I. ii. 80] and that "tyrants feare Decrease not, but grow faster then the yeares" [I. ii. 84-5] . . . , one suspects that the metaphor of vegetation persists, especially when Pericles says that Antiochus will "lop that doubt" [I. ii. 90] . . . , suggesting axe or pruning hook. Figurative uses of the words *lop* and *crop* are frequent in the early Shakespeare; and a closely kindred simile appears a little later on in *Pericles:* the griefs of starving Tarsus "like to Groues, being topt, they higher rise" [I. iv. 9]. . . .

This second scene of *Pericles,* in which Helicanus is the "Physition" who saves the prince from death from overindulgence in grief, the sin which nearly costs him his life in act V . . . , apparently is entirely original with the playwright, having no counterpart in the known sources. It is admirably conceived, however immature in execution, and is quite undeserving its reputation for corruption. Its integrity is emphasized by the leitmotiv of iterative imagery, whose consistency argues for an underlying original composition as against corrupting reconstruction. No scene in Shakespeare illustrates better how a major image, once introduced, is apt to persist in the poet's mind, determining subsidiary figures and thus infecting the diction. (p. 241)

The culmination of the tree image in the first part of *Pericles* occurs in the jousting scene at the court of King Simonides, when Pericles, entering the lists, presents his emblem.

> A withered Branch, that's onely greene at top,
> The motto: *In hac spe viuo.* . . .
>   [II. ii. 43-4]

King Simonides, interpreting Pericles' heraldic device to his daughter, echoes Antiochus' "hope succeeding from so faire a tree":

> . . . from the deiected state wherein he is,
> He hopes by you, his fortunes yet may flourish.
>   [II. ii. 46-7]

A royal grafting, a frequent image in Shakespeare, is here prefigured. The hope is fulfilled in his union with Thaisa and in the blossoming Marina of the second half of the play. (pp. 242-43)

Shakespeare's mature hand is regarded as unmistakable in at least two scenes of [the last three acts of] *Pericles*: III. i. in which Marina is born and Thaisa is committed to the sea, and V. i. in which Pericles and Marina are reunited. The image of the tree is not used in these scenes as a symbol for Pericles, but it seems to appear elsewhere, submerged and mixed. When Pericles is taking leave of Cleon and Dionyza, to whose care he is entrusting the infant Marina, Cleon says

> Your shakes of fortune, though they hant you mortally
> Yet glaunce full wondringly on vs.
>   [III. iii. 6-7]

Editors of *Pericles,* who often have been disinclined to let well enough alone, have pronounced this passage extremely corrupt and have emended it extensively. In view, however, of the metaphors of the storm of fortune elsewhere in the play . . . and of Shakespeare's habitual association of *shake* with storms, we may well have here, in the cryptic style found in the tragic period, his figure of the tree tossed and denuded. The meaning: Your shaking storms of fortune, which persecute you mortally, rebound upon us, filling us with wonder. Thaisa, who has been cast from him by a storm, is the subject of the lines that follow. The image seems to reappear, again sunken and mixed, in the Epilogue. . . . (p. 248)

Pericles himself, however, is not in the center of interest in the greater part of [the last three acts of *Pericles*]. For Thaisa and Marina, another set of metaphors of growing things are appropriate. As Cerimon's ministrations restore Thaisa to life, he says, "See how she ginnes to blow into lifes flower againe" [III. ii. 94-5]. . . . A few tree images, however, are associated with Marina. One, whose power is enhanced by the mysterious word *whirring,* is found in her first speech: ". . . this world to me is a lasting storme whirring me from my friends" [IV. i. 19-20]. . . . That which the wind snatches from its fellows and hurries along "with a rushing or vibratory sound" (*OED* [*Oxford English Dictionary*], *whirr*, 1b) is of course a leaf from a tree. . . . The Bawd, as she introduces Marina to the brothel, says, "Come you'r a young foolish sapling, and must be bowed as I would haue you" [IV. ii. 87-8]. . . .

Marina is associated, in fact and metaphor, with flowers. She first appears . . . with a bouquet, whose summer flowers she names over. Dionyza remarks on her pallor, and fears that her father will return to "find our Paragon to all reports thus blasted" [IV. i. 34-5]. . . . In the epitaph fabricated for her by Dionyza she "withered in her spring of yeare" [IV. iv. 35]. . . . (pp. 248-49)

The picture of [a] garden is made more explicit by Lysimachus, who speaks of the Bawd as "your hearbe-woman, she that sets seeds and rootes of shame and iniquitie" [IV. vi. 85-6]. . . . Boult enters with spirit into the role of gardener: "And if shee were a thornyer peece of ground then shee is, shee shall be plowed" [IV. vi. 144-45]. . . . The Bawd justifies the epithet of "hearbe-woman" with unexpected grace: "Marry come vp my dish of chastitie with rosemary & baies" [IV. vi. 150-51]. . . . Surely one of Shakespeare's happiest thoughts is the removal of Marina from this hothouse to "the leauie shelter that abutts against the Islands side" [V. i. 51-2]. . . . (pp. 249-50)

In the brothel scenes the clarity and consistency of the garden figure, together with the general moral simplicity and the ambiguity of Lysimachus' intentions in the brothel, ally this part to Shakespeare's early work. These features distinguish it, as indications of the author's immaturity, from the scenes in *Measure for Measure* with which it has often been compared. . . .

My intention has been to show that the first two acts of *Pericles* and portions of the last three are compatible in running imagery with Shakespeare's early work and that his late plays may have been influenced in metaphor by his engagement with this play.

It will be remembered that Dryden said *Pericles* was the first offspring of the poet's muse. The prevailing modern opinion, formed subjectively, [is] that this play shows Shakespeare's partial revision, in his mature period, of the work of another. . . . (p. 250)

At this juncture one may advance the simple hypothesis, which must be tested by further studies, that Dryden was right and that in *Pericles* we have a play from Shakespeare's apprentice hand, of which he partially revised the last three acts in his maturity, leaving the first two virtually unchanged. (p. 251)

> *James O. Wood, "The Running Image in 'Pericles'," in* Shakespeare Studies: An Annual Gathering of Research, Criticism, and Reviews, *Vol. V, 1969, pp. 240-52.*

W. B. THORNE (essay date 1971)

[*In the excerpt below, Thorne examines the similarities between Shakespeare's early comedies and his romances, such as* Pericles, *and concludes that these "late plays deepen and intensify a comic vision evolved directly from the early comedies."*]

In *Pericles* and the other late plays of reconciliation, there is a curious shift of emphasis from the young to the old, though the traditional structural polarity of the folk oppositions and the rebellion of the young against their elders and the dictates

of society are retained. The late plays represent, therefore, a sophisticated extension of the themes and devices of the early plays, not a venture into the unknown, as has so often been argued, and they place their emphasis, not upon the joyous and successful rebellion of young lovers but upon the ritual significance of the King, the central character, whose figure symbolizes the health and well-being of his whole kingdom. The corollary in the late comedies to the early comedies' view of the necessary regenerative qualities of love and springtime in youth is the concept of the King as scapegoat, as King of the Waste Land, who must bear a sterile period in his life which will be ultimately beneficial to his kingdom. Pericles, Leontes [*The Winter's Tale*], and Cymbeline suffer a bitter winter of separation from all that is humanly dear to them; they experience a penance which has considerable effect upon their communities, Pericles especially acting as the kingly scapegoat for his subjects. The focus of these late plays is, therefore, not only upon the effect of love upon young lovers but also upon the effect of the young and their love upon the entire continuum of life, so that the whole community benefits from the action dramatized.

This change in the late plays, so frequently assumed to be the result of a tired and bored dramatist toying with the themes which had engrossed him in his youth, seems rather to be a deliberate artistic shift in emphasis, an extension of the searching beam of the dramatist's world vision, and not a metamorphosis or a development of a radically new method or style. Previously, in the early comedies, the focal point of interest had been in the young and the social reconciliation which they make with their society, after they have had their brief fling of romantic misrule. In the later plays, even as early as *As You Like It,* Shakespeare extends the field of interest to embrace the older generation, which had formerly occupied a more or less flat role, stereotyped and virtually unchanging. In doing so, he retains the familiar situations of the early comedies, so that the comparisons between them and the late plays may be virtually endless.

Whereas the early plays had illustrated the vital forces of life acting upon the young and invigorating them with all that is admirable in human life, the late plays repudiate the romantic notion that this phenomenon is limited only to the young, and display its operation in both generations, bringing both towards a central reconciliation, a personal, as well as a social one. To achieve this end, *Pericles* and *The Winter's Tale* dramatizes not only the youth but also the maturity of the central character, the King who must play a symbolic role in the archetypal struggle between the forces of winter and summer in the life of his kingdom. . . . Whereas the early plays celebrate the natural and the healthy, the late plays punish the unnatural, and the father himself usually acts for a time as the kill-joy, who had been a stereotyped comic figure in the early comedies. These plays of reconciliation still include, however, the struggle between the young and age, winter, asceticism, or society, and the setting up of an artificial world apart from the normal. Like the early plays, their resolution is always the same; the unity and health of the community are assured for yet another year.

Pericles and the other late comedies are, therefore, remarkable not for their differences from the early comedies, but rather for their basic similarities to them, for their mature reassessment and enlargement of basic themes from folk and classical drama. These late plays deepen and intensify a comic vision evolved directly from the early comedies. They take as their

W. B. Thorne, " 'Pericles' and 'Incest-Fertility' Opposition," in Shakespeare Quarterly, Vol. XXII, No. 1, Winter, 1971, pp. 43-56.

ALAN R. VELIE (essay date 1972)

[*Velie argues that* Pericles *is more akin to a "romantic melodrama" than a romance, and he identifies a number of melodramatic characteristics in the play.*]

[Although] *Pericles, Cymbeline,* and *The Winter's Tale* are undeniably romantic in subject and treatment—as are many of Shakespeare's earlier plays—the term "romance" does not describe them adequately, since it tells us nothing about the form of the play. If we are to use the term "romance" to describe the last plays, it would be better to use the adjectival form "romantic," and couple it with a term designating the genre. This is in line with traditional description of Shakespeare's earlier plays. *As You Like It, Twelfth Night,* and *Much Ado about Nothing* are traditionally called "romantic comedies." No term exactly fits Shakespeare's last plays, but the one that comes the closest is "romantic melodrama." (p. 65)

Shakespeare first experimented with melodrama in *Pericles* (1607 or 1608). The play is clearly inferior to his other works. Indeed, scholars believe that he was not the sole author but merely a collaborator. Yet, although the play is poor, and although it has no serious theme itself, Shakespeare evidently saw that its form might, with some changes, provide a better medium than comedy for dealing with the theme of sin and repentance.

Pericles has much in common with Elizabethan melodramas. The play opens on a melodramatic note. Pericles comes to the court of King Antiochus to woo the King's daughter. This is a courtship common to fairy tale, in which the suitor must solve a riddle in order to win the lady. Since the answer to the riddle is that the king is living incestuously with his daughter, an accurate guess is just as hazardous as an inaccurate one; the penalty for both is death. Prior suitors have guessed wrong, and their heads, hanging on the walls, serve as a gruesome warning to Pericles. Shakespeare had used the marriage guessing game before in *The Merchant of Venice,* but there the penalty for guessing wrong was taking a vow of celibacy. This is nothing trivial, of course, but it is still appropriate to comedy. But in *Pericles* the decaying heads on the walls are the stuff of melodrama. (pp. 67-8)

As we can see, from the opening spectacle of the throne room with its severed heads to Cleon and Dionyza's violent end, *Pericles* is melodrama. Clearly it is no tragedy. The happy ending for Pericles and his family precludes this. Just as clearly, the play is not a comedy; the villains die. Most anthologies of Shakespeare's plays group *Pericles* with the comedies, but it is obvious from the opening scene that the play is not comic. The perilous guessing game strikes a note too sinister for comedy.

Pericles is filled throughout with the sensational incidents common to melodrama: Pericles' flight and shipwreck; Thaisa's apparent death and resurrection; Marina's imprisonment in a brothel.

Furthermore, the play employs the usual melodramatic appeals to the emotions. The audience trembles for Marina when an assassin tries to murder her, and suffers with her in the brothel. The audience fears for Pericles when he flees from Antiochus,

Act II. Scene i. Pericles and Fishermen. From the Art Collection of the Folger Shakespeare Library.

province, however, an examination of a larger portion of the continuum of life, and provide a larger perspective from which the audience may evaluate the action, for they suggest that the various seasons and stages of life are necessary for continued life, that a temporary withdrawal or change has vitalizing and regeneratory results. They acknowledge from the outset the central tenet—which the early comedies had been dedicated to illustrate—that youth must have its day, that spring must inevitably follow upon winter, and that love's regenerative qualities cannot safely be denied; but, like the songs of winter and summer in *Love's Labour's Lost,* they remind us that there is a place for all the seasons, that each has its validity and significance, and that the seasonal metaphor may be seen operating throughout all of man's life. In their dénouements, and frequently earlier, they illustrate a spring-like *renouveau* ["renewal"] of the spirit, paralleling the tremendous vitality of youth during the season of love, and they suggest that this experience is equally valuable and equally decisive in the totality of human affairs. The late plays therefore include the love-experience of the young, but they do not wait until the dénouement to set this vital element in perspective to the continuum of life. The young are apparently regarded as the old reborn, and the continuity of life becomes one of the central interests in the late plays. In these plays, the two generations are balanced equally in the dramatist's scale and found equally desirable and equally necessary in the wheel of life, and they recognize a process of "continuing accommodation" which is symbolized in the concluding scenes by marriage and feasting. (pp. 55-6) and pities him when he despairs over the death of Marina. And they hate Antiochus and Dionyza.

Finally, the characters are the stereotypes of melodrama. Pericles is an all-wise ruler and peerless warrior, but hardly distinguishable from other melodramatic heroes. (pp. 69-70)

Both Thaisa and Marina are, of course, virtuous and beautiful, but totally faceless. Neither possesses a single discernible fault. This perfection differentiates them from the heroines of Shakespeare's comedies, who are indubitably attractive, but possess normal human frailties. Antiochus and Dionyza are stage villains.

The people of *Pericles,* wooden characters of melodrama, seldom have convincing motives for their actions. For instance, when Cerimon brings Thaisa back to life, we might logically expect her to take the first boat for Tyre to join her husband and child. Instead, she enters a convent. Pericles' handing over his daughter, whom he loves, to foster parents is equally puzzling. (p. 70)

It may be contended . . . that Shakespeare is not experimenting with a new form, but simply following his source. The evidence does not support this. Shakespeare had dealt with tales like Gower's and Twine's before, changing details in their plots to suit his purpose. (p. 71)

In *Pericles,* on the other hand, Shakespeare leaves the story as he finds it. He could easily have made some minor changes and spared the villains. Had he done this, and had he lightened the tone by cutting down the bathos and by interjecting more humor, the play would have been a comedy. That he did neither is significant. Never before had he written a melodrama; in *Pericles* he does. In his next plays, *Cymbeline* and *The Winter's Tale,* he continues to use elements of melodrama, although he transforms them into a new kind of drama. It seems clear, then, that in *Pericles* he was experimenting with a dramatic form that was new to him, but for which he had ample precedent on the Elizabethan stage. (pp. 71-2)

> *Alan R. Velie, " 'Pericles' and 'Cymbeline' as Elizabethan Melodramas," in his* Shakespeare's Repentance Plays: The Search for an Adequate Form, *Fairleigh Dickinson University Press, 1972, pp. 61-90.*

PHILIP EDWARDS   (essay date 1976)

[*In his analysis of* Pericles, *Edwards raises questions about Lysimachus's behavior in the brothel and the importance of verisimilitude in the play, noting "the striking lack of connexion between character, deed, and event." Edwards states that* Pericles *does not finally assert "how things run in this world," and he concludes, after a consideration of the play's authorship, that there "is no solution to the problems" the play presents.*]

[When] we talk about *Pericles* as it was acted by Shakespeare's company in its heyday, we are talking about a hidden play, a play concealed from us by a text full of confusion and with a clumsiness and poverty of language unrivalled in the Shakespeare canon. Yet, encrusted and deformed though it is, this hidden play reveals itself in glimpses as a work of remarkable beauty and power. . . . It happened, as it often happens with [Henrik] Ibsen or Greek drama in English, that stage action was somehow able to re-create the true effectiveness of scenes which an impoverished language quite spoils for a reader. (p. 8)

It would be a great mistake to see Gower's manipulation of his three kinds of exposition (narrative, mime, and full stage action) as a reflection of the play's simple-mindedness. The effect indeed is of something primitive and quaint, but that effect must have been seriously intended. The interchange of devices seems to be an attempt to deepen the power of romance by giving it the vividness of performance without losing the indispensable relaxed air of a story-telling which takes a long time and treats of many years. An atavism of technique casts over the whole the sentimental glow of times past so important for the nostalgic Elizabethans. The more primitive the dumb shows seem, the more they serve the purpose of a play which is determined to be an antique. . . . The slow-moving pageantry of the parade of the knights at Pentapolis, each one in full armour with his page carrying an emblematic shield, and the jousting which follows are inventions of the dramatist. But the story as a whole is not placed within the age of chivalry. The worship of Diana at Ephesus at the end of the play and the founding of Antioch at the beginning contrast strikingly with the medieval note and help to give the feeling of all-time and no-time which we assume was intended.

From what has already been said, it will be seen that much importance is given in *Pericles* to the fact of a stage which, as Gower's words guide the imagination of the audience, is transformed into a succession of different, widely-separated places. *Pericles* insists on its locations, insists that they are physically there while agreeing with us that they are not. It is not wrong to think of the play as a series of composed spectacles, almost tableaux, each in its given and proper place. . . . Particularly interesting in this demand that we see the stage both as a stage and as another place is the repeated use which seems to have been made of the curtained recess in the rear wall of the stage (what used to be called the inner stage). This is first used when Lychorida draws back the curtains to show Pericles the dead body of Thaisa . . . ; it is used again for the tomb of Marina at Tarsus in the dumb show . . . ; and finally it is used to reveal the inert figure of Pericles himself in the harbour at Mytilene. . . . Wife, daughter, husband; each, in a sense, shown for dead in that curtained space, and each later made alive. The same curtained recess is made to travel widely in place and function but the unity of its uses is proclaimed by its being after all the same curtained recess.

There is, then, an emphasis in the scenes of *Pericles* on physical place, on a formality in grouping, and a certain ceremony in the action. To these we must add music as a presence in the play. . . . Music, ceremony, grouping, location: the mind of the audience is approached physically; the words of the actors are given a kind of visual, aural, tactile frame. This is as it should be when enactment on a stage is offered as a deliberate alternative to the more mental or subjective creation of a story told only by a narrator. *Pericles* is a statuesque sort of play, and its scenes remain strongly in the mind as sculpted groups. (pp. 11-13)

Pericles suggests that in the unrealistic adventures of romance, the journeyings, the shipwrecks, the restoring of the dead, uniting of the sundered, there can be found images of human life as compelling as in the severer naturalism of satirical comedy or the intenser articulation of conflict and catastrophe in tragedy. The play is quite ridiculous seen from any standard of probability or the expectations of ordinary life. Its unlifelikeness is not only in its coincidences and marvels, like the 'saving' of Marina by the pirates, or her being brought face to face with her father, but in the extreme simplification of character and of human encounter. The good are good and the bad are bad. Changes of moral state (Dionyza, Lysimachus, Boult) are as uncomplicated and unconvincing as the moral states themselves.

The striking lack of connexion between character, deed, and event in *Pericles* is perhaps less an offence against life than against art. Many commentators, conditioned to find in drama a full relationship between what people are and what they do and what happens to them, have tried to create a moral meaning for *Pericles* by relating the hero's sufferings and rewards to his sins and his virtues. Although these patterns are not absent from the play, they cannot be made to account for its structure. *Pericles* is a string of adventures, mostly misfortunes, ending in a climax of happiness. It does not have an inevitable and inexorable movement which can only be explained in the light of the hero's temperament and deeds. . . . *Pericles* is a profoundly moral work, and may well seem too one-sided in its views on culpability and responsibility, but it does not obtrude its moral views as principles or causes of the action. To account for Pericles' sufferings in terms of his rashness in casting Thaisa to the waves or of his neglect in leaving Marina to be brought up by Dionyza is quite to miss the mark.

A good Renaissance writer used romance with full consciousness of the extravagance and absurdity of its conventions. Its quests, its infatuations, its coincidences, its simplification of people and moral issues and conflicts, were employed not because the writer thought life was like that but because he knew it was not. It was the freedom from verisimilitude that attracted the writer. (pp. 13-15)

Although the brothel incident is in the play's source, and although virgins courageously defending their honour are a very common theme in romance, it might seem in *Pericles* that the stark and deeply etched realism of the brothel makes it simply the wrong place for a creature of fairy tale like Marina; that Boult and Marina belong to two different conventions of art and that to mix them is to mix Walter Scott and William Burroughs, or Jane Austen and Zola. There *is* a mixture of genres, but it is a purposeful and important mingling. The brothel-keepers balance the fishermen of Act II (almost certainly the parts were doubled) as creatures from a more 'real' world than the world of the rest of the characters. As the fishermen represent the rough good-heartedness of the rural poor, the brothel people represent the corruption, disease, and cruelty of urban life. Figures of romance, the noble prince in the first place and the virgin princess in the second, are thrust among creatures of naturalism whom they thoroughly bewilder. The achievement of this perhaps risky juxtaposition of earth and air is that the audience is made aware that the dramatist knows of another world and they can see him testing the different valuations of experience contained within different conventions of art, testing ideals against knowledge. (p. 20)

The contest between Marina and Lysimachus is the hub of this matter, and in many ways the hub of the whole play. It is the greatest misfortune that what our text gives us looks like a clumsy abbreviation of the original exchanges. Lysimachus, the governor of Mytilene, enters the brothel, disguising himself from the eyes of the people. He is well known to the three keepers and he cheerfully numbers himself among the house's 'resorters'. He is anxious that the girl he has should not be diseased, and his flippant reaction to the sight of Marina is 'Faith, she would serve after a long voyage at sea' [IV. vi. 44-5]. When they are alone, he chats to her with an off-hand condescension that shows no recognition of her as a person:

'Now, pretty one, how long have you been at this trade?' [IV. vi. 66-7]. He is quite uninterested in her replies and says impatiently 'Come, bring me to some private place' [IV. vi. 90]. Marina rather briefly appeals to him and laments her misfortune. There is a strong possibility that the 1609 text at this point misrepresents Lysimachus's behaviour.

> I did not think thou couldst have spoke so well,
> Ne'er dreamt thou couldst.
> Had I brought hither a corrupted mind,
> Thy speech had altered it. Hold, here's gold for thee. . . .
> For me, be you thoughten
> That I came with no ill intent; for to me
> The very doors and windows savour vilely. . . .
>
> [IV. vi. 102-10]

This moment is of great importance. The natural interpretation of Lysimachus's words is that he never had any designs on Marina and that his threatened assault was all a pretence. Is Lysimachus arranging an ordeal, like the Green Knight in the medieval poem, or is he a part of the ordeal? Is the encounter between Marina and Lysimachus an image of the purification of a man who sins through thoughtlessness, or a testing of Marina's virtue by a prince who has no thought of violating her? Either way, the brothel is Marina's ordeal; but is the climax of that ordeal real or faked? (pp. 21-2)

The moral issue is not easy. If, as I have argued, the idea that Lysimachus never intended to have sexual relations with Marina is repugnant on the grounds that it involves a cruel deception of Marina and an irritating deception of the audience, we then have to meet the argument that it is repugnant that a prince who has sought his gratifications in such a horrible place as this brothel, and has there met and been shamed by Marina, should then be presented as a suitable husband for her. Yet Shakespeare thought Angelo a fit husband for Mariana [*Measure for Measure*], and Angelo's intentions against Isabella were worse than Lysimachus's against Marina. It is true that the crudeness of the Quarto in the last act does not help Lysimachus to appear as successfully in his role as princely suitor as he did in his role as flippant whoremonger. Much depends on the actor in a stage presentation, but the *idea* of the whoremonger becoming a bridegroom is surely not offensive. Marina's transformation of the man who casually sought her as a prostitute into a man who woos her for his wife, and her acceptance in marriage of the man whose sexual advances she spurned in the brothel, are her victory. . . . The difference in the situation is not a promise of marriage but an attitude towards sexual relations. For Lysimachus, Marina was first simply an object to satisfy his sexual desire. Because of her response to him and the force of her very being, he recognizes her as a person and by that recognition is himself an altered being. The alteration shows not in the abandonment of his desire for her but in its transmutation, so that he seeks her love and not just her body. There is a similar though much less sharply presented alteration in Pericles. He pursued Antiochus's daughter with a kind of lust; he is not for that reason disqualified as the bridegroom of Thaisa. It is generous of Marina not to despise Lysimachus, but her acceptance of his love is a measure of the alteration of his nature which she has brought about, and such power as hers seems to me a main subject of the play. If we take it that Marina does not alter Lysimachus, because he never was an irresponsible sinner, we have taken much of the heart out of the play. (pp. 25-6)

What it seems *Pericles* tries to achieve is a vision (it is hardly anything else) of the sexual relationship contained within marriage, and of the generations joined by a link of affection even stronger and more spiritual than the relation of husband and wife, namely the relation of parent and child.

The concord of relationships at the end of *Pericles* is something which the characters do not so much achieve as reach, at the end of a long and difficult journey that had no destination. It is time to turn back to the sea, and to the difficult question how far *Pericles* is to be read as a spiritual journey, and how far the characters are under the direction of spiritual forces. 'The gods' are on everyone's lips in *Pericles*, appealed to for help or pointed to as the cause of what is happening. (pp. 28-9)

But it must be said that in the play taken as a whole divine guidance and direction seem fitful and inconstant. To see the entire play as a representation of a pattern of perceived and understood providence would be as wrong as to see it as a kind of *Pilgrim's Progress* in which the characters persevere towards a known goal of redemption and salvation. There is no pattern, either of providence or of redemption. (p. 30)

In the end, simplicity of the relationships in *Pericles,* the un-likelihood of the events, the lack of cause-and-effect in the plot, make the play a presentation of images which, while individually they expand into wide and general meanings, yet as a whole sequence withdraw from asserting how things run in this world. We are offered ideas or propositions about love and suffering and chastity, and the relation of them to a divine will, but we are not offered a clue to any meaning lying in the progression of events. The sea, therefore, remains a mystery. Neptune and Aeolus, the waves and the wind, are a great force and our lives are in their hands. We have the suggestion of divine control but we never understand its pattern. On this sea, two human forces, wisdom and chastity, seem to show divine investment, seem to show that the terrible power of the sea can be brought to help the fulfilment of the great triangle of affection represented by Pericles, Thaisa, and Marina. (p. 31)

Much of the energy and time spent on the subject of Who wrote *Pericles*? has been wasted, because the language of the Quarto has been used as the basis for testing authorship. The Quarto is a debased text and its language is the language of the pirates who got the text together. (p. 33)

It is an arguable theory, then, that the text of *Pericles* as we have it is an assemblage by two different 'reporters'. The first tried to create a 'literary' wholeness from his notes or memory by refashioning what he had into a rather feeble verse. The second had a livelier understanding and better notes or recol-lection and has given us material which, while it is extremely irregular as verse, preserves more of the original wording than the rewriting of Acts I and II does. Only in the first scene of Act III, where the verse is fairly regular, does one have the feeling that we may be very near the original text. Many would say that it is the best scene in the play; it would be more cautious to say that it is the best-reported. (p. 38)

I do not think it can be maintained that the whole of the original *Pericles* as acted was by Shakespeare. But it must always be borne in mind that there is a wholeness in the design of the play, a consistency in its method and a unity in its meaning, which powerfully suggests that the play was conceived as a whole by a single mind. And [a] comparison with *The Winter's Tale* and *The Tempest* leaves me in no doubt whatsoever that that mind was Shakespeare's. A second proposition which may be borne in mind is this. It has been argued that the verse of Acts I and II is a reworking of verse which was once much

better. Now, while such archaeological work is very tricky and uncertain, a reader must often have the feeling that what lay behind the different individual scenes of the first two acts was not all of the same quality. And he may feel that there are some scenes in the later acts which, while much higher in quality than the general run of Acts I and II, are still without much evidence of being by Shakespeare. (p. 39)

One has to admit, regretfully, that the problem is insoluble because the authentic text is irrecoverable. But that Shake-speare had a large share in the conception of the play and in the writing of it seems indisputable. The objection to the view that he revised an earlier play by another dramatist and confined his rewriting largely to the last three acts is that the archaic naivety which he is thus supposed to have started to brush up is part and parcel of the very meaning of the play. It would be curious indeed if Shakespeare had discovered, in a poor play that he started tinkering with, the kind of plot, the kind of art, the kind of theme, which he was to spend all the en-deavour of the last years of his writing life trying to develop. It would be curious, but it has to be admitted it would not be impossible. There is no solution to the problems of *Pericles.* (p. 41)

Philip Edwards, in an introduction to Pericles Prince of Tyre *by William Shakespeare, edited by Philip Edwards, Penguin Books, 1976, pp. 7-42.*

PHYLLIS GORFAIN   (essay date 1976)

[*In the following excerpt, Gorfain presents a structuralist inter-pretation of* Pericles, *emphasizing the ritual nature of Antiochus's riddle and defining that riddle's importance, specifically in its relation to the themes of incest and kinship, as the structural motif which unifies the play. Thus, Gorfain maintains that* Pericles *is not the "rambling" work determined by earlier critics, but instead is a play which exhibits "an analogical coherence" derived from its "transformations of the same deep structure"—namely, the "timeless" pattern of separation, loss, and recovery. For another consideration of the significance of incest in* Pericles, *see the comments above by C. L. Barber (1969).*]

Because of an apparently corrupt text and problematic author-ship for its first three acts, *Pericles,* among the late plays, has attracted the least critical attention. Yet a structural approach especially suits this work, particularly since it may be applied independently of textual issues. Accordingly, in the last two decades the play has inspired a number of structural studies centering on the meaning of its rambling form. We now rec-ognize that the implausibly ordered episodes produce an ana-logical coherence distinct from the causality of Aristotelian plotting. Recurrent and inverted outlines of action emerge as transformations of the same deep structure, which conveys a message about its own timeless rhythm of separation, loss, and recovery.

Because the play demands our participation and belief in that cosmic scheme, critics have characterized *Pericles* as ritualis-tic; they also note its folklore elements, but do not fully com-prehend the connection between the folkloric forms and rit-ual. . . .

The odd riddle which opens the action provides a useful ex-ample of an important folkloric device which critics have ne-glected. (p. 11)

Why does the marriage test in Antioch take the particular form of a riddle? Is the enigma really so transparent? Does the structure of this folkloric device have any relevance to its subjects, incest and the destruction of motherhood? Conversely, does riddling bear any relationship to familial reunion and legitimate procreation? The family romance in *Pericles* brings together a separated father, mother, and daughter only to divide the generations again for reproduction and rule. When Pericles and Thaisa inherit the rule of Pentapolis, Marina and Lysimachus assume reign over Tyre. That comedic resolution overturns the horror of the first incident in which overrating of blood relations requires the deathly riddle and tyranny of Antioch. (pp. 11-12)

Critics have frequently stressed the metatheatrical functions of Gower's stilted choruses. Yet they fail to recognize that the seemingly minor riddle is a complicated folkloric form which also distills a process of disorder and order to criticize the uses of fictions. Exciting parallels between the riddling, the choruses and dumb shows, and ritual emerge when one considers their structural significance.

The riddle invites and then frustrates formal expectations, and uses ambiguity to point up the necessary but arbitrary ways we organize experience. As fictions about artificiality, all the formal devices oscillate between contraries—their own concreteness and the abstract process of their own representing. Thus they stand at and for the point of coincidence where boundaries are defined and violated. Here they embody the inexorable truth that social and cognitive order is contrived. Exploring the epistemological problem that knowledge may be no more than perception yields both doubt and celebration in *Pericles*. The mixed genre of tragicomedy fittingly encloses both. Like a hall of mirrors, *Pericles* reproduces our endless substitutions of one fiction for another. The self-reflecting art and artifice unfold a secret order of the universe, but as an admitted illusion controlled by Gower. The inescapability of such magic portrays man as an artist who creates multiplying forms as he imitates the source of creativity, a prolific power which always eludes the metaphors by which he strives to replicate it. (p. 12)

The explicit motivation behind the marriage riddle suggests a latent incestuous impulse behind other such trials, both in this play and in other works of folklore and literature. Ordinarily when a deserving suitor passes a marriage test, the device frees the filial generation from both parental bonds and the social restrictions the test embodies. Traditionally, a riddle trial in folklore or literature transforms our vision as it creates new relationships through marriage. But in this perverse marriage riddle, the device breeds only the hollow skulls to which Gower points.

We may consider the riddle a false artifice, for its end is deception, not revelation. Antiochus uses it as he does oaths, to dictate a world to suit his desire rather than to disclose a hidden order in the universe. (p. 13)

The outright description of incest in the riddle has misled readers who miss the real question because they do not understand riddles. To solve a riddle, one must identify the hidden referent. Here the hidden term reveals to whom 'I' refers. The statement of illicit sexuality does not quibble about the relationship it details, only about who participates in it. Put another way, the solution to the riddle is not 'Incest,' but the name of Antiochus's nameless daughter.

Pericles alters its written sources in having the 'I' in this traditional puzzle refer to the daughter rather than to the father. The modification sharpens the focus on the princess, and accentuates her contrast to Thaisa and Marina later. All three

princesses employ either riddling or deceptive remarks. But the latter two use indirection to sanctify, not desecrate, bonds with fathers and lovers; their reunion ultimately breaks the destructive mother-daughter link provided in the riddle, and establishes a gentle bond between the formerly divided figures. Marina's wordplay transforms the effects of the nameless daughter. That princess becomes a symbol of disorder because of her undifferentiated anonymity and the silence her riddle imposes. Correspondingly, her incest blurs kinship categories, the most fundamental distinctions in human culture. (pp. 13-14)

Answering such a fake riddle solves nothing. To dissolve the fraudulent riddle, one must expose it as a fabrication. Yet to do this is as dangerous as to reply or to keep silent. Antiochus's pretext for murder tolerates no distinctions between winning and losing, and therefore creates an absurd universe. The end results of the counterfeit test match those of the incest it pictures; as incest denies clear categories, the sham test reduces every alternative to the same conclusion. (p. 14)

The power of curative art to reorder relationships becomes clear when Marina's riddling and her story open Pericles's portals of hearing and speech. He himself then speaks paradoxically of rebirth as he ends the silence and death caused by the false speech of Antioch and the misleading statue of Tharsus. . . . His reversal of roles then reconstitutes normal family ties and substitutes wonder for horror.

Marina represents the answer to all her father's queries. But she is also a question, for she presents herself as a puzzle; thereby she also teaches Pericles to riddle safely. . . . Although born on no shore, she is mortal. Her name later closes the opposition; it reveals she was born at sea. At the same time Marina's enigmatic reply also suggests that her birth was fatal to her mother. Her next line does not reconcile that antithesis; she implicitly warns Pericles she is not the one he seems to recognize. The line also claims that appearances reflect reality, and reassures Pericles not only that she is real, but also that her beauty is true. Taken all ways at once, Marina's completed riddle cancels the debts of Antioch.

Pericles's reply does not yet solve Marina's riddle; but it foresees that the answer will resemble birth. Pericles responds to Marina's puzzle by depicting himself pregnant with grief; 'I am great with woe, and shall deliver weeping.' . . . The anticipated delivery will bring forth joy as it frees Pericles from the immobility of mourning. In his poetry, Pericles usurps the female role; yet in his conceit rests the tragicomic thesis that art can include actions of both suffering and recovery. In the Antioch riddle, the daughter 'feed[s] on mother's flesh'; Pericles's paradox inverts the roles of father and daughter without consuming maternity and creativity. Metaphor and paradox now support reunion and yet also retain distinctive identities to recreate rather than abort relationships. (pp. 14-15)

Recognizing Marina's admittedly incredible tale as the corollary to his own history brings Pericles back to life; realizing Pericles's story complements her own restores Thaisa as mother and wife. All their tales compose Gower's song, which he offers us as a restorative. When we leave the theatre, the play may truly restore us to life if we choose to understand its directions, to see in it a riddle which reflects our own histories. (p. 15)

Phyllis Gorfain, "Puzzle and Artifice: The Riddle As Metapoetry in 'Pericles'," in Shakespeare Survey:

An Annual Survey of Shakespearian Study and Production, *Vol. 29, 1976, pp. 11-20.*

NONA FIENBERG (essay date 1982)

[*Focusing on the brothel scenes in the fourth act of* Pericles, *Fienberg examines the economic metaphors and Marina's relation to the commercial market Shakespeare was depicting. Fienberg states that by selling moral discourse instead of her body, "Marina acknowledges the market system, yet remains uncorrupted by it."*]

In his essay, "Of Truth" (1625), Francis Bacon distinguishes between "theological and philosophical truth" and the truth of "civil business." While he further distinguishes between the poets, whose harmless lies give pleasure, and the merchants, who lie "for advantage," both stand in the second category of the truth of civil business, since both participate in the nascent spirit of capitalism of seventeenth-century London. . . . But if the world of civil business where even truth has its price informs his essay, Bacon grants us, in the heart of the essay, a vision of truth "in varied lights," the spiritual truth that does not change with market prices: "Certainly it is heaven upon earth to have a man's mind move in charity, rest in providence, and turn upon the poles of truth." Bacon's simultaneous complicity in the world of economic values and vision of a "heaven on earth" provides an analogy to the complexity of Shakespeare's vision in *Pericles.* In the play world, Pericles' lost daughter Marina, while initially subject to the selfish, mutable truth of civil business, ultimately triumphs over the marketplace. Through her mastery of the linguistic act Marina not only controls audience response to her value, but also shapes her own destiny. Through Marina's eloquence, *Pericles* becomes a celebration of action carried out in a spirit of charity. (pp. 153-54)

Act Four and particularly Marina's role in it serve as the thematic and structural pivot between two contrasting economies, that which values women as a commodity to exploit and that which values their wholeness and integrity. In the debased economy of Antiochus' court, the king himself exploited his daughter as a sexual object. When Act Four begins, Marina has reached puberty, the marriageable, that is, marketable, age in Renaissance England. Dionyza, her surrogate mother, plots to have her killed in order to enhance the marriage value of Philoten, her own daughter. As long as praises are, as Gower says, "paid as debts" [IV. i. 34] to Marina, Philoten's worth suffers. Abandoned at the seaside to the savage Leonine, whose only incentive to murder is profit, Marina is powerless to save herself. Once the pirates capture her, however, she enters a world where the debased economy implicit in Antiochus' and Dionyza's courts becomes explicit. In the brothel, Marina challenges the truth of civil business with her spiritual truth; she sets her value system against their market economy.

The pirates' cries as they seize Marina declare how they value her. One calls, "A prize, a prize!" [IV. i. 93]; another claims his share in the profits, "Half-part, mates, half-part" [IV. i. 94]. They treat her as they would gold, silver, ivory, or pearls, purely as coin in the marketplace. When they sell Marina into the brothel, they drive a hard bargain but gain their price, "one thousand pieces" [IV. ii. 51]. In the world of Pander, Boult and Bawd, such objectification of women becomes even more reductive. The three take inventory, find that their stock in trade is low, and determine to replenish it. Pander's complaint pertains to quantity, "We lost too much money this mart by

being too wenchless" [IV. ii. 4-5], while Bawd's assessment concerns quality, "The stuff we have, a strong wind will blow it to pieces, they are so pitifully sodden" [IV. ii. 18-20]. By reducing a girl or young woman to a "wench" and further diminishing her to fabric to be worked, blown upon, or sold, they reveal the moral bankruptcy of their commerce. But as long as the accounting remains general, an audience can be amused by the spectacle of a brothel's financial concerns. The reductive language they apply both to their "goods" and their customers is itself richly metaphorical and solidly Anglo-Saxon: "Ay, she quickly poop'd him, she made him roast-meat for worms" [IV. ii. 24-5]. Until Marina enters this world, its moral emptiness matters less than its linguistic richness.

Marina, however, insists on the bond between the inherent value of a person and the moral content of language. In her dialogue with Bawd, for example, the term "woman" is at issue:

Mar.   Are you a woman?
Bawd. What would you have me be, and I be not a
         woman?
Mar.   An honest woman, or not a woman.

                                                   [IV. ii. 82-5]

To Marina, the word contains a moral value, as a woman expresses wholeness and integrity. To Bawd, a woman's value lies in her use. When she instructs Boult to cry their wares in the marketplace, she describes Marina by means of a *blazon*: "Boult, take you the marks of her, the color of her hair, complexion, height, her age, with warrant of her virginity, and cry, 'He that will give most shall have her first.' Such a maidenhead were no cheap thing, if men were as they have been" [IV. ii. 57-61]. In effect, Bawd shatters Marina into pieces, hair, height, complexion, age, maidenhead, in order to recover their one thousand piece investment. Such a process continues the violent assaults on Marina threatened by Leonine and the pirates. Bawd breaks her up into parts, with an aggressive, appropriative purpose. In that economy, Marina's sense of her integrity as a "woman" constitutes a danger.

Yet, in the brothel, Marina herself learns how to use her exchange value in a way quite at odds with what her masters intended. She finds, that is, another commodity to trade. Instead of selling the virginity for which she can gain a greater prize, she creates a market for her moral discourse. Through the art of her speech, moreover, she transforms the brothel customers into generous spirits. . . . Although Gower has just warned us that we must watch Marina in her "unholy service," presumably her performance of a prostitute's part, we see, in contrast, a "holy service." Marina has preached divinity so convincingly that the Gentlemen determine to "hear the vestals sing."

The testimony of the two Gentlemen prepares us for the more complex encounter between Marina and Lysimachus, the Governor of Mytilene. If she has opened the Gentlemen's ears to the worth and beauty of the Vestals' song, she educates the Governor's ears to her moral discourse. When Lysimachus enters her company, he calls her a "creature of sale" [IV. vi. 78], expecting to pay for his sexual pleasure. Moreover, he addresses her in prose speeches appropriate to the setting. Marina, however, both confounds his expectations that he is meeting an object for sexual exploitation and counters his prose with her poised, imaginative verse. When he leaves her company, he communicates in the verse appropriate to his own social position, to his inherent nobility, and to his teacher, Marina.

To effect such a conversion and to reveal her value she uses an integrated myth of her own identity:

> For me,
> That am a maid, though most ungentle fortune
> Have plac'd me in this sty, where since I came,
> Diseases have been sold dearer than physic—
> That the gods
> Would set me free from this unhallowed place,
> Though they did change me to the meanest bird
> That flies i' th' purer air!   [IV. vi. 95-102]

Through this myth of mysterious origins, present alienation, providential intercession and metamorphosis, Marina tames the rude Lysimachus. Despite its brevity and general outline, the myth describes accurately her subjection to a debased society and a corrupt economy. (pp. 154-56)

Lysimachus does not merely declare his transformation through the moral speech of Marina; he shapes his new measure of himself as a man and a governor into the measure of blank verse. He completes the unfinished last line of her myth with his praise:

> I did not think
> Thou couldst have spoke so well, ne'er dreamt thou
>   couldst.
> Had I brought hither a corrupted mind,
> Thy speech had altered it.   [IV. vi. 102-05]

Yet her story also commands a high exchange value. Because Lysimachus learns of Marina's integrity through her myth, he values her not in pieces, but, he says, as "a piece of virtue" [IV. vi. 111]. Nonetheless, he presses coin on her, "Hold, here's gold for thee" [IV. vi. 105] and "Hold, here's more gold for thee" [IV. vi. 113]. Just as he would have paid for the sexual pleasure he expected to purchase, Lysimachus pays for his pleasure in her narrative. Indeed, he may pay more for Marina's myth of selfhood and her redefinition of his moral role than he would have paid for a "creature of sale."

Ironically, the moral discourse which earns a good price resembles the skills Bawd so wanted her protégée to learn. Appropriately using the rhetorical figure of *gradatio*, in which one word is exchanged for another of greater value in a climactic sequence, Bawd tutors Marina in the strategy of earning a high price for her favors, "to weep that you live as you do makes pity in your lovers; seldom but that pity begets you a good opinion, and that opinion a mere profit" [IV. ii. 116-21]. To Bawd, the tears serve merely as counters in a commercial transaction, like the pieces into which she shatters Marina through the *blazon*. (p. 157)

When Boult vows to rape [Marina], he speaks of the act as a robbery, threatening "To take from you the jewel you hold so dear" [IV. vi. 154] and hoping to subject her through violence to the brothel's market economy. But Marina, who failed to tame Leonine, now tames this savage. She determines both her persuasive strategies and the commodities she will sell. First, she engages Boult in a dialogue where she controls the terms. She asks a riddle, "What canst thou wish thine enemy to be?" [IV. vi. 158]. The answer that Boult is his own enemy emerges from the truth-telling portrait Marina paints of him, "Thou art the damned doorkeeper to every / Custrel that comes inquiring for his Tib" [IV. vi. 165-66]. Then, she slips Boult some money, echoing Lysimachus, "Here, here's gold for thee" [IV. vi. 172]. Finally, she convinces him that she can support the brothel through singing, dancing, and embroidery. The combination of moral discourse and financial considerations persuades Boult. In this exchange, Marina acknowledges the market system, yet remains uncorrupted by it. Gower celebrates her new role as both an aesthetic success, a happy reconciliation of nature and art, and an economic triumph, a profitable enterprise:

> . . . pupils lacks she none of noble race,
> Who pour their bounty on her; and her gain
> She gives the cursed bawd.   [V. Gower. 8-10]

Like the art of the narrator of the play, Gower himself, Marina's arts now have exchange value. Although she still gives the brothel all her gold, she has retained the chastity which serves as a synecdoche for her inner value as well as her value in the marriage market. (p. 158)

> *Nona Fienberg, "Marina in 'Pericles': Exchange*
> *Values and the Art of Moral Discourse, in* Iowa State
> Journal of Research, *Vol. 57, No. 2, November, 1982,*
> *pp. 153-61.*

Act II. Scene ii. Simonides, Thaisa, and Knights. By H. Corbould (n.d.). From the Art Collection of the Folger Shakespeare Library.

ADDITIONAL BIBLIOGRAPHY

Allen, Percy. "The Authorship of *Pericles*." In his *Shakespeare, Jonson, and Wilkins As Borrowers: A Study in Elizabethan Dramatic Origins and Imitations*, pp. 185-223. London: Cecil Palmer, 1928.

   Seeks to prove that Wilkins wrote *Pericles*, suggesting that the play is merely a pastiche of other Shakespearean works. Allen gives instances where Wilkins lifted metaphors, situations and direct passages from *Macbeth, Richard II* and other plays to embellish his *Pericles* plot.

Arthos, John. "*Pericles, Prince of Tyre:* A Study in the Dramatic Use of Romantic Narrative." *Shakespeare Quarterly* IV, No. 3 (July 1953): 257-70.

   General analysis of the dramatic elements in *Pericles*, with emphasis on dramatic form and character development.

Boas, Frederick S. "Appendix B: 'Pericles,' 'Henry VIII,' 'The Two Noble Kinsmen'." In his *Shakespeare and His Predecessors*, pp. 540-50. New York: Charles Scribner's Sons, 1902.
> Discusses Wilkins's role in the authorship of *Pericles* and claims that the play is "too much of a patchwork to offer much scope for aesthetic criticism."

Boyle, Robert. "On Wilkins's Share in a Play Called Shakspere's *Pericles*." In *The New Shakspere Society's Transactions: 1880-5, Part II*, pp. 323-40. London: Trübner & Co., 1885.
> Discusses George Wilkins's role in the authorship of *Pericles*.

Collier, J. Payne. *Further Particulars Regarding Shakespeare and His Works*. London: Thomas Rodd, 1839, 68 p.
> Examines Shakespeare's reliance on Laurence Twine's novel *Apollonius King of Tyre* in his composition of *Pericles*.

Edwards, Philip. "An Approach to the Problem of *Pericles*." *Shakespeare Survey* 5 (1952): 25-49.
> A delineation of the flaws in the 1609 quarto *Pericles*. Edwards advances the theory that two reporters of differing ability transcribed the *Pericles* text by reconstructing some of the more abstruse lines and by closely analysing the verse and prose passages.

Empson, William. "Hunt the Symbol." *The Times Literary Supplement*, No. 3243 (23 April 1964): 339-41.
> Speculates on Shakespeare's motives in writing *Pericles*.

Flower, Annette C. "Disguise and Identity in *Pericles, Prince of Tyre*." *Shakespeare Quarterly* XXVI, No. 1 (Winter 1975): 30-41.
> Studies the recurring motif of disguise in *Pericles* through which the identity and location of "lost" and "dead" characters are hidden.

Greenfield, Thelma N. "A Re-Examination of the 'Patient' Pericles." *Shakespeare Studies* III (1967): 51-61.
> Questions the popular critical interpretation of Pericles as the embodiment of patience. Greenfield believes that "too often the play emphasizes his avoidance of and retreat from misfortunes than his patient endurance of them," thereby rejecting the theories of Hoeniger, Arthos, and Danby.

Haight, Elizabeth Hazelton. "*Apollonius of Tyre* and Shakespeare's *Pericles, Prince of Tyre*." In her *More Essays on Greek Romances*, pp. 142-90. New York: Longmans, Green and Co., 1945.
> Elucidates the dramatic elements of the Greek Apollonius legend used by Shakespeare in *Pericles*.

Kermode, Frank. "Introduction" and "*Pericles, Prince of Tyre*." In his *William Shakespeare, The Final Plays*, pp. 7-11, pp. 12-19. London: Longmans, Green and Co., 1963.
> Discusses similarities, such as the use of allegory, between *Pericles* and Edmund Spenser's *Faerie Queen*.

McManaway, James G. Introduction to *Pericles Prince of Tyre*, by William Shakespeare, edited by Alfred Harbage, pp. 1259-61. Baltimore: Penguin Books, 1969.
> Discusses the dramatic conventions experimented with in *Pericles*, especially the dumb show and the chorus/presenter.

Mowat, Barbara A. "The Romances as Open Form Drama." In her *The Dramaturgy of Shakespeare's Romances*, pp. 95-110. Athens: The University of Georgia Press, 1976.
> The audience relationship in *Pericles* seen as precursing that of the later romances.

Muir, Kenneth. "*Pericles*." In his *Shakespeare As Collaborator*, pp. 77-97. New York: Barnes & Noble, 1960.
> Compares *Pericles* to several other Shakespearean plays and concludes that while in this play the protagonist's misfortunes are "undeserved," in the later plays "Shakespeare set out to eliminate accident, and to infuse the restoration theme with ethical meaning."

Munro, John. "Some Matters Shakespearian—III: *Pericles*." *The Times Literary Supplement*, No. 2384 (11 October 1947): 528.

Argues that Wilkins's novel, *The Painfull Adventures of Pericles Prince of Tyre*, was the source for a Wilkins play, which was later revised by a playwright of the King's Men. Munro attempts to show that the "ordinary course of dependence of the play on the novel" was followed in the case of *Pericles*. Unfortunately, Munro offers no evidence to substantiate his claims.

Quiller-Couch, Arthur. "*Pericles* and *King Henry VIII*." In his *Shakespeare's Workmanship*, pp. 241-58. London: T. Fisher Unwin, 1918.
> Evidence supporting Shakespeare as the author of *Pericles'* last three acts and as the reviser of the first two. Quiller-Couch was an important early twentieth-century editor of Shakespeare, who also championed him as the author of the brothel scenes in the face of the moral reservations of Victorian critics.

Robertson, J. M. "Further Problems: *Pericles*." In his *Shakespeare and Chapman*, pp. 185-92. 1917. Reprint. St. Clair Shores, Mich.: Scholarly Press, 1971.
> Proposes Chapman as a possible collaborator on *Pericles*. Robertson cites Ben Jonson's *Ode to Himself* and Chapman's rebuttal *Invective Against Mr. Ben Jonson* as evidence supporting his theory.

Saintsbury, George. "Shakespeare: Life and Plays." In *The Cambridge History of English Literature, Vol. V*, edited by A. W. Ward and A. R. Waller, pp. 211-12. Cambridge: Cambridge University Press, 1910.
> Refers to efforts to attribute some of *Pericles* to other dramatists as a "hazardous . . . piece of 'hariolation'."

Schiffhorst, Gerald J. "The Imagery of *Pericles* and What It Tells Us." *Ball State University Forum* 8, No. 3 (Summer 1967): 61-70.
> Studies three types of imagery apparent in *Pericles*: that "concerned with nature and those concerned with daily life and customs."

Scott, W.I.D. "*Pericles*—The Schizophrenic." In his *Shakespeare's Melancholics*, pp. 131-44. London: Mills & Boon, 1962.
> A psychological character study delineating supposed schizophrenic tendencies in Pericles.

Semon, Kenneth J. "*Pericles*: An Order Beyond Reason." *Essays in Literature* I, No. 1 (Spring 1974): 17-27.
> Sees *Pericles* as an affirmation of the status quo, universal order and the sense of human wonder.

Smyth, Albert H. *Shakespeare's "Pericles" and Apollonius of Tyre: A Study in Comparative Literature*. Philadelphia: MacCalla & Co., 1898, 112 p.
> A history of the Apollonius of Tyre legend from its origins in antiquity to Shakespeare's *Pericles*. Smyth includes eleven different versions of the story, each in different languages, and reiterates the critical debate over authorship.

Spiker, Sina. "George Wilkins and the Authorship of *Pericles*." *Studies in Philology* XXX, No. 3 (July 1933): 551-70.
> Postulates Wilkins's novel as succeeding the production of Shakespeare's play by demonstrating examples where the novel clarifies corrupt passages in the play. Spiker believes that Wilkins wrote with a play before him "and that he was following it—not with the intimacy of its own author—very likely from memory instead of from a manuscript copy."

Taylor, Michael. "Innocence in Shakespeare's *Pericles*." *ARIEL* 13, No. 3 (July 1982): 3-19.
> Discusses the problem of the innocence of various characters in *Pericles*, especially Marina.

Traversi, Derek. "*Pericles, Prince of Tyre*." In his *Shakespeare: The Last Phase*, pp. 19-42. New York: Harcourt, Brace & Co., 1955.
> Defines the plot of *Pericles* as a "function of imagery." Traversi also expounds on the importance of the play's poetic symbolism.

Welsh, Andrew. "Heritage in *Pericles*." In *Shakespeare's Late Plays*, edited by Richard C. Tobias and Paul G. Zollbrod, pp. 89-113. Athens: Ohio University Press, 1974.

Cites four different literary conventions operating simultaneously in *Pericles,* including the tale itself, the importance of riddles, the ''seven capital sins,'' and the appearance of the ''flourishing emblem.'' In discussing Shakespeare's use of these literary conventions, Welsh says that the Pericles story ''brought to him [Shakespeare] basic, archaic patterns of the story-telling imagination.''

Wood, James. O. ''The Shakespearean Language of *Pericles*.'' *English Language Notes* XIII, No. 2 (December 1975): 98-103.
Traces the evolution of Shakespearean and non-Shakespearean passages in *Pericles* through the first and second printings, often proposing variations for supposed compositor errors.

Appendix

The following is a listing of all sources used in Volume 2 of *Shakespearean Criticism*. Included in this list are all copyright and reprint rights and acknowledgments for those essays for which permission was obtained. Every effort has been made to trace copyright, but if omissions have been made, please let us know.

THE EXCERPTS IN SC, VOLUME 2, WERE REPRINTED FROM THE FOLLOWING PERIODICALS:

The Adventurer, n. 113, 116 and 132, December 4, 1753, December 15, 1753 and January 5, 1754.

American Journal of Insanity, July, 1844.

The American Political Science Review, v. LI, June, 1957. Copyright, 1957, by The American Political Science Association. Reprinted by permission.

Anglia, v. 98, 1980. © Max Niemeyer Verlag Tubingen 1980. Reprinted by permission.

Blackwood's Magazine, v. V, May, 1819.

Bucknell Review, v. XX, Winter, 1972. Copyright © by *Bucknell Review* 1972. Reprinted by permission.

Bulletin of the John Rylands Library, v. 21, April, 1937; v. XXI, October, 1937.

The Censor, n. 10, May 2, 1715.

Comparative Drama, v. 8, Fall, 1974. © copyright, 1974, by the Editors of *Comparative Drama.* Reprinted by permission./ v. 11, Summer, 1977. © Copyright 1977, by the Editors of *Comparative Drama.* Reprinted by permission of the Editor of *Comparative Drama.*

The Craftsman, n. 72, November 18, 1727.

Critical Quarterly, v. 2, Winter, 1960 for "The New 'King Lear'" by Barbara Everett. Reprinted by permission of the author.

The Durham University Journal, n.s. v. IX, December, 1947. Reprinted by permission.

ELH, v. 15, June, 1948./ v. 42, Spring, 1975. Reprinted by permission.

THE EXCERPTS IN SC, VOLUME 2, WERE REPRINTED FROM THE FOLLOWING BOOKS:

Bagehot, Walter. From *Shakespeare, the Man: An Essay*. The University Society, 1901.

Barber, C. L. From *Shakespeare's Festive Comedy: A Study of Dramatic Form and Its Relation to Social Custom*. Princeton University Press, 1959. Copyright © 1959 by Princeton University Press. All rights reserved. Excerpts reprinted by permission of Princeton University Press.

Bertram, Paul. From "Shakespeare: 'Henry VIII', the Conscience of the King," in *In Defense of Reading: A Reader's Approach to Literary Criticism*. Edited by Reuben A. Brower and Richard Poirier. Dutton, 1962. Copyright © 1962 by Reuben A. Brower and Richard Poirier. All rights reserved. Reprinted by permission of the publisher, E. P. Dutton, a division of New American Library.

Boas, Frederick S. From *Shakspere and His Predecessors*. Charles Scribner's Sons, 1896.

Bradbrook, M. C. From *The School of Night: A Study in the Literary Relationships of Sir Walter Ralegh*. Cambridge at the University Press, 1936.

Bradbrook, M. C. From *Shakespeare and Elizabethan Poetry: A Study of His Earlier Work in Relation to the Poetry of the Time*. Chatto and Windus, 1951.

Bradley, A. C. From *Shakespearean Tragedy: Lectures on "Hamlet," "Othello," "King Lear," "MacBeth."* Second edition. Macmillan and Co., Limited, 1905.

Brandes, George. From *William Shakespeare: A Critical Study, Vols. I & II*. Translated by William Archer, Mary Morison, and Diana White. William Heinemann, 1898.

Brooke, Stopford A. From *Ten More Plays of Shakespeare*. Constable and Company Ltd., 1913.

Bucknill, John Charles. From *The Psychology of Shakespeare*. Longman, Brown, Green, Longmans & Roberts, 1859.

Burckhardt, Sigurd. From *Shakespearean Meanings*. Princeton University Press, 1968. Copyright © 1968 by Princeton University Press. All rights reserved. Excerpts reprinted by permission of Princeton University Press.

Bush, Geoffrey. From *Shakespeare and the Natural Condition*. Cambridge, Mass.: Harvard University Press, 1956. © 1956 by the President and Fellows of Harvard College. Copyright © 1984 by Geoffrey D. Bush. Excerpted by permission.

Calderwood, James L. From *Shakespearean Metadrama: The Argument of the Play in "Titus Andronicus," "Love's Labour's Lost", "Romeo and Juliet", "A Midsummer Night's Dream" and "Richard II"*. University of Minnesota Press, 1971. © copyright 1971 by the University of Minnesota. All rights reserved. Reprinted by permission.

Campbell, Oscar James. From *Shakespeare's Satire*. Oxford University Press, 1943. Copyright 1943 by Oxford University Press, Inc. Renewed 1971 by Mrs. Robert L. Goodale, Mrs. George W. Meyer, & Robert F. Campbell. Reprinted by permission.

Capell, Edward. From an introduction to *Mr. William Shakespeare: His Comedies, Histories, and Tragedies, Vol. I*. By William Shakespeare, edited by Edward Capell. J. & R. Tonson, 1768.

Capell, Edward. From *Notes and Various Readings to Shakespeare, Vol. I*. Henry Hughes, 1779.

Capell, Edward. From *Notes and Various Readings to Shakespeare, Vol. II*. Edited by John Collins. n.p., 1779-80.

Carroll, William C. From *The Great Feast of Language in "Love's Labour's Lost"*. Princeton University Press, 1976. Copyright © 1976 by Princeton University Press. All rights reserved. Excerpts reprinted by permission of Princeton University Press.

Chalmers, George. From *A Supplemental Apology for the Believers in the Shakspeare-Papers*. T. Egerton, 1799.

Chambers, E. K. From *Shakespeare: A Survey*. Sidgwick & Jackson, 1925.

Chambers, R. W. From *King Lear*. Jackson, Son & Company, 1940.

Chambers, R. W. From *Man's Unconquerable Mind: Studies of English Writers, from Bede to A. E. Housman and W. P. Ker*. Jonathan Cape, 1939.

Clemen, Wolfgang. From *The Development of Shakespeare's Imagery*. Second edition. Methuen, 1977. © 1951 and 1977 Wolfgang Clemen. Reprinted by permission of Methuen & Co. Ltd.

Coleridge, Samuel Taylor. From *The Literary Remains of Samuel Taylor Coleridge, Vol. 2*. Edited by Henry Nelson Coleridge. W. Pickering, 1837.

Coleridge, Samuel Taylor. From *Shakespearean Criticism, Vol. 1*. Edited by Thomas Middleton Raysor. Cambridge, Mass.: Harvard University Press, 1930.

Coleridge, Samuel Taylor. From a detached memoranda of December 23, 1810, in *Shakespearean Criticism, Vol. II*. Edited by Thomas Middleton Raysor. Constable & Co. Ltd., 1930.

Colman, George. From a preface to *The History of King Lear, As It Is Performed at the Theatre Royal in Covent Garden*. By William Shakespeare. R. Baldwin, 1768.

Cope, Walter. From a letter to Lorde Vycount Cranborne in 1604, in *Reports of the Royal Commission on Historical Manuscripts,* 1872.

Danby, John F. From *Poets on Fortune's Hill: Studies in Sidney, Shakespeare, Beaumont & Fletcher*. Faber and Faber, 1952.

Deighton, K. From an introduction to *The Works of Shakespeare: Pericles, Vol. 28*. By William Shakespeare, edited by K. Deighton. Methuen & Co. Ltd. 1907.

Dowden, Edward. From *Shakspere*. Macmillan and Co., 1877.

Dowden, Edward. From *Shakspere: A Critical Study of His Mind and Art*. Third edition. Harper & Brothers Publishers, 1881.

Dryden, John. From an epilogue to *Miscellany Poems*. By the Most Eminent Hands [John Dryden & others]. Jacob Tonson, 1684.

Eagleton, Terence. From *Shakespeare and Society: Critical Studies in Shakespearean Drama*. Chatto and Windus, 1967. © Terence Eagleton, 1967. Reprinted by permission of the author and Chatto & Windus.

Edwards, Philip. From an introduction to *Pericles Prince of Tyre*. By William Shakespeare, edited by Philip Edwards. Penguin Books, 1976. Introduction and notes copyright © Philip Edwards, 1976. Reprinted by permission of Penguin Books Ltd.

Ellis-Fermor, Una. From *The Jacobean Drama: An Interpretation*. Revised edition. Methuen & Co. Ltd., 1953.

Elze, Karl. From *Essays on Shakespeare*. Translated by L. Dora Schmitz. Macmillan and Co., 1874.

Empson, William. From *The Structure of Complex Words*. New Directions, 1951. All rights reserved. Reprinted by permission of New Directions Publishing Corporation.

Evans, Bertrand. From ''The Poem of 'Pericles','' in *The Image of the Work: Essays in Criticism*. Bertrand Evans, Josephine Miles, William R. Steinhoff, eds. University of California Press, 1955.

Evans, Bertrand. From *Shakespeare's Comedies*. Oxford at the Clarendon Press, Oxford, 1960. © Oxford University Press 1960. Reprinted by permission of Oxford University Press.

Farmer, Richard. From *An Essay on the Learning of Shakespeare*. J. Archdeacon, 1767.

Feltham, Owen. From *Resolves*. Eighth edition. N.p., 1661.

Fleay, F. G. From *Shakespeare Manual*. Macmillan and Co., 1876.

Foakes, R. A. From an introduction to *King Henry VIII*. By William Shakespeare, edited by R. A. Foakes. Revised edition. Methuen, 1957. Reprinted by permission of Methuen & Co. Ltd.

Foakes, R. A. From *Shakespeare, the Dark Comedies to the Last Plays: From Satire to Celebration*. University Press of Virginia, 1971. Copyright © R. A. Foakes 1971. Reprinted by permission.

Freud, Sigmund. From ''The Theme of the Three Caskets,'' translated by C.J.M. Hubback, in *Collected Papers: Papers on Metapsychology, Papers on Applied Psycho-analysis, Vol. 4*. Authorized translation under the supervision of Joan Riviere. The International Psycho-analytical Press, 1925.

Fripp, Edgar I. From *Shakespeare: Man and Artist, Vol. II*. Oxford University Press, 1938.

Frye, Northrop. From *Fools of Time: Studies in Shakespearean Tragedy*. University of Toronto Press, 1967. © University of Toronto Press 1967. Reprinted by permission.

Frye, Northrop. From *A Natural Perspective: The Development of Shakespearean Comedy and Romance*. Columbia University Press, 1965. Copyright © 1965 Columbia University Press. Reprinted by permission of the publisher.

Gerard, Alexander. From *An Essay on Genius*. N.p., 1774.

Gervinus, G. G. From *Shakespeare Commentaries*. Translated by F. E. Bunnètt. Revised edition. Smith, Elder, & Co., 1877.

Gildon, Charles. From ''Remarks on the Plays of Shakespear,'' in *The Works of Mr. William Shakespear, Vol. 7*. By William Shakespeare. E. Curll and E. Sanger, 1710.

Granville-Barker, Harley. From *Prefaces to Shakespeare* in first series. Sidgwick & Jackson, Ltd., 1927.

Griffith, Mrs. Elizabeth. From *The Morality of Shakespeare's Drama Illustrated*. T. Cadell, 1775.

Hallam, Henry. From *Introduction to the Literature of Europe in the 15th, 16th, and 17th Centuries, Vols. III & IV*. A. and W. Galignani and Co., 1837-39.

Halliwell-Phillipps, J. O. From *Memoranda on 'Love's Labour's Lost', 'King John', 'Othello', and on 'Romeo and Juliet'*. James Evan Adlard, 1879.

Harris, Bernard. From '' 'What's Past Is Prologue': 'Cymbeline' and 'Henry VIII','' in *Later Shakespeare*, Stratford-Upon-Avon Studies, No. 8. Edited by John Russell Brown and Bernard Harris. Arnold, 1966. © Edward Arnold (Publishers) Ltd. 1966. Reprinted by permission.

Harris, Frank. From *The Women of Shakespeare*. Methuen & Co. Ltd. 1911.

Hawkes, Terence. From *Shakespeare's Talking Animals: Language and Drama in Society*. Edward Arnold, 1973. © Terence Hawkes 1973. All rights reserved. Reprinted by permission of the author.

Hazlitt, William. From *Characters of Shakespear's Plays*. C. H. Reynell, 1817, Taylor and Hessey, 1817.

Heilman, Robert Bechtold. From *This Great Stage: Image and Structure in ''King Lear.''* Louisiana State University Press, 1948. Copyright, 1948, by Louisiana State University Press. Renewed 1976 by Robert Bechtold Heilman. Reprinted by permission of the author.

Hoeniger, F. D. From an introduction to *Pericles*. By William Shakespeare, edited by F. D. Hoeniger. Revised edition. Methuen, 1963. Editorial matter copyright © 1963 by Methuen & Co. Ltd. Reprinted by permission of Methuen & Co. Ltd.

Holloway, John. From *The Story of the Night: Studies in Shakespeare's Major Tragedies*. Routledge & Kegan Paul, 1961. © John Holloway 1961. Reprinted by permission of Routledge & Kegan Paul PLC.

Hudson, Rev. H. N. From *Shakespeare: His Life, Art, and Characters, Vol. I*. Revised edition. Ginn & Company, 1872.

Hudson, Rev. H. N. From *Shakespeare: His Life, Art, and Characters, Vol. II*. Revised edition. Ginn & Company, 1872.

Hugo, Victor. From *William Shakespeare*. Translated by Melville B. Anderson. A. C. McClurg and Co., 1887.

Huston, J. Dennis. From *Shakespeare's Comedies of Play*. Columbia University Press, 1981. Copyright © 1981 J. Dennis Huston. All rights reserved. Reprinted by permission of the author.

James, D. G. From *The Dream of Learning: An Essay on "The Advancement of Learning," "Hamlet," and "King Lear."* Oxford at the Clarendon Press, Oxford, 1951.

James, D. G. From *Scepticism and Poetry: An Essay on the Poetic Imagination*. George Allen & Unwin Ltd., 1937.

Jameson, Mrs. Anna Brownell. From *Characteristics of Women: Moral, Poetical & Historical*. Second edition. n.p., 1833.

John, Lord Chedworth. From *Notes upon Some of the Obscure Passages in Shakespeare's Plays*. W. Bulmer and Co., 1805.

Johnson, Samuel. From notes on "Henry VIII," in *The Plays of William Shakespeare*. By William Shakespeare, edited by Samuel Johnson. J. & R. Tonson, 1765.

Johnson, Samuel. From notes "Love's Labour's Lost," in *The Plays of William Shakespeare*. By William Shakespeare, edited by Samuel Johnson. J. & R. Tonson, 1765.

Johnson, Samuel. From notes on "King Lear," in *The Plays of William Shakespeare, Vol. VI*. By William Shakespeare, edited by Samuel Johnson. J. & R. Tonson, 1765.

Johnson, Samuel. From *The Yale Edition of the Works of Samuel Johnson: Johnson on Shakespeare, Vol. VII*. Edited by Arthur Sherbo. Yale University Press, 1968. Copyright © 1968 by Yale University. All rights reserved. Reprinted by permission.

Jonson, Ben. From *Ben Jonson: The Complete Poems*. Edited by George Parfitt. *Penguin English Poets*. Penguin Education, 1975. Reprinted by permission of Penguin Books Ltd.

Jorgensen, Paul A. From *Lear's Self-Discovery*. University of California Press, 1967. Copyright © 1967 by the Regents of the University of California. Reprinted by permission.

Keats, John. From a letter to George Keats and Thomas Keats on January 23, 1818, in *The Letters of John Keats*. Edited by Maurice Buxton Forman. Third edition. Oxford University Press, 1947.

Kemble, Frances Anne. From *Notes upon Some of Shakespeare's Plays*. Richard Bentley & Son, 1882.

Kernan, Alvin B. From "Formalism and Realism in Elizabethan Drama: The Miracles in 'King Lear'," in *Renaissance Drama, Vol. IX*. Edited by S. Schoenbaum. Northwestern University Press, 1966. Copyright © 1967 by Northwestern University Press, Evanston, Il. Reprinted by permission.

Kernodle, George R. From "The Symphonic Form of 'King Lear'," in *Elizabethan Studies and Other Essays in Honor of George F. Reynolds*. University of Colorado, 1945.

Knight, Charles. From "Supplementary Notice: 'Measure for Measure'," in *The Comedies, Histories, Tragedies, and Poems of William Shakspere, Vol. III*. By William Shakespeare, edited by Charles Knight. Second edition. Charles Knight and Co., 1842.

Knight, Charles. From "Supplementary Notice: 'King Henry VIII'," in *The Comedies, Histories, Tragedies, and Poems of William Shakspere, Vol. VII*. By William Shakespeare, edited by Charles Knight. Second edition. Charles Knight and Co., 1843.

Knight, Charles, From *Studies of Shakspere*. Charles Knight, 1849.

Knight, G. Wilson. From *The Crown of Life: Essays in Interpretation of Shakespeare's Final Plays*. Oxford University Press, 1947.

Knight, G. Wilson. From *Myth and Miracle: An Essay on the Mystic Symbolism of Shakespeare*. E. J. Burrow & Co., 1929.

Knight, G. Wilson. From *The Wheel of Fire: Interpretations of Shakespearian Tragedy*. Methuen & Co. Ltd., 1949.

Knights, L. C. From *Some Shakespearean Themes*. Stanford University Press, 1960. © 1959 by L. C. Knights. Reprinted with the permission of the publishers, Stanford University Press.

Kott, Jan. From *Shakespeare, Our Contemporary*. Translated by Boleslaw Taborski. Doubleday, 1964. Copyright © 1964, 1965, 1966 by Doubleday & Company, Inc. In Canada by Jan Kott. Reprinted by permission. Originally published as *Szkice o Szekspirze*. Panstwowe Wydawnictwo Naukowe, 1964. Copyright © 1964 Panstwowe Wydawnictwo Naukowe. Reprinted by permission.

Kreyssig, Friedrich. From an extract, translated by Horace Howard Furness, in *A New Variorum Edition of Shakespeare: King Lear, Vol. 5*. By William Shakespeare, edited by Horace Howard Furness. J. B. Lippincott Company, 1880.

Lamb, Charles. From "On the Tragedies of Shakespeare," in *Critical Essays of the Early Nineteenth Century*. Edited by Raymond Macdonald Alden. Charles Scribner's Sons, 1921.

Langbaine, Gerard. From *An Account of the English Dramatick Poets; or, Some Observations and Remarks on the Lives and Writings of All Those That Have Publish'd Either Comedies, Tragedies, Tragi-Comedies, Pastoral, Masques, Interludes, Farces, or Operas in the English Tongue*. George West and Henry Clemens, 1691.

Lawrence, William Witherle. From *Shakespeare's Problem Comedies*. Second edition. Ungar, 1960. Copyright 1960 by Frederick Ungar Publishing Co. Reprinted by permission.

Lee, Sidney. From an introduction to *Shakespeare's "Pericles:" Being a Reproduction in Facsimile of the First Edition 1609*. By William Shakespeare. Oxford at the Clarendon Press, Oxford, 1905.

Leech, Clifford. From *Shakespeare's Tragedies: And Other Studies in Seventeenth-Century Drama*. Chatto and Windus, 1950.

Leech, Clifford. From *William Shakespeare, the Chronicles: "Henry VI," "Henry IV," "The Merry Wives of Windsor," "Henry VIII."* Longmans, Green & Co., 1962. © Clifford Leech 1962. Reprinted by permission of Profile Books Limited.

Leggatt, Alexander. From *Shakespeare's Comedy of Love*. Methuen, 1974. © 1973 Alexander Leggatt. Reprinted by permission of Methuen & Co. Ltd.

Lennox, Charlotte. From *Shakespear Illustrated; or, The Novels and Histories, on Which the Plays of Shakespear Are Founded, Vol. 1*. A. Millar, 1753.

Lennox, Charlotte. From *Shakespear Illustrated; or, The Novels and Histories, on Which the Plays of Shakespear Are Founded, Vol. 3*. A. Millar, 1754.

Lever, J. W. From an introduction to *Measure for Measure*. By William Shakespeare, edited by J. W. Lever. Revised edition. Methuen, 1965. Editorial matter © 1965 Methuen & Co. Ltd., London. All rights reserved. Reprinted by permission of Methuen & Co. Ltd.

Lillo, George. From an extract from a prologue to *Marina: A Play of Three Acts, Taken from "Pericles, Prince of Tyre"*. By George Lillo. J. Gray, 1738.

Lloyd, William Watkiss. From *Essays on the Life and Plays of Shakespeare*. C. Whittingham, 1858.

Malone, Edmond. From a note on "Pericles," in *The Plays and Poems of William Shakspeare, Vol. 3*. By William Shakespeare, edited by Edmond Malone. J. Rivington and Sons, 1790.

Malone, Edmond. From "An Attempt to Ascertain the Order in Which the Plays Attributed to Shakspeare Were Written," in *The Plays of William Shakspeare*. By William Shakespeare, edited by George Steevens. Second edition. C. Bathurst, 1778.

Malone, Edmond. From an essay in *Supplement to the Edition of Shakspeare's Plays Published in 1778 by S. Johnson and G. Steevens*. Edited by Edmond Malone, C. Bathurst, W. Straham, etc. N.p., 1780.

McElroy, Bernard. From *Shakespeare's Mature Tragedies*. Princeton University Press, 1973. Copyright © 1973 by Princeton University Press. All rights reserved. Excerpts reprinted by permission of Princeton University Press.

Montégut, Émile. From an extract, translated by Horace Howard Furness, in *A New Variorum Edition of Shakespeare: Loves Labour's Lost, Vol. XIV*. Edited by Horace Howard Furness. J. B. Lippincott Company, 1904.

Muir, Edwin. From *Essays on Literature and Society*. Revised edition. Cambridge, Mass.: Harvard University Press, 1965, Hogarth Press, 1965. © copyright Edwin Muir 1949 and The Hogarth Press Ltd. 1965. Excerpted by permission of the President and Fellows of Harvard College. In Canada by The Hogarth Press and the Literary Estate of Edwin Muir.

Murry, John Middleton. From *Shakespeare*. Jonathan Cape, 1936. Reprinted by permission of The Society of Authors as the literary representative of the Estate of John Middleton Murry.

Noble, Richmond. From *Shakespeare's Use of Song*. Oxford at the Clarendon Press, Oxford, 1923.

Ornstein, Robert. From *A Kingdom for a Stage: The Achievement of Shakespeare's History Plays*. Cambridge, Mass.: Harvard University Press, 1972. Copyright © 1972 by the President and Fellows of Harvard College. All rights reserved. Reprinted by permission of the author.

Ornstein, Robert. From *The Moral Vision of Jacobean Tragedy*. The University of Wisconsin Press, 1960. Copyright © 1960, by the Regents of the University of Wisconsin. Reprinted by permission.

Palmer, John. From *Comic Characters of Shakespeare*. Macmillan and Co. Limited, 1946.

Parrott, Thomas Marc. From *Shakespearean Comedy*. Oxford University Press, 1949. Copyright 1949 by Thomas Marc Parrott. Renewed 1976 by Frances M. Walters. Reprinted with the permission of Russell and Russell.

Pater, Walter. From *Appreciations: With an Essay on Style*. Macmillan and Co., 1890.

Pepys, Samuel. From a diary entry of January 1, 1664, in *Diary and Correspondence of Samuel Pepys, Esq., F.R.S.* 1875-1877.

Pettet, E. C. From *Shakespeare and the Romance Tradition*. Staples Press, 1949.

Purdom, C. B. From *What Happens in Shakespeare: A New Interpretation*. John Baker, 1963. © C. B. Purdom 1963. Reprinted by permission of the Literary Estate of C. B. Purdom.

Quiller-Couch, Sir Arthur. From an introduction to *Measure for Measure*. By William Shakespeare. Cambridge at the University Press, 1922.

Raleigh, Walter. From *Shakespeare*. Macmillan Publishing Company, 1907.

Reibetanz, John. From *The "Lear" World: A Study of "King Lear" in Its Dramatic Context*. University of Toronto Press, 1977. © University of Toronto Press 1977. Reprinted by permission.

Richardson, William. From *Essays on Shakespeare's Dramatic Characters of Richard the Third, King Lear, and Timon of Athens*. J. Murray, 1784.

Riemer, A. P. From *Antic Fables: Patterns of Evasion in Shakespeare's Comedies*. St. Martin's Press, 1980. © A. P. Riemer 1980. All rights reserved. Reprinted by permission of St. Martin's Press, Inc.

Roderick, Richard. From "On the Metre of 'Henry VIII'," in *The Canons of Criticism, and Glossary: Being a Supplement to Mr. Warburton's Edition of Shakespear*. By Thomas Edwards. Sixth edition. C. Bathurst. 1758.

Rowe, Nicholas. From "Some Account of the Life, &c. of Mr. William Shakespear ," in *The Works of Mr. William Shakespear, Vol. I*. By William Shakespeare, edited by Nicholas Rowe. Jacob Tonson, 1709.

Schanzer, Ernest. From an introduction to "Pericles, Prince of Tyre," in *The Complete Signet Classic Shakespeare*. Sylvan Barnet, General Editor. Harcourt Brace Jovanovich, 1972. © 1965 by Ernest Schanzer. Reprinted by arrangement with The New American Library, Inc., New York, NY.

Schanzer, Ernest. From *The Problem Plays of Shakespeare: A Study of "Julius Caesar," "Measure for Measure," "Antony and Cleopatra."* Routledge and Kegan Paul, 1963. © Ernest Schanzer 1963. Reprinted by permission of Routledge & Kegan Paul PLC.

Schlegel, Augustus William. From *A Course of Lectures on Dramatic Art and Literature*. Edited by Rev. A.J.W. Morrison, translated by John Black. Revised edition. Henry G. Bohn, 1846.

Schücking, Levin L. From *Character Problems in Shakespeare's Plays: A Guide to the Better Understanding of the Dramatist*. Henry Holt & Company, 1922.

Sen Gupta, S. C. From *Shakespearian Comedy*. Oxford University Press, London, 1950.

Sewall, Richard B. From *The Vision of Tragedy*. Yale University Press, 1959. © 1959 by Yale University Press, Inc. All rights reserved. Reprinted by permission.

Sewell, Arthur. From *Character and Society in Shakespeare*. Oxford at the Clarendon Press, Oxford, 1951.

Shelley, Percy Bysshe. From *A Defence of Poetry*. Edited by Mrs. Shelley. The Bobbs-Merrill Company, 1904.

Sheppard, Samuel. From *The Times Displayed in Six Sestyads*. N.p., 1646.

Snider, Denton J. From *The Shakespearian Drama, a Commentary: The Comedies*. Sigma Publishing Co., 1890?.

Snider, Denton J. From *The Shakespearian Drama, a Commentary: The Histories*. Sigma Publishing Co., 1890.

Snider, Denton J. From *The Shakespearian Drama, a Commentary: The Tragedies*. Ticknor & Co., 1887.

Spencer, Theodore. From *Shakespeare and the Nature of Man*. Macmillan, 1942. Copyright 1942, 1949, 1977 by Macmillan Publishing Company. Renewed 1970 by Eloise B. Bender and John Spencer. All rights reserved. Reprinted with permission of Macmillan Publishing Company.

Spurgeon, Caroline F. E. From *Shakespeare's Imagery and What It Tells Us*. Cambridge at the University Press, 1935.

Squire, Sir John. From *Shakespeare As a Dramatist*. Cassell and Company, Limited, 1935.

Stauffer, Donald A. From *Shakespeare's World of Images: The Development of His Moral Ideas*. Norton, 1949. Copyright 1949 by W. W. Norton & Company, Inc. Copyright renewed 1977 by Ruth M. Stauffer. Reprinted by permission of W. W. Norton & Company, Inc.

Steevens, George. From an extract from a head-note to "Measure for Measure," in *The Plays of William Shakespeare, Vol. II*. By William Shakespeare. Edited by Samuel Johnson and George Steevens. N.p., 1773.

Steevens, George. From an essay in *Supplement to the Edition of Shakspeare's Plays Published in 1778 by S. Johnson and G. Steevens*. Edited by Edmond Malone, C. Bathurst, W. Straham, etc. N.p., 1780.

Stoll, Elmer Edgar. From *From Shakespeare to Joyce: Authors and Critics; Literature and Life*. Doubleday, Doran and Company, Inc., 1944.

Suddard, S. J. Mary. From *Keats, Shelley, and Shakespeare: Studies & Essays in English Literature*. Cambridge at the University Press, 1912.

Swinburne, Algernon Charles. From *A Study of Shakespeare*. Chatto & Windus, 1880, R. Worthington, 1880.

Sykes, H. Dugdale. From *Sidelights on Shakespeare*. The Shakespeare Head Press, 1919.

Tate, Nahum. From a dedication to *The History of King Lear*. Revised edition. E. Flesher, 1681.

Tathem, Joseph. From an extract from a preface to *A Joviall Crew; or, The Merry Beggars*. By Richard Brome. N.p., 1652.

Theobald, Lewis. From notes to "Measure for Measure," in *The Works of Shakespeare, Vol. I*. By William Shakespeare, edited by Lewis Theobald. A. Bettesworth & C. Hitch, 1733.

Theobald, Lewis. From a note on "Love's Labour's Lost," in *The Works of Shakespeare, Vol. II*. By William Shakespeare, edited by Lewis Theobald. A. Bettesworth & C. Hitch, 1733.

Tillyard, E.M.W. From *Shakespeare's Early Comedies*. Chatto and Windus, 1965. © Stephen Tillyard 1965. Reprinted by permission of the author's Literary Estate and Chatto and Windus.

Tillyard, E.M.W. From *Shakespeare's Last Plays*. Chatto and Windus, 1938.

Tillyard, E.M.W. From *Shakespeare's Problem Plays*. University of Toronto Press, 1949.

Tofte, Robert. From *Alba: The Month's Minde of a Melancholy Lover*. Matthew Lownes, 1598.

Tolstoy, Leo. From *Tolstoy on Shakespeare: A Critical Essay on Shakespeare*. Translated by V. Tohertkoff and I.F.M. Funk & Wagnalls Company, 1906.

Ulrici, Hermann. From *Shakspeare's Dramatic Art: And His Relation to Calderon and Goethe*. Translated by Rev. A.J.W. Morrison. Chapman, Brothers, 1846.

Van Doren, Mark. From *Shakespeare*. Henry Holt and Company, 1939.

Velie, Alan R. From *Shakespeare's Repentance Plays: The Search for an Adequate Form*. Fairleigh Dickinson University Press, 1972. © 1972 by Associated University Presses, Inc. Reprinted by permission.

Verplanck, Gulian C. From introductory remarks to ''Pericles,'' in *Shakespeare's Plays, with His Life, Vol. III*. Edited by Gulian C. Verplanck. Harper & Brothers, Publishers, 1847.

Warburton, William. From an extract in *The Works of Shakespear, Vol. II*. By William Shakespeare, edited by William Warburton. J. and P. Knapton, 1747.

Welsford, Enid. From *The Fool: His Social and Literary History*. Faber and Faber, 1935.

West, Robert H. From *Shakespeare & the Outer Mystery*. University of Kentucky Press, 1968. Copyright © 1968 by the University Press of Kentucky. Reprinted by permission.

Willcock, Gladys Doidge. From *Shakespeare As Critic of Language*. Oxford University Press, London, 1934.

Wilson, J. Dover. From *The Essential Shakespeare: A Biographical Adventure*. Cambridge at the University Press, 1932.

Wilson, John Dover. From *Shakespeare's Happy Comedies*. Faber and Faber, 1962. © 1962 by John Dover Wilson. Reprinted by permission of Faber and Faber Ltd.

Wotton, Sir Henry. From a letter to Sir Edmund Bacon on July 2, 1613, in *Reliquiae Wottoniae*. By Sir Henry Wotton, edited by Izaak Walton. Fourth edition. B. Tooke and T. Sawbridge, 1685.

Yates, Frances A. From *Shakespeare's Last Plays: A New Approach*. Routledge & Kegan Paul, 1975. © Frances A. Yates 1975. Reprinted by permission of A. D. Peters & Co. Ltd.

ISBN 0-8103-6126-4

90000

REFERENCE